LONGMAN

Collocations Dictionary and Thesaurus

Pearson Education Limited
Edinburgh Gate
Harlow
Essex CM20 2JE
England, UK
and associated Companies throughout the world

Visit our website: http://www.pearsonlongman.com/dictionaries

© Pearson Education Limited, 2013
All rights reserved; no part of this publication may be reproduced, stored in a retrieval system, or transmitted in any form or by any means, electronic, mechanical, photocopying, recording or otherwise, without the prior written permission of the publishers.

First published 2013

Words that editors have reason to believe constitute trademarks have been described as such. However, neither the presence not the absence of such a description should be regarded as affecting the legal status of any trademark.

ISBN 978 1 4082 5225 3 (Cased edition + online access)
ISBN 978 1 4082 5226 0 (Paperback edition + online access)

Set in Whitney by Letterpart, UK
Printed in China SWTC/01

Acknowledgements

Editorial Director
Michael Mayor

Managing Editor
Chris Fox

Senior Editor
Rosalind Combley

Editors
Karen Cleveland-Marwick
Lucy Hollingworth
Elizabeth Manning
Michael Murphy
Howard Sargeant
Dr Martin Stark
Laura Wedgeworth

Thesaurus Entries & Language Notes
Chris Fox

Project Management
Alan Savill

Computational Linguist
Allan Ørsnes

Online Development
Andrew Roberts

Senior Project Editor
Alice Willoughby

Proofreaders
Pat Dunn
Isabel Griffiths
Alison Sadler
Nicky Thompson

Production
Keeley Hill
Susan Braund

Design
Matthew Dickin

Project and Databases Administrator
Denise McKeough

Academic Collocations List
Kirsten Ackermann
Yu-Hua Chen
Professor Douglas Biber
Bethany Gray
Andrew Roberts

The publishers and editors of the *Longman Collocations Dictionary and Thesaurus* would like to thank the many people who have contributed ideas, suggestions and feedback during the creation of this new dictionary, in particular:

Professor the Lord Quirk, chair of the Linglex Advisory Committee
Professor Geoff Leech
Professor David Crystal
Professor John Wells
Della Summers
Diane Schmitt, Nottingham Trent University
Professor Norbert Schmitt, Nottingham Trent University
Dr Ron Martinez

The publishers and editors would also like to thank all the teachers and students who contributed to the research for the *Longman Collocations Dictionary and Thesaurus*.

Contents

How to use the Dictionary

Words from the Academic Word List are marked **Ac**

Collocations are arranged according to their part of speech, so that you can see all the adjectives, all the verbs etc, together.

Collocations are listed in order of frequency, so that you can see the most common collocations first.

The meanings of difficult collocations are explained in brackets.

research **Ac** *n*
serious study to discover new facts or test new ideas

ADJECTIVES/NOUNS + research

scientific/medical research *The university is an important centre for scientific research.*

cancer/AIDS etc research *She is raising money for cancer research.*

the latest research (=the most recent research) *The latest research is published in this month's 'Nature' magazine.*

pioneering/groundbreaking research (=producing completely new information) *Watson and Crick did pioneering research into DNA.*

basic research *He wants to conduct b...*

Labels tell you if the collocation is only used in formal or informal English.

Error notes warn about common mistakes with collocations.

painstaking historical research.

VERBS

do research/carry out research (*also* **conduct research** *formal*): *The research was carried out by a team of scientists at Tokyo University.*

⚠ Don't say 'make research'.

undertake research *formal* (=do research, or start doing research, especially into a complicated subject) *They are plannin...*

Words that have the same spelling, but have different parts of speech, are listed separately, and given different numbers.

Meanings of the word are listed in frequency order.

Every collocation, or group of collocations, has an example, so that you can see how it is used in a sentence. The examples are taken from the Longman Corpus Network: a database of over 450 million words of written and spoken English.

respect[1] *v*

1 to admire someone because you think they are very good, fair etc

ADVERBS

respect sb greatly *I admire her and respect her greatly.*

highly respected *The author is a highly respected historian.*

widely respected (=by many people) *The general is widely respected in the army.*

well respected *She was well respected by her colleagues.*

Grammar notes give information about how the word is used, for example whether it is usually plural or usually passive.

country and can be used to increase its wealth

Grammar
Often plural in this meaning.

ADJECTIVES/NOUNS + resource

natural resources *The country has always relied on coal and other natural resources.*

famous *adj*
known about by a lot of people in a country or in the world, especially because someone or something is very good or impressive

NOUNS

a famous writer/actor/singer/artist *Leonardo was one of the most famous artists who has ever lived.*

a famous book/story/poem/painting *'Nineteen Eighty-Four' was Orwell's most famous book.*

famous phrase/words *In John Donne's famous phrase, "No man is an island".*

VERBS

become famous *She became famous for the gardens she created.*

make sb famous *The song made him famous.*

Thesaurus entries show other words which have a similar meaning, so that you can compare the collocations and develop your vocabulary.

THESAURUS: famous

legendary
singer | musician | performer | player | figure | name | reputation | ability | courage
very famous and greatly admired for a long time – used especially about a singer, musician, or performer, often one who has died:
The album features songs by legendary guitar player Jimi Hendrix. | Her courage was legendary. | Newman was ***legendary for*** *his good looks.*

The words that a word is most commonly used with are listed before the definition.

The definition gives information about the nuance of the word, and shows how it is different from the other words.

Common prepositions and adverbs that you use with the word are shown in bold.

eminent
scientist | historian | scholar | professor | doctor | surgeon | economist | member
used about scientists and experts who are

British and American spellings of the word are shown.

realize (*also* **realise** *BrE*) *v*
1 to begin to understand, notice, or know something that you did not understand etc before

ADVERBS

suddenly realize *I suddenly realized I was late*

2 to achieve what you wanted

There are cross-references to words that appear in a Thesaurus box at another word.

THESAURUS: realize

accomplish, attain, reach, realize → **achieve**

reason *n*

Introduction

The aim of this book

When I'm writing in a foreign language, there is often a feeling of doubt in my mind. How can I be sure that the combination of words I'm using sounds natural? Is this what a native speaker would say in this situation? I need someone to tell me that I am on the right track. The aim of this book is to help students of English with exactly this sort of problem, so that they can quickly find the most typical word combination used by native speakers.

For example, when writing about **research**, which verb should you use? Do you 'make research' or 'do research'? The *Longman Collocations Dictionary and Thesaurus* gives the following information:

> *painstaking historical research.*
>
> **VERBS**
>
> **do research/carry out research** (*also* **conduct research** *formal*): *The research was carried out by a team of scientists at Tokyo University.*
>
> ⚠ Don't say 'make research'.
>
> **undertake research** *formal* (=do research, or start doing research, especially into a complicated subject) *They are planning to undertake research into the genetic causes of the disease.*
>
> **publish research** *His research was published in the 'New England Journal of Medicine'.*
>
> **present research** (=tell people the results of

The entry tells you the most common verbs used with **research**. It also tells you which word combinations to avoid - this can be very important for students, in order to avoid common errors such as 'make research'. There is also information about more formal word combinations, which are useful for academic writing. Here **conduct research** is often used in more formal contexts instead of **do research** or **carry out research**.

For each word combination there is an example, so that you can see how it is used in a sentence, and get a feeling for the most typical context. The examples are based on lines from the Longman Corpus Network, which is a 450 million word database of both written and spoken English. There are more examples in the online version of the book.

The collocations are listed according to their frequency on the Longman Corpus Network, with the most frequent collocations shown first. We think that the collocations that are most commonly used are also likely to be the first ones that people will want to look up.

What is a collocation?

In this book, a collocation is a word that you often use with another word. This can be an adjective used with a noun - for example when talking about the **rain**, you use **heavy rain** when there is a lot of rain, or when talking about the **wind**, you use **high winds** about winds that are very strong. It can be a verb used with a noun - for example when talking about a **decision** you can **make a decision**, **take a decision**, or **reach a decision**. It can also be an adverb used with an adjective - for example when you want to emphasize that something is **obvious**, you can say that it is **perfectly obvious**, **patently obvious**, or **glaringly obvious**.

Prepositions such as **about** and **over** are often not considered to be 'true' collocations, but we have included them in this book, because they are often the word that a student most needs to know and often the biggest cause of errors.

Some people make a distinction between 'transparent' collocations, where you can easily guess the meaning, for example **serious crime**, and 'opaque' collocations, where the meaning of the word is less obvious, for example **petty crime** (=crime that is not very serious, such as stealing small amounts of money). In this book we show both types of collocations, because they are both useful to students. If the meaning of the word is difficult to understand, we explain what it means after the collocation.

What makes this book special?

Apart from showing the collocations for each word, there are also Thesaurus sections, where you can compare words that have a similar meaning and see which collocations go with each word. For example, at **famous** you can see other similar words such as **legendary**, **eminent**, or **notorious**. Each of these words is used about a particular type of famous person - you use **legendary** especially about musicians and performers, **eminent** about scientists and historians, and **notorious** about criminals.

Similarly, if you are talking about things that are **empty**, there is a range of other words you can use, depending on the kind of thing you are talking about. And each of the synonyms has a fixed set of collocations. You can use **vacant** about a seat or a room at a hotel, **blank** about a computer screen, or **deserted** about a street or a beach. If you are talking about things that are **interesting**, you can use **stimulating** about a debate, **intriguing** about a question, or **absorbing** about a hobby.

Students sometimes overuse simple words like **famous** or **interesting**, when often there is a more specific and more natural-sounding word combination, depending on the kind of person or thing you are talking about. The Thesaurus sections will help you to improve your spoken and written English, making it sound more like that of a native speaker.

Native speakers often do not think of each individual word. They tend to use ready-made 'chunks' of language, such as a **notorious criminal** or an **eminent scientist**. This is the first book that makes a link between these chunks of language and groups them according to their meaning. We think this is very important for language learning.

Going beyond collocations

The key aim of this book is to help students produce natural English. In order to do this, you need to be aware of the nuances of a word. There is help with this in the definitions for the words and collocations. At **eminent** the definition says this is "used about scientists and experts who are greatly respected because of their knowledge". At **legendary** the definition says "very famous and greatly admired for a long time - used especially about a singer, musician, or performer, often one who has died".

Register is also very important. You need to know if the word is mainly used in formal or informal situations. This dictionary helps you to choose between similar word combinations, where there is a difference in formality, for example at **task**:

> **carry out/do a task** (*also* **perform a task** *formal*): *We don't have enough staff to carry out this task.*

This shows you that you usually say **carry out a task** or **do a task**, but in formal situations you say **perform a task**.

You also need to know about the grammar of the word - for example whether it is usually used in the plural, or in the passive. At **accommodation** there is the following note:

> **Grammar**
> In American English, the plural form **accommodations** is often used. In British English, however, people only use the uncountable form **accommodation**.

Collocations and Native Speaker Competence

People sometimes ask me how well I can speak a foreign language. Working with collocations has made me realize how much more I need to learn. Reaching native speaker competence in a language is not just about learning lists of words and grammar. Making the connections between the individual words of the language is equally important. We hope that the new *Longman Collocations Dictionary and Thesaurus* can help students have better access to this network of connections, so that they can make the links between words and improve their spoken and written fluency.

As always, we welcome comments on our work from students and teachers.
Please email us at:

chris.fox@pearson.com

A a

abandon [Ac] *v*

1 to leave someone or something completely

NOUNS

abandon a car/ship *The thieves abandoned the car when it ran out of fuel.*

abandon a building *We had to abandon the building when the roof began to collapse.*

abandon a child/family *The child was found abandoned outside a hospital.*

ADVERBS

quickly/hastily abandon sb/sth *They had to hastily abandon the ship when it started sinking.*

largely/virtually abandon sb/sth (=almost completely) *Her family had largely abandoned her, and she only saw her son occasionally.*

temporarily abandon sb/sth (=for a short time) *Residents were forced to temporarily abandon their homes due to a flood warning.*

VERBS

be forced to abandon sth *Guests were forced to abandon the hotel because of the fire.*

have to abandon sth *The soldiers had to abandon the tanks which had become bogged down in the mud.*

PHRASES

abandon sb to their fate (=leave someone in a bad situation with no one to help them) *The wounded soldier had been abandoned to his fate.*

2 to decide not to do something because you are unlikely to succeed

NOUNS

abandon an attempt/effort *Poor weather forced them to abandon their attempt to climb the mountain.*

abandon a search *When night fell, the police decided to abandon their search for the missing boy.*

abandon a plan/policy *The government was forced to abandon its economic policies.*

abandon an idea *Helen abandoned the idea of becoming a doctor, and studied law instead.*

abandon a decision *He showed no sign of abandoning his decision to earn a living as a writer.*

abandon your principles *The party was accused of abandoning its principles in order to win votes.*

abandon hope *She never abandoned hope of seeing him again.*

ADVERBS

abandon sth altogether/completely/totally *They abandoned their plans to start up a business altogether.*

largely/virtually abandon sth (=almost completely) *She appeared in a few films in the 1990s, but has largely abandoned her acting career.*

finally/eventually abandon sth *The police finally abandoned their hunt for the man when all sign of him had disappeared.*

temporarily abandon sth (=for a short time) *The rescue attempt was temporarily abandoned until the weather improved.*

VERBS

be forced to abandon sth *Severe storms forced them to abandon the expedition.*

have to abandon sth *He had to abandon the idea of travelling to Italy on account of his ill health.*

PHRASES

abandon sth in favour of sth else (=use something else instead) *The original plan was abandoned in favour of a cheaper one.*

abbreviation *n*

a group of letters used as a short way of saying or writing a word or group of words

VERBS

use an abbreviation *People often use the abbreviation 'US' instead of saying the 'United States'.*

ADJECTIVES

a written abbreviation *'BTW' is a written abbreviation which means 'by the way'.*

a common abbreviation *At the back of the book there is a list of common abbreviations used in English.*

the standard abbreviation *The standard abbreviation for 'for example' is 'e.g.'.*

PREPOSITIONS

the abbreviation for/of sth *'PC' is the abbreviation for 'personal computer'.*

PHRASES

an abbreviation is short for sth *The abbreviation 'WHO' is short for 'World Health Organization'.*

an abbreviation stands for sth *The abbreviation 'mph' stands for 'miles per hour'.*

ability *n*

someone's level of skill at doing something

ADJECTIVES

great/considerable ability *These drawings required considerable ability on the part of the artist.*

remarkable/outstanding/exceptional ability *The company aims to select people of outstanding ability.*

high/low/average ability *Many of these students are of above average ability.*

A

mixed ability (=with students who have different levels of ability) *It can be difficult to teach a mixed ability class.*
natural ability (*also* **innate ability** *formal*) (=one that you are born with) *The human body has a natural ability to fight infection.*
physical/athletic ability *He has considerable athletic ability.*
mental ability *The exercises are supposed to help you improve your mental ability.*
intellectual/academic ability *No one doubts his intellectual abilities.*
artistic/creative/musical ability *You do not need to have any artistic ability to do the course.*
an uncanny ability (=one that is unusual and difficult to explain) *He has an uncanny ability for spotting investment opportunities.*

VERBS

have the ability to do sth (*also* **possess the ability to do sth** *formal*): *She has the ability to make people feel relaxed.*
develop/acquire an ability to do sth *Students are encouraged to develop an ability to work independently.*
show/demonstrate the ability to do sth *Jones quickly demonstrated his ability to score goals.*
lack the ability to do sth *As a young man, he lacked the ability to communicate his feelings.*
lose the ability to do sth *Roger lost the ability to walk following a horrific accident.*
affect sb's ability to do sth *The noise was affecting her ability to concentrate.*
limit/reduce sb's ability to do sth *He has a medical condition which limits his ability to work.*
improve/increase sb's ability to do sth *Surely anything which improves your ability to learn is a good thing.*

PREPOSITIONS

ability in sth *Applicants for the job need to demonstrate an ability in English.*
ability as sth *She thought they were criticizing her ability as a mother.*

PHRASES

sb's level of ability/ability level *The children were of the same age and ability level.*
a range of ability/ability range *There is a wide range of ability within the class.*
a test of ability/ability test *Examinations are not always a good test of ability.*
an ability group (=a group that students are taught in, based on their level of ability) *Children are divided into different ability groups.*
play/perform/do sth to the best of your ability (=as well as you can) *Players must perform to the best of their ability every week.*

abnormal *adj*

not normal, especially when this seems strange or has a bad effect

NOUNS

abnormal behaviour *BrE*, **abnormal behavior** *AmE*: *A reduction in oxygen reaching the brain can cause changes in mood and abnormal behaviour.*
abnormal cells *Doctors can detect abnormal cells that may become cancerous.*
abnormal conditions *The damage was caused by abnormal weather conditions.*
abnormal signs/symptoms (=unusual things that show that something may be wrong) *Patients should report any abnormal symptoms to their doctor.*
something/nothing/anything abnormal *There was nothing abnormal about him – he was just like anyone else.*

ANTONYMS **abnormal → normal**

abort *v* THESAURUS **stop[1] (3)**

abortive *adj* THESAURUS **unsuccessful**

absence *n*

1 a situation in which someone is not at their school, office, a meeting etc

ADJECTIVES

a long absence *Henry returned to school after a long absence.*
a lengthy/prolonged absence (=unusually long) *Her prolonged absences were causing concern among her colleagues.*
a brief/short absence *He had a brief absence from work after his first child was born.*
a temporary absence *No one noticed her temporary absence from the meeting.*
frequent absences *His job involves frequent absences from home.*
repeated absences *Ian's repeated absences from work got him into trouble with his boss.*

VERBS

explain your absence *He explained his absence from class by saying that he had not been feeling well.*
apologize for your absence *Jim apologized for his absence from last week's meeting.*

PREPOSITIONS

absence from school/work etc *His absence from work was due to illness.*
during/in sb's absence *During my absence, Sally Greene will be in charge of the office.*

PHRASES

a week's/month's absence *After several weeks' absence, he returned home.*
a period of absence *Workers receive sick pay for each period of absence caused by illness.*
a reason/explanation for your absence *His explanation for his absence was not very convincing.*

be conspicuous by your absence (=be absent from somewhere, in a way that seems very noticeable) *The US ambassador was conspicuous by her absence at the conference.*

2 a situation in which someone or something does not exist

ADJECTIVES

a complete/total absence of sth *There was a complete absence of windows and very little light entered the room.*

a virtual absence of sth (=almost none) *There is still a virtual absence of female employees.*

a relative/comparative absence of sth *There is a relative absence of trees in this city.*

a notable/conspicuous/marked absence of sth (=very noticeable) *Despite a conspicuous absence of information to support his theories, many people accepted them as being true.*

PREPOSITIONS

an absence of sth *An absence of clean water has meant that the disease is very common in this part of the world.*

in the absence of sth *In the absence of any other evidence, they assumed that the man was innocent.*

absolutely *adv* THESAURUS ▶ very[1]

absorbing *adj* THESAURUS ▶ interesting

abstract[1] Ac *adj*

1 based on ideas rather than specific examples or real events

abstract + NOUNS

an abstract idea/concept/principle *Children gradually learn the words they need to deal with abstract ideas such as time.*

abstract thought *Do you think animals are capable of abstract thought?*

ADVERBS

highly abstract *People often regard philosophy as a highly abstract subject.*

PHRASES

in abstract terms *We've discussed the subject in abstract terms, but haven't made any concrete suggestions.*

2 abstract art consists of shapes and patterns that do not look like things or people

abstract + NOUNS

abstract art *The gallery is holding an exhibition of abstract art.*

an abstract painting/picture *The room was decorated with brightly coloured abstract paintings.*

an abstract pattern/design *The wallpaper comes in various abstract designs.*

an abstract artist/painter *Miró was famous as an abstract artist.*

abstract[2] Ac *n*

a written summary of an article or speech

VERBS

write an abstract *Write the abstract in a less formal style than the article itself.*

provide/submit an abstract *Editors of journals will expect you to provide an abstract of the article.*

publish an abstract *The magazine publishes abstracts of all the presidents' speeches to Congress.*

PREPOSITIONS

in sb's abstract *In your abstract, you should outline the main points of the paper you have written.*

abuse *n*

1 rude, offensive, or cruel words

ADJECTIVES

racial/racist abuse *Some of the children had experienced racial abuse at school.*

VERBS

shout/scream/hurl abuse *The other driver started hurling abuse at me* (=shouting abuse).

shower sb with abuse/heap abuse on sb (=give someone a lot of abuse) *Workers who refused to join the strike were showered with abuse.*

PHRASES

a term of abuse (=an offensive word or phrase) *In Australia, 'Pom' is a term of abuse for someone from the UK.*

a torrent/stream of abuse (=a lot of offensive words) *When I disagreed, he directed a stream of abuse at me.*

a target for/of abuse *Williams became a target for abuse when he failed to stop the opposing team's winning goal.*

2 cruel, violent, or unfair treatment of someone

ADJECTIVES

physical abuse *He experienced physical abuse when he was a child.*

verbal abuse *I was subjected to verbal abuse on many occasions.*

domestic abuse (=abuse inside the home) *Doctors see evidence of domestic abuse when women are treated for bruises and broken bones.*

sexual abuse *In his book, he revealed that he was a victim of sexual abuse as a teenager.*

emotional/psychological abuse *Constant criticism can be a form of emotional abuse.*

VERBS

suffer/experience/endure abuse *Women who suffer abuse may still be unwilling to leave their violent husbands.*

be subjected to abuse (=be made to suffer abuse by someone) *He was subjected to constant abuse by his older brother.*

A

NOUNS + abuse

child abuse *The man was arrested for child abuse.*

wife abuse *Wife abuse is more common than people imagine.*

elder abuse (=of old people) *Cases of elder abuse have increased as more people live to an advanced age.*

PHRASES

a victim of abuse *Children who have been victims of abuse sometimes grow up to be abusers themselves.*

abysmal *adj* THESAURUS ▶ terrible

academic [Ac] *adj*

relating to education, especially at college or university level

NOUNS

academic research/study *He has been carrying out academic research into the effects of computer games on children.*

an academic subject (*also* **academic discipline** *formal*): *Linguistics is a well-established academic discipline in universities.*

academic qualifications *What academic qualifications do you need for the job?*

academic achievements *Girls' academic achievements are better than those of boys in some subjects.*

academic success *Academic success is important, but it's not the only reason for studying hard at school.*

academic ability *The students are placed in groups according to academic ability.*

academic standards *The college prides itself on its high academic standards.*

the academic year *The academic year starts in October.*

an academic institution *The university is one of the oldest academic institutions in Britain.*

academic freedom *Universities want to protect the academic freedom of both staff and students.*

PHRASES

in academic circles (=among people who study at university or do research) *His name is well known in academic circles.*

> You can also use **academic** to describe a person who likes studying and is good at subjects that people study at school or university: *My brother is much more **academic** than I am – he studied law at Harvard.*

accent *n*

the way someone pronounces the words of a language, showing which country or which part of a country they come from

VERBS

have an accent *The girl had a Russian accent.*

speak with an accent *The old man spoke with an accent which I couldn't recognize.*

pick up an accent *He used to work in Sydney and picked up an Australian accent while he was over there.*

lose your accent *Although she was born in the US, Sally had lost her American accent after living in London for over 30 years.*

put on an accent (=deliberately speak with a different accent from your usual one) *Some people put on an accent when they're speaking on the phone.*

ADJECTIVES/NOUNS + accent

a strong/broad/thick/heavy accent *Claude speaks English with a strong French accent.*

a slight/faint accent *He has a very slight Irish accent which you can hardly notice.*

a French/American etc accent *He introduced himself in a strong American accent.*

a New York/London etc accent *The man I met had a Chicago accent.*

a foreign accent *The waitress spoke with a foreign accent.*

a regional accent *Some people try to hide their regional accents because they feel embarrassed about them.*

an upper-class/middle-class/working-class accent *The woman spoke with an upper-class accent.*

PREPOSITIONS

with an accent *She spoke English with a slight foreign accent.*

in an accent *Costas read out his speech in a thick Greek accent.*

> **Strong, broad, thick, or heavy accent?**
>
> You use all these words when saying that someone's accent is very noticeable. **Strong** is the most common word: *The man had a **strong** German accent.*
>
> You use **thick** or **heavy** when someone's accent is very strong and difficult to understand: *The teacher had a **thick** Scottish accent, and some of the students had difficulty following what he said.*
>
> You use **broad** when someone has an accent from a particular part of the UK or the US: *She spoke with a **broad** Yorkshire accent.*

> **Accent or pronunciation?**
>
> Your **accent** shows which country, or which social group you come from. **Pronunciation** is a more general word meaning the way in which a language or a particular word is pronounced.

PHRASES

a hint/trace of an accent *I could detect the hint of a German accent in her voice.*

accept *v*

1 to take something that someone offers you, or to agree to do something that someone asks you to do

NOUNS

accept an offer/invitation *I decided to accept their offer of a job.*

accept a gift/present/bribe *I wasn't sure whether I could accept such a generous gift.*

accept an award *He had to give a speech when he accepted the award.*

accept help/aid/assistance *He has always been reluctant to accept help from other people.*

accept an apology *Please accept my apologies for cancelling our meeting.*

accept sb's resignation *The manager refused to accept her resignation.*

accept a challenge *Paul accepted the challenge to run in the London Marathon.*

ADVERBS

gladly/willingly/readily accept sth *He invited her to dinner and she gladly accepted.*

gratefully accept sth *Any information you can let me have would be gratefully accepted.*

graciously accept sth (=in a polite and kind way) *She accepted her gift graciously.*

reluctantly accept sth *He handed the book to James who reluctantly accepted it.*

PREPOSITIONS

accept sth from sb *He accepted an invitation from the president to visit France.*

2 to decide that there is nothing you can do to change a bad situation

NOUNS

accept a situation *You'll just have to accept the situation – there's nothing you can do about it.*

accept reality (=accept the real situation) *He was unwilling to accept reality and kept calling his ex-girlfriend.*

accept defeat *Woods refused to accept defeat and came back to win the competition.*

accept the consequences *They will have to accept the consequences of their actions.*

accept your fate *Rather than accept their fate, the workers went on strike in protest at the job cuts.*

accept the inevitable *He had to accept the inevitable and close down his business.*

accept the fact (that)... *The team has had to accept the fact that it is not good enough to win the league.*

VERBS

be forced to accept sth *I was forced to accept defeat.*

learn/come to accept sth (=gradually accept something) *Eventually my parents came to accept our marriage.*

3 to agree that something is right or true

NOUNS

accept an idea/principle/notion *It took his parents a long time to accept the idea that he wanted to be a dancer.*

accept a view *This view is now generally accepted among scientists.*

accept an argument *I accept the argument that violence is sometimes necessary.*

accept an explanation *He accepted her explanation without question.*

accept a proposal *The committee voted to accept the proposals.*

accept a claim *A scientist wouldn't accept claims like this without proper evidence.*

accept a recommendation *The company accepted all the recommendations that were made in the report.*

accept the need for sth *The authorities say they accept the need for an investigation into the matter.*

ADVERBS

be generally/widely/commonly accepted (=by many or most people) *It is widely accepted that the Earth's climate is changing.*

be universally accepted (=by everyone) *This point of view was almost universally accepted in the nineteenth century.*

fully accept sth (=completely) *I fully accept that I was wrong and I apologize.*

readily/happily accept sth *Most people readily accept that learning a foreign language is difficult.*

reluctantly/grudgingly accept sth (=unwillingly) *She didn't like him, but she grudgingly accepted that he did a good job.*

blindly/unquestioningly accept sth *disapproving* (=without thinking or asking questions) *You shouldn't blindly accept what other people say.*

PHRASES

accept sth at face value (=accept something without thinking that there may be a hidden meaning) *He accepted this information at face value.*

have no choice but to accept sth *I had no choice but to accept the judge's decision.*

acceptable *adj* good enough or satisfactory

ADVERBS

completely/totally/entirely/fully acceptable *His suggestion sounds totally acceptable to me.*

quite acceptable *If you can't get fresh mangoes, then dried ones are quite acceptable.*

perfectly acceptable (=completely acceptable – often used when you disagree with

A

someone) *Some people think that it is perfectly acceptable to wear shorts to work when it's hot.*
generally/widely acceptable (=most people think it is acceptable) *This idea has now become widely acceptable.*
mutually acceptable (=acceptable to both people or groups) *The talks are aimed at finding a mutually acceptable solution.*
socially/culturally acceptable *In Britain, it is socially acceptable to live with someone before you get married.*
morally/ethically acceptable *I don't think that testing drugs on prisoners is morally acceptable.*

VERBS
prove acceptable *formal* (=be found to be acceptable) *None of the solutions proved acceptable.*
make sth acceptable *They changed the ending of the movie, to make it more acceptable to young children.*
find/consider sth acceptable (*also* **deem sth acceptable** *formal*) (=think it is acceptable) *What level of pollution would you deem acceptable?*

NOUNS
an acceptable standard/level *Teaching at the school is of an acceptable standard.*
acceptable behaviour *He seems to think that it is acceptable behaviour to sleep in class.*
an acceptable solution *Building another road is not an acceptable solution for traffic problems.*
an acceptable way *We are trying to find an acceptable way of dealing with the problem.*
an acceptable alternative *We will soon run out of oil and we need to find an acceptable alternative.*

PREPOSITIONS
acceptable to sb *We want to reach a solution that is acceptable to both sides.*
acceptable for sth *A suit is acceptable clothing for a business interview.*

PHRASES
be the acceptable face of sth (=be acceptable to people who do not usually approve of that type of thing) *The singer is the acceptable face of hip-hop music.*

access [Ac] *n*
the ability to enter a place, get information or other things, or talk to someone

VERBS
have access *Everyone needs to have access to clean drinking water.*
gain/get access *The thieves used a ladder to gain access to the back of the house.*
give/offer (sb) access *I was given access to secret files.*
provide (sb with) access *They want to provide access to the internet for everyone.*
allow/grant sb access *The men should have been allowed access to a lawyer.*
deny/refuse sb access *His family have been denied access to him in jail.*
improve access *The college needs to improve access for disabled students.*
limit/restrict access *The authorities are trying to restrict access to websites which show these images.*

ADJECTIVES
immediate/quick/instant access *The card gives you instant access to up to $10,000.*
direct access *Patients should have direct access to their medical records.*
easy access *The new road gives easy access to the city centre.*
free access *There is free access to the museum.*
unlimited/unrestricted/open access *The ticket gives you unlimited access to the palace.*
good access *The airport has good access by public transport and there are buses every 10 minutes.*
full access *I was given full access to all the documents about the case.*
equal access *All groups in society should have equal access to cancer care.*
limited/restricted access *In some countries, women have limited access to education.*
unauthorized access (=access which is not officially allowed) *The lock code can be changed very simply to prevent unauthorized access.*
public access *The company tried to restrict public access to this information.*

NOUNS + access
internet/Web access *More than 25 million homes in western Europe now have internet access* (=they can use the internet).
wheelchair/disabled access (=access for people using wheelchairs or disabled people) *The cinema only has limited wheelchair access.*

PREPOSITIONS
access to sth *Hotel guests have access to the swimming pool.*

PHRASES
freedom of access *American companies want greater freedom of access to Chinese markets for their goods.*

accident *n*
a situation in which someone is injured or something is damaged

ADJECTIVES
a bad/serious accident *The road is closed after a serious accident.*
a terrible/horrific/nasty accident *Janet was badly hurt in a horrific accident a couple of years ago.*
a tragic accident *Her son was killed in a tragic accident when he was only 21.*

a major accident *News is coming in of a major rail accident.*

a minor accident *His car was involved in a minor traffic accident.*

⚠ Don't say 'a small accident'.

a fatal accident (=in which someone is killed) *Police are at the scene of a fatal accident involving a lorry and a cyclist.*

a freak accident (=a very unusual accident) *She was injured in a freak accident when she was struck by lightning.*

a hit-and-run accident (=an accident in which someone is hit by a driver who does not stop) *Her son was killed in a hit-and-run accident.*

an industrial accident *He injured his hand in an industrial accident when it was crushed by a machine.*

a nuclear accident *There was a very serious nuclear accident in Fukushima.*

VERBS

have an accident *He had an accident while cleaning his gun.*

be involved in an accident *formal*: *Two women were taken to hospital after their car was involved in an accident.*

be hurt/injured/killed etc in an accident *Several coach passengers were injured in the accident.*

prevent an accident *Steps have been taken to prevent a similar accident happening again.*

survive an accident *She was lucky to survive the accident.*

an accident happens (*also* **an accident occurs** *formal*): *No one saw the accident happen.*

NOUNS + accident

a car accident *He was badly injured in a car accident.*

a road/traffic accident *They were killed in a traffic accident in France.*

a rail accident/a train accident *It was the country's most serious rail accident.*

a plane accident/an air accident *Holly died in a plane accident.*

accident + NOUNS

accident rates/statistics *Jets have one of the worst accident rates among military aircraft.*

an accident investigation/inquiry *Accident investigations often take months.*

accident prevention *The local authorities have just introduced an accident prevention scheme.*

PHRASES

the scene of an accident (=the place where it happened) *An ambulance soon arrived at the scene of the accident.*

the cause of the accident *The cause of the accident is thought to have been engine failure.*

at the time of the accident *At the time of the accident, 135 men were underground.*

THESAURUS: accident

crash
car crash | **plane crash** | **train crash**
a serious accident involving a car, plane, train etc:
His sister died in a car crash. | *Seven people have been injured in a train crash.*

collision
an accident in which two or more cars, trains etc hit each other:
Their car was involved in a ***head-on collision*** *with a lorry.* | *There have been reports of a* ***mid-air collision*** *between a military plane and an airliner.* | *He escaped unhurt from a* ***high-speed collision*** *with another racing driver.*

disaster
a serious accident involving a train, plane, or boat, in which a lot of people are killed or injured:
The Munich ***air disaster*** *took place on 6 February 1958.* | *Police are interviewing the driver of the train blamed for the Belgian* ***rail disaster****.*

wreck *AmE*
an accident in which a car or train is badly damaged:
He was killed in a ***car wreck*** *in Arizona.* | *This is the country's fourth fatal* ***train wreck*** *in three and a half years.*

pile-up
an accident that involves several cars or other vehicles:
Four people were injured in a ***multiple pile-up*** *involving a minibus and five cars in thick fog.* | *There was a 12-car pile-up on the motorway.*

accidental *adj*

happening without being planned or intended

NOUNS

accidental damage *It is difficult to see how this damage could have been accidental.*

accidental death *The court recorded a verdict of accidental death.*

accidental loss *The insurance policy protects you against accidental loss.*

accidental killing/shooting *He expressed deep regret over the accidental killing of innocent civilians.*

accidental injury *The insurance policy covers you against accidental injury.*

an accidental discovery *The invention was an accidental discovery.*

ADVERBS

purely/completely accidental *Do you think it was purely accidental, or do you think she wanted to cause trouble?*

A

THESAURUS: accidental

unintentional
comedy | humour | irony | death
unintentional means the same as **accidental**, but is more formal:
The film is full of unintentional humour. | The nets caused widespread unintentional deaths of dolphins and other sea creatures. | The company was committing an offence, even if it was unintentional.

unintended
consequence | effect | impact | result | outcome
unintended consequences and results are accidental:
Government decisions can sometimes have unintended consequences. | The new tax may have the unintended effect of making unhealthy foods cost less. | The unintended result of building bigger roads is that people use their cars more.

inadvertent *formal*
error | omission | use
accidental - often used about mistakes:
The problem was caused by an inadvertent error. | The paper apologized for the inadvertent omission of his name from the article. | The inadvertent use of an incorrect word can lead to serious misunderstandings.

In everyday English you often say that someone did something **by accident** or **accidentally**: *She found out about it* ***by accident***.
You can also say that something **was an accident**: *Investigators believe that her death was an accident.*

ANTONYMS **accidental → deliberate**

accommodation [Ac] *n*

a place for someone to stay, live, or work

Grammar
In American English, the plural form **accommodations** is often used. In British English, however, people only use the uncountable form **accommodation**.

ADJECTIVES

rented accommodation *It can be difficult to find cheap rented accommodation in the middle of the city.*
furnished/unfurnished accommodation (=with or without furniture) *More cheap furnished accommodation is required for the town's student population.*
living/residential accommodation (=a place where people can live) *We obtained permission to convert the barn into living accommodation.*
sleeping accommodation *There is sleeping accommodation for 25 people at a small hotel in the village.*
temporary accommodation *He will have to stay in temporary accommodation until permanent housing can be provided for him.*
free accommodation *Although the job is not very well paid, the employers do provide free accommodation.*
suitable accommodation *It can be problematic finding suitable accommodation for physically disabled people.*
alternative accommodation *If your hotel room is not satisfactory, the company will do its best to provide alternative accommodation of a similar standard.*

NOUNS + accommodation

hotel accommodation *He gave us a list of hotel accommodation.*
student accommodation *The university provides some student accommodation on campus.*

VERBS

look for/seek accommodation *Ideally, we're looking for accommodation within travelling distance of the conference centre.*
find accommodation *Our guide found some accommodation for us in the village.*
rent accommodation *Students rent accommodation in the streets around the university.*
provide/offer accommodation *The city provides accommodation for homeless people.*

accommodation + NOUNS

accommodation costs/expenses *When planning your holiday, you need to budget for accommodation costs as well as food and travel.*

In everyday English, people often say **I'm looking for somewhere to live/stay** instead of 'I'm looking for accommodation'.

accomplish *v* THESAURUS achieve

accomplished *adj* THESAURUS skilful

account *n*

1 a written or spoken description of a situation or of something that happened

VERBS

give an account (*also* **provide an account** *formal*): *He gave an account of his meeting with the prime minister.*
write an account *Greene wrote an entertaining account of the affair.*
publish an account *Orwell's account of the war was published in his book 'Homage to Catalonia'.*

ADJECTIVES/NOUNS + account

a detailed account *The book contains a detailed account of the history of the island.*

a full account (=including everything) *It is not possible to give a full account of everything that happened on that day.*

a short/brief account *He gave a brief account of his recent visit to Budapest.*

a true/accurate account *Do you think the article is an accurate account of what happened?*

a vivid account (=one that is so clear that it seems real) *The movie gives a vivid account of life in India.*

a graphic account (=one that gives clear and shocking details) *She published a graphic account of her experiences during the civil war.*

a first-hand account (=from someone who has experienced something) *The author gives us a first-hand account of life in the refugee camps.*

an eye-witness account (=from someone who saw an event) *The man gave an eye-witness account of the explosion.*

a blow-by-blow account (=one describing everything that happened in the order it happened) *She gave us a blow-by-blow account of her meeting with the boss.*

PREPOSITIONS

an account of sth *He was too shocked to give an account of what had happened.*

in an account *He includes these details in his account of the battle.*

2 an arrangement in which a bank keeps your money for you

VERBS

have an account *Do you have a bank account?*

open/close an account *She opened an account at her local bank.*

pay money into an account *Terry said he would pay the money into my account.*

take money out of an account/withdraw money from an account *When was the last time you took money out of your account?*

credit an account (=the bank pays money in) *The interest on your investment will be credited to your account.*

debit an account (=the bank takes money out) *Please authorize the bank to debit your account.*

ADJECTIVES/NOUNS + account

a bank account *He had $850 in his bank account.*

a current account *BrE*, **a checking account** *AmE* (=one that you can take money out of at any time) *I paid the money into my current account.*

a savings/deposit account (=one in which you keep money for a long time) *I think you should put the money in a savings account.*

a joint account *She has a joint account with her husband.*

a personal account *He withdrew £40 from his personal account.*

an account is overdrawn (=you have taken out more money than is in the account) *Your account is overdrawn by $50.*

account + NOUNS

an account number *Write your account number on the reverse of the cheque.*

an account holder *You have to be an account holder in order to use this service.*

an account balance/the balance on your account (=the amount of money in an account) *Your account balance is £656.78.*

account details *Never give your account details over the phone.*

PREPOSITIONS

an account at/with a bank *He opened an account with the Royal Bank of Scotland.*

accuracy Ac *n*

the ability to do something in an accurate or exact way

> **Grammar**
> **Accuracy** is often used in the phrase **with accuracy**.

VERBS

measure sth with accuracy *These tiny movements can be measured with incredible accuracy.*

predict sth with accuracy *It is impossible to predict with complete accuracy what will happen next.*

determine/establish sth with accuracy *Satellite navigation equipment makes it possible to determine your position with great accuracy.*

check/verify/assess the accuracy of sth *How can we check the accuracy of these figures?*

question/doubt the accuracy of sth *Some people questioned the accuracy of the research on climate change.*

improve/increase the accuracy of sth *The new equipment will greatly improve the accuracy of the data.*

ADJECTIVES

with great/remarkable accuracy *He described the symptoms of the disease with great accuracy.*

with complete/absolute accuracy *They predicted the result of the game with complete accuracy.*

with deadly accuracy (=very accurately, causing death or a lot of damage) *The planes hit their target with deadly accuracy.*

with pinpoint accuracy (=finding or hitting something with very great accuracy) *The device helps you find your location with pinpoint accuracy.*

with unerring accuracy (=always very accurately) *He always hits the ball with unerring accuracy.*

historical/scientific/technical accuracy *There is a lack of scientific accuracy in some news reports.*

PREPOSITIONS

with accuracy *It is impossible to predict the weather with complete accuracy.*

PHRASES

a degree/level of accuracy *Teachers can predict who will pass an exam with a high degree of accuracy.*

accurate [Ac] *adj*

correct and true in every detail

NOUNS

accurate information/data/figures *Not all the information that you read on the internet is accurate.*

an accurate description/account/record *The brochure tries to give a fair and accurate description of each hotel.*

an accurate picture/reflection/representation of sth (=show accurately what something is like) *These statistics give an accurate picture of the problem of unemployment.*

an accurate assessment of sth *He was able to give an accurate assessment of the situation.*

an accurate way/method of doing sth *There is no accurate way of knowing if she is telling the truth.*

an accurate measurement *Make sure that all your measurements are accurate.*

an accurate estimate/prediction *It is difficult to make an accurate estimate of the number of illegal workers.*

ADVERBS

very/highly/remarkably accurate *The scientists used a highly accurate measuring system.*

fairly/reasonably/pretty accurate *The measurements are usually fairly accurate.*

not strictly/completely/entirely accurate (=not exactly accurate) *The evidence she gave to the court was not strictly accurate.*

factually accurate (=the facts are all correct) *Everything in the article is factually accurate.*

historically accurate (=exactly like something that existed in the past) *The costumes designed for the film were historically accurate.*

broadly accurate (=mostly accurate) *His account is broadly accurate.*

VERBS

prove accurate (=be shown to be accurate) *The scientists' forecasts about global warming have proved accurate.*

PREPOSITIONS

accurate to (within) a millimetre/a second etc *The clock is accurate to one thousandth of a second.*

THESAURUS: accurate

accurate, undeniable/indisputable → **true (1)**

accusation *n*

a statement saying that someone is guilty of a crime or of doing something wrong

VERBS

make an accusation *A number of serious accusations have been made.*

bring an accusation against sb (=make an accusation, especially in a court) *The accusation against him was brought by one of his employees.*

level an accusation against sb *formal* (=make an accusation - used especially when someone is criticized for what they have done) *The accusation often levelled against bankers is that they get paid far too much money.*

face an accusation *The mayor faces accusations of corruption.*

deny an accusation *He denied accusations that he had cheated.*

reject/dismiss an accusation *Smith rejects accusations that he was involved in the man's disappearance.*

prove/support an accusation *There were very few facts to support the accusation against him.*

ADJECTIVES

a serious accusation *The accusations which the senator faces are extremely serious.*

a false accusation *Teachers sometimes have false accusations made against them by students.*

an unfounded/groundless/baseless accusation (=untrue and made without good reason) *The company insists that all the accusations are unfounded.*

a wild accusation (=one made without thought or without knowing all the facts) *He dismissed their claims as wild accusations.*

bitter accusations *There were bitter accusations from both sides of the dispute.*

PREPOSITIONS

accusations of sth *Three police officers face accusations of brutality.*

an accusation against sb *She rejects all of the accusations against her.*

accuse *v*

to say that you believe someone is guilty of a crime or of doing something bad

ADVERBS

wrongly/falsely accuse sb *Nichols claims that he was wrongly accused.*

unfairly/unjustly accuse sb *He is an innocent man who has been unjustly accused.*

wrongfully accuse sb (=in a way that is unfair or illegal) *The actress plays an innocent woman* *who is wrongfully accused of murdering her husband.*

publicly/openly accuse sb *She publicly accused the president of lying to voters.*

repeatedly accuse sb (=accuse someone many times) *These firms have been repeatedly accused of polluting the environment.*

practically accuse sb (=almost accuse someone) *Rebecca practically accused me of starting the fire.*

PREPOSITIONS

accuse sb of sth *The two men are accused of murder.*

accuse sb of doing sth *He accused them of stealing his work.*

PHRASES

stand accused of sth (=be accused of doing something) *Several members of the committee stand accused of taking bribes.*

accustomed *adj*

if you are accustomed to something, you have experienced it many times before, or for a long time, so that it seems normal

VERBS

become/get/grow accustomed to sth *Her eyes quickly became accustomed to the dark.*

ADVERBS

quite/well accustomed (=very accustomed) *She was obviously well accustomed to being the centre of attention.*

long accustomed (=for a long time) *He had long been accustomed to criticism of his work.*

PREPOSITIONS

accustomed to sth *I'm accustomed to criticism of my work.*

achieve Ac *v*

to succeed in doing or getting what you wanted, especially by working hard

NOUNS

achieve your goal/target/aim *He had achieved his goal of teaching at a university.*

achieve your ambition/dream *She has at last achieved her ambition of becoming world champion.*

achieve success *Streisand achieved success as a singer.*

achieve a standard/level *Students are expected to achieve high standards.*

achieve a result/effect *He achieved the result he had intended.*

achieve a feat (=achieve something very impressive) *Redgrave achieved the remarkable feat of winning five gold medals.*

achieve independence *Venezuela achieved independence from Spain in 1830.*

achieve your potential (=achieve the level of skill that it is possible for you to achieve) *We try to help young people achieve their full potential.*

VERBS

fail to achieve sth *The sales team failed to achieve their objectives.*

help sb (to) achieve sth *I love helping brides achieve their dreams.*

PHRASES

be difficult/hard/impossible to achieve *Political progress is going to be very difficult to achieve.*

it is possible to achieve sth *It might be possible to achieve greater efficiency.*

THESAURUS: achieve

accomplish
goal | aim | objective | task | feat | mission
to achieve something, especially something difficult. **Accomplish** is more formal than **achieve** and is used especially in written English:
To accomplish this goal, he brought together thousands of the country's top scientists and engineers. | *He scored over 2,000 goals. No other player has accomplished this feat* (=used when someone has done something very impressive). | *The soldiers have less than two months in which to accomplish their mission.*

attain *formal*
level | grade | standard | degree | rank | goal | objective
to achieve something, especially a level or goal. **Attain** is more formal than **achieve** or **accomplish**:
Over half of boys leave school without attaining a basic level of written English. | *Most of the students attained a grade C or higher.* | *You need to be very determined if you want to succeed in attaining your goals.*

reach
target | goal | decision | verdict | agreement | compromise
to achieve a target or goal, or to achieve something after discussing or thinking about it:
The university will reach its target of having over 5,000 students. | *The company hopes to reach its goal of a 10% increase in sales.* | *They were unable to reach a decision.* | *The jury took two hours to reach a verdict.* | *The two sides have finally reached an agreement.*

realize (*also* **realise** *BrE*)
ambition | dream | vision | potential
to achieve something, especially something that you wanted to do:
Gandhi was close to realizing his dream of leading his country to independence. | *It is only now that she is beginning to realize her full potential as a player* (=achieve the level of skill that it is possible for her to achieve).

A

achievement *n*

something important that you succeed in doing

ADJECTIVES

a great/fine/impressive achievement *His greatest achievement was to win an Olympic gold medal.*

a major/important/significant achievement *Writing the book was a major achievement.*

a remarkable/extraordinary/amazing achievement *The victory was an extraordinary achievement.*

VERBS

be an achievement *She came second out of 1,000 people, which is an amazing achievement.*

represent an achievement *formal* (=be an achievement) *The increase in profits represents a great achievement in such difficult economic times.*

recognize/acknowledge sb's achievements (=notice and reward them) *Her achievements were never recognized in her lifetime.*

celebrate sb's achievements *Prize Day is an occasion to celebrate students' achievements.*

acquaintance *n*

someone you know, but who is not a close friend

ADJECTIVES/NOUNS + acquaintance

an old acquaintance *I met an old acquaintance outside the museum.*

a casual acquaintance *He nodded at her, as if she was just a casual acquaintance.*

a personal acquaintance *Many people said that they obtained their jobs through a personal acquaintance.*

a mutual acquaintance (=someone you both know separately) *They were introduced to each other by a mutual acquaintance.*

a business acquaintance *We are business acquaintances of your husband.*

PHRASES

an acquaintance of mine/his etc *He introduced me to an acquaintance of his, who had visited Tokyo.*

friends and acquaintances *Ask your friends and acquaintances if they know of any job vacancies.*

acquire [Ac] *v formal* to get or buy something

ADVERBS

sb recently acquired sth *The gallery recently acquired a painting by Picasso.*

newly acquired *She was trying to decide what to do with her newly acquired wealth.*

acquire sth easily *Extremist groups can easily acquire materials for making a bomb.*

suddenly acquire sth *When his mother married again, he suddenly acquired a new family.*

THESAURUS: acquire

receive, obtain, acquire, gain, win, earn, inherit, get hold of sth → **get (1)**

action *n*

1 the process of doing something, especially in order to achieve a particular thing

VERBS

take action (=do something) *The government must take action to control inflation.*

call for/demand action *Voters are demanding tougher action on gun crime.*

swing/spring/leap into action (=suddenly start doing something) *The fire crew immediately swung into action.*

put sth into action (=start doing something you have planned to do) *She was looking forward to putting her plans into action.*

ADJECTIVES

immediate/prompt/swift action *Without immediate action, the company will go bankrupt.*

firm/tough action *Environmental groups want tougher action on pollution.*

decisive action (=that has a big effect on the way something develops) *We are urging the international community to take decisive action on debt relief.*

drastic action (=that has a very severe effect) *The president decided to take drastic action.*

further action *No further action is necessary.*

appropriate action (=that is suitable for the situation) *Schools should take appropriate action to deal with bullying.*

direct action (=things that people to do in order to protest about something, especially in order to prevent a government or company from doing something) *Local people are preparing to take direct action to prevent any mining on the island.*

political action *Some forms of political action are more effective than others.*

joint action (=that two or more countries, organizations etc take together) *Community leaders agreed to take joint action on scientific, social, and environmental issues.*

PREPOSITIONS

action on sth *Action on global warming requires international cooperation.*

action against sth *An agreement to take joint action against drug trafficking was signed last year.*

PHRASES

a course of action (=something that you decide to do) *Have you decided on a course of action?*

a plan of action/an action plan *The general outlined his plan of action for the campaign.*

2 something that someone does

VERBS

perform an action *formal* (=do it) *This action was performed without any concern for his own safety.*

defend/justify sb's actions *The chief of police tried to justify his actions.*

ADJECTIVES

prompt/swift actions (=quick actions) *Her prompt actions probably saved my life.*

PHRASES

hold sb responsible for their actions (=decide that someone can be punished if they have done anything wrong) *The child was too young to be held responsible for his actions.*

activity *n* things that people do

ADJECTIVES/NOUNS + activity

leisure activities (=things that you do for enjoyment) *She doesn't have much time for leisure activities.*

cultural activities *There is plenty of opportunity for children to get involved in cultural activities.*

classroom/school activities *Amelia had lost interest in school activities and didn't attend the school prom.*

outdoor activities *The college is well situated for students who are interested in outdoor activities.*

physical/mental activity *Regular physical activity helps to control your weight.*

criminal/illegal activity *The bar was being used for illegal activities.*

political/economic activity *Political activity is closely controlled by the government.*

business/commercial activity *Internet shopping is a rapidly developing area of business activity.*

military activity *There has been an increase in military activity in the area.*

human activity *There was no sign of any human activity.*

VERBS

take part in an activity *The children were encouraged to take part in several different activities.*

engage in/participate in an activity *formal* (=take part) *Police suspect he may have engaged in criminal activities.*

be involved in an activity *The men were involved in terrorist activities.*

do an activity *He doesn't do a lot of physical activity.*

⚠ Don't say 'make an activity'. Say **take part in an activity** or **be involved in an activity**.

PHRASES

the level of activity *The level of economic activity has increased.*

a flurry of activity (=a time when people are suddenly very busy) *The morning passed by in a flurry of activity.*

a burst of activity (=a sudden increase in activity) *Your muscles need to be strong enough to handle sudden bursts of activity.*

a hive of activity (=a place where people are busy doing something) *The kitchen was a hive of activity.*

actor *n*

someone who performs in plays or films

ADJECTIVES

a good/fine/great actor *He had a reputation as a fine actor.*

a talented/accomplished actor (=very good) *Daniel Radcliffe is a talented young actor.*

a well-known/famous actor *Tom Cruise is a very famous actor.*

a struggling actor (=one who is not getting many jobs) *We shared a house when we were both struggling actors.*

an aspiring actor (=someone who wants to be an actor) *Every year aspiring actors arrive in Hollywood looking for work.*

a professional actor *The plays will be recorded in a studio with professional actors.*

an amateur actor (=one who is not paid) *The play will be performed by local amateur actors.*

the leading/principal actor (=the person playing the most important part) *Who was the leading actor in 'The Sound of Music'?*

a supporting actor (=the person playing the second most important part) *She was awarded an Oscar for Best Supporting Actor.*

NOUNS + actor

a film/movie actor *Joe wanted to be a movie actor from an early age.*

a television/TV actor *For several years he had small parts as a television actor.*

a stage actor *Stage actors are often badly paid.*

a Hollywood actor *Hollywood actor Michael Douglas will be on the show to talk about his latest movie.*

a character actor (=one who plays unusual characters, rather than the most important characters) *As a character actor you get to play some interesting parts.*

a child actor *As a child actor, he played the role of Harry Potter.*

a comedy actor (=one who acts in funny plays and films) *Jason was voted top TV comedy actor.*

VERBS

an actor plays a part/role/character *The 31-year-old actor plays the role of Albert.*

an actor performs a play/scene *The actors performed the scene in full costume.*

an actor rehearses (for) sth (=practises for a play or film) *The actors are busy rehearsing for the opening night of the play.*

A

A

Actor or actress?
The word **actor** can be used about both men and women. Women who appear in plays and films prefer to be called **actors**. However, in everyday English, many people often still use **actor** about a man, and **actress** about a woman.

actress *n*

a woman who performs in plays or films

ADJECTIVES

a good/fine/great actress *Judy Garland was a truly great actress.*

a talented/accomplished actress (=very good) *Hurley is a highly talented actress.*

a well-known/famous actress *Lenya became a famous actress in the 1930s.*

a professional actress *She has been a professional actress for over thirty years.*

the leading/principal actress (=the woman playing the most important part) *Zhou Xun won the Best Leading Actress Award for her role in the film.*

a supporting actress (=a woman playing the second most important part) *Huston won an Oscar as best supporting actress in 1985.*

an aspiring actress (=someone who wants to be an actress) *Marilyn was an aspiring young actress.*

NOUNS + actress

a film/stage/television actress *Gish was the finest film actress of her generation.*

a Hollywood actress *She looked like a glamorous Hollywood actress.*

a child actress *Susan was a former child actress, making her first film at the age of four.*

a comedy actress (=one who acts in funny plays and films) *The film stars comedy actress Goldie Hawn.*

VERBS

an actress plays a part/role/character *Lynd is played by French actress Eva Green.*

acute *adj* THESAURUS ▶ **bad (2)**

adapt *v* THESAURUS ▶ **change[1] (1), (2)**

addict *n*

1 someone who likes something very much and does it a lot

NOUNS + addict

a (computer) games addict *Ken is a computer games addict and he spends most evenings on his computer.*

a chocolate/caffeine addict *Some caffeine addicts will drink eight or ten cups a day.*

a TV addict *The British are a nation of TV addicts.*

a news addict *The show is aimed at news addicts.*

a soap opera addict *She is a soap opera addict and she always knows what has been happening to all the characters.*

THESAURUS: addict

junkie
news junkie | political junkie | media junkie | sports junkie
someone who is very interested in a particular subject and is always watching programs or reading about it:
a 24 hour news channel for news junkies | Political junkies will be staying up all night to watch the election results come in.

Junkie, **fanatic**, and **~aholic** all sound rather informal.

fanatic
fitness fanatic | sports fanatic | baseball fanatic | football fanatic | cricket fanatic | crossword fanatic
someone who likes something very much, especially sports or games, and does it a lot:
He is a fitness fanatic and he spends three hours a day at the gym. | Our family are all sports fanatics.

~aholic
workaholic | shopaholic | chocoholic
used in words about people who do something too much:
My dad was a workaholic and he sometimes worked 80 hours a week (=someone who is always working). *| Shopaholics will love the new shopping mall* (=someone who loves shopping). *| Don't leave the box anywhere near Kevin – he's a chocoholic and it will be gone in a few minutes* (=someone who loves eating chocolate).

~aholic comes from **alcoholic**.

2 someone who is unable to stop taking drugs

ADJECTIVES/NOUNS + addict

a drug addict *The project helps drug addicts to find their way back into normal society.*

a cocaine/heroin addict *Heroin addicts often steal to get money to buy drugs.*

VERBS

treat/help an addict *The charity runs a home for treating drug addicts.*

address *n*

the details of where someone lives, where a company, school etc is, or the details of someone's email account

ADJECTIVES/NOUNS + address

sb's old/new address *What's your new address?*

sb's email address *My email address is chrisfox@pearson.com.*

sb's home/private address *I sent the letter to his home address.*

sb's work/business/school address *My business address is on my card.*

a web/website address *Just type in the web address.*

a full address *You need to give your full address, including the postcode.*

a forwarding address (=a new address for sending mail to when you move from your old address) *They moved without leaving a forwarding address.*

a false/fake address *He gave the police a false address.*

VERBS

give sb your address *She refused to give me her address.*

have/know sb's address *Do you know Helen's address?*

lose sb's address *I wanted to write to him, but I've lost his address.*

change your address *Please notify the school if you change your address.*

PREPOSITIONS

at an address *We've been at this address for over ten years.*

the address of sb/sth *Do you know the address of the school?*

adequate Ac *adj*

enough for a particular purpose

ADVERBS

barely/hardly adequate (=not really adequate) *The roads are barely adequate to cope with the amount of traffic.*

quite adequate/perfectly adequate (=completely adequate – used for emphasis) *The amount of food was quite adequate for the number of guests.*

more than adequate *The safety measures were found to be more than adequate.*

VERBS

consider sth to be adequate/regard sth as adequate *Thirty minutes of gentle exercise each day is considered to be adequate by most doctors.*

PREPOSITIONS

adequate for sth *The house was small, but it was perfectly adequate for my needs.*

THESAURUS: adequate

sufficient, adequate, ample, plenty → **enough**

adjourn *v*

to stop an official meeting for a short time

Grammar
Usually passive.

NOUNS

adjourn a meeting *We decided to adjourn the meeting until the following week.*

adjourn a trial/case/hearing *The judge can adjourn the trial to allow the prisoner to receive medical treatment.*

ADVERBS

adjourn sth indefinitely (=used when you do not know when something will start again) *The case has been adjourned indefinitely while new evidence is being examined.*

PREPOSITIONS

adjourn sth until tomorrow/next week etc *The meeting will be adjourned until next month.*

adjust *v* THESAURUS change[1] (2)

admiration *n*

a feeling of great respect and liking for something or someone

ADJECTIVES

great/deep admiration *I have great admiration for his work.*

profound admiration (=very great admiration) *Bacon expressed his profound admiration for Picasso's paintings.*

genuine/real admiration *"Your mother is a remarkable woman," said John with genuine admiration in his voice.*

grudging/reluctant admiration (=unwilling admiration) *She has won grudging admiration from her rivals.*

a sneaking admiration for sb (=you secretly admire someone) *He had always had a sneaking admiration for his opponent.*

open admiration (=you do not try to hide your admiration) *Her father looked at her in open admiration.*

mutual admiration (=that two or more people feel for each other) *Their friendship was based on mutual admiration.*

VERBS

have great/deep etc admiration *They have the greatest admiration for his music.*

be filled with admiration/be full of admiration *I'm full of admiration for what you've done.*

win/earn sb's admiration *His films have won him the admiration of the critics.*

express/show your admiration *The mayor expressed his admiration for the Cuban leader.*

PREPOSITIONS

admiration for sb/sth *His son was full of admiration for him.*

A

in/with admiration *Daniel gazed at her in admiration.*

admire *v*

to think that someone or something is good

> **Grammar**
> **Admire** is not used in the progressive. Don't say 'I am admiring him.' Say **I admire him.**

ADVERBS

greatly admire (=very much) *He greatly admired Wordsworth's poems.*
be much admired *Her books are much admired in the US.*
be widely/universally admired (=by many people) *Hunt was widely admired by his fellow pilots.*
secretly admire *Although what he did was wrong, many people secretly admired him.*
particularly admire *We contacted artists whose work we particularly admired.*

PREPOSITIONS

admire sb/sth for sth *He admired them for their determination.*

PHRASES

you can't help but admire/you have to admire (=used when saying that someone or something deserves to be admired) *You can't help but admire his courage.*

admirer *n* THESAURUS fan

admission *n*

1 the act of going into a place, or the amount that you pay to go in

ADJECTIVES/NOUNS + admission

free admission *Admission is free on Sundays.*
half-price admission *There is half-price admission for children.*

VERBS

refuse/deny sb admission *He was refused admission to law school.*
seek admission (=ask to enter) *She was advised by her doctor to seek admission to hospital.*
gain admission (=succeed in entering a place) *A large crowd was struggling to gain admission to the exhibition.*
include admission *The ticket price includes admission to the museum.*
apply for admission *The document explains how to apply for admission to a university.*

admission + NOUNS

an admission charge/fee *There is an admission charge to go into the gallery.*
the admission price/price of admission *The admission price includes a ride on the steam train.*
the admissions criteria (=the set of rules used to decide who can join a college or other organization) *The college changed its admissions criteria to encourage a wider range of students to study there.*

PREPOSITIONS

admission to sth *Admission to the gallery is £2.*
on admission (=when you go in) *You can pay on admission.*

2 a statement in which you admit that something is true or that you have done something wrong

PHRASES

an admission of guilt/failure/defeat/responsibility/liability *His statement was an admission of guilt.*
by/on sb's own admission (=based on someone's own words) *By her own admission, she lied about the incident.*

ADJECTIVES

a frank admission *We weren't expecting such a frank admission from him.*

VERBS

make an admission *I have an admission to make – I didn't tell you everything that happened last night.*

admit *v*

to agree that something is true, especially when you do not want to do this, or to say that you have done something wrong or illegal

ADVERBS

freely/openly/readily admit sth (=admit something without being ashamed) *The star freely admits that he has made mistakes in the past.*

VERBS

have to admit/be forced to admit sth *In the end, she had to admit that she was wrong.*
refuse to admit sth *The company refused to admit that they had caused the problem.*

PREPOSITIONS

admit to sb *He later admitted to me that he was lying.*
admit to (doing) sth *People will not admit to illegal activities because they are afraid of being punished.*

PHRASES

be willing/prepared/ready to admit sth *The chairman said he was willing to admit that there had been some problems.*
be ashamed to admit sth *David was ashamed to admit that he had lied to his parents.*
be reluctant/loath to admit sth (=not want to admit something) *I'm loath to admit it, but you're probably right.*

I must admit/I have to admit *spoken* (=used when saying that you admit that something is true) *I must admit, I had my doubts at first.*

I hate to admit it, but... *spoken: I hate to admit it, but her cake tastes better than mine.*

adolescent *adj* THESAURUS ▶ **young**

adopt *v*

1 to start to use a plan or method

> **Grammar**
> Often passive.

NOUNS

adopt an approach *It's a shame that this approach isn't adopted by more companies.*

adopt a method *We got better results when a different method of raising money was adopted.*

adopt a policy/strategy *The protesters adopted a policy of non-violence.*

ADVERBS

be widely/generally adopted (=be adopted by many people) *Her classic costume designs were widely adopted throughout Hollywood.*

be universally adopted (=be adopted by everybody) *This method of teaching children to read was soon universally adopted.*

be enthusiastically adopted *The policy was enthusiastically adopted by the new government.*

2 to accept a proposal at a meeting

> **Grammar**
> Often passive.

NOUNS

adopt a proposal/motion/resolution *The motion to go on strike was adopted by a clear majority of workers.*

ADVERBS

be officially/formally adopted *Resolutions are formally adopted by a simple majority vote.*

be adopted unanimously (=by everyone at a meeting) *A proposal must be adopted unanimously in order to become company policy.*

adult[1] Ac *n*

a fully grown person or animal

ADJECTIVES

a young adult *The novel is aimed at young adults.*

a healthy adult *The risk of catching the disease is rare for healthy adults.*

a responsible adult (=someone who can be trusted to look after someone) *Children can watch the movie, if they are accompanied by a responsible adult.*

a mature adult (=one who behaves sensibly) *Let's discuss this like mature adults.*

VERBS

become an adult *When we become adults we tend to think we've learnt everything we need to know.*

adult + NOUNS

sb's adult life *She spent most of her adult life in Africa.*

adult education/training *The demand for evening classes and other forms of adult education has increased.*

adult supervision (=adults watching children to make sure they are safe and behave well) *Young children are not allowed to play on the beach without adult supervision.*

adult[2] Ac *adj* fully grown or developed

NOUNS

an adult male/female *One in three adult males in this area is unemployed.*

an adult man/woman *Nine out of ten adult women work or study full-time outside the home.*

the adult population *Smokers have been a minority in the adult population since 1976.*

an adult child/son/daughter *She is married, with four adult children.*

advance *n*

a change or discovery that brings progress

ADJECTIVES

a great/huge/major advance *The discovery represents a major advance in cancer treatment.*

an important/significant advance *The school has made important advances in dealing with deaf children.*

a medical/scientific/technological/technical advance *The development of the drug has been a huge medical advance.*

VERBS

make an advance *The two groups have made an important advance towards working together.*

PREPOSITIONS

advances in science/technology etc *Communication has been transformed by advances in technology.*

advanced *adj*

1 using very modern technology and ideas

NOUNS

advanced technology/techniques *The company uses the most advanced technology available.*

an advanced country/society/civilization *Pay is higher in advanced industrial countries.*

an advanced economy *The US has a greater capacity to create jobs than any other advanced economy.*

an advanced system *The ship is equipped with an advanced missile defense system.*

A

advanced features *The phone has several advanced features, including a high-resolution video camera.*

advanced equipment *Advanced equipment is used at airports to check people's bags.*

advanced weapons *Britain has been supplying the country with advanced weapons including fighter aircraft.*

ADVERBS

highly advanced *The communications system is highly advanced.*

technologically/technically advanced *Japan is one of the world's most technologically advanced countries.*

THESAURUS: advanced

sophisticated
equipment | technology | system | way | method | approach | technique | weapon
advanced - used about equipment, systems etc that are cleverly designed but also complicated:
Sophisticated medical equipment saved his life. | This technique requires extremely sophisticated methods of analysis. | The weapons used by terrorists are becoming more and more sophisticated.

highly developed
economy | society | industry | system | sense | skill | understanding
good and effective compared to other countries, people, or animals:
It is a feature of highly developed societies that they place great value on educating young people. | New Zealand has a highly developed tourism industry. | The dog has a highly developed sense of smell.

high-tech/hi-tech
equipment | device | goods | products | weapons | industry | company | firm | business
using very advanced technology, especially electronic equipment and computers:
High-tech listening equipment was used to find survivors from the earthquake. | Many hi-tech industries are based in Silicon Valley.

state-of-the-art
technology | equipment | software | facilities | system | drug | kitchen
using the newest and most advanced features, ideas, and materials that are available:
Its factory uses state-of-the-art technology. | The football club has invested £40 million in state-of-the-art training facilities. | The sound system is state-of-the-art.

cutting-edge
technology | research | design
cutting-edge technology or research is the most advanced that there is at this time:
The building uses cutting-edge technology to cut energy consumption. | He has been involved in cutting-edge medical research.

THESAURUS: advanced

advanced, up-to-date, high-tech/hi-tech, state-of-the-art, new-fangled → modern (2)

2 studying a subject at a high level, or having a high level of skill

NOUNS

an advanced student *The class is for advanced students of English.*

an advanced course *The college has an advanced course in jewellery design.*

advanced level *At six he could solve complicated mathematical equations and play chess at an advanced level.*

an advanced certificate/diploma/qualification *Staff have to take an advanced certificate in food hygiene.*

advantage *n*

something good that helps someone or something to be more successful than others

ADJECTIVES

a big/great/major advantage *It's a great advantage to be able to speak some Spanish.*

a slight advantage (=a small one) *Karpov enjoyed a slight advantage over his opponent.*

an unfair advantage *Companies that receive government subsidies have an unfair advantage.*

an important/significant advantage *This software has a significant advantage in that it is easy to use.*

a definite/distinct/obvious advantage *Electronic trading has a number of distinct advantages.*

a real advantage (=a definite advantage) *The new system has some real advantages.*

the main advantage *The main advantage of digital photography is that there is no film to process.*

an added advantage (=an extra advantage) *Candidates with experience in Sales and Marketing would have an added advantage.*

a political/military/financial advantage *Republicans have a political advantage in most of those areas.*

a psychological advantage *Winning the first game gives you a psychological advantage over your opponent.*

a competitive advantage (=one relating to competition) *The company's longer opening hours give it a competitive advantage.*

⚠ Don't say 'a good advantage'. Say **a big advantage** or **a real advantage**.

VERBS

have an advantage (*also* **enjoy an advantage**

formal): *Western countries enjoyed considerable advantages in terms of technology.*

get/gain an advantage *Both teams tried to get an advantage.*

give sb an advantage *His height gives him a big advantage.*

work to your advantage (=make you have an advantage - often used when this is unexpected) *Sometimes a lack of experience can work to your advantage.*

PREPOSITIONS

the advantage of sth *The advantage of this method is that it is much quicker.*

be an advantage to sb *Playing at our own stadium in front of our own fans will be an advantage to us.*

have an advantage over sb/sth *This printer has several advantages over conventional printers.*

be at an advantage (=have an advantage) *Younger workers tend to be at an advantage when applying for jobs.*

to your advantage (=in a way that helps you) *She used the information to her advantage.*

there is an advantage in doing sth *There are advantages in using rewards rather than punishments in controlling children's behaviour.*

PHRASES

the advantages and disadvantages of sth *What are the advantages and disadvantages of living in a big city?*

the advantages outweigh the disadvantages (=the advantages are more valuable) *Working from home can be lonely, but, for me, the advantages outweigh the disadvantages.*

THESAURUS: advantage

benefit
a feature of something that has a good effect on people's lives:
Regular exercise has ***great benefits****, including reducing the risk of heart disease.* | *Tourism has brought considerable* ***economic benefits*** *to the island.*

merit
a good feature that something has, which you consider when you are deciding whether it is the best choice:
The committee will ***consider the merits of*** *the proposals.* | *We discussed the* ***merits and demerits of*** *the two systems* (=their good and bad features). | *The chairman* ***saw no great merit in*** *this suggestion* (=he did not think that it was a good idea).

virtue
an advantage that makes you believe that something is a good thing:
They believed in the ***virtues of*** *culture, civilization, and reason.* | *He's always* ***extolling the virtues*** *of hard work* (=saying that hard work is a good thing).

the good/great/best thing about sth
especially spoken
used when mentioning a good feature of something. This phrase is rather informal and you should not use it in formal essays:
The good thing about *cycling is that you don't have to worry about getting stuck in a traffic jam.*

ANTONYMS **advantage → disadvantage**

adventure *n*

an exciting experience in which dangerous or unusual things happen

ADJECTIVES

an exciting adventure *In the story, he has many exciting adventures.*

a great adventure *Climbing Everest was a great adventure and a massive challenge.*

a big adventure *For the children, the holiday was all one big adventure.*

a new adventure *He was always looking for new adventures and new countries to visit.*

VERBS

be looking for/searching for/seeking adventure *India is a great place to visit if you're looking for adventure.*

tell sb about your adventures (*also* **recount your adventures** *formal*): *He recounted his adventures in China.*

start/set out on an adventure (*also* **embark on an adventure** *formal*): *I was ready to embark on another adventure.*

share an adventure (with sb) *He wished Jane was with him to share his adventures.*

adventure + NOUNS

an adventure story/novel *The writer is best known for his adventure stories.*

an adventure film/movie *I like watching adventure films, like 'Indiana Jones'.*

an adventure holiday *The company specializes in adventure holidays in faraway countries.*

PHRASES

the adventure of a lifetime *The family are setting out on the adventure of a lifetime - a journey by sea from France to Kenya.*

a sense/spirit of adventure *He loves travelling and has a keen sense of adventure.*

adventurous *adj*

THESAURUS **brave**

advertise *v*

to tell people about a product or service, in order to persuade them to buy it

ADVERBS

be heavily advertised (=be advertised a lot) *People are more likely to choose the brands that are heavily advertised.*

be widely advertised (=a lot and in many places) *Details of the concert were widely advertised.*

A

advertise nationally *The big supermarkets can afford to advertise nationally.*
advertise locally *Some employers advertise locally for new staff.*

PREPOSITIONS

advertise sth in a newspaper/magazine *I saw the course advertised in a magazine.*
advertise (sth) on TV/the internet *The games are advertised on the internet.*
be advertised as sth *The drug was advertised as a miracle cure.*
advertise for sb/sth *The college is advertising for a new principal.*

advertisement *n*

a picture, set of words, or a short film, which is intended to persuade people to buy a product or use a service

ADJECTIVES/NOUNS + advertisement

a newspaper/magazine advertisement *She saw a newspaper advertisement for a job in a design company.*
a television/radio advertisement *When a television advertisement is shown in the evening, it might be seen by up to 10 million people.*
a job advertisement *There are not many job advertisements in today's paper.*
a car/coffee etc advertisement *The magazine is full of car advertisements.*
a misleading advertisement (=making you believe something that is not true) *There are lots of misleading advertisements for beauty products, which claim they will make you stay young forever.*
a full-page/half-page advertisement *The company took out a full-page advertisement in the 'New York Times'.*
a pop-up advertisement (=one that suddenly appears on your computer screen when you are looking at a website) *The software blocks unwanted pop-up advertisements.*

VERBS

see an advertisement *I saw an advertisement for the exhibition on my way to work.*
answer an advertisement/reply to an advertisement *He answered an advertisement in 'The Times'.*
publish an advertisement *The newspaper refused to publish the advertisement.*
put/place an advertisement in a newspaper/magazine *She placed an advertisement for a cleaner in the local newspaper.*
take out an advertisement (=arrange for an advertisement to appear in a newspaper or magazine) *Their record company took out full-page advertisements in the music press to promote the album.*
an advertisement appears in sth *The advertisement appeared in 'Newsweek' magazine.*

PREPOSITIONS

an advertisement in a newspaper/magazine *Car advertisements in glossy magazines are aimed at men, not women.*
an advertisement on the television/the internet/a website *I wish they didn't have all those annoying advertisements on the internet.*
an advertisement for sth *I saw an advertisement for the course on a website.*

⚠ Don't say 'an advertisement about'.

advice *n*

an opinion you give someone about what they should do

ADJECTIVES

good/excellent/useful/helpful advice *The book is full of good advice.*
sound advice (=sensible) *I thought that this was sound advice.*
bad/poor advice *Financial advisers can be fined if they give bad advice to a client.*
advice is wrong *Unfortunately all the advice they gave me was wrong.*
practical advice *The programme aims to offer practical advice on healthy eating.*
detailed advice *The website gives detailed advice about making bombs.*
professional/expert/specialist advice *It's advisable to get professional advice before starting any building work.*
legal/medical/financial etc advice *Good legal advice can be expensive.*
independent/impartial advice (=from someone who is not involved and will not get an advantage) *The banks claim to offer independent financial advice.*

VERBS

give sb some advice *My father gave me some useful advice.*
get some advice *I decided to get some advice from a specialist.*
ask sb's advice *Can I ask your advice about something?*
ask for advice *If in doubt, always ask for advice.*
take/follow sb's advice (*also* **act on sb's advice** *formal*) (=do what someone advises you to do) *He followed his doctor's advice and went on a low-fat diet.*
listen to sb's advice (*also* **heed sb's advice** *formal*) (=pay attention to someone's advice) *I wish I had listened to her advice.*
ignore/disregard sb's advice (=not do what someone tells you) *The accident happened because she ignored their advice.*
go/turn to sb for advice *People often go to him for advice about their problems.*
seek advice (=try to get some advice) *If you have any of these symptoms, you should seek urgent advice.*

offer advice *They can offer advice to those who wish to quit drinking.*

NOUNS + advice

career(s) advice *We offer career advice and information for graduates.*

business advice *Business advice from an expert is invaluable if you are starting a company.*

PREPOSITIONS

advice on/about sth *The nurse will give you some advice on diet and exercise.*

advice from sb *You should seek professional advice from a lawyer.*

on sb's advice (=because someone has advised it) *On his lawyer's advice, he pleaded guilty to the crime.*

against sb's advice (=ignoring someone's advice) *Eva travelled to India against the advice of her doctor.*

PHRASES

a piece of advice (*also* **a bit of advice** *informal*): *Let me give you a piece of advice.*

a word of advice *spoken* (=used when advising someone what to do) *A word of advice: look at the small print in the contract very carefully.*

advise *v*

to tell someone what you think they should do

> **Grammar**
> The most common way of using **advise** is in the phrase **advise sb to do sth**: *My lawyer **advised** me **to** plead guilty. | People are **advised not to** keep large sums of money at home.*

ADVERBS

strongly advise sb to do sth *There is a limited number of seats and we strongly advise customers to buy their tickets in advance.*

be badly/wrongly advised *She now feels that she was wrongly advised by her doctor.*

be legally advised to do sth *The men have been legally advised not to say anything to the press.*

PREPOSITIONS

advise (sb) against sth (=advise someone not to do something) *The authorities are advising people against traveling to the area.*

affair *n*

1 events or activities

> **Grammar**
> Always plural in this meaning.

ADJECTIVES/NOUNS + affair

world/international/global affairs *Are you interested in international affairs?*

current affairs (=important events that are happening now) *The BBC launched a 24-hour news and current affairs channel.*

political/economic/military affairs *He was appointed Minister of State with responsibility for economic affairs.*

foreign/external affairs (=events in other countries) *She is the Secretary of State for Foreign Affairs.*

domestic/internal affairs (*also* **home affairs** *BrE*) (=events inside a country) *He said that the US should not try to interfere in his country's domestic affairs.*

public affairs (=events that affect the people of a country) *In the past, women had little role in public affairs.*

sb's private affairs (=things that are personal and not for other people to know about) *He never discussed his private affairs in public.*

financial/business affairs *They offer advice on managing your financial affairs.*

religious affairs *Jones reports on religious affairs.*

VERBS

interfere/meddle in sb's affairs *China doesn't want other countries meddling in its domestic affairs.*

PHRASES

affairs of state (=the business of the government) *The church played no role in the affairs of state.*

2 something that happens

> **Grammar**
> Usually singular in this meaning.

VERBS

deal with/handle an affair *The chairman was criticized for the way he handled the affair.*

be involved in an affair *Several leading politicians were involved in the affair.*

ADJECTIVES

a private affair *He felt that his marriage was a private affair and he didn't want any press reporters there.*

the whole affair *The whole affair has been very embarrassing for the government.*

affect Ac *v*

to cause a change in something or someone

ADVERBS

badly/seriously/severely affect *The city was badly affected by the earthquake.*

greatly/significantly affect *The attitude of the parents can greatly affect a child's progress at school.*

deeply/strongly/profoundly affect *She was deeply affected by her parents' divorce.*

directly/indirectly affect *People living near the building works will be directly affected by the extra noise and dirt.*

adversely/negatively affect (=have a bad

A

effect on something) *Sales have been adversely affected by the weather.*

hardly/barely affect (=almost not at all) *The recession has barely affected us.*

disproportionately affect (=affect one person or group much more than other people) *The tax will disproportionately affect people on low wages.*

affection *n*

a feeling that you like or love someone or something and care about them

ADJECTIVES

great/deep/strong affection *Bart had great affection for the old man.*

real/genuine affection *They treat each other with genuine affection.*

mutual affection (=between two people) *Mutual respect and affection are very important in a marriage.*

special affection *She would always think of Nigel with special affection.*

warm affection *He felt a warm affection for his cousin.*

growing affection *There was a growing affection between them.*

brotherly/sisterly/fatherly etc affection *In a burst of sisterly affection, Dana hugged me.*

VERBS

show/display/express affection *Their father never showed much affection to his children.*

give sb affection *Joe never gave her the affection she needed from him.*

feel affection/have an affection for sb *It was obvious that Simon had a great affection for her.*

be held in great affection by sb *The ancient tree was held in great affection by the people of the town.*

need/want affection (*also* **crave affection** *formal*): *The little boy craved affection from his mother.*

return sb's affection *She was in love with someone who did not return her affection.*

win/gain sb's affection (=make someone like you) *He did his best to win her affection.*

PREPOSITIONS

affection for sb/sth *He had a deep affection for his wife.*

affection towards sb *The family members do not display much affection towards each other.*

with affection *She remembered her teachers with affection.*

PHRASES

a display/show/sign/expression of affection *People often give flowers as a sign of affection.*

a feeling of affection *You could see that he still had feelings of affection for her.*

the object of sb's affection (=the person someone loves) *In the film, the object of his affection is a shy girl who works in his office.*

love and affection *Children respond much more to love and affection than they do to punishment.*

affectionate *adj*

showing that you love someone or something and care about them

ADVERBS

deeply/highly affectionate *His letters were always deeply affectionate.*

PREPOSITIONS

affectionate towards/to/with sb *Jo is very affectionate towards her brother.*

affluent *adj* THESAURUS ▶ rich (1)

affordable *adj* THESAURUS ▶ cheap

afraid *adj*

frightened or worried that something bad may happen

ADVERBS

terribly/deeply/desperately afraid *She was terribly afraid that she would forget the lines of her speech.*

always afraid *Lionel was always afraid that she would find someone else.*

deathly afraid *AmE* (=extremely afraid) *He is deathly afraid of heights.*

VERBS

be/feel afraid *I am always afraid she is going to hurt me.*

look/sound afraid *He stood up straight and tried not to look afraid.*

make sb afraid *The accident made her afraid to get in a car again.*

PREPOSITIONS

afraid of sb/sth *Many people are afraid of the dark.*

afraid for sb (=worried that something bad will happen to someone) *She was afraid for her children.*

PHRASES

don't be afraid *Don't be afraid. It's only a little dog.*

there's nothing to be afraid of/there's no need to be afraid *There's nothing to be afraid of – it's just a small injection.*

be half afraid that (=a little afraid that something might happen) *I was half afraid that she would say 'no'.*

afternoon *n*

the part of the day after the morning and before the evening

ADJECTIVES/NOUNS + afternoon

good afternoon (=used when meeting someone in the afternoon) *Good afternoon everyone!*

this/that afternoon *I have a French class this afternoon.*

tomorrow/yesterday afternoon *What are you doing tomorrow afternoon?*

Monday/Friday etc afternoon *I have arranged to meet her next Saturday afternoon.*

early/late afternoon *Mike arrived in Boston in the early afternoon.*

a sunny/hot/wet etc afternoon *It was a lovely sunny afternoon.*

a summer/spring etc afternoon *One hot summer afternoon she decided to go for a walk.*

afternoon + NOUNS

an afternoon nap (=a short sleep in the afternoon) *Dad was having his Sunday afternoon nap.*

afternoon tea *My grandma always has afternoon tea at 4 o'clock.*

VERBS

spend the afternoon *He decided to spend the afternoon in town.*

PREPOSITIONS

in the afternoon *We went swimming in the afternoon.*

on Monday/Friday etc afternoon *There's a meeting on Thursday afternoon.*

⚠ Don't say 'On the afternoon I went to Pam's house.' Say **In the afternoon I went to Pam's house.**

PHRASES

the middle of the afternoon *By the middle of the afternoon, she was tired and wanted to go home.*

take the afternoon off *I'm taking tomorrow afternoon off to do some Christmas shopping.*

age *n*

1 how old someone is

ADJECTIVES/NOUNS + age

old age *Loneliness affects many people in old age.*

middle age (=between about 40 and 60) *Smoking kills a fifth of all smokers in middle age.*

a great/advanced age (=a very old age) *My aunt died at a great age.*

a difficult/awkward age (=used mainly about the time when people are teenagers) *13-16 is often a difficult age.*

retirement age *The risk of experiencing poverty is much greater for those over retirement age.*

school age *Children should start doing homework as they approach high school age.*

school-leaving age BrE: *The government is proposing to raise the minimum school-leaving age.*

the legal age *In the UK, the legal age for buying alcohol is 18.*

the minimum age *The minimum age for driving a car is 17.*

the voting age *There are plans to bring down the voting age from 18 to 16.*

age + NOUNS

an age group/bracket/range *Men in the 50-65 age group are most at risk from heart disease.*

an age limit *There's no upper age limit for drivers.*

an age gap/difference *There's a five-year age gap between me and my husband - he's 35 and I'm 40.*

VERBS

get to/reach/live to an age *One in three children died before they reached the age of 5.*

lower/raise the age (=at which something can be done) *The voting age was lowered from 21 to 18.*

look/feel your age (=look or feel as old as you really are) *The singer is 46, but she doesn't look her age at all.*

act your age (=behave in the way that a person of your age should behave) *It's time he started acting his age.*

ask sb his/her age *It's rude to ask a woman her age.*

PREPOSITIONS

at an age *At your age, you shouldn't have any problem walking.*

of this/that/sb's age *Children of this age learn very quickly.*

by the age of *I could read by the age of five.*

the age of 5/65 etc *She left school at the age of 15.*

under/below the age of *The film is not suitable for children under the age of twelve.*

over the age of *It is difficult to get travel insurance if you are over the age of 80.*

for your age *She looks very good for her age.*

PHRASES

from an early/young age *She'd been playing the piano from a very early age.*

at an early/young age *Kids can start learning a second language at a young age.*

sb (of) your own age *He needs to play with children of his own age.*

the age of consent (=when you are legally allowed to marry or have sex) *At 15, the girl was under the age of consent.*

2 a particular period of history

ADJECTIVES/NOUNS + age

a new age *We are now entering a new age in world history.*

a golden age (=a very good or successful time) *This is a television show from the golden age of American comedy.*

a bygone age (=a time in the past, which no longer exists) *The building has the elegance and grace of a bygone age.*

A

A

the modern age *In the modern age, the British monarch does not have any real power.*
the space age *The 1960s was the dawn of the space age.*
the nuclear age *The nuclear age began in the middle of the 20th century.*
the digital age *In the digital age, people can access information from a range of different sources.*

PREPOSITIONS

in an age *We are living in the age of technology.*
the age of sth *In the age of the internet, information is very easy to find.*
through the ages *The exhibition shows the development of the castle through the ages.*

PHRASES

in this day and age (=now - used when you do not think that something should still happen or exist now) *Racist comments are not acceptable in this day and age.*

agenda *n*

1 a list of things that need to be discussed or dealt with, or that someone plans to do - used especially about politics and business

PHRASES

an item on the agenda *What is the next item on the agenda for today's meeting?*
be (at the) top of the agenda *Energy efficiency is top of the agenda.*
be high on the agenda *Dealing with terrorism is high on the government's agenda.*
be on the political agenda *Reforming the healthcare system has been on the political agenda for many years.*

VERBS

set the agenda (=decide what needs to be dealt with or achieved) *The report set the agenda for the debate.*
agree an agenda *We need to agree an agenda for the next meeting.*
put sth on the agenda *This incident has put the issue of racism firmly back on the agenda.*
establish/create/provide an agenda *The scientists were able to establish an agenda for future research.*

ADJECTIVES

the political agenda *The political agenda was dominated by the world economic crisis.*
an ambitious agenda *The new government had an ambitious agenda when they first came to power.*

PREPOSITIONS

be on the agenda *The environment is still on the agenda.*
be off the agenda (=not on it) *Women's issues are off the agenda.*

2 secret reasons for doing something or things you secretly want to achieve

ADJECTIVES

a secret/hidden agenda *When the reforms were first announced, people suspected that the government had a hidden agenda.*
your own (personal) agenda *She had her own agenda when she agreed to accept the job.*
a political agenda *There is a small group of union leaders with a political agenda who are causing trouble.*

VERBS

have an agenda *The makers of the film clearly have an agenda.*

aggression *n*

angry or threatening behaviour or feelings that often result in fighting or wars

ADJECTIVES

military aggression *China suffered under military aggression from other countries in previous centuries.*
external/foreign aggression (=attacks from other countries) *States must be allowed to defend themselves against external aggression.*
naked/open/overt aggression (=very obvious aggression) *In some countries there is naked aggression towards foreigners.*
pent-up aggression (=angry feelings that you do not express) *Sports are a good way to release all your pent-up aggression.*

VERBS

control your aggression *He sometimes struggled to control his aggression.*
take out your aggression (=get rid of your aggressive feelings) *I know she feels strongly, but she shouldn't take out her aggression on me.*
channel your aggression (=use your aggression in a different way, which does not hurt other people) *To stay out of trouble, he began to channel his aggression into boxing.*
show/display aggression *Our dogs have never shown aggression towards other dogs.*

PREPOSITIONS

aggression against sb *The UN said the country had engaged in aggression against its neighbours.*
aggression towards sb *Unfortunately, it has become more common for pupils to show aggression towards teachers.*

PHRASES

an act of aggression *The invasion of Kuwait was an obvious act of aggression.*

aggressive *adj*

behaving in an angry threatening way, as if you want to attack someone or have a big argument with them

ADVERBS

highly aggressive *The man was behaving in a highly aggressive manner.*

openly aggressive (=in a way that is easy to notice) *He was not openly aggressive, but I felt uncomfortable with him.*

increasingly aggressive *The political candidates are becoming increasingly aggressive towards each other.*

VERBS

become aggressive *The man suddenly became aggressive and started shouting at me.*

PREPOSITIONS

aggressive to/towards sb *Some dogs are aggressive towards children and are not good pets.*

You can use **aggressive** about people, animals, countries, and companies.

agony *n* great pain or suffering

ADJECTIVES

great agony *She appeared to be in great agony.*

absolute agony *informal* (=very great pain) *I woke up in absolute agony, with a terrible pain in my leg.*

mental agony *It's hard to imagine the mental agonies suffered by someone wrongly accused of murder.*

VERBS

scream with agony *He screamed with agony when he caught his hand in the car door.*

writhe in agony (=twist your body violently because you are in pain) *She was writhing in agony, with tears running down her cheeks.*

prolong the agony (=make someone suffer any longer) *It would be unkind to prolong the agony and not tell him the test results.*

PREPOSITIONS

in agony *By the time she reached the hospital, she was in agony.*

the agony of sth *The country is recovering from the agonies of the recent civil war.*

PHRASES

a scream/cry of agony *He let out a scream of agony.*

days/weeks/months of agony *He suffered months of agony after damaging his foot during a soccer match.*

it is agony *spoken* (=it causes you a lot of worry and suffering) *It was agony not knowing if she would live.*

agree *v*

1 to have the same opinion as someone else

ADVERBS

completely/totally/entirely agree *He thinks that we should cancel the party and I completely agree with him.*

agree wholeheartedly (=agree completely – more formal) *The speaker said that she agreed wholeheartedly with the prime minister.*

unanimously agree (=used when everyone in a group agrees) *The committee unanimously agreed it was too much to pay.*

generally agree *People generally agree that education is important.*

broadly agree (=agree with most of something) *Most scientists broadly agree with the professor's views.*

PREPOSITIONS

agree with sb/sth *I think most people would agree with you. | I agree with what you're saying.*

agree about/on sth *My husband and I agree about most things.*

PHRASES

I agree with sb up to a point (=used when you partly agree with someone) *I agree with you up to a point, but I think there are some exceptions.*

I quite agree (=used when saying that you definitely agree with someone) *"It's a really good restaurant." "I quite agree."*

I couldn't agree more/I absolutely agree (=used when saying strongly that you completely agree) *"We need a new government." "I couldn't agree more."*

ANTONYMS **agree → disagree**

2 to say that you will do what someone asks, or allow something to happen

ADVERBS

reluctantly agree (=agree, although you do not really want to allow something) *I begged my parents to let me go, and they reluctantly agreed.*

happily/readily agree (=agree because you think something is a good idea) *She suggested that they go out for a meal and he happily agreed.*

unanimously agree (=everyone in a group agrees) *The three judges unanimously agreed to let the appeal go ahead.*

PHRASES

sb has kindly agreed to do sth (=a polite phrase used when saying that someone has agreed to do something) *The school has kindly agreed to let us use the hall for our meeting.*

sb would never agree to sth *The painting's owners would never agree to sell it.*

3 to make a decision with someone about something

NOUNS

agree a time/place/date *We still need to agree a time for our next meeting.*

agree a deal *The government and unions have agreed a deal setting a maximum 48-hour working week.*

agree a price/fee *They agreed a price of $3,500 for the job.*

A

Grammar
You can **agree** a time, place, price etc, or **agree on** a time, place, price etc: *Have you agreed (on) a date for the meeting?*

agreeable *adj* THESAURUS > enjoyable

agreement *n*

1 an arrangement or promise to do something, made by two or more people, companies, countries etc

ADJECTIVES

a legal agreement *He had signed a legal agreement to repay the money.*

an international agreement *We need an international agreement to deal with climate change.*

a written agreement *There is usually a written agreement between the borrower and the bank.*

a verbal agreement (=agreed in words, but not written down) *The doctor needs to have a verbal agreement from the patient.*

a formal/informal agreement *Two years of negotiation led to a formal agreement.*

a binding agreement (=an official agreement that must be obeyed) *Lawyers are in the process of drafting a legally binding agreement between both parties.*

a multilateral agreement *formal* (=involving several countries or groups) *They negotiated a multilateral agreement between all World Trade Organization members.*

a bilateral agreement *formal* (=between two countries or groups) *A bilateral agreement between the UK and Korean governments was signed last year.*

NOUNS + agreement

a trade agreement *The administration has signed a multi-billion dollar trade agreement with Colombia.*

a peace agreement (=a permanent agreement to stop fighting) *The five countries in the region signed a peace agreement.*

a ceasefire agreement (=a temporary agreement to stop fighting) *A ceasefire agreement was signed between the government and the rebels.*

a draft agreement (=one that is not yet in its finished form) *The government of Iraq refused to accept the wording of the draft UN agreement.*

a gentleman's agreement (=an agreement that is not written down, and is based only on trust) *The candidates seemed to have a gentleman's agreement not to criticize each other.*

VERBS + agreement

make an agreement *We made an agreement not to tell anyone.*

enter into an agreement *formal* (=make an official agreement, which has legal responsibilities) *In 2006, the city authorities entered into an agreement with a private firm to build a thousand new homes.*

sign an agreement *The two countries have signed an agreement on military cooperation.*

have an agreement *They have an agreement that all workers should be union members.*

reach/come to an agreement (*also* **conclude/secure an agreement** *formal*): *The two sides failed to come to an agreement.*

break/violate an agreement *The UN accused the country's leaders of breaking international agreements.*

keep/honour an agreement (*also* **stick to an agreement** *informal*) (=do what you have agreed) *Employers must honour an agreement to increase salaries.*

go back on an agreement (*also* **renege on an agreement** *formal*) (=not do what you agreed to do) *Republican leaders accused Democrats of trying to renege on an agreement to have a vote.*

be bound by an agreement (=have to obey the conditions of an official agreement) *India is bound by the agreements signed under the World Trade Organization.*

negotiate an agreement (=discuss particular things in order to reach an agreement) *They have been trying to negotiate an agreement with a Chinese company.*

hammer out an agreement (=decide on an agreement after a lot of discussion and disagreement) *Republicans and Democrats are hammering out an agreement to balance the federal budget.*

agreement + VERBS

an agreement breaks down/fails (=it stops working) *The agreement broke down almost immediately.*

an agreement comes into effect/force (=it starts being used) *It cannot be done until the agreement comes into force next month.*

PREPOSITIONS

an agreement with sb/sth *The German car maker signed an agreement with the state government to build a new factory.*

an agreement between sb (and sb) *A military cooperation agreement between the two countries was signed last year.*

under an agreement *Under the agreement, most agricultural prices will remain at the same level.*

an agreement on sth *They signed an agreement on military cooperation.*

PHRASES

the terms of an agreement (=the conditions that people agree on) *Under the terms of the agreement, the debt would be repaid over a 20-year period.*

a breach of an agreement (=an act of breaking an agreement) *Both sides were accusing each other of breaches of the agreement.*

be close to an agreement (=have almost reached an agreement) *Management and unions are close to an agreement about pay.*

2 a situation in which people have the same opinion

ADJECTIVES

unanimous agreement (=everyone agrees) *There was unanimous agreement that the plan was a good idea.*

general/broad/widespread agreement (=most people agree) *There is broad agreement that something needs to be done.*

mutual agreement (=two people or groups agree) *The decision to separate was arrived at by mutual agreement.*

PREPOSITIONS

be in agreement *We were all in agreement that changes needed to be made.*

agreement on sth *There is little agreement on what to do about the problem.*

agreement among sb *There is widespread agreement among scientists on how the disease is spread.*

aid Ac *n*

help, such as money or food, given by an organization or government to a country or to people who are in a difficult situation

ADJECTIVES/NOUNS + aid

foreign/international/overseas aid *The country is very poor and relies on foreign aid.*

government/federal/state aid *The school receives government aid.*

legal aid (=free legal services) *People on low incomes can get legal aid.*

financial/economic aid *The government provides financial aid for farmers.*

military aid *The US sent military aid to Pakistan.*

medical aid *The refugees are in urgent need of food and medical aid.*

food aid *We need to provide food aid for over 60,000 people.*

humanitarian aid (=given to people living in very bad conditions) *Ministers agreed to send humanitarian aid, including food and medical supplies.*

emergency aid *The government sent emergency aid to the victims of the earthquake.*

VERBS

give/provide aid *The United States continues to give aid to Israel.*

send aid *EU ministers agreed to send aid.*

ask for/appeal for/call for aid *The Pakistan authorities have asked for aid to help the flood victims.*

get/receive aid *The country is very poor and receives a lot of foreign aid.*

depend on/rely on aid *Millions of people rely on food aid.*

cut off/withdraw aid (=stop giving aid) *The US has threatened to cut off aid to the region.*

qualify for aid (*also* **be eligible for aid**) (=have the right to be given aid) *The project is eligible for aid from the government.*

promise aid *The president promised additional aid for the victims of the hurricane.*

aid + NOUNS

an aid worker *Aid workers warned that the situation was getting worse.*

an aid agency/group *The sanctions could prevent international aid agencies from delivering food and medicine.*

an aid programme/scheme/package *He works for a UN aid programme which helps street children.*

PHRASES

an appeal/request for aid *International aid agencies launched an appeal for emergency aid.*

aim *n*

something you hope to achieve by doing something

ADJECTIVES

the main aim (*also* **the principal/primary aim** *formal*): *The government's main aim is to stay in power.*

a key aim (=used when emphasizing that an aim is very important) *One of the key aims is to help people find work.*

the ultimate/long-term aim (=that you hope to achieve at some time in the future) *The ultimate aim is to produce vehicles that run on clean sources of energy.*

the immediate/initial aim (=that you hope to achieve first) *Their immediate aim was to pay off their debts.*

the general/broad/overall aim *The overall aim of the course is to help students improve their reading and writing skills.*

a common aim (=that people, countries, or organizations share) *The two groups share a common aim.*

the underlying aim (=basic aim, which lies behind all the other things you do) *The government's main underlying aim is now to get growth back into the economy.*

VERBS

sb's aim is to do sth *Our aim is to win the competition.*

have an aim *The scientists all have the same aim – to find a cure for the disease.*

achieve your aim *She achieved her aim of becoming a doctor.*

meet/realize/fulfil/accomplish your aim (=achieve your aim – more formal) *They hope to meet their aim of reducing world poverty within the next five years.*

set out/state the aims of sth *They set out their aims in the party manifesto.*

A

pursue your aims *formal* (=try to achieve them over a long period of time) *The men worked closely together to pursue their aims.*

further your aims *especially disapproving* (=help them to be successful) *The group is prepared to use violence to further its political aims.*

PREPOSITIONS

the aim of sth *The aim of the investigation is to find out what caused the crash.*

with the aim of doing sth *The project was set up with the aim of helping disabled people find places to live.*

PHRASES

aims and objectives (=the things you hope to achieve) *I've written down a list of aims and objectives for the meeting.*

sb's aim in life *His main aim in life is to avoid doing any work.*

THESAURUS: aim

goal
something important that you hope to achieve in the future, even though it may take a long time:
*The country can still **achieve** its **goal** of reducing poverty by a third. | Their **ultimate goal** is to become an independent country. | His **long-term goal** is to win the world championship.*

target
a particular amount or total that you want to achieve:
*The company is on track to **meet** its **target** of increasing profits by 10%. | He **set** himself a **target** of losing 10 kilos.*

objective
the specific thing that you are trying to achieve - used especially about things that have been officially discussed and agreed upon in business, politics etc:
*Their **main objective** is to halt the flow of drugs. | We met to **set** the business **objectives** for the coming year.*

ambition
something that you very much want to achieve in your future career:
*Her ambition was to go to law school and become an attorney. | Earlier this year, he **achieved** his **ambition** of competing in the Olympic Games.*

THESAURUS: aim

aim, goal, objective, the object of sth, the point, intention, ends → **purpose**

air *n*

the mixture of gases around the Earth, that we breathe

ADJECTIVES

fresh air *She opened the window to let in some fresh air.*

clean air *The air is much cleaner next to the sea.*

warm/hot air *Warm air rises and is replaced by cooler and denser air.*

cool/cold air *I could feel the cold air coming in under the door.*

crisp air (=pleasantly cool) *She breathed in the crisp autumn air.*

clear air *I looked up to the stars in the clear night air.*

damp/humid/moist air *Damp air can be bad for your breathing.*

dry air *Dry air and blazing sun made the soil crack.*

polluted air *The air in many cities is heavily polluted.*

stale air (=not fresh and often full of smoke) *The room was full of stale air and tobacco smoke.*

the air is thin (=there is less oxygen because you are in a high place) *People cannot live up there because the air is too thin and there is not enough oxygen to breathe.*

NOUNS + air

the morning/evening/night air *He stepped out and breathed in the cold morning air.*

the sea/mountain/country air *I love the salty smell of the sea air.*

air + NOUNS

air pollution *Most air pollution is caused by cars.*

the air quality *The air quality is very poor on hot days.*

VERBS

breathe in the air *She breathed in the cool mountain air.*

fight/gasp for air (=try to breathe with difficulty) *He clutched his throat as he fought for air.*

let in some air (=let fresh air into a room) *It would be nice to open the door and let in some air.*

put/pump air into sth (=fill a tyre, balloon etc with air) *I need to put some air in the tyres.*

sth fills the air *A smell of freshly brewed coffee filled the air.*

the air turns cooler/warmer (=it becomes cooler or warmer) *In the spring, the air turns warmer.*

PREPOSITIONS

in the air *There was a strong smell of burning in the air.*

PHRASES

a breath of air *I went outside for a breath of air.*

a current of air *The birds are able to glide on a current of warm air.*

a rush/blast/stream of air *There was a cold rush of air as she wound down her window.*

the air is thick with sth (=there is a lot of something in it) *The air was thick with smoke.*

airline *n*

a company that takes passengers and goods to different places by plane

ADJECTIVES/NOUNS + airline

a big/major airline *Several major airlines fly between London and New York.*

the national/state airline *KLM is the national airline of the Netherlands.*

a low-cost/budget/no-frills airline (=which has cheap flights) *Low-cost airlines are offering tickets for as little as 20 euros.*

an international airline *The airport is used mainly by international airlines.*

a domestic/regional airline *The domestic airline has a good safety record.*

a commercial airline *Last year, 1.6 billion passengers were carried by commercial airlines.*

VERBS

fly with an airline *"Which airline are you flying with?" "British Airways."*

an airline flies somewhere *The airline flies to Morocco twice a day.*

an airline operates somewhere *The airline operates mainly between Florida and Puerto Rico.*

an airline carries people *Last year, the airline carried over 2 million passengers.*

airline + NOUNS

an airline company *She worked as a pilot for a well-known airline company.*

the airline industry/business *The airline industry faces a challenging time.*

an airline passenger *Airline passengers face a 10 percent increase in air fares.*

alarm *n*

1 a piece of equipment that makes a loud noise to warn you of danger

ADJECTIVES/NOUNS + alarm

a fire/smoke alarm *If the fire alarm goes off, leave the building immediately.*

a security alarm *The building has a system of security alarms.*

a burglar alarm (*also* **an intruder alarm** *formal*) (=that tells you when someone is getting into a building without permission) *Neighbours heard the burglar alarm and called the police.*

a car alarm *I was woken by a car alarm in the middle of the night.*

a personal alarm (=that you carry with you in case you are attacked) *If you are nervous, buy a personal alarm.*

VERBS

an alarm goes off (*also* **an alarm sounds** *formal*) (=it suddenly makes a noise) *The thieves fled when an alarm went off.*

set off/trigger/activate an alarm (=make it start working) *A window blew open, setting off the alarm.*

set the alarm (=make it ready to operate) *Did you set the burglar alarm?*

switch off/turn off the alarm *The owner of the shop arrived and switched off the alarm.*

install an alarm (*also* **fit an alarm** *BrE*): *After our neighbours were burgled, we installed a burglar alarm.*

alarm + NOUNS

an alarm button *He hit the alarm button under the desk.*

an alarm system *They have installed an electronic burglar alarm system.*

2 a feeling of fear or worry because something bad or dangerous might happen

ADJECTIVES

great/considerable alarm *When the announcement was made, there was great alarm.*

growing alarm *There is growing alarm in the region over the situation in Iraq.*

sudden alarm *"Don't do that," Matt said in sudden alarm.*

unnecessary/undue alarm *His claims have caused unnecessary alarm among millions of parents.*

public alarm *The radiation leak caused considerable public alarm.*

VERBS

express alarm *Police expressed alarm at the level of drug use.*

cause/create alarm *The proposal has caused great alarm and anxiety.*

PREPOSITIONS

alarm at/over/about sth *There is alarm at the level of pollution.*

with alarm *Britain viewed this development with alarm.*

in alarm *The girl cried out in alarm.*

to sb's alarm *He noticed to his alarm that the fuel tank was nearly empty.*

PHRASES

there is no cause/need for alarm *The minister insisted that there was no cause for alarm.*

alarming *adj* THESAURUS ▸ **frightening**

alien *adj* THESAURUS ▸ **foreign**

alive *adj* living and not dead

> **Grammar**
> **Alive** is not used before a noun.

ADVERBS

still alive *Her grandparents are still alive.*

barely alive (=only just alive) *By the time she was rescued, she was barely alive.*

A

very much alive *He is very much alive and enjoying his retirement in Florida.*

VERBS

keep sb alive *The patient is being kept alive on a life-support machine.*

stay/remain alive *The explorers managed to stay alive in the jungle by eating berries and leaves.*

escape/get out alive *Fortunately, everyone escaped alive from the burning building.*

be found alive *The missing child was found alive and well at a neighbour's house.*

be buried alive *Two skiers were buried alive in an avalanche.*

see sb alive *She was the last person to see him alive.*

PHRASES

alive and well *He's alive and well, and currently living in Australia.*

lucky to be alive *She was lucky to be alive after being involved in a serious car accident.*

more dead than alive *The child was found lying on the ground, more dead than alive.*

THESAURUS: alive

living

thing | **relative** | **artist** | **writer** | **poet** | **songwriter** | **filmmaker**

if someone is living, he or she is alive now. **Living** is also used in the phrase **a living thing** (=an animal or plant that is alive): *All living things need oxygen.* | *Her son is her only living relative.* | *He is probably the greatest living American filmmaker.*

live

animals

live animals are not dead: *Many people are against scientists doing experiments on live animals.* | *Protesters want to stop the export of live sheep and cattle.* | *The children were excited at seeing* ***real live*** *elephants.*

Live is only used before a noun.

animate *formal*

object

an **animate object** is alive and able to move, and therefore different from other types of things: *Young children eventually learn the difference between an animate object, such as a cat, and an inanimate one, such as a ball.*

ANTONYMS **alive → dead**[1]

allegation *n*

a statement saying that you think someone has done something wrong or illegal, although this has not been proved

Grammar
Usually plural.

ADJECTIVES/NOUNS + allegation

a serious allegation *Some serious allegations have already been made against him.*

a damaging allegation *One of the most damaging allegations was that the airline did not care about passenger safety.*

a false allegation *She claims the allegations against her are all false.*

a wild allegation *The press have been making wild allegations.*

an unfounded/unsubstantiated allegation (=there is no evidence to support it) *The allegations are unfounded and will easily be disproved in court.*

an allegation is true/untrue *If these allegations are true, they could ruin his career.*

fresh/further allegations (=new allegations) *The newspaper is planning to publish fresh allegations.*

widespread allegations (=by many people) *There were widespread allegations of cheating.*

VERBS

make an allegation *In his article, he makes a number of allegations.*

deny an allegation *The mayor denies all the allegations that have been made against him.*

reject/dismiss an allegation *The company reacted by rejecting all the allegations.*

refute an allegation *formal* (=prove that it is wrong) *He has taken steps to refute the allegations publicly.*

face an allegation *The player faces allegations that he cheated in last week's game.*

publish an allegation *The newspaper published allegations that the president was involved with the Mafia.*

investigate/look into an allegation *The police are investigating allegations of fraud.*

withdraw/retract an allegation (=say that your allegation was a mistake) *They were forced to withdraw their allegations.*

support an allegation *There was no evidence to support these allegations.*

an allegation is levelled against sb *formal* (=it is made against someone) *The same allegation could not be levelled against her husband.*

allergy *n*

a medical condition that makes you ill when you eat, touch, or breathe a particular thing

VERBS

have an allergy (to sth) *She has an allergy to nuts.*

suffer from an allergy *Only a small number of people suffer from this type of allergy.*

cause an allergy *Some food colourings can cause allergies.*

A

NOUNS + allergy

a food allergy *Food allergies are becoming more common in young children.*

a peanut/milk allergy *Peanut allergies can be very serious.*

a skin allergy (=which makes your skin feel painful or uncomfortable) *Perfumes can cause skin allergies.*

allergy + NOUNS

an allergy test *The doctor sent her to a specialist to have an allergy test.*

alleviate *v* THESAURUS **reduce**

alliance *n*

an arrangement in which two or more countries, groups, or people agree to work together or support each other

ADJECTIVES

a military alliance *Greece was a useful member of the military alliance.*

a political alliance *Three parties have formed a political alliance.*

a strong/close alliance *He forged a strong alliance between his state and the church.*

a loose alliance (=not strong) *A loose alliance of opposition groups formed in 1990.*

a broad alliance (=involving very different groups) *We need a broad alliance of colleges, communities, and businesses.*

an unholy alliance (=very surprising because the people, groups etc have very different opinions) *Politicians on the left and the right have joined together in an unholy alliance against the reforms.*

VERBS

form/make an alliance *In 1902, Japan made an alliance with Britain.*

enter into an alliance with sb *formal* (=make an alliance) *Spain then entered into an alliance with France.*

forge/build an alliance (=work to make an alliance) *They won the election by forging an alliance with the Social Democrats.*

strengthen/cement an alliance (=make it stronger) *He cemented his alliance with France by marrying the French king's daughter.*

join an alliance *Two more countries have been invited to join the alliance.*

PREPOSITIONS

an alliance with sb *Most of the people approve of their country's political alliance with the United States.*

an alliance between sb and sb *There was an alliance between Spain and Portugal.*

in alliance with sb *They have been campaigning in alliance with other organizations.*

allocate Ac *v*

to officially give something to someone, or decide that something should be used for a purpose

allocate + NOUNS

allocate resources *The government will allocate more resources to regions with serious housing problems.*

allocate money/funds *More funds should be allocated for training.*

allocate an amount/number *Each police officer is allocated a certain number of streets to patrol.*

allocate time *How much time has been allocated for the meeting?*

allocate a space/area/land *Not enough space has been allocated for car parking.*

allocate work/a task *Tasks are allocated according to each worker's skills and experience.*

PREPOSITIONS

allocate sth to sb/sth *More government money will be allocated to repairing old buildings.*

allocate sth for sth *Thirty minutes is the amount of time allocated for lunch.*

allocate sth between/among sb/sth *The resources are allocated between the city's schools.*

allocate sth according to sth *In an election, the seats are allocated according to the proportion of votes each party receives.*

ally *n*

a person or country that helps and supports another person or country

ADJECTIVES

a close ally *Britain is a close ally of the United States.*

an old ally (=allies for a long time) *The two leaders are old allies.*

a former ally *Mr Rutskoi is a former ally of the president.*

a political ally *The senator is a close friend and political ally of the president.*

an important/key ally *He lost the support of one of his most important allies.*

sb's main ally *Beijing, North Korea's main ally, is being put under pressure by the US.*

a powerful ally *The prince has some powerful allies who he can ask for help.*

a great ally *The two countries were once great allies.*

a staunch ally (=a very loyal ally) *The congresswoman is normally a staunch ally of the administration.*

VERBS

win/gain an ally *He is hoping that he can win new allies by offering to cut taxes.*

find an ally in sb/sth *General de Gaulle found an ally in Konrad Adenauer.*

A

alter [Ac] *v*

to change, or to make something change

ADVERBS

alter (sth) slightly/a little *His face altered slightly when he saw me.*

alter (sth) completely *This event completely altered his career.*

alter (sth) dramatically (=a lot in a surprising way) *The situation has altered dramatically.*

alter (sth) considerably *People's tastes in food have altered considerably in recent years.*

alter (sth) radically/fundamentally (=completely) *His doctor told him that he would have to radically alter his diet.*

alter (sth) drastically (=in an extreme and sudden way) *The accident drastically altered her life.*

alter (sth) significantly/substantially (=in a very noticeable way) *Property prices did not alter significantly through the year.*

THESAURUS: alter

alter, turn, adapt, evolve, mutate, fluctuate, alternate → **change¹ (1)**

alter, adapt, adjust, turn sth up/down, reform, revise, restructure, transform, revolutionize, distort, twist, misrepresent → **change¹ (2)**

alteration [Ac] *n*

a change, especially a small one

ADJECTIVES

a slight/minor/small alteration *The editor made a few minor alterations to the text.*

a major/significant alteration *The last major alteration to the law was made in 2009.*

extensive/radical alteration (=one that has a big effect) *The system is in need of radical alteration.*

⚠ Don't say 'a big alteration'. Say **a major alteration** or **a significant alteration**.

VERBS

make an alteration *He made a few alterations to his speech.*

carry out an alteration (=make an alteration – used about big changes to buildings and designs) *The alterations were carried out by a firm of local builders.*

need/require some alterations *The software requires one or two alterations to improve its performance.*

undergo some alterations (=have some alterations – more formal) *The building has undergone several alterations during its long history.*

PREPOSITIONS

an alteration to sth *We need to make a few alterations to the dress before it is ready to wear.*

an alteration in sth *Have you noticed any alteration in his behaviour recently?*

THESAURUS: alteration

alteration, reform, shift, swing, fluctuation, transformation, revolution, shake-up, U-turn → **change²**

alternate *v* THESAURUS ▶ change¹ (1)

alternative¹ [Ac] *n*

something you can choose to do or use instead of something else

ADJECTIVES

a good/attractive alternative *If you don't want curtains, blinds are a good alternative.*

a possible/acceptable/satisfactory alternative *I'm busy tomorrow but Wednesday is a possible alternative.*

a cheap alternative *Plastic is a cheap alternative to wood.*

a practical/effective alternative *This treatment represents a practical alternative to surgery.*

the only alternative *If this doesn't work, the only alternative is to buy a new battery.*

a real/serious alternative *Do you think that wind power is a real alternative to other sources of energy?*

a viable alternative (=one that will work because it is as good as something else) *They want to make public transport a viable alternative for car owners.*

a clear/obvious alternative *It's not an ideal solution, but there is no obvious alternative.*

a safe alternative *Will there ever be a safe alternative to nuclear power?*

a healthy alternative *Low-fat cookies are a healthy alternative to cake.*

VERBS

have an alternative *We don't have to stay here – we have alternatives.*

suggest/provide/offer an alternative *I'd like to suggest some alternatives.*

seek/look for an alternative *People are seeking alternatives to meat-based dishes.*

consider/look at the alternatives *We have carefully considered all the alternatives.*

find an alternative *The aim of the research is to find alternatives to oil and natural gas.*

PREPOSITIONS

an alternative to sth *We need more alternatives to imprisonment.*

PHRASES

have no/little alternative (but to do sth) *He had no alternative but to resign.*

leave sb with no alternative (but to do sth) *I was left with no alternative but to seek legal advice.*

alternative² Ac *adj*

1 different and able to be used instead of something else

alternative + NOUNS

an alternative way/approach/method *Maybe there is an alternative way of dealing with the problem.*

an alternative idea/suggestion/proposal *She put forward an alternative suggestion which would cost less money.*

an alternative explanation/interpretation *I can't think of any alternative explanation.*

an alternative solution *The engineers quickly came up with an alternative solution.*

an alternative route *There is an alternative route which avoids all the traffic.*

alternative arrangements *Our flight was cancelled so we had to make alternative arrangements.*

2 different from the normal or traditional type of thing

alternative + NOUNS

alternative medicine/treatment/therapies *Various forms of alternative medicine, including acupuncture, may bring pain relief.*

alternative music/theatre/comedy *The festival is aimed at fans of alternative music.*

alternative energy sources *The need for alternative energy sources such as wind and solar power is now greater than ever.*

alternative lifestyles *In the 1960s, many young people experimented with alternative lifestyles.*

amazed *adj* very surprised

ADVERBS

absolutely/totally/utterly amazed *Her parents were absolutely amazed when they saw the change in her.*

always/constantly/continually amazed *I'm always amazed by how much food gets wasted.*

⚠ Don't say 'very amazed'. Say **absolutely amazed**.

VERBS

look/seem amazed *His friends all looked amazed when they saw him.*

continue to be amazed/never cease to be amazed *I never cease to be amazed by the amount of money she spends on clothes.*

PREPOSITIONS

amazed at sth *The doctors were amazed at how quickly he recovered from his illness.*

amazed by sth *She was amazed by the news.*

amazement *n* a feeling of great surprise

PHRASES

look at/stare at/watch sb in amazement *His friends all stared at him in amazement when told them how much he had won.*

shake your head in amazement *"Wow!" said Jack, shaking his head in amazement.*

a look of amazement *I'll never forget the look of amazement on his face when I told him my news.*

a cry/gasp of amazement *There were cries of amazement when she brought in the birthday cake.*

ADJECTIVES

complete/utter/sheer amazement *To his utter amazement, his application was accepted.*

genuine amazement *"Have you read all those books?" she said with genuine amazement.*

VERBS

express (your) amazement *He expressed amazement at the number of people who had come to help.*

PREPOSITIONS

in amazement *"How did you get here?" she asked in amazement.*

with amazement *I listened with amazement to his story.*

to sb's amazement *To my amazement, he burst into tears.*

amazement at sth *Peter was unable to hide his amazement at how Carla was dressed.*

amazing *adj* THESAURUS ▶ **excellent**

ambiguous Ac *adj*

if something is ambiguous, it is confusing, especially because it can be understood in two very different ways

ADVERBS

highly/very ambiguous *The book's title 'Closing Time' is highly ambiguous.*

somewhat/rather/slightly ambiguous *The law is somewhat ambiguous about this issue.*

deliberately ambiguous *The film has a deliberately ambiguous ending.*

NOUNS

an ambiguous word/term/phrase *'Different' is an ambiguous word – it can be used to praise or to criticize.*

ambiguous language *The language in the minister's statement is highly ambiguous.*

an ambiguous sentence/statement/message *His statement was ambiguous and I wasn't sure what he meant.*

an ambiguous concept *'Privacy' is an ambiguous concept.*

VERBS

leave sth ambiguous *The ending of the story is left deliberately ambiguous.*

A

remain ambiguous *The reasons behind his decision remain ambiguous.*

ambition *n*

a strong desire to achieve something

ADJECTIVES/NOUNS + ambition

sb's main ambition *What's your main ambition in life?*

sb's great ambition *He didn't achieve his greatest ambition – to be Wimbledon Champion.*

a lifelong/long-held ambition (=one that you have had all your life) *It's been her lifelong ambition to work with horses.*

a personal ambition *Crossing the Sahara was a personal ambition of mine.*

a secret ambition *His secret ambition was to become a pilot.*

a burning/driving ambition (=a very strong ambition) *She had a burning ambition to become a racing car driver.*

career ambitions *The course is designed to help you achieve your career ambitions.*

VERBS

sb's ambition is to be/do sth *My ambition was to be a journalist.*

have an ambition *He had an ambition to be a top cello player.*

achieve/fulfil/realize your ambition (=do what you wanted to do) *It took her ten years to achieve her ambition.*

lack ambition/have no ambition *Many of the students lack ambition.*

nurse/harbour/cherish an ambition (=have it for a long time, especially secretly) *He had nursed an ambition to become a writer for many years.*

end sb's ambition *An injury ended his ambitions of becoming a professional footballer.*

PHRASES

sb's lack of ambition *I was frustrated by their apparent lack of ambition.*

be full of ambition *She was full of ambition when she joined the company.*

sb's dreams and ambitions *He told her all about his dreams and ambitions.*

THESAURUS: ambition

goal, target, objective, ambition → **aim**

ambitious *adj*

1 determined to be successful, rich, powerful etc

ADVERBS

very/highly ambitious *Thompson was highly ambitious and later became Director General of the BBC.*

extremely/fiercely/intensely ambitious *Alfred was intensely ambitious and obsessed with the idea of becoming rich.*

ruthlessly ambitious (=so ambitious that you do not care about the effects on other people) *Stalin was ruthlessly ambitious in his pursuit of power.*

PREPOSITIONS

ambitious for sb (=wanting another person to be very successful) *His mother was ambitious for him and gave him constant encouragement with his studies.*

PHRASES

ambitious for power (=wanting to get power) *Kim was ambitious for power and wanted to become president one day.*

2 trying to do something difficult

ADVERBS

very/highly/hugely/extremely ambitious *The programme of reform is highly ambitious.*

extremely/hugely/enormously/extraordinarily ambitious *The project to build the stadium was enormously ambitious and very expensive.*

over-ambitious/overly ambitious *If you set yourself over-ambitious targets, you will end up feeling a failure.*

NOUNS

an ambitious plan/project/scheme/programme *The company has ambitious plans for expansion.*

an ambitious target/goal *It is an ambitious target, but Leblanc believes it is attainable.*

an ambitious attempt *The crash ends an ambitious attempt to break the world record for flying round the world.*

ambulance *n*

a special vehicle that is used to take people who are ill or injured to hospital

VERBS

call an ambulance/phone for an ambulance *She looked very ill and we decided to call an ambulance.*

send for an ambulance *Send for an ambulance immediately.*

an ambulance arrives/comes *He died before the ambulance arrived.*

an ambulance takes sb somewhere *An ambulance took her to Colchester General Hospital.*

ambulance + NOUNS

the ambulance service *The ambulance service denies it took too long for the ambulance to arrive.*

an ambulance crew *The ambulance crew removed him from the wreckage.*

PREPOSITIONS

by ambulance *Mr Brock was taken to hospital by ambulance.*

PHRASES

an ambulance is on its way (=it is coming soon) *Don't worry – the ambulance is on its way.*

ambush *n*

a sudden attack on someone by people who have been hiding and waiting for them

VERBS

set up/lay an ambush (=prepare an ambush) *The kidnappers had set up an ambush on the road.*

lie/wait in ambush *Armed police lay in ambush behind the hedge.*

stage/carry out an ambush *The rebels staged an ambush that killed 14 soldiers.*

be/get caught in an ambush *The police officers were caught in an ambush when they responded to a call.*

walk/run into an ambush *The soldiers had accidentally walked into an ambush.*

draw/lure sb into an ambush (=make someone come into the place where you have prepared an ambush) *Their plan was to lure the men into an ambush and then kill them.*

PREPOSITIONS

in an ambush *Their leader was shot dead in an ambush last week.*

an ambush on sb *He took part in an ambush on a US patrol.*

amendment Ac *n*

a change that is made to a law or document

VERBS

make an amendment *He asked his lawyer to make some amendments to the document.*

introduce an amendment *The party wants to introduce an amendment to the bill.*

table an amendment *BrE* (=suggest an amendment, especially in Parliament) *A group of MPs will table an amendment to remove the ban.*

pass/accept/approve/adopt an amendment *The amendment was eventually passed by 11 votes.*

reject/defeat an amendment *The Senate rejected the amendment.*

vote on an amendment *Parliament will vote on the amendment next week.*

support/oppose an amendment *Several members of the committee supported the amendment.*

ADJECTIVES

a constitutional amendment *A constitutional amendment does not need the Governor's signature.*

a minor/major amendment *A number of minor amendments have been made to the agreement.*

the First/Second etc Amendment (=in the US Constitution) *Freedom of speech is protected by the First Amendment.*

PREPOSITIONS

an amendment to sth *They introduced an amendment to the building regulations.*

amiable *adj* THESAURUS ▸ **friendly**

amount *n* a quantity of something

ADJECTIVES

a large amount *They still have a large amount of work to do.*

a great amount *I have a great amount of respect for his work.*

a huge/enormous/vast/massive/tremendous amount *A huge amount of progress has already been made.*

a considerable/substantial/significant amount *The house must have cost a considerable amount of money.*

a small/tiny amount *Mix a small amount of flour and water in a bowl.*

a certain amount *You need to have a certain amount of self-discipline to work on your own.*

a surprising amount *There is a surprising amount of agreement among scientists about climate change.*

the full amount *The company agreed to pay her back the full amount.*

the maximum/minimum amount *The maximum amount of luggage allowed is 22 kilos.*

the right/correct amount *It is your responsibility to pay the correct amount of tax by the correct date.*

an equal amount *They spend equal amounts of time in California and New York.*

copious amounts *formal* (=large amounts) *The trees absorb copious amounts of moisture from the soil.*

an inordinate amount *formal* (=too much) *She spends an inordinate amount of time doing simple things like pouring hot water into a teapot.*

Amount or quantity?

You often use **amount** about things that you cannot measure or count. For example, you say: *The team had a certain* ***amount*** *of luck* (not 'quantity'). *She has a tremendous* ***amount*** *of confidence* (not 'quantity').

You use **quantity** about things you can measure or count: *The plant produces large* ***quantities*** *of seeds.* You can also use **amount** in the same way: *The plant produces a large* ***amount*** *of seeds.*

A

A

THESAURUS: amount

quantity
a particular amount of food, liquid, or another substance that can be measured - used especially in written descriptions and instructions:
They buy the wood ***in large quantities****.* | *Make sure that you add* ***the right quantity of*** *milk.* | *A loaded pistol and a* ***small quantity of*** *explosives were found in his apartment.*

volume
the amount of something such as business activity or traffic, especially when this is large or increasing:
The ***volume of traffic*** *on our roads has risen sharply.* | *There is a huge* ***volume of trade*** *with China.* | *They are finding it hard to cope with the* ***high volume of business****.*

level
the exact amount of something at one time, especially when this varies and can go up or down:
They measured the ***level of*** *alcohol in his blood.* | *There is a* ***high level*** *of unemployment.* | *Rainfall is well above the* ***average level*** *for this time of year.*

proportion
the amount of something, compared with the whole amount that exists:
A ***high proportion of*** *the students were from poor families.* | *The study examined* ***the proportion of*** *road accidents caused by drunk drivers.* | *Only a* ***low proportion of*** *girls received places on training schemes.*

quota
a maximum or minimum amount of something that can be produced, sold, brought into a country etc:
The government wanted to ***impose import quotas on*** *foreign goods.* | *There are* ***strict fishing quotas on*** *the amount of fish that can be caught.* | *There is an* ***annual quota for*** *the number of permits that can be issued.*

yield
the amount of something that is produced, or the amount of profit that you get from an investment:
Farmers were able to obtain ***high*** *crop* ***yields****.* | *Shareholders are getting a* ***low yield*** *on their investment* (=not get much money).

ample *determiner* THESAURUS enough

amused *adj*
if you are amused by something, you think it is funny

ADVERBS

very/highly amused *Her father was highly amused when he saw the article.*

much/greatly amused (=very amused) *They were much amused to hear he had formed his own pop group.*

quite/rather amused *We were quite amused when we heard about it.*

faintly/slightly/mildly amused (=a little amused) *The man looked faintly amused.*

quietly amused *Sandra was quietly amused by their comments.*

genuinely amused *He seemed genuinely amused that anyone could believe such a story.*

VERBS

seem/look/sound amused *Ellen seemed amused by the whole situation.*

NOUNS

an amused expression/look/voice *Douglas felt uncomfortable until he saw Jean's amused expression.*

PREPOSITIONS

amused by/at sth *They seemed amused by his appearance.* | *Harry was amused at the suggestion.*

amusement *n*
the feeling you have when you think something is funny

ADJECTIVES

great/much amusement *It caused great amusement when he told us what had happened.*

mild/faint amusement *Daniel looked at her with mild amusement.*

genuine/real amusement *He laughed out loud with genuine amusement.*

VERBS

cause sb amusement *The memory seemed to cause him great amusement.*

show your amusement *James looked down to avoid showing his amusement.*

hide/conceal your amusement *She did not make any attempt to hide her amusement.*

PREPOSITIONS

in/with amusement *The others watched with amusement as she tried the strange food.*

(much) to sb's amusement *He got up and sang 'Yellow Submarine', much to everyone's amusement.*

PHRASES

a source of amusement (=something that continues to amuse you) *Geoff seemed to find life a source of constant amusement.*

amusing *adj* funny and entertaining

ADVERBS

very/highly/most amusing *Their attempts at skating were highly amusing to watch.*

extremely/hugely/wonderfully amusing *I always find it extremely amusing that people complain about these programmes but still watch them.*

quite/rather amusing *Initially she found being the centre of attention quite amusing.*

mildly/vaguely amusing (=slightly amusing) *The film is mildly amusing in an old-fashioned way.*

PHRASES

find sth amusing *George seemed to find the idea amusing.*

THESAURUS: amusing

amusing, humorous, light-hearted, witty, comic, comical, hilarious, hysterical → **funny (1)**

analogy *n*

a comparison showing that two situations are very similar

ADJECTIVES

a close analogy *There is a close analogy between the two cases.*

a useful/helpful analogy *A useful analogy can be drawn between the human brain and a computer.*

a good/better analogy *I wish that I could think of a better analogy.*

VERBS

draw/make an analogy (=say that two things are similar) *She draws an analogy between politics and soccer.*

use an analogy *The writer uses the analogy of a sudden change in the weather.*

give an analogy *One scientist gives the analogy of somebody trying to stop a ship from sinking.*

PREPOSITIONS

an analogy between sth (and sth) *He drew an analogy between the economic situation in the 1920s and the situation now.*

an analogy with sth *The physicist Richard Feynman used to make an analogy with a game of chess.*

the analogy of sth *He uses the analogy of someone pedalling on a bicycle up a steep hill.*

analyse *BrE*, analyze *AmE v*

to examine something carefully in order to understand it

NOUNS

analyse data/information/evidence *Experts will analyse evidence from the crash to establish its cause.*

analyse the results/findings of sth *We learn more about each substance by analysing the results of several chemical experiments.*

analyse a problem *You have to analyse the problem before you can begin to solve it.*

analyse the causes/effects of sth *Scientists have analysed the effects of heat on a range of materials.*

ADVERBS

analyse sth carefully *Information from the survey is analysed carefully to give an accurate picture of voters' opinions.*

analyse sth in detail *We analyse each situation in detail before giving advice.*

analysis Ac *n*

a careful examination of something in order to understand it or find out about it

ADJECTIVES

a detailed/in-depth/close analysis (=one in which you look carefully at every part) *The researchers carried out a detailed analysis of the students' performance.*

a careful/thorough analysis *After a careful analysis of the issues, he made his decision.*

a brief analysis *Let's start with a brief analysis of the situation.*

further analysis *The samples were kept for further analysis.*

economic/political/scientific etc analysis *His book provided a scientific analysis of human behaviour.*

a critical analysis (=involving judgements about how good or bad something is) *Write a critical analysis of the following poem.*

statistical analysis *Their research was based on statistical analysis.*

forensic analysis (=done to find out about a crime) *Samples from the crime scene were sent for forensic analysis.*

VERBS

do/carry out an analysis (*also* **perform/conduct an analysis** *formal*): *We have done an analysis of the data.*

provide/produce an analysis *The report provided an analysis of the problems we need to address.*

an analysis shows sth *DNA analysis showed that both blood samples came from the same person.*

an analysis suggests/indicates sth *Our analysis suggests that there is a bigger problem.*

be based on an analysis of sth *The study is based on an analysis of figures for the years 2011 and 2012.*

NOUNS + analysis

data analysis *Our research involves a lot of data analysis.*

DNA analysis *DNA analysis had shown that the baby was Gilbert's.*

computer analysis (=done by computer) *Computer analysis of the figures suggests that the election result will be very close.*

ancient *adj* THESAURUS ▶ **old (1)**

anger *n*

a strong feeling you have when someone has done something bad

A

PHRASES

be filled with anger/be full of anger *His voice was full of anger.*

be seething with anger (=be extremely angry) *Seething with anger and frustration, Polly stood up.*

be shaking/trembling with anger *My aunt was shaking with anger as she left the room.*

a feeling of anger *He was overcome by a sudden feeling of anger against the people who had put him there.*

a fit/outburst of anger (=an occasion when someone suddenly expresses anger) *His occasional outbursts of anger shocked those around him.*

a surge/wave of anger (=a sudden feeling of anger) *She felt a surge of anger.*

VERBS + anger

feel anger *He felt no anger, just sorrow.*

express/show your anger (*also* **vent your anger** *formal*): *Demonstrators expressed their anger by burning American flags.*

cause/provoke/arouse/stir up anger (=make people angry) *The referee's decision provoked anger among the fans.*

fuel anger (=make people even more angry) *The announcement fuelled public anger against the government.*

control/contain your anger *I could not control my anger any longer.*

hide your anger *For a second she was unable to hide her anger.*

anger + VERBS

sb's anger goes away/subsides/fades (=it stops) *I counted to ten and waited for my anger to go away.*

sb's anger grows/rises *Her anger and resentment grew as she drove home.*

ADJECTIVES

deep/great/fierce anger *There is deep anger against the occupying forces.*

growing/rising/mounting anger *There is growing anger among drivers over the rise in fuel prices.*

widespread anger (=among many people) *The decision to build the airport has provoked widespread anger.*

real anger *There is real anger about the amount of money that has been wasted.*

public/popular anger *By now public anger in the US was mounting.*

righteous anger (=anger felt when you think something should not be allowed to happen) *The speech was full of righteous anger against the West.*

PREPOSITIONS

anger at sth/sb *Her anger at him was obvious from her voice.*

anger over/about sth *There was widespread anger over the government's decision to increase taxes.*

anger against/towards sb *All his anger against Edward had gone.*

in anger (=when you are angry) *He said it in anger, and regretted it later.*

angle *n*

the shape that is formed when two straight lines or surfaces meet each other

ADJECTIVES

a right angle (=an angle of 90°) *A square has four right angles.*

a 45 degree/60 degree etc angle *The two lines are at a 45 degree angle.*

a steep/sharp angle *The plane flew upwards at a steep angle into the sky.*

a slight angle *The tool should be held at a slight angle to the surface.*

an acute angle (=an angle of less than 90°) *The rays of the evening sun shone down at an acute angle.*

VERBS

measure/calculate the angle *Measure the angle between the two lines.*

change/adjust the angle of sth *You can adjust the angle of the screen.*

PREPOSITIONS

an angle of 45 degrees/90 degrees etc *Raise the other leg slowly to an angle of 45°.*

the angle between sth *The angle between the two lines should be 60 degrees.*

at an angle *The posts are pushed into the ground at an angle.*

angry *adj*

feeling or showing strong emotions because you think someone has behaved badly, or because a situation seems bad or unfair

ADVERBS

very/really/extremely angry *His comments made me really angry.*

increasingly angry/more and more angry *Passengers became increasingly angry as the delays continued.*

visibly angry (=in a way that is easy to see) *He was visibly angry when a reporter asked another question.*

justifiably angry (=having a good reason to be angry) *Mark was justifiably angry at his punishment.*

NOUNS

people are angry *People are still angry at the way they have been treated.*

an angry man/woman *Henry was a very angry man.*

an angry crowd/mob *An angry crowd gathered outside City Hall.*

angry customers/fans/parents/residents etc *Angry customers demanded their money back.*

an angry face/expression/voice *His voice sounded angry on the phone.*

an angry protest/demonstration *There were angry protests outside government buildings.*

an angry response/reaction *His comments brought an angry response from opposition politicians.*

an angry argument/exchange *The meeting ended in an angry argument.*

an angry scene (=a situation in which people become very angry and often shout at each other) *There were angry scenes outside the court as the prisoner arrived.*

an angry outburst (=when someone suddenly says something in an angry way) *He later apologized for his angry outburst.*

angry words *The two men exchanged angry words.*

an angry letter/phone call *He wrote an angry letter complaining about the service he had received.*

VERBS

get/become angry *The children were misbehaving, and I was starting to get angry.*

feel angry *I felt so angry with her for leaving me.*

look/sound angry *Tony suddenly sounded angry.*

make sb angry *Jesse laughed, which made him even angrier.*

PREPOSITIONS

angry with sb *"Please don't be angry with me," she said.*

angry about/over/at sth *He's still angry about the way the company has treated him.*

PHRASES

angry and frustrated/upset *Anne was angry and upset when she heard the news.*

THESAURUS: angry

annoyed
if you are annoyed about something, you feel a little angry:
*I was annoyed because no one had told me the class was cancelled. | She was **annoyed with** him for being late.*

> **Annoyed** is not usually used before a noun.

irritated
annoyed and impatient, especially because something keeps happening or someone keeps saying or doing something:
*I was **irritated by** their stupid questions. | I **get irritated** when I hear people saying that teachers don't work hard. | "Please speak more clearly," she said in a very **irritated voice**.*

mad *informal*
very angry:
*Dad was **mad at** me for damaging his car.*

> **Mad** is not used before a noun in this meaning.

bad-tempered
a bad-tempered person becomes angry or annoyed easily and behaves in an unfriendly way:
The caretaker was a bad-tempered old man. | She's always bad-tempered when she doesn't get what she wants.

> **Bad-tempered** can also be used about situations or events in which people often become angry: *It was a **bad-tempered** game, and three players were sent off.*

grumpy *informal*
a grumpy person becomes annoyed easily. **Grumpy** is more informal than **bad-tempered**, and sounds less serious:
My husband's always grumpy first thing in the morning. | You sound like a grumpy old woman.

in a bad/foul mood
feeling a little angry for a period of time, often for no particular reason. **Foul** sounds more informal than **bad**:
I woke up in a bad mood. | She's been in a foul mood all morning.

furious
argument | row | debate | attack | reaction | response
extremely angry:
*The couple had a furious argument. | The minister's comments provoked a furious reaction. | She was **furious with** him when she found out he'd been lying to her. | Ella was absolutely **furious at** this news.*

irate
customer | boss | husband | father | parents | resident | voice | letter | (phone) call
extremely angry, especially because you think you have been treated badly or unfairly:
*Irate customers rang the store to complain. | He wrote an irate letter to the editor of the newspaper. | Passengers were **irate at** the delay.*

> **Irate** is often used before a noun.

heated
debate | discussion | argument | row | exchange | talks
a heated argument, debate etc is one in which people have strong opinions and become angry:

A

After a heated debate, councillors voted to accept the proposal. | He was having a heated argument with the referee.

Heated is usually used before a noun.

livid
if someone is livid, they are extremely angry: *Her father was* ***livid with*** *her. | He looked absolutely livid.*

Livid is not usually used before a noun.

outraged
very angry and shocked by something you think is unfair or wrong:
Most people were ***outraged by*** *the attacks. | The director said he was* ***outraged at*** *the ban on the film. |* ***Outraged viewers*** *complained about the programme.*

animal *n*

a living creature such as a dog or cat, that is not an insect, plant, bird, fish, or person

ADJECTIVES/NOUNS + animal

a wild animal *We have laws which prevent the killing of many wild animals.*

a dangerous animal *Australia is home to some of the world's most dangerous animals.*

an exotic animal *The jungle is full of tigers and other exotic animals.*

a farm animal *Generally speaking, it is better for farm animals to have plenty of space.*

a domestic animal (=kept as a pet or on a farm) *The disease affects sheep and other domestic animals.*

a land animal *The cheetah is the fastest land animal in the world.*

a marine animal (=living in the sea) *Many marine animals are poisonous.*

a furry animal *Children love little furry animals.*

animal + NOUNS

animal rights *Animal rights protesters want the laboratory to be closed.*

animal welfare (=providing good care and living conditions for animals) *People are becoming much more concerned about animal welfare.*

animal products *I always check the label to make sure that it does not contain animal products.*

an animal lover *The actress is an animal lover who keeps her own chickens and goats.*

the animal kingdom/world *The creature had the largest known eyes in the whole animal kingdom.*

an animal species/a species of animal (=a type of animal) *There are over 50 animal species on the island.*

animal experiments/testing (*also* **experiments/testing on animals**) *I disagree with animal testing – I think it is cruel and unnecessary.*

VERBS

keep animals *We're not allowed to keep animals in our apartment.*

test sth on animals *Many people are against testing beauty products on animals.*

kill an animal *They believe it is morally wrong to kill any animal.*

slaughter an animal (=kill an animal, especially for its meat) *Some religions have rules about the way animals should be slaughtered.*

hunt an animal *The animals were hunted for their fur.*

animate *adj* THESAURUS alive (1)

anniversary *n*

a date on which something important happened in a previous year

ADJECTIVES/NOUNS + anniversary

a wedding anniversary *It's my parents' wedding anniversary today.*

first/fifth/twentieth etc anniversary *The Society had a party for its 20th anniversary.*

silver/golden/diamond anniversary *They celebrated their golden wedding anniversary last September.*

A **silver anniversary** is after 25 years, a **golden anniversary** is after 50 years, and a **diamond anniversary** is after 60 years.

VERBS

celebrate an anniversary *The school is celebrating its 150th anniversary this year.*

mark/commemorate an anniversary (=remember an anniversary, especially by doing something special) *An exhibition will be held next year to mark the 100th anniversary of his birth.*

an anniversary falls on a particular day *Our wedding anniversary falls on Easter Sunday this year.*

anniversary + NOUNS

an anniversary celebration *There will be a special concert as part of the school's 350th anniversary celebrations.*

an anniversary party/dinner *The couple are having a twenty-fifth wedding anniversary party.*

sth's anniversary year *This history of the university is being published in its 500th anniversary year.*

PREPOSITIONS

the anniversary of sth *That day is the anniversary of the country's independence.*

on the anniversary of sth *A memorial service was held on the anniversary of the disaster.*

A

announce *v*
to officially tell people some news

ADVERBS

officially/formally announce sth *His death was officially announced on Tuesday morning.*

publicly announce sth *She has not publicly announced that she is willing to accept the job.*

triumphantly announce sth (=in a way that shows you are very pleased or proud) *The doctors triumphantly announced that they had found a cure for the disease.*

sth will be announced shortly/will shortly be announced (=soon) *The details of the agreement will be announced shortly.*

PREPOSITIONS

announce sth to sb *I announced to my parents that I wanted to stop eating meat.*

announcement *n*
an official public statement

ADJECTIVES/NOUNS + announcement

an official announcement *No official announcement is expected until next year.*

a formal announcement *A formal announcement will be made in Parliament.*

a government announcement *He welcomed a recent government announcement that an extra £25 million would be made available.*

a public announcement *He got in touch with me several days before the public announcement was made.*

an important announcement *He said he had an important announcement to make.*

a surprise/unexpected announcement *The senator made the surprise announcement that he will not be seeking re-election.*

a dramatic announcement (=sudden and important) *The dramatic announcement came after a cabinet meeting on Tuesday.*

VERBS

make/issue an announcement *He made the announcement to reporters at a press conference.*

hear an announcement *Everyone was shocked when they heard the announcement.*

greet an announcement *formal* (=react to it in a particular way) *The announcement was greeted with cheers.*

an announcement comes (=happens) *His announcement came after two days of peace talks.*

> **Make or issue an announcement?**
> **Make** is much more common than **issue**. **Issue** is used especially about companies and organizations making an announcement to the media: *The government is expected to **issue** a formal **announcement** soon.*

PREPOSITIONS

an announcement about sth *An announcement about the future of the festival will be made shortly.*

the announcement of sth *The announcement of his death sent everyone into shock.*

an announcement by/from sb *An announcement by the minister is expected within days.*

annoyed *adj* slightly angry

VERBS

get/become annoyed *Some of the passengers were beginning to get annoyed because of the delay.*

feel annoyed *She felt annoyed with herself for making such a silly mistake.*

ADVERBS

very/really annoyed *If you don't clear this mess up, I will be very annoyed.*

a little/slightly/a bit annoyed *I was a bit annoyed because I had to wait for him.*

clearly/visibly annoyed *The coach was clearly annoyed at his team's performance.*

PREPOSITIONS

annoyed about/by/at sth *He feels annoyed about the way he has been treated.*

annoyed with/at sb *She was annoyed with Duncan for forgetting to phone.*

> **THESAURUS: annoyed**
> annoyed, irritated, mad, cross, bad-tempered, grumpy, in a bad/foul mood, furious, irate, heated, livid, outraged, indignant → **angry**

annoying *adj*
making you feel slightly angry

ADVERBS

very/really/extremely annoying *I found the whole situation extremely annoying.*

slightly/a little/a bit annoying *It was a little annoying when I found out that the time of the meeting had changed.*

rather annoying *They asked some rather annoying questions.*

particularly annoying *The delay was particularly annoying because I needed to get home early that night.*

NOUNS

an annoying habit *She has an annoying habit of whistling while she does things.*

the annoying thing *The most annoying thing is that he is usually right.*

an annoying problem *My computer seems to have developed an annoying problem.*

an annoying man/woman/person *Her husband is probably the most annoying person I've ever met.*

A

VERBS

become/get annoying *The sound of the music was starting to become annoying.*

find sth annoying *I found his attitude to women really annoying.*

PHRASES

How annoying! *"He keeps making a funny noise through his nose." "How annoying!"*

it's so annoying when... *"My computer has just crashed." "It's so annoying when that happens."*

THESAURUS: annoying

irritating
noise | habit | mannerism
annoying – used especially about something that keeps happening or something that someone often does:
The bedside light kept making an irritating buzzing noise. | She has some rather irritating little mannerisms – she keeps saying 'like' all the time (=she has some rather annoying little habits). | I ***found*** *their constant questions* ***intensely irritating****.*

tiresome
business | task | woman | man
annoying, especially in a way that makes you feel bored or impatient:
Getting all the necessary documents is a tiresome business. | They began the tiresome task of pulling up all the weeds. | One tiresome woman kept asking endless questions.

infuriating/maddening
thing | smile | habit
very annoying:
The maddening thing was that it was too late to change my ticket. | He had an infuriating habit of not always telling the truth. | It was maddening to be treated like a child.

frustrating
experience | time | morning | afternoon | day | business
annoying because it is difficult or impossible for you to do what you want:
Searching for information on the internet can be an extremely frustrating experience. | I spent a frustrating afternoon trying to fix the car. | Trying to speak to someone at the bank is a frustrating business. | He ***found*** *his inability to speak* ***deeply frustrating****.*

trying
time | day | morning | afternoon | experience
annoying because you cannot do what you want, or because of being difficult to deal with:
He had just had rather a trying day at the office. | Applying for a visa can be a very trying experience. | Young children can be extremely trying and you need a lot of patience.

annul *v* THESAURUS ▸ cancel

answer[1] *n*

1 something you say or write as a reply

ADJECTIVES

a short/long answer *During the interview, he mostly gave short answers to my questions.*

a one-word answer *It's not very helpful to just give one-word answers such as 'yes' or 'no'.*

an honest/straight answer *The honest answer is that I don't know.*

a definite answer *Can you give me a definite answer tomorrow?*

a satisfactory answer *I didn't get a satisfactory answer from the company.*

VERBS

give sb an answer *I'll give you an answer tomorrow.*

get/receive an answer *She wrote to him, but she never got an answer.*

wait for an answer *Kate was looking at me, waiting for an answer.*

think of an answer *She couldn't think of a suitable answer to his question.*

demand an answer *He demanded an answer to his question.*

PREPOSITIONS

the answer to a question *These are important questions, and we want answers to them.*

in answer to your question *In answer to your question, yes, you can go.*

PHRASES

the answer is no/yes *If it's money that you want, the answer is no.*

the short answer is... (=used when giving a simple, honest, or direct answer to a difficult question) *The short answer is that it can't be done.*

2 something that you write or say in reply to a question in a test or competition

ADJECTIVES

the right/wrong answer *Do you know the right answer to this question?*

the correct/incorrect answer *You get 5 points for each correct answer.*

VERBS

know the answer *Put up your hand if you know the answer.*

guess the answer *If you don't know the answer, try guessing it.*

write the answer *Write your answer in the space provided.*

give/put an answer *I think I gave the wrong answer to question 6.*

PREPOSITIONS

the answer to a question *What was the answer to question 4?*

3 the solution to a problem

ADJECTIVES

a simple/easy answer *I'm afraid there are no easy answers in this type of situation.*

the obvious answer *The obvious answer is to raise taxes, but that would be very unpopular.*

the only answer *Military force is not the only answer.*

the perfect answer (=one that is certain to succeed) *It sounded like the perfect answer.*

the long-term answer (=which will solve problems in the future as well as now) *He believes that wind power is the long-term answer to our growing energy crisis.*

a possible answer *In the next chapter we will discuss a number of possible answers to this problem.*

VERBS

have the answer *He thinks he may have the answer to their problems.*

be the answer *Spending more money is not always the answer.*

look/search for an answer *People have been searching for an answer for years.*

find/come up with an answer *Scientists believe they have found an answer to the problem of climate change.*

know the answer *If anyone knows the answer, it's her.*

the answer comes to sb *The answer to her problem suddenly came to her.*

the answer lies somewhere (=you can find it there) *A lot of people seem to think the answer lies in technology.*

PREPOSITIONS

the answer to a problem *Maybe he has the answer to our problem.*

PHRASES

have all the answers *I wish I had all the answers, but I don't.*

answer² *v*

to give an answer to a question

ADVERBS

answer correctly *You have to answer 80% of the questions correctly in order to pass the test.*

answer honestly *"I don't know where he is," she answered honestly.*

answer fully (=completely) *I hope that I have fully answered your question.*

answer directly (=say what you mean without trying to hide anything) *He didn't answer directly when asked if he knew who had stolen the money.*

VERBS

refuse to answer (*also* **decline to answer** *formal*): *The man shook his head and refused to answer any more questions.*

try/attempt to answer *Sandra tried to answer her daughter's question as honestly as she could.*

anticipation *n*

excited or nervous feelings about something that is going to happen

ADJECTIVES

great anticipation *There was a feeling of great anticipation before the game.*

eager/keen anticipation (=very enthusiastic anticipation) *The crowd waited with eager anticipation for their heroes to arrive on stage.*

growing anticipation *There was growing anticipation among students as the day for exam results approached.*

PREPOSITIONS

in/with anticipation *I was licking my lips in anticipation.*

PHRASES

await/look forward to sth with anticipation (=feel excited because you know something is going to happen soon) *The birth of the baby was awaited with great anticipation.*

antiquated *adj* THESAURUS ▶ **old-fashioned**

antique *adj* THESAURUS ▶ **old (1)**

anxiety *n*

the feeling of being very worried because you think something bad might happen

ADJECTIVES

great/considerable anxiety *There is considerable anxiety about job losses.*

acute/deep anxiety (=which affects someone very strongly) *His enthusiasm was followed by deep anxiety about what lay ahead of him.*

constant anxiety *We lived in a state of constant anxiety about money.*

increasing/growing/mounting anxiety *There is growing anxiety about the rise in violent crime.*

VERBS

cause/create anxiety (*also* **arouse anxiety** *formal*): *The lack of rain is causing anxiety among farmers.*

lead to anxiety/give rise to anxiety (=cause it to happen later) *Stress at work can lead to anxiety and even depression.*

feel/suffer from anxiety *Children often feel anxiety when they are leaving home for the first time.*

reduce/relieve anxiety *The drug helps to reduce anxiety and make you feel more relaxed.*

anxiety grows *As the storm got worse, anxiety grew among the passengers on the ship.*

A

anxiety + NOUNS

an anxiety attack (=a sudden very strong feeling of fear) *Two-thirds of all people who suffer from anxiety attacks are women.*

PREPOSITIONS

anxiety about/over sth *There is a lot of anxiety about the future.*

anxiety among a group of people *The disease is causing anxiety among the local population.*

PHRASES

feelings of anxiety *Feelings of anxiety are natural in this kind of situation.*

a state of anxiety *His mother lived in a constant state of anxiety about what was going to happen to her family.*

a source of anxiety *For many people, the main source of anxiety is work.*

apartment *n*

a set of rooms on one floor of a large building, where someone lives

ADJECTIVES/NOUNS + apartment

a large/spacious apartment *Aida's family own a large apartment near the city centre.*

a small/tiny/cramped apartment (=one that has very little space) *It is tough bringing up a family in a cramped apartment.*

a one-bedroom/two-bedroom etc apartment *A tiny one-bedroom apartment was all she could afford.*

a studio apartment (=with just one main room, which you use for sleeping, cooking, and eating) *She had just moved from her small studio apartment.*

a first-floor/second-floor etc apartment *He climbed the stairs to his fourth-floor apartment.*

a luxury apartment *The school has been converted into luxury apartments.*

a penthouse apartment (=on the top floor of a building - used especially about a large expensive apartment) *She bought a penthouse apartment in Santa Monica.*

VERBS

live in an apartment *He lived in a small apartment on the third floor.*

share an apartment *I'm sharing the apartment with a group of friends.*

buy/rent an apartment *He rented an apartment for forty dollars a month.*

own an apartment *My parents own an apartment in Madrid.*

move into/out of an apartment *They moved into the apartment last Easter.*

apartment + NOUNS

an apartment building (*also* **an apartment block** *BrE*, **an apartment house** *AmE*): *They lived in the same apartment building.*

an apartment complex (=a group of buildings containing apartments)

Apartment or flat?

British people usually say **flat**. **Apartment** is used in British English, but it sounds bigger and more impressive than a **flat**. It is often used in advertisements.

American people say **apartment**. An **apartment** that you own yourself, in a building with several other apartments, is called a **condominium** (or **condo**) in American English.

apologize (*also* apologise *BrE*) *v*

to tell someone that you are sorry that you have done something wrong

ADVERBS

sincerely apologize *We sincerely apologize for the delay.*

humbly apologize (=apologize in a way that shows you know you were wrong) *I humbly apologize for any offence I may have caused.*

apologize profusely (=apologize a lot) *He apologized profusely for arriving so late.*

apologize publicly *The company apologized publicly for the way customers had been treated.*

PREPOSITIONS

apologize to sb *I think you should apologize to your brother.*

apologize for sth *The airline apologized for the mistake.*

apologize on behalf of sb *I'd like to apologize on behalf of the company for what has happened.*

PHRASES

I want to apologize/I'd like to apologize *I want to apologize for the other night. I'm afraid I drank too much.*

there's no need to apologize *"I'm sorry about your plate." "There's no need to apologize. It could happen to anyone."*

apology *n*

something that you say or write to show that you are sorry for doing something wrong

ADJECTIVES

a public apology *The company published a public apology in the newspaper.*

a formal apology *The document contained a formal apology for the suffering that has been caused.*

an official apology *The government has made an official apology and is offering compensation.*

a personal apology *The chief executive made a personal apology to customers.*

a written apology *The police sent a written apology to the family.*

a full apology *He is insisting on a full apology.*

a sincere/profound/heartfelt apology (=when you are genuinely very sorry) *I want to offer you a sincere apology.*

an abject apology *formal* (=one that shows that you are very sorry) *The newspaper was forced to issue an abject apology.*

VERBS

make an apology *I hope you are going to make an apology for what you said.*

issue an apology (=make an official public apology) *North Korea issued an official apology for the incident.*

get/receive an apology *He received a formal apology from the company.*

offer an apology *We would like to offer our sincere apologies for the delay.*

accept sb's apology *Please accept my apologies for having to cancel our meeting.*

demand an apology *China continued to demand a full apology from the US.*

owe sb an apology *I'm afraid I owe you an apology.*

publish an apology *The newspaper group was forced to publish a full apology.*

PREPOSITIONS

an apology for (doing) sth *He offered an apology for his remarks.*

an apology to sb *She made an apology to her colleagues.*

an apology from sb *The people of Wales deserve an apology from the government.*

You often use **my apologies** when saying politely that you are sorry about something: *Firstly,* ***my*** *sincere* ***apologies*** *for not having contacted you earlier.*

PHRASES

a letter of apology *She received a letter of apology from the hospital.*

appalling *adj* THESAURUS ▸ **terrible**

appeal *n*

1 an urgent request, especially one in which you ask people to help you or give money

ADJECTIVES

an urgent/desperate appeal *The family made a desperate appeal to their daughter to come home.*

a direct appeal *The police have issued a direct appeal to the witness to come forward with information.*

a personal appeal *Political leaders made a personal appeal for the hostage's freedom.*

an international appeal *The organization has now launched an international appeal for volunteers.*

a nationwide appeal *The missing 15-year-old was found yesterday after a nationwide appeal.*

a public/official appeal *The girl's family have made a public appeal for help to try to catch her killer.*

a fresh appeal (=one that you make again) *The growing violence in the country has led to fresh appeals for calm.*

VERBS

make/issue an appeal *The police have made an appeal for information about the robbery.*

launch an appeal (=make a public appeal about something important, in a carefully planned way) *The charity launched an appeal for money to help the victims of the floods.*

renew an appeal (=make an appeal again) *Detectives renewed their appeal for help from the public.*

give/donate/contribute to an appeal *People gave very generously to the appeal.*

an appeal raises money *The appeal raised over a million dollars.*

NOUNS + appeal

an emergency appeal *An emergency appeal for blankets has been issued.*

a fund-raising appeal (=to get money to pay for something) *A fund-raising appeal was launched to pay for a new school gym.*

a charity appeal *He often gives money to charity appeals.*

a television appeal *There was a television appeal for the victims of the floods.*

a disaster/earthquake/flood etc appeal *You can now give money online to disaster appeals.*

PREPOSITIONS

an appeal to sb *The university has made an urgent appeal to the government, asking for extra funding.*

an appeal for sth *They launched an appeal for money to help people who had been affected by the earthquake.*

2 a formal request to a court or to someone in authority asking for a decision to be changed

ADJECTIVES

a formal appeal *She decided to make a formal appeal through her lawyer.*

VERBS

make an appeal *His lawyer said that he was planning to make an appeal.*

file/lodge/bring an appeal (=make an appeal in a court) *She lodged an appeal against the court's decision.*

consider an appeal *The US Supreme Court is considering the men's appeal.*

hear an appeal (=listen to all the facts) *The Committee will hear the club's appeal against the fine next week.*

win/lose an appeal *Unless she wins her appeal, she will be imprisoned.*

uphold/allow an appeal (=give permission for a decision to be changed) *Judge Gabriel Hutton upheld Smith's appeal.*

A

A

dismiss/throw out/turn down an appeal (=not give permission for a decision to be changed) *His appeal was dismissed and he was sent to prison.*

an appeal fails/succeeds *If the appeal fails, he will serve his full sentence.*

appeal + NOUNS

the appeal process *The appeal process could take as long as three years.*

PREPOSITIONS

an appeal to a court *They made an appeal to the European Court of Human Rights.*

an appeal against a decision/fine/sentence *He made an appeal against the judge's decision.*

on appeal (=after making an appeal) *The sentence was reduced to three years on appeal.*

PHRASES

the right of appeal *He used his right of appeal against the demand for money from the tax department.*

grounds for an appeal (=reasons for making an appeal) *You need to have reasonable grounds for your appeal.*

pending appeal (=until an appeal can take place) *Both men were under house arrest, pending appeal of their convictions.*

3 a quality that makes people like something or someone

ADJECTIVES

great/considerable/a lot of appeal *This film will have considerable appeal for science fiction fans.*

(a) wide appeal (=it attracts many types of people) *The programme has a very wide appeal.*

(a) universal appeal (=everyone likes something) *The Harry Potter books have a universal appeal.*

(an) immediate/instant appeal *Their music had an instant appeal for me when I was young.*

(an) enduring appeal (=continuing for a long time) *The book has had an enduring appeal and it is just as popular now as it was when it was first written.*

VERBS

lose its appeal *The job had lost its appeal and she was starting to get bored.*

have an appeal (*also* **hold an appeal** *formal*): *Being rich and famous held no appeal for him – he just wanted to write songs.*

increase/add to the appeal of sth *The new design adds to the car's appeal.*

give sth appeal *It is the original design that gives the building its appeal.*

understand the appeal of sth *I must admit I have never understood the appeal of golf.*

the appeal lies in sth *The country's appeal lies in its lakes and rivers.*

PREPOSITIONS

the appeal of sth *What is the particular appeal of this island?*

appeal for sb *The programme has great appeal for young audiences.*

appear *v*

1 to start to be seen

NOUNS

a man/woman/boy/girl etc appears *A young man appeared at the door and asked to speak to my sister.*

sb's face/hand appears *The dog's sleepy face appeared in the back window.*

a car/ship/plane appears *A police car suddenly appeared in his rearview mirror.*

the sun/moon/clouds appear *A pale sun had appeared in the sky.*

flowers/leaves/shoots appear (=they start to grow) *The first flowers appear in the spring.*

a crack/hole appears *Cracks are starting to appear in the ceiling.*

a report/study/article/story/picture etc appears (=it is published or shown) *The study first appeared in the 'New England Journal of Medicine'.*

a box/menu appears (=on your computer screen) *A box appears, which contains the following message: 'An error has occurred in your application'.*

ADVERBS

first/originally appear *This article first appeared in the 'New Yorker' magazine.*

suddenly appear *A big hole suddenly appeared in the street.*

magically appear *These genes did not just magically appear – they developed over millions of years.*

PHRASES

appear out of nowhere (=suddenly in a surprising way) *A group of masked men appeared out of nowhere and told him to get in the car.*

THESAURUS: appear

pop up
face | head | name | menu | sign | restaurant
to appear suddenly. **Pop up** sounds rather informal:
A woman's face popped up from the other side of the fence. | His name keeps popping up in music reviews. | When you press this button, a menu pops up. | Michael suddenly popped up and asked us what we were doing.

come into view
house | building | castle | ship | mountain | coast
if something comes into view, you start to

see it as you get closer to it, or as it gets closer to you:
At that moment the castle came into view. | The coast of France came into view.

come out
sun | moon | stars
to appear in the sky:
The sun came out from behind a cloud. | I sit by my window watching the stars come out.

loom/loom up
face | figure | shape | building | mountain
to suddenly appear in a frightening way:
A face loomed up out of the darkness. | They both looked up as the tall figure of Hassan loomed over them. | The dark shape of the castle loomed out of the mist. | A huge grey building loomed over the avenue like an enormous battleship. | The mountain looms over this small mining town.

resurface
to appear again after being lost or missing – used especially about people or problems:
The girl's father has resurfaced after six years of no contact. | The issue of inaccurate news reports resurfaced last week.

If you start to be able to see something, you can say it becomes **visible**: *The shape of the baby's head gradually became* ***visible*** *on the screen.*

ANTONYMS **appear → disappear**

2 to seem

Grammar
This meaning of **appear** is usually used with an adjective, or with the verb **to be**: *She* ***appeared*** *calm at first. | The paintings* ***appear to be*** *by the same person.*

PHRASES

it appears (that)... *It appears that all the files have been deleted.*

what appears to be *Police have found what appear to be human remains.*

3 to be seen in public, in a court case, or in a movie, play etc

PHRASES

appear in public *The emperor rarely appears in public.*

appear in court/appear before a judge *Griffiths is due to appear in court next month, charged with murder.*

appear in a film/movie/play/show etc *She first appeared in the movie 'Taxi Driver'.*

appear on television/on screen *The president will appear on national television to talk about the decision.*

appearance *n*

the way someone or something looks to other people

ADJECTIVES

general/overall appearance *They want to improve the town's overall appearance.*

physical appearance *We are often attracted to somebody first by their physical appearance.*

personal appearance *Some men don't care very much about their personal appearance.*

odd/strange/bizarre appearance *Children sometimes stared at him because of his odd appearance.*

distinctive/striking appearance (=unusual and interesting) *The unusual leaves give the plant a distinctive appearance.*

attractive/handsome/pleasing appearance *The hotel didn't have a very attractive appearance.*

the outward appearance (=how a person or situation seems to be, rather than how they really are) *Beneath the outward appearance of confidence, she is very shy.*

youthful appearance (=someone looks young, especially when they are older) *She was no longer a young woman, despite her youthful appearance.*

VERBS

have a ... appearance *The restaurant has a pleasant appearance.*

improve the appearance (*also* **enhance the appearance** *formal*): *Fresh air improves the appearance of the skin.*

spoil the appearance *The metal posts spoiled the appearance of the garden.*

change/alter the appearance *The new factory will change the appearance of the area enormously.*

give sb/sth a ... appearance *His uniform gave him an official appearance.*

give the appearance of doing sth *He likes to give the appearance of being hard-working.*

PREPOSITIONS

the appearance of sb/sth *They've changed the appearance of the whole building.*

PHRASES

take pride in your appearance (=make an effort to look good) *She's the kind of woman who takes pride in her appearance.*

judge by appearances (=make judgements based on the way someone or something looks) *You shouldn't judge by appearances.*

to all appearances (=used when saying how someone or something looks, especially when this is different from the real situation) *He was, to all appearances, a respectable businessman.*

appearances can be deceptive (=the way something seems to be may not be how it really is) *The pupils looked well-behaved – but appearances can be deceptive.*

A

appetite *n* a desire for food

ADJECTIVES

a good/healthy appetite *Growing children should have a healthy appetite.*

a big/huge/enormous/hearty appetite *Most small boys have enormous appetites.*

a voracious/ravenous appetite (=you want a very large amount of food) *The dog had a voracious appetite and was asking for more food.*

a poor appetite (=a desire for less food than you need) *A poor appetite may be a sign of illness.*

a small appetite *If your child has a small appetite, give him or her smaller meals more frequently.*

VERBS

have an appetite *There's lots of food – I hope you have a good appetite.*

lose your appetite *She was so miserable that she completely lost her appetite.*

regain your appetite *He is feeling better and has regained his appetite.*

give sb an appetite (*also* **stimulate your appetite** *formal*): *The exercise and fresh air had given us an appetite.*

work up an appetite (=become hungry by being active) *We went for a long walk to work up an appetite.*

satisfy sb's appetite (=stop someone feeling hungry) *At each mealtime, eat enough to satisfy your appetite.*

spoil/ruin sb's appetite (=make someone not feel like eating a meal) *Don't give the children any more sweets – it will spoil their appetite.*

suppress/take away sb's appetite (=make someone not feel hungry) *The drug helps suppress your appetite.*

PHRASES

loss/lack of appetite *Symptoms include fever and loss of appetite.*

appetizing *adj* THESAURUS ▸ **delicious**

applause *n*
the sound of many people hitting their hands together to show that they have enjoyed something

ADJECTIVES

loud applause *There was loud applause as the young man received his award.*

deafening/thunderous/tumultuous applause (=very loud applause) *The band came on stage to thunderous applause.*

wild/rapturous applause (=very excited applause) *The audience burst into wild applause.*

polite applause *There was polite applause from some members of the audience.*

VERBS

break/burst/erupt into applause (=suddenly begin to applaud) *The excited crowd broke into loud applause.*

get/receive/win applause *He got more applause than any other player.*

draw applause (=receive applause – more formal) *Clapton's playing drew applause from the audience.*

applause dies down/away (=people stop clapping) *The applause died down as the curtains began to close.*

PREPOSITIONS

applause for sb *Can we please have a round of applause for our speaker, Mr John Richmond?*

PHRASES

a round of applause (=a short period of applause) *She got a round of applause when she finished.*

a burst of applause (=a short sudden period of applause) *A burst of applause greeted the band as they walked on stage.*

a roar of applause *The models came into the room to a roar of applause.*

a ripple of applause (=applause that comes from only some of the people in the audience) *A ripple of applause followed his remark.*

appliance *n* THESAURUS ▸ **machine**

applicable *adj* THESAURUS ▸ **relevant**

application *n*
a formal, usually written, request for something such as a job, place at university, or permission to do something

NOUNS + application

a job application *He's made 23 job applications and had 5 interviews.*

a visa application *It can take several weeks for your visa application to be processed.*

a planning application (=asking for permission to build something) *They put in a planning application for a new housing development.*

a loan/grant/mortgage application *His loan application was rejected by the bank.*

ADJECTIVES

a formal application *Turkey made a formal application to join the European Union.*

VERBS

make an application *Students usually make their applications for university in September.*

fill out/fill in an application *I filled out an application for a secretarial job.*

put in/send in/submit an application *The company has submitted a planning application.*

consider an application (=think about it before deciding) *The licensing committee met to consider his application.*

grant/approve an application (=say yes) *Your mortgage application has been approved.*

refuse/reject/turn down an application *He*

received a letter saying that his application had been rejected.

process an application *When I contacted the embassy, they said they were still processing my visa application.*

withdraw your application *The company withdrew its application to build the bridge.*

application + NOUNS

an application form *Simply fill in the application form and return it to your bank.*

PREPOSITIONS

an application for sth *We have put in an application for a grant to repair the roof.*

an application from sb *The university welcomes applications from overseas students.*

PHRASES

a letter of application *The purpose of your letter of application is to get an interview.*

apply *v*

1 to formally ask for something, for example a job

> **Grammar**
> You usually **apply for** something or **apply to** do something.

NOUNS

apply for a job/post *She enjoys working with children so she's applied for a job as a teacher.*

apply for a course *More students are applying for science courses than arts courses.*

apply for permission *We've applied to the council for permission to knock down a wall.*

apply for a licence/passport/visa *Have you applied for a visa for your trip to India?*

apply for a loan/grant *He doesn't have enough money for a new car, but he could apply for a loan.*

ADVERBS

apply directly *If the flight is cancelled, you have to apply directly to the airline to get your money back.*

apply online *To open a bank account, visit your local branch or apply online.*

2 to use something

> **THESAURUS: apply**
> utilize, employ, apply, draw on sth, exploit, resort to sth, exercise, exert → **use**[1]

appointment *n*

an arrangement to see someone, for a professional or medical reason

ADJECTIVES/NOUNS + appointment

a hospital appointment *BrE: My hospital appointment lasted half an hour.*

a doctor's appointment *What time is your doctor's appointment?*

a dentist's/dental appointment *She has a dental appointment, so she won't be in until later.*

a medical appointment *Children sometimes miss school because of medical appointments.*

a business appointment *Dennis had an early morning business appointment with a client.*

a morning/afternoon appointment *I asked for a morning appointment.*

VERBS

have an appointment *She has an appointment with the dentist at 5 o'clock.*

make/arrange an appointment *Can you phone the hairdresser and make an appointment?*

book an appointment *BrE*, **schedule an appointment** *AmE* (=make an appointment) *I've scheduled your appointment for 9.30.*

get an appointment (=succeed in arranging one) *It's difficult to get an appointment on Monday morning.*

cancel an appointment *He had to cancel all his afternoon appointments.*

miss an appointment (=not go to an appointment you have arranged) *The train was late so I missed my appointment.*

keep an appointment (=go to an appointment that you have arranged) *Please let us know if you cannot keep your appointment.*

PREPOSITIONS

an appointment with sb *I have an appointment with my lawyer this afternoon.*

an appointment at the doctor's/the hospital etc *Have you booked another appointment at the clinic?*

by appointment (=if you have made an appointment) *The collection can be viewed by appointment only.*

appreciate *v*

1 to realize something or understand that it is important or useful

NOUNS

appreciate the importance/significance/value of sth *To avoid disease in this area, you have to appreciate the importance of clean drinking water.*

appreciate the fact *Younger students don't always appreciate the fact that teachers are trying to help them.*

appreciate the difference *A good manager appreciates the difference between helpful and hurtful criticism.*

ADVERBS

fully appreciate sth *I didn't fully appreciate the dangers of traveling on my own.*

2 if you appreciate something, you are grateful for it

A

NOUNS

appreciate sb's support/help/efforts *It would be difficult to do the job on my own, so I really appreciate your help.*

appreciate sb's concern *I appreciate your concern but you needn't worry – I'm perfectly safe.*

ADVERBS

greatly/deeply appreciate *We greatly appreciate all the work you've done.*

really appreciate *She really appreciates all the time you've spent helping her.*

genuinely/truly appreciate *I genuinely appreciate the opportunity they've given me to start a new career.*

You use the phrase **I would appreciate it if** when telling someone firmly (not) to do something: *I'm trying to study, so **I'd appreciate it if** you'd make less noise!*

appreciation *n*

1 grateful feelings

ADJECTIVES

deep appreciation *I'd like to express my deep appreciation for all your support.*

genuine appreciation *She thanked him warmly, with genuine appreciation in her voice.*

VERBS

show/express your appreciation *The audience showed their appreciation by cheering loudly.*

2 the act of understanding something and realising that it is important

ADJECTIVES

a great/deep appreciation *She developed a deep appreciation of classical music at an early age.*

a good/full appreciation *To be a good diver you need a full appreciation of the dangers of the sea.*

a growing appreciation *In the West, there is a growing appreciation of the economic importance of China.*

VERBS

have an appreciation of sth *The prince doesn't have an appreciation of the problems that poor people face.*

develop/gain an appreciation of sth *I only developed an appreciation of the difficulties of the job after a few months.*

show/demonstrate an appreciation of sth *The article shows an appreciation of the complex political situation in the country.*

approach¹ [Ac] *n*

a method of doing something or dealing with a problem

ADJECTIVES

a different/alternative approach *Asking a direct question did not work, so I tried a different approach.*

a new/fresh approach *This is a new approach to teaching languages.*

a traditional approach *Their textbooks follow a very traditional approach.*

a similar approach *They both have a similar approach to management.*

the general/overall approach *Both research projects follow the same general approach.*

a flexible approach (=able to change according to circumstances) *Nowadays, our approach to learning is more flexible.*

a systematic/scientific approach (=following a careful method) *It's best to follow a systematic approach to problem-solving.*

a pragmatic/practical approach (=concerned with practical results, rather than theories or principles) *My approach to my job is very pragmatic.*

a cautious approach (=very careful) *When working with dangerous chemicals, a cautious approach is best.*

VERBS

take/follow/use an approach (*also* **adopt an approach** *formal*): *This book takes an unusual approach to art criticism.*

try an approach *Let's try a new approach.*

prefer/favour an approach *There are signs that the government prefers a radical approach.*

PREPOSITIONS

approach to sth *What is your approach to dealing with difficult behaviour in the classroom?*

approach² [Ac] *v*

1 to start to talk about, think about, or deal with something

NOUNS

approach a subject/issue *The film approached the subject in an interesting way.*

approach a problem *There are many different ways to approach the problem.*

approach a task *Each candidate approached the task in a slightly different way.*

ADVERBS

approach sth cautiously/carefully *He approached the subject of her divorce very carefully.*

PHRASES

approach sth with care/caution *This is a difficult subject and it needs to be approached with caution.*

approach sth in a different way/from a different viewpoint *Maybe we should try and approach the problem in a different way.*

2 to move towards or nearer to someone or something

A

ADVERBS

slowly approach sb/sth *A truck was slowly approaching them along the highway.*

approach sth cautiously/with caution *She approached cautiously and patted the horse's nose.*

approach sth closely *The animals should not be approached too closely.*

approval *n*

1 the fact of liking someone or something, and believing that they are good

ADJECTIVES

public approval *The policy won a lot of public approval.*

universal approval (=from everyone) *His decision has been met with almost universal approval.*

general approval (=from most people) *McGill's views did not gain general approval in the company.*

VERBS

meet with sb's approval (=be approved of by someone) *Her boyfriend did not meet with her mother's approval.*

win/gain approval *His condemnation of the war won widespread approval.*

seek sb's approval *He constantly sought his father's approval.*

look to sb for approval *They all admired Gordon and looked to him for approval.*

PREPOSITIONS

in/with approval *They clapped their hands in approval.*

approval from sb *Teenagers are desperate for approval from people their own age.*

PHRASES

a look/smile/nod of approval *"You've thought of everything," she said with a look of approval.*

a roar/murmur/chorus of approval (=noises showing approval from a group) *There were murmurs of approval from the crowd.*

2 an occasion when a plan, decision, or person is officially accepted

ADJECTIVES/NOUNS + approval

official/formal approval *Finance ministers gave their formal approval in July.*

final approval *The EU has still not granted final approval for the scheme.*

government approval *It can take years for a new drug to receive government approval.*

parental approval (=from someone's parents) *Students must first obtain parental approval.*

VERBS

give (your) approval to sth/give sth your approval *The president has already given his approval to the plan.*

get/win approval (*also* **receive/obtain approval** *formal*): *NASA finally got approval for the mission.*

approval is granted (for sth) (=it is approved) *Approval was granted for the construction work to go ahead.*

require/need approval *A multi-million pound project will require approval by the board of directors.*

seek approval *You will need to make an appointment with the bank to seek approval for the loan.*

submit sth for approval *The final design will be submitted for approval next month.*

PREPOSITIONS

with/without sb's approval *A company cannot be sold without the approval of the shareholders.*

approval by sb *The bill will be submitted for approval by Congress.*

PHRASES

be subject to approval (=need someone's approval before it can happen) *The merger is subject to approval by shareholders.*

sb's seal/stamp of approval (=someone's official approval) *You must not make decisions without your manager's seal of approval.*

approve *v*

1 to think that someone or something is good

> **Grammar**
> In this meaning, you usually say that you **approve of** someone or something.

ADVERBS

very much approve *His parents very much approved of his new girlfriend.*

thoroughly/wholeheartedly/heartily approve (=approve very strongly) *I thoroughly approve of the decision to give the money to charity.*

PHRASES

don't altogether approve (=not completely) *I don't altogether approve of zoos – I think animals are happier living in the wild.*

sb would never approve *My mother would never approve of me staying out so late.*

ANTONYMS **approve → disapprove**

2 to officially accept a plan, proposal etc

NOUNS

approve a bill/amendment/resolution (=vote to accept something) *Congress is expected to approve the bill.*

approve a plan/scheme/proposal *If the board approves the plan, construction work will start next month.*

approve a deal/sale/merger *A majority of the shareholders must approve the deal.*

ADVERBS

approve sth unanimously (=everyone in a

A

group approves something) *The conference unanimously approved a motion condemning the government's actions.*

overwhelmingly approve sth (=almost all of a group approve something) *Parents overwhelmingly approved the proposal to bring back school uniform.*

PREPOSITIONS

approve sth by 100 votes/a large majority etc *The committee approved the plan by 12 votes to 5.*

THESAURUS: approve

pass
law | bill | amendment | resolution
to approve a law or proposal, especially by voting:
The law was passed by a huge majority in Parliament. | Congress passed a bill which made the drug illegal.

ratify
treaty | agreement | deal
to make a written agreement official by signing it or voting about it:
The treaty was ratified by the Senate in 1988. | Australia plans to ratify the deal.

archive *n*

a place where a large number of historical records are stored, or the records that are stored

Grammar
Often plural.

ADJECTIVES/NOUNS + archive

the national archive *The film has been stored in the National Archives in Washington, DC since 1978.*

a digital/electronic archive *There is an electronic archive of all the previous editions of the newspaper.*

an online archive *The online archive can be accessed by internet users all over the world.*

a film/video/music archive *I spent an afternoon looking through the German National Film Archives.*

a literary archive *The letters formed part of a literary archive of the writer's work.*

a large/huge archive *The museum has a huge archive of the artist's paintings and drawings.*

VERBS

be held/stored/kept in an archive *The documents are held in the national archives.*

search/look through an archive *She spent hours searching the archives for information about her family history.*

create/set up an archive *The National Film Archive was set up in 1952.*

an archive contains sth (*also* **an archive houses sth** *formal*): *The archive contains over 50,000 photographs.*

PREPOSITIONS

in an archive *The records are kept in the national archive in Vienna.*

area Ac *n*

1 a particular part of a country, town etc

ADJECTIVES

a large/vast/huge area *Large areas of rainforest have been destroyed.*

the local area *He quickly made friends in the local area.*

the surrounding area *The tourist office will have a map of the surrounding area.*

a rural area (=in the countryside) *Schools in rural areas are often very small.*

an urban area (=in a town or city) *Ninety percent of the English population live in urban areas.*

a remote/isolated area (=a long way from towns and cities) *The animal has been discovered in a remote area of China.*

a wooded/mountainous area *The plane crashed into trees in a heavily wooded area.*

a coastal area *The bird is found mainly in coastal areas.*

a low-lying area *Low-lying areas are likely to be flooded.*

a residential area (=a part of a town where people live) *They had a large house in a pleasant residential area.*

an industrial area *People living in industrial areas are exposed to these types of chemicals.*

a built-up area *BrE* (=with a lot of buildings close together) *New development will not be allowed outside the existing built-up area.*

a deprived area (=where many poor people live) *He grew up in one of the toughest and most deprived areas of Glasgow.*

an inner-city area (=the central part of a city, where many poor people live) *When will something be done to improve our inner-city areas?*

a geographical area (=one that is shown on a map) *The survey took place in three geographical areas.*

a no-smoking/no-parking etc area (=where people are not allowed to smoke, park etc) *The airport terminal is a no-smoking area.*

VERBS

cover an area *The forest covers a big area of the country.*

live in an area *We live in a nice area of the city.*

move into/out of an area *She had just moved into the area and knew very few people.*

A

THESAURUS: area

region
a large area of a country or the world:
The ***entire region*** *was covered in snow. | The earthquake shook China's* ***northern region****. | The soldiers are fighting in a* ***mountainous region*** *of eastern Afghanistan. | They travelled through the* ***desert regions*** *of Ethiopia. | Confucius was walking through a* ***remote region*** *of China* (=far from other places).

zone
a special type of area, especially one where something happens, or where there are special rules:
The country is now a ***war zone****. | California is in an* ***earthquake zone****. | I didn't realise that it was a* ***no-parking zone****. | We crossed two different* ***time zones*** (=areas where there is a particular time compared to the rest of the world).

district
one of the areas a city or town is officially divided into, or an area of a city where a particular group lives or an activity happens:
They live in the Chelsea district of Manhattan. | The ***financial district*** *of London is known as 'the City'.*

neighbourhood *BrE*, **neighborhood** *AmE*
an area of a town where people live:
Payne was born in a ***poor neighborhood*** *of Newark. | I have a decent job, live in a* ***nice neighborhood****, and have a nice home. | This is a friendly neighbourhood and people often stop to talk to each other in the street. | There are lots of trees* ***in our neighborhood****.*

suburb
an area outside the centre of a city, where people live:
We moved to a ***quiet suburb*** *of Boston. | The school is in a* ***leafy suburb*** *of Paris* (=one with a lot of trees).

2 a particular subject or type of activity

ADJECTIVES/NOUNS + area

a subject area *The course covers four main subject areas.*

an important/key area *Customer service is a key area for improvement.*

the main area *His main area of interest is how young children learn foreign languages.*

a problem area *First they must identify the problem areas in the industry.*

a sensitive/difficult area *Serious illness within a family is a sensitive area.*

a broad area *A broad area of agreement has emerged.*

PHRASES

an area of activity/work/business *There are many laws relating to this area of activity.*

an area of research/study *Genetics is a flourishing area of research.*

an area of life *Communication is important in most areas of life.*

an area of interest *The people taking part in the conference have different areas of interest.*

an area of responsibility *The matter does not fall within my area of responsibility.*

an area of concern (=something someone is worried about) *Crowd violence towards players is another area of concern.*

argue *v*

1 to disagree with someone in words, often in an angry way

ADVERBS

be always/constantly arguing (=argue a lot) *She split up with her boyfriend because they were always arguing.*

PREPOSITIONS

argue about/over sth *The children were arguing about which TV programme to watch.*

argue with sb *Gallacher continued to argue with the referee throughout the game.*

2 to say that you think something is true or that people should do something

ADVERBS

rightly/correctly argue *She rightly argues that it is too soon to judge the success of the project.*

convincingly/persuasively argue (=in a way that makes people believe that what you are saying is right) *He convincingly argued that it would have been impossible for his client to commit the crime.*

NOUNS

argue your case/point/position (=explain the reasons why you think that something is true) *You will have the chance to argue your case in front of the committee.*

argument *n*

1 a situation in which two or more people disagree, often angrily

ADJECTIVES

a big/huge/massive/terrible argument *There was a big argument about whether we should move to a new house.*

a long argument *After a long argument, the guard agreed to let us into the building.*

a heated argument (=involving very strong feelings) *Someone was having a heated argument with a police officer.*

a bitter argument *There are bitter arguments about whether he was a hero or a war criminal.*

a violent argument *The singer was hurt in a violent argument with her husband.*

A

VERBS

have an argument *I could hear my parents having an argument downstairs.*

get into an argument (*also* **become involved in an argument** *formal*): *She didn't want to get into another argument about money.*

start an argument *He was deliberately trying to start an argument.*

cause an argument *Money often causes arguments.*

stop/end an argument *He tried to stop an argument between his brother and a police officer.*

settle an argument (=stop an argument, especially by showing who is right) *We settled the argument by looking the answer up on the internet.*

avoid an argument *I was anxious to avoid an argument.*

win/lose an argument *The party hopes to win the argument about how to reform the health system.*

an argument breaks out (=it starts) *The men were drunk and an argument soon broke out.*

an argument rages (=people argue with a lot of feeling) *An argument is raging about which is the better system.*

PREPOSITIONS

an argument with sb *She had an argument with her best friend.*

an argument between sb and sb *My mother tried to stop the arguments between my brother and me.*

an argument about/over sth *He left after an argument about playing loud music.*

2 a set of reasons that show that something is true or untrue, right or wrong etc

ADJECTIVES

a good/strong/powerful argument *There is a good argument for leaving things as they are.*

a convincing/persuasive/compelling argument (=one that makes you sure that something is right) *He will have to come up with some very convincing arguments.*

a valid argument (=based on good reasons) *I believe this argument is a valid one.*

a reasonable/plausible argument *Their arguments seemed perfectly reasonable to me.*

a weak/flawed/spurious argument (=one that does not work) *I was surprised he offered such a weak argument.*

an unconvincing argument (=one that does not make you believe that something is right) *I found his arguments unconvincing.*

VERBS

put forward/present/offer an argument *I have considered the arguments put forward by both sides.*

make an argument *A similar argument could be made in the case of elderly people.*

come up with an argument (=think of an argument) *Aristotle came up with many arguments for slavery being justified.*

develop an argument *He developed this argument further in later papers.*

support/strengthen/bolster an argument *There is not the slightest scientific evidence to support such arguments.*

undermine/weaken an argument (=make it appear weaker) *This evidence undermines the argument that companies need to offer high pay to attract good staff.*

refute/rebut/counter an argument (=show that it is wrong) *It is hard to refute these arguments.*

reject/dismiss an argument (=say that you are not convinced by it) *The court rejected these arguments.*

accept/agree with an argument *Not everyone accepts these arguments.*

PREPOSITIONS

an argument for/in favour of sth *There is a strong argument for reforming the law.*

an argument against sth *He put forward a powerful argument against the keeping of animals in zoos.*

arid *adj* THESAURUS **dry (1)**

arise *v* THESAURUS **happen**

arm *n*

one of the two long parts of your body between your shoulders and your hands

ADJECTIVES

sb's left/right arm *He had a tattoo on his left arm.*

a broken arm (=with a broken bone) *He can't play, as he has a broken arm.*

bare arms (=not covered by clothes) *She wore a dress which left her arms bare.*

strong arms *His arms were strong and muscular.*

VERBS

wave your arms (=move them from side to side to attract attention) *The man was waving his arms and shouting.*

raise your arm (=lift it up) *Raise one arm above your head.*

break your arm (=break a bone in it) *She broke her arm in a riding accident.*

fold/cross your arms (=bend both arms in front of your body) *He folded his arms across his chest and waited.*

stretch/hold out your arms *She held out her arms and the child ran towards her.*

put/wrap your arms around sb *I put my arms around Bobby and gave him a hug.*

take sb by the arm (=lead someone somewhere holding their arm) *"It's this way," he said, taking me by the arm.*

take/hold sb in your arms (=gently put your arms around someone) *She held a little baby in her arms.*

grab sb's arm (=take hold of it with a sudden movement) *He grabbed my arm and told me to wait.*

PREPOSITIONS

under your arm *Pat was carrying a box under his arm.*

in your arms (=held or carried using your arms) *He had a pile of books in his arms.*

PHRASES

arm in arm (=with your arm linked to someone else's arm) *There were several young couples, walking arm in arm.*

with outstretched arms *He came forward with outstretched arms to welcome her.*

army *n*

the part of a country's military force that is trained to fight on land in a war

VERBS + army

join/go into/enter the army *At 18, I decided to join the army.*

serve in the army (=be a soldier in an army) *He had served in the Indian army.*

leave the army *Why did you leave the army?*

lead/command an army *The general led an army of 18,000 men.*

be drafted into/conscripted into the army (=be made to join the army) *All the young men were drafted into the army.*

be discharged from the army (=be officially allowed to leave your job in the army) *He was discharged from the army because he became mentally ill.*

army + VERBS

an army attacks *The king's army attacked the castle.*

an army fights *When armies fight, it is mostly young men who get killed.*

an army advances *The army advanced slowly towards the village.*

an army withdraws/retreats (=it moves back) *The British army was forced to withdraw from France.*

an army invades sth *The Soviet army invaded Afghanistan in 1979.*

an army marches *The army marched through the town.*

ADJECTIVES/NOUNS + army

a powerful army *China has one of the most powerful armies in the world.*

a small army *The prince had a small army of a few hundred men.*

a private army *The prince has his own private army.*

a standing army (=permanent and existing whether there is a war or not) *The country has a standing army of over 100,000 men.*

the victorious army (=who have won) *Two days later, the victorious German army entered Paris.*

the defeated army *The defeated army were forced to leave the city.*

a foreign/enemy army *Foreign armies have been trying to take control of the country for hundreds of years.*

an occupying/invading army (=an army that enters a place in order to control it) *The invading army attacked the town.*

army + NOUNS

an army officer *Army officers must be good leaders.*

an army base/camp *There is an army base about 5 miles outside the town.*

an army helicopter/truck etc *Army helicopters can take supplies to places that are difficult to reach by road.*

PREPOSITIONS

in the army *Her father was in the army.*

PHRASES

be in command of an army *Wellington was placed in command of the army.*

aroma *n* THESAURUS smell[1]

arrange *v*

1 to organize or make plans for something to happen

ADVERBS

hastily arrange to do sth (=quickly) *They hastily arranged a press conference to explain the situation.*

PREPOSITIONS

arrange for sth to happen/for sb to do sth *She arranged for him to get some work experience in her office.*

PHRASES

as arranged (=in the way that was arranged) *Matthew arrived at 2 o'clock as arranged.*

2 to put things in a particular order or position

ADVERBS

arrange sth carefully *She picked some flowers and arranged them carefully in a vase.*

arrange sth alphabetically *He arranges all his CDs alphabetically according to their titles.*

be neatly arranged *Several pairs of shoes were neatly arranged at the bottom of the wardrobe.*

be beautifully/tastefully arranged *Plates of sandwiches and cakes were beautifully arranged on the tables.*

PHRASES

arrange sth/sb in order of sth *He arranged the children in order of size for the photograph.*

A

arrangement *n*
plans and preparations so that something can happen, or a way of doing something that has been agreed

Grammar
Usually plural in this meaning.

VERBS

make the arrangements *She is busy making the arrangements for her trip.*

change/alter the arrangements *Two people couldn't come on Friday, so we had to change the arrangements.*

cancel the arrangements *The arrangements had to be cancelled after the speaker developed flu.*

discuss the arrangements *We need to discuss the wedding arrangements.*

finalize the arrangements (=decide what you are going to do) *I'm meeting him tomorrow to finalize the arrangements.*

confirm the arrangements (=decide what they will be) *We can confirm the arrangements for the trip later.*

upset the arrangements (=spoil them) *I don't want to upset your arrangements.*

ADJECTIVES

a good/sensible/satisfactory arrangement *Leaving the children with a babysitter seemed like a sensible arrangement.*

a temporary/permanent arrangement *Fran is living with us at the moment, but this is a temporary arrangement.*

a flexible arrangement *I think it is better to keep the arrangement flexible, in case something happens.*

alternative arrangements *If the flight is delayed, you'll have to make alternative arrangements.*

special arrangements *Please inform us if any guests have disabilities or need any special arrangements.*

the necessary arrangements *You should have plenty of time to make the necessary arrangements.*

financial arrangements *As treasurer, you're responsible for all the financial arrangements.*

NOUNS + arrangement

travel arrangements *I'll make my own travel arrangements.*

seating/sleeping arrangements (=where people will sit/sleep) *What are the seating arrangements for dinner?*

wedding/funeral/holiday arrangements *A death certificate was issued so that funeral arrangements could be made.*

PREPOSITIONS

arrangements for sth *They met to discuss arrangements for the trip.*

according to/under an arrangement *Under the arrangement, each shareholder will receive an extra payment.*

PHRASES

come to an arrangement (=agree a way of dealing with a problem) *I'm sure we can come to an arrangement if you can't pay all the money back immediately.*

arrest *n*
if someone is under arrest, the police take them to a police station, because they may have done something illegal

VERBS

make an arrest *The police made several arrests.*

resist arrest *He was charged with resisting arrest and assaulting a police officer.*

avoid arrest *The Mafia boss managed to avoid arrest for many years.*

lead to sb's arrest *The new information led to his arrest.*

arrest + NOUNS

an arrest warrant/a warrant for sb's arrest (=an official order that allows the police to arrest someone) *The authorities issued arrest warrants for two men in their early 20s.*

ADJECTIVES

wrongful/unlawful/false arrest (=arrest without good reason) *He sued the police for wrongful arrest.*

PREPOSITIONS

be under arrest *A man is under arrest, following the suspicious death of his wife.*

arrest for murder/robbery etc *He is under arrest for murder.*

an arrest on charges of sth/on suspicion of sth *Pound was put in prison after his arrest on treason charges.*

PHRASES

put/place/keep sb under arrest *The two agents showed him their badges and placed him under arrest.*

arrival *n*
when someone or something arrives somewhere

ADJECTIVES

late arrival *We would like to apologize for the late arrival of Flight 502 from Los Angeles.*

safe arrival *They gave thanks for their safe arrival, after a long and difficult journey.*

VERBS

announce an arrival *The airline announced the arrival of Flight 702 from Bangkok.*

herald/mark/signal an arrival (=show that someone or something will arrive soon) *The storm clouds signalled the arrival of the summer rains.*

await sb/sth's arrival *The travellers were awaiting the arrival of the ferry.*

arrival + NOUNS

the arrival time/date *Due to work on the tracks, departure and arrival times of some trains may be delayed.*

PREPOSITIONS

on/upon arrival (=when someone arrives somewhere) *You will be met on arrival.*

arrival in a city/country *Shortly after our arrival in London, I received an offer of a job.*

arrival at an airport/school/office *He was arrested soon after his arrival at Chicago's O'Hare Airport.*

the arrival of sb/sth *Older children may misbehave after the arrival of a new baby.*

ANTONYMS **arrival → departure**

arrive *v*

to get to the place where you are going

ADVERBS

arrive late *Jo arrived late, as usual, and missed the first class.*

arrive on time *He never arrives on time for meetings.*

arrive early *We arrived early for our plane.*

arrive shortly (=soon) *My parents are due to arrive shortly.*

arrive safely *She phoned to say she had arrived safely.*

finally/eventually arrive *We finally arrived in Perth after 10 days' driving.*

arrive unannounced (=without anyone expecting or knowing you were coming) *He arrived unannounced yesterday and stayed the night.*

PREPOSITIONS

arrive at a station/airport/hotel/house *We arrived at the station just in time.*

arrive in a city/country *He arrived in New York with very little money.*

arrive on an island *The first Europeans arrived on the island in the 17th century.*

⚠ Don't say 'I arrived to my home.' Say **I arrived home** or **I arrived at my house.**

PHRASES

be due to arrive *The next train is due to arrive at 11.04.*

be the first/last (one) to arrive *Billy is always the first to arrive at the office.*

arrive safe and sound (=safely) *It was a great relief when he arrived back safe and sound.*

arrive on the scene (=at the place where an accident, crime etc has just happened) *Two more police cars arrived on the scene.*

as soon as sb arrives *Call me as soon as you arrive.*

THESAURUS: arrive

get
to arrive somewhere. **Get** is more informal than **arrive**:
What time do you usually ***get to*** *work? | I'll call you as soon as I* ***get there****. | We didn't* ***get home*** *till 5 o'clock the next day.*

come
if someone comes, they arrive at the place where you are:
What time did the plumber say he would come? | She ***came home*** *yesterday.*

reach
to arrive somewhere, especially after a long journey:
They ***finally reached*** *Hong Kong at midnight. | We were looking forward to* ***reaching our destination****.*

get in
plane | train | bus
to arrive somewhere:
What time does your plane get in? | The train gets in at 6.15. | I usually get in from work at around 6 o'clock.

land
plane
to arrive on the ground:
The plane landed about an hour ago. | We finally landed at 2 a.m.

pull in
train | bus | coach
to arrive at a station, or the place where you are waiting, and stop there:
Hundreds of people watched the train pull in. | As we left, another coach pulled in behind us.

dock
ship
if a ship docks, it arrives at a port and stops there, so that it can unload the passengers or goods:
The ship docked at Southampton with 400 passengers on board.

ANTONYMS **arrive → leave[1]**

art *n*

the use of painting, drawing, sculpture etc to represent things or express ideas

ADJECTIVES

modern/contemporary art (=from the late 19th century until now) *I think a lot of modern art is rubbish.*

contemporary art (=that is being created now, usually very recently) *There is an exhibition of contemporary Japanese art at the gallery.*

Western art (=art in Europe and North America) *He studied both Chinese and Western art.*

fine art (=art, especially painting, which is

A

made to be beautiful or affect your emotions, rather than to be useful) *He studied fine art at college.*

abstract art (=that consists of lines and shapes and is not of people, objects etc) *Kandinsky was famous for his abstract art.*

figurative art (=of people, objects, places etc) *Many people prefer figurative art because it is easier to understand than abstract art.*

primitive art (=art by people who live in societies where there is a very simple way of life and no modern technology or industry) *The interest in primitive art came about largely through the work of Gauguin.*

art + NOUNS

art school/college/student *I studied ceramics at art college.*

art history/historian *She teaches art history and women's studies at Sheffield University.*

an art gallery/museum *We spent the day looking around art galleries.*

an art exhibition *There is a big art exhibition in the city hall.*

an art collection *The museum has an interesting art collection including works by Henry Moore and Max Ernst.*

PHRASES

a work of art *Picasso's painting is one of the great works of art of the 20th century.*

article *n*

a piece of writing about a particular subject in a newspaper or magazine

ADJECTIVES/NOUNS + article

a newspaper/magazine article *I saw a newspaper article about the college.*

a good/excellent article *I read a good article about him in 'The Observer'.*

an interesting article *There was an interesting article on building your own home.*

a thought-provoking article (=one that is interesting because it makes you think) *I don't agree with everything she says, but it certainly is a thought-provoking article.*

a long/short article *She wrote a short article for the school newspaper.*

a recent article *In a recent article in the Times, she accuses the government of hypocrisy.*

a front-page article *They published a front-page article about the scandal.*

the leading/lead article (=the main article) *The paper's leading article described the government as weak.*

a feature article (=a special article, usually over several pages) *There's a feature article on women business leaders.*

an in-depth article (=which contains a lot of information about someone or something) *There was an in-depth article about the origins of the war.*

VERBS

read/see an article *Did you see the article about him in 'The Independent'?*

write an article (*also* **do an article** *informal*): *'The Times' asked him to do an article on the election.*

publish/carry/run an article (=print it in a newspaper or magazine) *The magazine carried an article on the dangers of being overweight.*

an article appears somewhere *The article appeared in a local paper.*

PREPOSITIONS

an article on/about sth *an article on environmental issues*

an article by sb *I enjoyed that article by the mayor of New York.*

in an article *In a recent article, she described herself as 'madly in love'.*

articulate *adj* THESAURUS > **eloquent**

artificial *adj* not real or not natural

NOUNS

artificial light/lighting *They use artificial lighting when there isn't enough daylight.*

artificial flowers *There was a vase of artificial flowers on the table.*

an artificial leg/limb/heart etc *He has an artificial leg because he lost a leg in a road accident.*

artificial sweeteners/colours/preservatives/additives *Diet drinks contain artificial sweeteners.*

an artificial environment/situation *An interview is a very artificial situation and people don't react in a natural way.*

artificial fibres *Artificial fibres such as nylon are cheap to produce.*

artificial grass/turf *The baseball game was played on artificial turf.*

an artificial lake/harbour *York University is built around a large artificial lake.*

artificial snow *Some ski resorts use huge amounts of artificial snow.*

VERBS

look artificial *The apples were so shiny that they looked artificial.*

THESAURUS: artificial

man-made
fibre | material | chemical | lake | reservoir | island | snow
man-made materials are made by people. You can also use **man-made** about geographical features such as lakes: *Polyester is a man-made fibre. | The town has its own man-made lake, which is popular with swimmers.*

synthetic
fibre | material | fabric | chemical | drug | fuel | rubber

synthetic materials and substances are made using chemical processes or substances, not natural ones:
The sweater is made from synthetic fibres which are designed to be light but very warm. | Amphetamine is a synthetic drug that stimulates the nervous system.

imitation
leather | silk | gold | diamond | pearl | gun | firearm | weapon
imitation materials and objects are made to look like the real thing:
Her shoes were made of imitation leather. | Only an expert can tell if the pearls are imitation.

Imitation can also be used as a noun: *The watch was **an imitation**.*

fake
fur | jewellery | pearl | tan | blood
made to look or seem like something else, especially in order to deceive people:
The collar is made of fake fur. | The actors' faces were covered in fake blood.

false
teeth | eyelashes | moustache | leg | nose
artificial – used about parts of the body that are made to look like the real thing:
My dad has false teeth. | The man was wearing a false moustache.

simulated
conditions | effect | flight | tour
not real, but made to look, sound, or feel real, by using special computers or machines:
Soldiers' reactions are tested under simulated combat conditions. | Training for astronauts involves a simulated space flight.

virtual
world | reality | tour
made or experienced using computers, rather than in the real world:
The online club is a virtual world for children where they can chat with each other. | Virtual reality games are becoming more and more popular. | Our website offers customers a virtual tour of the hotel.

ANTONYMS **artificial → real (1)**

artist *n*

someone who produces art, especially paintings or drawings

ADJECTIVES

a famous/well-known artist *The exhibition includes pictures by Andy Warhol and other famous artists.*

a great artist *Picasso was the greatest artist of the 20th century.*

a major/important/leading artist *Diego Rivera was one of Mexico's leading artists of the time.*

a distinguished artist (=respected by a lot of people) *She was painted by several distinguished artists, including Gabriel Rossetti.*

a talented/gifted artist *Her son is a talented young artist who hopes to study at the Royal College of Art.*

a living artist *He is regarded as one of Germany's most important living artists.*

a modern/contemporary artist *Modern artists use a range of different art forms, including film and video.*

a male/female artist *Tracey Emin is one of my favourite female artists – I love all her work.*

an amateur/professional artist *The paintings are mostly by amateur artists.*

a fine artist (=one who creates works of art, not someone who does pictures for magazines, books etc) *It is difficult for fine artists to make enough money to live on.*

a real/serious/true artist *His paintings are very popular, but until now many art critics didn't consider him to be a real artist.*

a struggling artist (=one who is trying to be successful) *When I first met him, he was a struggling artist, and his pictures weren't very expensive.*

an up-and-coming artist (=one who is likely to become successful) *The show features work by up-and-coming artists from China.*

a local artist *The show will feature works by local artists.*

artistic *adj*

relating to art, or relating to people's ability to paint, draw etc

NOUNS

artistic talent/ability/flair *She showed considerable artistic talent at an early age.*

artistic expression (=the expression of ideas or feelings in art) *The school tries to encourage artistic expression among its students.*

artistic freedom *In Russia at that time, there was very little artistic freedom.*

an artistic work *Her artistic works include both paintings and drawings.*

artistic merit (=the quality of being a good work of art) *His paintings have no artistic merit whatsoever.*

artistic temperament (=a type of character that artists are supposed to have, that allows them to feel emotions deeply) *She seems very sensitive to criticism. Perhaps it is part of her artistic temperament.*

ascend *v* THESAURUS climb

ashamed *adj*

feeling very guilty and sorry because of something you have done, or something that someone in your family, group etc has done

Grammar
Ashamed is not used before a noun.

A

ADVERBS

deeply ashamed *She was deeply ashamed of the way she had behaved.*

bitterly ashamed (=very ashamed, in a way that makes you very unhappy) *He was bitterly ashamed when his parents found out what he had done.*

thoroughly ashamed (=very ashamed – used especially when you think someone deserves to feel ashamed) *He should be thoroughly ashamed of what he's done to that poor girl.*

slightly ashamed/a little ashamed *I felt slightly ashamed that I had laughed when she fell over.*

VERBS

feel ashamed *I felt ashamed that I had not helped them.*

look ashamed *Kerry looked ashamed and started to apologize.*

make sb ashamed *When I hear about the behaviour of some English fans, it makes me ashamed to be English.*

PREPOSITIONS

ashamed of sb/sth *Rick felt ashamed of the things he had said. | Her parents said they were ashamed of her for what she had done.*

ashamed at sth *I am ashamed at what I did today.*

PHRASES

it's nothing to be ashamed of (=you do not need to feel ashamed) *Everyone cries sometimes – it's nothing to be ashamed of.*

be ashamed to admit sth *She was ashamed to admit that she had never read any of his books.*

I'm ashamed to say *I lied about that too, I'm ashamed to say.*

> **Ashamed or embarrassed?**
> You use **ashamed** when you feel guilty and sorry because you have done something bad or wrong: *Ella was* ***ashamed*** *of her behaviour at the party.*
> **Embarrassed** is used when you feel uncomfortable, and worry that people will think you are silly: *Boys often feel* ***embarrassed*** *when talking about their feelings.*

ask *v*

to speak or write to someone in order to get an answer or in order to get something that you want

NOUNS

ask a question *You can ask questions at the end of the talk.*

ask (for) permission *Don Amato asked permission to marry Candida.*

ask for advice/help/assistance *They were too proud to ask for help.*

ask for sb's opinion *It is always best to ask people for their opinion first.*

ADVERBS

often/frequently ask *Parents often ask me: "How can we teach our children to write?"*

always/constantly ask *People always ask how to spell my name.*

ask politely *"Did you sleep well?" she asked politely.*

ask quietly/softly *"Are you awake?" he asked softly.*

ask hopefully *"Will you be able to fix it?" he asked hopefully.*

ask anxiously/nervously/suspiciously *She asked anxiously whether anything was wrong.*

PREPOSITIONS

ask (sb) about sth *Visitors often ask about the history of the town.*

ask (sb) for sth *He asked his boss for permission to go home early.*

> ⚠ Don't say 'She asked to him to be quiet.' Say **She asked him to be quiet.**

PHRASES

if you don't mind me asking/my asking spoken (=used when politely asking a question) *Are you married, if you don't mind me asking?*

asleep *adj* sleeping

ADVERBS

fast asleep/sound asleep (=sleeping and not easily woken) *The children were fast asleep in their beds.*

half asleep (=almost asleep) *He was lying on the sofa, half asleep.*

dead asleep *AmE* (=completely asleep) *She was dead asleep within five minutes.*

VERBS

fall asleep (=start sleeping) *He rolled over and fell asleep quickly.*

ANTONYMS **asleep → awake**

aspect Ac *n*

one part of a situation, idea, plan etc that has many parts

ADJECTIVES

an important/significant aspect *A person's nationality is an important aspect of their identity.*

a key/fundamental aspect (=very important) *Helping people with their problems is one of the key aspects of the job.*

a positive/negative aspect *Tourism has its negative aspects, for example the damage caused to the environment.*

a worrying/disturbing/alarming aspect *The worrying aspect is that the situation is getting worse every year.*

the technical/practical/legal/financial etc aspects *The course focuses on the practical aspects of farm work.*

various/different aspects *We studied various aspects of language development.*

certain aspects *Certain aspects of his plays attracted criticism.*

VERBS

deal with an aspect *The book only deals with one aspect of American history.*

look at/consider/examine/explore an aspect *Managers were asked to look at every aspect of their work.*

cover an aspect (=include it as one of the things that are dealt with) *The training course covers all aspects of business.*

concentrate/focus on an aspect *People tend to concentrate on the political aspect of his films.*

highlight an aspect (=make it easy to notice) *The book highlights the negative aspects of the oil industry.*

PREPOSITIONS

an aspect of sth *Alcoholism affects all aspects of family life.*

assemble *v* THESAURUS ▸ **build**[1]

assess *v*

to make a judgment about a person or situation after thinking carefully about it

NOUNS

assess a situation *We'll have to assess the situation carefully, and then decide what to do next.*

assess a student *Students are assessed every six weeks.*

assess sb's performance/progress *The test is intended to assess your performance.*

assess sb's needs *Social workers visit the patients to assess their needs.*

assess the damage *Someone from the insurance company came to assess the damage to the car.*

assess the effect/impact *It is too early to assess the impact of the changes.*

assess the extent of sth *It is difficult to assess the extent of the problem.*

ADVERBS

assess sth carefully *Investors should assess the risk carefully before they invest their money.*

assess sth fully/thoroughly *The authorities have not yet had time to fully assess the situation.*

assess sth accurately *It is important to assess the patient's symptoms accurately.*

assess sth internally (=the grade is decided by a teacher at the same school or university) *The course is assessed internally.*

assess sth externally (=the grade is decided by someone from outside a school or university) *The written part of the test will be assessed externally.*

assessment Ac *n*

a process in which you make a judgment about a person or situation, or the judgment you make

ADJECTIVES

a general/overall/broad assessment (=that covers the main features or parts of something, not the details) *The doctor must make a general assessment of the patient's health.*

a detailed assessment *We need a detailed assessment of what this will cost.*

an accurate assessment *It is too early to make an accurate assessment of the situation.*

sb's personal assessment *What's your personal assessment of the risks?*

a fair assessment *I think the event was a success. Do you think that's a fair assessment?*

an objective assessment (=based on facts, not on feelings or beliefs) *The test results will provide an objective assessment of how much you have improved.*

a realistic/honest assessment *You should not start a business without a realistic assessment of the risks involved.*

an initial assessment (=that is done before anything else) *An initial assessment of the building's condition was carried out by a surveyor.*

VERBS

make/carry out an assessment (*also* **conduct an assessment** *formal*): *The engineers will make an assessment of the damage, and decide what needs to be done.*

do an assessment *more informal* (=make an assessment) *The teacher does a yearly assessment of each child's progress.*

give/provide an assessment *He gave an honest assessment of the risks.*

NOUNS + assessment

a risk assessment *Teachers have to do a risk assessment before taking students on a trip.*

a needs assessment (*also* **an assessment of sb's needs**) *The authorities did a needs assessment to find out what kind of housing was required.*

asset *n*

1 the things that a company owns, that can be sold to pay debts

> **Grammar**
> Usually plural in this meaning.

ADJECTIVES

total assets *The company has total assets of over £2 billion.*

financial assets *The value of the Trust's financial assets has risen by almost 30%.*

liquid assets (=the money that a company or person has, and anything else they can easily

A

exchange for money) *The company has very few liquid assets that it can use to pay back the loan.*
net assets (=assets after tax has been taken away) *When he died, his net assets amounted to £320,000.*

VERBS

have/own/hold assets *She has financial assets worth £250,000.*
buy assets *Foreign investors need dollars to buy American assets.*
sell off assets (*also* **dispose of assets** *formal*): *The firm will have to sell off some of its assets to pay its debts.*
seize/confiscate sb's assets (=take them from someone officially) *The court can seize the assets of criminals.*
freeze sb's assets (=legally prevent money in a bank from being spent, property from being sold etc) *The company's assets were frozen while the investigation was carried out.*
protect/safeguard your assets *The firm's directors failed to take proper action to protect the assets of the company.*

PHRASES

the value of sb's assets *The value of his assets was calculated at over $1 million.*

2 something or someone that is useful because they help you succeed or deal with problems

ADJECTIVES

a great/considerable/major asset *His greatest asset is his sense of humour.*
a valuable/useful asset *A respected brand name is a valuable asset.*
a real asset *Knowledge of the local language is a real asset when you're working abroad.*

PREPOSITIONS

be an asset to sb/sth *She works hard, and is an asset to the firm.*

assignment [Ac] *n*

1 a piece of work that a student is asked to do as part of their studies

NOUNS + assignment

a homework/school assignment *Don't watch TV until you've done your homework assignments!*
a writing/maths/science etc assignment *The maths assignment was hard.*

VERBS

give sb an assignment (*also* **set sb an assignment** *BrE*): *Our English teacher always gives us a lot of assignments. | The teacher set the students an assignment to do in the school holidays.*
do an assignment *Everyone in the class had done the assignment.*
complete/finish an assignment *Most of the students complete their assignments on time.*
hand in an assignment *Could everyone please hand in their homework assignments by Friday?*

PREPOSITIONS

an assignment on sth *He's doing an assignment on the history of his local area.*

2 a piece of work that someone is asked to do as part of their job

ADJECTIVES

a special assignment *He had been sent on special assignment to help the head of security.*
a tough assignment *It's a tough assignment but we think you can do it.*

VERBS

sb's assignment is to do sth *Their assignment was to guard the palace.*
give sb an assignment *Magazines regularly call her to give her assignments.*
carry out an assignment *You can claim for any expenses you have while carrying out the assignment.*

PREPOSITIONS

on (an) assignment *The reporter was on assignment in South America.*

assistance [Ac] *n* help or support

ADJECTIVES/NOUNS + assistance

financial/economic assistance *The council provided financial assistance for the project.*
technical assistance *Most of our time is spent providing technical assistance to companies.*
legal/medical assistance *It was difficult to get good legal assistance.*
government assistance (*also* **federal assistance** *AmE*): *The president pledged federal assistance to rebuild the town.*
military assistance *They appealed to the French government for military assistance.*
emergency assistance *The aid will provide emergency assistance for 2,000 families.*

VERBS

provide/offer assistance *We would be happy to provide assistance.*
give (sb) assistance *Our staff can give assistance with any problems that may arise.*
get/receive assistance *She got no assistance from her family.*
need assistance (*also* **require assistance** *formal*): *Call this number if you need any assistance.*
seek assistance *If side-effects are severe, seek medical assistance.*
ask for assistance (*also* **request assistance** *formal*): *Police are at the scene and have requested assistance.*
promise/pledge assistance *The government has promised financial assistance for victims of the floods.*

PREPOSITIONS

be of assistance *formal* (=help) *"Can I be of assistance?" the receptionist asked.*

assistance to sb/sth *The department provides financial assistance to universities.*

assistance for sth/sb *We need more assistance for people caring for sick relatives.*

assistance from sb *The agency receives no assistance from the government.*

assistance with (doing) sth *He requires assistance with washing and dressing.*

assistance in doing sth *We offer assistance in finding suitable accommodation.*

PHRASES

come to sb's assistance (=help someone) *One of her fellow passengers came to her assistance.*

turn to sb for assistance (=ask them to help) *The elderly sometimes have no one to turn to for assistance.*

with the assistance of sb/sth *He started the business with the assistance of his parents.*

association *n*

1 an organization that consists of people, countries, or groups who have similar interests or aims

ADJECTIVES

an international association *The international association of firefighters will hold a meeting next month.*

a local association *They set up a local association of small businesses.*

a community association *Community associations have said they will fight plans to build a new airport in the area.*

a professional association *Most diving instructors belong to a professional association.*

a public/private association *Public associations such as Trade Unions had their freedom limited.*

VERBS

join an association *He joined the Architects' Association in 2010.*

belong to an association *They belong to the professional basketball players' association.*

set up/form/found an association *The International Air Transport Association was founded in 1945.*

an association meets *The association meets once a year in London.*

PREPOSITIONS

the association of sb *She is a member of the National Association of Social Workers.*

PHRASES

a member of an association/an association member *Association members have to pay a fee every year.*

2 a relationship between people, groups, countries etc

ADJECTIVES

a close association *He has a close association with the town and went to school there many years ago.*

a personal association *She did not investigate the case because of her personal association with Mr Brown.*

a long/long-standing association *He has a long association with the football club.*

a loose association (=not working closely together) *The bombing suspect appears to have only a loose association with terrorist groups.*

VERBS

have an association *She claimed that she had no association with any political organization.*

maintain an association *The group maintains a loose association with the Republican party.*

PREPOSITIONS

an association with sb/sth *He studied at Leyden and maintained a close association with that university.*

the association between sb/sth *The association between the two men led to several scientific discoveries.*

in association with sb/sth *The concerts are sponsored by the Arts Council in association with local businesses.*

PHRASES

freedom of association *Freedom of association is an important civil right.*

assume Ac *v*

to think that something is true, although you do not have definite proof

ADVERBS

automatically assume (=without thinking carefully) *I automatically assumed she would be like her sister, but she was not.*

naturally assume *As the boy looked about ten, I naturally assumed that he should be in school.*

generally/usually/commonly assume *People generally assume that I will not want to work full-time after the baby is born.*

mistakenly/wrongly assume *They wrongly assumed that he wouldn't ask them for money.*

PHRASES

it seems reasonable to assume/we can reasonably assume *It seems reasonable to assume that the two events are connected.*

it is safe to assume/you can safely assume (=be almost certain) *I think it is safe to assume that they won't come back.*

it is widely assumed (=by many people) *It was widely assumed that the bomb was planted by al-Qaeda.*

let us assume *Let us assume for a moment that the average temperature will rise by 5 degrees.*

it is wrong/a mistake to assume *It is a mistake*

A

to assume that sleep is a time when the brain is not active.

people tend to assume *Men tend to assume that the woman should do all the housework.*

assume the worst (=think that the worst possible thing has happened) *When it got to midnight and Paul was still not back, I began to assume the worst.*

assumption Ac *n*

something that you think is true although you have no definite proof

ADJECTIVES

a reasonable/valid assumption *I thought he must have forgotten our meeting – it seemed like a reasonable assumption.*

a common/general/widespread assumption (=made by many people) *There's a common assumption that science is more difficult than other subjects.*

a basic/fundamental assumption *There is a basic assumption in international law that a state will protect its citizens.*

a correct assumption *Many people acted on the correct assumption that interest rates would rise.*

a false/mistaken assumption *People often make the false assumption that all homeless people are alcoholics.*

an underlying assumption (=a belief that is used as the basis for an idea, but which may not be correct) *There seems to be an underlying assumption in what he says that women are weak.*

a tacit/unspoken assumption (=one that people believe but do not actually express) *Everyone seemed to make a tacit assumption that they would get married.*

an implicit assumption (=one that is suggested or understood without being stated directly) *Implicit assumptions about how women should behave affect all areas of life.*

VERBS

make an assumption *You're making a lot of assumptions for which you have no proof.*

work/operate on an assumption (=act according to something that may not be true) *The police seemed to be working on the assumption that he was guilty.*

be based on/rest on an assumption *Our plans were based on the assumption that everyone would be willing to help.*

question/challenge an assumption *The report challenges common assumptions about what is a 'normal family'.*

PREPOSITIONS

an assumption about sth *The article makes assumptions about older people which are clearly not correct.*

on the assumption that (=based on an assumption) *On the assumption that he would be late, we set off late too.*

asylum *n*

protection given to someone by a government because they have escaped from fighting or political trouble in their own country

ADJECTIVES

political asylum *The dancer asked for political asylum in the West.*

VERBS

seek asylum (=try to get asylum) *The refugees are seeking asylum in Britain.*

apply for/request asylum *Last year around 600,000 people applied for asylum in European countries.*

grant/give sb asylum *He was granted asylum in France.*

offer sb asylum *He was offered political asylum in the US.*

refuse/deny sb asylum *He was denied asylum by the Dutch authorities.*

NOUNS + asylum

an asylum seeker (=someone who wants asylum) *Failed asylum seekers are sent home.*

an asylum application/claim/request *He is still waiting for a decision about his asylum claim.*

atmosphere *n*

the feeling that an event or place gives you

ADJECTIVES

the general atmosphere *There was a general atmosphere of fun and excitement.*

a good/great atmosphere *The club has a great atmosphere.*

a happy/cheerful atmosphere *It's a good school and it has a very happy atmosphere.*

a friendly/welcoming atmosphere *The bar provides a welcoming atmosphere for a relaxing drink.*

a relaxed/informal atmosphere *We're trying to create a more relaxed atmosphere at work.*

a cosy atmosphere *With its low ceilings and open fire, the house has a cosy atmosphere.*

a strained/tense atmosphere (=when people are angry or not relaxed) *The atmosphere at home was rather tense.*

the atmosphere is electric (=people are very excited) *The atmosphere was electric as the game began.*

NOUNS

a family atmosphere (=in which people like and care for each other) *The school has a real family atmosphere.*

a carnival/party atmosphere (=one in which people are having fun and enjoying themselves) *Outside the stadium, there was a carnival atmosphere.*

VERBS

have an atmosphere *The church has a peaceful atmosphere.*

create an atmosphere *We try to create an atmosphere in which students feel relaxed.*

lighten the atmosphere (=make it less serious or sad) *He attempted a joke to lighten the atmosphere.*

add to the atmosphere *Cheerleaders add to the atmosphere of the game.*

the atmosphere changes *New owners bought the company and the whole atmosphere changed.*

attack[1] *n*

1 the act of using weapons against an enemy in a war

ADJECTIVES

a military attack *The US launched a military attack on Iraq.*

a nuclear attack *They would not risk a nuclear attack on the United States.*

an armed attack *Armed attacks against villagers are on the increase.*

a surprise attack *They launched a surprise attack on the camp just before dawn.*

a devastating attack (=causing a lot of damage) *It was a devastating attack against a civilian target.*

an all-out attack (=using a lot of force, soldiers, or weapons, or using everything that you have) *General Smith was in favour of an all-out attack on the enemy.*

a full-scale attack (=using all the available soldiers and weapons) *German troops launched a full-scale attack on the city.*

NOUNS + attack

a missile/rocket/mortar attack *There were 15 dead and 20 wounded in a missile attack on the capital.*

an air attack (=an attack from a plane using bombs) *Malta was under heavy air attack.*

VERBS

launch/mount an attack *Napoleon's army launched an attack on Russia.*

lead an attack *The general himself led the attack.*

an attack happens/takes place (*also* **an attack occurs** *formal*): *The attacks had taken place at night.*

an attack kills sb *The missile attack killed several innocent people.*

PREPOSITIONS

an attack on/against sb *The planes were used in the missile attack against southern Iraq.*

be under attack *The base was under attack from enemy fire.*

PHRASES

come under attack *Camps in the south came under attack from government forces.*

ANTONYMS **attack → defence (1)**

2 an act of violence that is intended to hurt a person or damage a place

ADJECTIVES

a violent/vicious/brutal attack *Police described it as an extremely violent attack.*

an unprovoked attack (=in which the victim did nothing to cause the attack) *The man was knocked to the ground and kicked in an unprovoked attack.*

VERBS

carry out an attack *The man who carried out the attack has been described as tall and 25 to 30 years old.*

be subjected to an attack (=be attacked) *He was subjected to a brutal attack.*

survive an attack *She survived the attack despite being stabbed 17 times.*

foil an attack (=prevent one that has been planned) *The attack was foiled by security guards.*

an attack happens/takes place (*also* **an attack occurs** *formal*): *The attack took place at around 10 p.m. on Thursday.*

NOUNS + attack

a bomb attack *Extremists are believed to have carried out the bomb attack.*

a terrorist attack *The accused men went on trial on Monday for America's worst ever terrorist attack.*

a suicide attack (=one in which the attacker deliberately kills himself or herself as well as other people) *The bomber carried out a suicide attack on a bus.*

PREPOSITIONS

an attack on sb *He was jailed for an attack on a police officer.*

an attack by sb *She is recovering after an attack by a dog.*

be behind an attack (=be responsible for organizing it) *It is not known who was behind the attack or what the motive was.*

PHRASES

a series/wave/spate of attacks (=several attacks occurring in a short period of time) *The killing follows a series of brutal attacks on tourists.*

the victim of an attack *She was the victim of an attack in her own home.*

3 a strong criticism of someone or something

ADJECTIVES

a direct attack *The comments were seen as a direct attack on the president's leadership.*

a strong attack *Milliband made his strongest attack yet on the government's economic policy.*

a bitter attack (=full of strong angry feelings) *He launched a bitter attack on the company, accusing them of incompetence.*

a scathing/blistering/stinging attack (=very strong) *The senator delivered a blistering attack on the president's plans for welfare reform.*

a vitriolic attack *formal* (=extremely strong

A

and angry) *Last week she launched a vitriolic attack on her former colleagues.*
a personal attack (=which criticizes someone's character, especially in an unfair and unkind way) *The debate included some bitter personal attacks.*

VERBS

launch/mount/make/deliver an attack (=make an attack) *He gave a press conference in which he launched a fierce attack upon the Democrats.*

PREPOSITIONS

an attack on sb/sth (*also* **an attack upon sb/sth** *formal*): *The article contained a scathing attack on the leadership of the party.*

PHRASES

be/come under attack (=be criticized) *Plans to reform the education system have come under attack from teachers.*
go on the attack (=start to criticize someone, especially after they have criticized you) *Khan went on the attack, accusing his political opponents of corruption.*

ANTONYMS **attack → defence (2)**

attack² *v*

1 to deliberately use violence to hurt a person or damage a place

ADVERBS

viciously/savagely/brutally attack sb *The woman was brutally attacked in her own home.*
physically attack sb *Hospital staff have been physically attacked by patients.*

PREPOSITIONS

attack sb/sth with sth *He was attacked with a broken bottle.*

PHRASES

vulnerable to attack (=easy to attack) *The tanks are vulnerable to attack from the air.*

ANTONYMS **attack → defend**

2 to criticize someone or something very strongly

ADVERBS

strongly/vigorously attack sb/sth *Opponents have strongly attacked the bill.*
openly/publicly attack sb/sth *In his article, he openly attacked the government.*
repeatedly attack sb/sth (=many times) *The minister has been repeatedly attacked in the media.*

ANTONYMS **attack → defend**

attain *v* THESAURUS **achieve**

attempt *n*

an act of trying to do something

ADJECTIVES

an unsuccessful/failed/abortive attempt *All attempts to find a cure have been unsuccessful.*
a vain attempt (=that does not succeed) *The teacher made a vain attempt to separate the two boys.*
a doomed/futile attempt (=certain to fail) *His attempt to reach the Pole was doomed from the beginning.*
a brave/bold/valiant attempt (=one that you admire, but that is unsuccessful) *She made a valiant attempt to continue playing, but the pain was too much.*
a successful attempt *The writer has made a successful attempt at showing the panic the characters felt.*
a determined/deliberate/conscious attempt *This was a deliberate attempt to mislead the public.*
a concerted attempt (=in which people work together in a determined way) *The party has made a concerted attempt to have more women candidates.*
a serious/genuine attempt *This is the first serious attempt to tackle the problem.*
a desperate/frantic attempt *Doctors made a desperate attempt to save his life.*
a feeble/weak attempt *She ignored David's feeble attempt at humour.*
a half-hearted attempt (=not trying hard, because you do not think you can succeed) *She made a half-hearted attempt to mop up the spilled milk.*
a blatant attempt (=an obvious attempt to do something bad) *It was a blatant attempt to hide the truth.*
a final/last attempt *The deal is a final attempt to save 5,000 jobs.*
a last-ditch attempt (=a final attempt to achieve something before it is too late) *Negotiators are making a last-ditch attempt to save the agreement.*
repeated attempts *I made repeated attempts to contact her, but without success.*

VERBS

make an attempt *She made several attempts to escape.*
abandon/give up an attempt *The climbers had to give up their attempt to reach the summit.*
fail in an attempt *He failed in his attempt to set a new Olympic record.*
succeed in an attempt *The 16-year-old succeeded in his attempt to sail across the Atlantic Ocean.*
foil/thwart an attempt *formal* (=make it fail) *Alert passengers foiled his attempt to set off a bomb on the airplane.*
an attempt fails/succeeds *All attempts to find a cure have failed.*

NOUNS + attempt

a rescue attempt *Two firefighters were hurt in the rescue attempt.*

an assassination attempt (=an attempt to kill a leader) *A bodyguard was wounded in an assassination attempt on the president.*

an escape attempt *The prisoner has made two previous escape attempts.*

a suicide attempt (=an attempt to kill yourself) *He was admitted to hospital after a suicide attempt.*

a coup attempt (=an attempt to change the government, usually by force) *The rebels left the country after the failed coup attempt.*

PREPOSITIONS

on the first/second etc attempt (*also* **at the first/second etc attempt** *BrE*): *They reached the top of the mountain on their second attempt.*

an attempt at sth *She made an attempt at a smile.*

in an attempt to do sth *She began to run in an attempt to get away.*

despite sb's attempts *The engine refused to start despite all our attempts to make it work.*

attention *n*

1 the activity of listening to, looking at, or thinking about someone or something carefully

VERBS

pay attention to sth/sb *He read the final page, paying particular attention to the last paragraph.*

devote attention to sb/sth *He needs to devote more attention to his schoolwork.*

turn your attention to sth/sb (=start thinking about something or someone else) *She quickly put away the shopping and then turned her attention to preparing dinner.*

focus your attention on sb/sth *I tried to focus my attention on my book.*

give sth/sb your attention (=think about something or someone so that you can deal with a problem) *She promised to give the matter her attention the next day.*

keep/hold sb's attention *This game is fun and is sure to keep the attention of young students.*

bring sth to sb's attention (=tell someone about something so they can deal with it) *Thank you for bringing the problem to my attention.*

attract/catch sb's attention (=make someone see you) *We tried to attract the waiter's attention.*

escape sb's attention (=not be noticed by someone) *Even the tiniest details did not escape her attention.*

sb's attention wanders (=someone stops listening, watching etc carefully) *During the meeting, her attention began to wander.*

ADJECTIVES

sb's full/complete/undivided attention *He gave the task his undivided attention.*

close attention *They listened to the speech with close attention.*

particular/special attention *You should pay special attention to spelling in this exercise.*

scant attention (=not much or not enough) *Merrill paid scant attention to their conversation.*

attention + NOUNS

attention span (=the length of time when you continue to be interested in something) *Young children often have a short attention span.*

PREPOSITIONS

sb's attention is on sth/sb *My attention wasn't really on the game.*

PHRASES

attention to detail *Attention to detail is essential in this job.*

care and attention *The care and attention that has gone into this work is amazing.*

2 interest that people show in someone or something

VERBS

receive/get/attract/draw attention *His books received little attention while he was alive.*

capture sb's attention *The trial captured the attention of the whole country.*

enjoy sb's attention *He was enjoying the attention of his female fans.*

divert/deflect attention away from sth (=make people interested in something else instead) *This story has diverted attention away from his private life.*

command attention (=cause people to show interest) *A comment from a famous actor can command worldwide media attention.*

deserve/merit attention *His work is finally getting the attention it deserves.*

lavish attention on sb/sth (=show a lot of interest in them) *She had been jealous of the attention lavished on Sophie.*

attention turns/shifts (=it moves to someone or something else) *Attention has now shifted to the problems in other European countries.*

ADJECTIVES/NOUNS + attention

public attention *We hope the event will attract public attention.*

media/press attention *The princess received a lot of press attention.*

international/national/world attention *His novel attracted international attention.*

widespread attention *The dispute did not receive widespread attention.*

unwanted/unwelcome attention *He wanted to avoid unwanted attention from the authorities.*

PHRASES

be the focus of attention (*also* **be the centre**

A

of attention) *She became the focus of media attention after winning the prize.*

3 the activity of looking after or dealing with someone or something

ADJECTIVES

medical attention *Luke needs medical attention for a leg injury.*

urgent/immediate/prompt attention (=as soon as possible) *This matter needs your urgent attention.*

ADJECTIVES

need/require/demand attention *Let me know if you see anything that requires my attention.*

attitude [Ac] *n*

your general opinions and feelings about something, often shown in your behaviour

ADJECTIVES

a positive/negative attitude *A positive attitude is essential if you want to be successful in business.*

a different attitude *Nowadays there is a very different attitude towards mental illness.*

sb's whole attitude *As you get older, your whole attitude to life changes.*

general attitude *His general attitude to our situation was unsympathetic.*

public attitude (=among ordinary people) *There has been a shift in public attitudes to nuclear power.*

political attitude *The researchers did a survey of political attitudes among young people.*

mental attitude *There is a strong connection between health and mental attitude.*

a relaxed/tolerant/laid-back attitude *On the island of Bali, there is a more relaxed attitude to life.*

a favourable attitude *BrE*, **a favorable attitude** *AmE* (=having a good opinion of something or someone) *Older people tend to have a favourable attitude to the police.*

a critical attitude (=showing you disagree with or disapprove of someone or something) *People's attitude towards US foreign policy has become increasingly critical.*

an ambivalent attitude (=not sure if you approve of something) *The public have a rather ambivalent attitude towards science.*

a patronizing/condescending attitude (=showing that you think you are more important or intelligent than someone) *She didn't like his patronizing attitude towards women.*

an aggressive/hostile attitude *Their attitude suddenly became more aggressive.*

a healthy attitude (=a good and sensible attitude) *She now has a healthier attitude towards food and eating.*

a cavalier attitude (=very careless, especially about something serious or important) *It was an indication of his cavalier attitude that he had not bothered to sign the contract.*

> **A good/bad attitude**
> Someone who has a **bad attitude** behaves badly and does not seem interested in what they are doing: *He is a lazy student with **a bad attitude**.*
> Someone has a **good attitude** seems very interested in what they are doing and wants to do well: *Greg is a great player with a lot of talent and a **good attitude**.*

VERBS

have/take/adopt an attitude *Not everyone takes a positive attitude towards modern art.*

an attitude exists *This attitude no longer exists in the church.*

sb's attitude changes *As you get older, your attitude changes.*

sb's attitude hardens (=they feel less sympathy and they want to be stricter or firmer) *People's attitudes towards sex offenders have hardened.*

change/influence attitudes *We have got to change people's attitudes to the disease.*

PREPOSITIONS

sb's attitude to/towards sb/sth *Their attitude to work is excellent.*

PHRASES

people's attitudes *People's attitudes to divorce have changed.*

sb has an attitude problem (=someone is not helpful or pleasant to be with) *Some of the male students have a real attitude problem.*

attraction *n*

1 something interesting or enjoyable to see or do

ADJECTIVES/NOUNS + attraction

a tourist/visitor attraction *Buckingham Palace is one of London's most important tourist attractions.*

the main/star attraction *The painting of the Mona Lisa is the main attraction.*

a local attraction *There are a number of local attractions, including a 15th-century castle.*

VERBS

visit an attraction *There are plenty of attractions you can visit.*

2 a feature that makes people want to do something, because it seems good or enjoyable

ADJECTIVES

a big/great/huge attraction *For me, the free food was one of the biggest attractions.*

the main attraction *The software's main attraction is that it is very easy to use.*

VERBS

sth has its attractions *The work has its attractions and you get to meet some interesting people.*

sth loses its attraction *Camping soon lost its attraction when it started raining and the tent collapsed.*

increase/add to the attraction *The low price will add to the attraction for many people.*

understand the attraction of sth *I've never understood the attraction of golf – it looks really boring.*

the attraction lies in sth *It is difficult to see where the attraction lies in some horror movies.*

attractive *adj*

1 good-looking

NOUNS

an attractive woman/girl/man *Miss Fraser was an attractive woman in her early 30s.*

an attractive town/city/village *Nearby is the attractive town of Burford, built of golden Cotswold stone.*

an attractive area/place/part *The city is located in one of the most attractive parts of the country.*

an attractive building *The college is an attractive building, dating from the 17th century.*

an attractive design *It is important that the magazine has an attractive design.*

ADVERBS

extremely attractive *As well as being clever, she was also extremely attractive.*

stunningly attractive (=extremely attractive) *Marianne was a stunningly attractive woman.*

sexually/physically attractive *Some women say they find him physically attractive.*

VERBS

find sb attractive *Women seem to find him attractive.*

look attractive *Why do you wear clothes that make you look less attractive?*

THESAURUS: attractive

handsome, good-looking, pretty, attractive, cute, lovely, gorgeous, glorious, picturesque, magnificent, stunning, breathtaking/spectacular, exquisite → **beautiful**

2 used about something that people want to have or do

NOUNS

an attractive offer/proposition *It sounded like a very attractive offer.*

an attractive investment *For many people, houses are an attractive investment.*

an attractive feature *The car's most attractive feature is its powerful V8 engine.*

an attractive option *She wanted to take a walk, but in this weather it was not an attractive option.*

an attractive prospect (=something that seems like a good thing to happen or do) *A holiday in Vietnam seems like a very attractive prospect.*

VERBS

find sth attractive *I found the idea of backpacking attractive, but I wasn't sure I could afford it.*

sound attractive *His invitation sounds attractive. Perhaps I should go.*

PREPOSITIONS

attractive to sb *The rich soil made the area attractive to settlers.*

THESAURUS: attractive

nice, fine, sound, attractive, desirable, favourable, positive, beneficial → **good (1)**

audience *n*

1 a group of people who come to watch and listen to someone speaking or performing in public

ADJECTIVES

a big/large/small audience *The band regularly attract big audiences for their concerts.*

a live audience (=who are watching a performance in the place where it happens) *The show was filmed in front of a live audience.*

a packed audience (=the place is full) *He played to a packed audience.*

an enthusiastic/appreciative audience *They performed in front of enthusiastic audiences at Europe's biggest rock festival.*

a captive audience (=people who listen to or watch someone or something because they have to, not because they are interested) *His family were a captive audience for his jokes.*

NOUNS + audience

a studio audience (=in the studio where a programme is being recorded) *The studio audience mainly consisted of teenage girls.*

VERBS + audience

perform/play/sing to an audience *The band played to huge audiences in America.*

speak to an audience (*also* **address an audience** *formal*): *He spoke to an audience of young students.*

entertain an audience *The singer has entertained audiences all over the world.*

thrill/delight/captivate an audience (*also* **wow the audience** *informal*) (=do something that they enjoy very much) *The magician delighted the audience with some amazing tricks.*

attract/draw/pull in an audience *The concert attracted an audience of over 20,000 people.*

A

audience + VERBS

an audience claps (*also* **an audience applauds** *formal*): *The audience clapped at the end of the movie.*

an audience laughs *He has the ability to make an audience laugh.*

an audience cheers *The audience cheered loudly when he came on stage.*

an audience boos (=they say 'boo' because they do not like the performance) *The play wasn't very good and some of the audience started booing.*

audience + NOUNS

audience participation *The show involves a lot of audience participation and people are asked to come on stage.*

PREPOSITIONS

in front of/before an audience *He is used to performing in front of a live audience.*

in the audience *There must have been at least 200 people in the audience.*

an audience of *An audience of about 50 people came to the talk.*

PHRASES

a member of the audience *Several members of the audience left the film early.*

2 the people who watch or listen to a programme or film, read a magazine etc

ADJECTIVES

a big/large/huge/vast audience *Messages posted on the internet can attract a huge audience.*

a small audience *The show only gets a small audience.*

a young/teenage audience *This is a magazine with a young audience.*

an older audience *The programme mainly appeals to an older audience.*

a worldwide/international audience *Soccer has an ever-increasing worldwide audience.*

a wide/broad/diverse audience (=consisting of many different types of people) *He is an author who appeals to a wide audience.*

a mass audience (=a very large number of people) *Television brought entertainment to a mass audience.*

a mainstream audience (=ordinary people, not people with specialized interests) *The film is aimed at a mainstream audience.*

a viewing audience (=the people who watch a programme) *The show has a viewing audience of 2 million.*

VERBS

have/get an audience *The programme has a big audience every week.*

attract/draw/pull in an audience *The first show attracted an audience of more than 2 million.*

reach an audience *Advertisers use television to reach a large audience.*

appeal to an audience (=be interesting to them) *Teenage actors were used in the film in order to appeal to a younger audience.*

NOUNS + audience

a television/radio audience *Radio audiences have gone down in recent years.*

the target audience *The target audience is mostly men aged 28 to 35.*

audience + NOUNS

audience share (=a part of the total number of people who watch television or listen to the radio) *The TV has 12% of the audience share.*

authentic *adj* THESAURUS ▸ **real (1)**

author Ac *n*

someone who writes books, or someone who has written a book, article, or report

ADJECTIVES

a famous/well-known author *The famous author Ernest Hemingway stayed at the hotel in the 1920s.*

a best-selling author *Ian McEwan is a best-selling author, whose books have been translated into many languages.*

a children's author *'Matilda' was written by Roald Dahl, the famous children's author.*

your favourite author *"Who's your favourite author?" "I really like Charles Dickens."*

a prolific author (=one who writes many books) *She is a prolific author who has published more than 70 books.*

a contributing author (=someone who writes articles for a newspaper or magazine, or who writes part of a book, report etc) *Ms Gomez was a contributing author to Chapter 1 of the report.*

an acclaimed author (=one whose work is admired by many people) *Margaret Atwood is a highly acclaimed author, who has won many awards for her work.*

first author *formal* (=the first of two or more authors, who are mentioned as having written something) *My supervisor was listed as first author, even though I did most of the work.*

PREPOSITIONS

the author of sth *Professor Jones was one of the authors of the report.*

Author or writer?

You use **writer** about anyone who writes books. You usually use **author** about someone whose books are considered to be works of literature.

Author is also used when talking about the person who wrote something: *She is* ***the author of*** *a study of childhood illnesses.*

authoritarian *adj* THESAURUS ▸ **strict (1)**

authority Ac *n*

1 the power you have because of your official position

ADJECTIVES

full/complete/total authority *The manager has full authority to make decisions.*

absolute authority (=complete authority over everyone – used especially about the leader of a country) *In those days, the emperor had absolute authority.*

legal authority *US agents have legal authority to bring criminals back from overseas.*

moral authority *The government lacks the moral authority to regenerate the country.*

parental authority *The older children are more likely to resist parental authority.*

VERBS

have authority *Only the head of the department has the authority to make that decision.*

give sb authority *The department was given authority over highways and waterways.*

exercise/exert your authority (*also* **wield authority** *formal*) (=use your authority) *In practice it's very difficult for the president to exercise his authority.*

abuse/misuse your authority (=use your authority in a bad way) *The mayor was accused of abusing his authority and taking bribes.*

exceed/overstep your authority (=do more than you have the power or right to do) *A higher court decided that the judge had exceeded his authority.*

establish/assert your authority (=show people that you have authority) *The new manager was anxious to establish her authority.*

stamp/impose your authority on sth (=show people that you have authority over something) *Robertson quickly stamped his authority on the team.*

lose your authority *He's worried that he is losing his authority over the party.*

undermine/weaken sb's authority (=make someone's authority weaker) *I wasn't trying to undermine your authority.*

challenge sb's authority (=try to take power away from someone) *There had been no one to really challenge his authority.*

question sb's authority (=express doubt about someone's authority or decisions) *Students in secondary schools are more likely to question authority.*

authority + NOUNS

an authority figure (=someone who has the power to tell young people what they can do) *The teacher is an authority figure, like the parent.*

PREPOSITIONS

authority over sb/sth *He has no authority over us.*

in authority (=in a powerful position) *You need to speak to someone in authority.*

PHRASES

be in a position of authority *I've never been in a position of authority before.*

have an air of authority (=look like you have authority, in a way that makes people obey you) *The commander had an unmistakeable air of authority.*

a challenge to sb's authority *The leadership saw the demonstrations as a challenge to their authority.*

2 someone who knows a lot about a subject

ADJECTIVES/NOUNS + authority

a great authority *Jourdain was a great authority on English furniture and wrote several books on the subject.*

a world authority *He is a world authority on climate change.*

a leading/noted authority *They consulted leading authorities on the disease.*

the foremost authority (=the one who knows most) *He was considered to be the foremost authority on Spanish paintings.*

a respected authority *She is a highly respected authority on medieval church architecture.*

PREPOSITIONS

an authority on sth *Sue is an authority on Chinese cooking – she used to live in China.*

authorization (*also* **authorisation** *BrE*) *n*

official permission to do something, or the document giving this permission

ADJECTIVES

official authorization *The two men did not have official authorization to enter the country.*

special authorization *In Britain, the police need special authorization to carry guns.*

written authorization *If you want to go on the school trip, you'll need written authorization from your parents.*

prior authorization (=authorization before something happens) *Under Turkish law, protests must have prior authorization.*

proper authorization *In order to use the computer room, you will need the proper authorization.*

VERBS

have authorization *For security reasons, only certain people have authorization to enter the building.*

A

get authorization (*also* **obtain authorization** *formal*): *The university obtained authorization to build a new library.*

receive authorization *They have received authorization to publish the documents.*

ask for authorization (*also* **request/seek authorization** *formal*): *The pilot requested authorization to land the plane.*

give sb authorization (*also* **grant sb authorization** *formal*): *He was granted authorization to work in the United States.*

PREPOSITIONS

authorization for sth *The city council has given authorization for the concert to take place.*

authorization from sb/sth *The company has received authorization from the Ministry of Health to sell the drug.*

without authorization *Can a bank withdraw money from your account without authorization?*

autumn *n*

the season between summer and winter, when leaves change colour and the weather becomes cooler

ADJECTIVES

early autumn *We were enjoying the hazy sunshine of early autumn.*

late autumn *It was late autumn, almost winter.*

autumn + NOUNS

autumn leaves *The sun was shining through the red and gold autumn leaves.*

the autumn sun/sunlight/sunshine *The fallen leaves glowed in the autumn sun.*

the autumn colours *Visitors came to enjoy the rich autumn colours of the trees.*

autumn + NOUNS

an autumn day/morning *It was a beautiful autumn day.*

PREPOSITIONS

in the autumn *Charles returned to university in the autumn.*

during the autumn *She began writing the novel during the autumn of 1938.*

In American English, people usually say **fall**: *He plans to go back to school in the* ***fall***.

available Ac *adj*

something that is available is able to be used or can easily be bought or found

NOUNS

available evidence/data/information *All the available evidence suggests that the Earth's climate is getting warmer.*

available source/supply *The researchers consulted all the available sources of information.*

available resources/materials *The products are handmade using locally available materials.*

available space/land/room *Make sure that you have enough disk space available on your computer.*

available alternative/choice *There were no other available alternatives at the time.*

available opportunity/chance *You should practise speaking the language at every available opportunity.*

ADVERBS

easily/readily/freely available (=easy to get) *Timber is cheap and readily available.*

widely/commonly available (=available in many places) *Organic food is now widely available in the US.*

universally available (=available to everyone) *This information should be universally available.*

publicly available *The information was taken from publicly available documents.*

commercially available (=available to buy) *The game has been commercially available in Japan since last year.*

currently available *The product is currently available in all of our stores.*

available online *This software is available online.*

VERBS

become available *A place on the trip became available at the last minute.*

make sth available *The government will make more money available for research.*

have sth available *They said that they didn't have any more tickets available.*

PREPOSITIONS

available from somewhere *The book is available from all good bookstores.*

available to sb *I had used all the money that was available to me.*

available for use/rent/collection etc *The house is available for rent from next month.*

PHRASES

in the time available *Answer as many questions as you can in the time available.*

the best available *We use the best available technology.*

the only available *One small tree was the only available protection from the sun.*

the nearest available *Ruth sat down on the nearest available chair.*

THESAURUS: available

free
seat | room
not being used by anyone:
Excuse me, is this seat free? | The hotel has a couple of rooms free.

vacant
seat | chair | land | site | lot | apartment | room | job | position
available for someone to use, rent, or do:

She put her bag down on a vacant seat. | West Hollywood is becoming a town of vacant apartments. | The position of principal remains vacant.

On toilets in public places, there is often a sign that says either **vacant** (=no one is using it) or **engaged** (=someone is using it).

avenue *n* THESAURUS **road**

average[1] *n*

the amount calculated by adding together several quantities, and then dividing this amount by the total number of quantities

ADJECTIVES

the national average *Cancer rates in this area are 3% higher than the national average.*

VERBS

calculate/find the average *To calculate the average, add all the prices together, then divide by the number of prices you have.*

PREPOSITIONS/ADVERBS

on average *Women's earnings are on average lower than men's.*

above/below (the) average *His scores were well above average in science.*

higher/lower than (the) average *Unemployment is almost 50% higher than the national average.*

by an average of sth *Pay increased by an average of 17% in just one year.*

the average of sth *The average of 3, 8, and 10 is 7.*

average[2] *adj*

1 the average amount is the amount you get when you add together several quantities and divide this by the total number of quantities

average + NOUNS

average size/height/weight/length *He is of average height and weight.*

average age *The average age of the students is 19 years old.*

average cost/price *The average cost of making a movie has risen by 15%.*

average number/amount *The average number of workers on farms has gone down.*

average income/earnings/wage/salary *The average house price is nearly four times the average annual wage.*

average level/rate/speed *The average level of unemployment stood at 4%.*

average intelligence *The child seemed to be of above average intelligence.*

ADVERBS

above average *He is above average height for his age.*

below average *The economy grew at below average rates during this period.*

PHRASES

of average height/ability/intelligence etc *Most of the pupils are of average ability.*

longer/shorter/higher/lower etc than average *Last winter was colder than average.*

2 having qualities that are typical of most people or things

average + NOUNS

the average person/man/woman *A good diet will provide enough iron for the average person.*

the average family *The average family spends a lot of time watching television.*

an average week/month/year *In an average week I drive about 250 miles for my job.*

avert *v* THESAURUS **avoid (1)**

avid *adj* THESAURUS **enthusiastic**

avoid *v*

1 to prevent something bad from happening

NOUNS

avoid an accident/collision *The driver braked suddenly in order to avoid an accident.*

avoid a disaster/catastrophe *A major ecological disaster was avoided when the oil began drifting out to sea.*

avoid a war/strike *Chamberlain was anxious to avoid another world war.*

avoid the risk/danger/threat of sth *Smoking is forbidden, in order to avoid the risk of fire.*

avoid a repeat/repetition of sth (=prevent something bad from happening again) *The police are anxious to avoid a repeat of last year's violence.*

avoid a problem *There are a number of ways in which you can avoid this problem.*

avoid an argument/conflict/confrontation *She preferred to avoid conflict whenever she could.*

avoid confusion/misunderstanding *The name of the film was changed in order to avoid confusion with another film.*

avoid disappointment/embarrassment *Book early, to avoid disappointment.*

ADVERBS

narrowly avoid sth (=only just avoid something happening) *She narrowly avoided being hit by a bullet.*

PHRASES

avoid sth at all costs (=try as hard as you can to prevent something from happening) *They wanted to avoid a scandal at all costs.*

THESAURUS: avoid

avert *formal*
disaster | war | strike | crisis | threat
to prevent something bad from happening:

A

Disaster was averted only by quick thinking by the plane's captain. | *A teachers' strike was* **narrowly averted** *in January* (=it was only just averted). | *Some scientists believe that nuclear energy is the only way to avert the threat of global warming.*

2 to escape having to do something or deal with something

NOUNS

avoid work *His son would do anything to avoid work.*

avoid a question *Politicians are very good at avoiding difficult questions.*

avoid your responsibility/duty *The federal government is trying to avoid any responsibility for dealing with the problem.*

avoid the issue *It was impossible to avoid the issue any longer.*

THESAURUS: avoid

evade *formal*
taxes | **responsibility** | **question** | **payment** | **justice** | **issue** | **problem**
to avoid having to do something or deal with something:
Companies often hide their profits in order to evade taxes. | *The government cannot evade its responsibility to help the refugees.* | *She skilfully evaded all questions about where she had been the night before.*

Evade or avoid?
Evade means the same as **avoid**. **Evade** is more formal and is often used about taxes and responsibilities.

get out of *informal*
agreement | **contract**
to avoid doing something you should do or something you promised to do. **Get out of** is more informal than **avoid**:
The country is trying to get out of its agreement to pay back the money. | *We promised we'd go – we can't get out of it now.*

3 to not go near a person or place, or not talk about a subject

ADVERBS

carefully avoid *They carefully avoided each other's eyes.*

deliberately avoid *He had a feeling that she was deliberately avoiding him.*

studiously avoid *formal* (=make a deliberate effort to avoid someone or something) *The government has studiously avoided public debate about this subject.*

PHRASES

avoid sb/sth like the plague *informal* (=avoid someone or something as much as you can) *Why did you want to speak to him? You usually avoid him like the plague.*

awake *adj* not sleeping

ADVERBS

be wide/fully awake (=completely awake) *I had been in bed for an hour but was still wide awake.*

be half awake (=not fully awake) *Most of the people on the train were only half awake.*

be hardly/barely awake (=almost sleeping) *George was barely awake and he almost fell down the stairs.*

still awake *It was 11.30, but the children were all still awake.*

VERBS

stay/keep awake (*also* **remain awake** *formal*): *I was tired and it was hard to stay awake.*

lie awake *Kate lay awake worrying about the test.*

keep sb awake *The noise of the planes kept me awake.*

shake sb awake *Ben shook me awake and told me the news.*

jerk awake (=wake with a sudden movement) *There was a bang on the door, and he jerked awake.*

award[1] *n*

a prize or money that someone gets for something they have achieved

ADJECTIVES

a special award *He will receive a special award for his bravery.*

a national/international award *The programme was nominated for two national awards.*

a prestigious award (=a very important and well-respected award) *The Heisman Trophy is US college football's most prestigious award.*

a top/major award *The car won the top award at the British International Motor Show.*

the highest award *The Medal of Honor is the highest military award in the US.*

a literary award *He received numerous state and literary awards, both in Romania and Hungary.*

an annual award *They won the company's annual award for consistent high quality service to customers.*

NOUNS + award

a film/music/poetry award *The winners of this year's music awards have just been announced.*

VERBS

win an award *Tom Cruise won the award for best actor.* | *We had dinner at an award-winning restaurant.*

get/receive an award *The film has received many awards.*

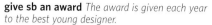

give sb an award *The award is given each year to the best young designer.*

present sb with an award *The college principal presented the students with their awards.*

be nominated for an award (*also* **be up for an award** *informal*) (=be chosen as one of the people, books etc that could receive an award) *The book has been nominated for several awards.*

pick up/scoop an award (=get an award – used especially in news reports) *The band scooped the award for best album.*

the award goes to sb/sth *The Team Of The Year Award went to the Ladies' England Cricket Team.*

award + NOUNS

an awards ceremony *She received her prize at an awards ceremony.*

an award winner *The four award winners received a total of £1,000 prize money.*

an award scheme *BrE: The award scheme aims to encourage young golfers to improve their technique.*

PREPOSITIONS

an award for sth *The actress won an award for her performance in the film.*

an award from sb/sth *He received the award from the British Academy of Film and Television Arts.*

award[2] *v* THESAURUS **give (1)**

aware Ac *adj*

1 knowing about or realizing something

ADVERBS

well/fully aware *He is an experienced climber and he is well aware of the dangers that he faces.*

acutely/keenly aware (=very aware, in a way that has a strong effect on your behaviour) *I'm acutely aware of the huge amount of work that still needs to be done.*

more/increasingly aware *People are becoming increasingly aware of the need to protect the environment.*

painfully/uncomfortably aware *He was painfully aware that everyone was looking at him.*

dimly/vaguely aware (=a little aware, although you are not completely sure) *I was dimly aware of the sound of an approaching car.*

suddenly aware *She suddenly became aware of a strange smell.*

VERBS

make sb aware of sth *It is important that young people are made aware of the dangers of taking drugs.*

become aware *He became aware that he was being watched.*

remain aware *Try to remain aware of the risks involved.*

PREPOSITIONS

aware of sth *The company says that it is aware of the problem and it will deal with it soon.*

PHRASES

as you are aware *As you are aware, funds for this project are very limited.*

ANTONYMS **aware → unaware**

2 knowing about a subject and realizing its importance

ADVERBS

politically aware *Schools must encourage students to become politically aware members of society.*

socially aware *He had become more socially aware and was now doing more things to help other people.*

environmentally aware *We are an environmentally aware company with excellent recycling facilities.*

awareness *n*

knowledge or understanding of a particular subject or situation

ADJECTIVES

growing/increasing awareness *There is an increasing awareness of the effects of mankind's activities on the environment.*

increased awareness (*also* **heightened awareness** *formal*): *There was an increased awareness of the need for education.*

general/public awareness *Public awareness of crime has increased.*

great awareness *There is great awareness of the need for reform.*

keen/acute awareness (=a very strong awareness) *A good teacher has a keen awareness of the needs of his or her students.*

little/no awareness *He has little awareness of the effect of his words on other people.*

VERBS

raise/increase awareness *The government wants to raise awareness about the dangers of smoking.*

create awareness *Companies use advertising to create awareness of their products.*

heighten awareness *formal* (=increase awareness, especially about a problem) *The campaign is intended to heighten people's awareness of the disease.*

have no/some/any awareness *The authorities had no awareness that a problem existed.*

PREPOSITIONS

awareness of/about sth *We want to develop an awareness of the benefits of eating healthy foods.*

awareness among sb *Awareness among the general public of the dangers of drink-driving has definitely increased.*

A

PHRASES

a lack of awareness *There is still a lack of awareness about the disease, even among some medical professionals.*

awesome *adj* THESAURUS ▸ excellent

awful *adj* THESAURUS ▸ terrible

awkward *adj*

1 difficult, embarrassing, or inconvenient

awkward + NOUNS

an awkward question *They asked me a lot of awkward questions.*

an awkward subject/topic *Money was an awkward subject between Steve and his wife.*

an awkward situation/position *It is a very awkward situation and there is no obvious solution.*

an awkward time/moment *You're calling at rather an awkward time – can you call back later?*

an awkward fact *The awkward fact remains that he is not a popular leader.*

an awkward silence/pause *There was a long and awkward silence, and neither of us knew what to say.*

an awkward customer *informal* (=someone who is difficult to deal with) *He is an awkward customer and you have to be careful what you say to him.*

ADVERBS

slightly/a little/rather awkward *There was one slightly awkward moment when he forgot what he was going to say.*

extremely awkward *You are putting me in an extremely awkward position.*

PREPOSITIONS

awkward for sb *I realise this must be very awkward for you.*

awkward about sth (=unhelpful and not doing what you want) *I hope she isn't going to be awkward about the money.*

PHRASES

make things awkward *I don't want to make things awkward for anybody.*

THESAURUS: awkward

hard, tough, demanding, challenging, daunting, awkward, tricky, delicate → **difficult**

awkward, uncomfortable, humiliating → **embarrassing**

2 embarrassed or not relaxed

VERBS

feel awkward *I sometimes feel awkward when I have to give a speech.*

PREPOSITIONS

awkward about sth *I felt awkward about asking her some rather personal questions.*

awkward with sb *We were strangers and felt awkward with each other.*

Bb

baby *n* a very young child

PHRASES

a baby is born *Let me know as soon as the baby is born.*

a baby is due (=is expected to be born) *When is your baby due?*

give birth to a baby *Sue gave birth to a baby boy.*

VERBS + baby

have a baby *She had her first baby when she was 16 years old.*

be having/expecting a baby (=be pregnant) *My wife's expecting a baby.*

deliver a baby (=help a woman to give birth to a baby) *Usually your baby will be delivered by a midwife.*

change a baby (=change its nappy) *Could you change the baby for me?*

feed a baby *She picked up the baby and began to feed her.*

⚠ Don't say 'She is waiting a baby.' Say **She is expecting a baby**.

Have a baby or be having a baby?

If a woman **has a baby**, it is born: *She had the baby at home* (=it was born at home). You often use **having a baby** when saying that a woman is pregnant: *My sister is having a baby and she has to go to hospital for regular check-ups.*

baby + VERBS

a baby arrives (=it is born) *I'd like to decorate the nursery before the baby arrives.*

a baby is conceived (=the woman becomes pregnant) *The baby was conceived soon after they were married.*

a baby cries/screams *The baby cried all night.*

a baby is teething (=teeth are appearing in its mouth) *If your baby starts crying a lot, he or she may be teething.*

ADJECTIVES

a young/small/little/tiny baby *Young babies need a lot of sleep.*

a two-day-old/six-month-old etc baby *You can't go into work with a three-month-old baby.*

a newborn baby (=recently born) *There's plenty of help and advice for people with newborn babies.*

a healthy baby *She gave birth to a healthy baby girl.*

a contented baby (=usually happy) *Danielle was a lovely contented baby.*

sb's first/second etc baby *Is this your first baby?*

a premature baby (=born before the normal time) *Lesley's baby was three weeks premature.*

an unwanted baby *Unwanted babies were frequently abandoned in the streets.*

baby + NOUNS

a baby boy/girl *She's just had a baby girl.*

a baby son/daughter/brother/sister *The little boy now has a baby sister.*

the baby boom (=the period when a lot of babies are born) *He was born in the baby boom of the 1960s.*

baby food/milk/clothes/seat/blanket etc *The baby likes his new baby food.*

back[1] *n*

1 part of the body on the opposite side from the stomach and chest

ADJECTIVES

a bad/sore/aching back *He suffers from a bad back.*

a stiff back *I was suffering from a stiff back and needed to get some treatment.*

sb's lower/upper back *He felt a sharp pain in his lower back.*

a strong back *He had a strong back and was used to carrying heavy loads.*

VERBS

your back hurts/aches *My back aches when I've been sitting in front of my computer for a long time.*

hurt/injure your back *He hurt his back while playing basketball.*

lie on your back *She was lying on her back, staring at the ceiling.*

massage sb's back *She gently massaged his back.*

hit/pat/slap sb on the back *My father slapped me on the back to congratulate me.*

straighten your back *She stood up and straightened her back.*

back + NOUNS

a back pain/injury/problem *More working days are lost in Britain through back problems than through any other single health problem.*

back trouble *She's still experiencing back trouble after the accident.*

a back muscle *He was suffering from a strained back muscle.*

a back exercise *I'll have to do some back exercises in the gym.*

a back massage/rub *She gave him a back massage to relieve the pain.*

PREPOSITIONS

on your back *She was carrying a small child on her back.*

a pain in your back *She complained of a pain in her back.*

with your back to sb/sth *He was standing with his back to the wall.*

PHRASES

keep your back straight *Keep your back straight and bend your knees when lifting things.*

turn your back on/to sb/sth *She turned her back on him.*

give sb a pat/slap on the back *He gave her a slap on the back and wished her luck.*

sit/stand back to back *The two boys were standing back to back.*

2 the part of something that is furthest from the front

PREPOSITIONS

the back of sth *I can see the back of their house from my window.*

at the back *I could see a tin of tomatoes at the back of the cupboard.*

in the back *We put our luggage in the back of the truck.*

down the back *She found some coins that had fallen down the back of the sofa.*

around/round the back *The incident had taken place around the back of the Berkeley cinema.*

to/towards the back *She went towards the back of the hall.*

PHRASES

back to front (=the wrong way round so the back is where the front should be) *He was wearing his pullover back to front.*

THESAURUS: back

rear

the back part of a building or vehicle. **Rear** is more formal than **back**:

*The carpark is situated **at the rear of** the hotel. | They went around **to the rear of** the house.*

ANTONYMS **back → front¹**

back² *adj*

at, on, or in the back of something

NOUNS

the back page *The sport is on the back page of the newspaper.*

the back row *We were sitting in the back row of the cinema.*

the back door/entrance *The thieves broke in through the back door.*

the back garden *She was sitting in the back garden.*

the back end *The back end of the truck hit our car.*

an animal's back leg/paw *The dog stretched out his back legs.*

a vehicle's back seat *She was sitting in the back seat of the car.*

THESAURUS: back

rear

seat | entrance | door | window | wall | wheel | end | part

in the back part of a building or vehicle. **Rear** is more formal than **back**:

The rear seats of the car are very comfortable. | A quiet street led to the rear entrance of her apartment block. | There was some damage to the rear end of the truck.

ANTONYMS **back → front²**

backfire *v* THESAURUS **fail (1)**

background *n*

1 the kind of family that someone has, or the kind of work or education experience someone has had

ADJECTIVES/NOUNS + background

different backgrounds *The two women come from totally different backgrounds.*

social background *Universities aim to attract students from a wide range of social backgrounds.*

ethnic/cultural/religious background (=which race, culture, or religion your family comes from) *London has people from every ethnic background.*

class/socio-economic background (=the kind of class you come from) *Smokers often come from poorer socio-economic backgrounds.*

a working-class/middle-class/upper-class background *She came from a comfortable middle-class background and she had never had to deal with these problems.*

a poor/deprived/disadvantaged background (=from a poor family) *The school has a high percentage of children from disadvantaged backgrounds.*

a wealthy/privileged background (=from a rich family) *All the top jobs were taken by people from privileged backgrounds.*

family background *Many kids lack a stable family background.*

professional background *Managers can come from a wide range of professional backgrounds.*

educational/academic background *The interviewer will ask you about your educational background and work experience.*

VERBS

have a background *She has a scientific background, but is very interested in the arts.*

PREPOSITIONS

from a ... background *Young people from a wealthy background are more likely to go to university.*

a background in sth *Students with a background in chemistry will probably find the course easier.*

PHRASES

come from a background *Mark and I came from very similar backgrounds.*

a range of backgrounds *People from a wide range of backgrounds go to watch football.*

2 the events and facts that explain why something happens in the way it does or why something is like it is

VERBS

give the background (*also* **provide the background** *formal*): *The guide gives a detailed background to the history of the area.*

form the background *The work I did in 2005 forms the background to this research.*

explain the background *Let me explain the background to the decision.*

ADJECTIVES

the historical/political background *The article provides the historical background to the war.*

background + NOUNS

background information/details *He was able to give background information about the events leading up to the accident.*

background knowledge *The students did not have any background knowledge of the subject.*

background reading *This book is good background reading for anyone interested in military history.*

PREPOSITIONS

the background to sth *The background to these concerns has been a deepening crisis in the economy.*

the background for sth *His experiences during the war provided the background for much of his work.*

against a background of sth *The decision was made against a background of political tension.*

backlog *n*

a large amount of work that you need to deal with, which should have been dealt with earlier

ADJECTIVES

a large/huge/enormous/massive backlog *The courts have a large backlog of cases.*

a growing backlog *We have a growing backlog of problems.*

VERBS

have a backlog *I have a huge backlog of work to do.*

clear a backlog (=finish dealing with it) *He had to stay late at the office to clear a backlog of paperwork.*

deal with a backlog *The company is trying to deal with the backlog of orders as soon as possible.*

a backlog builds up (=it develops) *A backlog of questions had built up.*

bad *adj*

1 not good

NOUNS

a bad time/day/year *It has been a bad time for many businesses.*

a bad situation/experience *The situation was so bad that they didn't know what to do.*

bad news *I'm afraid I have some bad news.*

the bad thing/aspect/point *The bad thing is the widening gap between rich and poor.*

a bad effect *Alcohol has a very bad effect on your liver.*

a bad idea/decision *I knew this was a bad idea.*

a bad mood/temper *He was in a bad mood all morning.*

a bad grade/mark *I got bad marks in my test.*

bad weather *The plane was delayed by bad weather.*

bad luck *It was bad luck that it rained on the day of our picnic.*

ADVERBS

pretty bad *It has been a pretty bad week.*

unbelievably/incredibly bad *It is an unbelievably bad state of affairs.*

notoriously bad (=everyone knows that something is bad) *Food at the restaurant is notoriously bad.*

VERBS

get worse *The situation is getting worse.*

PREPOSITIONS

bad for sb/sth *Some people say that meat is bad for your health.*

PHRASES

sth is in (a) bad condition/a bad state *The table was in bad condition.*

THESAURUS: bad

poor

quality | **standard** | **condition** | **design** | **workmanship** | **performance** | **health** | **eyesight** | **diet** | **hygiene**

bad – used especially when something is not as good as it should be. **Poor** is more formal than **bad**:

There were complaints about the poor quality of the materials. | *People criticized the government's poor performance.* | *A poor diet can lead to ill health.* | *The disease spread because of poor hygiene.*

B

disappointing
start | end | result | performance | sales | response | news | year | season
not as good as you hoped or expected:
It was a disappointing start to the campaign. | Her exam results were disappointing. | The team has had a disappointing season.

unpleasant
experience | surprise | shock | task | feeling | sensation | smell | taste | memory
not pleasant or enjoyable:
Many people think a trip to the dentist is an unpleasant experience. | Changing a baby's diaper is often an unpleasant task. | There was a rather unpleasant smell coming from the bin.

negative
impact | effect | results | consequences | reaction | feedback | publicity
bad – used especially about effects or people's reaction to something:
The bad publicity had a negative impact on sales. | We are starting to see the negative effects of climate change. | There was a lot of negative feedback from viewers when the programme was shown.

grim
news | future | prospect | reality | picture | reminder | warning | task
bad and worrying or depressing:
Workers were given the grim news of the job losses. | His films show the grim reality of war. | The report paints a grim picture of conditions for women in the country (=it describes a bad situation).

undesirable *formal*
behaviour | consequences | outcome | effects | side-effects
bad and not wanted:
The school works to reduce undesirable behaviour. | The policy had some undesirable consequences.

detrimental
effect | impact | influence | consequences
a detrimental effect is bad because it causes harm:
The detrimental effects of tourism can easily be seen. | The changes could have a detrimental impact on staff morale.

unfavourable *formal*
conditions | circumstances | climate | response | reaction
unfavourable conditions are not good for doing something. An unfavourable reaction shows that you do not like or agree with something:
The conditions are unfavourable for an agreement. | Their request received an unfavourable response.

You can also say that something is **not very good**: *The restaurant looked nice but the food wasn't very good.*

ANTONYMS **bad → good (1)**

2 having a serious effect and causing problems, harm, or injury

NOUNS

a bad accident *Dan was injured in a bad accident on the freeway.*
a bad mistake *Marrying him was the worst mistake she had ever made.*
a bad problem *People don't realise how bad the problem is.*
a bad injury/cut *The player suffered a bad leg injury.*
a bad cold *He had a bad cold and was sneezing.*

VERBS

look/sound bad *The injury looked quite bad.*

Describing things that are bad
Bad is a very common word. In more formal English, it is usually better to use more formal words such as **serious**, **severe**, or **grave**.

THESAURUS: bad

serious
problem | accident | injury | illness | disease | damage | crime | danger | trouble | consequences | blow | mistake | error | omission
bad – used especially when you want to emphasize how bad something is:
Obesity is becoming a serious problem in many Western countries. | Her car was involved in a serious accident. | He has a serious illness that prevents him from working. | The fire caused serious damage. | Kidnapping is a serious crime.

Don't say 'a bad crime'. Say **a serious crime**. Don't say 'a bad disease/illness'. Say **a serious disease/illness**.

severe
damage | problem | blow | pain | injury | depression | illness | flooding | drought
very serious – used about problems, injuries, and illnesses:
The building suffered severe damage in the explosion. | Her father's death was a severe blow to her. | The disease causes severe pain in the chest.

grave
danger | risk | threat | mistake | error | situation | consequences | problem | injustice
very bad and worrying, especially because people are in danger and the situation may get worse. **Grave** is more formal than **serious** or **severe**:

The building is in grave danger of collapse. | *The decision was a grave error.* | *If the trade negotiations fail, this could have grave consequences for the world economy.*

desperate
situation | **shortage** | **need** | **battle** | **struggle**
a desperate situation is very bad and it does not seem possible that it will improve:
We were in a desperate situation with no house and very little money. | *There is a desperate shortage of food and medicine.*

acute
pain | **illness** | **shortage** | **problem** | **anxiety**
very bad – used about a problem or about an illness that becomes bad very quickly:
He was suffering from acute chest pains. | *There is an acute shortage of nurses.*

3 not skilful

NOUNS

a bad player/driver/singer *There are a lot of bad drivers on the roads.*

a bad student/teacher *He was a bad student who never did any work.*

a bad cook *Not all men are bad cooks.*

bad French/Spanish etc *The waiter's English was as bad as my Spanish.*

a bad game/performance/speech etc *He had one bad game for England but that doesn't make him a bad player.*

a bad grade/mark *I got a bad grade in English.*

a bad job (=used when someone did not do something well) *The mechanics did a bad job on the engine.*

ADVERBS

really bad *He's a really bad swimmer.*

rather/pretty bad *The singing was pretty bad.*

unbelievably/incredibly bad *Her spelling is unbelievably bad.*

PREPOSITIONS

bad at (doing) sth *Scientists are often bad at communicating the importance of their work.*

THESAURUS: bad

poor
performance | **management** | **student** | **leader** | **manager** | **English** | **pronunciation** | **spelling** | **grammar**
bad. **Poor** is more formal than **bad**:
The team gave a poor performance in Saturday's game. | *He was a very poor student in high school.* | *His English was poor and it was difficult to understand what he was saying.*

ANTONYMS **bad → good (2)**

4 behaving in a way that is morally wrong, or doing things that you should not do

NOUNS

a bad man/woman *He was a bad man and I knew I couldn't trust him.*

a bad boy/girl/child/dog *Don't do that, you bad boy!*

bad behaviour *You shouldn't reward bad behaviour.*

a bad habit *It's difficult to break bad habits.*

THESAURUS: bad

naughty
child | **boy** | **girl** | **schoolboy** | **schoolgirl** | **dog**
a naughty child or pet behaves badly:
The children have been very naughty all morning. | *Get down, you naughty dog!*

immoral
behaving in a way that is morally wrong:
They believe that homosexuality is immoral. | *Having a mistress is usually considered to be immoral.*

evil
man | **woman** | **person** | **spirit** | **dictator** | **tyrant** | **genius** | **mastermind** | **empire** | **deed** | **plan** | **intentions**
doing things that are very bad or cruel:
The charm is believed to keep away evil spirits. | *He was an evil dictator, responsible for the deaths of millions.* | *One day he will be punished for his evil deeds.*

wicked
witch | **man** | **woman** | **person** | **stepmother** | **thought** | **plan** | **thing**
doing things that are very bad or cruel:
The wicked witch turned him into a frog. | *He was, in the judge's words, a very wicked man.* | *His mind was full of wicked thoughts.* | *How dare you say such a wicked thing!*

Wicked or **evil?**
Wicked and **evil** are very similar. **Evil** sounds even stronger than **wicked**. **Wicked** is often used in stories: *a* ***wicked*** *witch*
The main difference is collocation – you say an **evil spirit** (not a 'wicked' one) or an **evil genius/mastermind/dictator** (not a 'wicked' one).

ANTONYMS **bad → good (3)**

baffling *adj* THESAURUS **confusing, mysterious**

bag *n*

a container made of paper, cloth, plastic etc, used for carrying things

ADJECTIVES/NOUNS + bag

a plastic/paper bag *Store the mushrooms in a paper bag in the fridge.*

B

a leather bag *She was carrying a smart leather bag.*

a carrier bag (=for carrying shopping, usually made of plastic) *The supermarket no longer gives free carrier bags.*

a shopping bag *BrE*, **a grocery bag** *especially AmE: She loaded her shopping bags into the back of the car.*

a school bag *Hey, don't forget your school bag!*

a sports bag *I noticed that the man was wearing trainers and carrying a sports bag.*

a travel bag (=a suitcase or bag you take when travelling) *Your travel bag must not weigh more than 15 kilos.*

a shoulder bag (=one that you carry over your shoulder) *Big shoulder bags are fashionable this year.*

an overnight bag (=a small suitcase or bag for a short stay somewhere) *I put some clothes in an overnight bag and got in the car.*

an evening bag (=a small bag that a woman takes out with her in the evening) *She put her lipstick in a black velvet evening bag.*

Handbag is written as one word.

VERBS

carry a bag *Let me carry the bags.*

put sth in a bag *She put her make-up in her bag.*

open/close a bag *The customs officer opened my bag.*

pack a bag (=put things in it preparing to go somewhere) *Mum packed a bag for a day at the beach.*

unpack a bag *She unpacked her bags and put her clothes away.*

empty a bag *I've emptied my bags and I still can't find it.*

look/search/rummage (around) in a bag (=search for something in a bag) *Ivor was rummaging in the bag for his camera.*

a bag contains sth *The bag contained some old clothes.*

a bag holds sth *I don't think that bag will hold all those books.*

PREPOSITIONS

in a bag *What's in the bag?*

a bag of sth *There was a bag of potatoes on the kitchen counter.*

baggage *n*

the cases, bags etc you carry when travelling

Grammar
Baggage is an uncountable noun. It is not used in the plural. Don't say 'baggages'.

ADJECTIVES/NOUNS + baggage

hand baggage (=bags that you are allowed to carry with you onto a plane) *You are only allowed one item of hand baggage on the plane.*

excess baggage (=baggage that weighs more than you are allowed to take on a plane) *Passengers will be charged for excess baggage.*

VERBS + baggage

check (in) your baggage (=take it to the desk at an airport when you confirm your arrival for a flight) *I checked in my baggage and waited for my flight.*

carry your baggage *Passengers have to carry their baggage onto the ship.*

pick up/collect your baggage *After picking up our baggage, we went to the arrivals hall to meet my parents.*

search/go through your baggage *Customs officers went through everyone's baggage.*

baggage + NOUNS

baggage allowance (=the amount of baggage you are allowed to take on a plane) *There's a 20 kilo baggage allowance.*

the baggage compartment (=the place on a plane, train, bus, or ship where baggage is carried) *I put my briefcase into the overhead baggage compartment.*

baggage reclaim (*also* **baggage claim** *AmE*) (=the place where you collect your baggage after a flight) *We waited for almost an hour in baggage reclaim.*

PHRASES

an item/piece of baggage *How many pieces of baggage do you have?*

bail *n*

money left with a court of law to make sure that a prisoner will return when his or her trial starts

PHRASES

be released/freed on bail (*also* **be remanded on bail** *BrE*) (=be given bail and allowed to stay out of prison, usually until a trial takes place) *The men were released on police bail after spending 24 hours in custody.*

apply/ask for bail *The defendant did not apply for bail during the 15-minute court hearing.*

be held without bail *The judge ordered that Jones be held without bail.*

VERBS

be granted/given bail *Smith was granted bail when magistrates adjourned the case.*

be refused bail *Carter has been refused bail and will remain in custody.*

get bail *His wife says he hopes to get bail.*

jump bail (*also* **skip bail** *BrE*) (=not return for your trial as you promised) *He jumped bail and fled the country.*

bake *v*

to cook bread, cake, and other food in an oven, using dry heat

ADVERBS

freshly/newly baked *I love the smell of freshly baked bread.*

Bake or roast?
You usually use **roast** about meat. When you **roast** potatoes or other vegetables, you cook them in an oven using oil or fat from meat. You usually use **bake** about bread and cakes. When you **bake** potatoes, you cook them in an oven using dry heat only.

THESAURUS: bake
make, prepare, fix, rustle up, bake, roast, fry, sauté, stir-fry, deep fry, grill, broil, boil, steam, poach, barbecue, microwave → **cook¹**

balance *n*

1 your ability to stand or walk steadily, without falling

VERBS

lose your balance (=become unsteady) *He suddenly felt weak and he lost his balance and fell over.*

keep your balance (=stay steady) *The sea was so rough that it was hard to keep my balance.*

regain/recover your balance (=become steady again) *He held on to the rope until he regained his balance.*

knock/throw sb off balance *The punch was hard enough to knock him off balance.*

PREPOSITIONS

off balance *The branch knocked him off balance and he fell off his bicycle.*

PHRASES

a sense of balance *Cats have a good sense of balance.*

2 a situation in which there is the right relationship between things

ADJECTIVES

a good/healthy balance *I try to eat a good balance of fish, meat, and fresh vegetables.*

a fine balance (=hard to achieve) *She manages to strike the fine balance between being a boss and being a mom.*

a delicate balance (=easily damaged) *Too much carbon dioxide in the atmosphere upsets the delicate balance of gases.*

the right/proper/correct balance *With sport, you have to find the right balance between competition and fun.*

the natural balance *These chemicals will upset the natural balance of the pond.*

VERBS

get/find/achieve/strike a balance (=succeed in getting the balance right) *Finding the right balance between home and work is difficult.*

keep/maintain/preserve a balance *Try to keep a balance between your spending and your earnings.*

upset/disturb/disrupt the balance (=make it less equal or correct) *They don't want to upset the delicate balance of power in the region.*

change/alter/shift the balance *Will this election alter the balance of power in the Senate?*

redress/restore the balance (=make it equal or correct again) *What can be done to redress the balance in favour of the victims of crime?*

the balance changes/alters/shifts *After the strike, the balance of power had changed in favour of the workers.*

PREPOSITIONS

a balance between things *You won't be happy unless you keep a balance between work and leisure.*

PHRASES

the balance of power *The US wants to see the balance of power in Asia maintained.*

the balance of nature *Cutting down the forests seriously upsets the balance of nature.*

your work-life balance (=between your work and the rest of your life) *He is finding it difficult to get a good work-life balance.*

balanced *adj* THESAURUS ▸ **fair**, **healthy (2)**

bald *adj*

having little or no hair on your head

VERBS

go bald *He started going bald when he was in his thirties.*

bald + NOUNS

a bald head *The professor was a small man with a bald head.*

a bald patch/spot *He had a bald patch at the back of his head.*

ADVERBS

completely/totally bald *My father went completely bald when he was in his early forties.*

almost bald *His head was almost bald, except for a few hairs at the back.*

prematurely bald (=bald at an unusually young age) *He was tall and prematurely bald.*

ball *n*

a round object that is thrown, kicked, or hit in a game or sport

VERBS + ball

throw a ball *Suzy threw the ball to Matthew.*

catch a ball *He's useless at baseball; he can't even catch a ball.*

play with a ball *The dog was playing with a tennis ball.*

bounce a ball *He was in the yard bouncing a ball against the wall.*

B

hit/kick/strike a ball *He swung the bat and hit the ball as hard as he could.*

head the ball (=hit a ball with your head in a game of football) *Rooney headed the ball into the top corner.*

pass a ball (=kick or throw it to someone) *He passed the ball to his team-mate.*

get/win the ball *Then the Cowboys managed to get the ball again.*

miss the ball (=not catch or hit it) *I was trying hard but I kept missing the ball.*

drop the ball *He ran in to score when the keeper dropped the ball.*

ball + VERBS

a ball rolls *The ball rolled just past the hole.*

a ball bounces *In tennis, the ball must only bounce once.*

a ball flies/sails/soars (=moves through the air) *The ball flew over the goalkeeper's head and into the net.*

a ball rebounds (=hits something and moves back and away from it again) *The ball hit the goalpost and rebounded.*

a ball hits/strikes sth *The ball hit the ground once before bouncing over the line.*

NOUNS + ball

a tennis/cricket/golf/rugby/soccer ball *She was practising hitting golf balls.*

ball + NOUNS

a ball game *I'm not very good at ball games.*

> In American English, a **ball game** means a baseball game: *We watched the* ***ball game*** *on TV.*

ballet *n*

a performance in which dancing and music tell a story without any speaking

ADJECTIVES

classical ballet *I love watching classical ballet, because the dancers always look so graceful.*

modern ballet *In modern ballet, the dancers do not have to wear special ballet shoes.*

VERBS

go to the ballet *I sometimes go to the ballet at Covent Garden.*

perform a ballet *Tchaikovsky's ballet was performed for the first time in 1877.*

study/learn ballet *He won a scholarship to study ballet in London.*

ballet + NOUNS

a ballet dancer *She trained as a classical ballet dancer.*

ballet dancing *Ballet dancing is much less popular among men.*

a ballet class/lesson *When I was a child, my mother sent me to ballet lessons.*

a ballet school *He studied at the Royal Ballet School.*

a ballet teacher *Volkova was the best ballet teacher in London.*

a ballet company (=a group of dancers who perform together) *The National Ballet Company will give a performance of 'Sleeping Beauty'.*

ballet shoes *She needs a new pair of ballet shoes.*

balloon *n*

1 a small rubber bag that is filled with air and used as a decoration or toy

VERBS

blow up a balloon (*also* **inflate a balloon** *formal*): *She helped me blow up the balloons for the children's party.*

burst a balloon *He burst the balloon with a pin.*

a balloon floats *I watched the balloon float up into the air.*

2 a large thing that is filled with gas, which flies in the sky

NOUNS + balloon

a hot-air balloon *He wants to go for a trip in a hot-air balloon.*

PHRASES

go up in a balloon *We went up in a balloon over the mountains.*

a balloon comes down *The balloon came down in the middle of a field.*

ban *n*

an official order that prevents something from being used or done

VERBS

put a ban on sth (*also* **place/impose a ban on sth** *formal*): *The government imposed a ban on smoking in public areas.*

lift a ban (=end it) *Following protests, the ban was lifted.*

support/oppose a ban *Would you support a ban on plastic bags?*

give sb a ban/get a ban *He was given a three-match ban after being sent off against Cologne.*

face a ban *He faced a four-year ban after failing a drugs test.*

enforce a ban (=make sure that people obey it) *The police don't seem to be enforcing the ban.*

break/defy a ban (=not obey it) *They have openly defied the international ban on torture.*

comply with a ban (=obey it) *Some countries refused to comply with the ban.*

ADJECTIVES/NOUNS + ban

a complete/total ban *They are seeking a complete ban on nuclear testing.*

an outright/all-out ban (=a complete ban – used for emphasis) *An outright ban on gun* *ownership would not prevent gun crimes, because many guns are owned illegally.*

a blanket ban (=including all possible cases or types) *They imposed a blanket ban on beef products from Europe.*

a permanent ban (=forever) *Many people think there should be a permanent ban on whale hunting.*

a lifetime ban *He faces a lifetime ban from athletics.*

an immediate ban *The group has called for an immediate ban on fur farming.*

a three-year/six-month etc ban *She got a twelve-month ban for drinking and driving.*

a temporary ban *There is a temporary ban on fishing in the area, in order to give fish stocks a chance to recover.*

an international/worldwide/global ban *He called for an international ban on landmines.*

a nationwide ban (=everywhere in a country) *There was a nationwide ban on strikes.*

an export/import ban *There is an export ban on this type of technology.*

PREPOSITIONS

a ban on sth *They want a total ban on cigarette advertising.*

PHRASES

call for a ban (=say there should be one) *Senators called for a ban on French products.*

a ban comes into effect/force (=it starts being used) *The ban will come into force on March 29th.*

band *n*

a group of musicians, especially a group that plays popular music

ADJECTIVES/NOUNS + band

a rock/jazz/pop/blues etc band *Charlie was a drummer in a jazz band before he joined the Rolling Stones.*

the school band *Helen plays the trumpet in the school band.*

a live band (=one that is actually playing music, not a recording of someone playing music) *There's a live band at the club on Saturday nights.*

a boy band/girl band (=consisting of attractive teenage boys or girls) *He used to sing in a boy band.*

a brass band (=a band of brass instruments such as trumpets and trombones) *A brass band was playing in the park.*

VERBS + band

play/sing in a band (=be a musician or singer in a band) *Budd played in a rock band.*

join a band *He started learning the saxophone and joined the school band.*

form a band (=start one) *They formed their own band and released a single.*

⚠ Don't say 'make a band'.

lead a band (=be the lead singer, musician, or conductor of a band) *He led his own blues band in Memphis during the 1950s.*

conduct a band (=stand in front and direct how they play) *During the set, he was invited up to conduct the band.*

leave/quit a band *Brian quit the band halfway through the tour.*

band + VERBS

a band performs/plays *The band is performing live on Saturday night.* | *The band was playing a song by the Beatles.*

a band strikes up (=starts playing) *The band struck up the national anthem.*

a band records sth *The band has finished recording several songs for the new album.*

a band releases a song/record etc (=makes it available for people to buy) *The band has just released a new song.*

a band tours (=plays in several different cities or countries) *The band plans to tour the UK next summer.*

band + NOUNS

a band member/member of a band *He was one of the original band members.*

a band leader (=the conductor of a brass band, military band, or big band) *Glenn Miller was one of America's favorite big band leaders.*

PREPOSITIONS

in a band *All the guys in the band had long hair.*

with a band *We were the backing singers with his original band.*

bang *n* a sudden loud noise

ADJECTIVES

a loud bang *I was woken by a loud bang on the front door.*

a big bang *There was a big bang, followed by a cloud of smoke.*

a huge/massive/terrific/tremendous bang (*also* **an almighty bang** *BrE*): *The bomb exploded with a massive bang.*

VERBS

make a bang *The washing machine made a loud bang and stopped working.*

go bang (=make a sudden loud noise) *I was driving along the road when the engine suddenly went bang!*

hear a bang *She heard a sudden loud bang outside her window.*

PREPOSITIONS

with a bang *The door shut with a bang.*

bank *n*

1 a business that keeps and lends money

ADJECTIVES/NOUNS + bank

a big/large/major bank *Deutsche Bank is one of Germany's major banks.*

B

B

a high street bank (=one of the ordinary banks that most people use) *There's a lot of competition between the major high street banks.*

a commercial bank (=an ordinary bank, or one that deals with large businesses) *What was the role of UK commercial banks in the debt crisis?*

an investment/merchant bank (=one that buys and sells stocks and shares etc) *Investment banks are able to earn huge amounts of money.*

VERBS + bank

go to the bank *I have to go to the bank at lunchtime.*

pay sth into the bank *She paid the cheque into the bank.*

take sth out of the bank *He took 1,000 euros out of the bank on Friday.*

borrow sth from a bank *You may be able to borrow some money from the bank.*

rob a bank *They killed four policemen while robbing a bank.*

bail out a bank (=give it financial help to stop it failing) *Is it right that governments use taxpayers' money to bail out banks?*

bank + VERBS

a bank lends/loans sth *The bank lent me £10,000 to help me start the business.*

a bank charges (sb) sth *Banks charge interest on bank loans.*

a bank collapses/crashes (=it suddenly fails) *They lost all their savings when the bank collapsed.*

bank + NOUNS

a bank account *I'll put the money into my bank account today.*

your bank balance (=the amount of money in your bank account at a particular time) *You can check your bank balance online.*

a bank statement (=a list showing all the payments into and out of a bank account) *I used to get a written bank statement once a month, but now I have to look online.*

a bank loan *What's the interest rate on your bank loan?*

a bank robber/robbery *The bank robbers were never caught.*

a bank card *You can withdraw money using your bank card.*

a bank note (=a piece of paper money) *He paid with a $10 bank note.*

a bank manager *Could I make an appointment with the bank manager, please?*

a bank clerk (=a junior worker in a bank) *He began his career as a bank clerk.*

bank charges *Will I have to pay bank charges on this account?*

PREPOSITIONS

in a bank *We have very little money in the bank.*

2 land along the side of a river, lake, or canal

ADJECTIVES/NOUNS + bank

a river/canal bank *He runs along the canal bank every morning.*

the far/opposite/other bank (=the one furthest from you) *There was no bridge to get to the opposite bank.*

VERBS

a river bursts its banks (=the banks collapse and water comes over them) *The river had burst its banks and water was pouring down the streets.*

PREPOSITIONS

on the banks of sth *He enjoys fishing on the banks of the River Tees.*

along the banks of sth *A row of houses was built along the banks of the river.*

bankrupt *adj*

without enough money to pay what you owe

VERBS

go bankrupt *The firm went bankrupt before the building work was completed.*

be made bankrupt (*also* **be declared bankrupt** *formal*) (=a court officially says someone is bankrupt) *Her father was made bankrupt and they had to move out of their home.*

ADVERBS

almost/nearly/virtually bankrupt *The country was virtually bankrupt when he took over.*

> In everyday English, you say that a company **goes out of business** when it cannot continue trading.
> In more formal or technical English, you say that a company or person is **insolvent** (=they do not have enough money to pay their debts). You can also say that a company **goes into liquidation** (=it closes and sells off everything it has in order to try to pay off its debts).

bankruptcy *n*

the state of being officially unable to pay your debts

VERBS

face bankruptcy *The company now faces bankruptcy.*

be forced into/driven into bankruptcy *Many small firms are being forced into bankruptcy.*

avoid bankruptcy *The airline narrowly avoided bankruptcy.*

PHRASES

be close to bankruptcy *The company was close to bankruptcy following a massive drop in profits.*

be on the verge/brink/edge of bankruptcy (=close to bankruptcy) *He was on the verge of bankruptcy, with debts of over £800,000.*

go into bankruptcy *The business went into*

bankruptcy, owing their customers more than 12 million dollars.

file for bankruptcy (=officially ask to be declared bankrupt) *The company filed for bankruptcy, revealing a net debt of more than $18 billion.*

bar *n*

a place where alcoholic drinks are served

VERBS

go to/into a bar *Tony went into the bar and ordered a drink.*

drink in a bar *He spent all day drinking in a bar.*

hang out in a bar *informal* (=spend a lot of time in a bar) *I was lonely, so I started hanging out in my local bar.*

run a bar (=be in charge of a bar) *Mr Mills and his wife had been running the bar for two years.*

NOUNS + bar

a hotel bar *Would you like to have a drink in the hotel bar?*

a cocktail bar *We arranged to meet in a cocktail bar before going out to dinner.*

a wine bar *He took me to a trendy wine bar.*

bar + NOUNS

bar staff *The bar staff began clearing up at the end of the evening.*

a bar owner/manager *A bar owner can lose their licence for selling alcohol to someone under 18.*

a bar fight *He got in a bar fight over a girl.*

PREPOSITIONS

in a bar *I ended up in a bar near the station.*

at the bar *Several people were at the bar, waiting to be served.*

> **Bar** or **pub**?
> In American English, people usually say **bar**.
> In British English, people usually say **pub**.
> A **bar** is used about part of another building such as a hotel or restaurant: *They arranged to meet in the hotel* ***bar***. The **bar** also means the counter where you can go to buy drinks: *He went over to the* ***bar*** *and ordered another pint of beer.*

> **THESAURUS: bar**
> bit, lump, scrap, strip, sheet, slice, chunk, hunk, block, slab, cube, wedge, bar, segment, rasher, fragment, crumb, speck, drop → **piece**

barbaric *adj* THESAURUS **cruel (1)**

bare *adj* THESAURUS **empty**, **naked (1)**

bargain *n*

something you buy very cheaply or for much less than its usual price

ADJECTIVES

a good/great bargain *I got some great bargains in the sales.*

an amazing/incredible/fantastic/terrific bargain *The house they bought was an amazing bargain.*

a real bargain *You can sometimes pick up a real bargain in the local market.*

an absolute bargain *I think £100 for a year's membership at a gym is an absolute bargain.*

VERBS

look/search/hunt for a bargain *In January the stores are full of people looking for bargains.*

get a bargain *Shoppers always like to think they are getting a bargain.*

find a bargain *If you shop around, you might find a bargain.*

pick up/snap up a bargain *informal* (=find one) *You can often pick up a bargain at an auction.*

bargain + NOUNS

a bargain price *In the sales you can get a fully fitted kitchen at a bargain price.*

a bargain hunter (=someone looking for a bargain) *Bargain hunters queued for hours before the store opened.*

bargain hunting *We went bargain hunting in the January sales.*

barrier *n*

a problem, rule etc that prevents people from doing something, or limits what they can do

> **Grammar**
> Often plural.

ADJECTIVES/NOUNS + barrier

trade barriers *Removing trade barriers helps to create a free market.*

the language barrier (=the problem of not understanding people who speak a different language) *Living in China was hard for me at first because of the language barrier.*

cultural/racial/class/social barriers *Dr King helped African Americans overcome the racial barriers that held them back for so long.*

artificial barriers *I think the artificial barriers created by society lead to conflict between the sexes.*

a psychological barrier *Being unemployed for a long time creates a psychological barrier to getting a job.*

technical/legal/political barriers *Most of the technical barriers have been solved.*

VERBS

put up/build barriers (*also* **erect barriers** *formal*): *Sometimes managers put up barriers, which can make it hard for staff to communicate with them.*

create/set up barriers *Creating trade barriers may protect jobs in the short term, but will eventually lead to job losses.*

remove/eliminate/get rid of/lift barriers *Will changing the law remove all the barriers to trade?*

break down/tear down barriers *The social barriers between the two communities have gradually broken down.*

cross barriers (*also* **transcend barriers** *formal*) (=avoid barriers that usually exist) *Music has this wonderful ability to cross cultural barriers.*

reduce/lower barriers *We should be trying to reduce barriers between social classes, not create them.*

overcome barriers (=deal with them successfully) *There are still many barriers to overcome.*

PREPOSITIONS

a barrier to sth *The high cost of childcare remains the biggest barrier to women returning to work.*

a barrier between sb/sth *His stupid pride had become a barrier between them.*

base[1] *n*

1 the bottom part of something

ADJECTIVES

a heavy base *The lamp's heavy base prevents it from tipping over.*

a round/square/triangular/circular base *Each of the columns supporting the wall stands on a square base.*

a metal/wooden/concrete base *You need a frying pan with a solid metal base.*

PREPOSITIONS

the base of sth *The base of the statue is made of stone.*

2 a place from where an organization or group does its activities

ADJECTIVES/NOUNS + base

a military/naval/air/air-force base *Clark Air Base was the largest air base outside the US.*

sb's home base *The company controls its world operations from its home base in Detroit.*

VERBS

have a base *The airline has its base in London.*

establish a base *The company wants to establish a base in Europe.*

build a base *The US began building military bases inside Afghanistan.*

base + NOUNS

base camp *The mountaineers set up base camp at the foot of the mountain.*

3 a starting point for doing something

ADJECTIVES

a good/excellent base *His work provided a good base for other scientists.*

a solid/firm/strong base (=one that you can build upon) *Learning to play the piano gave me a solid base for learning other instruments.*

a sound/secure base (=one that is dependable and will not change) *A degree provides you with a sound base on which to build your career.*

a broad base (=one that includes many different things or people) *The first year of the course aims to provide students with a broad base of knowledge.*

VERBS

have a base *The family now have a solid base on which to build for the future.*

provide a base *This report will provide the base for future discussions.*

build a base *The company aims to build its customer base by 50%.*

give sb a base/provide sb with a base *His research provided us with a good base for our work.*

PREPOSITIONS

a base for sth *Their manufacturing industry should provide a secure base for future growth.*

base[2] *v* to use something as a basis

> **Grammar**
>
> **Base** is usually used in the passive, and is always followed by **on** (or **upon** in more formal English).

ADVERBS

base sth mostly/mainly/largely on sth *The students' grades are based mostly on test scores.*

base sth solely/entirely/exclusively on sth (=only on something) *The case against him is based solely on a single complaint from one customer.*

base sth partly on sth *The decision will be based partly on the candidate's qualifications and partly on their interview.*

base sth loosely on sth (=in a way that is not exact) *The movie is based loosely on his life.*

NOUNS

base a decision/judgment/conclusion on sth *I prefer to make a decision based on all the facts.*

base an argument on sth *His argument is based on a misunderstanding of the situation.*

base figures/calculations on sth *These figures are based on data from the Bank of England.*

base results/findings/observations on sth *They based their findings on the statements of people who had witnessed the accident.*

base an assumption/belief/opinion on sth (=something you believe to be true is based on something) *Many of their beliefs seemed to be based on superstition.*

baseball *n*

an outdoor game between two teams of nine

players, in which players try to get points by hitting a ball and running around four bases

ADJECTIVES

professional/amateur baseball *He started playing professional baseball after high school.*

major-league/minor-league baseball *Some kids dream of becoming a major-league baseball player.*

VERBS

play baseball *He plays baseball for the New York Yankees.*

watch baseball *I enjoy watching baseball on TV.*

baseball + NOUNS

a baseball game *Do you want to go to the baseball game?*

a baseball player *Babe Ruth was probably the most famous baseball player of all time.*

a baseball team *He is captain of the Texas Rangers baseball team.*

a baseball fan *58,000 baseball fans crowded into Candlestick Park.*

a baseball bat/cap/glove *He was wearing his baseball cap back to front.*

a baseball stadium/park/field *They're building a new major-league baseball stadium.*

a baseball league *The Chinese Professional Baseball League was formed in 2002.*

basic *adj*

1 used about the most important or necessary part of something, or about something that you need to know in order to understand something

NOUNS

the basic idea/concept *The basic idea is easy to explain.*

basic information/facts *Customers are looking for basic information about the products.*

basic knowledge/understanding/skills *The book assumes that the reader has a basic knowledge of the subject.*

a basic question *The interviewer will ask you some basic questions about your education and work experience.*

a basic part/element of sth *He showed me the basic elements of the system.*

basic rules/principles *Most people understand the basic rules of healthy living.*

a basic right *People have a basic right to control their own lives.*

basic needs (*also* **basic requirements** *formal*): *The body has several basic needs including food, sleep, and exercise.*

basic research/education/training *We need basic research into the causes of mental illness.*

the basic structure/pattern/framework *All computers have the same basic structure.*

basic pay/salary/pension (=the money you get before any special payments) *On top of the basic salary, there are numerous other benefits.*

PREPOSITIONS

basic to sth *These medical techniques are basic to the control of infection.*

THESAURUS: basic

fundamental
principle | belief | values | problem | question | issue | difference | right | aim
more important than anything else - used for emphasis:
Freedom of speech is a fundamental principle of any democracy. | The fundamental problem is a lack of resources. | There are some fundamental differences between their philosophies. | The fundamental aim of education is to prepare students for life. | These values are ***fundamental to*** *our society. | This issue* ***is of fundamental importance****.*

core
business | issue | belief | values | skill | area | part | element | teaching | concern
more important than anything else - used for emphasis:
The company's core business is selling food and household products. | The party has abandoned its core values (=the things that it believes to be most important). *| Information technology is a core part of our work. | The great world religions share many of the same core teachings.*

Core or **fundamental?**
These words mean the same thing and are used with many of the same collocations. **Fundamental** sounds more formal.

essential
part | element | ingredient | point | feature | aspect | characteristic | difference | problem
used when saying that something is very important, especially because you cannot do something without it, or something cannot exist without it:
Meetings and discussions are an essential part of many jobs. | The essential point is this: either we act now, or the whole future of our planet is uncertain. | One of the essential differences between humans and computers is that humans are more likely to make mistakes. | The essential problem is that we don't have enough time.

central
role | issue | theme | part | question | concern
very important and having a lot of influence or receiving a lot of attention:
Religion plays a central role in her life. | Personal responsibility is a central theme in his work. | For many economists, the central question is how to create a free market which is also a fair one. | Creating jobs is ***central to*** *government policy.*

B

underlying
cause | aim | objective | principle | factor | problem
underlying causes, aims etc are basic and important, but are not immediately obvious, or not stated directly:
When treating any health problem, it's always important to consider the underlying causes. | Their underlying aim was to increase profits. | Painting and photography are very different, but many of the underlying principles are the same.

THESAURUS: basic
plain, crude → **simple**

2 not high level, or not advanced

NOUNS

a basic knowledge/understanding *I only have a very basic knowledge of the Chinese language*
a basic skill *Students learn basic skills such as reading and writing.*
a basic technique *The course covers the basic techniques of sailing.*
basic training *The new police officers receive three months of basic training.*
basic equipment/tools *Hospitals are short of basic equipment such as needles and bandages.*
a basic model *The basic model only costs $100, but it has a very small memory.*

THESAURUS: basic

elementary
course | level | textbook
elementary courses, books etc teach students about the most basic parts of a subject:
I only took an elementary course in biology. | The book is designed for adults at elementary level. | He published a series of elementary textbooks on astronomy.

rudimentary
knowledge | skills | training | tools | equipment
if you have a rudimentary knowledge of something, you know a little about it. Rudimentary tools and equipment are very basic and can only be used for doing very simple things:
She only had a rudimentary knowledge of the sport when she started playing. | The soldiers are given rudimentary training in handling explosives. | Many of the schools are without rudimentary equipment such as blackboards.

Rudimentary or basic?
Rudimentary sounds a little more formal than **basic**. **Rudimentary** is often used about the simplest and most basic things.

plain
language | English
plain language uses simple and clear words, so that you cannot misunderstand the meaning:
The poem uses plain language which anyone can understand. | She explained what the document meant in plain English.

primitive
method | technology | tools | weapons | form
primitive methods, tools etc are very basic compared to more modern ones, and are usually not as good:
The primitive methods of construction meant that houses only lasted for a few years. | The recording was made using very primitive technology. | The workers had to use very primitive tools when building the temple. | Their primitive weapons were useless against tanks and machine guns. | The people got food from hunting and from primitive forms of agriculture.

crude
method | attempt | version | form | shelter
made or done using very basic methods or materials, and therefore not very accurate or effective:
The researchers used a rather crude method of measuring productivity. | The myths were a crude attempt to explain the origins of the universe. | The plant breeders used a crude form of genetic engineering. | They made a crude shelter out of a few branches and some leaves.

basis *n*

the facts, ideas, or things from which something can be developed

ADJECTIVES

a good basis *Love and trust form a good basis for marriage.*
a sound/firm/solid basis *Drama school may provide a sound basis for an acting career.*

VERBS

be/form the basis of sth *This research will form the basis of a book.*
provide a basis for sth *The poem provided the basis for an interesting class discussion.*
become the basis of/for sth *His design became the basis for the new engine.*
serve as a basis for sth *The document will serve as a basis for negotiations.*
establish/lay the basis for sth (=create something from which something can be developed) *The agreement established a sound basis for international commerce.*

PHRASES

on the basis of sth (=because of a particular fact or situation) *A decision will be made on the basis of your answers to a number of questions.*
have no basis in fact (=not be true) *Many of these rumours have no basis in fact.*

basket *n*

a container made of thin pieces of plastic, wire, or wood woven together, used to carry things or put things in

ADJECTIVES/NOUNS + basket

a shopping basket *She paid for the apples and put them in her shopping basket.*

a wastepaper basket *BrE*, **a waste basket** *AmE*: *He threw her letter in the wastepaper basket.*

a picnic basket *We took a picnic basket and a rug.*

a laundry/clothes basket (=for dirty clothes) *Will you please put your dirty socks in the laundry basket?*

a bread/fruit/flower basket *There was a bread basket on the table.*

a dog basket *The puppies were sleeping in the dog basket.*

VERBS

put sth in/into a basket *Put the fruit in the basket on the table.*

take sth from/out of a basket *We were all surprised when she took a little dog out of her basket.*

carry/hold a basket *She was carrying a basket of flowers.*

a basket is filled with sth *The basket was filled with loaves of bread.*

PREPOSITIONS

a basket of sth *A basket of logs sat next to the fire.*

in a basket *Is the dog in his basket?*

PHRASES

a basket full of sth *She prepared baskets full of food.*

basketball *n*

a game played indoors between two teams of five players, in which each team tries to win points by throwing a ball through a net

VERBS

play basketball *She has been playing basketball since she was 12.*

watch basketball *I often watch basketball on TV.*

basketball + NOUNS

a basketball game/match *Are you going to the basketball game?*

a basketball player *He dreams of becoming a professional basketball player one day.*

a basketball team *He plays for the New York Knicks basketball team.*

a basketball court *The college has several indoor basketball courts.*

a basketball league *She plays in the American Basketball League.*

a basketball tournament/competition *The Philadelphia 76ers won a four-team basketball tournament.*

a basketball coach *My dad used to be a high school basketball coach.*

ADJECTIVES/NOUNS + basketball

professional/amateur basketball *Professional basketball players can earn a lot of money.*

college/high school basketball *Joe used to play college basketball and he's very fast on the court.*

Basketball or basket?

⚠ Don't confuse **basketball** (=the game) and **basket** (=the thing that you throw the ball into). Don't say 'I like playing basket'. Say **I like playing basketball.**

bath *n*

1 an occasion when you wash your body in a bath

VERBS

have a bath *BrE*, **take a bath** *AmE*: *She usually has a bath in the evening.*

give sb a bath *He's upstairs giving the baby a bath.*

need a bath *After a week of camping, I really needed a bath.*

run a bath (=put water in a bath) *I went upstairs and ran a bath.*

ADJECTIVES/NOUNS + bath

a quick bath *Do I have time for a quick bath?*

a long bath *A long hot bath is a great way of relaxing.*

a hot/warm/cool bath *Why don't you have a nice warm bath?*

a relaxing/soothing/luxurious bath (=which makes you feel relaxed or very comfortable) *Treat yourself to a long luxurious bath.*

bath + NOUNS

bath time (=the time when someone usually has a bath) *Come on, Lucy, it's bath time.*

bath water *The bath water is getting cold.*

a bath towel *She handed him a soft white bath towel.*

2 *BrE* a long container for washing yourself in

VERBS

get in/into the bath *Old people often have difficulty getting into the bath.*

get out of the bath *I had to get out of the bath to answer the phone.*

soak in the bath *Try soaking in the bath to ease your aching muscles.*

lie in the bath *He's been lying in the bath for an hour.*

fill/empty the bath *I forgot to empty the bath.*

PREPOSITIONS

in the bath *"Where's Ben?" "He's in the bath."*

This meaning of **bath** is used in British English. In American English, people say **bathtub**.

B

battery *n*
an object that provides a supply of electricity for something such as a radio, car, or toy

ADJECTIVES

a flat battery *BrE*, **a dead battery** *AmE* (=with no more electricity in it) *The car's got a flat battery.*

a low battery (=with little electricity in it) *He could see the battery was low on his laptop.*

a rechargeable battery (=one that you can use again after putting more electricity in it) *The camera uses rechargeable batteries.*

a spare battery (=an extra one, in case you need it) *Take a torch and spare batteries.*

NOUNS + battery

a car/torch/phone battery *Have you checked your mobile phone battery?*

VERBS + battery

change/replace the battery (=put a new battery in something) *You may need to change the battery in the smoke alarm.*

charge/recharge a battery (=put more electricity in it) *It takes eight hours to fully recharge the battery.*

use batteries (*also* **run on batteries**) *The clock runs on two 9-volt batteries.*

put a battery in sth *She had put new batteries in the radio.*

drain/discharge a battery (=make it lose electricity) *If you forget to turn your car's lights off, it drains the battery.*

disconnect a battery *We had to disconnect the battery to stop the burglar alarm from ringing.*

battery + VERBS

a battery runs out/runs down (=there is no more electricity in it) *I think the batteries are running out.*

battery + NOUNS

battery power *You can plug your laptop in or use it on battery power.*

a battery charger (=a piece of equipment for charging batteries) *Don't forget to pack your battery charger.*

battle *n*

1 a fight between opposing people or armies

ADJECTIVES/NOUNS + battle

a fierce battle *They captured the town after a fierce battle with government soldiers.*

a bloody battle (=with a lot of killing and injuries) *The temple was the scene of a bloody battle in 1984.*

a pitched battle (=a violent battle between groups of people, usually not soldiers) *Students fought pitched battles with police during the demonstrations.*

a gun battle *Two men were left wounded after the gun battle.*

a street battle *He was killed in a street battle in 1998.*

VERBS

fight a battle (*also* **engage in/wage a battle** *formal*): *He pretended he was a soldier, going to war and fighting battles.*

do battle (=fight) *The army was ready to do battle again.*

win/lose a battle *Who won the Battle of Gettysburg?*

a battle rages (=a fierce battle happens) *People hid in basements while the battle was raging.*

PREPOSITIONS

a battle between sb *He was injured in a battle between rival gangs.*

a battle against sb *Why did the Celts lose the battle against the Romans?*

the battle for sth *The battle for the Atlantic intensified.*

in battle *Richard III was killed in battle in 1485.*

PHRASES

lead/send sb into battle *He died leading his men into battle.*

prepare (sb) for battle *Every general has his own method for preparing his troops for battle.*

ready for battle *Every ship was ready for battle.*

the field of battle *They showed great courage on the field of battle.*

2 an attempt to solve a difficult problem or change an unpleasant situation

ADJECTIVES/NOUNS + battle

a long/lengthy battle *His long battle with alcoholism is no secret.*

a tough/hard battle (=difficult) *He faces a tough battle to prove his innocence.*

a fierce/bitter battle *The two companies fought a bitter battle to win the contract.*

a running battle (=that continues or is repeated over a long time) *Her running battle with mice has not yet ended.*

an uphill battle (=very difficult) *For most people losing weight is an uphill battle.*

a constant battle *As a student, life was a constant battle against debt.*

a losing battle (=one that is going to fail) *She was fighting a losing battle to stop herself from crying.*

a legal/courtroom battle *They wanted to avoid an expensive courtroom battle.*

VERBS

fight a battle (*also* **wage a battle** *formal*): *The police are fighting a tough battle against crime.*

do battle with sb *They had to do battle with producers to keep the scene in the movie.*

win/lose a battle *It's essential to win the battle against inflation.*

face a battle *Paul faces a frantic battle to be fit for the match in November.*

PREPOSITIONS

a battle with sth *She died after a long battle with cancer.*

a battle against sth *The battle against car crime continues.*

a battle between sb *The battle between James and his insurance company has not yet been resolved.*

a battle for sth *Scientology has fought long battles for acceptance as a religion.*

a battle over sth *There would be a battle over who paid for dinner.*

beach *n*

an area of sand or small stones at the edge of the sea or a lake

ADJECTIVES

a crowded beach *In the summer the beaches get very crowded.*

a quiet beach (=with few people on it) *The beaches on this side of the island are quieter.*

a deserted/empty beach (=with no one on it) *We took a boat to a deserted beach.*

a sandy/rocky beach *Corfu is known for its sandy beaches.*

a white/golden beach (=with white or golden sand) *The house was beside a dazzling white beach.*

a private/public beach *The hotel has its own private beach.*

a secluded beach (=one that is peaceful, has few people, and is not near other places) *We had a picnic on a small secluded beach.*

an unspoilt beach (=not made worse by tourism) *The island is famous for its unspoilt beaches.*

VERBS

lie on the beach *I find it boring just lying on the beach all day.*

go to the beach *They've gone to the beach for the weekend.*

walk on/along the beach *She loved to walk along the beach in the early morning.*

beach + NOUNS

a beach holiday *BrE*, **a beach vacation** *AmE* (=spent mainly at the beach) *She loves beach holidays, while he prefers city breaks.*

a beach resort (=a place near a beach where people go on holiday) *This is one of the most popular beach resorts in Greece.*

PREPOSITIONS

on the beach *We've been on the beach all day.*

at the beach *They spent the morning at the beach.*

bear *v*

to bravely accept or deal with a painful, difficult, or upsetting situation

PHRASES

can't bear/be unable to bear sth *Fiona was unable to bear the thought of selling the house.*

can hardly bear sth (=find something very difficult or upsetting to do) *He was so ashamed that he could hardly bear to look at her.*

be hard to bear *The situation was very hard to bear.*

be more than sb can bear *He sometimes felt the grief was more than he could bear.*

as hot/long/much etc as you can bear *Make the water as hot as you can bear.*

bear + NOUNS

bear the pain *He knew that he couldn't bear the pain much longer.*

bear the heat/cold *Some people find it hard to bear the heat in the summer.*

bear the strain/pressure *Mark couldn't bear the pressure of the job any longer.*

bear the thought *I can't bear the thought of living without you.*

beard *n*

hair that grows around a man's chin and cheeks

ADJECTIVES

a long/short beard *The old man had a long white beard.*

a pointed beard *He had a small moustache and a pointed beard.*

a full/luxuriant beard (=with a lot of hair) *He wore a luxuriant beard that was red in colour.*

an unkempt beard (=not neat or clean) *His beard was tangled and unkempt.*

a straggly beard (=long and not neat) *The young man had a scraggly red beard.*

a neatly/closely trimmed beard *His closely trimmed beard had turned the color of snow.*

VERBS

have a beard *Karl Marx had a beard.*

wear/sport a beard (=have a beard - used in written descriptions) *The actor sported a neat black beard.*

grow a beard *He's not old enough to grow a beard.*

shave (off) your beard *When he shaved off his beard, he looked a lot younger.*

trim your beard (=cut it, especially to make it look neat) *He trimmed his beard in the mirror.*

stroke your beard *Karlinsky stroked his beard and smiled.*

beat *v*

to defeat someone in a game, race, election etc, especially by getting more points, votes etc than them

ADVERBS

easily beat sb *Jason easily beats me at chess every time we play.*

narrowly beat sb (=by only a few points, votes etc) *New Zealand narrowly beat South Africa.*

comfortably beat sb (=by more than a few points, votes etc) *He comfortably beat the other candidates in the election.*

comprehensively beat sb (=in a clear and definite way that leaves no doubt) *It was only the second time we had been so comprehensively beaten.*

soundly beat sb (=in a clear and definite way that leaves no doubt) *In each event she soundly beat her opponents.*

PREPOSITIONS

beat sb at tennis/golf/chess etc *My brother always beats me at chess.*

beat sb by 3 points/2 goals/20 votes etc *The Italian team beat France by two points.*

PHRASES

beat sb into second/third etc place *He was beaten into second place in the Monaco Grand Prix.*

beat sb hands down *informal* (=beat someone very easily) *He should be able to beat them all hands down.*

> **Beat** or **defeat?**
> **Beat** is more informal and is the usual word to use in everyday spoken English. **Defeat** is more formal and is the usual word to use in writing.
> When talking about wars and fighting, you usually use **defeat**: *The Greeks* ***defeated*** *the Persians in a famous battle.*

beautiful *adj*

very nice to look at, or giving you a lot of pleasure

NOUNS

a beautiful woman/girl/baby *Marilyn Monroe was one of the world's most beautiful women.*

beautiful face/hair/eyes *She has beautiful blonde hair.*

a beautiful place/country/city *South Africa is a very beautiful country.*

beautiful countryside/scenery/view *From the terrace there is a beautiful view over Sorrento.*

beautiful day/morning/weather (=with blue skies and a lot of sunshine) *The weather was beautiful and the sky was blue all day.*

beautiful music *The music was so beautiful that it almost made me want to cry.*

a beautiful book/film/poem *He wrote some of the most beautiful poems ever written.*

a beautiful flower *Her husband bought her some beautiful flowers for her birthday.*

a beautiful voice *He sings with a beautiful deep voice.*

a beautiful sound/smell/taste *The roses have a beautiful smell.*

VERBS

look beautiful *Diana looked beautiful in a long silk dress.*

ADVERBS

really/absolutely beautiful *Thank you for the flowers. They're absolutely beautiful.*

incredibly/extraordinarily beautiful (=extremely beautiful) *Fall in New England is incredibly beautiful.*

stunningly/breathtakingly beautiful (=extremely beautiful in a surprising way) *The Arctic dawn is stunningly beautiful.*

hauntingly beautiful (=beautiful, and often a little sad, in a way that you remember for a long time) *The singer had a hauntingly beautiful voice.*

exquisitely beautiful (=beautiful in a delicate way) *An exquisitely beautiful butterfly landed on the leaf.*

> **Describing men**
> You don't normally use **beautiful** about men. You use **good-looking** or **handsome**.

THESAURUS: beautiful

handsome

man | boy | prince | face | features

a handsome man or boy looks very attractive:

Dan was a strong handsome man. | *She dreamt that a handsome prince would marry her.*

> **Handsome** is also sometimes used in literature, to describe a good-looking woman who has a strong face: *His mother was a tall* ***handsome*** *woman.*

good-looking

man | woman | boy | guy | girl | couple | face

a good-looking person looks attractive. **Good-looking** is much more common in spoken English than **handsome** or **beautiful**:

There are no good-looking men in our office. | *Her husband is* ***incredibly good-looking*** *– he looks like a movie star.* | *Do you* ***think he's*** *good-looking?*

pretty

girl | woman | child | baby | face | dress | clothes | flower | village | town | garden | colour

a pretty woman, girl, or baby looks nice and has a nice face. A pretty thing or place looks nice, but is usually not very big:

What a pretty little baby! | *She has a very pretty face.* | *That's a pretty dress you're wearing.* | *They stayed in a pretty little village in the mountains.* | *The curtains are a very pretty colour.*

> You can also use **pretty** about names that sound nice: *Annalise? That's a* ***pretty name.***

attractive
woman | man | girl | town | location | appearance
an attractive person looks nice, in a way that makes you want to have a relationship with him or her. An attractive place or thing is nice to look at:
*I think she's a very attractive woman. | It is an attractive town and there are plenty of things to see. | If food has an attractive appearance, it often seems to taste better as well. | A lot of men **found** her **attractive**.*

cute *informal*
baby | kid | boy | girl | animal | dog | puppy | picture | face
nice to look at - used about animals, babies, and children:
The baby is very cute. | What a cute little dog! | There was a cute picture of a kitten.

> In informal American English, people also use **cute** about someone who looks attractive in a way that makes you want to have a relationship with him or her:
> *I think Joe's really **cute**!*

lovely *BrE spoken*
place | house | garden | view | smile | colour | picture | day | weather | name
very nice:
*They have a lovely house in the country. | He has a lovely smile. | The weather has been **absolutely lovely**. | I think Natasha is a lovely name. | She **looks lovely** in her wedding dress.*

gorgeous *spoken*
dress | man | woman | girl | place | colour | flowers | day | weather
extremely nice to look at - used mainly by women:
I love your dress. It's gorgeous! | He is always surrounded by gorgeous women. | His eyes are a gorgeous blue colour. | The weather has been gorgeous all week.

glorious
weather | day | morning
glorious weather is very good, with blue sky and a lot of sunshine:
Everyone was at the beach, enjoying the glorious weather. | It was a glorious sunny day. | It was a glorious September morning.

picturesque
village | town | surroundings | setting | view | house | cottage | harbour | landscape | countryside
a picturesque place is pleasant to look at, especially because it is old and interesting:
We stayed in the picturesque village of Herisau. | The hotel is situated in picturesque surroundings. | Picturesque cottages surround the village green.

magnificent
view | scenery | setting | surroundings | building | palace | animal | horse
very big, beautiful, and impressive:
There were magnificent views over the old city. | The train travels through some magnificent scenery. | The Bengal tiger is a magnificent animal.

stunning
view | scenery | countryside | setting
used about people who look very beautiful, or about places that are very beautiful and impressive:
*There is a stunning view of the city. | Alaska has some stunning scenery. | The whole place is **simply stunning**. | You **look stunning** in that outfit.*

breathtaking/spectacular
view | scenery | landscape | beauty
a breathtaking or spectacular view is very beautiful and impressive in a surprising way:
There are breathtaking views from the top of the mountain. | The river flows through some spectacular scenery.

exquisite
object | flower | jewellery | detail | beauty
used about things that have very beautiful small details:
The museum is full of exquisite objects that were made by skilled craftsmen. | The plants have exquisite blue flowers. | The statues are carved in exquisite detail.

ANTONYMS **beautiful → ugly (1)**

beauty *n*

a quality that makes someone or something very nice to look at or listen to

ADJECTIVES

great beauty *She was a woman of great beauty.*

natural beauty *Visitors are attracted by the island's natural beauty.*

breathtaking/stunning beauty (=great and surprising beauty) *The region is famous for the breathtaking beauty of its mountains.*

exquisite beauty (=great beauty because something is very delicately made) *Visitors are impressed by the exquisite beauty of the carving.*

sheer beauty (=the fact that something is so beautiful) *The sheer beauty of the music made him want to cry.*

unspoilt beauty *They want to protect the unspoilt beauty of the desert.*

feminine beauty *She represented the ideal of feminine beauty at the time.*

VERBS + beauty

admire/enjoy the beauty of sb/sth *He was admiring the beauty of the stars in the night sky.*

preserve the beauty of sb/sth *All visitors are asked to follow the rules and regulations in order to preserve the beauty of the park.*

be fascinated/captivated/entranced by the beauty of sb/sth (=feel that you like someone or something very much because they are very beautiful) *He was captivated by her beauty, and fell in love with her immediately.*

B

beauty + VERBS

sb's/sth's beauty fades (=it goes away slowly) *Over the years her beauty had faded a little.*

beauty + NOUNS

a beauty product *The shop mainly sells beauty products such as make-up and lipstick.*

a beauty contest/competition (=a competition in which women are judged on how attractive they look) *When she was younger, she won several beauty competitions.*

a beauty queen (=the winner of a beauty contest) *She used to be a beauty queen before she became a film actress.*

PREPOSITIONS

the beauty of sth *They want to protect the beauty of the English countryside.*

> **Beauty** is also used to mean a woman who is very beautiful: *She had been a great* ***beauty*** *and had appeared in movies.*

become *v*

to start to have a feeling or quality, or to start to develop into something or do a job

ADJECTIVES

become accustomed *His eyes were becoming accustomed to the dark.*

become famous *Everyone wants to become famous.*

become popular/fashionable *Cycling became popular at the beginning of the last century.*

become interested/excited *He became interested in philosophy at university.*

become angry/worried/unhappy etc *Pauline became concerned about her health and decided to see a doctor.*

become tired/weak/ill *I became very tired and I could not swim any more.*

become confident *She says the course has helped her become more confident as a businesswoman.*

become certain/sure/inevitable *War was becoming inevitable.*

become quiet/silent *The teacher waited for the class to become quiet.*

become hot/cold/warm/cool *The climate is likely to become warmer.*

become red/green/blue etc *His cheeks became red.*

NOUNS

become a teacher/doctor/writer etc *She wants to become a doctor.*

become president/chairman/king/queen *Obama became president when he was 47.*

become a man/woman/adult *At 18, you legally become an adult in the UK.*

become a member *Latvia became a member of the European Union.*

become a part/feature *Chips became part of the British diet during the 19th century.*

become a problem *Pollution has become a major problem.*

THESAURUS: become

get
better | worse | used to | angry | upset | bored | worried | confused | interested | excited | old | tired | ill | sick | rich | hot | cold | wet | dark | late | difficult
to start to have a feeling or quality. **Get** is more informal than **become** and is used especially in spoken English:
The team is getting better and better (=they keep getting better all the time). | *She soon got used to living in a foreign country.* | *Please don't get angry with me.* | *It's getting hot in here.* | *It gets dark at about eight o'clock.*

> **Get or become?**
> **Get** is more commonly used in informal contexts, for example when talking about your feelings, the temperature, or the weather: *I'm* ***getting tired****.* | *It's* ***getting*** *very hot.*
> **Become** is the usual word to use in more formal English, for example in essays and reports.
> With some adjectives, you can only use **become**. You say **become clear/obvious/apparent** (not 'get'): *It soon* ***became clear*** *she was lying.* You say **become certain/sure/inevitable** (not 'get'): *It* ***became certain*** *they would win the election.* You say **become extinct** (not 'get'): *Dinosaurs* ***became extinct*** *millions of years ago.*
> Both **get** and **become** are often used with comparative forms: *Things are slowly* ***getting better****.* | *The disease is* ***becoming more common****.*

grow
old | accustomed | impatient | bored | tired | concerned | rich
to become, especially gradually. **Grow** sounds rather formal and is used especially in written descriptions:
Some people are afraid of growing old. | *We have all grown accustomed to using credit.* | *She*

grew bored, and gazed out of the window. | He was growing tired of politics. | The city grew rich from the tourist trade.

turn
red | green | blue | brown | grey | black | cold | cooler | warmer | nasty | violent
to become - used especially when something changes and becomes a different colour:
His face turned red. | The water had turned bright green. | Apples quickly turn brown after the skin is peeled off. | The weather is expected to turn cold again. | The demonstration turned violent, and several protesters were killed.

go
crazy | mad | quiet | silent | blind | dark | red | green | blue | brown | grey | black
to become - used especially about people's behaviour or about colours:
The world is going crazy. | Everyone went quiet when we walked in. | The sky suddenly went dark. | His face went bright red. | Your hair is going grey.

come
undone | loose | apart
to become - used when something becomes separated or broken:
Her shoelace came undone. | The screws had come loose. | His marriage was coming apart.

bed *n*

1 a piece of furniture that you sleep on

VERBS

go to bed *What time do you go to bed at night?*

get into bed/get out of bed *She got into bed and turned out the light.*

climb/crawl into bed *Lucy climbed into bed and fell asleep straight away.*

jump into/out of bed *I jumped out of bed and ran over to the window.*

lie in bed *Simon lay in bed thinking.*

stay in bed (=not get up early or at the usual time) *At the weekend it's really nice to be able to stay in bed.*

put sb to bed (=put a child in their bed) *I put the baby to bed at 7 o'clock as usual.*

send sb to bed (=make a child go to bed as a punishment) *She was sent to bed without any dinner.*

be tucked up in bed *The children were all tucked up in bed.*

share a bed with sb *Do you mind sharing a bed with your sister?*

make the bed (=tidy the sheets and covers after you get up) *Don't forget to make your bed before you go out!*

change the bed (=put clean sheets on it) *You should change the beds every two weeks.*

take to your bed *written* (=go to bed because you feel ill) *Guy had a stomach ache and took to his bed.*

ADJECTIVES/NOUNS + bed

a warm/comfortable/cosy bed *I wish I was back home in my nice comfortable bed.*

a soft/hard bed *It was difficult to sleep on the hard bed.*

a narrow bed *A child lay sleeping on a narrow bed.*

an unmade bed (=one that has not had its sheets and covers tidied) *He threw his clothes on the unmade bed.*

a spare bed (=a bed for visitors to your home) *Come and stay any time - we have a spare bed.*

a single bed (=for one person) *There was only a single bed.*

a double bed (=a large bed for two people) *Would you like a double bed or twin beds?*

twin beds (=two single beds in a room) *The hotel room had twin beds.*

a king-size/queen-size bed (=a very big double bed) *I need a duvet cover for a king-size bed.*

bunk beds (=two single beds joined together one above the other) *The kids love sleeping in bunk beds.*

bed + NOUNS

bed covers/clothes (=sheets, blankets etc) *She pulled the bed covers up to her chin.*

bed sheets *The bed sheets need changing.*

bed linen (=sheets, pillow cases and duvet covers) *Where do you keep the clean bed linen?*

PREPOSITIONS

in bed *"Where are the children?" "They're in bed."*

out of bed *I'll speak to him about it when he's out of bed.*

before bed (=before you go to bed) *I always have a drink of warm milk before bed.*

PHRASES

the foot of the bed (=the bottom of the bed) *I woke up to find someone standing at the foot of the bed.*

(it's) time for bed *She sat and sewed until it was time for bed.*

2 the area at the bottom of the sea, a river etc

PHRASES

the sea/river/ocean/lake bed *Starfish live on the sea bed.*

Seabed and **riverbed** are often written as one word.

bedroom *n* a room for sleeping in

ADJECTIVES/NOUNS + bedroom

the main bedroom (*also* **the master bedroom** *formal*) (=the biggest bedroom in a house) *The master bedroom has a view of the sea.*

the spare bedroom (=for visitors) *She set up a home office in the spare bedroom.*

your own bedroom (=that you do not have to

share) *I want my own bedroom – I hate sharing with my sister.*
a hotel bedroom *All the hotel bedrooms have a telephone and a balcony.*
separate bedrooms *She and her husband have separate bedrooms.*
a single bedroom (=with a bed for one person) *We have one single bedroom and two doubles.*
a double bedroom (=with a big bed for two people) *I'd like to book a double bedroom for two nights, please.*
a twin bedroom (=with two single beds) *Would you prefer a double or a twin bedroom?*
an en suite bedroom (=with its own bathroom) *The hotel has 100 en suite bedrooms.*

VERBS

share a bedroom with sb *He shares a bedroom with his two brothers.*

bedroom + NOUNS

the bedroom door/window/wall/floor etc *Did you shut the bedroom window?*

bee *n*

a black and yellow flying insect that makes honey

VERBS

a bee buzzes *Bees buzzed around the flowers, collecting pollen.*
a bee stings (=it makes a hole in your skin which is often painful) *She was stung by a bee as she walked through the field.*
a bee flies somewhere *A bee flew in through the open window.*
keep bees *My dad used to keep bees and sell the honey.*

bee + NOUNS

a bee sting *For most people, a bee sting is painful, but not serious.*

PHRASES

a swarm of bees (=a large group of bees) *A swarm of bees flew out of the hive.*

begin *v* THESAURUS **start¹ (1), (2)**

beginner *n*

someone who has just started to do or learn something

ADJECTIVES

an absolute/complete/total beginner *I was a complete beginner and I had never played golf before.*
a real beginner *If you are a real beginner, you won't understand even the most basic words of the language.*
a false beginner (=someone who has studied before, but is still at a low level) *The course is for students who are false beginners.*

beginning *n*

the start or first part of an event, story, period of time etc

VERBS

mark the beginning of sth (=be the beginning of something) *This event marked the beginning of a ten-year worldwide depression.*
signal/herald the beginning of sth (=show that something will happen soon) *The release of Mandela signalled the beginning of the end of South Africa's racist system.*
see the beginning of sth (=be the time when something important starts to happen) *The 1970s saw the beginning of a technological revolution.*

ADJECTIVES

a new beginning *The country needed a new government and a new beginning.*

⚠ Don't say 'a fresh beginning'. Say **a new beginning** or **a fresh start**.

PREPOSITIONS

at the beginning *The store opened at the beginning of February.* | *There is a quotation at the beginning of the book.*
in the beginning *In the beginning I found the work quite hard.*
since the beginning *Since the beginning of the year, 238 soldiers have been killed.*
from the beginning *I opposed this war from the beginning.*

PHRASES

right from/at the beginning from/at the very beginning (=used for emphasis) *He had been lying to me from the very beginning.*
from beginning to end *This piece of work was a challenge from beginning to end.*
start at the beginning (=start a story or activity at the first part) *Just start at the beginning and tell us exactly what happened.*
sth is just/only the beginning (=used to emphasize that many more things will happen) *Signing the contract is just the beginning of a long process.*

THESAURUS: beginning

start

the beginning of something, or the way something begins. **Start** is a little less formal than **beginning**:

*Tomorrow marks **the start of** the presidential election campaign.* | *It was not a **good start to** the day.* | *The runners lined up for **the start of** the race.* | *We wanted to give our marriage a **fresh start*** (=one in which you forget about all the problems and bad things that have happened). | *I **knew from the start** that it wasn't going to be an easy climb.*

commencement *formal*
the beginning of something - used especially in official contexts:
*Tomorrow **marks the commencement of** the academic year. | The **commencement of** the contract is on January 1st.*

origin
the point from which something starts to exist:
*He wrote a book about **the origins of** the universe. | One idea concerning **the origin of** human language is that humans began to copy the sounds of nature. | The tradition **has its origins** in medieval times.*

Origin is often used in the plural.

the onset of sth
the time when something bad begins, such as illness, old age, or cold weather:
*An active lifestyle can delay the **onset of** many **diseases** common to aging. | The weather became colder, marking the **onset of winter**.*

dawn *literary*
the beginning of an important period of time in history:
*People have worshipped gods **since the dawn of civilization**. | Apples have been with us **since the dawn of time**. | Here we are, at the **dawn of a new age** of genetics and the biosciences. | At the **dawn of** the 21st **century**, nations depend more on each other than at any other point in human history.*

birth
the beginning of something important that will change many people's lives:
*We have seen the **birth of democracy** in South Africa. | The **birth of** the environmental **movement** was in the 1960s. | This was the **birth of** a new **nation**.*

ANTONYMS **beginning → end[1] (1)**

behave *v*
to do things that are good, bad, sensible etc

ADVERBS

behave badly/disgracefully/outrageously *I think he behaved very badly towards you.*

behave differently *Children sometimes behave completely differently at home and at school.*

behave oddly/strangely *The dog's owner noticed that it was behaving oddly.*

behave sensibly/responsibly *I'm sure you'll behave sensibly while I'm away.*

behave properly *These kids don't know how to behave properly in restaurants.*

behave impeccably (=extremely well) *We expect you to behave impeccably when you are on a field trip representing your school.*

PREPOSITIONS

behave with dignity/courage etc *These people behaved with great dignity even when they were abused and insulted.*

PHRASES

behave like/as if/as though (=as if a particular thing is true, usually when it is not) *He behaved as if he had never met me before.*

behaviour *BrE*, behavior *AmE n*
the way that someone behaves and the things that they do

ADJECTIVES

good/bad behaviour *It is important to reward good behaviour.*

normal/abnormal behaviour *They thought their son's behaviour was perfectly normal.*

aggressive/violent/threatening behaviour *His behavior became increasingly violent.*

strange behaviour *What could be causing her strange behaviour?*

antisocial behaviour *Antisocial behaviour such as spitting and swearing in public will not be tolerated.*

acceptable/unacceptable behaviour *This sort of behavior is completely unacceptable.*

appropriate/inappropriate behaviour *formal* (=suitable/not suitable in a situation) *Inappropriate behaviour must not be ignored.*

human/animal behaviour *The scientific study of human behaviour is known as psychology.*

criminal behaviour *There are many theories as to what causes criminal behavior.*

behaviour + NOUNS

behaviour problems *She teaches children with behaviour problems.*

VERBS

change your behaviour (*also* **modify your behaviour** *formal*): *He has no reason to change his behaviour.*

affect/influence sb's behaviour *The genes we inherit influence our behaviour.*

examine/observe sb's behaviour *Scientists examined the behaviour of mice injected with the drug.*

explain sb's behaviour (=be or give a reason for it) *That's the only way I can explain her behaviour.*

excuse sb's behaviour (=make someone's bad behaviour acceptable) *He's very tired, but that doesn't excuse his behavior.*

apologize for sb's behaviour *David apologized for his behaviour towards me.*

sb's behaviour gets better/improves *His behaviour in school has improved.*

sb's behaviour gets worse (*also* **sb's behaviour deteriorates** *formal*): *Children's behaviour often deteriorates when they are anxious about something.*

PREPOSITIONS

sb's behaviour towards/toward sb *She complained about her boss's inappropriate behavior towards her.*

PHRASES

standards of behaviour *The school expects certain standards of behaviour from its students.*

a pattern of behaviour *Different patterns of behaviour exist in different cultures.*

be on your best behaviour (=be behaving as well and politely as you can) *I want you both to be on your best behaviour at Grandad's.*

belief *n*

the feeling that something is definitely true or definitely exists

ADJECTIVES

a firm/strong belief *It is still my firm belief that we did the right thing.*

a strongly/deeply held belief (=that you believe very much) *Many strongly held beliefs have been proved wrong.*

a common/popular/widespread/widely held belief (=that a lot of people believe) *There is a common belief that educational standards are getting worse.*

a mistaken/false belief *There is a mistaken belief that being famous is the most important thing in life.*

a sincere belief (=based on what you really feel is true) *We have a sincere belief in the power of art to enhance human life.*

a passionate belief *He had a passionate belief in justice.*

religious/political beliefs *People of all religious beliefs come here to pray.*

VERBS

have a belief (*also* **hold a belief** *formal*): *You must always have the belief that you can succeed.*

share sb's belief *She does not share my belief that things will improve.*

respect sb's beliefs *It is important to respect other people's beliefs.*

defy/beggar belief (=be extremely surprising) *It beggars belief that something like this could happen.*

belief + NOUNS

a belief system *His political views are an important part of his belief system.*

PREPOSITIONS

a belief in sth *She has a strong belief in God.*

beliefs about sth *Our beliefs about women in the workplace are very different.*

PHRASES

it is my belief that *It is my belief that technology makes life better.*

contrary to popular belief (=opposite to what most people think) *Contrary to popular belief, boys are not usually better at maths than girls.*

be based on the belief that *Our policies must be based on the belief that the planet's resources are finite.*

do sth in the belief that (=do it because you believe something is true) *Thieves broke into the building in the mistaken belief that there was expensive computer equipment inside.*

believe *v*

1 to be sure that something is true or that someone is telling the truth

ADVERBS

strongly/firmly believe *I strongly believe that all children deserve a good education.*

passionately/fervently believe (=be extremely sure) *She passionately believes that what she is doing is important.*

genuinely/honestly/sincerely believe *Do you honestly believe it was an accident?*

wrongly/mistakenly believe *Many people wrongly believe that the disease can be caused by eating too much sugar.*

it is generally/widely believed that (=most or many people believe that) *It is generally believed that stress can affect the heart.*

PHRASES

(I) don't believe a word of it (=used to say strongly that you do not believe something) *He says he'll have the money ready for me tomorrow, but I don't believe a word of it.*

2 to believe that someone or something exists

PREPOSITIONS

believe in God *He started to pray, even though he did not believe in God.*

believe in miracles/ghosts etc *Hearing that she was alive was almost enough to make me believe in miracles.*

bell *n*

an object or piece of equipment that makes a ringing sound, usually as a signal

bell + VERBS

a bell rings *I could hear the church bells ringing in the distance.*

a bell rings out (=rings loudly) *The bells rang out to celebrate the end of the war.*

a bell sounds/goes (=a bell makes a sound, especially an electric bell or warning bell) *He raced for the school gates when the bell went.*

a bell chimes (=rings several times, especially in order to tell you the time of day) *The bells of Princeton University chimed the hour.*

a bell tolls (=rings slowly, when someone has died) *The church bell was tolling in the distance.*

VERBS + bell

ring a bell *She rang the bell, and a maid opened the door.*

press the bell (=press a button to ring a bell)

Irina pressed the bell for the nurse (=to call the nurse).

answer the bell (=go and see who is ringing the bell) *He dashed downstairs to answer the front door bell.*

NOUNS + bell

the door bell *At that moment the door bell rang and Sophia went to answer it.*

a church/temple bell *She woke on Sunday morning to the sound of church bells.*

belongings *n*

the things you own, especially things that you can carry with you

ADJECTIVES

personal belongings *All students have a locker where they can store their personal belongings.*

sb's most precious belongings (=the things which are the most important to you) *She kept her most precious belongings in a box under her bed.*

VERBS

take your belongings with you *Don't forget to take all your belongings with you when you get off the train.*

pack/pack up your belongings (=put them in a bag or suitcase) *She packed all her belongings into an old suitcase.*

collect/gather your belongings *Joe gathered his belongings and got ready to leave.*

go through/sort through your belongings (=search through them) *He went through all his belongings trying to find his passport.*

rifle through sb's belongings (=quickly and carelessly search through them) *The man was rifling through my belongings, looking for something to steal.*

PREPOSITIONS

among your belongings *They found the letter among his other belongings.*

belt *n*

a band of leather, cloth etc that you wear around your waist

VERBS

wear a belt *She was wearing a belt with a gold-plated buckle.*

buckle/fasten/do up your belt *She put the robe on and fastened the belt.*

unbuckle/unfasten/undo your belt *He unbuckled his belt and took his jeans off.*

loosen your belt *After he finished eating, he loosened his belt a little.*

tighten your belt *She tightened the belt of her coat and turned up the collar.*

bend *n*

a curved part of something, especially a road or river

ADJECTIVES

a sharp/tight bend (=that changes direction suddenly) *Drivers usually slow down when approaching a sharp bend.*

a hairpin bend (=a very sharp bend in a road) *The road wound up the mountain in a series of hairpin bends.*

a slight/gentle/wide bend (=that changes direction slightly or gradually) *Ahead of us there was a wide bend in the river.*

a blind bend (=that you cannot see around when you are driving) *Never overtake another car on a blind bend.*

a left-hand/right-hand bend (=going towards the left or the right) *Take the turning just after the left-hand bend in the road.*

the first/next/final bend *They rounded the final bend in the long drive and the house came into view.*

VERBS

come around/round a bend *Suddenly a motorbike came around the bend at top speed.*

round/take a bend *He rounded the bend much too fast.*

negotiate a bend (=go round a sharp and difficult bend) *The lorry knocked the sign over while trying to negotiate the bend.*

PREPOSITIONS

a bend in sth *There's a bend in the pipe.*

beneficial *adj* THESAURUS ▸ **good (1)**

benefit Ac *n*

an advantage or improvement that you get from something, especially one that helps you in your life

ADJECTIVES/NOUNS + benefit

a great/major/substantial benefit *The changes have brought great benefits to the organization.*

a real benefit *To get some real benefit from the exercise, you should continue for at least half an hour.*

a direct benefit *The money raised has been of direct benefit to the students.*

a lasting benefit *These plans are likely to result in lasting benefit to the whole of our district.*

the full/maximum benefit of sth *They will have the full benefit of our facilities.*

economic/social/environmental etc benefits *Tourism has brought considerable economic benefits to the island.*

health benefits *We all know the health benefits of eating green vegetables.*

mutual benefit (=for both people, companies etc involved) *Our two companies are working together for mutual benefit.*

potential benefits (=that you might get) *The potential benefits of the scheme must be weighed against the costs involved.*

B

VERBS

get/gain a benefit (*also* **gain/derive a benefit** *formal*): *If you do not exercise regularly, you are unlikely to get any benefit.*

enjoy the benefits *We're enjoying the benefits of living in a warm climate.*

have the benefit of sth *I never had the benefit of a university education.*

reap the benefits (=enjoy the advantages of something you have worked hard to get) *He was looking forward to reaping the benefits of all his hard work.*

bring/provide benefits *The new bridge has brought considerable benefits.*

have benefits *Breastfeeding has health benefits for both baby and mother.*

see/appreciate the benefit of sth (=realize that it brings advantages) *Some English people can't see the benefit of learning another language.*

sth outweighs the benefits (=something is more important than the benefits) *Make sure that the risks don't outweigh the benefits.*

PREPOSITIONS

the benefits of sth *What are the benefits of wearing contact lenses?*

benefit for/to sb *This project will have benefits for everyone involved.*

the benefit from sth *Some patients will get no benefit from this treatment.*

with/without the benefit of sth *Most people manage without the benefit of servants.*

PHRASES

be of benefit to sb (=be useful or helpful to someone) *His coaching has been of benefit to all the players.*

be to sb's benefit (=be helpful to someone) *They oppose all change unless it is to their benefit.*

for the benefit of sb (=for someone to use) *There is also a gym for the benefit of staff.*

for your own benefit (=for yourself) *He used the money for his own benefit, instead of using it to help other people.*

THESAURUS: benefit

benefit, merit, virtue, the good/great/best thing about sth, the beauty of sth is that → advantage

benevolent *adj* THESAURUS **kind²**

best *adj, n*

better than anything else or anyone else

Grammar

As a noun, **best** is always used in the phrase **the best**.

PHRASES

one of the best *It's one of the best restaurants in New York.*

easily the best/by far the best (=much better than the others) *The series was easily the best TV drama this year.*

the very best (=the best – used for emphasis) *The very best athletes compete at the Olympics.*

the best in the world/the country *The university is one of the best in the world.*

NOUNS

the best way *The best way to learn a language is to live in a country where it is spoken.*

the best thing (to do) *The best thing to do is to apologize immediately.*

the best place to be/live *London is the best place to be if you like going to the theatre.*

the best person for the job *I've worked with her before and I believe she's the best person for the job.*

best + ADJECTIVES

the best possible *We sold the house at the best possible time.*

the best available *The tuition we offer here is the best available.*

ANTONYMS **best → worst**

best-selling *adj* THESAURUS **successful (3)**

bet *n*

an agreement that someone will be given money if something happens, and lose money if it does not happen

VERBS

put/place/lay a bet *She placed a bet on a horse called Lucky.*

make a bet *He made a bet with her that she couldn't be silent for three hours.*

win/lose a bet *France won the game and I won my bet.*

have a bet *Are you going to have a bet on the race?*

put a bet on (sth) *He asked his brother to put a bet on for him.*

take/accept a bet (=accept someone's money as part of a bet) *They're taking bets on the result of the election now.*

ADJECTIVES/NOUNS + bet

a £50 bet/$100 bet etc *Someone placed a £1,500 bet on the horse at odds of 14-1.*

a big/small bet *He felt confident enough to make a big bet.*

PREPOSITIONS

a bet on sth *I put a bet on a race and I lost my money.*

for a bet *He dived off the bridge for a bet.*

better *adj, adv*

the comparative form of 'good' or 'well'

ADVERBS

much better/a lot better *The weather is much better today.*

slightly better/a little better (*also* **a bit better** *informal*): *She woke up feeling slightly better.*

infinitely better (=very much better) *The new system is infinitely better than the old one.*

marginally better (=only very slightly better) *The team did marginally better in the next game.*

even better *The show was even better than I expected.*

VERBS

get better *The situation should get better soon.*

feel better *Are you feeling any better?*

PHRASES

there is nothing better than sth *There is nothing better than having praise from someone whose work you respect.*

ANTONYMS **better → worse**

bewildering *adj* THESAURUS **confusing**

bias Ac *n*

an unfair attitude which makes you treat one person or group better or worse than another

ADJECTIVES/NOUNS + bias

political bias *New reporting is often affected by political bias.*

personal bias *During the job interview, you should be careful to avoid personal bias towards or against the candidate.*

ideological bias (=a bias that comes from a particular way of thinking about the world) *Historical accounts often contain some political or ideological bias.*

liberal/right-wing/left-wing etc bias *Many Republicans claim that the US media has a liberal bias.*

a strong/marked bias *There is a strong bias against older women.*

a clear/obvious/blatant bias *The press showed a clear bias towards the ruling party.*

racial/cultural bias *There is evidence of racial bias in some court cases.*

gender bias (=a bias concerning men and women) *There is a gender bias in many toys: pink kitchens for the girls, blue cars for the boys.*

patriotic bias (=a bias in favour of your country) *There is a patriotic bias in favour of the England team.*

media bias *The candidate complained of media bias against him in the run-up to the election.*

VERBS

have a bias against/in favour of sb *The college has a bias in favour of middle-class students.*

show/display/demonstrate bias *The referee is not allowed to show any bias toward either team.*

accuse sb of bias *He accused the newspaper of having a liberal bias.*

avoid bias *Teachers are careful to avoid bias towards any student.*

PREPOSITIONS

a bias against sb *The article shows a bias against women.*

a bias towards/toward/in favour of sb *An analysis of national television news revealed a significant bias towards the government.*

without bias *The information must be presented without bias.*

PHRASES

be free from bias *The news is supposed to be free from bias.*

anti-American/anti-intellectual etc bias *He accused the newspaper of having an anti-French bias.*

pro-British/pro-government etc bias *Israel accused them of a pro-Arab bias in their Middle East policies.*

bicycle *n*

a vehicle with two wheels that you ride by pushing its pedals with your feet

VERBS

ride a bicycle *Riding a bicycle is very good exercise.*

⚠ Don't say 'drive a bicycle'.

get on/get off your bicycle *I got on my bicycle and cycled over to Rob's house.*

mount your bicycle *formal* (=get on it) *Sara mounted her bicycle and rode off.*

pedal a bicycle *I used to see her pedalling her bicycle around town.*

fall off/be knocked off your bicycle *He was knocked off his bicycle by a careless driver.*

bicycle + NOUNS

a bicycle ride *They went for a 50 km bicycle ride.*

a bicycle helmet *Always wear a bicycle helmet.*

PREPOSITIONS

on a bicycle *They saw a few boys on bicycles.*

by bicycle *In many cities, it is too dangerous for children to travel by bicycle.*

> **Bicycle** or **bike**?
> In everyday English, people usually say **bike**: *I ride my **bike** to work.* **Bicycle** sounds rather formal.

bid *n*

1 an offer to pay a particular price for something, especially at an auction

ADJECTIVES/NOUNS + bid

a high/low bid *There were several high bids for the painting.*

an opening bid (=the first bid at an auction) *The opening bid was only $10.*

a final bid *She was successful with a final bid of £9,500.*

the winning bid *A wealthy Chinese businessman made the winning bid for the painting.*

a rival/competing bid (=competing with someone else's bid) *Shareholders will have to choose between two rival bids for the football club.*

B

VERBS

make a bid *A film company made a bid for the film rights to the book.*

put in a bid/place a bid (*also* **submit a bid** *formal*) (=officially make a bid) *Property developers have put in a bid for the land.*

receive a bid *They received four bids for the company.*

attract a bid *The business attracted bids of over £2 billion.*

accept a bid *An auctioneer may refuse to accept any bid below a certain price.*

reject a bid *The team has rejected a bid for its top player.*

PREPOSITIONS

a bid for sth *They put in a bid for the house.*

a bid by/from sb *The company rejected a bid by US Airlines.*

2 an attempt to do or get something

ADJECTIVES/NOUNS + bid

a successful bid *The agency made a successful bid for funding.*

an unsuccessful/failed bid *He made a failed bid for the presidency.*

a desperate bid *Knox made a desperate bid to stop the ball reaching the goal.*

a rescue/escape bid *Helicopters were brought in to help with the rescue bid.*

a takeover bid (=an attempt to buy another company) *Staff are afraid that the takeover bid will threaten their jobs.*

a hostile bid (=an attempt to buy another company that does not want to be bought) *The company faces a hostile bid from a major US firm.*

VERBS

make a bid *The party is making a serious bid for power.*

launch/mount a bid *The city launched a bid to host the 2012 Olympic Games.*

succeed/fail in a bid to do sth *We succeeded in our bid to reach the final.*

a bid succeeds/fails *The bid failed when officials rejected the plan.*

PREPOSITIONS

a bid for sth *The ex-president made another bid for power.*

in a bid to do sth *Stores installed cameras in a bid to reduce crime.*

PHRASES

a bid for freedom (=an attempt to escape) *The prisoners made a bid for freedom but they were soon recaptured.*

big *adj*

1 large in size

NOUNS

a big house/building *They live in a big house in New York.*

a big country/city/place *Canada is a big country.*

a big road/river *There is a big road outside the school.*

a big company/organization *His father works for a big oil company.*

a big smile/grin *She came out of the room with a big smile on her face and said "I've got the job!"*

> **Using big about people**
>
> When you use **big** about people, it usually means that they have a lot of muscles, or they are fat: *He was accompanied by two* ***big*** *bodyguards.* | *I'm getting too* ***big*** *for these jeans.*
>
> You also use **big** about people in your family who are older than you: *She's my* ***big*** *sister* (=my older sister).

ANTONYMS **big → small (1)**

2 very noticeable, important, or serious

NOUNS

a big effect/impact *The internet has had a big effect on our lives.*

a big difference *There is a big difference in the price.*

a big change *It was a big change in my life.*

a big advantage/disadvantage *Our team had a big disadvantage, because we had never played together before.*

a big problem *Don't worry – it's not such a big problem.*

a big mistake *Marrying him was the biggest mistake she had ever made.*

> **THESAURUS: big**
>
> big, significant, major, notable, key, essential, vital, crucial/critical, paramount, historic, landmark, momentous → **important (1)**

ANTONYMS **big → small (1)**

3 large in number or amount

NOUNS

a big increase/decrease *There has been a big increase in the number of people looking for work.*

a big cut/reduction/fall *The sign says there are big price reductions.*

a big profit/loss *The company announced big profits.*

a big population *The city has a big population.*

You usually say a **large amount**, not a 'big' one. You also usually say **large numbers** of people/things, not 'big' ones.

THESAURUS: big

Senses 1, 2, & 3

Academic Writing
In academic writing, it is better to use a more formal word instead of **big**. For example, you can say *a* ***large*** *area* instead of 'a big area' or *a* ***major*** *cause* instead of 'a big cause'. You can find more information about these alternative words below.

large
number | amount | quantity | proportion | increase | profit | area | man | woman
large means the same as **big**, but is more formal. You use **large** when talking about the size, number, or amount of something:
The museum attracts a large number of visitors. | The computer can store large amounts of data. | Large areas of the forest have been destroyed. | He pointed to a large man in dark glasses.

Big or large?
You don't use **large** when talking about the importance or seriousness of something.
For example, you say *a* ***big*** *problem* (not a 'large' one), *a* ***big*** *mistake* (not a 'large' one), and *a* ***big*** *effect* (not a 'large' one).

great
success | change | difference | number | variety | advantage | honour | mistake
very big - often used when something is very impressive, important, or serious:
The show was a great success. | We are living in a time of great change. | The store sells a great variety of household goods. | It is a great honour to receive this award.

major
part | role | factor | problem | issue | change | cause | source | contribution | impact
big and important:
Women's health is a major part of our work. | He played a major role in the team's success. | Pollution is a major problem. | There has been a major change in government policy. | Long working hours are a major cause of stress.

considerable
amount | number | degree | proportion | part | interest | importance | influence | success | progress
large in amount, number, or degree. **Considerable** is used especially in formal English:
They have already spent a considerable amount of money. | A considerable number of children live in one-parent families. | His writings are of considerable importance.

substantial
amount | number | part | proportion | increase | progress | change
large in amount or number. **Substantial** is used especially in formal English:
They invested a substantial amount of money. | A substantial number of his poems were written there. | The disease affects a substantial proportion of the population. | Substantial progress has been made in the last twenty years.

ANTONYMS **big → small (1)**

4 famous

THESAURUS: big
well-known, legendary, eminent, celebrated, big, renowned, notorious, infamous, unknown, little-known, obscure, minor → **famous**

Words meaning 'very big' see → **huge**

bike *n* a bicycle

VERBS

ride a bike *I learned to ride a bike when I was six.*

go somewhere by bike/on a bike *I usually go to work by bike.*

get on/off a bike *He got off his bike and walked with her for a while.*

rent a bike (*also* **hire a bike** *BrE*): *You can rent bikes and explore the island's cycle paths.*

NOUNS + bike

a racing bike *He bought a cool new racing bike.*

a mountain bike (=a strong bicycle for riding over rough ground) *They went out for a ride on their mountain bikes.*

an exercise bike (=used for exercising indoors) *I usually go on the exercise bike first at the gym.*

bike + NOUNS

a bike ride *I like going for long bike rides in the country.*

a bike race *The Tour de France is a famous bike race.*

a bike rack (=a metal frame that you can attach your bike to) *All stations should provide bike racks for passengers.*

a bike shed (=a small building for keeping

bikes in) *They used to meet behind the bike sheds at school.*

a bike lane (=a part at the side of a road for bikes to ride in) *He was riding in the bike lane.*

PREPOSITIONS

by bike *You can explore the area by bike.*

on a bike *Ben came past the house on his bike.*

B

bill *n*

1 a written list showing how much you have to pay for something

ADJECTIVES/NOUNS + bill

a big/huge bill *We got a huge bill for the repairs to the house.*

an electricity/gas/phone etc bill *The gas bill keeps going up every year.*

legal/medical bills *If you have no insurance, how do you pay your medical bills?*

a hotel bill *He paid the hotel bill by credit card.*

a tax bill *There are various ways you can reduce your tax bill.*

an unpaid bill *She had unpaid bills amounting to £3,000.*

an itemized bill (=giving details about each thing on it) *An itemized phone bill lists every call you have made.*

VERBS

pay a bill *Have you paid the phone bill?*

settle a bill (=pay all the money that you owe) *She went down to the lobby to settle the bill for their rooms.*

foot the bill/pick up the bill (=pay for something, especially when you do not want to) *Taxpayers will probably have to foot the bill for the project.*

ask for the bill (=ask for the bill in a restaurant) *If you're ready to go, I'll ask for the bill.*

get/receive a bill *They'll have a shock when they get the bill.*

run up a bill (=have to pay a lot of money for using or doing something) *It's easy to run up a big bill on your mobile phone.*

send sb a bill *Send me your bill and I will pay you in full.*

face a bill (=have a lot to pay on a bill) *They were facing a mounting legal bill.*

cut/reduce a bill *We need to find a way to cut our fuel bill.*

share the bills (=each pay part of them) *My housemates and I share the bills.*

a bill comes to sth (=it is for that amount) *The bill came to $60.*

PREPOSITIONS

the bill for sth *The bill for the repairs came to $650.*

> In American English, people often use **check** about a bill in a restaurant: *The waiter brought the **check**.*

2 a written proposal for a new law

ADJECTIVES/NOUNS + bill

a defence/finance/education etc bill *Monday's debate on the defence bill lasted all night.*

a controversial bill (=causing a lot of disagreement) *There is a controversial bill to increase taxes on pensions.*

VERBS

pass/approve a bill (=accept it so it becomes law) *The Senate passed the bill by 96 votes to 3.*

vote for/against a bill *The opposition parties are planning to vote against the bill.*

veto a bill (=not allow it to become law) *The president said he would veto the bill.*

reject/throw out a bill *They rejected a bill to limit arms exports.*

introduce/bring in a bill (=start using it) *The government introduced a bill to provide stiffer penalties for terrorists.*

propose a bill (=suggest it) *He proposed a bill to ban smoking in public areas.*

debate a bill *The bill is still being debated in Parliament.*

PHRASES

a bill becomes law *It will be several months before the bill becomes law.*

a bill goes through Parliament *We want this bill to go through Parliament as quickly as possible.*

bin *n BrE*

a container for putting waste in

NOUNS + bin

a rubbish/waste bin *The rubbish bin needs emptying.*

a wastepaper bin (=for paper you throw away) *I threw the letter straight in the wastepaper bin.*

a litter bin (=a bin in a public place) *Please put all your rubbish in the litter bin.*

a recycling bin (=for rubbish that you can recycle) *Those plastic cartons can go in the recycling bin.*

a wheelie bin (=a big bin on wheels kept outside a house) *They come to empty the wheelie bins on Friday.*

VERBS

put/throw sth in the bin (*also* **chuck sth in the bin** *informal*): *Just put the wrapper in the bin.*

bingo *n*

a game played for money or prizes, in which numbers are chosen by chance and called out, and if you have the right numbers on your card, you win

VERBS

play bingo *My sister likes to play bingo.*

win money at bingo *Vera won £20 at bingo.*

bingo + NOUNS

a bingo hall (*also* **a bingo parlor** *AmE*): *The old cinema had been made into a bingo hall.*

a bingo game/a game of bingo *They raised money for charity by organizing bingo games.*

a bingo card *I crossed off all the numbers on the top line of the bingo card.*

bird *n*

a creature with wings and feathers that can usually fly

ADJECTIVES/NOUNS + bird

a wild bird *There are hundreds of different kinds of wild birds in the area.*

a migratory bird (=that moves to different regions for summer and winter) *Migratory birds stop here on their way to Africa.*

a flightless bird (=that cannot fly) *The emu is a large flightless Australian bird.*

a wading bird (=a bird with long legs that stands in water to catch fish) *The lake is home to many different types of wading birds.*

a game bird (=that people shoot and eat) *They hunt game birds such as ducks and pheasants.*

> **Songbird** and **seabird** are usually written as one word.

VERBS

a bird flies *Some birds fly incredible distances.*

a bird soars (=flies very high in the sky) *We watched birds soar in the blue sky above.*

a bird swoops (=it suddenly flies down) *The bird swoops on its prey.*

a bird flaps its wings (=it moves its wings up and down) *The baby birds were trying to flap their wings.*

a bird sings (=makes musical sounds) *I woke up to hear the birds singing outside.*

a bird chirps/twitters (=makes short high sounds) *Birds chirped to one another from different branches of the tree.*

a bird squawks (=makes a loud unpleasant sound) *The bird in the cage started squawking.*

a bird nests (*also* **a bird builds a nest**) *Many birds are nesting on the river banks.*

a bird lays its eggs *The bird lays a single egg on the ground.*

a bird pecks (at) sth (=makes small movements with its beak) *Some birds were pecking at the remains of a sandwich.*

a bird perches (=stands on something above the ground) *Beautiful white birds perched on the tree's branches.*

a bird migrates (=flies to different regions for summer and winter) *The birds migrate from South America to North American breeding grounds.*

a bird hops (=makes small jumping movements) *A small bird was hopping across the grass.*

bird + NOUNS

a bird species/a species of bird *Many of the island's bird species need protection.*

a bird reserve/sanctuary (=a place where birds are protected) *This part of the coast is now a bird sanctuary.*

> **Birdwatcher**, **birdwatching**, and **birdsong** are usually written as one word.

PHRASES

a flock of birds (=a large number of birds together) *Suddenly a flock of birds flew up into the sky.*

a bird of prey (=that hunts and eats small animals) *A big bird of prey was circling over our heads.*

birth *n*

the time or process when a baby comes out of its mother's body

PHRASES

sb's date of birth *especially BrE*, **sb's birth date** *especially AmE* (=the day, month, and year you were born) *Please give your name, address, and date of birth.*

sb's place/country of birth *I wanted to find out my father's place of birth.*

the time of birth *They believe that the position of the planets at the time of birth determines a person's fate.*

birth + NOUNS

the birth rate (=the number of babies born somewhere) *The country's birth rate has decreased dramatically.*

a birth defect (=something wrong with a baby when it is born) *About 11% of babies have birth defects.*

a birth certificate (=an official document showing when and where you were born) *Her birth certificate says she was born in 1972.*

VERBS

give birth (=produce a baby from your body) *Most women in Britain give birth in hospital.*

celebrate sb's birth *They are celebrating the birth of their first child.*

register a birth (=officially tell a government department that a baby has been born) *Failing to register a birth is illegal.*

attend a birth *In Britain most fathers attend the birth of their children.*

ADJECTIVES/NOUNS + birth

a premature birth (=when a baby is born before the normal time) *Smoking in pregnancy has been linked to premature birth.*

a multiple birth (=when a woman has two or more babies at the same time) *The chance of a multiple birth is about 1 in 100 for the average woman.*

a home birth (=when a woman gives birth at

home, not in a hospital) *I decided I wanted a home birth for my second child.*

a hospital birth *Many women choose hospital births.*

a natural birth (=one that does not involve medical assistance or drugs) *She wanted a natural birth.*

a difficult/easy birth *It was a difficult birth and she took a long time to recover.*

PREPOSITIONS

at birth *He only weighed 2 kilos at birth.*

from birth *Henry has been blind from birth.*

the birth of sb *My husband was there at the birth of both our children.*

THESAURUS: birth

start, commencement, origin, the onset of sth, dawn, birth → **beginning (1)**

birthday *n*

the day that is an exact number of years after the day you were born

ADJECTIVES

Happy Birthday! (=said to someone on their birthday) *Happy Birthday, Linda!*

sb's 1st/18th/40th etc birthday *It's Mum's 50th birthday tomorrow.*

sb's next birthday *She'll be 18 on her next birthday.*

VERBS

have a good/nice etc birthday *Did you have a nice birthday?*

get sth for your birthday *What did you get for your birthday?*

give sth to sb for their birthday *I never know what to give him for his birthday.*

celebrate sb's birthday *He will celebrate his 90th birthday on August 25th.*

remember sb's birthday (=remember to send a card or present) *She always remembers my birthday.*

forget sb's birthday (=forget to send a card or present) *Oh no! I forgot his birthday.*

mark sb's birthday (=celebrate it by doing something) *The book was published to mark his 70th birthday.*

birthday + NOUNS

a birthday card *Don't forget to send her a birthday card.*

a birthday present *Have you got Lou a birthday present yet?*

a birthday party *Can you come to my birthday party next Saturday?*

birthday celebrations *the president's 60th birthday celebrations*

a birthday treat (=something special you do on your birthday) *What would you like to do for a birthday treat?*

a birthday meal *Where are you going for your birthday meal?*

a birthday cake *She had a birthday cake with 21 silver candles on it.*

PREPOSITIONS

on sb's birthday *That photo was taken on my birthday.*

for sb's birthday *He always buys her expensive presents for her birthday.*

bit *n informal*

1 a small piece of something

ADJECTIVES

a little/tiny/small bit *The floor was covered in tiny bits of glass.*

PREPOSITIONS

a bit of sth *He wedged the door open with a bit of wood.*

PHRASES

fall/come to bits (=separate into many different parts because of being old or damaged) *The book was so old that I was afraid it would fall to bits.*

take sth to bits (=separate the parts of something) *Tony loves taking old radios and computers to bits.*

break/smash (sth) to bits *The vase fell and smashed to bits on the concrete floor.*

rip/tear sth to bits *She grabbed the letter and ripped it to bits.*

be blown to bits (=be completely destroyed by a bomb) *The aircraft was blown to bits.*

THESAURUS: bit

bit, lump, scrap, strip, sheet, slice, chunk, hunk, block, slab, cube, wedge, bar, segment, rasher, fragment, crumb, speck, drop → **piece**

2 a little or a small amount

ADJECTIVES AND PHRASES

a little bit *She only ate a little bit.*

just a bit *Just a bit of sugar for me.*

not the faintest/slightest bit (=not at all) *They didn't seem the faintest bit surprised.*

bite[1] *v*

to use your teeth to cut, crush, or chew something

PREPOSITIONS/ADVERBS

bite into sth *When he bit into the apple, he found it had a delicious taste.*

bite off sth *She bit off a piece of bread.*

bite through sth *The mice had bitten through one of the power cables.*

bite sb on the leg/hand etc *The dog bit the boy on his leg.*

be badly bitten (=in a way that causes a serious injury) *The child was lucky not to have been badly bitten.*

NOUNS

bite your nails *I wish I could stop biting my nails.*

> You also use **bite** about insects and snakes making a hole or mark on someone's skin: *I got **bitten** by a mosquito.*

bite² *n*

1 the act of using your teeth to cut or crush food, so that you can eat it

ADJECTIVES

a big/large bite *Pierce took a large bite of his sandwich.*

a small/little bite *She ate her food in little bites.*

VERBS

take a bite *She picked up the sandwich and took a bite.*

have a bite *Can I have a bite of your apple?*

PREPOSITIONS

a bite of sth *Chew each bite of food slowly.*

a bite from/out of sth *The dog had taken a bite out of the roast beef.*

PHRASES

in one bite *Antonio can eat a burger in one bite.*

2 an injury caused by an animal or insect biting you

NOUNS + bite

an insect/mosquito etc bite *My arm was covered in insect bites.*

a dog/snake etc bite *Thousands of people die from snake bites every year.*

ADJECTIVES

a nasty bite *BrE*: *It looks like a nasty bite.*

VERBS

give sb a bite *Some fish can give you a nasty bite.*

PREPOSITIONS

a bite from an insect/animal *The disease is passed through a bite from an infected mosquito.*

bitter *adj*

1 having or causing strong feelings of anger, unhappiness, or disappointment

VERBS

feel bitter *Patsy feels very bitter about losing her job.*

sound bitter *Howard was trying hard not to sound bitter.*

ADVERBS

increasingly bitter *He became increasingly bitter about what had happened.*

NOUNS

a bitter battle/dispute *He was involved in a bitter dispute with his former employer.*

a bitter fight/struggle *There was a bitter struggle between them for control of the company.*

a bitter debate *The country now faces a bitter debate over the issue of abortion.*

a bitter disappointment *The result was a bitter disappointment for us.*

a bitter blow (=something that affects you very badly) *His death was a bitter blow to her.*

a bitter memory *She had bitter memories of her relationship with Alan.*

bitter rivals *The two businessmen are bitter rivals.*

PREPOSITIONS

bitter about sth *He was still bitter about the way he had been treated.*

PHRASES

know/learn/find out sth from bitter experience (=because of unpleasant experiences in the past) *Jane had learned from bitter experience that love doesn't always last.*

2 having a strong taste which is not sweet

NOUNS

a bitter taste *The medicine had a bitter taste.*

bitter oranges/lemons *Bitter oranges are good for making marmalade.*

black *adj, n*

the darkest colour, like the sky at night

ADJECTIVES AND ADVERBS

completely black *The screen went completely black.*

deep/dark black *The adult birds have deep black feathers.*

jet black (=very dark – used especially about someone's hair) *He had jet black hair.*

pitch black (=a place is completely dark, so that you cannot see anything) *It was pitch black inside the cave.*

matt black (=black that is not shiny) *The board was painted with matt black paint.*

PREPOSITIONS

in black *Fenella was dressed entirely in black.*

PHRASES

as black as night/coal/pitch/ebony *Her eyes were as black as coal.*

black with soot/dirt/smoke *His face and hands were black with dirt.*

black and white *A black and white dog was sitting outside the shop.*

blade *n*

the flat cutting part of a tool or weapon

ADJECTIVES

a sharp blade *Be careful – the blade is very sharp.*

a blunt/dull blade (=not sharp) *This blade is too blunt to cut anything.*

NOUNS + blade

a razor blade (=for removing hair from your face or body) *I need to buy some razor blades.*

PREPOSITIONS

the blade of a knife/sword/saw *She rinsed the blade of the knife under running water.*

B

blame[1] *v*

to say or think that someone or something is responsible for something bad

PREPOSITIONS

blame sb for sth *Marie still blames herself for Patrick's death.*

blame sth on sb *Don't try to blame everything on me.*

ADVERBS

always blame sb/sth *You can't always blame other people for what happens.*

unfairly blame sb *I felt that I was being unfairly blamed for their problems.*

be widely blamed (=by many people) *The authorities have been widely blamed for making the situation worse.*

PHRASES

be the one to blame (=be the person who should be blamed) *I'm the only one to blame for what has happened.*

be partly to blame *Some people think that television is partly to blame for the increase in violence among young people.*

have no one to blame but yourself *He should have checked that there was enough fuel in the car, so he has no one to blame but himself.*

blame[2] *n*

responsibility for a mistake or for something bad

VERBS

get the blame (=be blamed) *I always get the blame for his mistakes!*

take/accept the blame (*also* **shoulder the blame** *formal*) (=say that something is your fault) *No one was prepared to take the blame for the disaster.*

put/pin the blame on sb (*also* **lay/place the blame on sb** *formal*) (=blame someone, especially when it is not their fault) *Don't try to put the blame on me.*

shift the blame (onto sb) (=blame someone for something you did) *She always tried to shift the blame onto her brother.*

apportion/assign blame *formal* (=find someone to blame for something) *He seemed to want to apportion blame for her death.*

absolve sb from blame *formal* (=say that something is not their fault) *He was absolved of all blame.*

the blame lies with sb (=used to say that someone is responsible for something bad) *In this case, the blame lay with the police.*

PREPOSITIONS

the blame for sth *Much of the blame for the current crisis lies with the government.*

PHRASES

accept your share of the blame *The media must accept its share of the blame for this problem.*

place the blame squarely/firmly on sb (=blame someone in a very definite way) *The investigation placed the blame squarely on the mayor.*

blank *adj* with nothing on it

NOUNS

a blank sheet of paper *He was staring at a blank sheet of paper, wondering what to write.*

a blank screen *When I turned on my computer, all I got was a blank screen.*

a blank space *Write your answer in the blank space under the question.*

a blank expression/look/face (=showing no emotion) *She was looking out of the window with a blank expression on her face.*

VERBS

go blank (=become blank) *The screen suddenly went blank.*

leave sth blank *You can leave the last page blank - I'll fill it out later.*

PHRASES

my mind went blank (=you suddenly can't remember something) *In the interview my mind went blank and I couldn't think of anything to say.*

THESAURUS: blank

bare, blank, hollow, free, vacant, deserted, uninhabited, unoccupied → **empty**

blanket *n*

a cover for a bed, usually made of wool

ADJECTIVES

a thick/heavy/warm blanket *She gave me a thick blanket to keep me warm.*

VERBS

wrap sb in a blanket *The baby was wrapped in a blanket.*

cover sb/sth with a blanket *His mother covered him with a blanket and put a cushion behind his head.*

throw a blanket over sb/sth *She threw a blanket over the sleeping child.*

pull a blanket up/over you *He pulled the blanket over his head and went to sleep.*

huddle under the blankets (=lie under the blankets with your body curled up) *He lay huddled under the blankets, his eyes closed.*

PREPOSITIONS

under/beneath a blanket *They were nice and warm under the blankets.*

blaze¹ *n*

a big dangerous fire - used especially in news reports

ADJECTIVES

a huge/massive blaze *Four people died in a huge blaze at the factory.*

VERBS + blaze

put out a blaze (*also* **extinguish a blaze** *formal*) (=stop it burning) *Staff managed to put out the blaze before firefighters arrived.*

fight/battle/tackle a blaze *Nearly 80 firefighters fought the blaze for three hours.*

control a blaze (*also* **bring a blaze under control**) *It took several hours to control the blaze at the hotel.*

start a blaze *The blaze was started accidentally.*

cause/spark a blaze *An electrical fault sparked the blaze.*

blaze + VERBS

a blaze breaks out (*also* **a blaze starts**) *The blaze broke out on the third floor of the building.*

a blaze spreads *The blaze quickly spread to a neighbouring house.*

a blaze destroys sth *The blaze destroyed most of the school.*

blaze² *v* THESAURUS **burn¹ (1)**

bleak *adj*

without anything to make you feel happy or hopeful

NOUNS

a bleak future/prospect/outlook *My father lost his job and we faced a bleak future.*

a bleak picture/impression *The report painted a bleak picture of life in this war-torn country.*

a bleak vision/view *Orwell's book contains a very bleak vision of the future.*

a bleak place/landscape *The landscape is very bleak in winter, when there are no leaves on the trees.*

a bleak look/smile/expression (=without any hope) *She came out of the hospital with a bleak look on her face.*

bleak despair *His mood was one of bleak despair.*

VERBS

look/seem bleak *The company has lost a lot of money and the future looks bleak for the workforce.*

remain bleak *The economic situation remains bleak.*

ADVERBS

pretty bleak (=rather bleak) *Things are pretty bleak at the moment.*

THESAURUS: bleak

grim, gloomy, bleak, drab, dreary, disheartening → **depressing**

B

bleed *v* to lose blood from your body

ADVERBS

bleed heavily/profusely (=a lot) *He was bleeding heavily and he looked very pale.*

bleed easily *She bleeds easily and she has to be careful not to cut herself.*

PREPOSITIONS

bleed from a wound/a part of your body *The boy was bleeding from a cut on the side of his head.*

PHRASES

stop the bleeding *If you hold up your arm, it will help to stop the bleeding.*

bleed to death *She bled to death before the doctors could save her.*

blessing *n*

1 something that is good about a situation, which makes you feel pleased

ADJECTIVES

a great blessing *Having my parents living nearby has been a great blessing, as they often take care of the children while I work.*

a real blessing *The dishwasher has been a real blessing!*

a mixed blessing (=it has both good and bad effects) *Living next to a supermarket is rather a mixed blessing.*

VERBS

count your blessings (=think about how lucky you are) *The weather is terrible and we're counting our blessings that we decided to cancel our trip.*

sth can/could be a blessing (=it can/could be a good thing) *Not being able to speak the language can be a blessing sometimes.*

PREPOSITIONS

sth is a blessing for sb *The higher prices for corn have been a blessing for farmers.*

PHRASES

it's a blessing (that)... *It's a blessing no one was badly hurt.*

sth is a blessing in disguise (=something that seems unlucky, but actually has a good effect) *The fire was a blessing in disguise, as the insurance paid for the house to be completely redecorated.*

sth is a blessing and a curse (=something has very bad effects, as well as good ones) *The invention of the petrol engine has been both a blessing and a curse.*

2 someone's approval or encouragement for a plan, activity, idea etc

ADJECTIVES

sb's official blessing *The plan now has the official blessing of the principal.*

sb's full blessing (=complete approval) *The author gave his full blessing to the film version of his book.*

VERBS

give your blessing to sth *The board has given its blessing to the scheme.*

ask (for) sb's blessing *Eileen wrote to her father to ask his blessing.*

receive sb's blessing *The plans have not yet received an official blessing.*

PREPOSITIONS

with sb's blessing *The aid operation began, with the blessing of the United Nations.*

without sb's blessing *They were determined to marry, with or without their parents' blessing.*

blind *adj* unable to see

VERBS

go blind (=become blind) *My aunt was slowly going blind.*

ADVERBS

almost/nearly blind *She's almost blind in her right eye.*

totally/completely blind *He had measles as a boy, and it left him totally blind.*

partially blind *She is 78 and partially blind.*

half blind *The sun on the snow was so bright that he was half blind by the time he reached the town.*

blind + NOUNS

a blind man/child/person *He goes to a school for blind children.*

PHRASES

blind in one eye/your left eye/your right eye *The accident left him blind in one eye.*

(as) blind as a bat *humorous informal* (=unable to see things very well) *I'm as blind as a bat without my glasses.*

THESAURUS: blind

visually impaired *formal*
unable to see very much, or unable to see at all. **Visually impaired** is used especially in official contexts, and is the politically correct use:
Visually impaired students can record lectures and listen to them at home.

partially sighted
only able to see a little:
My grandmother is partially sighted and she can't really read books anymore.

blinding *adj* THESAURUS ▸ bright (1)

blissful *adj* THESAURUS ▸ happy

block *n*

a piece of hard material such as wood or stone with straight sides

ADJECTIVES

a big/large/huge/massive block *Huge blocks of stone were transported from the quarry.*

a solid block *The guitar was carved from a solid block of wood.*

a concrete/stone/wooden block *The street ended at a wall of grey concrete blocks.*

PHRASES

a block of stone/marble/granite *The Pyramids were built from massive blocks of stone.*

a block of wood *Carefully position the base on the blocks of wood.*

a block of ice *It was freezing and my feet felt like blocks of ice.*

THESAURUS: block

bit, lump, scrap, strip, sheet, slice, chunk, hunk, block, slab, cube, wedge, bar, segment, rasher, fragment, crumb, speck, drop → **piece**

blockade *n*

the use of soldiers or ships to surround an area, in order to stop people or supplies entering or leaving

ADJECTIVES

an economic/financial blockade *The economic blockade was lifted in April.*

a naval blockade *A naval blockade was imposed to prevent supplies reaching the country.*

VERBS

impose a blockade *A blockade was imposed on the Spanish port of Cádiz.*

end/lift/remove a blockade *He urged the US to lift its blockade of Cuba.*

PREPOSITIONS

a blockade of/on sth *President John F. Kennedy ordered a naval blockade of the island.*

blockage *n*

a situation in which things are unable to pass through a pipe, tube etc

ADJECTIVES

a complete blockage *Heart attacks are usually caused by a complete blockage of the coronary arteries.*

a partial blockage *The patient had a partial blockage of the intestine.*

a temporary blockage *The condition is caused by a temporary blockage of the blood flow to the brain.*

VERBS

cause a blockage *The blockage was caused by bits of food which had got stuck in the pipe.*

clear a blockage *The plumber came to clear the blockage under the sink.*

blog *n*

a web page containing information or opinions from a particular person or about a particular subject, to which new information is added regularly

VERBS

write/keep a blog *He writes a blog about his life as a professional gambler.*

read a blog *A lot of people read her blog.*

start/create a blog *I decided to create a blog and share my passion for food with other people.*

post a blog (=write entries for a blog on the internet) *He began posting a blog last year that criticised the government.*

update a blog (=add new things to it) *I update my blog every week.*

blog + NOUNS

a blog entry/post *Have you read his latest blog entry?*

blood *n*

the red liquid inside your body

blood + NOUNS

blood pressure *High blood pressure increases the risk of a heart attack.*

sb's blood type/group *The most common blood type is O positive.*

a blood cell *The red blood cells carry oxygen.*

a blood vessel (=a tube in your body through which blood flows) *The blood vessels that lead to the heart were damaged.*

the blood supply *If the blood supply to the brain decreases, you feel dizzy.*

the blood flow *Fat reduces the blood flow to the surface of the skin.*

a blood test *Blood tests proved he was not the father.*

a blood sample *The doctor took a blood sample and sent it away for analysis.*

a blood transfusion (=putting more blood in someone's body for medical reasons) *The patient needed a blood transfusion after the operation.*

a blood donor (=someone who provides blood from their body for the medical treatment of other people) *Blood donors normally give blood without expecting to be paid for it.*

a blood clot (=a mass formed when blood dries or sticks together) *Blood clots in the legs are potentially fatal.*

blood poisoning (=a serious illness in which an infection spreads through your body) *If the cut is not treated, he could die of blood poisoning.*

VERBS + blood

give/donate blood (=provide it from your body for the medical treatment of other people) *The Health Service is asking for more people to donate blood.*

lose blood *He had lost a lot of blood and was very weak.*

draw blood (=make someone bleed) *I got scratched by my kitten, but luckily it didn't draw blood.*

blood + VERBS

blood flows *A quick walk will get the blood in your legs flowing again.*

blood circulates (=moves around your body) *A special machine keeps the blood circulating while the organs are removed.*

blood trickles (=moves slowly in a thin stream) *The blood was beginning to trickle down his leg.*

blood oozes (=comes out slowly) *Blood oozed from a cut on his forehead.*

blood gushes/streams (=comes out very quickly) *Blood was gushing from a cut on his wrist.*

blood clots (=it forms a solid mass and stops flowing) *The blood should clot and stop the wound from bleeding.*

PHRASES

be covered in blood *His face was covered in blood.*

be spattered/splattered with blood (=covered with small spots of blood) *Today the only sign of violence is the walls spattered with blood.*

loss of blood *She suffered a massive loss of blood.*

a drop of blood *Police found tiny drops of blood in the apartment.*

a pool of blood *The body was surrounded by a pool of blood.*

blood pressure *n*

the pressure with which blood flows from your heart around your body

ADJECTIVES

high/low blood pressure *If you have high blood pressure, you are more likely to have a stroke.*

sb's blood pressure is normal *The doctor said that his blood pressure was normal for someone of his age.*

VERBS

take/check sb's blood pressure (=measure it) *The nurse will take your blood pressure.*

blossom *n*

a flower or the flowers on a tree or bush

NOUNS + blossom

cherry/apple/orange/peach blossom *The cherry blossom is very beautiful at this time of year in Japan.*

PHRASES

sth is in blossom (=it has flowers on it) *I visited when the apple trees were in blossom.*

sth is in full blossom (=it has a lot of flowers on it) *The cherry tree was in full blossom.*

the blossom comes out (=it appears) *The blossom usually comes out in May.*

the blossom is out (=it has appeared) *The orange blossom is out already.*

blow *n*

1 something bad that causes difficulty, sadness, or disappointment for someone

ADJECTIVES/NOUNS + blow

a big/major blow *Not being selected for the team came as a big blow.*

a serious/heavy blow *The banking crisis was a serious blow to the economy.*

a severe/terrible/awful blow *The news was a terrible blow for his family.*

a bitter/cruel blow *Their defeat was a bitter blow.*

a devastating/crushing/shattering blow (=one that has an extremely bad effect) *Losing her husband was a devastating blow.*

a body blow (=a very severe blow, which makes someone or something very likely to fail) *The scandal could be a body blow to his political career.*

a mortal/fatal/death blow (=one that causes something to finish or fail completely) *The star's departure dealt a mortal blow to the show.*

the final blow *The final blow was when the company announced that it was closing down.*

VERBS

suffer/receive/take a blow *The team suffered a blow when they lost their best player.*

deal a blow to sb/sth *The 1982 drought dealt a devastating blow to the country.*

deliver a blow *Opinion polls delivered a nasty blow to the Tory leader.*

inflict a blow *The arrests inflicted a serious blow to the organization.*

soften/cushion the blow (=make it easier to deal with) *To soften the blow, the company agreed to pay them a year's salary.*

PREPOSITIONS

a blow to sth/sb *He had suffered a blow to his pride.*

a blow for sb/sth *The closure of the school will be a big blow for the students.*

PHRASES

come as a blow to sb (=be a blow) *His sudden death came as a huge blow to us all.*

be a bit of a blow *BrE informal* (=be disappointing) *The result was a bit of a blow for the team.*

2 the act of hitting someone or something hard

ADJECTIVES

a heavy/hard/powerful blow *The injury was caused by a heavy blow to the chest.*

a glancing blow (=hitting someone or something on the side) *Their car was struck a glancing blow by a big truck.*

the fatal blow (=which kills someone) *They could not prove which of his attackers struck the fatal blow.*

VERBS

receive/take a blow *During the game, he received a blow to the head.*

give sb a blow *The other boxer gave him a powerful blow to the jaw.*

strike/deliver a blow *Who struck the first blow?*

aim a blow at sb/sth *I aimed a blow at his nose.*

land a blow (=succeed in hitting someone when you try to) *She managed to land one blow on the side of his head.*

dodge a blow (=move so that a blow does not touch you) *I managed to dodge the blow.*

exchange blows (=hit each other) *The girl watched as the two men exchanged blows.*

rain blows on sb (=hit someone many times) *Terrified and angry, she rained blows on him.*

PREPOSITIONS

a blow to/on sth *He died from a blow to the back of the head.*

a blow from sth/sb *A blow from someone's elbow broke his nose.*

PHRASES

come to blows (=start hitting each other as a result of an argument) *They often argued and on one occasion almost came to blows.*

with one blow/with a single blow *He knew how to kill a man with a single blow.*

blue *adj, n*

the colour of the sky or the sea on a fine day

TYPES OF BLUE

dark/deep blue *She had deep blue eyes.*

pale/light blue *He was wearing a pale blue shirt.*

bright/brilliant blue *The sky is bright blue.*

navy blue (=very dark blue) *I bought a navy blue sweater.*

sky blue (=blue like the colour of the sky) *The staff wear sky blue uniforms.*

electric blue (=very bright blue) *The fish were electric blue.*

PREPOSITIONS

in blue *Who's the woman in blue?*

PHRASES

a shade of blue *The room is decorated in different shades of blue.*

blunt *adj* THESAURUS **honest**, **sharp (1)**

board *n*

1 a flat vertical surface used for writing or showing information on

VERBS

write sth on the board *The teacher wrote the word 'democracy' on the board.*

put sth (up) on the board *She put a notice on the board saying when the next meeting would be.*

> **Noticeboard** is usually written as one word: *There was a message pinned on the noticeboard.* **Noticeboard** is used in British English. In American English, people say **bulletin board**.
>
> **Blackboard** and **whiteboard** (=used by a teacher for writing on in a classroom) are usually written as one word. **Scoreboard** (=used for showing the score in a game) and **billboard** (=a big board for advertisements) are written as one word.

2 a flat piece of wood that you do something on

NOUNS + board

a cutting/drawing/ironing etc board *I need a cutting board for the bread.*

> **Breadboard**, **skateboard**, **chessboard**, and **surfboard** are written as one word.

boat *n*

a vehicle that travels across water

ADJECTIVES/NOUNS + boat

a small/little/tiny boat *They left me alone in a small boat in the middle of the ocean.*

a fishing boat *The fishing boats go out to sea early in the morning.*

a sailing boat *BrE*, **a sailboat** *AmE*: *The lake was full of sailing boats.*

a rowing boat *BrE*, **a rowboat** *AmE*: *We took a rowing boat out on the river.*

a canal boat (*also* **a narrow boat** *BrE*) (=for use on canals) *We had a holiday on a canal boat in France.*

a pleasure boat (=a small boat that people use on a lake, river etc) *The river is frequently used by pleasure boats, particularly in the summer.*

VERBS + boat

sail a boat *We sailed the boat across the ocean.*

row a boat *They were rowing the boat as fast as they could.*

take a boat out *Why don't we take the boat out on the river?*

get/climb/step onto a boat *I helped her get onto the boat.*

get/jump/step off a boat *He jumped off the boat into the water.*

launch a boat (=put it in the water) *Where's the best place to launch the boat?*

steer a boat (=control it so that it goes in a particular direction) *She steered the boat towards the shore.*

tie up/moor a boat (=tie it to something so that it stays in that place) *The boy jumped on to the bank and tied up the boat.*

anchor a boat (=put a metal object attached to the boat by a rope into the water, so that the boat stays in that place) *He anchored his boat about 25 metres from the beach.*

meet sb off the boat *Her family were waiting to meet her off the boat.*

boat + VERBS

a boat sails somewhere *The boat sailed into the harbour.*

a boat sinks *Our boat sank in a storm.*

a boat capsizes/overturns (=turns over in the water) *He stood up suddenly and the boat capsized.*

a boat rocks (=moves from side to side in the water) *The little boat was rocking in the wind.*

a boat drifts (=moves without any power) *The boat drifted out to sea.*

boat + NOUNS

a boat trip *You can take a boat trip to the islands.*

a boat race *There's a boat race on the river tomorrow.*

PREPOSITIONS

by boat *The beach can only be reached by boat.*

in a boat *I've never been in a boat before.*

on a boat *Everyone on the boat was seasick.*

> **Boat** or **ship**?
> A **boat** is smaller than a **ship**.

body *n*

the physical structure of a person or animal

ADJECTIVES

the human body *There are billions of cells in an adult human body.*

the female/male body *Many of his pictures are of the female body.*

the upper/lower body *This is a good exercise to strengthen the upper body.*

a good/great/fantastic body *He was tall and had a great body.*

a muscular body *Brad had a lean muscular body.*

sb's thin/slim/slender body *She wrapped the robe around her slim body.*

a dead body *She had never seen a dead body before.*

B

sb's whole body *Her whole body was shaking with fear.*

VERBS

sb's body aches *He was exhausted and his body ached all over.*

sb's body shakes/trembles *Her body trembled because she was so nervous.*

sb's body lies somewhere *Her body was lying on the floor.*

body + NOUNS

body weight *You have exactly the right body weight for your height.*

body size/shape *We encourage women to accept their body shape.*

body temperature *His body temperature was dangerously low and they wrapped him in a foil blanket.*

body language (=the movements and expressions that show what you feel) *If you look at his body language, you can see that he is lying.*

body fat *Males have less body fat than females.*

PHRASES

all over sb's body *I had bruises all over my body.*

boil *v* THESAURUS ➔ cook[1]

boiling *adj* THESAURUS ➔ hot

bold *adj*

showing that you are not afraid of taking risks and making difficult decisions

NOUNS

a bold move/step *The newspapers described her resignation as a bold move.*

a bold decision *People praised his bold decision to cut income tax by 5%.*

a bold attempt *It was a bold attempt to win back public confidence.*

a bold statement/assertion/claim *She makes the bold claim that many of his poems were in fact written by his wife.*

a bold initiative *Investors welcome the company's bold initiatives.*

a bold experiment *Telling the story from his point of view was a bold experiment, and it worked.*

THESAURUS: bold

courageous, heroic, bold, daring, valiant, adventurous, intrepid, fearless → **brave**

bomb *n*

a weapon that explodes and causes a lot of damage

ADJECTIVES/NOUNS + bomb

a huge/massive bomb *The building was destroyed by a massive bomb.*

a terrorist bomb *The aircraft was blown apart by a terrorist bomb.*

an unexploded bomb *The workmen found an unexploded bomb.*

a homemade bomb *Officers discovered several homemade bombs in the trunk of his car.*

a car bomb *The car bomb killed 21 shoppers.*

a roadside bomb (=left next to a road) *The vehicle was totally destroyed by a roadside bomb.*

a nuclear/hydrogen/atomic/atom bomb *The US dropped atomic bombs on two Japanese cities.*

a time bomb (=that is set to explode at a particular time) *The time bomb was planned to cause the maximum carnage.*

bomb + VERBS

a bomb explodes/goes off *A 200-pound bomb went off in the car park.*

a bomb blows sth up (=destroys it completely) *A bomb blew up flight 103, killing 270 people.*

a bomb falls on sth *A bomb fell on the cathedral during the war.*

VERBS + bomb

set off/let off a bomb (*also* **detonate a bomb** *formal*) (=make it explode) *The area was cleared and the army detonated the bomb.*

drop a bomb (=from a plane) *Enemy planes dropped over 200 bombs during the raid.*

plant a bomb (=put one somewhere) *It is thought that right-wing extremists planted the bomb.*

make/build a bomb *He had enough explosives to make about 80 bombs.*

defuse a bomb (=make it safe so that it does not explode) *Police closed off the area while they defused the bomb.*

bomb + NOUNS

a bomb blast/explosion *The restaurant was destroyed in a massive bomb blast.*

a bomb attack *No one has yet claimed responsibility for the bomb attack.*

bomb damage *The building suffered extensive bomb damage during the war.*

a bomb scare (=when people think there might be a bomb somewhere) *There was a bomb scare and we all had to leave the building.*

a bomb site (=a place destroyed by a bomb) *They've pulled down so many buildings around here it looks like a bomb site.*

bomb-making equipment *Police found guns and bomb-making equipment in the house.*

bond Ac *n*

something that unites two or more people or groups, such as love or a shared interest

ADJECTIVES

a close/strong bond *A strong bond had developed between the members of the team.*

a common bond (=one that people share) *They shared a common bond - a love of music.*

a special bond *There was a special bond between Alan and his brother.*

an emotional bond *He finds it difficult to form emotional bonds with other people.*

VERBS

form/forge a bond (=begin to have a bond, which then grows) *Most dogs form a strong bond with their owner.*

create/establish a bond (=cause one to form) *He told his problems to his friend and this established a close bond between them.*

have a bond *Twins often have a very special bond.*

feel a bond *The people of the island feel a strong bond.*

strengthen a bond *Sharing common aims has strengthened the bond between our two nations.*

break/destroy a bond *The years spent apart had not broken the bonds of affection between them.*

develop a bond (=gradually form a bond over a long period) *Over the six years we worked together, we developed a very close bond.*

a bond exists *The bond that existed between my parents made me feel safe and secure.*

be linked/joined/united by a bond *The two countries are linked by bonds of language, religion, and culture.*

PREPOSITIONS

a bond of friendship/affection/trust etc *The president spoke about the lasting bond of friendship between the US and the UK.*

a bond between people *There is a strong emotional bond between a mother and her child.*

bone *n*

one of the hard white parts inside the body that form a skeleton

ADJECTIVES

a broken bone *The X-ray showed that I had a broken bone in my wrist.*

strong/healthy bones *Vitamin C is essential for healthy bones, teeth, and gums.*

brittle/fragile bones (=easily damaged or broken) *Old people often have fragile bones.*

NOUNS + bone

sb's thigh/hip/ankle etc bone *He fell off the horse, fracturing his collar bone.*

chicken/fish etc bones *She got a fish bone stuck in her throat.*

animal/human bones *The team found stone tools and animal bones at the site.*

VERBS

break a bone *Most rugby players end up breaking a bone or two during their career.*

fracture a bone (*also* **crack a bone** *informal*) (=partly break it so that a line appears on the surface) *Sally fell, fracturing a bone in her leg.*

PHRASES

pieces/fragments/splinters of bone (=small pieces that have broken off a larger piece) *The small fragments of bone and pottery found at the site are hundreds of years old.*

B

bonus *n*

1 an extra amount of money given to someone, especially as a reward for good work in their job

ADJECTIVES/NOUNS + bonus

a big/huge bonus *Bankers get paid big bonuses if the bank has a good year.*

an annual bonus *Each worker receives an annual bonus.*

a special bonus *The company paid its top trader a special bonus of $1.2 million.*

a cash bonus *Long-term savers qualify for a cash bonus.*

a Christmas bonus *Employees receive a Christmas bonus.*

VERBS

get/earn/receive a bonus *You will receive a bonus if you finish the work on time.*

give/pay/award sb a bonus *A £2 million bonus was awarded to the chief executive.*

qualify for a bonus *To qualify for this bonus, you must keep the money in your account for a year.*

bonus + NOUNS

a bonus system/scheme *The company offers a profit-related bonus scheme.*

2 something good that you did not expect

ADJECTIVES

an unexpected bonus *The money was an unexpected bonus.*

an added/extra/additional bonus *The free drink that came with the meal was an added bonus.*

a big/real/great bonus *His skills will be a big bonus for the team.*

a welcome bonus *The sunny weather was a welcome bonus.*

book[1] *n*

a set of printed pages that are held together in a cover so that you can read them

NOUNS + book

a history/travel/science/poetry etc book *Not much is written about her in the history books.*

a library book *I need to return my library books.*

a recipe book (=which tells you how to cook different foods) *I got the idea from a recipe book.*

a paperback book (=with a thin card cover) *She took a paperback book out of her bag and began to read.*

a hardback book (=with a thick stiff cover) *Hardback books are often very heavy.*

a paper book (=one that is printed on paper, not electronically) *Paper books are less tiring for your eyes.*

> You use **e-book** about an electronic book that you can read on a screen: ***E-books** are now becoming more popular than paper books.*

> **Textbook**, **schoolbook** and **phonebook** are usually written as one word.
> **Cookbook** (= a book that tells you how to cook different foods) is written as one word. It is used especially in American English. British people usually say **cookery book**.

B

VERBS + book

read a book *What book are you reading at the moment?*

look through a book *I looked through the book until I found the right section.*

write a book *He's written several interesting travel books.*

publish a book *The book is published by Penguin.*

borrow a book (*also* **take out a book** *BrE*) (=from a library) *You can borrow up to six books from the library.*

return a book (=give it back) *Please return all your books before the end of term.*

book + VERBS

a book comes out (=it is published for the first time) *The book first came out about a year ago.*

book + NOUNS

a book review *She had a book review published in the student magazine.*

PREPOSITIONS

a book about sth/sb *She wrote a book about her experiences.*

a book on a subject *This section has books on politics and economics.*

in a book *In his latest book, he tackles the subject of climate change.*

PHRASES

the cover of a book *His picture is on the cover of the book.*

the back of the book *It tells you the price on the back of the book.*

a chapter/section of a book *The first chapter of the book is about his childhood.*

> **Bookshop**, **bookstore**, **bookseller**, and **bookshelf** are usually written as one word.

book² *v*

to arrange to stay in a hotel, eat in a restaurant, go to a theatre, or travel on a plane etc at a particular time in the future

ADVERBS

book early/in advance/ahead *The restaurant is very popular, so it's a good idea to book ahead.*

book online (=on the internet) *It's much easier to book tickets online.*

be fully booked (=all the seats, tickets etc are sold) *I'm afraid that show is fully booked.*

be booked solid (=all the seats, tickets etc are sold for a long period) *The hotel is booked solid for the whole of August.*

book + NOUNS

book a holiday/vacation *People often book their holidays in January.*

book a trip/flight *I booked the whole trip on the internet.*

book a ticket *It's cheaper if you book your train ticket in advance.*

book a table (=in a restaurant) *I'll book a table for 7.30 tomorrow evening.*

book a room/hotel *Ross found a good hotel and booked a room.*

book a seat *She booked me a seat on the 9 a.m. flight.*

booking *n*

an arrangement to travel by train, use a hotel room, eat at a restaurant etc at a particular time in the future

ADJECTIVES/NOUNS + booking

a hotel/room booking *I'll make the hotel booking today.*

an online/phone/postal booking *Most hotels take online bookings.*

early/late booking *Early booking is recommended because places are limited.*

advance booking *The cinema charges £1 a ticket for advance booking.*

a group booking (=a booking for a large number of seats, rooms etc) *There's a 20% discount for group bookings.*

VERBS

make a booking *I made a booking for two nights.*

confirm a booking (=say definitely that you are going to travel etc) *Please confirm your booking 48 hours before your flight.*

cancel a booking *If you cancel the booking, there will be a small charge.*

take/accept a booking *Postal bookings are only accepted up to three days before the event.*

have a booking *The hotel clerk asked me if I had a booking.*

change a booking *I'll phone the airline and try to change the booking.*

booking + NOUNS

a booking form *You can complete the booking form online.*

a booking fee *Ticket agencies charge a booking fee.*

a booking system *The airline uses an automated booking system.*

boom *n*

a sudden increase in business activity

ADJECTIVES/NOUNS + boom

an economic boom *The country is experiencing an economic boom.*

a great boom *The great stock market boom ended and many people lost all their savings.*

a property/housing boom (=a sudden increase in house prices) *People made a lot of money in the 1980s property boom.*

a consumer/spending boom (=a sudden increase in the amount people spend) *The consumer boom was followed by a deep recession.*

a credit boom (=when people borrow a lot) *He was worried that the credit boom could result in a financial crisis.*

an investment boom *The investment boom is over.*

a building/construction boom *There's been a recent construction boom in the area.*

VERBS

experience/enjoy a boom *China has been enjoying a remarkable economic boom.*

cause/lead to a boom *The tax cuts led to an economic boom.*

fuel a boom (=add to it) *The energy crisis is fuelling a boom in alternative energy.*

boom + NOUNS

the boom years/times *The development was planned during the boom years of the late 1980s.*

PREPOSITIONS

a boom in sth *The company has enjoyed a boom in sales.*

booming *adj* THESAURUS **successful (3)**

boost[1] *v*

1 to make someone feel more confident

NOUNS

boost sb's confidence/self-confidence *The victory boosted the team's confidence.*

boost sb's morale *The president's visit was intended to boost morale.*

boost sb's ego (=make someone feel good about themselves) *David did his best to boost my ego, and told me that I could easily find another girlfriend.*

boost hopes of sth *The good news about exports boosted hopes of an economic recovery.*

2 to make something more successful

NOUNS

boost the economy *The government cut taxes in order to boost the economy.*

boost sales/profits/trade *The agreement will boost trade between the two countries.*

boost earnings *She worked extra hours to boost her earnings.*

boost production *The introduction of new technology should help to boost production.*

boost growth *They want to boost economic growth.*

ADVERBS

boost sth greatly/considerably/significantly *The deal will significantly boost the firm's position in the market.*

boost sth dramatically (=in a great and sudden way) *The party's share of the vote was boosted dramatically.*

boost sth artificially *The drug can artificially boost energy levels.*

VERBS

help boost sth *An attractive cover can help boost sales of a book.*

boost[2] *n*

something that helps someone feel more confident, or helps something be more successful

ADJECTIVES

a big/major/significant boost *Her acting career got a big boost when she was chosen to appear in the film.*

a huge/great/tremendous boost *The new factory will give the town's economy a tremendous boost.*

a real boost *The money will be a real boost to the local area.*

a financial boost *Advertising offers a financial boost for free internet services.*

a psychological boost *Saturday's win was a huge psychological boost.*

a welcome/much-needed boost *The new laws will give a much-needed boost to the police in their fight against crime.*

an extra/further boost *Give your body an extra boost by eating more fresh fruit and vegetables.*

NOUNS + boost

a morale boost (=something that gives you encouragement) *The prime minister's visit was intended to give the troops a morale boost.*

a confidence boost (*also* **a boost to your confidence**) *The team needed a confidence boost after last week's 4–0 defeat.*

an ego boost (=something that makes you feel that you are very important or special) *It's a real ego boost when people recognize you in the street.*

VERBS

give sb/sth a boost *Winning the competition has given his confidence a boost.*

provide a boost to sb/sth *The good news provided a significant boost to Japan's stock market.*

B

get/receive a boost *The island's tourism industry received a major boost with the building of a new airport.*
need a boost *His self-confidence needed a boost after his girlfriend left him.*

PREPOSITIONS

a boost to sb/sth *The discovery of oil gave a major boost to the country's economy.*

B

boot *n*

a type of shoe that covers your whole foot and the lower part of your leg, or that you use for a game or activity

ADJECTIVES/NOUNS + boot

football/rugby/riding/ski boots *We can hire ski boots at the ski resort.*
walking/hiking boots *In the mountains you'll need some strong walking boots.*
leather/suede boots *Long leather boots are in fashion this autumn.*
muddy/dirty boots *Take off your muddy boots before you come in the kitchen.*
heavy boots *They heard the sound of heavy boots in the street below.*
stout/sturdy boots (=strong and well-made) *I was glad of my stout walking boots as I climbed up the hill.*
wellington boots *BrE*, **rubber boots** *AmE* (=rubber boots that stop your feet and legs getting wet) *The kids put on their rubber boots and went out in the rain.*
ankle boots (=women's boots that are only as high as your ankles) *Ankle boots look good with skirts or trousers.*

VERBS

wear boots *The workmen wear special boots.*
put on/pull on your boots *He put on his boots and went out.*
take your boots off (*also* **remove your boots** *formal*): *He bent to take off his boots.*
lace your boots up (=tie the laces) *She laced up her walking boots.*
unlace your boots (=unfasten the laces) *Martin sat down and began unlacing his boots.*

PHRASES

a pair of boots *I really need a new pair of boots this winter.*

border *n*

a line separating two countries or areas

ADJECTIVES

the Canadian/Mexican etc border *I had reached the Swiss border.*
the southern/eastern etc border *They renewed their attacks on Ethiopia's northern border.*
a disputed border *Fighting broke out along the disputed border between Thailand and Cambodia.*

VERBS

cross/go across a border *To cross the border, you will need a valid passport.*
flee/escape across the border *Over 100,000 civilians fled across the border.*
open/close the border *After fifty years the border was finally opened.*
form the border *The river forms the border between the two countries.*
straddle the border (=cover land on both sides of it) *This small village straddles the border between the West Bank and Jerusalem.*

border + NOUNS

a border dispute *The border dispute between Iraq and Iran was resolved.*
a border town *She lives in the Chinese border town of Shenzhen.*
a border area/region *The Afghan border area is open and wild.*
a border crossing *There are problems of delays at border crossings.*
a border guard *The North Korean border guards will kill anyone who tries to cross.*
border controls (=controls on who crosses a border) *Hungary tightened its border controls.*

PREPOSITIONS

the border between sth and sth *We arrived at the border between the US and Mexico.*
the border of sth and sth *Liechtenstein lies on the border of Switzerland and Austria.*
the border with sth *We live in northern Sweden, near the border with Norway.*
on/along the border *Chester is a town on the border of England and Wales.*
across/over the border (=on the other side of it) *It happened hundreds of miles away, across the border.*

bored *adj*

tired and impatient because you do not think something is interesting, or because you have nothing to do

VERBS

get/become bored (*also* **grow bored**) *formal*: *I get bored if I'm at home on my own all day.*
feel bored *If you feel bored, you're welcome to turn on the television.*
look/sound bored *The children were starting to look bored.*

NOUNS

a bored look/expression *He sat in front of his computer screen with a bored expression on his face.*
bored children/teenagers/pupils *The park was full of bored teenagers.*

PREPOSITIONS

bored with sth *He is bored with the job already.*
bored of (doing) sth *I'm bored of going to the same places every weekend.*

PHRASES

bored stiff/bored rigid (=very bored) *The audience looked bored stiff.*

bored to tears/bored to death (=very bored – more informal) *I was bored to tears by the end of the film.*

bored out of your mind/bored witless (=very bored – more informal) *After a week in the country she was bored witless.*

ANTONYMS **bored → interested**

boredom *n*

the feeling you have when you are bored

VERBS

be dying of boredom (=very bored) *By the end of the film I was dying of boredom.*

relieve/alleviate the boredom (=stop yourself from feeling bored) *We played games in the back of the car to relieve the boredom.*

ADJECTIVES

sheer/utter boredom (=used when emphasizing that someone is very bored) *He gave up his job because of sheer boredom.*

terminal boredom *often humorous* (=a situation in which you are too bored to do anything) *Occasional jokes saved us from terminal boredom.*

PHRASES

have a low boredom threshold (=become bored very easily) *She has a low boredom threshold and wants new challenges.*

THESAURUS: boredom

monotony
a bored feeling, caused by the same thing happening again and again, or something always looking the same:
There were no trees or houses to ***break*** *the endless* ***monotony*** *of the landscape.* | *He was longing to* ***escape*** *the dull* ***monotony*** *of his job.*

tedium
a very boring feeling. **Tedium** is more formal than **boredom**, and is used especially when something very boring continues for a long time:
To ***relieve*** *the* ***tedium*** *of the days, they sang or told stories.* | *For the workers, the meal-breaks are a release from the tedium of their jobs at the factory.*

boring *adj* not interesting

NOUNS

a boring job *I had a boring job in a bank and I couldn't wait to leave.*

boring work *She was fed up with doing the same boring work every day.*

a boring person/man/woman *Her husband is the most boring person I've ever met – all he wants to talk about is football.*

a boring subject *I always thought that physics was a boring subject when I was at school.*

a boring book/film/programme *The book was so boring that she never finished it.*

a boring life *My life is never boring!*

a boring place/town *It's a boring town with nothing for teenagers to do.*

a boring day/evening/morning *He arrived home after another boring day at the office.*

a boring meeting *The meeting was long and boring.*

boring details *I'm not interested in all the boring details.*

the boring bits *informal* (=the boring parts of something) *He didn't bother to read the boring bits.*

ADVERBS

really boring *I think golf is really boring.*

incredibly boring (=very boring) *The work is incredibly boring.*

mind-numbingly boring (=extremely boring) *The meeting was mind-numbingly boring and I fell asleep halfway through.*

dead boring *informal* (=very boring) *The film sounds dead boring.*

VERBS

get boring *The game gets boring after a while.*

find sth boring *Some people find her books really boring.*

sound boring *I know it sounds boring, but I'd like to see the film again.*

⚠ Don't say 'I feel boring.' Say **I feel bored.**

PREPOSITIONS

boring for sb *The concert was very boring for the children.*

PHRASES

dull and boring *Life seemed very dull and boring.*

the same boring things *We always talk about the same boring things.*

You use **boring** when expressing your feelings very strongly and directly, usually in more informal English, for example when talking to someone you know well.
Instead of saying **boring**, you can say that something **isn't very interesting**. This sounds gentler and less direct: *The story* ***wasn't very interesting****.*

THESAURUS: boring

dull
film | **place** | **routine** | **life** | **job** | **man** | **day** | **affair**
rather boring, especially because nothing

exciting happens. **Dull** is more formal than **boring** and is used mainly in writing:
The film was rather dull and I wished I had stayed at home. | A world without music would be a very dull place. | Derby was a dull man who spent most of his life in business meetings. | It looks like another dull day outside (=the sky is grey and there is no sunshine). | *We have five children, so* ***there's never a dull moment*** *in our house.*

You can use **dull** about colours that are not very bright or exciting: *The room was painted a* ***dull*** *dark green colour.*

tedious
process | task | job | work | journey | wait | paperwork | debate | business
very boring and taking too long, so that you feel impatient:
Applying for a visa is a long and tedious process. | Jake began the tedious task of sorting through his papers. | After a tedious journey, we finally arrived in Paris. | Checking that all the names are correct is a tedious business (=a tedious thing to have to do).

monotonous
voice | work | job | task | diet | routine | existence
something that is monotonous is boring because it is always the same and does not change:
The speaker's voice was very monotonous and I found myself falling asleep. | Factory work is monotonous and unchallenging. | He ate a monotonous diet of fish and rice. | Her life followed the same monotonous routine of making meals and taking the children to school. | He has won the race every year, ***with monotonous regularity*** (=used when the same thing keeps happening and you know it will happen again).

mundane
matter | issue | task | details | world
relating to ordinary things that you do every day, rather than more exciting things:
Instead of philosophy and politics, he preferred to talk about more mundane matters. | His duties included mundane tasks such as getting us out of bed in the mornings. | Her boss wasn't interested in the mundane details of her life. | Our world must seem very mundane compared to hers.

humdrum
life | existence | routine | job | work
boring because nothing new or interesting ever happens:
He wanted to escape from his humdrum life at the office. | Yasmin saw travel as a way out of her humdrum existence. | When the excitement was over, he could get back to his humdrum routine.

dry
subject | topic | report | debate | reading
a dry subject, piece of writing etc is boring because it is very serious and does not contain any humour:
Economics can be rather a dry subject and it is difficult to make it interesting for students. | Books on statistics are usually dry reading.

dreary
place | town | suburb | landscape | life | weather
not interesting, and making you sad or bored:
The town is a dreary place in the winter. | Films were a way of escaping from their dreary lives. | The English weather was cold and dreary (=very grey and with no sunshine).

ANTONYMS **boring → interesting**

bottle *n*

a plastic or glass container with a narrow top, used for keeping liquids in

ADJECTIVES/NOUNS + bottle

a plastic/glass bottle *The countryside is littered with old plastic bottles.*

a water/beer/wine/milk etc bottle *Bring a water bottle in case you get thirsty.*

a medicine/perfume/shampoo bottle *It's important to keep medicine bottles away from children.*

an empty bottle *There were empty bottles all over the floor.*

a bottle is half-full/half-empty *The bottle was already half-empty.*

VERBS

open a bottle *Do you want me to open another bottle of beer?*

drink a bottle *I was so thirsty that I drank the whole bottle.*

fill a bottle with a liquid *She filled the bottle with water.*

pour liquid into/out of a bottle *He carefully poured the sauce out of the bottle.*

bring a bottle *Come to my party, and bring a bottle.*

bottle + NOUNS

a bottle bank (=a place where bottles are collected for recycling) *I usually take our bottles to the bottle bank.*

a bottle top *Don't just throw the bottle top on the floor.*

a bottle opener *I need a bottle opener to open this bottle of wine.*

PREPOSITIONS

a bottle of sth *Do you want another bottle of beer?*

bottom[1] *n*

1 the lowest part of something

ADJECTIVES

the very bottom (=the lowest part – used for emphasis) *It is a day's ride down to the very bottom of the Canyon.*

VERBS

sink to the bottom *The ship sank to the bottom of the sea.*

PREPOSITIONS

the bottom of sth *The bottom of the bath is very dirty.*

at the bottom *I parked at the bottom of the hill and walked up to the top. | There is a note at the bottom of the page.*

on the bottom *Lobsters live on the bottom of the ocean. | The skin on the bottom of my feet is very hard.*

to the bottom *She slid to the bottom of the slope.*

PHRASES

right at/to the bottom (=at or to the lowest part – used for emphasis) *My name was right at the bottom of the list.*

THESAURUS: bottom

the underneath/the underside
the bottom surface on the outside of something:
You will find the serial number ***on the underneath*** *of the computer. | The mechanic checked* ***the underside of*** *the car.*

the foot
stairs | staircase | steps | ladder | mountain | hill | cliff | wall | page | statue | tree
the bottom of the stairs, a mountain, a page etc:
She had just reached the foot of the stairs when she saw Ben entering the yard. | There was a small village at the foot of the mountain. | The note at the foot of the page says where the quote is from.

base
statue | lamp | spine | back | neck | skull | tree | column | wall
the lowest part of something, or the wide part on which something stands:
Flowers were left at the base of the statue. | The lamp has a square base. | She felt a slight pain at the base of her spine.

bed
sea | river | lake | ocean
the ground at the bottom of an area of water:
The fish feed mainly on the sea bed. | They found some interesting stones on the river bed.

Seabed and **riverbed** are often written as one word.

foundations
building | house
the layer of cement and stones that forms the bottom of a building:
The earthquake shook the foundations of the building. | The builders have begun laying the foundations for the house.

ANTONYMS **bottom → top[1] (1)**

2 the least successful or important position in an organization or group

ADJECTIVES

the very bottom *He's a man who has gone from the very top to the very bottom.*

VERBS

start at the bottom *He started at the bottom and worked his way up to become managing director.*

PREPOSITIONS

the bottom of sth *The school is near the bottom of the league table.*

at the bottom *We must help those at the bottom of society to cope.*

PHRASES

second/third etc from (the) bottom (=in a list or table showing results) *The team is currently fourth from bottom.*

the bottom of the ladder/pile/heap (=used especially to describe the poorest or least powerful people in a group) *Welfare cuts have reduced the income of those at the bottom of the pile.*

ANTONYMS **bottom → top[1] (2)**

bottom[2] *adj*

at a lower level than the other one or other ones

NOUNS

the bottom drawer/shelf *My passport is in the bottom drawer of my desk.*

the bottom layer/row *The bottom layer must be strong enough to support the layers of bricks above it.*

the bottom half/part *There were only two windows in the bottom half of the building.*

the bottom step/stair *Jenna sat on the bottom step.*

the bottom corner *Look at the bottom left-hand corner of your screen.*

sb's bottom lip *Her bottom lip trembled and she started to cry.*

ANTONYMS **bottom → top[2] (1)**

boundary *n*

1 the real or imaginary line that marks the edge of a country or area of land

ADJECTIVES/NOUNS + boundary

a national/international boundary *In the age*

B

of the internet, national boundaries are becoming less important.

a state boundary *The train crossed the state boundary.*

a city boundary *The new housing estates stretch beyond the old city boundaries.*

the northern/southern etc boundary *The road runs along the southern boundary of the city.*

a political/geographical/administrative boundary *Reforms could extend the geographical and political boundaries of the EU.*

a natural boundary *Here, the Andes forms a natural boundary between Argentina and Chile.*

VERBS

mark/form a boundary *The River Jordan marks the boundary between Israel and Jordan.*

cross a boundary *At the river, we crossed the boundary into the next county.*

extend a boundary *He extended the boundaries of his empire.*

draw/redraw a boundary *In the mid-1990s the government redrew the country's internal boundaries.*

boundary + NOUNS

a boundary dispute *They were involved in a boundary dispute with a neighbour.*

PREPOSITIONS

the boundary between sth and sth *The road marks the boundary between the two districts.*

within a boundary *They are not allowed to graze their cattle within park boundaries.*

2 the limit of something

ADJECTIVES

a clear boundary *They attempt to maintain clear boundaries between their working and family lives.*

traditional boundaries *These women were willing to take risks and step outside traditional boundaries.*

cultural boundaries *Silent films can cross cultural boundaries.*

VERBS

cross/cut across a boundary *This work crosses the boundary separating poetry and prose.*

push back/extend the boundaries (=do things that have not been done before) *Science has pushed back the boundaries of human knowledge.*

establish/set/define a boundary *When raising a child, it is important to set boundaries regarding acceptable behaviour.*

PREPOSITIONS

the boundary between sth and sth *The boundary between art and advertising is not always clear.*

within the boundaries of sth *Politicians must act within the boundaries of the law.*

bow[1] *v*

to bend the top part of your body forward after you finish a performance or as a greeting

NOUNS

bow your head *In Japan, it is polite to bow your head when you meet someone.*

ADVERBS

bow deeply *He walked to the front of the stage and bowed deeply.*

bow politely/respectfully *"Good evening Sir," she said, bowing respectfully.*

PREPOSITIONS

bow to sb *At the end of the show the actors bow to the audience.*

bow[2] *n*

the act of bending the top part of your body as a sign of respect or at the end of a performance

ADJECTIVES

a deep bow *He made a deep bow and left the room.*

a slight bow *The servant gave a slight bow and handed him the letter.*

VERBS

give/make a bow *She gave a bow when she met him.*

take a bow (=make a bow at the end of a performance) *The actors came back on stage to take a bow.*

box *n*

a container for putting things in, especially one with four straight sides

ADJECTIVES

a cardboard/wooden/plastic/metal box *We packed all our things into big cardboard boxes.*

an empty box *He lifted the lid and found the box was empty.*

NOUNS + box

a lunch box (*also* **a sandwich box** *BrE*): *His mum always put an apple in his lunch box.*

a storage box (=for storing things in) *The house was full of plastic storage boxes.*

a money box (=used by a child for keeping money in) *How much have you got in your money box?*

cash box (=used especially by a shop for keeping money in) *Thieves stole £100 from a cash box at the school.*

a jewellery box *BrE*, **a jewelry box** *AmE*: *She kept all her rings in a jewellery box by her bed.*

Toolbox and **shoebox** are usually written as one word.

VERBS

open a box *You can open the box to check the contents.*

shut/close a box *He shut the box and locked it.*

empty a box *The robbers emptied all the boxes, which contained cash and jewellery.*

a box contains sth *The box contained old letters and other documents.*

PREPOSITIONS

in/inside a box *He put the machine back in its box.*

a box of sth *He produced a box of matches and lit the candle.*

PHRASES

the lid of a box *She closed the lid of the box.*

a box full of sth/filled with sth *I have boxes full of old toys in the garage.*

boy

n a male child or a young man

ADJECTIVES

a little/small boy *Little boys love toy trains.*

a young boy *My family moved to Britain when I was a young boy.*

a baby boy (=a son) *Lucy has had a baby boy.*

a teenage boy *The movie is about the adventures of two teenage boys.*

a 10-year-old/12-year-old etc boy *A 14-year-old boy has won an award for bravery.*

a good/nice boy (=a well-behaved boy) *Kevin is a good boy who never gets in trouble.*

a bad/naughty boy *That naughty boy has spilt water all over the floor!*

a clever/smart boy *Some of the boys in my class are really clever.*

a big boy (=an older boy - used especially when saying that someone is old enough not to need help or advice from an adult) *You don't need me to go with you - you're a big boy now.*

sb is the golden boy (=the one who everyone admires) *Peter was always the golden boy at school.*

> **Little boy** or **small boy?**
> You use **little boy** especially when showing your feelings about the boy, for example when you think he is cute. You use **small boy** especially about a boy who is small in size.

boy + NOUNS

boy band/boyband (=a pop group that consists of attractive teenage boys) *He used to be a singer in a boy band.*

> **Paperboy** (=a boy who delivers newspapers) and **choirboy** (=a boy who sings in a choir) are usually written as one word.

PHRASES

become interested in boys *Girls become interested in boys at a very young age.*

boys will be boys (=used when saying that you expect boys and young men to behave a little badly sometimes) *Boys will be boys and it's normal for there to be some fighting in the playground.*

boycott

n

a form of protest in which people refuse to buy a country's or company's goods, or refuse to take part in something

ADJECTIVES/NOUNS + boycott

an economic/trade boycott *It's not clear whether economic boycotts really work.*

an international boycott *North Korea has been the subject of an international boycott for many years.*

a nationwide boycott (=in all of a country) *They organized a nationwide boycott of the movie.*

a mass boycott (=involving a large number of people or organizations) *There was a mass boycott of the election.*

VERBS

put a boycott on sth (*also* **impose a boycott on sth** *formal*) (=start a boycott) *The United States imposed a boycott on trade with Cuba.*

organize a boycott *The students organized a boycott of the company's products.*

call for a boycott *The senator called for a boycott on all French goods.*

end/lift a boycott *He hopes to persuade Western countries to lift their boycott.*

threaten a boycott *Athletes are threatening a boycott of the Olympic Games.*

support a boycott *Many people do not support the boycott.*

PREPOSITIONS

a boycott of sth *In 1955 Martin Luther King organized a boycott of the city's bus services.*

a boycott on/against sth *They want a boycott on all Canada's seafood products.*

boyfriend

n

a man that you are having a romantic relationship with

ADJECTIVES

sb's first boyfriend *Josh was my first boyfriend.*

sb's new boyfriend *Her parents were anxious to meet her new boyfriend.*

a steady/long-term boyfriend (=that you have had a long relationship with) *I asked if she had a steady boyfriend.*

an old boyfriend/ex-boyfriend/former boyfriend (=someone who was your boyfriend before) *I met an old boyfriend from college.*

VERBS

have a boyfriend *I have a boyfriend in the US.*

split up with your boyfriend *Helen has just split up with her boyfriend.*

leave your boyfriend *She left her boyfriend because he was boring.*

be sb's boyfriend *I told her that I wanted to be her boyfriend.*

brain *n*

1 the thing inside your head that you use for thinking, feeling, and controlling your body

ADJECTIVES

the human brain *The human brain is extremely complex.*

brain + NOUNS

brain damage/a brain injury *The baby suffered permanent brain damage.*

brain cells *The disease destroys brain cells.*

a brain tumour *BrE*, **a brain tumor** *AmE*: *He died of a brain tumour at the age of 49.*

PHRASES

the left/right side of the brain *Damage to the left side of the brain can cause problems with language.*

2 the ability to think clearly and learn quickly

ADJECTIVES/NOUNS + brain

a good/quick brain *It was obvious that Ann had a good brain.*

a business brain (=the ability to make good business decisions) *We need someone who has a business brain.*

VERBS

have brains (=be intelligent) *She had more brains than her husband.*

use your brain *It's easy if you just use your brain.*

rack your brains (=try very hard to think of something) *If we all rack our brains, we should come up with some ideas.*

pick sb's brains (=ask someone for ideas) *I thought I'd pick Greg's brains about what to take with us.*

brainy *adj* THESAURUS **intelligent**

branch *n*

1 a part of a larger organization

ADJECTIVES/NOUNS + branch

the London/New York etc branch *He works for the Paris branch of an American bank.*

the main branch *The main branch of the New York Public Library was officially opened in 1911.*

a local/regional branch *Her father had got a job in the local branch of a building society.*

a high street branch (=on one of the main streets in a town or city) *The increase in online banking has led to the closure of many high street branches.*

the nearest branch *The website tells you where the nearest branch of the store is.*

an overseas branch (=in a foreign country) *The company has just opened its first overseas branch in Paris.*

VERBS + branch

have a branch *The bank has branches all over the country.*

open/close a branch *The store opened its first branch in 1959.*

a branch opens/closes *Many local branches are having to close.*

establish a branch *The university wants to establish a branch in Australia.*

branch + NOUNS

a branch office *They have just set up a branch office in Boston.*

a branch meeting *The next branch meeting will be on May 5th.*

PREPOSITIONS

a branch of sth *He was the secretary of the local branch of the union.*

2 a part of a tree that grows out from the trunk

ADJECTIVES

a low/high branch *The bird flew down onto the lowest branch of the tree.*

the top/upper branches *The top branches were swaying in the wind.*

an overhanging branch *The overhanging branches of the tree formed a tunnel.*

the spreading branches *They sat under the spreading branches of an oak tree.*

VERBS

prune/cut back a branch *Prune the branches of the tree in winter.*

chop off a branch *We could chop off some branches to make a fire.*

brand *n*

a type of product which has its own name and is made by a particular company

ADJECTIVES/NOUNS + brand

a leading/top brand *Choose one of the leading brands of paint.*

a popular brand *The store has all the popular brands of breakfast cereal.*

sb's favourite brand *BrE*, **sb's favorite brand** *AmE*: *The shop no longer sells my favourite brand of soap.*

a well-known/famous brand *A dangerous chemical has been found in a well-known brand of bottled water.*

a global/international brand *The fashion company attempted to build a global brand.*

a luxury/premium brand (=an expensive brand) *Cheap copies pose a threat to some luxury brands.*

own brand *BrE*, **store brand** *AmE* (=sold by a particular store under its own name) *A supermarket's own brand should cost less than the nationally advertised brands.*

brand + NOUNS

a brand name *The brand name is well known to the public.*

a brand image (=the way a product or organization seems to the public) *A company carefully protects its brand image.*

brand loyalty (=the tendency to always buy a particular brand) *Advertising is used to sell a product and create brand loyalty.*

brand awareness (=the number of people who have heard of a brand) *The aim of the campaign is to increase brand awareness.*

the brand leader (=the brand that sells the most) *It is the brand leader for herbs and spices in the UK.*

brave *adj*

showing that you are not afraid to do things or be in situations that other people find dangerous or difficult

NOUNS

a brave man/woman/girl etc *The firefighters were all brave men.*

a brave soldier *Brave soldiers have given their lives to defend our country.*

a brave smile *Her tears were replaced by a brave smile.*

brave words *Despite these brave words he felt very frightened.*

a brave attempt/effort *He made a brave attempt to deal with the problem.*

a brave fight/battle *Sadly, Mr Shaw died last week after a brave fight against cancer.*

a brave decision *It was a brave decision to start again in a new country.*

a brave step/move *Trying to enter this market is a brave move for the company.*

a brave act/deed (=something brave you have done) *There were many stories about his brave deeds.*

a brave soul *often humorous* (=brave person) *A few brave souls were making their way through the deep mud.*

ADVERBS

incredibly/amazingly/exceptionally brave *I think he was incredibly brave to do a parachute jump.*

PHRASES

put a brave face on (sth) (=pretend that you are happy when you are upset) *The team tried to put a brave face on their defeat.*

> You can also use **brave** as a noun: *The United States is the land of the free and the home of* ***the brave****.*

THESAURUS: brave

courageous

man | woman | person | leader | decision | act | action | effort | stand | battle

very brave – used especially about someone who does something because they believe it is right, or who fights against a disease for a long time:

She was a courageous leader who fought for democracy all her life. | Their courageous actions saved many lives. | Her father died after a long and courageous battle with Parkinson's disease.

heroic

effort | attempt | achievement | act | deed | struggle | resistance | figure

very brave and admired by many people:

The team made a heroic effort to rescue the miners. | Rebuilding the city after the floods was a heroic achievement. | Mandela is a heroic figure for millions.

bold

move | step | decision | attempt | initiative

showing that you are willing to take risks, especially by making difficult decisions or suggesting things that other people may disagree with:

It was a bold move to set up his own company. | We need someone who is not afraid to make bold decisions. | None of his colleagues is ***bold enough*** *to say it in public, but there is a widespread feeling that the president has failed.*

daring

raid | mission | rescue | escape | exploits | robbery | pilot

brave because you are willing to take great risks:

They set off on a daring mission to free the hostages. | The men made a daring escape from prison. | Many people have seen films about the daring exploits of James Bond (=daring and exciting actions).

valiant

effort | attempt | fight | struggle | defender

brave. **Valiant** is often used when someone is unsuccessful, even though they try hard:

The cinema was forced to close down, despite all their valiant efforts. | The team put up a valiant fight, but they lost 2-1.

> **Valiant** is only used before a noun.

adventurous

traveller | visitor | spirit | life

an adventurous person likes going to new places and trying new things, even though they seem unusual or far away:

Jordan has a lot to offer the adventurous traveller. | The old lady has certainly led an adventurous life. | If you are ***feeling adventurous****, there are many unusual dishes you can try.*

intrepid

explorer | traveller | pilot | aviator | astronaut | reporter

willing to go on a dangerous journey or do dangerous things. **Intrepid** sounds rather

formal and is used especially in written descriptions. It is also sometimes used humorously:
A team of intrepid explorers will travel across 5,000 km of unexplored territory. | We sent our intrepid reporter to find out what was going on.

Intrepid is usually used before a noun.

fearless
defender | campaigner | critic | climber | rider | disregard
not frightened of anything or anyone:
A fearless critic of the government, Madhuku has been jailed several times. | He is known for his fearless disregard for his own safety. | They were ***absolutely fearless*** *and had no sense of danger.*

B

bread *n*

a type of food made from flour and water that is mixed together and then baked

ADJECTIVES/NOUNS + bread

white/brown bread *Would you like white bread or brown bread?*
wholemeal bread *BrE* (*also* **wholewheat bread** *AmE*) (=bread made with flour that contains all of the grain) *Wholemeal bread is good for you.*
fresh bread *There's nothing better than the smell of fresh bread.*
stale bread (=hard and no longer fresh) *This bread's stale – shall I throw it away?*
crusty bread (=having a hard crust that is nice to eat) *Serve the soup with crusty bread.*
sliced bread (=cut into pieces when you buy it) *If you buy sliced bread, you don't need a bread knife.*
homemade bread *Homemade bread always tastes better than shop-bought bread.*
artisan bread (=made by a skilled baker, not in a factory) *You can buy delicious artisan bread at the farmers' market.*

VERBS

make/bake bread *We usually make our own bread.*
cut/slice bread *Could you cut me some more bread?*
butter bread (=spread butter on it) *You butter the bread and I'll make up the sandwiches.*

NOUNS + bread

a bread roll *Would you like a bread roll with your soup?*

Breadknife, **breadboard**, and **breadcrumbs** (=small pieces of bread) are usually written as one word.

PHRASES

a loaf of bread *He's gone to buy a loaf of bread.*
a slice/piece of bread *Can I have another slice of bread?*
a hunk/chunk of bread (=a piece that you pull off a loaf) *He tore off a chunk of bread and dipped it in the sauce.*
bread and butter *We had bread and butter with the meal.*
bread and cheese *Lunch was bread and cheese.*

break[1] *v*

1 to damage something, so that it separates into pieces, or to become damaged

break + NOUNS

break your leg/arm etc *She broke her leg while skiing.*
break a cup/dish/plate etc *His mother shouted at him when he broke a cup.*
break a window/mirror *The burglar broke a window to get in.*

ADVERBS

break easily *Old people's bones are fragile and break easily.*

PHRASES

break (sth) in half/two *He broke the biscuit in half and handed one piece to me.*
break (sth) into pieces *Break the chocolate into pieces and melt it over a pan of hot water.*
break off a piece of sth *She broke off a piece of bread.*

THESAURUS: break

smash
to break (something) with a lot of force:
The plate smashed on the stone floor. | Someone smashed his camera.

shatter
to break (something) into a lot of small pieces:
The glass shattered all over the pavement. | The explosion shattered the windows of the building.

crumble
to break (something) into a powder or a lot of very small pieces:
The wood just crumbled in my hand. | Crumble the yeast with your fingers.

split
to separate (something) into two pieces along a straight line:
The wood ***split down the middle****. | Using a sharp knife,* ***split*** *the melon* ***in half****.*

snap
rope | string | cord | stick | branch | twig
to break (something) into two pieces, making a loud noise:
The rope suddenly snapped. | He ***snapped*** *the sticks* ***in two****. | The branch snapped under his weight.*

crack
ice | glass | mirror

if something cracks, a line appears on the surface, which means that it could later break into separate pieces:
The ice was starting to crack. | The glass cracked in the heat. | Do not overtighten the screws or you could crack the mirror.

fracture
arm | leg | wrist | bone | skull
to damage a bone, especially so that a line appears on the surface:
I fell over and fractured my wrist. | Schwarzenegger fractured his thigh bone while skiing in Idaho.

tear
paper | letter | page | photograph | jacket | dress | trousers
to damage paper or cloth by pulling it so that it separates into pieces:
Joe ***tore*** *the paper* ***into*** *tiny* ***pieces****. | She* ***tore up*** *the letter and put it in the bin. | The man* ***tore off*** *a page from his notebook and handed it to me. | I* ***tore*** *my jacket* ***on*** *a piece of metal.*

burst
pipe | balloon | bubble | tyre | dam
if something bursts, it gets a hole in it, and air or liquid suddenly comes out:
The pipes had burst and there was water all over the kitchen floor. | He burst the balloon with a pin.

THESAURUS: break

break, defy, flout, violate, contravene → **disobey**

2 to fail to obey a rule or law, or fail to do something you promised to do

NOUNS

break the law *He said he didn't know he was breaking the law.*

break a rule/regulation *If you break the rules, you can expect to be punished.*

break the speed limit (=drive faster than the speed that is allowed) *He was fined for breaking the speed limit.*

break a promise/vow *I'll never forgive him for breaking his promise to me.*

break your word (=break a promise you made) *I said I would do it and I never break my word.*

break an agreement/contract *He took the company to court for breaking the contract.*

break² *n*

a period of time when you stop doing something before starting again

ADJECTIVES/NOUNS + break

a short/quick break *Shall we have a quick break?*

a five-minute/two-week etc break *The workers were only allowed a 20-minute break.*

a lunch/coffee/tea break *What time's your lunch break?*

a morning/afternoon break *I don't usually have time for a morning break.*

a well-earned break (=one that you deserve) *Everyone's looking forward to a well-earned break when the exams are over.*

VERBS

have/take a break *After two hours, she took a break and switched on the radio.*

need/want a break *I'm sorry, I can't do any more – I need a break.*

PREPOSITIONS

a break from sth *He said he needed a break from politics.*

a break for tea/coffee etc *During the afternoon, there was a break for refreshments.*

a break in sth *The actor was interviewed during a break in filming.*

on a break *Stuart's on his lunch break.*

without a break *Do not work for long periods without a break.*

breakable *adj* THESAURUS ▸ fragile

breakdown *n*

1 a time when a relationship, arrangement, process etc ends because of problems, or becomes very bad

ADJECTIVES/NOUNS + breakdown

a complete/total breakdown *The dispute led to a complete breakdown of their business relationship.*

an irretrievable breakdown *formal* (=one that is impossible to put right again) *The irretrievable breakdown of a marriage can be grounds for divorce.*

marriage/relationship breakdown (*also* **marital breakdown** *formal*): *Violence is sometimes a factor in marital breakdown.*

family breakdown *A growing proportion of children are affected by family breakdown.*

a communication breakdown *The misunderstanding was the result of a communication breakdown.*

VERBS

cause/lead to a breakdown *Money problems often cause marriage breakdown.*

PREPOSITIONS

a breakdown of/in sth *Fighting started again after a breakdown in peace negotiations.*

2 a time when someone becomes mentally ill and is unable to deal with life

ADJECTIVES

a nervous breakdown *I think she's heading for a nervous breakdown.*

a mental/emotional breakdown *Clearly, he is having some kind of mental breakdown.*

a complete breakdown *She had a complete breakdown and had to be admitted to a mental hospital.*

a severe/serious breakdown *He suffered a severe mental breakdown in 1959.*

VERBS

have/suffer a breakdown *After months of stress, he had a breakdown.*

be heading for a breakdown (=be likely to have one soon) *Jo is heading for a breakdown if she doesn't take some time off work.*

PHRASES

on the verge of a breakdown (=very close to having a breakdown) *Amy was on the verge of a nervous breakdown and needed rest and quiet.*

breakfast *n*

the meal you have in the morning

ADJECTIVES

a big breakfast *Most people don't eat a big breakfast nowadays.*

a light breakfast (=a small one) *She ate a light breakfast of toast and coffee.*

a good/proper breakfast (=with plenty of food) *I think kids need a good breakfast before they go to school.*

a quick/hasty/hurried breakfast *I grabbed a quick breakfast and ran to the bus stop.*

a leisurely breakfast (=not hurried) *On Sunday mornings I like to have a leisurely breakfast.*

an early/late breakfast *We had an early breakfast and left before 7.30.*

a full English breakfast (=a big hot breakfast with bacon, egg, toast etc - used especially in hotels) *I'll have the full English breakfast.*

a continental breakfast (=coffee and bread with butter and jam - used especially in hotels) *The charge for the room includes a continental breakfast.*

a cooked/fried breakfast (=bacon, egg, toast etc) *She likes to start the day with a cooked breakfast.*

NOUNS + breakfast

a buffet breakfast (=one in a hotel, where you serve yourself from a range of dishes) *A buffet breakfast is served in the hotel's elegant dining room.*

VERBS

have/eat breakfast *Paul got up and had breakfast.*

have sth for breakfast *I usually have toast for breakfast.*

make breakfast *She wandered into the kitchen to make breakfast.*

finish your breakfast *Hurry up and finish your breakfast.*

skip/miss breakfast (=not eat breakfast) *Be sure to eat at least three meals a day and don't skip breakfast.*

breakfast + NOUNS

the breakfast things/dishes (=plates, spoons, bread etc that you have used at breakfast) *Dad was clearing away the breakfast things.*

(a) breakfast cereal *Many breakfast cereals are high in sugar.*

breakthrough *n*

an important discovery or achievement that happens after trying for a long time

VERBS

make a breakthrough *Detectives think they may have made a breakthrough in their hunt for the murderer.*

achieve a breakthrough *We achieved this breakthrough almost by accident.*

represent a breakthrough *This discovery represents a major breakthrough in the search for a cure.*

a breakthrough comes *The breakthrough came after a day of meetings between management and workers.*

ADJECTIVES

a big/major breakthrough *Researchers believe they are on the verge of a big breakthrough.*

a significant/important breakthrough *The agreement is seen as a significant breakthrough in relations between the two countries.*

a technological/scientific/medical breakthrough *Recent medical breakthroughs have brought fresh hope to people with the disease.*

a historic breakthrough *The president described the trade agreement as a historic breakthrough.*

PREPOSITIONS

a breakthrough in sth *Scientists have made significant breakthroughs in the treatment of breast cancer.*

breath *n*

the air that you take into or send out of your lungs when you breathe

ADJECTIVES

a deep breath (=in which you breathe a lot of air in slowly) *She took a deep breath and knocked on the door.*

a shallow breath (=a quick one that is not deep) *She was taking quick shallow breaths and seemed to be in pain.*

bad breath (=that has an unpleasant smell) *Smoking gives you bad breath.*

VERBS

take a breath (=breathe in) *Pause at the end of the sentence and take a breath.*

hold your breath (=not breathe out for a few seconds or minutes) *How long can you hold your breath underwater?*

let your breath out *Let your breath out slowly and relax.*

draw breath *formal* (=breathe) *I hid behind the door, hardly daring to draw breath.*

get your breath back (*also* **catch your breath**) (=start breathing normally again, especially after resting for a short time) *He had to sit down until he'd got his breath back.*

be gasping for breath (=have difficulty breathing, especially because you have been using a lot of effort) *By the time I reached the bus stop, I was gasping for breath.*

be fighting/struggling for breath (=find it very difficult to breathe) *He stumbled through the smoke, fighting for breath.*

pause for breath (=stop doing something, especially talking) *She talked solidly for five minutes, hardly pausing for breath.*

PHRASES

be out of breath (=have difficulty breathing after running, hurrying etc) *Andrew hurried in, slightly out of breath.*

be short of breath (=be unable to breathe easily, because you are ill) *She was so short of breath that it was an effort to speak.*

shortness of breath (=when you are unable to breathe easily) *Symptoms include dizziness and shortness of breath.*

a sharp intake of breath (=when you breathe in very quickly and suddenly, especially because of shock) *Richard took a sharp intake of breath as the hot cheese burned his tongue.*

breathe *v*

to take air into your lungs and send it out again

ADVERBS

breathe deeply (=take long slow breaths of air) *She breathed deeply in the cool night air.*

breathe heavily/hard (=breathe loudly, especially after exercise) *He was breathing hard by the time he reached the top of the hill.*

breathe fast/rapidly (=breathe quickly because of illness, fear etc) *I noticed that Freddie was breathing rapidly just before he fainted.*

breathe slowly *Breathe slowly and try to relax.*

breathe softly/gently *His wife lay next to him, breathing softly.*

breathe steadily/evenly/regularly *He forced himself to breathe steadily and remain calm.*

breathe normally/properly *The patient said that he felt a sharp pain in his chest and was unable to breathe normally.*

breathe easily *Sucking a mint may help you breathe more easily when you have a cold.*

NOUNS

breathe (in) some air *It was wonderful to be outside and breathe some fresh air.*

breathe (in) fumes (=breathe harmful gas or smoke) *These children are breathing traffic fumes all day long.*

PREPOSITIONS/ADVERBS

breathe in (=take air into your lungs) *It felt good to breathe in some country air.*

breathe out (=send air out) *Breathe out slowly, and relax.*

PHRASES

can/cannot breathe *He held her so tight that she could not breathe.*

can hardly breathe (=breathe with great difficulty) *It was so hot that I felt as though I could hardly breathe.*

breathe through your nose/mouth *This cold makes it hard to breathe through my nose.*

have trouble/difficulty breathing (*also* **struggle to breathe**) *In high altitudes some people have trouble breathing.*

breathing *n*

the process of breathing air in and out

ADJECTIVES

deep breathing *The yoga class starts with some deep breathing exercises.*

shallow breathing (=with small breaths) *She was very ill and her breathing became more shallow.*

heavy breathing (=loud breathing, especially by someone who is sexually excited) *When I picked up the phone, all I heard was heavy breathing.*

sb's breathing is regular *Walk around until your breathing becomes regular again.*

NOUNS

breathing exercises *Breathing exercises can help you relax.*

breathing difficulties/problems *If you develop breathing difficulties, go and see your doctor.*

breathing apparatus/equipment *Firefighters use special breathing apparatus when they go into burning buildings.*

breathtaking *adj* THESAURUS ▸ **impressive**

breeze *n* a gentle wind

ADJECTIVES/NOUNS + breeze

a cool breeze *It was bright and sunny with a cool breeze.*

a warm breeze *The warm breeze blew into the room.*

a gentle/soft/mild breeze *It was a beautiful day with a blue sky and a gentle breeze.*

a light/slight/faint breeze *The curtains moved slightly in the light breeze.*

a stiff/strong breeze *There was a stiff breeze that morning, just right for sailing.*

a cold/chilly breeze *A cold breeze blew off the water.*

a sea/ocean breeze *The boats were moving up and down in the sea breeze.*

a summer breeze *He felt the soft summer breeze against his skin.*

VERBS

a breeze blows *There was a strong breeze blowing when I went out.*

a breeze drifts/wafts (=blows very gently) *A cool breeze drifted through the window.*

a breeze rustles/ruffles/stirs sth (=blows something, making a slight noise) *A light breeze ruffled the leaves in the trees.*

a breeze comes off/from/into etc *There was just a very faint breeze coming off the ocean.*

THESAURUS: breeze

breeze, draught, gale, hurricane, typhoon, tornado, cyclone → **wind**

breezy *adj* THESAURUS **windy**

bribe *n*

money or a gift that you give someone to persuade them to do something for you, especially illegally

VERBS

offer (sb) a bribe *Some of the team were offered bribes to perform badly.*

accept/take a bribe *The judge was charged with taking bribes.*

pay a bribe *It was claimed that the company paid bribes to win the contract.*

give (sb) a bribe *He was arrested for trying to give the policeman a bribe.*

bridge *n*

a structure built over a river, road etc that allows people or vehicles to cross from one side to the other

NOUNS + bridge

a railway bridge *BrE*, **a railroad bridge** *AmE*: *Go under the railway bridge and turn right.*

a road bridge *The government plans to construct a new road bridge to the island.*

a suspension bridge (=one that hangs from strong steel ropes) *San Francisco has a famous suspension bridge.*

a toll bridge (=one that you pay to go across) *There is a toll bridge across the River Severn when you go into Wales.*

VERBS

build a bridge (*also* **construct a bridge** *formal*): *The bridge was built in 1902.*

cross a bridge *An estimated 150,000 cars cross the bridge each day.*

a bridge crosses sth *A pretty stone bridge crosses the little river.*

a bridge spans sth *formal* (=crosses a wide area) *By 1875 a railroad bridge spanned the Missouri.*

a bridge links/connects sth with sth *There's a bridge linking the island with the mainland.*

PREPOSITIONS

a bridge across/over sth *We walked across one of the bridges over the River Avon.*

over/across a bridge *We drove around the harbour and came back over the bridge.*

brief Ac *adj* continuing for a short time

NOUNS

a brief period/time *He lived there all his life, apart from a brief period during the war.*

a brief spell (=a short time) *After a brief spell in teaching, Sarah started her own business.*

a brief moment *The old lady's gaze rested on her for a brief moment.*

a brief pause *There was a brief pause before he replied.*

a brief visit/stay *The president met other world leaders during a brief visit to Geneva.*

a brief look/glance/glimpse *He gave her a brief look.*

a brief appearance *He made a brief appearance in front of reporters outside his home.*

VERBS

keep/make sth brief *Let's keep this conversation brief – I have a plane to catch.*

ADVERBS

relatively brief *The relatively brief period of time he spent in Australia changed his life.*

THESAURUS: brief

brief, quick, temporary, short-lived, short-term, fleeting, momentary, passing, ephemeral → **short (1)**

brief, concise, succinct, pithy → **short (3)**

bright *adj*

1 shining strongly, or with plenty of light

NOUNS

bright light *The bright light hurt his eyes.*

bright sunlight/sunshine/sun *He walked out into the bright sunlight.*

a bright day/morning *It was a bright sunny morning.*

a bright sky *Ella loved the bright skies of southern Australia.*

a bright room (=with plenty of light) *The room is bright and spacious.*

a bright star *Betelgeux is one of the brightest stars in the night sky.*

a bright flash *There was a bright flash in the sky and then a rumble of thunder.*

ADVERBS

blindingly/dazzlingly bright (=in a way that hurts your eyes) *The sun was already dazzlingly bright.*

THESAURUS: bright

strong
light | **sunlight**
strong light is very bright:
The plant grows best in strong light. | *Photographs fade if they are exposed to strong sunlight.*

brilliant
light | **sunshine** | **sun** | **moon**
brilliant light is extremely bright:
Brilliant light streamed through the window. | *The garden was full of brilliant spring sunshine.*

Brilliant is only used before a noun.

dazzling
light
a dazzling light is so bright that you cannot look at it:
The dazzling light of a torch shone in his eyes.

blinding
light | **flash** | **glare**
a blinding light is very bright and makes you unable to see for a short time after you have looked at it:
There was a sudden blinding light, followed by a huge explosion. | *A blinding flash lit up the sky.*

harsh
light | **sunlight** | **glare**
a harsh light is too bright and is unpleasant to look at:
In the harsh light of the kitchen, she looked older than she was. | *The goggles protect your eyes from the harsh glare of the snow.*

light
room | **space**
a light building or room is bright because there are big windows:
The dining room was light and airy. | *I need a nice light space in which to work.*

well-lit
area | **room** | **street** | **office**
a well-lit place has plenty of light and it is easy to see clearly, usually because of electric lights:
Always park in a well-lit area. | *The well-lit streets were full of people.*

THESAURUS: bright

good, fine, nice, bright, beautiful/glorious, clear, cloudless, dry → **sunny**

2 bright colours are strong and not pale

NOUNS

a bright colour *The room was painted in bright colours.*

bright red/yellow/blue etc *Wendy always wears bright red lipstick.*

a bright shade *His face went a bright shade of purple.*

THESAURUS: bright

brilliant
very bright:
Dancers dressed in ***brilliant colours*** *filled the stage.* | ***Brilliant white*** *walls give the room a light feel.*

Brilliant is only used before a noun.

vivid
very strong and bright, especially in a way that is attractive:
The sky was a ***vivid blue****.* | *Fish have such beautiful* ***vivid colours****.*

vibrant
very strong and bright, especially in a way that is exciting:
These rich ***vibrant colours*** *look lovely with dark hair.* | *The room was decorated in* ***vibrant reds*** *and greens.*

dazzling
a dazzling white colour is extremely bright to look at:
The boy had ***dazzling white*** *teeth.* | *The beach is famous for its* ***dazzling white*** *sands.*

garish
too bright and unpleasant to look at:
He uses rather ***garish colours*** *in his paintings.* | *The door was painted a* ***garish yellow****.* | *Her clothes* ***looked garish*** *and cheap.*

3 intelligent

THESAURUS: bright

clever, smart, bright, brilliant, gifted, wise, cunning, brainy → **intelligent**

brilliant *adj* THESAURUS **bright (1)**, **(2)**, **clever (2)**, **intelligent**

brisk *adj* THESAURUS **fast[1] (1)**

brittle *adj* THESAURUS **fragile**, **hard (1)**

broad *adj*

1 measuring a long distance across

THESAURUS: broad

broad, thick → **wide (1)**

2 consisting of a lot of different types of things

THESAURUS: broad

broad → **wide (2)**

B

broadband *n*

a system for using the internet that allows you to stay connected all the time

ADJECTIVES

high-speed broadband *With high-speed broadband you can download films and videos very quickly.*

VERBS

have broadband *Do you have broadband at home?*

broadband + NOUNS

a broadband provider (=a company that provides broadband) *Which is the cheapest broadband provider?*

a broadband connection *I can't send the email because my broadband connection isn't working.*

broadband speed *My broadband speed is really slow.*

broadband access *Some areas do not have broadband access.*

broadcast *n*

a programme on the radio or on television

ADJECTIVES/NOUNS + broadcast

a live broadcast (=one shown at the same time as events are happening) *NBC produced a 30-minute live broadcast from the White House.*

a radio/television broadcast *The president addressed the nation in a live television broadcast.*

a satellite broadcast *The match was shown live in a worldwide satellite broadcast.*

a news broadcast *His death was reported on the BBC's evening news broadcast.*

an election broadcast (=one shown before an election to persuade people to vote for a party) *The Labour Party's election broadcast was seen by an audience of 10 million.*

a party political broadcast (=made in order to advertise a political party) *That was a party political broadcast on behalf of the Conservative Party.*

> An **internet broadcast** is often called a **webcast**: *The **webcast** is aimed at young people.*

VERBS

make/do/produce a broadcast *The charity made a television broadcast appealing for money.*

give a broadcast *The Queen gives a television broadcast to the nation every Christmas.*

watch/hear/listen to a broadcast *Most viewers who watched the broadcast agreed with the president.*

brochure *n*

a thin book giving information or advertising something

ADJECTIVES

a free brochure *Would you like a copy of our free brochure?*

a colour brochure *Please write or call for our colour brochure.*

a glossy brochure (=with shiny pages) *Products always look nice in glossy brochures.*

NOUNS + brochure

a travel/tourist brochure (*also* **holiday brochure** *BrE*): *We've looked in all the travel brochures, but can't decide where to go on our vacation.*

a company/college/hotel brochure *I'll send you a copy of our company brochure.*

a sales brochure *The kitchen looks just like the one in the sales brochure.*

a course brochure *You'll find details about the English class in the course brochure.*

VERBS

read a brochure *The first step is to read the course brochure, then complete the application form.*

flick through a brochure (=look at the pages quickly) *She was flicking through a brochure about kitchen products.*

it says in the brochure (that)... *It says in the brochure that the price includes all your meals and accommodation.*

broken *adj*

1 damaged and split into pieces

NOUNS

a broken leg/arm/nose/bone *A broken arm can take several weeks to heal.*

broken glass/a broken window *He stepped on some broken glass and cut his foot.*

a broken bottle/cup/plate *I tried to glue the broken plate together.*

broken furniture/chair *We repair broken furniture.*

VERBS

get broken *How did the window get broken?*

2 if a machine is broken, it does not work: *The washing machine is broken. | My watch is broken.*

THESAURUS: broken

down
computers | system | network
if a computer system is down, it is not working, usually for a short period:
Our computers are down at the moment, so I can't check. | The system was down all afternoon, so we went home. | The network went down at 11.00 p.m.

out of order
toilet | elevator | lift | photocopier
not working – used about things that are used by the public:
The toilets were all out of order. | We had to use the stairs because the elevator was out of order.

You can say that a machine **doesn't work** or **won't work**: *The photocopier* ***won't work****.*

You say that an engine or car **won't start**: *I was late for work because the car* ***wouldn't start****.*

In spoken English, you can also say that part of a machine or vehicle **has gone**: *The hard drive on my laptop* ***has gone****.*

brother *n*

a boy or man who has the same parents as you

ADJECTIVES/NOUNS + brother

an older/elder brother *I have two older brothers.*

a big brother (=older brother - more informal) *Jake was my big brother and I admired him.*

a younger brother *Do you have any younger brothers?*

a little/kid brother (=younger brother - more informal) *My little brother was always annoying me.*

a baby brother (=one who is a baby, or who is much younger) *Mum let me hold my new baby brother.*

a twin brother *Luke and his twin brother Sam went everywhere together.*

a half-brother (=the son of just one of your parents) *I never really liked my half-brother.*

brown *adj, n*

the colour of earth, wood, or coffee

TYPES OF BROWN

light/pale/soft brown *Her hair was light brown.*

dark/deep brown *He removed his dark brown jacket.*

rich brown *Cook the butter and sugar until the mixture turns a rich brown colour.*

dull/muddy brown *The carpet is a rather unattractive dull brown.*

reddish brown *Some of the leaves had reddish brown spots.*

golden brown *Cook until the cheese on top is golden brown.*

chestnut brown (=a red-brown colour) *She had glossy chestnut brown hair.*

chocolate brown (=dark brown) *He was dressed in a chocolate brown suit.*

PREPOSITIONS

in brown *He was dressed in brown.*

brush[1] *n*

a tool with hairs or plastic threads fastened to a handle, used for cleaning, painting, making your hair tidy etc

ADJECTIVES

a fine brush (=a thin brush) *Using a fine brush, paint eyes and a mouth on the doll.*

a soft brush *I clean my teeth with a very soft brush.*

a stiff brush *Scrub the wood thoroughly with water and a stiff brush.*

NOUNS + brush

a clothes brush *BrE* (=used for removing dust from clothes) *He used a clothes brush to remove the dust from his jacket.*

a scrubbing brush *BrE*, **a scrub brush** *AmE* (=a stiff brush used for cleaning things) *I had to get down on my knees with a scrubbing brush to clean the floor.*

Paintbrush, **toothbrush**, **hairbrush**, and **nailbrush** are usually written as one word.

VERBS

use a brush *If you look at the painting closely, you can see how the artist uses his brush.*

clean sth with a brush *Houseplants can be cleaned with a soft brush.*

put sth on with a brush (*also* **apply sth with a brush** *formal*): *The paint is applied with a brush or a roller.*

brush + NOUNS

a brush stroke (=a mark made with a paintbrush) *You can see the brush strokes when you look closely at the painting.*

PHRASES

a dustpan and brush (=a special container for putting dust etc in and a brush) *She got a dustpan and brush and swept up the broken glass.*

brush[2] *v* THESAURUS clean[2]

brutal *adj* THESAURUS cruel (1)

bubble *n* a ball of air or gas

NOUNS + bubble

an air/gas bubble *Gas bubbles in any liquid tend to rise to the surface.*

bubble + VERBS

a bubble bursts/pops *The bubble got bigger and bigger until it burst.*

a bubble forms *Bubbles began to form as the liquid started to boil.*

a bubble floats *The bubbles are floating on the surface of the water.*

VERBS + bubble

blow bubbles *The children were blowing bubbles in the air.*

form bubbles *The gas in the beer forms bubbles.*

burst a bubble *He burst the bubble with his finger.*

budget *n*

the money that is available to someone, or a plan of how it will be spent

B

ADJECTIVES/NOUNS + budget

an annual/monthly/weekly budget *The organization has an annual budget of $24 million.*

a big/large budget *He does not have enough experience to manage a large budget.*

a small/low/limited budget *If you have a limited budget, this is a good machine to buy.*

a tight budget (=small for what you want to do) *Most young people have to live within a tight budget.*

a fixed budget *Our clients usually have a fixed budget.*

a shoestring budget (=very small) *The film had been made on a shoestring budget.*

a total/overall budget *The National Institute of Health had a total budget of $11 billion.*

the family/household budget *Often the husband and wife contribute equally to the family budget.*

the government/national/federal/state budget *He has a plan to balance the federal budget.*

the defence/education/welfare etc budget *The government had to make cuts in the defence budget.*

the training/advertising/research etc budget *Most of the advertising budget is spent on TV promotion.*

VERBS

have a budget *I have a budget of 5,000 euros to buy a new car.*

give sb/get a budget *They were given a budget of $20 million.*

overspend your budget *The school has overspent its budget by £10,000.*

keep/stay within a budget (=spend only the money that is available) *Further cuts are needed in order to keep within the budget.*

balance the budget (=spend only the money that is available) *They have to save 8 million euros to balance the budget.*

manage/control a budget *In many homes, it is the woman who controls the budget.*

set a budget (=decide how much it will be) *We set the budget at the beginning of the financial year.*

reduce/increase a budget *The health budget was increased by 6%.*

budget + NOUNS

budget cuts *The department has suffered severe budget cuts.*

a budget deficit/shortfall (=when a government has spent more money than it has) *The country has a budget deficit of over $4 billion.*

PREPOSITIONS

a budget for sth *We only have a small budget for furniture.*

within budget (=not spending more than you planned) *The project was completed within budget.*

under budget (=spending less than you planned) *If you come in under budget, everyone will be very impressed.*

over budget (=spending more than you planned) *Feature movies always run over budget.*

on a budget of $100/£50/€1,000 etc *She has to feed her family on a budget of less than £50 per week.*

on a budget (=with only a small amount of money) *We'll show you how to arrange a wedding on a budget.*

buff *n* THESAURUS ▸ fan

bug *n* a fault in a computer program

ADJECTIVES

a serious/major bug *There have been reports of serious bugs in the latest version of the software.*

a minor bug *The program has several minor but annoying bugs.*

NOUNS + bug

a software/computer bug *Software bugs threaten the safety of the country's nuclear power stations.*

VERBS

sth has a bug (in it) *The software had a bug in it.*

fix a bug *They have now fixed all the bugs in the system.*

PREPOSITIONS

a bug in the software/a program/the system etc *The error was caused by a bug in the software.*

build[1] *v*

to make a building, bridge, road etc

NOUNS

build a house/home *Hundreds of new houses are being built.*

build a road/railway line *Instead of building more roads, we should be encouraging people to use public transport.*

build a bridge/tunnel *A Japanese company won the contract to build the bridge across the harbour.*

build a factory/school/hospital/airport etc *The firm is building a $20 million factory in Fremont, California.*

build a wall/fence/barrier *Qin Shi Huang unified China and began to build the Great Wall.*

Other things that you build

Build is also used about making other things such as cars and boats: *Jaguar **cars** are **built** in the UK. | The 'Titanic' was the largest **ship** ever **built**.*

You also use **build** about birds making their

nests: *The birds* **build** *their* **nests** *high up on the cliffs.*

When talking about tents, you say **put up** a **tent** (not 'build' it).

PREPOSITIONS

be built of/from/out of sth (=using a particular material) *The houses were built of stone.*

build sth on sth *People built their homes on land near the river.*

THESAURUS: build

construct *formal*
building | **house** | **bridge** | **tunnel** | **road** | **railway line** | **airport** | **school** | **factory**
to build something, especially a large building, a bridge etc. **Construct** is more formal than **build**:
The present building was constructed in 1860. | *They are planning to construct a bridge across the River Thames.* | *The authorities have approved a plan to construct a new airport.* | *The houses were* **constructed out of** *bricks.*

put up
fence | **wall** | **barrier** | **tent** | **statue** | **monument** | **memorial**
to build or put something somewhere:
The neighbours have put up a new wooden fence. | *Can you help me put up the tent?* | *They are planning to put up a statue in Bradman's honour.*

erect *formal*
statue | **monument** | **memorial** | **barrier** | **fence** | **wall** | **tent** | **building**
to build or put something somewhere:
The city authorities erected a statue in his honour. | *The Berlin Wall was erected in August 1961.* | *The army began erecting tents for the refugees.*

Erect or **put up?**
These words mean the same. **Erect** is more formal, and is often used about statues and other public monuments: *A monument* **was erected** *in the city's main square.* **Erect** is often used in the passive.
Put up is not normally used in the passive, and is the normal word to use in everyday conversation, especially when talking about fences and tents: *Do you know how to* **put up** *a tent?* (You wouldn't use 'erect' when asking someone about this in everyday English.)

assemble
cars | **trucks** | **computers** | **products** | **furniture**
to put all the parts of something such as a machine or piece of furniture together:
BMW has announced plans to assemble cars in India. | *The instructions tell you how to assemble the furniture.*

You can also say that new houses/hotels etc are **going up** or **springing up** (=a lot of them are being built): *Fancy new homes are* **going up** *everywhere.* | *New hotels and businesses are* **springing up** *all along the coast.*

build² *n*

the shape and size of someone's body

Grammar
Build is most commonly used in the phrase **of medium/heavy/slim etc build**.

ADJECTIVES

medium/average build *The thief was of medium build and wearing a light-coloured jacket.*

heavy build (=big and fat) *The floor will not support someone of heavy build.*

slim/slender/slight build *She was very strong despite her slender build.*

muscular/powerful/athletic build *These exercises will help you achieve a muscular build.*

PHRASES

have the build of an athlete/rugby player/wrestler etc *He had the build of a wrestler so I didn't try to push past him.*

building *n*

a structure such as a house, church, or factory

ADJECTIVES/NOUNS + building

a tall building *Central Park is surrounded by tall buildings.*

a high-rise building (=with many levels) *There are a lot of high-rise buildings in Hong Kong.*

a low-rise building (=with only a small number of levels) *Most people prefer to live in low-rise buildings.*

a two-storey/three-storey etc building (=with two, three etc levels) *Our villa was a delightful two-storey building.*

a single-storey/one-storey building (=with only one floor) *The village school was a one-storey building made of stone.*

a brick/stone/wooden building *The farmhouse is a long stone building about a century old.*

an office/school/hospital etc building *Our office building is close to where I live.*

a public building *The town has a number of interesting public buildings, including the old town hall.*

a beautiful/fine/handsome building *The old station was a fine building, but has sadly been demolished.*

B

a historic building (=an old building of historical interest) *Most of the historic buildings are from the 18th century.*
a derelict building (=empty and in very bad condition) *Near the canal there are a number of derelict buildings.*

VERBS

design a building *He wanted to design a building that people would enjoy visiting.*
put up a building (*also* **erect a building** *formal*) (=build it) *They're putting up a lot of new buildings around here.*
convert a building (=change it so it can be used for something different) *The building has been converted into apartments.*
demolish a building (*also* **pull down/knock down/tear down a building** *more informal*): *All the old buildings were demolished.*

bullet *n*

a small piece of metal that you fire from a gun

VERBS + bullet

fire a bullet *Police fired rubber bullets into the crowd.*
spray bullets (=fire a lot of bullets) *The soldier lifted the machine gun and sprayed bullets at the wall.*

bullet + VERBS

a bullet hits/strikes sb/sth *The first bullet hit him in the back.*
a bullet misses sb/sth *The bullet narrowly missed her heart.*
a bullet flies somewhere *Bullets were flying around our heads.*
a bullet whistles past (=moves fast making a noise) *I heard a bullet whistle past me.*
a bullet ricochets off sth (=hits something and moves away from it again) *The bullet ricocheted off a wall.*

bullet + NOUNS

a bullet wound *He was brought into hospital with a bullet wound in his leg.*
a bullet hole *There were two bullet holes in the windscreen.*

ADJECTIVES

a stray bullet (=one that is not intended to hit that person or thing) *He was tragically killed by a stray bullet.*

PHRASES

a hail/volley of bullets (=a lot of bullets fired together) *Officers were met by a hail of bullets from the house.*
be riddled with bullets (=be hit by a lot of bullets) *The car was riddled with bullets.*

bulletin *n*

a short news report, or a short statement giving information

NOUNS + bulletin

a news bulletin *We interrupt this program to bring you a special news bulletin.*
an information bulletin *The club produces a weekly information bulletin.*
a radio/television bulletin *The standard television bulletin lasts 15 minutes.*
a weather bulletin *The weather bulletin said it was going to rain.*

ADJECTIVES

an electronic/online bulletin *The college's online bulletin is updated every few days.*
an official bulletin *An official bulletin will be released to the press later today.*
an hourly/daily/weekly/monthly etc bulletin *They broadcast an hourly news bulletin about the storm.*
a regular bulletin *The club produces a regular bulletin informing members about interesting events.*
the latest bulletin *The latest bulletin is now available online.*

VERBS

issue/release/put out a bulletin *The office issued a bulletin warning people about the storm.*
broadcast a bulletin *National television broadcast regular bulletins about the president's medical condition.*

bumpy *adj* THESAURUS rough (1)

bunch *n*

a group of things that are fastened, held, or growing together

PHRASES

a bunch of flowers/roses/herbs etc *I picked a bunch of flowers from the garden.*
a bunch of grapes/bananas/fruit *She served the cheese with a bunch of black grapes.*
a bunch of keys *A bunch of keys dangled from his belt.*

burden *n*

something difficult or worrying that you have to deal with

ADJECTIVES

a heavy/great/huge/terrible burden *Caring for elderly relatives can be a heavy burden.*
an intolerable burden (=one that is too hard for someone to deal with) *Too many exams can place an intolerable burden on young people.*
an unfair/undue burden *The new legislation put an unfair burden on employers.*
a financial burden *Paying for extra staff would impose too great a financial burden on schools.*

NOUNS + burden

the tax burden *These changes will ease the tax burden for small businesses.*

VERBS

be/become a burden *I don't want to be a burden to my children when I'm old.*

bear/carry a burden (=have something difficult or worrying to deal with) *At the age of 16, Suzy bore the burden of providing for her family.*

shoulder/take a burden (=accept responsibility for something) *Why should taxpayers shoulder this burden?*

place/put a burden on sb (*also* **impose a burden on sb** *formal*): *This situation places the main burden of family care on women.*

share the burden *I was glad my brother was there to share the burden.*

shift the burden onto sb (=put it onto someone else) *These changes are intended to shift the burden of paying for pollution from the taxpayer to the polluter.*

ease/reduce/lighten the burden *Smaller classes would ease the burden for teachers.*

a burden falls on/upon sb *The tax burden falls most heavily upon the poorest people.*

PREPOSITIONS

the burden on sb *This would reduce the burden on those least able to pay.*

be a burden to sb *The house is a burden to us and I don't think we can keep paying for it.*

PHRASES

the burden of responsibility *He felt unable to cope with the burden of responsibility.*

a burden of guilt *She carried a heavy burden of guilt for not having been able to protect her child.*

lift the burden from sb's shoulders (=take it away or make it less severe) *I feel as if a great burden has been lifted from my shoulders.*

bureaucracy *n*

a very complicated official system with a lot of rules

ADJECTIVES

unnecessary/excessive bureaucracy *People are always complaining about the amount of unnecessary bureaucracy in local government.*

a faceless bureaucracy (=in which you do not have human contact with someone) *Many big organizations seem like faceless bureaucracies.*

NOUNS + bureaucracy

government/state bureaucracy *There is so much government bureaucracy that it is difficult for people to set up their own business.*

VERBS

cut/reduce bureaucracy *Teachers want to cut bureaucracy in schools.*

increase/create more bureaucracy *The new system will only create more bureaucracy for farmers.*

deal with bureaucracy *Small businesses have to deal with a lot of bureaucracy.*

In more informal English, people often use the phrase **red tape** when talking about unnecessary rules and regulations: *There's a mountain of* ***red tape*** *to get through, before you can get a visa.*

burn[1] *v*

1 to produce flames

NOUNS

a fire burns *There was a wood fire burning in the front room.*

a candle/cigarette burns *She left a candle burning next to her bed.*

a house/building/forest/car etc burns *The trees were still burning.*

ADVERBS

burn down (=be destroyed by fire) *If your house burned down, would the insurance cover it?*

burn brightly *A coal fire was burning brightly in the kitchen.*

burn fiercely *Many buildings were burning fiercely.*

burn steadily *The candle burned steadily.*

burn merrily (=in a way that looks cheerful) *A fire burned merrily in the grate.*

PHRASES

burn to the ground (=be completely destroyed by fire) *The building burned to the ground after it was struck by lightning.*

burn out of control *The fire has been burning out of control for three days.*

THESAURUS: burn

blaze
fire
to burn very brightly with a lot of flames and heat:
They had their meal in the dining room, where a lovely fire was blazing.

flicker
flame | candle | fire
to burn with an unsteady light that appears and disappears quickly:
They watched the flames flicker in the fireplace. | The candle flickered in the wind. | The fire flickered and then went out.

smoulder *BrE*, **smolder** *AmE*
cigarette | cigar | fire
to burn slowly and continuously, producing smoke but no flames:
A cigarette smouldered in the ashtray. | The fire was still smouldering a week later.

B

You can also say that a building, vehicle etc is **on fire**: *Someone said our house was **on fire**.* If something is burning with a lot of flames, you can say that it is **ablaze** or **alight**: *Soon, the whole city was **ablaze**. | By the time the fire engines got there, the factory was **alight**.*

B

2 to hurt someone or damage something with fire or something hot

NOUNS

burn your hand/fingers/tongue etc *She burned her hand on a hot pan.*

burn a letter/document etc *Burn this letter after you read it.*

burn a hole in sth *The cigarette had burned a hole in the carpet.*

ADVERBS

be badly/severely burned *His face had been badly burned in the fire.*

burn a house/building etc down (=destroy it with fire) *They threatened to burn our house down.*

PHRASES

be burned to the ground (=be completely destroyed by fire) *The entire village was burned to the ground.*

be burned to death *Anyone inside the truck would have been burned to death.*

be burned at the stake (=be burned in a fire as a punishment) *In those days, witches were burned at the stake.*

THESAURUS: burn

set fire to sth (*also* **set sth on fire**)
to make something start burning so that it gets damaged:
Protesters set fire to cars. | Sparks from the fireplace could have set the rug on fire.

scorch
to damage the surface of something by burning it so that a dark mark is left on it:
I accidentally scorched my shirt with the iron. | The heater was left on all night and it scorched the wall.

scald
yourself | tongue | mouth | skin
to burn yourself with very hot liquid or steam:
I scalded myself with boiling water. | The coffee was so hot it scalded his tongue.

singe
hair | eyebrows | moustache | beard | fingers | fur
to damage something by burning it slightly so that the ends or edges are burned:
I singed the hairs on my arm. | The flames were hot enough to singe your eyebrows.

ignite *technical*
fuel | oil | petrol | fire | gas | fumes | vapour
to make something start to burn:
The gas is ignited by an electrical spark. | It appears that he lit a cigarette which ignited the petrol fumes.

burn² *n*

an injury caused by fire, heat, or chemicals

ADJECTIVES/NOUNS + burn

serious/severe/terrible burns *The man suffered serious burns.*

minor/superficial burns (=not serious) *She is being treated for minor burns.*

a cigarette burn *His body was covered in cigarette burns.*

first-degree burns/second-degree burns/third-degree burns *He has third-degree burns and will spend months in hospital.*

Different levels of burns
First-degree burns are not serious and the skin is red and a little painful. **Second-degree burns** are more serious and there are blisters on the skin. **Third-degree burns** are extremely serious and painful, and the skin is badly damaged.

VERBS

have burns *He had burns to his legs.*

suffer/receive burns *A firefighter suffered serious burns when he tried to rescue two people from a burning house.*

cause burns *Some chemicals can cause burns if you spill them on your skin.*

burn + NOUNS

a burn mark *You can still see the burn mark on my hand.*

burst *v* THESAURUS **break¹ (1)**

bus *n*

a large vehicle that people pay to travel on

VERBS

go/travel by bus *I usually go to work by bus.*

go on the bus/use the bus (=travel by bus) *It's easier to go on the bus than to drive.*

get/take/catch a bus *I took a bus to San Francisco.*

ride a bus *AmE*: *It was the first time Craig had ridden a bus downtown by himself.*

get on/off a bus *Several more passengers got on the bus.*

wait for a bus *We were waiting for the bus for half an hour.*

miss the bus (=be too late to get on it) *He woke up late and missed the bus.*

a bus goes/leaves *The last bus went ten minutes ago.*

a bus comes/arrives *I waited and waited but the bus didn't come.*

buses run (=go at regular times) *The buses run less frequently on a Sunday.*

ADJECTIVES

a bus is full *The bus was full, so we had to wait for the next one.*

a bus is late *Sometimes the bus is late, and we're late for school.*

a crowded bus *He made his way to the front of the crowded bus.*

the last bus *The last bus is at midnight.*

a double-decker bus (=one with two levels for passengers) *London is famous for its red double-decker buses.*

NOUNS + bus

a school bus *I saw her waiting for the school bus.*

a shuttle bus (=one that makes regular short journeys between two places) *There's a shuttle bus between the hotel and the beach.*

bus + NOUNS

a bus ride/journey/trip *It's a 20-minute bus ride into town.*

a bus lane (=a part of the road where only buses are allowed to drive) *You can be fined for driving in a bus lane.*

a bus service *It's a small village but there is a good bus service.*

a bus driver *The bus driver asked everyone to move down the bus.*

a bus stop *Let's get off at the next bus stop.*

a bus station *Dad met me at the bus station.*

a bus ticket *He checked our bus tickets.*

a bus pass (=a card that allows you to make several bus journeys) *Most of the students have a monthly bus pass.*

a bus fare (=the money you pay for a bus journey) *I didn't have enough money for my bus fare.*

a bus timetable *BrE*, **a bus schedule** *AmE*: *The bus timetable changes on January 31st.*

PREPOSITIONS

by bus *The best way to get there is by bus.*

on a bus *There were a lot of people on the bus.*

the bus to/from a place *The bus to the beach takes 10 minutes.*

the bus for a place (=that you use to go there) *Is this the bus for the city centre?*

business *n*

1 the activity of making money by producing or buying and selling goods, or providing services

VERBS

do business *They are starting to do business in China and India.*

conduct/carry on business *formal* (=do business) *I like the way they conduct their business.*

go into business (=start working in business) *A lot of university graduates want to go into business.*

set up/start up in business *The bank gave me a loan to help me set up in business.*

stay in business (=continue operating) *Some stores are finding it hard to stay in business.*

go out of business (=stop doing business because of financial problems) *In a recession, smaller firms often go out of business.*

⚠ Don't say 'make business'. Say **do business**.

business + NOUNS

a business deal *She was just about to complete a big business deal.*

a business meeting *He was late for an important business meeting.*

a business trip *Her father was frequently away on business trips.*

business activities *Her family did not know anything about her business activities.*

business interests (=business activities, or shares in companies) *Both companies have substantial business interests in Indonesia.*

a business plan *Together, they came up with a business plan.*

a business venture (=a new business activity that involves taking risks) *It is unwise to invest all your money in one business venture.*

a business leader *Business leaders have said that barriers to trade should be removed.*

NOUNS + business

the music/entertainment/computer etc business *She has been in the music business for thirty years.*

PREPOSITIONS

in business *By his early twenties he was in business as a printer.*

on business (=in connection with your work) *Are you here on business?*

THESAURUS: business

trade
the buying and selling of goods and services, especially between countries:
Trade between European countries became easier after the introduction of the euro. | The two countries signed a ***trade agreement***.

commerce
the buying and selling of goods and services. **Commerce** is more formal than **business**, and is used when talking about business activities in general:
One of the roles of the federal government is to regulate commerce. | London became a great ***centre of commerce***. *| the local* ***chamber of commerce*** (=an organization which the companies and shops in an area belong to)

B

e-commerce
the buying and selling of goods and services on the internet:
E-commerce is a fast-growing part of the US economy.

2 an organization that produces or sells goods or provides a service for money

VERBS + business

have/own a business *He had always wanted to have his own business.*

run a business *His daughter Susan now runs the business.*

start/set up a business *When you're starting a business, you have to work long hours.*

establish a business *She overcame many financial difficulties to establish her business.*

build (up)/develop a business *He spent years trying to build a business in Antigua.*

grow a business (=make it larger) *We borrowed money to help us grow the business.*

expand a business *He has had to expand his business to cope with demand.*

take over a business (=take control of it) *When my father retired, I took over the business.*

business + VERBS

a business does well/thrives/flourishes (=it is successful) *The business thrived, and they opened two more stores.*

a business collapses/fails *Thirty percent of small businesses fail in the first year of operation.*

ADJECTIVES/NOUNS + business

big business (=big companies in general) *Big business does so much damage to the environment.*

a small/medium-sized business *Hundreds of small businesses have closed.*

a successful/profitable/thriving business *Within a few years she had established a thriving business in London.*

a software/publishing/construction/furniture etc business *He and his brother run a construction business.*

an import/export business *Kingwell had an export business in New Zealand.*

a family business (=owned and controlled by one family) *For many years the hotel was a family business.*

business + NOUNS

a business partner *Margie was his wife and also his business partner.*

a business manager *We need to take on a business manager.*

3 the amount of work a company does

ADJECTIVES

business is good/brisk *People want our products and business is good.*

business is bad/slow *During the recession, business was very bad.*

business is down (=not as good as before) *Business is down over last year.*

new business *What is the best way to get new business for your company?*

business + VERBS

business is booming (=is very good and increasing) *Business is booming for mobile phone companies.*

business picks up (=becomes better) *Hopefully, business will pick up soon.*

VERBS + business

do good/brisk business (=sell a lot) *The fish market does brisk business every morning.*

get/win/attract business *They have been cutting their prices to win business.*

generate business *Karen will focus on generating new business from existing clients.*

drum up business (=try to get more work) *She took her product to shows and exhibitions to drum up business.*

compete for business *The two companies were competing for business.*

lose business *Local shops lost business when the road was temporarily closed.*

businessman/businesswoman *n*

a man or woman who works in business

ADJECTIVES

a successful businessman/businesswoman *Her aim was to become a successful businesswoman.*

a wealthy/rich businessman/businesswoman *The ship was owned by a wealthy businessman.*

a good businessman/businesswoman (=good at doing business) *She had researched the costs, like any good businesswoman.*

a shrewd/astute businessman/businesswoman (=able to understand situations in business and make good decisions) *Are you a shrewd businessman, quick to see how to make a profit?*

a leading/prominent businessman/businesswoman *In many cities, prominent businessmen financed city centre improvements.*

busy *adj*

1 if you are busy, you have a lot to do

NOUNS

a busy person/man/woman *He's a very busy man and he doesn't have much free time.*

a busy day/week/weekend *You look like you've had a busy day.*

a busy time *The start of term is always a busy time for teachers.*

a busy life *I sometimes wish my life wasn't so busy.*

a busy schedule *The president has a very busy schedule.*

ADVERBS

too busy *Many people say they are too busy to do any exercise.*

really/extremely busy *I've been really busy recently, and haven't had time to write to him.*

VERBS

keep sb busy *I have enough work to keep me busy.*

PREPOSITIONS

busy with sb/sth *Mr Haynes is busy with a customer at the moment.*

THESAURUS: busy

hectic
day | morning | week | schedule | life | lifestyle | round
used about a time when you are very busy:
It's been a very hectic day at the office. | She has taken some time out of her hectic schedule to be here with us today. | Her life was a hectic round of parties (=she had to go to a lot of them). | ***Things have been hectic*** *all day.*

THESAURUS: busy

packed, busy, overcrowded, teeming → **crowded**

2 full of people or vehicles and a lot of activity

NOUNS

a busy road/street *Take care when crossing busy roads.*

a busy intersection/junction *The two cars collided at a busy intersection.*

a busy place *Hospitals are busy places.*

a busy city/town *London is a huge busy city.*

a busy airport/station/port *Chicago is known for its busy port.*

a shop/store/restaurant is busy *The stores are always busy just before Christmas.*

VERBS

get busy *It was 8 p.m. and the restaurant was getting busy.*

THESAURUS: busy

crowded
room | hall | shop | store | street | city | train | bus | boat | station | airport | restaurant
full of people:
She looked around the crowded room for her friend. | He pushed his way through the narrow crowded streets. | We met in a crowded sushi restaurant. | The town is always ***crowded with*** *visitors in summer.*

congested
road | street | city | area
full of traffic, so that cars can only move slowly:
The congested roads and lack of parking spaces are putting off visitors. | The area is ***heavily congested*** (=badly congested).

The time when the trains and roads are busy with people travelling to work is called **the rush hour**: *The trains are really crowded in* ***the rush hour****.*

B

button *n*

1 a small round flat object on your shirt, coat etc that you pass through a hole to fasten it

ADJECTIVES/NOUNS + button

a shirt/skirt/coat etc button *I'm not very good at fastening shirt buttons.*

the top/bottom button *He was wearing a white shirt with the top button undone.*

VERBS

fasten/do up a button *He quickly did up the buttons on his shirt.*

unfasten/undo a button *I can't undo the buttons on the back of this dress.*

a button is missing *Two of the buttons on the jacket were missing.*

a button comes off sth *A button has come off my skirt.*

sth has lost a button *His favourite shirt had lost a button.*

sew on a button *It only takes a minute to sew on a button.*

PREPOSITIONS

the buttons of/on sth *He undid the buttons of his shirt.*

2 a small part of a machine that you press to make it do something

VERBS

press/push a button *He pressed a button and the doors slid open.*

hit a button (=quickly press a button) *He hit the alarm button by the door.*

ADJECTIVES/NOUNS + button

the on/off button *When one of her songs comes on the radio, I reach for the off button.*

the record/play/pause button *Can you press the pause button?*

PREPOSITIONS

the button on sth *I could see him pressing the buttons on his phone.*

PHRASES

at the touch/push of a button (=just by pressing a button) *You can access any information at the touch of a button.*

buy *v*
to get something by paying money for it

ADVERBS

buy sth cheaply *Houses can be bought cheaply in the area.*
buy sth direct *They buy the carpets direct from the manufacturer.*
buy sth in bulk (=in large quantities) *It's usually cheaper to buy in bulk.*
buy sth online/on the internet *More and more people are buying their groceries online.*

Cc

cab *n* a taxi

VERBS

take/get/catch a cab *Why don't we take a cab to the airport?*

call/order a cab (*also* **phone for a cab** *BrE*) (=telephone for one to come) *Here's the phone number if you want to call a cab.*

get into/in a cab *I just saw Fiona getting into a cab.*

get out of a cab *He got out of the cab and walked up to the hotel entrance.*

hail a cab *written* (=wave to make a cab stop for you) *Martin put his hand out and hailed a cab.*

⚠ Don't say 'get on a cab'. Say **get into a cab** or **get in a cab**.

cab + NOUNS

a cab ride *It's only a short cab ride to Georgetown.*

a cab driver *The cab driver didn't speak any English.*

a cab fare (=the money you pay to travel in a cab) *My dad gave me the money for my cab fare.*

cake *n*

a sweet food made by baking a mixture of flour, butter, sugar, and eggs

ADJECTIVES/NOUNS + cake

a birthday/Christmas/wedding cake *Lucy had twelve candles on her birthday cake.*

a chocolate/lemon/coffee etc cake *His favourite food is chocolate cake.*

a fruit cake (=one with dried fruit in it)

a sponge cake (=one made from flour, butter, sugar, and eggs)

a cream cake (=one with thick cream inside it)

VERBS

make/bake a cake *I've made a chocolate cake.*

decorate a cake *We decorated the cake with sugar flowers.*

ice a cake *BrE*, **frost a cake** *AmE* (=cover a cake with fine sugar mixed with a liquid) *She iced her own wedding cake.*

cut the cake *He took a photo of the bride and groom cutting the cake.*

⚠ Don't say 'cook a cake'. Say **make a cake** or **bake a cake**.

PHRASES

a piece/slice of cake *Would you like a slice of cake?*

calculate *v*

to find out how much something will cost, the amount of time, the distance, or size of something etc

ADVERBS

calculate sth exactly/precisely/accurately *The computer calculates exactly how much fuel the car has used.*

carefully calculate *We carefully calculated how much food we would need for twelve days.*

correctly calculate *She correctly calculated the total cost to be £53.50.*

you can easily calculate sth *You can easily calculate the number of calories in a meal using this guide.*

PHRASES

calculate sth to within a millimetre/an inch etc (=used to talk about how accurately something is calculated) *Satellite tracking devices can calculate your position to within a few metres.*

calculate sth to the nearest centimetre/second etc (=used when something is calculated approximately, using the nearest whole amount) *Calculate the amount of money to the nearest dollar.*

calculate sth with great accuracy/great precision *This method allows us to calculate the age of rocks with great accuracy.*

calculation *n*

the action of adding, multiplying etc numbers in order to get an answer

ADJECTIVES

a simple calculation *A simple calculation will show that these figures are incorrect.*

a rough calculation (=not very detailed or exact) *I made a few rough calculations of how much it would cost.*

a quick/rapid calculation *He did a rapid calculation.*

complex calculations *Computers can be used to handle complex calculations.*

mathematical/numerical/statistical calculations *She was studying a page of mathematical calculations.*

a mental calculation (=one that you do without writing the figures down) *I am not much good at mental calculations.*

sb's calculations are right/correct/accurate *Fortunately his calculations were accurate.*

sb's calculations are wrong/inaccurate *Some of our calculations were wrong.*

VERBS

do/make a calculation (*also* **perform a calculation** *formal*): *Computers can perform calculations very quickly.*

PREPOSITIONS

by/according to sb's calculations *By my calculations, we need to raise about £10,000.*

call[1] *v*

1 to say or shout something

ADVERBS

call softly (=quietly) *He called softly into the darkness.*

call loudly *She called loudly enough for everyone at the bar to hear.*

call sb over (=call someone to come to you) *He called the waitress over and ordered a cup of coffee.*

call sb back (=call someone to come back) *I was just about to leave when he called me back.*

call out (=to shout something or say it aloud, rather than saying it quietly or in your head) *He kept calling out in his sleep.*

NOUNS

call sb's name *I called her name but she didn't hear me.*

call the register *BrE* (=say the names of students in a class, to check who is there) *At the beginning of each day, the teacher calls the register.*

PREPOSITIONS

call to sb *In the distance, someone was calling to her.*

call for sb/sth *Your mother's been calling for you – didn't you hear her?*

call sb into your office/study/room etc *The head teacher called me into her office.*

2 to use a telephone to contact someone or something

NOUNS

call sb's number *I called your number, but there was no reply.*

call (sb) a cab (*also* **call (sb) a taxi** *BrE*): *Would you like me to call you a cab?*

call (for) a doctor/ambulance *There was no time to call a doctor.*

call (for) the police *Get off my land or I'll call the police!*

ADVERBS

call back (=call again) *Sam's not here at the moment – can you call back later?*

call (sb) collect *AmE* (=the person receiving the call pays for it) *He was calling collect from a pay phone.*

In British English, you say **reverse the charges**.

PHRASES

call sb on the phone *He called me on the phone and said "You've got the job!"*

wait for sb to call *She sat by the phone waiting for Dan to call.*

call[2] *n*

an occasion when you speak to someone on the telephone

ADJECTIVES/NOUNS + call

a phone/telephone call *I had a phone call from Barbara in Australia.*

a quick call *This is just a quick call to make sure you're OK.*

a local call *Local calls are free at weekends.*

a long-distance call *I'd like to make a long-distance call.*

an international call *International calls are getting much cheaper these days.*

a collect call *AmE* (=one paid for by the person who receives it) *Can I make a collect call to Florida, please?*

an emergency call (=to the police, fire service, or ambulance service) *The police normally respond immediately to an emergency call.*

VERBS

give sb a call (=phone someone) *I'll give him a call later today.*

make a call *He made three calls, the first of which was to Lily.*

get/receive/have a call *At 11 in the evening we got a call from the police.*

there is/was a call *There was a call for you while you were out.*

answer a call *We're sorry that we cannot answer your call right now.*

take a call (=answer one) *Monica took the call upstairs.*

return sb's call (=call someone after they have tried to call you) *I left a message for her but she didn't return my call.*

expect a call *She's expecting a phone call from Matt.*

calm[1] *adj*

1 relaxed and quiet, not angry, nervous, or upset

VERBS

remain/stay/keep calm *I tried to stay calm and ignore their comments.*

feel calm *He felt calm and in control.*

look/seem calm *She always looks so calm.*

NOUNS

a calm person *My dad's a very calm person.*

a calm voice *She spoke in a calm voice to reassure the child.*

a calm manner *Karen answered in her usual calm manner.*

calm confidence/assurance/authority *He spoke with the calm confidence of a priest.*

calm determination *Her worry was replaced by calm determination.*

calm discussion *We need calm discussion to solve these problems.*

ADVERBS

perfectly calm (=completely calm) *James felt perfectly calm as he walked into the room.*

remarkably calm *Ella had seen the accident but she seemed remarkably calm about it.*

PHRASES

beneath sb's calm exterior (=used when someone seems calm but is not really calm) *Beneath the calm exterior is a very troubled man.*

THESAURUS: calm

sleepy, peaceful, tranquil, calm, dead → **quiet (3)**

2 not affected by strong wind

ADVERBS

perfectly calm (=completely calm) *The sea was perfectly calm.*

calm² *n*

1 a situation in which people are not angry, upset, or excited and everything is quiet

ADJECTIVES

an uneasy calm (=which could end at any moment) *An uneasy calm settled over the country as the peace talks continued.*

relative/comparative calm *The relative calm is slowly attracting more tourists back to the area.*

VERBS + calm

maintain calm *Police were brought in to maintain calm on the streets.*

restore calm (=bring back calm) *The government is struggling to restore calm after several days of violent protests.*

keep your calm (=not become angry or upset) *She kept her calm and said, "We had better call for a doctor."*

bring calm *It is hoped that the peace talks will bring calm to the region.*

call/appeal for calm *The president appealed for calm following a series of bombings.*

break/shatter the calm (=end it) *The calm was suddenly shattered by a loud explosion.*

calm + VERBS

calm descends on sth *formal* (=a place becomes calm) *The crowds went home and calm descended on the streets.*

calm returns *Calm returned after a week of violence and rioting.*

PHRASES

an appeal for calm *Political leaders made an appeal for calm.*

a period of calm *The city is enjoying a brief period of calm after days of fighting.*

an oasis of calm (=a calm place that is very different from everything around it) *The park provides an oasis of calm in the centre of the city.*

2 the feeling you have when you are very relaxed and not worried about anything

ADJECTIVES

deep calm *He closed his eyes and felt a sense of deep calm.*

inner calm *She turned to religion in search of some kind of inner calm.*

PHRASES

a feeling/sense/state of calm *These breathing exercises can create a sense of calm and well-being.*

a moment of calm *He had the chance to sit down and enjoy a rare moment of calm.*

calorie *n*

a unit for measuring the amount of energy that food will produce

ADJECTIVES

low-calorie *She's on a low-calorie diet at the moment.*

high-calorie *You mustn't eat too many high-calorie foods.*

sb's daily calories *Americans get 22% of their daily calories from snacks.*

extra/excess calories *Exercise burns up extra calories.*

VERBS

have/contain calories *These yoghurts have approximately 90 calories per pot.*

count calories (=control your weight by eating fewer calories) *Women tend to count calories more than men.*

burn/burn up/burn off calories (=use up the calories you have eaten) *Even gentle walking will help you to burn up calories.*

eat calories (*also* **consume calories** *formal*): *The best way to lose weight is to eat fewer calories.*

calorie + NOUNS

calorie intake (=the amount of calories someone eats) *There are several ways you can reduce your calorie intake.*

calorie content *The calorie content of the food is listed on the package.*

PHRASES

be high/low in calories (=contain a lot of calories/a few calories) *Peanuts are very high in calories.*

a calorie-controlled diet *I went on a sensible calorie-controlled diet to try to lose weight.*

camera *n*

a piece of equipment used to take photographs or make films or television programmes

ADJECTIVES/NOUNS + camera

a digital camera *I uploaded the pictures from my digital camera.*

a good/expensive camera *You don't need an expensive camera to take good photos.*

a hidden/secret camera *He was filmed on a secret camera accepting bribes.*

a security/surveillance camera (=one that films or photographs people in public places) *Security cameras have been installed in the store to prevent theft.*

a television/film/movie camera *He never felt comfortable in front of television cameras.*

a video camera (=one that records moving pictures) *They hired a video camera to use at their wedding.*

VERBS + camera

pose for the camera (=sit or stand in a position in order to be photographed) *Come on everyone, pose for the camera!*

be caught on camera (=be photographed or filmed, especially doing something wrong) *The boys were caught on camera leaving the store.*

set up a camera (=make it ready to use) *The team set up their cameras some distance from the animals.*

camera + VERBS

a camera films/records sth *There were two cameras filming the action.*

a camera catches/captures sth (=films or photographs a particular event or scene) *A car park security camera captured the attack.*

a camera zooms in/out (=moves closer to or further away from the subject) *The camera zoomed in for a close-up of his face.*

camera + NOUNS

a camera crew (=the people who operate the cameras for a film or programme) *The camera crew were ready to start filming.*

camera equipment *He has all the latest camera equipment.*

a camera lens *A good camera lens can cost hundreds of dollars.*

PREPOSITIONS

on camera *I can never catch him laughing on camera.*

off camera *He continued to speak in the character's accent off camera.*

in front of the camera *She's very natural in front of the cameras.*

camp *n*

1 a place where people stay in tents or shelters

ADJECTIVES/NOUNS + camp

an army/military camp *The soldiers were from the army camp on the other side of town.*

base camp (=the main camp for people climbing a mountain) *The expedition's base camp was 6,000 feet below the summit.*

a training camp *They found a terrorist training camp in the hills.*

a temporary camp *We set up a temporary camp in the forest.*

a makeshift camp (=made from whatever is available rather than with proper tents or equipment) *The families are living in makeshift camps with no water or electricity.*

a refugee camp *Hundreds of people have fled their homes and are now living in refugee camps.*

VERBS

set up/make/pitch camp (=put up your tents) *It was dark by the time we pitched camp.*

break camp (=take down your tents ready to move to a new place) *Early the next morning we broke camp.*

PREPOSITIONS

at a camp *The men were trained at a camp in the desert.*

Campfire, **campsite**, and **campground** are usually written as one word.

2 a prison, especially one run by soldiers during a war

NOUNS + camp

a prison camp *Life in the prison camp was unbearable.*

a detention/internment camp (=a prison camp) *They held him in a detention camp for three months.*

a prisoner of war camp (=where soldiers captured in war are held) *My grandad spent a year in a prisoner of war camp.*

a concentration camp (=where a lot of people who are not soldiers are kept and treated cruelly) *Anne Frank died in a German concentration camp in 1945.*

campaign *n*

a series of organized actions intended to achieve a particular result or persuade people about something

ADJECTIVES/NOUNS + campaign

an advertising/marketing/sales campaign *The store ran a television advertising campaign just before Christmas.*

a publicity campaign (=to tell the public about something) *The interview was the start of a publicity campaign for his new book.*

a political campaign *She was involved in many political campaigns.*

an election campaign *He was a candidate in the 2008 election campaign.*

a presidential campaign *In his presidential campaign speeches he promised that he would not raise taxes.*

an anti-smoking/anti-bullying etc campaign *How effective has the anti-smoking campaign been?*

a fund-raising campaign (=to get money for something) *The church is launching a £50,000 fund-raising campaign for the renovation work.*

a media/press campaign *The government spent thousands of pounds on a media campaign.*

a national/nationwide campaign *The walk was part of a national campaign to raise £900,000.*

a worldwide/global/international campaign *a worldwide campaign for peace*

an effective/successful campaign *The Conservatives failed to mount an effective campaign.*

a deliberate/concerted campaign (=done by people in a determined way) *There was a concerted campaign to attract more women into the armed forces.*

a determined campaign *His wife waged a determined campaign for his release.*

a smear campaign (=in which unpleasant or untrue stories are spread about an important person) *He claims he was the victim of a smear campaign.*

VERBS

launch/mount a campaign (=begin a campaign) *They have launched a campaign to end world poverty.*

organize/wage a campaign (*also* **conduct a campaign** *formal*): *William Wilberforce waged a successful campaign to end slavery.*

run a campaign (=organize a campaign, especially in politics or advertising) *The Republicans ran a successful campaign.*

lead a campaign *The government is leading a 'walk to school' campaign.*

spearhead a campaign (=lead a campaign that involves a lot of people, organizations etc) *The campaign was spearheaded by the Students' Union.*

⚠ Don't say 'make a campaign'. Say **organize a campaign**.

campaign + NOUNS

campaign funds/money *He was found guilty of using campaign funds illegally.*

campaigner *n*

someone who tries to persuade governments and other public organizations to change what they are doing in order to achieve a particular aim

ADJECTIVES/NOUNS + campaigner

a leading/prominent campaigner (=an important one) *He was a leading campaigner against the war.*

a great campaigner *She's a great campaigner, combining exceptional energy with a real knowledge of the issues.*

a lifelong campaigner (=all his or her life) *Anderson was a lifelong campaigner for African development.*

a veteran campaigner (=who has had a lot of experience of campaigning) *Helen Suzman, a veteran campaigner for human rights in South Africa, has died at the age of 91.*

a tireless campaigner (=one who tries very hard for a long time) *He was a tireless campaigner for peace.*

a civil rights/human rights/animal rights campaigner *Civil rights campaigners were put in jail.*

a peace campaigner *Peace campaigners organized protest marches.*

a green/environmental campaigner *Environmental campaigners are trying to stop farmers from growing GM crops.*

an anti-nuclear/anti-drugs etc campaigner *Anti-nuclear campaigners say there is a risk of another nuclear accident.*

PREPOSITIONS

a campaigner for sth *Shelley was well known as a campaigner for women's rights.*

a campaigner against sth *He has been an active campaigner against the death penalty.*

campus *n*

the land and buildings of a university or college, including the buildings where students live

NOUNS + campus

a university/college campus *The swimming pool is located on the college campus.*

campus + NOUNS

campus life *She was looking forward to experiencing campus life.*

the campus buildings *The campus buildings are very modern.*

PREPOSITIONS

on campus *Most students live on campus.*

off campus *We moved off campus in the second year of our course.*

cancel *v*

to decide that something that was officially planned will not happen

NOUNS

cancel a meeting/class/appointment *Please accept my apologies for having to cancel our meeting on January 24th.*

cancel a flight *Flight 1098 was canceled due to an engine problem.*

cancel a concert/show/performance *The show was canceled because of poor ticket sales.*

cancel an event/competition/game/race/wedding etc *Wednesday's event was cancelled due to bad weather.*

cancel your plans *The company was forced to cancel its plans to export cars to the United States.*

cancel a project *The project had been cancelled due to lack of funds.*

C

C

THESAURUS: cancel

call off
strike | protest | talks | deal | search | game | match | meeting | party | wedding
to cancel something that has been planned to happen. **Call off** sounds more informal than **cancel** and is often used in news reports:
The union refused to call off the strike. | The deal was called off at the last minute. | Julia called off their wedding because she wasn't sure he was right for her.

postpone
meeting | game | match | show | concert | trial | election | trip | decision
to decide to do something at a later time, instead of the time that was officially planned:
Tonight's town council meeting has been postponed until next Tuesday. | Liverpool's match against Arsenal was postponed because of fog. | Defence lawyers asked for the trial to be postponed.

shelve (*also* **put sth on ice** *informal*)
plan | proposal | idea | project | programme | report
to decide not to continue with something that has been planned, although it may be considered again at some time in the future:
The plan was shelved to save money. | The company decided to put the project on ice.

lift
ban | sanctions | restriction | blockade | curfew | martial law
to end an official order that stops or limits someone from doing something:
The state lifted its ban on gambling in casinos. | They want the US to lift economic sanctions against Cuba.

repeal
law | act | bill | legislation | amendment | statute
to officially end a law, so that it no longer has any authority:
They want Parliament to repeal the laws on hunting. | The act was repealed by the new socialist government.

annul *formal*
election | result | marriage
to officially decide that something has no legal authority and is therefore cancelled:
Opposition parties have asked the Supreme Court to annul the election. | In 1960, he married a 15-year-old, but the marriage was annulled because of the bride's age.

In informal English, people say that something **is off** (=it has been cancelled): *I'm afraid the party* ***is off***.

cancer *n*

a very serious disease in which cells in one part of the body start to grow in a way that is not normal

ADJECTIVES/NOUNS + cancer

lung/stomach/breast/bowel etc cancer *He died of stomach cancer.*

skin cancer *Australia has one of the highest rates of skin cancer.*

terminal cancer (=cancer that cannot be treated, which will cause you to die) *My aunt has terminal cancer and she is not expected to live very long.*

VERBS

have/suffer from cancer *Her father suffers from a rare form of cancer.*

get/develop cancer (*also* **contract cancer** *formal*): *One in three people will develop cancer at some stage in their lives.*

die of/from cancer *He died of cancer last year.*

treat cancer *The drug is used to treat cancer.*

cause cancer *Everyone knows that smoking causes cancer.*

prevent cancer *The new treatment may be used to prevent cancer.*

screen sb for cancer (=check to see if someone has cancer) *Doctors are encouraging people to get screened for cancer regularly.*

be diagnosed with cancer (=a doctor says that someone has cancer, after examining them and doing tests) *Each year 40,000 women are diagnosed with breast cancer in the UK.*

survive cancer (*also* **beat cancer** *informal*): *Many people survive cancer.*

a cancer spreads *The cancer had spread to his stomach.*

cancer + NOUNS

cancer research *Millions of dollars are spent each year on cancer research.*

cancer cells *Chemotherapy is treatment with drugs which destroy cancer cells.*

a cancer patient *Less than 8% of lung cancer patients are alive five years after diagnosis.*

cancer treatment *The Christie Hospital is one of the foremost cancer treatment hospitals in the UK.*

a cancer ward (=a part of a hospital for cancer patients to stay in) *He was moved to a cancer ward in the local hospital.*

PHRASES

the risk of cancer *Smoking increases the risk of cancer.*

a type/form of cancer *There are over 200 different types of cancer.*

treatment for cancer *The drug can be used as a treatment for cancer.*

sb's fight/battle/struggle against cancer *He died after a long struggle against cancer.*

candid *adj*

THESAURUS honest

candidate *n*

someone who is competing in an election or being considered for a job

ADJECTIVES

a suitable candidate *No suitable candidate could be found.*

the successful/winning candidate *The successful candidate will start on a salary of £25,000.*

a good/strong/promising candidate *He looks like a very strong candidate for the job.*

a possible/potential/prospective candidate (=who might be given a job or position) *There were two women who were possible candidates.*

a likely candidate *His recent experience makes him a likely candidate for the post.*

the ideal/perfect candidate *The ideal candidate will have experience of leading a sales team.*

an obvious candidate *There is no obvious candidate for the position of Chairman.*

a presidential candidate *What is the system for selecting presidential candidates?*

a parliamentary candidate (=for the job of Member of Parliament) *He was selected as his local party's parliamentary candidate.*

a Republican/Democratic/Labour etc candidate *This part of Florida usually supports Republican candidates.*

VERBS

stand as a candidate (=compete in an election) *Lee stated that he did not intend to stand as a candidate in the presidential elections.*

nominate/put up a candidate (*also* **put sb forward as a candidate**) (=suggest someone for election) *The protest group has put up its own candidate for the election.*

interview a candidate (=for a job) *The human resources manager will interview the candidates first.*

choose a candidate (*also* **select a candidate** *formal*): *We will choose the best candidate, regardless of age.*

vote for a candidate *How many people voted for each candidate?*

PREPOSITIONS

a candidate for sth *There are only three candidates for the job.*

candle *n*

a stick of wax with a string through the middle, which you burn to give light

VERBS + candle

light a candle *She lit a candle in the church.*

blow out a candle *Can you blow out all the candles on your birthday cake?*

put out a candle (*also* **extinguish a candle** *formal*) (=make it stop burning) *Always make sure that you put out all the candles.*

candle + VERBS

a candle burns (=it gives out light) *The house was dark except for one candle burning in a window.*

a candle flickers (=the flame moves in an unsteady way) *As the door opened, the candles flickered.*

a candle goes out (=it stops burning) *There was a sudden gust of wind, and all the candles went out.*

a candle lights sth *The bedroom was lit by a single candle.*

ADJECTIVES

a lighted/burning candle *A procession moved through the village carrying lighted candles.*

a flickering candle *The church was full of white flickering candles.*

a scented candle (=one that smells nice) *Scented candles keep the air smelling sweet.*

candle + NOUNS

a candle flame *The candle flame flickered.*

candle wax *There were drops of candle wax all over the table.*

a candle holder *She used an old wine bottle as a candle holder.*

> **Candlelight** and **candlestick** are usually written as one word.

candy *n AmE*

a sweet food made from sugar or chocolate

VERBS

eat candy *Eating too much candy is bad for your teeth.*

buy/get candy *He wanted money to go to the store and buy some candy.*

candy + NOUNS

a candy bar *She was eating a candy bar.*

a candy wrapper (=the paper that covers the candy) *You shouldn't throw candy wrappers in the street.*

a candy store *The family ran a candy store in Brooklyn.*

ADJECTIVES/NOUNS + candy

chocolate candy *Do you like chocolate candy?*

PHRASES

a piece of candy *Would you like a piece of candy?*

a box of candy *He gave me a box of candy as a present.*

> **Candy** is used in American English. In British English, people say **sweets**.

cap *n* a hat

ADJECTIVES/NOUNS + cap

a baseball cap *He was wearing a sweater and a baseball cap.*

a swimming/bathing cap (*also* **a swim cap** *AmE*): *A swimming cap will stop water getting in your ears.*

a flat cap (*also* **a cloth cap**) *BrE* (=made of cloth with a stiff piece that sticks out at the front) *We saw an old man in a jacket and a brown flat cap.*

a school cap (=worn as part of a school uniform) *He looked very smart is his little blazer and school cap.*

a peaked cap (=a cap with a part at the front which goes over your eyes, usually worn as part of a uniform) *She wore a sailor's peaked cap.*

C

VERBS

wear a cap *He was wearing a baseball cap.*

put on a cap *Put on your swimming caps before you get in the pool.*

take off a cap (*also* **remove a cap** *formal*): *He opened the door, took off his cap, and threw it on a hook.*

capability *n*

the skill or power to do something, especially something difficult

VERBS

have the capability to do sth (*also* **possess the capability to do sth** *formal*): *North Korea has the capability to produce a nuclear bomb.*

demonstrate a capability *The video is intended to demonstrate the capabilities of the company's products.*

develop/expand/increase a capability *The company needs to develop the capability to assemble products quickly in response to customers' orders.*

ADJECTIVES/NOUNS + capability

mental/intellectual capability *The chimpanzee's intellectual capabilities are similar to those of a young child.*

technical/technological capability *The process requires a high level of technical capability.*

human capability *The device can perform tasks with a speed and reliability beyond human capabilities.*

nuclear capability (=the ability to use nuclear weapons) *They want the country to have its own nuclear capability.*

PREPOSITIONS

be beyond sb's capabilities (=someone cannot do something) *The task was beyond his capabilities as a programmer.*

be within sb's capabilities (=someone can do something) *The job is well within the capabilities of the average person.*

capacity [Ac] *n*

the amount that something can contain or produce

VERBS

have a capacity of 10 litres/25 gallons etc *The fuel tank has a capacity of 40 litres.*

increase/expand the capacity of sth *The college is planning to increase its capacity to 16,000 student places.*

reduce the capacity of sth *The capacity of the warehouse has been slightly reduced.*

ADJECTIVES

limited/unlimited capacity *The clinic only has a limited capacity for treating patients.*

excess/spare capacity *They could sell spare capacity on their trucks to other companies.*

full/maximum capacity *They loaded the ship to maximum capacity.*

sufficient/adequate capacity *The factory has sufficient capacity for 10,000 kilos of laundry.*

NOUNS + capacity

storage/memory capacity (=how much information a computer disk can hold) *The storage capacity is about 250 megabytes.*

seating capacity (=how many seats there are) *The largest hall in the university has a seating capacity of over 1,500.*

production/manufacturing capacity (=the amount of something that a factory, country etc is able to produce) *Over the next few years manufacturing capacity will expand.*

PHRASES

be filled/packed to capacity (=be completely full) *The courtroom was filled to capacity.*

work/operate at full capacity (=produce the maximum possible amount) *The factory is not yet operating at full capacity.*

capital *n*

1 an important city where the main government of a country or state is

capital + NOUNS

the capital city *They live a long way from the capital city.*

ADJECTIVES/NOUNS + capital

the Spanish/French etc capital *The Spanish capital Madrid has a population of over 3 million people.*

the regional/state capital *Austin is the state capital of Texas.*

the financial capital *Is London's position as the financial capital of Europe under threat?*

PREPOSITIONS

the capital of a country *Warsaw is the capital of Poland.*

2 money or property, especially when it is used to start a business or to produce more wealth

ADJECTIVES/NOUNS + capital

foreign capital *Sales of agricultural products are the country's largest source of foreign capital.*

private capital *The film was made with private capital.*

working capital (=money used by a business to carry on production and keep trading) *The firm needs more working capital to pay for the introduction of new technology.*

VERBS

raise/generate capital (=get capital) *They want to raise capital for a new business venture.*

accumulate capital (=get more and more of it) *The family had accumulated enough capital to set up their own bank.*

borrow capital *The cost of borrowing capital has increased.*

invest capital *The organization only invests capital in companies whose activities do not harm the environment.*

inject capital (=put large amounts of money into something) *The European Union plans to inject more capital to save the country's banking system.*

PHRASES

the movement of capital *There is no restriction on the movement of capital.*

car *n*

a vehicle with four wheels and an engine that can carry a small number of passengers

ADJECTIVES/NOUNS + car

a sports car *He was driving a red sports car.*

a racing car (*also* **a race car** *AmE*): *The racing cars go around the track at over 200 miles an hour.*

a police car *The vehicle was being chased by a police car.*

an electric car *Electric cars are better for the environment.*

a hire car *BrE*, **a rental car** *AmE*: *We picked up a rental car at the airport.*

a used/second-hand car (=one that is not new) *The company sells used cars.*

an estate car *BrE* (=one with a door at the back and folding seats) *Once you have children, an estate car is very useful.*

VERBS + car

drive a car *In the UK you can learn to drive a car when you are 17.*

have/own a car *Do you have a car?*

go/travel by car *The children now walk to school instead of going by car.*

get in/into a car *The man stopped and she got into the car.*

get out of a car *He got out of the car and went into the newsagent's.*

take the car (=use a car to go somewhere) *Is it all right if I take the car this evening?*

run a car (=have a car and pay for the petrol, repairs etc it needs) *People on low incomes can't afford to run a car.*

park a car *She parked the car by the side of the road.*

back/reverse a car (=make it move backwards) *Suzy backed the car into the driveway.*

lose control of a car (=no longer be able to control its direction) *He lost control of the car on a sharp bend.*

car + VERBS

a car passes/overtakes sb *I didn't want to let the other car overtake me.*

a car drives off/away *The police car drove off at top speed.*

a car slows down *The car slowed down and stopped outside our house.*

a car accelerates (=goes faster) *She watched the car accelerate down the road.*

a car pulls out (=moves away from the side of the road) *A car suddenly pulled out in front of me.*

a car pulls up (=stops) *They heard a car pull up outside their house.*

a car hits sth/crashes into sth *I saw the car leave the road and hit a tree.*

a car skids (=slides sideways in a way you cannot control) *If it's icy, the car might skid.*

a car breaks down (=stops working because something is wrong with it) *On the way home, the car broke down.*

car + NOUNS

a car crash/accident (*also* **a car wreck** *AmE*): *He was involved in a car crash.*

a car park *BrE*: *She couldn't find a space in the car park.*

a car door/engine/key etc *She left the car engine running.*

a car driver *Car drivers in large urban areas now spend a third of their time driving at below 5 miles per hour.*

the car industry *especially BrE*: *The car industry suffers in times of economic decline.*

a car maker/manufacturer *Volkswagen is the biggest car manufacturer in the world.*

a car dealer (=someone who buys and sells used cars) *Car dealers reported a 4% drop in sales.*

a car chase *The best bit in the movie was the car chase through the city.*

car crime *BrE* (=stealing or damaging cars) *Car crime in the area has gone down.*

a car bomb (=a bomb hidden in or under a car) *A car bomb exploded in the city's main square.*

> **Car industry** and **car maker** are more common in British English. In American English, people usually say **auto industry** and **auto maker**.
>
> British people say **car park**, American people say **parking lot**.

carbon *n*

a chemical substance that is found in coal, oil etc

carbon + NOUNS

carbon emissions (=the amount of carbon gases that are produced by cars, factories etc) *In recent years carbon emissions have increased dramatically, because more and more people are using cars.*

sb's carbon footprint (=the amount of carbon gases that a person or organization produces through their activities) *The company wants to reduce its carbon footprint.*

carbon credits (=permission to produce a particular amount of carbon gases, which countries and companies can buy and sell as a way of reducing the damage to the environment) *Countries that meet their emissions targets can sell carbon credits to those falling behind.*

carbon trading (=the buying and selling of permissions to produce carbon gases) *The Australian prime minister supports carbon trading to reduce greenhouse gases.*

carbon offsetting (=a system in which you can balance the amount of carbon gases you produce, by contributing to schemes that will reduce the overall amount of carbon that is produced) *You can use carbon offsetting schemes to reduce the amount of damage caused to the environment, for example when you are flying.*

carbon polluter *The US is the world's biggest carbon polluter.*

PHRASES

a low-carbon economy (=an economy that produces very little carbon dioxide) *The president wants the US to change to a low-carbon economy.*

carbon-neutral (=taking the same amount of carbon gases out of the atmosphere as the amount you produce) *A carbon-neutral home produces its own energy and stores it to heat the home.*

card *n*

1 a small piece of plastic which you use to pay for goods or to get money

ADJECTIVES/NOUNS + card

a credit card (=one you use to buy things and pay later) *He put all the shopping on his credit card.*

a debit card (*also* **a check card** *AmE*) (=one you use to pay for things directly from your account) *I paid for the tickets by debit card.*

a cash card (*also* **an ATM card** *especially AmE*) (=one you use to get cash from a machine) *You should report stolen cash cards immediately.*

a valid card (=one with dates etc that are legal and correct) *We accept cash and valid cards.*

a phone card (=one that you can use in some public telephones) *You can use this phone card in several countries.*

a store/charge card (=one that allows you to buy things from a particular shop and pay for them later) *Store cards often have high rates of interest.*

a stolen card *The man tried to pay using a stolen card.*

VERBS

pay by card *Can I pay by card?*

put sth on your card (=pay using a credit card) *I'll put the restaurant bill on my card.*

use your card *I don't use my card if I can pay by cash.*

accept/take a card (=allow you to pay by card) *Big hotels will accept most cards.*

apply for a card *How do I apply for a debit card?*

issue a card *Please contact the bank that issued your card.*

cancel a card *If your card is stolen, you must cancel it immediately.*

card + NOUNS

sb's card number/details *Enter your card number here.*

the card holder (=the person that a card belongs to) *One in ten store card holders owes more than £500.*

2 a small piece of plastic or paper containing information

ADJECTIVES/NOUNS + card

an identity card/ID card (=one that proves who you are) *All US citizens must carry an identity card.*

a membership card *Do you have a membership card for the library?*

a student card (=that proves you are a student) *Entrance is free if you have a student card.*

a business card (=with your name and company details on it, for giving to people to keep) *I'm having 100 business cards printed.*

a smart card (=one with an electronic part that records information) *Using a smart card with all your personal data on it, you can travel anywhere in the world.*

a swipe card (=one that you slide through a machine) *You need a swipe card to get into the gym.*

a SIM card (*also* **a Sim card**) (=one in a mobile phone that stores your information and allows you to use a network) *You can put your old SIM card into your new phone so you don't lose all your numbers.*

VERBS

carry a card (=have one with you) *Motorists could soon be forced to carry an ID card.*

show a card *You have to show your student card at the door.*

flash a card (=show one very quickly) *He*

flashed his card at the guard and walked straight in.

swipe a card (=slide it through a machine) *When you swipe your card, the door opens.*

3 a piece of folded card with a picture on the front that you give to people on special occasions

NOUNS + card

a birthday card *I must remember to send him a birthday card.*

a greetings card *BrE*, **a greeting card** *AmE* (=a card you give to people on special occasions) *They sell greetings cards and small gifts.*

a Christmas/Eid/Diwali etc card *We got over 100 Christmas cards last year.*

a thank-you card *She gave me a box of chocolates and a thank-you card.*

a get-well card (=for someone who is sick) *Katie's in hospital so I'm going to send her a get-well card.*

a leaving card *He was so unpopular that no one wanted to sign his leaving card.*

VERBS

send (sb) a card *Sally always sends me a card on my birthday.*

give (sb) a card *I like giving cards at Christmas.*

get/receive a card (from sb) *Did you get a card from David?*

sign a card *Everyone in the office signed his leaving card.*

write/put sth on a card *I can't think of anything funny to write on her card.*

4 a small piece of stiff paper with pictures and signs on, for playing a game

ADJECTIVES/NOUNS + card

playing cards *Five playing cards were laid out on the table.*

a high/low card *The person with the highest card goes first.*

the winning/losing card *He put down the winning card and punched the air with delight.*

a trump card (=one chosen to have a higher value than other cards) *You have to play a trump card if you have one.*

VERBS

play cards *Four men were playing cards in the bar.*

deal cards (=give some to each player) *Deal seven cards to each player.*

shuffle cards (=mix them up) *Who wants to shuffle the cards?*

cut the cards (=divide a pack of cards into two) *First, ask someone to cut the cards.*

put down/play a card *The first card he put down was the three of clubs.*

card + NOUNS

a card game *My favourite card game is poker.*

a card trick *Let me show you a card trick.*

a card player *Rose was a skilful card player.*

PHRASES

a game of cards *Let's have a game of cards.*

a pack of cards *BrE*, **a deck of cards** *AmE* (=a set of 52 cards) *He took out a pack of cards.*

a suit of cards (=one of the four types of cards) *The four suits of cards are hearts, diamonds, clubs, and spades.*

a hand of cards (=a set of cards that a player has to play in a game) *This is a terrible hand of cards.*

C

care¹ *n*

1 the process of looking after someone, especially because they are ill, old, or very young

ADJECTIVES/NOUNS + care

health care/medical care *Our patients get good standards of medical care.*

child care *Mothers are usually responsible for child care.*

patient care (=care of someone who is ill) *The changes should lead to better patient care.*

specialist care *Her father is very ill and needs specialist care.*

proper care *It's important to give your pets proper care.*

intensive care (=in a special part of a hospital, for very seriously ill people) *He was rushed to the intensive care unit at Alder Hey Hospital.*

constant/round-the-clock care (=all day and all night) *He cannot do anything for himself and needs round-the-clock care.*

day care (=care of people, especially children, during the day) *Some businesses provide day care for the children of employees.*

residential care (=for ill or old people in a place where they stay) *Residential care for the elderly can be very expensive.*

short-term/long-term care *The home provides long-term care for people with severe disabilities.*

VERBS

provide care *The charity provides care and shelter for homeless people.*

need care (*also* **require care** *formal*): *She had an aging mother who required constant care.*

receive care *Every citizen has the right to receive health care.*

PREPOSITIONS

in sb's care *It was better for him to be in the care of someone who loved him.*

under sb's care (=officially looked after or treated by someone) *She is under the care of a top heart specialist.*

care + NOUNS

a care worker *BrE* (=someone whose job is looking after people) *She's a part-time care worker in a nursing home.*

care services/facilities *How much money is spent on health care services?*

PHRASES

take care of sb *She wanted to stay home and take care of her children.*

2 when you are careful to avoid damage, mistakes etc

ADJECTIVES

great care *He takes great care with his work.*

extra care *Take extra care on icy roads.*

special/particular care *Make sure that you take special care with your spelling.*

extreme care *Extreme care is needed when flying at high speeds.*

meticulous care (=paying great attention to every detail) *The journey had been planned with meticulous care.*

VERBS

take care *Take care not to let the soup boil.*

exercise care *formal* (=do something with care) *You have a duty to exercise reasonable care in carrying out your job.*

care is needed *Great care is needed when handling the vase.*

PREPOSITIONS

with care *She chose her clothes for the interview with care – she didn't want to look too casual.*

care[2] *v*

to think that something or someone is important and be concerned about what happens to them

ADVERBS

really care *You really care about her, don't you?*

genuinely/truly care *The teachers genuinely care about their students.*

care a lot/very much *When we're young, we care a lot about how others see us.*

care deeply *She cares deeply about environmental issues.*

care passionately *I cared passionately about improving women's lives.*

not really care/not care much *I don't really care what happens to him.*

care little *formal: She cared little about her own safety.*

PREPOSITIONS

care about sth/sb *These people care about the future of their country.*

PHRASES

all/the only thing sb cares about is... *All he cares about is money.*

career *n*

a type of job which you do for a long period of your life

ADJECTIVES

a long/short/brief career *He has received dozens of awards in the course of his long career.*

a political/military/academic etc career *The scandal ruined his political career.*

a teaching/acting/sporting career *Her acting career lasted for more than 50 years.*

a professional career *He scored over 100 goals during his professional career.*

a successful career *David had a successful career in banking.*

a promising career (=likely to be successful) *She gave up a promising career in advertising in order to look after her children.*

a distinguished/brilliant/illustrious/glittering career (=very successful) *She retired last year after a distinguished career as a barrister.*

a rewarding/fulfilling career (=one that brings you satisfaction) *Teaching can be a very rewarding career.*

sb's career is over (=it has ended) *When I broke my leg, I was afraid my career was over.*

VERBS + career

have a career *Both my parents had careers in education.*

make/follow a career (*also* **pursue a career** *formal*): *She left teaching to pursue a career as a psychologist.*

begin/start a career (*also* **embark on a career** *formal*): *Jacobs started his banking career in 1990.*

launch sb's career *Rita went to New York, where she launched her dancing career.*

change career *People may change careers several times in their lives.*

end sb's career *The scandal ended his political career.*

career + VERBS

sb's career takes off (=starts to be successful) *His career took off and he started making a lot of money.*

sb's career ends/comes to an end *After his football career ended, he became a TV presenter.*

career + NOUNS

careers advice/guidance *Most universities offer professional careers advice.*

career opportunities/prospects *Students often know little about the career opportunities available to them.*

the career ladder (=the way to higher positions in a career) *Having children can disturb your progress up the career ladder.*

a career path (=a way of making a career) *There's no fixed career path for actors.*

a career change/move *After ten years in the job, I wanted a career change.*

career development/advancement/progression *A good job offers a programme of training and career development.*

PREPOSITIONS

a career in journalism/politics/teaching etc *At the age of 15, he knew he wanted a career in politics.*

a career as a teacher/lawyer/singer etc *What made you decide on a career as a lawyer?*

careful *adj*

paying a lot of attention in order to avoid mistakes, problems, or danger

NOUNS

careful thought/consideration *After careful thought, he decided to accept their offer.*

careful attention *Careful attention has been paid to the security arrangements at the airport.*

careful study/examination/scrutiny *Careful examination of the pipe revealed a small crack.*

careful observation/monitoring *The patient's condition requires careful monitoring.*

careful analysis *The findings were based on careful analysis of the data.*

careful planning/preparation *School trips need very careful planning.*

a careful look *She took a careful look around the house, to make sure she hadn't forgotten anything.*

ADVERBS

extra careful/particularly careful (=more than usual) *Be extra careful when carrying pans of hot liquid.*

scrupulously careful (=extremely careful) *Paul was always scrupulously careful in what he said or did.*

PREPOSITIONS

careful about sth *I'm very careful about what I eat.*

careful with sth *Try to be more careful with your punctuation.*

careful in sth *He had been very careful in his choice of words.*

PHRASES

make/take a careful note of sth *She made a careful note of all the details.*

you can't be too careful *It is always best to lock the door – you can't be too careful.*

THESAURUS: careful

cautious

approach | attitude | outlook | response | optimism | welcome

careful to avoid danger or risks, or careful when giving your opinion:

*The government adopted a cautious approach to economic reform. | The researchers expressed cautious optimism about the future. | The plan was given a cautious welcome. | It's always best to be **cautious about** lending people money.*

thorough

investigation | examination | inspection | check | search | analysis | study | assessment | research | review | job

careful to check everything, so that you do not miss anything important:

There will be a thorough investigation into the circumstances of her death. | The police carried out a thorough search of the building. | Our mechanics will check everything – they're very thorough.

methodical

approach | way | manner | study | search | research

always doing things in a careful and well-organized way:

*The data is collected in a methodical way. | He is very **methodical in** his work and likes to plan everything in advance.*

systematic

way | manner | approach | analysis | study | review | research | search

using a fixed plan, so that you do things carefully in a particular order:

The book presents the arguments in a clear and systematic way. | The researchers conducted a systematic review of all the scientific evidence.

meticulous

care | attention | record | detail | notes | planning | preparation | research | work

very careful about every small detail, in order to make sure everything is done correctly:

*The equipment is cleaned with meticulous care. | She keeps meticulous records of each student's progress. | Each part of the plant is shown in meticulous detail. | Robert was **meticulous about** his appearance.*

painstaking

work | task | job | effort | research | search | process | attention | care | detail

very careful and taking a lot of time and effort to do something:

They began the long and painstaking task of translating his work into English. | The book is the result of ten years of painstaking research. | The painting had been done with painstaking attention to detail.

careless *adj*

not paying enough attention to what you are doing, so that you make mistakes, damage things etc

NOUNS

a careless mistake *The essay was full of careless mistakes.*

careless attitude/approach *Her son seemed to have a careless attitude to money.*

careless words/talk *His careless words had upset her.*

careless driving *The man was found guilty of careless driving.*

C

careless use *Careless use of chemicals can be dangerous.*

careless handling *The government was criticized for its careless handling of the crisis.*

a careless driver *My aunt was hit by a careless driver and she had to go to hospital.*

VERBS

get/become/grow careless *People get careless about mixing drink and pills.*

PREPOSITIONS

be careless about (doing) sth *Some restaurant workers are careless about washing their hands.*

be careless with sth *Journalists are often careless with the facts.*

be careless of sth *He was careless of his own safety.*

it is careless of sb (to do sth) *It was careless of him to leave the door unlocked.*

THESAURUS: careless

clumsy
attempt | handling | fingers | hands | movements
not doing something skilfully, or moving in a careless way so that you break or drop things:
He made a clumsy attempt to apologize. | The government's clumsy handling of the affair has only made the problem worse. | With cold clumsy fingers she began fastening her coat. | I'm so clumsy, I spilt milk all over the floor.

sloppy
work | job | thinking
careless and lazy in the way you do your work, or in your behaviour generally. **Sloppy** sounds rather informal and is used mainly in spoken English:
The teacher said she didn't want any more sloppy work. | The previous builder did a very sloppy job. | The government had been in power for too long and they started to ***get sloppy***.

reckless *especially written*
driving | disregard | behaviour | spending
doing dangerous or stupid things without thinking about your own or other people's safety:
The driver of the car was arrested for reckless driving. | His actions showed a reckless disregard for human life.

irresponsible
behaviour | owner | lending
careless in a way that might affect other people, especially when this could cause serious accidents or problems:
Crew members could have lost their lives due to his irresponsible behaviour. | Some irresponsible owners allow their dogs to wander around the streets on their own. | It's irresponsible for parents to let their children smoke.

thoughtless
remark | comment
not thinking about the effects of your actions on other people, in a way that seems rather careless:
With that one thoughtless remark, she had got them all into trouble. | She realised ***it was thoughtless of*** *her not to say where she was going.*

tactless
remark | thing to say | question
carelessly saying something that upsets or embarrasses someone, without intending to do this:
He kept making tactless remarks about her appearance. | I'm sorry – it was a tactless question. | ***It was tactless of*** *her to say that it had been a boring evening.*

casual
attitude | way | manner
showing that you do not care very much about something and do not think it is important:
Nigel has a very casual attitude towards his work. | She mentioned the incident in a casual way. | They seem very ***casual about*** *what time people come into work.*

negligent
conduct
careless about something that you are responsible for, so that serious mistakes are made – used especially when someone will be officially punished for this:
He was found guilty of negligent conduct and was dismissed from his post. | The court decided that the doctor was negligent.

caring *adj*
THESAURUS ▸ **kind²**

carpet *n*
heavy woven material for covering floors, or a piece of this material

ADJECTIVES/NOUNS + carpet

a thick carpet *The thick carpet felt warm under her feet.*

a threadbare/worn carpet (=very thin and in bad condition) *She gazed gloomily at the dirty walls and the threadbare carpet.*

the bedroom/living room etc carpet *The bedroom carpet was brown.*

VERBS

fit/lay a carpet (=cut it to fit a room and fix it to the floor) *Will it cost extra to have the carpet fitted?*

make/weave a carpet *Young girls were trained to weave carpets.*

carry out *v*
THESAURUS ▸ **do**

cartoon *n*

a funny drawing or set of drawings in a newspaper or magazine, or a short film that is made by photographing a series of drawings

cartoon + NOUNS

a cartoon character *The little mouse is one of the world's most famous cartoon characters.*

a cartoon strip *The 'Peanuts' cartoon strip was created by Charles M. Schulz.*

a cartoon series *'The Simpsons' is a very popular cartoon series.*

VERBS

watch a cartoon *He's in the living room, watching a cartoon on TV.*

draw a cartoon *She draws cartoons for one of the national newspapers.*

ADJECTIVES

a political cartoon *Political cartoons are often very cruel.*

an animated cartoon *formal* (=a cartoon film) *There is a large selection of animated cartoons produced for children.*

carve *v* THESAURUS cut[1] (1)

case *n*

1 a matter that is dealt with by a law court or by the police

ADJECTIVES/NOUNS + case

a court case *There was a lot of publicity surrounding the court case.*

a criminal case *It was the longest and most expensive criminal case in US history.*

a murder/fraud/robbery etc case *He had been a witness in a murder case.*

a libel case (=when someone claims that something that has been written about them is untrue) *A libel case was brought against the newspaper.*

a divorce case *Things can get nasty in a divorce case.*

a civil case (=involving a disagreement between people, not a crime) *He is involved with civil cases, not criminal ones.*

a landmark case (=one that establishes a principle for the first time) *It was a landmark case in the regulation of the internet.*

a high-profile case (=one that gets a lot of attention) *They consulted a lawyer who has handled some high-profile cases.*

VERBS

bring a case (against sb) *There was not enough evidence to bring a case against him.*

hear/try a case (=listen to the evidence before making a judgment) *The case will be heard by a federal judge.*

decide a case *A panel of judges will decide his case.*

settle a case (=end it finally) *He paid a $15,000 fine to settle the case.*

prosecute/defend a case (=try to prove that someone is guilty or not guilty) *He defended his case himself.*

win/lose a case (=be successful or unsuccessful in proving someone guilty or not guilty) *Lomax was a brilliant lawyer who had never lost a case.*

adjourn a case (=stop it for a short time) *The case was adjourned until next month for further reports.*

dismiss/throw out a case (=officially stop it from continuing) *The case was thrown out by New York State's highest court.*

investigate a case *The police investigating the case had missed vital evidence.*

drop a case (=not continue with it) *The case was dropped because of a lack of evidence.*

solve a case *The police are making efforts to solve the case.*

PREPOSITIONS

a case against sb *She lost her case against the newspaper.*

PHRASES

a case comes/goes to court *When the case finally came to court, they were found not guilty.*

a case comes/goes to trial *By the time her case went to trial, her story had changed.*

2 an example of a particular situation, problem etc

ADJECTIVES

a clear case *It was a clear case of poor management.*

a simple case *His action appeared to be a simple case of cowardice.*

a classic case (=a very typical example) *This is a classic case of blaming the victim.*

an extreme case *In extreme cases, the building may have to be demolished.*

a special case *Farm workers say they must be treated as a special case.*

a rare/isolated case *There are rare cases of people being attacked by these animals.*

a similar case *I know of two similar cases.*

PREPOSITIONS

a case of sth *This is another case of science being misrepresented.*

in one case/in this case etc *In one case, a woman had to wait four hours for treatment.*

3 a set of reasons why something should happen or be done

ADJECTIVES

a good/strong/powerful case *There is a good case for caution.*

a convincing/compelling/persuasive case *He makes a convincing case for change.*

C

a weak case *His case is weak because he should have complained earlier.*

VERBS

have a case *We believe we have a strong case.*

present/put a case *You will have an opportunity to present your case.*

plead your case (=present your case) *They pleaded their case to US officials.*

make a case *I could make a case for both sides.*

support/strengthen/bolster a case *The discovery of this document strengthened the case for war.*

weaken/undermine a case (=make it appear weaker) *This information could undermine your case.*

PREPOSITIONS

a case for/against sth *I am aware of the case against nuclear energy.*

cash *n*

1 money

ADJECTIVES

spare cash *You should put any spare cash into a savings account.*

ready cash (=money that you can spend immediately) *If I'm short of ready cash, I can always borrow money from my parents.*

hard cash (=actual money, rather than a promise or possibility of payment) *No one was prepared to back his business with hard cash.*

VERBS

have any/enough etc cash *I'd love to come, but I don't have enough cash.*

raise cash (=get money) *She organized a series of events to raise cash for cancer charities.*

generate cash (=make money from business activities) *The website generates cash from advertising.*

provide cash *Campaigners are urging the government to provide more cash for health care.*

cash + NOUNS

a cash prize *The winner will get a cash prize of £10,000.*

cash flow (=the amount of money coming into a business compared to money going out) *The company was having a few problems with cash flow.*

PHRASES

be strapped for cash *informal* (*also* **be short of cash**) (=not have enough money) *Many airlines are strapped for cash at the moment.*

2 money in the form of coins or notes

VERBS

pay cash (=using money, not a credit card) *They won't take credit cards, so you will have to pay cash.*

have some/any etc cash *Do you have any cash with you?*

carry cash *I don't usually carry cash – I just use my credit card.*

withdraw/deposit cash (=take it out of a bank account, or put it into one) *There is a charge for withdrawing cash from the machine.*

cash + NOUNS

a cash machine (=a machine where you can get cash from your account with a plastic card) *There was a long line of people at the cash machine.*

a cash withdrawal/deposit *formal* (=money that is taken out of or put into a bank account) *There is a limit on cash withdrawals.*

PREPOSITIONS

in cash *The thieves stole over £200 in cash.*

cast *n*

all the people who perform in a play, film etc

ADJECTIVES

a large/small cast *The show required a large cast of dancers and singers.*

a strong/excellent/impressive cast (=with a lot of good actors) *The play has a strong cast of young actors.*

a talented cast *It's a fantastic production with an enormously talented cast.*

an all-star/star-studded/stellar cast (=with a lot of very famous actors) *The movie features an all-star cast.*

the supporting cast (=all the actors except the main ones) *There's also a fine supporting cast.*

VERBS

head the cast (=be the main actor) *Al Pacino heads the cast of this political thriller.*

have a cast (of people) *The play had a cast of almost unknown actors.*

cast + NOUNS

a cast member (*also* **a member of the cast**) *The members of the cast included Vanessa Redgrave and Judi Dench.*

the cast list (=the list of the actors in a film, play etc) *The movie has an impressive cast list.*

casual *adj*

1 not seeming to care or worry about something, or not treating something very seriously

NOUNS

a casual manner/attitude/way *Some students have a rather casual attitude to their studies.*

a casual glance/look *The man gave her a casual glance and then continued with his work.*

a casual remark/observation *It was just a casual remark, and not intended to be taken seriously.*

a casual conversation *They were having a casual conversation about the weather.*

VERBS

sound casual *She tried to sound casual when she was asking about the results of the test.*

PREPOSITIONS

casual about sth *She is very casual about most things, and doesn't often become stressed.*

> **THESAURUS: casual**
> clumsy, sloppy, reckless, irresponsible, thoughtless, tactless, casual, negligent → **careless**

2 casual clothes such as jeans are not suitable for a formal situation

NOUNS

casual clothes/dress/wear *She felt comfortable in casual clothes.*

a casual jacket *He was wearing jeans and a casual jacket.*

3 casual work is only for short periods of time and is not permanent

NOUNS

casual work *There are plenty of opportunities for casual work such as fruit picking.*

a casual worker *The farm employs casual workers during the harvest season.*

casual labour *BrE*, **casual labor** *AmE*: *The farmers depend on a supply of casual labour during the summer months.*

PHRASES

on a casual basis *At Christmas, the Post Office employs extra staff on a casual basis.*

casualty *n*

someone who is hurt or killed in an accident or war

ADJECTIVES/NOUNS + casualty

heavy/huge/massive casualties (=a lot of casualties) *There were heavy casualties on both sides.*

serious casualties (=badly injured people) *Serious casualties were taken to a nearby hospital.*

civilian casualties *The US forces are trying to avoid civilian casualties as much as possible.*

military casualties *His death brings the total number of military casualties to 5,000.*

road casualties (=people who are hurt or killed in road accidents) *The government is looking into ways of reducing road casualties.*

unnecessary casualties *The attack needs to be carefully planned in order to avoid unnecessary casualties.*

casualty + NOUNS

casualty figures *Official casualty figures put the number of people killed at 256.*

the casualty rate *Passenger casualty rates have fallen by 30 percent in the past five years.*

the casualty list *The casualty list of the war is long and growing.*

VERBS + casualty

suffer casualties *The British army suffered huge casualties in the battle.*

cause casualties *The bomb caused many casualties.*

PHRASES

the number of casualties *The number of civilian casualties is not known.*

cat *n*

a small animal with four legs that people often keep as a pet

ADJECTIVES

a pet cat *She has a pet cat called Snowy.*

a stray cat (=one that has lost its home) *He found a stray cat and started feeding it.*

a wild cat *If you are lucky, you might see a wild cat in the forests.*

a feral cat (=one that has no home and lives like a wild cat) *The fishing village was full of feral cats.*

a ginger cat (=with orange-brown fur)

a tabby cat (=with dark and light lines on brown or grey fur)

a tortoiseshell cat (=with yellow, brown, and black fur)

a domestic cat *formal* (=one that lives with people) *People have kept domestic cats for thousands of years.*

a pedigree cat *BrE*, **a pedigreed cat** *AmE* (=produced from other cats of the same type, over many years) *Pedigree cats can be very valuable, and should be insured against theft.*

> A male cat is called a **tom** or a **tom cat**, and a young cat is called a **kitten**.

cat + VERBS

a cat miaows/mews (=makes a noise) *The cat was miaowing outside the door.*

a cat purrs (=makes a soft noise that shows pleasure) *The cat purred as she stroked it.*

a cat hisses (=makes a noise that shows fear or anger) *Cats sometimes hiss at dogs.*

a cat scratches sb *He's been scratched by next door's cat.*

a cat jumps/leaps/springs somewhere *The cat leapt onto the bed.*

a cat pounces on sth (=jumps on something and catches it) *The cat pounced on the mouse and ate it.*

a cat is curled up somewhere *There was a cat curled up in the chair.*

VERBS + cat

have a cat (=keep one as a pet) *Mum, can we have a cat?*

feed a cat *She comes in while we're away to feed the cat.*

stroke a cat *She tried to stroke the cat, but it walked away.*

let/put the cat out (=let it go outside or make it go outside) *Can you let the cat out?*

cat + NOUNS

cat food *We need to buy some more cans of cat food.*

a cat flap (=a special small door for a cat to go in and out of a house) *The cat was getting too fat to fit through the cat flap.*

cat litter (=small grains for a cat to use as a toilet) *You should change cat litter daily.*

C

catalogue (*also* catalog *AmE*) *n*

a complete list of things that you can look at, buy, or use

NOUNS + catalogue

a clothes/furniture/gardening etc catalogue *She saw the sweater in a clothes catalogue.*

a mail order catalogue (=which allows you to buy goods by post, without going to a store) *He bought the coffee machine from a mail order catalogue.*

an exhibition catalogue *The exhibition catalogue tells you about the history of each picture.*

a library catalogue *I tried to find the book I wanted in the library catalogue.*

ADJECTIVES

a free catalogue *I asked them to send me a free catalogue.*

an online catalogue (=which you can look at on the internet) *The online catalogue shows all the books they have available.*

an illustrated catalogue (=with pictures) *The company has an illustrated catalogue of all their products.*

VERBS

look/flick/browse through a catalogue *She was flicking through a catalogue of women's fashions.*

order/buy sth from a catalogue *I was thinking of ordering the seeds from a catalogue.*

send off for a catalogue *You can send off for a free catalogue.*

produce/publish a catalogue *The company publishes a catalogue of all its products.*

catastrophe *n*

a terrible event in which there is a lot of destruction, suffering, or death

ADJECTIVES

a major catastrophe *The fire was a major catastrophe for the area.*

a terrible catastrophe *Then came the terrible catastrophe of 1914, when the First World War started.*

a global/world catastrophe *A nuclear war would be a global catastrophe.*

a national catastrophe *For fans, losing the game was a national catastrophe.*

an environmental/ecological catastrophe *A sudden rise in world temperatures could cause an environmental catastrophe.*

a natural catastrophe *Natural catastrophes such as floods and earthquakes cannot be prevented.*

an economic catastrophe *The country faces an economic catastrophe.*

a nuclear catastrophe *People are worried that there could be another nuclear catastrophe like the one at Chernobyl.*

a humanitarian catastrophe (=one which has a terrible effect on a lot of people's lives) *The earthquake caused a humanitarian catastrophe and thousands of people were left homeless.*

VERBS

cause/lead to/result in a catastrophe *The decision could lead to an economic catastrophe.*

prevent/avoid a catastrophe (*also* **avert a catastrophe** *formal*): *Firefighters prevented a catastrophe by putting out the fire before it could spread.*

face a catastrophe *The country is facing a catastrophe after being hit by three deadly storms.*

be heading for a catastrophe (=a catastrophe will happen soon) *According to some scientists, the planet is heading for a catastrophe because of the effects of global warming.*

a catastrophe happens/takes place (*also* **a catastrophe occurs** *formal*): *Fortunately, this kind of catastrophe occurs very rarely.*

category Ac *n*

a group of people or things that are all of the same type

ADJECTIVES

the main category *There are two main categories of evidence.*

a special category *Until very recently, female poets were placed in a special category.*

a distinct/separate category (=clearly different from others) *Drivers fall into two distinct categories.*

a broad/general category *Computer viruses fall into three broad categories.*

a major category *Theft is one of the major categories of crime.*

the same/a different category *In my opinion, this crime belongs in the same category as murder.*

VERBS

belong to/in a category *A lot of plants belong in this category.*

fall into/come into a category *The data we collected fell into two categories.*

fit into a category *There were classes for beginners and for advanced students, but I didn't fit into either category.*

put/place sb/sth in a category *I would put this book in the category of adventure story.*

group sb/sth into categories *The courses are grouped into three categories: basic, intermediate and advanced.*

divide/split sth into categories *The exhibition of 360 paintings is divided into three categories.*

create a category *The government wants to create a new category for this type of offence.*

form a category *This type of book forms the largest single category.*

a category includes sth *This category included skilled workers such as engineers, carpenters, and builders.*

PREPOSITIONS

in a category *The winner in each category will receive a prize.*

cause[1] *n*

1 a person, event, or thing that makes something happen

ADJECTIVES

a common cause of sth *Stress is a common cause of sleep problems.*

the main/primary cause of sth *Smoking is the main cause of lung disease.*

a major/leading cause of sth *In this country, debt is a major cause of homelessness.*

a direct/indirect cause *Government policies are the direct cause of the problems facing the economy.*

the root cause (=the most basic cause) *It is time to tackle the root causes of crime.*

the underlying cause (=the basic cause, especially one that is not obvious) *Current treatments deal with the symptoms rather than underlying causes of the disease.*

the probable/likely cause *The probable cause of the fire was an electrical fault.*

VERBS

find/discover the cause *The flight is being delayed while entineers try to discover the cause of the problem.*

determine/establish/identify the cause (=discover definitely what it is) *A team of experts is at the scene of the accident, trying to determine the cause.*

investigate the cause *Police are still investigating the cause of the fire.*

PHRASES

cause of death *The official cause of death was given as drowning.*

die of/from natural causes (=die of illness, old age etc, not because of an accident or crime) *He died from natural causes, probably a heart attack.*

cause and effect *The relationship between cause and effect in mental illness is complex.*

2 an aim, belief, or organization that a group of people support or fight for

ADJECTIVES

a good cause (=one that is worth supporting, for example a charity) *The money we are raising is for a good cause.*

a just cause (=one that is good and right) *The rebels believed that they were fighting for a just cause.*

a noble cause (=one that is morally good) *He died for a noble cause.*

a worthy/deserving cause (=a good cause which deserves people's support) *The Red Cross is a very worthy cause.*

the Nationalist/Republican etc cause *The election results were a serious blow to the Nationalist cause.*

VERBS

support a cause *Giving money is only one way of supporting a good cause.*

fight for a cause *Young people often want to fight for a cause.*

champion a cause (=publicly support it) *He has championed the cause of renewable energy since the 1980s.*

advance/further/promote a cause (=help to achieve an aim) *He did much to advance the cause of freedom.*

PHRASES

be committed to a cause (=support a cause very strongly) *We are committed to the cause of racial justice.*

be sympathetic to a cause (=understand it, and possibly support it) *They hope the new president will be sympathetic to their cause.*

all in a good cause (=done in order to help or raise money for people) *I didn't mind looking silly since it was all in a good cause.*

cause[2] *v*

to make something happen, especially something bad

NOUNS

cause a problem *Heavy rain has been causing serious problems on the roads.*

cause trouble *I decided not to complain because I didn't want to cause trouble.*

cause damage/injury *These insects can cause severe damage to crops.*

cause a disease *Scientists are trying to find out what causes the disease.*

cause pain *The infection can cause severe pain.*

cause death *The famine caused the death of 400,000 people.*

cause an accident *75% of accidents are caused by speeding.*

cause a delay *Bad weather caused delays at many airports.*

cause chaos/disruption *Floods caused chaos across much of the country.*

cause concern/alarm *The pollution in the area is causing concern among scientists.*

cause confusion/uncertainty *Teachers say the changes will cause confusion in schools.*

cause offence/embarrassment (=offend or embarrass someone) *How can I refuse the invitation without causing offence?*

THESAURUS: cause

result in sth
if an action or event results in something, it makes that thing happen:
The fire resulted in the deaths of two children. | The decision is likely to result in a large number of job losses. | Changes to the design of car engines could result in a significant reduction in air pollution.

lead to sth
to cause something to happen eventually after a period of time:
The information led to several arrests. | A poor diet in childhood can lead to health problems later in life. | Having more money does not necessarily lead to an increase in human happiness.

be responsible for sth
sb's death | bombing | killing | accident
if someone or something is responsible for something bad, they caused it to happen:
He was responsible for the deaths of thousands of people. | A small militant group was responsible for the bombing. | The court decided that the other driver was responsible for the accident.

bring about sth
change | improvement | sb's downfall | peace
to make something happen - used especially about changes or improvements:
The internet has brought about enormous changes in society. | Their system has not brought about any improvement in the conditions of the average worker. | He was very rich and had lots of money, but this helped bring about his downfail (=made him fail). *| It's important that we do everything we can to bring about peace.*

trigger
tsunami | earthquake | wave | protests | demonstrations | anger | outrage | alarm | crisis | heart attack
to make something suddenly happen, especially a natural disaster or strong angry feelings:
An earthquake off Java's southern coast triggered a tsunami. | The incident triggered a wave of violence. | Food price rises have triggered protests. | His heart attack was triggered by the physical and emotional pressure of his work.

precipitate *formal*
crisis | collapse | sb's fall | sb's resignation | war
to make a very serious event happen very suddenly, which will affect a lot of people:
The withdrawal of foreign investment would precipitate an economic crisis. | The government's actions precipitated a collapse in agricultural production. | The assassination of Archduke Franz Ferdinand precipitated World War I.

caution *n*

the quality of being very careful to avoid danger or risks

ADJECTIVES

great/considerable caution *With great caution he moved forward across the ice.*

extreme caution *Bears can be dangerous and walkers should proceed with extreme caution.*

the utmost caution *Such predictions should be treated with the utmost caution.*

VERBS

advise caution *We advise caution if you are buying a property overseas.*

urge caution *Scientists are urging caution in research involving genes.*

exercise caution (=be careful) *Travellers are advised to exercise caution while travelling in remote areas.*

caution is needed (*also* **caution is required** *formal*): *Caution is required when interpreting these figures.*

PHRASES

treat sth with caution *The results of the survey should be treated with caution.*

proceed with caution *formal*: *You should always proceed with caution in financial matters.*

err on the side of caution (=be more careful than may be necessary) *Doctors should err on the side of caution and do immediate tests on the child.*

cautious *adj*

careful to avoid danger or risks

NOUNS

a cautious approach *I think we need to take a cautious approach and not rush into a decision.*

a cautious attitude *Women tend to have a more cautious attitude than men, and they are less likely to take risks.*

cautious optimism *There is cautious optimism that the talks will result in an agreement.*

a cautious welcome/response *His suggestion received a cautious response from the other members of the group.*

a cautious driver *My aunt is a cautious driver and she always drives very slowly.*

VERBS

remain cautious *Companies remain cautious about using the new technology.*

ADVERBS

extremely/highly cautious *You need to be extremely cautious with this type of information.*

naturally cautious *Some investors are naturally cautious.*

PREPOSITIONS

cautious about sth *Banks are more cautious about lending people money.*

THESAURUS: cautious

cautious, thorough, methodical, systematic, meticulous, painstaking → **careful**

cave *n*

a large natural hole in the side of a cliff or hill, or under the ground: *the entrance to a cave*

ADJECTIVES

a dark cave *They walked out of the dark cave into the bright sunshine.*

a damp cave *The cave was cold and damp.*

a prehistoric cave (=which was used thousands of years ago) *These prehistoric caves were occupied by men and animals some 70,000 years ago.*

VERBS

enter a cave *I switched on my torch as we entered the cave.*

live in a cave *The old man lived in a cave on the side of the mountain.*

hide in a cave *She escaped being captured by hiding in a cave.*

cave + NOUNS

the cave entrance (*also* **the mouth of the cave**) *The mouth of the cave was hidden by some tall bushes.*

the cave floor (*also* **the floor of the cave**) *They crawled along the floor of the cave on their hands and knees.*

the cave walls/ceiling (*also* **the walls/ceiling of a cave**) *People drew pictures of animals on the cave walls.*

a cave system *The cave is part of a much larger cave system.*

a cave painting *Altamira is famous for its cave paintings.*

cave dwellers (=people who live in caves) *The first people who lived on the island were primitive cave dwellers.*

PREPOSITIONS

in a cave *Bats often live in caves.*

cease *v* THESAURUS stop[1] (1), (2)

ceasefire *n*

an agreement to stop fighting for a period of time

ADJECTIVES

a permanent/temporary ceasefire *The US called for a temporary ceasefire so food aid could be brought in.*

an immediate ceasefire *The president announced an immediate ceasefire.*

a unilateral ceasefire (=declared by one side only) *A unilateral ceasefire was announced by the government.*

VERBS + ceasefire

declare/announce a ceasefire *The two countries have declared a ceasefire.*

call for/demand a ceasefire *The United Nations called for a ceasefire in the region.*

agree to a ceasefire *The rebels eventually agreed to a ceasefire.*

negotiate a ceasefire *The African Union is attempting to negotiate a ceasefire.*

break a ceasefire *The ceasefire was broken when government troops invaded the area.*

observe a ceasefire *formal* (=obey it) *Both sides have observed a ceasefire for over two months.*

monitor a ceasefire (=check that it is being obeyed) *UN troops have been brought in to monitor the ceasefire.*

ceasefire + VERBS

a ceasefire comes into effect (=it starts) *As soon as the peace agreement is signed, a ceasefire will come into effect.*

a ceasefire breaks down *Fighting has begun again after a ceasefire broke down.*

a ceasefire holds (=it is not being broken) *The ceasefire is holding for now, but the situation could change at any moment.*

ceasefire + NOUNS

a ceasefire agreement *He was the first of the two leaders to sign the ceasefire agreement.*

PHRASES

the terms of a ceasefire *Under the terms of the ceasefire, it was decided that both armies would withdraw.*

a violation of a ceasefire (=an action that breaks a ceasefire) *The rocket attack was a clear violation of the ceasefire.*

ceiling *n*

the inner surface of the top part of a room

ADJECTIVES/NOUNS + ceiling

a high/low ceiling *The rooms have low ceilings and you need to be careful not to bang your head.*

the kitchen/bedroom etc ceiling *She looked up at the bedroom ceiling.*

a sloping ceiling *On the top floor the bedrooms have sloping ceilings.*

VERBS

hang from the ceiling *The lamp hung from the ceiling.*

PREPOSITIONS

on the ceiling *There was an enormous spider on the ceiling.*

from floor to ceiling *The bookcases covered the walls from floor to ceiling.*

celebrated *adj* THESAURUS ▶ famous

celebration *n*

an occasion or party when you celebrate something

ADJECTIVES/NOUNS + celebration

a big celebration *The big celebration usually takes place on Christmas Eve.*

a small/little celebration *We're having a small celebration for Dad's birthday.*

a special celebration *There's a special celebration tonight to mark the school's 50th anniversary.*

Christmas/New Year/wedding etc celebrations *They invited me to join in their New Year celebrations.*

a birthday/anniversary celebration *He is planning a very special 40th birthday celebration.*

a family celebration *Everyone's coming here for a family celebration.*

a victory celebration *Some football fans were arrested during the victory celebrations.*

a double celebration (=for two good things) *It's a double celebration for our first wedding anniversary and my birthday.*

VERBS

have a celebration *The villagers were having a celebration of some kind.*

hold/host a celebration *formal*: *The company is holding a celebration for its 75th anniversary.*

go to a celebration (*also* **attend a celebration** *formal*): *He was too ill to attend his son's birthday celebrations.*

join in the celebrations *You're welcome to come and join in the celebrations!*

celebration + NOUNS

a celebration dinner/meal/party *There will be a celebration dinner at the Red Lion Hotel.*

PREPOSITIONS

a celebration of/for sth *He took an active role in celebrations for the town's 50th anniversary.*

PHRASES

a celebration takes place *The celebrations took place in a stadium.*

a celebration to mark sth (=a celebration of something) *They are organizing celebrations to mark the completion of the building.*

celebrity *n* a famous living person

ADJECTIVES/NOUNS + celebrity

a TV/television celebrity *He is one of Britain's most famous TV celebrities.*

a major/minor celebrity *He became a minor celebrity after appearing on a reality TV show.*

a sports celebrity *Sports celebrities can make a lot of money from advertising.*

a media celebrity (=one who is seen a lot on television, in magazines etc) *She's a famous fashion model and media celebrity.*

a national/international celebrity *This exclusive resort attracts international celebrities.*

a local celebrity *They've invited a local celebrity to open the new shopping centre.*

celebrity + NOUNS

a celebrity guest *He has interviewed many celebrity guests on his radio show.*

celebrity status (=someone's position as a celebrity) *She used her celebrity status to raise money for charity.*

celebrity gossip (=stories about celebrities, especially about their private lives) *'NOW' magazine brings you the latest celebrity gossip.*

celebrity culture (=in which people pay a lot of attention to celebrities) *Magazines, TV, and the internet are obsessed with celebrity culture.*

cell *n*

the smallest part of a living thing that can exist independently

ADJECTIVES/NOUNS + cell

a blood/nerve/brain/muscle etc cell *No new brain cells are produced after birth.*

a human/animal/plant cell *How do viruses get inside plant cells?*

a living/dead cell *Every living cell has a nucleus.*

a normal/abnormal cell *The test enables doctors to detect abnormal cells.*

a cancer cell *Already there are many treatments which destroy cancer cells.*

a healthy cell *Drugs that kill cancer cells also kill healthy cells.*

a stem cell (=one that divides and repairs the body, and may be used in medical treatment) *Stem cells could be used to replace any body part.*

VERBS

a cell divides *White blood cells divide rapidly.*

cell + NOUNS

the cell wall (=the outside part of a cell) *The cell walls of plants are made from a tough material called cellulose.*

cell division *The embryo grows by cell division.*

cell phone, cellphone *n AmE*

a small phone that you can carry with you

VERBS

call sb on his/her cell phone *Why don't you call him on his cell phone?*

use a cell phone *It is illegal to use a cell phone while driving.*

a cell phone rings *Her cell phone started ringing in the middle of the meeting.*

switch on/off a cell phone *Please make sure that your cell phone is switched off.*

charge a cell phone (=put electricity into it) *How often do you charge your cell phone?*

cell phone + NOUNS

a cell phone number *What is your cell phone number?*

a cell phone company *Which cell phone company do you use?*

a cell phone call *The company is offering unlimited free cell phone calls at weekends.*

PREPOSITIONS

on a cell phone *She was speaking on her cell phone.*

from a cell phone *I can't make calls from my cell phone.*

> **Cell phone** is used in American English. In British English, people say **mobile phone**, or **mobile** (informal).
>
> In more formal American English, people say **cellular phone**. In informal American English, people say **cell**.

censor *v*

to remove parts of books, films, letters etc, because they are considered unsuitable for political, moral, or religious reasons

ADVERBS

be heavily censored (=a lot of parts have been removed) *The report had been heavily censored by the authorities.*

censorship *n*

removing parts of books, films, letters etc, because they are considered unsuitable for political, moral, or religious reasons

ADJECTIVES/NOUNS + censorship

government censorship *Newspaper reports about the war are subject to government censorship.*

political censorship *The decision to ban the film resulted in accusations of political censorship.*

strict/heavy censorship *There was heavy censorship of all letters sent by prisoners.*

press/media censorship (=censorship of newspapers, television etc) *I don't agree with press censorship – I think it goes against the right to free speech.*

film censorship *Film censorship was controlled by a special government department.*

VERBS

impose censorship on sth (=start controlling what is said or written and remove parts that are considered unsuitable) *The authorities imposed strict censorship on all newspapers and television networks.*

PREPOSITIONS

censorship of sth *In some countries there is strict censorship of the media.*

PHRASES

the abolition of censorship *Some people are calling for the abolition of censorship.*

central *adj* most important

NOUNS

a central role/part *The report emphasizes the central role of science in industry.*

a central feature *This mix of cultures is a central feature of modern British society.*

a central issue *Education is a central issue for the government.*

a central concern *Environmental problems are now a central concern.*

a central theme/idea *What would you say is the central theme of the book?*

a central figure *During this time he was a central figure in American politics.*

the central question *The central question is: could this accident have been prevented?*

the central argument *Let's consider the central argument for reducing the voting age.*

PREPOSITIONS

central to sth *Her religion was central to her life.*

PHRASES

of central importance *The mining industry was of central importance to the country's economy.*

> **THESAURUS: central**
>
> principal/chief, primary, core, central, prime, predominant → **main**

centre *BrE*, center *AmE n*

1 the middle of an area or object

NOUNS + centre

the city/town centre *The government has its main offices in the city centre.*

ADJECTIVES

the very centre *In the very centre of the room was a large round table.*

the exact centre *She placed the cake in the exact centre of the plate.*

PREPOSITIONS

the centre of sth *Check that the centre of the cake is cooked.*

in the centre *There was a fountain in the centre of the courtyard.*

at the centre *People used to believe that the Earth was at the centre of the universe.*

through the centre *10,000 protesters marched through the centre of London.*

PHRASES

right in the centre *The hotel is right in the centre of the village, close to all the shops.*

2 a place where there is a lot of a particular type of business or activity

ADJECTIVES/NOUNS + centre

a financial centre *Boston is a leading financial centre.*

a business/commercial centre *The company has branches worldwide in 15 major business centres.*

a trading centre *The town was a trading centre for the Romans.*

a cultural centre *Paris was then the cultural centre of Europe.*

a tourist centre *Our destination was Queenstown, a tourist centre set amid mountains and lakes.*

a major/important centre *The region has been named as a major centre of international terrorism.*

a world/international/national centre *The Asian Pacific Rim is a world centre of economic activity.*

PREPOSITIONS

a centre of/for sth *Zurich is an international centre of finance. | The city became a centre for the paper industry.*

3 a building which is used for a particular purpose or activity

ADJECTIVES/NOUNS + centre

a shopping centre *They are building a huge new shopping centre just outside the town.*

a sports centre *You could join an exercise class at your local sports centre.*

an arts centre (=for art, music, theatre, film etc) *Shall we go to the concert at the arts centre on Saturday?*

a conference centre *Westgate Hotel has 60 bedrooms and a conference centre.*

a tourist information centre *For further details contact the Tourist Information Centre.*

a visitor centre *The forest has a visitor centre with a shop and café.*

a research centre *A new research centre has just been opened at King's College Hospital.*

a training centre *He was a new recruit at the police training centre.*

a health/medical centre *The village has a small school and a health centre.*

a community centre (=where people can go for social events, classes etc) *The church is used as a community centre.*

a youth centre *BrE* (=where young people can go to meet and take part in activities) *The money will be used to provide a youth centre.*

a leisure centre *BrE* (=for sport and other leisure activities) *There's a leisure centre with a swimming pool, a sauna, and a gymnasium.*

a day centre/day care centre *BrE* (=where old, sick etc people can go during the day to be looked after) *A new day centre for the over 70s has recently opened.*

PREPOSITIONS

a centre for sth *He is a senior economist at the Centre for Economic and Business Research.*

century *n*

one of the 100-year periods before or after the year of Christ's birth, or any period of 100 years

ADJECTIVES

the 18th/20th etc century *The movie is set in the 18th century. | He has a collection of 19th-century art.*

the early/mid/late 18th/20th etc century *By the late nineteenth century, the town had a population of over 10,000.*

the last/next century *The house was built in the early part of the last century.*

this century (*also* **the present century** *formal*): *The present century has seen a big rise in international terrorism.*

> ⚠ Don't say 'in this century'. Just say **this century**.

VERBS

date from the 15th/18th etc century (=something was built, made, or started at that time) *The present church dates from the 13th century.*

a century sees something (=used when saying that something happens during that century) *The nineteenth century saw major developments in science.*

PREPOSITIONS

in the 18th/20th etc century *The game was invented in the sixteenth century.*

for centuries *This plant has been used for centuries to reduce pain.*

during a century *During this century, the US became the most powerful nation on earth.*

PHRASES

the beginning of the century *At the beginning of the century, there were more single than married people.*

the end of the century *He wrote his books towards the end of the 19th century.*

the turn of the century (=the time when one century ends and another begins) *The town was expanding at the turn of the century.*

the first/second half of the century *In the second half of the century, people's wages began to rise.*

the early/latter part of the century *The latter part of the century saw great progress in organic chemistry.*

half a century/a quarter of a century *The civil war lasted for half a century.*

ceremony *n*

a formal event, when people say or do special or traditional things

ADJECTIVES/NOUNS + ceremony

a religious ceremony *Did you have a religious ceremony when you got married?*

a special ceremony *The winners will receive their awards at a special ceremony in London.*

a short/brief ceremony *He became acting president in a brief ceremony yesterday.*

a simple ceremony *The gymnasium was opened in a simple ceremony on 26 May.*

a grand/elaborate ceremony *The inhabitants of the town organized a grand ceremony to mark the occasion.*

a solemn ceremony (=a very serious one) *There was a solemn ceremony in the city cathedral.*

a traditional ceremony *African traditional marriage ceremonies were not recognized by the state.*

a wedding/marriage ceremony *It was a beautiful wedding ceremony.*

a funeral ceremony *Funeral ceremonies have been held since ancient times.*

the opening/closing ceremony (=at the beginning or end of a special event) *I stayed for the closing ceremony.*

a prize-giving/awards ceremony *A prize-giving ceremony will take place tomorrow night at the university.*

a graduation ceremony *His proud parents attended his graduation ceremony.*

VERBS

hold a ceremony *A ceremony was held in Berlin to mark the occasion.*

attend a ceremony (=be at it) *I attended the ceremony at the cathedral.*

perform/conduct a ceremony (=be in charge of it) *The Bishop of Louisiana performed the ceremony.*

PHRASES

a ceremony takes place *The ceremony took place on 13 June at 2.30.*

take part in a ceremony *Women will be taking part in the ceremony for the first time.*

be present at a ceremony *The French ambassador was present at the ceremony.*

certain *adj*

1 confident and sure, without any doubts

ADVERBS

absolutely/completely certain *He was absolutely certain that he was right.*

almost certain *I'm almost certain I left my keys on the kitchen table.*

fairly certain (*also* **pretty certain** *informal*): *The team was fairly certain they would win.*

VERBS

feel certain *She felt certain that he did not intend to harm her.*

PREPOSITIONS

certain about/of sth *You can't be certain about anything these days.*

2 if something is certain, it will definitely happen or is definitely true

ADVERBS

almost/virtually certain *It is almost certain that she is innocent.*

VERBS

it seems certain (that)... *It now seems certain that he will have to resign.*

seem/look/appear certain to do sth *The mission seemed certain to end in failure.*

NOUNS

certain death *They escaped certain death by jumping out of the car before it went over the cliff.*

certain defeat *The team seemed to be heading for certain defeat.*

PHRASES

by no means certain/far from certain (=not certain at all) *Victory was by no means certain.*

certainly *adv* without any doubt

ADVERBS

almost certainly *They have almost certainly gone home.*

most certainly (=used when you are very sure about something) *"Giving up smoking has made a real difference." "It most certainly has."*

Certainly not! *"Are you going with him?" "Certainly not!"*

certificate *n*

an official document that states information about someone or something, or shows that someone has a qualification

ADJECTIVES/NOUNS + certificate

a birth/marriage/death certificate *In order to get a passport, you'll need your birth certificate.*

a medical certificate *In the UK, you need to produce a medical certificate if you are off work for more than a week.*

a degree certificate (=showing that someone has a degree)

a teaching certificate (=showing that someone is qualified to teach)

VERBS

have a certificate (*also* **hold a certificate** *formal*): *Do you have a teaching certificate?*

issue a certificate *The certificate will be issued upon payment of the fee.*

receive a certificate *Everyone who takes part in the race receives a certificate.*

PREPOSITIONS

a certificate of sth *The diamonds have a certificate of origin.*

chair *n*

a piece of furniture for one person to sit on, which has a back

VERBS

sit in/on a chair *She sat in her favourite chair.*

pull/draw up a chair (=move a chair nearer someone or something) *Pull up a chair and look at these pictures.*

take a chair (=sit down in one in a particular place) *Brian took a chair beside his wife.*

sink/slump/flop into a chair (=sit down in a tired or unhappy way) *Greg groaned and sank into his chair.*

collapse in/into a chair (=sit down suddenly because you are very tired or upset) *Eileen collapsed into a chair and burst out crying.*

get up from your chair (*also* **rise from your chair** *formal*): *He got up from his chair and walked to the window.*

lean back in your chair *He leant back in his chair and took out his pipe.*

ADJECTIVES

a comfortable chair (*also* **a comfy chair** *informal*): *There was a low glass table surrounded by comfortable chairs.*

a hard chair *I sat on a hard chair in the corridor and waited.*

an empty chair (=with no one using it) *He put his feet on an empty chair.*

chair + NOUNS

a chair leg/arm/back/seat *The chair leg has broken.*

> **Prepositions with chair**
> You sit **on** a hard chair. You sit **in** a soft comfortable chair.

chairman *n*

the person who is in charge of an organization, committee, or meeting

VERBS

appoint sb chairman *He was appointed Chairman of the World Cup Organizing Committee.*

elect sb chairman *The board of directors elected her chairman.*

take over as chairman *He will take over as chairman of the airline SpiceJet.*

serve as chairman *He has served as chairman of the US firm since 2010.*

a chairman resigns/stands down *The chairman was forced to resign following the scandal.*

ADJECTIVES/NOUNS + chairman

a company/committee/club chairman *The club chairman is responsible for hiring and firing managers.*

a party chairman *She was elected party chairman by a large majority.*

the deputy/vice chairman (=the position directly below the chairman) *She is deputy chairman of the school's Parent-Teacher Association.*

the executive chairman *The executive chairman is involved in the company's day-to-day management.*

PREPOSITIONS

the chairman of a company/committee/meeting *He became chairman of the company about five years ago.*

> **Chairman, chairwoman, chairperson, or chair?**
> **Chairman** is used about both men and women. People often use **chairperson** or **chair** instead of **chairman**, to avoid the reference to men.
> You can also call a female **chairman** a **chairwoman**.

challenge Ac *n*

something that tests your ability or skill, especially in a way that is interesting

ADJECTIVES

a big/great/huge/major challenge *The bridge will be a major challenge for the engineers.*

biggest/greatest challenge *Our biggest challenge is finding the money.*

a new/fresh challenge *Ross is looking for a fresh challenge.*

a tough/formidable/daunting challenge (=a very difficult one) *The mountain presents a formidable challenge to climbers.*

a real challenge *Winning the championship will be a real challenge.*

an intellectual/physical/technical etc challenge *I enjoy the intellectual challenge of solving problems.*

VERBS

face a challenge *The new government faces some difficult challenges.*

meet a challenge (=deal with it successfully) *I am confident that we can meet the challenge.*

rise to the challenge (=find the skills, abilities etc you need to deal with it successfully) *It was a difficult project but we rose to the challenge.*

deal with/tackle a challenge *Governments have only just begun to deal with the challenge of global warming.*

accept/take up a challenge *The new team captain says he is ready to take up the challenge.*

like/love/enjoy a challenge (*also* **relish a challenge** *more formal*): *She is relishing the challenge of learning a new language.*

present/pose a challenge (=be a difficult challenge) *Large classes present a challenge for teachers.*

challenging *adj* THESAURUS ▶ difficult

champion *n*

someone or something that has won a competition, especially in sport

ADJECTIVES/NOUNS + champion

a world/European/national champion *At 22, he was the youngest world champion in the history of the game.*

an Olympic champion *She's a top international athlete and an Olympic champion.*

the defending/reigning champion (=the one who won last time) *He defeated the defending champion in the National Grand Prix.*

a former champion *He is a former world heavyweight champion.*

a great champion *Like all great champions, he is dedicated to his sport.*

a worthy champion (=one who deserves to be champion) *The Australians played well and are worthy champions.*

a junior champion (=in a young age group) *The cycling team includes the British junior champion, Andrew Wright.*

a boxing/tennis/golf etc champion *He became the world boxing champion at the age of 22.*

the 100/200 etc metres champion *She is the world 100 metres champion.*

champion + NOUNS

a champion swimmer/boxer/cyclist etc *Dan had been a champion swimmer in high school.*

VERBS

become champion *It took him only three years to become champion.*

be crowned champion (=become champion) *The next year, the team were crowned rugby champions of the world.*

championship *n*

a competition to find which player or team is the best in a particular sport

ADJECTIVES/NOUNS + championship

the world championship *Twenty-nine nations competed in the world championship.*

a national/international championship *It was the final game of the international championship.*

the British/European etc championship *The team failed to qualify for the European Championship.*

a golf/swimming/tennis championship *The Women's Golf Championship was won by Paula Creamer.*

the league championship (=in which a group of soccer teams play against each other) *Arsenal are expected to win the League Championship this year.*

a major championship *He has never won a major championship.*

a junior championship (=for younger players or teams) *She reached the final of the junior championship when she was 15.*

VERBS

win/lose a championship *He won three national championships at Oklahoma.*

compete in/take part in a championship *Players from all over the world will be taking part in the championship.*

qualify for a championship (=be good enough to be in it) *Only 26 players will qualify for the World Championship.*

a championship is held/takes place *The championships are being held next Sunday at the San Jose Arena.*

championship + NOUNS

a championship game/race/fight *He was playing in his first championship game of the season.*

the championship finals *His team lost in the European Championship finals.*

a championship competition/tournament *When is the next motorcycling championship competition?*

PREPOSITIONS

in a championship *He came second in the championship.*

chance *n*

1 the possibility that something will happen, especially something you want

ADJECTIVES

a good/strong chance (=something seems likely) *I think there is a good chance that he will say yes.*

a high chance (=something seems very likely) *These diseases have a high chance of being passed on to the next generation.*

a small/slight/slim chance *He only has a very small chance of being elected.*

little/not much chance *The prisoners knew there was little chance of escape.*

no chance *There is no chance of the same thing happening again.*

a real/realistic chance *Only go to court if you think you have a realistic chance of winning.*

a reasonable/decent chance *If you study, you have a reasonable chance of passing the test.*

a one in three/four/ten etc chance *People in their 30s have a one in 3,000 chance of getting the disease.*

a 50-50 chance/an even chance (=an equal chance that something will or will not happen)

I'd say there is a 50-50 chance that the deal will go through.

a million-to-one/one in a million chance (=something is extremely unlikely) *It must have been a million-to-one chance that we'd meet.*

a sporting chance (=a fairly good chance) *The proposals had at least a sporting chance of being accepted.*

an outside/remote chance (=a very small chance) *He still has an outside chance of winning the championship.*

C

VERBS

have a chance of doing sth *I think you have a good chance of getting the job.*

give sb a chance *These treatments give the patient a high chance of survival.*

increase/improve the chance of sth *The book shows you how to improve your chance of success.*

reduce/lessen the chance of sth *The talks were aimed at reducing the chance of war.*

jeopardize the chance of sth (=make something much less likely to happen) *This could jeopardize any chance of peace.*

PHRASES

sb's chances of success *What are the team's chances of success?*

sb doesn't stand a chance (=they do not have a chance) *I didn't think that we stood a chance against such an experienced team.*

be in with a chance (=it is possible that someone can win, succeed etc) *He knows that he is still in with a chance of winning the election.*

2 an opportunity to do something

VERBS + chance

get/have the chance to do sth *I'd like a job in which I get the chance to travel.*

give sb/offer/provide the chance to do sth *I was given the chance to play the main part in the play.*

take a chance (=accept an opportunity) *If I was offered the chance to be in the team, I'd take it.*

deserve a chance *Every kid deserves a chance in life.*

wait for a chance *Ralph was waiting for a chance to introduce himself.*

jump at a chance (=use an opportunity eagerly) *Ed jumped at the chance to earn some extra money.*

grab/seize a chance (=quickly use an opportunity) *As soon as she stopped speaking, I grabbed the chance to leave.*

deny sb the chance (=stop someone having an opportunity) *She could not deny him the chance of becoming a father.*

miss/lose a chance *He missed a chance to score just before half time.*

throw away/squander a chance (*also* **blow a chance** *informal*) (=not accept or use an opportunity by being careless or stupid) *Your parents will be angry if you throw away the chance to go to college.*

chance + VERBS

a chance comes up (*also* **a chance arises** *formal*) (=it happens) *When the chance came up, we took it.*

ADJECTIVES/NOUNS + chance

another chance/a second chance *The interview went badly, and I didn't think they would give me a second chance.*

sb's last/only chance *This is my last chance to try to pass the exam.*

a good/great chance *Temporary work gives you a good chance to try out different jobs.*

a real chance *I haven't yet had a real chance to talk to her about it.*

sb's big chance (=a good and important one) *This is your big chance to show everyone how good you are.*

a fair chance *Did everyone have a fair chance to express their opinion?*

a rare chance *Visitors will get a rare chance to see inside a working mine.*

PREPOSITIONS

a chance for sth *The event provides a chance for open discussion.*

PHRASES

the chance of a lifetime (=one that you are very unlikely to have again) *If you don't decide soon, you'll have missed the chance of a lifetime.*

now is your chance (=you have the opportunity to do something now) *If you ever wanted to be in a movie, now's your chance.*

given half a chance/given a chance (=if there is any opportunity to do something) *Goats will eat anything, given half a chance.*

change[1] *v*

1 to become different

ADVERBS

change a lot/a great deal/considerably *The town has changed a lot since I was last here.*

change completely/totally *His life had completely changed since he met Anya.*

change dramatically (=a lot, especially in a surprising way) *The landscape has changed dramatically over the past hundred years.*

change fundamentally/radically/drastically (=completely, in a way that has a big effect) *The political situation has fundamentally changed since the election.*

change slightly/a little *After she died, the world seemed to change slightly. | The wind changed slightly and there was a hint of rain in the air.*

change rapidly/quickly *The market for phones is changing rapidly.*

sb/sth has hardly changed (=they are almost the same as before) *In 60 years the school had hardly changed.*

change slowly/gradually *Working conditions are gradually changing, with an increase in the number of people working longer hours.*

change constantly/all the time *The English language is changing all the time.*

change permanently/forever *Something happened that would change her life forever.*

change overnight (=very suddenly) *My financial position changed overnight and I was suddenly trying to think of ways of spending money.*

PREPOSITIONS

change to/into sth *Hope changed to despair.*

change from sth *She has changed from a shy schoolgirl into a confident young woman.*

PHRASES

change for the better/worse (=in a way that is better or worse) *According to his teachers, his attitude has changed for the better recently.*

sb/sth has changed out of all recognition (=they seem completely different) *She has changed out of all recognition since she left home.*

times have changed (=the situation is different now) *Times have changed since you could go out without locking your doors.*

things change (=situations always change) *He used to love his work, but things change.*

THESAURUS: change

alter

situation | **position** | **attitude** | **voice** | **tone** | **face** | **expression**

to change. **Alter** sounds more formal than **change**. It is used especially about very small or very big changes, or in negative sentences:

The situation has ***altered dramatically*** *in recent weeks.* | *His attitude has altered a little and he seems more relaxed.* | *Her tone suddenly altered and she said, "Come as soon as you can."*

adapt

person | **species** | **company**

to change so that you can deal with a new situation:

Some people find it hard to adapt to living in a foreign country. | *Species have to adapt to different environments.* | *Companies that failed to adapt went bankrupt.*

evolve

species | **animal** | **humans** | **bird** | **plant** | **idea** | **plan** | **system**

if a species of animal or plant evolves, it gradually changes over a period of time and develops into a different species. If an idea, plan or system evolves, it gradually develops:

Many researchers believe our species evolved in Africa. | *The animal has evolved to survive under very difficult conditions.* | *Do you think that humans have stopped evolving?* | *The idea for the film was slowly beginning to evolve in his mind.* | *The plan evolved in discussions between various world leaders.* | *The Chinese writing system* ***evolved into*** *a complex system very different from picture writing.*

mutate

virus | **gene**

if a virus or gene mutates, it changes and becomes a different organism:

The virus has ***mutated into*** *a much more dangerous form of the disease.* | *Genes often mutate and change their characteristics.*

fluctuate

price | **value** | **number** | **rate** | **level** | **weight** | **speed** | **temperature**

to keep changing to a higher or lower level and then back again:

Share prices on the New York Stock Exchange ***fluctuated wildly****.* | *The number of students in the class* ***fluctuates between*** *about 8* ***and*** *15.* | *Her weight* ***fluctuated between*** *120* ***and*** *140 pounds.*

alternate

to keep changing from one thing to another and back again - used especially about people and their moods:

His parents ***alternate between*** *feelings of pride* ***and*** *moments of frustration and desperation.* | *Kate Winslet has* ***alternated between*** *big-budget Hollywood films* ***and*** *much smaller British films.*

2 to make something become different

NOUNS

change your name/address *Miriam changed her name to Mary.*

change your plans/decision *We had to change our plans at the last minute because of the strike.*

change the law/system/rules *The protesters want the law to be changed.*

change the way you do sth *Technology is changing the way people work.*

change your opinion/attitude/outlook *I've changed my opinion about her since then.*

change your mind (=decide to do something different) *I've changed my mind - I'm not going out tonight.*

change the subject/topic (=talk about something different) *"Let's change the subject," she said suddenly. "I don't want to talk about this any more."*

change jobs/career *I'm too old to change career now.*

change sb's life *You should read this book - it could change your life.*

change direction/course *The ship suddenly changed direction.*

change colour BrE, **change color** AmE: *It's autumn and the leaves are changing colour.*

change society/the world *She was young and idealistic, and wanted to change the world.*

ADVERBS

change sth completely/totally *I have completely changed my diet, and my weight is starting to come down.*

change sth forever *It was an event which changed our lives forever.*

PREPOSITIONS

change sb/sth into sb/sth *Farmland is being changed into housing estates.*

C

THESAURUS: change

alter
way | situation | position | structure | cells | character | shape | balance | law
to change something. **Alter** sounds more formal than **change**. It is used especially about very small or very big changes, or in negative sentences:
The government has agreed to alter the way judges are appointed. | There was nothing we could do to alter the situation. | The cells have been ***genetically altered*** *to produce proteins that protect the body's immune system. | This could* ***radically alter*** *the balance of power in the Arab World.*

adapt
equipment | room | film | recipe
to change something so that it can be used for a different purpose, or so that it is suitable for someone:
The bathroom has been ***specially adapted*** *for disabled people. | The film is adapted from a Michael Crichton novel about a theme park with real dinosaurs.*

adjust
volume | temperature | colour | brightness | position | level | rate
to make small changes so that something is more suitable or is more how you want it:
How do you adjust the volume on the television? | He tried to adjust the position of his chair.

reform
system | law | economy
to change a law, system, organization etc, so that it is fairer or more effective:
They want to reform the health care system. | There is urgent need to reform the law. | As president, Museveni reformed the police and the armed forces.

revise
plan | policy | opinion | idea | decision | constitution | rules | version | estimate
to change something because of new information and ideas:
The company has been forced to revise its business plans. | The court revised its opinion after hearing new evidence. | Parliament voted in January to revise the constitution. | The contract is a revised version of an earlier agreement.

restructure
company | business | economy | industry | operations
to make big changes to a company, organization etc in order to make it more efficient, often with the result that a lot of people lose their jobs:
The company has been ***restructured from top to bottom*** *in order to make it more competitive. | Government plans to* ***radically restructure*** *the economy were met with widespread opposition. | Amdahl Corporation is restructuring its European operations.*

to change something completely

transform
way | life | society | economy | country | region | image | character
to change something completely, especially so that it is much better:
His discovery ***completely transformed*** *the way we think about space and time. | Education can transform people's lives. | Putin transformed the Russian economy. | Bright colours can transform the character of a room.*

revolutionize (*also* **revolutionise** *BrE*)
way | understanding | industry | business | treatment | medicine
to completely and permanently change the way people do something or think about something. **Revolutionize** sounds even stronger than **transform**, and is often used about a new idea or invention:
The internet has revolutionized the way we shop. | The drug could revolutionize the treatment of HIV patients in developing countries.

to change something in order to deceive people

distort
truth | facts | argument
to explain facts, statements etc in a way that makes them seem different from what they really are:
He believes the film distorts the truth about what really happened that day. | There has been a deliberate attempt to distort the scientific facts about global warming.

twist
facts | truth | words | meaning
to explain facts, statements etc in a way that makes them seem different from what they really are. **Twist** is more informal than **distort** and is used especially when someone does this deliberately and dishonestly for their own advantage:
Defence lawyers twist the facts, and guilty men are allowed to go free. | When leaders twist the truth they should be held responsible. | He accused reporters of twisting his words.

change² *n*

a situation in which someone or something becomes different, or the act of making something different

ADJECTIVES

a big/major/huge/massive change *Going to a new school is a big change for children.*

a slight/small/minor change *A few minor changes were made to the programme.*

social/political/economic change *Demands for political and social change are growing.*

an important/significant/change *There have been some important changes to the law.*

a dramatic/drastic change (=very big, especially in a surprising way) *The Industrial Revolution was a period of dramatic change.*

a fundamental/radical change (=affecting the most basic parts of something) *Reducing waste requires a fundamental change in attitude.*

sweeping/far-reaching changes (=affecting many things or people) *There are likely to be sweeping changes in the company.*

a complete change *I've had the same hairstyle for years and want a complete change.*

a subtle change (=difficult to notice) *I sensed a subtle change in our relationship.*

gradual/rapid/sudden change *Industry was experiencing a period of rapid change.*

a marked change (=very noticeable) *There was a marked change in his behaviour.*

a pleasant/nice/refreshing change *It's a refreshing change to hear people saying good things about teenagers.*

a proposed change (=that has been suggested) *Not everyone is in favour of the proposed changes.*

NOUNS + change

climate change *The effects of climate change can be seen in Antarctica.*

a career change *The website has information for people considering a career change.*

a temperature change *Fish cannot cope with sudden temperature changes.*

a personality change *A head injury can cause a personality change.*

VERBS + change

make a change *We've had to make some changes to the design.*

cause a change *Pregnancy causes big changes in a woman's body.*

bring (about) change (=cause change) *The war brought about radical social change.*

introduce a change *A number of changes were introduced after the accident.*

undergo a change (=be affected by a change) *Farming was undergoing considerable change during this time.*

implement a change (=make the change that another person has suggested) *The changes suggested in the report still have not been fully implemented.*

see/notice/observe a change *I saw a big change in her when I met her again.*

deal with/cope with/adapt to change *She finds it hard to cope with change.*

feel like a change (=want to do something different) *I felt like a change, so I decided to walk to work.*

change + VERBS

change happens/takes place (*also* **change occurs** *formal*): *Language change is happening all the time.*

a change affects sb/sth *The changes affect both new and existing customers.*

PREPOSITIONS

a change in sth *A change in personality may mean a person is depressed.*

PHRASES

the pace/rate of change *People sometimes feel alarmed by the pace of technological change.*

a change for the better/worse (=it becomes better or worse) *There was a change for the better in the patient's condition.*

a sea change in sth (=a very big change) *There has been a sea change in attitudes to divorce over the past 50 years.*

THESAURUS: change

alteration
a change, especially a small one that happens naturally or gradually, or one that is made in order to improve something:
I noticed a ***slight alteration in*** *her behaviour. | They had to make some* ***alterations to*** *the design.*

reform
a change made to a system or law in order to improve it:
He called for a ***reform of*** *our outdated voting system. | Many people opposed the* ***economic reforms****.*

shift
a change, especially in people's attitudes or in the way they do things, or in the position of someone or something:
There has been a ***shift in*** *public opinion about the war. | There needs to be a major* ***shift away from*** *road transport to rail transport. | After he died, there was a* ***dramatic shift*** *in the balance of power.*

swing
a big change, especially in someone's opinions or moods:
The drug can cause ***mood swings****. | There has been a big* ***swing toward*** *the Democrats* (=many more people are supporting them).

fluctuation
a change in something – used when something changes often:
There are frequent ***fluctuations in*** *the value of the dollar.* | *The graph shows* ***temperature fluctuations*** *over the past month.* | *She was used to* ***fluctuations in*** *his mood.*

a great change

transformation
a change in which something or someone becomes completely different:
There has been a complete ***transformation in*** *his attitude since he became a father.* | *They watched her* ***transformation from*** *a shy local girl* ***to*** *a famous movie actress.*

revolution
a complete change in ways of thinking or working:
The 1970s saw the beginnings of a new ***technological revolution.*** | *Einstein's General Theory of Relativity* ***led to a revolution in*** *scientific thinking.*

shake-up
a situation in which a lot of changes are very quickly made in a system or organization in order to make it more effective:
The administration is planning a ***thorough shake-up of*** *the welfare system.* | *The department has not performed well and is badly in need of a shake-up.*

U-turn
a complete change, so that you do the opposite of what you said you were going to do before – used especially about politics:
The government was forced to ***do a U-turn*** *after angry protests about their taxation policy.*

channel Ac *n*
a television or radio station and all the programmes that it broadcasts

ADJECTIVES/NOUNS + channel

a television/radio channel *NTV is the country's most popular television channel.*

a news/movie/sports channel *What's on the movie channel tonight?*

a digital channel *You can watch digital channels on your computer.*

a commercial channel (=paid for by companies advertising on it) *On commercial channels they have advertisement breaks.*

a satellite channel (=using signals sent from a machine in space) *There are now dozens of satellite channels to choose from.*

a cable channel (=using signals sent through a wire) *ABC announced its plans for a new cable channel.*

a terrestrial channel (=not using satellite) *Channel 5 is the newest terrestrial channel.*

VERBS

watch a channel *The kids are always watching the cartoon channel.*

change/switch channels *He kept switching channels.*

PREPOSITIONS

a programme is on a channel *What channel is 'The Simpsons' on?*

chaos *n*
a situation in which everything is happening in a confused way and nothing is organized or arranged in order

ADJECTIVES/NOUNS + chaos

total/complete/utter chaos *When we arrived, there was total chaos.*

economic/political/social chaos *The country faced widespread famine and economic chaos.*

traffic chaos *The first day of the holidays often brings traffic chaos.*

VERBS

cause/create/bring chaos *Snow has caused chaos on the roads this morning.*

end in chaos *The game ended in chaos when supporters ran onto the pitch.*

be thrown/plunged into chaos *A serious accident has thrown the roads into chaos.*

descend/slip into chaos (=gradually become completely confused and disorganized) *After the invasion, the country descended into chaos.*

chaos ensues (=it happens as a result of something) *A decade of civil war and chaos ensued.*

chaos reigns (=there is chaos and everything is out of control) *Everyone was trying to talk at once and for a while chaos reigned.*

PREPOSITIONS

in chaos *The kitchen was in chaos.*

PHRASES

be in a state of chaos *Nick's bedroom is permanently in a state of chaos.*

a scene of chaos *I came home to a scene of chaos, with food and empty bottles everywhere.*

chaos and confusion *Heavy flooding has caused chaos and confusion throughout the country.*

be on the brink of chaos (=be about to become completely confused and disorganized) *The peace talks were on the brink of chaos.*

chapter Ac *n*
one of the parts into which a book is divided

ADJECTIVES

the first chapter (*also* **the introductory/opening chapter** *formal*): *The introductory chapter gives an outline of the subject matter.*

the last/final chapter (*also* **the concluding chapter** *formal*): *In the final chapter, you find out who the murderer is.*

the next chapter (*also* **the following chapter** *formal*): *This theme will be developed in the next chapter.*

earlier/later chapters (=ones before/after this one) *These points will be explored in more detail in later chapters.*

the previous/preceding chapter *The method is described in the previous chapter.*

VERBS

be divided into chapters *The book is divided into ten chapters.*

see chapter 2/3 etc (=used in books to direct a reader to a chapter) *His scientific claims were never justified (see Chapter 16).*

a chapter deals with/discusses sth *This chapter discusses power, and how people use it.*

PREPOSITIONS

a chapter about/on sth *There's a whole chapter about William Shakespeare.*

in a chapter *These points will be discussed in Chapter 8.*

PHRASES

the beginning/end of a chapter *His character is introduced at the beginning of the first chapter.*

character *n*

1 a person in a book, play, film etc

ADJECTIVES/NOUNS + character

the main/central/leading character *Alec is the central character in the play.*

a minor/supporting character *Two of the minor characters get killed.*

a male/female character *He is the most sympathetic male character in the book.*

a television/movie/cartoon character *Who's your favourite television character?*

a comic/tragic character (=a funny or sad one) *Homer Simpson is a great comic character.*

a fictional/fictitious character (=not existing in real life) *People sometimes forget that television characters are fictional.*

a believable/convincing character (=seeming like a real person) *The characters were totally convincing.*

a memorable character *The extraordinary Mrs Jewkes is the novel's most memorable character.*

a sympathetic character (=one you like) *In the book, Jeff isn't a sympathetic character.*

an interesting character *For me, the nurse is the most interesting character.*

VERBS

play a character *I wanted to play the character of Danny.*

create a character *He created several memorable characters.*

2 the qualities which make someone a particular kind of person

ADJECTIVES

a strong character *You need brains and a strong character to be a leader.*

sb's true character *She is unaware of his true character.*

character + NOUNS

a character trait (=a quality that someone has) *Your greatest character trait is your honesty.*

a character flaw (=a bad quality that someone has) *Few people have no character flaws at all.*

PHRASES

be in character/out of character (=be typical or untypical of someone's character) *His unkindness on that occasion was entirely out of character.*

a side of sb's character (=a part of someone's character) *He had revealed a side of his character I hadn't seen before.*

characteristic *n*

a quality or feature of something or someone that is typical of them and easy to recognize

ADJECTIVES

physical characteristics *I want you to describe the man's physical characteristics.*

personal/individual characteristics *What are the personal characteristics that a leader requires?*

a human characteristic *The power of speech is an entirely human characteristic.*

certain characteristics *Successful organizations all have certain characteristics in common* (=they have the same characteristics).

the main characteristic of sth *A new interest in art was one of the main characteristics of this period.*

an essential/important characteristic *An essential characteristic of good teaching is that it creates interest in the learner.*

a common/shared characteristic (=that people or things share) *There are some common characteristics between the two painters.*

a unique characteristic *Every city has its own unique characteristics.*

a distinguishing/distinctive characteristic (=separating someone or something from others of the same type) *The blue feathers are the distinguishing characteristic of the male bird.*

a defining characteristic (=one that makes someone or something the kind of person or thing that they are) *The democratic nature of local government is one of its key defining characteristics.*

VERBS

have a characteristic (*also* **possess a characteristic** *formal*): *He has all the characteristics of a great sportsman.*

show a characteristic (*also* **exhibit a characteristic** *formal*): *A material may exhibit the characteristics of both a liquid and a solid.*

share a characteristic *The group shared one characteristic – they were all under 25.*

inherit a characteristic (=get it from your parents) *We all inherit physical characteristics from our parents.*

charge¹ *n*

1 the amount of money you have to pay for goods or services

ADJECTIVES

a small charge *For a small charge you can use the hotel pool.*

high/low charges *Lawyers' charges can be very high.*

an extra/additional charge *He had to pay an extra charge because the equipment was damaged when he returned it.*

a fixed/standard charge *There's a fixed charge for having a dental check.*

a minimum charge *Some restaurants operate a minimum charge at busy times.*

a daily/monthly/annual charge *The daily charge for car rental is 50 euros.*

a one-off charge (=that you only pay once) *There is a one-off charge to have the service set up.*

hidden charges (=ones that are not immediately obvious) *Make sure there are no hidden charges.*

a nominal charge (=very small) *Residents can use the tennis courts for a nominal charge.*

NOUNS + charge

a service charge (=for service in a hotel, restaurant etc) *The bill for the meal includes a 10% service charge.*

an admission charge (=for being allowed to enter a place) *There is no admission charge to the museum.*

a delivery charge (=for taking goods somewhere) *How much is the store's delivery charge?*

VERBS

pay a charge *There will be a charge to pay if you return the car late.*

make a charge *We make no charge for this service.*

introduce/impose a charge *The government introduced a charge for visa applications.*

increase/reduce a charge *Unfortunately, it has been necessary to increase our charges.*

waive a charge (=say it does not have to be paid) *The bank has agreed to waive the charge this time.*

PREPOSITIONS

a charge for sth *There is a charge for the use of the swimming pool.*

PHRASES

free of charge (=with no cost) *Delivery is free of charge.*

at no (extra) charge (=with no cost) *Breakfast may be served in your bedroom at no extra charge.*

> **THESAURUS: charge**
>
> price, value, charge, fee, fare, rent, rate, toll → **cost¹ (1)**

2 an official statement by the police that someone may be guilty of a crime

ADJECTIVES/NOUNS + charge

murder/burglary/drugs charges *He appeared in court on drugs charges.*

criminal charges *The investigation resulted in criminal charges against three police officers.*

a serious charge *He was accused of dangerous driving, but the more serious charge of murder was withdrawn.*

a trumped-up charge (=based on false information to make someone seem guilty) *The opposition leader was arrested on trumped-up charges.*

VERBS

face charges *He faces charges of tax evasion.*

deny/admit a charge *All three men denied the charge of murder.*

plead guilty to a charge (=say formally in court that you are guilty) *The youth pleaded guilty to a charge of burglary.*

press/bring charges (=make someone be brought to court for a crime) *Sometimes the victim of an assault does not want to press charges.*

drop/withdraw the charges (=decide not to go on with a court case) *They will drop the charges if we pay them £10,000.*

dismiss the charges (=say that a court case should not continue) *If there is insufficient evidence, the court will dismiss the charges.*

PREPOSITIONS

charges against sb *The charges against him were eventually dropped.*

a charge of (doing) sth *She denied a charge of assaulting her husband.*

PHRASES

be released without charge *She had been arrested twice and released without charge.*

be convicted of/on a charge (=be judged to be guilty) *McCorley was convicted on a charge of assault.*

be acquitted of/on a charge (=be judged to be not guilty) *Both men were acquitted of all charges.*

charge² *v*

to ask someone for a particular amount of money for something

NOUNS

charge a fee *Lawyers charge high fees.*

charge a price *Some companies charge different prices for the same product.*

charge a rate *The club charges a higher rate for non-members.*

charge a fare *The airline charges the same fare for children and adults.*

charge interest *They charge a lower rate of interest than the other banks.*

charge commission (=charge money for selling something) *The gallery charges 50% commission on every painting.*

charge (sb) a fine/penalty *You will be charged a fine if you return your library book late.*

PREPOSITIONS

charge for sth *The hospital charges for parking.*

be charged at 2 dollars/25p etc *Calls will be charged at 44p per minute.*

charity *n*

1 an organization that gives money, goods, or help to people who are poor, sick etc

ADJECTIVES/NOUNS + charity

a cancer/animal/homeless etc charity *The event raised thousands of pounds for a cancer charity.*

a local charity *All the money raised goes to local charities.*

a national/international charity *The Red Cross is a well-known international charity.*

a registered charity (=an official one) *How can I check that it is a registered charity?*

VERBS

give/donate sth to charity *I like to give a small amount of what I earn to charity.*

go to charity (=be given to charity) *Any profit that she makes from her writing goes to charity.*

support a charity (=give money to one) *Do you support any charities?*

set up/establish a charity *We set up the charity soon after our son died of cancer.*

charity + NOUNS

charity work *She spends a lot of her time doing charity work.*

a charity worker *Charity workers say these reforms will not help the poor.*

a charity appeal *BrE*, **a charity drive** *AmE* (=an occasion when a charity asks for money) *The organization is launching a charity appeal for a new air ambulance.*

a charity shop *BrE* (=which sells things people have given to get money for a charity) *I usually give all our old clothes to the charity shop.*

a charity event (=one organized to collect money for a charity) *She spoke at a charity event in aid of famine relief.*

a charity concert/show *The band appeared at a charity concert for free.*

PREPOSITIONS

for charity *The festival raises a lot of money for charity every year.*

a charity for sb/sth *Shelter is a British charity for the homeless.*

2 money and help from other people, given to someone who is too poor to look after himself or herself

VERBS

rely on/depend on charity *She doesn't like to rely on charity from other people.*

ask for/accept charity *Some people are too proud to ask for charity.*

not want charity *The refugees say they do not want charity. They want to be back in their own homes.*

charm *n*

a special quality someone or something has that makes people like them

ADJECTIVES

great/considerable/immense charm *He was a man of great charm.*

personal charm *He has a lot of personal charm and he gets on well with people.*

boyish charm (=like a young man or boy) *Women seem to love his boyish charm.*

feminine charm (=that a woman has) *She decided to use a little feminine charm.*

special/unique charm *These old films have their own special charm.*

a certain charm (=some charm) *The idea of moving to a Greek island does have a certain charm.*

VERBS

have charm *Richard was clever and he had a lot of charm.*

use your charm *She knew when to use her charm in order to get what she wanted.*

turn on the charm (=deliberately show a lot of charm) *If you turn on the charm, I'm sure you'll get the job.*

lack charm (*also* **be lacking in charm**) *A lot of new buildings lack charm.*

sth loses its charm (=it no longer seems good or enjoyable) *He was getting older, and travel was losing its charm.*

PHRASES

be part of sb's/sth's charm *The house is a long way from anywhere and that is part of its charm.*

it is impossible to resist sb's charm *Women say that it was impossible to resist Clooney's charm.*

fall for sb's/sth's charms (*also* **succumb to sb's/sth's charms** *formal*) (=allow yourself to be influenced by their charms) *Thomas seemed to be succumbing to Sylvie's charms.*

C

charming *adj* very pleasant or attractive

NOUNS

a charming man/woman *Mr Benn is a very charming man.*

a charming smile *He gave her a charming smile.*

a charming manner *Her charming manner was irresistible.*

a charming village/town/place *The region has several charming villages, which date from the 15th century.*

ADVERBS

absolutely/perfectly/utterly charming (=very charming) *Mr Herzog was utterly charming and his guests soon felt relaxed.*

charming + ADJECTIVES

charming little *We ate in a charming little restaurant.*

charming old *The village is full of charming old cottages.*

chart Ac *n*

information shown in the form of a simple picture or a set of figures

NOUNS + chart

a weather chart *The latest weather chart shows that a storm is coming.*

a wall chart *The child can stick a star on the wall chart when she completes a task.*

a bar chart (=with bars of different heights representing different amounts)

a pie chart (=a circle divided into sections representing different parts of an amount)

a flow chart (=with shapes and lines showing different stages in a process)

VERBS

a chart shows sth *The chart shows the average temperature each month.*

PREPOSITIONS

on/in a chart *Energy is obtained from a number of sources, as shown in the chart below.*

charter *n*

an official document giving the aims, principles, rights etc of an organization

VERBS

draw up a charter (=create one) *the United Nations Charter was drawn up at a conference in San Francisco.*

sign a charter *More than 100 companies have already signed the charter.*

ratify a charter (=officially agree to the terms of a charter) *Britain refused to ratify the charter.*

PHRASES

be in breach of a charter *formal* (=someone has done something which disobeys a charter) *The government was in breach of the European charter of human rights.*

PREPOSITIONS

under/according to a charter *Under the charter, complaints must be dealt with within a month.*

chat *n*

an informal friendly conversation

ADJECTIVES

a friendly chat *They had a friendly chat and talked about the weather.*

an informal chat *Come and see me any time if you want an informal chat about jobs.*

a quiet chat (=one that other people will not interrupt) *Let's go and have a quiet chat over lunch.*

a nice/good chat *We had a really nice chat.*

a long chat *They sat down and had a long chat.*

a quick/brief chat *My manager said he wanted to have a brief chat with me.*

a private/confidential chat *I think you should have a confidential chat with the school nurse.*

a little chat *Why don't you call her and have a little chat?*

VERBS

have a chat *We were just having a chat.*

stop for a chat *He would have liked to stop for a chat.*

drop in for a chat (=visit someone informally for a chat) *She used to drop in for a chat if she was passing.*

PREPOSITIONS

a chat with sb *Lucy felt more cheerful after her chat with Bridget.*

a chat about sth *We had a nice chat about what our kids were doing.*

cheap *adj*

not at all expensive, or lower in price than you expected

NOUNS

a cheap ticket/fare/flight *The tickets were very cheap – they were only $20.*

a cheap hotel/restaurant *We stayed in a cheap hotel near the station.*

a cheap shop/store/supermarket *The shop is surprisingly cheap and you can find some real bargains.*

a cheap phone/camera/watch etc *I only want a cheap phone, not a fancy one.*

a cheap way/method/alternative *The cheapest way of buying plants is to grow them from seed.*

a cheap rate *You get a cheaper rate for calls in the evenings.*

ADVERBS

relatively cheap *The equipment is relatively cheap and simple to use.*

dirt cheap *informal* (=extremely cheap) *Wine is dirt cheap – you can get a bottle for less than $2.*

incredibly/surprisingly/ridiculously cheap *Their computers are incredibly cheap.*

VERBS

look cheap *The decoration is plain and simple, without looking cheap.*

PHRASES

cheap and nasty *BrE* (=cheap and bad quality) *The plastic strap looks cheap and nasty.*

cheap and cheerful *BrE* (=cheap, but not of bad quality) *a cheap and cheerful Italian restaurant*

THESAURUS: cheap

inexpensive
not expensive. **Inexpensive** is more formal than **cheap**:
The furniture is inexpensive, but well made. | *a simple inexpensive meal* | *Nets hung over beds are* ***an inexpensive way to*** *help prevent malaria.*

Inexpensive or cheap?
Inexpensive things are not necessarily cheap, but they are not as expensive as you expect and you get good quality for the price.
If something is **cheap**, it can also mean that it is not of good quality: ***cheap*** *plastic chairs* | *The man was wearing a* ***cheap*** *suit.* | *Beware of* ***cheap*** *imitations.*

low
price | **rent** | **fare** | **fee** | **cost**
low prices, rents etc are not a lot of money:
You can get good clothes at surprisingly low prices. | *The rents in this area are low because it's a long way from the city centre.* | *Their fares are extremely low.* | *The cost is relatively low (£300-£500).*

Low or cheap?
You usually say **low cost** or **low fees** (not **cheap**).
You also use **low** when talking about someone's **wages/salary/pay/income**: *The women are on very* ***low wages.*** You use **cheap labour** about workers who are not paid very much: *Some companies rely on* ***cheap labour*** *in poor countries.*

reasonable
price | **rent** | **rates**
fair and not too expensive:
The restaurant serves good food at reasonable prices. | *They are offering loans at reasonable interest rates.* | *Only £25 a night? That* ***sounds*** *very* ***reasonable.***

economical
car | **way of doing sth** | **alternative**
cheap because you do not need to use a lot of money or fuel:
The car is very economical and does 100 miles to the gallon. | *A wood-burning stove can be an economical way of heating your home.* | *It is usually more economical to buy in large quantities.*

affordable
housing | **homes** | **childcare** | **prices**
cheap enough for most people to be able to buy or pay for:
There is a shortage of affordable housing. | *Single mothers often have trouble finding affordable childcare.* | *The shop sells designer fashions at affordable prices.* | *Electronic book readers are* ***becoming*** *more* ***affordable.***

competitive
price | **rate**
competitive prices and rates are as low as those charged by other shops or companies:
I think you'll find our prices are extremely competitive. | *The hotel offers a high standard of service at very competitive rates.*

budget
airline | **flight** | **hotel** | **accommodation**
having specially low prices:
Budget airlines are offering cheap tickets to New York. | *You can get a budget flight to Spain for only £50.* | *I found a list of budget hotels for under $90 a night.* | *They have budget accommodation for families with young children.*

Budget is only used before a noun.

Other ways of saying that something is cheap
You can say that something **is a bargain**: *The tickets* ***are a*** *real* ***bargain*** *at only $99 return.* You can also say that something **is good/great/excellent value**: *The hotel is very* ***good value.***

ANTONYMS **cheap → expensive**

check[1] *v*

to do something in order to find out whether something really is correct, true, or in good condition

ADVERBS

check sth carefully/thoroughly *Carefully check your work before you hand it in.*

check first/beforehand *He put the money in his pocket, checking it first to make sure it was all there.*

be checked regularly/daily/every week etc *The water quality in the pool is checked regularly.*

always check *We always check that all the children are on the bus before driving off.*

PREPOSITIONS

check (sth) for mistakes/errors/damage *She re-read the letter, checking for mistakes.*

check sth against sth (=compare two things

to check they are the same) *The company's figures are checked against the official data.*

check² *n*

the process of finding out if something is safe, correct, true, or in the condition it should be

ADJECTIVES

a quick check *A quick check showed that the car had been stolen.*

a thorough/careful check *An engineer gave the computer a thorough check.*

a regular check *Despite regular checks, the drains had become blocked.*

a routine check (=happening as a normal part of a process) *I went to the doctor for a routine health check.*

a random check (=done without any definite pattern) *Customs officials were carrying out random checks on cars.*

a spot check (=a quick check of one thing in a group, done to obtain information) *They do spot checks to make sure that all the products leave the factory in good condition.*

a medical check *People over 60 should have regular medical checks.*

NOUNS + check

a safety/security check *Airport security checks can take a long time.*

a health check *The dog was given a thorough health check.*

a background check (=done to get information about someone's previous work, education, family etc) *The company conducts background checks on its employees.*

a credit check (=done to get information about someone's financial history) *Banks usually do a credit check before they give you a loan.*

a virus check (=for computer viruses) *The computer is running a virus check.*

> **Check** or **checkup**?
> When talking about a medical examination to find out if you are healthy, you often say **checkup**: *When was your last dental* ***checkup****?*

VERBS

do/make a check *I did a quick check to make sure all the lights had been switched off.*

carry out/run a check (*also* **conduct a check** *formal*) (=do a check, especially one that you often do) *The police carried out a check on the car's registration number.*

have a check *BrE*: *Always have a final check to make sure you've got your ticket and passport.*

give sth a check *I'd like you to give the car a careful check.*

PREPOSITIONS

a check on sb/sth *There should be more checks on the performance of doctors.*

PHRASES

keep a (close) check on sb/sth (=check someone or something regularly) *His teacher was keeping a close check on his progress.*

checkup, check-up *n*

a general medical examination that a doctor gives you, to make sure you are healthy

ADJECTIVES/NOUNS + checkup

a medical/dental checkup *The doctor will see her for a general medical checkup.*

a regular checkup *Dentists recommend regular checkups.*

a routine checkup (=one that is done regularly, not because there is a particular problem) *Don't worry – it's just a routine checkup.*

an annual/yearly/monthly etc checkup *She went for her annual checkup at the hospital.*

a health checkup *You should get a health checkup before travelling.*

VERBS

have a checkup *It is important to have regular checkups.*

go for a checkup *I went for a checkup at the dentist.*

give sb a checkup *The doctor gave him a checkup and said he was fine.*

cheek *n*

the soft round part of your face below each of your eyes

ADJECTIVES

pink/rosy cheeks *She was a cheerful girl with rosy cheeks.*

red cheeks *His cheeks were all red and he looked embarrassed.*

flushed cheeks *Her cheeks were flushed and her eyes sparkled when she saw him.*

pale cheeks *Tears ran down her pale cheeks.*

chubby cheeks (=rather fat cheeks) *The little boy had chubby cheeks.*

hollow/sunken cheeks *His dull skin and hollow cheeks made him look ill.*

> **Different kinds of cheeks**
> **Pink** or **rosy cheeks** look healthy. **Red cheeks** look embarrassed. **Pale cheeks** look worried or ill. **Chubby cheeks** look a little fat – used especially about babies. **Flushed cheeks** mean you look hot, excited, embarrassed, or you have been using a lot of effort. **Hollow** or **sunken cheeks** look very ill, for example because you have not eaten for a long time.

VERBS

sb's cheeks flush (=they become red) *Joanna's cheeks flushed with embarrassment.*

sb's cheeks burn (=they feel hot) *Her cheeks burned as she remembered his kiss.*

kiss sb on the cheek/kiss sb's cheek *He leant over and kissed her on the cheek.*

touch/stroke sb's cheek *She stroked his cheek gently.*

cheerful *adj* THESAURUS ▶ **happy**

cheese *n* a solid food made from milk

ADJECTIVES/NOUNS + cheese

a strong cheese *This is one of the strongest French cheeses.*

a mild cheese *The cheese is mild and creamy.*

a hard/soft cheese *Camembert is my favourite soft cheese.*

goat's/sheep's cheese *Goat's cheese often has a surprisingly strong taste.*

grated cheese (=cut into small pieces) *Sprinkle the grated cheese over the pasta.*

PHRASES

a piece/slice of cheese *Would you like a piece of cheese?*

bread and cheese *Lunch was bread and cheese.*

chef *n* THESAURUS ▶ **cook**[2]

chemical Ac *n*

a substance used in chemistry or produced by a chemical process

ADJECTIVES

dangerous/harmful/hazardous chemicals *The sign on the truck said that it was carrying hazardous chemicals.*

toxic/poisonous chemicals (=harmful to people and other living things) *The chemicals that were released were highly toxic.*

industrial/agricultural chemicals *Some deaths from cancer are related to industrial chemicals.*

household chemicals (=used for cleaning etc in the home) *Keep household chemicals out of reach of children.*

VERBS

use chemicals *Farmers use chemicals to kill insects that would destroy their crops.*

produce chemicals *Some plants produce toxic chemicals to protect themselves.*

release chemicals *When we laugh, our brains release chemicals that make us feel good.*

contain chemicals *Tobacco smoke contains thousands of different chemicals.*

be exposed to chemicals *Many of the workers at the factory were regularly exposed to dangerous chemicals.*

a chemical reacts with another chemical *In a rocket, two chemicals react with each other to provide a great deal of heat.*

chemical + NOUNS

a chemical reaction *The carbon dioxide is produced as a result of a chemical reaction.*

a chemical element (=a basic substance that consists of one type of atom) *Silver is a chemical element whose symbol is Ag.*

a chemical compound (=a substance that consists of two or more elements) *DNA is a complex chemical compound.*

a chemical symbol *The chemical symbol for Hydrogen is H.*

the chemical industry *The chemical industry is one of the most important industrial sectors.*

a chemical plant/factory *There has been an explosion at a chemical plant in Germany.*

chemical weapons (=poisonous chemicals used as weapons) *The treaty banned chemical weapons.*

chess *n*

a board game for two players, in which you try to trap one of your opponent's pieces, called the king

VERBS

play chess *Do you want to play chess?*

chess + NOUNS

a chess match/game *He could play four chess matches at the same time.*

a chess set *She gave him a beautifully carved wooden chess set.*

a chess player *Even good chess players make mistakes.*

a chess piece (=one of the objects that you move around the board) *Some of the chess pieces were missing.*

a chess championship/tournament *Ray's taking part in a chess tournament.*

a chess club *Paul was a member of the school chess club.*

a chess move *You first have to learn the basic chess moves.*

Chessboard is usually written as one word.

PHRASES

a game of chess *Perhaps we could have a game of chess later.*

chest *n*

the front part of your body between your neck and your stomach

ADJECTIVES

a broad chest *He was a tall man with a broad chest.*

a powerful/muscular chest *His arms were folded across his powerful chest.*

a hairy chest *His shirt was unbuttoned, revealing a hairy chest.*

a bare chest *The workmen all had bare chests.*

a bad chest *BrE* (=one that is making you cough or giving you pain) *I'm not going running today – my chest is bad.*

a weak chest (=one that often gets infections) *My sister had a weak chest and was often ill.*

chest + NOUNS

chest pain/pains *Infection in the lungs can cause chest pain.*

a chest infection *Every time I get a cold I get a chest infection too.*

a chest injury/wound *He suffered serious chest injuries in the accident.*

a chest X-ray *A chest X-ray showed that there was damage to his lungs.*

VERBS

puff out your chest (=make your chest bigger by breathing in) *He puffed out his chest proudly.*

chicken *n*

a common farm bird that is kept for its meat and eggs

VERBS + chicken

keep/raise chickens *More and more city-dwellers are keeping chickens.*

feed the chickens *I'm going out to feed the chickens.*

chicken + VERBS

a chicken lays eggs *The chickens lay their eggs every morning.*

a chicken clucks (=it makes the noise that chickens make) *The chickens started clucking as she approached with their food.*

a chicken pecks *Chickens pecked in the dusty yard.*

a chicken roosts (=it rests or sleeps) *He built a little hut for the chickens to roost.*

chief *adj* THESAURUS main

child *n*

someone who is not yet an adult

ADJECTIVES

a young child *Young children are naturally curious about the world.*

a small/little child (=a young one) *My family lived in France when I was a small child.*

a four-year-old/ten-year-old etc child *A four-year-old child should not be left on his or her own.*

a newborn child *He was holding the newborn child in his arms.*

an unborn child (=a baby that is still inside its mother) *Smoking can damage your unborn child.*

a good/bad child *Be a good child and sit down!*

a naughty child *Some parents don't know how to deal with naughty children.*

a spoilt/spoiled child (=allowed to do or have whatever he or she wants, and behaving badly) *He's behaving like a spoilt child.*

a bright child (=intelligent) *He was a bright child – always asking questions.*

a gifted child (=extremely intelligent) *She goes to a special school for gifted children.*

a difficult child (=difficult to deal with) *Marcus was a difficult child and his parents didn't know what to do with him.*

an adopted child (=legally made part of a family that he or she was not born into)

NOUNS + child

a problem child (=one who causes problems for the people looking after him or her) *Problem children may need to be removed from the classroom.*

street children (=who live on the streets because they have no homes) *The organization aims to help street children in Latin America.*

> **Schoolchildren** is more commonly written as one word.

VERBS

bring up a child *especially BrE*, **raise a child** *especially AmE*: *The cost of bringing up a child has risen rapidly.*

a child is born *Most children are born in hospital.*

a child grows up *One in four children is growing up in poverty.*

child + NOUNS

child abuse (=cruelty to children, especially involving sex with them) *He was arrested on suspicion of child abuse.*

child development *She's an expert in child development.*

child labour *BrE*, **child labor** *AmE* (=the use of children as workers) *The garments were made using child labour.*

child poverty *The city has one of the highest rates of child poverty in the developed world.*

PREPOSITIONS

children under/over five/eight etc *In the UK, it is illegal to sell tobacco to children under 16.*

a child of five/eight etc *For a child of five, this was a terrifying experience.*

as a child (=when you were a child) *I lived there for several years as a child.*

childhood *n*

the period of time when you are a child

ADJECTIVES

a happy/unhappy childhood *My sisters and I had a very happy childhood.*

a normal childhood *I think my childhood was fairly normal.*

a lonely childhood *An only child with few friends, Greg had a lonely childhood.*

a deprived childhood (=without enough money, food, or love) *Many children in this city have very deprived childhoods.*

early/middle/late childhood *The experiences you have in early childhood are very important.*

VERBS

have a happy/unhappy etc childhood *I had a wonderful childhood growing up on a farm.*

spend your childhood somewhere *This is the house where the artist spent most of his childhood.*

remember sth from (your) childhood *He remembered the place from his childhood.*

childhood + NOUNS

childhood memories *The photograph brought back happy childhood memories.*

a childhood friend *The two childhood friends became bitter enemies in later life.*

sb's childhood sweetheart (=the person they loved when they were very young) *Brian married his childhood sweetheart.*

sb's childhood home *Her childhood home in North Dakota is no longer there.*

childhood experiences *Our childhood experiences make us who we are as adults.*

sb's childhood dream (=something they really wanted to do when they were young) *Becoming world champion has been my childhood dream.*

a childhood illness/disease *There are vaccinations against measles and other childhood illnesses.*

PREPOSITIONS

since/from childhood *Anna and I have known each other since childhood.*

in/during childhood (=when you are a child) *The disease usually occurs in childhood.*

chilling *adj* THESAURUS **frightening**

chilly *adj* THESAURUS **cold[1]**

chin *n*

the front part of your face below your mouth

ADJECTIVES

a double chin (=fat or loose skin under someone's chin) *Frank was much fatter now and he had a double chin.*

a pointed/pointy chin *She had a narrow face and a pointed chin.*

a weak chin (=small, and not square in shape) *He's grown a beard to cover his weak chin.*

a square/strong chin *His dark eyebrows and square chin make him look rather rugged.*

VERBS

stroke/rub your chin (=stroke it in a way that shows you are thinking about something) *He stroked his chin and then seemed to come to a decision.*

lift/raise your chin *Michelle lifted her chin proudly and shook her head.*

rest your chin on/in sth *He pictured her sitting at the table, resting her chin on one hand.*

chip *n*

1 *BrE* a long thin piece of potato cooked in oil

PHRASES

fish and chips *We had fish and chips last night.*

⚠ Don't say 'chips and fish'.

American people say **fries**.

2 *AmE* a thin round piece of potato or corn

PHRASES

a bag of chips *We bought a big bag of tortilla chips.*

NOUNS + chip

potato/tortilla chips *Can I have some of your potato chips?*

British people say **crisps**.

3 a small piece of silicon with electronic connections on it, used in a computer

ADJECTIVES

a powerful chip *The new computer has an extremely powerful chip and can process huge amounts of data.*

NOUNS + chip

a computer chip *The engine is controlled by a computer chip.*

a silicon chip *The company manufactures silicon chips.*

a memory chip *You should choose a computer with a big memory chip.*

a processor chip *There was a problem with the processor chip, which caused the machine to keep crashing.*

chocolate *n*

a sweet brown food that you can eat as a sweet or use in cooking cakes etc

PHRASES

a bar of chocolate (=a long block) *He bought a bar of chocolate.*

a piece of chocolate *Would you like a piece of chocolate?*

a box of chocolates *I gave Mum a box of chocolates for her birthday.*

ADJECTIVES/NOUNS + chocolate

milk chocolate (=with milk added to it) *She was eating a bar of milk chocolate.*

dark chocolate (*also* **plain chocolate** *BrE*) (=without milk and not very sweet) *The strawberries were covered in dark chocolate.*

white chocolate (=white in colour, with a sweet milky taste)

chocolate + NOUNS

a chocolate cake/pudding/sauce *For her birthday he made her a chocolate cake.*

chocolate biscuits/cookies/brownies *You mustn't eat too many chocolate cookies.*

C

choice *n*

1 the action of choosing between different people or things, or the opportunity to choose between them

ADJECTIVES/NOUNS + choice

a difficult choice *He called his decision to leave "the most painful and difficult choice of my life."*

a stark choice (=a choice between two unpleasant things that you must make) *We faced a stark choice: steal or starve.*

(a) free choice (=you are free to choose any thing or person) *Students have an entirely free choice of what to study at university.* | *In most countries, marriage is based on free choice.*

an informed choice (=one in which you know enough about something to make a good decision) *The patient should have enough information to make an informed choice.*

consumer choice (=the opportunity for people to choose between a range of different things to buy) *If these shops close, it will limit consumer choice.*

parental choice (=the opportunity for parents to choose between a range of different schools for their children) *The aim is to extend parental choice in education.*

VERBS

have a choice *Students have a choice between German and Spanish.*

make a choice (=choose something) *One of our course advisers can help you to make your choice.*

exercise choice *formal* (=make a choice) *Everyone should have the right to exercise choice in matters of relationships.*

give/offer sb a choice *Her doctor gave her a choice: take medicine or lose weight.*

be faced with a choice *He was faced with a difficult choice.*

influence sb's choice *Many factors will influence your choice of career.*

have no choice/not have any choice (=have to do or accept something) *The men had no choice but to obey.*

leave sb with no choice *I was left with no choice but to resign.*

PREPOSITIONS

a choice between sth and sth *She was faced with a choice between her job and her husband.*

a choice of sth *You should take more care with your choice of clothes.*

by choice (=because you choose to) *Some people live alone by choice.*

PHRASES

freedom of choice *Patients should have more freedom of choice.*

sth is a matter of (personal) choice (=it depends on what you prefer) *The way you feed your baby is a matter of personal choice.*

given the choice (=if you had a choice) *Given the choice, I probably wouldn't work.*

2 the range of people or things that you can choose from

ADJECTIVES

a wide choice *There is a wide choice of designs.*

a good/excellent etc choice *It was a lovely hotel with a good choice of food.*

a limited choice *There used to be a limited choice of TV channels.*

VERBS

offer/provide a choice *Which university offers the widest choice of subjects?*

PHRASES

be spoilt for choice *BrE* (=have a lot of good things to choose from) *If you find old buildings fascinating, you'll be spoilt for choice in this area.*

3 the person or thing that someone chooses

ADJECTIVES

a good/great/excellent choice *This plant is a good choice if your garden is shady.*

the right/wrong choice *I think you've made the right choice.*

the perfect choice *This hotel is the perfect choice for those who like comfort.*

a sensible choice *They thought that he was a sensible choice for the job of captain.*

personal choice *I like strong colours, but that's just my own personal choice.*

sb's first/second choice (=what they like most, or like almost most) *Tennis was not his first choice of sport at school.*

NOUNS + choice

a career choice *Do we ask teenagers to make career choices too early?*

a lifestyle choice *Our lifestyle choices can affect how long we live.*

PREPOSITIONS

sb's choice of sth *The sofa can be covered in your choice of material.*

choose *v* to decide which one you want

ADVERBS

choose sth carefully/with care *I could tell he was choosing his words carefully as he spoke.*

PREPOSITIONS

choose between sth (and sth) *For dessert we could choose between ice cream and apple tart.*

choose from sth *You can choose from a wide range of options.*

choose sb/sth over sb/sth (=choose one person or thing instead of another) *London was chosen over all the other candidates to host the 2012 Olympics.*

choose sb for a job/post *Why did you choose him for the job?*

choose sth as sth *The company chose Seattle as its base.*

chop *v* THESAURUS ▶ cut[1] (1)

chore *n*

a small job that you have to do regularly, especially work that you do to keep a house clean

ADJECTIVES

household/domestic chores *I spend my day off doing household chores like washing and ironing clothes.*

the daily/everyday/day-to-day chores *When you're working it can be hard to find time for the daily chores.*

VERBS

do the chores *I stayed at home and did the chores.*

help (out) with the chores *Do your children help with the chores?*

become a chore (=become something boring, that you do not want to do) *Visiting his mother every week was starting to become a chore.*

Christmas *n*

the period of time around December 25th, the day when Christians celebrate the birth of Christ

ADJECTIVES/NOUNS + Christmas

Merry/Happy Christmas! (=something you say to people at Christmas) *Merry Christmas and a happy New Year everyone.*

a family Christmas *We always have a family Christmas at home.*

a traditional Christmas *Mum likes to have a traditional Christmas for all the family.*

a white Christmas (=with snow on the ground) *We haven't had a white Christmas in England for years.*

a good/nice Christmas *Did you have a good Christmas?*

VERBS

have/spend Christmas somewhere *No one wants to spend Christmas alone.*

celebrate Christmas *How does your family usually celebrate Christmas?*

give sb sth for Christmas *What can I give Dad for Christmas?*

get sth for Christmas *I got a new watch for Christmas.*

wish sb a happy Christmas (=say that you hope someone enjoys Christmas) *They called to wish us a happy Christmas.*

Christmas + NOUNS

Christmas Day (=December 25th) *We spent Christmas Day with my parents.*

Christmas Eve (=December 24th, the day before Christmas Day) *The children were too excited to sleep on Christmas Eve.*

the Christmas holiday(s) *The Christmas holiday starts next week.*

Christmas dinner/lunch *All the family come to our house for Christmas dinner.*

a Christmas party *What are you wearing to the Christmas party?*

a Christmas present/card *The children couldn't wait to open their Christmas presents.*

Christmas shopping (=the activity of buying Christmas presents) *Have you done your Christmas shopping yet?*

Christmas carols (=songs sung at Christmas) *Children go from door to door singing Christmas carols.*

a Christmas tree *There were lots of gifts under the Christmas tree.*

Christmas decorations *When do you put your Christmas decorations up?*

a Christmas stocking (=a long sock which children leave in their house on Christmas Eve to be filled with presents) *I put some small gifts in the children's Christmas stockings and hung them on the bedroom door.*

PREPOSITIONS

at Christmas *Hopefully, we'll see you at Christmas.*

for Christmas *Are you going home for Christmas?*

chubby *adj* THESAURUS ▶ fat[1] (1)

chunk *n* THESAURUS ▶ piece

church *n*

1 a building where Christians go to worship

ADJECTIVES/NOUNS + church

the local church *He plays the organ in his local church.*

a parish church *BrE* (=the main Christian church in a particular area) *St Luke's is the parish church for all the villages in this area.*

a Catholic/Protestant/Baptist/Methodist church *I went to Mass at the nearest Catholic church.*

VERBS

go to church (*also* **attend church** *formal*) (=go to a regular religious ceremony in a church) *My parents didn't go to church.*

church + NOUNS

a church service (=a religious ceremony in a church) *There's a church service at 10.30 every Sunday morning.*

a church hall (=a large room in or next to a church) *The dance was held in the church hall.*

church bells *I could hear the church bells ringing.*

church music *His music is strongly influenced by the church music he heard as a child.*

a church wedding (=in a church) *She wants to have a church wedding.*

C

a church tower *I looked at the clock on the church tower.*

the church choir (=a group of people who lead the singing in a church)

PREPOSITIONS

in (a) church *Did you get married in church?*

at church *I made the Sunday dinner while my mother was at church.*

2 an organization which is part of the Christian religion and has its own beliefs and ceremonies

NOUNS + church

the Catholic/Protestant/Mormon etc Church *The group split from the Mormon Church more than a hundred years ago.*

the Christian Church (=the Christian religion) *St Peter founded the Christian Church.*

church + NOUNS

Church leaders/elders (=the people in official positions of authority) *Church leaders have called for an end to the fighting.*

the Church authorities *The Church authorities refused to comment on the allegation.*

Church members *Church members donate a part of their salary to charity.*

cigarette *n*

a thin tube of paper filled with finely cut tobacco that people smoke

VERBS

smoke a cigarette *Some of the boys were smoking cigarettes.*

light a cigarette *He went outside and lit a cigarette.*

put out a cigarette (*also* **extinguish a cigarette** *formal*) (=stop it burning) *The man asked him to put out his cigarette.*

pull on/drag on/draw on a cigarette (=smoke a cigarette with deep breaths) *Ed pulled on his cigarette and coughed.*

roll a cigarette (=make your own cigarette using special paper) *My grandad used to roll his own cigarettes.*

cigarette + NOUNS

cigarette smoke *The room was full of cigarette smoke.*

cigarette smoking *Everyone knows that cigarette smoking is bad for you.*

a cigarette butt (*also* **a cigarette end** *BrE*) (=the part that remains when someone has finished smoking a cigarette) *The ashtray was full of old cigarette butts.*

cigarette ash *She flicked her cigarette ash onto the ground.*

cigarette advertising *All TV cigarette advertising has been banned.*

ADJECTIVES

a lit/lighted/burning cigarette *The fire was started by someone dropping a lit cigarette.*

PHRASES

a packet of cigarettes *BrE*, **a pack of cigarettes** *AmE*: *How much does a packet of cigarettes cost?*

cinema *n*

a building in which films are shown

ADJECTIVES

sb's local cinema *We usually go to our local cinema.*

a multiplex cinema (=with several different screens for showing films) *Multiplex cinemas have a big choice of films for people to see.*

VERBS

go to the cinema *Why don't we go to the cinema tonight?*

be showing at/in cinemas *The film is showing in cinemas from this Friday.*

cinema + NOUNS

a cinema audience (=the people who watch a film) *His new movie is sure to bring in big cinema audiences.*

the cinema screen *The film was much better on the cinema screen than on TV.*

PREPOSITIONS

be on at the cinema *Do you know what's on at the cinema?*

> In American English, people usually say **movie theater**.

circular *adj* THESAURUS **round¹**

circumstance Ac *n*

the conditions that affect a situation

> **Grammar**
> Usually plural.

ADJECTIVES

exceptional/special circumstances *Students are not allowed to miss classes, except under special circumstances.*

unforeseen circumstances (=that you did not expect) *The tragedy was the result of a series of unforeseen circumstances.*

normal circumstances *In normal circumstances, a child's language will develop naturally.*

the present/current circumstances *I can't see them giving us the money – not in the present circumstances.*

particular/certain circumstances *There may be particular circumstances in which these rules can be ignored.*

difficult circumstances *These teachers are doing a very good job under difficult circumstances.*

unusual circumstances *Occasionally you hear of unusual circumstances where this kind of thing happens.*

suspicious/mysterious circumstances *The police said there were no suspicious circumstances surrounding his death.*

tragic circumstances (=when extremely sad things happen) *Both parents died in tragic circumstances.*

mitigating/extenuating circumstances (=conditions that make it reasonable for someone to break the rules or law) *His lawyer will try to argue that there were mitigating circumstances for the crime.*

VERBS

circumstances change *If circumstances change, we might decide to cancel our holiday.*

circumstances exist (*also* **circumstances prevail** *formal*): *A good army officer bases his decisions on the circumstances that exist at the time.*

circumstances dictate/require sth (=make something necessary) *Unfortunately, circumstances dictated that we left the party early.*

PREPOSITIONS

in/under ... circumstances *Under certain circumstances, prisoners may be allowed to leave prison early, for example if they are very ill.*

PHRASES

the circumstances surrounding sth *The book examines the circumstances surrounding Britain joining the war.*

the circumstances leading to sth *The police are investigating the circumstances leading to his death.*

depending on the circumstances *The club may, depending on the circumstances, ask members to pay more.*

in/under certain circumstances (=if particular circumstances exist) *In certain circumstances, people may travel without a passport.*

under/given the circumstances (=in this situation) *Under the circumstances, you were right to call the police.*

a set/combination of circumstances *An unusual combination of circumstances caused me to miss my train.*

due to circumstances beyond sb's control *Occasionally flights are cancelled due to circumstances beyond our control.*

if circumstances allow/permit *formal* (=if it is possible in that situation) *Letters can be sent to prisoners and, if circumstances permit, visits may also be arranged.*

citizen *n*

someone who has the right to live in a particular country

ADJECTIVES

a British/American/French etc citizen *Her husband is a British citizen.*

a good citizen *The education system is designed to produce good citizens.*

a second-class citizen (=someone who is treated badly and feels unimportant) *Compared to men, women footballers are treated as second-class citizens.*

sb's fellow citizens *70% of our fellow citizens live in poverty.*

a private citizen (=an ordinary person who is not famous or powerful) *The former prime minister is enjoying life as a private citizen.*

a law-abiding citizen (=someone who does not do anything illegal) *Most people who live here are law-abiding citizens.*

VERBS

become a citizen *To become a UK citizen, you have to be able to read English.*

PREPOSITIONS

a citizen of a country *We are proud to be citizens of the United States of America.*

citizenship *n*

the legal right to live in a country

ADJECTIVES

US/British/Chinese etc citizenship *The men all have British citizenship.*

full citizenship *Foreigners can acquire full citizenship after living in the US for a number of years.*

dual citizenship (=the right to live in two different countries) *Mexican law prohibits its citizens from having dual citizenship.*

VERBS

have/hold citizenship *She was born in Brazil, but she also holds US citizenship.*

apply for citizenship *After living in England for five years, he applied for British citizenship.*

acquire/obtain/gain citizenship *She acquired Spanish citizenship last month.*

give/grant sb citizenship *The French government refused to grant him French citizenship.*

deny/refuse sb citizenship *She was continuously denied US citizenship.*

strip sb of citizenship (=take away someone's right to live in a country) *He was stripped of his Turkish citizenship.*

city *n* a large important town

ADJECTIVES

a big/large/major city *I had never lived in a big city before.*

a great city *Cairo is one of the world's great cities.*

a capital city (=where the government of a country or state is) *Cuba's capital city is Havana.*

a country's second city (=the next largest after the capital) *Bergen is Norway's second city.*

sb's home/native city (=where they were born or grew up) *He said that he never wanted to leave his home city.*

an industrial city *Sheffield is an industrial city in the north of England.*

an ancient/historic city *The statue was found near the ancient city of Ephesus.*

a cosmopolitan city (=full of people from different parts of the world) *San Francisco is a very cosmopolitan city.*

city + NOUNS

the city centre *BrE*, **the city center** *AmE*: *The hotel is in the city centre.*

a city street *Traffic was moving slowly along the city streets.*

the city limits *AmE* (=the edge of a city) *New developments are being built outside the city limits.*

city life *He was tired of city life.*

PHRASES

in the heart of a city *The cathedral is right in the heart of the city.*

on the outskirts of a city (=on the edge) *There were several bombings on the outskirts of the city.*

civil Ac *adj*

relating to the people who live in a country

NOUNS

civil rights (=rights to vote, be treated fairly etc that everyone should have) *African-Americans marched in defence of their civil rights.*

civil liberties/liberty (=the right to be free to do what you want within the law) *Detention without trial threatens our civil liberties.*

civil war (=fighting between groups from within the same country) *His family fled Spain during the Spanish civil war.*

civil disobedience (=the refusal to obey some laws as a protest, usually without violence) *Gandhi was known for advocating non-violent civil disobedience.*

civil unrest/disturbances (=when people protest or behave violently) *Troops have been called in to deal with civil disturbances.*

civilization (*also* **civilisation** *BrE*) *n*

a society that is well organized and developed

ADJECTIVES

an ancient/early civilization *The achievements of Egypt's ancient civilization were remarkable.*

modern civilization *Technology is one of the benefits of modern civilization.*

a great civilization *History students read about the great civilizations of India and China.*

human civilization *Art was important in the development of human civilization.*

Western civilization (=of Europe and North America) *They were interested in the spread of Western civilization.*

VERBS

a civilization flourishes (=is very successful) *Ancient Greek civilization flourished for more than a thousand years.*

PHRASES

a threat to civilization *Climate change could be the greatest threat to our civilization.*

since the dawn of civilization *formal* (=since when civilizations started to exist for the first time) *Wars have happened since the dawn of civilization.*

the decline of a civilization (=a situation in which it stops being successful) *They are concerned about the decline of western civilization.*

claim[1] *v*

to state that something is true

> **Grammar**
> **Claim** is often used with **that**: *He **claims** **that** he has done nothing wrong.* You can also use **claim** with an infinitive: *They **claim to be** the world's largest music company.* | *He **claimed to have earned*** over $5 million.

ADVERBS

rightly/rightfully claim sth (=claim something that is true) *This hotel can rightly claim to have the best views on the island.*

justifiably/legitimately claim sth (=rightly claim) *The factory can justifiably claim to be one of the most modern in Europe.*

falsely/wrongly claim sth *Some companies falsely claim that their products have health benefits.*

VERBS

try/attempt to claim sth *She tried to claim that she had never seen him before in her life.*

NOUNS

claim responsibility for sth (=say that you are responsible for something bad) *A terrorist group called a newspaper claiming responsibility for the attack.*

claim (the) credit for sth (=say that you are responsible for something good) *Political parties always claim the credit for economic growth.*

claim victory (=say that you are the winner) *The president will not be able to claim victory until all the votes are counted.*

claim your innocence *Hussain has always claimed his innocence, saying Khan died when his own gun went off.*

> Instead of saying **claim your innocence**, you can say **maintain your innocence**: *Davis has always **maintained his innocence**.*

claim[2] *n*

a statement that something is true

ADJECTIVES

a false claim *The company was making false claims about the effectiveness of its products.*

a claim is untrue *A lot of the claims you read on the internet are untrue.*

a claim is unfounded/unsubstantiated *formal* (=not based on truth or evidence) *Workers' claims of cruel treatment are completely unfounded.*

extravagant/ridiculous/outrageous claims *formal* (=clearly not true) *Companies try to sell more products by making extravagant claims about them.*

competing/conflicting claims (=saying that different things are true) *Voters are confused by the competing claims of the different political parties.*

VERBS

make a claim *They make ridiculous claims about the benefits of the diet.*

bring/lodge a claim (=claim something officially or legally) *She's bringing a claim of unfair dismissal against her employer.*

deny/reject/dismiss a claim *Government officials denied claims that the country possessed chemical weapons.*

accept a claim *Some people refuse to accept the claim that sunlight is bad for your skin.*

support a claim (*also* **back up a claim**) *The court found no evidence to support his claim.*

challenge a claim *The article challenges the claims companies make for their skincare products.*

investigate a claim *Detectives are investigating claims of dishonesty by government officials.*

base a claim on sth (=use something to show that a claim is true) *She has no evidence on which to base her claim that she deserves special treatment.*

PREPOSITIONS

claims about/of sth *His friends didn't believe his claims about having no money.*

PHRASES

a claim does not stand up (=it is clearly not true) *The government's claims to have solved the problem simply don't stand up.*

clammy *adj* THESAURUS **damp (1)**

clandestine *adj* THESAURUS **secret**[1]

class *n*

1 a period of time during which someone teaches a group of people

ADJECTIVES/NOUNS + class

a French/history/music/dance etc class *I learned something interesting in my psychology class today.*

a beginners'/intermediate/advanced class *He started with a general computer course and then took some more advanced classes.*

an evening class/a night class *Mum goes to an evening class on Tuesdays.*

VERBS

go to a class (*also* **attend a class** *formal*): *You could try attending a yoga class.*

have a class *What classes do you have this morning?*

take a class (=go to classes as a student) *I'm taking some art classes at the moment.*

teach a class *One of the other teachers was ill so I taught her class.*

miss a class *Students who miss classes fall behind with their work.*

a class is held/takes place *The classes are held in a local school.*

PREPOSITIONS

in class *He was a shy boy who rarely spoke in class.*

PHRASES

be late for class *David was late for class again.*

2 one of the groups in a society that people are divided into according to their jobs, income, education etc

ADJECTIVES

the middle class *Most people say they belong to the middle class.*

the working/lower class *At this time most of the working class was very poor.*

the upper class *Members of the upper classes didn't have to work.*

social class *He belonged to a higher social class than his colleagues.*

the ruling/dominant class (=the people who have power) *For a long time, French was the language of the ruling class.*

the professional class (=people with professional jobs) *Doctors, lawyers, and teachers are all members of the professional class.*

a privileged class (=people who have advantages because of their wealth, social position etc) *Holidays abroad used to be only for the privileged classes.*

VERBS

belong to a class *We asked people what class they belonged to.*

class + NOUNS

the class system *He felt he was a victim of the class system.*

classified *adj* THESAURUS **secret**[1]

clause *n*

1 a group of words that contains a subject and a verb, but which is usually only part of a sentence

ADJECTIVES

a main clause (=giving the main information of the sentence) *The main clause can be a sentence on its own.*

a relative clause (=connected to another clause by 'who', 'why,' 'which,' 'that' etc) *In the sentence "The man who stole the money was punished", the relative clause is 'who stole the money'.*

a subordinate clause (=one that gives extra information to the main clause) *Any clause containing the word 'because' is a subordinate clause.*

C

2 a part of a written law or legal document covering a particular subject of the whole law or document

VERBS

have/include/contain a clause *The bill is 93 pages long and contains over 100 clauses.*

add/insert/introduce a clause *They want to add another clause to the agreement.*

draft a clause (=write it) *Our lawyer suggested drafting an extra clause to the contract.*

ADJECTIVES

a special clause *A special clause was introduced to cover this type of case.*

an exclusion/exemption clause (=allowing some people to ignore a rule) *There is an exemption clause for people who are over 65.*

an escape/get-out/opt-out clause (=which you can use to avoid obeying the conditions of an agreement) *They are trying to find a get-out clause so that they don't have to pay the money.*

PREPOSITIONS

a clause in sth *Is there a clause in the contract covering payments to lawyers?*

under clause 4/23 etc of sth *Under clause 5 of the agreement, each partner is responsible for the company's debts.*

claw *n*

the sharp curved nail on the toes of animals such as cats or bears, or the sharp curved part that a crab, scorpion etc uses to attack other animals

> **Grammar**
> Usually plural.

ADJECTIVES

sharp claws *Lizards have very sharp claws.*

powerful claws *Crabs are equipped with powerful claws.*

VERBS

dig/sink its claws into sth *The parrot dug its claws into my arm.*

sharpen its claws *Our cat likes to sharpen its claws on our best furniture.*

claw + NOUNS

claw marks *If you see claw marks on the trees, you know there are bears nearby.*

clean[1] *adj*

1 without any dirt, marks etc

NOUNS

clean clothes *He changed into some clean clothes.*

a clean shirt/sheet/towel *I put on a clean white shirt.*

clean hands/face/teeth *Make sure you have clean hands before you eat.*

a clean room/house/apartment *Her mother always kept the house very clean.*

clean air/water (=free from dirt or pollution) *The air is much cleaner outside the city.*

clean energy (=which does not cause pollution) *Wind power is an excellent source of clean energy.*

a wound/cut is clean (=with no bacteria or infection)

a clean needle/bandage (=unused and without blood, bacteria etc)

VERBS

keep sth clean *You should always keep your kitchen clean.*

get sth clean *It took me ages to get the tiles clean.*

wipe sth clean (=with a cloth) *He started to wipe the blackboard clean.*

sweep/scrub sth clean (=with a brush) *She quickly swept the floor clean.*

ADVERBS

spotlessly/immaculately clean (=completely clean - used for emphasis) *The floor was spotlessly clean.*

completely/perfectly clean *It is almost impossible to get the glass completely clean.*

scrupulously clean (=very carefully cleaned) *Hospitals must be kept scrupulously clean.*

PHRASES

nice and clean *Their job is to keep the streets nice and clean.*

clean and tidy *BrE*, **neat and clean** *especially AmE*: *Her kids were always neat and clean.*

THESAURUS: clean

spotless
room | kitchen | house | clothes | blouse | uniform | apron
completely clean, especially because someone takes great care:

Her kitchen is always spotless. | *She was wearing a spotless white blouse.*

Spotless means the same as **spotlessly clean**.

immaculate
condition | **clothes** | **suit** | **uniform** | **hair** | **teeth** | **room** | **house**
completely clean, especially because someone takes great care:
The car was in immaculate condition and had obviously been well looked after. | *The man wore an immaculate dark grey suit.* | *Her black hair was immaculate.* | *Rachel keeps the house immaculate.*

Immaculate means the same as **spotless**. It is most commonly used in the phrase **in immaculate condition**.

spick and span
clean and tidy, especially after having just been cleaned. **Spick and span** sounds rather informal:
By the end of the day, the whole place was ***spick and span****.*

pure
air | **water**
pure air and water does not contain any harmful substances at all:
I breathed in the pure mountain air. | *The water in the stream is pure and safe to drink.*

pristine
condition | **beaches** | **lakes** | **forest** | **desert** | **wilderness** | **countryside** | **beauty** | **house** | **shirt**
if something is pristine, it is so clean it looks like new. **Pristine** is also used about natural places that have no litter or other damage caused by humans:
The painting was in pristine condition. | *People come to the island for its pristine beaches and beautiful clear water.* | *He wore a pristine white shirt.*

sterile
needle | **bandage** | **dressing** | **conditions**
completely clean, with no bacteria, and therefore safe for medical or scientific use:
The needles are heated to make them sterile. | *Place a sterile bandage on the wound.* | *The samples must be kept in sterile conditions.*

hygienic
conditions | **way**
clean and not likely to cause the spread of disease:
The food is kept in hygienic conditions. | *The most hygienic way to dispose of diapers is to burn them.* | ***It's not hygienic to*** *eat things that everyone has touched.*

ANTONYMS **clean → dirty**

2 not causing harm to the environment

THESAURUS: clean

eco-friendly, green, clean, renewable, sustainable, carbon-neutral, low-carbon, low-energy → **environmentally friendly**

clean² *v*

to remove dirt from something by rubbing or washing

NOUNS

clean a house/room/floor *My mother used to spend hours cleaning the house.*

clean a window/wall *The windows had not been cleaned in years.*

clean your teeth/hands *I always clean my teeth after meals.*

clean your shoes/clothes/glasses *Your shoes need cleaning.*

clean a wound *The nurse cleaned the wound and put a bandage on it.*

PREPOSITIONS/ADVERBS

clean out the cupboard/refrigerator *It took me all morning to clean out the kitchen cupboards.*

clean off the dirt/mud/blood etc (=remove it) *You can use a damp cloth to clean off the dirt.*

clean up the mess *Who is going to clean up all this mess?*

clean sth thoroughly *It is important to clean the brushes thoroughly after you use them.*

PHRASES

clean sth from top to bottom (=clean all of a place very thoroughly) *They cleaned the house from top to bottom.*

THESAURUS: clean

wipe
table | **hands** | **face** | **nose**
to remove dirt or liquid from something using a damp cloth, or your fingers:
The waiter wiped the table and brought the menu. | *She wiped her hands on her apron.* | *He wiped his face with his napkin.* | *The head teacher wiped her nose on a handkerchief.* | *Lucy* ***wiped the tears from her eyes****.* | *The man* ***wiped*** *the paint* ***off*** *his hands.*

brush
hair | **teeth** | **shoes** | **clothes**
to clean something using a brush:
She was brushing her hair in front of the bedroom mirror. | *He went to the bathroom to brush his teeth.* | *Paul* ***brushed*** *the mud* ***off*** *his coat.*

C

C

scrub
floor | pan | hands | (finger)nails
to clean something by rubbing it hard with a brush and some water:
*She was on her knees, scrubbing the floor. | I worked in the kitchen scrubbing the pans. | I **scrubbed** the dirt **off** my hands.*

polish
shoes | glasses | car | table | furniture | floor
to rub something in order to make it shine, usually with a cloth:
*His shoes were always **well polished**. | She polished the glasses until they sparkled.*

dust
furniture | chair | shelves
to remove dust from somewhere using a cloth:
She found the letter when she was dusting some shelves in his study. | Don't forget to dust on top of the cupboards.

vacuum
carpet | rug | floor | house | room | car
to clean something using a special machine that sucks dirt off the floor:
It took me nearly an hour to vacuum the carpets. | She had vacuumed the whole house before her mother arrived.

rinse
hair | hands | mouth | clothes | cloth | plate | dish | glass | cup | vegetables | lettuce
to wash something quickly by pouring water on it, in order to remove soap, shampoo, dirt etc:
*Rinse your hair thoroughly to get rid of the shampoo. | She **rinsed out** her dirty clothes. | Polly went into her little kitchen and **rinsed out** two glasses. | I **rinsed off** the soap.*

You use **rinse out** about using water to clean the inside of a cup, pan etc, or to clean a cloth, some clothes etc. You also **rinse out** your mouth with a liquid to make it clean.

cleanse *formal*
skin | wound
to clean your skin or a wound thoroughly:
The cream is good for cleansing the skin. | Use salt water to cleanse the wound.

disinfect
surface | wound | equipment | shoes | clothing | hands | house | room
to use chemicals to clean something, in order to prevent the spread of disease:
It is important to disinfect the wound. | Staff must disinfect their hands before they go into the operating theatre. | I had to disinfect the room with bleach.

sterilize (*also* **sterilise** *BrE*)
needle | instrument | equipment | milk | water
to make something safe to use by heating it or using chemicals, by killing all the bacteria:
Always use sterilized needles, and only use them once. | Make sure that you sterilize the water before you drink it.

cleanse *v* THESAURUS ▸ clean[2]

clear *adj*

1 easy to understand

NOUNS

clear instructions *The instructions are clear and easy to follow.*

a clear explanation *His explanation wasn't very clear and I wasn't sure what to do.*

clear advice/guidance *The doctor's advice was very clear: lose weight.*

a clear warning *Police must give a clear warning before firing their weapons.*

a clear message/signal/indication *The voters have sent a clear message to the government.*

a clear statement *You should give a clear statement of your intentions.*

sb's position is clear *My position is absolutely clear: I am not in favour of these changes.*

ADVERBS

absolutely/perfectly clear *Their answer was perfectly clear.*

crystal clear (=extremely clear) *The instructions on the packet are crystal clear.*

VERBS

make sth clear *Children may have difficulty in making their feelings clear.*

PREPOSITIONS

clear about/on sth *The law is very clear on this point.*

PHRASES

make it clear that... *She made it clear that she did not want any help.*

make yourself clear (=express yourself in a way that is easy to understand) *Please tell me if I'm not making myself clear.*

far from clear/by no means clear (=very unclear) *Her explanation was far from clear.*

2 used when saying that someone is sure about something and understands it well

NOUNS

a clear idea/understanding/picture *This booklet will give you a clear idea of what the course involves.*

a clear sense of sth *She had a very strong will and a clear sense of purpose.*

a clear objective/aim *The US entered the war without any clear objectives.*

VERBS

get sth clear (=understand something properly) *I'm just trying to get clear exactly what you mean.*

PHRASES

be clear in sb's mind *The layout of the house was still clear in his mind.*

3 impossible to doubt, question, or make a mistake about

NOUNS

clear evidence/signs *There is clear evidence that smoking is bad for health.*

a clear case/example of sth *It was a clear case of theft.*

a clear distinction *There used to be a clear distinction between work and leisure.*

a clear winner/victory *He is the clear winner.*

ADVERBS

not entirely clear *Sam's reasons for leaving were not entirely clear.*

painfully clear (=very clear - used especially about something that causes problems or is embarrassing) *It became painfully clear that I had got it wrong.*

abundantly clear *formal* (=extremely clear) *By July the scale of the problem had become abundantly clear.*

PHRASES

as clear as day/daylight (=extremely clear) *His reason for contacting me was suddenly as clear as day.*

4 easy to see through, rather than coloured or dirty

NOUNS

clear water/liquid *The water was so clear that you could see down to the bottom of the lake.*

clear glass *The walls are made of clear glass.*

ADVERBS

crystal clear (=extremely clear) *You can go diving in crystal clear water.*

THESAURUS: clear

transparent
plastic | silk | varnish | film | tape | screen
clear - used about materials and solid things. **Transparent** is a little more formal than **clear**:
*The bottles are made of transparent plastic. | a transparent silk nightdress | The cream forms a transparent film on your skin. | Fry the onions until they are **almost transparent**.*

see-through
dress | blouse | top | bag
made of a very thin material that you can see through - used especially about clothes:
She wore a black see-through dress. | He kept the map in a see-through plastic bag.

You use **opaque** about something that is difficult to see through: *The bathroom windows are made of **opaque** glass.*

5 if the sky is clear, there are no clouds

THESAURUS: clear

good, fine, nice, bright, beautiful/glorious, clear, cloudless, dry → **sunny**

clever *adj*

1 a clever person is intelligent and good at thinking of ideas and ways of doing things

NOUNS

a clever boy/girl/man/woman *My uncle is a very clever man.*

a clever person *She was surrounded by clever people when she was at college.*

a clever politician/lawyer *Smith escaped going to prison because he had a clever lawyer.*

Clever is often used to describe people who are good at tricking other people, for example lawyers and politicians. It is also used to describe people who you admire for their intelligence, especially in British English. In American English, people usually say **smart**.

ADVERBS

how clever *How clever of you to remember!*

THESAURUS: clever

clever, smart, bright, brilliant, gifted, wise, cunning, brainy → **intelligent**

2 a clever idea, plan, method etc is interesting or unusual and works well

clever + NOUNS

a clever idea *What a clever idea!*

a clever way of doing sth *The brochure suggests several clever ways in which you can save energy in your home.*

a clever use of sth *There is a clever use of space in the kitchen.*

a clever trick *He used a clever trick to confuse his opponent.*

a clever gadget/device *They use a clever little gadget for peeling the oranges.*

a clever piece of software *He wrote a clever piece of software which can find the information you want for you.*

ADVERBS

extremely/really clever *She came up with an extremely clever way of solving the problem.*

fiendishly clever (=extremely clever in a surprising way) *The design is fiendishly clever.*

THESAURUS: clever

ingenious
way | method | idea | solution | explanation | device | experiment
very clever:
Many fish have ingenious ways of protecting their eggs from attack. | The people developed a ***highly ingenious*** *method of freeze-drying potatoes, to provide food throughout the winter months. | He used an ingenious experiment to test his theory.*

brilliant
idea | suggestion | solution
a brilliant idea, suggestion etc is extremely good and very clever. **Brilliant** sounds rather informal and is used especially in spoken English:
It sounded like a brilliant idea at the time. | Thanks again for your brilliant suggestion! | Archimedes came up with a brilliant solution to the problem.

cunning
plan | trick | way
clever – used about ways of tricking people and getting advantages for yourself:
Bill thought of a cunning plan to make them reduce their prices. | He used a cunning trick to defeat his opponent. | It was a cunning way of making people think he was trying to help them.

cliché *n*

a phrase that has been used too often

ADJECTIVES

an old cliché *He seemed to believe that old cliché about a woman's place being in the home.*

a tired/worn-out cliché (=boring because it has been used so often) *Try to think of fresh ways of describing things rather than using tired clichés.*

the usual clichés *The Chairman's statement contained the usual clichés.*

VERBS

use a cliché *'Time marches on', to use the old cliché.*

PHRASES

be full of clichés *Sports reporting tends to be full of clichés.*

sth has become a cliché *The phrase 'going forward' has become a cliché.*

THESAURUS: cliché

expression, idiom, cliché, saying/proverb, slogan, motto → **phrase**

client *n*

someone who gets services or advice from a professional person, company, or organization

ADJECTIVES/NOUNS + client

an important/major client *She is an important client and we do not want to lose her.*

a satisfied client *Satisfied clients will recommend your company to their friends.*

a new client *Most firms are desperate for new clients.*

a potential/prospective client (=someone who might become a client) *Make sure potential clients know about all of your services.*

an existing client *We are very keen to keep our existing clients happy.*

a private client (=a person rather than a business) *He designs and builds houses for private clients.*

VERBS

meet (with) a client *He has gone to meet a client.*

advise a client *The surveyor will advise his client on the value of the property.*

act for/on behalf of a client *The lawyer will write confirming that he agrees to act for his client.*

represent a client *Mead was a top attorney representing major corporate clients.*

deal with a client *They receive training to help them deal with difficult clients.*

client + NOUNS

a client base/list (=all the people, companies etc that are your clients) *The company quickly expanded its client base in the US.*

cliff *n*

a high area of rock or a mountain with a very steep side, often by the sea or a river

ADJECTIVES

a high/low cliff *The cliffs here are the highest in Britain.*

a steep cliff *The cliffs were steep and dangerous.*

a sheer/vertical cliff (=going straight up or down) *The sheer cliff looked impossible to climb.*

a rocky cliff *The stream then tumbles down a rocky cliff.*

a jagged cliff (=with a lot of sharp rocks) *This is an area of spectacular gorges and jagged cliffs.*

a towering cliff (=very high) *The towering cliffs of Gibraltar were visible in the distance.*

a rugged/craggy cliff (=rough and uneven) *Huge Atlantic waves were breaking against the rugged cliffs.*

dramatic cliffs (=very impressive) *The west coast has dramatic cliffs and a spectacular rock arch.*

cliff + NOUNS

the cliff face (=the side of a cliff) *Some climbers were scrambling up the steep cliff face.*

the cliff edge *Keep away from the cliff edge.*

the cliff top *There was a lovely view from the cliff top.*

a cliff ledge (=a flat narrow piece that sticks out from a cliff) *The sheep got stuck on a cliff ledge and he had to carry it down.*

a cliff path *I followed the cliff path down to the bay.*

VERBS

the cliffs rise (up) *literary: The cliffs rose up ahead of us.*

PREPOSITIONS

off a cliff *I was worried that he was going to jump off the cliff.*

over a cliff *The car went over a cliff.*

PHRASES

the top of a cliff *We climbed to the top of the cliff.*

the bottom/foot/base of a cliff *His body was found at the foot of the cliff.*

the edge of a cliff *Don't stand too near the edge of the cliff.*

be perched (high) on a cliff (=be situated on a cliff) *An 11th-century castle is perched high on the cliff.*

climate *n*

the typical weather conditions in a particular area

ADJECTIVES

a warm/hot climate *Many people prefer to live where the climate is warm.*

a cold/cool climate *Scotland's climate is too cold for these plants to survive.*

a mild climate *The region's climate is mild all the year round.*

a dry climate (=with little rain) *She loves the dry climate of southern California.*

a wet/damp climate *A damp climate can damage buildings.*

a humid climate (=with hot and wet air) *Florida has a humid climate.*

a tropical climate *Their thick clothing was not suitable for the tropical climate of Brazil.*

a harsh climate (*also* **an inhospitable climate** *formal*) (=uncomfortable and difficult to live in) *He endured the harsh climate of Siberia for three years.*

an extreme/severe climate (=extremely cold or hot) *The region has a very severe climate, with temperatures falling below -30°C in winter.*

an arid climate (=very dry) *The desert has a very arid climate and few plants can grow there.*

a temperate climate (=never very hot or very cold) *Europe's climate is temperate.*

the global/world climate *This temperature rise will change the global climate.*

climate + NOUNS

climate change (=a permanent change in weather conditions) *These fish are under threat as a result of climate change.*

THESAURUS: climate

climate, conditions, the outlook, the elements
→ **weather**

climax *n*

the most exciting or important part of a story, event, or time, which usually comes near the end

VERBS

reach/come to a climax *The film reaches its climax in the final scene.*

build (up) to a climax *The music was getting louder and building up to a climax.*

lead to a climax *The earlier scenes lead logically to the climax in Act Three.*

near/approach a climax *One of the most important trials in recent history is nearing its climax today.*

bring sth to a climax *He scored again, bringing the game to a climax.*

mark the climax of sth *This painting marked the climax of his career.*

the climax comes *The climax came when the president ordered an air strike on the capital.*

ADJECTIVES

a thrilling/dramatic/exciting climax *The Round the World yacht race is reaching a dramatic climax.*

a big climax *The big climax is when the magician makes the woman appear again.*

a sensational/spectacular climax *The match was a sensational climax to the season.*

a fitting climax (=a very suitable one) *The concert was very successful and a fitting climax to the school year.*

PREPOSITIONS

the climax of/to sth *The harvest was the climax of the rural year.*

climb *v*

to move up, down, or across something using your feet and hands, especially when this needs a lot of effort

NOUNS

climb a mountain/hill/peak/slope *Hillary and Tenzing climbed the mountain in 1953.*

climb the stairs/steps/staircase *The old man slowly climbed up the stairs.*

climb a tree/ladder/wall *Kids love climbing trees.*

climb a rope *In order to reach the sails, you had to climb a rope.*

VERBS + climb

go climbing *We used to go climbing together in the Alps.*

C

PREPOSITIONS/ADVERBS

climb up/down/over sth *She climbed down the ladder.*

climb out of/off sth *He climbed out of the pool and sat down.*

climb onto sth *Fans climbed onto the roof to get a better view.*

THESAURUS: climb

ascend *formal*
stairs | steps | staircase | mountain | hill | ladder
to climb up something:
Diana ascended the stairs to her room. | They ascended the mountain by the light of the moon.

Ascend or climb?
Ascend is much more formal than **climb** and is used mainly in written descriptions. **Ascend** is only used about going up, whereas **climb** can be used about going up, down, or over something.

go up
stairs | steps | staircase | mountain | hill | ladder | tree
to move up something:
The three children went noisily up the stairs. | The car went up the hill.

mount
stairs | steps | stage | platform | horse
to climb up something, or climb onto something. **Mount** sounds rather formal:
The women watched them curiously as they mounted the stairs. | The audience cheered as the band mounted the stage. | The prince mounted his horse and rode off.

scale *formal*
wall | fence | mountain | peak | cliff
to climb to the top of something very high:
The prisoners escaped by scaling a high barbed wire fence. | She was the youngest person ever to scale the mountain.

scramble
to climb somewhere quickly and with difficulty, using your hands to help you, especially when you are walking:
They ***scrambled up*** *the steep rocky bank.*

clamber
to climb somewhere with difficulty, using your hands to help you:
At last we saw the two girls ***clambering down*** *the slope to safety. | Everyone* ***clambered onto*** *the back of the truck.*

clinic *n*

a place people can visit to get medical treatment or advice

ADJECTIVES/NOUNS + clinic

a health/medical clinic *Children are given vaccinations at their local health clinic.*

a hospital clinic *You can be tested for infection at a special hospital clinic.*

a private clinic *Fees at private clinics are usually very high.*

an outpatient clinic (=in a hospital, for people who do not need to stay there) *There's an outpatient clinic for people with diabetes.*

VERBS

go to a clinic (*also* **attend a clinic** *formal*): *Pregnant women should attend an antenatal clinic at least once a month.*

hold a clinic (=arrange for a clinic to take place) *The hospital holds vaccination clinics once a fortnight.*

PREPOSITIONS

at/in a clinic *I have an appointment at the clinic.*

clock *n*

an instrument that shows what time it is

VERBS

look/glance at the clock *She looked at the clock. It was eight thirty.*

wind (up) a clock (=turn a key to keep it working) *It was one of those old clocks that you have to wind up.*

the clock says eight/nine etc (=shows a particular time) *The clock said five so I went back to sleep.*

a clock strikes eight/nine etc (=makes a number of sounds to show the hour) *I heard a church clock strike eleven.*

a clock ticks (=makes regular quiet sounds) *There was no sound in the room apart from a clock ticking.*

a clock stops (=stops working) *My bedside clock had stopped at 6 a.m.*

an alarm clock goes off (=rings at a particular time) *What time do you want the alarm clock to go off tomorrow?*

set an alarm clock (=move the controls so that it will make a noise at a particular time) *She set her alarm clock for 7.15.*

ADJECTIVES

a clock is fast/slow (=shows a later or earlier time than the real time) *There's no need to hurry – that clock's fast.*

ADJECTIVES/NOUNS + clock

an alarm clock (=that makes a noise to wake you up) *He forgot to set his alarm clock.*

a grandfather clock (=an old-style tall clock that stands on the floor)

a digital clock (=that shows the time as numbers that keep changing)

PHRASES

the hands of/on a clock (=the long thin pieces that point at the numbers) *The hands on the clock moved so slowly.*

the face of a clock/the clock face (=the front part that you look at) *I couldn't see the clock face from where I was sitting.*

close[1] *v*

to make something stop being open, or to stop being open

close + NOUNS

close your eyes/mouth/lips *I closed my eyes and tried to sleep.*

close a door/window/gate *Don't forget to close the gate.*

close the curtains/blinds *Can you close the curtains for me?*

close a book *Harry closed the book and put it back on the shelf.*

close a bag/suitcase/purse *It's difficult to close the suitcase.*

close a box/jar *He put the letter in the box and closed it.*

close a drawer/lid *He carefully closed the drawer.*

NOUNS + close

a door/gate closes *The door slowly closed behind him.*

sb's eyes close *His eyes closed and he fell asleep.*

ADVERBS

close sth firmly *Maggie closed the door firmly and went through to the kitchen.*

close sth tightly/tight (=used especially about your eyes) *He closed his eyes tightly and pulled the trigger.*

close sth carefully *Sabine closed her bag carefully.*

sth closes shut *The door suddenly closed shut.*

sth does not close properly (=not completely) *The car door doesn't seem to close properly.*

PREPOSITIONS

close (sth) behind you *She heard the door close behind her.*

THESAURUS: close

shut
door | eyes | window | gate | drawer | book | box | suitcase | lid
to close something:
She shut the door with a loud bang. | He told the audience to shut their eyes. | She shut the book and got up.

> **Shut** or **close**?
> **Shut** and **close** mean the same. Because they have different vowel sounds, they can have a slightly different feeling. **Shut** is used more when the action is quick, firm, or noisy. **Close** is used more when the action is slow, careful, or gentle.
> With some words you can only use **close**. You **close the curtains** (not 'shut' them). You **close a bag/wallet/jar/container** (not 'shut' it).

slam
door | gate | lid
to close a door or lid quickly and noisily, especially because you are angry:
She left the room, slamming the door behind her. | The boy slammed the lid of his desk.

> You can also say **slam sth shut**: *He* ***slammed*** *the drawer* ***shut***.

draw
curtains | blind
to close curtains or a blind by pulling them along a rail:
I drew the curtains and went upstairs to bed. | The blinds were still drawn in his office.

lock
door | gate | box | drawer | safe | car | room | house
to close something with a key or a special number or code, so that other people cannot get in:
She locked the front door behind her. | Don't forget to lock the car.

seal
jar | bag | box | container | hole | gap | chamber
to close something so that no air or liquid can get in or out:
Seal the jars and store them in a cool place. | The uranium is stored in ***hermetically sealed*** *containers* (=completely sealed, so no air at

C

all can get in or out). | *It is better to seal gaps in window frames, in order to avoid loss of heat.*

> **Seal** is most commonly used as an adjective participle: *The vegetables are sold in* ***sealed*** *containers, in order to keep them fresh.*
> If you **seal** an **envelope**, you stick down the top part, so that it is completely closed.

C

ANTONYMS **close → open² (1)**

close² *adj, adv*

1 not far away

PHRASES

close at hand (=very near) *If there are any problems, the library staff are always close at hand.*

in close proximity to sb/sth *formal* (=close to someone or something) *In this city, the rich live in close proximity to the poor.*

at close quarters (=when you are very close) *The picture looks even more magnificent at close quarters.*

at close range (=firing a gun from very close) *He was shot in the head at close range.*

VERBS

get/come close (*also* **draw close** *written*): *She felt a little afraid as they drew close to the house.*

PREPOSITIONS/ADVERBS

close to sb/sth *The hotel is close to the railway station.*

close together *They sat close together on the sofa.*

close behind/beside sb *The rest of the group followed close behind him.*

close by (=near to a place) *All her relatives live close by.*

> **THESAURUS: close**
> close, nearby, neighbouring, surrounding, local → **near**

2 if you are close to doing something, you are very likely to do it soon

PHRASES

close to tears (=very nearly crying) *She was exhausted and close to tears.*

close to death *He was close to death, but his condition has improved a little.*

close to extinction *The Hawaiian crow is close to extinction.*

close to retirement *Several of the firm's employees are close to retirement.*

close to collapse/bankruptcy *One of the big investment banks was rumoured to be close to collapse.*

VERBS

come close to (doing) sth *Only once has he come close to losing his temper.*

bring sb/sth close to (doing) sth *His speech brought me close to tears.*

ADVERBS

perilously/dangerously close *Three years ago, the theatre came perilously close to closure.*

agonizingly/tantalizingly close (=extremely close to achieving something) *The French came agonizingly close to winning the match.*

3 used when talking about looking at, thinking about, or watching something very carefully

NOUNS

a close look *She moved forward to take a close look at the painting.*

a close examination *A closer examination of the facts soon solved the mystery.*

close attention *Pay close attention when the teacher reads the instructions.*

close scrutiny (=careful and thorough examination) *The investigation included close scrutiny of video images of the incident.*

close inspection *Closer inspection revealed that the rocks were from an earlier period.*

close supervision *Initially there will be close supervision of the trainee.*

a close study *Their research involved a close study of two communities.*

PHRASES

keep a close eye/watch on sb/sth (=watch someone or something carefully) *They have to keep a close eye on their finances.*

4 used when talking about a good relationship between people

NOUNS

a close friend *He is a close friend of Prince Charles.*

a close colleague/associate *He discussed the problem with some of his close colleagues.*

a close friendship/relationship *He found it hard to form close relationships with other people.*

close ties/links *The president has said that he wants closer ties with China.*

a close bond *There has always been a close bond between the sisters.*

close cooperation *Close cooperation is needed between team members.*

PREPOSITIONS

close to sb *Guy was very close to his older sister.*

closed *adj*

1 not open

NOUNS

a door/gate is closed *The bedroom door was closed.*

a window/shutter is closed *All the windows were closed when they left the house.*

a curtain/blind is closed *She kept the curtains closed during the daytime.*

sb's eyes are closed *His eyes were closed and he looked like he was asleep.*

sb's mouth is closed *It is polite to eat with your mouth closed.*

ADVERBS

tightly/firmly closed *Her mouth was tightly closed.*

partially/partly closed *One eye was partly closed.*

fully closed *I checked that all the windows were fully closed.*

VERBS

keep sth closed *He always keeps the door of his office closed.*

remain closed *His eyes remained closed while he listened to her.*

> **Closed** or **shut?**
> **Shut** means the same as **closed**. You can say that a door, gate, or someone's mouth or eyes are **shut** or **closed**. You don't usually use **shut** about curtains or blinds. You don't say that something is 'partly shut'. You say that it is **partly closed**.
> You don't use **shut** before a noun. **Closed** is sometimes used before a noun: *He listened with **closed** eyes.*

ANTONYMS **closed → open¹ (1)**

2 if a store, bank, museum etc is closed, it is not open and people cannot enter or use it

NOUNS

a shop/store/bank/office is closed *The flower shop is closed on Sunday.*

a gallery/museum is closed *The museum is closed for a few days at Christmas.*

a market is closed *Japanese financial markets remained closed for a national holiday.*

ADVERBS

temporarily closed *The palace is temporarily closed for structural repairs.*

permanently closed *The bridge is permanently closed because it is unsafe.*

VERBS

remain closed *The park will remain closed until the end of the month.*

PHRASES

closed to the public/visitors *The church is currently closed to the public because of restoration work.*

closed for repairs/maintenance/refurbishment *The Grand Opera House remains closed for repairs.*

> **Closed** or **shut?**
> **Shut** means the same as **closed**. **Shut** is mainly used in spoken English. Signs on buildings say **closed**, not 'shut'. You usually say **temporarily/permanently closed**, not 'temporarily/permanently shut'.

ANTONYMS **closed → open¹ (2)**

cloth *n*

1 material used for making things such as clothes

ADJECTIVES/NOUNS + cloth

woollen/linen/silk cloth *His suit was made of dark grey woollen cloth.*

fine cloth *His waistcoat was made of fine cloth.*

coarse cloth (=rough cloth made from thick threads) *The shawl was made of coarse cloth.*

VERBS

make/manufacture/produce cloth *The cloth is made on a machine called a loom.*

weave cloth *The cloth is woven by hand.*

dye cloth *The cloth is dyed and then washed.*

cloth + NOUNS

a cloth cap/coat/bag *A tall man wearing a cloth cap suddenly appeared.*

a cloth merchant *Her family were wealthy cloth merchants.*

2 a piece of cloth used for a particular purpose

ADJECTIVES

a damp/wet cloth *She cleaned the surfaces with a damp cloth.*

a clean cloth *Cover the wound with a clean cloth.*

VERBS

clean/wipe sth with a cloth *The waitress was wiping the tables with a damp cloth.*

wrap sth in a cloth *He wrapped the gun in a cloth.*

cover sth with a cloth *The body was covered with a cloth.*

lay/put/spread a cloth over sth *The priest laid a linen cloth over the altar.*

> **Tablecloth** (= which you put on a table), **facecloth** (=which you use for washing your face), and **dishcloth** (=which you use for washing plates) are usually written as one word.

clothes *n* the things that people wear

ADJECTIVES/NOUNS + clothes

new/old clothes *I like your new clothes.*

clean/dirty clothes *I can't wait to get out of these dirty clothes.*

good/nice/beautiful/expensive/fashionable clothes *The magazine was full of pictures of people wearing expensive clothes.*

warm/dry/wet clothes *It's cold in the mountains and you'll need plenty of warm clothes.*

designer clothes (=made by a well-known designer) *She spends hundreds of pounds on designer clothes.*

work/school/sports clothes *He changed out of his work clothes.*

formal clothes *It's best to wear formal clothes for an interview.*

smart clothes *BrE* (=nice neat clothes that you wear for formal occasions) *Do you have to wear smart clothes to work?*

casual clothes *Most people feel more comfortable in casual clothes.*

sb's best clothes *They wore their best clothes for the photograph.*

ordinary/everyday clothes *Everyone else was wearing ordinary clothes.*

second-hand clothes (=not new) *Charity shops sell second-hand clothes at low prices.*

children's clothes/baby clothes *You don't have to pay tax on children's clothes in the UK.*

winter/summer clothes *The shops are already full of winter clothes.*

baggy clothes (=that do not fit tightly) *She always wears baggy clothes that hide her figure.*

scruffy/shabby clothes (=dirty and untidy) *I didn't want to go to the restaurant in scruffy clothes.*

VERBS

wear clothes *She always wears beautiful clothes.*

be dressed in ... clothes *The man was dressed in ordinary clothes.*

put your clothes on *I told him to get up and put some clothes on.*

take your clothes off (*also* **remove your clothes** *formal*): *She took off her clothes and slipped into bed.*

change your clothes *I usually change my clothes as soon as I get home from work.*

PHRASES

a change of clothes (=another set of clothes to put on) *He only took a small bag with a change of clothes.*

THESAURUS: clothes

clothing
used when talking in general about a type of clothes, or about making or selling clothes. Also used in the phrase **a piece/item/article of clothing** (=one of the things that someone wears):
*You'll need to take some **warm clothing**. | It is important to wear **protective clothing** at all times. | a clothing manufacturer | a clothing retailer | Police found **a piece of clothing** in the bushes. | I took **a change of clothing** with me.*

garment *formal*
something that you wear. Garment is often used when talking about people and companies that make clothes, or when talking about a type of clothes:
*They work in the **garment industry**. | **Garment workers** are often poorly paid. | The clothes are made in **garment factories** in Asia. | The burqa is a garment worn by some Muslim women, which covers the head and body.*

dress
a particular style of clothes:
***Casual dress** is not appropriate for an interview. | The picture shows a group of men **in evening dress**. | You have to wear **fancy dress** for the party* (=clothes that make you look like a particular type of person, which you wear for fun). *| The local people were wearing their **traditional dress**.*

> **Dress** is not used on its own in this meaning – it needs to have an adjective before it.

wear
used about types of clothes sold in a shop, in the following phrases. Don't use **wear** on its own:
*The shop sells **children's wear**. | Can you tell me where the **women's wear** department is? | **Designer wear** can be very expensive. | He preferred **casual wear** to formal clothes.*

> **Wear** is often used to form nouns, for example **sportswear** and **menswear**. **Wear** is not used on its own.

gear *informal*
clothes for a particular sport or activity:
*She was wearing her **running gear**. | Have you got all your **sports gear**?*

wardrobe
all the clothes that you own, or all the clothes that you wear at a particular time of year:
*Her wardrobe consisted mainly of smart clothes for work. | I will need a new **summer wardrobe**. | You could win a complete **new wardrobe**!*

clothing *n* the things that people wear

ADJECTIVES/NOUNS + clothing

warm clothing *The flood victims need shelter and warm clothing.*

light clothing (=made from thin material) *You'll only need light clothing during the day.*

waterproof clothing *Always take a map and waterproof clothing when walking on the hills.*

protective clothing *Laboratory technicians have to wear special protective clothing.*

loose clothing (=that does not fit tightly) *Wear loose comfortable clothing when travelling.*

tight clothing *Tight clothing may show your underwear.*

outdoor clothing *The shop sells ski-wear and other outdoor clothing.*

outer clothing (=that you wear over other clothes) *They were getting hot, so they stopped to remove their outer clothing.*

designer clothing (=made by a well-known designer) *She had been to all the designer clothing stores in London.*

sports clothing *The shop has a range of sports equipment and sports clothing.*

winter/summer clothing *It was cold, and they had not brought any winter clothing.*

clothing + NOUNS

the clothing industry *There are plenty of job opportunities in the clothing industry.*

a clothing manufacturer/company *He works for a large clothing manufacturer.*

a clothing store *She stopped to look in the window of a clothing store.*

a clothing factory *She worked in a clothing factory.*

> **Clothing** or **clothes**?
>
> **Clothing** sounds more formal. It is often used when talking about the business of making and selling clothes. For example, you usually say *a* ***clothing*** *manufacturer* or *the* ***clothing*** *industry*. (It is much less common to use **clothes** with these words.)
>
> **Clothes** is the usual word to use in everyday conversation. For example, when talking about your feelings about someone's clothes, you say *I like your* ***clothes***. and *She always wears really nice* ***clothes***. (not 'clothing').
>
> When talking about clothes in general, you can say either *warm/dry/clean* ***clothes*** or *warm/dry/clean* ***clothing***. **Clothing** sounds a little more formal and less personal than **clothes**.

PHRASES

a piece of clothing *There were pieces of clothing scattered around the room.*

an item/article of clothing *formal* (=a piece of clothing) *All items of clothing should be clearly labelled.*

> **THESAURUS: clothing**
>
> clothing, garment, dress, wear, gear, wardrobe
> → **clothes**

cloud *n*

1 a white or grey mass in the sky formed from very small drops of water

ADJECTIVES/NOUNS + cloud

a dark/grey/black cloud *Dark clouds usually mean rain.*

a white cloud *There was a bright blue sky with a few white clouds.*

heavy/thick cloud *By midday, heavy cloud had spread across the sky.*

low/high cloud *Low cloud spoiled our view from the top of the hills.*

storm/rain clouds *Dark storm clouds were moving in from the Atlantic.*

VERBS

clouds gather/form *The sky had darkened and clouds had gathered.*

clouds cover/hide sth (*also* **clouds obscure sth** *formal*): *The moon was now hidden by clouds and the sky was dark.*

clouds clear/lift (=disappear) *At last the rain had stopped and the clouds had cleared.*

clouds drift/float (=move slowly) *A few clouds drifted across the top of the mountains.*

clouds race/scud (=move quickly) *A strong wind was blowing and the clouds were scudding across the sky.*

clouds hang above/over a place *Heavy grey clouds hung over the town.*

PHRASES

a bank/mass of cloud (=a large amount of cloud) *A heavy bank of cloud was creeping across the sky.*

a blanket/veil of cloud (=a layer of cloud which stops you being able to see something) *In the morning, a blanket of cloud still covered the hills.*

a break/gap in the cloud(s) *The moon was visible through breaks in the cloud.*

the sun breaks through the clouds (=it starts to be seen) *The late morning sun was beginning to break through the clouds.*

2 a mass of dust, smoke etc in the air

PHRASES

a cloud of dust/ash (*also* **a dust/ash cloud**) *The car disappeared down the road in a cloud of white dust.*

a cloud of smoke/steam/gas *The fire sent up a huge cloud of smoke.*

ADJECTIVES/NOUNS + cloud

a great/big/huge/vast cloud of sth *Where the bomb had landed, there was a great cloud of dust.*

a thick/dense cloud of sth *These volcanic eruptions throw up dense clouds of ash.*

a swirling cloud (=moving around and around) *A swirling cloud of smoke hid everything.*

VERBS

a cloud rises *When I turned over, a big cloud of dust rose from the mattress.*

cloudless *adj* THESAURUS > **sunny**

C

cloudy *adj*

if the weather is cloudy, there are a lot of clouds in the sky

VERBS

become cloudy *It became cloudy later in the day.*

the sky grew cloudy *especially literary* (=became cloudy) *The sky grew cloudy and it started to rain.*

ADVERBS

mostly/partly cloudy *The weekend will be mostly cloudy, with a chance of thunderstorms.*

C

THESAURUS: cloudy

foggy
weather | day | morning | afternoon | night | conditions | road
if the weather is foggy, there is a lot of thick low cloud that is difficult to see through. You use **foggy** especially about cities, roads, and low-lying places:
It was a foggy day in London in November. | His car went off the road one foggy night.

misty
weather | day | morning | afternoon | night | mountain | hills | sky | air | darkness | rain | conditions
if the weather is misty, there is a lot of light low cloud that is difficult to see through. You use **misty** especially about places that are next to water or in the mountains:
We went out on the lake one misty morning to catch some fish. | The town is surrounded by misty mountains.

hazy
sky | sunshine | morning | afternoon | day | outline | horizon
if the sky is hazy, the air looks cloudy and it is difficult to see clearly, because there is smoke, dust, or mist in it:
The sun was a dull glow in the hazy sky. | Hazy sunshine streamed in through the living room window. | Every now and then, the hazy outline of a castle would appear on the horizon.

overcast
sky | day | morning | afternoon | conditions
if the sky is overcast, it is dark and completely covered with clouds, and it will rain soon:
The sky became overcast and it looked like it was going to rain. | It was a damp overcast day.

grey *BrE*, **gray** *AmE*
sky | weather | day | morning | afternoon
if the sky is grey, there are a lot of dark clouds:
She stared out of the train window at the grey sky. | The weather was cold and grey. | It's a very gray day.

dull
weather | day | morning | afternoon | sky
dull weather is cloudy and with no sunshine – used especially when this looks rather miserable:
It's nice to see some sunshine, after all the dull weather we've been having. | The plane's landing lights blazed against the dull sky.

gloomy
weather | day | morning | afternoon | night | sky
gloomy weather is dark and cloudy, in a depressing way:
The gloomy weather is set to continue over the next few days. | I couldn't see the moon or the stars, only the gloomy sky.

leaden *literary*
sky
a leaden sky is grey and full of dark clouds:
Snow fell from a leaden sky.

Leaden means 'looking like lead', which is a heavy grey-coloured metal.

club *n*

an organization for people who share a particular interest or enjoy similar activities

ADJECTIVES/NOUNS + club

a sports club *Why don't you join one of the school sports clubs?*

a tennis/chess/gardening etc club *She is the secretary of the local tennis club.*

a fan club *I used to be a member of the Take That fan club.*

a youth club *The youth club is on Thursday nights in the village hall.*

a social club *Older people may benefit from joining a social club.*

a health club *The hotel has its own health club with a range of exercise equipment.*

VERBS

belong to a club *Do you belong to any university clubs or societies?*

join a club *I decided to join the computer club.*

form/start a club *It's always possible to form your own club.*

run a club *My dad helps to run the rowing club.*

a club meets *The club meets every Monday evening at 6.30 p.m.*

club + NOUNS

a club member *There's a monthly magazine for club members.*

the club chairman/president/secretary *Reg took over as club chairman three years ago.*

PHRASES

a member of a club *They are members of the sailing club.*

clue *n*

an object or piece of information that helps someone solve a crime or mystery

ADJECTIVES

an important/useful/valuable clue *The car used in the robbery may provide important clues.*

a vital clue (=very important) *A videotape could hold vital clues to the criminal's identity.*

VERBS

look/hunt/search for clues *The detectives are looking for clues which could help them find the killer.*

hold a clue *formal* (=contain a clue) *The poem itself holds a clue about who it was written for.*

give/provide/offer a clue (*also* **yield a clue** *formal*): *These old documents may provide a clue to the building's origin.*

find a clue *He searched through old newspapers, hoping to find some clue as to what had happened to his father.*

leave a clue *The robber got away but he may have left a vital clue.*

piece the clues together (=put them together in order to find out the truth) *We can piece together clues from a variety of research studies.*

PREPOSITIONS

a clue to/as to/about sth *So far there are no clues as to what caused the crash.*

coach *n*

1 someone who trains a person or team in a sport

ADJECTIVES/NOUNS + coach

a football/basketball/tennis etc coach *Jody became the women's basketball coach.*

the head coach *Jim was head coach of the Dallas Mavericks.*

an assistant coach *He took a job as an assistant coach at the college.*

the national coach (=for a country's team) *Davies was the national coach in the World Cup.*

a professional coach *The tennis club has a professional coach.*

a top coach *He's one of America's top coaches.*

2 a bus used for long journeys

VERBS

go/travel by coach *We travelled by coach to London.*

get on/get off a coach *A group of tourists were getting on the coach.*

board a coach *formal* (=get on one) *When everyone was there, we boarded the coach for the journey home.*

ADJECTIVES/NOUNS + coach

an express coach (=one that does not stop often) *There is an express coach service to the airport.*

an air-conditioned coach *Travel is by air-conditioned coach.*

coach + NOUNS

a coach trip *The two-night coach trip to Paris will cost £149.*

a coach tour *How about going on a coach tour around Europe this year?*

a coach excursion (=a relatively short coach journey to visit a place) *There are coach excursions to the great classical site at Ephesus.*

a coach party (=a group of people who travel by coach) *We're organizing a coach party to the theatre.*

a coach driver *He worked as a part-time coach driver.*

a coach station *You will go from Victoria Coach Station to Amsterdam.*

PREPOSITIONS

by coach *The capital is just three hours away by coach.*

on a coach *I didn't like the idea of sitting on a coach for four hours.*

> **Coach** is used with this meaning especially in British English. In American English, people usually say **bus**.

coarse *adj* THESAURUS ▸ **rough (1)**

coast *n*

the area where the land meets the sea

ADJECTIVES/NOUNS + coast

the east/west etc coast *We stayed on the south coast of the island.*

the French/English etc coast *There have been storms along the Spanish coast.*

the Atlantic/Pacific etc coast *This wine is from the Mediterranean coast of Spain.*

a rocky/rugged coast (=with a lot of big rocks or cliffs) *On the horizon appeared the outline of a rocky coast.*

coast + NOUNS

a coast road *In summer the coast road is very crowded.*

a coast path *There were wonderful views from the coast path.*

VERBS

follow the coast (=stay close to the coast) *The path follows the coast.*

hug the coast (=follow it very closely) *A small railway hugs the coast.*

PREPOSITIONS

the coast of France/California etc *They landed on the coast of Italy.*

along the coast *We drove east along the coast.*

up/down the coast (=north or south along the coast) *They sailed up the coast to Newcastle.*

on the coast (=on the land near the sea) *We stayed in a village on the coast.*

off the coast (=in the sea near the land) *The ship sank off the coast of Ireland in 1588.*

PHRASES

a stretch of coast (=a long area of coast) *The 13th-century chapel lies on a spectacular stretch of coast.*

(from) coast to coast (=across a country, or all over a country) *He has been giving talks from coast to coast.*

coat *n*

a piece of clothing with buttons and long sleeves that is worn over your other clothes

ADJECTIVES

a warm coat *You'd better bring a warm coat.*

a heavy/thick coat *She was wearing a heavy coat and a thick scarf.*

a light coat (=a thin coat) *I took a light coat in case the weather got cooler in the evening.*

a long coat *He was wearing a long black coat.*

a leather/fur etc coat *She was wearing a fake fur coat.*

a white coat (=worn by medical or laboratory staff to protect their clothes) *The hospital doctors all wore white coats.*

NOUNS + coat

a winter coat *You need a good winter coat in Canada.*

> **Raincoat**, **overcoat** (=a long warm coat worn in cold weather), and **greatcoat** (=a big thick coat worn by soldiers) are written as one word.

VERBS

wear a coat *The men wore long coats.*

put on your coat (*also* **pull on your coat** *written*): *Mark stood up and put on his coat.*

take off your coat (*also* **remove your coat** *formal*): *She took off her coat and went into the kitchen.*

button (up)/do up your coat *She shivered as she buttoned up her coat.*

unbutton/undo your coat *He was hot, so he undid his coat.*

hang up your coat *We hung up our coats and went through to the lounge.*

coat + NOUNS

sb's coat pocket *I thought my wallet was in my coat pocket.*

sb's coat sleeve/collar *The little boy was pulling at his mother's coat sleeve.*

code *n*

1 a set of rules, laws, or principles for behaviour

ADJECTIVES/NOUNS + code

a moral/ethical code *Children learn their parents' moral code.*

a strict code *Companies have to follow a strict code on the treatment of workers.*

a voluntary code (=one that people are not legally obliged to follow) *The newspaper industry is governed only by a voluntary code.*

a dress code (=rules about what you must wear) *Some of the more expensive clubs have a dress code.*

the penal/criminal code (=laws relating to the punishment of criminals) *At that time the penal code allowed the death penalty.*

VERBS

have a code *Most professional organizations have a code of ethics.*

draw up/lay down a code *TV companies have drawn up their own code relating to advertising.*

adopt/introduce/establish a code *The company has introduced a dress code for employees.*

follow a code (*also* **comply with a code** *formal*): *When using dangerous chemicals, it's important to follow a basic safety code.*

break a code (*also* **breach/violate/contravene a code** *formal*): *Travel agents can be fined if they break the code.*

enforce a code (=make sure that people follow it) *A code of practice is useless if it isn't enforced.*

PHRASES

a code of practice/conduct/ethics (=rules for people in a particular profession) *There is a strict code of conduct for doctors.*

a code of behaviour *BrE*, **a code of behavior** *AmE*: *Each society follows its own code of behaviour.*

a code of honour *BrE*, **a code of honor** *AmE* (=a moral code about the best way to behave) *The soldiers' strict code of honour means that they all support each other.*

2 a system of signs or symbols for sending secret messages

ADJECTIVES/NOUNS + code

a secret code *We can't understand the message - it must be some sort of secret code.*

a security code *Only senior employees know the security code for the gate.*

Morse code (=a system of short and long sounds, or flashes of light) *Soldiers used radios to communicate in Morse code.*

VERBS

break/crack a code (*also* **decipher a code** *formal*) (=discover how to understand it) *My job in the army was deciphering the codes used by the enemy.*

code + NOUNS

a code word (=a secret word that you must say in order to get information or enter a place) *He gave me the code word so I showed him the map.*

a code name (=a secret name used for referring to something or someone) *The attack was always referred to by the code name 'Operation Overlord'.*

PREPOSITIONS

in code *Secret agents sent messages to each other in code.*

code for sth *'We're Oscar Mike' is code for 'we're on the move'.*

coffee *n*

a hot dark brown drink with a slightly bitter taste

ADJECTIVES

strong coffee *I need some strong coffee to wake me up.*

fresh coffee *The room was filled with the delicious smell of fresh coffee.*

black coffee (=without milk) *I've ordered two black coffees.*

white coffee (=with milk) *I'd like a tea and a white coffee, please.*

decaffeinated coffee (*also* **decaf coffee** *informal*) (=without any caffeine in it) *The restaurant didn't serve decaf coffee so I had tea instead.*

VERBS

have (a) coffee *She always has coffee with her breakfast.*

go for (a) coffee (=go out to drink coffee) *Let's go for a coffee and discuss your idea.*

make coffee *I'll make some coffee.*

drink coffee *I don't drink coffee in the evening because it keeps me awake.*

pour the coffee *He poured the coffee into mugs.*

sip coffee (=drink it slowly) *Dad sat in his chair, peacefully sipping his coffee.*

coffee + NOUNS

a coffee break (=a break from work to have some coffee) *Shall we stop for a coffee break?*

a coffee cup/mug (=a cup or mug for drinking coffee) *The café has run out of coffee cups.*

a coffee pot (=a pot for making coffee in) *She lifted the coffee pot and poured herself some coffee.*

a coffee machine (=that makes coffee) *Instead of working, he stands at the coffee machine talking to friends.*

a coffee shop/bar (=a café) *There's a coffee shop inside the hospital.*

PHRASES

take/like your coffee black/white/with sugar etc (=prefer to drink it with or without milk and sugar) *I take my coffee black. | How do you like your coffee?*

a cup/mug of coffee (=a cup or mug containing coffee) *He usually has a cup of coffee after lunch.*

coffee with/without milk (=used instead of saying white or black coffee) *Can I have two coffees with milk?*

coin *n*

a flat round piece of metal, used as money

ADJECTIVES/NOUNS + coin

a gold/silver etc coin *In his hand there was a silver coin.*

a pound/dollar etc coin *The machine will only accept pound coins.*

a Roman/Greek/Egyptian etc coin *Roman coins showed the head of the emperor.*

VERBS

toss a coin *BrE*, **flip a coin** *AmE* (=throw it up in the air to decide something) *The referee tossed a coin at the beginning of the match.*

put a coin in the slot (=put it into a thin hole in a machine, so that you can pay for something) *She put a coin in the slot of the vending machine and selected a chocolate bar.*

coincidence *n*

a situation in which two things happen together in a surprising or unusual way because of chance

ADJECTIVES

pure/sheer/mere coincidence (=just coincidence and nothing else) *It was pure coincidence that we both arrived on the same plane.*

a happy/lucky/fortunate coincidence *By a happy coincidence I met an old friend at the conference.*

an unfortunate coincidence *By a very unfortunate coincidence, she didn't get either of his emails.*

a strange/curious/odd coincidence *What a strange coincidence that they were born on the same day!*

a remarkable/amazing/extraordinary coincidence *It was an extraordinary coincidence seeing him there.*

a complete coincidence (=used when emphasizing that something was a coincidence) *It was a complete coincidence – I wasn't planning to see her again.*

PREPOSITIONS

by a ... coincidence (*also* **by coincidence**) *By a remarkable coincidence, his new boss has the same name as him.*

PHRASES

What a coincidence! *It's your birthday today too! What a coincidence!*

it is a coincidence that *It was a remarkable coincidence that two people with the same name were staying at the hotel.*

it is no coincidence that (=it is deliberate) *It's no coincidence that the government made the announcement today.*

be more than (a) coincidence *When I saw him a third time, I realized it was more than just coincidence.*

a string/series of coincidences *The accident happened because of a string of unfortunate coincidences.*

cold[1] *adj* having a low temperature

NOUNS

cold weather/climate *More cold weather is expected later this week.*

a cold night/day *It was a cold night in December.*

a cold winter *In a cold winter, we have the heating on all day.*

a cold wind *A cold wind was blowing from the north.*

cold water *He fell into the cold water of the North Sea.*

a cold drink/beer *I need a nice cold drink.*

cold food *The café only serves cold food at lunchtime.*

a cold meal/dish *You can choose from a range of hot and cold dishes.*

a cold floor/surface *We had to spend the night on the cold floor.*

a cold country/place/house *The bears live mainly in cold countries.*

a cold spell/snap (=a short period of cold weather) *A lot of plants died during the cold snap.*

ADVERBS

freezing cold (=extremely cold) *Take your gloves – it's freezing cold out there.*

bitterly cold (=extremely cold, in a way that hurts your skin) *It was a bitterly cold day in January.*

unusually/exceptionally cold *Crops have suffered during this period of unusually cold weather.*

ice cold *His skin was ice cold.*

VERBS

feel cold *I feel really cold – can we put the heating on?*

get cold (*also* **turn/grow cold** *more formal*) (=become cold) *The birds fly south before the weather turns cold.*

eat sth cold/serve sth cold *You can eat the beans cold.*

PHRASES

it's cold *It's cold in here – do you mind if I put the heating on?*

THESAURUS: cold

a little cold

cool
drink | place | breeze | air | weather | day | evening | morning
a little cold, especially in a way that feels pleasant:
He poured himself a cool drink. | Store the seeds in a cool place. | There was a nice cool breeze coming up from the river. | The air-conditioning ***keeps*** *everyone* ***cool****.*

chilly
weather | wind | breeze | air | day | night | evening | room
a little cold, especially in a way that feels rather uncomfortable:
In November the weather began to ***turn chilly*** (=become chilly). *| It's* ***getting*** *a bit* ***chilly*** *in here.*

draughty *BrE*, **drafty** *AmE*
room | house | corridor | hall | platform | window
with cold air blowing in from outside, in a way that feels uncomfortable:
Old houses can be very draughty. | They waited for over an hour on a cold and draughty platform.

crisp
day | morning | evening | air | weather
cold, dry, and clear, in a way that seems pleasant:
I love these crisp autumn mornings. | The clean crisp air in the mountains is good for your health.

frosty
weather | day | morning | evening | ground
in frosty weather, the ground is covered in frost (=a white powder which consists of very small pieces of ice):
The frosty weather made the countryside look even more beautiful. | It was a bright frosty morning.

very cold

freezing *spoken*
weather | wind | water | night | day | evening | morning | house | room
very cold – used when this makes you feel very uncomfortable:
A freezing wind howled across the mountain. | Sally lay in bed in a ***freezing cold*** *room. | It's freezing cold outside. | You look* ***absolutely freezing****!*

icy
water | weather | conditions | wind | air | blast
very cold, especially when the temperature is below zero:
The boat sank in the icy waters of the lake. | She shivered in the icy wind and pulled her hat down over her ears. | An icy blast came through the trees (=a sudden very cold wind).

arctic
conditions | weather | wasteland
extremely cold and unpleasant, with snow and ice:
He would not survive for long in the arctic conditions.

ANTONYMS **cold → hot**

cold² *n*

1 a common illness that makes it difficult to breathe through your nose

ADJECTIVES

a bad cold *If you have a bad cold, just stay in bed.*

a nasty cold (*also* **a heavy cold** *BrE*) (=a very bad one) *He sounded as if he had a heavy cold.*

a streaming cold *BrE* (=a cold in which a lot of liquid comes from your nose) *You shouldn't go to work if you've got a streaming cold.*

a slight cold *It's only a slight cold – I'll be fine tomorrow.*

the common cold *There are hundreds of viruses that cause the common cold.*

VERBS

have a cold (*also* **have got a cold** *spoken*): *She's staying at home today because she's got a cold.*

be getting a cold (=be starting to have a cold) *I think I might be getting a cold.*

catch a cold *I caught a cold and had to miss the match.*

come/go down with a cold (=catch a cold) *A lot of people go down with colds at this time of year.*

suffer from a cold *He was suffering from a cold and feeling rather miserable.*

2 a situation in which the temperature is low

ADJECTIVES

the bitter/freezing/biting cold (=extreme cold) *We stood outside for hours in the freezing cold.*

extreme cold *Extreme cold will damage these plants.*

the winter cold *The animal's thick fur protects it from the winter cold.*

VERBS

feel the cold (=feel uncomfortable because of the cold) *I feel the cold more as I get older.*

shiver/shake with cold *He awoke at dawn, shivering with cold.*

keep out the cold *They wrapped old sacks round themselves to keep out the cold.*

PREPOSITIONS

in the cold *They waited in the cold outside the cinema.*

out of the cold *She told him to come in out of the cold.*

against the cold (=in order to protect yourself from the cold) *The spectators were well wrapped-up against the cold.*

PHRASES

blue with cold *Her hands were blue with cold.*

numb with cold (=so cold you can't feel anything) *He tried to light a cigarette, but his fingers were numb with cold.*

collapse *v* THESAURUS fail (1)

colleague Ac *n*

someone who you work with in a company or organization, for example someone working in the same office, or someone teaching in the same school

ADJECTIVES

a former colleague *Friends and former colleagues described him as a kind and caring man.*

a close colleague (=one who you know very well) *The two men were close colleagues and shared the same office for many years.*

a junior/senior colleague *Junior colleagues often came to her for advice.*

a male/female colleague *She discovered that her male colleagues were earning more than she was.*

a trusted colleague *He only told his most trusted colleagues about his plans.*

PHRASES

a colleague of mine/hers etc *He is a colleague of mine from work.*

collection *n*

a set of things that are kept or brought together

ADJECTIVES/NOUNS + collection

a large/vast/extensive collection *The museum has an extensive collection of Greek statues.*

a fine collection (=a very good collection) *The palace has the finest collection of Scottish paintings in the world.*

a fascinating/remarkable collection *You can see a fascinating collection of historic vehicles at the Transport Museum.*

a complete/comprehensive collection *She has a complete collection of his novels.*

a private collection *Many of the paintings are now in private collections.*

a museum/library collection *The museum collection contains objects from all over the world.*

a permanent collection (=one that is permanently kept at a particular museum etc) *The art gallery hosts touring exhibitions and a permanent collection.*

an art collection *The National Gallery has an excellent art collection.*

a music/record/CD collection *Her enormous CD collection fills an entire room.*

a stamp/coin/book collection *My uncle gave me his stamp collection.*

VERBS

have/own a collection *She has an amazing collection of Chinese vases.*

start a collection *I decided to start a coin collection.*

build up/assemble a collection *He gradually built up a collection of plants from all over the world.*

hold/house a collection *formal* (=contain a collection) *The museum holds a remarkable collection of 19th-century photographs.*

boast a collection *formal* (=have a very impressive one) *The park boasts a fine collection of trees.*

add sth to your collection *She bought him another hat to add to his collection.*

a collection consists of sth *The collection consists of over 500 pictures.*

a collection contains/includes sth *Her collection includes both oil and watercolour paintings.*

collector *n*

1 someone who collects things that are interesting or attractive

ADJECTIVES

a keen/enthusiastic/avid collector *She's an avid collector of vintage movie posters.*

a great collector (=someone who collects a lot of things) *He was a great collector of Chinese ceramics.*

a serious collector *If you are a serious collector, the money is not important.*

a private collector *The painting was bought by a private collector for £1.5 million.*

a wealthy collector *Wealthy collectors will pay up to $10 million for one of his pictures.*

NOUNS + collector

an art collector *My uncle is an art collector and he has dozens of paintings in his house.*

a stamp/book/record etc collector *Record collectors will pay hundreds of dollars for one of his early records.*

PHRASES

a collector's item (=an object that people want to have because it is interesting or rare) *Tiffany lamps are now a real collector's item.*

2 someone whose job is to collect things

NOUNS + collector

a tax/debt/rent collector *He worked as a tax collector for the government.*

a ticket collector *The ticket collector asked for my ticket.*

a refuse/rubbish collector *BrE*, **a garbage collector** *AmE*: *The rubbish collectors have to pick up all the litter.*

college *n*

a place where people can study after they leave school

ADJECTIVES/NOUNS + college

art/music/drama etc college *David loves painting and he hopes to go to art college after he finishes school.*

an agricultural/secretarial/technical etc college *I wanted a job in farm management so I went to agricultural college.*

a Further Education/FE college *BrE* (=where adults can go to study, especially part-time) *She studied business studies at an FE college.*

a teacher training college (=where you learn to be a teacher) *At teacher training college we studied a lot about child psychology.*

a military college (=where you learn to be an officer in the army) *He left military college and joined the army as a junior officer.*

a sixth form college *BrE* (=a college for students between the ages of 16 and 18 in the British school system) *She is studying for her A-levels at sixth form college.*

VERBS

go to (a) college (*also* **attend college** *formal*): *After university I went to teacher training college for a year.*

start college (*also* **enter college** *formal*): *My daughter will start college next fall.*

leave/finish college *What are you going to do when you leave college?*

graduate from college (=leave with a degree) *Her son had just graduated from college.*

drop out of college (=leave before getting a qualification) *She dropped out of college after the first year.*

college + NOUNS

a college student *Many college students are unprepared for the world of work.*

a college graduate *College graduates earn more than people who have not been to college.*

a college education *My father didn't have a college education.*

PREPOSITIONS

at college (*also* **in college** *especially AmE*): *I met him when I was at college.*

> **College or university?**
> When British speakers use **college**, they usually mean a place where people study after secondary school, which is not a university and does not give degrees.
> American speakers usually use **college** to mean a university.

collision *n*

an accident in which two or more people or vehicles hit each other while moving in different directions

ADJECTIVES

a head-on collision (=between vehicles moving towards each other) *Three people died in a head-on collision between a car and a minibus.*

a high-speed collision *Both drivers escaped unhurt from a high-speed collision in the final race of the season.*

a fatal collision (=in which someone is killed) *The number of fatal collisions has gone down since the new speed limits were introduced.*

a mid-air collision *The aircraft was involved in a mid-air collision with a military jet.*

VERBS

be involved in a collision *The badly damaged car had clearly been involved in a collision.*

avoid/prevent a collision *The bus driver swerved to avoid a collision.*

a collision takes place (*also* **a collision occurs** *formal*): *More collisions occur at night when drivers are tired.*

PREPOSITIONS

a collision with sth *The truck was involved in a collision with a bus.*

a collision between sth and sth *There was a collision between a train and a car stuck on the crossing.*

THESAURUS: collision

crash, collision, disaster, wreck, pile-up → **accident**

colossal *adj* THESAURUS **huge**

colour *BrE*, color *AmE n* red, blue, yellow etc

ADJECTIVES

a bright/strong colour *The house is painted in bright colours.*

a dark colour *People tend to wear dark colours at work.*

a light/pale colour (=not dark or strong) *Light colours make a room look larger.*

a rich colour (=strong and beautiful or expensive-looking) *I love the rich colours in oriental rugs.*

a deep colour (=dark and attractive) *Her eyes were a deep brown colour.*

a bold/vivid/vibrant colour (=bright in a way that is exciting) *His paintings are known for their use of bold colours.*

a loud colour (=very bright in a way that looks unpleasant or funny) *He liked to wear ties in loud colours.*

a primary colour (=red, yellow, or blue) *Children's clothes are often in primary colours.*

a gaudy/garish colour (=very bright and usually showing bad taste) *The owners of the restaurant had painted it in gaudy colours – the walls were bright orange.*

a neutral colour (=white or cream and other colours that match other colours easily) *People usually use neutral colours in offices.*

a pastel colour (=pale blue, pink, yellow, or green) *The bedroom was painted in pastel colours.*

contrasting colours (=ones that are different from each other in a way that looks attractive) *You need to have one or two contrasting colours in the room.*

complementary colours (=ones that look nice together) *Garden designers like to use plants which have complementary colours.*

a matching colour (=one that is the same as something else) *I bought some gloves and a scarf in a matching colour.*

a red/green/blue etc colour *Our door was painted a bright green colour.*

a reddish/greenish/bluish etc colour (=slightly red, green, blue etc) *The glass used for bottles is often a greenish colour.*

VERBS

a colour fades (=becomes less bright) *The colour of the curtains had faded in the sun.*

a colour matches sth (=it is the same colour) *The colour in this tin of paint doesn't match the walls.*

a colour clashes (with sth) (=it looks very unattractive when next to another colour) *Do you think the colour of this tie clashes with my shirt?*

colour + NOUNS

a colour scheme (=the colours used in a room, painting etc) *Have you decided on a colour scheme for your new house?*

a colour combination/combination of colours *We looked at various colour combinations and in the end we decided to have a cream carpet and pale blue walls.*

PHRASES

a range of colours (=a number of colours that you can choose from) *There's a wide range of colours to choose from.*

column *n*

a regular article by a particular writer in a newspaper or magazine

ADJECTIVES/NOUNS + column

a newspaper column *His newspaper column is read by thousands of people.*

a weekly/daily/monthly column *She writes a weekly column on gardening for a national newspaper.*

a regular column *His views on religion are well known from his regular column in the magazine.*

a gossip column (=about the private lives of famous people) *There were stories about their affair in all the gossip columns.*

a financial/sports/gardening etc column (=about a particular subject) *My father is interested in business and he usually reads the financial column first.*

an obituary column (=about people who have

C

just died) *I spotted an old friend's name in the obituary column.*

the agony column *BrE* (=one that gives advice to readers about personal problems) *I always read the agony column first.*

a lonely hearts column *BrE* (=with advertisements from people looking for a new lover or friend) *She met him after placing an advertisement in a lonely hearts column.*

VERBS

write a column *He writes a column on food for the 'Daily News'.*

have a column (=write one) *My wife had a weekly column in a Sydney newspaper.*

publish/run a column (=include it in a newspaper or magazine) *Several of the papers run her cookery column.*

combat[1] *n*

fighting, especially during a war

ADJECTIVES/NOUNS + combat

hand-to-hand combat/close combat (=in which the opponents are very close) *He was killed in hand-to-hand combat.*

unarmed combat (=without weapons) *The soldiers are trained in the techniques of unarmed combat.*

ground combat (=on land) *This is the biggest ground combat operation in NATO's history.*

mortal combat *literary* (=until one opponent is killed) *The two men found themselves locked in mortal combat.*

VERBS

be locked in combat (=be fighting hard with someone) *Their troops were locked in combat.*

be engaged in combat *formal* (=be fighting an enemy) *Our troops are engaged in combat in the south of the country.*

send sb into combat *The president's most difficult task is sending soldiers into combat.*

see combat (=have the experience of fighting as a soldier) *She was in the army for three years but never saw combat.*

combat + NOUNS

combat operations/missions *He flew 280 combat missions in two wars.*

combat troops/soldiers/forces/units *US combat troops are being sent to the region.*

a combat zone (=an area where there is fighting) *A group of reporters flew over the combat zone.*

combat planes/aircraft/vehicles *Very few combat aircraft have been destroyed.*

combat readiness (=the state of being ready to fight) *Their army has thousands of troops in combat readiness.*

PREPOSITIONS

in combat *They risk being injured or killed in combat.*

combat against sb *France sent more troops into combat against the rebels.*

combat[2] *v* THESAURUS **fight[1] (4)**

combination *n*

two or more different things that exist together or are used together

ADJECTIVES

a good combination *The computer offers a good combination of price and performance.*

the perfect/ideal combination *The town has the perfect combination of beautiful beaches and a lively nightlife.*

the right/best combination *You need to find the right combination of colours for you.*

a unique/rare/unusual combination *She uses a unique combination of flavours.*

a particular combination *The crisis was caused by a particular combination of events.*

a powerful/potent combination *Music and drama can be a powerful combination.*

a winning/unbeatable/irresistible combination *He spent hours testing out various recipes before discovering the winning combination.*

a bad combination *Pilots know that low and slow is a bad combination.*

a lethal/deadly combination (=one that can kill you or that is very effective) *Mixing alcohol and drugs can be a lethal combination.*

VERBS

make a good/excellent combination *I think that Steve and Anna make a good combination.*

involve a combination *Accidents usually involve a combination of driver error and dangerous driving conditions.*

NOUNS + combination

colour combination *Do you think that purple and green is a good colour combination?*

PREPOSITIONS

a combination of sth *Before the race she felt a combination of fear and excitement.*

in combination (with sth) *The drugs are normally used in combination with each other.*

PHRASES

a combination of factors/things *The team's success is due to a combination of factors.*

a combination of circumstances *The fire appears to have resulted from an unfortunate combination of circumstances.*

come *v* THESAURUS **arrive**

comeback *n*

a time when someone is successful or popular again

ADJECTIVES

a remarkable/amazing comeback *When her career seemed finished, she staged a remarkable comeback to win another Olympic gold medal.*

a dramatic/spectacular comeback *A spectacular comeback in the last ten minutes of the game earned the team a victory.*

a big/great comeback *This tour might be the singer's chance for a big comeback.*

a political comeback *When opinions changed after the war, the party made a remarkable political comeback.*

VERBS

make/stage a comeback *The band are making a comeback after an absence of two years.*

comeback + NOUNS

a comeback tour *The singer is on the first night of a comeback tour of the US.*

comedy *n*

1 entertainment that is intended to make people laugh

ADJECTIVES/NOUNS + comedy

stand-up comedy (=one person telling jokes on stage) *He's developing a new stand-up comedy act.*

slapstick comedy (=in which the performers do silly things like falling over) *The tradition of slapstick comedy goes back to the early days of cinema.*

black/dark comedy (=about subjects that are usually sad or serious, especially death) *The film contains many moments of black comedy.*

comedy + NOUNS

a comedy series *He appeared in the popular comedy series 'Friends'.*

a comedy show *She has her own comedy show on TV.*

a comedy film *Chaplin made some of the most successful comedy films of all time.*

a comedy star/actor/actress *The main role in the film is played by comedy star Whoopi Goldberg.*

a comedy sketch (=a short funny performance that is part of a longer show) *There is a famous comedy sketch by Monty Python about a man buying a dead parrot.*

2 a funny film, television programme, or play

ADJECTIVES

a TV comedy *The actor became famous for his part in the TV comedy 'Frasier'.*

a romantic comedy *The American actor is best known for his roles in romantic comedies.*

a musical comedy (=with music and singing) *She has produced a string of successful musical comedies on Broadway.*

a sentimental comedy (=about emotions such as love and sadness) *The film is one of those tearful sentimental comedies.*

a situation comedy (=a regular comedy TV programme about the same characters) *She stars in a situation comedy about a family with teenage kids.*

a black comedy (=about serious subjects, especially death) *There are several murders in this black comedy set in Florida.*

comfort *n*

1 a feeling of being physically relaxed and without any pain or unpleasant sensations

ADJECTIVES

great comfort *After weeks of travelling, he was enjoying the great comfort of his own bed.*

maximum comfort *You can adjust the heating for maximum comfort.*

PREPOSITIONS

in comfort *The car can seat five people in comfort.*

PHRASES

be built/made/designed for comfort *The tennis shoe is designed for comfort and performance.*

in the comfort of your own home (=without having to leave your home) *The internet lets you do your grocery shopping in the comfort of your own home.*

2 a feeling of being less worried or unhappy, or something that creates this feeling

ADJECTIVES

great comfort *Her letters were a great comfort.*

little/small/cold comfort (=not much comfort) *The tax cuts will be cold comfort for people without jobs.*

VERBS

be a comfort to sb (=be someone or something that brings comfort) *His daughter was always a comfort to him.*

take comfort from sth *The family has taken comfort from the support of friends.*

draw/derive comfort from sth *formal* (=take comfort from something) *The government will draw comfort from the latest economic figures.*

find/take comfort in sth *She finds comfort in the fact that others have suffered similar problems.*

offer (sb) comfort *Volunteers are available to offer comfort to victims of crime.*

give (sb) comfort *She was so upset that it was impossible to give her any comfort.*

bring/provide comfort *Religious faith can bring comfort during difficult times.*

comfort + NOUNS

comfort food (=food that you eat to make you feel relaxed and happy) *To cheer me up, my mother would make me chicken soup or some other comfort food.*

C

PHRASES

a source of comfort *His happy memories were a source of comfort in difficult times.*

a word of comfort *He tried to find some words of comfort that would help her.*

comfortable *adj*

making you feel physically relaxed, without any pain or without being too hot, cold etc

NOUNS

a comfortable chair/sofa/bed *This chair is nice and comfortable.*

a comfortable room/bedroom/lounge *The rooms are very comfortable and have their own shower and bathroom.*

a comfortable house/hotel/apartment *We stayed in a comfortable hotel not far from the city centre.*

comfortable clothes/clothing/shoes *These shoes aren't very comfortable – they're too tight.*

a comfortable position *Make sure that you are sitting in a comfortable position.*

comfortable surroundings *You can relax in the comfortable surroundings of the hotel.*

VERBS

feel comfortable *Does the jacket feel comfortable?*

look comfortable *The bed looks very comfortable.*

make sb/sth comfortable *Sit down and make yourself comfortable.*

PHRASES

comfortable to wear/use/ride *My bike isn't very comfortable to ride.*

warm and comfortable *The house is warm and comfortable, even in winter.*

nice and comfortable *It's nice and comfortable in here.*

You also use **comfortable** when saying that someone has a nice easy life and plenty of money to live: *She left her **comfortable** life in New Jersey in order to become a songwriter.* | *Richard had a **comfortable** job and a good salary.*

THESAURUS: comfortable

comfy *informal*
shoes | **slippers** | **chair** | **armchair** | **sofa**
comfortable – used about chairs, clothes and people:
*These shoes are **nice and comfy**.* | *You look very comfy in that chair.*

cosy *BrE*, **cozy** *AmE*
room | **lounge** | **bedroom** | **bed** | **fire** | **house** | **apartment** | **home** | **cabin** | **restaurant** | **bar** | **suburb** | **atmosphere**
used about places that are comfortable and warm or friendly, which are often small. **Cosy** is more informal than **comfortable**:
There's a cosy lounge with a real fire. | *They live in a **cozy little** house in the country.* | *Marion loved her home and its cosy atmosphere.*

snug
warm and comfortable, especially in a way that makes you feel protected. Small places can be **snug**, or people can feel **snug**:
*It was very cold outside, but our tents were **snug and warm**.* | *I'm **snug as a rug** in here!* (=very snug – used in informal British English)

smooth
flight | **crossing** | **ride** | **journey**
comfortable because your car or plane does not shake, the sea is not rough, or there are no other problems:
The flight was very smooth. | *The car is designed to give a smooth ride.* | *I hope you have a smooth journey.*

comic *adj*

THESAURUS ▸ **funny (1)**

comical *adj*

THESAURUS ▸ **funny (1)**

command *n*

1 an order that should be obeyed

VERBS

give a command (*also* **issue a command** *formal*): *Which officer gave the command to advance?*

obey a command (=used about people or animals) *Your dog will soon learn to obey your commands.*

carry out a command (=obey it – only used about people) *The men carried out the command immediately.*

ignore/disobey a command *I ignored his command and ran after him.*

PREPOSITIONS

at sb's command (=when someone gives an order) *At his command, the men lowered their weapons.*

2 the control of a group of people or a situation

ADJECTIVES

complete/full command *The authorities say that they now have full command of the situation.*

military command *A large area was already under US military command.*

sole command (=not shared with anyone) *He was in sole command of a small military unit.*

VERBS

have command *US planes now had command of the skies.*

take command (=begin controlling a group or situation) *Captain Kent took command of the Emergency Control Centre.*

lose command *The enemy was losing command of the situation.*

assume command *formal* (=start to be in

charge of a group of people) *He assumed command of all the troops in the Washington area.*

be given command *He was given command of another ship.*

put/place sb in command *A third goal put Brazil in command of the game.*

PREPOSITIONS

in command (of sb/sth) (=controlling people or things) *Admiral Sir James Somerville was in command of the operation.*

under sb's command (=being controlled by someone) *Massive forces were assembled in the south of England under the command of General Eisenhower.*

at sb's command (=available to be given orders) *He had thousands of troops at his command.*

PHRASES

the chain of command (=a system in which decisions are passed from people at the top to the bottom) *The order came from someone high up in the chain of command.*

commemorate *v*

to show in a public way that you remember and respect a person or an event

commemorate + NOUNS

commemorate a victory *This grand monument was built to commemorate a famous military victory.*

commemorate an event *Public celebrations are held every year to commemorate the event.*

commemorate the 25th/100th etc anniversary of sth *To commemorate their 100th anniversary, the organisation has opened a new office in Glasgow.*

commemorate sb's life/death *The ceremony commemorates the deaths of soldiers in all recent wars.*

commemorate the victims of sth *Candles were lit across the country to commemorate the victims of the disaster.*

NOUNS + commemorate

a statue commemorates sth *A statue was built to commemorate those who died in the war.*

a plaque commemorates sth (=a piece of stone or metal with writing on it) *A plaque was unveiled to commemorate the princess's visit.*

commence *v* THESAURUS **start[1] (1), (2)**

commencement *n* THESAURUS **beginning (1)**

comment Ac *n*

something you say or write that expresses your opinion

ADJECTIVES

a brief/quick comment *I just want to make a very brief comment.*

an interesting comment *The students made some interesting comments on the poem.*

a positive/favourable/appreciative comment (=that shows you like something) *There were some very positive comments in the report.*

a negative/critical comment (=that shows you don't like it) *The school has received critical comments from inspectors.*

helpful/useful comments *Let us know if you have any helpful comments or suggestions.*

a constructive comment (=one that is intended to help someone do something better) *I always try to give constructive comments to students.*

a rude comment *He is always making rude comments about me.*

a sarcastic comment (=in which you say the opposite of what you mean, as an unkind joke) *I tried to stay calm, despite his sarcastic comments.*

a snide comment (=unkind but indirect) *I ignored his snide comments about my cooking.*

fair comment (=criticism that seems reasonable) *What he says is fair comment - he's right.*

a casual comment (=not very serious or important) *I only made a casual comment about finding the work a bit boring.*

a passing comment (=a quick comment made without thinking about it very carefully) *She got upset about a passing comment I made about her clothes.*

VERBS

make a comment *The teacher made some very positive comments about his work.*

post a comment (=put it on the internet) *I posted a comment on the newspaper's website.*

have a comment (=want to make a comment) *Do you have any comments on that, David?*

pass comment *BrE* (=give an opinion) *He looked at my photos but he didn't pass comment.*

invite comment(s) (=ask people to give an opinion) *The website invites comments from people who visit it.*

welcome comments (=be glad to hear people's opinions) *We would welcome your comments and suggestions.*

receive comments *It is very helpful to receive comments from the public.*

PREPOSITIONS

a comment on/about sth *I listened to their comments on the plan.*

commentary Ac *n*

a spoken description of an event, given while the event is happening, especially on the television or radio

ADJECTIVES/NOUNS + commentary

a live commentary (=given at the time the event is happening) *He got into trouble for a remark he made during a live commentary.*

a running/nonstop commentary (=a continuous commentary) *The coach driver gave us a running commentary on the places we passed.*

a radio/television commentary *A radio commentary on the funeral was broadcast live.*

the football/baseball etc commentary *I could hear the TV football commentary in the next room.*

C

VERBS

give/provide a commentary *His job is to give a non-stop commentary on each moment in the game.*

listen to a commentary *I was listening to the football commentary on the radio.*

PREPOSITIONS

commentary on sth *Radio 5 will have full commentary on the match.*

commerce *n*

the buying and selling of goods and services

ADJECTIVES

international/global commerce *Good relations between countries are important for global commerce.*

e-commerce (=selling goods using the internet) *E-commerce is becoming popular, and more and more people are buying goods on the internet.*

VERBS

encourage/promote commerce *The way to make people richer is to promote commerce in the region.*

PHRASES

a chamber of commerce (=a local organization that works to improve business) *She wrote to the Boston Chamber of Commerce complaining about lack of support for small companies.*

THESAURUS: commerce

trade, commerce, e-commerce → **business (1)**

commercial *adj*

related to business and the buying and selling of goods and services

NOUNS

commercial success *The book was a great commercial success.*

commercial interests *The US wants to protect its commercial interests.*

commercial activity *The town was a major centre of commercial activity.*

commercial use *The building was intended for commercial use.*

a commercial organization *As a commercial organization we exist to make money.*

commercial value *Is this data of commercial value?*

a commercial transaction *formal* (=a business deal) *Commercial transactions are often done over the internet.*

commercial reasons/considerations *The decision should not be based purely on commercial considerations.*

commercial development (=the building of houses, hotels, restaurants etc) *It was felt that further commercial development in the village should be restricted.*

PHRASES

for commercial purposes *Ships originally built for commercial purposes had to be adapted for military ones.*

commission *n*

a group of people who have been given the official job of finding out about something or controlling something

ADJECTIVES/NOUNS + commission

a special commission *A special commission was set up to investigate the killings.*

an independent commission *The plan requires approval by an independent commission.*

an international commission *A new international commission on climate change is being established.*

a joint commission (=involving two or more countries or groups) *The two leaders agreed to set up a joint commission examining the issue.*

a parliamentary/government commission *A report was made by a special parliamentary commission.*

a national/federal commission *According to the National Commission on Children, one in four children is living in poverty.*

a royal commission (=set up by the UK government) *The royal commission called for major changes to the criminal justice system.*

VERBS + commission

set up/establish/create a commission *They set up a commission to investigate the problem of youth crime.*

appoint a commission (=choose the members of a commission) *The president appointed a commission to raise standards in hospitals.*

commission + VERBS

a commission examines/looks into sth *The commission will look into possible sites for the new airport.*

a commission recommends sth *The commission recommended that the government changes the way it measures inflation.*

a commission approves sth *The commission approved the plan.*

PREPOSITIONS

a commission on sth *He was a member of the Commission on Environmental Pollution.*

PHRASES

a member of a commission *Each member of the commission must be a resident of this state.*

a commission of inquiry/investigation *There have been calls for a commission of inquiry into the incident.*

commit *v*

to do something wrong or illegal

NOUNS

commit a crime/offence *People who commit crimes usually end up in jail.*

commit (a) murder/robbery etc *She later admitted committing the robbery.*

commit an error *formal: She has committed a serious error of judgement.*

commit a sin (=do something that is wrong according to your religion) *He thought that God would punish him for the sins he had committed.*

People also say **commit suicide**, even though killing yourself is no longer a crime in most places.

THESAURUS: commit

make, give, take, commit, carry out, conduct, perform, undertake, implement → **do**

commitment *n*

1 a promise to do something, or something that you promised to do or must do

ADJECTIVES

family/work/teaching commitments *I was unable to go on the trip because of work commitments.*

financial commitments *Many people are struggling to meet their financial commitments.*

an existing/prior commitment *Do the hours of the course fit in with your existing commitments?*

a big/major commitment *Marriage is a big commitment.*

a firm commitment *They want a firm commitment from the government to provide more resources.*

a clear commitment *The party made a clear commitment to improve public services.*

a long-term/lifelong commitment *Her boyfriend is not ready for a long-term commitment.*

VERBS

make a commitment *People had to make a commitment to pay regular contributions for five years.*

give a commitment *The government gave a commitment to withdraw all its forces.*

meet/fulfil/honour a commitment (=do what you promised) *I promised to help, and I intend to meet this commitment.*

PREPOSITIONS

a commitment to sb *I made a commitment to my students and I won't let them down.*

a commitment from/by sb *The government wants a commitment from the rebels to end the violence.*

a commitment on sth *We have received a fresh commitment on funding.*

2 a willingness to work hard to support or achieve something

ADJECTIVES

real/genuine/serious commitment *The job demands real commitment.*

strong/deep/passionate commitment *She's known for her strong commitment to women's rights.*

full/total commitment *The treatment demands full commitment from the patient.*

continuing/long-term/lifelong commitment *She was careful to stress her party's continuing commitment to the European Union.*

VERBS

show/demonstrate your commitment *Throughout her life, she demonstrated her great commitment to helping the poor.*

have a commitment to sth *He has a deep commitment to social justice.*

sth needs/requires/demands commitment *Nursing as a profession demands genuine commitment.*

lack commitment *I never get promoted because they think I lack commitment.*

PREPOSITIONS

commitment to sth *These schools deserve the highest praise for their commitment to excellence.*

PHRASES

a lack of commitment *His lack of commitment to the project was easy to see.*

a level of commitment *This post demands a high level of commitment.*

committed *adj*

willing to work hard to support or achieve something

ADVERBS

fully/totally/wholly committed *Both sides claim to be fully committed to the peace process.*

highly committed *Our schools have highly committed teachers.*

deeply/strongly/firmly committed *He was deeply committed to his faith.*

passionately/fiercely committed (=with very strong feelings) *We are all passionately committed to our work in Africa.*

politically/ideologically committed *They were ideologically committed to democratic principles.*

irrevocably committed *formal* (=in a way that cannot be changed) *By now the US was irrevocably committed to the war.*

NOUNS

a committed supporter *He remains a committed supporter of the present government.*

a committed member of sth *She is a committed member of the Scottish Socialist Party.*

a committed Christian/Muslim/pacifist/feminist etc *They consider themselves to be committed Christians.*

VERBS

remain committed to sth *The government remained committed to the treaty.*

PREPOSITIONS

committed to (doing) sth *We are committed to building a better society.*

committee *n*

a group of people chosen to do a particular job, make decisions etc

ADJECTIVES/NOUNS + committee

a government committee *A government committee is looking into drug laws.*

a special committee *A special committee of scientists was set up to study the disease.*

the finance/education etc committee *He served on the finance committee.*

an executive/management committee (=that manages an organization and makes decisions for it) *He sat on the firm's Executive Committee.*

an advisory committee *The government is following the advice of the Food Advisory Committee.*

a joint committee (=involving two or more groups) *The two schools have set up a joint committee to look into the proposal.*

a select committee (=of politicians and advisers who examine a particular subject, especially in the UK) *The government appointed a select committee to look into the issue of press freedom.*

VERBS + committee

set up/form/appoint a committee *The council appointed a special committee to study the issue.*

appoint/elect sb to a committee *Mr D Pugh was elected to the committee, replacing Mr A J Taylor.*

serve/sit on a committee (=be a member of an important committee) *Our organization is always in need of volunteers to serve on the committee.*

chair/head a committee (=be in charge of a committee) *Professor Peacock was appointed to chair the committee.*

committee + VERBS

a committee meets *The committee meets once a month.*

a committee approves/rejects sth *The committee has approved the idea.*

committee + NOUNS

a committee meeting *There's a committee meeting once a month.*

a committee member (*also* **a member of a committee**) *Four committee members did not attend the meeting.*

a committee chairman (*also* **a chairman of a committee**) *There will be a new committee chairman next year.*

PREPOSITIONS

a committee on sth *She was a member of the Senate committee on welfare reform.*

be on a committee (=be a member of a committee) *I was on the parents' committee at my kids' school.*

commodity *n*

something that is bought and sold, especially a substance

ADJECTIVES

an important commodity *Crude oil is the world's most important commodity.*

an expensive commodity *Consumers began to find that they could afford more expensive commodities.*

a valuable/precious commodity *Land is an extremely valuable commodity.*

a rare/scarce commodity *Soap was a scarce commodity during the war.*

agricultural commodities *The falling prices of agricultural commodities such as coffee have severely affected the economy.*

industrial commodities *Sales of the old industrial commodities of iron and coal are still important.*

commodity + NOUNS

commodity prices *Commodity prices are very high in the UK.*

a commodity market *The price of coffee on the commodity market had risen.*

THESAURUS: commodity

goods, commodity, merchandise, wares, export, import → **product**

common *adj*

1 happening often and to many people or in many places, or existing in many places

NOUNS

a common cause/reason *Heart disease is one of the most common causes of death.*

a common type/form of sth *Many common forms of cancer can be treated if detected early.*

a common name *Jones is a very common name in the UK.*

a common flower/plant/bird/animal *Daisies are very common flowers.*

a common problem *Lack of sleep is a common problem among older people.*

a common illness/disease *The drug is used to treat a range of common illnesses.*

a common belief/view *There is a common belief that unemployment causes crime.*

common practice *It was common practice for girls to be married as soon as possible.*

a common mistake/error *Confusing 'it's' and 'its' is a common error among students.*

a common feature *Windmills used to be a common feature of the landscape.*

a common sight (=something you often see) *Street dentists are a common sight in Pakistan.*

a common occurrence (=something that often happens) *Flooding is a common occurrence in the area.*

ADVERBS

increasingly common *Living together before marriage has become increasingly common.*

particularly common *The disease is particularly common among young children.*

extremely common *Skiing injuries are extremely common.*

relatively common (=quite common) *This situation is relatively common with small businesses.*

VERBS

become common *It's becoming more and more common for women to keep their family name when they get married.*

remain common *The problem remains common in some areas.*

PREPOSITIONS

sth is common among sb/sth *Bad dreams are fairly common among children.*

it is common for sb to do sth *It is common for people to be afraid of the dark.*

THESAURUS: common

widespread
support | agreement | belief | concern | criticism | condemnation | use | practice | corruption | dissatisfaction | discontent | acceptance
used when a lot of people think or say the same thing, or something happens in a lot of places:
There is widespread agreement on the need for prison reform. | The widespread use of chemicals in agriculture is causing permanent damage to the soil. | Corruption in government was widespread.

commonplace
if something is commonplace, it happens a lot somewhere – used especially about things that are shocking or surprising, or things that have changed because of new technology:
*Violence was commonplace. | It is **becoming increasingly commonplace** to see young people sleeping on the streets of London. | Electric cars are likely to **become** more **commonplace** over the next few years.*

Commonplace is less commonly used before a noun.

rife
if an illness or problem is rife, it is very common:
*AIDS is **rife in** some parts of the world. | He claimed that racism was **rife among** police officers. | The city's streets are still **rife with** violent crime.*

Rife is not used before a noun.

prevalent *formal*
used when saying that many people have an idea or belief, or an illness or problem is common:
*This belief is more **prevalent among** men than women. | Suicide is less **prevalent in** rural societies.*

Prevalent is less common before a noun.

ubiquitous *formal*
very common and seen in many different places – often used humorously in written descriptions:
These cameras are ubiquitous in our cities.

You often say **the ubiquitous...**: *She was wearing **the ubiquitous** little black dress. | The film features **the ubiquitous** Scarlett Johansson.*

ANTONYMS **common → rare**

2 shared by two or more people, countries, or groups

NOUNS

a common aim/goal/purpose *We're all working together towards a common goal.*

a common interest *Dating agencies try to match people with common interests.*

a common language *English is their common language.*

common ground (=things that people agree about) *I'm hoping that we might be able to find some common ground.*

a common enemy *They were fighting against a common enemy.*

PHRASES

have sth in common (=have something that you both share or are interested in, so that you like or know each other) *The two men had a lot in common – they were both lawyers in their mid-30s.*

by common consent (=with everyone's agreement) *She was chosen as captain by common consent.*

communicate Ac *v*

to exchange information or conversation with other people, using words, signs, writing etc

ADVERBS

communicate directly (=by talking, writing etc to someone yourself) *Television gave political leaders a way to communicate directly with their people.*

communicate effectively (=in a way that gets good results) *We need to learn to communicate effectively with our colleagues.*

PREPOSITIONS

communicate with sb/sth *Advertising involves communicating with customers.* | *The crew on the ground were trying to communicate with the spacecraft.*

communicate by email/phone/letter etc *We communicate mostly by email.*

communicate sth to sb (=give someone particular information) *The baby cries as a way of communicating to you that she needs something.*

communication *n*

the process of exchanging information or telling people about your thoughts and feelings

ADJECTIVES

good communication *It is vital to have good communication between doctors and patients.*

effective communication *Effective communication is important in my job.*

poor communication *Poor communication can be a problem in large companies.*

mass communication (=to large numbers of people at the same time) *Television is a powerful form of mass communication.*

direct communication *Business success requires direct communication between staff and their customers.*

open communication (=being honest) *Open communication between couples is essential in a successful relationship.*

two-way communication (=when each person or side tells things to the other) *We want to make sure that there is two-way communication between teachers and students.*

verbal communication (=using language) *People don't just use verbal communication when they are talking to each other, they also use body language.*

non-verbal communication (=using hand movements and facial expressions rather than language) *Non-verbal communication includes gestures and facial expressions.*

VERBS

improve communication *We need to improve communication between company departments.*

establish communication *The scientists succeeded in establishing communication with the spacecraft.*

promote communication (=encourage it) *The aim is to promote better communication between employees.*

facilitate communication (=make it easier) *The internet has facilitated communication between people in different countries.*

communication + NOUNS

communication skills *You need to have good communication skills if you want to be a team leader.*

a communication system *The country's telephone and other communication systems were inadequate.*

a communication breakdown *There was a communication breakdown between the teenager and his parents.*

PREPOSITIONS

communication between sb *Communication between central government and local authorities needs improvement.*

communication with sb *We want to establish good communication with our customers.*

PHRASES

a means/method/form/system of communication (=a way of communicating) *Text messaging is an important means of communication.*

lines/channels of communication (=ways that information can be passed between groups) *It's vital to have clear lines of communication between management and staff.*

a lack of communication *A lack of communication between crew members played a critical role in the accident.*

a breakdown in communication (=when people stop communicating well) *There was a breakdown in communication between the team management and the players.*

community *n*

1 the people who live in the same area, town etc

ADJECTIVES/NOUNS + community

the local community *A school is often the centre of the local community.*

the whole community *These issues affect the whole community.*

the international community (=all the countries of the world) *The president appealed to the international community for help.*

the wider community (=all the other people

who live in an area) *The sports centre is open to both the university and the wider community.*

a small/large community *75% of the population live in small communities of fewer than 450 people.*

a close/close-knit/tight-knit community (=where all the people know each other well) *His disappearance shocked the close-knit community where he lived.*

a thriving community (=very successful) *In the past, the village was a thriving community with a number of shops.*

a farming/mining/fishing community *She lives in a small mining community in North Wales.*

VERBS

serve a community *The new arts centre will serve the whole community.*

help/support a community *He wanted to use the money to help the local community.*

benefit a community *The new bus service will benefit the whole community.*

unite/divide a community *The bombing had united rather than divided the community.*

create/build a community *We want to create a community, not just a row of houses.*

community + NOUNS

a community group *A local community group wants to take over the building.*

a community leader *Community leaders meet regularly to discuss local problems.*

community services (=schools, hospitals, libraries etc) *Some tax goes towards paying for your community services.*

community relations (=between people in a community) *Poor community relations are more common in cities than in rural areas.*

community spirit (=support and friendship between people in an area) *There is great community spirit in the area where I live.*

community work (=work to help the people in an area) *She does a lot of voluntary community work.*

a community centre *BrE*, **a community center** *AmE* (=where people can go for social events, classes etc)

PREPOSITIONS

in/within a community *How can you help stop crime in your community?*

PHRASES

a member of a community *It's good to feel that you are a member of a community.*

a part/section of the community *No other section of the community has been treated this way.*

sb is a pillar of the community (=he or she is very well respected there) *The doctor was regarded as a pillar of the local community.*

the heart of the community (=the centre of it) *The church used to be the heart of the community.*

a sense of community (=a feeling that you belong to a community) *There is a real sense of community here.*

2 a group of people who have the same interests, religion, race etc

ADJECTIVES/NOUNS + community

the business community *The idea has aroused a lot of interest from the business community.*

the academic/scientific community *Many people in the academic community do not agree with his views.*

Jewish/Christian/Muslim etc community *The mosque serves the local Muslim community.*

black/white/Asian etc community *The city has a large Asian community.*

ethnic community (=people of a particular race, especially not the main one in a country) *Black and other ethnic communities make up 47% of the city's population.*

commuter *n*

someone who travels a long distance to work every day

ADJECTIVES/NOUNS + commuter

a daily commuter *Thousands of daily commuters pour into the city.*

a regular commuter *He was a regular commuter between Cambridge and London.*

a long-distance commuter *The fare increases will be bad news for long-distance commuters.*

a morning/evening commuter *By 7.30 the roads are jammed with the usual morning commuters.*

a rush-hour commuter (=one travelling at the busiest time of the day) *The station was busy with rush-hour commuters.*

a rail commuter (=one who travels by train) *Rail commuters face severe delays because of engineering works.*

commuter + NOUNS

a commuter train/bus *Several commuter trains were delayed because of the bad weather.*

commuter traffic *How can we reduce commuter traffic in the capital?*

commuter services (=trains or buses for commuters) *More money is needed to improve commuter services in the region.*

a commuter line (=a railway line for commuter trains) *There's a fast and reliable commuter line across the county.*

a commuter route (=a road or railway line that commuters use) *This stretch of motorway is one of the country's busiest commuter routes.*

a commuter town/village (=one from which a lot of people travel to a big city for work every day)

the commuter belt *BrE* (=an area around a large city, from which many people travel to work every day) *House prices in the commuter belt are much higher than those outside it.*

compact *adj* THESAURUS ▶ small (1)

companion *n*

someone you spend a lot of time with, especially a friend

ADJECTIVES

a close companion *At school, we were close companions.*

a loyal/faithful companion *His dog had been a loyal companion for years.*

a female/male companion *He arrived with a female companion.*

a constant/inseparable companion (=who you spend most or all of your time with) *The two boys became constant companions.*

a lifelong companion (= throughout your life) *Lucinda was her best friend and lifelong companion.*

a good/wonderful companion *For older people, a pet cat can be a very good companion.*

ideal/perfect companion *Who would be your ideal dinner companion?*

a travelling/dining/drinking companion *I knew that Dave would be a good travelling companion.*

PREPOSITIONS

a companion to sb *She became an inseparable companion to my uncle.*

a companion for sb *We bought the dog as a companion for my mother.*

company *n*

1 a business organization

ADJECTIVES

a big/large company *She has a senior position in a large manufacturing company.*

a small company *His father is the director of a small company.*

a medium-sized company *The firm is a medium-sized company, employing just over 300 workers.*

a leading/major company *Apple is one of the world's leading computer companies.*

a reputable company (=with a good reputation) *Choose a reputable company to do the building work.*

a profitable/successful company *How can we make this company more profitable?*

a foreign company *There are many opportunities for foreign companies here.*

an international/multinational company (=with offices in different countries) *She works for a major international company.*

a local company *The new development will bring more business to local companies.*

a private company *It is private companies that create wealth in a society.*

a public/listed company (=one that offers its shares for sale on the stock market) *They are on the index of the top 100 listed companies.*

a limited company (=one whose owners only have to pay a limited amount if it gets into debt) *We decided it would be safer to change our business into a limited company.*

a state-owned/publicly owned company (=owned by the government) *The state-owned company was very inefficient.*

NOUNS + company

an internet company *He started his own internet company when he was only 15.*

an oil/drug/insurance/phone etc company *The oil company is paying for the clean-up operation.*

a manufacturing/publishing/shipping etc company *She works for a publishing company editing textbooks.*

a utility company (=a company that provides water, gas, or electricity to homes) *The utility companies have made huge profits.*

a water/electricity/gas company *The water company says it is not responsible for the burst pipe.*

a subsidiary company (=one that is owned or controlled by a larger company) *It is a large organization with several subsidiary companies.*

a parent company (=one that owns or controls a smaller one) *The firm's parent company is in the US.*

a sister company (=one that belongs to the same organization as another company) *Many of the flights will be operated by our sister company.*

a blue-chip company (=a very important and successful one) *He only invests in blue-chip companies.*

VERBS + company

work for a company *She works for a publishing company.*

run/manage a company *Nick runs an internet company.*

join/leave a company *Sara joined the company in 2008 as a software developer.*

resign from a company *I resigned from the company when they refused to promote me.*

set up/start/form/found/establish a company *The company was set up just after the war.*

own a company *The company is owned by an Indian businessman.*

buy/sell a company *They sold the company for a million dollars.*

take over a company (=buy it and run it) *The company was taken over by an Indian construction firm.*

company + VERBS

a company makes/manufactures/produces sth *The company manufactures parts for car engines.*

a company sells sth *What does your company sell?*

a company specializes in sth (=it mainly makes or sells a particular product) *We are a small company specializing in organic cotton clothing.*

a company grows/expands *The company has expanded since last year.*

a company goes bankrupt/fails (=stops doing business after losing too much money) *He lost everything when his company went bankrupt.*

a company merges with another company (=they join together to become one company) *What happened when the oil companies merged?*

company + NOUNS

a company director/executive *The company directors have awarded themselves a massive pay increase.*

a company spokesman/representative *A company spokesman denied that there had been a secret deal.*

company policy *It is not company policy to give that information.*

PHRASES

a company goes bust/goes under/goes to the wall *informal* (=it becomes bankrupt) *They were worried that the company was about to go bust.*

a company goes into liquidation (=it is closed and sold in order to pay its debts) *The company was forced to go into liquidation.*

2 the fact that you are with another person

ADJECTIVES

sb is good/pleasant company (=it is enjoyable being with them) *I always liked seeing Rob - he was such good company.*

sb is poor company (=it is not enjoyable being with them) *She apologized for being poor company on the journey.*

mixed company (=when men and women are together) *Most of us are happy in mixed company.*

the assembled company *formal* (=the people who are together in a place) *He gazed at the assembled company.*

VERBS

enjoy sb's company *Steve was fun and she clearly enjoyed his company.*

keep sb company (=be with someone so that they do not feel lonely) *Mum was out so I stayed at home to keep my younger sister company.*

have company (=have a person or people with you) *I'm sorry, I didn't realize you had company.*

need/want company *Children need the company of other kids their age.*

be expecting company (=be waiting for a visitor or visitors to arrive) *You look very nice - are you expecting company?*

PREPOSITIONS

for company *She only had her cat for company.*

in the company of sb (=when you are with someone) *I felt nervous in the company of such an important man.*

in company (=when with other people) *He finds it hard to speak to people and is awkward in company.*

PHRASES

like/prefer your own company (=prefer to be alone) *She's not unfriendly - she just prefers her own company.*

seek (out) the company of sb *formal: He has never sought the company of women.*

have the pleasure of sb's company *formal* (=used especially to say or ask whether someone will be attending something) *Will we have the pleasure of your company this evening?*

the company sb keeps (=the people someone spends time with) *You can tell a lot about someone by the company they keep.*

get into bad company (=start spending time with bad people)

you're in good company (=used to tell someone that other people also do, think, or experience something)

comparison *n*

a statement or examination of how similar or different two people or things are

VERBS

make/do a comparison (*also* **perform a comparison** *formal*): *Using the internet is an easy way to make comparisons between prices. | They did comparisons of three different types of camera.*

draw a comparison (=say in what way people or things are similar) *The writer draws a comparison between the 1950s and the present day.*

a comparison shows/reveals sth *Further comparison revealed that the pictures were by the same artist.*

ADJECTIVES/NOUNS + comparison

a direct comparison *You can't really make a direct comparison between the two schools.*

an interesting comparison *The exhibition provides an interesting comparison of the artists' works.*

a valid/useful/meaningful comparison (=a reasonable one, based on sensible information) *There is not enough data for a valid comparison to be made.*

a fair/unfair comparison *A fair comparison between the two firms is extremely difficult.*

a favourable/unfavourable comparison (=in which one thing or person is judged to be better/worse than another) *My aunt was always making unfavourable comparisons between me and my cousin.*

a detailed/close comparison *Students had to write a detailed comparison of the two writers.*

PREPOSITIONS

a comparison of sth *The table shows a comparison of pollution levels in Chicago and Detroit.*

a comparison between sth (and sth) *The comparison between Picasso and Matisse has been made before.*

a comparison with sth *Comparisons with other countries show big variations.*

by/in comparison (=when you compare two things) *The next test will be easy by comparison.*

PHRASES

for (the) purposes of comparison *Each child is given a score, simply for purposes of comparison.*

a basis for comparison (=something that can be used for comparing things) *The test results serve as a basis for comparison.*

compassion *n* strong feelings of sympathy

ADJECTIVES

great compassion *He had great compassion for animals.*

human compassion (=which people expect other people to have) *Judges are often criticised for lacking human compassion.*

genuine compassion *The country needs a leader with genuine compassion for the suffering of the people.*

VERBS

show compassion *The company showed no compassion towards him and fired him because he was too ill to work.*

feel compassion *Helen felt compassion for her friend and wanted to help her.*

treat sb with compassion *Criminals should always be treated with compassion.*

have compassion for sb *It is difficult to have compassion for people who are just lazy.*

lack compassion *His boss was a cold woman who lacked compassion.*

be filled with compassion *They were filled with compassion for their son.*

PREPOSITIONS

compassion for sb *He had no compassion for them and thought they deserved to be punished for what they had done.*

compassion towards sb *She felt great compassion towards the poor.*

PHRASES

a lack of compassion *The authorities showed a lack of compassion.*

a sense of compassion *Only someone with no sense of compassion could treat another person so badly.*

compassionate *adj* THESAURUS ▸ kind[2]

compensation Ac *n*

money paid to someone because they have suffered injury or loss, or because something they own has been damaged

ADJECTIVES

financial compensation *He applied for financial compensation from the government.*

full/maximum compensation *Full compensation is only paid very rarely.*

partial compensation (=partly covering the loss, damage etc) *The woman received partial compensation of £5,000.*

substantial compensation (=a lot of money) *She may be entitled to substantial compensation.*

record compensation (=more than has ever been paid before) *The company agreed to pay record compensation of $1 billion.*

VERBS

apply for/claim compensation (=ask for it because you have a right to it) *You can claim compensation for unfair dismissal from your job.*

get/receive/win compensation *Some people have received compensation from the government for the loss of their homes.*

pay/give (sb) compensation *Passengers will be paid compensation if their baggage is lost or damaged.*

award (sb) compensation (=say someone has a right to get it) *Many victims have been awarded compensation by the courts.*

offer sb compensation *The health authority offered compensation to the families.*

deny/refuse sb compensation (=not allow them to have it) *The released prisoners were denied compensation.*

be entitled to/be eligible for compensation (=be able to get it) *If you have lost money, you may be entitled to compensation.*

seek compensation (=try to get it) *Survivors of the rail disaster are seeking compensation.*

demand compensation (=ask for it in an angry way) *The people whose houses were damaged are demanding financial compensation.*

fight for compensation (=try hard to get it) *Alan, who hurt his back and hasn't worked since, is still fighting for compensation.*

compensation + NOUNS

a compensation claim *He was seeking legal advice on a compensation claim.*

a compensation payment *UK farmers may get compensation payments.*

PREPOSITIONS

compensation for sth *You can get compensation for injuries at work.*

compensation from sb *She received compensation from the government for damage to her property.*

in compensation *The jury awarded Tyler $1.7 million in compensation.*

as compensation *The workers were given 30 days' pay as compensation.*

competition *n*

1 an organized event in which people or teams compete against each other

ADJECTIVES/NOUNS + competition

a major/big competition *She has won several major sports competitions.*

a national/nationwide competition *He entered a nationwide competition to find the country's best storyteller.*

an international competition *Her oldest daughter has taken part in international competitions.*

an annual competition *Last year he won the magazine's annual photo competition.*

a writing/painting/dancing etc competition *Greg took part in the school public-speaking competition.*

a sports/football/basketball etc competition *There is an increasing demand to watch sports competitions.*

a music/essay/poetry etc competition *There's a music competition in the town on June 12th.*

an open competition (=that everyone can take part in) *An open competition is to be held at the tennis club.*

a knock-out competition *BrE* (=in which if you lose one part, you are no longer in the competition) *The singing contest is a knock-out competition, and no one wants to be the first to leave.*

a newspaper/magazine competition (=organized by a newspaper/magazine) *I entered a newspaper competition for young writer of the year.*

VERBS

enter a competition *You must be over 16 to enter the competition.*

take part in a competition (*also* **participate in a competition** *formal*): *Ten schools took part in the competition.*

win a competition *I was really happy when I heard I had won the competition.*

come first/second/third etc in a competition *Stuart came second in the swimming competition.*

have/hold a competition *Each year the school holds a painting competition.*

run a competition (=organize it) *The company is running a competition to come up with a new invention.*

judge a competition (=decide who has won) *A panel of five will judge the competition.*

withdraw from/retire from a competition (=not take part because you are no longer able to) *He had to withdraw from the competition because of an injury.*

be disqualified from a competition (=not be allowed to continue in it because of doing something wrong) *Anyone found taking drugs will be disqualified from the competition.*

PREPOSITIONS

be in a competition *She's in a dancing competition this weekend.*

be out of a competition (=no longer be in a competition because you have been defeated) *Our team scored the fewest points so we were out of the competition.*

a competition for sth *There's a competition for the best photograph.*

a competition between sb (and sb) *We decided that a competition between the boys and girls would be fun.*

PHRASES

the results of a competition *The results of the competition will be announced on April 3rd.*

the winner of a competition *Jane was the clear winner of the competition.*

the rules of a competition *Make sure you understand the rules of the competition.*

a competition is open to sb (=used to say who can enter a competition) *The competition is open to artists between 16 and 25 years old.*

2 a situation in which people or organizations are trying to be more successful than others

ADJECTIVES

strong/serious competition (=a lot of people, companies etc are competing) *The company is facing strong competition in the market.*

stiff/tough/keen competition (=strong competition) *There is stiff competition for places at the top universities.*

fierce/intense competition (=very strong) *There is fierce competition between the three leading manufacturers.*

cut-throat competition (=very strong and unpleasant) *The cut-throat competition in the airline industry kept prices low.*

fair/unfair competition *Fair competition offers the best guarantee of good services and low prices.*

open competition (=everyone has a chance to be successful) *We welcome open competition in the software market.*

healthy competition (=it is a good thing) *There has always been healthy competition between the two athletes.*

friendly competition *There's nothing wrong with a little friendly competition.*

increasing/growing competition *There is increasing competition for school places.*

VERBS

be up against/face competition (=other people or organizations are competing with you) *They are up against stiff competition.*

beat off/fight off competition (=be more successful than others) *She beat off competition from dozens of other candidates to get the job.*

go into competition with sb (*also* **enter into competition with sb**) (=start competing with them) *He never forgave his business partner for breaking away and going into competition with him.*

create competition *The proposals were intended to create more competition.*

encourage/stimulate competition *They want to encourage greater competition in the banking sector.*

increase/reduce competition *We need to increase choice and competition.*

competition increases/grows/intensifies *It is likely that competition will grow in the next few months.*

PREPOSITIONS

competition for sth *Competition for the job was intense.*

competition between sb (and sb) *Sometimes there's a lot of competition between brothers and sisters.*

competition among people/organizations *This price reduction is due to competition among suppliers.*

competition from sb *We face strong competition from foreign firms.*

be in competition with sb *Government departments are in direct competition with each other for limited resources.*

PHRASES

in the face of competition (=in a situation where you are competing to be successful) *They won the contract in the face of tough competition.*

competitive *adj* THESAURUS **cheap**

competitor *n*

a person, team, company etc that is competing with another

ADJECTIVES

sb's main/chief/biggest competitor *They sold many more phones than their main competitor.*

a major competitor *Japan soon became a major competitor in the electronics industry.*

a strong/serious competitor (=one that you have to compete hard with) *The company has become a strong competitor in the market.*

a top competitor (=one of the best, especially in a sport) *The race attracted top competitors from all over the world.*

sb's closest competitor (*also* **sb's nearest competitor** *BrE*) (=the one most likely to beat you) *He had five times as many votes as his nearest competitor.*

a direct competitor (=someone competing in exactly the same activity as you) *He knew she was a successful businesswoman and a direct competitor.*

a potential competitor (=a person, company etc that might compete with you) *He sees me as a potential competitor for the job.*

foreign/international/overseas competitors *Foreign competitors can make the same goods at lower prices.*

VERBS

beat a competitor *To stay in business you have to beat your competitors.*

outperform a competitor (=do better than them) *The company has consistently outperformed its competitors.*

switch to a competitor (=start doing business with a competitor) *If we do not provide good service, customers will switch to a competitor.*

complain *v*

to say that you are annoyed or not satisfied with something

ADVERBS

sb is always complaining *English people are always complaining about the weather – it's always too cold or too hot.*

complain bitterly (=in a very angry way) *My grandfather's always complaining bitterly about how expensive things are.*

complain loudly *The kids were complaining loudly about the heat.*

constantly complain *She is constantly complaining about her job.*

formally/officially complain *The club has officially complained about the referee's decision.*

complain publicly *People were unhappy with the government, but did not dare to complain publicly.*

PREPOSITIONS

complain about sth *There's no point complaining about the weather.*

complain to sb *She complained to her boss about the behaviour of a colleague.*

complain of sth (=say that something is annoying or hurting you) *She went to bed early, complaining of a headache.*

PHRASES

I can't complain *spoken* (=used to say that you are reasonably happy with something) *My job is pretty easy, so I can't complain.*

be the first to complain (=be quick to complain) *He's the first to complain if he thinks something is unfair.*

have (good) reason to complain *We felt we had good reason to complain about the food at the hotel.*

complaint *n*

a statement in which someone complains about something

ADJECTIVES/NOUNS + complaint

a formal/official complaint *The man has made a formal complaint against the police.*

a common/widespread/frequent complaint *A common complaint of children is that parents do not listen to them.*

a legitimate complaint (=reasonable) *In my view, it is a legitimate complaint.*

a customer/consumer complaint *As a result of the improvements, customer complaints went down by 70%.*

VERBS

make a complaint (to sb) (=complain formally to someone) *The manager of the team made a complaint about the referee.*

file/lodge/register a complaint (with sb) *formal* (=make a complaint) *She filed a complaint with her boss against several of her colleagues.*

bring a complaint against sb *formal* (=complain in a formal, legal way) *Higgins brought a complaint against his former manager.*

have a complaint (=want to complain about something) *Please let us know if you have any complaints about our service.*

get/receive a complaint *Our department has received a number of complaints from the public.*

deal with/handle a complaint *Police officers came to the house to deal with a complaint about noise.*

investigate a complaint *The dog was rescued after officials investigated a complaint of neglect.*

resolve a complaint (=deal with it in a satisfactory way) *The branch manager should be able to investigate and resolve your complaint.*

uphold a complaint (=say it is reasonable) *The complaint was upheld and the advertisement was withdrawn.*

PREPOSITIONS

a complaint about sth/sb *His manager had received a complaint about his behaviour.*

a complaint against sb (=about someone) *Complaints against doctors continue to rise.*

a complaint from/by sb *They were getting complaints from their customers.*

a complaint to sb *The matter was investigated following a complaint to the police.*

PHRASES

cause/grounds for complaint (=a good reason to complain) *I do not think that he has any cause for complaint.*

a letter of complaint *I wrote a letter of complaint to the hospital manager.*

a complaints procedure (=a system for dealing with complaints) *There is no formal complaints procedure for patients.*

complete *v* THESAURUS ▸ **finish[1] (1)**

complex[1] Ac *adj*

consisting of many different parts and often difficult to understand

ADVERBS

highly/extremely complex *Dreaming is a highly complex brain activity.*

increasingly complex *Modern weapons are becoming increasingly complex and difficult to handle.*

overly/unnecessarily complex (=more complex than it needs to be) *The payment system is unnecessarily complex.*

NOUNS

a complex system *A complex system of pipes is used to carry water to the building.*

a complex process *This guide takes you through the complex process of buying a home.*

a complex problem/issue *International trade is a highly complex issue.*

a complex subject *This is a very brief description of a complex subject.*

a complex situation *It is a complex situation with no easy answer.*

a complex relationship *The book explores the complex relationship between science and religion.*

a complex pattern/structure *The tropical rainforest has a complex structure, with many levels.*

a complex series of events *The French Revolution was a complex series of events.*

the complex nature of sth *This view does not take into account the complex nature of the human mind.*

THESAURUS: complex

complex, elaborate, intricate, involved, convoluted, tortuous → **complicated**

complex[2] Ac *n*

1 a large building or group of buildings used for a particular purpose

ADJECTIVES/NOUNS + complex

a large/vast complex *The company headquarters are situated in a vast complex of buildings.*

a leisure/entertainment complex *The new leisure complex includes a cinema and a bowling alley.*

a sports complex *Their local sports complex has good tennis facilities.*

an office complex *They rent some spaces in an office complex in Los Angeles.*

a shopping complex *A huge shopping complex was built on the old football ground.*

a housing complex (*also* **a residential complex** *formal*) *AmE: We lived in a rented unit in a single-story housing complex near the center of Phoenix.*

an apartment complex *AmE*: *He lives in a luxury apartment complex.*

an industrial complex *Kaesong is an industrial complex located in North Korea.*

2 an emotional problem that causes someone to worry a lot

NOUNS + complex

a guilt complex (=strong feelings of guilt) *After surviving the plane crash, he suffered from a guilt complex.*

an inferiority complex (=when you think you are not as good as other people) *When I first went to university, I had a real inferiority complex and I thought the other students were much smarter than I was.*

a persecution complex (=when you think other people are trying to harm you) *Doctors say she's developed a persecution complex.*

ADJECTIVES

a huge/massive/terrible complex *Our teenage son developed a huge complex about his weight.*

an acute complex (=a very serious one) *The woman was suffering from an acute anxiety complex.*

VERBS

have a complex (*also* **suffer from a complex**) *She has a complex about her height.*

get/develop a complex *You don't want your child to develop a complex about food.*

PREPOSITIONS

a complex about sth *I used to have a complex about being in large crowds.*

complexion *n*

the natural colour or appearance of the skin on your face

ADJECTIVES

a fair complexion (=light in colour) *People with a fair complexion should use plenty of sunscreen.*

a dark complexion *Bright colours may suit you if your complexion is dark.*

a pale complexion (=very light) *Red hair often goes with a pale complexion.*

a clear/fresh/healthy complexion (=without any spots) *Eating fresh fruit will keep your complexion clear.*

a bad complexion (=with spots or marks on it) *Teenagers often suffer from a bad complexion.*

a glowing/rosy/pink complexion (=healthy and pink) *His mother has the rosy complexion of a much younger woman.*

a flawless/perfect complexion (=perfect, with no marks or spots) *Good make-up gives the appearance of a flawless complexion.*

VERBS

have a ... complexion *She has bright blue eyes and a rosy complexion.*

complexity *n*

a complicated state, or a feature that makes something complicated

ADJECTIVES

great/considerable/enormous complexity *This is a problem of considerable complexity.*

increasing/growing complexity *The growing complexity of new technology makes it impossible for ordinary people to understand.*

sheer complexity (=used when emphasizing that something is very complex) *The sheer complexity of the process made it very expensive.*

technical complexity *For reasons of its technical complexity, the full details of this research cannot be covered in this book.*

VERBS

understand/grasp the complexity of sth *You can't solve the problem until you fully understand its complexity.*

cope with the complexity of sth (=deal with it successfully) *Visitors to Korea often can't cope with the complexity of its cultural rules.*

reduce the complexity of sth *She is more relaxed now that she has managed to reduce the complexity of her life.*

PHRASES

a level/degree of complexity *His recent paintings show a level of complexity not found in his earlier work.*

complicated *adj*

consisting of many parts or details, and difficult to understand or deal with

NOUNS

a complicated system/process *The United States has a very complicated voting system.*

a complicated problem/issue/matter/subject *Unemployment is an incredibly complicated issue.*

a complicated situation/case *She found herself in an extremely complicated situation.*

a complicated relationship *The film is about the complicated relationship between a patient and her doctor.*

a complicated story *It's a long and complicated story about a man who is sent to prison for a crime that he did not commit.*

a complicated explanation/complicated instructions *The instructions are too complicated for children.*

a complicated calculation *The deal involved some complicated financial calculations.*

ADVERBS

extremely/highly/enormously complicated *The situation in South Africa is highly complicated.*

fiendishly complicated (=extremely complicated – used when you want to emphasize how difficult something is to understand) *The rules of the game are fiendishly complicated.*

unnecessarily complicated *The current system of taxation is unnecessarily complicated.*

VERBS

look/seem complicated *The recipe looks complicated, but it's easier than it sounds.*

get complicated (=become complicated) *This is the part where it gets complicated.*

PHRASES

sth is a complicated business (=it is a complicated thing to do - a rather informal use) *Developing a new drug is a complicated business.*

things get complicated (=a situation becomes complicated - a rather informal use) *If there is an error in the software, things can get rather complicated.*

THESAURUS: complicated

complex
system | process | structure | relationship | problem | subject | issue | situation | set | series | network | nature
complicated - often used when something consists of a lot of parts that are connected in different ways:
Companies have to deal with a complex system of government regulations. | Viruses have a complex structure in which many different proteins are arranged around a piece of DNA or RNA. | This is a complex problem and there is no simple single solution. | Inflation is caused by a complex set of factors. | The war was caused by a complex series of events.

Complex or complicated?
These words are very often used in the same meaning, with the same words. You can say a **complex system/process/situation** etc, or a **complicated system/process/situation** etc.
Sometimes, the emphasis of the meaning is different. If something is **complicated**, it seems difficult to understand: *The rules of cricket are very **complicated*** (=difficult to understand). If something is **complex**, it has a lot of different parts, which are all connected with each other in different ways: *The molecules have a **complex** structure* (=one that consists of a lot of different parts, which are all connected to each other).
Complex is more common than **complicated**, especially in more formal English.

elaborate
plan | system | scheme | method | design | theory
having a lot of parts or details and very carefully planned. You often use **elaborate** when something seems more complicated than is necessary:
He came up with an elaborate plan to steal nuclear weapons so that he could use them to threaten an American city. | People in the Middle Ages constructed elaborate theories about the causes and treatment of disease.

intricate
pattern | design | carving | drawing | detail | system | structure
an intricate pattern or system is cleverly designed or made, and has a lot of parts or details which all connect with each other. You often use **intricate** when you admire what someone has done:
Persian carpets have beautifully intricate patterns. | She describes their lives in intricate detail. | From an intricate system of pipes, water flowed everywhere, in fountains and little artificial streams.

involved
discussion | debate | process | system
complicated and taking a long time to explain or understand:
They were having a long and involved discussion about the best way to cook lasagne. | The system for choosing candidates is very involved, and I won't go into it here.

too complicated

convoluted *disapproving*
plot | story | sentence | language | explanation | logic | structure | system | way
too complicated and difficult to understand:
The audience found it hard to follow the film's convoluted plot (=story). | Legal documents frequently consist of long paragraphs and convoluted sentences.

tortuous *disapproving*
route | journey | process | explanation | negotiations | argument | analogy | attempt | history
extremely complicated - used when something takes a long time and effort, and is not direct enough:
They came by a tortuous route, in order to avoid the mountains. | Taking a case to court can be a long and tortuous process.

Tortuous is related to **torture**, and it has the same idea of being very painful and slow.

ANTONYMS **complicated → simple**

compliment *n*
a remark or action that shows you admire someone or something

ADJECTIVES

a great/big/huge compliment *He said he loved my paintings, which was a great compliment.*

C

the highest/the ultimate compliment (=the best thing you can say or do) *The highest compliment you can pay an actor is to say they don't look as if they are acting.*

a backhanded compliment *BrE*, **a left-handed compliment** *AmE* (=something that someone says which is nice and not nice at the same time) *The reviewer said it was better than his last two films, which was rather a backhanded compliment.*

VERBS

pay/give sb a compliment *He was always paying her compliments.*

get/receive a compliment *The exhibition has received a lot of compliments from the public.*

accept a compliment (=show that you are pleased to have been given a compliment) *She accepted his compliment graciously.*

mean sth as a compliment *When I said she'd lost weight, I meant it as a compliment.*

take sth as a compliment (=be pleased about it, even though it may not have been meant as a compliment) *She said he was aggressive, and he took it as a compliment.*

fish for compliments (=try to make someone say something nice about you) *When she asked if I liked her dress, she was obviously fishing for compliments.*

PREPOSITIONS

a compliment on sth *I have had a lot of compliments on my cooking.*

component Ac *n*

one of several parts that together make up a whole machine or system etc

ADJECTIVES

an important/key component *Tourism is becoming an important component of the economy.*

the main/principal component *The course has four main components.*

an essential/vital/necessary component *The drug remains an essential component in many forms of cancer treatment.*

a basic/fundamental component *The first chapter of the book describes the basic components of the system.*

an electronic component *The factory produces electronic components for car engines.*

VERBS

assemble components *The components are made abroad and assembled in this country.*

comprehensive Ac *adj*

including all the necessary details or items

comprehensive + NOUNS

a comprehensive list *We publish a comprehensive list of the good hotels in the area.*

a comprehensive guide *The university's booklet is a comprehensive guide to the courses they offer.*

a comprehensive study/survey/review *She planned to publish a comprehensive survey of English literature.*

a comprehensive account/report *He's written a comprehensive account of animal life on the islands.*

a comprehensive assessment/analysis *We begin with a comprehensive assessment of the client's needs.*

a comprehensive range/set *The college has a comprehensive range of sports facilities.*

a comprehensive picture (=an understanding or explanation of all aspects) *The police still do not have a comprehensive picture of what happened.*

comprehensive information *The information we have is fairly comprehensive.*

ADVERBS

fully comprehensive *The report does not claim to be fully comprehensive.*

extremely/remarkably comprehensive *The instruction manual is extremely comprehensive.*

fairly/reasonably comprehensive *They supplied a reasonably comprehensive description of the job.*

compromise[1] *n*

an agreement in which all people accept less than they really want in order to end a dispute

ADJECTIVES

a good compromise *Eventually we came up with a good compromise.*

an acceptable/reasonable/satisfactory compromise *An acceptable compromise has been reached and the dispute has ended.*

a sensible compromise *Starting half an hour later would be a sensible compromise.*

an uneasy compromise (=one that people are not very happy with) *The deal represented an uneasy compromise.*

VERBS

reach a compromise *After a bitter political fight, a compromise was finally reached.*

come to a compromise (*also* **arrive at a compromise**) (=reach a compromise) *I'm sure we can come to some sort of compromise.*

make a compromise *Marriage involves being patient and making compromises.*

work out/find a compromise *Workers and management eventually worked out a compromise.*

accept a compromise (*also* **agree on a compromise**) *If you would accept a compromise, we could end this disagreement now.*

look for a compromise (*also* **seek a compromise** *formal*): *It's easier to seek a compromise than a perfect solution.*

negotiate/broker a compromise *Advisers have failed to negotiate a compromise, so the strike continues.*

lead to a compromise *Discussions between the residents and the council led to a compromise.*

compromise + NOUNS

a compromise solution *The prime minister may soon reach a compromise solution with his political opponents.*

a compromise deal/agreement *There is hope that a compromise deal can be reached to end the war.*

a compromise position *We need to find a compromise position.*

PREPOSITIONS

a compromise with sb *I made a compromise with my wife that we would each go out on alternate Fridays.*

a compromise between sb/sth (and sb/sth) *The agreement is a compromise between the president and the Senate.*

a compromise on/over sth *There is unlikely to be a compromise on the issue of pay.*

compromise² *v*

1 to reach an agreement by accepting less than you really want

PHRASES

be prepared/willing/ready to compromise *I'm willing to compromise if you think it costs too much.*

be unprepared/unwilling to compromise *He criticized the government for being unwilling to compromise.*

refuse to compromise *I offered to come home earlier, but Dad refused to compromise.*

PREPOSITIONS

compromise on sth *Are you prepared to compromise on the issue of pay?*

compromise with sb *You have to be able to compromise with your co-workers.*

2 if you compromise your principles or your beliefs, you do something that is against them

compromise + NOUNS

compromise your principles *The government says the plans will not compromise its environmental principles.*

compromise your integrity *The journalist would not compromise his integrity by revealing the source of the information.*

compromise your beliefs/convictions/ideals *Protesters were put in prison for refusing to compromise their beliefs.*

compromise your standards *Universities should not have to compromise their academic standards.*

PHRASES

compromise on safety/security *The company had compromised on safety in order to save money.*

compromise on quality *We're trying to reduce the prices of our goods without compromising on quality.*

compulsory *adj*

if something is compulsory, you must do it, because of a law or rule, or because someone in authority orders you to do it

VERBS

make sth compulsory *The government is planning to make the test compulsory.*

NOUNS

compulsory attendance *Attendance is compulsory for all students.*

compulsory education *Compulsory education was first introduced in England in 1870.*

compulsory retirement *She works for an organisation that has a compulsory retirement age of 65.*

compulsory military service *All men are obliged to do two years' compulsory military service.*

compulsory testing *Experts argue that compulsory testing of all cattle for the disease is unnecessary.*

PHRASES

it is compulsory for sb to do sth *Since 1983 it has been compulsory for car drivers to wear seat belts.*

THESAURUS: compulsory

obligatory

if something is obligatory, you must do it because of a rule or law. **Obligatory** is more formal than **compulsory**:

***It is obligatory for** all drivers to have car insurance.* | ***It is obligatory to** pay tax on imported goods.* | *The new regulations **made it obligatory for** students to do physical exercises before classes.* | *Shaving was obligatory.*

Obligatory is not usually used before a noun.

mandatory

sentence | **penalty** | **limit** | **ban** | **requirement** | **retirement age** | **testing**

if something is mandatory, you must do it because it is the law. **Mandatory** is more formal than **compulsory** or **obligatory** and sounds stronger:

There is a mandatory sentence of life in prison for murder (=a punishment in which someone must stay in prison for a period of time). | *There will be mandatory limits on carbon emissions.* | *Companies have a mandatory requirement to provide a safe working environment.* | *Helmets are **mandatory for** cyclists in some countries.*

computer Ac *n*

an electronic machine that stores and handles information

ADJECTIVES/NOUNS + computer

a powerful/fast computer *He decided he needed a more powerful computer.*

a home/personal computer *Most of the children have a home computer.*

a computer is down (=is not working) *I can't give you that information because the computer is down.*

a computer is slow *Why is the computer so slow today?*

VERBS + computer

switch on/off a computer (*also* **turn on/off a computer**) *Always switch off your computer at the end of the day.*

log onto a computer (=start using it by typing a password) *Next time you log onto your computer, you will have to use a new password.*

start up/boot up a computer (=make it start working) *He sat down at his desk and booted up his computer.*

shut down a computer (=close the programs and make it stop working until you need to use it again) *I saved the file and shut down the computer.*

program a computer (=give it instructions so that it will do a particular job) *You can program a computer to pay your monthly bills.*

download sth onto a computer (=move it from the internet onto your computer) *I downloaded the video onto my computer.*

hold/store sth on a computer *This data is all held on a central computer.*

computer + VERBS

a computer crashes/goes down (=suddenly stops working) *My computer crashed and I lost all the work I'd done.*

computer + NOUNS

a computer screen/monitor *Make sure your computer screen is at the right height.*

a computer game *Kids love playing computer games.*

a computer system/network *Our office is installing a new computer system.*

a computer program *At school, we're learning how to write simple computer programs.*

computer software (=computer programs)

computer technology *Advances in computer technology have changed the way people work.*

a computer programmer (=someone who writes the instructions a computer uses to do a particular job) *He is looking for work as a computer programmer.*

a computer language (=a system of instructions used to program a computer) *You need to be able to use computer languages such as Java.*

a computer error *The mistake was caused by a computer error.*

PREPOSITIONS

on (a) computer *We have all that information on computer now.*

> Instead of saying that you 'work on a computer', you often say that you **work on screen**.

concentrate Ac *v*

1 to think very carefully about something that you are doing

ADVERBS

concentrate hard/intensely *I concentrated hard on what he was telling me.*

concentrate fully/totally *He closed his eyes so he could concentrate fully.*

concentrate only on sth *Try to concentrate only on the music, and not on the words.*

PREPOSITIONS

concentrate on sth *It's difficult to concentrate on one thing for longer than an hour.*

VERBS

try to concentrate *Please can you be quiet – I'm trying to concentrate.*

PHRASES

find it difficult to concentrate *I find it difficult to concentrate if I sit by the window.*

find it impossible to concentrate *She finds it impossible to concentrate when people are talking.*

be unable to concentrate *If the radio is on, I'm completely unable to concentrate.*

2 to give most of your attention or effort to one thing

NOUNS

concentrate your efforts *Tackle one problem at a time, so you can concentrate your efforts.*

concentrate your attention *I tried to concentrate my attention on what the teacher was saying.*

concentrate your energy *She decided to continue to concentrate her energies on what she knew best.*

concentrate resources *We identify the areas of greatest need so we know where to concentrate resources.*

concentrate your mind *It took a lot of effort to concentrate his mind that morning.*

ADVERBS

concentrate solely/exclusively on sth (=only on it) *In future the company will concentrate exclusively on the luxury market.*

concentrate mainly/primarily on sth *To begin with, we concentrated mainly on short-term objectives.*

PREPOSITIONS

concentrate your efforts/attention/energies etc on sth *It would be better to concentrate your thoughts on your immediate problems.*

concentration Ac *n*

the ability to think about something carefully or for a long time

ADJECTIVES

deep/intense concentration *The work of a surgeon demands intense concentration.*

total/absolute/utter concentration *There was a look of total concentration on her face.*

poor concentration *The girl behaved badly in class and suffered from poor concentration.*

VERBS

sth takes/demands/requires concentration (=needs concentration) *Playing a musical instrument takes a lot of concentration.*

lose (your) concentration *Halfway through the game, he seemed to lose concentration.*

break/disturb/affect sb's concentration (=stop someone concentrating) *The telephone rang and broke my concentration.*

increase/improve sb's concentration *Getting enough sleep will improve your concentration.*

concentration + NOUNS

concentration span (=the length of time that you are able to concentrate) *Young children have a short concentration span.*

PHRASES

powers of concentration (=the ability to concentrate) *The best athletes have great powers of concentration.*

a lapse in/of concentration (=a short time when you do not concentrate) *Their brief lapse of concentration allowed the other team to score.*

concept Ac *n*

an idea of what something is, or how something should be done

ADJECTIVES

a basic/fundamental concept *The children learn the basic concepts of mathematics.*

a key/central/important concept *The title tells you something about the central concept of the poem.*

a difficult concept *Difficult concepts can sometimes be explained with diagrams or graphs.*

a simple concept *Cause and effect is a fairly simple concept.*

an abstract concept *He finds it hard to grasp abstract concepts.*

a legal/mathematical/political etc concept *The right to remain silent is a very important legal concept.*

a general/broad concept *The book begins with some general historical concepts.*

a theoretical concept *The theoretical concepts of psychology are also useful in the study of literature.*

a vague/ambiguous concept (=one that is not clear or is hard to define) *Trust is rather a vague concept.*

a clear concept *When I paint, I have a very clear concept of what I am trying to communicate.*

VERBS

understand/grasp a concept *The class will help you grasp the basic concepts of physics.*

have no concept of sth *Young children have no concept of the value of money.*

define a concept *First, we need to define the concept of reasonable force.*

examine/explore a concept *In his book, Sartre explores the concept of individual freedom.*

explain a concept *Please can you explain the concept of 'a just war'?*

develop a concept *The Greeks developed the concept of democracy.*

PREPOSITIONS

the concept of sth *They do not understand the concept of social class.*

concern *n*

1 a feeling of worry about something, or something that makes you worried

ADJECTIVES

great/considerable concern *The spread of the disease is an issue of considerable concern.*

deep/serious/grave concern *There is deep concern about the proposals among local people.*

widespread concern (=among many people) *There is widespread concern about the state of our hospitals.*

public concern *The government is ignoring public concern about the safety of nuclear energy.*

real/genuine concern *His teachers expressed real concern about his behaviour.*

sb's main/major/biggest concern *The aid workers' main concern is the lack of clean drinking water.*

growing/increasing/mounting concern *Growing concern has been expressed over pollution in the North Sea.*

a legitimate concern (=a reasonable thing to be worried about) *Voters have legitimate concerns about the level of taxes.*

VERBS

cause/raise concern *The announcement will cause concern in the Arab World. | The incident has raised concern over safety at the power station.*

feel concern/have concerns about sth *He had some concerns about his health.*

share sb's concern *We share your concern about the lack of training.*

express/voice concern (=say that you are

C

worried) *He expressed concern that the incident would harm the UK's image abroad.*

raise your concerns (=mention something that is worrying you) *He intends to raise his concerns at the next staff meeting.*

allay sb's concern(s) *formal* (=make someone feel less worried) *The head teacher attempted to allay parents' concerns.*

NOUNS + concern

security/safety/health concerns *The airport was closed because of safety concerns.*

PREPOSITIONS

concern about/over sth (*also* **concern regarding sth**) *The president expressed concern over the situation.*

concern for/to sb *The high cost of living is a concern for many people.*

PHRASES

a cause for concern *Rising global temperatures are a cause for serious concern.*

a matter/issue/area of concern *The long hours worked by hospital doctors have been a matter of concern for many years.*

2 something that is important to you or that involves you

PHRASES

sth is not sb's concern (*also* **sth is none of sb's concern**) *His personal life is not my concern.*

be of concern to sb (=to interest or involve someone) *Politicians should focus on issues that are of concern to the public.*

ADJECTIVES

sb's main/biggest concern *Their main concern is to make money.*

sb's primary/chief/principal concern (=main concern - more formal) *The president said his primary concern was the welfare of the American people.*

sb's only/sole concern *Rick's only concern was having a good time at the weekend.*

sb's present/immediate concern *Her two immediate concerns were to find a home and a job.*

sb's overriding concern (=much more important than anything else) *As an artist, his overriding concern is to communicate.*

3 a feeling of wanting someone to be happy and healthy

ADJECTIVES

genuine concern *He showed a genuine concern for the welfare of his crew.*

tender/loving concern *I want to thank my parents for their loving concern.*

VERBS

show/demonstrate concern *He had not shown the slightest concern for her.*

PREPOSITIONS

concern for sb/sth *She had great concern for the poor.*

out of concern for sb/sth *He had sent his children abroad out of concern for their safety.*

PHRASES

concern for sb's health/welfare/safety *My employers had no concern for my safety.*

concerned *adj*

1 worried about something

ADVERBS

very/deeply/extremely concerned *She is deeply concerned about her son's behaviour.*

increasingly concerned *The girl has been missing for five days, and her family are becoming increasingly concerned.*

particularly concerned *Hotel owners are particularly concerned about the impact on tourism.*

naturally/understandably concerned (=used when you can understand the reasons why someone is concerned) *Local people are naturally concerned about pollution from the factory.*

PREPOSITIONS

concerned about sb/sth *She's concerned about her father. | We are very concerned about the current situation.*

concerned at/by sth *The authorities are deeply concerned by the increase in violence.*

concerned for sb/sb's safety *His family are all very concerned for him.*

2 caring about something and thinking that it is important

ADVERBS

mainly/primarily concerned *The organization is mainly concerned with protecting the rights of its members.*

solely/exclusively concerned (=only concerned) *We are solely concerned with finding out the truth.*

genuinely concerned *He seems genuinely concerned about our problems.*

PREPOSITIONS

concerned with/about sth *She is too concerned with her appearance.*

concert *n*

a performance given by musicians or singers

ADJECTIVES/NOUNS + concert

a pop/rock/jazz/classical concert *There were 150,000 people at the rock concert in Frankfurt.*

an orchestral concert/a symphony concert (=one in which an orchestra plays) *Tickets for orchestral concerts range from $15 to $35.*

a live concert (=that people are there to watch

and listen to) *Attending a live concert is more exciting than listening to a CD.*

an open-air/outdoor concert *He is playing a big outdoor concert in Hyde Park next week.*

VERBS

go to a concert (*also* **attend a concert** *formal*): *I love music and often go to concerts.*

give/do a concert *The group gave concerts for charity throughout Europe.*

play/perform a concert *The band still plays 100 concerts a year.*

put on a concert (*also* **stage a concert** *formal*) (=arrange one) *The music club puts on regular concerts throughout the year.*

concert + NOUNS

a concert performance *She gave a number of concert performances in Berlin.*

a concert hall *On the last night, the concert hall was packed.*

concession *n*

something that you agree to in order to end a disagreement

ADJECTIVES

a major/important concession *We made some major concessions in order to reach an agreement.*

a further concession *Britain agreed to further concessions.*

a minor/small concession *Washington made a few minor concessions in the climate talks.*

a significant/substantial concession *This offer was viewed as a significant concession.*

a political concession *The mayor was forced to make some political concessions.*

VERBS

make a concession *The government made some concessions in order to get the law passed.*

offer a concession *The king was prepared to offer some concessions to France.*

win/obtain/gain a concession *In the end, the strikers returned to work having won few concessions.*

extract a concession from sb (*also* **wring a concession from sb**) (=make someone give you one) *They failed to extract significant concessions from the government.*

PREPOSITIONS

a concession on sth *The company made some concessions on pay.*

a concession to sb *This reversal of policy represented a significant concession to the opposition.*

a concession by/from sb *We cannot reach a solution without concessions from all sides.*

concise *adj* THESAURUS **short (3)**

conclude *v* THESAURUS **finish[1] (1)**

concluding *determiner* THESAURUS **last[1] (1)**

conclusion Ac *n*

something you decide after considering all the information you have

ADJECTIVES

the same/a similar conclusion *The two teams of scientists reached the same conclusion.*

a different/the opposite conclusion *A lot of scientific evidence supports the opposite conclusion.*

the right/correct conclusion *I am sure that you came to the right conclusion.*

the wrong/an incorrect conclusion *Reporters saw the couple together and leapt to the wrong conclusion.*

an obvious conclusion *The conclusion was obvious: he had stolen the money.*

the inescapable/inevitable conclusion (=one that is very obvious, although you may not like it) *The inescapable conclusion was that the country needed a change of leadership.*

the logical conclusion *The logical conclusion is that short commercials are just as effective as longer ones.*

a firm/definite conclusion *We still haven't reached a firm conclusion about what to do.*

a hasty conclusion (=one that you reach too quickly) *We must not leap to hasty conclusions on the basis of one study.*

a surprising/startling conclusion *After years of research, he reached the startling conclusion that Einstein's theory was wrong.*

VERBS

come to/arrive at/reach a conclusion *I came to the conclusion that I would never be a writer.*

draw a conclusion (=decide something from what you learn or see) *We tried not to draw any conclusions too early in the investigation.*

jump to/leap to a conclusion (=decide without knowing all the facts) *Everyone jumped to the conclusion that we would get married.*

base a conclusion on sth *Your conclusion is based on a rather small sample.*

lead to/point to a conclusion (=make you decide that something is true) *All the facts point to only one conclusion.*

support/reinforce a conclusion *This evidence supports the conclusion that his death was an accident.*

condemn *v*

to say publicly and very strongly that you do not approve of something

ADVERBS

strongly/roundly condemn sth *The president strongly condemned the attack.*

be widely condemned (=by many people or groups) *The laws have been widely condemned by human rights groups.*

vehemently/vigorously/fiercely condemn sth (=in a very strong or angry way) *Teachers have* *vehemently condemned the changes to the education system.*

utterly/totally/unequivocally condemn sth (=very definitely and with no doubts) *We utterly condemn any acts of terrorism.*

publicly/openly condemn sth *Army officers openly condemned the war.*

unanimously condemn sth (=all members of a group condemn something) *The committee unanimously condemned his remarks.*

be rightly condemned by sb *The attack has been rightly condemned by world leaders.*

PREPOSITIONS

condemn sth as sth *The move was condemned as a waste of time.*

condemn sb for (doing) sth *Farmers have condemned the government for doing too little too late.*

condition *n*

1 the state that something is in

PHRASES

in bad/poor/terrible condition *Some of these old buildings are in terrible condition.*

in good/excellent condition *She keeps her hair in good condition.*

in reasonable condition (=quite good) *The car is in reasonable condition, considering its age.*

in perfect condition *The goods were in perfect condition when they left the factory.*

in mint/pristine/immaculate condition (=as good as when it was new) *A copy of this book in mint condition is very valuable.*

2 the state that someone is in

ADJECTIVES

sb's physical/mental condition *I am very concerned about his mental condition.*

a serious/critical condition *Doctors described the injured man's condition as serious.*

a satisfactory/comfortable condition *His life was in danger at one point, although his condition is now satisfactory.*

a stable condition (=not getting worse) *He is in a serious but stable condition.*

VERBS

sb's condition improves *Her condition is improving, but she remains seriously ill.*

sb's condition deteriorates/worsens *His condition deteriorated, and he died yesterday.*

sb's condition stabilizes (=stops getting worse) *After his condition stabilized, he was transferred to St Andrew's Hospital.*

3 the situation somewhere, especially when someone is doing something

> **Grammar**
> Always plural in this meaning.

ADJECTIVES

good conditions/the right conditions *In the right conditions, cooking can be very enjoyable.*

ideal/perfect conditions *Conditions were ideal for diving.*

bad/poor conditions *The game was stopped because of the poor conditions.*

difficult conditions *She played well in spite of the difficult conditions.*

appalling/dreadful conditions (=very bad) *The prisoners were being kept in appalling conditions.*

normal conditions *Under normal conditions, there shouldn't be a problem.*

cold/wet/windy etc conditions *It's not easy playing golf in windy conditions.*

overcrowded/crowded conditions *The families are living in dirty overcrowded conditions.*

NOUNS + condition

weather conditions *The rescue was delayed because of the extreme weather conditions.*

working conditions *A factory must provide safe working conditions.*

living/housing conditions *Living conditions in the camp were appalling.*

driving/road conditions *Drivers should take care because road conditions are very bad, with ice and fog.*

VERBS

conditions improve *Economic conditions are improving.*

conditions get worse (*also* **conditions deteriorate** *formal*): *The weather conditions deteriorated until the rescue workers were forced to stop.*

PREPOSITIONS

in ... conditions *They live in very cold conditions.*

under ... conditions *The doctors are having to work under terrible conditions.*

PHRASES

in/under laboratory conditions *The test was carried out under laboratory conditions.*

in/under controlled conditions *All this work must be done under carefully controlled conditions.*

4 something that you must agree to in order for something to happen

ADJECTIVES

a strict condition *The US agreed to give financial aid, with a number of strict conditions.*

VERBS

lay down/set/impose conditions (=say that something must happen before you agree to do something) *They laid down certain conditions before agreeing to the ceasefire.*

agree to/accept conditions *He refused to accept the conditions set by union leaders.*

meet/satisfy/fulfil a condition (=be or do what has been agreed) *In order to get a state pension, you must satisfy certain conditions.*

comply with/observe a condition (=act according to a condition) *You must agree to comply with the bank's conditions before you can get a loan.*

PHRASES

the terms and conditions (=what a contract says must be done) *Before you buy online, make sure you read the terms and conditions.*

on condition that *formal*: *The police released him on condition that he return the following week.*

on one condition *You can go, but only on one condition – you must be back by eleven.*

on certain conditions *He said we could rent the house from him on certain conditions.*

5 a health problem that someone has for a long time

ADJECTIVES/NOUNS + condition

a medical condition *She has an unusual medical condition.*

a heart/lung/skin etc condition *I'm taking some medicine for a heart condition.*

a common condition *Depression is a very common condition.*

a rare condition *He had a rare condition which made all his hair fall out.*

an incurable condition *I'm afraid the condition is incurable.*

a genetic/hereditary condition (=that is passed from parent to child) *The disease is a genetic condition that eventually causes blindness.*

a life-threatening condition (=that may cause death) *The surgery repaired a potentially life-threatening heart condition.*

a chronic condition (=that continues for a long time and cannot be cured) *People with chronic medical conditions need long-term care.*

VERBS

have a condition *The baby has a rare skin condition.*

suffer from a condition *He has suffered from this condition for many years.*

conduct[1] Ac *v formal* to do something

NOUNS

conduct research *He's conducting educational research at the University of Washington.*

conduct a test/experiment *Investigators will be conducting tests to determine how the man died.*

conduct a study/review *Scientists conducted a study of the area affected by the disaster.*

conduct a survey/poll *She is conducting a survey to see what shops people want in the area.*

conduct an investigation/inquiry *Experts conducted an investigation into the causes of the crash.*

conduct a search *The authorities conducted a nationwide search for the girl.*

conduct an interview *Here are a few guidelines on how to conduct an interview.*

conduct a campaign *The party was criticized for the way it had conducted its election campaign.*

conduct your affairs (=organize your activities) *We have no right to tell them how to conduct their affairs.*

conduct business *The company had been conducting a lot of business in Latin America.*

PHRASES

conduct sth in accordance with sth *He said the elections had been conducted in accordance with the rules.*

Conduct is a formal word. In everyday English, people usually say **do** or **carry out**: *I've* ***done*** *a lot of research into this.* | *We need to* ***carry out*** *some more tests.*

THESAURUS: conduct

make, give, take, commit, carry out, conduct, perform, undertake, implement → **do**

conduct Ac *n formal*

the way someone behaves, especially in public or in their job

ADJECTIVES

good conduct *One boy was given a book as a reward for good conduct.*

bad/disgraceful conduct *I thought the other team's conduct was disgraceful.*

improper/inappropriate conduct (=not acceptable) *There was no evidence of improper conduct on the part of the police.*

unprofessional conduct (=not acceptable for someone in a particular job) *Members of the Institute can be suspended or expelled for unprofessional conduct.*

moral conduct *Children should be taught about the basic rules of moral conduct.*

ethical conduct (=concerning the way people should be treated) *Standards of ethical conduct have got worse.*

professional conduct (=by someone when they are doing their job) *There are strict rules that regulate lawyers' professional conduct.*

disorderly conduct (=behaving in a noisy or violent way in public) *Her husband was arrested for drunkenness and disorderly conduct.*

PHRASES

a code of conduct (=a set of rules stating how you must behave) *All professions have a code of conduct.*

rules/standards of conduct *In war, there are established rules of conduct.*

confer *v* THESAURUS give (1)

conference Ac *n*

a large formal meeting where a lot of people discuss an important subject

ADJECTIVES/NOUNS + conference

a world/international conference *She spoke at an international conference on human rights.*

a national/regional conference *The teachers' national conference will start next week.*

an annual conference *It is the biggest annual conference for people who work in the advertising industry.*

a peace conference *The two sides agreed to hold a peace conference.*

a sales conference *He was looking forward to the company's annual sales conference.*

a party conference (=for a political party) *The prime minister will give a speech at the party conference.*

a summit conference (=for the leaders of governments) *The heads of the Arab states met in Amman for a summit conference.*

VERBS

go to a conference (*also* **attend a conference** *formal*): *Over 500 scientists attended the conference.*

hold a conference *The dentists' annual conference was held in Chicago.*

host a conference (=have it in your country, city, university etc) *In June, Japan hosted a peace conference.*

organize a conference *The administration organized a conference on Africa.*

chair a conference (=be the person who is in charge and introduces the speakers) *The conference was chaired by Professor James Murray.*

address a conference (=give a speech at a conference) *He received a warm welcome when he addressed the conference.*

conference + NOUNS

a conference centre *BrE*, **a conference center** *AmE*: *The conference centre is about a mile from the station.*

a conference hall *Thousands of people demonstrated outside the conference hall.*

a conference delegate *Most of the conference delegates were staying at the same hotel.*

PREPOSITIONS

a conference on sth *She is attending a conference on linguistics.*

at a conference *There were over 10,000 people at the conference.*

confession *n*

a statement in which you admit that you have done something wrong, illegal, or embarrassing

ADJECTIVES

a full confession *The killer had made a full confession to the authorities.*

a written confession *His written confession was produced as evidence.*

a false confession *She made a false confession to protect her son.*

VERBS

make a confession *He made a confession after he was arrested.*

sign a confession *He had signed a confession in front of witnesses.*

retract a confession (=say that a confession you made was not true) *Though he had confessed to the police, Gerrards later retracted his confession.*

get/obtain a confession *Threats must not be used in order to obtain confessions.*

extract a confession (=get one with difficulty, or by using force) *Confessions extracted under torture are unreliable.*

PHRASES

have a confession (to make) (=used humorously when you want to admit to doing something) *I have a confession to make – I've eaten all the chocolates.*

a confession of guilt *If I say I was there when the robbery happened, it could be seen as a confession of guilt.*

a confession of weakness/ignorance *I was touched by his confession of weakness.*

confidence *n*

1 belief in your own ability to do things well

VERBS + confidence

have confidence *As a teenager, she didn't have a lot of confidence.*

give sb confidence *I had really good teachers who gave me confidence in myself.*

boost/increase sb's confidence (=make someone feel more confident) *One of my stories was published, which really boosted my confidence.*

lose (your) confidence *He started to lose his confidence in his abilities as a singer.*

lack confidence (*also* **be lacking in confidence**) *Beth lacked the confidence to talk to people she didn't know.*

gain confidence (*also* **grow/gain in confidence**) (=become more confident) *He's gaining in confidence now that he's enjoying some success.*

exude/radiate confidence *formal* (=show it in a very noticeable way) *As the leader, you have to exude confidence and authority.*

be brimming with confidence (=have a lot of confidence) *His opponent was brimming with confidence.*

destroy/shatter sb's confidence *When she failed her degree, it shattered her confidence.*

build up sb's confidence (=gradually increase it) *When you've had an accident, it takes a while to build up your confidence again.*

undermine/shake/dent sb's confidence (=make it less strong) *A bad experience like that can undermine your confidence.*

ADJECTIVES

quiet/cool/calm confidence (=confidence that is strong but not shown in an obvious way) *She has a quiet confidence that other players admire.*

unshakeable/unwavering confidence *formal* (=so strong that nothing can reduce it) *We were impressed by his unshakeable confidence.*

confidence + VERBS

sb's confidence grows/increases *Since she started her new school, her confidence has grown a lot.*

sb's confidence goes (=they stop being confident) *She made a series of mistakes and her confidence went.*

confidence + NOUNS

a confidence boost/booster *They offered me the job immediately, which was a real confidence boost.*

confidence building (=making it develop) *Training for a big match is all about confidence building.*

PREPOSITIONS

with confidence *She speaks with great confidence and audiences like her.*

PHRASES

be full of confidence (=have a lot of confidence) *The team are full of confidence after winning their last three games.*

a lack of confidence *She suffers from a lack of confidence and she hates giving talks.*

a loss of confidence *The team were suffering from a loss of confidence.*

2 the feeling that you can trust someone or something to do something well

ADJECTIVES

great confidence *She has great confidence in her doctors.*

little/no confidence *He had little confidence in the government.*

public confidence *The changes should improve public confidence in the system.*

NOUNS + confidence

business confidence (=the feeling in business that the economic situation is good) *The region has gained 46,000 jobs and business confidence is high.*

investor/market confidence (=the feeling of investors that the economic situation is good) *A fall in the value of shares damages investor confidence.*

consumer confidence (=the feeling among ordinary people that the economic situation is good) *Consumer confidence has fallen to its lowest for two years.*

customer confidence (=people's feeling that they can trust a company or a type of goods or service) *It is hoped that the new regulations will increase customer confidence in internet shopping.*

VERBS + confidence

have confidence *I had no confidence at all that they would do anything about my problem.*

lose confidence *Employees are losing confidence in the company.*

gain/win sb's confidence *As team captain, he soon won the confidence of the players.*

inspire/breed confidence (=make people have confidence) *We need an education system that inspires public confidence.*

restore/rebuild confidence (=make people have confidence again) *A few victories would restore the fans' confidence.*

boost confidence (=make people have more confidence) *The government's decision was intended to boost consumer confidence.*

shake/undermine sb's confidence (=make them have less confidence) *The low value of the stock market has shaken the confidence of investors.*

destroy/shatter confidence in sb/sth *The scandal destroyed public confidence in the bank.*

express confidence in sb/sth (=say or show that you have confidence) *The teacher expressed confidence in her ability to pass the exam.*

confidence + VERBS

confidence falls (*also* **confidence wanes/declines** *formal*) (=people become less confident) *Since the election, confidence in the party has waned.*

confidence increases/rises (*also* **confidence soars** *formal*): *A positive financial report made confidence in the company soar.*

PREPOSITIONS

confidence in sb/sth *Public confidence in politicians has never been lower.*

confidence among people *These results reveal a lack of confidence among voters.*

confidence about sth *They are full of confidence about the future.*

say/predict/state etc with confidence *We can now say with confidence that this is going to be the company's best ever year.*

PHRASES

have every/complete/absolute confidence (=be very confident) *The head teacher has complete confidence in his staff.*

a lack of confidence *Among the team, there is clearly a lack of confidence in the manager.*

a crisis of confidence (=a situation in which people no longer have confidence) *We are seeing a crisis of confidence over food safety.*

a vote of confidence (=a sign that people are confident) *The decision to build the factory in Britain is a vote of confidence for the UK economy.*

C

C

confident *adj*

1 sure that you have the ability to do things well or deal with situations successfully

ADVERBS

extremely/supremely confident *When she climbed up on to the stage, she looked supremely confident.*

VERBS

look confident *It is important to try to look confident at a job interview.*

feel confident *I've always been shy, and I wish I felt more confident.*

NOUNS

a confident smile *She gave Jack a confident smile.*

a confident voice *He read his speech in a strong confident voice.*

PHRASES

confident in your ability *He was very confident in his own abilities.*

confident in yourself *They try to make young people feel more confident in themselves.*

2 sure that something will happen in the way that you want or expect

VERBS

feel confident *We feel confident that the project will be a success.*

remain confident *He remains confident about the company's long-term future.*

sound/seem confident *His agent sounded confident that a deal would be worked out.*

NOUNS

a confident mood *The team are in a very confident mood after their win last night.*

a confident prediction *It is hard to make a confident prediction about the economy.*

ADVERBS

reasonably/fairly/pretty confident *I'm fairly confident that they'll get married eventually.*

completely confident *Police were completely confident that they had found the right man.*

quietly confident (=sure in your mind that you can succeed, even though you do not tell everyone about it) *They were quietly confident of winning the game.*

PREPOSITIONS

confident of (doing) sth *The president was confident of winning the election.*

confident about sth *I feel quite confident about the future.*

PHRASES

confident in the knowledge that *You can buy this car, confident in the knowledge that it has everything you will need.*

confidential *adj* THESAURUS ➤ **secret**[1]

conflict Ac *n* arguments or fights

VERBS

cause/create/provoke/lead to conflict *Worries about their child caused conflict within their marriage.*

resolve/end/settle a conflict *Legal advice may be needed to resolve a conflict between neighbours.*

avoid/avert/prevent a conflict *The prime minister wants to avoid a conflict over the issue.*

a conflict begins (*also* **a conflict arises/erupts** *formal*): *When conflict arises, try to remain calm.*

a conflict escalates/intensifies *formal* (=gets worse) *If the conflict intensifies, war could break out.*

ADJECTIVES

bloody/violent conflict (=involving violence) *The attack was followed by a bloody conflict that lasted for months.*

bitter conflict (=very angry) *The new tax provoked bitter conflict.*

political/social conflict *Widespread unemployment often leads to social conflict.*

armed/military conflict *We are concerned about the use of children in armed conflicts.*

conflict + NOUNS

conflict resolution (=finding a way to end a conflict) *It's important to teach children methods of conflict resolution.*

PREPOSITIONS

conflict with sb *They were engaged in a conflict with a neighbouring region.*

conflict between people *There was angry conflict between members of the party.*

conflict over/about sth *A conflict over pay is likely.*

PHRASES

come into conflict with sb *Local people have come into conflict with planning officials over plans for a new road.*

bring sb into conflict with sb *Her aggressive manner has brought her into conflict with managers.*

a source of conflict *Lack of money is often a source of conflict between husband and wife.*

an area of conflict (=a subject that causes conflict) *One potential area of conflict is where exactly to build the new store.*

confrontation *n*

an angry argument or a fight

ADJECTIVES

direct/open confrontation (=very angry disagreements) *The decision to strike brought workers into open confrontation with management.*

major confrontation *Political differences are a source of major confrontation.*

a violent/physical confrontation *Several people died in violent confrontations between rival gangs.*

armed/military confrontation *Politicians are working hard to avoid military confrontation in the region.*

VERBS

avoid (a) confrontation *I knew she was upset, and I wanted to avoid confrontation with her if at all possible.*

lead to (a) confrontation (*also* **provoke a confrontation** *more formal*): *His unpleasant behaviour seemed deliberately intended to provoke a confrontation.*

get into a confrontation *He didn't want to get into a confrontation with the soldiers.*

bring/lead sb into confrontation *His strong opinions on religion would often lead him into confrontation.*

PREPOSITIONS

confrontation with sb *The event brought protesters into direct confrontation with police.*

confrontation between sb and sb *There was an armed confrontation between the rebels and government forces.*

confrontation about/over sth *There were sometimes confrontations about money.*

confused *adj*

unable to understand or think clearly about what someone is saying or what is happening

VERBS

get/become confused *Because she is old, she gets confused from time to time.*

feel confused *When he read the instructions again, he felt more confused than ever.*

look/seem/appear confused *The waitress spoke to him in Italian, and he replied in English. She looked completely confused.*

remain confused *Many voters remain confused about the party's policies.*

leave sb confused *The book contains so much information that it can leave you feeling rather confused.*

ADVERBS

totally/completely/utterly confused *Polly stared at him, totally confused.*

hopelessly confused (=used when emphasizing that someone is completely confused and does not know what to do) *Now he was hopelessly confused and lost.*

somewhat confused/a little confused *I was somewhat confused by this statement.*

NOUNS

a confused state *Dirk was wandering around in a confused state.*

a confused expression/look *"What do I do now?" she asked with a confused expression.*

confused thoughts *His mind was full of confused thoughts.*

PREPOSITIONS

confused about sth *Customers are often confused about which product to choose.*

confused by sth *I was rather confused by his question.*

PHRASES

dazed and confused (=confused and unable to think clearly, especially because you have just had a big shock) *She got out of the car looking dazed and confused.*

confusing *adj*

unclear and difficult to understand

VERBS

find sth confusing *Many people find the new tax forms confusing.*

make sth confusing *To make matters more confusing, the two girls both have the same name.*

sth gets/becomes confusing *The film gets confusing towards the end.*

NOUNS

a confusing situation *The change in rules has created a very confusing situation.*

confusing messages/signals *We get confusing messages about what kinds of foods are healthy or unhealthy.*

a confusing mixture *She had a confusing mixture of feelings.*

a confusing mess/jumble *The website was a confusing mess.*

a confusing array of sth (=a confusing range of different things) *There is a confusing array of products to choose from.*

ADVERBS

extremely/highly confusing *The way the report is written is highly confusing.*

rather/somewhat/slightly confusing *The layout of the store is rather confusing if you've never been there before.*

PREPOSITIONS

confusing to/for sb *Product labels are often confusing for shoppers.*

THESAURUS: confusing

puzzling (*also* **perplexing** *formal*)
if something is puzzling, it seems confusing or difficult to understand, especially because it is different from what you expect:
I ***found*** *the ending of the book rather* ***puzzling****. | The results of these experiments were, to say the least,* ***puzzling to*** *the researchers. | Gandhi presented a* ***deeply perplexing problem*** *to the British authorities in India.*

baffling
case | mystery
extremely difficult to understand, even though you try for a long time:

Police are close to solving one of Australia's most baffling murder cases. | *This is one of science's most baffling mysteries.* | *Westerners often **find** the Japanese writing system **utterly baffling*** (=completely baffling).

bewildering
number | **variety** | **range** | **array** | **choice** | **experience** | **complexity**
extremely confusing, especially because there are so many different things:
There is a bewildering number of books on the subject. | *The geologist is faced with a bewildering array of rock types* (=a lot of different rock types). | *The bewildering complexity of the tax system causes problems for many people.*

C

Collocations of words meaning **confusing**
If something seems confusing to you, you say that you **find** it **confusing/puzzling/perplexing/baffling/bewildering**.
Instead of saying that something is very confusing, you can say that it is **deeply puzzling/perplexing**, **utterly baffling** or, **utterly bewildering**.

confusion *n*

when you do not understand what is happening or what something means

ADJECTIVES

great confusion (*also* **considerable confusion**) *The movie jumps around in time, which causes considerable confusion.*

complete/total/utter confusion *The child's face showed total confusion.*

general/widespread confusion *There is general confusion about how the new rules will operate.*

understandable confusion *Different groups received different advice, which led to understandable confusion.*

VERBS + confusion

cause/create confusion *English spelling often causes confusion for learners.*

lead to/result in confusion *Different sets of instructions led to confusion.*

add to the confusion (=make something more confusing) *There were a lot of rumours, which added to the confusion.*

throw/plunge sb into confusion (=make someone very confused) *The unexpected news threw us all into confusion.*

clear up the confusion (=explain something more clearly) *More accurate information would help to clear up the confusion.*

avoid/prevent confusion *Try to avoid confusion by giving simple advice.*

confusion + VERBS

confusion arises (=starts to exist) *The confusion arose because we both have the same name.*

confusion reigns (=there is a lot of confusion) *Confusion reigned, with nobody understanding what they were supposed to do.*

PREPOSITIONS

confusion over/about sth (*also* **confusion as to sth**) *The party cannot blame voters for the confusion over its policies.*

confusion among people *There's considerable confusion among parents about the school's rules on uniform.*

PHRASES

a state of confusion *They were in a state of confusion because of unclear advice.*

to avoid (any) confusion *To avoid any confusion, let me state exactly what my views are.*

the confusion surrounding sth *There is a lot of confusion among shoppers surrounding new food labels.*

a source of confusion (=something that confuses people) *A possible source of confusion is that the two words sound very similar.*

congested *adj* THESAURUS **busy (2)**

Congress *n*

the group of people elected to make laws for the US, consisting of the Senate and the House of Representatives

VERBS

Congress votes *Congress voted to go to war.*

Congress passes a bill/law/amendment *Congress passed a law making this practice illegal.*

Congress approves/authorizes sth *Last month Congress approved a $100 million aid package.*

Congress considers sth *Congress is considering new legislation.*

Congress rejects sth *Congress rejected the bill.*

Congress convenes (=meets) *The new Congress will convene in January.*

Congress adjourns (=takes a break) *Congress adjourned in the fall.*

sb is elected to Congress *He was first elected to Congress in 1994.*

a party controls Congress/has control of Congress *The Democrats still control Congress.*

PREPOSITIONS

in Congress *Democrats in Congress have proposed alternative plans.*

PHRASES

a member of Congress *They are trying to persuade members of Congress to vote 'No'.*

both houses of Congress (=the Senate and the House of Representatives) *The bill must be approved by two-thirds of both houses of Congress.*

a session of Congress *He promised to change the law during the next session of Congress.*

an act of Congress *The organization was created by an act of Congress in 1991.*

a seat in Congress *She won a seat in Congress in 2008.*

connection *n*

a relationship between facts, ideas, events, or people

ADJECTIVES

a direct connection *Poverty has a direct connection with ill health.*

a close connection (*also* **an intimate connection** *formal*): *She sees a close connection between maths and music.*

a clear/obvious connection *There is an obvious connection between this painting and his earlier works.*

a strong connection *I still feel a strong connection with the country where I was born.*

a loose connection (*also* **a tenuous connection** *formal*) (=not strong, close, or obvious) *There seemed to be only a loose connection between the questions and the answers.*

VERBS

have a connection *Police do not think the two murders have any connection.*

see a connection *It's easy to see a connection between stress and illness.*

make/form a connection (=see or show that there is one) *In learning to read, children make a connection between a written sign and a sound or word.*

establish a connection (=show that there is one) *Studies have established a connection between ill health and pollution.*

discover/find a connection *Investigators found a connection between the two men: they worked for the same company.*

break a connection (*also* **sever a connection** *formal*): *We must break the connection between money and politics.*

maintain a connection *After retiring as a player, he maintained a close connection to the football club.*

PREPOSITIONS

a connection between sth (and sth) *The book suggests a close connection between war and oil.*

in connection with sth *There have been no further reports in connection with the attack.*

conscience *n*

your feelings about whether your behaviour is morally right or wrong

ADJECTIVES

a guilty/bad conscience (=the knowledge that you have done something wrong) *His guilty conscience kept him awake at night.*

a clear/easy conscience (=the knowledge that you have done nothing wrong) *I was able to answer his questions with a clear conscience.*

a moral conscience (=an idea of what is right and wrong) *At what age do children develop a moral conscience?*

a social conscience (=a moral sense of what society should be like) *The writer's strong social conscience is obvious in all his novels.*

VERBS + conscience

have a guilty/clear etc conscience *He may have a guilty conscience about his role in the accident.*

wrestle/struggle with your conscience (=struggle to decide whether it is right or wrong to do something) *She wrestled with her conscience for weeks before joining the protest.*

examine your conscience (=ask yourself whether something is right or wrong) *After examining his conscience, he still felt he was right.*

prick sb's conscience (=make someone feel guilty) *Some of the things he did in his youth still prick his conscience.*

ease sb's conscience (=make you feel less guilty) *Returning some of the money helped to ease her conscience.*

follow your conscience (=do what you think is morally right) *A good leader will always follow his or her conscience.*

conscience + VERBS

your conscience tells you to do sth *They offered me a lot of money, but my conscience told me to refuse.*

your conscience troubles/bothers you (=you feel that something is morally wrong) *His conscience continued to bother him and he decided to tell her the truth.*

PHRASES

be a matter of conscience (=be something that you must make a moral judgment about) *Whether you vote or not is a matter of conscience.*

a crisis of conscience (=a situation in which it is very difficult to decide what is right) *The minister had a crisis of conscience about whether to give this information to journalists.*

the voice of conscience (=something in your mind that tells you what is right) *If you listen to the voice of conscience, you will know what to do.*

an attack of conscience (=a sudden strong feeling that you should do what is right) *He finally had an attack of conscience and decided to admit what he had done.*

a prisoner of conscience (=someone who is in prison because they have followed their beliefs about what is right) *The men claim that they are prisoners of conscience.*

conscious *adj*

aware of something or concerned about something

ADVERBS

acutely/deeply conscious of sth *formal* (=very conscious) *She was acutely conscious of the dangers of working with wild animals.*

fully conscious of sth *He did not seem to be fully conscious of the consequences of his decision.*

painfully conscious of sth (=very conscious of something unpleasant) *I was painfully conscious of the fact that I had failed.*

barely/hardly conscious of sth *She felt so ill that she was barely conscious of where she was.*

socially/politically/environmentally etc conscious *Environmentally conscious companies are reducing the amount of energy they use.*

C

NOUNS + conscious

health conscious *People who are health conscious are careful about what they eat.*

fashion conscious *Like many young girls, she is very fashion conscious.*

security/safety conscious *After the attacks, most airports became extremely security conscious.*

consciousness *n*

the normal condition of being awake and aware of things that are happening

VERBS

lose consciousness (=stop being awake and aware) *She hit her head and lost consciousness for several minutes.*

regain/recover consciousness (=start to be awake and aware again) *I wanted to stay by his bedside until he regained consciousness.*

bring sb back to consciousness *The doctors have been unable to bring her back to consciousness.*

PHRASES

drift in and out of consciousness (=change between being and not being awake and aware) *He had a high temperature and was drifting in and out of consciousness.*

consensus [Ac] *n*

an opinion that everyone in a group agrees with or accepts

ADJECTIVES

general/broad consensus *There was a general consensus that he should be replaced.*

clear consensus (=that everyone agrees on) *There was no clear consensus about the future direction of the company.*

growing/emerging consensus (=that more people are agreeing on) *The growing consensus is that the UK economy is getting stronger.*

strong consensus *There is a strong consensus that the party needs a new leader.*

political/scientific etc consensus *The scientific consensus is that global warming is already occurring.*

national/international consensus *There was no international consensus on how to deal with the situation.*

VERBS + consensus

there is a consensus *There is a consensus among scientists that something needs to be done.*

reach/achieve a consensus (*also* **arrive at a consensus**) *The committee found that it was unable to reach a consensus.*

build/forge/develop a consensus (=gradually achieve one) *Leaders are trying to build a consensus among governments in the region.*

consensus + VERBS

a consensus exists *A clear consensus exists that women should have equal opportunities at work.*

a consensus emerges (=it is reached after people talk about something) *No consensus emerged from these discussions.*

a consensus breaks down (=people stop agreeing) *One angry comment could cause the consensus to break down.*

PREPOSITIONS

consensus on/about sth *There is little consensus on the best method of teaching languages.*

consensus among/between people *There is general consensus among drivers that petrol is too expensive.*

PHRASES

a consensus of opinion *After days of talks, no consensus of opinion has been reached.*

a lack of consensus *Nothing was decided because of a lack of consensus among scientists.*

a degree of consensus (=some consensus) *There is now a degree of consensus about this issue.*

consent [Ac] *n* permission to do something

VERBS

give your consent *The child's parents have to give their consent for the operation.*

have sb's consent *You need to have the consent of the car's owner before you carry out the repair.*

get/obtain sb's consent *Police officers got her consent to search her house.*

sth requires sb's consent *The lawyer requires your consent to make any changes to your will.*

grant consent *formal* (=give it formally) *The local council has granted consent to the project.*

refuse (your) consent (*also* **withhold (your) consent** *formal*): *A patient can refuse consent for treatment if they don't want it.*

ADJECTIVES

written consent *If you are under 18, you need your parents' written consent to get married.*

sb's prior consent (=consent before you do something) *Do not photograph people without their prior consent.*

parental consent (=from someone's parents) *Students may not be absent from school without parental consent.*

informed consent (=based on full information about what will happen) *We took part in this study after giving our informed consent.*

PREPOSITIONS

consent to/for sth *I did not give my consent for the work to be done.*

consent to sb *The patient gave his consent to the doctors for the operation to be carried out.*

PHRASES

by mutual consent (=because both people agree) *He and his wife have separated by mutual consent.*

by common/general consent (=because everyone agrees) *By common consent, the committee decided to meet only once a month.*

the age of consent (=the age at which someone can legally marry or have sex) *She was under the age of consent when she became pregnant.*

consequence Ac *n*

something that happens as a result of something else

> **Grammar**
> Usually plural

ADJECTIVES

serious consequences *A nuclear accident would have serious consequences for the environment.*

important/major consequences *Their decision had some important consequences.*

disastrous/dire consequences *Rising temperatures could have disastrous consequences for agriculture.*

a negative/adverse consequence *formal* (=a bad effect on something) *Heavy drinking has negative consequences for people's health.*

unintended consequences *Changing the voting system has had unintended consequences.*

the possible/likely consequences *We need to think about the possible consequences of such an approach.*

an inevitable consequence (=that you cannot avoid) *Ill health is not an inevitable consequence of old age.*

a direct consequence of sth *The accident was a direct consequence of his actions.*

long-term consequences (=that last a long time, or appear after a long time) *If you smoke, it may have long-term consequences for your health.*

far-reaching consequences (=important and affecting many things) *New laws on tax will have far-reaching consequences.*

social/political/economic consequences *A rise in food prices has political consequences.*

a natural/logical consequence *Disappointment is a natural consequence of defeat.*

VERBS

have consequences (=cause problems) *Taking financial risks can have serious consequences.*

face/suffer the consequences (=experience something bad as a result of what you have done) *If you break the law, you have to face the consequences.*

accept/take the consequences *I'm prepared to accept the consequences of my decision.*

think about/consider the consequences *She jumped into the river without considering the consequences.*

escape the consequences (=avoid them) *I knew I'd made a mistake and that I couldn't escape the consequences.*

consequences follow/arise (=happen as a result of something) *If we fail to tackle the problem, serious consequences will arise.*

PREPOSITIONS

a consequence of sth *You need to think about the consequences of your actions.*

a consequence for sth *There could be serious consequences for his future career.*

PHRASES

as a consequence (=used for saying what happens as a result of something) *He ate nothing on the journey and, as a consequence, was starving when he arrived.*

conservation *n*

the protection of countryside, wild animals, and other natural things

ADJECTIVES/NOUNS + conservation

nature conservation *She is a government adviser on nature conservation.*

wildlife conservation *Woodland is important for wildlife conservation.*

environmental conservation *Schools are educating children in environmental conservation and awareness.*

marine conservation (=relating to the sea and to plants and animals in it) *She works as a diver in the area of marine conservation.*

conservation + NOUNS

a conservation area (=an area where animals and plants are protected) *The mountains are a wildlife conservation area.*

conservation measures/policies/efforts/work *We welcome the government's new conservation policies.*

a conservation programme/project *Our conservation programme has already protected dozens of beaches.*

PREPOSITIONS

the conservation of sth *The conservation of these wetland areas is our main aim.*

consider *v*
to think about something carefully, especially before making a choice or decision

ADVERBS
consider sth carefully *You should carefully consider the impact on your family before taking the job.*
consider sth fully/in detail *After fully considering all the options, we have reached a decision.*
consider sth separately/individually *The results should be considered separately because they are based on different types of data.*
seriously consider doing sth (=think about it as a very strong possibility) *At one point, she seriously considered emigrating to Australia.*
briefly consider doing sth (=think about doing it for a short time, then decide not to) *I briefly considered phoning Matty, but it was very late.*

PREPOSITIONS
consider sb for a job *You need to be fluent in Spanish to be considered for the job.*

PHRASES
be worth considering (=used to say that something might be the right choice or decision) *If your children have left home, renting out one of your rooms is worth considering.*

considerable *adj* THESAURUS **big (3)**

considerate *adj* THESAURUS **kind**²

consist of Ac *v*
if something consists of people or things, it has them in it

ADVERBS
consist mainly/mostly of sb/sth *Their diet consists mainly of fish.*
consist largely/predominantly/chiefly/principally/primarily of sb/sth (=mainly – more formal) *The audience consisted largely of women.*
consist entirely/wholly of sb/sth *These organizations usually consist entirely of older people.*
consist only/solely/exclusively of sb/sth *Your password should not consist solely of letters.*
usually/typically consist of sb/sth *A brigade typically consists of 3,000 to 5,000 soldiers.*

conspiracy *n*
a secret plan made with other people to do something harmful or illegal

ADJECTIVES
a political conspiracy *Were the killings part of a political conspiracy?*
a criminal conspiracy *There was no evidence of a criminal conspiracy between them.*
an international/worldwide/global conspiracy *Some people believe there is a worldwide conspiracy to keep fuel prices high.*
an alleged conspiracy *The police want to speak to him about an alleged conspiracy to commit fraud.*

VERBS
be part of a conspiracy (*also* **be involved in a conspiracy**) *The minister was part of a conspiracy to cover up the truth.*
be charged with conspiracy *The women were charged with conspiracy to supply drugs.*
be convicted of conspiracy *He was convicted of conspiracy to carry out terrorist attacks.*
uncover/discover/expose a conspiracy (=find out about it) *Journalists realized that they had uncovered a conspiracy and published their story.*

conspiracy + NOUNS
a conspiracy charge (*also* **a charge of conspiracy**) *Three men have been convicted on fraud and conspiracy charges.*
a conspiracy theory *President Kennedy's assassination inspired a lot of conspiracy theories.*

PREPOSITIONS
a conspiracy against sb *He believed his opponents were involved in a conspiracy against him.*
a conspiracy between people/groups *She alleged that there was a conspiracy between the police and the politicians.*

constant *adj* THESAURUS **continuous**

constitution Ac *n*
a set of laws and principles governing a country or organization

VERBS + constitution
draw up/draft a constitution (=write one) *The American constitution was drafted in 1787.*
amend/change the constitution *Congress amended the constitution more than 300 times during 1992.*
adopt/approve a constitution (*also* **ratify a constitution** *formal*) (=agree one and start to use it) *In 1994, the South African government adopted a new constitution.*
violate the constitution *formal* (=do something that is against it) *Such unfair treatment of workers violates the constitution.*
be enshrined in a constitution *formal* (=used about rights and principles protected by a constitution) *The right to practise your religion is enshrined in the country's constitution.*

constitution + VERBS
a constitution says/states sth *Peru's constitution says that only a Peruvian can hold the highest elected office.*
a constitution guarantees sth (=says that it must happen or exist) *The country's constitution guarantees freedom of speech.*

ADJECTIVES

the US/Russian etc constitution *The US constitution states that all men are created equal.*

a written constitution *The UK has no written constitution.*

a democratic constitution *After the king died, the people voted for a new democratic constitution.*

a draft constitution (=not yet in its final form) *The new committee has produced a draft constitution to be considered by members.*

PREPOSITIONS

under/according to the constitution *Under our constitution, the president has the power to get rid of any officer.*

PHRASES

an amendment to the constitution (=a change) *Any amendment to the constitution must be agreed by at least 70% of the members.*

a clause in the constitution (=a rule or section in it) *There was a clause in the constitution that prevented women from joining the armed forces.*

constraint Ac *n*

something that limits what you are able to do

Grammar
Usually plural.

ADJECTIVES/NOUNS + constraint

a major/important constraint *Shortage of water is a major constraint on farming here.*

a serious/severe constraint *Lack of land puts a serious constraint on development.*

tight constraints *There are tight financial constraints on what we are able to do.*

financial/economic constraints *Financial constraints prevented us from carrying out some of our plans.*

political constraints *The government faces certain political constraints when making decisions.*

legal constraints *There are many legal constraints on trade union activities.*

time constraints *Exams are always done under time constraints.*

VERBS

impose/place/put constraints on sb/sth *Lack of funding is putting severe constraints on research.*

free sb/sth from constraints *The summer holidays free children from the constraints of the school timetable.*

overcome constraints (=achieve something in spite of constraints) *We overcame many constraints to complete the work on time.*

relax/remove constraints (=get rid of them) *The government is relaxing constraints on international trade.*

PREPOSITIONS

constraints on sth/sb *He is very busy and there are severe constraints on the amount of time he has available.*

within constraints *Alcohol advertising operates within tight legal constraints.*

PHRASES

be subject to constraints (=be limited by them) *Teachers are subject to the constraints of the examination system.*

be free from constraints *No government is free from the constraints of its budget.*

given the constraints on sth (=because there are particular constraints on something) *Given the constraints on space in the city, most people live in tiny apartments.*

construct *v* THESAURUS build[1]

construction Ac *n*

the process of building things such as houses and roads

VERBS

begin/start construction *They will soon begin construction on a major new housing development.*

finish/complete construction *We expect to complete construction of the shopping mall in May.*

construction + NOUNS

the construction industry/sector *The construction industry always suffers during difficult economic times.*

a construction project/programme *The new hotel is one of the biggest construction projects in the city.*

a construction company/firm *He runs a large construction company in Mexico.*

a construction worker *Thousands of construction workers are out of work.*

construction work *Construction work on the new road is expected to take two years.*

a construction site (=an area where something is being built) *Safety is very important on construction sites.*

construction materials *Steel and concrete are expensive construction materials.*

PREPOSITIONS

the construction of sth *The government is funding the construction of a new national sports stadium.*

sth is under construction (=it is being built) *A new road is currently under construction.*

consultant Ac *n*

someone whose job is to give advice

ADJECTIVES/NOUNS + consultant

a business consultant *She's worked for several top London companies as a business consultant.*

a management consultant (=advising a company on its management) *A team of management consultants advised the company to restructure.*

a political/financial/legal etc consultant *He is a leading speech writer and political consultant.*

a marketing consultant *The new advertising campaign was designed by a team of marketing consultants.*

a media consultant (=giving advice on how to deal with journalists) *Every detail of the interview was discussed with the star's media consultant.*

an outside/independent consultant (=one who does not belong to your organization) *The school brings in outside consultants from time to time.*

VERBS

act/work as a consultant *He acted as a historical consultant on the film.*

hire/employ a consultant (*also* **bring in a consultant**) *The company hired an outside consultant to help improve efficiency.*

PREPOSITIONS

a consultant to sb *She's a marketing consultant to several major supermarket chains.*

a consultant on sth *He was employed by the government as a consultant on cultural issues.*

consultation Ac *n*

a discussion in which people can give their opinions

ADJECTIVES

public consultation (=asking for ordinary people's views) *There should be formal public consultations before the new road is built.*

full/proper consultation (=including as many people and questions as necessary) *No decision will be made until there has been full consultation with farmers.*

close consultation (=in which people or groups discuss something carefully together) *The changes followed close consultation with parents and teachers.*

prior consultation (=happening before something is done) *We will not make any changes to your job description without prior consultation.*

further consultation *The committee recommends that further consultation should take place between both groups.*

widespread/extensive consultation (=involving a lot of people or groups) *After widespread consultation, important changes were made to the design of the park.*

formal consultation *The meetings are part of a formal consultation.*

VERBS

hold/carry out a consultation *The police are holding further consultations with local residents.*

begin consultations (*also* **launch a consultation** *formal*): *Officials from the US began consultations with the European nations.*

consultation + NOUNS

a consultation paper/document (=a formal report on a subject that needs to be discussed) *Researchers produced a consultation document on public transport in the city.*

the consultation process/period *This meeting is the start of an eight-week consultation process.*

PREPOSITIONS

consultation on/about sth *Will there be public consultation on the design of the building?*

consultation with sb *There was no time for consultation with the public.*

consultations between people *There were several months of consultations between community groups in the area.*

in consultation with sb (=involving someone in deciding or planning something) *The decision was taken in consultation with members of the club.*

consumer Ac *n*

someone who buys and uses products and services

consumer + NOUNS

consumer goods/products *In richer countries, there is greater demand for consumer goods.*

consumer demand *Consumer demand decreases as unemployment rises.*

consumer spending (*also* **consumer expenditure** *formal*): *Higher taxes will reduce consumer spending.*

consumer choice *Competition between businesses leads to more consumer choice.*

a consumer society (=a society of people who want to buy a lot of things) *In the West, we live in a consumer society and we have lost our spiritual values.*

consumer confidence *The economy was growing and consumer confidence returned.*

ADJECTIVES

the biggest/largest consumer of sth *The US is the world's biggest consumer of oil.*

the average consumer *The average consumer cares a lot about the price of goods.*

VERBS

warn consumers *Experts are warning consumers to cook meat thoroughly.*

reassure consumers (=make them less worried) *The government has tried to reassure consumers that the products are safe.*

mislead consumers *The advertisement was deliberately intended to mislead consumers.*

consumption Ac *n*

the amount of something that is used or the act of using or buying something

NOUNS + consumption

energy/electricity/fuel/water etc consumption *There are many ways to reduce your energy consumption.*

tobacco/cigarette/alcohol consumption *The doctor says you need to cut your alcohol consumption.*

ADJECTIVES

high/low consumption (=using a lot or very little of something, especially petrol) *He drives a big car with a high petrol consumption.*

excessive/excess consumption (=too much) *Excessive consumption of alcohol is harmful to your health.*

moderate consumption (=some, but not too much) *Moderate consumption of coffee during pregnancy is fine.*

total/overall consumption *Our total consumption of electricity has risen by 20%.*

domestic consumption (=in the country where something is produced) *Most of the crop is grown for domestic consumption.*

per capita consumption (=per person) *Turkey has the highest per capita consumption of tea in the world.*

VERBS

reduce/lower/cut consumption *We want to reduce electricity consumption by up to 30%.*

increase consumption *The 'Five-a-Day' promotion is meant to increase the consumption of fruit and vegetables.*

stimulate/encourage consumption (=make it increase) *Government spending encourages consumption and hence economic growth.*

consumption rises/increases/goes up *Consumption of unleaded fuel rose by 17%.*

consumption falls/decreases/goes down *His cigarette consumption has fallen dramatically.*

PHRASES

fit/unfit for human consumption (=suitable/not suitable to be eaten by people) *The meat is not fit for human consumption.*

for personal/private consumption (*also* **for your own consumption**) (=for yourself to use, not to give or sell to others) *You can bring alcohol into the country for your personal consumption.*

contact[1] Ac *v*

to telephone, email, or write to someone, so that they speak to you or read your message

ADVERBS

contact sb directly *It was the first time that Helen had contacted him directly since they had separated.*

PREPOSITIONS

contact sb by phone/email/letter *He contacted the other members of the club by email.*

contact sb at an address/at home etc *You can contact him at the usual address.*

PHRASES

do not hesitate to contact sb/feel free to contact sb *Please do not hesitate to contact me if you have any queries.*

contact[2] Ac *n*

1 communication with a person, organization, country etc

PHRASES

be in contact (with sb) (=have regular communication) *He's been in contact with his lawyer about the situation.*

get in contact (with sb) (=manage to communicate) *Where can I get in contact with you while you are away?*

a point of contact (=a person or place you go to when you want to use a service) *Your family doctor is the first point of contact for most medical services.*

VERBS

make contact (*also* **establish contact** *formal*) (=communicate with someone for the first time) *We'd like to make contact with other schools in the area.*

have contact with sb *I haven't had any contact with her for over a year.*

stay/keep in contact (*also* **maintain contact** *formal*): *We've stayed in contact since we met on holiday.*

lose contact (=no longer see someone or hear from them) *She went to live in Australia and he lost contact with her.*

put sb in contact with sb (=give someone the name, telephone number etc of another person) *I can put you in contact with a friend of mine in Paris.*

break off/sever contact with sb (=refuse to have any contact with someone) *After the divorce, she severed all contact with her husband.*

ADJECTIVES/NOUNS + contact

direct contact (=spending time with someone) *Our volunteers work in direct contact with people who need help.*

close contact (=communicating with someone often) *I like to stay in close contact with my parents.*

personal contact (=seeing and speaking to someone yourself) *She never comes into personal contact with senior managers.*

social/human contact (=spending time with other people) *He lived alone and had little human contact.*

regular/frequent contact *All students have regular contact with their tutor.*

constant contact *Police negotiators were in constant contact with the gunman.*

radio/telephone/email contact (=using a particular method) *Air traffic control had lost radio contact with the pilot.*

day-to-day/daily contact *I like my job because it involves day-to-day contact with clients.*

contact + NOUNS

sb's contact details (=an address, telephone number etc on which someone can contact you) *Please leave your contact details and we will write to you.*

PREPOSITIONS

contact between sb and sb *There is very little contact between the two tribes.*

contact with sb *Many of us have no direct contact with elderly people.*

in contact (with sb) *We stay in contact by email.*

2 the fact that people or things touch one other

PHRASES

be in contact (with sth) (=be touching) *For a second, our hands were in contact with each other.*

VERBS

make contact (=touch something at a particular moment) *He reached out and his fingers made contact with a wall.*

come into contact (=touch, especially when this produces a particular result) *When water comes into contact with air, carbon dioxide is released.*

keep contact (*also* **maintain contact** *formal*): *Make sure you keep eye contact all the time.*

avoid contact *It is sensible to avoid contact with other people's blood.*

prevent contact *How can we prevent contact with harmful germs?*

ADJECTIVES/NOUNS + contact

direct contact *Some skin diseases are spread by direct contact.*

prolonged contact (=for a long time) *Prolonged contact with a wet nappy makes a baby's bottom sore.*

eye contact (=looking directly at someone who is looking at you) *He was shy and always avoided eye contact with people.*

physical contact *Children need physical contact with a caring adult.*

contact + NOUNS

contact sports (=sports in which players have physical contact) *Rugby and American football are contact sports.*

PREPOSITIONS

contact with sth *You can catch the disease through contact with contaminated material.*

on contact (=when something touches something) *The chemical explodes on contact with water.*

container *n*

something such as a box or bowl that you use to keep things in

ADJECTIVES

a plastic/glass/metal etc container *A lot of food is sold in plastic containers.*

a large/small container *He brought out a large container of ice.*

a shallow container (=not deep) *Fill a shallow container with soil.*

an empty/full container *I need an empty container to put blackberries in.*

an airtight/watertight/sealed container (=not allowing air or water in) *Seeds are best stored in airtight containers.*

a childproof container (=that children cannot open) *Always store medicines in a childproof container.*

VERBS

keep/store sth in a container *Carrots from the garden were stored in containers of sand.*

put sth in a container *The food is then put in special containers.*

fill a container *First, fill a container with water.*

seal a container (=close it so that no air or water can get in) *Seal the container by closing the lid firmly.*

a container holds/contains sth *How much liquid will this container hold? | Each container contains 100 ml of paint.*

PREPOSITIONS

in a container *I keep my keys in a container on the top shelf.*

contaminated *adj* THESAURUS ▶ **dirty**

contemporary Ac *adj*

belonging to the present time

contemporary + NOUNS

contemporary society *What is the role of religion in contemporary society?*

contemporary life/culture *Technology is a vital part of contemporary culture.*

the contemporary world *The environment is a major issue in the contemporary world.*

contemporary Britain/America etc *The book moves from the late 19th century to contemporary America.*

contemporary issues (=subjects or problems that a lot of people are talking about) *Some film-makers tackle contemporary issues such as terrorism and climate change.*

contemporary debate (=discussion about things people are interested in now) *The electoral system is a subject of contemporary debate.*

contemporary art *He collects contemporary art.*

contemporary writing/literature/poetry *Students study contemporary writing as well as pre-20th-century literature.*

contemporary music/dance *There is a contemporary music festival in town every spring.*

a contemporary artist/writer/composer *Paintings by contemporary artists covered the walls.*

THESAURUS: contemporary
contemporary, modern-day → **modern (1)**

contempt *n*
a feeling that someone or something is not important and deserves no respect

ADJECTIVES

utter/total/complete contempt *Sally looked at him with utter contempt.*

great/deep contempt (*also* **profound contempt** *formal*): *He seemed to have a deep contempt for women.*

the utmost contempt (=great contempt) *Many people regarded the government with the utmost contempt.*

open/undisguised contempt (=that you do not try to hide) *Her expression was one of open contempt.*

barely/thinly disguised contempt (=obvious because someone is not hiding it very well) *He corrected my mistake with barely disguised contempt.*

cold/icy contempt (=that shows in a very unfriendly way) *I noticed the icy contempt in his voice.*

VERBS

treat sth with contempt *The opinions of the public should not be ignored or treated with contempt.*

have/feel contempt for sth *He had a deep contempt for authority.*

view/regard sb with contempt (=feel contempt for them) *Anyone who did not have a job was regarded with contempt.*

hold sb in contempt (=feel contempt for them) *He holds us in contempt because we do not agree with him.*

show contempt for sb *Throwing litter on the floor shows total contempt for other people.*

express contempt for sth *In public he expressed great contempt for the government.*

PREPOSITIONS

contempt for sb/sth *He could not hide his contempt for his boss.*

with contempt *She looked at me with contempt.*

beneath contempt (=very bad and not deserving any respect at all) *That sort of behaviour is simply beneath contempt.*

PHRASES

a look of contempt *He gave her a look of contempt.*

have/feel nothing but contempt for sb *I have nothing but contempt for people who treat animals badly.*

treat sth with the contempt it deserves *She treated these accusations with the contempt they deserved.*

familiarity breeds contempt (=if you know someone very well, you may respect them less)

Contempt (of court)
This phrase is used about the crime of not doing what a court of law has ordered you to do: *He was fined for* ***contempt of court****, after he failed to attend the trial.*

C

content *n*
the things that something contains

PHRASES

the contents of a bag/suitcase/desk/room etc *He tipped the contents of her bag all over the floor.*

the content of a course/film/programme *The website provides details about the content of each course.*

the contents of a letter/book/article *He read the contents of the letter out loud to her.*

NOUNS + content

salt/sugar/alcohol content *Fast food such as burgers and sausages generally have a high salt content.*

fat/protein/vitamin content *If you boil vegetables, they may lose some of their vitamin content.*

moisture/water content *The maximum moisture content in air varies with temperature.*

VERBS

examine the contents *She opened the suitcase and carefully examined its contents.*

empty the contents *She emptied the contents of her handbag onto the table.*

pour the contents *He poured the contents of the bottle into his glass.*

reveal/disclose the contents (=tell people about them) *The report is confidential, and we cannot disclose its contents.*

The list of the chapters or sections that a book contains is called **the contents, the contents page**, or in more formal English **the table of contents**.

contented *adj* THESAURUS **happy**

contentious *adj* THESAURUS **controversial**

contentment *n* THESAURUS **satisfaction**

contest *n*
a competition or a situation in which two or more people are competing with each other

ADJECTIVES

a close/tight contest (=one which someone wins by a very small amount) *The race was a close contest between two very good teams.*

a good/exciting/interesting contest *This is going to be a really good contest.*
a fair contest *Divide the class into groups in a way that will make it a fair contest.*
a one-sided contest (*also* **an uneven/unequal contest** *BrE*) (=one of the people, groups etc is much more likely to win) *Given their military strength, the war was a pretty unequal contest.*
an even/equal contest *BrE* (=everyone has the same chance of winning) *One of the men was much bigger so it was not an even contest.*
a hard-fought contest (=both sides try hard to win) *The game was a hard-fought contest.*
a leadership contest *He is expected to win the leadership contest.*
a beauty contest (=to find the most beautiful person) *Miss Colombia won the beauty contest.*
a talent contest (=to find the best performer) *She's singing a song in the school talent contest.*
a popularity contest (=to decide which person people like the most) *If there was a popularity contest, I don't think my boss would win.*
an election/electoral contest *What will be the outcome of the electoral contest?*
a sports/sporting contest *The Highland Games is a sporting contest held in Scotland.*

VERBS

enter a contest (=arrange to take part in one) *Anyone over 18 years old can enter the contest.*
take part/compete in a contest *Twenty-five countries took part in the contest.*
win/lose a contest *Who do you think will win the contest?*
withdraw from a contest (=stop taking part in one) *Two candidates had withdrawn from the contest.*
have/hold a contest *They decided to hold a contest to see who could write the best song.*
a contest takes place *The contest took place in Berlin.*

PREPOSITIONS

a contest for sth *There was a contest for the post of party leader.*
a contest between sb and sb *Everyone remembers the 1960 contest between Kennedy and Nixon.*
a contest with/against sb *Tomorrow's contest with Canada should be very exciting.*
be in a contest *I've never been in a talent contest before.*

PHRASES

the winner of a contest *The winner of the contest wins a recording contract with a record company.*
a contest is open to sb (=particular people or groups can enter it) *The talent contest is open to all teenagers.*

context Ac *n*

the situation, events, or information that are related to something and that help you to understand it

ADJECTIVES

the general context *I will start by explaining the general context behind these events.*
a broader/wider/larger context *It is important to think about what he says in a broader context.*
the right/correct/appropriate context *Students learn to use words in the right context.*
a narrow/limited context *This is true, but only in a very narrow context.*
historical/political/economic context *These events must be considered in their historical context.*
the cultural context *You often need to understand the cultural context of jokes.*
a moral context *There is a deeper moral context to this question.*

VERBS

put sth in/into context (*also* **place/set sth in context** *formal*) (=consider something together with its context) *These statistics need to be put into context.*
see sth in the context of sth (=consider and understand something in relation to a particular situation) *His life and work must be seen in the context of his youth.*
examine/look at sth in context (=together with its context) *This may seem a bad result, but let's examine it in context.*
take sth out of context (=not consider the situation in which something is said) *His comments, taken out of context, seem harsh.*
give a context for sth (*also* **provide a context for sth** *formal*): *The research provides a context for developing a new curriculum.*
create/establish a context *This creates a context in which successful teaching can take place.*

PREPOSITIONS

the context of/for/behind sth *What was the context for these remarks?*

continual *adj* THESAURUS continuous

THESAURUS: continual

continual, constant, incessant, persistent, unbroken, non-stop → **continuous**

continue *v*

1 to not stop doing something, or to start doing something again after you have stopped

Grammar

You usually use an infinitive after **continue**: *Sheila* ***continued to*** *work after she had her baby.* | *The economy* ***continued to*** *grow.* You can also use a participle in the same meaning: *Sheila* ***continued*** *working after she had her baby.* | *The economy* ***continued*** *growing.* The infinitive use is more common.

continue + NOUNS

continue your work/studies/education *Students may choose to continue their studies at an advanced level.*

continue your efforts/fight/struggle/campaign *We will continue our efforts to find a solution.*

continue your journey *They spent the night in Chicago and continued their journey the following morning.*

PREPOSITIONS

continue with sth *He continued with his work despite his illness.*

THESAURUS: continue

go on (*also* **carry on** *especially BrE*)
to continue to do something. **Go on** and **carry on** are more informal than **continue**:
Dan ***went on*** *talk****ing****, but she was no longer listening. | Many people* ***carry on*** *smok****ing****, even though they know it is bad for their health. | Sheehan has* ***carried on with*** *her campaign.*

keep (on) doing sth
to continue doing something for a long time - especially so that you feel tired or annoyed:
We ***kept on*** *walk****ing*** *until we got to the top of the hill. | The man* ***kept*** *star****ing*** *at me. | My computer* ***keeps*** *crash****ing****.*

persevere
to continue trying to do something in a very patient and determined way, in spite of difficulties. **Persevere** sounds rather formal:
I'm sure that if you persevere, you will succeed in the end. | Despite his early disasters, he decided to ***persevere with*** *photography and learn as much about it as he possibly could.*

2 to not stop happening or existing

NOUNS

a trial/case continues *The trial continues tomorrow when the defence will begin their evidence.*

the war/fighting/violence continues *As the war continued, the number of civilians killed rose to over a million.*

a show/exhibition continues *The exhibition continues until 17 May.*

a game continues *The game continues until there is only one person left.*

work continues *Work continues on the tunnel.*

a trend/process continues *If this trend continues, more than 15% of the island will be under water.*

ADVERBS

continue forever *The rise in profits cannot continue forever.*

continue all day/night/week *The wind continued all night.*

continue indefinitely (=you do not know when something will end) *The strike will continue indefinitely.*

PREPOSITIONS

continue for 2 hours/10 years etc *The rain continued for an hour.*

continue until tomorrow/next week etc *Work will continue until next March.*

THESAURUS: continue

last
to continue - used when saying how long something continues for:
The trial ***lasted for*** *six days. | The meeting lasted until lunchtime. | The training* ***lasts from*** *July 2nd* ***to*** *August 25th. | How long does suncream protection last?*

go on
to continue, especially for a long time:
The film goes on for over two hours. | Disputes between neighbours can go on for years. | The war ***went on and on*** (=it continued for much too long).

drag on
to continue for much longer than necessary or for longer than you want:
The case has dragged on for more than two years. | Presidential campaigns ***seem to drag on*** *forever.*

persist *formal*
problem | symptoms | pain | conditions
if something bad or unwanted persists, it continues to exist or happen:
If the problem persists, we may have to change our approach. | See your doctor if the symptoms persist (=signs that someone may have an illness). *| The cloudy weather conditions are expected to persist into the evening.*

continuous *adj*

continuing for a long time without stopping

NOUNS

a continuous process *Learning is a continuous process - you don't stop learning when you leave school.*

continuous improvement/development/growth *It was a period of continuous economic growth.*

continuous flow/supply *The system provides a continuous flow of information.*

a continuous line/stream of sth *There was a continuous stream of traffic.*

a continuous series *A continuous series of meetings took place.*

continuous use *The battery allows 2.5 hours of continuous use.*

continuous employment/service *She has been in continuous employment since she left school.*

continuous assessment *Teachers carry out continuous assessment of students' work.*

ADVERBS

almost/virtually continuous *We had a week of almost continuous sunshine.*

PHRASES

the longest/oldest continuous *This summer was the longest continuous period of hot weather since records began.*

C

THESAURUS: continuous

continual
process | improvement | use | state | reminder | threat | fear | struggle | conflict | problem
continuing for a long time without stopping:
There has been a continual improvement in standards. | The country lives with the continual threat of terrorism. | There were continual problems with mud and rain.

> **Continuous** or **continual?**
> In many situations, you can use either **continuous** or **continual** with the same meaning: *There has been a* ***continual/ continuous*** *improvement in standards.*
> **Continual** is used more often when something keeps happening in a way that is annoying or causes problems: *There were* ***continual problems*** *with leaking windows. | He lived in* ***continual fear*** *of being attacked.*

constant
pressure | attention | worry | fear | threat | reminder | source | struggle | battle | speed | temperature | rate | flow | stream
continuing for a long time without stopping – used especially about things that are worrying, or when something continues to be at the same temperature, speed, rate etc:
I'm under constant pressure from my family to get married. | Young children always want constant attention. | Her sister was a constant source of irritation. | His illness makes life a constant struggle for him and his parents. | The car was traveling at a constant speed of 80 kilometres an hour.

incessant *formal*
rain | noise | roar | traffic | questions | demands | chatter | whining
continuing for a long time without stopping – used about something that makes you feel annoyed:
I was tired of the incessant rain. | She was kept awake by the incessant roar of the ship's engines. | The incessant demands of a small child can test anyone's patience.

persistent
problem | reports | allegations | rumours | refusal | failure | doubt | cough | infection
continuing to exist for a long time and difficult to get rid of or ignore:
Violence in the city has been a persistent problem. | There were persistent rumours about the president's private life. | You should consult your doctor if you have a persistent cough.

unbroken
run | series | string | record | rule | sleep
continuing for a long time – used especially when someone keeps being successful:
The team's unbroken run of wins came to an end on Saturday. | Brazil maintained their unbroken record of success against Italy. | It was the first night of unbroken sleep he had had in months.

non-stop *informal*
flight | service | entertainment | fun | action | work | rain
continuing for a long time or a long way without stopping:
The airline has launched a new non-stop service between London and Hong Kong. | The concert will be seven hours of non-stop entertainment. | We have had two days of non-stop rain. | They ***worked non-stop****.*

contract Ac *n*

an official agreement between two or more people, stating what each will do

ADJECTIVES/NOUNS + contract

a one-year/two-year etc contract *He signed a five-year contract worth $2 million.*

a short-term/long-term contract *A lot of the workers are on short-term contracts.*

a written contract *All employees should have a written contract.*

a binding contract (=one that must be obeyed) *Our lawyer believes it is a binding contract.*

a recording/building etc contract *The band was soon offered a recording contract with Columbia Records.*

VERBS

sign a contract *He signed a contract to become vice-president of the football club.*

make a contract (*also* **enter into a contract** *formal*): *Did he know this when he made the contract?*

negotiate a contract (=agree the conditions of a contract with someone) *Your lawyer will assist you in negotiating a contract.*

draw up a contract (=write one) *The two sides drew up a contract.*

have a contract *The company had a contract to build a new hotel there.*

break a contract (=do something that your contract does not allow) *She broke her contract and left the job after only six months.*

fulfil/honour a contract (=do what you have agreed to do) *If you have signed a contract, you have to fulfil it.*

win/get a contract *They won a contract to supply 37 passenger trains to Regional Railways.*

give/award sb a contract *He was given a new two-year contract in March.*

cancel/end/terminate a contract *The buyer has three days in which to cancel the contract.*

renew sb's contract (=give someone another contract when their old one ends) *I hope they will renew my contract at the end of the year.*

extend a contract *His original two-year contract was extended.*

a contract expires (=ends at an agreed time) *Her five-year contract expires at the end of June.*

PREPOSITIONS

a contract with sb *He is expected to sign a contract with a new club soon.*

a contract between sb and sb *There is a contract between buyer and seller.*

PHRASES

a contract of employment (*also* **an employment contract**) *Make sure you fully understand your contract of employment.*

the terms of a contract (=the conditions that are part of the contract) *He explained the terms of the contract.*

breach of contract *formal* (=an action that your contract does not allow) *They are suing the building company for breach of contract.*

contradict Ac *v*

to show that the opposite is true, or say the opposite of what someone says

NOUNS

contradict yourself/each other *She contradicted herself several times when she was interviewed by the police.*

contradict a view/idea/notion *Some scientists say that the Earth's temperature is not changing, but recent research contradicts this view.*

contradict a claim *The new evidence contradicts his claim that he did not know about the plan.*

contradict a statement/assertion *A spokesman for the company was quick to contradict this statement.*

contradict reports *His latest remarks contradict reports that he was planning to resign.*

contradict a theory *The research appears to contradict previous theories about the origins of the universe.*

ADVERBS

completely contradict *His evidence completely contradicts what the other witness was saying.*

directly contradict *A report into the incident directly contradicted the government's account of it.*

flatly contradict sb (=completely - used for emphasis) *This study flatly contradicts the old idea that thin people live longer.*

VERBS

seem/appear to contradict sth *The survey appears to contradict claims that speed is the most important thing when you are choosing a car.*

contradiction Ac *n*

a very great difference between two statements, ideas, facts etc, so it seems they cannot both be true or possible

ADJECTIVES

a major contradiction *If we look more closely, we can see major contradictions in the evidence from the two witnesses.*

a basic/fundamental contradiction *There is a fundamental contradiction between the official figures and the experiences of people looking for work.*

an obvious contradiction *I noticed some obvious contradictions in his story.*

an apparent contradiction (=one that seems likely) *There's an apparent contradiction between wanting to help people and wanting to make a profit.*

a curious/strange contradiction *One of the curious contradictions about him was that he loved the countryside but he chose to live in the city.*

an inherent contradiction *formal* (=one that forms an important part of something) *There is an inherent contradiction between a one-party state and mass democracy.*

VERBS

there is a contradiction *There is an obvious contradiction in his argument.*

seem/sound (like) a contradiction *This may seem like a contradiction, but sometimes the easy questions are the hardest ones to answer.*

contain a contradiction *The present law contains many contradictions.*

see/notice/observe a contradiction *They do not see a contradiction between individual freedom and the freedom of the other members of a society.*

highlight a contradiction (=make it very noticeable) *The case has highlighted some contradictions in the present system.*

resolve a contradiction (=stop it being a problem) *I can't see any way of resolving this contradiction.*

PREPOSITIONS

a contradiction between sth (and sth) *Do you think there is a contradiction between these two statements?*

C

contradictions in/within sth *There are some strange contradictions in the law.*

PHRASES

be full of contradictions *Some people are full of contradictions.*

contraption *n* THESAURUS machine

contrast Ac *n*

a difference between people or things that are being compared

ADJECTIVES

a complete/total contrast *The modern buildings are a complete contrast to those in the old town.*

a sharp/stark/strong contrast (=very big) *There is a sharp contrast between the typical readers of these newspapers.*

a great contrast *There is a great contrast between the countryside here and in other parts of England.*

a dramatic/startling contrast (=big and surprising) *Alaska is a land of dramatic contrasts.*

an obvious/clear/marked/striking contrast (=very noticeable) *I noticed a marked contrast in his behaviour after his parents' divorce.*

a direct contrast *She's warm and amusing – in direct contrast to James.*

VERBS

make a contrast *The fruit and the meat make a delicious contrast of flavours.*

draw a contrast (=say there is a contrast) *It is tempting to draw contrasts between religion and science.*

provide/offer contrast (=be different in a way that is interesting) *The plant is very attractive, and provides excellent contrast to other plants.*

highlight a contrast (=make it very obvious) *The research will highlight the contrasts between different approaches to taxation.*

PREPOSITIONS

in contrast to/with sth (=unlike something) *In contrast to his father, Joe was a very sociable person.*

a contrast between sth and sth *She describes the contrast between the two women's lifestyles.*

a contrast with sth *The smooth marble makes a strong contrast with the rough stone around it.*

by/in contrast (=used when giving a different situation) *The birth rate for older women has fallen, but, by contrast, births to teenage mothers have increased.*

contravene *v* THESAURUS disobey

contribute *v* THESAURUS give (1)

contribution Ac *n*

something that you give or do in order to help something be successful

ADJECTIVES

a major/great/huge contribution *Tourism makes a major contribution to the island's economy.*

a significant/important contribution *All of you can make a significant contribution to the company.*

a useful/valuable contribution *The book is a valuable contribution to the study of modern American history.*

a vital/invaluable contribution (=very important) *Foreign workers make a vital contribution to the economy.*

an outstanding contribution (=very good) *He won an award for his outstanding contribution to cinema over many years.*

a positive contribution *We want kids to grow up to make a positive contribution to society.*

a small contribution (*also* **a modest contribution** *formal*): *It made only a small contribution to the company's profits.*

a financial contribution *Some parents cannot afford to make a financial contribution when their kids go to college.*

VERBS

make a contribution *I'd like everyone to make a contribution towards the discussion.*

acknowledge/recognize sb's contribution (=say that you are grateful for what someone has done) *He acknowledged the contribution of many individuals in writing the report.*

value sb's contribution (=think someone's contribution is important) *My co-workers didn't seem to value my contribution.*

pay a contribution (=pay part of the money for something) *Parents are being asked to pay a small contribution towards the trip.*

PREPOSITIONS

a contribution to/towards sth *He was awarded a prize for his contribution to sport.*

a contribution from sb *The journal has contributions from well-known writers.*

control[1] *v*

1 to have the power to make the decisions about how a country, place, company etc is organized or what it does

NOUNS

control a city/country/area *The area is now controlled by rebels.*

control a company/business *His family has controlled the company for 150 years.*

control a party/union/organization *The party was controlled by a small group of extremists.*

control an industry *The oil industry was controlled by five multinational companies.*

control the media (=newspapers, television, radio etc) *The government should not attempt to control the media.*

control the budget/finances *Often, it is the woman who controls the household budget.*

ADVERBS

directly control sth *The bank is no longer directly controlled by the government.*

effectively control sth (=be really in control, when this is not what is intended or believed) *His son effectively controls the company.*

be centrally controlled *The Chinese economy is centrally controlled.*

THESAURUS: control

be in charge
to have the authority to control what happens, and tell other people what to do:
*She **is in charge of** training new employees. | I left him **in charge of** the children while I was out. | He asked to speak to the person who **was in charge**.*

be in power
to be the leader or government of a country:
The former prime minister resigned after less than a year in power. | It was the first time a democratically elected government had been in power.

run
company | organization | school | hospital | hotel | country | economy | industry | world
to make the important everyday decisions concerning a company, organization, country etc, so that it can continue to operate:
It was unusual for a woman to run a company in those days. | The parents want to run the school themselves. | The military ran the country until 1974. | The book is about a world run by robots.

manage
company | business | firm | store | hotel | team
to organize and control the work of a company or organization:
*Her father used to manage the company. | The business had been **poorly managed**, and owed a large amount of money* (=badly managed). | *Sir Alex Ferguson managed the team for a long time.*

rule
country | world
to control a country or place and make all the important political decisions:
The president ruled the country for almost 30 years. | In those days, Britain ruled the world. | Japan was ruled by the same party for a long time.

supervise
work | activities | operation | project | team | students | employees
to be in charge of a group of workers, students etc, and make sure that they do their work properly, or behave properly:
I'm supervising the building work myself. | The Policing Board supervises the activities of the police. | There aren't enough teachers to supervise the students.

2 to limit the amount or growth of something

ADVERBS

carefully control sth *Costs need to be carefully controlled.*

strictly/tightly/rigidly control sth *The sale of handguns is very strictly controlled.*

adequately/effectively control sth *It is important to control inflation effectively.*

NOUNS

control costs/prices/wages *All businesses have to control their costs.*

control spending (*also* **control expenditure** *formal*): *If you want to save money, you have to control your spending.*

control inflation *They may have to increase interest rates in order to control inflation.*

control pollution/crime/disease *The state has strict laws to control pollution.*

control immigration *He argued for the need to control immigration more strictly.*

control the growth/spread of sth *Education is the best way of controlling the spread of AIDS.*

control pain *There are many ways to help control pain in childbirth.*

control the bleeding *To control the bleeding, press a clean bandage firmly against the wound.*

control your weight *She exercises to control her weight.*

3 to make something operate in a particular way

ADVERBS

automatically control sth *Your body automatically controls its own temperature.*

electronically control sth *The car's locking system is electronically controlled.*

manually control sth *The machine can be controlled manually or automatically.*

control sth remotely (=from a distant place) *The heating in some bank branches is controlled remotely.*

be easily controlled *Fuel flow is easily controlled using this switch.*

PHRASES

remote-controlled (*also* **remote-control**) (=controlled from a distant place using an electronic device) *They use remote-controlled robots to clean radioactive surfaces.*

radio-controlled (=controlled from a distant place using radio signals) *He was given a radio-controlled toy car for his birthday.*

C

control² *n*

1 the ability or power to make someone or something do what you want or make something happen in the way you want

ADJECTIVES/NOUNS + control

complete/total control *The editor has complete control over everything that is published.*

full/absolute control (=complete) *We are never in full control of our own lives.*

effective control (=used for saying who is really in control, when this may not be what is intended or believed) *The rebels are now in effective control of the city.*

C

overall control *Managers make many decisions, but the chairman has overall control.*

direct control *The country was now under the direct control of the army.*

financial/political/social control *The new CEO was given complete financial control.*

central control (=in which one main part of an organization or system controls the rest of it) *Local governments increasingly came under central control.*

government/state control *I am against government control of the media.*

military control (=by the armed forces) *The town is under military control.*

self-control (=the ability to control your emotions and behaviour) *Small children do not have the same self-control as adults.*

VERBS

take control (*also* **assume/assert control** *formal*): *Students are encouraged to take control of their own learning.*

seize control (=take control quickly or violently) *About 400 prisoners had seized control and were smashing up the jail.*

get/gain control *He felt himself wanting to laugh and struggled to gain control.*

have control *She's a good teacher who always has control of her class.*

keep control (*also* **maintain/retain control** *formal*): *Some people don't know how to keep control of their dogs.*

lose control *It is important to stay calm and not lose control of the situation.*

regain control *How can the government regain control of the economy?*

give sb control *His parents gave him control of his own finances.*

exercise control *formal* (=have control, or use the control that you have) *Her parents no longer exercise any control over her life.*

give up control (*also* **relinquish control** *formal*): *She relinquished control of the company to her three sons.*

control + NOUNS

a control freak *informal* (=someone who wants to control every situation they are in) *She's a complete control freak and she won't let anyone help her do anything.*

PREPOSITIONS

control of/over sth *Schools were given control over their own budgets.*

be in control *He always drives because he says he likes to be in control.*

under sb's control *He has a large organization under his control.*

be outside/beyond sb's control (=be impossible for someone to control) *Flight delays do occur, for reasons that are outside our control.*

be out of control *The fire was getting out of control.*

be under control *The flu outbreak is now under control.*

PHRASES

keep sth under control *Dogs are allowed on the trails if they are kept under control.*

fight/battle/struggle for control *The rebels battled for control of the city.*

2 a way of limiting something, often using an official rule or law

ADJECTIVES

strict/tight controls *There are strict controls on the kind of goods you can bring into the country.*

lax controls (=not strict enough) *The banks admitted that controls on lending had been lax.*

NOUNS + control

import/export controls *Import controls were introduced on farm products.*

arms control (=limits on the weapons countries can have) *The two countries signed an arms control agreement.*

wage/price/rent controls *Rent controls were introduced to stop landlords from making huge profits.*

gun control (=limits on who can buy and own guns) *Many people in the US are against gun control.*

VERBS

introduce controls *The government introduced strict controls on imported goods.*

strengthen/tighten controls (=make them stricter) *Some people say we need to tighten controls on the internet.*

relax controls (=make them less strict) *Wage controls have been relaxed.*

remove/lift controls *They have removed price controls on a number of basic goods.*

enforce controls (=make people obey them) *The department is responsible for enforcing controls on the sale of protected animals.*

PREPOSITIONS

a control on sth *There are tight controls on the number of foreign workers.*

controversial Ac *adj*

causing a lot of disagreement and argument

NOUNS

a controversial issue/topic/subject *Gay marriage remains a controversial issue.*

a controversial figure (=a person who many do not agree with) *He is a controversial figure because of his extreme views.*

a controversial decision *The judge's decision to release the prisoners was highly controversial.*

a controversial plan/proposal/policy *There is a controversial plan to build a new airport.*

a controversial measure (=an official action that is controversial) *Charging people to drive into the city was a controversial measure.*

a controversial book/film/play *The film was extremely controversial and some people wanted it to be banned.*

controversial remarks/comments *His talk contained some controversial remarks about religion.*

ADVERBS

highly/deeply/extremely controversial *This policy proved highly controversial.*

politically controversial *The area of workers' rights remains politically controversial.*

potentially controversial *The issue was a potentially controversial one for the government.*

VERBS

remain controversial *The treatment remains controversial because it is expensive and not always effective.*

prove controversial (=be controversial) *The plans have proved controversial with local people.*

THESAURUS: controversial

contentious *formal*
issue | subject | topic | area | question | proposal | debate | claim
Contentious means the same as **controversial**, but is more formal:
Water has been a contentious issue between the country and its neighbours for years. | This is a contentious area of the law. | His comments sparked a contentious debate over nationalism. | These claims are ***highly contentious****.*

controversy Ac *n*

a serious argument about something that involves many people and continues for a long time

ADJECTIVES

great/much/considerable controversy *The article has caused considerable controversy.*

fierce/intense/bitter controversy (=very great) *Her remarks have been at the centre of a fierce controversy.*

a major controversy *That decision was the second major controversy of the prime minister's career.*

public controversy *His book sparked public controversy about the issue.*

the latest controversy *The scandal is the latest controversy to hit the government.*

growing/increasing controversy *There is growing controversy over the decision.*

political/religious/financial controversy *The agreement attracted a lot of political controversy.*

international controversy (=in many countries) *The politician's remarks aroused international controversy.*

VERBS + controversy

cause/create controversy *His speech caused a lot of controversy.*

arouse/provoke/spark controversy (=cause it) *The judges' decision provoked controversy.*

run into controversy *BrE* (=cause it without intending to) *The band ran into controversy over the video for their single.*

fuel controversy (=add to it) *England's manager fuelled controversy with his criticism of the referee.*

controversy + VERBS

controversy arises *formal* (=it starts to happen because of something) *Some controversy arose over the safety of the vaccination.*

controversy exists *Controversy exists over the use of the drug.*

controversy surrounds sth *Much controversy surrounds the issue of genetically modified crops.*

controversy rages (=there is a lot of controversy) *Controversy was raging about smoking in public places.*

PREPOSITIONS

controversy about/over sth *There has been a lot of controversy over the decision.*

controversy among/between sb *He has provoked controversy among party members.*

PHRASES

a storm of controversy (=a lot of controversy) *Since its release, the film has met a storm of controversy.*

be the centre of a controversy *The book became the centre of a bitter controversy.*

a matter/subject of controversy *The right age to have children is a matter of controversy.*

convention Ac *n*

1 a large formal meeting for people who belong to the same profession or organization or who have the same interests

ADJECTIVES/NOUNS + convention

an annual convention *The church has an annual convention each July.*

C

a national/international/European convention *Leaders attended an international convention on climate change.*

a political convention *The hall is used for political conventions.*

a party convention (=of a political party) *He was elected leader at the party convention.*

VERBS

hold/have a convention *The party will hold its annual convention next week.*

arrange/organize a convention *She is busy organizing the company's sales convention.*

go to a convention (*also* **attend a convention** *formal*): *Teachers from all over the country went to the convention.*

speak at a convention (=make a speech there) *Thank you for the invitation to speak at your convention.*

address a convention (=make a speech to the people at a convention) *He addressed the national convention in 2008.*

a convention takes place *Our 20th annual convention takes place in March.*

convention + NOUNS

a convention centre *BrE*, **a convention center** *AmE* (=a building where conventions are held) *The party conference will take place at the International Convention Centre in Birmingham.*

a convention organizer *Convention organizers are expecting around 2,000 people.*

a convention delegate (=someone who goes to a convention) *Convention delegates must register on arrival.*

PREPOSITIONS

at a convention *He gave an excellent speech at the convention.*

a convention on sth *She will speak at a convention on higher education next week.*

2 a formal agreement, especially between countries, about particular rules or behaviour

ADJECTIVES/NOUNS + convention

an international convention *There is an international convention banning land mines.*

a European convention *The dumping of waste at sea was banned under a European convention.*

VERBS + convention

sign a convention *Twenty-five countries have signed the convention.*

ratify a convention (=make it official by signing it) *He called on all states to ratify the convention.*

adopt a convention (=start using it) *They adopted a convention banning the import of nuclear waste.*

breach/violate a convention (=not do what it says you must do) *The proposals would violate the European Convention on Human Rights.*

adhere to/comply with a convention (=do what it says you must do) *The court heard that members of the assembly had not complied with the convention.*

be bound by a convention (=have to do what it says) *Countries are not bound by the convention unless they have signed it.*

convention + VERBS

a convention bans sth *The convention bans the production of chemical weapons.*

a convention governs sth *The convention governs the treatment of political prisoners.*

PREPOSITIONS

a convention on sth *They signed a convention on the rights of the child.*

a convention between countries *A convention between Italy and Turkey was signed in 1932.*

under a convention *Torture is not allowed under the convention.*

PHRASES

a signatory of/to a convention (=a country that has signed it) *The UK and the US were signatories to the convention.*

the terms of a convention (=things a convention states must happen) *The terms of the convention still apply.*

article/paragraph ... of a convention *Article 3 of the convention states the following.*

be in breach of a convention (=have done something that is not allowed by it) *His treatment was in breach of the Convention on Human Rights.*

3 the way something is usually done, or people's attitudes about what is the most normal and correct way to do something

> **Grammar**
> This meaning of **convention** can be countable or uncountable.

ADJECTIVES

the normal/usual convention *The normal convention is to reply to an invitation.*

an established convention (=one that has been used for a long time) *There are established conventions for how you should end a letter.*

an accepted convention *This way of referring to an unknown person as 's/he' is a widely accepted convention.*

a social/cultural convention *Each society has its own cultural conventions.*

VERBS

follow convention (=do what is accepted and normal) *If everyone followed convention, life would be very dull.*

break (with) convention (=not do what is accepted or normal) *She broke with convention and chose a pink wedding dress.*

use/adopt/follow a convention *We will use the usual convention of representing an unknown number as x.*

defy/flout convention (=deliberately not do what is accepted or normal) *He loved to flout convention by his eccentric behaviour.*

be bound by convention (=have to do something in a particular way because of convention) *You do not need to be bound by convention and wear black to a funeral.*

convention demands/dictates sth (=says that something should happen in a particular way) *Convention dictates that children take their father's family name.*

PREPOSITIONS

according to convention *Society expects us to act according to convention.*

by convention (=according to convention) *By convention, the bride's father gives her away at her wedding.*

PHRASES

sth is a matter of convention *It is a matter of convention for business people to wear suits.*

a set of conventions *In a different culture, you will have to learn a different set of conventions.*

rules and conventions *Women were expected to behave according to certain rules and conventions.*

a break with convention *In a break with convention, women were allowed into the club.*

conversation *n*

an informal talk in which people exchange news, feelings, and thoughts

ADJECTIVES

a short/brief/quick conversation *We only had time for a brief conversation.*

a long conversation *Joe had several long conversations with Maureen and she told him about her feelings.*

a serious/intelligent/meaningful conversation *He's always making jokes, and it's difficult to have a serious conversation with him.*

an informal/casual conversation *I heard someone say something about it in an informal conversation.*

a private conversation *Is there somewhere near here where we can have private conversation?*

an animated/lively conversation (=in which people get excited) *They seemed to be having an animated conversation about who was responsible for the accident.*

an after-dinner conversation *The scandal was the subject of many after-dinner conversations.*

a face-to-face conversation *I don't like sending emails. I much prefer to have a face-to-face conversation.*

NOUNS + conversation

a phone/telephone conversation *The president had a phone conversation with the German chancellor.*

VERBS + conversation

have a conversation with sb *She was having a conversation with one of her friends on her phone.*

hold/conduct/carry on a conversation (=have a conversation - more formal) *The noise of the traffic made it difficult to hold a conversation.*

get into/enter into a conversation (=become involved in a conversation with someone) *I was at my daughter's school and I got into a conversation with her teacher.*

join in/take part in a conversation *I didn't know anything about baseball, so it was hard for me to join in their conversation.*

strike up a conversation with sb (=start talking to someone) *She struck up a conversation with one of the other passengers.*

engage sb in conversation/initiate a conversation with sb *formal* (=make someone have a conversation with you) *He is very shy and it can be difficult to engage him in conversation.*

make (polite) conversation (=talk to someone about unimportant things so that you can have a conversation) *"Nice weather, isn't it?" he said, trying to make conversation.*

overhear a conversation (=hear someone else's conversation) *I overheard the conversation in the dressing room next to me.*

interrupt sb's conversation *Sorry – I hope I'm not interrupting your conversation.*

conversation + VERBS

a conversation takes place *The conversation took place in the early hours of the morning.*

the conversation turns to sth (=people start talking about something) *The conversation turned to politics.*

PREPOSITIONS

a conversation about sth *We had a conversation about the best way to cook rice.*

a conversation with sb *He paused then continued his conversation with her.*

a conversation between sb (and sb) *There was a telephone conversation between the two leaders.*

PHRASES

be deep in conversation (=be having a serious conversation, so that you do not notice what is happening around you) *The two men appeared to be deep in conversation about something.*

a topic/subject of conversation *The only topic of conversation was food.*

convey *v*

to communicate or express something, with or without using words

NOUNS

convey a message *The poem conveys a message about war.*

convey information/facts *All this information can be conveyed in a simple diagram.*

convey meaning *Children sometimes find it easier to use pictures to convey meaning.*

convey a sense/an impression of sth *The music conveys a sense of sadness and despair.*

convey an idea *In her portrait, I was trying to convey the idea of dignity.*

convey an image *Make sure your clothes convey the right image for a job interview.*

convey a feeling/an emotion *How could he convey his feelings for her?*

ADVERBS

clearly convey sth *His tone of voice clearly conveyed his disgust.*

adequately convey sth *Words cannot adequately convey how relieved I am.*

effectively/successfully convey sth *The novel effectively conveys some of the country's problems.*

powerfully/vividly convey sth (=in a way that affects you or makes you take notice) *The sense of desperation is powerfully conveyed in the music.*

PREPOSITIONS

convey sth to sb *We use words to convey our thoughts to other people.*

convincing [Ac] *adj*

making you believe that something is true, real, or right

NOUNS

convincing evidence/proof *There is now convincing evidence that the Earth's climate is changing.*

a convincing argument/case *One of the most convincing arguments against the death penalty is that an innocent person could be killed.*

a convincing explanation *I can't think of a more convincing explanation.*

a convincing reason *There are no convincing reasons to believe this story.*

ADVERBS

totally/completely/entirely/utterly convincing *His portrayal of the ageing boxer is entirely convincing.*

far from convincing/not remotely convincing (=not at all convincing) *Their explanation was far from convincing.*

VERBS

seem/sound/look convincing *This idea sounds convincing at first.*

find sth convincing *Many people found his arguments convincing.*

convoluted *adj* THESAURUS **complicated**

convoy *n*

a group of vehicles or ships travelling together, sometimes in order to protect one another

ADJECTIVES/NOUNS + convoy

an aid/relief/humanitarian convoy (=taking food, clothes, medicine etc to people in disaster areas) *A relief convoy was turned back at the border.*

a food convoy *Troops guard the food convoys.*

a military/army convoy *The military convoy moved towards Budapest.*

a naval convoy *The ship is part of a US naval convoy.*

a troop convoy *Twenty-eight soldiers were killed in an attack on a troop convoy.*

a police convoy (=of police vehicles) *He was driven off at speed in a police convoy.*

an armed convoy *The president travelled to the meeting in an armed convoy.*

a refugee convoy (=of people trying to escape from a war, disaster etc) *The refugee convoy consisted of several hundred buses and 3,000 people.*

VERBS

join a convoy *Three more cars joined the convoy.*

lead a convoy *Alan led the convoy in his blue sports car.*

escort a convoy (=go with a convoy) *Troops will escort convoys of emergency food through the war zone.*

ambush a convoy (=hide and then attack as it passes) *Gunmen ambushed a convoy of trucks heading north.*

a convoy carries/transports sth *The military convoy was carrying supplies to a NATO base.*

a convoy arrives/leaves *The convoy arrived carrying 450 tonnes of food.*

a convoy reaches sth *When is the convoy expected to reach its destination?*

PREPOSITIONS

a convoy of sb/sth *A convoy of military vehicles rumbled past.*

be in a convoy *There were seven cars in the convoy.*

in convoy (=travelling together, in separate vehicles) *We all drove to the beach in convoy.*

cook[1] *v*

to prepare food for eating using heat

NOUNS

cook rice/vegetables/meat etc *Cook the onion until it is soft.*

cook food *She tends to cook very spicy food.*

cook a meal *David cooks all his own meals.*

cook (sb) breakfast/lunch/dinner *He offered to cook me dinner one evening.*

VERBS

learn to cook *She learned to cook from her mother.*

like/love to cook *My dad loves to cook.*

ADVERBS

cook sth slowly *The pumpkin has to be cooked slowly.*

cook sth gently (=on a low heat) *Cook the sauce gently for about 5 minutes.*

cook sth thoroughly *Cook food thoroughly to destroy bacteria.*

be well cooked (=cooked for a long enough time, or cooked skilfully) *Always make sure your food is well cooked.*

be perfectly/beautifully cooked *The fish was perfectly cooked.*

PREPOSITIONS

cook sth in the oven/in a pan *Mushrooms can be fried, grilled, or cooked in the oven.*

cook for sb *I've offered to cook for some friends.*

PHRASES

be cooked to perfection (=cooked perfectly) *All the dishes were cooked to perfection by the French chef.*

THESAURUS: cook

make a meal

make
breakfast | **lunch** | **dinner** | **supper** | **meal** | **salad** | **sandwich** | **pasta** | **pizza** | **curry**
to cook a meal or a kind of food, or get all the parts of it ready:
It's your turn to make breakfast. | *I made some supper for the children.* | *He made us a fantastic meal.* | *I think I'll make a salad for lunch.* | *She makes her own pasta.*

> **Make** or **cook?**
> When talking about meals such as breakfast, lunch or dinner, you usually use **make**.
> When you use **cook**, the focus is on heating food, usually in a pan, so that it is ready to eat.
> You can use **make** about foods that do not need heat, such as salads or sandwiches.

prepare
meal | **food** | **dish** | **vegetables** | **sauce**
to get a meal or a kind of food ready to eat. **Prepare** is more formal than **make**:
She had prepared a delicious meal for them. | *The dish takes a long time to prepare.*

fix *AmE informal*
meal | **something to eat** | **breakfast** | **lunch** | **dinner** | **supper** | **sandwich**
to make a meal quickly:
I'll fix us something to eat. | *Mom fixed me a sandwich.*

rustle up *informal*
meal | **breakfast** | **supper**
to cook a meal or dish quickly using whatever is available:
The book tells you how to rustle up an inexpensive meal in a few minutes. | *If friends arrived unexpectedly, could you rustle up some supper?* | *I'm not sure what we have in the fridge, but I'm sure I can* **rustle something up**.

different ways of cooking something

bake
bread | **cake** | **pie** | **potato** | **fish** | **apple**
to cook food in an oven:
She bakes her own bread. | *I ordered baked potato topped with cheese.*

roast
turkey | **chicken** | **beef** | **pork** | **meat** | **potato**
to cook meat in an oven, usually in its own juice. You can also roast potatoes in an oven, often using the juices from the meat:
Roast the meat for 20 minutes. | *Roast the potatoes in a hot oven.*

> Don't say 'roasted potatoes/beef/chicken'. Say **roast potatoes/beef/chicken.**

fry
vegetables | **onion** | **mushroom** | **egg** | **bacon** | **chicken** | **rice**
to cook food in hot oil or fat in a pan:
First of all, fry an onion in some olive oil. | *I ordered fried eggs.*

sauté
vegetables | **potato** | **onion** | **mushroom** | **chicken** | **beef**
to fry vegetables or meat for a short time in a small amount of butter or oil:
Sauté the mushrooms for two minutes. | *I had sautéed chicken and rice.*

stir-fry
vegetables | **beef** | **chicken** | **prawns** | **noodles**
to fry small pieces of food while moving them around continuously:
The prawns were served with stir-fried vegetables and noodles.

deep fry
vegetables | **fish** | **prawns**
to cook food under the surface of hot oil or fat:
The vegetables are dipped in batter and then deep fried.

grill
cheese | **chicken** | **meat** | **steak** | **fish** | **vegetables** | **onion** | **tomato**
to cook food over or under strong heat:
I'll have a grilled cheese sandwich. | *Grill the tomatoes until they turn brown.*

broil *AmE*
chicken | **fish** | **beef** | **steak**
to cook food under heat, especially fish or chicken:
They have the best broiled chicken in town.

boil
egg | **potato** | **rice**
to cook food in very hot water:
He doesn't even know how to boil an egg. | *The dish was served with boiled potatoes.*

steam
vegetables | rice | couscous
to cook food using steam:
Steam the vegetables until they are tender.

poach
egg | fish | pear
to cook food slowly in hot water, wine, or milk:
We had poached eggs on toast. | You can poach the pears in white wine.

barbecue
chicken | fish | beef | ribs
to cook food on a metal frame over a fire outdoors:
Most American restaurants serve barbecued chicken. | They barbecued the fish on a grill.

microwave
to cook food in a microwave oven:
Food that has been microwaved is often very hot in the middle.

C

cook² *n*

someone who prepares and cooks food

ADJECTIVES

a good cook *My mother is a very good cook.*

a great/excellent/fantastic cook *Thanks for a lovely meal - you're an excellent cook.*

a bad/terrible cook *I admit I'm a terrible cook.*

a professional cook (=someone who cooks as their job) *These knives are used by professional cooks.*

an amateur cook (=someone who cooks for their family or for fun, not as their job) *The book has lots of advice for the amateur cook.*

⚠ Don't say 'He is a good cooker.' Say **He is a good cook**.

THESAURUS: cook

chef
a professional cook, especially one who works in a restaurant or hotel:
The ***head chef*** *at the hotel is from France. | The restaurant is owned by* ***celebrity chef*** *Gordon Ramsay* (=a well-known chef who often appears on television).

cooking *n*

the act of making food and cooking it

ADJECTIVES/NOUNS + cooking

home cooking (=food cooked at home, not in a restaurant) *Home cooking always tastes best.*

Italian/French/Mexican etc cooking *Fresh herbs are used a lot in Thai cooking.*

regional cooking (=food cooked in a particular area) *Italy is famous for its superb regional cooking.*

traditional cooking *Traditional Japanese cooking has five distinctive types of dishes.*

vegetarian cooking *I bought a book on vegetarian cooking.*

VERBS

do the cooking *Who does the cooking in your house?*

share the cooking *Pete and I usually share the cooking.*

like/enjoy cooking *I enjoy cooking at the weekend.*

cooking + NOUNS

cooking facilities (=somewhere to cook, with the equipment you need) *There are cooking facilities in the apartments.*

cooking utensils (=pots, spoons, knives etc) *The kitchen has all the cooking utensils you will need.*

cooking time (=the time a particular thing takes to cook) *Adjust the cooking time according to the size of the chicken.*

cooking instructions *Follow the cooking instructions on the box.*

cool *adj* THESAURUS ▶ cold¹

cooperate [Ac] *v*

to work together with someone, in order to achieve something

ADVERBS

cooperate closely *The two governments are cooperating closely with each other in the fight against terrorism.*

cooperate fully (=completely) *We will, of course, cooperate fully with the inquiry.*

PREPOSITIONS

cooperate with sb *The US troops will continue to cooperate with local forces.*

PHRASES

be willing/ready/prepared to cooperate *He says he is willing to cooperate with the police and help them find the killer.*

agree to cooperate *The countries all agreed to cooperate in protecting the environment.*

refuse/fail to cooperate *People who refuse to cooperate could face prosecution.*

cooperation [Ac] *n*

working together with someone to achieve something that you both want

ADJECTIVES

complete/full cooperation *We hope to have your complete cooperation.*

close cooperation *We work in close cooperation with many local agencies.*

better/greater cooperation *Without better cooperation from students, we will not succeed.*

effective cooperation *He criticized a lack of effective cooperation among the staff.*

mutual cooperation (=when both people, groups etc cooperate) *Because of the size of the task, mutual cooperation was essential.*

political/economic/military cooperation *The association deals with trade and economic cooperation.*

international cooperation *We need greater international cooperation to solve the problem.*

VERBS

have sb's cooperation *He promised we would have his full cooperation.*

get sb's cooperation (*also* **gain/secure sb's cooperation** *formal*): *If we can gain the cooperation of other users, we are much more likely to succeed.*

give/offer (sb) your cooperation *Many local businesses have offered their cooperation.*

need/require sb's cooperation *Schools need the cooperation of parents.*

improve/increase cooperation *We need to improve cooperation with foreign governments in the fight against drugs.*

encourage/promote cooperation *The programme will promote cooperation between universities and industry.*

PREPOSITIONS

cooperation with sb *Cooperation with other countries is important.*

cooperation between/among sb *There should be more cooperation between management and workers.*

cooperation from sb *The school got no cooperation from her parents.*

with/without sb's cooperation *Without your cooperation we would not have succeeded.*

in cooperation with sb *A study was done in cooperation with oil companies.*

PHRASES

a lack of cooperation *There was a lack of cooperation among the staff at the hospital.*

coordination Ac *n*

1 the activity of making sure that people or organizations work together well

ADJECTIVES

close coordination *The police are working in close coordination with the army.*

good/effective coordination *There is very good coordination between local community groups.*

poor coordination *Poor coordination is preventing supplies from getting through to the people who need them.*

overall coordination (=general coordination) *Who is in charge of overall coordination of the work?*

VERBS

improve/strengthen coordination *The group was set up in order to improve coordination between schools and universities.*

PREPOSITIONS

coordination between sb/sth (and sb/sth) *He is in charge of coordination between the government and the aid organizations.*

coordination with sb *Coordination with officials in other countries is not always easy.*

in coordination with sb *The program is being carried out in coordination with the United Nations High Commissioner for Refugees.*

PHRASES

lack of coordination *Local officials began to complain about the lack of coordination between federal agencies.*

2 the way in which your muscles move together when you perform a movement

ADJECTIVES

good coordination *He's good at sports because he has good coordination.*

poor coordination (=not good) *People who have the illness often have poor coordination and they are unable to do simple tasks.*

physical coordination *She lacks the physical coordination needed to put her shoes on the right way.*

hand-eye/hand-to-eye coordination *Computer games help to develop your hand-eye coordination.*

VERBS

improve/develop your coordination *Dancing is an excellent way of improving your coordination.*

lose your coordination *As the illness progressed, he lost his coordination and he found it difficult to walk in a straight line.*

copy[1] *n*

1 something that is made to be exactly like another thing

ADJECTIVES/NOUNS + copy

a good/close/accurate copy (=very like the original) *It's not an original painting, but it's a very good copy.*

a faithful copy (=accurate) *The statue is a faithful copy of one in the palace gardens.*

an exact/identical/perfect copy *She had a ring made that was an exact copy of her grandmother's.*

a bad/poor copy *All he has done is produce poor copies of other people's work.*

a cheap copy *A market stall was selling cheap copies of designer handbags.*

an illegal copy *They warned us about buying illegal copies of the software.*

hard copy (=information from a computer printed on paper) *I like to see hard copy of important documents.*

C

a back-up copy (=made in case the original is lost) *Be sure you regularly make back-up copies of your data.*

a draft copy (=a version of a document that is not the final version) *He showed me a draft copy of the contract.*

an electronic copy (=on computer) *We keep electronic copies of all the documents.*

a paper/printed copy *I need a paper copy of the email.*

C

VERBS

make/create a copy of sth *Make a copy of the letter before you send it.*

take a copy (=make a copy of a document) *He asked his secretary to take a copy of the letter.*

keep/save a copy of sth *Did you keep a copy of the email?*

send/email (sb) a copy of sth *Could you send me a copy of the agreement?*

attach a copy of sth (=put it with an email) *I'm attaching a copy of the schedule.*

enclose a copy (=put it in a letter) *I enclose a copy of my resume.*

download a copy of sth *You can download a copy of the contract from our website.*

print a copy (*also* **run off a copy** *informal*): *She printed a copy of the email and put it in a file.*

PREPOSITIONS

a copy of sth *The rug is a copy of a fine Chinese carpet.*

2 one of many books, magazines, DVDs etc that are all exactly the same

VERBS

sth sells hundreds/thousands etc of copies *The book has sold millions of copies.*

print/produce copies of sth *The publishers printed 30,000 copies of the magazine.*

distribute/circulate copies of sth (=give them to a group of people) *Someone has been circulating copies of the leaflet among students.*

ADJECTIVES/NOUNS + copy

a free copy (*also* **a complimentary copy** *formal*): *He was handing out free copies of his latest book.*

a spare copy *Do you have a spare copy of the disk?*

your own/personal copy *Each student has their own copy of the book.*

a hardback/paperback copy (=a book with a hard cover or a paper cover) *Paperback copies are available from bookshops.*

a signed copy (=signed by the author) *She sent me a signed copy of her autobiography.*

an advance copy (=given to someone before it is available to the public) *The publishers sent me an advance copy of the book.*

copy[2] *v*

1 to deliberately make or produce something that is exactly like another thing

NOUNS

copy a file/CD/DVD *Press control and 'C' on your keyboard to copy a file.*

copy a letter/document/photograph *Please could you copy this letter for me?*

copy a painting/sculpture *I tried to copy his paintings to learn how to paint.*

ADVERBS

copy sth illegally *The films they were selling had been copied illegally.*

be widely copied (=by many people) *Michelangelo's statues were widely copied.*

PREPOSITIONS

copy sth onto sth *Copy the file onto your hard disk.*

copy sth from sth *DNA is copied from one cell to another.*

THESAURUS: copy

photocopy
to copy a document, picture, article etc onto a piece of paper, using a special machine:
I'll photocopy the article for you.

You can also say **make/take a photocopy (of sth)**: *The customs officer* ***made a photocopy*** *of my passport.*

reproduce
to print a copy of a picture or document, especially in a book or newspaper:
The image was reproduced in magazines and newspapers around the world. | *The paintings are* ***reproduced by kind permission of*** *the Tate Gallery* (=used when saying that someone has allowed you to print a copy of something).

forge
signature | **note** | **bill**
to illegally copy something written or printed:
He forged my signature in order to get money out of my account (=he copied the way I sign my name). | *Police found thousands of pounds of forged £10 notes.*

2 to use someone else's words, answers, or ideas instead of your own

NOUNS

copy sb's idea *Be creative – don't just copy other people's ideas.*

copy sb's work *If the teacher sees you copying anyone else's work, you will be in trouble.*

copy sb's style *Many young photographers have copied his style.*

ADVERBS

blatantly copy sth (=in an obvious way, without trying to hide it) *The idea was blatantly copied from the company's competitors.*

blindly/slavishly copy sth (=exactly, without thinking for yourself) *His designs have been slavishly copied by other fashion designers.*

VERBS

accuse sb of copying sb *They have been accused of copying other bands.*

catch sb copying sb (=notice someone looking at someone else's work and copying it) *Any student caught copying will fail the test.*

PREPOSITIONS

copy from sb (=cheat by copying someone else's work) *David had copied from the girl next to him.*

THESAURUS: copy

plagiarize (*also* **plagiarise** *BrE*)
work | **book** | **essay** | **speech**
to copy things that other people have written and pretend that they are your own work:
He denied that he had plagiarized the work of other scientists. | *The book was* ***plagiarized from*** *another book by Sir Everard Digby.*

The activity of copying other people's work is called **plagiarism**: *There have been accusations of* ***plagiarism****.*

steal
idea | **design**
to take someone else's ideas and use them without permission, in order to make money from them. You use **steal** especially when this seems shocking:
He was worried that someone else would steal his idea. | *The inventor claims that the company stole his design for a vacuum cleaner.*

3 to write down words or numbers exactly as you read or hear them

NOUNS

copy an address/phone number *I copied the address in my notebook.*

copy information/details *She copied all the relevant information from the website.*

ADVERBS

copy sth carefully *He copied her name carefully into his address book.*

copy sth laboriously/meticulously (=very carefully) *He had meticulously copied hundreds of names.*

copy sth faithfully (=so it is exactly like the original) *I have faithfully copied his words.*

copy sth accurately *It is important to copy the place names accurately.*

copy sth word for word/verbatim (=using someone's exact words) *Students need to learn to write using their own words, rather than just copying verbatim from books.*

PREPOSITIONS

copy (sth) from sth *Copy the vocabulary list from the whiteboard.*

copy sth into a book/notebook *He copied the number into his notebook.*

cordial *adj* THESAURUS ▸ **friendly**

core *adj* THESAURUS ▸ **basic (1)**, **main**

corner *n*

1 a point or place where two lines, edges, walls etc meet

ADJECTIVES

the top/bottom corner *The ball flew straight into the top corner of the net.*

the far/opposite corner (=furthest from where you are) *Something was moving in the far corner of the garden.*

the right-hand/left-hand corner *We followed the path to the left-hand corner of the field.*

a quiet/dark corner (=in a room, garden etc) *He sat on his own in a quiet corner of the library.*

a shady corner (=protected from the sun in a garden) *Plant the herbs in a shady corner of the garden.*

PREPOSITIONS

in a/the corner *They had a red flag with a golden star in the corner.*

on the corner *She sat on the corner of her bed.*

2 the point where two roads meet

ADJECTIVES/NOUNS + corner

a street corner *She waited for her friend on the street corner.*

a tight/sharp corner (=very curved and difficult to drive around) *Go slowly because there's a sharp corner up ahead.*

a blind corner (=one that you cannot see around) *The car had come around a blind corner much too fast.*

VERBS

turn the corner (=go around a corner) *I walked on and turned the corner into Church Road.*

come/go around a corner *At that moment, a police car came around the corner.*

approach a corner *Reduce your speed as you approach the corner.*

PREPOSITIONS

on a corner *They stood on the corner chatting.*

at the corner *We met in the café at the corner of the street.*

around the corner (=very near here) *There's a postbox just around the corner.*

C

corporate Ac *adj*
belonging to or relating to a corporation

NOUNS

corporate headquarters (=a big company's main offices) *The company is moving its corporate headquarters from New York to Houston.*

corporate profits *US corporate profits were higher than expected.*

the corporate sector (=the area of business involving big companies) *The UK corporate sector is very competitive.*

the corporate world *After 15 years, I really wanted to escape the corporate world.*

corporate culture (=the way the people in a big company think and behave) *We need to change the corporate culture to accept family-friendly policies.*

the corporate ladder (=the levels in a big company, that you move up in your career) *He climbed up the corporate ladder until he became vice-president.*

corporate identity/image (=the way a company presents itself to the public) *Companies are always anxious to protect their corporate image.*

corporate hospitality (=entertainment provided by companies for their customers) *The castle can be hired for corporate hospitality.*

correct *adj* having no mistakes

ADVERBS

absolutely/perfectly/entirely correct (=correct in every way) *What he said was perfectly correct.*

broadly/essentially/basically correct (=in most ways) *The results of his research are essentially correct.*

grammatically correct (=written or spoken with correct grammar) *The sentence is grammatically correct, but doesn't sound natural.*

factually correct (=having all the correct facts) *Newspaper articles are not always factually correct.*

technically correct (=according to the exact details of a rule or law) *The referee was technically correct in not allowing the goal.*

not strictly correct (=not completely) *It's not strictly correct to say he lied.*

partially/partly correct *Her answer was only partially correct.*

politically correct (=used to describe language and behaviour that are carefully chosen so they do not offend anyone) *It's not politically correct to describe people as 'disabled'.*

NOUNS

the correct answer *Score one point for each correct answer.*

correct information *I'm not sure that I've been given the correct information.*

the correct address/phone number *Make sure you have the correct address before you set off.*

the correct size/temperature/position *He cut the wood to the correct size.*

the correct order *Put these numbers in the correct order.*

a correct entry (=answer in a competition) *The first five correct entries will win a prize.*

correct spelling/grammar/pronunciation *I'm never sure of the correct spelling of words like 'accommodation'.*

the correct term (=the correct word) *What is the correct term for someone who is from the Netherlands?*

the correct way of doing sth *She asked me about the correct way of replying to a wedding invitation.*

VERBS

prove correct (=be shown to be true) *Fortunately, my memory proved correct.*

correlation *n*
a connection between two ideas, facts etc, especially when one may be the cause of the other

ADJECTIVES

a significant correlation *There is no significant correlation between age and work performance.*

a strong/high/close correlation (=things are closely related) *They found a high correlation between drinking alcohol and violence.*

a poor/weak correlation (=things are not closely related) *The graph shows whether there is a strong or weak correlation between two values.*

a general/broad correlation (=in most situations, but not all) *There is a general correlation between body size and the size of our brains.*

a direct correlation *Research showed a direct correlation between TV viewing and poor academic work.*

a clear/obvious correlation *There is a clear correlation between carbon dioxide emissions and global warming.*

a positive correlation (=if one thing increases, the other also increases) *They found a positive correlation between income and health.*

a negative/inverse correlation (=if one thing increases, the other decreases) *Is there an inverse correlation between a person's weight and the distance they walk on an average day?*

VERBS

show a correlation (*also* **demonstrate a correlation** *formal*): *Studies have shown a correlation between crime and poverty.*

find a correlation (*also* **identify/establish a correlation** *formal*): *Researchers failed to find any correlation between the two.*

observe a correlation *A correlation has been observed between untidiness and creativity.*

a correlation exists/there is a correlation *A strong correlation exists between social class and exam success.*

PREPOSITIONS

a correlation between sth and sth *Is there a correlation between health and happiness?*

a correlation with sth *He noticed a correlation with the time of year.*

correspondent *n*

a journalist reporting news from a particular area or on a particular subject

ADJECTIVES/NOUNS + correspondent

a foreign correspondent (=reporting on other countries) *She works as a foreign correspondent for the 'New York Times'.*

a political correspondent *The report was from their political correspondent in Washington.*

a newspaper/television/radio correspondent *The president told newspaper correspondents about his plans last night.*

a sports/education/health/science etc correspondent *Here is our sports correspondent with all the details of yesterday's game.*

a war correspondent *A war correspondent from 'The Sunday Times' was killed by rebel soldiers.*

a diplomatic correspondent (=who reports about relations between countries) *The BBC's diplomatic correspondent is in Beijing to cover the story.*

a special correspondent (=one with a special area of responsibility) *She is the paper's special correspondent for the environment.*

the Beijing/Cairo/Washington etc correspondent (=sending reports from a particular place) *This report comes direct from our Tel Aviv correspondent.*

PREPOSITIONS

a correspondent for/with sth *She is a political correspondent with 'The Washington Post'.*

corrupt *adj*

dishonest and immoral, because people use power to get advantages for themselves

NOUNS

a corrupt official/politician/police officer etc *Corrupt judges have taken millions of dollars in bribes.*

a corrupt government/regime *The government is completely corrupt and it is impossible to get anything done without paying bribes.*

corrupt practices *The police were found to be guilty of bribery and other corrupt practices.*

ADVERBS

deeply corrupt (=very corrupt) *The book examines the deeply corrupt relationship between corporations and the government.*

totally/completely/utterly corrupt *The elections will not be fair, because the government is totally corrupt.*

politically corrupt *The country has a reputation for being politically corrupt.*

morally corrupt *The mine owners were wicked and morally corrupt.*

inherently corrupt (=corrupt because of the way it is organized) *The present system of giving honours is inherently corrupt.*

THESAURUS: corrupt

corrupt, devious, sneaky, sly, underhand, unscrupulous, fraudulent, deceitful → dishonest

corruption *n*

dishonest or immoral behaviour by people with power

ADJECTIVES/NOUNS + corruption

political/financial corruption *The country has a long history of political corruption.*

government/police corruption *There will be an inquiry into police corruption.*

widespread corruption (=in many areas) *There is widespread corruption in government.*

corruption is rife (=it is very common) *Corruption is rife among government officials.*

rampant corruption (=it is common, especially in a way that seems shocking) *The country faced major problems, including rampant corruption.*

high-level corruption (=among senior officials) *The new minister has promised to end high-level corruption.*

VERBS

fight/tackle corruption (=try to stop it) *He criticized the minister for failing to fight corruption within government.*

root out/weed out corruption (=find and stop it) *The president is launching a new campaign to root out corruption.*

stamp out/eradicate corruption (=stop it completely) *The party's chairman called for action to stamp out corruption.*

expose/uncover corruption (=show that it exists) *He wrote a newspaper article exposing corruption in government.*

corruption + NOUNS

a corruption scandal *All the newspapers are reporting the latest government corruption scandal.*

a corruption investigation/probe *She is the officer in charge of the corruption investigation.*

C

PHRASES

allegations/charges of corruption *The club's chairman has strongly denied allegations of corruption.*

bribery and corruption *It seems that bribery and corruption were widespread in the council.*

cost[1] *n*

1 the amount of money that you have to pay in order to buy, do, or produce something

ADJECTIVES

high/low cost *Drivers are angry about the high cost of fuel.*

the average cost of sth *The average cost of a wedding is around $25,000.*

the total/full cost *The total cost of the project was over $30 million.*

the annual/monthly cost *The annual cost of membership has increased.*

the estimated cost *The estimated cost of the repairs was £3,000.*

exorbitant/extortionate cost (=much too high) *The cost of court cases is exorbitant.*

prohibitive cost (=so high that people cannot afford to buy or do something) *People in poor countries are dying because of the prohibitive cost of drugs.*

the rising cost of sth *Older people are worried about the rising cost of electricity.*

the final cost *No one knows what the final cost will be.*

VERBS + cost

pay/cover the cost (*also* **meet/bear the cost** *formal*): *His parents have offered to meet the cost of his college fees.*

afford the cost *Many people cannot afford the cost of the treatment.*

cut/reduce/lower/bring down the cost *If you go later in the year, it will bring down the cost of your holiday.*

keep the cost down (=make the cost as low as possible) *Companies are using fewer workers in order to keep their employment costs down.*

increase/push up the cost *The new tax will increase the cost of owning a car.*

cost + VERBS

the cost rises/goes up *The cost of electricity has risen again.*

the cost falls/goes down *The average cost of a flight has fallen considerably.*

NOUNS + cost

labour/production/transport etc costs *The company employs hundreds of workers, so labour costs are very high.*

running/operating costs (=the amount it costs to run a machine, system, or business) *The new technology is cheaper and the running costs are lower.*

administrative costs (=the cost of running an organization or for paying for things to be done as part of an official system) *There have been complaints about poor customer service and high administrative costs.*

PHRASES

the cost of living (=the amount you need to pay for food, clothes etc) *People are complaining about the rising cost of living.*

at a cost of (=used for saying what the cost of something is) *They've built a new factory, at a cost of £10 million.*

at no extra cost (=without having to pay more money) *Many of these services are available to guests at no extra cost.*

Cost or price?

You use **price** when talking about the exact money that you have to pay when you buy something in a shop, or pay to use something: *The* ***price*** *is on the back cover of the book.* | *The* ***price*** *includes breakfast.*

You often use **cost** when talking in a general way about whether something is expensive or cheap, rather than the exact price: *The* ***cost*** *of living in Sweden is very high.* | *The* ***cost*** *of insurance keeps going up.*

Costs is also used about the total amount of money that a company or organization spends: *Companies are always trying to find ways of cutting* ***costs****.*

THESAURUS: cost

price
the amount of money you must pay for something that is for sale:
Prices were ***lower*** *in those days.* | *Stores are charging* ***higher prices*** *for electronic goods.* | *They sell good-quality clothes at* ***reasonable prices****.* | *How much is the* ***price of*** *a plane ticket to New York?*

value
the amount of money that something is worth:
A new kitchen can ***increase*** *the* ***value*** *of your home.* | *The* ***value*** *of your investment can* ***go down*** *as well as up.*

charge
the amount that you have to pay for a service or to use something:
Bank ***charges*** *have increased.* | *There is a small* ***delivery charge****.* | *Hotel guests may use the gym* ***for a small charge****.*

fee
the amount you have to pay to enter a place or join a group, or for the services of a professional person such as a lawyer or a doctor:
There is no ***entrance fee*** *to get into the museum.* | *The* ***membership fee*** *is £125 a year.* | *We had to pay a lot of money in* ***legal fees****.*

fare
the amount you have to pay to travel somewhere by bus, plane, train etc:
*I didn't even have enough money for my **bus fare**. | The train company has announced big **fare increases**. | The **air fare** to London is just under $500.*

rent
the amount you have to pay to live in or use a place that you do not own:
*The **rent on** his apartment is $800 a month. | Rents are **high** in this area. | People are attracted by the **low rents**.*

rate
a charge that is set according to a standard scale:
*Most TV stations offer **special rates** to local advertisers. | Banks are able to charge **high rates** of interest.*

toll
the amount you have to pay to travel on some roads or bridges:
*You have to pay **tolls on** many French motorways. | The government is planning to introduce **road tolls** to reduce traffic congestion.*

2 the damage, losses, or other bad effects that are caused by something

ADJECTIVES

great/huge/enormous/heavy/terrible cost *They succeeded in capturing the city at great cost in terms of human life.*

personal cost *He was determined to continue with his work, regardless of the personal cost.*

the social cost *The social cost of their policies was enormous and many people lost their jobs.*

the human cost *His photographs show the human cost of war.*

the environmental cost *In spite of the benefits they bring, cars carry a massive environmental cost.*

the full cost *The full cost of the disaster may never be known.*

VERBS

pay the cost *Future generations will have to pay the cost of our failure to protect the environment.*

sth comes at a cost/carries a cost *Her success as a singer came at a huge cost to her personal life.*

PREPOSITIONS

the cost to sb/sth *The cost to local wildlife was enormous.*

at a cost *The Russians defeated the invasion at the cost of millions of lives.*

PHRASES

at any cost/at all costs (=even though it may cause a lot of problems) *He wanted to win, at any cost.*

find/learn/discover sth to your cost (=to realise something because of a bad experience) *Superior strength does not necessarily mean victory, as the US learned to its cost in Vietnam.*

cost² *v* to have a particular price

PHRASES

cost a lot *The course is good but it costs a lot.*

cost a fortune/cost the earth *informal* (=have a very high price) *The ring must have cost a fortune.*

not cost (very) much *The drug does not cost very much.*

cost sth per minute/hour/year etc *Calls cost only 2p per minute.*

not cost (sb) a penny (=cost nothing) *Using the internet, you can make phone calls that don't cost a penny.*

cost sth per person (*also* **cost sth per head** *formal*): *A meal costs £80 per person.*

costly *adj* THESAURUS **expensive**

costs *n* THESAURUS **spending**

costume *n*

a set of special clothes - used especially about clothes worn by actors, traditional clothes worn by people who live in a place, or clothes worn by people who lived at a time in the past

ADJECTIVES/NOUNS + costume

the traditional costume *The local women were dressed in their traditional costumes.*

the national costume (=the clothes that are traditionally worn in a country) *The men were wearing the Japanese national costume.*

period costume/historical costume (=clothes like those worn at a particular time) *The play is set in the 1700s, and the actors wear period costumes.*

a clown/fairy/rabbit etc costume *He wore a red-striped clown costume and big shoes.*

a fancy-dress costume *BrE*: *The shop hires out fancy-dress costumes for parties.*

a colourful costume *BrE*, **a colorful costume** *AmE*: *The actors wore colourful costumes.*

an elaborate/lavish costume (=expensive and detailed) *The film features lavish costumes and spectacular sets.*

an outlandish costume (=very strange) *He used to play guitar and wear outlandish costumes in a punk band.*

VERBS

wear a costume/be dressed in a costume *The children wore witch costumes for Halloween.*

PHRASES

in full costume *The rehearsal will be in full costume.*

cosy *adj* THESAURUS **comfortable**

cottage *n* a small house in the country

ADJECTIVES/NOUNS + cottage

a little/small/tiny cottage *He lived all his life in a small cottage by the river.*

a country cottage (=in the countryside) *We dreamed of leaving the city and buying a country cottage.*

a thatched cottage (=with a roof made from dry straw) *The village is full of traditional thatched cottages.*

a holiday cottage *BrE* (=that people use or rent for holidays) *We rented a holiday cottage in Wales.*

a weekend/summer cottage (=that the owners go to at weekends or in the summer) *They live in London but they also have a weekend cottage by the sea.*

VERBS

live in a cottage *She lives in a pretty little cottage in the country.*

rent/hire a cottage (*also* **take a cottage** *formal*): *We've rented a cottage in the Highlands for New Year.*

have/own a cottage *It would be nice to have a weekend cottage.*

cough[1] *n*

1 a medical condition that makes you cough a lot

VERBS

have (got) a cough *I've had a cough for weeks now.*

get/develop a cough *A lot of people get coughs at this time of year.*

relieve/soothe/treat a cough (=make it less severe) *This medicine will help to relieve your cough.*

ADJECTIVES

a bad/nasty/terrible cough *She had a bad cough and a sore throat.*

a slight cough (=one that is not very serious) *He has a slight cough but I don't think he's really ill.*

a smoker's cough (=one caused by smoking) *He's a heavy smoker and has the typical smoker's cough.*

a tickly cough (=one that keeps irritating your throat) *I had a tickly cough, a runny nose and a high temperature.*

a violent cough (=one in which someone coughs very loudly) *The symptoms include a violent cough.*

cough + NOUNS

cough medicine/syrup/mixture *You should take some cough medicine.*

a cough drop (*also* **a cough sweet** *BrE*) (=a sweet you suck to make a cough less severe) *He was sucking on a cough sweet.*

2 the action of coughing

ADJECTIVES

a loud cough *There was a loud cough from someone in the audience.*

a quiet/little cough *His friend gave a little cough, to attract his attention.*

VERBS

give a cough *Stuart gave an embarrassed cough.*

cough[2] *v*

to suddenly push air out of your throat with a short sound, often repeatedly

ADVERBS

cough politely/discreetly *She coughed politely to get their attention.*

cough nervously *He coughed nervously and changed the subject.*

cough loudly *He walked into the doctor's room, coughing loudly.*

VERBS

make sb cough *The dust in the air made him cough.*

PHRASES

be coughing and sneezing *I think I'm getting a cold – I've been coughing and sneezing all day.*

be coughing and spluttering *BrE* (=coughing a lot) *She woke up coughing and spluttering.*

a coughing fit (=a long period of continued coughing) *He had a terrible coughing fit.*

council *n*

1 a group of people chosen to make rules or decisions

ADJECTIVES/NOUNS + council

the executive/ruling/governing council (=the most important council) *He is a member of the union's national executive council.*

the school/student council *Members of the student council had discussions with the principal of the university.*

an advisory council (=which gives advice) *The report was issued by the Advisory Council on Science and Technology.*

council + NOUNS

a council member *School council members are elected by their fellow students.*

2 an organization providing services in a local area

ADJECTIVES/NOUNS + council

the city/county/district council *The city council is responsible for making sure that the roads are in good condition.*

the local council *Schools are managed by the local council.*

council + NOUNS

a council house *BrE* (=owned by a council and rented to people) *She's lived in a council house all her life.*

a council estate *BrE* (=an area of houses owned by a council and rented to people) *The road runs through the middle of a large council estate.*

a council meeting *Council meetings are open to the public.*

PREPOSITIONS

on the council *The Conservatives are the largest group on the council.*

count *n*

the process of counting, or the total number counted

VERBS

do/make a count *She did a count to make sure that there were enough chairs.*

keep (a) count (=keep checking so that you know how many people or things there are) *He kept a count of the number of correct answers.*

lose count (=forget how many, especially because there are a lot) *I've lost count of the number of times I've seen this film.*

ADJECTIVES

a quick count *He did a quick count of the number of people in the room.*

a rough count (=not exact) *I made a rough count of the houses in the street.*

a word/page count (=of the number of words or pages) *Your computer can do an automatic word count.*

a head count (=of the number of people who are there) *Make sure you do a head count before the children get back on the bus.*

counterfeit *adj* THESAURUS **false**

country *n*

1 an area of land that has its own government, president, king etc

ADJECTIVES

an independent country *Malaysia has been an independent country since 1963.*

sb's home/native country *After five years in the US, she returned to her home country, Japan.*

a foreign country *How many foreign countries have you visited?*

a rich/wealthy/prosperous country *Germany is one of the richest countries in the world.*

a poor/developing country *Many developing countries rely on foreign aid.*

a developed/industrialized/advanced country (=rich, with a lot of industry and trade) *Developed countries are responsible for most of the world's pollution.*

a democratic country *In a democratic country, everyone has the right of free speech.*

a neighbouring country *BrE*, **a neighboring country** *AmE* (=next to another country) *People are worried that the fighting could spread to neighbouring countries.*

a Western/European/African/Asian etc country *The president will be visiting four European countries.*

sb's adopted country (=that they have chosen to live in permanently) *She loved France, her adopted country.*

NOUNS + country

a member country *There were talks between the member countries of the European Union.*

the host country (=where an event is held) *They will meet to decide which will be the host country for the next World Cup.*

VERBS

rule/run/govern a country *The country has been ruled by the same party for over 20 years.*

lead the country *She became the first woman to lead the country.*

leave the country *Foreign journalists were given 24 hours to leave the country.*

flee the country (=leave it quickly to avoid trouble) *At the outbreak of the war, many people fled the country.*

serve your country *These soldiers have served their country bravely.*

represent your country *It is a great honour to represent your country in a sport.*

PREPOSITIONS

in/into a country *They are one of the top companies in the country.*

across/through a country (=from one side to the other) *It took us three days to drive across the country.*

throughout/across/around a country (=in many places in a country) *The new bank has opened branches all across the country.*

PHRASES

the country of origin *The fruit must be labelled with its country of origin.*

THESAURUS: country

nation

a country, considered especially in relation to its people, or its political and economic structure:
*The events shocked **the whole nation**. | The US is the most **powerful nation** in the world. | **Developing nations** receive huge amounts of aid from Western countries. | Leaders of the world's major **industrialized nations** attended the meeting.*

state

a country considered as a political organization with its own government:
*They believe that Scotland should be an **independent** sovereign **state**. | In a **democratic state**, people are free to criticize the government. | Most European states joined the Council of Europe.*

C

power
a country that is very strong and important: *China is now a major* ***world power****. | There was a meeting of the* ***great powers****, including Russia, the United States, Britain, and France.*

superpower
one of the most powerful countries in the world:
During the Cuban Missile Crisis there was a real danger of conflict between the two ***world*** *superpowers.*

land
a country or region - used especially in stories:
He told them about his journeys to ***foreign lands****. | I met a traveller from a* ***far-off land****. | She hopes one day to return to her* ***native land*** (=the place where she was born).

C

2 a type of area

ADJECTIVES/NOUNS + country

farming/walking country *This is farming country and all you see is mile after mile of agricultural land.*

open country (=with few buildings, walls, trees etc) *We left the city and headed towards the open country in the north.*

wild country (=not used or farmed by people) *I love the wild country of the Scottish Highlands.*

rough country (=difficult to travel over) *Here, you need a vehicle specially designed for rough country.*

mountain/mountainous country *The town is on the edge of a vast stretch of mountain country.*

PHRASES

a stretch/piece of country *The new road will go right through this beautiful stretch of country.*

countryside *n*

land that is outside cities and towns

ADJECTIVES

beautiful/lovely/stunning countryside *The countryside between the mountain villages is stunning.*

open countryside (=with few buildings, walls, trees etc) *The farmhouse has views over open countryside.*

the surrounding countryside *Both the town and the surrounding countryside are worth exploring.*

rolling countryside (=with hills) *They live in a valley surrounded by rolling countryside.*

unspoilt countryside (=with natural beauty not spoiled by buildings) *We walked through miles of unspoilt countryside.*

VERBS

protect/conserve the countryside (=stop people building on it or spoiling its beauty) *How can we protect the countryside for future generations?*

spoil/ruin the countryside *Too many tourists can spoil the countryside.*

PREPOSITIONS

the countryside around/near a place *The countryside around London is surprisingly pretty.*

coup *n*

a sudden and sometimes violent attempt to take control of the government

ADJECTIVES

a military/army coup *The general seized power in a military coup.*

an attempted coup *There was an attempted coup against the country's military dictator.*

a failed/unsuccessful coup (*also* **an abortive coup** *formal*): *The men were jailed for taking part in a failed coup.*

a successful coup *The armed forces are too weak to mount a successful coup.*

a bloodless coup (=without killing or violence) *The regime was overthrown in a bloodless coup.*

a presidential coup (=in which power is taken from a president)

VERBS

plan/plot a coup *They were accused of plotting a coup against the leader.*

stage/mount/launch a coup *formal* (=attempt one) *Later that year, the rebels staged an unsuccessful coup.*

foil/crush a coup *formal* (=stop it from succeeding) *The government foiled an armed coup by rebel soldiers.*

be overthrown in a coup (*also* **be deposed in a coup** *formal*): *The prime minister was deposed in a coup by the armed forces.*

PREPOSITIONS

a coup against sb *She was accused of plotting a coup against the government.*

coup + NOUNS

a coup attempt *There have been repeated coup attempts against the government.*

the coup leader *Most of the rebels were arrested but the coup leader escaped.*

couple Ac *n*

two people who are married or having a sexual or romantic relationship

ADJECTIVES

a young couple *A young couple with a baby moved into the house next door.*

a middle-aged couple/an elderly couple *The only other people in the train carriage were an elderly couple.*

a married couple *The tax laws are different for married couples.*

an unmarried couple *It is common nowadays for unmarried couples to live together.*

a childless couple (=without children)

Childless couples tend to have plenty of money to spend.

a retired couple *These small houses are suitable for retired couples.*

a perfect couple (=a couple that seem very suited to each other) *I'm surprised they split up – they seemed like the perfect couple.*

the happy couple (=a bride and bridegroom at their wedding) *Guests congratulated the happy couple.*

PHRASES

make a lovely couple (=be suited to each other as romantic partners) *Everyone who knows them thinks that they would make a lovely couple.*

courage *n*

brave behaviour in a difficult situation

ADJECTIVES

great/remarkable/extraordinary courage *The soldiers fought with great courage.*

enough/sufficient courage *Not many politicians have enough courage to vote against their own party.*

personal courage (=the courage of one particular person) *She showed enormous personal courage during her illness.*

VERBS

have the courage to do sth *He didn't have the courage to say what he really thought.*

sth takes courage (=it needs courage) *It takes courage to disagree with your friends.*

show courage (*also* **demonstrate courage** *formal*): *The pilot showed enormous skill and courage.*

find/pluck up/summon up the courage to do sth (=get enough courage to do something that you do not want to do) *He was trying to pluck up the courage to end their relationship.*

lack the courage to do sth *I lacked the courage to tell her the truth.*

give sb the courage to do sth *My friends and family gave me the courage to carry on with my work.*

PHRASES

have the courage of your convictions (=be brave enough to do what you have decided or think is right) *We want a government that has the courage of its convictions.*

courageous *adj* THESAURUS **brave**

course *n* a series of lessons

ADJECTIVES/NOUNS + course

a language/art/business etc course *The school runs language courses in the summer.*

a full-time/part-time course *We also offer part-time courses for mature students.*

a short course *I did a short course on website design.*

a one-year/two-year etc course *She did a one-year teacher training course.*

a college/university course *Students who fail their college courses still have to pay the fee.*

a degree course *BrE* (*also* **an undergraduate course**) (=a first course at a university, which usually lasts three years) *The college offers degree courses in nursing.*

a postgraduate course *BrE* (=one you do after your first degree course) *After graduating, she did a two-year postgraduate course.*

a beginner's/intermediate/advanced course *She is taking an advanced course in art and design.*

an introductory course *She decided to do an introductory computing course.*

an intensive course (*also* **a crash course** *informal*) (=in which you learn a lot in a short time) *Workers who are moving to the Moscow office are sent on an intensive Russian course.*

a training course *Before you start the job, you will attend a two-week training course.*

a vocational course (=that trains you to do a particular job) *The local college offers a number of vocational courses.*

VERBS + course

do/take a course *I decided to do a Spanish course.*

go on a course *My company wanted me to go on a course in time management.*

enrol on a course (*also* **sign up for a course** *informal*) (=officially put your name on the list of students for the course) *He enrolled on a cookery course.*

apply for/to do a course (=ask to join a course) *She applied for a nursing course.*

pass a course (=complete it successfully) *If you pass the course, you get a diploma.*

fail a course *If she fails the course, she may lose her job.*

finish/complete a course *I went back to university to finish my degree course.*

run a course (=organize a course) *The course is run by the British Council.*

teach a course *He is teaching an introductory course in Russian.*

drop out of a course (=leave without finishing it) *She dropped out of the course after a few weeks.*

course + VERBS

a course covers/includes sth *The course covers all aspects of wine-making.*

a course focuses/concentrates on sth *The course focuses on European history.*

course + NOUNS

a course tutor *BrE*: *I discussed the essay with my course tutor.*

the course syllabus (=the plan of what is taught on a course) *The history department has recently introduced a new course syllabus.*

PREPOSITIONS

a course on/in a subject *We run a six-month course on car maintenance.*

court *n*

the place where a trial is held, or the people who make decisions there

ADJECTIVES/NOUNS + court

a criminal court (=which deals with crimes) *The case will go to a criminal court.*

a civil court (=which deals with disagreements between people rather than crimes) *Family disputes are dealt with by civil courts.*

the Supreme Court (=the most important court in some countries or states) *Thomas was the only African-American judge on the Supreme Court.*

the High Court (=an important court, with more power than an ordinary court) *Their convictions were overturned in the High Court.*

a federal court *A federal court reached a similar conclusion.*

an appeals court/court of appeal (=one that deals with cases in which people are not satisfied with a decision) *The appeals court rejected the defence's argument.*

a kangaroo court *disapproving* (=an unofficial court that punishes people unfairly) *Innocent civilians were dragged before a kangaroo court and sentenced to death.*

a higher/lower court (=a more important or less important one) *His appeal was rejected by a higher court.*

VERBS + court

go to court (=take legal action) *The costs of going to court are very high.*

take sb to court (=take legal action against someone) *She took the company to court for sex discrimination.*

bring sb/sth to court (*also* **bring sb/sth before a court**) *He died before the case could be brought to court.*

appear in court *The men will appear in court on Monday.*

settle sth out of court (=reach an agreement without using a court) *The matter was finally settled out of court.*

a case comes to court/comes before the court *The case came to court 21 months later.*

court + VERBS

a court finds sb guilty/innocent *The court found him guilty of all the charges.*

a court clears/acquits sb (=says that they are not guilty) *A US court cleared him of bribery allegations.*

a court convicts sb (=says that they are guilty) *A New York court convicted her as a tax cheat.*

a court orders sth *The court ordered that the men should be released.*

a court hears a case (=they listen to all the evidence before making their decision) *The county court will hear the case next month.*

a court rules sth (=it decides something) *The court ruled that the penalty was not excessive.*

a court adjourns/is adjourned (=it stops for a period of time) *The court adjourned until Tuesday.*

a court overturns/quashes sth (=it says that an earlier decision was wrong) *A Brazilian court has quashed his sentence.*

a court dismisses/throws out sth (=refuses to allow or consider something) *The court dismissed his appeal against conviction.*

court + NOUNS

a court case *He was involved in a famous court case.*

a court battle *He faces a lengthy court battle.*

a court hearing (=a meeting of a court) *A court hearing is scheduled for February 14th.*

a court order *A court order specified that the money must be paid back over six months.*

court action *They were threatened with court action if they did not go back to work.*

a court ruling (=an official decision) *The company appealed against the court ruling.*

court proceedings (=the processes that are part of a court case) *The court proceedings were over in a day.*

a court appearance (=when someone accused of a crime appears in court) *He refused to speak during his court appearance.*

PHRASES

a court of law *You may be asked to give evidence before a court of law.*

courtesy *n*

polite behaviour and respect for other people

ADJECTIVES

great courtesy *They welcomed us with great courtesy and kindness.*

VERBS

treat sb with courtesy *He treated everyone with courtesy.*

behave/act with courtesy *She behaved with great courtesy towards us.*

show courtesy towards sb *The staff are trained to show courtesy towards customers at all times.*

have the courtesy to do sth (=be polite enough to do something - used especially when criticizing someone for being rude) *He didn't even have the courtesy to call and say he couldn't come.*

PREPOSITIONS

with courtesy *They always spoke to one another with courtesy.*

PHRASES

it is (only) common courtesy to do sth *It is only common courtesy to hold the door open for other people.*

as a courtesy (*also* **as a matter of courtesy**) *As a courtesy to other diners, we ask that all cell phones be switched off.*

out of courtesy (=in order to be polite) *I don't think she really wanted us to come and stay with her, she just offered out of courtesy.*

cover[1] *v*

1 to be over the surface of something, or to put something over the surface of something

ADVERBS

cover sth completely/entirely *We need a bigger tablecloth, one that covers the table completely.*

barely cover sth (=only just cover something) *The hat was too small, barely covering the top of his head.*

partly/partially cover sth *The path was partially covered with snow.*

PREPOSITIONS

cover sth with sth *She covered her face with her hands.*

2 to deal with or include something

NOUNS

cover a topic/subject *The course covers topics such as financial planning and IT skills.*

cover an issue *It is the job of a newspaper to cover the political issues of the day.*

cover aspects of sth *These lectures will cover all major aspects of European art.*

cover a range/variety of things *Her photographs cover a huge range of subjects.*

cover costs/expenses (=provide enough money to pay for what something costs) *The money he makes only just covers his living expenses.*

ADVERBS

cover sth fully/comprehensively/in full (=include everything) *Students need a textbook that covers the subject in full. | The major issues of the day are all comprehensively covered by the magazine.*

cover sth in depth/detail (=cover all aspects) *The report covers the incident in great detail.*

cover[2] *n*

1 something that you put over something to protect it

ADJECTIVES

a glass/plastic/leather etc cover *I bought a plastic cover for my phone.*

a protective cover *The sewing machine has a protective cover.*

VERBS

take off/remove the cover *Now that winter is over, people are taking the covers off their garden furniture.*

put the cover on *I put a clean cover on the duvet.*

lift the cover *She took the container and lifted the cover carefully.*

replace the cover (=put it back on) *After using the camera, always replace the lens cover.*

PREPOSITIONS

a cover for sth *The company makes covers for chairs and sofas.*

2 the outside part of a book or magazine

ADJECTIVES/NOUNS + cover

a book/magazine cover *The magazine cover says 'How to lose five kilos in a month'.*

the front/back cover *The price of the book is on the back cover.*

cover + NOUNS

a cover story (=the main story mentioned on the front of a magazine) *The editor decides what the cover story will be.*

PREPOSITIONS

on the cover *Her face was on the cover of every magazine.*

PHRASES

read sth from cover to cover (=read a book, magazine etc very thoroughly) *I read the book from cover to cover in one day.*

crack[1] *n*

a very narrow space or thin line on a surface, or between two things or two parts of something

ADJECTIVES

a deep crack *I noticed a deep crack in the pavement.*

a narrow crack *She squeezed through a narrow crack between two rocks.*

a small/thin crack *They reduced the price of the vase because it had a small crack in it.*

a hairline crack (=extremely thin) *The X-ray revealed a hairline crack in the bone.*

VERBS

a crack appears/forms *A large crack had appeared in the concrete.*

fix/mend/repair a crack *There's a crack in the windscreen that needs repairing.*

fill/seal a crack *Fill all the cracks in the wall before painting it.*

fall into/down a crack *My credit card has fallen down a crack in the floorboards.*

PREPOSITIONS

a crack in sth *This plate has a crack in it.*

a crack between sth and sth *She stuffed the money into a crack between the bricks.*

through a crack *He could see them through a crack in the fence.*

crack[2] *v* THESAURUS > **break[1] (1)**

C

craft *n*
an activity in which you make something skilfully with your hands. Objects made in this way are called **crafts**

ADJECTIVES

a traditional/ancient craft *You can learn traditional crafts such as weaving and pottery.*

a local craft *The village shop sells local crafts as well as food.*

a rural/country craft *The museum contains exhibits of old rural crafts.*

a skilled craft *Building stone walls is a highly skilled craft.*

C

VERBS

learn a craft *As a girl, she had to learn the craft of hand sewing.*

practise a craft *BrE*, **practice a craft** *AmE* (=make something skilfully with your hands) *They use traditional tools to practise their ancient crafts.*

craft + NOUNS

craft work (=things made by hand) *Craft work, such as hand-knitted items or decorated cakes, often sells well.*

a craft fair (=an event where people buy and sell crafts)

a craft shop (=that sells things made by hand)

PHRASES

arts and crafts (=art and beautiful things produced by hand) *We went to an exhibition of Indian arts and crafts.*

craftsmanship *n*
skill at making something in a beautiful or detailed way

ADVERBS

fine/good craftsmanship *The chair is truly an example of the finest craftsmanship.*

superb/exquisite/superior craftsmanship *The watch is well-made and the craftsmanship is superb.*

skilled/expert craftsmanship *The local people have a reputation for skilled craftsmanship.*

traditional craftsmanship *We use traditional craftsmanship, and every puppet is carved by hand.*

PHRASES

the quality of the craftsmanship *The quality of the craftsmanship is very impressive.*

the standard of craftsmanship *In Japan, the standard of craftsmanship is very high.*

a fine/superb etc piece of craftsmanship *The carving is a superb piece of craftsmanship.*

cramped *adj* THESAURUS **small (1)**

crash *n*
an accident in which a vehicle violently hits something else

ADJECTIVES/NOUNS + crash

a car/train/plane crash *He was badly hurt in a car crash.*

an air/rail/road crash *There will be an investigation into the cause of the air crash.*

a fatal crash *There have been several fatal crashes on this road.*

a horrific/terrible/appalling crash *She was left paralysed after a horrific crash.*

a head-on crash (=in which the front parts of two vehicles hit each other) *He died in a head-on crash with a lorry.*

a high-speed crash *In a high-speed crash, this kind of seat belt is not adequate.*

VERBS

have a crash (*also* **be involved in a crash**) (=in a car) *I've been nervous about driving since I had a crash last year.*

survive a crash *The pilot and one passenger survived the crash.*

cause a crash *So far, there are no clues as to what caused the crash.*

a crash happens/occurs *The crash happened on the corner of Ongar Road.*

a crash involves sth *Two women were taken to hospital after a crash involving a bus and a car.*

a crash kills sb *The crash killed the two crew members and three people on the ground.*

crash + NOUNS

a crash victim *Families of the crash victims want to know what happened.*

the crash site/scene *The authorities closed off a five-mile area around the crash site.*

a crash investigator *Crash investigators spent several days examining the scene.*

PREPOSITIONS

a crash with sth *A motorcyclist has been killed in a crash with a stolen car.*

a crash between sth and sth *Fifty people were taken to hospital after a crash between a coach and a lorry.*

THESAURUS: crash

crash, collision, disaster, wreck, pile-up → **accident**

crater *n*
a round hole in the ground made by something that has fallen on it or by an explosion

ADJECTIVES/NOUNS + crater

a deep crater *The explosion left a deep crater.*

a large/huge/massive crater *The large craters were formed by volcanic activity.*

a bomb crater *The road was dotted with bomb craters.*

a volcanic crater *There are more than 400 volcanic craters in the region.*

a lunar crater (=on the moon) *You can look at lunar craters through a telescope.*

VERBS

leave a crater *The blast left a 10-foot crater in the car park.*

PHRASES

the rim of a crater (=the edge of a crater) *You can walk around the rim of the crater.*

crazy *adj informal*

very strange or not at all sensible

NOUNS

a crazy person/man/woman *There are some crazy people out there.*

a crazy idea/thought/suggestion *It sounds like a crazy idea to me.*

a crazy plan/scheme *Her father had lots of crazy schemes for making money.*

a crazy world *We're living in a crazy world.*

a crazy thing *When you're young, you do all kinds of crazy things.*

ADVERBS

absolutely/totally/completely crazy *You're absolutely crazy to trust someone like him.*

VERBS

sound/seem crazy *It seems crazy to spend all that money on one meal.*

think sb is crazy *My parents think I'm crazy to leave my job.*

THESAURUS: crazy

mad *BrE informal*
idea | scheme | suggestion | world
crazy:
Whose mad idea was that? | Sometimes I think we are living in a mad world. | ***You must be mad*** *to go out in weather like this. | At first, everyone thought he was* ***completely mad****.*

insane *informal*
look | grin | desire
completely crazy:
The man had an insane grin on his face. | Steiner had an insane desire to laugh. | I know it ***sounds insane****, but it's true. | My friends all* ***think*** *I'm* ***insane****.*

eccentric
person | character | millionaire | family | behaviour | habits
behaving in a way that seems a little strange or unusual to other people:
The professor was a rather eccentric person who never wore matching socks. | Hughes was an eccentric millionaire who designed his own plane. | Her friends became worried about her increasingly eccentric behaviour.

create *v* THESAURUS **invent**, **make (1)**

creative *adj*

involving the use of imagination to produce new ideas or things

ADVERBS

highly/extremely creative *They came up with some highly creative solutions.*

NOUNS

the creative process *He talks about the creative process of writing a poem.*

a creative genius *Picasso was a creative genius.*

a creative idea/solution *We need some good creative ideas.*

creative thinking *I wanted to be alone so that I could do some creative thinking.*

creative writing *I teach creative writing at Trinity College.*

creature *n*

anything that is living and is not a plant

ADJECTIVES/NOUNS + creature

a living creature *He was always careful not to hurt any living creature.*

a wild creature *Damage to the environment affects all wild creatures.*

a sea/marine creature *They catch fish and other sea creatures in their nets.*

a woodland creature *Rabbits, foxes, and other woodland creatures regularly came into the garden.*

a little/small/tiny creature *Not all small creatures are pests.*

a furry creature *My cats kill birds and small furry creatures.*

a strange creature *A lot of strange creatures live in the depths of the sea.*

a beautiful/magnificent creature *The buffalo is a magnificent creature.*

a shy creature *These shy creatures are rarely seen.*

a mythical creature (=of a type that exists only in stories) *The unicorn is a mythical creature that looks like a horse with a single horn.*

credible *adj*

deserving or able to be believed or trusted

ADJECTIVES

highly credible (=very credible) *His story is highly credible.*

scarcely/barely credible *Her excuse was barely credible.*

wholly credible (=completely credible) *I find his version of what happened to be wholly credible.*

NOUNS

a credible witness *The judge refused to accept her as a credible witness.*

credible evidence/information *There is no credible evidence that ghosts exist.*

a credible report/account *His account of the accident seemed very credible.*
a credible explanation/excuse/story *He was unable to give a credible explanation for his behaviour.*
a credible threat/challenge (=something or someone that could possibly create a danger, defeat someone etc) *Arsenal are a credible threat to Manchester United's chances of winning the league.*
a credible alternative *Does the party provide a credible alternative to the current government?*

C

credit *n*

1 an arrangement with a shop, bank etc that allows you to buy something and pay for it later

VERBS

give sb credit (*also* **extend credit to sb** *formal*) (=allow customers to buy things on credit) *He seems to know how to get people to give him credit.*
let sb have credit *The store agreed to let him have credit.*
refuse/deny sb credit *You may be refused credit if you have a bad financial record.*
get/obtain credit (=be allowed to buy something on credit) *The economic situation is making it more difficult for people to get credit.*
pay by credit *We accept cash, cheques, or you can pay by credit.*

credit + NOUNS

a credit card (=a plastic card that you use to buy things and pay for them later) *Can I pay by credit card?*
a credit agreement (=an arrangement to allow or receive credit) *People sometimes sign credit agreements and then realize they can't afford the payments.*
credit terms (=how much you must pay back and when) *The credit terms were a deposit of £1,000 and two later instalments of £900.*
a credit arrangement/facility *The company announced that it has received a credit facility of approximately $12 million from China.*
sb's credit limit *The amount you can withdraw depends on your credit limit.*
sb's credit history/credit rating (=how likely a bank etc thinks someone is to pay their debts) *If you have a poor credit rating, you will have a hard time getting a mortgage.*
a credit risk (=a risk that a bank etc may not get back the money it lends) *Banks first have to assess whether a borrower is a credit risk.*

NOUNS + credit

consumer credit (=the amount of credit used by consumers) *Consumer credit has risen substantially during this period.*

PREPOSITIONS

on credit (=using credit) *Most new cars are bought on credit.*

2 approval or praise that you give to someone for something they have done

VERBS

get the credit *She got the credit even though Steve did most of the work.*
give sb the credit *They never give Martin any credit for the extra work he does.*
take the credit *He took the credit for his team's work.*
claim the credit *The US and NATO claimed the credit for ending the Bosnian war.*
deserve the credit *Who really deserves the credit for the company's success?*

ADJECTIVES

great credit *She deserves great credit for trying her best.*
due credit (=credit owed to someone) *He has never received due credit for his achievements.*

PREPOSITIONS

the credit for (doing) sth *The credit for preparing such an excellent meal goes to the kitchen staff.*
to sb's credit (=used when saying that someone deserves to be praised) *To his credit, he remained calm.*

PHRASES

all the credit goes to sb/sb gets all the credit *All the credit goes to Tony who has done a wonderful job.*
credit must go to sb *It was a thrilling game to watch and full credit must go to both sets of players.*
give credit where it is due (=used to say that someone deserves to be praised for the good things they have done) *You have to give credit where it is due - he did all the work on time.*

creepy *adj* THESAURUS ▸ **frightening**

crest *n* THESAURUS ▸ **top[1] (1)**

crime *n*

something that is against the law, or illegal activities in general

ADJECTIVES/NOUNS + crime

(a) serious crime *Armed robbery is a very serious crime.*
(a) violent crime *There has been a rise in violent crime.*
a terrible/horrific crime (*also* **a dreadful crime** *BrE*): *What made him commit such a terrible crime?*
petty crime (=crime that is not very serious, such as stealing small amounts of money) *There has been an increase in petty crime.*

car crime *BrE*: *The latest figures show that car crime has gone down.*

gun/knife crime *There is far less gun crime in Europe than in the US.*

street crime *Cameras can help to reduce street crime.*

juvenile/youth crime (=committed by children and teenagers) *Police say gangs are responsible for a third of all juvenile crime in the city.*

organized crime (=committed by large organizations of criminals) *The recent killings have been linked to organized crime.*

a war crime (=a serious crime committed during a war) *The country's president will be charged with war crimes.*

computer crime *It is usually companies that are the victims of computer crime.*

VERBS

commit (a) crime *He has committed a serious crime and he deserves to be punished.*

carry out a crime (=commit a crime. especially one that you have planned) *The police are not sure how the crime was carried out.*

⚠ Don't say 'do a crime'. Say **commit a crime** or **carry out a crime**.

turn to crime (=start committing crimes) *Youngsters who are bored sometimes turn to crime.*

fight/combat/tackle crime *How can the public help the police fight crime?*

solve a crime *It took ten years for the police to solve the crime.*

report a crime *I immediately telephoned the police to report the crime.*

crime + NOUNS

the crime rate *Japan's crime rate is relatively low.*

the crime figures/statistics *The new crime figures are not good.*

a crime wave (=a sudden increase in crime in an area) *The village has suffered a crime wave recently, with more than 30 burglaries.*

crime prevention *The police can give you advice on crime prevention.*

a crime story/novel/writer *Ian Rankin writes crime stories that are set in Edinburgh.*

PREPOSITIONS

a crime against sb *There has been an increase in crimes against women.*

PHRASES

a victim of crime *More help should be offered to victims of crime.*

the scene of the crime (*also* **the crime scene**) (=the place where a crime was committed) *Detectives were already at the scene of the crime.*

be tough on crime (=punish crime severely) *Politicians want to appear tough on crime.*

criminal[1] *n*

someone who is involved in illegal activities or has been proved guilty of a crime

ADJECTIVES/NOUNS + criminal

a violent/dangerous criminal *He believes there should be tougher sentences for violent criminals.*

a petty criminal (=one who commits crimes that are not very serious) *How much time should the police spend dealing with petty criminals?*

a convicted criminal (=someone who has been found guilty of a crime) *The president pardoned a number of convicted criminals.*

a habitual/hardened/career criminal (=someone who often commits crimes) *Young offenders should not be put in the same prison as hardened criminals.*

a common criminal (=one who is not special) *He was treated like a common criminal.*

a known criminal *Some of this man's friends are known criminals.*

a suspected criminal *It is right that the police should keep information on suspected criminals.*

a notorious criminal (=one who is famous for their crimes) *The prison houses some of Britain's toughest and most notorious criminals.*

a wanted criminal (=who the police want to arrest) *He is one of the ten most wanted criminals in the United States.*

a war criminal (=one who committed serious crimes during a war) *They believed that all Nazi war criminals should be prosecuted.*

VERBS

catch a criminal (*also* **apprehend a criminal** *formal*): *Information from the public helps the police catch criminals.*

arrest a criminal *Within hours of the incident, the criminals had been arrested.*

prosecute a criminal *The United Nations wanted to prosecute these war criminals.*

jail a criminal *More criminals than ever are being jailed.*

PHRASES

bring a criminal to justice (=put them on trial) *We will make every effort to bring these criminals to justice.*

criminal[2] *adj*

1 used to describe something that is a crime

NOUNS

a criminal offence/act *Driving without insurance is a criminal offence.*

criminal activity/behaviour *There was no evidence of any criminal activity.*

criminal wrongdoing *AmE* (=actions that are illegal) *The investigation cleared him of any criminal wrongdoing.*

criminal damage *BrE* (=damaging someone's property illegally) *He was charged with criminal damage to his boss's car.*

C

criminal negligence (=not taking enough care to protect people you are responsible for) *Charges of criminal negligence were brought against senior staff.*

2 relating to actions of lawyers or the police that are concerned with crime

NOUNS

a criminal charge *He faces criminal charges under the Official Secrets Act.*

a criminal conviction (=an official decision that someone is guilty of a crime) *He had a criminal conviction for fraud.*

a criminal investigation *The FBI is conducting a criminal investigation into the bombing.*

a criminal record (=the fact that someone has committed crimes in the past, which the police have a record of) *It can be difficult for someone with a criminal record to find work.*

the criminal justice system *How effective is our criminal justice system?*

a criminal case *These courts deal with the overwhelming majority of criminal cases.*

a criminal trial *His year-long criminal trial ended in October.*

a criminal court (=that deals with crimes) *The trial will take place in an international criminal court.*

criminal law *The basic principle of English criminal law is that a person is presumed innocent until they have been shown to be guilty of an offence.*

> **Criminal** or **civil?**
> You use **criminal** when talking about crimes, for example robbery or crimes of violence. You use **civil** about cases involving legal disagreements about property, business etc, rather than crimes: *The case will be heard in a **civil court**. | The magistrate deals with **civil** cases.*

crisis *n*

a very bad situation, especially one that must be dealt with quickly

ADJECTIVES/NOUNS + crisis

a major/serious/deep/severe crisis *The company is in the middle of a major financial crisis.*

the worst/biggest crisis *This is the worst crisis the industry has ever faced.*

an economic/political/financial etc crisis *Europe was hit by an economic crisis.*

an energy/fuel/debt etc crisis *The rising cost of oil could create another energy crisis.*

a worsening/deepening crisis *The strikes came during a worsening economic crisis.*

a personal/family crisis *She had to take time off work because of a family crisis.*

a constitutional crisis (=relating to the way a country is governed) *President Nixon's involvement in the Watergate Affair led to a constitutional crisis.*

a midlife crisis (=when someone is in their 40s or 50s and realises they are no longer young) *Some men have a midlife crisis and start dating women half their age.*

VERBS

create/cause a crisis *The people fled the country, creating a huge refugee crisis.*

face a crisis *Many families are facing a debt crisis.*

go through/experience a crisis *The company is going through a serious financial crisis.*

deal with/handle a crisis *Many voters thought the president handled the crisis badly.*

tackle/resolve a crisis (=deal with it successfully) *We still hope that the hostage crisis can be resolved by negotiation.*

avert a crisis *formal* (=stop it happening) *More talks were proposed in an attempt to avert a crisis.*

a crisis is looming (=seems likely to happen soon) *There is a crisis looming for the European Union.*

crisis + NOUNS

a crisis situation *We could end up in a crisis situation.*

(a) crisis point (=the point at which a problem becomes a crisis) *Events were now reaching crisis point.*

crisis management *Most of my job consists of crisis management.*

crisis talks (=discussions about a crisis) *The prime minister went back to London for crisis talks.*

PREPOSITIONS

in crisis *The country is in crisis.*

during a crisis *During the oil crisis, American companies began producing smaller cars.*

in a crisis *We want a leader who can keep calm in a crisis.*

PHRASES

a time of crisis *The countries provide support for each other in times of crisis.*

a way out of a crisis *There appears to be no way out of the current financial crisis.*

crispy *adj* THESAURUS ▸ **hard (1)**

criterion Ac *n*

a standard that you use to judge something or make a decision about something

> This word is usually used in the plural, which is **criteria**. The singular word **criterion** sounds very formal.

ADJECTIVES/NOUNS + criterion

the main/key criteria *What are your main*

criteria when you are choosing someone for the job?

the sole criterion (=the only one) *Examination results are still seen as the sole criterion for success in education.*

objective criteria (=based on fact and not opinion) *Are there objective criteria for deciding whether a work of art is good or bad?*

strict criteria *All the cars are tested to make sure they meet strict criteria.*

basic/essential criteria *The form sets out the basic criteria for applying for a loan.*

selection criteria (=for choosing someone or something) *Our two main selection criteria were the skill of the artists, and their ability to teach.*

VERBS

meet/satisfy/fulfil the criteria *I hope my experience meets the criteria for the job.*

use/apply criteria *What criteria do we use to decide whether one book is better than another?*

be based on criteria *The judge's decisions are based on clear criteria.*

establish/set out/lay down criteria *The criteria are laid down in the official guidelines.*

PREPOSITIONS

criteria for (doing) sth *The document gives the criteria for assessing students' work.*

PHRASES

a set/list of criteria *There is a list of criteria that you must meet in order to pass your driving test.*

critic *n*

1 someone whose job is to write or broadcast giving their opinion of new plays, films, exhibitions etc

ADJECTIVES/NOUNS + critic

a film/art/music etc critic *Film critics say that it is his best film for a long time.*

a literary critic *Literary critics were shocked by the novel when it first appeared.*

a theatre/restaurant/food critic *One restaurant critic said that the food was overpriced.*

a distinguished critic (=well known and very respected) *She is one of the country's most distinguished art critics.*

VERBS

a critic reviews sth (=writes or says what they think of it) *The critics who reviewed the play said that it wasn't very good.*

a critic praises sth *The play was highly praised by critics.*

a critic pans sth *informal* (*also* **a critic slates sth** *BrE informal*) (=criticizes something strongly) *The film was panned by critics but was a commercial success.*

a critic hails sth as sth (=describes something as very good) *Critics hailed the film as a triumph.*

2 someone who criticizes a person, organization, idea etc

ADJECTIVES

a fierce/harsh/sharp/strong critic *He is one of the president's fiercest critics.*

a leading/prominent critic (=one who is well known for criticizing someone or something) *She has been among the leading critics of the theory.*

an outspoken/vocal critic (=one who often criticizes very openly and directly) *Her father, an outspoken critic of the regime, was killed by police.*

a frequent critic *He has been a frequent critic of the government.*

a longtime critic (=one who has been criticizing someone or something for a long time) *The senator is a longtime critic of the war.*

VERBS

answer your critics *How would you answer your critics?*

silence your critics (=make them stop criticizing you) *The regime tried to silence its critics.*

confound your critics (=do well after being criticized) *She confounded her critics and the show was a great success.*

PREPOSITIONS

a critic of sth *The senator is well-known as a critic of the president's economic policies.*

PHRASES

prove your critics wrong *She was desperate to prove her critics wrong.*

sth has its critics (*also* **sth is not without its critics**) (=it is criticized by some people) *This policy was not without its critics within the party.*

critical *adj*

1 if you are critical, you criticize someone or something

ADJECTIVES

highly critical *He made some highly critical remarks.*

strongly critical *Many parents are strongly critical of the school.*

openly critical *She was openly critical of the government's decision.*

PREPOSITIONS

critical of sth/sb *The teacher was rather critical of my essay.*

NOUNS

a critical comment/remark *He made some very critical comments about the prime minister.*

a critical report *She wrote a highly critical report about the country's prison system.*

a critical assessment *The book provides a critical assessment of the poet's major works.*

C

2 extremely important

ADJECTIVES

absolutely critical *It's absolutely critical that we find out the truth.*

NOUNS

a critical factor *Temperature is the most critical factor in food storage.*

a critical issue *We need an immediate decision on this critical issue.*

a critical moment/time *Right now he faces the most critical time in his career.*

a critical period/stage in sth *The negotiations have reached a critical stage.*

a critical need for sth *There is a critical need for food and clean water in the disaster area.*

PHRASES

of critical importance *Foreign trade is of critical importance to the country.*

C

criticism *n*

remarks that say what you think is bad about someone or something

ADJECTIVES

strong/severe/heavy criticism *The decision to build the road received strong criticism from environmental groups.*

fierce/harsh/sharp/bitter criticism (=involving angry feelings) *The prison system has been the object of fierce criticism.*

main criticism *My main criticism is that the film is too long.*

a major criticism *One major criticism is that the system is very complicated.*

a minor criticism *A minor criticism of the book is that the sections are not numbered.*

a valid criticism *In his article, he made a number of valid criticisms.*

unfair criticism *I feel young people come in for a lot of unfair criticism.*

constructive criticism (=that will help you improve something) *I welcome constructive criticism of my work.*

public criticism (=in public) *As a politician, you have to get used to public criticism.*

widespread criticism (=from many different people) *There was widespread criticism of his speech.*

growing/mounting criticism *The government last night faced mounting criticism over its plans to introduce a new higher rate of tax.*

outspoken criticism (=said very openly and directly) *I was surprised by his outspoken criticism of the system.*

scathing criticism (=attacking someone or something very strongly) *The minister came in for scathing criticism from the press.*

VERBS

make a criticism *The only criticism I would make is that the film was a little too long.*

express/voice a criticism *The report expressed criticism of the way the police handled the situation.*

face criticism *The United States faces international criticism because of its refusal to take part in the talks.*

come under criticism/come in for criticism (*also* **be subjected to criticism** *formal*) (=be criticized) *The new law came under fierce criticism.*

receive/meet with criticism (=be criticized) *His theory met with harsh criticism from colleagues.*

draw/attract/provoke criticism (=be criticized) *The plan has drawn criticism from environmental groups.*

accept/take criticism (=listen to it and learn from it) *I am not very good at taking criticism.*

level/direct criticism at sb/sth (=criticize someone or something) *A great deal of criticism was levelled at the manager.*

single sb out for criticism (=criticize one person in particular) *The goalkeeper was singled out for criticism.*

answer/address a criticism *How would you answer their criticisms?*

PREPOSITIONS

criticism of sb/sth *There has been much criticism of the government's housing policy.*

PHRASES

be the subject/object of criticism (=be criticized by people) *The club has been the subject of criticism since last October.*

be open to criticism (=be able to be criticized) *The magazine is open to criticism for printing the article.*

be sensitive to criticism (=care about or be upset by criticism) *He was highly sensitive to criticism in the press.*

a storm/barrage of criticism (=a lot of criticism) *His comments provoked a barrage of criticism.*

criticize (*also* criticise *BrE*) *v*

to say that you think someone has done something badly, or that something has been badly done

ADVERBS

strongly/severely/heavily criticize sb/sth *The president was strongly criticized for the way in which he handled the crisis.*

sharply/harshly criticize sb/sth (=in an angry way) *The report sharply criticized the behaviour of some banks.*

criticize sb unfairly *He feels that he has been criticized unfairly.*

be widely criticized (=by many people) *The research has been widely criticized, because of the methods that were used.*

publicly criticize sb/sth *The coach publicly criticized the referee's decision.*

openly criticize sb/sth (=in a public and direct way) *People who openly criticize the government are likely to end up in prison.*

PREPOSITIONS

criticize sb/sth for (doing) sth *He criticized the president for failing to send aid.*

be criticized as sth *The system has been criticized as undemocratic.*

PHRASES

be quick to criticize sb/sth *Their opponents were quick to criticize the plan.*

criticize sb/sth on the grounds that (=for the reason that) *The survey was criticized on the grounds that the sample was too small.*

crop *n*

1 a plant such as wheat, rice, or fruit that is grown by farmers

ADJECTIVES/NOUNS + crop

the wheat/cereal/rice etc crop *In January, farmers prepare the ground for the potato crop.*

a food crop *The land is unfit for food crops.*

a staple crop (=an important one that forms a big part of people's diet) *In Japan, rice has been the staple crop for centuries.*

a cash crop (=grown to be sold rather than used) *Cotton is grown here as a cash crop.*

an export crop (=grown to be exported) *Cocoa is the country's main export crop.*

genetically modified crops (*also* **GM crops**) (=ones that have had their genetic structure changed) *GM crops could cause huge problems for the environment.*

VERBS + crop

grow a crop (*also* **cultivate a crop** *formal*): *They grow crops such as beans and maize.*

plant/sow a crop *They cleared the ground and planted crops.*

spray crops *Crops are sprayed with chemicals to protect against insects and disease.*

irrigate crops (=water them) *Water from the river was used to irrigate crops.*

rotate crops (=regularly change the crops grown on a piece of land) *Crops are sometimes rotated with grass.*

sth destroys/damages a crop *The crops were destroyed by insects.*

crop + VERBS

a crop grows *They prayed for rain that would help the crops grow.*

a crop fails (=does not grow or produce food properly) *The drought meant the crops failed and food was scarce.*

crop + NOUNS

crop production *The area is mostly unsuitable for crop production.*

crop failure (=failure to grow or produce food) *Ethiopia's 1989 crop failure was disastrous.*

crop damage *The storms caused crop damage across the country.*

crop rotation (=the practice of not growing the same crops in the same place each year) *Crop rotation helps build up soil fertility.*

2 the amount of wheat, rice, fruit etc that is produced in a season

ADJECTIVES

a good/heavy/big crop *We had a good crop this year.*

a bumper crop (=a very large amount) *They will have to find somewhere to store their bumper crop.*

a record crop (=the largest amount ever) *They had a record crop of grapes last year.*

a poor crop *Food prices rose last spring as a result of poor crops.*

VERBS

produce/yield a crop *Olive trees usually produce a big crop every two years.*

harvest/bring in/gather a crop *Brazil's coffee crop begins to be harvested in May.*

PREPOSITIONS

a crop of sth *If you follow these instructions, you should get a good crop of apples next year.*

cross[1] *v*

to go from one side of something to the other

NOUNS

cross a road/street *Always look carefully when you are crossing the street.*

cross a river *We decided to cross the river lower down.*

cross the ocean/sea *They crossed the Atlantic Ocean in a small sailing ship.*

cross a border *The men had crossed the border illegally.*

cross a bridge *After crossing the bridge, follow the path on your right.*

cross a line *He crossed the finish line in under 10 seconds.*

cross[2] *adj* THESAURUS ▸ **angry**

crowd *n*

a large group of people who have gathered together to do or watch something

ADJECTIVES/NOUNS + crowd

a big/large/huge crowd *A big crowd gathered outside the parliament building.*

a good crowd (=a big one at an event) *There was a good crowd on the first night of the show.*

a 5,000-strong/15,000-strong etc crowd *The match took place in front of a 30,000-strong crowd.*

a record crowd (=the biggest one there has

ever been) *They were playing before a record crowd of 50,000.*

a capacity crowd (=the largest number that a place can hold) *The band performed brilliantly to a capacity crowd.*

a sellout crowd (=one at an event where every ticket has been sold) *The team won in front of a sellout crowd of 17,765.*

an angry/hostile crowd *The president's car was attacked by an angry crowd.*

an excited/enthusiastic/appreciative/ adoring crowd *Clinton was greeted by an enthusiastic crowd.*

C

the home crowd (=the supporters of the team who are playing in their own town or country) *There was a roar from the home crowd as he scored.*

crowd + VERBS

a crowd gathers *A large crowd had gathered to watch the procession.*

a crowd cheers *The crowd cheered as the team came onto the pitch.*

a crowd roars (=shouts loudly in a very excited way) *As the band appeared, the crowd roared in approval.*

a crowd disperses/breaks up (=goes away in different directions) *The speech finished and the crowd began to disperse.*

crowds line the street/route etc *Huge crowds lined the streets on the day of the royal wedding.*

VERBS + crowd

attract/draw a crowd *The ceremony is expected to draw a crowd of more than 1,000.*

pull in a crowd (=attract a lot of people) *Low prices always pull in the crowds.*

disperse/break up a crowd (=make a crowd go away in different directions) *Troops fired warning shots in an attempt to disperse the crowd.*

address a crowd (=speak to them) *He went up onto the platform and addressed the crowd.*

mingle/mix with the crowd (=join a crowd to be friendly or in order not to be noticed) *Police officers in plain clothes were sent to mingle with the crowd.*

PHRASES

a crowd of people/supporters/demonstrators *I pushed my way through the crowd of people.*

a crowd of onlookers (=people who stop to watch something that is happening) *A crowd of onlookers had gathered to see what the argument was about.*

crowded *adj*

if a place is crowded, there are a lot of people and it is difficult to move around

NOUNS

a crowded train/bus *The train was very crowded, and we had to stand.*

a crowded restaurant/bar/room etc *We were in a crowded bar, full of English soccer fans.*

a crowded street *She pushed her way through the narrow crowded streets.*

a crowded station/airport *The stations are always crowded during the rush hour.*

PREPOSITIONS

crowded with people/traffic/shoppers *The narrow streets were crowded with holiday traffic.*

ADVERBS

densely crowded *The people live in densely crowded conditions.*

increasingly crowded *The roads are becoming increasingly crowded and we all need to use our cars less.*

THESAURUS: crowded

packed
train | house | hall | courtroom
you use **packed** about trains, theatres, and other public places that are very crowded:
The trains are always packed at this time of day. | On the first night of the play, the house was packed (=the theatre was completely full). *| He spoke to a packed lecture hall. | There was silence in the packed courtroom. | The bus was* **packed with** *people returning from their holidays.*

busy
road | street | intersection | town | station | airport | shopping centre
a busy road, town etc is full of people or vehicles:
He was crossing a busy street and got hit by a car. | Skipton is a busy market town. | The group exploded a bomb outside a busy railway station. | At this time of day, the city centre is **busy with** *shoppers.*

overcrowded
cities | prison | train | conditions
if a place is overcrowded, there are too many people in it and it feels uncomfortable:
More and more people are choosing to leave Japan's overcrowded cities. | The country's prisons are terribly overcrowded. | Perry was fed up with travelling on overcrowded trains to a boring bank job. | The workers live in overcrowded conditions.

teeming
streets | cities
full of people who are all moving around – used to describe a place where there is a lot of activity:
He got lost in the teeming streets of Cairo. | In the teeming cities of Asia, car pollution is becoming more and more of a problem. | The border area is **teeming with** *soldiers.*

THESAURUS: crowded

crowded, congested → **busy (2)**

crucial Ac *adj*

extremely important, especially because other things depend on it

NOUNS

a crucial factor/part/element *Timing was a crucial factor in the company's success.*

a crucial point *They forget to mention one crucial point – how are we going to pay back the money?*

the crucial thing *The crucial thing is not to start until you are completely ready.*

a crucial issue/question *They will be focusing on the crucial issue of the economy.*

a crucial moment/time/point/stage *He withdrew his support at a crucial moment.*

a crucial difference *There is a crucial difference between British and American attitudes.*

a crucial step *The talks are a crucial step towards peace.*

crucial information/evidence *The government did not share this crucial information.*

a crucial decision *This is a crucial decision which needs a lot of careful thought.*

ADVERBS

absolutely crucial *Technology has an absolutely crucial role in modern medicine.*

VERBS

prove crucial (=be crucial) *His appointment was to prove crucial to the organization's success.*

remain crucial *Oil remains crucial to the country's economy.*

regard/consider sth as crucial *The city was regarded as crucial to the area's defence.*

PREPOSITIONS

crucial to/for (doing) sth *In some countries, money is crucial to success in politics.*

crucial in doing sth *Ted's mother was crucial in forming his outlook on life.*

PHRASES

play a crucial role/part in sth *Parents play a crucial role in preparing their children for adult life.*

be of crucial importance *Good leadership is of crucial importance in motivating staff.*

THESAURUS: crucial

big, significant, major, notable, key, essential, vital, crucial/critical, paramount, historic, landmark, momentous → **important (1)**

crude *adj* THESAURUS simple

cruel *adj*

1 very unkind – used when someone deliberately causes suffering to a person or an animal

NOUNS

a cruel man/woman/person *The king was a cruel man and everyone hated him.*

a cruel joke/trick *Simon made cruel jokes about her appearance.*

cruel treatment *There are laws against the cruel treatment of prisoners.*

a cruel punishment *The death penalty is an unnecessarily cruel punishment.*

a cruel sport *Many people think hunting is a cruel sport.*

a cruel act *He deserves to be punished for this cruel act.*

a cruel streak (=a cruel part of your character) *My boss had a cruel streak and she loved to humiliate people.*

ADVERBS

unnecessarily cruel *His reaction seemed unnecessarily cruel.*

unspeakably/hideously cruel (=in an extreme and shocking way) *The press were unspeakably cruel about her.*

PREPOSITIONS

cruel to sb *Children can be very cruel to each other sometimes.*

THESAURUS: cruel

heartless

not feeling any pity and not caring about other people or their problems:

*He was **cold and heartless** and had no concern for the welfare of his employees. | How could you be so heartless? | Heartless thieves stole all the old lady's money.*

sadistic

pleasure | treatment | violence | killer | crime | streak

getting pleasure from making other people suffer:

The guards took sadistic pleasure in abusing prisoners. | The judge described him as a sadistic killer who showed no mercy to his victims. | He had a sadistic streak in him which frightened her.

barbaric

act | practice | murder | crime | sport | punishment

extremely cruel, in a way that shocks people:

The bombing was a barbaric act. | Keeping chickens in tiny cages is a barbaric practice. | We have all been profoundly shocked by this barbaric crime.

vicious

attack | assault | war | fight | dog | killer

very violent and cruel, especially by suddenly

attacking someone and causing injury to them:
It was a vicious attack on an innocent man. | A vicious war broke out between terrorist groups. | Some dogs can be vicious.

Vicious is also used when someone says or writes cruel things: *The newspaper launched a* ***vicious attack*** *on him. | I don't know who was responsible for these* ***vicious rumours****.*

brutal
assault | attack | murder | killing | violence | treatment | dictator | regime | honesty | criticism
very cruel and violent, in a way that shows no human feelings:
He was the victim of a brutal assault. | Many people died under his brutal regime (=political system). | *One of the judges is known for his brutal honesty* (=honesty that might upset people).

inhumane
treatment | act | conditions
inhumane conditions, treatment etc cause too much suffering and should not be allowed:
The prisoners were subjected to inhumane treatment. | The animals had been kept in inhumane conditions. | The punishments were inhumane and degrading (=showing no respect).

cold-blooded
murder | killing | massacre | killer | murderer | psychopath
extremely cruel and showing no pity or emotion when killing or attacking someone:
Bates was charged with the cold-blooded murder of his girlfriend. | Prosecutors say the brothers are cold-blooded killers.

2 used when something happens that makes someone suffer or feel very unhappy

NOUNS

a cruel blow *His death was a cruel blow.*
a cruel irony (=situation that is cruel and unusual or the opposite of what you expect) *It's a cruel irony that a woman who has helped so many cancer sufferers should die from cancer herself.*
a cruel twist (of fate) (=a cruel situation that you were not expecting) *He considered his illness to be a cruel twist of fate.*
a cruel world *It's a cruel world out there.*
a cruel death *His cruel death from a brain tumour at the age of 35 devastated his parents.*

cruelty *n*

behaviour or actions that deliberately cause pain to people or animals

ADJECTIVES

deliberate cruelty *This was an act of deliberate cruelty which deserves the most severe punishment allowed.*
terrible/unimaginable cruelty *The prisoners were treated with unimaginable cruelty.*
extreme cruelty *The film contains scenes of extreme cruelty.*
mental cruelty (=involving the mind rather than the body) *The most common reason women give for leaving their husbands is mental cruelty.*

VERBS

inflict cruelty on sb (=do something cruel to someone) *The court found him guilty of inflicting cruelty on a child.*
suffer cruelty *Animals should not be allowed to suffer cruelty.*

NOUNS + cruelty

animal/child cruelty *Her ex-partner was convicted of child cruelty.*

PREPOSITIONS

cruelty to/towards sb *Cruelty towards slaves was common.*

PHRASES

an act of cruelty *formal*: *He was charged with committing an act of cruelty.*

cruise *n*

a holiday on a boat, or a journey by boat for pleasure

ADJECTIVES/NOUNS + cruise

a luxury cruise *He went on a luxury cruise to Alaska.*
a Mediterranean/Caribbean/Nile etc cruise *On our Mediterranean cruise, we visited Italy, Greece, and Turkey.*
a world cruise (=around the world) *How much would a world cruise cost?*
a river cruise *We all enjoyed the river cruise on the Rhine.*
a pleasure cruise *I wanted to take a pleasure cruise on the lake.*

VERBS

go on a cruise *What about going on a cruise down the Nile?*
take a cruise *We thought about taking a ten-day cruise in the Caribbean.*

cruise + NOUNS

a cruise ship/liner *It is the largest cruise ship ever built.*
a cruise line/operator (=a company that provides cruises) *Many cruise lines offer short cruises out of Florida.*

crumb *n* THESAURUS **piece**

crumble *v* THESAURUS **break[1] (1)**

crunchy *adj* THESAURUS **hard (1)**

cry[1] *v*

1 to produce tears, usually because you are unhappy or hurt

ADVERBS

cry quietly/softly/silently *The woman was crying softly to herself in a corner of the room.*

cry loudly *The little boy cried loudly and refused to go up to his room.*

cry uncontrollably *When she saw him, she started to cry uncontrollably.*

cry hysterically (=very loudly and uncontrollably) *The girl cried hysterically and her friends tried to calm her.*

VERBS

make sb cry *The end of the book was so sad that it made me cry.*

PREPOSITIONS

cry about/over sth *I didn't know what he was crying about.*

cry for sb (=because you feel sorry for them, or want them) *She cried for herself and for all those who had suffered like her.*

cry with rage/pain/relief etc *I was almost crying with rage.*

PHRASES

can't stop crying *She was so unhappy, she couldn't stop crying.*

feel like crying (=used when something makes you feel very upset) *Today's been a really bad day. I just felt like crying.*

cry your eyes out/cry your heart out (=cry a lot) *Lucy read the letter and cried her eyes out.*

cry all the time *When my girlfriend left me, I cried all the time.*

cry like a baby (=cry a lot and without control) *I cried like a baby when I heard the news.*

cry yourself to sleep (=cry until you fall asleep) *That night, in his lonely room, he cried himself to sleep.*

2 to shout or say something loudly: *"Someone please help us!" he cried.* | *I heard someone cry my name.*

cry[2] *n*

a shout or a loud sound expressing pain, fear, pleasure etc

ADJECTIVES/NOUNS + cry

a loud cry *There were loud cries of protest when he said this.*

a great cry (=a loud cry by a lot of people) *With a great cry, they charged into battle.*

a small/little cry *She gave a small cry and ran towards me.*

a low cry (=not loud or high) *I heard a long low cry of despair.*

a sharp cry (=loud, short, and sudden) *He gave a sharp cry of pain.*

a muffled/faint cry (=that cannot be heard clearly) *I thought I heard a muffled cry from the next room.*

a plaintive cry (=a high sad cry) *They could hear the plaintive cries of the wounded.*

a battle/war cry (=used in a battle to show courage and frighten the enemy) *They charged forward, shouting their battle cry.*

VERBS

give/let out/utter a cry *The woman looked up and gave a cry of fear.*

PREPOSITIONS

a cry of pain/despair/delight etc *He fell with a sharp cry of surprise.*

a cry for help/mercy etc *Two walkers heard his cries for help.*

a cry of "No"/"Stop" etc *There were cries of "No!" from the crowd.*

cube *n* THESAURUS **piece**

cult[1] *adj*

popular and fashionable, often among a small group of people

cult + NOUNS

a cult film/book/show/TV programme *'Easy Rider' became a cult film in the late 1960s.*

a cult object *The Mini is a classic car, cult object, and lifestyle symbol.*

a cult hero *The actor James Dean acquired the status of a cult hero.*

a cult figure *His sense of humor and fondness for simple rock and roll helped make him a cult figure.*

a cult following (=small group of people who admire someone or something) *The band soon acquired a cult following.*

cult status *The actress gained cult status for her role in the 1965 Russ Meyer movie 'Faster, Pussycat! Kill!'*

cult[2] *n*

a small religious group with extreme beliefs

VERBS

join a cult *He joined a strange religious cult.*

belong to a cult *She belongs to a cult, having abandoned her family many years ago.*

ADJECTIVES/NOUNS + cult

a religious cult *It is surprisingly easy for people to become involved in religious cults.*

cult + NOUNS

a cult leader *The cult leader ordered his followers to commit suicide.*

a cult member (*also* **a member of a cult**) *Cult members are not allowed to read or watch anything not produced by the cult itself.*

C

cultural Ac *adj*

relating to a particular society and its way of life

NOUNS

cultural heritage (=ideas, customs etc that have existed for a long time) *Greeks are proud of their cultural heritage.*

cultural life *The festival is a major event in British cultural life.*

cultural values (=ideas of what is right and wrong in a culture) *It is important to be aware of local cultural values.*

C

cultural identity (=a feeling of belonging to a group and sharing its values) *Children develop a sense of their cultural identity at a young age.*

cultural differences *People should be tolerant of cultural differences.*

cultural diversity (=including people from many different cultures) *We all benefit from the cultural diversity of British society.*

cultural background *People from different cultural backgrounds had the chance to exchange ideas.*

cultural tradition *The city has a proud cultural tradition and there are lots of theatres, concert halls, and museums.*

cultural factors/influences *Cultural factors are important in a child's ability to learn foreign languages.*

cultural context (=the culture at a particular place or time) *This chapter looks at the cultural context in which the French Revolution took place.*

culture Ac *n*

1 the ideas, beliefs, and ways of behaving of people in a particular society or organization

ADJECTIVES

national culture *Sport is part of our national culture.*

local culture *The local culture of the island has much to interest visitors.*

traditional/ancient culture *They have a traditional culture which has hardly changed in 500 years.*

Western/American/Japanese etc culture *Modern Korean society is heavily influenced by American culture.*

youth culture (=of young people) *Music and clothes are very important in youth culture.*

modern culture *Technology is a vital part of modern culture.*

human culture *Stories about how the earth was created are found in every human culture.*

a common culture (=one that different societies or people share) *Many European countries share a common culture.*

the dominant culture (=the one that has the most influence) *Youth culture is the dominant culture in Western society.*

culture + NOUNS

culture shock (=confusion or shock that you may feel in a very different place) *During my first weeks in Britain, I experienced huge culture shock.*

culture clash (=problems between people or groups because of different cultures) *There was a culture clash when the companies merged.*

VERBS

create/build a culture *The head teacher wants to create a culture of honesty and openness among staff.*

PHRASES

be part of sb's culture *The car is so much part of American culture.*

a culture of fear/blame/secrecy etc *It is clear that a culture of secrecy existed within the company.*

2 art, music, and similar activities

ADJECTIVES/NOUNS + culture

popular culture (*also* **pop culture** *informal*) (=enjoyed by a lot of ordinary people) *She writes about movies, pop music, and other aspects of popular culture.*

high culture (=enjoyed by highly educated people) *The government still gives money to support ballet, opera, and other high culture activities.*

folk culture (=traditional among a group or in a region) *Nursery rhymes and children's songs are part of folk culture.*

PHRASES

a man/woman/person of culture (=one who likes and understands art, music etc) *She is a woman of great culture and refinement.*

cunning *adj*

1 a cunning plan is clever and often involves tricking other people in order to get what you want

cunning + NOUNS

a cunning plan/plot *They used a cunning plan to get him out of prison.*

a cunning trick/ploy/ruse (=a clever trick or plan) *My uncle thought it was a cunning ploy intended to get money from him.*

a cunning strategy *The king won the battle by means of a cunning strategy, in which his men pretended they were about to surrender.*

THESAURUS: cunning

ingenious, brilliant, cunning → **clever (2)**

2 a cunning person is good at tricking people in a clever way in order to get what he or she wants

ADVERBS

very/extremely cunning *These people are very cunning and they will do everything they can to protect those closest to them.*

PHRASES

a cunning old devil *What is he doing now, the cunning old devil?*

as cunning as a fox *The old man was as cunning as a fox and it would be difficult to catch him.*

THESAURUS: cunning

clever, smart, bright, brilliant, gifted, wise, cunning, brainy → **intelligent**

cup *n*

a small round container for drinking coffee, tea, and similar drinks, or the amount of coffee, tea etc a cup contains

ADJECTIVES/NOUNS + cup

a full cup *The cup was full of hot tea.*

an empty cup *A girl was clearing away the empty cups.*

a whole cup *I spilled the whole cup on my skirt.*

a paper/plastic/china cup *The tea was served in plastic cups.*

a coffee cup *He picked up the coffee cups and took them into the kitchen.*

Teacup is usually spelled as one word.

VERBS

fill a cup *She filled the cup and handed it to him.*

drink/have a cup (of sth) *I drink two or three cups of coffee a day.*

drain/empty a cup (=drink all the coffee, tea etc in it) *He lifted his cup of coffee and drained it.*

drink out of/from a cup *He drinks from a cup placed next to his bed.*

make (sb) a cup of sth *I'll make you a cup of tea.*

pick up a cup (*also* **lift a cup**) *The woman lifted the cup and took a sip.*

put down a cup (*also* **set/lay down a cup** *formal*): *There was a mark on the table where someone had put a hot cup down on it.*

pour (sb) a cup *Pour yourself a cup from the teapot.*

order a cup of sth *She ordered a cup of coffee.*

PREPOSITIONS

a cup of sth *Two cups of tea, please.*

PHRASES

a cup and saucer *Do you prefer a mug or a cup and saucer?*

a set of cups *They bought a set of beautiful blue coffee cups.*

cupboard *n*

a piece of furniture for storing things, with doors and usually shelves

ADJECTIVES/NOUNS + cupboard

the kitchen/bathroom/bedroom etc cupboard *The kitchen cupboards were empty.*

the food/clothes/medicine etc cupboard *BrE*: *The medicine cupboard is in the bathroom.*

a built-in/fitted cupboard *BrE* (=that is there permanently and cannot be moved) *The kitchen has built-in cupboards.*

a storage cupboard *BrE* (=for storing things) *There was a storage cupboard under the stairs.*

the airing cupboard *BrE* (=a warm cupboard for sheets and towels) *She looked in the airing cupboard for a fresh towel.*

VERBS

keep sth in a cupboard *They keep coats in a cupboard in the hall.*

put sth in a cupboard *Please put your toys back in the cupboard.*

look in a cupboard *They looked in all the cupboards but could not find the camera.*

take sth out of a cupboard *We took all the dishes out of the cupboard so we could clean it.*

cupboard + NOUNS

a cupboard door *She pulled open the cupboard door.*

cupboard space (=space that cupboards provide for storing things) *It was a lovely big house with plenty of cupboard space.*

PREPOSITIONS

in a cupboard *Is there any flour in the cupboard?*

Cupboard is used especially in British English.

curb *v* THESAURUS stop[1] (3)

cure[1] *v*

to make an illness or medical condition go away

ADVERBS

be completely/fully cured *Her illness is now fully cured.*

be partially cured *His condition was only partially cured.*

be miraculously cured (=be cured in a very unexpected way, or be cured by an act of God) *The people who drank the water claimed that they had been miraculously cured.*

sth can easily be cured *The disease can easily be cured, providing you have access to modern medical treatment.*

sth can now be cured *Many types of cancer can now be cured.*

VERBS + cure

can cure sb/sth *The old man claims he can cure illness without using medicine.*

PREPOSITIONS

cure sb of sth *She was treated and cured of cancer by a team of German doctors.*

You can also use **cure** about dealing successfully with problems: *Installing new software could help to* ***cure*** *the* ***problem****.*

C

cure^2 *n*

a medicine or medical treatment that makes an illness go away

ADJECTIVES/NOUNS + cure

an effective cure *A few decades ago there was no effective cure for the disease.*

a miracle cure (=a very effective one that cures a serious disease) *People always hope for a miracle cure.*

a possible/potential cure *The drug is being tested as a possible cure for AIDS.*

an instant/quick cure (=one that works very quickly) *The treatment is offered as an instant cure for short sight.*

VERBS

find/discover a cure *Scientists have still not found a cure for the common cold.*

develop a cure *It will be at least ten years before a cure is developed.*

search/look for a cure (*also* **seek a cure** *formal*): *Millions are spent every year searching for a cure for cancer.*

PREPOSITIONS

a cure for sth *What is the best cure for a headache?*

PHRASES

no known cure *At present there is no known cure for this virus.*

the search for a cure *Scientists worldwide are involved in the search for a cure.*

curiosity *n*

the desire to know about something

ADJECTIVES

great/intense curiosity *The arrival of the foreigners caused great curiosity in the town.*

insatiable curiosity (=a lot of curiosity about everything) *He learned the job quickly, thanks to his insatiable curiosity.*

natural curiosity *A good teacher will encourage children to follow their natural curiosity.*

idle curiosity (=curiosity for no particular reason, for example because you are bored) *Out of idle curiosity, I opened the book.*

intellectual curiosity (=wanting to understand and learn about ideas) *He was an intelligent man, full of intellectual curiosity.*

scientific curiosity *Their scientific curiosity led to the development of the vaccine.*

mild curiosity *I watched what was happening with mild curiosity.*

morbid curiosity (=about death or other unpleasant things) *Ken used to enjoy listening to murder trials – he had some kind of morbid curiosity.*

VERBS

arouse sb's curiosity (*also* **pique sb's curiosity** *formal*) (=make someone want to know about something) *New people arriving in the village always aroused our curiosity.*

satisfy sb's curiosity (=find out something that you want to know) *I decided to call him in order to satisfy my curiosity.*

PREPOSITIONS

out of curiosity (=because you are curious) *She saw the door and, out of curiosity, opened it.*

curiosity about sth *Children have a natural curiosity about animals and nature.*

PHRASES

be an object/subject of curiosity *Anyone new was always the object of our curiosity.*

be burning with curiosity (=want to know about something very much) *She was burning with curiosity about this strange man.*

curiosity gets the better of sb (*also* **curiosity overcomes sb**) (=you decide to do something because you are curious, even though you feel you should not do it) *Curiosity got the better of me and I read her diary.*

curious *adj*

1 wanting to know about something

ADVERBS

deeply/intensely/extremely curious *He began to feel intensely curious about Anna. Why was she here?*

a little/mildly/rather curious *Colin was a little curious about the reasons for her visit.*

naturally curious *Children are naturally curious and they like to find out why things happen.*

genuinely curious *She seemed genuinely curious about my work.*

just/merely curious *"Why do you want to know?" "I'm just curious, that's all."*

curious + NOUNS

a curious look/glance/stare *Her shouting attracted some curious glances from other people in the restaurant.*

curious onlookers (=people watching because they want to know what is happening) *Curious onlookers watched as the car started to roll back down the hill.*

VERBS

make sb curious *She had told me just enough to make me curious.*

feel curious *He felt slightly curious, and went for a closer look.*

grow curious (=become curious) *When nothing happened, people began to grow curious.*

PREPOSITIONS

curious about sth *He was curious about the money.*

curious as to sth *I am curious as to why she left.*

PHRASES

curious to know/find out/hear etc *Mandy was curious to know what happened.*

THESAURUS: curious

inquisitive
mind | stare | look | crowd | animals | nature
curious – used when someone always wants to find out more about things, or when describing someone's expression:
She had an inquisitive mind and asked her parents many questions. | *The man gave her an inquisitive look when she asked if the painting was genuine.* | *Cats are inquisitive animals.* | *He was born with an inquisitive nature.*

inquiring
mind | look
wanting to find out more about things – used especially in the following phrases:
The young scientist had an inquiring mind. | *The president gave him an inquiring look.*

Inquiring is only used before nouns.

nosy *disapproving*
neighbour | question
always wanting to find out about things that do not concern you, especially other people's private lives:
Our neighbours are very nosy and they always want to know what we're doing. | *I'm sorry if this is a nosy question.* | *"Who were you talking to on the phone?" "**Don't be so nosy!**"*

In informal English, you call a nosy person who annoys you **a nosy parker**.

2 strange or unusual

VERBS

look/seem/sound curious *It all looks very curious to me.*

curious + NOUNS

a curious thing *A curious thing happened to me the other day.*

a curious way *In a curious way, the argument had actually made them feel closer to each other.*

a curious mixture *He felt a curious mixture of excitement and anxiety.*

a curious fact *It is a curious fact that Lee wrote no other books after the success of her first novel.*

a curious coincidence *It was a curious coincidence that the couple were both born on the same day.*

a curious sensation/feeling *She had a curious sensation in her legs.*

currency Ac *n*

the money that is used in a country

ADJECTIVES

local currency *You can change money into local currency at the airport.*

foreign currency *They make an extra charge for transactions in foreign currency.*

the national currency *The national currency of Zambia is the 'kwacha'.*

hard currency (=unlikely to lose its value because it is from a country with a strong economy) *Some goods have to be paid for in hard currency.*

a strong/weak currency (=whose value is currently high or low compared with others) *The central bank tried to prevent the already weak currency from falling further in value.*

a stable currency (=not likely to rise or fall suddenly) *The government wants to maintain a stable currency.*

a single currency (=one currency used by many countries in Europe) *He argued against the creation of a single currency.*

VERBS

change/exchange/convert currency *Unlike most banks, we make no charge for exchanging currency.*

devalue a currency (=reduce its value in relation to other currencies) *The finance minister was forced to devalue the currency.*

a currency rises/falls *If the currency falls much more, the economy will be in serious trouble.*

currency + NOUNS

currency exchange *Banks make good profits on currency exchange.*

currency movements/fluctuations (=changes in values of currencies) *Global trends such as oil prices influence currency movements.*

currency reserves (=money that a government saves for use in difficult economic times) *The country's currency reserves are running low.*

the currency markets (=financial markets where currencies are bought and sold) *Experts were suprised to see the dollar's recent fall on currency markets.*

current *n*

a continuous movement of water in the sea or a river

ADJECTIVES/NOUNS + current

a strong current *On surfing beaches, strong currents are common.*

a dangerous/treacherous current *Beaches usually have signs warning of dangerous currents.*

a fast/fast-flowing/swift current *He was swept away by a fast-flowing current.*

an ocean/sea current *Ocean currents carry young fish out to sea.*

a river current *A small boat can be carried away by a strong river current.*

a tidal current (=caused by the movement of the tides) *Tidal currents make the seas around the islands very rough.*

C

VERBS

a current flows *Sea currents flow at up to 12 miles per hour around parts of the coast.*

a current carries sb/sth *Their boat was moving fast, carried by the current.*

a current sweeps sb/sth away (=carries them away very powerfully) *The treacherous currents have swept away many swimmers.*

PREPOSITIONS

against the current (=in the opposite direction) *These fish swim upstream, against the current, to lay their eggs.*

with the current (=in the same direction) *We stopped rowing and allowed the boat to drift with the current.*

C

curriculum *n*

subjects that are taught, or things that are studied in a particular subject

ADJECTIVES/NOUNS + curriculum

the school curriculum *Helping with community projects is part of the new school curriculum.*

the science/maths/English etc curriculum *The English curriculum is divided into Language and Literature.*

the National Curriculum (=the curriculum set by the government for schools in England and Wales) *Most independent schools also follow the National Curriculum.*

the academic curriculum *Some schools are moving away from teaching the traditional academic curriculum.*

a broad/broad-based/wide curriculum (=involving a wide range of different types of subjects) *The school offers a broad curriculum with a rich choice of learning opportunities.*

the core/common curriculum (=subjects that everyone must study because they are considered important) *English, Maths, and Science are the main elements of the core curriculum.*

VERBS

develop/design/plan a curriculum *The government has spent five years developing the new school curriculum.*

follow a curriculum *Five-year-olds now follow the National Curriculum.*

change/revise the curriculum *The education minister wants to revise the curriculum to include more practical subjects.*

introduce sth into a curriculum (=start to teach it as part of the curriculum) *Some parents objected when sex education was introduced into the curriculum.*

PREPOSITIONS

on the curriculum *Is the study of other religions on the curriculum?*

across the curriculum (=in all or many subjects) *Our exam results this year improved across the whole curriculum.*

PHRASES

be part of the curriculum *Moral education should be an important part of the school curriculum.*

curtain *n*

a piece of hanging cloth that covers a window, divides a room etc

VERBS

draw/close/shut the curtains (=move them to cover a window) *The room was dark because the curtains were drawn.*

open/draw (back)/pull back the curtains (=move them so that they do not cover a window) *He opened the curtains to let the sunlight in.*

put up/hang curtains (=fix new curtains) *She was standing on a ladder hanging some new curtains.*

curtains hang *Bright red curtains hung at all the windows.*

ADJECTIVES/NOUNS + curtain

heavy/thick curtains *Heavy curtains help to keep the house warm.*

curtain + NOUNS

curtain fabric/material *During the war, women made dresses out of old curtain material.*

curve *n*

a line that gradually bends like part of a circle

ADJECTIVES

a gentle curve (=one that turns gradually) *From the hilltop, we could see the river's gentle curves.*

a sharp/tight curve (=one that turns suddenly) *There's a tight curve in the road up ahead.*

an upward/downward curve *Her eyes followed the upward curve of the bird's flight.*

a graceful curve *Her arm arched over her head in a graceful curve.*

a sweeping curve (=wide and gentle) *The road follows the sweeping curve of the bay.*

a smooth curve *We admired the smooth curves of the aircraft's design.*

curved *adj* THESAURUS ▸ **round[1]**

cushy *adj* THESAURUS ▸ **easy**

custom *n*

something that is traditionally done by people in a particular society

ADJECTIVES/NOUNS + custom

a local custom *We were unfamiliar with the local customs.*

an old custom *We still follow the old custom of hiding a coin in the Christmas pudding.*

a traditional custom *The children learn about traditional customs, crafts, music, and dance.*

an ancient/age-old custom *The coming of spring is celebrated with many ancient customs.*

a French/Greek/Spanish etc custom *The Japanese custom is to take off your shoes when you enter someone's house.*

an established custom *This behaviour has become the established custom.*

a social custom *The length of people's hair varies according to social custom.*

a tribal custom (=of a tribe) *He knows a lot about African tribal customs.*

a quaint custom (=amusing and rather old-fashioned) *My father observed the quaint custom of standing up whenever a woman came into the room.*

VERBS

follow/observe a custom *He follows the Chinese custom of writing his family name first.*

respect a custom *Strangers should respect the customs of the country they are in.*

a custom survives *These old customs still survive in some rural areas.*

a custom dies out/disappears *Many of the region's ancient customs have died out.*

PREPOSITIONS

the custom of doing sth *Where did the custom of eating cheese with apple pie come from?*

according to custom (*also* **in accordance with custom**) (=because it is a custom) *According to Norwegian custom, the couple shared a bed the night before their wedding.*

PHRASES

it is the custom to do sth *In Korea, it is the custom to bow your head slightly when saying 'hello'.*

as is the custom (=because it is a custom) *We covered our heads with scarves before entering the church, as was the custom.*

customer *n*

someone who buys goods or services

ADJECTIVES/NOUNS + customer

a regular customer *Our regular customers are particularly important to us.*

a major/big/large customer *The bank is one of our biggest customers.*

a good customer (=one who buys a lot of goods or services from a company) *He was a very good customer for local restaurants.*

a loyal customer *Some of our loyal customers have been coming here since the store opened.*

a potential/prospective customer (=who might become a customer in the future) *It is important for any company to make contact with potential customers.*

existing/current customers *We want to improve our service for both new and existing customers.*

a satisfied/happy customer *Satisfied customers will return again and again.*

a dissatisfied/unhappy customer *They received hundreds of calls from dissatisfied customers.*

a business/corporate customer *The bank has a separate department for dealing with business customers.*

VERBS

deal with a customer *He has a lot of experience in dealing with customers.*

serve a customer *Every day the shop serves around 800 customers.*

attract customers (*also* **bring in customers**) *The internet is a great way to attract new customers.*

keep/retain customers *Keeping prices low helps to retain customers.*

lose a customer *If we do not resolve this problem, we could lose customers.*

customer + NOUNS

customer service/care *Our aim is always to raise the level of customer service.*

customer relations *Staff are given training in customer relations.*

customer complaints *My job is to handle customer complaints and enquiries.*

customer base (=a company's group of customers) *The company aims to increase its customer base.*

cut[1] *v*

1 to use a knife, scissors, or another sharp tool to divide or remove something, make something look neat etc

NOUNS

cut (sb) a piece/slice of sth *Can I cut you another slice of pizza?*

cut food/bread/cake etc *The picture shows her cutting their wedding cake.*

cut wood/metal etc *The blade needs to be strong to cut metal.*

cut a hole in sth *They had to cut a hole in the kitchen wall for the water pipe.*

cut sb's nails *Her nails were cut very short.*

cut the grass/lawn/hedge *The grass needs cutting – it's getting very long.*

cut sb's hair *"Who cuts your hair? It looks really nice."*

PHRASES

cut sth in half *Cut the melon in half and remove the seeds.*

cut sth into pieces/slices/quarters *She cut the bread into thin slices.*

cut sth to size/length (=so that it is the size or length you need) *The shop will cut the wood to size for you.*

⚠ Don't say 'I cut my hair.' Say **I have my hair cut**: *She usually has her hair cut once every six weeks.*

C

PREPOSITIONS/ADVERBS

cut sth down *The trees were cut down and used for timber.*

cut sth off (=remove something by cutting) *Cut off all the dead branches.*

cut sth away (=remove part of the surface) *Cut away the peel from the grapefruit.*

cut sth open *She cut open the avocado and removed the stone.*

cut through sth *The knife is so sharp that it will cut through anything.*

cut sb free (=cut something, so that someone can escape) *Firefighters had to cut him free from his car using special equipment.*

C

THESAURUS: cut

saw
wood | logs | timber
to cut wood, metal etc, using a saw (=a long tool with a row of sharp points):
Saw the wood ***in half****. | They* ***sawed through*** *the bars of the windows.*

chop
wood | firewood | vegetables | onion | tomato | herbs | meat
to cut wood, vegetables, meat etc into pieces, using a heavy knife or an axe:
We need to chop some more wood for the fire. | Chop the onion into small pieces. | He ***chopped down*** *the old tree. | Bill was outside* ***chopping up*** *firewood with an axe* (=cutting it into pieces). *| They* ***chopped off*** *the king's head.*

slice
bread | vegetables | tomato | onion | fruit | apple | meat | chicken | ham
to cut something – used especially about cutting food into thin pieces:
Slice the bread thinly. | She sliced the tomatoes and arranged them on the top of the dish. | He took his sword and ***sliced*** *the knot* ***in half****. | Careful that you don't* ***slice off*** *your finger.*

carve
meat | chicken | turkey | beef | joint
to cut thin pieces from a large piece of meat:
Uncle Ray carved the turkey. | A sharp knife is essential when carving any joint of meat.

You also use **carve** about cutting wood or stone into a particular shape: *The statue was* ***carved*** *out of solid marble.*

snip
thread | tape | hair
to cut something by making quick movements, especially using scissors:
She snipped the thread with a pair of scissors. | The hairdresser snipped away at her hair (=she or he kept snipping at it). *| I* ***snipped off*** *the top of the packet.*

slit
envelope | bag | throat | wrist
to make a long narrow cut through something, especially using a knife:
She ***slit*** *the envelope* ***open*** *with a penknife. | They threatened to slit his throat if the police came any closer.*

slash
tyre | wrist | face | painting | seat
to cut something quickly and violently with a knife, making a long thin cut:
Someone had slashed the tyres on his new car. | Her son tried to slash his wrists.

dice
carrot | onion | apple | pineapple | chicken | ham | bacon
to cut vegetables, meat etc into small square pieces:
Add one cup of diced carrots. | First dice the apple into cubes.

grate
cheese | lemon | carrot | onion
to cut cheese, vegetables, fruit etc by rubbing it against a special tool:
Grate the cheese and sprinkle it over the vegetables.

peel
potato | onion | tomato | apple | banana | orange | grapefruit | skin
to cut the outside part off vegetables or fruit:
I peeled the potatoes and put them in a saucepan. | Clarisa peeled a banana and handed half of it to him. | I don't bother to ***peel off*** *the skin* (=the outer part of vegetables or fruit).

trim (*also* **clip**)
hair | beard | moustache | fat | end | edge | grass | hedge
to cut a small amount off something, especially to make it look neater:
His white hair was always ***neatly trimmed****. | The old man's beard was long and needed trimming. | Trim the excess fat off the meat.*

shave
face | head | legs
to cut the hair off your face or your body, using a razor:
He shaved his face and combed his hair. | The monk had shaved his head completely. | Nigel had ***shaved off*** *his beard* (=removed it). *| I shaved and went down to breakfast.*

mow
lawn | grass
to cut the grass in a garden, park etc:
The gardener was mowing the lawn.

THESAURUS: cut

cut, lower, bring sth down, slash, cut sth back, downsize, relieve/ease, alleviate → **reduce**

2 to injure yourself by touching something sharp

NOUNS

cut yourself (on sth) *I cut myself on a piece of glass.*

cut your finger/hand/leg etc *She cut her foot on a sharp stone.*

ADVERBS

cut sth badly *He fell off his bike and cut his legs rather badly.*

3 to reduce the price, number, or amount of something

NOUNS

cut prices *Shops have been forced to cut their prices after very slow sales.*

cut costs (=reduce the amount of money you spend running a business, a home etc) *They cut costs by getting rid of staff.*

cut taxes/rates *The government is expected to cut interest rates next month.*

cut spending/borrowing *In the 1990s, governments worldwide cut military spending.*

cut jobs (*also* **cut the workforce**) *The bank announced that it was cutting 500 jobs.*

cut crime *Cameras have helped to cut crime in the town centre.*

ADVERBS

cut sth sharply/severely/drastically (=cut something a lot) *Budgets for local councils have been sharply cut.*

PREPOSITIONS

cut sth from... to... *The department's budget has been cut from £2 million to £1.5 million.*

PHRASES

be forced to cut sth *If the company loses more orders, it will be forced to cut jobs.*

cut sth to the bone (=reduce it to the lowest level possible) *Funding for art and music in schools has been cut to the bone.*

cut[2] *n*

1 a reduction in an amount or number, for example in an amount of money available to spend

> **Grammar**
> Usually plural in this meaning.

ADJECTIVES

big/deep/severe cuts *Deep cuts were made in research spending.*

drastic/sharp cuts (=big and sudden) *The minister resigned over drastic cuts in the education budget.*

swingeing cuts *formal* (=so big that they cause harm) *Universities are worried about swingeing cuts.*

VERBS

make cuts *The country needs to make cuts in the carbon dioxide it produces.*

impose cuts (=officially force people to accept them) *The government may impose cuts on public spending.*

announce cuts *A major engineering company has announced big job cuts.*

propose/threaten cuts *The manager is proposing cuts in working hours.*

face cuts *The education department is facing cuts to its budget.*

NOUNS + cut

tax cuts *The president announced tax cuts.*

price cuts *The company announced big price cuts on all its computers.*

pay/wage cuts *Millions of workers face pay cuts.*

job/staff cuts *There have been falling sales and job cuts at the company.*

spending cuts *His proposals could involve spending cuts of up to £12 billion.*

budget cuts *There are likely to be further budget cuts in several departments.*

defence cuts *BrE*, **defense cuts** *AmE*: *Further proposals for defence cuts were announced.*

PREPOSITIONS

cuts in sth *Will there be any cuts in public spending?*

cuts to sth *If there are cuts to pay, employees will be unhappy.*

PHRASES

a round of cuts (=one of several occasions when cuts are made) *This next round of cuts could be even more severe.*

> **THESAURUS: cut**
> fall/drop, decline, reduction, cut → **decrease[1]**

2 a wound that is caused when something sharp cuts your skin

VERBS

have a cut *He had a cut on his forehead.*

get a cut *How did you get that cut on your hand?*

suffer a cut *formal*: *The cyclist suffered cuts to his face and neck.*

bandage/dress/cover a cut *The nurse will bandage that cut for you.*

clean/wash a cut *Use warm water to clean any cuts.*

a cut bleeds *The cut on her knee was still bleeding.*

a cut heals *Lift the bandage carefully to check if the cut has healed.*

ADJECTIVES

a minor/small/slight cut *Two passengers had to be treated for minor cuts.*

a superficial cut (=not deep) *I'm fine – just a few superficial cuts.*
a bad/nasty cut (=wide or deep and bleeding a lot) *How did you get that nasty cut?*
a deep cut *She fell and got a deep cut on her leg.*

PREPOSITIONS

a cut on sth (*also* **a cut to sth** *formal*): *He was treated in hospital for cuts to his head.*

PHRASES

cuts and bruises (=cuts and dark marks on the skin) *He escaped the crash with just a few cuts and bruises.*

C

cute *adj* THESAURUS > **beautiful**

CV *n BrE*

a document giving details of your qualifications and work experience, which you send to companies when applying for a job

ADJECTIVES

an impressive CV *His CV looks very impressive and he has a lot of experience.*
a full CV *They asked me to send a full CV with my application form.*
an up-to-date CV/a CV is up to date (=including all the latest information) *Always make sure that your CV is up to date.*

VERBS

send a CV *Please send your CV to the following address.*
enclose a CV (=include it with your letter) *I am interested in applying for the post of sales manager and I enclose my CV.*
write a CV *When you write your CV, you list your academic qualifications and the companies you have worked for.*
update a CV (=change it to include the latest information) *The last time I applied for a job was three years ago and my CV needs updating.*

> **CV** is short for **curriculum vitae**.
> British people say **CV**. American people say **resume**.

cycle Ac *n*

1 a set of related events that are repeated

ADJECTIVES/NOUNS + cycle

the natural cycle *All creatures go through the natural cycle of birth and death.*
the complete/whole/full cycle *This is the complete cycle of operations that make the engine work.*
the yearly/monthly/weekly etc cycle *People lived according to the yearly cycle of planting and harvesting crops.*
the economic/business cycle *Every country's economy goes through periods of growth and decline – it's all part of the economic cycle.*
sth's life cycle (=the stages of life that happen in order) *The insects develop wings in the last stage of their life cycle.*

VERBS + cycle

follow a cycle *Human sleep patterns follow a natural cycle.*
go/pass through a cycle (=follow a cycle) *Economies seem to go through a regular cycle.*
break a cycle (=stop a bad cycle happening) *If people can get jobs, they can break the cycle of poverty and debt.*
reverse a cycle (=stop a bad cycle and make good things happen) *Exercise can actually reverse the cycle of poor sleeping and tiredness.*
complete a cycle *We protect the birds to allow them to complete their breeding cycle.*

cycle + VERBS

a cycle begins/ends *Winter snow disappears, plants grow, and the cycle of nature begins again.*
a cycle repeats itself *She wakes in the night, then falls asleep during the day, and this cycle repeats itself.*

PHRASES

the cycle of life (*also* **the cycle of birth and death**) *Getting old is all part of the cycle of life.*
the cycle of the seasons *Agricultural societies are very dependent on the cycle of the seasons.*
a cycle of poverty/violence/addiction *We want to help these people out of their cycle of addiction.*
be trapped in a cycle *The country is trapped in a cycle of poverty and underdevelopment.*
a stage/phase of a cycle *We are now in the recovery phase of the economic cycle.*

2 a bicycle or motorcycle

cycle + NOUNS

a cycle lane (=a part of a road that only bicycles can use) *Cars are not allowed in the cycle lanes.*
a cycle path/track (=a path for bicycles in a park, wood etc, or beside a road) *The forest is full of beautiful cycle paths.*
a cycle route (=a way of getting somewhere on a bicycle) *I bought a map of all the cycle routes in the area.*
a cycle ride (=a trip on a bicycle for pleasure) *We went for a 20 km cycle ride.*
a cycle race *The Tour de France is the annual cycle race around France.*
a cycle helmet (=a hat to protect your head) *You should always wear a cycle helmet.*
cycle hire *BrE*: *Cycle hire is available in the town centre.*

> **Grammar**
> **Cycle** is used mainly in compounds such as **cycle lane** or **cycle path**. In other situations, you normally use **bicycle** or **bike**.

cyclone *n* THESAURUS **wind**

cynicism *n*
an unwillingness to believe that people have good or sincere reasons for doing something

ADJECTIVES

bitter cynicism *The writer is known for his bitter cynicism.*

deep cynicism (*also* **profound cynicism** *formal*): *The actions of the government met with deep cynicism across the community.*

general/widespread cynicism *There is widespread cynicism regarding the behaviour of professional sportsmen.*

growing/increasing cynicism *Research indicates a growing cynicism among the public about how they are governed.*

public cynicism *Are the media responsible for public cynicism about Congress?*

healthy cynicism (=natural, normal, and sensible cynicism) *He still has a healthy cynicism about big business.*

VERBS

breed cynicism (=cause it) *Old age very often breeds cynicism - most of us have heard it all before.*

PREPOSITIONS

cynicism about sth *There is a lot of cynicism about politics these days.*

PHRASES

a hint/touch/trace of cynicism (=a little cynicism) *I detected a hint of cynicism in his reply.*

Dd

dam *n*

a big wall built across a river to stop the water from flowing, especially in order to make a lake or produce electricity

VERBS

build/construct a dam *They are planning to build a dam across the river.*

a dam bursts/breaks *The dam burst and flooded the surrounding villages.*

a dam holds back water *The dam holds back millions of cubic metres of water.*

ADJECTIVES

a hydroelectric dam *Hydroelectric dams use water to generate electricity.*

dam + NOUNS

a dam project *The dam project will cost millions of dollars.*

damage[1] *n* harm to something

ADJECTIVES/NOUNS + damage

serious/severe damage *The earthquake caused severe damage to a number of buildings.*

extensive/widespread damage (=covering a large area) *Because of the size of the bomb, the damage was extensive.*

permanent/irreparable/irreversible damage (=that cannot be repaired) *Smoking can cause irreversible lung damage.*

minor damage *Fortunately, the fire caused only minor damage.*

physical damage *There is considerable evidence that the drug can cause physical damage.*

structural damage (=to the structure of a building) *After the earthquake, the building was checked for structural damage.*

environmental damage *The programme will concentrate on reducing environmental damage and pollution.*

fire/storm/flood etc damage (=caused by fire, storm, flood etc) *The campsite suffered extensive flood damage.*

brain/liver/nerve etc damage *If you drink a lot of alcohol, it can cause liver damage.*

accidental damage (=caused by an accident) *The insurance covers you for accidental damage to your possessions while you are on holiday.*

criminal damage (=caused by someone committing a crime) *The man was charged with criminal damage after setting fire to his girlfriend's house.*

VERBS

cause damage *The explosion caused damage over a wide area.*

do damage *Too much sun can do permanent damage to your skin.*

inflict damage (=make someone or something suffer damage) *The bombers intended to inflict maximum damage.*

suffer/sustain damage *formal: She sustained brain damage in the accident.*

repair the damage *The cost of repairing the damage could be around £300 million.*

prevent/avoid damage *Young trees need protecting to prevent damage from the wind.*

limit/reduce/minimize damage *We need to limit the damage done to the area by mining.*

inspect/survey the damage (=look at it) *He got out of his car to inspect the damage after hitting another car.*

assess the damage (=make a judgment about what has been damaged) *Once the fire was put out, the immediate task was to assess the damage.*

PREPOSITIONS

damage to sth *Biofuels cause less damage to the environment.*

damage from sth *$50,000 was spent on repairing damage from the fire.*

PHRASES

the (full) extent of the damage *It is too soon to assess the full extent of the damage.*

the cost of the damage *The cost of the damage was over £300,000.*

damage[2] *v*

to cause harm or have a bad effect on something

ADVERBS

badly damage *The explosion badly damaged the boat.*

seriously/severely damage *Smoking can severely damage your health.*

slightly damage *The chairs were slightly damaged, so we got them at a bargain price.*

be heavily damaged *The building was so heavily damaged it had to be demolished.*

be extensively damaged (=damaged in many different parts or ways) *The town's main shopping mall had been extensively damaged in a fire.*

be irreparably/irreversibly damaged (=so badly that it cannot be repaired) *Relations between them were irreparably damaged by the disagreement.*

be permanently damaged *If we don't take action now, the company's reputation could be permanently damaged.*

be psychologically damaged (=a person's mental health has been damaged) *These are* *people who have been psychologically damaged by childhood abuse.*

NOUNS

damage a building/house/car/plane etc *The attack damaged airport buildings.*

damage sb's health *Drinking too much alcohol will damage your health.*

damage sb's image/reputation/good name (=have a bad effect on people's opinion about someone or something) *The incident seriously damaged the country's image abroad.*

damage sb's credibility (=make people less likely to believe someone or take them seriously) *The president's credibility was damaged by his failure to act.*

damage sb's confidence/morale *The leader of the rail workers' union said that the plan would badly damage morale.*

damage the economy/business *They argued that high public spending was damaging the economy.*

damp *adj*

1 slightly wet, often in an unpleasant way

NOUNS

a damp cloth/towel *Wipe the leather with a damp cloth.*

damp hair *Meg's hair was still damp from her shower.*

damp clothes *The room smelled of damp clothes.*

damp earth/soil/ground/grass *Worms crawled through the damp earth.*

damp air/atmosphere *The damp air is bad for my lungs.*

a damp wall/surface *Paper was peeling off the damp walls.*

a damp patch *There were damp patches on the ceiling where water had leaked through.*

ADVERBS

slightly damp *The towel was still slightly damp.*

VERBS

feel/smell/look damp *The air felt damp.*

PHRASES

cold and damp *The church was cold and damp.*

damp with sweat/tears *His T-shirt was damp with sweat.*

THESAURUS: damp

moist
soil | earth | lips | eyes | skin | cake | air
slightly wet in a pleasant way, or in the way that something should be:
The cream helps to keep your skin moist. | The cake was beautifully moist. | Warm moist air is flowing from the Gulf of Mexico.

clammy
hands | skin | palm
clammy hands or skin feel slightly wet and sticky, in an unpleasant way:
Ben was nervous and his hands felt clammy. | Her skin was hot and clammy after all the exercise.

dank *literary*
room | corridor | tunnel | basement | smell | air
unpleasantly damp and cold – used especially about rooms and smells:
The dank corridors led to a courtyard. | It was a small dark room with a dank smell. | The cold dank air chilled him.

2 if the weather is damp, it often rains and there is a lot of moisture in the air

NOUNS

a damp day *It was a cold damp day in November.*

damp weather/conditions *The weather was too damp for drying clothes outside.*

damp climate *The damp climate made the land less suitable for growing wheat.*

PHRASES

dark and damp *It was a dark and damp November morning.*

THESAURUS: damp

humid
weather | climate | air | atmosphere | heat | summer | night | day
humid weather or air is very hot and damp:
The hot and humid weather was making him feel tired. | It gets very humid in Tokyo in the summer.

muggy
night | day | afternoon | weather | air | heat
muggy weather is warm and damp, and makes you feel uncomfortable:
It was a hot and muggy night, and it was difficult to sleep. | The muggy weather gives me a headache. | It's really muggy – I wish it would rain.

Muggy or humid?
These words are very similar in meaning. You use **humid** especially when talking about places that are very hot and damp in summer, for example Tokyo or Hong Kong. You use **muggy** especially when talking about the weather in places such as England, where the weather is less hot.
Muggy is always used when saying that the weather makes you feel uncomfortable. **Humid** can be used in a more neutral way – you can say *This plant prefers* ***humid*** *conditions.* You wouldn't use **muggy** in this sentence.

THESAURUS: damp

wet, damp, showery, drizzly, grey → **rainy**

D

dance *n*

1 movements performed to music, for pleasure or as a form of entertainment

ADJECTIVES

a traditional dance *The drum is often used to accompany traditional dances.*

a folk dance (=typical of the ordinary people who live somewhere) *This is one of the oldest folk dances in Greece.*

a national dance *The tango is Argentina's national dance.*

modern/contemporary dance *She teaches contemporary dance at a local college.*

classical dance *Do you know anything about Indian classical dance?*

VERBS

do a dance *I couldn't do any of the dances they taught us.*

perform a dance *We watched the group perform some traditional Spanish dances.*

dance + NOUNS

dance music *There was a band at the party playing dance music.*

a dance step (=a movement in a dance) *Lou taught me a few dance steps.*

a dance routine/sequence (=a set of movements that are part of a dance) *She was practising a complicated dance routine.*

the dance floor (=a special floor for people to dance on) *When we heard the song starting we rushed onto the dance floor.*

a dance class *We took dance classes for a few months before the wedding.*

a dance teacher/instructor *His dance teacher gave him some stretching exercises to do.*

a dance company *He worked as a choreographer with a top Paris dance company.*

2 a social event where people dance

VERBS

go to a dance *We're going to a dance at the Park Hotel.*

have/hold a dance *They're having the dance in the church hall.*

PREPOSITIONS

at a dance *We met at a dance when we were both 17.*

danger *n*

a situation in which something bad may happen or someone or something may be harmed, destroyed, or killed

PHRASES

be in danger *The public was not in danger at any time.*

be in danger of doing sth *It was clear that the ship was in grave danger of sinking.*

put sb/sb's life in danger *Firemen put their own lives in danger as part of their job.*

be fraught with danger (=involve a lot of danger) *Their journey was long and fraught with danger.*

be out of danger (=no longer be in danger) *John is still in hospital but he is out of danger.*

ADJECTIVES

great danger *Soldiers in the area are in great danger.*

grave/serious danger (=very great) *People are putting themselves in grave danger by taking illegal drugs.*

real danger *There is a real danger that the disease will spread.*

mortal danger *literary* (=danger of death) *The plane's crew were now in mortal danger.*

immediate/imminent danger (=likely to happen very soon) *The passengers on the boat were not in immediate danger.*

potential danger (=possible but not definite) *Gloves should be worn because of the potential danger of infection.*

constant danger (=continuing all the time) *They are in constant danger of attack.*

physical danger (=danger to your body) *Many sports involve some physical danger.*

an obvious danger *Some sports have obvious dangers.*

a hidden danger (=one that is not easy to notice) *Many parents of young children don't recognize the hidden dangers in their own homes.*

VERBS

face danger *Today's police officers face danger every day.*

avoid danger *To avoid danger of torn muscles, you must warm up properly before exercising.*

sense danger (=feel that there is danger) *The animal lifted its head, sensing danger.*

pose a danger (=be something that can harm someone or something) *The chemical poses a danger to human health.*

highlight the dangers (=emphasize that something can harm someone or something) *The report highlights the dangers of alcohol.*

danger threatens (=seems likely) *Most birds will warn other birds when danger threatens.*

danger lurks (=it exists but you may not see it or know about it) *My mother was very anxious, and danger lurked everywhere for her.*

danger lies in sth (=it exists) *The river's danger lies in its depth and strong undercurrents.*

danger passes (=there is no longer any danger) *At last the sound of bombing had stopped and the danger had passed.*

danger + NOUNS

a danger area/zone (=an area that could be dangerous) *People living in the danger area have been told to leave.*

PREPOSITIONS

the danger of sth *The danger of a fire in the home increases during the holidays.*

danger from sth *The public was not aware of the danger from nuclear tests in Nevada.*

a danger to sb/sth *Smoking is a danger to health.*

dangerous *adj*

likely to harm or kill someone, or cause very serious problems

NOUNS

a dangerous situation/position *The situation was extremely dangerous and someone could have been killed.*

a dangerous place/road/area *The mountains are a dangerous place for walkers because the weather changes quickly.*

dangerous job/work *Police work can be dangerous.*

a dangerous sport/activity *Parachute diving is an extremely dangerous sport.*

a dangerous chemical/substance/drug *US troops were exposed to nerve gas and other dangerous chemicals.*

a dangerous weapon *Police have the power to stop and search people for dangerous weapons such as knives.*

a dangerous level of sth *They found dangerous levels of pollution in the city air.*

a dangerous man/criminal/offender *He is one of the most dangerous criminals in the country.*

a dangerous animal/dog *There have been several cases of dangerous dogs attacking young children.*

dangerous driving *He was charged with causing death by dangerous driving.*

ADVERBS

extremely/highly dangerous *The drug is highly dangerous if misused.*

increasingly dangerous *The political situation has made her work increasingly dangerous.*

potentially dangerous *High blood pressure is potentially dangerous as it can lead to a heart attack.*

downright/positively dangerous (=used to emphasize that something is dangerous) *Driving without lights is downright dangerous.*

inherently dangerous (=in a way that is a natural part of something) *Firefighting is an inherently dangerous job.*

VERBS

make sth dangerous *Snow and ice are making driving conditions very dangerous.*

PREPOSITIONS

dangerous for sb/sth *Plastic bags can be dangerous for very young children.*

dangerous to sb/sth *Smoking is dangerous to health.*

PHRASES

sth is a dangerous business (=a job or activity is dangerous) *Politics is a dangerous business in some countries.*

THESAURUS: dangerous

risky
business | situation | strategy | proposition | move | venture | activity | operation | investment
if something is risky, something bad could easily happen or you could easily make a mistake:
Buying a second-hand car can be a risky business. | It's a risky strategy trying to blame the previous government. | Doctors said it was ***too risky*** *to operate.*

high-risk
strategy | approach | business | venture | enterprise | behaviour | sport | activity
a high-risk activity, plan etc is one in which something bad could very easily happen:
Borrowing so much money to buy the club was a high-risk strategy. | High-risk sports are excluded from many insurance policies.

High-risk is usually used before a noun.

hazardous
waste | chemical | substance | material | journey | job | occupation | business | conditions
dangerous, especially to someone's health or safety:
Governments need to decide how to deal with hazardous waste. | The journey through the desert was extremely hazardous. | Take care when driving in hazardous conditions.

unsafe
building | road | water | conditions | level | mine
a place that is unsafe is dangerous because someone is likely to be hurt there. Water that is unsafe is likely to make someone ill:
The building was unsafe because it had been damaged by the earthquake. | The road is unsafe for children. | Millions of people die from diseases caused by unsafe drinking water. | The roof was ***declared unsafe****.*

treacherous *literary*
conditions | road | surface | terrain | waters | sea | currents | journey
treacherous places or conditions are very dangerous for anyone who is walking, driving, climbing etc in them:
The snow turned to ice, making conditions treacherous for walkers. | Ahead are 1,700 miles of treacherous mountain roads. | The boat sank in the treacherous waters of the North Atlantic Ocean.

perilous *literary*
journey | crossing | trip | position | situation | state
a perilous journey or situation is very dangerous:

He was the first person to make the perilous journey to the South Pole. | The club has no money and is still in a perilous position. | The economy is in a perilous state and we need some imaginative changes.

ANTONYMS **dangerous → safe (2)**

dank *adj* **THESAURUS** **damp (1)**

daring *adj* **THESAURUS** **brave**

dark *adj*

1 with little or no light

NOUNS

a dark place/room *The curtains were drawn and the room was dark.*
a dark corner/recess *He hid in a dark corner.*
a dark street/alley *The thief escaped down a dark alley.*
a dark tunnel/corridor *She walked down endless dark corridors.*
a dark night *It was a cold dark night in November.*

ADVERBS

completely dark *The room was completely dark.*
pitch dark (=used to emphasize that a place is completely dark and you cannot see anything) *The country lanes are pitch dark at night.*

VERBS

go dark (=become dark) *Suddenly, the room went dark.*

PHRASES

it is dark *It was dark by the time we arrived home.*
it gets dark *It gets dark around 5 p.m. in winter.*

THESAURUS: dark

gloomy
room | office | place | corridor | street
a gloomy place or room is not at all bright or cheerful:
We sat in a gloomy waiting room. | His childhood memory of the house was of a dark and gloomy place. | The bar was rather gloomy and smelled of stale cigar smoke.

shady
spot | place | corner | garden | woods
a shady place is cooler and darker than the area around it, because the light of the sun cannot reach it:
They found a shady spot for a picnic. | It was nice and shady under the trees.

murky
water | darkness | light
dark and difficult to see through:
The fish were barely visible in the murky water. | A man appeared out of the murky darkness.

dimly lit
room | corridor | hall | hallway | street | church
a dimly lit building or place is fairly dark because the lights there are not very bright:
She showed us into a dimly lit room. | The church was dimly lit.

unlit
area | room | staircase | passage | road
dark because there are no lights or because the lights are not switched on:
Don't park your car in an unlit area. | We drove along narrow unlit roads.

darkened
room | hall | house | building | theatre
a darkened room or building is darker than usual, especially because its lights have been turned off or the curtains have been drawn:
He lay down in a darkened room because his headache was so bad. | The car stopped outside a darkened house.

pitch-dark/pitch-black
completely dark, so that nothing can be seen:
It was pitch-dark inside the shed.

2 a dark colour is not pale and is closer to black

NOUNS

a dark colour *Lena always wears dark colours.*
dark brown/blue/green/red etc *Her hair is dark brown.*
dark clouds *Dark clouds moved across the sky.*
a dark sky *The sky grew dark and it looked like it was going to rain.*

THESAURUS: dark

deep
blue | red | yellow | green | purple | orange | brown | colour
deep colours are strong and dark, especially in a way that is attractive:
She looked at him with her deep blue eyes. | The house was painted in deep colours.

rich
colour | blue | red | yellow | green | purple | orange | brown
rich colours are strong and dark, and give a feeling of luxury and comfort:
The cushions were all in rich jewel colours. | She admired the rich purple curtains.

ANTONYMS **dark → pale (1)**

darkness *n* when there is no light

ADJECTIVES

complete/total darkness *It was late and the village was in total darkness.*
pitch darkness (=complete darkness) *We*

ended up coming down the mountain in pitch darkness.

semi-darkness *I could see the figure of a man in the semi-darkness.*

VERBS

darkness falls/comes (*also* **darkness descends** *literary*): *As darkness fell, rescue workers had to give up the search.*

darkness closes in *literary* (=it becomes darker outside) *The rain turned to snow and darkness closed in.*

PREPOSITIONS

in darkness *All the lights went out, leaving the room in complete darkness.*

into the darkness *The car disappeared into the darkness.*

out of the darkness *The house seemed suddenly to appear out of the darkness.*

PHRASES

the hours of darkness (=the night) *Desert animals come out during the hours of darkness when it's cool.*

under cover of darkness (=when darkness makes you less likely to be seen) *The attack took place under cover of darkness.*

be plunged into darkness (=be suddenly in darkness because the lights go out) *Suddenly the electricity went off and we were plunged into darkness.*

be shrouded in darkness (=be very dark) *When I arrived, the apartment was shrouded in darkness.*

data Ac *n* information or facts

ADJECTIVES/NOUNS + data

accurate data *It's important that the data we collect is accurate.*

reliable data *Some of the data isn't very reliable.*

historical/financial/scientific etc data *My research involves analyzing historical data.*

raw data (=that has been collected, but not organized or studied) *We have plenty of raw data, but we don't yet know what it means.*

available data *Unfortunately, the available data was incomplete.*

personal data *The company has very secure systems for storing customers' personal data.*

computer data *Digital cameras transfer pictures and sound into computer data.*

electronic data *These tiny devices can store huge amounts of electronic data.*

statistical data *It is difficult to compare statistical data from different countries.*

empirical data (=based on real tests and experience, not on theories) *The theory is supported by empirical data.*

VERBS + data

collect data *The survey data has been collected over the last three decades.*

store data *The data is stored on a computer in our central office.*

process data (=store and organize it using computers) *Newer computers can process data much more quickly.*

analyze data *The researchers then began analyzing the data.*

access data (=get it so you can use it) *The website has been improved so that users can access the data they need more easily.*

input/enter data (*also* **feed in data**) (=put it onto a computer) *His job is to input the data into the main computer system.*

retrieve/extract data (=get it from a computer or other place where it is stored) *The search program makes it very quick to retrieve data.*

data + VERBS

data shows/reveals sth *The data shows that suicide rates among young men have increased.*

data indicates/suggests sth *Our data indicates that weather patterns are likely to get more extreme.*

data + NOUNS

data collection/capture *Choosing the right method of data collection is important.*

data processing (=using computers to store and organize information) *They've got a very efficient system for data processing.*

data protection (=the process of keeping people's personal information safe) *This information cannot be published because of European laws on data protection.*

data analysis *Computers are increasingly used for data analysis.*

a data bank (=a large amount of data stored in a computer system) *We can compare insurance prices from different companies on the data bank.*

PREPOSITIONS

data on sth *We did not have any data on people's alcohol use.*

data for sth *Some of the data for the period 2002–2004 was not reliable.*

PHRASES

a set of data *The three sets of data produced very different results.*

a piece/item of data *Every single piece of data is important.*

a body of data (=a large amount of data) *There is an enormous body of data supporting the theory.*

database *n*

a large amount of information that is stored on a computer

ADJECTIVES/NOUNS + database

a computer database/an electronic database *Patient records are kept on a computer database.*

an online database *This website provides an online database of jobs in the computer industry.*

a big/huge database *The company have a big database which has the details of all their products.*

a national database *The ID cards will contain data which will be stored on a national database.*

a central database *The police have a central database of criminal fingerprints.*

a customer database *Your customer database can be used as a mailing list of clients.*

VERBS

have/keep a database *The library has a database of over 21 million book titles.*

build/create a database *After you've created a database, simply enter or import your information into the fields.*

put sth in/into a database *You want to be able to retrieve every single piece of data you put into a database.*

hold/keep sth on a database *Some argue that everyone's DNA should be kept on a database to help fight crime, do you agree?*

update a database *The database will be updated to a new version.*

search a database *You can search the database online.*

access/use a database *The library database can be accessed by all students registered at the college.*

a database contains sth *The database contains over 100,000 names.*

database + NOUNS

database management *The IT manager is responsible for database management.*

a database system *The company is planning to update its database system.*

PREPOSITIONS

be on a database *Customer details are held on a database.*

a database of sb/sth *The National Insurance Crime Bureau has access to a database of vehicles which have been reported as stolen.*

date *n*

1 a particular day of the month or year, especially shown by a number

ADJECTIVES

the exact/precise date *I can't remember the exact date we moved into this house.*

the due date (=the date by which something is due to happen) *Payment must be made by the due date.*

the closing date (=the last day you can officially do something) *The closing date for applications is April 30th.*

a provisional date (=one that may change later) *The provisional date for the meeting is August 24th.*

a start date *Setting a start date for the negotiations has been difficult.*

the sell-by date *BrE* (=a date on a food product after which it should not be sold) *Those yoghurts are a week past their sell-by date.*

the agreed date *BrE*, **the agreed upon date** *AmE* (=one that people have agreed on) *The work was not finished by the agreed date.*

NOUNS + date

a start date *Setting a start date for the negotiations has been difficult.*

the completion date (=a date when work will be finished) *The completion date for the work is early October.*

the delivery date (=a date on which goods will be delivered) *The delivery date should be around 23 August.*

the expiry date *BrE*, **expiration date** *AmE* (=a date on a product after which it cannot be used) *Check the expiry date on your credit card.*

the departure date (=the date when someone leaves) *My departure date was only a few days away.*

the launch date (=the date when a new product or system is available) *The proposed launch date for the software is next December.*

a wedding date *The couple are engaged but have not yet set a wedding date.*

the publication date (=the date when something is published) *We are aiming at a publication date of mid-November.*

VERBS

set/decide on/fix a date (=decide the date when something will happen) *Have you set a date for the wedding yet?*

change a date *They've changed the date of the show from March 6th to March 9th.*

confirm a date (=say that something will definitely happen on a particular day) *The company called to confirm the delivery date for our sofa.*

announce a date (=tell people when something will happen) *The band has announced the dates of their European tour.*

PREPOSITIONS

a date for sth *A date for the trial will be set later this year.*

the date of sth *What's the date of the next meeting?*

on a date *The ship sank on this date in 1912.*

before/after a date *You should apply at least 8 weeks before your date of departure.*

PHRASES

today's date *Don't forget to put today's date at the top of the letter.*

sb's date of birth (*also* **sb's birth date**) (=the day and year when someone was born) *What's your date of birth?*

the date of publication/issue/departure etc *formal*: *The insurance will only cover costs incurred on or after the date of departure.*

at a future/later date (=at some time in the future) *We planned to extend the house at a later date.*

2 an arrangement to meet someone, especially someone you have a romantic relationship with

VERBS

have a date *Ben had a date with a woman from work.*

go on a date *She agreed to go on a date with him.*

ADJECTIVES

a first date *He had kissed her on their first date.*

a blind date (=an arranged meeting for two people who have not met each other before) *I've only been on a blind date once.*

a hot date *informal* (=a meeting with someone who you are very sexually attracted to) *He had a hot date with the woman of his dreams.*

PREPOSITIONS

a date with sb *She has a date with John tonight.*

on a date *I always feel nervous on a first date.*

dated *adj* THESAURUS → **old-fashioned**

daunting *adj* THESAURUS → **difficult**

dawn *n*

the beginning of the day when it starts to get light

VERBS

dawn breaks *As soon as dawn broke, they set off on their journey.*

dawn comes (up) *Unfortunately as the dawn came up, so did the clouds.*

ADJECTIVES

the grey dawn *He woke early to a grey dawn.*

the early dawn *By early dawn they had reached the coast.*

NOUNS + dawn

the dawn chorus (=sound of many birds singing at dawn) *He was woken up by the dawn chorus.*

a dawn raid (=an attack at dawn) *The police carried out a dawn raid on the house of a suspected drug dealer.*

PREPOSITIONS

at dawn *She would be up at dawn and away before he woke.*

PHRASES

at the crack of dawn (=very early in the morning) *I had to get up at the crack of dawn to catch a plane.*

from dawn till dusk *She used to work in the fields from dawn till dusk.*

the light of dawn *The light of dawn was beginning to brighten the sky.*

THESAURUS: dawn

start, commencement, origin, the onset of sth, dawn, birth → **beginning (1)**

day *n*

1 a period of 24 hours

ADJECTIVES/NOUNS + day

every/each day *The museum is open to visitors every day.*

the same day *Similar protests took place on the same day in other towns.*

the next/following day (=the day after something happened in the past) *The story was in the newspaper the following day.*

the previous day (=the day before something happened in the past) *I had been to the doctor the previous day.*

a big day (=a day when something important is planned) *The team was training hard to prepare for the big day.*

a historic day (=when a historically important event happens) *The moon landing was a historic day.*

a school/working/trading etc day (=a day when children go to school, people go to work etc) *She has to get up at 7 a.m. on school days.*

election/market etc day *Election day is on May 2nd.*

a holy day *Friday is the Muslim holy day.*

Christmas/Easter/Independence etc Day *What day of the week is Christmas Day this year?*

sb's wedding day (=the day when someone gets married) *She wanted everything to be perfect for her wedding day.*

VERBS

a day comes (=it happens) *The war will end and, when that day comes, everyone will be happy.*

a day passes/goes by *The day passed uneventfully.*

PREPOSITIONS

on a day *On days when I have to work, I leave the house at 8 a.m.*

the day of sth (=the day when a particular thing happens) *They all looked forward to the day of the wedding.*

for ... days (=used for saying how many days something lasts) *It rained heavily for three days.*

in ... days (*also* **in ... days' time**) (=used for counting a number of days into the future) *In six days' time they will be in San Francisco.*

PHRASES

the day before yesterday *We arrived in France the day before yesterday.*

the day after tomorrow *They have agreed to meet for lunch the day after tomorrow.*

the other day (=a few days ago) *Mark called the other day.*

day by day (*also* **by the day**) (=as time passes) *She gets more beautiful day by day.*

24 hours a day (=during the whole day and night) *In Cairo, the streets are busy 24 hours a day.*

one/some day (=at some time in the future) *They knew they would see each other again some day.*

2 the time during the day when it is light, or when you are working or doing things

ADJECTIVES

a beautiful/lovely/glorious day (=with very nice weather) *It was a beautiful day for a wedding.*

a sunny/rainy/cloudy day *They hoped for a sunny day for the picnic.*

a nice/lovely/happy day *The family enjoyed a lovely day at the beach.*

a good day (=in which things have happened in the way you want) *She had another good day at work.*

a bad day (=in which things have happened in a way you do not want) *You look as if you've had a bad day.*

a hard day (=in which you work hard) *A hot bath is nice after a hard day.*

a long day *They've been working since 6 a.m., so it's been a long day.*

VERBS

have a ... day *Simon had had a difficult day at the office.*

spend the day (doing sth) *I spent the day shopping with my friends.*

start the day (=do something at the beginning of a day) *You should start the day with a good breakfast.*

end the day (=do something at the end of a day) *We ended the day at a little restaurant by the beach.*

a day goes well/badly etc *Although they had expected problems, the day went very well.*

PREPOSITIONS

by day (=during the period that is not night) *This shy creature sleeps by day and feeds at night.*

per day (=for each period of one day) *Workers on the farm are paid about £45 per day.*

PHRASES

all day (long) (=throughout the whole of a day) *The sun continued to shine all day.*

Have a nice/good day! *spoken* (=used when saying goodbye to someone in a friendly way) *"Bye Sam! Have a good day!"*

one of those days *spoken* (=a day when there are problems) *"I'm sorry I'm late. I've had one of those days."*

day and night (=for many hours, including periods during the night) *They would have to work day and night to get the project finished.*

dazzling

adj THESAURUS ▶ **bright (1)**, **(2)**, **impressive**

dead

adj no longer alive

NOUNS

a dead body *A dead body has been found in the woods.*

a dead man/woman/person etc *Police are trying to contact the family of the dead man.*

sb's dead husband/wife/son etc *She had a photograph of her dead husband next to her bed.*

a dead animal/bird/cat *You often find dead animals on the road.*

a dead tree/plant/leaves *Dead trees are cut down and used for firewood.*

VERBS

drop dead (=die suddenly) *He dropped dead from a heart attack at the age of 52.*

find sb dead *A man was found dead in the apartment.*

lie dead *He lay dead for several days before being discovered by one of the neighbours.*

shoot sb dead *She shot him dead with a single bullet to the heart.*

sth leaves sb dead (=an event results in someone dying - used especially in news reports) *The explosion left at least 28 people dead.*

leave sb for dead (=leave someone to die) *The men beat him and ran away, leaving him for dead.*

pronounce/declare sb dead (=say officially that someone is dead) *She was pronounced dead at the scene of the accident.*

be presumed dead (=used when someone is missing and the police think they are certainly dead) *The two boys have not been seen since they fell into the river, and are now presumed dead.*

be feared dead (=used especially in news reports when people have probably been killed in an accident or attack) *Hundreds of people are feared dead in a ferry disaster.*

ADVERBS

clinically dead (=dead based on medical checks) *A person is declared clinically dead when the brain stops working.*

long dead (=dead for a long time) *Her grandparents were long dead.*

PHRASES

dead and gone *informal* (=dead and no longer here) *Let's face it, we'll all be dead and gone soon.*

dead or alive/alive or dead *The president said he wanted the men caught, dead or alive.*

more dead than alive (=very badly hurt or ill

and almost dead) *He was swept up onto a beach after three days at sea, more dead than alive.*

Grammar
You can also use **dead** as a noun: *The names of* ***the dead*** *were read out at the memorial service. | Ten children were among* ***the dead*** *and injured.*

THESAURUS: dead

late *formal*
husband | wife | father | mother | sister | brother
dead – use this as a polite way of talking about someone who has died, especially recently:
Her late husband started the business 20 years ago. | The book was a present from his late father.

Late is only used before a noun. You often use **the late** before someone's name: *The play was written by* ***the late*** *Harold Pinter.*

deceased *formal*
person | partner | husband | wife | brother | sister
dead. **Deceased** is very formal and is often used in legal situations:
A deceased person's assets will be distributed according to his or her will. | The house had belonged to her deceased husband. | Her parents, now deceased, disapproved of her marriage.

Deceased can also be used as a noun: *It is important to check whether* ***the deceased*** *had already made arrangements for their own funeral.*

lifeless *literary*
body | fingers
dead or seeming to be dead:
His lifeless body was eventually taken from the river. | The scissors fell from her lifeless fingers and skidded across the floor. | She was lying there, apparently lifeless.

ANTONYMS **dead → alive**

deadline *n*

a date or time by which you have to do or complete something

VERBS

meet a deadline (=finish something by a deadline) *Everyone's working extremely hard to meet the deadline.*

miss a deadline (=fail to finish something by a deadline) *There will be penalties if the government misses the deadline to cut air pollution.*

have a deadline *It's easier to work hard if you have a deadline.*

work to a deadline (=have to finish something by a deadline) *We're all under pressure and working to deadlines.*

beat a deadline (=finish or do something before a deadline) *Five thousand applicants rushed to beat Wednesday's deadline for applications.*

set a deadline (=decide on a date when something must be finished) *The deadline has been set at January 31st.*

give sb a deadline (*also* **impose a deadline** *formal*) (=make someone have a deadline) *NATO has imposed a deadline of two weeks for a deal to be reached.*

extend a deadline (=make the date or time later than it was before) *My editor agreed to extend the deadline by two weeks.*

a deadline approaches/looms *Things began to get more frantic as the deadline loomed.*

a deadline passes (=the date or time by which you must do something goes past) *The deadline had already passed for him to raise the money.*

ADJECTIVES/NOUNS + deadline

a tight deadline (=one that is difficult because it does not allow much time to do something) *As a journalist, you have to be able to work to tight deadlines.*

a strict deadline (=a time or date when something must definitely be finished) *We're working to a very strict deadline.*

a self-imposed deadline (=one that you have set for yourself) *The government has missed a self-imposed deadline to solve the problem.*

the Friday/December etc deadline *The project went on long after the December deadline.*

PREPOSITIONS

a deadline for (doing) sth *The deadline for registration on the course is 23 January.*

a deadline of sth *A deadline of 3 May was set.*

deadly *adj* THESAURUS poisonous

deaf *adj*

physically unable to hear anything or unable to hear well

ADVERBS

totally deaf (=completely deaf) *My grandmother is totally deaf.*

partially deaf (=partly deaf) *The accident left him partially deaf in his left ear.*

stone deaf *informal* (=completely deaf) *She must be stone deaf if she didn't hear all that noise!*

profoundly deaf (=completely deaf) *Many profoundly deaf children have difficulty in learning to read.*

VERBS

go deaf (=become deaf) *By the time he was 50 he had begun to go deaf.*

be born deaf *If the mother gets the disease, her baby may be born deaf.*

leave sb deaf (=cause someone to become deaf) *A blow on the head left him permanently deaf.*

THESAURUS: deaf

be hard of hearing
to have difficulty hearing things, for example because you are old:
You'll have to speak up – she's ***a little hard of hearing****. | The programme has subtitles for* ***the hard of hearing****.*

hearing-impaired *formal*
having a permanent physical condition which makes it difficult for you to hear things. **Hearing-impaired** is used especially in official contexts, and is the politically correct use:
Not all ***hearing-impaired people*** *are completely deaf.*

D

deafening *adj* THESAURUS loud

deal *n*

an agreement or arrangement, especially in business or politics, that helps both sides involved

NOUNS + deal

a business deal *Branson and Wilson discussed a possible business deal together.*

a trade deal *The two countries are hoping to negotiate a trade deal.*

a pay deal (=one that involves an agreement about how much people will be paid) *They are currently negotiating a new pay deal.*

a record deal (=one between a singer or band and a recording company) *It's hard for a band to get a record deal.*

a sponsorship deal (=when a company gives money to an event or organization as a form of advertising) *His football club has just signed a sponsorship deal with a soft drinks company.*

an arms/weapons deal (=one which involves selling weapons) *A number of recent arms deals have embarrassed the government.*

a peace deal (=an agreement to end fighting between countries) *Hopes of a peace deal are fading.*

ADJECTIVES

a financial/political etc deal *After weeks of negotiation, the chances of a political deal seemed increasingly unlikely.*

a good deal (=a good price, offer, or arrangement) *You can buy two for £10, which sounds like a good deal.*

a shady deal (=dishonest or illegal) *Some senior members of the party were involved in shady deals and bribery.*

a secret deal *A secret deal was struck with the US to release the prisoners.*

a lucrative deal (=one that will give you a lot of money) *She's just signed a lucrative deal to host the show.*

a one-year/two-year etc deal (=one that will be fixed for one year, two years etc) *The five-year deal is estimated to be worth $17.2 million.*

VERBS + deal

make/do a deal *They made a deal to sell the land to a property developer.*

reach/strike a deal (=agree a deal after a lot of discussions) *The two countries reached a deal to reduce the number of nuclear weapons.*

clinch/secure a deal (=finally agree on a deal, especially one that is good for you) *The salesman was eager to clinch the deal.*

cut a deal *informal* (=agree a deal, especially when it is difficult or you have to accept some things you would rather not accept) *His lawyer thinks they can cut a deal, so that he only has to go to prison for a couple of years.*

sign a deal *The singer has signed a $20 million deal with an American TV network.*

negotiate a deal (=agree a deal by discussing over a long period) *We have negotiated a special deal with one of the world's leading car hire companies.*

close/conclude a deal *formal* (=agree a deal formally) *A deal between the two parties has now been concluded.*

offer (sb) a deal *Stores are offering good deals to attract customers.*

have a deal (=have made or agreed on a deal) *Do we have a deal?*

back out of/pull out of a deal (=decide not to make a deal after discussing one) *Twenty-five jobs were lost after their partner pulled out of the deal.*

get a good deal (=buy something at a good price) *He thought he had got a good deal.*

deal + VERBS

a deal goes through/ahead (=it happens as arranged) *It's 99% certain that the deal will go through.*

a deal falls through (=does not happen as arranged) *The cost was simply too high, so the deal fell through.*

PREPOSITIONS

a deal with sb *They signed a deal with a multinational company.*

a deal between sb and sb *Twelve US soldiers were released after a deal between the army and the guerrillas.*

a deal on sth *The company offered a better deal on pay and working hours.*

under a deal *Under the deal, the production of the engines will be moved to China.*

PHRASES

part of the deal *I got free accommodation as part of the deal.*

the terms of a deal (=the details or conditions in it) *The hotel group refused to release the financial terms of the deal.*

a done deal *informal* (=something that has been completely agreed) *The takeover has been described as a done deal.*

a deal worth sth (=used for saying how much money someone will get from a deal) *He has just signed a deal worth £2 million.*

deal with *v*

1 to take action to solve or get rid of a problem

NOUNS

deal with a problem/issue/matter *We are currently looking at ways of dealing with the problem.*

deal with a situation *At first I had no idea how to deal with the situation.*

deal with a crisis *The president has flown home to deal with the crisis.*

deal with an emergency *All our ambulance drivers are trained to deal with emergencies.*

deal with a complaint *Working in the Customer Service Department, you become an expert in dealing with complaints.*

deal with a question/enquiry *Our staff will be happy to deal with any enquiries.*

ADVERBS

deal with sth effectively *The company did not deal with the problem of bullying very effectively.*

deal with sth successfully *Most of these issues have now been successfully dealt with.*

deal with sth adequately/satisfactorily *Do you think our Health Service deals adequately with the needs of older people?*

deal with sth speedily/promptly (=quickly) *The organization deals with complaints very promptly.*

deal with sth properly/appropriately *If the police had dealt with the case properly, we would not be in this situation.*

deal with sth fairly *We felt that the court had not dealt with our case fairly.*

2 to be about a subject

NOUNS + deal with

a book/article/report/essay etc deals with sth *She has written several books dealing with the history of medicine.*

a chapter/section etc deals with sth *The first chapter deals with his early work.*

ADVERBS

deal with sth fully/comprehensively *It is the first book to deal comprehensively with this topic.*

deal with sth separately *My essay will deal with these three questions separately.*

deal with sth at length (=writing or speaking about it a lot, giving a lot of detail) *The article deals at length with the question of guilt.*

3 to successfully control your feelings about an emotional problem

NOUNS

deal with stress *Different people have different ways of dealing with stress.*

ADVERBS

deal with sth well *The family has dealt with this tragedy remarkably well.*

deal with sth bravely *People admired the way she dealt with the illness so bravely.*

death *n* the end of someone's life

ADJECTIVES

sudden death *Monroe's sudden death shocked the world.*

tragic death *The newspapers carried the story of the tragic death of a child.*

violent death *There is a high rate of violent death in the city.*

early death (=at a young age) *His first marriage ended with the early death of his wife.*

untimely death *formal* (=at a young age, when this seems very sad and unexpected) *He remained in charge of the company until his untimely death in 2004.*

premature death (=earlier than people usually die) *Smoking is a significant cause of premature death.*

accidental death *The court decided that it was an accidental death.*

a suspicious/mysterious death *The police are investigating a suspicious death in the village.*

a lingering death (=lasting a long time) *We do not want the animal to suffer a lingering death.*

certain death (=definitely going to happen) *Many of the prisoners faced certain death.*

VERBS

cause (sb's) death *Police still don't know what caused his death.*

lead to (sb's) death (*also* **result in (sb's) death**) *The delay in calling an ambulance may have resulted in her death.*

mourn sb's death (=feel very sad after someone has died) *The entertainment world was last night mourning the actor's death.*

meet your death *formal* (=die) *He met his death tragically while on holiday in Greece.*

risk death *She risked death to save the lives of others.*

escape death (=avoid being killed) *He narrowly escaped death when he fell from a cliff while climbing.*

death + NOUNS

the death toll (=the number of people who die

in an accident or disaster) *The death toll from the earthquake could be as high as 3,000.*
the death rate (=the number of people who die each year from something) *The death rate from heart attacks is about 50% higher for smokers.*
the death penalty (=the legal punishment of death) *In the West, most countries have abolished the death penalty.*
a death sentence (=the legal punishment of death) *Because of his young age, the judge decided not to impose a death sentence.*
a death threat (=a threat to kill someone deliberately) *The writer had received a number of death threats.*
a death wish (=a desire to die) *He drank more than two bottles of whisky a day, as if he had some kind of death wish.*

D

PREPOSITIONS

the death of sb *The death of the princess caused a huge display of public grief.*
death from sth *The number of deaths from cancer is falling steadily.*

PHRASES

bleed/freeze/burn/starve to death *Thousands of people are starving to death.*
stab/beat/kick sb to death *He was stabbed to death in an attack outside his home.*
be put to death (=be killed as a punishment) *The rebels were defeated and their leaders put to death.*
sentence/condemn sb to death (=decide someone must die as an official punishment) *Two men were sentenced to death for the killings.*
the cause of death (=used especially in legal or medical contexts) *The cause of death was gunshot wounds.*
a matter of life and/or death (=a very important matter) *The decision to go to war is literally a matter of life and death.*
be close to death (=almost dead) *She was close to death when the doctor arrived.*

debate Ac *n*

discussion of a particular subject in which people express different opinions

ADJECTIVES

a heated/fierce/impassioned debate (=in which people express strong opinions in an angry way) *There has been a fierce debate over the reasons for the war.*
lively debate (=interesting and involving a lot of different opinions) *The conference produced some lively debate.*
intense debate (=in which people put forward strong and different arguments) *Nuclear power has been the subject of intense debate.*
considerable/great debate *There has been considerable debate about the best way to pay for university education.*
a wider debate (=involving more people or a more general discussion) *The issue of an ageing population should be part of a wider debate about health care.*
a public debate *He called for a public debate on racism in society.*
a national debate *It is time to start a national debate on the future of education.*
political debate *There was much political debate on pensions reform.*
a long-running debate *His comments are part of a long-running debate about religious freedom.*
ongoing debate (=still continuing) *There is an ongoing debate about the benefits of nuclear power.*
endless debate (=continuing for so long that it becomes annoying) *The newspapers are continuing the endless debate over the future of the royal family.*
open/honest debate *What we need is an open debate on voting reform.*

VERBS + debate

have a debate *I think we should have a proper debate about population growth.*
get into a debate *I don't want to get into a debate about the details of the plan.*
be drawn/dragged into a debate *The president's wife refused to be drawn into the debate.*
provoke/spark/trigger debate (*also* **stimulate/fuel debate** *formal*) (=cause a debate to start) *The episode provoked fierce debate about freedom of speech.*
stifle debate (=prevent people from having a debate) *He was accused of trying to stifle debate about the war.*

debate + VERBS

a debate centres on sth *The debate centred on the question of whether he was responsible for his actions.*
a debate rages (=happens over a period of time and involves strong feelings) *A national debate is now raging over the level of youth crime.*
a debate continues *The debate continues over whether the government should send more troops to the region.*

PREPOSITIONS

debate on/about/over sth *There continues to be much debate about the safety of the nuclear industry.*
debate between people *There is likely to be fierce debate between the main parties on this issue.*
debate among people *The minister's comments are likely to fuel the debate among teachers.*

PHRASES

be the subject of debate/be a matter of debate *Teaching methods have long been the subject of debate.*
sth is a matter for debate (=it is something

that people should discuss) *The future of the police force is a matter for public debate.*

be open to debate (=be something that people can have very different opinions about) *The precise cause of the problem is open to debate.*

there is debate as to sth (=people are not sure about something) *There is some debate as to the exact number of people killed.*

debate surrounding/concerning sth *There is considerable debate surrounding the manager's decision to resign.*

debt *n*

1 an amount of money that a person or organization owes

ADJECTIVES/NOUNS + debt

a big/large debt *The debts got bigger and bigger.*

huge/massive debts (=very big) *Young people often leave university with huge debts.*

heavy debts (=big debts) *The company wanted to reduce its heavy debts.*

a crippling debt (=big and causing a lot of problems) *Her husband left her with crippling debts.*

an unpaid/outstanding debt (=not yet paid) *The average outstanding debt on credit cards in the UK is now over £3,000.*

a bad debt (=one that is unlikely to be paid back) *Companies lose millions of pounds each year from having to write off bad debts.*

a credit card debt *I want to pay off my credit card debt.*

gambling debts *His gambling debts had become so large that he had to sell his home.*

the national debt (=the total amount that is owed by the government of a country) *Their national debt is the third largest in the world.*

VERBS

have debts *The company has debts of over $200 million.*

run up debts (*also* **amass/accumulate debts** *formal*) (=borrow more and more money) *At that time, he was drinking a lot and running up debts.*

pay off a debt (=pay the money back) *The first thing I'm going to do is pay off my debts.*

repay/settle a debt *formal* (=pay the money back) *He was hoping he would soon have enough money to settle his debts.*

clear your debts (=repay all of them) *It took her three years to clear her bank debts.*

service a debt (=pay the interest on a debt, but not pay it back) *By then, she was borrowing more money just to service her debts.*

write off/cancel a debt (=say officially that it does not have to be paid) *The bank finally agreed to write off the debt.*

be burdened with/saddled with debts (=have big debts) *Many poor countries are saddled with huge debts.*

reduce a debt *The programme aims to reduce the debt of the world's poorest countries.*

debt + NOUNS

debt relief/forgiveness (=when a country or bank says that money paid to a poor country does not need to be paid back) *We need a programme of debt relief for the world's poorest countries.*

debt reduction *The government has a target for debt reduction.*

a debt burden/load (=money that someone owes which must be paid back) *The country's debt burden became even heavier.*

a debt collector (=someone whose job is to get back money that people owe to a bank or company) *They were chased by debt collectors after failing to pay their household bills.*

PREPOSITIONS

a debt of £5,000/$700 etc *She had debts of over £100,000.*

2 a situation in which you owe money

VERBS

be in debt *He had lost his job and was already in debt.*

get/run/fall/go into debt *Eva got deeper into debt through gambling.*

get out of debt *Borrowing more money is not the way to get out of debt.*

PHRASES

be heavily/deeply in debt (=owe a lot of money) *The country remains heavily in debt.*

be £2,000/$50,000 etc in debt (=owe £2,000 etc) *By the time they leave university, many students are £30,000 in debt.*

3 a feeling of being grateful because someone has helped you or influenced you

ADJECTIVES

a huge/immense/great debt *Betty later acknowledged her huge debt to her mother.*

VERBS

owe a debt *I owe an immense debt to my parents.*

acknowledge a debt *He acknowledged a debt to previous researchers.*

repay a debt (=do something for someone who has helped you) *Paul had helped me immensely and it was now time to repay the debt.*

PREPOSITIONS

a debt to sb *The singer acknowledged her debt to Marilyn Monroe.*

PHRASES

be in sb's debt (=feel that someone has helped you and that you owe them something) *He saved my life and I'll be forever in his debt.*

a debt of gratitude/thanks *I owe a debt of gratitude to my old teacher who encouraged me to go to university.*

decade Ac *n* a period of ten years

ADJECTIVES

the last/past decade *The number of Americans with the disease has doubled in the last decade.*

the previous decade *Darwin had been working on his theory for much of the previous decade.*

preceding decades (=previous decades) *The economy grew much more quickly than in the preceding decades.*

the next/following decade *China will become even more powerful in the next decade.*

the present/current decade *By the beginning of the present decade, the city's population had increased to over six million.*

recent decades *Universities have changed a lot in recent decades.*

PREPOSITIONS

during/throughout a decade *During the next decade, the world's population will continue to grow.*

for decades *This problem has been going on for decades.*

in a decade *In a decade from now, scientists will have found a cure for the disease.*

PHRASES

the beginning/middle/end of the decade *The city's population will approach 12 million by the end of the decade.*

the first half/second half of the decade *The number of violent crimes had dropped steadily during the second half of the decade.*

decay *n*

changes that cause something to be slowly destroyed

ADJECTIVES/NOUNS + decay

natural decay *The damage to the wood is caused by natural decay.*

slow/rapid decay *The houses were all neglected and in a state of slow decay.*

tooth decay *Eating too much sugar causes tooth decay.*

economic decay *Many parts of the country are now suffering the signs of economic decay.*

VERBS

cause decay *Bacteria in food will cause decay.*

prevent decay *Using a preservative on the wood prevents decay.*

allow sth to decay *Buildings are standing empty and being allowed to decay.*

PHRASES

in a state of decay *Most of the wooden floorboards were in an advanced state of decay.*

signs of decay *The house is old and showing signs of decay.*

a stage of decay *Apples lay on the ground in various stages of decay.*

the process of decay *Fungi play an important part in the natural process of decay.*

deceased *adj* THESAURUS ▸ **dead**[1]

deceitful *adj* THESAURUS ▸ **dishonest**

decent *adj* THESAURUS ▸ **good (3)**

decide *v*

to make a choice or judgment about something, especially after considering all the possibilities or arguments

ADVERBS

suddenly decide *Why did you suddenly decide to leave?*

wisely decide *He was tempted to argue, but wisely decided to say nothing.*

eventually decide *I thought long and hard, and eventually decided not to accept their offer.*

PREPOSITIONS

decide in favour of sb/sth (=choose a person, thing, action etc) *After long discussions, they decided in favour of doing nothing at all.*

decide between (=choose one of two or more people or things) *He was trying to decide between strawberry jam and honey.*

decide against sth (=choose not to do or have something) *I had planned to walk, but decided against it because it was raining.*

PHRASES

decide for yourself (=without being influenced or controlled by others) *I can't tell you which career to take – you must decide for yourself.*

decide among/amongst yourselves (=used when a group of people decide something together) *The team were left to decide among themselves who should take each role.*

decision *n*

a choice or judgment that you make after a period of discussion or thought

ADJECTIVES

an important/big/major decision *My father made all the important decisions.*

a difficult/hard/tough decision *In the end, I took the difficult decision to retire early.*

an easy decision *It was an easy decision to leave because I hated my job.*

a good/wise decision *It was a good decision to change the name of the product.*

a bad/poor decision *I think he made a bad decision.*

the right decision *She chose to study Engineering and it was definitely the right decision.*

the wrong decision *I thought she'd made the wrong decision marrying Jeff.*

a conscious/deliberate decision (=one that you have thought about clearly) *Belinda had made a conscious decision not to have children.*

a clear/firm decision (=a definite one) *It's now time to come to a clear decision on this.*

a final decision (=one that will not be changed) *The council will make a final decision in four months.*

an informed decision (=one based on knowledge and correct information) *The information in this leaflet is intended to help you make an informed decision about which treatment to choose.*

a snap decision (=one that you make extremely quickly) *Police officers often have to make snap decisions on how to act.*

a hasty decision (=one that you make without enough thought) *Don't let yourself be forced into making hasty decisions.*

a controversial decision (=that people disagree about) *A controversial decision was taken to close the school.*

a joint decision (=one that two people make together) *Jo and I made a joint decision that we should separate.*

a collective decision (=one that a group of people make together) *Society should take collective decisions about individual rights and responsibilities.*

a unanimous decision (=one that everyone agrees about) *The unanimous decision to remove the ban was greeted with applause.*

VERBS

make a decision *I want to think about it a bit longer before I make a decision.*

take a decision *BrE* (=make an important or formal decision) *I fully accept the decision taken by the committee.*

reach/come to/arrive at a decision (=make a decision after a lot of thought) *We hope they will reach their decision as soon as possible.*

announce a decision *The minister announced his decision to resign.*

face a decision (=have to make one) *Tom is facing a difficult decision about whether to have the operation.*

regret a decision (=wish you had not made a particular decision) *I was already regretting my decision to go on holiday with him.*

reconsider a decision (=think about changing a decision you have made) *She said she wasn't prepared to reconsider her decision.*

reverse a decision (=change a decision) *They want him to reverse his decision to quit.*

overrule/overturn a decision (=officially change a decision made by another person or group) *A director of the company had overruled that decision.*

postpone/delay a decision (=not make a decision until later) *The government has postponed its decision about when to hold the election.*

welcome a decision (=be pleased about it) *Environmental campaigners welcomed the decision to cancel the road building project.*

defend a decision (=argue to try to show that a decision is right when people are criticizing it) *The airline defended its decision to charge passengers for carrying wheelchairs.*

PREPOSITIONS

a decision on/about/over sth *A decision on whether to accept the proposal will be made next week.*

a decision by sb *The decision by the committee to reject the application was welcomed.*

declaration *n*

an important or official statement about a plan, intention, or belief

ADJECTIVES/NOUNS + declaration

a formal declaration *The king responded with a formal declaration of war.*

a joint declaration (=by two or more people, groups, countries etc) *The leaders of North and South Korea signed a joint declaration calling for a permanent peace deal.*

a unilateral declaration (=by one side only) *The country became an independent state by unilateral declaration in 1975.*

a final declaration *At the end of the meeting, the heads of government issued a final declaration.*

a ceasefire declaration (=an agreement to stop fighting) *A ceasefire declaration by the rebels was rejected by the government.*

VERBS

make a declaration *The president made a declaration to the nation.*

issue a declaration *Two hundred scientists issued a declaration urging politicians to agree on targets for dealing with climate change.*

sign a declaration *On December 10th, 1948, 48 countries signed the Universal Declaration of Human Rights.*

PHRASES

a declaration of independence *The United States Declaration of Independence was signed in 1776.*

a declaration of war *Britain issued a declaration of war against Germany.*

a declaration of intent (=which explains your plans) *The two countries signed a declaration of intent to increase trade with each other.*

decline Ac *n*

a decrease in the quality, quantity, or importance of something

ADJECTIVES

a rapid decline *We noticed a rapid decline in his energy level.*

D

a sharp/steep decline (*also* **a precipitous decline** *formal*) (=by a large amount) *The higher prices caused a sharp decline in sales.*
a dramatic decline (=extremely fast, and by a large amount) *There has been a dramatic decline in the number of tigers in the area.*
a marked decline (=very noticeable) *Hunting led to a marked decline in bird numbers.*
a gradual/slow decline *After 1870, there was a gradual decline of the disease.*
a steady/progressive decline (=gradual but continuous) *There has been a steady decline in club membership.*
a long-term decline *The long-term decline of manufacturing industry is still continuing.*
a terminal decline (=which continues until something stops existing) *After this, his health went into a terminal decline.*
economic/industrial decline *This area has been severely affected by long-term industrial decline.*

VERBS

cause a decline (*also* **lead to a decline**) *The use of agricultural chemicals has led to a decline in water quality.*
go/fall into decline (=become less important, successful etc) *At the beginning of the century the cloth trade was going into decline.*
suffer/experience a decline *The firm suffered a sharp decline in its profits.*
stop/halt a decline (=stop it from continuing) *These measures are intended to halt the decline in fish populations.*
reverse a decline (=make something start to improve again) *The main aim is to reverse the economic decline.*
accelerate a decline (=make it happen faster) *Supermarkets are being blamed for accelerating the decline of local shopping.*

PREPOSITIONS

a decline in sth *Has there really been a decline in the standard of education?*
the decline of sth *The decline of shipbuilding led to the closure of steel factories.*
be in decline (*also* **be on the decline**) *We do not accept the view that the car industry is in decline.*

THESAURUS: decline

fall/drop, decline, reduction, cut → **decrease**[1]

decoration *n*

1 something pretty that you use to make something look more attractive, or to celebrate something

VERBS

use sth as a decoration *You can use the ribbon as a decoration.*
put up decorations *We used to put up the Halloween decorations at the beginning of October.*
take down a decoration *In France they traditionally take down the Christmas decorations on January 6th.*

NOUNS + decoration

Christmas/birthday etc decorations *The children helped to put up the Christmas decorations.*
a cake decoration *The bakery specializes in wedding cake decorations.*
a table decoration *They decided to use candles as table decorations.*

2 the way in which a house is decorated

ADJECTIVES

interior decoration (=of the inside of a house) *The interior decoration of the house is magnificent and it is surrounded by Italian-style gardens.*

decrease[1] *n*

the process of becoming less, or the amount by which something becomes less

ADJECTIVES

a significant/substantial/considerable decrease *There has been a significant decrease in the number of road accidents.*
a dramatic/sharp decrease (=a very big and surprising decrease) *The figures show a dramatic decrease in violent crime.*
a marked decrease (=a very noticeable decrease) *The new treatment has resulted in a marked decrease in the number of deaths from the disease.*
a slight/small decrease *The company reported a slight decrease in profits.*
a steady/gradual decrease *There has been a steady decrease in the number of visitors to the island.*
a general/overall decrease *The graph shows a general decrease in fuel prices.*
a large decrease *There has been a large decrease in the amount of water resources available.*

PREPOSITIONS

a decrease in sth *There was a decrease in the number of people who were unemployed.*

THESAURUS: decrease

fall/drop
a decrease, especially by a large amount. **Fall** and **drop** are less formal than **decrease**: *There has been a sharp* ***fall in sales*** *of CDs.* | *The US auto maker reported a huge* ***drop in profits****.* | *There was a dramatic* ***fall*** *in share* ***prices*** *on the New York Stock Exchange.* | *There was a* ***fall in demand*** *for beef because of concerns about food safety.* | *Last night there was a big* ***drop in temperature****.*

decline
a decrease in the number, amount, level, or standard of something, especially one that happens gradually:
There has been a ***decline in the number*** *of young workers. | Farmers have seen a* ***decline in*** *their* ***incomes****. | The country has experienced a gradual* ***decline in population****. | There was a* ***decline in the price*** *of corn from $5 to $4.*

reduction
a decrease in the price, amount, or level of something:
The company announced significant ***price reductions****. | Stores are offering big reductions on electronic goods. | A small* ***reduction in costs*** *can mean a large increase in profits. | Have you noticed any* ***reduction in*** *your* ***earnings****? | There has been a significant* ***reduction in the volume*** *of traffic. | The firm saw a dramatic* ***reduction in the number*** *of complaints.*

cut
a decrease in the price, amount, or level of something, because a company or government has reduced it. **Cut** is more informal than **reduction**, and is often used in news reports and on advertisements:
The bank announced a 1% ***cut in*** *interest* ***rates****. | He called for drastic* ***cuts in*** *government* ***spending****. | The website is offering big* ***price cuts*** *on a range of goods. | The government has promised* ***tax cuts*** *for families with children. | The company has already made significant* ***job cuts****.*

decrease² *v*

to become less in number, amount, or level

NOUNS

the number/rate/level/amount of sth decreases *The number of farmers is decreasing year by year.*

the price/value/cost of sth decreases *The price of gold decreased to 618.50 dollars per ounce.*

crime/violence/unemployment decreases *Crime has decreased by 70% since the cameras were installed.*

ADVERBS

decrease significantly/considerably/substantially (=a lot) *Violent crime has significantly decreased over the last ten years.*

decrease rapidly (=very quickly) *Since then, elephant numbers have been decreasing rapidly.*

decrease dramatically (=suddenly by a large amount) *The survival rate decreases dramatically as the disease progresses.*

decrease slightly *Population levels have slightly decreased.*

decrease steadily (=gradually and continuously) *The number of cigarette smokers has been steadily decreasing.*

PREPOSITIONS

decrease from... to... *The amount of debt decreased from £63 million to £58 million.*

decrease by sth *The population decreased by almost 50%.*

In more formal English, people often use **decline** instead of **decrease**: *Living standards* ***declined****. | Agricultural exports have* ***declined****, and food imports are increasing at 7% a year.*

In more informal English, people often use **go down**: *The price of computers has* ***gone down****.*

ANTONYMS **decrease → increase¹ (1)**

dedicated *adj*

someone who is dedicated works hard, tries hard, or is very interested in something, and cares about it a lot

ADVERBS

highly dedicated *He is a highly dedicated member of staff.*

absolutely/totally dedicated *She was totally dedicated to her children.*

NOUNS

dedicated staff *We have friendly dedicated staff who are happy to help in any way they can.*

a dedicated team *Our dedicated team provides excellent customer service.*

a dedicated fan/follower *The most dedicated football fans spend an average of £97,500 following their team during a lifetime.*

a dedicated teacher/doctor *She is a dedicated and hard-working doctor.*

a dedicated professional *He is a dedicated professional with a huge passion for his sport.*

PREPOSITIONS

dedicated to sth *She was a very good teacher who was dedicated to helping students.*

deed *n*

something someone does, especially something that is very good or very bad

ADJECTIVES

a good deed *He did many good deeds without expecting any kind of reward.*

a heroic/brave/noble deed *Hercules was a strong courageous hero who was known for his strength and his heroic deeds.*

a great deed *She has ambitions to do great deeds in her life.*

an evil/wicked deed *The man will be punished for his evil deeds.*

a dastardly deed (=a wicked deed - often used humorously) *The book is full of tales of pirates and their dastardly deeds.*

a dirty deed (=a bad thing that is done

secretly) *The management get him to do their dirty deeds, such as firing people.*

VERBS

do a deed *Some people choose to do a good deed because it makes them feel better.*

perform a deed *formal* (=do a deed) *The award is given to people who perform heroic deeds, such as saving someone's life.*

Deed is a rather old-fashioned sounding word, used especially about brave things that people did in the past. Nowadays it is mostly used in the phrase **your good deed for the day**, which is a rather humorous expression, used when someone has done something kind and helpful: *I've made the dinner and washed the dishes – I've done* ***my good deed for the day****.*

D

deep *adj*

1 measuring a long distance to the bottom

NOUNS

deep water *The submarine was found by scuba divers in deep waters off the coast of Australia.*

deep ocean/sea *These creatures live in deep oceans.*

a deep river/lake *For most of the year the river is deep, wide and impossible to cross.*

a deep valley/gorge/canyon *There are snow-capped mountains and deep valleys.*

a deep hole/cave/well/mine *The explosion blew a deep hole in the road.*

deep snow *The north of the country was covered with deep snow.*

a deep cut/gash *He had a deep cut in his arm.*

the deep end (=of a swimming pool) *She dived in at the deep end.*

ADVERBS

deep enough (*also* **sufficiently deep** *formal*): *The canal is not deep enough or wide enough for larger boats.*

PHRASES

waist-deep/knee-deep *The water was only waist-deep and I walked ashore.*

six inches/three metres etc deep *In places, the lake is more than twenty metres deep.*

ANTONYMS **deep → shallow**

2 used about strong feelings

NOUNS

a deep feeling/emotion *A deep feeling of sadness washed over her.*

a deep sense of sth *They felt a deep sense of shock when they heard the news.*

deep love/admiration *He has a deep love for classical music.*

deep desire/yearning *There was a deep desire for political change.*

deep concern/anxiety *They expressed deep concern about the economic situation.*

deep shock *Everyone is in deep shock and we can't believe such a thing could happen.*

deepest sympathy/apologies *You have my deepest sympathy.*

deep hatred/distrust *These young people have a deep distrust of the police.*

deep despair/frustration/disappointment *The failure to end the violence is causing deep frustration.*

deep gratitude *I want to express my deep gratitude for what you've done.*

PHRASES

run deep (=be felt very strongly) *When it comes to religion, feelings run deep in this area.*

THESAURUS: deep

profound
admiration | respect | concern | shock | hatred | distrust | apologies | sympathy | disappointment | gratitude | belief | sense of sth
profound means the same as **deep** but is more formal:
Atkinson expressed profound admiration for her work. | There is an atmosphere of profound distrust between the two countries. | There is a profound belief that gambling is wrong. | She felt a profound sense of shame.

3 thinking a lot about something or understanding it very well

NOUNS

deep thought/contemplation *Holmes looked at him in deep thought.*

deep understanding *You need to develop a deep understanding of local culture.*

deep interest *She had a deep interest in psychology.*

deep insight *His work provided some deep insights into the human mind.*

THESAURUS: deep

profound
understanding | insight
profound means the same as **deep** but is more formal:
Shakespeare's greatness lies in his profound understanding of the human heart. | He offers some profound insights into our current economic problems (=new and original ideas which help you understand something better).

4 used when a situation is very bad, or something has a very big effect

NOUNS

deep trouble *These animals are in deep trouble because of climate change.*

deep crisis *The farming industry is in deep crisis.*

deep recession (=when there is very little money in an economy) *The economy is in deep recession.*

a deep effect/impact/influence *His friend's death had a deep effect on him.*

ADVERBS

unusually deep *Experts are saying that the current economic crisis is unusually deep.*

THESAURUS: deep

profound
effect | impact | influence | consequences | implications
used when something has a very big effect. **Profound** is more formal than **deep**:
Parents have a profound effect on children's early development. | The war had a profound impact upon public opinion. | Japanese prints had a profound influence on Western art. | The change in the law could have profound consequences for business. | The case has profound implications for freedom of expression on the internet.

THESAURUS: deep

deep, powerful, intense → **strong (3)**

5 used about someone's voice

THESAURUS: deep

deep, husky, gravelly → **low (3)**

6 used about colours

THESAURUS: deep

deep, rich → **dark (2)**

defeat[1] *v*

to win a victory over someone in a war, competition, game, or election

NOUNS

defeat an enemy *The king was able to defeat his enemies.*

defeat an army *Napoleon's army was defeated at the battle of Waterloo.*

defeat an opponent/rival *Williams defeated her opponent easily.*

defeat a team *The team was defeated in the finals of the competition.*

defeat a government *The government could be defeated in tomorrow's election.*

defeat a party *The Socialists have defeated the ruling Nationalist Party.*

ADVERBS

narrowly defeat sb (=only just defeat someone) *Kennedy narrowly defeated Nixon for the presidency in 1960.*

easily defeat sb *The Yankees easily defeated the Boston Red Sox 12–3.*

decisively/comprehensively defeat sb (=in a clear and definite way that leaves no doubt) *The Arab armies decisively defeated the Persians in the battle.*

be soundly defeated (=in a clear and definite way that leaves no doubt) *The English army were soundly defeated by the Scots.*

be heavily defeated (=be defeated easily or by a large number of votes, points etc) *The party was heavily defeated in the election.*

be completely/totally defeated *Austria was totally defeated by Prussia at the battle of Sadowa.*

Defeat or **beat?**

Defeat is more formal and is the usual word to use in writing. **Beat** is more informal and is the usual word to use in everyday spoken English: *Manchester City* ***beat*** *Liverpool. | The Democrats* ***beat*** *the Republicans at the last election.*

When talking about wars and fighting, you usually use **defeat**: *The Greeks* ***defeated*** *the Persians in a famous battle.*

defeat[2] *n* a failure to win or succeed

ADJECTIVES/NOUNS + defeat

a serious/heavy/bad/big defeat *This was a serious defeat for the government.*

a humiliating defeat (=very embarrassing) *They are still bitter about their humiliating defeat.*

a crushing/resounding defeat (=by a very large amount) *He quit as prime minister following a crushing defeat in regional elections.*

a disastrous defeat (=very big, and with a very bad result) *The party suffered a disastrous defeat in the 2006 election.*

a narrow defeat (=by a small amount) *Following their narrow 17–15 defeat by Wales last year, England are hoping to do better this time.*

an election/electoral defeat *It was their worst general election defeat since 1982.*

a military defeat *The president resigned following a series of military defeats.*

a shock defeat *BrE* (=very unexpected) *Arsenal are now out of the competition, following their shock defeat by Torquay Town.*

VERBS

suffer a defeat (=be defeated) *The party suffered a defeat in the state elections.*

inflict a defeat on sb (=defeat someone,

D

especially easily) *The army inflicted a heavy defeat on the English.*

admit defeat *If I left my job, I would be admitting defeat.*

accept defeat *It can be very hard to accept defeat.*

concede defeat (=formally accept that you have lost in a game, election etc) *His opponent conceded defeat.*

face defeat (=be likely to be defeated) *In May 1945 Germany faced defeat at the hands of the Allies.*

PREPOSITIONS

a defeat in sth *The party suffered its worst defeat in a general election since 1912.*

a defeat against sb *Pakistan had suffered a shock defeat against Ireland in last Saturday's game.*

D

defect *n*

a fault or a lack of something that means that something or someone is not perfect

ADJECTIVES/NOUNS + defect

a serious defect *The movie has a few serious defects.*

a major defect (=very serious) *They have found a major defect in the program.*

a slight/minor defect *There are one or two minor defects on the car's paintwork.*

a physical defect *Doctors examined the baby and could find no physical defects.*

a structural defect *Older buildings are bound to have some structural defects.*

a genetic/inherited defect (=one that is passed to you in your genes) *The condition is caused by a genetic defect.*

a birth defect (=one that you are born with) *About 11% of children have birth defects.*

a character defect (=a fault in your character) *Laziness was just one of his character defects.*

VERBS

have a defect *The old system had some serious defects.*

correct a defect *She had surgery to correct a defect in her right eye.*

test sth for defects *All the cars are tested for defects before they leave the factory.*

defence *BrE*, defense *AmE n*

1 things that are done to protect someone or something from attack

PHRASES

come to sb's defence *Luckily a passing driver came to his defence and chased the gang away.*

leap/spring/rush to sb's defence *His wife rushed to his defense and hit his attacker in the face.*

put up/mount/offer a defence *The old man was too weak to put up much of a defence.*

act as a defence (=be used as a defence) *The huge wall acted as a defense against the sea.*

sb's defences are vulnerable to attack (=they are easily attacked) *The city's defences are vulnerable to attack.*

VERBS

build/put up a defence (*also* **construct/erect a defence** *formal*): *They erected defences against the foreign invaders.*

break through a defence (*also* **penetrate a defence** *formal*): *The Russian tanks easily broke through the German defenses.*

strengthen/weaken sb's defences *The attack had weakened the city's defences.*

2 something you say to support someone or something that is being criticized

PHRASES

come to sb's defence *None of his friends came to his defence.*

leap/spring/rush to sb's defence *She immediately leaped to her colleague's defense.*

speak in defence of sb/sth *The minister spoke in defence of the government's plans to cut the education budget.*

put up/mount/offer a defence *They are sure to put up a strong defence of their policies.*

speak in sb's defence *His lawyer spoke in his defense.*

ADJECTIVES

a strong/powerful/effective/good defence *He put up a strong defence of his arguments.*

a spirited/robust defence (=strong and impressive) *Thatcher made a spirited defence of her own record and expressed her determination to defeat any opponents.*

3 relating to a country's armies and weapons that it uses to protect itself from attack by other countries

defence + NOUNS

the defence budget (=amount of money a government makes available for defence) *They have called for the defence budget to be increased.*

defence spending/expenditure *There are plans to cut defense spending.*

the defence force(s) (=group of soldiers, pilots etc trained to defend a country) *The country's defence forces are on standby in case of an attack.*

a defence policy *Ministers in Brussels have been discussing a possible European defence policy.*

the Defense Department (=part of the government dealing with defence – used especially about the US) *This is secret information, known only to the Defense Department.*

the Defence Secretary (=the person in a government in charge of defence – used especially about the UK) *The Defence Secretary is under pressure to resign.*

defend *v*

to try to protect someone or something from being attacked or criticized

ADVERBS

bravely/valiantly defend *These men died bravely defending their country.*

fiercely/vigorously defend (=with a lot of energy and determination) *She gave a lecture in which she vigorously defended her theory.*

resolutely defend (=in a very determined way) *Our party has always resolutely defended the freedom of the press.*

strenuously defend (=very strongly) *His lawyer said that his client intended to strenuously defend himself against the charges.*

successfully defend *They successfully defended the city against the attack.*

publicly defend *Few people would be willing to publicly defend his comments.*

be heavily defended (=be protected by a lot of soldiers, weapons etc) *The port is heavily defended by anti-aircraft guns and tanks.*

PREPOSITIONS

defend sth/sb/yourself from attack/criticism *I was constantly having to defend myself from criticism.*

defend sth/sb/yourself against sb/sth *They were trying to defend their territory against the Romans.*

PHRASES

be determined to defend sb/sth *We are determined to defend our hard-won rights and freedoms.*

deficit *n*

the difference between the amount of money that a country, organization etc spends and the amount that it earns

ADJECTIVES/NOUNS + deficit

a huge/massive deficit (=very big) *These economic problems left the government with a massive deficit.*

a trade deficit (=the difference between the amount of goods a country imports and the amount it exports) *Last year the country had its largest trade deficit in recent history.*

a budget deficit *Last year there was a budget deficit of $700 billion.*

a projected deficit (=which people expect in the future) *The UK is facing a projected deficit of several billion pounds.*

a federal deficit *AmE* (=of the US government) *The president should do more to tackle the federal deficit.*

a public-sector deficit (=relating to government departments and government-owned industries) *There is concern about Germany's growing public-sector deficit.*

VERBS

have a deficit *The UK had a trade deficit of more than £4 billion.*

show a deficit *Friday's trade figures showed a €10 billion deficit.*

face a deficit *The company is facing a deficit of £1.3 million for this year.*

reduce/cut a deficit *We must drastically cut our budget deficit to help economic growth.*

deal with/tackle a deficit *Conditions will not improve unless the government tackles the huge deficit.*

finance/fund a deficit (=use money to prevent it from getting bigger) *This money is no longer available to fund the deficit.*

eliminate/correct a deficit (*also* **wipe out a deficit** *informal*): *It will take years to wipe out the deficit.*

deficit + NOUNS

deficit reduction *There needs to be a greater emphasis on deficit reduction.*

PREPOSITIONS

a deficit of €1 million/$1 billion etc *How will the government deal with a deficit of over a billion dollars?*

in deficit *If a country finds itself in deficit, action should be taken early.*

definition Ac *n*

a phrase explaining what a word means or what something is

ADJECTIVES/NOUNS + definition

a good/satisfactory definition *Can we come up with a good definition of intelligence?*

a clear/precise definition *There is no precise definition of a storm.*

the dictionary definition *The dictionary definition of a phobia is 'an irrational fear of something'.*

the legal definition *What is the legal definition of murder?*

the usual/traditional/accepted definition *People who do not fit the traditional definition of a refugee may not be allowed to stay in a country.*

a broad/general definition (=including a lot of things) *This is a very broad definition of what poetry is.*

a narrow/strict definition (=including only a few things) *Some psychiatrists still use a very narrow definition of mental illness.*

a simple definition *There is no simple definition of 'culture'.*

VERBS

give/offer a definition *Can you give me a definition of 'psychology'?*

come up with a definition (=think of a definition) *The committee tried to come up with a definition of mental illness.*

fit a definition *These objects did not fit the traditional definition of art.*

D

extend/broaden/widen a definition (=make it include more) *The new law broadened the definition of terrorism.*

PREPOSITIONS

a definition of sth *There are many definitions of 'risk'.*

the definition of sth as sth *Do you agree with his definition of leadership as 'the ability to influence others'?*

by/according to a definition *By this definition, the country is not a democracy.*

defy *v* THESAURUS ▸ disobey

degree *n*

1 a course of study at a university or college, or the qualification that you get

ADJECTIVES/NOUNS + degree

a university/college degree *For many jobs you need to have a university degree.*

a science/history/law etc degree *I decided to do a maths degree.*

an arts degree (=in a subject that is not science) *What kind of jobs are open to people with arts degrees?*

an honours degree (=a British university degree that is above pass level) *The ideal candidate will have an honours degree.*

a bachelor's/undergraduate degree (=a first university degree, which usually takes three or four years study) *He has a bachelor's degree in French.*

a higher/postgraduate/graduate degree (=one that you take after a first degree)

a master's degree (=a higher degree for which you study for one or two years) *She decided to stay on and do a master's degree.*

a first-class/second-class/third-class degree *She was very bright and was expected to get a first-class degree.*

a joint degree *BrE* (=in which you study two subjects) *a joint degree in economics and politics*

an honorary degree (=given as an honour to an important person, not to a student) *Last year, the actress received an honorary degree from Queen's University.*

VERBS

have a degree (*also* **hold a degree** *formal*): *You will earn more if you have a college degree.*

do/take a degree *Not enough students are taking degrees in physics.*

study/work/read for a degree *He is studying for a degree in law.*

get/obtain a degree *She worked hard and got a good degree.*

be awarded/receive a degree *At the end of the three years, he was awarded a first-class honours degree.*

degree + NOUNS

a degree course *I didn't enjoy the first year of my degree course.*

degree level *Candidates should be educated to degree level.*

PREPOSITIONS

a degree in history/economics/chemistry etc *Applicants should have a degree in biochemistry.*

a degree from a university/college *He holds an engineering degree from the University of Nebraska.*

2 a level or amount of a quality

ADJECTIVES

a high/large/great degree *These investments involve a high degree of risk.*

a considerable/significant/substantial degree *The king depended to a considerable degree on his advisers.*

a remarkable/extraordinary degree *When we were children, we were allowed a remarkable degree of freedom.*

a fair/reasonable degree (=quite a lot) *We can predict the result of the election with a fair degree of confidence.*

a certain degree/some degree *There is a certain degree of truth in what he says.*

an unusual degree *He enjoyed an unusual degree of financial success for a painter.*

a marked degree (=a noticeable level or amount) *The dog showed a marked degree of aggression.*

a small/limited/low degree *You need only a limited degree of fitness to do this job.*

a sufficient degree *formal* (=enough) *Does the child have a sufficient degree of understanding to make that decision?*

a moderate degree *The curtains between the beds give patients a moderate degree of privacy.*

an unprecedented degree (=more than ever before) *With this new system we get an unprecedented degree of flexibility.*

PHRASES

to a degree/to a certain degree (=partly but not completely) *To a degree, he succeeded.*

to a lesser degree *His illness affected his wife badly, and, to a lesser degree, his children.*

to a greater degree *They were concerned to a greater degree about the effect on the business.*

to a greater or lesser degree (=sometimes more, sometimes less) *We all depend on other people to a greater or lesser degree.*

delay *n*

a situation in which something happens later than it could have or should have

ADJECTIVES

a long/lengthy delay *Patients often face long delays in getting the treatment they need.*

a considerable/serious delay (=very long) *After a considerable delay, the report was finally published.*

a slight/short delay *He rang the bell and there was only a short delay before a woman opened the door.*

a 20-minute/6-month etc delay *A train had broken down, causing a two-hour delay.*

an unavoidable delay *He announced that there would be a slight but unavoidable delay due to engine difficulties.*

unnecessary delays *They want to avoid unnecessary delays.*

NOUNS + delay

traffic delays *The roadworks are likely to cause serious traffic delays.*

flight delay(s) *Unfortunately, flight delays do sometimes occur.*

VERBS

cause/lead to/result in a delay *The bad weather caused a three-hour delay in sending out rescue helicopters.*

experience delays *People are experiencing considerable delays in receiving their mail.*

face delays (=be likely to experience them) *Commuters face long delays as a result of the rail strikes.*

reduce/minimize delays (=make them shorter and less frequent) *The new rules should reduce delays in bringing prisoners to trial.*

PREPOSITIONS

a delay in (doing) sth *I apologize for the delay in replying.*

a delay of 20 minutes/3 hours etc *After a delay of ten minutes, the game started again.*

without delay (=immediately) *Fill in the form and return it to us without delay.*

PHRASES

a series of delays *After a series of delays and setbacks, the project was finally approved.*

deliberate *adj* intended or planned

NOUNS

a deliberate attempt/effort *His comments had been a deliberate attempt to embarrass her.*

a deliberate act/action/move *It was a deliberate act of cruelty.*

a deliberate choice/decision *She made a deliberate choice to remain single.*

a deliberate intention *They have to show that there was a deliberate intention to mislead the public.*

a deliberate policy/strategy/campaign *Some companies have a deliberate policy of delaying payments for as long as possible.*

a deliberate ploy (=a clever but dishonest trick) *It was a deliberate ploy to make them think he didn't have any money.*

a deliberate attack *It was a deliberate attack on unarmed civilians.*

a deliberate lie *Would you ever tell a deliberate lie in order to get a job?*

a deliberate insult *They saw it as a deliberate insult to their religion.*

a deliberate provocation (=a deliberate attempt to make someone angry or upset) *The bombing was a deliberate provocation.*

the deliberate use of sth *The deliberate use of torture to obtain information is legal in some countries.*

ADVERBS

quite/completely deliberate *The use of the word 'unhelpful' in the report was quite deliberate.*

THESAURUS: deliberate

intentional
killing | act
deliberate. **Intentional** is more formal than **deliberate**:
We believe that the intentional killing of another person is wrong. | Lying is an intentional act. | Do you think it was intentional, or do think it was a mistake? | There are some funny moments in the movie, but you wonder how many of them were actually intentional.

calculated
attempt | plan | act | move | insult | murder | killing
planned in a careful and deliberate way, especially in order to hurt or cause problems for someone:
The speech had been a calculated attempt to discredit the president. | Every word he spoke was a calculated insult. | This was a cold calculated killing.

premeditated
murder | killing | attack | assault | act | crime
a premeditated crime or attack is deliberate and has been planned:
He was found guilty of premeditated murder. | Jones was the victim of a premeditated attack. | He admits killing her but denies that it was premeditated.

In everyday English you often say that someone did something **on purpose**: *I think she said it **on purpose**, in order to make me feel uncomfortable.* **On purpose** is less formal than **deliberate**.

ANTONYMS **deliberate → accidental**

delicate *adj*

1 attractive and graceful – used especially when something is not big or heavy, or is easily damaged

D

NOUNS

delicate features *She had a pretty face with delicate features.*

a delicate face *Long blonde hair framed her delicate face.*

delicate hands/fingers *Her delicate fingers moved gracefully over the guitar strings.*

delicate skin *The sun can easily damage a child's delicate skin.*

a delicate flower/delicate leaves *This tall plant has delicate leaves.*

a delicate touch *Playing the piano requires a delicate touch.*

delicate beauty *When he first saw her, he was struck by her delicate beauty.*

ADVERBS

extremely delicate *Silk is an extremely delicate material.*

surprisingly delicate *For such a large man, his movements were surprisingly delicate.*

THESAURUS: delicate

delicate, brittle, breakable, flimsy → **fragile**

2 needing to be dealt with carefully or sensitively in order to avoid problems or failure

NOUNS

a delicate matter/issue/question/subject *She was wondering how to approach the delicate question of asking her boss for a pay rise.*

a delicate balance *There is a delicate balance between meeting your customers' expectations and remaining a profitable operation.*

delicate negotiations *Following delicate negotiations, a peace deal was finally agreed.*

a delicate task/operation *He faced the delicate task of deciding who deserved promotion.*

a delicate process *They have begun the delicate process of negotiating a peace agreement.*

a delicate business *Persuading him to give us permission was a delicate business.*

ADVERBS

highly/extremely delicate *This is an extremely delicate matter that needs to be handled carefully.*

particularly delicate *Immigration control is a particularly delicate issue which the government has to face.*

politically delicate *Increasing tuition fees is a politically delicate matter.*

THESAURUS: delicate

hard, tough, demanding, challenging, daunting, awkward, tricky, delicate → **difficult**

delicious *adj*

very pleasant to taste or smell

NOUNS

delicious food *The restaurant serves delicious food at surprisingly reasonable prices.*

a delicious meal/lunch/dinner *Thanks for a delicious meal.*

a delicious dish *Our recipes will show you ways of creating simple and delicious dishes.*

a delicious smell *The delicious smell of apple pie was coming from the kitchen.*

a delicious taste/flavour *Fresh basil adds a delicious flavour when used in salads.*

a delicious recipe *You'll find lots of delicious recipes in this week's magazine.*

VERBS

taste delicious *Blueberries are good for your health and they taste delicious.*

smell/look delicious *The pizza smells delicious.*

sound delicious *Everything on the menu sounded delicious.*

ADVERBS

absolutely delicious *The chocolate cake was absolutely delicious.*

⚠ Don't say 'very delicious'.

THESAURUS: delicious

tasty
food | meal | dish | morsel | treat
if food is tasty, it has a good strong taste. **Tasty** is more informal than **delicious**:
He can make a tasty meal using just a few vegetables. | *The mother bird was holding a tasty morsel in her beak* (=small piece of delicious food). | *I liked the onion soup – it was really tasty.*

mouth-watering
aroma | food | dish | selection | variety | sauce
looking or smelling delicious:
There was a mouth-watering aroma coming from the kitchen (=a delicious smell). | *The chef had prepared a selection of mouth-watering dishes.*

appetizing
food | meal | colour
appetizing food looks or smells good to eat. **Appetizing** is often used in negative sentences:
The hospital food didn't ***look*** *very* ***appetizing***. | *You should be able to prepare a healthy appetizing meal in ten minutes.*

juicy
orange | peach | melon | strawberry | pineapple | tomato | meat | steak
juicy fruit or meat contains a lot of juice and tastes good:
The oranges are lovely and juicy. | *I picked some juicy tomatoes from the garden.* | *The meat was juicy and tender.* | *They served us a big juicy steak.*

succulent
meat | pork | beef | chicken | fruit | peach | pear | flesh | flavour
succulent fruit or meat contains a lot of juice and tastes good:
The succulent meat melted in his mouth. | The tree produces small succulent fruit in August. | She bit into the succulent flesh of the chicken. | The guests loved the succulent flavour of the tender meat.

Succulent or **juicy?**
Succulent is more formal than **juicy** and is mainly used in written descriptions. You use **succulent** when emphasizing the pleasure something gives you when you put it in your mouth and bite or suck on it. You use **juicy** when saying that fruit or steak contains a lot of juice.

You can say that food **melts in your mouth** (=it is very soft and delicious): *The delicate butter pastry* ***melts in your mouth****.* You can also say that food **is bursting with flavour** (=it is delicious and has a lot of flavour): *The cherry tomatoes are* ***bursting with flavour****.*

delight *n*
a feeling of great pleasure and satisfaction

ADJECTIVES

great delight *It gave her great delight to tease him about his girlfriends.*

sheer/pure delight (=very great) *She opened the present and laughed with sheer delight.*

obvious/evident delight *The children were watching the show with obvious delight.*

VERBS

take/find delight in (doing) sth (=enjoy something a lot) *He took delight in cooking for his friends.*

squeal/scream with delight *Lucy saw the sea and screamed with delight.*

PREPOSITIONS

to sb's delight *To my delight, dolphins came and swam alongside the boat.*

in/with delight (=because of feeling very happy) *He clapped his hands in delight.*

sb's delight at sth *He could not hide his delight at being invited.*

PHRASES

a squeal/gasp/cry etc of delight *The child gave a squeal of delight.*

a source of delight *This beautiful park is a source of delight to many visitors.*

delighted *adj* THESAURUS **happy**

delivery *n*
the act of bringing things to a particular person or place, or the things that are brought

ADJECTIVES/NOUNS + delivery

free delivery *Delivery is free for purchases over £20.*

next-day/overnight delivery *You have to pay extra for next-day delivery.*

immediate/prompt delivery *The software may not be available for immediate delivery.*

special/express delivery (=a service that delivers mail and packages very quickly) *A brown package arrived by special delivery.*

recorded delivery *BrE* (=when a record is kept of posting and safe delivery) *I'd better send my passport recorded delivery.*

milk/fuel/pizza etc delivery *I gave the kids some money for a pizza delivery.*

VERBS

make/do a delivery *I'm afraid we don't make deliveries on Saturdays.*

have a delivery *The store has just had a delivery of tiles from Italy.*

take delivery of sth (=receive something that has been delivered) *The airline has just taken delivery of three new passenger jets.*

accept/receive a delivery *Someone must be at home to accept the delivery.*

expect (a) delivery *She wanted to know when to expect delivery of the fabric.*

await (a) delivery *They could not do the repair because they were awaiting delivery of some engine parts.*

delivery + NOUNS

a delivery charge *There is no delivery charge on goods over £20.*

a delivery date/time *The normal delivery time is 7 to 10 days after you place your order.*

a delivery service *The store has a delivery service.*

a delivery truck/van *Just then a delivery truck stopped outside.*

delusion *adj* THESAURUS **untrue**

demand *n*
1 the need or desire that people have for particular goods and services

ADJECTIVES/NOUNS + demand

high/strong demand (=a lot of people want something) *Demand for housing is higher than ever.*

low demand (=not many people want something) *Recently the demand for new cars has been relatively low.*

a big demand *There's always a big demand for photographs of celebrities.*

a great/huge demand (=very big) *There is a huge demand for business software and services.*

D

increased/increasing/growing demand *One of the problems is the growing demand for housing.*
falling demand (=decreasing) *The falling demand for coal has put many coal merchants out of business.*
global/international/world demand *There is a huge global demand for specialist skills.*
consumer/customer demand (=people's desire to buy goods) *Consumer demand for new technology is strong.*

VERBS

meet/satisfy demand (=supply as much as people need or want) *Companies must be able to satisfy demand.*
keep up with demand (*also* **keep pace with demand**) (=satisfy the demand) *Public funding for higher education has not kept up with demand.*
cope with demand (=satisfy demand) *The existing services were not capable of coping with the demand for advice.*
increase/boost demand *A very hard winter boosted the demand for natural gas.*
reduce demand *Higher prices could have the effect of reducing the demand for oil.*
demand rises/increases/grows *Demand for energy has continued to rise.*
demand falls (=becomes lower) *Demand for the products has fallen in the last six months.*

PREPOSITIONS

the demand for sth *The demand for new housing has risen.*

PHRASES

be in demand (=people want someone or something) *As a speaker he was always in demand.*
be much in demand (*also* **be in great demand**) (=be wanted by a lot of people) *Fuel-efficient cars are now much in demand.*
supply outstrips/exceeds demand (=more is available than people need or want) *In the 1980s, the supply of grain far exceeded the demand.*
a lack of demand *Many factories closed through lack of demand.*
a surge in demand (=a sudden increase) *There's often a surge in demand for the internet at the weekend.*

2 a firm request for something

VERBS

make a demand *The kidnappers made a demand for over $1 million.*
face a demand *The president is facing demands for him to resign.*
reject a demand *The government rejected demands for a general election.*
resist a demand *It can be difficult for parents to resist the demands of children for the latest toys.*
ignore a demand *He was arrested after ignoring police demands to stop.*
agree to a demand *Employers won't agree to demands for such big pay increases.*
accommodate/satisfy a demand *formal* (=do what someone asks) *This strategy will satisfy Iraqi demands for power.*

ADJECTIVES

an unreasonable demand *It is not an unreasonable demand to want a higher salary.*
an impossible demand *I'm afraid this is an impossible demand.*

PREPOSITIONS

a demand for sth *The government is facing demands for political change.*

3 a situation in which someone or something has to use a lot of effort or do a lot of work

> **Grammar**
> Usually plural in this meaning.

ADJECTIVES

heavy/great demands *Being overweight makes heavy demands on your heart.*
growing/increasing demands *Increasing demands are being placed on police officers.*
excessive demands (=too many) *Teachers argue that the new exam system is placing excessive demands on students.*
conflicting/competing demands (=things which are very different and difficult to combine) *Working mothers face competing demands on their time.*

VERBS

place/put demands on sb/sth *The demands placed on athletes these days are incredibly tough.*
make demands on sb/sth *The new curriculum makes great demands on teachers.*
juggle/balance the demands of sth (=do two difficult things successfully) *It can be very difficult to juggle the demands of being a father and a successful politician.*
cope with/deal with the demands of sth *Being fit and healthy helps you to cope with the demands of life.*

PREPOSITIONS

the demands of sth *Mary was finding it difficult to cope with the demands of being a doctor.*
demands on sb *Demands on students are greater than ever.*

demanding *adj* THESAURUS ▸ **difficult**

demonstrate *v*

to show or prove something clearly

ADVERBS

demonstrate sth clearly *The study clearly demonstrates the connection between smoking and heart disease.*

amply demonstrate sth (=show something more than enough) *These figures amply demonstrate the financial problems which the company faces.*

demonstrate sth conclusively (=show that something is definitely true) *Research has conclusively demonstrated that the drug does not cause cancer.*

vividly/graphically demonstrate sth (=show something in a very clear way) *This selection of Hoffmann's finest short stories vividly demonstrates his intense imagination.*

demonstration Ac *n*

1 an event at which a large group of people meet to protest or to support something in public

ADJECTIVES/NOUNS + demonstration

a big/large demonstration *Opponents of the new law are planning a big demonstration next week.*

a huge/massive demonstration (=very big) *Thousands of people took part in a series of massive demonstrations against the war.*

a mass demonstration (=involving a very large number of people) *There have been mass demonstrations in several American cities.*

a peaceful demonstration *Everyone has the right to take part in peaceful demonstrations.*

a violent demonstration *Nine people have been killed during violent demonstrations.*

a street demonstration (=in the streets of a city) *A street demonstration completely blocked the centre of the city.*

a student demonstration (=by students) *In France, student demonstrations were disrupting university teaching.*

a political demonstration (=to protest about the government or a political policy) *She was arrested twice for her part in political demonstrations.*

a public demonstration (=by members of the public) *A series of public demonstrations have been held in cities across the country.*

a protest demonstration (=in which people protest against something) *The price increases were met by a series of strikes and protest demonstrations.*

an anti-government/pro-democracy etc demonstration *There have been further violent anti-government demonstrations this week.*

VERBS

hold/stage a demonstration (=organize and take part in one) *Protesters staged angry demonstrations outside government buildings.*

organize a demonstration *A large demonstration was organized by the opposition.*

take part in a demonstration (*also* **participate in a demonstration** *formal*): *As many as 400,000 people took part in the demonstration.*

go on a demonstration *BrE* (=take part in a demonstration) *I've never been on a demonstration before.*

join a demonstration *They were prevented by police from joining the demonstration.*

break up a demonstration (=prevent it from continuing) *Police moved in to break up the demonstration.*

provoke/spark a demonstration (=cause it) *The incident sparked a demonstration of 2,000 people.*

a demonstration takes place *Violent street demonstrations took place in the capital.*

PREPOSITIONS

a demonstration against sth *Students took part in a demonstration against changes to university funding.*

PHRASES

a demonstration in support of sth/sb *Public demonstrations took place in support of the rebels.*

a demonstration in protest at sth *There were demonstrations in protest at the food shortages.*

2 something that shows that something is true

ADJECTIVES

a clear demonstration *This study provides the clearest demonstration yet that passive smoking can cause cancer.*

a vivid/graphic demonstration (=very clear and often unpleasant) *Her death was a graphic demonstration of the dangers facing journalists in the country.*

PREPOSITIONS

a demonstration of sth *The high number of calls received is a clear demonstration of the need for this service.*

denial Ac *n*

a statement saying that something is not true

VERBS

issue a denial (=deny something publicly or officially) *Immediately the government issued a denial of the rumours.*

make a denial *He made no public denial of the allegations against him.*

ADJECTIVES

a strong/firm denial *Her accusation against the company met with a strong denial.*

an angry denial *There were angry denials of corruption in the police force.*

an official/public denial *The Army has consistently issued official denials that they were involved.*

a categorical/flat denial (=saying very definitely that something is not true) *Her response to the allegation was a categorical denial.*

a vehement/vigorous denial (=very strong) *The report led to vehement denials from the minister.*

deny Ac v

to say that something is not true, or that you do not believe something

ADVERBS

strongly/firmly/emphatically deny sth *Reports of government corruption have been strongly denied.*

vehemently/vigorously/strenuously deny sth (=very strongly) *He vehemently denied that he had ever been to her house.*

flatly/categorically deny sth (=very definitely and directly) *In the interview, he flatly denied knowing the woman.*

angrily deny sth *The singer angrily denied the allegations.*

hotly deny sth (=in an angry or excited way) *She hotly denied ever having taken drugs.*

repeatedly/consistently deny sth *King has repeatedly denied being a gang member.*

NOUNS

deny a charge/allegation/accusation *Officials denied allegations that torture was used.*

deny a claim *Claims that money had been wasted were denied by the chairman.*

deny a report/rumour *Their chief executive denied rumours of the company's decline.*

deny any involvement in sth *The minister denied any involvement in the affair.*

deny any wrongdoing *formal* (=say that you have not done anything wrong) *The White House denied any wrongdoing.*

deny all knowledge of sth *CIA officers denied all knowledge of the operation.*

deny the existence of sth *The government has denied the existence of chemical weapons in the country.*

PHRASES

refuse to confirm or deny sth (=say whether something is true or not) *He refused to confirm or deny the story.*

department n

one part of a large organization such as a hospital, university, company, or government

ADJECTIVES/NOUNS + department

a government/federal department *The Ministry of Arts & Culture was the government department responsible for museums.*

a university department *University departments are generally judged by the quality of their research.*

the biology/English/history etc department (=in a university or school) *He joined the German Department at Stirling University in 1972.*

the finance/sales/personnel etc department (=in a company) *She worked in the sales department of a software company.*

the police/fire department *AmE: He is a narcotics officer with the San Francisco Police Department.*

PHRASES

the Department of Health/Trade/Education etc (*also* **the Department for Health etc** *BrE*) (=in a government) *My brother works for the Department of Health.*

the head of a department *The current head of department is Professor Mary Keen.*

a member of a department *Meetings are open to all members of the department.*

departure n

the act of leaving a place, organization, or job

ADJECTIVES/NOUNS + departure

sb's sudden/abrupt departure (=done suddenly, without being planned) *I didn't know the reason for his abrupt departure.*

a hasty/speedy departure (=done very quickly and suddenly) *The room showed signs of a hasty departure.*

sb's imminent/impending departure (=going to happen soon) *They were feeling sad about their son's imminent departure for university.*

a flight/train/coach departure *All flight departures have been delayed due to fog.*

departure + NOUNS

the departure date/time (*also* **the date/time of departure**) *You cannot make a change to your booking within six weeks of your departure date.*

a departure lounge (=airport room where people wait before their flights) *We sat in the departure lounge for over an hour.*

a departure gate (=an exit from an airport to get on a particular plane) *It was a long walk to the departure gate.*

the departures board (=a board showing the times of planes or trains) *I checked the departures board for details of my flight.*

VERBS

delay sb's departure *She decided to delay her departure by a few days.*

hasten sb's departure (=make it happen sooner) *This defeat in parliament hastened the prime minister's departure.*

PREPOSITIONS

sb's departure for a place (=when they leave to go to a place) *She came to visit us shortly before her departure for France.*

sb's departure from a place/organization *He began making arrangements for his departure from the city.*

PHRASES

on the eve of sb's departure (=the day before they leave) *He stayed at the Adelphi Hotel on the eve of his departure for America.*

the day of departure *As the day of departure drew closer, we became more and more excited.*

depend *v*

1 to be affected by something else

> **Grammar**
> **Depend** is used with **on** or **upon**, except in the phrase **it/that depends**.

ADVERBS

sth very much/greatly depends on sth *The cost of accommodation very much depends on where you live.*

sth mainly/largely depends on sth *Whether they succeed or not will mainly depend on their own efforts.*

sth entirely/completely depends on sth *It entirely depends on each individual couple how they conduct their relationship.*

sth partly depends on sth *The result partly depends, of course, on the conditions at that particular time.*

sth rather depends on sth (=partly – often used ironically to mean that something has a large effect) *"Is it easy?" "That rather depends on what you mean by 'easy'!"*

sth ultimately depends on sth *His future ultimately depended on whether the court believed his story.*

PREPOSITIONS

depend on/upon sth *The outcome depends on several economic factors.*

PHRASES

it (all) depends on sth (=something will affect what will happen or what you choose) *Several different scenarios are possible. It all depends on the weather.*

it/that depends (=used when saying that you are not sure what will happen) *"How are you going to get there?" "It depends."*

everything depends on sth *Everything depends on how the team plays on the day.*

depend on sth to some extent (=be partly affected by something, but not completely) *Your answer will depend to some extent on the type of person you are.*

2 to need someone or something in order to be able to do something

ADVERBS

depend heavily on sb/sth *She finds it difficult to walk, and depends heavily on her children.*

depend entirely on sth/sb *The industry depends entirely on exports.*

PREPOSITIONS

depend on/upon sb for sth *We all depend upon one another for survival.*

deposit *n*

money that you pay when you rent something such as an apartment or car, which will be given back if you do not damage it

VERBS

pay a deposit *Car hire firms may ask you to pay a deposit in advance.*

get your deposit back *You'll get your deposit back when all the bills have been paid.*

give sb their deposit back (*also* **return sb's deposit** *formal*): *When I left, the landlord refused to give me my deposit back.*

lose your deposit *If there is any damage to the car, we could lose our deposit.*

ADJECTIVES

a refundable/returnable deposit (=that you get back later if there is no damage) *You can hire a bicycle with a refundable deposit of 100 euros.*

depressed *adj*

very unhappy, either because something bad has happened or because of a medical condition

VERBS

be/feel depressed *People who feel depressed often have difficulty sleeping.*

get/become depressed *She became depressed after her husband left her.*

look/sound depressed *I was worried about him because he had sounded so depressed on the phone.*

make sb depressed *Losing his job made him even more depressed.*

ADVERBS

deeply/terribly depressed *Helen sat at home all day feeling deeply depressed.*

severely/seriously depressed (=very depressed, so that you are ill or almost ill) *He became severely depressed after his wife died.*

clinically depressed *technical* (=depressed in a way that doctors recognize as an illness) *His medical records show that he was suicidal and clinically depressed.*

slightly/mildly depressed *I was slightly depressed when we lost.*

PREPOSITIONS

depressed about/at sth *He was depressed about the break-up of his marriage.*

> **THESAURUS: depressed**
> unhappy, homesick, gloomy, glum, dejected/downcast, mournful, wistful, down, miserable, depressed, heartbroken, distressed, devastated
> → **sad (1)**

depressing *adj* making you feel sad

NOUNS

a depressing experience *Being unemployed is a very depressing experience.*

a depressing thought *"Maybe life will always be like this." "What a depressing thought!"*

D

a depressing prospect (=something that seems likely to be depressing) *Working until I'm 70 is rather a depressing prospect.*

a depressing sight *The building was a depressing sight, with water leaking through the roof.*

a depressing picture (=a depressing idea of what something is like) *The latest report paints a depressing picture of Britain.*

depressing news *There was more depressing news about the economy.*

a depressing place *The walls were painted grey and it looked like a depressing place to live.*

a depressing story *He told me a depressing story about a man who died on the subway without anyone even noticing.*

D

VERBS

find sth depressing *He found the news very depressing.*

ADVERBS

very/really/deeply depressing *The article was deeply depressing.*

PHRASES

sth makes depressing reading (=it is bad and makes you feel depressed when you read it) *The crime statistics make depressing reading.*

THESAURUS: depressing

grim
reality | **reminder** | **news** | **picture**
depressing, especially because something unpleasant happens:
His films show the grim reality of war and its effect on people's lives. | *The bombings are a grim reminder of the threat of terrorism* (=something that makes you remember an unpleasant event or situation). | *A police officer told them the grim news about the accident.*

gloomy
news | **picture** | **prediction** | **forecast** | **outlook** | **prospect** | **assessment**
showing that things are not going well and not making you feel hopeful about the future:
The news about the economy is always gloomy. | *In his book, he paints a gloomy picture of the future of our planet.* | *People are making gloomy predictions about the future of the company.* | *The coach gave a gloomy assessment of the team's chances.*

bleak
picture | **future** | **prospect** | **vision** | **outlook** | **day**
if something seems bleak, there is nothing at all to make you feel happy or hopeful. **Bleak** sounds even more miserable than **gloomy**:
He gives a bleak picture of his lonely life. | *The country faced a bleak economic future after the war.* | *Many people face the bleak prospect of losing their jobs.* | *It was another bleak day for English football fans.*

drab
office | **building** | **surroundings** | **existence**
if something seems drab, there is nothing exciting or interesting about it – used especially about places:
I waited for hours in a drab government office. | *The town is full of drab concrete factory buildings.* | *He was tired of his drab surroundings.* | *She wanted to escape from her drab existence and become an actress.*

dreary
day | **life** | **monotony** | **routine** | **tale** | **place**
if something seems dreary, there is nothing exciting or interesting about it – used especially about situations that continue for a long time in a boring way:
I came home, after another dreary day at the office. | *My own life seemed very dreary compared to theirs.* | *She hated the dreary monotony of her work.* | *Every day, he would tell me the same dreary tale.* | *The town is a dreary place in winter, when all the tourists have gone away.*

disheartening
depressing and making you want to give up what you are doing:
It was disheartening for fans to see their team lose again. | *I found the attitude of some students very disheartening – they didn't seem to care about their work.*

THESAURUS: depressing

depressing, dismal, tragic, heartbreaking, pathetic → **sad (2)**

depression *n*

1 a medical condition that makes you very unhappy and anxious and often prevents you from living a normal life

ADJECTIVES

deep depression *She sank into a deep depression.*

severe depression *Severe depression requires medical treatment.*

mild depression *I have been suffering from mild depression for the last year.*

post-natal depression (=depression after giving birth) *Post-natal depression can affect women in different ways.*

clinical depression (=severe depression which requires medical help) *How do you tell the difference between clinical depression and normal sadness?*

manic depression (=a mental illness that causes someone to feel very strong emotions of happiness and sadness in a short period of time) *Manic depression affects one in 200 people, both men and women alike.*

VERBS

suffer from/have depression *He's been suffering from depression since his wife died.*

treat depression *Some doctors think that exercise is useful in treating depression.*

diagnose depression (*also* **diagnose sb with depression**) (=find out that someone has depression) *Most people diagnosed with depression are successfully treated.*

PHRASES

symptoms of depression *Sleeplessness is one of the symptoms of depression.*

a bout of depression (=a period during which someone is depressed) *He suffered bouts of depression throughout his adult life.*

feelings of depression *A poor diet can result in tiredness and feelings of depression.*

2 a long period during which there is very little business activity and a lot of people do not have jobs

ADJECTIVES

the Great Depression *The Great Depression began in 1929 with the Stock Market crash.*

an economic depression *The economic depression is likely to worsen.*

a worldwide depression *The Great Depression of 1929 was a worldwide depression that lasted for ten years.*

a major/severe depression *The economy collapsed and the country entered a major depression.*

the worst depression *The United States is suffering the worst depression since the 1930s.*

VERBS

go into a depression *The economy went into a depression.*

come out of a depression *There are signs that the country is beginning to come out of the depression.*

a depression deepens/gets worse *The depression deepened and people felt increasingly desperate.*

PREPOSITIONS

during a depression *A lot of people were out of work during the depression.*

PHRASES

be in the middle/midst of a depression *The UK is in the middle of a depression with few signs of recovery.*

be in the grip of a depression (=be experiencing a depression) *The entire country is in the grip of a depression.*

deprived *adj* THESAURUS ▸ **poor (1)**

describe *v*

to say what someone or something is like by giving details about them

ADVERBS

describe sb/sth accurately *Which of the following words most accurately describes you?*

describe sb/sth perfectly *This passage perfectly describes the way you feel on a hot humid day.*

describe sb/sth vividly (=with a lot of details, so you can imagine them very clearly) *Victorian London is vividly described in the novels of Charles Dickens.*

describe sb/sth fully *Can you describe the man you saw more fully?*

describe sth briefly *The introduction briefly describes how and why the two men began their research.*

PREPOSITIONS

describe sb/sth to sb *When she described him to me, I immediately realized who she was talking about.*

describe sb/sth as sth *Colleagues describe her as 'dynamic' and 'highly focused'.*

PHRASES

be difficult/hard/not easy to describe *My feelings at the time are very difficult to describe.*

describe sth in great detail *The article describes in great detail how the device works.*

description *n*

a piece of writing or speech that gives details about what someone or something is like

ADJECTIVES

a good description *There is a good description of life in ancient Egypt.*

a clear description *She gave the police a clear description of the car.*

a detailed/full description *Please give a full description of your responsibilities in your present job.*

an accurate description *I don't think the hotel's description of its facilities was very accurate.*

a perfect description (=a very suitable description) *When they said it was like being in paradise, it was a perfect description of the place.*

a long/lengthy description *I didn't want to hear a lengthy description of their holiday.*

a brief/short description *There's only a brief description of the company on the internet.*

a general description (=not detailed) *He started by giving us a general description of the manufacturing process.*

a vivid description (=very clear and interesting) *The book contains some vivid descriptions of his childhood.*

a graphic description (=very clear and containing a lot of details, usually about something unpleasant) *The book has some graphic descriptions of life in the prison camp.*

D

VERBS

give (sb) a description *He was able to give the police a good description of his attackers.*

provide a description *formal: The diary provides a clear description of farming life in the 1850s.*

issue a description (=formally give a description of someone to the public) *Police have issued a description of the two men they are looking for.*

fit/match a description (=be like the person in a police description) *The first man they arrested did not fit the description given by the victim.*

sb answering a description (=a person who looks like someone in a police description) *A young girl answering this description has been seen in Spain.*

D

desert *n*

a large area of land where it is always very dry

ADJECTIVES/NOUNS + desert

a vast desert (=extremely big) *To the south is a vast desert.*

an arid desert (=with very little rain) *Very little can grow in this arid desert.*

empty/open desert (=with no buildings) *Outside the city there was nothing but empty desert.*

an inhospitable desert (=not easy to live or stay in) *The interior of the country is an inhospitable desert.*

a barren desert (=where no plants can grow) *Years of intensive farming have turned the area into a barren desert.*

the Sahara/Gobi/Australian etc desert *The Gobi desert is the largest desert in Asia.*

desert + NOUNS

a desert area/region *A hot dry wind blows from the desert areas of North Africa.*

a desert landscape *She found the flat desert landscape uninteresting.*

desert country/land *Large parts of Oman are desert country.*

the desert sun/heat *Animals shelter from the desert sun during the day.*

desert plants/animals *Many desert plants have small leaves.*

desert conditions *These frogs have adapted to hot desert conditions.*

VERBS

a desert stretches (=covers a large area) *The desert stretches for hundreds of miles.*

PREPOSITIONS

in the desert *He got lost in the desert.*

across/through the desert *They travelled across the desert for three days.*

PHRASES

a stretch/expanse of desert (=a very large area of desert) *In front of us was nothing but a vast expanse of desert.*

deserted *adj* THESAURUS **empty**

deserve *v*

if you deserve something, it is right that you get it or experience it

ADVERBS

thoroughly/fully deserve sth *He did no work, so he thoroughly deserved his poor marks.*

richly deserve sth (=deserve something very much, especially something good) *She finally got the success that she richly deserved.*

really/truly deserve sth *He played well and truly deserved to win.*

well deserved *The restaurant has a well deserved reputation for excellent fish.*

NOUNS

deserve a rest/break/holiday etc *Now that the students have done their exams they deserve a break.*

deserve a chance *Everybody deserves a second chance.*

deserve credit/praise/respect *The team played really well and they deserve credit for it.*

deserve your reputation *The hotel thoroughly deserves its reputation for good food.*

deserve sb's attention *This issue deserves the government's attention.*

deserve (a) punishment *He got the punishment he deserved and he was put in prison for the rest of his life.*

PHRASES

deserve better (=deserve to be treated better or to be in a better situation) *They treated him badly at work and I thought he deserved better.*

get what you deserve (=experience something bad after you have behaved badly) *I like films where the bad guys get what they deserve.*

design[1] Ac *n*

the form of something, or the way it has been made or will be made

ADJECTIVES

(a) good design *Good design is very important in a house.*

a modern design *Many people were against such a modern design in the old city centre.*

a simple design *The latest model of the car has a much simpler design.*

an innovative design (=new and different) *The company has won several prizes for innovative designs.*

an elegant/stylish design *We chose this bath because of its elegant design.*

a traditional design *The furniture they make is known for its traditional design.*

a classic design (=traditional design that always looks good) *The jacket has a simple classic design that goes with anything.*

the basic design (=not including all the small details) *The basic design of the two churches is very similar.*

VERBS

do/create/produce a design *Who did the design for the princess's wedding dress?*

come up with a design (=think of one) *We asked the architect to come up with another design.*

change/improve a design *How can we improve the design of safety belts?*

design + NOUNS

a design feature (=something interesting or attractive that is part of the design) *The aircraft has some special design features.*

a design fault/flaw (=a part of something that does not work well or look good) *The main design fault with this washing machine is that it makes too much noise.*

design² Ac *v*

to draw or plan something that will be made, built, done etc

ADVERBS

well designed *The furniture was attractive and well designed.*

badly/poorly designed *Their ships were poorly designed and very slow.*

specially designed *The chemicals are transported in specially designed vehicles.*

carefully designed *The questions have been carefully designed to test your understanding of the subject.*

cleverly designed *The kitchen is small but has many cleverly designed cupboards.*

originally designed *The cell was originally designed to hold around 20 prisoners.*

be specifically designed for sb/to do sth *The game was specifically designed for children.*

PREPOSITIONS

be designed for sth *The sofa is designed for three people to sit on comfortably.*

be designed as sth (=was intended to be something) *The building was not designed as a place for people to live permanently.*

designer *n*

someone whose job is to design clothes, furniture, equipment etc

ADJECTIVES/NOUNS + designer

a top designer (=a very good and famous designer of clothes) *She always wore clothes by top designers.*

a fashion designer (=who designs clothes) *The fashion designer will be showing his latest collection next week.*

an interior designer (=who chooses colours, furniture etc for people's homes) *The apartment's previous owners had hired an expensive interior designer.*

a web designer (=who designs websites) *A good web designer will create a website that is easy to use.*

desirable *adj* THESAURUS good (1)

desire *n*

a strong wish to have or do something

ADJECTIVES

a great/strong desire *His one great desire in life was to be famous.*

a deep/fierce/passionate desire (=very strong) *The victim's family felt a deep desire for revenge.*

a burning desire (=extremely strong) *You could sense the team's burning desire to win.*

an overwhelming/irresistible desire (=so strong that it is hard to fight it) *He felt an overwhelming desire for a cigarette.*

a sudden desire *I had a sudden desire to escape.*

a natural desire *Kids have a natural desire to find out about new things.*

a genuine/real/sincere desire *Everything she did was motivated by a genuine desire to help the poor.*

an insatiable desire (=a desire that cannot be satisfied) *She had an insatiable desire to be admired.*

a desperate desire *Who knows what they will do in their desperate desire to hold on to power?*

VERBS

have/feel a desire *Milly had a sudden strong desire to laugh.*

express a desire *Many political leaders have expressed their desire for peace.*

show a desire (*also* **indicate a desire** *formal*): *He had shown no desire to get involved in the project.*

satisfy/fulfil a desire *Companies aim to satisfy people's desire for variety.*

fight/resist/suppress a desire *She fought the desire to go back to him.*

PREPOSITIONS

a desire for sth *We seem to be born with a desire for knowledge.*

in your desire to do sth (=as a result of your desire) *In our desire to be fair to women, we must not be unfair to men.*

PHRASES

an object of desire (=something that someone wants very much) *This car is an object of desire for many drivers.*

have/feel no desire to do sth (=used to emphasize that you do not want to do something) *It was raining outside and I had no desire to go out.*

desk *n*
a piece of furniture like a table that you sit at to write and work

VERBS

sit at a desk *I don't want a job in which I'm sitting at a desk all day.*

get up from your desk *He got up from his desk to welcome the visitors.*

tidy your desk *I need to tidy my desk.*

clear your desk (=remove all the papers etc from it) *He was told to clear his desk and leave the building.*

ADJECTIVES/NOUNS + desk

a tidy desk *Try to keep your desk tidy.*

a cluttered desk (=covered with papers, books etc in an untidy way) *His desk is so cluttered he can't find anything.*

an empty desk (=that no one is using) *There are one or two empty desks in the office.*

an office desk *I got back from holiday to find piles of papers on my office desk.*

a school desk *The children are at their school desks by 8.30 in the morning.*

a writing desk (=that you use for writing letters etc) *Under the window was a small writing desk.*

desk + NOUNS

a desk job (=working mostly at a desk in an office) *He left his desk job to become a gardener.*

PREPOSITIONS

at your desk *He said he would be back at his desk at 3 o'clock.*

despair *n*
a very unhappy feeling, because you think there is no hope at all

ADJECTIVES

deep/great despair *Losing his job had left him in a state of deep despair.*

complete/total/utter despair *I was in complete despair and I didn't know what to do next.*

PREPOSITIONS

out of despair (=because of despair) *Out of despair he banged his fists against the wall.*

to sb's despair *To the despair of his parents, he refused to study for his exams.*

PHRASES

be in despair *I was in despair and I didn't know who I could ask for help.*

be filled with despair *Jane was filled with despair when her husband left her.*

be in the depths of despair *Her business was losing money and she was in the depths of despair.*

be close to despair *She was close to despair when she received the tax bill.*

drive sb to despair *Their son's behaviour drove them to despair.*

throw up your hands in despair *The England manager threw up his hands in despair.*

shake your head in despair *She stared at the broken vase, shaking her head in despair.*

cry in despair *She cried in despair when no one believed her story.*

fall into despair *formal* (=become very unhappy) *He fell into despair when his wife died.*

a feeling/mood/note of despair *A feeling of despair came over him when he realized that he had missed his flight.*

a cry of despair *She gave a cry of despair when she realised that there was nothing she could do.*

a sense/feeling of despair *He looked around the dark prison cell with a sense of despair.*

a moment/state of despair *He tore up the painting in a moment of despair.*

the edge/point/verge of despair *Noisy neighbours were driving her to the edge of despair.*

desperate *adj* THESAURUS bad (2)

destination *n*
the place that someone or something is going to

ADJECTIVES

sb's/sth's final destination (*also* **sb's/sth's ultimate destination** *formal*): *We should arrive at our final destination around 1 p.m.*

a popular/favourite destination *Switzerland is a popular destination for skiing.*

a top/major destination *This ancient city is a major tourist destination.*

an exotic/far-off destination (=a place that is far away and exciting) *The company arranges tours to exotic destinations such as Nepal.*

sb's/sth's intended destination *The parcel never reached its intended destination.*

NOUNS + destination

a tourist destination *Las Vegas is the country's top tourist destination.*

a holiday destination (*also* **a vacation destination** *AmE*): *If you like the sun, Egypt is the ideal holiday destination.*

VERBS

reach your destination/arrive at your destination/get to your destination *It had taken us six hours to reach our destination.*

⚠ Don't say' reach to your destination'.

destroy *v*
to damage something so badly that it no longer exists or cannot be used or repaired

ADVERBS

completely/totally/utterly destroy sth *The house was completely destroyed.*

partially destroy sth (=destroy part of something) *The fire partially destroyed the prison.*

almost/nearly/practically/virtually destroy sth *A 15-year civil war has virtually destroyed the country.*

effectively destroy sth (=used when saying that this was the real result of someone's actions) *He was the man who effectively destroyed the Italian Socialist party.*

NOUNS

destroy a building/house/city etc *The explosion destroyed the building.*

destroy the world/planet *No one wants another war, which might destroy the world.*

destroy the evidence (=deliberately destroy evidence of a crime) *They set light to the car to destroy the evidence.*

destroy sb's career/reputation *The scandal destroyed his political career.*

destroy sb's hopes/dreams *That defeat destroyed the team's hopes of reaching the semi-finals.*

destroy the myth (=show that something is completely untrue) *The Vietnam war destroyed the myth that the United States could not be defeated.*

VERBS + destroy

threaten to destroy sth (=used especially when saying something is likely to destroy something) *Our dependence on oil threatens to destroy our planet.*

set out to destroy sth (=deliberately try to destroy) *He set out to destroy his opponent's political reputation.*

destruction *n*

the act or process of destroying something or of being destroyed

ADJECTIVES

great/massive destruction *The bombing caused massive destruction.*

widespread destruction (=over a big area) *There was widespread destruction to crops as a result of the storms.*

total/complete destruction *The earthquake resulted in the total destruction of the town.*

the wholesale destruction of sth *formal* (=the destruction of every part of something - used especially when you strongly disapprove of what is being done) *These people are facing the wholesale destruction of their way of life.*

wanton destruction *formal* (=done in a very careless and stupid way, without any good reason) *People were shocked by the wanton destruction that occurred during the riots.*

partial destruction *He ordered the partial destruction of the castle.*

deliberate destruction *They were accused of the deliberate destruction of official company records.*

environmental destruction *The islands are threatened by environmental destruction.*

VERBS

cause/lead to/bring about destruction *The bomb was clearly intended to cause death and destruction.*

wreak destruction *formal* (=cause it) *The destruction wrought by the hurricane left thousands of people homeless.*

save sth from destruction *Protests alone will not save the rainforest from destruction.*

prevent/stop destruction *Action is needed to prevent widespread destruction of the animal's habitat.*

PREPOSITIONS

the destruction of sth *The government has done little to prevent the destruction of the rainforest.*

PHRASES

a trail/path of destruction (=a long series of things that have been destroyed) *The accident left a trail of destruction on the motorway.*

D

detail *n*

1 a piece of information

Grammar
Often plural in this meaning.

ADJECTIVES

a small/minor/tiny detail *Don't waste time examining every minor detail.*

further/more details *Check our website for more details.*

full details *The police have not yet disclosed the full details of the case.*

precise/exact details *Precise details of what happened may never be known.*

every detail *He remembers every detail of the accident.*

sb's personal details (=your name, address, and other information about you) *Please make sure that all your personal details are correct.*

the gory details (=the full details about an unpleasant or interesting event - often used humorously) *She wanted to hear all the gory details about Tina's date with Nigel.*

VERBS

give details *She refused to give any details about what had happened.*

provide/supply details *He did not provide details of the government's plans.*

disclose/reveal/release details (=make secret information public) *The magazine revealed details of her relationship with the musician.*

ask for details *I went into the bank to ask for details about their savings accounts.*

send (off) for details (=write asking for information) *Why don't you send for details of the course?*

send your details (=send your name and

address to someone) *For a free sample, send your details to us at this email address.*
confirm the details (=make sure that they are correct) *Could you confirm the details of your reservation in writing?*
announce/publish details *Further details of the band's tour will be announced later.*

PREPOSITIONS
details of/about sth *Details of the course can be found on our website.*

2 detailed information which concerns all the parts or features of something

Grammar
Always uncountable in this meaning.

ADJECTIVES
in great/considerable detail *The subject has already been discussed in great detail.*
enough/sufficient detail *The government was criticized for not giving sufficient detail about the proposed tax changes.*
little detail (=not much detail) *Maps of the area contain very little detail.*
fine/minute/precise detail (=very exact detail) *We've been through all the arrangements for the wedding in minute detail.*
meticulous detail (=very careful detail) *His books describe the mountains and their paths in meticulous detail.*
graphic detail (=a lot of very clear and often unpleasant detail) *He told the police in graphic detail about his involvement in the murders.*
vivid detail (=so clear that they seem real) *The three characters in the novel are described with vivid detail.*

VERBS
go into detail (=give a lot of details) *He refused to go into detail about what had been said at the meeting.*
describe/explain sth in detail *The doctor spent time describing the treatment in detail to me.*
discuss sth in detail *His report discusses the problem in detail.*
examine/consider/study sth in detail *I asked my lawyer to examine the contract in detail.*
be set out in detail (=be written down and described in detail) *The changes to the system are set out in detail in the next paragraph.*
plan sth in detail/work sth out in detail *I haven't worked our trip out in detail yet.*

PHRASES
attention to detail (=care that all the small features of something are correct) *Editing requires great attention to detail.*
an eye for detail (=the ability to notice all the small features) *He's a brilliant photographer with a fantastic eye for detail.*
every last detail (=all the details, including the small things) *He wanted to know every last detail of my personal life.*
a wealth of detail (=a lot of useful detail) *The records provide a wealth of detail about people's lives.*

detailed *adj*
giving a lot of information about every part of something

ADVERBS
highly/extremely/immensely detailed *The book includes highly detailed colour illustrations.*
incredibly detailed (=extremely detailed) *The spacecraft sent back some incredibly detailed images of the surface of Mars.*
minutely/meticulously detailed (=very carefully done and containing a lot of small details) *Her paintings are minutely detailed and you can see every leaf on the trees.*
finely/exquisitely detailed (=very beautiful because you can see a lot of small details) *The carving is exquisitely detailed.*
richly detailed (=with many interesting details) *She gives a richly detailed account of her life in Paris.*

NOUNS
detailed information *The guide gives detailed information about setting up a website.*
a detailed study/examination *The scientists are doing a detailed study of the effects of climate change.*
detailed research/analysis *The report contains a detailed analysis of the country's economic situation.*
a detailed report *They published a detailed report about their findings.*
a detailed description/account/record/picture of sth *He gave the police a detailed description of his attacker.*
a detailed plan/proposal *The government has published detailed plans to cut emissions of greenhouse gases.*
detailed instructions *He's left detailed instructions on how to take care of the animals.*
a detailed knowledge *The job requires a detailed knowledge of international law.*

deteriorate *v* to become worse

ADVERBS
deteriorate rapidly/suddenly *Ethel's health deteriorated rapidly and she died soon afterwards.*
deteriorate sharply/dramatically (=suddenly and a lot) *The situation in the country has deteriorated sharply since yesterday.*

determination *n*
the quality of trying to do something even when it is difficult

ADJECTIVES
great determination *She showed great determination to succeed.*

D

sheer determination (=nothing except great determination) *He had survived by sheer determination.*

fierce determination (=involving strong feelings) *They fought with fierce determination.*

dogged/steely/grim/gritty determination (=very strong determination) *As a politician she was known for her dogged determination.*

single-minded determination (=having one clear aim and working very hard to achieve it) *She tackled every task with the same single-minded determination.*

ruthless determination (=that involves not caring about hurting other people) *His ruthless determination took him to the top, but it also made him many enemies.*

VERBS

have ... determination *To become a professional musician, you need to have a lot of determination.*

show determination (*also* **demonstrate determination** *formal*): *Yuri shows great determination to learn English.*

sth requires determination *Success requires hard work and determination.*

express your determination to do sth *He made a speech expressing his determination to rebuild the economy.*

PREPOSITIONS

with determination *He gripped the rope with grim determination.*

determined *adj*

having a strong desire to do something and not letting anyone or anything stop you from doing it

NOUNS

a determined man/woman/character *My mother was a very determined woman and she wasn't going to let her illness prevent her from attending the wedding.*

a determined effort/attempt/bid *George made a determined effort to get a job.*

a determined campaign *There was a determined campaign to protect the forest.*

a determined attack *The rebels launched a determined attack on the town.*

determined opposition/resistance *Leopold 's plan soon ran into determined opposition and he was forced to abandon it.*

a determined mood *The team started the game in a determined mood.*

a determined look/expression *He walked into the office with a determined look on his face.*

ADVERBS

absolutely determined *Paul is absolutely determined to win.*

fiercely determined *She was fiercely determined to be financially independent from her husband.*

grimly determined (=serious and determined) *Nathan's expression was grimly determined.*

THESAURUS: determined

stubborn
refusal | resistance | determination | pride | insistence | man | child | streak
You use **stubborn** when you think someone is being unreasonable, because they refuse to listen to other people and change what they are doing. You can also use **stubborn** when you admire someone because they refuse to give up, in spite of all the difficulties they face:
Her stubborn refusal to admit the truth irritated me. | The defenders put up stubborn resistance. | Hutchings had a stubborn streak and he refused to be rushed into making a decision (=he had a stubborn character). | *I wish you would **stop being so stubborn!***

single-minded
determination | pursuit | devotion | dedication | obsession | commitment | attitude | approach
working very hard in order to achieve one particular thing, and thinking that everything else is much less important:
*He tackled the task with single-minded determination. | The single-minded pursuit of profits is likely to be harmful to the public interest. | He was very **single-minded about** his career.*

tough
negotiator | businessman | businesswoman | leader
having a strong character and determined to succeed, even in difficult situations:
*He is known as a tough negotiator. | In competitive sports, you need to be **mentally tough** as well as physically fit.*

firm
leadership | management | voice | grip
showing by your behaviour that you are determined not to change your mind, especially when you are telling someone what to do:
What this country needs is firm leadership. | Use a firm voice when issuing instructions. | He has a firm grip on power (=he is determined to keep it). | *You have to be **firm with** young children. | I always try to be **firm but fair**.*

resolute *formal*
action | opposition | leadership | determination | defence
very determined and refusing to change your opinions or change what you are doing, especially because you believe firmly that you are right:
*The government must take resolute action to tackle this problem. | China expressed its resolute opposition to the proposal. | They **remained resolute** in spite of the terrorist threat.*

tenacious *formal*
efforts | hold | grip | belief
determined and refusing to give up:
Thanks to their tenacious efforts the building was saved from the fire. | The doctors were amazed at her tenacious hold on life. | He is ***tenacious in*** *fighting for the rights of his members.*

dogged
determination | persistence | refusal | resistance | insistence | pursuit
dogged behaviour shows that you are very determined and will not give up, over a long period of time:
I admired him for his dogged determination to learn the language. | With dogged persistence, she eventually gained access to the records.

D

persistent
efforts | attempts | offender | critic
someone who is persistent keeps trying to do something or keeps asking something:
The scheme was set up mainly because of Wilson's persistent efforts. | Persistent offenders will receive severe punishments (=people who keep committing crime). *| The journalist was very persistent and he refused to leave until he got an answer.*

ruthless
dictator | leader | determination | efficiency | ambition | streak
extremely determined to get what you want, and not caring if you harm other people:
Stalin was a ruthless dictator, responsible for the deaths of millions. | He carried out the task with ruthless efficiency. | She was driven by ruthless ambition to become the biggest star in the world. | She was completely ***ruthless in*** *her approach to management.*

feisty
woman | heroine | kid
determined and energetic, and not afraid to say what you think and argue with people:
The group is led by a feisty 65-year-old woman. | Fonda plays the feisty heroine of the film. | He is a feisty kid with a mind of his own.

strong-willed
always very determined to do what you want to do, even if other people think it is not a good idea to do it:
Young children are often very strong-willed and will make a fuss if they don't get what they want. | My grandmother was a strong-willed and ambitious woman.

headstrong
determined to do what you want, without listening to other people's advice or thinking about the results of your actions – used especially about young people:
He had many arguments with his headstrong young daughter about her behaviour. | Her brother was ***headstrong and impulsive****, and always went out whenever and wherever he liked.*

deterrent *n*

something that makes someone less likely to do something, by making them realize it will be difficult or have bad results

ADJECTIVES

a good/effective/powerful deterrent *Street cameras have been shown to be a powerful deterrent against crime.*

a real/significant deterrent *Burglar alarms are a real deterrent to thieves.*

a major/great deterrent *The high degree of risk is a major deterrent to investors.*

the ultimate deterrent *The death penalty is the ultimate deterrent.*

a sufficient deterrent (=enough of a deterrent) *Is the cost of cigarettes a sufficient deterrent to teenage smoking?*

a general deterrent *The threat of prison may act as a general deterrent.*

a nuclear deterrent (=nuclear weapons, which are kept in order to stop other countries attacking your country) *The prime minister has said that there will be no reduction in Britain's nuclear deterrent.*

VERBS

act as/be a deterrent (*also* **serve as a deterrent** *more formal*): *The small fines for this type of crime do not act as much of a deterrent.*

provide a deterrent *Experts do not agree about whether the death penalty provides a deterrent.*

be intended as a deterrent *Speed cameras are intended as a deterrent against speeding to improve road safety.*

deterrent + NOUNS

a deterrent effect *There is no hard evidence that proves the death penalty has a deterrent effect on criminal violence.*

the deterrent power/value of sth *World war may be prevented by the deterrent power of nuclear weapons.*

PREPOSITIONS

a deterrent against sth/sb *Window locks are a cheap and effective deterrent against thieves.*

a deterrent to sth/sb *Is capital punishment a deterrent to murder?*

a deterrent for sb *The study demonstrated that longer prison sentences can be a deterrent for some offenders.*

detrimental *adj*

THESAURUS bad (1)

devastated *adj*

THESAURUS sad (1)

develop *v*

to grow or change into something bigger, stronger, or more advanced, or to make someone or something do this

ADVERBS

develop rapidly/quickly *Vietnam's economy has been developing quite rapidly.*

develop sth further *If you want to develop your talents further, you should consider going to art college.*

fully developed *Once the product is fully developed, he hopes to find more investors.*

highly developed *Japan's electronics and automobile industries are highly developed.*

recently/newly developed *Tests on newly developed drugs can take several years.*

develop + NOUNS

develop a plan/strategy *We had to develop a strategy that could handle the rapidly changing situation.*

develop a system *Staff at the hospital developed a system for sharing information.*

develop a product *The company will have to develop new products to stay competitive.*

develop an idea *Watching the programme helped us to develop ideas for our own house.*

develop your skills *These lessons help young children develop their reading skills.*

NOUNS + develop

a friendship/relationship develops *Our relationship first began to develop when we were at college.*

technology develops *Some people believe that as technology develops, cars will become less damaging to the environment.*

PREPOSITIONS

develop into sth *Chicago developed into a big city in the late 1800s.*

develop from sth *Isn't it amazing that a tree develops from a small seed?*

THESAURUS: develop

create, do, produce, manufacture, mass-produce, develop, form, generate → **make (1)**

developing *adj* THESAURUS **poor (1)**

development *n*

1 the process of increasing business, trade, and industrial activity

ADJECTIVES

economic/industrial development *The US has been keen to encourage economic development in Egypt.*

business/trade development *The organization promotes trade development in Asia.*

regional development (=of particular regions of a country or area) *The area received European Union funding for regional development.*

sustainable development (=that is able to continue without damaging the environment) *There should be more emphasis on sustainable development.*

overseas development (=in other countries, especially poor ones) *The Overseas Development Minister announced a £7 million emergency aid programme for Somalia.*

VERBS

support/assist/further development *They want the Arts Council to support the development of the European film industry.*

encourage/promote development (=help it) *Projects which could have encouraged economic development have been abandoned.*

stimulate development (=actively help it grow) *We are looking at measures to stimulate economic development and create jobs.*

development + NOUNS

a development plan/project/programme *The region receives aid from the United Nations Development Programme.*

development work (=the work of helping development in poor areas) *The development work can only continue if we get more funds.*

a development grant (=money, usually from a government, to help development) *Blackpool Pleasure Beach received a large development grant from the English Tourist Board.*

development aid (=money given to help development in poor areas) *The region has received huge amounts of development aid from the European Union.*

2 the process of gradually improving or becoming more advanced

ADJECTIVES/NOUNS + development

human development *Forming strong family bonds is vital for human development.*

child development (=from being a small baby to becoming a young adult) *We can observe stages of child development by simply watching children at play.*

language development *Language development is a gradual process that begins at birth.*

personal development (=in your personal life or in your job) *Activities such as music and sport are an important part of students' personal development.*

career development *Are there good opportunities for career development within your company?*

professional development (=in a professional job) *The school is committed to providing continuing professional development for all staff.*

skills development *These exercises are aimed at vocabulary expansion and skills development.*

VERBS

promote/encourage development (=help it) *The government is keen to promote the development of IT skills.*

D

hinder/impede/inhibit development (=make it difficult) *We want to remove the barriers that hinder language development.*

influence development (=affect its progress) *We studied the main factors influencing adolescent development.*

PREPOSITIONS

the development of sb/sth *The test allows us to check the development of each student's writing skills.*

device Ac *n*

a machine or tool that does a special job

ADJECTIVES

a simple device *He invented a simple device for chopping onions.*

a labour-saving device *BrE*, **a labor-saving device** *AmE* (=one that reduces the amount of work you have to do) *Most households have labour-saving devices like washing machines and vacuum cleaners these days.*

a clever/ingenious device *This clever little device rings to tell you where you left your keys.*

an electronic device (=something such as a computer) *The shops are always full of new electronic devices.*

a mechanical device (=a machine or piece of equipment that is powered by an engine or by electricity) *One day it may be possible to replace a human heart with a mechanical device.*

a handheld device (=a small electronic device that you hold in your hand) *This new handheld device for playing electronic games is very popular.*

a mobile device (=an electronic device that is small enough to carry around with you) *They make chips for personal computers, mobile devices and video game systems.*

NOUNS + device

a security device (=that protects against crime) *Modern cars have better security devices, making them much harder to steal.*

a safety device (=that keeps you safe) *The accident happened because a simple safety device wasn't properly fitted.*

VERBS

be fitted with a device *From 2010, all new cars had to be fitted with this safety device.*

PREPOSITIONS

a device for doing sth *The ships are fitted with a device for detecting submarines.*

THESAURUS: device

appliance, device, gadget, contraption → machine

devious *adj* THESAURUS **dishonest**

devise *v*

to plan or invent a new way of doing something

NOUNS

devise a method/way *We have devised a way to improve quality and reduce costs.*

devise a means (=think of a way) *We need to devise a means of getting aid to the most remote villages.*

devise a system *How do you devise a system of testing students that is completely fair?*

devise a plan/scheme *Together they devised a plan to escape.*

devise a strategy (=plan a series of actions for achieving something) *The region is keen to devise a strategy to develop tourism.*

devise a solution *No one has yet devised a long-term solution to the problem.*

devise a programme *BrE*, **devise a program** *AmE*: *Your trainer will devise an exercise programme for you to follow.*

devise an experiment/test *He devised a series of experiments to test his theory.*

THESAURUS: devise

create, devise, come up with sth, make sth up, coin, fabricate, dream sth up → invent

devoted Ac *adj*

giving someone or something a lot of love and attention

ADVERBS

completely/utterly/absolutely devoted *The researchers are absolutely devoted to their work.*

passionately devoted *He loves soccer and is passionately devoted to the game.*

NOUNS

a devoted husband/wife *She was a devoted wife who had spent her lifetime taking care of her husband.*

a devoted father/mother *He was the devoted father of three young children.*

a devoted fan *Devoted fans of the singer regularly travel hundreds of miles to see her perform.*

a devoted following (=a loyal group of fans) *The band has gained a devoted following since the release of their first CD last year.*

a devoted follower *He became a devoted follower of Buddhism.*

PREPOSITIONS

devoted to sb *David is devoted to his wife and children.*

devotion Ac *n*

great love or loyalty, which shows that you care about someone or something a lot

ADJECTIVES

great/deep devotion *Shah Jahan showed his great devotion to his wife by building a great palace in her honour.*

total/complete devotion *The monks lead a life of total devotion to God.*

lifelong devotion *She received an award for her lifelong devotion to her work.*

undying devotion (=someone never stops being devoted to someone or something) *I remember his undying devotion to his students.*

selfless devotion (=great devotion that shows you care about other people more than yourself) *Churchill was famous for his selfless devotion to his country.*

fanatical devotion (=very strong devotion, which makes you do crazy things) *The band inspire fanatical devotion amongst their followers.*

blind devotion *especially disapproving* (=devotion without thinking about whether this is the right thing to do) *The leader expected his followers to show blind devotion toward him.*

religious devotion *Praying is an act of religious devotion.*

VERBS

show your devotion *He shows his devotion to his religion by praying every day.*

inspire devotion (=make people feel devotion) *There are few leaders today who inspire as much devotion as Nelson Mandela.*

PREPOSITIONS

devotion to sb/sth *a mother's devotion to her children*

PHRASES

an act of devotion *Taking care of her husband was an act of devotion.*

an object of devotion *The cross is an object of devotion in the Christian religion.*

devotion to duty/your work/a cause *He was praised for his devotion to duty.*

devout *adj*

THESAURUS **religious (2)**

diagnosis *n*

a statement saying what medical condition or disease someone has, or the process of discovering what is wrong with someone by examining them closely

ADJECTIVES

a correct/accurate diagnosis *It is impossible to make an accurate diagnosis without a thorough examination.*

an incorrect/wrong diagnosis *The doctors apparently made an incorrect diagnosis.*

an early diagnosis (=at an early stage of a disease) *Successful treatment is dependent on early diagnosis.*

a definite/firm diagnosis (=that doctors are sure is correct) *With this disease it can be very difficult to make a firm diagnosis.*

a medical/clinical diagnosis *Computer-based systems are being used in medical diagnosis.*

a final diagnosis (=after a series of examinations or tests) *It took several weeks of tests to arrive a final diagnosis of his condition.*

VERBS

make a diagnosis *The doctor examined him before making her diagnosis.*

arrive at/reach a diagnosis (=find out the reason why someone is ill) *It is important to arrive at a diagnosis and begin treatment as soon as possible.*

give (sb) a diagnosis *They will give me a diagnosis when they get the scan results.*

confirm a diagnosis (=show that it is definitely true) *The blood tests confirmed the diagnosis.*

diagram *n*

a simple drawing or plan that shows what something is like or how something works

ADJECTIVES

a simple diagram *The whole process can be summarized in a simple diagram.*

a rough diagram *The teacher drew a rough diagram of a molecule.*

a detailed diagram *On page 14 there is a detailed diagram of the human eye.*

VERBS

a diagram shows/illustrates/represents sth *This diagram shows how this process works.*

draw a diagram *He drew a quick diagram to explain how the parts of the system were connected with each other.*

see diagram *The plant uses sunlight to make energy (see diagram on page 268).*

ADVERBS

the diagram above/below *The diagram below illustrates the life cycle of a butterfly.*

dialogue (*also* dialog *AmE*) *n*

a discussion between two groups or countries

ADJECTIVES

political dialogue *Only political dialogue can bring an end to the crisis.*

peaceful dialogue *The Chinese president wants to settle the dispute through peaceful dialog.*

open dialogue (=a dialogue in which people are free to say what they want) *Staff meetings aim to encourage open dialogue and the sharing of ideas.*

constructive dialogue (=dialogue in which you are trying to reach an agreement about something, not just criticizing each other) *The government said that it was involved in a constructive dialog with the US.*

direct dialogue *Ministers refused to enter into direct dialogue with the terrorists.*

D

VERBS

have a dialogue *The leaders had a dialogue about relations between their countries.*

be engaged/involved in a dialogue *formal* (=be having a dialogue) *The parties are currently engaged in a political dialog.*

start/open a dialogue *The union says it wants to start a dialogue with the management.*

enter into/establish a dialogue *formal* (=start a dialogue) *The United States entered into a dialog with Russia about nuclear weapons.*

engage in a dialogue *formal* (=take part in a dialogue) *The artist was happy to engage in a dialogue about her work.*

maintain a dialogue *The two countries are keen to maintain a dialog with each other.*

encourage/promote dialogue *He hopes to encourage dialogue between parents and their children.*

D

PREPOSITIONS

a dialogue with sb *Pakistan has restarted a dialogue with China.*

a dialogue between sb *There is little prospect of dialogue between the government and the rebels.*

a dialogue about sth *The two countries were continuing a dialogue about trade.*

through dialogue (=by discussion) *The dispute should be settled through dialogue.*

diary *n*

a book in which you write down the things that happen to you each day

VERBS

keep/write a diary (=write regularly in a diary) *While I was travelling, I kept a diary every day.*

write (sth) in your diary *He wrote in his diary that he was planning to visit her.*

record sth in your diary (*also* **note sth in your diary**) *James Alvin recorded the incident in his diary.*

read a diary *I wish my sister would let me read her diary.*

ADJECTIVES/NOUNS + diary

sb's personal/private diary *She later agreed to the publication of parts of her personal diary.*

a detailed diary *For years she had kept a detailed diary.*

a daily/weekly diary *Clarke kept a daily diary of life in San Francisco.*

a travel diary *His travel diary makes fascinating reading.*

a secret diary *He found his girlfriend's secret diary.*

diary + NOUNS

a diary entry (=a piece of writing in a diary) *His last diary entry was on June 14th.*

a diary extract/excerpt (=a short part of a diary entry) *A newspaper printed diary extracts in which he called the president 'arrogant'.*

PREPOSITIONS

in a diary *He records in his diary his arrival in New York as a young man.*

die *v*

to stop living and become dead

ADVERBS

die suddenly *Jack died suddenly of a heart attack.*

die instantly (=as soon as an accident, injury etc happens) *He was shot in the head and died instantly.*

die peacefully (=calmly and without pain) *My grandmother died peacefully in her sleep.*

die tragically *His wife had died tragically in an accident.*

die young *They had seven children and three of them died young.*

die alone *It's very sad to think of someone dying alone in hospital.*

die penniless (=without any money) *Van Gogh died penniless, but his paintings were later worth millions.*

PREPOSITIONS

die of/from sth *His mother died of cancer.*

die in a fire/crash/fall etc *Her father died in a car crash when she was only ten.*

die for your country/beliefs/principles etc (=be killed while fighting to defend something) *Would you be willing to die for your beliefs?*

PHRASES

die aged 35/50 etc *Her father died aged 84.*

die in your sleep *We would all prefer to die peacefully in our sleep.*

die in suspicious/mysterious circumstances (=used to say that someone may have been killed) *He got involved with drugs and died in mysterious circumstances.*

die from natural causes (=not because of being killed by someone else) *The coroner concluded that Wilks had died from natural causes.*

die a sudden/violent/slow etc death *At the end of the play, the main character dies a violent death.*

die a hero/a rich man etc *He died a hero on the battlefield.*

die in childbirth (=giving birth to a baby) *In the 19th century, it was fairly common for women to die in childbirth.*

until/til the day I die (=for someone's whole life) *Their screams will haunt me until the day I die.*

sb's dying wish (=someone's last wish) *It was my father's dying wish to be buried with my mother.*

sb's dying breath (=someone's last breath,

before they die) *With her dying breath, she cursed the soldiers.*

diet *n*

1 a plan of eating only certain foods, in order to lose weight or improve your health

PHRASES

be on a diet (=be only eating certain foods, in order to lose weight) *She didn't have a dessert because she was on a diet.*

⚠ Don't say 'I'm doing a diet.' Say **I'm on a diet.**

go on a diet (=start eating less or only some types of food) *I really ought to go on a diet.*

stick to a diet (=continue to follow a diet) *Most people find it hard to stick to a diet.*

VERBS

follow a diet (=only eat certain types of food) *You will feel better if you follow a low-fat diet.*

ADJECTIVES

a strict diet (=in which you eat a very limited amount or range of food) *She followed a strict diet for several weeks.*

a crash diet (=a very sudden and strict attempt to lose weight) *It's better to lose weight gradually than to go on a crash diet.*

a low-calorie/low-fat etc diet *A low-calorie diet should solve your weight problem.*

a starvation diet (=in which you eat very little) *A starvation diet can have negative health effects.*

2 the kind of food that a person or animal eats each day

ADJECTIVES

a healthy/good diet *A healthy diet includes plenty of fresh fruit and vegetables.*

a poor/unhealthy diet *Diseases like this are caused by poor diet.*

a nutritious diet (=that provides you with the substances your body needs) *The mothers provide a nutritious diet for their children.*

a balanced diet (=including all the types of food that people need) *A balanced diet is important for a child's development.*

a varied diet (=including many different foods) *Provide your fish with a varied diet of worms, insects, and dried food.*

a sensible/proper diet *Students don't always eat a sensible diet.*

sb's staple diet (=the food that a group of people or type of animal normally eats) *For hundreds of years potatoes were their staple diet.*

a diet high/rich in sth (=which contains a lot of something) *In the West many people eat a diet high in fat and salt.*

a vegetarian diet *A vegetarian diet is good for protecting against cancer and heart disease.*

VERBS

eat/have a diet *People in Mediterranean areas generally have a very good diet.*

live/exist on a diet of sth *The people lived on a diet of fish and rice.*

feed sb (on) a diet of sth *Kids should not be fed a diet of hamburgers and sugary snacks.*

sb's diet consists of sth *Their diet consists mainly of wild fruit and shellfish.*

PREPOSITIONS

in sb's diet *You should include more vegetables in your diet.*

differ *v*

to be different from something in some way

ADVERBS

differ greatly/enormously/considerably *Modern teaching methods differ greatly from those fifty years ago.*

differ slightly/somewhat *Prices differ slightly from one shop to another.*

differ significantly/substantially *The second set of test results did not differ significantly from the first.*

differ widely (=used to say that there are many very different things) *Opinions differ widely on the best approach to the problem.*

differ sharply/noticeably/markedly/dramatically (=in a very noticeable way) *Opportunities for women differed markedly from those enjoyed by men.*

differ radically/fundamentally (=in a very basic and important way) *The new car differed radically from the earlier model. | These paintings differed fundamentally from his earlier work.*

differ little (=not much) *The system differs very little from state to state.*

PREPOSITIONS

differ from sb/sth *People differ from one another in their ability to handle stress.*

differ between places/people etc *Business practices differ between countries.*

differ in sth *They differ in their views on religion.*

PHRASES

opinions/views differ *Opinions differ greatly as to whether the government's strategy will work.*

difference *n*

a way in which two or more people or things are not like each other

ADJECTIVES/NOUNS + difference

a big/great/huge/enormous etc difference *There is a big difference between a musical and a Shakespeare play.*

the main difference *The main difference between African and Asian elephants is the size of the ears.*

D

an important/key/significant/crucial difference *A study of the two groups of students showed a significant difference.*
a considerable/major/substantial difference *He points out two major differences.*
a slight/small/minor difference *There's only a slight difference between the male and the female bird.*
the only difference *The only difference is that this apartment has two bedrooms, not one.*
a real difference *Voters believe there is no real difference between the parties.*
an obvious/clear/noticeable difference *One obvious difference between these systems is their size.*
a marked/striking/dramatic difference (=very noticeable) *There was a marked difference between the two sets of results.*
a subtle difference (=not obvious) *There's a subtle difference in flavour between these coffees.*
an essential/fundamental/basic difference *The fundamental differences between the two sides slowly emerged.*
the age/price/temperature etc difference *Despite the big age difference, they fell in love.*
individual differences (=between one person and another) *We respect the children's individual differences.*
cultural/political differences *The book examines cultural differences between the East and the West.*
national/regional differences (=between different countries or areas) *It is vital for a businessman to have an understanding of national differences.*

VERBS

notice a difference *She has noticed a dramatic difference in her energy levels.*
spot the difference (=see the difference) *It's easy to spot the difference between real and imitation leather.*
can tell/see the difference (=can recognize how two things are different) *I can't really see the difference between these two colours.*
know the difference *If you don't know the difference between two words, your dictionary can help.*
show a difference *Our data showed considerable national differences.*
highlight/emphasize a difference (=make it noticeable or draw attention to it) *The report also highlighted the difference in attitudes between men and women.*
explain the difference (=help someone understand it, or be a reason for it) *Can you explain the difference between psychiatry and psychology?*

PREPOSITIONS

a difference between sth and sth *There are many differences between British English and American English.*
a difference in age/price/quality etc *There is little difference in price between these two cars.*

PHRASES

there is a world of difference (=there is a very big difference) *There's a world of difference between being alone and being lonely.*

different *adj*

not like something or someone else, or not like before

ADVERBS

completely/totally/entirely different *From now on, Tess's life was to be completely different.*
slightly different/a little different *They decided to use a slightly different approach.*
rather/somewhat different *In New Zealand for example, the situation is somewhat different.*
fundamentally/radically different (=extremely different in very basic ways) *Their world was radically different from ours.*
significantly different (=very different in an important and noticeable way) *The results from the two groups of patients were significantly different.*
refreshingly different *North Africa offers a fascinating and refreshingly different style of holiday.*

NOUNS

a different way/approach/method *Women are treated in a different way from men.*
a different kind/type/sort of sth *Obama promised that he would be a different kind of leader.*
a different view/perspective/outlook *Other scientists take a different view.*
a different world *My parents seemed to live in a different world.*
a different person *When she came back from college, she was a different person.*
a different direction/angle *He approaches the subject from a different angle.*
a different colour/taste/smell *Her left eye is a slightly different colour.*

PREPOSITIONS

different from sb/sth *Health care is different from producing cars or selling food.*
different than sb/sth *especially AmE: Boys are often different than girls.*

Grammar
In spoken British English, you will also sometimes hear people say **different to**. In written English it is better to use **different from** or **different than**.

PHRASES

be no different (=not different in any way) *He is no different than any other pop star.*

ANTONYMS **different → same**

difficult *adj*

hard to do, understand, or deal with

NOUNS

a difficult job/task *Peter had the difficult task of judging the competition.*

a difficult question *There were some difficult questions in the test.*

a difficult situation/position *The country is in a difficult economic situation.*

difficult circumstances/conditions *Staff are doing a good job in difficult circumstances.*

a difficult problem/issue *Anti-social behaviour is a difficult problem for the police to deal with.*

a difficult decision/choice *The government is facing some difficult decisions.*

a difficult time/period/day/year *Gina has had a difficult time recently – she has just lost her job.*

a difficult person/man/child etc *Joe was a very difficult man to live with.*

difficult words/language *Lawyers tend to use a lot of long and difficult words.*

ADVERBS

extremely/incredibly/extraordinarily difficult *The past week has been an incredibly difficult time.*

fiendishly difficult (=used to emphasize that something is difficult) *This piece of music is fiendishly difficult to play.*

increasingly difficult/more and more difficult *As the disease develops, walking becomes increasingly difficult.*

notoriously difficult (=in a way that many people know about) *Mountain weather is notoriously difficult to predict.*

doubly difficult (=much more difficult than usual) *If you have sensitive skin, finding suitable skin products can be doubly difficult.*

VERBS

make sth difficult *Shortages of food during the war made life very difficult.*

find sth difficult *He's finding it difficult to get a job.*

prove difficult (=be difficult) *The task was proving more difficult than she had imagined.*

become/get difficult *When things get difficult, I know I can always ask him for help.*

look difficult *The puzzle looks more difficult than it really is.*

PREPOSITIONS

difficult for sb *Talking about personal problems is very difficult for many people.*

PHRASES

it is difficult to understand/imagine *It's difficult to imagine what life was like in the 18th century.*

it is difficult to know/say/see *It's difficult to see how peace can be achieved in the region.*

THESAURUS: difficult

hard

job | work | time | day | decision | choice | question | test | problem | life | part

difficult:

It's a hard job and some of the drivers work seven days a week. | I was having a hard time finding a place at university. | The test was really hard. | You can see from her face that she has had a hard life. | ***It was hard to*** *forgive him after what he had done.*

> **Hard or difficult?**
>
> **Hard** is less formal than **difficult** and is very common in spoken English.
>
> If something is tiring and you have to use a lot of effort, you usually use **hard** rather than **difficult**: *It was a* ***hard*** *race. | It was a long* ***hard*** *climb to the summit.*
>
> You say **a difficult problem/issue** or **a difficult situation**, not a 'hard' one.

tough

time | decision | choice | question | game | challenge | competition | life

very difficult, because you have to use a lot of effort, or because it affects you emotionally:

James has had a tough time at home recently – his parents have just got divorced. | Doctors had to make tough decisions about who to treat first. | The team faces some tough competition. | Life is tough sometimes.

demanding

job | task | work | schedule | day

difficult and tiring, because it takes a lot of effort:

Being a nurse in a busy hospital is a demanding job. | He was exhausted after a busy and demanding day at work. | It can be very demanding bringing up young children.

challenging

task | work | job | role | position | situation

difficult in an interesting or enjoyable way:

This was a challenging task even for an experienced manager. | I wanted a job that was more challenging. | The course is meant to be ***intellectually challenging****.*

> You sometimes use **challenging** when you want to politely avoid using the word **difficult**: *Some of the students can be rather challenging to teach.*

daunting

task | prospect | challenge | problem | experience

if something seems daunting, you think that it will be difficult and you do not feel confident about being able to do it:

D

We are faced with the daunting task of raising $5 million. | *Your first solo performance may seem a daunting prospect* (=an idea of something that will happen, which worries you). | *The aim is to make a visit to the hospital less daunting for children.*

awkward
question | **position** | **situation** | **problem** | **moment** | **silence**
rather difficult to deal with – used especially when something could be embarrassing:
They started asking awkward questions about where the money had gone. | *You've put me in a very awkward position.* | *There was an awkward moment during the meal when she asked him about his family.* | *It was getting dark and foggy, which made the rescue even more awkward.*

D

tricky
situation | **business** | **task** | **job** | **operation** | **question** | **subject** | **issue** | **problem**
difficult because it is complicated and full of problems. **Tricky** is more informal than **awkward** and is used especially in spoken English:
She had helped him out of a tricky situation. | *Fixing up a curtain rail can be a tricky business* (=a tricky job). | *It was a tricky operation to move the barrels.* | *Then there is the tricky issue of who is going to pay for the wedding.* | *Merging the two companies was bound to be tricky.*

delicate
balance | **matter** | **subject** | **issue** | **question** | **task** | **operation** | **process** | **situation** | **negotiations**
needing to be dealt with carefully or sensitively, especially in order to avoid offending people or causing problems:
There is a delicate balance between treating every student equally and rewarding those who do better. | *I need to speak to you about a rather delicate matter.* | *The country is beginning the delicate task of maintaining peace.*

If something is difficult and needs a lot of time and effort, you say that it is an **uphill battle/struggle/task**: *For a long time, it was an* ***uphill struggle*** *and we didn't think we would succeed.* If you are impressed that someone has done something very difficult, you say that it is **no mean feat**: *Sailing across the Atlantic Ocean is* ***no mean feat***. You can also use negative sentences, and say that something is **not easy**: *It's* ***not easy*** *bringing up three children on your own.*

ANTONYMS **difficult → easy**

difficulty *n*
a problem, or the situation of having a problem

ADJECTIVES

great/considerable/enormous difficulty *Many deaf children have great difficulty in learning to read.*

a major/serious/severe difficulty *Making sure the rules were obeyed remained a major difficulty.*

the main difficulty *The main difficulty was in finding the right actor to play the title role.*

a real difficulty *The real difficulty was finding suitably qualified staff.*

technical difficulties *The flight was delayed due to technical difficulties.*

financial/economic difficulties *The company is facing serious financial difficulties.*

practical difficulties *It's a great idea, but there will be a number of practical difficulties.*

VERBS + difficulty

have difficulties/difficulty *Robbie was having difficulty with reading.*

face difficulties *The hotel's owners were facing financial difficulties.*

experience/encounter difficulties *formal*: *Graduates often experience considerable difficulties in getting their first job.*

run into/get into difficulties (=find yourself in a difficult situation) *Three people were rescued from a boat that had got into difficulties.*

deal with/tackle a difficulty *What is the best way to deal with this difficulty?*

overcome/resolve difficulties (=deal with them successfully) *We are confident that we can overcome these difficulties.*

present/pose difficulties (=be something that is difficult to deal with) *English spelling may present some difficulties for learners.*

cause/lead to difficulties *Stress and worry both cause sleep difficulties.*

difficulty + VERBS

difficulties arise (=happen) *The student should feel able to discuss difficulties as they arise.*

difficulties face sb (=exist for someone) *He stressed the difficulties facing the government.*

the difficulty lies in sth (=used to say what the problem relates to) *The difficulty lies in heating the fuel to a high enough temperature.*

PREPOSITIONS

a difficulty with sth *There are a couple of difficulties with this argument.*

with difficulty *He heaved himself out of the chair with difficulty.*

without difficulty *She found the hotel without difficulty.*

be in difficulty *They help people who are in difficulty.*

PHRASES

a lot of/a great deal of difficulty *I had a great deal of difficulty in hearing what they were saying*

be fraught with difficulties (=involve a lot of them) *The whole plan was fraught with difficulties.*

dig *v*

to move earth, snow etc, or to make a hole in the ground, using a spade or your hands

NOUNS

dig a hole *The turtles dig a small hole in the sand to bury their eggs.*

dig a tunnel/trench/ditch *A tunnel had to be dug through the hillside for the railway.*

PREPOSITIONS/ADVERBS

dig for sth (=try to find it by digging) *The apes use sticks to dig for insects and roots.*

dig (sth) up (=remove it from earth etc by digging) *Someone had dug up all the flowers in the garden.*

dig down *Archaeologists dug down to uncover the original foundations of the temple.*

dig deep *If you dig deep enough into the snow, you will find plants living underneath.*

dignified *adj*

behaving in a calm and serious way, so that people respect you

VERBS

look/sound dignified *She looked very dignified in her uniform.*

remain dignified *Her father remained calm and dignified throughout the trial.*

NOUNS

a dignified man/woman/lady *His grandfather was a dignified man who always wore a suit.*

a dignified figure *She sat alone on the platform, a silent but dignified figure.*

a dignified manner/way *The minister answered their questions in a dignified manner.*

a dignified silence *The princess maintained a dignified silence and refused to speak to reporters.*

a dignified exit/departure (=leaving in a dignified way) *He tried to make a dignified exit, but he fell over a chair.*

PHRASES

quietly dignified *Colin Firth gives a quietly dignified performance.*

dignity *n*

1 calm behaviour, even in difficult situations, which makes people respect you

ADJECTIVES

great dignity *He acted with great dignity throughout the crisis.*

quiet dignity *Her quiet dignity impressed everyone.*

a certain dignity *The refugees have a certain dignity about them.*

VERBS

maintain/retain/keep your dignity *He managed to maintain his dignity, and refused to become angry or upset.*

show dignity *She has shown remarkable dignity throughout this awful time.*

PREPOSITIONS

with dignity *She faced her death with dignity.*

PHRASES

an air of dignity (=a calm appearance or way of behaving) *He always had an air of dignity.*

2 the feeling that you deserve respect from other people

ADJECTIVES

human dignity *Respect for human dignity is one of our basic principles.*

VERBS

treat sb with dignity *All the prisoners are treated with dignity.*

lose your dignity *Old people are often afraid of losing their dignity.*

respect sb's dignity *Every society should respect the dignity of the individual.*

die with dignity *Patients should be allowed to die with dignity.*

recover/regain your dignity (=get it back) *He got up off the floor and tried to recover his dignity.*

have your dignity *We still have our dignity and self-respect.*

give sb (a sense of) dignity *Having a job gives people a sense of dignity.*

lend dignity to sth *formal* (=make people respect this position or occasion) *They want someone who will lend dignity to the office of head of state.*

PHRASES

a sense of dignity *Being a grandmother gave her a sense of dignity.*

sth is beneath your dignity (=it is something that is for people who are less important than you) *They do jobs that the local people think are beneath their dignity.*

a loss of dignity *Patients fear the loss of dignity that may come with their illness.*

be an affront to sb's dignity *formal* (=be something that shows no respect for someone) *His unpleasant remark is an affront to the dignity of every woman in this town.*

with dignity and respect *All employees should be treated with dignity and respect.*

dilemma *n*

a situation in which it is very difficult to decide what to do, because all the choices seem equally good or equally bad

VERBS

face a dilemma (*also* **be faced with a dilemma**) *Many women are faced with the dilemma of choosing between work and family.*
be in a dilemma/have a dilemma *I'm in a dilemma about whether to accept their job offer.*
pose/create/present a dilemma (=exist and cause problems) *The economic situation poses a dilemma for investors.*
put sb/place sb in a dilemma *The disagreement between his advisers placed the president in a dilemma.*
resolve/solve a dilemma *People often need help resolving their dilemmas.*
explain your dilemma (=talk about it) *He explained his dilemma to me.*

D

ADJECTIVES

a difficult/serious dilemma *He was in a serious dilemma as he risked upsetting either his mother or his wife.*
a terrible dilemma *Knowing that her son had committed a crime put her in a terrible dilemma.*
a moral/ethical dilemma *Doctors face a moral dilemma over whether to prolong a suffering patient's life.*
a legal/political dilemma *My political dilemma was whether to support my party or stick to my principles.*
a personal dilemma *The men had a personal dilemma over whether to join the strike.*
a painful dilemma (=a very difficult one) *She had the painful dilemma of having to choose which friend to believe.*
a common/familiar dilemma (=one that a lot of people have) *Deciding whether to put an elderly relative in a nursing home is a common dilemma.*
the central dilemma (=the main one) *The country's central dilemma is how to increase its own security without seeming to threaten its neighbours.*

PREPOSITIONS

the dilemma of sth *The dilemma of having to choose was too much, so I bought them both.*
a dilemma over sth *Parents are in a dilemma over which school to choose for their children.*
a dilemma about sth *We face a dilemma about negotiating with terrorists in the interests of peace.*
a dilemma between sth and sth *He was faced with a dilemma between his religious beliefs and his professional duties.*

PHRASES

a way out of a dilemma (=a way to solve it) *There seemed to be no way out of the dilemma.*
a solution to a dilemma (=a way to solve it) *One possible solution to the dilemma is to divide the money equally between them.*

dim *adj*

not very bright, or difficult to see because there is not much light

NOUNS

a dim light *The dim light made it difficult to read.*
dim lighting *Dim lighting on stairs and in passageways can be dangerous.*
a dim glow *I watched her standing in the dim glow of a street lamp.*
a dim shape/outline *He could see a dim shape on the other side of the room.*
a dim figure *There was a dim figure standing next to his bed.*

PHRASES

the sky grew dim *especially literary* (=it became dark) *The evening sky grew dim and the people returned to their homes.*

THESAURUS: dim

faint
light | glow/glimmer | star
a faint light is not very bright, especially because it is a long distance away:
In the distance I could see a faint light. | There was a faint glimmer of light from her window. | Above them there was a faint star in the night sky.

weak
light
weak light is not strong enough for you to see clearly:
The frosted windows let in a weak light.

pale
light | moonlight | sunlight | glow
pale light is not bright and has very little colour:
The pale light of morning crept in through the window. | His white shirt gleamed in the pale moonlight. | The pale winter sunlight falls on stone farmhouses and walls.

poor/bad
light | lighting
poor or bad light is not at all bright, so that you cannot see well enough to do things:
The game was finally abandoned because of bad light. | Poor lighting makes the streets dangerous to cycle on at night.

soft
light | lighting | glow
soft light is pleasant and relaxing because it is not too bright:
The antique furniture glowed in the soft light. | Soft lighting is used to create a feeling of relaxation. | He switched on the bedside lamp and the room was filled with a soft glow.

low
light | lighting
low light is rather dark for seeing or photographing things. **Low lighting** is not

bright and gives a room a pleasant and relaxing feeling:
Owls' eyes are adapted for seeing in very low light. | *Low lighting, lots of couches, and excellent music produce a great atmosphere.*

ANTONYMS **dim → bright (1)**

dimension Ac *n*

a part of a situation or a quality involved in it

ADJECTIVES

a new/different dimension *Her experience will bring a new dimension to the team.*

an extra/added/additional dimension *Add an extra dimension to your holiday by hiring a car.*

a social/political/cultural/historical dimension *His writing has a strong political dimension.*

a moral/ethical dimension *The book discusses the ethical dimension of genetic engineering.*

a spiritual dimension *People need to have a spiritual dimension to their lives.*

a human dimension *Statistics alone cannot show us the human dimension of the disaster.*

VERBS

add/give/bring a ... dimension (to sth) *Digital cameras have added a new dimension to photography.*

have a ... dimension *Learning a language has an important cultural dimension.*

take on a ... dimension (=develop in a particular way) *Since I met her, my life has taken on a completely different dimension.*

PREPOSITIONS

a dimension to sth *His argument added a religious dimension to the debate.*

diminutive *adj* THESAURUS **short (4)**

dinner *n*

the main meal of the day, eaten in the middle of the day or the evening

VERBS

have/eat dinner *We had dinner at a nice local restaurant.*

have sth for dinner *I thought we might have pasta for dinner tonight.*

finish your dinner *She was so upset she couldn't finish her dinner.*

make/cook/prepare dinner *I offered to cook dinner.*

have sb for/to dinner *We're having a few friends round to dinner.*

ask/invite sb to dinner *Let's ask Kate and Mike to dinner.*

come for/to dinner *Mark is coming over for dinner.*

go out for/to dinner (=go and eat in a restaurant) *Would you like to go out for dinner on Saturday?*

serve dinner (=start giving people food) *Dinner is served between 7 and 11 p.m. in the hotel restaurant.*

ADJECTIVES/NOUNS + dinner

a three-course/four-course etc dinner *The cost of the hotel includes a three-course dinner.*

Sunday/Christmas/Thanksgiving dinner (=a special meal eaten on Sunday etc) *We usually have a walk after Christmas dinner.*

a good/excellent dinner *They were relaxing after a good dinner.*

a quiet dinner *He was having a quiet dinner with a couple of friends.*

a romantic dinner (=for two people in a romantic relationship) *Clive and Denise were enjoying a romantic dinner for two in a quiet French restaurant.*

a leisurely dinner (=not hurried) *I enjoy having a leisurely dinner with some friends at the weekend.*

a formal/official dinner *A formal dinner was held to celebrate the 150th anniversary of the college.*

school dinners *BrE* (=meals provided at school in the middle of the day) *School dinners are served in the canteen.*

dinner + NOUNS

dinner time *He said he would be back by dinner time.*

a dinner party (=when someone's friends are invited for a special evening meal) *We are having a dinner party on Saturday.*

a dinner guest *The dinner guests began arriving at about seven o'clock.*

diploma *n*

a document showing that someone has successfully completed a course of study or passed an examination

In American English people usually use **diploma** when talking about a high school or college diploma.

ADJECTIVES/NOUNS + diploma

a teaching/engineering/banking etc diploma *BrE: Do you have a teaching diploma?*

a college/university diploma *Having a college diploma no longer guarantees you a job.*

a high school diploma *AmE: More women than men have a high school diploma.*

a professional diploma *BrE: If you want to be a chef, you need to have a professional diploma.*

an advanced/higher diploma *BrE: She is working for an advanced diploma in educational management.*

a one-year/two-year/three-year diploma *BrE: I am thinking of taking a two-year diploma in hairdressing.*

D

VERBS

have a diploma (*also* **hold a diploma** *formal*): *She has a diploma in fashion design.*

get/obtain/receive a diploma (*also* **gain/ attain a diploma** *formal*): *He went back to college and got a diploma in business studies.*

take a diploma (*also* **do a diploma** *BrE*): *Two years ago he took a diploma in leisure management at Southampton University.*

study for a diploma *BrE*: *I am currently studying for a teaching diploma.*

receive a diploma (*also* **be awarded a diploma** *BrE*): *She received a diploma from the Institute of Management.*

a course leads to a diploma *BrE*: *Some courses lead to a diploma.*

diploma + NOUNS

a diploma course/programme *BrE*: *The diploma course lasts nine months.*

PREPOSITIONS

a diploma in sth *She is studying for a diploma in nursing.*

a diploma from a college/university etc *He has a diploma from the London College of Technology.*

diplomacy *n*

the activity of dealing with relationships between countries or groups of people

ADJECTIVES

international diplomacy *Before he became president, he had little experience of international diplomacy.*

secret diplomacy *There are rumours of secret diplomacy between the US and Iran.*

quiet diplomacy *A lot of quiet diplomacy has been going on behind the scenes.*

clever/skilful diplomacy *Through skilful diplomacy, they succeeded in reaching an agreement that was acceptable to both sides.*

careful diplomacy *This is a very sensitive situation that needs careful diplomacy.*

high-level diplomacy *The hostages were released as a result of high-level diplomacy in Washington.*

NOUNS + diplomacy

shuttle diplomacy (=diplomacy in which someone travels between countries and talks to leaders there) *The Japanese prime minister was leading a round of shuttle diplomacy, traveling first to China and then to South Korea.*

gunboat diplomacy *disapproving* (=the threat of force against another country) *The British used gunboat diplomacy to make the Chinese agree to their terms.*

telephone diplomacy *There was some intense telephone diplomacy between Moscow and Paris.*

VERBS

conduct diplomacy (=talk to other countries on behalf of a country) *Congress does not have the power to conduct diplomacy.*

use diplomacy *It is always better to use diplomacy rather than military force.*

PHRASES

a round of diplomacy (=one of several periods of diplomacy) *The two sides began a new round of diplomacy aimed at achieving a ceasefire.*

a flurry of diplomacy (=a situation in which there is suddenly a lot of diplomacy) *There was a flurry of diplomacy after two weeks of heavy fighting.*

diplomatic *adj*

relating to or involving the work of diplomats

NOUNS

diplomatic relations/ties (=between governments that have an embassy in each other's country) *We hope to restore diplomatic relations between our two countries.*

diplomatic activity *The attacks led to intensive international diplomatic activity.*

diplomatic efforts *Diplomatic efforts to end the fighting began on October 15th.*

diplomatic pressure *There was diplomatic pressure on the president to step down.*

a diplomatic initiative (=plan to achieve something) *Havana launched a diplomatic initiative to establish ties with Latin American governments.*

diplomatic channels (=diplomatic methods for achieving something) *The president said that he hoped the situation could be resolved through diplomatic channels.*

a diplomatic solution *UN delegates met to find a diplomatic solution to the crisis.*

a diplomatic row/incident (=disagreement) *The affair led to a diplomatic row between Russia and China.*

a diplomatic mission (=a group of diplomats sent somewhere) *He was sent to France three times on diplomatic missions.*

diplomatic immunity (=the right not to obey a country's laws, which foreign diplomats have) *The two men had diplomatic immunity and were released from police custody.*

dire *adj*

THESAURUS terrible

direct *adj*

done without any other people, actions, or processes coming between

NOUNS

direct access *Very few people have direct access to the president.*

direct contact *The disease is only spread by direct contact between people.*

a direct link/connection *There is a direct link between poverty and ill-health.*

a direct relationship *Performing live helps build a direct relationship between a band and its fans.*

a direct effect/impact *These government spending cuts will have a direct impact on children's lives.*

a direct result/consequence *The decision to close the hospital is a direct result of government policy.*

a direct influence/bearing *The price of a barrel of oil has a direct bearing on the price drivers pay at the pumps.*

direct evidence *There is no direct evidence that the substance causes cancer.*

direct control *The Bank of England has direct control over interest rates.*

direct experience *He had no direct experience of managing a football club before he took over here.*

THESAURUS: direct

truthful, sincere, frank, straight, open, candid, direct, blunt, forthright, outspoken, upfront → **honest**

direction *n*

1 the way something or someone moves, faces, or is aimed

ADJECTIVES

the right/wrong direction *Are you sure this is the right direction for the airport?*

the opposite/other direction *The car crashed into a truck that was coming in the opposite direction.*

a different direction *They attacked us from different directions.*

the same direction *The sheep were all moving in the same direction.*

a southerly/westerly etc direction *A strong wind was blowing from an easterly direction.*

VERBS

go in a direction *Which direction did they go in?*

move/head/travel in a direction *The car was last seen heading in the direction of Miami.*

look/glance in a direction *She looked in the direction that Jeremy was pointing.*

face (in) a direction *He turned around until he was facing the opposite direction.*

turn in a direction *The men turned in the direction of Mecca and began praying.*

change direction (=start to go in a different direction) *Suddenly the flock of birds changed direction.*

PREPOSITIONS

from a ... direction *There was a loud scream from the direction of the children's pool.*

the direction of sth *It was hard work rowing against the direction of the river's current.*

PHRASES

in each/every direction (*also* **in all directions**) *From the top of the tower, there are splendid views in every direction.*

in both directions *The traffic in both directions was at a complete standstill.*

in different directions *They said goodbye and walked off in different directions.*

in the general direction of sth (=approximately where something is) *He pointed in the general direction of the village.*

in a clockwise/anticlockwise direction (=like or unlike the movement of the hands of a clock) *The cars go round the track in a clockwise direction.*

a sense of direction (=the ability to judge which way you should be going) *I have a terrible sense of direction so Mike usually drives.*

2 instructions about how to get from one place to another

Grammar
Always plural in this meaning.

VERBS

give sb directions *Luke gave me directions to his house.*

follow directions *You can't get lost if you follow my directions.*

ask (sb) for directions *Let's stop and ask someone for directions.*

get directions (=ask someone for directions) *I went into a petrol station to get directions.*

ADJECTIVES

clear/good directions *His directions were very clear and easy to follow.*

PREPOSITIONS

directions to sth *He gave me directions to his apartment on Boylston Street.*

3 instructions about how to do something

Grammar
Usually plural in this meaning.

VERBS

follow the directions *Always follow the manufacturer's directions when using this product.*

read the directions *I wish that I'd read the directions properly before starting!*

ADJECTIVES

clear directions *There are clear directions on their website telling you how to download the software.*

step-by-step directions *The software comes with step-by-step directions for installing it.*

director *n*

1 the person who gives instructions to the actors and other people working on a film or play

ADJECTIVES/NOUNS + director

a film/movie director *The film director Stephen Spielberg is expected to win the award.*

D

a theatre director *BrE*, **a theater director** *AmE*: *Laura Thompson is a theatre director, currently rehearsing 'Romeo and Juliet'.*
an artistic director (=who controls which plays a theatre produces and how they are produced) *He returned to the theatre as artistic director in 2008.*
a musical director (=who controls which music is performed and how it is performed) *He later became musical director of the London Symphony Orchestra.*
a television/TV director *She worked as a television director for the BBC.*
a Hollywood director *Martin Scorsese is a famous Hollywood director.*

D

2 a person who controls and manages a company or a department of a company

ADJECTIVES/NOUNS + director

a company director *Mr Eaton and the other company directors will be attending the meeting.*
a managing director *BrE* (=the person who is in charge of a large company) *The managing director may have to resign.*
the finance/marketing/sales etc director (=of a particular department) *The sales director explained the new marketing strategy.*
an executive director (=who is involved in the daily management of a company) *Bill was promoted to executive director.*
a non-executive director (=who gives advice but is not involved in the daily management of a company) *She is a non-executive director for several big companies.*

VERBS

appoint a director (=choose someone to become a director) *She was appointed a director of DBCM in June 2009.*

PREPOSITIONS

a director of sth *Her husband is a director of a small publishing company.*

PHRASES

the board of directors *His appointment to the board of directors was confirmed by the chairman.*

dirt *n*

1 any substance that makes things dirty, such as mud or dust

PHRASES

be covered with/in dirt *The kitchen floor was covered with dirt.*
be black with dirt (=be very dirty) *His hands were black with dirt after work.*
a speck of dirt (=a very small piece of dirt) *Their house was so clean – there wasn't a speck of dirt anywhere.*

VERBS

remove the dirt (from sth) *First, remove any dirt from the cut and then put a bandage on it.*
wash off/clean off/scrub off the dirt *I washed the dirt off my hands and sat down to eat.*
brush off/rub off the dirt *Brush the dirt off those boots before you come into the house.*
sth shows the dirt (=something looks dirty – used about colours) *These white jeans really show the dirt.*

2 *especially AmE* earth or soil

dirt + NOUNS

a dirt road *We drove down a dirt road until we came to the lake.*
a dirt track/path *There are several dirt tracks through this part of the forest.*
a dirt floor *They slept on mats on a dirt floor.*

PREPOSITIONS

in the dirt *The children had been playing in the dirt.*

PHRASES

a pile of dirt *There was a pile of dirt next to the hole.*
a handful of dirt *His sister threw a handful of dirt onto his coffin.*

dirty *adj* not clean

NOUNS

dirty clothes/socks/sheets etc *My son leaves his dirty clothes all over the bedroom floor.*
dirty laundry/washing *She put the dirty laundry in the washing machine.*
dirty dishes/plates *There was a stack of dirty dishes in the sink.*
dirty hands/fingernails *Don't eat food with dirty hands.*
a dirty city/street/room/place *They lived in a poor part of London, in a dirty street full of cheap bars.*
a dirty mark *The coal had left a dirty mark on her white shirt.*
a dirty nappy *BrE*, **a dirty diaper** *AmE*: *You should dispose of dirty nappies in a bin and not down the toilet.*
dirty water *Drains carry the dirty water underground to the sewer.*
dirty work/job (=which makes you dirty) *Working in the fields is hot dirty work.*

VERBS

get dirty *How did you get so dirty?*
get/make sth dirty *Don't walk in the mud – you'll get your shoes dirty.*

THESAURUS: dirty

filthy
clothes | streets | hands | room | window | water | river | conditions
very dirty:
His clothes were filthy, covered in dirt and blood. | The mayor plans to get citizens to clean

up the city's filthy streets. | She fell into the filthy water. | The animals were being kept in filthy conditions.

squalid *formal*
conditions | camp | housing | prison | room | mess | shanty town | slum | neighbourhood
extremely dirty and unpleasant. **Squalid** sounds very disapproving and is used about the place or conditions in which someone lives:
People are living in squalid conditions, with little water and no sanitation. | The refugees were forced to live in squalid camps.

polluted
air | water | river | lake | land | soil | city | area | environment
dirty and dangerous because of unwanted chemicals and gases from cars, factories etc:
*The air is **heavily polluted** because of all the fumes from the traffic. | The river is polluted and many fish have died. | Reducing car usage will help to clean up Britain's polluted cities.*

contaminated
land | soil | water | food | meat | milk | site | area | needle | blood
made dirty by a dangerous substance or bacteria:
Cleaning up contaminated land is very expensive. | Thousands of people die every year from drinking contaminated water. | He became infected with HIV after being given contaminated blood.

unhygienic *formal*
conditions | practice | method | premises
dirty in a way that is likely to cause diseases to spread:
The food was prepared under unhygienic conditions. | Officials have blamed the infections on unhygienic practices at the hospital. | Wiping tables with a dirty cloth is unhygienic.

unsanitary *formal* (*also* **insanitary** *BrE*)
conditions | housing
used about dirty conditions that are likely to cause diseases to spread, especially because there is not a good system for getting rid of waste:
They work for long hours in unsanitary conditions. | People's health is being threatened by overcrowded and insanitary housing.

muddy
boots | shoes | footprints | water | puddle | field | track | path | road
covered with mud:
She left her muddy boots by the door. | There were muddy footprints all over the white carpet. | It had been raining hard and the path was muddy.

grubby
hands | fingers | face | handkerchief | clothes | mark
fairly dirty and needing to be cleaned or washed:
The children put their grubby hands on the walls. | He pulled a grubby handkerchief out of his pocket.

grimy
window | glass | face | street | city
covered with thick dirt or dirt that has been there for a long time:
I couldn't see much out of the grimy windows of the train. | They spent the day walking round the cold grimy streets.

greasy
hair | skin | hands | fingers | overalls | mark
covered with oil or grease:
If your hair is greasy, you may need to wash it every day. | She wiped her greasy hands on the towel. | There was a greasy mark on his shirt.

dingy
room | office | hotel | basement | apartment | building
a dingy place looks dark, dirty, and unpleasant:
The room had a small window and was rather dingy. | We worked in a dingy little office behind the station.

dusty
road | street | track | town | room | book | shelf
covered with dust:
He cycled up the narrow dusty road. | The books were dusty and looked as though they hadn't been read for a long time.

soiled *formal*
nappy | diaper | clothes | sheets | bedding | linen | mattress | dressing
made dirty, especially by waste from your body:
Soiled nappies should be changed as quickly as possible. | The dressing was heavily soiled with blood.

ANTONYMS **dirty → clean[1] (1)**

disability *n*

a physical or mental condition that makes it difficult for someone to use a part of their body properly, or to learn normally

ADJECTIVES/NOUNS + disability

a learning disability *He goes to a special school for people with learning disabilities.*

a physical disability *She manages to lead a normal life in spite of her physical disabilities.*

a mental disability *Someone may be born with a mental disability or may acquire it through brain damage.*

a language disability *Behaviour problems are common in children with speech and language disability.*

a permanent/long-term disability *He was in a car accident that left him with a permanent disability.*

D

a severe disability *She teaches children with severe learning disabilities.*

a mild disability *Colour blindness is usually classed as a mild disability.*

VERBS

have a disability *The university welcomes applications from students who have a disability.*

suffer from a disability *In Florida alone, there are more than half a million people who suffer from a disability.*

disability + NOUNS

disability benefits/payments *Seven percent of Britons of working age receive disability benefits.*

PREPOSITIONS

with a disability *Public places are becoming more accessible to people with disabilities.*

D

disabled *adj*

someone who is disabled cannot use a part of their body properly, or cannot learn easily

ADVERBS

severely disabled *Elaine is severely disabled and relies on 24-hour care.*

partially/temporarily disabled *He was partially disabled as a result of the accident.*

physically disabled *If you are physically disabled, you can get help with your living accommodation.*

NOUNS

a disabled person *Disabled people should have the same rights and choices as everyone else.*

a disabled adult/child *a support group for parents of disabled children*

a disabled toilet *The nearest disabled toilet is in the hall.*

VERBS

be born disabled *Her son was born disabled.*

leave sb disabled *The accident left him disabled and unable to use his legs.*

disadvantage *n*

something that causes problems, or that makes someone or something less likely to be successful or effective

ADJECTIVES

a big/great/major disadvantage *This method has one major disadvantage: its cost.*

the main disadvantage *The main disadvantage of iron as a material is its weight.*

a serious/severe disadvantage *Public transport is very bad here, which is a serious disadvantage.*

a significant disadvantage *This approach does have a number of significant disadvantages.*

a slight/minor disadvantage *Children who are young in their school year sometimes have a slight disadvantage.*

a further/additional/added disadvantage *It's a very small garden and it has the further disadvantage of facing north.*

an unfair disadvantage *This arrangement would put the UK citizen at an unfair disadvantage.*

social/economic/educational disadvantage *Unemployment often leads to social disadvantage.*

a competitive disadvantage (=one relating to a situation in which people or companies are competing) *Firms that are not part of the group would be at a competitive disadvantage.*

VERBS

have a disadvantage *Cars have many disadvantages and they cause a lot of pollution.*

suffer (from) a disadvantage *formal*: *Working-class boys suffer disadvantages in the educational system.*

overcome a disadvantage (=succeed in spite of a disadvantage) *She was able to overcome the disadvantages of poverty.*

PREPOSITIONS

the disadvantage of doing sth *This medicine has the disadvantage of working slowly.*

disadvantages to sth *There are some disadvantages to the plan.*

PHRASES

sb/sth is at a disadvantage (=they have a disadvantage compared to other people, companies etc) *The company was at a disadvantage compared with its competitors.*

put/place sb at a disadvantage (=make someone less likely to be successful than others) *Not speaking English might put you at a disadvantage.*

be/work to the disadvantage of sb (=make someone unlikely to be successful) *This system works to the disadvantage of women.*

advantages and disadvantages (=the good and bad features of something) *Both methods have their advantages and disadvantages.*

the advantages outweigh the disadvantages (=there are more advantages than disadvantages) *The advantages of building the new road would outweigh the disadvantages.*

THESAURUS: disadvantage

drawback

a bad feature that something has, especially when it has other features that seem good: *One of the* ***main drawbacks*** *is the price. | The* ***only drawback*** *that I can think of is that the house is next to a busy road. | The system has one* ***slight drawback*** *– it's rather complicated to use.*

the downside

the disadvantage of a situation that in most other ways seems good or enjoyable: *It's a great job.* ***The only downside is*** *that I don't get much free time. |* ***There is a downside to*** *all this success – you can't have any privacy. | Can you think of a* ***potential downside*** (=something that might cause problems)?

bad point *especially spoken*
a bad feature that something has:
*All of these designs have both their **good points** and **bad points**.*

disadvantaged *adj*

having social problems, such as a lack of money or education, which make it difficult for you to succeed

NOUNS

a disadvantaged group/community *The college has announced plans to increase the number of students from disadvantaged groups.*

a disadvantaged area/region *Fewer than one in five young people from the most disadvantaged areas enters higher education.*

a disadvantaged background *Despite coming from a disadvantaged background, he was a millionaire by the age of 30.*

disadvantaged people/students/children *Britain's education and welfare system is failing disadvantaged children.*

disadvantaged families *The charity raised £30,000 for disadvantaged families in Birmingham.*

ADVERBS

seriously/severely disadvantaged *Many of the girls are severely disadvantaged and their families do not have any money to pay for their education.*

economically/socially disadvantaged *The government provides training programs for economically disadvantaged young people.*

doubly/further disadvantaged *Children from poor families are further disadvantaged due to a lack of home internet access.*

THESAURUS: disadvantaged

developing, deprived, disadvantaged, needy, destitute, impoverished, poverty-stricken, penniless, broke/hard up → **poor (1)**

disagree *v*

to have or express a different opinion from someone else

ADVERBS

completely/totally/entirely disagree *Some people say that this is his best film. I completely disagree.*

strongly/profoundly disagree *Although we strongly disagree about politics, we are still friends.*

sharply disagree (=strongly, and in an important way) *The prime minister and foreign minister sharply disagreed on the best way to handle the crisis.*

fundamentally disagree (=disagree about the most basic aspects of something) *John and I fundamentally disagree about the role of women in society.*

violently disagree (=very strongly and angrily) *The brothers had violently disagreed over what should be done with their parents' estate.*

PREPOSITIONS

disagree with sb/sth *I totally disagree with the decision to close the hospital.*

disagree about/on/over sth *Experts disagree on how much the program will cost.*

ANTONYMS **disagree → agree**

disagreement *n*

a situation in which people have different opinions or argue about something

ADJECTIVES

considerable/substantial disagreement (=people have very different opinions) *There is considerable disagreement among teachers about the value of the tests.*

deep/profound disagreement (=people have extremely different opinions) *The issue has caused deep disagreement among local people.*

bitter/sharp disagreement (=people have very different opinions and argue a lot about something) *There was bitter disagreement between the EU and the US over farming subsidies.*

widespread disagreement (=among many people) *The judge's decision was a source of widespread disagreement.*

fundamental disagreement (=about the most basic parts of something) *There is fundamental disagreement about the nature of history.*

a serious/major disagreement (=a situation in which people argue about something because they strongly disagree) *If you have a serious disagreement at work, you should talk to your manager.*

a minor/slight disagreement (=about something that is not very important) *There was a slight disagreement about where we should eat.*

VERBS

cause disagreement *The decision has caused an enormous amount of disagreement.*

have a disagreement *We've had a few disagreements, but we're still good friends.*

resolve/settle a disagreement (=end it by finding a way in which you can agree) *Negotiations failed to resolve the disagreement.*

express/voice disagreement (=say that you disagree) *She wrote to the newspaper expressing her disagreement with the article.*

disagreements arise/occur *formal* (=they happen) *Disagreements often arise because of misunderstandings.*

disagreement exists *Disagreement still exists over who is to blame.*

PREPOSITIONS

a disagreement with sb *I had a minor disagreement with my parents.*

disagreement between/among people *There is deep disagreement between ministers on how to tackle the problem.*

disagreement about sth *They found themselves in sharp disagreement about policy.*

in disagreement *The meeting ended with the two sides in disagreement.*

PHRASES

a cause/source of disagreement *The issue has become a cause of disagreement between the airline and the union.*

an area of disagreement (=an idea or subject that people disagree about) *Substantial areas of disagreement still exist between scientists.*

a point of disagreement (=a particular thing that people disagree about) *One point of disagreement between the two parties concerns the future of nuclear power.*

room/scope for disagreement (=the possibility that people will disagree about something) *There is room for disagreement about how much independence to give children.*

D

disappear *v*

to become impossible to see any longer, or be impossible to find

NOUNS

a man/woman/boy/girl etc disappears *The man disappeared on the day after the murder.*

a car/ship/plane/train disappears *He stood there watching until the little car had disappeared.*

the sun/moon/cloud disappears *The sun disappeared behind a cloud.*

sb's money/savings disappear *It is impossible to know how the money disappeared.*

sb's hopes/anger/worries disappear *The team's hopes of winning disappeared.*

ADVERBS

disappear completely/altogether *The next day, the pain had completely disappeared.*

mysteriously disappear *Several reporters in the area have mysteriously disappeared.*

sth has almost/virtually/practically disappeared *Dolphins have virtually disappeared from this part of the ocean.*

PHRASES

disappear without trace (=disappear without leaving any signs that you were there) *Hundreds of people disappear without trace every year.*

disappear from view/sight *The train went around a bend and disappeared from view.*

disappear into thin air (=completely disappear in way that seems mysterious) *The money had somehow disappeared into thin air.*

disappear from/off the face of the earth (=disappear completely – a rather informal phrase, used for emphasis) *As far as I knew, he had disappeared off the face of the earth.*

disappear into a crowd *The thief ran away and disappeared into the crowd.*

disappear over the horizon (=disappear after passing the place where the sky seems to meet the sea or the land) *The ship slowly disappeared over the horizon.*

THESAURUS: disappear

vanish

to disappear very suddenly, especially in a mysterious way:

When I looked again, the boy had vanished. | *His smile vanished and he looked worried.* | *Her plane* ***vanished without trace*** *in the middle of the Indian Ocean* (=disappeared completely, without leaving any signs that it was there). | *The bird flew up and* ***vanished from sight*** (=it could not be seen). | *It seems impossible for a whole continent to just* ***vanish from the face of the earth****.*

go away

pain | headache | hunger | problem | issue | threat | question

to disappear and stop causing problems:

The doctor gave me an injection, and the pain went away. | *We can't just wait for the problem to go away.* | *The threat of another attack has never completely gone away.*

fade (away)

sound | voice | laughter | light | anger | hope | power

to gradually become less clear, strong, or bright, and finally disappear:

The sound of the city faded away. | *The light faded away, and they found themselves in complete darkness.* | *The power of the state is beginning to fade away, because of the internet.*

melt away

crowd | anger | tension | opposition | support | doubt

to disappear, especially gradually. **Melt away** is used about groups of people or feelings, especially in written descriptions:

The concert ended and the crowd slowly started to melt away. | *When she apologized, his anger melted away.* | *Public opposition to the plan melted away.*

die out

species | animal | plant | custom | tradition | practice | language | disease

to stop existing after gradually becoming more and more rare:

Scientists estimate that between 15 and 20 species are dying out every year (=types of animal or plant). | *Sometimes the streets are decorated with flower petals, although this custom is dying out.* | *Wolves had died out in much of Europe.*

If a type of animal or plant stops existing because they have all died, you can say that it becomes **extinct**: *Dinosaurs became **extinct** millions of years ago.* | *The rocks contain the bones of **extinct** species of animals* (=types of animals that no longer exist).

ANTONYMS **disappear → appear (1)**

disappearance *n*

a situation in which someone or something disappears

ADJECTIVES

strange/mysterious disappearance *The film is about the mysterious disappearance of several teenage girls on a school trip.*

gradual disappearance *The gradual disappearance of the forests in the region is cause for extreme concern.*

sudden disappearance *Mystery surrounds the sudden disappearance of a wealthy businessman.*

rapid disappearance *Destruction of the rainforest has led to the rapid disappearance of many animals.*

virtual disappearance (=someone or something has almost completely disappeared) *Improvements in medicine have resulted in the virtual disappearance of the disease in most parts of the world.*

complete/total disappearance *The treatment resulted in the complete disappearance of the cancer cells.*

VERBS

investigate/look into sth's/sb's disappearance *Police are looking into the woman's disappearance.*

be linked/connected to sb's disappearance *A Dutchman linked to the disappearance of an American teenager five years ago was arrested on Thursday.*

disappointed *adj*

unhappy because something you hoped for did not happen, or because someone or something was not as good as you expected

ADVERBS

bitterly disappointed (=extremely disappointed, in a way that makes you very unhappy) *Local residents were bitterly disappointed with the decision.*

deeply/extremely/terribly/incredibly disappointed *The team were deeply disappointed that they didn't win.*

a little/slightly disappointed *I think my parents were a little disappointed in me.*

sadly disappointed (=used when saying that someone will be disappointed, because what they want is not going to happen) *If people think the country will change overnight, they are going to be sadly disappointed.*

NOUNS

a disappointed customer/fan *Thousands of disappointed customers were kept waiting for free tickets.*

a disappointed look/expression/face *She gave me a long disappointed look.*

VERBS

look/sound/feel disappointed *He looked disappointed when I told him the news.*

PREPOSITIONS

disappointed with sb/sth *I was a little disappointed with the film.*

disappointed by sth *They are disappointed by the lack of progress.*

disappointed at sth *He was disappointed at not being selected for the team.*

disappointed in sb/sth *I'm disappointed in you, Mervyn. I thought you had more intelligence.*

disappointing *adj* THESAURUS **bad (1)**

disappointment *n*

1 a feeling of unhappiness because something is not as good as you expected, or has not happened in the way you hoped

ADJECTIVES

great/huge/deep disappointment *There was great disappointment among the fans when England lost.*

bitter disappointment (=in which you feel very unhappy and upset) *She could not hide her bitter disappointment at not being chosen for the job.*

extreme disappointment *She expressed her extreme disappointment at the court's decision.*

obvious disappointment *"Are you leaving?" he asked with obvious disappointment.*

VERBS

feel disappointment *It's only natural to feel disappointment when this sort of thing happens.*

express disappointment (=say that you are disappointed) *They expressed disappointment at the company's pay offer.*

hide/conceal your disappointment *She turned away quickly to hide her disappointment.*

avoid disappointment *We recommend that you book early to avoid disappointment.*

overcome your disappointment (=stop feeling disappointed) *He eventually overcame his disappointment.*

share sb's disappointment *We all shared her disappointment when she didn't get the job.*

PREPOSITIONS

to sb's disappointment *To Edward's disappointment, Gina was not at the party.*

disappointment at sth *The victim's family expressed anger and disappointment at the verdict of 'not guilty'.*
disappointment with sth/sb *He was painfully aware of his father's disappointment with him.*
disappointment over/about sth *There was a lot of disappointment over the cancellation of the project.*

PHRASES

a sense/feeling of disappointment *There is a sense of deep disappointment at the team's performance.*
a look of disappointment *She couldn't hide the look of disappointment on her face.*
a twinge of disappointment (=a small feeling of disappointment) *She felt a twinge of disappointment at not getting first prize.*

D

2 someone or something that is not as good as you hoped or expected

ADJECTIVES

a big disappointment *I was a big disappointment to my parents.*
a huge/great/massive disappointment *His latest film is a massive disappointment.*
a bitter disappointment *Not getting into university was a bitter disappointment to my brother.*
a terrible disappointment *It must be a terrible disappointment to lose a final.*
a severe/grave disappointment *The unemployment figures are a grave disappointment for the government.*

VERBS

come as a disappointment *If you are looking for quiet beaches, the island may come as a disappointment.*
prove/turn out to be a disappointment (=be shown to be a disappointment) *The job proved a disappointment and she left after only six months.*

PREPOSITIONS

a disappointment to/for sb *The cut in funding came as a huge disappointment to us. | The concert was a real disappointment for many fans.*

PHRASES

be something of a disappointment (=be rather disappointing) *After her brilliant last novel, this one was something of a disappointment.*

disapproval *n*

the feeling when you do not like or agree with someone or something

ADJECTIVES

strong/deep/intense disapproval *The president faces strong disapproval of his war strategy.*
widespread/general disapproval (=among many people) *There is widespread international disapproval of the way the country has treated its citizens.*
public disapproval *The company decided not to go ahead with the plan, because of public disapproval.*
official disapproval *His behaviour was the subject of official disapproval.*
universal disapproval (=by everyone) *There is almost universal disapproval for the scheme.*

VERBS

express/show/voice your disapproval *Britain and the United States expressed their disapproval by withdrawing their offer of substantial economic aid.*
look at sb/look upon sth with disapproval *Isaac looked at his son with disapproval.*
meet with disapproval/be greeted with disapproval (=people disapprove of something) *The decision met with widespread public disapproval.*

PHRASES

a chorus of disapproval (=a lot of people saying that they do not agree with something) *This suggestion was met by a chorus of disapproval from other party members.*
much to sb's disapproval (=used when saying that someone strongly disapproves of something) *She decided to study art, much to her parents' disapproval.*

disapprove *v*

to think that someone or something is bad or wrong

ADVERBS

strongly disapprove of sb/sth *Her parents strongly disapproved of the marriage.*
thoroughly disapprove of sb/sth (=completely) *I thoroughly disapprove of hunting in any form.*

ANTONYMS **disapprove → approve (1)**

disarmament *n*

when a country reduces the number of weapons it has, or the size of its army, navy etc

ADJECTIVES

nuclear disarmament *The campaign for nuclear disarmament began in the 1960s.*
multilateral disarmament (=involving several different countries) *Some form of multilateral disarmament would benefit everyone.*
unilateral disarmament (=involving only one country) *The British prime minister is not in favour of unilateral disarmament.*

disarmament + NOUNS

disarmament negotiations/talks *United Nations disarmament negotiations started today.*
a disarmament treaty/agreement *There will be talks on a new disarmament treaty.*

disaster *n*

1 a sudden event such as a flood, storm, or accident which causes great damage or suffering

ADJECTIVES/NOUNS + disaster

a natural disaster (=one caused by nature, such as a storm or earthquake) *The island has been hit by storms and other natural disasters.*

a terrible disaster *The nation suffered a terrible disaster and thousands were killed.*

the worst disaster *The earthquake was the worst disaster in the country's history.*

a national disaster (=one affecting the whole of a country) *The president called the flooding a national disaster.*

an ecological/environmental disaster (=one causing great damage to nature) *This region is facing an ecological disaster as oil continues to wash up on our coastline.*

a humanitarian disaster (=in which a lot of people die) *The prime minister appealed for international aid to avert a humanitarian disaster.*

a nuclear disaster (=an accident involving nuclear power or weapons) *People are worried that there could be another nuclear disaster like the one in Fukushima.*

an air/rail disaster (=a bad air or rail accident) *The crash was the worst rail disaster in Pakistan's history.*

a ferry disaster *His parents were both drowned in a ferry disaster in the Greek islands.*

a mining disaster *83 coal miners have been killed in the country's worst ever mining disaster.*

VERBS

a disaster strikes (=happens suddenly) *No one knows where the next natural disaster will strike.*

a disaster happens/takes place *We moved out of New Orleans shortly after the disaster happened.*

prevent/avert a disaster *Luckily the pilot saw the other plane just in time, and a disaster was averted.*

spell disaster (=mean that a disaster will happen) *The drought could spell disaster for wildlife.*

disaster + NOUNS

a disaster area/zone (=area where a disaster has happened) *Military planes flew food supplies to the disaster area.*

a disaster victim (*also* **a victim of a disaster**) *Aid is being given to the disaster victims.*

PHRASES

the aftermath of a disaster (=the time after a disaster when people are still dealing with its effects) *In the aftermath of the disaster, disease and starvation killed many people.*

THESAURUS: disaster

crash, collision, disaster, wreck, pile-up → **accident**

2 something that is very bad or a failure, especially when this is very annoying or disappointing

ADJECTIVES

a complete/total disaster *It rained all day and the parade was a complete disaster.*

a financial/economic disaster *The project was a financial disaster.*

an unmitigated disaster (=a complete failure) *The movie was an unmitigated disaster, hated by critics and the public.*

a potential disaster (=one that could happen) *Always save a backup copy of your work to avoid potential disasters.*

impending disaster (=one that is going to happen soon) *She had a sense of impending disaster.*

a near disaster (=almost a complete failure) *The election proved to be a near disaster for Labour.*

VERBS

end in disaster *The scheme ended in disaster and they lost all their money.*

spell disaster (=cause something to end badly or fail) *Bad luck and the recession spelt disaster for her business.*

be courting disaster (=be behaving in a way that makes a bad thing more likely to happen) *By having an affair with his boss, he was courting disaster.*

become a disaster *The crisis was quickly becoming a political disaster.*

PREPOSITIONS

be a disaster for sb *This year has been a disaster for the team.*

PHRASES

be on the brink of disaster (=almost in a very bad situation) *Once again the peace process was on the brink of disaster.*

be a recipe for disaster (=very likely to end badly) *Getting married too young is a recipe for disaster.*

sth is a disaster waiting to happen (=used to say that something is bad and will fail) *The government's health service reforms are a disaster waiting to happen.*

disbelief *n*

the feeling when you cannot believe someone or something or are very surprised

ADJECTIVES

complete/total/utter/absolute disbelief *My mother looked at me in total disbelief.*

D

VERBS

look/stare/watch in disbelief *When he said he didn't know the answer, she stared at him in disbelief.*

express disbelief (=say that you cannot believe that something is true) *The school expressed disbelief when he scored zero marks in his English exam.*

discipline *n*

control of your own or other people's behaviour so that rules are obeyed

ADJECTIVES/NOUNS + discipline

strict discipline (=very firm and not always reasonable or kind) *Some parents complained about the school's strict discipline.*

strong/firm/good discipline (=clear rules that people understand and must obey) *Without good discipline in the classroom, learning suffers.*

harsh discipline (=severe or cruel) *Discipline is harsh, and can include physical punishment.*

rigid discipline (=always strictly maintained) *The rigid discipline of life in a monastery was not for him.*

poor discipline (=not firm enough) *Problems tend to arise in families where there is poor discipline.*

military discipline (=the kind of strict discipline imposed in the army) *I hated the army and the routine of military discipline.*

school/classroom discipline *The committee looked at ways to improve school discipline.*

VERBS

maintain/keep discipline (=make people obey rules) *A good teacher can maintain discipline without shouting.*

enforce/impose discipline (=make people obey rules, especially by using punishment) *Discipline in the army is very strictly enforced.*

need/require discipline *The children needed firm discipline.*

restore discipline (=bring it back) *The General wanted to restore discipline among the troops.*

PHRASES

a lack of discipline *The principal never tolerated a lack of discipline.*

a breach of discipline *formal* (=an act of not obeying the rules) *Being absent without permission was a breach of discipline.*

discount *n*

a reduction in the usual price of something

ADJECTIVES

a special discount *Some hotels offer special discounts during the winter.*

a big/large/huge discount *If you spend over £500, you get a big discount.*

a generous discount (=larger than normal) *Some students may qualify for generous discounts on fees.*

a substantial/good discount (=fairly big) *Insurance companies give substantial discounts to mature drivers.*

a 10%/40% etc discount *The gym is offering a 15% discount to members who renew their membership.*

a small discount *They offer a small discount to people who pay their bills online.*

a staff discount *BrE*, **an employee discount** *AmE*: *The employee discount can be up to one-third of the sale price.*

VERBS

get/receive a discount *You get a small discount if you book more than ten tickets.*

give (sb) a discount *Many theatres give discounts to students.*

offer (sb) a discount *The store is offering a 50% discount on some toys.*

ask for a discount *I asked for a discount because the vase was slightly damaged.*

be entitled to a discount (*also* **qualify for a discount**) (=have the right to get a discount) *Staff are entitled to a 20% discount.*

discount + NOUNS

a discount price *You can buy books online at discount prices.*

a discount fare *The bus company offers discount fares to pensioners.*

PREPOSITIONS

a discount on sth *This card gives you a discount on all rail travel.*

a discount of 5%/10% etc *Season ticket holders get a discount of between 10 and 15%.*

at a discount *Employees can buy books at a discount.*

discovery *n*

something that is discovered, or the act of discovering something

ADJECTIVES

a scientific/medical etc discovery *The book covers the major scientific discoveries of the last century.*

an important/significant/major discovery *The archaeologists had made an important discovery.*

a great discovery *The truly great discoveries are the ones that are perfectly obvious after someone has pointed them out to us.*

an exciting/interesting discovery *The existence of a new planet was a very exciting discovery.*

a remarkable/amazing discovery *It was a remarkable discovery.*

a surprising/unexpected/startling discovery *Their work led to some surprising discoveries.*

a new discovery *New discoveries are being made all the time.*

an accidental/chance discovery *All these were chance discoveries by scientists working on other things.*

VERBS

make a discovery *He made some interesting discoveries in the course of his research.*

lead to a discovery *It was pure chance that led to the discovery.*

PREPOSITIONS

the discovery of sth *I'm reading a book about the discovery of America.*

discrimination *n*

the practice of treating one person or group differently from another in an unfair way

ADJECTIVES/NOUNS + discrimination

racial/race discrimination *Racial discrimination is against the law.*

sex/sexual discrimination *She had been the victim of sex discrimination.*

age discrimination *Many older job candidates face age discrimination.*

religious discrimination *Religious discrimination was widespread in northern Ireland.*

job/employment discrimination (=not giving someone a job because of their race, sex etc) *We are making progress in reducing job discrimination.*

widespread discrimination (=happening in many places) *There was widespread discrimination against women in the job market.*

positive discrimination/reverse discrimination (=giving jobs or positions to a group who have been discriminated against in the past) *Positive discrimination will help to get more women into parliament.*

VERBS

experience/face/suffer discrimination *Women faced discrimination when applying for jobs.*

fight/oppose discrimination *The Senator opposed discrimination against gays in the military.*

prevent discrimination *By speaking out, he hopes to prevent discrimination against people suffering with AIDS.*

end discrimination *We want to end discrimination against older people at work.*

tackle discrimination (=try to deal with it) *The law can now be used to tackle discrimination on the grounds of religion.*

PREPOSITIONS

discrimination against sb *He fought discrimination against homosexuals.*

PHRASES

discrimination on the grounds of sth *Discrimination on the grounds of nationality is prohibited.*

a victim of discrimination (=someone who has experienced discrimination) *Victims of discrimination have the right to compensation.*

an act of discrimination *formal*: *We condemn all acts of discrimination on the ground of race, colour, and ethnic origin.*

discuss *v*

to talk about something with another person or a group in order to exchange ideas or decide something

ADVERBS

discuss sth at length (=for a long time) *The committee has discussed the problem at length.*

discuss sth briefly *We only discussed sales briefly at our last meeting.*

discuss sth openly/publicly (=in a way that does not hide your opinion or feelings) *With John, she felt that she could discuss her feelings openly.*

discuss sth fully/thoroughly/in detail (=discuss everything about something) *The surgeon and I discussed the operation thoroughly before I made my decision.*

discuss sth informally *It's a place where mothers can meet and discuss their problems informally.*

discuss sth sensibly/rationally (=in a way that is calm and thoughtful) *Surely we can discuss this rationally, like adults.*

NOUNS

discuss a question/subject/topic *We'd never discussed the question of having children.*

discuss a matter/issue *formal*: *The two leaders met to discuss the issue further.*

discuss a problem *I suggested meeting her to discuss the problem.*

discuss the situation *They held a three-hour meeting to discuss the situation.*

discuss a possibility *Government officials were seriously discussing the possibility of war.*

discuss a plan/idea/policy *It's a good idea to discuss your plans with your parents.*

VERBS + discuss

meet to discuss sth *We met to discuss arrangements for the wedding.*

refuse to discuss sth (*also* **decline to discuss sth** *formal*): *Colonel Simpson refused to discuss the military operation in detail.*

need to discuss sth *There are still a few minor things that we need to discuss.*

wish to discuss sth *We certainly don't wish to discuss family matters with someone we hardly know.*

be willing/prepared to discuss sth *I don't know if she will be willing to discuss this with me.*

agree to discuss sth *The principal has agreed to discuss the matter.*

PREPOSITIONS

discuss sth with sb *My accountant discussed the changes with me.*

D

discussion *n*

an occasion when people discuss something, or the process of discussing something

ADJECTIVES

a long/lengthy discussion *After a long discussion, they decided that she should go back to work.*

a short/brief/quick discussion *The book starts with a brief discussion of how people might live without modern technology.*

much discussion *There has been much discussion recently of the role of religion in the modern world.*

a general discussion *There will be a general discussion about the situation in Afghanistan.*

an informal/private discussion *The two leaders had informal discussions over the phone.*

an interesting/fascinating/useful discussion *Thank you all very much - it has been a very interesting discussion.*

a serious/intense discussion *There needs to be a serious discussion about the future of our planet.*

a heated discussion (=one in which people have very strong feelings) *There were a number of heated discussions between the actor and the director of the film.*

a high-level discussion (=by people in very important positions) *There have been high-level discussions between the US and Russia.*

a detailed/in-depth/extensive discussion *For a more detailed discussion of this issue, see Chapter 12.*

a wide-ranging discussion (=about many things) *They had wide-ranging discussions covering political, financial, and strategic matters.*

an online discussion (=on the internet) *There will be an online discussion and everyone will get a chance to express their views.*

VERBS + discussion

have a discussion *They were having a discussion about the best place for the conference.*

hold a discussion *formal* (=people have a discussion) *Discussions were held in Geneva about a possible peace agreement.*

join in/take part in/participate in a discussion *He is an enthusiastic student who always joins in class discussions.*

start/open a discussion *The president will start discussions on Monday with political leaders to form a new government.*

enter into a discussion (=start a discussion in order to reach an agreement about something) *The two companies have agreed to enter into discussions aimed at resolving the issue.*

continue a discussion *I hope we can continue this discussion at a later date.*

lead a discussion (=be the main speaker in a discussion about something) *Timothy Garton Ash led a discussion about Britain's place in the world.*

encourage/promote/stimulate discussion *We hope the book will encourage discussion on the development of Asian cities.*

come up for discussion (=be something that people discuss) *The subject of who owns the islands is likely to come up for discussion.*

facilitate a discussion (=help people to have a successful discussion) *His role is to facilitate discussions between the two opposing groups.*

discussion + VERBS

a discussion takes place *Discussions took place about the types of restaurants and shops that would be most appropriate for the area.*

a discussion arises/ensues (=people start to discuss something) *Considerable discussion arose over the role played by the US in the war.*

a discussion centres on/focuses on sth *The discussion centred on the best way to use the money.*

NOUNS + discussion

a group discussion *Students are expected to take part in group discussions about a range of different topics.*

a class discussion *We had a class discussion about the death penalty.*

PREPOSITIONS

a discussion about/on sth *There has been a lot of discussion about racism in sport recently.*

a discussion with sb *He visited Paris for discussions with the French president.*

a discussion between sb *There have been discussions between the two companies about a possible merger.*

sth is under discussion (=people are discussing it) *The subject is still under discussion and no agreement has been reached.*

be in discussion with sb (=be discussing something with someone) *We are currently in discussion with his lawyer.*

PHRASES

a subject/topic for discussion (*also* **a subject/topic of discussion**) *The main topic for discussion in Britain is usually the weather.*

the outcome of a discussion (=what is decided as the result of a discussion) *The main outcome of the discussions was a trade agreement between the two countries.*

use sth as the basis for discussion *The teacher used the film as a basis for discussion about women's issues.*

throw the subject open for discussion (=allow people to discuss something and give their opinions about it) *The chairman threw the subject open for discussion and asked people for their comments.*

bring the discussion to an end/close (=end the discussion) *We're running out of time and I think we had better bring the discussion to a close.*

a discussion is going nowhere (=it is not achieving anything useful) *I don't see any point in continuing – this discussion is going nowhere.*

a full and frank discussion (=a discussion in which people say what they really think and often strongly disagree) *Let's just say we had a full and frank discussion about why we lost the game.*

disease *n*

an illness which affects a person, animal, or plant

ADJECTIVES/NOUNS + disease

a common disease *Measles is a common disease among children.*

a rare disease *She suffers from a rare bone disease.*

a serious disease *He was worried that he might be suffering from a serious disease.*

a fatal/deadly disease (=that causes death) *If left untreated, the disease can be fatal.*

an incurable disease (=that cannot be cured) *Diseases that were once thought incurable can now be treated with antibiotics.*

an infectious/contagious disease (=that spreads quickly from one person to another) *The disease is highly contagious.*

heart/blood/skin etc disease *He is being treated for kidney disease.*

a hereditary/inherited/genetic disease (=that is passed from parent to child) *Should people with a serious hereditary disease have children?*

a tropical disease (=one that occurs in hot countries) *Malaria is the commonest of the tropical diseases.*

a degenerative disease *formal* (=one that gradually gets worse and makes your body weaker over a long time) *She was suffering from a degenerative disease that confined her to a wheelchair.*

VERBS

have a disease *How long have you had the disease?*

suffer from a disease *About three million people suffer from the disease.*

catch/get a disease (*also* **contract a disease** *formal*): *He caught the disease while travelling in Africa.*

die of/from (a) disease *Many of the prisoners died of disease.*

pass on a disease (*also* **transmit a disease** *formal*): *They may pass the disease on to their children.*

carry a disease (=have it and able to give it to people) *They tried to kill the insects that carried the disease.*

cause a disease *Smoking is probably the major factor causing heart disease.*

prevent a disease *It has been claimed that fibre in the diet could help prevent many serious diseases.*

treat a disease *The disease can be treated with antibiotics.*

cure a disease *The plant was believed to cure diseases in humans and cattle.*

fight/control a disease *Some bacteria help the human body fight disease.*

a disease spreads *The disease spread quickly throughout Europe.*

PREPOSITIONS

a disease of the lungs/liver/spine etc *He suffers from a disease of the liver.*

PHRASES

a cure for a disease *There is no known cure for this disease.*

the symptoms of a disease (=physical signs that someone has a disease) *To begin with, there are often no symptoms of the disease.*

an outbreak of a disease (=an occasion when a lot of people or animals get it) *There has been an outbreak of the disease in Wales.*

the spread of a disease *Knowing the facts about AIDS can prevent the spread of the disease.*

disgust *n*

a very strong feeling of dislike or disapproval

VERBS

look at sb/sth with disgust *She looked at him with disgust.*

feel disgust (*also* **experience disgust** *formal*): *He felt disgust at seeing his daughter's killer in court.*

show/express your disgust *The player showed his disgust by throwing his shirt to the ground as he left the pitch.*

hide your disgust *She made no effort to hide her disgust.*

ADJECTIVES

obvious disgust *She was staring at him with obvious disgust.*

utter disgust *He had a look of utter disgust on his face.*

PREPOSITIONS

in disgust *Sam threw his books down in disgust and stormed out of the room.*

with disgust *She shook her head with disgust.*

disgust at/with sb/sth *The fans didn't hide their disgust at the referee's decision.*

PHRASES

a look/expression of disgust *He reached into the bin with a look of disgust on his face.*

feelings of disgust *People who are extremely overweight often experience feelings of disgust about their own bodies.*

(much) to sb's disgust *Much to my disgust, I found that there were no toilets for the disabled.*

be full of disgust *His voice was full of disgust and anger.*

turn up your nose in disgust (=reject something because you feel disgust) *The dog turned up its nose in disgust at the bowl of food.*

disgusting *adj*

extremely unpleasant and making you feel sick

ADVERBS

absolutely disgusting (=completely disgusting) *The soup tasted absolutely disgusting.*

⚠ Don't say 'very disgusting'.

THESAURUS: disgusting

awful, appalling/atrocious/horrendous, horrible, horrific, hideous, disgusting, dire, lousy, ghastly, vile, diabolical, abysmal → terrible

D

dish *n*

1 a type of food that is served as one part of a meal

ADJECTIVES/NOUNS + dish

a French/Greek/Mexican etc dish *Mexican dishes are often very spicy.*

a local dish *When I'm visiting a place, I like to try the local dishes.*

a country's national dish *Fish and chips is Britain's national dish.*

a traditional/classic dish *Sushi is a traditional Japanese dish.*

a meat/fish/vegetable etc dish *This herb is used in many meat dishes.*

a vegetarian dish *Most restaurants now have vegetarian dishes on the menu.*

a delicious/tasty dish *They serve a wide range of tasty dishes.*

a hot/cold dish *I prefer to eat hot dishes in the winter.*

a simple dish *This simple dish only takes a few minutes to prepare.*

a main dish *The main dish was fish stew.*

a side dish (=a small amount of food such as vegetables or salad, that you eat with a main dish) *I ordered the salad as a side dish.*

VERBS

prepare/make a dish *Most of these dishes can be prepared in advance.*

serve a dish *This dish can be served as a first course.*

create a dish *The dish was created by a French chef.*

PHRASES

a variety/range/selection/choice of dishes *The restaurant offers a delicious range of homemade dishes.*

2 the dishes are the plates, bowls, pans etc that have been used when making and serving a meal

Grammar
Always plural in this meaning.

VERBS

do/wash the dishes *I was in the kitchen doing the dishes.*

clear the dishes (=take them off the table) *He stood up and began clearing the dishes.*

dry the dishes *Gloria helped dry the dishes after dinner.*

put away the dishes *I'll do the washing-up and then you can put away the dishes.*

ADJECTIVES/NOUNS + dish

dirty dishes *He used to leave dirty dishes in the sink.*

the breakfast/supper/lunch dishes *Mike offered to wash the breakfast dishes.*

disheartening *adj* THESAURUS

depressing

dishonest *adj*

behaving in a way that is intended to deceive people, for example by lying, cheating, or stealing

Grammar
Dishonest is most commonly used after the verb **be**: *Are you accusing me of being* ***dishonest****? | Not all politicians are* ***dishonest****.*

ADVERBS

deliberately dishonest *When he said he knew nothing about it, he was being deliberately dishonest.*

patently dishonest (=obviously dishonest) *He described the government's attitude as patently dishonest.*

fundamentally/basically dishonest *There is something fundamentally dishonest about this policy.*

downright dishonest *informal* (=completely dishonest) *It was downright dishonest of him to sign the contract when he knew that he couldn't do what was agreed.*

NOUNS

a dishonest person *There are dishonest people in every area of society.*

dishonest tactics/methods *They used dishonest tactics to get what they wanted.*

a dishonest claim *The company made dishonest claims about its products.*

dishonest conduct *formal* (=dishonest behaviour) *He was found guilty of dishonest conduct.*

THESAURUS: dishonest

corrupt
official | politician | leader | government | regime | police officer | cop | practice | system | country
using your official power in a dishonest way to get advantages for yourself:
Corrupt officials have been accepting bribes. | There was an international campaign against Burma's corrupt military regime (=government – used to show disapproval). *| The justice system is* ***notoriously corrupt*** (=everyone knows it is corrupt).

devious
way | means | scheme | tactics | mind
dishonest in a clever way, and good at thinking of ways of secretly tricking people in order to get what you want:
Using various devious means, they can trick people into paying hundreds of dollars for things they don't want. | You have a very devious mind! | Be careful what you tell her – she can be very devious.

sneaky *informal*
trick | way
secretly tricking people in order to get what you want:
What a sneaky trick! | Companies have all kinds of sneaky ways of getting information about their customers. | It was ***a bit sneaky*** *not telling him that you already had a boyfriend.*

> **Sneaky** or **devious?**
> These words are similar in meaning. **Sneaky** is much more informal than **devious**. You say a **sneaky trick** (not a 'devious' one). **Devious** sounds more serious and is often used when someone carefully plans what they are doing.

sly
smile | grin | look | fox | way
deliberately behaving in a way that hides what you are really thinking or doing, and is often slightly dishonest:
The old man had a sly grin on his face, as if he knew something that we didn't. | He's a sly old fox (=a sly person). *| Lucy was very sly and didn't tell him where she was going.*

underhand *BrE*, **underhanded** *AmE*
tactics | method | means | manner | way | dealings
underhand methods involve secretly deceiving people in order to get what you want:
The other candidate used underhand tactics to win the election.

unscrupulous
employer | landlord | lender | dealer | trader | seller | owner | politician | company | person
an unscrupulous person uses dishonest and unfair methods to get what they want, without caring about the effects of their actions on other people:
Some unscrupulous employers try to avoid paying pensions to their workers. | The new rules are intended to prevent unscrupulous landlords from overcharging tenants.

fraudulent *formal*
claim | practice | activity | conduct | transaction | use | accounting
deliberately deceiving people, especially in order to get money – used when this is against the law or the official rules:
You will be prosecuted if you make a fraudulent claim on your insurance policy. | The stolen credit card had been used to carry out fraudulent transactions (=for buying things or getting money in a dishonest way).

deceitful *formal*
way | politician
telling lies or tricking people, especially in order to get what you want:
He won the race in a deceitful way. | The company were deliberately ***deceitful about*** *their intentions when they bought the land.*

ANTONYMS **dishonest → honest**

disinfect *v* THESAURUS **clean²**

dislike¹ *v*
to think someone or something is unpleasant and not like them

ADVERBS
strongly/heartily dislike *Many people strongly dislike being contradicted.*
particularly dislike *He was not fond of fish, and particularly disliked shellfish.*
instinctively dislike (=without thinking about why) *Parents instinctively dislike the government telling them how to raise their children.*
dislike sb/sth intensely (=very strongly) *She had to work with a man who she disliked intensely.*
be widely/generally disliked (=by many people) *As a leader, he was widely disliked.*

ANTONYMS **dislike → like**

dislike² *n*
a feeling of not liking someone or something

ADJECTIVES
a deep/strong/great dislike *He took a strong dislike to his piano teacher.*
an intense/violent dislike *She has an intense dislike of the media.*
a hearty dislike (=a very strong dislike) *Doctors have a hearty dislike of this kind of advertising, which encourages people to eat unhealthy food.*
a personal dislike *I allowed my personal dislike of the man to influence my decision.*

D

VERBS

have a dislike of/for sb/sth *I have a particular dislike of modern jazz.*

feel dislike of/for sb/sth *I don't feel any dislike for him – we're just very different.*

take a dislike to sb/sth (=start to dislike someone or something) *My sister took an instant dislike to him.*

show/express your dislike of/for sb/sth *Arthur tried hard not to show his dislike of the meal.*

hide/conceal your dislike of/for sb/sth *He didn't bother to hide his dislike for me.*

PREPOSITIONS

a dislike of sth/sb *Denise shared her mother's dislike of housework.*

a dislike for sb/sth *He always had a deep dislike for authority.*

D

dismal *adj* THESAURUS ▸ **sad (2)**

dismiss *v*

1 to refuse to consider someone's idea, opinion etc, because you think it is not serious, true, or important

NOUNS

dismiss an idea *Both actors dismissed any idea of a romantic relationship between them.*

dismiss a suggestion/proposal *He dismissed suggestions by his rival that he should resign.*

dismiss a possibility *The prime minister dismissed the possibility of an early election.*

dismiss a claim *An industrial tribunal dismissed his claim of unfair dismissal.*

dismiss an allegation/charge *She dismissed all the allegations against her, saying they were completely unfounded.*

dismiss a thought *I tried to dismiss the thought that he could be lying to me.*

dismiss fears *The Transport minister dismissed fears that the railway line would close.*

dismiss criticism *He dismissed criticism of the country's human rights record.*

ADVERBS

dismiss sth easily/lightly (=without much thought) *This is a question that cannot be dismissed lightly.*

quickly dismiss sth *He quickly dismissed the idea as unworkable.*

casually dismiss sth (=without thinking about it seriously enough) *You can't just casually dismiss her opinion like that.*

PHRASES

dismiss sth out of hand (=immediately, without thinking about it) *It's an interesting idea so don't dismiss it out of hand.*

dismiss sth as unrealistic/false/ridiculous etc *We dismissed his proposal as completely unworkable.*

dismiss sth as nonsense/a fake/a joke etc *She dismissed the comments as 'a joke'.*

2 to make someone leave their job, usually because they have done something wrong

PREPOSITIONS/ADVERBS

dismiss sb from their job/post/position *He was dismissed from his post as chairman of the party.*

dismiss sb for sth/on the grounds of sth (=for a particular reason) *The senior nursing officer was dismissed for misconduct.*

be unfairly dismissed *The tribunal decided that she was unfairly dismissed from her job.*

disobedient *adj* THESAURUS ▸ **naughty**

disobey *v*

to refuse to do what someone with authority tells you to do, or refuse to obey a rule or law

NOUNS

disobey sb's orders/instructions *He had disobeyed the captain's orders.*

disobey the law/rules *If you disobey the rules, you can expect to be punished.*

disobey an officer *In the army, it is a crime to disobey a superior officer.*

disobey your father/mother/parents etc *You know what will happen, if you continue to disobey your father.*

ADVERBS

wilfully disobey (=deliberately disobey) *The charges against him include making false official statements and wilfully disobeying orders.*

THESAURUS: disobey

break
law | rule | regulations | guidelines | limit | agreement | promise
to not obey a law or rule, or not do what you have agreed or promised:
The government will deal harshly with anyone who breaks the law. | The minister was caught breaking the speed limit by the police. | Both sides accused each other of breaking their agreement. | She said she would come to the party and then she broke her promise.

defy
law | order | ban | father | parents
to deliberately refuse to do what someone in authority tells you to do, especially in a way that shows you do not agree with them and have no respect for them:
Supermarkets are defying the law by opening on national holidays. | The police arrested the youth for defying a court order. | Protesters defied the ban on demonstrations (=defied an order that forbids you from doing something). *| John had always argued with his father and defied him.*

flout
law | rules | regulations
to deliberately disobey a rule or law in a very public way, especially in a way that shows you do not care about it:
Some drivers regularly flout the law and drive at speeds of over 180 kilometres per hour. | We need tougher action against companies who flout the rules. | For too long, people have blatantly flouted building regulations (=in a very obvious way).

violate
law | rules | regulations | rights | agreement | treaty | terms | principle
to disobey a law, or do something that is against an agreement or principle:
Capone was arrested for violating US tax laws. | The government has violated the basic human rights of its citizens. | He denied that Britain had violated its agreement. | She violated the terms of her contract by working for another company. | Giving government money to a company violates the principle of free competition.

contravene *formal*
law | act | guidelines | rules | agreement | treaty | resolution | convention | section | article
to be against a law, rule, or agreement, or do something that is against a law, rule, or agreement:
Some people say that the US invasion contravened international law. | The deal did not contravene any existing trade agreements. | The British government may have contravened the European Convention on Human Rights.

ANTONYMS **disobey → obey**

disorder *n*

a mental or physical illness which prevents part of your body from working properly

ADJECTIVES/NOUNS + disorder

a common/rare disorder *The doctor said that it was a very common skin disorder.*

a genetic disorder (=caused by a gene from your parents) *This genetic disorder speeds up the process of ageing.*

a mental/psychiatric/psychological disorder (=affecting the mind) *He was diagnosed with a severe psychiatric disorder.*

a blood/brain/heart/liver etc disorder *She suffers from a rare blood disorder.*

an eating disorder (=in which someone stops eating a normal amount of food) *Eating disorders can be very difficult to treat.*

a sleep/sleeping disorder *Sleep disorders such as insomnia affect huge numbers of people.*

a personality disorder (=that stops someone having normal relationships) *The study suggested that 84% of prisoners have some sort of personality disorder.*

VERBS

have a disorder *The singer admitted she had an eating disorder.*

suffer from a disorder *People who are suffering from psychological disorders often fail to get treatment.*

develop a disorder *Women are more likely to develop this disorder than men.*

treat a disorder *The drug is used to treat lung disorders.*

a disorder affects sb/sth *Many genetic disorders affect only girls or only boys.*

PREPOSITIONS

a disorder of sth *He suffers from a rare disorder of the liver.*

display Ac *n*

a show or an arrangement of things for people to look at or buy

ADJECTIVES

a fine/magnificent/superb display (=a very good one) *The museum has a magnificent display of medieval jewellery.*

a spectacular/dazzling/eye-catching display (=very impressive to look at) *The gymnastic team put on a dazzling display.*

VERBS

create a display *She created an award-winning display at the national garden show.*

have a display *The gallery has a superb display of modern art.*

go on/be on display *The vase will go on display to the public from today.*

PREPOSITIONS

a display of sth *I was amazed at the dazzling display of talent on show.*

disposal Ac *n*

the process of getting rid of something

ADJECTIVES/NOUNS + disposal

safe disposal *The US and Russia held talks on the safe disposal of nuclear weapons.*

illegal disposal *People were put at risk by the illegal disposal of clinical waste.*

waste disposal (=of unwanted materials or substances) *Most countries have improved their standards of waste disposal.*

refuse/rubbish/garbage disposal (=of things people throw out of houses, shops etc) *Refuse disposal is the responsibility of county councils.*

sewage disposal (=of waste water and waste products from toilets etc) *The city invested heavily in improved sewage disposal.*

bomb disposal (=of bombs before they explode) *The building was evacuated and a bomb disposal team moved in.*

PREPOSITIONS

the disposal of sth *There are strict rules governing the safe disposal of hazardous waste.*

dispute *n*

a serious argument or disagreement

ADJECTIVES/NOUNS + dispute

a bitter/fierce/acrimonious dispute (=very angry) *It caused a bitter dispute between the neighbouring republics.*

a major/serious dispute *He had major disputes with several players.*

a minor dispute *A minor dispute about homework became a violent confrontation.*

a long-running/long dispute *They now have a chance to end this long-running dispute.*

an industrial dispute *BrE*, **a labor dispute** *AmE* (=between workers and employers) *A lot of working days are lost through industrial disputes.*

a pay dispute (=about how much money employees are paid) *The pay dispute involved 450 staff.*

a trade dispute *The countries were involved in a trade dispute over imports of bananas.*

a political/legal dispute *There was a long legal dispute between the two companies.*

a domestic dispute *formal* (=between people who live together) *The court heard that he had been stabbed during a domestic dispute.*

a border dispute (=about where the border between two countries is) *The border dispute between Argentina and Chile was resolved.*

a territorial dispute (=about which country land belongs to) *The war started as the result of a territorial dispute.*

VERBS

be involved in/have a dispute *The US government was involved in a dispute with China.*

be locked in a dispute (=be involved in one that is difficult to resolve) *Workers and management are locked in a bitter dispute.*

get into a dispute (=become involved) *We don't want to get into a dispute with them.*

be in dispute with sb *He was in dispute with the company about his contract.*

resolve/settle/end a dispute *It is hoped that the dispute can be resolved peacefully.*

deal with/handle a dispute *The court can deal with disputes between member states.*

sth leads to a dispute *Decisions about education can lead to disputes between parents.*

a dispute arises (=starts) *Sometimes a dispute arises between the seller and the buyer.*

PREPOSITIONS

a dispute over/about sth *There was a dispute over pay.*

a dispute between sb and sb *It is a typical dispute between two former business partners.*

a dispute with sb *He was involved in a dispute with his employer.*

dissertation *n*

a long piece of writing on a particular subject, especially one written for a university degree

ADJECTIVES/NOUNS + dissertation

a 3,000-word/15,000-word etc dissertation *Courses are assessed by written examination and by a 15,000-word dissertation.*

a PhD/MA etc dissertation *I wrote my MA dissertation on Japanese phonetics.*

an undergraduate dissertation *BrE*: *More and more colleges are requiring undergraduate dissertations that demonstrate a student's abilities.*

a research dissertation *He is collecting data for his research dissertation.*

VERBS

write/do a dissertation *Students have to write a 10,000-word dissertation.*

hand in your dissertation (*also* **submit your dissertation** *formal*): *You must submit your dissertation by the deadline date.*

dissertation + NOUNS

a dissertation topic *You should select a dissertation topic that can be completed within a two-year time frame.*

PREPOSITIONS

a dissertation on sth *She wrote her dissertation on Charles Baudelaire, the French poet.*

distance *n*

the amount of space between two places or things

ADJECTIVES

a long/great/considerable distance *The sound of guns seemed a long distance away.*

vast distances (=very long distances) *The aircraft is able to carry huge loads over vast distances.*

a short distance *I quickly walked the short distance to the car.*

a good distance (=quite a long distance) *He was a good distance ahead of us.*

some distance (=quite a long distance) *He heard a scream some distance away.*

a safe distance (=enough space to be safe) *You should keep a safe distance from the car in front.*

the right/correct distance *Are you the right distance from your computer screen?*

VERBS

travel a great/long etc distance *In some countries children must travel great distances to school each day.*

cover a distance (=go a particular distance) *I don't know how he covered the distance so quickly.*

measure the distance between things *Now we are able to measure the distances between the planets.*

judge/estimate a distance *Animals that hunt can judge distances very well.*

PREPOSITIONS

the distance between sth and sth *He judged the distance between the boat and the river bank wrongly.*

the distance from sth to sth *The distance from London to Weymouth is 143 miles.*

at a distance of two feet/ten metres etc *I followed him at a distance of about ten yards.*

from a distance of two feet/ten metres etc *She could read the sign from a distance of 20 feet.*

over a long/short etc distance *We can now communicate easily over long distances.*

PHRASES

within (easy) walking distance (=near enough to walk to easily) *There are lots of restaurants within walking distance.*

within travelling/commuting/driving distance of sth (=near enough to make travel to or from a place possible) *The job was not within travelling distance of my home.*

within striking distance of sth (=not far from something, especially something you are going to attack) *Their troops had advanced to within striking distance of the town.*

distant *adj, adv* THESAURUS ▸ **far**

distinction Ac *n*

1 a clear difference or separation between two similar things

ADJECTIVES

a clear distinction *The legal system makes a clear distinction between adults and children.*

a fine/subtle distinction (=small) *Language enables us to make fine distinctions between similar ideas.*

a sharp distinction (=very clear) *The president drew a sharp distinction between his party and the Republican Party.*

an important/crucial distinction *There is an important distinction between these two types of cancer.*

a fundamental distinction (=a basic one) *There is a fundamental distinction between authors and readers.*

a useful distinction *He makes a useful distinction between the two theories.*

VERBS

make a distinction (*also* **draw a distinction** *formal*) (=say or show that one exists) *It isn't easy to make a distinction between these two words.*

see a distinction (=recognize that one exists) *He saw no distinction between religious beliefs and superstition.*

blur the distinction between sth and sth (=make it less clear) *The distinction between military and civilian targets has become blurred.*

PREPOSITIONS

a distinction between sth *There is often no clear distinction between an allergy and food intolerance.*

2 the quality of being special in some way

VERBS

have/enjoy the distinction of doing sth *Philadelphia has the distinction of being the largest city in Pennsylvania.*

achieve/earn the distinction of doing sth *He had achieved the rare distinction of being the only driver to win both races.*

ADJECTIVES

a rare distinction *Ahmed had achieved the rare distinction of qualifying for all four championships.*

a dubious distinction (=a special quality that is not good) *The country has the dubious distinction of having the highest proportion of its population in prison.*

distort *v* THESAURUS ▸ **change[1] (2)**

distress *n*

1 great unhappiness or suffering

ADJECTIVES

great/considerable/deep distress *This type of crime can cause great distress.*

acute/severe distress (=which you feel very strongly) *She was clearly suffering from acute distress after the death of her husband.*

emotional/mental/psychological distress *Some people eat too much as a way of dealing with emotional distress.*

financial/economic distress (=difficulties caused by money problems) *The charity helps families who are in financial distress.*

further distress *I was anxious to avoid causing them any further distress.*

VERBS

cause sb distress *I'm sorry if I caused you any distress.*

feel distress *I know that he feels great distress as a result of losing his job.*

suffer/experience distress *She claimed that she suffered emotional distress because of the company's actions.*

show signs of distress *Did your pet show any signs of distress when you moved home?*

add to sb's distress *I don't want to add to your distress by giving you more things to worry about.*

PREPOSITIONS

in distress *The girl was crying and clearly in distress.*

sb's distress at/over sth *We share their distress at what has happened.*

to sb's distress *To the distress of his parents, he showed no interest in getting a job.*

PHRASES

a state of distress *The women was in a state of distress.*

2 a situation when a ship or aircraft is in danger and needs help

distress + NOUNS

a distress call/signal *The ship sent out a distress signal because it was sinking.*

PREPOSITIONS

in distress *We stopped to help another boat in distress.*

distressed *adj* THESAURUS ▶ **sad (1)**

distribute *v* THESAURUS ▶ **give (1)**

district *n*

an area of a town or the countryside, especially one with particular features

ADJECTIVES/NOUNS + district

an urban district (=in a town) *By 1911 over three-quarters of British people lived in urban districts.*

a rural district (=in the countryside) *There are few schools in the rural districts of Bangladesh.*

the surrounding districts (=in the area around or next to something) *The market attracts farmers from the surrounding districts.*

a financial/business/commercial district (=where there are a lot of banks and other businesses) *He works in San Francisco's financial district.*

a shopping district *The bomb exploded in a crowded shopping district.*

an entertainment district (=where there are a lot of bars, clubs etc) *The West End is London's entertainment district.*

a theatre district *BrE*, **a theater district** *AmE*: *The restaurant is located in the middle of New York's theater district.*

a residential district (=where people live rather than work) *The residential districts are much quieter than the city centre.*

a poor/wealthy district (=where a lot of people are poor or wealthy) *He lived in one of London's poorest districts.*

a fashionable district (=popular with rich or well-known people) *She lives in a fashionable district of the city.*

PREPOSITIONS

in a district *The apartment is in a wealthy district of Cairo.*

> **THESAURUS: district**
>
> region, zone, district, neighbourhood, suburb, quarter, slum, ghetto → **area (1)**

distrust *n*

a feeling that you cannot trust someone

ADJECTIVES

deep/profound distrust (=great distrust) *Dylan's deep distrust of journalists made him difficult to interview.*

mutual distrust (=both people, countries etc distrust each other) *The two countries are locked in a relationship of mutual distrust.*

popular/public distrust *A new study shows that public distrust of the media has increased.*

widespread/general distrust (=among many people) *The financial crisis has led to widespread distrust of the banking industry.*

growing distrust *The poll reveals a growing distrust of business among the public.*

healthy distrust (=distrust for good reasons) *He has always had a healthy distrust of authority.*

VERBS

feel distrust *Eighty percent of American citizens feel distrust of politicians.*

create distrust *Lies create distrust in a relationship between two people.*

PREPOSITIONS

distrust of sb/sth *Will the country ever overcome its distrust of foreigners?*

distrust between sb and sb *The book discusses the origins of the distrust between the Arab World and the West.*

distrust towards/toward sb/sth *There is growing distrust toward the government.*

with distrust *Local people regard the police with suspicion and distrust.*

PHRASES

a climate/atmosphere of distrust *There remains a climate of distrust between the management and the workers.*

feelings of distrust *She has had feelings of distrust for her husband ever since he admitted to having an affair.*

disturb *v*

to interrupt someone or interfere with something so that it cannot continue in the same way

NOUNS

disturb sb's concentration *I couldn't work with the kids disturbing my concentration.*

disturb sb's sleep *Local people said their sleep was being disturbed by noise from aircraft.*

disturb sb's thoughts *A gentle knock on the door disturbed his thoughts.*

disturb the balance (*also* **disturb the equilibrium** *formal*): *His arrival disturbed the delicate balance of their marriage.*

> **Disturb the peace** is used in legal contexts, to refer to the crime of making a loud noise, fighting etc in a public place: *He was found guilty of* ***disturbing the peace.***

PHRASES

sorry to disturb you *spoken*: *Sorry to disturb you, but could you sign this letter, please?*

disturbance *n*

a situation in which people behave violently in public

ADJECTIVES

a violent disturbance *Over a hundred people were injured during violent disturbances in the capital.*

a serious disturbance *There were serious disturbances in a number of British cities.*

a public disturbance *Many people were unhappy with the government's plans but there were no reports of public disturbances.*

civil disturbances (=fighting between different groups of people in a country) *Two men had already been killed in civil disturbances.*

political disturbances *There were political disturbances following the announcement.*

VERBS

cause/create a disturbance *Several people were arrested for creating a disturbance outside the embassy.*

quell a disturbance *formal* (=stop one) *Extra police were called to quell the disturbances.*

be involved in a disturbance *He was involved in a disturbance with journalists waiting outside his house.*

a disturbance breaks out (=starts) *A disturbance broke out between local youths and a group of soldiers.*

dive *n*

when something moves down through the air or water

ADJECTIVES

a steep dive (=going down suddenly) *The fighter plane went into a steep dive.*

a vertical dive (=going straight down) *His actions sent the plane into a near vertical dive.*

a shallow dive (=going down slowly rather than suddenly) *The bird captures its prey on the ground after a long shallow dive.*

VERBS

go into a dive (=start to move downwards) *The plane was in trouble, then it went into a dive.*

pull out of a dive (=stop a plane going down) *He tried to pull out of the steep dive before hitting the ground.*

diverse *adj*

including many different things or types of people

ADVERBS

highly/incredibly diverse (=extremely diverse) *India is an incredibly diverse country.*

ethnically/culturally diverse *New York is one of the most culturally diverse cities in the world.*

NOUNS

a diverse range/group *The college has students from a diverse range of social and economic backgrounds.*

a diverse population/community/society *The rainforest is home to a diverse population of animals and plants.*

a diverse workforce *The advantage of having a diverse workforce is that staff can relate to a wide range of customers.*

diverse backgrounds/cultures *University gives you the opportunity to meet people from diverse backgrounds.*

diverse interests *He was a man of remarkably diverse interests and achievements.*

diverse needs *Teachers have to take account of the diverse needs of their students.*

diversity Ac *n*

a situation in which something includes many different types of people or things

ADJECTIVES

great/considerable/enormous diversity *There was considerable diversity of opinion among the experts.*

rich diversity *The region is known for the rich diversity of its wildlife.*

incredible/extraordinary diversity *Iran is a country of incredible diversity.*

the sheer diversity of sth (=the surprisingly great diversity) *The sheer diversity of the courses available is amazing.*

cultural diversity *Because of its cultural diversity, Malaysia has many festivals throughout the year.*

ethnic/racial diversity *The huge number of different restaurants reflects the ethnic diversity of the city.*

biological diversity (=the fact that there are many different types of plant and animal) *Human society is having a major effect on the biological diversity of the Earth.*

genetic diversity (=the fact that there are many different genes) *Genetic diversity is vital for maintaining disease resistance in crops.*

VERBS

encourage/promote diversity *Creating a pond in your garden encourages wildlife diversity.*

maintain/protect/preserve diversity *It is important to maintain diversity among the plant population.*

increase/reduce diversity *Governments often try to reduce diversity in education.*

reflect the diversity of sth *The school is keen to reflect the diversity of the community.*

PREPOSITIONS

diversity of sth *Because of our members' diversity of experience, our debates are interesting and well-informed.*

diversity in sth *The diversity in the size and shape of animals' horns is remarkable.*

divide *v*

1 to separate something into two or more parts

> **Grammar**
> You can also say **divide sth up**, with the same meaning.

ADVERBS

be broadly/roughly divided (up) into sth (=in a way that is not exact) *The research can be broadly divided into three main categories.*

be neatly divided (up) into sth *In those days, the world was neatly divided into friends and enemies.*

be conveniently divided (up) into sth *The book is conveniently divided into three parts.*

PREPOSITIONS

divide sth in two *The room was divided in two by a plastic partition.*

divide sth (up) into sth *Divide the class into groups of four.*

2 to share something between people or things

> **Grammar**
> You can also say **divide sth up**, with the same meaning.

ADVERBS

divide sth (up) equally *We need to divide the work equally.*

divide sth (up) fairly *The other family members complained because they didn't think the money was being divided up fairly.*

be evenly divided *The eight-member panel was evenly divided between Republicans and Democrats.*

PREPOSITIONS

divide sth (up) between/among sb *They planned to divide the money between them.*

3 to make a group of people disagree with each other

> **Grammar**
> This meaning of **divide** is often passive.

ADVERBS

be deeply divided *Politically, the city is deeply divided.*

be bitterly divided *The country was bitterly divided over the war.*

sharply divided (=very clearly divided) *Opinion is sharply divided on this issue.*

be evenly divided *Voters are evenly divided over the plan.*

VERBS

remain divided *Experts remain divided about whether the drug is harmful or not.*

NOUNS

divide the country/nation *We need a leader that can unite this divided country.*

divide the community *We risk dividing the community even further.*

divide the party *The issue continues to divide the party.*

divide opinion *The war has divided public opinion.*

PREPOSITIONS

be divided over/on/about sth *The people are divided over the future of their country.*

divorce *n*

the legal ending of a marriage

VERBS

get a divorce *After five unhappy years they decided to get a divorce.*

ask (sb) for a divorce *She asked her husband for a divorce after he had been unfaithful.*

want a divorce *She told him she wanted a divorce.*

a marriage ends in divorce *One in three marriages ends in divorce.*

file/petition for (a) divorce (=start the legal divorce process) *The next day I saw a lawyer and filed for a divorce.*

be granted a divorce (=be legally given one) *Mullaney's wife was granted a divorce on grounds of his adultery.*

ADJECTIVES

a bitter/painful divorce *After a long and bitter divorce, Wendy was looking forward to starting a new life.*

a messy divorce (=complicated and unpleasant to deal with) *For the children's sake we want to avoid a messy divorce.*

divorce + NOUNS

the divorce rate (=the number of people who get a divorce) *The country has a high divorce rate.*

a divorce case (=a legal case dealing with a divorce) *It was the biggest divorce case that an English court has dealt with.*

a divorce settlement (=the amount of money, property etc each person gets in a divorce) *She received a $10 million divorce settlement from her first husband.*

PHRASES

grounds for divorce (=acceptable reasons for divorce, according to the law) *Violence and neglect are grounds for divorce.*

do *v*

to perform an action or activity

do + NOUNS

do a job/task *Machines are doing jobs that humans used to do.*

do work/housework/homework *She was too tired to do any work.*

do business *The company does a lot of business in China.*

do something/nothing/anything *My son lies on the sofa and does nothing all day.*

do sports/exercise *The doctor says I need to do more exercise.*

do a test/exam/course/class *Everyone has to do a fitness test.*

do an essay/report *I'm doing an essay on Jane Austen.*

do research/an experiment/a study *A lot of experiments have been done by psychologists on this topic.*

do a talk/presentation *I was asked to do a talk at the conference.*

do a check/inspection/search *Customs officers are doing a check on the company.*

do an investigation/survey *The police did a thorough investigation but they found no new evidence.*

do a calculation *She did a quick calculation on a piece of paper.*

do a drawing/painting/picture/sketch *He did a picture of an old farmer.*

You often use **do** when talking about everyday household tasks – **do the shopping/cleaning/ironing/cooking**: *Who **does the cooking** in your family?* **do the dishes/laundry**: *Can you **do the dishes** for me* (=wash them)? **do your hair/make-up**: *She's upstairs **doing** her **make-up*** (=putting it on).

THESAURUS: do

make
decision | choice | mistake | speech | statement | announcement | suggestion | progress | change
used with certain nouns when saying that someone does something, for example decides, says, or changes something:
The committee will make its final decision tomorrow. | The newspaper admitted that it had made a mistake. | He made a speech about the need for more nurses. | Can I make a suggestion? | His teacher says he has made good progress at school. | Companies are having to make major changes to adjust to new market conditions.

give
speech | talk | presentation | class | lecture | performance
to do something such as talk or perform in front of an audience:
Chris will give an illustrated talk on his expedition to Greenland. | Nicole Kidman gave a brilliant performance in the film.

take
test | exam | bath | shower | walk | drive | ride | swim
to do something – used about tests and everyday actions such as going for a walk or having a shower:
Kate's taking her driving test tomorrow. | I think I'll go and take a shower. | They took long walks in the woods.

British speakers often use **have** instead of **take**, and say **have a bath/shower/walk/swim**.
You can also say **go for a walk/drive/swim**.

commit
crime | offence | murder | robbery | act | suicide | sin | atrocity
to do something that is a crime, or something that people strongly disapprove of:
The crime was committed in the early hours of Sunday morning. | He was one of the men who committed the robbery. | She tried to commit suicide because she was being bullied at school (=tried to kill herself).

You don't say 'do a crime/offence'. However, when you are talking about a particular crime, you can say that someone was *the person who **did the murder/robbery/burglary***.

carry out
work | task | duties | research | study | test | experiment | operation | investigation | search | survey | business | attack | robbery | punishment | execution
to do something, especially in a carefully planned way:
The work is being carried out in the university laboratory. | They carried out a survey on people's attitudes to work. | The group has carried out a number of bomb attacks.

You also use **carry out** when you do what you have said you will do: *The union **carried out their threat** and went on strike.* You also use it when you do what another person has told you to do: *I was only **carrying out your orders**. | The staff **carried out her instructions**.*

conduct *formal*
research | study | test | experiment | investigation | inquiry | search | survey | ceremony | business | operation | interview
to do something, especially in a carefully planned way. **Conduct** means the same as **carry out**, but it sounds more formal and official:
North Korea announced that it had conducted a nuclear test. | The police are conducting an investigation into the cause of the fire. | They

D

conducted a survey of approximately 2,000 people living in the area. | The interview was conducted in English.

perform *formal*
task | duties | operation | surgery | ceremony | analysis | research | study | experiment | calculation | action
to do something:
The job mostly involves performing administrative tasks. | Surgeons performed an emergency operation to save the baby. | We asked our local priest to perform the ceremony. | Do you think it is right to perform experiments on animals?

undertake *formal*
investigation | inspection | review | research | study | survey | project
to do something, especially something complicated or something that needs a lot of effort, which you are responsible for:
The company is undertaking a full investigation into the allegations. | All final year students have to undertake a research project.

implement
policy | plan | system | programme | decision | recommendation | proposal | change | reform | measure
to do something that has been officially planned or agreed:
The government continued to implement its policy of radical economic reform. | Managers are expected to implement decisions rather than deciding on the overall direction of the company. | Schools will have three months in which to implement the changes.

Formality
Often the same noun can be used with a range of different verbs, depending on the formality. For example ***carry out*** *research/a study/an experiment/an operation* sounds neutral. ***Do*** *research/a study/an experiment/an operation* sounds more informal and is typically used in spoken English. ***Perform*** *research/a study/an experiment/an operation* sounds more formal and is typically used in written English.

doctor *n*

someone who is trained to treat people who are ill

VERBS + doctor

go to the doctor *I'd been having bad headaches so I went to the doctor.*

see/visit a doctor (=go to the doctor) *A friend urged me to see a doctor about my breathing problems.*

ask a doctor (*also* **consult a doctor** *formal*): *If you have any of these symptoms, you should consult a doctor.*

call a doctor (=telephone one and ask them to come to you) *His mother was very worried and called the doctor.*

send for/get a doctor (=arrange for one to come to you) *In the middle of the night we decided to get the doctor.*

qualify as a doctor *He studied medicine, and qualified as a doctor in 2008.*

doctor + VERBS

a doctor examines sb *The doctor examined her and said she had a chest infection.*

a doctor treats sb *The doctors who treated her say she will recover.*

a doctor prescribes sth (=writes an order for medicine for someone) *My doctor prescribed me some painkillers.*

ADJECTIVES/NOUNS + doctor

a qualified/trained doctor *The operation must be performed by a qualified doctor.*

a junior doctor *BrE* (=a doctor who has finished their medical training, who works in a hospital to get experience) *She worked as a junior doctor at South Tyrone Hospital.*

sb's local doctor *You should go and see your local doctor.*

a family doctor (=who treats all the members of a family) *We've had the same family doctor for 15 years.*

a hospital doctor *BrE*: *Hospital doctors have to work very long hours.*

PHRASES

a doctor's appointment *I have a doctor's appointment this afternoon.*

the doctor's surgery *BrE*, **the doctor's office** *AmE* (=where a doctor works) *Parents usually accompany children on visits to the doctor's surgery.*

document [Ac] *n*

a piece of writing on paper or on a computer

ADJECTIVES

a legal document *Legal documents are often written in a way that is difficult to understand.*

an official document *His name is mentioned in an official document.*

an important document *Your birth certificate is an important document, so keep it safe.*

a secret/confidential document *This document is strictly confidential.*

a leaked document (=a secret document that is made public in a newspaper, on the internet etc) *The paper published a leaked document which showed that the company knew the equipment was unsafe.*

an electronic document *You can send electronic documents by email.*

the original document *A photocopy will not be accepted – we need to see the original document.*

VERBS

sign a document *I had to sign a document to say that I had received my money.*

print/publish a document *The final document was published the following year.*

NOUNS + document

travel documents *I've lost my passport and all my travel documents.*

a draft document (=an early version of a document, which will be changed later) *This is only a draft document.*

a discussion/consultation document (=a document that asks people's opinions about something) *We all have to comment on the proposals in the consultation document.*

documentary *n*

a television or radio programme that gives detailed information about a subject

ADJECTIVES/NOUNS + documentary

a television/radio documentary *There is an interesting television documentary about the effects of climate change.*

a wildlife/science documentary *He likes watching wildlife documentaries.*

a fly-on-the-wall documentary (=a documentary showing people's daily lives using a secret camera) *The programme is filmed in the style of a fly-on-the-wall documentary.*

documentary + NOUNS

a documentary film/programme *He has just completed a documentary film about Thomas Jefferson.*

a documentary series *There was a BBC documentary series about the history of art.*

a documentary filmmaker *The American documentary filmmaker Michael Moore has won several awards.*

VERBS

make a documentary *A local film crew is making a documentary about volcanoes.*

see/watch a documentary *I watched a really interesting documentary last night.*

show/broadcast a documentary *The documentary was first shown on Channel 4.*

PREPOSITIONS

a documentary about/on sth *I remember seeing a documentary about Picasso's early life.*

dog *n*

a common animal with four legs, fur, and a tail. Dogs are kept as pets or trained to guard places, find drugs etc

ADJECTIVES/NOUNS + dog

a pet dog (=that you keep in your house) *Some owners give their pet dogs too much food.*

a wild dog *Packs of wild dogs roamed the countryside.*

a stray dog (=a pet dog that is lost) *He was always bringing home stray dogs.*

a guide dog *BrE*, **a seeing eye dog** *AmE* (=trained to guide a blind person) *No dogs except guide dogs are allowed in the store.*

a guard dog (=trained to guard a building) *The guard dog growled at him.*

a police dog (=trained to help the police) *Police dogs helped in the search for the missing child.*

a sniffer dog *BrE* (=trained to find drugs or bombs) *Police and sniffer dogs have become a regular presence at the airport.*

a dangerous dog *There have been several tragic cases of young children being attacked by dangerous dogs.*

dog + VERBS

a dog barks (=makes short loud sounds) *The dog barks every time someone comes to the door.*

a dog yaps (=barks – used of small dogs) *A little dog was yapping at her heels.*

a dog growls (=makes a long deep angry sound) *The dog growled at me as I walked towards it.*

a dog snarls (=shows its teeth and makes an angry sound) *When a dog snarls, it is threatening attack.*

a dog whines (=makes a long high sound because it is unhappy or in pain) *I could hear the dogs whining outside the door.*

a dog howls (=makes a long loud sound like a wolf) *We knew something was wrong because the dogs were howling.*

a dog bites sb *The dog bit me on the leg.*

a dog wags its tail (=moves its tail from side to side to show pleasure) *The dog bounded towards me, wagging its tail.*

VERBS + dog

have a dog (=keep one as a pet) *We have one dog and two cats.*

walk a dog/take a dog for a walk *She loves walking her dogs on the beach.*

feed a dog *Feeding a dog of that size costs a lot of money.*

train a dog (=teach it to do something) *The dogs are trained to sniff out drugs.*

dog + NOUNS

dog food *Ella opened a can of dog food.*

a dog owner *Dog owners are responsible for controlling their animals.*

a dog lover (=someone who likes dogs) *Britain is a nation of dog lovers.*

PHRASES

a breed of dog (=a type of dog) *The corgi is a small breed of dog.*

a pack of dogs (=a group of wild dogs or stray dogs) *There are packs of wild dogs in the mountains.*

Good dog! (=said to a dog when it obeys you) *Sit! Good dog!*

Beware of the dog! (=a sign warning people that there is a dog inside a place) *There was a sign on the gate saying 'Beware of the dog!'*

domestic [Ac] *adj*

1 relating to or happening in one particular country and not involving any other countries

NOUNS

domestic affairs (=public and political events inside a country) *Colombia rejected any interference in its domestic affairs.*

domestic policy (=policy relating to your own country) *The president's foreign and domestic policies have been criticized.*

the domestic market (=buying of goods inside a country) *The French domestic market is the largest consumer of champagne.*

the domestic economy (=production, sales etc inside a country) *Japan's domestic economy expanded greatly during this period.*

domestic demand (=the amount of something that people want to buy in a country) *Exports fell by 0.5 percent while domestic demand grew.*

domestic consumption (=the amount of something that people use in a country) *Are the goods for domestic consumption or for export?*

domestic flights (=that stay inside a country) *London's airports handle 100,000 domestic flights a year.*

2 relating to family relationships and life at home

NOUNS

domestic violence/abuse (=in a family, especially by a husband towards his wife) *The organization supports women who are victims of domestic violence.*

domestic problems (=problems in the home and with family relationships) *He never spoke about his domestic problems at work.*

a domestic dispute (=an argument between people who live together, especially when it involves violence) *Police are often called to domestic disputes.*

domestic life *She enjoyed domestic life and bringing up her children.*

domestic tasks/chores (=small jobs at home such as cleaning and washing) *How many hours do you spend on domestic tasks each week?*

domestic responsibilities *It can be hard to balance your work and your domestic responsibilities.*

domestic waste (=food, paper, containers etc from a house that are thrown away) *More domestic waste needs to be recycled.*

domestic help (=help with cleaning, washing etc) *People in well-paid jobs can afford domestic help.*

domestic service *formal* (=the work of a servant in a large house) *His mother went into domestic service at the age of 15.*

dominant *adj* THESAURUS ▶ **powerful (1)**

donate *v* THESAURUS ▶ **give (1)**

donation *n*

something, especially money, that you give to a person or an organization in order to help them

ADJECTIVES

a big/large/substantial donation *The Princeton Public Library received a large donation from the Kenderick family.*

a generous donation *A generous donation of £800 was received from a local company.*

private/individual donations *It is unrealistic to expect the political parties to give up large private donations unless funding needs are met from other sources.*

public donations *Over £900,000 has been raised through public donations.*

political donations *Big companies spend a lot of money on political donations.*

corporate donations (=from big companies) *The party gets a lot of money from corporate donations.*

an anonymous donation (=when the person giving money does not say who they are) *Hundreds of patients will be helped by a £400,000 anonymous donation to the hospital.*

charitable donations (=to charities) *The company makes a number of charitable donations every financial year.*

VERBS

make/give a donation *Would you like to make a donation to our charity appeal?*

send a donation *Please send all donations to the following address.*

get/receive a donation *Any donation, however small, will be gratefully received.*

appeal for/ask for donations *The Disasters Emergency Committee is appealing for donations to help people caught up in the floods.*

be funded by donations (*also* **rely on donations**) *The charity receives no government help and relies entirely on donations from the public.*

PREPOSITIONS

a donation to sb/sth *He made a large donation to Cancer Research.*

a donation from sb *The party receives huge donations from the big tobacco companies.*

donor *n*

1 someone who gives money or goods to help an organization or country

ADJECTIVES

an anonymous donor (=one whose name is not known) *An anonymous donor has given $5 million to the museum.*

a private/individual donor *Some of the money came from the Arts Council, and the rest from private donors.*

a corporate donor *The company is one of the Republican Party's biggest corporate donors.*

a generous donor *The refugees have received help thanks to generous donors.*

a big/major donor (=someone who gives a lot of money) *Most of the party's campaign costs were paid for by big donors.*

PREPOSITIONS

a donor to sth *Mr James was known as a major donor to the Conservative party.*

2 someone who gives blood or a body organ so that it can be used in the medical treatment of someone else

ADJECTIVES/NOUNS + donor

a blood donor *Are you willing to register as a blood donor?*

an organ donor *He carried a card showing that he was willing to be an organ donor.*

a heart/liver/kidney etc donor *There is a desperate shortage of kidney donors.*

a suitable donor *The doctors think that his brother may be a suitable donor.*

VERBS

find a donor *It can take several months to find a suitable donor.*

doom *n*

failure, destruction, or death that is certain to happen

ADJECTIVES

impending doom (=likely to happen soon) *With a terrible sense of impending doom, he opened the door.*

certain/inevitable doom (=sure to happen) *Some environmentalists have concluded that Earth faces certain doom.*

VERBS

spell doom (=mean that something will not continue to exist) *Many people predicted that the internet would spell doom for traditional media.*

meet your doom (=die in an unpleasant way) *Thousands of soldiers met their doom on this very field.*

PHRASES

a sense/feeling of doom *Rachel was filled with a terrible sense of doom.*

doom and gloom (*also* **gloom and doom**) (=bad things that may happen in the future) *The newspapers are always full of doom and gloom.*

it's not all doom and gloom (=there are some positive features) *Despite unemployment rising, it's not all doom and gloom for the economy.*

a prophet of doom (=someone who says that something bad is going to happen) *In this electronic age, the prophets of doom are predicting the end of the paper book.*

a harbinger of doom *formal* (=a sign that something bad is going to happen) *In ancient times, comets were seen as harbingers of doom.*

doomed *adj* THESAURUS ▸ **unsuccessful**

door *n*

the thing you open or close when entering a building, room, vehicle etc, or using a cupboard

ADJECTIVES/NOUNS + door

the front/back/side door *I heard someone knocking at the front door.*

the main door *The main door to the hotel is on Queen Street.*

the kitchen/bedroom/bathroom etc door *Jake opened the kitchen door to let the steam out.*

the oven/fridge/cupboard door *Smoke poured out when I opened the oven door.*

a car/train door *She heard a car door slamming.*

the passenger door (=for the person in a car who sits beside the driver) *The taxi driver was holding open the passenger door.*

the rear door (=at the back of something, especially a vehicle) *The kids opened the rear doors and climbed in.*

a sliding door (=one that slides rather than swings open) *Glass sliding doors opened onto the roof terrace.*

VERBS + door

open the door *I opened the door and Dad was standing there.*

close/shut the door *Can you close the door as you go out?*

slam/bang the door (=shut it noisily) *He strode out of the room, slamming the door behind him.*

knock on/at the door *Who's that knocking at the door?*

bang/hammer on the door (=hit it very loudly and urgently) *We banged on the door but no one answered.*

answer the door (*also* **get the door** *informal*): *Lucy ran downstairs to answer the door.*

lock/unlock the door *I locked the door and turned out the lights.*

bolt the door (=slide a metal bar across to fasten it) *She locks and bolts the front door at night.*

door + VERBS

a door opens *We were still waiting for the train doors to open.*

a door closes/shuts *The door closed behind him with a bang.*

a door slams/bangs (=shuts loudly) *I heard the front door slam.*

a door flies/bursts open (=opens very suddenly and quickly) *Suddenly the door burst open and two men pushed their way in.*

a door swings open/shut (=moves forward to open or backwards to shut) *The door swung shut behind me.*
a door slides open/shut (=moves smoothly to the side or back again) *The lift doors slid open and we got in.*
a door leads somewhere *The kitchen door leads into the garden.*

door + NOUNS
a door handle (=that you move up or down to open a door) *Ella reached for the door handle.*
a door key *She was looking in her bag for her door key.*
a door knocker (=a metal object on a door that you use to knock with) *There was a brass door knocker in the shape of a lion's head.*

> **Doorbell**, **doormat**, and **doorknob** (= a round object that you turn to open a door) are usually written as one word. **Doorstep** is always written as one word.

PHRASES
the key to a door *I've lost the key to the back door.*

dose *n*
an amount of a medicine or a drug that someone takes or should take

ADJECTIVES
a high/large/massive dose *High doses of the drug can have bad side effects.*
a low/small dose *You should only take the drug in small doses.*
a daily dose *The study shows that a daily dose of aspirin may reduce the risk of heart disease.*
the recommended dose *The recommended dose is 250 mg a day.*
a lethal/fatal dose (=an amount that kills you) *He died after taking a lethal dose of painkillers.*
a single dose *The medicine is given as a single dose.*

VERBS
take a dose of sth *He had taken his usual dose of sleeping pills.*
give sb a dose of sth *A nurse came in to give me a dose of antibiotics.*
exceed the dose (=take more than you should) *You should take care not to exceed the recommended dose of paracetamol.*
increase/reduce the dose *He was in a lot of pain, and doctors decided to increase the dose of morphine.*
prescribe a dose (=a doctor says that someone should have an amount of a drug) *The doctor prescribed a higher dose of the drug.*

PREPOSITIONS
a dose of sth *She was given another dose of painkillers.*

doubt[1] *v*
to think that something may not be true or that it is unlikely

ADVERBS
doubt sth very much *"Do you think you will ever go back there again?" "I doubt that very much."*
seriously doubt (=doubt something very much) *I seriously doubt that such a meeting would take place in the near future.*

PHRASES
I doubt it (=I don't think so) *"Do you think there'll be any tickets left?" "I doubt it."*
I never doubted sth (for one minute) (=you were completely sure about it) *I never doubted for one minute that we would win.*

doubt[2] *n*
a feeling of being not sure about something

ADJECTIVES
serious/grave doubts *They have some serious doubts as to his honesty.*
considerable doubts *He had considerable doubts about accepting the job.*
a lingering/nagging doubt (=that does not go away) *I still had a nagging doubt that there might be something seriously wrong.*
growing/increasing doubts *There have been growing doubts about the accuracy of the test results.*

VERBS
have doubts (*also* **harbour doubts** *formal*): *Scientists still have some doubts about the theory.*
feel doubt *He felt some doubt about whether the treatment would work.*
express/voice doubts (=say that you have doubts) *Many people expressed doubts about the necessity of the war.*
raise doubts (=make people unsure about something) *The disaster raised doubts about the safety of nuclear power.*
cast/throw doubt on sth (=make people unsure about something) *Research has cast doubt on the safety of mobile phones.*

PREPOSITIONS
doubt about sth *There is no doubt about what he wants.*
doubt over sth *There are continuing doubts over his fitness.*
doubt as to sth *Some government ministers had serious doubts as to whether the policy would work.*
in doubt (=not sure) *If in doubt, ask your teacher.*
without doubt *She is, without doubt, the most beautiful woman I have ever seen.*
beyond doubt (=definitely) *The test proved beyond doubt that Paul was her father.*

PHRASES

have no/little doubt (=be completely sure) *I have no doubt that you are right.*

be in no doubt/not be in any doubt (=be completely sure) *The government is in no doubt about the seriousness of the situation.*

leave no/little doubt (=make people sure or almost sure about something) *The evidence left no doubt that he was the murderer.*

there is no/little/some doubt (=used to talk about how sure people are about something) *There is little doubt that he will play for England one day.*

without/beyond a shadow of a doubt (=without any doubt) *I knew without a shadow of a doubt that I was going to win.*

not the slightest doubt (=no doubt at all) *There's not the slightest doubt in my mind about it.*

an element of doubt (=a slight doubt) *There's an element of doubt about his true age as he doesn't have a birth certificate.*

downfall *n*

a complete failure or the complete loss of money, position, power etc

ADJECTIVES

the ultimate/eventual downfall of sb/sth *There were various causes which led to the eventual downfall of the Roman Empire.*

the inevitable downfall of sb/sth *The economic crisis resulted in the inevitable downfall of the government.*

VERBS

lead to/cause sb's downfall *The scandal led to the president's downfall.*

sth is sb's downfall (=it causes someone's downfall) *Gambling was his downfall.*

prove (to be) sb's downfall (=eventually cause it) *An addiction to alcohol proved to be her downfall.*

contribute to sb's downfall (=help to cause it) *Several factors contributed to his downfall.*

plot sb's downfall (=plan it) *He plotted the downfall of his hated rival.*

sb's downfall comes *Her downfall came through being overconfident.*

download *v*

to get something from the internet or a computer system and put it onto your computer, phone etc

NOUNS

download music/a song/a film/a game etc *He often downloads films onto his computer.*

download software/a program/a file etc *You can download the software for free.*

PREPOSITIONS

download sth from sth/off sth *I downloaded the camera software from the internet.*

download sth to sth *A salesman can write an order and download it to his company's main computer at the end of the day.*

download sth onto sth *I downloaded the songs onto my phone so I could listen to them on the train.*

drab *adj* THESAURUS **depressing**

draft Ac *n*

a piece of writing or a plan that is not yet in its finished form

ADJECTIVES

the first/second etc draft *The second draft of the agreement contained a few important changes.*

the final draft (=the finished form) *All parties eventually approved the final draft of the peace treaty.*

a rough draft (=not the finished form) *Could you let me see a rough draft of your report?*

the original draft (=the first one) *The hero had a different name in the original draft of the story.*

an early/earlier draft (=written before others) *In earlier drafts of the speech, he criticized the pace of political progress.*

a preliminary draft (=coming before others) *A preliminary draft of the charter has been issued.*

a revised draft (=changed from an earlier form) *The US circulated a revised draft last week.*

VERBS

write/draw up/prepare a draft *Always write a rough draft of your essay first.*

approve a draft (=officially accept one) *The draft was approved by the Senate.*

draft + NOUNS

a draft proposal *The committee was discussing draft proposals to restructure the organization.*

drama Ac *n*

a play or a film that tells a dramatic story, usually a serious one

ADJECTIVES/NOUNS + drama

a TV/television/radio drama *The book has been made into a television drama.*

a romantic drama *The film is a romantic drama about two young people who fall in love.*

a comedy drama *There is a new comedy drama on TV.*

a historical drama *She starred in a historical drama about Marie Antoinette.*

a costume drama (=about events in history, in which people wear costumes from that time) *The series is a costume drama set in Victorian England.*

a medical/hospital drama *He played a doctor in the US medical drama 'ER'.*

a courtroom drama *Perry Mason was the hero of 82 courtroom dramas.*

D

a crime drama *'American Gangster' is a crime drama set in 1970s New York.*
a police drama *'The Bill' was a popular police drama.*
a powerful drama (=having a strong emotional effect on viewers) *'Scum' was a powerful drama about the treatment of young prisoners.*

VERBS

write/produce a drama *He has written a new drama about life in prison.*
a drama is set in sth (=it happens in a particular place or time) *'Washington Square' is a drama set in the 1850s.*

drama + NOUNS

a drama series/serial *The show is one of the longest-running drama series on Japanese television.*

PREPOSITIONS

a drama about sth *He is starring in a new drama about prison life.*

D

draught *n* THESAURUS wind

draughty *adj* THESAURUS cold[1]

draw *v*

to produce a picture, pattern etc using a pen or pencil

NOUNS

draw a picture *Can you draw a picture of a cat?*
draw a map/graph/diagram *Keith was drawing a complicated-looking graph.*
draw a sketch *She drew a sketch of how she wanted the room to look.*
draw a circle/line etc *The teacher drew a circle on the blackboard.*

THESAURUS: draw

shut, slam, draw, lock, seal → **close[1] (1)**

drawback *n*

a disadvantage of a situation, plan, product etc

ADJECTIVES

the main/major/biggest drawback *One of the major drawbacks of being famous is the lack of privacy.*
the only/one drawback *It's a good-looking car – the only drawback is the price.*
a slight drawback *A slight drawback with this phone is that the keyboard is a bit small.*
a serious drawback *A serious drawback to solar energy is that it's only available to us for a certain number of hours per day.*
a real drawback *I can't think of any real drawbacks.*
the obvious drawback *The obvious drawback of this method is that it takes a long time.*
a possible drawback *I think we've considered all the possible drawbacks.*

VERBS

have a drawback *This approach has a number of drawbacks.*
suffer from a drawback *The car suffers from one major drawback: there is not enough luggage space.*
overcome a drawback *In order to overcome this drawback, we would like to make the following suggestion.*

drawer *n*

part of a piece of furniture, such as a desk, that you pull out and push in and use to keep things in

ADJECTIVES/NOUNS + drawer

the top/bottom/middle drawer *He opened the bottom drawer and got out a T-shirt.*
a desk/table etc drawer *The passports are in my desk drawer.*
the kitchen drawer (=in a piece of kitchen furniture) *There's some string in the kitchen drawer.*

VERBS

open a drawer *Jonathan opened the drawer and took out a fork.*
close/shut a drawer *She shut the drawer and locked it with a small key.*
go/look/search through drawers (=look in drawers for something) *I've gone through all the drawers and I can't find it.*
rummage/rifle through drawers (=search in them by moving things around in an untidy way) *Someone had been in my bedroom and rummaged through the drawers.*

PREPOSITIONS

in a drawer *You can put the papers in that drawer.*

drawing *n*

a picture that you draw with a pencil, pen etc

VERBS

do a drawing *Sammy was doing a drawing of his sister.*
make a drawing *In ancient times, people made drawings of animals on cave walls.*
a drawing shows sth *The drawing showed a castle surrounded by woods.*

Do or make a drawing?

Do is more common than **make**. **Make** sounds more formal.

ADJECTIVES/NOUNS + drawing

a pencil/ink/charcoal etc drawing *I like to do a few pencil drawings when I travel anywhere.*
a detailed drawing *He made detailed drawings of plants and flowers.*
a scale drawing (=showing the correct relative

sizes of things) *The architect made a scale drawing of the new room.*

PREPOSITIONS

a drawing of sth/sb *I did a drawing of the front of the house.*

dream *n*

1 thoughts, images, and feelings you experience when you are asleep

ADJECTIVES

a bad dream (=unpleasant or frightening) *The movie gave the kids bad dreams.*

a strange/weird dream *Sometimes I have a strange dream in which I try to speak but I can't.*

a vivid dream (=very clear) *The dream was so vivid I thought it was real.*

a recurring/recurrent dream (=that you have many times) *I have a recurring dream that I'm trying to escape from somewhere.*

VERBS

have a dream *I had a dream about you last night.*

wake from a dream (*also* **awake from a dream** *formal*): *Suddenly she awoke from her dream.*

remember a dream *It's hard to remember your dreams if you don't write them down.*

PREPOSITIONS

a dream about sth *I often have this dream about falling down the stairs.*

in a dream *In my dream I flew to a forest of enormous trees.*

PHRASES

be/seem like a dream (=seem unreal) *That summer was so wonderful it seemed like a dream.*

Sweet dreams! (=said to someone who is going to bed) *Good night, Sam! Sweet dreams!*

2 something that you want very much

ADJECTIVES/NOUNS + dream

big/great dreams (=a wish to achieve great things) *She was a little girl with big dreams.*

an impossible dream (=about something that cannot happen) *Having a number one record had seemed an impossible dream.*

a childhood dream (=that you had when you were a child) *I had a childhood dream of becoming an actor.*

a lifelong dream (=that you have had all your life) *His lifelong dream had been to write a novel.*

a distant dream (=that it will take a long time to achieve) *Peace in this area may still be a distant dream.*

VERBS

have a dream/dreams *I had dreams of becoming a doctor.*

sb's dream is to do sth *Her dream is to make a movie.*

achieve/fulfil/realize a dream (=do or get what you want) *He had finally achieved his dream of winning an Olympic gold medal.*

live the dream (=be as famous or successful as you have always wanted to be) *I'm living the dream, and I don't want it to ever end.*

pursue/follow a dream (=try to do or get what you want) *She left her home town to pursue her dreams.*

shatter sb's dreams (=end someone's hopes of doing or getting what they want) *Injury shattered his dreams of being able to play in the World Cup final.*

dream + NOUNS

a dream home/holiday/job etc (=one you would very much like to have) *Here's how you can win a dream kitchen.*

a dream world *You're living in a dream world if you think this is going to work.*

PREPOSITIONS

dreams of sth *She had dreams of going to university.*

PHRASES

a dream comes true (=something you want happens) *I'd always wanted to go to Africa and at last my dream came true.*

the man/woman/house etc of your dreams (=the perfect one for you) *We can help you find the house of your dreams.*

beyond your wildest dreams (=better or more than you ever hoped for) *Suddenly he was wealthy beyond his wildest dreams.*

never/not in your wildest dreams (=used to say that you had never expected something to happen) *Never in my wildest dreams did I think I would win the competition.*

dreary *adj* THESAURUS ▸ **depressing**

drenched *adj* THESAURUS ▸ **wet[1] (1)**

dress[1] *v*

to put clothes on yourself or someone else

> **Grammar**
>
> In everyday spoken English, you usually say **get dressed**: *I **got dressed** and went down for breakfast.* **Dress** on its own sounds more formal, and is mainly used in written descriptions: *That evening, Julia **dressed** for dinner with unusual care.*
>
> You also **dress** children and other people who cannot put on their own clothes: *I usually have to **dress** the kids in the mornings.*

ADVERBS

dress quickly/hurriedly *She quickly got dressed and went out of the house.*

D

dress² *n*

1 a piece of clothing worn by a woman or girl that covers the top of her body and part or all of her legs

ADJECTIVES/NOUNS + dress

a beautiful/pretty dress *That's a pretty dress you're wearing!*

a silk/cotton/velvet etc dress *Ellie chose a green silk dress.*

a long/short dress *Most of the women were wearing long dresses.*

a wedding dress *Have you chosen your wedding dress yet?*

an evening dress (=a formal dress to wear in the evening) *She arrived in a red evening dress.*

a cocktail dress (=a formal dress which is not usually very long) *She wore a little black cocktail dress.*

a party dress *I need a new party dress for Christmas.*

a summer dress *The weather wasn't warm enough for a summer dress.*

VERBS

wear a dress *Sheila wore a long red dress.*

make a dress *She has made dresses for the Queen.*

design a dress *The dress was designed by Vera Wang.*

PREPOSITIONS

in a dress (=wearing a dress) *Who's that woman in the green dress?*

THESAURUS: dress

clothing, garment, dress, wear, gear, wardrobe → clothes

2 clothes of a particular type or for a particular occasion

Grammar

Always uncountable in this meaning.

ADJECTIVES/NOUNS + dress

evening dress (=formal clothes for an important social event) *Everyone was in evening dress.*

formal dress *This kind of formal dress is worn at very traditional weddings.*

casual dress (=not formal) *Casual dress is now acceptable in many British workplaces.*

traditional dress *Women in traditional Tibetan dress lined the streets.*

modern dress *They performed Shakespeare plays in modern dress.*

fancy dress *BrE* (=clothes that you wear for fun, which make you look like someone else or like an animal or object) *Party guests have been asked to wear fancy dress.*

military dress *The prince often wears military dress.*

dress + NOUNS

a dress code (=a standard of what people must wear) *The school has a strict dress code.*

PREPOSITIONS

in ... dress *The dancers were in traditional dress.*

PHRASES

full evening dress/full military dress etc (=completely dressed in evening clothes, military clothes etc) *The others were all wearing full evening dress.*

dressed *adj*

having your clothes on or wearing a particular type of clothes

ADVERBS

well-dressed (=wearing nice clothes of good quality) *The restaurant is full of well-dressed couples.*

smartly/neatly dressed *There was a smartly dressed man with a briefcase at the door.*

immaculately/impeccably dressed (=perfectly dressed in smart clothes) *He was immaculately dressed in a grey suit and a blue tie.*

fashionably dressed *Most teenagers want to be fashionably dressed.*

elegantly/beautifully dressed *Even in her eighties, my grandmother was always elegantly dressed.*

fully dressed (=with all your clothes on) *She was so tired that she went to bed fully dressed.*

half dressed (=not having finished putting your clothes on) *Don't come in – I'm only half dressed!*

casually dressed (=wearing informal clothes) *Luke was casually dressed in jeans and a T-shirt.*

properly/suitably/appropriately dressed (=wearing suitable clothes for something) *It's important to be properly dressed when walking in the mountains.*

badly dressed (=not well dressed) *The prime minister has been criticized for being badly dressed.*

PREPOSITIONS

be dressed in jeans/shorts/a suit etc *She was dressed in a skirt and jacket.*

dressed as sb/sth *The children came to the party dressed as pirates.*

drift *v*

to move slowly from one place or condition to another

NOUNS

a boat drifts *A boat had come loose and was drifting down the river.*

cloud/smoke/mist drifts *Cloud drifted across the sky.*

a sound/sb's voice drifts *Joe's voice drifted to where we were standing.*

a smell drifts *The smell of freshly baked bread drifted into the room.*

sb's gaze drifts/sb's eyes drift *His gaze drifted to the wedding ring on her finger.*

sb's mind drifts/sb's thoughts drift (=start thinking about other things) *The meeting was rather boring and her mind started to drift.*

ADVERBS

drift slowly *The boat drifted slowly down the river.*

drift aimlessly (=do one thing after another, without any definite purpose) *Some people drift aimlessly through life without knowing what they really want to do.*

drift apart (=gradually end your relationship) *Some couples get bored with each other and slowly drift apart.*

drink[1] *v*

1 to take liquid into your mouth and swallow it

NOUNS

drink some water/coffee/beer etc *You should drink plenty of water.*

drink a glass/bottle of sth *He drank another glass of orange juice.*

PREPOSITIONS/ADVERBS

drink sth quickly/slowly *She drank her tea slowly because it was hot.*

drink sth down/up (=finish your drink) *Drink up your coffee – it's time to go.*

drink out of/from sth *We had to drink out of plastic cups.*

PHRASES

something to drink *Take a seat while I get you something to drink.*

2 to drink alcohol

ADVERBS

drink heavily/excessively (=drink a lot of alcohol often) *After his wife left him, he started drinking heavily.*

drink sensibly/in moderation (=not drink too much) *The advertisement warns people to drink sensibly.*

drink too much *Don't drink too much at the party!*

PHRASES

drink like a fish *informal* (=often drink a lot of alcohol) *She drinks like a fish – she says it helps her to relax.*

drink and drive *We all know the dangers of drinking and driving.*

sb can drink sb under the table *informal* (=someone can drink much more than another person without getting drunk) *My sister can drink me under the table anytime.*

sb has had too much to drink *The man had had too much to drink and he couldn't walk in a straight line.*

binge drinking (=drinking a lot of alcohol in a short time, so that you get very drunk) *Binge drinking is a problem among students.*

drink[2] *n*

liquid that you drink, or the act of drinking something

ADJECTIVES

a hot/warm drink *Come inside and I'll make you a hot drink.*

a cool/cold drink *You can relax by the pool with a nice cool drink.*

a soft drink (*also* **a non-alcoholic drink** *formal*) (=one that does not contain alcohol) *I'm driving, so I had better have a soft drink.*

an alcoholic drink (=one that contains alcohol) *Beer, wine, and other alcoholic drinks will be available.*

a fizzy drink *BrE*, **a carbonated drink** *especially AmE* (=with bubbles of gas) *Fizzy drinks are bad for children's teeth.*

a refreshing drink (=making you feel less tired or hot) *You can enjoy a refreshing drink in our lakeside café.*

strong drink (=strong alcohol) *His breath smelled of tobacco and strong drink.*

a stiff drink (=a glass of strong alcohol) *He needed a stiff drink to calm himself down.*

a quick drink (=one or two drinks in a pub or bar) *Why don't we go for a quick drink after work?*

a quiet drink (=alone or with a small group of people) *We went for a quiet drink, just the two of us.*

a farewell drink (=in order to say goodbye to someone) *When someone leaves the company, they usually organize a farewell drink.*

VERBS

have a drink *Can I have a drink of water?*

take a drink *She took a drink of her coffee.*

pour (sb) a drink *She got out two glasses and poured us a drink.*

make (sb) a drink *Shall I make you a hot drink?*

buy/get sb a drink *It's my turn to buy you a drink.*

go for a drink (=go to a bar or pub for an alcoholic drink) *Why don't we go for a drink after work?*

sip your drink (=drink it in very small amounts) *Connie was sitting at the table, sipping her drink slowly.*

spill sb's drink *He split his drink all over the floor.*

spike sb's drink (=secretly add alcohol or a drug to it) *She suspects that someone spiked her drink.*

drink + NOUNS

a drink problem *BrE* (=when someone often drinks too much alcohol) *Their marriage ended because of her husband's drink problem.*

drink driving *BrE* (=driving after having drunk too much alcohol) *He was arrested for drink driving.*

a drinks cabinet *She took a bottle of whisky out of the drinks cabinet.*

PREPOSITIONS

a drink of sth *Would you like another a drink of coffee?*

PHRASES

sb has had a few drinks (=someone has been drinking alcohol) *He looked like he had had a few drinks.*

the drinks are on sb (=used when saying that someone will pay for the drinks) *I've just got my bonus, so the drinks are on me!*

D

drinker *n* someone who drinks something

ADJECTIVES/NOUNS + drinker

a heavy drinker (*also* **a big drinker** *informal*) (=someone who drinks a lot of alcohol) *Journalists are often heavy drinkers.*

a hard drinker (=someone who drinks a lot of strong alcohol such as whisky or brandy) *He had a reputation for being a hard drinker.*

a moderate drinker (=someone who does not drink too much alcohol) *Moderate drinkers have a lower chance of heart trouble than heavy drinkers.*

a coffee/beer/wine etc drinker *The company varies its instant coffee to suit the tastes of coffee drinkers in different countries.*

drive¹ *v*

1 to make a car move

ADVERBS

drive fast *She was driving too fast, and lost control of the car.*

drive slowly *Stevie drove slowly along the narrow streets.*

drive safely/carefully *Drive safely, and let me know when you've got home.*

drive dangerously *Teenage drivers are more likely to drive dangerously and go over the speed limit.*

drive recklessly (=badly and without caring that you might cause an accident) *The man who caused the accident admitted that he had been driving recklessly.*

drive erratically (=in a way that is not safe, for example because you do not drive in a straight line or you do not obey the traffic rules) *He was driving erratically and appeared to have been drinking.*

PHRASES

drink and drive (=drink alcohol and then drive) *It is against the law to drink and drive.*

2 to make someone or something get into a bad or extreme state, usually an emotional one

PHRASES

drive sb crazy/mad/insane *spoken* (*also* **drive sb nuts** *spoken informal*) (=make someone feel very annoyed) *The continuous noise was driving me crazy.*

drive sb crazy/wild (=make someone feel very excited) *The handsome singer is known for driving women wild.*

drive sb up the wall/round the bend/out of their mind *spoken informal* (=make someone feel very annoyed) *The sound of her voice drives me up the wall.*

drive sb to despair/desperation (=make someone feel despair) *Problems with debt have driven many people to despair.*

drive² *n* a journey in a car

ADJECTIVES

a long/short drive *It's only a short drive to the airport.*

an easy drive *The town isn't far – it's an easy drive.*

a five-hour drive/20-minute drive *I was very tired after our five-hour drive.*

an hour's drive *The nearest hospital is an hour's drive from here.*

a pleasant drive *It takes longer along the coast road, but it's a pleasant drive.*

VERBS

go for a drive/take a drive *Let's go for a drive along the coast.*

take sb for a drive *Taylor took me for a drive through the town.*

driver *n*

someone who drives a car, bus etc

ADJECTIVES

a good driver *He thinks he's a very good driver.*

a careful/safe driver *Since I had the accident, I'm a much more careful driver.*

a bad driver *There are a lot of bad drivers on the roads.*

a dangerous/reckless driver *Some young men tend to be dangerous drivers.*

a reckless driver (=dangerous and taking risks) *Reckless drivers should be given more severe punishments.*

a drunk driver *Her husband was killed by a drunk driver.*

a hit-and-run driver (=a driver who hits someone and does not stop) *The boy was in hospital after being knocked down by a hit-and-run driver.*

an experienced/inexperienced driver *Young drivers are much more likely to have accidents than experienced drivers.*

NOUNS + driver

a taxi/bus/truck/car driver *Car drivers will have to pay a charge to enter the city.*

a racing driver *He wanted to be a world famous racing driver like Lewis Hamilton.*

a delivery driver (=delivering goods to a place) *He's a delivery driver for a pizza takeaway restaurant.*

a learner driver *BrE* (=who is learning to drive) *Learner drivers spend a lot of money on driving lessons.*

driver + NOUNS

a driver's license *AmE: The police officer asked to see his driver's license.*

driver error (=when a driver makes a mistake) *Most road accidents are caused by driver error.*

driver fatigue (=when a driver is tired) *Motorists need to be warned about the dangers of driver fatigue.*

driving *n*

the activity of driving a car or truck

driving + NOUNS

driving conditions *Icy roads have made driving conditions dangerous.*

a driving lesson *Jane is having driving lessons.*

a driving test *He passed his driving test first time.*

a driving instructor *It's important to feel comfortable with your driving instructor.*

a driving licence *BrE: When hiring a car, you must bring your driving licence.*

a driving ban *After the accident he faced a three-year driving ban.*

a driving offence *He had to appear in court for a driving offence.*

ADJECTIVES/NOUNS + driving

careless/dangerous/reckless driving *He faces charges of reckless driving.*

bad driving *Accidents are often caused by bad driving.*

drink-driving *BrE* (=the offence of driving after drinking too much alcohol) *Len was convicted on a charge of drink-driving.*

VERBS

go driving *We went driving in the mountains.*

be banned/disqualified from driving (=not be allowed to drive any more as a punishment) *If you are caught speeding, you could be banned from driving.*

drop[1] *v*

1 to fall to a lower level or amount

ADVERBS

drop sharply/dramatically (=suddenly and by a large amount) *Figures showed that inflation had dropped sharply.*

drop significantly (=by a large and noticeable amount) *The number of refugees arriving has dropped significantly.*

drop rapidly *The temperature drops rapidly at night.*

drop steadily *Sales have been dropping steadily.*

drop slightly *Her blood pressure has dropped slightly with the new medication.*

PREPOSITIONS

drop by sth *The number of people attending church has dropped by 30%.*

drop below sth *Temperatures regularly drop below zero during the winter.*

drop from sth to sth *In this national park, the rhino population has dropped from 150 to 16.*

2 to stop doing something, discussing something, or continuing with something

NOUNS

drop the charges/a case (=stop a legal process against someone) *Both men have been released and the charges have been dropped.*

drop the subject/matter (=stop talking about it) *I think we've said enough – can we drop the subject?*

drop a subject (=stop studying it at school or university) *Students may choose to drop a subject in their second year.*

drop a plan/scheme/proposal *The company has dropped its plan to build a hotel on the site.*

drop a demand *They agreed to drop demands for compensation.*

drop the idea *The project was going to be too expensive so the idea was dropped.*

drop everything (=completely stop everything you are doing) *When my mother was sick, I dropped everything and flew to be with her in Seattle.*

ADVERBS

quietly drop sth (=in a way that does not attract attention) *The proposal was quietly dropped earlier this year.*

PHRASES

let sth drop (=agree not to talk about something any more) *"What about the money?" "We've agreed to let it drop."*

drop[2] *n* THESAURUS ▸ **piece**

drought *n*

a long period of dry weather when there is not enough water for plants and animals to live

ADJECTIVES

the worst drought *Australia suffered the worst drought in its history.*

a severe drought *A severe drought has caused most of the corn crop to fail.*

a prolonged drought (=continuing for an unusually long time) *This part of Africa has been hit by a prolonged drought.*

D

the summer drought *The summer drought is threatening Britain's fruit and vegetable crops.*

VERBS

experience/suffer a drought *The country experienced its worst drought this century.*
be affected by drought/be hit by drought *The area has been severely affected by drought.*

drought + NOUNS

drought conditions *Drought conditions have spread to nearly all of the country.*

PHRASES

a period of drought *Some trees survive long periods of drought by storing water internally.*

drug *n*

1 a medicine

ADJECTIVES/NOUNS + drug

a strong/powerful drug *Morphine is a very powerful drug.*
a miracle/wonder drug (=a very effective drug that cures a serious disease) *When penicillin first appeared, it was seen as a miracle drug.*
a life-saving drug *People are being denied life-saving drugs because they don't have enough money.*
a pain-killing drug *A pain-killing drug was injected into the man's leg.*
a prescription drug (=that you can only have if a doctor writes an official note for it) *Not everyone can afford the cost of prescription drugs.*
an over-the-counter drug (=which is available without special permission from a doctor) *Some over-the-counter drugs can have serious side effects.*
a performance-enhancing drug (=taken by a sportsperson to make them perform better) *Seven of the twelve winners tested positive for performance-enhancing drugs.*

VERBS

take a drug *There are certain drugs you should not take when you are pregnant.*
give (sb) a drug *They gave him all sorts of drugs.*
prescribe a drug (=a doctor writes an official note saying that someone can receive it) *Doctors won't prescribe drugs if you don't need them.*
test a drug (*also* **trial a drug** *BrE*): *They tested the drug for five years before using it on humans.*

drug + NOUNS

a drug company *The big drug companies make huge profits.*

PREPOSITIONS

a drug for sth *There's a new drug for breast cancer.*
a drug against sth *Some drugs against the disease have strong side effects.*

PHRASES

be on a drug (=be taking it regularly) *How long have you been on this drug?*
a drug is used to treat sb/sth *The drug is used to treat heart disease.*
the side-effects of a drug (=the bad effects it can have) *One of the side effects of the drug is headaches.*

2 an illegal substance such as marijuana or cocaine

PHRASES

be on drugs (=take drugs regularly) *Sometimes she looks as though she's on drugs.*
be addicted to drugs (=be unable to stop taking drugs) *People who are addicted to drugs need help.*
come off/get off drugs (=stop taking drugs permanently) *It was years before I was able to come off drugs.*
be high on drugs (*also* **be under the influence of drugs** *formal*) (=be experiencing the effects of a drug) *He was high on drugs when he was arrested.*
the war on drugs (=a long struggle by the authorities to control drugs) *The war on drugs continues.*

VERBS

take/use drugs (*also* **do drugs** *informal*): *When did he start taking drugs?*
experiment with drugs (=try taking drugs) *She admitted that she had experimented with drugs.*
smuggle drugs (=take drugs illegally from one country to another) *She was caught trying to smuggle drugs into the country.*
seize drugs (=take possession of drugs) *The police seized drugs worth over £1 million.*

drug + NOUNS

drug abuse (=taking illegal drugs) *She is being treated for drug abuse.*
drug addiction (=the problem of not being able to stop taking drugs) *He wrote a book about his struggle with drug addiction.*
a drug addict (=someone who cannot stop taking drugs) *He is a former drug addict who has been in prison twice.*
a drug user (=someone who takes drugs) *We set up a counselling service for drug users.*
a drug problem/habit (=the problem of being addicted to drugs) *His daughter has a drug problem.*
a drug overdose (=taking too much of a drug at one time) *She died from a drug overdose.*
a drug dealer/pusher (=someone who sells drugs) *The city's streets are full of drug dealers.*
drug trafficking/smuggling (=the crime of bringing drugs into a country) *The maximum penalty for drug smuggling was 25 years in jail.*
a drug trafficker/smuggler (=someone involved in bringing drugs into a country) *US*

efforts against drug traffickers are beginning to work.

the drug trade *The international drug trade is worth billions of dollars.*

a drug test *She was banned from the Olympics after failing a drug test.*

ADJECTIVES

illegal drugs *A lot of crime is connected to illegal drugs.*

hard drugs (*also* **class A drugs** *BrE*) (=strong drugs such as heroin, cocaine etc) *He was in prison for dealing hard drugs.*

soft drugs (=less strong drugs such as marijuana) *Soft drugs are legal in some countries.*

recreational drugs (=taken for pleasure) *Ecstasy was first used in Britain as a recreational drug in the 1980s.*

drunk *adj*

having drunk too much alcohol so that your behaviour and mental processes are affected

VERBS

get drunk *I just hope they don't get drunk and start fighting.*

get sb drunk (=deliberately try to make someone drunk) *She was trying to get him drunk.*

make sb drunk *The wine had made her drunk.*

feel drunk *I started to feel a bit drunk.*

look/sound drunk *Both men sounded drunk.*

ADVERBS

slightly drunk *He was slightly drunk and his face was pink.*

completely/very drunk *By 10 p.m., she was completely drunk and I had to take her home.*

roaring/blind drunk *informal* (=very drunk) *They were not just happy, they were roaring drunk.*

too drunk *She was too drunk to stand up.*

NOUNS

a drunk man/woman *We found a drunk man lying in a bush.*

a drunk driver *Their daughter had been killed by a drunk driver.*

drunk driving *He was arrested for drunk driving.*

> **Driving when drunk**
> You say that someone is arrested for **drink driving** (BrE) or **drunken driving** (AmE), or in official contexts **driving under the influence (of alcohol)**.

PHRASES

drunk and disorderly (=used in legal situations when someone is drunk and behaving badly) *She admitted two charges of being drunk and disorderly.*

THESAURUS: drunk

drunken *especially written*
stupor | **state** | **behaviour** | **rage** | **brawl** | **driving** | **rampage** | **party** | **night** | **man** | **soldier** | **sailor** | **yob** | **reveller**
drunk, or behaving in a way that shows you are drunk – usually used in the following phrases:
We found him lying by the roadside in a drunken stupor (=almost unconscious as a result of being drunk). | *She was injured during a drunken brawl outside a bar.* | *He was arrested for drunken driving* (=driving after you have drunk alcohol – used in American English). | *On New Year's Eve, the streets are full of drunken revellers* (=people who are enjoying themselves by getting drunk, especially in order to celebrate something).

> **Drunken** is always used before a noun. Don't say 'He is drunken.' Say **He is drunk.**

intoxicated *formal*
drunk – used especially in legal or official situations:
He was arrested for driving while intoxicated.

> **Intoxicated** is not usually used before a noun.

tipsy
slightly drunk:
After the second glass of wine I was ***feeling*** *a little* ***tipsy***. | *He* ***got*** *a bit* ***tipsy*** *and started saying some embarrassing things.*

dry *adj*

1 without any water or moisture

NOUNS

dry clothes *I need to change into some dry clothes.*

dry grass/leaves *There had been no rain and the grass was very dry.*

dry mouth/tongue/throat/lips *My mouth is getting dry – can I have a glass of water?*

> **Dry land** is used especially when someone has been on the sea or a river in a boat, and comes back onto the land: *It was good to get off the ship onto* ***dry land*** *again.*

VERBS

keep/stay dry *We managed to keep dry inside an old farm building.*

get dry (=become dry) *Come inside and get dry.*

shake/rub/wipe etc sth dry *He wiped his hands dry with a handkerchief.*

ADVERBS

completely dry *Don't put clothes away until they are completely dry.*

PHRASES

(as) dry as a bone/bone dry (=completely dry and with no moisture at all) *These plants need some water – the soil is as dry as a bone.*

a river runs dry (=it becomes dry) *The Yellow River has run dry twice in the last few years.*

THESAURUS: dry

arid
region | area | land | landscape | conditions | environment | climate | desert | plain | wastes
an arid region is extremely dry because it rarely rains, which makes it difficult to grow crops:
Scorpions are able to survive in some of the world's most arid regions. | The organism evolved in order to cope with the hot and arid conditions of the desert. | The people live in the arid wastes of the Tibetan plateau.

parched *literary*
throat | skin | lips | land | earth | soil | landscape | region
completely dry and needing water or rain: *Her throat was parched with thirst. | The earth was so parched that there were huge cracks in it.*

In informal English, you say *I'm* ***parched.*** when you are very thirsty.

ANTONYMS **dry → wet[1] (1)**

2 if the weather is dry, there is very little rain

NOUNS

dry weather *Water the rose bushes regularly in dry weather.*

a dry spell (=a period when there is no rain) *The country has enjoyed a long dry spell.*

a dry summer *Two dry summers in succession have caused low water levels.*

dry conditions *The plants prefer warm dry conditions.*

dry season (=period of the year in some countries when it never rains) *In many climates there are long dry seasons followed by long wet seasons.*

THESAURUS: dry

good, fine, nice, bright, beautiful/glorious, clear, cloudless, dry → **sunny**

ANTONYMS **dry → rainy**

3 not interesting

THESAURUS: dry

dull, tedious, monotonous, mundane, humdrum, dry, dreary → **boring**

dull *adj* THESAURUS ▸ **boring, cloudy**

dust[1] *n*

dry powder consisting of extremely small bits of dirt

PHRASES

be covered in dust *All the furniture was filthy and covered in dust.*

a layer of dust *I brushed away the thin layer of dust which covered the picture.*

a cloud of dust *A truck roared past, sending a large cloud of dust into the air.*

a particle of dust (*also* **a dust particle**) (=a small piece of dust) *The air is full of dust particles.*

a speck of dust (=a tiny piece of dust) *By the time I'd finished cleaning, there wasn't a speck of dust anywhere.*

VERBS

gather/collect dust (=become covered with dust – especially because something has not been used for a long time) *Piles of old books lay on the floor gathering dust.*

NOUNS + dust

house/household dust *Some people are allergic to house dust.*

coal/brick/chalk dust *There was brick dust everywhere while the building work was being done.*

dust[2] *v* THESAURUS ▸ **clean[2]**

dustbin *n BrE*

a large container for waste outside your house

VERBS

put sth in the dustbin *Don't put plastic bottles in the dustbin – recycle them!*

empty the dustbin *The dustbins are emptied once a week.*

NOUNS

a dustbin lid *When he took off the dustbin lid, a mouse jumped out.*

a dustbin man (=the men who take away the waste) *The dustbin men come on Thursdays.*

Dustbin is used in British English. American people say **garbage can**.

dusty *adj* THESAURUS ▸ **dirty**

duty *n*

1 something that you have to do because it is morally or legally right

VERBS

have a duty to do sth *Parents have a duty to make sure that their children receive an education.*

do your duty *I felt I had done my duty by voting.*

fulfil your duty *BrE*, **fulfill your duty** *AmE* *formal* (=do the things you are officially supposed to do) *The school has failed to fulfil its legal duty towards students.*

have/owe a duty to sb *A tenant owes a duty to the landlord to keep the house in reasonable condition.*

fail in your duty (=not do something that you should do) *I would be failing in my duty if I didn't warn you of the dangers.*

ADJECTIVES

a legal duty *Employers have a legal duty to ensure the safety of their workers.*

a moral duty *She felt it was her moral duty to care for her mother.*

a religious duty *For many Muslim women, covering their hair is a religious duty.*

a public duty *The media has a public duty to report the truth.*

a statutory duty (=according to the law) *Local authorities have a statutory duty to keep public parks clean.*

PHRASES

it is your duty to do sth *We feel it is our duty to help her.*

because of/out of a sense of duty *He visited them out of a sense of duty rather than love.*

be under a duty to do sth *formal* (=have a duty to do something) *The committee is under a duty to act fairly.*

be duty-bound to do sth (=have a duty to do something) *If you know a colleague is breaking the law, you are duty-bound to report it.*

2 something you have to do as part of your job

> **Grammar**
> Usually plural in this meaning.

VERBS

carry out your duties (*also* **perform/discharge your duties** *formal*) (=do your job) *She has always carried out her duties efficiently.*

take up your duties (=start doing a new job) *Neale has agreed a three-year contract and takes up his duties on March 1st.*

report for duty (=arrive and be ready to start work) *You must report for duty at 8.30 tomorrow morning.*

resume your duties (=start doing your job again) *She hopes to be well enough to resume her duties next week.*

neglect your duties (=not do your job properly) *They accused him of neglecting his duties as a parent.*

sb's duties include sth *John's duties included cleaning the cars.*

ADJECTIVES/NOUNS + duty

official duties *The new president will take up his official duties next month.*

household/domestic duties (=jobs you have to do around the house) *My husband and I share most of the household duties.*

light duties (=not involving hard physical work) *He'd been wounded, sent home, and put on light duties.*

guard duty *There were two soldiers on guard duty outside the embassy.*

PHRASES

beyond the call of duty (=more than you have to do as part of your job) *She's a doctor who has gone beyond the call of duty in her care for her patients.*

in the course of duty (=while doing your job, especially for your country) *Stewart received a medal for outstanding bravery in the course of duty.*

a tour of duty (=a period of working in another country as a soldier, government officer etc) *He became a General, and his tours of duty included Korea and Vietnam.*

dynamic *adj*

THESAURUS ▸ **energetic**

Ee

eager *adj* THESAURUS ▸ **enthusiastic**

ear *n*
one of the two parts on the side of your head that you use for hearing

ADJECTIVES

sb's left/right ear *She is deaf in her right ear.*
big/small ears *African elephants' ears are bigger than those of Indian elephants.*
long/short ears *Why do some dogs have long ears?*
floppy ears (=soft and hanging down loosely) *She brought out a rabbit with big floppy ears.*
pointy/pointed ears *The cat has short pointy ears.*
sb's inner/middle ear (=the parts inside your ear, which you use to hear sounds) *I've got an infection in my middle ear.*

VERBS

say/whisper sth into sb's ear *He whispered something into his wife's ear.*
cover your ears (=put your hands over your ears) *She covered her ears and said, "I'm not listening."*
have your ears pierced (=have a hole put into the skin, so that you can wear an earring) *I had my ears pierced when I was quite young.*
an animal pricks up its ears (=it makes them upright when listening carefully) *The horse pricked up its ears and set off in the direction of its master's voice.*
sb's ears stick out *If my hair is too short, you can see that my ears stick out.*
sb's ears pop (=the pressure in them changes suddenly, for example when you go up or down quickly in a plane) *My ears finally popped when the plane landed.*

ear + NOUNS

an ear infection *He's taking medicine for an ear infection.*

> **Earphones**, **earrings** (=jewellery that you wear on your ears), **earache**, **earlobe** (= the soft part at the bottom of your ear), and **eardrum** (= the part inside your ear that vibrates with sounds) are written as one word.

PREPOSITIONS

in your ear *It feels like there's something in my ear.*
behind your ears *She tucked her hair behind her ears.*

early *adj, adv*

1 arriving or happening before the usual or expected time

VERBS

arrive early/be early *Some of the guests arrived early.*
leave early *I had to leave early, so I missed the end of the party.*
be/get/come home early *Your father said he'd be home early.*
get up/wake up/be up early *Set the alarm for six - I have to be up early tomorrow.*
go to bed early *I think I'll go to bed early tonight.*

NOUNS

an early lunch/dinner *Let's have an early lunch before we go.*
an early night (=when you go to bed earlier than usual) *I need an early night because I'm tired.*
an early start (=when you have to get up earlier than usual in the morning) *I should go to bed. I've got an early start in the morning.*
early retirement *She took early retirement at the age of 52.*
sb's early death (=when someone is not very old) *The early death of her father at the age of 45 had a profound effect on her.*

PREPOSITIONS

early for sth *I arrived early for my appointment.*

PHRASES

five minutes/three hours etc early *The bus left five minutes early, and I missed it.*

ANTONYMS **early → late (1)**

2 in the first part of a period of time, event, or process

NOUNS

early morning/afternoon/evening *The lake looked beautiful in the early morning light.*
early spring/summer/autumn *The plants produce flowers in the early spring.*
early August/January etc *Italy is lovely in early June, before it gets too hot.*
the early days/weeks/months/years of sth *In the early years of our marriage, we lived with my wife's parents.*
the early 1870s/1920s etc (=1870-73, 1920-23 etc) *He lived in London in the early 1980s.*
the early 17th/20th etc century *She was born in the early 19th century.*
the early part of sth *I was doing quite well in the early part of the race.*
an early stage *His illness is at an early stage.*
sb's early childhood/life *We've known each other since early childhood.*

sb's earliest memory *One of my earliest memories is of sitting on the beach with my dad.*
sb's early work *The artist's early work focused on nature.*
an early sign *Chest pains can be an early sign of heart disease.*

PREPOSITIONS

early in sth *We set off early in the morning.*
in early May/June etc *They decided that the wedding would be on a Saturday in early July.*
in early 1998/2004 etc *We moved to Tokyo in early 2004.*
be in your early twenties/forties etc (=aged 20–23, 40–43 etc) *Both men are in their early twenties.*

PHRASES

at/from an early age *He played the piano from a very early age.*
as early as *The money could be paid as early as next week.*
early yesterday/today *Mike called me earlier today.*
these are (still) early days (=used when it is too soon to say what will happen) *We have made a lot of progress, but these are still early days.*

ANTONYMS **early → late (2)**

earn *v*

1 to receive a particular amount of money for the work that you do

NOUNS

earn money *I'd like to earn more money than I do now.*
earn a ... wage/salary *You are more likely to earn a decent wage if you have a degree.*
earn a living (*also* **earn your living**) (=earn the money you need to live) *She earns a living by giving music lessons.*
earn £30,000 a year/$200 a week/£5 an hour etc *Newly qualified teachers earn a minimum of £24,000 a year.*
earn good money *informal* (=earn a lot of money) *She was earning good money at the bank.*
earn a fortune *informal* (=earn an extremely large amount of money) *Footballers at the top clubs earn a fortune these days.*

THESAURUS: earn

receive, obtain, acquire, gain, win, earn, inherit, get hold of sth → **get (1)**

2 to get something as a result of your efforts – used especially when saying that someone deserves to get something

Grammar

In this meaning, **earn** is often used with **himself/herself**: *He had* ***earned himself*** *a reputation as a great artist.*

NOUNS

earn (sb) a reputation *The company has earned a reputation for excellent customer service.*
earn (sb) a nickname/title *Ray Charles's song-writing skills earned him the nickname of 'the Genius'.*
earn (sb's) respect/praise/admiration *He quickly earned the respect of his colleagues.*
earn (sb) the right to sth *I feel I've worked hard and have earned the right to a good pension.*
earn (sb) a place in sth *His performance earned him a place in the national team.*

PHRASES

well-earned *He is taking a well-earned rest from work.*
hard-earned *People spend a lot of their hard-earned money on holidays.*

earnings *n*

the money that you receive for the work that you do

ADJECTIVES/NOUNS + earnings

average earnings *Average earnings for teachers are around $70,000.*
hourly/weekly/monthly earnings *Some football players have weekly earnings of over £50,000.*
high earnings *Professional people pay more tax, because of their higher earnings.*
low earnings *The new government policy is designed to help people on low earnings.*
annual earnings *His annual earnings are over £1 million.*
future earnings *With serious injuries, the court may award substantial damages for loss of future earnings.*
gross earnings (=before tax has been paid) *You can usually borrow up to three times the value of your gross earnings per year.*
net earnings (=after tax has been paid) *The company's net earnings have fallen over the last two years.*
export earnings (=money a company earns by exporting goods or services) *Export earnings from oil bring valuable overseas currency into the country.*

PHRASES

loss of earnings *The insurance policy covers you for loss of earnings due to illness.*

THESAURUS: earnings

pay, wages, income, earnings, the money → **salary**

earring *n*

a piece of jewellery that you wear on your ear

PHRASES

a pair of earrings *She was wearing a pair of beautiful diamond earrings.*

VERBS

wear earrings *We are not allowed to wear earrings at school.*

put on/take off your earrings *I forgot to put on my new earrings.*

earth *n*

1 the planet that we live on

In this meaning **earth** is often used in the phrase **the Earth**, which is often spelled with a capital 'E'.

PHRASES

the Earth's surface *Over 70% of the Earth's surface is covered by ocean.*

the Earth's atmosphere *The Earth's atmosphere blocks off all radiation from space other than light and radio waves.*

the Earth's climate *The level of carbon dioxide in the atmosphere has an influence on the Earth's climate.*

the Earth's gravity *The continual pull of the Earth's gravity on the Moon has affected the way that it has evolved.*

the Earth's orbit (=a regular movement around it) *The rocket left the Earth's orbit and set off to Mars.*

the Earth's crust *Volcanoes and earthquakes occur where there is movement in the Earth's crust.*

the Earth's core (=the central part) *The Earth's inner core is almost entirely composed of iron.*

VERBS

the Earth orbits sth (=it moves around it) *The Earth orbits the Sun once a year, and the Moon orbits the Earth approximately every 27 days.*

sth orbits the Earth *A space satellite was orbiting the Earth.*

the Earth revolves/rotates *Because of the direction in which the Earth revolves, the Sun always rises in the east and sets in the west.*

fall to earth *The rocket fell back to earth.*

NOUNS + earth

planet Earth *I'm reading a book about the origin of life on planet Earth.*

PREPOSITIONS

on earth *Mount Everest is the highest mountain on earth.*

2 the substance that plants grow in

ADJECTIVES

wet/damp/moist earth *His feet were slipping on the damp earth.*

dry earth *She picked up a handful of the dry earth.*

bare earth (=not covered by trees or grass) *There were no flowers or grass in the yard, just bare earth.*

soft earth *The wheels got stuck in the soft earth.*

the earth is hard *It hadn't rained for weeks and the earth was hard.*

freshly dug earth *We planted seeds in the freshly dug earth.*

PHRASES

a mound of earth (=a pile of earth that looks like a small hill) *A mound of earth lay beside the grave.*

a clod/clump/lump of earth (=a piece of earth) *The horse's hooves kicked up great clods of earth.*

earthquake *n*

a sudden shaking of the Earth's surface that often causes a lot of damage

ADJECTIVES

a big/large/major earthquake *The city was hit by a big earthquake.*

a powerful/strong earthquake *A powerful earthquake shook the northwest of the country.*

a great/massive/huge earthquake *San Francisco was destroyed by the great earthquake of 1906.*

a small/minor earthquake *Minor earthquakes are relatively common.*

a devastating earthquake (=causing a lot of damage) *The whole town was flattened by a devastating earthquake.*

VERBS

an earthquake happens (*also* **an earthquake occurs** *formal*): *Scientists cannot predict when an earthquake will occur.*

an earthquake hits/strikes a place (=happens in a particular place) *A huge earthquake hit Japan in March 2011.*

an earthquake destroys/damages sth *The earthquake completely destroyed most of the town.*

an earthquake shakes sth *A powerful earthquake shook buildings across a large region of western Indonesia.*

earthquake + NOUNS

an earthquake zone *The city is in an earthquake zone.*

PHRASES

an earthquake measures 5/6.4 etc on the Richter scale *The earthquake, which measured 7.6 on the Richter scale, left more than 20,000 people homeless.*

the magnitude of an earthquake (=how powerful it is) *The magnitude of the earthquake was 5.8.*

the epicentre of an earthquake (=the exact place on the Earth's surface above where an earthquake begins) *The town was close to the epicentre of the earthquake.*

ease[1] *n*

if you do something with ease, you do it easily

PHRASES

with ease *He passed the test with ease.*

for ease of sth (=in order to make something easy) *The boxes can be fitted together for ease of storage.*

ADJECTIVES

with great/considerable ease (=very easily) *The car handles these mountain roads with great ease.*

with surprising ease *We were impressed by the surprising ease with which she completed the tasks.*

with relative/comparative ease (=seeming easy, especially considering how difficult something is) *Most modern laptops can store large amounts of data with relative ease.*

with apparent ease (=seeming easy, although this may not be the case) *I was amazed by the apparent ease with which the thieves got through the security system.*

with consummate ease *formal* (=in a way that shows great skill and so makes something difficult look very easy) *She defeated her opponent with consummate ease.*

with practised ease (=with great skill that comes from doing something many times) *He hits the ball with practised ease.*

ease[2] *v* THESAURUS **reduce**

east *adj, adv, n*

the direction from which the sun rises, or the part of a place that is in this direction

east + NOUNS

the east side/end *We live on the east side of the city.*

the east coast *There are some lovely beaches on the east coast.*

the east bank *The village of Skelton lies on the east bank of the River Ouse.*

an east wind (=a wind from the east) *The weather will be cold, with a bitter east wind.*

ADVERBS

further east *I had never been further east than Brooklyn.*

due east (=directly east) *The village lies about five miles due east of York.*

VERBS

go/travel/head east *They travelled east until they reached the border with Hungary.*

face east *The garden faces east.*

PREPOSITIONS

in the east *The sun rises in the east.*

to/towards the east *Berlin is 50 miles from here, to the east.*

from the east *The road enters the city from the east.*

the east of a place *The east of Australia has all the major cities.*

> **The East**
>
> When people talk about **the East**, they mean countries in Asia such as India and China. **The East** sounds exotic – a place with traditions and customs that are very different from **the West**.
>
> The **Far East** includes Japan, Korea, and China. The **Middle East** includes Egypt, Israel, Saudi Arabia, and Iran.

easy *adj*

not difficult to do, and not needing much effort or not causing any problems

NOUNS

an easy job/task (=often used in negative sentences) *Persuading John to come with us is not going to be an easy task.*

an easy question *All you have to do is answer a few easy questions and you could win a prize.*

an easy test/exam *The test was really easy and I got 100%.*

an easy solution/answer *It's a problem which has no easy solution.*

the easy way *The easiest way to reach the island is by boat.*

the easy option (=the easiest thing you can do) *It is human nature to take the easy option.*

an easy time/day *It is not an easy time to be looking for a job.*

an easy target (=one that is easy to attack) *The bird flies very slowly, which makes it an easy target for hunters.*

easy access *The town has easy access to London.*

an easy decision *Moving to a different country was not an easy decision for either of us.*

an easy life *I just wanted an easy life with no worries.*

an easy victory/win *The team had an easy victory on Saturday.*

ADVERBS

quite/fairly/pretty easy *It is fairly easy to create your own website.*

relatively/comparatively easy *The drug is relatively easy to produce.*

surprisingly/remarkably easy *He had a surprisingly easy victory over Federer.*

VERBS

find sth easy *I find it easy to talk to her.*

make sth easy *The software makes it easier to download music.*

look/sound easy *She makes dancing look so easy.*

become/get easier *The exercise is difficult but it does get easier with practice.*

PREPOSITIONS

easy for sb *It's easy for you – you're good at maths.*

PHRASES

it is easy to see/understand *It is easy to see why he is so popular.*

sth is easy to use/make/find *Good software should be easy to use.*

as easy as pie/as easy as ABC *informal* (=very easy) *It's as easy as pie to order from the website.*

nice and easy *I love spaghetti! It's so nice and easy to cook.*

THESAURUS: easy

simple
answer | question | explanation | instructions | thing | solution | way | method | system | terms | rules | idea | test
easy to understand or do, because there are no complicated words, processes, or actions involved:
I just want a simple answer – yes or no. | Patients need a simple explanation of how the disease is likely to affect them. | Vaccination is such a simple thing, and it can save many lives. | The simplest solution would be to cancel the event. | They developed a simple system for sending messages over long distances. | The guide explains in simple terms how to use the dictionary. | This book gives you plenty of simple ideas for healthy meals.

> **Simple or easy?**
> If something is **simple**, it is not complicated: *The book is written in* ***simple*** *language, which anyone can understand.* If something is **easy**, it is not difficult to do: *The program is very* ***easy*** *to use.*

straightforward
matter | task | approach | process | explanation | answer | question | case
easy to understand or do, and unlikely to cause you any problems:
Applying for a licence is a relatively straightforward matter. | The most straightforward approach is to ask the customer exactly what they want. | I asked a straightforward question, and I'd appreciate a straightforward answer. | When she explained how to fill in the form, it all sounded ***perfectly straightforward*** (=completely straightforward).

user-friendly
guide | computer | software | website | interface | product | car | camera | phone | feature
easy to use:
The book is a user-friendly guide to setting up your own business. | The company's website is now much more user-friendly. | Their products are designed to be user-friendly.

undemanding
job | role
easy because it does not take a lot of effort:
The job was undemanding, but it didn't pay very well. | It was an undemanding role for someone of his experience.

mindless
job | task
so easy that you can do it without thinking – used especially when it makes you feel bored:
I got a mindless job in a factory.

painless
without any difficulties or problems – used especially when you expected something to be much worse:
Finding the car hire place at the airport was ***relatively painless****. | There is no quick fix or painless solution to this problem.*

cushy *informal*
job
a cushy job is easy to do and needs very little effort – often used when you are envious of the person who has it:
It's a pretty cushy job – all she has to do is drive a nice car around. | He earns £5,000 a week for two days' work – most people would consider that a very ***cushy number*** (=a very easy job).

> **Other ways of saying that something is easy**
> There are many other ways of saying that something is **easy**. You can say that something is **plain sailing**, if there are no problems: *If you get the measurements right, the rest is* ***plain sailing****.* If something is not complicated to do, you can say that it is **not rocket science**: *Building a wind turbine is* ***not*** *exactly* ***rocket science****.* If something is surprisingly easy to do, you can say that it is **child's play**: *Woods makes the game look like* ***child's play****.* In informal English, if something is very easy, you can say that it is a **piece of cake**: *"How was the interview?" "It was* ***a piece of cake****."*

ANTONYMS **easy → difficult**

eat *v*

to put food in your mouth and chew and swallow it

NOUNS

eat food *Is your baby eating the right food?*

eat meat (=include it in your diet) *She doesn't eat meat, so I made her a tomato omelette.*

eat a healthy/balanced/vegetarian etc diet *It's important to eat a balanced diet.*

eat breakfast/lunch/dinner/supper *What time do you usually eat lunch?*

ADVERBS

eat well (=have enough food, or have good food) *The people work hard, but they eat well.*

eat healthily/sensibly *If you eat healthily and exercise regularly, you'll look and feel a lot better.*

eat properly *BrE*, **eat right** *AmE* (=eat food that will keep you healthy) *He hadn't been eating properly and looked very thin.* | *I exercise and eat right and get plenty of sleep.*

eat hungrily/ravenously (=eat a lot quickly, because you are very hungry) *The children ate hungrily, devouring everything on their plate.*

eat heartily (=eat a lot of food) *We ate heartily every evening.*

eat sparingly (=eat very little) *Carter joined us for lunch, but ate sparingly.*

PHRASES

something to eat *I'm sure you can get something to eat on the train.*

a bite to eat (=a small meal or snack) *We should have time for a bite to eat before we set out.*

nothing to eat *I've had nothing to eat all day.*

have enough/plenty to eat *Have you had enough to eat?*

go out to eat (=eat at a restaurant) *Would you like to go out to eat?*

eat like a horse (=eat a lot) *She eats like a horse but never puts on any weight.*

eat like a bird (=eat very little) *Ever since she was a child, Jan had always eaten like a bird.*

Eat or **have?**

You use **eat** when talking about having food in your mouth and biting or chewing it: *He was **eating** a banana.* You can use **eat** when talking about someone's diet: *She doesn't **eat** meat.* You can also use **eat** about the time when you eat: *We usually **eat** at about 1 o'clock.*

You use **have** when talking about eating a particular food for a meal: *We usually **have** porridge for breakfast.* | *I think I'll **have** a cheese sandwich.*

When talking about meals, it is more common to say **have breakfast/lunch/dinner**: *You must **have** lunch with us some time.*

eater *n*

used when talking about how much someone eats, or what kinds of things someone eats

ADJECTIVES

a big eater (=someone who usually eats large meals) *I'm not a very big eater.*

a good eater (=someone who eats plenty of food and is not difficult to please) *All her children were good eaters.*

a healthy eater (=someone who eats healthy food) *Do you think healthy eaters live longer?*

a picky/fussy eater (=someone who will only eat particular things, and is difficult to please) *My son's a very picky eater, and only eats bread and peanut butter.*

a messy eater (=someone who drops food and makes a mess when they eat) *He's a very messy eater – he leaves crumbs all over the floor.*

a noisy eater (=someone who makes unpleasant noises with their mouth as they eat) *I can't stand noisy eaters!*

a compulsive eater (=someone who cannot stop themselves eating too much) *Most compulsive eaters suffer from a range of psychological problems.*

NOUNS + eater

a meat eater (=a person or animal that eats meat) *I'm not a big meat eater, but I do like chicken.*

a plant/fruit eater (=an animal that only eats plants, fruit etc) *Most insects are plant eaters.*

eccentric *adj*

behaving in a way that is unusual and different from most people

ADVERBS

a little eccentric (*also* **a bit eccentric** *especially BrE*): *Aunt Nessy is a little eccentric and she keeps all her money under her bed.*

rather/somewhat eccentric *He has his own rather eccentric taste in furniture.*

highly eccentric *The writer has a highly eccentric view of the world.*

increasingly eccentric *His behaviour became increasingly eccentric and his family were worried about him.*

eccentric + NOUNS

eccentric behaviour/habits *He has a number of eccentric habits, including keeping cockroaches as pets.*

eccentric personality *Some Hollywood actors are known for their eccentric personalities.*

eccentric appearance *She was wearing an enormous straw hat, which added to her eccentric appearance.*

VERBS

consider sb/sth (to be) eccentric (=think that someone or something is eccentric) *In those days it was considered rather eccentric for a woman to be a farmer.*

regard sb/sth as eccentric (=think that someone or something is eccentric) *He always wore the same jacket and his colleagues regarded him as somewhat eccentric.*

E

THESAURUS: eccentric

mad, insane, eccentric → **crazy**

rare, exotic, exceptional, out of the ordinary, freak, unprecedented, unheard of, eccentric, unconventional, unorthodox → **unusual**

echo[1] *v*

if a sound echoes, it is repeated, especially because it hits a surface and comes back again

ADVERBS

echo faintly *Their voices echoed faintly in the distance.*

echo strangely/eerily *His words echoed eerily around the darkened room.*

echo back *The sound echoed back from the bottom of the well.*

PREPOSITIONS

echo around sth *The applause was still echoing around the auditorium.*

echo off sth *Her voice echoed off the walls of the cave.*

echo through sth *The sound echoed through the empty building.*

echo across sth *The call of the ducks echoed across the lake.*

echo[2] *n*

a sound that is repeated, especially because it hits a surface and comes back again

ADJECTIVES

a faint echo *I heard a faint echo from the other side of the cave.*

a distant echo *The distant echo of thunder came from the mountains.*

VERBS

an echo dies away/fades (=it disappears) *The echo of their voices slowly died away.*

an echo comes back *The echo came back from the bottom of the cave.*

send an echo *The sound of the explosion sent echoes around the valley.*

eclipse *n*

an occasion when the Sun or the Moon cannot be seen because of the position of the Earth

ADJECTIVES

a solar eclipse (=one in which the Sun is hidden behind the Moon) *You need to wear protective glasses to view a solar eclipse.*

a lunar eclipse (=one in which the Moon is hidden behind the Sun) *If it's cloudy, it may not be possible to see the lunar eclipse.*

a partial eclipse (=one in which the Sun or Moon is not completely hidden) *A partial eclipse of the Sun will occur on August 28th.*

a total eclipse (=one in which the Sun or Moon is completely hidden) *The best places to witness the Sun's total eclipse are in southern Africa and South America.*

PREPOSITIONS

an eclipse of the Sun/Moon *They were able to see a partial eclipse of the Moon.*

eco-friendly *adj* THESAURUS

environmentally friendly

economic Ac *adj*

relating to trade, industry, and the management of money

NOUNS

economic growth/development *We have enjoyed a period of steady economic growth.*

economic performance *The country's economic performance this year has been better than expected.*

the economic conditions/situation/climate *In the current economic climate, a lot of people are trying to save more and spend less.*

economic activity *This year we have seen an increase in economic activity.*

the economic system *There are fears that the country's whole economic system could collapse.*

economic policy/strategy *Controlling inflation is the main aim of the government's economic policy.*

economic reform *The government agreed to a programme of economic reform.*

economic problems *The country's continuing economic problems could lead to recession.*

an economic crisis *The economic crisis continues to worsen.*

an economic recovery *There are now signs of economic recovery in the region.*

an economic slowdown/downturn (=when the economy stops growing as quickly) *Experts are predicting an economic slowdown at the beginning of next year.*

the economic outlook (=future economic conditions) *Many experts are saying that the economic outlook is good.*

economical *adj* THESAURUS **cheap**

economy Ac *n*

the system by which a country's money and goods are produced, or a country considered in this way

ADJECTIVES/NOUNS + economy

a strong/powerful economy *The government's main aim is to build a strong economy.*

a big/large economy *Germany has one of the world's biggest economies.*

a booming economy (=extremely strong and successful) *What can we learn from China's booming economy?*

a weak/fragile/depressed economy *The president's main problem is the continuing weak economy.*

the world/global economy *Rising oil prices threaten the world economy.*

the US/German etc economy *The Japanese economy is showing signs of recovery.*

the national/local economy *The new factory is good news for the local economy.*

the agricultural economy (=the business of farming) *The early 1920s saw a rapid expansion in the American agricultural economy.*

the rural economy (=business in the countryside) *The rural economy was badly hit by the weather.*

a capitalist/free-market/market economy (=in which companies produce and sell products freely, without restrictions) *The country changed to a free-market economy in the 1990s.*

VERBS

boost/stimulate the economy (=make there be more activity and money in it) *People are hoping that the Olympic Games will boost the country's economy.*

kick-start the economy (=make there be more activity and money in it when there has been very little) *Congress hopes the tax cut will kick-start the economy.*

manage the economy *Governments are judged on how well they manage the economy.*

harm/damage the economy *The rise in oil prices could harm the economy.*

economy + VERBS

the economy grows/expands *The economy grew by 3% last year.*

the economy slows down/contracts (=there is less activity and money in it) *The economy is slowing down after a long period of growth.*

the economy collapses (=fails completely) *In 1929, the US economy collapsed.*

the economy recovers *The economy is beginning to recover from the recession.*

PHRASES

a slowdown/downturn in the economy (=a reduction in activity and money in it) *The continuing slowdown in the economy is giving cause for concern.*

an upturn in the economy (=an increase in activity and money in it) *New figures showed the first signs of an upturn in the economy.*

a sector of the economy (=part of it) *Levels of pay are low in this sector of the economy.*

ecosystem *n*

all the animals and plants in a particular area, and the way in which they are related to each other and to their environment

ADJECTIVES/NOUNS + ecosystem

a natural ecosystem *The lake has an amazingly complex natural ecosystem.*

a fragile/delicate ecosystem *The tourists may be damaging the island's fragile ecosystem.*

VERBS

damage/disrupt/destroy an ecosystem *They are worried that the dam will severely disrupt the river's ecosystem.*

ecstatic *adj*

feeling extremely happy and excited

ADVERBS

absolutely ecstatic *I was absolutely ecstatic when I found out that I had passed my exam.*

not exactly ecstatic/less than ecstatic *spoken* (=not pleased at all) *She wants to marry him, but her parents are not exactly ecstatic about the idea.*

PREPOSITIONS

ecstatic about/over/at sth *Thompson is ecstatic about receiving the award.*

THESAURUS: ecstatic

cheerful, contented, pleased/glad, delighted, thrilled, overjoyed, ecstatic, blissful → **happy**

E

edge *n*

1 the part of an object that is furthest from its centre

ADJECTIVES

the top edge *I gripped the top edge of the door and pulled myself up.*

the bottom/lower edge *The lower edge of the window frame was starting to rot.*

the front/back edge *I banged my elbow on the front edge of the desk.*

the inside/inner edge *He painted carefully around the inner edge of each door.*

the outside/outer edge *The airport is located on the outer edge of the town.*

the northern/southern etc edge (=used about a part near the end of an area of land, city etc) *There's a ridge of hills on the northern edge of the county.*

PREPOSITIONS

at the edge *The bird has black wings that are yellow at the edges.*

the edge of sth *We walked to the far edge of the wood.*

on the edge *He stood on the edge of the harbour wall.*

around/round the edge *There is a large square of grass with flowers around the edges.*

over the edge *Her feet were dangling over the edge of the bed.*

PHRASES

the edge of the sea *BrE*, **the edge of the ocean** *AmE* (=the land next to the sea) *The castle stands on the edge of the sea.*

the water's edge (=the land next to a river, the sea etc) *We sat down at the water's edge.*

2 the thin sharp part of a blade or other tool that cuts

ADJECTIVES

a sharp edge *You need a blade with a really sharp edge.*

a jagged edge (=with a series of uneven sharp points) *The stone had a dangerous jagged edge like broken glass.*

a rough edge *He cut his hand on the rough edge of the wall.*

a serrated edge (=with a row of sharp points for cutting) *The bread knife has a serrated edge.*

edition Ac *n*

the form that a book, newspaper, magazine etc is produced in

ADJECTIVES/NOUNS + edition

a new edition *They published a new edition of his poems.*

a revised edition (=one that has more information than a previous edition, or contains corrections) *The revised edition includes a chapter on modern art.*

the first/second/third etc edition (=the first, second etc set of copies to be published) *The first edition of the novel was published in 2010.*

a later edition *The mistake was corrected in a later edition of the book.*

a special edition *They produced a special edition of the magazine, to celebrate its 50th anniversary.*

a limited edition (=only a limited number of copies are produced) *The band has released a new limited edition CD.*

an online edition (=published on the internet) *The article was only available in the online edition of the newspaper.*

the hardback/paperback edition *The paperback edition costs £7.99.*

an abridged edition (=shorter because some original sections have been removed) *An abridged edition of the book was produced for children.*

VERBS

publish an edition *The first edition of the book was published in 1982.*

produce/release/bring out an edition *A special edition of the paper was produced.*

an edition comes out/appears (=is published or produced) *An English edition of the poems appeared in the same year.*

PREPOSITIONS

an edition of sth *The article appeared in the US edition of the paper.*

education *n*

the process of teaching and learning

ADJECTIVES/NOUNS + education

a good education *It is important to get a good education.*

a poor education (=not very good) *She had a poor education, and left school without qualifications.*

an all-round education (=including a balance of lots of different subjects) *The school offers a good all-round education.*

full-time education (=spending every weekday in a school or college) *Children must stay in full-time education until the age of 16.*

state education *BrE*, **public education** *AmE* (=provided by the government) *The state of California guarantees free public education to all children.*

private education (=that people have to pay for) *I don't agree with the principle of private education.*

formal education (=from teachers at school or college, rather than learning by yourself) *She had no formal education and was brought up by her grandmother.*

higher education (=at universities) *When he starts university in October, he will be the first member of his family to go into higher education.*

further education *BrE* (=at colleges after leaving school) *The government aims to provide further education for everyone.*

secondary education (=for students between 11 and 18 years old) *She hopes to start a teaching career in secondary education.*

primary education *BrE*, **elementary education** *AmE* (=for children aged between 5 and 11) *The government has announced plans to improve the quality of primary school education.*

nursery/pre-school education (=for children aged under 5) *The funding will provide nursery education for all four-year-olds.*

adult education (=for adults) *They run adult education classes at the local community college.*

vocational education (=relating to skills needed for a particular job) *We offer vocational education and job training.*

a university/college education *Did you have a university education?*

VERBS

have an education *Most teachers have had a university education.*

get/receive an education *Some children grow up without receiving any education.*

give/provide an education *The school aims to provide a good general education.*

stay in education *He decided to get a job rather than stay in education.*

continue your education *I hope to continue my education after high school.*

complete/finish your education *He went back to the US to finish his education.*

deny sb an education *Young people are being denied a good education.*

enter education *formal: The number of students entering higher education has risen.*

education + NOUNS

the education system *Japan's education system is very different from that of Britain.*

education policy *The teaching unions are calling for the government to review its education policy.*

education reform *They talked about the government's programme of education reform.*

the local education authority *BrE: The school is funded by the local education authority.*

PREPOSITIONS

the education of sb *The education of women was inadequate.*

eerie *adj* THESAURUS ▸ frightening

effect *n*

a change that is caused by something

ADJECTIVES

a big/major effect *The increase in oil prices will have a big effect on the economy.*

an important/significant/substantial effect *Climate change will have a significant effect on agriculture.*

a powerful/profound/strong effect *My father's death had a profound effect on me.*

a dramatic effect (=very big and sudden) *The treatment had a dramatic effect.*

a good/positive effect (*also* **a beneficial effect** *formal*): *The holiday had a good effect on him and he felt much more relaxed.*

a bad/negative effect *Stress has a very negative effect on people's health.*

a detrimental/adverse effect *formal* (=a bad effect) *Any tax increase will have an adverse effect on economic growth.*

a harmful/damaging effect (=causing harm or damage to something or someone) *We all know about the harmful effects of drinking too much alcohol.*

an immediate effect *The painkillers had an immediate effect.*

a visible/noticeable/marked effect (=that you can clearly see) *The punishment didn't seem to have any visible effect on his behaviour.*

the long-term/short-term effect (=for a long or short time) *The disease can have serious long-term effects.*

the full effect *People are starting to feel the full effect of the world economic crisis.*

a knock-on effect (=an effect on one thing which then affects other things) *The strike could have a knock-on effect at other airports.*

a cumulative effect (=the effect of many things happening one after the other) *The cumulative effect of the government's policies will be to push up inflation.*

the desired effect (=the effect you want) *His team talk had the desired effect because the team went on to win the game.*

VERBS

have an effect *The war had a big effect on people's lives.*

produce an effect *If you mix the two colours together, it produces an interesting effect.*

feel an effect (=notice it) *Small companies will feel the effect of the recession first.*

suffer (from) the effects of sth *The people in this area are still suffering from the effects of the famine.*

lessen/reduce/minimize an effect (=make an effect smaller or less severe) *The government must take action to reduce the effects of pollution.*

an effect lasts (=continues) *The effect of the drug lasts about six hours.*

an effect wears off (=gradually stops) *The effect of the anaesthetic was beginning to wear off.*

cushion the effect of sth (=make it less bad) *A tax cut helped cushion the effect of rising fuel prices.*

deal with the effects of sth *These people are already dealing with the effects of climate change.*

PREPOSITIONS

an effect on sth *What is the effect of a rise in temperature on the plant?*

PHRASES

have the effect of doing sth *The news had the effect of making everyone feel better.*

have little or no effect *The treatment had little or no effect and he went back to his doctor.*

cause and effect (=when one thing directly causes another) *History is more than a simple case of cause and effect.*

a domino effect (=when one event or action causes several other things to happen, one after the other) *If a major bank fails, we could see a domino effect leading to a global banking crisis.*

the greenhouse effect (=the gradual warming of the air surrounding the Earth as a result of heat being trapped by pollution) *Car exhaust fumes add to the greenhouse effect.*

effective *adj*

successful, and working in the way that was intended

ADVERBS

extremely/highly/superbly effective *The company launched a highly effective advertising campaign.*

remarkably/surprisingly/amazingly effective *The cleaning fluid he was using had been remarkably effective.*

reasonably/moderately effective *The advertisements were only moderately effective.*

increasingly/more and more effective *American industries faced increasingly effective competition from other countries.*

devastatingly effective (=extremely effective)

E

It was a devastatingly effective argument, superbly supported by facts and logic.

NOUNS

an effective way/method/means *What's the most effective way to control crime?*

an effective method/means *Exams are not the most effective method of assessing students' abilities.*

an effective solution *The most effective solution to traffic congestion is to build more roads.*

an effective treatment *Antibiotics are still the most effective treatment for this disease.*

an effective system *There needs to be a more effective system of financial management.*

effective action *The police must take effective action to protect the public.*

VERBS

prove effective *formal* (=be shown to be effective) *A new antibiotic may prove effective in fighting the disease.*

PHRASES

sth is just as effective *The other treatment was just as effective, but much cheaper.*

> **THESAURUS: effective**
>
> effective, fruitful → **successful (1)**

efficiency *n*

the quality of doing something well and effectively, without wasting time, money, or energy

ADJECTIVES/NOUNS + efficiency

greater/increased efficiency *In a search for greater efficiency, the two departments have merged.*

maximum efficiency *The boat's design helps it to move with maximum efficiency.*

high efficiency (=used about machines) *The diesel engine offers high efficiency and low fuel consumption.*

fuel/energy efficiency *Better fuel efficiency can be achieved by driving more slowly.*

VERBS

improve/increase efficiency *The company is taking steps to improve efficiency and reduce costs.*

promote efficiency (=develop or encourage it) *A competitive market helps to promote efficiency.*

efficiency + NOUNS

efficiency savings (=money saved by being more efficient) *Efficiency savings in the industry will inevitably lead to job losses.*

efficiency gains/improvements *New technology introduced by the company has brought efficiency gains.*

efficiency measures (=changes introduced to make something more efficient) *The new efficiency measures are designed to improve the health service.*

efficient *adj*

if someone or something is efficient, they work well without wasting time, money, or energy

ADVERBS

extremely/highly/incredibly efficient *The factory is modern and highly efficient.*

economically efficient *We needed a more economically efficient way of transporting our goods.*

relatively efficient *The failing company has transformed itself into a relatively efficient business.*

ruthlessly efficient (=achieving success with a determined attitude that could seem cruel) *She was known to be a ruthlessly efficient manager.*

efficient + NOUNS

an efficient way *Email is an efficient way of contacting a large number of people.*

an efficient method/means *They need a secure and efficient method of storing data.*

an efficient system *He introduced a more efficient system for collecting payments.*

an efficient service *We aim to provide our clients with an efficient and friendly service.*

the efficient use of sth *We should work towards the more efficient use of natural resources.*

the efficient operation/running of sth *The law must protect investors without interfering with the efficient operation of the market.*

an efficient solution *Using mobile phones to communicate was the most efficient solution.*

efficient management *Accurate records are essential for the efficient management of any business.*

NOUNS + efficient

energy/fuel efficient (=not wasting any fuel or energy) *We installed a more energy efficient heating system.*

cost efficient (=costing or spending as little as possible) *The larger a firm becomes, the more cost efficient it can become.*

PREPOSITIONS

efficient at doing sth *As we get older, our bodies become less efficient at using the food we eat.*

efficient in sth *The kitchen is very efficient in its use of space.*

effort *n*

1 an attempt to do something

> **Grammar**
>
> Always countable in this meaning.

ADJECTIVES/NOUNS + effort

a big/great effort to do sth *The government has made a big effort to tackle the problem of poverty.*

a supreme/tremendous effort (=a very big effort) *It was only with a supreme effort that Roger controlled his temper.*

a successful/unsuccessful effort *Their efforts were successful, and they won the contract.*

a futile effort (=with no chance of success) *Doctors knew that any effort to save his life would be futile.*

a special effort *I made a special effort to be nice to the children.*

a determined effort *She had made a determined effort to lose weight.*

a deliberate/conscious effort *He made a conscious effort to become a better person.*

a desperate effort *The prisoners made a desperate effort to escape.*

a heroic effort (=used when you admire someone for their great efforts) *Thanks to the heroic efforts of the firefighters, the building was saved.*

a superhuman effort (=using all your strength and power) *It took a superhuman effort to get the car back on the road.*

a joint/collaborative effort (=with different people or groups working together) *This was a collaborative effort involving the three largest energy companies.*

a team effort (=in which many people work together as a team) *We had many fine performances but the win was a real team effort.*

a concerted effort (=determined and well-organized) *It will take a concerted effort to get rid of this problem.*

a sustained effort (=one that you continue making for a long time) *It will take a sustained effort over the next five years to achieve our objectives.*

a final effort *I made one final effort to open the door.*

a last-ditch effort (=a last desperate effort, even though you think you probably will not succeed) *The team made a last-ditch effort to score a goal.*

VERBS

make an effort (=try to do something) *I made an effort to be polite.*

abandon your efforts *Bad weather forced them to abandon their efforts to sail across the Atlantic.*

continue your efforts *We will continue our efforts towards peace.*

PREPOSITIONS

effort at sth *They all laughed at her efforts at skiing.*

through sb's efforts (=because of someone's efforts) *Through scientists' efforts, we have learnt a lot about disease.*

despite sb's efforts *Despite all our efforts, we lost the game 1–0.*

in an effort to do sth (=in order to try to do something) *He bought an expensive car in an effort to impress her.*

PHRASES

make the effort (=try especially hard to do something that you do not usually do) *She always makes the effort to talk to the children.*

make every effort to do sth (=try very hard) *I made every effort to see their point of view.*

make no effort to do sth (=not try at all) *They make no effort to learn the local language.*

2 the physical or mental energy needed to do something

> **Grammar**
> Always uncountable in this meaning.

ADJECTIVES

great/considerable/huge effort *The police put considerable effort into finding his car.*

physical/mental effort *Digging requires a lot of physical effort.*

hard/strenuous effort *After a lot of hard effort, we got the sofa up the stairs.*

a constant effort (=you have to keep using a lot of effort) *Walking was a constant effort.*

the extra effort *It's a long way to the top of the hill, but it is worth the extra effort.*

VERBS

sth takes effort (*also* **it takes effort to do sth**) (=you have to try hard) *It takes so much effort to interest audiences in new shows.*

sth requires/involves effort *formal* (=it takes effort) *Trying to get my mother to change her mind requires considerable effort.*

take the effort out of sth (=make it easy) *An automatic car takes the effort out of driving.*

put effort into (doing) sth (=try hard to do something) *Frank put a lot of effort into the party.*

use effort *You need to use your time and effort efficiently.*

focus your efforts on sth *The company is focussing its efforts on Asia.*

effort goes into sth *A lot of effort goes into organising a football team.*

PREPOSITIONS

with effort *With great effort, he managed to keep quiet.*

without effort *Her horse jumped the fence without any effort.*

PHRASES

a great deal/a lot of effort *I eventually found the house, but it took a great deal of effort.*

be (well) worth the effort (=be worth doing even though it is hard) *It's a difficult place to get to, but it's well worth the effort.*

be a waste of effort *I could have told him it was a waste of effort.*

time and effort *You can save time and effort by booking your holiday online.*

egg *n*

1 a round object that contains a baby bird, snake, insect etc

VERBS

lay an egg *Blackbirds lay their eggs in March.*

fertilize an egg (=provide the male cell that will help create a baby bird, snake etc) *After the female fish has laid the eggs, the male comes along and fertilizes them.*

incubate an egg (=keep it warm so that it will hatch) *The female bird incubates the eggs.*

an egg hatches (=it opens and the baby bird, snake etc comes out) *The eggs hatch after 26 days.*

2 an egg, especially one from a chicken, that is used for food

ADJECTIVES

free-range eggs (=from chickens that are not kept in cages and are able to move freely outside) *The restaurant uses only free-range eggs.*

organic eggs (=from chickens that are not kept in cages and that are fed foods without chemicals) *Organic eggs are usually more expensive, but you know the chickens are well looked after.*

a boiled egg *We sometimes have boiled eggs for breakfast.*

a fried egg *I'm having fried eggs and hash brown potatoes.*

a poached egg (=cooked in a little water) *She made us poached eggs on toast.*

scrambled egg (=cooked with the yellow and white parts mixed together) *He had a quick meal of scrambled eggs and coffee.*

a raw egg (=not cooked) *Some raw eggs contain a bacteria called salmonella.*

a bad/rotten egg *The crowd threw rotten eggs at the stage.*

> **Easter eggs**
> These are usually made of hollow chocolate, with small pieces of chocolate or candy inside.

egg + NOUNS

an egg yolk (=the yellow part of an egg) *The little boy dipped his toast into the egg yolk.*

an egg white (=the part that is not the yolk) *Add the egg whites to the icing sugar and beat them together.*

VERBS

boil/fry/cook an egg *Boil the eggs for four minutes.*

break/crack an egg *Rodney broke two eggs into the frying pan.*

beat/whisk an egg *Beat the eggs in a bowl, then add the milk and flour.*

PHRASES

eggs over easy *AmE* (=eggs that have been fried on both sides) *He orders eggs over easy, bacon, and sliced tomatoes.*

bacon and eggs/ham and eggs *We had a quick meal of bacon and eggs.*

> You usually say **bacon and eggs,** or **ham and eggs**, rather than 'eggs and bacon' or 'eggs and ham'.

ego *n*

the opinion that you have about yourself

ADJECTIVES

a big/large/huge/enormous/massive ego (=when you think you are very intelligent or important) *Richard has the biggest ego of anyone I've ever met.*

a fragile ego (=when you lose confidence easily) *She works with actors and is used to dealing with fragile egos.*

the male ego *I didn't want to hurt his feelings, as I know how fragile the male ego is.*

VERBS

have a big/large etc ego *Unfortunately, Carson has a big ego but no talent.*

boost/build up/bolster sb's ego (=make someone feel more confident about their abilities) *The promotion really boosted her ego.*

ego + NOUNS

an ego trip *disapproving informal* (= a situation in which someone feels pleased because they think they are important and other people admire them) *The film is a huge ego trip for the director.*

an ego boost (=something that makes you feel much more confident about yourself) *Getting the prize was a real ego boost.*

PHRASES

be good for sb's ego *Someone said she looked ten years younger, which was very good for her ego.*

it's an ego thing *informal* (=it is caused by someone worrying about their ego) *Men want to be best at everything – I guess it's an ego thing.*

elaborate *adj* THESAURUS **complicated**

elder *adj* older

elder + NOUNS

an elder brother/sister *He has two elder brothers.*

an elder daughter/son/child *Her elder son Liam became a lawyer.*

an elder sibling *formal* (=elder brother or sister) *His elder siblings looked after him.*

an elder statesman (=an old and respected politician) *Deng is one of China's leading elder statesmen.*

> You can also use **elder** as a noun: *Sarah is the elder of the two.*

> **Elder** or **older**?
> **Elder** and **older** mean the same. **Elder** is more formal and is usually used about family members. The same is true of **eldest** and **oldest**.

elderly *adj*

old - often used about an old person who is weak or has bad health because of their age

elderly + NOUNS

an elderly man/woman/lady/gentleman *I stood up and offered my seat to an elderly gentleman on the bus.*

an elderly person *There are more elderly people attending the church than there are young people.*

an elderly mother/father/parent *She has to take care of her elderly parents.*

an elderly relative *Elderly relatives are often put in retirement homes.*

an elderly couple *An elderly couple sat drinking tea at one of the tables.*

ADVERBS

very elderly *His aunt is very elderly and she needs full-time care.*

> You can also use **elderly** as a noun: *She works in a home for* ***the elderly****.*

> **Elderly** or **old**?
> **Elderly** sounds more formal than **old**. It makes the person sound weak and needing help. Some people consider that **elderly** is not politically correct.

> **THESAURUS: elderly**
> elderly, aging, aged, ancient, antique, historic, vintage, age-old → **old (1)**

elect *v*

to choose someone for an official position by voting

NOUNS

elect sb (as) leader/president/mayor etc *Chavez was elected president in 1998.*

elect a government *Voters will elect a new government on November 26.*

elect a representative/elect sb as a representative *Lucio was elected as a state representative in 2006.*

> **Grammar**
> The passive form **elected** is often used before nouns, like an adjective: *Rebels tried to overthrow the* ***elected government****. |* ***Elected officials*** *are not allowed to accept money from the public.*

ADVERBS

democratically elected *This is the country's first democratically elected government.*

freely elected (=elected in a fair election) *He is the Congo's first freely elected president in more than 40 years.*

newly elected *What would be your advice to the newly elected president?*

duly elected (=as people expected) *Edwards was duly elected as treasurer at the next annual meeting.*

elect sb unanimously (=all of the people in a group vote for someone) *The new chairman was elected unanimously by the members of the board.*

PREPOSITIONS

be elected to Parliament/Congress etc *He was the first Muslim to be elected to Congress.*

elect sb as leader/president/chairman etc *The people elected her as their leader.*

> **THESAURUS: elect**
> cast your vote, go to the polls, elect, re-elect, ballot, veto → **vote[1]**

election *n*

an occasion when people vote to choose someone for an official position

ADJECTIVES/NOUNS + election

a general/national election (=in which the whole country votes to elect a government) *The party's victory in the general election gave them a huge majority.*

a local/regional election *The Green Party increased its share of the vote in the French regional elections.*

a presidential election (=for electing a new president) *He is the Democrat Party's candidate for the next presidential election.*

a leadership election (=for electing a new leader for a political party) *The result of the leadership election will be announced today.*

a mayoral election (=for electing a new mayor) *The mayoral elections are due to take place next month.*

fair/democratic elections *We are confident we can win, if the elections are fair.*

free elections (=with everyone allowed to vote for who they want) *These will be the country's first free multi-party elections.*

a congressional/parliamentary election (=for electing people to Congress or Parliament) *The Republican Party had considerable success in the congressional elections.*

a federal election (=for electing a federal government) *The federal elections are scheduled for May 2nd.*

VERBS

vote in an election *People under 18 years of age cannot vote in elections.*

have/hold an election *The government plans to hold an election in November.*
call an election (=decide that one should happen) *The prime minister would be unwise to call an election now.*
win/lose an election *Who do you think will win the election?*
fight an election *BrE* (*also* **contest an election** *BrE formal*) (=take part in it and try to win) *Three independent candidates are also planning to contest the election.*
run for election (*also* **stand for election** *BrE*) (=try to become elected) *Three candidates are running for election.*
rig an election (=dishonestly arrange the result) *He accused the ruling party of rigging the elections.*
boycott an election (=refuse to take part in it as a protest) *Opposition parties have threatened to boycott the elections.*
an election takes place *The last election took place four years ago.*

E

election + NOUNS

the election results *The election results have been coming in all night.*
an election victory/defeat *The party suffered its worst election defeat.*
an election campaign *The election campaign has already started.*
an election candidate *BrE* (=someone trying to be elected in an election) *Local party members choose the election candidates.*
an election manifesto (=a written statement by a political party, saying what they will do if they win the election) *In the party's election manifesto, they said they would cut taxes.*
an election promise/pledge *The government has broken all its election promises.*
election day/night/year/time *We urge all our supporters to get out and vote on election day.*
an election rally (=a public meeting to support a politician or party before an election) *The party leader spoke at an election rally in Manchester.*
an election broadcast *BrE* (=a programme by a party saying why people should vote for them in an election) *The next programme will be an election broadcast by the Green Party.*

PREPOSITIONS

in an election *He lost power in the last election.*
at an election *We're hoping to do better at the next election.*
an election for sth *Elections for the state governorship will be on November 25th.*

PHRASES

the result/outcome of an election *Which factors will decide the outcome of the election?*
the run-up to the election (=the period of time before an election) *There have been violent street protests in the run-up to the elections.*
win an election by a large/small etc majority (=win by a lot of votes or a small number of votes) *The Labour Party won the 2001 election by a huge majority.*

electric *adj*

relating to electricity - used especially about something that works using electricity, or about power produced by electricity

electric + NOUNS

an electric light/kettle/fan/guitar etc *She filled the electric kettle to make tea.*

⚠ Don't say 'electrical kettle'.

an electric car *The electric car has a range of about 100 miles.*

⚠ Don't say 'electrical car'.

electric power *Most of the country's electric power comes from nuclear energy.*
an electric wire/cable *The battery was connected to a thin electric cable.*
electric wiring (=the wires that carry electricity in a building or machine) *The electric wiring is old and needs replacing.*
electric current *The weapon can send 50,000 volts of electric current through your body.*
an electric charge *In an atom, a proton has a positive electric charge.*
an electric shock *Be careful not to touch the bare wire, or you will get an electric shock.*

THESAURUS: electric

electrical
goods | equipment | appliances | fault | storm | engineer
used about goods that use electricity, problems caused by electricity, or people whose job is to make or repair things that use electricity:
The store sells electrical goods. | The problem was caused by an electrical fault. | Electrical storms can cause a lot of damage (=storms with lightning). *| Michael is training to be an electrical engineer.*

Electric or electrical?
You can say an **electric charge** or an **electrical charge**: *The proton has a positive electric/electrical charge.*
You can say **electric power** or **electrical power**: *The generator produces electric/electrical power.*
You can say **electric wire/cable** or **electrical wire/cable**: *Don't touch the electric/electrical wires.*
You say an **electrical fault**. Don't say an 'electric fault'.

electronic
equipment | device | calculator | message | game | book | music | database | voting
used about equipment such as computers and televisions that work by using tiny electrical parts, or about things that you do using computers:
All electronic equipment such as mobile phones should be turned off. | Kids love electronic games. | The band plays electronic music. | The information is stored on an electronic database. | The winner of the competition will be chosen by electronic voting.

Electronic is often shortened to just '**e**', for example **email** (=electronic mail), **e-book** (=electronic book), and **e-commerce** (=electronic commerce).

electricity *n*

power that is carried by wires, cables etc

VERBS

generate/produce electricity *We need to find cleaner ways of generating electricity.*

provide/supply electricity *The dam will provide water and electricity for 30 million people.*

use electricity *The system uses electricity to heat the water.*

save/conserve electricity (=not waste it) *To save electricity, turn the lights out when you leave a room.*

have electricity *The farm didn't have electricity and we used candles for lighting.*

be powered by electricity *In an emergency, the hospital can be powered by electricity from a generator.*

cut off the electricity (=stop the supply of electricity) *You risk having your electricity cut off if you fail to pay the bill.*

waste electricity *Am I wasting electricity if I keep my computer on all day?*

conduct electricity (=electricity can travel along or through something) *Some metals conduct electricity better than others.*

electricity + NOUNS

the electricity supply *The storms have affected the electricity supply in some areas.*

electricity consumption (=the amount of electricity that is used) *Our target is to cut electricity consumption by 10%.*

an electricity bill *Have you paid the electricity bill?*

an electricity company *Contact the electricity company to see if you can move onto a cheaper plan.*

ADJECTIVES/NOUNS + electricity

mains electricity *BrE* (=supplied to a building from the national electricity supply) *The cottage has no mains electricity.*

static electricity (=that collects on a surface, for example on your clothes or a balloon) *He touched the door handle, and felt a jolt of static electricity.*

electronic *adj* THESAURUS ▸ **electric**

elegance *n*

the quality of being beautiful and graceful

ADJECTIVES

great elegance *She danced with great elegance.*

simple elegance *The simple elegance of the design will appeal to many people.*

classical elegance *The sofa combines classical elegance and modern style.*

understated elegance (=something is attractive because it is simple and does not have too many decorations) *The hotel has an understated elegance with its white marble floors and its high ceilings.*

a certain elegance *The café is informal, but has a certain elegance.*

great elegance *The women danced with great elegance.*

PREPOSITIONS

with elegance *Each bedroom has been furnished with elegance and style.*

PHRASES

a touch of elegance *Lace curtains add a touch of elegance to any room.*

elegant *adj*

an elegant person dresses in an attractive and graceful way. An elegant building has a beautiful design, or is decorated in a way that looks beautiful

VERBS

look elegant *The guests, who all wore evening dress, looked very elegant.*

ADVERBS

beautifully/wonderfully elegant *The beautifully elegant church tower rises to a height of 200 feet.*

supremely elegant (=extremely elegant) *Morris's designs look supremely elegant in any room.*

NOUNS

an elegant woman/lady/man *Mark looked up at the tall elegant man in his long black coat.*

an elegant hotel/restaurant *We stayed at an elegant hotel in Manhattan, overlooking Central Park. | The hotel has an elegant restaurant, with a terrace facing the harbour.*

an elegant building/house/room *We enjoyed a fine meal in the hotel's elegant dining room.*

elegant clothes/dress/suit/shoes *Italian people are often admired for their elegant clothes.*

elegant surroundings *We dined in the elegant surroundings of the royal palace.*

You can also use **elegant** about a solution that you admire because it is very simple and effective: *The French mathematician Pascal came up with an* ***elegant solution*** *to the problem.*

element Ac *n*

one part or feature of a whole system, plan, piece of work etc

ADJECTIVES

an important element *This one fact is the most important element of his theory.*

a key/major element (=very important and necessary) *Trust is a key element in any relationship.*

a vital/essential/crucial/critical element (=extremely important and necessary) *Her determination is a vital element of her success.*

the main element *The reform programme has three main elements.*

a basic/fundamental element *Milk and butter are the basic elements of these sauces.*

VERBS

contain/include/incorporate an element *For a joke to be funny, it must contain an element of truth.*

consist of elements *Any successful method will consist of these three elements.*

introduce an element *By offering a prize for the best design, you introduce an element of competition.*

PREPOSITIONS

an element of sth *Music is an important element of these TV shows.*

an element in sth *Marketing is an essential element in the success of any business.*

elementary *adj*

1 very simple or basic

NOUNS

an elementary mistake/error *The team made a number of elementary mistakes.*

the elementary principles/rules/laws of sth *The article shows an ignorance of even the most elementary principles of physics.*

elementary level *The coursebook is designed for students at elementary level, who want to improve their language skills.*

an elementary course *She did an elementary course in mathematics at school.*

elementary science/maths/biology etc *I took elementary science for two terms.*

THESAURUS: elementary

plain, crude → **simple**

2 relating to the first six years of a child's education

NOUNS

an elementary school *She went to the local elementary school.*

an elementary teacher *After college, I decided I wanted to become an elementary teacher.*

elementary education *The children spend six years in elementary education and three years in junior high school.*

In British English, people usually say **primary**: *a* ***primary*** *school* | ***primary*** *education*

elevator *n AmE*

a machine that takes people and goods from one level to another in a building

VERBS

take the elevator *My office is on the fourth floor, so I usually take the elevator.*

ride the elevator (=take the elevator) *Glen walked through the lobby, and rode the elevator to the eleventh floor.*

use the elevator *Do not use the elevators in the event of a fire.*

get into/out of/off the elevator *I did not want to get into an elevator crowded with people.*

step into/out of/off the elevator *As he stepped into the elevator, the doors closed behind him.*

the elevator goes up/down *The elevator only goes up to the 23rd floor, and then you have walk up to the top floor.*

Elevator is used in American English. British people say **lift**.

eliminate Ac *v*

to completely get rid of something that is not needed or wanted

ADVERBS

eliminate sth completely/totally/entirely *Their aim is to completely eliminate the disease.*

be largely/virtually eliminated (=almost completely eliminated) *The use of these chemicals has now been virtually eliminated.*

effectively eliminate sth *The company has effectively eliminated all the competition and they now dominate the market.*

VERBS

try to eliminate sth (*also* **seek to eliminate sth** *formal*): *They are trying to eliminate the risk of people catching the disease.*

help to eliminate sth *Better lighting would help to eliminate the problem.*

be designed to eliminate sth *The bank's security measures are designed to eliminate fraud.*

NOUNS

eliminate the need for sth *The new system will eliminate the need for people to buy tickets from a ticket office.*

eliminate the risk *It is impossible to eliminate the risk of an accident completely.*

eliminate the problem *The engineers think that they have eliminated the problem.*

eliminate the possibility of sth *If you save the file on an external hard drive, this will eliminate the possibility of losing data.*

eliminate poverty *The government wants to eliminate child poverty.*

eliminate waste *We are always looking for new ways to eliminate waste and make the company more efficient.*

THESAURUS: eliminate

murder, assassinate, execute, eliminate, slay, massacre, slaughter, exterminate, wipe out, commit suicide, take your own life → **kill**

eloquent *adj*

able to express your ideas and opinions well when you are speaking in public, especially in a way that influences people

NOUNS

an eloquent speaker *The president is an eloquent speaker and he is good at persuading people to accept his arguments.*

an eloquent speech *She gave an eloquent speech about the need for reform.*

an eloquent appeal/plea *The head of the Red Cross made an eloquent appeal for aid to help the survivors.*

PHRASES

wax eloquent about sth *formal* (=talk a lot about something, in a very enthusiastic way) *The critics waxed eloquent about the show, and praised the actors for their performances.*

THESAURUS: eloquent

articulate
able to talk or write about your ideas or feelings easily and effectively:
Girls are often more articulate and better at expressing their ideas than boys. | *Jones emerged as the most articulate spokesman for the group.*

flowery
language | prose
flowery language uses words or phrases that are rare or difficult to understand, instead of simple clear language:
His books are full of flowery language and they can be rather hard to read. | *It's best not to use flowery prose in a formal report.*

You can also say that someone **has a way with words**, when you think that they are good at speaking or writing: *He **has a** wonderful **way with words**, and describes everyday events in a unique and interesting way.*

email, e-mail *n*

a system that allows you to send and receive messages by computer, or a message sent using this system

VERBS

send (sb) an email *I'll send you an email with all the details.*

get/receive an email *Didn't you get my email?*

read an email *It took most of the morning to read my emails.*

write an email *Jack spent the evening writing emails and surfing the internet.*

reply to/answer an email *She did not bother replying to his email.*

check your email(s) *The first thing I do every morning is check my email.*

delete an email *I accidentally deleted your email.*

forward an email (=send an email you have received to someone else) *Can you please forward this email to Chris?*

ADJECTIVES

a long email (*also* **a lengthy email** *formal*): *He sent me a long email explaining how I could improve my performance.*

email + NOUNS

an email address *What's your email address?*

an email message *I can send email messages on my phone.*

an email attachment (=a computer file sent in an email) *Don't open an email attachment unless you know who sent it.*

an email account *Kevin showed her how to open an email account.*

email confirmation (=an email that tells you something is definitely booked, ordered etc) *The airline sent email confirmation of our flights.*

PREPOSITIONS

by email *It's best to contact him by email.*

embargo *n*

an official order to stop trade with another country

ADJECTIVES/NOUNS + embargo

a trade embargo *The EU threatened to impose a trade embargo.*

an arms embargo (=that stops weapons being sold or sent to a country) *Ministers knew that the arms embargo was being broken.*

an oil embargo *Some Middle Eastern countries were threatening an oil embargo.*

an economic embargo *He asked for an immediate end to the economic embargo.*

a financial embargo *Some countries wanted to tighten the financial embargo on Syria.*

an international embargo (=one that a group of countries agree to impose together) *Under the terms of the international embargo, medical aid can still be flown into the capital.*

a complete/total embargo (*also* **a blanket embargo**) (=on all of something) *There is a complete embargo on arms sales to governments that violate human rights.*

a strict embargo *There is a strict embargo on arms exports.*

an air embargo (=stopping aircraft from flying into or out of a country) *An air embargo in Iraq was agreed by five members of the Security Council.*

E

VERBS

impose/place/put an embargo on sth *The UN imposed an embargo on trade with the military regime.*

lift/end an embargo *We should lift the embargo because people are suffering.*

break an embargo (*also* **violate an embargo** *formal*) (=break the rules forbidding trade) *It has been almost impossible to stop countries breaking the arms embargo.*

tighten an embargo (=make it stricter and more difficult to break) *We are taking further action to tighten the embargo.*

PREPOSITIONS

an embargo on sth *The country imposed an immediate embargo on US goods.*

an embargo against sb *The UN ordered an international arms embargo against Iraq.*

embarrassed *adj*

feeling uncomfortable or nervous, and worrying about what people think of you

ADVERBS

terribly/deeply embarrassed (=very embarrassed) *I was deeply embarrassed to see my mother arrive in a very short skirt.*

acutely/highly embarrassed (=extremely embarrassed) *The government must be acutely embarrassed by the minister's behaviour.*

slightly/a little embarrassed *Tom looked slightly embarrassed when his name was called out.*

somewhat embarrassed (=rather embarrassed) *His family seemed somewhat embarrassed to be there.*

clearly/obviously embarrassed *He was clearly embarrassed about what had happened.*

easily embarrassed *My sister was easily embarrassed.*

VERBS

feel embarrassed *I felt embarrassed that he had seen me cry.*

seem/look/sound embarrassed *The judge seemed embarrassed to be asking her such personal questions.*

get/become embarrassed *Sometimes I get embarrassed, and I start to stutter.*

make sb embarrassed *Don't say that! You're making me embarrassed!*

NOUNS

an embarrassed silence *There was an embarrassed silence, then Gina laughed loudly.*

an embarrassed smile/laugh/grin *Lucy gave an embarrassed smile and looked down at her feet.*

PREPOSITIONS

embarrassed by sth *I felt embarrassed by my own lack of knowledge about the subject.*

PHRASES

embarrassed and ashamed *I was embarrassed and ashamed of your behaviour.*

embarrassing *adj*

making you feel ashamed, nervous, or uncomfortable

NOUNS

an embarrassing situation *I was in a very embarrassing situation and I didn't know what to do.*

an embarrassing position *John's refusal to attend his brother's wedding put the rest of his family in an embarrassing position.*

an embarrassing question *The media began asking embarrassing questions about his private life.*

an embarrassing silence *There was a long and embarrassing silence after she asked the question.*

an embarrassing experience *Discussing your personal problems with a complete stranger can be an embarrassing experience.*

VERBS

find sth embarrassing *Men often find it embarrassing to talk about their problems.*

prove embarrassing (=be embarrassing for someone) *Rumours about his affair with a glamour model proved highly embarrassing.*

ADVERBS

highly/deeply/extremely embarrassing *This incident is highly embarrassing for the college.*

acutely/excruciatingly embarrassing (=extremely embarrassing) *She had never asked her family for money before, and she found the whole situation acutely embarrassing.*

rather/somewhat/quite embarrassing *Meeting my old boyfriend at the party was rather embarrassing.*

a little embarrassing (*also* **a bit embarrassing** *spoken especially BrE*): *It was a bit embarrassing when he started to cry.*

potentially embarrassing (=could be embarrassing in the future) *The timing of his resignation is potentially embarrassing for the government.*

How embarrassing! *"I suddenly realised I had forgotten her name." "How embarrassing!"*

PREPOSITIONS

embarrassing to/for sb *This news will be embarrassing to the government.*

THESAURUS: embarrassing

awkward
situation | position | moment | question | silence | pause
rather embarrassing, so that you do not feel relaxed when you are talking to someone or dealing with someone. **Awkward** sounds less strong than **embarrassing**:
Because he is my brother, it puts me in rather an awkward position. | There was an awkward moment when she asked him why he was being so rude. | "Hi David!" There was an awkward pause and then he said, "Actually, my name is Daniel."

uncomfortable
position | experience | silence | reminder | truth | fact
used about things that make people feel nervous and not relaxed. **Uncomfortable** is similar in meaning to **awkward**:
She found herself in the uncomfortable position of criticizing people who used to be her friends. | Watching yourself on camera can be a very uncomfortable experience. | There was a long uncomfortable silence and people tried to avoid looking at each other. | The documents are an uncomfortable reminder of the past (=they make you remember something embarrassing). | *The uncomfortable truth was that he did not love her any more.*

humiliating
defeat | experience | climbdown
making you feel very ashamed and embarrassed, because you have been made to look stupid or weak in front of other people:
The team suffered a humiliating defeat. | It was the most humiliating experience of my life. | The government has been forced into a humiliating climbdown about its economic policy (=an embarrassing situation, in which someone in authority has to admit they were wrong and change their plans). | *It was* ***humiliating for*** *her to admit she had lied to the court.*

embarrassment *n*

1 the feeling you have when you are embarrassed

ADJECTIVES

great/huge/severe embarrassment *To my great embarrassment, my dad started dancing.*

acute/intense embarrassment *formal*: *The incident has caused acute embarrassment for the minister.*

considerable embarrassment *His behaviour was a source of considerable embarrassment to his family.*

further/fresh embarrassment (=more) *His resignation should save the government any further embarrassment.*

potential embarrassment (=possible) *By leaving the competition, he was spared the potential embarrassment of losing.*

political embarrassment *Her remarks caused considerable political embarrassment to the party.*

VERBS

cause embarrassment *Some of his jokes caused embarrassment to the older members of the audience.*

avoid embarrassment *This solution could help both countries avoid embarrassment.*

hide your embarrassment *She started laughing in an attempt to hide her embarrassment.*

spare/save sb embarrassment (=allow them to avoid it) *If he goes, it will save us the embarrassment of asking him to leave.*

feel embarrassment *She seems incapable of feeling embarrassment.*

PREPOSITIONS

embarrassment at/over sth *I was amused by his embarrassment over one little kiss.*

with/in embarrassment *He smiled with embarrassment as he admitted the truth.*

PHRASES

a source of embarrassment (=a cause of embarrassment) *His views on immigration were a constant source of embarrassment to the party.*

(much) to sb's embarrassment (=which makes someone feel embarrassed) *Much to my embarrassment, my parents kissed each other.*

nearly/almost die of embarrassment (=feel extremely embarrassed) *I almost died of embarrassment when photos of me as a baby were brought out.*

2 a feature or event that makes people stop respecting a person, an organization etc

ADJECTIVES

a major/huge/big embarrassment *If the story is true, it could be a huge embarrassment for the government.*

a severe/serious embarrassment *The scandal was a serious embarrassment for the club.*

E

an acute embarrassment (=extremely severe) *The newspaper stories were an acute embarrassment to the president.*

a potential embarrassment (=something that could be an embarrassment) *The party is anxious to avoid a potential embarrassment just before the elections.*

VERBS

be/become an embarrassment *Your behaviour is becoming an embarrassment to the school.*

consider sb/sth an embarrassment (=think they are embarrassing) *His colleagues considered him an embarrassment and they decided to get rid of him.*

prove an embarrassment *formal* (=be an embarrassment) *The publication of the documents proved a severe embarrassment to the company.*

PREPOSITIONS

an embarrassment to/for sb *The scandals came as an embarrassment to the government.*

E

embassy *n*

a group of officials who represent their government in a foreign country, or the building they work in

ADJECTIVES

the Chinese/French/British etc Embassy *I went to the American Embassy to get a visa.*

a foreign embassy *There are many foreign embassies in central London.*

embassy + NOUNS

an embassy official *Embassy officials have urged tourists not to travel to the region.*

embassy staff *The government ordered the Iranian ambassador and two other embassy staff to leave the country.*

an embassy spokesperson *An embassy spokesperson insisted that the story was not true.*

the embassy compound (=the embassy buildings and land) *People were trying to climb over the wall to get into the embassy compound.*

VERBS

open/close an embassy *Italy decided to close its embassy and withdraw its ambassador.*

take/seek refuge in an embassy (=go there and ask to be protected) *The man was forced to seek refuge in the US embassy.*

emergency *n*

an unexpected and dangerous situation that must be dealt with immediately

ADJECTIVES

a serious emergency *The police usually respond quickly to serious emergencies.*

an extreme emergency *These weapons should be used only in an extreme emergency.*

a major emergency *In a major emergency, the national guard may be called in.*

a sudden/unexpected/unforeseen emergency *I left early in case of traffic jams or any unforeseen emergency.*

a national emergency *With food supplies running dangerously low, the government declared a national emergency.*

a medical emergency *The patient's condition represented a serious medical emergency.*

VERBS

deal with an emergency *Several fire crews were called to deal with the emergency.*

cope with an emergency *Do you think that you could cope with an emergency?*

handle an emergency *There is always a doctor on call to handle emergencies.*

respond to an emergency (=go to the place where it happens and deal with it) *How long does it take an ambulance crew to respond to an emergency?*

declare an emergency (=say officially that there is an emergency situation and the government is taking action to deal with it) *The storm caused a lot of damage and the president declared a national emergency.*

emergency + NOUNS

the emergency services (=the police, fire service, and ambulance service) *There have been pay cuts for members of the emergency services.*

an emergency vehicle (=an ambulance or fire engine) *Emergency vehicles rushed to the scene.*

an emergency situation *The pilot and crew must stay calm in an emergency situation.*

an emergency landing *The plane made an emergency landing on the Hudson River.*

emergency treatment *The driver is receiving emergency treatment at Park Royal Hospital.*

an emergency operation *He had an emergency operation to save his sight.*

emergency aid/relief/help *The charity made a television appeal for emergency aid to the region.*

an emergency meeting/session *The government held an emergency meeting earlier today.*

emergency powers *The army was given emergency powers to help tackle the rising violence.*

emergency measures (=official actions in order to deal with an emergency situation) *The president announced emergency measures to deal with the financial crisis.*

PREPOSITIONS

in an emergency *She is able to stay very calm in an emergency.*

for emergencies *They keep extra supplies of food and fuel in the basement for emergencies.*

PHRASES

in case of emergency/in the event of an emergency (=if there is an emergency) *The* *fire-exit doors should only be opened in case of emergency.*

eminent *adj* THESAURUS famous

emissions *n*

gases in the air that come from cars, factories etc

> **Grammar**
> Usually plural in this meaning, except in some noun phrases such as **emission levels**.

ADJECTIVES/NOUNS + emissions

carbon/carbon dioxide/greenhouse gas etc emissions *The treaty calls for a 30% reduction in carbon emissions.*

harmful emissions (=likely to cause harm to people or the environment) *The law is designed to limit harmful emissions.*

toxic emissions (=poisonous) *By the end of the decade, we could reduce toxic emissions by half.*

vehicle emissions (=from cars, lorries etc) *California has introduced tough new standards for vehicle emissions.*

industrial emissions (=from factories) *The trees are being killed by acid rain and other industrial emissions.*

VERBS

cut/reduce emissions *These countries signed an agreement to cut emissions of gases which contribute to global warming.*

control/limit emissions *Efforts to control carbon dioxide emissions have not been very effective.*

monitor emissions (=officially check how much pollution is being produced) *The department monitors emissions from factories around the country.*

emissions + NOUNS

emission levels (=the amount of emissions) *We want to see much lower emission levels throughout the industry.*

emissions targets (=a level that emissions should be reduced to) *Too many companies are failing to meet their emissions targets.*

emission(s) standards (=official rules or agreements about how much pollution can be produced) *There are strict emission standards for new vehicles.*

emission reduction/cuts *The government will continue to work towards emission reduction.*

emission controls *With stricter emission controls, we could see major improvements in air quality.*

emissions trading (=a system in which companies pay money if they produce more pollution than an official level) *We would like to see more industries joining the emissions trading scheme.*

PREPOSITIONS

emissions of sth *Since the new engine was introduced, there has been a sharp fall in emissions of carbon monoxide.*

emissions from sth *Experts are concerned about emissions from the power station.*

emotion *n*

a strong human feeling such as love, hate, or anger

ADJECTIVES

a strong/intense emotion *The death penalty is a topic which arouses strong emotions.*

a powerful emotion *Grief is a very powerful emotion.*

a deep emotion (=strongly felt, but not always expressed) *He had never revealed these deep emotions to anyone.*

great emotion *She sings with great emotion.*

real/true/genuine emotion *There was real emotion in his voice.*

raw emotion (=shown clearly without any attempt to hide it) *The film is full of raw emotion.*

human emotions *We express human emotions through music and poetry.*

a painful emotion *Painful emotions, stored away in the patient's memory, can suddenly come flooding back.*

mixed/conflicting emotions (=a mixture of very different feelings) *She had mixed emotions about starting a new school.*

pent-up/suppressed emotions (=that someone feels but does not express) *Crying can release pent-up emotions.*

a positive emotion (=love, happiness, hope etc) *Try to focus on your positive emotions.*

a negative emotion (=anger, fear, hate etc) *It's not easy learning how to deal with negative emotions.*

VERBS

show/display emotion *He didn't show any emotion when I told him I was pregnant.*

express an emotion (=show or talk about it) *He had always found it difficult to express his emotions.*

feel/experience an emotion *Meeting his new wife, she felt a mixture of emotions.*

have emotions *Young people have strong emotions that they don't always know how to express.*

hide your emotions (*also* **conceal/suppress your emotions** *formal*): *Laura could not hide her emotions on seeing him again.*

control your emotions *She was behaving like a teenager who couldn't control her emotions.*

arouse/provoke emotions (=cause people to feel them) *Abortion is a subject that arouses strong emotions.*

stir up people's emotions (=deliberately try to make people full of anger and hate) *He accused politicians of trying to stir up people's emotions.*

PREPOSITIONS

with emotion *His voice was shaking with emotion.*

PHRASES

full of emotion (=showing or feeling strong emotions, especially sadness) *When she spoke, her voice was full of emotion.*

overcome with emotion (=feeling it so strongly that you cannot behave normally) *As soon as I heard that song, I was overcome with emotion.*

choked with emotion (=feeling so much that you cannot speak normally) *Mr Ford's voice was choked with emotion as he addressed the mourners.*

devoid of emotion *formal* (=not showing or feeling any emotion) *I find his books completely devoid of emotion.*

a lack of emotion *I was shocked by her apparent lack of emotion.*

a display/expression of emotion *Open displays of emotion made him uncomfortable.*

a sign of emotion *He showed no sign of emotion as the guilty verdict was read out.*

a wave/flood/surge/rush of emotion (=a sudden very strong emotion) *A great surge of emotion swept through her when she learnt that he was safe.*

emotions are running high (=people in a particular situation have very strong feelings, especially feelings that could lead to violence) *The police were aware that emotions in the city were running very high.*

emotional *adj*

1 feeling or causing strong feelings of sadness or happiness

ADVERBS

very/highly emotional *It was a highly emotional moment when they renewed their wedding vows.*

quite/pretty emotional *He became quite emotional at the end of his speech.*

VERBS

feel emotional *I felt very emotional when I returned to the house where I was born.*

get/become emotional *Everyone got quite emotional when he left.*

NOUNS

an emotional experience *The funeral was a very emotional experience for his family.*

an emotional reunion (=a meeting in which you cry because you have not seen someone for a long time) *She had an emotional reunion with her father, who she had not seen for over ten years.*

an emotional farewell *Fans gathered outside the church to bid an emotional farewell to the singer who died last week.*

an emotional moment *It was a very emotional moment and they both wept tears of joy.*

an emotional scene *There were emotional scenes in the court as the killer was led away to prison.*

an emotional speech/appeal/plea *The parents of the missing girl made an emotional appeal for her return.*

an emotional roller coaster (=a situation which causes you to feel very happy, then very sad) *Her relationship with the singer was an emotional roller coaster.*

THESAURUS: emotional

emotive
issue | subject | word | language
making people have strong feelings, so that they want to argue with each other:
Fox hunting is a very emotive issue in Britain. | Animal experiments are a highly emotive subject. | 'Propaganda' is a highly emotive word. | His speech was full of emotive language.

moving
story | account | film | experience | tribute
making you have strong feelings, especially of sadness, sympathy, or pity:
The book is a moving story about a young boy's search for his mother. | I found the film ***deeply moving****. | Jeremy paid a moving tribute to his wife.*

touching
story | gesture | faith
affecting your emotions and making you feel sympathy, especially because someone shows how much they care about another person or animal. **Touching** is less strong than **moving**:
She wrote a touching story about a little girl and her dog. | My son phoned me to wish me good luck, which was a touching gesture. | I found his faith in his parents rather touching. | There was something rather touching about the letter.

poignant
reminder | memory | moment | image
making you feel strong feelings of sadness or pity, especially because you remember something in the past:
The ruins are a poignant reminder of the city's glorious past. | The visit clearly brought back poignant memories. | There are some poignant moments in the film.

sentimental
film | song | comedy | story
dealing with emotions such as love and sadness in a way that seems silly:
I found the film too sentimental. | The play is a sentimental comedy. | Her stories have been criticized for being too sentimental.

highly charged
atmosphere | meeting | debate | topic | issue
full of strong emotions, so that people often argue with each other:

The trial took place in a highly charged atmosphere. | After a highly charged meeting, the council eventually voted by 459 votes to 403 to accept the deal.

2 relating to your feelings, and the way in which they affect your life

NOUNS

emotional problems *The patient has a long history of emotional problems.*

sb's emotional state *Her parents were worried about her emotional state.*

emotional support *His friends gave him a lot of emotional support during the breakup of his marriage.*

emotional needs *It is important to pay attention to the emotional needs of the child.*

emotional well-being/welfare (=the state of feeling happy and not worried about your life) *Physical and emotional well-being are closely linked.*

emotional strain/distress/trauma (=very unpleasant feelings after a bad experience) *She has been under a great deal of emotional strain lately.*

an emotional scar (=a permanent bad effect on someone, caused by a bad experience) *His childhood had left deep emotional scars.*

emotional turmoil (=strong and confused feelings) *When you're going through emotional turmoil, you can't concentrate on anything.*

the emotional impact *They were worried about the emotional impact of their divorce on the children.*

emotional involvement/attachment (=a feeling of liking or loving someone or something) *A nurse has to avoid emotional involvement with patients.*

emotional baggage (=feelings about the past which affect your life now) *He was carrying a lot of emotional baggage from a previous relationship.*

emotive *adj* THESAURUS **emotional (1)**

emphasis Ac *n*

special attention or importance

VERBS

put emphasis on sth *The airline is accused of putting more emphasis on profit than on safety.*

place/lay emphasis on sth *formal* (=put emphasis on something) *The school places a lot of emphasis on sports.*

give emphasis to sth *We need to give greater emphasis to cancer prevention.*

shift the emphasis (=change it to something else) *With drug addiction, we are shifting the emphasis from punishment to treatment.*

the emphasis shifts/moves (=changes) *The emphasis is now shifting away from oil towards renewable sources of energy.*

add emphasis (=make an opinion or fact seem more important) *Some punctuation marks are used to add emphasis.*

ADJECTIVES

great emphasis *The company places great emphasis on customer care.*

strong/heavy emphasis *There is a strong emphasis on research in the university.*

considerable emphasis *Most religions put considerable emphasis on the importance of marriage.*

the main emphasis *The main emphasis must be on quality, not quantity.*

particular/special emphasis *The new legislation places particular emphasis on energy conservation.*

increasing/growing emphasis *Recently, there has been an increasing emphasis on creating more jobs.*

undue emphasis (=too much emphasis) *In our society, we place undue emphasis on wealth and possessions.*

PREPOSITIONS

emphasis on sth *In many Asian cultures, there is a lot of emphasis on politeness.*

PHRASES

a change of emphasis (*also* **a shift in emphasis**) *There has been a change of emphasis in the government's foreign policy.*

emphasize Ac (*also* **emphasise** *BrE*) *v*

to say something in a strong way

NOUNS

emphasize the importance/significance/value of sth *The report emphasizes the importance of improving safety standards.*

emphasize the need for sth *I would emphasize the need for further research before we can reach a definite conclusion.*

emphasize sb's/sth's role *His work emphasized the role of psychological factors in physical illness.*

emphasize a point/fact *She emphasized her point by giving several shocking examples.*

ADVERBS

strongly emphasize *The report strongly emphasizes the need for better communication between teachers and parents.*

repeatedly/constantly emphasize *They repeatedly emphasized the government's failure to deal with unemployment.*

PHRASES

be keen to emphasize/be at pains to emphasize (=make a lot of effort to emphasize something) *He was keen to emphasize that the situation was getting better.*

it is worth emphasizing that *It is worth emphasizing that this man is innocent until proved guilty.*

E

empire *n*

1 a group of countries that are all controlled by one ruler or government

ADJECTIVES

a large/vast/huge empire *The Emperor Claudius ruled a vast empire stretching from Persia to Britain.*

a great empire (=large and powerful) *The city was the centre of a great empire.*

the Roman/British/Ottoman etc Empire *The Barbarians finally overthrew the Roman Empire.*

a colonial empire (=a group of countries ruled by another country that is far away) *France had a huge colonial empire.*

VERBS

found/establish an empire (=start an empire) *The Persian Empire was founded by Cyrus the Great.*

expand an empire (=increase its size) *Spain wanted to expand its empire north.*

destroy an empire *Crusades and civil wars gradually destroyed the Byzantine Empire.*

an empire grows/expands *The empire grew to include many new territories.*

an empire falls/collapses (=loses power suddenly) *In AD 476, the western part of the empire collapsed.*

an empire crumbles (=loses power gradually) *The vast empire was beginning to crumble.*

PHRASES

the decline of an empire (=the gradual decrease in its power) *The next two hundred years saw the gradual decline of the Roman Empire.*

the fall/collapse of an empire (=its sudden end) *After the Battle of Waterloo, the collapse of Napoleon's empire was inevitable.*

2 a group of organizations controlled by one person

ADJECTIVES

a large/vast/huge empire *He created a vast financial empire worth billions of dollars.*

a business/financial/media etc empire *His business empire is now worth over $20 billion.*

VERBS

build (up) an empire *She built her clothing empire from one small shop to an international chain.*

an empire collapses *When the business empire collapsed, thousands of employees lost their jobs.*

PHRASES

the collapse of an empire *He left the country after the collapse of his construction empire.*

employ *v* THESAURUS **use**[1]

employee *n*

someone who is paid to work for someone else

ADJECTIVES

a full-time/part-time employee *We now have 110 full-time employees.*

a permanent/temporary employee *Some of the temporary employees were later hired as permanent staff.*

a senior/junior employee *The company offers large bonuses to senior employees.*

a male/female employee *Many female employees earn less than men doing similar jobs.*

a former employee *The company is being sued by three former employees.*

a disgruntled employee (=who is annoyed by the way their company has treated them) *A disgruntled employee revealed secret information to a national newspaper.*

VERBS

have ... employees *The Birmingham-based company has over 200 employees.*

recruit employees (=offer them jobs) *We are recruiting employees for our IT division.*

lay off employees (*also* **make employees redundant** *BrE*) (=stop employing them because there is no work for them to do) *Unions fear that many part-time employees will be laid off.*

dismiss/fire an employee (*also* **sack an employee** *BrE*) (=stop employing them, usually because they have done something wrong) *Seven employees were dismissed for misconduct.*

an employee joins a company/firm etc *Employees who join the firm after April will be on the new contracts.*

an employee leaves *A number of employees have left the company in recent months.*

PREPOSITIONS

an employee of sth *Employees of the bank were given the bad news this morning.*

employer *n*

a person, company, or organization that employs people

ADJECTIVES

a big/large/major employer *The company is one of the state's biggest employers.*

a local employer *A number of local employers are involved in the scheme.*

sb's former/previous/last employer *His former employer described him as an excellent worker.*

a future/prospective/potential employer (=someone who might employ you) *It is important to be able to prove to prospective employers that you have the relevant experience for the job.*

sb's present/current employer *Try to persuade your current employer to give you more training.*

sb's new employer *She hoped that she wouldn't be a disappointment to her new employer.*

a good employer *The company has a reputation as a good employer.*

an unscrupulous employer (=an unfair or dishonest employer) *Unscrupulous employers forced children to work for up to 16 hours a day.*

VERBS

an employer hires sb (=gives someone a job) *The government wants to encourage employers to hire more workers.*

an employer fires/sacks/dismisses sb (=stops employing someone, usually because they have done something wrong) *His employer fired him for taking too much time off.*

work for an employer *My father has worked for the same employer since he was 19.*

employment *n*

the condition of having a paid job

ADJECTIVES

full-time/part-time employment *Mike is in full-time employment, but his wife is not working.*

permanent/temporary employment *The staff are mainly university graduates entering permanent employment for the first time.*

long-term/regular employment (=working for the same company for a long time) *She finally found regular employment at a hospital in York.*

continuous employment *You can join the pension scheme after two years of continuous employment with the company.*

alternative employment *After leaving his job in a tax office, he found alternative employment in a restaurant.*

gainful employment *formal* (=which provides money for you to live) *He has had no gainful employment for the last five years.*

VERBS

look for/seek employment *My son had to leave the farm and seek employment elsewhere.*

give/offer sb employment *He was offered employment in the company's main office.*

provide employment *The new power station will provide employment for around 400 people.*

create/generate employment *The government is trying to stimulate the economy and create employment.*

find/get/obtain employment *The men hope to find employment in the construction industry.*

terminate sb's employment *formal* (=end it) *After he arrived at work drunk several times, the decision was taken to terminate his employment.*

employment + NOUNS

the employment figures/statistics *The latest employment figures will be embarrassing for the government.*

employment opportunities *There are very few employment opportunities in the area.*

employment prospects (=someone's chances of getting a job) *Better qualifications will improve your employment prospects.*

employment rights (=the rights that someone has in their job) *Part-time workers now have the same employment rights as full-time staff.*

an employment contract *There is a clause in your employment contract covering holiday entitlement.*

employment practices (=a company's treatment of its workers) *The company was accused of unfair employment practices.*

employment legislation/law *The government is supporting changes to European employment law.*

an employment agency (=an organization that finds jobs for people) *After losing his job, he signed on with several employment agencies.*

PREPOSITIONS

in employment (=in the position of having a paid job) *He has been in employment for the last three years.*

PHRASES

sb's place of employment *formal: They had a long journey to their place of employment.*

loss of employment *The insurance policy pays your rent in the event of loss of employment.*

the terms of employment (=the rules or conditions relating to someone's job) *It's in the terms of their employment that they can't go on strike.*

empty *adj*

if something is empty, there is nothing or no one in it

NOUNS

an empty bottle/can/box/packet *Can you put the empty bottles in the recycling bin?*

an empty cup/glass/plate *A girl cleared away the empty cups.*

an empty cupboard/fridge/shelf *The food had all gone and the cupboard was empty.*

an empty tank *The fuel tank is almost empty.*

an empty room/hall/corridor *His voice echoed through the empty room.*

an empty house/hotel/restaurant/building *The hotel was completely empty when they arrived.*

an empty seat/chair/bed *People began filling up the empty seats.*

an empty street *The rain fell on the empty streets.*

an empty train/bus *The trains are empty at the weekends.*

an empty space *There was an empty space where his chair had been.*

an empty landscape (=with no trees, houses, hills etc) *She stared out of the window at the bleak empty landscape.*

ADVERBS

completely empty *The shelves were completely empty.*

almost/nearly/virtually/practically empty *The restaurant was dark and almost empty, except for four men at a table.*

half-empty *A half-empty bottle of red wine stood on the table.*

VERBS

a building stands/stays/lies empty (=no one lives there) *The house stood empty for over a year.*

leave sth empty *Holiday homes are sometimes left empty for months.*

PREPOSITIONS

empty of people/traffic *The streets were still empty of traffic.*

THESAURUS: empty

with nothing in it or on it

bare
room | cupboard | landscape | tree | branch
used about a room or cupboard that has very little in it:
The room was bare, except for a small table. | *She was hungry, but the cupboard was bare.* | *I looked out at the bare trees in the snow* (=with no leaves).

blank
sheet | page | screen | space | disk | tape
used about a computer screen or a piece of paper that has no writing or pictures on it, or a disk or tape with nothing recorded on it:
Fontaine handed her a pen and two sheets of blank paper. | *The screen suddenly went blank* (=became blank). | *I've left a blank space for your signature.*

hollow
tree | tube | cylinder | piece of wood
used about something that has an empty space inside:
The insects make their nests in hollow trees.

not being used

free
seat | table | room | parking space
available and not being used:
There is a seat free by the window. | *"Is the meeting room free?" "I'm sorry, it's being used right now."* | *There are never any parking spaces free at this time of day.*

> **Free** is less commonly used before a noun.

vacant
room | seat | chair | table | building | house | apartment | land | lot
available and not being used. **Vacant** is more formal than **free** and is used especially about places you pay to use or buy:
I asked the hotel if they had any vacant rooms. | *He was lucky enough to find a vacant seat.* | *They bought a vacant lot for $40,000* (=a small area of land).

> On toilets in public places, there is often a sign which says **vacant** (=empty) and **engaged** (=someone is using it).

with no people there

deserted
street | road | beach | city | town | village | station | platform | place
a deserted place is quiet because there is no one there, or because the people who used to be there have left:
It was three o'clock in the morning and the streets were deserted. | *We went for a walk along the deserted beach.*

uninhabited
island | area | region
used about a place that has no people living in it, especially permanently:
Cousin Island is a beautiful uninhabited island which is home to many rare birds. | *The rocket fell in an uninhabited region of the Negev desert.*

unoccupied
house | apartment | flat | building | property | room
used about a house or room that no one is living in or using at the moment:
Burglaries frequently happen when people are on holiday and their house is unoccupied. | *There was no noise and the building appeared to be unoccupied.*

> **Unoccupied** is less commonly used before a noun.

ANTONYMS **empty → full (1)**

encounter Ac *n formal*

an occasion when you meet someone or experience something, especially for the first time

ADJECTIVES

sb's first/next/last encounter *This was my first encounter with Shakespeare.*

a chance/unexpected encounter *A chance encounter in a restaurant led to a profitable business partnership.*

a casual encounter *He tried to suggest it was a casual encounter, but Claire guessed he had been waiting for her.*

a brief encounter *That brief encounter changed my life forever.*

sb's previous/last encounter *He had not yet fully recovered from their last encounter.*

a recent encounter *He remembered the anxiety she had shown during their recent encounter in the church.*

a personal/face-to-face encounter *In my personal encounters with Italians, I have found them very friendly.*

a direct encounter *It was not until many years later that I had my first direct encounter with the organization.*

a close encounter *He looked very shaken after his close encounter with a shark.*

a violent encounter *The film begins with a violent encounter between people in a Paris street.*

an unpleasant encounter *One evening I had an unpleasant encounter on the bus.*

a strange encounter *He had a strange encounter with a man who was dressed as a woman.*

a dangerous encounter *After some dangerous encounters with pirates, they finally find the treasure.*

VERBS

have an encounter *On their travels, they have one strange encounter after another.*

survive an encounter *He was lucky to survive his encounter with the snake.*

remember/recall an encounter *I remember my first encounter with him.*

an encounter takes place/occurs *On May 6th 1999 an unlikely encounter took place in Downing Street.*

NOUNS + encounter

an alien encounter (=an encounter with creatures from space) *He claimed he had had an alien encounter.*

PREPOSITIONS

an encounter with sb/sth *I told her about my encounter with the priest.*

an encounter between people *There was a violent encounter between police and protesters.*

encourage *v*

to give someone more confidence or desire to do something, or to make something easier or more desirable to do

ADVERBS

actively/positively encourage sth/sb *The teachers actively encourage independent decision-making.*

strongly/greatly encourage sb *Language students are strongly encouraged to study abroad for one semester.*

deliberately encourage sb *He had deliberately encouraged the other boy to throw stones.*

PREPOSITIONS

encourage sb in sth *We want to encourage young people in whatever they choose to do.*

PHRASES

designed to encourage sth/sb (*also* **aimed at encouraging sth/sb**) *There are various incentives designed to encourage participation in the program.*

try to encourage sb/sth *The government is trying to encourage more schools to manage their own budgets.*

encouragement *n*

something that helps someone feel that they can do something

ADJECTIVES

great/considerable encouragement *It was a great encouragement to hear these words.*

a little encouragement *I'm sure he can become a good player – he just needs a little encouragement from us.*

strong encouragement *A new organization is to be established, with strong encouragement from the government.*

active encouragement *The scheme was set up with the active encouragement of the local authority.*

gentle encouragement *I find that gentle encouragement often works better than criticism.*

every encouragement *Every encouragement should be given to those trying to bring peace to the region.*

VERBS

give sb encouragement *My friends gave me a lot of encouragement.*

offer encouragement *My parents offered encouragement and support.*

provide encouragement *The scheme is intended to provide encouragement for young writers.*

shout encouragement *The fans shouted encouragement to the team.*

get/receive encouragement *We have received tremendous encouragement from the Australian people.*

take/draw encouragement from sth (=you feel encouraged because of something) *The coach will have taken encouragement from the way his team performed.*

need encouragement *Young boys often need help and encouragement.*

PREPOSITIONS

encouragement from sb *Stephen received a lot of encouragement from his parents.*

with sb's encouragement *With her husband's encouragement, she became a teacher.*

PHRASES

words of encouragement *The rest of the team shouted out words of encouragement.*

encouraging *adj*

giving you hope and confidence

ADVERBS

very/most/highly encouraging *The first results look very encouraging.*

extremely/tremendously/immensely encouraging *I'm pleased with his progress – it all sounds extremely encouraging.*

quite encouraging *The news so far is quite encouraging.*
hardly encouraging/far from encouraging (=not at all encouraging) *The latest sales figures were far from encouraging.*

NOUNS

encouraging news *There is some encouraging news about the economy.*
an encouraging sign *His breathing was now normal, which was an encouraging sign.*
encouraging results *Scientists are reporting encouraging results from early tests of a vaccine.*
an encouraging response (=many people have replied) *The police have had an encouraging response to their appeals for information.*
encouraging noises (=say some encouraging things) *After making some encouraging noises, they eventually rejected his request.*
an encouraging start *The team had an encouraging start to the season when they won their first two games.*
an encouraging development *Despite these encouraging developments, the situation is still not satisfactory.*

PREPOSITIONS

encouraging for sb *It is encouraging for students to get nice comments about their work.*

ANTONYMS **encouraging → discouraging**

end[1] *n*

1 the last part of a period of time, event, activity, or story

PHRASES

the end of the day/week/month etc *Karen will return to the US at the end of the month.*
the end of March/July/December etc *My visa runs out at the end of May.*
from beginning to end *Michael Jones led the race from beginning to end.*

ADJECTIVES

the very end *Save the best joke for the very end of the speech.*
a fitting end (=a very suitable one) *Winning the championship a fifth time was a fitting end to his career.*

PREPOSITIONS

the end of sth *The end of the match was very exciting.*
at the end *At the end of the book they get married.*
until the end *You have to wait until the end of the movie to find out what happens.*
by the end *It was a good performance but by the end some people were getting bored.*
towards/near the end *Her character only appears towards the end of the film.*

ANTONYMS **end → beginning (1)**

2 a situation in which something is finished or no longer exists

VERBS

come to an end (=finish) *The team's series of victories came to an end when they lost 3-2.*
draw to an end (*also* **near an end**) (=be close to the end) *My holiday was drawing to an end.*
get to the end of sth (*also* **reach the end of sth**) *The 40-year-old power station has now reached the end of its life.*
put an end to sth (=make something stop) *A shoulder injury put an end to his baseball career.*
bring an end to sth (*also* **bring sth to an end**) (=make something stop) *They began talks aimed at bringing an end to the war.*
call for/demand an end to sth (=publicly ask for something to stop) *The union is calling for an end to discrimination.*
mark/mean/spell the end of sth (=show that something is ending) *These disappointing sales figures could spell the end of the company.*

ADJECTIVES

a sudden/abrupt end (=sudden and unexpected) *After the news leaked out, his political career came to a sudden end.*
an early end *Hopes of an early end to the conflict are fading.*
a tragic end (=when something ends in a very sad and upsetting way, usually with the death of someone) *His promising acting career came to a tragic end.*
a premature/untimely end (=when something ends too soon) *The event came to an untimely end when a fire broke out inside the stadium.*

PREPOSITIONS

an end to sth *We are hoping for an early end to the dispute.*

PHRASES

sth is at an end (=it has ended) *Now that the war is at an end, the country can begin the task of rebuilding itself.*
the end is in sight (=you know that something will end soon) *After a nine-month wait for her operation, the end is finally in sight.*
to/until the bitter end (=until it is not possible to do something any longer, even though you are in a very difficult situation) *They will remain loyal to their leader to the bitter end.*

3 the part of a place or object that is furthest from its beginning or centre

ADJECTIVES

the opposite/other end (of sth) *The two men were sitting at opposite ends of the bar.*
the far end (of sth) (=furthest from you) *He walked to the far end of the room and sat down.*

the very/extreme end of sth *Our room was at the very end of the corridor.*

the deep/shallow end (=used about the parts of a swimming pool where the water is deepest or least deep) *The kids were splashing about in the shallow end.*

PREPOSITIONS

the end of sth *The hairdresser snipped off the ends of her hair.*

at the end of sth *The school is just at the end of the street.*

on the end of sth *On the end of the chain was a bell.*

PHRASES

lay/place sth end to end (=in a line, with the ends touching) *The roof tiles are laid end to end.*

from end to end (=from one end to the other) *The animal measures over four metres from end to end.*

4 an aim or purpose

ADJECTIVES

political/military financial etc ends *The government used the situation for political ends.*

a common end (=which you all want to achieve) *We felt we were all working together towards a common end.*

a desired end *People want democracy but how can they bring about this desired end in that country?*

a noble/worthy end (=one that you admire) *Finding a cure for cancer seems a very worthy end.*

VERBS

achieve your own ends *disapproving* (=get what you want) *Some people would do almost anything to achieve their own ends.*

PHRASES

to that/this end (=with that/this aim or purpose) *Our first priority is safety, and the airline is working to that end.*

the end justifies the means *disapproving* (=you believe that doing something bad is acceptable, if it achieves a good result) *The terrorists believe that the end justifies the means, and it doesn't matter how many people are killed.*

a means to an end (=something that you do because it is a way of getting something else) *To Joe, work was a means to an end, nothing more.*

end² *v*

1 if something ends, it reaches its final point

NOUNS

a meeting/game/trial ends *The meeting ended in the late afternoon, without any agreement.*

a class/course/term ends *When the class ended, the teacher said she wanted to talk to me.*

a show/exhibition/concert/festival ends *The audience clapped when the show ended.*

a period/year/day/week etc ends *For the three-month period ending December 31st, the company made £24.8 million.*

a story/movie/film/play ends *The story ends with the couple getting married.*

war/fighting ends *The Vietnam War ended in 1975.*

conversation/talks/negotiations end *The talks ended in failure.*

a marriage/relationship ends *Her marriage ended seven years ago, when her husband suddenly left home.*

sb's life ends (=used especially when someone's life suddenly stops being happy or interesting) *Just because you have children, it doesn't mean that your life ends.*

ADVERBS

end well/badly *I knew it would end badly.*

end happily *Cinema audiences like films that end happily.*

PREPOSITIONS

end with sth *The day ended with a trip to a local restaurant.*

end in sth *The game ended in a draw.*

PHRASES

end in failure/defeat/disaster/success *Every attempt has ended in failure.*

end in divorce *One in three marriages ends in divorce.*

end in tears *informal* (=end with people being unhappy) *I hope that it won't all end in tears.*

end on a high/positive/happier note (=end with something good happening) *The story ends on a happier note, with Sally recovering from her illness.*

THESAURUS: end

finish

meeting | **concert** | **show** | **exhibition** | **race**

to end – use especially when saying what time an organized event ends:

The meeting will finish at 7 p.m. and refreshments will be provided. | *The exhibition finishes on March 7th.*

> You can also use **end** in all these sentences. **End** is more common than **finish** in this meaning.

come to an end

time | **period** | **year** | **career** | **war** | **ordeal** | **holiday** | **contract** | **relationship**

to finally end – used about something that has continued for a long time:

Her time in Africa was coming to an end. | *The war finally came to an end six years later.* | *We'd love to stay here longer, but* ***all good things must come to an end.***

draw to a close/an end
year | century | day | afternoon | season | career | campaign | war | game | conversation
if a period of time or an activity draws to a close, it gradually ends. **Draw to a close/end** is rather formal and is mainly used in written descriptions:
The weather turned colder as the year drew to a close. | The 20th century was drawing to an end. | Lowe's international playing career was drawing to a close.

run out
time | money | luck | supply | visa | contract | agreement | lease | ticket | guarantee
if time, money etc runs out, there is no more available. If an official document runs out, the period of time when you can use it has ended:
You'd better hurry – time is running out. | His luck ran out and he lost the next game by one point. | Her boyfriend must go home because his visa has run out. | The five-year guarantee runs out this October.

expire
visa | contract | agreement | lease | card | ticket | passport | guarantee | warranty
if something expires, the period of time when you can use it has ended. **Expire** is more formal than **run out**:
She had to leave when her visa expired. | My season ticket is about to expire and I need to get a new one. | If your passport expires this year, now is a good time to renew it.

You can say that something **is over** (=it has definitely ended): *The war* ***was over****. | His political career* ***is over****. | I will be glad when all this* ***is over****.*
You can also say that something is **at an end** (=it has ended, or nearly ended): *Laura realised that her marriage* ***was at an end****. | He thought his life* ***was at an end****.*
You say that **time is up** when the time that you are allowed has officially ended: *Stop writing and put down your pens. Your* ***time is up****.*

ANTONYMS end → **start¹ (2)**

2 to make something stop permanently

NOUNS

end a war/conflict *In 1975 a treaty was signed, which ended the war in Vietnam.*
end the violence/fighting/killing *The only way to end the violence is for everyone to be involved in the peace process.*
end a strike/dispute *The workers voted to end their strike.*
end a situation/problem/crisis *We need to find a way of ending the current economic crisis.*
end sb's career *The scandal effectively ended his political career.*
end the use/sale of sth *Governments have promised to end the use of these weapons.*

ending *n*

the way that a story or film finishes, or the way something that you are describing finishes

ADJECTIVES

a happy ending *I like stories with happy endings.*
a sad/unhappy/tragic ending *The story has a sad ending, and the girl never sees her family again.*
a dramatic ending *The movie has a dramatic ending in which both the main characters are killed.*
a surprise ending *I think a good detective story should have a surprise ending.*
a good ending *A joke makes a good ending to a speech.*
the perfect ending *The walk home under the stars was the perfect ending to the evening.*
a fairy-tale ending (=a good and happy ending that seems unlikely) *The story has a fairy-tale ending, and the two enemies become close friends.*
a disappointing ending *It was a disappointing ending for Castrale, who managed only third place.*
a different/alternative ending *The author invites readers to choose between three different endings.*

VERBS

have a happy/sad ending *The story has a happy ending: the dog survived and now has a new owner.*
give away the ending (=tell someone what the ending of a story will be) *The title of the story gives away the ending.*

PREPOSITIONS

an ending to sth *It was a disastrous ending to his career.*
the ending of a film/story/book/poem *He changed the ending of the book.*

endless *adj*

used when saying that there seem to be a very large number of something, or something seems to continue for a very long time, especially when this makes you surprised, annoyed, or bored

NOUNS

an endless series/succession *We had to sit through an endless series of talks.*
an endless stream *An endless stream of trucks went to and from the harbour.*
an endless supply *Our host seemed to have an endless supply of amusing stories.*
an endless round of meetings/parties *Life was an endless round of picnics and parties.*
an endless variety *The fish display an almost endless variety of colors and patterns.*

endless problems/difficulties/trouble *They had endless trouble with the water supply.*

endless questions *She patiently answered her son's endless questions.*

endless meetings *They had endless meetings with the producer.*

endless cups of tea/coffee *He drank endless cups of tea as he worked.*

the possibilities are endless *I could start a business of some kind. The possibilities are endless.*

the list is endless *There are so many courses to choose from – the list is endless.*

ADVERBS

almost/virtually/practically endless *The possible colour combinations are almost endless.*

seemingly/apparently endless *He had a seemingly endless list of demands.*

VERBS

seem endless *The journey home seemed endless.*

ends *n*

THESAURUS purpose

enduring *adj*

THESAURUS long (2), permanent

enemy *n*

someone who hates you and wants to harm you

ADJECTIVES

a great enemy *Henry prepared to fight his great enemy, the king of France.*

main/biggest/greatest enemy *He sees terrorism as his country's main enemy.*

an arch enemy/arch-enemy (=main enemy, used for emphasis) *The comic book character Lex Luthor is Superman's arch enemy.*

bitter enemies (=enemies who hate each other very much) *When these former friends quarrelled over money, they became bitter enemies.*

a political enemy *The prime minister keeps these political enemies at a safe distance.*

sworn enemies (=enemies who will always hate each other) *The men have been sworn enemies for many years.*

a common enemy (=shared by more than one person or group) *They were all united against the common enemy of fascism.*

a formidable enemy (=a very powerful enemy) *The North Vietnamese army proved to be a formidable enemy.*

deadly enemies (=enemies who try to harm each other as much as possible) *France and Germany, once deadly enemies, are now partners in the European Union.*

an old/traditional enemy (=that has been an enemy for a long time) *In 1548, Scotland moved towards an alliance with her traditional enemy, England.*

VERBS

have enemies *Everybody loved her – she didn't have any enemies.*

make enemies (=become unfriendly with people) *During her long political career, she made many enemies.*

defend/protect yourself from your enemies *Our country has a right to protect itself from its enemies.*

defeat an enemy *His opponent will be a hard enemy to defeat.*

face/confront an enemy *We must confront the real enemy, which is poverty and disease.*

engage/meet the enemy (=start fighting them) *For these young soldiers, this will be the first time they engage the enemy.*

enemy + NOUNS

enemy forces *The town is occupied by enemy forces.*

enemy soldiers/aircraft *He shot down over forty enemy aircraft.*

an enemy position (=a place controlled by an enemy army) *General Hunt ordered an air strike on the enemy positions.*

PHRASES

behind enemy lines (=behind the edge of an area that is controlled by an enemy army) *Men from the First Airborne Division were dropped behind enemy lines.*

energetic Ac *adj*

having or needing a lot of energy or determination

VERBS

feel energetic *If you're feeling energetic, we could go out for a run.*

NOUNS

an energetic person/man/woman/child *The hotel is run by a friendly and energetic woman.*

energetic activity *Guests can relax by the pool or take part in more energetic activities.*

energetic efforts *Kim made energetic efforts to improve that situation.*

an energetic campaign *Despite an energetic campaign, the Republicans lost the election.*

an energetic performance *All the dancers gave energetic performances.*

ADVERBS

very/highly energetic *She is at home all day with three highly energetic children.*

PHRASES

young and energetic *The players are young and energetic.*

THESAURUS: energetic

dynamic
leader | performer | person | performance
very energetic – used especially about

E

someone who does a lot of new or exciting things:
Margaret Thatcher was a very dynamic leader. | Robbie Williams is a powerful and dynamic performer.

hyperactive
child | son | daughter
a hyperactive child has too much energy and cannot keep still or quiet for very long:
Our youngest son was hyperactive, and it had a damaging effect on the whole family.

tireless
campaigner | worker | advocate | supporter | efforts | work | campaigning | dedication
working with a lot of energy in a determined way in order to achieve something:
She was a tireless campaigner for women's rights. | The president praised the tireless efforts of the rescue team.

Other ways of saying that someone is energetic
You can also say that someone is **full of energy** or **bursting with energy**: *At the beginning of the year, the students are* ***full of energy*** *and enthusiasm.*

E

energy Ac *n*

1 power used to provide heat, operate machines etc

ADJECTIVES/NOUNS + energy

solar energy (=from the sun) *The water is heated using solar energy.*

nuclear/atomic energy *The problem with nuclear energy is dealing with the waste.*

wind/wave energy *The windmill uses wind energy to crush grain and pump water.*

renewable energy (=energy such as solar or wind energy that can be replaced naturally) *Switching to sources of renewable energy will reduce carbon emissions.*

alternative energy (=from sources other than oil, coal, or nuclear energy) *It is the first form of public transport to be powered by alternative energy.*

clean/green energy (=causing no pollution) *The aim is to provide 80% of electricity from clean energy sources.*

VERBS

generate/produce energy *It is possible to generate energy from waste.*

supply/provide energy *The wind farm will provide enough energy for 100,000 homes.*

use energy *Washing machines use a lot of energy.*

save/conserve energy (=not waste it) *An efficient boiler will conserve energy and save you money.*

store energy *Batteries store the energy from the solar panels.*

harness energy (=get energy from somewhere and use it) *The system is designed to harness the energy of the waves.*

energy + NOUNS

energy use (*also* **energy consumption** *formal*): *We all need to reduce our energy consumption.*

energy production *Energy production has fallen.*

energy conservation (=preventing it from being wasted) *There will be taxes to encourage energy conservation.*

energy efficiency *This guide provides advice on ways of improving energy efficiency.*

energy needs/requirements *Sixty percent of the country's energy needs are met by imported oil.*

energy supplies/resources *The world's energy resources are being used up at an alarming rate.*

an energy source *Nuclear power is one of the few energy sources that does not pollute the atmosphere.*

an energy shortage *California experienced energy shortages that in turn led to power outages.*

an energy crisis *Europe could soon face an energy crisis.*

an energy bill *We are looking at ways of cutting our energy bill.*

energy prices *Energy prices keep going up.*

an energy company/the energy industry *Energy companies are making massive profits.*

PREPOSITIONS

energy from sth *The water is heated using energy from the sun.*

PHRASES

a source/form of energy *Coal is more expensive than other sources of energy.*

the demand for energy *The demand for energy in developing countries will continue to grow.*

2 the physical and mental strength that makes you able to do things

PHRASES

be full of energy/be bursting with energy (=have a lot of energy) *The children were all bursting with energy.*

a lack of energy *Common symptoms include a loss of appetite and a lack of energy.*

a burst of energy (=a short sudden increase in energy) *He tried to summon up one final burst of energy, but his legs wouldn't respond.*

VERBS

have a lot of/little/no etc energy *He always has plenty of energy!*

lack energy (=have no energy) *She lacked the energy to continue.*

put energy into sth *I really put a lot of energy into what I do.*

channel your energy into sth (=use your energy doing something, rather than other things) *She should channel more of her energy into her studies.*

devote your energy to sth (=use most of your energy doing something) *Models devote all their energy to looking perfect.*

conserve energy (=use as little as possible) *The lions spend much of the day sleeping, conserving energy for the hunt.*

waste energy *Don't waste energy making excuses.*

run out of energy (=have none left) *The players seemed to be running out of energy.*

drain/sap your energy (=make you tired) *The long walk in hot weather sapped our energy.*

summon up/find the energy to do sth (=manage to do something even though you feel tired) *I couldn't even summon up the energy to make a cup of tea.*

sth takes energy (*also* **sth requires energy** *formal*): *Climbing with a full backpack takes a lot of energy.*

ADJECTIVES

boundless energy (=that seems to have no limit) *Her boundless energy and lively personality make her a great kids TV presenter.*

youthful energy (=energy that young people naturally have) *She is very talented and full of youthful energy.*

creative energy (=that makes you want to write, draw, paint etc) *We have seen an explosion of creative energy from the band this year.*

nervous energy (=energy that comes from being nervous or excited) *She seems to thrive on nervous energy.*

excess/surplus energy *Kids need an opportunity to use up their excess energy.*

pent-up energy (=used especially when someone feels frustrated because they have a lot of unused energy) *He needed an outlet for all his pent-up energy.*

energy + NOUNS

energy levels (=the amount of energy someone has) *Regular exercise increases your energy levels.*

enforce Ac *v*

to make people obey a rule or law

NOUNS

enforce a law *He wants the police to enforce the law and arrest the men.*

enforce a rule/regulation *The rules are strictly enforced.*

enforce an agreement *The president called for UN action to enforce the agreement.*

enforce discipline *A school must enforce discipline in the classroom.*

enforce a ban *A ban on arms sales can only be enforced with international cooperation.*

ADVERBS

be strictly/rigorously/rigidly enforced *The new parking restrictions will be strictly enforced.*

be properly/fully enforced *Rules are only effective if they are properly enforced.*

be effectively enforced *Many members think that the regulations cannot be effectively enforced.*

be legally enforced *Most of the social rules and customs we follow are not legally enforced.*

engagement *n*

1 an agreement between two people to marry, or the period of time they are engaged

VERBS

announce your engagement (=tell people about it) *The couple are expected to announce their engagement today.*

break off an engagement (=suddenly end it) *Were you surprised when she broke off the engagement?*

engagement + NOUNS

an engagement ring *Jerry bought her a beautiful sapphire engagement ring.*

PREPOSITIONS

sb's engagement to sb *He announced his engagement to the actress last week.*

2 *formal* an official arrangement to do something, especially one that is related to your work

ADJECTIVES

an official engagement *This is the prime minister's first official engagement since the elections.*

a public engagement *She appeared with her husband at many public engagements.*

an important engagement *He had an important engagement with his solicitor.*

a pressing engagement (=something important that must be done now) *He left in a hurry, claiming to have a pressing engagement elsewhere.*

a previous/prior engagement (=one that is already arranged) *I'm sorry I can't be there, but I have a previous engagement.*

a speaking engagement (=one in which you give a speech) *I've been turning down speaking engagements to concentrate on writing my memoirs.*

VERBS

have an engagement *I don't have any engagements tomorrow.*

keep an engagement (=do the thing that you have arranged to do) *The prime minister will be unable to keep this engagement.*

carry out an engagement *Last year, the princess carried out over 300 official engagements.*

cancel an engagement *He instructed his secretary to cancel all his engagements.*

PREPOSITIONS

an engagement with sb *He had an engagement with the French president.*

engine *n*

the part of a vehicle that produces power to make it move

VERBS

start an engine (*also* **switch on/turn on an engine**) *I fastened my seat belt and turned on the engine.*

switch off/turn off an engine *Maggie pulled over and switched off the engine.*

rev (up) an engine *BrE*, **gun an engine** *AmE* (=make an engine run very fast, usually when the vehicle is not moving) *He waits at the red light, impatiently revving the engine.*

leave/keep the engine running (=not turn it off) *He parked outside the bank and kept the engine running.*

an engine runs on sth (=it uses a kind of fuel) *The engine runs on ordinary petrol.*

ADJECTIVES/NOUNS + engine

a big/powerful engine *The newer model has a more powerful engine.*

a small engine *The engine is small, so it's quite cheap to run.*

a petrol/diesel engine *The van has a 2.5 litre diesel engine.*

a jet engine *We could hear the plane's powerful jet engines.*

a car/motorbike etc engine *Modern car engines are highly efficient and use much less gas.*

engine + NOUNS

engine trouble *When the boat developed engine trouble, the crew had to abandon ship.*

engine failure *Their aircraft suffered engine failure and crashed into the sea.*

the engine capacity (=the size of the engine) *The car has a small engine capacity but it produces a lot of power.*

engineer *n*

someone whose job is to design, build, or repair things such as machines, bridges, or roads

ADJECTIVES/NOUNS + engineer

a civil engineer (=an engineer who designs and builds roads, bridges etc) *The bridge was designed by the famous civil engineer, Thomas Telford.*

a mechanical engineer *He was a mechanical engineer, and he knew everything there was to know about car engines.*

an electrical/electronic engineer *He works as an electronic engineer for a phone company.*

an aircraft engineer *The plane had been checked by aircraft engineers.*

a mining engineer *Mining engineers were constructing a new mine shaft.*

a qualified/trained engineer *The oven should be installed by a qualified engineer.*

a chartered engineer *BrE* (=a qualified engineer) *She is training to become a chartered engineer.*

VERBS

work as an engineer *He works as an engineer at a nuclear power plant.*

an engineer designs/develops sth *A British engineer has designed a car made of wood especially for use in Africa.*

English *n*

the language used in Britain, the US, Australia, and some other countries

ADJECTIVES

good/excellent English *You speak very good English.*

perfect English *His English was perfect, with no trace of an accent.*

fluent English (=very good English, without any mistakes or hesitations) *She studied in the United States, and she speaks fluent English.*

poor English (=very bad) *He had only recently arrived in Britain, and his English was poor.*

British/American/Australian etc English *The spelling 'color' is used in American English.*

non-standard English (=English which some native speakers say, but which is not considered to be correct) *'There ain't no bread' is non-standard English.*

correct/standard English *The correct English phrase is 'There isn't any bread.'*

pidgin English (=English consisting of a few simple English words mixed with another language) *They were able to communicate by means of pidgin English.*

Instead of saying that someone's English is 'bad', you usually say that it is **not very good**, **poor**, or **terrible** if it is very bad.

⚠ Don't say 'His English is broken.' Say **His English isn't very good.** You only use **broken** in this meaning in the phrase **in broken English**.

VERBS

speak English *Does anyone here speak English?*

understand English *Most people can understand English because they study it at school.*

use English *The children all use English at home.*

learn English *I came here because I wanted to learn English.*

practise your English *BrE*, **practice your English** *AmE*: *She was glad of a chance to practise her English.*

improve your English *Hiroshi hopes to improve his English.*

translate sth into English *Some of her books have been translated into English.*
be published in English *His books are being published in English for the first time.*

English + NOUNS

an English word/phrase *The English word 'landscape' comes from the Dutch word 'lanschap'.*
English grammar *A good knowledge of the rules of English grammar is essential.*
an English course/class/lesson *I'm thinking of taking English classes this summer.*
an English teacher *His English teacher says his English is getting better.*

PREPOSITIONS

in English *The sign was written in English.*

PHRASES

be fluent in English (=be able to speak English well, without mistakes or hesitation) *He spent a year in England and became fluent in English.*
have a good command/knowledge of English (=be able to speak English well) *The book is aimed at those who already have a good command of English.*
not speak a word of English (=does not speak any English at all) *He doesn't speak a word of English.*
in plain English (=in simple clear English) *Could you explain, in plain English, what that means?*
in broken English (=speaking English with a lot of mistakes) *A waitress came and took their order in broken English.*
learners of English *Pronunciation is a problem for many learners of English.*

> **The Queen's English**
> People sometimes talk about **the Queen's English**, meaning 'standard British English'. This phrase now sounds rather old-fashioned.

enigmatic *adj* THESAURUS > mysterious

enjoy *v*

1 to get pleasure from something

ADVERBS

enjoy sth very much/very much enjoy sth *It's a very funny book and I enjoyed it very much.*
enjoy sth a lot *I've enjoyed my trip a lot.*
really/thoroughly enjoy sth *She really enjoys cooking.*
enjoy sth immensely/enormously/tremendously/hugely *The audience enjoyed the show immensely.*
greatly enjoy sth *The children's teacher said they had greatly enjoyed the visit.*
particularly/especially enjoy sth *I particularly enjoyed the article about space travel.*
quite/rather enjoy sth *He quite enjoys being alone.*
actually enjoy sth (=used when you think it is surprising) *I actually enjoy being out in the rain.*

NOUNS

enjoy your job/work *He clearly enjoys his job.*
enjoy a holiday/trip *Did you enjoy your holiday?*
enjoy a day/evening *We enjoyed our day in London.*
enjoy a meal *The waiter brought their food and said "Enjoy your meal".*
enjoy life *I'm enjoying life more than ever before.*
enjoy an experience *I enjoyed the experience of being part of a team.*
enjoy sb's company (=enjoy being with someone) *He was an interesting man and she enjoyed his company.*
enjoy the view *They sat outside, enjoying the view across the lake.*
enjoy your freedom *Enjoy your freedom while you can.*

PHRASES

enjoy yourself (=do things that make you happy) *People come here to relax and enjoy themselves.*
enjoy every minute *I enjoyed every minute of the trip.*

> **Grammar**
> **Enjoy** is usually used transitively and usually has an object after it. Don't say 'I enjoyed very much.' Say **I enjoyed it very much.** People sometimes say **Enjoy!** on its own, meaning "I hope you enjoy it!", especially when they are serving you a meal.

THESAURUS: enjoy

have fun *informal*
to enjoy doing something relaxing or not serious:
*See you soon. **Have fun!** | We all **had a lot of fun** when we were in Paris.*

> **Have fun** is usually used on its own. You can also use it with a participle: *They **had fun** shopping together.*

get pleasure from/take pleasure in
to enjoy something:
*She **gets a lot of pleasure from** her job. | They **took great pleasure in** each other's company.*

> These phrases are sometimes used when talking about people who enjoy causing suffering or problems: *Some people **get pleasure from** hurting other people. | I shall **take** great **pleasure in** telling him that I'm resigning.*

E

revel in sth
to enjoy every moment or part of something very much:
The rest of the family were ***revelling in*** *the glorious hot weather.* | *He was* ***positively revelling*** *in his new-found freedom* (=enjoying it very much).

relish
prospect | **chance/opportunity** | **challenge** | **thought/idea**
to enjoy the thought that something is going to happen:
He is relishing the prospect of playing against some of the best players in the world. | *I relished the chance to learn all about the local culture.* | *It'll be tough, but I'm relishing the challenge.* | *I don't relish the thought of leaving all my friends.*

savour *BrE*, **savor** *AmE*
moment | **memory** | **victory** | **prospect**
to enjoy something as it happens and spend time thinking about how enjoyable it is:
He paused to savour the moment of being on top of the world's highest mountain. | *He had little time to savour his victory.* | *Fans are savouring the prospect of a great match.*

bask in
glory | **publicity** | **attention**
to enjoy the approval or attention that you are getting from other people:
He smiled for the cameras, basking in the glory of a job well done. | *Robertson basks in the attention such stories bring.*

wallow in
misery | **self-pity** | **the past**
to enjoy being sad and feeling sorry for yourself, especially in order to make people notice you and pay attention to you:
His songs are depressing and he seems to enjoy wallowing in misery. | *Since his girlfriend left him, he's been wallowing in self-pity.* | *Some people like to wallow in the past* (=they enjoy saying how much better things were in the past than they are now).

2 to have something good

NOUNS

enjoy an advantage *These children do not enjoy the same advantages that we have.*

enjoy a benefit *Other countries want to share the benefits that Western countries now enjoy.*

enjoy good health *My aunt Eileen is enjoying good health at the age of 84.*

enjoy support *The police service still enjoys the support of the public.*

enjoy success *The team enjoyed some success.*

enjoy popularity *The magazine enjoyed enormous popularity in the early 20th century.*

enjoy a good reputation *The hotel enjoys a good reputation.*

enjoy a good/close relationship *The two men enjoyed a good relationship.*

enjoy freedom *Students enjoy considerable freedom.*

enjoyable *adj* giving you pleasure

ADVERBS

very/really/highly/most enjoyable *We all had a very enjoyable time.* | *This has been a most enjoyable evening.*

extremely/hugely/immensely enjoyable *The film is a hugely enjoyable romantic comedy.*

quite/rather enjoyable *Learning new skills can be quite enjoyable.*

NOUNS

an enjoyable experience *I wanted the holiday to be an enjoyable experience for us.*

an enjoyable activity *Cooking should be an enjoyable activity.*

an enjoyable day/evening/afternoon *We had an enjoyable day at the beach yesterday.*

an enjoyable time *They all had a really enjoyable time.*

an enjoyable holiday *It is the perfect place for a relaxing and enjoyable holiday.*

an enjoyable game *It was certainly an enjoyable game to watch.*

an enjoyable way of doing sth *Sailing is an extremely enjoyable way of learning teamwork skills.*

VERBS

find sth enjoyable *I found the task quite enjoyable.*

make sth enjoyable *How can teachers make learning enjoyable?*

THESAURUS: enjoyable

agreeable *formal*
experience | **evening** | **place**
pleasant and enjoyable:
I wished that my visit had been a more agreeable experience. | *They had an agreeable evening at the theatre.* | *Cambridge is an agreeable place to live.*

rewarding
experience | **job** | **occupation**
enjoyable because it gives you a lot of satisfaction:
Finding your new home can be a rewarding experience. | *The teacher likes the children and says she finds her job rewarding.*

entertaining
film | **book** | **story** | **account** | **programme** | **evening**
enjoyable because it is interesting, exciting, or funny:
It is a ***highly entertaining film.*** | *The book is an entertaining account of his travels in China.* | *We*

watched an entertaining programme about penguins. | *Thank you for a most entertaining evening.*

fun *informal*
time | **day**
enjoyable:
We all had a fun time. | *I had a fun day with the kids.* | ***It was fun while it lasted**, but I'm back at college tomorrow* (=used when saying that you enjoyed something, but now it has finished).

enjoyment *n* a feeling of pleasure

ADJECTIVES

great/huge/tremendous enjoyment *Three boys had been watching my struggles with great enjoyment.*

maximum enjoyment *The trip is planned to give maximum enjoyment.*

obvious enjoyment (*also* **evident enjoyment** *formal*): *He was eating a vast breakfast with evident enjoyment.*

VERBS

get enjoyment out of/from sth (*also* **derive enjoyment from sth** *formal*): *I get a lot of enjoyment out of painting.*

find enjoyment in sth *I was finding enjoyment in discovering London on foot.*

bring/give enjoyment to sb *His music has brought enjoyment to millions.*

add to/increase sb's enjoyment (*also* **enhance sb's enjoyment** *formal*): *Knowing about the poet's life can add to our enjoyment of the poem.*

spoil/interfere with sb's enjoyment *The behaviour of a few fans spoiled the enjoyment of the other people watching the game.*

take away/detract from sb's enjoyment (=make someone enjoy something less) *He had a bad headache and this rather detracted from his enjoyment of the film.*

PHRASES

for your own (personal) enjoyment *She cooks for friends, and for her own enjoyment.*

a source of enjoyment *Music can be more than just a source of enjoyment.*

a sense/feeling of enjoyment *He still plays the game with a sense of enjoyment.*

enormous *adj* THESAURUS **huge**

enough *determiner, pronoun*

as many or as much as is needed or wanted

NOUNS

enough time/money *We had just enough time to catch the train.*

enough food/water *There should be enough food for everyone.*

enough space/room *He left enough room on the sofa for Anna to sit down.*

enough evidence/information *There is enough evidence to suggest that this drug is potentially harmful.*

enough experience/practice *She doesn't have enough experience for the job.*

enough sense/courage *Luckily, Marija had enough sense not to panic.*

PREPOSITIONS

enough for sb/sth *There weren't enough chairs for everyone.*

PHRASES

more than enough *They've had more than enough time to make all the preparations.*

nowhere near/not nearly enough (=much less than is needed) *The money I had was nowhere near enough to buy a car.*

barely enough (=only with great difficulty) *There was barely enough room for them to pass each other.*

just enough *The lamp gave just enough light to see what we were doing.*

quite enough (=definitely enough) *You've spent quite enough money already.*

enough to go round (=enough for everyone) *They took pain-relieving drugs to the refugees but there weren't enough to go round.*

Someone has **had enough**
This phrase has two meanings. It can mean you don't want any more: *"Do you want any more pizza?" "No thanks, I've* ***had enough****."* It can also mean that you are annoyed with someone or something, and you don't want the situation to continue any longer: *"I've* ***had enough*** *of this job. I need a change."*

THESAURUS: enough

sufficient *formal*
evidence | **time** | **funds** | **resources** | **information** | **data** | **detail** | **reason** | **interest** | **number** | **amount**
enough for a particular purpose:
The police did not have sufficient evidence to charge her. | *Allow sufficient time to get there.* | *If there is sufficient interest, we might organize another workshop next year.* | *Three kilos should be* ***sufficient for*** *our needs.*

adequate *formal*
supply | **provision** | **resources** | **funding** | **support** | **protection** | **explanation** | **information** | **training** | **time** | **preparation**
enough in quantity or good enough in quality for a particular purpose:
We try to make sure the refugees have adequate supplies of food. | *Your insurance policy should give you adequate protection.* | *All staff must be given adequate training in health and safety.* | *The heating system was* ***barely adequate*** (=only just adequate). | *This printer is* ***perfectly adequate*** *for most purposes* (=completely adequate).

E

ample
opportunity | time | evidence | proof | reason | warning | space | room | parking | scope
more than enough for what is needed:
Local residents will be given ample opportunity to express their views. | If we leave at 3 o'clock, that should allow ample time to get to the airport. | The dining room has ample space for a large table. | There's ample parking at the hotel. | People used to think that 1 GB of memory was ***ample for*** *the average personal computer.*

plenty
an amount that is enough or more than enough:
Allow yourself ***plenty of*** *time to get to the airport. | Your daughter won't need much cash at camp ($20-25 will be plenty).*

enterprise *n formal*

1 companies and businesses in general

ADJECTIVES/NOUNS + enterprise

private enterprise (=companies that are not owned by the government) *The government feels it cannot interfere in private enterprise.*

state/state-owned/public enterprise (=companies owned by the government) *New Zealand Rail is a state-owned enterprise.*

local enterprise (=businesses in a particular area) *The council is helping to support local enterprise.*

enterprise + NOUNS

an enterprise zone (=an area created by the government to attract businesses) *Many firms relocate to enterprise zones because of tax advantages.*

2 a company or business

ADJECTIVES/NOUNS + enterprise

a large/large-scale enterprise *The company has grown into a large-scale enterprise.*

a small/small-scale enterprise *The tax will affect owners of small-scale enterprises consisting of up to ten people.*

a successful enterprise *She is the owner of an extremely successful enterprise.*

a commercial/business enterprise *If you are setting up your own business enterprise, your bank can help.*

3 an activity that someone is involved in

ADJECTIVES

a dangerous/hazardous enterprise *He was probably involved in a dangerous enterprise of some kind.*

a criminal enterprise *In these countries, the government is secretly involved in large-scale criminal enterprises.*

an exciting enterprise *She knew the trip would be an exciting enterprise.*

VERBS

undertake an enterprise (=do it) *Why did you agree to undertake such a hazardous enterprise?*

embark on an enterprise (=start doing it) *A few months after first discussing it, they were embarking on this most exciting of enterprises.*

entertaining *adj* enjoyable

ADVERBS

highly/very entertaining *The novel is highly entertaining and I would recommend it to anyone.*

hugely/enormously/wonderfully entertaining (=extremely entertaining) *This hugely entertaining play was a big hit on Broadway.*

mildly entertaining (=not very entertaining) *The film is mildly entertaining in parts.*

VERBS

find sb/sth entertaining *The children certainly found him entertaining.*

THESAURUS: entertaining

agreeable, rewarding, entertaining, fun → **enjoyable**

entertainment *n*

things such as films, television, performances etc that are intended to amuse or interest people

ADJECTIVES/NOUNS + entertainment

live entertainment (=performed while people watch, not recorded and watched later) *There are three bars on the ship, all with live entertainment.*

family entertainment (=suitable for children and adults) *The holiday village has plenty of family entertainment on offer.*

mass/popular entertainment (=popular with large numbers of people) *Reality TV has been a very successful form of mass entertainment.*

light entertainment (=shows that are funny and easy to understand rather than serious) *He believes that children can appreciate more than just light entertainment.*

home entertainment (=provided by machines such as televisions, DVD players, and music systems) *A TV that connects to the internet will become a standard part of home entertainment.*

a day's/afternoon's/evening's entertainment *The evening's entertainment concluded with a firework display.*

VERBS

provide entertainment *Dancers and musicians were on hand to provide entertainment.*

put on/lay on entertainment (=organize and provide it) *The organizers laid on some entertainment for the children.*

entertainment + NOUNS

the entertainment business/industry *The union represents people who work in the entertainment industry.*

entertainment value (=how enjoyable something is to watch) *The films have great entertainment value for kids.*

an entertainment venue (=a place such as a concert hall where there are performances) *Most entertainment venues have a licence to sell alcohol.*

an entertainment complex (=a group of buildings providing a range of entertainment) *The hotel is next to a large entertainment complex.*

PREPOSITIONS

for sb's entertainment *formal: After dinner, there will a musical performance for your entertainment.*

PHRASES

a form of entertainment (=a type of entertainment) *Video games are a popular modern form of entertainment.*

a place of entertainment *formal: Clubs and other places of entertainment must close by 3 a.m.*

a source of entertainment *The only source of entertainment was a piano.*

enthralling *adj* THESAURUS **interesting**

enthusiasm *n*

strong feelings of interest in something, and a desire to be involved in it

ADJECTIVES

great/much/considerable enthusiasm *There was considerable enthusiasm for the idea of a picnic.*

enormous/tremendous enthusiasm *He always plays with tremendous enthusiasm.*

genuine/real enthusiasm *She talked about the project with genuine enthusiasm.*

boundless/unbounded/unbridled enthusiasm *formal* (=very great) *I'd like to thank the organizers for their boundless enthusiasm.*

infectious enthusiasm (=spreading from one person to another) *Her enthusiasm was infectious.*

little enthusiasm (=not much enthusiasm) *In the nearby villages, there's little enthusiasm for the new airport.*

initial enthusiasm (=happening at first, but not lasting) *After a few months, their initial enthusiasm had started to wane.*

renewed enthusiasm (=starting again, with increased energy or interest) *After lunch, she went about the task with renewed enthusiasm.*

youthful enthusiasm (=that is typical of young people) *The team has just the right mix of youthful enthusiasm and experience.*

VERBS

have enthusiasm *He never had much enthusiasm for work.*

show enthusiasm *The younger children showed little enthusiasm for the game.*

lose (your) enthusiasm *The diet started well, but I lost enthusiasm after a while.*

lack enthusiasm *The audience seemed to lack enthusiasm.*

dampen sb's enthusiasm *formal* (=stop them feeling enthusiastic) *The bad weather had dampened our enthusiasm.*

fire sb's enthusiasm (=make someone feel very enthusiastic) *The teacher really fired their enthusiasm for history.*

arouse/generate enthusiasm *formal* (=make people feel enthusiastic) *The new system failed to arouse enthusiasm amongst the staff.*

retain enthusiasm (=still have it) *We want children to retain this enthusiasm for sport in their adult lives.*

share sb's enthusiasm *I don't share my husband's enthusiasm for camping.*

enthusiasm wears off/wanes/fades (=becomes less strong) *After years of doing the same job, your enthusiasm tends to wane.*

PREPOSITIONS

with/without enthusiasm *The proposal has been greeted with enthusiasm by both parties.*

enthusiasm for/about sth *He has great enthusiasm for all types of sport.*

enthusiasm among people *There was not much enthusiasm for the plans among local people.*

PHRASES

full of enthusiasm (=very enthusiastic) *He entered politics full of enthusiasm, but that gradually disappeared.*

brimming/bursting/bubbling with enthusiasm (=very excited and enthusiastic) *Her voice was brimming with enthusiasm when she told us her plans.*

fired (up) with enthusiasm (=very enthusiastic and keen to do something) *She came back from the course fired up with enthusiasm.*

a wave/burst/surge of enthusiasm (=a sudden feeling of enthusiasm) *The new year began with a fresh wave of enthusiasm.*

a lack of enthusiasm *My lack of enthusiasm for his suggestion upset him.*

enthusiast *n* THESAURUS **fan**

enthusiastic *adj*

feeling or showing a lot of interest and excitement about something

ADVERBS

very/highly/extremely enthusiastic *The children are very enthusiastic about the holiday.*

wildly enthusiastic (=extremely enthusiastic) *The audience burst into wildly enthusiastic applause.*

overly enthusiastic (=too enthusiastic) *An overly enthusiastic child had rung my doorbell five times.*

VERBS

be/feel enthusiastic *They felt enthusiastic about moving to another country.*

get/become enthusiastic *He got very enthusiastic while he was telling the story.*

seem/appear enthusiastic *I wanted to go, but Helen seemed less enthusiastic.*

sound/look enthusiastic *"I'm sure we can do it," she said, trying to sound enthusiastic.*

NOUNS

enthusiastic support *His policies won him the enthusiastic support of middle-income voters.*

an enthusiastic supporter *He is an enthusiastic supporter of the war.*

an enthusiastic response *The proposal has received an enthusiastic response from students.*

an enthusiastic reception/welcome *The audience gave him an enthusiastic reception.*

an enthusiastic crowd/audience *An enthusiastic crowd cheered the team onto the pitch.*

enthusiastic applause *His speech was greeted by enthusiastic applause.*

an enthusiastic amateur (=someone who tries hard but is often not very skilful) *There are a few professionals in the race, but most are enthusiastic amateurs.*

an enthusiastic review *The play received enthusiastic reviews.*

PREPOSITIONS

enthusiastic about sth *All the staff are enthusiastic about the project.*

THESAURUS: enthusiastic

eager

anticipation | expectation | audience | fans | customers | hands | face | smile

wanting to do something or know about something very soon:

We waited in eager anticipation. | Eager fans waited for hours to hear him play. | The child's eager hands tore the wrapping paper off the gift. | The classroom was full of eager young faces. | He was eager to hear every detail of her day.

keen

eager to work or learn:

She hasn't much experience but she's very keen. | John was a keen student who worked very hard.

In British English, **keen** can also be used before a noun when someone is very enthusiastic about a particular activity and does it a lot: *Pat is a very* ***keen*** *gardener. | I'm a* ***keen*** *golfer and play twice a week.*

avid

reader | collector | fan | supporter | golfer | skier | interest

used when you want to emphasize that someone does something a lot or is very interested in something:

She was an avid reader all her life. | I've become an avid collector of his work. | As a schoolboy he had an avid interest in birds.

Avid is only used before a noun.

Avid or keen?

In British English **avid** or **keen** can be used before a noun to describe someone who does something a lot or is very interested in it. **Avid** is more formal than **keen**: *He is a* ***keen/avid*** *skier.*

In American English, **keen** is not usually used in this sense and **avid** is the usual word to use: *He is an* ***avid*** *skier.*

zealous

doing something in a very enthusiastic way, especially supporting something or making sure that people obey rules:

She was a zealous supporter of the revolution. | The company has been extremely zealous in defending its interests. | Officials have been very zealous in the application of the new regulations.

fervent *written*

supporter | admirer | proponent | believer | belief | support | prayer | wish

believing or feeling something very strongly and sincerely:

Galinsoga was one of Franco's most fervent supporters. | He was a fervent admirer of Margaret Thatcher. | It was her fervent belief that she could achieve anything.

Fervent is usually used before a noun.

In informal English, if you are very eager to do something, you can use the phrase **can't wait to do sth**: *I* ***can't wait to*** *see him again.*

If you are pleased and excited because you know something is going to happen soon, you can say that you **are looking forward to something**: *I'm* ***looking forward to*** *visiting Japan next month.*

E

entrance *n*

a door, gate etc that you go through to enter a place

ADJECTIVES/NOUNS + entrance

the main entrance *She found a parking space close to the hospital's main entrance.*

a front/back/rear/side entrance *Steps lead up to the front entrance.*

a narrow entrance *I could see part of the yard through the narrow entrance.*

a wide entrance *There was a wide entrance at the front of the building.*

a grand/impressive/imposing entrance *She was photographed in front of the museum's imposing entrance.*

the hotel/hospital/museum etc entrance *Our taxi pulled up outside the hotel entrance.*

the tunnel/cave entrance *The tunnel entrance is halfway up the mountain.*

the harbour entrance *BrE*, **the harbor entrance** *AmE*: *We watched as the ferry approached the harbour entrance.*

VERBS

use an entrance *It's quicker to use the side entrance.*

come/go/pass etc through an entrance *People passed in single file through the narrow entrance.*

block the entrance *A large stone blocked the entrance to the tomb.*

entrance + NOUNS

the entrance hall (=a room at the entrance to a building) *He walked through the front door into the entrance hall.*

the entrance gate/door *Soldiers were guarding the entrance gate.*

entry *n*

1 the act of going into a place

VERBS

gain entry (=succeed in going into a place) *Burglars use various methods to gain entry to houses.*

force an entry (=get into a building by breaking a door, window etc) *The church was locked, but he managed to force an entry.*

make your entry (=enter in a way that makes other people notice you) *She waited until everyone was sitting down before she made her entry.*

ADJECTIVES

illegal entry (=when someone enters a building illegally) *The two men were later arrested and charged with illegal entry.*

unauthorized entry (=when someone enters a place without permission) *There was a big sign on the door saying 'No Unauthorized Entry'.*

forced entry (=when someone gets into a building illegally by breaking a door, window etc) *There were no signs of a forced entry, but several paintings were missing.*

entry + NOUNS

an entry point (*also* **a point of entry**) (=a place where people can enter a country) *This mountain pass is the main entry point into the country for refugees.*

PREPOSITIONS

entry into a place *This is where the thieves made their entry into the building.*

2 the right to go into a place

VERBS

allow (sb) entry (*also* **grant (sb) entry** *formal*) (=let someone enter a place) *Citizens of most EU countries are allowed automatic entry into Britain.*

refuse/deny (sb) entry (=stop someone entering) *He was refused entry to the club because he was wearing trainers.*

apply for entry *The number of people applying for entry into the country is increasing every year.*

restrict/limit entry *We have to restrict entry to the first 300 people who apply.*

ADJECTIVES

free entry *Guests have free entry to the hotel spa and gym.*

entry + NOUNS

an entry visa (=a visa which allows you to enter a country) *Visitors to the United States must first obtain an entry visa.*

an entry fee *Do visitors to the castle pay an entry fee?*

an entry ticket *The price of the holiday includes a two-day entry ticket to the Disneyland Theme Park.*

PREPOSITIONS

entry to/into a place *Entry to the palace gardens is included in the price of admission.*

PHRASES

no entry (=written on signs to show that you are not allowed to go somewhere) *The door had 'No Entry' written in large letters.*

right of entry *Mexican citizens do not have automatic right of entry into the United States.*

3 when someone becomes a member of a university, an organization etc or starts to take part in a system, a particular kind of work etc

VERBS

gain entry (=be allowed to do something or join something) *You need good exam results to gain entry to the best universities.*

restrict entry (=stop someone from doing something or joining something) *Tariffs on trade have the effect of restricting entry into the market.*

NOUNS + entry

university/college/school entry *Japan has one of the highest rates of college entry in the world.*

entry + NOUNS

entry requirements *Applicants must satisfy the normal entry requirements for the school.*

entry qualifications *What are the entry qualifications for the course?*

an entry form *New members have to fill in a ten-page entry form.*

PREPOSITIONS

entry into/to sth *This is the minimum height for entry into the police force.*

4 a piece of information written in a book, on a list, on a website etc

VERBS

write/make an entry *She was asked to write an entry on karate for a new sports dictionary.*

post an entry (=on a website) *An unhappy customer posted an angry entry on the company's website.*

read an entry *If you read any entry on the American Revolution, it will mention George Washington.*

NOUNS + entry

an encyclopedia/dictionary entry *The encyclopedia entry for him is over two pages long.*

a diary entry *This was the last diary entry she made before she died.*

a blog entry (=on a website) *In a recent blog entry, she criticized government policy on education.*

PREPOSITIONS

an entry in sth *There's no entry in her diary for that date.*

an entry for sth *Look at the entry for 'Russia' in the encyclopedia.*

envelope *n*

a thin paper cover in which you send a letter

ADJECTIVES

a stamped-addressed envelope (=with a stamp and an address already on it) *A copy of the rules can be obtained by sending a stamped-addressed envelope to the above address.*

a self-addressed envelope (=with your own name and address on) *Enclose a self-addressed envelope with your application form.*

a sealed envelope (=firmly closed) *The contract was delivered by special messenger in a sealed envelope.*

VERBS

open an envelope *I opened the envelope and pulled out the document.*

seal an envelope (=close it) *She sealed the envelope and stuck on a stamp.*

an envelope contains sth *Does the envelope contain any money?*

PREPOSITIONS

in/into an envelope *I put the card in a small envelope.*

PHRASES

on the back of an envelope (=used to describe a calculation or plan that is written down quickly on any available small piece of paper) *She scribbled a few ideas on the back of an envelope.*

envious *adj*

wanting something that someone else has

VERBS

be/feel envious *He felt envious of his friends who had children.*

get envious *I get envious when other people talk about their holidays in exotic places.*

look/sound envious *"How nice!" she said, trying not to sound envious.*

make sb envious *He showed us his new sports car, which made us all very envious.*

NOUNS

envious looks/glances *She was aware of the envious looks of other women as she began to dance with him.*

envious friends/colleagues *Envious colleagues wondered how he had got such a big office.*

envious eyes *The other players have been watching him win every game with envious eyes.*

PREPOSITIONS

envious of sb/sth *She was very envious of her brother.*

environment Ac *n*

1 the air, water, and land on Earth

VERBS

protect the environment *You can help protect the environment by recycling your waste.*

conserve the environment (=protect it and prevent it from changing or being damaged) *People need to live in harmony with nature and conserve the environment.*

harm/damage the environment *The government insists that the dam will not harm the environment.*

destroy the environment *We need to find ways of producing energy without destroying the environment.*

affect the environment *Tourism affects the environment in several ways.*

pollute the environment *Nuclear waste will pollute the environment for centuries.*

clean up the environment *It's about time that we started cleaning up the environment.*

⚠ Don't say 'hurt the environment'. Say **harm the environment** or **damage the environment**.

E

PHRASES

be good/bad for the environment *Plastic bags are bad for the environment.*

be harmful/damaging to the environment *Some of these chemicals are very damaging to the environment.*

protection of the environment *In developing countries, protection of the environment is not a primary concern.*

conservation of the environment *There are many organizations dedicated to conservation of the environment.*

damage/harm to the environment *A lot of chemicals used in industry cause harm to the environment.*

the destruction of the environment *How can we prevent the destruction of the natural environment?*

pollution of the environment *The waste material must be stored safely to avoid pollution of the environment.*

the effect/impact on the environment *The building's design will minimize its impact on the environment.*

ADJECTIVES

the natural environment *Current methods of farming are damaging the natural environment.*

the marine environment (=the sea and the creatures that live there) *Fish farming poses a threat to the marine environment.*

2 the people and things that are around you in your life

ADJECTIVES/NOUNS + environment

the physical environment (=the place where you live or work, including buildings, furniture etc) *Improvements to the physical environment range from removing graffiti to planting trees.*

the immediate environment (=the building in which you live or work, and the area very close to it) *Most accidents happen to young children within the immediate environment of their home.*

a safe environment *The playground provides a safe environment for children.*

a stable environment (=without any big changes) *They argued that being married helps provide a stable environment for bringing up children.*

a friendly/pleasant environment *The restaurant offers a stylish and friendly environment with first-class service.*

a clean/dirty environment *No-one wants to live in a dirty environment.*

a competitive environment (=where everyone is trying to be the best) *Our business has to operate in an increasingly competitive environment.*

an unfamiliar environment (=one that you do not know very well) *I find it difficult to sleep in an unfamiliar environment.*

a working/learning environment *Most people prefer a quiet working environment.*

the home/family environment (*also* **the domestic environment**) *A lot of children suffer because of problems in their home environment.*

the economic/political/business environment *The economic environment has changed, and many countries are sliding into recession.*

VERBS

create an environment *We want to create an environment where children can learn happily.*

provide an environment *The government should provide an economic environment which encourages enterprise.*

improve an environment (*also* **enhance an environment** *formal*): *They do not take pride in their area, and do nothing to improve their environment.*

PREPOSITIONS

in an environment *Children should not be growing up in this environment.*

an environment for sth *The spa provides a pleasant environment for relaxation.*

an environment of sth *Important decisions must be discussed in an environment of understanding.*

3 the natural features of a place, for example its weather, land, and plants

ADJECTIVES

a harsh/hostile environment (*also* **an inhospitable environment**) (=with many difficulties and dangers) *How can anything can survive in such a hostile environment?*

a fragile environment (=easily damaged) *Many people are worried about the impact of tourism on the region's fragile environment.*

a coastal/desert/mountain etc environment *The storm caused significant damage to the coastal environment.*

VERBS

adapt to an environment (=change in order to become suitable for it) *Darwin studied how organisms adapt to their environment.*

PREPOSITIONS

in an environment *Foxes and rabbits are often found in a forest environment.*

environmental Ac *adj*

concerning or affecting the air, land, or water on Earth

NOUNS

environmental issues *Environmental issues, such as air pollution, directly affect people's lives.*

environmental damage *She wrote a famous book about the environmental damage caused by the use of chemicals in agriculture.*

environmental pollution *Power stations cause a lot of environmental pollution.*

environmental protection *Is environmental protection more important than economic growth?*

an environmental group *Environmental groups have launched a campaign to protect the Antarctic.*

the environmental movement (=all the groups concerned about the environment) *There are differences of opinion about nuclear power within the environmental movement.*

environmental problems *Acid rain is one of the major environmental problems associated with burning coal.*

the environmental impact/effect *Pollution from cars is having a serious environmental impact.*

environmental concerns (=worries about the environment) *Residents have raised some valid environmental concerns about the nuclear plant.*

environmental awareness *Schools are crucial in helping to raise environmental awareness.*

environmentally friendly *adj*

not harmful to the environment

E

NOUNS

environmentally friendly products *The company claims that all its products are environmentally friendly.*

an environmentally friendly car/vehicle/form of transport *Battery-powered cars are supposed to be environmentally friendly, but where does the electricity come from?*

environmentally friendly methods/practices/ technology *Farmers are using more environmentally friendly farming methods, and there are more birds and butterflies in the fields.*

an environmentally friendly alternative *Parents of babies should consider using an environmentally friendly alternative to disposable nappies.*

environmentally friendly paper/packaging/ washing powder etc *All their books are printed on environmentally friendly paper.*

THESAURUS: environmentally friendly

eco-friendly

products | house | home | car | light bulb | technology | lifestyle

eco-friendly means the same as **environmentally friendly**. People often use **eco-friendly** because it is shorter and easier to say:

We always use eco-friendly cleaning products. | The book offers advice on how to make your home more eco-friendly.

green

energy | technology | products | building | party | movement | campaigner | politician | Member of Parliament | issues | image | credentials

not harmful to the environment. You also use **green** about the people and issues that are concerned with protecting the environment:

The electricity will come from green energy sources such as wind farms. | The US leads the world in green technology. | Green campaigners are opposed to the building of a new airport. | The company is anxious to maintain its green credentials (=its reputation for not harming the environment).

clean

energy | fuel | technology | alternative

clean energy and fuels do not release any harmful substances into the atmosphere:

Hydrogen could be a fantastic source of clean energy. | Gas is a cheaper and cleaner alternative to oil.

renewable

energy | power | fuel | source | resource | technology

renewable energy comes from sources that can be easily replaced naturally, so that there is always more available:

The building is heated using renewable energy from the sun. | Trees can be a renewable resource if forests are managed properly.

sustainable

development | growth | agriculture | farming | tourism | source | resource | lifestyle

using the earth's resources, without causing damage to the environment – used especially about farming, ways of living, and development:

The government wants to encourage sustainable development of the areas around our cities. | Sustainable farming is much more cost-effective in the long term. | All our timber products come from sustainable sources.

carbon-neutral

city | home | company | strategy

balancing the amount of carbon gases that you put into the earth's atmosphere with other activities that will effectively reduce the amount of carbon gases, for example by planting trees:

This is the world's first carbon-neutral city. | All new homes will have to be carbon-neutral.

low-carbon

economy | technology | electricity

producing only a small amount of carbon:

The paper examines ways of developing a low-carbon economy. | The use of wind farms and other low-carbon technology could reduce energy bills.

low-energy

light bulb | house | building | housing

using very little energy:

Low-energy houses are designed to keep the heat from escaping.

envy *n*
the feeling of wanting something that someone else has

VERBS

be filled with envy *All the other boys were filled with envy when they saw his new computer.*

be consumed with envy *formal* (=very envious) *She was consumed with envy when she heard the news.*

feel envy *I sometimes feel envy when I see how much money he earns.*

arouse envy *formal* (=make someone feel envy) *His achievements aroused envy among his classmates.*

PREPOSITIONS

with envy *Other countries look with envy at our excellent education system.*

PHRASES

green with envy *informal* (=very envious) *My friends are green with envy.*

a twinge/tinge/touch/stab of envy (=a sudden short feeling of envy) *As he talked about his happy childhood, I felt a twinge of envy.*

an object of envy *Enzo Ferrari's cars have become objects of envy.*

episode *n*
one of a series of television or radio programmes, in which the same story is continued each week

ADJECTIVES

the next episode *The next episode of the series will be shown on Tuesday.*

the last/previous episode *I missed the last episode.*

the final episode *You don't find out who the killer is until the final episode.*

last week's episode/next week's episode *Did you see last week's episode?*

an exciting/thrilling episode *Don't miss next week's thrilling episode.*

a classic episode *The DVD contains classic episodes of the show.*

VERBS

watch/see an episode *She always watches every episode of the programme.*

show/broadcast an episode *The first episode was shown last Monday.*

an episode is repeated *Today's episode will be repeated on Wednesday.*

equal *adj*
1 the same in size, number, amount, value etc as something else

NOUNS

an equal number/amount *Both candidates received an equal number of votes.*

an equal chance *Everyone has an equal chance of winning the lottery.*

ADVERBS

about/almost equal *The two objects are about equal in height and weight.*

roughly/approximately equal (*also* **more or less equal**) (=about equal) *The number of buyers and sellers must be roughly equal before trading begins.*

exactly equal *The food is shared out in exactly equal portions.*

PHRASES

be equal to sth *The rent was equal to half his monthly income.*

of equal size/length/value etc *Draw two lines of equal length.*

equal in size/length/value etc *The population of each town is roughly equal in size.*

2 having or involving the same rights, opportunities etc as everyone else, whatever your race, religion, or sex

NOUNS

equal rights *In many countries, women do not have equal rights with men.*

equal opportunities *The government must make sure that all children have equal opportunities in education.*

equal pay *The workers' demands include equal pay for equal work.*

equal access (=the same right to do or receive something) *The law states that disabled people must have equal access to employment.*

equal treatment *Everyone should get equal treatment under the law.*

equal status *Meetings are held at a round table, emphasising the equal status of everyone present.*

an equal partner *She never felt she was an equal partner in their marriage.*

VERBS

be considered equal *Different classes of people were not considered equal in public life.*

be born equal *It is a myth that all men are born equal.*

be created equal *They believe that everyone is created equal by God.*

ADVERBS

genuinely/truly/really equal *For women to be genuinely equal, they must receive equal pay.*

PHRASES

on equal terms/on an equal footing (=in conditions that are the same for everyone) *If one player has better equipment, they are not competing on equal terms.*

equality *n*
a situation in which people have the same rights, advantages etc

ADJECTIVES/NOUNS + equality

complete/full/absolute equality *Women have not yet achieved full equality with men.*

racial/race equality *The minister is a well-known campaigner for racial equality.*
sexual/gender equality *How can we have sexual equality if women cannot choose whether to have children?*
social/political/economic equality *African Americans fought for social and economic equality with whites.*
genuine/real equality *There is still no genuine equality for people with disabilities.*

VERBS

achieve equality *He praised previous generations who struggled to achieve racial equality.*
demand equality *Disabled people are demanding equality under the law.*
fight for equality *Women fought for equality throughout the twentieth century.*
promote equality (=help it to happen) *The organization's aim is to promote equality for people of all religions.*

PREPOSITIONS

equality for sb *We want equality for all groups in society.*
equality between/among people *Can there ever be true equality between men and women?*
equality with sb *They are asking for equality with people of other faiths.*

PHRASES

the struggle/fight for equality *The film is about the people who led the struggle for equality in the United States.*
the campaign for equality *She is one of the leaders of the campaign for equality for gay women.*
equality of opportunity *The government must ensure equality of opportunity for all children.*

equation Ac *n*

a statement in mathematics that shows that two amounts or totals are equal

ADJECTIVES

a mathematical equation *Look at the set of mathematical equations printed below.*

VERBS

solve an equation *For homework, solve the equations on page 56.*
work out an equation *I spent over an hour trying to work out the equation.*

equipment Ac *n*

the tools, machines etc that you need to do a particular job or activity

ADJECTIVES/NOUNS + equipment

special equipment *You don't need any special equipment, just a pair of running shoes.*
the right/proper equipment *We need the right equipment to do the job properly.*
modern/up-to-date equipment *The factory has some of the most up-to-date equipment available.*
essential/necessary/vital equipment *A compass is essential equipment when hiking.*
heavy equipment *The truck has to be able to carry tanks and other heavy equipment.*
standard equipment (=that comes with a car or other product, and does not cost extra) *Standard equipment on this model includes airbags, climate control, and cruise control.*
camping/skiing/climbing etc equipment *Can you help me load the camping equipment into the car?*
sports/gym equipment *The shop sells a wide range of sports equipment.*
electrical/electronic/computer equipment *The thieves stole thousands of pounds of computer equipment.*
medical equipment *The ambulance carries life-saving medical equipment.*
office equipment *The company supplies office equipment such as photocopiers and printers.*
military equipment *The sale of military equipment to the country is banned.*
safety/protective equipment *Employers must provide safety equipment and make sure it is used.*

VERBS

use equipment *I will now demonstrate how to use the equipment safely.*
provide/supply equipment *Our firm won the contract to supply drilling equipment to the mine.*
install equipment (=put it in a place so that it is ready to use) *We are installing new computer equipment in place of the old machines.*
need/require equipment *For scuba diving, you'll need specialized equipment.*
test equipment *All the equipment has been tested by our engineers.*

PREPOSITIONS

equipment for sth *Equipment for golf can be very expensive.*

PHRASES

a piece of equipment (*also* **an item of equipment** *formal*): *When you buy an expensive piece of equipment, you need to insure it.*

equitable *adj* THESAURUS **fair**

equivalent Ac *n*

something that has the same value, purpose, meaning etc as something else

ADJECTIVES/NOUNS + equivalent

a direct/exact equivalent *The word has no direct equivalent in English.*
the nearest/closest equivalent *In those days, the grocer's shop was the closest equivalent to a supermarket.*
the modern/modern-day equivalent (of sth) *Boxers are the modern-day equivalent of Roman gladiators.*

E

an English/American/French etc equivalent *Savings and loan associations are the American equivalent of building societies in Britain.*

the musical/literary etc equivalent of sth *It is a loud and overpowering song, the musical equivalent of cheap perfume.*

VERBS

have an equivalent *This institution has no equivalent in any other European country.*

PREPOSITIONS

the equivalent of sth *He had drunk the equivalent of half a bottle of whisky.*

an equivalent to sth *The disease is the human equivalent to the cattle disease known as BSE.*

era

n a period of time in history

ADJECTIVES/NOUNS + era

the modern/present era *Kennedy was probably the greatest president of the modern era.*

a new era *They hope the talks will be the start of a new era in relations between the two countries.*

a bygone era (=a time in the past, usually when something was good) *The hotel belongs to a bygone era and has a beautiful marble staircase.*

a golden era (=a time when something is at its most successful) *The album features songs from the golden era of rock 'n' roll.*

the Obama/Thatcher etc era (=when a particular political leader was in power) *The end of the Bush era was defined by the war in Iraq.*

VERBS

enter an era/move into an era *We have entered an era of instant global communication.*

usher in an era *formal* (=to be the start of a new era) *His death ushered in an era of political instability.*

herald/mark/signal an era *formal* (=show that it is beginning) *Her election heralded an era of social change.*

recreate/recapture an era (=allow people to experience it again) *This marvellous ship recreates the era of luxury ocean travel.*

evoke/recall an era (=make people remember it) *The black and white pictures of the hotel recall a bygone era.*

an era begins/ends *The era of cheap oil has ended.*

PREPOSITIONS

in an era *We live in an era of rapid technological change.*

an era of sth *People in the region are hoping for a new era of peace.*

PHRASES

the end/passing of an era *The closure of the last coal mine marked the end of an era in Wales.*

the dawn/beginning of a new era *The fall of the Berlin Wall heralded the dawn of a new era in Europe.*

erect

v THESAURUS ▶ **build**[1]

erosion

Ac *n*

1 the process by which rock or soil is gradually destroyed by wind, rain, or the sea

ADJECTIVES/NOUNS + erosion

serious/severe erosion *Some areas of the coast have suffered severe erosion.*

significant erosion (=quite severe) *This system of cultivation leads to significant erosion of the subsoil.*

soil erosion *Soil erosion is worse in areas where trees have been cut down.*

marine/coastal erosion (=on land that is close to the sea) *Some of these homes are at risk from coastal erosion.*

water/wind erosion (=caused by water or wind) *Trees help to reduce the effect of wind erosion.*

VERBS

cause erosion *Acid rain has caused serious erosion in the area.*

lead to erosion *Poor farming practices have led to erosion of the soil.*

contribute to erosion (=be one of the causes of it) *High levels of rainfall can contribute to erosion.*

suffer (from) erosion *Many areas of farmland have suffered severe erosion.*

reduce erosion *They introduced new measures designed to stop flooding and reduce erosion.*

prevent erosion *Planting this grass along coastlines helps to prevent erosion.*

erosion happens/occurs *The worst erosion occurs where soil is exposed to drought.*

erosion + NOUNS

erosion damage *Volunteers are building stone walls to prevent further erosion damage.*

PREPOSITIONS

erosion of sth *If sea levels continue to rise, there will be more erosion of coastlines.*

PHRASES

the rate of erosion (*also* **the erosion rate**) *The maps show that the average rate of coastal erosion is about four metres per year.*

2 the process by which something is gradually reduced or destroyed

ADJECTIVES

gradual/steady erosion *There has been a steady erosion of the courts' powers over the last ten years.*

serious/significant erosion *The demonstrators were protesting about the serious erosion of individual freedoms.*

VERBS

see/witness an erosion of sth *We have seen a gradual erosion of these rights over the last 40 years.*

lead to/result in an erosion of sth *The government's policies have led to a serious erosion of freedom of speech.*

PREPOSITIONS

erosion of sth *We are seeing a gradual erosion of our civil liberties.*

erosion in sth *There has been considerable erosion in support for the government.*

error Ac *n* a mistake

ADJECTIVES

a common error *Writing 'recieve' instead of 'receive' is a common error.*

a serious/grave error *The hospital admitted they had made a serious error.*

a small/minor error *The letter contained some minor spelling errors.*

a glaring error (=very bad and very noticeable) *There is a glaring error on page 15.*

a spelling/grammatical/typing error *The article was full of spelling errors.*

a factual error (=which includes a fact that is wrong) *The article contains many factual errors.*

a fatal error (=extremely serious, so that you are certain to fail) *It was a fatal error, which ended his political career.*

an unfortunate error *An unfortunate error resulted in confidential information being released to the press.*

a clerical/administrative error (=relating to office work) *The application forms were sent to the wrong addresses due to a clerical error.*

a tactical error (=a mistake in someone's planning which could cause them to fail) *The decision to wait before attacking was a tactical error.*

NOUNS + error

computer error *It is unlikely that the accident was caused by computer error.*

human/driver/pilot error (=errors made by people, drivers etc) *Automatic checks reduce the danger of human error.*

VERBS

make an error *The bank made an error, and added $10,000 to her account instead of $100.*

commit an error *formal* (=make an error, especially one that has very serious effects) *He knew he had committed a serious error of judgment.*

contain an error/have an error in it *If the data contains errors, the results will be wrong.*

find/spot/notice an error *His teacher spotted several errors in his work.*

correct an error (*also* **rectify an error** *formal*): *We will rectify the error as soon as possible.*

realize your error *By the time she realized her error, it was too late.*

avoid errors *How can we avoid similar errors in the future?*

compound an error *formal* (=make it worse) *He refused to listen to our advice, which compounded the error.*

PREPOSITIONS

an error in sth *There must be an error in our calculations.*

PHRASES

an error of judgment *The decision to lie on the application form was an error of judgment.*

a margin of error (=an amount by which something may be different from the correct amount, without causing problems) *We have to allow for a small margin of error in the calculations.*

be in error (=have made a mistake) *The doctor admitted he was in error.*

do sth in error (=do something by mistake) *The wrong man was arrested in error.*

escalator *n*

a set of moving stairs that take people to different levels in a building

VERBS

take the escalator *They took the escalator to the second floor.*

use the escalator *It is quicker to use the escalator.*

ride (up/down) the escalator *AmE: They rode the escalator down to the first level of the mall.*

get on/off the escalator (*also* **step on/off the escalator**) *She fell over when she was stepping off the escalator.*

an escalator takes/brings/carries sb to sth *The escalator takes you to the menswear department.*

ADJECTIVES

the up escalator/the down escalator *We couldn't find the down escalator, so we took the stairs.*

a moving escalator *You should always be careful when getting on or off a moving escalator.*

PHRASES

at the top of an escalator *Turn right at the top of the escalator.*

at the bottom/foot of an escalator *She was standing at the foot of the escalator.*

the escalator is out of order (=it is not working) *The escalator was out of order, so we had to use the stairs instead.*

escape[1] *v*

1 to leave a place when someone is trying to catch you or stop you, or when there is a dangerous or unpleasant situation

VERBS

try/attempt to escape *Some prisoners tried to escape, but they were quickly recaptured and taken back to the prison.*

manage to escape (=succeed in escaping) *I managed to escape when the guards weren't looking.*

PREPOSITIONS

escape from somewhere *Three men have escaped from prison.*

escape to somewhere *They escaped to South America.*

escape by doing sth *I escaped by jumping out of a window.*

PHRASES

escape with your life/escape alive (=escape and not be killed) *When the tunnel collapsed, the men were lucky to escape with their lives.*

escape sb's clutches *especially literary* (=not be caught be someone) *She managed to escape the clutches of the secret police.*

2 to avoid having something bad happen to you

NOUNS

escape injury (=not be hurt) *Both drivers were lucky to escape serious injury.*

escape punishment (=not be punished) *The people responsible for this crime will not escape punishment.*

escape justice (=not be caught and punished) *These terrorists must not be allowed to escape justice.*

escape capture (=not be captured) *We are not sure how the men continue to escape capture in an area flooded with police officers.*

escape detection (=not be noticed) *Some insects manage to escape detection by merging with the background.*

escape sb's attention (=not be noticed, contacted, or talked to by someone) *His criminal activities had so far escaped the attention of the police.*

escape the ravages of sth (=not be spoiled by the effects of something) *Her face, still beautiful, had escaped the ravages of old age.*

ADVERBS

narrowly/barely escape (=only just avoid having something bad happen to you) *The firefighters narrowly escaped being killed by the explosion.*

miraculously escape (=be very lucky to escape) *The bomb fell just a few yards away but our house miraculously escaped damage.*

escape unharmed/unhurt (*also* **escape unscathed** *formal*) (=not be harmed or hurt in an accident or attack) *Two bodyguards were killed, but the president escaped unharmed.*

escape scot-free (=not be punished) *Victims are angry when they see criminals escape scot-free.*

escape[2] *n*

1 the act of getting away from a place, or away from a dangerous or bad situation

VERBS

make your escape *I had to make my escape before the guards returned.*

plan an escape *We planned our escape carefully and waited for just the right moment.*

prevent an escape (*also* **foil an escape** *formal*) (=stop an escape) *He grabbed her by the wrist, preventing any chance of escape.*

block sb's escape *I rushed towards the door but two large men blocked my escape.*

ADJECTIVES

a daring escape *Two prisoners made a daring escape in a helicopter.*

a quick escape *I saw him walking towards me so I decided to make a quick escape.*

escape + NOUNS

an escape attempt/bid *She made several unsuccessful escape attempts before finally getting away.*

an escape plan *You should have an escape plan in the event of a fire.*

an escape route *All their escape routes had been blocked.*

PREPOSITIONS

an escape from sth *There have been no escapes from the prison in its history.*

an escape to sth *They made their escape to freedom.*

PHRASES

a means of escape (=a way of escaping) *She searched in vain for a means of escape.*

a chance/hope/possibility of escape *The river represented our only hope of escape.*

2 a situation in which you avoid something bad happening to you

ADJECTIVES

a lucky escape *The report tells of the family's lucky escape when a tree crashed onto their car.*

a miraculous escape (=when you are extremely lucky to escape or avoid harm) *Ellie had a miraculous escape after a firework exploded in her hand.*

a narrow escape (=when you only just avoid danger or difficulties) *The team had a narrow escape from disaster last season.*

a remarkable escape *The city was heavily bombed but the cathedral had a remarkable escape.*

essay *n*
a short piece of writing about a subject

ADJECTIVES/NOUNS + essay

an English/history/politics etc essay *Have you done your economics essay yet?*

a 10,000-word/20-page etc essay *Students have to write a 3,000-word essay on a subject of their choice.*

a critical essay (=that judges how good a book, writer etc is) *The book contains critical essays by Kael, Graham Greene and others.*

an academic essay *Mature students often need practice writing academic essays.*

a literary essay *In a literary essay, you should explore the meaning and construction of the text.*

VERBS

write/do an essay *I'm writing an essay about Alexander Fleming.*

give in/hand in an essay (*also* **submit an essay** *formal*): *Make sure that you hand in your essay on time.*

mark an essay *BrE*, **grade an essay** *AmE*: *I still have a pile of essays to mark this evening.*

read an essay *Did you read her essay on 'The Waste Land'?*

an essay discusses/examines/explores sth *This essay discusses the causes of the Spanish Civil War.*

sb argues sth in an essay *In his essay, he argues that true equality is impossible.*

an essay is entitled sth *She wrote an essay entitled 'The Theory of Democracy'.*

essay + NOUNS

an essay question *We practised essay questions from previous exam papers.*

an essay title *You will find a list of essay titles on the noticeboard.*

an essay topic *Students will be given six essay topics, from which they must choose two.*

PREPOSITIONS

an essay on/about sth *We had to write an essay on the causes of the Russian Revolution.*

in an essay *She mentions this research in her essay.*

PHRASES

a collection of essays *She published a collection of essays on philosophy.*

essential *adj* very important and basic

ADVERBS

absolutely/really essential *Regular checks at the dentist are absolutely essential if you want healthy teeth.*

NOUNS

an essential part/feature *Practical study forms an essential part of the course.*

an essential ingredient/element/component (=a part that is essential for something to succeed) *Most people believe that love is an essential ingredient in a marriage.*

the essential difference *The essential difference between people and machines is that people sometimes make mistakes.*

the essential point *I think they have missed the essential point.*

an essential requirement *Knowledge of the financial markets was an essential requirement of her job.*

an essential tool *A camera is an essential tool for all kinds of work.*

an essential item *Mothers are given money so they can buy clothes and other essential items for their babies.*

essential information *You can get essential travel information from the website.*

essential reading (=something you must read) *The journal is essential reading for doctors.*

essential services (=organizations such as the police or the fire or health service) *The law prohibits workers in essential services from striking.*

VERBS

be seen/regarded as essential *These measures are seen as essential for national security.*

be considered essential *Air conditioning is considered essential in some parts of the world.*

PREPOSITIONS

essential for sb/sth *Change is essential for the survival of the company.*

PHRASES

play/perform an essential role in sth *Antibiotics play an essential role in controlling infection.*

by no means essential (=certainly not essential) *The equipment is useful but by no means essential.*

THESAURUS: essential

fundamental, core, essential, central, underlying → **basic (1)**

big, significant, major, notable, key, essential, vital, crucial/critical, paramount, historic, landmark, momentous → **important (1)**

establish Ac *v* **THESAURUS** **start[1] (3)**

established Ac *adj*
already in use or existing for a long period of time

Grammar
Established is usually used before a noun with this meaning.

E

ADVERBS

well established (=existing for a long time and respected or trusted by people) *As an author, McCarthy is well established.*

long established *The right to remain silent is a long-established principle of British justice.*

> You write **well-established** and **long-established** with a hyphen when you use them before a noun.

NOUNS

an established business *He wanted to buy an established business, rather than start his own.*

an established institution *The new prime minister criticized many established government institutions.*

an established brand/product *The company plans to make major changes to its established products.*

an established reputation *This firm has an established reputation for quality.*

an established tradition *The custom of sending Christmas cards was an established tradition by 1900.*

established practice (=a particular way of doing something that is accepted as the best way) *Not allowing patients to eat before surgery is established practice.*

an established part/feature of sth *The tomato has become an established part of the British diet.*

an established writer/artist/composer etc (=one that is already successful) *The exhibition includes work by art students as well as by more established artists.*

the established order (=the people and organizations that have power) *The revolutionaries posed a serious threat to the established order.*

establishment Ac *n*

the group of people in a society or profession who have a lot of power and influence, and are often opposed to any kind of change

> **Grammar**
> In this meaning, you always say **the establishment**. You usually use it when you disapprove of the people who control what happens in a society.

PHRASES

a member of the establishment *Most male members of the establishment resisted equal rights for women.*

a pillar of the establishment (=an important and respected member) *Though a rebel in his youth, he became a pillar of the establishment.*

estimate Ac *n*

a calculation of the probable cost, size, or amount of something

ADJECTIVES

a rough/approximate estimate (=not exact) *Can you give me a rough estimate of how long this is going to take?*

an accurate/reliable estimate (=fairly exact) *It's hard to put an accurate estimate on the number of people who have been affected by the disaster.*

a conservative estimate (=deliberately low) *By conservative estimates, 2.5 million people die each year from smoking cigarettes.*

an official estimate (=accepted by people in authority) *According to official army estimates, more than 500 rebels had been killed.*

current/recent estimates (=ones that are accepted now) *According to current estimates, the country can expect 200,000 visitors in the next three years.*

the latest estimates (=most recent) *The latest estimates are that sea levels could rise by about 20 cm by 2050.*

earlier/previous estimates *These amounts are much higher than those given in previous estimates.*

the original estimate (=the one given at the beginning of a process) *The final cost of the project was nearly three times the original estimate.*

a revised estimate (=changed from the previous one) *If the time starts to exceed this estimate, we will let you know and give you a revised estimate.*

VERBS

make an estimate *If you don't know the exact figure, make a rough estimate.*

give (sb) an estimate (*also* **provide (sb with) an estimate** *formal*) (=tell them approximately how much something will cost) *The builder's going to give us an estimate for the work.*

put an estimate on sth (=say the amount that you think something is) *It is impossible to put an estimate on the value of the jewellery.*

exceed an estimate (=be more than it) *The final price cannot exceed the estimate.*

base an estimate on sth (=use something as information to give an estimate) *The government based its estimate on data from the 2008 census.*

an estimate puts sth at sth *Independent estimates put the number of refugees at 50,000.*

estimates range/vary from sth to sth *Estimates of the number of homeless people in the city range from 6,000 to 10,000.*

PREPOSITIONS

an estimate of sth *We need an estimate of the number of people who will come.*

E

an estimate for sth *How much was their estimate for the work?*

according to an estimate *According to some estimates, an acre of rainforest is cleared every minute.*

eternal *adj* THESAURUS **permanent**

ethics Ac *n*

moral rules or principles of behaviour

ADJECTIVES/NOUNS + ethics

professional ethics *He said professional ethics did not allow him to give me the information.*

business ethics *Business ethics may vary from one country to another.*

medical ethics *Not giving a patient full information about their treatment is against medical ethics.*

journalistic/media ethics *It is a violation of journalistic ethics to let your own opinions influence a news report.*

PHRASES

a code of ethics (=a set of ethics, usually an official one) *Members are required to abide by the code of ethics.*

a system of ethics *This philosopher offered a new system of ethics.*

a breach/violation of ethics (=doing something that is not morally acceptable) *He was accused of a breach of journalistic ethics.*

ethnic Ac *adj*

relating to a particular race or group of people with the same culture and traditions

NOUNS

an ethnic group *People from India form the city's largest ethnic group.*

an ethnic minority (=a small ethnic group living within a much larger group) *There should be no discrimination against those from ethnic minorities.*

ethnic origin/background *The students are from a variety of ethnic backgrounds.*

an ethnic identity (=the feeling of belonging to an ethnic group) *These small tribal communities share a common ethnic identity.*

ethnic diversity (=the fact of including people from many different ethnic groups) *Chicago prides itself on its ethnic diversity.*

an ethnic mix (=a mixture of people from different ethnic groups) *The school has a wonderful ethnic mix.*

the ethnic composition/make-up of sth (=how many members of different ethnic groups something contains) *The ethnic composition of the population has changed.*

ethnic violence/conflict (=fighting between different ethnic groups) *There have been outbreaks of ethnic violence.*

ethnic tension *It is feared that the growing ethnic tension could lead to civil war.*

ethnic divisions (=disagreements between members of different ethnic groups) *There are deep ethnic divisions in the country.*

ethnic cleansing (=the action of forcing people to leave an area or country because of their ethnic group) *The first time we heard about ethnic cleansing was in Yugoslavia.*

an ethnic Russian/Albanian etc (=someone whose family is Russian etc, but who is living in another country) *There are about 1.4 million ethnic Hungarians in Romania.*

PHRASES

along ethnic lines (=according to the ethnic groups that people belong to) *They are planning to divide the country along ethnic lines.*

evade *v* THESAURUS **avoid (2)**

evaluate *v*

to judge how good, useful, or successful something is

ADVERBS

carefully evaluate sth *The research data is carefully evaluated.*

critically evaluate sth *There is a constant need to critically evaluate and improve the systems we use for our work.*

properly evaluate sth *There was a failure to properly evaluate the evidence available at the time.*

fully/thoroughly evaluate sth *The project's effect on criminal behaviour has not yet been thoroughly evaluated.*

continually/constantly evaluate sth *The relationship between doctors and other health workers needs to be continually evaluated.*

PHRASES

be difficult/hard to evaluate *It is difficult to evaluate the effectiveness of the drug based on a small number of patients.*

evaluation *n*

the process of making a judgment about what something is like or how good it is

VERBS

make/carry out/do an evaluation (*also* **conduct an evaluation** *formal*): *The doctors are carrying out an evaluation of the patient's condition.*

undergo an evaluation *formal*: *Every new product has to undergo a safety evaluation before it is allowed to be sold.*

ADJECTIVES/NOUNS + evaluation

a full/comprehensive evaluation *A decision will be taken after a full evaluation of all the possible options.*

a critical evaluation *The students were asked to write a critical evaluation of the poem.*

a proper evaluation *Nobody has yet provided a proper evaluation of the risks involved.*

PREPOSITIONS

for evaluation *Some samples were sent to the laboratory for evaluation.*

under evaluation (=being examined and judged) *The new drug is currently under evaluation to make sure that it is safe.*

PHRASES

sb's evaluation of the situation *His evaluation of the situation is much the same as mine.*

even *adj*

THESAURUS **flat**[1]

evening *n*

the early part of the night between the end of the day and the time you go to bed

ADJECTIVES/NOUNS + evening

good evening (=used when meeting someone in the evening) *Good evening, officer.*

this/that evening *I'll phone you this evening.*

tomorrow/yesterday evening *Would you like to come over tomorrow evening?*

Monday/Friday etc evening *By Sunday evening, all the snow had gone.*

early/late evening *By the time we arrived, it was late evening.*

all evening/the whole evening *They watched television all evening.*

a fine/warm/cool etc evening *It was a fine evening, so we decide to eat outside.*

a spring/summer etc evening *On a summer evening, the streets are full of people.*

a lovely/wonderful/pleasant evening *I thanked them for a lovely evening.*

a romantic evening *Tonight the couple are having a romantic evening to celebrate their anniversary.*

evening + NOUNS

an evening meal *I was just preparing the evening meal when the phone rang.*

the evening paper/news *There was a report about the fire on the evening news.*

evening dress (=formal clothes that people wear to social events in the evening) *The men all wore evening dress.*

VERBS

spend an evening *He spent many evenings alone in his room.*

have a nice/wonderful etc evening *Have a nice evening. See you tomorrow.*

PREPOSITIONS

in the evening *We met up again later in the evening.*

for the evening *Her parents had gone out for the evening.*

on Monday/Friday etc evening *They were due to leave on Sunday evening.*

⚠ Don't say 'On the evening we went to a party.' Say **In the evening we went to a party.**

event *n*

something that happens, especially something important, interesting, or unusual

ADJECTIVES

an important event *It's natural to be nervous before such an important event.*

a big/major/significant event (=important) *Getting married is a major event in anyone's life.*

a political/historical event *The French Revolution was the result of a complex series of historical events.*

a historic/momentous event (=very important and having a big effect) *The signing of the peace treaty was a historic event.*

a dramatic event (=very exciting) *The dramatic events were broadcast live all over the world.*

a terrible/tragic event *The court heard evidence of the tragic events that led to his death.*

current events (=happening now) *The website has news of current events in the US.*

recent events/the latest events *Recent events in the country have caused great concern.*

the day's/week's etc events *We sat down to discuss the day's events.*

a traumatic event (=very upsetting) *He was forced to relive the traumatic events of his kidnap.*

a rare/unusual event *A sighting of a white deer is a rare event.*

an unlikely event *Should this unlikely event take place, they want to be prepared.*

a common/everyday event *The death of a child was a common event in those days.*

VERBS

an event happens/takes place (*also* **an event occurs** *formal*): *When traumatic events happen, we need our families around us.*

events unfold (=happen, usually in an exciting or unexpected way) *I watched the dramatic events unfold from my window.*

events lead (up) to sth (=cause it) *His assassination was one of the events that led to the First World War.*

celebrate/commemorate/mark an event *Fans observed a minute's silence to commemorate the tragic event.*

witness an event (=see it happen) *Luckily, a film crew was there to witness the event.*

PHRASES

a series/sequence of events (=related events that happen one after the other) *The book describes the sequence of events leading up to the war.*

a chain of events (=a series of events where each one causes the next) *He set in motion a chain of events that he couldn't control.*

the course of events (=the way in which a series of events happens) *Nothing you could have done would have changed the course of events.*

the events surrounding sth (=the events that are closely related to it) *The events surrounding her death remain a mystery.*

everlasting *adj* THESAURUS ▶ **permanent**

evidence [Ac] *n*

facts or signs that show something is true

ADJECTIVES

good/clear/strong/firm evidence *There is clear evidence that smoking causes heart disease.*

convincing/compelling evidence (=making you feel sure that something is true) *The data provides compelling evidence that the climate is changing.*

conclusive/incontrovertible/irrefutable evidence (=showing that something is definitely true and cannot be proved false) *We need irrefutable evidence before making an arrest.*

overwhelming evidence (=so much that you are sure something is true) *The evidence against him was overwhelming.*

hard evidence (=facts that show something is true, rather than ideas and things that people say) *They have no hard evidence to support their claim.*

reliable/credible evidence *Do you think their evidence is reliable?*

flimsy evidence (=not good enough to make you believe something) *Their conclusions are drawn from some very flimsy evidence.*

vital evidence (=very important) *Vital evidence was ignored.*

fresh evidence (=new evidence) *The police have found fresh evidence which proves Tom was at the scene of the crime.*

medical/scientific evidence *The eating guidelines are based on the latest scientific evidence.*

damning evidence (=proving that someone has done something wrong) *Her testimony proved to be the most damning evidence against him.*

incriminating evidence (=making someone seem guilty of a crime) *The robbers were careful not to leave any incriminating evidence behind.*

circumstantial evidence (=that makes something seem likely, but does not prove it) *His barrister claims the case against him is based on circumstantial evidence.*

anecdotal evidence (=based on what people believe, rather than on facts) *Anecdotal evidence suggests that gang-related violence is on the increase.*

VERBS + evidence

look for/search for evidence *The investigation will look for evidence of financial mismanagement.*

gather/collect evidence *Police experts are still collecting evidence at the scene of the crime.*

find/obtain evidence *The authorities failed to obtain enough evidence to convict him.*

consider/examine/study the evidence *Having considered all the evidence, the court found him not guilty.*

have evidence *Do you have any evidence that this treatment works?*

hide/destroy evidence *The killer may have tried to burn the bodies in an attempt to hide the evidence.*

plant evidence (=deliberately put it somewhere to make someone look guilty) *He claims the evidence was planted there by the police.*

give evidence (=tell a court about what you have seen or know to be true) *Ms White has agreed to give evidence at their trial.*

evidence + VERBS

evidence shows sth *Evidence shows that most accidents are the result of human error.*

evidence confirms/proves/supports sth *All the evidence supports this theory.*

evidence points to/suggests sth *Police say evidence suggests there was a third man involved.*

PREPOSITIONS

evidence of sth *At present we have no evidence of life on other planets.*

evidence for sth *There is no evidence for these claims.*

evidence about/on sth *He has vital evidence about what happened that night.*

evidence against sb *Do the police have any evidence against him?*

PHRASES

a piece of evidence *They found an important piece of evidence.*

evidence comes to light *There could be a re-trial if new evidence comes to light.*

be used in evidence (=be used as evidence) *The photographs may be used in evidence against him.*

evil[1] *adj*

deliberately doing things that are bad or cruel

NOUNS

an evil man/woman/person *These evil men want to destroy our society.*

an evil dictator/tyrant *He was an evil dictator, responsible for the deaths of millions.*

an evil genius/mastermind *Who was the evil genius behind this terrible plan?*

an evil spirit *The charm is believed to keep away evil spirits.*

evil forces *He warned that evil forces were at work.*

an evil deed *One day he will be punished for his evil deeds.*

an evil plan *Although he beat her, she refused to help him with his evil plan.*

evil intentions *He was unaware of her evil intentions.*

E

ADVERBS

totally/utterly/truly evil *These crimes are carried out by people who are truly evil or sick.*

inherently/intrinsically evil (=naturally and always evil) *I don't believe that these killers are inherently evil.*

THESAURUS: evil

naughty, immoral, evil, wicked → **bad (4)**

evil² *n*

1 something that is very bad or harmful

ADJECTIVES/NOUNS + evil

a great evil *He saw fascism as the greatest evil of his times.*

a lesser evil (*also* **the lesser of two evils**) (=a bad thing, but not as bad as something else) *She had chosen what she thought was the lesser evil.*

a necessary evil (=something that is bad but necessary) *Most businesses see government regulation as a necessary evil.*

a social evil *They battle against social evils such as poverty and drug abuse.*

a moral evil *Mental or physical torture is a moral evil, and it can never be justified.*

PREPOSITIONS

the evils of sth *He knew all about the evils of war.*

2 cruel or morally bad behaviour in general

ADJECTIVES

pure evil *In the film, the killer is a symbol of pure evil.*

VERBS

fight/combat evil *They swore to fight evil in all its forms.*

PHRASES

good and evil *You have to teach your kids about right and wrong, good and evil.*

the forces of evil *literary* (=the people or things that increase the amount of evil in the world) *The superhero fights the forces of evil that are threatening mankind.*

sth is the root of all evil (=something is the main cause of bad things) *Love of money is the root of all evil.*

evolution Ac *n*

the gradual development of something – used about animals and plants, and also about ideas, systems, countries etc

ADJECTIVES

gradual/slow evolution *The book traces the gradual evolution of the modern state.*

continuous evolution *Computer technology is in a process of continuous evolution.*

cultural/social/political etc evolution *Prime Minister Nehru played a significant role in the political evolution of India.*

human evolution *Our ancestors reached a key stage in human evolution when they began to stand upright.*

biological evolution *Every living creature has been formed by the slow process of biological evolution.*

VERBS

evolution takes place (*also* **evolution occurs** *formal*): *We can see signs of evolution taking place in the world around us.*

trace sth's evolution (=find how it developed) *The show traced the evolution of black American music from gospel through soul to hip-hop.*

PREPOSITIONS

sth's evolution from sth to/into sth *These photographs show Tucson's evolution from small frontier town to thriving modern city.*

PHRASES

the theory of evolution *Many Christians find it impossible to accept Darwin's theory of evolution.*

a stage in the evolution of sth *The crucial stage in the evolution of writing occurred when pictures were replaced by symbols representing sounds.*

evolve *v* THESAURUS **change¹ (1)**

exact *adj*

completely correct or the same, in every detail

NOUNS

the exact amount/number/figure *I don't know the exact amount, but it cost a lot.*

the exact size *You need a piece of paper about 10 cm x 25 cm – the exact size doesn't matter.*

the exact date/time etc *He plans to retire soon, but the exact date is not fixed.*

the exact position/location/spot etc *Satellite pictures showed the enemy's exact location.*

the exact cause *An investigation will be held to determine the exact cause of death.*

the exact details (=details that are correct in every way) *Nobody knows the exact details of what happened.*

sb's exact words (=the words someone actually said) *I can't remember his exact words, but he basically refused.*

the exact wording (=the words that were used in a letter, speech etc, with nothing changed) *What was the exact wording of the message?*

an exact copy/replica (=something which has been made, that is exactly like another thing) *The boat is an exact replica of an ancient Greek ship.*

an exact equivalent *There is no exact equivalent in English for the phrase.*

ANTONYMS **exact** → **rough (2)**

exaggerate *v*

to say that something is greater, worse etc than it really is

NOUNS

exaggerate the importance/significance of sth *I think people sometimes exaggerate the importance of his work.*

exaggerate the impact/effect of sth *It is important not to exaggerate the impact of this legislation.*

exaggerate the danger/threat/risk *Newspapers were accused of exaggerating the danger of the virus.*

exaggerate the size of sth *I'm sure the government is exaggerating the size of the problem.*

exaggerate the extent of sth *The extent of the damage has been exaggerated.*

E

ADVERBS

greatly exaggerated *He claimed that the risks had been greatly exaggerated.*

wildly exaggerated (=by a very large amount, in a way that is not at all realistic) *Wildly exaggerated reports about the singer's private life began appearing in the press.*

highly exaggerated *Their claims were highly exaggerated.*

grossly exaggerated (=by a very large amount, in a way that is wrong) *The damage the animals did to crops was grossly exaggerated.*

slightly exaggerate sth *I may have slightly exaggerated my ability as a cook.*

deliberately exaggerate sth *Did government officials deliberately exaggerate the threat to national security?*

PHRASES

it is difficult/hard/impossible to exaggerate sth (=used to emphasise that something is very big, important etc) *It is difficult to exaggerate the strength of people's feelings on this matter.*

it is easy to exaggerate sth *It is easy to exaggerate the threat of terrorism.*

exaggeration *n*

a statement or way of saying something that makes something seem better, larger etc than it really is

ADJECTIVES

a great/huge exaggeration *Some people say the painting is worth over $1 million - this is a great exaggeration.*

a gross exaggeration *formal* (=very great and untrue) *His comments were a gross exaggeration.*

a wild exaggeration *The claim that 100,000 people attended the concert was a wild exaggeration.*

a slight exaggeration (*also* **a bit of an exaggeration** *informal*): *It's a slight exaggeration, but it's not far from the truth.*

PHRASES

without exaggeration *I can say without exaggeration that he is one of the finest writers of his generation.*

a degree/an element of exaggeration (=some exaggeration) *There may be a degree of exaggeration in her story, but basically it is true.*

it is no exaggeration to say that... (=it is definitely true, even though it may seem surprising) *It is no exaggeration to say that this is the best film so far this year.*

sb is prone to exaggeration (=they often exaggerate) *My aunt was prone to exaggeration and I did not always trust what she said.*

exam *n*

a test of knowledge, usually taken in a school, college, or university

ADJECTIVES/NOUNS + exam

a chemistry/French/music etc exam *She scored 80% in her history exam.*

a written exam *There is a written exam at the end of the course.*

an oral exam (=in which you answer questions by speaking) *I have my French oral exams next week.*

a final exam (=at the end of a course) *The students take their final exams in June.*

an entrance exam (=in order to enter a school or university) *Her son failed the entrance exam to a national university.*

high school exams *Greg got good grades in all of his high school exams.*

a mock exam *BrE* (=as practice for a real exam) *He did well in the mock exams.*

VERBS

take/do an exam (*also* **sit an exam** *BrE*): *We have to take exams at the end of each year.*

⚠ Don't say 'make an exam'.

pass an exam (=succeed in it) *You need 50% or more to pass the exam.*

fail an exam (*also* **flunk an exam** *AmE informal*): *If you fail the exam, you can retake it.*

do well/badly in an exam *BrE*, **do well/badly on an exam** *AmE*: *Maria always did well in her exams at school.*

study for an exam (*also* **revise for an exam** *BrE*): *She has to study for her exams.*

sail though an exam (=pass it easily) *Don't worry - I'm sure you'll sail through all your exams.*

scrape through an exam (=only just pass it) *He managed to scrape through the exam and stay on the course.*

cheat in an exam *BrE*, **cheat on an exam** *AmE*: *She was caught cheating in the exam.*

retake an exam (*also* **resit an exam** *BrE*) (=take it again because you did not do well the first time) *If you don't do well, you'll have to resit the exam in January.*

set an exam *BrE* (=write the questions for it) *Set the students an exam and see how well they do.*

mark an exam *BrE*, **grade an exam** *AmE* (=see how well someone has done) *Which teacher will be marking the exam?*

exam + NOUNS

an exam paper *I've still got dozens of exam papers to mark.*

an exam question *Read the exam questions carefully before writing your answers.*

exam results *The school achieves consistently good exam results.*

exam marks *BrE*, **exam score** *AmE*: *Her exam marks have improved since last year.*

exam revision *BrE*: *I have to do my exam revision this weekend.*

exam technique (=good ways to succeed in exams) *Mr Frasier gave us some useful tips on exam technique.*

PREPOSITIONS

in an exam *BrE*, **on an exam** *AmE*: *In his chemistry exam, he got 68%.*

examination *n*

1 a test of knowledge, usually taken in a school or college

> **Examination** is a formal word. In everyday English, people usually say **exam**.

ADJECTIVES/NOUNS + examination

a chemistry/French/music etc examination *Most of the students passed the science examination.*

a written examination *Assessment is by coursework and written examinations.*

an oral examination (=in which you answer questions by speaking) *For French, there is an oral and a written examination.*

a final examination (=at the end of a course) *My final examinations are in June.*

an entrance examination (=to enter a school or university) *He failed the college entrance examination twice.*

a mock examination (=a practice examination to prepare for the real one) *We have our mock examinations in March, and the real ones in June.*

VERBS

take an examination (*also* **sit an examination** *BrE*): *Do you have to take an examination in every subject?*

pass an examination *I really hope that Suzie passes the examination.*

fail an examination *Michael had never yet failed an examination.*

study for an examination (*also* **revise for an examination** *BrE*): *I have been studying all week for the examination.*

do well/badly in an examination *BrE*, **do well/badly on an examination** *AmE*: *He did well in his examinations, and went on to study at MIT.*

cheat in an examination *BrE*, **cheat on an examination** *AmE*: *Any student caught cheating in an examination will be suspended.*

set an examination *BrE* (=write the questions for it) *The people who set the examinations are usually former teachers.*

examination + NOUNS

examination results *The examination results will be announced in September.*

an examination paper *There will be a choice of questions on the examination paper.*

an examination question *Read the examination questions carefully before starting to write.*

examination marks *BrE*, **examination grade** *AmE*: *On average, girls achieved higher examination marks than boys.*

PREPOSITIONS

in an examination *BrE*, **on an examination** *AmE*: *In this examination, students may use a calculator.*

2 the process of looking at something carefully in order to see what it is like

ADJECTIVES

a careful examination *After a careful examination of the evidence, we find the defendant guilty.*

a detailed examination *Investigators have carried out a detailed examination of the scene.*

a close/thorough examination (=very careful and detailed) *A close examination of the figures raised some questions.*

a brief examination (=quick, and not very detailed) *In chapter one, there is a brief examination of the economic situation at the time.*

a cursory examination (=very quick and not careful or detailed) *Even a cursory examination of the documents would reveal some serious problems.*

a preliminary/initial examination (=done before something is examined more closely) *An initial examination of the car showed no mechanical fault.*

further examination (=a more detailed or careful examination) *The results of the experiment merit further examination.*

VERBS

carry out an examination (*also* **conduct an examination** *formal*) (=examine something) *The police are carrying out an examination of the crime scene.*

an examination shows sth (*also* **an examination reveals sth** *formal*): *Closer examination reveals the difference between the two insects.*

PREPOSITIONS

an examination of sth *An examination of the figures shows that sales have been falling.*

under examination *The way the matter was handled is under examination by investigators.*

PHRASES

on closer examination *On closer examination, I could see a slight crack in the vase.*

3 a set of medical tests

ADJECTIVES

a medical examination *We need to do a further medical examination.*

a physical examination *All patients are given a complete physical examination.*

a routine examination (=one that is done regularly) *I made an appointment at the dentist's for a routine examination.*

a clinical examination (=by a doctor) *The clinical examination did not reveal anything abnormal.*

a post-mortem examination (=of a dead body to discover why the person died) *The post-mortem examination showed that he died from heart failure.*

VERBS

have an examination (*also* **undergo an examination** *formal*): *He was examined by Dr Bower yesterday and will have another examination today.*

conduct/perform an examination *The doctor will perform an examination in order to assess the problem.*

an examination shows sth (*also* **an examination reveals sth** *formal*): *A second examination showed a small growth in his stomach.*

examine *v*

to look at something carefully and thoroughly because you want to find out more about it

ADVERBS

examine sth carefully/closely *The doctor examined his ears carefully, and told him there was no damage.*

examine sth thoroughly/fully *These important archaeological remains will be thoroughly examined by experts.*

examine sth briefly *In this section we briefly examine the evidence so far.*

PREPOSITIONS

examine sth for sth (=look at it carefully trying to find something) *The police have examined the weapon for fingerprints.*

PHRASES

examine sth in detail *Hegel's philosophy will be examined in detail in Chapter 4.*

example *n*

1 something that explains or supports an idea or is typical of something

ADJECTIVES

a good/typical example *This painting is a good example of his early work.*

a fine/excellent example *Cairo has many fine examples of Arab architecture.*

an outstanding example (=extremely good) *The garden is one of the most outstanding examples of traditional Japanese garden design.*

a classic/perfect/prime example (=very typical) *This is a classic example of how not to run a business.*

an obvious example *The most obvious example of an information source is a dictionary.*

a blatant/glaring example (=very obvious and very bad) *His case is a blatant example of the unfairness of the current system.*

an extreme example *To give you an extreme example, one lady called the police 15 times in a single evening.*

a graphic example (=very clear and full of unpleasant details) *The film is full of graphic examples of what can go wrong if safety procedures are not followed.*

VERBS

give/provide an example *Can anyone give me an example of a transitive verb?*

take an example (=consider it or talk about it) *Let's take the example of a family with two school-age children.*

use an example *He used several examples to illustrate his point.*

cite an example (=mention one) *The report cites the example of Sweden, where there is a complete ban on advertising on children's television.*

find an example *We found examples of people being overcharged by as much as 50%.*

an example shows/illustrates sth *These examples show how the disease can be passed on to humans.*

2 a person or behaviour that people copy

ADJECTIVES

a good/positive example *The older children should set a positive example for the rest of the school.*

a bad example *Stop it – you're setting a bad example to your little brother.*

a shining example (=a very good example) *Professor Squires was a shining example of what a good teacher should be.*

an inspiring example (=who makes people want to do something great or good) *She remains an inspiring example of love and self-sacrifice.*

VERBS

set an example (=show by your own behaviour how other people should behave) *Parents should set an example for their children.*

follow sb's example (=copy their behaviour) *I suggest you follow Rosie's example and start doing regular exercise.*

lead by example (=show people what they should do by doing it yourself) *The captain of the team should lead by example.*

hold sb up as an example (=use someone as a good example of something) *He was held up as an example to the younger athletes.*

PREPOSITIONS

an example to sb *Her courage is an example to us all.*

excellent *adj*

extremely good or of very high quality

NOUNS

excellent condition *The car is in excellent condition.*

excellent value *The hotel was excellent value.*

an excellent example *The palace is an excellent example of late 17th-century architecture.*

an excellent idea/suggestion/choice *I think the award is an excellent idea.*

an excellent job/piece of work *She does an excellent job of describing the problems that young people face.*

an excellent student/player/cook *Maria was an excellent student and passed all her exams easily.*

an excellent book/film/song *He wrote an excellent book about child psychology.*

excellent English/French/German etc *The hotel staff all speak excellent English.*

an excellent article/report/paper *The paper has an excellent article on the current political situation in Greece.*

ADVERBS

really excellent *His wife was a really excellent cook.*

absolutely excellent *I loved the speech – it was absolutely excellent.*

truly excellent *We increased our profit by 40% – a truly excellent performance!*

⚠ Don't say 'very excellent'.

THESAURUS: excellent

great *spoken*
extremely good. **Great** is more informal than **excellent**, and is very common in everyday spoken English:
The kids had a great time. | He did a great job as captain. | It sounds like a great idea.

wonderful
extremely good – used especially when you are very pleased or excited:
"She's having a baby." "That's wonderful news." | There are some wonderful moments in the film.

fantastic/terrific *spoken*
extremely good – used especially when you are very pleased or excited:
The music was fantastic – it's one of the best concerts I've ever been to. | He's a terrific tennis player.

awesome *informal*
very good – used especially when you are very pleased or excited. **Awesome** is a very informal word, which is used mainly by young people:
The band were awesome.

amazing/incredible
extremely good in a surprising and exciting way:
The hotel has an amazing view of Tokyo. | The trip was an incredible experience.

superb
extremely good – used especially when you are very impressed by something:
The acting was superb. | There is a superb range of cheeses.

first class
food | service | meal | hotel | restaurant | accommodation | facilities
of a high quality and much better than most others:
The service at the hotel is first class. | The school has first-class sports facilities.

> You write **first-class** with a hyphen when you use it before a noun.

outstanding
example | achievement | success | performance | player | feature | natural beauty
extremely good – used especially when saying that someone has done something very well:
The painting is an outstanding example of early Italian art. | Winning the championship three times was a ***truly outstanding*** *achievement. | The Lake District is an area of outstanding natural beauty.*

exceptional
talent | ability | skill | value | player | artist | performance | quality
unusually good – used when saying that someone or something is much better than any others:
He is an artist of exceptional talent. | The café offers exceptional value for money.

E

If something is extremely good, you can say that it is **out of this world**: *The food is out of this world.*

exception *n*

something or someone that is not included in a general statement or does not follow a rule or pattern

ADJECTIVES

an important/significant exception *The treaty was signed by all the EU member countries with one significant exception: Britain.*

a major exception (=very important) *Most industries are struggling but the tourist industry is a major exception to this.*

a notable exception (=one that is very interesting, excellent, or unusual) *The houses along the river are all modern, with the notable exception of the old mill.*

an obvious exception *The earliest historical records are written in Indo-European languages, with the obvious exception of Chinese.*

a minor exception (=not important) *Everyone was in agreement, with a few minor exceptions.*

a single/sole exception (=one on its own) *All the men were killed, with the sole exception of Captain Jones.*

a rare exception *Books on philosophy can be quite dull, but this is a rare exception.*

VERBS

make an exception (=deal with someone or something in a different way from usual on a particular occasion) *We usually require a 10% deposit, but I'll make an exception in this case.*

PREPOSITIONS

an exception to sth *There are some exceptions to this rule.*

without exception *Without exception, all the children were well behaved and polite.*

with the exception of sth/sb *We all laughed, with the exception of Miss Smith.*

PHRASES

be no exception *The river floods every winter, and this year was no exception.*

be the exception to the rule/that proves the rule (=be different from most other people or things) *Most of the boys were shy, but Larry was the exception to the rule.*

be the exception, not the rule (=used to emphasize that something is unusual) *Staying married for life seems to be the exception, not the rule these days.*

with the possible exception of sb/sth *Scientists say that Mercury is the least understood planet, with the possible exception of Uranus.*

exceptional *adj*

1 unusually good

ADVERBS

quite exceptional (=very exceptional) *Her memory for facts is quite exceptional.*

truly exceptional (=really or extremely exceptional) *The film features a truly exceptional cast, including Oscar winner Denzel Washington.*

NOUNS

exceptional talent/ability/skill *He showed exceptional talent even as a youngster.*

exceptional quality *This is a wine of exceptional quality.*

exceptional bravery/courage *Fire crews showed exceptional bravery.*

an exceptional performance *He left the field to cheers from the fans, after another exceptional performance.*

exceptional value *The hotel offers exceptional value.*

an exceptional person/player/student etc *He was an exceptional manager, and all the staff liked him.*

THESAURUS: exceptional

great, wonderful, fantastic/terrific, awesome, amazing/incredible, superb, first class, outstanding, exceptional → **excellent**

2 unusual and likely not to happen often

NOUNS

an exceptional case *Students are only allowed to take time off from their studies in exceptional cases.*

an exceptional event *If an exceptional event occurs, such as the death of a family member, you can ask for the court case to be postponed.*

an exceptional situation *It was an exceptional situation so the usual rules didn't apply.*

the exceptional nature of sth (=the very unusual qualities or features that something has) *In view of the exceptional nature of his crime, he was sentenced to 20 years in prison.*

ADVERBS

most exceptional (=very exceptional) *A child will only be removed from the parental home in the most exceptional cases.*

highly exceptional (=extremely exceptional) *A loan of this size is highly exceptional.*

PHRASES

in exceptional circumstances (=when a situation is extremely unusual) *The US will only issue a visitor visa at short notice in exceptional circumstances.*

THESAURUS: exceptional

rare, exotic, exceptional, out of the ordinary, freak, unprecedented, unheard of, eccentric, unconventional, unorthodox → **unusual**

excessive *adj*

much more than is reasonable or necessary

ADVERBS

rather/somewhat excessive *$20 for two beers seems rather excessive.*

grossly excessive (=extremely excessive) *The punishment was grossly excessive and totally unfair.*

NOUNS

excessive use of sth *Farmers have been criticized for their excessive use of chemical fertilizers.*

excessive force *The men claim that the police officers used excessive force.*

excessive amounts of sth *I was staying up late, consuming excessive amounts of coffee.*

excessive drinking/eating *His liver problems had been caused by excessive drinking.*

excessive speed *Excessive speed is a major cause of road accidents.*

exchange *n*

1 the act of giving someone something and receiving something from them

ADJECTIVES

a fair exchange *Two of his computer games for two of mine seemed like a fair exchange.*

PREPOSITIONS

an exchange of sth *We hope to have an exchange of ideas on how to deal with the problem.*

in exchange for sth *The country agreed to give up its nuclear program in exchange for energy benefits and other aid.*

2 an arrangement in which a student, teacher etc visits another school or university to work or study

ADJECTIVES/NOUNS + exchange

a student exchange *Our college arranged student exchanges with four colleges in France.*

a language exchange (=done for the purposes of learning a foreign language) *A German girl is coming to stay with us on a language exchange.*

a Spanish/French/German etc exchange (=in order to learn a particular language) *I'm going to Madrid on a Spanish exchange.*

a cultural/scientific/academic exchange *The mayors of Tokyo and New York signed an agreement to encourage cultural exchanges between the cities.*

VERBS

go on an exchange (*also* **take part in an exchange**) *Students have the opportunity to go on exchanges.*

exchange + NOUNS

an exchange programme *BrE*, **an exchange program** *AmE*: *The University of Stirling has undergraduate exchange programmes with several institutions.*

an exchange visit *He had gone to France on an exchange visit.*

an exchange student *We have a German exchange student in our class.*

an exchange partner *We are going to Rome in March, then our Italian exchange partners are coming over in June.*

PREPOSITIONS

on an exchange *I went to Japan on an exchange.*

an exchange with sb/sth *I'm here for one term, on an exchange with Dr Fisher.*

an exchange between sb/sth *Her visit is part of an exchange between students from the two universities.*

3 a process in which you change money from one currency to another

ADJECTIVES/NOUNS + exchange

foreign exchange (=money in a foreign currency, that a country gets by selling goods abroad) *Oil is a vital source of foreign exchange earnings for the country.*

exchange + NOUNS

the exchange rate *What's the current exchange rate between the dollar and the euro?*

the exchange markets (=a financial market where different currencies are bought and sold) *The pound rose against the dollar on the world foreign currency exchange markets.*

exchange controls (=limits on the amount of a currency people are allowed to exchange) *The government is going to impose stricter exchange controls.*

excite *v*

to cause a particular feeling or reaction

NOUNS

excite interest/attention *She is a talented young actress who has excited a lot of interest.*

excite curiosity *Rumours of hidden treasure excited our curiosity.*

excite sympathy *She sought to excite the jury's sympathy at every opportunity.*

excite anger *The government's proposals have excited anger among teachers.*

excite hatred/hostility *He accused sections of the media of trying to excite racial hatred.*

excite suspicion *He tried not to do anything to excite the suspicion of the police.*

excite a reaction *Her comments did not excite any reaction from her listeners.*

excite comments *The film excited a lot of favourable comments, both here and in America.*

excite rumours *BrE*, **excite rumors** *AmE: These photographs have excited rumours that their marriage is over.*

excite speculation (=encourage people to discuss something when they do not know the facts) *The cut in US interest rates excited speculation of a similar cut in the UK.*

excited *adj*

happy, interested, or hopeful because something good has happened or will happen

VERBS

get/become excited *They got really excited about the idea.*

feel/sound/look excited *She looked very excited when I told her the news.*

NOUNS

an excited voice/face *Loud excited voices could be heard outside the room.*

an excited crowd *The streets were full of excited crowds.*

excited anticipation (=excited feelings because you know something will happen soon) *We waited with excited anticipation for the band to come on stage.*

ADVERBS

wildly excited *They played in front of a wildly excited crowd.*

PREPOSITIONS

excited about sth *The governors were very excited about the scheme.*

excited by sth *Many people were excited by what he had to say.*

excited at sth *I was excited at the thought of seeing her again.*

excitement *n* the feeling of being excited

ADJECTIVES

great/tremendous/enormous excitement *There is great excitement about the Pope's visit.*

growing/mounting excitement *The children waited with growing excitement.*

sheer excitement (=used when emphasizing that something is very exciting) *Nothing can beat driving a racing car for sheer excitement.*

intense excitement (=a very strong feeling of excitement) *The trial created intense excitement.*

real/genuine excitement *There is genuine excitement about what we can achieve together.*

nervous excitement *Before the race I was full of nervous excitement.*

VERBS + excitement

feel excitement *I remember the excitement I felt as I approached the house.*

cause/generate/create excitement *The arrival of a stranger caused some excitement in the village.*

hide/conceal your excitement *He tried to hide his excitement, but his voice was shaking.*

control/contain your excitement *She could hardly control her excitement when I told her the news.*

tremble with excitement *Her hands were trembling with excitement as she opened the letter.*

be bursting with excitement (=be feeling extremely excited) *I was bursting with excitement and I couldn't wait to tell them the news.*

excitement + VERBS

the excitement grows/mounts/builds (=it increases) *Her excitement grew as the day of the wedding came nearer.*

the excitement wears off (=it gradually becomes less) *The initial excitement of my new job was starting to wear off.*

the excitement dies down (=people stop feeling excited) *The excitement after last month's elections is beginning to die down.*

PREPOSITIONS

excitement at sth *You can imagine my excitement at the thought of visiting Antarctica.*

the excitement of (doing) sth *He loved the excitement of flying his own plane.*

with excitement *We waited with great excitement but nothing happened.*

PHRASES

a sense/feeling of excitement *He woke up that morning with a feeling of excitement.*

a state of excitement *It seemed that the whole country was in a state of excitement.*

an air of excitement (=a general feeling of excitement among a group of people) *There was a real air of excitement before the game.*

be full of excitement/filled with excitement *They were full of excitement at the thought of meeting a real movie star.*

be wild with excitement *Cathy was wild with excitement at the idea.*

a flicker of excitement (=a feeling of excitement that lasts a very short time) *He felt a flicker of excitement when he heard someone mention his name.*

exciting *adj* making you feel excited

VERBS

find sth exciting *He found it very exciting to ride a horse at such speed.*

make sth exciting *We want to make politics more exciting to young people.*

ADVERBS

very/really exciting *It's a really exciting time for us.*

tremendously/incredibly exciting *This has been a tremendously exciting project.*

NOUNS

an exciting opportunity *The new post offers an exciting career opportunity.*

exciting news *I've got some very exciting news for you.*

an exciting story/film/game *The story was so exciting that I forgot about the time.*

an exciting event *Eva felt very tired after the exciting events of the weekend.*

an exciting possibility *Penny considered the exciting possibility that Jack might be at the party.*

an exciting time *It was the most exciting time of my life.*

an exciting development (=a change that makes a product, situation etc better) *This exciting development could mean the end of the long-running conflict.*

an exciting prospect (=a future event, or a person who is likely to be successful) *For the team, there's the exciting prospect of travelling all over the world.*

an exciting life *She leads a glamorous and exciting life in New York.*

an exciting discovery *This Roman coin was a very exciting discovery for archaeologists.*

PHRASES

new and exciting *At that time the internet was all new and exciting.*

an exciting new... *There are some exciting new developments in cancer research.*

something exciting *Philip could see that she had something exciting to tell him.*

exclude Ac *v*

to deliberately not include someone or something

ADVERBS

specifically/expressly exclude sb/sth (=exclude them in particular) *The insurance policy specifically excludes dangerous sports such as rock climbing.*

completely/totally exclude sb/sth *These people are completely excluded from our society.*

automatically exclude sb/sth *Prisoners are automatically excluded from voting.*

VERBS

decide/choose to exclude sb/sth *The researchers chose to exclude these figures from their calculations.*

seek/try/attempt to exclude sb/sth *The contract seeks to exclude liability for all such claims.*

feel excluded *Writers and artists often feel excluded from the world around them.*

PREPOSITIONS

exclude sb/sth from sth *Women were excluded from the top levels of decision-making and power.*

exclusive Ac *adj*

1 available or belonging only to particular people, and not shared

NOUNS

exclusive rights to sth *BSkyB had exclusive rights to all the live matches.*

exclusive access to sth *Regulations prohibit anyone having exclusive access to the data.*

the exclusive use of sth *We had exclusive use of the house while he was away.*

an exclusive report/interview/picture (=appearing in only one newspaper or magazine) *The newspaper featured exclusive pictures of the couple's new baby.*

exclusive coverage (=by only one newspaper or TV channel) *You can watch exclusive coverage of all the matches on BBC1.*

an exclusive deal/contract (=one that says that no other person or company can do the same job) *Our firm has an exclusive contract to handle the company's legal affairs.*

an exclusive club (=only open to particular people) *Unfortunately, I'm not a member of the exclusive club of millionaires.*

PREPOSITIONS

exclusive to sb *This offer is exclusive to club members.*

2 exclusive places, organizations, clothes etc are so expensive that not many people can afford to use or buy them

NOUNS

an exclusive suburb/area *They live in an exclusive suburb on the north side of the city.*

an exclusive neighbourhood *BrE*, **an exclusive neighborhood** *AmE*: *Some of these kids are from the most exclusive neighbourhoods.*

an exclusive hotel *With its marble columns and crystal chandeliers, the Crillon is one of the most exclusive hotels in Paris.*

an exclusive school *Marjorie went to an exclusive girls' school.*

an exclusive shop (*also* **an exclusive store** *AmE*): *I walked along Bond Street, past all the exclusive shops.*

excuse *n*

a reason that you give to explain something you do

ADJECTIVES

a good excuse *I hope you have a good excuse for keeping me waiting.*

a wonderful/great excuse (=a very good excuse to do something) *A wedding is a wonderful excuse to buy a new set of clothes.*

the perfect excuse *The phone call gave me the perfect excuse to leave.*

a reasonable/legitimate/valid excuse (=one that is true and that other people cannot

E

criticize) *He didn't have a legitimate excuse for being late.*

a lame/feeble/weak/flimsy excuse (=not good) *Joe muttered some feeble excuse about having a headache.*

a pathetic excuse (=very weak) *That's the most pathetic excuse I've ever heard.*

the usual excuse/the same old excuse *He made the usual excuses for not coming.*

a convenient excuse *The rioting provided the government with a convenient excuse not to hold an election.*

VERBS

give/offer an excuse *I'll have to give my boss some kind of excuse.*

make an excuse *I made an excuse and left.*

make up/think up/invent an excuse *I made up some excuse about my car breaking down.*

find an excuse *You must find an excuse to go back there.*

have an excuse *Companies have no excuse for breaking the law.*

use sth as an excuse *She never complained or used her illness as an excuse.*

look for an excuse *I began to look for excuses to avoid seeing him.*

believe/accept an excuse *She didn't believe his excuse for one minute.*

listen to sb's excuses *The teacher didn't want to listen to his excuses.*

run out of excuses (=have made a lot of excuses before, so that you cannot think of any more) *The government has run out of excuses for its failure to fix the economy.*

make excuses for sb/sth (=try to explain why someone has made a mistake or behaved badly) *His mother was always making excuses for her son's behaviour.*

sth gives sb/provides an excuse *Drinking provides an excuse for behaving badly.*

PREPOSITIONS

an excuse for (doing) sth *What was his excuse for not calling you?*

PHRASES

at the slightest excuse (=for any reason, however unimportant) *She comes to our house at the slightest excuse.*

execute *v* THESAURUS ▸ kill

execution *n*

the act of killing someone, especially as a legal punishment

ADJECTIVES

a public execution (=which ordinary people can watch) *The last public execution in England was held in 1868.*

a mock execution (=in which people pretend they are going to kill someone) *The guards gave him a mock execution.*

a political execution *During the 1930s political executions were common in Stalin's Russia.*

a mass execution (=in which many people are killed at the same time) *Evidence of a mass execution of young men has been found.*

summary execution (=in which someone is killed immediately, without a trial) *Churchill demanded the summary execution of Nazi leaders.*

VERBS

carry out an execution *The execution was carried out early the next morning.*

face execution *He faces execution for the murder of his brother.*

await execution *formal* (=be waiting to be executed) *More than 3,300 prisoners currently await execution in US prisons.*

order sb's execution *The judge ordered his execution.*

watch/witness an execution *A crowd had gathered to witness the execution.*

delay an execution *The court agreed to delay the execution while they looked at new evidence.*

stop/halt an execution *The US Supreme Court stopped his execution, just minutes before he was to be killed.*

escape execution *The man was lucky to escape execution.*

an execution takes place *The execution took place the following day.*

PHRASES

a stay of execution (=an order that an execution should be delayed) *Saddam's lawyers asked a US judge for a stay of execution.*

death by execution *They face death by execution.*

exercise *n*

physical activities or movements that you do in order to stay healthy and become stronger

ADJECTIVES

good exercise *Swimming is very good exercise for all your muscles.*

regular/daily exercise *Taking regular exercise is the best way to improve your overall health.*

physical exercise *Physical exercise keeps you fit and helps to reduce stress.*

hard/strenuous/vigorous exercise (=involving a lot of physical effort) *Pregnant women should avoid strenuous exercise.*

gentle/light/moderate exercise *Try to do some gentle exercise as part of your daily routine.*

aerobic exercise (=in which you breathe deeply and your heart beats faster) *Aerobic exercise, such as jogging or cycling, is a great way to stay in shape.*

NOUNS + exercise

keep-fit exercises *I couldn't get to the gym, so I did a few keep-fit exercises in my bedroom.*

a warm-up exercise (=in order to make your muscles ready for doing an activity) *The* *athletes were doing their warm-up exercises before the race.*

stretching exercises (=in order to stretch your muscles and make you healthy) *My grandfather was doing his stretching exercises.*

leg/chest/arm exercises *Repeat this series of leg exercises three times.*

VERBS

do some exercise (*also* **take some exercise** *BrE*): *I don't do enough exercise.*

do an exercise *She does exercises to strengthen her legs.*

get some exercise *I work in an office, so I don't get enough exercise.*

exercise + NOUNS

an exercise programme *BrE*, **an exercise program** *AmE*: *The athletes follow an intensive exercise programme.*

an exercise routine/regime (*also* **an exercise regimen** *AmE*): *His exercise routine includes weight training and running ten kilometres a day.*

an exercise class *I usually go to my exercise class on Wednesdays.*

PHRASES

lack of exercise *Children are becoming overweight through lack of exercise.*

a type/form of exercise *This type of exercise is great for your upper body.*

exert *v*

to use your power, influence etc in order to make something happen

NOUNS

exert pressure *Environmental groups are exerting pressure on the government to tighten pollution laws.*

exert influence *Large companies exert considerable influence over the government.*

exert control *The state should not exert control over the media.*

exert power *He exerts a lot of power within the family.*

exert authority *Parents sometimes need to exert their authority by establishing firm rules.*

exert discipline *Exerting discipline with these problem students is essential.*

exert effort *We exerted every effort to get there on time.*

exert your will (=make something happen in the way that you want) *The people used the elections to exert their will.*

THESAURUS: exert

utilize, employ, apply, draw on sth, exploit, resort to sth, exercise, exert → **use[1]**

exhausted *adj* extremely tired

ADVERBS

absolutely exhausted *I was absolutely exhausted by the time we got home.*

totally/completely/utterly exhausted *Looking after a baby on my own left me feeling totally exhausted.*

mentally exhausted *When I got to the end of my exams, I was mentally exhausted.*

physically exhausted *After the climb, both men were physically exhausted.*

emotionally exhausted *She was emotionally exhausted, and the strain was affecting her job.*

VERBS

feel exhausted *He felt exhausted, as though he had just run a marathon.*

look exhausted *You look absolutely exhausted.*

PREPOSITIONS

exhausted by/from sth *I was exhausted by the journey.*

exhausting *adj* THESAURUS › tiring

exhaustion *n* extreme tiredness

VERBS

suffer from exhaustion *The singer was suffering from exhaustion and she had to cancel the concert.*

collapse with/from exhaustion *They kept on dancing until they collapsed from exhaustion.*

be overcome by exhaustion (=be so exhausted that you cannot continue) *Overcome by exhaustion, she fell asleep at her desk.*

ADJECTIVES/NOUNS + exhaustion

complete/total/utter exhaustion *Henry returned home late from work in a state of complete exhaustion.*

sheer exhaustion (=used to emphasize that someone is very tired) *I eventually fell asleep from sheer exhaustion.*

nervous exhaustion (=exhaustion caused by worrying a lot) *The actor said he was suffering from nervous exhaustion.*

mental/emotional exhaustion *He was forced to give up teaching because of mental exhaustion.*

physical exhaustion *She can no longer deal with the physical exhaustion of doing two full-time jobs.*

heat exhaustion (=caused by very hot weather) *Several elderly people were treated for heat exhaustion.*

PHRASES

close/near to exhaustion *The men were close to exhaustion, having walked for over 36 hours.*

weak with exhaustion *The long climb had left him weak with exhaustion.*

on the edge of exhaustion *I could see that she was on the edge of exhaustion and she needed to rest.*

be in a state of exhaustion *The long journey had left him in a state of exhaustion.*

exhibition Ac *n*

a show of paintings, photographs, or other objects that people can go to see

ADJECTIVES/NOUNS + exhibition

an art/photography/sculpture exhibition *The museum houses temporary art exhibitions.*

a big/large/small exhibition *This is the largest exhibition of its kind that we have ever seen in London.*

an important/major exhibition *His work is the subject of a major new exhibition at the National Gallery.*

a permanent exhibition *The museum has a permanent exhibition of paintings by local artists.*

a temporary exhibition *The space is used for temporary exhibitions.*

a touring/travelling exhibition (=one that moves from place to place) *The touring exhibition is scheduled to be in Dallas from March until June.*

a retrospective exhibition (=one that shows work from the past) *It was a retrospective exhibition celebrating 150 years of photography.*

VERBS + exhibition

go to/visit an exhibition *We went to an exhibition at the National Gallery.*

see an exhibition *Did you see any exhibitions when you were in Paris?*

have an exhibition *The college is having an exhibition of the students' work in April.*

hold/mount/stage an exhibition *formal* (=have an exhibition) *The Hayward Gallery is mounting an impressive exhibition of new British artists.*

put on an exhibition (=arrange for an exhibition to take place) *Last summer the museum put on some wonderful exhibitions for children.*

organize/arrange an exhibition *The exhibition was organized by the Getty Foundation.*

exhibition + VERBS

an exhibition opens/closes (=it starts or ends) *The exhibition opens on May 2nd.*

an exhibition includes sth *The exhibition includes some little-known works by Picasso.*

exhibition + NOUNS

an exhibition centre *BrE*, **an exhibition center** *AmE* (=a large building for holding exhibitions) *The exhibition will be held in the National Exhibition Centre in Birmingham.*

an exhibition hall *There's a large exhibition hall on the ground floor.*

an exhibition catalogue *BrE*, **an exhibition catalog** *AmE* (=a list or book giving information about all the things in an exhibition) *The exhibition catalogue contained some interesting information about the artists.*

PREPOSITIONS

an exhibition of sth *We're going to see an exhibition of Victorian photography.*

in an exhibition *All the paintings in the exhibition are for sale.*

on exhibition (=being shown in an exhibition) *Ancient musical instruments are on exhibition at the Institute.*

> **American English**
> US speakers often say **exhibit** instead of **exhibition**.

exile *n*

a situation in which you are forced to leave your country and live in another country, especially for political reasons

VERBS

go into exile *Napoleon's wife went into exile in Austria.*

live in exile *The Guatemalan writer has lived in exile in Mexico for over 40 years.*

be sent into exile *The old leaders were removed from power and sent into exile.*

be forced/driven into exile *Many of his political opponents have been forced into exile.*

flee/escape into exile *Hundreds of people fled into exile or were jailed.*

die in exile *He never returned to his own country, but died in exile.*

return from exile *Martinez returned from exile in 1990 and was later elected president.*

ADJECTIVES

long exile *These refugees have finally returned home from a long exile in Senegal.*

permanent exile *The king threatened her with permanent exile.*

enforced exile (=when someone is forced to go into exile) *After 12 years of enforced exile abroad, Almeyda returned home to Salvador.*

self-imposed/voluntary exile (=when someone goes into exile willingly, without being forced) *He spoke to the media from his self-imposed exile in the United States.*

PREPOSITIONS

in exile *Sharif began a new life in exile.*

exile from a place *During his exile from Russia, he took up art as a hobby.*

exist *v*

to happen or be present in a particular situation or place

ADVERBS

really/actually exist *Do you think ghosts really exist?*

already exist *Legislation to protect us from terrorists already exists.*

currently exist *No treaty currently exists between the two countries.*

E

still exist (=existing in the past and continuing to exist) *A number of his early photographs still exist.*

VERBS

continue to exist *The same problems continue to exist.*

cease to exist (=stop existing) *The club will cease to exist if financial help is not found.*

be known to exist *Seven copies of the original book are still known to exist.*

existence *n*

1 the state of existing

ADJECTIVES

a brief/short existence *The band had rather a brief existence.*

human existence *Darwin's theory of natural selection changed our view of human existence forever.*

sth's continued existence *The city's continued existence is threatened by rising water levels.*

sth's very existence (=the fact that it exists at all) *The university's very existence is in doubt.*

VERBS

come into existence (=start to exist) *Pakistan came into existence as an independent country in 1947.*

bring sth into existence *formal* (=make something start to exist) *This is the treaty that brought our state into existence.*

go out of existence (=stop existing) *If a buyer isn't found, this famous old club could go out of existence.*

acknowledge/recognize/accept the existence of sth (=agree that something exists) *The company finally acknowledged the existence of a problem.*

prove/confirm/establish the existence of sth *The images confirm the existence of water on the planet's surface.*

deny the existence of sth *He immediately denied the existence of any deal.*

doubt the existence of sth *He began to doubt the existence of God.*

threaten/jeopardize the existence of sth (=make it likely that something will stop existing) *The strike could jeopardize the existence of his company.*

owe your existence to sth (=be able to exist because of something) *The birds owe their existence to the fact that they have no natural enemies on the island.*

PREPOSITIONS

the existence of sth *Between the ages of two and five, children usually become aware of the existence of rules.*

in existence *The organization has been in existence for 25 years.*

2 the type of life that someone has, especially when it is bad or unhappy

ADJECTIVES

everyday/daily/day-to-day existence (=someone's normal life that is the same most days) *He saw drugs as a way of escaping the tedium of his everyday existence.*

a lonely/solitary existence *Male bears live a mostly solitary existence, away from the female and cubs.*

a miserable existence *The refugees had to endure a miserable existence in the desert.*

a dull/routine existence *I was happy to leave my routine existence behind.*

a frugal existence (=without much money) *He led a hard and frugal existence.*

a hand-to-mouth existence (=with just enough food or money to live) *The survivors lived a hand-to-mouth existence until they were rescued.*

a precarious existence (=only just managing to live) *The islanders, who rely on the sea to provide food, have a precarious existence.*

a comfortable existence (=with plenty of food and money) *He left behind his comfortable existence to become a monk.*

a peaceful existence *The different tribes in the area enjoyed a relatively peaceful existence.*

VERBS

lead/live a ... existence *The family lived a pretty miserable existence.*

enjoy a peaceful/quiet etc existence *They enjoy a comfortable existence.*

eke out an existence (=manage to live with very little money) *She eked out a miserable existence in a dreary apartment.*

exit *n*

1 a door or space through which you can leave a public room, building etc

ADJECTIVES/NOUNS + exit

a fire/emergency exit (=a special door, used if there is an emergency or a fire) *Fire exits should not be locked.*

the front/rear/side exit *When the lights dimmed, she slipped out by the rear exit.*

the nearest exit *Please leave the building in an orderly fashion, using the nearest exit.*

VERBS

head for/make for the exit (=go to the exit) *Disappointed fans began heading for the exits.*

use an exit *In the event of a fire, please use the emergency exit nearest to you.*

block an exit *Two men were blocking the exit.*

exit + NOUNS

an exit door *Exit doors shouldn't be blocked at any time.*

an exit route (=a way out of a building, plane etc, used in an emergency or a fire) *Staff*

E

must become familiar with the building's exit routes.

an exit sign (=one showing where an exit is) *There was a red glowing exit sign over the door.*

2 when you leave a room or building

ADJECTIVES

a quick/fast exit *I made a quick exit before the speeches began.*

a hurried/swift exit (=very quick) *The family made a hurried exit, leaving many of their belongings behind.*

a dignified exit (=when someone leaves in a way that makes people respect them) *Marco did his best to make a dignified exit.*

an undignified exit (=when someone leaves in a way that is embarrassing or makes them look silly) *She made a rather undignified exit, tripping down the step.*

VERBS

make an exit/make your exit (=leave) *And then, kissing them both goodbye, he made his exit.*

exotic *adj* THESAURUS **unusual**

expand Ac *v*

to become larger in size, or to make something become larger in size

ADVERBS

expand (sth) rapidly *The population is expanding rapidly.*

expand (sth) greatly *Japan's domestic economy expanded greatly during this period.*

expand (sth) significantly (=in an important way) *The United Nations significantly expanded its peacekeeping force in the region.*

expand (sth) dramatically (=in a great and sudden way) *Wine production has expanded dramatically.*

expansion Ac *n*

when something increases in size, range, amount etc

ADJECTIVES/NOUNS + expansion

a rapid expansion *During the 1990s, there was a rapid expansion in student numbers.*

a steady expansion *There has been a steady expansion of the self-employed sector of the economy.*

a big expansion *This week the company announced a big expansion of its European workforce.*

a great/huge/massive expansion *There are plans for a massive expansion of the oil and gas industries.*

a major/significant expansion (=large and important) *The company is planning a major expansion of its retail outlets.*

economic/business/commercial expansion *Economic expansion in India and China is set to continue.*

further expansion *Investors think the hotel chain is ready for further expansion.*

expansion + NOUNS

expansion plans *The city's ambitious expansion plans will require major investment.*

PREPOSITIONS

expansion of sth *The rapid expansion of cities can cause social and economic problems.*

expansion in sth *There was a huge expansion in the size of the school.*

PHRASES

the rate of expansion *The rate of expansion was slightly slower last year.*

expect *v*

to think that something will happen because it seems likely or has been planned

ADVERBS

fully expect sth (=completely) *We fully expected to win.*

confidently expect sth (=with a feeling of confidence) *He confidently expected to be elected again.*

half expect sth (=partly, but not completely) *He walked slowly towards the box, half expecting it to explode.*

really/honestly expect sth *I didn't really expect her to come.*

realistically/reasonably expect sth *You need to ask yourself what you want and what you can realistically expect.*

rightly expect sth (=with good reason) *The public rightly expects government officials to be honest.*

hardly expect sth (=used to say that it is not reasonable to expect something) *You can hardly expect a child of three to understand such a difficult concept.*

be widely expected to do sth (=many people think something will happen) *The Democrats are widely expected to win the election.*

PHRASES

as expected *As expected, the chairman resigned from his post.*

sth is (only) to be expected (=used to say that you are not surprised by something unpleasant) *A little nervousness is only to be expected when you are starting a new job.*

it is reasonable/unreasonable to expect sth *It's unreasonable to expect a tenant to pay for repairs to the outside of the house.*

sth happens when you least expect it *Bad luck tends to happen when you least expect it.*

expectation *n*

what you think or hope will happen

ADJECTIVES/NOUNS + expectation

high expectations (=expecting that someone or something will be very good) *Like most parents, we have high expectations for our children.*

great expectations (=very high) *Emigrants sailed to America with great expectations.*

low expectations (=expecting that someone or something will not be very good) *Their expectations of success were pretty low.*

growing/rising/increased expectations *China's growing economy will bring rising expectations of wealth.*

realistic/reasonable expectations *The disease is not curable, and patients must have realistic expectations.*

unreasonable/unrealistic expectations *I think you had unrealistic expectations of what could be done in the time.*

a general/widespread expectation (=shared by a lot of people) *The general expectation was for married couples to have children.*

VERBS

have expectations *People often have high expectations when they first arrive in the US.*

raise sb's expectations (=make people expect that something good will happen) *The government raised expectations, then failed to keep its promises.*

lower sb's expectations (=expect that something will not be as good) *If you can't afford your dream home, you may have to lower your expectations.*

come up to/live up to sb's expectations (=be as good as someone hoped) *The match was boring, and didn't live up to expectations at all.*

meet/satisfy/fulfil sb's expectations (=be as good as someone hoped) *The concert failed to meet the fans' expectations.*

exceed/surpass (sb's) expectations (=be even better than someone hoped) *The holiday exceeded all our expectations.*

create expectations (=make people expect that something will happen) *His remarks created expectations that the couple would soon announce their marriage.*

PREPOSITIONS

above/below expectations *Economic growth last month was above expectations.*

beyond all expectations (=greater or better than someone expected) *The plan succeeded beyond all expectations.*

against/contrary to expectations (=very different from what someone expected) *Contrary to our expectations, the share price actually increased.*

in/with the expectation that *The weapons had been developed in the expectation that they would be used.*

PHRASES

fall below/fall short of (sb's) expectations (=be worse than someone hoped) *Our profits last year fell below expectations.*

in line with expectations (=the same as you expected, or similar to what you expected) *Results were in line with expectations.*

expedition *n*

1 a long and carefully organized journey, especially to a dangerous or unfamiliar place

ADJECTIVES

a scientific expedition *He led the first major British scientific expedition to the Amazon.*

a military expedition *The generals decided to launch a military expedition to the region.*

an Arctic/Antarctic expedition *I accompanied him on one of his Arctic expeditions.*

VERBS

go on an expedition *Swainson went on an expedition to Patagonia.*

make an expedition (=go on an expedition) *The men made expeditions to Spain, Greece, and Asia Minor to find fossils.*

set off on an expedition (*also* **embark on an expedition** *formal*): *Trent set off on a botanical expedition with other students.*

mount/launch an expedition (=plan, organize, and begin an expedition) *Scientists are mounting an expedition to the island to study its wildlife.*

lead an expedition *Scott led an expedition to the South Pole.*

expedition + NOUNS

an expedition leader *Bonington was the expedition leader.*

PREPOSITIONS

an expedition to a place *He led an expedition to Borneo.*

on an expedition *What equipment should we take with us on the expedition?*

2 a short journey in order to do something

NOUNS + expedition

a shopping expedition (=when you go shopping) *I took Mary and the kids on a shopping expedition into Manchester.*

a fishing expedition *We're organizing a fishing expedition to the lake for next week.*

a hunting expedition *He was joined on his hunting expedition by two local guides.*

VERBS

go on an expedition *We decided to go on a shopping expedition to London.*

take someone on an expedition *He's taking the boys on a camping expedition next weekend.*

expenditure *n*

the total amount of money that a government, organization, or person spends during a particular period of time

ADJECTIVES/NOUNS + expenditure

public/government/state expenditure (=money a government spends on the services it provides for people) *The Conservatives want to maintain a firm control on public expenditure.*

national/local expenditure (=money spent by national or local government) *There have been cuts in local expenditure on education.*

military/defence expenditure (=money that a government spends on the armed forces) *Military expenditure has been growing each year.*

health/welfare/education expenditure *There has been a steady rise in welfare expenditure.*

household expenditure (=the money the people in a house spend on food, heating etc) *The figures show that household expenditure on fuel has risen.*

total/overall expenditure *The company's total expenditure rose by 19%.*

additional/extra expenditure *Businesses have been forced to pass on the additional expenditure to customers.*

capital expenditure (=money that a company spends on buildings, machinery etc) *Capital expenditure on IT equipment will come from a different budget.*

gross/net expenditure (=the total amount a company spends before/after tax or costs have been taken away) *Spending on research and development represents 13% of our gross expenditure.*

VERBS

increase expenditure *The company plans to increase capital expenditure by 20% this financial year.*

cut/reduce expenditure *The school has been told it must cut expenditure.*

control expenditure *The government intends to strictly control public expenditure.*

incur expenditure *formal* (=have to spend money) *They will incur additional expenditure on architects' fees.*

expenditure rises *As public expenditure has risen, so have taxes.*

expenditure falls *Government expenditure on scientific research has fallen in the last few years.*

PREPOSITIONS

expenditure on sth *Expenditure on education has increased.*

expenditure of £5 million/$4 billion etc *The government proposed expenditure of £10 billion on modernizing the rail network.*

PHRASES

an increase/rise in expenditure *The government has announced a planned 4.4% increase in public expenditure.*

a cut/reduction in expenditure *There has been a significant cut in expenditure on social and welfare services.*

an item of expenditure (=something a government or person spends money on) *Housing is the biggest single item of expenditure in most household budgets.*

the level of expenditure *The level of expenditure on military equipment was too high.*

THESAURUS: expenditure

expenditure, costs, expenses, outgoings, outlay, overheads → **spending**

expense *n*

1 the amount of money that you spend on something

ADJECTIVES/NOUNS + expense

the extra/additional expense *Is it worth the extra expense to get a room with a sea view?*

an unnecessary expense *Paying extra for leather seats seemed like an unnecessary expense.*

living/household expenses (=money that you spend on basic things such as rent, food, and electricity) *She receives £80 a week, from which she must pay for all her living expenses.*

legal/medical expenses *We had to get a loan to pay for my husband's medical expenses.*

VERBS

meet the expenses *formal* (=pay the necessary money) *She did not have enough money to meet household expenses.*

incur an expense *formal* (=have to pay for something) *He did not want to incur the expense of upgrading his computer.*

cover an expense (=be enough to pay for something) *The payments he gets barely cover his expenses.*

PHRASES

at great/huge/considerable/vast expense (=used when saying that something costs a lot of money) *The tiles were imported at great expense from Italy.*

at your own expense (=used when saying that you pay for something yourself) *He had copies of the book printed at his own expense.*

at (the) public expense (=paid for by the public through taxes) *The bridge was built at public expense.*

go to the expense of doing sth (=do something that costs a lot of money) *He didn't want to go to the expense of buying a suit, so he hired one.*

spare no expense (in doing sth) (=spend a lot of money to buy the best things) *Her parents spared no expense in arranging the wedding.*

2 things that you pay for when you are doing your job, which you can ask your employer to pay you back for

> **Grammar**
> Always plural in this meaning.

ADJECTIVES/NOUNS + expense

travel/travelling expenses *The company will pay the travelling expenses involved in getting to and from the meeting.*

business expenses *She receives an allowance for business expenses.*

entertainment expenses (=expenses for meals, trips etc with people who you are doing business with) *When I take clients out for a meal, I can put it on entertainment expenses.*

relocation/moving expenses (=expenses when changing where you live or work) *We are prepared to pay the relocation expenses of successful candidates.*

reasonable/legitimate expenses *All reasonable interview expenses will be reimbursed.*

VERBS

pay sb's expenses *They agreed to pay my travel expenses.*

claim expenses *If you have to stay overnight, you will be able to claim expenses.*

claim/put sth on expenses (=claim money from your employer for it) *He claimed the meal on expenses.*

fiddle your expenses *BrE informal* (=deliberately make a false claim for money) *Several MPs were accused of fiddling their expenses.*

reimburse sb's expenses (=pay the money someone has spent for business purposes back to them) *Your expenses will be reimbursed within one month of receiving the claim.*

expenses *n* THESAURUS ▸ **spending**

expensive *adj* costing a lot of money

NOUNS

expensive clothes/furniture/equipment *She spent all her money on expensive clothes.*

an expensive car/camera/watch/phone *There was a big expensive car parked outside their house.*

an expensive gift/present *Her boyfriend was always buying her expensive presents.*

an expensive hotel/restaurant *We stayed at the most expensive hotel in town.*

an expensive place/area/part *Tokyo is one of the world's most expensive places to live.*

⚠ Don't say an 'expensive price'. Say a **high price**.

ADVERBS

rather expensive (*also* **quite expensive** *BrE*): *The food's quite expensive.*

too expensive *Private medical insurance is too expensive for many people.*

ridiculously/outrageously/horrendously expensive (=extremely expensive, in a way that seems shocking) *Room service in the hotel was ridiculously expensive.*

astronomically/phenomenally expensive (=extremely expensive) *The drug is phenomenally expensive.*

prohibitively expensive (=too expensive, with the result that most people cannot afford to buy something) *HIV medicines are still prohibitively expensive for sufferers in Africa.*

VERBS

look/seem/sound expensive *At £75, the concert tickets seemed rather expensive.*

PHRASES

sth is expensive to make/produce/buy *Handmade furniture is expensive to produce.*

sb has expensive tastes (=they want to have things that are very expensive) *His wife has very expensive tastes.*

sth was an expensive mistake (=it resulted in someone having to spend a lot of money) *Choosing the wrong builder turned out to be an expensive mistake.*

E

THESAURUS: expensive

high
rent | fee | price | cost | tax
high rents, fees, taxes etc cost a lot of money:
Rents are very high in Manhattan. | Lawyers charge high fees. | Drivers are complaining about the high price of fuel. | Students have problems because of the high cost of accommodation.

> **High** is the usual word to use before these nouns, not **expensive**.

> You also use **high** when talking about someone's **wages/salary/pay/income**: *Bankers are paid* ***high salaries****.*

pricey *informal*
expensive – used when something costs more than you want to pay:
She looked at the menu. Everything was very pricey. | The clothes are beautiful but pricey.

overpriced
too expensive and not worth the price:
The restaurant was overpriced and the food wasn't very good. | The tickets are ***ridiculously overpriced****. | The shop sells overpriced souvenirs.*

costly
mistake | failure | business | exercise | process | lawsuit | legal battle | delay
if something is costly, it results in you having to pay a lot of money:

The decision turned out to be a costly mistake. | Caring for all these animals is a costly business. | They were hoping to avoid a costly legal battle.

astronomical
price | cost | amount | sum | rate | fee
extremely expensive:
The painting was sold for an astronomical price. | Housing costs are astronomical here. | His paintings sell for astronomical sums of money.

exorbitant
fee | price | rent | amount of money | rate
much too expensive:
Some accountants charge exorbitant fees. | It's a nice hotel, but the prices are exorbitant. | The call cost an exorbitant amount of money.

If something is too expensive for someone, you can say they **cannot afford** it: *Young people* ***cannot afford*** *to live in the area.*
If something looks expensive, you can say that it **must have cost a lot of money**: *The house looked like* ***it must have cost a lot of money****.*

ANTONYMS **expensive → cheap**

experience *n*

1 knowledge or skill that you gain from doing a job or activity, or the process of doing this

ADJECTIVES/NOUNS + experience

considerable/extensive experience *Margaret has considerable experience of hospital work.*
long experience *His long experience of management enabled him to give us some useful advice.*
useful/valuable experience *That summer he got some valuable experience working in a tax office.*
relevant experience (=that directly relates to a job, subject, or problem) *Applicants need a degree and two years of relevant experience.*
past/previous experience *He had no previous experience of running a farm.*
practical/hands-on experience (=gained from doing something, not from books or study) *The classes provide students with some practical experience of computers.*
direct/first-hand experience (=gained by doing something yourself) *She has no first-hand experience of dealing with sick children.*
teaching/nursing etc experience *Preference will be given to candidates with teaching experience.*
work experience *Students will spend three months doing work experience.*

VERBS

have experience *You must have experience of working with children.*
get experience (*also* **gain experience** *formal*): *He suggested that I should gain some experience in the travel industry.*
lack experience (=not have enough experience) *Some students lack experience writing essays.*
broaden/widen your experience (=increase the amount of different experience you have) *After six years with the bank, he went to work in New York to broaden his experience.*
use your experience *She was able to use her experience in public relations to promote the event.*

PREPOSITIONS

experience of sth *Bella had ten years' experience of team management.*
experience in sth *She lacked experience in the entertainment industry.*
experience as a teacher/salesperson/manager etc *Firaz has considerable experience as a journalist.*

PHRASES

two years'/50 years' etc experience *Carla has over 25 years' experience in the IT industry.*
lack of experience *My colleagues kept making comments about my lack of experience.*
a wealth of experience (=a lot of useful experience) *Between them, the team members have a wealth of experience.*

2 knowledge that you gain about life and the world by being in different situations and meeting different people, or the process of gaining this

ADJECTIVES/NOUNS + experience

personal experience *She spoke from personal experience about the harmful effects of taking drugs.*
first-hand experience (=gained from doing something yourself) *Her father had been badly affected by his first-hand experience of living in a war zone.*
bitter experience (=that makes you feel disappointed or upset) *I knew from bitter experience how unreliable she could be.*

VERBS

know/learn from experience *Janet knew from experience that love doesn't always last.*
speak from experience *The miners spoke from experience about the dangers of their work.*
lack experience *These young men lack experience and social skills.*
experience suggests/shows sth *Experience suggests that many criminals commit crimes from an early age.*
experience teaches sb sth *Experience has taught me to read a document carefully before signing it.*

use your experience (*also* **draw on (your) experience** *formal*): *He has over 50 years of experience that he can draw on.*

PREPOSITIONS

through/from/by experience *Good judgment comes gradually through experience.*

in sb's experience *In my experience, children like getting muddy.*

PHRASES

lack of experience *He was embarrassed about his lack of experience with women.*

3 something that happens to you or something you do, especially when this has an effect on what you feel or think

ADJECTIVES/NOUNS + experience

a good/pleasant/enjoyable experience *We want to make the experience as enjoyable as possible.*

a bad/unpleasant experience *I've had some bad experiences when I've been travelling on my own.*

a positive/negative experience *Many people reported having negative experiences when dealing with their local council.*

an interesting experience *I had an interesting experience yesterday.*

a memorable/unforgettable experience (=one that you will remember for a long time) *Meeting the Queen was a memorable experience.*

a painful experience *Her family supported her through the painful experience.*

a frightening/terrifying experience *The attack was truly a terrifying experience for her.*

a traumatic/harrowing experience (=extremely shocking and upsetting) *Having an operation can be a traumatic experience for a child.*

an everyday/commonplace experience (=one that is typical of normal life) *The sound of gunfire is an everyday experience in the city.*

a new experience *Life in London was a whole new experience for me.*

childhood experiences *Our childhood experiences make us what we are as adults.*

VERBS

have an experience *I had a similar experience last year.*

talk about/share your experiences *They meet monthly to share their experiences.*

relive an experience (=remember or imagine it so that you have the same feelings again) *He had been forced to relive the experience in court.*

PREPOSITIONS

experience of (doing) sth *This was my first experience of living on my own.*

a bad/interesting etc experience for sb *We want to make reading an enjoyable experience for children.*

PHRASES

be quite an experience *BrE* (=used when something had a strong effect on you) *Meeting him was quite an experience.*

experienced *adj*

having skills or knowledge because you have done something often or for a long time

NOUNS

an experienced player/skier/rider *Mick is a very experienced player and will be an excellent addition to the team.*

an experienced driver/pilot/sailor *It's better to travel with an experienced driver.*

an experienced teacher/manager/politician *Experienced teachers know what kind of behavior to expect.*

an experienced member *Yvonne is one of the most experienced members of the crew.*

an experienced user *The books are written by experienced users.*

experienced staff/workforce/team/crew *Classes are led by experienced staff.*

ADVERBS

very/highly experienced *The company has a highly experienced workforce of engineers.*

extremely/vastly experienced *They have a number of vastly experienced players.*

PREPOSITIONS

be experienced in/at (doing) sth *They are experienced in running training courses.*

THESAURUS: experienced

veteran
politician | leader | campaigner | player | actor | fighter | member | broadcaster
used about someone who has been doing something for a very long time and is respected by other people:
He is a veteran politician and a former ambassador to the United Nations. | Sister Christine is a veteran campaigner against corruption. | The film stars veteran Hollywood actor Dustin Hoffman.

seasoned
traveller | professional | performer | campaigner | observer
used about someone who has done something regularly for a long time, and knows all the problems involved:
It's best to take as little luggage as possible, as every seasoned traveller knows. | The two candidates are both seasoned campaigners.

hardened
criminal | terrorist | professional | politician | reporter
used about someone who has committed a lot of serious crimes, or someone who has a

E

lot of experience and is not easily shocked or affected by something:
Seven men, some of them hardened criminals, have escaped from jail. | The ambulance workers are hardened professionals.

practised *BrE*, **practiced** *AmE*
eye | ease
good at doing something, because you have a lot of experience:
He looked at the painting with a practised eye (=he had a lot of experience and was good at noticing things). | *Ben turned the boat around with practised ease.* | *They were* ***practised in the art of*** *negotiation* (=good at negotiating, because you have a lot of experience).

In more informal English you can also say that someone is an **old hand** (=he or she has a lot of experience): *The rest of the team are all* ***old hands****.*

E

experiment *n*

a test that is done in order to discover something

ADJECTIVES

a scientific/medical/psychological experiment *Astronauts performed scientific experiments during the flight.*

a simple experiment *In a simple experiment, he gave yellow and green grasshoppers a choice between yellow and green backgrounds.*

a practical experiment (=one that relates to real situations or events, not scientific theories) *The research team compiled a set of practical experiments in Modern Astronomy.*

a controlled experiment (=one that is done using correct scientific methods) *The theory has not yet been tested by a properly controlled experiment.*

NOUNS + experiment

a laboratory experiment (=one that takes place in a laboratory) *They did a series of laboratory experiments on human sleep patterns.*

animal experiments (=experiments using animals) *I think most animal experiments are cruel and unnecessary.*

VERBS

do/carry out an experiment *They carried out a series of experiments to test their theory.*

⚠ Don't say 'make an experiment'.

perform/conduct an experiment *formal* (=do an experiment) *The laboratory began conducting experiments on rats.*

try an experiment *He decided to try a simple experiment.*

repeat an experiment *The researchers obtained similar results when they repeated their experiment.*

an experiment shows/proves/demonstrates sth *His experiment showed that lightning was a kind of electricity.*

an experiment suggests/indicates sth *Experiments suggest that the disease is carried by flies.*

an experiment to test/measure/find out sth *We did an experiment to test the acidity of the soil.*

PREPOSITIONS

an experiment on sb/sth *I don't agree with experiments on animals.*

an experiment with sb/sth *In 1936 he had started his experiments with wheat-free diets.*

PHRASES

the results of an experiment *The results of the experiment supported her theory.*

THESAURUS: experiment

work, study, experiment → **research**

expert[1] [Ac] *n*

someone who has special knowledge of a subject, or a special skill

ADJECTIVES/NOUNS + expert

a leading/top expert *He is one of the country's leading experts on climate change.*

a world/international expert *She is a world expert on tropical diseases.*

a great expert *I'm not really a great expert on Japanese food.*

a medical/legal/financial etc expert *Medical experts agree that screening can prevent deaths from breast cancer.*

a health/safety/computer etc expert *Some air safety experts have expressed concern.*

an acknowledged/recognized expert (=someone who people agree is an expert) *The authors are acknowledged experts in this field.*

an independent expert (=someone who is not connected with an organization or the government) *The authorities called in an independent expert to advise them.*

a so-called expert (=someone who says they are an expert, but who you do not respect very much) *There are many so-called experts willing to tell you how to bring up your children.*

VERBS

talk to/consult an expert *If cracks appear in your house, you should consult an expert to find out what is causing the problem.*

experts advise/recommend sth *Most financial experts recommend that you don't borrow money on credit cards.*

NOUNS

expert advice/help *Get some expert advice before investing in a property.*

expert knowledge *He has expert knowledge of the plants and animals in this area.*

expert opinion *Expert opinion on the matter is deeply divided.*

PREPOSITIONS

an expert on/in sth *He is an expert on beetles.*

PHRASES

a team/panel of experts *You can get advice from our panel of gardening experts.*

the advice of an expert *The government has ignored the advice of its own experts.*

expert² *adj* THESAURUS ▸ **skilful**

expertise Ac *n*

special skills or knowledge in a particular subject, that you learn by experience or training

ADJECTIVES/NOUNS + expertise

considerable/extensive/great expertise (=a lot) *The Marine Pollution Control Unit has considerable expertise in dealing with oil spills.*

professional expertise (=skills requiring education and special training) *A health and safety inspector will be glad to give you the benefit of his professional expertise.*

special/specialist expertise (=a lot of knowledge about a particular subject) *Our haulage company has specialist expertise in transporting hi-tech products.*

medical/scientific/technical/legal expertise *How can an individual without medical expertise make such a decision?*

managerial/management expertise *Does he have the management expertise required to make the department more productive?*

business expertise (=skill at operating a business or company) *She was employed because of her business expertise.*

relevant expertise *All the applicants had the relevant expertise for the job.*

VERBS

have expertise *The rescue workers have a lot of expertise in dealing with this type of emergency.*

need/require expertise (=used about a job, task etc) *It's a specialist job that requires expertise.*

lack expertise *The country lacks the expertise, equipment, and funds to deal with the disaster.*

develop expertise (*also* **acquire/gain expertise** *formal*): *Many administrators develop great expertise within their specialized areas.*

share/pool expertise *By sharing knowledge and expertise we can make the town a better place to live.*

use sb's expertise (*also* **draw on sb's expertise** *formal*): *The course draws on the expertise of lecturers at the city's three universities.*

PREPOSITIONS

expertise in sth *The inspection will be carried out by someone with expertise in language teaching.*

PHRASES

sb's area/field of expertise (=the subject or activity that someone is skilled in) *She is a historian whose area of expertise is the Roman Empire.*

degree/level of expertise *Different financial advisers will have different levels of expertise.*

range of expertise *The committee hopes to draw on a wide range of expertise from different institutions.*

a lack of expertise *His lack of expertise in running such a large factory led to serious problems.*

expire *v* THESAURUS ▸ **end² (1)**

explain *v*

to tell someone about something in a way that is clear and easy to understand

ADVERBS

carefully explain sth *He carefully explained the situation to me.*

politely/patiently explain sth *She politely explained that she could not give out any information about a client.*

briefly explain sth *Could you just explain briefly why you are here?*

clearly explain sth *The meanings of technical terms are clearly explained in the glossary at the back.*

PREPOSITIONS

explain sth to sb *If you explain the problem to your teacher, she may be able to help.*

explain about sth *Would you explain about this equipment – what is it for?*

PHRASES

I can explain (=used when you want the chance to explain a situation that seems bad) *Tony, please calm down. I can explain.*

let me explain (=used when you are going to explain something that seems complicated, surprising, or bad) *It's really quite simple. Let me explain...*

be hard/difficult to explain *It's hard to explain why it upset me so much.*

explain sth in a few words (=briefly) *I'll start by explaining in a few words what my research is about.*

explanation *n*

the reason for something happening, or a reason that someone gives

ADJECTIVES

a good explanation *Can you think of a good explanation why this happens?*

a satisfactory/adequate explanation *No satisfactory explanation has been found for this decline.*

the most likely/probable explanation (=one that is probably true) *The most likely explanation is that John missed the bus.*

a possible explanation *One possible explanation is that he may have forgotten that there was a meeting today.*

a plausible/convincing/reasonable explanation (=one that seems likely to be true) *Pilot error is the most plausible explanation for the crash.*

an alternative/different explanation *This led us to consider an alternative explanation.*

an obvious explanation *There is no obvious explanation for his strange behaviour.*

a simple explanation *He has a simple explanation for the book's success.*

a logical/rational/scientific explanation *There is no logical explanation for this feeling.*

an innocent explanation (=an explanation in which someone is not involved in doing something bad) *She insists there is a more innocent explanation.*

further explanation *No further explanation is necessary.*

VERBS

give/offer/provide an explanation *The police gave no explanation for their actions.*

put forward/propose an explanation *Another team of researchers proposed a different explanation.*

find/think of/come up with an explanation *Scientists have been unable to find an explanation for this phenomenon.*

ask for/demand/want an explanation *Furious parents are demanding an explanation from the school.*

have an explanation *I don't have any explanation for his behaviour.*

owe (sb) an explanation (=should give someone an explanation) *I think you owe me some kind of explanation.*

accept an explanation (=believe that it is true or correct) *The court accepted her explanation.*

need/require an explanation *We think the minister's decision requires an explanation.*

the explanation lies in sth (=is related to something) *The explanation lies in the structure of atoms.*

PREPOSITIONS

an explanation for/of sth *They were not satisfied with his explanation of events.*

without explanation *He used to disappear for long periods without explanation.*

PHRASES

by way of explanation (=as an explanation) *"I had a train to catch," she said by way of explanation.*

exploit *v* THESAURUS ▸ use[1]

explorer *n*

someone who travels through an unknown area to find out about it

ADJECTIVES/NOUNS + explorer

a European/Spanish/French etc explorer *European explorers discovered the temple in the 19th century.*

a great explorer *Marco Polo was the great explorer who travelled across Asia.*

the first explorers *He was one of the first explorers to see an American buffalo.*

an early explorer *The early explorers were looking for new lands and trading opportunities.*

an intrepid explorer (=an explorer who is willing to go to dangerous places) *The two intrepid explorers became the first people to travel across the US.*

an Arctic/Antarctic/Polar explorer *Perry was following in the footsteps of other Arctic explorers.*

a space explorer *One day space explorers will set up a base on Mars.*

explosion *n*

1 a loud sound and the energy produced by something such as a bomb bursting into small pieces

ADJECTIVES/NOUNS + explosion

a huge/massive/tremendous explosion *A huge explosion tore the roof off the building.*

a powerful explosion *A powerful explosion took place outside an army training center.*

a loud explosion *We heard several loud explosions followed by a long silence.*

a muffled explosion (=one that is not heard very clearly) *He reported hearing a muffled explosion from deep inside the mine.*

a bomb explosion *He was fatally injured in a bomb explosion.*

a nuclear/atomic explosion *This is the site of the first ever nuclear explosion.*

VERBS

cause an explosion *The police do not yet know what caused the explosion.*

set off/trigger an explosion (=cause an explosion) *Investigators believe a fuel leak may have triggered the explosion.*

an explosion shakes sth *A series of explosions shook the building.*

an explosion destroys sth *Seven people died when an explosion destroyed the bus.*

carry out an explosion (=cause one deliberately) *By 1942, the United States had carried out test explosions with nuclear bombs.*

2 a sudden or quick increase in the number or amount of something

ADJECTIVES

a sudden explosion *There was a sudden explosion of interest in the sport.*

NOUNS + explosion

a population explosion *At the turn of the century, the city saw a population explosion.*

PHRASES

an explosion of interest in sth *There has been an explosion of interest in his work.*

an explosion of violence *The army had to cope with the explosion of violence that followed the elections.*

an explosion of anger *The verdict was greeted by an explosion of public anger.*

export Ac *n*

the business of selling and sending goods to other countries, or a product that is sold to another country

ADJECTIVES/NOUNS + export

a country's major/main/principal export *Coffee is the country's main export.*

oil/agricultural/manufacturing exports *Oil exports from Iraq have resumed.*

British/US etc exports *British exports to Europe are at their lowest level since April.*

invisible exports (=exports of services such as banking or insurance, rather than of goods) *Most of the country's earnings come from invisible exports such as banking services.*

exports are up/down (=they have increased or decreased) *Exports to China are up by 25%.*

export + VERBS

exports increase/rise/grow *Electronics exports grew more slowly than in previous years.*

exports fall/decline/drop *Exports of gas and oil continued to fall.*

VERBS + export

boost exports (=make them increase) *The government wants to boost exports and create employment.*

ban exports *The government banned exports of wood from the rainforest.*

export + NOUNS

an export market *The US is our second largest export market.*

export earnings/revenue (=money made from exports) *Oil and gas provide 40% of Norway's export earnings.*

export sales/figures *Export sales are down on last year.*

an export licence *BrE*, **an export license** *AmE* (=an official document giving you permission to sell something to another country) *You will have to submit an application for an export licence.*

PREPOSITIONS

exports to the US/Japan/Germany etc *Exports to the US were up by 50%.*

for export *They produce goods for export.*

PHRASES

a growth/rise/increase in exports *The electronics sector has seen a 16% growth in exports.*

a fall/decline/drop in exports *There has been a decline in exports and an increase in oil prices.*

THESAURUS: export

goods, commodity, merchandise, wares, export, import → **product**

ANTONYMS **export → import**

express[1] *v*

to tell or show people what you are feeling or thinking by using words, looks, or actions

ADVERBS

express sth openly (=express a feeling in a way that is obvious to other people) *They expressed their anger openly in the meeting.*

express sth publicly *Republicans have publicly expressed their concerns about his appointment.*

express sth clearly *He expresses his views very clearly.*

express sth freely *I'm proud of living in a country where ideas and beliefs can be freely expressed.*

NOUNS

express your views/opinions/ideas *Everyone who attends the meeting will be given the opportunity to express their opinions.*

express your feelings *He found it difficult to express his feelings.*

express an interest in sth *Many property developers have expressed an interest in buying the land.*

express concern (=say or show that you are worried) *Economic analysts have expressed concern about the possibility of a recession.*

express regret *He has expressed regret over the remarks he made.*

express doubts/reservations *Environmentalists began to express doubts about the benefits of biofuels.*

express surprise/shock *She expressed surprise that anyone thought he was guilty.*

express anger *Teachers have expressed anger at the government's education reforms.*

express your thanks/gratitude/appreciation (=say thank you to someone, in a speech) *On behalf of the team, I'd like to express our appreciation for all your efforts.*

express your support/opposition *The Israeli leader expressed his support for the US plan.*

PREPOSITIONS

express sth in/by/through sth *She expressed her disgust in a letter to a national newspaper.*

E

PHRASES

express yourself (=say or show what you think or feel) *Young people like to express themselves through the way they dress.*

a chance/opportunity to express sth *The debate will give MPs an opportunity to express their views.*

words cannot express sth (=it is impossible to describe something) *Words can't express how much I miss her.*

express² *adj* THESAURUS **fast¹ (1)**

expression *n*

1 a look on someone's face that shows what they are thinking or feeling

ADJECTIVES

sb's facial expression (=the expression on someone's face) *Victor's facial expression never changed throughout the interview.*

a thoughtful expression *She listened to his story with a thoughtful expression on her face.*

a blank/vacant expression (=one that shows no emotion or interest) *He said nothing in class – he just sat there with a blank expression.*

a serious/worried/anxious expression *"Is there any news?" she asked with an anxious expression.*

a surprised/shocked expression *He didn't need to speak – his shocked expression said it all.*

an angry/furious expression *Her father rushed into the room with an angry expression on his face.*

a puzzled/baffled/bewildered expression (=one that shows you are confused) *Dan looked at the sign with a puzzled expression.*

a stern expression (=very strict) *I saw from Aunty Kitty's stern expression that she was not amused.*

an innocent expression *"It was so late," she continued with an innocent expression, "I had to stay the night."*

a pained expression (=one that shows you are upset or hurt) *A pained expression crossed Rory's face when he saw them together.*

VERBS

have an expression (on your face) (*also* **wear an expression** *formal*): *He had a puzzled expression on his face.*

change your expression *The child did not cry or change her expression.*

watch sb's expression *"Why do you want to know?" Elizabeth asked, watching his expression closely.*

see sb's expression *You should have seen the expression on his face when I said I was leaving!*

sb's expression changes *Suddenly, her expression changed.*

an expression crosses sb's face (=it appears on their face) *Dean looked towards Meredith, and a surprised expression crossed his face.*

PREPOSITIONS

an expression of surprise/shock/anxiety etc *He looked at me with an expression of shock.*

the expression on sb's face *I could tell by the expression on her face that she was angry.*

PHRASES

a lack of expression *I was surprised at the lack of expression on his face.*

be devoid of expression *formal* (=have no expression on your face) *His face was totally devoid of expression, but I could sense his anger.*

THESAURUS: expression

expression, idiom, cliché, saying/proverb, slogan, motto → **phrase**

2 a word or group of words with a particular meaning

ADJECTIVES

a common expression *'Out to lunch' is a common expression which means 'crazy'.*

an old-fashioned/outdated expression *'In the family way' is an old-fashioned expression which means 'pregnant'.*

an idiomatic expression *Try to avoid using idiomatic expressions in essays.*

a figurative expression (=one in which words are not used with their literal meaning) *'Boiling with rage' is a figurative expression which means 'very angry'.*

a coarse/vulgar expression (=rude) *He came out with some vulgar expressions that I couldn't possibly repeat.*

VERBS

use an expression *Lawyers often use expressions that are hard for ordinary people to understand.*

coin an expression (=invent it) *He coined the expression 'war on terror'.*

an expression means sth *Do you know what the expression 'go ballistic' means?*

PHRASES

if you'll pardon/forgive the expression (=used when you have said a word or phrase that might offend someone) *He didn't seem to give a damn, if you'll pardon the expression.*

exquisite *adj* THESAURUS **beautiful**

extent *n*

how large or serious something such as a problem, injury, or crime is

ADJECTIVES

the full extent *He refused to reveal the full extent of his debts.*

the actual/true extent *Rescue workers still do not know the true extent of the disaster.*

VERBS

know/realize the extent of sth *We do not yet know the extent of the damage.*

understand the extent of sth *Other people didn't seem to understand the extent of his disability.*

discover/find out the extent of sth *We were shocked when we discovered the extent of the fraud.*

assess/establish/determine the extent of sth *We are still trying to assess the extent of the problem.*

show/reveal the extent of sth *These pictures show the extent of the devastation caused by the earthquake.*

PHRASES

to some extent/to a large extent etc (=used when saying how much something is true or how much something is affected by another thing) *What he says is true to some extent. | The materials we use will depend to a considerable extent on what is available.*

extinct *adj*

if a type of animal or plant is extinct, it has stopped existing

ADVERBS

almost/virtually/practically extinct *The grey whale was almost extinct because of hunting.*

completely/totally extinct *Wolves became totally extinct in Scotland.*

VERBS

become extinct *There are fears that the polar bear could become extinct because of climate change.*

be thought to be extinct *The orchid was so rare it was thought to be extinct.*

extinction *n*

a situation in which a particular type of animal or plant stops existing

ADJECTIVES

total/complete extinction *Polar bears may face total extinction if nothing is done to protect them.*

mass extinction *We do not know what caused the mysterious mass extinction of the dinosaurs.*

VERBS

face extinction (=be likely to stop existing soon) *The red squirrel faces extinction in England and Wales.*

lead to/cause extinction *Hunting has caused the extinction of several species.*

save sth from extinction *Conservationists are trying to save the whale from extinction.*

be threatened with extinction (=likely to stop existing) *Hundreds of species of birds are now threatened with extinction.*

be hunted to extinction (=hunted so much that extinction is the result) *The wolves were hunted to extinction in the 1920s.*

PREPOSITIONS

extinction of sth *Climate change could lead to the mass extinction of many species.*

PHRASES

in danger of extinction *The species is in danger of extinction in the UK.*

be on the verge/brink of extinction (=at the point of almost not existing) *The Siberian crane is on the verge of extinction.*

extravagant *adj*

spending or costing a lot of money, especially more than is necessary or more than you can afford

ADVERBS

wildly extravagant *$300,000 for a car sounds wildly extravagant, but you do get a lot for your money.*

a little extravagant *I know it's a little extravagant, but I wanted to get him something special for his birthday.*

rather extravagant *It does seem rather extravagant to have three houses.*

extravagant + NOUNS

an extravagant lifestyle *He enjoyed an extravagant lifestyle of luxury holidays and fast cars.*

an extravagant taste in sth (=you like buying expensive things) *His wife had a rather extravagant taste in clothes.*

extravagant spending *Instead of extravagant spending on unnecessary weapons systems, we should use the money to help the poor.*

an extravagant present/gift *He often bought the children extravagant presents.*

PREPOSITIONS

extravagant with sth *She is very extravagant with her money, and is always buying new clothes.*

Extravagant is also used about **claims** and **promises** which are not true because someone is exaggerating: *The company makes* ***extravagant claims*** *about its beauty products. | The party made* ***extravagant promises*** *before the elections.*

extreme *adj*

1 very great in degree

NOUNS

extreme care/caution *It is necessary to use extreme caution when handling chemicals.*

extreme difficulty *He had extreme difficulty finding the book she wanted.*

extreme importance *The article emphasizes the extreme importance of good family relationships.*

extreme poverty *Extreme poverty still exists in many rural areas.*

extreme pressure *They are working under extreme pressure.*

E

extreme violence *Many of the refugees had witnessed extreme violence.*

extreme cold/heat *Most plants are not able to withstand extreme cold.*

extreme pain *He was rushed to hospital in extreme pain.*

2 very unusual and severe

NOUNS

an extreme case *In extreme cases, the illness can cause death.*

an extreme example *This incident is an extreme example of poor management.*

extreme circumstances *The use of force is only justified in extreme circumstances.*

an extreme situation *In extreme situations, children may be removed from their parents.*

an extreme measure (=a very unusual or severe action taken to try to solve a problem) *He hoped that such extreme measures would not be necessary.*

an extreme form of sth *Racially motivated attacks are the most extreme form of discrimination.*

extreme weather/conditions *The search had to be abandoned because of the extreme conditions.*

extreme temperatures *Extreme temperatures had caused the pipes to burst.*

PHRASES

go to extreme lengths (=do things that are very unusual) *Criminals will go to extreme lengths to smuggle drugs into the country.*

3 having very strong political or religious opinions which seem unreasonable

NOUNS

extreme views/opinions *Some party members have extreme right-wing views.*

extreme policies *Their policies on immigration seem very extreme.*

an extreme nationalist *The most extreme nationalists wanted complete separation from England.*

ANTONYMS **extreme → moderate**

eye *n*

one of the two parts of the body that you use to see with

COLOUR

brown/blue/grey/green eyes *Both their children have blue eyes.*

dark eyes *She looked into his dark eyes.*

hazel eyes (=pale brown and slightly green or golden) *He was a quiet kindly man, with hazel eyes.*

red/bloodshot eyes (=red because you are upset, tired, ill etc) *My mother's eyes were red from crying.*

⚠ Don't say 'black eyes' when you mean **dark eyes**. If someone has a **black eye**, they have a bruise around their eye after being hit.

SHAPE/POSITION

big/small eyes *She looked at me with those big brown eyes.*

narrow eyes *He has a thin face and narrow eyes.*

deep-set eyes (=deep in your face) *It was difficult to see his deep-set eyes.*

close-set eyes (=close together) *He had a small nose and close-set eyes.*

sb's eyes are open/closed/shut *His eyes were closed and he seemed to be asleep.*

ABILITY TO SEE

sharp/keen eyes (=good at seeing or noticing things) *Her sharp eyes had missed nothing.*

beady eyes (=small and good at noticing a lot of things) *His beady eyes darted around the room.*

SHOWING YOUR FEELINGS/CHARACTER

tired/sleepy eyes *He rubbed his tired eyes and yawned.*

sad eyes *He smiled, but his eyes were sad.*

misty/moist eyes (=almost crying) *Her eyes grew moist at the memory.*

bright eyes (=happy or excited) *Her eyes were bright with hope.*

cold eyes (=unfriendly and not showing any emotion) *Her eyes were cold and uncaring.*

wild/mad/staring eyes (=very angry, afraid etc) *The old man stared at them with wild eyes.*

VERBS + eye

open/close/shut your eyes *Joe closed his eyes and tried to get back to sleep.*

rub/wipe your eyes *Anna rubbed her eyes wearily.*

lower your eyes (=look down at the ground) *Instead of answering the question, he lowered his eyes.*

raise your eyes (=look up at someone or something) *She raised her eyes towards the sky.*

narrow your eyes (=partly close them, especially to show that you do not trust someone) *The woman narrowed her eyes at him suspiciously.*

roll your eyes (=move your eyes up to show you are annoyed, bored, frustrated etc) *When I asked her to tidy her room, she rolled her eyes and sighed.*

shade/shield your eyes (=protect them from a bright light or the sun) *They gazed out to sea, shielding their eyes from the sun.*

avert your eyes *literary* (=look away from something) *He averted his eyes from the body.*

eye + VERBS

sb's eyes open/close *I shook him, and his eyes opened.*

sb's eyes shine/sparkle/twinkle (=are bright because they are very happy) *Jenny's eyes sparkled with excitement.*

sb's eyes light up (=suddenly show excitement or happiness) *His eyes lit up when I mentioned the word 'money'.*

sb's eye/eyes fall on sth (=they suddenly notice it) *My eye fell on a piece of paper on the desk.*

sb's eyes glaze (over) (=they show no expression, because they are very bored or tired) *As I talked, I could see his eyes begin to glaze over.*

two people's eyes meet (=they look at each other's eyes) *Our eyes met across a crowded room.*

eye + NOUNS

eye contact (=when you look directly at someone at the same time as they are looking at you) *Make eye contact with the person interviewing you.*

an eye test (*also* **an eye exam** *AmE*) (=to find out how well you can see) *You should have an eye test every couple of years.*

PHRASES

sb's eyes are full of tears/hatred etc *When she put the phone down, her eyes were full of tears.*

sb's eyes are glued to sth/fixed on sth (=they are watching something with all their attention) *Ted sat with his eyes glued to the television.*

can't take your eyes off sb/sth (=be unable to stop looking at someone or something) *She was so beautiful I couldn't take my eyes off her.*

look into sb's eyes *She looked into his eyes and said "Don't worry".*

look sb in the eye (=look directly at someone when speaking to them) *I knew he was lying because he didn't look me in the eye.*

see sth with your own eyes (=see something yourself) *I know he took the money – I saw him with my own eyes.*

before/in front of sb's very eyes (=while someone is watching) *Their homes were destroyed before their very eyes.*

eyesight *n* someone's ability to see

ADJECTIVES

good/better eyesight *Your eyesight is much better than mine.*

bad/poor eyesight *Moles have very poor eyesight.*

perfect eyesight *People think that you need to have perfect eyesight to become a pilot.*

keen eyesight (=extremely good) *Eagles are known for their extremely keen eyesight.*

failing eyesight (=becoming worse) *In his later years, he suffered from failing eyesight.*

VERBS

have good/bad etc eyesight *She has very good eyesight.*

lose your eyesight *He lost his eyesight as the result of an accident.*

sb's eyesight fails *She's over 80 now, and her eyesight is beginning to fail.*

sb's eyesight deteriorates/gets worse *People's eyesight gradually deteriorates with age.*

eyesight + NOUNS

eyesight problems *Many older people suffer from eyesight problems.*

Ff

face¹ *n*
the front part of your head, or your expression

ADJECTIVES

a pretty/beautiful/handsome/nice face *She has a pretty face – she could be a model.*

an ugly face *I never want to see his ugly face again!*

a round/oval/square face *The woman's face was round and jolly.*

a thin/narrow/long face *The girl had a thin face and big dark eyes.*

a wrinkled/lined face (=with a lot of small lines, especially because someone is old) *The old man looked at me with his wrinkled face.*

a craggy/rugged face (=strong-looking, with deep lines) *Jake looked like a cowboy, with his tanned rugged face.*

a haggard/gaunt/drawn face (=looking very tired or ill) *Her face was haggard and she had not slept for two nights.*

a happy/smiling face *It was good to see the children's happy faces.*

a sad/serious/grim face *Maggie looked at him with a sad face.*

a long face (=an unhappy expression) *I could see from his long face that he wasn't happy with the decision.*

an angry/scowling face *He looked around and saw his boss's scowling face behind him.*

an anxious/worried/puzzled face *The woman glanced up at Kathleen, her face puzzled.*

a shocked/horrified face *"You are not going out in that dress!" my father said with a horrified face.*

a blank/impassive face (=showing no emotion or thoughts) *What was she really thinking behind that blank face?*

> **How the colour of someone's face shows their feelings**
> If someone's face is **red** or **scarlet**, they are embarrassed.
> If someone's face is **pale** or **white**, they are very worried or afraid.
> If someone's face is **grey** or **ashen**, they are very worried, ill, or in pain.

VERBS

pull/make a face (=make a silly expression or make an expression that shows you are unhappy about something) *The kids were pulling faces for the camera.*

sb's face goes red/white etc (*also* **sb's face turns red/white etc**) (=it becomes red, white etc) *When he heard the news, his face suddenly went pale.*

sb's face falls (=they look sad or disappointed) *Her face fell when she found out that she hadn't got the job.*

sb's face lights up/brightens (=they start to look happy) *Denise's face lit up when she heard the news.*

sb's face darkens (=they start to look angry) *She handed him the letter and his face darkened.*

sb's face glows (=they look healthy or happy) *Her face was glowing with happiness.*

PHRASES

a look/expression on sb's face *She had a rather surprised look on her face.*

a smile/grin/frown on sb's face *There was a mischievous grin on her face.*

sth is written all over sb's face (=their feelings can be seen very clearly in their expression) *You're jealous – it's written all over your face!*

a sea of faces (=the faces of a very large number of people) *She walked onto the platform and looked out at the sea of faces.*

you should have seen sb's face (=used to say that someone was very angry, surprised etc) *You should have seen his face when I told him that I was resigning.*

sb has a face like thunder (=they have a very angry expression)

face² *v*
1 to have to deal with a difficult situation that is likely to happen

NOUNS

face a problem/difficulty *She told me about some of the problems she was facing.*

face opposition/criticism *The government faced opposition from the courts.*

face a challenge *The coal industry faces serious challenges.*

face the task of doing sth *He faced the task of preparing a three-course meal for 50 people.*

face a dilemma (=have a difficult choice) *The manager is facing the dilemma of who to select for the team.*

face charges/prosecution/trial (=be accused of a crime and have to go to a court of law) *The former chairman faces charges of fraud and theft.*

face the risk/threat of sth *The factory is facing the threat of closure.*

face the prospect of sth (=something bad is likely to happen to you in the future) *Many coastal cities face the prospect of disastrous flooding.*

face starvation *A million people across the country face starvation.*

face extinction (=used when all of a type of animal could die, so that it no longer exists) *The polar bear could face extinction if global warming continues.*

face competition *We are facing strong competition from Chinese companies.*

2 to accept that a bad situation exists

NOUNS

face the truth *Doctors told him he was dying but he just couldn't face the truth.*

face facts *Face facts, Peter, she doesn't love you any more.*

face reality *It's time she faced reality and accepted that it will not be easy to find a job.*

PHRASES

face the fact that... *I had to face the fact that I would never see my mother again.*

(let's) face it (=used when saying that something is true, although it may be hard to accept) *She is quite pretty but let's face it, she's never going to be a model.*

facilitate Ac *v formal*

to make it easier for something to happen

VERBS

help to facilitate sth *The African Trade Office helps to facilitate trade between the US and countries in Africa.*

be designed to facilitate sth *The course is designed to facilitate language learning.*

ADVERBS

greatly facilitate sth *The internet has greatly facilitated the movement of ideas.*

facility Ac *n*

1 facilities are rooms, equipment, or services that are provided for a particular purpose

Grammar
Always plural in this meaning.

ADJECTIVES/NOUNS + facility

modern facilities *The Grand Hotel offers many modern facilities and there is internet access in every room.*

state-of-the-art facilities (=with the most modern equipment) *The college has state-of-the-art recording facilities.*

sports facilities *Have you checked out the local sports facilities?*

leisure/recreational facilities (=for activities that you do for pleasure) *The leisure facilities include a sauna and a gym.*

training facilities *The company plans to set up in-house training facilities.*

cooking/washing etc facilities *The rooms all have cooking facilities and a fridge.*

parking facilities *The building has parking facilities for 20 cars.*

hotel facilities *Make use of the hotel facilities, which are excellent.*

medical facilities *The university has its own medical facilities.*

childcare facilities *More women would work if there were better childcare facilities.*

toilet facilities *Toilet facilities are available at the bus station.*

VERBS

provide/offer facilities *Recycling facilities are provided by the local council.*

use the facilities *Guests are welcome to use all the hotel's facilities.*

PREPOSITIONS

facilities for sb *The sports centre has facilities for disabled people.*

facilities for sth *Some campsites have facilities for barbecues.*

PHRASES

a range of facilities *The range of facilities offered by this hotel is superb.*

2 *formal* a factory

THESAURUS: facility
facility, plant, works, mill, refinery, foundry, assembly line/production line, sweatshop → **factory**

fact *n* a piece of true information

ADJECTIVES

the basic/key/central facts *The report outlines the basic facts of the case.*

an important/crucial fact *You seem to have forgotten one important fact.*

an interesting/fascinating fact *The research revealed some interesting facts about the behaviour of cats.*

a curious/remarkable/amazing etc fact *The book is full of all kinds of curious facts.*

a well-known/little-known fact *It is a well-known fact that smoking is bad for you.*

a relevant fact *Have we been told all the relevant facts?*

an obvious fact *The writer ignores the obvious fact that not everyone has a car.*

hard facts (=information that is definitely true and can be proven) *His theory is supported by hard facts.*

the bare facts (=only the basic general facts of a situation) *We know the bare facts of his life, but nothing about what he was really like.*

the full facts *I can't give my opinion until I know the full facts.*

a historical/scientific fact *I'm not making this up – it's a historical fact.*

an inescapable/undeniable/indisputable fact (=one that is definitely true and has a big effect) *It's an undeniable fact that none of us is getting younger.*

VERBS

give/present/provide the facts *Newspapers have a duty to give their readers the facts.*

tell sb the facts/let sb have the facts *If you let him have the facts, he can make his own decision.*

state the facts (=say what you know is true) *I'm not exaggerating – I'm just stating the facts.*

stick to the facts (=say only what you know is true) *Just stick to the facts when the police interview you.*

look at/examine the facts *I decided to examine the facts for myself.*

ignore/overlook a fact *He chose to ignore the fact that his wife was having an affair.*

PREPOSITIONS

a fact about sth *Here are some fascinating facts about sharks.*

PHRASES

be aware of a fact *I was aware of the fact that the company was in trouble.*

get your facts right/straight (=make sure that what you say or believe is correct) *You should get your facts straight before making accusations.*

the facts of the case *Let us look at the actual facts of the case.*

facts and figures *The book is packed with facts and figures about the island.*

F

factor Ac *n*

one of several things that influence or cause a situation

ADJECTIVES/NOUNS + factor

an important/significant factor *Peace is the most important factor for economic development.*

a big/major/key factor (=a very important one) *Training is a key factor in the team's success.*

a crucial/critical factor (=an extremely important one) *Timing is often a crucial factor with any business venture.*

the deciding/decisive factor (=the one that has the biggest effect) *The support of women voters could be the deciding factor in the election.*

a contributing factor (=one that helps to make something happen) *Stress is a contributing factor in many illnesses.*

economic/social/environmental factors *The crisis was caused by a wide range of social and economic factors.*

genetic factors *Genetic factors may play a role in who gets the disease.*

a risk factor (=something that makes a bad thing such as an illness more likely) *The highest risk factor for heart disease was found to be smoking.*

VERBS

factors cause sth *The increase in the number of accidents was caused by several factors.*

factors influence/affect/determine sth *Various factors influenced the government's decision.*

depend on factors *How well you do in the test depends on a variety of different factors.*

identify factors *Our aim was to identify key factors that affect crime rates.*

consider a factor *The judge also considered other factors, including the man's previous criminal record.*

a factor contributes to sth *A number of factors have contributed to the country's economic problems.*

PREPOSITIONS

a factor in sth *It is estimated that alcohol is a factor in a third of all accidents.*

a factor behind sth *His concern about his health was one of the main factors behind his decision to retire.*

PHRASES

a variety/number of factors *There are a number of factors that need to be considered.*

a combination of factors *A combination of factors led to the factory closing.*

take certain factors into account (=consider them) *You should take all these factors into account.*

factory *n*

a place where goods are produced in large quantities using machines

NOUNS + factory

a car/textile/chemical/chocolate etc factory *The company plans to build the biggest car factory in Europe.*

ADJECTIVES

a modern factory *There are pictures of workers assembling electronic equipment in modern factories.*

a disused factory (=not used any more) *The apartments will be built on the site of a disused paint factory.*

VERBS

work in a factory *My dad works in a carpet factory.*

open a factory *The company opened a new factory in India last year.*

close/shut down a factory *They are planning to shut down the factory and make everyone redundant.*

a factory makes/produces/manufactures things *The factory produces sports shoes.*

factory + NOUNS

a factory worker *Factory workers are usually well paid.*

a factory owner/manager *The factory owner placed a large order for some new equipment.*

a factory closure *Further factory closures have been announced.*

on the factory floor (=among the workers in a factory) *A manager should spend time on the factory floor, as well as in his office.*

THESAURUS: factory

facility
manufacturing facility | research facility | weapons facility
a factory. **Facility** is more formal than **factory** and is used mainly by people in business and in news reports:
The company plans to set up a big new manufacturing facility in Mexico. | The satellite pictures are of a nuclear weapons facility. | The facility will provide work for over 400 people.

plant
car plant | chemical plant | power plant | water treatment plant
a large factory, especially one where energy, cars, or chemicals are produced:
Workers at the car plant produce over 1,200 cars every day. | Two people were killed in an explosion at a chemical plant.

works
steelworks | brickworks | chemical works | cement works | printing works
a factory where steel, chemicals, cement etc are produced, or where books are printed:
The steelworks specialized in the manufacture of rails made from Bessemer steel. | He owns the city's oldest-established printing works.

mill
textile mill | cotton mill | paper mill
a factory that produces cloth or paper:
The wool was exported to British textile mills in Lancashire.

refinery
oil refinery | sugar refinery
a factory where things are removed from oil, sugar etc to make them pure:
The new oil refinery can process 200,000 barrels per day.

foundry
a factory where things are made out of metal using moulds:
The bells were made in a foundry just outside Paris.

assembly line/production line
a system in a factory, in which the products move past a line of workers who each do one part of the work:
Over 1,000 cars come off the assembly line each day.

sweatshop
a factory where people work very hard in bad conditions for little money:
The shoes are made in sweatshops by child workers.

fail *v*

1 to not succeed

Grammar
You often use **fail** with an infinitive verb in this meaning: *The climbers* ***failed to*** *reach the top of the mountain. | The team* ***failed to*** *win the competition.*

NOUNS + fail

a plan fails *Their plan failed and they had to start again.*

an attempt fails *The prisoners' attempt to escape failed.*

an experiment fails *Ulrich later admitted that his experiment had failed.*

a company/business fails (=it is unable to make a profit and has to close) *The company failed and the investors lost all their money.*

a marriage fails *Some marriages fail after only a few months.*

talks/negotiations fail *The peace talks failed and the fighting continued.*

crops fail (=they do not grow) *The crops failed and the people went hungry.*

ADVERBS

fail completely/totally/altogether *Unfortunately our plan failed completely.*

fail badly *Critics say that the current system is failing badly.*

fail miserably/dismally (=very badly) *We have failed miserably to stop climate change.*

fail spectacularly (=extremely badly) *The plan failed spectacularly and the terrorists blew themselves up.*

narrowly fail (=only just fail) *The team narrowly failed to win the game.*

PREPOSITIONS

fail in an attempt/effort/bid to do sth *The two sides failed in their attempt to reach an agreement.*

PHRASES

be doomed to fail (=be certain to fail) *The talks seem doomed to fail before they start.*

sb/sth can hardly fail (=it seems certain they will succeed) *He is the best player and he can hardly fail to win.*

if all else fails (=if every other method fails) *If all else fails, you can borrow some money off your parents.*

THESAURUS: fail

flop/bomb *informal*
movie | show | record | product
if a movie, show etc flops, it is unsuccessful because people do not like it. **Bomb** is more informal than **flop**:

The show bombed and ended after only a couple of weeks. | *His first record flopped and only sold a few copies.*

You can also say that a movie, show etc was **a flop**.

fall through
deal | **plan** | **sale**
if a deal, plan etc falls through, it is unsuccessful and fails to happen:
They were hoping to buy a house, but the deal fell through at the last minute. | *His great ambition was to travel around the world by bus. Those plans fell through.*

backfire
plan | **strategy** | **scheme** | **tactic**
if a plan backfires, it has the opposite effect of what it was intended to do:
Her plan to get attention backfired, and instead of being promoted she lost her job. | *The company's tactic backfired and they were forced to admit publicly that they were wrong.*

collapse
system | **economy** | **talks**
to fail suddenly and completely, especially with the result that there is a very serious situation:
People are worried that the banking system could collapse. | *In 1929 the US economy collapsed and millions of people lost their jobs.* | *The talks with the union collapsed and workers went back on strike.*

break down
talks | **negotiations** | **communication** | **relationship** | **marriage**
to fail, with the result that you are unable to continue:
Talks broke down between unions and employers. | *Communication sometimes breaks down between couples.* | *Unfortunately, his marriage had broken down and he and his wife had separated.*

companies/businesses

go bankrupt
company | **firm** | **business**
if a company or person goes bankrupt, they cannot pay their debts and they have to stop trading permanently:
My father's company went bankrupt, with debts of over $15 million. | *The reason he went bankrupt, he says, is that there weren't enough customers.*

go bust *informal*
company | **firm** | **business**
if a company goes bust, they cannot pay their debts and they have to stop trading permanently:
A record number of companies are going bust every week. | *His business went bust and he owes £120,000.* | *The store went bust and 200 staff lost their jobs.*

Another way of saying that someone or something fails

You can use other parts of speech to say that someone or something **failed**. For example, you can say that someone or something was **unsuccessful**: *Unfortunately, on this occasion your application was **unsuccessful**.* | *He was **unsuccessful in** his attempt to reach the South Pole.*

You can also say that something was **a failure**: *The experiment was **a failure**.*

If something failed very badly, you can say that it was **a complete failure**, or **a disaster**: *I burnt the pizza and the meal **was a disaster**.*

Finally, you can say that someone tried **in vain** to do something (=they tried unsuccessfully): *Rescue workers tried **in vain** to save the ship.* | *All her efforts had been **in vain**.*

Another way of saying that a company or business fails

There are many expressions you can use when talking about a company having to close its business.

You can say that a company **closes down**: *The steel plant **closed down**, with the loss of 2,500 jobs.*

You can say that a company **goes under**: *More than 7,000 firms have **gone under** in the last three months* (=they had too many debts to be able to continue trading).

Finally, you can say that a company **goes to the wall**: *Many small firms will **go to the wall*** (=have to close because of difficult financial conditions).

ANTONYMS **fail → succeed**

2 to not pass a test

fail + NOUNS

fail a test/exam *If you fail the test, you can always take it again.*

fail an interview *They told her that she had failed the interview.*

ADVERBS

fail sth badly *I failed the test badly.*

(only) just fail sth *His son just failed the entrance exam.*

ANTONYMS **fail → pass (1)**

failure *n*

a lack of success in doing something, or something that is not successful

ADJECTIVES

complete/total/utter failure *The project ended in total failure.*

(an) abject/dismal failure (=used to emphasize how bad a failure is) *The experiment was considered a dismal failure.*

a disastrous failure *This approach was a disastrous failure.*

a costly failure (=one that results in a lot of money or many lives being lost) *The war came to be seen as a costly failure.*

a personal failure (=a failure that is someone's personal fault) *He considered his inability to form long-term relationships to be a personal failure.*

a commercial failure (=something that does not make much money) *The film was a commercial failure.*

economic/political failure *Economic failure drove the government out of office.*

VERBS

end in/result in failure *A series of rescue attempts ended in failure.*

be doomed to failure (=be certain to fail) *The rebellion was doomed to failure from the start.*

admit failure *He was too proud to admit failure.*

accept failure *Being able to accept failure is part of life.*

avoid failure *She was anxious to avoid failure.*

failure + NOUNS

the failure rate *There is a high failure rate in the restaurant industry.*

PHRASES

fear of failure *Fear of failure should not deter you from trying.*

the risk/possibility of failure *The risk of failure for a new product is very high.*

an admission of failure *Dropping out of college would be an admission of failure.*

a history/record of failure (=when someone has failed many times in the past) *Some children have a history of failure at school.*

a string of failures (=a series of failures) *The team has had a string of failures in recent games.*

a sense/feeling of failure *He felt a sense of failure when he lost he job.*

ANTONYMS **failure → success**

faint[1] *adj*

1 difficult to see, hear, or smell

faint + NOUNS

a faint noise/sound *He could hear the faint sound of voices in the room next door.*

a faint light/glow *I could see a faint light in the distance.*

a faint smell/scent/aroma *When I got into the car, I noticed the faint smell of perfume.*

a faint smile *A faint smile crossed his face.*

a faint trace of sth *There was a faint trace of a foreign accent in his voice.*

the faint outline of sth *I could just see the faint outline of the town.*

a faint memory *Her childhood was now only a faint memory.*

VERBS

become faint *The sound became fainter.*

sound faint *His voice sounded faint on the telephone.*

THESAURUS: faint

faint, weak, pale, poor/bad, soft, low → **dim**

low, soft, silent, hushed, faint, muffled, dull, inaudible → **quiet (1)**

2 very small or slight

faint + NOUNS

a faint hope *There is still a faint hope that the men may be alive.*

a faint possibility *There is only a faint possibility that he will be fit enough to play.*

a faint chance *The team has a faint chance of winning the competition.*

faint[2] *v*

to suddenly become unconscious for a short time

PHRASES

be going to faint/be about to faint *She turned pale and looked as if she was about to faint.*

be close to fainting *He was so hungry, he was close to fainting.*

faint at the sight of blood *Are you one of those people who faint at the sight of blood?*

faint from hunger/exhaustion *He fainted from exhaustion.*

Faint is often used when saying that someone was very shocked: *She* ***almost/nearly fainted*** *when she saw the bill.*

fair *adj*

treating people equally or in a way that is right

NOUNS

fair treatment *They are demanding fair treatment for all workers.*

a fair chance *Everyone should have a fair chance of winning.*

a fair wage *Women workers do not receive a fair wage.*

a fair share of sth (=as much as other people) *He insisted that he had always paid his fair share of taxes.*

a fair system *Do you think the current voting system is fair?*

a fair election *The country's first free and fair elections were held last year.*

F

a fair trial *The men may be guilty, but they deserve a fair trial.*

a fair hearing (=a chance for you to talk about something, so that your opinions can be considered) *He claimed he was not given a fair hearing and that his views were ignored.*

fair competition *There should be fair competition between US companies and foreign companies.*

fair trade (=in which workers are treated well and there are no unfair taxes or laws which give one country an advantage) *Denying fair trade to developing countries is a major cause of poverty.*

ADVERBS

completely/totally/entirely fair *I don't think this statement is completely fair.*

absolutely/perfectly fair (=completely fair – used for emphasis) *It seems perfectly fair that she should get paid the same as everyone else.*

scrupulously fair (=very careful to treat people fairly) *The judge was scrupulously fair to both sides in the dispute.*

PREPOSITIONS

fair to sb *The referee has to be fair to everyone.*

fair on sb *It's not fair on him, if he has to do all the work.*

You use **fair on sb** especially in negative sentences, when you think someone is being treated badly compared to other people.

PHRASES

it is fair *It's not fair that she gets paid more than me.*

it is only fair *I thought it was only fair to let you know what happened to your money.*

to be fair *To be fair, it is the first time he has ever played the game.*

THESAURUS: fair

reasonable
amount | price | offer | excuse | grounds
fair and sensible according to most people's standards:
It is important to give children a reasonable amount of freedom of choice. | Twenty dollars sounds like a **perfectly reasonable** *price for a meal to me. | The police officer must have reasonable grounds for stopping and searching someone* (=a good reason for doing this).

just *formal*
punishment | cause | war | society | reward
morally right and fair:
We believe our cause is just. | Do you think there is such a thing as a just war? | He will receive his just reward when the time comes.

impartial
advice | account | observer | judge
able to make fair comments or decisions, because you do not support anyone who is involved in a situation:
Our staff can offer impartial advice on choosing the best investment. | Journalists have a duty to be impartial. | The scientist is supposed to be an impartial observer.

balanced
view | reporting | account
giving fair and equal treatment to all sides of an argument or subject:
The movie gives a balanced view of the situation in Iraq. | Balanced reporting of the news is essential to a democracy.

even-handed
approach | attitude | criticism
giving fair and equal treatment to everyone, and not favouring one particular group:
Schools are expected to have an even-handed approach when they are punishing students. | The author is even-handed in his criticism of both sides.

equitable *formal*
distribution | treatment
giving equal treatment to everyone involved:
In his speech, he called for a more equitable distribution of wealth. | the equitable treatment of all members of society

ANTONYMS **fair → unfair**

faith *n*

1 a strong feeling of trust or confidence in someone or something

ADJECTIVES

great/enormous faith *He had great faith in his team.*

complete/total/absolute faith *The owners have complete faith in Sam as manager.*

blind/unquestioning faith (=trusting someone or something without thinking) *Most people just have blind faith that they will have enough money when they retire.*

unshakeable/firm faith (=that nothing can make weaker) *Her parents had unshakeable faith in her ability.*

VERBS

have faith *They no longer have faith that the police will protect them.*

put/place your faith in sb/sth *People seem less and less inclined to put their faith in science.*

show faith in sb/sth *The club have shown faith in the young goalkeeper by offering him a permanent contract.*

lose faith *After more broken promises by the government, people are starting to lose faith.*

destroy sb's faith in sb/sth *Terry's lies had destroyed Liz's faith in men.*

shake/undermine sb's faith in sb/sth (=make it weaker) *Bad decisions by judges shake the public's faith in the legal system.*

F

restore sb's faith in sb/sth (=make it return) *His kindness had restored her faith in human nature.*

sb's faith is misplaced (=they are wrong to trust someone or something) *I hope their faith in him is not misplaced.*

PREPOSITIONS

faith in sb/sth *After so many disappointments, my faith in him was almost gone.*

PHRASES

have every faith in sb/sth (=trust them completely) *We have every faith in your ability to solve the problem.*

a leap of faith (=something risky that someone does, believing that it may have a good result) *She took a leap of faith and lent him the money he needed to start the company.*

2 a belief in a god or gods

ADJECTIVES

religious faith *Yousuf put his success down to his religious faith.*

deep faith *He is a man of deep faith.*

VERBS

lose faith *Her experience of war led her to lose her faith in God.*

find faith *Christians of all nations have found faith in Christ.*

PREPOSITIONS

faith in God *My first priority has always been my faith in God.*

3 a religion

ADJECTIVES/NOUNS + faith

a religious faith *It is easy to concentrate on the differences between the religious faiths and forget what they have in common.*

the Christian/Jewish/Hindu/Muslim etc faith *She was brought up in the Jewish faith.*

a world faith *It is important for students to study other world faiths apart from their own.*

VERBS

practise your faith *BrE*, **practice your faith** *AmE* (=do the things that it is your duty to do, according to your religion) *Everybody should be allowed to practice their faith.*

spread the faith *Their mission was to spread the faith.*

faith + NOUNS

a faith community/group (=a group of people living somewhere who belong to a particular religion) *He will meet the leaders of the different faith communities.*

a faith school (=which is based on a particular religion) *Parents want to have the choice of sending their children to a faith school.*

PHRASES

of all faiths/of every faith/of different faiths *People of all faiths are welcome.*

fake *adj* THESAURUS **artificial**, **false**

fall[1] *v*

1 to become less

ADVERBS

fall dramatically (=by a very large amount) *The number of deaths has fallen dramatically.*

fall sharply/steeply (=quickly and by a large amount) *Share prices fell sharply today, leading to fears of recession.*

fall slightly *Sales fell slightly this quarter, from $5.3 million to $5.1 million.*

fall significantly (=enough to make a big difference) *The price of corn has fallen significantly.*

fall gradually *The population fell gradually, because fewer people were having children.*

PREPOSITIONS

fall to sth *In winter, the temperature can fall to 20 degrees below zero.*

fall below sth *Unemployment has fallen below one million for the first time in ten years.*

PHRASES

be expected/likely to fall *Interest rates are expected to fall over the coming months.*

2 to move or drop down from a higher position to a lower position

PREPOSITIONS/ADVERBS

fall off sth *Careful you don't fall off your bike.*

fall down/over *He fell over and hurt his leg.*

fall on sth *I fell on a loose stone and went flying through the air.*

fall down *She fell down at school today and grazed her knees.*

fall badly *The old lady fell badly and injured her ankle.*

PHRASES

fall down on your knees *She fell down on her knees and begged him to stay.*

fall[2] *n*

1 a decrease in the price, amount, level etc of something

ADJECTIVES

a big/huge fall *The study shows a big fall in the number of people who die from the disease.*

a slight fall *A slight fall in fuel prices has been predicted.*

a sudden/rapid fall *There was a sudden fall in the value of the US dollar.*

a sharp/steep fall (=a sudden big fall) *There has been a sharp fall in the price of electricity.*

F

PREPOSITIONS

a fall in sth *There was a sudden fall in temperature.*

THESAURUS: fall

fall/drop, decline, reduction, cut → **decrease**[1]

2 an occasion when someone or something goes down onto the ground

ADJECTIVES

a bad/nasty/terrible fall *My aunt had a nasty fall and she had to go to hospital.*

a heavy fall *There was a heavy fall of snow.*

VERBS

have a fall *The old lady had a fall and hurt her leg.*

break/cushion sb's fall (=make someone fall more slowly and not get badly hurt) *He fell off a cliff, but luckily some trees below broke his fall.*

survive a fall *His friends were amazed that he had survived the fall.*

3 *AmE* autumn

ADJECTIVES

early/late fall *The fruit is ready in early fall.*

PREPOSITIONS

in the fall *New England looks beautiful in the fall.*

false *adj* not true or not real

NOUNS

a false name/address *The man used a false name and address.*

false teeth/eyelashes/moustache *My grandmother had false teeth.*

false information *The company gave clients false information about their investments.*

false charges/allegations *He claims that all the charges against him are false.*

a false idea/impression/assumption *The 'local' label gives a false impression about where the food is from.*

false hopes/expectations *The team had false hopes of an easy victory.*

a false premise/argument (=a false principle that you base your ideas on) *The theory is based on a false premise.*

a false smile *She looked at me with a false smile.*

false modesty *If I say it was a lucky choice, it sounds like false modesty.*

ADVERBS

completely/entirely/absolutely false *This story is completely false.*

patently/clearly false (=obviously false) *Some of their claims are patently false.*

blatantly false (=obviously false in a shocking way) *I am continually amazed by how much blatantly false information is on their website.*

PHRASES

a false sense of security *The gun gave him a false sense of security.*

under false pretences (=used when someone gets something by deceiving people) *She had obtained the money under false pretences.*

THESAURUS: false

fake

passport | ID | painting | fur | jewellery | pearls | tan

made to look like something else, especially in order to deceive people:

The men were able to enter the country using fake passports. | The collar is made of fake fur. | You can use the cream to give yourself a fake tan.

Fake can also be used as a noun: *The painting is* ***a fake****.*

phoney/phony *disapproving informal*

accent | smile | story | excuse | name | address | certificate | passport

false. You use **phoney** about what someone says or does, or about a name or document that is not real:

He spoke with a phony American accent. | I made up some phony excuse about having problems with my car. | He gave the hotel a phoney address so that they could not contact him later. | She was caught using a phoney medical certificate.

Phoney is also used as a noun: *I knew the guy was* ***a phony*** (=he was not who he said he was).

imitation

leather | silk | diamonds | pearls | gun

imitation materials and objects are made to look like the real thing, especially something that is much more expensive:

The shoes are made of imitation leather. | Only an expert can tell if the pearls are imitation. | The robbers used an imitation gun. | He was wearing an imitation Rolex watch.

Imitation can also be used as a noun: *The watch was* ***an imitation****.*

counterfeit

money | note | dollar bill | goods | tickets | drugs | medicines | cigarettes

counterfeit money and goods are produced in large quantities by criminals in order to deceive people:

The bank has issued a warning about counterfeit notes. | Police seized thousands of pounds worth of counterfeit goods. | The authorities are concerned about the production of counterfeit medicines such as fake antibiotics. | About a third of the vodka that is sold is counterfeit.

forged
document | passport | evidence | letter | signature | cheque | banknote
a forged document, letter etc is made to look like a real one in order to deceive people:
He is charged with using forged documents to get a work permit. | The evidence against him was all forged. | The passport had a forged signature on it.

You can also say that something is **a forgery**: *The passport was **a forgery**.*

insincere
if someone is insincere, he or she is not being honest about their true feelings:
*His apology **sounded insincere** and I didn't believe a word of it. | He knew that her compliments were insincere.*

Insincere is not usually used before a noun.

empty/hollow
promise | threat | gesture
used when you do not believe that someone will do what they say:
She accused the government of making empty promises in order to get votes. | He looked serious and I knew this was not a hollow threat.

spurious
claim | argument | reason | excuse | charges | allegations
used when you do not believe that what someone says is true, especially when it stops you from thinking about the real situation:
Food manufacturers often make spurious claims about the health benefits of their products. | People say that the Earth's climate is always changing, but that is a spurious argument. | The charges against him were spurious.

THESAURUS: false

false, misleading, trumped-up, myth, illusion, misconception, delusion, fallacy → **untrue**

incorrect, inaccurate, false, untrue, misleading, misguided, mistaken → **wrong (1)**

ANTONYMS false → **real**

ANTONYMS false → **true**

fame *n*

the state of being known about by a lot of people because of your achievements

ADJECTIVES

international/worldwide fame *The Beatles were the first British group to achieve international fame.*

national fame *Her oil paintings won her national fame.*

local fame *The restaurant rapidly acquired local fame for its excellent food.*

lasting/enduring fame (=used when someone is famous for a very long time) *Beatrix Potter gained lasting fame for her children's books.*

brief fame *Ed achieved brief fame as a pop singer in the late 1980s.*

instant fame (=used when someone suddenly becomes famous) *The success of her first novel brought her instant fame.*

great fame *His acting ability brought him great fame.*

new-found fame (=used when someone has just become famous) *Anna was finding it difficult to get used to her new-found fame.*

VERBS + fame

win/gain fame *He won fame when he appeared in the film 'The Graduate'.*

achieve/find fame *Amy Johnson found fame as a pilot when she became the first woman to fly from Britain to Australia.*

bring/win sb/sth fame *Chomsky's theories about language brought him fame.*

rise/come to fame (=become famous) *She rose to fame during the early sixties.*

shoot to fame (=become famous very suddenly) *She shot to fame as a result of her victory in the Olympics.*

seek fame (=try to become famous) *He sought fame in the jazz clubs of New York.*

enjoy fame (=be famous) *The town briefly enjoyed fame as the location of a popular television series.*

fame + VERBS

sb's fame spreads/grows *By this time his fame had spread throughout the islands.*

sb's fame rests on sth (=used to say what someone is famous for) *His fame rests on his achievements as an engineer.*

PREPOSITIONS

fame as sth *She later achieved fame as a writer.*

of ... fame (=used to show what someone is famous for) *The film was produced by George Lucas, of 'Star Wars' fame.*

PHRASES

sb's/sth's rise to fame *Her rise to fame has been astonishingly rapid.*

at the height of his/her fame (=when someone was most famous) *At the height of his fame, he could earn $5,000 a day.*

sb's/sth's claim to fame (=reason for being famous) *One of his main claims to fame is having invented the electric light bulb.*

fame and fortune (=being rich and famous) *He came to London to seek fame and fortune.*

familiar *adj*

if you are familiar with someone or something, or if they are familiar to you, you have seen, read, or used them before

VERBS

look/sound/seem familiar *Her face looks familiar and I'm sure I've seen her somewhere before.*

ADVERBS

strangely/oddly familiar *The writing on the envelope looked strangely familiar.*

slightly/vaguely familiar *Her face is vaguely familiar, but I can't remember her name.*

depressingly/painfully familiar *Those problems sound depressingly familiar.*

reassuringly familiar (=familiar in a way that makes you feel relaxed) *His hometown looked reassuringly familiar.*

sth is all too familiar (=you have experienced the same thing many times before) *The problem is all too familiar to many people.*

NOUNS

a familiar face/voice *I recognized a familiar face - it was one of my old school friends.*

a familiar figure (=someone you often see somewhere) *The local policeman became a familiar figure in our school.*

familiar surroundings (=a place you know well) *It was good to be back home in more familiar surroundings.*

a familiar landmark (=a famous building that people can recognize easily) *St Paul's Cathedral is one of London's most familiar landmarks.*

a familiar sight (=something that you often see) *Beggars on the street are a familiar sight.*

a familiar name/word *The company name sounds familiar.*

a familiar refrain (=something that you often hear people say) *Parents hear the familiar refrain from their children "I'm bored!"*

PREPOSITIONS

sth is familiar to sb *The name will be familiar to many people.*

sb is familiar with sth *Are you familiar with his books?*

> **Familiar** sounds a little formal. In everyday English, you often say that you **know** someone or something: *Do you* ***know*** *Los Angeles? | She* ***knew*** *him well.*
> You can also say that you have **heard of** someone or something, when you are familiar with their name: *I'm sure that I've* ***heard of*** *him from somewhere.*

family *n*

a group of people who are related to each other

ADJECTIVES/NOUNS + family

a large/big/small family *He came from a large family and had four sisters.*

a wealthy/rich/well-off family *She was from a wealthy family and did not need to work.*

a poor/low-income/disadvantaged family *Children from poor families are less likely to go to university.*

a young family (=with young children) *It's not easy bringing up a young family on your own.*

the whole family/the entire family/all the family *We have invited the whole family to our house for Christmas.*

the Smith/Jones/Brown etc family *The Smith family are living in temporary accommodation.*

the royal family (=the king or queen and their family) *The royal family have large estates in Scotland.*

sb's immediate family (=closest relations) *What if one of your immediate family were disabled?*

sb's extended family (=including not only parents and children, but also grandparents, aunts etc) *She gets a lot of help from her extended family.*

a one-parent/single-parent family *Many of the kids are from one-parent families.*

a nuclear family (=a family consisting of a mother, a father, and their children) *Not everyone lives in a typical nuclear family.*

a close/close-knit family (=spending a lot of time together and supporting each other) *Laura's family are very close.*

a dysfunctional family *formal* (=a family with bad relationships between the members) *Children from dysfunctional families need special help.*

VERBS

come from a family *He comes from a family of doctors.*

start a family (=start to have children) *She wanted to get married and start a family.*

bring up/raise a family (=look after children until they are grown up) *You can work as well as bringing up a family.*

support your family (=provide the money and things they need) *He works hard to support his family.*

sth runs in the family (=used to say that many members have an illness, feature, ability etc) *Depression runs in my family.*

family + NOUNS

a family member/a member of the family *He lost two members of his family in the disaster.*

sb's family background *He comes from a stable family background.*

family life *Some people believe that television is destroying family life.*

a family business (=one run by members of a family) *My parents expected me to join the family business.*

a family car (=one designed for families with children) *It's a practical family car that is also fun to drive.*

a family holiday *BrE*, **a family vacation** *AmE*: *Most of our family holidays were spent in the south of France.*

a family resemblance (=when members of the same family look like each other) *There's a strong family resemblance between all the sisters.*

PREPOSITIONS

a family of four/five etc *This house isn't big enough for a family of seven.*

in sb's family *Everyone in my family is smarter than me.*

⚠ Don't say 'My family is five.' Say **There are five people in my family**.

famine *n*

a situation in which a large number of people have little or no food for a long time and many people die

ADJECTIVES

a severe/terrible famine *The country suffered a severe famine last year.*

a devastating famine (=it causes a lot of damage) *A devastating famine killed over one million people.*

widespread famine *Lack of rain produced widespread famine in Africa.*

the worst famine *In Sudan the year 1888 is remembered as the worst famine in history.*

VERBS

suffer a famine *When the potato crop failed, the people of Ireland suffered a terrible famine.*

be hit by famine *The charity continues to support food distribution in the areas hit by famine.*

be facing famine *Millions of people in West Africa are facing famine.*

cause a famine *The poor harvest caused a famine.*

relieve a famine (=end it) *Donations of grain from Western nations gradually relieved the famine in Ethiopia.*

famine + NOUNS

famine victims (*also* **victims of famine**) *The organization was founded to provide aid to famine victims.*

famine relief (=help for people suffering from famine) *A concert was organized to raise money for famine relief.*

famine areas *The worst famine areas are in the north of the country.*

famous *adj*

known about by a lot of people in a country or in the world, especially because someone or something is very good or impressive

NOUNS

a famous writer/actor/singer/artist *Leonardo was one of the most famous artists who has ever lived.*

a famous person/man/woman *Many famous people are buried there, including Oscar Wilde and Jim Morrison.*

a famous book/story/poem/painting *'Nineteen Eighty-Four' was Orwell's most famous book.*

a famous name/brand *The company owns some famous names, including Johnnie Walker whisky and Gordon's gin.*

famous phrase/words *In John Donne's famous phrase, "No man is an island".*

a famous example/case *The painting is probably the most famous example of his work.*

a famous victory *The Democrats were celebrating a famous victory by Barack Obama.*

VERBS

become famous *She became famous for the gardens she created.*

make sb famous *The song made him famous.*

ADVERBS

internationally famous *The internationally famous Munich beer festival is held in the autumn.*

If something is famous all over the world, you say that it is **world-famous**: *Cheddar cheese is* ***world-famous***.

PREPOSITIONS

famous for sth *France is famous for its wine.*

famous as sth *He is famous as the man who invented the internet.*

THESAURUS: famous

well-known

brand | book | story | play | poem | artist | writer | actor | figure | company

used about things and people that many people know about:

a well-known brand of breakfast cereal | The film is based on a well-known children's book. | Michael appeared in many shows and concerts and was a well-known figure in the theatre in Bradford, (=someone who people know well). *| He works for a well-known insurance company. | She is* ***well known for*** *her views. | His work is* ***well known among*** *people who collect modern art.*

You write **well-known** with a hyphen before a noun: *a* ***well-known*** *poem.* You write **well known** without a hyphen when you use it on its own: *He became very* ***well known*** *for his paintings.*

legendary

singer | musician | performer | player | figure | name | reputation | ability | courage

very famous and greatly admired for a long time – used especially about a singer,

F

musician, or performer, often one who has died:
*The album features songs by legendary guitar player Jimi Hendrix. | Her courage was legendary. | Newman was **legendary for** his good looks.*

eminent
scientist | historian | scholar | professor | doctor | surgeon | economist | member
used about scientists and experts who are greatly respected because of their knowledge:
Professor Dawkins is one of the most eminent scientists in his field. | This is the view taken by the eminent American economist J. K. Galbraith.

celebrated
case | example | artist | writer | painter | study | experiment | collection
famous and often mentioned:
In one celebrated case, the jury decided that a man was not guilty, because he was asleep at the time when the crime was committed. | Frida Kahlo is one of Mexico's most celebrated artists. | Kenneth Clark is famous for his celebrated study of Western Civilization.

big
name | brand
famous and very popular or important. **Big** sounds rather informal:
*Some big names will be at the concert, including Coldplay and Beyoncé. | People tend to choose the big brands, which they know they can rely on. | The band is **big in** America.*

renowned
famous for something:
*The British are **renowned for** their love of animals. | Colombia is **world-renowned** for its coffee. | The city has an **internationally renowned** art school.*

You can also talk about someone being **famous** using the noun **fame**, for example: *The book **brought** him worldwide **fame*** (=it made him famous). | *She **achieved/gained fame** for her discoveries* (=she became famous). | *The band **enjoyed fame** during the 1990s* (=they were famous).

famous for doing something bad

notorious
criminal | killer | gang | case | example | reputation
used about people, places, and cases that are famous for bad reasons:
*Al Capone was one of America's most notorious criminals. | In one notorious case, a police officer was allowed to go free after shooting an innocent man in the street. | The city is **notorious for** its level of violence.*

infamous
case | event | incident | words
famous for being extremely bad - used especially about something that is very shocking:
*The massacre was one of the most infamous events of the Vietnam War. | He uttered his now infamous words "Read my lips. No new taxes." | The country became **infamous for** its treatment of political prisoners.*

not famous

unknown
not famous:
*The painting is by an **unknown** Scottish **artist**. | The singer is **virtually unknown** outside the US* (=almost unknown). | *Her work **remained unknown** for many years.*

little-known
only known about by a few people:
*Phyllis Pearsall was the **little-known artist** who created the A–Z map of London. | The film featured a **little-known** young Scottish **actor**.*

obscure
only known about by a very small number of people, especially people who have special knowledge or interest in a subject:
*They listened to Guitar Gabriel, Big Boy Henry, and other **obscure** recording **artists**. | He bought shares in an **obscure** software **company**, which made him very rich.*

minor
not famous or important:
*The pictures are mainly by **minor artists**. | This is one of Beethoven's **minor works**.*

fan *n*

someone who likes a famous person or a particular kind of sport, music, film etc very much

NOUNS + fan

a football/tennis/baseball etc fan *Jack is a keen football fan.*

a music/jazz/rock etc fan *Every year jazz fans come to the Montreux Jazz Festival.*

a film/movie fan *This book about Hollywood is essential reading for film fans.*

a Manchester United/Red Sox/Colts etc fan *Manchester United fans were delighted with their team's victory.*

a Beatles/Bob Marley etc fan *I didn't know you were a Lady Gaga fan!*

ADJECTIVES

a big/great/huge/massive fan *Elizabeth is a massive fan of Elton John.*

a keen/avid/ardent fan *He is an avid tennis fan and has been to all the major tournaments.*

a devoted/dedicated fan (=a very strong supporter or admirer) *Devoted fans from all over the country have travelled to the concert.*

a loyal fan (=who always supports someone) *He will be playing to hundreds of loyal fans on Sunday.*

a lifelong fan (=someone who has been a fan since they were young) *Like his father, he was a lifelong fan of Liverpool football club.*

adoring fans (=who like and admire someone very much) *She's surrounded by adoring fans wherever she goes.*

sb's number one fan *She told the singer that she was his number one fan.*

rival/opposing fans (=who support different teams) *There were fights between rival fans outside the stadium.*

VERBS

fans cheer/applaud (sb/sth) *Fans on both sides applauded their skill and spirit.*

fans chant sth (=keep shouting something) *England fans chanted his name.*

delight/please fans *He delighted his fans by coming back on stage and singing three more songs.*

disappoint fans *The concert was cancelled, disappointing hundreds of fans.*

fan + NOUNS

fan mail/letters *The band receives lots of fan mail.*

a fan club *Her fan club has 25,000 members in the UK.*

THESAURUS: fan

admirer
someone who admires a famous writer, leader, painter, or performer, especially with the result that this influences what they do:
President Obama is a ***great admirer of*** *Abraham Lincoln. | The artist was a* ***keen admirer of*** *Picasso's work and you can see this in his paintings* (=he liked Picasso's work very much).

lover
a music/opera/jazz etc lover | an animal/dog/cat etc lover | a nature lover
someone who likes a particular subject, activity, or animal very much:
Opera lovers have been waiting for the concert for months. | The British are a nation of animal lovers. | This book is the ideal present for ***lovers of*** *gardening.*

supporter
a Manchester United/Liverpool etc supporter | a football/soccer supporter
someone who likes a particular soccer team and often goes to watch them play:
Manchester United supporters cheered when Rooney scored the winning goal. | Hundreds of football supporters were making their way to the stadium. | His son is a keen supporter of Barcelona.

buff
a film/movie buff | a jazz/opera buff | a wine buff | a history buff
someone who is interested in a particular subject and knows a lot about it:
My brother is a movie buff and he can tell you all the movies that a director has made.

addict
a TV addict | a news addict | a chocolate addict | a computer games addict
someone who watches, eats, or does something too much, because they like it a lot:
She's a TV addict and she spends half her life in front of the television. | Are we becoming a nation of chocolate addicts? | We're both ***addicts of*** *the show and we watch it every Saturday night.*

enthusiast
a car/motoring enthusiast | a railway/aircraft enthusiast | a DIY enthusiast | a sports enthusiast
someone who is very interested in a subject, and often has a lot of technical knowledge about it:
The exhibition will be of interest to classic car owners and other motoring enthusiasts. | My dad was a keen model railway enthusiast and had his own model railway in his garden. | She's a great sports enthusiast.

F

fanatic *n*

1 *disapproving* someone who has very extreme political or religious ideas, which you strongly disagree with

ADJECTIVES

a religious fanatic *He was murdered by a religious fanatic.*

a crazed fanatic *A bunch of crazed fanatics tried to blow up a crowded subway train.*

a right-wing/left-wing fanatic *The party is full of right-wing fanatics who want to start another war.*

2 *informal* someone who likes doing something very much

Grammar
Fanatic is usually used after a noun in this meaning.

NOUNS + fanatic

a sports/football/baseball fanatic *The family are all sports fanatics and they love watching games on TV.*

a fitness fanatic *He is a fitness fanatic and he is in the gym every morning at 6 a.m.*

a crossword/chess fanatic *The website is aimed at crossword fanatics, and there are thousands of puzzles on it.*

fantastic *adj* THESAURUS ▶ excellent

fantasy *n*
something that you imagine happening to you, which is extremely unlikely

ADJECTIVES/NOUNS + fantasy

a childhood fantasy *The story is just a childhood fantasy.*

a romantic fantasy *She started having romantic fantasies about her boss.*

sth is pure/sheer fantasy (=it is not really true) *None of this will ever happen – it's all pure fantasy.*

VERBS

have fantasies about sth *He had fantasies about being a famous actor.*

act out/play out/live out your fantasies (=do what you imagine you would like to do) *For many people, computer games are a way of acting out their fantasies.*

fantasy + NOUNS

a fantasy world *She created a fantasy world, in order to escape from her job at the factory.*

a fantasy novel/story/tale *The book is a fantasy tale about a boy and his dragon.*

a fantasy figure *Marilyn Monroe was a real person, not just a Hollywood fantasy figure.*

a fantasy life *He lived in a fantasy life where he thought he was a kind of superhero.*

PHRASES

the realms of fantasy (=used when you think someone's ideas are completely wrong and not based on reality) *The idea belongs in the realms of fantasy.*

sb is living in (a) fantasy land (=they are imagining something that will never happen) *If he thinks he can persuade them, he's living in fantasy land.*

far *adj, adv*
a long distance from somewhere

PREPOSITIONS/ADVERBS

far from sth *He was far from home.*

far away *They could hear the sound of water not far away.*

Grammar
Far is not used before a noun. You use **distant**, **remote**, or **faraway** instead.

⚠ Don't say 'My house is far.' Say **My house is a long way from here. Far** is not usually used on its own. **Far** is most commonly used in questions and in negative sentences: *"How far is it to the station?" "It's not very far."*

THESAURUS: far

a long way
if something is a long way, it is a long distance from a place. **A long way** is much more common than **far**:
*It's **a long way to** the next town. | The school is **a long way from** her house. | The airport is **a long way away** – over 50 miles.*

miles *informal*
very far:
*I was **miles from** the nearest hospital. | We had been walking **for miles** and needed a rest.*

distant *especially literary*
sound | **voice** | **star** | **planet** | **galaxy** | **horizon** | **land** | **thunder** | **gunfire**
a long distance away, and often difficult to see or hear:
*I could hear the distant sound of thunder. | On the distant horizon they saw a small fishing boat. | **Several miles distant** was the border with Switzerland.*

remote
village | **island** | **area** | **place** | **location** | **part** | **corner**
a very long distance away from the nearest town or city, so that few people go there:
*He comes from a remote mountain village in Nepal. | They travelled to one of the most remote corners of the world to make this film. | This area is **physically remote from** the rest of the USA* (=used to emphasize that a place is remote).

faraway *especially literary*
place | **land** | **country** | **kingdom**
a very long distance away:
a traveller from a faraway land | He lay in bed dreaming of faraway countries. | Her home was in faraway Australia.

Far away is written as two words when it is used as an adverbial phrase: *Her only living relative lived **far away** in America.*

faraway *adj, adv* THESAURUS ▶ far

fare *n*
the price you pay to travel somewhere by bus, train, plane etc

ADJECTIVES/NOUNS + fare

an air fare/a plane fare *Air fares are becoming much cheaper.*

a train fare (*also* **a rail fare** *BrE*): *Train fares are too expensive.*

a bus/coach fare *The coach fare is only £20.*

a taxi fare *The taxi fare from the airport is €25.*

a one-way fare (*also* **a single fare** *BrE*): *A one-way fare costs £75.*

a return fare *BrE*, **a round-trip fare** *AmE*: *The airline is offering a $99 round-trip fare.*

cheap/low fares *Several companies offer cheap fares to Barcelona.*
high fares *People are fed up with paying high fares for short flights.*
full fare *If you are not a student, you have to pay full fare.*
half fare *Children can travel half fare.*
the normal/standard fare *The standard fare is £30, but you pay less if you book early.*
the first-class/second-class fare *How much is the first-class fare to London?*

fare + NOUNS

a fare increase/rise *People who travel to work by train are complaining about the fare increases.*

VERBS

pay a fare *You get on the bus, pay your fare, then sit down.*
cut/lower/reduce fares *If train companies reduce their fares, it will encourage people to use their cars less.*
increase/put up fares *The airline plans to increase its fares by 10%.*
fares increase/go up *Fares have gone up three times in the last two years.*

PREPOSITIONS

the fare to a place *How much is the fare to Boston?*

THESAURUS: fare

price, value, charge, fee, fare, rent, rate, toll → **cost[1] (1)**

farm *n*

an area of land used for growing crops or keeping animals

ADJECTIVES/NOUNS + farm

a sheep/cattle/pig farm *His family owns a sheep farm in Australia.*
a dairy farm (=a farm that has cows and produces milk) *The milk comes from local dairy farms.*
an arable farm (=where crops such as wheat or corn are grown) *The wheat is grown on huge arable farms in Canada.*
a fruit farm *He lives on a fruit farm and helps to pick apples.*
an organic farm (=where artificial chemicals are not used) *Organic farms are better for the environment.*
a factory farm (=where many animals are kept inside, in small spaces, and made to grow or produce eggs very quickly) *It is cruel to keep animals on factory farms.*
a 300-hectare/400-acre etc farm *He bought a 300-hectare farm in Shropshire.*

VERBS

work on a farm *I used to work on a farm when I was younger.*
live on a farm *She lives on a farm in Wiltshire.*
own/have a farm *The family owned a small farm in Suffolk.*
manage/run a farm *He manages a large dairy farm.*
grow sth on a farm *They grew wheat and barley on their farm.*

farm + NOUNS

farm produce (=things that are produced on a farm, such as vegetables or eggs) *The local shop sells farm produce.*
farm animals *This crop is used mainly for feeding farm animals.*
a farm worker/labourer *They employ temporary farm workers to pick the fruit.*

farmer *n*

someone who owns or manages a farm

ADJECTIVES/NOUNS + farmer

an organic farmer *Organic farmers don't use chemicals that damage the environment.*
a local farmer *We buy our eggs from a local farmer.*
a dairy farmer (=farmers who keep cows for their milk) *He is a dairy farmer with a herd of 100 cows.*
a sheep/pig/cattle/chicken farmer *Sheep farmers have been keeping sheep here for hundreds of years.*
a rice/wheat/cotton/tobacco farmer *In Japan, rice farmers receive a lot of money from the government.*
a livestock farmer (=farmers who keep animals) *Livestock farmers need to get their animals to market.*

farming *n*

the activity of growing crops or keeping animals to produce food

ADJECTIVES/NOUNS + farming

organic farming *Organic farming does not use chemicals that will harm the environment.*
sheep/pig farming *There is a lot of sheep farming in central Australia.*
dairy farming (=keeping cows for their milk) *The grass makes the area suitable for dairy farming.*
arable farming (=in which you grow crops such as wheat) *There is a big difference between arable farming and keeping animals.*
intensive farming (=in which large numbers of animals are kept together in crowded conditions) *Many people think that intensive farming is bad for humans as well as the animals.*
subsistence farming (=in which the farmer can only produce enough food to feed his or her family) *The region is poor and relies heavily on subsistence farming.*

farming + NOUNS

the farming industry *The farming industry gets huge amounts of money from the government.*

F

farming methods *Modern farming methods make it possible to grow far more food than ever before.*

fascinating *adj* THESAURUS ➤ interesting

fascination *n*

the feeling of being extremely interested in something

ADJECTIVES

great fascination *The children listened with great fascination to the story.*

a particular fascination *There was one painting in the gallery that held a particular fascination for me.*

a morbid/unhealthy fascination (=that seems unusual and bad for you) *He developed an unhealthy fascination with guns.*

an enduring/abiding fascination (=it lasts a long time) *Venice has always held an enduring fascination for artists.*

a lifelong fascination *She has had a lifelong fascination with the islands.*

continued/constant/endless fascination *The Loch Ness Monster is a subject of endless fascination.*

VERBS

sb has a fascination with sth *The boy had a fascination with all forms of transport.*

sth has/holds a fascination for sb *She studied in the US as a teenager, and American culture has held a fascination for her ever since.*

watch (sb/sth) with fascination *They watched with fascination as the turtle laid its eggs.*

sth retains its fascination (=it continues to be fascinating) *The Lake District retains its fascination for people from all over the world.*

sth's fascination lies in sth (=used when saying why something is fascinating) *Much of the film's fascination lies in the fact that it is based on true events.*

PREPOSITIONS

a fascination with/for sth *He's had a fascination with trains ever since he was a child.*

PHRASES

sth is a source of fascination (=it is fascinating) *Her life has been a source of fascination to French writers from Voltaire to the present day.*

a subject/object/topic of fascination *The royal family has always been a subject of fascination throughout history.*

fashion *n*

1 a style of clothes that is popular at a particular time

ADJECTIVES

the latest fashion *The store sells all the latest fashions.*

⚠ Don't say 'the last fashion'.

men's/women's fashions *Men's fashions have not changed much in the last 50 years.*

high fashion (=fashion by top designers) *She longed to be involved in the glamorous world of high fashion.*

fashion-conscious (=very interested in the latest fashions, and always wanting to wear fashionable clothes) *Fashion-conscious people can't get enough of these new designs.*

VERBS

keep up with fashion (=make sure that you know about the most recent fashions) *Lucy likes to keep up with the latest fashions.*

follow fashion (=wear what is fashionable) *Don't follow fashion blindly, but think about what suits you.*

fashion + NOUNS

the fashion industry/world *London is the centre of the British fashion industry.*

a fashion model *Fashion models are usually very tall.*

a fashion magazine *She's the editor of a leading fashion magazine.*

a fashion show *Calvin Klein's fashion show featured suits and sportswear.*

fashion design/designer *Her favourite fashion designers include Giorgio Armani and Gianfranco Ferré.*

fashion photograph/photography/photographer *a book of Avedon's fashion photographs*

a fashion shoot (=an occasion when photographs are taken of fashion models) *She was asked to star with top model Naomi Campbell in a fashion shoot.*

a fashion victim *informal* (=someone who always wears what is fashionable, even if it makes them look bad) *I didn't want to look like a fashion victim.*

2 a situation in which something is popular for a period of time

PHRASES

be in fashion (=be fashionable) *Gangster movies are in fashion again this year.*

be out of fashion (=no longer fashionable) *His teaching methods are now out of fashion.*

go/fall out of fashion (=stop being fashionable) *The Beatles' songs will never go out of fashion.*

come back into fashion (=become fashionable again) *Her paintings have come back into fashion.*

be the height of fashion (=be very fashionable) *Wigs were considered to be the height of fashion.*

VERBS

fashions change (*also* **fashions come and go**) *Fashions change at an alarming rate.*

F

start/set a fashion *Prince Albert started the fashion for having trees at Christmas.*

PREPOSITIONS

a fashion for sth *There was a fashion for big cars in the 1950s.*

fashions in sth *Fashions in education come and go.*

THESAURUS: fashion

vogue *formal*
if there is a **vogue for** something, or it is **in vogue**, it is fashionable:
*There was a **vogue for** cream furniture in the 1920s. | His pictures are very much **in vogue** these days.*

trend
a way of doing something or a way of thinking that is becoming fashionable or popular:
*The magazine focuses on the **latest trends in** contemporary design. | **The trend is for** people to wait longer to marry and have children.*

craze/fad *informal*
a fashion, activity, type of music etc that suddenly becomes very popular, but only remains popular for a short time - often used about things that you think are rather silly:
*It's the new **fitness craze** from America. | I'm sure it's just a **passing fad*** (=something that will soon stop being fashionable). | ***Fad diets** can be dangerous.*

sth is all the rage
used when saying that something is very popular and fashionable for a short time:
The game was all the rage at her school.

fashionable *adj*

modern and popular at the present time

NOUNS

fashionable clothes *She likes her clothes to look young and fashionable.*

a fashionable store/restaurant/club *Rodeo Drive is full of fashionable stores.*

a fashionable area/district/resort *Acapulco become a fashionable resort in the 1950s.*

a fashionable address (=a fashionable place to live) *Mayfair is London's most fashionable address.*

a fashionable idea/view/theory *He doesn't agree with all these fashionable teaching ideas.*

a fashionable design/style *The house was built in a fashionable modern style.*

a fashionable word/term/phrase/topic *'Diversity' has become a fashionable word.*

VERBS

become fashionable *Long before it became fashionable, the restaurant only served locally produced food.*

make sth fashionable *The town was made fashionable by Hollywood stars such as Frank Sinatra.*

ADVERBS

very/highly fashionable *Their clothes look good, as well as being highly fashionable.*

no longer fashionable *His ideas are no longer fashionable these days.*

PREPOSITIONS

be fashionable among/with a group of people *Tight jeans were fashionable among teenagers.*

it is fashionable for sb to do sth *It was fashionable for women to wear huge hats covered with bird feathers.*

Instead of saying that something is **fashionable**, you can say that it is **in fashion**: *Short hair was **in fashion**.*

Instead of saying that something **becomes fashionable**, you can say that it **comes into fashion**: *Their music is **coming** back **into fashion**.*

Instead of saying that something is **no longer fashionable**, you can say that it has **gone out of fashion**: *His work has never gone out of fashion.*

ANTONYMS **fashionable → unfashionable**

fast[1] *adj*

1 moving quickly or able to move quickly

NOUNS

a fast car/train/plane/boat *Her husband liked driving fast cars.*

a fast runner/walker/driver *Bolt is the fastest runner in the race.*

a fast pace *They were walking at a fast pace and she found it hard to keep up.*

a fast time *The fastest time for the 100 metres is under 10 seconds.*

the fast lane (=the part of a road for vehicles that can go fast) *He pulled out into the fast lane to go past a truck.*

a fast road (=where people drive fast) *Be careful when driving in the rain on fast roads.*

ADVERBS

extremely/incredibly/unbelievably fast *The plane is incredibly fast and can reach speeds of over 1,500 miles an hour.*

PHRASES

the fastest ... in the world/on earth *The cheetah is the fastest animal in the world.*

Fast or quick?

Fast is the usual word to use when talking about speed of movement. You say *a **fast** train* or *a **fast** runner* (not a 'quick' one).

Quick is the usual word to use when something takes a short time. You say *a **quick** shower* or *a **quick** meal* (not a 'fast'

F

one). However, food that is made and eaten quickly is called *fast food*.
When talking about the speed at which someone can do something, you can use either **fast** or **quick**. You can say *She's a **fast** learner*, or *a **quick** learner*. However, you say *a **fast** computer* (not a 'quick' one).

THESAURUS: fast

high-speed
train | line | service | rail link | collision | chase
able to travel very quickly, or happening when someone is travelling very quickly:
High-speed trains can travel from London to Paris in just over two hours. | The bus was involved in a high-speed collision but luckily no one was hurt. | The police caught up with the gang after a high-speed chase.

supersonic
aircraft | plane | jet | airliner | fighter | bomber | speed | flight
a supersonic aircraft can travel faster than the speed of sound:
Concorde was the world's first supersonic passenger aircraft. | The plane was travelling at supersonic speed.

express
train | bus | coach | service
an express train or bus travels quickly because it does not stop at many places:
An express train suddenly came rushing past. | The airport express service operates every 15 minutes.

You can also use **express** as a noun: *It's quicker if you take **the express**.*

swift
movement | kick | stroke | water | current
moving quickly. **Swift** sounds rather formal and is mainly used in written English:
With a sudden swift movement, he seized the shotgun with his left hand. | She gave the door a swift kick. | The water was very swift, shallow, and rocky.

brisk
walk | pace
quick and energetic:
They went for a brisk walk in the countryside. | We set off at a brisk pace.

fast-flowing
river | stream | water | current
fast-flowing water moves quickly:
He fell into the fast-flowing river.

ANTONYMS **fast → slow**

2 able to do something quickly

NOUNS

a fast computer/processor/chip *Computer companies want faster chips, and faster means smaller.*
a fast machine *It is one of the fastest machines on the market.*
a fast worker/learner/reader *He's a fast worker and he should have it done by lunchtime.*

THESAURUS: fast

quick
learner | worker | reader | mind | brain
able to do something quickly:
He was a quick learner and his English seemed to get better every day. | His mind was surprisingly quick for someone of his age.

high-speed
broadband | internet access
high-speed internet connections operate very quickly:
Do you have a high-speed broadband connection at home? | All rooms have high-speed internet access.

ANTONYMS **fast → slow**

3 taking only a short time to do something

THESAURUS: fast

fast, rapid, speedy, prompt, hasty, cursory → **quick (1)**

fast² *adv* at a high speed

VERBS

go/drive/travel fast *You're driving too fast – slow down.*
run/walk fast *You can run much faster than I can.*
move fast (=take action quickly) *The rescue workers knew that they had to move fast.*
work fast *There's a lot to do – we need to work fast.*
learn fast *In this job, you have to learn fast.*
be falling/sinking fast *The temperature was falling fast.*
be growing/rising fast *Inflation is rising fast.*

fasten *v*

to join together two sides or ends of something in order to close it, or join together two things so they are attached

ADVERBS

fasten sth tightly/securely *The gate was fastened securely with a padlock and chain.*
fasten sth together *A paperclip is for fastening pieces of paper together.*

NOUNS

fasten your belt/seat belt *Please fasten your seat belts ready for landing.*

fasten your coat/tie/shoes *I stopped to fasten my shoe.*

fasten a rope/chain *He fastened the rope to a metal ring on the harbor wall.*

PREPOSITIONS

fasten sth to sth *A name badge was fastened to his jacket with a safety pin.*

fasten sth around sth *She fastened a silk scarf around her neck.*

fat[1] *adj*

1 weighing too much because you have too much flesh on your body

> **Be careful when you use fat**
> **Fat** is a very direct word. You might use it about yourself, but it will usually cause offence if you use it about someone else. The same is true about other words meaning **fat**.

ADJECTIVES

a fat man/woman/boy/girl *He was a short fat man in his early fifties.*

a fat person *The number of fat people in Britain is rising.*

a fat baby/child/teenager *People made fun of him at school because he was a fat child.*

a fat stomach (*also* **a fat belly** *informal*): *The exercise is good for getting rid of a fat stomach.*

a fat face *She was a small woman with a fat face.*

fat hands/fingers *His fat fingers made playing the guitar difficult.*

fat legs/thighs/bottom *He ran as fast as his fat legs would carry him.*

VERBS

get/become fat (*also* **grow fat** *formal*): *You'll get fat if you eat too much chocolate.*

look fat *Do I look fat in this dress?*

make sb fat *Eating too much fast food will make you fat.*

ADVERBS

extremely/enormously/incredibly fat *I was incredibly fat in those days.*

PHRASES

big fat *informal*: *He had a big fat stomach.*

THESAURUS: fat

overweight
weighing more than you should:
One in three Americans is overweight. | *She was several* ***kilos overweight****.* | *Diabetes is particularly common among* ***overweight people****.* | *He is* ***grossly overweight*** (=extremely overweight).

big/large
man | **woman** | **boy** | **girl** | **person** | **bottom** | **stomach**
used when saying that someone has a big body. **Large** is more common than **big** in written English:
My father was a big man. | *These chairs have been specially designed for large people.* | *Does my bottom look big in these trousers?*

obese
person | **child** | **teenager** | **patient**
extremely fat in a way that is dangerous to your health:
Obese people cannot control their desire for fattening foods. | *Obese patients are put on a special diet.* | *Her son was* ***clinically obese*** (=obese according to official medical standards). | *a* ***morbidly obese*** *woman* (=extremely obese)

chubby
baby | **child** | **boy** | **girl** | **cheeks** | **face** | **arms** | **legs** | **hands** | **fingers**
slightly fat in a nice-looking way:
A chubby little baby was playing on the rug. | *He was a chubby boy of about 16.* | *His cheeks were slightly chubby.*

plump
woman | **baby** | **child** | **body** | **face** | **cheeks** | **arms** | **chicken**
a plump woman, baby, or bird has a pleasantly round fat body:
Her mother was a plump cheerful woman. | *She was holding a plump baby in her arms.* | *She had plump cheeks and pretty brown hair.* | *The chickens were getting plump.*

flabby
stomach | **arms** | **legs** | **body**
having soft loose skin that looks unattractive:
Lack of physical exercise can lead to a flabby stomach. | *She was waving her flabby arms in the air.* | *He looked down at his flabby body.*

portly *literary*
man | **figure** | **frame**
a portly person has a fat round body - used especially about middle-aged men:
The farmer was a portly man with a long beard. | *She saw a portly figure standing by the gate.* | *He had difficulty getting his portly frame through the narrow door.*

ANTONYMS **fat** → **thin (1)**

2 thick

THESAURUS: fat

fat, chunky, heavy → **thick (1)**

fat[2] *n*

1 an oily substance in some foods

PHRASES

be low/high in fat (=contain very little fat or a lot of fat) *Cheese is very high in fat.*

ADJECTIVES/NOUNS + fat

low-fat/high-fat (=containing very little fat or a lot of fat) *A low-fat diet with plenty of vegetables is good for you.*
animal/vegetable fat *It is a good idea to cut down on the amount of animal fat that you eat.*
saturated/unsaturated fat *Saturated fat is found mostly in animal products such as meat.*

VERBS

contain fat *The cake contains a lot of fat.*

fat + NOUNS

fat intake (=the amount of fat that you eat) *You should reduce your fat intake.*
fat content (=the amount of fat that a food contains) *There have been calls for manufacturers to reduce the fat content in fast foods.*

2 a substance under the skin of people and animals, that helps to keep them warm

ADJECTIVES/NOUNS + fat

body fat *Women tend to have more body fat than men.*
excess/surplus fat (=extra fat) *He needs to lose some of that excess fat.*

VERBS

lose/shed fat *The best way to lose fat is to do some exercise.*
burn off fat (=get rid of fat by exercise) *Jogging helps to burn off fat.*

PHRASES

a roll of fat *There was a big roll of fat around her stomach.*

F

fatal *adj* resulting in someone's death

ADVERBS

often/sometimes/rarely fatal *This type of cancer is often fatal.*
potentially fatal (=used when something can cause someone to die) *Snake bites are potentially fatal.*
invariably fatal (=almost always fatal) *The disease is invariably fatal.*

VERBS

prove fatal (=be fatal) *If it is not treated correctly, the condition can prove fatal.*

NOUNS

a fatal accident *The number of fatal accidents has gone down.*
a fatal crash/collision *Diana died in a fatal car crash in Paris.*
a fatal injury/wound *The cyclist received fatal injuries.*
a fatal disease/illness *The disease can be fatal in young children.*
a fatal shooting *There have been several fatal shootings this year.*
the fatal shot *It was Oswald who fired the fatal shot.*

PREPOSITIONS

fatal to sb *The disease can be fatal to cats.*

THESAURUS: fatal

terminal
illness | cancer | condition
a terminal illness cannot be cured and will cause someone to die:
He has a terminal illness and only has a few months left to live. | Her husband suffers from terminal cancer. | The doctors say his condition is terminal.

mortal *literary*
wound | danger
causing death:
The hero receives a mortal wound to his chest. | The crew of the spacecraft were in mortal danger (=they were in danger of dying).

Mortal is only used before a noun.

fate *n*

the things that happen to someone or something, especially an unpleasant death or end

ADJECTIVES

the same/a similar fate *He did not intend to meet the same fate as his companion.*
a terrible/horrible/grim fate *The crew of the ship met a terrible fate.*
a sad/tragic fate *The play is about the tragic fate of two lovers.*
a cruel fate *She suffered a cruel fate at the hands of her captors.*
sb's ultimate fate (=what finally happens to someone) *The ultimate fate of the refugees is in our hands.*
an uncertain fate (=not clear, definite, or decided) *The bill faces an uncertain fate in the Senate.*

VERBS + fate

suffer a fate *We must prevent other children from suffering the same fate.*
face a fate *Other army bases are facing a similar fate.*
meet your/a fate *This is the battlefield where he met his fate.*
share sb's fate (=have the same fate) *She had no desire to share Linda's fate.*
decide/determine sb's/sth's fate *The meeting will decide the fate of the factory.*
seal sb's fate (=make it certain that something bad will happen to someone, especially that they will die) *Engine failure sealed the pilot's fate.*
leave/abandon sb to their fate (=leave someone in a bad situation) *The abandoned sailors were left to their fate on the island.*

resign yourself to/accept your fate *I had no choice but to resign myself to my fate.*

deserve a fate *These people deserve a better fate.*

discover/find out sb's fate *He only discovered his sister's fate after the war.*

fate + VERBS

sb's/sth's fate depends on sth *The company's fate depends on a decision by the bank.*

a fate awaits sb *formal* (=something will happen to someone) *A terrible fate awaited any soldier who was captured.*

a fate befalls sb *formal* (=something happens to someone) *I wondered what fate would befall me.*

PHRASES

your fate is in sb's hands (=someone will decide what happens to you) *His fate is now in the hands of the judge.*

father *n* a male parent

ADJECTIVES/NOUNS + father

a good/better father *I hope I've been a good father to you.*

a loving/devoted father *He said he was lucky to have such a loving father.*

a proud father *Steve recently became the proud father of a baby girl.*

an absent father (=who has left the family home) *Absent fathers are being made to pay to support their children.*

a single/unmarried/lone father (=who has to bring up a child without the help of a mother) *The evidence suggests that lone fathers are more likely to work than lone mothers.*

sb's real/birth/biological father *He never knew who his real father was.*

sb's foster father (=a man who looks after a child instead of its real father) *His uncle became his foster father.*

sb's late father (=who has died) *The picture was given to him by his late father.*

VERBS

become a father *Andrew was very excited about becoming a father.*

resemble/take after your father (=be like your father) *They are worried that John will take after his father and start gambling.*

NOUNS + father

a father figure (=someone who seems like a father to you and who you ask for advice) *Mitchell has been a father figure to Reid since he was ten.*

PHRASES

a father of two/three etc *The driver of the car was a father of four.*

be like a father to sb *The coach was like a father to him.*

fault *n*

1 something that is wrong with something, especially something that prevents it from working properly

ADJECTIVES/NOUNS + fault

a small/minor/slight fault *It's only a minor fault – it shouldn't take long to fix.*

a serious/major fault *If the product has a serious fault, you should be able to get your money back.*

an electrical fault *The fire was caused by an electrical fault.*

a design fault *The car had a design fault and thousands of vehicles had to go back to the factory.*

VERBS

find/discover/detect/identify a fault *It took them a couple of minutes to find the fault.*

develop a fault *The phone developed a fault and I had to take it back.*

fix/deal with/rectify/cure a fault *I've managed to fix the fault and the computer works OK now.*

PREPOSITIONS

a fault in/with sth *There was a fault in one of the engines.*

PHRASES

for all its faults (=even though there are things wrong with something) *For all its faults, we love this city.*

2 if something is your fault, you made it happen and you are responsible

PHRASES

say/claim that sth is sb's fault *The other driver said it was my fault, because I should have stopped in time.*

the fault lies with sb/sth (=that person or thing should be blamed) *Everyone always thinks that the fault lies with the parents.*

sth is sb's own fault *It's my own fault – I should have made sure the store was open on Sundays.*

sth is sb's stupid fault *It's his own stupid fault for drinking too much last night.*

favour *BrE*, favor *AmE n*

something that you do for someone in order to help them or be kind to them

ADJECTIVES

a big/great/huge favour *I've got a big favour to ask of you. | He acted as though he'd done us a great favor by coming.*

a small/little favour *Can you do me a small favour?*

a special favour *As a special favour, we were allowed to watch the players training.*

a personal favour (=something you do specially for a particular person) *As a personal favor, he let us use the hall to rehearse.*

a political favour *He was accused of granting political favours in return for illegal payments.*

VERBS

do sb a favour *Could you do me a favour and lend me £5?*

ask sb a favour (*also* **ask a favour of sb** *formal*): *I felt nervous about asking Stephen a favour.*

owe sb a favour (=feel that you should do something for someone because they have done something for you) *I owe you a favour for all the help you've given me.*

return a favour (=do something for someone because they have done something for you) *He helped me in the past and now he wanted me to return the favor.*

grant sb a favour *formal* (=do them a favour) *Female soldiers do not wish to be granted any special favors.*

PHRASES

as a favour to sb (=because you want to be kind, not because you have to) *She delivered the parcel as a favour to her sister.*

do yourself a favour (=do something good for yourself) *Do yourself a favour and get a good night's rest before the exam.*

F

favourable *BrE*, favorable *AmE adj*

THESAURUS **good (1)**

favourite[1] *BrE*, favorite *AmE adj*

your favourite thing or person is the one that you like more than others

NOUNS

sb's favourite food *What's your favourite food?*

sb's favourite book/film/website etc *One of my favourite books as a child was R. L. Stevenson's 'Treasure Island'.*

sb's favourite place *The writing room was her favourite place in the house.*

sb's favourite subject/topic *English was my favorite subject at school.*

sb's favourite pastime (=the thing that someone likes doing the most) *Her favourite pastime is golf.*

sb's favourite kind of sth *He says his favourite kind of music is jazz.*

sb's favourite time of (the) year *Autumn is my favourite time of the year.*

ADJECTIVES

least favourite *Cleaning the shower is one of my least favorite jobs.*

favourite[2] *BrE*, favorite *AmE n*

1 something that you like more than others

ADJECTIVES

a great/big favourite (=used when saying that a lot of people like something) *The area is a great favourite with tourists.*

an old/traditional favourite (=popular for a long time) *The CD contains all the old favorites plus some new additions.*

sb's own/personal favourite *This poem is one of my personal favourites.*

a particular favourite *Their songs were all good – my particular favourite was 'Mamma Mia'.*

a firm favourite (=used when saying that someone likes something very much) *Dahl's books are firm favourites with children.*

an all-time favourite (=your favourite of all the ones that have existed) *This song is one of my all-time favourites.*

a perennial favourite (=something that is always a favourite) *The film is a perennial favourite at Christmas time.*

NOUNS + favourite

a family/crowd favourite *The game quickly became a family favorite.*

VERBS

choose/pick a favourite *All his books are good and it is difficult to choose a favourite.*

remain a favourite *The Empire State Building remains a favorite with visitors to New York.*

PREPOSITIONS

sth is a favourite of sb's *The poem is a favourite of my father's.*

sth is a favourite with a group of people *The bar is a favourite with students.*

2 the team or player that is expected to win a game or competition

ADJECTIVES

the clear/strong favourite *At this stage, the US team looked clear favourites.*

the odds-on favourite (=the one that is most likely to win) *Serena is the odds-on favourite to win.*

the overwhelming favourite (=the one that is much more certain to win than any of the others) *This horse is the overwhelming favourite in tomorrow's race.*

the hot favourite *informal* (=the one that most people think will win) *The team are hot favourites to win the competition.*

joint favourites (=used when two teams or players are both the favourites) *France and Spain are joint favourites.*

fear[1] *n*

the feeling you have when you are afraid, or something bad that you are afraid will happen

ADJECTIVES

(a) great/deep/terrible fear *I had a terrible fear that I was going to die.*

(a) genuine/real fear *There was a look of genuine fear on her face.*

constant fear (=all the time) *During the war, we lived in a state of constant fear.*

sb's worst/greatest fear *Her worst fear was that she would never see her children again.*

an irrational fear (=one that is not reasonable) *He grew up with an irrational fear of insects.*

a deep-seated fear (=very strong and difficult to change) *He exploited people's deep-seated fears about strangers.*

sb's fears are groundless/unfounded (=there is no good reason for someone to be afraid) *As it turned out, these fears were groundless.*

VERBS

have no fear (of sth) *He had no fear of death.*

feel fear *For the first time, Peter felt fear.*

show your fear *She was determined not to show her fear.*

shake/tremble with fear *He was shaking with fear after being held at gunpoint.*

be gripped/overcome by fear (=be very afraid) *We were gripped by fear as the boat was tossed around by the waves.*

conquer/overcome your fear (=stop being afraid) *She managed to conquer her fear of flying.*

create/cause fear *The purpose of the terrorist attack was to create fear among the local population.*

confirm sb's fears (=show that what you were afraid of has actually happened) *The look on Colin's face confirmed all my worst fears.*

calm/ease/allay sb's fears (=make someone less afraid) *Frank eased my fears about not being able to speak the local language.*

dispel sb's fears (=make someone stop being afraid) *The announcement failed to dispel fears that jobs would be cut.*

raise fears (=make people feel afraid) *The attack has raised fears of increased violence against foreigners.*

⚠ Don't say that someone 'has fear'. Say that someone **is frightened** or **is afraid**. However, you can say that someone **has a great/terrible fear** of something, or **has no fear** of something.

PREPOSITIONS

fear of sth/sb *Fear of failure should not stop you trying.*

fear about sth *There were fears about the possibility of the disease spreading.*

fears for sb (=worries that something bad might happen to someone) *She spoke of her fears for her children.*

in/from/out of fear (=because you are afraid) *One of the women cried out in fear.*

for fear of doing sth/for fear that sth might happen (=because you are afraid something might happen) *They do not go out alone for fear of being kidnapped.* | *I didn't want to leave the path, for fear that I might get lost.*

without fear *People should be able to go about without fear of attack.*

PHRASES

filled with fear/full of fear *Mark sat in silence, his eyes filled with fear.*

be white/pale with fear *His face was pale with fear.*

be paralysed with fear (=be so afraid that you cannot move) *Bruce was paralysed with fear when he saw the snake.*

be/live in fear of sth (=be always afraid of something) *They were constantly in fear of an enemy attack.*

be in fear of/for your life (=be afraid that you may be killed) *Celia was in fear of her life when she saw the truck coming toward her.*

strike fear into the heart of sb (=make someone feel afraid) *Their shouts struck fear into the hearts of their enemies.*

a state of fear *People are living in a constant state of fear.*

a sense/feeling of fear *There is a great sense of fear and tension in the area.*

a climate/atmosphere of fear (=when everyone in a place feels afraid) *The killings have created a climate of fear.*

fear[2] *v*

to feel afraid or worried that something bad may happen

ADVERBS

secretly fear *He secretly feared that he wouldn't be brave enough to do the jump.*

greatly fear *The disease was greatly feared at the time.*

initially fear *Doctors initially feared he had suffered a heart attack.*

PREPOSITIONS

fear for sb *We fear for him and we're worried that he might be killed.*

fear for sth *She has lost her job and now fears for her future.*

PHRASES

sth is not as bad as you had feared *Luckily, the news was not as bad as we had first feared.*

be feared dead (=be thought to have died – used in news reports) *Hundreds of people are feared dead after a big earthquake hit northern Turkey.*

have nothing to fear (=you do not need to be worried or afraid) *You have nothing to fear in the test if you have studied hard.*

have reason to fear sth (=a good reason to fear it) *He had reason to fear that someone was trying to kill him.*

fear the worst (=think that something very bad has happened) *When Jake didn't return, I started to fear the worst.*

feast *n*
a large meal where a lot of people celebrate a special occasion

ADJECTIVES/NOUNS + feast

a great feast (=large and impressive) *A great feast took place at the palace.*
a sumptuous/lavish feast (=very large and impressive) *A hundred guests were treated to a sumptuous feast.*
a wedding/marriage feast *This dish is traditionally served at wedding feasts.*
a midnight feast (=snacks eaten late at night, usually by children in secret) *I slept over at my friend's house and we had a midnight feast.*

VERBS

have a feast *They decided to have a feast to celebrate the victory.*
hold/give a feast (=arrange for a feast to take place) *The feast was held in the college dining hall.*
prepare a feast *A catering company was hired to prepare the feast.*
attend a feast *The men of the village were attending a feast given by the chief.*

F

feature Ac *n*
1 an important or interesting part of something

ADJECTIVES

a common feature *In the 1920s, suburbs became a common feature of many American cities.*
an interesting/attractive/useful feature *The building has some interesting features, including a natural climate control system.*
an important/major/significant/key feature *One of the key features of the phone is its size.*
the main feature *The main feature of the square is the Gothic cathedral.*
a striking/distinctive/notable feature (=noticeable and interesting) *The most striking feature of this design is its simplicity.*
an unusual/unique feature *A unique feature of this guitar is its shape.*
a distinguishing feature (=one that makes something different from others of the same type) *The bird's main distinguishing feature is its curved beak.*
a regular/recurring feature (=one that happens often) *Delays and cancellations are a regular feature of air travel.*
a redeeming feature (=a good feature of something that is otherwise bad) *The hotel's only redeeming feature was its view of the bay.*
a standard feature *Airbags are now a standard feature on most cars.*

NOUNS + feature

a design feature *The building has many interesting design features.*
a safety feature *The car has more safety features than its rivals.*

2 a part of someone's face

ADJECTIVES

regular features (=not an unusual shape or size) *She was attractive rather than beautiful, with regular features and dark hair.*
strong features *He was good-looking, with strong features and even teeth.*
small/large features *Her small pretty features twisted into a frown.*
fine/delicate features *The girl had fine features and a long slender neck.*
handsome/pretty features *A scar spoiled his otherwise handsome features.*
sb's best feature *Her large brown eyes were her best feature.*

fee Ac *n*
an amount of money that you pay to do something or that you pay to a professional person for their work

ADJECTIVES/NOUNS + fee

a high fee *The school fees are extremely high.*
a small/low/modest fee *For a small fee, the shop will wrap the gift for you.*
an annual/monthly fee *An annual fee of £150 has been introduced.*
a flat/fixed/set fee (=a fee that is the same in every case) *You pay a flat fee for all the services that are provided.*
an entrance/entry fee (=a fee to enter a place) *The gallery charges an entrance fee.*
a membership fee (=a fee to become a member of a club or organization) *The gym's annual membership fee is £250.*
school/college/university fees *She paid for her college fees by taking a part-time job as a waitress.*
tuition fees (=money paid for being taught) *Many universities now charge tuition fees for these courses.*
doctor's/lawyer's/accountant's etc fees *We need to find the money for the doctor's fees somehow.*
legal/medical fees *She received £300 compensation after legal fees had been deducted.*
a booking fee (*also* **a service fee** *AmE*) (=a charge you pay when buying a ticket) *Tickets for the concert are £45, plus a booking fee.*

VERBS

charge a fee *The accountant charged a big fee for his services.*
pay a fee *You have to pay a fee for the course.*

THESAURUS: fee

price, value, charge, fee, fare, rent, rate, toll → **cost[1] (1)**

feeble *adj* THESAURUS **weak (1)**, **(3)**

feedback *n*

advice or criticism about how successful or useful something is

ADJECTIVES

positive/good feedback (=people say they like something) *We have had some positive feedback on our courses.*

negative feedback (=people say they dislike something) *Try not to be discouraged by negative feedback.*

constructive feedback (=which helps someone to improve what they are doing) *It's important to give constructive feedback.*

useful/valuable feedback *Thank you for your feedback. It was most useful.*

detailed feedback *Your tutor will provide detailed feedback on your essay.*

written feedback *You will be given written feedback on your interview.*

immediate/instant feedback *The coach is able to give the players immediate feedback on how they are playing.*

VERBS

give sb feedback *You have to be careful not to upset people when giving them feedback.*

ask for/request feedback *She asked for feedback on her work.*

get/receive/have feedback *It is useful to get feedback on your performance.*

welcome/appreciate feedback *The museum welcomes feedback from visitors.*

NOUNS + feedback

customer/user feedback *Customer feedback is very useful to businesses.*

PREPOSITIONS

feedback on sth *We welcome feedback on our products.*

feel[1] *v*

1 to experience a particular physical feeling or emotion

ADJECTIVES

feel angry/happy/guilty/frightened etc *She felt angry with herself.*

feel hungry/cold/ill/strange etc *I was feeling hungry, so I made myself a sandwich.*

feel good (=happy or physically comfortable) *Sunshine makes people feel good.*

feel better *You'll feel better in the morning after you've slept.*

feel bad/terrible etc (=unhappy, guilty, or ill) *She felt bad about leaving without saying goodbye.*

NOUNS

feel pain *The doctor asked if I felt any pain.*

feel an emotion *I felt a mixture of emotions as I prepared to leave.*

feel anger/fear/relief/excitement etc *He remembered the fear he felt that night.*

PHRASES

feel as if/as though/like *He felt as if he were drowning.*

how sb feels *The nurse asked me how I was feeling.*

2 to have a particular opinion or think that something is true

ADJECTIVES

feel sure/certain *Harry felt sure something was terribly wrong.*

feel confident *I felt confident we would find her.*

ADVERBS

feel strongly *Many people feel strongly about this issue.*

PHRASES

how sb feels about sb/sth *I know how you feel about him - he can be rather scary.*

feel[2] *n*

the way that something seems to you

ADJECTIVES

the overall/general feel *The overall feel of the place is very modern.*

a different feel *The two hotels have a completely different feel - one is very traditional, while the other is very new.*

a good/nice feel *The house has a good feel about it.*

a friendly/relaxed/warm feel *The restaurant has a nice relaxed feel and the staff are friendly.*

a homely feel (=it feels like a nice home) *A log fire will give your house a homely feel.*

a modern/contemporary feel *The camera work gives the film a contemporary feel.*

a traditional feel *The bar has a traditional feel.*

an authentic feel *Italian-speaking waiters give the restaurant an authentic feel.*

VERBS

have a feel *Despite their age, the photographs have a modern feel.*

give sth a feel *Silk sheets give the room a luxurious feel.*

create/provide a feel *Soft lighting creates a nice feel to the restaurant.*

add/bring a feel *The colour adds a warm feel to the room.*

retain/maintain a feel (=keep it, in spite of other changes) *The house has retained the feel of being a family home.*

feeling *n*

1 an emotion that you feel

ADJECTIVES

a good/great/wonderful etc feeling *It's a great feeling when you try something new and it works.*

a terrible feeling *I had a terrible feeling of guilt.*
a strong/deep/intense feeling *A deep feeling of sadness came over her.*
an overwhelming feeling (=very great) *When I heard the news, I just had an overwhelming feeling of relief.*
a slight/vague feeling *He didn't know how to explain his slight feeling of unease.*
positive/negative feelings *These women had negative feelings about their bodies.*
mixed/ambivalent feelings (=used when you have doubts about whether something is a good idea) *Her parents had mixed feelings about the marriage.*
bad feeling (=the feeling that you hate someone because of what has happened) *There is still a lot of bad feeling toward the soldiers.*
sb's true/real feelings *He never revealed his true feelings.*

VERBS

have/experience a feeling *I remember experiencing a feeling of tremendous excitement.*
give sb a feeling *My work gives me a feeling of achievement.*
arouse/cause a feeling *The music aroused a feeling of calm within him.*
show your feelings *I know you find it embarrassing to show your feelings.*
express your feelings/put your feelings into words (=tell other people about them) *Children sometimes find it difficult to put their feelings into words.*
hide/conceal/disguise your feelings *She could no longer hide her feelings.*
control/suppress your feelings (=not feel something, or not show your feelings) *She struggled to control her feelings.*
hurt sb's feelings (=make someone feel upset) *I hope I didn't hurt your feelings.*
a feeling comes/sweeps over sb *Suddenly, a feeling of joy came over him.*

PREPOSITIONS

a feeling of guilt/panic/relief etc *Stephen had a sudden feeling of panic.*
sb's feelings about sth/sb *He wrote a poem about his feelings about the death of his father.*
sb's feelings towards/toward sb *She had made her feelings towards him very clear.*
sb's feelings for sb (=especially feelings of love) *Tom's feelings for her hadn't changed.*

PHRASES

feelings are running high (=people have strong feelings, especially of anger) *It was the last game of the season, and feelings were running high.*

2 an idea or opinion about something, especially one that is influenced by your emotions

ADJECTIVES/NOUNS + feeling

a strong feeling *Mary has very strong feelings on the subject of women's rights.*
a vague feeling *I had a vague feeling that I had seen him somewhere before.*
a distinct/definite feeling (=used when you feel sure that something is true) *He had a distinct feeling that he was being tricked in some way.*
a good feeling *I had a good feeling about the race* (=I thought I would probably win).
a bad feeling *He had a bad feeling about the project from the start.*
a strange/funny feeling (=not easily explained) *I had the strange feeling that we had met before.*
an uneasy/uncomfortable feeling (=used when you feel a little worried about something) *She had the uneasy feeling that something was wrong.*
a sinking feeling (=a sudden bad feeling that something is true) *I realized with a sinking feeling that I had left my keys at the office.*
a sneaking feeling (=a slight feeling that something is true, without being sure) *I have a sneaking feeling that this band will do very well.*
sb's personal feeling *My personal feeling is that it would be a very good idea.*
a gut feeling (=an opinion based on emotion, not facts) *I had a gut feeling that something very unusual was about to happen.*

VERBS

have a feeling *He has strong feelings about the war.*
get the feeling that *I got the feeling that he didn't like me much.*

PREPOSITIONS

sb's feelings about/on sth *What are your feelings about this subject?*

feisty *adj* THESAURUS › **determined**

fertile *adj* able to produce good crops

NOUNS

fertile soil *Farmers use the fertile soil to grow huge quantities of rice and vegetables.*
fertile land *On this side of the island, the land is more fertile.*
fertile farmland *Ukraine has vast stretches of fertile farmland.*
a fertile valley/plain *The wheat is grown on the fertile plains of Canada.*
a fertile area/region *This is one of the most fertile areas of the country.*

> You can also use **fertile** about situations that are likely to be interesting or useful for someone: *This is particularly **fertile ground** for future research.* | *The country is now **fertile territory** for extremists.*

F

Fertile is also used about people, animals, or plants that are able to produce babies, animals, or plants: *The seeds are still* ***fertile****.*

fervent *adj* THESAURUS enthusiastic

festival *n*

1 a series of performances or special events in a place

ADJECTIVES

an international festival *They will be taking part in an international festival of drama and dance.*

a cultural festival *A cultural festival will celebrate the traditions of the local people.*

a literary festival *He will be speaking at the town's literary festival.*

NOUNS + festival

a music/rock/pop/folk etc festival *He's appeared at folk festivals all over Europe.*

a film/theatre/music/arts etc festival *The movie won an award at the Cannes Film Festival.*

a beer/wine/food festival *the famous Munich beer festival*

VERBS

have/hold/stage a festival *Tucson had a film festival last month.*

organize a festival *She has organized the annual theatre festival for ten years.*

go to a festival (*also* **attend a festival** *formal*): *An estimated 20,000 people attended the festival.*

perform/play/appear at a festival *The singer is scheduled to appear at a festival in Amsterdam next month.*

take part in a festival (=perform there) *She is one of the performers taking part in the festival.*

a festival takes place (=happens) *The festival takes place once a year, usually in March.*

a festival opens/starts *The festival opens on June 17th.*

festival + NOUNS

a festival organizer *Festival organizers say they expect more than 50,000 visitors.*

a festival programme *BrE*, **a festival program** *AmE* (=a series of events at a festival) *This year's festival programme includes musicians from all over the world.*

PREPOSITIONS

at a festival *There were lots of people at the festival.*

2 an important religious celebration

VERBS

celebrate a festival *Muslims will celebrate the festival of Eid ul-Fitr on Tuesday.*

have/hold a festival *The festival is held in the middle of summer.*

a festival marks/celebrates sth *Christmas celebrates the birth of Christ.*

PREPOSITIONS

the festival of Easter/Eid/Obon etc *Tomorrow is the start of the festival of Diwali.*

feud *n*

an angry argument between two people or groups that continues for a long time

ADJECTIVES

a bitter feud *There had been a long and bitter feud between the two families.*

a bloody feud (=a violent feud) *The dispute caused a bloody feud between the two groups.*

a long-running feud (=continuing for a long time) *The quarrel developed into a long-running feud.*

a personal feud *The dispute is part of a personal feud between two of the country's most powerful men.*

an internal feud (=between people in an organization) *The party was split by internal feuds.*

VERBS

have a feud *He and his uncle Alfred had a long-running feud.*

be involved in a feud (*also* **be engaged in a feud** *formal*): *The two men have been engaged in a bitter public feud.*

settle a feud (=agree to end it) *The families eventually settled their feud.*

end a feud *I wish they would end this ridiculous feud.*

a feud breaks out/erupts (=it suddenly starts) *A feud erupted between the neighbours about who owned the land.*

a feud escalates (=it becomes worse) *The feud escalated in the years that followed.*

NOUNS + feud

a family feud *She refuses to speak to her parents because of a family feud.*

a blood feud (=in which people have been killed or injured) *The groups have continued a blood feud for generations.*

PREPOSITIONS

a feud between two people/groups *There was a feud between the two families.*

a feud with sb *They are involved in a continuing feud with neighbours.*

a feud over sth *The murder followed a feud over money.*

fever *n*

an illness in which you have a high temperature

VERBS

have a fever *I had a fever and my muscles ached.*

⚠ Don't say 'I have fever.' Say **I have a fever.**

F

be running a fever (=have a fever, usually a serious one) *The little boy was running a fever for several days.*
develop a fever *Some people develop a slight fever after having the injection.*
catch a fever (*also* **contract a fever** *formal*): *In 1821, he caught a fever and died.*
cause fever *The disease often causes fever.*

ADJECTIVES

a high fever (=a very high temperature) *He is in bed with a high fever.*
a raging fever *especially literary* (=a very serious fever) *He was admitted to hospital with a raging fever and a temperature of 106 degrees.*
a slight fever *It is nothing to worry about – it's just a slight fever.*
a mild fever (=one whose effects are not serious) *Symptoms often include a mild fever.*

PHRASES

a bout of fever (=an occasion when you have a fever) *My mother was recovering from a bout of fever.*

> You can also say that someone **has a temperature** (=their body temperature is too high): *He doesn't look very well – I think he has a temperature.*

F

fiction *n*

books and stories about imaginary people and events

ADJECTIVES/NOUNS + fiction

modern/contemporary fiction *I like reading modern American fiction.*
historical fiction *She writes historical fiction.*
science fiction *Arthur C. Clarke wrote science fiction books.*
romantic fiction *Men don't usually like reading romantic fiction.*
crime/detective fiction *Agatha Christie was a crime fiction writer.*
literary fiction (=fiction that is considered to be literature) *The book will appeal to readers of both popular and literary fiction.*
popular fiction (=fiction that is read by large numbers of people, but is not usually considered to be literature) *Many supermarkets now sell popular fiction.*
pulp fiction (=fiction that is not very good and is often about sex and violence) *The novel could be described as pulp fiction.*

VERBS

write fiction *Ruth Rendell writes detective fiction.*
read fiction *She mostly reads fiction.*
publish fiction *Penguin publish fiction and non-fiction books.*

fiction + NOUNS

a fiction writer *Henry James was best known as a fiction writer.*

field *n*

1 an area of grass or crops with a border around it

ADJECTIVES/NOUNS + field

green/grassy fields *All around the house were green fields and rolling hills.*
open fields (=with nothing growing or built on them) *I saw a fox run across the open field.*
a corn/wheat/cotton etc field *There were corn fields on both sides of the road.*
a playing/sports field (=on which sport is played) *There's a large playing field at the back of the school.*
a rugby/football/cricket etc field *The garden is the size of a football field.*

> **Battlefield** and **minefield** are written as one word.

VERBS

work in the fields (=do farm work) *Most villagers work in the fields during the day.*
plough a field (=make long deep lines in the ground so that you can grow crops) *The farmer was using a tractor to plough the field.*
cultivate a field (=use it for growing crops and plants) *By clearing woods and cultivating fields, man has changed the environment.*

PREPOSITIONS

in a field (=used about fields in the countryside) *The children spent hours playing in the fields.*
on a field (=used about sports fields) *It was one of the best games ever seen on a rugby field.*
a field of corn/wheat/rice etc *The sun set over the fields of corn.*

2 an area of activity that someone is involved in

ADJECTIVES/NOUNS + field

sb's chosen field *He is extremely talented in his chosen field.*
a specialist/specialized field *The academic study of music is a specialist field.*
a related field *Graduates with degrees in languages, philosophy, and related fields are invited to apply.*
a research field *The subject has now become a major research field.*
a new field *Human genetics is a relatively new field of research.*

VERBS

work in a field *Many former students are now working in the field of mechanics.*
open up a field (=create it) *New technologies open up new fields of research.*

lead the field (=be the best or most advanced) *US companies lead the field in biotechnology.*

PREPOSITIONS

a field of sth *This is a very exciting field of research.*

in sb's field *He couldn't find a job in his field.*

outside sb's field *I don't know much about physics – it's outside my field.*

PHRASES

an expert in the field *Cole is the most noted expert in the field.*

a pioneer in the field (=someone who discovered new and important things) *He was a pioneer in the field of telecommunications.*

sb's field of expertise (=the subject or activity they are skilled in) *We're looking for a historian whose field of expertise is the Roman Empire.*

fight¹ *v*

1 if two people fight, they hit each other and try to hurt each other

PREPOSITIONS

fight with sb *Dean was fighting with his brother.*

fight over/about sth *People were so hungry that they were fighting over food.*

> Instead of saying that people are fighting, you can say that they are **having a fight**.

2 to take part in a war or battle

ADVERBS

fight bravely (*also* **fight valiantly** *formal*): *They fought valiantly to defend their country.*

NOUNS

fight a war *The two countries have been fighting a long war.*

fight a battle *His army fought several battles against the English.*

fight the enemy *They had the guns and equipment needed to fight the enemy.*

PREPOSITIONS

fight against sb *The Greeks fought against the Turks.*

fight with sb (=fight together with someone against another country or group) *He fought with the US forces in Vietnam.*

fight alongside sb (=fight and help another group of people) *Polish airmen fought alongside British pilots in World War II.*

fight over/about sth *The two sides are fighting over land.*

fight for sth *They fought for control of the islands.*

PHRASES

fight to the death (=keep fighting until you are killed) *They say they will fight to the death against the invaders.*

fight to the last man (=fight until there is only one soldier who is still alive) *His soldiers fought to the last man.*

3 to try hard to achieve something

ADVERBS

fight hard (=using a lot of effort) *The people have fought hard for independence.*

fight tirelessly/ceaselessly (=for a long time, without stopping) *He has fought tirelessly for justice for the victims.*

fight desperately (=in a very determined way, even though you know you are unlikely to succeed) *The sailors fought desperately to save the ship.*

fight stubbornly/tenaciously/doggedly (=in a very determined way) *She fought tenaciously to keep her children.*

PREPOSITIONS

fight for sth *At that time, women were fighting for the right to vote.*

4 to try hard to stop something

NOUNS

fight crime/corruption/terrorism *We are determined to fight terrorism.*

fight poverty *Oxfam raises money to fight poverty around the world.*

fight disease *You need your immune system to help you fight disease.*

fight discrimination/prejudice/racism *Dr King fought against racism all his life.*

fight injustice (=fight situations that are not fair) *The organization is dedicated to fighting injustice.*

PHRASES

fight sth tooth and nail (=in a very determined way) *We will fight the proposals tooth and nail.*

THESAURUS: fight

combat

crime | terrorism | disease | poverty | discrimination | racism | inflation | unemployment | climate change | problem | threat

to try to stop something bad from happening, or a problem that affects a large number of people. **Combat** sounds more formal than **fight** and is often used in news reports: *Police are being given new powers to combat crime. | New drugs are being developed to combat the disease. | To help combat climate change we are being encouraged to use our cars less. | How can we combat the problem of identity theft?*

wage war on sth

illegal drugs | corruption | terrorism | poverty

to make a determined and organized effort in

order to try to stop something bad from happening, over a long period:
The government says it will wage war on corruption. | Campaigners talked about the need to wage war on poverty.

fight² *n*

1 a situation in which two people or groups hit, push, or hurt each other

ADJECTIVES

a big fight *There was a big fight outside the pub.*
a fair fight *It was a fair fight – two against two.*
a fierce fight *The city was the scene of a fierce fight between armed gangs.*
a bloody fight (=when many people die or are wounded) *After a bloody fight, government troops forced them back.*

NOUNS + fight

a street fight *There were reports of street fights every night in the local newspaper.*
a fist fight (=when people hit each other with their closed hands) *A fist fight broke out after the match.*
a knife/sword fight *There have been several arrests, following knife fights between drunken fans.*

Gunfight and **firefight** (=a fight in which groups of soldiers fire bullets at each other) are written as one word.

F

VERBS + fight

have a fight *I didn't want to have a fight with him.*
get into a fight (=become involved in a fight) *The two men got into a fight over a girl.*
start a fight *They started a fight in the crowded bar.*
pick a fight (=deliberately start a fight) *The guy tried to pick a fight with Jack.*
stop/break up a fight *The police were called in to break up a fight outside a nightclub.*
win/lose a fight *He always won every fight he was in at school.*
be spoiling for a fight (=be very eager to fight with someone) *The kids went round in gangs, all spoiling for a fight.*

fight + VERBS

a fight breaks out/erupts (=suddenly starts) *A fight broke out and one man was struck on the head.*
a fight takes place (=happens) *The fight took place outside a nightclub.*

PREPOSITIONS

a fight with sb *He had a fight with an older boy.*
a fight between people *There were fights between rival fans.*
a fight over/about sth *He was knifed in a fight over some drugs.*

2 the process of trying hard to achieve, get, or prevent something

ADJECTIVES

a long fight *They won their case after a long fight in the courts.*
a tough/hard fight *We are prepared for a hard fight if necessary.*
a brave/valiant fight *She died yesterday, after a brave fight against cancer.*
a desperate fight *This is the story of their desperate fight for survival.*
a legal fight *A 14-year-old girl won a legal fight to be allowed to wear trousers in school.*

VERBS

win/lose a fight *The islanders won their fight for independence.*
lead a fight *Nelson Mandela led the fight for freedom in South Africa.*
face a fight *The men faced a long hard fight to prove their innocence.*
wage a fight (=try hard to achieve something) *It is over 100 years since Lincoln waged his fight to end slavery.*
continue a fight *The protesters vowed to continue their fight.*
give up a fight *They refused to give up the fight for justice.*
join (in) a fight *He urged others to join the fight to change the law.*

PREPOSITIONS

a fight for sth *We will continue our fight for justice.*
(in) the fight against sth *Schools have an important part to play in the fight against drugs.*

PHRASES

put up a fight (=try very hard to win or achieve something) *The team put up a good fight, but in the end they lost the game 3–2.*
have a fight on your hands (=used to say that someone will find it difficult to do something) *The government is determined to bring in this law, but it has a fight on its hands.*

fighting *n*

a situation in which people or armies attack each other

ADJECTIVES

heavy/fierce/intense fighting *They finally took the town after nine days of heavy fighting.*
violent fighting *There was violent fighting between rebel and government forces.*
hand-to-hand fighting *There was fierce hand-to-hand fighting and hundreds of people were killed.*
sporadic fighting (=occasional fighting) *Sporadic fighting was reported during the rest of October.*

VERBS + fighting

stop/halt/end the fighting *Talks were held to halt the fighting.*

flee/escape the fighting *People fled the fighting and crossed the border into Jordan.*

fighting + VERBS

fighting breaks out/erupts (=it suddenly starts) *Fighting broke out between the army and the rebels.*

fighting continues/goes on *The fighting went on for almost a week.*

fighting stops/ceases/ends *The fighting finally ended and a peace agreement was signed.*

PREPOSITIONS

fighting between/among sb *More than 35 people were killed in fighting between religious groups.*

PHRASES

an outbreak of fighting (=a situation in which fighting suddenly starts) *There are still sometimes outbreaks of fighting along the border.*

figure *n*

a number representing an amount

ADJECTIVES/NOUNS + figure

a high/low figure *1,000 calories a day is quite a low figure.*

the exact figure *What is the exact figure for the number of foreign workers in the country?*

an approximate/rough/ballpark figure (=not exact) *He gave us an approximate figure for the cost of the repairs.*

the final/total figure *The final figure is expected to be much higher than this.*

a target figure *The government set a target figure of 6.2%.*

a realistic figure *A more realistic figure for energy saving would be 20%.*

the latest figures *The latest figures show that crime is down slightly.*

official figures *According to official figures, almost one million people are unemployed.*

government figures *Government figures suggest the economy is recovering.*

sales/unemployment/crime etc figures *We exceeded our target sales figures.*

trade figures (=showing the value of a country's exports compared to imports) *The trade figures were down compared to the previous year.*

attendance figures (=how many people went to an event) *Last year's fair saw attendance figures of 32,000.*

VERBS

calculate a figure *The figures were calculated based on the number of cancer cases at 212 hospitals.*

add up the figures *I must have made a mistake when I added up the figures.*

estimate a figure *We estimate the figure to be around 15%.*

reach a figure *The population reached a figure of over 100 million.*

exceed a figure (=be more than it) *The total figure must not exceed £75,000.*

PREPOSITIONS

in figures *Write the amount in words and in figures.*

according to the figures *According to official figures, exam results have improved again this year.*

PHRASES

in single figures (=less than 10) *Women senior managers in the company are in single figures.*

in double figures (=between 10 and 99) *Only two students in the class achieved scores in double figures.*

four-figure/five-figure/six-figure etc (=in the thousands/ten thousands/hundred thousands etc) *He earns a six-figure salary* (=more than £100,000).

facts and figures *The report contains some interesting facts and figures.*

file Ac *n*

1 information on a computer that you store under a particular name

VERBS

open/close a file *You may need to close the file and restart the computer.*

save a file *I saved the file to my hard drive.*

create a file *She created a file of useful contacts for work.*

delete a file *I accidentally deleted the wrong file.*

access a file *You won't be able to access the file if another user has opened it.*

edit a file *After you've finished editing a file, always remember to save it.*

copy a file *I copied the file onto a memory stick.*

move a file *He was trying to move the file from one folder to another.*

send/email sb a file *Do you want me to send you the file?*

attach a file (=send it with an email) *Sorry, I forgot to attach the file.*

download a file (=copy it from the internet so that you can use it) *It just takes a few seconds to download the file.*

upload a file (=send a file from your computer onto another computer system using the internet) *Save your work, then upload the file.*

NOUNS + file

a computer file *I've just deleted all my old computer files.*

a backup file (=a copy of a file, which is made in case the original becomes lost or damaged) *It's always a good idea to have a backup file.*

F

2 a set of paper documents or records with information about someone or something

VERBS

files are kept/stored somewhere *The patients' files are stored in the basement.*

keep/store sth on file (=put information in a special file) *Customers' details are kept on file.*

keep/retain a file (=save it and not get rid of it) *Lawyers have to retain their files for several years.*

open/close a file *There was no more evidence and the police closed the file on the case.*

find/lose a file *The passport office said they had lost my file.*

PREPOSITIONS

a file on sb/sth *The government has hundreds of files on suspected terrorists.*

on file *The information is kept on file in case it is needed later.*

fill *v*

to put things or liquid into something, so that it is full

NOUNS

fill a container *Fill the container with water.*

fill a bag/suitcase *She filled her suitcase with clothes.*

fill a bottle/jug/kettle *He filled the jug with fruit juice.*

fill a glass *The waiter filled our glasses with champagne.*

fill a tank *I filled the tank with fuel.*

fill a space/gap *He filled the space with a new sofa.*

PREPOSITIONS/ADVERBS

fill sth with water/oil etc *She filled his glass with wine.*

fill sth up (=completely) *She filled the bottle up.*

fill sth completely *It cost me £70 to fill the tank completely.*

PHRASES

fill sth to the brim (=fill a glass, bucket etc up to the top) *He filled the glass right to the brim.*

be filled to capacity (=be completely full) *The tank was filled to capacity.*

THESAURUS: fill

pack
bag | suitcase | case
to fill a bag or case with clothes and other things that you need when travelling:
I packed a small bag to take with me to Paris. | I usually pack the suitcase the day before we leave. | Ellie was packing the case for her trip.

load/load up
car | truck | ship | plane
to fill a vehicle with goods:
She loaded up the car with all the bags for their trip. | Tell the men to start loading the ship.

top sth up *BrE especially spoken*
glass | cup
to fill a glass or cup that still has some liquid in it:
Can I top up your glass of wine? | She topped up his cup of tea.

You can also say **give sb a top-up**: *Do you want me to* ***give you a top-up****?* (=fill your glass or cup)

replenish/recharge *formal*
glass
to fill someone's glass again:
Our host came and replenished our glasses.

fill out *v* THESAURUS write (1)

film *n*

moving pictures shown at a cinema or on television

ADJECTIVES/NOUNS + film

an action/adventure/war film *Boys like action films.*

a horror film *The old house looked like something out of a horror film.*

a science fiction film *My favourite science fiction film was '2001: A Space Odyssey'.*

a documentary film *We watched a documentary film about China.*

a wildlife/nature film *I've seen lions in wildlife films.*

a cartoon film/animated film *Disney started making cartoon films in the early 1920s.*

a classic film *Bogart and Bergman starred in the classic film 'Casablanca'.*

a cult film (=one that a small group of people like very much and watch often) *'The Blues Brothers' was a cult film when I was at college.*

a big-budget/low-budget film (=that costs a lot/a little to make) *Big-budget Hollywood films can cost over $200 million.*

an art-house film (=made by a small company for artistic reasons, not to earn lots of money) *It's a small cinema which shows mainly art-house films.*

a black-and-white film *I love those old black-and-white films.*

a silent film (=made in the time before films had sound) *He started his career in silent films.*

VERBS + film

watch a film *He stayed in and watched a film on TV.*

see a film *We saw a good film last night at the cinema.*

appear in/be in a film *She once appeared in a film with Al Pacino.*

star in a film (=be one of the main characters) *Robert Mitchum starred in a film called 'River of No Return' with Marilyn Monroe.*

make/shoot a film *She is making a film for Australian TV.*

direct/produce a film *The film was directed by Jean-Luc Godard.*

show/screen a film *The film is being shown in cinemas all across the country.*

film + VERBS

a film stars sb *The film starred Brad Pitt.*

a film comes out/is released (=it starts to be available for people to see) *The film is due to come out in May.*

a film is showing/is on somewhere (=it is being shown at a cinema) *The film is on at the Odeon cinema.*

a film is set somewhere (=it takes place in a place or at a time) *The film is set in Paris in the 1950s.*

sth is made/turned into a film *The story was made into a highly successful film.*

film + NOUNS

a film actor/star *She dreamed of being a film star.*

a film director *This year's festival includes a tribute to the French film director Bertrand Tavernier.*

a film crew/unit *The film crew are making a documentary about village life.*

the film industry *Scorsese is a highly respected figure in the film industry.*

a film company *Many film companies are based in Hollywood.*

a film studio (=a company that makes films, or a building where films are made) *The scenes were all shot in a film studio.*

a film premiere (=the first showing of a film) *Film premieres tend to be glamorous occasions.*

PREPOSITIONS

a film about sb/sth *He wanted to make a film about a boxer.*

Film is used especially in British English. In American English, people usually say **movie**.

filthy *adj* THESAURUS ▸ dirty

final *adj* THESAURUS ▸ last[1] (1)

finance Ac *n*

1 the management of money, especially by governments or large organizations

ADJECTIVES/NOUNS + finance

international finance *The City of London is still the world's leading centre of international finance.*

high finance (=business activities involving very large amounts of money) *He is a key figure in the world of high finance.*

corporate/business finance (=involving big companies) *I was trying to get a job in corporate finance.*

personal/consumer finance (=relating to borrowing and saving by ordinary people) *This month's personal finance feature looks at retirement planning.*

finance + NOUNS

a finance minister *Finance ministers from around Europe are meeting in Luxembourg.*

a finance director *She joined the company as finance director.*

the finance department *The finance department has no record of your invoice.*

2 the money that is needed to pay for something, especially a big project

ADJECTIVES

public finance (=money that governments need for their activities) *Taxation is a central part of modern public finance.*

private finance (=money from private companies, rather than government) *The bridge was built using private finance.*

finance + NOUNS

finance costs *The finance costs are high for this type of loan.*

a finance company (*also* **a finance house** *BrE*) (=a company that lends money) *He got a loan from a finance company to buy the car.*

VERBS

get/raise/secure finance (=get the money to do something) *It took a long time to raise the necessary finance.*

provide finance *Who is providing the finance for the project?*

PREPOSITIONS

finance for sth *They had difficulty getting finance for the scheme.*

financial Ac *adj*

relating to money or the management of money

NOUNS

a financial institution (=an organization such as a bank, which lends money) *The agency is responsible for regulating the activities of banks and other financial institutions.*

the financial markets (=stock markets and other markets) *India's financial markets were closed on Monday for a national holiday.*

the financial year *They reported an increase in profits at the end of the financial year.*

financial support/assistance/aid *The Japanese government gives financial support to farmers.*

financial problems/difficulties *The company faces serious financial problems.*

financial adviser/advice *An independent financial adviser told me to put my money in stocks and shares.*

financial services *Steve has over 32 years experience in the financial services industry.*

financial resources *Big companies have the financial resources to invest in research and development projects.*

a financial transaction (=the action of buying or selling something) *Police are investigating illegal financial transactions involving millions of dollars.*

a financial incentive (=money offered to someone in order to encourage them to do something) *There should be more financial incentives for people to save.*

financial success *Financial success is important, but it is not the only thing that matters.*

finding *n*

information that someone has discovered as a result of their study or work

> **Grammar**
> Often plural.

ADJECTIVES/NOUNS + finding

research findings *Her research findings will be published next month in the 'British Medical Journal'.*

the main findings *There is a summary of the main findings at the end of the report.*

an important finding *His study contained some important findings.*

an interesting finding *Another interesting finding is that many of these patients were women.*

a surprising/unexpected finding *These unexpected findings could change the way doctors treat the disease.*

new/recent findings *This view is supported by recent findings.*

worrying/disturbing findings *One of the most worrying findings was that many young people believe they have no hope of getting a job.*

early/preliminary findings (=before you have completely finished your report) *The research team published some of their early findings after the first six months.*

VERBS + finding

present/report your findings *We had to present our findings to the class.*

publish your findings *His findings were published in the 'International Journal of Linguistics'.*

be based on findings *The report is based on the findings of a team which visited the country last year.*

discuss sb's findings *Ministers will be discussing the findings of the report.*

PREPOSITIONS

the findings of sth *We are waiting for the findings of the research team.*

findings from sth *The findings from their study are very interesting.*

findings on/about sth *Recent findings on depression have greatly increased our understanding of the condition.*

fine[1] *adj*

1 very good

NOUNS

a fine performance *Congratulations on a fine performance.*

a fine player/musician/soldier *Many fine musicians never become famous.*

fine wine/food *He likes fine wine and beautiful women.*

a fine collection/selection *The museum has a fine collection of Roman coins.*

a fine example of sth *The church is a fine example of Gothic architecture.*

a fine shot/goal/save *A fine save by the goalkeeper kept the score level.*

fine quality *Our modern factory produces fine quality carpets.*

> **Fine art**
> You use this phrase about paintings, sculptures etc that are made by artists for people to look at: *She is studying **fine art** at college.*

PHRASES

in fine form *He was in fine form and scored three times.*

in fine style *They began their journey in fine style, taking a limousine to the airport.*

> **THESAURUS: fine**
> nice, fine, sound, attractive, desirable, favourable, positive, beneficial → **good (1)**

2 healthy: *She had a bad cold, but she's fine now. | "How are you?" "I'm fine."*

> **I'm fine**
> You say **I'm fine** when someone asks "How are you?" It means "I'm healthy and everything is OK." Often though, it is just something you say automatically, without thinking.
> Don't say 'I'm very fine.'

3 sunny and with no rain

NOUNS

a fine day/morning/afternoon (=bright and sunny, with no rain) *It's going to be a fine day tomorrow.*

fine weather *The weather was fine, so they decided to go sailing.*

THESAURUS: fine

good, fine, nice, bright, beautiful/glorious, clear, cloudless, dry → **sunny**

4 thin or narrow

NOUNS

fine hair/thread/wire *They use fine gold thread to make the jewellery.*

a fine needle/tube *A fine tube is inserted into the body.*

a fine brush *She used a fine brush to paint the grass.*

fine lines *As we get older, our skin starts to develop fine lines.*

a fine layer/coating *The table was covered with a fine coating of dust.*

fine rain/drizzle (=consisting of very small drops of rain) *A fine rain was falling.*

the fine print (=small writing that gives important information which people often miss) *Always read the fine print before you sign anything.*

THESAURUS: fine

thin, fine → **narrow (1)**

fine[2] *n*

money that you have to pay as a punishment

ADJECTIVES/NOUNS + fine

a large/heavy fine *There are heavy fines for people who break the law.*

a stiff/hefty fine (=a large fine) *The men face stiff fines and a possible jail sentence.*

a $100/£50 etc fine *He got a thousand dollar fine.*

the maximum fine *The maximum fine for dropping litter is £200.*

a parking/speeding fine *You can get a parking fine if you park outside the police station.*

an on-the-spot fine (=a fine that you have to pay immediately to the person who gives it) *If you are caught speeding, you have to pay an on-the-spot fine.*

an unpaid fine *There are companies that collect unpaid fines.*

VERBS

pay a fine *He refused to pay the fine.*

get/receive a fine *I got a fine for paying the bill late.*

face a fine *The company could face fines of up to a million dollars.*

give sb a fine (*also* **impose a fine** *formal*): *Should parents be responsible for fines imposed on their children?*

PREPOSITIONS

a fine for sth *People should get fines for dropping litter.*

finger *n*

one of the four long thin parts on your hand

ADJECTIVES/NOUNS + finger

long fingers *You need to have long fingers to play the piano.*

small/little/tiny fingers *The baby had tiny fingers.*

thin/slim fingers (*also* **slender fingers** *literary*): *She had long slender fingers.*

fat fingers *He held his cigar with two big fat fingers.*

chubby/pudgy fingers (=a little fat) *The baby touched her hand with his pudgy fingers.*

nimble fingers (=skilful fingers) *Surgeons need to have nimble fingers.*

index finger (=the finger next to your thumb) *You point with your index finger.*

middle finger *He clicked his thumb and middle finger.*

third finger (=the third finger from your thumb)

little finger (=the fourth finger from your thumb, which is your smallest finger)

VERBS

put/dip/stick/poke your finger in sth *He dipped his finger in the water to see how cold it was.*

point your finger at sb/sth *The man pointed his finger at my shoes.*

prick your finger (=make a small hole in it) *She pricked her finger when she was pruning the roses.*

click/snap your fingers (=make a noise by rubbing them together) *She was clicking her fingers in time to the music.*

drum/tap your fingers on sth (=tap one finger after another against something, especially in an impatient way) *He waited, drumming his fingers on the desk.*

run your fingers through sb's hair (=gently pass your fingers through someone's hair) *She ran her fingers through his hair.*

cross your fingers (=put one finger over another as a way of wishing for good luck) *I crossed my fingers, hoping the letter would be for me.*

wag your finger (=shake your finger from side to side to show disapproval) *"You naughty girl!" she said, wagging her finger.*

fingernail *n*

the hard flat part near the top of your finger

ADJECTIVES

long/short fingernails *The woman had long fingernails.*

dirty/clean fingernails *I cleaned my dirty fingernails with a nailbrush.*

sharp fingernails *Careful you don't tear the fabric – you have sharp fingernails.*

painted fingernails *She had red lipstick and red painted fingernails.*
manicured fingernails (=carefully cut and shaped) *Sally always has perfectly manicured fingernails.*

VERBS

cut your fingernails *She was cutting her fingernails with some scissors.*
file your fingernails *He was filing his fingernails with a nail file.*
paint your fingernails *She likes to paint her fingernails in different colours.*
bite your fingernails *Don't bite your fingernails!*
break a fingernail *I broke a fingernail trying to fix my bike.*
grow your fingernails *I want to grow my fingernails but I can't stop biting them.*

Instead of **fingernail**, in everyday English people usually just say **nail**.
The nails on your toes are called **toenails**.

fingerprint *n*

a mark made by the pattern of lines at the end of someone's finger

VERBS

leave fingerprints *The burglar was careful not to leave any fingerprints.*
take sb's fingerprints (=make a copy of them) *The police will take his fingerprints and compare them with ones found at the crime scene.*
look for fingerprints *They went round the whole house looking for fingerprints.*
find fingerprints *The police found no fingerprints except those of the owner.*

PHRASES

a set of fingerprints *Every set of fingerprints is unique.*

finish[1] *v*

1 to do all of something

Grammar
Finish is often followed by a participle in this meaning: *Have you **finished** eating?*
Don't say 'Have you finished to eat?'

NOUNS

finish your work/homework *The work was finished four months ahead of schedule.*
finish your meal/food/drink *You stay and finish your meal.*
finish a book/article/report *She is finishing her first book, which will be published this autumn.*
finish your course/studies/education *I had just finished my university course, and was wondering what to do next.*
finish school/university *He didn't have the money to finish high school.*

ADVERBS

almost/nearly/just about finished *We've nearly finished making the cakes.*

VERBS

let sb finish (=allow someone to finish speaking) *Just let me finish, and then you can make your point.*
wait for sb to finish *We all had to wait for her to finish eating.*

PHRASES

sb will be finished in no time *informal* (=they will have finished very soon) *Don't worry, we'll be finished in no time.*

THESAURUS: finish

complete
work | task | job | project | course | studies | PhD | training | education | journey | investigation | sale | term of office
to finish doing something, especially something that takes a lot of time and effort. **Complete** is more formal than **finish**:
Marx died before he could complete the work. | She started a new job as a computer technician after completing her course. | The president has just completed his term of office (=the period when he or she has the position of president).

conclude *formal*
agreement | deal | negotiations | work | study | investigation | interview | argument
to finish something, especially an agreement or an investigation:
The US concluded a trade agreement with Mexico. | Police concluded their investigation and a 39-year-old man was charged with the murder.

finalize (*also* **finalise** *BrE*)
agreement | deal | negotiations | sale | details | plans | arrangements
to do the last things that are necessary in order to finish an agreement or plan:
The agreement was finalized during ten hours of talks at the presidential mansion. | We have an agreement in principle and we are finalizing the details. | The arrangements are still being finalized.

wrap sth up *informal*
agreement | deal | negotiations | investigation | game | match | victory | win
to finish something successfully. **Wrap up** is rather informal and is often used in news reports:
Negotiators are meeting on Friday to wrap up the deal. | The police have a few more days in which to wrap up their investigation. | The game was wrapped up by half-time, with Rooney scoring twice.

round off *BrE*, **round out** *AmE*
evening | day | year | season | meal | visit | meeting | interview | game
to finish something by doing one final thing, especially something enjoyable:
You can round out the evening with a trip to a local nightclub. | The day was rounded off with a picnic. | We rounded off the meal with some Irish coffee.

When saying that you **have finished** doing something in everyday English, you often say that you **have done** it: *Have you* ***done*** *your work/homework/essay? | I've* ***done*** *the washing/ironing/cleaning.* This is much more common than saying "I/you have finished".
In informal spoken English, people also say **I'm done** (=I have finished).

ANTONYMS **finish → start[1] (1)**

2 to end

THESAURUS: finish
finish, come to an end, draw to a close/an end, run out, expire → **end[2] (1)**

finish[2] *n*

the end or last part of something

ADJECTIVES/NOUNS + finish

an early/late finish *On Fridays we have an early finish, and can go home at three o'clock.*

an exciting/dramatic/nail-biting finish *The race had an exciting finish.*

a strong finish *A performance needs a strong finish that leaves the audience wanting more.*

a close/tight finish (=when two competitors finish very close to each other) *Jack came second, but it was a close finish.*

a photo finish (=in which the winner is decided by looking at a photo because it is very close) *His horse was announced to be the winner, after a photo finish.*

finish + NOUNS

the finish line *Bolt was first across the finish line.*

PREPOSITIONS

the finish of sth *We usually have a party to celebrate the finish of filming.*

at the finish *There was a sprint for second place at the finish.*

to/until the finish *She stayed to the finish.*

PHRASES

from start to finish *The whole day was a disaster from start to finish.*

ANTONYMS **finish → start[2]**

fire *n*

1 flames, light, and heat that destroy and damage things

ADJECTIVES

a big/major/serious fire *The house was destroyed by a big fire.*

a small fire *It was only a small fire and we quickly put it out.*

NOUNS + fire

a forest fire *There have been a lot of forest fires this summer in Greece.*

a brush fire/bush fire (=a very large fire in a wild area of bushes and small trees) *There were frequent brush fires during the hot dry summers.*

a house fire (=a fire that starts inside a house) *Faulty electrical wiring is being blamed for a house fire.*

VERBS + fire

start a fire *The fire may have been started by a cigarette.*

set fire to sth/set sth on fire (=make something start burning) *A candle fell over, setting fire to the curtains.*

sth catches fire (=starts burning) *The boat caught fire and sank.*

put out a fire (*also* **extinguish a fire** *formal*) (=stop a fire burning) *Firefighters successfully extinguished the fire.*

fight a fire (=try to make a fire stop burning) *Further attempts to fight the fire were abandoned.*

fire + VERBS

a fire burns *The fire was burning more strongly every minute.*

a fire breaks out (=starts suddenly) *A fire broke out in the engine room.*

a fire goes out (=stops burning) *After several hours, the fire eventually went out.*

a fire rages/blazes (=burns strongly for a long time over a large area) *Fires were raging in the forest near Magleby.*

a fire spreads *The fire spread to the house next door.*

a fire destroys/damages sth *The school was badly damaged by fire.*

fire + NOUNS

the fire brigade/service *BrE*, **the fire department** *AmE* (=the organization that works to prevent fires and stop them burning) *Someone had seen the smoke and called the fire brigade.*

a fire fighter/firefighter (=someone whose job is to stop fires burning) *Firefighters rescued ten people from the burning building.*

a fire engine (*also* **a fire truck** *AmE*) (=a large vehicle used by firefighters) *The fire engine arrived within a few minutes.*

a fire station (=a building where firefighters are based) *The nearest fire station is over 20 kilometres away.*

a fire extinguisher (=a metal container with water or chemicals in it, used for stopping small fires) *He grabbed a fire extinguisher and put the fire out.*
a fire alarm (=a piece of equipment that makes a loud noise to warn people of a fire in a building) *When the fire alarm went off, we all went outside.*
a fire escape (=metal stairs on the outside of a tall building that people can use to escape if there is a fire) *They rushed down the fire escape.*

PHRASES
be on fire (=be burning) *The whole house was on fire within minutes.*
bring a fire under control *Firefighters took more than an hour to bring the fire under control.*

2 burning material used to heat a room, cook food etc, or get rid of things you do not want

ADJECTIVES
an open fire (=a fire in a room that is not inside a stove etc) *Sophie warmed herself by the open fire.*
a (nice) warm fire *There was a nice warm fire burning in the fireplace.*
a roaring/blazing fire (=one that is burning strongly) *I sat by the roaring fire and dried off.*

NOUNS + fire
a coal/wood/log/gas fire *She lit the gas fire and settled in front of the TV.*

Campfire is written as one word.

VERBS + fire
make/build a fire *He found wood to make a fire.*
start/light a fire *She struck a match and lit the fire.*
stoke a fire (=put more wood or coal on it) *I stoked the fire and boiled some water.*
put sth on the fire *Put another log on the fire.*
cook sth over a fire *They cooked strips of meat over a wood fire.*

fire + VERBS
a fire burns/blazes *A fire was burning merrily in the sitting room.*
a fire smoulders *BrE*, **a fire smolders** *AmE* (=a little smoke comes from a fire when it has almost gone out) *The fire was smouldering in the grate and the room was getting cold.*
a fire dies down (=it burns less strongly) *The fire slowly died down.*

PREPOSITIONS
by/in front of the fire *Vernon was sitting in his armchair by the fire.*

PHRASES
the embers of a fire (=pieces of wood, coal etc that have almost been completely burned) *He stared at the glowing embers of the fire.*

firework *n*

an object that burns or explodes to produce coloured lights and noise in the sky

Grammar
Often plural.

VERBS
watch the fireworks *We can watch the fireworks from our bedroom window.*
let off/set off a firework (=make it explode) *People were letting off fireworks in the street.*
light a firework *You need to be careful when lighting fireworks.*
a firework goes off (=it explodes) *There were fireworks going off outside.*

firework + NOUNS
a firework display/show *Every year there is a huge firework display in the park.*
a firework party *We're having a firework party in our garden.*

British people associate **fireworks** with November 5th, which is called Bonfire Night. It was on this night in 1605 that Guy Fawkes tried to blow up the Houses of Parliament. There are **firework** parties and shows on this night each year.

firm[1] *adj*

1 not soft

PHRASES
nice and firm *Make sure that the apples are nice and firm.*
firm to the touch (=firm when you touch them) *The pears should be firm to the touch.*

NOUNS
a firm base/foundation *The bricks need to have a firm base made of concrete.*
a firm mattress *A firm mattress is good for your back.*
firm ground *The ground is firm enough for the horses to race on.*
firm stomach/thighs/buttocks *If you want a firm stomach you have to do a lot of exercise.*
firm flesh *The melons have firm yellow flesh.*

THESAURUS: firm
firm, stiff, solid, rigid, crispy, crunchy, tough, rubbery, brittle → **hard (1)**

2 not changing your decision, or not likely to change

NOUNS
a firm promise/commitment *The company has made a firm commitment to clean up the oil spill.*
a firm decision/intention *No firm decision has yet been made.*

F

a firm offer *I will not leave my job until I get a firm offer from the other company.*

a firm date *We should set a firm date for the wedding.*

firm plans *She had no firm plans for the next day, so she agreed to go out with him.*

a firm conclusion *It is difficult to reach a firm conclusion without knowing all the facts of the case.*

firm evidence *There is not enough firm evidence to find him guilty.*

a firm belief/conviction *It is her firm belief that women are better than men.*

a firm believer/supporter *John is a firm believer in natural medicine.*

firm friends *We met three years ago and have been firm friends ever since.*

VERBS

stand/hold firm (=not change your decision) *He is standing firm and refusing to sell his land to developers.*

PHRASES

be firm in your beliefs *She is firm in her belief that she will never have children.*

THESAURUS: firm

stubborn, single-minded, tough, firm, resolute, tenacious, dogged, persistent, ruthless, feisty, strong-willed, headstrong → **determined**

3 strict

NOUNS

firm discipline/control *This school believes in firm discipline and students who break the rules will be dealt with immediately.*

firm leadership/government *The country needs firm leadership.*

firm action *The police should take firm action against people who break the law.*

a firm stance/stand *We fully support their firm stand against racism.*

a firm voice *"We're going now," he said in a firm voice.*

a firm hand (=firm treatment) *He believes that children need a firm hand.*

PREPOSITIONS

be firm with sb *You must be firm with her.*

be firm about sth *She is very firm about us doing our homework on time.*

PHRASES

firm but fair *A good manager needs to be firm but fair.*

take a firm line (=deal with something in a very strict way) *The school takes a firm line about smoking.*

THESAURUS: firm

firm, tough, harsh, stern, authoritarian → **strict (1)**

4 holding or pressing something strongly

NOUNS

a firm grip/hold/grasp *He kept a firm grip on his wallet.*

a firm handshake *Mr Smith welcomed me with a firm handshake.*

firm pressure *Apply firm pressure to the wound.*

firm² *n* a business or company

ADJECTIVES/NOUNS + firm

a large/small/medium-sized firm *He is managing director of a large firm.*

an international/multinational firm *They want to encourage more multinational firms to establish factories in Spain.*

a local firm (=based nearby) *The equipment was supplied by a local firm.*

a family firm *The business grew from a small family firm into a large company.*

a foreign/overseas firm *There has been renewed competition from foreign firms.*

a leading firm *The building was designed by a leading firm of American architects.*

a reputable firm (=a firm that people say is good) *Make sure you choose a reputable firm to fit your new windows.*

a rival firm *They didn't want rival firms to know what they were planning.*

a law/accountancy/consultancy firm *She was offered a job with a top law firm.*

an engineering/electronics/advertising firm *Fred worked for an electronics firm.*

VERBS + firm

work for a firm *Chris has been working for this firm for nearly 20 years.*

join a firm *She joined the firm when she was 20.*

set up/start/found a firm *Hanson decided to start his own management consulting firm.*

manage/run a firm *We need someone younger to run the firm.*

take over a firm (=buy it and start to run it) *They expanded by taking over existing firms.*

firm + VERBS

a firm employs sb *The firm employs more than 200 people.*

a firm goes bankrupt (*also* **a firm goes bust/under** *informal*) (=it cannot continue because it cannot pay what it owes) *Unfortunately, the firm went bankrupt before the work was completed.*

PREPOSITIONS

a firm of solicitors/accountants/architects etc *Ms Shaw is a partner in a firm of solicitors.*

be with a firm (=be working for a firm) *He has been with the same firm for many years.*

first[1] *adj, determiner*

coming before all the other things or people in a series

NOUNS

the first time *It was the first time she had been on a plane.*

the first day/month/year etc *Today is the first day of spring.*

the first part/section/chapter/stage *The first part of the report dealt with the school's history.*

the first half/quarter *The custom began in the first half of the 19th century.*

sb's first book/film/record etc *Shakespeare's first play was 'Henry VI, Part One'.*

sb's first boyfriend/wife/child etc *Her first husband died when he was very young.*

sb's first reaction/response/instinct *My first reaction was surprise.*

the first thing *I just said the first thing that came into my head.*

the first step *The first step is to get the evidence.*

the first sign/indication *Chest pain can be the first sign of a heart attack.*

PHRASES

the first (one) of its kind *The service is believed to be the first of its kind.*

THESAURUS: first

initial

reaction | response | shock | impression | assessment | stage | phase | period | cost

at the beginning, when something starts or has just happened. **Initial** is more formal than **first**:

Her initial reaction was to laugh. | The investigators will be carrying out an initial assessment of the damage. | Parents are very important in the initial stages of learning. | The initial cost is higher than we expected.

preliminary

results | findings | report | investigation | inquiry | test | study | research | work | hearing | discussion

coming before the main one:

The preliminary findings were that 10% of Europe's forests have been damaged by pollution. | The FBI announced that it was opening a preliminary investigation into the matter. | Preliminary tests have shown no evidence of dangerous levels of radiation.

opening

day | night | ceremony | session | stages | address | speech | words | lines | sentence | chapter | scene | bars

happening at the beginning of an event, book, film, piece of music etc:

Tomorrow is the opening day of the conference. | I hope you will be coming to the opening night of the play (=the first performance). *| In his opening speech, he warned about the threat of another nuclear war. | The opening sentence of George Orwell's book 'Nineteen Eighty-Four' is "It was a bright cold day in April and the clocks were striking 13." | The opening scene of the film shows American soldiers arriving on the Normandy beaches. | The orchestra began playing the opening bars of Beethoven's 5th symphony.*

introductory

chapter | paragraph | section | essay | course | lecture | talk

written, said, or done as an introduction:

The introductory chapter opens with a general statement of the problem. | Michael was asked to give the introductory lecture at an engineering conference.

ANTONYMS **first** → **last[1] (1)**

first[2] *adv*

before anything or anyone else

VERBS

do sth first/finish first *An extra five points will be given to the team that finishes first.*

arrive/get somewhere first *Cindy and Joe arrived first.*

first discover/find out about/hear about sth *The disease was first discovered in 1986 in the UK.*

PHRASES

first of all *First of all we'd better make sure we've got everything we need.*

first and foremost (=first and most importantly) *He is first and foremost a brilliant engineer.*

first class *adj* THESAURUS **excellent**

fish *n*

1 an animal that lives in water, and uses its fins and tail to swim

ADJECTIVES/NOUNS + fish

freshwater fish (=that live in rivers or lakes) *The pools are home to frogs and freshwater fish.*

marine/saltwater fish (=that live in seas or oceans) *Marine fish are difficult to breed in captivity.*

tropical fish *There was a tank full of tropical fish in the waiting room.*

VERBS

catch a fish *Pete caught a really big fish.*

keep fish (=have them as pets) *We used to keep tropical fish when I was young.*

fish + NOUNS

fish stocks (=the quantity of fish in the sea) *Fish stocks have declined dramatically.*

F

a fish tank (=a glass container for keeping fish indoors) *He keeps several kinds of tropical fish in his fish tank.*

a fish pond (=for keeping fish outdoors, in a garden) *We're thinking of building a fish pond in the back garden.*

a fish farm (=an area of water used for breeding fish as a business) *The salmon comes from fish farms in Scotland.*

A **fish tank** is also called an **aquarium**.

PHRASES

a shoal/school of fish (=a large group swimming together) *Shoals of little fish were swimming around her.*

2 the flesh of a fish used as food

ADJECTIVES

fresh fish *The market sells an amazing variety of fresh fish.*

frozen fish *I stopped at the supermarket to buy some frozen fish.*

raw fish (=not cooked) *In Japan, people eat raw fish.*

PHRASES

fish and chips *Why don't we stop off for some fish and chips on the way home?*

⚠ Don't say 'chips and fish'.

fishing *n*

the sport or business of catching fish

VERBS

go fishing *We used to go fishing in the lake.*

take sb fishing *My dad promised to take me fishing at the weekend.*

NOUNS + fishing

salmon/trout/tuna etc fishing *He and his wife share a passion for trout fishing.*

(deep) sea fishing *We went deep sea fishing in my uncle's boat.*

river fishing *People go to the area for river fishing.*

fly fishing (=fishing with hooks that look like flies) *It was my first experience of fly fishing for salmon.*

ADJECTIVES

good/excellent fishing (=good opportunities for catching fish) *There is good fishing out in the bay.*

commercial fishing (=catching fish in large quantities as a business) *There is a ban on commercial fishing in these waters.*

coarse fishing *BrE* (=the sport of catching fish, except for trout or salmon, in rivers and lakes) *The new coarse fishing season starts next Wednesday.*

fishing + NOUNS

a fishing boat/vessel *There were a few small fishing boats in the bay.*

a fishing village/port *The resort was once a tiny fishing village.*

the fishing industry *The oil spill caused problems for the local fishing industry.*

a fishing rod/line/net *He tied a hook to the end of the fishing line.*

fishing tackle/gear (=equipment for fishing) *The shop sells fishing tackle and bait.*

a fishing trip/expedition *Their boat sank when they were on a fishing trip.*

a fishing fleet (=a group of fishing boats) *The harbour provides shelter for a small fishing fleet.*

fishing grounds (=an area where fish can be caught) *The ship headed out to the fishing grounds off the coast of Canada.*

PREPOSITIONS

fishing for cod/tuna etc *There may have to be a ban on fishing for cod in the North Sea.*

fist *n*

your hand when it is tightly closed

ADJECTIVES

a clenched fist (=in which you hold your fingers tightly, especially because you are angry or want to hit someone) *The two men took their jackets off and stood there with clenched fists.*

sb's left/right fist *I hit him with my right fist.*

a big/huge/massive fist *The gorilla held the banana in his huge fist.*

a small/little/tiny fist *The baby waved its tiny fists around.*

VERBS

bang/slam/beat/pound/smash your fist on sth (=hit something hard with your fist) *Helen banged her fist on the table.*

shake your fist (=move your fist in the air to show your anger) *She stood there, shaking her fist at the departing van.*

clench your fist (*also* **clench your hand into a fist**) (=close your hand tightly) *He clenched his fists in frustration and annoyance.*

raise your fist *He raised his fist in victory as the judge read her decision.*

pump your fist *informal* (=move your fist up and down to show you are pleased) *Hassan pumped his fist in the air as he crossed the finish line.*

make a fist (=close your hand into a fist) *The doctor asked me to make a fist with my injured hand.*

close your fist over sth *Jack picked up the flower and closed his fist slowly over it.*

use your fists *Some men use their fists to settle arguments.*

put up your fists (=put them in a position ready for fighting) *She put up her fists like a boxer.*

fists fly (=people fight with their fists) *There was an angry argument and fists started flying.*

PREPOSITIONS

in your fist *He crumpled the note up in his fist.*

with your fist *She pounded on the door with her fist.*

fist + NOUNS

a fist fight *He got into a fist fight with another teenager who had insulted his girlfriend.*

a fist bump *informal* (=when you touch someone's fist with yours as a greeting) *He said "Hi!" and gave me a fist bump.*

fit[1] *v*

1 to be the right size and shape to go on or in something

ADVERBS

fit well *It's important to buy shoes that fit well.*

fit perfectly (=very well) *The dress fitted perfectly.*

fit tightly/closely/snugly *The ring fitted snugly on her finger.*

fit loosely *The jacket fitted loosely around his waist.*

fit properly *The lid doesn't fit properly.*

fit exactly *The piece of wood fitted exactly in the space.*

fit neatly/nicely *Trim the circle of paper so that it fits neatly into the baking tin.*

fit easily/comfortably *The notebook will fit easily into a handbag.*

PHRASES

fit (sb) like a glove (=very well) *The expensive jacket fitted him like a glove.*

2 to match or be similar to something in some way

ADVERBS

fit sth well/perfectly *The man fitted her description perfectly.*

PREPOSITIONS

fit (in) with sth *Their view fits in with mine.*

PHRASES

the punishment should fit the crime *They believe that the punishment should fit the crime and that murderers should be killed.*

fit[2] *adj*

healthy and able to do physical exercise

VERBS

get fit *I need to get fit before we go for any long walks.*

keep sb fit *Cycling keeps you fit.*

keep/stay fit *She tries to keep fit by going swimming twice a week.*

look fit *Keith doesn't look very fit – he needs to do some exercise.*

feel fit *Do you feel fit enough to do the race?*

ADVERBS

really/incredibly fit *My dad's really fit for someone of his age.*

physically fit *You need to be physically fit to join the army.*

fully/perfectly fit *It could take months before he is fully fit again after his injury.*

PHRASES

(as) fit as a fiddle (=completely fit) *I feel as fit as a fiddle now.*

fit[3] *n*

1 a short time during which you cannot control your emotions or actions

ADJECTIVES

an epileptic fit (=caused by epilepsy) *I was worried that she was having an epileptic fit.*

a sudden fit *The woman slammed the door in a sudden fit of rage.*

occasional/periodic fits *He has periodic fits of depression.*

VERBS

have a fit *Nina had a coughing fit.*

cause/trigger a fit *Flashing lights can trigger a fit.*

PREPOSITIONS

a fit of sth *He had a sudden fit of anger.*

in a fit of sth *Paul collapsed in a fit of laughter.*

2 the way in which something fits on or into something

ADJECTIVES

a good/perfect fit *The shoes look a good fit.*

a poor/bad fit *The door was a poor fit and there was a big gap underneath.*

a tight/snug/close fit *We got all the furniture in the van, but it was a tight fit.*

a loose fit *I like skirts with a loose fit.*

a comfortable fit *The dress has an elastic waist for a comfortable fit.*

fitness *n*

how healthy and strong someone is, especially when doing sports or exercise

ADJECTIVES

physical fitness *You need a reasonable level of physical fitness for this job.*

general fitness *Swimming is good for your general fitness.*

full/peak fitness (=maximum fitness) *He has six weeks to get back to peak fitness before the race.*

VERBS

improve/increase your fitness *I'm trying to improve my fitness by playing tennis.*

build up your fitness (=improve it, especially gradually) *Start with a lot of walking to build up your fitness.*

maintain your fitness (=stay fit) *She worked hard to maintain her fitness while pregnant.*

get back to fitness (*also* **regain your fitness** *formal*) (=become fit again) *She gradually regained her fitness after her injury.*

fitness + NOUNS

a fitness test (=a test to see if a sports player is fully fit) *He failed a fitness test and will not be playing in tomorrow's match.*

fitness levels *His fitness levels are as good as someone half his age.*

fitness training *The players have to do a lot of fitness training.*

a fitness instructor *He works as a fitness instructor at a local gym.*

a fitness fanatic *informal* (=someone who likes exercising a lot) *He's a fitness fanatic who works out every day.*

fix *v*

THESAURUS **repair**[1]

flag *n*

a piece of cloth that represents a country or organization, or is used as a signal

ADJECTIVES

the national flag *People were waving the national flag.*

the American/British/Spanish etc flag *The American flag is known as the Stars and Stripes.*

a white flag (=a sign that you do not want to fight) *They raised a white flag, and the police stopped firing.*

the chequered flag *BrE*, **the checkered flag** *AmE* (=a flag with black and white squares, waved at the end of a motor race) *The race official waved the checkered flag to signal the end of the race.*

VERBS

wave a flag *People cheered and waved flags as the parade came by.*

carry/hold a flag *The solder in front was carrying the French flag.*

fly a flag (=have a flag on a pole) *The ships flew the Spanish flag.*

raise/hoist a flag (*also* **run up a flag**) *The Marines hoisted the American flag above the embassy.*

lower a flag *The flag is ceremonially lowered at the end of each day.*

hang a flag/put up a flag *They hung a big flag over the entrance to the shop.*

unfurl a flag (=open out a flag) *People in the crowd started unfurling red flags.*

drape a flag over sth/be draped with a flag (=used when people cover something with a flag) *His coffin was draped with a Mexican flag.*

salute the flag *The soldiers stood still and saluted the flag.*

a flag flies somewhere *There was a Red Cross flag flying from the rooftop.*

PHRASES

a flag flies at half-mast (=halfway up a pole, not at the top) *Flags are flying at half-mast today as a sign of respect.*

pledge allegiance to the flag (=swear that you will be loyal to your country) *I pledge allegiance to the flag of the United States of America.*

flame *n*

hot bright burning gas that you see when something is on fire

ADJECTIVES/NOUNS + flame

bright flames *Bright flames were coming from the fire.*

roaring flames (=very bright and hot and making a loud noise) *A firefighter shouted over the sound of the roaring flames.*

a naked/open flame (=not enclosed with a cover) *Never use a naked flame near spray paint.*

a candle flame *He lit the fire with the candle flame.*

a gas flame *The glass is heated over a gas flame.*

VERBS + flame

put out the flames (*also* **extinguish the flames** *formal*) (=make them stop burning) *Firefighters are still trying to put out the flames.*

light the flame (*also* **ignite the flame** *formal*) (=make it start burning) *The spark had ignited the flame.*

flame + VERBS

a flame burns *A flame will burn hotter and faster in pure oxygen.*

flames die down (*also* **flames subside** *formal*) (=burn less strongly) *By evening, the flames had died down.*

a flame goes out (=stops burning) *Try not to let the flame go out.*

flames flicker (=move unsteadily) *He watched the flames flickering in the fireplace.*

flames engulf sth (=completely surround and burn it) *Flames quickly engulfed the building.*

PHRASES

burst into flames (=suddenly start burning with big flames) *The plane had crashed and burst into flames.*

go up in flames (=be destroyed by fire) *The whole town went up in flames.*

in flames (=being destroyed by fire) *He returned home to find his house in flames.*

flash[1] *v*

1 to shine brightly for a very short time, once or many times

NOUNS

a light flashes *A police car sped past with its lights flashing.*

lightning flashes *Lightning flashed across the sky.*

a sign flashes *A big neon sign flashed outside the hotel.*

PHRASES

flash on and off *The lights flash on and off in time with the music.*

2 to make something shine

NOUNS

flash your headlights *The other driver flashed his headlights and let me go first.*

flash a torch *She flashed her torch along the corridor.*

3 to smile or look at someone quickly

NOUNS

flash a smile/grin *She flashed him a smile and drove off.*

flash a look/glance *My mother flashed a warning glance at me.*

flash your teeth (at sb) *He was very pleased and he flashed his teeth in a big smile.*

flash[2] *n*

1 a bright light or colour that appears for a very short time

ADJECTIVES

a bright flash *There was a bright flash of light.*

a brilliant flash (=very bright) *We saw a brilliant flash.*

a blinding flash *There was a blinding flash as the rockets exploded.*

VERBS

a flash lights up/illuminates sth *The night sky was lit up by flashes of light from the explosions.*

a flash illuminates sth *formal* (=makes it be clearly seen) *A brilliant flash of lightning illuminated the house.*

PHRASES

a flash of light *They saw a big flash of light in the sky.*

a flash of lightning (*also* **a lightning flash**) *There was a flash of lightning and a crash of thunder.*

2 an occasion when you suddenly feel or experience something for a short time

ADJECTIVES

a sudden flash of sth *She had a sudden flash of inspiration.*

a blinding flash (=when you suddenly realize something which surprises you) *In a blinding flash, she realized what he had meant.*

a rare/occasional flash of sth *He had one of his occasional flashes of brilliance.*

PHRASES

a flash of inspiration *He was sitting in the bath when he suddenly had a flash of inspiration.*

a flash of brilliance *The player has shown flashes of brilliance this season.*

a flash of anger/temper *"That's ridiculous!" he said with a flash of anger.*

a flash of humour *BrE*, **a flash of humor** *AmE*: *It is a dark film, but there are a few flashes of humour.*

a flash of insight (=when you suddenly realize something) *With a flash of insight, he realized that she didn't hate him at all.*

flat[1] *adj, adv* not sloping or curving

NOUNS

a flat surface *Lay the cloth on a flat surface.*

a flat roof *The shed has a flat roof.*

flat land/ground *The land near the coast is mostly flat.*

a flat stone/rock *He sat down on a flat rock.*

a flat screen *Modern TVs have flat screens.*

a flat bottom/base/top *Use pans with flat bottoms.*

a flat stomach *He started exercising because he wanted a flat stomach.*

ADVERBS

completely/perfectly/absolutely flat *The field is perfectly flat.*

as flat as a pancake (=completely flat) *The sea was as flat as a pancake.*

VERBS

lie (down) flat *Peter lay down flat on his towel.*

lay/spread sth (out) flat *She laid the map out flat on the table.*

fold (sth) flat *The table and chairs fold flat for easy storage.*

keep sth flat *Bend your legs, keeping your feet flat on the floor.*

press sth flat *He pressed his nose flat against the window.*

THESAURUS: flat

level
surface | ground | floor
a level surface does not slope in any direction, so that every part is at the same height:
Press the soil down to make a firm level surface. | The pilot was looking for an area of level ground so that he could land the plane. | Make sure that the floor is level before you lay the tiles. | The base needs to be ***absolutely level.***

even
surface | ground
without any holes or raised areas:
Spread the rug out on an even surface. | The ground isn't very even and you can't play soccer on it. | The walls look nice and even.

smooth
skin | surface | wall | water
without any holes or raised areas – used

F

especially when saying how something feels when you touch it:
Her skin was as smooth as a child's. | She looked out over the smooth water of the lake. | He rubbed the wood until it was ***perfectly smooth****.*

You also use **smooth** about a journey which is comfortable and without any sudden movements or problems: *Did you have a* ***smooth flight/crossing****?*

horizontal
line | stripe | band | layer | position
going straight across and not sloping:
The paper had horizontal lines printed on it. | The sweater has horizontal stripes. | Keep your body in a horizontal position.

ANTONYMS **flat → rough (1)**

flat² *n BrE*

a home consisting of a set of rooms that are part of a larger building

ADJECTIVES/NOUNS + flat

a small/tiny flat *The flat was too small for the three of them.*

a big/spacious flat *It is a big flat with eight or nine rooms.*

a one-bedroom/two-bedroom etc flat *She lived in a one-bedroom flat in North London.*

a studio flat (=a small flat with one main room) *I might just be able to afford a tiny studio flat.*

a ground-floor/first-floor/second-floor etc flat *We're moving into first-floor flat.*

a basement flat (=below ground level) *They lived in a basement flat in South London.*

a furnished/unfurnished flat (=rented with or without furniture) *We rented a furnished flat in the city centre.*

a luxury flat (=large and expensive) *They're building some luxury flats next to the harbour.*

high-rise flats (=flats in a very tall building) *Many high-rise flats are now having to be knocked down.*

VERBS

live in a flat *Terry lived in a flat on the second floor.*

move into a flat *They move into their new flat next week.*

buy a flat *I'm planning to buy a flat with my girlfriend.*

rent a flat (=pay money to live in someone else's flat) *Renting a flat can be very expensive in this part of town.*

own a flat *They live in London but also own a small flat in Oxford.*

make/convert sth into flats *The hospital is being converted into flats.*

PHRASES

a block of flats (=a large building divided into separate flats) *I live on the fourth floor of a block of flats.*

American speakers say **apartment**.

flavour *BrE*, flavor *AmE n*

the particular taste of a food or drink

ADJECTIVES/NOUNS + flavour

a strong flavour *The flavour of the sauce was quite strong.*

a mild flavour *I prefer a cheese with a milder flavor.*

a delicious flavour *Mango gives the pudding a delicious flavour.*

a spicy/bitter/salty etc flavour *The flavor was too bitter for me.*

a delicate/subtle flavour (=pleasant and not at all strong) *If you serve the wine too cold you will not appreciate its delicate flavour.*

a rich flavour (=strong and pleasant) *Brown sugar gives the candy a lovely rich flavor.*

a full flavour (=having a strong and satisfying taste) *The beer is brewed longer with reduced sugar to give a fuller flavor.*

a distinctive/unique flavour (=very different from other foods or drinks) *The berries give the drink its distinctive flavour.*

a chocolate/strawberry etc flavour *Does this milkshake come in a chocolate flavor?*

VERBS

have a ... flavour *The sauce has an interesting flavour.*

add/give flavour to sth *Herbs add flavor to a salad.*

bring out the flavour (=make the flavour more noticeable) *The fruit is cooked to bring out the flavour.*

improve/enhance the flavour *Salt is used to enhance the flavour of other foods.*

PHRASES

be full of flavour *The soup was full of flavour.*

flaw *n*

a mistake, fault, or weakness in something or in someone's character

ADJECTIVES

a serious/major flaw *There are some serious flaws in the design.*

a fundamental/basic flaw *The theory has some fundamental flaws.*

a fatal flaw (=a very serious flaw which makes someone or something certain to fail) *He has a fatal flaw for a politician: he has no idea how to reach compromises.*

the main/biggest flaw *The main flaw in this argument is that not everyone is motivated by money.*

a small/little/tiny flaw *It's a small flaw in an otherwise impressive film.*

a minor/slight flaw *I wouldn't worry about it – it's only a minor flaw.*

an obvious/glaring flaw *You don't have to be an expert in statistics to see the obvious flaw in this analysis.*

NOUNS + flaw

a character flaw *He seemed to have no character flaws.*

a design flaw *The type of reactor used at Chernobyl had a design flaw.*

VERBS

have a flaw *The system has some serious flaws.*

find/discover a flaw *Scientists have found flaws in the theory.*

expose/reveal a flaw *The drought of 1976–77 exposed a design flaw in the dam.*

correct a flaw *What would be the cost of correcting the flaws in the software?*

PREPOSITIONS

a flaw in sth *There is a flaw in this argument.*

despite its/his flaws *Despite its flaws, the book is a remarkable achievement.*

flight *n*

a journey in a plane or space vehicle, or the plane or vehicle that is making the journey

ADJECTIVES

a good/pleasant/comfortable flight *Have a good flight!*

a long/short flight *I was very tired after the long flight.*

a cheap flight *I found a cheap flight on the internet.*

a direct/non-stop flight (=going straight from one place to another without stopping) *She got on the next direct flight to Tokyo.*

a connecting flight *We flew to New York before catching a connecting flight to Chicago.*

a long-haul/long-distance flight (=one travelling a long distance) *You should wear comfortable clothes on a long-haul flight.*

an international flight *The number of international flights increased by over 5% last year.*

a domestic/internal flight (=within a country) *Is there a domestic flight between Boston and Portland?*

a return flight *BrE*, **a round-trip flight** *AmE* (=to a place and back again) *The holiday cost nearly £1,000, including a return flight and accommodation.*

a scheduled flight (=a plane service that flies at the same time every day or every week) *There is only one scheduled flight per day between the islands.*

a charter flight (=a plane service that is arranged for a particular group or purpose) *The company is operating charter flights to Crete.*

VERBS + flight

book a flight (=reserve a seat on a particular plane) *I booked a flight to Paris over the internet.*

catch a flight (=be in time to get on a plane) *They caught a flight that night to Frankfurt.*

get a flight (=book it or catch it) *I'll be there tomorrow morning if I can get a flight.*

board a flight (=get on a flight) *We arrived at the departure lounge to board the flight to Madrid.*

get on/off a flight *She'd just got off a flight from Buenos Aires.*

miss your flight (=arrive too late for a flight) *Jack overslept and missed his flight.*

operate flights (=make flights available for people to use) *The airline operates three flights a day between London and New York.*

flight + VERBS

a flight leaves (*also* **a flight departs** *formal*): *By the time we got to the airport, our flight had already left.*

a flight arrives/lands *The flight landed 30 minutes late.*

a flight is cancelled *All flights have been cancelled due to fog.*

a flight is delayed *She called to say her flight was delayed.*

a flight is diverted (=it has to change direction and land at a different airport) *Our flight was diverted to Luton because of poor weather.*

a flight is bound for London/New York etc (=it is going there) *Johnson boarded a flight bound for Caracas.*

flight + NOUNS

flight time (=how long it takes to fly somewhere) *Our estimated flight time is 3 hours and 15 minutes.*

the flight number (=the number given to the flight by the airline or airport) *Write the flight number on all your luggage labels.*

a flight attendant (=a person who looks after passengers on a plane) *The flight attendant asked me if I wanted a drink.*

the flight crew (=the pilot and all the other people working on a plane) *The flight crew helped passengers board the plane.*

PREPOSITIONS

a flight to a place *There are three flights a day to Logan Airport from Heathrow.*

a flight from a place *Has the flight from Sydney landed yet?*

flood *n*

a very large amount of water that covers an area that is usually dry

ADJECTIVES

a big/huge/massive flood *There was a huge flood and many people lost their homes.*

a devastating/disastrous/catastrophic flood (=which affects a place very badly) *The country* *is still recovering from devastating floods that killed more than 700 people.*

the great flood (of 1947/2010 etc) (=a very famous flood) *People still talk about the great flood of 1826.*

the worst flood *Last winter the town suffered the worst floods for 50 years.*

a flash flood (=a sudden flood) *The thunderstorm caused flash floods on some roads.*

a spring/summer/winter flood *The highways were damaged by winter floods.*

flood + NOUNS

flood water/floodwater *The kitchen was full of flood water.*

flood damage *The town suffered extensive flood damage.*

a flood victim *Helicopters were sent to rescue flood victims.*

a flood warning *The National Weather Service has issued a flood warning.*

flood defences/barriers *People living near the river were warned to prepare flood defences.*

a flood plain/floodplain (=an area of land that is often flooded by a river) *You shouldn't build houses on a flood plain.*

VERBS

a flood hits sth (=it affects a place) *In 2010, the area was hit by massive floods.*

a flood destroys sth *The floods destroyed the crops completely.*

a flood sweeps away sth *The bridge had been swept away by floods.*

be cut off by floods (=people are unable to leave a place because of floods) *The village was cut off by floods.*

a flood subsides (=it goes away) *After the flood had subsided, the new seed was sown in the dark fertile soil.*

floor *n*

1 the flat surface that you stand on inside a building

ADJECTIVES/NOUNS + floor

the bathroom/kitchen/bedroom etc floor *I've still got to clean the bathroom floor.*

a wooden/concrete/stone etc floor *He slipped on the marble floor.*

a tiled floor (=covered with tiles) *Tiled floors can be cold to walk on.*

a bare floor (=not covered by anything) *The room had a bare floor and a simple bed.*

a dance floor *Ray and Lisa were the first ones on the dance floor.*

VERBS

clean/wash the floor *Take your shoes off – I've just cleaned the floor.*

scrub the floor (=clean it by rubbing it hard with a stiff brush) *She was on her hands and knees scrubbing the kitchen floor.*

sweep the floor (=clean it with a brush with a long handle) *He grabbed a broom and began sweeping the floor.*

fall/drop/sink to the floor *He took off his jacket and let it fall to the floor.*

hit the floor/land on the floor *She fainted, and hit the floor with a thud.*

look at the floor *She had her head down, looking at the floor.*

floor + NOUNS

floor space *There's not enough floor space for another bed.*

floor polish *The room smelt of floor polish.*

> **Floorboard** is usually written as one word.

PHRASES

from floor to ceiling *Books covered the walls from floor to ceiling.*

PREPOSITIONS

on the floor *The children can sit on the floor.*

all over the floor *There were toys all over the floor.*

2 a level in a building

ADJECTIVES/NOUNS + floor

the top floor *He lives on the top floor of a block of flats.*

the first/second/third etc floor *The fire started on the eighth floor of the hotel.*

the ground floor *BrE* (=at the same level as the ground) *They got in through a ground floor window.*

the next floor (=the one above) *Menswear is on the next floor.*

PREPOSITIONS

on a floor *There are 17 rooms on this floor.*

up/down a floor *He took the lift up three floors.*

> **First floor or ground floor?**
> In British English, the **ground floor** is the floor at ground level. In American English, this is the **first floor**. In British English, the **first floor** is the floor above the one at ground level.
> The floor under the ground is called the **basement**.

3 the bottom of the sea or the ocean

NOUNS + floor

the sea/ocean floor *These creatures live close to the ocean floor.*

flow[1] *v*

to move in a steady continuous stream

ADVERBS

flow fast/swiftly *The stream was flowing fast over the stones.*

F

flow freely/easily *If the windows are shut, air cannot flow freely through the building.*

flow smoothly *Keeping to the speed limit helps traffic to flow smoothly.*

PREPOSITIONS

flow into/out of sth *These gates regulate the amount of water flowing into the canal.*

flow through sth *The blood flowing through your veins transports nutrients around your body.*

flow past sb/sth *A constant stream of cars flowed past them.*

flow² *n*

a steady movement of something such as water, people, vehicles, or information

ADJECTIVES

a steady/constant/continuous flow *There has been a steady flow of customers into the store.*

a free flow of sth *There needs to be a free flow of air around the room.*

NOUNS + flow

the water/blood flow *You can adjust the water flow.*

the air flow *If there is too much air coming out, you can reduce the air flow.*

the traffic flow *The new road system has improved the traffic flow.*

VERBS

control the flow of sth *It is impossible to control the flow of information on the internet.*

increase/improve the flow of sth *Exercise improves the flow of blood to the brain.*

reduce/restrict/slow the flow of sth *The dam helps to restrict the flow of water.*

maintain/ensure the flow of sth *More planes were brought in, to maintain the flow of supplies.*

stem the flow of sth (=stop it or make it less) *She tightened the bandage to stem the flow of blood.*

interrupt the flow of sth *They want to interrupt the flow of illegal drugs.*

PREPOSITIONS

the flow of sth *He held up his arm to stop the flow of blood.*

against the flow *The salmon have to swim against the flow of the river.*

flower *n*

a plant which has coloured parts called petals, from which its seeds or fruit develop, or this part of the plant

ADJECTIVES/NOUNS + flower

a wild flower *The meadow was full of wild flowers.*

spring/summer/autumn/winter flowers *The mountains were covered with spring flowers.*

a lovely/pretty/beautiful flower *He gave me a bunch of beautiful flowers.*

a delicate flower *The bush produces delicate pink flowers.*

a garden flower *Roses have become one of the best-loved garden flowers.*

cut flowers *Cut flowers last longer if you change the water in the vase.*

dried flowers *She brightened up the room with an arrangement of dried flowers.*

flower + VERBS

a flower grows *Flowers were growing along the side of the road.*

a flower blooms (=it appears on a plant) *Spring flowers bloomed in the meadows.*

a flower appears *The first flowers appear in the early spring.*

a flower opens *As the weather gets warmer, the flowers open.*

a flower wilts (=it bends and starts to die) *The flowers began to wilt in the hot sun.*

VERBS + flower

pick flowers *I'll pick some flowers to put on the table.*

give/send sb flowers *He sent his daughter flowers and a birthday card.*

produce flowers *During spring, the plant produces beautiful purple flowers.*

grow flowers *He grows flowers as well as vegetables.*

be covered in flowers (=have flowers on every part) *The fields are covered in wild flowers.*

flower + NOUNS

a flower pot *The terrace was covered in flower pots.*

a flower bed (=an area for growing flowers in a garden) *The flower beds had not been weeded for a long time.*

PHRASES

a bunch of flowers *He picked a bunch of flowers and gave them to her.*

a bouquet of flowers (=a carefully arranged bunch) *The bride held a bouquet of flowers.*

a vase of flowers *There was a vase of flowers on each table.*

the flowers are in bloom (*also* **the flowers are out**) (=they appear on a plant) *At this time of the year, most of the flowers are in bloom.*

be in flower (=have flowers) *The roses are in flower throughout the summer.*

be in full flower (=have a lot of flowers) *By May, the trees are in full flower.*

flowery *adj* THESAURUS **eloquent**

flu *n*

a common illness in which you have a high temperature, a sore throat, cough a lot etc

VERBS

have flu *He can't come to school because he has flu.*

get/catch flu *I don't want you to get my flu.*

come/go down with flu (=start to have flu) *Half the people in the office have come down with the flu.*

recover from flu/get over flu *It was several weeks before she recovered from her flu.*

ADJECTIVES

bad flu *I had really bad flu and I was off work for two weeks.*

mild flu *The illness feels like mild flu.*

flu + NOUNS

a flu virus (*also* **a flu bug** *informal*): *I picked up a flu bug from someone at work.*

a flu jab *BrE*, **a flu shot** *AmE* (*also* **a flu vaccination** *formal*): *Have you had your flu shots?*

a flu outbreak (=when a lot of people get the flu) *Britain was in the midst of its worst flu outbreak in a decade.*

a flu epidemic (=when an extremely large number of people get the flu) *Doctors now fear a flu epidemic.*

a flu strain (=a type of flu virus) *Five hundred chickens died from the H5N1 flu strain.*

PHRASES

be in bed with flu *Steven is still in bed with flu.*

be laid up with flu (=have flu and be unable to work or do anything) *Johnson took over for Ben Miller while he was laid up with flu.*

a case of flu *There have been a number of cases of flu at the college.*

a bout of flu (=an occasion when you are affected by flu) *This is her second bout of flu this winter.*

> **Flu** or **the flu**?
> In British English, people often just say **flu**: *She's off work with* ***flu***. In American English, people always say **the flu**: *She's off work with* ***the flu***. Don't say 'a flu'.

> **Flu** or **influenza?**
> **Flu** is the usual word to use in everyday English. **Flu** is short for **influenza**, which is more formal: *Millions of people died in the great* ***influenza*** *epidemic after the war.*

fluctuate Ac *v*

to keep changing between a high and a low amount or number

ADVERBS

fluctuate wildly *Oil prices fluctuated wildly.*

fluctuate significantly/considerably *The number of visitors fluctuates considerably, depending on the time of year.*

fluctuate sharply (=change suddenly by a large amount) *The value of the dollar fluctuated sharply.*

PREPOSITIONS

fluctuate between sth and sth *Her weight fluctuated between 50 and 60 kilos.*

fluctuate by sth *The temperature can fluctuate by as much as 30 degrees in one day.*

fluctuate with/according to sth *His mood seemed to fluctuate according to the weather.*

fluctuate from day to day/week to week etc *Prices fluctuate from day to day.*

> **THESAURUS: fluctuate**
> alter, turn, adapt, evolve, mutate, fluctuate, alternate → **change[1] (1)**

fluctuation *n*

a change in a price, amount, or level

ADJECTIVES

minor fluctuations *The number of masters degrees awarded by the college shows only minor fluctuations over the past ten years.*

wild fluctuations (=large changes that are difficult to predict) *The illness can cause wild fluctuations in blood pressure.*

seasonal fluctuations *Many types of businesses experience seasonal fluctuations in sales.*

PREPOSITIONS

fluctuation in sth *Fluctuation in the price of oil can damage the world economy.*

PHRASES

be subject to fluctuation (=something may change) *Prices are subject to fluctuation.*

> **THESAURUS: fluctuation**
> alteration, reform, shift, swing, fluctuation, transformation, revolution, shake-up, U-turn → **change[2]**

fluent *adj*

able to speak a language very well

NOUNS

fluent English/Chinese etc *She speaks fluent Italian and spends part of each year in Rome.*

a fluent speaker *Collins, a fluent Japanese speaker, acted as our interpreter.*

ADVERBS

very fluent *She is very fluent in Spanish.*

completely/totally fluent *He lived in the US and his English is completely fluent.*

VERBS

become fluent *It is very difficult to become fluent in a language.*

PREPOSITIONS

be fluent in English/Chinese etc *She was fluent in several European languages.*

fly[1] *v*

to travel through the air – used about planes, people in planes, birds, and insects

PREPOSITIONS/ADVERBS

fly to/from a place *We flew from London to New York.*

fly over/across an area of land/ocean *The plane flies over Greenland on its way to Toronto.*

fly past *I saw a flock of pigeons flying past.*

fly high/low *They watched the birds flying high above them in the sky.*

fly direct/nonstop (=without stopping) *She flew nonstop to Singapore.*

fly solo (=fly a plane alone) *He bought a small plane which he flew solo from Los Angeles to Miami.*

fly[2] *n*

a small flying insect with two wings

VERBS

a fly buzzes *A few flies buzzed around the kitchen.*

a fly lands *A fly landed on his arm and he waved it away.*

attract flies *If you leave food out, it will attract flies.*

PHRASES

a swarm/cloud of flies *A swarm of flies was buzzing around my head.*

focus[1] Ac *v*

to give special attention to one particular person or thing, or to make people do this

> **Grammar**
> **Focus** is usually used with **on** or **upon** (in more formal English).

ADVERBS

focus mainly/primarily/largely on sth *This essay will focus mainly on the work of European philosophers.*

focus heavily on sth (=focus a lot on something) *The book focuses heavily on the artist's eccentric personality.*

focus especially/particularly/specifically on sth *I would like to focus particularly on the moral aspects of this issue.*

focus only/exclusively/solely on sth *Try to focus only on those things which you can easily change.*

focus entirely/completely on sth *The programme focused entirely on the problems of nuclear energy.*

be narrowly/sharply focused on sth (=giving attention to only one thing) *Companies are often narrowly focused on making profits.*

be firmly/intensely focused on sth *She was firmly focused on her exams.*

VERBS

stay/remain/keep focused *He was finding it hard to stay focused on the game.*

help/allow sb to focus *Breathe slowly – this will help you to focus better on the task.*

PREPOSITIONS

focus on/upon sth *He wants to focus more on his career.*

focus[2] Ac *n*

1 the thing, person, situation etc that people pay special attention to

ADJECTIVES

the main/central/primary focus *The film's central focus is the relationship between the two women.*

a clear/sharp focus *Lessons should have a clear focus.*

a narrow/tight focus (=attention to only one thing or a few things) *Within the narrow focus of this book, the treatment is detailed and full.*

VERBS

become the focus *When you give a talk you become the focus of attention.*

provide a focus *The church provided a focus for the community.*

shift the focus (=move it to something else) *They accused the prime minister of trying to shift the focus onto other issues.*

bring sth into focus (=make people start paying attention to it) *9/11 brought the issue of terrorism into sharp focus.*

come into focus (=start having attention paid to it) *In the 1960s a new set of problems came into focus.*

lose focus (=stop paying attention to something you should be concentrating on) *You won't win the game if you lose focus.*

the focus changes/shifts *The focus of the negotiations shifted to working conditions.*

PREPOSITIONS

the focus is on sth *The focus is now on improving students' communication skills.*

the focus of sth *The focus of the project is literacy.*

a focus for sth *Now he had a focus for his investigation.*

PHRASES

the focus of attention *In this section the focus of attention will be on statistics.*

a focus of interest *Animal behaviour has always been a focus of interest for scientists.*

the focus of debate (=the thing which people are discussing) *The strike became the focus of debate in the media.*

the focus of concern (=the thing which people are worried about) *The spread of the disease has become the main focus of concern.*

a change/shift of focus *Over the years, there has been a change of focus from treatment to prevention.*

2 the clearness of an image

VERBS

come into focus (=become clear) *When I put my glasses on everything came into focus.*

adjust the focus *You can adjust the focus on the binoculars manually.*

ADJECTIVES

sharp focus (=very clear) *Objects closer to the camera are seen in sharp focus.*

PREPOSITIONS

in focus (=showing an image clearly) *It's a good photograph with the main building in focus.*

out of focus (=not showing an image clearly) *The picture is a little out of focus.*

fog *n*

cloudy air near the ground which is difficult to see through

ADJECTIVES/NOUNS + fog

thick/heavy/dense fog *Heavy fog is making driving conditions dangerous.*

freezing fog (=which forms ice) *Flights were cancelled due to freezing fog.*

swirling fog (=which blows around) *She could not see through the swirling fog.*

patchy fog (=in some areas but not in others) *Mist and patchy fog will form tonight.*

hill/sea/ground fog *Rain was forecast, along with hill fog.*

VERBS

be covered in fog *The mountains were covered in fog.*

be shrouded in fog *literary* (=be covered in fog, so that it is difficult to see) *The streets of London were shrouded in fog.*

fog comes down (*also* **fog descends** *literary*) (=it appears) *Suddenly the fog came down and covered the valley.*

fog rolls in (=it arrives from the mountains, the sea etc) *The fog rolled in from the ocean.*

the fog lifts/clears (=it disappears) *He sat and waited for the fog to lift.*

PHRASES

a blanket of fog (=a large area of fog) *A blanket of fog lay over the town.*

a bank of fog (=a large mass of fog) *As we approached the coast, we ran into a dense bank of fog.*

patches of fog (=fog in some places but not in others) *Patches of fog are expected later today.*

foggy *adj* THESAURUS **cloudy**

fold *v*

to bend something such as paper or cloth, so that one part covers another part

ADVERBS

fold sth neatly *Molly shook the crumbs off the tablecloth and folded it neatly.*

fold sth carefully *He folded his clothes carefully and put them on the chair.*

fold sth tightly *The note was written on a tightly folded piece of paper.*

PREPOSITIONS/ADVERBS

fold sth up *Fold up your clothes – don't just leave them on the floor.*

fold sth over/under/down etc *Fold the paper over, so that you make the shape of a triangle.*

fold sth away (=fold something and put it away) *I folded away the blankets.*

fold sth in half/two *The letter will fit in the envelope if you fold it in half.*

follow *v*

1 to move along behind someone else

ADVERBS

follow (sb) closely *A woman walked down the street with her children following closely behind.*

follow quickly/slowly etc *Dad went indoors and Frankie and I followed quickly.*

follow shortly (=follow soon) *Tom's already gone out to Rome and his wife and children will follow shortly.*

PREPOSITIONS

follow sb to/into/out of sth *Peggy followed her out into the hall.*

follow sb down/along sth *I followed him down the stairs.*

2 to happen or come after something else

ADVERBS

follow soon/closely after sth *The next earthquake followed soon after the first one.*

follow quickly/swiftly *This announcement was followed swiftly by the news that the chairman was planning to resign.*

follow immediately *As soon as he had asked the question, the answer followed immediately.*

PHRASES

there follows sth *After weeks of intense fighting, there followed a brief period of calm.*

the days/years/weeks that followed *Over the years that followed, friendship turned into love.*

follow (hot/hard) on the heels of sth (=happen very soon after another related thing) *The band's success follows hard on the heels of their recent US tour.*

follow in the wake of sth (=happen after another related thing, especially one that helps cause it to happen) *The economic crisis followed in the wake of a sudden rise in the price of oil.*

3 to do what someone tells you to do

NOUNS

follow sb's advice *He followed the doctor's advice and had no further trouble.*

follow instructions/directions/guidelines *Follow the instructions very carefully when filling out the form.*

follow the rules *The game is more fun if you follow the rules.*

follow orders *The soldiers are trained to follow orders without questioning them.*

follow your instinct *Cats will follow their natural instinct to hunt, even if they are not hungry.*

ADVERBS

obediently follow sb/sth *The men obediently followed his orders.*

dutifully follow sb/sth (=carefully do what someone says you should do) *The cookbook said to use 300 grams of chocolate, and I dutifully followed these instructions.*

blindly follow sb/sth *disapproving* (=do what someone says without questioning it or thinking for yourself) *I don't just blindly follow everything the boss says I should do.*

F

THESAURUS: follow

follow, abide by, comply with, respect → **obey**

4 to do the same thing or do something in the same way as someone else

NOUNS

follow sb's example (=do the same thing after another person has done something) *The younger children learned how to behave by following the example of the older ones.*

follow sb's lead (=do the same thing after another person, company etc has done something, especially because you think it is the best thing to do) *If one energy company puts up the price of electricity, the other companies are sure to follow their lead.*

ADVERBS

faithfully follow sth *The TV version faithfully follows the book.*

slavishly follow sb/sth *disapproving* (=do exactly what other people do, without thinking for yourself) *Some people slavishly follow all the latest fashions, with the result that they end up looking silly.*

PHRASES

follow in sb's footsteps (=do the same type of work or achieve the same success as someone else) *She hopes to follow in her father's footsteps and become a lawyer.*

follow suit (=do the same thing that a group of other people, companies etc have just done) *When one supermarket lowered prices, the others felt they had to follow suit.*

follow the family tradition *He followed the family tradition and became a farmer.*

follow the crowd *disapproving* (=do the same as everyone else does - used especially when you think this is a boring thing to do) *She has her own unique style of clothes - she doesn't just follow the crowd.*

be a hard act to follow (=have done something so well that other people will have difficulty doing it to the same standard) *Her sisters had done very well in school, so they were a hard act to follow.*

5 to understand a story, an explanation, or what someone says

PHRASES

be hard/difficult/impossible to follow *The story was really complicated and hard to follow.*

be easy to follow *The instructions are easy to follow.*

not quite follow sb/sth *especially BrE*: *I'm afraid I don't quite follow you - can you explain the rules again?*

fond *adj*

liking someone or something very much, and caring about them a lot

ADVERBS

very/deeply/extremely fond of sb/sth *She was deeply fond of her two nieces.*

quite/rather fond of sb/sth *It was an old car and he was quite fond of it.*

genuinely fond of sb/sth *The boy's nanny seemed genuinely fond of him.*

increasingly fond of sb/sth *He found himself growing increasingly fond of her.*

VERBS

grow fond of sb/sth (=become fond of them) *Over the years we've grown very fond of each other.*

PREPOSITIONS

be fond of sb/sth *He was fond of Lily and wished he could help her.*

food *n*

things that people and animals eat

ADJECTIVES

good/delicious/tasty food *Thanks for dinner - the food was delicious.*

fresh food *He buys fresh food from a local farm.*

frozen/canned/processed food *Some people claim that frozen food is just as healthy as fresh food.*

healthy/nutritious food *We try to give the kids good healthy food.*

spicy food (=with a hot taste) *I like spicy food with a lot of chilli in it.*

plain/simple food *He liked eating simple food, nothing spicy.*

hot/cold food *She wanted a rest and some hot food.*

organic food (=produced without using chemicals) *Organic food is better for the environment.*

vegetarian food (=food that does not contain meat) *The restaurant specializes in vegetarian food.*

fatty/salty/sugary/starchy foods *I try to avoid eating fatty foods.*

junk food (=full of sugar or fat, and bad for your health) *Eating too much junk food makes you fat.*

fast food (=food you buy which is prepared quickly and which you can take away with you to eat) *He cooked hamburgers in a fast food restaurant.*

VERBS + food

eat food *He sat in the corner and ate his food.*

have food *Sit down and have some food.*

cook/prepare food *I have to cook some food for this evening.*

serve food *The waitress was serving food to the customers.*

enjoy your food *I've never seen anyone enjoy their food so much.*

chew food *He chewed the food slowly and carefully.*

swallow food (=make it go down your throat) *She had difficulty swallowing her food.*

digest food *If you drink plenty of water, it helps you digest your food.*

food + VERBS

food tastes good/delicious etc *The food at Jan's house always tastes delicious.*

food smells good/delicious etc *The food smelt good to her.*

food + NOUNS

the food industry *The food industry has responded to consumer concerns about health.*

food prices *Food prices have increased rapidly in recent months.*

a food shortage *He remembered the food shortages of the war years.*

food additives (=chemicals that are added to improve the taste or appearance of food) *Biscuits and cakes often contain a lot of food additives.*

fool *n* a stupid person

ADJECTIVES

a silly/stupid fool *Why did you do that, you silly fool?*

a complete/utter/absolute/awful fool *I felt like a complete fool when I found out that I had been cheated out of my money.*

an old/young fool *You old fool! Why don't you watch where you're going!*

a crazy fool *The crazy fool ran right out into the street in front of the cars!*

PHRASES

make a fool (out) of sb (=make someone look stupid) *I'm always afraid I'll make a fool of myself when I have to give a speech.*

feel like a fool *I felt like a fool when I found out she wasn't really a famous singer.*

like a fool *She said she loved me, and like a fool, I believed her.*

> **Fool** or **idiot?**
> **Fool** seems a little old-fashioned, and people usually use a slightly stronger word such as **idiot**: *You **stupid idiot**! What did you do that for?*

foolish *adj* stupid and not sensible

VERBS

feel foolish *She felt foolish because she didn't know the answer.*

look foolish *He was certain that he would look foolish if he tried to dance.*

sound foolish *I wanted to ask a question, but I was afraid I'd sound foolish.*

seem/appear foolish *It seems foolish to plan a holiday when we haven't yet saved the money.*

PHRASES

it is foolish to do sth *It would be foolish to ignore her advice.*

sth is foolish of sb *The man started shouting at the police officer, which was very foolish of him.*

be foolish enough to do sth *I was foolish enough to believe him, even though he had lied to me before.*

young and foolish *We were young and foolish and we wanted to enjoy ourselves.*

foot *n*

1 the part of your body that you stand on and walk on

ADJECTIVES

sb's left/right foot *He kicked the ball with his left foot.*

front foot (=of an animal) *A tiger has five claws on each of its front feet.*

back/hind foot (=of an animal) *The horse lifted its back foot.*

big/small feet *He has very small feet for a man.*

bare feet *The marble floor felt cold under his bare feet.*

dainty feet (=small and pretty) *She was sitting on the couch, her dainty little feet tucked under her.*

flat feet (=a medical condition in which your feet rest flat on the ground, with no curved part) *The doctor says I have flat feet.*

F

VERBS

injure/hurt your foot *Simon injured his foot while playing rugby.*

wipe your feet (=wipe your shoes on a mat to remove dirt) *Be sure to wipe your feet before coming into the house.*

stamp your feet (=hit them on the ground loudly) *He stamped his feet to keep warm.*

tap your feet (=hit the ground with your toes, making a short sound) *She was tapping her feet in time with the music.*

shuffle your feet (=make small movements with them, because you are nervous or impatient) *The boy shuffled his feet and looked down at the floor.*

sb's foot hurts *These boots make my feet hurt.*

PREPOSITIONS

at sb's feet (=on the ground, near your feet) *The dog was sitting at his master's feet.*

under/beneath sb's feet *The sand was hot under her feet.*

PHRASES

the sole of your foot (=the base of it, that you walk on) *The soles of her feet were aching from the long walk.*

2 the lowest part of something, or the end of something

PHRASES

the foot of the stairs/staircase/steps/ladder *Perry stood at the foot of the stairs, looking up at her.*

the foot of the hill/mountain/cliff/slope *The museum is at the foot of the hill.*

the foot of the page *There was a note at the foot of the page.*

the foot of a statue/tree *At the foot of the statue was a big iron candleholder.*

the foot of the bed *She sat at the foot of the bed and took off her shoes.*

football *n*

1 a game played by two teams of eleven players who try to kick a round ball into the other team's goal

> This meaning of **football** is used in British English. In American English, people say **soccer**. **Soccer** is also used in British English, but it is less common.

VERBS

play football *The boys are playing football in the garden.*

watch football *He likes to spend Saturday afternoon watching football.*

football + NOUNS

a football match/game *Do you often go to football matches?*

a football team/club *Which football team do you support?*

a football player/star *As a boy, his ambition was to be a football player.*

a football manager/coach *Football managers shouldn't complain about referees' decisions.*

a football fan (=someone who likes football a lot) *Pat is a keen football fan.*

a football supporter (=someone who likes a particular football team and goes to see them play) *After the game, 55 football supporters were arrested.*

a football hooligan (=someone who behaves in a noisy or violent way when they go to watch a football match) *There were fights between gangs of football hooligans.*

a football pitch (=an area of grass where football is played) *An area of waste ground had been turned into a football pitch.*

a football ground/stadium (=a place where people can watch football being played) *Hundreds of fans were making their way towards the football ground.*

the football season (=the period in a year when football is played) *The new football season is just over a week away.*

> Instead of **football player**, people often say **footballer**.

ADJECTIVES/NOUNS + football

professional football *It was his dream to play professional football one day.*

international football (=played by teams representing their country) *He will retire from international football after the World Cup.*

2 a game played in the US by two teams of eleven players who try to carry or kick an oval ball into the other team's goal

> British people call this sport **American football**.

VERBS

play football *He played football in college.*

watch football *I like watching football on TV.*

football + NOUNS

a football team *The Dallas Cowboys are a great football team.*

a football player/star *Simpson was a former professional football player.*

a football coach *He is the head football coach at UCLA.*

a football fan *The stadium was crowded with 75,000 football fans.*

a football game *I went to a football game at the University of Arizona last week.*

a football field (=an area of grass where football is played) *Brad was a hero on the football field.*

a football stadium (=a place where people can watch football being played) *The football stadium was filled to capacity.*

the football season (=the period in a year when football is played) *We're coming to the end of the football season.*

ADJECTIVES/NOUNS + football

professional football *I always wanted to play professional football.*

college/high school football *It's the best team in college football.*

footpath *n*

a narrow path for people to walk along, especially in the country

ADJECTIVES

a public footpath *A public footpath crosses the field.*

a narrow footpath *There is a narrow footpath up the mountain.*

a muddy footpath *At this time of year the footpaths are all muddy.*

VERBS

follow/take/use a footpath *We followed a winding footpath through the woods.*

keep/stick to the footpath (*also* **stay on the footpath**) *It's important to keep to the footpath, otherwise you'll get lost.*

a footpath leads to sth *The footpath leads to the top of the hill.*

a footpath runs between sth *A footpath runs between the school and Church Street.*

footpath + NOUNS

a footpath sign *Follow the footpath signs to the church.*

PREPOSITIONS

on a footpath *They walked through the woods, staying on the footpaths.*

along a footpath *We walked along a footpath beside the river.*

a footpath across/through sth *She took the footpath across the field.*

forbid *v*

if something is forbidden, it is not allowed

> **Grammar**
> **Forbid** is usually used in the passive.

ADVERBS

sth is strictly forbidden *Smoking is strictly forbidden in the mine.*

sth is absolutely/completely/totally forbidden *It was absolutely forbidden to talk to the other prisoners.*

be expressly/explicitly/specifically forbidden from doing sth (=a particular thing is forbidden) *The jury are expressly forbidden from discussing the case outside the court.*

PREPOSITIONS

sb is forbidden from doing sth *Women are forbidden from going out without a veil.*

PHRASES

it is forbidden to do sth *Under Islamic law, it is forbidden to receive interest from savings accounts.*

sth is forbidden by law *Discrimination is forbidden by law.*

force *n*

1 physical power or violence

ADJECTIVES

physical force *They had to use physical force to get into the building.*

great/considerable force *The rock had been thrown with considerable force.*

brute force (=force rather than intelligence or careful thinking) *He got the box open using sheer brute force.*

the full force of sth *He slammed the full force of his body into the man to stop him.*

excessive force (=too much force) *The police should not use excessive force when arresting suspects.*

reasonable force (=no more than is necessary) *You have the right to defend yourself with reasonable force.*

VERBS

use force *The police used force to overpower the demonstrators.*

resort to force (=use it because every other method has failed) *The government is prepared to resort to force if negotiations fail.*

PREPOSITIONS

by force (=using force) *He had to be thrown out of the house by force.*

the force of sth *The force of the explosion smashed all the windows.*

with great/considerable etc force *He raised his hand and hit her with terrifying force.*

PHRASES

the use of force *On this occasion, the use of force was fully justified.*

2 a group of people, especially soldiers or police officers

> **Grammar**
> You usually say **forces** when talking about a group of soldiers.

ADJECTIVES/NOUNS + force

the armed forces (=the army, navy, and air force of a country) *Representatives from the armed forces attended the ceremony.*

military forces *US military forces will remain for as long as they are needed.*

the police force *I'm thinking of joining the police force.*
government forces (=soldiers fighting for the government) *Fighting between government forces and the rebels continues.*
security forces (=who protect a country against people who are fighting the government) *The security forces destroyed the rebels' headquarters.*
defence force *BrE*, **defense force** *AmE* (=the armed forces of a country or other area) *Should the European Union have its own defence force?*
enemy forces *Enemy forces now occupy large areas of the city.*
rebel forces (=those fighting against the government) *The village was attacked by rebel forces.*
a peacekeeping force *A UN peacekeeping force is being sent to the region.*
special forces (=who are specially trained to fight against guerrilla or terrorist groups) *Bin Laden was killed by US special forces.*

VERBS

join the forces (=become a soldier, sailor etc) *He was too young to join the forces.*
serve in the forces (=be a soldier, sailor etc) *Both my brothers served in the forces.*
withdraw your forces (=take them out of a place) *The US began withdrawing its forces from the country.*

PREPOSITIONS

in the forces (=in the army, navy, or air force) *Her husband is in the forces.*

forecast *n*

a description of what is likely to happen

ADJECTIVES

an economic forecast *The Bank of England has revised its economic forecast.*
an accurate/reliable forecast *Long-range weather forecasts are often not very reliable.*
a pessimistic/gloomy forecast (=expecting bad things to happen) *Scientists have produced a gloomy forecast on the effects of global warming.*
an optimistic/upbeat forecast (=expecting good things to happen) *In his speech, the president gave an optimistic forecast for the economy.*
a long-term/long-range forecast (=for a long time from now) *In their long-term forecast, they projected that sugar imports would double in the coming year.*
a short-term/short-range forecast (=for a short time from now) *The short-term forecast looks good.*

NOUNS + forecast

the weather forecast *The weather forecast for the weekend is fine and dry.*
the shipping forecast (=about weather conditions at sea) *According to the shipping forecast, strong winds can be expected later today.*
a sales/profit forecast *The company has cut its profit forecast to £57 million.*

VERBS

make a forecast *It is too early to make a forecast on what will happen.*
give/provide a forecast *Economists gave an upbeat forecast for the world economy.*
revise a forecast (=change it because of new information) *The company has revised its sales forecast.*

PREPOSITIONS

a forecast for sth *The forecast for the weekend is not very good.*
a forecast of sth *Forecasts of future prices were of little use.*

PHRASES

sth is in line with forecasts (=it is the same as predicted) *The rise in inflation has been roughly in line with forecasts.*

foreign *adj*

from or relating to another country

NOUNS

a foreign language *How many foreign languages can you speak?*
a foreign country *It takes a long time to get used to living in a foreign country.*
a foreign student/worker/visitor *She teaches English to foreign students.*
a foreign national *formal* (=a person who was born in a foreign country, or who is living in or visiting another country) *Foreign nationals need to have a permit in order to work.*
a foreign company/bank etc *US car-makers face tough competition from foreign companies.*
foreign currency/exchange *formal* (=money from other countries) *Customers can buy foreign exchange at most banks.*
foreign investment *The government wants to attract foreign investment.*
foreign aid *The government relies heavily on foreign aid.*
foreign affairs (=things that happen in other countries) *Most people aren't very interested in foreign affairs.*
foreign policy *US foreign policy toward the region has changed.*
the foreign ministry (*also* **the foreign office** *BrE*) (=the government department that deals with matters involving other countries) *I applied to work at the Foreign Office because I wanted a career abroad.*
the foreign minister (*also* **the foreign secretary** *BrE*): *The Japanese foreign minister is visiting the UK.*

F

a foreign correspondent (=a journalist who lives in a foreign country and reports on it) *He works as a foreign correspondent in China.*

THESAURUS: foreign

overseas *especially BrE*
market | trade | investment | aid | company | student | visitor | player | trip
from or connected with a foreign country, especially one that is a long distance away: *The company has increased its sales to overseas markets. | Much of the land is owned by overseas companies. | The university welcomes applications from overseas students. | This is his first overseas trip.*

Grammar
The adjective **overseas** is always used before a noun.
Overseas is also used as an adverb: *Her parents lived* ***overseas****.*

alien *formal*
culture | species | country | land
from or relating to another country, race, or society, especially one that seems strange: *He had difficulty adapting to an alien culture when he was living in Australia. | The introduction of an alien species has often proved ecologically disastrous. | My parents were worried about me moving to an alien country.*

In everyday English, you can also use the phrase **from abroad** when talking about someone or something from another country, for example: ***Visitors from abroad*** *have become the island's main source of income. | The flow of* ***money from abroad*** *to Thailand has increased. | Companies face increased* ***competition from abroad****.*

forest *n*

a large area of land covered with trees

ADJECTIVES

thick/dense forest (=with trees growing close together) *The island was once covered in thick forest.*

a tropical forest *Many areas of tropical forest have been cleared.*

virgin forest (=forest that has not been used or changed by people) *Canada has huge areas of virgin forest.*

a primeval forest (=forest which has existed since ancient times) *One of Europe's last areas of primeval forest is threatened with destruction.*

NOUNS + forest

a pine/oak etc forest *A narrow path led through the pine forest.*

Rainforest is usually written as one word.

VERBS

cut down/clear a forest *The forest was cut down to make way for housing.*

plant a forest (=plant new trees to create a forest) *Large areas of forest have been planted.*

be covered in forest *The mountain slopes were covered in forest.*

forest + NOUNS

a forest fire *A forest fire destroyed thousands of trees.*

the forest canopy (=the area at the top of the trees) *He could see the sky through the gaps in the forest canopy.*

PREPOSITIONS

in a forest *Many types of animals live in the forest.*

PHRASES

in the depths of a forest (=deep inside it) *In the depths of the forest there is a beautiful waterfall.*

forget *v*

to not remember facts, information, people, or things from the past

ADVERBS

completely/totally forget *I'm so sorry I'm late – I completely forgot that we'd changed the time of the meeting.*

never forget *He never forgets my birthday.*

almost/nearly forget *I almost forgot my keys, but remembered them just as I was leaving.*

conveniently forget (=in a way that is probably deliberate, because it gives a good result for you) *She conveniently forgot to mention all the help she had had from her family.*

sth is largely forgotten (=most people do not know about it now) *His poetry is now largely forgotten.*

PREPOSITIONS

forget (all) about sb/sth *Sorry I didn't come to the meeting! I forgot all about it!*

PHRASES

can't/couldn't forget *We can't forget what happened that terrible day.*

keep forgetting *I keep forgetting to ask him about the money.*

sth is easy/hard to forget *It is easy to forget that she is not English.*

sb never forgets a face (=someone is good at remembering people who they have met) *I recognized you at once – I never forget a face.*

ANTONYMS **forget → remember**

forgive *v*

to stop being angry with someone and stop blaming them, although they have done something wrong

VERBS

can/can't forgive sb *I can't forgive her for what she did.*

ask/beg sb to forgive you *The man begged my mother to forgive him for what he had done.*

PREPOSITIONS

forgive sb for sth *She never forgave him for what he said.*

PHRASES

be hard/difficult/impossible to forgive *I found it hard to forgive him for lying to me.*

be prepared/ready/willing to forgive *She was willing to forgive his mistake.*

forgive and forget (=forgive someone and no longer think about it, so that you no longer feel angry) *He didn't seem the type of man who could forgive and forget easily.*

forgiveness *n*

when someone forgives another person

VERBS

ask for (sb's) forgiveness (*also* **ask (sb's) forgiveness**) *He admitted that he had been rude, and asked for her forgiveness.*

beg (for) forgiveness *She apologized and begged him for forgiveness.*

pray for forgiveness *I prayed for forgiveness for the things I had done.*

seek forgiveness (=look for it) *He sought forgiveness from his wife.*

show (sb) forgiveness *She showed him forgiveness and support.*

PREPOSITIONS

forgiveness for sth *He begged forgiveness for the mistakes he had made.*

form[1] *n*

1 a particular type of something that exists in many different varieties

ADJECTIVES

a common form of sth *Breast cancer is the most common form of cancer among women.*

a simple/basic/primitive form of sth *Flags were used as a simple form of communication.*

a new form of sth *He created a new form of music.*

a different form of sth *There are many different forms of government.*

various forms of sth *The painter uses various forms of technique.*

an early form of sth *Pascal invented a calculating machine that was an early form of computer.*

sth's final form of sth *The report is not yet in its final form.*

a traditional form of sth *Bowing is the traditional form of greeting in Japan.*

the standard form of sth *'BBC English' is often regarded as the standard form of the language in the UK.*

a mild/severe form of sth *She suffers from a mild form of the illness.*

NOUNS + form

an art form *Music is an art form that has existed since the beginning of time.*

a life form (=a type of living thing) *Do you think we will find life forms on other planets?*

PREPOSITIONS

a form of sth *Poetry is a form of expression.*

in the form of sth *Peace is represented in the form of a dove.*

PHRASES

take the form of sth (=used when saying what something is like) *The examination took the form of an interview.*

in solid/liquid/tablet etc form *The medicine is available in tablet form.*

in any form/in all its forms *He opposed the use of violence in all its forms.*

in some form (or other) *We all need help in some form or other.*

in its original form *In its original form, the building only had three rooms.*

in its present/current form *The organization cannot continue in its present form.*

2 an official document with spaces where you write information

VERBS

fill out a form (*also* **fill in a form** BrE): *If you want to become a member, you need to fill out a form.*

complete a form *formal*: *Please complete the form below and we will respond to your request as soon as possible.*

sign a form *The person who signs the form should be 18 or over.*

send in/off a form *I sent in my application form last week.*

return a form *formal* (=send it back) *You should return the form to the above address.*

NOUNS + form

an application form *Please complete this application form in block capitals.*

a tax form *The tax form must be submitted before the end of the month.*

an order form *Send your completed order form together with your payment to the address below.*

a booking form (=a form you use to reserve something) *Have you filled out a hotel booking form?*

a registration form *On arrival at the hotel, the guest must complete a registration form.*

an online form (=on the internet) *It's easier to fill out an online form.*

an entry form (=to take part in something) *If you wish to take part in the competition, please fill out an entry form.*

form² *v*

1 to establish something

NOUNS

form a company/organization/society/party etc *The World Trade Organization was formed in 1995.*

form a government *The party has enough votes to form a government.*

form an alliance/partnership *The two countries formed an alliance.*

form a relationship/friendship *The two men formed a close relationship.*

form a band/group *He formed his first band at the age of 14 with three friends from high school.*

> **THESAURUS: form**
>
> open, establish, found, set up, form → **start¹ (3)**

2 to make something start to exist

> **THESAURUS: form**
>
> create, do, produce, manufacture, mass-produce, develop, form, generate → **make (1)**

3 to make a shape or line

NOUNS

form a circle/square etc *The teacher asked the children to form a circle.*

form a line/queue *The visitors had formed a queue outside the museum.*

formal *adj*

1 formal language or behaviour is used with people who you do not know well, or at important official occasions

NOUNS

formal language *It's best to use formal language when you're writing an essay.*

a formal word *'Acquire' is a formal word for 'get'.*

formal behaviour *BrE*, **formal behavior** *AmE*: *His mother's behaviour towards the children was rather formal.*

a formal manner *"Am I speaking to Miss Price?" he asked in a very formal manner.*

VERBS

seem/sound formal *Her voice sounded very formal on the phone.*

ANTONYMS **formal → informal**

2 made or done officially or publicly

NOUNS

a formal announcement/statement *The chairman will make a formal announcement about the company's future.*

a formal request/invitation *You have to make a formal request to see the documents.*

a formal complaint *She intends to make a formal complaint against the police.*

a formal agreement *The two companies have signed a formal agreement to merge with each other.*

a formal system/procedure *There is a formal procedure for dealing with complaints.*

a formal meeting *The committee held a formal meeting to discuss the issue.*

a formal occasion/event *He only wears his suit at formal occasions such as weddings and funerals.*

a formal investigation/inquiry *The authorities have launched a formal investigation into the accident.*

formal approval *Parliament gave its formal approval to the bill.*

formal education/training/qualifications (=in a school or college) *His father had no formal education after the age of 14.*

ANTONYMS **formal → informal**

format Ac *n*

the way in which something is arranged, organized, or presented

ADJECTIVES

a new format *The magazine hopes to attract younger readers with its new format.*

a different format *The movie is available in several different formats.*

digital/electronic format *The pictures are sent in digital format.*

a standard/common format *They usually use a standard format for writing business letters.*

the usual/traditional format *The meeting will follow the traditional format, with a speech by the chairman at the end.*

a large/small format *The book was published in a large format with pictures for children.*

a similar format *The August event will follow a similar format to the spring event.*

VERBS

change the format *The TV company has changed the format of the show.*

use a format *This time we're using a slightly different format.*

follow a format *When you're writing an essay, it's best to follow the usual format.*

adopt a format (=start using a format) *The two companies have agreed to adopt a common format for their products.*

PREPOSITIONS

the format for sth *The format for the event is the same as last year.*

in a ... format *The paper is available in a larger format.*

F

formula Ac *n*

1 a series of numbers or letters that represent a mathematical or scientific rule

ADJECTIVES

a chemical formula *CO_2 is the chemical formula for carbon dioxide.*

a mathematical formula *Richter used a mathematical formula to calculate the size of the earthquake.*

a complex/complicated formula *Insurance companies use a complex formula to calculate risk.*

a standard formula *There is a standard formula for doing this type of calculation.*

VERBS

devise/work out/come up with a formula (=think of a formula) *He worked out a formula for measuring the distance around the earth.*

PREPOSITIONS

the formula for sth *The chemical formula for water is H_2O.*

2 a method that you can use in order to do something successfully

ADJECTIVES

a magic formula (=a method that is certain to be successful) *There is no magic formula for success.*

a winning/successful formula *The company's winning formula includes excellent service and quality products.*

the same formula *Both books use the same basic formula.*

the right formula *After years of trying to win the championship, he finally found the right formula.*

a simple formula *The authorities found a simple formula to deal with the problem.*

VERBS

use/follow a formula *Many Hollywood films follow the same successful formula.*

search for a formula *The team has been searching for a winning formula, but so far without success.*

find/discover a formula *He discovered the formula for getting votes easily and winning elections.*

PREPOSITIONS

a formula for sth *She found the formula for the perfect crime novel.*

fortune *n*

1 a very large amount of money

> This meaning of **fortune** is used in two ways. You use it when talking about the amount of money someone has, or gets from their work: *She will inherit her father's* ***fortune****.* | *He made his* ***fortune*** *in the oil industry.*
>
> You also use it in informal English, when saying that something costs a lot of money, or someone spends or earns a lot of money: *The ring must have cost a* ***fortune****.* | *Lawyers earn a* ***fortune****.*

ADJECTIVES

a large/substantial/considerable fortune *She made a considerable fortune as an author.*

a huge/vast/immense fortune *When he died, his vast fortune went to his daughter.*

an absolute fortune *informal* (=used when you want to emphasize how much something costs, someone earns etc) *The ring must have cost an absolute fortune.*

a small fortune *informal* (=a surprisingly large amount of money) *My first painting sold for £25, which was a small fortune for an art student.*

sb's personal/private fortune (=how much money someone has - used about someone who had a lot of money) *Her personal fortune was estimated at £37 million.*

VERBS

cost a fortune *informal* (=be very expensive) *It'll cost a fortune if we go by taxi.*

make a fortune *informal* (=get a lot of money) *He sold the business and made a fortune.*

make your fortune (=become rich) *She made her fortune in the fashion industry.*

earn a fortune *informal* (=get a lot of money from your job) *Some bankers earn a fortune.*

amass a fortune *formal* (=gradually get a lot of money) *His family amassed a fortune during that period.*

lose a fortune *informal*: *Her father lost a fortune on the stock market.*

spend a fortune *You don't have to spend a fortune to have a good holiday.*

pay a fortune *informal*: *We had to pay a fortune in rent.*

save a fortune *informal*: *You can save a fortune by buying online.*

leave sb a fortune (=arrange for someone to receive a lot of money after you die) *The old man left his wife a fortune.*

PHRASES

be worth a fortune *informal*: *The painting is worth a fortune.*

fame and fortune (=a situation in which someone is rich and famous) *He came to London to seek fame and fortune.*

be heir to a fortune (=be the person who will get a lot of money from someone after they die) *Joseph was heir to a vast fortune.*

2 luck

ADJECTIVES

good fortune *His success was mainly due to good fortune.*

bad fortune (*also* **ill fortune** *formal*): *No-one deserves such ill fortune.*

VERBS

bring (sb) fortune *In Britain, it is believed that if a black cat crosses your path, it will bring good fortune.*

fortune smiles on sb *literary* (=they are lucky) *Fortune smiled on me that night, and I escaped unharmed.*

PHRASES

have the good fortune to do sth *I did not have the good fortune to know your father.*

a change of fortune (*also* **a reversal of fortune** *formal*) (=from good to bad luck, or bad to good) *Some internet firms have suffered a painful reversal of fortune.*

a piece/stroke of good fortune *It really was an extraordinary piece of good fortune.*

3 your fortunes are the good or bad things that happen to you

> **Grammar**
> Always plural in this meaning.

ADJECTIVES

changing fortunes *The book is the story of a family's changing fortunes over the years.*

flagging/declining fortunes (=something is becoming less successful) *The new leader claims he can revive the party's flagging fortunes.*

mixed fortunes (=some good things and some bad) *It has been a week of mixed fortunes for the British team.*

economic fortunes *The economic fortunes of companies can change.*

political fortunes *There has been a revival in the political fortunes of the Liberal Party.*

VERBS

sb's fortunes change *Then, a year later, his fortunes changed and he was offered a job at the United Nations.*

improve sb's fortunes *They moved to New York in the hope of improving their fortunes.*

restore/revive sb's fortunes (=make them successful again) *He was working in a bank, desperately trying to restore the family fortunes.*

reverse sb's fortunes (=change them from good to bad, or bad to good) *Those companies need government help to reverse their fortunes.*

follow the fortunes of sb (=pay attention to how successful they are) *Since then I have always followed the fortunes of Manchester United.*

PHRASES

a change in sb's fortunes *The defeat marked a change in the team's fortunes.*

a revival in sth's fortunes (=it starts being successful again) *A decision to change the product's name brought an instant revival in its fortunes.*

the fortunes of war (=the things that can happen during a war) *The position of the frontier changed with the fortunes of war.*

found *v* THESAURUS ▶ start[1] (3)

foundation Ac *n*

1 something from which another thing can develop and become successful

ADJECTIVES

a strong/solid/firm/sound foundation *His research provided a strong foundation for the work of other scientists.*

a good foundation *The course is designed to give students a good foundation for a career in design.*

shaky/weak foundations *The country's economic recovery rests on shaky foundations.*

a scientific foundation *There is no scientific foundation for their claims.*

a theoretical foundation *This book presents the theoretical foundations of modern psychology.*

the economic foundations *The crisis rocked the economic foundations of the country.*

VERBS

lay the foundations for sth *His training at drama school laid the foundations for his acting career.*

provide a foundation for sth *Investment in new technology provides a foundation for the future growth of the company.*

build the foundations for sth *By doing these exercises, you will be building the foundations for your future health and fitness.*

shake/rock the foundations of sth *Freud's writings shook the foundations of psychology.*

PREPOSITIONS

a foundation for sth *The previous manager laid a sound foundation for the firm's future.*

2 the solid layer of cement, bricks, stones etc that is put under a building to support it

> **Grammar**
> Usually plural in this meaning.

ADJECTIVES/NOUNS + foundation

deep foundations *Tall buildings need to have deep foundations.*

stone/concrete foundations *You can still see the stone foundations of the temple.*

VERBS

lay the foundations *The foundations of the building were laid in the first week of May.*

build the foundations *We have already built the foundations and walls for four new classrooms.*

dig the foundations *Workmen damaged an underground pipe while digging the foundations of the new hotel.*

F

foundation + NOUNS

the foundation stone *The foundation stone was laid in 1829.*

foundry *n* THESAURUS **factory**

fracture *v* THESAURUS **break[1] (1)**

fragile *adj*

easily broken or damaged – used about physical objects, and also about abstract things

NOUNS

glass is fragile *The glass is extremely fragile.*

fragile bones *Her bones were old and fragile.*

a fragile relationship *He didn't want to create distrust in an already fragile relationship.*

a fragile state *Her health was in a fragile state.*

a fragile ecosystem/habitat *The oil could damage the island's fragile ecosystem.*

a fragile economy *The fragile economy cannot keep up with population growth.*

a fragile democracy *The country's fragile democracy is under threat.*

a fragile peace/truce/ceasefire *A fragile peace has been in place since the war ended.*

fragile health *She wasn't able to travel because of her fragile health.*

F

THESAURUS: fragile

delicate
cup | flower | necklace | fabric | skin
easily damaged – used especially about things that are made from thin material and look attractive:
The tea was served in delicate little china cups. | The plant has delicate yellow flowers. | People with delicate skin should not go out in strong sunlight.

Delicate is also used about hands or features that are small or thin and look pretty: *The dancers had* ***delicate features****.* It is also used about people who are weak and in poor health: *He was a* ***delicate child*** *and was often ill.*

brittle
bones | nails | hair | material
if something is brittle, it has a hard surface that breaks easily:
An unhealthy diet can lead to the development of brittle bones. | The shampoo is good for brittle hair. | Glass is a brittle material.

breakable
object | ornament
breakable objects must be handled carefully because they will break easily:
Breakable objects should be carefully wrapped in newspaper. | It's best to keep breakable ornaments away from animals and children.

flimsy
shirt | dress | material | wall | furniture | structure
made of thin or light material which is easily damaged or badly made:
His flimsy cotton shirt did not give him much protection from the cold. | The hotel walls were so flimsy that you could hear everything in the next room. | The hut was a flimsy structure that looked like it would collapse at any moment.

fragment *n* THESAURUS **piece**

fragrance *n* THESAURUS **smell[1]**

frail *adj* THESAURUS **weak (1)**

framework [Ac] *n*

a set of ideas, rules, or beliefs from which something is developed, or on which decisions and actions are based

ADJECTIVES

a basic framework *This course provides a basic framework for understanding the issues involved.*

a general/broad framework *The meeting established a broad framework for the negotiations.*

a legal/political/social framework *Services must operate within the current legal framework.*

a conceptual/theoretical framework (=a set of ideas that are used as a basis for understanding or doing something) *Scientists are trying to develop a single theoretical framework which explains everything that happens in the universe.*

VERBS

provide/offer a framework *The previous research programme provides a framework for further studies.*

create/build/develop/establish a framework *The aim is to create a framework for discussion.*

introduce/implement a framework *The government has introduced a new framework for inspecting schools.*

use a framework *We use the same framework for all our research.*

PREPOSITIONS

a framework for sth *The data will be used to develop a framework for future policies.*

frank *adj* THESAURUS **honest**

freak *adj* THESAURUS **unusual**

free *adj*

1 something that is free does not cost you any money

ADVERBS

completely/absolutely free *The design service is absolutely free.*

VERBS

be free *There's a concert in the park, and it's free.*

come free (=be given free when you get or buy something else) *Drinks come free with your meals.*

NOUNS

a free copy *Call us for a free copy of our brochure.*

a free ticket *I was given two free tickets for the concert.*

a free gift *There's a special free gift with this month's magazine.*

free parking *The hotel offers free parking.*

free admission/entry *There is free admission to the gardens for all members.*

free delivery *There is free delivery on all orders over £50.*

free software *You can download free software from this site.*

a free service *We offer a free legal advice service.*

free advice *The police will give you free advice on preventing crime.*

2 not kept as a prisoner

VERBS

set sb/sth free *Stolen cattle were returned to their owners or set free.*

break/struggle/pull free *After a struggle she managed to break free.*

roam/run free (=move around freely - used especially about animals) *Outside, ducks and chickens roam free.*

walk free (=not be sent to prison) *The charges were dropped and he walked free from court.*

remain free *Lozano was allowed to remain free while appealing against his conviction.*

3 not being used

THESAURUS: free

free, vacant → **available**

bare, blank, hollow, free, vacant, deserted, uninhabited, unoccupied → **empty**

freedom *n*

the right to do what you want without being controlled or restricted

ADJECTIVES

total/complete freedom *Riding a motorbike gives me a feeling of total freedom.*

great/considerable freedom *Teachers are given considerable freedom to choose their teaching methods.*

personal/individual freedom *Our personal freedom is being restricted more and more.*

new-found/new freedom (=which someone has been given only recently) *She loved the new-found freedom her car provided.*

a basic/fundamental freedom (=which everyone deserves to have) *Our economy should give all people the fundamental freedom to work.*

political/religious freedom *The people were given political freedom for the first time in the country's history.*

academic freedom (=for people studying at university or doing research) *She wants to teach at a university that provides complete academic freedom.*

artistic freedom *Banning the film would be an unacceptable restriction on artistic freedom.*

VERBS

have freedom *If you had your own apartment you would have more freedom.*

enjoy freedom (=have it - more formal) *Filmmakers today enjoy more freedom than in the past.*

give sb freedom *Our flexible programme gives you the freedom to study when and where you like.*

defend/protect freedom *People have fought wars to defend the freedom that we enjoy.*

value your freedom *I didn't want to get married because I valued my freedom.*

limit/restrict/curb sb's freedom *The new laws would limit our freedom of speech.*

PHRASES

the struggle/fight for freedom *The student movement played an important role in the struggle for political freedom.*

freedom of speech/expression (=the legal right to say what you want) *We will defend freedom of speech and oppose censorship.*

freedom of choice *If more companies come into the market, that gives customers greater freedom of choice.*

the freedom of the press *The freedom of the press is guaranteed by the constitution.*

freedom of movement (=the right or ability to travel, or the ability to move your body freely) *The tight uniforms restrict their freedom of movement.*

freedom of religion/worship *Freedom of religion is threatened in many countries.*

freeway *n AmE*

a very wide road in the US, built for fast travel

ADJECTIVES

a major freeway *The motel is near a major freeway.*

a crowded/congested freeway *Interstate 15 is the most congested freeway in the county.*

VERBS

come off/get off/exit a freeway *He got off the freeway and called police.*

get on a freeway *We need to get on the freeway.*

PREPOSITIONS

on a freeway *There was an accident on the freeway.*

NOUNS

a freeway system *Los Angeles has an increasingly crowded freeway system.*

freeway traffic *We were stuck in freeway traffic.*

freeze *v*

if a liquid or something wet freezes or you freeze it, it becomes solid because it is very cold

ADVERBS

freeze solid *The water had frozen solid in the pipes.*

freeze over (=freeze across its entire surface) *It was so cold that the lake froze over.*

fresh *adj*

1 prepared or picked recently

NOUNS

fresh fruit/vegetables/milk/fish/eggs etc *You should eat two or three pieces of fresh fruit every day.*

fresh bread *Let's eat the bread today, while it's fresh.*

fresh produce (=food grown on a farm) *The market sells fresh produce.*

fresh ingredients (=fresh things used to make a meal) *Italian cooking is based on simple fresh ingredients.*

VERBS

keep sth fresh *Store apples in the bottom of the fridge to keep them fresh.*

stay fresh *Milk does not stay fresh for long in the heat.*

2 new and interesting

NOUNS

fresh ideas *We need some fresh ideas.*

a fresh perspective/insight (=a new way of thinking about something) *Reading this book gave me a fresh perspective on the subject.*

a fresh approach *The new director has brought a fresh approach to the job.*

fresh talent (=new people with skills) *The company needs to attract fresh talent.*

PHRASES

take a fresh look at sth *You need to take a fresh look at your wardrobe, and throw out things you never wear.*

THESAURUS: fresh

recent, latest, original, fresh, novel, innovative, revolutionary, new-fangled → **new (1)**

friend *n*

someone who you know and like, and enjoy spending time with

ADJECTIVES/NOUNS + friend

a good/close/great friend (=one of the friends you like the most) *The owner of the restaurant is a good friend of mine.*

your best friend (=the friend you like the most) *She asked her best friend to help her.*

an old friend (=someone who has been your friend for a long time) *We are staying with some old friends.*

a dear friend (=a friend who is very important to you) *I'd like you to meet a dear friend of mine.*

a lifelong friend (=all your life) *The two men met during the war and became lifelong friends.*

a childhood friend (=someone who was your friend when you were a child) *I had lost touch with all my childhood friends.*

a school/college/university friend *I met some old school friends for lunch.*

a family friend *He's visiting family friends.*

a personal friend *Mr Hutton is a close personal friend of my father.*

a mutual friend (=someone who is a friend of both you and someone else) *They went to a mutual friend's home for dinner.*

firm friends (=friends who like each other a lot and want to stay friends for a long time) *They have remained firm friends for over 20 years.*

a true friend *A true friend will always tell you the truth.*

a loyal friend *She has always been a loyal friend to me.*

a trusted friend *She told only a few trusted friends.*

VERBS

have a friend *Suzie is a popular student who has lots of friends.*

become friends *Liz and Vanessa soon became friends.*

make friends (=make someone your friend) *He found it hard to make friends.*

remain/stay friends *We have remained friends despite some difficult times.*

PHRASES

a friend of mine/yours/Bill's etc *A friend of mine is going to Tokyo next week.*

a friend of a friend *I managed to get tickets from a friend of a friend.*

sb's circle of friends (=all the friends someone has) *She has a wide circle of friends.*

friendly *adj*

behaving in a pleasant and helpful way towards someone, or making someone feel comfortable and relaxed

ADVERBS

genuinely friendly *The staff seem genuinely friendly.*

F

overly friendly (=too friendly, usually because someone wants something from you) *Beware of overly friendly strangers offering to help with your bags.*

NOUNS

a friendly smile *She greeted us with a friendly smile.*

a friendly voice *Talk to the dog in a calm friendly voice.*

a friendly atmosphere *The café has a friendly atmosphere.*

a friendly welcome *We received a friendly welcome when we arrived.*

friendly service *The service at the restaurant is always friendly.*

a friendly chat *They were enjoying a drink and a friendly chat.*

a friendly manner *I liked Ben's open friendly manner.*

a friendly place/city/hotel etc (=a place where the people are friendly) *This is a friendly family-run hotel.*

PREPOSITIONS

friendly to/towards sb *The other students were very friendly to me.*

THESAURUS: friendly

nice *especially spoken*
guy | man | woman | girl | person
friendly and kind:
You'll like him – he's a nice guy. | A nice man helped me put my bike on the train.

warm
welcome | reception | hospitality | smile | personality
friendly and caring about other people, in a way that makes them feel comfortable when they are with you:
We received a warm welcome from the staff at the hotel. | She thanked them for their warm hospitality. | My aunt had a wonderfully warm personality.

welcoming
smile | atmosphere
friendly to someone who has just arrived somewhere:
He greeted me with a welcoming smile. | The hotel has a warm and welcoming atmosphere.

hospitable
person | people | country | welcome
friendly and wanting to make visitors feel comfortable:
The Japanese are a very hospitable people. | Thank you for your kind and hospitable welcome. | They are always very ***hospitable to*** *strangers.*

amiable
man | mood | nature
friendly and easy to like:
He was an amiable man who was well liked by his students. | Flynn was in an amiable mood and offered to buy us all a drink.

genial
smile | host
behaving in a cheerful and friendly way:
He answered her question with a genial smile. | "Glad you could come," said our genial host.

cordial
relations | relationship | ties | atmosphere | welcome | reception | meeting | invitation | greetings
friendly and polite but formal:
The two nations have always maintained cordial relations. | The meeting was held in a cordial atmosphere. | He received a cordial invitation to dine at the White House.

approachable
easy to talk to – used especially about people who are important or famous:
Even though she is an international star, she is still very approachable.

ANTONYMS **friendly → unfriendly**

friendship *n*

a relationship between friends

ADJECTIVES

a close friendship *Ron had formed a close friendship with Andrea.*

a firm friendship *Our working relationship developed into a firm friendship.*

a lasting friendship *This began a lasting friendship between the two women.*

a long-standing friendship (=that has existed for a long time) *There is a long-standing friendship between our two countries.*

a lifelong friendship *The two men formed a lifelong friendship.*

an unlikely friendship *Many people were surprised by this unlikely friendship between a teenager and an elderly man.*

true/real friendship *There is respect and real friendship between the two leaders.*

VERBS

start/form/strike up a friendship *He and Matthew struck up a friendship.*

renew a friendship (=become friends again) *They renewed their friendship after the war.*

destroy/spoil a friendship *An argument about a boy destroyed their friendship forever.*

strengthen a friendship *Having disagreements and talking about them can strengthen a friendship.*

lose sb's friendship *I don't want to lose your friendship.*

value sb's friendship *If she really valued your friendship she wouldn't behave this way.*

a friendship develops *Friendships often develop on the basis of shared interests.*

PREPOSITIONS

a friendship with sb *Her parents disapproved of her friendship with John.*

a friendship between sb and sb *The friendship between Jane and Sarah was as strong as ever.*

PHRASES

the start/end of a friendship *We met at work and that was the start of a long friendship.*

a gesture of friendship (=an action which shows that someone is a friend) *He invited us to his house as a gesture of friendship.*

bonds/ties of friendship (=things that connect friends) *They were united by deep bonds of friendship.*

frighten *v* to make someone feel afraid

PHRASES

(almost) frighten sb to death *informal* (=make someone very frightened) *You almost frightened me to death!*

frighten the life out of sb *informal* (=make someone very frightened) *When I felt his hand on my neck, it frightened the life out of me.*

frightened *adj*

worried that you might be hurt, or that something bad might happen

VERBS

be/feel frightened *Don't be frightened. We're not going to hurt you.*

look/sound frightened *"What are those men doing here?" Garry sounded frightened.*

get frightened (=start to feel frightened) *He used to get frightened when the boys from the village asked him to play with them.*

make sb frightened *The big waves are making me frightened.*

PREPOSITIONS

frightened of sth *Many animals are frightened of fireworks.*

frightened about sth *There's nothing to be frightened about. It'll be all right.*

frightened at sth *She was frightened at the thought of going back there again.*

PHRASES

frightened to death/frightened out of your wits *informal* (=extremely frightened) *I was frightened to death that I was going to make a mistake.*

like a frightened rabbit/animal *The young woman just stared at me like a frightened rabbit.*

Frightened, scared, or afraid?
Scared is a little more informal than **frightened**, and is very common in spoken English. In written English, **frightened** is more commonly used. **Afraid** is more formal than **frightened** and often sounds more serious.

frightening *adj* making you feel afraid

NOUNS

a frightening experience *Going skiing for the first time can be a frightening experience.*

a frightening place *The forest is a frightening place at night.*

a frightening moment *It was the most frightening moment of my life.*

a frightening film/book/story *There are some frightening stories about people getting lost in the mountains.*

a frightening thought/prospect (=something frightening that you imagine happening) *They faced the frightening prospect of having no money.*

ADVERBS

extremely/truly/genuinely frightening *The whole building was shaking – it was truly frightening.*

PHRASES

find sb/sth frightening *I found him a little frightening at first.*

it is frightening to think/imagine... *It's frightening to think what could happen if terrorists got hold of nuclear materials.*

THESAURUS: frightening

scary *especially spoken*
movie | **film** | **story** | **experience** | **moment** | **place** | **monster** | **feeling** | **thought**
frightening. **Scary** is more informal than **frightening** and is very common in spoken English:
I don't like watching scary movies. | The subway can be a scary place. | Maybe they're watching us right now – it's a scary thought.

spooky *informal*
atmosphere | **house** | **place** | **story** | **tale** | **feeling** | **coincidence**
frightening and strange, especially because something involves ghosts or powers that people do not understand:
The dark shadows created a spooky atmosphere. | They live in a spooky old house in the country. | By some spooky coincidence, they had been born in the same hospital at the same time.

creepy *informal*
feeling | **place** | **house** | **guy** | **film**
frightening because you think there is something strange and unpleasant about someone or something, especially when you are not exactly sure what it is:
Do you know that creepy feeling when you think that someone's watching you? | With the wind whistling through the trees and the cries of the owls, Park House could be a creepy place for a child. | There was ***something creepy about*** *him.*

eerie *especially literary*
silence | stillness | feeling | sensation | sound | effect | light | glow | coincidence
strange and frightening:
An eerie silence descended on the house after the soldiers had gone. | She began to get an eerie feeling that something terrible was about to happen.

chilling
tale | account | story | thought | reminder | moment | words | message | facts | discovery | performance
frightening, especially because violence, cruelty, or danger is involved:
The book is a chilling tale of murder and revenge. | The camps are a chilling reminder of the country's past (=they make you remember something terrible that happened).

intimidating
place | experience | atmosphere | presence | man | woman
making you feel frightened or nervous - used when something makes you lack confidence, or when you feel someone wants to hurt you:
Big schools can be intimidating places for young children. | The city remains calm, in spite of the intimidating presence of large numbers of soldiers.

menacing
way | manner | look | presence | tone
behaving in a frightening way - used when someone looks like they are about to hurt you:
The bull started to move towards her in a rather menacing manner. | The boy had a menacing look on his face.

alarming
rate | increase | rise | decline | number | proportions
very worrying and frightening:
Violent crime is increasing at an alarming rate. | He noticed an alarming rise in the numbers of children with the disease.

daunting
task | challenge | experience | prospect | thought
if something is daunting, you are worried because you think it may be too difficult:
Dealing with climate change is an incredibly daunting task. | Your first solo show can be a very daunting experience.

very frightening

terrifying
experience | ordeal | moment | prospect | thought | situation
extremely frightening:
Crossing the ocean alone must have been a ***truly terrifying*** *experience. | For one terrifying moment, he thought he was going to be killed.*

hair-raising
adventure | story | ride | experience | encounter
very frightening and involving danger, in a way that is exciting:
The film tells the story of his hair-raising adventures in the jungles of South America. | They went on a hair-raising ride through the mountains.

spine-chilling
story | tale | novel | movie | film | music | moment | experience
a spine-chilling story, film etc is very frightening, because very violent and cruel things happen:
The book is a spine-chilling tale of obsession and murder. | He wrote the spine-chilling music for Hitchcock's film 'Psycho'.

blood-curdling *especially literary*
scream | howl | sound
a blood-curdling sound is very frightening:
I heard a blood-curdling scream in the middle of the night.

front[1] *n*

the part of something that is furthest forward

VERBS

face the front *Turn around and face the front.*
reach/get to the front *There was a long queue and we waited an hour to get to the front.*

PREPOSITIONS

the front of sth *The front of the house is painted white.*
on the front *It's a thick book with a picture of a soldier on the front.*
on your front (=on the front part of your body) *She was lying on her front on the bed.*
at the front *The photographer asked the smallest kids to stand at the front.*
in the front *Adam was sitting in the front, next to the driver.*
down the front (=across the front surface of something such as a shirt) *His sweater had ice cream all down the front.*
in front (=directly ahead) *Don't get too close to the car in front.*
in front of sb (=directly ahead of someone) *I can't see if you stand in front of me.*

At, on, or in the front?
At the front is used to talk about a forward position in a group, the front part of a building or place, or the beginning part of a book: *There's a small garden* ***at the front of*** *the house. | The contents list is* ***at the front***.
On the front is used to talk about the front surface or cover of something, such as a book: *The magazine has a famous actor's face* ***on the front***.

> **In the front** is used to talk about the forward part inside something, especially a vehicle: *She let me sit* ***in the front****.*

ANTONYMS **front → back[1] (2)**

front[2] *adj*

at, on, or in the front of something

NOUNS

the front page/cover *The story is on the front pages of all the newspapers.*
the front row *When we went to the theatre, we had seats on the front row.*
the front door/entrance/bedroom (=at the front of a building) *She knocked on the front door, but no-one answered.*
the front garden/lawn *The house has a large front garden and a field at the back.*
the front end/edge/side *The pilot sits in the front end of the plane.*
an animal's front leg/paw *The dog had injured his front leg.*
a vehicle's front seat/wheel/headlights *A woman was sitting in the front passenger seat.*
the front desk/office (=one that people see when they come into a building) *He works at the front desk of a hotel.*

ANTONYMS **front → back[2]**

frontier *n* the border of a country

VERBS

cross the frontier *They crossed the frontier into Switzerland.*
reach the frontier *Alexander's armies reached the frontier of India.*

ADJECTIVES

the northern/southern/eastern/western frontier *The Great Wall protected the northern frontier of China.*
the Russian/Chinese etc frontier *The town is not far away from the Russian frontier.*

PREPOSITIONS

the frontier between sth and sth *The town is close to the frontier between France and Belgium.*
the frontier with sth *Pakistan has a 1,500 mile frontier with Afghanistan.*
on/at the frontier *They were delayed at the frontier by security checks.*
along the frontier *Fighting continues along the frontier.*

frost *n*

very cold weather, when water freezes

ADJECTIVES

a severe/hard/heavy frost *Many plants were damaged by the hard frost.*
a sharp frost (=sudden and severe) *There had been a sharp frost overnight.*
ground frost (=that forms on the ground) *Tonight will be cold, with clear skies and a ground frost in most areas.*
an early/late frost *I hoped the early frost wasn't a sign of a bad winter to come.*

VERBS

the frost melts *The frost was gradually melting.*
be covered in/with frost *The lawn was covered in frost.*
protect sth against frost *The plants need to be protected against frost.*
withstand/survive frost *Can the plants withstand frost or will it be too cold for them?*

frost + NOUNS

frost damage *Some crops have suffered frost damage.*

PHRASES

a risk/danger of frost *There is a risk of frost from September onwards.*

frosty *adj* **THESAURUS** **cold[1]**

frown[1] *v*

to move your eyebrows together and make an angry or unhappy face

ADVERBS

frown angrily/irritably/impatiently *He frowned angrily as he listened to her excuse.*
frown disapprovingly *She didn't speak, she just frowned disapprovingly.*
frown slightly/a little *He looked at the letter and frowned slightly.*

VERBS

make sb frown *She couldn't see without her glasses, which made her frown with frustration.*

PREPOSITIONS

frown at sb *"What's all this mess?" she said, frowning at him.*

frown[2] *n*

an angry, unhappy, or confused expression

VERBS

have a frown on your face *His sister always had a frown on her face.*
wear a frown (=have a frown on your face) *Lucy, wearing a worried frown, asked where Joe was.*
give a frown *The teacher gave a frown and told him not to be so rude.*
a frown crosses sb's face *Suddenly, a frown crossed Anna's face.*

ADJECTIVES

an angry/irritated frown *I could see from his angry frown that something was wrong.*
a worried/puzzled frown *She had a puzzled frown on her face.*
a slight/small frown *A slight frown crossed his face when he read the letter.*

PREPOSITIONS

with a frown *"Are you still here?" he said with a frown.*

fruit *n*

food such as apples, bananas, and grapes

ADJECTIVES/NOUNS + fruit

fresh fruit *Try to eat plenty of fresh fruit.*

canned fruit (*also* **tinned fruit** *BrE*): *Canned fruit is on the bottom shelf, next to the sugar.*

dried fruit *The cake is made with sultanas, currants, and other dried fruit.*

ripe fruit *When the fruit is ripe, it smells sweet.*

citrus fruit (=lemons, oranges, limes etc) *The drink has a sharp taste, like citrus fruit.*

tropical/exotic fruit *He likes tropical fruits such as pineapples and bananas.*

soft fruit (=small fruits with no skin or large seed) *She made a dessert out of strawberries, raspberries, and other soft fruit.*

VERBS

pick fruit *You can pick the fruit in October.*

a tree bears fruit (=produces fruit) *It was too cold for the trees to bear fruit.*

grow fruit *I'm growing fruit in my greenhouse.*

peel fruit (=take off the outer part) *Use a sharp knife to peel the fruit.*

fruit + NOUNS

a fruit tree *They have fruit trees in the garden.*

fruit juice *She always has a glass of fruit juice for breakfast.*

fruit salad (=a dish of many kinds of fruit cut into small pieces) *Fruit salad is a very healthy dessert.*

a fruit pie *For dessert, we're having fruit pie.*

a fruit bowl (=a bowl for holding fruit) *There was a fruit bowl full of oranges in the middle of the table.*

Fruitcake is usually written as one word.

PHRASES

fruit and vegetables *People buy fruit and vegetables in the local market.*

a piece of fruit (=a whole apple, pear etc, or a piece cut from it) *Lunch is usually a sandwich and a piece of fruit.*

fruitful *adj* THESAURUS **successful (1)**

frustrating *adj* THESAURUS **annoying**

frustration *n*

the feeling of being annoyed or impatient, because you cannot control or change something

ADJECTIVES

deep frustration (=a lot of frustration) *Children feel deep frustration if they can't communicate.*

growing/increasing/mounting frustration *He could not hide his growing frustration.*

sheer frustration *Jack wanted to shout in sheer frustration.*

bitter frustration *If patients recover much more slowly than they hoped, this can lead to bitter frustration.*

VERBS

feel frustration (*also* **experience frustration** *formal*): *It's natural to feel frustration if you can't do something.*

lead to/cause frustration *The ferry only takes a limited number of cars, and this can lead to frustration for drivers.*

express/vent your frustration *The fans expressed their frustration at their team's poor performance.*

take your frustration out on sb (=be angry with other people because of your frustration with yourself) *Don't take your frustration out on other people.*

hide your frustration *In the end she could not hide her frustration any longer.*

understand sb's frustration *I understand your frustration, but please try to be patient.*

PREPOSITIONS

frustration at/over sth *She feels frustration at her own helplessness.*

frustration with sb/sth *She tried not to show her frustration with him as he struggled to understand.*

do sth in frustration (=showing frustration) *He sighed in frustration.*

do sth through/out of frustration (=because of frustration) *Many people leave their jobs through frustration.*

PHRASES

a sense of frustration *People often feel a sense of frustration that they are not progressing at work.*

a source of frustration *Her son is a constant source of frustration to her.*

tears of frustration *She cried tears of frustration.*

fuel *n*

a substance such as coal, gas, or oil that can be burned to produce heat or energy

VERBS

use fuel *Our car uses a lot of fuel.*

run on fuel (=use fuel as the source of power) *Will this engine run on unleaded fuel?*

run out of fuel (=have no more left) *The ship ran out of fuel and drifted helplessly.*

fill up with fuel (=put fuel in a vehicle's fuel tank) *Before leaving, I filled up with fuel at the local petrol station.*

save fuel *You can save fuel by driving more slowly.*

ADJECTIVES/NOUNS + fuel

a fossil fuel (=a fuel such as coal or oil, produced by the gradual decaying of plants and animals) *Global warming may be caused by burning fossil fuels.*

nuclear fuel *What do we do with the spent nuclear fuel?*

solid fuel (=a solid substance, such as coal, that is used as a fuel) *The number of homes using solid fuel for heating has decreased.*

domestic/household fuel (=used in a house) *There has been a sharp rise in domestic fuel costs.*

a clean fuel (=that does not harm the environment) *The proposal is to cut tax on cars that run on clean fuel.*

smokeless fuel (=that burns without producing smoke) *The government is trying to encourage the use of environmentally friendly smokeless fuels.*

fuel + NOUNS

fuel costs/prices *The increase in fuel costs is causing problems for many old people.*

sb's fuel bill *I wish there was some way to cut our fuel bill.*

a fuel tank *The fuel tank holds 14 gallons of petrol.*

a fuel gauge *I noticed the fuel gauge was on empty so I pulled into the nearest gas station.*

fuel consumption (=the amount used) *Fuel consumption averages 54 miles per gallon.*

fuel economy/efficiency *Modern cars have much greater fuel economy.*

PHRASES

sth is running low on fuel (=it does not have much fuel left) *The plane was running low on fuel.*

full *adj*

1 containing as much or as many things or people as possible, so there is no space left

> **Grammar**
> **Full** is usually used after the verb **be** in this meaning.

NOUNS

a plane/train/bus/car is full *The train was completely full.*

a hotel/restaurant is full *All the hotels are full in August.*

a course/class is full *The college said the course was full and that I'd have to apply again next year.*

a glass/cup/plate is full *He kept pouring until the glass was full.*

a box/bag/suitcase is full *The suitcase was full of clothes.*

a cupboard is full *There was a cupboard full of toys.*

sb's mouth is full (=full of food) *You shouldn't talk with your mouth full.*

a full tank *The car has a full tank of gas.*

ADVERBS

completely full *Each day the café was completely full.*

almost/nearly/virtually/practically full *The bus was almost full and we had to sit separately.*

half full/three-quarters full *The cups are only half full.*

PHRASES

crammed/stuffed/packed full of sb/sth (=very full of people or things) *The hall was crammed full of people.*

chock full of sb/sth *informal* (=containing a lot of people or things) *The book is chock full of useful information.*

full to the brim (=full to the top with liquid) *The bath was full to the brim with hot water.*

full to bursting (with sth) (=extremely full) *The fridge is full to bursting with pies, cakes, and drinks.*

> **Full of**
> You often use **full of** when saying that something contains a lot of things or people: *The book is **full of** fascinating information.*

> **Full up**
> You say that hotels, restaurants, courses etc are **full up**, when there are no more places available: *The hotel is **full up** for the next three weeks.*

THESAURUS: full

packed
street | **road** | **room** | **store** | **restaurant** | **hall** | **house** | **theatre** | **train** | **bus** | **plane** | **audience**
completely full of people. **Packed** is a little informal:
*The streets are **packed with** late night shoppers.* | *The restaurant is packed on Friday nights.* | *Wherever they play, the house is always packed* (=the concert hall or theatre is full). | *He gave a speech to a packed audience of students* (=a hall full of people who have come to watch or listen to something).

bursting with sth
extremely full of something:
Her wardrobe was bursting with coats and shoes. | *At this time of year, the garden is bursting with flowers.*

crammed with sb/sth
so full that you cannot fit anyone or anything else in - often used when you think there are too many people or things:
In summer, the hotels are crammed with tourists. | *The shelves are crammed with books on art and design.*

F

teeming with sth
full of people, animals etc that are all moving around:
*The rivers are teeming with fish. | The town is teeming with tourists. | The rainforest is **teeming with life*** (=many different animals live there).

overflowing
so full of things, liquid, or people that some of them come outside:
*Heavy rains and overflowing rivers have flooded hundreds of towns and villages. | The drawers were **overflowing with** magazines. | The little meeting hall was **overflowing with** people.*

overloaded
used about a vehicle or a ship which has too many people or things in it:
*an overloaded fishing boat | The trucks are often **grossly overloaded*** (=far too overloaded).

Half full or **half empty**?
If you say that someone's **glass is always half empty**, you mean that this person is a pessimist, and is never happy with his or her situation.
Someone who thinks their **glass is half full** has a more positive attitude to life.

ANTONYMS **full → empty**

2 including all of something

Grammar
Full is always used with **the** in this meaning.

NOUNS

the full amount/length/extent (of sth) *The insurance company agreed to pay the full amount.*
the full cost/price (of sth) *The full cost of the repairs could be over $30,000.*
the full range (of sth) *Patients will have access to the full range of services.*
the full effect/impact (of sth) *People are starting to feel the full impact of the recession.*
the full force *The building suffered the full force of the bomb.*

fun *n, adj*

an experience or activity that is very enjoyable

ADJECTIVES

good fun *BrE*: *It was good fun working with him.*
great/tremendous fun *The show is great fun for all the family.*
harmless fun (=not likely to upset or offend anyone) *People say these video games are just harmless fun, but some parents disagree.*

VERBS

have fun *Did you have fun at the party?*
join in the fun *On festival days the whole village joins in the fun.*
sth sounds (like) fun *A picnic sounds like fun.*
spoil/ruin the fun *It was cold on the beach but we didn't let that spoil the fun.*

fun + NOUNS

a fun time (=an enjoyable experience) *Everyone had a really fun time at the beach.*

PHRASES

just for fun/just for the fun of it (=because you enjoy it) *She's the kind of person who learns a new language just for the fun of it.*
a lot of fun (*also* **lots of fun**) *The kids had a lot of fun singing and dancing.*
sth is no fun/not much fun (=not enjoyable) *Being stuck in a traffic jam for three hours was no fun.*
sth is not sb's idea of fun (=something is not the kind of thing you enjoy) *Camping in the rain is not my idea of fun.*
sth is half the fun (=it is a very enjoyable part of something) *Planning a vacation is half the fun.*
have a sense of fun *Children like her because she has a great sense of fun.*
a fun thing to do *We're planning lots of fun things for the children to do.*
in fun (=with the intention of being funny, not of upsetting someone) *We teased her, but just in fun.*

THESAURUS: fun
agreeable, rewarding, entertaining, fun → **enjoyable**

F

function[1] Ac *n*

the purpose or job that something or someone has

ADJECTIVES

an important/key function *Your kidneys have an important function – they remove waste from your blood.*
a basic function *The most basic function of a home is to provide shelter.*
a useful function *These rules serve no useful function.*
a special/particular/specific function *Each part of the machine has a special function.*
the main/primary function *The main function of a business is to make money.*
a dual function (=two purposes) *School has a dual function: to educate children and help them to become good citizens.*
bodily functions (=eating, breathing, going to the toilet etc) *The nervous system regulates our bodily functions.*

VERBS

have a function *The two switches have different functions.*
fulfil/serve a function (=have a function) *Singing seems to serve two functions for birds – defending territory and attracting females.*

carry out/perform a function *In her new role she will perform a variety of different functions.*

PREPOSITIONS

the function of sth *The function of the courts is to maintain the rule of justice.*

function² Ac *v*

to work in the correct or intended way

ADVERBS

function correctly/properly *Check that all the equipment is functioning correctly.*

function well/effectively/successfully *No factory can function effectively without a happy workforce.*

function efficiently/smoothly *Everyone wants to see the economy functioning smoothly again.*

function normally *Flights in and out of Heathrow are functioning normally again.*

function perfectly *All systems are functioning perfectly.*

function independently *We teach people who have been involved in serious accidents to function independently again.*

barely function (=almost not function at all) *He was so tired he could barely function.*

VERBS

be able/unable to function *Without support staff, a hospital would be unable to function.*

cease to function *Her legs have now ceased to function.*

fail to function *What happens if the reserve parachute fails to function?*

continue to function/keep functioning *His brain continued to function even though he could not move or speak.*

enable/allow sth to function *Every organization has rules which allow it to function.*

PREPOSITIONS

function as sth *The library will function as an extra classroom.*

fund Ac *n*

1 an amount of money that is collected and kept for a particular purpose

NOUNS + fund

an emergency fund *We keep an emergency fund in case we have unexpected bills to pay.*

an investment fund (=which buys shares, property etc in order to make a profit for investors) *The building is currently owned by an investment fund.*

a pension fund (=which pays for people's pensions) *He had been paying into a pension fund for the whole of his working life.*

a campaign fund (=used to help a political party or a politician to get elected) *These social events help to raise campaign funds.*

a memorial fund (=for remembering the life of someone who has died) *They launched a memorial fund for Olivia, to support children's art projects in her name.*

a disaster fund (=used to help people who have been affected by a disaster) *There was a disaster fund for victims of the earthquake.*

an appeal fund *BrE* (=one that asks people to give money to help someone, save or repair something etc) *The appeal fund for the church roof has now reached £65,000.*

a trust fund (=money that belongs to one person, but is controlled by another) *The money from the sale of the house will go into a trust fund for the children.*

VERBS

set up/establish/launch a fund (=start it) *They have set up a fund to repair the church roof.* | *They plan to launch an investment fund by raising $40 million from investors.*

2 money that a person or organization needs or has

> **Grammar**
> Always plural in this meaning.

ADJECTIVES/NOUNS + fund

available funds *All the available funds have now been used.*

sufficient/insufficient funds *formal* (=enough or not enough) *The bank will only transfer the money if there are sufficient funds in your account.*

limited/unlimited funds *Many organizations are fighting for limited funds.*

surplus funds (=extra and not needed for a particular purpose) *Surplus funds can be invested.*

government/public funds (*also* **federal funds** *AmE*): *There have been claims that ministers misused public funds.*

private funds (=from individuals or companies, not the government) *The school was paid for entirely by private funds.*

church/school etc funds *A total of $5,800 in church funds has been used to help local people.*

VERBS

raise funds (=get money for something) *The event was held to raise funds to promote AIDS awareness.*

provide funds *Critics claim the scheme did not provide sufficient funds to help those in need.*

misuse funds (=use them in a dishonest way) *He was found guilty of misusing public funds.*

PHRASES

a lack/shortage of funds *The park remains unfinished due to a lack of funds.*

be short of funds (=not have enough money) *The museum is so short of funds it may have to sell the painting.*

PREPOSITIONS

funds for sth *The government will provide the funds for this research.*

funds from sth *Political parties are not allowed to accept funds from abroad.*

fundamental Ac *adj*

relating to the most basic and important parts of something

PHRASES

sth is of fundamental importance (=it is extremely important) *This issue is of fundamental importance.*

THESAURUS: fundamental

fundamental, core, essential, central, underlying → **basic (1)**

funding Ac *n*

money that is provided by an organization for a particular purpose

ADJECTIVES/NOUNS + funding

government funding *We need more government funding for the arts.*

federal funding (=from the government, especially in the US) *The agency has federal funding from the US government.*

public funding (=from the government) *The charity receives no public funding.*

private funding (=from people and companies, rather than the government) *Many top universities rely heavily on private funding.*

adequate/sufficient funding *The main problem was a lack of adequate funding.*

research funding *They have applied for research funding for the project.*

extra/additional funding *The organization requires additional funding of between £8 and £10 million in order to continue its work.*

external funding (=funding from outside an organization) *We have been successful in attracting external funding.*

VERBS

get/receive funding *The museum receives funding from the government.*

get/obtain/find funding (=succeed in getting it) *They were unable to get funding for their idea.*

secure funding (=succeed in getting it – 'secure' sounds more formal and more definite than 'get') *We hope to secure funding for the project from local businesses.*

apply for funding *The group successfully applied for funding to build a new youth centre.*

provide funding *The university has provided funding for the project.*

cut funding *The government cut funding for sport.*

attract funding *They are looking at new ways of attracting funding for the school.*

seek funding *The scientists are seeking funding for their research work.*

need funding *Theatre groups always say that they need more funding.*

funding comes from sb/sth *The funding comes from the local authority.*

funding + NOUNS

a funding crisis *Universities are facing a serious funding crisis.*

a funding gap (=a difference between the amount of money someone has and the amount they need) *The group faces a funding gap of more than £500 million.*

funding arrangements *The government has changed the funding arrangements for schools.*

a funding application *We have submitted several funding applications, so far without success.*

a funding body/agency/council (=an organization that provides funding) *The Science Research Council is a research-funding body in the UK.*

PREPOSITIONS

funding for sth *Funding for the project comes from the government.*

PHRASES

a source of funding *The shops are the charity's main source of funding.*

funeral *n*

a religious ceremony for burying or cremating (=burning) someone who has died

ADJECTIVES/NOUNS + funeral

a big/elaborate funeral *There was a big funeral in Westminster Abbey after he died.*

a small/simple funeral *She asked to have a simple funeral with a few close family members.*

a public/private funeral *A public funeral will be held for the singer in her hometown.*

a state funeral (=a very big funeral that is arranged by the government for a very important person) *A state funeral will be held for the former US president.*

VERBS

a funeral is held/takes place *The funeral will be held at St Martin's Church.*

go to a funeral (*also* **attend a funeral** *formal*): *Hundreds of people attended the funeral of the two boys.*

funeral + NOUNS

a funeral service/ceremony *A priest conducted the funeral service.*

a funeral procession (=the line of people, vehicles etc going to a funeral with the body) *We watched the funeral procession as it went through London.*

PREPOSITIONS

be at a funeral *All his family were at the funeral.*

a funeral for sb *There will be a state funeral for the former president.*

funny *adj*

1 making you laugh

NOUNS

a funny story *The book is a funny story about a young robot called Tonk.*
a funny joke *Someone told me a really funny joke.*
a funny book/film/play etc *'Shrek' is such a funny film.*
a funny scene/line/part *The play has some funny lines in it.*
a funny moment *There were several funny moments during the trip.*

VERBS

find sth funny (=think that something is funny) *I didn't find the video funny at all.*
look/sound funny *John looked funny in his new hat.*

ADVERBS

hilariously/hysterically/outrageously funny (=extremely funny) *The film is hilariously funny.*
wickedly funny (=very funny but slightly cruel) *He did some wickedly funny impressions of his classmates.*
wonderfully/brilliantly funny *This is a wonderfully funny book.*
wildly funny *The kids all seemed to think it was wildly funny.*
genuinely funny *He was a genuinely funny man.*
unintentionally funny *Some parts of the film are unintentionally funny.*
not that funny *A lot of his jokes aren't that funny.*

PHRASES

see the funny side (=see that something is partly funny) *Luckily, when I explained the situation, he saw the funny side.*

THESAURUS: funny

amusing
anecdote | story | incident | tale | moment | company | spectacle
funny and enjoyable. **Amusing** is more formal than **funny**. It is often used when something is a little funny and makes you smile, rather than laugh:
The book contains many amusing anecdotes about his time in the army (=interesting stories about things that happened to you). | *He recalled an amusing incident which happened on his wedding day.* | *There are some* ***highly amusing*** *moments in the film.* | *He is very amusing company* (=he says things that make you smile and you enjoy being with him). | *His parents didn't* ***find*** *the situation very* ***amusing***.

humorous
look | story | tale | account | anecdote | moment | speech | verse | style
intended to be funny - used about stories, films, articles etc that have situations that are a little funny:
The novel takes a humorous look at relationships. | *It's a humorous short story set in New York.* | *There were some mildly humorous moments in the film.* | *He gave a humorous speech at the wedding.* | *She has written a book of humorous verse.*

light-hearted
look | comedy | fun | conversation | banter
done for amusement or enjoyment, and not intended to be serious:
The programme is a light-hearted look at recent political events. | *The film is a light-hearted comedy.* | *The jokes were all good light-hearted fun.* | *There was some light-hearted banter between Kim and Frank* (=conversation in which friends or colleagues gently tease each other).

witty
remark | comment | conversation | repartee | dialogue | line | script | comedy | riposte
using words in a funny and clever way:
Dan often makes witty remarks. | *He had some jokes and witty repartee to entertain us* (=conversation in which someone gives clever funny answers). | *The movie contains some witty lines.* | *He managed to come up with a witty riposte* (=a witty reply).

comic
opera | novel | tale | drama | performer | performance | character | genius
a comic opera, novel etc is intended to be funny. **Comic** is also used about performers and characters:
This comic novel is about the daily life of the Slivenowicz family. | *The film is a comic drama starring Penélope Cruz.* | *Walt Disney created some famous comic characters.* | *Charlie Chaplin was a comic genius* (=a brilliantly funny performer).

comical
funny in a strange or silly way, especially without intending to be funny:
There was something rather comical about the situation. | *He plays a comical little man who is full of his own self-importance.*

hilarious
story | tale | show | parody | moment | scene | consequences
extremely funny:
She told me a hilarious story about how they met each other. | *It was a hilarious parody of a cowboy movie* (=a funny film, book etc that copies another more serious film, book etc). | *There is one particularly hilarious moment in the play.* | *In the film, she starts her own restaurant, with hilarious consequences.*

F

hysterical *informal*
extremely funny:
You should have seen the look on his face. It was hysterical!

Hysterical is used in informal spoken English. It does not have any strong collocations, and is often used after the verb **be**.

2 a little strange

VERBS

seem funny *It seems funny that he didn't call.*
sound/look/smell/taste funny *The milk tasted funny.*
feel funny *I feel a bit funny – I need to sit down.*

NOUNS

a funny feeling *I had a funny feeling that I'd seen her somewhere before.*
a funny situation *No one knew what to do – it was a funny situation.*
a funny sound/noise *There was a funny sound coming from the engine.*
a funny smell/taste *What's that funny smell?*

furious *adj* THESAURUS angry

fury *n*

extreme, often uncontrolled, anger

PHRASES

be shaking with fury *Her face had turned bright red, and she was shaking with fury.*
sb's face is twisted/contorted with fury *The man was so angry that his face was twisted with fury.*

VERBS

cause/provoke fury *The decision caused fury among local people.*
vent your fury (=express it) *He vented his fury by kicking over a wastepaper basket.*

ADJECTIVES

pent-up/suppressed fury (=which has not been expressed) *All her pent-up fury came pouring out.*

PREPOSITIONS

in fury *She began screaming at her husband in fury.*

fuss *n*

a lot of worry, anger, or excitement, usually about unimportant things

ADJECTIVES

a big/great/huge fuss *There was a big fuss when he couldn't find the keys.*
unnecessary fuss *I can't understand all this unnecessary fuss.*

VERBS

make/kick up/create a fuss *There's no need to make such a fuss.*
cause a fuss *The new rules caused a lot of fuss.*
fuss surrounds sth *After all the fuss that surrounded the film, I expected it to be really shocking.*

PREPOSITIONS

without (any) fuss *The children went upstairs quietly and without any fuss.*
a fuss about/over sth *There was a big fuss about who was going to sit at the head of the table.*

PHRASES

a (big) fuss about nothing *People complained that the buildings would spoil the view, but it was all a big fuss about nothing.*
what all the fuss is about (=why people are worried, angry, or excited) *It's just a football game – I don't understand what all the fuss is about.*
with the minimum of fuss/with minimum fuss (=with hardly any problems or interruptions) *The workmen did the job quickly and with the minimum of fuss.*

futile *adj* THESAURUS useless

future[1] *n*

the time after the present, or what will happen to someone or something then

PHRASES

in the near future (=soon) *We're planning to move house in the near future.*
in the immediate future (=very soon) *There will be no major changes in the immediate future.*
in the distant future (=a very long time from now) *I don't worry about what might happen in the distant future.*
in the not too distant future (=quite soon) *We're planning to go there again in the not too distant future.*
for the foreseeable future (=for as long as you can imagine) *The population is expected to keep growing for the foreseeable future.*
sb's plans/hopes for the future *What are your hopes for the future?*
what the future holds/will bring (=what will happen) *No one knows what the future holds for the company.*
sb has a great/bright future ahead of them *He's a fantastic actor and has a great future ahead of him.*
sb's/sth's future is in sb's hands (=they will decide or control it) *The corporation's future is in the hands of a new management team.*

ADJECTIVES

a great/good future *The country has a great future.*

the long-term future (=a long time from now) *The long-term future of the collection remains uncertain.*

a bright/promising/rosy future (=likely to be good or successful) *Her future as a tennis player looks promising.*

a bleak/grim/dark future (=without anything to make you feel hopeful) *The theatre is losing money and its future looks bleak.*

an uncertain future (=not clear or decided) *The college's future is now uncertain.*

VERBS + future

predict the future *No one can predict the future.*

foretell the future (=say what will happen in the future, especially using magical powers) *The god Apollo gave her the power to foretell the future.*

see/look into the future (=know what will happen in the future) *I wish I could see into the future.*

plan/make plans for the future *As soon as she knew she was pregnant, she started to plan for the future.*

have a ... future *The company has a great future.*

face a bleak/grim etc future *Many pensioners face a bleak future.*

threaten sb's/sth's future *Global warming is threatening the future of life on this planet.*

future + VERBS

the future looks good/bright etc *The future looks good for the company.*

sb's/sth's future lies in/with sth (=is related to a particular thing) *The country's economic future lies with its skilled workforce.*

PREPOSITIONS

in the future *This lack of control may cause problems in the future.*

In British English, **in future** is used to mean "from now": *I will be more careful* ***in future.***

future² *adj*

likely to happen or exist at a time after the present

future + NOUNS

future generations *It is important to preserve the countryside for future generations.*

future plans *I don't know what my future plans are at the moment.*

future events *The leaflet has details of future events at the college.*

future development/direction *He feels uncertain about the future direction of his career.*

future growth *Research is vital for the future growth of the company.*

a future role *There has been a lot of discussion about the future role of the monarchy.*

future research/work *This is a topic for future research.*

future prospects (=what is likely to happen to someone or something) *The team's future prospects look good.*

future success *We're looking forward to the future success of the team.*

sb's future wife/husband (=the person who you later marry) *She met her future husband while they were at university.*

PHRASES

in future years *We are hoping the birds will survive, and breed in future years.*

at a future date (=at some time in the future) *The decision will be made at some future date.*

for future use *They kept the other bottles for future use.*

for future reference (=for you to look at for information in the future) *He took some notes for future reference.*

F

Gg

gadget *n*

a small, useful, and cleverly designed machine or tool

ADJECTIVES/NOUNS + gadget

a useful/handy gadget *This handy gadget tells you when the meat is cooked.*

the latest gadget *The kitchen has all the latest gadgets.*

an electronic/electrical gadget *The building is full of electronic gadgets for controlling the lighting and the temperature.*

a high-tech gadget *The car has all kinds of high-tech gadgets.*

a kitchen/household gadget *He loves buying household gadgets.*

PREPOSITIONS

a gadget for doing sth *I bought a clever little gadget for sharpening knives.*

THESAURUS: gadget

appliance, device, gadget, contraption → **machine**

gain¹ *v* to get or achieve something

NOUNS

gain control/power *The army had already gained control of the city.*

gain independence *In 1962, Jamaica gained independence from Britain.*

gain a reputation *He had gained a reputation as a hard worker.*

gain support/acceptance *The proposal failed to gain much support.*

gain experience/knowledge *Voluntary work is a good way of gaining experience.*

gain confidence *As you gain confidence you will become a better driver.*

gain momentum (=make progress and become more successful) *His campaign to become president was starting to gain momentum.*

ADVERBS

quickly/rapidly gain sth *Adam quickly gained the respect of the soldiers under his command.*

steadily gain sth *The party was steadily gaining more support.*

gradually gain sth *He is gradually gaining confidence in his own abilities.*

PREPOSITIONS

gain in popularity/confidence/strength/size etc (=become more popular, confident etc) *The sport seems to be gaining in popularity.*

gain (sth) from sth *Children gain a lot from reading books.*

PHRASES

stand to gain (sth) (=used when someone is likely to gain advantages from something) *The rich stand to gain the most from the tax cuts.*

have a lot/much to gain (from sth) *Schools have much to gain from adopting new technologies.*

have little/nothing to gain (from sth) *He has nothing to gain from lying about the situation.*

have something to gain (from sth) *Is there anyone who had something to gain from her death?*

THESAURUS: gain

receive, obtain, acquire, gain, win, earn, inherit, get hold of sth → **get (1)**

gain² *n*

an improvement, an increase, or a benefit

ADJECTIVES

a big/significant/substantial gain *The company has achieved significant gains in productivity.*

a modest gain (=fairly small) *Buyers expect to make a modest gain over time, and not become rich overnight.*

potential gain (=possible) *A businessman saw the potential gain and decided to support the idea.*

immediate gain *Sometimes you have to sacrifice immediate gain for long-term advantage.*

short-term gain (=in the period not very far into the future) *Political parties are only interested in short-term gain.*

long-term gain (=in the distant future) *Are you prepared to suffer short-term pain for long-term gain?*

economic/financial/political gain *Criminals should not receive financial gain from writing about their crimes.*

personal/private gain (=for yourself) *She is motivated entirely by personal gain.*

net gain (=after considering all you have lost and gained) *Labour made a net gain of 39 seats in the election.*

VERBS

make/achieve a gain *The party made considerable gains at local elections.*

result in a gain *Leg exercises can also result in gains in the upper body.*

show a gain *February sales showed a gain of 0.4%.*

report/post a gain (=announce a gain in profits) *Stores posted big gains over the Christmas period.*

PREPOSITIONS

gains in sth *There have been substantial gains in efficiency.*

gallery *n*

a building where people can see pieces of art

ADJECTIVES/NOUNS + gallery

an art gallery *I first saw his paintings in an art gallery in Spain.*

a picture gallery *The picture gallery is full of treasures.*

a portrait gallery (=showing paintings of people) *The latest painting of Queen Elizabeth is on display at the National Portrait Gallery.*

a private gallery (=owned by a private person) *The drawing was sold to a private gallery.*

a national gallery (=owned by a country) *Edinburgh has three national galleries.*

VERBS

visit/go to a gallery *The children visited the gallery on a school trip.*

a painting hangs in a gallery *Many of her pictures hang in the National Gallery of Canada.*

a gallery shows sth (*also* **a gallery exhibits sth** *formal*): *The gallery is showing a series of watercolour works.*

a gallery contains sth (*also* **a gallery houses sth** *formal*): *Today the gallery houses a fine collection of photographs and paintings.*

exhibit sth in/at a gallery *It was the first time that the paintings had been exhibited in a gallery.*

gallery + NOUNS

gallery space (=an area for displaying art) *She exhibited her work in the gallery space of the Institute of Art and Technology.*

PREPOSITIONS

at a gallery *More of his work is on show at the gallery.*

in a gallery *It is one of my favourite pictures in the gallery.*

gamble *n*

an action or plan that involves a risk but that you hope will succeed

ADJECTIVES

a big/huge/enormous gamble *Giving him the job seemed like a big gamble.*

a calculated gamble (=in which you consider the risks very carefully) *He made a calculated gamble that an early election would return his party to power.*

a desperate gamble *The parents took a desperate gamble by throwing their baby out of the burning building.*

a reckless gamble (=not at all careful) *He described the spending cuts as a reckless gamble with people's livelihoods.*

a political gamble *The decision was a huge political gamble.*

VERBS

take a gamble *He was never afraid to take a gamble.*

a gamble pays off (=succeeds) *She gave up a career in law to become an actor, but the gamble has paid off.*

a gamble fails *You must prepare for the possibility that a gamble might fail.*

PREPOSITIONS

a gamble on sth/sb *The publishers' gamble on an unknown author paid off.*

PHRASES

be something of a gamble (*also* **be a bit of a gamble** *spoken*) (=involve an amount of risk) *A few years ago, launching a weekly magazine for men would have been something of a gamble.*

gambler *n*

someone who likes to risk money on the result of card games, races etc

ADJECTIVES

a heavy gambler (=someone who gambles a lot and loses a lot of money) *Her father was a heavy gambler and he was always in debt.*

a compulsive gambler (=someone who cannot stop gambling) *The organization was set up to help compulsive gamblers.*

a professional gambler *Many professional gamblers owe great sums of money to other gamblers.*

game *n*

an activity in which you try to win according to agreed rules, or an occasion when a game is played

VERBS

play a game *They explained how to play the game.*

have a game *BrE*: *They were having a game of golf.*

see/watch a game *Did you see the game last night?*

win/lose a game *Our team won the game with a last-minute goal.*

draw a game *BrE* (=end the game with the same score as the opposing team or player) *We played badly and were lucky to draw the game.*

the game is tied (=both teams or players have the same score) *The game was tied 10-10 at half-time.*

ADJECTIVES/NOUNS + game

a close/tight game (=when both teams or players play equally well and might win) *It was a close game and we should have won it.*

a tough/hard game (=one that is hard to win) *They are a good team, and it will be a very tough game for us.*
a card/board/ball game *Bridge is a card game for four people.*
a computer/video game *He was up all night playing computer games.*
a team game *I wasn't very good at team games when I was at school.*
a party game *The kids had fun playing party games.*
indoor games *There is a hall for indoor games and social functions.*
a basketball/baseball/football etc game *AmE: He was watching a baseball game on TV.*
a home game (=played at a team's own sports field) *Next Saturday Liverpool have a home game against Manchester United.*
an away game (=played at an opposing team's sports field) *We didn't win any away games last season.*

PREPOSITIONS

a game of tennis/football etc *We played another game of chess.*
a game against/with sb *I watched their last game against Holland.*

PHRASES

the rules of the game *It's against the rules of the game to pick up the ball.*

gang *n*

a group of young people who spend time together, often one that fights against other groups

ADJECTIVES/NOUNS + gang

a criminal gang *He had links with a criminal gang.*
a rival gang (=that another gang competes or fights with) *Fighting between rival gangs left dozens of people injured.*
a street gang (=which spends a lot of time on the streets) *He belonged to a notorious street gang in Chicago.*
an armed gang (=with guns) *An armed gang stole jewels worth more than five million pounds.*
a masked gang (=wearing masks to cover their faces) *She woke up to find a masked gang in her bedroom.*
a teenage gang *Teenage gangs often carry knives to make themselves look tough.*

VERBS

join a gang *He was only eight when he joined the gang.*
belong to a gang *Eleven men belonging to a local gang were arrested.*

gang + NOUNS

a gang member (*also* **a member of a gang**) *Shootings by gang members have increased.*
a gang leader *Gang leaders used cellphones to order the attacks.*
gang violence *Local people say that gang violence is common.*
gang crime (=crime committed by gangs) *Most gang crime happens between gang members.*
gang warfare (=fighting between gangs) *Gang warfare is wrecking the neighborhood.*
gang culture *Tattoos have become an important part of gang culture.*

PREPOSITIONS

a gang of kids/youths etc *There are always gangs of kids hanging around.*
be in a gang (=be a member of a gang) *Has he ever been in a gang?*

gap *n*

1 a big difference between two situations, amounts, groups of people etc

ADJECTIVES

a big/large/wide gap *There is a big gap between our system and theirs.*
a huge/enormous gap *A huge gap still exists between rich and poor.*
a yawning gap (=a very big difference) *There was a yawning gap between the earnings of men and women.*
a narrow gap *The gap between the two candidates is very narrow.*
a growing/widening gap *There is a growing gap in the academic performance of boys and girls.*
a cultural gap (=a difference between cultures) *There is a cultural gap between Europe and America on this subject.*

NOUNS + gap

an age gap (=a difference in age between two people) *There is a big age gap between them – she's 17 and he's 52.*
a generation gap (=the difference in attitudes between older and younger people) *One reason for the generation gap is that younger people have been brought up in a very different way from their parents.*
the gender gap (=the difference between the situation of men and women) *The gender gap was visible in the way men and women voted during the presidential elections.*
the trade gap (=the difference between the amounts a country imports and exports) *Britain's trade gap almost doubled last month.*

VERBS

bridge/close/narrow the gap (=make it less big) *The book aims to bridge the gap between theory and practice.*
widen the gap *Technology has widened the gap between people with and without computer skills.*
the gap narrows/widens (=gets smaller or bigger) *The gap is widening between rich and poor.*

G

a gap exists *A cultural gap exists between the older and the younger generations.*

PREPOSITIONS

a gap between sth and sth *The gap between rich and poor has grown wider.*

2 a space between two things

ADJECTIVES

a narrow/small/little/tiny gap *She has a small gap between her front teeth.*

a big/wide/enormous/massive gap *There is a big gap in the fence.*

VERBS

fill in/seal a gap *We filled in the gaps around the windows.*

a gap opens up *A gap had opened up between the wall and the ceiling.*

PREPOSITIONS

a gap between *There are gaps between the floorboards.*

3 a situation in which there is something missing

ADJECTIVES

a big/large/huge/great gap *There were huge gaps in his story.*

an important/major gap *The present study aims to fill an important gap in the research.*

VERBS

leave/create a gap *His mother's death left a big gap in his life.*

fill/plug a gap *This machine has been designed to fill a gap in the market.*

identify/spot a gap *Losey had identified a gap in the existing research.*

PREPOSITIONS

a gap in sth *There are still many gaps in our knowledge of the laws of physics.*

garbage *n AmE*

waste material, such as paper, empty containers, and food thrown away

VERBS

take/put the garbage out *Can you take the garbage out for me?*

dump garbage (=leave it in a place, especially where it should not be) *At the time, the city dumped surplus garbage into the bay.*

collect the garbage *They come to collect the garbage once every week.*

ADJECTIVES/NOUNS + garbage

household garbage (=produced by people at home) *Here are some ideas for reducing your household garbage.*

kitchen garbage *How can I keep the kitchen garbage from smelling bad?*

recyclable garbage (=that can be treated and used again) *The blue box is for recyclable garbage.*

rotting garbage (=decaying) *The smell of rotting garbage was overpowering.*

garbage + NOUNS

a garbage can (=a container with a lid for holding waste until it can be taken away) *Go and put it in the garbage can.*

a garbage truck *The garbage truck had already taken the bags away.*

a garbage collector (*also* **a garbage man** *informal*): *She didn't want the garbage collectors seeing what she'd thrown out.*

garbage collection *People want more frequent garbage collection.*

a garbage bag/sack (=a large plastic bag for putting garbage in) *Vegetable waste should be put in the green garbage bag.*

a garbage dump (=a place where garbage is taken and left) *I'm going to take these old toys to the garbage dump.*

PREPOSITIONS

in the garbage *Don't throw glass in the garbage – recycle it.*

In British English, people usually say **rubbish**.

garden *n especially BrE*

the area of land next to a house, where there are flowers, grass, and other plants

ADJECTIVES/NOUNS + garden

a beautiful/lovely garden *The cottage has a beautiful garden with lots of pretty flowers.*

the front garden (=at the front of a house) *Our house only has a small front garden.*

the back garden (=at the back of a house) *The children are playing in the back garden.*

a flower/rose/vegetable/herb garden *The vegetable garden has rows of cabbages and lettuces.*

a well-kept/tidy/neat garden *The hotel is set in a well-kept garden.*

an overgrown garden (=covered with plants that have grown in an uncontrolled way) *The garden is getting rather overgrown.*

a secluded garden (=private and quiet) *There is a secluded garden where patients can sit.*

VERBS

water the garden *I need to water the garden – the soil is really dry.*

weed the garden (=remove unwanted wild plants) *She was outside weeding the garden.*

do the garden *informal* (=take care of it by doing gardening) *Grandad is too old to do the garden himself.*

plant a garden *They planted a beautiful rose garden in her memory.*

design a garden *Ask a professional to design your garden.*

garden + NOUNS

a garden centre (=a shop selling plants and things for the garden) *She has gone to the garden centre to get some new plants.*

a garden shed (=a small building in the garden for storing tools and equipment) *The lawnmower is kept in the garden shed.*

a garden path/gate/wall *Martin was waiting by the garden gate.*

garden waste (=grass, leaves etc that you have cut and do not want) *You can use garden waste to make compost.*

PREPOSITIONS

in the garden *She is outside in the garden.*

PHRASES

(at) the bottom of the garden (=the part furthest from the house) *There was a big apple tree at the bottom of the garden.*

In American English, people usually say **yard**.

garment *n* THESAURUS clothes

gas *n*

1 a substance such as air, which is not solid or liquid, and usually cannot be seen

ADJECTIVES/NOUNS + gas

natural gas (=gas from under the earth, used for cooking and heating) *Russia supplies huge amounts of natural gas to European countries.*

a poisonous/toxic/noxious gas (=a harmful gas) *The factories send toxic gases into the atmosphere.*

greenhouse gas (=a gas that traps heat above the Earth, causing the surface to become warmer) *If we don't reduce greenhouse gas emissions, we can expect more extreme weather events.*

tear gas (=a gas that stings your eyes, used by the police to control crowds) *Police fired tear gas into the crowd.*

VERBS

gas escapes/leaks (out) *Ammonia gas leaked out of a broken pipe at the factory.*

smell gas *I'm sure I can smell gas. Can you?*

produce gas *The chemical reaction produced a toxic gas.*

release/emit/give off gas (=let it flow out) *Burning waste releases harmful gases into the atmosphere.*

breathe in gas (*also* **inhale gas** *formal*): *Many protesters were suffering the effects of inhaling tear gas.*

gas + NOUNS

a gas cooker/oven/stove *Do you use a gas or an electric cooker?*

a gas fire/heater (=an object that burns gas to heat a room) *She turned on the gas fire to warm up the room.*

a gas leak (=gas that comes out through a hole in something) *If you suspect a gas leak, do not turn on an electric light.*

the gas supply (=the system for supplying gas to someone's house) *Engineers have finally restored the gas supply to the estate.*

a gas pipeline *Building the gas pipeline was a joint project involving China and Russia.*

2 *AmE* liquid used to power cars and other vehicles

VERBS

fill (a vehicle) up with gas *I filled up with gas before leaving Fresno.*

run out of gas (=have no more gas) *We've run out of gas on Route 12. Can you come get us?*

gas + NOUNS

a gas station (=a place where you take your car to fill it with gas) *I pulled into the gas station and filled up.*

a gas pump (=a machine for putting gas into cars at a gas station) *There were long lines at the gas pumps.*

In British English, people say **petrol**.

gate *n*

the part of a fence or outside wall that you can open and close to enter or leave a place

ADJECTIVES/NOUNS + gate

the front/back/side gate *She stood outside the front gate of the cottage.*

the school/factory/prison etc gates *Parents were waiting outside the school gates.*

the main gate/the entrance gate *Soldiers were guarding the main gate.*

the garden gate *Ellie ran down the path towards the garden gate.*

VERBS + gate

open a gate *He heard Jack open the gate.*

close/shut a gate *Please close the gate behind you.*

go through a gate *They went through the gate into the field.*

lock a gate (=close it with a key) *The gate was locked, so he climbed over it.*

leave a gate open *Someone left the gate open, and the dog got out.*

gate + VERBS

a gate opens *The gate opens automatically when you approach it.*

a gate closes/shuts *The gates shut behind him with a loud bang.*

a gate swings open/shut (=it opens or shuts quickly and smoothly) *As the gate swung open, it hit me in the face.*

a gate leads to sth *She ran through the gate leading to the station.*

PREPOSITIONS

through a gate *Go through the gate and turn left.*

PHRASES

a set of gates *We passed through a second set of gates.*

gather *v*

1 to get things from different places and put them together

NOUNS

gather information/data/statistics *We hope to gather information about people's eating habits.*

gather evidence *Police have not yet gathered enough evidence to prosecute him.*

gather intelligence (=secretly collect information about someone or something) *They were attempting to gather intelligence on US military operations.*

gather material *The research was based on material we had gathered from interviews.*

gather views/opinions/ideas *The meeting aimed to gather the views of local people.*

gather support *He met with other leaders to gather support for military action.*

2 to come together and form a group

NOUNS

people gather *Thousands of people gathered outside the embassy.*

a crowd/group gathers *A crowd gathered to watch the fight.*

friends/family gather *Friends and family gathered to celebrate her 21st birthday.*

supporters/fans gather *His supporters gathered outside the High Court.*

PREPOSITIONS/ADVERBS

gather around/round *Gather round, everyone, so that you can see the screen.*

gather together *Could the bride's family all gather together for a photo?*

quickly/hastily/hurriedly gather *They hastily gathered around the television, to see if there was any news about the storm.*

VERBS

begin to gather *A crowd began to gather outside the building.*

3 to increase in speed, development etc

NOUNS

gather speed/pace *The train started to gather speed.*

gather momentum (=make progress and become more successful) *The campaign is gathering momentum.*

G

gaze[1] *v*

to look at something for a long time

ADVERBS

gaze longingly (=showing you want something very much) *She was gazing longingly at the cakes.*

gaze wistfully (=in a thoughtful and slightly sad way) *She sat gazing wistfully at photographs of her family far away.*

gaze lovingly/fondly *The old man gazed lovingly at his grandchildren.*

gaze absently/blankly/vacantly (=without paying attention, while thinking about something else) *He sat gazing blankly at the screen.*

PREPOSITIONS

gaze at sb/sth *I gazed at her with admiration.*

PHRASES

gaze into sb's eyes *The two lovers gazed into each other's eyes.*

gaze out of the window *He gazed out of the window at the rain.*

gaze into the distance (=at a point far away, without paying attention) *She just gazed into the distance and gave no answer.*

gaze in awe/wonder at sth *They gazed in awe at the beauty of the landscape.*

gaze[2] *n*

the action of looking at someone or something, especially for a long time

gaze + VERBS

sb's gaze falls on sb/sth (=someone looks at someone or something) *My gaze fell on a photograph on the table.*

sb's gaze moves/travels/shifts *His gaze moved around the room.*

VERBS + gaze

lower/drop your gaze (=look down) *Her eyes met his and she immediately dropped her gaze.*

avert your gaze (=stop looking at someone or something) *He averted his gaze from the beggars that lined the streets.*

meet sb's gaze (=look at someone who is looking at you) *He said nothing, but met her gaze.*

hold sb's gaze (=keep looking at someone who is looking at you) *He held her gaze for a few seconds, then continued eating.*

fix your gaze on sb/sth (*also* **keep your gaze (fixed) on sb/sth**) (=look at someone or something continuously) *He fixed his gaze on the clock behind her.*

PHRASES

under sb's watchful gaze (=with someone watching carefully) *Little children play in the sand under the watchful gaze of their parents.*

gear *n*

1 the machinery in a vehicle such as a car, truck, or bicycle that you use to go comfortably at different speeds

ADJECTIVES

first/second/third etc gear *The traffic was so bad that we never got out of second gear.*

a low gear (=first or second gear, for going slowly) *You should use a low gear when going up a hill.*

a high gear (=third, fourth, or fifth gear, for going fast) *Put the car into a higher gear.*

top gear *BrE* (=the highest gear) *Hamilton slipped effortlessly into top gear.*

bottom gear *BrE* (=the lowest gear) *The car trundled slowly forward in bottom gear.*

the wrong gear *The straining noises from the engine told him that he was in the wrong gear.*

reverse gear (=for driving backwards) *He put the truck into reverse gear.*

VERBS

change gear (*also* **switch/shift gears** *AmE*): *It takes some time to learn when to change gear.*

put a car into (first/second/third etc) gear *He put the car into gear, and they moved slowly forwards.*

gear + NOUNS

a gear lever (*also* **a gear stick** *BrE*), **a gear shift** *AmE* (=the stick you move to change gears) *She pushed the gear lever into first gear.*

gear change *A rapid gear change gave them speed on the corner.*

PREPOSITIONS

in first/third etc gear *Andy drove cautiously along in second gear.*

in gear (=with one of the gears connected) *Don't turn off the engine while you're still in gear.*

out of gear (=with no gear connected) *It's a good habit to take the car out of gear while you're at a stoplight.*

2 equipment or clothes for a particular activity

ADJECTIVES/NOUNS + gear

protective gear *Police officers wore protective gear including vests and helmets.*

climbing/walking gear *I changed out of my walking gear into some jeans.*

outdoor gear *The store sells waterproof jackets, backpacks, and other outdoor gear.*

camping/fishing gear *We packed all the camping gear into the car.*

combat/battle gear *Armed troops in full battle gear were seen entering the camp.*

riot gear (=worn by police dealing with violent crowds) *70 police officers in riot gear raided the site.*

THESAURUS: gear

clothing, garment, dress, wear, gear, wardrobe
→ **clothes**

gender Ac *n*

the fact of being male or female

gender + NOUNS

a gender difference *There are gender differences in the way alcohol affects the brain.*

a gender gap (=a difference between how men and women behave or how they are treated) *A gender gap still exists between men and women's pay.*

gender roles (=the positions of men and women in society) *It is a country where gender roles have remained largely unchanged.*

gender bias/inequality/discrimination (=when one gender is treated unfairly) *Her research investigates gender bias in the classroom.*

gender equality (=when men and women are treated in the same way) *Organizations have a duty to promote gender equality.*

a gender stereotype (=a fixed idea of what men or women are like) *The characters in the novel were criticized for being gender stereotypes.*

PHRASES

on (the) grounds of gender (=because of gender) *Discrimination on grounds of race or gender is forbidden.*

gene *n*

a part of a cell in a living thing that controls what it looks like, how it grows, and how it develops. People get their genes from their parents

ADJECTIVES

a dominant gene (=a gene that has its effect when there is only one copy of it) *The disease occurs when a child inherits a single dominant gene from a parent with the disease.*

a recessive gene (=a gene that has its effect only when there are two copies of it) *The gene for blue eyes is recessive.*

a defective/faulty gene (=a gene that does not work properly) *The disease is caused by a defective gene.*

VERBS

carry a gene (=have a gene that causes a medical condition which you can pass on to your children) *Some women carry a gene which makes them more likely to develop breast cancer.*

inherit a gene (=get a gene from your parents) *Children who inherit the gene may be born with physical abnormalities.*

pass on a gene (=have it inherited by your children) *All animals try to maximize their chances of passing on their genes to the next generation.*

identify/discover a gene (=find a particular gene which is responsible for something) *Scientists have identified a gene which seems to protect against some types of cancer.*

gene + NOUNS

the gene pool (=all the genes in a particular species) *It is hoped that these new wolves will mate with the native population and increase the gene pool.*

gene therapy (=using genes to treat diseases) *Scientists have successfully treated the disease using gene therapy.*

PREPOSITIONS

a gene for sth *Matt carries the gene for Huntington's disease.*

general *adj*

1 describing or relating to only the main features or parts of something, not the details

NOUNS

a general description/account/overview/outline *There is a general description of the company's work.*

general information *The website gives you some general information about the area.*

a general introduction *This book is a good general introduction to the subject.*

a general idea/impression *I hope you get the general idea of what we are trying to do.*

a general comment/remark/point/observation *I will start by making a few general comments.*

a general discussion *There will be a general discussion about the situation in the Middle East.*

the general principle/approach *The general principle is that you can use enough force in order to defend yourself.*

PHRASES

in a general way/in general terms *We began talking in a general way about the project.*

ANTONYMS **general → specific**

2 among most people, or concerning most things or situations

NOUNS

a general belief/feeling *There is a general belief that economic growth is more important than protecting the environment.*

a general sense of sth *The general sense of optimism is very noticeable.*

the general conclusion *The general conclusion from the research is that cellphones are not harmful to health.*

general support/agreement/praise *There was general support for the idea.*

general concern/confusion *There is general concern about the impact of the changes.*

a general lack of sth *In the US there is a general lack of interest in global politics.*

a general trend/pattern/direction *The general trend is for oil prices to increase.*

a general improvement/decline *We have seen a general decline in the size of families.*

PHRASES

as a general rule (=used when saying that something is usually true) *As a general rule, vegetable oils are better for you than animal fats.*

generalization (*also* generalisation *BrE*) *n*

a statement about all the members of a group that may be true in some or many situations, but is not true in every case

ADJECTIVES

a broad generalization (=one that is only partly true and not true in every case) *As a broad generalization, you can say that people who go to good universities tend to get better jobs.*

a sweeping/gross generalization (=one that is very exaggerated and obviously untrue) *The article makes a number of sweeping generalizations about the attitudes of young people.*

a dangerous generalization *It's a dangerous generalization to say that change is always a good thing.*

VERBS

make a generalization *People are always making generalizations about what men and women are like.*

PREPOSITIONS

a generalization about sth *It's best to avoid making generalizations about people from different cultures.*

PHRASES

a generalization is based on sth *None of these generalizations is based on good evidence.*

generate *v* THESAURUS **make (1)**

generation Ac *n*

all people of about the same age

ADJECTIVES/NOUNS + generation

my/your/their etc generation *He was the greatest actor of his generation.*

future generations *We need to preserve the planet for future generations.*

the younger generation *We want to encourage the younger generation to take an interest in politics.*

the older generation *These beliefs were common among the older generation.*

the new generation (=younger people, especially people who use new ways of doing something) *He is one of the new generation of English players.*

the next generation *People want to pass on money to the next generation when they die.*

successive/succeeding generations (=generations that follow one another) *This* *textbook has been used by successive generations of medical students and doctors.*

earlier/previous generations *Compared with previous generations, we eat more and do less.*

later generations *For later generations, the chances of getting work on leaving school were much lower.*

generation + NOUNS

the generation gap (=the difference in attitudes between older and younger people) *This study explores the generation gap between parents and their teenage children.*

VERBS

belong to a generation *Cho belonged to a new generation of Koreans who did not remember the war.*

PREPOSITIONS

in/of sb's generation *Most people in my generation feel the same as I do.*

PHRASES

hand sth down from generation to generation *Native Australians hand down stories and songs from generation to generation.*

pass sth from one generation to the next *Traditional customs are passed from one generation to the next.*

generous *adj*

kind because you are very willing to give people things

ADVERBS

extremely/incredibly generous (*also* **exceedingly generous** *formal*): *Church members have been extremely generous with the money they have given.*

overly/excessively generous (=too generous) *A £20 tip seems excessively generous.*

NOUNS

a generous person/man/woman *Her father was a warm and generous man who was always willing to help other people.*

a generous gift/donation *She felt she could not accept such a generous gift.*

a generous offer *I was thankful for my employer's generous offer to pay all my expenses.*

generous support *He thanked the members for their generous support.*

PREPOSITIONS

be generous to sb *He is very generous to his friends.*

be generous with sth *Jim is generous with his time.*

it is generous of sb to do sth *It was generous of them to offer to help.*

PHRASES

be generous to a fault (=always extremely generous) *Harry was generous to a fault; he'd always help out when his friends needed money.*

kind and generous *Mrs Lyndham had been so kind and generous to her.*

THESAURUS: generous

generous, considerate, thoughtful, caring, sympathetic, compassionate, warm-hearted/kind-hearted, benevolent, benign, nice, good, sweet → **kind²**

genius *n*

1 someone who is extremely intelligent or skilful at doing something

ADJECTIVES/NOUNS + genius

an artistic/musical/literary/creative genius *He argued that James Joyce was the greatest literary genius of the 20th century.*

a scientific/mathematical genius *You don't need to be a mathematical genius to do this calculation.*

a great genius *Picasso was the greatest genius of the century.*

a real/true genius *Hendrix was a true genius, who created his own unique style of guitar playing.*

an evil genius *In the movie he plays an evil genius who wants to take over the world.*

a boy genius (=a boy or young man who is extremely clever or good at something) *The chess championship was won by a Russian boy genius.*

2 a very high level of intelligence, mental skill, or ability, which only very few people have

ADJECTIVES

artistic/musical/literary/creative genius *The music was written when Mozart was at the peak of his creative genius.*

great genius *He has been described as a man of great genius.*

pure/sheer genius (=used when emphasizing how good something is) *The film is a work of pure genius.*

real/true genius *During the painter's lifetime, few people recognized his true genius.*

VERBS

show sb's genius *The performance showed his musical genius at its greatest height.*

sb's genius lies in sth *The author's genius lies in his ability to make memorable characters.*

PREPOSITIONS

a genius for sth *She is a kind woman who has a genius for friendship.*

PHRASES

a stroke/touch of genius (=a very clever idea) *Adding cinnamon to the chocolate mixture was a stroke of genius – the cake tasted wonderful.*

a work of genius *The building is beautiful, a work of genius.*

a man/artist/writer etc of genius *P. G. Wodehouse was a comic writer of genius, whose books still make us laugh.*

genre *n*

a style of writing, art, film, music etc

ADJECTIVES

literary/musical/artistic genre *Writers such as Virginia Woolf created a new literary genre.*

a particular genre *Lucas is a master of his own particular genre of film-making.*

a popular genre *A popular genre within the children's publishing market is that of 'real life' teenage fiction.*

VERBS

create/invent/develop a genre *Tarantino has created his own genre of movies.*

mix/combine genres *The book was a fun way to combine two genres that I've always liked: the action thriller and the horror story.*

gentle *adj*

1 kind, and careful not to hurt anyone or anything

NOUNS

a gentle man/woman/person *My mother was a kind gentle woman.*

gentle fingers/hand *Her gentle hand stroked my hair.*

a gentle smile *He looked up at her with a gentle smile.*

a gentle touch *He felt his mother's gentle touch on his shoulder.*

a gentle voice *"Where does it hurt?" she asked in a gentle voice.*

gentle persuasion (=speaking kindly in order to persuade someone) *With a little gentle persuasion, the boy's mother got him to go into the classroom.*

PREPOSITIONS

gentle with sb/sth *Be gentle with the baby.*

2 not strong, loud, or extreme

NOUNS

gentle exercise *Gentle exercise will help you feel better more quickly.*

a gentle breeze *There was a gentle breeze, just enough to move the curtains slightly.*

a gentle rain *A gentle rain began to fall.*

gentle pressure *Apply gentle pressure to the wound to stop the bleeding.*

PREPOSITIONS

gentle on sth *Use a soap that is gentle on your skin.*

genuine *adj*

1 if a thing or person is genuine, they really are what they seem to be

NOUNS

a document/letter/signature etc is genuine *The historians believe that the documents are genuine.*

a painting/work of art is genuine *An art expert confirmed that the painting was genuine.*

a genuine attempt/effort *There was a genuine attempt to improve living conditions for the working classes.*

a genuine mistake *It wasn't clear if this was a genuine mistake, or a deliberate action.*

ADVERBS

absolutely genuine (=completely genuine) *They are sure that the pictures are absolutely genuine.*

PHRASES

sb/sth is the genuine article (=they really are as good as people say they are) *He was the genuine article, a great champion who never did anything but his best.*

THESAURUS: genuine

genuine, authentic, true, bona fide/bonafide, hard → **real (1)**

2 genuine feelings are sincere

NOUNS

genuine concern *There is genuine concern about the safety of nuclear energy.*

genuine interest/enthusiasm *The students seem to have a genuine interest in the subject.*

a genuine desire *She was motivated by a genuine desire to help the poor.*

a genuine love/affection/respect *Wilentz is a fine scholar, and I have a genuine respect for his work.*

a genuine belief *There was a genuine belief that she was the best person for the job.*

genuine surprise/fear *The decision was greeted with genuine surprise by many older members.*

a genuine person (=someone who is honest about their feelings) *Although she is a famous movie star, she is also a very genuine person.*

ADVERBS

perfectly genuine (=completely genuine) *Their surprise seemed perfectly genuine.*

germ *n*

a type of bacteria that spreads disease

VERBS

spread germs *Cover your mouth when you cough so that you don't spread germs.*

protect against germs *Washing your hands will help protect you against germs.*

kill germs *Bleach is good for killing germs.*

be exposed to germs (=be in a place where there are germs) *We are constantly exposed to germs and the possibility of infection.*

contain germs *She is worried that the dirt contains germs that will harm her children.*

ADJECTIVES

deadly germs (=germs that can kill people) *Terrorists could use deadly germs to carry out an attack on a population.*

nasty/harmful germs *There are some nasty germs around.*

germ + NOUNS

germ warfare (=the use of harmful bacteria in war to cause illness and death among the enemy) *The Biological Weapons Convention is a treaty that bans germ warfare.*

PHRASES

the spread of germs *Good hygiene has a major role to play in preventing the spread of germs.*

gesture *n*

1 something that you say or do to show how you feel about someone or something

ADJECTIVES

a nice gesture *It would be a nice gesture if we gave them something to say 'thank you'.*

a friendly gesture *Ella bought him a drink as a friendly gesture.*

a generous gesture *Giving all that money was a very generous gesture.*

a grand gesture (=something you do to impress people) *Love is not about grand gestures and expensive gifts.*

a dramatic gesture *In politics, dramatic gestures are sometimes necessary.*

a bold gesture (=that shows you are not scared of taking risks) *Appointing one of his opponents to the government was seen as a bold gesture.*

a token gesture (=done to pretend that you are dealing with a problem) *The inclusion of one woman on the committee was seen as a token gesture.*

a symbolic gesture (=that is intended to show how you feel) *In a symbolic gesture, he gave up his $10,000 monthly presidential salary.*

an empty gesture (=that does not achieve anything important) *Sacking his deputy was an empty gesture which failed to satisfy his critics.*

a futile gesture (=that is not likely to have any effect) *Sending extra troops was a futile gesture.*

a conciliatory gesture (=that shows you want to solve an argument or disagreement) *The government made several conciliatory gestures to the protesters.*

VERBS

make a gesture *Shouldn't we make some gesture to show we appreciate what she's done?*

PREPOSITIONS

a gesture towards/toward sth *The visit was regarded as a gesture towards repairing relations between the two countries.*

PHRASES

a gesture of goodwill (*also* **a goodwill gesture**) (=done to show you want to be helpful) *As a gesture of goodwill, customers will be offered a full refund.*

a gesture of friendship *He invited the two men to his house as a gesture of friendship.*

a gesture of support *She wrote a letter to the prime minister as a gesture of support.*

a gesture of solidarity (=done to show loyalty and support) *People sent food parcels to the strikers in a gesture of solidarity.*

a gesture of defiance (=done to show that you will not do what someone tells you to do) *The rebels launched an attack as a gesture of defiance.*

2 a movement of part of your body, especially your hands or head, to show what you mean or how you feel

VERBS

make a gesture *He made a gesture to the waiter.*

ADJECTIVES

a rude/obscene gesture *Luke made a rude gesture with his finger.*

an angry/threatening gesture *One of the men made a threatening gesture and I decided to leave.*

G

get *v*

1 if you get something, you are given it or buy it, or you find it or succeed in having it through your efforts

> **Grammar**
> **Get** is rarely used in the passive. **Obtain** and **acquire** are often used in the passive.

NOUNS

get a present/some clothes/some food etc *I got some nice presents for my birthday.*

get a letter/email/phone call/message etc *She gets hundreds of emails every day.*

get a job/get work *It is hard for young people to get jobs.*

get a degree *Sachs got his degree in biology from Yale University.*

get money/get a loan *I don't know where he gets his money from.*

get information/details/sb's address etc *You can get more information from the Tourist Office.*

get an answer/reply/reaction *Hopefully we'll get an answer later today.*

get an invitation/offer/complaint *I got an offer of a place on a course.*

get a ticket/table/room/seat *They managed to get a table at an Italian restaurant.*

get a surprise/shock *I got a shock when I opened the front door.*

get a husband/girlfriend etc *He was worried that he would never get a girlfriend.*

PREPOSITIONS

get sth from sb/sth *We get all our food from our local supermarket.*

get sth for sb/sth *Where did you get the idea for the book?*

> **Get or have got?**
> Don't confuse *I* ***got*** *some money* (=I received it) and *I* ***have got*** *some money* (=I have it). **Have got** is only used in the present tense. If you want to talk about having something in the past, you say **I had**, not 'I had got'.

THESAURUS: get

receive
prize | award | present | money | attention | support | letter | message | email | call | answer | invitation | offer | complaint
to be given something, or to get something that someone has sent you. **Receive** is more formal than **get**:
The winner will receive a prize of $500. | The case received a lot of attention in the media. | The police received a phone call from someone who said they had some information. | I called her name, but received no answer.

obtain *formal*
information | document | copy | result | sample | loan | permission | degree
to get something, especially by asking officially, or by studying or examining something. **Obtain** is also used about something that is difficult to get:
More information may be obtained from Cambridge Computers Ltd. | Journalists were able to obtain top secret government documents. | You will need to obtain permission from the author, if you want to publish part of the book. | She obtained a master's degree in German.

acquire *formal*
company | business | land | property | painting | collection | skill | knowledge | reputation | information | language
to get something, especially something big or expensive, or to get skills, knowledge etc:
The investment group acquired the company for $18 a share. | The Museum of Modern Art acquired a collection of Warhol's work. | The course is for students who want to acquire computer skills. | They are studying how children acquire language.

gain
control | power | independence | reputation | support | popularity | experience | confidence | understanding | strength | momentum
to get or achieve something. **Gain** is more formal than **get**:
The army has already gained control of the city. | Algeria gained independence from France in 1962. | Gubbay gained a distinguished reputation as a lawyer. | The sport began to gain popularity in the 1950s. | He gained more confidence in his abilities as a public speaker.

win
prize | award | medal | right | reputation | support | respect | admiration | trust | confidence
to get something as a result of your efforts:
He won the prize for best new writer. | The men are hoping to win the right to stay in the US. | The party won support by promising tax cuts.

earn
reputation | right | respect | praise | title | admiration
to get something as a result of your efforts, especially because people think you deserve it:
Johnson earned a reputation as one of the hardest-working players in the game. | The team played well and they have earned the right to be in the final of the competition. | She earned the respect of all her colleagues.

> **Earn** is often used with **himself/herself**:
> *He had* ***earned himself*** *a reputation as a great artist.*

inherit
money | house | estate | jewellery | fortune | wealth | property
to get someone's money or property after they die:
Jo inherited a lot of money from her mother. | Who will inherit the house when he dies? | She felt guilty about her inherited wealth, and gave most of it away.

get hold of sth *informal*
to get something that is difficult to find:
I have been trying to get hold of a map of the area.

2 to become

THESAURUS: get
get, grow, turn, go, come → **become**

3 if you get to a place, you arrive there

THESAURUS: get
get, come, reach, show up, get in, land, pull in, dock → **arrive**

G

ghost *n*

the spirit of a dead person that some people think they can feel or see in a place

VERBS

see a ghost *People say they have seen the ghost of a young girl in the room.*

believe in ghosts *Do you believe in ghosts?*

a ghost haunts a place *The house is supposed to be haunted by ghosts.*

a ghost appears *A ghost appeared through the wall.*

a ghost disappears/vanishes *The ghost suddenly vanished into thin air.*

ghost + NOUNS

a ghost story *'The Turn of the Screw' is a ghost story by Henry James.*

ADJECTIVES

a friendly ghost *Don't be scared – he's a friendly ghost.*

PREPOSITIONS

the ghost of sb *The ghosts of the dead are believed to come out on that night.*

gift *n*

1 something that you give someone, usually on a special occasion

ADJECTIVES/NOUNS + gift

a birthday/wedding/Christmas etc gift *The camera was a birthday gift from his parents.*

a free gift (=something that a shop or business gives you) *If you spend over £50, you get a free gift.*

the perfect/ideal gift *This book is the perfect gift for anybody with an interest in birds.*

a suitable gift *What would be a suitable gift for a ten-year-old boy?*

an expensive gift *His wife always gives him expensive gifts.*

a generous gift *She thanked them for such a generous gift.*

a lavish gift (=a large, impressive, or expensive gift) *She received lavish gifts of jewellery and clothes.*

an unwanted gift *You can return any unwanted gifts if you have the receipts.*

a parting gift (=a gift that you give someone when you leave) *Before boarding the train, he gave her the ring as a parting gift.*

a small gift *I decided to give my hosts a small gift.*

VERBS

give sb a gift *We gave her a gift on her birthday.*

receive a gift *He received a lot of gifts from clients.*

accept a gift *Sam accepted the gift on behalf of the school.*

exchange gifts (=people give each other gifts) *It's traditional to exchange gifts at Christmas.*

wrap (up) a gift *We were wrapping gifts for the children.*

make sb a gift of sth *formal* (=give someone something as a gift) *She had always admired the painting so I made her a gift of it.*

sth makes a good/ideal/unusual etc gift *A recipe book makes an ideal gift for someone who likes to cook.*

shower sb with gifts (=give someone a lot of gifts) *She has a rich boyfriend who showers her with gifts.*

PREPOSITIONS

a gift for/to sb *The money was intended as a gift for the children.*

a gift from sb *The bike was a gift from his grandparents.*

as a gift *Please accept the tickets as a gift.*

> **Gift** or **present?**
> **Present** is the usual word to use in everyday conversation. **Gift** sounds more formal. Companies give away **free gifts** (not 'presents').

2 a natural ability to do something well

VERBS

have a gift (*also* **possess a gift** *formal*): *She has a gift for making people feel happy.*

ADJECTIVES

a great gift *Being able to get on with all kinds of people is a great gift.*

a special/remarkable gift *The boy has a remarkable gift for music.*

a natural gift (*also* **a God-given gift** *literary*): *She has a natural gift for all sports.*

PREPOSITIONS

a gift for sth *Because of his gift for languages, he loves to travel.*

gifted *adj* THESAURUS > **intelligent**, **skilful**

gigantic *adj* THESAURUS > **huge**

giggle¹ *v*

to laugh quickly in a high voice, especially because you are excited or nervous

ADVERBS

giggle nervously *Instead of answering my question, the girl giggled nervously.*

PREPOSITIONS

giggle at sb/sth *The couple stopped kissing and were giggling at each other.*

giggle² *n*

a quick, quiet laugh, in a high voice

ADJECTIVES

a nervous giggle *She gave a nervous giggle before answering.*

a little giggle *Angela nodded politely with a little giggle.*
a hysterical giggle (=that someone cannot control) *The children were all in hysterical giggles.*
a high-pitched giggle (=with a very high sound) *The young woman gave a high-pitched giggle.*
helpless giggles (=that you cannot control) *She tried to answer him through helpless giggles.*

VERBS

give a giggle (=laugh) *She gave a little giggle.*
give sb the giggles (=make someone laugh) *The way he was waving his arms around gave us the giggles.*
burst into/collapse into giggles (=suddenly start laughing) *When I said I was their new teacher, the class suddenly all collapsed into giggles.*
stifle/suppress a giggle (=try to not laugh) *Britta covered her mouth to stifle a giggle.*
get/have the giggles (=laugh in a way that is difficult to control) *Now every time he looks at me I get the giggles.*

PREPOSITIONS

with a giggle *"Catch me if you can," she said with a giggle.*

PHRASES

a fit of giggles (= an occasion when you suddenly start laughing a lot) *Her remark sent Danny off into another fit of giggles.*

G

girl *n* a female child

ADJECTIVES/NOUNS + girl

a pretty/beautiful/cute girl *She is a pretty girl with dark brown long hair.*
a little/small girl (=one who is under 10 years old) *I've known Mollie ever since I was a little girl.*
a young girl (=one aged from about 5 to about 16) *Young girls in school uniform were walking to school.*
a baby girl *She just had a baby girl!*
a five-year-old girl/a ten-year-old girl etc *The picture was of an eight-year-old girl.*
a teenage girl *His fans are mainly teenage girls.*
a good/bad girl (=one who behaves well or badly) *Have you put all your toys away? That's a good girl.*
a big girl (=one who is old enough to behave in a sensible way) *She's a big girl; she can take care of herself.*

PHRASES

a girl of three/seven etc (=aged three, seven etc) *The patient was a girl of 12.*
boys and girls *Both boys and girls can apply to join the choir.*

girlfriend *n*

a girl or woman that you are having a romantic relationship with

ADJECTIVES

sb's first girlfriend *Beth was his first girlfriend.*
a steady/long-term girlfriend (=that you are having a long relationship with) *I asked him if he had a steady girlfriend.*
sb's new girlfriend *His parents were looking forward to meeting his new girlfriend.*
an old girlfriend/ex-girlfriend/former girlfriend (=someone who was your girlfriend before) *His old girlfriends were all very glamorous.*

VERBS

have a girlfriend *Paul had never had a girlfriend before.*
split up with your girlfriend *He's just split up with his girlfriend.*
leave your girlfriend *Sam left his girlfriend because they kept arguing.*
be sb's girlfriend *She told him that she wanted to be his girlfriend.*

gist *n*

the main idea and meaning of what someone has said or written

> **Grammar**
> **Gist** is always used in the phrase **the gist**.

VERBS

get the gist (=understand the main meaning) *She knew enough of the language to get the gist of what people were saying.*
give sb the gist (=tell someone the main ideas) *I don't need to know everything that was said – just give me the gist.*

PREPOSITIONS

the gist of sth *The gist of his argument is that full employment is impossible.*

PHRASES

the gist of the conversation *I don't speak a lot of Spanish, but I got the gist of the conversation.*
the gist of the/sb's argument *The gist of her argument is that books give children a wider experience of the world.*
the gist of the story/report/article etc *The gist of the newspaper's story is that people were tricked into working for very low wages.*

give *v*

1 to let someone have something, or put something in someone's hand

NOUNS

give sb a present/gift *At Christmas people give each other presents.*
give sb a prize/award/medal *The judges gave the prize to an Egyptian writer.*
give sb some money/a loan/a grant *She asked her father to give her the money.*

give help/support/backing *The Venezuelan president gave his support to the plan.*

give advice *They can give expert advice on career opportunities for students.*

give an answer *Think carefully before you give your answer.*

give your name/address/phone number *The form asks you to give the address where you are staying.*

give sb a drug/some medicine *The doctor gave him a drug which made him feel sleepy.*

give sb a chance/opportunity *Give me the chance to explain.*

ADVERBS

give generously *The refugees need your help, so please give generously.*

PREPOSITIONS

give sth to sb/sth *The ring was given to her by her grandmother.*

give sb sth for their birthday/for Christmas etc *What did Bob give you for your birthday?*

THESAURUS: give

donate
money | blood | organ | kidney | egg
to give money or other things to an organization to help with their work. You also use **donate** about giving blood or part of your body to help save someone's life:
Lawrence sold everything and ***donated*** *the money* ***to*** *charity. | Large numbers of volunteers came to the main hospital to donate blood.*

distribute
leaflet | pamphlet | questionnaire | food | aid | copies
to give things to a large number of people:
Anti-war protesters were distributing leaflets. | United Nations agencies are ***distributing*** *aid* ***to*** *the refugees. | Afterwards, police distributed 2,500 copies of a letter explaining their actions to local residents.*

contribute
money | funds | troops
to give money, goods etc in order to help to achieve something, especially when other people, organizations, or countries are also doing this:
Some of America's biggest companies ***contributed*** *money* ***to*** *his election campaign. | Canada* ***contributed*** *troops* ***to*** *the UN peace-keeping force.*

award
prize | medal | degree | damages
to officially give something such as a prize to someone:
Doris Lessing was awarded the Nobel Prize for Literature. | She was awarded a law degree at Yale University. | The court awarded him damages of $500,000 (=they said he should receive this money because of the harm done to him).

leave (*also* **bequeath** *formal*)
house | money | painting | collection | estate
to officially arrange for someone to have something that you own after your death:
He ***left*** *his house* ***to*** *his children in his will. | An uncle left her enough money to travel to Europe. | The estate was* ***bequeathed to*** *the nation.*

lavish *formal*
praise | gifts | money | attention
to give someone a lot of something:
The French press ***lavished*** *praise* ***on*** *the book when it was published. | She was* ***lavished with*** *gifts including airline tickets and jewellery. | He was jealous of all the attention that was* ***lavished on*** *his sister.*

> **Lavish** is used in two ways. You can ***lavish*** *praise/attention etc* ***on*** *someone*, or ***lavish*** *someone* ***with*** *praise/attention etc.*

confer *formal*
right | power | status | privilege | benefit | title | honour | degree
to officially give someone a special right, power, or honour:
The Constitution ***conferred*** *equal rights* ***on*** *all US citizens. | In many societies, being a doctor confers special status. | She received the highest honour that her country could* ***confer on*** *her. | The university will* ***confer*** *the degree of Doctor of Law* ***on*** *Professor Gregory.*

bestow *formal*
honour | gift | title | name | privilege | right | citizenship | favour
to give someone something to show how much they are respected – a very formal use:
Churchill was awarded the Congressional Gold Medal, the highest civilian honour that America can bestow. | The king ***bestowed*** *many precious gifts* ***upon*** *her.*

to put something in someone's hand

hand
to put something in someone's hand:
She ***handed*** *a note* ***to*** *the waiter and asked him to give it to the person at the next table. | He handed her his coat.*

> If you **hand** something **out**, you give it to a group of people: *The teacher was* ***handing out*** *forms to the students.*
> If you **hand** something **over**, you give it to someone, especially when you do not want to: *The police officer ordered him to* ***hand over*** *the gun.*

G

pass
to move something so that someone can have it, by putting it in their hand, or by putting it next to them:
Can you pass me my glasses? | She passed him the paper and said "Read this!"

You often ask someone to **pass** you something when you are eating: *Can you pass me* ***the salt/sugar/water****?*
Pass is also often used in sport, when one player throws or kicks the ball to another player: *He* ***passes the ball*** *to Johnson, who scores.*

present
prize | award | cup | cheque
to formally or officially give something to someone by putting it in their hands, especially at a formal ceremony:
The award will be presented by Michelle Obama. | The head of the school ***was presented with*** *flowers and gifts by the students.*

2 to do something such as make a speech in front of an audience

THESAURUS: give
make, give, take, commit, carry out, conduct, perform, undertake, implement → **do**

G

give up *v* THESAURUS stop[1] (1)

glad *adj* THESAURUS happy

glance[1] *v*

to quickly look at someone or something

ADVERBS
glance up/down/across (at sb/sth) *She glanced up at him before continuing to read.*
glance away *Blushing, Polly glanced away.*
glance back *He walked away, and this time he didn't glance back.*
glance over (at sb/sth) *I saw him glance over at his friend.*
glance sideways *She glanced sideways to see Neil's expression.*
glance nervously/anxiously *Rosa glanced nervously at the door.*
glance quickly/briefly *He glanced quickly around the room again.*
glance surreptitiously (=quickly and secretly so that other people do not notice) *Maria glanced surreptitiously at the papers on his desk.*
barely glance at sb/sth (=almost not look at someone or something) *He had barely glanced at her all evening.*

PREPOSITIONS
glance at sb/sth *Shelley glanced at the clock.*
glance towards sb/sth *Everyone glanced towards the door.*
glance around/round sth *He glanced around the restaurant before sitting down.*

glance[2] *n* a quick look

ADJECTIVES
a quick/brief glance *I had little time for more than a quick glance around the house.*
a cursory glance (=a very quick look without much attention to details) *I cast a cursory glance over the document.*
a fleeting glance (=a very quick look) *Stephen caught a fleeting glance of his father in the crowd.*
a furtive glance (=a quick secret look) *I sneaked a furtive glance at the letter on her desk.*

VERBS
give sth/sb a glance *He gave me a brief glance, then nodded.*
cast/take/have a glance at sth (=have a quick look at something) *Can you cast a glance at this report?*
steal/sneak a glance (=look quickly and secretly) *Alice stole a quick glance in the mirror to check her hair.*
exchange glances (=look at each other quickly) *The two brothers exchanged glances.*
sb's glance falls on sth (=someone looks at something) *Geoff's glance fell on the broken vase.*

PREPOSITIONS
a glance at sb/sth *A glance at my watch showed that it was still only 9.30.*
a glance towards/over/across etc sth *After a glance through the window, Mary started to worry.*

PHRASES
at a glance (=by looking at something or someone very quickly) *I could tell at a glance what it was.*
at first glance (=when you first look at something or someone) *At first glance everything looked normal.*

glare[1] *v*

to look angrily at someone or something for a long time

ADVERBS
glare angrily/furiously *He stood up, still glaring angrily at his mother.*
glare fiercely *The two men stood glaring fiercely at each other.*
glare accusingly *She turned and glared accusingly in Lindsey's direction.*

PREPOSITIONS/ADVERBS
glare at sb *"Where did he go?" Katherine demanded, glaring at her daughter.*
glare back *Ebert was glaring back at him, his hands shaking with anger.*

glare² *n*

1 an angry look

ADJECTIVES

an angry/furious/hostile glare *He fixed his audience with an angry glare.*

a steely/icy glare (=a very determined glare) *Her eyes narrowed into a steely glare.*

VERBS

give sb a glare *Instead of answering his question, she gave him a hostile glare.*

fix sb with a glare (=look at someone very closely in an angry way) *Her mother fixed her with a glare as soon as she entered the room.*

2 very bright light which is unpleasant to look at

ADJECTIVES

the harsh/intense/brilliant glare (=very strong and unpleasant) *The sun came up, giving the snow the harsh glare of desert sand.*

the blinding glare (=so strong that it is difficult for you to see) *They shielded their eyes against the blinding glare of the sun.*

VERBS

reduce/stop/eliminate glare *These sunglasses help to reduce glare.*

reflect the glare *The whitewashed houses reflected the glare of the sun.*

glass *n*

a transparent solid substance used for making windows, bottles etc

VERBS

glass breaks *This type of glass doesn't break easily.*

glass shatters (=breaks into small pieces) *When glass shatters, it leaves jagged edges.*

glass cracks *Glass will crack if too much pressure is put on it.*

PHRASES

a piece of glass *He cut his foot on a piece of glass.*

a shard/splinter of glass (=a sharp piece of broken glass) *People were injured by shards of glass following the explosion.*

a fragment of glass (=a small piece of glass that has broken off) *Fragments of glass covered the floor near the broken window.*

a pane of glass (=a piece of glass used in a window) *There was a broken pane of glass in the kitchen window.*

a sheet of glass (=a piece of flat glass) *Sheets of glass were used as shelves.*

glasses *n*

two pieces of specially cut glass or plastic in a frame, which you wear in order to see more clearly

VERBS

wear glasses *I didn't know you wore glasses.*

put on your glasses *He put on his glasses and read through the instructions.*

take off/remove your glasses *Elsie took off her glasses and rubbed her eyes.*

wipe/clean your glasses *Harry wiped his glasses with the corner of a handkerchief.*

break your glasses *I broke my glasses when I accidentally sat on them.*

ADJECTIVES/NOUNS + glasses

dark glasses (=sunglasses) *She wore a scarf over her head and dark glasses.*

thick glasses (=with lenses that are thick) *The old man looked up at them through thick glasses.*

reading/driving glasses (=for reading or driving) *I can't find my reading glasses.*

PHRASES

a pair of glasses *She was wearing a new pair of glasses.*

glide *v*

to move smoothly and quietly, as if without effort

ADVERBS

glide along/over *The couples glided over the dance floor.*

glide away/down/up/through etc *Sea birds glided through the air, suddenly diving into the ocean for fish.*

glide effortlessly *Experienced skiers glided effortlessly down the slopes.*

glide gracefully *Skaters were gliding gracefully over the ice.*

glide smoothly *Sailing boats glided smoothly over the calm surface of the lake.*

glimpse *n*

1 a quick look at someone or something that does not allow you to see them clearly

VERBS

catch/get a glimpse *They caught a glimpse of a dark green car.*

have a glimpse *Stephen had a glimpse of a man running past the car.*

ADJECTIVES

a brief/quick/fleeting glimpse (=lasting a very short time) *We only had a fleeting glimpse of the river.*

an occasional glimpse (=one that does not happen often) *The sky was often cloudy, and we caught only occasional glimpses of the sun.*

a tantalising glimpse (=one that makes you want to see more) *She gave us a tantalising glimpse of the cake.*

sb's first glimpse of sth (=the first time someone sees something) *I got my first glimpse of the sea when I was seven, on a school outing.*

2 a short experience of something that helps you understand it

ADJECTIVES

a rare glimpse *The programme gives you a rare glimpse into the private life of the royal family.*

a fascinating glimpse *The exhibition provides a fascinating glimpse of how people lived in ancient Egypt.*

VERBS

give/allow sb a glimpse *We were given a glimpse of the team's preparations for the Olympic Games.*

provide/offer a glimpse *The court case offers a glimpse into the top-secret world of medical research.*

show/reveal a glimpse *The young player struggled at times, but showed glimpses of the great sportsman he could become.*

get/have a glimpse *We got a few glimpses of how well she could play.*

PREPOSITIONS

a glimpse of sth *Visit the weekly market to get a glimpse of traditional Italian life.*

a glimpse into the future/the past/sb's world *The film offers a glimpse into the future of our planet.*

global *adj*

affecting or including the whole world

NOUNS

the global economy *The financial problems in the US affected the global economy.*

global trade *There is a growing global trade in hazardous waste, which needs regulation.*

the global market *The company has a large share of the global market for computers.*

the global village/community (=the world considered as a place where all people live closely together) *In today's global village, events in small countries can affect events worldwide.*

ADVERBS

increasingly global (=involving more of the world's countries) *The economy is increasingly global, so events worldwide have an effect on it.*

truly global (=really including every country in the world) *The internet is a truly global network that links millions of people.*

global warming *n*

a general increase in world temperatures caused by increased amounts of carbon dioxide around the Earth

VERBS

cause global warming *Burning fossil fuels such as coal causes global warming.*

reduce/curb global warming *They failed to agree on actions to curb global warming.*

stop/prevent global warming *Larger countries should do more to stop global warming.*

deal with/tackle global warming *Urgent action is needed to tackle global warming.*

fight/combat global warming *The leaders are meeting to discuss ways to combat global warming.*

contribute to global warming (=help cause global warming) *Gases such as carbon dioxide contribute to global warming by trapping heat in the atmosphere.*

sth is caused by global warming *The rise in sea levels is caused by global warming.*

sth is linked/related to global warming *The recent floods have been linked to global warming.*

PHRASES

the effects/consequences of global warming *One of the effects of global warming has been the melting of the glaciers.*

the threat of global warming *To deal with the threat of global warming, countries must work together on clean energy.*

globe Ac *n* the world

PHRASES

halfway around the globe *We had gone halfway around the globe, only to find shops selling the same things we could buy at home.*

on/to the other side of the globe *The internet allows information to be sent to the other side of the globe with just the click of a button.*

in/from every corner of the globe (=in or from every part of the world) *Scientific information has come in from every corner of the globe.*

ADJECTIVES

the entire/whole globe *These lines circle the entire globe, allowing information to travel quickly around the world.*

VERBS

circle the globe (=go around the globe) *They were the first to circle the globe in a hot-air balloon.*

span the globe (=include all the countries in the world) *His publishing businesses span the globe.*

spread across the globe *The slowdown in the economy spread across the globe.*

PREPOSITIONS

around/across the globe *The book includes stories from writers around the globe.*

all over the globe *Millions of people all over the globe use the internet to keep in touch.*

gloom *n*

1 a feeling of great sadness and lack of hope

PHRASES

be filled with gloom *She was filled with gloom when she heard the news.*

G

be sunk/shrouded in gloom (=feel very sad and hopeless) *The boy was sunk in gloom and would not speak.*

cast (a) gloom over sth (=make people feel sad) *Her father's illness cast a gloom over the holidays.*

add to the gloom (=make people feel more sad) *To add to the gloom, the team's best player is injured.*

doom and gloom (=when there seems no hope) *The economic situation is not all doom and gloom – some industries are doing very well.*

an atmosphere of gloom *They laughed, and the atmosphere of gloom lightened a little.*

a sense of gloom *He had a sense of gloom about the test.*

VERBS

gloom descends (=people start to feel sad) *Gloom descended on the crowd when the news was announced.*

gloom deepens (=people feel more sad) *The party's gloom deepened as the election results came in.*

gloom lifts (=people stop feeling sad) *Germany's gloom lifted when Stallkamp scored a goal.*

dispel/lift the gloom (=make people feel less sad) *Now for some good news to dispel the gloom.*

ADJECTIVES

economic gloom *It was a year of economic gloom for the car industry.*

deep gloom *There was deep gloom about the future.*

deepening gloom (=becoming worse) *There is deepening gloom over the country's economic prospects.*

the general gloom (=when many people feel there is not much hope) *Amid the general gloom, there are some positive signs.*

PREPOSITIONS

gloom about/over/at sth *There is deepening gloom over the lack of progress in the peace negotiations.*

2 almost complete darkness – used especially in literature

PHRASES

sb's eyes become accustomed to the gloom (=they start to be able to see in the darkness) *My eyes gradually became accustomed to the gloom.*

be shrouded in gloom *The ballroom was empty and shrouded in gloom.*

peer into the gloom *"Who's that?" the old woman asked, peering into the gloom.*

ADJECTIVES

deep gloom *They wandered through the deep gloom of the forest.*

deepening/gathering gloom (=becoming darker) *We drove through the deepening gloom.*

damp/cold gloom *The two men stood in the chilly damp gloom.*

PREPOSITIONS

in the gloom *All she could see in the gloom was the high wall of a building.*

through the gloom *Through the gloom, he could just make out the figure of a man.*

into/out of the gloom *I stared into the gloom.*

gloomy *adj*

THESAURUS **cloudy**, **dark (1)**, **depressing**, **sad (1)**

glorious *adj*

THESAURUS **beautiful**

glory *n*

1 praise and admiration from people

PHRASES

sb's moment of glory *His moment of glory came in the second half of the game when he scored.*

a blaze of glory (=when someone or something is praised a lot) *The film opened in a blaze of glory with rave reviews from critics.*

sb's dreams of glory *His dreams of glory were shattered when he lost to Federer.*

VERBS

win glory *These men had won glory in battle.*

bring glory to sb/sth *Locals hope the discovery will bring prosperity and glory to the town.*

cover yourself in glory (=do something that makes people admire you) *As team captain, he hasn't covered himself in glory.*

bask/bathe/revel in the glory of sth (=enjoy the fame and admiration you get) *He basked in the glory of his achievement.*

steal sb's glory (=do something that makes you more admired than someone else doing something similar) *She played brilliantly, but Shaw stole all the glory by scoring three times.*

ADJECTIVES

reflected glory (=fame that you get because you are close to someone admired) *She basked in the reflected glory of her daughter's marriage to such a famous actor.*

personal glory *She put the team's interests above personal glory.*

past glory (=past successes) *Journalists only ever talk about past glories and no one thinks of the future.*

glory + NOUNS

glory days/years (=a time in the past when someone or something was admired) *The team's glory days are over.*

2 great and impressive beauty

PHRASES

restore sth to its former glory (=make something impressive and beautiful again) *This*

17th-century house has been restored to its former glory.

in all its/their etc glory *Charles had longed to see Venice in all its glory.*

ADJECTIVES

sth's full glory *Roses reach their full glory in June.*

3 something's most impressive feature

ADJECTIVES

sth's great glory *The castle's great glory is its massive twin-towered gatehouse.*

sth's crowning glory (=the thing that is the most impressive and beautiful) *The stunning gardens are the hotel's crowning glory.*

glossy *adj* THESAURUS **shiny**

glove *n*

a piece of clothing that you wear on your hand in order to protect it or keep it warm

PHRASES

a pair of gloves *Forbes pulled on a pair of black leather gloves.*

VERBS

wear gloves *I usually wear gloves when gardening.*

put on your gloves *Put on your gloves, children – it's cold outside.*

take off your gloves *He took off his gloves and hat.*

G

glow *v*

1 to produce or reflect a soft steady light

NOUNS + glow

the sun glows *The evening sun glowed in the sky.*

a lamp/light glows *The lights of the city glowed in the distance.*

a fire glows *The fire still glowed in the fireplace.*

a cigarette glows *The men stood around, their cigarettes glowing in the dark.*

ADVERBS

glow softly/faintly/dimly *The bedside lamp glowed dimly.*

glow brightly/brilliantly *The lights inside the shop were glowing brightly.*

glow warmly *A candle glowed warmly in its holder.*

glow briefly *The sun glowed briefly on the horizon and was gone.*

glow steadily *The power light on the computer glowed steadily.*

PREPOSITIONS

glow with sth *The windows were glowing with a warm yellow light.*

PHRASES

glow red/orange/pink *The end of her cigarette was glowing red.*

2 to look very happy and healthy

NOUNS + glow

sb's face glows (*also* **sb's cheeks glow**) *Her face was glowing as we talked.*

sb's eyes glow *Her eyes glowed with delight when she saw him.*

sb's skin glows *To make your skin glow, eat plenty of fresh fruit and vegetables.*

ADVERBS

positively glow (=used to emphasize how happy and healthy someone looks) *Rachael was positively glowing at her birthday party on Saturday.*

PHRASES

glow with health *He returned from his holiday glowing with health.*

glow with pride/pleasure/happiness *She gazed up at him, glowing with happiness.*

glum *adj* THESAURUS **sad (1)**

goal Ac *n*

1 something that you hope to achieve in the future

ADJECTIVES

the main goal (*also* **the primary goal** *formal*): *My main goal is to win this race.*

the ultimate goal (=that you hope to achieve eventually) *The ultimate goal is a fairer and more democratic society.*

a long-term goal (=that you hope to achieve after a long time) *The organization's long-term goal is to gain a strong position in the European market.*

an immediate goal (=that you want to achieve very soon) *Our immediate goal is to cut costs.*

an ambitious goal (=difficult to achieve) *The agreement set ambitious goals to cut greenhouse gas emissions worldwide.*

sb's personal goal *They had to sacrifice personal goals for their family life.*

a common goal (=shared by more than one person or organization) *Iran and Turkey shared common goals in their handling of the refugee crisis.*

a realistic/achievable goal *Students are encouraged to set themselves realistic goals for academic improvement.*

a modest goal (=not too difficult to achieve) *Don't try to lose a lot of weight quickly; set yourself a more modest goal.*

VERBS

achieve/attain/reach your goal *She worked hard to achieve her goal of becoming a doctor.*

set a goal (=decide what you want to achieve) *It helps if you set yourself clear goals.*

have a goal *Henry had one goal in life: to make a lot of money.*

work towards a goal *We are all working towards similar goals.*

pursue a goal *Have we gone too far in pursuing the goal of national security?*

NOUNS + goal

a career/business goal *The plan sets out our business goals and targets.*

THESAURUS: goal

goal, target, objective, ambition → **aim**

aim, goal, objective, the object of sth, the point, intention, ends → **purpose**

2 the action of making the ball go into a goal in a game such as soccer

VERBS

score a goal *Robbie Keane scored a goal just before half-time.*

get a goal *It was great that he got that goal so late in the game.*

head a goal (=score a goal by hitting the ball with your head) *Peter Crouch headed England's equalizing goal.*

concede a goal/let in a goal (=let the other team score a goal) *Arsenal conceded a goal in the final minute of extra time.*

disallow a goal (=not allow a goal to be counted because a rule has been broken) *The goal was disallowed by the referee.*

ADJECTIVES

a spectacular/superb goal (=very good) *He has scored some spectacular goals this season.*

the winning goal *The winning goal came three minutes before the end.*

an own goal (=when a player accidentally puts the ball into his or her own net) *Dixon scored an unfortunate own goal against West Ham.*

a last-minute goal (=one that happens just before the game ends) *Italy won with a last-minute goal.*

goal + NOUNS

a goal scorer *He is the team's top goal scorer.*

go away *v* THESAURUS **disappear, stop[1] (2)**

god *n*

1 the spirit or being who Christians, Jews, Muslims etc pray to, and who they believe created the universe

This sense is usually written with a capital letter as **God**.

VERBS

believe in God *Do you believe in God?*

pray to God *They prayed to God for forgiveness.*

worship God (=show love and respect for God) *On this day, people worship God and thank Him for the harvest.*

praise God *They came to the church to praise God.*

find God (=start to believe in God) *He was an armed robber before he found God.*

God exists *I believe that God exists.*

PHRASES

belief/faith in God *Her faith in God helped her deal with her illness.*

God's will/the will of God (=what God wants to happen) *He believed it was God's will that they should suffer.*

Almighty God/God Almighty (=used to emphasize God's power) *He swore by Almighty God to tell the truth.*

the word of God (=what God says) *Missionaries travelled the world to tell people the word of God.*

a gift from God *Life is a gift from God.*

God's existence/the existence of God *Philosophers argued about the existence of God.*

2 a male spirit who is believed by some religions to control the world or part of it, or who represents a particular quality

ADJECTIVES

a Greek/Roman/Egyptian/Norse god *Janus is one of the most important Roman gods.*

PREPOSITIONS

the god of sth *Eros is the Greek god of love.*

gold *n*

a very valuable soft yellow metal

ADJECTIVES/NOUNS + gold

solid gold *The chain was made of solid gold.*

pure gold *Pure gold can be beaten out to form very thin sheets.*

9/18/24 carat gold (=a measurement used to show how pure gold is) *These earrings are 18 carat gold.*

gold + NOUNS

a gold chain/ring/watch/coin etc *He wore a gold ring on the third finger of his left hand.*

gold jewellery *BrE*, **gold jewelry** *AmE*: *She likes wearing chunky gold jewellery.*

a gold medal (=for first place in a race etc) *She dreams of winning an Olympic gold medal.*

gold leaf (=a very thin sheet of gold) *The picture frame was covered with gold leaf.*

gold bullion (=bars of gold) *Gold bullion worth £26 million was taken in the robbery.*

a gold bar/ingot (=a piece of gold the size of a brick) *The bank keeps the gold bars locked in its vault.*

a gold mine *Her father worked in a gold mine.*

a gold rush (=a time when people hurry to a place where gold has been found, hoping to find gold themselves) *People headed west in the days of the California gold rush.*

VERBS

prospect for gold (=try to find gold) *The company had prospected for gold in China, with some success.*

pan for gold (=wash soil in order to find small pieces of gold in it) *Every day he went down to the river to pan for gold.*

find gold (*also* **strike gold**) *The French came to America in the hope of finding gold there.*

> **Using gold when saying that something is very valuable**
>
> If you say something is **(like) gold dust**, you mean it is difficult to get and people will pay a lot of money for it: *Tickets for the show are* ***like gold dust***.
>
> A **gold mine** is often used about something that makes a lot of money for someone: *The shop turned out to be a* ***gold mine*** *for us.*
>
> **Strike gold** originally meant "to find gold". It is now usually used when someone has discovered or created something very valuable: *The company that makes the drug thinks it has* ***struck gold***.

golden *adj*

having a bright yellow colour like gold

NOUNS

golden hair *She had golden hair and blue eyes.*

a golden beach *The Costa del Sol has almost two hundred miles of golden beaches.*

golden sand *The resort has a long beach of fine golden sand.*

golden light *In the evening, the front of the house is bathed in golden light.*

a golden glow *The interior was lit only by the golden glow of the fire.*

a golden colour *BrE*, **a golden color** *AmE*: *This soup is a beautiful golden color.*

> **Golden or gold?**
>
> **Golden** is the usual word to use when talking about colour: *She has beautiful* ***golden*** *hair.* | *the island's* ***golden*** *beaches*
>
> **Gold** is the usual word to use when saying that something is made of gold: *a* ***gold*** *bracelet.* **Golden** is rarely used in this meaning, but you will sometimes see it in stories: *the goose that lays the golden eggs* | *The Man with the Golden Gun.* In these phrases the idea of the colour and the material are mixed together.

golf *n*

a game in which you hit a small white ball into holes in the ground

VERBS

play golf *I often play golf at the weekends.*

take up golf (=start playing golf) *She took up golf as a way of getting more exercise.*

golf + NOUNS

a golf course (=an area of land designed for playing golf) *The hotel has an 18-hole golf course.*

a golf club (=an organization that runs a golf course, or the building where members meet) *Keith is a member of the Royal Aberdeen Golf Club.*

golf clubs (=long thin sticks for hitting the ball in golf) *She bought a new set of golf clubs.*

a golf tournament/championship *He will play in the British Open golf championship.*

ADJECTIVES/NOUNS + golf

amateur/professional golf *The standard of amateur golf is improving.*

tournament/championship golf *The course is suitable for world-class championship golf.*

PHRASES

a game/round of golf *He invited me to join him for a round of golf.*

good *adj*

1 used about things that you like, or about things that are useful, suitable, or of high quality

NOUNS

a good time/day/year *We had a really good time at the party.*

good news *I have some good news – you've passed your exam.*

a good idea/suggestion *It's a good idea to take some warm blankets if you're driving in snow.*

good advice *The book offers plenty of good advice on buying a house.*

the good thing/aspect/point *The good thing about this car is that it is cheap to run.*

a good reason/excuse/argument *Is there a good reason why you haven't done your homework?*

a good effect *The changes had a good effect on the economy.*

a good example/illustration *The church is a good example of early English architecture.*

good luck *Some people believe that black cats bring good luck.*

good weather *I hope we have good weather for our picnic next week.*

good food *The restaurant serves good food at a reasonable price.*

a good book/film/song *Have you read any good books recently?*

ADVERBS

really good *I thought the play was really good.*

rather/quite/pretty good *The facilities at the school are quite good.*

particularly/especially good *The food was nice and the dessert was especially good.*

outstandingly/exceptionally good *2009 had been an exceptionally good year for the company.*

PHRASES

be of good quality *The carpets are of good quality and are very expensive.*

THESAURUS: good

nice
day | place | house | hotel | feeling | idea | surprise | meal | weather
pleasant and enjoyable. **Nice** is very common in spoken English. In essays and formal written English, it is better to use other words:
Have a nice day. | Heidelberg is a nice place to live. | What a nice surprise! I wasn't expecting to see you. | ***It will be really nice*** *to meet your brother.*

fine
view | food | example | performance | painting | collection | building | church | piece of work
very good and impressive:
The hotel has fine views of the old town. | This restaurant serves some of the finest food in Italy. | The house is a fine example of a Tudor building. | The museum has a fine collection of clocks dating back to 1658.

Fine can be used to talk about good weather: *If it's* ***fine*** *tomorrow, we'll go for a walk.*
You can also use **fine** to say that your health is good, especially when you were ill before: *I'm* ***fine*** *now.*

sound
advice | reason | judgment | decision | strategy | investment
good and sensible:
The book is full of sound advice. | There is a very sound reason for this decision. | Property always makes a sound investment.

Sound is often used after an adverb: **financially/theoretically/morally/ecologically etc sound**: *The product is easy to use and is* ***environmentally sound****.*

attractive
offer | idea | prospect | opportunity | proposition | option | alternative | deal | price | rate | feature | argument | investment | target
if something is attractive, it seems good and makes you feel that you want to do something:
It was a very attractive offer and I was tempted by it. | Setting up your own business may seem like an attractive proposition, but you need to be aware of the risks involved. | The product is available at a very attractive price.

desirable *formal*
quality | feature | attribute | place | location | area | aim | goal | outcome | state of affairs
used about things that you want to have, places where you want to live, or things that you want to happen:
Most drivers put safety at the top of the list of desirable features in a car. | California remains a desirable place to live. | Getting rid of all nuclear weapons sounds like a very desirable aim. | Clearly, this situation is not a desirable state of affairs.

favourable *BrE*, **favorable** *AmE*
response | reaction | reception | impression | reviews | comments | conditions | climate | position | result | outcome
good – used especially when people like something, or when the conditions are suitable for success:
The new style of exam received a favourable response from teachers. | She wanted to make a favourable impression at the interview (=she wanted people to like her and think she was suitable for the job). *| Conditions are favourable for sailing. | There was little hope of a favourable outcome.*

positive
effect | influence | impact | experience | step | aspect | feedback | response | reaction | comments | results | contribution
good – used especially when something has a good or useful effect, or shows that you like something:
Exercise has a positive effect on health. | Working here has been a very positive experience for me. | There are a lot of positive aspects to retirement, but there is a negative side too. | The response from our customers has been very positive.

beneficial
effect | impact | influence | consequences | change | arrangement | role
having a good effect:
Drinking plenty of water has a beneficial effect on your skin. | Aspirin has a potentially beneficial role in preventing heart attacks.

ANTONYMS **good → bad (1)**

2 doing something in a skilful way

NOUNS

a good player/team *The team has some really good players.*

a good actor/singer/painter/writer *He's a very good actor and he's been in a lot of films.*

a good swimmer/skier/driver/teacher *I'm not a very good swimmer.*

a good student *Amelie's teachers say she is a good student who asks intelligent questions.*

a good cook *Eva was a good cook and often made cakes for us.*

G

good English/French/Japanese etc *Your French is really good – have you lived in France?*
a good game *It was a good game and the players played well.*
a good performance/speech *We want to put on a good performance.*
a good job/good work *Ken did a good job of painting the house.*
a good grade/mark *Svetlana always gets good grades in English.*

⚠ Don't say 'I want to be a good English speaker.' Say **I want to speak English well/fluently/like a native speaker.**

ADVERBS
really good *Daniel is really good at tennis.*
rather/quite/pretty good *I'm quite good at art.*
exceptionally/outstandingly good *Mike has done an outstandingly good job and I'd like to thank him.*
good enough *The team are not good enough to win the competition.*

PREPOSITIONS
good at (doing) sth *Ella is very good at making clothes.*

PHRASES
be good with your hands (=be good at making things) *My dad was very good with his hands and made some beautiful things for the house.*
be good with figures (=be good at doing calculations) *You should ask Steve – he's very good with figures.*
be good with words *Some sports players aren't very good with words.*
be good with people/children *He is very good with children and knows how to talk to them.*

ANTONYMS **good → bad (3)**

3 behaving in a way that is morally right, or in the way that you should behave

NOUNS
a good man/woman/person *Ford was a good man who was well respected by voters.*
a good boy/girl/child/dog *Have you been a good boy at school today?*
good behaviour *BrE*, **good behavior** *AmE*: *It is important to reward good behaviour.*
good manners (=polite behaviour) *It is only good manners to obey the traffic regulations wherever you are.*
good intentions *She was full of good intentions when she started her job.*
a good deed (=a good thing that you do) *I feel like I've done my good deed for today.*

PHRASES
as good as gold (=very well behaved) *The children were as good as gold.*
be on your best behaviour *BrE*, **be on your best behavior** *AmE* (=behave as well and politely as you can) *You'd better be on your best behaviour when your grandmother comes to visit.*
it is good of sb to do sth (=it is kind) *It was good of them to offer to lend us the money.*

THESAURUS: good

nice
person | man | guy | bloke | woman | child | kid
good, kind, and friendly. **Nice** is very common in spoken English. In written English, it is better to use other words:
Dave's a really nice guy. | ***It was nice of*** *him to help.*

well behaved
child | pupil | dog | pet | crowd
behaving in a polite calm way, and doing what you are told to do:
The children were very well behaved all day. | *Well-behaved dogs are welcome at the hotel.* | *A police spokesman said the crowd was remarkably well behaved.*

You write **well-behaved** before a noun. You write **well behaved** if there is no following noun.

decent
person | man | woman | guy | bloke | chap | citizen
good and honest, and treating people in a fair and kind way:
My parents were decent hard-working people. | *Hopefully the kids will grow up to be decent citizens.* | ***It's decent of*** *you to join us.*

honourable *BrE*, **honorable** *AmE*
man | woman | thing | history | profession | war | defeat | surrender | settlement | compromise
morally correct and showing that you have high moral standards, especially when you do something that you feel is your duty:
Her father was a brave and honourable man. | *In the circumstances, the only honourable thing she can do is to resign.* | *The country has a long and honourable history.*

respectable
man | woman | person | family | citizen | business | occupation
behaving and living your life in a way that most people think is morally correct – this use seems rather old-fashioned these days:
The bar was no place for a respectable married man. | *His mother wants him to marry someone from a respectable family.*

virtuous *formal or humorous*
man | woman | life | conduct
behaving in a morally correct way and having very high moral standards:

Everybody agreed that Senator Daley was a wise and virtuous man. | *She* ***felt very virtuous*** *because she hadn't drunk any alcohol for a year.*

upright *formal*
citizen | **member of the community** | **man**
having high moral standards and always obeying the law:
Wordsworth was a man of integrity, an upright citizen. | *He was a good honest upright man.*

dutiful *formal*
wife | **daughter** | **son** | **husband** | **servant**
careful to do what people expect you to do, especially people in your family – this use seems rather old-fashioned these days:
She remained the dutiful wife, never complaining about her husband.

THESAURUS: good

generous, considerate, thoughtful, caring, sympathetic, compassionate, warm-hearted/kind-hearted, benevolent, benign, nice, good, sweet → **kind²**

ANTONYMS **good → bad (4)**

good-looking *adj* **THESAURUS** **beautiful**

goods *n*

things that are produced in order to be sold

ADJECTIVES/NOUNS + goods

electrical goods *People spend more money on electrical goods than on clothing.*

household goods (=which you use in your home) *The high street has several shops selling household goods.*

consumer goods (=televisions, washing machines etc) *The market for consumer goods is huge.*

white goods *BrE* (=large electrical equipment such as washing machines and refrigerators) *Sales of white goods have increased by 15%.*

luxury goods *People are getting richer and the demand for luxury goods is growing.*

imported goods *The government raised taxes on imported goods.*

manufactured goods (=made in large quantities using machines) *Imports of manufactured goods have increased rapidly.*

damaged/defective/faulty goods (=that have something wrong with them) *Faulty goods can be returned to the manufacturer for a refund.*

stolen goods *The police charged him with handling stolen goods.*

VERBS

produce/manufacture goods *The company produces goods for export.*

import goods *Huge quantities of goods are imported from China.*

export goods *We export our goods all over the world.*

supply goods *The firm supplies goods and services to Europe.*

deliver goods *We promise to deliver the goods in time for Christmas.*

transport goods *Companies are still choosing to transport most of their goods by road.*

THESAURUS: goods

goods, commodity, merchandise, wares, export, import → **product**

gorgeous *adj* **THESAURUS** **beautiful**

gossip *n*

conversation or information about other people's private lives

ADJECTIVES/NOUNS + gossip

the latest gossip *Annie told me all the latest gossip from work.*

juicy gossip *informal* (=interesting gossip) *Do you want to hear some juicy gossip?*

hot gossip *informal* (=new and interesting) *The magazine features hot gossip from the world of show business.*

idle gossip (=not based on facts) *I'm not interested in idle gossip.*

malicious gossip (=unkind and intending to upset or harm someone) *Criticisms of him were based on malicious gossip.*

office gossip *He told her a few bits of office gossip which he thought might interest her.*

VERBS

spread gossip *Someone's been spreading gossip about Lucy and Ian.*

gossip goes around (=it is told by one person to another) *It was a small village, and any gossip went around very quickly.*

gossip + NOUNS

a gossip column (=a regular article in a newspaper or magazine about the private lives of famous people) *The princess often appeared in the gossip columns.*

PREPOSITIONS

gossip about sb/sth *There is always a lot of gossip about professional football players.*

PHRASES

a piece/bit/snippet of gossip *I've got a piece of gossip which might interest you.*

be the subject of gossip (=be talked about) *His close friendship with Carol was the subject of gossip.*

government *n*

1 the group of people who govern a country or state

ADJECTIVES/NOUNS + government

the UK/Japanese etc government *The UK government has offered to send aid.*

the Labour/Conservative etc government *In August 1931, the Labour government collapsed.*
a left-wing/right-wing government *The new left-wing government restructured the economy.*
central/national government (=that deals with national rather than local things) *Funding will continue to be available from central government for further education for adults.*
federal government (=of the whole of the US rather than of the individual states) *The state, rather than the federal government, would have to pay the extra cost.*
local/state/city government (=in a particular area) *Libraries are the responsibility of local government.*
a democratic government/a democratically elected government *A military group tried to overthrow the democratically elected government.*
an authoritarian government (=a strict one which forces people to obey it) *An increasingly authoritarian government is threatening people's political freedom.*
a coalition government (=one made up of members of more than one political party) *The country has had a succession of weak coalition governments.*

government + NOUNS

a government minister *A government minister said that there would be an inquiry.*
a government official (=someone who works for a government in an official position) *He had a meeting with French scientists and government officials.*
a government department/agency/body *The Ministry of Justice is the government department responsible for prisons in England and Wales.*
government policy *Government policy on education has been criticized.*
government spending *Government spending on health care totals about $60 billion a year.*
government cuts (=a reduction in the amount of money a government spends) *Many research centres will close because of government cuts.*

VERBS + government

elect a government *A new government was elected last October.*
form a government *Neither party had the majority necessary to form a government.*
bring down a government (=force it to lose power) *It was a major scandal that nearly brought down the government.*
overthrow/topple a government (=remove it, especially by force) *Soldiers made an unsuccessful attempt to overthrow the government.*

government + VERBS

a government comes to power/takes office (=it starts to have power) *The new government took office in May.*
a government falls/collapses (=it suddenly fails and cannot continue) *The government collapsed after only nine months.*

PREPOSITIONS

under a government *Structural reforms are unlikely under the present government.*

PHRASES

a member of the government *The prime minister and other members of the government travelled to Davos for the meeting.*
a change of government *I hope that we will have a change of government soon.*

2 the process, method, or system of governing a country or state

ADJECTIVES

strong/firm government *We need a leader who can provide strong government.*
good/effective government *The lack of effective government has caused problems over many years for the country.*
democratic government *He promised more democratic government for the island.*
authoritarian government *Powers were limited to prevent authoritarian government.*
big government (=when the government has a lot or too much control over people's lives) *President Clinton declared an end to big government.*
small government (=when the government does not have too much control over people's lives) *The party has traditionally supported the idea of small government.*

graceful *adj*

moving in a smooth and attractive way, or having an attractive shape

NOUNS

a graceful movement *He watched her graceful movements as she came towards him.*
sb's graceful neck/legs/arms *She had slender graceful arms.*
sth's graceful lines (=graceful shape) *People admire the building's graceful lines.*

grade Ac *n*

a number or letter that a student is given for their work or for an examination

ADJECTIVES

a good grade *If you study hard, you will get good grades.*
a bad grade *Matt was disappointed because he got a bad grade.*
a high grade *She got high grades in all her science subjects.*
a low grade *These boys receive low grades because they fail to turn in assignments.*

G

the top grade *Ted's was the top grade in the maths exam.*

grade + NOUNS

grade A/B/C etc BrE: *Applicants must have Grade A, B, or C in two GCSE subjects.*

VERBS

get/receive a grade *He had always received good grades.*

achieve a grade BrE: *Rick had achieved good exam grades.*

give/award sb a grade *A quarter of all students were given a grade A.*

improve your grades *She's working hard to improve her grades.*

gradual *adj*

happening slowly over a long period of time

NOUNS

a gradual change/shift *Over the last ten years, there has been a gradual change in people's attitudes.*

a gradual process *Learning is a gradual process.*

a gradual increase in sth *One symptom is a gradual increase in your weight.*

a gradual decline/reduction/decrease in sth *There was a gradual decline in the birthrate during that decade.*

a gradual improvement/deterioration *There has been a gradual improvement in girls' performance in mathematics.*

the gradual development of sth *A long novel is able to show the gradual development of a character.*

a gradual loss of sth *There is a gradual loss of function of some brain cells which can result in forgetfulness.*

THESAURUS: gradual

gradual, leisurely, unhurried, measured, sluggish, lethargic, languid, glacial → **slow**

graduate *n*

someone who has completed a university degree

ADJECTIVES/NOUNS + graduate

a university/college/art school etc graduate *Many university graduates are facing unemployment.*

a history/science etc graduate *They want to persuade more science graduates to become teachers.*

a recent/new graduate *The firm hires 100 new graduates every year.*

a Cambridge/Harvard/Bristol University etc graduate *The head teacher was a Cambridge graduate.*

In American English, **college graduate** is used more often than **university graduate**, and someone who has completed their studies at high school is a **high school graduate**.

graduate + NOUNS

a graduate trainee/recruit BrE: *He joined the newspaper as a graduate trainee.*

a graduate engineer/teacher/nurse BrE: *The number of jobs for graduate engineers in Scotland has almost doubled in the past 18 months.*

graduate recruitment BrE (=employing new graduates) *Businesses have found it increasingly difficult to maintain their level of graduate recruitment.*

a graduate student especially AmE: *He worked on the project while a graduate student at Yale.*

a graduate degree AmE (=one you take after your first degree) *She has a graduate degree in education from Ohio State.*

a graduate program AmE (=a course or courses for graduates) *She hopes to continue her Arabic studies in a graduate program at Georgetown University.*

graduate school AmE (=a college where graduates can study) *After graduation, Karen and Jess are planning to go to graduate school.*

PREPOSITIONS

a graduate of/from York University/Boston University etc *Terry is a graduate of York University.*

a graduate in engineering/philosophy etc *The ideal candidate will be a graduate in electronic engineering.*

graduation *n*

the time when you complete a university degree course, or your education at an American high school

graduation + NOUNS

a graduation ceremony *She had come to attend her sister's graduation ceremony.*

graduation day *That photo was taken on graduation day.*

a graduation present/gift *His parents gave him a car as a graduation gift.*

NOUNS + graduation

college/high school graduation AmE: *He had been with the bank since college graduation.*

PREPOSITIONS

graduation from college/high school/Yale etc *He went to work for the company after his graduation from Syracuse University.*

after graduation *After graduation, he moved to Washington.*

grammar *n*

the way the words of a language are combined into sentences and can change their forms

ADJECTIVES

English/French etc grammar *The students have been taught the basics of English grammar.*

bad/poor grammar *Bad grammar is not acceptable in essays.*

good grammar *A secretary should have good grammar and spelling.*

correct/proper grammar *They provide examples of correct grammar for students to use.*

grammar + NOUNS

a grammar book *They all opened their grammar books.*

grammar rules *Understanding grammar rules can help with fluency and accuracy.*

> **Grammar or grammatical?**
> You can say **grammar rules** or **grammatical rules**. It is much more common to say a **grammatical error/mistake** than a 'grammar error/mistake'.

VERBS

learn grammar *I need to learn some grammar.*

teach (sb) grammar *He taught us Latin grammar.*

use grammar *It's important for journalists to use proper grammar.*

correct sb's grammar *His mother used to correct his grammar when he talked.*

grant Ac *n*

an amount of money given to someone, especially by the government, for a particular purpose

NOUNS + grant

a government grant *The school has won a £25,000 government grant for new sports equipment.*

a research grant *He received a research grant to study the effect of pollution on the environment.*

a student grant *If you are on a low income, you may be able to get a student grant.*

a block grant AmE (=money given by the central government to state governments to pay for particular services) *Congress approved block grants for education, health, and social services.*

VERBS

get/receive a grant *It is likely that you will receive a grant to pay for your tuition.*

get/obtain a grant *We may be able to get a grant to put a new roof on the building.*

give/award sb a grant *He has been awarded a grant to study in Paris.*

apply for a grant *If you wish to apply for a grant, write to the Treasurer.*

qualify for a grant (*also* **be eligible for a grant**) (=be allowed to receive a grant) *This booklet explains who is eligible for a grant.*

PREPOSITIONS

a grant of £5,000/$8,000 etc *The library received a grant of $20,000 to improve its computer facilities.*

a grant from sb *Training was funded by a grant from the Sports Council.*

a grant for sth *People on low incomes can be given a grant for home improvements.*

graph *n*

a drawing that uses a line or lines to show how two or more sets of measurements are related to each other

VERBS

a graph shows sth *The graph shows the increase in blood pressure.*

draw a graph *Draw a graph to show changes in the temperature over this period.*

plot sth on a graph (=show facts, numbers etc as points on a graph) *The different values can be plotted on a graph.*

grasp *v*

1 to take and hold something firmly

ADVERBS

grasp sth firmly *He was sitting down, grasping the box firmly in his hands.*

grasp sth tightly *She grasped her bag tightly and pressed it to her chest.*

PHRASES

grasp sb by the hand/arm/wrist *She grasped the screaming child by the arm.*

grasp hold of sth/sb *The goalkeeper managed to grasp hold of the ball.*

2 to completely understand a fact or an idea

ADVERBS

fully grasp sth *They did not fully grasp the seriousness of the problem.*

easily grasp sth *This course will help you to easily grasp the basics of the language.*

VERBS

try to grasp sth *The students were asked to try to grasp the meaning of the poem.*

fail to grasp sth *The government failed to grasp the severity of the financial crisis.*

struggle to grasp sth *He was struggling to grasp what he had done wrong.*

PHRASES

difficult/hard to grasp *Some pupils find even basic concepts in mathematics difficult to grasp.*

grasp the fact that *My boyfriend won't grasp the fact that he needs to be a bit more romantic.*

grateful *adj*

feeling or showing that you want to thank someone for something that they have done

ADVERBS

very/really/deeply grateful *We are deeply grateful for their support.*

extremely/immensely/enormously grateful *I am extremely grateful to him for getting me out of a very awkward situation.*

so grateful (*also* **most grateful** *formal*): *If you could help me, I would be so grateful.*

eternally grateful (=grateful forever) *He gave me my first job, and for that I will be eternally grateful.*

just grateful *I'm just grateful to have the chance to put things right.*

NOUNS

a grateful look/smile *The woman gave him a grateful look.*

grateful thanks *formal*: *Our grateful thanks go to everyone who helped to organize the event.*

PREPOSITIONS

be grateful for sth *I am grateful for the opportunity to explain my work.*

be grateful to sb *He was grateful to Sam for his advice.*

gratitude *n* the feeling of being grateful

ADJECTIVES

sb's deep/profound/immense/heartfelt gratitude (=which someone feels very strongly) *My only emotions afterwards were relief and deep gratitude.*

sb's eternal/undying gratitude (=forever) *The doctors who saved my daughter have my undying gratitude.*

sb's sincere gratitude *First, I must express our sincere gratitude for all you have done.*

VERBS

show your gratitude *He bought them a present to show his gratitude.*

express your gratitude *We would like to express our gratitude to everyone for their generous donations.*

feel gratitude *He felt some gratitude to Eleanor for giving him this idea.*

earn sb's gratitude (=make someone feel grateful) *Her willingness to help earned the gratitude of her colleagues.*

PREPOSITIONS

gratitude to/towards sb *I would like to express my gratitude to all the people who have helped us.*

gratitude for sth *Maureen ought to show some gratitude for what Dean has done.*

with gratitude *She accepted his offer with gratitude.*

in gratitude for sth *We'd like to take you out to dinner in gratitude for what you've done.*

PHRASES

a feeling/sense of gratitude *She had a sudden feeling of gratitude towards him.*

a gesture/token of (sb's) gratitude (=something you do to show you are grateful) *I think I deserve a small gesture of gratitude for my efforts, don't you?*

owe sb a debt of gratitude (=someone deserves your gratitude) *I owe my former teacher a deep debt of gratitude.*

grave¹ *adj* THESAURUS ▸ **bad (2)**

grave² *n*

the place in the ground where a dead body is buried

ADJECTIVES/NOUNS + grave

a shallow grave (=not very deep in the ground) *The body of a woman was found in a shallow grave in the woods.*

a mass grave (=filled with many people) *Victims of the disease were buried in mass graves.*

an unmarked grave (=one that does not have anything to show where it is or who is in it) *Until 1855, poor people here were buried in unmarked graves.*

a family grave (=one where members of a family are buried together) *Walter was buried in the family grave in Finchley cemetery.*

a war grave (=one where a soldier killed in a war is buried) *He has gone to visit the war graves in Flanders.*

VERBS

dig a grave *In the churchyard, a man was digging a grave.*

mark a grave *The stone marked her grave.*

bury sb in a grave (=put someone in a grave) *She was buried in a grave next to her older sister.*

visit sb's grave *I always visit my mother's grave on her birthday.*

desecrate a grave (=deliberately damage it) *More than 300 graves had been desecrated.*

greasy *adj* THESAURUS ▸ **dirty**

great *adj* THESAURUS ▸ **big (3)**, **excellent**, **powerful (1)**

greed *n*

a strong desire for more food, money, power, possessions etc than you need

ADJECTIVES

human greed *We can all see the damage that human greed has done to the environment.*

corporate greed (=greed by big companies or people who work for them) *Critics saw the large bonuses as evidence of corporate greed.*

personal greed *The country's leaders are motivated mainly by personal greed.*

insatiable greed (=that can never be satisfied) *His insatiable greed was his downfall.*

pure/simple greed *Why have they increased their prices? Pure greed.*

VERBS

be driven/motivated by greed (=greed is the reason for doing something) *The people who are developing this land are driven by greed.*

satisfy your/sb's greed (=get as much of something as you can for yourself, even though this harms other people) *Some people will do anything in their power to get what they want, and to satisfy their greed.*

PREPOSITIONS

greed for sth *There appeared to be no end to the man's greed for power.*

greedy *adj*

always wanting more food, money, power, possessions etc than you need

NOUNS

a greedy person/child/relative etc *Greedy relatives wanted to get their hands on the old lady's money.*

greedy banks/corporations *This ruling will hurt the customer and increase profits for greedy corporations.*

greedy eyes *He looked at the gold with greedy eyes.*

greedy hands *Greedy hands grabbed at the cakes on the plate.*

a greedy pig *informal* (=someone who is greedy) *Have you eaten them all, you greedy pig?*

PREPOSITIONS

greedy for sth *The company was greedy for profits.*

green *adj, n*

1 the colour of grass or leaves

TYPES OF GREEN

pale/light/soft green *The room had pale green walls.*

dark/deep green *The plant has dark green leaves and white flowers.*

bright green *She dyed her hair bright green.*

lime green (=bright light green) *The lime green sofa contrasted with the red carpet.*

emerald green *The sea was a beautiful emerald green.*

PREPOSITIONS

in green *Fiona was dressed in green.*

PHRASES

a shade of green *Her eyes were an odd shade of green.*

2 harming the environment as little as possible, or connected with protecting the environment

NOUNS

green products *There is an increasing market for green products.*

green energy/fuels *The school is switching to green energy by installing solar heating panels.*

green technology *Car makers are investing in green technology.*

a green car/vehicle *They are funding research into greener cars.*

green transport *BrE*, **green transportation** *AmE*: *Mountain bikes are a popular method of green transport.*

green issues *The group has been campaigning on green issues for ten years.*

the Green Party *I usually vote for the Green Party.*

VERBS

go green (=change in order to harm the environment less) *We're always being told that we must go green.*

THESAURUS: green

eco-friendly, green, clean, renewable, sustainable, carbon-neutral, low-carbon, low-energy → **environmentally friendly**

greeting *n*

1 something you say or do when you meet someone

ADJECTIVES

a friendly/warm greeting *He didn't respond to my friendly greeting.*

a polite greeting *We exchanged the usual polite greetings.*

a formal greeting *After formal greetings, they were invited to sit down and watch the ceremony.*

a traditional greeting *A bow is the traditional Japanese greeting.*

VERBS

exchange greetings (=greet each other) *We exchanged greetings if we met in the street.*

shout/call out a greeting *One of the boys shouted a greeting.*

give/offer sb a greeting *He always gave her a friendly greeting.*

nod/wave a greeting *The man nodded a greeting to us.*

acknowledge/return sb's greeting (=greet someone who has greeted you) *She acknowledged their greetings with a wave.*

ignore sb's greeting *The old woman ignored his greeting and continued talking to her friend.*

PREPOSITIONS

in greeting *Jack raised a hand in greeting as they drove past.*

2 a friendly message that you send someone, for example on their birthday or at Christmas

NOUNS + greeting

birthday/Christmas etc greetings *He sent her some flowers with birthday greetings.*

holiday greetings *AmE: The president sent holiday greetings to Muslims in the United States and across the world.*

season's greetings *The Christmas card said "Season's Greetings" inside.*

VERBS

send greetings *At Christmas some people just send greetings by email.*

greeting + NOUNS

a greetings card *BrE*, **a greeting card** *AmE: The shop sells a range of greetings cards for all occasions.*

PREPOSITIONS

greetings from sb *Greetings from the whole family.*

greetings from somewhere *Greetings from sunny Cornwall.*

greetings to sb *Greetings to all the family.*

grey *adj* THESAURUS › **cloudy**, **rainy**

grief *n*

extreme sadness, especially because someone you love has died

ADJECTIVES

deep/great grief *She expressed deep grief at his death.*

terrible/overwhelming grief *Childlessness brings feelings of terrible grief.*

public grief *There was a great public grief when Princess Diana died.*

private/personal grief *Too often the media intrudes on private grief.*

VERBS

feel grief *When her father died, she felt no grief.*

deal with/cope with your grief *People deal with their grief in different ways.*

come to terms with your grief (=accept the sad event and not be upset any more) *Counselling helped her come to terms with her grief.*

PREPOSITIONS

grief at/over sth *Her grief at his death was deep and sincere.*

grief for sb *He had been driven mad by grief for his son.*

PHRASES

be overcome/overwhelmed with grief (=feel it so strongly that you feel you cannot continue) *When his wife died, he was overcome with grief.*

be racked/wracked with grief (=feel extremely deep grief) *She was so racked with grief that she couldn't sleep.*

mad with grief *Her poor husband was mad with grief.*

an outpouring of grief (=the strong expression of a lot of grief) *The tragedy prompted a national outpouring of grief.*

feelings of grief *In his poems, he writes about his feelings of grief for his mother.*

grievance *n*

a belief that you have been treated unfairly, or a complaint that you have been treated unfairly

ADJECTIVES

a genuine grievance (=a real one) *He felt that he had a genuine grievance and was prepared to take the company to court.*

a legitimate grievance (=one that is reasonable) *Many people feel that the rebels have a legitimate grievance.*

an old/long-standing grievance (=one that you have felt unhappy about for a long time) *Years later, we became friends again and sorted out our old grievances.*

a personal grievance *He had turned the dispute into a personal grievance.*

VERBS

have a grievance (against sb) *I had no grievance against him.*

air your grievances (=tell people you think you have been treated unfairly) *There must be an opportunity for both sides to air their grievances.*

nurse/harbour a grievance (=think about it a lot or for a long time) *He was nursing a grievance about not being picked for the team.*

settle a grievance (=solve one) *The union decided to settle its grievance in the law courts.*

PREPOSITIONS

a grievance against sb/sth *If you have a grievance against a company, then you must go through a formal complaints procedure.*

PHRASES

a sense of grievance (=a feeling that you have been treated unfairly) *Anti-Americanism in these countries comes from a deep sense of grievance against the United States.*

grill *v* THESAURUS › **cook[1]**

grim *adj* THESAURUS › **bad (1)**, **depressing**

grimy *adj* THESAURUS › **dirty**

grin[1] *v*

to smile widely, showing your teeth

ADVERBS

grin broadly/widely *She was grinning broadly when she opened the letter.*

grin sheepishly (=in a way that shows you are embarrassed) *"Sorry about that!" he said, grinning sheepishly.*

grin mischievously (=in a naughty way) *She grinned mischievously at me and I wondered what she was planning to do.*

grin inanely (=in a way that makes you look stupid) *The picture shows him grinning inanely at the camera.*

PREPOSITIONS

grin at sb *He grinned at me and said "I've passed my test!"*

PHRASES

be grinning from ear to ear (=in a way that shows you are very pleased) *He came out of the interview grinning from ear to ear.*

be grinning like an idiot (=in a way that makes you look stupid) *Her friend was still grinning like an idiot.*

grin² *n* a wide smile

ADJECTIVES

a wide/broad/big grin *She opened the door with a wide grin.*

a mischievous grin *"Let's play a trick on her," he suggested, with a mischievous grin.*

a sheepish grin (=embarrassed because you have done something silly or wrong) *"Sorry," he said with a sheepish grin.*

a silly grin *"Wipe that silly grin off your face!" the teacher shouted.*

VERBS

give a grin *He gave a big grin when she walked into the room.*

a grin spreads over/across sb's face *A self-satisfied grin spread across his face.*

sb's face breaks/splits into a grin *The old man's face broke into a grin.*

PHRASES

a grin on sb's face *He looked at me with a big grin on his face.*

grip¹ *n*

1 the action of holding something tightly

> **Grammar**
> Usually singular in this meaning.

ADJECTIVES

a firm/tight grip *The streets were crowded and she kept a tight grip on her bag.*

a strong grip *Maggie took the boy's arm in a strong grip.*

a good grip (=with which you can keep hold of something) *The rocks were wet and slippery and it was difficult to get a good grip.*

an iron/vice-like grip (=very strong) *Victor was holding her wrist in an iron grip.*

VERBS

keep a grip on sth (*also* **maintain a grip on sth** *formal*): *Alain kept a firm grip on the bag.*

tighten your grip (=hold something more tightly) *Holding her son's hand, she tightened her grip as they crossed the road.*

loosen/relax your grip (=hold something less tightly) *Lee loosened his grip on the dog's collar.*

have a grip on sth *You need to have a good grip on your tennis racket.*

get a grip on sth (=hold something that is hard to hold firmly) *I got a grip on the rope and pulled myself up.*

lose your grip (=accidentally let go of something) *As he was climbing up he lost his grip and fell.*

release your grip/let go of your grip (=stop holding something) *The guard released his grip on the prisoner and pushed him into the cell.*

sb's grip tightens *His grip tightened on the steering wheel.*

PREPOSITIONS

sb's grip on sth *I felt her grip on my wrist.*

2 power or control over someone or something

> **Grammar**
> Always singular in this meaning.

ADJECTIVES

a tight/firm/strong/powerful grip *She kept a firm grip on her voice, trying to hide her fear.*

an iron grip (=very strong) *Previously the government had kept an iron grip on national spending.*

a tenuous grip (=not strong) *He is losing support and has only a tenuous grip on the presidency.*

VERBS

have a grip on/over sth *The president has a firm grip on power.*

lose your grip *The government seems to be losing its grip on the economic situation.*

tighten your grip (=start to have more power and control) *The army tightened their grip on the area.*

relax/loosen your grip (=start to have less power or control) *The movie is a powerful drama which never loosens its grip on you.*

keep/maintain your grip *Voters will decide whether the Republicans maintain their grip over the Senate.*

break sb's/sth's grip (=stop someone or something having power or control) *Police and community groups are working to break the grip of gangs in the city.*

PREPOSITIONS

a grip on/over sth *Religion had a powerful emotional grip over people's lives.*

PHRASES

be in the grip of sth (=be in a bad situation that you cannot control) *Europe is in the grip of the worst economic recession for 50 years.*

grip² *v* to hold something tightly

ADVERBS

grip sb tightly/firmly/hard *The little boy gripped his mother's arm tightly.*

gripping *adj* THESAURUS ▸ **interesting**

groan *n*

a long deep sound that you make when you are in pain or do not want to do something

ADJECTIVES

a low/deep groan *He gave a low groan when he saw the mess in the kitchen.*

a loud groan *There was a loud groan of disappointment from the crowd.*

a little/small groan *She let out a little groan of frustration as she struggled to open the door.*

VERBS

give a groan *He gave a groan when I asked him to wash the dishes.*

let out a groan *She tried to sit up, let out a groan of pain, and collapsed again.*

hear a groan *He could hear groans of pain coming from the patient in the next bed.*

PREPOSITIONS

a groan of protest/disappointment etc *The announcement was met with groans of protest.*

with a groan *With a small groan of annoyance, he got up to answer the door.*

PHRASES

moans and groans (=complaints about unimportant things) *Everything I ask her to do is met with moans and groans.*

grotesque *adj* THESAURUS ugly (1)

ground *n*

1 the surface of the earth

ADJECTIVES

muddy ground *They were picking up potatoes from the muddy ground.*

firm/soft ground *We managed to get the car back onto firm ground.*

frozen ground *Snow fell on the frozen ground.*

dry/wet ground *The ground is so dry that the dirt turns to dust.*

VERBS

fall to the ground *The tree fell to the ground.*

hit the ground *I caught the ball just before it hit the ground.*

leave the ground *The plane left the ground and went up into the air.*

PREPOSITIONS

on the ground *She lay on the ground and looked up at the stars.*

above/below the ground *The miners work thousands of feet below the ground.*

2 a subject that people are talking about or dealing with

ADJECTIVES

new/fresh ground *The research covers some interesting new ground.*

the same (old) ground *I don't want to have to go over the same ground again.*

familiar ground *If you have read any of his other books, you will be on familiar ground.*

dangerous/shaky ground *When I saw her face suddenly change, I knew that we were on dangerous ground.*

safe ground *I think the author decided to stick to safe ground.*

common ground (=things that you agree about or share an interest in) *There is some common ground between the two political parties.*

VERBS

cover/go over ground *In her speech she covered a lot of ground.*

break new/fresh ground (=deal with something that people have not dealt with before) *The film broke new ground and was the first film to be shown in 3-D.*

3 your grounds for doing something are your reasons for doing it

> **Grammar**
> Always plural in this meaning.

ADJECTIVES

good/strong/reasonable/valid grounds for sth *There are strong grounds for believing that the same thing could happen again.*

on medical/legal/financial/moral grounds *Ethan was forced to give up work on medical grounds.*

on compassionate grounds (=because something bad has happened in your life) *When my dad died, I was allowed time off work on compassionate grounds.*

VERBS

have grounds for sth *He may have grounds for a claim against the company.*

give grounds for sth *The latest news about the US economy gives grounds for optimism.*

PREPOSITIONS

on ... grounds *I don't agree with animal experiments on moral grounds.*

on the grounds that *His application was turned down on the grounds that he didn't have enough experience.*

grounds for sth *The court decided that she had grounds for divorce.*

group *n*

several people or things together

VERBS

join a group *I asked him if he wanted to come over and join our group.*

belong to a group *Snakes belong to the same group of animals as lizards and crocodiles.*

put/divide/organize sth/sb into groups *The children were divided into groups according to their age.*

get into groups *The teacher told the students to get into groups.*

leave a group *Rebecca left the group following a disagreement.*

ADJECTIVES/NOUNS + group

an age group *The show appeals to people from all age groups.*

a social group (=from a particular part of society) *The researchers studied the health of different social groups.*

an ethnic/racial group (=who belong to a particular race) *The university welcomes applications from all ethnic groups.*

a minority group (=who belong to a different race, religion etc from most people in a place) *Conditions for some minority groups have got worse in recent years.*

a terrorist group *A terrorist group has claimed responsibility for the bombing.*

a splinter/breakaway group (=that has separated from another political or religious group) *The Social Democratic Party (SDP) was formed as a splinter group of the main Socialist Party.*

a pressure group (=one that tries to make the government do something) *Friends of the Earth is a leading environmental pressure group.*

a close-knit/tightly knit group (=in which everyone knows each other well and supports each other) *The young artists in Paris formed a close-knit group.*

G

group + NOUNS

a group discussion *The course includes both individual work and group discussions.*

a group decision *It wasn't just my idea – it was a group decision.*

PREPOSITIONS

a group of sb/sth *A group of teenagers were standing on the street corner.*

as a group *The team work well as a group.*

in/within a group *People in lower income groups will be worst affected by the new tax.*

outside a group *They weren't allowed to speak to people outside the group.*

PHRASES

a member of a group *She's a member of a Christian group at the school.*

THESAURUS: group

a group of things

bunch
flowers | roses | keys | fruit | grapes | bananas
a group of things that are held or tied together, or that grow together on a plant:
He handed me a bunch of roses. | The manager took out a huge bunch of keys and unlocked the door. | I've brought you a bunch of grapes.

bundle
papers | clothes | letters | documents | newspapers | sticks
a group of things that have been put or tied together, often in an untidy way:
Bundles of papers and files filled the shelves. | The room was untidy and a large bundle of clothes lay near the wardrobe door. | The old woman was carrying a bundle of sticks. | She tied the letters into a bundle.

sheaf *especially literary*
papers | letters | notes | documents
a lot of pieces of paper held or fastened together in a flat pile:
He produced a sheaf of papers and asked Harry to sign every one. | She sat down at the desk, pulling a sheaf of notes towards her.

cluster
houses | buildings | shops | trees | stars | galaxies | islands | cells
a group of things of the same kind that are close together in a place:
The track ended at a cluster of farm buildings. | Near to the house was a cluster of small trees. | The Faroes are a cluster of islands between Scotland and Iceland. | They found a small cluster of cancer cells.

a group of animals

herd
cows | deer | elephants
a group of cows, deer, or elephants:
A herd of cows was blocking the road.

flock
sheep | birds | seagulls | geese | crows | pigeons
a group of sheep or birds:
The farmer has over 100 sheep in his flock. | A flock of seagulls landed on the ocean.

pack
dogs | wolves | hounds
a group of dogs or wolves:
The dogs work in packs. | According to legend, the children were raised by a pack of wolves.

school/shoal
fish | dolphins
a group of fish or dolphins:
Piranha fish live in shoals in the wild. | A school of dolphins swam alongside our boat.

litter
puppies | kittens
a group of baby animals born at one time to a particular mother:
He was one of a litter of seven puppies.

grow *v*

1 to increase in amount, size, number, or strength

ADVERBS

grow rapidly/fast *The city grew rapidly.*

grow slowly *The business grew slowly at first.*
grow steadily *The economy has grown steadily.*
grow significantly *They have seen the value of the shares grow significantly over five years.*
have grown considerably *Since then, the number of students has grown considerably.*
grow dramatically *British exports grew dramatically at the end of the eighteenth century.*
grow exponentially (=keep growing at increasing speed) *Computer speed is growing exponentially.*

PREPOSITIONS

grow by... *Sales are expected to grow by six percent this year.*
grow (from...) to... *The population of the village grew from 3,000 to over 20,000.*
grow in size/number/popularity etc *Farms have been growing in size.*

2 if a living thing grows, it becomes bigger

NOUNS

a child/animal grows *The children have all grown since I last saw them.*
sb's hair grows/nails grow *Don't worry – your hair will grow back.*
a plant/tree grows *The plant grows rapidly.*
grass grows *In spring, the grass starts to grow.*

ADVERBS

grow quickly/rapidly/fast *The weeds are growing fast.*
grow well *There are many plants that will grow well in shade.*
grow tall/long *The trees have grown so tall they hide the house. | I'm going to let my hair grow long.*
grow 3 inches/30 centimetres etc *I had grown six inches since he had last seen me.*

PREPOSITIONS

grow into sth *He had grown into a tall strong youth.*

Grow up means to develop from being a child to being an adult: *Their children have **grown up** and left home.*

PHRASES

grow to 12 feet/40 metres etc *This fish can grow to 12 feet.*
grow to a height of 20 inches/3 metres etc *The plant grows to a height of 20 inches.*

3 to look after plants

NOUNS

grow crops/food *Farmers have cleared the land to grow crops.*
grow plants *If you haven't got much space, you can grow plants in containers.*
grow flowers/vegetables/fruit/herbs etc *She grew the flowers for the wedding herself.*

ADVERBS

be locally grown *All the vegetables are locally grown.*
grow sth organically (=without using chemicals) *Many people choose to buy vegetables that have been grown organically.*

PHRASES

grow your own vegetables/food *He likes gardening and grows his own vegetables.*
grow sth from seed *You can grow herbs from seed.*

THESAURUS: grow

cultivate
to grow a crop. **Cultivate** is more formal than **grow**:
*The Mayans were the first people to **cultivate** cocoa. | When did people begin to keep livestock and **cultivate crops**?*

4 to become

THESAURUS: grow

get, grow, turn, go, come → **become**

growth *n*

1 an increase in the success, importance, or size of something

ADJECTIVES/NOUNS + growth

economic/industrial growth *China enjoyed a long period of economic growth.*
population growth *The country has one of the highest population growth rates in the world.*
rapid growth *During this period there was rapid growth in the economy.*
strong growth *Many industries are expecting strong growth this year.*
steady growth *There has been a steady growth in employment.*
slow/sluggish growth *Economists are forecasting a period of slow growth.*
exponential growth (=becoming much faster very quickly) *Internet advertising has experienced exponential growth in the last few years.*
zero growth (=no growth) *The company recorded zero growth this quarter.*
annual growth *Mexico achieved a remarkable annual growth rate of 8%.*

VERBS

stimulate/encourage/promote growth (=make it more likely to happen) *Greater government spending may stimulate economic growth.*
maintain/sustain growth *Governments that want to survive have to maintain growth.*
achieve growth *After the war, Europe achieved remarkable economic growth.*

growth slows (down) *Economic growth slowed last year.*

growth + NOUNS

a growth area/industry (=a type of activity that is increasing) *Recycling waste is a huge growth industry.*

the growth rate *The economic growth rate averaged only 1.4 percent.*

PREPOSITIONS

the growth of sth *The growth of the internet has allowed more people to work from home.*

growth in sth *There has been a growth in the number of elderly people.*

2 the development of the physical size of a person, animal, or plant

ADJECTIVES

normal growth *This protein is essential for normal growth.*

healthy growth *Make sure your children get all the right vitamins for healthy growth.*

abnormal growth *The gene causes abnormal growth in the cells.*

VERBS

stimulate/encourage growth (=make it more likely to happen) *This process produces nutrients that stimulate the growth of new grasses.*

stunt/inhibit growth (=stop someone or something from growing as much as they should) *Seckel syndrome is a rare disease that stunts growth.*

G

grudge *n*

a feeling of dislike for someone because you cannot forget that they harmed you in the past

VERBS

bear/carry a grudge (=have a grudge) *I try not to bear grudges.*

have/hold a grudge *The police asked if anyone might have had a grudge against the victim.*

harbour a grudge *BrE*, **harbor a grudge** *AmE* (=have a grudge for a long time) *He was the sort of person who would harbour a grudge for years.*

nurse a grudge (=have a grudge and keep finding reasons for it) *She was still nursing a grudge against her former boss.*

ADJECTIVES/NOUNS + grudge

a personal grudge *It is known that the man had a personal grudge against his co-worker.*

an old/ancient/long-standing grudge *He said they should celebrate their achievements, not nurse old grudges.*

a childhood grudge (=from when someone was a child) *Police hinted that Robert's crime was motivated by a childhood grudge.*

PREPOSITIONS

a grudge against sb/sth *Do you have some sort of grudge against her?*

PHRASES

bear/hold etc no grudge *He insisted that he held no grudge against Taylor.*

someone with a grudge *The bomb could be the work of someone with a grudge against the company.*

grumpy *adj* THESAURUS angry

guarantee[1] [Ac] *v*

1 to promise that something will happen

NOUNS

guarantee sb's safety/security *New measures will help guarantee the safety of passengers.*

guarantee sb's rights/freedom *The law guarantees equal rights for men and women.*

guarantee standards/quality *Companies must be able to guarantee the quality of their products.*

guarantee the accuracy of sth *We cannot guarantee the accuracy of this information.*

ADVERBS

personally guarantee *I can personally guarantee that you will have the delivery on Thursday.*

effectively guarantee (=used when saying what the real situation is, even though it may seem different officially) *The bank has effectively guaranteed to lend him the money.*

2 to make something certain to happen

NOUNS

guarantee success *There is no way of guaranteeing success.*

guarantee a place *A win today will guarantee the team a place in the final.*

guarantee (sb) a job *Training programmes do not guarantee a job, but they do provide necessary skills.*

ADVERBS

almost/practically/virtually guarantee *The island has beautiful beaches and friendly people, so a good time is virtually guaranteed.*

automatically guarantee *Having a lot of money does not automatically guarantee happiness.*

sth is by no means guaranteed (=it is not certain to happen, even though some people think that it is) *Victory is by no means guaranteed.*

guarantee[2] [Ac] *n*

1 a company's formal promise to repair or replace a product if it breaks

ADJECTIVES/NOUNS + guarantee

a one-year/two-year etc guarantee *The washing machine has a five-year guarantee.*

a full guarantee (=one that covers all problems) *All our bathrooms come with a full guarantee.*

a lifetime guarantee *They say that their furniture has a lifetime guarantee.*

a money-back guarantee (=one that gives you back the money you paid if there is a problem) *The company offers a 30-day money-back guarantee on all its products.*

VERBS + guarantee

have a guarantee *All our boots have a five-year guarantee.*

come with/carry a guarantee *The building work comes with a 30-year guarantee.*

extend a guarantee (=make it last for a longer period) *For an extra £20 you can extend the guarantee to two years.*

guarantee + VERBS

a guarantee covers sth (=it includes something) *The guarantee doesn't cover accidental damage.*

a guarantee runs out/expires (=it ends) *Customers have to pay for repairs after the guarantee runs out.*

PREPOSITIONS

a guarantee on sth *The company offers a five-year guarantee on all new cars.*

a guarantee against sth *There is a guarantee against all electrical faults.*

be under guarantee (=be protected by a guarantee) *We paid for the repair because the computer was no longer under guarantee.*

2 a person's firm promise to do something

VERBS

give/offer sb a guarantee (*also* **provide sb with a guarantee**) *He gave me a guarantee that the work would be finished next week.*

get/receive a guarantee *I received a guarantee that prisoners would be treated fairly.*

demand a guarantee *Customers are demanding guarantees that their goods will be delivered on time.*

ADJECTIVES

a cast-iron guarantee (*also* **an absolute guarantee**) (=one that is completely definite) *The manager has given him a cast-iron guarantee that he will be promoted.*

sb's personal guarantee *I give you my personal guarantee that I will be at the meeting.*

PHRASES

a guarantee of satisfaction (=a promise that someone will be pleased with something you are giving them) *Each of our products comes with a guarantee of complete satisfaction.*

guard[1] *n*

someone whose job is to protect a place or person, or prevent someone from escaping

ADJECTIVES

an armed guard *Armed guards stood in front of the gate.*

NOUNS + guard

a security guard *There were two security guards on duty outside the building.*

a border guard *We were stopped by border guards.*

a prison guard *Prison guards patrolled the jail.*

> **Bodyguard** (= someone whose job is to protect an important person) is written as one word.

VERBS

a guard escorts sb (=goes with someone) *Six guards escorted the men into court.*

a guard patrols somewhere (=a guard walks regularly around) *Guards patrolled the area with dogs.*

post/station a guard somewhere (=make a guard stand somewhere) *Armed guards were posted by the exit.*

PHRASES

be on guard duty (=be standing as a guard somewhere) *Two men were on guard duty at the gate.*

guard[2] *v*

1 to stand next to someone or something to protect them or prevent them from escaping

ADVERBS

be heavily/closely/tightly guarded (=with a lot of soldiers or weapons) *The US embassy is heavily guarded.*

PREPOSITIONS

guard sth from/against sth *The missiles are there to guard the city from attack.*

2 to prevent someone from taking something or finding out about something

ADVERBS

be closely/carefully/tightly guarded *The name of the new car is a closely guarded secret.*

jealously/fiercely guard sth (=in a way that shows you care a lot about something) *Universities have jealously guarded their independence.*

guess[1] *v*

to try to answer a question or form an opinion when you are not sure whether you will be correct

ADVERBS

guess right/correctly *The first team to guess correctly wins the game.*

guess wrong/incorrectly *If they guess incorrectly, the other team gets the points.*

NOUNS

guess the answer *You can probably guess the answer to that question.*

PREPOSITIONS

guess at sth *We can only guess at the cause of the crash.*

PHRASES

be difficult/hard/easy to guess *It was difficult to guess his age.*

let me guess *What star sign are you? Let me guess.*

guess² *n*

an attempt to answer a question or make a judgment when you are not sure whether you will be correct

ADJECTIVES

a rough guess (=one that is not exact) *This is just a rough guess, but I think it would cost about $50.*

a wild guess (=one made without much thought or information) *I made a wild guess and I got the answer right first time.*

a lucky guess *"How did you know?" "It was just a lucky guess."*

a good/fair/reasonable guess (=one that is likely to be right) *I'm not sure how old she is, but I can make a good guess!*

sb's best guess (=one that you think is most likely to be right) *My best guess is that it will take around six months.*

an educated/informed guess (=a guess based on things that you know are correct) *Stockbrokers try to make educated guesses as to which stocks will do well.*

G

VERBS

make a guess *I didn't know the answer to question 7, so I just had to make a guess.*

have a guess *BrE*, **take a guess** *AmE*: *Go on, have a guess at how much it cost.*

hazard a guess (=guess something, when you feel very uncertain) *No one at this stage is prepared to hazard a guess about the outcome of the elections.*

PHRASES

my guess is (that)... *My guess is there won't be many people there.*

at a guess *BrE* (=used when saying that you are making a guess) *I'd say the house was built around 1900, at a guess.*

I'll give you three guesses (=used when you think it will be easy for someone to guess something) *"Where is he?" "I'll give you three guesses."*

guest *n*

someone who is invited to your home or to an event or special occasion

ADJECTIVES/NOUNS + guest

a wedding/party/dinner guest *We need to send out invitations to all the wedding guests.*

the main/chief/principal guest *The prime minister was one of the main guests at the event.*

an uninvited guest *She was surprised when an uninvited guest arrived at the door.*

an unwelcome guest (=one who is not wanted) *Security guards were employed to keep out unwelcome guests.*

a regular/frequent guest *The Johnsons were regular guests at Eric's house.*

an honoured guest *BrE*, **an honored guest** *AmE* (=one who is given special respect and treatment) *They were the honoured guests of the Queen at the Royal Garden Party.*

a distinguished guest (=one who people respect or admire a lot) *Many distinguished guests were invited to the opening ceremony.*

VERBS

have guests (=have people visiting you in your house) *We had guests over Christmas, and the house was full.*

invite a guest *The guests were invited to a dinner at his country house.*

greet/welcome the guests *Roger was busy greeting the guests as they arrived.*

entertain guests (=have guests at your house or another place for a meal or party) *Their garden is a wonderful place to entertain guests.*

guest + NOUNS

the guest list (=a list of the people invited to an event) *The guest list included many of his old school friends.*

a guest speaker/lecturer (=one who is invited to an event from another organization, university etc) *The guest speaker at the conference was Dr Kim.*

PHRASES

the guest of honour *BrE*, **the guest of honor** *AmE* (=the most important guest) *The senator was guest of honor at a reception held at the embassy.*

guide *n*

1 someone whose job is to show people around a place

ADJECTIVES

a local guide *If you are going into the jungle, you need to hire the services of a local guide.*

NOUNS + guide

a tour guide *A group of teenagers were listening to their tour guide.*

a mountain guide *They went climbing with a mountain guide.*

a museum guide *The museum guide explained about the history of the coins.*

a tourist guide *She works as a tourist guide in her vacation.*

VERBS

hire a guide *You can hire a guide for $30 a day.*

act as a guide *The hotel owner acted as our guide.*

work as a guide *He works as a guide for Japanese tourists.*

2 something that provides information and helps you to form an opinion or make a decision

ADJECTIVES

a good/reliable/accurate guide *The weather forecast is not always a very reliable guide to the weather.*

a rough guide (=not exact) *These figures are only meant to be a rough guide.*

a general guide *As a general guide, you need one kilo of sugar for every kilo of fruit.*

VERBS

use sth as a guide *This information should only be used as a general guide.*

provide/offer a guide *The tests offer a guide to students' abilities.*

act/serve as a guide *His paintings act as a guide to how he was feeling at the time.*

3 a book or piece of writing that gives information about something

ADJECTIVES

a useful/handy guide *The website also includes a useful guide for writing research papers.*

a practical guide *This book is a practical guide to designing your own website.*

a detailed guide *There is a detailed guide of the best walks in the area.*

a brief/quick/short guide *The article includes a brief guide to local restaurants.*

a comprehensive guide (=including all the information you need) *The tourist office produces a comprehensive guide to the city.*

the definitive guide (=the best guide) *He wrote the definitive guide to photography.*

an introductory guide *The book is intended as an introductory guide to the subject.*

a step-by-step guide (=a guide that clearly explains each stage in a process) *The magazine offers a step-by-step guide to making wine.*

NOUNS + guide

a travel guide *I read about the beach in the travel guide.*

a study guide *You can use study guides to help you prepare for your exam.*

a reference guide *The book is intended as a reference guide for students.*

VERBS

produce/publish a guide *They produced a handy guide to identifying butterflies.*

PREPOSITIONS

a guide to sth *There is a short guide to hotels in the area.*

a guide for sb *This is a useful guide for walkers.*

Guidebook is written as one word.

guidelines Ac *n*

rules or instructions about the best way to do something

ADJECTIVES

new guidelines *The government has announced new guidelines for food safety.*

strict guidelines *There are strict guidelines on how the money can be used.*

clear guidelines *Students should be given clear guidelines on which books they need to study.*

simple/basic guidelines *Here are some simple guidelines to help you when you are choosing a pet.*

general/broad guidelines *The committee produced a set of general guidelines.*

detailed/specific guidelines *Detailed guidelines are available for students who are planning to take the exam.*

NOUNS + guidelines

government guidelines *Under government guidelines, everyone can have free emergency treatment.*

policy guidelines *We need to establish clear policy guidelines.*

safety guidelines *Try to follow these basic safety guidelines.*

VERBS

follow guidelines *You must follow these guidelines when you are writing your application.*

meet guidelines (*also* **comply with guidelines** *formal*) (=obey them) *All new vehicles must meet the guidelines on emissions.*

issue/lay down guidelines *The hospital has issued strict new guidelines on the treatment of mentally ill patients.*

provide/offer guidelines *They should provide some sort of guidelines which tell you how to fill out the form.*

introduce/implement guidelines (=start to use guidelines for the first time) *The new guidelines will be introduced next year.*

establish/draw up guidelines *The school has drawn up guidelines for teachers.*

produce/publish/bring out guidelines *Guidelines have been published on prevention and treatment of the disease.*

adopt guidelines (=start to use them) *Many states have adopted the guidelines.*

revise guidelines (=change them) *The guidelines are being revised.*

PREPOSITIONS

under guidelines *Under current guidelines, the treatment is not offered to people over 65.*

guidelines on/about sth *There are new guidelines on the employment of children.*

PHRASES

a set of guidelines *We have developed a new set of guidelines.*

guilt *n*

1 the feeling you have when you have done something you know is wrong

VERBS

have/feel guilt *She didn't feel any guilt; she had done nothing wrong.*

be consumed with/racked with/overwhelmed by guilt (=feel very guilty) *After he hit his son he was racked with guilt.*

assuage sb's guilt *formal* (=make someone feel less guilty) *I was not there when he died, and there was nothing I could do to assuage my guilt.*

guilt + NOUNS

a guilt complex (=when you cannot stop feeling guilty, although it is unnecessary) *Some of the survivors developed a guilt complex about living when others had died.*

a guilt trip *informal* (=an unreasonable feeling of guilt) *My parents like to give me a guilt trip about not studying enough at college.*

PREPOSITIONS

guilt over/about sth *He felt some guilt over the accident.*

out of guilt (=because you feel guilty) *I think he married her out of guilt.*

without guilt *Now the children are older, we can take time to relax without guilt.*

PHRASES

a feeling/sense of guilt *I had a permanent feeling of guilt that I didn't see Mum and Dad as often as I should.*

a pang/twinge/stab of guilt (=a sudden feeling of guilt) *Richard felt a pang of guilt for forgetting her birthday.*

a burden of guilt (=a strong feeling of guilt) *Many children feel responsible when their parents divorce, and carry a burden of guilt.*

2 the fact that you have committed a crime or done something wrong

VERBS

admit your guilt *Athletes who are caught using drugs rarely admit their guilt.*

deny your guilt *He has always denied his guilt.*

prove sb's guilt *Lawyers said Jackson's behaviour after the killing was enough to prove his guilt.*

PHRASES

an admission of guilt (=something that you say or do, which shows you know that you have done something wrong) *His resignation was seen as an admission of guilt.*

evidence of guilt *Silence should not be used as evidence of guilt.*

ANTONYMS **guilt → innocence (1)**

guilty *adj*

1 if someone is guilty of a crime or doing something wrong, they did it, and they should be punished for it

VERBS

find sb guilty (=decide that someone is guilty) *He was found guilty of murder.*

declare sb guilty (=say that someone is guilty) *The jury declared the defendants guilty on all charges.*

prove sb guilty *A person is regarded as innocent until they are proved guilty.*

plead guilty (=say in court that you committed a crime) *The men pleaded guilty to the robbery.*

NOUNS

a guilty man/woman *The guilty men will go to prison for a long time.*

the guilty party (=the person or people who made something bad happen) *She appeared to be the guilty party, so everyone blamed her.*

a guilty verdict (=a decision that someone is guilty) *Simpson escaped a guilty verdict in his criminal trial.*

a guilty plea (=a statement to a court, in which someone admits they are guilty of a crime) *In exchange for his guilty plea, the government dropped the other charges against him.*

PREPOSITIONS

guilty of sth *The soldiers were guilty of war crimes.*

ANTONYMS **guilty → innocent**

2 if you feel guilty, you feel sorry or ashamed because you think you have done something wrong

VERBS

feel guilty *I feel guilty about leaving my family.*

make sb feel guilty *She's always trying to make other people feel guilty.*

look guilty *Lisa looked a little guilty.*

NOUNS

a guilty feeling *I had a guilty feeling that somehow I was responsible for what happened.*

a guilty conscience (=guilty feelings, because you regret doing something) *He had a guilty conscience and decided to give them back the money.*

a guilty secret (=something that you feel bad about, which you do not tell other people about) *She must have carried that guilty secret all her life.*

a guilty pleasure *especially humorous* (=something that you enjoy, even though you know you should not do it) *She says her guiltiest pleasure is eating chocolate cookies.*

PREPOSITIONS

guilty about sth *Do you ever feel guilty about what you did?*

gun *n*

a weapon that fires bullets or shells

VERBS

fire/shoot a gun *Someone fired a gun into the air.*

point a gun at sb/sth *The man was pointing a gun at me.*

have a gun *If someone has a gun, you don't argue with them.*

be carrying a gun/be armed with a gun *The terrorists were armed with guns and grenades.*

pull a gun on sb (=take it out and threaten to use it to kill someone) *One of the men pulled a gun on the clerk and told him to hand over all the money.*

load a gun (=put bullets in it) *He loaded the gun and got ready to shoot.*

draw a gun (=pull it out so it is ready to use) *The police officer drew his gun from his belt.*

turn a gun on sb/sth (=move a gun so that it points at someone) *The man turned the gun on himself and tried to kill himself.*

lay down/put down your gun (=put it down on the ground) *The police ordered the robbers to lay down their guns.*

a gun goes off (=it fires a bullet, usually by mistake) *The gun went off accidentally in his hand.*

gun + NOUNS

gun crime *Gun crime in the city has increased.*

a gun battle/attack *Two gang members were killed in a gun battle.*

gun laws/control *Britain has stricter gun laws than the US.*

gun culture *disapproving*: *Gangs and gun culture have had a terrible impact on many lives.*

> **Gunshot** is written as one word.

ADJECTIVES

a loaded gun (=with bullets in it) *He kept a loaded gun under his bed.*

NOUNS + gun

a machine gun (=that fires a lot of bullets very quickly) *He began to fire a machine gun into the crowd.*

a toy gun *Do you think children should be allowed to play with toy guns?*

> **Handgun** (= a small gun that you can fire with one hand) and **shotgun** (= a long gun, used especially for hunting) are written as one word.

gusty *adj*

THESAURUS ▸ **windy**

G

Hh

habit *n*

something you do regularly, often without thinking about it

ADJECTIVES/NOUNS + habit

a bad habit *Some children develop bad habits and always leave their room in a mess.*

an annoying/unpleasant/nasty habit *He had an annoying habit of eating with his mouth open.*

a dirty/filthy habit *We all know smoking is a filthy habit.*

a good habit *Exercising every day is a good habit to get into.*

a strange/peculiar/odd habit *Amy had a lot of peculiar habits, one of them being to stare at you without blinking.*

a disconcerting habit (=making you feel slightly worried or embarrassed) *The president has a disconcerting habit of saying exactly what he is thinking.*

an unfortunate habit (=one that you wish was different) *She had an unfortunate habit of forgetting what she wanted to say.*

eating/drinking habits (=the kinds of things you eat or drink regularly) *You need to change your eating habits and start eating healthy foods.*

buying/spending habits (=the kinds of things you buy regularly) *People are changing their spending habits because they are worried about their jobs.*

VERBS

have a habit (of doing sth) *He has a habit of being late.*

sth becomes a habit *Thinking negatively can become a habit.*

get into a habit (=start doing something regularly or often) *Try to get into the habit of walking for 30 minutes each day.*

get out of a habit (=stop doing something regularly or often) *I was busy at work and got out of the habit of exercising.*

break/kick a habit (=stop doing something that is bad for you) *I've smoked for years, but I really want to kick the habit.*

develop/form a habit *He felt very uncomfortable in social situations and had developed the habit of avoiding them.*

change your habits *It's sometimes difficult for people to change their habits.*

make a habit of (doing) sth (=start doing something regularly) *You can leave work early today as long as you don't make a habit of it.*

PREPOSITIONS/ADVERBS

out of/from habit (=because you have been doing something regularly for a long time) *I always go to the same supermarket, out of habit.*

PHRASES

be in the habit of doing sth *On Friday evenings, Carrie was in the habit of visiting her parents.*

(by/from) force of habit (=used about a habit that is difficult to change) *I still think about her every day – force of habit, I suppose.*

change/break the habits of a lifetime (=stop doing the things you have done for many years) *It is hard to change the habits of a lifetime, but you must eat more healthily.*

habitat *n*

the natural home of a plant or animal

ADJECTIVES/NOUNS + habitat

sth's natural/native habitat (=the type of place where an animal or plant usually lives or grows) *She studies gorillas in their natural habitat.*

a wildlife habitat *The area has a rich variety of wildlife habitats.*

an important habitat *The island is an important habitat for exotic animals.*

a fragile habitat (=that could easily be damaged) *The forest has become an increasingly fragile habitat.*

an endangered/threatened habitat (=that is in danger of being destroyed) *These wetlands are one of Britain's most endangered habitats.*

a suitable habitat *The land provides a suitable habitat for many types of birds.*

VERBS

damage/destroy a habitat *Widening the road will damage the habitat of many birds.*

threaten a habitat (=be likely to damage it) *Huge out-of-town developments are threatening wildlife habitats.*

protect/conserve/preserve a habitat *These laws will protect the habitat of endangered species such as wolves.*

provide a habitat (=be suitable and available as a habitat) *Marshes provide a habitat for many species of wading birds.*

create a habitat *The aim is to create a suitable breeding habitat for rare birds.*

a habitat disappears *The number of bears is falling because their natural habitat is disappearing.*

PREPOSITIONS

a habitat for sth *The woods provide an excellent habitat for dozens of small mammals.*

PHRASES

loss of habitat *The elephants are threatened by loss of habitat.*

the destruction of sth's habitat *The destruction of the bird's habitat has been worst in the south.*

hair *n*

the mass of things like fine threads that grow on your head

Grammar

When talking about the mass of things on your head, **hair** is always uncountable. You say *He has got brown* ***hair***. Don't say 'He has got a brown hair.'

The countable form **a hair** is used when talking about a single piece of hair: *I found a* ***hair*** *in the sink.*

ADJECTIVES - COLOUR

dark hair *He's about six feet tall, with dark hair and brown eyes.*

fair hair *Her long fair hair fell untidily over her shoulders.*

black/brown hair *Her long black hair hung down her back.*

blond/blonde hair (=pale yellow in colour – 'blonde' is used especially about women) *Anneka has short blonde hair and blue eyes.*

red/ginger hair (=orange-brown in colour) *The boy had red hair and his friends called him 'carrot'.*

grey/white/silver hair (=used about old people's hair) *She was about 70, with grey hair.*

Other hair colours

Jet black hair is completely black. **Chestnut hair** is dark brown. **Sandy hair** is pale brown. **Mousy hair** is an unattractive pale brown colour. **Auburn hair** is brownish-red. **Golden hair** is a beautiful yellow colour.

ADJECTIVES - LENGTH

short hair *I like your hair when it's short like that.*

long hair *A few of the boys had long hair.*

shoulder-length/medium-length hair *He had shoulder-length brown hair.*

ADJECTIVES - TYPE

straight hair *Bella has long straight hair.*

curly hair *When he was young, his hair was thick and curly.*

wavy hair (=with loose curls) *Her golden wavy hair fell around her shoulders.*

thick hair *She had thick hair down to her waist.*

spiky hair (=stiff and standing up on top of your head) *Billy had black spiky hair.*

ADJECTIVES - CONDITION

glossy/shiny hair *She combed her hair until it was all glossy.*

greasy hair (=containing too much oil) *This shampoo is ideal for greasy hair.*

dry hair (=lacking oil) *Use a shampoo for dry hair.*

sb's hair is in good/bad/terrible etc condition *How do you keep your hair in such perfect condition?*

VERBS

have ... hair *She has beautiful blonde hair.*

brush/comb your hair *He cleaned his teeth and brushed his hair.*

wash your hair *He showered and washed his hair.*

do your hair (*also* **fix your hair** *AmE*) (=arrange it in a style) *She's upstairs doing her hair.*

have your hair cut/done/permed (*also* **get your hair cut etc**) (=by a hairdresser) *I need to get my hair cut.*

cut sb's hair *My mum always cuts my hair.*

dye your hair (blonde/red etc) (=change its colour, especially using chemicals) *Craig has dyed his hair black.*

wear your hair long/in a ponytail etc (=have that style of hair) *He wore his hair in a ponytail.*

grow your hair (long) (=let it grow longer) *I'm growing my hair long, but it's taking forever.*

lose your hair (=become bald) *He was a small round man who was losing his hair.*

run your fingers through sb's hair (=touch someone's hair in a loving way) *He ran his fingers through her smooth silky hair.*

⚠ Don't say 'I cut my hair' if another person cut your hair for you. Say **I had my hair cut.**

hair + NOUNS

hair colour *BrE*, **hair color** *AmE*: *You've changed your hair colour!*

hair products (=products such as shampoo that you use to make your hair look nice) *The company has launched a new range of hair products.*

hair loss *The drug can cause hair loss.*

Hairstyle, **haircut**, and **hairdresser** (=someone who cuts people's hair as a job) are written as one word.

PHRASES

a strand/wisp of hair (=a thin piece of hair) *She brushed away a strand of hair from her eyes.*

a lock of hair (=a fairly thick piece of hair) *She tossed a stray lock of hair back off her forehead.*

a mop of hair (=a large amount of thick untidy hair) *He had an unruly mop of brown hair.*

have a full head of hair (=used to say that a man has not lost any hair) *Even though he is 70, he still has a full head of hair.*

haircut *n*

1 if you have a haircut, someone cuts your hair for you

VERBS

have a haircut *How often do you usually have a haircut?*

get a haircut *She went to get a haircut.*

H

need a haircut *Your hair is too long – you need a haircut.*

give sb a haircut *Last time they gave me a terrible haircut.*

2 the style your hair is cut in

ADJECTIVES

a new haircut *I like your new haircut.*

a short haircut *A short haircut really suits him.*

a good/decent haircut *A good haircut can make you look ten years younger.*

a stylish haircut *The band all have stylish haircuts.*

a bad haircut *He had a bad haircut and wore unfashionable clothes.*

half *n*

one of two equal parts of something

ADJECTIVES

the top/bottom half *The bottom half of the wall is painted blue.*

the first/second half *Profits doubled in the first half of the year.*

the northern/southern half *The northern half of the city is more industrial.*

the other half *Half the patients were given the drug and the other half were given a sugar pill.*

the last/latter half *He had a lot of illness in the latter half of his life.*

VERBS

break/cut/tear sth in half *He tore the paper in half.*

divide/split sth in half *Divide the dough in half.*

reduce/cut sth by half *The company has reduced the number of staff by half.*

decrease/fall by half *Share prices fell by half.*

increase/rise by half *The number of passengers using the service has increased by half.*

PHRASES

one/two etc and a half *"How old is she?" "Five and a half."*

halt[1] *n* a stop or pause

ADJECTIVES

a sudden halt (*also* **an abrupt halt** *formal*): *My happiness was brought to a sudden halt by the death of my father.*

an immediate halt *The government called for an immediate halt to the fighting.*

a complete halt *Traffic on the busy motorway has slowed almost to a complete halt.*

a temporary halt *The game was brought to a temporary halt when the floodlights failed.*

a grinding halt (=one in which all of a system stops completely) *One accident can bring the whole road system to a grinding halt.*

VERBS

bring sth to a halt (=make it stop moving or operating) *The city was brought to a halt by the transport strike.*

sth/sb comes to a halt (=they stop moving or operating) *The bus came to a halt right outside the school.*

call for a halt to sth (=publicly ask for something to stop) *The government has called for a halt to the violence.*

call a halt to sth (=stop doing it) *University officials have asked the students to call a halt to their protest.*

order a halt to sth (=officially say that something must stop) *The president ordered a halt to nuclear tests on the islands.*

demand a halt to sth (=firmly ask for something to stop) *Irish farmers demanded a halt to imports of British cattle.*

put a halt to sth (=stop something) *The bad news put a halt to our celebrations.*

sth grinds to a halt (=it stops slowly – used for emphasis) *If the computer system fails, the entire banking system could grind to a halt.*

sth draws to a halt (=a vehicle slows down and stops) *As the train drew to a halt, people started to get off.*

sth screeches to a halt (=a vehicle stops very quickly with a loud high sound) *A police car screeched to a halt and two officers jumped out.*

PREPOSITIONS

a halt to sth *The government has agreed to meet protesters if there is an immediate halt to the violence.*

halt[2] *v* THESAURUS **stop[1] (3)**

hand[1] *n*

the part of your body at the end of your arm, including your fingers and thumb, that you use to hold things

ADJECTIVES

sb's right/left hand *She held the book in her right hand.*

big/small hands *He has very big hands and feet.*

strong hands *His strong hands gripped her shoulders.*

delicate hands (=small and thin) *Ben has very delicate hands for a man.*

clammy/sweaty hands (=with a lot of sweat) *His hands get clammy when he's nervous.*

rough hands *The farmer had big rough hands.*

gnarled hands (=rough and twisted because of old age) *The photograph showed the gnarled hands of the old man.*

sb's free hand (=the hand someone is not already using) *Amy was stroking the dog with her free hand.*

an outstretched hand (=stretched out towards someone or something) *She took her father's outstretched hand and began to walk from the room.*

VERBS + hand

wave your hand *Marta waved a hand to attract his attention.*

clap your hands *They were singing and clapping their hands.*

wash your hands *Go wash your hands before dinner.*

hold hands (with sb) *Joanne and Kevin held hands on the sofa.*

shake sb's hand (*also* **shake hands with sb**) *"Nice to meet you," he said, as they shook hands.*

take sb's hand (=hold someone's hand) *He reached across the table and took her hand in his.*

join hands (=take hold of the hands of people on either side of you) *They stood in a circle and joined hands.*

clasp your hands (=hold them together tightly) *Emily clasped her hands together and stood there nervously.*

raise your hand (*also* **put your hand up**) (=lift your hand, especially when you want to ask or answer a question) *If you know the answer, raise your hand.*

hand + VERBS

sb's hands shake/tremble *His hands trembled as he lifted the cup.*

sb's hand holds sth *His other hand was holding his mobile phone.*

sb's hand touches sth *Daniel's hand touched mine.*

sb's hand grips/clutches sth (=holds something firmly) *Her hands gripped the steering wheel very tightly.*

hand + NOUNS

a hand movement *The disease means she has trouble controlling her hand movements.*

a hand gesture/signal (=a movement of your hand to show what you mean) *He made a rude hand gesture at the other driver.*

hand cream/lotion *If your hands feel rough, put some hand cream on them.*

PREPOSITIONS

in sb's hand *In her hand was a tattered old photograph.*

with your hands *I grasped the vase with both my hands.*

by hand (=done or made by a person and not a machine) *You should wash delicate clothes by hand.*

PHRASES

hand in hand (=holding hands with each other) *The couple left the building hand in hand.*

the palm of your hand (=the inside surface of your hand) *The phone could fit into the palm of his hand.*

the back of your hand (=the outside surface of your hand) *Let a dog sniff the back of your hand, rather than your fingers.*

with your bare hands (=without using a tool, weapon, machine etc) *With his bare hands, he forced the doors apart.*

on your hands and knees (=in a crawling position) *They got down on their hands and knees to search.*

hand² *v*

THESAURUS ▸ **give (1)**

handicap *n*

a situation that makes it difficult for someone to do what they want

ADJECTIVES

a real handicap *Not speaking the language is a real handicap.*

a major/big handicap *The lack of an industrial sector in the country is a major handicap to improving its economy.*

a serious/severe handicap *His old age proved to be a serious handicap to being elected president.*

VERBS

have a handicap *The English team had a big handicap because several of their best players were injured.*

overcome a handicap *She had to work hard to overcome the handicap of coming from a very poor family.*

PREPOSITIONS

a handicap to sth *Being a small country is not necessarily a handicap to economic success.*

a handicap for sb *Shyness can be a handicap for anyone who wants to become an actor.*

> **Handicapped**
> This word was used in the past about disabled people. It is now becoming old-fashioned and is considered offensive by many people.

handle *n*

the part of something used for opening it or holding it

VERBS

turn the handle *She turned the handle and went inside.*

try the handle (=try to turn it) *He tried the handle, but the door was locked.*

hold the handle *Hold the handle of the basket carefully so that you don't drop it.*

grab/grasp the handle *I grabbed the handle of the door and pulled it open.*

NOUNS + handle

a door handle *He put his hand on the door handle and tested it.*

handshake *n*

the act of taking someone's right hand and shaking it

ADJECTIVES

a firm handshake *He greeted me with a firm handshake.*

a farewell handshake (=when saying 'goodbye') *After a brief farewell handshake, he boarded the train.*

a secret handshake (=done in a special way as a secret signal) *Club members greet each other with a secret handshake.*

VERBS

give sb a handshake *The women hugged me and the men gave me a handshake.*

greet sb with a handshake *He greeted all of his guests with a handshake.*

exchange handshakes *The teams exchanged handshakes at the end of the game.*

handsome *adj*

1 a handsome man is good-looking

NOUNS

a handsome man/boy *Your husband is a very handsome man.*

a handsome prince *A handsome prince kissed her and she woke up.*

a handsome face *His handsome face looked sad for a moment.*

handsome features *His handsome features are framed by thick dark hair.*

> **Handsome** is normally only used about men. It is sometimes used in literature about a woman, especially an older woman with very strong or noticeable features: *She was a tall* **handsome** *woman dressed in riding clothes.*

ADVERBS

strikingly handsome (=in a very noticeable way) *He is a strikingly handsome young man.*

devastatingly handsome (=extremely handsome) *A smile passed across his devastatingly handsome face.*

darkly handsome (=handsome, with dark hair and skin) *He was lively, funny, and darkly handsome.*

ruggedly handsome (=handsome, with strong features) *I like men who are ruggedly handsome, not pretty boys.*

classically handsome (=handsome in a way that has always been considered to be handsome) *His face is interesting, rather than classically handsome.*

VERBS

look handsome *You look very handsome in your new suit.*

PHRASES

tall (dark) and handsome *Jack is very tall and handsome.*

young and handsome *She likes working with men, particularly if they are young and handsome.*

> **THESAURUS: handsome**
>
> handsome, good-looking, pretty, attractive, cute, lovely, gorgeous, glorious, picturesque, magnificent, stunning, breathtaking/spectacular, exquisite → **beautiful**

2 large or impressive

NOUNS

a handsome profit *He sold the house at a handsome profit.*

a handsome sum *£10,000 is a handsome sum.*

a handsome reward *She received a handsome reward for finding the wallet.*

PHRASES

pay handsome dividends (=have very good results later) *Being well prepared will pay handsome dividends in a job interview.*

handwriting *n*

the style of someone's writing

ADJECTIVES

neat/clear handwriting *Your handwriting is much neater than mine.*

legible/illegible handwriting (=written clearly, or not written clearly enough for you to read) *He writes very quickly and his handwriting is almost illegible.*

small/tiny handwriting *Her handwriting was so tiny I couldn't read it without my glasses.*

bad/poor/terrible/awful handwriting (=untidy and difficult to read) *Like many doctors, she has terrible handwriting.*

good/lovely/beautiful handwriting *I received a postcard in her familiar lovely handwriting.*

sb's best handwriting *The teacher encouraged pupils to do the test in their best handwriting.*

VERBS

have neat/small etc handwriting *Yu Yin has tiny handwriting.*

recognize sb's handwriting *I didn't recognize the handwriting on the envelope.*

read sb's handwriting *I left her a note and hoped she would be able to read my handwriting.*

handwriting + NOUNS

a handwriting expert (=someone who studies people's handwriting) *A handwriting expert is sure that the letter was written by the suspect.*

PHRASES

in (sb's) handwriting *Entry forms must be completed in the candidate's own handwriting.*

handy *adj* THESAURUS **useful**

happen *v*

used when saying that there is an event, especially one that is not planned

H

NOUNS

an accident/incident/event happens *The accident happened at 6.15 a.m.*

an attack/explosion/murder etc happens *Neighbours are shocked that such an attack could happen in their village.*

a change happens *They don't believe that climate change is really happening.*

a disaster/earthquake happens *The question is, could an earthquake like this happen in California?*

a miracle happens *I was hoping that a miracle would happen.*

a ... thing happens *A funny thing happened last week when I was on the subway.*

something/nothing happens *If something happens, call me immediately.*

VERBS

make sth happen *It's up to you – only you can make it happen.*

let sth happen *The authorities are determined not to let the same thing happen again.*

predict/know that sth will happen *It's impossible to predict what will happen next.*

ADVERBS

happen quickly/slowly/gradually *It all happened so quickly that there was nothing I could do.*

happen overnight (=immediately) *Change doesn't happen overnight.*

PREPOSITIONS

happen to sb *The same thing happened to my sister.*

PHRASES

sth is bound to happen (=certain to happen) *An accident was bound to happen sooner or later.*

sth happens all the time/every day (=it happens often) *This kind of thing happens all the time where I live.*

whatever happens *We'll still be friends, whatever happens.*

THESAURUS: happen

take place
meeting | conference | ceremony | marriage | competition | game | race | demonstration | change | accident | incident | attack | murder
to happen. **Take place** is often used about things that have been planned:
The meeting took place in Paris on January 12th. | The ceremony will take place in Westminster Abbey. | Important changes were taking place across the Arab World. | They want to avoid the kind of accident that took place at Three Mile Island in the US.

occur *formal*
problem | accident | incident | attack | explosion | situation | case | disease | condition
to happen. **Occur** is used about events that have not been planned, especially bad events. **Occur** is more formal than **happen**:
Problems might occur if there is a big rise in sea levels. | The accident occurred on the northbound No. 3 Freeway. | A similar situation occurred in Thailand in 2004.

come up
question | opportunity | chance | problem
to happen – used especially about problems, questions, and opportunities:
This question often comes up when I'm talking to students. | After a year, an opportunity came up to move to Vienna. | There aren't any jobs at the moment, but we'll let you know if ***something comes up*** (=if there are any opportunities for jobs).

arise *formal*
problem | difficulty | question | opportunity | chance | circumstance | need | dispute | conflict | doubt | concern
to happen – used especially about problems, questions, and opportunities. **Arise** is more formal than **come up**. It is often used when talking about dealing with possible problems:
There may be financial problems ***arising from*** *the patient's illness. | The question arose as to who the money belonged to. | Charles decided to talk to her about it, when the opportunity arose. | The lifeguard will be there to rescue you,* ***should the need arise*** (=if necessary). *| A dispute arose between the steel companies and their employees.*

crop up
problem | issue | emergency | question
to happen suddenly or often – used especially about less serious problems that can easily be dealt with:
Traditionally, if a problem crops up, a manager goes in and tells people what to do. | The same issues always keep cropping up on every project. | Here is my phone number, just in case ***something crops up****.*

strike
disaster | tragedy | earthquake | tsunami | hurricane | storm | drought
to happen suddenly – used about very bad events:
They were coming down the mountain when disaster struck. | I was on the 38th floor of an office building when the earthquake struck.

turn out
well | fine | okay | badly | as planned
used when saying whether something happens successfully, in the way that you wanted:
Luckily, everything turned out well in the end. | Things don't always turn out as planned. | How did it all turn out?

materialize (*also* **materialise** *BrE*) to happen – used when saying that something did not happen, even though people expected it to: *The rains **failed to materialize** last year. | The violence the newspapers had predicted **did not materialize**.*

Instead of saying that something **happened**, you often use **there is/was**: *The leaflet tells you what to do if **there is** an accident* (=if an accident happens).
You say that **there is something going on**, when you know that something is happening, but you are not sure what it is: ***There's something going on** outside our house.*

happiness *n* the state of being happy

ADJECTIVES

great happiness *His grandchildren bring him great happiness.*

true/real happiness *She found true happiness with a man she loved.*

perfect/pure/sheer happiness *The birth of my child was a moment of sheer happiness.*

personal happiness *People are realizing that wealth and success do not always bring personal happiness.*

future happiness *Your future happiness depends on this decision.*

lasting happiness (=that continues for a long time) *In her second marriage, she found lasting happiness.*

VERBS

find happiness (*also* **achieve happiness** *formal*): *His ambition was to be a musician but he unexpectedly found happiness as a teacher.*

bring (sb) happiness *She wrongly believes that money can bring happiness.*

be filled with happiness *She ran towards me, her eyes filled with happiness.*

PHRASES

a feeling of happiness *Being by the ocean gave her a feeling of great happiness.*

the pursuit of happiness (=the act of trying to achieve happiness) *Life, liberty, and the pursuit of happiness are seen as basic rights.*

I wish you every happiness (=used to say that you hope someone will have a happy life) *I wish you both every happiness in your new life together.*

happy *adj*

having feelings of pleasure, for example because something good has happened to you or you are very satisfied with your life

VERBS

be/feel happy *It's a lovely house and we've been very happy here.*

look happy *They looked so happy and proud of their son.*

make sb happy *I loved her and thought I could make her happy.*

NOUNS

a happy ending *The story has a happy ending and the baby bear finds his mother again.*

a happy man/woman/couple/family *If we win, I'll be a very happy man.*

a happy face/smile *I looked around at the happy faces of the children.*

a happy child/boy/girl *Nigel was a happy boy with lots of friends.*

a happy childhood/marriage *Although we were poor, we had a very happy childhood in many ways.*

a happy time/occasion/experience *Floyd's farm was a place where I spent many happy times.*

a happy life *We hope you have a long and happy life together.*

happy memories *The film brought back many happy memories.*

happy birthday/Christmas/New Year (=used as a greeting on someone's birthday, at Christmas etc) *I wanted to wish you a very happy birthday.*

the happy news (=often used when someone has a new baby or is going to have one) *She couldn't wait to tell her friends the happy news.*

PREPOSITIONS

happy with sth (=used especially when saying someone is satisfied) *I'm happy with the situation.*

happy about sth *When I talked to her about the idea, she seemed very happy about it.*

happy for sb *I'm so happy for you both.*

happy in your job/work/marriage/life *He is happy in his job and has no intention of leaving.*

ADVERBS

blissfully/deliriously happy (=extremely happy) *Ronni had never been so deliriously happy in her life.*

perfectly happy (=completely happy and not wanting anything to change) *I'm perfectly happy here – I don't want to move.*

fairly/reasonably happy (=fairly satisfied) *He was reasonably happy with his performance in the competition.*

genuinely happy *She seemed genuinely happy to be there.*

PHRASES

happy as can be/happy as anything *especially spoken* (=extremely happy) *His parents are as happy as can be.*

H

THESAURUS: happy

cheerful
voice | smile | face | expression | manner | mood | atmosphere | woman | man | room | place | colour
looking or sounding happy:
"Great to see you!" he said in a cheerful voice. | It was the end of term and everyone was in a cheerful mood. | Mrs Johnson was a cheerful woman with enormous energy. | The room was painted in bright cheerful colours. | He seems a lot more cheerful today.

contented
smile | expression | silence | sigh | mood | man | woman | baby | cat
feeling happy with your life, job, situation etc. **Contented** sounds a little formal and is mainly used in written English:
There was a contented smile on the little boy's face. | He was a contented man, with a good wife and a prosperous farm. | She was ***contented with*** *her job at the university.*

> **Contented** or **content?**
> You can also use **content** to mean "satisfied with your life": *Henry was happy and if he was* ***content****, so was Diana.*
> However, usually **content** means that someone does not want to do anything else, or have anything else: *He was* ***content to*** *just sit back and wait. | The team had to be* ***content with*** *second place.*

pleased/glad
happy because something good has happened:
I'm pleased I passed my exam. | He was glad to see someone that he knew.

> **Pleased** and **glad** are not usually used before a noun.

> If someone seems happy, you can also say that he or she is **in a good mood**.

very happy

delighted
very happy because something good has happened:
The doctors say they are ***delighted with*** *her progress.*

thrilled
very happy and excited about something:
He's ***thrilled at*** *the idea of going to Disneyworld.*

overjoyed
very happy because you have heard some good news:
She was overjoyed when she found out that her son was safe.

> **Delighted**, **thrilled**, and **overjoyed** are not used before a noun.

ecstatic
fans | crowd | welcome | review
extremely happy and feeling very excited:
The crowd were ecstatic, and cheered wildly. | The play received ecstatic reviews. | The coach said he was simply ***ecstatic about*** *yesterday's result.*

blissful
smile | weeks | hours
extremely happy, especially because something gives you a lot of pleasure:
The man lay asleep, a blissful smile on his face. | For two blissful weeks we explored the islands. | It sounded blissful – sea, sun, and good food.

> If someone is extremely happy because something good has happened, you can say that he or she is **on top of the world** or **over the moon**: *I was* ***over the moon*** *when I found out that I'd passed my exam.*

ANTONYMS **happy → sad**

harassment *n*

unpleasant or threatening behaviour towards someone

ADJECTIVES/NOUNS + harassment

sexual harassment *The woman accused her boss of sexual harassment.*

racial harassment *At school he was the victim of bullying and racial harassment.*

frequent/continual harassment (=happening often) *Female students experience frequent harassment.*

police harassment *African-Americans have been complaining about police harassment for years.*

VERBS

suffer/experience harassment *Employees can take legal action to protect themselves if they have suffered harassment.*

be subjected to harassment (=suffer harassment) *Opposition party members have been subjected to harassment and death threats.*

accuse sb of harassment *Under the new law, an employee who keeps making remarks about a woman's appearance could be accused of sexual harassment.*

complain of harassment *The group was set up to protect journalists, who often complain of harassment by the authorities.*

PREPOSITIONS

harassment of sb *Sexual harassment of women is still a problem.*

harassment against sb *There have been reports of threats and harassment against human rights groups.*

PHRASES

a victim of harassment *Victims of harassment in the workplace can take their company to court.*

accusations/allegations of harassment *False accusations of harassment can destroy people's lives.*

a campaign of harassment *She was accused of carrying out a campaign of harassment against her ex-husband.*

hard *adj*

1 having a surface that is difficult to press down, cut, or break

NOUNS

a hard chair *She was sitting on a hard wooden chair.*

a hard bed *The beds were hard and uncomfortable.*

a hard floor *The plate smashed on the hard stone floor.*

the hard ground *Players can easily injure themselves on the hard ground.*

a hard surface *The birds drop shellfish onto hard surfaces in order to break them open.*

a hard material/substance *Diamonds are the hardest substance known to man.*

a hard case (=used to protect something from being damaged) *I keep my guitar in a hard case when I'm travelling.*

hard metal/stone *The steps were made of hard stone.*

hard skin *The skin on his feet had become very hard.*

cheese/bread/potatoes etc are hard *The bread was old and very hard.*

ADVERBS

extremely/incredibly hard *The pan is made of an extremely hard type of metal.*

rock hard (=extremely hard and very difficult to break) *The ice was rock hard.*

VERBS

set hard *It takes a few days for the concrete to set hard.*

go hard (=become hard) *The bread had gone hard.*

THESAURUS: hard

firm
mattress | cushion | texture | pear | apple | tomato | muscles
not easy to press or bend, but not completely hard – used especially when this seems a good thing:
I like to sleep on a firm mattress. | This particular cheese has a good firm texture. | It's best to buy pears when they are still firm. | These exercises will make your stomach muscles nice and firm.

stiff
collar | cardboard | card | paper | material | cotton | body | brush
difficult to bend and not changing shape:
The collar of the shirt felt stiff and uncomfortable. | The box was made out of stiff cardboard. | His body was stiff and motionless.

solid
gold | silver | iron | metal | wood | oak | pine | rock | stone | block of sth
consisting of a thick hard material and not hollow or liquid:
She was wearing a solid gold bracelet. | All the rooms have solid wood floors. | The sculpture was carved out of solid rock. | During winter the lake became a solid block of ice.

rigid
frame | structure | case | container
having a structure that is made of a material that is difficult or impossible to bend:
The tent is supported by a rigid frame. | The camera is supplied with a rigid case. | Carry sandwiches in a rigid container.

crispy
bacon | chicken | duck | lettuce | pancake
used about thin pieces of food that are pleasantly hard, which make a noise when you bite them:
They had fried eggs and crispy bacon for breakfast. | It's best to use crispy lettuce leaves for the salad. | Fry the potato slices until they are nice and crispy.

crunchy
carrots | vegetables | lettuce | salad | biscuit | toast | peanut butter | texture
food that is crunchy makes a noise when you bite on it – used especially about things that are fresh, for example fruit, vegetables, and nuts:
The carrots are nice and crunchy. | I made a delicious crunchy salad. | The beans have a crunchy texture.

tough
meat | steak | leaves
meat, vegetables, or plants that are tough are difficult to chew or cut:
The meat was tough and flavourless. | The steak I had yesterday was a bit tough. | The outer leaves of the cabbage can be rather tough.

rubbery
chicken | texture
having a rather hard surface which bends like rubber, and seems unpleasant:
The chicken was a bit rubbery. | The cheese has a mild flavour, and a slightly rubbery texture.

brittle
bones | nails | hair | material
if something is brittle, it has a hard surface that breaks easily:
Old people often have brittle bones. | The shampoo is good for brittle hair. | Glass is a brittle material.

H

ANTONYMS **hard → soft (1)**

2 difficult

THESAURUS: hard

hard, tough, demanding, challenging, daunting, awkward, tricky, delicate → **difficult**

3 tiring

THESAURUS: hard

exhausting, hard, gruelling, punishing, backbreaking, wearing → **tiring**

hardened *adj* THESAURUS **experienced**

hard-hearted *adj* THESAURUS **unkind**

harm[1] *n*

damage, injury, or trouble caused by someone or something

VERBS

cause (sb/sth) harm *We try not to use chemicals that cause harm to the environment.*

do (sth) harm *The scandal did a lot of harm to his reputation.*

suffer harm *formal: Luckily, no one suffered any serious harm.*

prevent harm *Pregnant women should stop smoking in order to prevent harm to their unborn babies.*

reduce/minimize harm *The new law aims to reduce the harm caused by drugs.*

protect/shield sb/sth from harm *They offer advice on how to protect children from harm when using the internet.*

⚠ Don't say 'give harm' or 'make harm'. Say **do harm** or **cause harm**.

ADJECTIVES/NOUNS + harm

great/serious/significant harm *If you drink too much alcohol, you can do yourself serious harm.*

lasting/permanent harm *The doctor says that there is no permanent harm to his legs.*

irreparable harm (=which cannot be made better) *The stories in the newspapers caused irreparable harm to her career.*

untold harm *formal* (=very great harm) *Bullying causes untold harm and can affect a child for the rest of his or her life.*

potential harm *People need to be more aware of the potential harm of some foods.*

physical harm (=to someone's body) *Too much exercise can cause physical harm.*

psychological/emotional harm (=to someone's mind) *Some of these children have suffered serious emotional harm.*

PREPOSITIONS

harm to sb/sth *Plastic bags cause a lot of harm to the environment.*

PHRASES

mean no harm (=not intend to hurt or upset someone) *He apologized and assured me that he meant no harm.*

come to no harm/not come to any harm (=not be hurt or damaged) *She was pleased her car had come to no harm.*

do more harm than good *Vitamin pills sometimes do more harm than good.*

out of harm's way (=in a place where something cannot cause harm or be harmed) *If you have children, make sure you keep medicines out of harm's way.*

harm[2] *v*

to have a bad effect on something or someone

ADVERBS

seriously/severely harm sb/sth *The incident has seriously harmed his chances of winning the election.*

deliberately/intentionally harm sb/sth *They had been accused of deliberately harming their children.*

irreparably harm sth (=in a way that cannot be repaired) *Environmentalists said the area's wildlife would be irreparably harmed by the building work.*

physically harm sb (=harm someone's body) *Prisoners will not be physically harmed in any way.*

harmful *adj* causing harm

NOUNS

a harmful effect *We all know about the harmful effects of smoking, so why do so many people still smoke?*

a harmful side effect *The drug appears to have no harmful side effects.*

harmful consequences *She was unaware of the harmful consequences of her actions.*

a harmful substance *The workers may have been exposed to harmful substances.*

harmful bacteria *Cooking should kill any harmful bacteria.*

ADVERBS

extremely harmful *Smoking is extremely harmful to your health.*

potentially harmful (=could be harmful) *Many natural foods are potentially harmful.*

positively harmful (=very harmful - often used when this is the opposite of what people expect) *Hiding your true feelings can be positively harmful.*

PREPOSITIONS

harmful to sb/sth *These chemicals are harmful to the environment.*

harmless *adj*

unable or unlikely to hurt anyone or cause damage

ADVERBS

completely/totally/perfectly harmless *Don't be frightened – the dog is perfectly harmless.*

relatively harmless (=not very harmless) *The drug is relatively harmless if taken in small amounts.*

seemingly/apparently harmless *This seemingly harmless mushroom is actually very poisonous.*

sb/sth is harmless enough (=used when emphasizing that someone or something is harmless) *John shouts a lot, but he's harmless enough.*

NOUNS

harmless fun *The children are just having a bit of harmless fun.*

a harmless substance *Some substances are harmless to humans, but they can be harmful to other animals.*

a drug is harmless *We need to know that the drug is harmless.*

VERBS

look/seem harmless *Smoking may seem harmless, but it is very bad for your health.*

render sth harmless *formal* (=make something harmless) *Medical advances mean that some diseases have been rendered harmless.*

PREPOSITIONS

harmless to sth *Most spiders are harmless to humans.*

harmony *n*

when people live or work together without fighting or disagreeing

ADJECTIVES

perfect/complete harmony *The brothers work together in perfect harmony.*

relative/reasonable harmony (=quite friendly and peaceful when compared to something else) *These neighbouring peoples have lived together in relative harmony for years.*

racial/social/political harmony *We aim to promote racial harmony through shared sporting activities.*

domestic harmony (=in the home) *There was a lot of tension beneath the impression of domestic harmony.*

inner harmony (=a feeling of being peaceful and calm) *His search for inner harmony led him to Buddhism.*

VERBS

live in harmony *We want a society in which people of all races and religions can live in harmony.*

work in harmony *The president urged all Americans to work in harmony to solve the nation's problems.*

achieve harmony *After years of tension, it will be difficult to achieve racial harmony in the city.*

promote harmony (=do things that help it develop or improve) *We need to develop ways of promoting harmony between nations.*

create harmony *The aim is to create better harmony within the community.*

PREPOSITIONS

harmony between/among people *Leaders appealed for harmony between Christians and Muslims in the region.*

PHRASES

peace and harmony *He longed for peace and harmony to return.*

a sense of harmony *There was a quiet sense of harmony between them as they walked along.*

harsh *adj*

1 unkind or cruel, especially in a way that seems unfair

harsh + NOUNS

harsh criticism *Politicians have to learn to live with harsh criticism.*

a harsh punishment *There are harsh punishments for drug smugglers.*

harsh treatment *He experienced particularly harsh treatment in prison.*

harsh discipline *Their father believed in harsh discipline and beat them with a stick.*

harsh words *She has some harsh words to say about her ex-husband.*

a harsh tone/voice *"You don't know what you're doing," he said in a harsh tone.*

a harsh decision *The referee's decision seemed very harsh.*

ADVERBS

a little harsh (*also* **a bit harsh** *BrE spoken*): *Maybe I'm being a bit harsh, but I think he deserved to be expelled from school.*

rather harsh/particularly harsh *Making him take the test again because of one small mistake seemed rather harsh. | Some of the prisoners are given particularly harsh treatment.*

unduly harsh (=unreasonably harsh) *It is unduly harsh to criticise him for doing what he was told to do.*

VERBS

sb is being harsh *"I think you're being a bit harsh," she objected.*

seem/sound harsh *I am sorry if I sound harsh, but I don't trust him at all.*

PREPOSITIONS

be harsh on sb *Don't be too harsh on him, he's only a child.*

H

THESAURUS: harsh

firm, tough, harsh, stern, authoritarian → **strict (1)**

tight, tough, harsh, stringent → **strict (2)**

2 difficult or unpleasant

harsh + NOUNS

a harsh climate/harsh weather *Siberia has a very harsh climate and the temperature can go below minus 30 degrees.*

a harsh winter *Some plants may not survive the harsh winter.*

harsh conditions *Conditions in the camp were particularly harsh.*

a harsh environment *The city is a harsh environment for any child to grow up in.*

a harsh world *He sees himself as a victim of a cruel harsh world.*

the harsh facts *Don't wait to find out these harsh facts the hard way.*

the harsh truth *The harsh truth is, he is not good enough to be a professional footballer.*

the harsh reality/realities of sth *The only way he could escape the harsh realities of life was to lose himself in books.*

harsh light (=too strong, especially in a way that makes it difficult to see) *He shielded his eyes from the harsh light.*

harvest *n*

the gathering of crops from the fields, or the amount of crops that are gathered

ADJECTIVES

a good harvest *Farmers are hoping for a good harvest this year.*

a bumper harvest (=very good) *Thanks to a good summer, there will be a bumper harvest.*

a poor/bad harvest *There were food shortages because of last year's poor harvest.*

a disastrous harvest (=very bad) *The disastrous harvest of 1948 caused widespread famine.*

VERBS

bring in/gather in/get in the harvest (=collect the crops from the fields) *They worked late into the night to bring in the harvest.*

help with the harvest *He goes back home in late summer to help with the harvest.*

the harvest fails (=there are no crops or only poor crops) *The potato harvest failed that year.*

NOUNS + harvest

the grain/potato/grape etc harvest *This year's grain harvest is expected to be well over 85 million tons.*

harvest + NOUNS

harvest time *He hired extra workers to help at harvest time.*

the harvest season *The harvest season is in October.*

a harvest festival (=celebration to give thanks for the harvest) *Many churches and schools hold a harvest festival in September.*

hasty *adj* THESAURUS ▸ **quick (1)**

hat *n*

a piece of clothing that you wear on your head

ADJECTIVES

a fur/straw/paper etc hat *She was wearing a thick coat and a fur hat.*

a woolly hat *BrE informal* (=made of wool) *Wear a woolly hat to keep your head warm.*

a sun hat *In hot weather, make sure the kids wear sun hats.*

a riding/swimming hat *He got off the horse and took off his riding hat.*

a hard hat (=worn by workers to protect their heads) *Hard hats must be worn on the building site at all times.*

a floppy hat (=made of soft material that bends easily) *She was wearing a flowery dress and a big floppy hat.*

a silly hat *The people at the party were all wearing silly hats.*

VERBS

wear a hat *The man was wearing a cowboy hat.*

have a hat on *especially spoken* (=be wearing a hat) *His mother had her best hat on.*

put your hat on *She fastened her coat and put her hat on.*

take off your hat (*also* **remove your hat** *formal*): *It is polite to take your hat off when you go into someone's house.*

raise your hat (=lift it up as a greeting) *He always raised his hat when he saw me.*

PREPOSITIONS

in a hat *A man in a fur hat came over to me.*

hate[1] *v*

to dislike something or someone very much

ADVERBS

really/absolutely hate sb/sth *I absolutely hated sport when I was at school.*

secretly hate sb/sth *One in ten people admitted to secretly hating their boss.*

PREPOSITIONS

hate sb for (doing) sth *She hated her husband for what he had done.*

PHRASES

hate to see sth *Her mother hated to see good food being wasted.*

I hate it when... *I hate it when we argue with each other.*

I hate to say/admit it *I hate to admit it, but you're right.*

H

hate² *n*

the angry feeling that someone has when they hate someone

PHRASES

be full of hate/be filled with hate *Her eyes were full of hate.*

a look of hate *He gave me a look of pure hate as I entered the room.*

a love-hate relationship (= in which you sometimes like and sometimes hate someone or something) *She had a love-hate relationship with her mother.*

ADJECTIVES

absolute/pure hate *There was a look of pure hate in his eyes.*

hate + NOUNS

a hate figure (=someone who a lot of people hate) *He became a national hate figure because of his remarks.*

hate mail *She began receiving hate mail and abusive phone calls after she appeared on the show.*

a hate crime (=crime that is committed by someone because they hate a particular group of people and want to hurt them) *Most hate crimes are based on race or ethnicity.*

a hate campaign *Barker was the victim of a vicious hate campaign.*

You say that something is a **pet hate** when you particularly dislike it: *Rice pudding has always been one of my* ***pet hates****.*

Hate or hatred?

Hatred and **hate** both mean "the feeling of hating someone". **Hatred** is more common. **Hate** is often used in compounds such as **hate figure**, **hate mail**, or **hate crime**, and often has the feeling that you want to harm someone because you hate them so much.

hatred *n*

an angry feeling of extreme dislike for someone or something

ADJECTIVES/NOUNS + hatred

deep/bitter/passionate/intense hatred (=that you feel very strongly) *What had she done to provoke such deep hatred?*

pure hatred (=complete hatred) *The child opened her eyes and stared at Juliet with pure hatred.*

irrational hatred (=very unreasonable) *Some drivers seem to have an irrational hatred of cyclists.*

pathological hatred (=very strong and unreasonable, and impossible to change) *My sister had a pathological hatred of men.*

racial hatred *The attack was motivated by racial hatred.*

religious/sectarian hatred (=between different religious groups) *The law makes it an offence to stir up religious hatred.*

VERBS

have a hatred of sb/sth *Gang members have a hatred of the police.*

feel hatred *I just feel hatred for the evil person who killed my brother.*

incite/stir up hatred (=encourage people to hate each other. 'Incite' is more formal than 'stir up') *He faces criminal charges for inciting racial hatred.*

fuel hatred (=make hatred stronger) *The government's policy will only fuel racial hatred.*

preach hatred (=try to persuade other people to hate a particular group of people) *They continue to preach hatred in the name of religion.*

PREPOSITIONS

hatred of sth *Racism and hatred of foreigners is on the increase in some countries.*

hatred for sb/sth *Abby made no secret of her hatred for her father.*

hatred towards sb *It is terrifying to know that someone can feel such hatred towards another person.*

PHRASES

full of/filled with hatred *She told me, in a voice full of hatred, that I meant nothing to her.*

feelings of hatred *It will take a long time for their feelings of hatred to go away.*

hazard *n*

something that may be dangerous, or cause accidents or problems

ADJECTIVES/NOUNS + hazard

a serious/major/real hazard *Fumes from the factory posed a serious hazard to the health of people living in the area.*

a potential/possible hazard (=something is likely to be a hazard) *Microwave ovens are a potential hazard if not used properly.*

a fire hazard *Christmas lights and decorations pose a potential fire hazard.*

a health hazard *The waste needs to be removed before it becomes a health hazard.*

a safety hazard *Protesters claim that the nuclear reactor is a safety hazard.*

an occupational hazard (=a hazard that always exists in a particular job) *Catching frequent colds is an occupational hazard when working with young children.*

a natural hazard (=caused by nature) *One of the most widespread natural hazards is flooding.*

an environmental hazard *Oil from the tanker caused an environmental hazard.*

VERBS

cause/create a hazard *There was concern that overhead power lines could cause a health hazard.*

pose/present/constitute a hazard (=be a possible hazard) *It was not known whether radiation from the weapons posed any hazard to soldiers.*

eliminate a hazard (=get rid of a hazard) *They took steps to eliminate all potential fire hazards.*

reduce a hazard *The authorities are trying to reduce the hazard of flooding by building new flood defences.*

avoid a hazard *The road safety classes aim to help children to avoid hazards while crossing the road.*

PREPOSITIONS

a hazard to sth/sb *The chemical is present at levels which are likely to be a hazard to health.*

a hazard for sb *Icy paths are a hazard for elderly people.*

the hazard from sth *The hazard from lead in water is very serious.*

hazardous *adj* THESAURUS ▸ **dangerous, poisonous**

hazy *adj* THESAURUS ▸ **cloudy**

head *n*

1 the top part of your body that has your face at the front and is supported by your neck

ADJECTIVES

a bare head (=not covered with a hat) *The sun beat down on her bare head.*

a bald head (=with no hair) *His bald head shone with sweat.*

a shaved/shaven head (=with the hair removed from it using a razor) *He has a shaved head and a small beard.*

VERBS + head

turn your head *John turned his head to look at the boy.*

shake your head (=move it from side to side, especially to show disagreement) *"It's too much," he said, shaking his head.*

nod your head (=move it up and down, especially to show agreement) *The audience nodded their heads enthusiastically.*

raise/lift your head (=look up) *Tom raised his head to listen, then went back to his book.*

bow/bend/lower your head (=look down) *He bowed his head and tried not to look at her.*

scratch your head (=especially because you do not understand something) *He scratched his head and started looking through the drawers again.*

bang/bump your head *He fell over and banged his head.*

head + VERBS

sb's head hurts/aches *Dan's head was aching and he was tired.*

sb's head rests on sth *Tom's head was resting on her shoulder.*

head + NOUNS

head injury *Wearing a helmet reduces the risk of head injuries.*

PHRASES

a shake of your head *He answered with a shake of his head.*

a nod of your head *With a nod of her head, she indicated that he should sit on the chair.*

dive head first into sth *They dived head first into the water.*

from head to toe (=over all your body) *She was dressed in black from head to toe.*

with your head held high (=with your head and neck straight, especially as a sign of confidence or pride) *Anne walked home with her head held high.*

THESAURUS: head

head, subconscious, psyche, mentality, the ego → mind

2 your mind and thoughts

VERBS

use your head (=think carefully) *If you used your head, you could do it without any problem.*

clear your head (=make yourself able to think more clearly) *All he wanted was some fresh air to clear his head.*

sb's head is spinning/reeling/swimming (=they cannot think clearly, especially because they are very tired, ill etc) *My head was spinning after the interview.*

ADJECTIVES

a cool head (=an ability to stay calm) *Sarah has a cool head, she won't panic.*

a clear head (=an ability to think clearly and sensibly) *I didn't drink any alcohol because I wanted to keep a clear head for the next day.*

a level head (=an ability to be calm and sensible) *Nursing is a job where a level head is essential.*

PREPOSITIONS

in your head *Bertie quickly did the calculation in his head.*

PHRASES

sth comes into/enters your head (=you think of something) *I said the first thing that came into my head.*

put sth into sb's head (=make someone think or believe something) *What put that idea into your head?*

get/put sth out of your head (=stop thinking or worrying about something) *I know you're worried about your exams but try to put them out of your head.*

get your head round sth *BrE* (=be able to understand something) *He just couldn't get his head round what he was supposed to be doing.*

get sth into your head (=realise that something is true) *Can't you get it into your head that he is never going to change?*

headache *n* a pain in your head

VERBS

have a headache (*also* **have got a headache** *spoken*): *If you have a headache, you should go and lie down.*

get headaches/suffer from headaches (=regularly have a headache) *He sometimes gets headaches at school.*

give sb a headache *The noise was starting to give her a headache.*

cause headaches *The drug can cause headaches.*

complain of a headache (=say that you have a headache) *The patient complained of headaches and had difficulty looking at bright objects.*

relieve a headache *formal* (=make it better) *Sleep sometimes relieves a headache.*

a headache goes away (=it stops) *She lay down until her headache went away.*

ADJECTIVES

bad/terrible/severe headache *I've got a really bad headache.*

⚠ Don't say 'a strong/heavy headache'.

a splitting/blinding headache (=a very bad headache) *The next day he woke up with a splitting headache.*

a throbbing/pounding headache (=a very bad headache with regular strong pains) *He had a throbbing headache, behind his nose and his eyes.*

a slight headache (*also* **a bit of a headache** *spoken*) (=one that is not very serious) *I'd rather stay at home – I've got a bit of a headache.*

⚠ Don't say 'a little headache'.

headline *n*

the title of a newspaper report, which is printed in large letters above the report

ADJECTIVES/NOUNS + headline

a newspaper headline *The story dominated newspaper headlines around the world.*

a front-page headline *The front-page headline was "Prime Minister resigns".*

a big headline *Sex scandals always get big headlines.*

a banner headline (=a very large headline across the top of the page) *The paper ran its famous banner headline "We are all Americans now".*

national/international headlines *The announcement made the national headlines.*

a tabloid headline (=in a newspaper that has a lot of stories about famous people, shocking events etc) *One tabloid headline read "Doctor of Death".*

a lurid/sensational headline (=one that is deliberately shocking) *There were lurid headlines about the singer's alleged sexual activities.*

PHRASES

be in the headlines (=be reported in many newspapers as an important story) *The case has been in the headlines all week.*

VERBS + headline

have/carry a headline *'The Times' carried the headline "Massive Earthquake hits Los Angeles".*

run a headline (=use a headline) *One newspaper ran the headline "Crime rate hits all-time low".*

read a headline *He picked up the paper and read the headlines.*

make/grab (the) headlines (=be reported in many newspapers as an important story) *The issue that has grabbed the headlines this year is food safety.*

hit the headlines (=be reported for the first time in many newspapers) *The woman hit the headlines after she was arrested for the murder of her husband.*

dominate the headlines (=be the story that is most often reported in newspapers) *The war continues to dominate the headlines.*

headline + VERBS

a headline reads/says *The next morning's headline read: "Missing boy found".*

a headline screams (=it states something unusual or shocking that is difficult to ignore) *"Dog ate my husband" screamed one headline.*

headline + NOUNS

headline news *The protests made headline news.*

a headline writer *He is the man that headline writers call "Mac the Knife".*

headstrong *adj* THESAURUS determined

health *n*

the general condition of your body and how healthy you are

ADJECTIVES

good/excellent health *Physical exercise is essential to good health.*

poor/bad health *He wanted to join the army but his health was too poor.*

ill health (=bad health – always used as a fixed phrase "ill health") *He retired early due to ill health.*

frail health (=when someone seems very weak) *The Pope's frail health was causing concern.*

failing/declining health (=someone's health is getting worse) *Despite failing health, she travelled to Australia to visit her son.*

physical health *Poverty affects children's physical health.*

mental health *The long hours of work were having an effect on his mental health.*

general health *A balanced diet will improve your general health.*

human health *Some chemicals pose a significant risk to human health.*

VERBS

have good/poor etc health (*also* **enjoy good/poor etc health** *formal*): *The study showed that happy people enjoy better physical health.*

damage your health *There is no doubt that smoking can seriously damage your health.*

endanger your health *formal* (=cause danger to your health) *Being overweight endangers your health.*

improve (sb's) health *Doing more exercise will improve your health.*

sb's health improves/gets better *Her health improved slowly after she came home from hospital.*

sb's health deteriorates/gets worse *Her health deteriorated rapidly and she died two days later.*

health + NOUNS

health care/healthcare *Many Americans cannot afford even basic health care.*

a health problem *He missed a lot of time at work through health problems.*

a health condition (=illness or health problem that affects you permanently of for a very long time) *The test can be used to test for specific health conditions such as diabetes.*

a health risk/hazard/threat (=something that could damage your health) *The report looked at the health risks linked to eating excess sugar.*

health benefits *There are many known health benefits of doing yoga.*

a health warning (=a warning printed on a product that could harm you) *There is a health warning on cigarette packets.*

health education *Health education is vital in helping to stop the spread of diseases.*

PHRASES

be good for your health *Eating plenty of vegetables is good for your health.*

be bad for your health *Smoking is bad for your health.*

be in good health (=be healthy) *Doctors who visited him said that he was in good health.*

be in rude health *formal* (=be very healthy) *Isabel had always been in rude health.*

be in poor health (=be unhealthy) *Her parents were elderly and in poor health.*

for health reasons *I don't eat meat for health reasons.*

sb's state of health *Your choice of exercise must depend on your general state of health.*

healthy *adj*

1 physically strong and not likely to become ill or weak

VERBS

stay/remain healthy *If you want to stay healthy, you should try to get plenty of sleep.*

look healthy *The children all looked happy and healthy.*

keep sb healthy *Exercise keeps you healthy.*

ADVERBS

perfectly healthy (=completely healthy, with no health problems) *I've always been perfectly healthy until now.*

NOUNS

a healthy baby/child/person *She gave birth to a healthy baby boy.*

a healthy body *Salt is essential for a healthy body.*

healthy skin/teeth *Vitamin A is good for healthy skin.*

healthy cells/tissue *The drug leaves healthy cells unharmed.*

a healthy plant/animal *Make sure that the plants are healthy when you buy them.*

2 good for your body and making you strong

NOUNS

a healthy diet *A healthy diet is one that contains lots of vitamins and minerals.*

healthy food *I try to eat plenty of healthy food, especially fresh fruit and vegetables.*

a healthy meal *Poor families find it difficult to afford healthy meals.*

healthy exercise *Cycling is good fun and healthy exercise.*

a healthy lifestyle *He has a very healthy lifestyle and goes to the gym three times a week.*

healthy living/eating *The booklet gives advice on healthy living.*

THESAURUS: healthy

nutritious
food | meal | snack
nutritious food contains substances that are good for your health:
Eggs are a ***highly nutritious*** *food. | The programme shows you how to make quick and nutritious meals.*

balanced
diet
a balanced diet contains the right amounts of the different types of foods that your body needs:
It is important to eat a balanced diet.

You can say that a food **is good for you**: *Peanut butter* ***is good for you****.* You can also say that a food **is low in** something: *Prawns* ***are low in*** *calories.*

H

hearing *n*

1 a meeting of a court or special committee to find out information

ADJECTIVES/NOUNS + hearing

a court hearing *At a court hearing last week, he was accused of hiding evidence.*

a public hearing *A public hearing on the proposal will be held next week.*

a congressional hearing *At a congressional hearing, the Secretary of State admitted that the case had been wrongly handled.*

a disciplinary hearing (=one to decide if someone should be punished) *A disciplinary hearing ruled that Mr Reid should be dismissed from his job.*

a preliminary hearing (=one happening before the main hearing) *He appeared in court for a preliminary hearing.*

an appeal hearing (=one to try to change an earlier decision) *At the appeal hearing, his lawyer argued that the conviction was unlawful.*

VERBS

hold/conduct a hearing *The committee promised to hold hearings on discrimination in the armed forces.*

attend a hearing *He was arrested after failing to attend a court hearing.*

tell a hearing sth *A doctor told the hearing that she could not say for certain when Ms Williams had died.*

open/close a hearing *The committee opened a hearing into the scandal yesterday.*

adjourn a hearing (=stop it until a later time) *The hearing was adjourned until January 23rd.*

a hearing takes place *The next hearing will take place on April 2nd.*

H

PREPOSITIONS

at a hearing *At the hearing, he denied lying about the money.*

2 the sense which you use to hear sounds

ADJECTIVES

good/sharp/acute hearing *My hearing isn't as good as it used to be.*

bad/poor hearing *You'll have to speak clearly – she has very bad hearing.*

VERBS

have good/bad etc hearing *Dogs have excellent hearing.*

lose your hearing (=become unable to hear) *He lost his hearing as a child after suffering scarlet fever.*

sb's hearing deteriorates/gets worse *Your hearing deteriorates as you get older.*

affect/impair your hearing (=make your hearing worse) *Listening to loud music will eventually impair your hearing.*

hearing + NOUNS

hearing loss *Many older people suffer from some degree of hearing loss.*

a hearing problem/difficulty/impairment *The phone is suitable for people with hearing difficulties.*

a hearing aid (=a piece of equipment worn in or around someone's ear to help them hear) *My grandfather wears a hearing aid.*

PHRASES

be hard of hearing (=not be able to hear well) *There is a subtitling service for people who are hard of hearing.*

heart *n*

1 the organ in your chest which pumps blood through your body

VERBS

sb's heart beats *Her heart was beating fast.*

sb's heart pounds/thuds/thumps (=it beats very strongly) *He reached the top of the hill, his heart pounding.*

sb's heart races (=it beats very fast) *Was there someone there in the dark? Joe's heart began to race.*

ADJECTIVES

a healthy heart *Eating oily fish can help maintain a healthy heart.*

a bad/weak heart *The effort proved too much for her weak heart.*

heart + NOUNS

a heart attack (=a sudden and very painful event in which your heart stops working) *Jim had a heart attack and died at the age of 55.*

heart disease *Smoking increases the risk of heart disease.*

heart trouble/problems *You should not take this medication if you have heart problems.*

heart failure (=when your heart stops working, either suddenly or gradually) *The cause of death was heart failure.*

a heart condition/defect (=something wrong with your heart) *The baby was born with a heart condition.*

sb's heart rate (=the number of times someone's heart beats per minute) *Your heart rate increases as you exercise.*

heart surgery/operation *Geoff is going into the hospital for a heart operation.*

a heart transplant (=a medical operation to put a heart from someone else into a person's body) *In 1967, Dr Barnard performed the first heart transplant.*

2 the part of you that feels strong emotions and feelings

ADJECTIVES

a big heart (=a kind and generous character) *She may be only small, but she has a big heart.*

a good/kind/warm heart (=a kind character) *My father had a good heart.*

a soft heart (=a kind and sympathetic character) *Julia's soft heart had been touched by Minnie's grief.*

a cold/hard heart (=used about someone who does not feel sympathy for other people) *It takes a hard heart not to be moved by these images of suffering.*

with a heavy heart (=feeling very sad) *She made her way to the hospital with a heavy heart.*

with a light heart (=feeling happy) *Paul left for home with a light heart.*

a broken heart (=when someone feels very sad, especially because a love affair has ended) *I wonder how many broken hearts Carlo was responsible for.*

VERBS + heart

break sb's heart (=make someone feel very sad) *It broke my heart to see him so sick.*

win sb's heart (=make someone love you) *The singer won the hearts of millions of teenagers.*

touch sb's heart (=make someone feel strong feelings, especially of sympathy) *The sight of starving children touched the hearts of people around the world.*

set your heart on sth (=want to do something very much) *She had set her heart on becoming an actor.*

follow your heart (= do what your emotions want you to do) *Follow your heart. Who cares what everyone else thinks?*

heart + VERBS

sb's heart aches (=they feel very sad) *It made his heart ache to look at her.*

sb's heart leaps/jumps/lurches *literary* (=you suddenly feel excited, frightened etc) *The unexpected sound of his voice made her heart leap.*

sb's heart sinks (=they suddenly feel very unhappy or lose hope) *My heart sank when I saw Richard's car outside the house.*

my heart bleeds (=you feel a lot of sympathy - often used ironically to mean that you do not have any sympathy for someone) *It makes my heart bleed to see them suffer.*

PREPOSITIONS

at heart (=used for saying what someone is really like even though they may seem different) *I'll always be a Canadian at heart even though I now live in Britain.*

from the heart *His comments were spoken from the heart.*

in your heart (=used for saying that you know something but do not want to admit it) *In my heart, I knew he didn't really love me.*

PHRASES

affairs of the heart (=matters relating to love) *I had little experience of affairs of the heart.*

a heart of gold (=a very kind character) *She was rather brisk in manner but with a heart of gold.*

a heart of stone (=a very cruel character) *You'd have to have a heart of stone not to feel sorry for them.*

with all your heart and soul (=used when you feel something very strongly) *She loved Peter with all her heart and soul.*

from the bottom of your heart (=used to emphasize that your feelings are sincere) *I thank you from the bottom of my heart.*

3 the most important or central part of something

> **Grammar**
> In this meaning, you always say **the heart of** something.

PHRASES

the heart of the matter/issue/problem *We need to get to the heart of the matter.*

be/lie at the heart of sth (=be the most important or central part) *Unemployment is at the heart of many of society's problems.*

go to the heart of sth (*also* **strike at the heart of sth**) (=involve or deal with the most important or central part) *These are difficult questions which go to the heart of the education process.*

ADJECTIVES

the very heart of sth *The hospital was built at the very heart of the community it serves.*

heartbreaking *adj* THESAURUS ▸ **sad (2)**

heartbroken *adj* THESAURUS ▸ **sad (1)**

heartless *adj* THESAURUS ▸ **cruel (1)**

heat *n*

1 very hot weather or conditions

ADJECTIVES/NOUNS + heat

the summer heat *Air-conditioning is great in the summer heat.*

the tropical/desert heat *He stepped off the plane into the tropical heat.*

burning/searing/blistering/scorching heat (=extreme heat) *The desert is a place of scorching heat by day and bitter cold by night.*

stifling/oppressive/sweltering heat (=extreme heat that makes you feel uncomfortable) *They spend the summer in the mountains to escape the oppressive heat.*

intense/extreme heat *People in the region are suffering from intense heat and continuing drought.*

dry heat *The garden soil had cracked in the dry heat.*

heat + NOUNS

a heat wave (=a period of unusually hot

H

weather) *In the summer of 2006, there was a heat wave in Britain.*

heat exhaustion (=weakness and sickness caused by doing too much in very hot weather) *Several players were suffering from heat exhaustion.*

a heat haze (=the effect when very hot weather makes it difficult to see things clearly) *A heat haze shimmered above the fields.*

PREPOSITIONS

in the heat *She was starting to sweat in the heat.*

PHRASES

the heat of the day *The locals retreat to their cool houses and sleep during the heat of the day.*

2 the warmth produced by something

VERBS

produce/generate heat *Lightbulbs generate heat as well as light.*

withstand heat *The material is capable of withstanding extreme heat.*

absorb heat *Stone absorbs the heat from the sun.*

conduct heat (=allow heat to move through) *Metals conduct heat better than other materials.*

retain heat (=keep heat) *Close the door to retain the heat in the room.*

NOUNS + heat

body heat *More than 30% of body heat can be lost through your head.*

heat + NOUNS

heat loss *Double glazing reduces heat loss through windows.*

a heat source (=something that produces heat) *Don't put a fridge next to a radiator or any other heat source.*

heated *adj* THESAURUS ▸ angry

heating *n*

a system for making a room or building warm

ADJECTIVES

central heating (=a system in which water or air is heated in one place and sent around a building) *Most houses now have central heating.*

gas/electric heating *Electric heating is the only source of hot water in the cottage.*

solar heating (=powered by the sun) *They've installed solar heating in the new house.*

VERBS + heating

put/switch/turn the heating on *Why don't you put the heating on if you're cold?*

switch/turn the heating off *We turn the heating off before bed.*

turn the heating down/up *Can you turn the heating down a bit?*

have the heating on (=use the heating) *It's getting colder, but we haven't had the heating on yet.*

leave the heating on (=continue to use the heating) *I don't like to leave the heating on at night.*

install heating *We're thinking of installing underfloor heating.*

heating + NOUNS

a heating bill *Many people can't afford to pay their heating bills.*

a heating system *The gas leak was caused by a faulty heating system.*

heavy *adj*

1 weighing a lot

NOUNS

a heavy bag/suitcase *He had a heavy bag on his back.*

a heavy load *If you have to carry a heavy load, divide the weight between two bags.*

a heavy weight *Take care when lifting heavy weights.*

heavy equipment/machinery (=large and powerful) *They used heavy machinery to clear the site.*

heavy artillery/weapons/guns (=large and powerful) *Troops with heavy weapons were advancing into the area.*

a heavy vehicle/lorry *The road is not suitable for heavy vehicles.*

heavy lifting (=lifting heavy objects) *He has a bad back and can't do any heavy lifting.*

ADVERBS

very/extremely heavy *The boy was very heavy to carry.*

quite/fairly/rather heavy *Her bag was quite heavy.*

THESAURUS: heavy

cumbersome
heavy and difficult to move or carry:
The old movie cameras were very big and cumbersome. | *He was carrying cumbersome diving equipment.*

weighty *literary*
tome | volume
heavy – used about books, especially ones that contain a lot of information about a serious subject:
This is a weighty tome that deals in depth with the subject (=a big book that contains a lot of information). | *The encyclopedia consists of twelve weighty volumes.*

If something is very heavy, you can also say that it **weighs a ton**: *This suitcase* ***weighs a ton*** *– I don't know if I can lift it.*

ANTONYMS **heavy → light² (1)**

2 great in amount or degree, or very severe

NOUNS

heavy traffic *We were late because we got stuck in heavy traffic.*

heavy rain/downpour/rainfall *Heavy rains had left the roads flooded.*

heavy snow/snowfall *Heavy snowfalls are expected in the north.*

heavy fighting (=a lot of fighting in a war, with many people hurt) *More than 100 people were killed in heavy fighting.*

heavy drinking/smoking (=drinking a lot of alcohol or smoking a lot) *Heavy drinking increases the risk of liver disease.*

a heavy drinker/smoker *Her father was a heavy smoker and died aged 58.*

heavy losses (=when someone loses a lot of something, usually money) *The company made heavy losses last year.*

heavy casualties (=a large number of people injured or killed) *Both armies suffered heavy casualties.*

heavy use/demand *The equipment is strong enough to withstand heavy use.*

a heavy fine/penalty *Those who break the law face heavy fines.*

a heavy burden (=a very difficult responsibility) *Looking after a sick relative is a heavy burden.*

heavy pressure *Businesses are under heavy pressure to cut costs.*

ADVERBS

unusually heavy *Unusually heavy rain has caused flooding in the area.*

PHRASES

pay a heavy price (=have to suffer or give up a lot for something) *Ordinary people pay a heavy price when their governments go to war.*

ANTONYMS **heavy → light² (3)**

hectic *adj* THESAURUS **busy (1)**

height *n*

1 how tall someone or something is

ADJECTIVES

of average/medium height *Nick was a slim man of average height.*

a considerable height (=a height that is quite tall) *The trees had grown to a considerable height.*

a maximum/minimum height *The plants reach a maximum height of 50 cm.*

VERBS

measure sb's/sth's height *The nurse measured his height.*

grow to/reach a height of sth *Sunflowers can grow to a height of 15 feet.*

reduce/increase sth's height *They decided to increase the height of the wall.*

PREPOSITIONS

in height *He was a small man, only 1.6 metres in height.*

2 the distance that something is from the ground

VERBS

reach a height *The plane reached a height of 500 metres before it came down.*

gain height (=become higher) *He liked to walk in the early morning before the sun had gained height.*

lose height (=become lower) *The plane suddenly lost height.*

ADJECTIVES/NOUNS + height

a great/considerable height *He had fallen from a great height.*

shoulder/waist/chest/head height (=the same level as someone's shoulder, waist etc) *He held the ball at waist height.*

help¹ *v*

to make it possible or easier for someone to do something by doing part of their work or by giving them something they need

ADVERBS

help considerably/enormously/tremendously *The sleeping pills helped considerably.*

greatly help *Of course, the money will greatly help.*

really help *It really helps if you can speak the local language.*

help a little *I'm glad I was able to help a little.*

definitely/certainly help *The trees definitely help to reduce the noise from the traffic.*

PREPOSITIONS

help (sb) with sth *Can you help with the washing up?*

PHRASES

anything/nothing I can do to help *If there's anything I can do to help, just give me a call.*

help² *n*

1 things you do to make it easier or possible for someone to do something

VERBS

ask (sb) for help *He asked for help with the cleaning.*

appeal for help (=publicly ask for help) *The police are appealing for help to track down the killer.*

seek help (=try to find help) *He decided to seek medical help for his drink problem.*

give sb help *Do you want me to give you some help?*

get/receive help *She gets no help from her husband.*

accept help *Her father was a proud man who wouldn't accept help from anyone.*

offer (your) help *The taxi driver offered his help and we accepted.*
provide help *The government should do more to provide help for people who are looking for work.*
need help *Some of the older patients need help with walking.*
enlist sb's help (=persuade someone to help you) *She enlisted the help of a private investigator to find her missing son.*
find help *To get it finished by tomorrow, we'll need to find help from somewhere.*
refuse help *She refused medical help despite being injured.*

ADJECTIVES

medical/financial/legal/technical help *We received a lot of financial help from my family.*
practical help *The organization offers practical help with finding accommodation.*
expert/specialist help *Expert help is available if you want to give up smoking.*
professional help *You need to seek some professional help.*
outside help (=from someone who is not in your organization, family etc) *Can you do it yourself or do you need outside help?*
extra help *Some of the younger children need extra help with writing.*

PREPOSITIONS

help with sth *Do you want any help with the washing up?*
help in doing sth *Our business advisers offer help in starting your own business.*
help from sb *Help from the public was essential in solving the crime.*
with sb's/sth's help *With the help of a dictionary, I managed to read the article.*

H

2 someone or something that helps

VERBS

a great/big help *Thank you. You've been a great help.*
a real help *Talking to someone can be a real help when you are worried.*

PREPOSITIONS

a help to sb *She was a great help to me when I was sick.*
be of help (=be something that helps) *This information may be of help to you.*

helpful *adj*

providing useful help in making a situation better or easier

ADVERBS

extremely helpful *The staff were extremely helpful and offered to carry our bags to our room.*
most helpful *formal, especially spoken* (=very helpful) *Thank you for your suggestions – you've been most helpful.*
especially/particularly helpful *The books are particularly helpful for parents with small children.*

NOUNS

helpful advice *He gave me some helpful advice about visiting Paris.*
a helpful hint *This website contains helpful hints on how to improve your grammar skills.*
a helpful suggestion *His colleagues had plenty of helpful suggestions.*
helpful information *The book is packed with helpful information and good ideas.*

VERBS

find sth helpful *I found his explanation very helpful.*
prove helpful (=be helpful when you are doing something) *Her language skills proved helpful when she was travelling around Europe.*

PREPOSITIONS

helpful to sb *They are trained to be polite and helpful to customers.*
helpful for sb/sth *Professor Taylor's book is very helpful for students who want a general introduction to the subject.*

THESAURUS: helpful

handy, helpful, worthwhile, valuable, invaluable, indispensable → **useful**

heritage *n*

customs, buildings, art etc which have existed for a long time and are important to a group of people or a place

ADJECTIVES/NOUNS + heritage

a rich heritage *The town has a rich heritage and there are many historic buildings.*
sb's common/shared heritage *The UK and the US share a common heritage and language.*
the national/nation's heritage *These works of art are considered of great importance to Russia's national heritage.*
cultural heritage *Cubans are proud of their cultural heritage.*
artistic/architectural/literary heritage *The city takes great pride in its architectural heritage.*

VERBS

preserve/protect sth's heritage *They want to preserve the country's heritage for future generations.*

PHRASES

sth is part of sb's/sth's heritage *The castle is part of the heritage of Wales and should be preserved for the Welsh people.*

hero *n*

1 someone, often a man, who is admired for doing something extremely brave or for a particular skill

ADJECTIVES/NOUNS + hero

a great hero *He finally got to meet his great hero, the footballer David Beckham.*

a real/true hero *Virginia Hall was a true hero of the French Resistance.*

a war hero *His father was a war hero, a former fighter pilot.*

a national/local hero *In Cuba, Fidel was seen as a national hero.*

a sporting hero *There are many female sporting heroes, for example Venus Williams.*

sb's boyhood/childhood hero (=when you were a boy or a child) *McEnroe had been one of his boyhood heroes.*

a cult hero (=someone who a particular group of people admire) *She became a cult hero for her role in the film.*

a folk hero (=an ordinary person who becomes a hero for a particular group) *He was a folk hero in his home country because of his escapes from the police.*

an unsung hero (=someone whose bravery or effort is not noticed or recognized) *These volunteers are the unsung heroes of the campaign.*

an unlikely hero (=someone who people did not expect to be a hero) *A taxi driver became an unlikely hero when he helped to get the woman to hospital.*

a reluctant hero (=someone who is a hero but does not want to be) *The reluctant hero did not want to talk to the press about how she prevented the robbery.*

VERBS

be sb's hero *Keith Richards was my hero and I wanted to play the guitar like him.*

become a hero *He became a national hero for his part in the war.*

be hailed (as) a hero (=people say you are a hero) *He was hailed a hero after saving the young girl's life.*

hero + NOUNS

hero worship (=admiration for someone, especially when it is extreme or unreasonable) *They treat her with a kind of hero worship.*

PREPOSITIONS

a hero to sb *Some called him a criminal, but he was a hero to many.*

PHRASES

receive/be given a hero's welcome (=be treated as a hero when you arrive somewhere) *The team were given a hero's welcome when they returned to the city.*

the hero of the hour (=someone who does something brave or admirable at a particular time) *The Russian president emerged as the hero of the hour.*

2 the main male character of a film, book etc

VERBS

play the hero *Sean Penn plays the hero of the film.*

ADJECTIVES

a romantic hero *The movie features Clark Gable as the romantic hero.*

a tragic hero *Othello is the tragic hero of Shakespeare's play.*

> **Hero** or **heroine?**
> When talking about people who are admired for their bravery, skill etc, you can use **hero** about both men and women. Women are also called **heroines**: *His grandmother was a national **heroine**.*
> When talking about films and books, you use **hero** for the main male character and **heroine** for the main female character.

heroic *adj* THESAURUS brave

hesitation *n*

a short pause before you do something, or the feeling that you should not do something

ADJECTIVES

a brief/momentary hesitation *After a brief hesitation, she answered "Yes".*

a little/slight hesitation *There was a slight hesitation in his voice.*

the slightest/least hesitation *They agreed to help without the slightest hesitation.*

PREPOSITIONS

without (any) hesitation/with no hesitation *He agreed without hesitation.*

after some hesitation *After some hesitation, one of the boys began to speak.*

hesitation over/about sth *There was some hesitation over who should take the penalty kick.*

PHRASES

have no hesitation in doing sth *I would have no hesitation in recommending her for the job.*

a moment's hesitation *After a moment's hesitation, she decided to accept their offer.*

show some/no hesitation *The judges showed no hesitation in declaring him the winner.*

a trace of hesitation (=a very small amount) *I could detect a trace of hesitation in her voice.*

hide *v*

to make sure that something cannot easily be seen or found

ADVERBS

be well hidden (=be very difficult to see or find) *The entrance to the cave was well hidden.*

be cleverly hidden *The money was cleverly hidden inside one of the books on the shelf.*

deliberately hide sth *The authorities deliberately hid the truth.*

PREPOSITIONS

hide sth in/under/behind sth *She quickly hid the bag behind the sofa.*

hide sth from sb *He was accused of trying to hide evidence from the police.*

PHRASES

keep sth hidden somewhere *I keep a spare key hidden under a plant pot.*

hideous *adj* THESAURUS **terrible, ugly (1)**

high *adj*

1 measuring a long distance from the bottom to the top, or in a position that is a long way from the ground

NOUNS

a high mountain/cliff *Mount Fuji is the highest mountain in Japan.*

a high wall/fence *The camp was surrounded by a high fence.*

a high tower *The high towers of the cathedral rose above them.*

a high ceiling *The rooms all had high ceilings.*

at high altitude (=a long distance from the ground, or in a place that is high above sea level) *The plane can fly at high altitude. | The athletes have been training at high altitude.*

a high shelf *Keep medicines on a high shelf where children cannot reach them.*

PHRASES

100 feet/40 metres etc high *The waves were up to 40 metres high.*

waist/chest/knee high (=as high as your waist etc) *The grass was knee high.*

> **Saying how high a place is in relation to other places**
> You say that a place is **800 feet/3,000 metres etc above sea level**: *Mexico City is situated 2,250 metres above **sea level**.*

THESAURUS: high

tall
man | woman | boy | girl | figure | grass | tree | building | column | pillar | chimney | glass
measuring a long distance from the bottom to the top – used about people, or about things that are high and narrow, such as trees, plants, and buildings:
He was a tall man with dark hair. | A tall figure appeared at the top of the stairs. | The house was surrounded by tall trees. | Her office is in a tall modern office building. | He poured the wine into a tall glass.

> **Tall or high?**
> You use **tall** about people (not 'high'). You use **high** about mountains (not 'tall').

majestic
mountain | landscape | scenery | building | arch | tree | animal | bird
very big, high, and impressive:
They could see the majestic mountains of the Himalayas. | The castle is a majestic building that overlooks the town below. | The garden contains some majestic oak trees. | The African elephant is a majestic animal.

soaring
mountain | cliff | skyscraper | tower
extremely high and impressive:
Soaring mountains give way to enormous glaciers. | Manhattan is famous for its soaring skyscrapers.

towering
figure | wall | skyscraper | mountain | peak | cliff | tree
extremely high, in a way that seems impressive, but also often rather frightening:
The other boxer was a towering figure of a man. | He looked up at the towering walls of the prison. | The old building sits among the towering skyscrapers of Hong Kong.

lofty *literary*
heights | mountain | peak | tower | tree | roof | ceiling
very high and impressive:
From the lofty heights of the church tower you have a superb view of the town. | He could see a chain of lofty mountains in the distance. | The paths are sheltered by lofty trees.

high-rise
building | apartment block | flat | office | development
used about tall modern buildings with many floors containing apartments or offices:
Old houses were knocked down and replaced by ugly modern high-rise buildings. | They live in a high-rise apartment block.

ANTONYMS **high → low (1)**

2 great, or greater than the usual amount, number, price etc

NOUNS

a high amount/proportion/percentage *People who eat high amounts of fat are more likely to suffer heart attacks.*

a high number/grade/score *The university has an unusually high number of part-time students.*

a high price/charge/fee *If you want the best, you have to be prepared to pay a high price for it.*

a high rent/tax *Taxes are much higher in Sweden.*

high salary/wages/pay/income *Doctors get paid high salaries.*

a high level/rate/degree *A high level of chemical pollution was found in the river water.*

a high standard *The school has very high academic standards.*

high speed *The train was approaching at high speed.*

a high temperature *Temperatures are likely to remain high this weekend.*

a high demand *There is a high demand for Chinese goods.*

a high profit/return *High profits from oil and gas have made Russia a rich country.*

high unemployment *The north east is an area of high unemployment.*

high inflation *The 1920s were a period of high inflation.*

a high risk/chance *There is a high risk of losing your money.*

THESAURUS: high

rising
price | cost | rate | level | demand | crime | unemployment | inflation
becoming higher than before:
Voters are concerned about the rising cost of living. | The nation's capital has been struggling with rising crime.

soaring
price | cost | rate | level | demand | unemployment | inflation
becoming very high:
The soaring cost of housing means that many young people cannot find a place to live. | The US has a soaring divorce rate. | Fuel companies will be unable to meet the soaring demand for energy.

rocketing
price | cost | rate | unemployment | inflation
very high and increasing very quickly. **Rocketing** sounds a little informal and is often used in news reports:
The rocketing price of oil will have a bad effect on the economy. | The police force is trying to cope with a rocketing crime rate.

record
number | amount | level | rate | profits | sales | demand | unemployment | inflation
the highest ever:
They received a record number of complaints. | Sales have reached record levels. | The economy is growing at a record rate.

ANTONYMS **high → low (2)**

3 near the top of the range of sounds

NOUNS

a high note *He had difficulty singing the high notes of the song.*

a high voice/sound *He spoke with an unusually high voice for a man.*

a high pitch *Her voice rose to a high pitch.*

THESAURUS: high

high-pitched
voice | sound | noise | cry | squeak | whine | whistle
a high-pitched voice or sound is very high:
She was speaking in an unnaturally high-pitched voice. | Dogs are able to hear high-pitched sounds which humans cannot hear. | Bats make high-pitched squeaks.

shrill
voice | cry | whistle | scream | laugh
a shrill voice or cry is high and unpleasant:
His boss had a rather shrill voice, which could be heard all over the office. | The bird has a shrill cry. | The woman gave a shrill laugh.

piercing
scream | shriek | noise | whistle
extremely high and loud, in a way that is unpleasant:
She let out a piercing scream.

squeaky
voice | floorboard | gate | noise | toy
making short high noises that are not very loud:
She spoke with a squeaky little voice. | He lived in an old house with squeaky floorboards. | The dog was playing with a squeaky toy.

ANTONYMS **high → low (3)**

4 costing a lot

THESAURUS: high

high, pricey, overpriced, costly, astronomical, exorbitant → **expensive**

highly *adv* THESAURUS **very[1]**

high-risk *adj* THESAURUS **dangerous**

high-speed *adj* THESAURUS **fast[1] (1), (2)**

high-tech (*also* **hi-tech**) *adj* THESAURUS **advanced (1)**

highway *n especially AmE*

a wide main road that joins one town to another

ADJECTIVES/NOUNS + highway

a main/major highway *He pulled off the main highway into a side road.*

a 4-lane/12-lane etc highway *There is a big new 8-lane highway from the airport into the city.*

an interstate highway *I drove my rental car at*

H

100 miles per hour along a straight stretch of interstate highway.

a federal highway *We were heading southwest on the busy federal highway.*

VERBS

drive along a highway *We were driving along the highway from Montreal to Ottawa.*

travel on/along a highway *I was traveling north along the highway.*

turn off/pull off a highway *Near the Oregon border, we turned off Highway 97 to Highway 161.*

build a highway *They are planning to build a highway across the country.*

highway + NOUNS

highway traffic *She decided to take the train in order to avoid the highway traffic.*

the highway patrol (=the police who control a highway) *Colorado Highway Patrol officers charged him with drunk driving.*

the highway system *In the 1950s, construction of the vast interstate highway system began.*

highway safety *We need to look at ways of improving highway safety.*

PREPOSITIONS

on a highway *There was a lot of traffic on the highway.*

along a highway *Port Arthur is just one mile along the highway to the west.*

a highway to/from somewhere *The road connects the village with the main highway to Veracruz.*

hilarious *adj* THESAURUS ▸ **funny (1)**

hill *n*

an area of land that is higher than the land around it, like a mountain but smaller

ADJECTIVES

a steep hill *She pushed her bicycle up the steep hill.*

rolling/gentle hills (=hills with slopes that are not steep) *He loved the green rolling hills of Dorset.*

a high/low hill *We climbed a very high hill today called An Teallach.*

green hills (=covered with grass) *New Zealand is a country of lush green hills.*

VERBS

climb a hill (=walk or drive up a hill) *She climbed the hill out of the village.*

go down a hill *It's best to use a low gear when you are going down steep hills.*

a hill overlooking sth *The castle is on a hill overlooking the town.*

sth nestles in/among hills *literary* (=it is surrounded by hills) *The farmhouse nestles in the hills of southern Spain.*

hill + NOUNS

a hill town *the hill towns of Tuscany*

a hill farm/farmer *They have a small hill farm in Devon.*

PREPOSITIONS

on a hill *Their house is on a hill overlooking the sea.*

PHRASES

the top of a hill *The view from the top of the hill was beautiful.*

the brow/crest of a hill (=the top part of a hill) *A car appeared over the brow of the hill.*

the bottom/foot of a hill *The house was at the bottom of a hill.*

hint *n*

1 something that you say or do to suggest something to someone, without telling them directly

VERBS

give (sb) a hint *Come on, what is it? Give me a hint.*

drop a hint (=give a hint) *She was dropping quite a few hints about what she'd like for her birthday.*

get the hint (=understand a hint) *I looked hopefully at the cake, but he didn't get the hint.*

take a/the hint (=understand a hint and do something) *Mark took the hint and stopped talking.*

ADJECTIVES

a broad/strong/heavy hint (=one that is very easy to understand) *He had dropped a heavy hint that they might get married.*

a subtle/gentle hint (=sometimes used ironically when someone is being very obvious) *Is your yawning a subtle hint that you're bored?*

a vague hint (=so general that it is not at all clear) *In his article, he gave only vague hints as to what he had actually done.*

PREPOSITIONS

a hint about sth *His wife kept dropping hints about all the work that needed to be done.*

PHRASES

I can take a hint (=used when you understand someone's hint) *All right, I can take a hint. I'm leaving.*

2 a useful piece of advice about how to do something

VERBS

give/offer hints *Can you offer some hints on what to look for when buying a car?*

ADJECTIVES

helpful/handy/useful hints *The book gives some handy hints on owning a dog.*

PREPOSITIONS

a hint on (doing) sth *There are some hints on decorating your home.*

historic *adj*

1 a historic building or place is important because it is old

NOUNS

a historic building/house/monument *The town has many historic buildings, including a 15th-century town hall.*

a historic town/city/capital/port *York is a beautiful and historic city.*

a historic place/site *There are many castles and other historic places which you can visit.*

a historic landmark (=a well-known place which is easy to recognize) *The Eiffel Tower is Paris's most famous historic landmark.*

sth's historic character *They say that the development would be harmful to the historic character of the town.*

PHRASES

of historic interest *The village of Hutton is over a thousand years old, and has many buildings of historic interest.*

of historic importance *The church is of historic importance and is an attraction for many tourists.*

> **THESAURUS: historic**
> elderly, aging, aged, ancient, antique, historic, vintage, age-old → **old (1)**

2 a historic event is very important and will be recorded as part of history

> In more formal English, people also say ***an historic*** *event, moment* etc.

NOUNS

a historic event *Neil Armstrong's walk on the moon was a historic event.*

a historic moment/day *The signing of the agreement was a historic moment in relations between the two countries.*

a historic opportunity *This is a historic opportunity to achieve peace.*

a historic victory *Switzerland won a historic victory over Spain in the World Cup.*

a historic role *President Yeltsin played a historic role in leading Russia to democracy.*

a historic agreement *He called the treaty a historic agreement.*

> **Historic** or **historical?**
> Don't confuse **historic** and **historical**. **Historic** is used about places that are important because they are old, or about important events. For example, you say *The city has many* ***historic*** *buildings* (not 'historical buildings').
> **Historical** just means relating to history. You say ***historical*** *evidence* (not 'historic evidence').

> **THESAURUS: historic**
> big, significant, major, notable, key, essential, vital, crucial/critical, paramount, historic, landmark, momentous → **important (1)**

historical *adj* relating to history

> **Grammar**
> **Historical** is usually used before a noun.

NOUNS

historical research/study/analysis *Historical research has shown that people have been living there for hundreds of years.*

historical evidence/facts/data *There is no historical evidence for the story.*

historical records/documents *According to the historical records, they moved to London in 1737.*

historical events/periods *The film is based on actual historical events.*

a historical figure *Robin Hood was a real historical figure.*

a historical novel/play/romance (=which takes place during a period in the past) *The book is a historical novel set in 18th-century Paris.*

a historical reason/explanation/connection *There are all sorts of historical reasons why the two countries are suspicious of each other.*

the historical background/context/perspective *You need to understand the historical background to the war.*

⚠ A book about history is a **history book**. Don't say 'a historical book'.

> A film, play, or programme which tells a story about people who lived in the past is often called a **period drama**.

history *n*

all the things that have happened in the past, or the study of these events

ADJECTIVES/NOUNS + history

American/Chinese/British etc history *We studied American history and the War of Independence.*

world history *The attack changed the course of world history.*

local history *The building is now a museum of local history.*

early/ancient history *I'm reading a book about ancient Roman history.*

modern/contemporary/recent history *For the first time in modern history, the country had a female leader.*

political/social/economic history *The 1780s were a dramatic time in French political history.*

art/music/sports etc history *The Beatles are an important part of Britain's music history.*

family history (=the history of one particular family) *My grandfather has researched our family history and discovered that we come from the south of Ireland.*
a long history (=something has existed for a long time) *The 1970s were the most successful years in the theatre's long history.*
a rich history (=an interesting and important history) *Greece has a very rich history.*
human history *It was the most destructive war in human history.*

VERBS
study/teach history *Paul studied history at Bristol University.*
trace the history of sth (=find out what the history of something is) *He traces the history of the game back to the late 1700s.*
be steeped in history (=be connected with many important events) *Cambridge is steeped in history and tradition.*
go down in history (=be remembered for many years) *She will go down in history as one of the greatest tennis players of all time.*
make history (=do something important that will be recorded and remembered) *Ordinary Berliners made history when they tore down the wall.*
shape history (=influence events) *He is one of the politicians who shaped 20th-century history.*
rewrite history (=change what we believe are the facts about the past) *Politicians often try to rewrite history to justify their actions.*
history shows/tells/teaches us (that)... *History teaches us that society is always changing.*

history + NOUNS
a history book *History books often don't tell you much about the lives of ordinary people.*
a history teacher/student *He gave a series of lectures to history students about the English civil war.*

PREPOSITIONS
the history of sth *The book is about the history of flying.*
in (sth's) history *This was the worst battle in the country's history.*
during sth's history (=during the time since something started) *During its 80-year history, the organization has undergone many changes.*
throughout history *Throughout history the achievements of women have often been ignored.*

PHRASES
a period of/in history *It was an interesting period in Japanese history.*
change the course of history *Roosevelt and Churchill helped to change the course of history.*
for the first time in history *For the first time in history, the US had a black president.*

hit[1] *v*

1 to touch someone or something quickly and hard with your hand, a stick etc

ADVERBS
hit sb/sth hard *He felt as though someone had hit him very hard in the stomach.*

PREPOSITIONS
hit sb/sth with sth *He accidentally hit his thumb with the hammer.*
hit sb/sth on sth *A small piece of rock flew off and hit me on the chin.*
hit sb/sth in sth *The door swung back and hit her right in the face.*
hit sth into/over sth *She hit the ball into the net.*
hit sb over the head (=hit someone on their head) *The robbers hit him over the head with a baseball bat.*

2 to have a bad effect on someone or something

ADVERBS
hit sb badly/severely/hard *Local farmers have been hit very hard by the dry weather.*
be worst hit (=be the most badly affected) *Unemployment increased in many areas of the country, with the North the worst hit.*

hit[2] *n*

something or someone that is very popular and successful

VERBS
become a hit *The TV series became a hit with viewers.*
prove (to be) a hit (=be a hit) *Patrick proved a big hit with the audience.*
have a hit *Michael Jackson had a big hit with the song.*

ADJECTIVES
a big/great/huge/massive hit *The new museum has been a big hit with families.*
sb's latest hit *She sang her latest hit.*
sb's greatest hits *The band released a record of their greatest hits.*
an instant hit *With his experience and enthusiasm, he was an instant hit.*
a runaway hit (=something that quickly becomes successful) *The film has become a runaway hit.*

NOUNS + hit
a number one hit (=a song that is number one on the weekly list of the most popular records) *Her single 'Crazy In Love' was a number one hit all over the world.*
a smash hit (=a very successful song, play, film etc) *They had a smash hit with their first single.*
a box office hit (=a play or film that is very

successful) *The film 'Mamma Mia' was a box office hit.*

hit + NOUNS

a hit movie/film *She worked on the hit movie 'Toy Story'.*

a hit show/musical/comedy *Gervais was co-writer of the hit comedy 'The Office'.*

a hit song/record/single *The band has had a couple of hit singles.*

a hit series *She took part in the hit series 'Who Do You Think You Are?'.*

PREPOSITIONS

a hit with sb *She was a popular politician and a huge hit with voters.*

hobby *n*

an activity that you enjoy doing in your free time

ADJECTIVES

an interesting/fascinating/absorbing hobby *Growing roses is a fascinating hobby.*

sb's favourite/main hobby *His favourite hobby is motor racing.*

a strange/unusual hobby *Keeping snakes may seem like an unusual hobby.*

an expensive hobby *Photography is an expensive hobby.*

VERBS

have a hobby *At the interview they asked me if I had any hobbies.*

take up a hobby (=start doing it) *If you are feeling bored, you should take up a hobby.*

sb's hobbies include sth *Susan's hobbies include reading, cooking, and drama.*

PHRASES

sth started as a hobby *It started as a hobby and then she decided to start her own cake-making business.*

> Instead of saying "What are your hobbies?", people often say **What do you do in your free time?**

hoist *v* THESAURUS lift[1] (1)

hold[1] *v*

to have something in your hand, hands, or arms

ADVERBS

hold sb/sth tightly *She took his hand and held it tightly.*

hold sb close (=put your arms around someone and hold them close to your body) *Max held her close and wiped away her tears.*

hold sth up *Hold the picture up so we can see it.*

hold sth out *He held out his hand to help her to her feet.*

PREPOSITIONS

hold onto sth *I walked carefully down the steps, holding onto the rail.*

hold sth for sb *Could you hold my bag for me?*

hold sth in your hand/hands/arms *I held the baby in my arms until she fell asleep. | He was holding a key in his hand.*

hold[2] *n*

the action of holding something with your hands

ADJECTIVES

a tight/firm hold *Rose had a tight hold of her hand.*

VERBS

tighten your hold *Luke tightened his hold on his wallet.*

loosen/relax your hold *Laughing, he loosened his hold until she could pull her arms free.*

release your hold (=stop holding something) *As soon as his fingers released their hold, Robyn turned and ran.*

PHRASES

keep hold of sth (=hold something without letting go) *I had to run to keep hold of the leather strap.*

get/take hold of sth (=start holding something) *Wallace took hold of Fred's jacket and pulled him roughly backwards.*

catch/grab/seize etc hold of sth (=start holding something quickly and firmly) *She grabbed hold of the letter and tore it open.*

have hold of sth (=be holding something) *Nathan had hold of her hand again.*

hold up *v* THESAURUS steal

hole *n*

an empty space in something solid

ADJECTIVES

a big/massive/great hole *There was a big hole in the middle of the field.*

a small/tiny hole *The plant's leaves are full of tiny holes.*

VERBS

dig a hole *I began digging a hole for the tree.*

make/cut a hole *Make a hole for the wire to go through.*

drill/bore a hole (=make a hole using a special tool) *The engineers began boring a hole in the side of the mountain.*

blow/blast a hole *The explosion blew a massive hole in the side of the building.*

burn a hole *The hot iron had burned a hole in the shirt.*

come in through a hole *Rain was coming in through a hole in the roof.*

fill in a hole *Can you help me fill in this hole?*

NOUNS + hole

a bullet hole *The car was full of bullet holes.*

a mouse/rabbit hole *We found a mouse hole behind the fridge.*

PREPOSITIONS

a hole in sth *There was a huge hole in the road.*

holiday *n*

1 *BrE* a period of time when you travel to another place for pleasure

> **Holiday** is used in British English. American speakers say **vacation**.

ADJECTIVES/NOUNS + holiday

a good/great/nice holiday *We had a great holiday in Austria.*

a summer/winter holiday *They were going to a house on the coast for their summer holidays.*

a skiing/camping/walking etc holiday *They went on a camping holiday in France.*

a beach holiday *The hotel is in the perfect place for a relaxing beach holiday.*

a foreign/overseas holiday *We couldn't afford to go on foreign holidays.*

a two-week/seven night etc holiday *The prize is a fabulous two-week holiday to Jamaica.*

a package holiday (=in which you pay a price that includes travel, room, and food) *The company organizes package holidays to Spain and Greece.*

a family holiday *I first visited Orkney on a family holiday when I was a boy.*

sb's dream holiday (=the best holiday you can imagine) *They won a dream holiday for two to the Caribbean.*

VERBS

go on holiday *The children were excited about going on holiday.*

have/take a holiday *We've had two lovely holidays in Italy.*

book a holiday *I booked the holiday online.*

plan a holiday *He and Marcia were planning a holiday in Japan.*

cancel a holiday *We had to cancel the holiday because my dad was ill.*

holiday + NOUNS

a holiday resort (=a place with many hotels where a lot of people go on holiday) *Benidorm is a terrific holiday resort with so much to do.*

a holiday destination (=a town or country where a lot of people go on holiday) *Marmaris is one of Turkey's most popular holiday destinations.*

a holiday home/house/cottage/apartment (=a house that someone owns and uses for holidays) *They bought a holiday home in France.*

holiday accommodation *The tourist office can give information about holiday accommodation in the area.*

the holiday season *The town is very busy during the holiday season.*

holiday photos (*also* **holiday snaps** *informal*) (=photographs that you take when you are on holiday) *Do you want to see our holiday snaps?*

PREPOSITIONS

on holiday *What did you do on holiday?*

PHRASES

a holiday abroad (=a holiday in a country other than the one you live in) *They were planning a holiday abroad that year.*

the holiday of a lifetime (=a very good or expensive holiday that you will only take once) *We took the family on a holiday of a lifetime to Orlando, Florida.*

2 *BrE* a time of rest from work or school

NOUNS + holiday

the school holidays *The school holidays start tomorrow.*

the summer holidays (=time during the summer when children do not go to school) *What are you doing in the summer holidays?*

ADJECTIVES

paid holiday (=when you are paid by your employer but do not have to go to work) *We get 25 days' paid holiday a year.*

VERBS

take a holiday *I'm taking a holiday on Tuesday next week.*

get/have holiday *How much holiday do you get?*

holiday + NOUNS

holiday pay (=money from your employer when you have a holiday) *Many workers do not get holiday pay.*

a holiday job (=a job you do when you have a holiday from school or college) *I had a holiday job working on a farm.*

PREPOSITIONS

(away) on holiday *I'm away on holiday until June 1st.*

in/during the holidays *He came to stay with us in the school holidays.*

PHRASES

a week's/two weeks' etc holiday *I get five weeks' holiday a year.*

3 a day fixed by law when people do not have to go to work or school

ADJECTIVES/NOUNS + holiday

a national/public/official holiday *July 4th is a national holiday in the US.*

a bank holiday *BrE* (=an official holiday when banks and some businesses are closed) *The last Monday in August is a bank holiday.*

a religious holiday *Christmas Day is a religious holiday.*

a Jewish/Muslim etc holiday *The family always observe the Jewish holiday Yom Kippur.*

H

the Passover/Thanksgiving etc holiday *The market was closed because of the Thanksgiving holiday.*

holiday + NOUNS

a holiday weekend *Many people travel during the Easter holiday weekend.*

the holiday season *AmE* (=time between Thanksgiving and New Year) *Sales of toys usually increase during the holiday season.*

VERBS

celebrate/observe a holiday *Jewish people were gathering to observe the Passover holiday.*

hollow *adj* THESAURUS ▸ **empty**

holy *adj*

if something is holy, it is treated with special respect, especially because it is connected with God or religion

NOUNS

a holy place/city/site *Jerusalem is regarded as a holy city by Jews, Christians, and Muslims.*

holy ground *You are standing on holy ground.*

the Holy Land (=Israel/Palestine) *Millions of people visit the Holy Land each year.*

a holy mountain/river *Kanchenjunga is regarded as a holy mountain.*

a holy man *Mount Koya is the burial place of Japan's great holy man, Kobo Daishi.*

a holy book *The holy book contains guidelines about the behaviour expected from Muslims.*

a holy war *He called for a holy war against the American invaders.*

a holy relic (=a holy object) *The box was used for storing holy relics.*

holy water *I dipped my fingers in the holy water and crossed myself.*

the holy month (of Ramadan) *The festival marks the end of the holy month of Ramadan.*

a holy day *They light the candle on Sundays and holy days.*

VERBS

be considered holy/be regarded as holy *This site is also considered holy by Muslims.*

Holy or **sacred?**

These words mean the same and have many of the same collocations. You can say a **holy place/city/mountain/relic** or a **sacred place/city/mountain/relic**.

There are some differences. You say a **holy man** and a **holy war** (not a 'sacred' one). It is more common to say a **holy book**, but a **sacred text**. It is more common to say **holy water**, but a **sacred flame**.

Holy is used with a capital letter about many things that are connected with the Christian religion – for example, the **Holy Bible**, the **Holy Spirit**, the **Holy Ghost**, the **Holy Father**, and the **Holy Cross**.

home *n*

the house, apartment, or place where you live

VERBS

live at home (=live with your parents) *More people in their twenties are still living at home because housing is so expensive.*

leave home *Lisa had left home at age 16.*

work from home/work at home (=instead of in an office) *I work at home three days a week.*

stay at home *BrE*, **stay home** *AmE*: *Last night we stayed at home and watched TV.*

head for home (=begin the journey to your home) *Tired and weary, they headed for home.*

make your home somewhere (=start living somewhere) *A family of birds made their home under the roof.*

ADJECTIVES/NOUNS + home

a nice/beautiful/luxurious home *We interviewed the star in her luxurious home.*

affordable homes (=that do not cost too much money) *We need to provide affordable homes for young people.*

a permanent/temporary home *Flood victims were offered temporary homes.*

a happy home (=a happy family) *We had a happy home when I was young.*

a secure/stable home (=a caring family without a lot of changes) *He had grown up in a stable home.*

sb's childhood/boyhood etc home (=where you lived as a child) *I had not been back to my childhood home for ten years.*

the family home (=where a family lives) *The house was once the family home of the Kennedys.*

a second home (=in addition to the one where you usually live, for holidays etc) *About 300,000 British people have a second home abroad.*

a holiday home *BrE*, **a vacation home** *AmE*: *They bought a luxury holiday home in Spain.*

home + NOUNS

home address/phone number *If you give me your home address, I'll send you a copy.*

a home owner *Home owners will be badly affected by the rise in mortgage rates.*

home comforts (=things at home which make your life pleasant) *I really missed my home comforts when I was travelling.*

PREPOSITIONS/ADVERBS

at home *I wasn't at home when he called.*

away from home *He was spending more and more time away from home.*

homely *adj* THESAURUS ▸ **ugly (1)**

homesick *adj* THESAURUS ▸ **sad (1)**

homework *n*

work that a student at school is asked to do at home

VERBS

do your homework *Paul, have you done your homework?*

give (sb) homework (*also* **set (sb) homework** *BrE*): *The teacher gave them some homework to do by Monday.*

get homework *I think we get too much homework.*

help sb with their homework *I often have to help her with her homework.*

hand in your homework (=give it to the teacher) *You must hand in your homework by Friday.*

finish your homework *You're not going out until you've finished your homework.*

NOUNS + homework

biology/history/French etc homework *The science homework was really hard.*

homework + NOUNS

a homework assignment *Students are given homework assignments to do.*

PREPOSITIONS

for homework *For homework, finish the exercise on page 14.*

⚠ Don't say 'make/write your homework'. Say **do your homework**.

PHRASES

a piece of homework *I still have one more piece of homework left to do.*

honest *adj*

if you are honest, you tell the truth and do not cheat or steal

NOUNS

an honest man/woman/person *He looked like an honest man, so she agreed to lend him the money.*

an honest face *The lady had a kind honest face.*

an honest answer/opinion *I'm going to ask you something and I want an honest answer.*

an honest mistake *Please believe me. It was an honest mistake.*

the honest truth (=used when emphasizing that this is the truth) *The honest truth is that nobody knows why he left his job.*

an honest debate/discussion *We need to have an honest debate about the future of the European Union.*

an honest assessment/appraisal *During his speech, the president gave an honest assessment of the current state of the economy.*

ADVERBS

completely/totally/absolutely/perfectly honest *I'll be perfectly honest with you – I don't really want to go to the party.*

scrupulously honest (=very careful to be honest) *Lawyers have to be scrupulously honest in their dealings with their clients.*

painfully honest (=in which you talk about things that are difficult or embarrassing to talk about) *This is a painfully honest account of her relationship with her parents.*

brutally honest (=in a way that may seem unkind) *To be brutally honest, she's too old for the job.*

refreshingly honest (=in a way that is unusual and good) *He is refreshingly honest about the mistakes he has made.*

PREPOSITIONS

honest with sb *I don't think you are being completely honest with me.*

honest about sth *It's always best to be honest about your feelings.*

PHRASES

let's be honest *Let's be honest, she only married him for his money.*

to be honest (=used when saying what you really think) *To be honest, I don't like her very much.*

THESAURUS: honest

truthful

answer | account

if you are truthful, you do not tell any lies: *The truthful answer is that we do not know. | It was a truthful account of life inside the camp. | To be truthful with you, I had to admire this guy. | I don't think she is being entirely truthful with us.*

sincere

apology | thanks | belief | desire | wish | hope

if you are sincere, you say what you really think or feel:

Please accept our sincere apologies for the delay. | We published the story in the sincere belief that the documents were genuine. | It was their sincere desire to make sure that no further lives were lost. | He ***sounded*** *so* ***sincere*** *that I forgave him at once.*

frank

discussion | debate | account | assessment | admission

speaking honestly and directly about something, especially something that people find difficult to discuss:

The programme contains a frank discussion about sex. | It was an unusually frank admission of guilt. | In her book, she is ***brutally frank*** *about their marriage* (=in a way that may shock people). *|* ***To be frank****, I have no idea where the money has gone.*

If you say that **there was a full and frank exchange of views**, this usually means that there was an angry argument, because people said what they really thought.

straight *informal*
answer | talking
saying what you really think:
*I need a straight answer. | After some straight talking by the manager, the team started to play better. | I can't help you if you're not **straight with** me.*

open
willing to talk about your feelings and opinions in an honest way, rather than trying to hide them:
*American people tend to be more **open about** their feelings. | She's very easy to talk to because she's so open.*

Open is not used before a noun in this meaning.

candid *formal*
admission | interview | discussion | statement | assessment
honest about the facts, or about your opinions and feelings, even if other people disapprove of them:
*It was an unusually candid admission for a politician. | In a candid interview, he talks about his reasons for resigning. | The actor has always been completely **candid about** his past.*

direct
answer | manner | way
saying exactly what you think in a clear way, even when this might annoy or upset people:
When I asked him what he thought of my work, I got a surprisingly direct answer. | Not everyone liked her direct manner. | The boss can be very direct.

blunt
message | warning | statement | answer | language | words
saying exactly what you think in a few words without trying to be careful or polite, even when this might annoy or upset people:
*He gave them a blunt warning – either go back to work, or face the consequences. | Diplomats expressed surprise at the blunt language of the text. | Sorry if I was a bit **blunt with** you earlier.*

forthright *formal*
manner | way | views | statement | speech | attack | rejection
saying exactly what you think, without being afraid of what other people will think:
Her husband told her in a forthright manner where he thought she was going wrong. | The Chief Executive Officer issued a forthright statement in which he described the company's financial position as "deeply worrying".

outspoken
critic | opponent | advocate | supporter | views | opinions | comments | criticism | opposition
expressing your opinions publicly in a very direct way, which may offend or annoy some people:
Ozawa is an outspoken critic of the government. | The senator is an outspoken advocate of tax cuts (=someone who strongly supports an idea). *| Professor Dawkins is known for his outspoken views on religion.*

ANTONYMS **honest → dishonest**

honesty *n* the quality of being honest

ADJECTIVES

complete/total honesty *I want complete honesty from you.*

brutal honesty (=honesty that might hurt someone) *Sometimes brutal honesty is necessary to get someone to change.*

painful honesty (=about something that is upsetting or embarrassing for you) *"I don't know," she said with painful honesty.*

refreshing honesty (=that you like because it is unusual) *He admitted, with refreshing honesty, that the team hadn't deserved to win.*

PREPOSITIONS

with honesty *He talked with complete honesty about his drink problem.*

PHRASES

in all honesty (=used to emphasize that you are being honest) *In all honesty, I found it a bit boring.*

honour *BrE*, honor *AmE n*

1 something that makes you feel very proud

ADJECTIVES

a great honour *It was a great honour to meet my hero in person.*

a rare honour (=a very special honour that is not given to many people) *Being asked to paint a portrait for the Queen is a rare honour for any artist.*

a dubious honour (=something that you are not sure that you should be proud of) *The city has the dubious honor of being the smoggiest city in the world.*

a signal honour *formal* (=a great honour) *He received the signal honour of becoming an Honorary Fellow of the college.*

VERBS

have the honour *formal*: *As a young man, he had the honour of meeting Winston Churchill.*

do sb the honour *formal* (=make someone proud and happy by doing something for

H

them) *Will you do me the honour of becoming my wife?*

PREPOSITIONS

the honour of doing sth *Over 100 players competed for the honour of representing the county in the national finals.*

PHRASES

it is an honour to do sth (=used as a polite way of saying that you are pleased to do something) *It is an honour to have you here, sir.*

2 the respect that you, your family, your country etc receive from other people, which makes you feel proud

VERBS

bring honour to sb/sth (=make people respect someone or something) *The bravery of these men has brought honour to their regiment.*

defend sb's/sth's honour (=do something to protect it when it is being attacked) *To defend his honour and his business interests, he was prepared to go to court.*

save the honour of sb/sth (=stop it being lost) *He saved the team's honour by scoring a goal in the final minute.*

uphold the honour of sb/sth (=defend it) *She felt duty bound to uphold the honour of her country.*

restore the honour of sb/sth (=make it return to its former state) *He would be forced to restore the honor of his family name.*

ADJECTIVES/NOUNS + honour

national honour *For the French team, winning tomorrow's game is a matter of national honour.*

family honour *Refusal of a marriage offer is seen as an attack on the family honour.*

PHRASES

sb's/sth's honour is at stake (=someone may lose their honour) *People believed that the country's honor was at stake over the incident.*

3 strong moral beliefs and standards of behaviour that make people respect and trust you

PHRASES

a man of honour *I know Tom to be a man of honour and integrity.*

a matter/point/question of honour (=something you feel you must do because of your moral beliefs) *To my mum, paying bills on time is a point of honour.*

a code of honour (=a set of moral rules, laws, or principles that people follow) *We abide by a strict military code of honor.*

a sense of honour (=a desire to do what is morally right) *Is he marrying her out of some misplaced sense of honour?*

a badge of honour (=something that shows you have honour) *He wore his battle scars as a badge of honour.*

sb's word of honour (=a promise based on strong moral beliefs) *I give you my word of honour that you will not be harmed.*

be/feel honour bound to do sth (=feel that you should do something, because it is morally right or your duty to do it) *My father felt honour bound to help his sister.*

4 a prize or title given to someone for an achievement

ADJECTIVES

highest honour *The Victoria Cross is Britain's highest honour for bravery.*

a top honour *Joey was awarded the top honour in recognition of his work.*

a major honour *The team last won a major honour in 2001.*

VERBS

win/receive an honour *The company has won several honours including the Queen's Award for Export.*

give/award (sb) an honour *Many people who are awarded this honour go on to win the Nobel Prize.*

bestow an honour on sb *formal* (=give it to them) *The honour is normally bestowed on someone who has done something for the city.*

accept an honour *Paltrow accepted the honor at a city hall ceremony.*

PREPOSITIONS

an honour for sth *The Hero Star medal is Russia's top honour for bravery.*

hope¹ *v*

to want something to happen or be true and to believe that it is possible or likely

ADVERBS

really/very much hope *I really hope things get better.*

secretly hope *She had secretly hoped to marry him.*

sincerely hope *We sincerely hope that you enjoy your stay with us.*

desperately hope *The team desperately hopes to win the match.*

fervently hope *formal* (=very much want something to happen) *He fervently hopes to be picked for the team.*

PREPOSITIONS

hope for sth *They are hoping for good weather.*

PHRASES

hope for the best *We shall continue to hope for the best and prepare for the worst.*

be hoping against hope (=hope for something that is very unlikely to happen or be true) *She glanced about the hall, hoping against hope that Richard would be waiting for her.*

hope and pray *They were hoping and praying for a better future.*

sth is too much to hope for *We might win the competition, but I guess that is too much to hope for.*

hope² *n*

the feeling that what you want will happen, or something that you want to happen

VERBS + hope

have hope *The situation looked bad, but we still had hope that things would get better soon.*

give/offer hope *The research has given hope to thousands of people who have the disease.*

lose/give up/abandon hope (=stop hoping) *After six weeks, she had abandoned hope of finding him alive.*

raise sb's hopes (*also* **get/build sb's hopes up**) (=make someone feel that what they want is likely to happen) *I don't want to raise your hopes too much.*

pin your hopes on sth (=hope for one thing that everything else depends on) *After a difficult year, the company is pinning its hopes on its new range of products.*

cling to the hope that (=keep hoping that something will happen, even though it seems unlikely) *They clung to the hope that one day a cure would be found.*

dash/shatter sb's hopes (=make what someone wants seem impossible) *The ending of the talks has dashed any hopes of peace.*

live in hope (=keep hoping) *We haven't had any success yet, but we live in hope.*

hope + VERBS

hopes are fading (=people have much less hope of doing something) *Hopes are fading that rescuers will find any more survivors.*

sb's hope lies in/with sth (=something gives people hope) *Our real hope lies with a vaccine.*

ADJECTIVES

fresh/renewed hope *The news has given the family renewed hope that their daughter may still be alive.*

false hope *We don't want to give people false hopes.*

a vain/forlorn hope (=hope for something that is impossible) *He traveled south in the vain hope of finding work.*

sb's only/one hope *My only hope is that someone may have handed in the keys to the police.*

sb's last hope (=the only person or thing left that can help someone) *No one else would lend us the money - you are our last hope.*

hopes are high (=people think that something good will happen) *Hopes are high that the hostages will be released soon.*

PREPOSITIONS

hope for/to sb *This drug offers new hope for breast cancer sufferers.*

hope for sth *The Pope has voiced hope for peace.*

hopes of (doing) sth *Rita has hopes of becoming a nurse.*

in the hope of doing sth (=because you hope that you will do it) *Shoppers flocked to the sales in the hope of finding a bargain.*

in the hope that (=because you hope that something will happen) *We went for a picnic anyway, in the hope that the weather would improve.*

PHRASES

be full of hope *His voice sounded full of hope.*

a glimmer/ray of hope (=a little hope, or something that gives you a little hope) *The new treatment gives patients a glimmer of hope.*

sb's hopes and dreams/fears *We talked about all our hopes and dreams for the future. | The crew members have different hopes and fears about the trip.*

keep sb's hopes alive (=make someone still have hope) *A goal in the 33rd minute kept England's hopes alive.*

hopeless *adj* THESAURUS ▸ **useless**

horizon *n*

1 the line where the land or sea seems to meet the sky

ADJECTIVES

the distant/far horizon *Beyond the thick forests lie the Rocky Mountains on the distant horizon.*

VERBS

scan the horizon (=examine it carefully but quickly) *He scanned the horizon for any sign of the boat.*

dominate the horizon (=be the biggest and most noticeable thing on the horizon) *The castle dominates the horizon.*

appear on the horizon *Clouds had begun to appear on the horizon.*

disappear over the horizon *She watched the car until it disappeared over the horizon.*

PREPOSITIONS

on the horizon *They could see a ship on the horizon.*

above/below the horizon *The sun disappeared below the horizon.*

over/beyond the horizon *He saw the moon rising up over the horizon.*

2 your horizons are the limits of your ideas, knowledge, and experience

> **Grammar**
> Always plural in this meaning.

VERBS

broaden/expand sb's horizons *Which books would you say have broadened your horizons?*

H

ADJECTIVES

limited/narrow horizons *They are incapable of seeing beyond their own narrow horizons.*

horizontal *adj* THESAURUS ▶ flat[1]

horrible *adj* THESAURUS ▶ terrible

horrific *adj* THESAURUS ▶ terrible

horror *n*

1 a strong feeling of shock and fear

ADJECTIVES

absolute/sheer/abject horror (=great horror) *There was a look of sheer horror on her face.*

mock horror (=horror that is not real) *Grandma raised her hands in mock horror.*

VERBS

fill sb with horror *The idea of killing an animal filled him with horror.*

imagine sb's horror *Imagine his horror when he found the body.*

PREPOSITIONS

in horror *Ashley stared in horror at the black hairy spider.*

with horror *Staff watched with horror as he set the documents on fire.*

to sb's horror *To my horror, I realized my shirt was wet with blood.*

horror at sth *He was filled with horror at the thought of what he had to do.*

PHRASES

a look of horror *Suddenly, a look of horror spread over his face.*

H

2 something that is very shocking and terrible

ADJECTIVES

the true/full horror of sth *He suddenly realized the true horror of what he was doing.*

unspeakable/unimaginable horror (=used when emphasizing how bad something is) *The refugees had suffered unspeakable horrors.*

VERBS

experience/suffer a horror *His grandfather had experienced the horror of the First World War.*

hospitable *adj* THESAURUS ▶ friendly

hospital *n*

a large building where sick or injured people receive medical treatment

> **Grammar**
> In British English, people usually miss out **the** before **hospital** and say **go to hospital**. In American English, people say **go to the hospital**.

VERBS

go to (the) hospital *The pain got worse and she had to go to the hospital.*

go into (the) hospital (=go to hospital and stay for treatment which has already been planned) *He's going into hospital for an operation next week.*

be taken/rushed to (the) hospital *Three people were taken to hospital after a crash on the motorway.*

be airlifted to (the) hospital (=be taken there in a plane or helicopter) *A man was airlifted to hospital with serious injuries.*

be admitted to (the) hospital (=be taken into the hospital) *He was admitted to hospital suffering from chest pain.*

leave/come out of (the) hospital *He is expected to come out of hospital later this week.*

be discharged/released from (the) hospital (=be allowed to leave a hospital because you are better) *It was several weeks before he was released from hospital.*

ADJECTIVES/NOUNS + hospital

a general hospital (=one that treats many different types of disease and injury) *The injured were taken to Bristol General Hospital.*

a psychiatric hospital (*also* **a mental hospital** *old-fashioned*) (=for people with mental illnesses) *He was admitted to a secure psychiatric hospital.*

a maternity hospital *BrE* (=for women having babies) *Many maternity hospitals have been forced to close.*

a children's hospital *They are trying to raise money to build a children's hospital.*

a military hospital *Injured soldiers were taken to a nearby military hospital.*

a teaching hospital (=one where medical students receive practical training) *The nurse had trained at a London teaching hospital.*

a private hospital *BrE: The operation was carried out at a private hospital.*

hospital + NOUNS

hospital treatment/care *He is badly hurt and needs urgent hospital treatment.*

a hospital stay (=the period someone spends in hospital) *New surgical techniques mean a hospital stay of less than 48 hours.*

a hospital bed *There is a shortage of hospital beds.*

a hospital ward (=a room for patients staying in a hospital) *She works on a busy hospital ward.*

hospital doctor/nurse/staff *Hospital doctors often work long hours.*

PREPOSITIONS

in (the) hospital *His wife visited him in hospital.*

at a hospital *She's a doctor at Addenbrooke's Hospital.*

hostage *n*

someone who is kept as a prisoner by an enemy in order to force people to agree to their demands

VERBS

take sb hostage (=force someone to be a hostage) *The bank robbers took three customers hostage and threatened to shoot them.*

seize a hostage *Rebel gunmen seized 30 more hostages in Chechnya.*

keep/hold sb hostage *They kept him hostage for nine months in the jungle.*

hold a hostage *Police have surrounded the house where the hostages were being held.*

rescue a hostage *US special forces attacked the bus and rescued the hostages.*

release/free a hostage *The terrorists have agreed to release all the hostages.*

hostage + NOUNS

a hostage crisis *Diplomatic talks have begun to bring the hostage crisis to an end.*

hostage-taking *They use hostage-taking as a way of getting money to buy weapons.*

PHRASES

the release of the hostages *The government is continuing its efforts to secure the release of the hostages.*

hostile *adj*

1 angry and deliberately unfriendly towards someone

ADVERBS

openly hostile (=used when someone does not try to hide their unfriendly feelings) *The guards were openly hostile to him.*

increasingly hostile *The boy became increasingly hostile to his parents and refused to talk to them.*

downright hostile (=extremely hostile in a very unpleasant way) *She was downright hostile towards us.*

NOUNS

a hostile welcome/reception (=people are hostile to someone when they arrive somewhere) *The visiting team received a hostile reception from the crowd.*

a hostile attitude *Some young people have a very hostile attitude to the police.*

a hostile crowd/audience *A hostile crowd of protesters gathered outside the parliament building.*

a hostile atmosphere *There was a hostile atmosphere at the match, and the police made several arrests.*

VERBS

become hostile *The neighbours became hostile and started shouting at her.*

PREPOSITIONS

hostile to/towards sb *The local people are often hostile to foreigners.*

2 opposing something very strongly

ADVERBS

deeply hostile *They were deeply hostile to any kind of change.*

bitterly hostile *Public opinion is bitterly hostile to tax increases.*

hostile + NOUNS

a hostile response/reaction *The plan met with a hostile response from the workers.*

VERBS

remain hostile to sth *UK shoppers still remain hostile to genetically modified foods.*

PREPOSITIONS

hostile to/towards sth *They became hostile to the war when they realised how many soldiers were being killed.*

hostility *n*

unfriendly and angry feelings, or strong opposition

ADJECTIVES

deep hostility *There was deep hostility to the changes among the workforce.*

open hostility (=not trying to hide your feelings of hostility) *The two women looked at each other with open hostility.*

outright hostility (=complete hostility) *The mood in the village had changed to outright hostility.*

great/considerable hostility *The reforms were greeted with considerable hostility.*

widespread hostility (=among many people) *There is widespread hostility towards the foreign soldiers in the country.*

growing hostility *He had noticed a growing hostility towards refugees.*

personal hostility *The writer seems to have a personal hostility to Mary Kingsley.*

mutual hostility (=between two people or groups) *The mutual hostility between the two groups seems to be deep-rooted.*

VERBS

face hostility *Foreigners often face hostility from the local population.*

meet sb/sth with hostility (*also* **greet sb/sth with hostility**) *The idea was met with hostility when it was first suggested.*

feel hostility *I felt no hostility towards him – I just felt sorry for him.*

arouse/provoke hostility *formal* (=cause hostility) *The speaker aroused hostility among some members of the audience.*

PREPOSITIONS

hostility to/towards sb/sth *The plans had to be abandoned because of hostility to them.*

hostility against sb *There have been reports of violent hostility against foreigners.*

hostility between sb *There is a lot of hostility between the two groups.*

hot *adj* having a high temperature

NOUNS

hot weather/climate *In hot weather, the plants need to be watered every day.*

a hot day/evening/summer *It was a hot day and everyone was wearing T-shirts.*

a hot country *The bird normally lives in hot countries.*

hot drink/food/meal *A hot drink will help to warm you up.*

hot water/bath/shower *There is hot water in all the rooms.*

ADVERBS

incredibly hot (=very hot) *Tokyo gets incredibly hot in summer.*

boiling hot (=very hot) *The car is boiling hot.*

scorching hot (=extremely hot) *The drill gets scorching hot.*

blazing hot (*also* **baking hot** *BrE*) (=extremely hot - used about the weather) *It was a baking hot week in August.*

scalding hot (=extremely hot - used about liquids) *The coffee was scalding hot.*

burning hot (=used about someone's skin or the weather) *His forehead was burning hot.*

steaming hot (=used about drinks or the weather) *The waitress put a steaming hot cup of coffee on the table.*

piping hot (=very hot - used about food and drink) *The fruit pie was covered with piping hot custard.*

red hot (=so hot that it glows red, or extremely hot to touch) *Take care - the iron is red hot.*

white hot (=white hot metal has been heated to a very high temperature) *He held the metal in the flame until it became white hot.*

uncomfortably hot *The sweater made her feel uncomfortably hot.*

unbearably/oppressively hot (=so hot that it is very uncomfortable) *The office gets unbearably hot in summer.*

VERBS

be/feel hot *I was hot and tired after the journey.*

become/get hot *The water gets hot very quickly.*

keep sth hot *The flask will keep the tea hot.*

serve sth (while it is) hot *Serve the soup hot with fresh bread.*

PHRASES

hot and cold *The bar serves hot and cold food.*

> **Hot** is also used about food that is very spicy: *I like a nice* ***hot*** *curry.*

THESAURUS: hot

warm
weather | climate | day | evening | summer | water | air | wind | clothes | bed | fire | bed
a little hot, especially in a way that seems pleasant:
Florida is full of British people who are attracted by the warm climate. | Scrub your hands with soap and warm water. | I was looking forward to being in a ***nice warm*** *bed. |* ***It's lovely and warm*** *in here. | He moved his legs in order to try to* ***keep warm****.*

boiling *spoken*
very hot:
It's boiling *in my office. | You must be* ***absolutely boiling*** *in that sweater!*

> **Boiling** is not usually used before a noun. You use **boiling hot** before a noun: *a* ***boiling hot*** *day.*

scorching
heat | sun | weather | day | summer | desert
extremely hot, especially because the sun is shining very strongly:
The local people are accustomed to the scorching heat of the desert. | When we got to Spain, the weather was scorching.

humid
weather | climate | conditions | air | atmosphere | night | day | morning | summer
hot and with a lot of moisture in the air:
The night was hot and humid, and she was unable to sleep. | Hong Kong ***gets very humid*** *at this time of year.*

feverish
feeling very hot because you are ill:
His head ached and he ***felt feverish****.*

> **Feverish** is not usually used before a noun.

Another way of saying that something is hot

You can also say that a room, car etc **is like an oven**: *It's* ***like an oven*** *in here.*

If part of your body feels very hot and painful, you say that it is **burning**: *His forehead was* ***burning****. | I had a* ***burning*** *sensation in my mouth.*

ANTONYMS **hot → cold[1]**

hotel *n*

a building where people pay to stay and eat meals

VERBS

stay at/in a hotel *We stayed at a hotel near the airport.*

check into a hotel (*also* **book into a hotel** *BrE*): *He checked into the hotel a little after 2 p.m.*

check out of a hotel (=leave a hotel) *We packed and checked out of the hotel.*

book a hotel *BrE* (=arrange to stay in it) *Have you booked the hotel yet?*

run/manage a hotel *They run a small hotel in Cornwall.*

ADJECTIVES/NOUNS + hotel

a two-star/five-star etc hotel *On our honeymoon, we stayed in a four-star hotel in Paris.*

a luxury hotel *He took her to a luxury hotel in central London.*

a comfortable hotel *The Beau Rivage is a comfortable hotel on the lakeside.*

a budget hotel (=with rooms at low prices) *The chain now has 200 budget hotels in Europe.*

a country hotel (=a hotel in the countryside) *They chose a quiet country hotel for their honeymoon.*

hotel + NOUNS

a hotel room *She was watching TV in her hotel room.*

a hotel suite (=a set of rooms in a hotel) *The singer was staying in a luxury hotel suite.*

a hotel guest *Hotel guests have free use of the gym and pool.*

the hotel manager/receptionist/porter *Speak to the hotel manager if you are not happy with your room.*

the hotel restaurant/bar/gym *The hotel bar was empty.*

the hotel reception/lobby *She waited for him in the hotel lobby.*

a hotel chain/group (=a group of hotels owned by the same company) *The building has been bought by the Hilton Hotels chain.*

PREPOSITIONS

at/in a hotel *I'll meet you at the hotel.*

hour *n*

a unit for measuring time. There are 60 minutes in one hour, and 24 hours in one day

PHRASES

half an hour (*also* **a half hour**) (=30 minutes) *I'll meet you in half an hour.*

(a) quarter of an hour (=15 minutes) *She was only gone for about a quarter of an hour.*

three quarters of an hour (=45 minutes) *The journey takes three quarters of an hour.*

miles/kilometres an hour (=used in speeds) *The speed limit is 65 miles an hour.*

£10/$7 etc an hour (=used to say how much someone is paid or something costs) *I earn £5 an hour babysitting.*

an hour's walk/drive etc *Frankfurt is about three hours' drive away.*

VERBS

sth takes an hour (*also* **it takes an hour to do sth**) *It took about three hours to paint the whole wall.*

spend an hour *I spent an hour reading.*

last (for) an hour *The meeting lasted almost two hours.*

an hour goes by/passes *Six hours had passed since he left, and I was starting to get worried.*

PREPOSITIONS

for an hour/for two hours etc *I study for an hour every evening.*

in an hour/in two hours etc (=one hour etc from now) *We'll have to leave in an hour.*

within an hour/within two hours etc (=before one hour etc has passed) *I should be back within an hour.*

over an hour/over two hours etc (=more than an hour etc) *It took us over three hours to get there.*

under an hour/under two hours etc (=less than an hour etc) *You can be in Amsterdam in under an hour.*

an hour/two hours etc of sth *After ten hours of work, I was very tired.*

by the hour (=according to the number of hours) *You can hire a boat for a whole day or by the hour.*

house *n*

a building that someone lives in

ADJECTIVES/NOUNS + house

a small/big/huge etc house *They live in a huge house in London.*

a beautiful/nice/lovely house *Her family has a beautiful house overlooking the bay.*

a three-bedroom/four-bedroom etc house *A four-bedroom house in this area costs around £350,000.*

a semi-detached house *BrE* (=one that is joined to another house on one side) *It was a semi-detached house with a very small garden.*

a detached house *BrE* (=that is not joined to other houses) *Fontaine lives in a large detached house.*

a terraced house *BrE*, **a row house** *AmE* (=joined to other houses on two sides) *They lived with their four children in an old row house.*

a country house (=a very large house in the countryside) *After the war, many big country houses had to be sold because the owners could not afford to maintain them.*

a council house *BrE* (=one owned by a local council that people can rent cheaply) *There are not enough council houses available for people to live in.*

a derelict house (=that no one lives in and is in very bad condition) *Some derelict houses in our street are being knocked down.*

VERBS

live in a house *The star lives in a big house in Hollywood.*

buy a house *We bought this house when Liam was just a baby.*

rent a house (=pay rent to live in it) *They decided to rent a house in the suburbs.*

sell a house *We decided to sell the house and move back to Seattle.*

move into/out of a house *We're moving into our new house next week.*

build a house *The family is building a house on land overlooking Galway Bay.*

put up houses (=build houses, especially quickly) *I think they've ruined the village by putting up these new houses.*

decorate a house (=put paint or wallpaper on the inside walls of a house) *The couple are busy decorating their new house.*

renovate a house (=repair a house so that it is in good condition again) *He makes money by renovating old houses and selling them.*

house + NOUNS

house prices *House prices have tripled over the last ten years.*

house hunting (=the activity of looking at houses that you might buy) *Have you had any success with your house hunting?*

housework *n*

work that you do to take care of a house, for example washing, cleaning etc

VERBS

do the housework *Women usually do the housework.*

help sb with the housework *Her husband sometimes helps her with the housework.*

share the housework *We share the housework – I do the cleaning and he washes the dishes.*

hug[1] *v*

to put your arms around someone and hold them tightly to show love or friendship

ADVERBS

hug sb tightly *She hugged her daughter tightly and said goodbye.*

hug sb close (=hug someone tightly) *Sarah kissed him and hugged him close.*

hug[2] *n*

the action of putting your arms around someone to show affection

VERBS

give sb a hug *Mary gave him a friendly hug and got onto the train.*

ADJECTIVES

a big hug *She came over to him and gave him a big hug.*

a quick hug *He gave her a quick hug and said goodbye.*

huge *adj* extremely big

NOUNS

a huge amount/quantity *There is a huge amount of work to be done.*

a huge number *Huge numbers of people use the airport each year.*

a huge increase *There has been a huge increase in the number of cars on our roads.*

a huge profit/loss/debt *The company made a huge profit last year.*

a huge impact/effect *The new technology will have a huge impact on people's lives.*

a huge success *The book was a huge success and sold millions of copies.*

a huge difference *There is a huge difference between acting and directing.*

ADVERBS

absolutely huge *The task ahead of them is absolutely huge.*

⚠ Don't say 'very huge'.

THESAURUS: huge

enormous

enormous means the same as **huge**, and can be used with the same collocations:

The building cost an enormous amount of money. | She gets enormous pleasure from her work. | The impact of his discovery was absolutely enormous.

massive

massive means the same as **huge** and **enormous**, and can be used with the same collocations. It sounds a little more informal:

There was a massive increase in food prices. | The company is massive, operating in 150 countries. | They heard a massive explosion.

When you use **massive** about objects and buildings, it has the feeling of being very solid or heavy: *The castle is surrounded by a **massive** stone wall. | a **massive** wooden table*

giant

giant things are much bigger than other things of the same kind:

There is a giant TV screen on the wall. | He works for a giant electronics corporation.

Giant is often used about animals and plants: *a **giant** snake | a **giant** mushroom*

Giant is only used before a noun.

vast

amount | quantity | number | range | area | distance | majority

vast amounts, numbers, areas, or distances are extremely big:

A vast amount of energy is wasted. | Sweet foods like ice cream contain vast quantities of sugar. | The gallery has a vast number of paintings. | The fire spread over a vast area. | The vast majority of children did not go to school.

colossal
statue | amount | bill | mistake | waste
a colossal object or amount is extremely big. A colossal mistake is a very serious. **Colossal** sounds even bigger than **huge**:
In the middle of the square there is a colossal statue. | There is still a colossal amount of work to be done. | She received a colossal phone bill. | The war was a colossal mistake.

gigantic
creature | snake | wave | proportions | scale
extremely big and very frightening or worrying. **Gigantic** sounds even bigger than **huge**:
The earth was once inhabited by strange gigantic creatures. | The debt has now increased to gigantic proportions. | This is corruption on a gigantic scale.

immense
satisfaction | pleasure | respect | relief | importance | value | power | problems | difficulties | amount
immense feelings are very strong. **Immense** is also used about something that is very important or serious:
Her job gives her immense satisfaction. | The forest is of immense importance because of its wildlife. | The country faces immense economic problems. | The book contains an immense amount of information about China.

tremendous
change | opportunity | impact | difference | pressure | effort | amount | respect | achievement
having an extremely big effect. You also use **tremendous** when you think someone or something is very impressive:
There have been some tremendous changes in our society. | My parents had a tremendous impact on me. | The organization does a tremendous amount of good work. | I have tremendous respect for him as a scientist. | Four Olympic gold medals is a tremendous achievement.

monumental
task | effort | struggle | mistake | error | moment | significance
needing a very large amount of effort, or very serious or important. **Monumental** sounds even bigger than **huge**:
Clearing up all the mess will be a monumental task. | There was a monumental struggle for power. | Releasing the terrorists was a monumental mistake. | It was a monumental moment when Obama became president.

mega-
megastore | megacity | megacorporation | megastar
used as a prefix, in the names of very big or important things:
Huge megastores have been built on the edge of town. | The singer is now a megastar (=she is very famous).

whopping *informal*
used before a number, when you want to emphasize that it is extremely big:
He lost a whopping 23 kilos. | The film cost a whopping $200 million to make.

human *adj*

belonging to or relating to people, especially as opposed to machines or animals

NOUNS

the human body *The diagram shows all the organs in the human body.*

the human mind/brain *Distances in space are too great for the human mind to comprehend.*

human life *I believe that all human life is precious.*

the human race (=all people as a group) *We are all members of the human race.*

human rights *It is important to respect the prisoners' basic human rights.*

human error (=a mistake made by a person) *Investigators concluded that the crash was caused by human error.*

human behaviour *BrE*, **human behavior** *AmE*: *We study aspects of human behaviour that result from our social upbringing.*

human relationships *Trust is an essential ingredient in all human relationships.*

the human spirit *The film is about the triumph of the human spirit.*

PHRASES

fit for human consumption/habitation (=suitable to be eaten or lived in by people) *This meat is not fit for human consumption.*

humdrum *adj* THESAURUS **boring**

humid *adj* THESAURUS **damp (1)**, **hot**

humiliating *adj* THESAURUS **embarrassing**

humorous *adj* THESAURUS **funny (1)**

humour *BrE*, humor *AmE n*

the quality of being funny or being able to find things funny

PHRASES

a sense of humour (=the ability to make people laugh, or to laugh at funny things) *I'm afraid my dad doesn't have a very good sense of humour.*

sb's brand of humour (=the type of jokes etc

H

that a particular person likes or tells) *His brand of humour is not enjoyed by everyone.*

ADJECTIVES/NOUNS + humour

gentle/subtle humour *His novels are full of gentle humor.*
black/dark humour (=about unpleasant things such as death) *The film is a light comedy but there are moments of black humour.*
dry/deadpan humour (=in which someone appears to be serious but is really being funny) *Sometimes people don't understand his deadpan humour.*
wry humour (=making something seem both funny and sad) *He wrote with wry humour about his time in prison.*

VERBS

see/appreciate the humour (=understand that something is funny) *I was covered in mud, but I could still see the humour in the situation.*

hunger *n*

lack of food, especially for a long period of time, that can cause illness or death

VERBS

die from/of hunger *Thousands of people are dying from hunger every day.*
suffer from hunger *He experienced a hard life in the desert, suffering from hunger, thirst, and loneliness.*
fight hunger *The organization aims to fight hunger, poverty, and disease.*
alleviate hunger *formal* (=make the problem of hunger less serious) *Billions of dollars have been spent on alleviating hunger in Africa.*
satisfy sb's hunger (=stop someone feeling hungry) *Sugary foods are high in calories and do not satisfy your hunger for long.*

⚠ Don't say 'I have hunger.' Say **I'm hungry.**

hunger + NOUNS

a hunger strike (=refusal to eat food as a protest, especially by a prisoner) *He was on a hunger strike in prison.*
hunger pangs (=sudden feelings of hunger) *I was getting hunger pangs and my stomach was rumbling.*

PHRASES

be weak from hunger *I hadn't eaten for two days and was weak from hunger.*

hungry *adj*

1 wanting to eat something, or ill because of lack of food

VERBS

be/feel hungry *I'm hungry – can we stop for a meal?*
get hungry (=become hungry) *If you get hungry, there's some salad in the fridge.*
go hungry (=not get anything to eat) *Life was not easy and we often went hungry.*

ADVERBS

always/constantly hungry *We were always hungry in wartime.*
desperately hungry *The people are desperately hungry and they need our help.*

2 wanting something very much

> **Grammar**
> In this meaning, you usually say **hungry for** sth.

PHRASES

hungry for success/victory/power/profit *He has been training hard and is hungry for success.*
hungry for news/information/knowledge *The media are hungry for news about the royal family.*
hungry for love/affection *The little boy was hungry for love.*
hungry for justice/revenge *The team will be hungry for revenge on Saturday.*

hunk *n* THESAURUS ▸ piece

hunky *adj* THESAURUS ▸ strong (1)

hurricane *n* THESAURUS ▸ wind

hurry *n*

if you are in a hurry, you want to go somewhere or do something quickly

> **Grammar**
> The noun **hurry** is usually used in the phrase **be in a hurry**.

ADVERBS

be in a big/great hurry *She was in a big hurry to get home.*
be in a terrible/frightful/desperate hurry *I can't talk to you now – I'm in a terrible hurry.*
be in no hurry *"Take your time – we're in no hurry."*

hurt[1] *v*

1 to injure yourself or someone else

ADVERBS

hurt sb/sth badly *Luckily, nobody was badly hurt in the accident.*
seriously/severely hurt sb/yourself *A fall like that could kill or seriously hurt someone.*
intentionally/deliberately hurt sb *I would never intentionally hurt anyone.*

NOUNS

hurt your leg/arm/finger/back etc *Ouch! I think I've hurt my back.*
hurt yourself *She hurt herself when she fell over.*

2 if part of your body hurts, it feels painful

H

ADVERBS

hurt a lot *If your stomach hurts a lot, see a doctor.*

really hurt *My ankle really hurts when I walk.*

hurt badly *His head was hurting quite badly, and he wanted to lie down.*

hurt like hell *informal* (=very very much) *It was only a little knock, but it hurt like hell.*

PHRASES

it hurts when/if (=it feels painful) *It hurts when I lift up my arm.*

hurt² *adj*

1 suffering pain or injury

ADVERBS

badly/seriously hurt *Fortunately, no one was seriously hurt.*

slightly hurt *A driver was slightly hurt after two cars collided.*

VERBS

get hurt *Sometimes players get hurt in training.*

2 upset because someone has done something unkind or unfair

ADVERBS

deeply hurt *She was deeply hurt that Gabriel no longer loved her.*

terribly hurt *My mother would be terribly hurt if I didn't call and see her when I was in London.*

slightly hurt *He felt slightly hurt that Ella had forgotten his birthday.*

easily hurt *Be careful what you say to her – she's very easily hurt.*

VERBS

get hurt *Some people don't want a serious relationship because they fear getting hurt.*

feel hurt *I felt hurt that he had not bothered to call me.*

look hurt *He looked hurt when she didn't join him.*

sound hurt *"Don't you like it?" he asked, sounding hurt.*

NOUNS

hurt feelings *David bravely hid his hurt feelings.*

hurt pride *It was hurt pride that made me behave so coldly towards you.*

a hurt look/expression *He saw Tom standing at the door with a hurt look.*

a hurt voice *"Why don't you want me to come?" she asked in a hurt voice.*

hurtful *adj* THESAURUS **unkind**

husband *n*

the man that a woman is married to

ADJECTIVES

a good husband *He's a very good husband and father.*

a devoted/loving husband *Paul was a devoted husband and he often bought her gifts.*

sb's first/second/third etc husband *Stuart is her second husband.*

sb's new husband *She and her new husband bought a house in the country.*

sb's ex-husband (*also* **sb's former husband** *formal*): *My children live with my ex-husband.*

sb's future husband *I met my future husband when we worked together.*

sb's late husband (=someone's husband who is now dead) *Her late husband had been a police officer.*

sb's estranged husband *formal* (=someone's husband that they no longer live with – used especially in newspapers) *She and her estranged husband rarely speak.*

a faithful/unfaithful husband *Unfaithful husbands are often very good at telling lies.*

VERBS

have a husband *She had a husband who loved her very much.*

find a husband *Magazines used to give women advice on how to find a husband.*

meet your husband (=meet the man who will become your husband) *I met my husband at university.*

leave your husband (*also* **walk out on your husband**) (=decide you do not want to live with your husband any longer) *She left her husband after two years of marriage.*

lose your husband (=your husband dies) *Jill lost her husband last year.*

be divorced/separated from your husband *Joanna is divorced from her husband.*

NOUNS + husband

a house husband (=a husband who does not have a paid job, but cleans the house and looks after the children while his wife works) *More and more men are becoming house husbands.*

PHRASES

husband and wife *It is a small company that is run by husband and wife.*

husky *adj* THESAURUS **low (3)**

hygiene *n*

the practice of keeping yourself clean and the things around you clean, in order to prevent the spread of disease

ADJECTIVES/NOUNS + hygiene

personal hygiene *A healthy lifestyle includes having a nutritious diet and good personal hygiene.*

good/proper hygiene *Schools should have policies to ensure good hygiene in kitchen areas.*

bad/poor/inadequate hygiene *Poor hygiene leads to the spread of disease.*

basic hygiene *A lack of basic hygiene causes a wide range of illnesses.*

food hygiene *Anybody who handles food as part of their job must be trained in food hygiene.*

hygiene + NOUNS

hygiene standards *Food factories must meet strict hygiene standards.*

hygienic *adj* THESAURUS ▶ **clean[1] (1)**

hyperactive *adj* THESAURUS ▶ **energetic**

hypothesis Ac *n*

an idea that is suggested as an explanation for something, but that has not yet been proved to be true

VERBS

test/examine a hypothesis *He set up an experiment to test his hypothesis.*

support a hypothesis (*also* **be consistent with a hypothesis** *formal*): *The test results supported her hypothesis.*

put forward a hypothesis (*also* **propose a hypothesis** *formal*): *This hypothesis was first put forward by Einstein in the early 20th century.*

be based on a hypothesis *The theory is based on the hypothesis that man first appeared in Africa more than 100,000 years ago.*

develop/form a hypothesis (*also* **formulate a hypothesis** *formal*): *Researchers developed the hypothesis that there was a link between diet and blood pressure.*

prove/confirm a hypothesis *There is no way of proving this hypothesis.*

accept/reject a hypothesis *Most scientists accept the hypothesis that the universe began between 10 and 20 billion years ago.*

a hypothesis explains sth *The hypothesis explains the observed facts.*

ADJECTIVES

a working hypothesis (=a hypothesis that can be used now, but you may have to change later) *He developed a working hypothesis.*

an alternative hypothesis *No one has been able to suggest an alternative hypothesis.*

a plausible hypothesis (=one that can be believed) *I have yet to see a plausible hypothesis which can explain why this happens.*

PREPOSITIONS

a hypothesis about sth *His research tests a hypothesis about a possible cause of the disease.*

hypothetical *adj*

based on a situation that is not real, but that might happen

ADVERBS

purely hypothetical *The question is purely hypothetical.*

NOUNS

a hypothetical situation/scenario *Imagine the hypothetical situation of going to live alone on an island. Which books would you take with you?*

a hypothetical question *Let me ask a hypothetical question. What would you do if you saw a UFO?*

a hypothetical example/case *He brought up a hypothetical case to make his point.*

a hypothetical problem *The students were given a number of hypothetical problems to solve.*

hysteria *n*

uncontrolled excitement or fear

ADJECTIVES/NOUNS + hysteria

mass/public hysteria (=among a lot of people) *There was mass hysteria when she died.*

anti-communist/anti-British etc hysteria *During the 1950s, the US was gripped by anti-communist hysteria.*

media/press hysteria *Much unnecessary anxiety about the disease has been caused by media hysteria.*

VERBS

create/provoke hysteria *The terrorists are trying to create hysteria and make people frightened to go to work.*

whip up hysteria (=encourage it) *Extremists have been whipping up hysteria in the local community.*

border on/verge on hysteria (=be close to hysteria) *He arrived in a state of excitement bordering on hysteria.*

PREPOSITIONS

hysteria about/over sth *There is a lot of hysteria about bird flu at the moment.*

PHRASES

be in a state of hysteria *Her family were in a state of hysteria because they did not know where she was.*

a mood/atmosphere/climate of hysteria *The government was accused of creating a mood of hysteria about the crisis.*

a wave/tide/outbreak of hysteria *A wave of hysteria about communism was sweeping the country.*

be on the verge/edge of hysteria (=be nearly hysterical) *She was deeply upset and on the verge of hysteria.*

hysterical *adj* THESAURUS ▶ **funny (1)**

H

Ii

ice *n* water that has frozen

ADJECTIVES

thick ice *Thick ice was preventing the ship from moving.*

thin ice *The ice is too thin to skate on.*

black ice (=a thin layer of ice on a road, which is difficult to see) *Black ice on the roads is making driving conditions very dangerous.*

crushed ice (=broken into small pieces, for example to add to a drink) *Serve the cocktail with crushed ice.*

VERBS

be covered in ice *Our driveway was covered in ice.*

ice melts *The ice in my glass had begun to melt.*

ice forms *Ice was forming on the surface of the lake.*

ice cracks *We could feel the ice cracking beneath our feet.*

scrape the ice off sth *He scraped the ice off the car windscreen.*

ice + NOUNS

an ice cube (=a small square piece of ice that you add to a drink) *She put a couple of ice cubes in her glass.*

an ice rink (=a specially prepared surface of ice where you can skate) *The floor was as slippery as an ice rink.*

the ice cap (=an area of thick ice that permanently covers the North and South Poles) *As the polar ice caps melt, sea levels will rise.*

an ice floe (=a large flat piece of ice that has broken off and is floating in the sea) *We could see penguins standing on the ice floes.*

PHRASES

a block of ice *The fish were packed in blocks of ice, ready for transportation.*

a sheet of ice *A thin sheet of ice had formed over the surface of the pond.*

A very large mass of ice floating in the sea is called an **iceberg**. A long thin pointed piece of ice that hangs from something is called an **icicle**.

icy *adj* **THESAURUS** **cold**[1]

idea *n*

1 a plan or suggestion that someone thinks of

ADJECTIVES

a good/bad idea *"Let's have a party!" "Good idea!"*

a great/brilliant/excellent etc idea *It sounds like a great idea to me!*

a nice idea *It's a nice idea, but I don't think we have enough money.*

an interesting idea *The idea sounded interesting, but I didn't think it would work.*

a simple idea *His idea was simple but effective.*

a bright idea (=a very good idea - often used in a joking way to mean a stupid idea) *Whose bright idea was it to build the school next to a busy road?*

a new/original/fresh idea *The company is looking for people who can come up with fresh ideas for selling its products.*

a radical idea (=very new and different, so that people may not agree with it) *He has some radical ideas about reforming the healthcare system.*

a stupid/silly/crazy etc idea *The idea sounded crazy to me, and I told him so.*

a half-baked idea (=one that has not been carefully thought about) *His speech was full of half-baked ideas about borrowing money to help to pay off the country's debts.*

a big idea (=an idea for a big change, or for something new and important) *The government has some big ideas for improving schools.*

the basic idea *The basic idea is that freedom is not free and we must always work hard to protect it.*

the whole idea *I think we should forget the whole idea and start again.*

VERBS + idea

have an idea *He thought he would never be able to escape. Then he had an idea.*

come up with an idea (=think of an idea) *Why don't you ask Helen? She's always coming up with interesting ideas.*

hit on an idea *informal* (=suddenly think of an idea) *Then we hit on the idea of having the concert on the beach.*

conceive an idea *formal* (=first think of an idea) *Edison conceived the idea of a machine that could record sounds.*

get an idea *Martha got the idea from an article in a magazine.*

give sb an idea *What gave you the idea for the book?*

toy with an idea (=think about doing something, but not very seriously) *I'm toying with the idea of going back to college.*

abandon/give up/forget an idea *He abandoned the idea of studying medicine and decided to be an actor.*

reject/dismiss an idea *The committee rejected the idea.*
share/exchange ideas (=talk to each other about your ideas) *It will be an opportunity for local business people to share ideas.*
bounce ideas off each other (=discuss each other's ideas and think of good new ones) *The students work in groups and bounce ideas off each other.*
brainstorm ideas (=get a group of people to all try and think of ideas) *We had a meeting to brainstorm ideas for the new advertising campaign.*

idea + VERBS

an idea comes to/occurs to sb (=someone suddenly thinks of an idea) *The idea came to me while I was having a bath.*

PREPOSITIONS

the idea of (doing) sth *Who first had the idea of preserving food in cans?*
the idea for sth *The idea for the poem came from an experience he had while travelling.*

PHRASES

be full of ideas (*also* **be bursting with ideas**) (=have a lot of ideas) *The children were enthusiastic and full of ideas.*
have the right idea (=be planning or doing something that will probably have a good result) *He has the right idea, but how would it work in practice?*

2 an image in your mind or an understanding of something

ADJECTIVES

a clear/definite idea *John had a very clear idea of how he wanted the house to look.*
a rough/general idea *Can you give me a rough idea of the cost?*
a vague idea *She had only a vague idea of how much her husband earned.*
a fixed idea *I certainly had no fixed idea of what to do when I graduated from college.*
the very idea (=just the idea) *The very idea of eating meat made her feel ill.*

VERBS

have an idea/some idea/no idea *When she woke, she had no idea what time it was.*
give sb some/an idea *I wanted to give you a clearer idea of the business.*
get the idea (=begin to understand something or how to do something) *I'm not explaining it very well, but you get the idea.*

PREPOSITIONS

an idea of sth *We try to give the children an idea of what things were like in the past.*

PHRASES

not have the faintest/slightest/foggiest idea (=not know at all) *I haven't the faintest idea where he is.*

3 an opinion or belief

ADJECTIVES

an old/traditional idea *They have some very traditional ideas about women's role in society.*
a strange/funny idea *I had the strange idea that I could eat and not get fat.*
a false/mistaken idea *He thought it would be easy to do, but he soon realised that this idea was mistaken.*
strong ideas *Parents have strong ideas about what their children should and should not eat.*

VERBS

have an idea *My mother had the idea that being in the cold air was good for you.*
express an idea *Students are taught how to express their ideas clearly.*
support an idea *The statistics supported the idea of a link between smoking and cancer.*
reinforce an idea (=make someone believe it more strongly) *These TV programmes reinforce the idea that architects only design spectacular buildings.*
challenge an idea (=say or show that it might be wrong) *She challenged the idea that housework is women's work.*

PREPOSITIONS

ideas about/on sth *People have funny ideas about computers.*

PHRASES

get/have the wrong idea (=think that something is true when it is not) *You seem to have got the wrong idea about me.*

ideal *n*

a principle about what is morally right, or a perfect standard that you hope to achieve

ADJECTIVES

a high ideal (*also* **a lofty ideal** *formal*): *Most politicians start out with high ideals about changing the world.*
a noble ideal (=good and impressive) *A united and peaceful country remains a legitimate and noble ideal.*
a romantic ideal *Paul gave up his romantic ideal of love at the age of nineteen.*
political ideals *Are you willing to fight for your political ideals?*
democratic/socialist/liberal ideals *The authorities put her in prison, but she refused to abandon her democratic ideals.*
revolutionary ideals *He still believed in the revolutionary ideals of equality and justice.*

VERBS

believe in an ideal *We believe in the ideal of justice for all.*
be committed to an ideal (=believe in it strongly) *Everyone in the party is committed to the same ideals.*

meet/live up to your ideals (=reach the standard of your ideals) *We still have not met our ideal of liberty for all.*

fall short of your ideals (=not be as good as you think something should be) *In appearance, she fell somewhat short of his ideals.*

be true to your ideals (=behave in the way that you believe is right) *Stick to your principles and be true to your ideals.*

cling to your ideals (=continue to believe them even when real life seems very different) *He still clings to ideals of loyalty and friendship.*

abandon your ideals (=stop believing in them) *Have these young people abandoned the ideals of the Civil Rights Movement?*

betray your ideals (=do something that is not acceptable according to them) *He refused to betray his socialist ideals.*

identical Ac *adj*

exactly the same, or very similar

VERBS

look/sound identical *The phones look identical and it is difficult to tell them apart.*

ADVERBS

completely/absolutely identical *The cells are completely identical in all respects.*

almost/nearly/virtually/practically identical *Last week, two different groups of scientists presented virtually identical results.*

identical + NOUNS

an identical twin *Identical twins share the same genes.*

an identical copy *Cloning is a process where an identical copy of an original organism or thing can be created.*

PREPOSITIONS

identical to sth *His laptop is identical to mine.*

identical in size/shape/appearance *The boxes are identical in size.*

identity Ac *n*

someone's identity is their name or who they are

ADJECTIVES

sb's real/true identity *The true identity of the author was not revealed until 100 years later.*

a new/different identity *He avoided arrest by adopting a new identity.*

a false identity (=when someone pretends to be another person) *He used a fake passport to assume a false identity.*

VERBS

find out/discover sb's identity *The police have yet to discover the victim's identity.*

hide/conceal sb's identity *She used a false name to conceal her identity.*

protect sb's identity (=make sure no one finds out who someone is) *Journalists frequently protect the identity of their sources.*

reveal/disclose sb's identity (=show or say who a person is) *The company did not reveal the identity of the prospective buyer.*

steal sb's identity (=pretend to be another person) *Someone had stolen my identity and taken money out of my bank account.*

prove your identity *I have lost all my documents so I can't prove my identity.*

identity + NOUNS

identity card/papers/documents (=documents that show who you are) *Each member of staff is issued with an identity card.*

identity theft/fraud (=the crime of stealing another person's personal details in order to pretend to be that person) *Identity theft is becoming more and more common because of the internet.*

PHRASES

proof of identity (=something that proves you are who you say you are) *You will need proof of identity, such as a driving licence.*

a case of mistaken identity (=when people think that someone is a different person) *When he was arrested, he said it was a case of mistaken identity.*

idiom *n* THESAURUS ▸ **phrase**

ignite *v* THESAURUS ▸ **burn[1] (2)**

ignorance Ac *n*

lack of knowledge or information about something

ADJECTIVES

complete/total/sheer ignorance *Her comments were based on total ignorance.*

widespread ignorance (=among many people) *There is widespread ignorance about where our food comes from.*

general/public ignorance *Many people are unaware that they have diabetes because of public ignorance about the disease.*

blissful ignorance (=happy because you do not know about something) *Isabel remained in blissful ignorance of her husband's affair.*

VERBS

show/display/demonstrate ignorance *His remarks showed a complete ignorance about politics.*

reveal/betray your ignorance *I kept quiet, because I didn't want to reveal my ignorance.*

admit your ignorance *He was too embarrassed to admit his ignorance.*

plead/claim ignorance (=say you have no knowledge of something and you cannot be blamed) *The children pleaded ignorance when I asked where the chocolate had gone.*

PREPOSITIONS

ignorance of sth *Ignorance of the law is no excuse.*

ignorance about sth *Fear was made worse by ignorance about how the disease spread.*

ignorance among sb *There is much ignorance among the public about these issues.*

PHRASES

the level of ignorance *I am always surprised at the level of ignorance about scientific matters.*

ignorant Ac *adj*

not knowing facts or information that you ought to know

ADVERBS

totally/completely/wholly ignorant *He is totally ignorant of the facts.*

blissfully ignorant (=happy because you do not know about something unpleasant) *Many people remain blissfully ignorant about the dangers of too much sun.*

largely ignorant (=ignorant about most of something) *Her mother was largely ignorant of the situation.*

woefully/grossly ignorant *disapproving* (=used when you are very shocked that someone does not know about something) *People are woefully ignorant of other cultures.*

wilfully ignorant *disapproving* (=deliberately not trying to find out about something) *Politicians seem wilfully ignorant about the effects of the war on ordinary people's lives.*

VERBS

remain ignorant *There are still many people who remain ignorant of their rights.*

keep sb ignorant *Anna had been kept ignorant about her father's poor health.*

PREPOSITIONS

ignorant of/about sth *As a city girl, I was completely ignorant about country life.*

I

ignore Ac *v*

1 to not consider or obey something because you do not think it is important

ADVERBS

completely/totally ignore sth *Their evidence was completely ignored at the trial.*

deliberately/wilfully ignore sth *The company deliberately ignored the laws about dumping waste.*

blatantly ignore sth (=deliberately ignore something in a shocking way that shows you do not care) *Some motorists blatantly ignore the speed limits.*

blithely ignore sth (=not take any notice of something in a way that seems rather careless) *The government blithely ignored the facts about global warming.*

routinely/systematically/consistently ignore sth (=often ignore something- used when you disapprove of this) *Regulations about food safety are routinely ignored in some restaurants.*

NOUNS

ignore sb's advice *He ignored his doctor's advice and continued working.*

ignore a warning *Many people ignore warnings about the dangers of sunbathing.*

ignore the evidence *We cannot ignore the evidence about climate change.*

ignore the problem/issue *We cannot ignore the problem of homelessness.*

ignore the fact that... *It is impossible to ignore the fact that traffic congestion is getting worse.*

ignore a law/rule *Many employers are choosing to ignore the laws about maximum working hours.*

ignore a sign *Cyclists often just ignore road signs and go down streets the wrong way.*

ignore sb's wishes *The council has completely ignored the wishes of local residents.*

VERBS

choose to/decide to ignore sth *Some people have chosen to ignore their doctor's advice.*

tend to ignore sth *Such advice tends to be ignored.*

continue to ignore sth *The country continues to ignore international laws on human rights.*

PHRASES

sth is impossible to ignore *The problem is now so serious that it is impossible to ignore.*

sb cannot afford to ignore sth (=you must not ignore it, because there will be very serious problems) *The government cannot afford to ignore the increase in unemployment.*

2 to pretend not to notice or hear someone or something

ADVERBS

completely/totally ignore *I said hello but he completely ignored me.*

virtually ignore *She virtually ignored me.*

simply ignore *The troops either didn't hear, or simply ignored, the call.*

deliberately ignore *The children were deliberately ignoring me.*

studiously/pointedly ignore (=very deliberately) *He studiously ignored her question.*

politely ignore *Unpleasant questions are politely ignored.*

VERBS

choose/decide to ignore sth *Barker chose to ignore her comments.*

try to ignore sth *She tried to ignore the sound of his crying.*

ill *adj*

suffering from a disease or not feeling well

Grammar
You do not usually use **ill** before a noun, unless it has an adverb in front of it.

VERBS

feel ill *I've been feeling ill since I woke up this morning.*

look ill *He looked rather ill when I saw him.*

become ill (*also* **get ill** *informal*): *She became ill after eating oysters.*

fall ill *formal* (=become ill) *Louise fell ill while she was on holiday.*

be taken ill (=become ill suddenly) *Henry was suddenly taken ill and had to go to the hospital.*

make sb ill *I think it was the heat that made me ill.*

ADVERBS

seriously ill (=very ill) *Any seriously ill patients are usually sent to a state hospital.*

gravely ill *formal* (=extremely ill) *She went to visit her grandfather, who was gravely ill.*

critically/desperately/dangerously ill (=so ill that you might die) *He got news that his mother was critically ill in hospital.*

terminally ill (=with a very serious illness that you will die from) *He is terminally ill with cancer.*

chronically ill (=with a long-term illness that cannot be cured and will not get better) *Chronically ill patients often find it difficult to get travel insurance.*

mentally ill (=with an illness of your mind) *Caring for mentally ill people can be challenging.*

PREPOSITIONS

ill with flu/pneumonia/cancer etc *He became ill with pneumonia.*

Other ways of saying that someone is ill
You can say that someone is **sick**, especially in American English. You can also use **unwell**, which is formal and is not used before a noun.

illegal Ac *adj* not allowed by the law

NOUNS

an illegal weapon *He was charged with carrying an illegal weapon.*

illegal drugs *She was found guilty of possession of illegal drugs.*

an illegal substance (=an illegal drug) *Customs officials found an illegal substance in Smith's luggage.*

illegal parking/gambling/hunting etc *The fines for illegal parking are likely to increase.*

illegal activities *They were suspected of being involved in illegal activities.*

illegal use of sth *There has been an increase in the illegal use of guns.*

illegal possession of sth *Illegal possession of a weapon is punishable by a prison sentence.*

an illegal immigrant (=someone who enters a country illegally) *An estimated seven million illegal immigrants are brought into Europe each year.*

ADVERBS

highly illegal (=completely illegal) *He was driving at a speed which was highly illegal.*

completely/totally illegal *The deal was completely illegal.*

strictly illegal (=completely illegal - used for emphasis) *Copying music files is strictly illegal.*

technically illegal (=according to the exact details of a law) *This type of boxing, although technically illegal, remained popular until the 1880s.*

VERBS

become illegal *The drug did not become illegal until the 1970s.*

make sth illegal *She was involved in the campaign to make hunting illegal.*

declare sth illegal *The strike was declared illegal on July 7th.*

do something/anything illegal *I don't know why they're complaining - we're not doing anything illegal.*

PHRASES

it is illegal to do sth *It is illegal to sell tobacco products to anyone under the age of 16.*

THESAURUS: illegal

unlawful
killing | violence | arrest | detention | act | means | strike
illegal. **Unlawful** is more formal than **illegal**. It is used especially when a particular action is considered to be illegal, although there are some situations where such actions can be legal:
The soldiers were found guilty of the unlawful killing of an unarmed civilian. | Anyone who has been a victim of unlawful arrest has the right to compensation. | The money was obtained by unlawful means. | The judges said that the strike was unlawful.

illicit
drug | substance | alcohol | activity | trade | use | affair
illicit drugs, goods, or activities are illegal and are used or done secretly:
Illicit drugs are sometimes used by athletes to help improve their performance. | Some government officials were involved in illicit activities. | The poet had an illicit affair with his half-sister.

Illicit is usually used before a noun.

illegitimate *formal*
use | way
using your power or authority in a way that is not allowed or not acceptable according to rules or agreements:
The report warns about the illegitimate use of power by the US and other countries. | He ***declared*** *that the Council and its decisions were* ***illegitimate****.*

unconstitutional
not allowed by a country's constitution (=the set of rules and principles by which a country is governed):
The court ruled that the new law was unconstitutional. | Critics say that the president's decision was unconstitutional.

Unconstitutional is not usually used before a noun.

You can also say that an action is **against the law**: *Driving a car without insurance is* ***against the law****.*

ANTONYMS **illegal → legal (2)**

illness *n*

something wrong with your health, or the state of being ill

ADJECTIVES/NOUNS + illness

a serious/severe illness *His illness is more severe than the doctors first thought.*
a minor illness *He suffered a succession of minor illnesses.*
a terminal illness (=causing death eventually, and not possible to cure) *At that point the illness was thought to be terminal.*
a fatal illness (=causing death quite quickly) *She developed a fatal illness.*
an incurable illness (=not possible to cure) *The film tells the sad story of a young boy with an incurable illness.*
a life-threatening illness (=likely to cause death) *Doctors say that his illness isn't life-threatening.*
a long/short illness *She nursed him through his long illness.*
a childhood illness *Measles is a common childhood illness.*
mental/psychiatric illness *The man who attacked the painting had a history of mental illness.*
a chronic illness (=that lasts a long time, and cannot be cured) *Diabetes is a chronic illness.*

VERBS

have an illness *When did you first find out that you had the illness?*
suffer from an illness *She suffers from a rare illness.*
get/develop an illness *She developed the illness when she was in her 50s.*
contract an illness *formal* (=get an illness by catching it from another person) *He contracted the illness while he was working abroad.*
recover from an illness *It took several months for him to recover from his illness.*
die of/from an illness *His father had died of a mysterious illness.*
treat an illness *No one had any idea how to treat his illness.*
cure an illness *This isn't an illness that can be cured.*
prevent illness *Vaccines have been successful in preventing illness.*
cause/lead to illness *Inadequate hygiene can lead to illness.*
be diagnosed with an illness (=be found by doctors to have an illness) *Her husband had just been diagnosed with a terminal illness.*

PHRASES

the symptoms of an illness *Symptoms of the illness include vomiting and severe headaches.*
a stage of an illness *He was in the last stage of a terminal illness.*

illusion *n*

an idea about something that is not really true

PHRASES

be under an illusion (=believe something that is not true) *Some people are under the illusion that smoking is a harmless activity.*
have no illusions about sth (=used when you know that something is difficult) *She had no illusions about how difficult the job would be.*
sth is just an illusion *He says that for him, love is just an illusion.*

ADJECTIVES

a dangerous illusion *The idea that we can all stay young forever is a dangerous illusion.*
a grand illusion *Leaders sometimes have grand illusions about curing all the world's problems.*
a romantic illusion *People have all kinds of romantic illusions about life in the country, but the reality is very different.*
an optical/visual illusion (=an image or view that tricks your eyes into seeing something that is not there) *He thought he could see water in the distance, but it was just an optical illusion caused by the heat.*

VERBS

create/give an illusion *The white walls create the illusion of space.*
shatter/destroy/dispel an illusion *Their illusions of creating a perfect society were completely shattered.*
suffer from an illusion *Some people suffer from the illusion that money will solve all their problems.*

maintain an illusion *His parents tried to maintain the illusion that they were all one big happy family.*

foster an illusion (=encourage people to believe something that is not really true) *He believes that doctors have fostered the illusion of miracle cures.*

THESAURUS: illusion

false, misleading, trumped-up, myth, illusion, misconception, delusion, fallacy → **untrue**

image Ac *n*

1 the way a person, organization etc seems to the public

ADJECTIVES

a good/positive image *It is important to present a positive image of yourself at the interview.*

a bad/negative/poor image *It's difficult to explain why the industry has such a bad image.*

a glamorous image *These parties were part of Hollywood's glamorous image.*

a wholesome/clean-cut image (=morally good and never doing anything bad) *The recent scandal has damaged his clean-cut image.*

the traditional image of sth *They want to improve the traditional image of English food.*

sb's/sth's public image *Her public image does not reflect the way she behaves in private.*

the popular image of sb/sth (=that many people have) *The popular image of him as a quiet shy man is not entirely accurate.*

sth's corporate image (=a company's image) *The bank wanted to improve its corporate image.*

VERBS

have an image *In those days cigarettes had a rather glamorous image.*

give (sb) an image *You need to choose clothes that give the right image.*

create an image *The company is trying to create an image of quality and reliability.*

present/project/promote an image *He presented an image of himself as an energetic young leader.*

cultivate an image (=try to develop a particular image) *He was trying to cultivate an image of himself as an intellectual.*

improve/enhance sb's/sth's image *The casino industry was keen to improve its image.*

damage sb's/sth's image *Has this scandal damaged the company's image?*

tarnish sb's/sth's image (=damage it slightly) *His behaviour has tarnished the image of the sport.*

clean up your image (=improve your image after it has been damaged) *The pop star promised to clean up his image after he was released from prison.*

lose/shed an image (=get rid of it) *The party struggled to lose its image of being somewhat old-fashioned.*

THESAURUS: image

image, name, standing, prestige, stature → **reputation**

2 a picture that you see or that you have in your mind

ADJECTIVES

a visual image *Sounds and visual images are stored on the disk.*

a mental image *She had a sudden mental image of herself walking out onto the stage.*

a photographic/television image *His paintings are so detailed they look like photographic images.*

a powerful image *The man's face as he is shot is a powerful image.*

a clear image *I have a very clear image of how Miami looked that day.*

a vivid image (=very clear) *A series of vivid images came into her mind.*

disturbing/horrifying/horrific images *We were warned that the show has some disturbing images in it.*

VERBS

have an image (=have it in your mind) *She had an image of the bunch of flowers lying on the path.*

conjure up an image (=make you have it in your mind) *The word 'breakfast' conjures up the image of a steaming cup of coffee.*

imaginary *adj*

not real, but produced from pictures or ideas in your mind

imaginary + NOUNS

an imaginary world *In her books, she creates an imaginary world of magicians and wizards.*

an imaginary line *The equator is an imaginary line around the middle of the earth.*

an imaginary creature *The unicorn is an imaginary creature.*

an imaginary friend *Many young children have an imaginary friend.*

an imaginary conversation *She sat in the bedroom having imaginary conversations with her teacher.*

ADVERBS

completely/purely/wholly/entirely imaginary *The story was purely imaginary.*

imagination *n*

the ability to form pictures or ideas in your mind

ADJECTIVES

a vivid/fertile/lively imagination (=an ability to think of a lot of strange ideas and things

I

that could happen) *Carroll had a very vivid imagination, as can be seen in books like 'Alice's Adventures in Wonderland'.*

a good imagination *If you want to be a writer, you need to have a good imagination.*

great imagination (=a lot of imagination) *His paintings show great imagination.*

creative imagination *Reading depends greatly on the creative imagination of the reader.*

an overactive/fevered imagination (=a mind that imagines strange things that are not real – used especially when something seems crazy) *These stories are the product of an overactive imagination.*

VERBS

use your imagination *Musicians need to use their imagination as well as their technical skills.*

have (an) imagination *Her poems show that she has a lot of imagination.*

show/display imagination *His latest paintings display a vivid imagination.*

stimulate sb's imagination (=make someone use their imagination) *The aim of the exhibition is to stimulate people's imagination.*

sth takes imagination *It doesn't take much imagination to guess what would happen.*

PHRASES

be a figment of sb's imagination (=be something that someone imagines, not something real) *Were the lights in the sky real, or just a figment of my imagination?*

be a product of sb's imagination (=be something that is not real or true) *Professor Dawkins believes that religion is a product of the human imagination.*

let your imagination run wild/run riot (=think of many strange or wonderful things) *When he writes songs, he lets his imagination run riot.*

be full of imagination *Her stories are full of imagination.*

> **Lack imagination**
> If you say that someone's work **lacks imagination** or shows **a lack of imagination**, you mean that there is nothing new or original about it: *A lot of today's pop music seems to* ***lack imagination****.*

imagine *v*

to form a picture or idea in your mind about what something could be like

VERBS

can/can't imagine *Joe couldn't imagine life without his wife.*

ADVERBS

can easily imagine (*also* **can well imagine**) *I can easily imagine how frightening the accident must have been.*

can hardly/scarcely imagine (=find it difficult to imagine) *She could scarcely imagine what living in such conditions would be like.*

fondly imagine (=believe something because you want it to be true, when it is not true) *He had fondly imagined that she was in love with him.*

PHRASES

sth is difficult/hard to imagine *It is difficult to imagine being in a prison – it must be horrible.*

sth is easy to imagine *It was easy to imagine his father's reaction.*

be bigger/smaller/worse etc than sb imagined *The interview was much worse than I had imagined.*

be what/how sb imagined (=be what or how you thought something would be like) *The job was not what he imagined.*

sb is imagining things (=they think something is true when it is not true) *Am I imagining things or did I see you in town earlier?*

let us imagine... (=used to encourage someone to think about a possibility) *Let's imagine you could do any job in the world – what would you do?*

imbalance *n*

a situation in which there is not an equal balance between two things

ADJECTIVES/NOUNS + imbalance

a serious/dangerous imbalance *There is a serious imbalance between the rich and the poor in the world.*

a great/huge/major imbalance *There is a great imbalance between government spending on roads and public transport.*

a growing/increasing imbalance *The increasing imbalance of wealth in the global economy is becoming a problem.*

a chemical imbalance *Some mental illnesses are caused by a chemical imbalance in the brain.*

a power imbalance *A power imbalance exists between the north and the south of the country.*

VERBS

there is an imbalance/an imbalance exists *At the higher levels of management, there's definitely an imbalance between the number of men and women.*

cause/create an imbalance *Human activity has caused an imbalance in the climate system.*

correct/redress/counteract the imbalance (=make something more balanced) *Eighty per cent of our wealth belongs to five per cent of the people, and we need to counteract this imbalance.*

reduce the imbalance *The president stressed the need to reduce the trade imbalance.*

PREPOSITIONS

an imbalance between sth and sth *The economy is failing because of the great imbalance between imports and exports.*

an imbalance in sth *There is an imbalance in the country's population: for every seven women there are now only three men.*

imitation[1] *n*

something that is made to look like another thing, but is often not as good

ADJECTIVES

a cheap imitation *There are a lot of cheap imitations of the Swiss Army knife.*

a poor/pale imitation (=used when you are emphasizing that something is not nearly as good as another thing) *The new film is a pale imitation of the original movie.*

a good imitation *It's a remarkably good imitation of a real diamond.*

imitation + NOUNS

an imitation gun/weapon/firearm *He had used an imitation gun to rob the bank.*

an imitation diamond/stone *The diamonds were all imitation.*

imitation leather/wood/gold etc *The seats were imitation leather.*

imitation[2] *adj* THESAURUS **artificial**

immaculate *adj* THESAURUS **clean[1] (1)**

immense *adj* THESAURUS **huge**

immigrant Ac *n*

someone who enters another country to live there permanently

ADJECTIVES

European/African/Jewish etc immigrants *There has been a recent increase in the number of African immigrants.*

an illegal immigrant *Large numbers of illegal immigrants try to enter the country.*

a legal immigrant *720,000 legal immigrants were admitted to the United States in that year.*

a recent immigrant *The majority of workers at the factory are recent immigrants.*

a first-generation immigrant (=someone who came to a country as a child or adult) *Her parents were first-generation immigrants from Poland.*

a second-generation immigrant (=who was born in a country to parents who were immigrants) *The boys are second-generation immigrants who grew up speaking English.*

VERBS

welcome immigrants (=be pleased to accept them) *The US has always welcomed immigrants.*

immigrant + NOUNS

an immigrant family *A quarter of the school's students are from immigrant families.*

immigrant workers *Many immigrant workers live in poor areas of the city.*

an immigrant community/group *There are shops catering for various immigrant communities.*

an immigrant population *The immigrant population increased rapidly during the 1970s.*

PREPOSITIONS

immigrants from a country *His grandparents were immigrants from Mexico.*

immigrants to a country *Many immigrants to the United States are better educated than the average American.*

PHRASES

a wave/influx of immigrants (=a large number of them) *A new wave of immigrants arrived in the 1950s.*

a flood of immigrants *disapproving* (=a very large number that arrive at the same time - used especially when you think there are too many) *Some people are worried that there will be a flood of immigrants coming into their country.*

immigration *n*

the activity of entering another country in order to live there

ADJECTIVES

illegal immigration *The Coast Guard plays a critical role in fighting drug smuggling and illegal immigration.*

large-scale/mass immigration *Mass immigration helped to double the country's population.*

immigration + NOUNS

immigration policy *A large majority of Americans want to see the nation's immigration policy reformed.*

immigration controls/restrictions *The party is calling for immigration controls to be tightened.*

immigration law/rules/legislation *Under immigration law, foreign nationals have to register with the police once they arrive.*

the immigration issue *The immigration issue could greatly damage the party at the next general election.*

the immigration authorities/service *The journalists are being held by the immigration authorities, because they are suspected of entering the country illegally.*

sb's immigration papers *The police officer asked to see his immigration papers.*

sb's immigration status *Employers have a duty to check the immigration status of foreign workers before offering them a job.*

an immigration official/officer *Immigration officers stopped and arrested the man at JFK airport.*

the immigration minister *The immigration minister spoke about the government's plans to reduce immigration to more manageable levels.*

VERBS

control/limit/restrict immigration *The European Union has policies to control immigration from non-member countries.*

PREPOSITIONS

immigration from another country *When did immigration from Mexico to the US begin?*

PHRASES

a wave of immigration (=a sudden increase in the number of immigrants) *In the 1950s Britain experienced a wave of immigration from the West Indies.*

immoral *adj* THESAURUS ▸ **bad (4)**

impact Ac *n*

the effect or influence that an event, situation etc has on someone or something

ADJECTIVES

a big/great/profound impact *The internet has had a big impact on people's shopping habits.*

a huge/enormous/massive impact *Industry has made a huge impact on the environment we live in.*

a real impact *informal* (=big) *The film made a real impact on cinema audiences.*

a major/significant/strong impact (=important) *The war had a major impact on French domestic politics.*

little impact *New technologies have had little impact on the overall level of employment.*

a minimal/negligible/minor impact (=very small and not important) *The change in government had a minimal impact in rural areas of the country.*

a lasting impact (=one that lasts for a long time) *Karen made a lasting impact on everyone she met.*

the long-term/short-term impact (=over a long or short period) *Scientists are assessing the long-term impact of the floods.*

a negative/damaging impact (*also* **an adverse impact** *formal*): *The impact on the environment of a new airport would be negative.*

a positive impact *Cuts in interest rates should have a positive impact on spending.*

a disastrous/devastating impact (=very bad) *His leg injury had a disastrous impact on his footballing career.*

an immediate impact *The change in the law will have an immediate impact for consumers.*

the full impact of sth (=all the different effects) *It will take some time for the full impact of the disaster to be understood.*

the potential/likely impact *He's studying the potential impact of climate change.*

VERBS

have an impact *New technology has had a massive impact on our lives.*

make an impact *The product quickly made an impact on the market.*

feel the impact of sth *Many families are feeling the impact of rising food prices.*

assess/consider/examine the impact of sth *Further studies are needed to assess the impact of GM crops on the countryside.*

reduce/lessen/soften the impact (=make it less severe or unpleasant) *The chemical industry is looking at ways to reduce its impact on the environment.*

minimize the impact (=make it as little as possible) *We need to minimize the impact of tourism on the islands.*

increase the impact *Pictures and music will increase the impact of your presentation.*

PREPOSITIONS

an impact on sb/sth *We believe the smoking ban will have a massive impact on public health.*

impatience *n*

the feeling you have when you are annoyed because something has not happened or someone has not done something soon enough

ADJECTIVES

growing/mounting/increasing impatience *He listened to her explanation with growing impatience.*

VERBS

control your impatience (*also* **contain/curb your impatience** *formal*): *You must learn to control your impatience.*

hide your impatience *His mother was finding it increasingly difficult to hide her impatience.*

express/show/reveal impatience *He expressed his impatience at the delay.*

PREPOSITIONS

impatience at sth *He sighed with impatience at being made to wait.*

impatience with sb/sth *Sometimes Joe was unable to hide his impatience with his staff and started shouting at them.*

with impatience *She was waiting with impatience for her husband's return.*

impatient *adj*

annoyed because something has not happened, or wanting something to happen as soon as possible

VERBS

get/become/grow impatient *The band were over an hour late and the audience were starting to get impatient.*

seem/sound impatient *His voice was starting to sound impatient.*

ADVERBS

increasingly impatient *They are becoming increasingly impatient with the slow pace of change.*

PREPOSITIONS

impatient with sb *She was becoming impatient with her husband because she thought they would miss the plane.*

impatient with/at sth *There was no sign of the train and they were getting impatient at the delay.*

impatient for sth (=you want to have something soon) *He is impatient for news about the results of his test.*

If you feel **impatient** because you want something good to happen soon, you often say that you **can't wait** for it to happen: *I* ***can't wait for*** *the summer vacation.* | *She* ***can't wait to*** *see all her friends.*

impetus *n*

an influence that makes something happen or makes someone or something more likely to be successful

ADJECTIVES

new/fresh impetus *The rise in oil prices has given fresh impetus to research into alternative forms of energy*

further/added/extra impetus *We need to find a good team leader to give this project added impetus.*

the initial/original impetus *The initial impetus for the development of the railway came from plantation owners.*

the main impetus *The main impetus towards equal opportunity policies has come from female members of staff.*

a major/strong/great impetus *The construction of a power station will provide a major impetus for the local economy.*

real impetus *Shocking news reports gave real impetus to campaigns to protect children from abuse.*

the necessary impetus *Her earlier defeat could provide her with the necessary impetus to win this race.*

VERBS

give impetus to sth *We hope the new factory will give impetus to the local economy.*

provide impetus *The festival's success provided the impetus for the creation of the Southbank Centre.*

add impetus *The improvement in US-Soviet relations had added further impetus for a US policy revision.*

gain/receive impetus *The peace movement gained impetus after a civilian plane was attacked.*

lose impetus *The business began to lose its impetus.*

impetus comes from sth *The impetus to change a product may come from the customer.*

PREPOSITIONS

impetus for sth *The impetus for change must always come from within.*

the impetus behind sth *The impetus behind these cuts has been the need to reduce government spending.*

implication Ac *n*

1 a possible future effect or result of an action, event, decision etc

Grammar
Usually plural in this meaning.

ADJECTIVES

the financial/political/legal/social implications *Managers must be aware of the financial implications of their decisions.*

the possible/potential implications *He was worried about the possible implications of his illness.*

the wider implications (=affecting more people or society in general) *What are the wider implications of this change in the law?*

the practical implications *We discussed the practical implications of the decision.*

important/serious/profound implications *The results of the research could have important implications.*

major/huge implications (=very important or serious) *The lack of affordable housing has major implications for families in rural areas.*

far-reaching implications (=affecting a lot of things in an important way) *This trial could have far-reaching implications for the American justice system.*

the full implications (=all the different effects) *The full implications of the decision will become clear over the next few weeks.*

long-term implications *Eating a poor diet can have long-term health implications.*

VERBS

have implications *This is an environmental disaster which will have implications for more than one country.*

understand/realize/grasp the implications *The government has been slow to grasp the implications of the current teacher shortage.*

consider/assess the implications *Before you make your final decision, you should consider the implications carefully.*

study/examine the implications *He has studied the implications of recent technical innovations.*

discuss the implications *The paper discusses the implications of the agreement.*

PREPOSITIONS

the implications of sth *What are the implications of these proposals?*

implications for sth *This election has profound implications for the future of our democracy.*

2 something that you say in a way that is not direct

ADJECTIVES

a clear/obvious implication *There was a clear implication in what he said that I was lying.*

a strong implication *Police statements carried the strong implication that the man was guilty.*

VERBS

have/carry an implication *The word 'know-all' usually carries implications of disapproval.*

resent an implication (=be annoyed by it) *He resented the implication that he wasn't doing enough to help.*

PREPOSITIONS

by implication *The article examines the processes by which English, and by implication, any language, is learned.*

imply Ac *v*

to suggest that something is true, without saying this directly

ADVERBS

strongly imply sth *He strongly implied that he would like to leave.*

clearly imply sth *In the interview, she clearly implies that the minister lied.*

wrongly/falsely imply sth *The newspaper wrongly implied that he had been addicted to drugs.*

subtly imply sth (=in a very indirect way) *They subtly implied that she was not good enough to do the job.*

NOUNS

an implied criticism *He was a little hurt by her implied criticism.*

an implied threat *There seemed to be an implied threat that the company would close the factory if the workers went on strike.*

PHRASES

seem to imply sth *The advertisement seems to imply that taking vitamin tablets can prevent any illness.*

do/did not mean to imply sth *I'm sorry, I didn't mean to imply that it was your fault.*

be taken to imply sth (=be understood to imply something) *This statement should not be taken to imply that there will be no job cuts.*

as the name implies *The Cornmarket, as the name implies, was once the place where corn was bought and sold.*

import *n*

a product that is brought from one country into another so that it can be sold there, or the business of doing this

ADJECTIVES/NOUNS + import

Chinese/German etc imports *Japanese imports rose by 5% last year.*

foreign imports *Foreign imports into Britain continued to grow.*

cheap imports *Farmers are complaining about cheap imports flooding the market.*

oil/coal/food etc imports *Japan is dependent on oil imports for almost all its basic energy needs.*

agricultural imports *The country relies heavily on agricultural imports.*

luxury imports *Higher duties were placed on luxury imports.*

VERBS

imports increase/rise/grow *Imports increased by 13 percent last year.*

imports fall/drop *Imports of consumer goods fell sharply in December.*

ban imports (=officially order them to stop) *The organization wants the government to ban imports of exotic birds.*

control/restrict imports *The scheme aims to control imports of cheap goods.*

reduce/cut imports *New investment will reduce imports and save jobs.*

import + NOUNS

an import ban *The US imposed an import ban on several types of fish.*

import restrictions/controls *Strict import controls were introduced.*

import quotas (=limits on the number of imports allowed) *Import quotas restrict the number of foreign cars which can be sold in the country.*

import taxes/duties/tariffs *Import duty on cigarettes has increased by 5%.*

PREPOSITIONS

the import of sth *The import of weapons and explosives is forbidden.*

ANTONYMS **import → export**

importance *n*

the quality of being important

> **Grammar**
> **Importance** is often used in the phrase **be of ... importance**.

ADJECTIVES

great/considerable/enormous importance *Their friendship was of great importance to her.*

vital/crucial/critical importance (=very great) *This research is of vital importance.*

overriding importance (=greater than for anything else) *The question that will be of overriding importance is how you are going to finance your training.*

equal importance *When applying for a job, qualifications and experience are often of equal importance.*

particular importance *Tourism has particular importance in some regions.*

relative importance (=compared to other

things) *Discuss the relative importance of the factors affecting people's health.*

growing/increasing importance *This is evidence of the growing importance of the internet as a source of information.*

international/national/local importance *Crime is an issue of national importance.*

economic/political importance *The role of the police has great political importance.*

VERBS

have importance *This is an issue that has importance for all of us.*

attach importance to sth (=think it is important) *She attached great importance to loyalty.*

emphasize/stress the importance of sth *I'd like to emphasize the importance of reading exam questions carefully.*

exaggerate/overestimate the importance of sth *It is hard to exaggerate the importance of this development.*

recognize/realize the importance of sth *We all recognize the importance of his work.*

underestimate the importance of sth *Do not underestimate the importance of good illustrations.*

assume/take on importance (=become important) *The town assumed importance once it was connected to the rail system.*

lose its importance *The island lost its importance when trade routes changed.*

grow/increase in importance (=become more important) *The country's tourism industry has grown in importance.*

decline in importance (=become less important) *The party declined in importance as new parties were formed.*

PREPOSITIONS

the importance of sth *The article stresses the importance of regular exercise.*

importance to sb *These records are of importance to local historians.*

PHRASES

a sense/feeling of importance (=a feeling that you are an important person) *Sitting behind the big desk gave her a feeling of importance.*

matters of importance *He consulted Lansdowne on all matters of importance.*

be of little/no importance *Where the money came from is of no importance.*

be of the utmost importance/be of paramount importance (=be extremely important) *It is of the utmost importance that this matter is kept confidential.*

be of secondary importance (=be less important than another thing) *It is how confidently you speak that matters; what you say is of secondary importance.*

important *adj*

1 having a big effect or influence on people's lives, or on what happens in the future

NOUNS

an important event/occasion *The Civil War was the single most important event in American history.*

an important moment/time/day *Today is a very important day for her - she's getting married.*

an important decision *Choosing a home is one of the most important decisions of your life.*

an important meeting *He has an important business meeting.*

an important point/question/issue *The important point to remember is that language is constantly changing.*

an important part/feature/aspect *Music is an important part of the life of the community.*

an important role/contribution *Agriculture still has an important role in the country's economy.*

an important factor *Price is always an important factor.*

an important source of sth *Vegetables are an important source of vitamin C.*

the (most) important thing *spoken: You're safe - that's the most important thing.*

PREPOSITIONS

be important to sb/sth *My relationship with God is very important to me.*

be important for sth *Regular exercise is important for health.*

ADVERBS

extremely/highly important *The right to privacy is a highly important issue.*

tremendously/incredibly/hugely important *Radio still plays an incredibly important part in people's lives.*

vitally/crucially/critically important (=extremely important for someone or something to succeed) *It is vitally important for buyers to have accurate and independent information.*

particularly/especially important *Training is particularly important for young people who've never had a job.*

increasingly important *China now has an increasingly important role in world affairs.*

equally important *The father's role is equally important.*

strategically important (=important because of its position) *Turkey is strategically important, because of its border with Iran, Iraq, and Syria.*

VERBS

become important *Combining a career with a family is becoming important to more and more women.*

PHRASES

it is important (that)... *It is important that the patient understands the risks.*

most important of all *Most important of all, try to get as much information as you can about the universities you are considering going to.*

THESAURUS: important

big
day | occasion | moment | decision | game | problem | issue | mistake
important or serious:
The couple have spent months getting ready for the big day. | Choosing the right course is a big decision. | Crime is a big problem.

significant
difference | change | increase | reduction | improvement | progress | number | proportion | effect | impact | role | contribution
important enough to be noticeable or have a big effect. You often use **significant** about things that have been measured:
*There is no significant difference between the two groups. | The researchers found significant changes in the level of carbon in the atmosphere. | There have been a significant number of cases of the disease in Canada. | The results are not **statistically significant**.*

major
problem | issue | part | change | cause | factor | reason | contribution | source
one of the most important or serious things:
Homelessness continues to be a major problem. | Selling goods on the internet is now a major part of their business. | Smoking is a major cause of heart disease. | Oil is a major source of income for the government.

Major is always used before a noun.

notable *formal*
exception | feature | achievement | success | victory | example
important or interesting and deserving your attention:
*Apart from one or two notable exceptions, there are very few women in positions of power. | The Theory of Evolution was his most notable achievement. | The film is **notable for** its use of special effects.*

very important or extremely important

key
part | area | element | role | factor | point | issue | question | objective
extremely important:
Listening is a key part of communication. | Wheeler had a key role in the development of the atom bomb. | Training is a key factor in the team's success. | Cost is naturally a key issue. | One of their key objectives is to reduce the amount of waste. | Timing is key.

essential
part | element | aspect | feature | role | supplies
extremely important, because something cannot exist without it, or you cannot do something without it:
*Protein is an essential part of a healthy diet. | The US is sending essential supplies of food and medicine to the victims of the earthquake. | Oxygen is **essential for** life.*

vital
part | element | role | information | evidence | clue | source | resources
extremely important, because something cannot exist without it, or you cannot do something without it:
*Communication is a vital part of our business. | Forests play a vital role in reducing the impact of climate change. | His evidence was **vital to** the case.*

Vital or essential?
These words basically mean the same. **Essential** sounds more neutral: *Calcium is **essential** for healthy bones.* **Vital** sounds stronger and more urgent: *It is **vital** that he gets the money today.*

crucial/critical
role | part | factor | time | moment | stage | question | issue
extremely important, because without it there could be serious problems. You also use **crucial/critical** about times and questions that are extremely important:
Oil plays a crucial role in the country's economy. | He was worried about losing his voice at a crucial moment in front of an audience. | The critical question is whether this trend is likely to continue.

paramount *formal*
consideration | concern
more important than anything else, so that you must consider it when deciding what to do:
The safety of the child must be the court's paramount consideration (=the thing that most affects their decision). | *The needs of the students are paramount.*

In more formal English, if something is very important, you can say it is **of great/considerable importance**: *Tourism is **of great importance** to the local economy.* If something is extremely important, you can say that it is **of major/vital/crucial/paramount importance**: *Customer loyalty **is of paramount importance** to us.*

important in history

historic
moment | event | agreement | opportunity | victory
very important and having a great effect on future events:

Today is a historic moment for our country. | The politicians must seize this historic opportunity for peace.

landmark
decision | judgment | ruling | case | study | report | agreement | deal | victory | achievement | event | visit
very important and having a great effect on future events, or on the future development of something:
In a landmark decision, the Supreme Court said that students of all races should be able to attend the college. | They published a landmark study which showed that aspirin could reduce the risk of heart disease.

> **Landmark** is often used as a noun: *The case was **a landmark** for women's rights* (=an important event which had a great effect on the development of women's rights).

momentous *formal*
event | decision | occasion | change | consequences | victory | year
extremely important and having a very great effect on the future. **Momentous** sounds even more important than **historic** or **landmark**:
Momentous events were taking place across the Arab World. | This was to be a momentous decision, although he did not know it at the time. | The party won a momentous victory.

ANTONYMS **important → unimportant**

2 an important person, organization, or country has a lot of power or influence

NOUNS

an important person/man/woman *He is a very important man and he does not like to be kept waiting.*

an important customer/client *Japan Airlines is one of our most important customers.*

an important guest/visitor *We are expecting some important visitors tomorrow.*

an important friend/ally *Turkey is an important ally and a good friend of the United States.*

THESAURUS: important

top
man | woman | executive | scientist | expert | job
most important. **Top** sounds rather informal and is often used in news reports:
*He is the party's top man in the Senate. | In China, over 30 per cent of top executives are women. | Who is the **top dog** around here?* (=the most important person - an informal use)

key
player | member | personnel
a key person is very important to the success of a group or organization:
The team will be without one of their key players. | She is a key member of the laboratory staff, with over 28 years' experience.

leading
figure | member | expert | authority | scientist | intellectual | writer | artist | opponent
important and well respected:
His uncle was a leading member of the Egyptian Communist Party. | Professor Cole is one of the country's leading authorities on the subject (=he or she knows more about it than anyone). | *Gandhi **played a leading role** in India's struggle for independence.*

influential
figure | member | writer | artist | newspaper | magazine | journal
important and having a lot of influence:
She worked with some of Hollywood's most influential figures (=influential people). | *Another influential writer of the period was William Faulkner. | Stieglitz was the editor of the **highly influential** journal 'Camera Work'.*

prominent
figure | member | businessman | businesswoman | activist
important and well known:
The letter was signed by 34 prominent figures from the US entertainment industry. | Cox was a prominent member of the Campaign for Nuclear Disarmament.

valued
member | customer
very important to a company, team, or organization:
Her pleasant personality and hard work made her a valued member of staff. | As one of our most valued customers, we would be delighted to offer you our Gold Credit Card.

imposing *adj* THESAURUS ▸ **impressive**

impossible *adj*

something that is impossible cannot happen or be done

ADVERBS

absolutely impossible *It is absolutely impossible to predict the outcome of the election.*

almost/nearly impossible *He thought that winning would be almost impossible.*

virtually/practically impossible (=almost impossible) *Getting tickets for the concert is practically impossible.*

I

well-nigh impossible *formal* (=almost impossible) *It would be well-nigh impossible to police the whole coastline.*
physically impossible *It was physically impossible for him to climb over the wall.*

VERBS

seem impossible *Finding time to exercise can seem impossible when you have a demanding job.*
prove impossible (=be impossible because you have tried but not succeeded) *It proved impossible for the two sides to reach an agreement.*
become impossible *As it became darker, it became impossible for players to see the ball.*
find sth impossible *He found it impossible to sleep because of the heat.*
make sth impossible (*also* **render sth impossible** *formal*): *The loud music made conversation impossible.*

NOUNS

an impossible job/task *He faced the near impossible task of paying back huge debts.*
an impossible feat (=something that is impossible to do) *She achieved the seemingly impossible feat of breaking the world record.*
an impossible dream (=something you want, but will never happen) *For a small club, winning the cup final will always be an impossible dream.*

PREPOSITIONS

impossible for sb *Lifting such a heavy object would be impossible for anyone.*

PHRASES

it is impossible to do sth *It is impossible to know if this story is true.*

ANTONYMS **impossible → possible**

I

impression *n*

the opinion or feeling you have about someone or something because of the way they seem

ADJECTIVES

a good/favourable/positive impression *She wanted to make a good impression on her first day at college.*
the right impression *It is important to create the right impression for customers.*
a bad/unfavourable/negative impression *They say that the film gives people a negative impression of their religion.*
the wrong impression/a misleading impression *The advertisement gives a misleading impression of the product.*
a false/mistaken impression *He had the mistaken impression that Julia was married.*
sb's first/initial/immediate impression *My first impression was that he was rather arrogant.*
the overall/general impression *The general impression was of a well-run company.*
a strong/deep/big/great impression (=one that someone feels very strongly) *Vanessa made a strong impression on me the first time I met her.*
a clear/vivid impression *He had the clear impression that most people were in favour of the idea.*
the distinct impression (=used when something seems very clear to you) *We were left with the distinct impression that the contract was ours if we wanted it.*
the overwhelming/overriding impression (=an impression that is stronger than all others) *The overwhelming impression after the meeting was one of optimism.*
a lasting impression (=one that someone remembers for a long time) *Christina's performance had made a lasting impression on the audience.*
an indelible impression *formal* (=lasting forever and impossible to change) *Alan's wartime experiences had left an indelible impression on him.*
a vague impression (=not very clear) *Dave only had a vague impression of the man who had attacked him.*
sb's personal impression *My personal impression is that the new government has done a good job.*

VERBS

make an impression on sb *His father made a big impression on him when he was young.*
have/leave an impression on sb (=make an impression on someone) *The film left a lasting impression on me.*
give sb an impression/leave sb with an impression *The company gave the impression that they were interested in publishing her work.*
create an impression *Arriving late won't create a very good impression at an interview.*
get an impression (*also* **gain an impression** *formal*): *What sort of impression did you get of the city?*
form an impression *The coach had formed a very favourable impression of him.*
correct an impression *I'd like to correct a false impression I may have given.*

PHRASES

be under the impression (that)... (=believe that something is true when it is not) *I was under the impression that the museum opened at 9.30.*
first impressions count (=the impression you make when you first meet someone is important) *Always remember that first impressions count, so don't be late.*

impressive *adj*

something that is impressive makes you admire it because it is very good, large, important etc

NOUNS

an impressive achievement/feat *Winning the award at her age is an impressive achievement.*

impressive performance/display/results *The team gave an impressive performance.*

an impressive sight *The huge bridge is an impressive sight.*

an impressive victory/win *He won an impressive victory over his opponent.*

an impressive start/debut *The team have made an impressive start to the season.*

an impressive record *He has an impressive record of 21 goals in 27 games.*

an impressive list *The conference includes an impressive list of speakers.*

an impressive array of sb/sth *formal* (=an impressive group) *Among the guests was an impressive array of authors and critics.*

ADVERBS

pretty impressive *informal* (=rather impressive) *The results are pretty impressive.*

particularly impressive *The museum has a particularly impressive collection of modern art.*

highly impressive (=very impressive) *This is a highly impressive piece of work.*

hugely/tremendously/mightily impressive *It was a tremendously impressive performance.*

VERBS

look/sound/seem impressive *The figures certainly look impressive.*

PHRASES

far from impressive (=not impressive at all) *The results of the experiment were far from impressive.*

THESAURUS: impressive

spectacular
view | sight | display | success | result | goal | fashion | example
very impressive and exciting to look at or watch:
There are spectacular views of the ocean. | The book was a spectacular success. | Rooney scored a spectacular goal near the end of the match. | Bolt won the race in spectacular fashion (=in a spectacular way).

majestic
mountain | river | castle | scenery | view | sight | animal | bird
very impressive because of being big and beautiful:
The village is surrounded by majestic mountains. | The golden eagle is one of the most majestic of all birds.

imposing
building | figure | structure | entrance | door | edifice
big and impressive. **Imposing** sounds rather formal and is mainly used in written descriptions:
Delhi is full of wide avenues, beautiful gardens, and imposing buildings. | He looked an imposing figure in his official blue and gold uniform (=an imposing person).

breathtaking
view | scenery | sight | image | beauty | pace | speed
extremely impressive - used especially when something is very beautiful, very big, or very fast:
The hotel has a breathtaking view across the Bay of Naples. | Nepal is known for the breathtaking beauty of its mountains. | Everything seemed to be happening at a breathtaking speed.

awe-inspiring
sight | display | masterpiece
so impressive that you feel great respect and admiration, or you feel rather frightened:
The volcano was an awe-inspiring sight. | Michelangelo's masterpiece is awe-inspiring.

dazzling
smile | performance | sight | success | range
extremely impressive - used especially when someone does something very well or looks very beautiful:
She gave me a dazzling smile. | Uma Thurman gives a dazzling performance as Charlotte. | The show was a dazzling success.

glittering
career | success | prize
extremely impressive - used when someone is greatly admired for their achievements:
Hoffman has had a glittering career as an actor. | The record was a glittering success.

improve *v*

to become better, or to make something better

ADVERBS

a lot *The town has improved a lot since I was young.*

considerably/significantly/greatly *Doctors said yesterday his condition had improved significantly.*

dramatically *With regular exercise, your energy levels will improve dramatically.*

really improve (sth) *Your spelling has really improved.*

radically *The system needs to be radically improved.*

slightly/marginally *In the afternoon the weather improved slightly and we were able to go out.*

steadily/gradually/slowly *He believes the economic climate will gradually improve.*

rapidly *The quality of education is rapidly improving.*

PHRASES

improve with age/time/practice *The singer's voice has improved with age.*

new and improved *They produce a new and improved version of the software every eighteen months.*

improvement *n*

the act of improving something, or the state of being improved

ADJECTIVES

a big improvement *There's been a big improvement in the children's behaviour.*

a great/vast/major/massive improvement (=very big) *The new computer system was a vast improvement.*

a dramatic improvement (=very big and happening suddenly) *With the new treatment we saw a dramatic improvement in his condition.*

a significant/substantial/considerable improvement (=quite big) *There has been a considerable improvement in trading conditions.*

a marked/noticeable/distinct improvement (=easy to notice) *Joanna's work showed a marked improvement.*

a slight/modest improvement *Sales figures have shown a slight improvement this month.*

a gradual/steady improvement *There has been a gradual improvement in educational standards.*

a continuous improvement *The company is committed to continuous improvement of its service.*

a general improvement *The 1960s brought a general improvement in the standard of living.*

VERBS

carry out/make improvements *We need to carry out some improvements to the system.*

see/notice an improvement *Despite the changes, I hadn't noticed any improvement in the service.*

show an improvement *Patients showed significant improvement after taking the new drug.*

represent an improvement (=be an improvement) *A profit of £4.3 million represents a 15% improvement on last year.*

need improvement *The payment process needs improvement.*

bring (about)/produce an improvement *This policy has brought substantial improvements in some schools.*

PREPOSITIONS

an improvement in sth *Reducing car usage will result in significant improvements in air quality.*

an improvement on sth (=something that is better than something that existed before) *This version of the software is a big improvement on its predecessor.*

PHRASES

show signs of improvement *The patient is showing signs of improvement.*

there is room for (further) improvement (=something could be done better) *There's room for improvement in the way we run our business.*

impulse *n*

a sudden strong desire to do something without thinking about whether it is sensible

ADJECTIVES

a strong impulse *Harry often felt a strong impulse to stop and talk to her.*

an irresistible impulse (=very strong, so you cannot control it) *I felt an irresistible impulse to laugh.*

a sudden impulse *On a sudden impulse, he threw the book into the fire.*

sb's first/initial impulse *Her first impulse was to turn and walk away.*

a natural impulse *My natural impulse was to shout for help.*

VERBS

have/feel an impulse to do sth *Rosa had an impulse to tell Henry the truth.*

resist/control an impulse *Gerry couldn't resist the impulse to kiss her.*

do sth on impulse (=do something without having planned it) *Many people buy clothes on impulse and then find they never wear them.*

act on an impulse (*also* **obey an impulse** *formal*) (=do something because of a sudden desire to) *Acting on an impulse, he decided to visit his sister.*

impulse + NOUNS

an impulse buy (=something you buy because you see it and not because you planned to buy it) *She admitted that the shoes had been an impulse buy.*

inaccurate *adj* not accurate or correct

ADVERBS

totally/completely/wholly inaccurate *A lot of what has been written about him is totally inaccurate.*

grossly/wildly inaccurate *The report in 'The Times' was criticized for being wildly inaccurate.*

hopelessly inaccurate *In the 16th century, maps were often hopelessly inaccurate.*

slightly/somewhat inaccurate *The statement he gave to the police was somewhat inaccurate.*

historically inaccurate *Some of the events shown in the film are historically inaccurate.*

factually inaccurate *He complained that the article was factually inaccurate.*

notoriously inaccurate (=known by many people for being inaccurate) *Tabloid stories about celebrities are notoriously inaccurate.*

NOUNS

inaccurate information/data/figures/results *The report was based upon inaccurate information.*

an inaccurate claim/statement *An advertisement can be banned if it makes inaccurate claims about a product.*

an inaccurate picture/portrayal/representation of sth *The report paints an inaccurate picture of events.*

VERBS

prove inaccurate *formal* (=be inaccurate) *The original estimate of the cost proved inaccurate.*

THESAURUS: inaccurate

incorrect, inaccurate, false, untrue, misleading, misguided, mistaken → **wrong (1)**

inappropriate *adj* not suitable

ADVERBS

totally/completely/wholly inappropriate *His comments were wholly inappropriate on such a solemn occasion.*

highly inappropriate *He lost his job after making a series of highly inappropriate remarks about his female colleagues.*

particularly inappropriate (*also* **singularly inappropriate** *formal*): *Wearing red at a funeral is considered particularly inappropriate as it is a joyful color.*

clearly/obviously inappropriate *This is clearly inappropriate and unacceptable behaviour.*

somewhat/rather inappropriate *His somewhat inappropriate jokes managed to offend quite a few people.*

VERBS

seem/appear inappropriate *It seems inappropriate to ask her how old she is.*

be considered/judged inappropriate *This story contains language which may be considered inappropriate for more sensitive readers.*

be regarded as inappropriate (*also* **be deemed inappropriate** *formal*): *The college rules make clear what is regarded as inappropriate behaviour.*

make sth inappropriate *The violent scenes in the film make it inappropriate viewing for young children.*

PREPOSITIONS

inappropriate for sb/sth *It would be inappropriate for me to comment until we know more of the facts.*

THESAURUS: inappropriate

inappropriate, the wrong..., out of place, incompatible, incongruous, inconvenient, unfit → **unsuitable**

incentive Ac *n*

something that encourages you to work harder, start a new activity etc

ADJECTIVES/NOUNS + incentive

a strong/powerful incentive *Competition with others acts as a strong incentive for many people.*

a significant incentive *The high financial rewards are a significant incentive.*

a greater incentive *The scheme gives industry a greater incentive to tackle pollution.*

the main/biggest incentive *The main incentive is the high salary.*

an extra/added incentive *As an added incentive, there's a bottle of champagne for the best team.*

a financial/economic incentive (=money offered as an incentive) *Doctors are encouraged through financial incentives to work in poor areas.*

cash incentives *The scheme gives farmers cash incentives to manage the countryside for wildlife.*

tax incentives (=a reduction in tax, offered as an incentive) *Tax incentives are provided for employees to buy shares in their own companies.*

VERBS

give/offer sb an incentive *If you want people to change their behaviour, it's good to offer them some kind of incentive.*

provide (sb with) an incentive *Good teachers provide their students with incentives to learn.*

create an incentive *We need to create an incentive for people to recycle their rubbish.*

act as an incentive (=be an incentive) *The chance of promotion acts as an incentive for many employees.*

have an incentive *Companies have an incentive to cut their energy use.*

remove/take away an incentive *Some people believe that welfare benefits remove the incentive to work.*

lack an incentive *He lacked any incentive to try harder.*

incentive + NOUNS

an incentive scheme/system *The incentive scheme was introduced to promote renewable energy.*

PREPOSITIONS

an incentive for sb *Awards provide an incentive for young people to improve their skills.*

PHRASES

have little/no incentive to do sth *Poor farmers have little incentive to grow crops for export.*

incessant *adj* THESAURUS **continuous**

incident Ac *n*

an event, especially one that is unusual, important, or violent

ADJECTIVES

a major incident (=very serious) *The most*

recent major incident was an explosion at an oil refinery.

a small/minor incident *An apparently minor incident sparked off rioting.*

a serious incident *The road is closed following a serious incident earlier today.*

a dramatic incident (=unexpected and exciting) *Viewers watched the dramatic incident on the television news.*

the whole incident *The whole incident was caught on camera.*

a separate incident *Young men were killed in two separate incidents on the same day.*

an isolated incident (=one that happens on its own, not connected with others) *Luckily the attack turned out to be an isolated incident.*

a related incident (=connected to another incident) *The report describes a number of related incidents.*

the latest incident (=the most recent in a series) *In the latest incident two men were seriously hurt.*

an unfortunate incident *There was an unfortunate incident when someone dropped their wedding ring down the toilet.*

a strange/unusual/curious incident *Any unusual incidents should be reported to the police.*

VERBS

an incident happens/takes place/occurs *The incident happened as Mrs Edwards was walking her dog.*

cause an incident *His carelessness caused a major incident.*

be involved in an incident *All those involved in the incident were sacked.*

witness an incident (=see it) *Anyone who witnessed the incident should contact police.*

investigate an incident *Hospital officials are investigating the incident.*

PREPOSITIONS

without incident (=without anything unusual happening) *The plane landed without incident.*

I

income *n*

the money that you receive, for example as payment for working

ADJECTIVES/NOUNS + income

a high/large income *He has a relatively high income.*

a low/small income *Rent takes a large part of their small income.*

a fixed income *I'm retired and on a fixed income.*

sb's annual income *Brian's annual income is around £43,000.*

the average income *The report compares average incomes across different European countries.*

family/household income *She works in a shop to supplement the family income.*

disposable income (=your income after tax and necessary bills have been paid) *People are spending more of their disposable income on things like mobile phones and computers.*

gross income (=income before you have paid tax) *The family's gross income has increased by 5% this year.*

net income (=income after you have paid tax) *He was left with a net income of just £80 per week.*

sb's personal income *Average personal incomes rose by about 5% last year.*

a joint income (=that two or more people have) *Between them they have a joint income of less than £20,000.*

the national income (=the income of a country) *A large proportion of the national income comes from food exports.*

VERBS

have an income *He has an income of $80,000 a year.*

receive an income *The tax authorities need to know about any income you have received during the past year.*

provide (sb with) an income *The properties he rented out provided him with an income.*

generate an income (=provide one) *He decided to invest the money to generate an income for the future.*

increase your income *She took on extra work to increase her income.*

supplement/add to your income (=increase your income, for example by doing an extra job) *Ted supplemented his income by doing part-time work in the evenings.*

sb's income rises/increases/goes up *They saw their income rise considerably over the next few years.*

sb's income falls/goes down *Average income fell by one third during this period.*

income + NOUNS

an income group/bracket (=a group of people with roughly the same income) *In general, people in higher income brackets live longer.*

an income level *The tax rate rises with the individual's income level.*

income tax (=tax that you pay on your income) *The standard rate of income tax is to be cut by 0.5%.*

PREPOSITIONS

on a high/low etc income *People on low incomes will get help to pay their fuel bills.*

income from sth *Only 5% of this group had any income from paid employment.*

PHRASES

a source of income *His pension was his only source of income.*

loss of income *You can buy insurance to protect you against loss of income if you are ill.*

THESAURUS: income

pay, wages, income, earnings, the money → **salary**

incompatible *adj* THESAURUS **unsuitable**

incongruous *adj* THESAURUS **unsuitable**

inconsiderate *adj* THESAURUS **unkind**

inconvenient *adj* THESAURUS **unsuitable**

incorrect *adj* THESAURUS **wrong (1)**

increase¹ *v*

1 to become bigger in size, number, or amount

ADVERBS

greatly increase *The city has greatly increased in size.*

vastly increase (=by an extremely large amount or number) *The power of the state has vastly increased.*

increase significantly *The number of students is expected to increase significantly over the next few years.*

increase dramatically/sharply (=suddenly and by a large amount) *The population increased dramatically in the first half of the century.*

increase rapidly *Oil imports are increasing rapidly.*

increase gradually/slowly/steadily *After fourth grade, the amount of schoolwork continues to increase gradually.*

increase slightly *The prison population increased only slightly from 2,800 prisoners to 2,950.*

increase markedly (=enough to be easily noticed) *Violence in the city has increased markedly in recent days.*

increase exponentially *formal* (=used when something keeps increasing at a very fast rate) *Internet fraud has increased exponentially in the last few years.*

increase threefold/tenfold etc (=by three, ten etc times as many or as much as before) *Car production increased tenfold.*

NOUNS + increase

the number/rate/amount/level of sth increases *During this period, the number of car drivers increased by 8%.*

the price/value/cost of sth increases *The price of land continues to increase.*

crime/violence/unemployment increases *Crime has increased throughout the Western world during the past half century.*

sb's salary/income/pay increases *Doctors' salaries increased by 50 percent.*

sales increase/production increases *Sales have increased rapidly over the last few years.*

the population increases *The world's population is increasing at an alarming rate.*

the risk increases *The risk of getting the disease increases as you get older.*

sb's power/influence increases *The power of the unions increased.*

PREPOSITIONS

increase by 10%/£100/a large amount etc *Food prices increased by 10% in less than a year.*

increase to 1 million/£1,000/75% etc *The salary is £18,600 a year, increasing to £23,000.*

increase in value/size/importance etc *Investments are certain to increase in value.*

increase with age/time/speed etc *The risk of getting the disease increases with age.*

PHRASES

increase in real terms (=increase in amount when you consider all other things, especially when you include the rate of inflation) *Pensions have increased in real terms over the last twenty years.*

THESAURUS: increase

go up
price | **cost** | **tax** | **rate** | **sales**
to increase. **Go up** is less formal than **increase**, and is the usual verb to use in everyday English when talking about prices, taxes etc:
The price of coffee keeps going up. | *Costs have gone up by 15%.* | *Taxes will go up dramatically.* | *Sales have gone up this year.*

rise
level | **rate** | **unemployment** | **crime** | **price** | **inflation** | **production** | **demand** | **temperature** | **living standards**
to increase. **Rise** sounds a little formal and is often used when talking about the level of something increasing:
Income levels rose, as did prices. | *Unemployment has been rising in most European countries.* | *Crime has risen faster than at any time in our history.* | *Oil production rose by 24% to almost 26 million tonnes.* | *Living standards have risen dramatically.*

grow
number | **population** | **economy** | **sales** | **trade** | **imports** | **exports**
to increase, especially gradually over a period of time. **Grow** sounds a little formal and is used about numbers or amounts:
The number of people working from home has grown substantially. | *The town's population grew from 3,000 to over 20,000.* | *Vietnam's economy has grown by an average of more than 7% a year.* | *Sales grew slightly during the first quarter.* | *Since 1990, US imports of foreign goods have grown at a rate of 7.7% per year.*

I

escalate
violence | fighting | crime | cost | price
to increase to a high level - used about things that you do not want to increase:
Police statistics indicate that late-night violence has escalated. | The fighting has escalated in recent months. | The cost of the project has escalated from £457 million to £1.4 billion. | The price had escalated from $30 to over $60.

soar
price | profit | sales | temperature | unemployment | inflation | demand | confidence | popularity
to increase and reach a very high level - used about numbers and amounts, or about feelings:
Copper prices have soared due to strong demand from China's booming economy. | The company's operating profit soared by 150%. | The temperature soared to 36.6 degrees centigrade. | After winning the match his confidence soared. | The singer's popularity has soared.

shoot up
price | profit | sales | temperature | unemployment
to increase very quickly and suddenly:
Share prices shot up 30% over the last week. | Sales of their products have shot up by more than a third. | My body temperature shot up. | US workers have seen unemployment shoot up alarmingly in the past year.

ANTONYMS **increase → decrease[2]**

2 to make something become bigger in size, number, or amount

ADVERBS

greatly/substantially increase sth *Smoking greatly increases your risk of developing cancer.*

vastly increase sth (=by an extremely large amount or number) *Rapid economic development has vastly increased demand for water in recent years.*

dramatically/sharply increase sth (=suddenly and by a large amount) *The government was determined to dramatically increase the number of people going to university.*

significantly increase sth *The United States significantly increased the number of US military personnel in the area.*

increase sth threefold/tenfold etc (=by three, ten etc times as many or as much as before) *We have increased our online sales threefold since May.*

gradually/slowly/steadily increase sth *The union has steadily increased its membership, which now stands at over 5 million.*

increase sth slightly *There is a slightly increased risk of cancer.*

increase + NOUNS

increase the number/rate/amount/level of sth *The city authorities increased the number of police officers.*

increase the price/cost of sth *Businesses are expected to increase the price of their products.*

increase sales/production *The company changed their website in order to try to increase sales.*

increase the risk/chance/likelihood of sth (=make something more likely to happen) *Studying languages increases your chances of getting a good job.*

increase sb's power *The internet has increased the power of the people, because governments can no longer control the flow of information.*

increase production/demand *Saudi Arabia increased oil production to 1 million barrels a day.*

increase efficiency *Companies are always looking for ways of increasing efficiency.*

increase speed *He increased his speed to 50 miles an hour.*

PREPOSITIONS

increase sth by 10%/£100/a large amount etc *The bank increased its profits by 13.4%.*

THESAURUS: increase

put up
price | tax | rent | cost
to make prices, taxes etc increase. **Put up** is less formal than **increase**, and is the usual verb to use in everyday English when talking about prices, taxes etc:
They're always putting up gas prices. | Voters expect the government to put up taxes. | The landlord has put the rent up again.

raise
tax | rate | standard | level | awareness | tension
to increase something such as prices or taxes, or levels or standards. **Raise** is a little more formal than **increase**:
The Democrats want to raise taxes. | The bank has raised interest rates for the third time this year. | The new government wants to raise living standards. | The school aims to raise students' levels of achievement. | They are trying to raise awareness about the disease. | Recent events have raised tensions between different racial groups.

boost
sales | profits | output | revenue | imports | exports | hopes | confidence
to make something increase to a higher level:
The hot weather has boosted sales of ice cream. | Cost-cutting helped boost operating profits. | Expanding world trade will boost German exports. | The news boosted the party's hopes of winning the election. | The team's victory had boosted their confidence.

expand
business | operations | trade | range | scope
to increase something, especially the amount of business, or the range of something:
The South Korean firm has been expanding its business in the US. | They want to expand trade with China. | We have expanded the range of products and services we offer to customers.

grow
business | company | economy
to increase the size of a company or economy - used in business English:
He helped grow the business from three hotels to 63. | Cutting taxes would help to grow the economy and create new jobs.

extend
influence | power | dominance | role | range | scope | life
to increase something such as your power or influence, the range of something, or the time that something lasts:
China hopes to extend its influence in the region. | The company plans to extend the range of services that they offer. | The scientists extended the scope of the research. | One day we may be able to extend human life to up to 150 years.

step up
efforts | pressure | campaign | attacks | security | pace
to increase your efforts or activities:
All governments need to step up their efforts to fight global warming. | Congress stepped up pressure on the president to change his decision. | Local people have stepped up their campaign to prevent the airport being built in their neighbourhood. | Rebel forces stepped up their attacks against the government. | Security has been stepped up following the bombing. | The government has agreed to step up the pace of political reform.

heighten
tension | awareness | fears | worries | concerns | effect | interest | excitement
to increase a feeling or effect:
The presence of foreign troops has heightened tensions between the different groups. | The campaign is aimed at heightening awareness about the disease. | Unemployment rose, heightening fears of a slowdown in the US economy. | The attack has heightened concerns about gun crime. | Hunger can heighten the effect that alcohol has on you.

maximize (*also* **maximise** *BrE*)
profit | return | chance | benefit | impact | efficiency | savings
to increase something as much as possible:
Companies are always looking for ways to maximize profits. | He studied hard to maximise his chances of passing his exam. | You need to eat healthily in order to maximize the benefits of exercise. | TV advertising was used in order to maximize the impact of the campaign. | The organization is trying to maximize efficiency and cut costs.

ANTONYMS **increase → decrease²**

increase² *n*

a rise in amount, number, or degree

ADJECTIVES

a big/large/great increase *The company has announced a big increase in profits.*

a huge/massive increase *There was a huge increase in house-building after the war.*

a substantial/considerable increase *formal* (=big) *He negotiated a substantial increase in pay for the workers.*

a significant/marked increase (=definite and noticeable) *There has been a significant increase in violent crime over the past year.*

a dramatic/sharp increase (=large and sudden) *We have seen a sharp increase in the number of vehicle thefts in the area.*

a slight/small increase *The temperature increase was quite small.*

a modest increase (=small) *The figures reveal a modest increase in the birth rate.*

a rapid increase *Recently there has been a rapid increase in fish farming.*

a gradual increase *There was a gradual increase in the severity of her symptoms.*

a steady increase (=happening slowly but continuously) *The university has benefited from a steady increase in student numbers.*

a threefold/fourfold/fivefold etc increase (=by three, four etc times) *The figures show a threefold increase in passenger numbers.*

a 10%/50% etc increase *A 15% increase in oil prices is predicted.*

an annual increase *This is the smallest annual increase in wages since 1995.*

VERBS

lead to an increase *Government policies have led to an increase in unemployment.*

cause/bring about an increase *The heatwave brought about a massive increase in water consumption.*

see an increase *We've seen a huge increase in the number of insurance claims.*

NOUNS + increase

a price/fare/tax increase *The airline introduced a 10% fare increase.*

a wage/pay/salary increase *Canadian workers received a 5.4% wage increase.*

PREPOSITIONS

an increase in sth *School reforms were accompanied by an increase in funding.*

an increase of 10%/£500 etc *The proposed charge represents an increase of £45.*

an increase over/on sth *This is a 10% increase over last year's figure.*

PHRASES

the rate of increase *The rate of increase in the world population is worrying.*

sth is on the increase (=it is increasing) *Knife attacks are on the increase.*

THESAURUS: increase

growth
an increase in the number, size, or importance of something. **Growth** is also used when saying that a company or a country's economy becomes more successful:
Japan experienced a period of rapid ***economic growth***. | *Many people are concerned about the* ***exponential growth in*** *the world's population* (=used when something increases at an extremely fast rate). | *The astonishing* ***growth of*** *the internet has had a dramatic effect on people's lives.*

rise
an increase in the amount of something, or in the standard or level of something:
The latest figures show a sharp ***rise in unemployment*** *in the region* (=a sudden big rise). | *There was a big* ***rise in the number of*** *armed robberies.* | *The company reported a small* ***rise in profits***. | *The majority of families experienced a* ***rise in*** *living* ***standards***.

surge
a sudden increase in something such as profits, demand, or interest:
There was a huge ***surge in demand*** *for organically grown food.* | *The sudden* ***surge in*** *gas* ***prices*** *came at the worst possible time.* | *We have seen a tremendous* ***surge of interest*** *in Chinese medicine.* | *There has been a* ***surge in popularity*** *of this type of dancing.*

gain
an increase in the amount or level of something - used especially in business or political contexts, or when talking about an increase in someone's weight:
The party has experienced a significant ***gain in popularity***. | *There was a big* ***gain in productivity*** *after the new system was introduced.* | *The December job figures show a* ***net gain*** *of 81,000 jobs* (=a gain after other numbers or amounts have been taken away). | *The amount of* ***weight gain*** *during pregnancy varies.*

hike *informal especially AmE*
a large or sudden increase in prices, taxes etc - often used in newspaper reports:
Further ***price hikes*** *are expected.* | *The government is planning to introduce* ***tax hikes***. | *Further* ***wage hikes*** *could affect the company's ability to compete with foreign companies.* | *Despite a 25%* ***hike in*** *fuel costs, the airline made a profit last year.*

a very big increase

explosion
a sudden very large increase in the amount or number of something:
The country experienced a ***population explosion***. | *The book caused an* ***explosion of interest*** *in Renaissance Italy.* | *There has been an* ***explosion in the number of*** *fast food restaurants.*

boom
a sudden large increase in trade, profits or sales, with the result that a country, company, or industry becomes very successful. **Boom** is also used about a sudden increase in interest in something, with the result that it becomes very popular:
Japan experienced an ***economic boom*** *in the 1980s.* | *There has been a* ***boom in sales*** *of diet books and videos.* | *The* ***boom years*** *are over for construction companies.*

ANTONYMS **increase → decrease**[1]

independence *n*

political freedom from control by the government of another country

ADJECTIVES

full/complete independence *The country gained complete independence from Britain in the 1960s.*

political/economic independence *Zambia achieved political independence without a prolonged conflict.*

national independence *The struggle for national independence lasted over 20 years.*

local independence *The new constitution aims to strengthen local independence.*

VERBS

get independence *The country eventually got its independence in 1960.*

gain/achieve/win independence (=get independence) *Our aim was to achieve full independence.*

declare independence *Estonia declared independence on August 20th.*

grant sth independence (=allow a country to become independent) *It was General de Gaulle who granted Algeria independence.*

bring independence to sth *The rebels fought to bring independence to East Africa.*

move towards independence (=gradually achieve it over a period of time) *The country was slowly moving towards independence.*

independence + NOUNS

Independence Day (=a day on which a country's independence is celebrated) *The president was on television giving his Independence Day speech.*

independence celebrations *The region is preparing for Monday's independence celebrations.*

PHRASES

the struggle for independence *The struggle for independence continued for three decades.*

independent *adj*

1 able to do things by yourself, without needing help or advice from other people

ADVERBS

very independent *He is a very independent child and gets himself ready for school every morning.*

fiercely independent (=very determined to be independent) *She had worked hard all her life and was fiercely independent.*

financially/economically independent *His inheritance from his father left him financially independent.*

PREPOSITIONS

independent of sb *Almost every child eventually becomes independent of its parents.*

2 an independent country or organization is not controlled, owned, or paid for by another one

ADVERBS

fully independent *Bahrain became fully independent in 1971.*

newly independent *A trade agreement was signed with the newly independent state of Ukraine in late December.*

politically independent *It is important that our police service remains politically independent.*

VERBS

become independent (from France/the UK etc) *Mozambique became independent from Portugal in 1975.*

PREPOSITIONS

independent of sth *In some countries, central banks are completely independent of the government.*

index Ac *n*

an alphabetical list of names, subjects etc at the back of a book, with the numbers of the pages where they can be found

VERBS

look (sth up) in the index *She couldn't resist looking her name up in the index.*

appear in the index *The name 'Shakespeare' does not appear in the index.*

the index lists sth *At the back, an index lists all the artist's paintings.*

indication Ac *n*

a sign that something exists or is happening

ADJECTIVES

a good/fair indication *The presence or absence of wildlife gives a good indication of pollution levels.*

a clear indication *The heavy police presence was a clear indication that security concerns remained high.*

a strong indication *There were strong indications that the economy was recovering.*

an accurate/true indication *These figures do not give an accurate indication of the rate of volcanic activity.*

a general/rough/broad indication *These responses give us a rough indication of how many people to expect.*

an important indication *Her decision is an important indication of the minister's influence on her.*

a useful indication *This test will provide a useful indication of the child's linguistic ability.*

the first indication *The first indication of the disease is brown spots on the plant's leaves.*

an early indication (=a sign of something that comes some time before it happens) *This was an early indication of what the government would decide.*

every indication (=very clear signs) *There is every indication that the problem will get worse.*

VERBS

sb/sth gives an indication *He didn't give any indication that he knew she was there.*

sth provides an indication *The research provides an indication of what may happen if British summers get warmer.*

show no indication (*also* **not show any indication**) *None of them showed any indication of illness.*

be seen as an indication *A guilty plea is seen as an indication of remorse.*

PHRASES

(the) indications are that... *The indications are that people are becoming more cautious in their spending.*

PREPOSITIONS

an indication of sth *Strange behaviour can be an indication of stress.*

an indication from sb *They were anxious to get a clear indication from the player regarding his future.*

indifference *n* lack of interest or concern

ADJECTIVES

total/complete indifference (*also* **supreme indifference** *especially literary*): *They showed a total indifference to local cultural traditions.*

apparent/seeming indifference *Her apparent indifference to the situation was annoying.*

studied indifference (=deliberately seeming or pretending to be indifferent) *The girls, with studied indifference, avoided the eyes of the boys as they walked past.*

casual indifference *He treated his guests with*

casual indifference and they thought he was very rude.
public indifference *There was widespread public indifference to the president's visit.*

VERBS

show indifference *He has shown nothing but indifference towards his own children.*
express indifference *Thirty-one per cent of those polled liked the statue, while twenty-five per cent expressed indifference.*

PREPOSITIONS

indifference to/towards sth/sb *In spite of his indifference to her needs, Amy loved him.*
with indifference *All too often, elderly patients are treated with indifference.*

PHRASES

a matter of indifference (to sb) (=something that does not matter to someone) *It is a matter of complete indifference to me whether he comes or not.*

indignant *adj* THESAURUS ▶ angry

individual Ac *n*

a person, considered separately from the rest of the group or society that he or she lives in

ADJECTIVES

a private individual (=a person, not a government or company) *Most churches were built with donations from private individuals.*
a particular individual *The writer is addressing a general reader rather than a particular individual.*
a single individual (=one person on their own) *Equipment of this kind is not something a single individual could afford.*
an ordinary individual *Ordinary individuals need no more than 3-5 grams of salt per day.*
a talented/gifted individual *He had taken a group of talented individuals and built a superb team.*
an outstanding individual (=with unusually good qualities) *We need a few outstanding individuals to act as leaders.*
a wealthy individual (=rich person) *Large ranches are often owned by corporations or wealthy individuals.*
selected individuals (=ones who are specially chosen for something) *Selected individuals were invited to the dinner.*

VERBS

treat sb as an individual *Each student must be treated as an individual.*
individuals vary (=everyone is different) *Individuals vary in their ability to adapt to change.*

PHRASES

the rights of the individual *The rights of the individual must be protected.*
freedom of the individual *We live in a society which prizes the freedom of the individual.*
a group of individuals *We need to perform as a team rather than a group of individuals.*
the needs of the individual *The fitness program is adapted to the needs of the individual.*

industry *n*

the production of a particular type of goods or services

ADJECTIVES

an important/major industry *Whisky making is a major industry in Scotland.*
a thriving/booming industry (=very successful) *Software development soon became a thriving industry in the area.*
a growing industry *The company is part of a small but growing industry.*
a declining industry (=one that is less and less successful) *Coal and steel are declining industries in Britain.*
heavy industry (=industries that involve the production of large goods) *Shipbuilding and other heavy industry developed in the north of the country.*
light industry (=industries that involve the production of small goods) *Jobs in light industry are increasing.*
a global/international industry *Market research is becoming a global industry.*
local industry *Most of the people are employed in local industry.*
a traditional industry (=one that has been in a particular area for a long time) *The shipyards, the traditional industry in the Northeast, had closed.*

NOUNS + industry

the car/oil/food etc industry *He works in the car industry.*
the manufacturing/banking/advertising etc industry *The last twenty years have seen a decline in manufacturing industry.*
a service industry (=businesses that provide a service, such as banking and tourism) *Most of the new jobs are in service industries.*
the film/music/entertainment industry *She would really like to work in the music industry.*
the tourist/tourism/travel industry *The tourist industry earns billions of dollars per year.*

industry + VERBS

an industry grows/expands *The clothing industry grew rapidly during the 1960s.*
an industry declines (=becomes less successful) *The shipping industry declined after World War II.*
an industry employs sb *The industry currently employs 2.2 million people.*

inevitable *adj*

certain to happen and impossible to avoid

VERBS

seem/look inevitable *Defeat now seems inevitable.*

become inevitable *War was becoming inevitable.*

make sth inevitable *The country's huge debts made financial collapse almost inevitable.*

consider sth inevitable (*also* **see/regard sth as inevitable**) *An increase in oil prices is now considered inevitable.*

ADVERBS

almost/virtually inevitable *It was almost inevitable that he would resign from his job.*

perhaps inevitable *It was perhaps inevitable that she should see the accident as some kind of punishment.*

NOUNS

an inevitable consequence/result of sth *Disease was an inevitable consequence of poor living conditions.*

an inevitable part of sth *Leaving home is an inevitable part of growing up.*

the inevitable conclusion *The inevitable conclusion is that someone must have been lying about what happened.*

the inevitable question *There is always the inevitable question – how did he achieve his success?*

inevitable problems/delays *Heavy snowfall means that there will be inevitable delays for air passengers.*

inevitable decline *Lack of investment in new players led to the inevitable decline of the club.*

infamous *adj* THESAURUS > **famous**

infant *n formal* a baby or very young child

ADJECTIVES

a young infant *The never-ending demands of a young infant can be very stressful for parents.*

a newborn infant *Newborn infants only a few hours old can distinguish between different voices.*

an unborn infant *Unborn infants can hear some sounds while still in the mother's womb.*

a healthy infant *Healthy mothers are more likely to produce healthy infants.*

infant + NOUNS

infant mortality (=the number of infants who die) *The infant mortality rate doubled during the 1990s.*

infection *n*

a disease that affects a particular part of your body and is caused by bacteria or a virus

ADJECTIVES/NOUNS + infection

a chest/throat/eye etc infection *The doctor said he had a chest infection.*

a serious/severe infection *He was admitted to hospital with a serious infection.*

a slight/minor infection (=not serious) *Alice is suffering from a slight infection.*

a nasty infection *informal* (=serious) *He's got a really nasty infection.*

an acute infection (=one that is serious and develops quickly) *The disease usually occurs as an acute infection of the throat.*

a secondary infection (=an additional infection that happens as a result of the main illness) *He developed a secondary infection and had to go back to the hospital for treatment.*

VERBS + infection

have an infection *Your temperature is often high when you have an infection.*

suffer from an infection *He was suffering from an infection of the lungs.*

get/develop/catch an infection *She got a nasty throat infection which meant she couldn't sing.*

contract/acquire an infection *formal* (=get an infection) *They had contracted the infection through contaminated water.*

treat an infection *Antibiotics are used to treat the infection.*

fight/combat an infection *Your body is trying to fight the infection.*

spread an infection (*also* **transmit an infection** *formal*): *Pregnant women can transmit the infection to their unborn child.*

be exposed to an infection *He was exposed to the infection while he was travelling in India.*

infection + VERBS

an infection causes sth *The infection causes vomiting and diarrhoea.*

an infection spreads *The infection spread to her chest.*

an infection clears up (=goes away) *Usually the infection clears up in a few days.*

PHRASES

the source of an infection *Doctors are trying to locate the source of an infection.*

infectious *adj*

an infectious disease can be passed from one person to another, especially through the air you breathe

ADVERBS

highly/very infectious *The virus is highly infectious.*

NOUNS

an infectious disease *How can we prevent the spread of infectious diseases?*

inferior *adj*

not good, or not as good as someone or something else

ADVERBS

greatly inferior *Iron is greatly inferior to steel in many ways.*

far inferior (=greatly inferior) *He easily defeated a far inferior opponent.*

vastly inferior (=by a very great amount) *The*

I

original software was vastly inferior to the latest version.

considerably inferior (=by quite a large amount) *The product was replaced by one of a considerably inferior quality.*

slightly/somewhat inferior *I always felt slightly inferior to her.*

markedly inferior (=in a way that is easy to notice) *Our equipment was markedly inferior to that of the enemy forces.*

VERBS

feel inferior *She knows so much, she always makes me feel inferior.*

consider sb/sth inferior *Women were considered to be socially inferior to men.*

NOUNS

inferior quality *The poor soil produces wine of inferior quality.*

an inferior position/status *She refused to accept an inferior position in society.*

PREPOSITIONS

inferior to sb/sth *A fake diamond is inferior to the real thing.*

inflation *n*

a situation in which prices of goods in a country increase

ADJECTIVES/NOUNS + inflation

low inflation *France had achieved low inflation and steady growth.*

high inflation *Inflation remained high throughout this period.*

double-digit inflation (=over 10%) *There was a period of recession, with double-digit inflation.*

zero inflation *The government is committed to achieving zero inflation.*

rising inflation *The country was hit by rising inflation.*

soaring/spiralling inflation (=inflation that is increasing quickly and out of control) *Argentina was suffering from spiralling inflation.*

annual inflation *Annual inflation in 1990 was 8.1%.*

price/wage inflation (=increasing prices or wages) *Price inflation was running at about twelve percent last summer.*

inflation + NOUNS

the inflation rate (*also* **the rate of inflation**) *The current inflation rate stands at 4.1%.*

the inflation figures *April's inflation figures are likely to show a further fall.*

VERBS + inflation

cause/lead to inflation *Too much government borrowing can lead to inflation.*

fuel/push up/increase inflation (=make inflation worse) *The increase in food prices is fuelling inflation.*

control/curb inflation *These measures are designed to curb inflation.*

fight/combat/tackle inflation *An economic plan to combat inflation was drawn up.*

reduce inflation/get inflation down *The government has promised to reduce inflation to 3%.*

keep inflation down (=keep it at a low level) *These policies will help to keep inflation down.*

inflation + VERBS

inflation rises *Inflation rose steadily from the mid-1960s.*

inflation falls *Inflation fell by 0.5% last month.*

PHRASES

a rise/increase in inflation *There was a slight rise in inflation due to an increase in petrol prices.*

a fall/drop in inflation *They welcomed the fall in inflation.*

bring/keep inflation under control *They have made great progress in bringing inflation under control.*

influence[1] *n*

the ability to change what someone does or thinks, or how something develops, or a person or thing with this ability

VERBS + influence

have an influence *His works have had an influence on many modern writers.*

use your influence *She wasn't afraid to use her influence to get what she wanted.*

exercise/exert/wield influence *formal* (=have it or use it) *The Catholic Church still wields considerable influence. | He urged Mr Lang to exercise his influence on the government.*

gain influence *The movement grew and gained political influence.*

extend your influence (=make your influence affect more people or things) *Syria had the opportunity to extend its influence in the region.*

increase/strengthen sb's influence *Britain tries to increase its influence by placing its representatives in key posts.*

reduce/weaken sb's influence *The influence of priests has been reduced.*

come/fall under the influence of sb/sth (=be influenced by someone or something) *At university, he came under the influence of Professor Green.*

influence + VERBS

sb's/sth's influence grows/increases *His wealth and his influence grew.*

sb's/sth's influence wanes/dwindles/declines (=becomes less) *The unions are still important, but their influence has waned.*

sb's/sth's influence spreads *Martin Luther's influence spread beyond Germany.*

ADJECTIVES

a good/positive influence *Television can have a positive influence on young people.*

a bad/negative influence *He thought her friends were a bad influence.*

a big influence *The goalkeeper's injury had a big influence on the match.*

great/considerable/enormous/tremendous influence *He had great influence in the region.*

an important/significant/major influence *Parents have an important influence on children's development.*

a strong/powerful influence *The press can have a powerful influence on the way people vote.*

a deep/profound influence *His writings had a profound influence on the Romantic poets.*

the growing/increasing influence of sb/sth *Many people are worried about the growing influence of these websites.*

a lasting influence (=continuing for a long time) *His travels in Africa had a lasting influence on his work.*

a direct/indirect influence *The cubist painters had a direct influence on his work.*

a calming/soothing influence *The music seemed to have a calming influence.*

sb's personal influence *Frank used his personal influence to get his son a job at the newspaper.*

political/cultural/economic influence *French political influence began to dominate the country.*

PREPOSITIONS

influence over sb/sth *These newspapers have considerable influence over their readers.*

influence with sb *They used their influence with local officials to get the water supply reconnected.*

influence² *v*

to affect someone's thoughts or behaviour, or to affect a situation

ADVERBS

greatly influence sth *Living conditions greatly influence the spread of disease.*

deeply influence sb/sth (*also* **profoundly influence sb/sth** *formal*): *His writings deeply influenced many later scientists.*

strongly/heavily influence sb/sth *Marx was strongly influenced by the historian Niebuhr.*

significantly influence sth *His work significantly influenced modern educational theory.*

directly influence sb/sth *The environment a child lives in has been shown to directly influence its behaviour.*

unduly influence sb/sth (=influence them too much) *Critics say the president has been unduly influenced by his advisers.*

VERBS

try/attempt to influence sth/sb (*also* **seek to influence sb/sth** *formal*): *No one should attempt to influence the competition judges.*

influential *adj*

having a big effect on people's opinions and behaviour

ADVERBS

highly/extremely influential *He is a highly influential member of Hong Kong's banking community.*

immensely/hugely/enormously/profoundly influential *Aristotle was an immensely influential ancient Greek philosopher.*

widely influential (=in many places) *His research has been widely influential.*

particularly influential *Within political theory the work of John Dewey has been particularly influential.*

increasingly influential *Political advertisements have become increasingly influential in determining voters' decisions at the polls.*

politically influential *She was born into one of India's most politically influential families.*

NOUNS

an influential writer/artist/politician/member *He painted with a group of influential artists that became known as the New York School.*

an influential figure/voice *formal* (=an influential person) *He became an influential figure in world politics.*

an influential group/organization/body *An influential group of scientists has concluded that global warming is very likely to have a human cause.*

an influential book/magazine/paper/report *'Vogue' is a highly influential fashion magazine.*

an influential role/position *She has always had an extremely influential position within the party.*

an influential factor *According to the study, price is the most influential factor when deciding on which airline to use.*

PREPOSITIONS

influential on sb/sth *Picasso's work was influential on many other painters.*

influential in doing sth *Although she was not a professional politician, her views were influential in shaping government policy.*

I

THESAURUS: influential

top, key, leading, influential, prominent, valued → **important (2)**

influential, dominant, strong, great → **powerful (1)**

inform *v formal*

to officially tell someone about something or give them information

ADVERBS

officially inform sb *The school had been officially informed of this change.*

NOUNS

inform the police *He saw a man behaving suspiciously and informed the police.*

inform the authorities *Barker was released from prison on condition that he did not change his address without informing the authorities.*

inform the public *The public needs to be informed of the risk.*

VERBS

keep sb informed (=give them the latest information) *Keep the school informed of any change in circumstances.*

fail to inform sb *The bank had failed to inform customers of the change in interest rates.*

be required to inform sb *The head teacher is required to inform the parents of any child who will be excluded.*

PREPOSITIONS

inform sb of/about sth *Please inform us of any change of address as soon as possible.*

PHRASES

inform sb in writing *You must inform us in writing if you wish to close your account.*

I/we regret to inform you that... (=used in formal letters when rejecting or refusing someone) *We regret to inform you that your application has been unsuccessful.*

I am/we are pleased to inform you that... (=used in formal letters when giving someone good news) *We are pleased to inform you that you have been selected for interview.*

informal *adj*

1 relaxed and friendly, rather than following strict rules of correct behaviour

ADVERBS

relatively informal (=informal compared to similar things) *The meetings are usually relatively informal.*

fairly informal (*also* **pretty informal** *spoken*): *The atmosphere at work is fairly informal.*

NOUNS

an informal meeting/discussion *The chancellor had informal discussions with other European finance ministers.*

an informal chat/conversation *I managed to have an informal chat with some of the players after the game.*

informal talks *The two leaders held informal talks.*

an informal agreement/arrangement *We reached an informal agreement, but haven't yet signed a contract.*

an informal atmosphere *The hotel's relaxed and informal atmosphere makes it the perfect place for a weekend break.*

ANTONYMS **informal** → **formal**

2 informal language is language that you use when you are speaking to friends and people you know well

NOUNS

informal language/word *It's best not to use informal language in essays.*

ANTONYMS **informal** → **formal**

information *n*

facts about someone or something

ADJECTIVES/NOUNS + information

useful/valuable information *The information he gave me was very useful.*

correct/accurate information *Are you sure this information is correct?*

wrong/false information *He was jailed for providing false information to the police.*

relevant information (=about the subject you are interested in) *Some of the information in the article is not particularly relevant.*

important information *He said he had some important information for me.*

confidential/secret information *That information was confidential and should not have been passed on.*

more/further/additional information *For more information, visit our website.*

new information *The police have received new information about the case.*

the latest information (=information that has been discovered very recently) *We have access to all the latest information.*

the necessary information *This leaflet should provide you with all the necessary information.*

detailed information *More detailed information is available free on request.*

personal information (=information about yourself) *Be careful about putting personal information on the internet.*

financial/economic information *The financial information contained in the report is based on the company's accounts.*

background information (=information explaining what happened before the present situation) *He gave us some background information about the trial.*

VERBS

have information *Do you have any information about coach trips to Oxford?*

contain information *The documents contained top secret information.*

store information *The information is stored on computer.*

get/find/obtain information *She tried to get information about her husband's death.*

get/receive information (=be given it) *It is vital that people receive the information they need.*

collect/gather information *The job consisted of gathering information about consumer needs.*

look for information (*also* **seek information** *formal*): *Journalists going to the building to seek information were denied entry.*

ask for information (*also* **request information** *formal*): *I had written to them requesting further information.*

give/provide/offer information *The booklet gives information about local education services.*

⚠ Don't say 'tell someone information'. Say **give someone information** or **tell someone about something**.

exchange information (=give information to each other) *The meetings provided an opportunity to exchange information.*

reveal/disclose/divulge information (=give it to someone, rather than keeping it secret) *They didn't want to reveal too much information about the project.*

pass on information to sb (=give it to someone else) *He had passed that information on to the authorities.*

leak information (=deliberately give secret information to a newspaper, TV company etc) *A government official had leaked information to the press.*

withhold information (=not give it to someone) *Why did the banks withhold this information from the public?*

PREPOSITIONS

information about/on sth (*also* **information regarding sth** *formal*): *They gathered information about the firm.*

PHRASES

a piece/bit of information (*also* **an item of information** *formal*): *He provided me with several useful pieces of information.*

a source of information *Newspapers are valuable sources of information.*

ingenious *adj* THESAURUS ▶ clever (2)

inhabitant *n*

one of the people who live in a particular place

ADJECTIVES

a local inhabitant *Most of the local inhabitants worked down the mine.*

the early/original inhabitants *How did the early inhabitants of this area live?*

the indigenous/native inhabitants (=people who lived in a place before other people came there) *What effect will the project have on the forest's indigenous inhabitants?*

the present inhabitants *The village includes many writers and artists among its present inhabitants.*

rural inhabitants *The country's politicians have neglected the needs of rural inhabitants.*

the oldest inhabitant *At 98, he is the town's oldest inhabitant.*

PREPOSITIONS

an inhabitant of a place *Most of the inhabitants of the island were related to each other.*

a city/town/village of 1,500/60,000 inhabitants *The road will bring you to Weinfelden, a town of about 9,000 inhabitants.*

inherit *v* THESAURUS ▶ get (1)

inhumane *adj* THESAURUS ▶ cruel (1)

initial *adj* THESAURUS ▶ first[1]

injection *n*

an act of putting a drug into someone's body using a special needle

VERBS

give sb an injection *The nurse gave him an injection to relieve the pain.*

have an injection *I had an injection so that I wouldn't feel any pain.*

ADJECTIVES

a painkilling injection *I needed a painkilling injection in my elbow.*

an intravenous injection (=into a vein) *He had given the patient an intravenous injection to calm her down.*

PREPOSITIONS

an injection against sth *You may need to be given an injection against tetanus.*

injure Ac *v*

to hurt yourself or someone else, for example in an accident or attack

ADVERBS

be seriously/badly/severely injured *Fortunately, no one was seriously injured.*

be critically injured (=be very badly injured) *She was critically injured in a car crash two months ago and is still in hospital.*

be fatally injured (=when someone is so badly injured they die) *Three workers were hurt, one of them fatally injured.*

be slightly injured *The car turned over but, amazingly, he was only slightly injured.*

> **Grammar**
> These adverbs are usually used with **injure** in the passive.

NOUNS

injure your knee/ankle/back etc *I injured my knee playing football.*

injure yourself *You might fall and injure yourself.*

PREPOSITIONS

be injured in an accident/crash/fire etc *Her husband was injured in an accident at work.*

injury Ac *n*

a wound or damage to part of your body caused by an accident or attack

I

ADJECTIVES/NOUNS + injury

a serious/severe injury *Bella suffered serious leg injuries in the accident.*

a minor injury *A man was treated in hospital for minor injuries.*

a head/leg/shoulder etc injury *Thomas suffered a shoulder injury while playing rugby.*

a terrible/horrific injury (=very bad and shocking) *Some of the victims had terrible injuries.*

a nasty injury *The player is recovering from a nasty knee injury.*

a fatal injury (=that kills someone) *Fortunately, her injuries weren't fatal.*

a life-threatening injury (=that may kill someone) *He remains in hospital although his injuries are not life-threatening.*

permanent injury *Even a minor blow to the head can cause permanent injury.*

internal injuries (=injuries inside your body) *He was coughing blood, a sign that he had internal injuries.*

multiple injuries (=many different injuries) *The man was hit by a train, and died of multiple injuries.*

a sports injury (=one you get while doing sport) *She has vast knowledge of treating sports injuries.*

an industrial injury (=one that happens at work) *Victims of an industrial injury can claim compensation.*

VERBS + injury

have an injury *Tom had just a few minor injuries.*

suffer an injury (*also* **receive/sustain an injury** *formal*) (=get an injury) *Her brother suffered a serious leg injury in a motorcycle accident.*

treat an injury *The injury was treated at the local hospital.*

cause an injury *The injury was caused by flying glass.*

recover from an injury *It took her six months to recover from the injury.*

escape/avoid injury *Two workers narrowly escaped injury when a wall collapsed.*

injury + NOUNS

injury problems *BrE* (=when a sports player has injuries) *He suffered injury problems throughout his career as a footballer.*

PREPOSITIONS

an injury to sth *He gave up skiing after an injury to his leg.*

through injury (=because of injury) *Beckham has missed several games through injury.*

PHRASES

do yourself an injury *BrE informal* (=accidentally hurt yourself) *Be careful with that knife or you'll do yourself an injury.*

innocence *n*

1 the fact that someone is not guilty of a crime

VERBS

prove sb's innocence *I am determined to prove my innocence.*

protest your innocence (=say firmly that you are innocent) *When the police interviewed her, she protested her innocence.*

maintain your innocence (=keep saying that you are innocent) *He has maintained his innocence and is appealing against his conviction.*

establish sb's innocence (=prove it) *Doesn't the man deserve a chance to establish his innocence?*

be convinced of sb's innocence (=be sure that someone is innocent) *I am convinced of her innocence – she isn't capable of such a thing.*

PHRASES

proof/evidence of sb's innocence *After her execution, proof of her innocence was found.*

ANTONYMS **innocence → guilt (2)**

2 lack of experience of life, or of knowledge of the bad things in the world

VERBS

lose your innocence (=used when you become aware of what the world is really like) *We've lost our innocence, but not our hope.*

ADJECTIVES

childlike/childish innocence (=which is typical of a child) *Jackson had a childlike innocence about him which was appealing to his fans.*

wide-eyed innocence (=used to emphasize how innocent someone seems) *I'm not sure the character's wide-eyed innocence is convincing.*

PREPOSITIONS

in my/his etc innocence (=used when someone did not realize the truth about a situation) *In my innocence, I assumed that everyone obeyed the rules.*

PHRASES

an air/look of innocence (=an innocent appearance) *The boy had a touching air of innocence.*

the innocence of childhood *There is no return to the innocence of childhood.*

innocent *adj* not guilty of a crime

VERBS

find sb innocent (=decide that someone is innocent) *He was found innocent of all the charges against him.*

declare sb innocent (=say that someone is innocent) *The jury declared him innocent and he was allowed to go free.*

prove sb innocent *Even if I'm proved innocent, my reputation will be ruined.*

plead innocent *AmE* (=say in court that you

did not commit a crime) *He pleaded innocent to the charge of theft.*

be presumed innocent *formal* (=be considered to be innocent) *A person is presumed innocent until proven guilty.*

In Britain, a person does not **plead innocent**. They **plead not guilty**.

ADVERBS

completely/totally innocent *She claims her son is completely innocent.*

PREPOSITIONS

innocent of sth *She was innocent of the crime with which she was charged.*

ANTONYMS **innocent → guilty**

innovative *adj* THESAURUS ▸ **new (1)**

inquiring *adj* THESAURUS ▸ **curious (1)**

inquiry (*also* **enquiry** *BrE*) *n*

1 an official process designed to find out about something

VERBS

have/hold/conduct an inquiry *The government is planning to hold an inquiry into the incident.*

launch/set up an inquiry (=start one) *Police launched an inquiry yesterday after a man was hit by a patrol car.*

ask/call for/demand an inquiry *Members of both political parties are calling for an inquiry.*

announce an inquiry *The committee is expected to announce an inquiry into deaths at the hospital.*

ADJECTIVES/NOUNS + inquiry

an official/government inquiry *There will be an official inquiry into the causes of the riots.*

a public inquiry *MPs are demanding a public inquiry into the accident.*

an independent inquiry *The Labour Party is calling for an independent inquiry into the conduct of the police.*

a police inquiry *The case has been reopened with a police inquiry.*

a judicial inquiry (=led by a judge) *Some politicians are calling for a judicial inquiry into the affair.*

an accident/murder inquiry *The accident inquiry revealed that the accident had been caused by human error.*

PREPOSITIONS

an inquiry into sth *Will there be an inquiry into the plane crash?*

2 a question you ask in order to get information

VERBS

make an inquiry *The police are making inquiries in the area to see if anyone witnessed the incident.*

get/have/receive an inquiry *We've already had a lot of inquiries about the course.*

deal with/handle an inquiry *Staff will be available to deal with inquiries.*

answer an inquiry (*also* **respond to an inquiry** *formal*): *The company has not yet answered our inquiry.*

ADJECTIVES

a general inquiry *Reception staff can answer general inquiries only.*

a written inquiry *I made a written inquiry to the local council.*

PREPOSITIONS

inquiries about sth *We've received hundreds of inquiries about the new tax.*

inquiries from sb *Phone inquiries from members of the public come to this office.*

PHRASES

a flood/stream of inquiries *The special offer has produced a flood of inquiries from interested customers.*

inquisitive *adj* THESAURUS ▸ **curious (1)**

insane *adj* THESAURUS ▸ **crazy**

insect *n*

a small creature with six legs, such as a fly or an ant

ADJECTIVES

a small/tiny insect *The bird's natural diet mainly consists of small insects.*

a flying/winged insect *The air was filled with thousands of flying insects.*

VERBS

an insect flies *Insects were flying around the food on the counter.*

an insect crawls (=moves along the ground) *A tiny insect was crawling up his arm.*

an insect buzzes (=makes a continuous sound, like a bee) *In the forest, insects buzzed around our heads.*

insect + NOUNS

an insect bite/sting *He had a large red insect bite on his back.*

insect repellent (=a chemical to keep insects away) *If you go camping, you should take some insect repellent.*

inspection Ac *n*

an examination of something, usually to check that it is satisfactory

ADJECTIVES

a careful/detailed/thorough inspection *An architect will make a detailed inspection of the building.*

an official inspection *The school was preparing for an official inspection.*

an annual inspection *The building is due for its annual safety inspection.*

a routine inspection (=an ordinary one that happens regularly) *A routine inspection revealed that the machine was not functioning correctly.*

regular/frequent inspections *Restaurants are subject to regular health inspections.*

a full inspection *A full inspection of the site has been conducted.*

a brief inspection (*also* **a cursory inspection** *formal*) (=very quick and not very careful) *He gave the truck only a cursory inspection.*

a random inspection (=not done regularly, but at any time) *Random inspections are carried out on restaurants to ensure that they meet food hygiene standards.*

VERBS

do/make/carry out an inspection *Engineers had carried out an inspection on the plane.*

conduct/perform/undertake an inspection *formal* (=make an inspection) *Experts conducted a thorough inspection of the site of the crash.*

arrange/organize an inspection *The head teacher has arranged a uniform inspection.*

have an inspection (*also* **undergo an inspection** *formal*): *Boats carrying more than 12 passengers on international voyages must undergo an inspection each year.*

pass/fail an inspection *The shop will have to pass a hygiene inspection.*

complete/finish an inspection *When the inspection is finished, these forms must be filled in.*

an inspection shows/reveals sth *The inspection revealed several safety problems at the factory.*

NOUNS + inspection

a safety/health inspection *A safety inspection was carried out on the boiler system.*

inspection + NOUNS

an inspection visit *An inspection visit will be made by officials from the education department.*

an inspection team *The inspection team described the school as 'outstanding'.*

PHRASES

on close/closer/further inspection (=after examining something carefully) *On closer inspection, the painting turned out to be a fake.*

a tour of inspection (=an official visit to inspect something) *Building control officers arrived on the site for a tour of inspection.*

be available/ready for inspection *The troops are ready for inspection.*

inspiration *n*

a sudden good idea, or someone or something that gives you the idea

VERBS

get inspiration from sth *I got the inspiration for this dish from my holiday in Thailand.*

take/draw inspiration from sth (*also* **derive inspiration from sth** *formal*) (=get inspiration) *Many writers draw inspiration from old folk tales.*

find inspiration in sth *She often finds inspiration in nature.*

look for inspiration (*also* **seek inspiration** *formal*): *The artist sought inspiration in the medieval carvings in this cathedral.*

have an inspiration (=suddenly have an idea) *She had an inspiration while she was taking a walk.*

lack inspiration (=not have any good or interesting ideas) *He sat down to plan the party, but lacked inspiration.*

provide inspiration for sth *This landscape provided the inspiration for a famous children's book.*

sb's inspiration comes from sb/sth *Where did your inspiration for this design come from?*

ADJECTIVES

artistic/creative/poetic etc inspiration *Where do you get your artistic inspiration?*

a great inspiration *My mother was a great inspiration to me.*

a sudden inspiration *I had a sudden inspiration.*

fresh inspiration (=new inspiration) *Her travels provided fresh inspiration for her painting.*

direct inspiration (=in which someone takes an idea directly from a person or thing) *She took direct inspiration from the films of John Ford.*

divine inspiration (=inspiration from God) *He prayed for divine inspiration.*

PREPOSITIONS

inspiration for sth *Inspiration for the paintings came from a recent trip to New York.*

inspiration behind sth *Daniel Marks was the inspiration behind the show.*

an inspiration to sb (=giving someone ideas, confidence, or enthusiasm) *She's a wonderful teacher who has been an inspiration to many students.*

PHRASES

a flash/moment of inspiration (=a sudden good idea) *A sudden flash of inspiration came to him.*

a source of inspiration for/to sb *His success was a source of inspiration for many Africans.*

instance *n*

an example of a particular type of situation

ADJECTIVES

many/several instances (*also* **a number of instances**) *Several instances of theft from college buildings have been reported recently.*

countless/numerous/innumerable instances (=a very large number) *Countless instances of human rights abuses have occurred.*

a few instances *There have only been a few instances of students being caught cheating in exams.*

a rare/occasional instance (*also* **an isolated instance** *formal*): *The floods this month are unlikely to be an isolated instance.*

the only instance/a single instance *Fortunately that was the only instance of racism I came across.*

a particular/specific/certain instance *He couldn't think of any specific instances when she had been behaving strangely.*

VERBS

give/provide an instance of sth *History has provided many instances where technology has changed the way we communicate.*

remember/recall an instance *I remember an instance when he turned up two hours late for work.*

an instance occurs *formal*: *Whenever an instance of bullying occurs, it is taken very seriously by the college authorities.*

PHRASES

for instance (=used when giving an example) *We need to rethink the way we consume energy. Take, for instance, our approach to transport.*

in this instance *In this instance I think she was mistaken.*

in one instance *In one instance, a man was arrested for the theft of a bottle of whiskey from a liquor shop.*

instinct *n*

a natural tendency to behave in a particular way or a natural ability to know something

ADJECTIVES/NOUNS + instinct

a basic instinct *The will to survive is the most basic instinct that we have.*

sb's gut instinct (=one that you feel sure is right, although you have no reason for this) *Her gut instinct about Jimmy had been right - he was a liar.*

sb's first/initial instinct *His first instinct was to run away.*

a natural instinct *I thought I could find my way back using my natural instinct.*

a deep/strong/powerful instinct *A deep instinct told me not to trust him.*

human/animal instinct *It's a natural human instinct to comfort someone who is unhappy.*

the maternal instinct (=the instinct of a mother) *Your maternal instinct makes you want to care for a baby.*

VERBS

trust/rely on your instinct(s) *I've trusted my instincts in the past and they've usually been right.*

follow/obey your instinct(s) (*also* **go on your instincts** *informal*): *You should follow your instincts when dealing with strangers.*

have an instinct *She has a good instinct for business.*

your instinct tells you sth *Every instinct told her that he was not to be trusted.*

institution Ac *n*

a large organization such as a bank, university, or church

ADJECTIVES/NOUNS + institution

a national/international institution *Many national institutions and private galleries organize exhibitions of foreign works of art.*

a financial/economic/banking institution *They had received loans from several financial institutions.*

a government/state institution *Once in power, the armed forces immediately abolished all state institutions.*

a large/major/important institution *He has held key roles at major banking institutions.*

a powerful institution *The Catholic Church is the most powerful institution in the country.*

a prestigious/venerable institution (=a respected institution) *Its students were routinely accepted at Harvard and other prestigious institutions.*

an academic/educational institution *It was the first academic institution in Britain to offer a degree course in golf.*

a scientific/research institution *One of the UK's major scientific institutions, the Royal Society, was founded in 1660.*

a political/cultural institution *Each state has its own political institutions.*

a religious institution *Religious institutions such as monasteries were extremely powerful at that time.*

a public/private institution *Public institutions are suffering cutbacks.*

VERBS

found/set up an institution *The institution was founded in 1919 by Henry Huntington.*

fund an institution (=provide the money for it) *The College is a publicly funded institution.*

instruction Ac *n*

1 written information that tells you how to do or use something

> **Grammar**
> Usually plural in this meaning, except when used before another noun.

VERBS

follow the instructions (=do what they tell you to do) *You should follow the instructions on the packet.*

read the instructions *Always read the instructions before switching on the machine.*

come with instructions *The tent comes with instructions on how to put it up.*

the instructions say sth (*also* **the instructions tell you to do sth**) *The instructions say that you should take the tablets after meals.*

ADJECTIVES/NOUNS + instruction

clear instructions *The instructions that I got with the phone weren't very clear.*

detailed instructions *There are detailed instructions on the back of the box.*

written instructions *Each member of the team was issued with written instructions.*

full/comprehensive instructions (=very detailed) *There are comprehensive instructions for completing the new tax form.*

step-by-step instructions (=giving details of each thing you should do in order) *This book gives step-by-step instructions for making curtains.*

the manufacturer's instructions (=given by the company that made something) *Make up the mixture according to the manufacturer's instructions.*

the operating instructions *The operating instructions have been simplified so that they are easier to follow.*

instruction + NOUNS

an instruction book/manual *The instruction manual for the camera is over 150 pages long.*

an instruction booklet/leaflet/sheet *The washing machine comes with an instruction leaflet.*

PREPOSITIONS

instructions on (doing) sth *He gave us clear instructions on opening the parachute.*

instructions for (doing) sth *Where are the instructions for the printer?*

2 a statement telling someone what they must do

> **Grammar**
> Usually plural in this meaning.

VERBS

give sb instructions/issue sb with instructions *I gave him clear instructions not to spend any more money.*

follow/obey instructions (*also* **act on instructions**) (=do what someone tells you to do) *It was not my decision; I was simply following instructions.*

disobey/disregard sb's instructions *I was angry because she had deliberately disobeyed my instructions.*

leave instructions *He left strict instructions saying that he was not to be disturbed.*

receive instructions *The lawyer has received no instructions from his client.*

await instructions *formal* (=wait for someone to give you instructions) *The staff are awaiting instructions from the manager.*

ADJECTIVES

specific/explicit instructions (=clear and giving details) *I gave you explicit instructions about where to leave the package.*

strict instructions (=which must be followed) *Workers have received strict instructions not to speak to journalists.*

further instructions (=more instructions) *We were told to go home and await further instructions.*

PREPOSITIONS

instructions from sb *Military leaders have received no instructions from the president.*

be under instructions to do sth (=someone has told you that you must do something) *The players are under instructions to drink no alcohol for the next two weeks.*

instructor [Ac] *n*

someone who teaches a sport or practical skill

ADJECTIVES/NOUNS + instructor

a qualified instructor *She is a qualified aerobics instructor.*

a driving/riding/swimming/flying etc instructor *Her driving instructor told her she was driving too fast.*

a ski instructor *The ski instructor showed them how to go down the ski slope.*

an aerobics/yoga/fitness instructor *She now has her own personal fitness instructor.*

instrument *n*

an object used for producing music, such as a piano or violin

VERBS

play an instrument *Can you play a musical instrument?*

learn to play an instrument (*also* **learn an instrument**) *All students at the school have the opportunity to learn an instrument.*

tune an instrument (=make small changes so that it plays exactly the right notes) *The members of the orchestra were tuning their instruments before the concert.*

ADJECTIVES/NOUNS + instrument

a musical instrument *She owns a shop that sells musical instruments.*

a wind/woodwind instrument (=such as a flute or saxophone) *I like the sound of flutes and other wind instruments.*

a brass instrument (=such as a trumpet or trombone) *The tuba is the deepest of the brass instruments.*

a string/stringed instrument *He plays the violin and some other string instruments.*

an electronic instrument *An electronic instrument requires no tuning.*

THESAURUS: instrument
implement, instrument, utensil, gadget → **tool (1)**

insult *n*

a remark or action that is offensive or deliberately rude

VERBS

shout/hurl insults at sb *He was drunk and started shouting insults at us.*

take sth as an insult (=think it is an insult) *He took the comparison to the older writer as an insult.*

mean sth as an insult *I didn't mean it as an insult.*

people trade/exchange insults (=insult each other) *Supporters of both sides traded insults.*

ADJECTIVES

a personal insult *He took my remark as a personal insult.*

a great/terrible insult *In their culture, it is a great insult to refuse food that is offered to you.*

the ultimate/worst/greatest insult *Being called weak was the ultimate insult.*

a deliberate/calculated insult *It was a deliberate insult, and I will never forgive him for it.*

a racial/racist insult *Racial insults in sport will not be tolerated.*

PREPOSITIONS

an insult to sb/sth *Not preparing properly is an insult to your audience.*

PHRASES

an exchange of insults *The fight between the two men began with an exchange of insults.*

The final insult
You use this phrase about the last and most annoying of a series of things that happened to you: ***The final insult*** *was that they later claimed they had never received my complaint.*

insurance *n*

an arrangement in which a company pays you money if something bad happens

ADJECTIVES/NOUNS + insurance

health/medical insurance *Many families cannot afford private health insurance.*

life insurance (=paid to someone's family when they die) *When her husband died, she discovered that he had no life insurance.*

travel insurance *The bank can also arrange travel insurance.*

car/motor insurance *He was fined for driving without motor insurance.*

house/home insurance *The damage may be covered by your house insurance.*

VERBS

have insurance *Do you have insurance for your boat?*

get/take out insurance (=buy insurance) *It is wise to take out insurance on your house and its contents.*

claim on your insurance (=ask an insurance company to pay for something) *She has never claimed on her car insurance.*

insurance covers sth (=it includes something) *Flood damage isn't covered by the insurance.*

insurance pays for sth *His insurance paid for the damage to the car.*

insurance + NOUNS

an insurance policy (=an insurance agreement) *Check if your insurance policy covers damage to cameras.*

an insurance claim *She filed an insurance claim for the missing jewellery.*

insurance cover (=protection by insurance in case something happens) *The scheme provides full insurance cover for medical conditions.*

an insurance company *They are one of the biggest insurance companies in the country.*

an insurance scheme *An insurance scheme is available in case you lose your job.*

an insurance premium/payment (=money that you pay regularly to an insurance company) *Your insurance premium must be paid when you book your holiday.*

an insurance broker (=a person or firm that sells insurance to people on behalf of insurance companies) *Speak to an insurance broker about the right policy for you.*

intellectual[1] *adj*

relating to the ability to understand things and think intelligently

NOUNS

intellectual ability *Women were considered inferior in intellectual ability to men.*

sb's intellectual development *What factors influence children's intellectual development?*

intellectual curiosity *Learning by rote can kill students' intellectual curiosity.*

intellectual activity/work *All forms of intellectual activity were tightly controlled by the state.*

intellectual freedom *The universities were determined to defend their intellectual freedom.*

intellectual life *His work had a great influence on the intellectual life of Spain.*

an intellectual level *I knew I was not on the same intellectual level as her.*

an intellectual challenge *He enjoys the intellectual challenge of research.*

intellectual effort *Solving this puzzle requires a lot of intellectual effort.*

intellectual² *n*

a well-educated person who is interested in art, science, philosophy etc at a very high level

ADJECTIVES

a leading/prominent intellectual (=important and well known) *The plan was supported by leading intellectuals and religious figures.*

a dissident intellectual (=who disagrees with government policies) *Odinga was among six dissident intellectuals who were arrested by the police.*

a left-wing/right-wing intellectual *A group of 150 left-wing intellectuals announced plans to form a Marxist party.*

intelligence Ac *n*

the ability to learn, understand, and think about things

ADJECTIVES

great/considerable intelligence *His mother was a woman of great intelligence.*

high intelligence *He was of high intelligence and did well at school.*

average/normal intelligence *The forms should be able to be understood by a person of average intelligence.*

low/limited intelligence *He claimed that most criminals were of low intelligence.*

quick intelligence *Miller was impressed by his quick intelligence.*

native/natural intelligence (=that someone has naturally, not as a result of education or training) *He had arrived in California with nothing but his native intelligence and capacity for hard work.*

VERBS

use your intelligence *People had to use their intelligence in order to survive.*

have the intelligence to do sth *He had the intelligence to wait to see what their reaction would be.*

show intelligence *The fact that the animal is using a rock as a tool to break the nuts shows intelligence.*

intelligence + NOUNS

an intelligence test *He achieved high scores on intelligence tests.*

PHRASES

be a sign of intelligence *Asking lots of questions is a sign of intelligence in a child.*

a man/woman of intelligence (=an intelligent person) *He was obviously a man of intelligence.*

intelligent Ac *adj*

having a high level of mental ability and good at understanding difficult ideas

NOUNS

an intelligent man/woman/boy/girl/person *He was a well-educated and intelligent man with a sharp sense of humor.*

an intelligent animal/creature *Pigs are very intelligent animals.*

intelligent life/beings (=from another planet or universe) *Do you think there is intelligent life elsewhere in the universe?*

an intelligent question/conversation/comment (=which shows you understand something well) *The students asked some intelligent questions.*

ADVERBS

highly/extremely intelligent *People who are highly intelligent are not always good team workers.*

THESAURUS: intelligent

clever *especially BrE*
man | woman | boy | girl | child | idea | way | trick | lawyer | politician
good at learning and understanding things quickly, and using your intelligence to do things. You also use **clever** about ideas and ways of doing something that seem effective and good:
"He's a very clever man, and a dangerous enemy," said Holmes. | The book is full of clever ways of saving money. | She had a clever lawyer at her trial, and was never punished for the murder.

Intelligent or clever?
Intelligent sounds more neutral and is used when talking about someone's level of mental ability. You say *Chimpanzees are highly **intelligent** animals* (not 'clever' ones).
You use **clever** about someone who is good at using their intelligence to do things. **Clever** is often used about someone who is also slightly dishonest. You say *a **clever** lawyer/politician* (not an 'intelligent' one).
You use **clever** about ideas and methods. You say *What a **clever** idea!* (not an 'intelligent' one).

smart *especially AmE*
guy | kid | move | idea
smart means the same as **clever**:
My boss is a pretty smart guy. | He's a smart kid who works hard. | Selling the shares was a smart move (=a clever thing to do). | *Monroe was a **smart cookie**, even though she pretended to be dumb* (=a clever person - an informal use).

Smart or clever?
These words mean the same. **Clever** is more common in British English. In American English, people usually say **smart**.

bright
student | **pupil** | **young man** | **young woman** | **boy** | **girl** | **child** | **kid**
intelligent. **Bright** is more informal than **intelligent** and is used especially about young people:
Helen was the brightest student in her year. | *He is a bright young man with a great future.* | *Universities want to attract* ***the best and the brightest****.*

You can also say a **bright idea**. This means a **clever idea**, but it is also often used ironically in the opposite meaning: *Whose* ***bright idea*** *was this?* (=this idea seems stupid)

brilliant
scientist | **scholar** | **mathematician** | **student** | **engineer** | **linguist** | **mind**
extremely intelligent and good at the work you do:
The research team is led by one of the world's most brilliant scientists. | *He is a great writer, with a brilliant mind.*

gifted
child | **student**
a gifted child or student has a high level of intelligence or natural ability:
Her son goes to a special school for gifted children. | ***Academically gifted*** *students sometimes find it difficult to form relationships with people of their own age.*

wise
man | **woman** | **decision** | **choice** | **move** | **precaution**
able to make good decisions and give sensible advice, especially because you have a lot of experience. You also use **wise** about decisions that seem sensible:
A wise man once said that all political careers end in failure. | *I think you've made a wise decision.* | *Putting him in prison was not a wise move* (=was not a sensible thing to do).

cunning
plan | **strategy** | **way** | **politician**
good at using your intelligence to get what you want, often by making secret plans or tricking people:
It was just a cunning plan to make people feel sorry for him. | *Palin is a cunning politician. Even her enemies admit that.* | *He's a* ***cunning old devil!*** (=a cunning person - an informal use)

brainy *informal*
intelligent and good at studying:
I wish I was as brainy as he is. | *My sister is the brainy one in our family.*

intend *v*
to have something in your mind as a plan or purpose

Grammar
Intend is usually followed by an infinitive: *He* ***intends to*** *stay there for a year.* In more formal English, people say **It is intended that...**:*It is* ***intended that*** *these meetings will become a regular event.*

ADVERBS

fully intend to do sth (=definitely intend) *I fully intend to return home next year.*

originally intend to do sth *We spent much more than we originally intended.*

clearly intend to do sth *The bomb was clearly intended to cause as much damage as possible.*

sb never intended to do sth *I'm sure that she never intended to hurt anyone.*

In more informal English, you often use **mean to**, especially when saying that something was not what you intended: *I'm sorry – I didn't* ***mean to*** *hurt your feelings.*
When talking about your plans, you often use **going to** instead of **intend to**: *We're* ***going to*** *come back again next year.*

intense Ac *adj*
having a very strong effect or felt very strongly

NOUNS

intense pressure *The prime minister is under intense pressure to resign.*

intense competition *There is intense competition for places on the course.*

intense heat/cold *He could feel the intense heat of the desert sun.*

intense pain *She felt an intense pain in her right shoulder.*

intense feelings/emotion *Her lips trembled with intense emotion.*

intense dislike *I have an intense dislike of snakes.*

intense interest in sth *The police are aware of the intense media interest in the case.*

intense activity *There was a period of intense activity before the restaurant's opening night.*

intense debate/discussion *The war has become the subject of intense debate.*

intense scrutiny (=being examined very carefully) *The mining industry is coming under intense scrutiny over its environmental record.*

VERBS

become/grow intense *Fighting has become very intense in the south of the country.*

THESAURUS: intense
deep, powerful, intense → **strong (3)**

I

intention *n* what you are intending to do

ADJECTIVES

sb's real/true intention *He had made the mistake of revealing his true intentions.*

sb's only/sole intention *Their sole intention was to make a profit.*

good intentions (*also* **the best of intentions**) (=intentions to do something good or kind, especially when the result is not good) *I'm sure you acted with good intentions.*

sb's original intention *My original intention was to write four books, but I ended up writing seven.*

sb's stated/declared/avowed intention (=that someone has stated openly) *Their avowed intention is to get rid of the government.*

the firm intention of doing sth *He returned home to Yorkshire with the firm intention of becoming a farmer.*

VERBS

state/express your intention (=say what you intend to do) *They expressed their intention to work together.*

announce/declare your intention *The actor has announced his intention to do more comedy.*

indicate/signal your intention *formal* (=show it) *Several celebrities have already indicated their intention of taking part.*

PREPOSITIONS

with the intention of doing sth *They bought the building two years ago with the intention of turning it into an art gallery.*

the intention behind sth *The intention behind this policy is to reach a wider audience.*

PHRASES

sb's intention is to do sth *Her intention was to start her own business.*

have no intention of doing sth (*also* **not have the slightest intention of doing sth**) *I have no intention of leaving my job.*

have every intention of doing sth (=definitely intend to do something) *He had every intention of marrying Maria.*

make clear your intention *The education minister has made his intentions quite clear.*

> **THESAURUS: intention**
>
> aim, goal, objective, the object of sth, the point, intention, ends → **purpose**

intentional *adj* THESAURUS **deliberate**

interest *n*

1 if you have an interest in something or someone, you want to know or learn more about them

ADJECTIVES

great interest *The government has shown great interest in the idea.*

enormous/intense interest (=very great) *This tournament has created enormous interest.*

considerable/strong/keen interest *The results of the tests will be of considerable interest.*

special/particular interest *Natural history was a special interest of his.*

a personal interest in sth *He took a personal interest in the lives of his workers.*

renewed interest (=starting again after it had stopped) *There has been a renewed interest in the artist's work since her death.*

VERBS

have an interest in sth *Steve has a keen interest in birds.*

show an interest in sth *The child shows no interest in school.*

express an interest in sth (=say that you are interested) *Several film directors have expressed interest in the script.*

take an interest in sth (=be interested in something) *He first took an interest in golf when he was only six.*

arouse/generate/attract interest (=make people interested) *She is a young actor who has aroused great interest in Hollywood.*

lose interest in sth (=stop being interested) *I could see that she had lost interest in our conversation.*

maintain/keep up an interest in sth *After his retirement from the army, he maintained an interest in military affairs.*

feign interest *formal* (=pretend to be interested) *He feigned interest in her work just so he could spend time with her.*

interest grows *Interest in the show has steadily grown.*

interest wanes *formal* (=it becomes less) *After six months in the job, his interest waned.*

PREPOSITIONS

interest in sth *His interest in electronics helped him to get the job.*

out of interest (=because you want to know something, not because you need to know) *Just out of interest, what time did you leave the party?*

PHRASES

a lot of/a great deal of interest *There has been a lot of interest in the story.*

(a) lack of interest *The show was cancelled due to lack of interest from the public.*

2 things about something that make it seem good or interesting to someone

> **Grammar**
>
> In this meaning, you often say **of interest**.

PHRASES

sth is of great/considerable/huge interest *The book is of considerable interest to students of Indian culture.*

I

something/nothing/anything of interest *There was nothing of interest in the magazine.*

much/little of interest *There is much of interest on the island if you like wild flowers.*

of special/particular interest *There is one item of news of particular interest to me.*

of scientific/historical interest *The discovery is of huge scientific interest.*

VERBS

hold no/any interest *Does the movie hold any interest for lovers of sport?*

add interest to sth *A few more flowering plants would add interest to the garden.*

lack interest *This is an important historical document but it lacks interest as a human story.*

3 the things that bring advantages or benefits to someone or something

> **Grammar**
> Often plural in this meaning.

ADJECTIVES

sb's own interests *All they are interested in doing is looking after their own interests.*

sb's personal/private interests *Wasn't he allowing his personal interests and prejudices to cloud his judgement?*

political/economic interests *Her political interests may have influenced her decision.*

sb's selfish interests *disapproving*: *He had put his own selfish interests before those of the group.*

VERBS

look after/protect/safeguard sb's interests *We need to look after our own interests first.*

consider sb's interests *The company didn't seem to want to consider the interests of the local community.*

PREPOSITIONS

against sb's interests (*also* **contrary to sb's interests**) *He would never do anything that was against the interests of his family.*

PHRASES

be in sb's (best) interests (=bring an advantage or benefit to someone) *It would be in your best interests to accept the offer.*

have sb's (best) interests at heart (=try to do things that are best for someone) *As parents, we have our children's best interests at heart.*

in the interest(s) of sth (=in order to protect something or make something happen) *In the interest of safety, smoking is not allowed in the building.*

sth is in the national/public interest *The government will only reveal the information if it is in the public interest.*

interested *adj*

giving a lot of attention to something because you want to find out more about it or because you enjoy it

ADVERBS

very/really interested *My friends are all really interested in music.*

deeply interested *Herschel was also deeply interested in chemistry and other scientific subjects.*

particularly interested *Scientists are particularly interested in observing changes in sea level.*

genuinely interested *A good teacher is genuinely interested in his or her students.*

keenly/passionately interested *The whole family are passionately interested in sport.*

mainly/mostly/primarily interested *He was mainly interested in modern art.*

only interested *Adam is only interested in one thing - making money.*

not (even) remotely interested (=not at all) *I was never remotely interested in listening to their problems.*

VERBS

seem/look/sound/appear interested *The doctor seemed interested - he wasn't just being polite.*

become/get interested *She got interested in flying when she took a ride in a small plane for her sixth birthday.*

get sb interested (=make someone interested) *My dad got me interested in golf.*

keep sb interested *It is difficult to keep students interested for two hours.*

PREPOSITIONS

interested in sb/sth *She became interested in the work of Dr Ludwig Schmitt.*

ANTONYMS **interested → bored**

interesting *adj*

if something or someone is interesting, you give them your attention because they seem unusual or exciting, or provide information that you did not know about

NOUNS

an interesting book/film/programme *I saw an interesting programme about bees.*

an interesting story/article *There's an interesting article in today's paper.*

an interesting person/man/woman *He is one of the most interesting people I've ever met.*

an interesting question *The students asked some interesting questions.*

an interesting point/idea *You've raised an interesting point.*

an interesting example/case *This is a particularly interesting example of her work.*

an interesting experience *Travelling around India was an interesting experience for me.*

interesting results/findings *The report contained some interesting findings.*

an interesting feature/aspect *An interesting feature of the room is its circular window.*

ADVERBS

very/really interesting *The book sounds really interesting.*

particularly/especially interesting *This last statement is particularly interesting.*

quite interesting *His story is quite interesting.*

historically/geologically/architecturally etc interesting *The building is architecturally interesting because of the material it is built from.*

VERBS

find sth interesting *I found her talk really interesting.*

look/sound/seem interesting *Leigh's new movie sounds quite interesting.*

make sth interesting *Teachers need to make lessons interesting for students.*

PREPOSITIONS

interesting for sb *The film was interesting for me because I used to live in Japan.*

PHRASES

something/anything interesting *Is there anything interesting on television?*

sth makes interesting reading (=something is interesting to read) *The report makes interesting reading.*

the interesting thing is... *The interesting thing is that he wrote most of his poems before he was 20.*

nothing remotely interesting (=nothing interesting at all) *He had nothing remotely interesting to say.*

THESAURUS: interesting

fascinating
story | book | film | account | subject | place | history | collection | insight
extremely interesting:
*The film is the fascinating story of Mary Shelley, the woman who wrote Frankenstein when she was only 18 years old. | The origin of words is an **endlessly fascinating** subject. | New York is a fascinating place to visit. | The book gives some fascinating insights into Picasso's life* (=pieces of information that you did not know about).

intriguing
question | possibility | idea | story | aspect | results | mixture
interesting because of being unusual, mysterious, or unexpected, so that you want to find out more:
It's an intriguing question, but I'm not sure what the answer is. | This discovery raises the intriguing possibility that there may be life on other planets. | The book tells the intriguing story of a boy who was found in the desert. | Their research has produced some intriguing results. | The buildings were an intriguing mixture of old and new.

stimulating
debate | argument | conversation | ideas | book | experience | environment
giving you new ideas or experiences in a way that is interesting and enjoyable:
The programme provided the basis for a stimulating debate. | Frude's book brings together a range of stimulating ideas. | I found the trip an enjoyable and stimulating experience. | Children need a happy and stimulating environment.

absorbing/engrossing
hobby | book | account | contest | game | task
interesting in a way that keeps your attention completely or for a long time. **Engrossing** is more formal than **absorbing**:
Cooking can be an absorbing hobby. | It's an engrossing account of his time in India. | He defeated Jones in an absorbing contest.

gripping/riveting/compelling
story | account | tale | drama | book | film | performance | contest
used about a very interesting story, film etc that you feel you must keep reading or watching. **Compelling** is more formal than **gripping** and **riveting**:
*The book is a riveting story of love and power. | There's a gripping account of how the climbers got down from the mountain. | I couldn't put the book down - it was **absolutely riveting**. | The programme **makes compelling viewing*** (=you cannot stop watching it).

enthralling
match | game | contest | experience | climax
very interesting and exciting - used especially about a performance you are watching or listening to:
Germany won an enthralling match by three goals to two. | Visitors to the show will find it an enthralling experience.

spellbinding
tale | story | description | performance
very interesting because of being so strange, unusual, or wonderful:
The book is a spellbinding tale of her life in China. | The actor gives a spellbinding performance.

Collocations with words meaning interesting

You can use the verb **find** with all of these words, when talking about your personal opinion about something: *I **found** it fascinating/intriguing/stimulating/absorbing etc.*

I

ANTONYMS **interesting → boring**

interference *n*

an act of getting involved in a situation where you are not wanted or needed

ADJECTIVES/NOUNS + interference

outside/external interference (=from outside an organization, group, country etc) *Most governments resist outside interference in their internal affairs.*

foreign interference *They should be allowed to choose their own government without foreign interference.*

political/government interference *We cannot tolerate political interference with the workings of the law courts.*

unwarranted interference (=for no good reason) *They should be free to do their jobs without unwarranted interference from the head office.*

VERBS

resent sb's interference *It was her case and she resented Baxter's interference.*

not tolerate interference *He has made it clear that he will not tolerate any interference in the way he runs the team.*

PREPOSITIONS

interference in sth (=getting involved in something) *He thinks there is too much government interference in people's personal lives.*

interference from/by sb *He blamed interference from neighbouring states for his country's problems.*

without interference *Journalists should be allowed to report without interference.*

PHRASES

free from/of interference *Such organisations must be free from government interference or control.*

interminable *adj* THESAURUS **long (2)**

internet *n*

a system that allows millions of computer users around the world to exchange information

> **Punctuation**
>
> You can spell **internet** with or without a capital letter.

> **Grammar**
>
> You usually say **the internet**: *I bought it on the internet*. Don't say 'I bought it on internet.'
>
> The exception to this is when **internet** is used before another noun: *internet users* | *internet shopping*

VERBS

use the internet *He uses the internet for his work.*

go on the internet *I went on the internet to find some information for my assignment.*

access the internet/connect to the internet *You can access the internet from your mobile phone.*

surf the internet (=look at different websites) *She spends hours surfing the internet every evening.*

search/trawl/scour the internet *She immediately searched the internet for relevant information.*

download sth from the internet *I downloaded the file from the internet.*

buy sth on the internet *He bought the chairs on the internet.*

internet + NOUNS

an internet connection *You need a high-speed internet connection to play this game.*

internet access (*also* **access to the internet**) *Not everyone has internet access at home.*

an internet address *The company charges $100 to register a new internet address.*

internet shopping/banking *Internet banking saves customers a lot of time.*

an internet service provider *Your internet service provider should be able to solve the problem.*

an internet café *The message had been sent from an internet café in Leeds.*

PREPOSITIONS

on the internet *You can find this information on the internet.*

over/via the internet (=using the internet) *A lot of business is now done over the internet.*

⚠ Don't say 'You can pay bills by internet.' Say **You can pay bills online**.

> **The internet** is often shortened to **the net**, especially in informal English. *You can get the information off **the net**.*
>
> Instead of saying 'using the internet', you can say **online**: *We do most of our shopping **online**.*

interruption *n*

something that prevents someone from continuing to talk, or that prevents something from continuing to happen, usually for a short time

ADJECTIVES

constant/frequent interruptions *She was distracted from her studies by constant interruptions.*

numerous interruptions *His speech was marked by numerous interruptions from members of the opposition party.*

a brief/short interruption *An electrical failure caused a brief interruption to production at the factory.*

a temporary interruption *There will be a temporary interruption to the email service as necessary maintenance work is carried out.*

occasional interruptions *The radio station plays music continuously with only occasional interruptions by an announcer.*

further interruption(s) *She hoped that she would be able to finish her work without any further interruptions.*

a rude interruption *He switched off his mobile phone to avoid any rude interruptions during the meeting.*

an unwelcome interruption *The impression she gave was that she had better things to do and that our presence was an unwelcome interruption.*

VERBS

experience/suffer interruptions *The airport has been experiencing interruptions in operations due to the bad weather.*

avoid/prevent/reduce any interruption *The police were determined to prevent any interruption to the president's visit by protesters.*

ignore an interruption *She decided to ignore the interruption and carried on speaking.*

PREPOSITIONS

an interruption to sth *What should I do if there is an interruption to my electricity supply?*

without interruption *She let him speak without interruption.*

interval Ac *n*

the period of time between two events or activities

ADJECTIVES

at weekly/monthly/10-minute etc intervals *The treatment may have to be repeated at monthly intervals.*

at regular intervals *Feed your dog small quantities at regular intervals.*

at irregular/random intervals *The banging continued at irregular intervals.*

at frequent intervals (=often) *The patients were checked at frequent intervals.*

at fixed intervals *In some countries, elections are held at fixed intervals.*

a short/brief interval *After a short interval, the woman returned carrying a box.*

a long interval *There was a long interval before the next course.*

a decent interval (=a suitably long interval) *He waited for a decent interval before asking her friend out on a date.*

PREPOSITIONS

an interval of 4 weeks/6 years etc *There was an interval of eight years before I had another exhibition.*

an interval of time *Memory of an event can often improve after an interval of time has passed.*

the interval between sth and sth *The interval between taking and freezing the specimens was less than 30 minutes.*

at intervals (=sometimes, not continuously) *At intervals throughout the next months he worked on this material.*

at intervals of 10 minutes/20 years etc *Meetings were held at intervals of three months.*

in an interval *In that short interval, he had changed completely.*

interview *n*

1 a meeting at which someone is asked questions in order to find out whether they are suitable for a job, course of study etc

VERBS

have an interview *She has an interview next week for a teaching job in Paris.*

go for an interview (*also* **attend an interview** *formal*): *I went for an interview at a software company yesterday.*

get an interview *Only 5% of the applicants will get an interview.*

be called/invited for (an) interview *Applicants who are called for interview may be asked to have a medical exam.*

carry out/do an interview (*also* **conduct an interview** *formal*) (=ask questions) *The interview was conducted in French.*

give sb an interview (=ask someone questions) *We gave her an interview, but decided not to offer her the job.*

ADJECTIVES/NOUNS + interview

a job interview *Try to predict the questions you might get in your job interview.*

an informal/formal interview *Applicants will normally have an informal interview with the manager.*

a mock interview (=one that you do for practice, rather than a real interview) *Mock interviews are one way in which students can improve their job-seeking skills.*

a telephone interview *The first stage is a telephone interview.*

interview + NOUNS

the interview panel (=the group of people interviewing someone) *The interview panel were very impressed with her enthusiasm.*

interview technique *The book gives some useful advice on interview technique.*

PREPOSITIONS

an interview for a job/post etc *I have an interview for a job tomorrow.*

at (an) interview *She felt quite confident at the interview.*

2 an occasion when someone is asked questions for a newspaper, magazine, television programme etc

I

ADJECTIVES/NOUNS + interview

a newspaper/radio/television interview *She said in a recent television interview that she was enjoying life.*

an exclusive interview (=one that is given to only one newspaper, programme etc) *He gave the paper an exclusive interview.*

an in-depth interview (=one that finds out a lot of information) *This is his first in-depth interview since the death of his son.*

VERBS

do an interview *I have to do an interview with the principal for the school magazine* (=ask him or her questions in an interview). | *He's a very private person and rarely does interviews* (=answers questions in an interview).

give an interview (=answer someone's questions) *The minister agreed to give them an interview.*

carry out an interview (*also* **conduct an interview** *formal*) (=ask questions) *She had done her research before carrying out the interview.*

PREPOSITIONS

an interview with sb *He managed to get an interview with Madonna.* | *In an interview with reporters yesterday, he said he regretted his action.*

an interview for/with a newspaper/programme etc *He made the remarks in an interview for 'The Times'.*

intimidating *adj* THESAURUS **frightening**

intolerance *n* THESAURUS **prejudice**

intoxicated *adj* THESAURUS **drunk**

intrepid *adj* THESAURUS **brave**

intricate *adj* THESAURUS **complicated**

intriguing *adj* THESAURUS **interesting**

introduce *v*

to bring something into use or into a place for the first time

ADVERBS

sth was first/originally introduced *The programme was first introduced in 2004.*

gradually introduce sth *Try gradually introducing more healthy foods into their diets.*

quickly/rapidly introduce sth *Technical improvements are rapidly introduced.*

successfully introduce sth *Similar arrangements were successfully introduced in other prisons.*

PREPOSITIONS

introduce sth into/to/in sth *They are about to introduce the scheme into schools.*

introduction *n*

1 the first part of a book, essay, or talk

ADJECTIVES

a brief/short introduction *Each chapter begins with a brief introduction.*

PREPOSITIONS

in the introduction *Set out your intentions in the introduction.*

sb's introduction to sth *"It is the language that is the most important thing," says Anthony Burgess in his introduction to the book.*

2 something that gives general basic information about a subject

ADJECTIVES

a general introduction *'History of Music 1' is a general introduction to the subject.*

a good/useful/excellent introduction *He gives a useful introduction to business practice.*

PREPOSITIONS

an introduction to sth *This colourful book is an introduction to the geography and history of Russia.*

3 the act of bringing something into use for the first time

ADJECTIVES

the gradual introduction of sth *The government is planning the gradual introduction of tax increases.*

the recent introduction of sth *The recent introduction of wireless networks will mean easier access to information.*

the widespread introduction of sth *The widespread introduction of electric cars may simply transfer the problem of pollution somewhere else.*

PREPOSITIONS

with the introduction of sth *With the introduction of better street lighting, the number of accidents went down by 25%.*

introductory *adj* THESAURUS **first**[1]

invasion *n*

a situation in which the army of one country enters another country by force, in order to take control of it

ADJECTIVES/NOUNS + invasion

a foreign invasion *The role of the military is to protect the country from foreign invasion.*

a military invasion *He warned the US against any military invasion of Cuba.*

a full-scale invasion *The operation became a full-scale invasion.*

a land/ground invasion *Some called for air strikes followed by a land invasion.*

an alien invasion (=by creatures from another planet) *a science fiction movie about an alien invasion*

I

VERBS

launch/mount an invasion *He feared that the Spanish king might launch an invasion.*

resist/repel an invasion *Could they successfully resist an invasion?*

invent *v*

to think of a new type of thing, or think of an excuse

NOUNS

invent the telephone/the wheel/the motor car etc *Alexander Graham Bell invented the telephone in 1876.*

invent an idea/concept/theory *Newton was the man who invented the idea of gravity.*

invent a word/term/phrase/language *The word 'robot' was invented by a Czech writer.*

invent a game/sport *James Naismith invented the game of basketball.*

invent an excuse/reason *She didn't want to go to the party, so she decided to invent some kind of excuse.*

ADVERBS

newly invented *The first words ever spoken on the newly invented telephone were "Come here Watson, I want you."*

THESAURUS: invent

create
design | style | character | story | work of art | game | dish | product | look | world
to make or design something new and original:
Jacquie creates imaginative carpet designs in her London studio. | Picasso and Braque created a new style of painting, which became known as 'cubism'. | The character of Winnie-the-Pooh was originally created by A. A. Milne.

devise
way | method | system | strategy | scheme | technique | plan | test | program | solution
to invent a way of doing something:
Scientists devised a way of making energy from water. | They are hoping to devise a system that is fair for everyone. | He devised a simple solution to the problem.

come up with sth
idea | way | solution | plan | name | system | theory
to think of something, especially an idea or solution. **Come up with** is more informal than **devise** or **invent**:
It was Tony who first came up with the idea. | Scientists think they may have come up with a solution to the problem.

make sth up
excuse | story | song
to invent something, especially something that is not true, or is about imaginary things:
I made up an excuse and said that I had a cold. | The press are always making up stories about famous people. | He liked to make up songs for the children.

coin
term | word | name | phrase | expression | slogan
to invent a new word or phrase:
Apollinaire coined the word 'surrealism'. | William Gibson coined the phrase 'cyberspace' in his novel 'Neuromancer'.

fabricate
evidence | charges | allegations | confession | case | data
to invent things that are not true, in order to try to prove something:
Police officers later admitted fabricating evidence which was presented to the court. | The scientists were accused of fabricating their data about global warming.

dream sth up
idea | way | scheme
to think of an idea or plan that seems unusual or annoying. **Dream up** sounds rather informal:
Carrot ice cream? I wonder who dreamt up that idea! | Companies are constantly dreaming up new ways to sell us things we don't need.

invention *n*

a useful machine, tool etc that has been invented

ADJECTIVES

a new/recent/modern invention *The telephone was a recent invention then.*

a great invention *The internet is one of the world's greatest inventions.*

a wonderful/brilliant invention *The computer is a wonderful invention.*

an ingenious invention (=very clever) *No one knows who first made this ingenious invention.*

a technical/technological invention *In the textile industry, technical inventions produced an increase in output.*

VERBS

make an invention *Edison made a number of other important inventions.*

patent an invention (=get a special document which says that only you can use it) *He never thought of patenting his invention or trying to make any money out of it.*

PREPOSITIONS

an invention for doing sth *Thomas Edison's 1877 invention for recording sound was very simple.*

invest [Ac] *v*

to buy shares, property, or goods because you hope that the value will increase and you can make a profit

ADVERBS

invest heavily in sth (=invest a lot of money) *He had invested heavily in the bond market.*

PREPOSITIONS

invest (money) in sth *Oliver made a fortune by investing in antique furniture.*

investigation Ac *n*

an official attempt to find out about something

ADJECTIVES

an official/formal investigation *Federal agents have begun a formal investigation of the company.*

a full/full-scale investigation *A full investigation of the incident was continuing yesterday.*

a thorough/detailed investigation *There will be a thorough investigation into why, and how, this accident happened.*

a criminal/police investigation *The bank faces a criminal investigation by the Department of Justice.*

an internal investigation (=by other members of the same organization) *An internal investigation revealed that executives received £19 million in unauthorized payments.*

a preliminary investigation (=the first investigation, when more work will be done later) *A preliminary investigation showed the man was hit by two bullets fired at close range.*

an ongoing investigation (=one that is continuing) *He will continue to assist the police in their ongoing investigation.*

further investigation *Further investigation revealed that the brake cables had been cut.*

VERBS

carry out an investigation (=do one) *The Health and Safety Authority carried out an investigation into the accident.*

conduct/perform/undertake an investigation *formal* (=carry out an investigation) *I am sure the police will conduct a thorough investigation and bring him to justice.*

launch/open an investigation (=start an investigation) *An investigation has been launched into the fire.*

reopen an investigation (=start it again, usually after a long time) *Detectives have reopened an investigation into the disappearance of the two men.*

order/demand/call for an investigation *Congress has recently called for an investigation of the use of these chemicals.*

close an investigation *Police said on Friday they have closed their investigation into the matter.*

PREPOSITIONS

an investigation into sth *The army are carrying out an investigation into the shooting.*

be under investigation (=being investigated) *Several politicians are under investigation.*

PHRASES

the outcome of an investigation (=the final result) *We are pleased with the outcome of this investigation.*

investment Ac *n*

the use of money in order to make a profit, or to get benefits in the future

ADJECTIVES

a good investment *Property is usually a good investment.*

a bad/poor investment *The shares turned out to be a poor investment.*

a big/major/massive/huge investment *Developing a new computer system is always a big investment for an organisation.*

a safe investment (=in which you are unlikely to lose money) *Electricity shares are still a safe investment.*

a wise investment (=very sensible) *A pension might be a wise investment.*

a risky investment (=in which you are likely to lose money) *If you cannot afford to lose any money, choose less risky investments.*

a long-term/short-term investment (=one that will give you profit after a long time or a short time) *Buying a house is a long-term investment.*

foreign/overseas investment *The government is eager to attract foreign investment to fund building projects.*

private investment (=investment by companies or people, not the government) *The government is hoping to attract private investment for the project.*

VERBS

make an investment (in sth) *We have made a huge investment in our website.*

attract investment *The company is trying to attract investment from overseas.*

stimulate/encourage investment *The government has cut taxes in order to stimulate investment.*

protect your investment *A company will want to protect its investment in training, and discourage employees from leaving.*

investment + NOUNS

an investment opportunity *The salesman said it was a unique investment opportunity.*

PREPOSITIONS

investment in sth *We need increased investment in public services.*

as an investment *He bought the painting as an investment.*

PHRASES

the (rate of) return on an investment (=how much profit you will get) *We expect a high return on our investment.*

invisible [Ac] *adj*

something that is invisible cannot be seen

ADVERBS

almost/nearly invisible *The thread is so thin that it is almost invisible.*

virtually/practically invisible (=almost invisible) *Tigers are virtually invisible in the thick jungle.*

totally/completely invisible *The pipes are laid inside the wall, making them totally invisible.*

VERBS

become invisible *As morning approached, the stars faded and became invisible.*

PREPOSITIONS

invisible to sth *The plane is invisible to radar.*

invisible from sth *Because the house was surrounded by trees, it was almost invisible from the road.*

PHRASES

invisible to the naked/human eye *Using a telescope, Galileo discovered stars that were invisible to the naked eye.*

invitation *n*

a written or spoken request to someone, inviting them to go somewhere or do something

ADJECTIVES/NOUNS + invitation

a party/wedding invitation *He had a wedding invitation from Rob and Jen.*

a dinner/lunch invitation *Fred's wife has accepted the dinner invitation.*

a formal/official invitation *The president received a formal invitation to visit Nigeria.*

a personal invitation *Each parent was sent a personal invitation for the school's open day.*

a special invitation *We received a special invitation to attend a reception at the embassy.*

an open/standing invitation (=an invitation to do something at any time you like) *Phillip kindly gave me an open invitation to stay at his villa in Tuscany.*

VERBS

get/receive an invitation *Did you get an invitation to Janet's party?*

have an invitation *The following week, I had an invitation to give a talk in Cambridge.*

send (sb) an invitation (*also* **send out invitations**) *They must have forgotten to send me an invitation.*

give sb an invitation (*also* **issue/extend an invitation** *formal*): *He has issued an invitation to the Chinese president to come to Washington.*

accept an invitation *She accepted his invitation to dinner.*

take up sb's invitation/take sb up on their invitation (=accept someone's invitation) *I decided to take up Teresa's invitation and visit her.*

refuse/turn down an invitation (*also* **decline an invitation** *formal*): *She turned down an invitation to take part in a televised debate.*

thank sb for an invitation *I'll have to write a letter thanking Martha for the invitation to her wedding.*

invitation + NOUNS

an invitation card (=a card with an invitation printed on it) *Everyone entering will have to show an invitation card.*

PREPOSITIONS

an invitation to sth *She had an invitation to a party that Sunday.*

an invitation from sb *I received an invitation from my German pen friend to spend a week with her.*

at sb's invitation (=because someone has invited you) *He paid a visit to China at the invitation of the Chinese government.*

by invitation *formal* (=because someone has invited you) *We are here by invitation.*

PHRASES

a flood of invitations (=a lot of invitations) *He got a flood of invitations to appear on TV and radio shows.*

invite *v*

to ask someone to come to a party, wedding, meal etc

ADVERBS

formally/officially invite sb *The Pope has been formally invited to visit Ireland by the Irish bishops.*

kindly invite sb *She kindly invited me to come for the weekend.*

cordially invite sb *formal* (=in a friendly but polite and formal way) *Members are cordially invited to a special screening of the film on Monday evening.*

invite sb in (=ask someone to come into your home) *Mrs West invited her in for a cup of tea.*

invite sb over (*also* **invite sb round** *BrE*) (=ask someone to come to your house for a meal or a drink) *I rang a few friends and invited them over.*

invite someone out (=ask someone to go on a date with you) *He phoned to invite me out for dinner.*

invite sb along (=ask someone if they would like to go somewhere with you) *I invited Susie along to meet the director.*

invite sb back (=ask someone to come to your home after you have been out somewhere together) *I'd like to invite you back for coffee, but I have to be up early tomorrow.*

PREPOSITIONS

invite sb to a party/wedding/show etc *Are you inviting him to your birthday party?*

invite sb for dinner/a meal/a drink etc *Why don't you invite her for a drink at the club one evening?*

invoice *n*

a list of goods that have been supplied or work that has been done, showing how much is owed for them

VERBS

get/receive an invoice *After a month, he called to make sure they had received his invoice.*

send an invoice *Please send the invoice to me at our office in London.*

issue an invoice *When you issue the first invoice to a new customer, check that the name is correct.*

put in/submit an invoice (=give them to a company or organization, asking them to pay you money) *He submitted fake invoices and stole a total of £12,448.*

pay/settle an invoice *All invoices must be paid within a month.*

ADJECTIVES

an unpaid/outstanding invoice *They are taking him to court over an unpaid invoice.*

PREPOSITIONS

an invoice for sth *An invoice for the fees will be sent to you.*

involved *adj* THESAURUS complicated

irate *adj* THESAURUS angry

ironic (*also* ironical) *adj*

funny or sad because something happens that is the opposite of what you expect

ADVERBS

how ironic *"It was freezing cold in the desert." "How ironic!"*

somewhat/rather/a little ironic *The fact that he is seen as so typically English is somewhat ironic when you consider that he was actually born in the US.*

deeply ironic *Her colleagues find it deeply ironic that she should complain about other people's incompetence.*

particularly/especially ironic *Burning wood causes pollution, which is particularly ironic considering its natural origin.*

NOUNS

the ironic thing *The ironic thing is that I didn't really want to go to the party anyway.*

an ironic twist *In an ironic twist, the book he wrote about his job made so much money he was able to quit.*

irony *n*

the use of words that are the opposite of what you really mean, often in order to be amusing

ADJECTIVES

heavy irony *BrE* (=a lot of irony) *"Take your time. There's no hurry," he said with heavy irony.*

gentle irony *She pointed out with gentle irony that he was not in a position to criticize her.*

PREPOSITIONS

with irony *"Any more brilliant ideas?" he said with unpleasant irony.*

without irony *He told me, without irony, that everyone agreed with him.*

PHRASES

a trace/hint/touch of irony *Without a trace of irony, she told me she had done most of the work.*

irrational Ac *adj*

not based on a good reason

NOUNS

an irrational fear *She has an irrational fear of birds.*

an irrational hatred/prejudice *He had developed an irrational hatred of teenagers.*

irrational behaviour *BrE*, **irrational behavior** *AmE*: *His parents were becoming concerned about his increasingly irrational behaviour.*

an irrational belief/thought *Anxious people may have irrational beliefs about situations they fear.*

an irrational feeling *He had an irrational feeling that everything was about to go wrong.*

ADVERBS

completely/totally/quite irrational *These actions seem to me to be completely irrational.*

seemingly/apparently irrational *I finally understood the reason for his seemingly irrational behaviour.*

irrelevant Ac *adj*

not useful or not relating to a particular situation, and therefore not important

ADVERBS

completely/totally/entirely/utterly irrelevant (*also* **quite irrelevant** *BrE*): *His age is completely irrelevant. What matters is his ability to do the job.*

increasingly irrelevant *The country where a company is based is becoming increasingly irrelevant.*

largely irrelevant (=mostly irrelevant) *The precise timing of the meeting is largely irrelevant.*

VERBS

become irrelevant *People's social class is becoming irrelevant.*

seem irrelevant *The subject of pensions seems irrelevant to most teenagers.*

dismiss sth as irrelevant (=say that it is not worth considering something, because you think it is irrelevant) *The report's findings were dismissed as irrelevant at the time.*

I

consider sth irrelevant/regard sth as irrelevant *Nobody's feelings should be considered irrelevant.*

PREPOSITIONS

irrelevant to sb/sth *Politics is irrelevant to many young people.*

> In spoken English, people often say that something **has (got) nothing to do with** what you are talking about: *"What about the money?" "That* ***has got nothing to do with*** *it!"* This use sounds a little informal and very strong.
>
> In more formal English, people say that something **has no bearing on** another thing: *The court decided that the evidence* ***had no bearing on*** *the case* (=it had no effect on the case and should not be considered).

ANTONYMS **irrelevant → relevant**

irreplaceable *adj* THESAURUS **valuable (2)**

irresponsible *adj*

careless in a way that might affect other people, especially when this could cause accidents or serious problems

ADVERBS

highly irresponsible (=very irresponsible) *Driving with tyres in this condition is highly irresponsible.*

totally/completely/utterly irresponsible *The judge said that the company's behaviour was totally irresponsible.*

downright irresponsible *especially spoken* (=extremely irresponsible - used when you feel very strongly about this) *Selling cheap alcohol to teenagers is downright irresponsible.*

grossly irresponsible (=extremely irresponsible - used when you think something will have a very bad effect) *It would be grossly irresponsible for any government to cut taxes, when the economy is in such a bad state.*

> **THESAURUS: irresponsible**
>
> clumsy, sloppy, reckless, irresponsible, thoughtless, tactless, casual, negligent → **careless**

irritated *adj* THESAURUS **angry**

irritating *adj* THESAURUS **annoying**

island *n*

a piece of land completely surrounded by water

ADJECTIVES

a tropical island *They had their wedding on a tropical island.*

a desert island (=a tropical island that is far away and where nobody lives) *It is a story about a man shipwrecked on a desert island.*

a remote island (=far away) *The islands were so remote that they could only be reached at certain times of the year.*

an uninhabited island (=one where nobody lives) *There are over a thousand uninhabited islands in the seas around Greece.*

island + NOUNS

an island nation (=a country that is an island) *An island nation such as Britain needed a powerful navy.*

PREPOSITIONS

on an island *There are no motor vehicles allowed on the island.*

PHRASES

a chain/group of islands *Our destination was a chain of islands 60 miles east of Taiwan.*

issue *n*

a subject or problem that people discuss or argue about

ADJECTIVES

an important issue *The committee will meet this week to discuss the important issue of childcare.*

a key/major/big issue (=very important) *For most families, the big issue is cost.*

a fundamental issue (=basic and important) *Decisions still need to be made about some fundamental issues.*

a political/social/economic etc issue *Students hold regular meetings to discuss a range of political issues.*

a difficult/complex issue *He was able to grasp complex issues quickly.*

a controversial/sensitive issue (=causing strong feelings and arguments) *They discussed the controversial issue of abortion.*

a thorny issue (*also* **a vexed issue** *formal*) (=causing a lot of disagreement) *Immigration is always a thorny issue.*

a burning issue (=very important and urgent) *Transport is a burning issue for people in rural areas.*

wider/broader issues (=more general) *This is a question that raises much wider issues.*

the underlying issue (=the cause of something) *This research explores some of the underlying issues related to high unemployment.*

an unresolved issue (=not yet dealt with) *A number of unresolved issues are preventing the groups from reaching an agreement.*

a topical issue (=important at the present time) *The magazine discusses topical issues in science.*

VERBS + issue

discuss/debate an issue *They met to discuss the issue of working conditions at the factory.*

raise an issue (*also* **bring up an issue**) (=mention it) *Some important issues were raised at the meeting.*

deal with an issue *The school made a serious attempt to deal with the bullying issue.*

address/tackle an issue *The government must tackle the issue of knife crime.*

decide/settle/resolve an issue *The issue was settled after some tough negotiations.*

face an issue (=accept that it exists and deal with it) *Politicians seem reluctant to face the issue of child poverty.*

avoid/evade an issue (*also* **dodge an issue** *informal*) (=avoid discussing or dealing with it) *There is no point in evading the issue.*

issue + VERBS

an issue comes up (*also* **an issue arises** *formal*) (=people start to discuss it) *The issue arose during a meeting of the Budget Committee.*

an issue faces/confronts sb *The high cost of education is just one of many issues facing students today.*

an issue affects sb *Fuel prices are an issue that affects private individuals and companies alike.*

PHRASES

the issues surrounding sth *This chapter discusses the ethical issues surrounding genetically modified foods.*

a range of issues *A range of issues were debated at the meeting.*

sth is not the issue *spoken* (=something is not the most important problem or part) *The price of the service is not the issue.*

item Ac *n*

a single thing, especially one thing in a list, group, or set of things

ADJECTIVES/NOUNS + item

a particular item *The shop assistant can show you any particular item you are interested in.*

a single/individual item *This is the highest price ever paid for a single item of jewellery.*

an essential/important item *Salt was an important item in the Roman economy.*

a household item (=something that you often use in your home) *The shop stocks a wide variety of household items.*

a consumer item (=something that people often buy) *The government controls the import of hundreds of consumer items.*

a luxury item *Tea and coffee, once luxury items, began to be drunk by everyone.*

the offending item *humorous* (=something that is causing a problem) *I removed the offending item from my soup.*

a collector's item (=something interesting or valuable that a collector would want to own) *This record is so rare that it has become a collector's item.*

stolen items *The police have recovered most of the stolen items.*

miscellaneous items (=of lots of different types) *The cardboard box contained a number of miscellaneous items.*

PHRASES

an item of clothing/equipment/furniture *She still needs a few items of clothing for her trip.*

an item of food (*also* **a food item**) *The cupboard contained a few items of food.*

an item of jewellery *BrE*, **an item of jewelry** *AmE*: *Expensive items of jewellery should be insured.*

an item on a list *What's the next item on the list?*

an item on an agenda (=one of a list of things to be discussed at a meeting) *The next item on the agenda is the sales conference.*

a range of items (=different types of items) *Clay was used to make a wide range of items.*

Jj

jail (*also* **gaol** *BrE*) *n*

a building where people are kept as a punishment for a crime, or while they are waiting for their trial

VERBS

go to jail *They're going to jail for a long time.*

send sb to jail *The judge sent Meyer to jail for six years.*

put sb in jail *The government would put him in jail if he stayed in the country.*

throw sb in jail (=put someone in jail) *Drunks were thrown in jail for a few days.*

get out of/leave jail *He got out of jail after five years for armed robbery.*

release sb from jail *More than 30 of those arrested were released from jail for lack of evidence.*

escape from jail *The killer has escaped from jail.*

ADJECTIVES/NOUNS + jail

the local jail *The suspects were taken to the local jail.*

the town/city/county jail *He was held for 30 days in the county jail.*

a high-/top-/maximum-security jail *Some inmates at the high-security jail had been wrongfully imprisoned.*

jail + NOUNS

a jail sentence *He's serving a seven-year jail sentence.*

a jail term (=a period of time in jail) *He served only half of his three-month jail term.*

a jail cell *The suspect was found dead in his jail cell.*

PREPOSITIONS

in jail *He has been in jail for 14 years.*

out of jail *He has been trying to stay out of jail.*

PHRASES

spend time/six years etc in jail *Griffiths spent three days in jail after pushing a policeman.*

serve time/five years etc in jail (=spend time in jail) *He was finally released after serving 27 years in jail.*

jargon *n*

words used in a particular profession or by a particular group, which are difficult for others to understand

ADJECTIVES/NOUNS + jargon

technical jargon *We try to avoid using technical jargon in our instruction manuals.*

computer jargon *In computer jargon, a SAN is a 'storage area network'.*

legal/academic/scientific/medical/military jargon *The letter was full of legal jargon that I didn't understand.*

incomprehensible jargon (=jargon that is impossible to understand) *Their conversation was just incomprehensible jargon to everyone else.*

PHRASES

be full of jargon *The instructions are full of technical jargon.*

jealous *adj*

1 feeling unhappy because someone has something that you wish you had

VERBS

be/feel jealous *Fathers sometimes feel jealous of the attention given to a new child.*

get jealous *Parents get jealous of their children.*

ADVERBS

really jealous *"I wish I could have a house like that," he said. "I'm really jealous."*

a little jealous/rather jealous *I was always a little jealous of my older sister.*

bitterly jealous (=extremely jealous) *They were all bitterly jealous of her because she had a face like a film star.*

sb is just jealous *spoken: He's just jealous because each time the telephone rings it's for me and not for him.*

PREPOSITIONS

jealous of sb/sth *His wife was jealous of his success.*

2 feeling unhappy because someone you love is attracted to another person

VERBS

get jealous *He gets very jealous of other men looking at me.*

make sb jealous *I let you think she was my girlfriend, because I wanted to make you jealous.*

NOUNS

a jealous husband/wife/lover *A jealous husband tried to kill his wife and her new lover.*

ADVERBS

insanely jealous (=extremely jealous in a way that seems crazy) *When he heard of her wedding, he was insanely jealous.*

> **Jealous or envious?**
>
> You can use either **jealous** or **envious** when saying that you wish you had something that someone else has. **Jealous** sounds a little more informal.
>
> You only use **jealous** when saying that someone is unhappy because the person they love is attracted to another person. You say *a **jealous** husband* (not an 'envious' one).

jealousy
n a feeling of being jealous

ADJECTIVES

pure jealousy *The remark was motivated by pure jealousy.*

petty jealousy *disapproving* (=about unimportant things) *He quickly discovered the petty jealousy of village life.*

bitter jealousy (=strong and angry) *She felt nothing but bitter jealousy for her rival.*

VERBS

feel jealousy *I didn't feel any jealousy when I met her ex-husband.*

cause/provoke/arouse jealousy *A partner's close friendship with a colleague can cause jealousy.*

PHRASES

feelings of jealousy *Children may have strong feelings of jealousy about a new baby.*

in a fit of jealousy (=because of sudden strong feelings of jealousy) *In a fit of jealousy, he broke off their engagement.*

jewellery
BrE, **jewelry** *AmE n*
small things that you wear as a decoration, such as rings or necklaces

ADJECTIVES/NOUNS + jewellery

gold/silver/diamond jewellery *She looked very elegant in her black dress and silver jewellery.*

handmade jewellery *The shop sells beautiful handmade jewelry.*

expensive/cheap jewellery *The star always wears expensive jewellery.*

costume jewellery (=jewellery that is not valuable but looks expensive) *The company sells costume jewelry for teenagers.*

antique jewellery *The thieves stole antique jewellery worth thousands of pounds.*

VERBS

wear jewellery *She likes to wear a lot of jewellery.*

make/produce jewellery *Sarah makes her own jewelry.*

design jewellery *The jewelry is beautifully designed.*

jewellery + NOUNS

a jewellery box *I keep all my rings and necklaces in a jewellery box.*

a jewellery designer *The brooch was made by a famous jewellery designer.*

a jewellery store (*also* **a jewellery shop** *BrE*): *The jewellery shop was robbed.*

PHRASES

a piece of jewellery (*also* **an item of jewellery** *formal*): *This necklace is a very unusual piece of jewellery.*

⚠ Don't say 'jewelleries'. **Jewellery** is an uncountable noun and is not used in the plural.

jigsaw
n
a picture that consists of many pieces that you try to fit together, as a game

jigsaw + NOUNS

a jigsaw puzzle *She's very good at doing jigsaw puzzles.*

a jigsaw piece *One of the jigsaw pieces was missing.*

VERBS

do a jigsaw *I like doing jigsaws in the evenings.*

complete a jigsaw *He completed a 5,000-piece jigsaw.*

job
Ac *n*

1 the regular paid work that you do for an employer

ADJECTIVES/NOUNS + job

a part-time/full-time job *He had a part-time job in a restaurant.*

a temporary/permanent job *The job is only temporary, but I'm hoping it will be made permanent.*

a teaching/cleaning/engineering etc job *She was offered a teaching job at the local college.*

a well-paid/low-paid job *I used to have a well-paid job and a nice apartment.*

a steady job (=a job that is likely to continue) *I haven't had a steady job since last March.*

a good/decent job *If you work hard at school, you'll get a good job.*

a proper job *BrE* (=a good job that is likely to continue) *His parents wanted him to settle down and get a proper job.*

a high-powered job (=well paid and of high rank) *She had a high-powered job as a banker in London.*

a dead-end job (=low paid and with no chance of progress) *He had a series of dead-end jobs.*

a rewarding job (=one that makes you feel happy because you feel you are achieving something good) *She thinks that being a nurse is the most rewarding job in the world.*

an office job *She was fed up with her boring office job.*

a holiday job *BrE* (=done by a student during a holiday from school or university) *I once had a holiday job in a chocolate factory.*

VERBS

have a job *Mark doesn't have a job right now.*

look for a job *He left school and started looking for a job.*

apply for a job *I've applied for a job at the university.*

offer/give sb a job *After the interview, they offered me the job.*

get/find a job *Eventually, Mary got a job as a waitress.*

take a job (=accept a job you are offered)

I was so desperate that I took the first job that came along.

start a job *She will start her new job next week.*

do/carry out your job *The police officer said he was just doing his job.*

hold down a job (=keep a job) *He had never been able to hold down a job.*

leave/give up/quit your job *He gave up his job to look after his sick wife.*

lose your job *At least there's no danger of you losing your job.*

be fired/sacked/dismissed from your job (=lose your job, usually as a punishment) *He was fired from his job because of his drinking problem.*

create jobs *The government should encourage industry and create jobs.*

job + NOUNS

job losses/cuts *The factory is closing, with 600 job losses.*

job satisfaction (=the enjoyment you get from your job) *Levels of job satisfaction vary between departments.*

a job offer *He turned down a job offer from an American company.*

PREPOSITIONS

a job as sth *Wendy got a job as a receptionist in a dental surgery.*

in a job *He has been in the job for three years.*

out of a job (=without a job) *If the project fails, we're all out of a job.*

learn/be trained on the job (=learn skills by doing a job) *He doesn't have any cooking qualifications - he learned on the job.*

2 a particular thing that has to be done

ADJECTIVES

a hard/tough/tricky job *Bringing up a child is a tough job.*

an easy job *They had thought that building a shelter would be an easy job.*

a big job *It was a big job, and we only had three days to do it.*

a small/little job *I had some small jobs to do around the house.*

VERBS

have the job of doing sth *She has the job of carrying water home for her family.*

give sb the job of doing sth *I was given the job of dealing with customers' complaints.*

take on a job (=agree to do it) *He took on the job of looking after his little sister.*

do a job *They haven't got the tools they need to do the job.*

get on with a job (=continue doing it) *He quietly got on with the job.*

finish/complete a job *I am sure we can finish the job this week.*

PHRASES

do a good/great/fine etc job (=do something well) *I think our troops are doing a great job.*

make a good job of sth (=do something well) *He offered to cut our hedge, and made a good job of it.*

joke *n*

something that you say or do to make people laugh, especially a funny story or trick

ADJECTIVES

a good/funny joke *I heard a really good joke the other day.*

a bad/terrible/feeble/lame joke (=not funny) *Dad was known for his bad jokes.*

a cruel/sick joke (=very unkind) *When I heard he had cancer, at first I thought it was some kind of sick joke.*

an old joke *It reminded me of the old joke about the chicken crossing the road.*

a dirty joke (=about sex) *A bunch of boys were telling dirty jokes.*

a practical joke (=that involves tricking someone) *He set off the fire alarm as a practical joke.*

an inside/private joke (=that only a few people who are involved in something will understand) *After I'd worked there a while, I started to understand some of the inside jokes.*

a running joke (=in which people always laugh when the same situation happens, or when someone says something) *It's a running joke in our house that my husband can never find his keys.*

VERBS

tell a joke (=repeat a funny story) *He was always telling jokes and making people laugh.*

⚠ Don't say 'say a joke'. Say **tell a joke**.

make a joke (*also* **crack a joke**) (=say something intended to be funny) *He was cracking jokes and seemed relaxed and happy.*

get a joke (=understand a joke and find it funny) *She never gets my jokes.*

laugh at sb's jokes *A few people laughed at his jokes, but some didn't find them funny.*

play a joke on sb (=trick someone to make people laugh) *John's always playing jokes on his brothers.*

share a joke (with sb) (=laugh at a joke with someone else) *They seemed to be sharing a private joke.*

swap jokes (=tell each other jokes) *They spent the evening swapping jokes and stories.*

PREPOSITIONS

a joke about sb/sth *She made a joke about his unusual name.*

as/for a joke *He pretended to be choking, as a joke.*

J

PHRASES

a joke falls flat (=people don't find a joke funny) *His practical jokes usually fell flat.*

sb can take a joke (=someone can laugh at jokes about themselves and not get upset) *Luckily he can take a joke.*

mean sth as a joke *I meant it as a joke, but she thought I was being serious.*

be the butt of a joke (=be the person a joke is made about, so that people laugh at you) *Somehow he'd become the butt of all his classmates' jokes.*

make jokes at sb's expense (=make jokes about them in a way that makes them seem silly) *He had the unpleasant habit of making jokes at his wife's expense.*

journal Ac *n*

1 a magazine for professional people or for people who have a particular interest

ADJECTIVES

a scientific/medical/technical journal *The results were published in the medical journal 'The Lancet'.*

an academic journal *She often writes articles for academic journals.*

a specialist journal *The paper was published in a specialist journal for engineers.*

a professional journal *The 'Nursing Standard' is a professional journal for nurses.*

a leading/major journal (=an important journal) *The study first appeared in a leading academic journal.*

a prestigious journal (=one that is very well respected) *Prestigious journals such as 'Scientific American' reported on the importance of this research.*

an international journal *They produce an international journal called 'Waste and Environment Today'.*

an electronic/online journal *The company publishes a free online journal.*

NOUNS + journal

a trade journal (=for people involved in a particular profession or business) *'The Bookseller' is a trade journal for people who are involved in selling books.*

a science/law journal *The article appeared in a Dutch law journal.*

a research journal *The department publishes its own research journal.*

VERBS

publish/produce a journal *The journal is published monthly.*

appear in/be published in a journal *The research has appeared in specialist journals.*

write (sth) for a journal *He's writing an article for a scientific journal.*

subscribe to a journal (=pay to have copies of a journal sent to you regularly) *The college library subscribes to several journals.*

journal + NOUNS

a journal article/report *I read a journal article about this study.*

THESAURUS: journal

journal, periodical, supplement, comic/comic book, fanzine → **magazine**

2 a written record that you make of the things that happen to you each day

VERBS

keep a journal *Darwin kept a journal of his voyage.*

write sth in your journal *"Another dramatic day", she wrote in her journal.*

ADJECTIVES

an online journal *Blogs are a kind of online journal.*

journal + NOUNS

a journal entry *He quoted a journal entry by Victor Hugo for December 1847.*

Journal or diary?

A **journal** is often written by a famous or important person.

journey *n* a trip

ADJECTIVES/NOUNS + journey

a car/plane/bus etc journey *I often feel sick on car journeys.*

a long/short journey *They arrived tired from their long journey.*

a two-hour/forty-minute etc journey *It's a six-hour train journey from here to London.*

a six-mile/hundred-mile etc journey *The seven-mile journey down the river is an experience not to be missed.*

a difficult journey *It was a difficult journey, especially in the winter months.*

a dangerous/hazardous/perilous journey *They set off on the dangerous journey down the river.*

a safe journey (=used especially to wish someone a good journey) *Have a safe journey.*

a wasted journey (=not achieving the result you wanted) *To avoid a wasted journey, call first to check that the event is still on.*

an epic journey (=very long and eventful) *Lewis and Clark made their epic journey across the continental United States in the early 1800s.*

the outward journey/the journey there (=the journey to a place) *The outward journey seemed long and slow.*

the return journey/the journey back (=the journey back from a place) *The return journey was uneventful.*

VERBS

go on a journey (=travel somewhere, especially somewhere far away) *She doesn't like going on long journeys.*
make a journey (=go on a journey - used about a complete journey) *I still use my car, but now I make fewer journeys.*
begin/start a journey *He began the journey home across London.*
set off on a journey (*also* **embark on a journey** *formal*) (=start a long journey) *Before setting off on a journey, look at maps and guidebooks.*
break your journey (=make a short stop on a journey) *We broke our journey to have a picnic.*
continue your journey *We stopped for breakfast, then continued our journey.*

PREPOSITIONS

a journey to sth *The journey to work takes about an hour.*
a journey from sth *We started our journey from New York on May 1st.*
a journey across/along/around etc sth *The journey across Europe was long and hard.*
on a journey *We made many friends on our journey.*

PHRASES

a leg/stage of a journey (=one part of a journey) *We set off on the final leg of our journey.*

joy *n* great happiness and pleasure

PHRASES

be filled with joy (*also* **be full of joy**) *I was filled with joy at the thought of seeing her again.*
be jumping for joy (=be very pleased about something) *She tried to appear calm, but she was secretly jumping for joy.*
tears of joy *She began to cry again, but they were tears of joy.*
a feeling/sense of joy *A feeling of total joy swept over him.*
a look of joy *There was a look of joy on their faces.*
shouts/cries of joy *They greeted each other with cries of joy.*

ADJECTIVES

great joy *There was great joy in the town that day.*
pure/sheer/complete joy *The victory was a moment of pure joy.*
overwhelming joy *formal* (=very great joy) *He felt overwhelming joy at seeing her again.*
true/real joy *She is still trying to find true joy in her life.*

VERBS

give (sb) joy *His music has given people a lot of joy over the years.*
bring joy to sb (=make someone feel joy) *Her children have brought her great joy.*
feel/experience joy *I had never experienced such joy before.*
express your joy *It was nice to see the children express their joy so openly.*

PREPOSITIONS

joy at sth *The book describes the joy she felt at her children's happiness.*
to sb's joy (=used for saying that something makes someone very happy) *To my great joy, she agreed to marry me.*

judge[1] *n*

1 an important public official, whose job is to make decisions in a court

ADJECTIVES/NOUNS + judge

a high court judge *A high court judge ordered that the men should be released.*
a federal judge *AmE* (=a judge in a federal court) *A federal judge ruled that the land belonged to them.*
a trial judge *The trial judge instructed the jury to ignore what the witness had just said.*
a senior judge *He is Scotland's most senior judge.*
the presiding judge (=the most important judge in charge of the trial) *The presiding judge refused to accept his claim.*

VERBS

a judge orders sth *The judge ordered that she should pay a fine.*
a judge rules (that)... (=says that this is what he or she has decided) *The judge ruled that there was not enough evidence to prove him guilty.*
a judge finds sb innocent/guilty (=decide that someone is innocent or guilty) *The judges found her innocent of all charges.*
a judge sentences sb to 6 months/5 years etc in prison (=says that someone must go to prison as a punishment) *The judge sentenced the men to three years in prison.*
a judge imposes a fine/penalty/prison sentence (=gives someone a fine or punishment) *The judge can impose a fine of up to $1 million.*
a judge awards/grants sth *The judge awarded him £20,000 compensation.*
a judge hears a case/evidence/testimony (=considers it, in order to make a decision) *Three judges will hear the case.*
a judge throws out a case/the charges (=decides that there should not be a trial) *The judge threw out all the charges against him.*

a judge overturns/overrules sb/sth (=changes an earlier legal decision) *Two senior judges overturned the ruling.*

a judge dismisses/rejects sth (=refuses to accept something) *The judge rejected this argument.*

a judge instructs a jury (=advises the jury to do something) *The judge instructed the jury about the main legal points in the case.*

2 someone who decides who has won a competition

ADJECTIVES

an independent judge *The winner will be decided by a panel of independent judges.*

NOUNS + judge

a competition judge *The competition judges were impressed by her singing.*

VERBS

a judge awards (sb) a prize *The judges awarded him first prize.*

a judge decides sth *The judges decided that there were two winners.*

PHRASES

a panel of judges (=a group of judges) *Each competitor will cook their dish in front of a panel of judges.*

judge² *v*

to form or give an opinion after thinking carefully

PHRASES

sth is difficult/hard/impossible to judge *It is difficult to judge the size of the problem.*

judge sth a success/failure *The concert was judged a success.*

judge sth on its merits (=according to how good it is and nothing else) *The ideas should be judged on their merits, regardless of who suggested them.*

judge sth on the basis of sth (=using a particular thing to make your decision) *You can't judge someone's progress on the basis of a single exam.*

judge it best/better to do sth *The animal looked fierce, so I judged it best not to approach it.*

judge whether/if/how etc *It is impossible, at this early stage, to judge whether the experiment will work.*

judging by sth (=used for giving a reason for your opinion) *Judging by the smile on his face, I'd say he's had some good news.*

ADVERBS

judge sth objectively/fairly/impartially (=in a fair way, without being affected by your own personal feelings or interests) *Local people are worried that their protests will not be judged objectively.*

judge sb harshly (=in a severe or unkind way) *Do not judge her too harshly; she was very young at the time.*

judge sth correctly *It takes a lot of experience to judge correctly how hard to hit the ball.*

PREPOSITIONS

judge sb/sth on/according to sth (=by considering something) *Candidates are judged on their performance on the day.*

judge sth against sth (=by comparing one thing with another) *Readers will inevitably judge this new book against her earlier novels.*

judgment (*also* judgement) *n*

1 an opinion that you form, especially after thinking carefully about something

VERBS

make/form a judgment *I prefer to form my own judgments, rather than relying on other people's opinions.*

come to/reach a judgment (=make a judgment after considering all the facts) *The tribunal will examine all the evidence before coming to a judgment.*

pass judgment (on sth) (=give your opinion, especially a negative one) *Our aim is to help him, not to pass judgment on what he has done.*

base your judgment on sth *His judgment was based on the information available to him at the time.*

reserve judgment (=wait to decide until you have all the facts) *Why don't you reserve judgment until you have finished the book?*

ADJECTIVES

a moral judgment *You should always be careful when making moral judgments about other people's behaviour.*

a snap judgment (=made very quickly) *In business, you often have to make snap judgments.*

a balanced judgment *He interviewed as many people as possible so that he could form a balanced judgment.*

PREPOSITIONS

in sb's judgment *In my judgment, we should accept his offer.*

a judgment about/on sth *We won't make a judgment about the treatment until we have seen the full results.*

PHRASES

against sb's better judgment (=even though you think your action may be wrong) *I lent him the money, against my better judgment.*

2 the ability to make sensible decisions

VERBS

use your judgment *Officers have to use their professional judgment when handling a violent situation.*

trust/respect sb's judgment *I trusted Ben's judgment, so I asked his opinion.*

question sb's judgment (=have or express doubts about someone's decision) *She's the doctor – why should I question her judgment?*

affect/influence sb's judgment *Hill sometimes allowed his personal feelings to affect his judgment.*

cloud sb's judgment (=make someone less able to make good decisions) *Don't let your friends' comments cloud your judgment.*

impair your judgment (=stop it being as good as it should be) *Alcohol impairs your judgment, making you take risks you would not normally take.*

show good/bad etc judgment *I think his decision to sue the newspaper showed really poor judgment.*

rely on/upon sb's judgment *Business people are used to relying on their own judgment when making decisions.*

ADJECTIVES

good/sound judgment *They demonstrated good judgment in their choice of captain.*

bad/poor judgment *He showed poor judgment in discussing the affair with the press.*

sb's political judgment *Her handling of the matter has led people to question her political judgment.*

sb's personal judgment *Sometimes you have to rely on your own personal judgment.*

PHRASES

an error of judgment *In trusting him, Ellie had made a serious error of judgment.*

a lack of judgment *Doesn't that show a lack of judgment on your part?* (=show a lack of judgment by you)

sth is a matter/question of judgment *How you decide to proceed is very much a matter of personal judgment.*

juicy *adj* THESAURUS ▶ delicious

jungle *n*

a thick tropical forest with many large plants growing very close together

ADJECTIVES/NOUNS + jungle

dense jungle (=where trees grow close together) *The explorers walked through miles of dense jungle.*

remote jungle (=far from other places) *A new species of rat has been discovered in a remote jungle in Indonesia.*

tropical jungle *On the island of Timor there are large areas of tropical jungle.*

the Amazon/African etc jungle *The plane crashed in the Amazon jungle.*

PHRASES

deep in the jungle *They discovered a lost city deep in the jungle.*

junk *n*

unwanted objects that have no use or value

ADJECTIVES

old junk *The garage was full of old junk.*

useless/unwanted junk *I need to tidy the house and get rid of a lot of useless junk.*

household junk *Almost all your household junk can be re-used or recycled.*

PHRASES

a heap/pile of junk *There was a large pile of junk in the front garden that included an old cooker.*

a bit/piece of junk *The artist creates sculptures out of pieces of junk.*

jury *n*

a group of people in a court who decide whether someone is guilty or not

PHRASES

a member of the jury *Only three members of the jury were women.*

the foreman of the jury (=its leader, who announces its decision) *The foreman of the jury announced a guilty verdict.*

trial by jury *Defendants have a right to trial by jury.*

the jury finds sb guilty/not guilty (=says officially whether someone is guilty or not) *The jury found her not guilty of her husband's murder.*

the jury reaches a verdict (*also* **the jury arrives at a verdict**) (=decides if someone is guilty or not guilty) *The judge asked if the jury had reached its verdict.*

VERBS + jury

sit/serve on a jury (=be a member of a jury) *I've never served on a jury before.*

just *adj* THESAURUS ▶ fair

justice *n*

1 the system of judging people in courts of law and punishing criminals

VERBS

face justice *It is important that he faces justice for his crimes.*

escape justice (=escape being punished) *The thieves managed to escape justice.*

demand justice *The families of the murder victims are demanding justice.*

bring sb to justice (=catch and punish someone) *No one has been brought to justice for any of these killings.*

justice is done (=a case is judged fairly in a court of law, especially with the result that the person who committed a crime is punished) *We want to see that justice is done.*

administer/dispense justice *formal* (=to judge cases and decide if someone should be punished) *In wartime, the courts were closed and* *it was impossible to administer justice in the normal way.*

obstruct justice (=prevent a case from being judged fairly, usually by lying or hiding evidence) *She was charged with obstructing justice by lying to the police.*

justice + NOUNS

the justice system *The criminal justice system is in need of reform.*

the justice minister *The justice minister confirmed that a total of 5,200 prisoners had been released.*

the justice department *The Justice Department believes that it has now caught everybody involved in the fraud.*

PHRASES

a miscarriage of justice *formal* (=an occasion when justice is not done and someone is unfairly punished) *His lawyer claims that he is the victim of a miscarriage of justice and he was denied a fair trial.*

pervert the course of justice *formal* (=prevent justice from being done by lying, hiding evidence etc) *The men are accused of attempting to pervert the course of justice by threatening witnesses.*

2 fairness in the way people are treated

ADJECTIVES

social justice (=fair treatment for everyone in society, both rich and poor) *The government aims to improve social justice by providing better schools in poor neighbourhoods.*

rough justice (=punishment that is not decided in court in the usual legal way, and that is often severe or unfair) *Gangs practise a kind of rough justice on their members.*

poetic justice (=a situation in which something bad happens to someone, but they deserve it because they have done something bad) *After the way he treated her, it's poetic justice that she left him.*

PHRASES

a sense of justice *He has a strong sense of justice, and feels that people who work hard should be rewarded for their efforts.*

justification Ac *n*

a good and acceptable reason for doing something

PHRASES

there is no/little justification for doing sth *There is no justification for holding her in jail.*

use sth as a justification *The terrorists try to use religion as a justification for their crimes.*

with some justification *Hoggart felt, with some justification, that his friends had let him down.*

VERBS

provide/give/offer a justification *The company failed to provide a justification for its actions.*

see/find justification *I can see little justification for most of the changes.*

need justification (*also* **require justification** *formal*): *Spending money on such a project will require justification.*

ADJECTIVES

sufficient justification (=a good enough reason) *You can't put someone in prison without sufficient justification.*

ample justification (=more than enough good reasons) *If she was angry, she had ample justification.*

a reasonable/rational justification *He could provide no rational justification for his change of mind.*

legal/economic/scientific justification *I see no economic justification for investing in new equipment.*

moral justification *There was no moral justification for the war.*

theoretical justification (=theories that give a reason) *The article examines theoretical justifications for capital punishment.*

the main justification *The main justification for this policy is that it will save money.*

the only justification *He believed that profit was the only justification for being in business.*

further justification *He doesn't need to give any further justification of his decision.*

a possible justification *What possible justification can there be for sacking her?*

PREPOSITIONS

without justification *Police officers cannot stop and search people without justification.*

justification for sth *There is no justification for this belief.*

justification of sth *This gives a justification of the method used.*

juvenile *adj*

THESAURUS ▸ **young**

keen *adj* THESAURUS › **enthusiastic**

keep (on) doing sth *v* THESAURUS › **continue (1)**

key[1] *n*

1 a shaped piece of metal that fits into a lock to open a door etc

ADJECTIVES/NOUNS + key

a door/house key *I can't find my house keys.*
car keys *She left her car keys on the hall table.*
the ignition key (=the key that starts an engine) *She turned the ignition key and drove slowly away.*
a spare key *She hides her spare key under the doormat.*

VERBS

put the key in a lock/door (*also* **insert the key** *formal*): *I put the key in the lock and opened the door.*
turn the key *He climbed into his car and turned the key.*

PHRASES

a bunch/set of keys (=a group of keys kept together) *He had a huge bunch of keys hanging from his belt.*
get a key cut (=have a key made) *I got another key cut for my brother.*

2 a button that you press on a computer keyboard

NOUNS + key

the return/shift/control etc key *Use the Return key to move the cursor down to the next line.*

VERBS

press/hit a key *Press the Delete key to get rid of a word you have typed.*
hold down a key *Hold down the Control key while you press the Function key.*

3 the thing that makes something possible or successful

VERBS

hold/have the key (=be the person or thing that brings success) *He's the player who holds the key to victory in the World Cup.*

PREPOSITIONS

the key to sth *Money still seems to be the key to success in American politics.*

key[2] *adj* very important

NOUNS

a key factor *The weather could be a key factor in tomorrow's game.*
a key element/feature/component *Advertising is a key element in the success of a product.*
a key role/part *The captain played a key role in the team's winning season.*
a key area *What are the key areas of the government's economic policy?*
a key issue/question/point *The environment became a key issue during the election.*
a key figure (=person) *Adams was a key figure in the company's success.*
a key player (=a person, organization etc that has a very important role in a situation, or an important player in a team) *Germany is a key player within the EU.*
a key witness (=someone who can give important information about a crime) *She will be a key witness in the murder trial.*
a key decision *Women made most of the key decisions about money in these families.*

ADVERBS

absolutely key *For any business to succeed, timing is absolutely key.*
clearly/obviously key *His good looks have obviously been key to his success.*

PREPOSITIONS

key to sth *Finding a safe place to live is key to survival for these animals.*

THESAURUS: key

big, significant, major, notable, key, essential, vital, crucial/critical, paramount, historic, landmark, momentous → **important (1)**

top, key, leading, influential, prominent, valued → **important (2)**

kick[1] *v*

to hit something or someone with your foot

ADVERBS

kick sb/sth hard *Her brother kicked her leg hard under the table.*
kick sb/sth repeatedly *He had been repeatedly kicked as he lay on the ground.*

NOUNS

kick a ball/football *Billy was kicking a ball around the yard.*
kick the door down/open (=force it to open by kicking) *The police had to kick the door down.*
kick off your shoes *She kicked off her shoes and sat down.*

kick[2] *n*

an act of hitting something with your foot, or a movement of your leg that is like that

ADJECTIVES

a good/hard kick (=with a lot of force) *The machine only works if you give it a good kick.*

a swift kick (=done quickly and with force) *She gave me a swift kick on the shins.*

a well-aimed kick *He was knocked over by a well-aimed kick to his chest.*

VERBS

give sth a kick *He gave the door a kick.*

get a kick *While trying to get the ball, he got a kick on the ankle.*

kid *n informal* a child

ADJECTIVES/NOUNS + kid

a young kid *She has two young kids.*

a little kid (=a very young child) *He lived in Los Angeles when he was a little kid.*

a school kid *A group of school kids were being shown around the museum.*

a four-year-old/a five-year-old etc kid *Even a four-year-old kid knows that.*

VERBS

raise a kid (=look after a child) *After his wife died, he had to raise the kids on his own.*

PHRASES

a wife and kids *He had a wife and kids to support.*

be just a kid *She was just a kid and didn't know that she was doing anything wrong.*

kill *v* to make someone die

NOUNS

kill a man/woman/person *Police officers shot and killed a man in Los Angeles.*

kill an animal/insect/plant *I believe it is wrong to kill any animal.*

kill germs/bacteria/cancer cells *If you boil the water it will kill all the bacteria.*

kill yourself *She tried to kill herself by taking an overdose of sleeping tablets.*

ADVERBS

deliberately/accidentally kill sb *He accidentally killed one of his patients by giving them the wrong medicine.*

slowly kill sb *The disease was slowly killing him.*

kill sb/sth humanely (=in a way that does not cause unnecessary suffering) *Does it matter if a murderer is killed humanely?*

kill sb unlawfully *formal* (=illegally) *The journalist was unlawfully killed by US troops.*

be tragically killed (=used when this is very sad) *His son was tragically killed in a plane crash.*

be killed instantly (=immediately) *The driver of the car was killed instantly.*

be needlessly killed (=in a way that is unnecessary) *Our soldiers are being needlessly killed, in a war which cannot be won.*

kill (sb) indiscriminately *formal* (=without caring which person dies) *The terrorists kill indiscriminately.*

Be killed

Kill is often used in the passive, when saying that someone dies: *One **soldier** was **killed** and another seriously injured.*

THESAURUS: kill

murder
to deliberately kill someone - used when talking about this as a crime:
He was found guilty of murdering his wife. | Watson was brutally murdered by robbers in his own home.

assassinate
president | prime minister | king | leader | politician | judge
to deliberately kill an important person:
The president was assassinated on 22nd November 1963 in Dallas. | He was part of a plot to assassinate Hitler.

execute (*also* **put sb to death**)
prisoner | criminal | murderer | killer
to kill someone as a punishment for a crime:
85 prisoners were executed in the US in 2000. | McVeigh, who killed 168 people in a bombing attack, was executed by lethal injection.

slay
to kill someone or something in a violent way. **Slay** is an old-fashioned word which is used in old stories and in news reports:
The king was slain at the Battle of Hastings. | St George slew the dragon. | The victims were slain in their beds.

to kill a large number of people

massacre
to kill a large number of people in a violent way:
Hundreds of demonstrators were massacred in the city's main square. | The soldiers massacred men, women, and children.

slaughter
to kill animals for food, or to kill a large number of people in a cruel and violent way:
The pigs are slaughtered on the farm. | It is estimated that half a million people were slaughtered.

exterminate
to kill large numbers of a particular group of people or animals, so that they no longer exist:
The Nazis exterminated six million Jews. | They want to exterminate all the rats from the building.

wipe out
to kill all of a group of people, animals, or plants. **Wipe out** is more informal than **exterminate**:
Whole villages were wiped out. | It was not long before the species was wiped out.

to kill yourself

commit suicide
to kill yourself:
*He **tried to commit suicide** after the death of his girlfriend.*

take your own life
to kill yourself:
Ian Curtis tragically took his own life in 1980, after recording the song 'Love will tear us apart'. | Some people believe that it is a sin to take your own life.

Take your own life or commit suicide?
Take your own life sounds rather formal, and shows a feeling of sympathy for the person who died. **Commit suicide** sounds more neutral. **Take your own life** is also often used in moral discussions.

kind[1] *n*

one of the different types of a person or thing that belong to the same group

ADJECTIVES

all kinds/every kind of *You can buy all kinds of fruit at the market.*

different kinds of *The flowers attract many different kinds of insects.*

the same kind of *We both have the same kind of car.*

some kind of *Carved into the stone was some kind of design.*

(of) any kind *There was no television, no radio – no technology of any kind.*

the right/wrong kind of *It isn't the right kind of course for me.*

the best/worst kind of *The best kind of teaching is when the teacher also gets to learn from her students.*

a certain/particular/specific kind of *Certain kinds of cancer can be treated with drugs.*

various kinds *Students have to read various kinds of literature, including novels, plays, and poetry.*

ADVERBS

precisely/exactly the kind of *This was precisely the kind of advice she needed.*

PREPOSITIONS

a kind of sth *A vihuela is a kind of small guitar.*

PHRASES

what kind of *What kind of sandwich would you like?*

of its kind *It is the biggest shopping centre of its kind in the country.*

of this kind *How can we be sure a disaster of this kind will not happen again?*

of the worst/best etc kind *This is hypocrisy of the worst kind.*

that kind of thing *She usually wears trainers and jeans, that kind of thing.*

kind[2] *adj*

saying or doing things that show that you care about other people and want to help them or make them happy

NOUNS

a kind man/woman/person *The priest was a kind man and he took the trouble to sit and talk to her.*

a kind face/smile *The old lady had a kind face and gentle blue eyes.*

kind words *Thank you for your kind words about the magazine – I'm glad you like it.*

a kind offer/invitation/gift *Jenny wrote to say that she would be delighted to accept their kind offer.*

a kind thing *It was a kind thing to say.*

a kind letter *We cannot thank you all enough for the kind letters of support.*

ADVERBS

extremely/incredibly/really kind *The staff were really kind to me and they made me feel that they genuinely cared.*

most kind (=very kind – used when thanking someone politely) *Thank you for your help. You've been most kind.*

PREPOSITIONS

kind to sb *The local people were very kind to us.*

it is kind of sb (to do sth) *It was kind of him to offer to lend the money.*

THESAURUS: kind

generous
person | offer | gift | present | donation
kind because you give people money, presents etc:
*He's one of the most generous people I've ever met – he even offered me the use of his villa in Florida. | Dr Singer thanked the chairman for his generous gift. | "I'll pay for the meal." "That's very **generous of** you." | He was always very **generous with** his money.*

considerate
person | neighbour
thinking about other people's feelings, and careful not to do anything that will upset them:
*Our neighbours are very considerate and always keep their TV turned down. | He's always very polite and **considerate to** his guests. | "I didn't want to interrupt your conversation." "That was very **considerate of** you!"*

K

thoughtful
person | gift | present
thinking of things you can do to make other people happy or feel good – used especially when someone does something such as giving someone a present or helping someone:
Some thoughtful person had taken her bag to the lost property office. | I thanked him for his thoughtful gift. | It was ***thoughtful of*** *you to send him a card.*

caring
person | man | woman | husband | family | attitude | approach | society | environment
kind and wanting to help and look after people:
She's lucky to have such a loving and caring husband. | The British are well known for their caring attitude toward animals.

sympathetic
smile | look | listener | audience | attitude | manner
someone who is sympathetic cares about a person who has problems, and shows this by their behaviour:
She gave me a sympathetic smile and said "I know just how you feel!" | Her boss was very ***sympathetic towards*** *her and said she should take some time off work. | He was always ready to* ***lend a sympathetic ear*** (=listen to someone talk about their problems).

compassionate
person | man | woman | look
someone who is compassionate wants to help people who are suffering or having problems, and does not want to punish them or treat them badly:
Instead of getting angry, she gave her young friend a compassionate look. | The man was released from prison ***on compassionate grounds*** (=for compassionate reasons, for example because he was very ill).

warm-hearted/kind-hearted
person | man | woman
having a kind and friendly character, which makes other people like you:
She was a warm-hearted affectionate person and I shall always remain grateful to her.

benevolent *formal*
despot | dictator | ruler | dictatorship | God | uncle
kind and wanting to help people – used about someone who is important or well respected:
Ford was a benevolent despot who refused to allow labor unions, but paid his workers more than the national average (=a leader who had complete power, but who treated his or her people kindly). *| They believe that the universe was created by a wise and benevolent God. | He listened politely, like a benevolent uncle.*

saying someone is kind in spoken English

nice *especially spoken*
man | woman | thing
friendly and kind. **Nice** is very common in everyday spoken English and is often used instead of **kind**:
He seems such a nice man. | They said lots of nice things about you. | Everyone has been so ***nice to*** *me. |* ***It's nice of*** *you to invite me here.*

good *especially spoken*
man | woman | friend
kind and showing that you want to help:
He had been a good friend to her in the past. | ***It was good of you to*** *come and see me. | She's always been very* ***good to*** *us. | They were very* ***good about it*** *and gave me a new phone.*

sweet *especially spoken*
man | woman | lady | child | thing
very kind – used especially when you like someone very much, or you are very pleased because of something they have done:
I was given the flowers by a ***sweet little*** *old lady who lived next door. | What a sweet thing to say! |* ***It's sweet of*** *you to ask.*

ANTONYMS **kind → unkind**

kindness *n*
kind behaviour towards someone

ADJECTIVES

great kindness *His aunt had shown him great kindness when he was ill.*

unexpected kindness *Lisa felt touched by the girl's unexpected kindness.*

VERBS

thank sb for their kindness *We thanked him for his kindness in lending us the money.*

treat sb with kindness *Guests should be treated with kindness and respect.*

show sb kindness *The neighbours showed her a lot of kindness when she first moved in.*

appreciate sb's kindness *Thank you very much. I appreciate your kindness.*

repay sb's kindness *He wondered how he would ever be able to repay her kindness.*

PREPOSITIONS

kindness to/towards sb *She greatly appreciated his kindness to her.*

out of kindness/out of the kindness of your heart (=because you want to help someone) *He visited her out of kindness.*

PHRASES

an act of kindness *Paul remembered the many small acts of kindness she had done for him in the past.*

the kindness of strangers *If you get into trouble away from home, you often have to rely upon the kindness of strangers.*

king *n*

a man who is the royal ruler of a country

VERBS

become king *He will become king when the Queen dies.*

crown sb king (=officially give someone the position of king) *George was crowned king following the death of his father.*

depose/overthrow a king *formal* (=remove a king from power) *The Spanish king was deposed in 1931.*

a king rules/reigns *He was the king who reigned during the Second World War.*

a king abdicates (=gives up the position of being king) *It shocked the nation when King Edward VIII abdicated.*

ADJECTIVES

the future king *She married the future king of France, Philip Augustus.*

the rightful king (=the person who should be king) *The Duke of Gloucester claimed that he was the rightful king.*

PHRASES

a king's subjects (=the people he rules) *The new laws were very unpopular with the king's subjects.*

kiss[1] *v*

to touch someone or something with your lips, especially to show affection

ADVERBS

kiss sb gently/lightly *She smiled and kissed him gently on the cheek.*

kiss sb tenderly (=in way that shows you love someone) *He held her tightly against him, kissing her tenderly.*

kiss sb passionately *They looked at one another for a second and kissed passionately.*

PREPOSITIONS

kiss sb on the cheek/lips/mouth/hand *She kissed her husband on the cheek before leaving the house.*

> You can also say **kiss sb's cheek/lips/mouth/hand**: *He leant forward and kissed her hand.*

PHRASES

kiss sb goodbye/goodnight *He kissed her goodbye and watched her get on the train.*

kiss[2] *n* an act of kissing

ADJECTIVES/NOUNS + kiss

a big/little kiss *She put her arms around him and gave him a big kiss.*

a quick kiss *He gave her a quick kiss before leaving for work.*

your first kiss *Do you remember your first kiss?*

a farewell/goodnight kiss *Don't go to bed without your goodnight kiss!*

a gentle kiss *He gave her a gentle kiss on her cheek.*

a passionate kiss *He gave her a passionate kiss.*

VERBS

give sb a kiss *Come and give me a kiss.*

blow sb a kiss (=kiss your hand and then blow across it towards someone) *Joe blew her a kiss and waved goodbye.*

PHRASES

love and kisses (=used at the end of a letter) *See you soon. Lots of love and kisses from Anna.*

knock[1] *v*

1 to hit a door or window with your closed hand to attract the attention of the people inside

ADVERBS

knock hard/loudly *I knocked as hard as I could.*

knock gently *He knocked gently on her bedroom door.*

PREPOSITIONS

knock at/on the door *We knocked at the door but there was no-one there.*

knock at/on the window *I thought I could hear someone knocking on the window.*

2 to hit someone or something hard

ADVERBS AND PHRASES

knock sb unconscious/senseless (=hit someone so hard that they become unconscious) *The stone hit his head and knocked him unconscious.*

knock sb flying (=hit them so they fall or almost fall) *Ben ran through the door and knocked me flying.*

knock sb to the ground *He was punched twice and knocked to the ground.*

knock sb off balance *The blow almost knocked me off balance.*

PREPOSITIONS

knock sb/sth off sth *I accidentally knocked the plate off the table onto the floor.*

knock[2] *n*

the sound of someone hitting a door, window etc in order to ask to come into a house or room

ADJECTIVES

a loud/sharp knock *We heard a loud knock at the door.*

a gentle knock *I gave a gentle knock on the window.*

VERBS

hear a knock *When he heard a knock, he ran to the door.*

answer a knock *She answered a knock at the door and found a parcel on the doorstep.*

give a knock *He gave a knock, then walked in.*

PREPOSITIONS

a knock on/at the door/window *There was a knock at the window.*

knot *n*

a point where one or more pieces of string, rope, cloth etc have been tied or twisted together

VERBS

tie a knot *He taught me how to tie knots when I was a boy.*

untie/undo a knot *He managed to untie the knot and struggle free.*

loosen a knot (=make it less tight) *She loosened the knot in her shoelace.*

ADJECTIVES

a tight knot *The knot in my tie is really tight.*

a loose knot *She tied the scarf in a loose knot.*

PREPOSITIONS

a knot in sth *There's a knot in the string at one end.*

know *v*

to have information about something

ADVERBS

know how/why *Do you know how this works? | I don't know why I'm always so tired.*

know when/where *Nobody knows when he'll be back.*

know if/whether *Do you know if John is coming to the party?*

know beforehand (=before something happens or is done) *They always seemed to know beforehand precisely where I would be.*

VERBS

let sb know (=tell them) *If you let me know what time your plane arrives, I'll pick you up.*

want to know *I thought you'd want to know immediately.*

PREPOSITIONS

know about sth *I need to know more about the job before I decide whether to apply for it.*

know of sth *Do you know of any good places to eat?*

PHRASES

as you/we know *"I'm divorced, as you know," she said.*

if you must know (=used when you are angry because someone wants to know something) *If you must know, I was with James last night.*

knowledge *n*

information, skills, and understanding you have gained through learning or experience

ADJECTIVES/NOUNS + knowledge

considerable/extensive/vast knowledge *She had considerable knowledge of antiques.*

general knowledge (=about a lot of different subjects) *The questions are intended to test your general knowledge.*

scientific/technical knowledge *There have been great advances in scientific knowledge over the past 100 years.*

specialist/expert knowledge *Making profitable investments requires specialist knowledge.*

detailed knowledge *You need to have a detailed knowledge of criminal law.*

first-hand/personal knowledge (=from experiencing something yourself) *These soldiers have first-hand knowledge of war.*

basic knowledge (=of the basic aspects of something) *These things are obvious to anyone with even a basic knowledge of computers.*

in-depth/thorough knowledge (=detailed knowledge about all of a particular subject) *He demonstrated an in-depth knowledge of the subject matter.*

intimate knowledge (=knowledge about something because you are involved in it) *He seemed to have an intimate knowledge of prison life.*

inside knowledge (=that you have because you are part of a group) *His inside knowledge is gained from 20 years in the industry.*

background knowledge (=that you need before you can understand or do something) *The test will show what background knowledge a student brings to the course.*

VERBS

have some knowledge of sth *The book assumes that you already have some knowledge of physics.*

get knowledge (*also* **gain/acquire knowledge** *formal*): *He gets all his knowledge about politics from watching the television.*

⚠ Don't say 'learn knowledge'.

increase/improve your knowledge *If you want to improve your knowledge of the language, you should go and live in France.*

broaden/expand your knowledge (=increase your knowledge) *The course is designed to help students broaden their knowledge of modern American literature.*

show/demonstrate your knowledge *The test should be an opportunity for students to demonstrate their knowledge.*

use your knowledge (*also* **apply your knowledge** *formal*): *She decided to use her knowledge to set up her own business.*

test sb's knowledge *This quiz will test your knowledge of current events.*

PHRASES

a thirst for knowledge (=a desire to learn more) *She arrived at college with a thirst for knowledge.*

sb's breadth of knowledge (=knowledge about all the different parts of something) *They lack his breadth of knowledge about the industry.*

be common knowledge (=be known by most people) *It's common knowledge that he's gay.*

PREPOSITIONS

knowledge of/about sth *My knowledge of the subject is limited. | Young people's knowledge about the harmful effects of smoking is considerable.*

THESAURUS: knowledge

expertise
special knowledge about how to do something, that you get through experience, training, or study:
*The **technical expertise** was provided by a Japanese company. | The country needs people with **medical expertise*** (=doctors, nurses etc).

know-how
practical knowledge about how to do something. **Know-how** is more informal than **expertise**:
*They don't have the **technical know-how** to build a nuclear weapon. | You don't need any special know-how to install the program.*

grasp
the ability to understand a subject or situation:
*She speaks French well and **has a good grasp of** the language. | He's been praised for his **grasp of** the country's economic problems.*

wisdom
good sense and judgment, based on knowledge and experience:
*In these societies, people respect the wisdom of older family members | The book is full of **ancient wisdom**. | Thank you for all your **words of wisdom*** (=wise advice).

Ll

label [Ac] *n*

a piece of paper or another material that is attached to something and gives information about it

ADJECTIVES/NOUNS + label

a price label *The book still has the price label on it.*

a luggage label *It's a good idea to attach a luggage label to your suitcase in case it gets lost.*

a product label *According to the product label, the drink is full of vitamin C.*

a food label *Food labels should say exactly what's in the food.*

a warning label *Cigarette packets now have warning labels on them.*

a sticky label (=a label that has been glued onto something) *Each CD has a sticky label on the front.*

an address label *She stuck an address label on the envelope.*

VERBS

put/stick a label on sth *He put a label on each plastic container with a description of its contents.*

read/check the label *Always read the label on the bottle.*

have a label (*also* **carry/bear a label** *formal*): *The packet has a label with a picture of a happy cow on it.*

the label says *The label says that the jacket should be dry-cleaned.*

PREPOSITIONS

on the label *The country of origin is on the label.*

laboratory *n*

a special room or building used for research by scientists or engineers

laboratory + NOUNS

a laboratory experiment *Many people believe that animals should not be used in laboratory experiments.*

laboratory studies/research/analysis *Laboratory studies showed that the medicine was effective in 90% of cases.*

a laboratory technician/assistant *The laboratory technician set up the equipment.*

laboratory work *Students spend most of the course doing laboratory work.*

NOUNS + laboratory

a research laboratory *The company tests out its new products in a research laboratory.*

PHRASES

in the laboratory *The samples were tested in the laboratory.*

under laboratory conditions *The experiment was carried out under laboratory conditions.*

> In informal English, people use the short form **lab**: *The samples were sent off to the **lab** for analysis.*
> **Lab** is often used in compounds: **a lab coat**, **a lab technician**, **lab tests**, and **lab results**.

labour [Ac] *BrE*, **labor** *AmE n*

1 all the people who work for a company or in a country

ADJECTIVES/NOUNS + labour

skilled labour *There is a shortage of skilled labour in the country.*

unskilled labour *Wages for unskilled labor were the lowest.*

cheap labour (=workers who have low wages) *Women and children were used as cheap labour.*

casual labour (=workers who do jobs that are not permanent) *The industry makes use of a large supply of casual labor.*

child labour *The shoe company was accused of using child labour in its factory.*

slave labour *Cotton was grown using slave labor.*

migrant labour (=workers who move somewhere to work there) *Companies are relying on migrant labour rather than training domestic workers.*

labour + NOUNS

the labour force (=all the people who work in a country or for a company) *70% of the labor force are employed in agriculture.*

the labour supply (=all the people available to work) *What was the effect of the war on the labour supply?*

the labour market (=the people looking for work and the jobs available) *She had lost confidence after being out of the labour market for so long.*

a labour shortage *Immigrants came into the country to fill the labour shortage.*

labour costs *We need to reduce our labor costs.*

labour relations (=the relationship between employers and workers) *The company has fairly good labour relations.*

2 work, especially physical work

ADJECTIVES

manual labour (=work with your hands) *He's a builder, so he's used to manual labour.*

physical labour *Childhood was followed by hard physical labour in factories.*

hard labour (=hard physical work given as a punishment) *He was sentenced to 6 months hard labor.*

forced labour (=that prisoners or slaves are forced to do) *They were either executed or sentenced to long periods of forced labour.*

VERBS

withdraw your labour (=protest by stopping work) *Workers withdrew their labour for 24 hours.*

labour + NOUNS

a labour camp *Some were sent to prisons and some to labor camps.*

> If something needs a lot of work by a lot of people, you say that it is **labour-intensive**: *Picking strawberries is very* ***labour-intensive***.

lack[1] *v*

to not have something that you need, or not have enough of it

NOUNS

lack confidence *As a teenager I lacked confidence.*

lack experience *I found it hard to get a job after college because I lacked experience.*

lack the skills/knowledge/expertise *These children lack the language skills to communicate properly.*

lack resources/funds *The police lack the resources to tackle the problem.*

lack courage *He wanted to kiss her but lacked the courage to do so.*

lack ambition *My children all seem to lack ambition.*

lack imagination *His last novel lacked imagination.*

lack credibility (=be difficult to believe or trust) *The plot of the film lacks credibility.*

ADVERBS

be completely/totally/entirely lacking *The show is almost completely lacking in humour.*

be sorely lacking (=to a very great and serious degree) *I find his poetry sorely lacking in imagination.*

be sadly lacking (=be unfortunately lacking) *Marriage requires commitment, a quality sadly lacking in couples today.*

PREPOSITIONS

be lacking in sth *He is almost totally lacking in confidence.*

lack[2] *n*

a situation in which there is not enough or not much of something

ADJECTIVES

a complete/total lack of sth *I was amazed by his almost total lack of interest in music.*

a relative/comparative lack of sth (=when compared with other things) *The relative lack of progress in the peace talks is frustrating.*

a distinct/marked/conspicuous lack of sth (=very noticeable) *She showed a distinct lack of enthusiasm for his idea.*

a general lack of sth (=among most people) *There is a general lack of support for the war.*

a profound/serious/severe lack of sth (=very serious and bad) *His comments demonstrate a profound lack of understanding about the subject.*

an apparent lack of sth (=that seems to exist) *Adam's apparent lack of concern angered his brother.*

PREPOSITIONS

a lack of sth *Too often, teachers are treated with a lack of respect.*

for lack of sth (=because there is not enough) *The case against him was dropped for lack of evidence.*

PHRASES

there is no lack of sth (=there is plenty of it) *There was no lack of willing helpers.*

ladder *n*

a piece of equipment used for climbing, with bars for your feet

VERBS

climb/go up a ladder *He climbed the ladder up to the roof.*

go down a ladder (*also* **descend a ladder** *formal*): *It's important to go down the ladder slowly.*

fall off a ladder *One of the builders fell off a ladder and broke his leg.*

PHRASES

a rung/step of a ladder (=a bar that you put your foot on) *The first rung of the ladder was broken.*

the foot/bottom of a ladder *Get a friend to hold the bottom of the ladder for you.*

the top of a ladder *Tie the top of the ladder to something secure.*

lake *n*

a large area of water surrounded by land

PHRASES

the edge/shores/banks of a lake *The hotel is set on the shores of Lake Lugano.*

ADJECTIVES

a freshwater lake (=which does not contain salt water) *The crocodiles live in freshwater lakes in southern Pangaea.*

a man-made/artificial lake *There is a man-made lake where you can go fishing.*

a frozen lake *They skated with Edwin on the frozen lake.*

VERBS

go swimming/fishing in a lake *After breakfast, we went swimming in the lake.*

cross a lake *You can cross the lake by ferry.*

land *n*

1 an area of ground

ADJECTIVES

flat land *The airport was built on an area of flat grassy land.*

open land (=with no buildings on it) *In the middle of the city are several hundred acres of open land.*

agricultural land *Farmers are always complaining about the price of agricultural land.*

industrial land (=for factories and industry) *Industrial land is often polluted and not necessarily suitable for building houses.*

arable land (=for growing crops) *The forest was cleared to create arable land.*

fertile land (=good for growing crops) *The land near the river is very fertile.*

poor land (=not good for growing crops) *The land on the hills is too poor for farming.*

barren land (=with nothing growing on it) *There was not a single tree to protect him on this barren land.*

derelict land *BrE* (=not used and in bad condition) *There are plans to transform an area of derelict land into a new sports stadium.*

vacant land *BrE* (=available for use) *There are very few areas of vacant land left.*

> **Farmland**, **parkland**, **wasteland**, **swampland**, and **marshland** are usually written as one word.

PHRASES

a piece of land (=an area of land) *He built a house on a piece of land near the river.*

a plot/parcel of land (=a piece of land, especially one that someone buys or rents) *They bought a small plot of land next to their house.*

a strip of land (=a narrow piece of land) *They owned the strip of land between the forest and the sea.*

a tract of land (=a large area of land) *The Kalahari Desert is a vast tract of land.*

an acre/hectare of land *The family owned hundreds of acres of land.*

VERBS

own land *First, find out who owns the land.*

land belongs to sb (=they own it) *The land belonged to her cousin.*

buy/sell land *We're thinking of buying some land and building a house on it.*

clear land (=remove buildings, trees etc from it) *They cleared more land and made new villages.*

develop land (=build houses, factories etc on it) *Developing derelict land can only improve our cities.*

work/farm the land (=grow crops) *Many people were forced to give up working the land.*

live off the land (=grow or catch all the food you need) *A third of the region's population lives off the land.*

contaminate/pollute land (=spoil it with chemicals or poison) *Pollution from the factory is contaminating agricultural land.*

2 the part of the Earth's surface that is not covered in water

ADJECTIVES

dry land *It was good to get off the ship onto dry land.*

VERBS

reach land *The captain expects to reach land in about two days.*

see/sight land *After 21 days at sea, we sighted land.*

land + NOUNS

a land animal/bird *The white stork is one of the biggest land birds of the region.*

land forces (=soldiers who fight on land, not at sea or in planes) *Action by air, sea, or land forces may be necessary.*

PREPOSITIONS

on land *The crocodile lays its eggs on land.*

by land *All supplies are transported by land.*

3 a country or region

ADJECTIVES

a foreign land *Their journey took them to many foreign lands.*

a distant/far-off land *He fled to a distant land.*

sb's native land (=the country where someone was born) *She misses the beauty of her native land.*

the Holy Land (=the place where most of the events in the Bible happened) *People visit the Holy Land to see the sacred sites.*

VERBS

rule a land *There once was a king who ruled the land.*

conquer a land *Many armies have tried to conquer our land.*

PREPOSITIONS

in a land *It is the most important court in the land.*

PHRASES

a land of opportunity *Australia represented a land of opportunity for thousands of people.*

a land of freedom *The United States of America was seen as a land of freedom and justice.*

a land of plenty (=where people have a lot of money, food etc) *To many Africans, South Africa is a land of plenty.*

a land of milk and honey (=where you can get everything that you want) *People seem to think the island is the land of milk and honey, but it really isn't.*

THESAURUS: land

nation, state, power, superpower, land → **country (1)**

landmark *n*

1 a building or other large object in a landscape that is easy to recognize

ADJECTIVES/NOUNS + landmark

a famous/well-known landmark *The Eiffel Tower is probably the most famous landmark in Paris.*

an important/major/significant landmark *From Parliament Hill, you can see most of London's major landmarks.*

a historic landmark *Rome is crammed with historic landmarks such as the Colosseum.*

a prominent landmark (=one that is very noticeable) *The castle sits on a hill above the town and is a prominent landmark.*

a familiar landmark *It was so dark we could not see any familiar landmarks.*

a local landmark *This oddly shaped rock is a well-known local landmark.*

a London/New York/Paris etc landmark *Buckingham Palace is a major London landmark.*

landmark + NOUNS

a landmark building *The park is a lovely setting for this landmark building.*

2 an important event or item in the development of something

ADJECTIVES

an important/significant landmark *Mozart's first work is an important landmark in the history of opera.*

a historic landmark *The peace agreement was a historic landmark.*

landmark + NOUNS

a landmark case *The company was found guilty of fraud in a landmark case.*

a landmark decision/ruling *In a landmark ruling, the Supreme Court said that racially segregated schools were unconstitutional.*

a landmark agreement/truce *The USA and Russia signed a landmark agreement.*

landmark elections *Mandela became president following landmark elections in South Africa.*

PREPOSITIONS

a landmark in sth *The album is regarded as a landmark in the history of rock music.*

VERBS

be seen as a landmark *The Pope's visit was seen as a landmark.*

represent a landmark *President Obama's election represented a landmark in American history.*

THESAURUS: landmark

big, significant, major, notable, key, essential, vital, crucial/critical, paramount, historic, landmark, momentous → **important (1)**

landscape *n*

an area of countryside or land of a particular type

ADJECTIVES

beautiful landscape *The landscape around Siena is incredibly beautiful.*

dramatic landscape (=very impressive) *The picture shows a dramatic landscape of mountains and clear blue lakes.*

wild landscape *The Brontë sisters' books are set in the wild landscape of the Yorkshire moors.*

rugged landscape (=with a lot of rocks and hills or mountains) *The island's rugged landscape can only be crossed on foot.*

desolate/bleak landscape (=with no attractive features) *It is a desolate landscape, with no trees or signs of habitation.*

barren landscape (=with no plants, trees, or buildings) *Birds can be seen searching the barren landscape for food.*

natural landscape *The new buildings blend into the natural landscape.*

industrial landscape *The cotton mills are part of the familiar industrial landscape of this part of England.*

rural landscape (=in the countryside) *Wind farms will have a big effect on the rural landscape.*

urban landscape (=in a city) *Kuwait city is an urban landscape of huge modern buildings.*

desert landscape *The desert landscape is hot and dusty.*

lunar landscape (=on the moon, or looking like the surface of the moon) *The volcano is surrounded by a lunar landscape.*

VERBS

dominate the landscape (=be larger or more noticeable than any other thing) *The church dominates the landscape.*

conserve/preserve the landscape *We want to preserve this beautiful landscape so future generations can enjoy it.*

PHRASES

be/become part of the landscape *The mine has been here for 200 years and has become part of the landscape.*

be a feature of the landscape *The square fields have not always been a feature of this landscape.*

have an effect/impact on the landscape *Building hundreds of new homes will have a big impact on the landscape.*

be a blot on the landscape (=spoil a landscape by being ugly) *The protesters say the wind farms are a blot on the landscape.*

a landscape is dotted with sth (=it contains a lot of something) *The landscape is dotted with pretty villages.*

lane *n*

1 a narrow road in the countryside or away from the main streets in a town

ADJECTIVES/NOUNS + lane

a country lane *There are no streetlights on country lanes.*

a narrow lane *A truck got stuck in the narrow lane.*

a winding lane (=one that curves in different directions) *We cycled along the winding lanes down to the sea.*

a quiet lane *Her house is at the end of a quiet lane.*

VERBS

a lane leads somewhere *The lane leads to a farm.*

turn into a lane *We turned into a lane with fields on either side.*

PREPOSITIONS

along a lane *A little way along the lane is a bridge.*

down/up a lane *They carried on down the lane towards the village.*

THESAURUS: lane

street, avenue, boulevard, lane, cul-de-sac, track, ring road, bypass, dual carriageway, freeway/expressway, motorway, interstate, toll road, turnpike → **road**

2 one of the parts that a large road is divided into

ADJECTIVES/NOUNS + lane

the slow/fast lane (=for people driving slowly or quickly) *The driver pulled out into the fast lane and overtook us.*

the middle lane *Take the middle lane and go straight ahead at the roundabout.*

the left-hand/right-hand lane *The left-hand lane takes you towards Calais.*

the right/wrong lane *Make sure you are in the right lane as you approach the roundabout.*

a bus/cycle lane (=for buses/bicycles only) *Cars are not allowed to use the bus lane.*

VERBS

change lanes *Make sure you give a signal before you change lanes.*

take a lane (=go in a particular lane) *Take the left-hand lane for Cambridge.*

pull/move out into a lane *A big truck suddenly pulled out into my lane.*

language *n*

1 a system of words and grammar used by the people of a particular country or area

ADJECTIVES

a foreign language *He found learning a foreign language extremely difficult.*

sb's first/native language (=the language someone first learned as a child) *His first language was Polish.*

a second language (=a language you speak that is not your first language) *Most of the students learned English as their second language.*

modern languages (=ones that are spoken now) *The school has a good modern languages department.*

a dead language (=one that is no longer spoken) *She didn't see the point of learning a dead language.*

the official language (=the language used for official business in a country) *Canada has two official languages: English and French.*

a common language (=a language that more than one person or group speaks, so that they can understand each other) *Most of the countries of South America share a common language: Spanish.*

the local language *I had learned a few phrases of the local language.*

the indigenous language *formal* (=spoken by a group of people living in a country, before other people arrived there) *In Guatemala there are more than 20 indigenous languages.*

an international language *English has become an international language.*

VERBS

speak a language *Can you speak a foreign language?*

use a language *The children use their native language at home.*

learn a language *It is important to learn the local language when living abroad.*

master a language (=succeed in learning a language well) *She had had a long struggle to master the Russian language.*

know a language *He had lived in Japan, but did not know the language.*

language + NOUNS

the language barrier (=the problem of communicating with someone when you do not speak the same language) *Because of the language barrier, it was hard for doctors to give good advice to patients.*

a language student/learner *Language learners often have problems with tenses.*

a language teacher *She worked as a foreign language teacher in a secondary school.*

language teaching *The article is about recent developments in language teaching.*

PHRASES

sb's command of a language (=someone's ability to speak a language) *Does he have a good command of the language?*

2 words in general

ADJECTIVES

bad/foul/strong/obscene language (=rude words) *There is some bad language in the play.*

spoken/written language *There are some big differences between spoken and written language.*

formal/informal language *The word 'hitherto' is used in formal language.*

plain/simple/everyday language *The leaflet is written in simple everyday language.*

legal/technical language *Lawyers often use complicated legal language.*

suitable language/the right language *When you are writing an essay, you need to use the right language.*

poetic language *The author uses beautiful poetic language.*

VERBS

use language *Some people were offended by the language he used.*

learn language (*also* **acquire language** *formal*): *Children mainly acquire language from their mothers.*

mind/watch your language (=used when telling someone not to use rude words) *You'd better mind your language in front of the teacher.*

> **Body language**
> You use **body language** about communication using your body, rather than words: *If you study his **body language**, you can see that he is lying.*

large *adj* THESAURUS **big (3)**

last[1] *adj, determiner*

1 the last one of a series of things is the one at the end, with no others after

NOUNS

the last time *That was the last time we saw him.*

the last day/week/morning etc *Today is the last day of the competition.*

last chance *This may be our last chance to save our planet.*

the last train/bus/plane *The last train leaves just before midnight.*

the last game/race *This is the last game of the season.*

the last part/stage/section/chapter *He was born in the last part of the 19th century.*

last words/line/sentence *His last words were "Don't shoot!"*

the last thing *The last thing I do at night is lock the front door.*

the last one *Our house is the last one on the right.*

PHRASES

the very last (=used to emphasize that something is the last one) *This is the very last chocolate in the box.*

last but one (=the one before the last one) *This is my last assignment but one.*

the last remaining *The region's last remaining forest is now a national park.*

THESAURUS: last

final

day | week | year | stage | phase | round | part | chapter | version | game | race | exam | scene | report | result | score | outcome | decision | verdict | words | thoughts | advice

Final is used about the last one in a series of things. It is also used when talking about something such as a result, decision, or report, which comes at the end of an event or process:

On the final day of their visit, Melissa and her parents were invited to the White House. | Chan received the most votes in the final round of voting. | They kiss each other in the final scene of the film. | The final score was 4–3 to United. | The committee will give their final decision next month.

> **Final or last?**
> You use both **final** and **last** about the last one of a series of things. You can say *the **last** week* or *the **final** week.*
> You usually say the **last train/bus/plane** (not the 'final' one).
> You also use **final** about something important, that comes at the end of an event or process. You say: *the **final** decision/verdict* (not the 'last' one) | *the **final** result/score/outcome* (not the 'last' one) | *the **final** version* (not the 'last' one).
> **Final exams** are usually the most important exams, which you take at the end of a course.

closing

date | stages | minutes | days | weeks | months | years | session | scene | lines | words

happening at the end, or near the end:

The closing date for applications is June 30th. | We are now entering the closing stages of the competition. | The ship sinks in the closing scene of the film. | The closing words of her book are: "But enough about me".

concluding

section | remarks | chapter | paragraph | lines | sentence

happening at the end of something, especially a book, report, speech, or meeting:

In the concluding section, he considers the relationship between the artist and society. | The judge made his concluding remarks. | We will return to this issue in the concluding chapter.

penultimate
day | game | stage | round | chapter | paragraph | sentence
the one before the last one:
It rained on the penultimate day of the competition. | Tomorrow will be the penultimate game of the season.

Penultimate sounds rather formal. In everyday English you usually say **last ... but one**: *Tomorrow will be the **last** game **but** one.*

ANTONYMS **last → first[1]**

2 most recent, or nearest to the present time

NOUNS

last year/month/week/night *Did you see the game on TV last night?*

last July/January etc *The law was passed last August.*

last summer/winter etc *It was very cold last winter.*

last game/race/meeting *The team won their last game 3-0.*

sb's last book/film/record etc *She published her last book in 2010.*

the last time (=the most recent occasion) *The city has changed since the last time I was there.*

When talking about the morning/afternoon/evening before today, you say **yesterday morning/afternoon/evening**: *I spoke to her **yesterday morning**.*

PHRASES

the last five years/six months etc *The internet has grown rapidly in the last twenty years.*

the last few minutes/hours/days etc *The last few weeks have been very dry.*

last[2] *v*

to continue for a particular length of time

ADVERBS AND PHRASES

last forever *She wanted the day to last forever.*

last indefinitely (=for a period of time with no definite end) *The money won't last indefinitely.*

not last (for) long (=not last for a long time) *The ceasefire didn't last long.*

last (for) a lifetime *The material is so strong, it will last a lifetime.*

last (for) a long time *The war lasted a very long time.*

VERBS

be expected to last *The trial is expected to last ten weeks.*

be built/designed/made to last *The houses weren't built to last this long.*

PREPOSITIONS

last for an hour/a week/10 years etc *Each lesson lasts for an hour.*

last until Monday/next month/1950 etc *The job only lasts until the summer.*

last into the night/into January/into the next century etc *The rain lasted into the night.*

Grammar
The preposition **for** is often omitted. You can say that something **lasted for an hour/a week etc** or something **lasted an hour/a week etc**.

THESAURUS: last
last, go on, drag on, persist → **continue (2)**

lasting *adj*

THESAURUS **long (2)**, **permanent**

late *adj, adv*

1 happening, arriving, or done after the usual or expected time

VERBS

arrive late/be late *Helen arrived late for the meeting.*

get home/come home late *My dad always used to come home late.*

get up/wake up/be up late *We usually get up late on Saturdays.*

go to bed late *Did you go to bed late last night?*

stay late/work late *I have to work late this evening.*

PREPOSITIONS

late for sth *You don't want to be late for school.*

late with sth (=not paying or giving someone something when you should) *The family had very little money and they were often late with the rent.*

PHRASES

five minutes/three hours etc late *The plane was five hours late.*

leave it too late (=be unable to do something because you did not do it soon enough) *We couldn't buy tickets because we left it too late.*

ANTONYMS **late → early (1)**

2 in the final part of a period of time, event, or process

NOUNS

late morning/afternoon/evening *In the late afternoon, it started to get dark.*

late spring/summer/autumn *The plant continues flowering into late summer.*

late August/January etc *The school year ends in late June.*

the late 1920s/1870s etc (=1927-29, 1877-79 etc) *He lived in London in the late 1980s.*

the late 17th/20th etc century *The pictures were painted in the late 19th century.*

a late stage *The negotiations are at a late stage.*

a late goal (=near the end of a game) *United won with a late goal.*

PREPOSITIONS

late in sth *They arrived late in the evening.*

in late May/June etc *School starts in late September.*

in late 1962/2004 etc *He left in late 2010.*

be in your late twenties/forties etc (=aged 27-29, 47-49 etc) *She had her first baby when she was in her late twenties.*

PHRASES

late in the day (=used when someone should have done something much earlier) *It's a bit late in the day to change your mind.*

ANTONYMS **late → early (2)**

3 used about someone who has died

> **THESAURUS: late**
> late, deceased, lifeless → **dead**[1]

latest *adj* THESAURUS **new (1)**

laugh[1] *v*

to make sounds with your voice when you think something is funny

VERBS

begin/start to laugh *The audience began to laugh as soon as they heard his voice.*

make sb laugh *I like her - she always makes me laugh.*

want to laugh *They all looked so serious that I wanted to laugh.*

try not to laugh *"Are you all right?" she said, trying not to laugh.*

ADVERBS

laugh out loud (=laugh loudly, so people can hear you) *The book was so funny that it made me laugh out loud.*

laugh hysterically (=laugh a lot in a loud uncontrolled way) *When his trousers fell down, everyone started laughing hysterically.*

laugh uncontrollably/helplessly (=laugh a lot and in a way that you cannot control) *Laughing helplessly, she tried to pull me out of the mud.*

laugh nervously *A few people laughed nervously, not sure whether he was really angry.*

PREPOSITIONS

laugh at sth *She never laughs at my jokes.*

laugh at sb (=in a way that is not kind) *When he got the answer wrong, the other children laughed at him.*

laugh about/over sth *I can laugh about it now, but at the time it was rather frightening.*

PHRASES

burst out laughing (=suddenly start laughing) *She looked at his silly hat and burst out laughing.*

laugh till you cry (*also* **laugh till the tears run down your face**) *He leaned back in his chair and laughed till the tears ran down his face.*

laugh your head off *informal* (=laugh a lot) *It was really funny - we were all laughing our heads off.*

fall about laughing *BrE* (=laugh a lot) *He saw the look on my face and he just fell about laughing.*

laugh[2] *n*

the act of laughing or the sound you make when you laugh

ADJECTIVES/NOUNS + laugh

a loud laugh *There was a loud laugh from someone in the audience.*

a little/short/small laugh *When I asked her what happened, she let out a little laugh.*

a nervous laugh *"Don't be silly," she said with a nervous laugh.*

a big/huge laugh *The joke received the biggest laugh of the evening.*

a belly laugh (=a deep loud laugh) *It's the kind of comedy that raises a smile rather than a belly laugh.*

VERBS

give a laugh/let out a laugh *She saw the picture and let out a loud laugh.*

burst into a laugh (=start laughing) *He burst into a laugh when I asked if they paid well.*

get a laugh (*also* **raise a laugh** *BrE*) (=make people laugh) *Most of his jokes didn't even get a laugh.*

stifle/suppress a laugh (=stop yourself from laughing) *I had to stifle a laugh when I saw what she was wearing.*

have a (good) laugh about/at/over sth *The farmer had a good laugh at our attempts to catch the horse.*

get a laugh out of sb (=make someone laugh) *She will do anything to get a laugh out of her audience.*

PHRASES

be good for a laugh (=be enjoyable and amusing) *His films are always good for a laugh.*

laughter *n*

when people laugh, or the sound of people laughing

VERBS

burst into laughter (=suddenly start laughing) *She burst into laughter when I told her the joke.*

roar with laughter (=laugh very noisily) *The audience roared with laughter.*

shriek/scream with laughter (=laugh very noisily in a high voice) *The children shrieked with laughter as they watched the clown.*
shake with laughter *They were shaking with laughter and couldn't even speak.*
meet/greet sth with laughter (=react to something by laughing) *Her remarks were greeted with mocking laughter.*
stifle/suppress your laughter (=stop yourself from laughing) *When she almost fell over, I had to stifle my laughter.*
the laughter dies (down) (=it stops) *The laughter died instantly when the boss walked in.*

ADJECTIVES

hysterical/helpless laughter (=when you laugh a lot and for a long time) *The audience were in fits of helpless laughter.*
nervous laughter (=because someone is not sure how to react) *Nervous laughter greeted her remarks.*
raucous laughter (=very loud and rough-sounding) *His attempt to explain was greeted with raucous laughter.*
suppressed laughter (=when someone tries not to laugh) *He began to shake with suppressed laughter.*

PHRASES

a fit of laughter (=a period in which you laugh uncontrollably) *Her funny stories had us in fits of laughter.*
a burst of laughter (=a short period of loud laughter) *There was a loud burst of laughter behind me.*
hoots/peals of laughter (=a lot of loud laughter) *There were hoots of laughter from the audience.*

launch *v*

1 to start something big or important

NOUNS

launch a campaign *The police have launched a campaign to reduce car crime.*
launch an appeal *We have raised $150,000 since we launched the appeal.*
launch an attack/assault/offensive (=start attacking an area or group of people) *The army launched an assault on the eastern part of the country.*
launch a search/hunt *The police immediately launched a murder hunt.*
launch a project/initiative/scheme *The government has launched another initiative to help boost employment.*
launch a business/company *She launched her business in 2000.*
launch a product/range *They have launched a range of baby clothes made from organic cotton.*

ADVERBS

officially/formally launch sth *The scheme will be officially launched next month.*
successfully launch sth *Many graduates successfully launch their own businesses.*
launch sth nationally *When do they plan to launch the product nationally?*

PHRASES

plan/prepare to launch sth *We are planning to launch an exciting new range of products later in the year.*

THESAURUS: launch

begin, commence, set off, set out, get down to, take up, resume, launch, open, enter into, embark on → start[1] (1)

2 to send something into the sky, into space, or into the water

NOUNS

launch a rocket *The rocket was launched from Cape Canaveral.*
launch a missile *Two soldiers prepared to launch the missile.*
launch a satellite *The cost of launching a satellite is extremely high.*
launch a ship/boat *We watched as the ship was launched into the river.*

PREPOSITIONS

launch sth into sth *Hundreds of people gathered to watch the Space Shuttle be launched into space.*

laundry *n*

clothes and similar things that need to be washed or have just been washed

VERBS

do the laundry (=wash dirty clothes) *I cleaned the kitchen and did the laundry.*
hang out/up the laundry (=put it outside on a line to dry) *My mother was hanging out the laundry in the sun.*
fold the laundry (=fold clothes after they have been washed and dried) *He was folding the laundry and watching TV.*
put away the laundry (=put away clean dry clothes) *There's a big pile of laundry to be put away.*

ADJECTIVES

dirty laundry *There was a bag of dirty laundry in the kitchen.*
clean laundry *The clean laundry goes in this basket, ready to be ironed.*

laundry + NOUNS

the laundry room *There's a washing machine in the laundry room.*
the laundry basket *He's teaching the children to put their dirty clothes in the laundry basket.*
a laundry service *Does the hotel provide a laundry service?*
laundry facilities (=equipment for washing

and drying laundry) *Each block of flats has its own laundry facilities.*

PHRASES

a bundle/pile of laundry *At the weekend I was faced with a huge pile of dirty laundry.*

a load of laundry (=an amount that fits in a washing machine) *I do at least one or two loads of laundry every day.*

law *n*

the system of legal rules, or a particular rule

VERBS + law

obey the law *Most people obey the law.*

break/disobey the law (=do something illegal) *Is the company breaking the law?*

flout the law (=deliberately disobey a law) *Employers who flout the law should be properly punished.*

stay/act within the law (=not do illegal things) *The security forces must act within the law.*

make a law *Part of the function of parliament is to make laws.*

pass a law (=agree to make a law by voting) *Parliament passed a law banning smoking in public places.*

introduce a law *In 1989, a new law was introduced to protect the Polish language.*

become law (=officially be made a law) *For a bill to become law, it must be approved by both houses of Parliament.*

enforce a law (=make people obey a law) *It is the job of the police to enforce the law.*

repeal a law (=officially end a law) *Many people want the law to be repealed.*

law + VERBS

the law says/states that *The law states that you can use reasonable force to defend yourself.*

the law allows/permits sth *The law does not allow us to sell alcohol to persons under 18 years of age.*

the law bans/prohibits sth (=says that it is not allowed) *The law prohibits possession of these animals.*

ADJECTIVES/NOUNS + law

US/English/Chinese etc law *This is not an offence under English law.*

international law *Under international law, the countries must respect the treaty.*

federal law (=the law of the US, not a particular state) *Under federal law, it is illegal to discriminate against employees because of race or sex.*

state law (=the law in a US state) *Under state law, it was illegal for any public official to receive gifts worth more than $100.*

criminal law (=laws concerning crimes) *Criminal law contains definitions of such crimes as murder, rape, and robbery.*

civil law (=laws concerning disagreements between people, rather than crimes) *The punishment for breaking civil law is usually a fine.*

strict/tough laws *The country has strict anti-tobacco laws.*

tax/copyright/divorce etc law *You need an accountant who knows about tax law.*

PREPOSITIONS

by law (=according to a law) *By law, seat belts must be worn by all passengers.*

under American/international etc law (=according to the law in a country or area) *This is illegal under English law.*

the law(s) on sth *The laws on owning a gun are very strict.*

sth is against the law (=it is illegal) *Everyone knows that stealing is against the law.*

sth is within the law (=it is legal) *The court decided that the company's actions were within the law.*

sb is above the law (=they are too important to have to obey a law) *He seems to think he's above the law.*

lawful *adj* THESAURUS **legal (2)**

lawyer *n*

someone whose job is giving advice about laws and representing people in court

VERBS + lawyer

get a lawyer *If you are charged with breaking the law, you will need to get a lawyer.*

hire a lawyer (*also* **engage a lawyer** *formal*): *He's rich enough to hire a good lawyer.*

see a lawyer (*also* **consult a lawyer** *formal*): *She has consulted a lawyer about taking her case to court.*

talk/speak to a lawyer (=for advice) *Have you spoken to a lawyer?*

lawyer + VERBS

a lawyer represents sb (*also* **a lawyer acts for sb**) *He is one of the lawyers who are representing the airline.*

a lawyer argues sth *His lawyers argued that the company had treated him unfairly.*

a lawyer advises sb to do sth *My lawyers have advised me not to speak to reporters.*

ADJECTIVES/NOUNS + lawyer

a good/clever lawyer *A clever lawyer knows the answer to his question before he asks it.*

a hotshot lawyer *informal* (=very good, confident, and likely to succeed) *The company can afford to hire a whole team of hotshot lawyers.*

a defence lawyer (=who tries to prove in court that someone is not guilty) *Defence lawyers produced evidence to support their client's alibi.*

a prosecution lawyer (=who tries to prove in court that someone is guilty) *The prosecution lawyer summed up his case for the jury.*

L

a criminal lawyer *She is one of the country's leading criminal lawyers.*

layer *n*

an area of something on top of a surface, or between two surfaces

ADJECTIVES/NOUNS + layer

a thin layer *A thin layer of ice had formed on the windows.*

a fine layer (=very thin) *The copper wire is coated with a fine layer of gold.*

a thick layer *A thick layer of dust lay on the furniture.*

a protective layer *The cream forms a protective layer to stop the skin drying out.*

a single/double layer *It is very hot so you will only need a single layer of bed covers.*

the top/bottom layer *We've eaten all the chocolates in the top layer of the box.*

alternate layers *Put alternate layers of pasta and sauce in a dish.*

the outer layer *He took off the outer layers of the onion.*

the surface layer *Below the surface layer of the skin are several further layers of cells.*

the ozone layer (=a layer of gases in the sky that prevents the sun from damaging the Earth) *Scientists found a hole in the ozone layer over Antarctica.*

PREPOSITIONS

a layer of sth *Cover the seeds with a thin layer of soil.*

in layers *The peppers, garlic, and tomatoes are arranged in layers.*

between the layers *There is a padded material between the two layers of fabric.*

PHRASES

layer upon layer (=many layers) *He used layer upon layer of paint.*

lead *n*

the first position in a race or competition that has not finished

PHRASES

be in the lead (=be winning) *His horse was in the lead as they approached the last fence.*

VERBS

have the lead (=be winning) *She still had the lead as the runners began the last lap of the race.*

have a 3-point/5-second etc lead *The young golfer has a one-shot lead in her first tournament.*

take the lead (*also* **go into the lead**) (=start winning) *The British driver has just taken the lead in the Monaco Grand Prix.*

put sb in the lead (*also* **give sb the lead**) (=make someone start winning) *His goal put Portugal in the lead.*

extend/increase your lead (=get further ahead) *The Australian swimmer has now extended his lead to around ten metres.*

lose the lead *Chelsea lost their two-goal lead shortly after half-time.*

throw away the lead *informal* (=stop being ahead because you make a mistake) *They somehow managed to throw away a 22-point lead.*

share the lead (=two or more players or teams are winning) *At the end of the first round, the two American golfers share the lead.*

ADJECTIVES/NOUNS + lead

a clear/comfortable lead *The Boston team had a comfortable lead at half-time.*

a big/huge lead (*also* **a commanding lead** *formal*): *The Brazilian driver raced into a commanding lead.*

an early lead (=at an early stage of a game, race etc) *Liverpool took an early lead with a goal from their captain.*

a tiny/slender/slim lead (=small) *They managed to defend their slender lead until the end of the season.*

a one-shot/two-goal/30-point etc lead *The Labour Party had a ten-point lead in the opinion polls.*

PREPOSITIONS

lead over sb *Can they keep their lead over their closest rivals?*

leader *n*

the person who directs or controls a group, organization, country etc

ADJECTIVES

a good/effective leader *What characteristics make a good leader?*

a strong leader *Margaret Thatcher had a reputation as a strong leader.*

a weak leader *The country had a series of weak leaders.*

a natural/born leader (=someone who naturally has all the qualities needed to be a leader) *He has the confidence of a born leader.*

a charismatic leader (=who people like and admire, and want to follow) *Martin Luther King was one of the most charismatic leaders of the civil rights movement.*

a political leader *He became the country's most influential political leader.*

a military leader *Montgomery was one of the great military leaders of the Second World War.*

a religious/spiritual leader *The Pope is the spiritual leader for Roman Catholics throughout the world.*

NOUNS + leader

a world leader (=someone who is in charge of a country) *The president and other world leaders are meeting to discuss the environment.*

a government leader *He was the first EU government leader to visit the new US president.*

a party leader *The highlight of any political conference is the speech by the party leader.*

a team/group/project etc leader *Members of the sales team each report to their team leader.*

a union/business leader *Business leaders welcomed a cut in the interest rate.*

VERBS

choose a leader (*also* **choose sb as leader**) *The party is meeting to choose a new leader.*

elect a leader (*also* **elect sb as leader**) *He was elected leader of his country by a huge majority.*

appoint a leader (=officially announce that someone is leader) *His son was appointed leader after him.*

PREPOSITIONS

the leader of sth *She became the first female leader of her party.*

leadership *n*

the way someone leads a country or organization, or the people who are in the position of leader

ADJECTIVES/NOUNS + leadership

strong/firm leadership *Good schools need strong leadership.*

weak/poor/indecisive leadership *Because of poor leadership, the country now faces an economic crisis.*

clear leadership *He blames the company's problems on a lack of clear leadership.*

effective leadership *Good communication skills are essential for effective leadership.*

military/political leadership *The country's military leadership are against any kind of democratic reform.*

the party leadership (=the leaders of a political party) *The party leadership are divided on this issue.*

VERBS

take over the leadership (*also* **assume the leadership** *formal*) (=become the new leader) *A younger person should take over the leadership of the party.*

challenge sb's leadership *Three other candidates will challenge her leadership.*

show/demonstrate leadership *She showed great leadership in getting everyone into the lifeboats.*

provide leadership *We need someone who can provide strong leadership at this difficult time.*

resign your leadership *He was forced to resign his leadership as a result of the scandal.*

leadership + NOUNS

a leadership election *The leadership election is in November.*

a leadership contest/battle *Most people think he will win the leadership battle.*

leadership skills/qualities *The tasks were designed to test their leadership skills.*

sb's leadership style/style of leadership *The manager's leadership style is very informal.* | *The two managers have very different styles of leadership.*

a leadership position/role *Is Tom suitable for a leadership position?*

PREPOSITIONS

leadership of sth *Some people have criticized his leadership of the country.*

under sb's leadership (=when someone is leader) *Under her leadership, the school has improved considerably.*

PHRASES

a change of leadership *It is time for a change of leadership.*

leading *adj* THESAURUS ▶ **important (2)**

lead to sth *v* THESAURUS ▶ **cause²**

leaf *n*

one of the flat green parts of a plant that are joined to its stem or branches

VERBS

leaves turn red/brown etc (=become red, brown etc) *In late September, the leaves start to turn red.*

leaves fall *All the leaves had fallen off the tree.*

a tree loses/sheds its leaves (=the leaves come off the tree) *Most trees shed their leaves in the autumn.*

sweep (up) leaves (=tidy away fallen leaves using a brush) *She was sweeping leaves in the back garden.*

ADJECTIVES

a green/brown/yellow etc leaf *She loved the deep green leaves of the coconut trees.*

a dead leaf *The ground beneath the tree was covered in dead leaves.*

fallen leaves (=that have fallen off the trees) *The children were jumping in piles of fallen leaves.*

NOUNS + leaf

an oak/vine/spinach etc leaf (=from a particular plant or tree) *Vine leaves stuffed with rice is a typical Greek dish.*

autumn leaves (*also* **fall leaves** *AmE*): *Her photographs feature the rich colours of autumn leaves.*

PHRASES

be in leaf *literary* (=have leaves) *By this time, most of the trees were in leaf.*

come into leaf *literary* (=start having leaves) *The apple tree had finally come into leaf.*

leak *n*

a small hole that lets liquid or gas out, or the liquid or gas that is coming out

L

VERBS

spring a leak (=start to have a leak) *The boat had sprung a leak.*

stop a leak *Tightening the nut will sometimes stop the leak.*

check sth for leaks *Check the sides of the container for leaks.*

ADJECTIVES/NOUNS + leak

a gas/oil/fuel etc leak *The fire was caused by a gas leak.*

a radioactive/radiation leak *A radioactive leak was discovered at the nuclear reactor.*

PREPOSITIONS

a leak in sth *There is a leak in the mains pipe.*

lean[2] *adj* THESAURUS **thin (1)**

leap *n*

1 a big jump

ADJECTIVES

a huge/enormous leap *With a huge leap, he managed to catch the ball.*

a flying leap *He threw a stick in the river, and the dog went after it in a flying leap.*

VERBS

make/take a leap *Her horse took a leap over the fence.*

2 a large increase, improvement, or change

ADJECTIVES

a big/great/huge/enormous/giant leap *When Neil Armstrong landed on the moon, he famously said "That's one small step for man, one giant leap for mankind".*

a dramatic leap *Following her move to Los Angeles, her career in show business took a dramatic leap.*

a quantum leap (=a very great improvement in something) *There has been a quantum leap in our understanding of the disease.*

a sudden leap *A sudden leap in fuel prices has led to an increase in airfares.*

a technological/technical leap *Every ten years, there is a major technological leap in computer science.*

a mental/conceptual/imaginative leap (=used when something takes a lot of mental effort to understand) *The world was so different in those days that you have to make a big mental leap to imagine what it was like.*

VERBS

make/take a leap *The company was hoping it could make a technical leap that would give it a clear advantage over its competitors.*

require a leap *Reading his books does require an imaginative leap.*

PREPOSITIONS

a leap in sth *We weren't expecting such a big leap in costs.*

PHRASES

a leap forward *AIDS treatment has made a great leap forward in recent years.*

in leaps and bounds (=making a lot of progress very quickly) *Her English has improved in leaps and bounds.*

learn *v*

to gain knowledge of a subject or skill, by experience, by studying it, or by being taught

PHRASES

learn sth quickly/slowly *She moved to France and learned the language very quickly.*

soon learn sth (=learn it quickly, as a result of an experience) *You soon learn not to make the same mistake again.*

learn sth by heart (=learn something so you know it exactly without reading it) *Actors have to learn their lines by heart.*

learn sth from/through experience *Students will learn from experience the importance of planning.*

learn sth by/through trial and error (=by trying things and making mistakes) *When you start doing pottery, you learn mostly through trial and error.*

have a lot to learn *She still has a lot to learn about boys.*

be eager to learn *Young children are very eager to learn.*

PREPOSITIONS

learn about sth *He said he was too old to learn about computers.*

learn from sb *I learned a lot from my father.*

learn by doing sth *Babies learn by copying the people around them.*

learner *n*

someone who is learning to do something

ADJECTIVES/NOUNS + learner

a quick/fast learner *She was a quick learner, and her English got better day by day.*

a slow learner *The programme allows slow learners to get extra practice.*

an adult learner *Many adult learners also work full-time.*

a young learner *The activities are good for young learners.*

an intermediate/advanced learner *These exercises are designed for intermediate learners.*

a foreign learner *Many foreign learners find English pronunciation difficult.*

a language learner *She writes textbooks for language learners.*

learner + NOUNS

a learner driver *Learner drivers often grip the steering wheel too tightly.*

PHRASES

the needs of the learner *The coursebooks are designed to meet the needs of the learner.*

leave[1] *v*

1 to go away from a place or a person

NOUNS

leave the house/room/office/building *She said goodbye, and watched him leave the room.*

leave home/work *I usually leave home at 8.30.*

leave the country/city/area *The men have probably already left the country.*

leave town *His friends thought he had left town.*

leave hospital *BrE*, **leave the hospital** *AmE*: *Her mother will soon be well enough to leave hospital.*

leave your wife/boyfriend/family etc *She left her husband after she found out that he was having an affair.*

ADVERBS

leave suddenly *He left suddenly and without saying where he was going.*

VERBS

have to leave/be forced to leave *Thousands of people had to leave their homes because of the fire.*

refuse to leave *She refused to leave her injured friend.*

threaten to leave *The players are threatening to leave the team.*

PREPOSITIONS

leave at 10 o'clock/5.30 etc *The next plane leaves at 12.30.*

leave for somewhere *Edward left for America on business.*

PHRASES

leave on time *The train left on time.*

leave in a hurry *She left in a hurry, saying she had a plane to catch.*

be ready to leave *An hour later they were ready to leave.*

be about to leave (=be going to leave very soon) *I was about to leave when the phone rang.*

leave sb in peace (=go away and stop disturbing someone) *I wish you would all leave me in peace!*

leave sb to it *informal* (=leave someone and let them continue what they are doing) *You seem to have a lot of work, so I'll leave you to it.*

ANTONYMS **leave → arrive**

2 to officially arrange for someone to have something that you own after your death

THESAURUS: leave

donate, distribute, contribute, award, leave, lavish, confer, bestow, hand, pass, present → **give (1)**

leave[2] *n*

time that you are allowed to spend away from your work

ADJECTIVES/NOUNS + leave

annual leave (=total time allowed away from work each year) *Annual leave is 22 days plus public holidays.*

sick leave (*also* **medical leave** *AmE*) (=time allowed away from work because you are ill) *The form must be filled in as soon as you return from sick leave.*

maternity leave (=time that a mother is allowed away from work to have and take care of a baby) *Two teachers were off on maternity leave.*

compassionate leave (=time allowed away from work because someone in your family is very ill or has died) *She was given compassionate leave to go to the funeral.*

paid/unpaid leave *He took three months' unpaid leave in order to look after his mother.*

VERBS

get 10 days'/3 months' etc leave *We get 25 days' leave a year.*

take leave (=use the time you are allowed) *Staff will not be allowed to take any leave in January because the company is too busy.*

be entitled to leave (=be allowed to have leave) *All employees are entitled to 21 days' leave.*

go on leave (=start your time away from work) *She needs to finish the report before she goes on leave.*

give/grant sb leave *He was given compassionate leave.*

cancel sb's leave (=stop people taking leave) *The Police Department cancelled all leave because of the emergency.*

PREPOSITIONS

on leave *Who is doing her job while she is on leave?*

lecture *n*

a long talk given to a group of people

VERBS

give a lecture *She gives lectures on modern French literature.*

deliver a lecture *formal* (=give a lecture, especially in a particular place or about a particular subject) *He delivered the lecture at the London School of Economics.*

go to a lecture (*also* **attend a lecture** *formal*): *Have you been to any of Professor MacPherson's lectures?*

listen to a lecture *Students spend about a quarter of their time listening to lectures.*

have a lecture *I have lectures all morning.*

miss/skip a lecture (=not go to it) *It is important that students do not skip lectures.*

lecture + NOUNS

a lecture hall/room (*also* **a lecture theatre** *BrE*): *The lecture hall was packed.*

lecture notes *Can I borrow your lecture notes?*

a lecture tour *He's on a lecture tour of the US.*

ADJECTIVES/NOUNS + lecture

a history/politics/biology etc lecture *I'm late for my economics lecture.*

an interesting/fascinating/boring lecture *Her lectures are always very interesting.*

a public lecture (=for anyone to go to) *He's going to deliver a public lecture on politics in the Arab World.*

an illustrated lecture (=with pictures) *Mrs Robinson gave a fascinating illustrated lecture on Spanish history.*

PREPOSITIONS

a lecture on/about sth *I went to a very interesting lecture on Russian cinema.*

PHRASES

a series of lectures (*also* **a course of lectures** *BrE*): *She's giving a series of lectures on the history of art.*

leg *n*

one of the long parts of your body that your feet are joined to

ADJECTIVES

your left/right leg *My right leg hurts.*

back/hind legs (=of a four-legged animal) *The dog stood on its back legs.*

front legs (=of a four-legged animal) *The elephant had injured one of its front legs.*

long/short legs *Most models are very slim with long legs.*

good/nice legs (=attractively shaped) *If you have good legs, why not wear a skirt?*

a bad leg *informal* (=an injured leg) *He can't play football because of his bad leg.*

a broken leg *She can't walk because she has a broken leg.*

bare legs (=not covered by any clothing) *Her bare legs were a beautiful brown colour.*

leg + NOUNS

a leg injury/wound *A leg injury means he cannot play in tomorrow's match.*

leg muscles *Walking and cycling are good for strengthening the leg muscles.*

leg room (=space for your legs) *There was not much leg room on the plane.*

VERBS

cross your legs (=sit in a position with one leg over the other) *She sat down and crossed her legs.*

break your leg *He broke his leg skiing.*

raise/lift your legs *Lie on your back and raise your legs a few centimetres.*

bend your legs *Keep your back straight and bend your legs.*

straighten your legs *There wasn't enough room in the back of the car to straighten your legs.*

stretch out your legs *Curl up and then stretch out your legs.*

rest your legs (=have a rest) *They sat down to rest their legs.*

your legs ache *The children had walked a long way and their legs were aching.*

PHRASES

stand on one leg *She can balance standing on one leg.*

legal Ac *adj*

1 relating to the law

NOUNS

the legal system/framework *Under the English legal system, the accused person has the right to remain silent.*

a legal right *Women should have the same legal rights as men.*

legal action/charges/proceedings (=action in a court of law) *The paper cannot comment because of the threat of legal action.*

legal advice/services *You should get legal advice before signing any agreement.*

a legal battle/dispute/debate *The couple were involved in a bitter legal battle.*

legal aid (=money to pay your legal fees) *She applied for legal aid in order to pursue her case against the hospital.*

legal fees/costs *The company paid legal fees of $15.8 million.*

a legal document/contract *An insurance agreement is a legal document.*

a legal expert *Many legal experts believe that the law needs to be changed.*

a legal adviser *She worked as a legal adviser at the U.S. State Department.*

the legal profession (=lawyers, judges etc, considered as a group) *The first Congress of the United States was dominated by the legal profession.*

legal language/words *The document was written in complicated legal language.*

legal status *The organization has no formal legal status.*

PHRASES

take legal action (against sb/sth) (=bring a case in a court of law) *She is taking legal action against a British newspaper which secretly recorded her private phone conversations.*

2 used when saying that something is allowed by law, or you must do something because of the law

NOUNS

a legal duty/obligation/responsibility *It is your legal duty to report a crime to the police.*

the legal limit/minimum/maximum *He had twice the legal limit of alcohol in his blood.*

a legal requirement (=something that you must do because of the law) *Prices at gas stations have to be displayed as a legal requirement.*

legal tender (=forms of money that are legally accepted) *The coins are no longer considered legal tender.*

VERBS

make sth legal *They are campaigning to make the drug legal.*

become legal *Divorce finally became legal in 1992 in that country.*

ADVERBS

perfectly legal (=completely legal) *What the company has done is perfectly legal.*

THESAURUS: legal

lawful
business | manner | methods | use | means | excuse | purpose | owner
allowed by law or based on the law. **Lawful** is more formal than **legal**. It is used especially when comparing actions or methods with others that are not allowed by law:
The demonstrators were preventing other people from going about their lawful business. | The information was obtained in a lawful manner. | US citizens are permitted to keep firearms for lawful use. | The defendants argued that they had a lawful excuse for what they did. | The property was returned to its lawful owner.

legitimate
claim | right | reason | excuse | activities | business | president | leader | government | authority
based on or allowed by the normal laws or rules - often used when there is a disagreement about this:
The local people argue that they have a legitimate claim to the land. | I had a **perfectly legitimate** *reason or being there* (=a completely legitimate reason). | *The organization says all its money comes from legitimate activities. | His supporters regard him as the legitimate president of the country.*

statutory
rights | duty | requirement | power | authority | payment
used about something such as a right, duty, or power, which the law says you must have:
The law gives you certain statutory rights when you buy goods. | There is a statutory duty to investigate how the death occurred. | The officers who searched the house were using their statutory powers.

constitutional
right | reform | change | amendment | power | authority
relating to a country's constitution (=the set of rules and principles by which a country is governed):
Freedom of speech is one of our constitutional rights. | Constitutional amendments require the approval of two thirds of the House and the Senate. | Congress has the constitutional power to prevent the president from travelling abroad.

You can say that your actions are **above board** (=there is nothing illegal about them): *The firm says they have nothing to hide and everything they do is* **above board**. You can also say that someone **acts** or **stays/keeps/remains within the law** (=they do not do anything illegal): *The protesters were careful to* **remain within the law** *and not cause any damage to property.*

ANTONYMS **legal → illegal**

legend *n*

an old well-known story, often about brave people, adventures, or magical events

ADJECTIVES

an old/ancient legend *The story is based on an ancient legend.*

local legend *According to local legend, the cave was the home of a witch.*

a popular legend (=one that many people believe) *Many popular legends grew up about him.*

Greek/Roman etc legend *In ancient Greek legend, the Chimera was part lion, part dragon, and part goat.*

VERBS

become legend/pass into legend (=become a story that is told many times by many people) *The incident has since become legend.*

a legend grows (up) (=develops over time) *The legend of his bravery grew after the battle.*

(the) legend says *Legend says King Arthur's sword was thrown into one of these lakes.*

the legend tells how *The legend tells how the King of Troy offended Poseidon, the sea god.*

the legend goes (=says) *Spartacus refused to flee, or so the legend goes.*

a legend is attached to sth (=connected with it) *The forest has an unusual legend attached to it.*

PREPOSITIONS

the legend of sth *In class, we were told the legend of St George and the dragon.*

legends about sb/sth *Legends about her date from the dawn of Christianity.*

according to legend *According to legend, he escaped by leaping from the cliffs into the sea.*

PHRASES

legend has it that (=says that) *Legend has it that Rhodes was home to the sun god Helios.*

be the subject of legend (*also* **be the stuff of legend**) (=have stories told about it) *The island has long been the subject of legend.*

myths and legends *I read all the Greek myths and legends.*

legendary *adj* THESAURUS ▸ famous

legitimate *adj* THESAURUS ▸ legal (2)

leisure *n*

time when you are not working or studying and can relax and do things you enjoy

leisure + NOUNS

leisure time *My parents spend most of their leisure time gardening.*

a leisure activity/interest *Watching TV is now the nation's most popular leisure activity.*

leisure pursuits *formal* (=leisure activities) *Golfing and fishing were among his many leisure pursuits.*

a leisure centre/complex *BrE: The local leisure centre has a swimming pool and a sauna.*

leisure facilities *The leisure facilities in the town are very good.*

leisurely *adj* THESAURUS ▸ slow

length *n*

1 how long something is from one end to the other

ADJECTIVES

the total/overall length *The total length of the railway line is 650 kilometres.*

the average length *The worms grow to an average length of 10 cm.*

the whole/full/entire length *The camera looks down the full length of the street.*

a maximum/minimum length *The maximum length of a filename is 10 characters.*

medium length *She has medium length hair.*

VERBS

measure the length of sth *We measured the length of the room.*

adjust/alter the length of sth *You can adjust the length of the strap.*

grow to/reach a length of 2 metres/8 feet etc *A blue whale can reach a length of 30 metres.*

have a length of 1 metre/8 feet etc *These leaves have a length of about 7 cm.*

PREPOSITIONS

the length of sth *The average length of the snake is about 30 centimetres.*

> When talking about the length of something, you can say that it is **4 inches/10 centimetres etc long**.

PHRASES

be 100 metres/3 miles etc in length *The hotel pool is 15 metres in length.*

of different lengths *You'll need several pieces of string of different lengths.*

of equal/the same length *She drew two lines of equal length.*

cut sth to length (=so that it is the right length) *Use a saw to cut the wood to length.*

increase in length *The icicles increase in length as more water freezes.*

three/four/ten etc times the length of sth *Their garden is three times the length of this room.*

along the length of sth (=from one end of it to the other) *There are houses all along the length of the road.*

2 how much time something lasts from beginning to end

ADJECTIVES

the average length *What is the average length of a stay in hospital?*

the usual/normal length *The usual length of a movie is about two hours.*

the minimum/maximum length *Your presentation should have a maximum length of 20 minutes.*

VERBS

reduce/cut/shorten the length of sth *He decided to reduce the length of his speech.*

increase the length of sth *People try many things to increase the length of their lives.*

PHRASES

be 20 minutes/an hour etc in length *The test will be 30 minutes in length.*

a length of time *Next time, I'll stay for a shorter length of time.*

lengthy *adj* THESAURUS ▸ long (2)

lesson *n*

a period of time in which someone is taught a particular skill or subject

ADJECTIVES/NOUNS + lesson

a history/physics/maths etc lesson *I have a history lesson this afternoon.*

a piano/guitar etc lesson *You'll be late for your guitar lesson.*

a swimming/dancing/driving etc lesson *My sister is taking driving lessons.*

a private lesson (=when you pay someone to teach you alone or in a small group) *He gave private lessons in mathematics at the weekends.*

a good/interesting lesson *I'm always looking for ways to make lessons more interesting.*

extra lessons *Her father decided she needed extra maths lessons.*

VERBS

have a lesson *I have swimming lessons on Fridays.*

take lessons (=have them regularly - not used for saying where or when someone has lessons) *He started taking piano lessons at age four.*

go to a lesson (*also* **attend a lesson** *formal*): *I have to go to my French lesson now.*

miss/skip a lesson (=not go to it) *Her parents found out she had been skipping lessons.*

give lessons (=teach them) *She made extra money giving English lessons.*

teach a lesson (*also* **take a lesson**) *Which teacher taught the lesson?*

plan/prepare a lesson *Teachers spend a long time preparing their lessons.*

observe a lesson (=watch someone teach it) *The principal has come to observe the lesson.*

lesson + NOUNS

a lesson plan (=that a teacher uses to teach a lesson) *It is important to have a clear lesson plan.*

PREPOSITIONS

a lesson about/on sth *I enjoyed the lessons on art history.*

in/during a lesson *She was always talking during lessons.* | *The teacher spoke to every child in the lesson.*

lethargic *adj* THESAURUS ▸ slow

letter *n*

1 a message that you write to someone on paper

ADJECTIVES/NOUNS + letter

a long/short letter *She wrote me a long letter, telling me all her news.*

a business letter *In business letters, you often use phrases such as "I would be grateful if...".*

an official letter *I received an official letter thanking me for my enquiry.*

a formal/informal letter *The letter sounded very formal.*

a personal letter *I don't want him reading my personal letters.*

a love letter *A boy in my class wrote me a love letter.*

a thank-you letter *Mum made me write thank-you letters for all my birthday presents.*

a covering letter *BrE*, **a cover letter** *AmE* (=that you send with a job application) *Always enclose a cover letter with your resume.*

a strongly-worded letter (=expressing your disapproval in a very direct way) *I sent a strongly-worded letter to the manager, complaining about the service in his shop.*

VERBS

write a letter *He wrote a letter inviting her to visit.*

read a letter *May I read her letter?*

sign a letter *I forgot to sign the letter!*

send a letter *The school sent a letter to all the children's parents.*

post a letter *BrE*, **mail a letter** *AmE*: *Could you post this letter for me?*

get/receive a letter *I got a letter from my mother.*

open a letter *Bill opened the letter and read it.*

reply to/answer a letter *I never answered his letter.*

a letter is addressed to sb (=has their name and address on the envelope) *The letter was addressed to Mr John Appleby.*

a letter is dated sth (=has a particular date on it) *Thank you for your letter dated March 4th.*

a letter comes/arrives *The letter arrived the following day.*

PREPOSITIONS

a letter from sb *I've had a letter from Sam.*

a letter to sb *Someone had been reading her letters to her boyfriend.*

a letter about/concerning sth *I get a lot of letters about this subject.*

in a letter *He said in his letter that he was moving house.*

by letter *We only communicate by letter.*

a letter of complaint *I wasn't satisfied with the service I had received and I wrote the company a letter of complaint.*

⚠ Don't say a 'complaint letter'.

2 a sign used in writing to represent speech sounds

ADJECTIVES

capital letters (*also* **upper case letters** *formal*) (=A, B, C etc) *Fill out the form in capital letters.*

small letters (*also* **lower case letters** *formal*) (=a, b, c etc) *In McCartney, the first 'c' is written in small letters.*

double letters (=two of the same letter written together) *Words with double letters are often spelt wrong.*

a silent letter (=one which is written but not pronounced) *There is a silent letter in the word 'know'.*

the first letter *What's the first letter of his name?*

PHRASES

the letters of the alphabet *Songs can help children learn the letters of the alphabet.*

in capital/small/big etc letters *The title was printed in capital letters.*

level[1] *n*

1 the amount or degree of something

ADJECTIVES

a high/low level *The monkeys showed a high level of intelligence.*

a record level (=more than ever before) *Sales have reached record levels.*

the usual/normal level *The temperature has now returned to its usual level for this time of year.*

the minimum/maximum level *Companies try to pay the minimum level of tax.*

an average level *She has an average level of fitness for her age.*

the general/overall level *This will have no effect on the overall level of unemployment.*

the current/present level *The government's current level of borrowing is too high.*

the right level *Her report had just the right level of detail.*

an excessive level (=too much) *There was an excessive level of alcohol in his blood.*

the recommended/permitted level *His weight is above the recommended level.*

an acceptable level *Noise must be kept to an acceptable level.*

the desired level (=the level you want) *Change the volume on your phone to the desired level.*

VERBS + level

measure the level of sth *A special machine measures the level of radiation.*

monitor the level of sth (=check the level and how it changes) *The level of humidity in the room is constantly monitored.*

control/regulate the level of sth (=make it not fall or rise too much) *Your kidneys regulate the level of calcium in your blood.*

increase/raise/improve the level of sth *Healthy eating can increase your energy levels.*

reduce/lower the level of sth *You need to reduce your stress levels.*

achieve/reach a level *China's imports of wheat reached record levels.*

exceed a level (=be more than it) *Companies can be fined for exceeding permitted pollution levels.*

stay/remain at a level *The fees are likely to remain at current levels.*

maintain a level (=keep it the same) *It's difficult to maintain the same level of physical fitness.*

level + VERBS

a level rises/goes up/increases *The level of unemployment has increased.*

a level goes down/decreases/drops/falls *Pollution levels have fallen slightly.*

a level plummets (=it goes down very quickly) *His blood sugar level plummeted to 30.*

a level soars (=it increases to a very high level) *The level of unemployment soared to 25%.*

a level varies/fluctuates (=it changes) *Unemployment levels vary according to the time of year.*

NOUNS + level

noise levels *Noise levels at the factory are too high.*

price/income/wage levels *Wage levels had failed to keep up with inflation.*

pollution levels *We hope to reduce pollution levels.*

PREPOSITIONS

the level of sth *The level of pollution is much too high.*

at a level *Inflation is at a fairly low level.*

above/below a level *Prices dropped below the level of the previous year.*

PHRASES

be on a level with sth (=be the same as something) *Sales were roughly on a level with last month.*

THESAURUS: level

quantity, volume, level, proportion, quota, yield
→ **amount**

2 the height of something

NOUNS + level

water level *The water level is almost up to the deck.*

sea level (=the height on the Earth reached by the sea) *The highest point of the island is only 16 feet above sea level.*

ground level *Cut the plants to about an inch above ground level.*

street level *The front window was at street level.*

knee/waist/ankle level *Soon the snow was up to knee level.*

eye level *Hold the page at eye level.*

ADJECTIVES

a high/low level *The oil in the tank was at a low level.*

VERBS

change/adjust the level of sth *You can adjust the level of the shelves.*

lower/raise the level of sth *How do you lower the level of the chair?*

fall/rise to a level *The ski lift rises to a level of 3,250 metres.*

PREPOSITIONS

above a level *Hold your hands out above shoulder level.*

below a level *Part of the house is below ground level.*

PHRASES

be on a level with sth (=be at the same level) *Her eyes were on a level with his nose.*

3 a particular standard of skill or ability, for example in education or sport

ADJECTIVES/NOUNS + level

a high/low level *He plays football at a very high level.*

a basic level *She has a basic level of skill.*
elementary/intermediate/advanced level *The students have all reached an advanced level in English.*
degree level *She studied French to degree level.*
graduate/postgraduate level (=after completing a first degree) *Some students continue studying economics at postgraduate level.*

VERBS

achieve/reach/attain a level *Students can expect to achieve a high level of skill.*

PREPOSITIONS

level of sth *Her level of English is extremely high.*
at a level *Her reading skills are still at a low level.*
above/below a level *If you are above intermediate level, you might find some of these exercises too easy. | Is the course below degree level?*

PHRASES

at the highest/top level (=against the best teams or people) *You need a lot of determination to compete at the top level.*
at national/international level *She has played the sport at international level.*

4 a particular position in an organization, industry, or society

ADJECTIVES

a high/low level *He reached a high level in the company.*
the upper level *People at the upper levels of society do not always appreciate these problems.*
senior level (=a high level in an organization) *There are very few women managers at the most senior level.*

VERBS

reach a level *How long does it take to reach the level of senior nurse?*
rise to a level *He rose to the level of vice-president.*

PHRASES

at board level *BrE* (=by the directors and owners of a company) *The most important decisions are made at board level.*
at ministerial level (=by government ministers) *The project was approved at ministerial level.*
at an international/global level (=with people or organizations from other countries) *The company operates at an international level.*
at a local/regional level (=with people or organizations in the local area) *Committees were set up at a local level.*
at a grass-roots level (=the ordinary people, not the leaders) *We are hoping for full participation at the grass-roots level.*

level² *adj* THESAURUS ▸ **flat¹**

liar *n*

someone who deliberately says things that are not true

ADJECTIVES

a good/accomplished liar *He's a good liar and we didn't suspect a thing.*
a terrible/poor/rotten liar *I'm such a rotten liar, nobody believed me for a minute.*
a habitual/chronic liar *formal* (=who lies a lot) *Drug users are often habitual liars trying to cover up their addiction.*
a compulsive/congenital/pathological liar *formal* (=who lies a lot because it is part of their personality) *She seems to be a congenital liar who will say anything to stay out of trouble.*
you little/big liar *informal: I never said that, you little liar!*

VERBS

call sb a liar (=say that someone is lying) *Are you calling me a liar?*
accuse sb of being a liar *I'm not accusing you of being a liar, just of being mistaken.*

liberty *n*

the freedom to do what you want and not be controlled by others

ADJECTIVES

complete/perfect liberty *You have complete liberty to write whatever you like.*
basic/fundamental liberties (=freedoms that everyone has a right to) *Freedom of speech and freedom of religion are basic liberties.*
individual/personal liberty (=of ordinary people) *The new law is a threat to individual liberty.*
civil liberties (=the rights of all people to do what they want while respecting other people's rights) *He argues that secret cameras in public places threaten our civil liberties.*
religious/political liberty *The American Constitution protects religious liberty.*

VERBS

have the liberty to do sth *You have the liberty to leave whenever you like.*
give/allow sb the liberty to do sth *Should people be allowed the liberty to take their own lives?*
protect/defend/safeguard sb's liberty *The constitution exists to protect the liberty of the citizens.*
threaten/endanger sb's liberty *The government should not be so powerful that it threatens individual liberty.*

L

fight for liberty *They fought for liberty during the revolution.*

guarantee sb's liberty *The new government promised to guarantee civil liberty.*

take away sb's liberty/deprive sb of their liberty *He had been wrongly deprived of his liberty.*

lose your liberty *He would rather lose his liberty than pay the fine.*

infringe on/restrict sb's liberty (=limit it) *Will the new security measures infringe on our liberty?*

PHRASES

be at liberty to do sth (=be able to do something) *I am not at liberty to discuss the case.*

loss of liberty *He claimed that preventing people using their cars represented a loss of liberty.*

an attack on/a threat to sb's liberty *These new laws are an attack on our liberty.*

an infringement of sb's liberty (=something that takes away someone's liberty) *It is a serious infringement of their liberty.*

the right to liberty *Everyone has the right to liberty.*

library *n*

a room or building containing books that can be looked at or borrowed

ADJECTIVES/NOUNS + library

the school/university/college library *She was studying in the college library.*

a public library *Our public libraries need more support.*

your local library *This information is available at your local library.*

a reference library (=one that does not lend books, so you read them there) *The reference library contains a collection of documents relating to slavery.*

a lending library (=one that lends books) *Lending libraries became increasingly popular in Victorian times.*

a private library *He has his own private library at home.*

a well-stocked library (=with a lot of books) *The journals are available from any well-stocked library.*

VERBS

go to/visit the library *I need to go to the library to return some books.*

use the library *You can use the library before or after school.*

borrow sth from the library *Books, CDs, DVDs, and magazines can be borrowed from the library.*

take sth out of the library (*also* **check sth out of the library** *AmE*): *Someone took it out of the library on March 4th.*

take sth back/return sth to the library *Have you taken those books back to the library?*

library + NOUNS

a library book *She's gone into town to change her library books.*

a library card (=a card that proves you are a member of a library) *You need your library card in order to take out books.*

the library catalogue *BrE*, **the library catalog** *AmE* (=the list of books in a library) *Students need to be taught how to use the computerised library catalogue.*

PREPOSITIONS

at a library *I'll meet you at the library.*

in a library *There's a copy of that book in the school library.*

licence *BrE*, license *AmE n*

an official document giving you permission to own or do something for a period of time

VERBS + licence

have a licence (*also* **hold a licence** *formal*): *He doesn't have a licence to fish in the lake.*

apply for a licence *The company applied for an export licence for its products.*

get/obtain a licence *Pilots must fly for at least fifty hours before getting their licence.*

give sb a licence (*also* **grant sb a licence** *formal*): *He was granted his flying instructor's license.*

issue (sb with) a licence *They do thorough checks before issuing a gun licence.*

deny/refuse sb a licence *Why was she refused the licence?*

lose your licence *The police caught him driving while drunk and he will now lose his licence.*

take away sb's licence (*also* **revoke sb's licence** *formal*): *The doctor had his license taken away after he was found to be abusing drugs.*

renew a licence (=arrange for it to continue for longer) *My licence expired and I forgot to renew it.*

licence + VERBS

a licence runs out (*also* **a licence expires** *formal*) (=it officially ends and you can no longer use it) *Her driver's license had expired.*

a licence allows/permits sth *A marriage licence allows you to get married.*

ADJECTIVES/NOUNS + licence

a special licence *You need a special licence to keep dangerous dogs.*

a valid licence *He was charged with driving without a valid licence.*

a full licence (=not temporary and with no restrictions) *Make sure your adviser has a full operating licence.*

a temporary licence *The factory has operated under a temporary licence for 5 years.*
a driving licence *BrE*, **a driver's license** *AmE*: *Eighty per cent of 18 year olds have a driver's license.*
a pilot's licence *She became the youngest woman to hold a pilot's licence.*
a gun licence (*also* **a firearms licence** *formal*): *You don't need to be trained in shooting to get a gun licence.*
a fishing/hunting licence *He renewed his hunting license.*
an import/export licence *An export licence was issued in August last year.*

licence + NOUNS

the licence holder *BrE* (=the person who has a licence) *The licence holder can drive any vehicle.*
a licence fee *In the UK, all TV owners have to pay a licence fee.*
a licence agreement *People often don't bother to read software licence agreements.*

PREPOSITIONS

a licence for sth *He didn't have a licence for the gun.*
with/without a licence *He was arrested for driving without a license.*
under licence (=if you have a licence) *Certain types of goods can only be sold under licence.*

lid *n*

a cover for a container such as a pan or box

VERBS

put/place the lid on sth *Put the lid on the pan.*
close/shut the lid *I put the apple core in the bin and closed the lid.*
screw the lid on (sth) *Screw the lid on tightly.*
cover sth with a lid *Cover the rice with a lid and cook for 10 minutes.*
open the lid *She unlocked the old trunk and opened the lid.*
unscrew the lid *I can't unscrew the lid of this jam jar.*
take the lid off sth/remove the lid *He took off the saucepan lid and sniffed the contents.*
lift the lid *I lifted the lid of the box and looked inside.*
replace the lid (=put it back on) *Always remember to replace the lid.*

lie[1] *v*

1 to deliberately tell someone something that is not true

> **Grammar**
> In this meaning, the past tense and past participle are **lied**.

PREPOSITIONS

lie to sb *You lied to me!*
lie about sth *The man had lied about his qualifications on his application.*

PHRASES

be lying through your teeth (=be saying something completely untrue) *"How fast were you going?" "30 miles an hour," said Slater, lying through his teeth.*

2 to be in a position in which your body is flat on the floor, on a bed etc

> **Grammar**
> In this meaning, the past tense is **lay** and the past participle is **lain**.

ADVERBS

lie awake *That night, Alice lay awake for a long time.*
lie asleep *He went into the room where his children lay asleep.*
lie quietly/peacefully *The baby lay quietly in her room.*
lie unconscious *The two officers discovered a man lying unconscious on the living room floor.*
lie dead *She found her husband lying dead in the hallway.*
lie still (=not moving) *You won't get to sleep unless you lie still.*
lie motionless (=not moving - used when someone is dead or very badly hurt) *The body lay motionless on the ground.*

PREPOSITIONS

lie in bed *You're not going to lie in bed all day, are you?*
lie on the floor/ground/bed *She saw a man lying on the ground.*
lie on your back/side/stomach *She was lying on her back with her eyes closed.*

> **Lie in or lie on?**
> If you **lie in bed**, you have the sheets and blankets on top of you. If you **lie on the bed**, you lie on top of the sheets and blankets.

PHRASES

lie face down *He was lying face down on the grass.*
lie sleeping/dying/watching sth etc (=doing something while lying down) *I held his hand as he lay sleeping.*

lie[2] *n*

something you say that you know is untrue

ADJECTIVES

a complete/total/outright lie (=something that is completely untrue) *She didn't want to tell her mother an outright lie.*

a white lie (=a small lie that you tell someone for good reasons, for example to avoid hurting their feelings) *We all have to tell white lies sometimes.*

a downright lie (=used when something is clearly a lie, especially when you feel annoyed) *That's a downright lie. I never said any such thing!*

a vicious lie (=very unkind and very untrue) *He told the court that it was a vicious lie from beginning to end.*

a blatant lie (=obvious) *He felt sure Adams was not convinced by such blatant lies.*

a barefaced lie *BrE*, **a bald-faced lie** *AmE* (=an obvious lie that is told with no sense of shame) *How can you stand there and tell me such a barefaced lie?*

an elaborate lie *Her parents didn't realize that it was all an elaborate lie.*

a big lie *The lawyer said it was a "big lie" that Jones had not received the message.*

VERBS

sth is a lie *That's a lie – I didn't do it.*

tell (sb) a lie *He got into trouble for telling a lie.*

believe a lie *How could you believe his lies?*

spread lies (=tell them to a lot of people) *How dare you spread such vicious lies?*

live a lie (=pretend all the time that you feel or believe something when you do not) *I knew that I could not continue to live a lie.*

PREPOSITIONS

a lie about sth *She had told many lies about her past.*

⚠ Don't say 'say a lie'. Say **tell a lie**.

PHRASES

a pack of lies *informal* (*also* **a tissue of lies** *BrE formal*) (=a lot of lies) *Everything he had told me was a pack of lies.*

life *n*

1 the state of being alive

VERBS

save sb's life *The money you give will save the life of a child.*

risk your life *Two firefighters risked their lives to save the children.*

lose your life (=die) *Hundreds of people lost their lives on the first day of the fighting.*

take a life/take sb's life (=kill someone) *All cultures consider it wrong to take a life for no reason.*

take your own life (=kill yourself) *He was depressed and decided to take his own life.*

cost lives/cost sb their life (=result in someone's death) *That decision may have cost him his life.*

give your life/lay down your life (=die in order to save other people, or because of a strong belief) *These men gave their lives during the war to keep us free.*

endanger sb's life (=make someone likely to die because of your actions) *By driving too fast you are endangering the lives of yourself and other road users.*

spare sb's life (=not kill someone, when you could kill them) *She begged him to spare the life of her son.*

owe your life to sb (=be still alive because of someone's actions) *The victim said he owed his life to the stranger who helped him.*

PHRASES

show no signs of life (=seem to be dead) *She was taken to the hospital showing no signs of life.*

be fighting for your life (=be so ill or injured that you might die) *One badly burned man was fighting for his life in hospital.*

be in fear for/of your life (=be afraid that you might die) *He is in fear of his life after threats by former drug associates.*

loss of life *There was only minor damage to property and no loss of life.*

the right to life *The right to life is the most basic of human rights.*

life after death *Do you believe in life after death?*

2 the time someone is alive

ADJECTIVES/NOUNS + life

sb's whole/entire life *This is the best day of my whole life.*

sb's adult life *He spent his entire adult life in France.*

sb's early life *We don't know much about the poet's early life.*

a long life *We wish you a long and happy life.*

a short life *He spent all of his short life in hospital.*

a past/previous life *She believes she must have done something wrong in a previous life.*

VERBS

spend your life *I've spent my whole life in this town.*

end your life (=die or kill yourself) *What makes someone want to end their life?*

prolong (sb's) life (=make someone live longer) *Drugs against HIV can prolong life in a person with AIDS.*

shorten (sb's) life *Every cigarette you smoke can shorten your life by five minutes.*

life + NOUNS

a life member *He's a life member of the club.*

a life sentence/life imprisonment (=a punishment of life in prison) *He received a life sentence for the murder.*

life expectancy (=how long someone is likely to live) *In some areas, life expectancy is 49 years.*

sb's life story *She insisted on telling me her whole life story.*

PREPOSITIONS

in sb's life *For the first time in my life I was happy.*

throughout sb's life *Throughout her life she had always felt different from other people.*

for life (=for the whole of someone's life) *He was sent to prison for life.*

PHRASES

all your life *I've known John all my life.*

for the rest of your life *She knew she'd feel guilty for the rest of her life.*

late in life (=when someone is fairly old) *She married late in life.*

in later life (=when you are older) *Poor diet can lead to a whole range of diseases in later life.*

go through life doing sth *You can't go through life worrying what people think of you.*

dedicate/devote your life to sth (=spend your life doing a particular activity) *He dedicated his life to music.*

3 the way someone lives

ADJECTIVES

a normal life *After the operation, you should be able to lead a normal life.*

a happy/lonely/busy etc life *On the whole, Dad has an easy life.*

a hard life (=full of problems) *As a single mother of eight children, she had a hard life.*

a quiet life *He wants a quiet life, while she wants to go out partying.*

a full life (=with many different activities) *Before her illness, Rose enjoyed a full life.*

a sheltered life (=protected from unpleasant things) *She had lived a sheltered life, and was shocked by the things she saw.*

a double life (=having two homes, families, or sets of activities, one of which is kept secret) *Mary had no idea that her husband was leading a double life with another woman.*

VERBS

have/lead/live a ... life *She just wants to have a normal life.*

affect sb's life *These are decisions that affect people's lives.*

change sb's life *Having a baby changes your life completely.*

enrich sb's life (=make it better) *Education can greatly enrich your life.*

rule sb's life (=control and affect everything you do) *You shouldn't let your boyfriend rule your life.*

ruin sb's life *I'm not going to let this illness ruin my life.*

rebuild your life (=live normally again after something bad has happened) *She is beginning to rebuild her life without her husband.*

start a new life *They moved to Australia to start a new life.*

sb's life revolves around sth (=it is the most important thing in someone's life) *Ken's whole life revolved around surfing.*

PREPOSITIONS

a life of crime/poverty/misery etc *He had been drawn into a life of crime.*

PHRASES

a way of life *The tribe's traditional way of life is under threat.*

4 the activities that are typical of a situation or job

ADJECTIVES/NOUNS + life

daily/everyday life *Communication using the internet is now part of everyday life.*

married life *Are you enjoying married life?*

family life *She left work and she now has a happy family life.*

college/student life *Parties are an important part of student life.*

country/city/village etc life *I like the slow pace of island life.*

political life *Why do so few women enter political life?*

public life (=work, especially for the government, that makes you well known) *Her drink problem forced her to retire from public life.*

sb's social life (=the activities someone does to enjoy themselves) *He has a great social life and is always going to parties.*

sb's working life *I have been with the same company all my working life.*

sb's personal/private life (=involving close family and friends) *There's a lot going on in his personal life at the moment.*

sb's home life *She tried to find a balance between her home life and her career.*

PHRASES

from all walks of life/from every walk of life (=from many different jobs or positions in society) *Our volunteers come from all walks of life.*

lifeless *adj* THESAURUS ▸ dead[1]

lifestyle *n*

the way a person or group of people live

ADJECTIVES

a healthy/unhealthy lifestyle *A healthy lifestyle includes taking exercise and not smoking.*

an active lifestyle (=with a lot of activities and exercise) *There are many health benefits to an active lifestyle.*

a sedentary lifestyle (=with a lot of sitting down and not much exercise) *As a writer, he has a sedentary lifestyle.*

a busy lifestyle *Many people these days have a busy lifestyle.*

L

a hectic lifestyle (=very busy and full of activity) *She has a hectic lifestyle, juggling a career with family life.*

a stressful lifestyle *A stressful lifestyle may lead to illness.*

a comfortable lifestyle (=with enough money) *He enjoyed a comfortable lifestyle after he retired from work.*

an extravagant/lavish lifestyle (=in which you spend a lot of money) *How can he afford such an extravagant lifestyle?*

a simple lifestyle (=with few possessions or modern machines) *He admired the simple lifestyle of the people who lived on the island.*

an alternative lifestyle (=different from most people's) *We should respect people who choose alternative lifestyles.*

VERBS

have a ... lifestyle *We had very different lifestyles.*

live/lead a ... lifestyle (=live in a particular way) *I had enough money to live a comfortable lifestyle.*

change/improve your lifestyle *You can help prevent heart disease by changing your lifestyle.*

maintain a lifestyle (=keep it the same) *You cannot maintain this lifestyle on your income.*

fit/suit sb's lifestyle *Choose a hobby that suits your lifestyle.*

PHRASES

a change of/in lifestyle *Her new job meant a complete change in lifestyle.*

lifetime *n*

the period of time during which someone is alive or something exists

ADJECTIVES

a whole/entire lifetime *He has lived here throughout his entire lifetime.*

a short/long lifetime *She had learned a lot in her short lifetime.*

VERBS

spend a lifetime *I've spent a lifetime looking after other people.*

take a lifetime *It can take a lifetime to develop this skill.*

last a lifetime *Well-made golf clubs ought to last a lifetime.*

seem (like) a lifetime *It seemed a lifetime since she'd gone to bed the night before.*

> You often use **a lifetime** when you mean "a very long time": *There was enough food in the house to last* ***a lifetime***.

PREPOSITIONS

during/in sb's lifetime *Only about 100 of his poems were published in his lifetime.*

a lifetime of sth *They face a lifetime of misery.*

PHRASES

the chance/experience/holiday etc of a lifetime (=the best one you will ever have or do) *I'm offering you the chance of a lifetime.*

the habit of a lifetime (=a habit that someone has had all their life) *It isn't easy to break the habits of a lifetime.*

a lifetime's work *Almost a lifetime's work has been destroyed.*

a lifetime's experience *She had a lifetime's experience of cooking for people.*

once in a lifetime *It was the kind of discovery that a scientist makes only once in a lifetime.*

> The phrase **once in a lifetime** is often used before nouns: *This is a* ***once-in-a-lifetime*** *opportunity.*

lift[1] *v*

1 to move something or someone upwards or to another place

NOUNS

lift the lid/top/cover *She lifted the lid of the pan to see if the soup was ready.*

lift a suitcase/case/bag *My case was so heavy I could hardly lift it.*

lift a box/container/coffin *The last two boxes were lifted onto the ship.*

lift your head/hand/arm/leg/finger *Katie lifted her hand to shade her eyes.*

lift your glass/cup *His hand was shaking as he lifted the glass to his lips.*

ADVERBS

lift sb/sth carefully *Lift the jug carefully, so that you don't spill any of the liquid.*

lift sb/sth gently *David gently lifted the child onto his shoulders.*

PREPOSITIONS/ADVERBS

lift sb/sth up *They lifted up the stone, to see what was underneath.*

lift sb/sth down *Can you lift my bag down for me?*

lift sb/sth onto sth *The nurses lifted Andrew onto the bed.*

THESAURUS: lift

raise
head | hand | fist | finger | glass | cup | hat | gun | lid | bridge
to lift something to a higher position, usually for a short time before lowering it again. **Raise** is more formal than **lift**:
She raised her head and looked at him. | The man raised his fists as if he intended to hit me. | "Cheers, everyone!" said Larry, raising his glass. | Mr Rutherford always raised his hat when he saw me. | The bridge can be raised to allow ships to pass under it.

L

Raise or lift?

Raise is more formal than **lift**. You often use **raise** in certain fixed expressions. If you **raise your glasses**, you lift them up and then drink some alcohol, in order to celebrate something or wish someone good luck. If you **raise your eyebrows**, you move them up because you are surprised. If you **raise your hand**, you put it in the air, especially because you want to speak in class or vote.

You usually use **raise** when you lift something for a short time, for example your hat, your hand, a bridge etc. However, you can also use **raise** when talking about lifting up a ship that has sunk: *They are planning to **raise** the ship from the bottom of the ocean.*

When talking about lifting things so that you can carry them, you usually use **lift**. You say **lift a suitcase/bag** (not 'raise' it).

put your hand up/put up your hand
to lift your arm into the air, for example because you want to speak in class or when voting:
Put your hand up if you know the right answer.

hoist
to lift up something which is heavy and difficult to carry, or to lift someone up:
*Joe picked up the sack and **hoisted** it **onto** the truck. | The crowd **hoisted** him **onto** their shoulders and carried him down the main street.*

You also use **hoist** about pulling up a flag, sail etc using a rope: *They **hoisted** the flag up the pole.*

2 to end an official order that stops someone from doing something

THESAURUS: lift

call off, postpone, shelve, lift, repeal, annul → **cancel**

lift² *BrE n*

a machine that takes people and goods from one level to another in a building

VERBS

the lift goes up/down *The doors closed and the lift went down.*

take the lift *Take the lift to the fourth floor.*

use the lift *He decided to walk up the stairs instead of using the lift.*

get into/out of the lift *As I was getting into the lift, a voice shouted, "Wait for me!"*

Lift is used in British English. In American English, people say **elevator**.

light¹ *n*

1 brightness from the sun, a flame, a lamp etc

ADJECTIVES/NOUNS + light

bright/strong light *The light was so bright he had to shut his eyes.*

blinding/dazzling light (=extremely bright, so that you cannot see properly) *The white buildings reflected a blinding light.*

dim light (=not bright) *Gradually her eyes became accustomed to the dim light.*

poor/bad light (=not bright enough) *The light was too poor for me to read.*

good light (=bright enough) *Stand over here where the light is good.*

soft/warm light (=light that seems slightly yellow or orange) *Her face was beautiful in the soft light of the candles.*

cold/harsh light (=light that seems slightly blue) *Under the cold light of the moon, he built a fire.*

the morning light *The flowers glowed brightly in the morning light.*

natural light (=from the sun, not electric lights) *The only natural light came from two high windows.*

artificial light (=produced by electric lights) *The office was windowless, lit only by artificial light.*

Sunlight, **moonlight**, **firelight**, and **candlelight** are written as one word.

light + VERBS

light shines *Light from the sun shines on the earth.*

light comes from somewhere *The only light came from the fire.*

light streams/floods in (=a large amount of light comes in) *Light streamed in through the window.*

light falls on/across sth *The light of the moon fell on her face.*

the light is fading (=it is getting darker as the sun is going down) *The light was fading and we decided to go indoors.*

VERBS + light

produce light (*also* **emit light** *formal*): *The bulbs don't produce much light.*

reflect light *Snow reflects a lot of light.*

block (out) the light (=stop light reaching a place) *Move away from the window – you're blocking out the light.*

sth is bathed in light *literary* (=something has a lot of light shining on it) *The fields and woods were bathed in golden light.*

PREPOSITIONS

light from sth *The light from a torch was all they had to guide them.*

by the light of sth (=using a particular light to do something) *I read by the light of the fire.*

PHRASES

a beam/ray/shaft of light (=a thin line of light) *There was a shaft of light from the doorway.*

a flash of light (=a bright light that appears suddenly for a very short time) *A flash of light was followed by a deafening sound as the bomb exploded.*

a pool/circle of light (=an area of light) *They stood in the pool of light cast by the streetlamp.*

a source of light (*also* **a light source**) (=something that produces light) *The only source of light was a candle.*

2 something that produces light, especially electric light

ADJECTIVES/NOUNS + light

a light is on *All the lights in the house were on.*

a light is off/out *Most people sleep with the light off.*

the bedroom/kitchen/bathroom etc light *She could see that his bedroom light was on.*

an electric light *He fitted an electric light inside the cupboard.*

a bedside light *She switched off the bedside light and went to sleep.*

a warning light *A warning light comes on if the engine gets too hot.*

Streetlight, **headlight**, and **spotlight** are written as one word.

VERBS + light

turn on/switch on a light *Switch the light on, please.*

turn off/switch off the light *To save energy, turn the light off when you leave a room.*

leave the light on *You've left the bathroom light on.*

shine a light somewhere *The policeman shone a light down the hallway.*

light + VERBS

a light goes out/goes off *Suddenly all the lights in the house went out.*

a light comes on/goes on (=starts working) *The light comes on automatically when you open the fridge door.*

a light glows/shines *There were a few houses, their lights shining on the hillside.*

a light flashes *A police car arrived with its blue lights flashing.*

a light flickers (=goes on and off repeatedly) *The light flickered, and then came on.*

light² *adj*

1 not heavy

ADVERBS

very light *These scissors are very light and easy to use.*

quite/fairly light *When I swung the golf club, it felt quite light.*

relatively light *When you start training, use relatively light weights.*

surprisingly light *This guitar is compact and surprisingly light.*

VERBS

feel light *The box felt lighter than I expected.*

PHRASES

as light as a feather (=extremely light) *I'll carry you – you're as light as a feather.*

light in weight *This type of plastic is immensely strong but light in weight.*

THESAURUS: light

lightweight
material | fabric | nylon | plastic | aluminium | suit | jacket
lightweight materials, clothing, or equipment weigh less than average:
They wear special boots made of lightweight materials. | This bag is made from a strong lightweight nylon. | A lightweight linen suit is appropriate for a summer wedding.

ANTONYMS **light → heavy (1)**

2 not dark

VERBS

it is light *Let's go now, while it's still light.*

it gets light *It gets light very early at this time of year.*

the sky turns light (*also* **the sky grows light** especially literary): *It was 5 a.m. and the sky was just turning light.*

it stays light (*also* **remain light** *formal*): *In midsummer it stays light until nearly midnight.*

THESAURUS: light

strong, brilliant, dazzling, blinding, harsh, light, well-lit → **bright (1)**

ANTONYMS **light → dark (1)**

3 not severe, or not great in amount or degree

NOUNS

a light punishment/penalty *A small fine seems an extremely light punishment.*

a light sentence (=a light punishment given by a judge, usually a period of time in prison) *Burglars and muggers usually only get a light sentence.*

light rain/snow *There will be some light rain followed by sunny periods.*

light traffic *The traffic was surprisingly light in the rush hour.*

light casualties (=a small number of people injured or killed) *The US forces suffered only light casualties.*

light use *The equipment is only built for light use.*

ANTONYMS **light → heavy (2)**

light-hearted *adj* THESAURUS **funny (1)**

lightning *n*

a flash of light in the sky caused by electricity and usually followed by thunder

PHRASES

a flash of lightning *Suddenly there was a flash of lightning in the sky.*

a bolt of lightning (=a flash of lightning, especially one that hits something) *The house was struck by a bolt of lightning.*

thunder and lightning *The thunder and lightning began to move further away.*

VERBS

be hit/struck by lightning *The house had been hit by lightning.*

lightning flashes *Lightning flashed in the sky.*

ADJECTIVES

forked lightning (=with smaller lines coming off the main line) *There was a sudden flash of forked lightning.*

sheet lightning (=a sudden flash of brightness covering a large area of sky) *Sheet lightning lit up the sky.*

lightning + NOUNS

a lightning conductor *BrE* **a lightning rod** *AmE* (=a metal bar that protects a building from lightning) *The church has a lightning conductor on the roof.*

lightweight *adj* THESAURUS **light[2] (1)**

like *v*

to think someone or something is good

ADVERBS

like sb/sth very much/a lot *John's nice – I like him very much.*

like sb/sth best/better *He's been all over the world, but he likes Africa best.*

like sb/sth enormously *I knew Mary very well and liked her enormously.*

really like sb/sth *We really liked the film.*

quite like sb/sth *I quite like their new album.*

particularly like sth *It's a good magazine – I particularly like the arts section.*

always like sb/sth *She had always liked bright colours.*

be universally liked (=be liked by everyone) *He is well respected and almost universally liked.*

L

PHRASES

get to like sb/sth (=start to like someone or something) *We soon got to like each other.*

like sth more than anything (else) in the world *Some people like money more than anything else in the world.*

I don't like it when... *I don't like it when you get angry.*

ANTONYMS **like → dislike[1]**

likely *adj*

something that is likely will probably happen or is probably true

ADVERBS

very/extremely likely *It is very likely that he is still alive.*

highly likely (=very likely) *Snow showers are highly likely tomorrow.*

quite likely *BrE* (=very likely) *If the service is good, customers are quite likely to come back.*

fairly/reasonably likely *It seems fairly likely that he'll resign.*

more/most likely *Young drivers are far more likely to have accidents than older ones.*

less/least likely *The smallest puppies are the least likely to survive.*

hardly likely (=not very likely) *It seems hardly likely that she would tell her husband about it.*

increasingly likely *Rain looks increasingly likely.*

VERBS

seem likely (*also* **appear likely** *formal*): *Which candidate seems likely to win?*

look likely (=seem likely) *It looks likely that she'll leave.*

make sth likely *The attack made war even more likely.*

NOUNS

a likely explanation *What is the most likely explanation for her behaviour?*

a likely effect/impact *They discussed the likely impact of a new factory.*

a likely outcome/consequences (=what will happen as a result of something) *The most likely outcome of the contest is a draw.*

a likely cause/reason *The likely cause of the fire was a dropped cigarette.*

a likely possibility *The most likely possibility is that he will lose all his money.*

a likely scenario (=situation) *One likely scenario is that no one will get the job.*

PHRASES

more than likely (=very likely) *It is more than likely the votes will have to be counted again.*

sth is all too likely (=very likely – used especially about something bad) *His plan was all too likely to fail.*

sth is not at all likely/not remotely likely (=very unlikely) *He could win, but it's not at all likely. | That is not remotely likely to happen.*

limit¹ *v*

to stop an amount or number from being greater

ADVERBS

severely/greatly limit sth *The bad weather severely limited the amount of work that could be done.*

be strictly limited *Parking is strictly limited.*

PREPOSITIONS

limit sth to sth *Limit the amount of coffee you drink to two cups per day.*

limit² *n*

the greatest or least amount that is allowed, or that you have available

ADJECTIVES

a strict limit *There are strict limits on how much luggage you can take on the plane.*

the legal limit *The alcohol in his blood was four times over the legal limit.*

an upper/lower limit (=the highest/lowest amount allowed) *There is no upper limit on the amount you can borrow.*

NOUNS + limit

the speed limit *Too many people go over the speed limit in residential areas.*

a time limit *Is there a time limit for making an insurance claim?*

an age limit *The lower age limit for entering the army is 17.*

a weight/height limit *The weight limit per bag is 20 kilos.*

spending limits *The council has to save money to meet government spending limits.*

an overdraft limit (=the maximum amount you can owe a bank when you have spent more than you have in your account) *You will be charged if you go over your overdraft limit.*

VERBS

set a limit (*also* **impose a limit** *formal*): *Set a time limit for the completion of the task.*

put a limit on sth *They put a limit on the cost of tickets.*

go over/exceed a limit (=go faster, buy more etc than a limit allows) *Drivers often exceed the speed limit.*

PREPOSITIONS

a limit on/to sth *Is there a limit on how many books you can borrow?*

over/above the limit *Their luggage was over the limit when they tried to get on the plane.*

under/below/within a limit *He always drives below the speed limit.*

at/on a limit *She was at the limit of her patience.*

up to a limit *I had spent up to the limit on my credit card.*

> You say a driver is **over the limit** if they have more alcohol in their blood than is legally allowed: *He told the policeman that he did not realize he was* ***over the limit****.*

limited *adj* not very great

NOUNS

limited amount/number/range *There are a limited number of tickets still available.*

limited space *What should I plant in a small garden where space is limited?*

limited time *They have limited time to train new staff.*

limited resources *We must not waste our limited resources.*

limited success *They have had only limited success in reducing pollution.*

limited value *The information they provided was of limited value.*

ADVERBS

very/extremely limited *His knowledge was extremely limited.*

severely limited *Evidence from this period is severely limited.*

rather/quite/relatively limited *Most puppies have a rather limited attention span.*

PHRASES

of limited use (=not very useful) *This anti-missile system is of limited use against modern missiles.*

to a limited extent (=a little, but not very much) *The method has been used to a limited extent in some other schools.*

in a limited way *I contributed in a limited way to the success of the project.*

line *n*

1 a long thin mark on a piece of paper, the ground, or another surface

ADJECTIVES

a straight line *Draw a straight line across the top of the page.*

a horizontal/vertical/diagonal line *The bricks need to be in a vertical line.*

parallel lines (=equally distant from each other) *There were two parallel lines of stitches.*

a thick/thin line *A thin line of blood ran down his cheek.*

the dotted line (=one that consists of a series of dots) *Sign your name on the dotted line.*

the starting/finishing line (=at the start or end of a race) *The athletes were getting ready at the starting line.*

VERBS

draw a line *Draw a straight line between the two points on the graph.*

put a line through sth (=draw a line through something, especially because it is a mistake)

The teacher put a red line through the first sentence.
cross/go over a line *He crossed the finishing line in 3rd place.*
be covered in lines *The old man's face was covered in lines.*
a line shows/indicates sth *The line shows the average rise in temperature.*
a line separates/divides sth *The red line separates the two countries on the map.*

2 a row of people or things

PHRASES

stand in line *The passengers stood in line, waiting to board the plane.*
get in line *The teacher told us to get in line outside the classroom.*
form a line *The dancers formed a line on the stage.*

ADJECTIVES

a long/short line *There was a long line of traffic.*
a continuous line *The houses formed a continuous line up the hill.*

link[1] Ac *n*

a way in which two things or people are connected

ADJECTIVES

a direct link *There is a direct link between smoking and some forms of cancer.*
a close link *The university has close links with several universities in China.*
a strong link *There is a strong link between sport and health.*
a clear link *Official figures show a clear link between poverty and crime.*
a vital/important link *The team of doctors and nurses provides a vital link between the hospital and the local community.*
economic/trade links *Economic links between the two countries strengthened.*
international links *The organization has greatly benefited from its international links.*
a tenuous link (=one that is not strong) *He had only a tenuous link with the famous singer.*

VERBS

have links *Several members of the government have links with big companies.*
create a link *The program creates a link between teaching in schools and learning at home.*
establish/form/forge a link *He established links with writers and artists.*
develop/build links *Academics need to develop links with business.*
maintain a link *These immigrants maintain very close links with family back home.*
strengthen a link *The country was trying to strengthen its links with its neighbours.*
break a link (*also* **sever a link** *formal*): *She was reluctant to sever this last link with her former life.*
make a link (=realize or show that two things are connected with each other) *The Swedish scientist was the first person to make the link between climate change and greenhouse gases.*
find a link *The researchers found strong links between diet and health.*
show/establish a link *Other research has shown a link between crime and employment opportunities.*

PREPOSITIONS

a link between things *There is a link between stress and headaches.*
a link with sth/sb *They are hoping to establish links with local business.*

link[2] Ac *v*

1 if two things are linked, they are related or connected in some way

> **Grammar**
> This meaning of **link** is usually passive.

ADVERBS

be closely linked *The medical department is closely linked with the local hospital.*
be directly linked *They believe his death was directly linked to the scandal.*
be strongly linked *Educational achievement is strongly linked to social class.*
be clearly linked *Urban growth is clearly linked with population increase.*
be inextricably linked (=very closely, so you cannot separate them) *Physical and emotional well-being are inextricably linked.*

PREPOSITIONS

be linked to sth *Their wages are linked to the number of years they have been with the company.*
be linked with sth *Obesity is linked with many health problems.*

2 to join two or more things, people, or places

PREPOSITIONS/ADVERBS

link sth with/and sth *The new railway line will link London and Birmingham.*
link sth together *The scientists developed a network to link their computers together.*

liquid *n*

a substance that is not a solid or a gas, for example water or milk

ADJECTIVES

a hot/cold liquid *Be careful when dealing with hot liquids.*
a clear liquid *We were offered a clear liquid that looked like water.*
a colourless liquid *BrE*, **a colorless liquid** *AmE*: *The liquid was colourless and had no smell.*

L

a thick liquid *She stirred the thick liquid in the saucepan.*

VERBS + liquid

pour a liquid *The chef poured the liquid into a bowl.*

drink/swallow a liquid *He put the glass to his lips and drank the liquid.*

sth absorbs a liquid *Cook the sauce until all of the liquid has been absorbed.*

liquid + VERBS

a liquid flows *The liquid flowed down the pipe.*

a liquid oozes (=flows slowly because it is thick) *A red liquid oozed over the floor.*

> **Fluid** is used as a more formal word for **liquid**, especially in medical and technical contexts: *Drink plenty of clear* ***fluids****. | The car was leaking brake* ***fluid****.*

list *n*

a set of names, numbers etc written one below the other

ADJECTIVES/NOUNS + list

a long/short list *The teacher read out a long list of names.*

a complete/full/comprehensive list *The full list of winners is on page seven.*

a shopping list/grocery list (=a list of things or food you want to buy) *I didn't get everything on my shopping list.*

a price list *We'll send you a catalogue and price list.*

a wine list (=a list of wines available in a restaurant) *The restaurant has a good wine list.*

a guest list *The guest list for the wedding did not include me.*

a waiting list (=a list of people who are waiting for something) *If you don't get the class you want, you can put your name on a waiting list.*

a mailing list (=a list of people that a company sends information to) *If you do not want to be on our mailing list, please tick the box below.*

a to-do list (=a list of things you must do) *Painting the bedroom is at the top of my to-do list.*

> **Checklist** (=a list of things to do) and **shortlist** (= a list of the most suitable people for a job or prize) are usually written as one word.

VERBS

make/write a list *Make a list of all the things you have to do.*

draw up/compile a list (=make a list - more formal) *They've compiled a list of children's clubs and organizations.*

put sb/sth on a list *I was put on a waiting list to see a specialist at the hospital.*

add sb/sth to a list *I'll add those books to my list.*

join a list *Belgium has now joined the list of member countries.*

the list goes on (=used when saying there are many more people or things on a list) *You have to pay for flowers, the wedding dress, the church... the list goes on.*

PREPOSITIONS

a list of sth *There's a list of local restaurants in the back of the book.*

on a list *There are ten names on my list.*

PHRASES

at the top/bottom of a list *Her name was at the top of the list of students.*

first/last on a list *Why am I always last on the list?*

listen *v*

to pay attention to what someone is saying or to a sound that you can hear

ADVERBS

listen carefully/closely *If you listen carefully, you can hear the birds singing.*

listen hard (*also* **listen intently/attentively** *formal*) (=listen very carefully) *The students listened intently to her every word.*

listen politely/respectfully/patiently *He expects you to listen politely and agree with everything he says.*

listen sympathetically *Her boss listened sympathetically and told her not to worry.*

PREPOSITIONS

listen to sb/sth *I like listening to music when I'm driving.*

> ⚠ You always say **listen to** something. Don't say 'I like listening music'.

PHRASES

listen in silence *I told him my story and he listened in silence.*

listen with interest *The audience listened with interest to what she was saying.*

sb never listens to sb/sth (=they always ignore someone or something) *My son never listens to what I say.*

listen at the door/window (=stand next to it and secretly listen to someone or something) *One of the servants was listening at the door, and she heard everything that was said.*

literature *n*

books, plays, poems etc, especially ones that people think are important and good

ADJECTIVES

English/American/French etc literature *She took a degree in French literature.*

18th-/19th-/20th-century literature *This type of plot is common in 19th-century literature.*
modern literature *I haven't read much modern literature - I prefer the classics like Dickens and Thomas Hardy.*
contemporary literature (=modern literature, or literature of the time you are talking about) *The role of the individual was a common theme in contemporary literature.*
great literature *Teenagers should be introduced to the great literature of the past.*
popular literature *He made good money as a writer of popular literature.*
classical literature (=the literature of ancient Greece and Rome) *There are many references in classical literature to the Trojan War.*
medieval literature (=written between about the 11th and 15th centuries) *His principal area of research is medieval literature.*

VERBS

study literature *She studied medieval literature at the university.*
read literature *He reads German literature for pleasure.*
teach literature *He now teaches English literature at Cambridge University.*

PHRASES

a work/piece of literature *I admit the book is not a great work of literature.*

litter *n*

waste paper, cans etc that people have thrown onto the ground

VERBS

drop/throw litter *People who drop litter in the street should be fined.*
leave litter *Please do not leave litter. Use the bins provided.*
pick up/clear up/clean up/collect litter *Teams of volunteers regularly pick up litter that has been left on the beach.*
be strewn with litter (=covered with it) *The pavement was strewn with litter.*

litter + NOUNS

a litter bin/basket *Keep the park tidy and use the litter bins.*

PHRASES

a pile of litter *They left a pile of litter behind for us to clean up.*
a piece of litter *Over 373,000 pieces of litter were found on beaches in the UK last year.*
take your litter home with you *If there is no litter bin in the area, please take your litter home with you.*

little *adj* THESAURUS **small (1)**

little-known *adj* THESAURUS **famous**

live *adj* THESAURUS **alive (1)**

live[1] *v*

1 if you live in a place, you have your home there

ADVERBS

live together *They fell in love and started to live together.*
live alone *I'm quite happy living alone.*
live apart *Their busy schedules forced the couple to live apart.*
live nearby/close by *She was visiting her daughter who lives nearby.*

PREPOSITIONS

live in a house/town/country *Living in London is very expensive.*
live on a street *He lives on Queens Street.*
live at an address *They live at 1201 Columbia Drive, Los Angeles.*

PHRASES

live at home (=in your parents' home) *Most seventeen-year-olds still live at home.*
live next door *A rather odd family came to live next door to us.*
live just across the street/down the road from sb *He lives just across the street from me.*
live on the streets *There has been an increase in the number of mentally ill people living on the streets.*
a place to live/somewhere to live *They've finally found a place to live.*

2 to have a particular kind of life

ADVERBS

live well/comfortably/happily *They have enough money to live comfortably.*
live dangerously (=take a risk or do something new) *She decided to live dangerously and have her hair cut short.*

PHRASES

live in luxury *The president was living in luxury in a palace while his people starved.*
live frugally (=with only the things you need and no luxuries) *They lived frugally, eating only rice and beans.*
live below the poverty line (=with very little money, so you are officially considered to be very poor) *There are hundreds of families living below the poverty line.*
live in peace *It is time for the war to end and everyone to live in peace.*

3 to be alive

ADVERBS

live longer *People are living longer than ever before.*
live forever *No-one lives forever.*

PREPOSITIONS

live until you are 82, 96 etc *Her mother lived until she was 99.*

live for 60/70 etc years *Goldfish can live for 10 to 20 years in a garden pond.*

live through sth *During his life, he had lived through some very hard times.*

livid *adj* THESAURUS ▸ angry

living[1] *adj* THESAURUS ▸ alive (1)

living[2] *n*

the way that you earn money or the money that you earn

VERBS

earn/make a living *It's hard to make a living as a musician.*

do sth for a living (=work at something as your job) *What do you do for a living?*

eke out/scratch/scrape a living (=only just earn enough money to live) *They eke out a living selling whatever they can.*

provide a living *The industry provides a living for thousands of people.*

ADJECTIVES

a good/decent/comfortable living (=enough money) *Her husband makes a good living.*

an honest living *I'm just trying to earn an honest living.*

load[1] *n*

1 the quantity of something that a vehicle or person carries, especially a large quantity

ADJECTIVES

a heavy load *The road has been damaged by lorries carrying heavy loads.*

a light load *This van is ideal for transporting light loads.*

a full load *The plane was carrying a full load of fuel.*

the maximum load *The elevator carries a maximum load of 800 kg.*

VERBS

carry a load *The horse was carrying a heavy load.*

pull a load *The train can pull loads of hundreds of tons.*

shed a load (=used when a load falls off a lorry or truck) *Drivers suffered delays on the motorway after a lorry shed its load.*

> **A truckload/lorryload/carload/busload**
> You use this about the amount of things or people that will fit into a truck, car etc: *They used two* ***truckloads*** *of soil.* | ***Busloads*** *of tourists began arriving in the city square.*

> **Loads of**
> This phrase is used in informal English to mean "a lot of" things or people: *There were* ***loads of*** *mistakes.* | *She has* ***loads of*** *friends.*

2 the amount of work or responsibilities that someone has

VERBS

reduce/lighten the load *Companies can lighten the load on permanent staff by hiring extra workers during busy periods of the year.*

increase the load *Now that his colleagues have gone, this will increase the load on him.*

share the load *They shared the load by taking it in turns to drive the car.*

> **Workload** is usually written as one word.

load[2] *v* THESAURUS ▸ fill

loan *n*

an amount of money that you borrow

VERBS

get a loan *She got a loan from the bank.*

take out a loan (=borrow money) *I had to take out a loan to buy my car.*

repay/pay off/pay back a loan (=give back the money you borrowed, usually over a period of time) *It'll be years before we've paid off the loan.*

give/make sb a loan *We're hoping my dad will give us a loan.*

ask sb for a loan *He asked his father for a loan.*

apply for a loan (=officially ask for a loan) *To apply for a loan, fill out this online form.*

arrange a loan *Do you need help arranging a loan?*

refuse sb a loan *Did the bank say why they refused her the loan?*

ADJECTIVES/NOUNS + loan

a £20,000/$5,000 etc loan *The company asked for a £100,000 loan.*

a bank loan *If my parents won't lend me the money, I'll have to get a bank loan.*

a home/car loan *They took out a 30-year home loan.*

a business loan *The bank offers a range of business loans to meet the needs of small businesses.*

a student loan *Many college graduates are paying off huge student loans.*

local *adv* THESAURUS ▸ near

location Ac *n*

the place where someone or something is

ADJECTIVES

a good/great location *The apartment is in a good location.*

an ideal/perfect location *I've found the perfect location for our new store.*

a suitable location *They are still searching for a suitable location for the museum.*

a convenient location *The house is in a convenient location close to local shops.*

a prime location (=an extremely good location) *The hotel is in a prime location right by the sea.*

a central location (=near the centre of a town or area) *The park's central location makes it a popular meeting place.*

a remote location (=far from where most people live) *One proposal is to bury the waste deep underground in a remote location.*

a secret/unknown/undisclosed location *The talks were held at a secret location.*

exact/precise location *The exact location of his grave is not known.*

geographical location *The schools are grouped according to their geographical location.*

present location *The college moved to its present location in 1931.*

a new/different location *The store is moving to a new location.*

an exotic location *They like to have their holidays in exotic locations.*

VERBS

find the location of sth *I managed to find the location of the hotel on the map.*

PREPOSITIONS

in/at a location *The cottage is in a beautiful location.*

the location of sth *He wasn't sure about the precise location of the building.*

lock *v* THESAURUS ▸ close¹ (1)

logic *n*

a way of thinking about something that seems correct and reasonable, or a set of sensible reasons for doing something

VERBS + logic

understand/follow/see sb's logic *It's easy to understand his logic.*

explain the logic of sth *Can anyone explain the logic of this statement to me?*

use/apply logic *Why do we not apply the same logic in the way we treat animals as we do with humans?*

be based on logic *This view is not based on logic.*

accept the logic of sth (=agree that it is correct) *If we accept this logic, no one should pay tax.*

question/challenge the logic of sth (=say you do not agree with it) *People are questioning the logic of building more homes in an area that is already overcrowded.*

sth defies logic (=used when something does not seem reasonable) *It defies logic to import food that we can grow more easily and cheaply here.*

logic + VERBS

logic suggests sth (=means it is likely to be true) *Logic suggests that if an expert can't fix it, neither can you.*

logic dictates sth (=means it is definitely true) *Logic dictates that poorer people will be more affected by the rise in inflation.*

the same logic applies (=the same thing is also true about someone or something else) *The same logic applies to other prisoners.*

ADJECTIVES

the same logic *By the same logic, other harmful substances such as alcohol or tobacco should also be prohibited.*

a simple logic *The argument does have a simple logic.*

impeccable logic (=very good and difficult to criticize) *They argued, with impeccable logic, that if you were old enough to die for your country, you should have the right to vote.*

compelling logic (=seeming to be definitely right) *Few will argue with the compelling logic of his theory.*

twisted/warped logic (=wrong in a cruel or shocking way) *According to the terrorists' warped logic, we all deserve to be killed.*

flawed/faulty logic (=wrong) *Their arguments are full of flawed logic.*

the underlying logic (=which something is based on) *These word lists show students the underlying logic of English spelling.*

internal logic (=the logic that exists between the various parts of a system) *Every religion has its own internal logic.*

a certain logic (=used when something may seem wrong or strange, but there are understandable reasons for it) *With a certain logic, the child said that 'ten and one' would be the next number after ten.*

PREPOSITIONS

the logic of sth *I don't see the logic of your argument.*

the logic behind sth *The logic behind this statement is wrong.*

PHRASES

there is no logic in (doing) sth *There is no logic in telling a child not to swear if you do it yourself.*

a lack of logic *There seems to be a lack of logic in his remarks.*

logical Ac *adj*

seeming reasonable and sensible, or based on ideas that are connected in the right way

NOUNS

a logical reason/explanation *The only logical explanation is that he didn't receive the letter.*

a logical conclusion *If you take this argument to its logical conclusion, nobody would ever have children at all.*

a logical answer/solution *I can't think of any logical solution to the problem.*

the logical thing to do *The logical thing to do is to repeat the process and see if you get the same result.*

a logical choice *Because of his greater experience, he seemed a logical choice.*

a logical step *The next logical step would be to test the system.*

a logical result/consequence/outcome *The logical consequence of this view is to raise taxes.*

a logical order *Present the information in a logical order.*

a logical argument *I've tried to convince him with logical arguments.*

ADVERBS

perfectly/quite/entirely logical *This is a perfectly logical explanation from the child's point of view.*

highly logical *Like many ancient languages, it has a highly logical structure.*

only logical (=used to emphasize that something is logical) *It is only logical that the problem will become more serious as more people use the internet.*

VERBS

seem/sound logical *It seemed logical to suppose that the men were guilty.*

PREPOSITIONS

logical to sb *It may be logical to you, but it certainly doesn't sound very logical to me.*

lonely *adj*

unhappy because you are alone or do not have anyone to talk to

VERBS

be/feel lonely *She had been lonely all her life.*

get lonely (=become lonely) *Do you get lonely living here by yourself?*

NOUNS

a lonely man/woman/boy/girl *In her eyes, he was a sad lonely man who needed looking after.*

lonely people *These lonely unhappy people needed to know there was somebody who loved them.*

a lonely figure *At the end of his life, Wilson became a tragic lonely figure.*

a lonely place *The north coast is a wild and lonely place.*

lonely days/nights *There would be no more lonely nights in hotels.*

a lonely life/existence *Being a fisherman can be a hard lonely life.*

PHRASES

the lonely hearts column (=the part of a newspaper or magazine where people advertise for romantic relationships) *She answered an advert in a lonely hearts column.*

long *adj*

1 measuring many kilometres, metres, centimetres etc

NOUNS

a long distance/way *We were a long way from home.*

long hair/face/neck/body *The girl had long brown hair.*

long legs/arms/fingers/tail *Your arms are longer than mine – can you get it for me?*

a long road/river/bridge *Which is the longest river in the world?*

a long tunnel/corridor *The porter led us down a long corridor to our room.*

a long line/queue *A long line of people waited outside the museum.*

a long piece of sth *He tied the letters together with a long piece of string.*

long trousers/socks/boots/dress/coat etc *The older boys were allowed to wear long trousers.*

long sleeves *She always wore long sleeves which covered up her arms.*

> If something is very long, you can say that it **stretches for miles/hundreds of metres** etc: *The beach **stretches for** over four miles.*

ANTONYMS **long → short (2)**

2 continuing for many years, months, minutes etc

NOUNS

a long time/period *It's been a long time since we last met.*

a long delay/pause *There are long delays on the road due to an accident.*

a long story/film/play *It's a very long story – you wouldn't want to hear it all now.*

a long day/night/evening etc (=one that seems long because it is very tiring or busy) *I have a long day ahead of me tomorrow.*

a long life *We hope that you have a very long and happy life together.*

a long history *The university has a long and distinguished history.*

a long journey/trip/voyage *It is a long journey from New York to Mexico City.*

a long walk/ride/drive/flight *They went for a long walk along the river.*

a long meeting/discussion/conversation *Karen spent most of the day in a long meeting.*

a long speech/talk/lecture *The president gave a long speech about the need for reform.*

a long silence *There was a long silence before he spoke again.*

VERBS

get longer *Summer is coming and the days are getting longer.*

PHRASES

in the long term (=in the future a long time

from now) *No one knows what will happen in the long term.*

THESAURUS: long

long-running
show | programme | series | dispute | battle | argument | debate | campaign | saga
a long-running show, dispute, campaign etc continues for a long time:
She was the star of a long-running TV show. | He has been involved in a long-running dispute with his neighbour. | There has been a long-running campaign to save the forest.

long-term
effect | consequences | benefit | problem | relationship | solution | strategy | goal | investment | unemployment | growth | decline
used about something that is expected to continue for a long time into the future:
No one knows what the long-term effects of climate change will be. | Her job involves caring for people with long-term problems. | This is his first long-term relationship since he separated from his wife. | Can wind farms provide a long-term solution to our energy problems?

lasting
impression | effect | impact | influence | peace | damage | benefit | value | friendship | solution | achievement | memorial | reminder
strong enough or great enough to continue for a long time:
The book left a lasting impression on me. | The negotiations were aimed at achieving a lasting peace. | This affair has done lasting damage to his reputation. | The stone is a lasting memorial to those who died.

Lasting is always used before a noun.

lengthy
period | process | delay | discussion | negotiation | conversation | description | sentence
continuing for a long time, especially longer than you want or expect:
There was a lengthy period of economic decline. | Getting a visa can be a lengthy and time-consuming process. | He faces a lengthy prison sentence (=period in prison).

protracted
negotiations | debate | discussion | talks | dispute | struggle | battle | fight | stay | delay
continuing for a long time, especially an unusually long time. **Protracted** is more formal than **lengthy**:
Despite protracted negotiations, they were unable to reach an agreement. | The firm is anxious to avoid a protracted legal battle. | There were protracted delays during the trial.

prolonged
period | use | exposure | absence | recession | drought | illness
continuing for a long time - used especially about a bad situation or something that has a bad effect:
The country entered a prolonged period of economic and political crisis. | Prolonged use of the drug can cause harmful side effects. | His absences from work became more and more prolonged.

enduring
appeal | fascination | influence | memory | love | legacy
enduring feelings and memories continue for a long time without disappearing or being forgotten:
It is easy to understand the enduring appeal of the James Bond movies (=people continue to like something for a long time). | *His poems show his enduring love for Ireland.*

Enduring is always used before a noun.

extended
period | visit | stay | holiday | break | tour
used when someone stays somewhere or does something for longer than usual, or longer than was planned:
You shouldn't leave children on their own for extended periods. | She had to have an extended stay in hospital after the baby was born.

marathon
session | contest | journey | battle | effort
continuing for a very long time and needing a lot of effort or determination:
The doctors treated over a hundred patients in one marathon session. | He arrived after a marathon journey across Europe.

Marathon is always used before a noun.

interminable
argument | debate | meeting | delay | wait | journey
very long and boring - used especially when something makes you feel impatient because it continues for far too long:
There were interminable arguments about money. | The journey home was interminable.

ANTONYMS **long → short (1)**

3 consisting of many words, pages, or letters

NOUNS

a long book/article/report *Because his report was so long, few people bothered to read it.*

a long list *There is a long list of rules and regulations.*

a long word/name/title *Some people like to use long words because it makes them sound more intelligent.*

L

> **THESAURUS: long**
>
> **long-winded**
> **answer | question | story | discussion | speech | explanation | apology**
> using too many words and continuing for too long:
> *It was a very long-winded answer to a simple question. | He gave a long-winded speech about his vision for the company's future.*

ANTONYMS **long → short (3)**

long-term *adj* THESAURUS **long (2)**

look¹ *v*

to turn your eyes towards someone or something, so that you can see them

ADVERBS

look carefully/closely *If you look carefully, you can see small cracks in the ceiling.*

look suspiciously *He looked suspiciously at the strange pink food.*

look longingly/enviously (=in a way that shows you would like something) *A bird was looking enviously at her sandwich.*

PREPOSITIONS

look at sb/sth *"It's time we left," Ian said, looking at his watch.*

look towards sb/sth *Sue kept looking towards the door.*

look out of the window *"We can't go out in this weather," said Bob, looking out of the window.*

PHRASES

turn to look at sb/sth *The men all turned to look at her as she entered the room.*

look² *n*

1 an act of looking at something

> **Grammar**
> Usually singular in this meaning.

ADJECTIVES

a quick/brief look *After a quick look at the map, we set off.*

a long/lingering look *Sam took a long look at her face.*

a good/careful/close/proper look *I didn't get a good look at the man's face.*

VERBS

have/take a look *Let me have a look at that coat – I think it's mine.*

get a look *They moved to the front of the crowd to get a better look.*

sneak a look (=without wanting anyone to notice) *When the doctor wasn't looking, I sneaked a look at his notes.*

2 the expression on someone's face, which shows their feelings

ADJECTIVES

a frightened/worried/nervous look *His mother watched him with a worried look on her face.*

a funny/odd/strange/curious look *She gets some strange looks when she takes her cat for a walk.*

an angry look/a black look *"Where have you been?" he asked, with an angry look.*

a doubtful/puzzled/quizzical look *The wrong use of a word can cause puzzled looks.*

a dirty look (=disapproving) *She gave me dirty looks the whole time I was talking to her boyfriend.*

a frosty look (=unfriendly) *"You're late," said Simon, with a frosty look.*

a blank look (=showing no emotion, understanding, or interest) *Maria could see from his blank look that he didn't understand.*

VERBS

have a look (on your face) *He had a nervous look on his face.*

give sb a look *People keep giving her strange looks.*

exchange looks *The old woman and the young child exchanged looks.*

PREPOSITIONS

a look of surprise/despair/horror/satisfaction etc *She suddenly stopped, a look of surprise on her face.*

PHRASES

the look in sb's eyes *He could tell by the look in her eyes that she was upset.*

the look on sb's face *I can't wait to see the look on his face when he opens his present.*

loophole *n*

a small mistake in a law that makes it possible to avoid doing something that the law should make you do

VERBS

close/plug a loophole (=get rid of it) *The president wants to close tax loopholes for foreign companies.*

tighten (up) a loophole (=get rid of it or make it smaller) *The changes will tighten up loopholes in the law.*

find/discover a loophole *Some lawyers spend their time finding loopholes in contracts.*

leave a loophole *A Bill must be exact and not leave any loopholes.*

create a loophole *The company created a loophole in their terms in order to avoid giving refunds.*

use/take advantage of/exploit a loophole (=use it to get what you want) *Some people will take advantage of any loophole they can find.*

a loophole allows sb to do sth (*also* **a loophole enables sb to do sth** *formal*): *Security loopholes allowed thieves to copy the data.*

ADJECTIVES/NOUNS + loophole

a serious/major loophole *This is a major loophole in the system.*

a gaping/glaring loophole (=very large) *There is a gaping loophole in the ban on sales of these weapons.*

a possible/potential loophole *Beware of potential loopholes that an insurer could use to refuse to pay.*

a legal loophole *The new law closed a number of legal loopholes.*

a tax loophole *Because of a tax loophole, many high earners are not paying tax.*

PREPOSITIONS

a loophole in sth *A loophole in the law means this is not illegal.*

loose *adj*

not firmly fastened in place, or no longer fastened in place

VERBS

come loose *Some ropes had come loose and were swinging in the wind.*

work (itself) loose *One of the bolts had worked loose.*

break loose *On our way home, the canoe broke loose and came off the trailer.*

shake (sth) loose *A bookcase shook loose from my wall during the earthquake.*

tear (sth) loose *The wind tore a shutter loose from the front of the house.*

pry sth loose (*also* **prise sth loose** *BrE*) (=make it come loose by putting a tool under it) *He prised a brick loose.*

hang loose *He undid his tie so that it hung loose around his neck.*

leave sth loose *The gust blew around some papers that had been left loose on the desk.*

wear your hair loose (=hanging down, and not tied with anything) *Why don't you ever wear your hair loose?*

ANTONYMS **loose → tight[1] (1)**

loot *v* THESAURUS **steal**

lorry *n BrE*

a large vehicle for carrying heavy goods

VERBS

a lorry carries sth *The lorry was carrying a large quantity of parcels.*

drive a lorry *Her husband drives a lorry.*

load a lorry (with sth) (*also* **load sth onto a lorry**) *They began loading the lorry with timber.*

unload a lorry *I waited while the lorry was unloaded.*

ADJECTIVES/NOUNS + lorry

a heavy lorry *They are disturbed by heavy lorries going past their homes.*

a container lorry (=carrying goods in a very large metal box) *Huge container lorries transport the fish to the markets in the cities.*

an articulated lorry (=a long lorry formed of two parts connected together) *We got stuck behind an articulated lorry.*

an army lorry *The rebels blew up an army lorry.*

PREPOSITIONS

by lorry *Food and water supplies have been brought in by lorry.*

in/on a lorry *They took everything away in a lorry.*

NOUNS

a lorry driver *He now works as a lorry driver.*

a lorry load of sth (*also* **a lorryload of sth**) *I have to deliver a lorry load of stationery to York.*

PHRASES

a lorry loaded/laden with sth *A lorry loaded with bricks overturned.*

a convoy of lorries (=a group of lorries travelling together) *A convoy of UN lorries were held up at a checkpoint.*

Lorry is used in British English. In American English, people say **truck**.

loss *n*

1 a situation in which you do not have something any more, or you have less of something

ADJECTIVES

a great/severe loss *He suffered a severe loss of confidence after the accident.*

a significant/considerable loss *This could lead to a significant loss of income.*

a major loss *They have studied how people adjust to major losses in their lives.*

a total loss *There has been a total loss of trust.*

a temporary/permanent loss *He's suffering from a temporary loss of memory.*

a rapid/gradual loss *Rapid weight loss can cause health problems.*

financial loss *Several clients had suffered financial losses as a result of taking his investment advice.*

NOUNS + loss

weight loss *Weight loss should be gradual.*

hearing loss *Listening to loud music can result in permanent hearing loss.*

hair loss *Some men are embarrassed about their hair loss.*

heat loss *Insulation will reduce heat loss.*

job losses *Further job losses are expected.*

VERBS

suffer a loss of sth *They have suffered a loss of their traditional authority.*

result in/lead to/cause a loss of sth *The decision will result in the loss of 80 jobs.*

prevent/reduce the loss of sth *If you keep saving your files, this will prevent the loss of your work if there is a power failure.*

PHRASES

loss of memory (*also* **memory loss**) *Have you ever had a loss of memory as a result of a blow to the head?*

loss of blood (*also* **blood loss**) *She was weak from loss of blood.*

loss of appetite *Depression is a very common cause of loss of appetite.*

loss of confidence *She was bullied at school and she still suffers from a loss of confidence.*

loss of control *Drinking often results in loss of control over one's life.*

loss of earnings/income *The insurance policy compensates you for loss of earnings.*

2 if a business makes a loss, it spends more than it earns

ADJECTIVES

a big/huge/massive loss *Many football clubs have made big losses.*

a substantial loss *If we sell the property now, we will make a substantial loss.*

a small loss *Their small loss had turned into a very big one.*

a net loss (=after tax and costs are paid) *The company reported a net loss of $28 million.*

VERBS

make a loss (*also* **incur a loss** *formal*): *The restaurant made a loss last year.*

run/operate at a loss (=make a loss while operating as a business) *The business is currently running at a loss.*

report a loss *Last year the company reported a loss of £4.2 million.*

recoup your losses (=get money back) *The company will try to recoup its losses by charging customers more.*

PREPOSITIONS

a loss of £50,000/$10 million etc *The company is expected to make a loss of about £2 million.*

loud *adj*

a loud sound or voice makes a lot of noise

NOUNS

a loud voice/shout/cry/cheer *"Go away!" he said in a loud voice.*

a loud noise/sound *I heard a loud noise outside my window.*

loud music *Neighbours complained that the loud music was keeping them awake.*

a loud explosion/bang/crash *The book fell to the floor with a loud bang.*

loud applause/laughter *She received loud applause at the end of her speech.*

ADVERBS

extremely/incredibly loud *The roar of the engines was incredibly loud.*

deafeningly loud (=extremely loud, in a way that could cause damage to your hearing) *The music they play is deafeningly loud.*

PHRASES

loud and clear (=loud enough for other people to hear) *We can hear you loud and clear.*

turn sth up loud (=make something play loudly) *I turned the music up loud.*

THESAURUS: loud

noisy

neighbour | crowd | children | protest | demonstration | meeting | bar | restaurant | factory | office | road | traffic | engine

used about people, places, and machines that are too loud:

Their lives were being ruined by noisy neighbours. | I find it difficult to work in a noisy office. | Steam engines are incredibly noisy.

Noisy or loud?

You use **loud** when talking about sounds. You say **loud music** (not 'noisy' music) and ***loud** thunder* (not 'noisy' thunder).

You use **noisy** about a person who is making a lot of noise: *I was surrounded by a group of **noisy** children.* You use **loud** to describe a person who always speaks in a loud confident way, which you find rather annoying: *He is very **loud** and he always thinks he knows everything.*

rowdy

fans | crowd | teenagers | protesters | behaviour | party | pub | bar

a rowdy group of people behave in a noisy and uncontrolled way. A rowdy party or place is full of noisy people, often behaving badly: *The streets were full of rowdy soccer fans. | The police were called to the pub after customers complained about rowdy behaviour.*

raucous *formal*

laughter | celebration | demonstration | crowd | behaviour | shouting | song

very loud because people are excited:

The audience suddenly burst into raucous laughter. | The city is well known for its raucous New Year celebrations. | The teams played in front of a raucous crowd of 14,000 fans.

resounding

crack | thud | cheer

used to describe a loud noise when

something hits another thing, or a loud cheer that continues for some time:
The door shut with a resounding crack. | His remarks were met with a resounding cheer.

Resounding is only used before a noun.

very loud

deafening
roar | noise | sound | music | explosion | cheer | applause
so loud that you cannot hear anything else:
I shouted to make myself heard above the deafening roar of the wind. | The noise from the ship's engines was deafening.

You say there was a **deafening silence** when you are shocked because someone refuses to give an answer: *Demands for reform were met with a **deafening silence** from the military government.*

thunderous
applause | roar | cheer | noise | explosion | ovation
extremely loud – used about long deep sounds:
His remarks received thunderous applause from the audience (=people clapped very loudly). *| The thunderous roar from the waterfalls can be heard from far away.*

Thunderous is only used before a noun.

Thunderous or deafening?
Thunderous is the usual word to use with **applause**. It is used about long deep sounds: *the **thunderous** roar of the engines.* You use **deafening** when something is so loud that you cannot hear anything else, especially when you wish it would stop: *The music was **deafening**.*

ear-splitting
sound | noise | racket
so loud that your ears feel uncomfortable:
The ear-splitting sound of techno music was coming from the next room. | The scooter engines made an ear-splitting racket (=a very loud annoying noise – an informal use).

piercing
scream | cry | shriek | whistle | sound
extremely loud, high, and unpleasant to hear:
She let out a piercing scream and pushed the man away. | The bird has a high piercing cry. | The piercing sound of the alarm bell rang out.

If music or a radio, TV etc is very loud, you say that it is **at full volume**: *She has her television on **at full volume**.*

ANTONYMS **loud → quiet (1)**

lousy *adj* **THESAURUS** **terrible**

love[1] *v*

to like someone or something very much

ADVERBS

love sb very much *He loves his wife very much.*
love sb deeply/dearly/passionately *They both loved each other deeply.*
truly/really love sb *He suddenly realized that he truly loved Pat and wanted her back in his life.*

You can also say that someone is **in love with** another person: *Tracy **was in love** with a man who was much older than her. | The couple **are** very much **in love**. | She **fell in love** with a beautiful young prince* (=started to have feelings of love for him).

ANTONYMS **love → hate[1]**

love[2] *n*

1 a strong feeling of liking someone very much

ADJECTIVES

true love (=real love) *He felt that he had finally found true love.*
real love *You could see real love in their eyes.*
romantic love *Romantic love was not always the reason for marriage.*
passionate love *He wrote about his passionate love for her.*
young love (=between young people) *It's a story of young love in the 1950s.*
unrequited love *formal* (=love for someone who does not love you) *Shakespeare's play is a tale of unrequited love.*
undying love (=love that does not stop) *She wrote of her undying love for her children.*
unconditional love (=that continues whatever bad things someone does) *Their mother gave them unconditional love.*
brotherly love (=between brothers or like that of brothers) *They was no sign of any brotherly love between them.*

VERBS + love

show/express your love *He shows his love for her by buying her presents.*
declare your love (=say that you love someone) *At the age of 5, he declared his undying love for his teacher.*
find love (=meet someone to love) *I never thought I would find love.*
return sb's love (=love someone who loves you) *Estella does not return his love.*

love + VERBS

love grows/blossoms (=it becomes greater) *Their love blossomed when they went on holiday together.*
love dies (=it ends) *Our love will never die.*

L

love + NOUNS

a love song/story *The book is basically a love story.*

a love letter *She kept all their old love letters.*

a love affair (=a romantic relationship between people who are not married to each other) *He had a love affair with his wife's best friend.*

sb's love life (=someone's romantic relationships) *She's always asking about my love life.*

PREPOSITIONS

love for sb *Their love for each other grew deeper every day.*

love between sb *It was clear that there was no longer any love between them.*

out of/for love (=because you love someone) *She gave up her career for love.*

PHRASES

be in love (with sb) (=have feelings of love for someone) *You can see that she is very much in love with him.*

fall in love (with sb) (=start to love someone) *They fell in love and decided to get married.*

love at first sight (=when you love someone as soon as you meet them) *When I first met my wife, it was love at first sight.*

madly/deeply in love (=you love someone very much) *I married Dan because I was madly in love.*

head over heels in love *informal* (=you love someone very much) *The two of them fell head over heels in love.*

love is blind (=used to say that people do not notice the faults of the person they love) *I don't know what she sees in him, but I guess love is blind.*

the love of your life (= the person you have loved the most in your life) *She said that he was the love of her life.*

2 a strong feeling of enjoyment and interest in something

VERBS

have a love of sth *If you have a love of music, you will enjoy this course.*

develop a love of sth *This is where he first developed a love of the sea.*

share a love of sth *They both share a love of Shakespeare.*

fall in love with sth (=start liking it very much) *I fell in love with Amsterdam the first time I visited the city.*

ADJECTIVES

a lifelong love of sth *Her lifelong love of Brazil began during a visit to Rio de Janeiro.*

a secret love of sth *She confessed to a secret love of the Harry Potter books.*

PREPOSITIONS

a love of sth *He had a great love of music.*

a love for sth *He's a teacher with a love for sport.*

lovely *adj* THESAURUS ▸ **beautiful**

low *adj*

1 not high, or in a position that is not high

NOUNS

a low table/chair *There was a low table coffee table in front of the sofa.*

a low wall/fence *The yard was surrounded by a low fence.*

a low hill/mountain *The house stood on top of a low hill.*

a low house/building *The village consisted of a row of low wooden houses.*

a low branch *He picked an apple from one of the lower branches of the tree.*

a low roof *The houses in the mountains had low roofs.*

low ground *There is a risk of flooding on low ground.*

a low bridge *The bridge was too low for the ship to go under.*

a low door *There is a low door in the kitchen which leads to the cellar.*

THESAURUS: low

low-lying
area | region | place | part | land
a low-lying area is in a low position compared to the level of the sea or rivers:
People living in low-lying areas were forced to move to higher ground. | The river flooded vast areas of low-lying land.

low-rise
building | housing
low-rise buildings are only one or two floors high:
The complex consists of a group of low-rise office buildings. | People want low-rise housing made using traditional materials.

ANTONYMS **low → high (1)**

2 small, or smaller than usual, in amount, level, or value

NOUNS

a low price/cost *They sell good carpets at low prices.*

a low rent/tax *Rents are low in this part of the city.*

low salary/wage/pay/income *The workers are paid very low wages.*

a low level/rate/degree *The city has a relatively low level of pollution.*

a low amount/proportion/percentage *The amount of traffic is low.*
a low number/grade/score *A lower number of men are choosing teaching as a career.*
a low standard *His work has been of a low standard.*
a low speed *Both vehicles were travelling at low speed.*
a low temperature *The medicine needs to be stored at a low temperature.*
a low demand *Continuing low demand for new cars has led the company to cut production.*
a low profit/return *Restaurants complain about low profits and high food costs.*
low unemployment *Traditionally this part of the country has been an area of low unemployment.*
low inflation *The country has achieved low inflation and steady growth.*
a low risk/chance *There is only a very low risk of catching the disease.*

THESAURUS: low

falling/declining
value | price | number | rate | demand | sales | profits
becoming low. **Declining** is more formal than **falling**:
The falling value of the dollar will push up the price of imports. | A declining number of students are choosing to study history. | In Japan, people are worried about the declining birth rate.

3 near the bottom of the range of sounds

NOUNS
a low note *I can't sing the low notes.*
a low voice/sound *Boys' voices usually become much lower as they get older.*
a low whisper *They spoke in a low whisper, to avoid being heard.*
a low pitch *His voice dropped to a low pitch.*

THESAURUS: low

deep
voice | sound
a deep voice or sound is low, strong, and pleasant:
He has a lovely deep voice. | The engine has a wonderful deep sound.

husky
voice | whisper | laugh
a husky voice is deep, quiet, and rough-sounding, especially in a way that is attractive:
Jazz singers often have husky voices. | His voice dropped to a husky whisper.

gravelly
voice | tone
a gravelly voice is very low and rough-sounding:
John Wayne was famous for his gravelly voice. | His gravelly tones gave the report an air of seriousness.

THESAURUS: low

low, soft, silent, hushed, faint, muffled, dull, inaudible → **quiet (1)**

ANTONYMS low → **high (3)**

4 not expensive

THESAURUS: low

inexpensive, low, reasonable, economical, affordable, competitive, budget → **cheap**

lower *v* THESAURUS reduce

loyal *adj*

always supporting a person, organization etc

VERBS
remain/stay loyal *The army has remained loyal to the government.*

ADVERBS
fiercely/intensely loyal (=extremely loyal) *The football club has a fiercely loyal group of fans.*

NOUNS
a loyal customer *The hotel has many loyal customers who come to stay there every year.*
a loyal friend/ally *She has been a good and loyal friend to me.*
a loyal member *She is a very loyal member of the church.*
a loyal supporter/fan/follower *He has been a loyal supporter of the party for many years.*
loyal support *The head teacher thanked parents for their loyal support.*
a loyal following (=group of people who support or admire someone or something) *The band has built up a small but loyal following.*
a loyal servant *He was the king's most loyal servant.*
a loyal subject *formal* (=someone who is loyal to their country which is ruled by a king or queen) *They were loyal subjects of the Queen.*
loyal service *She has given many years of loyal service to the company.*

PREPOSITIONS
loyal to sb/sth *She was very loyal to her father, and never criticized him.*

loyalty *n*

the quality of being loyal to someone or something

L

ADJECTIVES

great/deep/strong loyalty *Why do you feel such deep loyalty to him?*

absolute/total/complete loyalty *She has always shown complete loyalty to the company.*

fierce/intense loyalty (=very great) *She was moved by her friend's fierce loyalty.*

unswerving/unwavering loyalty (=never changing) *He was rewarded for his unswerving loyalty.*

undying loyalty (=never ending) *I pledge my undying loyalty to you.*

blind/unthinking/unquestioning loyalty (=without thinking whether someone deserves it) *Sarah was criticized for her blind loyalty to her husband.*

divided/conflicting loyalties (=to more than one person or group, especially when this causes problems) *The war created divided loyalties in many families.*

NOUNS + loyalty

family/company/party loyalty (=to your family, company, or party) *Family loyalty prevented her from telling what she knew.*

customer loyalty (=to a company, so that you always buy its products) *The company relies on customer loyalty instead of using big advertising campaigns.*

VERBS

feel loyalty *Marco felt an intense loyalty to the country where he was born.*

show/demonstrate loyalty *He showed great loyalty to his wife during her long illness.*

prove your loyalty *He has proved his loyalty many times.*

swear/pledge loyalty (=promise to be loyal) *The president's assistants swore their loyalty to him.*

win sb's loyalty (=get it) *Steve had won her loyalty and trust.*

inspire/command loyalty (=make people feel loyal to you) *She inspires extraordinary loyalty among her staff.*

reward sb's loyalty *He rewarded his friends' loyalty by helping them in times of need.*

doubt/question sb's loyalty *Are you doubting my loyalty?*

test sb's loyalty *Perhaps she is trying to test your loyalty.*

shift/switch your loyalties (=start being loyal to a different person) *He would never shift his loyalties to another football team.*

PREPOSITIONS

loyalty to/towards sb/sth *Eva understood her husband's loyalty to his sister.*

out of loyalty (=because of loyalty) *She remained silent out of loyalty to her friend.*

PHRASES

a sense of loyalty *She had a strong sense of loyalty to her family.*

an oath of loyalty (=a promise to be loyal) *They swore an oath of loyalty to their king.*

a show of loyalty (=an action that shows someone is loyal) *He was hoping for a show of loyalty from his boss.*

where your loyalties lie (=who or what you are loyal to) *Decide where your loyalties lie – with your friends or your family.*

luck *n*

good or bad things that happen to you by chance

ADJECTIVES/NOUNS + luck

good luck *These birds are said to bring good luck.*

bad luck *His bad luck continued and he lost the next three games.*

sheer/pure luck (*also* **dumb luck** *AmE*) (=chance, and not skill or effort) *She managed to catch hold of the rope by sheer luck.*

beginner's luck (=good luck that happens when you first try something) *His first shot hit the centre of the target. "Beginner's luck, I guess," he said.*

bad/hard luck! (=used to show sympathy for someone who has not succeeded) *"I didn't get the job." "Oh, bad luck!"*

tough luck (=used when saying that you do not feel sorry for someone) *If they can't get to the airport in time for the plane, that's tough luck.*

VERBS + luck

have good/bad luck *He's had some bad luck lately.*

have no luck (*also* **not have much/any luck**) (=not be lucky or successful) *I'd been looking for a job for weeks, but had had no luck.*

have the (good/bad) luck to do sth *He had the good luck to meet a man who could help him.*

wish sb luck *I'm taking my driving test tomorrow – wish me luck.*

bring sb/give sb luck *He always carried the stone in his pocket; he thought it brought him luck.*

try your luck (=try something that involves a risk) *He decided to try his luck in management.*

push your luck (=do something that involves a risk, especially something you have successfully done before) *You're pushing your luck if you ask him for more money.*

luck + VERBS

sb's luck holds (=they continue having good luck) *Our luck held, and the weather remained fine.*

sb's luck runs out (=they stop having good luck) *Finally, my luck ran out and they caught me.*

PREPOSITIONS

by luck (=because of luck) *It was only by luck that I realized what had happened.*

for luck (=in order to have good luck) *She crossed her fingers for luck.*

with luck (=if someone is lucky) *With luck, we'll be home before dinner.*

PHRASES

a piece/stroke of luck (=something good that happens by chance) *What a piece of luck that he arrived when he did!*

be in luck (=be able to do or get something, especially when you did not expect to) *You're in luck – someone found your keys this morning.*

have a run of good/bad luck (=a series of good or bad things) *The team have had a run of bad luck lately, losing their last five games.*

can't believe your luck *I couldn't believe my luck when I heard I had got the job!*

sth is a matter of luck (=something that depends on chance) *Winning is a matter of luck.*

there is an element of luck (=an amount of luck is involved in something) *There is always an element of luck when hiring someone for a job.*

lucky *adj*

1 if you are lucky, something good happens to you by chance

VERBS

be/feel lucky *I feel very lucky to be here.*

get lucky *informal* (=be lucky) *They're not a great team – they just got lucky.*

strike lucky/strike it lucky *informal* (=be lucky) *I applied for twenty jobs before I struck lucky.*

count/think/consider yourself lucky (=think that you are lucky, considering the situation) *You should count yourself lucky you weren't seriously hurt.*

NOUNS

a lucky man/woman/boy/girl *Your son's a lucky man, having a father like you.*

a lucky winner *The lucky winner of the competition will be announced next week.*

a lucky escape *We had a lucky escape when our car crashed into a tree.*

a lucky chance/accident *It was discovered by a lucky chance.*

a lucky coincidence (=a situation when two things happen together unexpectedly) *By a lucky coincidence, Paul was in New York, too.*

a lucky break (=an opportunity that allows you to be successful) *Our band just needs a lucky break.*

a lucky guess *Did she really work out the answer, or was it just a lucky guess?*

a lucky win *England got a lucky win over France.*

PREPOSITIONS

lucky with sth *We've been lucky with the weather.*

lucky for sb *It's lucky for them that no one saw them.*

PHRASES

the lucky ones (=people who are lucky compared to others) *They considered themselves the lucky ones because they escaped with only minor injuries.*

a lucky few *It is a special quality that only a lucky few possess.*

be lucky enough to do sth (=have the good luck to do something) *I was lucky enough to be chosen for the school team.*

be born lucky (=always be lucky) *Some people seem to be born lucky.*

not be so lucky *One twin survived, but the other was not so lucky.*

you lucky thing! (=said when you are telling someone you think they are lucky) *You're going to the concert? You lucky thing!*

third time lucky (=when you succeed on the third time of trying) *Everyone is praying that this time it will be third time lucky.*

it is sb's lucky day *I found £10 – it must be my lucky day.*

> **Lucky or fortunate?**
> **Fortunate** is more formal than **lucky** and is the usual word to use in more formal contexts: *The university has been* ***fortunate*** *to attract a wide range of excellent speakers.*
> The difference is mainly about collocation. You say a **lucky winner/guess/break** (not a 'fortunate' one).
> You can say a **lucky coincidence/accident** or a **fortunate coincidence/accident**.

ANTONYMS **lucky → unlucky (1)**

2 something that is lucky is believed to bring good luck

NOUNS

a lucky number *In many cultures, 7 is a lucky number.*

a lucky charm (=a small object, often worn on a chain or bracelet, thought to bring good luck) *She was wearing a bracelet with lucky charms on it.*

ANTONYMS **lucky → unlucky (2)**

luggage *n*

the cases, bags etc that you carry when you are travelling

PHRASES

a piece of luggage (*also* **an item of luggage** *formal*): *Security officers checked every piece of luggage.*

> ⚠ Don't say 'luggages'. Say **pieces/items of luggage**. **Luggage** is an uncountable noun and is not used in the plural.

VERBS

carry luggage *Don't carry more luggage than you need.*

check in your luggage *BrE*, **check your luggage** *AmE*: *Some airlines charge you to check in your luggage.*
lose sb's luggage *The airline lost all my luggage.*
search sb's luggage *They searched his luggage for weapons.*

ADJECTIVES

heavy luggage *Take a taxi, especially if you have heavy luggage.*
hand luggage/carry-on luggage (=luggage that you take onto a plane with you) *You're not allowed to carry knives in your hand luggage.*
lost luggage (=luggage that an airline or a bus, train etc company has lost) *The insurance company will pay for any lost luggage.*
left luggage (=a place at a station etc where you can pay to leave luggage and collect it later) *Left luggage is situated next to the information desk.*

luggage + NOUNS

a luggage rack (=a shelf for putting luggage on) *He got on the train and put his case on the luggage rack.*
a luggage compartment (=a place in a vehicle for storing luggage) *The luggage compartment of the bus was full.*

PREPOSITIONS

in your luggage *The drugs had been hidden in his luggage.*

lump *n* THESAURUS ▶ piece

lunch *n*

a meal eaten in the middle of the day

VERBS

have/eat lunch *We'll have lunch around midday.*
have sth for lunch *I usually have sandwiches for lunch.*
take sb (out) to lunch (=pay for someone's lunch when you go to a restaurant) *He took her out for lunch at a local pub.*
go out for/to lunch (=have lunch at a restaurant) *I don't often go out to lunch, as it's expensive.*
come for/to lunch (=come to someone's house for lunch) *Can you come to lunch tomorrow?*
make lunch *You clear the table while I make lunch.*
break for lunch (=stop doing something in order to eat lunch) *Why don't we break for lunch at about 1 o'clock?*
meet for lunch (*also* **do lunch** *informal*): *We must meet for lunch sometime.*
serve lunch *Lunch is served in the main dining room.*

ADJECTIVES/NOUNS + lunch

a three-course/two-course etc lunch (=with three, two etc parts) *It costs 30 euros for a four-course lunch.*
a light lunch (=a small lunch) *After a light lunch, he would take a nap each afternoon.*
a hot/cold lunch (=consisting of hot or cold food) *At 1 o'clock, a cold lunch will be served.*
an early/late lunch (=eaten earlier/later than the usual time) *I'm not hungry – I had a late lunch.*
a school lunch (=provided by a school) *Free school lunches are provided for the poorest children.*
a business/working lunch (=a lunch during which you also do business) *She was having a business lunch with a customer.*
a packed lunch *BrE*, **a bag/sack lunch** *AmE* (=food such as sandwiches that you take to school etc) *Most of the children had brought packed lunches.*
Sunday lunch *BrE* (=a hot lunch eaten on Sunday) *Mum always makes a big Sunday lunch.*

lunch + NOUNS

the lunch hour *I try to go out for a walk during my lunch hour.*
a lunch break *We took a half hour lunch break.*

Lunchtime and **lunchbox** are usually written as one word.

PREPOSITIONS

for lunch *It's salad for lunch.*
at lunch *I'm afraid he's at lunch until two.*
over lunch (=while having lunch) *Shall we discuss this over lunch?*

luxury *n*

1 very great comfort and pleasure, for example from expensive food, beautiful houses, and comfortable cars

ADJECTIVES

great luxury *She was used to a life of great luxury.*
absolute/pure/sheer luxury (=used to emphasize that something is a great luxury) *The dress was made of Chinese silk, and felt like pure luxury.*

luxury + NOUNS

a luxury hotel/home/apartment *We stayed in a five-star luxury hotel.*
a luxury car *The company makes luxury cars.*
luxury goods *People are getting wealthier and spending more on luxury goods.*
a luxury item (=something that only rich people can afford) *In those days, a television was considered a luxury item.*
a luxury brand *It was no ordinary box of chocolates, but a luxury brand made by hand.*

PHRASES

sth is the height of luxury (=it is one of the most comfortable and pleasant things) *For many people, a Rolls-Royce is the height of luxury.*
the lap of luxury (=a situation that feels very

L

comfortable and full of luxury) *Millionaires live in the lap of luxury, while poor people starve on the city streets.*

feel/seem like luxury *The bed felt like luxury after a week spent sleeping in a tent.*

live in luxury (*also* **live/lead a life of luxury**) *Mick was leading a life of luxury in Florida.*

keep sb in luxury *He has to work hard to keep his wife in luxury.*

add a touch of luxury (=make something feel like luxury) *Leather chairs added a touch of luxury to the room.*

2 something that gives you pleasure and enjoyment but which is not necessary

ADJECTIVES

an expensive luxury *In those days, washing machines were an expensive luxury.*

an affordable luxury (=cheap enough for you to buy) *Chocolate is an affordable luxury.*

an unnecessary luxury *We stopped spending money on unnecessary luxuries.*

little luxuries *She loves life's little luxuries.*

a rare luxury *Clean water is still a rare luxury in some parts of the world.*

the ultimate luxury (=the greatest luxury) *A hot tub in your own back yard is the ultimate luxury.*

VERBS + luxury

afford luxuries *We can't afford luxuries like piano lessons any more.*

buy luxuries *She started saving her money rather than buying luxuries.*

spend sth on luxuries *How much money do you spend each month on luxuries?*

Mm

machine *n*

a piece of equipment with moving parts that uses power to do a particular job

VERBS + machine

use/operate/work a machine *Do you know how to use the machine?*

switch on/turn on a machine *Turn the machine on and slowly add the hot liquid.*

switch off/turn off a machine *Always make sure that the machine is switched off.*

stop/start a machine *Just hit that button to stop the machine.*

plug in/unplug a machine (=connect it to/disconnect it from the electricity supply) *The machine won't work if it's not plugged in.*

unplug a machine (=disconnect from the electricity supply) *Always unplug the machine before trying to do any repairs.*

install a machine (=put it somewhere and connect it so that it is ready to be used) *Three hundred new machines have been installed across the country.*

fix/repair a machine *Someone's coming to fix the washing machine tomorrow.*

load/unload a machine (=put things in or take things out) *First, load the machine with paper.*

machine + VERBS

a machine operates/works/runs *The machine works using solar power.*

a machine breaks down *The printing machine kept breaking down.*

a machine beeps (=makes a series of short high noises) *My washing machine beeps when it's finished.*

a machine is powered by sth *The early machines were powered by steam.*

NOUNS + machine

a washing/sewing/mixing etc machine *I've put your dirty clothes in the washing machine.*

a cash/ticket machine (=for getting money from your bank account) *I need to stop at a cash machine.*

a coffee/drinks machine *Could you get me a tea from the drinks machine?*

a vending machine *formal* (=which sells drinks, chocolate bars etc) *You can buy chocolate from the vending machine in the corridor.*

a cutting/sorting/printing machine *Steve's job is to operate the cutting machine.*

machine + NOUNS

a machine operator *He worked as a machine operator in a factory.*

machine parts *The boxes contained machine parts.*

machine code (=instructions in the form of numbers put into a computer) *The program was written in machine code.*

PREPOSITIONS

by machine *The letters are sorted by machine.*

on a machine *She makes sweaters on her knitting machine.*

a machine for (doing) sth *There was a machine for making pasta.*

You often use **machine** when talking about a computer: *My **machine** is running really slowly today* (=My computer is running slowly).

THESAURUS: machine

appliance *formal*
a machine or piece of electrical equipment, usually a large one, that people use in the home:
*The store sells **kitchen appliances** such as refrigerators, dishwashers, and toasters. | We carry out repairs on a range of **household appliances**.*

device
a piece of equipment, usually a small electronic one, that does a special job:
*Passengers must switch off all **electronic devices** when the plane is taking off and landing. | The car **is fitted with a device** which makes it brake automatically if it gets too close to the car in front.*

gadget
a small, useful, and cleverly designed tool or machine:
*She showed them a **useful little gadget** for peeling apples and potatoes. | The house is full of all the latest **electronic gadgets**.*

contraption
a machine or piece of equipment that looks strange or complicated:
*Seven of us squeezed into a **strange contraption**, which went along at about ten miles an hour, coughing blue fumes. | There was a **curious contraption** which consisted of lots of tubes and containers, which they used for making beer.*

machinery *n*

machines, especially large ones

ADJECTIVES/NOUNS + machinery

heavy machinery (=big heavy machines) *The workers had to use heavy machinery to dig the tunnel.*

M

agricultural machinery/farm machinery *The company sells agricultural machinery such as tractors.*

industrial machinery *He works for an engineering firm that specializes in industrial machinery.*

modern machinery *The job can be done much quicker using modern machinery.*

VERBS

operate machinery *Only trained workers are allowed to operate the machinery.*

use machinery *These days the furniture is made using modern machinery in a factory.*

sth drives/powers the machinery (=it provides the power that makes it work) *The river turns the waterwheel, which drives the machinery.*

PREPOSITIONS

machinery for sth *Windmills use the wind to drive machinery for grinding wheat into flour.*

PHRASES

a piece of machinery *He wasn't trained to operate this piece of machinery.*

mad *adj*

1 *informal* very angry

> **Grammar**
> **Mad** is not used before a noun in this meaning.

VERBS

go mad (=become angry) *My parents will go mad when they find out!*

get mad (=become angry - used especially when this seems unreasonable) *There's no need to get mad about it!*

make sb mad *It makes me mad when I see people being cruel to animals.*

drive sb mad (=make someone angry) *I wish they'd turn down that horrible music - it's driving me mad.*

ADVERBS

really mad *He was really mad and started shouting at me.*

hopping mad (=extremely angry) *Dino was hopping mad because we were so late.*

PREPOSITIONS

mad at/with sb *He was mad at me for driving into the back of his car.*

> **THESAURUS: mad**
> annoyed, irritated, mad, cross, bad-tempered, grumpy, in a bad/foul mood, furious, irate, heated, livid, outraged, indignant → **angry**

2 *BrE informal* crazy

> You often use **mad** in this meaning when you think someone or something seems strange or makes you annoyed.
> Originally **mad** was used to describe someone who was mentally ill. This use is becoming old-fashioned and is likely to be offensive.

NOUNS

a mad idea *Whose mad idea was this?*

a mad scientist/professor/genius *The book is about a mad scientist who is secretly planning to destroy the world.*

a mad world *Sometimes I think the world is going completely mad.*

VERBS

go mad (=start to feel crazy) *I'll go mad if I have to wait here much longer.*

drive someone mad (=make someone feel crazy) *Can you help me with this crossword? It's been driving me mad.*

think sb/sth is mad *My family think I'm mad, but I've always wanted to go sky-diving.*

ADVERBS

completely/quite/absolutely mad *The whole idea sounds completely mad to me.*

stark raving mad/barking mad (=completely crazy - used when you want to emphasize this very strongly) *My friends all think I'm stark raving mad.*

PHRASES

sb must be mad *He must be mad if he thinks he can get there by 4 o'clock.*

> **THESAURUS: mad**
> mad, insane, eccentric → **crazy**

madness *n*

1 something that seems crazy, because it could have a very bad effect

ADJECTIVES

sheer/absolute/complete/utter madness (=used for emphasis when you think something is crazy) *Cutting down the forest is sheer madness.*

VERBS

stop/end the madness *We must stop this madness now before more people are hurt.*

PHRASES

a moment of madness *In a moment of madness I agreed to give a speech at the wedding.*

2 serious mental illness

PHRASES

the first sign of madness *Some people say that talking to yourself is the first sign of madness.*

M

have a history of madness (=many people in your family have suffered from serious mental illness) *Her family has a history of madness.*

sb's descent into madness (=the process of becoming seriously mentally ill) *His descent into madness began after the death of his mother.*

magazine *n*

a large thin book with a paper cover that contains news stories, articles, photographs etc, and is sold weekly or monthly

ADJECTIVES/NOUNS + magazine

a music/computer/fashion etc magazine *I read an interview with Johnny Depp in a movie magazine.*

a news magazine *'Der Spiegel' is a German news magazine.*

a weekly/monthly/quarterly magazine *I received the January edition of the monthly magazine 'Birdwatch'.*

an online magazine (=on the internet) *They started an online magazine for people who love food.*

a national/international magazine *'Snip' is an international magazine for hairdressers.*

a glossy magazine (=printed on shiny paper, with a lot of pictures) *She appeared on the front cover of the glossy magazine 'Vogue'.*

a popular magazine *The story first appeared in a popular women's magazine.*

a men's/women's magazine *Women's magazines are full of articles about ways of losing weight.*

the school/college magazine *My friend edits the school magazine.*

a literary magazine *He writes for an American literary magazine.*

VERBS

read/look at a magazine *She was sitting on the sofa reading a magazine.*

flick/leaf through a magazine (=turn the pages without reading anything properly) *Anna was flicking through the magazines in the hospital waiting room.*

publish/produce a magazine *The magazine is published once a month.*

write for a magazine *She writes for a well-known fashion magazine.*

edit a magazine *Paul edits a student magazine.*

launch a magazine (=start a new magazine) *The company is launching a new fashion magazine.*

sth appears/is published in a magazine *The story was first published in the 'New Yorker' magazine.*

a magazine features sth (=it includes something) *The magazine features articles on a wide range of topics.*

magazine + NOUNS

a magazine article/feature *I'm reading a magazine article about global warming.*

a magazine interview *She said in a magazine interview that she planned to retire when she was 35.*

a magazine cover (=the front page of a magazine) *Her face was on every magazine cover.*

a magazine editor *She wrote to the magazine editor to complain about the article.*

PHRASES

an issue of a magazine *Have you read the latest issue of 'New Scientist' magazine?*

THESAURUS: magazine

journal
a serious magazine for people who are interested in a scientific, technical, or academic subject, or who do a particular job:
The research was published in a ***scientific journal****. | His office is full of* ***academic journals****. | 'The Bookseller' is the* ***trade journal*** *for the publishing industry* (=for people who are involved in a particular type of work).

periodical
a serious magazine which has long detailed articles about a particular academic or scientific subject:
She gives a long list of the ***academic periodicals*** *she consulted at the end of the article. | His publications included over 100 original papers in* ***scientific periodicals****.*

Periodical is similar in meaning to **journal** but sounds more formal.

magic *n, adj*

1 the power to make impossible things happen by saying special words or doing special actions

magic + NOUNS

a magic spell (=a piece of magic, or the words or actions used) *The witch put a magic spell on her.*

a magic trick (=a skilful trick done as entertainment) *He showed me how to do magic tricks.*

a magic show *The kids loved watching the magic show.*

magic powers *The ring was said to have magic powers.*

a magic wand (=a stick, usually black and white, used by a magician) *He waved his magic wand and the bird disappeared.*

the magic number/word *You have to say the magic word 'Abracadabra'.*

a magic potion (=a drink with magic powers) *She gives him a magic potion to make him disappear.*

M

VERBS

believe in magic *Do you believe in magic?*

use magic *The priests claim that they can cure people using magic.*

do magic (*also* **perform magic** *formal*) (=used especially about doing magic tricks for entertainment) *He learned to do magic and put on shows for his friends.*

ADJECTIVES

black magic (=intended to harm people) *The women were accused of using black magic to make people ill.*

PREPOSITIONS AND PHRASES

by magic (=using magic) *She claimed to be able to make things disappear by magic.*

as if by magic (=as though magic is being used) *As if by magic, Sara appeared by his side.*

2 a surprisingly effective way of making something good happen

magic + NOUNS

a magic formula/solution (=a way of achieving something quickly and easily) *There is no magic formula for making yourself look younger.*

a magic bullet (=something that cures an illness or problem quickly and easily) *Everyone wishes there was a magic bullet to cure cancer.*

VERBS

work like magic *This product works like magic to remove stains from your carpet.*

magnificent *adj* THESAURUS > **beautiful**

mail *n*

the letters and packages that are delivered to you, or the system of sending them

ADJECTIVES/NOUNS + mail

personal/private mail (=for one person to read and no one else) *He accused her of reading his private mail.*

junk mail (=that you do not want, especially advertisements) *I only ever get junk mail and bills.*

air mail/airmail (=sent by plane) *I sent the card by air mail.*

express mail *AmE* (=for delivering letters very quickly) *He sent me the contract by express mail.*

surface mail (=sent by land or sea) *Papers can be sent surface mail.*

internal mail (=sent within an organization) *I was sorting the internal mail for the office.*

fan mail (=from fans) *The band gets a lot of fan mail.*

hate mail (=expressing hate) *She got threatening phone calls and hate mail.*

snail mail *informal* (=letters rather than email) *Fewer and fewer people are using snail mail.*

direct mail (=advertisements sent to many people) *The marketing campaign began with newspaper advertising and direct mail.*

VERBS

the mail comes/arrives *The mail usually comes at about 8.30.*

get/receive mail *Did we get any mail this morning?*

send mail *Please do not send personal mail to my work address.*

read your mail *The first thing he did was read his mail.*

open your mail *She opened her mail as she ate her breakfast.*

deliver the mail *The postman had just delivered the mail.*

forward/redirect sb's mail (=send it to a new address) *The post office will forward your mail for a limited time.*

mail + NOUNS

a mail system/service *The company has its own internal mail system.*

mail delivery *There is only one mail delivery a day.*

mail order (=the system of ordering goods from home and having them delivered there) *The plants are available by mail order from Green Life Products.*

> **Mailbox**, **mailman**, and **mailbag** are written as one word.

PREPOSITIONS

by mail *He received a job offer by mail.*

in the mail *Your cheque is in the mail.*

through the mail *Customers can receive the goods through the mail.*

> **Mail** is used in British English and American English, but in British English people often say **post** instead.

main *adj* largest or most important

> **Main** is always used before a noun, usually with **the** or **our/my** etc.

NOUNS

the main entrance/door/gate *I'll meet you outside the main entrance.*

the main building/room *The main building dates from the 19th century.*

the main part/aspect/feature *The treaty can be divided into four main parts.*

the main reason/cause/function *The warm weather is the main reason for the large numbers of insects this year.*

sb's main problem/issue/concern *Our main problem was getting enough to eat.*

the main point *Start by making a list of the main points that you want to make in your essay.*

the main thing *especially spoken*: *The main thing is that it must be enjoyable.*

the main aim/purpose/objective *One of the main aims of the experiment was to find out if his theory worked.*

the main conclusion *The main conclusion of the report is that using any phone while driving is dangerous.*

the main difference *The main difference between scientists and engineers is that engineers want to make things and scientists want to understand them.*

THESAURUS: main

principal/chief
reason | cause | aim | objective | problem | difference | argument
most important. **Principal** and **chief** are more formal than **main**:
Most people work for the same principal reason – in order to make money. | Cutting down trees was the chief cause of floods and landslides. | Their chief problem was lack of funds.

primary
aim | objective | purpose | reason | function | role | concern | focus
most important – used especially about the reason why you are doing something. **Primary** is more formal than **main**:
The primary aim of the research is to find out more about the causes of the disease. | The primary function of government is to represent the wishes of the people. | His health is our primary concern.

core
business | beliefs | values | principles | skills | subject | issue | area
most important – used especially about the things that people pay most attention to:
The company needs to focus on its core business. | One of our core values is freedom of choice. | Students receive help with English, maths, and other core skills.

central
issue | theme | question | concern | role | part | feature | place
very important or most important:
Memory is a central theme in Proust's work. | Religion played a central role in all areas of life. | The central feature of the hotel is a magnificent Victorian staircase.

prime
example | target | suspect | concern | cause | reason
very important or most important:
Germany is often cited as the prime example of a successful industrial economy. | The Games could become a prime target for terrorists. | He is the prime suspect in the case.

predominant
feature | influence | colour | view | concern
most common or most typical:
The predominant feature of this condition is extreme changes of mood. | Yellow was the predominant colour in the fields. | This was the predominant view among scientists.

maintain Ac *v*

1 to keep a building, machine, road etc in good condition by checking it regularly and repairing it

ADVERBS

be well maintained *The house was very well maintained.*

be properly/adequately maintained *Keep the equipment clean and properly maintained.*

be poorly/badly maintained *Many of the country's roads are poorly maintained.*

be regularly maintained *The brakes were regularly inspected and maintained.*

be carefully/meticulously/immaculately maintained *The grounds are meticulously maintained.*

be beautifully maintained *The interior of the house is beautifully maintained.*

2 to make something continue in the same way or at the same standard as before

NOUNS

maintain contact *He left the country but maintained contact with his family.*

maintain a balance *It's important to maintain a balance between work and home life.*

maintain stability *Our first priority is to maintain economic stability.*

maintain control *The party will maintain control of Congress.*

maintain order/peace *Police were struggling to maintain order.*

maintain standards/quality *The hotel prides itself on maintaining high standards.*

maintain relations/a relationship *Businesses need to build and maintain a good relationship with customers.*

maintain an interest *Throughout his life, he maintained an interest in religion.*

maintain a position *Britain wants to maintain its position as a world power.*

maintain the status quo (=maintain the situation that exists now) *The government is struggling to maintain the status quo.*

VERBS

try to maintain sth *We try to maintain a high level of quality.*

struggle/strive to maintain sth *Schools are struggling to maintain standards.*

M

maintenance Ac *n*
the repairs, painting etc that are necessary to keep something in good condition

ADJECTIVES

regular maintenance *A car needs regular maintenance to keep it running smoothly.*

routine maintenance (=which is done regularly as part of the usual system) *They noticed the cracks during routine maintenance.*

basic/essential maintenance (=which has to be done to keep something working properly) *The swimming pool will be closed next week for essential maintenance.*

poor maintenance (=not done well or often enough) *Poor maintenance led to a gas leak at the factory.*

careful/proper maintenance *With proper maintenance, planes can be flown for many years.*

general maintenance *He is responsible for the general maintenance of the computer system.*

low maintenance (=not needing much maintenance) *The machine is very basic, but it has the advantage of being very low maintenance, because there is very little to go wrong.*

VERBS

do/carry out maintenance *Engineers are carrying out essential maintenance on the bridge.*

maintenance + NOUNS

maintenance work *Maintenance work is being carried out on the track.*

maintenance costs *Old houses often have high maintenance costs.*

majestic *adj* THESAURUS **high (1), impressive**

major *adj* THESAURUS **big (3), important (1)**

majority Ac *n*

1 most people or things in a group

ADJECTIVES

a large majority *A large majority of patients said they were satisfied with the treatment they had received.*

the vast/overwhelming majority (=almost all) *In the vast majority of cases, death is due to natural causes.*

the silent majority (=the ordinary people in a society, who do not make their opinions known) *She said she was speaking on behalf of the silent majority of ordinary people.*

VERBS

make up/form the majority *Foreign workers formed the majority of the labour force.*

represent the majority *This newspaper does not represent the majority of British people.*

majority + NOUNS

a majority decision *Everyone agreed to abide by the majority decision.*

a majority judgment/verdict (=a legal decision agreed by most members of a committee or jury) *The jury found him guilty by a majority verdict.*

the majority view (=what most people think) *The majority view was that he should resign.*

PREPOSITIONS

the majority of sb/sth *The majority of people agreed with the government's decision.*

be in a/the majority (=form the largest group) *In this city, Muslims are in a majority.*

2 the difference in the number of votes when a law or decision is made, or a person or government is elected

ADJECTIVES/NOUNS + majority

a large/huge/small majority *Parliament voted by a large majority to change the law.*

a narrow/slim majority (=very small) *The bill was passed by a narrow majority, by 151 to 144.*

an overwhelming majority (=very large) *The Senate approved the bill by an overwhelming majority.*

a landslide majority (=used when a government or leader wins by a very large majority) *Aristide was elected president with a landslide majority.*

a comfortable/solid majority (=rather large) *The government won the vote with a comfortable majority.*

an overall majority (=more votes than any other political party) *The party lost its overall majority in Parliament.*

an outright/clear/absolute majority (=one that makes a party or person clearly the winner of the election) *None of the parties had an outright majority.*

a two-thirds/three to one etc majority (=used when comparing the number of votes for and against someone or something) *A change in the constitution requires a two-thirds majority in both houses of Parliament.*

a Socialist/Republican/Democratic etc majority (=a situation in which the Socialists, Republicans etc have more votes than the other parties) *There was a Socialist majority in the national elections.*

a parliamentary majority (=a situation in which one party has more seats than others in a parliament) *The Conservative Party increased its parliamentary majority.*

VERBS

have/hold/command a majority *The Democratic party has a majority in the Senate.*

win/get/gain a majority *The Conservative Party failed to win a majority.*

increase a majority (=get more votes than you had before) *Labour increased its majority in the area.*

lose a majority *The Republicans lost their narrow majority in Congress at the midterm elections.*

retain your majority (=keep it) *They were able to retain their majority.*

defend a majority (=try not to lose it) *He is defending a majority of 400 against his Labour opponent.*

overturn a majority (=win a majority that previously belonged to someone else) *She hoped to overturn a Conservative majority of 2,221.*

majority + NOUNS

a majority vote (=a vote by more than half the group) *The union takes decisions by a majority vote.*

the majority party (=the political party with the most seats in a parliament) *At that time, Labour was the majority party in Parliament.*

a majority government (=with more than half the votes in an election) *They did not receive enough support to form a majority government.*

PREPOSITIONS

by a majority (=with a majority) *He won by a majority of 500.*

with a majority *She returned to power with a large majority.*

a majority over sb/sth *Her majority over the other candidate was 601.*

make *v*

1 if you make something, you cause it to start to exist, usually by putting different parts together

NOUNS

make clothes/furniture/jewellery etc *Anna makes her own clothes.*

make cars/planes/toys etc *Half of all American robots are used to make cars or trucks.*

make a film/movie *George Lucas made six 'Star Wars' movies.*

make a record/album *Elvis made his first record in 1954.*

make lunch/coffee/cake/a meal etc *I made some lunch for the children.*

make electricity *Most coal is used in power stations to make electricity.*

PHRASES

be easy/difficult/fun to make *Pretty decorations for cakes and desserts are easy to make.*

PREPOSITIONS

be made of sth *The shirt is made of silk.*

be made from sth *Wine is made from grapes.*

be made out of sth *The necklace was made out of little seashells.*

be made in China/a factory etc *Her shoes are made in Italy.*

make sth into sth *The play was made into a film.*

make sth by hand/machine *The candles are made by hand.*

⚠ Don't say 'The statue is made by wood.' Say **The statue is made of wood.**

Making things by hand

You use **handmade** about things that are made using your hands: ***Handmade** chocolates are very expensive.*

You use **homemade** about things that you make at home: *Fresh **homemade** bread always tastes better than shop-bought bread.*

You use **homegrown** about things you grow yourself: *The tomatoes are all **homegrown**.*

THESAURUS: make

create

design | style | character | picture | image | masterpiece | system | jobs | opportunities

to make something new, which did not exist before. **Create** is often used about using your imagination and skill to make new things:

Jacquie creates imaginative carpet designs in her London studio. | Brando created a whole new style of acting. | Leonardo created his masterpiece at the end of the 15th century. | They want to create a fairer tax system. | The programme will create over 100 jobs.

You can also **create a file/folder/document/database** (=make it on a computer): *If you **create** a new **document**, don't forget to save it.*

You can **create a mood/atmosphere/impression** (=make people feel it): *In his films Hitchcock **creates** an **atmosphere** of mystery and terror.*

do

picture | drawing | sketch | portrait | design | copy

to make something, especially a picture or a design:

He did a rough sketch to show how he wanted the room to look. | A French company did the design. | I did one copy for each student.

produce

oil | coal | steel | goods | cars | crops | food | wine

to make something in large quantities:

Saudi Arabia produces over 10% of the world's oil. | The company produces high-quality goods and services. | Farmers are able to produce more crops using modern farming methods.

You also use **produce** when saying that something is made as a result of a natural process: *When burned, hydrogen reacts with oxygen to **produce energy and water**. | The pancreas is a gland in your body which **produces hormones**. | Recycling saves energy and **produces** less **pollution**.*

M

manufacture
cars | engines | clothes | goods | products | equipment | parts | components
to make machines, cars, equipment etc in factories:
Renault announced plans to manufacture cars in India. | China manufactures and sells goods to over 100 countries. | The company manufactures parts for aircraft engines.

mass-produce
clothing | goods | products | cars | food | drugs | images
to make very large quantities of something in a factory:
Henry Ford started to mass-produce cars in the early part of the 20th century. | Mass-produced food doesn't taste as good as food you grow yourself.

develop
system | way | technology | product | machine | weapon | drug | treatment
to design and make a new way of doing something:
He developed a system which allowed people to communicate with each other electronically. | India and Pakistan have developed their own nuclear weapons. | Scientists are developing a new treatment for cancer.

form
water | liquid | gas | substance | planet | Earth | universe
to make something, especially as the result of a natural process or chemical reaction:
Hydrogen and oxygen combine to form water. | Scientists say that the Earth was formed 4.5 billion years ago.

generate
electricity | power | heat
to make electricity, power, or heat:
Wind can be used to generate electricity. | The plan was to build a dam on the Volta river to generate power. | A nuclear explosion generates enormous amounts of heat.

2 used with certain nouns when saying that someone does something

THESAURUS: make
make, give, take, commit, carry out, conduct, perform, undertake, implement → **do**

make sth up *v* THESAURUS invent

make-up, makeup *n*
substances that you put on your face, especially to make yourself look attractive

VERBS

wear make-up *I always wear make-up for work.*
put on make-up (*also* **apply make-up** *formal*): *Gloria watched her mother put on her make-up.*
do your make-up (=put on make-up - more informal) *Can you wait a moment - I'm just doing my make-up.*
use make-up *She rarely uses make-up.*
have make-up on (=be wearing make-up) *She had no make-up on.*
remove/take off make-up *Take off eye make-up gently, using a cotton ball.*

ADJECTIVES/NOUNS + make-up

eye make-up *She was wearing far too much eye make-up.*
stage make-up (=used by actors) *She was in her dressing room removing her stage make-up.*
heavy make-up (=a lot of make-up) *Heavy make-up can sometimes make you look older.*

malicious *adj* THESAURUS unkind

man *n* an adult male human

ADJECTIVES

a good-looking/handsome man *Adam was a good-looking man when he was young.*
a married/single/divorced man *My advice is stay away from married men.*
a rich/wealthy man *His grandfather became a very wealthy man.*
a young/middle-aged/old/elderly man *He was an old man with white hair.*
a strong man *The people wanted to have a strong man in charge of the country.*

PHRASES

a men's magazine *Men's magazines are becoming more like women's magazines.*
the men's team *The men's team lost.*

manage *v* THESAURUS control[1] (1), succeed

management *n*
1 the people who are in charge of a company or organization

ADJECTIVES

senior/top management *There was a meeting between senior management and union representatives.*
middle management *A whole layer of middle management lost their jobs.*
local management *Communication between the company's headquarters and local management is extremely important.*

management + NOUNS

the management team/committee *She is a member of the management team.*
a management buyout (=when the top managers of a company take control of it by buying all the shares) *They are planning a management buyout in order to save the company.*

a management shake-up (=big changes in the way the managers are organized) *He lost his job following a management shake-up.*

PHRASES

under sb's management *The department has been very successful under her management.*

be under new management *The restaurant is under new management and has improved considerably.*

2 the activity of managing an organization such as a company

ADJECTIVES

good management *The company's success is mainly due to good management.*

bad/poor management *Poor management has caused a lot of problems.*

efficient management *Efficient management of the company's budget is very important.*

financial/economic management *The government aims to keep tax levels as low as possible by careful financial management.*

general management *The company is looking for someone with general management experience.*

the day-to-day management (=the ordinary management that you do everyday, not big decisions about future plans) *His partner does most of the day-to-day management of the company.*

corporate management (=of large companies) *Shareholders should have more control over corporate management decisions.*

management + NOUNS

management skills *The course is designed to improve people's management skills.*

management training *The company has introduced a new management training program.*

a management course *He took a management course at Harvard Business School.*

management style *Individuals respond differently to different types of management style.*

management practice *We can learn a lot from Japanese management practice.*

a management consultant (=an adviser about how to improve the management of a company) *The firm employed management consultants to help develop a strategy for the future.*

NOUNS + management

business management *I studied business management at college.*

PREPOSITIONS

in management *He wants a career in management.*

manager *n*

someone who is in charge of an organization or part of an organization

ADJECTIVES

a senior manager *She has just been promoted to senior manager.*

a top manager (=one who has a very important position - a rather informal use) *Top managers enjoyed an average increase in earnings of 17.8% last year.*

a good/excellent/successful/effective manager *Karen has a reputation as a good manager.*

an assistant/deputy manager *The assistant manager will be in charge when I'm away.*

a junior manager *He started his career as a junior manager in an advertising firm.*

NOUNS + manager

a bank manager *She asked her bank manager for a loan.*

a hotel/store/hospital manager *They complained to the hotel manager.*

a branch manager (=manager of a local shop or business that is part of a larger business) *Each branch manager is responsible for selling the goods in his particular shop.*

sb's line manager (=the person directly above you in a company, who is in charge of your work) *I asked my line manager for permission to leave work early.*

a sales/marketing manager *He worked as a sales manager in a supermarket.*

a project manager *A project manager was appointed to supervise the building work.*

a team manager *The club is looking for a new team manager.*

a stage manager (=someone who manages the performers in a show) *She works as a stage manager at the local theatre.*

VERBS

appoint a manager/appoint sb as manager *Hopefully the board can appoint a new manager soon.*

take over as manager *Helen took over as manager earlier this year.*

PREPOSITIONS

the manager of sth *She is the manager of a software company.*

mandatory *adj* THESAURUS > **compulsory**

man-made *adj* THESAURUS > **artificial**

manner *n*

1 manners are polite ways of behaving in social situations

> **Grammar**
> Always plural in this meaning.

ADJECTIVES/NOUNS + manner

good manners *The children have very good manners and always say "please" and "thank you".*

M

bad manners *She apologized for her son's bad manners.*

perfect manners (*also* **impeccable manners** *formal*): *He is a handsome man, with impeccable manners.*

table manners (=the polite way of eating at a table) *My parents expected good table manners from all of us.*

VERBS

have good/bad/no etc manners *He has no manners and he eats like a pig.*

mind your manners (=used when telling a child to behave politely) *I frowned at him and told him to mind his manners.*

forget your manners (=behave in an impolite way) *Oh, I'm forgetting my manners. Let me introduce you to Suzanne.*

teach sb some manners (=teach someone how to behave properly - used when you think someone is behaving rudely) *Those girls need to be taught some manners!*

PHRASES

it is good/bad manners to do sth *It's bad manners to eat with your mouth open.*

2 a way of doing something

> **Grammar**
> In this meaning, **manner** is usually used with **in**, for example **in the usual manner**, or **in a similar manner**.

ADJECTIVES

in the normal/usual manner *I set off to work in the usual manner.*

in the correct/proper manner *The machine should last for several years if it is looked after in the proper manner.*

in a similar/different manner *The books are written in a similar manner.*

in a friendly/calm/confident manner *She greeted me in a friendly manner.*

in a suspicious manner (=as though doing something wrong) *A man was seen behaving in a suspicious manner.*

in a sensible/responsible/safe manner *Make sure razor blades are disposed of in a safe manner.*

in an appropriate manner *formal* (=suitable) *You must learn to express anger in a more appropriate manner.*

in a timely manner *formal* (=quickly) *We aim to deal with all complaints in a timely manner.*

in an orderly manner (=sensible and organized) *Please leave the building in an orderly manner.*

PREPOSITIONS

in a/the ... manner *He went about his work in the usual manner.*

in the manner of sb/sth (=like someone or something) *She was balancing in the manner of a circus tightrope walker.*

3 someone's way of behaving

ADJECTIVES

a pleasant/friendly/cheerful manner *The woman had a very pleasant manner.*

a relaxed manner *His relaxed manner put me at ease.*

a confident manner *For a second, her confident manner disappeared.*

an unassuming manner (=not wanting to be noticed or given special treatment) *With his unassuming manner, it is hard to believe he is one of the most powerful men in the world.*

an aggressive manner *The man had a red face and an aggressive manner.*

a direct manner (=saying what you mean, without worrying what people think) *Some people find her direct manner offensive.*

a businesslike manner (=effective and practical) *Her manner was very cool and businesslike.*

NOUNS + manner

sb's telephone manner (=how someone speaks on the phone) *A pleasant telephone manner is essential in this job.*

sb's bedside manner (=how a doctor speaks to sick patients) *The doctor had a very good bedside manner.*

VERBS

have a ... manner *She has a friendly manner.*

adopt a ... manner (=use a particular way of behaving) *He always adopts a patronizing manner when talking to women.*

manoeuvre *BrE*, **maneuver** *AmE n*

1 a skilful or careful movement that you make, for example in order to avoid something or go through a narrow space

ADJECTIVES

a difficult/tricky manoeuvre *Turning around on skis can be quite a difficult manoeuvre.*

a complex/complicated manoeuvre *The driving test requires drivers to perform some complex manoeuvres.*

a dangerous/risky manoeuvre *Bringing the ships together is a dangerous manoeuvre.*

VERBS

carry out a manoeuvre (*also* **perform/execute a manoeuvre** *formal*): *Pilots are trained to carry out various manoeuvres in a plane.*

2 something that you do in order to deal with a situation or get an advantage for yourself

ADJECTIVES

a political/legal manoeuvre *The delay in introducing the new law was widely seen as a political manoeuvre.*

a diplomatic manoeuvre *Britain used diplomatic manoeuvres to gain the support of other countries.*

a tactical manoeuvre *Football managers sometimes change players as a tactical manoeuvre.*

PHRASES

room to manoeuvre *The poor state of the economy gives the finance minister little room to manoeuvre as regards reducing tax.*

freedom of manoeuvre *The government must have some freedom of manoeuvre if it is to negotiate effectively.*

manual Ac *n*

a book that gives instructions about how to do something, especially how to use a machine

ADJECTIVES

a technical manual *The technical manual provides information about setting up and operating the equipment.*

a training manual *New staff are given a training manual when they start at the company.*

a comprehensive manual (=that covers a lot of subjects) *This book is a comprehensive manual of home cookery.*

NOUNS + manual

a user manual *The camera comes with a 300-page user manual.*

a computer/camera/car etc manual *I followed the instructions in the computer manual.*

an instruction manual *Read the instruction manual before using the product.*

a reference manual *This textbook is designed as a reference manual.*

the owner's/teacher's/employee's manual *She looked in the owner's manual, to see if there was any information.*

VERBS

read a manual/look in a manual *I never read the manual – I always try to work it out for myself.*

write a manual *He writes manuals for computer games.*

a manual describes/explains/shows sth *The manual describes how to install the software.*

PHRASES

it says in the manual *It says in the manual that the car needs to be serviced every 30,000 kilometres.*

manufacture *v* THESAURUS make (1)

map *n* a drawing of an area

ADJECTIVES

a detailed map *He bought a detailed map of the city.*

an accurate map *The map she drew me was not very accurate.*

a large-scale map (=showing a small area in a lot of detail) *On the wall was a large-scale map of Paris.*

NOUNS + map

a road/street map *There's a road map in the car.*

a tourist map *The museum is marked on most tourist maps.*

a tube/underground map *BrE*, **a subway map** *AmE* (=of an underground railway) *There are tube maps at every station.*

VERBS

look at a map *She stopped the car to look at the map.*

read a map (=look at and understand the information on a map) *I'm not very good at reading maps.*

study a map (=look carefully at a map) *They studied the map before setting out.*

draw a map *He drew me a map of the route.*

check a map (*also* **consult a map** *formal*) (=look at a map to get information) *I don't know how to get to Berlin without consulting a map.*

be marked on a map *The path is clearly marked on the map.*

find sth on a map *I managed to find the village on the map.*

spread out/unfold a map *We spread out our maps on the floor.*

PHRASES

the contours on a map (=the lines on a map showing the height of mountains and valleys) *Contours on the map are given in feet.*

PREPOSITIONS

a map of sth *Here's a map of the city centre.*

on a map *Where are we on the map?*

according to a map *According to the map, we should turn left.*

march *n*

an organized event in which many people walk together to protest about something

NOUNS + march

a protest march *The trades union organized a protest march through the city centre.*

a peace/anti-war march *Several people were arrested during yesterday's peace march.*

ADJECTIVES

a peaceful march *The organizers say the march will be a peaceful one.*

VERBS

hold/organize/stage a march *The workers held a march to show their opposition to the plan.*

take part in a march (*also* **attend a march** *formal*): *She took part in student marches when she was at university.*

go on a march *They went on a march to protest against cuts in government spending.*

M

join a march *Tens of thousands joined the protest march through Caracas.*

lead a march *Dr King led a famous march in Washington.*

ban a march *Anti-government marches have been banned.*

PREPOSITIONS

a march to/towards/from sth *More than 5,000 people took part in a protest march to the capital.*

a march through sth *The demonstrators are planning a march through the centre of London.*

a march against sth *They are planning a march against the war.*

mark[1] *n*

1 a spot or dirty area on something that spoils its appearance

ADJECTIVES

a black/red/white mark *There were black marks all over the floor.*

a dirty mark *What's that dirty mark on your coat?*

a greasy mark *The spray is good for getting greasy marks off carpet.*

a big mark *The TV screen has a big mark on it.*

a faint mark (=difficult to see) *There were faint marks on his arm where she had gripped it.*

a slight mark *You may be left with a slight mark on your skin, but it will fade.*

a stubborn mark (=difficult to remove) *Remove stubborn marks by scrubbing them lightly with a nailbrush.*

VERBS

make a mark *Her lipstick had made a mark on his collar.*

leave a mark (=make one) *The glass had left a mark on the table.*

get a mark out/off (*also* **remove a mark**) *I can't get these marks out of my T-shirt.*

a mark comes off/out *That mark will come out if you wash it with warm water.*

a mark fades (=gradually disappears) *Eventually the bite marks on his skin faded.*

NOUNS + mark

finger marks *There were finger marks all over the windows.*

a grease mark *Handle the photographs by their edges to avoid grease marks.*

a burn mark *There were burn marks on the carpet from cigarettes.*

a tyre mark *BrE*, **a tire mark** *AmE*: *The ground was pretty soft and there were tyre marks.*

2 *especially BrE* a letter or number given by a teacher to show how good a student's work is

ADJECTIVES/NOUNS + mark

a high mark *He got a very high mark in the last test.*

a low mark *Her marks have been a lot lower this term.*

a good mark *She always gets good marks.*

a bad/poor mark *My parents get angry if I get bad marks at school.*

the pass mark (=needed to pass an exam) *The pass mark was 75%.*

full/top marks (=the highest possible mark) *He managed to get top marks in maths.*

extra marks *You get no extra marks for including irrelevant information.*

the total marks *Add up the total marks then divide by two.*

the average mark *The average mark for this test was 52%.*

VERBS

get/receive a mark *You get one mark for each correct answer.*

give sb a mark *I'll give you three marks for that answer.*

take marks away/off (*also* **deduct marks** *formal*): *Marks will be deducted for poor presentation.*

lose a mark (=have it taken away) *If you do not complete the work on time, you could lose marks.*

PREPOSITIONS

marks in a subject *Her marks in science have improved.*

marks for sth *What mark did you get for the English essay?*

a mark out of 10/100 etc *You will be given a mark out of 100.*

> In American English, people usually say **grade**: *He got very **good grades** in school.*

mark[2] *v*

1 to write or draw letters, lines, or symbols on something for a particular purpose

ADVERBS

mark sth clearly *All books should be clearly marked with the student's name.*

mark sth carefully *Mark carefully where to drill the holes.*

NOUNS

mark a place/position *He marked the place where we were to meet on the map.*

mark a route *Someone had marked the route in red on the map.*

mark a page *I've marked the pages you need to look it.*

PREPOSITIONS

mark sth on sth *The walk is marked on the map.*

mark sth with sth *The envelope was marked with my name.*

PHRASES

mark sth urgent/confidential/personal etc *I forwarded the message to John, marked urgent.*

mark sth for sb's attention (=write someone's name on a letter, document etc so they can deal with it) *Send the contract to my office and mark it for my attention.*

2 to damage the surface of something

ADVERBS

badly mark sth *The table was badly marked.*

market *n*

1 a place where people buy and sell things, often outdoors

ADJECTIVES

an open-air/outdoor market (=outside) *There is an open-air market in the city's main square.*

an indoor/covered market *He has a stall at the covered market.*

NOUNS + market

a fruit/vegetable/flower market *There is a good flower market on Tuesdays.*

a craft market (=a market selling things people have made) *I bought a wooden carving at the craft market.*

a farmers' market (=where farmers sell their produce directly to the public) *He always buys his vegetables at the farmers' market.*

a flea market (=where you can buy old or used things) *Flea markets are good if you want to buy vintage clothes.*

VERBS

go to a market *He went to the market to buy some vegetables.*

hold a market *A market is held every Saturday.*

market + NOUNS

a market stall (=a covered table with goods for sale) *There were market stalls selling clothes and toys.*

the market square/place *There is a market every Saturday in the town's market square.*

a market town *Ashbourne is a pretty market town in Derbyshire.*

market day *Saturday is market day in Vevey.*

PREPOSITIONS

at the market *I bought these shoes at the market.*

to market *She was taking her chickens to market to sell them.*

2 trade in a particular type of goods

ADJECTIVES

the international/global market *There has been a fall in coffee prices on the global market.*

foreign/overseas markets *The majority of our sales are in overseas markets.*

the domestic market (=people in the same country) *They supply sugar to the domestic market.*

a competitive market *The sale of mobile phones is a very competitive market.*

a booming/thriving market (=in which a lot of goods are sold) *Car sales in China's booming market are expected to reach 7 million this year.*

an open/free market (=one where anyone is free to sell) *The airlines are competing in a free market.*

the financial markets (=trade in shares, currencies etc) *The world's financial markets were in chaos.*

NOUNS + market

the stock market *Shares on the New York stock market were down.*

the housing/property market *The property market crashed, and many builders went out of business.*

the export market *The cars are made for the export market.*

VERBS + market

enter the market (=start to sell a particular type of goods) *A lot of new companies have entered the market.*

dominate the market *US companies dominate the market.*

corner the market in sth (=sell much more of a product than anyone else) *The company had cornered the market in personal computers.*

flood the market (=make large quantities of something available to buy) *They flooded the market with cheap products, so that they could put the other companies out of business.*

regulate a market *The government is supposed to regulate the financial markets.*

market + VERBS

the market grows/expands *The market in organic produce grew by 13%.*

the market collapses/crashes (=it fails because people are not buying very much) *The property market collapsed.*

market + NOUNS

the market price/value (=the normal price paid for something) *Many people were not willing to pay the market price.*

market share *The company aims to increase its market share.*

the market leader *The firm is the market leader in this kind of advertising.*

PREPOSITIONS

the market in sth *The market in gold and other precious metals has grown.*

on the market (=available to buy) *There are a lot of new products on the market.*

PHRASES

on the black market (=illegally) *You can buy foreign cigarettes on the black market.*

3 the people who want to buy something

ADJECTIVES

a big/huge/large market *We think there is a huge market for this type of product.*

M

a growing market *There is a growing market for organic produce.*

a niche market (=a market that consists of a small group of customers who want to buy something) *It's a niche market and only a few people are able to afford this type of car.*

the mass market (=large numbers of people who buy something) *The magazine is aimed at the mass market.*

an emerging market (=one that is starting to buy more and more products) *Eastern Europe is an emerging market.*

a lucrative market (=one that makes a lot of money for a company) *The company believes it has found a lucrative market.*

VERBS

create a market *The company is trying to create a market for its products.*

target a market *The magazine targets the teenage market.*

cater for a market (=provide goods and services for a particular group of people) *This shop caters for a slightly different market.*

tap into a market (=start to sell something to a particular group of people) *This service aims to tap into a new market of young travellers.*

grow the market (=make it bigger - used in business English) *Companies are looking at new ways to grow the market.*

PHRASES

sb's share of the market *Ford wants to increase its share of the luxury car market.*

PREPOSITIONS

a market for sth *There was no market for the company's products.*

marriage *n*

the relationship between two people who are married

ADJECTIVES

a happy/unhappy marriage *Jack and Iris had a long and happy marriage.*

a successful marriage *The key to a successful marriage is friendship.*

a failed/broken marriage (=that ended in divorce) *After two failed marriages, she was not willing to risk marrying again.*

a loveless marriage *Why should I stay in a loveless marriage?*

sb's first/second etc marriage *She had two children from her first marriage.*

a previous marriage *Anne is his daughter from a previous marriage.*

an arranged marriage (=when your parents choose the person you will marry) *In our culture, there is a long tradition of arranged marriages.*

a mixed marriage (=between people of different races or religions) *Her parents disapproved of mixed marriages.*

a civil marriage (=a marriage ceremony that does not take place in a church) *Many young couples are now choosing to have civil marriages.*

VERBS + marriage

have a long/happy etc marriage *They had a very unhappy marriage.*

save your marriage (=do things to try to stay together as a married couple) *I will do anything I can to save my marriage.*

propose marriage *formal* (=ask someone to marry you) *How did your husband propose marriage to you?*

marriage + VERBS

a marriage ends *Her three marriages all ended in divorce.*

a marriage breaks down/up (=ends because of disagreements) *Liz's marriage broke up after only eight months.*

marriage + NOUNS

marriage breakdown/breakup *Marriage breakdown is difficult for the whole family.*

marriage guidance *BrE* (=help for people who are having problems in their marriage) *It might help to see a marriage guidance counsellor.*

a marriage ceremony *Over seventy guests attended the marriage ceremony.*

marriage vows (=the promises you make in a marriage ceremony) *Her marriage vows are important to her.*

a marriage proposal (=when someone asks another person to marry them) *At first, she refused his marriage proposal.*

a marriage licence/certificate *BrE*, **a marriage license** *AmE* (=a document that proves you are married) *We will need to see your marriage licence.*

⚠ Don't say 'marriage life'. Say **married life**.

PHRASES

the breakdown/breakup of sb's marriage (=the end of it) *She blamed herself for the breakup of their marriage.*

a proposal of marriage *formal* (=when someone asks you to marry them) *She rejected his proposal of marriage.*

be born outside marriage (=be born when your parents are not married) *Four in ten children are born outside marriage.*

sex before/outside marriage *She believes that sex before marriage is wrong.*

a marriage of convenience (=for political or economic reasons, not for love) *She admitted it was a marriage of convenience, to get her husband into the country.*

ask for sb's hand in marriage *old-fashioned* (=ask someone to marry you, or ask their parents for permission to marry) *He asked my father for my hand in marriage.*

M

PREPOSITIONS

marriage to sb *Her marriage to John lasted 50 years.*

marriage with sb *She tried to trick him into marriage with her.*

marriage between sb *Marriage between cousins is not illegal.*

by marriage *He is related by marriage to the King of Spain.*

in a marriage *Trust is important in any marriage.*

married *adj* having a husband or wife

ADVERBS

happily married *I have been happily married for nine years.*

unhappily married *They were behaving like an unhappily married old couple.*

newly/recently married (=married not long ago) *The newly married couple arrived at their hotel.*

legally married *Because they were not legally married, she was entitled to nothing when he died.*

NOUNS

a married man/woman *Married men shouldn't kiss other women.*

a married couple *Most of their friends are married couples.*

married life *Throughout her married life, her husband's interests had come first.*

sb's married name (=a woman's last name, when she has changed it to her husband's name) *Jones is her married name.*

VERBS

be married *Are you married or single?*

get married (=to have a wedding) *We're getting married next month.*

stay married (*also* **remain married** *formal*): *I cannot stay married to a man I do not love.*

PREPOSITIONS

married to sb *Nicole is married to my brother.*

PHRASES

be married with children *Kevin is married with four children.*

marry *v*

if you marry someone, you become their husband or wife

> **Marry** is most commonly used in the phrase **get married**: *My parents* **got married** *when they were young.* | *She wants to* **get married** *to someone she met at college.*

VERBS

get married *The couple are planning to get married next summer.*

ask sb to marry you *Philip asked her to marry him.*

agree to marry sb *She agreed to marry him, as soon as they could afford to live together.*

ADVERBS

marry young (=at a young age) *He knew he had made a mistake marrying young.*

marry late (=at an older age than is usual) *Martha had married late, at a time when she had almost given up hope of finding a husband.*

PHRASES

permission to marry sb *He had to ask her parents for permission to marry her.*

marry for love/money *He had married her for love, not for money.*

PREPOSITIONS

get married to sb *She got married to an Englishman.*

mask *n*

something that covers all or part of your face, to protect or to hide it

NOUNS + mask

a face mask *The diver was wearing a wetsuit and a face mask.*

an oxygen mask *The air steward showed the passengers how to use the oxygen masks.*

a gas mask *The soldiers were equipped with gas masks.*

VERBS

wear a mask *The robbers wore masks.*

have a mask on (=be wearing a mask) *The workers have masks on to protect them from the smoke.*

put on a mask *The children put on their Halloween masks.*

take off/remove a mask *He took off his ski mask.*

hide behind a mask *He kept his face hidden behind a mask so nobody would recognize him.*

use a mask *You should always use a face mask when spraying paint.*

PREPOSITIONS

in a mask (=wearing a mask) *We saw people in masks and wearing carnival costumes.*

with a mask (on your face) *A man with a mask on his face demanded money from the bank clerk.*

mass *n*

1 a large amount of a substance that does not have a definite or regular shape

ADJECTIVES

a great/huge/enormous/vast mass *A great mass of rock fell into the ocean.*

a solid mass *The Antarctic is covered in a solid mass of snow and ice.*

a dense mass *A dense mass of grey cloud hung over the bay.*

a shapeless mass *People who dislike the building have described it as a shapeless mass of concrete.*

M

2 a large number of things or people

ADJECTIVES

a great/huge/enormous/vast mass *There is a huge mass of evidence against him.*

a tangled mass (=a lot of things twisted together in an untidy way) *The garden was covered in a tangled mass of weeds.*

a seething/heaving/teeming mass (=a lot of people, insects etc, moving quickly in many different directions) *The station was a seething mass of people.*

> **Masses of**
> This phrase is used in informal English, when saying that there is a lot of something: *I have* ***masses of*** *homework to do.* | *There are* ***masses of*** *problems.*

massacre[1] *n*

an event in which a lot of people are killed violently, especially people who cannot defend themselves

ADJECTIVES

a bloody massacre (=very violent) *There was a bloody massacre in which over a hundred civilians lost their lives.*

VERBS

die/be killed in a massacre *Over thirty people were killed in a massacre by the army.*

carry out a massacre *The soldiers who carried out the massacre were never punished.*

order a massacre *Amin ordered the massacre of thousands of his countrymen.*

survive a massacre *A woman who survived the massacre was able to describe what happened.*

a massacre takes place *The massacre took place during the Second World War.*

PHRASES

the scene/site of a massacre (=the place where a massacre took place) *The town was the scene of one of the worst massacres of the civil war.*

a victim of a massacre *The victims of the massacre were buried in unmarked graves.*

be responsible for a massacre *The security forces were directly responsible for the massacre.*

massacre[2] *v* THESAURUS **kill**

massage *n*

the action of pressing and rubbing someone's body with your hands, to help them relax or to reduce pain

ADJECTIVES

a relaxing/soothing massage *What you need is a nice relaxing massage.*

NOUNS + massage

a foot/shoulder/back/body massage *A shoulder massage is good for getting rid of stress.*

VERBS

give sb a massage *Do you want me to give you a massage?*

have a massage *The players often have a massage after the game.*

massage + NOUNS

massage oil *She rubbed massage oil into my shoulders.*

> A **massage parlour** BrE/**massage parlor** AmE usually means a place where people pay to have sex, although it is supposed to mean a place where people go to have massages.

massive *adj* THESAURUS **huge**

mass-produce *v* THESAURUS **make (1)**

master *n*

1 someone who is very skilled at something

PHRASES

a master of the art of sth *He became a master of the art of diplomacy.*

a master of disguise (=someone who is very good at changing the way they look, so that they look like a different person) *The spy in this novel is a master of disguise who easily tricks his way into any building.*

be a past master at (doing) sth *disapproving* (=someone has always been good at doing something) *She is a past master at getting other people to do all the work.*

the old masters (=famous painters from the 15th to the 18th century) *His style of painting is heavily influenced by the old masters.*

> **Master** is often used as an adjective in this meaning: **a master craftsman**, **a master builder**, **a master chef**.

PREPOSITIONS

a master of sth *Parker is a master of his craft.*

2 the person who is in charge of someone, especially a servant or an animal

VERBS

serve your master *Benjamin served his master faithfully until the day he died.*

obey your master *Slaves had to obey their master at all times.*

ADJECTIVES

your political masters (=the politicians who are in charge of someone) *He can only say what his political masters allow him to say.*

sb's colonial masters (=the country that has taken control of another country) *In 1960, the country finally became independent from its old colonial masters.*

masterpiece *n*

a work of art, a piece of writing or music etc that is of very high quality or that is the best that a particular artist, writer etc has produced

ADJECTIVES

a great masterpiece *'War and Peace' is one of the great masterpieces of Russian literature.*

a literary masterpiece *Not all his books are literary masterpieces.*

a minor masterpiece *The play was a minor masterpiece.*

a musical masterpiece *His ninth symphony is a musical masterpiece.*

an architectural masterpiece *Gaudi's cathedral is an architectural masterpiece.*

a modern masterpiece *The museum is full of modern masterpieces.*

VERBS

be sb's masterpiece (=be someone's finest work) *This book is her masterpiece.*

create/produce a masterpiece *Picasso created some of the greatest masterpieces of the 20th century.*

write a masterpiece *In 1885, Twain wrote his masterpiece 'The Adventures of Huckleberry Finn'.*

paint a masterpiece *Van Gogh painted many of his masterpieces when he was in the asylum at Saint-Rémy.*

regard sth as a masterpiece/consider sth (to be) a masterpiece (=think that something is a masterpiece) *The poem is considered to be his masterpiece.*

hail sth as a masterpiece (=say that something is a masterpiece) *The movie is being hailed as a masterpiece by the critics.*

PREPOSITIONS

a masterpiece of sth *The novel is considered a masterpiece of European literature.*

a masterpiece by sb *A masterpiece by the painter Marc Chagall will be one of the highlights of the exhibition.*

match[1] *n*

1 *especially BrE* a sports event between two teams or people

NOUNS + match

a football/tennis/boxing etc match *My dad took me to my first football match when I was 8 years old.*

a chess match *A friend asked me if I wanted to have a chess match.*

a cup/championship match (=part of a competition) *The team lost their last two World Cup matches.*

ADJECTIVES

a good/great/brilliant match *We're sure it's going to be another great match.*

an exciting/thrilling match *That was the most exciting match I have ever seen.*

a close match (=one in which it is not sure who will win, because both teams or players play well) *Germany have a good team and it looks like a close match.*

a tough match (=difficult) *At this stage of the competition, every match is tough.*

an important match (*also* **a big match** *informal*): *They're preparing for a big match tomorrow.*

an international match (=against a team or player from a different country) *Before international matches, the national anthem is played.*

a practice match *Federer was injured in a practice match with his coach.*

a qualifying match (=to decide who plays in a competition) *They won all their qualifying matches.*

a live match (=shown on TV as it happens) *There is a live match on TV every Wednesday evening.*

a home match (=played at a team's own ground) *They have won their last five home matches.*

an away match (=played at the opponent's ground) *This is their last away match of the season.*

a friendly match (=not part of a competition) *England won a friendly match with Sweden.*

VERBS

watch a match *I watched the match on TV.*

go to a match *Are you going to the match on Saturday?*

play a match *We played the match in heavy rain.*

win/lose a match *The team lost the match 3-0.*

draw a match *BrE*, **tie a match** *AmE* (=finish with the score even) *United have drawn their last two matches.*

have a match *They have a match with Liverpool on Wednesday.*

postpone a match (=arrange for it to happen at a later time) *Our first match was postponed because of bad weather.*

miss a match *He missed two matches because of an injury.*

PHRASES

man of the match (=the best player in a match) *Henri was named man of the match.*

PREPOSITIONS

a match between two teams/players *We saw a great match between Nigeria and Ireland.*

a match against/with another player or team *Our next match is against UCLA.*

in a match *He was injured in a boxing match.*

during a match *Three players were sent off during the match.*

before/after a match *She gets nervous before a tennis match.*

M

This meaning of **match** is used especially in British English. In American English, people usually say **game**.

2 a small stick for lighting fires, cigarettes etc

VERBS

strike/light a match (=rub it against a rough surface to produce a flame) *Karen struck a match and lit the candle.*

blow out a match (=blow it so it stops burning) *I had to blow the match out because it was burning my fingers.*

put a match to sth (=light it with a match) *He turned on the gas and put a match to the stove.*

a match goes out (=stops burning) *Before he could light the fire, the match went out.*

PHRASES

a box of matches *He took a box of matches out of his pocket.*

a book of matches (=a small folded card containing matches) *I kept a book of matches with the name of the hotel on the front.*

match[2] *v*

if one thing matches another, or if two things match, they look attractive together because they are a similar colour, pattern etc

ADVERBS

match sth perfectly (=very well) *The scarf matched the colour of her eyes perfectly.*

PHRASES

to match (=used when things that you buy are in the same style, colour etc) *We bought a beech dining table with four chairs to match.*

material *n*

1 a substance, especially one that can be used for making things

ADJECTIVES/NOUNS + material

raw material *The island has to import oil and other raw materials.*

natural material *We only use natural materials in our products.*

a man-made/synthetic material *It looks like wood but has all the advantages of a modern synthetic material.*

local material *The houses are built using local materials.*

genetic material (=that consists of genes) *Scientists analyzed the genetic material in these cells.*

building/construction material *The company supplies bricks, concrete, and other building materials.*

radioactive material (=dangerous because it contains substances such as uranium) *A cloud of radioactive material had leaked from the nuclear reactor.*

2 cloth used for making clothes, curtains etc

Grammar
Always uncountable in this meaning.

NOUNS + material

dress/curtain material *She bought some pretty dress material.*

PHRASES

scraps of material (=little pieces) *I keep all the scraps of material that I don't use.*

a kind of material *She was wearing a scarf made of some kind of soft material*

matter[1] *n*

a subject or situation that you have to think about or deal with

ADJECTIVES

an important/serious matter *There are important matters we have to discuss.*

an urgent matter *I need to speak to him immediately about an urgent matter.*

a small/trivial matter (=not important) *Quitting your job over such a small matter is ridiculous.*

a simple/easy/straightforward matter (=easy to do) *Putting the bookcases together is a fairly simple matter.*

a complex/complicated matter *Since this is quite a complex matter, professional advice is essential.*

a different/separate matter *The next day he came to see me again, about a separate matter.*

a related/unrelated matter *Detectives investigating an unrelated matter found the gun.*

financial/business/legal/political/religious etc matters *Rick wasn't interested in financial matters.*

a personal/private matter *We never spoke about personal matters.*

a practical matter *He wrote to him several times about practical matters to do with the house.*

a delicate/sensitive matter (=needed to be dealt with carefully to avoid upsetting or offending someone) *There is something I need to speak to you about – it's rather a delicate matter.*

VERBS

discuss the matter *She refused to discuss the matter with her colleagues.*

raise/bring up the matter (=start a conversation about it) *I'll raise the matter at the next meeting.*

consider the matter (=think about it) *She considered the matter carefully before making a decision.*

look into/investigate the matter (=try to find out the truth) *The police said they were investigating the matter.*

deal with a matter *She usually deals with financial matters.*

settle/resolve a matter (=deal with it completely) *I hope this will settle the matter.*

improve/help matters (=make a situation better) *His aggressive attitude did not help matters.*

pursue the matter (=keep discussing or asking about it) *If he refuses to help, I see no point in pursuing the matter.*

complicate matters (=make a situation more difficult) *She didn't want to complicate matters by asking about her son.*

PREPOSITIONS

on/about a matter *She came to see me on a matter of some importance.*

a matter for sb (=someone should decide it) *This is a matter for the police.*

matters relating to sth *They do not comment on matters relating to security.*

matters arising from sth *formal* (=things that come from another thing) *Are there any matters arising from the report which you wish to discuss?*

PHRASES

the heart/crux of the matter (=the most important part of something) *The crux of the matter is this: how do we prevent these floods from happening again?*

a matter of importance (=something important) *He consulted her on all matters of importance.*

a matter of concern (=something that worries people) *Safety standards in the industry have become a matter of concern.*

a matter for discussion/negotiation/speculation etc *The exact figure is a matter for negotiation between the two companies.*

sth is a matter of/for debate (=people do not agree about it) *The Buddha's dates are a matter of debate.*

sth is no easy matter (=it is difficult) *Sorting out the family finances was no easy matter.*

the matter at/in hand (=the thing you are dealing with now) *We need to focus on the matter in hand.*

to make matters worse *I failed the test and, to make matters worse, all my friends passed.*

let the matter rest/drop (=stop discussing or worrying about it) *I think we should let the matter rest, don't you?*

that is the end of the matter *Mr Brown resigned and we thought that would be the end of the matter.*

matter² *v*

to be important to you, or to have an effect on what happens

ADVERBS

really matter *Your age doesn't really matter- it's whether you can do the job.*

hardly matter *My left foot is slightly bigger than the right, but the difference is so small that it hardly matters.*

matter most *What still matters most to shoppers is value for money.*

matter a lot *The poem matters a lot to me.*

matter less *Fame matters less and less to me as I get older.*

matter little *Helen's disappearance seemed to matter little to anyone but her parents.*

matter a great deal (=a lot) *The public's opinion about my work matters a great deal to me.*

not matter very much *I don't think it matters very much what you wear as long as you look clean and neat.*

not matter any more *All he wanted was to win – nothing else mattered any more.*

VERBS

cease to matter (=stop being important) *The reason why they'd argued ceased to matter – he just wanted her back.*

PHRASES

what matters *I don't care about the money – that's not what matters.*

all that matters/the only thing that matters *All that matters is that you're safe.*

nothing else matters *At last she was with the man she loved and nothing else mattered.*

the thing that matters *It's the little things that matter most.*

not that it matters *The landlord is going to raise the rent. Not that it matters very much because we are moving anyway.*

maximum Ac *n, adj*

the largest number or amount that is possible or is allowed

ADJECTIVES

the absolute maximum *5,000 words is the absolute maximum for the essay.*

the legal maximum *Many people work more than the legal maximum of 50 hours per week.*

the recommended maximum *The recommended maximum is six grams of salt per day.*

NOUNS

the maximum number/amount *The maximum number of students in a class is 15.*

the maximum speed/weight/temperature etc *The car has a maximum speed of 200 miles an hour.*

the maximum rate *He has to pay the maximum rate of tax.*

the maximum penalty/fine/sentence (=the largest punishment that someone can get) *The maximum penalty for this offence is life imprisonment.*

maximum effect/impact *She paused to give her words maximum effect.*

M

VERBS

rise to/reach a maximum *Temperatures in Dubai reach a maximum of around 39°C.*

achieve a maximum *You can achieve a maximum of 500 points.*

exceed the maximum (=be more than it) *You should not exceed the recommended maximum of four tablets per day.*

limit/restrict sth to a maximum *Places on the course are limited to a maximum of 24 people.*

allow a maximum (*also* **permit a maximum** *formal*): *The maximum allowed is four tickets per person.*

PREPOSITIONS

a maximum of 10/£500/40 degrees etc *You can take a maximum of 30 kilos of luggage.*

above/below a maximum *The temperature is kept below a maximum of 30 degrees.*

at the maximum *Interviews should last 30 minutes at the maximum.*

to the maximum (=as much as possible) *As a teacher she pushes her students to the maximum.*

ANTONYMS **maximum → minimum**

meal *n*

an occasion when you eat food, for example a dinner, or the food that you eat then

ADJECTIVES/NOUNS + meal

a delicious/lovely/excellent meal *"It was a delicious meal," Merrill said politely.*

a healthy/nutritious meal *You can make a healthy meal in just a few minutes.*

a balanced meal (=with some of each type of food, to keep you healthy) *Children need to eat balanced meals, not just sugary snacks.*

sb's main meal *We usually have our main meal in the evening.*

the evening/midday meal *The evening meal is served at 7.30.*

a three-course/five-course etc meal (=a meal with several separate parts) *The restaurant offers a three-course meal for $30.*

a big meal *We don't have a big meal at lunchtime, usually just sandwiches.*

a decent/square meal (*also* **a proper meal** *BrE*) (=with enough good food to satisfy you) *I hadn't had a decent meal in days.*

a heavy meal (=with a lot of rich food which makes you feel very full) *A heavy meal is likely to make you feel sleepy.*

a light meal (=with not a lot of food) *We just had a light meal of salad.*

a simple meal *He prepared a simple meal of soup and bread.*

a hot/cold meal *With a hot meal inside me, I began to feel better.*

a ready meal *BrE* (=one that you buy and heat in an oven) *British supermarkets sell a huge range of ready meals.*

school meals *Many of the children are receiving free school meals.*

VERBS

have a meal (=eat a meal) *We usually have our evening meal fairly early.*

⚠ Don't say 'take a meal'.

eat a meal *When they had eaten their meal, they went out for a walk.*

cook/make a meal (*also* **prepare a meal** *formal*): *Who cooks most of the meals in your house?*

serve a meal *The bar serves snacks and meals.*

go (out) for a meal *How about going out for a meal tonight?*

take sb (out) for a meal *He took Anna out for a meal and then to the theatre.*

meal + NOUNS

a meal break (=a time when you stop work to have a meal) *There is one meal break in the middle of the day.*

Mealtimes is written as one word.

mean *adj* unkind or cruel

NOUNS

a mean trick *Hiding your brother's homework was a mean trick to play on him.*

a mean thing to say/do *It was a mean thing to say.*

a mean look *The guard gave Joe a mean look, which made him feel nervous.*

a mean streak (=a cruel part to someone's character) *She seems friendly at first, but she has a mean streak.*

VERBS

feel mean *Later, Betty felt mean for what she'd said, so she phoned Mike to say sorry.*

seem mean *It seems mean not to let the children play together.*

ADVERBS

pretty/quite mean *If her husband has a bad day, he can be pretty mean to her when he gets home.*

a bit mean *BrE informal*: *I felt bad afterwards, because I thought I'd been a bit mean.*

PREPOSITIONS

mean to sb *The other boys were very mean to him and called him names.*

THESAURUS: mean

mean, nasty, hurtful, spiteful, malicious, unsympathetic, hard-hearted, inconsiderate, insensitive → **unkind**

meaning *n*

the thing or idea that a word, expression, or sign represents

ADJECTIVES

the original meaning *The original meaning of the word holiday was 'holy day'.*

the literal meaning *Idioms are groups of words that are used in a different way from their literal meaning.*

a precise/specific/exact meaning *The term 'stress' has a precise meaning to an engineer.*

a hidden meaning *She felt there was a hidden meaning behind his words.*

a double meaning (=two meanings at the same time) *Everything he said had a double meaning.*

the figurative/metaphorical meaning (=different from its usual or basic meaning) *'Heated' is most commonly used in a metaphorical meaning, when talking about angry arguments.*

the technical/scientific meaning *The word 'tolerance' also has a technical meaning.*

the ordinary meaning *Technical uses are often different from the ordinary meaning of the word.*

sb's/sth's true meaning *Children need to understand the true meaning of Christmas.*

VERBS

have a meaning *The same word may have several different meanings.*

take on a meaning (=begin to have a new meaning) *The word 'chaos' has taken on a special scientific meaning.*

understand the meaning *The pictures help the children understand the meanings of the words.*

know the meaning *Do you know the meaning of the word 'paraphrase'?*

grasp the meaning (=begin to understand the meaning) *She suddenly grasped the meaning of what they were saying.*

get sb's meaning *informal* (=understand what someone is saying in an indirect way) *He's not like other people, if you get my meaning.*

convey meaning *formal* (=express a meaning) *Hand signals can be used to convey meaning.*

PREPOSITIONS

the meaning of sth *You can look up the meaning of a word in a dictionary.*

means *n*

a way of doing or achieving something

ADJECTIVES

other/different/alternative means *If the airport was closed, they would have to get there by some other means.*

the normal/usual means (=that people usually use) *The horse was the normal means of transport in those days.*

the only/sole means *Writing letters became his sole means of communicating with his family.*

the main/principal means *Rivers and canals were the main means of carrying coal.*

a common means *The most common means of spreading infection is through breathing in other people's germs.*

a good/effective/reliable means *Is this really the best means of achieving our goal?*

a useful/important means *Local radio is a useful means of advertising.*

an ideal means *Graphs are an ideal means of presenting information.*

legal/lawful means *Their protests will continue, but only by legal means.*

legitimate means (=acceptable or legal) *Stealing someone's property is not a legitimate means of getting back money they owe you.*

illegal/unlawful means *He was accused of attempting to overthrow the government using unlawful means.*

conventional means (=not using special technology) *They claim that genetically modified tomatoes are as safe as tomatoes bred by conventional means.*

VERBS

use a means to do sth *He will use any means to get what he wants.*

have a means of doing sth *I had no means of telling him I would be late.*

PHRASES

a means of escape *The window was our only means of escape.*

a means of transport/transportation (=a car, bus, bicycle etc) *The car has become the main means of transportation.*

a means of communication (=telephone, email, speech etc) *The only means of communication was sign language.*

a means of expression (=a way of expressing your feelings or opinions) *Music and art are important means of expression.*

a means of identification (=an official document that shows who you are) *Do you have any means of identification?*

sth is a means to an end (=it is something you do to achieve a result, not because you want to do it) *Many of the students saw the course as a means to an end: a way of getting a good job.*

by any means necessary (=doing whatever you have to do in order to achieve something) *Their only goal was survival by any means necessary.*

the end justifies the means *disapproving* (=the result you want to achieve is the most important thing, even if other people are badly affected by your actions) *The terrorists believe that the end justifies the means and it does not matter who they kill.*

PREPOSITIONS

by ... means *They had entered the country by unlawful means.*

through ... means *Can the conflict be resolved through peaceful means?*

by means of sth (=using something) *The best way of understanding this is by means of an example.*

M

measure¹ *v*

to find the size, length, or amount of something

ADVERBS

measure sth accurately/precisely *Very small changes in weight are difficult to measure accurately.*

measure sth exactly *Unless we measure the distance exactly, our results will be inaccurate.*

NOUNS

measure the size/amount *The meter measures the amount of water you use.*

measure the weight/speed/temperature *They measure the baby's weight every month for the first year.*

measure the distance *We measured the distance between the two points with a ruler.*

measure the rate/level *The nurse measures the patient's heart rate.*

PHRASES

measure how much/how long/how big etc *Researchers measured how much carbon dioxide there was in the atmosphere.*

sth is difficult/hard/easy to measure *The long-term effects of taking the medication are difficult to measure.*

it is possible/impossible to measure sth *Using this method, it should be possible to measure the plant's growth rate.*

measure² *n*

an action, especially an official one, intended to deal with a particular problem

ADJECTIVES/NOUNS + measure

an extreme/drastic measure (=unusual and severe) *Drastic measures are needed if we are to fight global warming.*

a desperate measure (=one that you only use because you are in a very difficult situation) *The government was forced to take desperate measures to reduce its debts.*

a temporary/short-term measure (*also* **an interim measure** *formal*): *It's just a temporary measure until he finds somewhere else to live.*

an emergency measure *Emergency measures are needed to reduce the number of homeless people.*

appropriate measures *We will take appropriate measures to make sure the information remains private.*

all necessary measures *The army will take all necessary measures to protect the public.*

a precautionary/preventative measure (=in order to prevent something bad from happening) *He was kept in hospital overnight as a precautionary measure.*

a safety measure *New safety measures were introduced after the rail crash.*

a security measure *Cameras have been installed as a security measure.*

VERBS

take measures to do sth (=do something to deal with a problem) *We are taking measures to improve the situation.*

use a measure *The government has used various measures to silence the protests.*

introduce/bring in a measure *The authorities introduced tough new security measures.*

adopt a measure (=start using it) *They agreed to adopt measures to reduce pollution.*

announce a measure *Emergency measures have been announced.*

outline a measure (=describe it in general way) *He outlined the measures in his plan.*

PHRASES

a series of measures *They introduced a series of measures to encourage people to exercise more.*

measurement *n*

the length, height etc of something, or the activity of calculating this

ADJECTIVES

an accurate measurement *When making curtains, you need to have accurate measurements of the window.*

an exact/precise measurement *It's about 10 metres by 8 metres - I don't know the exact measurements.*

a careful measurement *Careful measurements of the human skull were taken and recorded.*

an objective measurement (=not influenced by opinions or feelings) *The test provides an objective measurement of the student's listening skills.*

NOUNS + measurement

sb's waist/chest/leg etc measurement *Her waist measurement is 28 inches.*

VERBS

take/make a measurement (=measure something) *Take measurements of the room before you buy any new furniture.*

take sb's measurements (=measure their body for a piece of clothing) *She was having her measurements taken for her wedding dress.*

get/obtain a measurement *In order to get an accurate measurement, you need to have the right equipment.*

record a measurement *The students recorded their measurements in their notebooks.*

medal *n*

a flat piece of metal, usually shaped like a coin, that is given to someone who has won a competition or who has done something brave

ADJECTIVES

a gold medal (=for first place) *He won the gold medal in the diving competition.*

a silver medal (=for second place) *She was awarded the silver medal for the 100 metres.*

a bronze medal (=for third place) *Morrell took the bronze medal in the long jump.*

an Olympic medal *He won a total of six Olympic medals.*

VERBS

win a medal *She won a medal at the Olympics.*

take a medal (=used when saying which person or team wins a medal) *German runner Stephan Freigang took the bronze medal.*

get/receive a medal *She received a medal from the Society of Arts.*

give/award sb a medal *He was given a medal for his courageous actions.*

be awarded a medal *The two women were awarded medals for services to the community.*

medal + NOUNS

a medal winner *Johnson was a silver medal winner at the Olympic Games.*

PREPOSITIONS

a medal for sth *The two boys were awarded medals for bravery.*

media Ac *n*

all the organizations, such as television, radio, and newspapers, that provide news and information for the public

> **Grammar**
>
> **Media** is often used in the phrase **the media**.
>
> Although **media** is a plural noun, you will often hear people use a singular verb after it: *The **media has** shown great interest in the story.*

ADJECTIVES/NOUNS + media

the national/local media (=for the whole country/part of a country) *The case received enormous publicity in the national media.*

the foreign media *The foreign media were very interested in these events.*

the news media *Do the news media have a role in forming public opinion?*

the mass media (=the media that large numbers of people watch, read etc) *The mass media has helped to call attention to environmental issues.*

the mainstream/popular media (=the media that most people watch, read etc) *Few of these events were reported in the mainstream media.*

online/digital media (=websites, blogs etc) *More and more people are using online media as their main source of news.*

media + NOUNS

media attention/interest *The story received worldwide media attention.*

media reports *Media reports suggest he is going to resign.*

media speculation (=reports in the media about what might happen or be true) *There was media speculation that the crisis would soon be at an end.*

media coverage (=how much something is reported in the media) *Media coverage of the case should have been restricted.*

media hype *disapproving* (=media attention making something seem better or more important than it is) *A great deal of media hype surrounded the release of the band's latest CD.*

a media campaign *The government launched a media campaign aimed at reducing drink driving.*

a media empire (=many newspapers, TV stations etc owned by someone) *Murdoch owns a global media empire.*

a media circus *disapproving* (=a situation in which there are too many reporters and people from the media trying to get news about something) *The trial has turned into a media circus.*

media studies (=the study of newspapers, radio, television etc) *She's doing a degree in media studies.*

PREPOSITIONS

in the media *There have been a lot of stories in the media about him.*

medical Ac *adj*

relating to medicine and the treatment of disease or injury

NOUNS

medical treatment/care/attention *Her son was ill and needed urgent medical treatment.*

medical advice/help *If you suffer from chest pains, you should seek medical advice immediately.*

medical research/science *Medical research may eventually lead to a cure for cancer.*

the medical profession (=doctors and other people whose work involves treating sick people) *A majority of the medical profession supports this view.*

medical supplies/equipment *Medical supplies are being flown out to victims of the earthquake.*

medical services/facilities *The country's medical services are among the best in the world.*

medical school *Sarah recently graduated from medical school.*

sb's medical history/record *The patient's medical history includes a number of heart-related problems.*

medical costs/expenses/bill *She couldn't pay her medical bills after a stay in hospital.*

medical insurance *Your medical insurance should cover the cost of the treatment.*

M

medication *n*

medicine or drugs given to people who are ill

PHRASES

be on medication (for sth) (=be taking a type of medicine) *He is on medication for his heart.*

VERBS

take medication (=regularly have it) *Are you taking any medication?*

go on medication (=start taking it) *Since I went on the medication, I've felt a lot better.*

come off medication (=stop taking it) *Her doctor told her to come off the medication as soon as she found out she was pregnant.*

put sb on (a course of) medication (=make someone start taking it) *He put me on a course of medication for my sleeping problems.*

a doctor prescribes medication (=arranges for someone to have it) *Doctors should explain the reasons for prescribing any medication.*

give sb medication (*also* **administer medication (to sb)** *formal*): *Teachers are not allowed to administer medication.*

change sb's medication *I started to feel worse after they changed my medication.*

respond to medication (=start to get better after taking it) *The study found that some patients responded better to medication than others.*

ADJECTIVES/NOUNS + medication

regular medication *He is on regular medication to control his blood pressure.*

long-term medication (=taken for a long time) *People with mental illness may require long-term medication.*

prescription medication (=for which you need a doctor's order) *In extreme cases, there are prescription medications for people who want to lose weight.*

PREPOSITIONS

medication for sth *She takes medication for high blood pressure.*

> **Medication or medicine?**
> **Medication** sounds more formal than **medicine**. You use **medication** about pills that a doctor gives you for a particular medical problem. **Medicine** is a more general word for any substance that is used to treat an illness: *Scientists are always trying to develop new* ***medicines****.*

medicine *n*

1 a substance used for treating illness

ADJECTIVES/NOUNS + medicine

a strong/powerful medicine *Patients were treated with a powerful medicine.*

an over-the-counter medicine (=one that you can buy without seeing a doctor) *Many people buy over-the-counter medicines to treat coughs and colds.*

a prescription medicine (=one that your doctor says you should have) *There are several prescription medicines that can be used to treat high blood pressure.*

VERBS

take a medicine *I have to take the medicine three times a day.*

give sb a medicine (*also* **administer a medicine (to sb)** *formal*): *The medicine is usually given to patients in tablet form.*

a doctor prescribes a medicine (=a doctor gives someone a piece of paper saying that they should have a medicine) *Your doctor can prescribe medicines which help treat allergies.*

PREPOSITIONS

a medicine for sth *The company has developed a new medicine for treating cancer.*

2 the treatment and study of illnesses and injuries

ADJECTIVES

modern medicine *Thanks to modern medicine, these babies will survive.*

Western medicine (=conventional medicine as developed in Western countries) *Many people turn to herbal remedies after Western medicine has failed.*

traditional medicine *The plant was used in traditional medicine for the treatment of stomach problems.*

conventional/orthodox medicine (=medicine based on modern medical science) *Patients should be able to choose between conventional medicine and other forms of medical treatment.*

alternative/complementary medicine (=medical treatments that are not part of modern medicine) *Various types of alternative medicine, particularly acupuncture, can give pain relief.*

herbal medicine (=medical treatments that use herbs) *Herbal medicine has been used for thousands of years.*

VERBS

study medicine *He went to study medicine at Leiden University.*

practise medicine *BrE*, **practice medicine** *AmE* (=work as a doctor) *Dr West has been practising medicine for 25 years.*

medium Ac *adj*

not large or small, long or short, high or low etc

PHRASES

of medium size *The town is of medium size.*

⚠ Don't say 'The town is medium size.'

of medium height/length *The girl was of medium height.*

of medium build (=used especially in

descriptions of people the police are looking for) *The police say that the man is of medium build.*

in the medium term (=in the next few months or years) *The future of the company looks good in the medium term.*

> **Medium** or **medium-sized?**
> You usually say **medium** when buying something in a shop or restaurant or when talking about your clothes size: *"What size sweater do you take?" "I'm a* ***medium****."*
> You use **medium-sized** especially about companies or places: *Many small and* ***medium-sized*** *companies have gone out of business.* | *York is a* ***medium-sized*** *city and it is easy to find your way around.*

meeting *n*

an event at which people meet to discuss and decide things

ADJECTIVES/NOUNS + meeting

a business meeting *He had to go into town for a business meeting.*

a formal/informal meeting *Trade had been discussed at an informal meeting of EU foreign ministers.*

a public meeting *A public meeting was held to discuss the proposal to build a new school.*

a private meeting *The senator attended a private meeting with the president.*

a general meeting *especially BrE* (=that anyone, or anyone in a particular organization, can go to) *The annual general meeting of the rugby club was held last night.*

a monthly/weekly meeting *I have my weekly meeting with the managing director.*

an annual meeting (=once a year) *The British Medical Association has its annual meeting tomorrow.*

an emergency meeting *The Council has called an emergency meeting to decide what action to take.*

a protest meeting *Anti-road campaigners are holding a protest meeting today.*

a committee/staff/board meeting *A staff meeting will be held at 3 p.m.*

a summit meeting (=between leaders of governments) *The prime minister is in Paris for a European summit meeting.*

VERBS + meeting

have a meeting *We're having a meeting next week to discuss the matter.*

hold a meeting (=have a meeting - more formal) *The meetings are usually held on a Friday.*

go to a meeting (*also* **attend a meeting** *formal*): *All staff members are expected to attend the meeting.*

arrange/organize a meeting *They hoped to arrange a meeting with the president.*

call a meeting (=ask for people to come to a meeting) *David Couper called a meeting to discuss the idea of a field laboratory.*

chair a meeting (=lead it) *The meeting was chaired by Professor Jones of the University of York.*

host a meeting (=provide the place and everything needed for a meeting) *King Abdullah will host a meeting between the two leaders.*

begin/open a meeting *She opened the meeting by welcoming everyone.*

close/end a meeting *Before I close the meeting, does anyone have any further questions?*

address a meeting (=speak to the people at a meeting) *A member of Greenpeace addressed the protest meeting.*

adjourn a meeting (=make it stop for a period of time) *This meeting is adjourned until tomorrow.*

> **Have a meeting** or **hold a meeting?**
> **Hold a meeting** sounds more formal and is often used in the passive when talking about the place or time at which the meeting happens.

meeting + VERBS

a meeting takes place (=it happens) *The meeting took place on September 26th.*

a meeting begins/starts *As soon as the meeting began, differences between the leaders began to emerge.*

a meeting ends *The meeting ended around 10.30.*

a meeting breaks up (=it ends and people leave) *The meeting broke up without a deal.*

meeting + NOUNS

a meeting room *The hotel has meeting rooms available to hire.*

PREPOSITIONS

in/at a meeting *She said that Mr Coleby was in a meeting.*

a meeting with sb *He had further meetings with Serbian officials.*

a meeting between sb (and sb) *The talks are the first formal meeting between the two leaders.*

a meeting of sb *The comments were made during a meeting of senior politicians.*

a meeting about/on sth *A public meeting about the future of the gallery will be held next week.*

PHRASES

the minutes of a meeting (=a written record of what people have discussed at a meeting) *The minutes of last week's meeting have now been distributed.*

a series of meetings *Managers have held a series of meetings to discuss the problem.*

M

melody *n*

a song or tune, or the main tune in a piece of music

ADJECTIVES

a strong melody (=good and easy to notice) *Beatles' songs usually have a strong melody.*

a haunting melody (=beautiful, in a sad way that you remember) *The song has beautiful words and a haunting melody.*

a good melody *What makes a good melody?*

a sweet/pretty/lovely melody (=pleasant to listen to) *She played a sweet melody on the violin.*

a simple melody *I like songs with a simple melody.*

a gentle melody *Irish folk songs often have gentle melodies.*

a catchy melody (=easy to remember) *A pop song needs to have a catchy melody.*

VERBS

have a melody *All his songs have good melodies.*

write/compose a melody *First we write the melody, then we think about the words.*

play/sing a melody *He was playing a gentle melody on his guitar.*

carry the melody (=play or sing it, while other voices or instruments play other notes) *The soprano voice carries the melody.*

whistle a melody (=produce it by blowing air through your lips) *Paddy whistled the melody while Katie danced.*

melody + NOUNS

the melody line (=the melody, rather than other parts of the music) *He played the melody line to me on the piano.*

member *n*

a person or country that belongs to a club, group, or organization

ADJECTIVES

a senior/junior member (=with a higher or lower rank) *A senior member of the government has resigned.*

a leading member (=an important member) *Lucas became a leading member of the Green Party.*

an active member (=one who takes part in many activities of an organization) *The couple are active members of the church.*

a full member (=one who has all the possible rights of a member) *At that time, women were not allowed to be full members of the club.*

an associate member (=one who has fewer rights than a full member) *Turkey is an associate member of the European Union.*

an honorary member (=one who has been given membership as an honour) *He was made an honorary member of the society.*

ADJECTIVES/NOUNS + member

a family/team/staff/committee/crew member *Close friendships developed between crew members on the ship. | He became a staff member of the Institute in 2002.*

a founder/founding member (=one who helped start an organization) *He was a founder member of the African National Congress.*

VERBS

be a member *Lisa is a member of the school hockey team.*

become a member *Germany became a member of NATO in 1954.*

recruit members (=get new members) *The club launched an advertising campaign to recruit new members.*

PHRASES

a member of staff *All members of staff have to attend regular training sessions.*

a member of the public *Members of the public were invited to put forward suggestions.*

a member of society (=a citizen) *We want our children to become productive members of society.*

a member of a family *I was the only member of our family who had been to university.*

member + NOUNS

a member state/country/nation (=a country that belongs to an international organization) *Some member states of the European Union opposed this policy.*

PREPOSITIONS

a member of sth *A few members of the audience laughed nervously.*

membership *n*

the right to be a member of a club, group, or organization

ADJECTIVES

annual membership *Annual membership of The Hilton Club is $200 per year.*

full membership (=with all the rights that are allowed to members) *Poland applied for full membership of the European Union.*

associate membership (=with only some of the rights allowed to members) *You have the choice of full club membership for $10,000 or associate membership for $2,500.*

free membership *Students get free membership of the tennis club.*

honorary membership (=given as an honour) *His work won him honorary membership of the London Medical Society.*

NOUNS + membership

club/party/gym etc membership *How much do you pay for your gym membership?*

life/lifetime membership *He was offered a lifetime membership of the society.*

VERBS

apply for membership (=officially ask to be a member) *To apply for membership, simply return the attached form.*

seek membership (=try to become a member) *The country is seeking membership of the European Union.*

qualify for membership (=be able to become a member) *To qualify for membership, you must be over 18 years of age.*

be granted membership (=be accepted as a member) *Montenegro was granted membership of the UN in 2006.*

be refused/denied membership *She was refused membership of the club because she was a woman.*

have/hold membership (=be a member) *Only 16% of people hold membership of a political party.*

renew your membership (=make it continue for a longer period) *I forgot to renew my club membership.*

cancel your membership *He cancelled his gym membership because he never used it.*

sb's membership expires/lapses (=it comes to an end) *We will send you a letter when your membership is about to expire.*

membership + NOUNS

a membership card *You will need to show your membership card when you enter the sports centre.*

a membership fee/subscription (=money you must pay to become a member) *The current annual membership fee is 20 euros.*

membership requirements (=the conditions needed to become a member) *She did not fulfil the membership requirements of the organization.*

PREPOSITIONS

membership of sth *He did not qualify for membership of the group.*

PHRASES

be eligible for membership (=have the right to ask to be member) *All former students of the university are automatically eligible for membership.*

memoir *n*

a book by a famous or important person, in which they write about their life and experiences

ADJECTIVES

a personal memoir *The book is a personal memoir of her childhood in Ireland.*

a political memoir *Political memoirs are often very long and dull.*

an unpublished memoir *She left an unpublished memoir after she died.*

VERBS

write your memoirs *He is planning to write his memoirs after he retires from politics.*

publish your memoirs *The famous biologist has just published his memoirs.*

read sb's memoirs *Anyone who has read Nelson Mandela's memoirs will know how much South Africa has changed.*

PREPOSITIONS

in your memoirs *He described the incident in his memoirs.*

memorable *adj*

very good, enjoyable, or unusual, and worth remembering

NOUNS

a memorable experience *The beautiful scenery made the boat trip a memorable experience.*

a memorable occasion *The concert should be a memorable occasion, with some of the world's top musicians playing together.*

a memorable moment *There are some memorable moments in the film.*

a memorable day/night/evening *Today is a memorable day in our country's history.*

a memorable performance *Brad Pitt gives a truly memorable performance.*

a memorable phrase/line *In Churchill's memorable phrase, "it was not the beginning of the end, but the end of the beginning."*

ADVERBS

truly memorable *We're hoping that the party will be a truly memorable occasion.*

particularly memorable *The principal of the college made a particularly memorable speech.*

VERBS

make sth memorable *The hotel does everything it can to make your stay memorable.*

prove to be/turn out to be memorable *The visit turned out to be memorable, but not in the way he had intended.*

PREPOSITIONS

be memorable for sth *The day was memorable for many reasons.*

memorial *n*

something, especially a stone with writing on it, that reminds people of someone who has died

ADJECTIVES

a national memorial *They want to establish a national memorial to the victims of the war.*

a permanent/lasting memorial *They honoured his bravery by erecting a permanent memorial.*

a fitting memorial (=a suitable memorial) *The statue will be a fitting memorial to the man who founded the college.*

VERBS

build a memorial (*also* **erect a memorial** *formal*): *The city authorities built a memorial in his honour.*

M

a memorial commemorates sb/sth (=it is built to show that you remember a person or event) *The memorial commemorates the soldiers who died during World War II.*

serve as a memorial *The park will serve as a memorial to the dead.*

NOUNS + memorial

a war memorial *The war memorial honours local people who lost their lives in World War I.*

memorial + NOUNS

a memorial stone *There is a memorial stone outside the church.*

PREPOSITIONS

a memorial to sb *Arlington House was originally built as a memorial to George Washington.*

a memorial for sb *We visited a memorial for the soldiers who died in the war.*

memory *n*

1 someone's ability to remember things, places, experiences etc

ADJECTIVES

a good/excellent memory *I wish my memory was as good as yours.*

a bad/poor/terrible memory *A student with a poor memory may struggle in school.*

short-term memory (=for things that you have just seen, heard, or done) *John has problems with short-term memory.*

long-term memory (=for things that happened a long time ago) *Most people's long-term memory is limited.*

a photographic memory (=the ability to remember every detail of things that you have seen) *He had a photographic memory for faces, for clothes, even for the way people walked.*

VERBS

remain/stay/stick in your memory (=be remembered for a long time) *That day will remain in my memory forever.*

refresh/jog your memory (=help someone to remember something) *Perhaps this photograph will refresh your memory?*

lose your memory (=become unable to remember things that happened in the past) *The blow on the head caused him to lose his memory.*

commit sth to memory *formal* (=make yourself remember something) *I've already committed his name to memory.*

memory + NOUNS

memory loss (*also* **loss of memory**) (=when you cannot remember things) *The condition can cause dizziness and memory loss.*

a memory lapse (*also* **a lapse of memory**) (=when you cannot remember something for a short time) *The alcohol seemed to make him suffer lapses of memory.*

PHRASES

have a memory like a sieve (=forget things very easily) *I'm sorry, I have a memory like a sieve. I forgot you were coming today!*

have a short memory (=if you have a short memory, you soon forget things) *Voters have short memories.*

have a long memory (=if you have a long memory, you remember things for a long time) *Football fans with long memories may remember what happened to the club in the early 1970s.*

sth is fresh in your memory (=you can remember it well because it happened recently) *The game is still fresh in my memory.*

sth is etched in your memory (=it is impossible to forget) *The date was etched in my memory.*

if my memory serves (me correctly/right) (=used to say that you are almost certain you have remembered something correctly) *If my memory serves me correctly, Johnson was also there.*

PREPOSITIONS

in your memory *She will always stay in my memory.*

from memory (=using your memory and not reading something) *The pianist played the whole piece from memory.*

a memory for sth *She has a terrible memory for names.*

2 something that you remember from the past about a person, place, or experience

ADJECTIVES/NOUNS + memory

good/bad etc memories *He left school with good memories of his time there.*

happy/unhappy memories *Many people have unhappy memories of being forced to play team sports.*

fond memories (=about someone or something you like) *She had fond memories of her aunt and uncle.*

a painful memory (=very upsetting) *He sobbed as he relived the painful memory.*

a vivid memory (=very clear and detailed) *I have vivid memories of that summer.*

a clear memory *I have a clear memory of the first time I met David.*

a dim/distant memory (=not clear, from a long time ago) *He had only dim memories of his father, who had died when he was four.*

a vague memory (=not clear) *I have a vague memory of visiting them when I was small.*

sb's earliest memory *My earliest memory is playing in my grandmother's garden, when I was three years old.*

an abiding/enduring/lasting memory (=that you will always have) *The children's abiding memory of their father is of his patience and gentleness.*

a childhood memory *Going to the farm brought back happy childhood memories.*

VERBS

have memories/a memory of sth (=remember something) *I have memories of walking up the street when I was a little boy.*

have no memory of sth (=not remember something) *She had no memory of the accident.*

relive a memory (=talk about past events so you remember them again) *Seeing her again was an excuse to relive old memories.*

bring back memories (*also* **rekindle/revive/evoke memories** *formal*) (=make you remember something) *For many older people, the film brought back memories of the war.*

erase/banish a memory (=get rid of a memory) *She spent several years trying to erase the memory of what had happened.*

cherish/treasure a memory (=the memory is very important to you) *I cherish the memory of our last day together.*

a memory fades (=becomes less clear and accurate) *The bad memories have faded with time.*

PHRASES

a place is full of memories (=makes you remember things that happened there) *My old home is full of unhappy memories.*

memories come flooding back (=you suddenly remember things clearly) *When I saw the pictures, the memories came flooding back.*

be haunted by the memory of sth (=be unable to forget something unhappy) *He is haunted by memories of his unhappy childhood.*

PREPOSITIONS

sb's memory of sth *She talked about her memories of the war.*

menacing *adj* THESAURUS **frightening**

mend *v* THESAURUS **repair**[1]

mental Ac *adj* relating to someone's mind

NOUNS

a mental illness *Many people suffer from mental illness at some time in their lives.*

mental health *Stress at work can affect your mental health.*

mental problems *John had to take time off college because of mental problems.*

sb's mental state/condition *His family were worried about his mental state.*

a mental hospital *Her mother received treatment in a mental hospital.*

a mental patient *Mental patients are more likely to harm themselves than other people.*

a mental picture/image *I have a mental image of the house where I grew up.*

a mental attitude *You need to develop a positive mental attitude.*

a mental scar (=a feeling of fear or sadness that remains with you for a long time after an unpleasant experience) *He still carries the mental scars from the attack.*

mental development *Some people say that television is harmful to children's mental development.*

mentality *n* THESAURUS **mind**

mention[1] *v*

to talk or write about something, usually quickly and without saying very much or giving details

ADVERBS

rarely/seldom mention sth/sb *She rarely mentions her parents.*

frequently mention sth/sb *Lucy frequently mentioned a man named Charles.*

repeatedly mention sth/sb *He repeatedly mentioned the fact that he needed money.*

barely/hardly mention sth/sb *He was a very important figure, but textbooks hardly mention him.*

mention sth/sb briefly *The subject is only mentioned briefly in the book.*

casually mention sth/sb (=as though they are not important) *He casually mentioned that he was leaving home.*

directly/specifically/explicitly mention sth/sb *Although he didn't mention my name directly, I knew he was talking about me.*

NOUNS

mention sb's name *Why does he look angry every time I mention Clare's name?*

mention a fact *He never mentioned the fact that he was married.*

mention a subject/topic *I won't mention the subject again.*

mention a word *Neither of them dares mention the word 'divorce'.*

mention the possibility of sth *She mentioned the possibility of moving back to Germany.*

VERBS

fail/neglect/omit to mention sth (=not mention something, especially something that you should have mentioned) *She omitted to mention that she had not been to university.*

forget to mention sb/sth *I forgot to mention something - the next meeting is on June 2nd.*

avoid mentioning sth *They both avoided mentioning John, though Anne longed to talk about him.*

happen to mention sth (=mention it by chance) *I happened to mention that my father was a doctor.*

PREPOSITIONS

mention sth/sb to sb *I mentioned the idea to Joan, and she seemed to like it.*

M

mention sth/sb as sth *He mentioned Mark as a possible candidate for the job.*

PHRASES

as I mentioned earlier (*also* **as I mentioned previously**) *As I mentioned earlier, there have been a lot of changes recently.*

it is worth mentioning that... (=it is important enough to mention) *It's worth mentioning that they only studied a very small number of cases.*

mention sth in passing (=without much detail, especially while you are talking about something else) *She mentioned in passing that she had an eight-year-old son.*

to mention but a few (=used when you are only giving a few examples) *She had taken photography, art, and pottery classes, to mention but a few.*

mention² *n*

when someone mentions something or someone in a conversation, piece of writing etc

ADJECTIVES

a brief/quick mention *Her research only gets a brief mention in his article.*

special/particular mention *Mrs McMillan deserves particular mention for all her hard work.*

explicit/specific mention (=a clear and direct mention) *Although there is no explicit mention of a wife, the implication is that he is married.*

a passing mention (=a brief mention, while you are talking about something else) *There was only a passing mention of the event in the paper.*

little mention *There has been little mention of the drug's side-effects.*

VERBS

get/receive a mention *They all get a mention in the book.*

give sb a mention *I'd like to give a special mention to Paul Smith, who made this event possible.*

deserve/merit a mention (=be good, large etc enough to get one) *There is one other person who deserves a mention.*

earn a mention (=be mentioned) *The factory even earned a mention in a famous song.*

hear mention of sth/sb (=hear them mentioned) *It was the first time I had ever heard mention of Socrates.*

PHRASES

make no/little/some mention of sth (=not mention it at all, not very much etc) *He made no mention of his wife's illness.*

be worthy of mention (=deserve to be talked about) *This book is particularly worthy of mention for the quality of its writing.*

the mere mention of sth (=the fact of saying something rather than discussing it in detail) *The mere mention of his name caused her to burst into tears.*

at the mention of sth (=when it is mentioned) *At the mention of a trip to the beach, the children got very excited.*

menu *n*

1 a list of all the kinds of food that are available for a meal, especially in a restaurant

ADJECTIVES/NOUNS + menu

the dinner/lunch/breakfast menu *The lunch menu is only $25.*

a two-course/three-course etc menu *We were hungry, so we chose the four-course menu.*

a set/fixed menu (=which only has certain dishes on it) *Dinner is three courses from a set menu.*

an à la carte menu (=with different dishes you can choose from) *In the evening there is a full à la carte menu.*

an extensive menu (=with many different dishes) *They have an extensive menu that includes Chinese, Thai, and Vietnamese food.*

a children's menu *I asked the waiter if there was a children's menu.*

a vegetarian menu *There's a good vegetarian menu for people who do not eat meat.*

the dessert menu (=with sweet food you eat after your main meal) *I chose apple pie from the dessert menu.*

VERBS

ask for the menu/ask to see the menu *We asked for the dessert menu.*

bring the menu *The waiter will bring you the menu.*

read/study the menu *Sam read the menu, but didn't see anything he wanted to eat.*

look at the menu (=read it) *She looked at the menu and decided to have the salad.*

choose/order sth from the menu *He ordered a chicken dish from the menu.*

have a menu *The restaurant has an excellent menu.*

a menu includes sth *The menu includes several vegetarian dishes.*

PREPOSITIONS

on the menu *She chose the most expensive dish on the menu.*

2 a list of choices on a computer screen

ADJECTIVES/NOUNS + menu

the main menu *To return to the main menu, click 'back'.*

the file menu *Save your file using the file menu.*

the start/help menu *Select 'help' from the start menu.*

a drop-down/pull-down menu (=that comes down from a word when you click on it) *The drop-down menu offers you a list of choices.*

a pop-up menu (=that appears on the screen when you click on a word) *Choose 'Contact us' from the pop-up menu.*

VERBS + menu

select/choose sth from the menu *You can save your favourite websites so you can select them instantly from a menu.*

go to the menu *Go back to the main menu.*

open the menu *He opened the menu and selected 'Exit'.*

call up the menu (=ask the computer to show the menu) *Click on the toolbar to call up the menu.*

merchandise *n* THESAURUS **product**

merchant *n*

someone whose job is to buy and sell wine, coal etc, or a small company that does this. **Merchant** is often used to talk about people who lived in past times

ADJECTIVES

a rich/wealthy/prosperous merchant *The house was originally built for a wealthy merchant.*

a local merchant *The square was filled with the stalls of local merchants.*

a foreign merchant *Many foreign merchants left after the fishing industry declined.*

NOUNS + merchant

a wool/cloth merchant *The wool merchants bought the wool from the farmers at a very low price.*

a wine/coal/timber merchant *You can find bottles of the wine at your local wine merchants.*

a builders' merchant *The builders' merchants sells bags of powder for making concrete.*

mercy *n*

forgiveness or kindness shown to someone you have the power to hurt or punish

VERBS

show mercy (to sb) *He showed no mercy to his enemies.*

have mercy (on sb) (=show mercy - often used in prayers) *"God have mercy on me!" she cried.*

ask/beg/plead for mercy *She continued the punishment, although they begged for mercy.*

scream/cry for mercy *He screamed for mercy, shouting "Don't shoot!"*

pray for mercy *She prayed for mercy and forgiveness.*

expect no mercy *The cold look in the guards' eyes told her she could expect no mercy.*

deserve mercy *The killers do not deserve any mercy.*

mercy + NOUNS

a mercy mission (=a journey to help people) *They made several mercy missions to the orphanage.*

PREPOSITIONS

have mercy on sb *The soldiers had no mercy on anyone they took prisoner.*

show mercy to sb *Please show mercy to my son.*

without mercy (=very severely) *They will be punished without mercy.*

PHRASES

an act of mercy *The men were to be released from jail as an act of mercy.*

throw yourself on sb's mercy (=hope that someone will show mercy to you) *He had to throw himself on the mercy of the court.*

merit *n*

an advantage or good feature of something, or the fact that someone or something is good

ADJECTIVES

great merit *It seems to me that the idea has great merit.*

considerable merit (=a lot of merit) *There is considerable merit in using this kind of approach.*

artistic/literary/technical etc merit *There was no literary merit in his poems.*

the relative/comparative merits of sb/sth (=used when comparing two things or people) *We have to consider the relative merits of the two candidates.*

of outstanding/exceptional merit (=unusually good) *The prize is for students whose work is of outstanding merit.*

of dubious/questionable merit (=not very good) *His early paintings are of dubious merit.*

VERBS

have merit *The painting had some artistic merit.*

have its merits (=have some good qualities) *Each idea has its merits.*

discuss/debate the merits of sth *They were discussing the merits of sending soldiers to the area.*

consider/judge the merits of sth *The committee is considering the merits of the proposal.*

weigh (up) the merits of sth (=consider whether something is a good idea) *The committee will weigh up the merits of the plan.*

question the merits of sth (=not be sure if it is a good idea) *People began to question the merits of nuclear energy.*

see/recognize the merits of sth *I can see the merits of this argument.*

see no/little/any merit in sth *She could see no merit in his suggestion.*

PREPOSITIONS

merit in sth *There is some merit in what he says.*

merit to sth *There was little merit to that argument.*

on merit (=based on how good you are) *Students are selected on merit.*

M

THESAURUS: merit

benefit, merit, virtue, the good/great/best thing about sth, the beauty of sth is that → advantage

mess *n*

a situation in which a place is dirty or untidy, or there are a lot of awkward problems

ADJECTIVES

a terrible/awful/horrible mess *The country is in a terrible mess.*

a big/huge mess *Why is my life such a big mess?*

a complete/total mess *I'm afraid my house is a complete mess.*

a real mess (*also* **a right mess** *BrE informal*): *The files were a real mess – it took me days to sort them out.*

a financial/economic mess *He made a lot of money but is now in a financial mess.*

A fine mess

People sometimes describe a very bad situation as a **fine mess**: *You've got yourself into a* ***fine mess*** *this time.*

VERBS

make a mess (*also* **create a mess** *formal*): *You can play in here, but try not to make a mess.*

make a mess of sth *The last government made a mess of the economy.*

leave a mess (*also* **leave sth in a mess**) *They left a terrible mess in the kitchen.*

clean up/clear up a mess *The previous manager made a lot of mistakes, and now I have to clear up the mess.*

look a mess *His face was covered with bruises and he looked a mess.*

deal with a mess *A waiter came to deal with the mess.*

sort out/fix a mess (=deal with it) *Don't worry – we'll sort this mess out.*

get (sb) into a mess *He borrowed a lot of money on his credit card, and got himself into a real mess.*

get (sb) out of a mess *My parents are going to help me get out of this mess.*

PREPOSITIONS

in a mess *especially BrE*: *The company is in a mess.*

PHRASES

a bit of a mess *Our records are in a bit of a mess.*

message *n*

1 a spoken or written piece of information that you send to another person or leave for them

ADJECTIVES/NOUNS + message

a brief/short message *She left a short message on his voicemail.*

an urgent/important/vital message *I have an urgent message for you from your mother.*

a personal message *The prime minister sent him a personal message of support.*

a text message *My phone beeps when I get a text message.*

a voicemail/answerphone message *I listened to his answerphone message several times.*

a telephone/phone message *There was a telephone message for her to call the office.*

a secret message *He'd been sending secret messages written in code.*

VERBS + message

give sb a message/pass on a message *Don't worry, I'll give him your message when I see him.*

send (sb) a message *Danny keeps sending me text messages asking me out.*

leave (sb) a message *He left a message saying he would probably be late.*

get/receive a message *Did you get my message?*

take a message (=write down a message from someone for someone else) *Ellen isn't here. Can I take a message?*

forward a message (=send it on to someone else – used especially about an email) *I'll forward her message to you when I log on.*

write (sb) a message *Annie wrote a message on Helen's Facebook page.*

read a message *It took me ages to read all my email messages when I got back from holiday.*

check your messages (=read or listen to them) *I checked my phone messages when I got home and there was a call from Eddie.*

message + VERBS

a message says sth *His message said that I should meet him here at one o'clock.*

a message is waiting for sb *She found a message waiting for her when she got back to the hotel.*

PREPOSITIONS

a message for sb *Chris, I've got a message for you from your mum.*

a message to sb *He is with a client at the moment, but I'll try to get a message to him.*

a message of support/sympathy/congratulations *Fans from all over the world have sent me messages of support.*

a message from sb *There's a message from your daughter on the answering machine.*

a message about sth *What was his message about anyway?*

2 the most important idea in a book, film, speech etc

ADJECTIVES

a strong/powerful message *He urged the UN to send a strong message to countries that support terrorism.*

a clear message *By raising interest rates, the*

M

Bank of England is sending out a clear message to the markets.

the basic/key/core/main/fundamental message (=the most basic and important one) *The main message is that we need to reduce the amount of waste we produce.*

conflicting/contradictory/mixed messages (=containing two different messages that cannot both be true or correct) *The public is getting contradictory messages from the government about immigration.*

a hidden/subliminal message (=that you are not conscious of) *He claims that the lyrics of the song contain subliminal messages.*

a positive/negative message *This sends a very negative message to investors.*

the right/wrong message *It's vitally important that we get the right message across to voters.*

a religious/social/political message *I think most of the film's audience will not understand its social message.*

a serious message *Behind the jokes there is a serious message in the speech.*

VERBS

get across/put across/convey a message *He failed to get his message across to voters.*

spread a message *We try to spread the Christian message through tolerance, not intolerance.*

send (out) a message (=make something clear to people in general) *The verdict sends out a clear message: the law applies to rich and poor alike.*

ram/drive/hammer/drum home a message (=emphasize a message by repeating it a lot) *The Chancellor's speech rammed home the message that cutting public spending is the government's top priority.*

preach a message *Why is he allowed to go around preaching a message of hate?*

PREPOSITIONS

a message about sth *The book sends a clear message about the evils of war.*

a message of sth *The president's speech carried a message of peace and hope.*

a message to sb *This sends out the wrong message to teenagers.*

method Ac *n*

a planned way of doing something, especially one that a lot of people know about and use

ADJECTIVES

a simple/cheap/quick method *Most people find cash the simplest method of payment.*

an effective/efficient method *Some methods are more effective than others.*

an ingenious method (=clever and unusual) *He devised some ingenious methods of raising money.*

a reliable method (=likely to give the result you want) *We need a more reliable method of predicting earthquakes.*

the usual method *The usual method is to cook the chestnuts in the oven.*

a common method (=often used) *Freezing is a common method of preserving food.*

an unusual/unorthodox method *Mr Bright has some very unusual teaching methods. | Some very unorthodox methods were being tried.*

an alternative method (=different from the usual one) *Try to use alternative methods of transport, such as cycling or taking the bus.*

the traditional/conventional method (=usual) *Farmers are being encouraged to return to more traditional methods of farming.*

modern methods *Modern methods of solving crime depend a lot on genetic evidence.*

a tried-and-tested/proven method (=that has been tried and definitely works) *Tried-and-tested methods must not be abandoned.*

a suitable method *No single method is suitable for all occasions.*

VERBS

use a method (*also* **employ a method** *formal*): *Let's try again using a different method.*

adopt a method (=start using it) *Other companies adopted Japanese business methods.*

devise a method (=invent one) *Scientists have devised a method of recycling contaminated oil.*

find/discover a method *They found new methods of protest.*

change a method *The company has changed its accounting methods.*

improve a method *We are working to improve our farming methods.*

NOUNS + method

working methods *We need to change our working methods.*

teaching methods *We're always interested in learning about new teaching methods.*

farming methods *Farming methods have changed a lot over the last 100 years.*

PREPOSITIONS

a method of (doing) sth *The doctors will decide on the best method of treatment.*

a method for (doing) sth *There are several methods for dealing with this type of situation.*

methodical *adj* THESAURUS > careful

meticulous *adj* THESAURUS > careful

microscopic *adj* THESAURUS > tiny

midday *n*

12 o'clock in the middle of the day

midday + NOUNS

a midday meal *She began to prepare the midday meal for herself and her mother.*

M

the midday sun *The inside of the car was hot from the midday sun.*

PREPOSITIONS

at midday *We stopped work at midday for lunch.*

midnight *n* 12 o'clock at night

PHRASES

two minutes etc past/to midnight *At twelve minutes past midnight he received a signal.*

at/on the stroke of midnight (=at exactly midnight) *The book will go on sale at the stroke of midnight.*

the clock strikes midnight (=the clock makes twelve sounds at midnight) *What will you be doing as the clock strikes midnight?*

midnight on Monday/Tuesday etc (*also* **midnight Monday/Tuesday etc** *AmE*): *Campaigning officially started at midnight on Friday.*

midnight + NOUNS

a midnight feast/snack *The children had planned to have a midnight feast.*

a midnight walk/stroll *I was just out for a midnight stroll.*

the midnight train *I'm catching the midnight train to Paris.*

PREPOSITIONS/ADVERBS

at midnight *The party began at 8 p.m. and finished at midnight.*

around/about midnight *The rain stopped around midnight.*

after/before midnight *He got back just after midnight.*

nearly/almost midnight *I look at my watch and I see it's nearly midnight.*

past/gone midnight (=after midnight) *It was past midnight and he was getting tired.*

by midnight *I'll be home by midnight.*

until midnight *The bar is open until midnight.*

> ⚠ Don't say 'in the midnight' or 'in midnight'. Say **at midnight** if you mean "at 12 o'clock": *I heard the clock strike at midnight.* If you mean "late at night", use the phrase **in the middle of the night**: *The telephone rang in the middle of the night.*

mild *adj*

1 mild weather is fairly warm

ADVERBS

very mild *The region is enjoying very mild weather.*

relatively mild *Denmark's relatively mild climate suits this tree.*

quite mild *It's going to be wet and windy, but quite mild.*

unusually/exceptionally mild *We have had an unusually mild winter.*

unseasonably mild (=warmer than usual at that time of year) *It was February and the weather was unseasonably mild.*

NOUNS

mild weather *The mild weather is expected to continue into December.*

a mild climate *The island has a mild climate.*

a mild winter *This plant may survive outside in a mild winter.*

a mild evening/night *It was a mild night, so I took the blanket off the bed.*

mild temperatures *Demand for heating fuel is lower than usual due to the mild temperatures.*

2 a mild illness, problem, feeling etc is not serious, severe, or strong

ADVERBS

very mild *The side effects were very mild.*

relatively mild *His punishment was relatively mild by the standards of the time.*

only mild *At first Sophie listened with only mild interest.*

fairly/pretty mild *His criticisms were pretty mild.*

NOUNS

a mild illness/disease/infection *Even relatively mild diseases can cause long-term damage.*

a mild punishment/criticism *Three months in prison seems a very mild punishment for such a serious offence.*

a mild form of sth *He has a mild form of the illness.*

a mild case of sth *As a child she had a mild case of polio.*

miles THESAURUS > far

military[1] Ac *adj*

relating to the army, navy, or air force

NOUNS

military action *They were right to take military action to stop the invasion.*

a military operation *The soldiers were taking part in a major military operation.*

military force *We will use military force to protect our country.*

military power *They were concerned about Germany's growing military power.*

military forces *Australia is ready to send military forces to the area if necessary.*

a military base *A US military base in Afghanistan has been attacked.*

a military aircraft/plane/helicopter *A military aircraft has been shot down.*

a military leader/commander/officer *He is the country's top military leader.*

military personnel (=people who are members of the army) *The police worked alongside military personnel to keep law and order.*

military service (=a period of time when every man in a country has to serve in the army, navy etc) *He avoided military service during the Vietnam War.*

a military government/regime/dictatorship *The country is run by a military government.*

military² Ac *n especially AmE*

the military forces of a country

ADJECTIVES

a strong/powerful military *We need a strong military to protect our country.*

the US/Russian etc military *The US military will drop aid supplies in the area.*

VERBS

join the military *They wanted to join the military to defend their country.*

serve in the military *He served in the military for eight years.*

leave the military *After leaving the military, he became a security guard.*

order the military to do sth *The president has ordered the military to continue its withdrawal.*

PHRASES

a member of the military *This was the first time that a member of the military had been found guilty of a human rights violation.*

PREPOSITIONS

in the military *Both my brothers are in the military.*

The military is used especially in American English. In British English, people often use **the (armed) forces** instead.

mill *n* THESAURUS ▸ **factory**

mind *n*

your thoughts or your ability to think, feel, and imagine things

ADJECTIVES

the human mind *Scientists still do not fully understand how the human mind works.*

a brilliant mind *Hawking has one of the most brilliant minds of his generation.*

a logical mind *You need to have a very logical mind to be a computer programmer.*

a suspicious mind *I have a naturally suspicious mind and I never trust anyone.*

an open mind (=without fixed opinions about something) *She went into the debate about nuclear energy with an open mind.*

a closed mind (=with fixed opinions and unwilling to change your ideas) *The people had closed minds and they would not listen to what he was saying.*

a curious/enquiring mind (=one that wants to find out more about things) *When she was young she had a curious mind and was hungry for knowledge.*

the subconscious/unconscious mind (=the part of your mind that you do not realize you have and which affects your behaviour) *These experiences are buried deep in the child's subconscious mind.*

a sick/twisted/warped/depraved mind (=a very strange and cruel mind) *The killer must have had a very sick mind.*

VERBS + mind

sth enters/comes into your mind (=you think of something) *The thought entered my mind that she might be lying.*

sth crosses/goes through your mind (=you think of something, especially for a short time) *The idea never crossed my mind.*

use your mind *Children should be taught to use their minds.*

keep your mind on sth (=keep your attention on something) *I found it hard to keep my mind on my work.*

concentrate/focus your mind (=make someone pay attention to something) *The attack concentrated people's minds on the dangers of religious extremism.*

lose your mind (=become crazy) *You think I'm losing my mind, but I'm not.*

get sb/sth out of your mind/off your mind (=stop thinking about someone or something) *I couldn't get that day out of my mind.*

broaden the mind (=develop your mind because you get new experiences) *They say that travel broadens the mind.*

control sb's mind *Do you think that advertisers are able to control people's minds?*

mind + VERBS

sb's mind wanders/drifts (=someone starts to think of other things) *Melissa looked out of the window and let her mind wander.*

sb's mind works *I really don't understand how that man's mind works.*

PHRASES

there is no doubt in sb's mind (=used when someone feels completely sure about something) *There was no doubt in my mind that it was the right decision to make.*

at the back of my mind (=used when you are aware of something, especially when you are not completely sure or clear about it) *At the back of my mind I had the funny feeling that I'd met her somewhere before.*

sb's state of mind (=how someone feels and whether he or she is upset, frightened etc) *Her family became worried about her state of mind.*

sb's frame of mind (=how someone feels – used especially about someone's attitude to something they are going to do) *You need to go into the exam in the right frame of mind.*

sb's mind is on sth (=someone is thinking about or paying attention to something rather than other things) *My mind is on my work.*

M

sth is on sb's mind/preys on sb's mind (=someone worries about something) *Her father's illness was on her mind.*

sb's mind is full of sth (=someone thinks a lot about something) *Her mind was full of big ideas about how she was going to change the world.*

sth is fresh in sb's mind (=someone remembers it clearly) *The event is still fresh in most people's minds.*

have a picture/image in your mind *Do you have a clear picture in your mind of what you want?*

know what's going on in sb's mind (=know what someone is thinking) *I never know what's going on in her mind.*

THESAURUS: mind

head
the place where someone's mind is – use this especially when talking about the thoughts that are in someone's mind:
*I can't **get** him **out of my head**. | You need to **get it into your head** that you've done nothing wrong. | To keep myself calm, I counted to ten in my head. | She's so quiet – you never quite know **what's going on inside her head*** (=what she is thinking).

subconscious
the part of your mind that influences the way you think or behave, even though you may not realize this is happening, and which makes you have dreams:
*She suddenly remembered a traumatic incident that had been **buried deep in her subconscious**. | During the daytime our conscious minds are active, but during the night **the subconscious** takes over.*

psyche *formal*
someone's mind, especially their feelings and attitudes, and the way these influence their character – used especially when talking about people's minds in general:
*Freud has provided an account of **the human psyche**'s stages of development. | The need for love is **deeply buried in our psyche**.*

mentality
a particular way of thinking that a group of people have, especially one that you think is wrong or bad:
*I just don't **understand the mentality** of these people. | They all seem to have a kind of **victim mentality**, which makes them think that the world is permanently against them.*

mine *n*

a deep hole in the ground that people dig so that they can remove coal, gold, tin etc

NOUNS + mine

a coal/gold/copper etc mine *More than a million people worked in Britain's coal mines.*

a salt mine *Political prisoners were sent to work in the salt mines.*

ADJECTIVES

a deep mine *The TauTona gold mine in South Africa is the deepest mine in the world.*

an opencast mine *BrE* (=one where coal is taken out of holes in the ground near the surface) *Opencast mines cause a lot of damage to the environment.*

mine + NOUNS

a mine shaft (*also* **a mineshaft**) (=a hole down into a mine) *The boy fell down an abandoned mine shaft.*

VERBS

a mine produces coal/gold etc *The mine will produce 9 million tonnes of coal a year.*

PREPOSITIONS

in a mine *Working conditions in these mines were terrible.*

down a mine *Have you ever been down a mine?*

People who work in **mines** are called **miners**.

miniature *adj* THESAURUS tiny

minimum Ac *n, adj*

the smallest amount or number that is possible, allowed, or necessary

ADJECTIVES

the bare minimum (=the very least amount or number) *She does the bare minimum of exercise.*

the absolute minimum *Bring enough money – $10 per day is the absolute minimum.*

the legal minimum (*also* **the statutory minimum** *formal*): *The wage was often well below the legal minimum.*

NOUNS

the minimum number/amount *The minimum number of students needed to run the course is 25.*

the minimum age *Eighteen is the minimum age for getting married.*

minimum standards *The company failed to meet the minimum safety standards.*

the minimum requirement *The minimum requirement for the job is a TOEFL diploma.*

the minimum period *The minimum period of study is normally 12 months.*

the minimum price/cost *The minimum cost of a room is $100 a night.*

the minimum wage (=the lowest amount of money that an employer can legally pay a worker) *Unions want an increase in the minimum wage.*

PHRASES

keep sth to a minimum *Keep the noise to a minimum, will you?*

reduce sth to a minimum *We want to reduce the environmental impact to a minimum.*

PREPOSITIONS

a minimum of sth *The contract will be for a minimum of two years.*

at a minimum (=at least) *At a minimum, there should be one teacher for every 20 students.*

below/above the minimum *His salary is above the minimum level.*

with a/the minimum of sth *They checked our passports with the minimum of fuss.*

ANTONYMS **minimum → maximum**

minister *n*

a politician who is in charge of a government department in Britain and some other countries

ADJECTIVES/NOUNS + minister

a government minister *A government minister will be appointed to lead the committee.*

the prime minister (=the leader of the government in the UK and some other countries) *Margaret Thatcher was Britain's first woman prime minister.*

the chief minister (=the leader of the government in some states or regions) *He is the chief minister of Maharashtra state in India.*

the health/finance/transport etc minister *I have written to the health minister about the matter.*

the foreign minister (=who deals with relations with other countries) *He will meet with the Japanese foreign minister on Monday.*

a cabinet minister (=an important minister in the UK government) *Two cabinet ministers have resigned over the issue.*

a senior/junior minister *A senior minister warned that Labour might lose the next election.*

a deputy minister *He was appointed deputy minister of culture.*

VERBS

appoint sb (as) minister *In 2000, he was appointed minister of health.*

serve as minister *He served as foreign minister between 1982 and 1986.*

resign as minister *He announced that he would resign as foreign minister.*

PREPOSITIONS

the minister of/for agriculture/health/education etc *He was brought in to advise the minister of education.*

ministry Ac *n* a government department

ADJECTIVES/NOUNS + ministry

the health/finance/transport etc ministry *The Defence Ministry refused to comment on the report.*

the foreign ministry (=which deals with relations with other countries) *The Russian Foreign Ministry issued a statement saying the meeting was "useful".*

the interior ministry (=which deals with law and order in some countries) *The interior ministry announced stricter immigration laws.*

ministry + NOUNS

a ministry official *A junior ministry official passed on the information to a national newspaper.*

a ministry spokesman/spokesperson *A ministry spokesman said no formal decision had been made.*

a ministry building *There have been attacks on interior ministry buildings.*

PREPOSITIONS

at/in a ministry *Sir Peter worked in the Ministry of Defence from 1985 to 1991.*

the Ministry of/for Agriculture/Health/Education etc *The Ministry of Agriculture represents the interests of farmers as well as the public.*

Ministry, Department, or Office?

The US government has **departments**, not ministries: *She works for the* ***Department*** *of Agriculture.* | *The announcement was made by a State* ***Department*** *official.*

Some parts of the British government are called **departments**, not ministries: *Funding for the study was provided by the* ***Department*** *of Education.* | *The* ***Department*** *of Health issued new guidelines.*

The part of the British government that deals with crime, justice, and the police is called the **Home Office**. The part that deals with relations with foreign countries is called the **Foreign Office**. The part that deals with financial matters is called the **Treasury**.

minor *adj*

THESAURUS **famous**, **small (1)**, **unimportant**

minority Ac *n*

a small group of people or things that form less than half of a larger group

ADJECTIVES

a small/tiny minority *She is one of a small minority of women working in engineering.*

a substantial/significant/large/sizeable minority (=less than half, but still a lot of people) *A significant minority of people alive today will live to be 100.*

VERBS

form a minority (*also* **constitute a minority** *formal*) (=be a minority) *Shiite Muslims form a minority in this mainly Sunni country.*

represent a minority (=be a minority) *The over-65s represent only a minority of the population.*

M

belong to a minority *People who belong to a minority community often stick closely together.*

minority + NOUNS

a minority group *Many of the company's employees are from minority ethnic groups.*

a minority interest *Jazz is a minority interest, but it is still an important part of musical studies.*

a minority opinion/view *This is a minority view among scientists.*

PREPOSITIONS

a minority of sb/sth *In a significant minority of cases, the virus can be deadly.*

be in a minority (=be less than half of the total) *Male students are in a minority in this class.*

minuscule *adj* THESAURUS ▶ tiny

minute[1] *n*

1 one sixtieth of an hour

VERBS + minute

take five/ten etc minutes *It takes 15 minutes to walk into town.*

last (for) five/ten etc minutes *The speech lasted exactly 45 minutes.*

spend five/ten etc minutes *Spend a few minutes thinking about your goals in life.*

wait (for) five/ten etc minutes *He waited five minutes and then dialed again.*

minute + VERBS

minutes pass (*also* **minutes elapse** *formal*): *He glanced at the clock. Less than two minutes had passed.*

the minutes go by/tick by (=they pass) *The minutes ticked by, but there was still no sign of the train.*

the minutes fly by (=they seem to pass quickly) *The minutes were flying by, and soon they would have to leave.*

ADJECTIVES

every (single) minute *It's a great film, and I loved every minute of it.*

a spare minute (=one when you are free to do other things) *There was so much to do, Sarah rarely had a spare minute.*

ADVERBS

five/ten etc minutes later *Five minutes later, the phone rang again.*

five/ten etc minutes earlier *He said that David had left a few minutes earlier.*

five/ten etc minutes ago *Mr Roberts arrived about five minutes ago.*

PHRASES

in the space of five/ten etc minutes (=within a period of five, ten etc minutes) *They scored two goals in the space of five minutes.*

PREPOSITIONS

for five/ten etc minutes *Cook the mushrooms for two minutes.*

in five/ten etc minutes *Meet me in my room in five minutes.*

after five/ten etc minutes *After ten minutes, I got up and left.*

⚠ When saying how soon something will happen, you usually say **in**, not 'after': *I'll be back in ten minutes.*

Saying what time it is

Minute is used especially when speaking in a very exact way: *It's 23* ***minutes*** *past 7.* Normally when you are saying what time it is, you use **5**, **10**, **quarter**, **20**, **25**, or **half**, without using the word **minutes**: *It's nearly 25 to 5. | It's just gone* ***half*** *past 12.*

2 a very short period of time

VERBS

take a minute *It'll only take a minute to fix.*

have a minute *Do you have a minute? I have a couple of questions to ask you.*

wait a minute/hold on a minute *Wait a minute – I've not finished explaining.*

ADVERBS

a minute ago *She was here a minute ago.*

just a minute (=used when telling someone to wait for you) *"Can you come downstairs?" "Just a minute! I'm getting dressed!"*

(not for) a single minute (=not for one moment) *I have never regretted it for a single minute.*

PREPOSITIONS

for a minute *I hesitated for a minute.*

in a minute *He'll be all right in a minute.*

in/within minutes *Within minutes, she was asleep.*

3 the minutes of a meeting are an official written record of what has been said and decided

Grammar

Always plural in this meaning.

VERBS

take the minutes (*also* **do the minutes** *informal*) (=write them down) *The secretary was away, so I took the minutes.*

read the minutes *The Honorary Secretary read the minutes of the previous meeting.*

approve the minutes (=formally accept them as the record of a meeting) *The minutes of the previous meeting were approved.*

circulate the minutes *All committee minutes are circulated to members of the Board.*

PHRASES

the minutes of a meeting *The minutes of the meeting reveal that several members of the committee disliked the idea.*

minute² *adj* THESAURUS ▸ tiny

miracle *n*

something very lucky or very good that happens, which you did not expect to happen or did not think was possible

PHRASES

it's a miracle (that)... *It's a miracle no one was killed.*

it will take a miracle (=used when saying that something is very unlikely) *It will take a miracle for us to get there on time.*

by some miracle (=through good luck and nothing else) *By some miracle, we managed to catch the plane.*

ADJECTIVES

a minor/small miracle *It was a minor miracle that the driver walked away from the crash unharmed.*

an economic miracle *Brazil seemed to be experiencing an economic miracle.*

VERBS

perform/work miracles (=make good things happen that did not seem possible) *The new coach has worked miracles, and the team have won their last four games.*

believe in miracles *Unless you believe in miracles, there is no way the situation is going to get any better.*

hope/pray for a miracle *The team are hoping for a miracle, but they don't really have a chance of winning.*

miracles can/do happen *Someone handed my wallet in to the police, which shows that miracles do happen.*

miracle + NOUNS

a miracle cure (=something that solves a problem very effectively) *Unfortunately, there is no miracle cure for baldness.*

a miracle drug *Why are all these miracle drugs so expensive?*

a miracle worker (=someone who performs miracles) *A doctor is just a person, not a miracle worker.*

mirror *n*

a piece of special glass that you can see yourself in

VERBS

look (at sb) in the mirror *She looked at herself in the mirror and smiled.*

see sth in the mirror *Do you like what you see in the mirror?*

be reflected in a mirror *The candles were reflected in the mirror over the fireplace.*

check your mirror (=when driving) *Check your mirrors before you pull out into the road.*

admire yourself/your reflection in the mirror *He's so vain – he's always admiring himself in the mirror.*

PREPOSITIONS

in the mirror *He examined his face in the mirror.*

in front of the mirror *She spends hours in front of the mirror every morning.*

PHRASES

a reflection/image in a mirror *I frowned at my reflection in the mirror.*

mischievous *adj* THESAURUS ▸ naughty

misconception *adj* THESAURUS ▸ untrue

miserable *adj* THESAURUS ▸ sad (1)

misery *n*

great unhappiness or suffering

ADJECTIVES

human misery *Wilberforce devoted his life to fighting human misery and ending the slave trade.*

abject/untold/great misery (=extreme misery) *The news of his son's illness had plunged him into abject misery.*

sheer misery *It is difficult for us to imagine the sheer misery of people living in that country.*

VERBS

live in misery *Millions of families are living in misery.*

suffer/endure misery *The population of this war-torn country have endured so much misery.*

cause (sb) misery *The court case caused untold misery to his family.*

bring sb misery *Her husband had brought her nothing but misery.*

add to sb's misery (=make it worse) *To add to our misery, it rained heavily all day.*

end the misery (*also* **put an end to the misery**) *The international community should do more to end the misery in these camps.*

PHRASES

a life of misery *He rescued them from a life of misery.*

years/a lifetime of misery *She had endured years of misery.*

put an animal out of its misery (=kill a sick or injured animal to end its suffering) *The vet said it was better to put the dog out of its misery.*

> In informal English, you tell someone to **put you out of your misery**, when asking them to tell you something, and when you have been waiting to find out the answer: *Come on, Rick!* ***Put us out of our misery****! Did you get the job or not?*

M

misfortune *n*

very bad luck, or something that happens to you as a result of bad luck

ADJECTIVES

a great/terrible misfortune *Everything they owned was lost in the fire, which was a great misfortune.*

VERBS

suffer misfortune (=experience it) *You are not the only person to have suffered misfortune in your life.*

be plagued by misfortune (*also* **be dogged by misfortune** *BrE*) (=have a lot of bad luck over a long period of time) *The project seemed dogged by misfortune.*

profit from sb's misfortune (=get advantages because of another person's bad luck) *It seems the banks always profit from farmers' misfortunes.*

a misfortune happens to sb (*also* **a misfortune befalls sb** *formal*): *He had lost his father at a young age, and didn't want the same misfortune to befall his children.*

PHRASES

have the misfortune to do sth/of doing sth *Last year, he had the misfortune to be involved in a car crash.*

a series/string of misfortunes *The team has suffered a series of misfortunes this year.*

misgiving *n*

a feeling of doubt or fear about what might happen or about whether something is right

> **Grammar**
> Usually plural.

VERBS

have misgivings *Her parents had some misgivings about the marriage. She was very young.*

allay sb's misgivings (=stop someone from being worried) *He tried to allay her misgivings about the idea, but with little success.*

express/voice your misgivings (=say that you are worried about something) *Only a few senators voiced their misgivings about the war.*

ADJECTIVES

grave/great/serious/severe misgivings (=used when you feel extremely worried about something) *Many people have grave misgivings about the idea of human cloning.*

deep/profound/considerable misgivings (=used when you feel very worried about something) *Teachers have deep misgivings about allowing business values to be used in schools.*

initial misgivings (=used when you feel worried at first, but later stop feeling worried) *He admits to having some initial misgivings about returning to Liverpool.*

PREPOSITIONS

misgivings about sth *I had some misgivings about leaving my job.*

despite/in spite of sb's misgivings *Despite her misgivings, she decided to support the proposal.*

misguided *adj* THESAURUS ▸ wrong (1)

misleading *adj* THESAURUS ▸ untrue, wrong (1)

misrepresent *v* THESAURUS ▸ change[1] (2)

miss *v*

1 to not hit something

ADVERBS

miss sth completely *The player completely missed the ball and it hit his chest.*

barely/narrowly/only just miss sth *The bullet narrowly missed her head.*

miss sth badly *His wild shot badly missed the net.*

PHRASES

miss sth by a mile (=miss by a long distance) *The arrow missed the target by a mile.*

2 to feel sad because someone is not with you

ADVERBS

really miss sb/miss sb a lot *especially spoken*: *He really misses her.*

greatly/deeply miss sb *She greatly misses her sister.*

desperately miss sb *I desperately missed my parents.*

miss sb dearly (=used especially about someone who is dead) *She missed her brother dearly.*

sb is sadly/sorely missed *He will be sadly missed when he retires.*

3 to fail to do something

NOUNS

miss a chance/opportunity *He didn't want to miss the chance of earning some extra money.*

miss an appointment *She missed her appointment because she could not leave her new job to come to the clinic.*

miss a deadline *He missed the deadline for handing in his essay.*

mission *n*

an important job that someone has been given to do, especially one that involves travelling somewhere

ADJECTIVES/NOUNS + mission

a secret mission (*also* **a covert mission** *formal*): *He volunteered for a secret mission behind enemy lines in North Korea.*

a dangerous mission *He knew very well that it was a dangerous mission.*

a successful mission *I am confident that the mission will be successful.*

a military/combat/bombing mission *In a daring military mission, their warplanes destroyed an unfinished nuclear reactor.*

a reconnaissance/spying mission *They flew reconnaissance missions over Cuba.*

a rescue mission *The first rescue mission had to be abandoned when the weather worsened.*

a fact-finding mission *A group of MPs have just returned from a fact-finding mission to India.*

a trade mission *The mayor is currently on a trade mission in Asia.*

a diplomatic mission *He was employed by King Henry III on diplomatic missions.*

a space mission *This is the most important space mission since the moon landings.*

a mercy mission (=a journey taken to bring help to people who are in a bad situation) *He is planning his eighth mercy mission to aid homeless refugees.*

VERBS

carry out/conduct a mission *He was selected to carry out a dangerous mission.*

accomplish/complete a mission (=do it successfully) *Do they have the resources they need to accomplish that mission?*

send sb on a mission *Oswald was sent on a mission to Russia by the CIA.*

fly a mission *His grandfather flew 280 combat missions in two wars.*

a mission fails/succeeds *The mission failed and they returned empty-handed.*

PHRASES

sb's mission is to do sth *Their mission is to gather information about the wildlife on the island.*

a mission ends in failure *Unfortunately the mission ended in failure and he was unable to secure the release of the hostages.*

PREPOSITIONS

be on a mission *They were on a mission of vital importance to their country.*

a mission to a place *He recently returned from a four-day mission to Israel.*

mist *n*

a light cloud low over the ground

ADJECTIVES/NOUNS + mist

a thick/heavy mist *Outside, a heavy mist obscured everything.*

a fine/light mist *A fine mist began to settle on the water.*

a white/grey mist *A layer of white mist hung over the valley.*

the morning/evening mist *The sun broke through the morning mist.*

autumn mist *The field looked magical in the autumn mist.*

VERBS

a mist comes down/in *The mist came down like a curtain.*

a mist rolls in (=moves along to a place) *A mist began to roll in off the sea.*

the mist clears/lifts (=goes away) *The mountains suddenly appeared as the mist lifted.*

PHRASES

be shrouded in mist *literary* (=be covered in mist) *The mountains were shrouded in mist.*

disappear/vanish into the mist *He passed me on the trail and disappeared into the mist.*

appear out of/emerge from the mist *Suddenly a man appeared out of the mist.*

loom out of the mist (=suddenly be seen, especially when still partly covered by mist) *Here and there, trees loomed out of the mist.*

mistake *n*

1 something that is done in the wrong way, for example when you are writing or calculating something

ADJECTIVES/NOUNS + mistake

a spelling mistake *There was a spelling mistake in the first paragraph.*

a grammatical mistake *Her French essay was full of grammatical mistakes.*

a common/classic mistake *A common mistake is to imagine that dogs think like humans.*

a little/small/slight/minor mistake *He made one or two little mistakes, but the rest was good.*

a silly/stupid/foolish/careless mistake *Don't worry – we all make silly mistakes sometimes.*

a serious/bad mistake *There was a serious mistake in the instructions.*

an honest/genuine/innocent mistake (=a mistake, and not a deliberate action) *Thomas admitted he had broken the law, but said that it had been an honest mistake.*

an easy mistake (to make) *She looks like her sister, so it's an easy mistake to make.*

a basic/elementary mistake *The most basic mistake that people make is to take too many vitamin pills, without considering which is going to help them most.*

a deliberate mistake *Did you spot the deliberate mistake?*

VERBS

make a mistake *The hotel made a mistake with the bill.*

correct a mistake (*also* **rectify a mistake** *formal*): *Luckily he was able to correct the mistake before his boss saw it.*

realize your mistake *She didn't realize her mistake until it was too late.*

find/discover/spot a mistake *Let me know if you spot any mistakes.*

admit your mistake *It is better to admit your mistake and apologize.*

M

mistakes happen *Doctors are always extremely careful, but mistakes can happen.*

⚠ Don't say 'do a mistake'. Say **make a mistake**.

PREPOSITIONS

a mistake in sth *There were a lot of mistakes in his essay.*

PHRASES

be full of mistakes *The article was full of mistakes.*

it is a mistake to think/assume etc sth *It is a mistake to assume that all snakes are dangerous.*

there must be some mistake (=used when you think someone has made a mistake) *There must be some mistake. I definitely booked a room for tonight.*

Mistake or error?

You can say a **spelling mistake** or a **spelling error**. The only difference is that **error** is more formal than **mistake**.

When talking about things you have done wrong, you usually use **mistake**: *I made some silly little **mistakes**.* (not 'errors'). **Error** sounds too formal for this type of situation.

You say **computer error**, **human error**, **driver error**, or **pilot error** (not 'mistake'): *The crash was caused by **pilot error**.*

2 something you do that is not sensible and has a bad result, which you regret later

ADJECTIVES

a big/great mistake *Buying the house was a big mistake.*

a bad/terrible/dreadful mistake *Marrying him was the worst mistake she had ever made.*

a serious/grave mistake *I warned him that I thought he was making a serious mistake.*

a fatal mistake (=a very bad mistake, especially one that causes you to fail) *His fatal mistake was trying to do everything by himself.*

a costly mistake (=that has a bad result or costs a lot of money) *Increasing taxes could be a costly mistake for the government.*

VERBS

make a mistake *I am worried that you are making a terrible mistake.*

learn from your mistakes *It is important to learn from your mistakes.*

repeat a mistake *No one wants to repeat the mistakes of the past.*

avoid a mistake *Town planners need to avoid the mistakes made in the 1960s.*

PHRASES

it is a mistake to do sth *It is a mistake to try to see everything in the museum in one day.*

mistaken *adj* THESAURUS **wrong (1)**

misty *adj* THESAURUS **cloudy**

misunderstanding *n*

a problem caused by someone not understanding a question, situation, or instruction correctly

ADJECTIVES

a serious/terrible misunderstanding *Through some terrible misunderstanding the wrong person had been arrested.*

a little/slight misunderstanding *We need to clear up a little misunderstanding over the bill.*

a simple misunderstanding (=one that is not serious and is easy to correct) *It was a simple misunderstanding: I got the day wrong.*

a complete/total misunderstanding *There seems to be a complete misunderstanding of how the changes will affect most taxpayers.*

a possible misunderstanding *To avoid any possible misunderstanding, both parties will sign a written contract.*

a widespread misunderstanding (=a misunderstanding that many people share) *There is a widespread misunderstanding of the purpose of the law.*

VERBS

cause/lead to (a) misunderstanding *The lack of clear information has led to misunderstanding among consumers.*

avoid a misunderstanding *State clearly what you want, to avoid misunderstandings later on.*

clear up/correct a misunderstanding *I want to talk to him, to try to clear up any misunderstandings.*

be based on a misunderstanding (=happen as a result of a misunderstanding) *The whole argument was based on a misunderstanding.*

a misunderstanding arises/occurs (=it happens) *Misunderstandings easily arise between people from different cultures.*

PREPOSITIONS

a misunderstanding about/over sth *There is a great deal of misunderstanding about his role in the company.*

a misunderstanding between people/countries *A minor misunderstanding between the two countries led to a diplomatic row.*

PHRASES

there has been a misunderstanding *There's been a misunderstanding about what I actually meant.*

there must be some misunderstanding (=used when you think someone has not understood something correctly) *There must have been some misunderstanding – I didn't order all these books.*

there is no misunderstanding *I am writing to make sure there is no misunderstanding between us.*

mixture *n*

a combination of two or more different things, feelings, or types of people

ADJECTIVES

an interesting/fascinating mixture *The town is an interesting mixture of the old and the new.*

a strange/curious/odd/weird mixture *She felt a strange mixture of excitement and fear.*

a unique mixture *Each person has a unique mixture of genes.*

a rich/eclectic mixture (=one that includes a lot of different types of things) *This performance was a rich mixture of musical styles, from jazz to hip-hop.*

a heady mixture (=one that has a powerful effect) *The novel is a heady mixture of drama and horror.*

PREPOSITIONS

a mixture of sb/sth *I experienced a mixture of emotions.*

mob *n*

a large noisy crowd, especially one that is angry and violent

ADJECTIVES

an angry mob *The speaker was surrounded by an angry mob.*

an unruly mob *disapproving* (=difficult to control) *The police did not know how to deal with the unruly mob.*

a baying mob *disapproving* (=shouting loudly in a frightening way) *A baying mob of reporters were waiting outside the courtroom.*

a lynch mob (=a group of people that want to kill someone by hanging them, without a legal trial) *The man was put in a police cell to save him from a lynch mob.*

VERBS

a mob gathers *A mob gathered in front of the government building.*

a mob surrounds sb/sth *His car was surrounded by a hostile mob.*

mob + NOUNS

mob rule (=when a mob controls the situation rather than the government or the law) *If leaders lose control, the result is mob rule.*

PREPOSITIONS

a mob of people *A mob of 150 people attacked police with petrol bombs, bottles, and bricks.*

model *n*

1 a copy of a building, vehicle, machine etc, usually a small copy

ADJECTIVES/NOUNS + model

a wooden/plaster/clay etc model *There was a wooden model of a sailing ship in a glass case.*

a full-size/full-scale model *A full-scale model of the shark was used for some of the filming.*

a scale model (=an accurate model in which every part is smaller than the real object by the same amount) *The ship is a one-fifth scale model of Captain Cook's ship 'Endeavour'.*

a working model (=one with parts that move) *The children built a working model of a windmill.*

VERBS

make a model *He made a model of St Paul's Cathedral.*

build/construct a model *The students were building complex models out of wood.*

assemble a model (=put the parts together) *To assemble the model, first attach the wheels to the base plate.*

model + NOUNS

a model aircraft/train/car etc *I loved making model aircraft when I was a boy.*

a model railway *BrE*: *He has a model railway in his back garden.*

PREPOSITIONS

a model of sth *She makes lifelike models of animals.*

2 a particular type of a vehicle or machine

ADJECTIVES

a new model *A new model will soon be available.*

the latest model *The latest models are much faster.*

an earlier model/the previous model *The earlier models were much less reliable.*

a popular model *The car is the most popular model in the Renault range.*

the basic/standard model *The motor is the same as in the basic model.*

a luxury/deluxe model *The luxury model has leather seats and a drinks cabinet.*

a top-of-the-range model *A top-of-the-range model will cost at least $7,000.*

a cheaper/more expensive model *The cheaper model does not have as many features.*

VERBS

produce/make a model *The company has stopped making this model.*

launch/introduce a model (=make it available for the first time) *They're launching the new model in the autumn.*

unveil a model (=show it for the first time) *The company unveiled its latest model at the Motor Show.*

3 someone whose job is to show clothes by wearing them at fashion shows or in photographs

ADJECTIVES/NOUNS + model

a fashion model *She looks like a fashion model.*

a top model *Even top models are often unhappy with their looks.*

a male model *Mike could get a job as a male model.*

a catwalk model *BrE*, **a runway model** *AmE* (=who walks on a special stage at a fashion show) *The average catwalk model is 5 ft 9 in tall.*

M

VERBS

work as a model *Her mother used to work as a model.*

a model poses *The models posed for the cameras.*

moderate *adj*

1 not very large or very small, hot or cold, fast or slow etc

ADVERBS

relatively/fairly moderate *A relatively moderate increase in the price of oil can have a big effect on the economy.*

NOUNS

a moderate increase/decrease *We have seen a moderate increase in prices.*

moderate growth *There has been moderate growth in the economy.*

a moderate amount/number *He only eats a moderate amount of sugar.*

moderate success *The show was a moderate success.*

a moderate heat (=not very hot or cold – used about cooking) *Heat the oil in a pan over a moderate heat.*

a moderate drinker *Moderate drinkers have a lower risk of heart disease than heavy drinkers.*

2 not having strong political or religious opinions

NOUNS

moderate opinions/views *His views are more moderate than some other members of his party.*

moderate policies *The party's policies on immigration are surprisingly moderate.*

a moderate politician/leader/government *He is regarded as a moderate politician.*

moderate voters *The party wants to attract moderate voters.*

Moderate is also used as a noun in this meaning: *The* ***moderates*** *are a small minority of the party* (=people with moderate views).

ANTONYMS **moderate → extreme**

modern *adj*

1 relating to the present or recent time

NOUNS

the modern world *In the modern world people can travel anywhere they want.*

modern society/civilization/culture *Smaller families are a feature of modern society.*

modern times *It was one of the greatest disasters of modern times.*

the modern age/era/period *Deaths from infections are much less common in the modern age.*

modern life *Computers are an essential part of modern life.*

modern medicine/science *Modern medicine has saved thousands of lives.*

modern art/painting/literature/poetry *We visited the Museum of Modern Art in New York.*

modern man (=people living now) *Modern man's knowledge of the universe is based mainly on the scientific discoveries of the last century.*

modern history *BrE* (=recent history, as a subject of study) *Chris has a degree in modern history.*

modern languages *BrE* (=languages that are spoken today, as a subject of study) *She studied modern languages at university.*

PHRASES

by modern standards (=when compared with what something is like now) *The first supermarkets were small by modern standards.*

the modern equivalent of sth *Sending an email is the modern equivalent of writing a letter.*

THESAURUS: modern

contemporary

art | music | dance | artist | writer | society | life | culture

relating to the present time – used especially about music, art etc. **Contemporary** is more formal than **modern**:

The museum had an exhibition of contemporary art. | We publish short stories by contemporary writers. | The media is very much a feature of contemporary life.

modern-day

reader | audience | visitor | version | equivalent | America | Europe

existing in the present time – used when comparing someone or something to a person or thing in the past:

Modern-day readers will have difficulty imagining how hard life was in those days. | His novel is a modern-day version of a Dickens novel. | She is the modern-day equivalent of Marilyn Monroe. | These stories are typical in modern-day America.

Modern-day is always used before a noun.

2 using the most recent designs or methods

NOUNS

modern technology *Modern technology has made it easier to work from home.*

a modern building/house *The building is modern, and made from steel and glass.*

a modern kitchen/bathroom *The house has a well-equipped modern kitchen.*

modern equipment *The army needs more modern equipment.*

modern facilities *All rooms in the hotel have modern facilities.*

modern architecture *Most of the architecture was very modern.*
modern methods/techniques *They use modern methods for analysing the information.*
a modern design *The chairs have a very modern design.*
a modern look/feel/style *The use of light colours gives the room a modern look.*

ADVERBS

thoroughly modern (=very modern in every way) *The hotel is thoroughly modern.*
ultra-modern (=extremely modern) *The house is ultra-modern, with high-tech gadgets built in everywhere.*
relatively modern (=fairly modern compared to other things) *Most of the jewellery on sale was relatively modern.*

THESAURUS: modern

advanced
technology | equipment | weapons | country | society | economy | system | technique
using very modern technology and ideas:
The company uses the most advanced technology available. | Pay is higher in advanced industrial countries. | We use the most advanced techniques in making our golf clubs.

up-to-date
equipment | methods | technology | facilities
using the most modern technology and ideas:
The hospital has the most up-to-date equipment in the country. | Up-to-date methods make lessons exciting and interesting.

high-tech/hi-tech
equipment | device | goods | products | weapons | industry | company | firm | business
using very modern technology, especially electronic equipment and computers:
High-tech listening equipment was used to find survivors in the rubble. | Many hi-tech industries are based in Silicon Valley.

state-of-the-art
technology | equipment | facilities | system | drug | kitchen | software
using the newest and most modern features, ideas, and materials that are available:
Its factory uses state-of-the-art technology. | The football club has invested £40 million in state-of-the-art training facilities. | The sound system is state-of-the-art.

new-fangled
idea | device | gadget | machine | technology | thing
used about something that is new and modern but which you disapprove of, especially because you are old and do not like change:
Some people didn't approve of these new-fangled ideas. | My grandfather refuses to use new-fangled devices such as cash machines. | I don't understand all this new-fangled technology.

New-fangled is always used before a noun.

ANTONYMS **modern → old-fashioned**

modest *adj*

1 someone who is modest does not want to talk about their abilities or achievements

ADVERBS

too modest *You are being too modest – you did a great job.*
surprisingly modest *Both men are surprisingly modest about their achievements.*
characteristically modest (=typically modest) *Her speech when she received the award was characteristically modest.*

NOUNS

a modest man/woman/person *He was a very modest man, who did not see himself as a hero.*
a modest smile *"I will do my best," he said with a modest smile.*

PREPOSITIONS

modest about sth *He was always incredibly modest about his talents.*

2 rather small

ADVERBS

relatively/comparatively modest *Rates of inflation have been relatively modest in recent years.*

NOUNS

a modest amount/sum *I borrowed a modest amount to buy my house.*
a modest increase/improvement *There was a modest increase in the number of births.*
a modest reduction/fall *The government was able to achieve a modest reduction in unemployment.*
a modest effect/impact *The changes will only have a modest effect on the global economy.*
a modest price/fee *His prints could be purchased at modest prices.*
a modest profit *Last year, the company made a modest profit of £602,000.*
a modest income/salary *His father was on a modest income, and he could not afford to send his son to university.*
modest success *She had some modest successes with her short stories.*

THESAURUS: modest

little, low, minor, slight, modest, compact, cramped → **small (1)**

M

modesty *n*
a modest way of behaving or talking

ADJECTIVES

great modesty *He spoke with great modesty about his achievements.*

natural modesty *His shyness and natural modesty prevented him from boasting about his success.*

false modesty (=when someone pretends to be modest) *This is no time for false modesty – you should be proud of your achievement.*

VERBS

modesty prevents sb from doing sth (*also* **modesty forbids**) *often humorous* (=you do not want to talk about something because you are too modest) *Modesty prevents me from mentioning my own part in the team's success.*

PHRASES

with typical/characteristic modesty *"Anyone else would have done the same thing," he said with typical modesty.*

moist *adj* THESAURUS **damp (1)**

moisture *n*
small amounts of water that are present in the air, in a substance, or on a surface

VERBS

absorb moisture *Plants use their roots to absorb moisture from the soil.*

hold/retain/conserve moisture (=keep moisture) *Creams can help your skin to retain moisture.*

lose moisture *The soil loses moisture and dries out.*

moisture evaporates (=it disappears into the air) *Hot sun makes the moisture evaporate.*

moisture gets into sth (*also* **moisture penetrates sth** *formal*): *Moisture can penetrate the wood if it isn't sealed properly.*

ADJECTIVES

excess moisture *Wash the leaves and shake to remove excess moisture.*

moisture + NOUNS

moisture content *Your skin's moisture content changes as you get older.*

moisture level *The moisture level has increased.*

moisture loss *Skin can become very dry because of moisture loss.*

PHRASES

a drop/droplet of moisture *Drops of moisture hung in the air.*

moment *n*

1 a particular point in time

ADJECTIVES

the right moment *I'm just waiting for the right moment to tell her.*

the perfect moment *Now would be the perfect moment to visit the area.*

a good/bad moment (*also* **an opportune/inopportune moment** *formal*) (=a good or bad time to do something) *The occasion provided an opportune moment for the couple to announce their engagement.*

the exact/precise moment *Her stomach chose that precise moment to make a loud noise.*

an important/crucial/critical moment *This was probably the most important moment in his life.*

a historic moment (=one that is important in history) *The fall of the Berlin Wall was a historic moment.*

a defining moment (=a very important moment which has a big effect on something) *The speech was a defining moment in her career.*

the worst moment of sth *Hearing that news was the worst moment of my life.*

sb's finest moment (=when someone was most successful or admired) *The performance was one of the band's finest moments.*

a special/memorable moment *It was a really special moment when my boyfriend asked me to marry him.*

an awkward/tense/difficult/embarrassing moment *There was an awkward moment when he didn't know what to say to her.*

VERBS + moment

enjoy the moment (*also* **savour the moment** *formal*): *She found herself laughing, enjoying the moment.*

capture the moment (=photograph or describe something in a way that shows exactly what something is like) *The film captures the moment when Kennedy first became president.*

choose a moment to do sth (=do something at a particular time) *Ellie wondered why he had chosen this moment to reveal his plans.*

moment + VERBS

a moment comes/arrives *Eventually the dreaded moment came, and I had to get up on stage and speak.*

a moment passes (=it is no longer the right time for something) *He tried to apologize but the moment had passed.*

PHRASES

at the moment/at the present moment (=now) *The situation is a little difficult just at the moment.*

at that/this moment *Just at that moment there was a knock on the door.*

from the moment (=from that time) *I could tell something was wrong from the moment I walked in through the front door.*

from that moment on (=after that time) *From that moment on we became firm friends.*

M

just this/that moment (=only a very short time ago) *I had just that moment got home.*

at any given moment (=at any particular time) *We knew exactly what we would be doing at any given moment of the week.*

from moment to moment/moment by moment (=used when emphasizing that something changes quickly) *The colours of the sunset changed from moment to moment.*

at this moment in time *formal* (=now) *At this moment in time it would be inappropriate to comment.*

> You can also use **very** with **moment**, when saying that something happens exactly at a particular time: *At that **very moment**, the doorbell rang. | He is with her at this **very moment**.*

2 a very short period of time

ADJECTIVES

a brief moment *For a brief moment, he looked directly at her.*

a fleeting moment (=a very short time) *For a fleeting moment she wanted to run away.*

a spare moment (= when you are not doing other things) *She spent every spare moment in the library.*

VERBS

take a moment *Can I ask you something? It will only take a moment, I promise.*

spend a moment *He spent a few moments thinking about what to do next.*

wait a moment *Wait a moment while I get my coat.*

pause/hesitate (for) a moment (=stop speaking or doing something for a short time) *Lisa paused a moment, then said yes.*

spare a moment (=used when asking someone if they have a short time available to spend with you) *Can you spare a moment to go through some figures with me?*

a moment passes *A few moments passed before he started to speak.*

PHRASES

a moment ago *I saw him outside just a moment ago.*

just a moment (=used when telling someone to wait) *Just a moment, I'll go and get her.*

when sb has a moment (=when someone has some free time to do something) *Can you call me when you have a moment?*

there's never a dull moment (=something is always exciting or full of activity) *There's never a dull moment with Chris around!*

PREPOSITIONS

for a moment *It was quiet for a moment, then Rae spoke.*

after a moment *After a moment, Rex came back into the room.*

in a moment/in a few moments (=very soon) *I'll come back to that point in a moment.*

a moment of sth *There was a long moment of silence.*

momentary *adj* THESAURUS > **short (1)**

momentous *adj* THESAURUS > **important (1)**

momentum *n*

the ability to keep increasing, developing, or being more successful

VERBS

gain/build (up)/gather momentum (=become more and more successful) *The campaign to change the law is gaining momentum.*

lose momentum *If a film loses momentum, the audience becomes bored.*

regain momentum (=make it start again) *The American economy was struggling to regain momentum.*

maintain momentum *It is essential to maintain the momentum of economic growth.*

keep the momentum going (*also* **sustain the momentum** *formal*) (=make it continue) *Hopefully we can keep the momentum going and win the next game as well.*

create/generate momentum *Winning this vote created the momentum to carry his election campaign forward.*

momentum builds/grows *Momentum is building for a review of the law.*

ADJECTIVES

political/economic momentum *Obama had political momentum because he symbolized something new.*

unstoppable/irresistible momentum (=that cannot be stopped) *The social changes began to gather irresistible momentum.*

new momentum *The agreement was small, but it gave new momentum to the talks.*

strong momentum *In Britain there has been strong momentum for reform.*

PREPOSITIONS

momentum for sth *There was an irresistible momentum for change.*

money *n*

what you use to buy things, in the form of notes or coins

VERBS + money

have ... money *I didn't have enough money to pay for it.*

make/earn money *Beth wanted to get a job and earn some money.*

spend money (on sth) *He spent all his money on computer equipment.*

M

cost money/cost a lot of money *Good food doesn't have to cost a lot of money.*
save money (=use less money) *Companies fired workers to save money.*
make money (=make a profit) *The farm was beginning to make money at last.*
lose money (=not make a profit, so that you then have less money) *The movie didn't attract audiences and lost money for the studio.*
pay money (for sth) *Has he paid the money he owes you?*
lend sb money *My dad lent me money to buy a car.*
borrow money *They arranged to borrow money from the bank to buy a house.*
owe sb money *He owes the bank a lot of money.*
waste money (on sth) *Don't waste your money on a computer that doesn't have enough memory.*
raise money (=do something to get money for a charity, school etc) *The Christmas fair raises money for the school.*
save up money *She had saved up enough money to buy a car.*
refund sb's money/give sb their money back (=give money back to a customer) *We regret that we are unable to refund money on tickets.*

⚠ Don't say 'gain money'. Say **make money**.

money + VERBS

money goes on sth (=is spent on something) *All the money went on doctor's bills.*
money comes from sth *Their money came from drugs.*
money comes in (=you get money, usually from working) *My husband lost his job, so we had less money coming in.*

ADJECTIVES/NOUNS + money

prize money *They won a million dollars in prize money.*
pocket money *BrE* (=a small amount of money that parents regularly give their children) *How much pocket money do you get?*
government/taxpayers'/public money *More government money should be spent on improving the railways.*
spending money *We had £500 spending money saved for our holiday.*

money + NOUNS

money problems/worries *She had a good job and no money worries.*
money laundering (=the crime of putting money that someone has got illegally into banks and businesses in order to hide where it came from) *Dawson was arrested for money laundering.*

PHRASES

a sum of money (*also* **an amount of money**) *£10,000 seemed a huge sum of money to me.*
be a waste of money *Fancy clothes for a baby are a waste of money.*
be value for money *BrE* (=used when saying that something is worth the amount of money you pay for it) *The holiday was excellent value for money.*

PREPOSITIONS

money for sth *They were so poor that they didn't have much money for food.*

monitor Ac *v*

to carefully watch and check a situation in order to see how it changes

ADVERBS

carefully/closely monitor sth *The temperature is carefully monitored.*
strictly monitor sth *Water usage is strictly monitored.*
constantly/continuously monitor sth *The situation is being constantly monitored.*
regularly/routinely monitor sth *The company regularly monitors the performance of managers.*
effectively monitor sth *Schools need to monitor student progress effectively.*

monopoly *n*

complete control of a business, industry, or activity, so that other organizations cannot compete

ADJECTIVES/NOUNS + monopoly

a virtual/near monopoly (=almost a complete monopoly) *The company had a virtual monopoly on this type of computer system.*
a state/government monopoly *They wanted to end the state monopoly of television.*
a local/national monopoly *The local monopoly has been opened up to new rivals.*

VERBS

have a monopoly (*also* **hold a monopoly** *formal*): *For years Bell Telephone had a monopoly on telephone services in the US.*
break/end a monopoly *The government wants to break the monopoly of the big energy companies.*
create a monopoly *There are fears that the merger between the two companies will create a monopoly.*

PHRASES

a monopoly of power (=the position of being the only person or organization that can have political power) *The people want an end to the ruling party's monopoly of power.*

PREPOSITIONS

a monopoly on/over sth *The firm had a monopoly on sugar processing.* | *They want to end the state's monopoly over broadcasting.*

monotonous *adj* THESAURUS ▸ **boring**

month *n*

one of the 12 periods of time that a year is divided into, or a period of about 4 weeks

ADJECTIVES/NOUNS + month

last month *The restaurant opened last month.*

the previous/preceding month *Sales were lower than in the previous month.*

next month *The movie will be released next month.*

the following month (=the month after the one you have just mentioned) *By the following month he had raised over £400.*

the coming months (=the next few months) *Further work is planned for the coming months.*

the past month *He had been off work for the past month.*

the summer/autumn etc months *It's very cold here during the winter months.*

VERBS

spend a month *I spent four months travelling around Europe.*

sth takes a month *It took several months to sort the problem out.*

a month passes (by)/goes by *Seven months went by before he returned.*

PHRASES

the beginning/end/middle of the month *You'll receive your wages at the end of the month.*

once/twice etc a month *We update the schedule at least once a month.*

in recent months *He had started to drink heavily in recent months.*

time of the month *This is the busiest time of the month.*

the month of April/June etc *It snowed heavily during the month of January.*

PREPOSITIONS

for a month *We stayed in Denver for a month.*

in/during a month *In that month he had only earned £150.*

monument *n*

1 something such as a statue that is built to remind people of an important event or famous person

ADJECTIVES

a national monument *In Amsterdam there is a national monument honoring Dutch victims of World War II.*

a fitting monument (=a suitable monument) *The statue is a fitting monument to Churchill.*

VERBS

build/erect/put up a monument *Local people have erected a monument on the spot where she died.*

a monument commemorates sb/sth (=it is there to make people remember someone or something) *The monument commemorates soldiers who gave their lives.*

PREPOSITIONS

a monument to sb/sth *Outside the gate is a monument to King Charles IV.*

2 a very old building or place that is important in history

ADJECTIVES

an ancient/historic/prehistoric monument *There are many castles, churches, and other ancient monuments to visit in the area.*

a famous/important monument *The Taj Mahal is one of the most famous monuments in the world.*

a national monument *Melrose Abbey is now a national monument.*

a public monument *The organization is responsible for preserving important public monuments.*

an industrial monument *The old mine has now become an industrial monument.*

mood *n*

the way you feel at a particular time

ADJECTIVES

a good/cheerful mood (=happy) *You're in a good mood this morning!*

a bad mood (=angry) *The news had put her in a bad mood.*

a foul mood (=very angry) *Watch what you say; he's in a foul mood.*

a black mood *BrE* (=very angry or sad) *His earlier black mood seemed to have gone.*

a confident/optimistic mood *He started the game in a confident mood.*

a relaxed mood *She was clearly in a relaxed mood as she chatted to friends.*

a festive mood (=a mood in which you want to enjoy yourself and celebrate something) *The fans were in a festive mood after their team won the championship.*

a sombre mood *BrE*, **a somber mood** *AmE* (=serious and rather sad) *His death has put the country in a sombre mood.*

the general mood (=the mood of a group of people) *One soldier expressed the general mood of fear and failure in a letter home.*

the public/national mood (=the mood of the people in a country) *The public mood was one of anger and frustration.*

the prevailing mood (=the one that exists in a group of people at a particular time) *The prevailing mood in the country was optimistic.*

mood + VERBS

sb's mood changes *Suddenly his mood changed, and he laughed.*

sb's mood improves *By the next morning, her mood had improved.*

M

VERBS + mood

match/suit sb's mood (=be like someone's mood) *The terrible weather matched their mood.*

reflect/capture sb's mood (=show what someone is feeling) *His comments reflected the national mood.*

lighten/lift sb's mood (=make someone feel happier) *The sun was streaming in the window, but it did nothing to lighten his mood.*

dampen sb's mood (=make someone feel less happy) *The thought that the holiday would end soon dampened her mood.*

gauge sb's mood (=try to decide what someone's mood is) *He looked at her for a moment, trying to gauge her mood.*

mood + NOUNS

mood swings (=sudden changes of mood) *Sudden mood swings can be a sign of mental illness.*

PREPOSITIONS

in a good/confident etc mood *John arrived for his interview in a confident mood.*

PHRASES

a mood of optimism/despair/excitement etc *There is a new mood of optimism.*

a change of mood *Michael underwent one of his sudden changes of mood.*

the mood of the time/moment (=the way people in general feel at a particular time) *The movie captured the mood of the moment.*

be in the mood (for sth) (=feel like doing something) *I don't want to go to the party. I'm not in the mood.*

moon *n*

the round object that you can see in the sky, which goes around the Earth every 28 days

ADJECTIVES/NOUNS + moon

a full moon (=with a completely round shape) *A full moon hung low in the sky.*

a half moon (=looking like half a circle) *A half moon was up now, pale and cool.*

a crescent moon (=with a thin curved shape) *The stars and thin crescent moon gave just enough light to see the path.*

a new moon (=a very thin moon which is just starting to get bigger) *It was twilight and a new moon was rising.*

a bright moon *The moon was very bright.*

a pale moon *Her face glowed in the light of the pale moon.*

a silver/silvery moon *It was a frosty night, with a cold silver moon.*

a harvest moon (=the full moon that appears in early autumn) *Over the potato fields a harvest moon was rising.*

VERBS

the moon shines *The moon shone through the window.*

the moon rises (*also* **the moon comes up**) *He watched the full moon come up over the trees.*

the moon appears *A brilliant moon appeared over the mountains.*

the moon comes out (=appears as it gets dark or a cloud moves) *The moon came out from behind the clouds.*

the moon hangs somewhere *literary* (=stays there for a long time) *The moon hung over the quiet sea.*

the moon sets (=goes down so that you cannot see it) *The moon had set, but the sky was clear.*

the moon waxes (=gets bigger each night) *The moon waxed larger over the next few days.*

the moon wanes (=gets smaller each night) *The August moon was waning.*

PHRASES

the light of the moon *The clouds blocked out the light of the moon.*

there is no moon *There was no moon, and the fields were completely dark.*

moral *adj*

relating to the principles of what is right and wrong behaviour, and to the difference between good and evil

NOUNS

moral standards *Has there been a decline in moral standards in our society?*

moral principles *He refused to lie - it was against his moral principles.*

moral values (=the types of behaviour that a society believes are good) *Schools teach moral values both by example and in lessons.*

a moral duty/obligation/responsibility (=something you should do for moral reasons) *If you have a child, you have a moral obligation to take care of him or her.*

a moral judgment *We shouldn't make moral judgments about the way other people live their lives.*

sb's moral authority (=influence that someone has because people believe their principles are right) *Corruption in government destroys its moral authority.*

a moral dilemma (=a difficult decision for moral reasons) *Doctors face a moral dilemma when a patient can be kept alive but has no chance of real recovery.*

a moral issue *There is a debate on the moral issues surrounding the use of animals in medical research.*

moral superiority (=the idea that you are morally right and other people are not) *People from rich countries have a sense of moral superiority.*

moral fibre *BrE*, **moral fiber** *AmE* (=the emotional strength to do what is right) *Some people say there is a lack of moral fibre in our society.*

PHRASES

on moral grounds (=for moral reasons) *He was opposed to hunting on moral grounds.*

morale *n*

the level of confidence and positive feelings that people have, especially people who work together, who belong to the same team etc

ADJECTIVES/NOUNS + morale

morale is high/good *Morale among the staff was high.*

low/poor morale *The pay levels have resulted in low morale within the company.*

staff/team morale *Positive feedback is good for staff morale.*

VERBS

raise/improve morale *The special meetings were intended to raise morale.*

boost/bolster morale (=improve morale) *The wins have boosted team morale.*

keep up/maintain morale (=keep morale high) *It was becoming difficult to keep up the morale of the troops.*

restore morale (=make people confident and positive again) *The new manager realized that his first job would be to restore morale.*

affect morale *The uncertainty has badly affected morale.*

lower/damage morale *We need to avoid damaging people's morale.*

morale + NOUNS

a morale booster/boost (=something that improves morale) *A letter from home was always a morale booster.*

PHRASES

a lack/loss of morale *Rising sickness levels among your employees may show a loss of morale.*

sth is good/bad for morale *Well-deserved praise is always good for morale.*

morals *n*

all of the basic ideas that a person or group of people has about what is morally good and right

ADJECTIVES

public morals (=the standards of behaviour, especially sexual behaviour, expected by people in a society) *They wanted to protect public morals and stop the film from being shown.*

high/strong morals *Her father had high morals and was very strict with his children.*

VERBS

have no morals/not have any morals *I don't think he has any morals at all.*

corrupt sb's morals *Magazines like this corrupt the morals of young people.*

PHRASES

a decline in public morals *Some people think there has been a decline in public morals in recent years.*

morning *n*

the early part of the day, from when the sun rises until 12 o'clock in the middle of the day

ADJECTIVES/NOUNS + morning

good morning (=used when meeting someone in the morning) *Good morning, class!*

Friday/Saturday etc morning *I'll see you on Monday morning.*

this/that morning *What did you do this morning?*

tomorrow/yesterday morning *Can you have the report ready by tomorrow morning?*

the next morning/the following morning *His meeting was not until the next morning.*

early/late morning *A light frost covered the fields in the early morning.*

all morning/the whole morning *It took me all morning to do the washing.*

a beautiful/sunny/cold etc morning *Hot coffee tastes good on a cold morning.*

a summer/spring etc morning *They set off on a beautiful spring morning.*

morning + NOUNS

the morning sun/light/mist *The morning sun was shining through the curtains of their bedroom.*

a morning coffee/run/swim *She read the paper while drinking her morning coffee.*

the morning paper/news *The story was in all the morning papers.*

the morning train/flight *She took the morning flight back to London.*

VERBS

spend the morning *She had planned to spend the morning shopping.*

PHRASES

early in the morning *He has to get up very early in the morning.*

first thing in the morning (=at the beginning of the morning) *I'll call him first thing in the morning.*

from morning till night (=all day) *He studied from morning till night every day.*

take the morning off *He got permission from his boss to take the morning off.*

PREPOSITIONS

in the morning *You'll feel better in the morning.*

during the morning *Were you allowed a break during the morning?*

on Monday/Friday etc morning *I left on Monday morning.*

on the morning of July 4th/May 12th etc *formal*: *She was reported missing on the morning of September 30th, 2008.*

⚠ Don't say 'I did some gardening on the morning.' Say **I did some gardening in the morning.**

M

M

mother *n*

a female parent of a child or animal

ADJECTIVES/NOUNS + mother

a good/better mother *I sometimes wish I'd been a better mother.*

a bad mother *Women who went out to work after having children were regarded as bad mothers.*

a loving mother *I was lucky to have such a loving mother.*

a single/unmarried/lone mother (=who has to bring up a child without the help of a father) *You can't blame all society's problems on single mothers.*

an unmarried mother *The rise in the number of unmarried mothers is most dramatic in Northern Europe and the United States.*

a widowed mother (=whose husband has died) *Keith shared the cottage with his widowed mother.*

sb's real/birth/biological mother *When she was 18, she was told the identity of her real mother.*

sb's foster mother (=a woman who looks after a child instead of its real mother) *Many women want to become foster mothers, but they are unable to because of unnecessary rules and regulations.*

a surrogate mother (=who gives birth to a baby for another woman) *There are a lot of ethical issues surrounding the use of surrogate mothers.*

a teenage mother *Teenage mothers often have a hard time.*

a full-time mother *She gave up job in order to become a full-time mother.*

sb's late mother (=who has died) *Her late mother was also an actress.*

VERBS

become a mother *Helen became a mother quite late in life.*

resemble/take after your mother (=be like your mother) *Boys often take after their mothers.*

mother + NOUNS

a mother figure (=someone who seems like a mother to you) *She was like a mother figure to Charles.*

PHRASES

a mother of two/three etc *Janet is a full-time teacher and a mother of two.*

motion *n*

1 the process or action of moving

ADJECTIVES

constant/perpetual/continuous motion (=moving all the time) *Her hands were in constant motion as she talked.*

a forward/backward motion *The sudden forward motion of the train caused him to fall.*

PREPOSITIONS

in motion (=moving) *Please remain seated while the bus is in motion.*

the motion of sth *The motion of the ship was making me feel ill.*

2 a formal suggestion made at a meeting, which is decided on by voting

VERBS

propose/put forward a motion (*also* **table a motion** *BrE*): *He put forward a motion to elect a new chairperson.*

debate/consider a motion *The party will debate a motion to legalize sales of the drug.*

support/back a motion *Several officials supported the motion.*

second a motion (=say officially that you support a motion made by someone else) *The motion was seconded by Ross.*

sign a motion *130 MPs signed a motion opposing the bill.*

vote on a motion (=vote to decide what will happen) *Party members will be asked to vote on the motion.*

vote for/against a motion *Most committee members voted against the motion.*

approve/pass/carry a motion *The motion was carried by 9 votes to 1.*

oppose a motion *Doherty opposed the motion.*

defeat/reject a motion *The motion was defeated by 104 votes to 147.*

a motion calls for sth *Politicians signed a motion calling for reforms.*

motivation Ac *n*

1 the reason why you want to do something

ADJECTIVES

the main/primary/prime motivation *The main motivation was a desire to improve the lives of ordinary people.*

a political/religious/financial motivation *He denied that there was any political motivation behind the investigation.*

a strong/powerful motivation *The desire to escape ordinary life can be a strong motivation for travel.*

an underlying motivation (=the real reason why someone did something, which is different from the reason that they say at the time) *The underlying motivation was to save money.*

VERBS

understand sb's motivation *I never understood his motivation for wanting the job.*

question sb's motivation *People started to question the company's motivation for offering to help.*

provide a motivation *The unusual situation provided a motivation to make changes.*

PREPOSITIONS

the motivation for (doing) sth *What was the motivation for changing the system?*

the motivation behind sth *The motivation behind the attack was not immediately clear.*

2 eagerness and willingness to do something without needing to be told or forced to do it

ADJECTIVES/NOUNS + motivation

strong/high motivation *Ella found learning difficult despite her strong motivation.*

poor/low motivation *Many of the children show poor motivation.*

employee/student motivation *A good choice of courses helps maintain student motivation.*

individual/personal motivation *We want to increase individual motivation and commitment.*

human motivation *Human motivation is complex.*

VERBS

lack motivation *Jack is an intelligent child, but he lacks motivation.*

lose motivation *Students quickly lose motivation if lessons are boring.*

improve/increase sb's motivation *The scheme is intended to improve employees' motivation.*

have motivation *You need to have a lot of motivation, if you want to succeed.*

show motivation *I wish he would show a little more motivation.*

PHRASES

a lack of motivation *Boredom and lack of motivation are difficult problems to overcome.*

sb's level of motivation *Mature students often have higher levels of motivation.*

motive Ac *n*

the reason that makes someone do something, especially when this reason is kept hidden

ADJECTIVES

the main/prime/primary motive *The main motive for the killings seemed to be revenge.*

sb's real/true motive *What were his true motives for offering her the job?*

a hidden/secret motive *She wondered if there was a hidden motive for his departure.*

an ulterior motive (=a different motive, which you do not tell other people about) *He had an ulterior motive for inviting her to his house.*

a political/economic/sexual/racial motive *The murders might have a political motive.*

a strong motive *Barbara had a strong motive for disliking Ben.*

a possible motive *Police have received information about possible motives for the attack.*

the underlying motive (=a motive that is not directly stated) *The treaty's underlying motive was to make Japan a strong ally of the US.*

have mixed motives (=have more than one motive) *He had mixed motives for joining the army: a desire to prove himself, but also the desire to get away from his family.*

VERBS

have a motive *The killer must have had a motive.*

find/establish a motive *So far the police have been unable to establish a motive for the attack.*

question/suspect/doubt sb's motives (=think that someone might have bad reasons for doing something) *He was quick to question the motives of those who publicly disagreed with him.*

PREPOSITIONS

a motive for sth *The motive for the attack is unknown.*

the motive behind sth *The main motive behind this research is a commercial one.*

motor *n*

the part of a machine that makes it work or move, by changing power, especially electrical power, into movement

ADJECTIVES/NOUNS + motor

a powerful motor *The cleaner has a powerful motor which sucks up the dust.*

an electric motor *The wheels were driven by an electric motor.*

an outboard motor (=attached to the back of a small boat) *He had an inflatable boat with an outboard motor.*

VERBS

start/switch on a motor *He pulled the cord to start the motor.*

stop/switch off/turn off a motor *She steered the boat to shore and then stopped the motor.*

a motor is powered by sth *The motor is powered by batteries.*

a motor runs (*also* **a motor operates** *formal*): *The motor had been running for twenty minutes.*

a motor drives sth (=a motor makes something work) *A small electric motor drives the pump.*

motorcycle (*also* motorbike *especially BrE*) *n*

a fast two-wheeled vehicle with an engine

ADJECTIVES/NOUNS + motorcycle

a big motorcycle *I've always wanted to ride on a big motorcycle.*

a powerful/high-performance motorcycle *The Honda Fireblade is an extremely powerful motorcycle.*

a 125 cc/750 cc etc motorcycle *He was riding a 250 cc motorcycle.*

a police motorcycle *Two police motorcycles rode in front of the president's car.*

VERBS

ride a motorcycle *He was riding a big motorcycle.*

use a motorcycle *Clayton uses a motorcycle to get to work.*

M

get on/off a motorcycle *She got on the motorcycle and rode off.*

fall off/come off a motorcycle *The rider came off his motorcycle and had serious leg injuries.*

build/produce/manufacture a motorcycle *The company has been building motorcycles since 1925.*

motorcycle + NOUNS

a motorcycle rider *Young motorcycle riders often ride very dangerously.*

a motorcycle accident/crash *The singer was badly hurt in a motorcycle accident.*

a motorcycle helmet *You should always wear a motorcycle helmet when riding.*

a motorcycle race *A Spanish rider won the motorcycle race.*

PREPOSITIONS

on a motorcycle/by motorcycle *They toured around the US on a motorcycle.*

PHRASES

on the back of a motorcycle *His girlfriend was on the back of his motorcycle.*

> **Motorcycle** or **motorbike?**
> American speakers usually say **motorcycle**. British speakers usually say **motorbike** or just **bike**.

motto *n*

a short sentence or phrase giving a rule, which expresses the aims or beliefs of a person or institution

ADJECTIVES/NOUNS + motto

a national motto *Jamaica's national motto is 'Out of Many, One People'.*

a family/school motto *The school motto was 'Through work to honour'.*

a state motto *'Live Free or Die' is New Hampshire's state motto.*

a personal motto *Her personal motto is 'Think positive'.*

a guiding motto *One of my guiding mottoes is, 'If you can't do a lot, do a little'.*

VERBS

have a motto *The school has a Latin motto.*

adopt a motto *In 1960, Atlanta adopted the motto 'The City Too Busy to Hate'.*

PREPOSITIONS

a motto of sb/sth *'Be prepared' is the motto of the Boy Scouts.*

a motto for sb *'The purer the better' might be a good motto for a water company.*

> **THESAURUS: motto**
> expression, idiom, cliché, saying/proverb, slogan, motto → **phrase**

mount *v* THESAURUS climb

mountain *n* a very high hill

ADJECTIVES

a high mountain *Mount Everest is the highest mountain in the world.*

a steep mountain *The village is surrounded by steep mountains.*

rugged mountains (=rough and steep) *The scenery varies from rugged mountains to gentle hills.*

a majestic mountain *literary* (=high and impressive) *The majestic mountains rise up to over 5,000 metres.*

a snow-capped mountain (=with snow on the top) *The hotel offers beautiful views of snow-capped mountains.*

a sacred/holy mountain *Mount Fuji is considered to be a sacred mountain.*

VERBS

climb a mountain (*also* **ascend a mountain** *formal*): *Hillary and Tenzing were the first people to climb Mount Everest.*

go up a mountain *We went up the mountain behind the house.*

go down a mountain (*also* **descend a mountain** *formal*): *She lost her way as she went down the mountain.*

cross the mountains *We crossed the mountains between Spain and France.*

mountains rise up/soar up (=go high into the sky) *The mountains rise up above the plains.*

a mountain towers above sb/sth (=is very high next to someone or something) *The great mountain towered above us.*

mountain + NOUNS

a mountain range/chain (=a line of mountains) *The Alps are the largest mountain range in Europe.*

a mountain top/peak *Until the end of June you may find snow on the mountain tops.*

a mountain slope *Snow lay on the steep mountain slopes.*

a mountain pass (=a path or road between mountains) *Their journey took them through river valleys and over mountain passes.*

a mountain stream *The water was as clear and cold as a mountain stream.*

a mountain village *Kaprun is a delightful mountain village in Austria.*

a mountain climber *Emerson was an experienced mountain climber.*

mountain rescue (=people who help people who are in difficulty on a mountain) *Mountain* *rescue teams were called out to search for the missing men.*

PHRASES

the top/summit of a mountain (=the highest point) *We climbed to the top of the mountain.*

the foot/bottom of a mountain (=the lowest part) *There are several villages at the foot of the mountain.*

the side of a mountain *The path wound up the side of the mountain.*

PREPOSITIONS

on a mountain *The hotel is located on a mountain overlooking the lake.*

up/down a mountain *He had never been up a mountain before.*

in the mountains (=in an area where there are a lot of mountains) *In the mountains, the air cools quickly in the evenings.*

mournful *adj* THESAURUS ▶ sad (1)

mouth *n*

the part of your face which you put food into, or which you use for speaking

ADJECTIVES

a big/large/wide mouth *Billy's wide mouth stretched into a grin.*

a full mouth (=with large attractive lips) *She had beautiful eyes and a full mouth.*

a generous mouth *literary* (=a large mouth that is attractive) *On her generous mouth was a smile.*

a dry mouth (=especially because someone is nervous or ill) *My mouth was dry and my hands were shaking.*

VERBS

open your mouth *He opened his mouth wide so the doctor could examine his throat.*

shut/close your mouth *Close your mouth when you chew, please, Michael.*

cover your mouth *She laughed, covering her mouth with her hand.*

wipe your mouth *He laid down his fork and wiped his mouth.*

kiss sb on the mouth *She walked boldly up to him and kissed him on the mouth.*

sb's mouth falls/drops open (=suddenly opens because they are very surprised) *"Me?" she said, her mouth dropping open.*

PHRASES

the corner/side of your mouth *A smile lifted the corners of her mouth.*

the roof of your mouth (=the top inside part) *He made a clicking sound with his tongue on the roof of his mouth.*

with your mouth open *He was chewing with his mouth open.*

PREPOSITIONS

in your mouth *The woman had a cigarette in her mouth.*

around your mouth *As you get older, you develop more lines around your mouth and eyes.*

mouth-watering *adj* THESAURUS ▶ delicious

move *n*

1 something that you decide to do in order to achieve something

ADJECTIVES/NOUNS + move

sb's next move *He wasn't sure what his next move should be.*

the first move *She waited for Michael to make the first move.*

a good/wise move (=sensible) *I'm not sure it was a good move giving him the job.*

a smart/shrewd/canny move (=good and clever) *It was a smart move to sell the company when they did.*

the right move *He hoped he had made the right move in telling his father.*

a bad move *It was a bad move letting him come here in the first place.*

a false/wrong move (=a mistake) *One wrong move and the business might never recover.*

a surprise move (=one people were not expecting) *In a surprise move, Dixon has been named as the team's new manager.*

a bold/daring move (=taking a lot of courage) *The writers made a bold move by killing off the main character.*

a drastic move (=one that seems very sudden and severe) *They were worried that such a drastic move could have a bad effect on the stock market.*

a tactical/strategic move (=carefully planned to achieve something) *The announcement was a tactical move to draw public attention away from more serious issues.*

a career move (=a decision that will improve the type of job you can do) *It looked like a good career move, with the possibility of promotion later.*

VERBS + move

make a move *They are worried about making the wrong move.*

welcome a move *Environmentalists welcomed the move to limit the length of fishing nets.*

support/back a move *The move was supported by the government.*

oppose/reject a move *Union members have opposed the move.*

move + VERBS

a move follows sth *The move follows complaints from local residents.*

M

a move is aimed at doing sth/is designed to do sth *The move is aimed at strengthening business in the region.*

PHRASES

make no move to do sth *The authorities have made no move to resolve the conflict.*

sth is a move in the right direction (=one that will help you achieve what you want) *The decision seemed to be a move in the right direction.*

PREPOSITIONS

a move towards sth *The country's first moves towards independence began in 1967.*

a move away from sth *A worldwide move away from the use of fossil fuels will cut carbon emissions.*

2 when someone moves for a short time in a particular direction

ADJECTIVES

a sudden move *Don't make any sudden moves, or you will frighten the horse.*

one false/wrong move (=in the wrong direction) *One false move, and she'd fall over the edge.*

VERBS

make a move *She made a move towards the door.*

make no move to do sth *He made no move to stop her.*

watch/follow sb's every move *His eyes followed Cissy's every move.*

movement *n*

1 when someone or something changes position or moves from one place to another

ADJECTIVES

a slight/small movement *He noticed a slight movement behind the bushes.*

a sudden movement *With a sudden movement, Ellen reached out and grabbed the letter.*

a quick/rapid movement *In one quick movement, he took her hand and pulled her up to dance.*

a slow movement *The old man's movements were painfully slow.*

a smooth/fluid movement (=graceful) *She admired his smooth movement as he jumped the fence.*

a jerky movement (=with many starts and stops) *Teresa's movements were jerky and nervous.*

a forward/backward movement *The forward movement of the boat stopped.*

an involuntary movement (=one that you cannot control) *The disease can cause involuntary movements of the muscles.*

NOUNS + movement

body movements *Babies communicate with body movements and facial expressions.*

hand/arm/leg etc movements *Students of kung fu have to learn many different hand movements.*

troop movements (=of soldiers) *There have been reports of troop movements in the area.*

VERBS

make a movement *He made a small movement with his head, to indicate the door.*

control sb's/sth's movement *The camera's movement is controlled by a computer.*

restrict/hinder sb's movement (=make movement more difficult) *Clothes should not be so tight that they restrict your movement.*

track/monitor sb's/sth's movements *Electronic tags are used to track the movements of prisoners.*

PHRASES

freedom of movement (=when people can go wherever they want) *The automobile gave people a freedom of movement previously unknown.*

ease of movement (=when someone or something can move easily) *Cyclists wear stretchy shorts for ease of movement.*

2 a group of people who have the same ideas or beliefs, and work together to achieve an aim

ADJECTIVES/NOUNS + movement

a growing movement *There is a growing movement against globalization.*

a mass movement (=one that involves a lot of people) *The scattered protests had been transformed into a mass movement.*

a political/religious movement *The group never became a serious political movement.*

the pro-democracy/anti-war etc movement *Protests by the pro-democracy movement ended in violence.*

the civil rights/animal rights/gay rights movement *Extremists from the animal rights movement were believed to be behind the attack.*

the feminist/women's movement *Despite the gains of the feminist movement, women are still earning less than men.*

the peace movement *Sheehan was heavily involved in the peace movement.*

the environmental movement *The environmental movement started to become popular in the 1970s.*

VERBS

start/launch/found a movement *They launched a movement to save the local language.*

join a movement *She joined the feminist movement in the 1960s.*

lead a movement *Havel led the movement against the communist government.*

support a movement *Police clashed with*

demonstrators supporting the anti-war movement.

crush a movement (=use violent or extreme methods to stop it) *The army attempted to crush the pro-democracy movement.*

a movement begins/starts *The civil rights movement began in the 1960s.*

PREPOSITIONS

a movement against sth *There was no well-organized movement against the war.*

movie *n*

moving pictures shown at a cinema or on television

ADJECTIVES/NOUNS + movie

an action/adventure/war movie *There have been so many war movies about Vietnam.*

a horror movie *The old house looked like something out of a horror movie.*

a science fiction movie *My favourite science fiction movie is 'Avatar'.*

a documentary movie *They showed a documentary movie about the 1920s.*

a cowboy movie *Clint Eastwood made a lot of cowboy movies.*

a classic movie *'Citizen Kane' was Orson Welles' classic movie about the life of a newspaper tycoon.*

a cult movie (=one that a small group of people like very much and watch often) *'Blade Runner' started as a cult movie before it became a worldwide hit.*

a hit movie (=a successful film) *The book was turned into a hit movie starring Liza Minnelli.*

a big-budget/low-budget movie (=one that costs a lot or very little to make) *Big-budget Hollywood movies can cost over $200 million.*

an independent movie (=a film made by a small film company) *Young directors began making small independent movies.*

an art-house movie (=made by a small company for artistic reasons, not to earn lots of money) *It's a small cinema which shows mainly art-house movies.*

a black-and-white movie *I love those old black-and-white movies.*

a silent movie (=made in the time before films had sound) *He started his career in silent movies.*

a foreign-language movie (=a film in a language that is not the audience's native language) *Foreign-language movies seldom do well at the box office.*

VERBS + movie

watch a movie *We watched an old movie on TV.*

see a movie *She had agreed to go and see a movie with him that evening.*

go to a movie *How about going to a movie?*

take in a movie *AmE* (=go to see a movie) *Maybe we could go out to dinner and take in a movie.*

appear in/be in a movie *She's also appeared in ten movies.*

star in a movie (=play one of the main characters) *Depp will star in director Tim Burton's next movie.*

make/shoot a movie *The children have made their own movies for the contest.*

direct/produce/edit a movie *He wrote and directed the movie.*

show/screen a movie *What movies are they showing this weekend?*

movie + VERBS

a movie stars/features sb *The movie stars Colin Firth as King George VI.*

a movie is released (=becomes available for the public to see) *The movie has already been released in the US.*

movie + NOUNS

a movie actor/star *She looked like a movie star.*

the movie industry *Steven Spielberg is a highly respected figure in the movie industry.*

a movie director *Hitchcock was one of the greatest movie directors of all time.*

a movie producer (=someone who controls the preparation of a film) *British movie producer Alexander Korda decided to make a movie about Vienna.*

a movie crew/unit *The movie crew are making a documentary about village life.*

a movie company *Many movie companies are based in Hollywood.*

a movie studio (=a company that makes films, or a building where films are made) *The scenes were all shot in a movie studio.*

a movie premiere (=the first showing of a film) *Movie premieres tend to be glamorous occasions.*

a movie critic *Movie critics said the movie was much too long.*

PREPOSITIONS

a movie about sb/sth *I like movies about detectives.*

> **Movie** is used especially in American English. In British English, people usually say **film**.

moving *adj*

making you feel strong emotions, especially sadness or sympathy

ADVERBS

very/deeply moving (*also* **profoundly moving** *formal*): *It is a beautiful and deeply moving film.*

intensely/incredibly moving *Her final words to me were incredibly moving.*

NOUNS

a moving story/account *It is a moving story of love and death.*

M

a moving speech/performance *He gave a moving speech at her funeral.*
a moving film/scene *In the film's most moving scene, she finally finds her mother.*
a moving experience *It is a moving experience to visit these wonderfully preserved Roman cities.*
a moving tribute (=a moving expression of admiration, especially about someone who has died) *He paid a moving tribute to his wife.*

VERBS

find sth moving *She found their singing so moving that tears came to her eyes.*

THESAURUS: moving

emotive, moving, touching, poignant, sentimental, highly charged → **emotional (1)**

mud *n*

wet earth that has become soft and sticky

ADJECTIVES

deep mud *The car was stuck in deep mud.*
thick mud *It had rained, and we had to wade through thick mud.*
soft mud *Her feet sank into the soft mud.*
wet mud *My boots were full of wet mud.*
dried mud *There was dried mud on the carpet.*

VERBS

be covered in mud *By the end of the game, all the kids were covered in mud.*
be caked in/with mud (=be covered with mud that has dried) *Our boots were caked with mud.*
be/get stuck in mud *It was impossible to move the car – its wheels had got stuck in the mud.*
wade through mud (=walk with difficulty through mud) *Residents had to wade through mud to get to their houses.*

mud + NOUNS

mud flats (=low areas of land with a lot of mud) *Along the shore of the river there are mud flats.*
a mud track *The streets of the town were rough mud tracks.*
a mud hut (=a house made from dried mud) *Many villages in Mali consist of mud huts.*
a mud slide (=the sudden movement of a large amount of mud) *The town was buried by a mud slide.*

PHRASES

a sea of mud (=a lot of mud) *Rain had turned the campsite into a sea of mud.*

muddle *n*

a confused or disorganized state or situation

PHRASES

be in a muddle *I'm in such a muddle, I'd completely forgotten you were coming today.*
get in/into a muddle *I got in a muddle when I tried to give them directions.*

ADJECTIVES

an awful/hopeless muddle *I'll get in a hopeless muddle if I don't put these papers in the right order.*
an embarrassing muddle *The grand opening event turned into an embarrassing muddle.*
a financial muddle *He was in a financial muddle because he hadn't kept his accounts up to date.*
a bureaucratic/administrative muddle (=confusion or mistakes by officials) *He hadn't yet received the money because of a bureaucratic muddle.*

PREPOSITIONS

a muddle over/about sth *There was a muddle over the arrangements for paying.*

muddy *adj*

covered with mud or containing mud

NOUNS

muddy water *His jeans were soaked with muddy water.*
a muddy puddle/pool/pond *There was a large muddy puddle outside the house.*
a muddy field *Their shoes sank into the muddy field.*
a muddy track/path/lane *She set off down the muddy track to the farm.*
muddy ground *The ground was very muddy.*
muddy boots/shoes *Please leave your muddy boots by the door.*

VERBS

get (sth) muddy *The golf course gets very muddy when it rains. | I tried not to get my trousers muddy.*
make sth muddy *Rain had made the track muddy.*

THESAURUS: muddy

filthy, squalid, polluted, contaminated, unhygienic, unsanitary, muddy, grubby, grimy, greasy, dingy, dusty, mucky, soiled → **dirty**

muffled *adj* THESAURUS ▸ **quiet (1)**

mug *v* THESAURUS ▸ **steal**

muggy *adj* THESAURUS ▸ **damp (1)**

mundane *adj* THESAURUS ▸ **boring**

murder[1] *n*

the crime of deliberately killing someone

VERBS

commit (a) murder (=kill someone deliberately and illegally) *Whoever committed these murders planned them carefully.*

convict sb of murder (=decide that someone is officially guilty of murder in a court of law) *Smith was convicted of murder and sentenced to life in prison.*

accuse sb of murder (=say that you think someone murdered a person) *He was accused of his wife's murder.*

charge sb with murder (=officially say that someone may be guilty of murder) *Is there enough evidence to charge her with murder?*

investigate a murder *The police are investigating the murder of a homeless man.*

solve a murder (=find out who murdered someone) *The murder has never been solved.*

a murder takes place/happens (*also* **a murder occurs** *formal*): *The murder took place inside a hotel room.*

ADJECTIVES

attempted murder (=the crime of trying to kill someone) *He could be charged with assault, or even attempted murder.*

mass murder (=of a large number of people) *Hitler was responsible for the largest mass murder in history.*

first-degree murder/murder in the first degree *AmE* (=the most serious type of murder under US law) *If convicted of first-degree murder, he could be executed.*

premeditated murder (=planned before it happens) *Prosecutors claimed that this was premeditated murder.*

a brutal/horrific murder (=violent and cruel) *He is wanted for the brutal murder of an elderly couple.*

cold-blooded murder (=cruel and without showing any emotion) *The terrorists were responsible for the cold-blooded murder of 50 people.*

an unsolved murder (=in which the killer has never been found) *Police are questioning a man about two unsolved murders.*

murder + NOUNS

the murder weapon *Police are searching for the murder weapon.*

a murder victim *The mother of the murder victim wept in court.*

a murder scene (=where a murder happened) *His fingerprints were found at the murder scene.*

a murder investigation/inquiry *Detectives have launched a murder investigation after a woman's body was found.*

a murder case *She is an experienced detective who has worked on several murder cases.*

a murder mystery (=a story about a murder) *Agatha Christie was famous for writing murder mysteries.*

a murder trial *The murder trial heard how the couple's relationship had always been violent.*

PHRASES

a motive for a murder (=a reason to kill someone) *Police believe the motive for the murders was robbery.*

be guilty of murder *He's certainly a strange man, but I don't think he's guilty of murder.*

murder² *v* THESAURUS ▸ kill

murky *adj* THESAURUS ▸ dark (1)

murmur *v*

to say something in a soft voice that is difficult to hear clearly

ADVERBS

murmur (sth) softly/quietly *The boy murmured softly as she lifted him onto his bed.*

murmur (sth) politely *"How do you do?" Fabia murmured politely.*

PHRASES

murmur (sth) under your breath *"Hurry up," he murmured under his breath.*

muscle *n*

one of the pieces of flesh inside your body that you use in order to move, and that connect your bones together

ADJECTIVES/NOUNS + muscle

arm/leg/stomach etc muscles *Her leg muscles ached after the run.*

strong muscles *You need strong muscles to lift the case.*

big muscles *He went to the gym every day and developed big arm muscles.*

rippling muscles (=muscles that move in a strong attractive way) *The sight of his rippling muscles sends women wild.*

sore muscles *A hot bath is good for sore muscles.*

a strained/pulled muscle (=one that has been injured by a sudden movement) *He cannot play because of a strained leg muscle.*

a torn muscle *Johnson suffered a torn calf muscle during training.*

VERBS + muscle

use your muscles *I don't really use my arm muscles very much.*

build up/strengthen muscles *Regular exercise will help to strengthen the muscles in your legs.*

pull/strain a muscle (=injure it) *Rooney has pulled a muscle and won't play tomorrow.*

flex your muscles (=bend your arm muscles so that people can see how strong you are) *He was lifting weights and flexing his muscles.*

relax your muscles *A hot bath will help relax sore muscles.*

tense/tighten your muscles *He tensed his stomach muscles, ready for the blow.*

muscle + VERBS

your muscles ache *I ran until my muscles ached.*

M

muscle + NOUNS

muscle strength/power *This exercise will help increase your muscle strength.*

muscle tone (=the firmness of your muscles) *Swimming is good exercise for improving muscle tone.*

a muscle spasm (=when your muscles tighten suddenly) *The drug can cause painful muscle spasms.*

muscle strain/injury *Robson has recovered from the muscle strain which kept him out of last week's game.*

muscular *adj* THESAURUS ▶ **strong (1)**

museum *n*

a building where important cultural, historical, or scientific objects are kept for the public to see

ADJECTIVES/NOUNS + museum

a history/science/art etc museum *The town has an interesting local history museum.*

a national/local/regional museum *We went to see an exhibition at the National Museum of Photography.*

VERBS

go to/visit a museum *We visited the Natural History Museum in Kensington.*

establish a museum *The museum was first established in 1857.*

be kept in a museum *The statues are kept in the British Museum.*

a museum has/contains sth (*also* **a museum houses sth** *formal*): *The museum houses a large collection of Egyptian art.*

museum + NOUNS

a museum collection *Many of his paintings are in museum collections.*

a museum curator (=the person in charge of the objects in a museum) *She is studying art history and she hopes to become a museum curator.*

a museum exhibit (=an object shown in a museum) *We looked round at the museum exhibits.*

PREPOSITIONS

in a museum *The coins are now in a local museum.*

a museum of sth *Have you been to the Museum of Modern Art in New York?*

music *n*

the sounds made by musical instruments or people singing

ADJECTIVES/NOUNS + music

pop/rock/jazz/soul/folk/country etc music *The Beatles were the most successful group in the history of pop music.*

classical music *My father listened a lot to classical music.*

⚠ Don't say 'classic music'.

traditional music *The band plays traditional Irish music.*

modern/contemporary music *A lot of modern music sounds the same to me.*

world music (=by people from different countries around the world) *The concert will feature many world music stars.*

recorded music *Live music can sound very different from recorded music.*

live music (=played by musicians on stage) *Most of the bars have live music.*

background music (=that you hear but do not listen to) *There was some background music playing in the restaurant.*

film music *Williams wrote the film music for films such as 'Star Wars'.*

loud music *They were kept awake by loud music from next door.*

dramatic music *His operas are full of dramatic music.*

soft/quiet music *James took her for a romantic dinner with candles and soft music.*

VERBS

listen to music *Ella liked to listen to music while she worked.*

play music *A small band was playing jazz music.*

write/compose music *He composed the music for the 'Lord of the Rings' films.*

read music (=understand music that is written down, so that you can play or sing the notes) *His father taught him to read music.*

perform music (=play or sing music) *The group will perform music from Germany and Austria.*

make music (=play or write music) *We began making music together about five years ago.*

record music *The singer is recording music for his new album.*

download music (=get music from the internet) *The research shows that many people are downloading music for free.*

music blares (out) (=music is loud and unpleasant) *Music blared out from the bar across the road.*

music fades (=becomes quieter gradually) *The music fades and the main character comes onto the stage.*

music + NOUNS

a music festival *The band played at an international music festival.*

the music industry/business *The music industry is having a hard time because people are getting music for free from the internet.*

a music scene (=activities relating to music, and the people involved in them) *The city has a* *lively music scene and there are lots of good local bands.*

a music lover *Music lovers have been waiting for this record for a long time.*

a music stand (=a metal frame for holding a musician's music while they play) *She propped the book on the music stand.*

PHRASES

a piece of music *It's a beautiful piece of music.*

musician *n*

someone who plays a musical instrument, especially very well or as a job

ADJECTIVES

a professional musician *Billy was a professional musician with his own band.*

an amateur musician (=one who plays for pleasure, not as a job) *He was an amateur musician who played in several local jazz bands.*

a young musician *The song was written by a young musician from Minnesota.*

a good/great/fine musician *Bob Marley was a great musician.*

a talented/gifted musician *His wife was a gifted musician.*

a famous/legendary musician *The record features songs by legendary blues musician Robert Johnson.*

an accomplished musician (=very skilful) *She was an accomplished musician as well as a painter.*

a classical musician *He was a classical musician who enjoyed playing Mozart's works.*

a serious musician (=one who plays a lot and thinks music is very important) *Serious musicians have always disapproved of his work.*

a backing musician (=who plays while another person sings) *He got work as a backing musician for Bob Dylan.*

NOUNS + musician

a jazz/rock/folk/pop musician *John Coltrane was a well-known jazz musician.*

a session musician (=who is not part of a band but records with different bands) *In the 1970s he worked as a session musician.*

a street musician (=who plays in the street, asking the public for money) *He liked listening to the street musicians who played in the city square.*

VERBS

a musician plays/performs (sth) *Many famous musicians will be playing at the festival.*

mysterious *adj*

difficult to explain or understand

mysterious + NOUNS

a mysterious man/woman/figure *Jim attracts the attention of a mysterious woman, who keeps sending him gifts.*

a mysterious stranger *A mysterious stranger saved her life.*

sb's mysterious death *Detectives are investigating the mysterious death of a young soldier.*

a mysterious illness/disease/accident *The doctor was unable to explain his patient's mysterious illness.*

sb's mysterious disappearance *The case ended after the mysterious disappearance of the main witness.*

mysterious powers *Scientists are often puzzled by the mysterious powers of nature.*

NOUNS + mysterious

something mysterious *There was something mysterious about him and she wanted to ask so many questions.*

PHRASES

die/disappear/vanish in mysterious circumstances *He disappeared in mysterious circumstances, just before the wedding.*

> If you cannot understand something and it seems strange, you can also say that it is **a mystery**: *His death **remains a mystery**. | The way his mind works **is a mystery to me**.*
>
> If you say that an event is **shrouded/veiled in mystery**, it seems very mysterious and no one knows exactly what happened: *The actor's death is still **shrouded in mystery**.*

THESAURUS: mysterious

puzzling

question | situation | phenomenon | aspect

difficult to explain or understand, especially so that you spend a long time thinking about something:

There was the puzzling question of where the money had gone. | The northern lights are a puzzling phenomenon (=a puzzling thing that happens). *| I **found** her attitude **deeply puzzling**.*

baffling

case | murder | mystery

impossible to understand or solve, so that you feel very confused:

*It was a baffling case for the police. | The ship's disappearance remained a baffling mystery. | Like many people, I **find** the whole thing **completely baffling**.*

inexplicable *formal*

reason | feeling | behaviour | event | phenomenon

impossible to explain:

For some inexplicable reason, her mind went completely blank. | Perhaps drink was the true explanation of his inexplicable behaviour.

enigmatic *formal*

smile | expression | figure | man | reply

mysterious and difficult to understand, but also often attractive or interesting:

M

M

When our eyes met, she gave me an enigmatic smile. | Throughout his life, the great writer remained an enigmatic figure.

cryptic *formal*
message | remark | comment | reference having a meaning that is difficult to understand, and is not expressed in a clear direct way:
I received a rather cryptic message, which said that the time for waiting was over. | She made a cryptic comment about the two of us being 'close friends'.

mystery *n*

something that people do not understand or cannot explain because they do not know enough about it

ADJECTIVES

a complete/total/real mystery *It's a complete mystery who this man is and where he is from.*

a big/great mystery *If scientists are right, they have solved one of the biggest mysteries in physics.*

an unsolved mystery *What happened to her is still an unsolved mystery.*

VERBS

sth remains a mystery *The cause of the accident remains a mystery.*

solve/unravel a mystery *The research could help solve the mystery of why some people develop the illness and not others.*

explain the mystery *No one has been able to explain the mystery of why so many ships have disappeared in this area.*

mystery surrounds sth *Mystery surrounded the death of a Russian spy in London.*

the mystery deepens (=it becomes more difficult to understand) *The mystery deepened with the discovery of a letter from his ex-wife.*

PREPOSITIONS

the mystery of sth *Scientists are trying to unravel the mystery of the origins of life on Earth.*

mystery about/as to sth *There is still the mystery about where all the money has gone.*

a mystery to sb *The way her mind worked was always a mystery to him.*

PHRASES

shrouded/veiled in mystery (=not able to be understood or explained) *The origins of this tradition remain shrouded in mystery.*

an element of mystery (=part of something that seems mysterious) *There is still an element of mystery about what really happened.*

an air/sense of mystery (=a mysterious quality) *The dark glasses gave her an air of mystery.*

sth is a bit of a mystery *informal* (=it seems strange and you do not understand it) *I don't know why he left – it's all a bit of a mystery.*

one of life's (little) mysteries *humorous* (=something that you will never understand) *Where socks disappear to is one of life's little mysteries.*

be something of a mystery (=a mystery) *The origin of the name St Kilda is something of a mystery.*

myth *n*

1 an idea or story that many people believe, but which is not true

VERBS + myth

believe a myth *People still believe the myth that money will bring them happiness.*

create a myth *Stalin created a lot of myths about himself.*

explode/dispel/debunk a myth (=show that it is not true) *Our goal is to debunk the myth that science is boring.*

perpetuate a myth (=make it continue) *Let's stop perpetuating this myth.*

myth + VERBS

a myth grows up (=starts) *A number of myths have grown up about their relationship.*

a myth persists (=it continues) *The myth still persists that we need to build more roads.*

myths surrounding sth (=myths about something) *There are a lot of myths surrounding mental illness which still persist.*

ADJECTIVES

a common/popular myth (=that many people believe) *Contrary to popular myth, most road accidents are not the result of speeding.*

a modern myth *Is it a modern myth that we are living in a classless society?*

a powerful myth (=that has a lot of influence on people) *There is a powerful myth that crime has increased – in fact there was much more crime 100 years ago.*

a dangerous myth (= that may cause problems) *The idea that a little alcohol is good for you is a dangerous myth.*

an old myth *It's amazing that some people still believe that old myth.*

sth is a complete/total myth (=it is completely untrue) *The idea that smoking calms your nerves is a complete myth.*

an enduring myth (=that has continued for a long time) *The idea that Kennedy was shot by the CIA is one of the enduring myths of our time.*

an urban myth (=an unusual or shocking story that a lot of people believe but it probably is not true) *The story of a man meeting a beautiful woman who drugged him and stole his kidneys was just an urban myth.*

PHRASES

it is a myth that... *It's a complete myth that eating carrots helps you to see in the dark.*

sth is a bit of a myth *informal* (=it is not really true) *The whole story is a bit of a myth.*

PREPOSITIONS

a myth about sth *Constantly repeated myths about the difficulties of having a female boss do not help women in the workplace.*

the myth of sth *The myth of happy animals down on the farm is often far from the truth.*

2 a story about people in ancient times

ADJECTIVES

an ancient myth *According to ancient myth, Chiron taught Achilles to run swiftly by making him chase wild deer.*

a classical myth *In classical myth, Dionysus marries Ariadne, who was princess of Crete.*

a Greek/Roman/Chinese etc myth *In the Roman myth, Romulus and Remus were brought up by wolves.*

PREPOSITIONS

myth of/about sth *The painting is based on the myth of Narcissus.*

Nn

N

nail *n*

your nails are the hard smooth layers on the ends of your fingers and toes

ADJECTIVES

long/short nails *Her long nails were painted a pearly pink.*

dirty/clean nails *How did you get such dirty nails?*

VERBS

cut your nails *Try to avoid cutting your nails too short.*

bite your nails *Eddie bit his nails nervously.*

trim your nails (=cut a small amount off) *His nails were neatly trimmed.*

file your nails *A girl was filing her nails on the bus.*

paint/polish/varnish your nails (=put coloured liquid on your nails) *Her nails were painted red.*

do your nails *informal* (=cut, file, or paint your nails) *She sat at her desk, doing her nails.*

break a nail *Oh, no, I've broken a nail.*

nail + NOUNS

nail varnish/polish *She took a bottle of purple nail varnish out of her make-up bag.*

> You write **fingernail** and **toenail** as one word.

naked *adj*

1 not wearing any clothes – used especially when this seems rather shocking

NOUNS

a naked man/woman/boy/girl *There is a picture of a naked man on the cover of this month's magazine.*

a naked body *A naked body was found on the beach.*

naked chest/breasts/skin/flesh *Sweat ran down his naked chest.*

> If you look at something with **the naked eye**, you look at it without a telescope or microscope: *The cells are invisible to **the naked eye**.*

ADVERBS

completely/totally naked *She had just got out of the shower, and she was completely naked.*

half naked (=wearing very few clothes) *It was very hot in the mine, and the men were all half naked.*

stark naked (*also* **buck naked** *AmE*) (=completely naked – used when this is very surprising or shocking) *The local people wander around stark naked.*

VERBS

pose naked (=sit or stand without any clothes, so that someone can paint a picture or take a photograph of you) *The actress posed naked for a men's magazine.*

strip (sb) naked (=take off all someone's clothes very quickly or roughly) *The police stripped him naked and beat him with sticks.*

run/walk/swim naked *The children ran naked into the sea.*

THESAURUS: naked

bare

foot | leg | arm | shoulders | chest | back | skin

a bare part of the body is not covered by clothes:

The sand was too hot to walk on in bare feet. | Lucy felt the sun on her bare arms.

nude

picture | portrait | photograph | scene | statue | woman | man | figure | body | beach

naked – used especially when talking about someone in a painting, film, or work of art:

*He painted a nude portrait of his wife. | There have been complaints about the nude scenes in the film. | The artist asked her to **pose nude** for him* (=sit or stand without any clothes, so that someone can paint a picture or take a photograph of you). *| She **appeared nude** in the film.*

> **Nude** is also used as a noun (=a picture of a naked person): *He often painted **nudes**.* It is also used in the phrase **in the nude** (=without any clothes): *Some people like to swim **in the nude**.*

topless

dancer | waitress | model | woman | sunbathing | bar | photo

a topless woman has no clothes on the upper part of her body, so that her breasts are not covered:

*She worked as a topless dancer in a nightclub. | You need to be careful about sunburn if you **go topless*** (=wear no clothes on the upper part of your body).

> Instead of saying that someone is **naked**, you can say that they **have no clothes on/nothing on**: *He was standing there with **nothing on**!*
>
> If someone takes off their clothes, you say that they **get undressed**: *I **got undressed***

and got ready for bed. **Get undressed** is the most commonly used form of the verb **undress**.

2 used about something which is not hidden, and seems shocking

NOUNS

naked ambition/aggression *There is naked aggression against foreigners.*

naked greed/hatred *The government tried to satisfy the naked greed of its rich supporters.*

the naked truth/reality *Maybe it's time to state the naked truth. Pop music is dead.*

name *n*

1 what someone or something is called

ADJECTIVES/NOUNS + name

first name (*also* **given name** *especially AmE*) (=the name chosen for you by your parents) *"What's your first name?" "Helena."*

Christian name (=first name - becoming old-fashioned) *"Roman is an unusual Christian name," she said.*

last/family name (=the name that you share with your family) *Her first name is Isabella, and her last name is Mullane.*

middle name (=the name between your first and last names) *Harry Potter's middle name is James.*

full name (=your first name, middle name, and last name) *Rhoda Anne Dent was her full name.*

maiden name (=a woman's family name before she married and began using her husband's name) *My mother's maiden name was Higgins.*

user name (=when using a computer program) *Enter your user name and password.*

pen name (=a name that a writer uses which is not his or her real name) *Mark Twain was his pen name. His real name was Samuel Clemens.*

scientific/medical/technical name *The medical name for high blood pressure is hypertension.*

sth's common name (=the name that most people use for something, which is not scientific) *The plant's common name is willow moss.*

sth's official name *The Democratic People's Republic of Korea is the official name for North Korea.*

a false name *When arrested, he gave a false name to the police.*

VERBS

have a name *A lot of people have the name 'Smith'.*

sign your name *Sign your name here, please.*

give sb a name *They gave their pets unusual names.*

know sb's name *His first name is Tom, but I don't know his last name.*

ask (sb) their name *The man asked me my name.*

tell sb your name *When he told me his name, I knew I had met him somewhere before.*

give (sb) your name (=tell someone your name, especially someone in an official position) *I gave my name to the receptionist.*

call sb's name (=say someone's name loudly, to get their attention) *He called Jean's name, but there was no answer.*

change your name *Many immigrants changed their names to seem more American.*

PREPOSITIONS

the name of sth *What's the name of the street?*

the name for sth *Edo was the ancient name for Tokyo.*

under the name (of) sth *I have a reservation under the name of Jackson.*

by the name of *formal* (=used for saying what someone's name is) *He married a young lady by the name of Sarah Hunt.*

PHRASES

know sb by name (=know their name) *The head teacher knew all the children by name.*

call sb by their first/family etc name (=use that name when you speak to them) *Everyone called him by his first name.*

go by the name of... (=be called something by people, often when that is not your real name) *As he had long red hair, he went by the name of Red.*

under an assumed name (=using a false name in order to hide your real name) *He had rented the car under an assumed name.*

your name and address *Write your name and address at the top of the form.*

2 *informal* a famous person, company, or product

ADJECTIVES/NOUNS + name

a big/top/great name *Many of the big names in hairdressing have their own range of shampoos and hair products.*

a famous/well-known name *The exhibition featured Rolls Royce, Ford, Toyota, and other famous names from the car industry.*

a household name (=one that most people know) *General Electric became a household name in the US for its appliances and lighting.*

a familiar name *Several familiar names attended the show.*

3 the opinion that people have about a person or organization

ADJECTIVES

a good name *The reports could damage the bank's good name.*

a bad name *The behaviour of some players has given the sport a bad name.*

VERBS

clear your name (=prove that you have not done something bad or illegal) *She was determined to clear her name.*

give sb/sth a bad name (=make someone or something have a bad reputation) *A scandal like this could give the university a bad name.*

You say that someone **makes** or **establishes a name for themselves**, when saying that they become well known and well respected for what they do: *He quickly* ***made a name for himself*** *in the art world.* | *The company has* ***established a name for itself*** *in Europe.*

THESAURUS: name

image, name, standing, prestige, stature → **reputation**

N

nap *n*

a short sleep, especially during the day

ADJECTIVES/NOUNS + nap

a short/little nap *A short nap may make you feel better.*

an afternoon/morning nap *She has her afternoon nap at about two.*

VERBS

have/take a nap *I took a nap after lunch.*

narrow *adj*

1 measuring only a small distance from one side to the other, especially in relation to the length

NOUNS

a narrow street/road/lane *We visited the lovely old town with its narrow winding streets.*

a narrow path/track/alley *There was a narrow path at the side of the house.*

a narrow passage/corridor/passageway *His office was at the end of a narrow passage.*

a narrow strip/band/stripe *She cut the ham into narrow strips.*

a narrow gap *Rosie peered through the narrow gap in the curtains.*

a narrow bed *The bed was narrow and uncomfortable.*

narrow stairs/a narrow stairway *She went ahead of him up the narrow stairs.*

a narrow valley/canyon *The stream is in a steep narrow valley.*

a narrow ledge *He fell from the cliff and landed on a narrow ledge.*

narrow hips *She had narrow hips like a boy.*

ADVERBS

very narrow *Cats can squeeze through very narrow gaps.*

quite/fairly/rather narrow *The streets are quite narrow and full of people.*

relatively/comparatively narrow *The path is relatively narrow.*

THESAURUS: narrow

thin

line | **slice** | **strip** | **layer**

measuring only a small distance from one side to the other:

She noticed a thin line of sweat on his upper lip. | *Ben cut a thin slice of bread.* | *Cut the peppers into thin strips.* | *The road was covered with a thin layer of ice.*

fine

hair | **thread** | **wire** | **needle** | **tip**

extremely narrow – used especially about hair, thread etc:

Polly felt the fine hairs on her arm rise. | *The cotton is spun to a fine thread.* | *The cloth is richly decorated with fine gold wire.* | *The plant's broad leaves curve to a fine tip.*

ANTONYMS **narrow → wide (1)**

2 limited and not including many things

NOUNS

a narrow range *The shop stocks a narrow range of products.*

narrow scope *The main weakness of the review is its narrow scope.*

a narrow focus *The report has an unnecessarily narrow focus.*

a narrow view *You have a very narrow view of what is normal.*

narrow limits *The date of the temple can be identified to within fairly narrow limits.*

narrow confines (=used to refer to something that does not include or allow many different things) *She was tired of the narrow confines of boarding school life.*

a narrow sense *In that narrow sense, Reagan was right.*

a narrow definition *This is a fairly narrow definition of income.*

ADVERBS

very narrow *This definition is a very narrow one.*

quite/fairly/rather narrow *The range of options is fairly narrow.*

relatively/comparatively narrow *The focus of this study was relatively narrow.*

ANTONYMS **narrow → wide (2)**

3 used when something could easily not have happened

NOUNS

a narrow escape *They had a narrow escape when their car suddenly burst into flames.*

a narrow victory *The result was a narrow victory for Arsenal.*

a narrow defeat *It was a narrow defeat for France.*

a narrow margin *Kennedy won the election by a narrow margin.*

nasty *adj* unpleasant or unkind

NOUNS

a nasty shock/surprise *I got a nasty shock when I discovered my phone was missing.*

a nasty habit *Drivers often have a nasty habit of driving too close to cyclists.*

a nasty accident/fall *Ella had a nasty fall and broke her leg.*

a nasty injury/cut/gash *That's a nasty cut you've got on your arm.*

a nasty cough/cold *He's had a nasty cough for a few weeks now.*

a nasty feeling *I have a nasty feeling that things are going to get worse.*

a nasty taste/smell *There's a nasty smell in here.*

nasty weather *The weather is going to be nasty tomorrow.*

a nasty business (=an unpleasant situation or activity) *War is a very nasty business.*

nasty things (*also* **nasty stuff** *informal*): *He wrote some nasty things about me.*

a nasty comment/remark *She made a nasty comment about my family.*

VERBS

turn/get nasty *When Harry refused, Don turned nasty and hit him.*

look/sound nasty *That cut looks nasty - you should go to the hospital.*

ADVERBS

very/really nasty *He was very nasty to me.*

downright/thoroughly nasty *Some of the comments were downright nasty.*

particularly nasty *It was a particularly nasty attack.*

pretty nasty *informal*: *It was a pretty nasty injury.*

rather nasty *We had a rather nasty surprise.*

PREPOSITIONS

be nasty to sb *She's always being nasty to her sister.*

THESAURUS: nasty

mean, nasty, hurtful, spiteful, malicious, unsympathetic, hard-hearted, inconsiderate, insensitive → **unkind**

nation *n*

a country, considered especially in relation to its people and its social or economic structure

ADJECTIVES

a great/powerful nation *China is one of the most powerful nations in the world.*

a rich/wealthy nation *Most tourists come from the wealthy nations of the world.*

a poor nation (*also* **an impoverished nation** *formal*): *The high cost of medicines in poor nations prevents many citizens from receiving health care.*

an independent/sovereign nation (=one that rules itself, rather than being run by another country) *We are a sovereign nation and do not accept interference in our internal affairs.*

an industrial/industrialized nation *The rich industrial nations dominate the global economy.*

a developed/advanced nation (=one that has many industries) *In the developed nations, many students stay in education after 18.*

a developing/emerging nation (=one that is starting to have more industry) *Food shortages are often a problem in developing nations.*

VERBS

lead the nation *He led the nation out of a depression.*

address the nation (=make an official speech to people in a country) *The president addressed the nation from outside the White House.*

unite the nation *The crisis seemed to unite the nation.*

divide the nation (=make people in a country disagree) *The war has divided the nation.*

create/build a nation *They worked together to build a new nation.*

shock the nation *This terrible crime has shocked the whole nation.*

a nation faces sth *The nation is facing its greatest challenge ever.*

THESAURUS: nation

nation, state, power, superpower, land → **country (1)**

national *adj*

related to a whole nation as opposed to any of its parts

NOUNS

national security *Officials believe this group is a threat to national security.*

the national average *The crime rate in the area is below the national average.*

a national team *He plays for the Danish national team.*

a national newspaper *His photo appeared in every national newspaper.*

national television/radio *The president appeared on national television.*

a national organization/charity/agency *It is a national organization which offers advice to consumers.*

a national campaign/survey/election *A national survey of teachers found that many are unhappy in their jobs.*

a national anthem (=a national song) *The national anthem of both teams was played at the start of the game.*

the national interest (=what is good or necessary for a country) *I believe these changes will be against our national interest.*

national pride *Jamaican music is a source of deep national pride.*

national identity *This tradition is part of our national identity.*

PHRASES

at a national level *Religion matters very much at a national level.*

national and international *The paper contains national and international news.*

nationality *n*

the state of legally being a citizen of a particular country

ADJECTIVES

a different nationality *The school has students of many different nationalities.*

dual nationality (=two nationalities) *He has dual nationality because he was born in France to Argentine parents.*

all nationalities/every nationality (=many different nationalities) *Her books are popular with people of all nationalities.*

VERBS

have British/US etc nationality (*also* **hold British/US etc nationality**) *Her husband has Japanese nationality.*

change nationality *She changed nationality twice.*

nationality + NOUNS

a nationality group *They examined the differences between nationality groups.*

PREPOSITIONS

of Chinese/Algerian/any etc nationality *We accept students of any nationality.*

PHRASES

on grounds of nationality *It is illegal to discriminate on grounds of nationality.*

native *adj*

1 your native country, town etc is the place where you were born

NOUNS

sb's native country *He moved back to his native country.*

sb's native land/soil *literary*: *I knew I would never see my native land again.*

sb's native city/town/village *She is proud of her native city.*

sb's native Australia/Poland etc *He left Hong Kong in August to return to his native Australia.*

2 native people, animals, or plants have always been in a particular place, rather than coming there from somewhere else

NOUNS

the native population/inhabitants *What impact did the Romans have on the native population?*

the native people *The native people lived in harmony with nature.*

a native New Yorker/Californian etc *Her husband was a native New Yorker and had never lived outside the city.*

a native species *These foreign species threaten the survival of native species.*

a native plant/tree *British scientists came here to study native plants.*

a native animal/fish/bird *The kiwi is New Zealand's most famous native bird.*

sth's native habitat (=the place where a plant or animal normally lives) *It was wonderful to see these creatures in their native habitat.*

PREPOSITIONS

native to a place *Chillies are not native to India, and probably came from South America.*

3 your native language is the first language you learned to speak

NOUNS

sb's native language *His native language was German.*

sb's native tongue *literary*: *The girls were singing in their native tongue.*

a native speaker *He had never spoken to a native speaker of English before.*

natural *adj*

1 existing in nature and not caused, made, or controlled by people

NOUNS

the natural world (=trees, flowers, animals, rivers etc) *We should be protecting the natural world, not destroying it.*

natural history (=the study of plants, animals, and minerals) *We went to the Natural History Museum, to see the dinosaurs.*

natural resources *Japan has few natural resources such as oil or coal, and has to depend on imports.*

natural beauty *The region is famous for its great natural beauty.*

a natural disaster/catastrophe (=a terrible event such as a flood or earthquake) *The earthquake was the country's worst natural disaster.*

a natural phenomenon (=something that happens in nature) *Some natural phenomena are difficult for scientists to explain.*

a natural lake/river/harbour *There are few natural lakes that can be used to supply drinking water.*

natural products/ingredients (=with no artificial chemicals) *We only use natural ingredients in our foods.*

natural fibres (=wool, cotton etc – not materials that are man-made) *Natural fibres such as cotton will help to keep you cool.*

natural light (=from the sun) *I prefer to use natural light when I'm taking photographs.*

natural causes (=used when someone dies because of an illness or accident, not because of human actions) *The police say the man died from natural causes.*

natural enemies/predators (=other types of animals that will attack an animal) *The bird has few natural enemies.*

sth's natural habitat/environment/surroundings (=the place where something usually lives) *You can observe the birds in their natural habitat.*

THESAURUS: natural

wild
flower | plant | herb | animal | bird | beauty | landscape
wild flowers, plants, and animals are not grown or kept by people. Wild areas of land do not have humans living there:
In spring, the fields are full of wild flowers. | Many wild plants are in danger of dying out, because of modern farming methods. | The Yorkshire moors are famous for their wild beauty.

pure
gold | silver | cotton | wool | silk | air | water | juice | alcohol
a pure substance or material is not mixed with anything else:
The necklace is made of pure gold. | The shirt is pure cotton. | The air is much purer in the mountains. | I'd like a glass of pure orange juice.

organic
food | farming | produce | vegetables | carrots | tomatoes | fruit | milk | eggs | meat | chicken | beauty products
organic food is grown or produced without using chemicals which harm the environment:
Do you think that organic food tastes better than ordinary food? | Scientific evidence has shown that organic farming is better for the environment. | Sales of organic produce have increased significantly in recent years. | You can buy organic vegetables at our local farmers' market.

unspoiled (*also* **unspoilt** *BrE*)
countryside | beaches | village | town | scenery | surroundings | beauty | charm | paradise
a place that is unspoiled is still beautiful because no one has built roads or buildings on it:
The countryside is ***remarkably unspoiled****. | The island has mile after mile of unspoiled beaches. | It is a pleasant unspoilt village. | Bali was once an unspoilt paradise.*

undeveloped
area | region | land | island | coast | coastline
an undeveloped area does not have towns, factories, or big roads built on it:
The south west is still an undeveloped area of the country. | Because they are so far away, the islands have ***remained relatively undeveloped****.*

untouched
wilderness | jungle | ecosystem
a place that is untouched has not been affected by human activity:
Europe's last untouched wilderness is to be preserved for future generations. | There are very few parts of the world that remain ***untouched by humans****.*

virgin
forest | rainforest | land | territory
virgin forest or land is still in its natural state and has not been spoiled or changed in any way by humans:
Thousands of acres of virgin rainforest are being destroyed each year. | He bought 14,000 acres of virgin land in Ontario.

Virgin is always used before a noun.

2 natural feelings and reactions are reasonable and what you would expect in that situation

NOUNS

a natural reaction/response *Of course you feel disappointed – it's a very natural reaction.*

a natural desire/wish/willingness *There is a natural desire to avoid change.*

ADVERBS

perfectly natural *When you feel sad, it is perfectly natural to cry.*

PHRASES

it is (only) natural *It is only natural to worry about your baby's health.*

sth is the most natural thing in the world (=it does not surprise or shock you at all) *His parents behaved as if it was the most natural thing in the world when he told them about it.*

3 a natural skill or feeling is one that you were born with

NOUNS

a natural skill/talent/ability/aptitude *She has a natural talent for the game.*

a natural instinct/feeling *His natural instinct was to defend himself.*

natural shyness/curiosity/interest *It was difficult for the prince to overcome his natural shyness.*

a natural distrust/suspicion *He had a natural distrust of reporters.*

a natural leader/artist/singer/actor (=someone who is born with the skill needed to be a leader etc) *Thatcher was a natural leader.*

You can also use **natural-born** in this meaning: *Thatcher was a* ***natural-born*** *leader.*

N

nature *n*

1 everything in the physical world that is not made by people, including plants and animals

nature + NOUNS

a nature reserve (*also* **a nature preserve** *AmE*) (=a natural area in which animals and plants are protected) *This area of rainforest is now a nature reserve.*

nature conservation (=protecting nature) *The government is committed to nature conservation.*

a nature lover (=someone who likes nature) *Canada is a great place for nature lovers.*

a nature trail (=a path through an area where you can see interesting animals and plants) *There is a nature trail through the woods.*

PREPOSITIONS

in nature *In nature, only the strongest animals will survive.*

PHRASES

the laws of nature *We have increased our understanding of the laws of nature.*

the forces of nature *The world's most powerful country is still vulnerable to the forces of nature.*

the wonders of nature (=the most impressive things or places in the natural world) *The Grand Canyon is one of the wonders of nature.*

the beauty of nature *Students are taught to appreciate the beauty of nature.*

sth is nature's way of doing sth *Pain is nature's way of telling us there's something wrong.*

get closer to nature/get back to nature *They moved to the countryside because they wanted to get closer to nature.*

Other ways of talking about nature

When you are talking about how a natural area looks, you often use **countryside**, for example: *The* ***countryside*** *around Oxford is very beautiful.* Don't say 'the nature is beautiful'.

Countryside is used especially about fields and low hills. If you want to talk about mountains, it is better to use **scenery**, for example: *Yosemite National Park has some amazing* ***scenery***. You can also say *There are some amazing* ***views***.

2 someone's character

ADJECTIVES

a kind/serious/happy etc nature *He has a kind nature and always wants to help people.*

sb's true nature (=what someone is really like) *After a few months we began to see her true nature.*

human nature (=what humans are usually like and why they behave in the way they do) *Freud's theory of human nature was very complex.*

PREPOSITIONS

by nature *I am by nature a shy person.*

sth is in sb's nature (=it is what someone is usually like) *It wasn't in his nature to be cruel.*

sth is against sb's nature (=it is not how someone usually behaves) *It was against her nature to tell lies.*

PHRASES

take advantage of sb's good nature (=try to get things from someone because you know they are a kind person and will do what you ask) *People took advantage of my father's good nature and borrowed money which they never paid back.*

3 the qualities or features that something has

ADJECTIVES

the true/real nature of sth *He refused to reveal the true nature of his work.*

the exact/precise nature of sth *The precise nature of their relationship remains unclear.*

the essential/fundamental/intrinsic nature of sth *This new rule will not change the essential nature of the game.*

of a general nature *I am able to answer questions of a general nature.*

of a different/similar nature *In the cities, the problem is of a different nature.*

of a personal nature (=concerning private details about someone) *Employee files contain information of a personal nature.*

complex nature *The complex nature of many frauds makes it difficult for the police to prepare a good case.*

sensitive nature *Because of its sensitive nature, access to the report was restricted to a few officials.*

VERBS

understand the nature of sth *I understand the nature of the risks involved.*

change the nature of sth *You have the power to change the nature of the relationships in your life.*

PREPOSITIONS

the nature of sth *He did not tell us about the nature of the discussions.*

PHRASES

by its very nature (=because of its nature) *The future is, by its very nature, uncertain.*

naughty *adj*

a naughty child or pet behaves badly and does not obey you

NOUNS

a naughty boy/girl/child *Don't do that, you naughty girl!*

a naughty dog/cat etc *That naughty cat has just eaten your food!*

naughty behaviour *BrE*, **naughty behavior** *AmE*: *How do you punish naughty behaviour?*

ADJECTIVES

naughty little *You are a naughty little boy!*

THESAURUS: naughty

bad *especially spoken*
boy | girl | dog | cat | behaviour
very naughty:
Have you been a bad boy? | No! Bad dog! | Children soon learn that bad behaviour is a good way of getting attention.

badly behaved
child | pupil | student
a badly behaved child does naughty things. **Badly behaved** is more formal than **naughty** or **bad**:
If a child is badly behaved, are the parents to blame? | Teachers know how to deal with badly behaved pupils.

disobedient
child | dog
a disobedient person or animal deliberately does not do what they are told to do:
She treated her husband like a disobedient child. | Disobedient dogs need to be carefully trained. | She was sent to her room for being disobedient. | The slaves were punished for being disobedient.

mischievous
grin | smile | look | boy | girl | child
doing naughty things, but in a way that makes people laugh rather then be angry - often used about someone's face or smile :
The boy was watching them with a mischievous grin on his face. | I remember her as a happy mischievous girl.

rebellious
teenager | adolescent | son | daughter | streak
deliberately not obeying people in authority:
He suddenly turned into a rebellious teenager who stayed up in his room all day. | Her rebellious daughter decided to leave home. | Young people with a rebellious streak may experiment with drugs (=young people with a tendency to be rebellious).

nausea *n formal*

the feeling that you have when you think you are going to vomit (=bring food up from your stomach through your mouth)

VERBS

suffer from nausea *Some patients suffer from nausea and headaches.*

cause nausea *The medicine can cause nausea and dizziness.*

nausea sweeps over/engulfs sb *formal* (=someone suddenly feels strong nausea) *Nausea swept over him when he tried to stand.*

PHRASES

a feeling of nausea *Many women have feelings of nausea in early pregnancy.*

a wave of nausea (=a sudden strong feeling of nausea) *When he tried to smoke the cigarette, a wave of nausea swept over him.*

near *adv, prep*

only a short distance from a person or thing

VERBS

go near sb/sth *She told the children not to go near the canal.*

come near sb/sth (*also* **draw near** *formal*): *The fox came near the house.*

live near sb/sth *The family lives near San Diego.*

get nearer (and nearer) *The sound got nearer and nearer.*

Near or **near to**?
You usually say **near sb/sth**, or **close to sb/sth**.
'Near to sb/sth' is possible, but less common.

THESAURUS: near

close
very near something or someone, or almost touching them:
The hotel is **close to** *the beach. | Nancy came and sat* **close beside** *me on the bed.*

nearby
town | city | village | street | building | hospital
near here or near a particular place:
They owned a shop in a nearby town. | Police closed some nearby streets to traffic. | He was taken by ambulance to a nearby hospital. | Her son **lives nearby**. *| Is there a post office nearby?*

Nearby is used as an adverb and an adjective.

neighbouring *BrE*, **neighboring** *AmE*
country | state | area | town | village | field
neighbouring countries, towns etc are next to or near a particular place:
Thousands of refugees escaped to neighbouring countries. | The rioting quickly spread to neighbouring areas.

surrounding
area | region | countryside | hills | mountains | villages
around a place:
There was a slight increase in radiation in the surrounding area. | The surrounding countryside is very beautiful.

local
school | hospital | library | shop | store | people | community | residents | inhabitants | farmer | government
in the area near where someone lives, or near where something happens:
The children go to the local school. | You can buy milk and eggs at the local store. | The police depend on the support of the local community.

When saying that something is **near** and easy to get to, you can also say that it is **a 2-minute walk**, **a 5-minute drive**, or that it is **within walking distance**.
You can also say that something is **in the area** (=near a place): *Are there any good restaurants **in the area**?* In more informal English, you can also say *Are there any good restaurants **around here**?*

nearby *adv* THESAURUS **near**

necessary *adj*
used to describe something that you need to have or do

ADVERBS
absolutely necessary *Force is only used when absolutely necessary.*
strictly necessary (=really necessary – used especially when saying that something is not necessary) *He spoke for longer than was strictly necessary.*

VERBS
become necessary *It became necessary to find another office.*
make it necessary to do sth *Larger ships made it necessary to create a new port.*
find it necessary to do sth *I rarely find it necessary to use a ruler.*
prove necessary *formal* (=be necessary) *It may prove necessary to increase the number of staff.*
consider sth necessary (*also* **deem sth necessary** *formal*): *The court may deem it necessary for the person to stay in prison.*

NOUNS
the necessary information *We couldn't make a decision, because we didn't have all the necessary information.*
the necessary skills/knowledge/experience *He lacks the necessary skills and experience.*
the necessary steps/arrangements/measures *People should take the necessary steps to protect themselves from burglars.*
the necessary changes *It will take up to two years to make the necessary changes.*
a necessary part of sth *Many people look on religion as a necessary part of life.*
a necessary evil (=someone or something that you must have, even though you do not want to) *Voters see taxation as a necessary evil.*

PREPOSITIONS
necessary for sth *Oxygen is necessary for life.*

PHRASES
it is necessary (for sb to do sth) *They try to only spend money when it is necessary.*
if necessary *We are willing to fight, if necessary.*
as necessary (=whenever necessary) *Repeat this process as necessary.*

ANTONYMS **necessary → unnecessary**

necessity *n*
1 a situation in which something is necessary

PHRASES
there is no necessity to do sth *The prime minister believes that there is no necessity to change the law.*
sth is a matter of necessity (=something needs to be done) *Building a high-speed rail system in the US is a matter of necessity.*
sth is born out of necessity (=something happens as a result of being necessary) *Labor unions were born out of necessity, to protect the health and well-being of American workers.*

ADJECTIVES
urgent/immediate necessity *Tax reform is an urgent necessity.*
practical necessity *Most car buying decisions made by UK families are born out of practical necessity.*
absolute necessity *Education is an absolute necessity for the economic and social development of any nation.*
sheer/great necessity *There is a great necessity to improve public transport in the area.*
economic/financial/political necessity *Economic necessity forced her to leave school at 16 and find work at a local factory.*

VERBS
avoid/remove/eliminate the necessity to do sth *Having a home gym eliminates the necessity to travel for your workout.*
feel the necessity to do sth *He didn't feel the necessity to move to London.*
emphasize/stress/highlight the necessity to do sth *The president stressed the necessity to invest in and develop the country's oil industry.*

PREPOSITIONS

out of necessity/through necessity *She sold the car out of necessity because it had become too expensive to run.*

without the necessity of sth *You can book a flight online without the necessity of using a paper ticket.*

2 something that you need to have

ADJECTIVES

the bare/basic necessities *Being unemployed makes it difficult to afford even the basic necessities.*

an absolute/vital necessity *Access to clean drinking water is an absolute necessity.*

a daily necessity *The majority of people consider their car to be a daily necessity for getting around.*

VERBS

have the necessities *Once you have the necessities in place, you should be able to make any business a success.*

lack the necessities *A large proportion of the population lack the necessities of life.*

sth has become a necessity *A fast internet connection has become a necessity these days.*

PHRASES

the necessities of life *An increasing number of people are unable to afford the necessities of life.*

neck *n*

the part that joins a person's or animal's head to their shoulders

ADJECTIVES

a long/short neck *Giraffes have long necks.*

a thick neck *He had a thick neck and muscular shoulders.*

a slender neck (=slim and attractive) *The girl had a long slender neck.*

a stiff neck *I woke up with a stiff neck.*

VERBS

injure/hurt your neck *She injured her neck while skiing.*

stretch your neck *The bird stretched its neck and flapped its wings.*

crane your neck (=stretch your neck so that you are more able to see something) *They craned their necks to see what was going on.*

PREPOSITIONS

around/round sb's neck *She wore a gold chain around her neck.*

PHRASES

hold/take/grab sb by the scruff of the neck (=hold someone by the back of their neck) *He grabbed me by the scruff of the neck and pushed me towards the door.*

a crick in your neck (=a pain in the muscles in your neck) *He had a crick in his neck after sleeping in his car.*

need[1] *v*

if you need something or someone, you must have them, because you cannot do something without them

ADVERBS

need sth urgently *The hospital needs supplies of blood urgently.*

need sth badly/desperately *Our company was growing and we needed an office badly.*

really need sth *I was tired and really needed a rest.*

only/just need sth *They only need another $100 to reach their target.*

still need sth *Do you still need a babysitter tomorrow night?*

no longer need sth *He threw away all the papers he no longer needed.*

hardly need sth (=almost not need something) *Bamboo plants hardly need any care.*

much-needed *They are going away for a much-needed holiday.*

sorely needed (=needed very much) *The team had lost four games in a row and sorely needed a win.*

PHRASES

all/everything you need *Are you sure that you have everything you need?*

need[2] *n*

1 a situation in which something is necessary, especially something that is not happening yet or is not yet available

ADJECTIVES

an urgent/pressing need *There is an urgent need for more teachers.*

a desperate/crying need (=very urgent) *There is a desperate need for more housing.*

a real/clear need *There is a real need for after-school care in our area.*

a growing/increasing need *There will be a growing need for experienced business people.*

VERBS

create a need for sth *The increase in the birthrate created a need for more schools.*

eliminate/remove/get rid of the need for sth (=make something unnecessary) *The new drug treatment eliminates the need for surgery.*

reduce/increase the need for sth *A good public transport system will reduce the need for car travel.*

stress/emphasize/underline the need for sth (=say how important it is) *He stressed the need for better health care.*

accept/recognize/acknowledge the need for sth *We fully recognize the need to improve communications.*

a need exists *New teaching materials must be created if a need exists for them.*

N

PREPOSITIONS

the need for sth *Most people recognize the need for change.*

in need (=who need help) *It is important that the money goes to those in need.*

PHRASES

be in need of sth (=need something) *The boy was in need of a haircut.*

there is a need for sth *Clearly there is a need for more research.*

as/if/when the need arises (*also* **should the need arise**) (=when something becomes necessary) *Team members move from job to job as the need arises.*

if need be (=if it is necessary) *I can work during my lunch break if need be.*

2 something that someone needs

Grammar
Usually plural in this meaning.

ADJECTIVES/NOUNS + need

basic needs *In some countries people do not earn enough to meet their basic needs.*

human needs *Energy for cooking is one of the biggest human needs.*

individual/specific needs *We make furniture to suit a customer's individual needs.*

financial/emotional/spiritual etc needs *The emotional needs of elderly patients are often ignored.*

energy/information etc needs *Solar power can meet all of the country's energy needs.*

VERBS

meet/satisfy/serve sb's needs (=provide what someone needs) *The success of the supermarket shows that it is meeting the needs of shoppers.*

address sb's needs (=deal with and try to satisfy needs) *It is vital for any health service to address the needs of people of all ages.*

respond to sb's needs *Parents should be able to respond to the needs of their children.*

ignore sb's needs *The government has been accused of ignoring the needs of refugees.*

consider sb's needs *He believes that companies should consider the needs of older people when designing goods and services.*

be tailored to sb's needs (=be designed for what a particular person or group needs) *We offer diet and fitness programmes which are tailored to your needs.*

balance sb's needs (=deal with the different needs of two people or groups) *Park rangers have to balance the needs of wildlife with the needs of local people.*

needy *adj*

THESAURUS poor (1)

negative *adj*

1 expecting that something bad will happen, or criticizing or disapproving of someone or something

NOUNS

a negative attitude/outlook *She seems to have a very negative attitude on life.*

a negative view *We need to move way from the negative view of children as troublemakers or victims.*

a negative response *The idea met with a negative response from the rest of the team.*

negative feedback *Too much negative feedback can have a bad effect on performance.*

VERBS

seem/sound negative *I wish you wouldn't always sound so negative about everything.*

PREPOSITIONS

negative about sth *She was very negative about my work.*

ANTONYMS **negative → positive (1)**

2 bad or harmful

NOUNS

a negative effect/impact *Pollution from cars has a negative effect on health.*

negative consequences/implications *The changes to the law could have negative consequences for democracy.*

a negative aspect/side *The news reports tended to focus on the negative aspects of the situation.*

THESAURUS: negative

poor, disappointing, unpleasant, negative, grim, undesirable, detrimental, unfavourable → bad (1)

ANTONYMS **negative → positive (2)**

negligence *n*

failure to take enough care over something that you are responsible for

ADJECTIVES

criminal negligence *The manager of the hotel has been charged with criminal negligence.*

professional negligence *The accountant was found guilty of professional negligence.*

medical negligence *She was brain-damaged at birth as a result of medical negligence.*

gross negligence (=very serious negligence) *He was dismissed for gross negligence after leaving the store unlocked.*

VERBS

accuse sb of negligence *He accused the rail company of negligence.*

sue sb for negligence (=bring a court case against someone for negligence) *When he was* *injured at work, he sued his employers for negligence.*

be caused by negligence *Damage caused by negligence is not covered by this insurance.*

prove negligence *It can be difficult to prove negligence on the part of the manufacturer.*

PREPOSITIONS

negligence by sb/on the part of sb *The cause of death was gross negligence on the part of the doctor treating the patient.*

PHRASES

be guilty of negligence *The captain of the ship was found guilty of negligence.*

a victim of negligence *Victims of negligence can claim compensation.*

negligent *adj* THESAURUS careless

negligible *adj* THESAURUS unimportant

negotiate *v*

to discuss something in order to reach an agreement, especially in business or politics

NOUNS

negotiate an agreement/treaty/settlement *The US negotiated a trade agreement with China.*

negotiate a contract/deal *The singer is in the middle of negotiating a new contract with her record company.*

negotiate terms *The two sides are still negotiating the terms of the agreement.*

negotiate a sale *Her father is negotiating the sale of his business.*

negotiate a price *We are in a good position to negotiate a lower price.*

negotiate peace *It took four years to negotiate peace in Vietnam.*

negotiate the release of sb *He helped negotiate the release of the hostages.*

ADVERBS

successfully negotiate sth *They successfully negotiated a contract for another movie.*

negotiate directly with sb *He said that he would negotiate directly with the two leaders.*

PREPOSITIONS

negotiate with sb *The government has refused to negotiate with the rebels.*

negotiation *n*

official discussions in which people try to reach an agreement, especially in business or politics

> **Grammar**
> Usually plural in this meaning. Used as an uncountable noun in phrases such as **be under negotiation**.

ADJECTIVES/NOUNS + negotiation

peace/trade etc negotiations *A new round of global trade negotiations is due to start next week.*

long/lengthy negotiations *After lengthy negotiations, a compromise was finally reached.*

difficult/tough negotiations *The agreement is the result of two years of long and difficult negotiations.*

direct negotiations *We hope to resolve the issue through direct negotiations.*

delicate negotiations *The company is about to start delicate negotiations with the union about next year's pay agreement.*

secret negotiations *After secret negotiations in Norway, the two leaders signed the Oslo agreement.*

VERBS + negotiation

enter into/open negotiations (=start negotiations) *They have entered into negotiations to acquire another company.*

conduct/hold negotiations *The country should conduct direct negotiations with its neighbours.*

break off negotiations (=stop them) *The two companies have broken off negotiations on the deal.*

resume negotiations (=start them again) *The pressure is on Israel and the Palestinians to resume peace negotiations.*

negotiation + VERBS

negotiations take place *The negotiations took place in Helsinki.*

negotiations break down/fail (=stop because of disagreement) *The negotiations broke down over a dispute about working conditions.*

PREPOSITIONS

negotiations with sb *Negotiations with the company had reached a crucial stage.*

negotiations between sb *Merger negotiations between the two companies started last year.*

negotiations on/over sth *He is trying to involve community leaders in negotiations on reform.*

by/through negotiation *The contract is renewable every two years by negotiation.*

PHRASES

sth is under negotiation (=it is being discussed) *The contract is currently under negotiation.*

sb is in negotiation with sb (=they are discussing something with someone) *We are currently in negotiation with the owners.*

sth is open to negotiation (=it can be discussed) *The price is usually open to negotiation.*

sth is subject to negotiation (=it is not fixed and must be discussed) *The pay is subject to negotiation.*

a round of negotiations (=one part of a series of negotiations) *The next round of negotiations on trade barriers will begin next week.*

a breakdown in negotiations (=an occasion when negotiations cannot continue because of a disagreement) *There has been a breakdown in negotiations with the union.*

neighbour *BrE*, **neighbor** *AmE n*

1 someone who lives next to you or near you

ADJECTIVES

sb's next-door neighbour *My next-door neighbour was having a party.*

sb's upstairs/downstairs neighbour *He could hear the voice of his downstairs neighbour.*

sb's new neighbour *We invited our new neighbours over for coffee.*

a good neighbour *She is a good neighbour and we've never had any arguments.*

a friendly neighbour *Ask a friendly neighbour to keep an eye on your house while you're away.*

noisy neighbours *Our lives are being ruined by noisy neighbours.*

a nosy neighbour (=one who is too interested in finding out about your private life) *She put up net curtains to stop nosy neighbours looking in.*

VERBS

disturb the neighbours *He put the radio on quietly so as not to disturb the neighbours.*

wake the neighbours *Stop that noise or you'll wake the neighbours!*

PHRASES

friends and neighbours *She received support from her friends and neighbours.*

2 a country that is next to another country

ADJECTIVES

a powerful neighbour *Nepal is surrounded by more powerful neighbours.*

a rich/poor neighbour *Unlike its poorer neighbours, the country has not really been affected by the economic crisis.*

a northern/southern neighbour *Oman differs from its northern neighbours.*

a European/Asian neighbour *The issue could affect Japan's relationship with its Asian neighbours.*

neighbourhood *BrE*, **neighborhood** *AmE n*

an area of a town or city where people live

ADJECTIVES

a good/nice neighbourhood *Everyone says this is a good neighbourhood.*

a quiet neighbourhood *We live in a nice quiet neighbourhood.*

a bad/rough/tough neighbourhood *The house was cheap because it was in a rough neighbourhood.*

a poor neighbourhood *She works in one of the city's poorest neighborhoods.*

the whole neighbourhood (=everyone who lives near here) *I'll make sure the whole neighbourhood knows about it.*

the immediate neighbourhood (=the area close to someone or something) *There was one shop in our immediate neighbourhood.*

VERBS

live in the neighbourhood *He has lived in the neighbourhood for years.*

move into/to the neighbourhood *She moved to the neighbourhood about two years ago.*

PREPOSITIONS

in the neighbourhood *It's nice to see you back in the neighbourhood.*

THESAURUS: neighbourhood

region, zone, district, neighbourhood, suburb, quarter, slum, ghetto → **area (1)**

neighbouring *adj* THESAURUS **near**

nerve *n*

1 nerves are feelings of being worried or frightened

Grammar
Always plural in this meaning.

VERBS

calm/steady sb's nerves (=make someone feel less worried or nervous) *She took a few deep breaths, trying to calm her nerves.*

settle/soothe sb's nerves (=make someone feel less worried or nervous) *A cup of tea will soothe your nerves.*

suffer from nerves (=experience feelings of worry or nervousness) *He suffered from nerves when he had to perform on stage.*

ADJECTIVES/NOUNS + nerve

exam nerves *It's quite normal for students to have exam nerves.*

first-night nerves (=before the first night of a performance) *She always suffered from first-night nerves.*

frayed nerves (=when someone is very worried or nervous) *She had a glass of wine to calm her frayed nerves.*

PHRASES

sb's nerves are on edge (=they feel slightly nervous or worried) *His nerves were on edge as he entered the dark room.*

be a bag/bundle of nerves (=feel extremely nervous or worried) *I was a bag of nerves during the interview.*

an attack of nerves (=a time when you feel very nervous) *Harrison had an attack of nerves before the match.*

2 courage and confidence in a dangerous, difficult, or frightening situation

Grammar
Always uncountable in this meaning.

VERBS

have the nerve to do sth *I just didn't have the nerve to tell them the truth.*

find the nerve to do sth *He couldn't find the nerve to ask her out.*

hold/keep your nerve (=remain calm and confident in a difficult situation) *The team held their nerve and went on to win.*

lose your nerve (=suddenly lose the courage or confidence to do something) *I wanted to ask him the question, but I lost my nerve.*

test sb's nerve (=test whether someone will have the courage to do something difficult) *The experience would test their nerve to the limit.*

sb's nerve fails (him/her) (=someone suddenly loses the courage or confidence to do something) *At the last moment, her nerve failed her and she refused to jump.*

PHRASES

it takes nerve to do sth (=something requires a lot of courage or confidence) *It takes nerve to stand up for what you believe in.*

a failure/loss of nerve (=a situation in which someone lacks the courage to do something) *They accused the government of a loss of nerve.*

nervous *adj*

worried or frightened about something, and unable to relax

VERBS

feel nervous *He looked at her for so long that she began to feel nervous.*

get/become nervous *Everyone gets nervous before a big game.*

seem/appear nervous *She seemed nervous at first, but her presentation was good.*

look/sound nervous *He sounded nervous and uncertain.*

make sb nervous *Being alone in the house made her nervous.*

ADVERBS

slightly nervous (*also* **a little nervous**) *Looking slightly nervous, Paul began to speak.*

extremely nervous *The policeman noticed that the driver seemed extremely nervous.*

understandably nervous *The musicians are understandably nervous about their first appearance on TV.*

NOUNS

a nervous smile/laugh/giggle *"It doesn't matter," she said, with a nervous smile.*

nervous laughter *His comment was met with nervous laughter.*

a nervous look/glance *Lucy swallowed as she sent him a nervous glance.*

nervous tension/excitement (=a feeling of being very tense or excited and nervous) *It was the play's opening night, and Gloria was in a state of nervous tension.*

a nervous wait (=a wait for something which makes you feel nervous) *They are facing a nervous wait for the results.*

PREPOSITIONS

nervous of sb/sth (=frightened) *We were all a bit nervous of him at first.*

nervous about sth *She was so nervous about her exams that she couldn't sleep.*

PHRASES

be a nervous wreck (=be so nervous or worried that you cannot deal with a situation) *By the time I got to the interview, I was a nervous wreck.*

people of a nervous disposition *formal* (=people who are easily frightened) *It's a horror movie which is definitely not for people of a nervous disposition.*

nest *n*

a place made or chosen by a bird or some insects to live in, and where a bird lays its eggs

VERBS

build/make a nest *In May the females build a nest and lay their eggs.*

leave the nest *Barn owls leave the nest at two to three months.*

net *n*

1 another name for the internet

> **Spelling**
> This meaning can be spelled **Net** or **net**.

VERBS

use the net *You can use the Net to find the answer to almost any question.*

surf the net (=look at information in different places on the internet) *He spends hours surfing the net.*

access the net *These boxes allow people to access the Net from their TV.*

PREPOSITIONS

on the net *I read about it on the net.*

over the net *You can deliver lectures over the Net.*

via the net *Many companies sell their products via the net.*

2 an object made of threads that is used for catching fish, insects etc

ADJECTIVES/NOUNS + net

a fishing net *The boy dipped his fishing net into the pond.*

salmon/tuna etc nets *They release the trapped dolphins from the tuna nets.*

a mosquito net (=a net placed over a bed as a protection against mosquitoes) *There is a mosquito net over the bed.*

VERBS

catch sth in a net *Turtles sometimes get caught in fishing nets.*

N

cast your net *They cast their nets and brought up hundreds of fish.*

haul in a net *We hauled the net into the boat.*

mend a net *The fishermen sat mending their nets.*

N

network Ac *n*

1 a system of things that are connected to each other

NOUNS + network

a computer network *Someone had gained access to the company's computer network.*

a telephone/phone network *The telephone network couldn't cope with the number of calls.*

a communications network *The police force requires a sophisticated communications network.*

a rail/road network *The money should be used to improve the rail network.*

a transport network *The city's transport network is out of date.*

a broadband network *The country has the fastest broadband network in Europe.*

ADJECTIVES

an international/global/worldwide network *The internet is an international network of computers.*

a national network *The rail line is the first part of a national network that will connect all the major cities.*

an extensive/large network *Germany, the Netherlands, and Denmark have extensive networks of cycle paths.*

a vast network *There is a vast network of tunnels under the city.*

a complex/complicated/elaborate network *The islands are separated by a complex network of rivers.*

VERBS

use a network *Some phone companies charge people too much for using their networks.*

operate/run a network *The government allowed private companies to operate the rail network.*

build/create/develop a network *They plan to build a global telecommunications network.*

PREPOSITIONS

a network of sth *Amsterdam has a network of canals.*

through/via a network *Local offices had become linked to the head office via computer networks.*

2 a group of people or organizations that have connections with each other

ADJECTIVES

a wide/extensive/large network (=consisting of a lot of people, companies etc) *I have an extensive network of contacts.*

a vast network *The security services relied on a vast network of informers.*

an international/global/worldwide network *Tim and Hedy are part of an international network of young people.*

a national network *There will also be a national network of debt counselling services.*

an informal network *An informal network of social organizations supported the poor.*

> The term **social networking** is used about communicating and forming relationships with people, especially using the internet.

NOUNS + network

a family network *We show the importance of the family network in providing financial backing.*

a support network *For some, their fellow women students provided a support network.*

a terrorist network *Were these men part of a terrorist network?*

VERBS

build (up)/develop a network *She has built up a network of contacts.*

establish/set up a network *They established a network of consultants and specialists.*

PREPOSITIONS

a network of friends/contacts/spies etc *She has a close network of friends.*

PHRASES

the old boy network (=the system by which men from the same school, club etc help each other) *Managers have been chosen through the old boy network.*

3 a group of radio or television stations, which broadcast in different parts of a country or area

NOUNS + network

a television/radio network *The game will be shown on all the big television networks.*

a cable network *The city has its own cable network.*

a news network *The ceremony was broadcast live on a Russian news network.*

ADJECTIVES

a major/big network *Teenagers had been largely ignored by the major networks.*

network + NOUNS

network television *It's like nothing you've ever seen before on network television.*

network news *The network news is at 7 o'clock.*

VERBS

a network shows/runs sth *The network showed a short part of the interview yesterday.*

a network broadcasts (sth) *The network will broadcast 24 hours a day.*

PREPOSITIONS

on a network *It's one of the most popular programmes on the network.*

neutral *adj*

not supporting any of the people involved in an argument or disagreement, or not involved in a war

VERBS

remain/stay neutral *The country stayed neutral throughout the entire conflict.*

ADVERBS

politically neutral *The newspaper claims that it is politically neutral.*

NOUNS

a neutral position *The organization has adopted a neutral position, neither supporting nor opposing a change in the law.*

a neutral observer (=someone who is not involved in a situation) *To a neutral observer, her decision may seem rather strange.*

a neutral country (=one that does not take part in a war) *Switzerland was a neutral country at the time of the Second World War.*

new *adj*

1 recently made, written, developed etc

NOUNS

a new book/film/song etc *His new book will be in bookstores next week.*

a new building/house/home *New buildings are often cheaper to heat.*

a new method/way *We need a new way of thinking about this issue.*

new technology *New technology has changed the way we work.*

a new product/drug *Scientists are developing new drugs to treat cancer.*

a new business/company *They plan to set up a new company.*

new law/rule/legislation *The new rules will start from next month.*

a new idea/theory *The discussion gave me some new ideas for a business.*

new research/a new study *According to a new study, 15% of children never do any exercise.*

a new edition *A new edition of her book will be published next month.*

ADVERBS

completely new *We have introduced a completely new range of products.*

brand new (=new and not yet used) *He was driving a brand new car.*

fairly/relatively new *This is a relatively new drug.*

VERBS

look new *The building looked fairly new.*

PHRASES

as good as new (=in good condition, even though something is not new) *The clothes were as good as new.*

You can use **new** about something that you got recently: *I wore my* ***new*** *dress to the party.* | *Have you seen their* ***new*** *baby yet?*
You can also use **new** about something that you have not experienced before: *Sailing was a* ***new*** *experience for me.* | *Learning a* ***new*** *language can be difficult.*

N

THESAURUS: new

recent
study | **research** | **survey** | **report** | **book** | **film** | **album** | **work** | **interview** | **event** | **development**
done or happening a short time ago:
A recent study showed that the drug was effective in most cases. | *Her most recent book has been a bestseller.* | *In a recent interview, the singer said she would like to have a baby.* | *Recent events have shown that we cannot ignore climate change.*

latest
news | **information** | **development** | **technology** | **version** | **figures** | **issue** | **book** | **film** | **album** | **report**
most recent:
I turned on the television to watch the latest news. | *The factory uses the latest technology.* | *The latest figures show that unemployment has risen by 2%.* | *The latest issue of the magazine has an article about him.*

original
idea | **design** | **work**
new and completely different from what other people have done or thought of before, especially in a way that seems interesting:
Some of his ideas are very original. | *The design for the building is* ***highly original****.* | *The essay must be your own original work, not something you have copied off the internet.*

Original is often used after the verb **be**.

fresh
ideas | **evidence** | **look** | **approach** | **perspective**
fresh ideas and ways of doing things are new and different from the old ones:
They want young people with fresh ideas. | *Police think they may have found some fresh evidence about the murder.* | *Take a fresh look at the way you live your life.* | *We need a fresh approach to the problem.*

Fresh is usually used before a noun.

novel
way | **method** | **approach** | **solution** | **idea** | **concept** | **experience** | **feature**
new and different in a surprising and unusual way:

The club has found a novel way of raising money. | He was rarely ill, so visiting a doctor was a novel experience for him.

innovative
idea | solution | approach | way | product | design | technology | project | scheme
completely new and showing a lot of imagination:
They need to develop an innovative solution to the problem. | The school has an innovative approach to language teaching. | The company worked hard to create a product that was innovative. | Our products have won several prizes for innovative design.

revolutionary
idea | concept | change | treatment
completely new in a way that has a very big effect:
Darwin's theory was a revolutionary idea, which changed how we think about the history of our planet. | These changes were revolutionary because they meant that women could receive equal pay. | This revolutionary treatment is changing the lives of many people with heart disease.

You can use the phrase **a revolutionary new...** with any type of product or method: *a* ***revolutionary new*** *drug/car/system/technique etc*

new-fangled
idea | device | gadget | machine | technology | thing
used about something that is new and modern but which you disapprove of, especially because you are old and do not like change:
Some people didn't approve of these new-fangled ideas. | My grandfather refuses to use new-fangled devices such as cash machines. | I don't understand all this new-fangled technology.

New-fangled is only used before a noun.

ANTONYMS **new → old (1)**

2 used about something or someone that replaces the one you had before

NOUNS

sb's new car/computer/house etc *Our new car is much bigger than our old one.*

sb's new number/address etc *I'll give you my new phone number.*

sb's new boss/manager/teacher etc *Our new teacher is very strict.*

the new government *The new government needs to make some big changes.*

the new owner *The club's new owner is a Russian billionaire.*

ANTONYMS **new → old (3)**

news *n*

1 information about something that has happened recently

Grammar
News is an uncountable noun, and is used with a singular verb.

ADJECTIVES

good news *He's feeling much better, so that's good news.*

great/wonderful news *They're getting married? That's wonderful news!*

welcome news (=good news that makes you happy) *The lower interest rates will be welcome news to home owners.*

positive/encouraging news *We are hoping for some more positive news.*

bad news *"I'm afraid I have bad news," said Jackson.*

terrible news (=very bad) *Have you heard the terrible news about Simon?*

sad/tragic news *I was in London when I received the sad news that Peter had died.*

the latest news *Mom sent a letter with all the latest news.*

old news (=news that you have already heard) *She wasn't surprised; it was old news to her.*

important news *I've got some important news to tell you.*

the big news *informal* (=the most important piece of news) *The big news is that Polly and Richard are getting married.*

VERBS

hear the news (=hear about something that has happened) *She was really upset when she heard the news.*

tell sb the news *Jack called him to tell him the good news.*

break the news (to sb) (=tell someone some bad news) *Two policemen came to the door to break the news about her husband.*

have some news (for sb) *I could tell by his face that he had some news.*

get/receive some news *They had recently received some good news about their investments.*

spread the news (=tell a lot of people the news) *After she had the baby, her husband made phone calls to spread the happy news.*

welcome the news (=say that you are pleased about some news) *Environmental groups welcomed the news that the road was not going to be built.*

news reaches sb/sth *The tragic news reached us the next day.*

news spreads (=a lot of people find out the news from other people) *News spreads fast in a small town.*

PREPOSITIONS

news about/on sb/sth *What's the latest news on your university application?*

news of sth/sb *News of his death shocked everyone.*

news from sb *Any news from your parents?*

PHRASES

a piece of news (*also* **a bit of news** *BrE*): *Leo thought about this piece of news carefully.*

the good news is...; the bad news is... *The good news is that most stores have the game in stock; the bad news is that it's not cheap.*

no news is good news *"Have you heard anything from the hospital yet?" "No, not yet. I suppose no news is good news."*

2 television, radio, or newspaper reports about events that have happened recently

> **Grammar**
> **News** is an uncountable noun and is used with a singular verb.

ADJECTIVES/NOUNS + news

the latest news *I watched the latest news about the war.*

local/national/international news *The paper covers a mixture of local and national news.*

sports/business/travel etc news *I often listen to the sports news on the radio.*

world news *The main part of the programme is about world news.*

television/radio news *The television news is always so depressing.*

the evening news/the 6 o'clock news *Good evening. Here is the 6 o'clock news.*

front-page news (=important news that is printed on the front page of a newspaper) *The scandal is front-page news in all the papers.*

headline news (=important news at the beginning of a television or radio news programme or at the top of a newspaper report) *The story was headline news around the world.*

breaking news (=news that is just being announced) *We interrupt this programme to bring you some breaking news.*

news + NOUNS

a news programme *BrE*, **a news program** *AmE*: *She presents a news programme on Channel 4.*

news headlines *The news headlines are at 12.30.*

a news bulletin (=a short news programme) *There is an hourly news bulletin.*

a news story/report/item *They were watching a news report about the earthquake.*

a news conference *The president told a news conference that he would continue the negotiations for peace.*

news coverage (=the way that news is reported in a newspaper, on television etc) *The newspaper won an award for its news coverage.*

a news blackout (=a time when news about a particular event is not allowed to be reported) *The government imposed a news blackout on the talks.*

a news channel *There are more details on this story on the BBC's news channel.*

a news agency/organization *The singer was having tests on his heart, according to one Italian news agency.*

VERBS

watch/listen to the news *Can we watch the news?*

report news *The local newspaper reported news of a traffic accident in the centre of the city.*

make/hit the news (=be reported in a newspaper, on television etc) *The family made the news when their daughter was kidnapped.*

sth dominates the news (=it is in many newspapers, news programmes etc) *At that time the swine flu outbreak was dominating the news.*

news breaks/emerges (=it starts to be reported) *News also emerged that 15 prisoners had escaped.*

PREPOSITIONS

in the news *Japan is in the news this morning.*

news on/about/of sth *We have all the latest news on what's happening around the world.*

newspaper *n*

a set of folded sheets of printed paper containing news

ADJECTIVES/NOUNS + newspaper

a national newspaper *The story was in all the national newspapers.*

a local newspaper *You could put an advertisement in the local newspaper.*

a daily/weekly/Sunday newspaper *Do you get a daily newspaper?*

today's/yesterday's/tomorrow's newspaper *You'll be able to read all about it in tomorrow's newspaper.*

a tabloid newspaper (=a small-sized newspaper, especially one with not much serious news) *Their wedding made the headlines in all the tabloid newspapers.*

a broadsheet/quality newspaper *BrE* (=a newspaper with a lot of serious news and good writing) *The story has not been given as much coverage in the quality newspapers.*

VERBS

read a newspaper *He sat in the garden reading his newspaper.*

get a newspaper (=buy one regularly) *We don't get a newspaper; we tend to watch the news on TV.*

see/read sth in the newspaper *I saw in the newspaper that he had died.*

N

appear in a newspaper *Her photo appeared in all the newspapers.*

deliver a newspaper *We have a newspaper delivered every Sunday.*

work for a newspaper (=work for an organization that produces newspapers) *She's worked for the newspaper for three years.*

a newspaper reports sth (=has an article on something) *The newspapers reported that the police were treating the death as a suicide.*

a newspaper comes out (=is published) *The newspaper comes out every weekday.*

N

newspaper + NOUNS

a newspaper article/report/story *Write a story in the style of a newspaper article.*

a newspaper headline *'Wine is good for you' announced a recent newspaper headline.*

a newspaper column (=a regular article in a newspaper written by a particular journalist) *She writes a regular newspaper column about gardening.*

a newspaper reporter *She was fed up with being followed by newspaper reporters.*

a newspaper editor *Newspaper editors have a lot of power.*

a newspaper proprietor *BrE* (=owner) *Ultimately, it's the newspaper proprietor who decides what goes into the paper.*

a newspaper clipping (*also* **a newspaper cutting** *BrE*) (=a story cut out of a newspaper) *I found some old newspaper cuttings of the band's first concert in Liverpool.*

PREPOSITIONS

in a newspaper *I read about it in the newspaper.*

⚠ Don't say 'I read about it on the newspaper.'

on a newspaper (=working for an organization that produces newspapers) *He's a reporter on a local newspaper.*

> **Paper** or **newspaper?**
> In everyday English, **paper** is much more common than **newspaper**. In some cases, though, you can only use one of these words.
> For example, you say a **paper boy/girl**, or a **paper shop**. (You do not use 'newspaper' in these phrases.)
> You say a **newspaper article**, a **newspaper headline**, a **newspaper column**, a **newspaper reporter** etc. (You do not use 'paper' in these phrases.)

New Year (*also* **New Year's** *AmE*) *n*

the time when people celebrate the beginning of a new year

ADJECTIVES

Happy New Year *He wished me a merry Christmas and a happy New Year.*

a prosperous New Year *formal* (=a successful New Year) *I wish you all a peaceful Christmas and a prosperous New Year.*

VERBS

see in the New Year (=celebrate the beginning of the year) *Our neighbours invited us round to see in the New Year.*

spend New Year *She will be spending New Year with her daughter.*

New Year + NOUNS

a New Year('s) resolution (=a promise to yourself that you will do something, which you make at the beginning of the year) *My New Year resolution is to give up smoking.*

the New Year celebrations *A huge fireworks show marked the start of the New Year celebrations.*

PREPOSITIONS

at New Year *At New Year we usually have a huge family meal.*

over New Year *I'm going to be relaxing over New Year.*

for New Year *What are you going to do for New Year?*

PHRASES

New Year's Day (=January 1st) *The museum is closed on New Year's Day.*

New Year's Eve (=December 31st) *We're having a party on New Year's Eve.*

nice *adj*

used when saying that you like something or someone

NOUNS

a nice day/time/holiday *Did you have a nice day at school?*

a nice house/place/car *She has a nice house and a good job.*

a nice person/guy/man/boy/woman *He seems like a nice guy.*

a nice idea *"We could have a pizza." "That sounds like a nice idea."*

a nice life *We have a nice life and lots of friends.*

nice clothes *She always wears nice clothes.*

nice weather (=sunny) *It is supposed to be nice weather this weekend.*

a nice feeling *It's a nice feeling waking up and knowing that I don't have to go in to work.*

VERBS

look/smell/taste/sound/seem nice *You look nice in that dress.*

ADVERBS

really nice *It's really nice to see you again.*

so nice *It's so nice to be back home.*

rather nice *especially BrE: A cup of tea would be rather nice.*

not very nice/not particularly nice *The food wasn't very nice.*

PHRASES

nice little... *Nice little place you've got here.*

nice big/long... *You need a nice long rest.*

nice and warm/cool/easy/clean/quiet/soft etc *It's nice and warm in front of the fire.*

how nice *"My parents want us to come and stay." "How nice!"*

have a nice day *AmE* (=used when saying goodbye to someone, especially a customer) *The woman at the bank said, "Have a nice day!"*

nice to meet you (=used when meeting someone for the first time) *Hi, I'm Sam. Nice to meet you!*

(it was) nice talking to you (=used at the end of a conversation with someone) *Well, it's been nice talking to you, but we have to get back home.*

one of the nice things about ... is... (=used when saying what you like about something) *One of the nice things about Christmas is having all the family together.*

> **Nice** is extremely common in everyday spoken English. In more formal English it is usually better to use another word such as **pleasant**, **enjoyable**, or **wonderful**. You can also say that a person is **charming**, when you like being with them.

THESAURUS: nice

nice, fine, sound, attractive, desirable, favourable, positive, beneficial → **good (1)**

nice, well behaved, decent, honourable, respectable, virtuous, upright, dutiful → **good (3)**

generous, considerate, thoughtful, caring, sympathetic, compassionate, warm-hearted/kind-hearted, benevolent, benign, nice, good, sweet → **kind²**

nice, warm, welcoming, hospitable, amiable, genial, cordial, approachable → **friendly**

good, fine, nice, bright, beautiful/glorious, clear, cloudless, dry → **sunny**

night *n*

the dark part of each 24-hour period, or the hours before you go to bed

ADJECTIVES/NOUNS + night

good night (=used when saying goodbye at night) *Good night, everybody. Sleep well.*

Monday/Friday etc night *I haven't seen him since Thursday night.*

that night *That night, she heard a strange noise.*

last night *It rained last night.*

tomorrow night *I should be back by tomorrow night.*

all night *He looked as if he'd been up all night.*

a winter/summer etc night *They spent the long winter nights telling stories round the fire.*

a clear/cold/stormy etc night *It was a clear night, with a full moon shining brightly.*

a dark/black night *I wouldn't like to walk down that path on a dark night.*

an early night (=when you go to bed early) *I'm really tired – I need an early night.*

a late night (=when you go to bed late) *You've had too many late nights recently.*

a long night *Everyone was tired and grumpy. It had been a long night.*

a sleepless/bad night *She had spent a sleepless night wondering what to do.*

> ⚠ Don't say 'We're having fish for dinner this night.' Say **We're having fish for dinner tonight.**

night + NOUNS

the night sky *We looked up at the stars in the night sky.*

the night air *The night air was cold.*

a night train/bus/flight *I took the night train to Fort William.*

VERBS

spend a night somewhere *We spent two nights at the Grand Hotel.*

stay the night (=sleep at someone's house) *You're welcome to stay the night if you like.*

night falls *written* (=it starts to become dark) *It grew colder as night fell.*

PREPOSITIONS

at night *Brush your teeth before you go to bed at night.*

by night (=used when saying what an animal or person does regularly at night) *Owls hunt by night and sleep in the daytime.*

in the night *He woke in the night feeling very hot.*

during the night *Do you often need a drink of water during the night?*

for the night *He stayed at a friend's for the night.*

on Monday/Friday etc night *The programme was broadcast on Thursday night.*

> When you are mentioning a time before midnight, you use **at night**: *We stayed until ten o'clock **at night**.* When you are mentioning a time after midnight, you use **in the morning**: *He came home at two **in the morning**.*

PHRASES

the night before *She had not slept much the night before.*

late at night *We often get to bed very late at night.*

last thing at night (=just before you go to bed) *Take regular physical exercise, but not last thing at night.*

late/far into the night (=until very late at

night) *Staff worked late into the night to get the system working again.*

in the middle of the night *She woke up suddenly in the middle of the night.*

in/at the dead of night *literary* (=in the middle of the night when it is quiet) *There was a sudden knock on the door in the dead of night.*

at this time of night (=used when it seems very late at night to do something) *Why are you calling me at this time of night?*

all night long *The noise continued all night long.*

day and night/night and day (=all the time) *The phones rang day and night.*

morning, noon, and night (=all the time) *She worked to care for him morning, noon, and night.*

a night out (=an evening when you go to a party, restaurant etc) *People come here for a good night out.*

nightmare *n*

a very difficult, unpleasant, or frightening experience or situation

ADJECTIVES

an absolute/complete nightmare *The whole day was an absolute nightmare.*

a real nightmare *The situation with our neighbours is a real nightmare.*

the ultimate nightmare (=the worst possible situation) *The ultimate nightmare for any parent is to suffer the loss of a child.*

sb's worst nightmare (=the worst possible thing someone can imagine) *Forgetting your lines is every actor's worst nightmare.*

VERBS

become/turn into a nightmare *Their honeymoon turned into a nightmare when they were involved in a car accident.*

a nightmare begins/ends *The nightmare began when her mother became ill.*

nightmare + NOUNS

a nightmare scenario (=a very bad situation) *The nightmare scenario would be if my wife and I both lost our jobs.*

a nightmare vision (=a very bad situation that might happen) *The book presents a nightmare vision of Britain in the next century.*

a nightmare world (=a situation in which everything is bad and there is nothing good) *It's hard to understand how people survived the nightmare world of the concentration camps.*

a nightmare journey/trip *Commuters are facing a nightmare journey to work due to the train drivers' strike.*

a nightmare day/week etc *The resignations end a nightmare week for the president.*

PREPOSITIONS

a nightmare for sb *The past year has been a nightmare for the family.*

the nightmare of sth *For some children the nightmare of abuse continues.*

noble *adj*

1 morally good and deserving praise or respect

NOUNS

a noble cause *They believe they are fighting for a noble cause.*

a noble goal/aim *Keeping unemployment as low as possible is a noble goal.*

a noble gesture *His family appreciated the government's noble gesture.*

a noble ideal *The health service has genuinely noble ideals.*

a noble enterprise *formal* (=a noble activity) *The peace process has been a noble enterprise.*

PHRASES

it/that is noble of sb *"I offered to give her my ticket." "That was very noble of you."*

2 belonging to the highest social class, with a title such as 'Duke' or 'Countess'

NOUNS

a noble family *He came from a noble family.*

noble birth *The Empress was served by ladies of noble birth.*

noble blood *She may have noble blood in her veins.*

a noble name *He had brought shame on his noble name.*

nod[1] *v*

to move your head up and down, for example to show agreement or understanding

ADVERBS

nod thoughtfully *He nodded thoughtfully, then smiled.*

nod vigorously *"Do you agree?" he asked. I nodded vigorously.*

nod sympathetically *The barman nodded sympathetically.*

nod approvingly *He wondered if he had said the wrong thing, but James was nodding approvingly.*

NOUNS

nod your head *"Of course," he said, nodding his head.*

PREPOSITIONS

nod to/at sb *They nodded to each other.*

nod towards/in the direction of sth/sb *"What's that?" asked Jack, nodding at the sack. | She nodded towards the shed. "He's in there."*

nod in agreement/approval etc *His brother nodded in agreement.*

nod[2] *n*

an act of moving your head up and down

ADJECTIVES

a friendly nod *The man turned and gave me a friendly nod.*

a little/small/slight nod *He gave a little nod, unable to speak.*

a brief/quick nod *Her teacher gave her a quick nod of encouragement.*

an approving nod *I got approving nods from my colleagues.*

VERBS

give a nod *She gave a satisfied nod.*

PHRASES

a nod of your head *He indicated Rachel with a nod of his head.*

a nod of approval/agreement/acknowledgement etc *My little speech was greeted with nods of approval.*

noise *n*

a sound, especially one that is loud, unpleasant, or frightening

ADJECTIVES/NOUNS + noise

a loud noise *He was woken by a loud noise in the kitchen.*

a deafening noise (=extremely loud) *Their conversation was drowned out by the deafening noise of an aircraft taking off.*

a strange/funny noise *What's that funny noise?*

a gurgling/whistling/clicking etc noise (=a particular kind of sound) *The water moved through the pipes with a loud gurgling noise.*

constant noise (=that does not stop) *She was fed up with the constant noise of traffic.*

background noise (=noise of things that are happening around you) *The background noise made it hard to hear what he was saying.*

traffic/aircraft/engine etc noise *It was peaceful there, with no traffic noise at all.*

VERBS

make a noise *The car engine was making a funny noise.*

hear a noise *She heard a strange noise.*

a noise comes from sth *The noise seemed to be coming from the kitchen.*

keep the noise down (=be or make something as quiet as possible) *We tried to keep the noise down so we wouldn't disturb her.*

reduce noise *The road is covered with a special surface which helps reduce noise.*

generate/create/produce noise *The noise generated by the air conditioner was keeping him awake.*

a noise stops *Suddenly the noise stopped.*

a noise dies down/away (=becomes quieter) *After a while, the noise died down.*

noise + NOUNS

noise levels *The hospital is trying to reduce noise levels to help patients sleep.*

noise pollution (=noise from traffic, building etc which has a bad effect on people's lives) *The new airport will increase noise pollution in the surrounding area.*

PREPOSITIONS

the noise of sth *The noise of the traffic made conversation impossible.*

the noise from sth *The noise from the house next door was keeping him awake.*

above/over the noise *Nothing could be heard above the noise of the engine.*

noisy *adj*

making a lot of noise, or full of noise

NOUNS

a noisy crowd/group *A noisy crowd of people gathered outside the embassy.*

noisy children *The park is full of noisy children.*

noisy neighbours *BrE*, **noisy neighbors** *AmE*: *Noisy neighbours are making our life miserable.*

noisy road/car/traffic *I couldn't sleep because of the noisy traffic.*

a noisy engine *The car has a noisy engine and it's difficult to talk when you're driving.*

a noisy room/office/factory etc *It can be hard to concentrate in a noisy office.*

a noisy demonstration/protest *The protesters held a noisy demonstration outside the factory.*

a noisy party/celebration *There were noisy celebrations which carried on all night.*

a noisy eater (=someone who makes too much noise when they eat) *My brother is a very noisy eater.*

ADVERBS

very/really noisy *The bar was very noisy and I couldn't hear what she was saying.*

extremely/incredibly noisy *The wind was extremely noisy that night.*

rather noisy/a little noisy (*also* **a bit noisy** *informal*): *It's a bit noisy in there, isn't it?*

THESAURUS: noisy

noisy, rowdy, raucous, resounding, deafening, thunderous, ear-splitting, piercing → **loud**

ANTONYMS **noisy → quiet**

nomination *n*

the act of saying that someone or something should be given an important job, a prize, or an award

VERBS

get/receive a nomination *The film got the nomination for Best Drama.*

win a nomination (=succeed in being nominated) *Do you think she has enough votes to win the nomination?*

make a nomination (=say that you think someone should be given a job or position) *The president has the right to make nominations for the Supreme Court.*

seek a nomination (=try to get it) *He is seeking the Republican nomination in the Senate race.*

accept a nomination (=agree to be nominated) *Lieberman accepted the nomination as the vice-presidential candidate.*

oppose sb's nomination (=say that someone should not get a job or position) *Senator Hatch said that he would oppose Lee's nomination to assistant attorney general.*

announce a nomination *The Academy Awards nominations were announced in Los Angeles yesterday.*

N

ADJECTIVES/NOUNS + nomination

the presidential nomination (=for the job of president) *He was unsuccessful in his campaign for the presidential nomination in 2008.*

the Republican/Democratic etc nomination (=to be the candidate for a party at an election) *Feinstein beat Van de Kamp for the Democratic nomination.*

PREPOSITIONS

a nomination for sth *Nominations for British Designer of the Year will be announced next week.*

sb's nomination as sth *She accepted the party's nomination as presidential candidate.*

sb's nomination to a post/committee/court *The judge's nomination to the Supreme Court was widely opposed.*

nonsense *n*

ideas, opinions, statements etc that are not true or that seem very stupid

ADJECTIVES

complete/total/utter nonsense *Most of what has been written on this subject is complete nonsense.*

absolute/sheer nonsense (=complete nonsense) *He said that the charges against him were absolute nonsense.*

superstitious nonsense (=based on ideas that some things bring good or bad luck) *He thought all this talk about black cats bringing good luck was superstitious nonsense.*

VERBS

talk nonsense *That's not true – he's talking nonsense!*

believe this/that nonsense *Don't tell me you believe all this nonsense about ghosts!*

PHRASES

that's nonsense (=used to emphasize that something is not true) *That's nonsense. I never said that at all.*

a load/lot of nonsense *informal* (=things that are completely untrue) *What she told you was a load of nonsense. Mark doesn't drink at all.*

non-stop *adj* THESAURUS ▸ **continuous**

norm Ac *n*

the usual situation, way of doing something, way of behaving etc

> **Grammar**
> You usually say **the norm**.

VERBS

be the norm *At that time, big families were the norm.*

become the norm *Owning a car has become the norm.*

accept sth as the norm *They encourage children to accept early bed times as the norm.*

establish the norm *Parents are responsible for establishing the norms within a family.*

conform to the norm (=behave or do something in the same way as everyone else) *Teenagers feel under pressure to conform to the norm.*

deviate from the norm (=be different from the norm) *It sounds like your experience deviated from the norm in every way.*

violate the norm (=do something that is against the norm) *People who violated norms of society were publicly punished.*

ADJECTIVES

social norms *Our behaviour is restricted by social norms.*

cultural norms *We must learn to work with people whose cultural norms are different from our own.*

the accepted/established norm *Behaviour that was different from the accepted norm was viewed with suspicion.*

the national norm *The school has a 30-hour week, five hours above the national norm.*

PREPOSITIONS

above/below the norm *Unemployment here is now 5%, which is far above the norm.*

the norm for sb/sth *This kind of behaviour is not the norm for a child of her age.*

PHRASES

different from the norm *I like being around people who are different from the norm.*

a departure/deviation from the norm *formal: This violence was an unexpected deviation from the norm.*

be the norm rather than the exception (=be what usually happens) *Going to university is the norm rather than the exception these days.*

normal Ac *adj* usual, typical, or expected

ADVERBS

completely normal *The test results came back, and everything was completely normal.*

perfectly normal (=completely normal) *Her reaction to the news was perfectly normal.*

quite normal (=completely normal) *Her room was untidy, but that was quite normal.*

fairly/pretty normal *They were a pretty normal family.*

NOUNS

a normal life *All I want is to lead a happy normal life.*

a normal conversation *You can't have a normal conversation if you know you're being recorded.*

a normal routine *The arrival of Celia had disrupted his normal routine.*

a normal day/week *On a normal day, Volker starts work at 7.30.*

a normal level/rate *His blood pressure returned to a normal level.*

normal practice/procedure *It is normal practice to appoint two or more directors.*

a normal process *Getting wrinkles is considered to be part of the normal process of ageing.*

normal size/weight *His legs had swollen to three times their normal size.*

the normal range/pattern *Her weight was within the normal range.*

the normal time *Alice woke at the normal time.*

VERBS

seem/look/appear normal *Fred seemed quite normal and gave no impression of being angry.*

sound normal *"Everything will be OK," she said, trying to sound normal.*

consider sth normal *In Britain, having a drink with your colleagues after work is considered normal.*

PREPOSITIONS

normal for sb/sth *The weather is normal for the time of year.*

PHRASES

as normal (=used to emphasize that something happens very regularly) *John and Liz were late, as normal.*

under normal circumstances *Under normal circumstances, you would have to pay to go into the exhibition.*

in the normal way *The results will be posted to you in the normal way.*

THESAURUS: normal

ordinary
house | car | day | person | man | woman | citizen | family
not special, unusual, or different from normal:
They live in an ordinary three-bedroomed house. | It looks like an ordinary car, but it uses solar power. | It was just an ordinary day – nothing special happened. | The book is written in a way that ordinary people can easily understand. | We need someone who knows about the needs of ordinary citizens.

regular *especially AmE*
guy | size | coffee
not special or unusual, or of the usual size or type:
He's just a regular guy. | I ordered a dozen regular-size cookies. | In Seattle, espresso is cheaper than regular coffee.

average
height | intelligence | price | cost
around the usual level or amount:
The robber was of average height and was wearing a black leather jacket. | The test showed that he was of ***above average*** *intelligence. | The average price of a pint of milk has gone up. | The noise level was* ***about average*** *for this type of machine.*

standard
practice | way | method | size | equipment | terms
normal – used about methods of doing something, or about the size, shape, features etc of products:
It is standard practice to X-ray hand-baggage at airports (=used when talking about the usual system for doing something). *| This method is still the standard way of making wine. | We stock shoes in all the standard sizes. | Airbags are standard equipment on all new cars* (=they are part of the usual equipment). *| The contract is subject to the standard terms and conditions.*

routine
check | inspection | examination | screening | maintenance | task
used about things that are usually done, often as part of a regular system :
The fault was discovered during a routine check of the plane. | The building is closed for routine maintenance. | His daughter helps him with routine tasks such as shopping and cooking. | The figures are updated every day ***on a routine basis*** (=as part of a regular system).

everyday
life | world | experience | existence | conversation | language | speech | event | occurrence | affairs | problem | work | things | objects | clothes
used about things that happen or that you use as part of normal life:
The artist painted scenes from everyday life in his hometown. | As we all know from our everyday experience, there are too many cars on our roads. | The word "yeah" is often used in everyday conversation to mean "yes". | She is good at making everyday events seem of interest to her reader. | Take time to look at and enjoy simple everyday things. | Sally was still dressed in her everyday clothes.

common
used about birds and plants that are of the most usual type:
Most people keep the common goldfish, but there are plenty of others. | The common daisy is a familiar sight in summer.

N

Common is also used in the phrases **the common people** or **the common man** (=people who are not rich and powerful): *Churchill had a great ability to communicate with* ***the common people.***

conventional
engine | medicine | treatment | approach | way | method | view
of the kind that is usually used, especially when you are comparing this with a different or special type:
The new engine is more efficient than a conventional diesel engine. | People sometimes turn to alternative therapies when conventional medicine has failed. | The teaching methods they use are very different from the conventional approach. | His hypothesis challenged the conventional view that life started in the ocean.

Conventional weapons are ones that are not nuclear, chemical, or biological: *The aircraft is capable of carrying* ***conventional*** *or nuclear* ***weapons.***

orthodox
medicine | approach | way | view
accepted by most people as being the right or usual way of doing something:
Some illnesses cannot be treated using orthodox medicine. | The orthodox economic approach is to give companies as much freedom as possible. | In those days, the orthodox view was that the earth was only a few thousand years old.

ANTONYMS **normal → abnormal**

normality *n*

a situation in which everything is normal

VERBS

return to normality (*also* **get back to normality** *informal*): *After the earthquake it took a long time for everything to return to normality.*

restore normality *The government is trying to restore normality to life in the country.*

ADJECTIVES

relative/comparative normality *The end of the war saw the town return to comparative normality.*

apparent normality *Despite his apparent normality, he was suffering from severe depression.*

PHRASES

a return to normality *Companies waiting for a return to normality following the recession may be disappointed.*

a sense/feeling of normality *After suffering a serious illness she is slowly getting a sense of normality back into her life.*

north *adj, adv, n*

the direction that is at the top of a map of the world, or the part of a place that is in this direction

north + NOUNS

the north side/end *Their house is on the north side of the square.*

the north coast *They landed on the north coast.*

the north bank *You can walk along the north bank of the river.*

the North Pole *It is very cold at the North Pole.*

a north wind (=a wind from the north) *The trees are bent by the north wind.*

ADVERBS

further north *A little further north is the small town of Leith.*

due north (=directly north) *He told us to head due north.*

ADJECTIVES

the far north *The birds breed in the far north.*

VERBS

go/travel/head north *We decided to go north.*

face north *The kitchen faces north.*

PREPOSITIONS

in the north *There has been fighting in the north of the country.*

to/towards the north *Port Meadow is situated to the north of Oxford.*

from the north *The wind was blowing from the north.*

the north of a place *I lived for many years in the north of England.*

nose *n*

the part of a person's or animal's face used for smelling or breathing

ADJECTIVES

a big/large nose *See that guy over there, the one with the big nose?*

a small/little nose *She had a cute little nose.*

a long nose *He looked down his long nose at me.*

a straight nose *Her nose was long, straight, and elegant.*

a broken nose *The boxer had a broken nose.*

a sharp/pointed nose *The rat had a long pointed nose.*

a red nose (=because you are cold or drunk, or have a cold) *His nose was red from the cold.*

a hooked nose (=one that curves down at the end) *An old man with a hooked nose pulled at her sleeve.*

a Roman/aquiline nose (=one that curves out near the top) *He had a thin face with an aquiline nose.*

a runny nose (=with liquid coming out) *I had a sore throat and a runny nose.*

a blocked nose (=so that you cannot breathe

easily) *My nose is really blocked and I can't smell anything.*

VERBS

blow your nose (=clear it by blowing strongly into a piece of soft paper or cloth) *She blew her nose on a large white handkerchief.*

wipe your nose (=wipe liquid away from your nose) *The boy sniffed and wiped his nose with the back of his hand.*

pick your nose (=remove substances from inside your nose with your finger) *His mother told him to stop picking his nose.*

breathe through your nose *Close your eyes and breathe through your nose.*

punch sb on the nose (=deliberately hit their nose) *He threatened to punch me on the nose.*

sb's nose is running (=liquid is coming out) *She was crying hard and her nose was running.*

PHRASES

the bridge of your nose (=the upper part, between your eyes) *Sam pushed his glasses up on the bridge of his nose.*

nostalgia *n*

a feeling that a time in the past was good, or a memory of a good time in the past

ADJECTIVES

great nostalgia *I read the college newsletter with great nostalgia.*

pure nostalgia *It was an evening of pure nostalgia, as the band played hits from the 1960s.*

VERBS

feel/have nostalgia *He didn't feel any nostalgia for his school days.*

wallow in nostalgia (=enjoy remembering a good time in the past) *It's fun to look back at old photos and wallow in nostalgia.*

PREPOSITIONS

nostalgia for sth *Many people feel nostalgia for the old days.*

PHRASES

a sense/feeling of nostalgia *It gave me a sense of nostalgia to hear him play the piano again.*

a pang of nostalgia (=a short feeling of nostalgia) *She felt a pang of nostalgia for the time when they were all children.*

a wave of nostalgia (=a sudden strong feeling of nostalgia) *As I drove into the village where I grew up, a wave of nostalgia swept over me.*

nosy *adj* THESAURUS ▶ **curious (1)**

notable *adj* THESAURUS ▶ **important (1)**

note *n*

1 a short message or piece of writing telling someone about something

ADJECTIVES/NOUNS + note

a brief/quick/short note *I wrote a short note telling him my plans.*

a handwritten note *The flowers had a handwritten note attached to them.*

a thank-you note *The children always write thank-you notes for their birthday presents.*

a delivery note *A delivery note is sent with the goods.*

VERBS

write a note *Do you think I should write a note to thank him for the flowers?*

leave (sb) a note *He had left a note for Sara in the kitchen.*

send (sb) a note *I sent a note of congratulations when their daughter was born.*

get/receive a note *Bella received a note asking her to attend a meeting.*

a note says sth *The note said that he would be back late.*

PREPOSITIONS

a note from sb *There was a note from her mother on the table.*

a note to sb *The note to his sister said that he wanted to help her.*

a note about sth *I've left him a note about tomorrow.*

in a note *In the note, he said that he would arrive at 10.*

PHRASES

a note of thanks/apology/congratulations *Tom wrote a note of apology to colleagues for his behaviour.*

2 words that you write down so that you can remember something

> **Grammar**
> Usually plural in this meaning.

ADJECTIVES/NOUNS + note

detailed notes *I always make quite detailed notes after important meetings.*

extensive/copious notes (=a very large amount) *She sat at the back of the hall and took copious notes.*

lecture notes (=that a student writes during a lecture) *I missed class today; can I borrow your lecture notes?*

medical notes (=notes that a doctor keeps about a patient) *I asked if I could see my medical notes.*

case notes (=notes that a doctor, social worker etc makes about someone) *The researchers looked at the case notes of 500 patients with this type of cancer.*

VERBS

make/take notes *The reporter took notes throughout the interview.*

make a note of sth *I'll just make a note of your name.*

jot down/scribble notes (=write them quickly) *The jurors were scribbling notes as the witness gave evidence.*

write up your notes (=write them again using full sentences and more details) *It's a good idea to write up your notes soon after a lecture.*

look/go/read through your notes *I read through my notes before the exam.*

keep a note *Keep a note of how much you have spent.*

N

3 a particular musical sound or a symbol that represents a musical sound

ADJECTIVES

a high/low note *Frankie has quite a deep voice and can't sing the high notes.*

VERBS

play/sing a note *He played the wrong note.*

hold a note (=make it continue) *She didn't have enough breath to hold the note.*

4 a type of mood or feeling

ADJECTIVES

a good/high note (=when you are pleased because something good has happened) *The season ended on a high note with a 5-0 win for the team.*

a happy/optimistic/positive note *I wanted to start the meeting on a happy note.*

a lighter/brighter note (=less serious) *On a brighter note, Jenni has invited us for dinner.*

a serious/sad note *On a more serious note, he said that there were still a lot of problems facing the company.*

VERBS

end/finish on a ... note *Despite the week ending on a sad note, he remains optimistic about the future.*

PREPOSITIONS

on a ... note *On a happier note, we are delighted to announce the birth of our first grandchild.*

a note of optimism/sadness/desperation etc *There was a note of sadness in his voice.*

nothing *pronoun* not anything

ADVERBS

absolutely nothing *I know absolutely nothing about baseball.*

nothing at all (*also* **nothing whatsoever**) *Her mother said nothing at all.*

almost/virtually/practically nothing *The two men have virtually nothing in common.*

nothing else/more *I have nothing more to say.*

nothing + ADJECTIVES

nothing wrong/new/special etc *There was nothing wrong with her hearing.*

nothing untoward (=nothing unusual, unexpected, or unwanted) *Police searched the house but found nothing untoward.*

VERBS

do nothing *We can't just sit here and do nothing.*

nothing happens *For a few seconds nothing happened, then the door started to open.*

nothing changes *I've told him a million times, but nothing changes.*

PHRASES

have nothing to say/hide/fear etc *I'm not worried about the investigation because I have nothing to hide.*

nothing of interest/value/importance etc *There was nothing of interest in the desk.*

have nothing to do with sth (=not have any connection with something) *His age has nothing to do with it.*

notice[1] *v*

if you notice something or someone, you realize that they exist, especially because you can see, hear, or feel them

ADVERBS

hardly/barely/scarcely notice sth (=almost not at all) *The mark was so tiny, I hardly noticed it.*

not really notice (=not notice - used for making what you say less definite) *I didn't really notice what they were doing.*

not even notice (=not notice, when this is surprising or annoying) *At first, he didn't even notice that she had left.*

never notice sth *Have you never noticed how annoying he is?*

immediately/instantly notice sth *He immediately noticed the missing picture.*

notice sth at once (=immediately) *When you enter the store you will notice at once that all the products are very good quality.*

PHRASES

can't help noticing sth (=notice something because it is obvious) *I can't help noticing that there are no women in this company.*

fail to notice sth *The driver failed to notice that his brake lights weren't working.*

seem/appear not to notice sth *The actor made a mistake, but the audience seemed not to notice.*

notice[2] *n*

1 a written statement about something

VERBS + notice

put up a notice *Someone had put up a notice on the board, which said that the lecture had been cancelled.*

see a notice *Did you see the notice about the staff meeting?*

notice + VERBS

a notice says/reads *The notice said 'No ball games'.*

a notice goes up *Notices were going up everywhere about the election.*

2 if you take notice of someone or something, you pay attention to them

VERBS

take notice (=pay attention to something) *I began to take notice when the subject of money came up.*

take no notice/not take any notice (=ignore someone or something) *The other passengers took no notice of what was happening.*

come to sb's notice (=used when someone notices something) *This problem first came to our notice last summer.*

escape sb's notice (=used when someone does not notice something) *It had somehow escaped his notice that Phil seemed interested in Jean.*

bring sth to sb's notice (=tell someone about something) *It has been brought to my notice that employees are smoking in the restrooms.*

attract notice (=be noticed by other people) *She didn't want to attract notice, so she dressed very plainly.*

3 information or a warning about something that is going to happen

VERBS

give (sb) notice *To withdraw money from this type of savings account, you must give the bank 30 days' notice.*

serve notice *formal* (=give official legal notice about something) *They have served notice that they intend to take legal action against the company.*

have/receive notice *If I had had more notice, I could have spent more time getting ready for their visit.*

need/require notice *The company requires a month's notice of any holiday time you would like to take.*

ADJECTIVES

advance notice (*also* **prior notice** *formal*) (=given before an event) *When you're on the mailing list, you'll receive advance notice of upcoming events.*

reasonable/sufficient notice *Did you have reasonable notice of the court case?*

ten days'/three months'/five minutes' etc notice *His contract said he must give three months' notice if he decides to leave.*

written notice *He gave written notice of his intention to sell the company.*

formal/official/legal notice *We expect to receive official notice of the transfer next week.*

PREPOSITIONS

without notice *Trains may be cancelled without notice.*

notice of sth *The bank must give you one month's notice of any changes.*

PHRASES

at short notice (=without much time to prepare) *Thank you for coming to help at such short notice.*

at a moment's notice (=very quickly) *He'd be ready to leave at a moment's notice.*

until further notice (=from now until you are told something else) *On the door was a sign: 'Library closed until further notice'.*

noticeable *adj* easy to notice

NOUNS

a noticeable change/improvement *There was a noticeable change in her attitude when she found out who I was.*

a noticeable difference *If you do these exercises daily, you will soon see a noticeable difference.*

a noticeable increase/reduction *There has been a noticeable increase in temperatures around the world.*

a noticeable effect/impact *He drank several glasses of wine, but it had no noticeable effect on him.*

a noticeable feature *These groups of trees are the most noticeable feature of the landscape.*

ADVERBS

hardly/barely noticeable *The scar was hardly noticeable.*

immediately noticeable *The effects of the poison are not immediately noticeable.*

particularly/especially noticeable *These changes were particularly noticeable in Africa.*

notion [Ac] *n* an idea, belief, or opinion

ADJECTIVES

a vague notion (=unclear) *He had only a vague notion of what might happen next.*

an absurd/ridiculous notion *The ridiculous notion crossed his mind that she might be in love with him.*

a preconceived notion (=an idea that you have before you have enough knowledge or experience, which is often wrong) *I didn't come to the job with any preconceived notions about what it would be like.*

an accepted/popular notion (=an idea that most people believe, and which is often wrong) *These women challenged accepted notions of female roles in society.*

the whole notion of sth *The movie makes us question the whole notion of what makes a hero.*

a romantic notion (=based on how you want something to be, not how it is in real life) *He rejected the romantic notion of pure art with no political or social influence.*

a traditional notion *This is a method which abandons the traditional notions of teaching and learning.*

VERBS

have a notion *He didn't have a clear notion of what to do.*

accept a notion *Probably 95% of scientists now*

N

accept the notion that human activity is causing climate change.

support a notion *There is no evidence to support the notion that girls are treated better than boys in school.*

reinforce a notion (=make an idea stronger or easier to believe) *The research reinforces the notion that fathers have an important role in their children's lives.*

N

challenge/dispute a notion *Copernicus challenged the notion that the Sun goes around the Earth.*

reject/dismiss a notion *Aristotle rejected the notion that the body and the soul are separate.*

dispel a notion (=show that it is not true) *He is keen to dispel the notion that he is a wealthy man.*

abandon a notion (=stop having it) *I thought the course would be easy but I soon abandoned that notion.*

PREPOSITIONS

the notion of sth *The notion of individual freedom dominated political debate.*

a notion about sth *He had preconceived notions about life in the country.*

notorious *adj* THESAURUS ▸ famous

nourishment *n*

substances that people and other living things need in order to grow and stay healthy

ADJECTIVES

enough/adequate/proper nourishment *You must ensure that the patient receives adequate nourishment.*

vital/essential nourishment *The outer part of wheat and rice contains vital nourishment.*

VERBS

provide nourishment *The baby's mother provides nourishment and security.*

get/receive/obtain nourishment *A plant gets all its nourishment from the soil.*

draw nourishment (=get nourishment. 'Draw' sounds more formal or technical than 'get') *The fungus draws its nourishment from the tree it grows on.*

need nourishment *After all that activity, you'll need some nourishment.*

PHRASES

lack of nourishment *He looked as if he might collapse from lack of nourishment.*

novel[1] *n*

a long written story in which the characters and events are usually imaginary

VERBS

read a novel *Have you read Anne Tyler's latest novel?*

write a novel *She writes historical novels.*

publish a novel *His first novel was published in 2005.*

be based on a novel *The film is based on a novel by Robert Harris.*

a novel is set somewhere (=the events in it take place there) *Many of her novels are set in Egypt.*

ADJECTIVES/NOUNS + novel

a great/good novel *She wanted to write a great novel.*

a classic novel *We will be discussing Aldous Huxley's classic novel 'Brave New World'.*

a best-selling novel (=one that a lot of people buy) *She is the author of several best-selling novels.*

a popular novel (=one that a lot of people like) *Spring became a writer of popular novels.*

a modern/contemporary novel *Too many students only read contemporary novels.*

sb's debut novel (=their first novel) *It's an impressive debut novel.*

a romantic novel *He was as handsome as the hero of a romantic novel.*

a historical novel (=one about a time in the past) *Graves wrote historical novels set in ancient Rome.*

an autobiographical novel (=one that is based on events in the writer's life) *Isherwood's 'Goodbye to Berlin' is an autobiographical novel about his time in Germany.*

a detective/crime novel *I like reading crime novels.*

PREPOSITIONS

a novel by sb *I'm reading a novel by D. H. Lawrence.*

the novels of sb *We're studying the novels of Jane Austen.*

a novel about sb/sth *He is writing a novel about the First World War.*

novel[2] *adj* THESAURUS ▸ new (1)

novelist *n* someone who writes novels

ADJECTIVES

a great novelist *He is related to Russia's greatest novelist, Tolstoy.*

a popular/successful novelist *She was a popular novelist of the 1920s and 30s.*

a best-selling novelist *My ambition is to be a best-selling novelist.*

a prolific novelist (=one who writes a lot of novels) *He was a prolific novelist and published over 60 books.*

a crime novelist *Crime novelists often research ways of murdering people.*

a romantic novelist (=one who writes romantic novels) *Barbara Cartland was a famous romantic novelist, who wrote more than 700 books.*

novelty *n*
the quality of being new, unusual, and interesting

VERBS

sth loses its novelty (=it stops seeming new and interesting) *His work has lost its novelty and it now seems rather old-fashioned.*

the novelty wears off (=used when something stops seeming new and interesting) *Once the novelty had worn off he didn't play with his new toy much.*

novelty + NOUNS

novelty value (=the quality that something has when it seems interesting and unusual) *Some people liked the phone because of its novelty value.*

ADJECTIVES

sheer novelty (=used when emphasizing how new and different something seems) *Few pieces of music can match the sheer novelty of Sibelius's Sixth Symphony.*

PREPOSITIONS

the novelty of (doing) sth *The novelty of travelling around the country was starting to wear off.*

PHRASES

be something of a novelty/be quite a novelty (=be something that seems new and different) *At that time, computers were still something of a novelty.*

noxious *adj* THESAURUS ▸ poisonous

nude *adj* THESAURUS ▸ naked (1)

nuisance *n*
a person, thing, or situation that annoys you or causes problems

ADJECTIVES

a real nuisance *Traffic noise is a real nuisance here.*

a great/terrible/awful nuisance *Slight deafness can be a great nuisance.*

such a nuisance *I'm sorry to be such a nuisance.*

a minor nuisance *The pain is now just a minor nuisance.*

VERBS

become a nuisance *The dog's behaviour was becoming a nuisance.*

cause a nuisance *Some of the boys were causing a nuisance during morning break.*

PREPOSITIONS

a nuisance to sb *She said she did not want to be a nuisance to her grown-up children.*

PHRASES

What a nuisance! *I've left my umbrella behind. What a nuisance!*

it's a nuisance *It's a nuisance having to sweep up leaves all the time.*

make a nuisance of yourself (=annoy other people with your behaviour) *He was very drunk and making a nuisance of himself.*

number *n*
1 a word or sign representing an amount

ADJECTIVES/NOUNS + number

a phone/house/flight etc number *Can I have your phone number?*

a lucky/unlucky number (=that you think gives you good or bad luck) *Three is my lucky number.*

an even number (=2, 4, 6, 8 etc) *All even numbers can be divided by 2.*

an odd number (=1, 3, 5, 7 etc) *You can't work in pairs if you've got an odd number of people.*

a whole number (=a number that is not a fraction) *Give your answer to the nearest whole number.*

a round number (=ending in zero) *A hundred is a nice round number.*

a prime number (=a number such as 13 that can be divided only by itself and 1) *After 7, what is the next prime number?*

VERBS

add numbers together/add up numbers *Add the two numbers together and divide by three.*

subtract one number from another *Subtract this number from the total.*

multiply one number by another *What happens if you multiply a positive number by a negative number?*

divide one number by another *Divide the top number of the fraction by the bottom number.*

2 an amount of something

ADJECTIVES

a large/huge/considerable etc number *We've had a huge number of complaints.*

⚠ Don't say 'a big number of people/things'.

a high number (=a lot) *There seems to be no reason for the high number of accidents.*

a good number (=quite a lot) *He has written a good number of books for children.*

a small/tiny number *The class had only a small number of students.*

a low number (=not many) *What is the reason for the low numbers of women involved in management?*

a limited number (=quite small) *A limited number of copies were printed.*

a growing/increasing number *An increasing number of women are entering the profession.*

the exact/precise number *No one knows the exact number of deaths.*

the approximate number *What's the approximate number of people on the course?*

the total/overall number *The overall number of divorces has gone up.*

N

the real/true number *The real number of drug users is much higher than the official figure.*

VERBS + number

increase the number of sth *The government plans to increase the number of police officers.*

reduce the number of sth *We need to reduce the number of cars on the road.*

control/limit the number of sth *They want to limit the number of foreigners entering the country.*

calculate a number *The program can calculate the number of words that will fit the space available.*

count/measure a number *We counted the number of children in the school hall.*

number + VERBS

a number increases/goes up/grows/rises *The number of mobile phones has increased dramatically.*

a number falls/drops/goes down/decreases/declines *The number of new houses being built is falling steadily.*

a number doubles (=becomes twice as big) *The number of road accidents has doubled in the last ten years.*

PREPOSITIONS

the number of sth *The number of cars on our roads is increasing.*

PHRASES

a number of sth (=several) *A number of different ideas were discussed.*

any number of sth (=a lot of something) *There have been any number of magazine articles about the celebrity couple.*

in large/increasing/limited etc numbers *Birds nest here in large numbers.*

sth are few/small/limited in number (=there are not many of something) *Jobs were few in number.*

a drop/decline in numbers *Whales have suffered a large decline in numbers.*

bring the number to 25/120 etc *This will bring the number of jobs lost at the company to 85.*

3 a telephone number

ADJECTIVES/NOUNS + number

the wrong number *I think you've got the wrong number.*

a work/home number *You can call me on my work number.*

a mobile number *BrE*, **a cell/cellphone number** *AmE*: *She gave him her mobile number.*

a contact number (=that someone can call if they need to speak to you) *They had no contact number for the child's parents.*

a number is engaged *BrE*, **a number is busy** *AmE*: *If the number is engaged, leave a message.*

VERBS

dial a number *Make sure you dial the number carefully.*

call/phone a number (*also* **ring a number** *BrE*): *Every time he called Sue's number, she didn't answer.*

give sb a number *She wouldn't give me her number.*

exchange numbers *We exchanged numbers at the end of the evening.*

PHRASES

sb's name and number *Take her name and number and tell her I'll call her back.*

nutritious *adj* THESAURUS ▸ **healthy (2)**

Oo

oath *n*

a formal and very serious promise

ADJECTIVES

a solemn oath *She swore a solemn oath never to tell anyone about their secret.*

the presidential oath (=sworn by a new president) *He was the oldest person ever to take the presidential oath.*

a sacred oath (=one you swear by God) *Stephen swore a sacred oath to recognize Matilda as Queen.*

VERBS

swear/take an oath *The witness has to swear an oath to tell the truth and nothing but the truth.*

break/violate an oath (=do something you promised not to do) *I know he will never break his oath.*

keep your oath (=do what you promised to do) *They doubted that the king would keep his oath.*

be bound by an oath (=have sworn an oath) *These chiefs were bound by oaths of loyalty.*

PHRASES

an oath of allegiance/loyalty/obedience (=saying that you will be loyal) *All American citizens have to take an oath of allegiance.*

an oath of secrecy *Anyone who joined the group had to swear an oath of secrecy.*

obedience *n*

when someone does what they are told to do, or what a law, rule etc says they must do

ADJECTIVES

absolute/complete/total obedience *The king demanded absolute obedience.*

blind/passive obedience (=without thinking about why) *I followed my father's commands with blind obedience.*

unquestioning obedience (=without questioning whether someone or something is right) *He is the type who expects unquestioning obedience from his employees.*

VERBS

demand/expect obedience *Parents should not demand unquestioning obedience from their children.*

owe sb obedience (=have a duty to obey someone) *The knights owed obedience to their king.*

swear obedience *Monks swore obedience to the Pope.*

PREPOSITIONS

obedience to sb/sth *Life in a monastery demands obedience to God's authority.*

obedience from sb *She expected obedience from all the children.*

obese *adj* THESAURUS ▸ fat[1] (1)

obey *v*

to do what someone in authority tells you to do, or what a law or rule says you must do

NOUNS

obey a law/rule *Most drivers obey the law.*

obey an order/command/instruction *The first duty of a soldier is to obey orders.*

obey your father/mother/parents etc *He was a good boy who always obeyed his parents.*

obey your master *Slaves had to obey their masters at all times.*

VERBS

must/have to obey sb/sth *She felt she had to obey her father, even though she thought he was wrong.*

refuse to obey *Many people felt the law was unfair, and refused to obey it.*

fail to obey *Employees failed to obey company regulations.*

ADVERBS

obey instantly/immediately *She said "sit!" and the dog obeyed instantly.*

blindly obey (=obey without thinking or asking any questions) *He expected his followers to blindly obey him.*

PHRASES

failure to obey *Failure to obey the court is a serious offence.*

obey sb/sth without question (=obey without asking why you should do this) *The staff were afraid of her and obeyed her without question.*

THESAURUS: obey

follow
rules | regulations | instructions | advice | suggestion | orders | directions
to do what a rule says you should do, or do what someone advises or suggests:
There are some simple rules which you should follow when handling electric equipment. | If you follow my advice, you shouldn't have any problems. | The soldiers claimed that they were only following orders.

abide by *formal*
rule | law | decision | agreement | deal | commitment | ceasefire
to accept and obey something:
Players have to abide by the rules of the game. | The company announced that it would abide by

the court's decision. | *The US will abide by its commitment to withdraw its soldiers from the country* (=do what it has officially promised).

comply with *formal*
law | regulation | rule | order | requirement | standard | agreement | terms
to do what someone or something says, or be according to a rule, law, or agreement:
Companies have a duty to comply with employment laws. | *The equipment does not comply with the new safety regulations.* | *About half of the beaches fail to comply with European standards.*

respect *formal*
law | rules | rights | principle
to behave in a way that shows that you understand the importance of something, and not do anything that is against it:
Both sides must respect international law and not attack civilians. | *Sweden has the reputation of being a democratic country that respects human rights.* | *The government should respect the principle of freedom of speech.*

You **obey** someone who has authority over you, for example a parent, army officer, or teacher. When talking about other people, you **do what sb says**: *My husband never **does what I say**.* You also **do what** instructions **say** you should do: *I did **what it said** on the washing instructions.*

ANTONYMS **obey → disobey**

object¹ *n*

1 a solid thing

ADJECTIVES

a small/large object *It can be used to store paperclips and other small objects.*

a metal/wooden/plastic object *The scanner can detect metal objects in passengers' bags.*

a heavy object *He was struck on the head by a heavy object.*

a sharp/blunt object *Keep sharp objects away from small children.*

an everyday/household object *Try to describe an everyday object such as a spoon.*

an inanimate object (=a thing that is not alive) *It's silly to be angry with an inanimate object like a computer.*

a solid/physical object *The boat seemed to bump against a solid object.*

a three-dimensional object *Drawing three-dimensional objects is quite difficult.*

a moving object *Cats can spot moving objects better than still ones.*

a foreign object *formal* (=something in someone's body or food that should not be there) *The infection was caused by a foreign object in the eye.*

2 the purpose of a plan, action, or activity

ADJECTIVES

the main/primary object *The main object of their expedition was to collect new plants.*

the sole object *I came here with the sole object of seeing you.*

the real object *What was the real object of his visit?*

the whole object (=the only purpose) *The whole object was to keep the kids busy.*

PREPOSITIONS

the object of sth *The object of the game is to capture your opponent's pieces.*

PHRASES

the object of the exercise (=the purpose of what you are doing) *The object of the exercise is to get people discussing the issue.*

defeat the object (=prevent you achieving your purpose) *If you have to go and collect the things you order online, that defeats the object.*

object² *v*

to say that you do not agree with something

ADVERBS

strongly/vigorously/strenuously object to sth *The Russian government strongly objected to the plan.*

loudly object to sth (*also* **vociferously object to sth** *formal*): *Conservative groups vociferously object to any change in the current tax system.*

PREPOSITIONS

object to sth *No one objects to companies making a profit.*

PHRASES

object on the grounds that *Local people objected to the scheme on the grounds that it would spoil the surrounding countryside.*

have the right to object/be entitled to object *You have the right to object if you think you are being treated unfairly.*

sb can hardly object/there is no way sb can object (=someone cannot object) *He can hardly object if other people use the same method as he used himself.*

I object (=used when you do not think someone should say something, especially in a court of law) *"How many other people has he murdered?" "I object, Your Honour!"*

objection *n*

a reason that you have for opposing or disapproving of something, or something you say that expresses this

VERBS

have an objection *Does anyone have any objections to the proposal?*

make/raise/voice an objection (=say that you have an objection) *The Parish Council made several objections to the changes.*

lodge an objection (=formally make an objection) *Residents have lodged an objection to the new development.*
withdraw an objection (=stop objecting to something) *The FBI withdrew its objections to publishing the information.*
overrule an objection (=order that people should ignore someone's objection) *The prime minister overruled the objections of two ministers.*
meet sb's objections (=change something so that someone will no longer object) *He altered the plans to meet the objections of community leaders.*

ADJECTIVES

a strong objection *Parents at the school have voiced strong objections to the closure.*
a serious/major objection *There were serious objections to using the videotaped evidence at the trial.*
the main/principal objection *One of the main objections was that classes were being taught by untrained staff.*
the fundamental objection *The fundamental objection to this scheme is that there is no way of making sure that people obey it.*
a moral objection *He had moral objections to killing animals for food.*

PREPOSITIONS

an objection to sth *We have strong objections to the use of drugs in sport.*
an objection from/by sb *The nightclub was built despite objections from local residents.*

objective[1] Ac *n*

something that you are trying hard to achieve, especially in business or politics

ADJECTIVES/NOUNS + objective

the main/principal/primary/prime objective *This research project has three main objectives.*
a key/major objective (=very important) *Their economic strategy was based on a number of key objectives.*
an overriding objective (=more important than others) *The overriding objective is to reduce our costs.*
an economic/military/business/political etc objective *We have made good progress towards meeting our business objectives.*
a clear objective *Managers must give their teams clear objectives to work towards.*
the ultimate objective (=the main one which will happen after a long process) *The ultimate objective of the treatment programme is a drug-free lifestyle.*
a long-term objective *His long-term objective was to have enough money to retire at 55.*
a common/shared objective (=one that people, countries etc share) *They have one common objective – to bring an end to the fighting.*

VERBS

have an objective *The degree program has two main objectives.*
set an objective (=decide what you are trying to achieve) *Students should be encouraged to set their own objectives.*
achieve/accomplish an objective (*also* **attain an objective** *formal*): *The plan will help us achieve our objective of reducing paper waste.*
reach/meet an objective (=achieve it) *We need to control spending in order to meet our financial objectives.*
pursue an objective (=try to achieve something) *War has always been a means of pursuing national objectives.*

PREPOSITIONS

an objective of sth *The objective of the research is to find out how cancer cells develop.*

PHRASES

aims and objectives (=all the things someone wants to achieve) *The department should clearly state its aims and objectives.*

THESAURUS: objective

aim, goal, objective, the object of sth, the point, intention, ends → **purpose**

objective[2] Ac *adj*

based on facts rather than on your feelings or beliefs

ADVERBS

completely/totally objective *It is not possible for anyone to be completely objective.*
purely objective *There is no purely objective way of assessing each claim.*

NOUNS

an objective assessment/evaluation/analysis *You should have carried out an objective assessment of the risk.*
an objective criterion/standard/measure *A decision is made on the basis of objective criteria such as the patient's age.*

ANTONYMS **objective → subjective**

obligation *n*

a moral or legal duty to do something

VERBS

have an obligation *Citizens have an obligation to obey the law.*
feel an obligation *When his mother died, he felt an obligation to continue her work.*
owe an obligation to sb *formal*: *He owed an obligation of loyalty to his king.*
meet/fulfil/honour an obligation (=do something that you have a duty to do) *The government failed to honour its obligations under the terms of the agreement.*

O

carry out an obligation *States will be punished if they do not carry out their obligations.*

impose an obligation on sb *formal* (=make someone have to do something) *A contract imposes certain obligations on employees and employers.*

ADJECTIVES/NOUNS + obligation

a legal/statutory obligation (=something that the law says must be done) *The local authority has a statutory obligation to provide education for children.*

a moral obligation *We have a moral obligation to take care of our environment.*

a financial obligation *The company has been unable to meet its financial obligations.*

a contractual/treaty obligation (=something that a contract or treaty says you must do) *He is looking for a way to get out of his contractual obligations.*

PREPOSITIONS

an obligation to/towards sb (=an obligation to do something for someone) *A university has an obligation to its students.*

an obligation on sb (=a obligation that someone has) *There is no obligation on the company to pay any compensation.*

be under an obligation to do sth (=have an obligation to do something) *The landlord is under an obligation to repair the house.*

be under no obligation to do sth (=not have an obligation to do something) *An accused person is under no obligation to say anything.*

PHRASES

a sense of obligation *They send back money because of their strong sense of obligation to their family.*

obligatory *adj* THESAURUS ▶ **compulsory**

obscure *adj* THESAURUS ▶ **famous**

observation *n*

the process of watching something or someone carefully for a period of time

ADJECTIVES

close/careful/detailed observation *A lot of useful knowledge is gained by careful observation of the world around you.*

casual observation (=not very careful or organized) *Even casual observation suggests that not all men behave like this.*

direct/personal/first-hand observation *Piaget developed his theories based on direct observation of children.*

scientific observation *Scientific observation led to the discovery of vaccines.*

VERBS

carry out observation(s) *The Pentagon was carrying out electronic observations of the Soviet Union.*

observation + NOUNS

an observation post/point (=a place from where you can watch something, especially below you) *The top of the mountain was a natural location for an observation post.*

PREPOSITIONS

from observation *We know from observation that this teaching method is effective.*

PHRASES

be under observation (=be in the process of being watched) *The police said that the house had been under observation.*

keep sb under observation *The doctor ordered that the patient be kept under observation.*

sb's powers of observation (=someone's ability to notice things) *In the past, people used their own powers of observation to forecast the weather.*

obsession *n*

an extreme unhealthy interest in something or worry about something

ADJECTIVES

an unhealthy obsession *Our society seems to have an unhealthy obsession with food.*

a dangerous obsession *Mark had a dangerous obsession with fast cars.*

a national obsession (=an obsession that the whole country has) *In Britain, the weather is a national obsession.*

a strange/weird obsession *Why do you have this strange obsession with trains?*

VERBS

have an obsession *The poet seems to have an obsession with death.*

become an obsession *For Rosie, losing weight had become an obsession.*

border on/upon obsession (=be almost as extreme as an obsession) *Sometimes his tidiness bordered on obsession.*

PREPOSITIONS

an obsession with sth *His obsession with mountain climbing caused the break-up of his marriage.*

PHRASES

be something of an obsession (=be almost as strong as an obsession) *The case became something of an obsession with him.*

to the point of obsession (=so much that it is an obsession) *She was protective of her children, to the point of obsession.*

be in the grip of an obsession *Ever since he met that woman, he has been in the grip of an obsession.*

obsolete *adj* THESAURUS ▶ **old-fashioned**

obstacle *n*

something that makes it difficult to achieve something

ADJECTIVES

a major/serious/big obstacle *Debt is a major obstacle to economic growth.*

a real obstacle *She has overcome some very real obstacles.*

the main/biggest/greatest etc obstacle *The biggest obstacle to change is people's attitudes.*

a formidable obstacle (=a very big one) *There are formidable obstacles to legal reform.*

an insuperable/insurmountable obstacle *formal* (=one that cannot be successfully dealt with) *We were faced with an apparently insuperable obstacle.*

a legal/political/technical etc obstacle *Despite technical obstacles, scientists at NASA are considering the project.*

VERBS

face an obstacle *The investigation has faced numerous obstacles.*

overcome an obstacle (*also* **surmount an obstacle** *formal*) (=deal with it successfully) *We need to help young people overcome the obstacles that poverty puts in their way.*

remove an obstacle *Opening the border removed all obstacles to travel between the two countries.*

create an obstacle *These regulations must not create unnecessary obstacles to international trade.*

present/pose an obstacle (=be or cause an obstacle) *Serious differences continue to present obstacles to an agreement.*

prove an obstacle (=be an obstacle) *The cost of taking legal action may prove an obstacle.*

PREPOSITIONS

an obstacle to sth *A lack of resources is the main obstacle to progress.*

PHRASES

an obstacle in the way/path *There were still a number of obstacles in the way of an agreement.*

put/place obstacles in the way (=try to stop someone from doing something easily) *Her father put several obstacles in the way of their marriage.*

obstruction *n*

the blocking of a road, tube etc, or the thing that blocks it

VERBS

cause an obstruction *The illegally parked car was causing an obstruction.*

remove/clear an obstruction *She had an operation to remove an obstruction from her throat.*

PREPOSITIONS

an obstruction in sth *He has an obstruction in his small intestine.*

an obstruction to sth *Clear the pipe so there is no obstruction to the free flow of water.*

obtain *v formal* to get something

ADVERBS

obtain sth illegally/legally *The guns were obtained illegally.*

sb recently obtained sth *She recently obtained a PhD in chemistry.*

PREPOSITIONS

obtain sth from sb/sth *You can obtain a list of recommended accommodation from the tourist information office.*

PHRASES

sth can easily be obtained *The data can easily be obtained from the internet.*

sth is difficult/hard to obtain *Nuclear material is hard to obtain.*

sth may be obtained (=you can get something) *Further details may be obtained by telephoning this number.*

THESAURUS: obtain

receive, obtain, acquire, gain, win, earn, inherit, get hold of sth → **get (1)**

obvious Ac *adj* easy to notice or understand

ADVERBS

perfectly obvious (=very obvious) *It was perfectly obvious what he was thinking.*

patently/blatantly obvious (=very obvious – used when something seems very bad or shocking) *It is patently obvious that this method is no longer effective.*

glaringly/blindingly obvious (=extremely obvious) *The book's faults are glaringly obvious.*

painfully obvious (=very obvious, and embarrassing or upsetting) *It became painfully obvious that she and Edward had nothing in common.*

immediately obvious *The cause of the pain was not immediately obvious.*

increasingly obvious *The effects of global warming are becoming increasingly obvious.*

far from obvious (=not at all obvious) *The benefits of the change are far from obvious.*

NOUNS

an obvious reason *For obvious reasons, I did not give my real name.*

an obvious example *Many children's books have been turned into successful films – 'Harry Potter' is an obvious example.*

an obvious question *The obvious question is why did she do it?*

an obvious fact *They ignored the obvious fact that they didn't have enough money.*

the obvious conclusion *The conclusion is obvious: he never intended to resign.*

the obvious answer/solution *There is no obvious answer to their problem.*

the obvious thing (to do) (=what clearly seems the best thing to do) *The obvious thing to do is to ask the boss what she wants.*

the obvious choice (=what clearly seems the best thing to choose) *Ruth was the obvious choice for this job.*

an obvious sign *There were no obvious signs that the fire was started deliberately.*

an obvious advantage/benefit *This system had obvious advantages for the government.*

an obvious difference/similarity *There are obvious differences between the two women in the play.*

O

VERBS

become obvious *It soon became obvious that the plan wasn't going to work.*

look/seem/sound/appear obvious *The solution seems obvious to us now.*

state the obvious (=say something that is obvious) *At the risk of stating the obvious, maybe making them angry is not a good idea.*

PREPOSITIONS

obvious to sb *It was obvious to me that he wasn't well.*

occasion *n*

1 a time when something happens

ADJECTIVES

several occasions *He has helped me on several occasions.*

many occasions *I have seen him drunk on many occasions.*

numerous occasions *She has been late on numerous occasions.*

a rare occasion (=used when something does not happen often) *Only on rare occasions did she ever receive a letter.*

a particular occasion *On that particular occasion, he greeted me by kissing my hand.*

a previous occasion *He insisted then, as on every previous occasion, that he was innocent.*

a separate occasion *I had heard this story on at least four separate occasions.*

a different occasion *The same person can react differently on different occasions.*

such occasions (=an occasion like the one mentioned or described) *He had a box of toys by his desk for such occasions.*

VERBS

recall/remember an occasion *Meyer recalls one occasion when the snow was so bad that he couldn't get home.*

PREPOSITIONS

on this/that/one etc occasion *She usually dressed in black, but on this occasion she was wearing a red dress.*

PHRASES

a number of occasions *The crowd interrupted her speech on a number of occasions.*

more than one occasion (=more than once) *She stayed out all night on more than one occasion.*

at least one occasion (=once, and probably more than once) *On at least one occasion he was arrested for robbery.*

on the odd occasion (=used when something does not happen often) *Being unable to sleep doesn't matter on the odd occasion, but it is a problem if it happens regularly.*

2 an important social event or ceremony

ADJECTIVES

a special occasion *I'm saving this bottle of champagne for a special occasion.*

a big/great/splendid occasion *The big occasion for country people was the Agricultural Fair.*

a formal occasion *He wore the suit on formal occasions.*

a social occasion *I prefer not to discuss business at social occasions.*

ceremonial occasions (=very formal official occasions) *The gowns are worn only on ceremonial occasions.*

a happy/joyful occasion *The wedding had been a joyful occasion.*

a sad/solemn occasion *He did not want his funeral to be a sad and solemn occasion, but a celebration of his life.*

a historic occasion (=important as part of history) *This is truly a historic occasion.*

a momentous occasion (=an important one that will have an influence on the future) *We all recognized that this was a momentous occasion.*

NOUNS + occasion

a family occasion *For many people, Christmas remains a family occasion.*

VERBS

celebrate an occasion *To celebrate the occasion, a small party was held at his home.*

mark an occasion (=do something special to celebrate an event) *The bells were rung to mark the occasion.*

suit the occasion *The table was decorated to suit the occasion.*

PREPOSITIONS

an occasion of sth *The wedding will be an occasion of joyful celebration.*

PHRASES

a sense of occasion (=a feeling that an event is very special or important) *The music gave the event a real sense of occasion.*

enter into the spirit of the occasion (=join in a social occasion in an eager way) *People entered into the spirit of the occasion by enjoying a picnic before the outdoor concert.*

occupation Ac *n formal*

1 a type of job

ADJECTIVES

a dangerous/hazardous occupation *Mining remains a hazardous occupation.*

manual/blue-collar occupations (=jobs in which you work using your hands) *People from manual occupations have seen their wages fall in recent years.*

professional/white-collar occupations (=jobs for which you need a lot of education) *Most people in professional occupations have been to university.*

skilled/unskilled occupations *Making jewellery is a highly skilled occupation which requires years of training.*

a male/female occupation *Agricultural work was considered to be a male occupation.*

a sedentary occupation (=in which you have to sit down) *Sedentary occupations can be bad for your health.*

VERBS

have an occupation *The people in the region have a variety of occupations.*

choose an occupation *Young people need help with choosing a suitable occupation.*

give your occupation (=say what your job is) *The form asks you to give your occupation.*

take up an occupation (*also* **enter an occupation** *formal*) (=start doing a type of job) *Many of his former colleagues have taken up another occupation.*

follow an occupation *formal* (=do a type of job) *The third son followed the same occupation as his brothers.*

2 a way of spending your time

ADJECTIVES

sb's favourite occupation *BrE*, **sb's favorite occupation** *AmE*: *Walking in the countryside near his home is one of his favourite occupations.*

a rewarding occupation (=one that you enjoy, especially because you feel you are doing something useful) *I don't find housework a very rewarding occupation.*

3 a situation in which a place is controlled by another country's army

ADJECTIVES

military occupation *The people want an end to US military occupation of their country.*

illegal occupation *The illegal occupation of the region caused a lot of bad feeling against the soldiers.*

PREPOSITIONS

be under US/German etc occupation *The island was under German occupation during the war.*

occur *v* THESAURUS **happen**

occurrence *n* something that happens

ADJECTIVES

a common/frequent/everyday occurrence *Forest fires are a common occurrence between November and February.*

a regular/daily occurrence *Kidnappings are a daily occurrence here.*

a rare/isolated occurrence *Thirty years ago, divorce was a fairly rare occurrence.*

a strange/odd/unusual/unexpected occurrence *What could be the reason for this strange occurrence?*

a freak occurrence (=extremely unusual) *You can't spend your life worrying about a freak occurrence.*

a natural/normal occurrence *The bird's loss of feathers is a natural occurrence.*

an unfortunate occurrence *The sport has been damaged by a number of unfortunate occurrences.*

ocean *n*

the great mass of salt water that covers most of the Earth's surface

ADJECTIVES

the deep ocean *Many strange creatures live in the deep ocean.*

the open ocean (=the part of the ocean that is away from land) *These sharks always stay out in the open ocean.*

a vast ocean *There is a vast ocean between the two countries.*

VERBS

cross the ocean *Could early settlers have crossed the ocean in boats like these?*

ocean + NOUNS

the ocean floor *The bodies of these creatures fall to the ocean floor when they die.*

ocean currents *The spilt oil was carried away by ocean currents.*

an ocean voyage *I was afraid I would get bored on a long ocean voyage.*

PREPOSITIONS

in the ocean *I love swimming in the ocean.*

by the ocean *I spent many afternoons sitting by the ocean.*

across the ocean *They sailed across the ocean.*

PHRASES

in the middle of the ocean (=in the part that is far from land) *We were in the middle of the ocean with no hope of being rescued.*

at/on the bottom of the ocean *The ship is now at the bottom of the ocean.*

the depths of the ocean (*also* **the ocean depths**) *They will explore the depths of the ocean.*

Ocean is used especially in American English. In British English, people usually say **sea**, except when they are talking about particular areas of water such as **the Atlantic Ocean** or **the Pacific Ocean**.

odour *BrE*, odor *AmE n*

a smell, usually an unpleasant one

ADJECTIVES

a strong/pungent odour *There was a strong odour of disinfectant in the room.*

a faint odour *The faint odor of cooked meat hung in the air.*

an unpleasant/bad odour *The local residents complained about an unpleasant odour coming from the factory.*

a foul odour (*also* **an offensive odour** *formal*) (=a very unpleasant smell) *The foul odour made her feel sick.*

a stale/lingering odour (=an old smell) *There was a lingering odour of tobacco and dogs.*

a musty odour (=a smell in which the air is not fresh, and is often a little damp - used about old rooms, books etc) *The apartment had been empty for months and had a musty odor.*

a familiar odour *She breathed in his familiar odour of beer and cigarettes.*

a strange odour *When she arrived in the country, she was struck by the intense heat and strange odors.*

a distinctive odour (=one that is easy to recognize) *The gas has a distinctive odour.*

VERBS

have a strong/unpleasant etc odour *The room had a strong odor.*

give off/produce a strong/unpleasant etc odour *This fungus gives off an unpleasant odour.*

cause an odour *What could be causing the odour?*

smell an odour (*also* **detect an odour** *formal*): *The pilot smelled an odd odor in the plane.*

remove/eliminate an odour *How can I remove odors from my refrigerator?*

an odour comes from sth (*also* **an odour emanates from sth** *formal*): *There was a bad odour coming from the river.*

NOUNS + odour

body odour (=a bad smell coming from someone's body) *The person sitting next to me had terrible body odor.*

cooking odours *She opened the window to get rid of the cooking odors.*

PREPOSITIONS

the odour of sth *I could smell the odour of rotting vegetables.*

THESAURUS: odour

scent, fragrance/perfume, aroma, whiff, odour, pong, stink/stench → **smell[1]**

Odour is more formal than **smell**.

offence *BrE*, offense *AmE n*

an illegal action or a crime

VERBS

commit an offence (=do something that is against the law) *If you lie to the court, you are committing a serious offence.*

charge sb with an offence *In that year, 367 people were charged with terrorist offences.*

convict sb of an offence (=say officially that they are guilty) *The number of women convicted of serious offences is fairly small.*

admit an offence *When questioned by police, he admitted the offense.*

make sth an offence (*also* **make it an offence to do sth**) *The Act made it an offence to sell cigarettes to children under 16.*

ADJECTIVES/NOUNS + offence

a criminal offence *It is a criminal offence to sell alcohol to someone under the age of 18.*

a serious offence *The prisoners have committed serious offenses such as murder or robbery.*

a minor/trivial offence *The police stopped him for a minor offence.*

a first offence *Because it was a first offence, she was not sent to prison.*

a driving/parking/traffic offence *Speeding is the most common traffic offence.*

drug/weapons/sex offences *He is serving 20 years for drug offenses.*

a capital offence (=one for which death is the punishment) *Drug smuggling was made a capital offense in 1987.*

PREPOSITIONS

an offence against sb *There is a high risk that he will commit further offenses against women.*

PHRASES

it is an offence to do sth *It is an offence to carry a weapon in a public place.*

offend *v*

to make someone angry or upset by doing or saying something that they think is rude

ADVERBS

deeply/greatly offend sb *He deeply offended his aunt by not inviting her to his wedding.*

personally offend sb *I was personally offended by his remarks about women.*

be easily offended *Don't go and see this comedian if you are easily offended.*

PHRASES

for fear of offending sb (=because you do not

want to offend someone) *They decided not to broadcast the programme, for fear of offending viewers.*

offer[1] *v*

to ask someone if they would like something, or to provide something

NOUNS

offer money/£1,000/a reward etc *A newspaper offered him money for his story.*

offer help/assistance/support etc *She offered practical help when I was ill.*

offer advice *He offered some advice on how to handle teenage children.*

offer sb a job/post/position *They had offered him the position of editor.*

offer sb a place *I was offered a place at Liverpool University.*

offer a service *There are many companies offering financial services on the internet.*

offer a course *His local university did not offer a course in architecture.*

offer sb an opportunity/chance *We are offering people the opportunity to express their views.*

offer sb a choice *Voters will be offered a choice between tax cuts and increased government spending.*

offer an explanation *She offered no explanation for her behaviour.*

ADVERBS

kindly/generously offer sth *They kindly offered to show me around their city.*

PREPOSITIONS

offer sth to sb *They offered the job to someone else.*

offer[2] *n*

a statement in which you say you will do or give something if someone wants you to

VERBS

accept an offer (=say yes to it) *I can't sell you the car because I've accepted another offer.*

take sb up on their offer (*also* **take up an offer** *BrE*) (=accept someone's offer) *I might take him up on his offer to babysit.*

turn down/refuse/reject an offer (=say no to it) *She turned down the job offer because she didn't want to move to London.*

decline an offer *formal* (=refuse it) *She declined the offer of a lift.*

make (sb) an offer (=offer something, especially money) *A Swedish firm has made an offer for the company.*

put in an offer (=offer money for something) *We have put in an offer for the house.*

get/receive/have an offer *He received the offer of a place at York University.*

withdraw an offer *They said I could stay with them, then suddenly withdrew their offer.*

consider an offer *He was given a week to consider the offer.*

ADJECTIVES

a kind/generous offer *He made a generous offer to let them use his house.*

a good offer *£100 for the bike is a good offer – you should accept it.*

sb's best offer (=the most that someone will offer to pay for something) *Is that your best offer? I was hoping for more money.*

an attractive/tempting offer *Another football club has made the player a tempting offer.*

a formal/written offer *They have not yet received a formal offer of funding.*

a firm offer (=a definite offer) *We hope to get a firm offer from them this week.*

NOUNS + offer

a job offer *He has had several interviews but no job offers.*

PREPOSITIONS

an offer of sth *Any offers of help would be appreciated.*

an offer from sb *She wanted him to accept a job offer from a bank.*

PHRASES

I appreciate your offer, but... (=I am grateful for it – used especially when politely refusing) *I appreciate your offer, but I don't need any help.*

be open to offers (=be ready to consider offers, especially of money for something) *The owners of the building are open to offers.*

office *n*

a building or room that belongs to a company or an organization, where people work at desks

ADJECTIVES

the head/main office *The firm moved its head office to Bristol.*

a local/regional/branch office *They plan to open a branch office in Mountain View this summer.*

an overseas office (=in a foreign country) *The bank has overseas offices in ten countries.*

a busy office *She works all day in a busy office.*

an open-plan office (=one without walls dividing it into separate rooms) *It can be hard to concentrate in an open-plan office.*

office + NOUNS

an office job/office work *He got an office job with a property company.*

an office worker/office staff *The park was full of office workers eating their lunch.*

an office building (*also* **an office block** *BrE*): *The development will include a 20-storey office building.*

office space *They rent 1,000 square feet of office space in the city.*

office hours (=the period in a day when

offices are open) *Call this number during office hours.*

office politics (=activities related to gaining personal advantage in an office) *You can escape office politics by working for yourself.*

VERBS

have an office somewhere *We have an office in San Francisco.*

open/close an office *The company has recently opened an office in Prague.*

run an office *Who's going to run the office when you're not there?*

PREPOSITIONS

in an office *Have you worked in an office before?*

at the office *They need to relax after a hard day at the office.*

to the office *I have to get back to the office.*

officer *n*

someone who is in a position of authority in the army, navy etc

ADJECTIVES/NOUNS + officer

a military officer *He is a senator and retired military officer.*

an army/air force/naval officer *His father was a French army officer.*

a senior/high-ranking officer *The strategy was criticized by several high-ranking officers.*

a junior officer *A junior officer was suspended from duty following the incident.*

a superior officer (=someone of a higher rank) *A soldier must salute a superior officer.*

sb's commanding officer *He was told his commanding officer wanted to see him.*

VERBS

serve as an officer *He served as an officer in the Royal Navy during World War II.*

PREPOSITIONS

an officer in the army, navy etc *Their grandfathers had been officers in the Confederate Army.*

PHRASES

the officer in command/in charge of sth *Who is the officer in command of this operation?*

officers and men *The British lost 1,654 officers and men.*

official[1] *adj*

1 produced or decided, by the government or by an organization such as a company

NOUNS

the official figures/statistics/data *Unemployment is going down, according to the latest official figures.*

the official records *The official records show that the economy grew by just over 1% last year.*

an official statement *The company will issue an official statement about the future of the factory.*

an official report *The official report said that the airline was not to blame for the accident.*

an official investigation/inquiry *There will be an official investigation into the accident.*

the official policy *The official policy is to cut spending in all government departments.*

the official language *Brazil's constitution says that Portuguese is the official language.*

official guidelines/regulations *All companies have to follow the official guidelines.*

sth's official name *Burma's official name is Myanmar.*

the official launch/opening of sth (=when something starts) *Tomorrow is the official launch of the election campaign.*

2 relating to someone in an important job or position

NOUNS

an official visit/tour *The prime minister is on an official visit to China.*

sb's official duties/responsibilities *He quietly carried out his official duties.*

sb's official residence *No. 10 Downing Street is the British prime minister's official residence.*

sb's official title *His official title is 'Professor the Lord Jones'.*

official[2] *n*

someone who is in a position of authority in an organization

ADJECTIVES/NOUNS + official

a senior/top/high official *A number of senior party officials resigned.*

a public official *Public officials are not allowed to accept gifts.*

an elected official *The mayor is an elected official.*

a government/administration/federal official *A government official denied the reports.*

a state/county/city official *City officials have asked for help from the government to deal with the flooding.*

a military official *Military officials said the fighting was still continuing.*

a party/union official *A union official announced that the strike had been canceled.*

an immigration official *He was stopped at the airport by US immigration officials.*

a court official *A court official read out the charges against him.*

old *adj*

1 having lived or existed for a long time

NOUNS

an old man/woman/lady/person *The old man was asleep in a chair.*

the older generation *The older generation didn't have all the advantages we have now.*

an old building/church/house *It costs a lot of money to repair old buildings.*
an old town/city *They visited the old city of Jerusalem.*
an old car/plane *He drives an old car.*
an old book/photograph/record *We looked at some old photographs from the 1930s.*
an old tradition/custom *It was an old tradition on the island to have a party on that day.*
an old saying/proverb *There's an old saying that you should never judge a book by its cover.*
old age (=the time when someone is old) *Heart disease is a common problem in old age.*

VERBS

get old (*also* **grow old** *formal*): *My parents are getting rather old now.*
look old *The lines on her face make her look old.*
feel old *Becoming a grandmother made me feel old.*

ADVERBS

too old *He was too old to serve in the army.*
very old *The building is very old.*
rather old (*also* **quite old** *BrE*): *Our dog is getting quite old now.*

PHRASES

the oldest known *She was the oldest known woman to give birth to a baby.*
as old as the hills (=extremely old) *That story's as old as the hills.*
old enough to be sb's father/grandfather etc *Her husband is old enough to be her father.*

You can also use **old** after another adjective, when saying that you like or dislike them: *The house belonged to my dear* ***old*** *dad.* | *He's a stupid* ***old*** *fool!* | *It's a funny* ***old*** *place, but we like living there.*

THESAURUS: old

elderly
person | **woman** | **man** | **parents** | **relative** | **couple** | **patient** | **resident** | **population**
a polite word used to describe a person who is old:
He was jailed for attacking an elderly woman. | *Finding suitable care for elderly relatives is a problem.* | *6.5% of the elderly population are aged over 85.*

The elderly is used to talk about old people as a group: *The disease is most common among* ***the elderly***.

aging (*also* **ageing** *BrE*)
population | **workforce** | **society** | **parents** | **mother** | **father** | **actor** | **rock star** | **aircraft** | **fleet**
becoming old:
The country has a rapidly ageing population. | *The band are now just a group of aging rock stars.* | *The airline intends to replace its ageing fleet of planes.*

Aging is only used before a noun.

aged
parent | **mother** | **father** | **aunt** | **relative**
aged relatives are very old - used mainly in written descriptions:
Many people in their 50s have aged parents to care for. | *An aged relative died and left him some money.*

Aged is only used before a noun.
The aged is used as a noun phrase, when talking about old people as a group: *He works in a home for* ***the aged***.

ancient
city | **town** | **civilization** | **world** | **monument** | **art** | **site** | **forest** | **woodland**
very old - used about places and things that existed thousands of years ago, or have existed for a very long time:
We visited the ancient city of Rome. | *China is an ancient civilization.* | *The area has many ancient monuments.*

In informal English, **ancient** can also be used about people, as a humorous way of saying they are old, especially when they are really not old: *I'll be 30 next year - it sounds really* ***ancient***!

antique
furniture | **clock** | **desk** | **table** | **jewellery** | **silver**
antique furniture, jewellery etc is old and often valuable:
The house is full of antique furniture.

Antique is normally used before a noun. Otherwise, you say that something *is an antique*.

historic
building | **town** | **city** | **monument** | **place** | **landmark**
a historic building or place is important because it is old:
The city is full of historic buildings. | *The leaning tower is the town's most famous historic landmark* (=place that is easy to recognize).

vintage
clothing | **clothes** | **dress** | **car** | **aircraft** | **vehicle**
vintage clothes and furniture are a little old, and people buy them because they are now fashionable again. You also use **vintage** about old cars:
The store sells vintage clothing. | *He owned a vintage car from the 1920s.*

Vintage is only used before a noun.

age-old
tradition | custom | problem | question | dilemma | phenomenon | conflict | mystery
used about traditions, problems, or situations that have existed for a very long time:
Open-air markets are an age-old tradition in most African countries. | The age-old problem of bullying in schools has never gone away. | The programme aims to answer the age-old question of whether money makes you happy. | Racism is an age-old phenomenon.

O

ANTONYMS **old → young**

ANTONYMS **old → new (1)**

2 used about someone you have known for a long time

NOUNS

an old friend *Tom is an old friend of the prince.*
an old acquaintance *I bumped into an old acquaintance outside the museum.*

You can also use **old** about things that you have owned for a long time: *I always wear **old** clothes when I'm painting.*

3 used about someone you knew or something you had in the past

NOUNS

an old boyfriend/girlfriend *She got an email from an old boyfriend.*
sb's old boss/teacher/colleague *My old boss used to say that I was lazy.*
sb's car/computer etc *My old computer was really slow.*
sb's old house/school etc *I've never been back to my old school.*

old-fashioned *adj*

not considered to be modern or fashionable any more

VERBS

seem old-fashioned *Some of their ideas about women seem rather old-fashioned.*
look old-fashioned *The design of the car now looks very old-fashioned.*

NOUNS

in the old-fashioned way *They still make the wine in the old-fashioned way.*
old-fashioned virtues/values *She says she believes in the old-fashioned virtues of honesty and reliability.*

PHRASES

good old-fashioned... *He doesn't like emails – he prefers good old-fashioned pen and paper.*
call me old-fashioned *spoken* (=used when saying that you do not care if other people think that you are old-fashioned) *Call me old-fashioned, but I think a lot of modern art is rubbish.*

THESAURUS: old-fashioned

out of date
information | statistics | map | book | guidebook
not containing the most recent information and therefore not useful:
*The information on the website is already out of date. | The map we were using was out of date. | Guidebooks quickly **go out of date*** (=become out of date).

Out of date is less common before a noun. If you use it before a noun, it needs to have hyphens: *an **out-of-date** map.*

dated
picture | music | song | book | decor
used about styles etc that were fashionable until recently but now look old-fashioned:
*The pictures in this book already look a bit dated. | Some of his music sounds **rather dated**. | I liked the food but the decor in the restaurant was very dated* (=the decoration looked old-fashioned).

Dated is less common before a noun.

outdated
equipment | methods | practices | technology | concept
used about machines, equipment, or methods that are old-fashioned and have been replaced by better, more recent ones:
The country has some of the world's most dangerous mines, due to outdated equipment and poor safety standards. | Businesses are still using outdated practices that prevent them from being competitive (=outdated ways of doing things). *| The royal family now seems an outdated concept in the modern world.*

obsolete
old-fashioned – used about machines and equipment that are no longer being produced because better ones have been invented:
*These days, you buy a computer and it **becomes obsolete** almost immediately. | The old type of cameras were **rendered obsolete** by the arrival of digital technology* (=made obsolete).

antiquated *formal*
system | method | equipment
old and not suitable for modern needs and conditions:
Banks are using a mixture of electronic and antiquated paper-based systems. | Unsafe and antiquated equipment was still in use at the factory until very recently.

passé *formal*
no longer fashionable – used especially about ways of doing and thinking about things: *The musicals and light comedies for which she was famous have* ***become passé****. | His designs now* ***seem a bit passé****.*

Passé is not usually used before a noun.

sth is so last year *informal*
used when saying that something is now very unfashionable – a very informal use: *Black is so last year. | Blogging is already starting to feel so last year.*

ANTONYMS **old-fashioned → modern (2)**

omission *n*

the act of not including someone or something, accidentally or deliberately

ADJECTIVES

a serious/major omission *There is no mention of the internet. This is a serious omission.*

a glaring omission (=one that is very bad and easily noticed) *There are some glaring omissions in the article.*

an important/significant/notable omission *The book has some important omissions.*

a surprising/curious omission *Critics commented on her surprising omission from the short-list.*

a deliberate omission *The omission of those details was deliberate.*

an accidental omission (*also* **an inadvertent omission** *formal*): *I meant to include your name – it was just an accidental omission.*

VERBS

correct/rectify an omission *The omission will be corrected when the book is reprinted.*

PREPOSITIONS

the omission of sth/sb *The omission of one word may change the meaning of a sentence.*

sth's/sb's omission from sth *There was controversy over his omission from the team.*

omit *v*

to not include someone or something, or not do something, either deliberately or because you forget

ADVERBS

deliberately omit sth/sb *The information had been deliberately omitted.*

inadvertently omit sth/sb (=accidentally) *His name was inadvertently omitted from the list.*

conveniently omit sth/sb (=because there is an advantage for you in not including something) *Dan conveniently omitted the fact that he had been at the pub.*

PREPOSITIONS

omit sth/sb from sth *There has been some surprise that McKenna has been omitted from the team.*

PHRASES

omit all/any reference to sb/sth *He had deliberately omitted any reference to the attack.*

omit to mention sth *Kazuo modestly omitted to mention that he had won the competition.*

opaque *adj* THESAURUS → clear[1] (4)

open[1] *adj*

1 not closed or fastened together

Grammar
Open is less common before a noun.

NOUNS

a door/gate is open *Becky's bedroom door was open.*

a window is open *We lay in bed with the window open.*

a drawer is open *He had left one drawer open.*

the curtains are open *The curtains were open and we could see in.*

sb's mouth is open *Don't eat with your mouth open.*

sb's eyes are open *I was so tired I couldn't keep my eyes open.*

sb's shirt/jacket/coat is open *His shirt was open at the neck.*

a box/bag/suitcase etc is open *Someone had left the box open.*

VERBS

push/pull sth open *She pushed the door open and went in.*

throw/fling sth open *I leapt from my bed and threw open the shutters.*

force/break sth open *The burglars used a spade to force open a window.*

tear sth open *I tore open the envelope.*

leave sth open *Who left the car window open?*

hold sth open *He held the door open for her.*

swing open *The castle gates swung open.*

fly/burst open (=suddenly become open) *The door flew open and Harriet burst in.*

sb's mouth falls/drops open (=it suddenly becomes open, especially because they are surprised) *My mouth fell open and I stared at him.*

a door stands open (=someone has left it open) *The back door stood open and he could see the garden beyond it.*

a book/case/bag etc lies open (=be open – used especially about something lying on a surface) *His guitar case lay open on the floor in front of him.*

slide open *The glass doors slid open.*

ADVERBS

wide open (=completely open) *Her eyes were wide open.*

fully open *He pushed the doors fully open.*

partly/partially/slightly open *A breeze came up through the partly open window.*

> Instead of saying that a door is slightly open, you can say that it is **ajar**: *I left the door* ***ajar****, so that I could listen to what they were saying.* You cannot use **ajar** before a noun.

ANTONYMS **open → closed (1)**

2 if a shop or a public building is open, people can enter or use it

NOUNS

a shop/store is open *I hope the shop is still open.*

a gallery/museum/office is open *The museum is open at weekends.*

VERBS

stay open *The bars stay open most of the night.*

declare sth open *The new hospital was declared open by the mayor.*

PREPOSITIONS

be open to the public/to visitors *The house and gardens are open to the public on Sundays.*

be open for business *The shop was open for business on every day of the year.*

ANTONYMS **open → closed (2)**

3 not hiding your feelings or what you really think, or not hiding information

ADVERBS

very open *She was very open about her feelings towards him.*

completely/quite open *I had always been completely open with the children in the past.*

NOUNS

open admiration *Jeff was looking at her with open admiration.*

open curiosity *She gazed with open curiosity at the other passengers.*

open hostility *Foreigners were greeted with open hostility.*

open defiance *Their actions were in open defiance of the Supreme Court.*

open government *We believe in open government, with greater access to official information.*

PREPOSITIONS

be open about sth *It is always better to be open about your feelings.*

be open with sb *Most people want doctors to be completely open with them.*

THESAURUS: open

truthful, sincere, frank, straight, open, candid, direct, blunt, forthright, outspoken, upfront → **honest**

open² *v*

1 to make something stop being closed, or to stop being closed

open + NOUNS

open a door/window/gate *I opened the door and went inside.*

open your eyes/mouth/lips *When she opened her eyes, it was daylight.*

open the curtains/blinds *He opened the curtains the next morning and the sun was shining.*

open a book/newspaper/magazine *The teacher opens a book and hands it to me.*

open a box/packet/container/bottle/jar *I opened the box and looked inside.*

open a bag/suitcase/purse *The woman opened her bag and took out some money.*

open a drawer *She opened the drawer where she kept all her letters.*

open a present/letter/envelope *The children wanted to open their presents immediately.*

open a lid *When the men opened the lid of the coffin, there was no one inside.*

NOUNS + open

a door/gate opens *James heard the door open and the sound of voices downstairs.*

sb's eyes open *His eyes slowly opened and he gave me a weak smile.*

ADVERBS

open sth carefully/cautiously *I carefully opened the box with a knife.*

open sth quietly *She opened the door quietly and checked to see that Julia was asleep.*

open sth wide *The dentist asked him to open his mouth wide.*

open sth at random (=without choosing a particular thing or page) *He opened the book at random, and began reading.*

sth opens automatically *The doors open automatically.*

THESAURUS: open

unlock
door | gate | box | drawer | safe | car | room | house
to open something with a key, or by using a special number or code:
She unlocked the door of the apartment and went inside. | You should never leave the car unlocked.

unscrew
lid | cap | top
to open the top part of a bottle, container etc by turning it:
She couldn't unscrew the lid of the jar. | Rory carefully unscrewed the top from the bottle.

unwrap
present | **gift** | **package**
to open a package by removing the paper that covers it:
I watched him unwrap his present. | *She started to unwrap the different packages of food.*

ANTONYMS **open** → **close**[1]

2 to start a company or organization

THESAURUS: open

open, establish, found, set up, form → **start**[1] **(3)**

3 to start happening

THESAURUS: open

begin, commence, resume, open, break out, kick off, get under way → **start**[1] **(2)**

opening *adj* THESAURUS **first**[1]

opera *n*

a musical play in which all of the words are sung

VERBS

write an opera *Beethoven only wrote one opera.*

produce/put on an opera *Producing an opera is expensive.*

sing (an) opera *The opera was sung in English.*

go to the opera *I like going to the opera.*

perform an opera *The opera was first performed in Paris in 1979.*

ADJECTIVES

a comic opera *His comic operas were very popular.*

opera + NOUNS

an opera singer *Opera singers have to take care of their voices.*

an opera house (=a theatre where operas are performed) *They will be performing at the Opera House in Milan.*

an opera company *She's a singer with an opera company.*

PREPOSITIONS

at the opera (=at the theatre where an opera is performed) *She was looking forward to her night at the opera.*

operation *n*

1 the process of cutting into someone's body to repair or remove a part that is damaged

ADJECTIVES/NOUNS + operation

a major/minor operation *The unit cares for patients recovering from major operations.*

an emergency operation *He had to have an emergency operation on his spine.*

a heart/stomach/knee etc operation *He is almost back to full fitness after a knee operation.*

a successful operation *The operation was successful, and she should make a complete recovery.*

a routine operation (=an operation that is often performed) *A hip replacement is now a routine operation.*

a life-saving operation *The child underwent a life-saving operation to remove a blockage in her stomach.*

a transplant operation (=when a part from another person's body is put into yours) *He is too weak to undergo a transplant operation.*

VERBS

have an operation (*also* **undergo an operation** *formal*): *Harris had a hip operation in October.*

do/carry out an operation (*also* **perform an operation** *formal*): *I spoke to the surgeon who performed the operation.*

⚠ Don't say 'make an operation'.

recover from an operation *A man is recovering from an emergency operation after his pet dog attacked him.*

PREPOSITIONS

an operation on your knee/nose/throat etc *He is waiting for an operation on his knee.*

an operation for cancer/an ulcer etc *Last year she had an operation for cancer.*

2 a set of planned actions, especially one involving a lot of people

ADJECTIVES/NOUNS + operation

a big/major/massive operation *The police mounted a major operation against drug dealers in the area.*

a joint operation (=involving two or more organizations, countries etc) *They were arrested following a joint operation by Czech and German police.*

a military/peace-keeping operation *It was the biggest military operation Iraqi forces have undertaken.*

a security operation *Police cleared the streets of the capital as part of a massive security operation.*

a rescue/search operation *A rescue operation was launched after two climbers were reported missing.*

a secret/covert/undercover operation *These planes are used by British Intelligence for covert operations.*

VERBS

carry out/conduct an operation *The operation was carried out in coordination with the Colombian police.*

mount/organize an operation *A huge security operation was mounted for the five-hour visit.*

launch an operation (=start it) *The police launched a search operation last night.*

plan an operation *They had information that another terrorist operation was being planned.*

PREPOSITIONS

an operation against sb *The authorities launched an operation against the gangs.*

PHRASES

take part in/be involved in an operation *More than 100 officers took part in the operation.*

be in charge of an operation *General Franks will be in charge of the operation.*

O

opinion *n*

your ideas or beliefs about a particular subject

ADJECTIVES

the general opinion (=that most people have) *The general opinion seems to be that the government has made a mess of the war.*

popular/public opinion (=what ordinary people think about something) *How much do newspapers influence popular opinion?*

sb's personal opinion *My personal opinion is that his first film was better.*

strong opinions *People have strong opinions about this subject.*

an honest opinion *I need your honest opinion about something.*

a high opinion of sb/sth *He has a high opinion of himself.*

a low/poor opinion of sb/sth *She had a low opinion of politicians.*

a second opinion (=an opinion from a second expert such as a doctor) *The patient asked for a second opinion.*

an expert opinion (=the opinion of someone who knows about the subject) *Before making important decisions, specialists are called upon to give their expert opinion.*

a professional opinion *It is my professional opinion that the house is not worth that amount.*

medical/legal/scientific opinion *Medical opinion is still divided on whether alcoholism is a disease.*

political opinions *His daughter did not share his political opinions.*

VERBS + opinion

have/hold an opinion *Everyone seemed to have a different opinion.*

share sb's opinion *There are many people who share his opinion about the war.*

give/express/offer an opinion (=say what your opinion is) *He gave his opinion only when asked.*

⚠ Don't say 'say your opinion'.

voice/state an opinion *written* (=give your opinion, especially in a formal situation) *Everyone will have the chance to voice their opinion.*

form an opinion (=decide what your opinion is) *I haven't had time to form an opinion about the matter.*

change your opinion *Later, he changed his opinion of the painting.*

ask (for) sb's opinion (*also* **ask sb (for) their opinion**) *Nobody asked my opinion.*

get an opinion (=especially from an expert) *He wanted to get my opinion on the book he was writing.*

opinion + VERBS

opinions differ/vary *Opinions differ as to whether the change is an improvement.*

PREPOSITIONS

sb's opinion of sb/sth *What is your opinion of him?*

sb's opinion on/about/regarding sth *I have no opinion on the matter.*

sb's opinion as to sth *People were defending their opinions as to the identity of the murderer.*

be of the opinion that (=think that) *Sarah was of the opinion that he drank too much.*

opinion + NOUNS

an opinion poll/survey (=when a number of people are asked the same questions to see what people think) *According to opinion polls, people trust the prime minister.*

PHRASES

in my/her etc opinion (=used when giving someone's opinion) *In my opinion, the law should be changed.*

⚠ Don't say 'according to my opinion'.

sth is a matter of opinion (=used to say that you disagree, or that people disagree about something) *Whether the treatment is effective is a matter of opinion.*

opinion is divided (=people have different opinions about it) *Opinion was divided about the issue.*

have a difference of opinion (=used to say that two people disagree) *He and Luke had a difference of opinion.*

a shift/change in opinion *There has been a huge shift in public opinion on this matter.*

contrary to popular opinion (=in spite of what most people think) *Contrary to popular opinion, many cats dislike milk.*

everyone is entitled to their opinion (=used especially when politely disagreeing with what someone says) *Of course, everyone is entitled to their opinion, but I can't accept what he is saying.*

Instead of saying **in my opinion**, people sometimes say **in my humble opinion**. This sounds rather formal and is often used when speaking in a slightly humorous way: *In my humble opinion, it is easily one of the best books of the year.*

The abbreviation of this phrase **IMHO** is often used in emails and when writing messages using the internet: ***IMHO** she's right.*

opponent *n*

1 someone who you try to defeat in a competition, game, fight, or argument

ADJECTIVES

a political opponent *He held on to power by jailing political opponents.*

sb's main/chief opponent *Who was her main opponent for the presidential nomination?*

a leading opponent *The authorities arrested two leading opponents of the government.*

a strong/tough opponent (=one that is difficult to defeat) *They are tough opponents, but I think we can beat them.*

a formidable/dangerous opponent (=a very strong opponent) *In debate, he was a formidable opponent.*

a worthy opponent (=one who deserves respect) *The Democratic Senator has shown himself to be a worthy opponent.*

VERBS

face an opponent *He knows he is facing a tough opponent.*

beat/defeat an opponent *She came within three points of defeating her opponent.*

crush an opponent (=defeat or stop them completely) *It is satisfying to end the game having crushed your opponents.*

2 someone who disagrees with a plan, idea, or system and wants to stop it or change it

ADJECTIVES

a leading opponent of sth *She was a leading opponent of gun control in the Senate.*

a strong opponent of sth (=one who strongly disagrees with something) *Brennan was a strong opponent of the death penalty.*

a fierce/bitter opponent of sth (=who disagrees very strongly and angrily) *She became well known as a bitter opponent of slavery.*

a vigorous opponent of sth (=who opposes something with a lot of energy) *He is a vigorous opponent of the new law.*

an outspoken/vocal/vociferous opponent of sth (=who often publicly expresses their disagreement) *He was a vocal opponent of closer relations with the United States.*

opportunity *n* a chance to do something

ADJECTIVES

a good/great/wonderful etc opportunity *It's a great opportunity to try new things.*

the ideal/perfect opportunity *I'd been wanting to try sailing, and this seemed like the ideal opportunity.*

a valuable opportunity *This is a valuable opportunity to cure yourself of a bad habit.*

a golden opportunity (=a very good opportunity) *The council has missed a golden opportunity to improve the town centre.*

a rare/unique opportunity *Visitors will have a unique opportunity to see how the programme is made.*

a once-in-a-lifetime opportunity (=a very good opportunity that you will only get once) *For many athletes, the Olympics are a once-in-a-lifetime opportunity.*

a wasted/lost/missed opportunity (=one you do not use) *Many people see the failed talks as a missed opportunity for peace.*

ample opportunity/plenty of opportunity (=a number of chances to do something) *There will be ample opportunity for shopping.*

little opportunity (=not many chances) *They had little opportunity to discuss the issue beforehand.*

educational/political/economic etc opportunities *She campaigned for better educational opportunities for women.*

VERBS + opportunity

have an opportunity *I was lucky enough to have the opportunity to travel.*

get an opportunity *I decided to go, as I might never get this opportunity again.*

take/use an opportunity (=do something you have a chance to do) *Several employees took the opportunity to retire early.*

seize/grasp/grab an opportunity (=do something very eagerly when you have the chance) *She saw an opportunity to speak to him, and seized it.*

welcome an opportunity *He welcomed the opportunity to give his version of events.*

miss/lose/pass up an opportunity (=not do something you have a chance to do) *Dwyer never missed an opportunity to criticize her.*

give sb an opportunity *The children should be given the opportunity to make their own choices.*

provide/present/open up an opportunity *The course also provides an opportunity to study Japanese.*

create an opportunity *A good player is always creating opportunities to score.*

see/spot an opportunity *We saw an opportunity to expand our business.*

opportunity + VERBS

an opportunity comes (along/up) *When an opportunity comes, grab it.*

an opportunity arises *Perhaps she would explain later, if the opportunity arose.*

NOUNS + opportunity

a photo opportunity (=a chance to take a

good photograph, especially of a particular person) *Parents will always look for good photo opportunities at their kid's graduation ceremony.*

a business opportunity *He realized that this was an excellent business opportunity.*

job/employment opportunities *There are better job opportunities in the south of England.*

PREPOSITIONS

(an) opportunity for sth *There was little opportunity for discussion.*

an opportunity for sb *This is a great opportunity for someone who likes being with animals.*

O

PHRASES

at the first/earliest opportunity (=as soon as possible) *He decided to leave school at the earliest opportunity.*

at every (possible) opportunity (=whenever possible) *She went to the museum at every opportunity.*

a window of opportunity (=a time when you can do something) *The other team started making mistakes, but we didn't take advantage of this window of opportunity.*

a land of opportunity (=a country where people have a lot of good opportunities) *America was then seen as a land of opportunity.*

the opportunity of a lifetime (=a very good opportunity that you will only get once) *The winner of the contest got the opportunity of a lifetime – the chance to work with a top fashion designer.*

opposed *adj*

if you are opposed to a plan or action, you disagree with it

ADVERBS

strongly opposed *He was strongly opposed to the idea.*

fiercely/bitterly opposed (*also* **vehemently opposed** *formal*): *They are fiercely opposed to the reforms.*

firmly opposed *The union was firmly opposed to the cuts.*

totally/completely opposed *They are totally opposed to the scheme.*

adamantly/resolutely opposed (=so strongly that you will never change your mind) *Her family was adamantly opposed to the marriage.*

VERBS

remain opposed to sth *Several council members remain opposed to the plan.*

PREPOSITIONS

opposed to sth *I am opposed to capital punishment.*

opposite[1] *adj*

as different as possible from something else

ADVERBS

totally/completely/quite opposite *They hold totally opposite views.*

diametrically opposite (=totally opposite) *They came to diametrically opposite conclusions.*

exactly opposite *The two forces are acting in exactly opposite directions.*

NOUNS

the opposite direction/way *She turned and walked off in the opposite direction.*

the opposite effect *He thought the news would cheer her up, but it had the opposite effect.*

the opposite view *The astronomer thought life on other planets was likely, but the biologist took the opposite view.*

the opposite conclusion *After I examined the facts I came to the opposite conclusion.*

the opposite problem *In English, the school has the opposite problem, with boys doing much worse than girls.*

the opposite way *The controls work in the opposite way to what you would expect.*

the opposite sex (=the other sex, that is not your own) *He found it hard to talk to members of the opposite sex.*

PREPOSITIONS

opposite to sth *Her character was completely opposite to her shy timid sister's.*

PHRASES

at the opposite end of the scale/spectrum (=used when comparing two things that are of very different types) *At the opposite end of the spectrum, there are some plants that can grow almost anywhere.*

the opposite way round/around *In a mirror, everything is the opposite way round.*

opposite[2] *n*

a person or thing that is as different as possible from someone or something else

> **Grammar**
> You usually say **the opposite**.

ADJECTIVES

the complete/total opposite *He and his brother are complete opposites.*

the exact/precise/direct opposite *The result was the exact opposite of what was intended.*

the very opposite *Exercise does not increase the appetite – in fact, the very opposite is true.*

polar opposites (=used when emphasizing that two things or people are completely opposite) *These two viewpoints seem like polar opposites.*

VERBS

do the opposite *Whatever I tell him to do, he does the exact opposite.*

mean the opposite *She claimed she meant the opposite of what she said.*

PREPOSITIONS

the opposite of sth *'Right' is the opposite of 'wrong'.*

PHRASES

exactly/precisely the opposite *It looks simple, but it is exactly the opposite.*

just/quite the opposite *He wasn't laughing. Quite the opposite – he was crying.*

the opposite is the case/is true *People believed the Sun moved around the Earth, but Copernicus showed that the opposite was the case.*

opposition *n*

strong disagreement with or protest against a plan, law, or system

ADJECTIVES

strong opposition *The scheme has met with strong opposition from local people.*

fierce/intense/stiff opposition (=very strong opposition) *It is certain that there will be fierce opposition to any change in the law.*

violent/vehement opposition (=involving extremely strong angry feelings) *There has been violent opposition to the airport from local environmental groups.*

considerable/much/a lot of opposition *The development was allowed despite considerable opposition.*

widespread opposition (=among many people) *There was widespread opposition to the plans.*

growing/mounting/increasing opposition *There was growing opposition to the war.*

public opposition *Public opposition has blocked the building of nuclear power stations.*

political opposition *There was very little political opposition to the war.*

local opposition *The company ignored local opposition to its plans.*

open opposition (=expressed in public) *The law was passed with little open opposition, although some privately had doubts about it.*

VERBS + opposition

face/encounter opposition *The proposal faced opposition from road safety campaigners.*

meet (with) opposition/run into opposition (=face opposition) *A new tax would meet a lot of opposition.*

arouse/draw/provoke opposition (=make people express disagreement) *A plan to build on the land aroused local opposition.*

overcome opposition (=deal with it successfully) *She overcame her mother's opposition and began training as a nurse.*

express/voice opposition (=say that you disagree) *Parents expressed their opposition to the tests.*

suppress/stifle opposition (=prevent it from being expressed) *The authorities are trying to suppress any opposition.*

drop your opposition to sth (=stop opposing something) *The United States agreed to drop its opposition to the plan.*

opposition + VERBS

opposition comes from sb *The strongest opposition came from Republican voters.*

PREPOSITIONS

opposition to sth *He declared his opposition to the proposed tax increases.*

opposition from sb *The airport was built despite opposition from environmentalists.*

PHRASES

in the face of opposition *The policy collapsed in the face of determined opposition.*

optimism *n*

a belief that good things will happen in the future

ADJECTIVES

great/considerable optimism *There was great optimism about the future.*

cautious/guarded optimism (=a feeling that good things may happen, although you realize that they may not) *The mood is one of cautious optimism and people know that the economic situation is only just beginning to get better.*

false/misplaced optimism (=based on wrong ideas) *In his speech he warned against false optimism.*

renewed optimism (=new optimism) *The new leadership has brought renewed optimism.*

VERBS

express optimism *Diplomats expressed optimism about the progress of the talks.*

share sb's optimism *After so many problems, I found it hard to share his optimism.*

dampen sb's optimism (=make people feel less optimistic) *The crisis dampened the optimism of those who had hoped for an end to the war.*

PREPOSITIONS

optimism about sth *There is a feeling of optimism about the company's future.*

PHRASES

a mood/sense/feeling of optimism *The release of Mandela created a mood of optimism.*

a wave/surge of optimism (=a sudden strong feeling of optimism) *The government was swept to power on a wave of optimism.*

be full of optimism *Economists are currently full of optimism.*

be grounds/cause/reason for optimism *The lower crime figures are certainly grounds for optimism.*

optimistic *adj*

believing that good things will happen in the future, or that someone can succeed

ADVERBS

very/extremely/highly optimistic *The chairman said that he was very optimistic about the future of the company.*

cautiously/guardedly optimistic (=optimistic, but careful not to be too optimistic) *She was cautiously optimistic about her party's chances of success.*

overly/unduly/wildly optimistic (=too optimistic) *You often hear overly optimistic claims about new medical treatments in the media.*

NOUNS

an optimistic view/attitude/outlook/assessment *He has an optimistic view of life, and always thinks that things will get better.*

an optimistic forecast/prediction *According to some optimistic forecasts, the economy will grow by 10%.*

an optimistic mood *I woke up in an optimistic mood.*

VERBS

sound/seem/appear optimistic *The doctor seems optimistic about her chances of recovery.*

remain optimistic *Despite all the difficulties, he remains optimistic.*

PREPOSITIONS

optimistic about sth *I am optimistic about the future of this great country.*

ANTONYMS **optimistic → pessimistic**

O

option Ac *n*

something you can choose to do or have

ADJECTIVES

a possible option *We should consider every possible option.*

an alternative option/a different option/another option *Another option is to reduce the number of staff.*

the only option *He was convinced that war was the only option.*

a good/attractive option *Selling work direct to the public is an attractive option for artists.*

a realistic/real/serious option *I wanted to start my own business, but financially it was not a realistic option.*

a viable/practical option (=something you can choose that will be successful) *Surgery may be a viable option in some cases.*

a safe option *The pilot decided that making an emergency landing was the safest option.*

an easy option (*also* **a soft option** *BrE*): *Divorce is never an easy option.*

sb's preferred option *formal*: *The new scheme appears to be the airport management's preferred option.*

an option is available (*also* **an option is open to sb**) *People may not know what options are available.*

VERBS

have an option *In a situation like this, you have two options.*

give/offer sb an option *Some employees were given the option of retiring early.*

choose an option (*also* **go for an option** *BrE*): *Fewer women are choosing the option of motherhood.*

take (up) an option (=choose an option) *America was persuaded not to take up the option of military action.*

consider/look at an option *You have to look at every option as your business develops.*

explore the options (=find out more about them) *Explore all the options before making a decision.*

limit your options *If you don't go to college, it may limit your options.*

NOUNS + option

a career option *Students need better information about career options.*

PREPOSITIONS

the option of doing sth *Until recently, students had the option of leaving school at 16.*

PHRASES

a range of options *The council is considering a range of options for improving the city's transport system.*

keep/leave your options open (=not make a firm decision about what you are going to do) *Studying a broad range of subjects helps to keep your options open.*

have no/little option but to do sth (=be obliged to do something) *I had no option but to fire him.*

optional *adj* THESAURUS ▸ **voluntary (1)**

oral *adj* THESAURUS ▸ **spoken**

orange¹ *n*

a round juicy fruit that has a thick orange skin

VERBS

peel an orange *Maria peeled herself an orange.*

squeeze an orange *They began squeezing oranges to make juice.*

orange + NOUNS

orange juice *Can I have a glass of orange juice?*

orange peel/rind *She carefully removed all the orange peel.*

an orange tree *The orange trees are in blossom.*

PHRASES

a piece of orange *Do you want a piece of orange?*

orange² *n, adj*

a colour that is between red and yellow

TYPES OF ORANGE

bright/brilliant orange *The male bird has a bright orange beak.*

deep orange *The western sky is already deep orange.*

pale/light orange *The lamps cast their pale orange light over the pavement.*

fluorescent orange (=very bright orange) *The workmen wore fluorescent orange jackets.*

orchestra *n*

a large group of musicians playing many different kinds of instruments and led by a conductor

VERBS + orchestra

conduct an orchestra (=stand in front of an orchestra and direct their playing) *Herbert von Karajan conducted the Berlin Symphony Orchestra for over 35 years.*

lead an orchestra *Conductor Esa-Pekka Salonen will lead the orchestra in works by Schubert and Beethoven.*

play (sth) in an orchestra *My sister plays the violin in the school orchestra.* | *Evitts studied at Pittsburgh State University, where he played in the orchestra.*

orchestra + VERBS

an orchestra plays/performs (sth) *The Russian orchestra will perform at the National Concert Hall.* | *The orchestra played Brahms' First Symphony.*

an orchestra strikes (sth) up (=starts playing) *The orchestra struck up Aaron Copland's 'Fanfare For The Common Man'.*

ADJECTIVES/NOUNS + orchestra

a live orchestra (=one that is playing front of an audience, not one that is recorded) *This is the first time she has sung in front of a live orchestra.*

a full orchestra (=a complete orchestra with all the usual players and instruments) *The opera has thirty singers and a full orchestra.*

a great/top orchestra *The London Philharmonic is one of the world's great orchestras.*

the school orchestra *I was in the school orchestra and I played the flute.*

PREPOSITIONS

in an orchestra *My father played the clarinet in an orchestra.*

an orchestra under sb (=conducted by someone) *The Prokofiev Piano Concertos were recorded with the Leipzig Gewandhaus Orchestra under Kurt Masur.*

PHRASES

a member of the orchestra *The 100 members of the orchestra perform under the direction of Leonard Slatkin.*

a 21-piece/50-piece etc orchestra (=with 21, 50 etc instruments) *Her New York concert will include a 58-piece orchestra.*

ordeal *n*

a terrible experience that continues for a period of time

ADJECTIVES

a terrible/dreadful/painful ordeal *The trial was a dreadful ordeal.*

a terrifying ordeal *The victim of the shark attack described his terrifying ordeal.*

a long ordeal *After thirteen months, the hostages' long ordeal finally ended.*

VERBS

go through an ordeal (*also* **undergo an ordeal** *formal*) (=experience an ordeal) *I'd already gone through the ordeal of a divorce once.*

face an ordeal *He faced the ordeal of caring for his dying wife.*

endure an ordeal *In his book, he describes how he endured the ordeal of prison life.*

survive an ordeal *The woman survived her ordeal and identified her attacker.*

recover from an ordeal *She took a long time to recover from her ordeal.*

subject sb to an ordeal (=make someone go through it) *He was subjected to a horrifying ordeal at gunpoint.*

PREPOSITIONS

the ordeal of (doing) sth *The girl will not have to undergo the ordeal of giving evidence in court.*

PHRASES

an ordeal is over (=it has finished) *The villagers thought their ordeal was over, but it was just beginning.*

order *n*

1 an arrangement of things, so that one thing is first, another thing is second etc

ADJECTIVES

the right/correct order *Of course, the notes must be played in the right order.*

the wrong order *The pages had been put in the wrong order.*

the same order *He always closed the windows in the same order.*

reverse order *They announced the results in reverse order, starting with the last.*

alphabetical order *List the names in alphabetical order.*

numerical order *The dogs are given numbers, and stand in numerical order while the judge looks at them.*

chronological order (=the order that things happened in time) *The paintings are arranged in chronological order.*

a logical order *Put the events of the story into a logical order.*

no particular order *Here are my ten favourite books, in no particular order.*

PREPOSITIONS

in order (=one after another, in the right order) *It is important to read the stories in order.*

PHRASES

put/arrange things in order *Decide what points you want to talk about, and put them in order.*

list/rank things in order *The candidates are listed in order of preference.*

in order of importance/priority/preference etc *The country's main exports were, in order of importance, coffee, sugar, and soya beans.*

O

2 an instruction to do something that is given by someone in authority

VERBS

give/issue an order *Do not fire until I give the order.*

obey an order *He refused to obey this order.*

follow orders/carry out orders (=obey them) *The men argued that they had only been following orders.*

take orders from sb (=be given orders by them and obey them) *I don't take orders from you!*

disobey/ignore an order *Anyone who disobeys these orders will be severely punished.*

have orders to do sth *The soldiers had orders to shoot anyone on the streets after 10 o'clock.*

get/receive an order *The general says he received no order to withdraw.*

ADJECTIVES

a direct order (=a clear order) *What happens to a soldier who disobeys a direct order?*

strict orders *The guards had strict orders not to allow anyone into the building.*

PREPOSITIONS

an order from sb *He disobeyed an order from his commanding officer.*

on sb's orders *The road was constructed on the orders of Mussolini in 1931–32.*

by order of sb *He was released from prison by order of the court.*

be under orders to do sth *They are under orders not to reveal the identities of their clients.*

3 a request by a customer for something to be supplied

VERBS

place/put in an order *They placed an order for over a thousand tiles.*

cancel your order *The airline has cancelled its order for the plane.*

get/receive sb's order *Your DVDs will be mailed to you on the day we receive your order.*

take sb's order (=write down what a customer in a restaurant wants) *The waiter came to take our order.*

fill/meet an order (=supply what someone wants) *The company does not have enough stock to fill the order.*

win an order *The company has just won a large order.*

lose/forget sb's order *I hope they haven't lost our order.*

ADJECTIVES

a big/large order *We have just had a big order from a Japanese company.*

order + NOUNS

an order form *Make sure that you write your address clearly on the order form.*

PREPOSITIONS

an order for sth *In May I placed an order for an expensive guitar.*

on order (=asked for, but not yet received) *Two new ships are on order.*

PHRASES

make/supply sth to order (=produce something when asked for it by a customer) *Special sizes of bed can be made to order.*

4 a situation in which rules are obeyed and people behave well

VERBS

keep/maintain order (*also* **preserve order**) *The police tried to keep order.*

restore order *When rioting started, troops were sent in to restore order.*

ADJECTIVES

public order *These measures are necessary to maintain public order.*

PHRASES

law and order *The forces of law and order are there to protect citizens.*

a breakdown of order *The government was concerned that there would be a breakdown of order.*

keep sb in order *Some teachers find it hard to keep teenagers in order.*

organ *n*

a part of the body that has a particular purpose

ADJECTIVES

internal organs (=organs inside your body) *She suffered serious damage to her internal organs.*

vital organs (=organs that you need to live) *Luckily, the bullet passed through his body without hitting any vital organs.*

major organs *The drug can cause bleeding in all the body's major organs.*

organ + NOUNS

an organ transplant (=an operation to put an organ from one person's body into another person's body) *Up to 5,000 people are waiting for an organ transplant.*

an organ donor (=someone who gives an organ for an organ transplant) *They are trying to find an organ donor.*

organic *adj*

relating to farming or gardening without using artificial chemicals

NOUNS

organic food/vegetables/wine etc *The restaurant uses only fresh organic vegetables.*

organic produce *formal* (=organic fruit and vegetables) *The store stocks a wide range of organic produce.*

organic farming/gardening *Organic farming is better for wild birds.*

organic methods *Many local farmers have adopted organic methods.*

an organic farmer/gardener *Organic gardeners do not use artificial insecticides.*

an organic farm *Chemical fertilizers are banned on organic farms.*

VERBS

go organic (=start buying only organic food, or using only organic methods) *Not all families can afford to go organic.*

ADVERBS

totally organic *All the ingredients are totally organic.*

THESAURUS: organic

wild, pure, organic, unspoiled, undeveloped, untouched, virgin → **natural (1)**

organism *n* a living thing

ADJECTIVES

a living organism *All living organisms are made up of cells.*

a microscopic organism (=so small it can only be seen using a microscope) *The water is full of microscopic organisms.*

a simple organism *These simple organisms appeared very early in the history of life.*

a complex organism *These creatures are complex organisms.*

a marine organism (=that lives in water) *The oil spill had a bad effect on marine organisms.*

organization (*also* **organisation** *BrE*) *n*

a group of people, businesses, countries etc that has formed for a particular purpose

ADJECTIVES/NOUNS + organization

a large/big organization *The public expect high standards from any large organization.*

a financial/business organization *Many business organizations are in trouble.*

a political organization *There will be a meeting of the country's main political organizations.*

an international/worldwide organization *Greenpeace is an international organization that works to protect the environment.*

a terrorist/terror organization *The men were charged with belonging to an illegal terrorist organization.*

a voluntary organization (=whose members work without being paid) *We are a voluntary organization which helps disabled people with their transport needs.*

a grass-roots organization (=which includes ordinary people and represents their views) *They set up a grassroots organization dealing with social issues affecting the poor.*

VERBS

join an organization *In June 1940, Joe joined a small organization called the Century Group.*

belong to an organization *Do you belong to any political organizations?*

work for an organization *She works for an organization called Amnesty International, which helps political prisoners.*

set up/found an organization *The organization was set up in the early 1950s.*

PHRASES

a member of an organization *Nigeria is a leading member of the Organization of Petroleum Exporting Countries (OPEC).*

the head of an organization (=the person who is in charge of it) *I asked to speak to the head of the organization.*

organize (*also* **organise** *BrE*) *v*

to make the necessary arrangements so that something can happen

ADVERBS

organize sth well/badly *The museum had organized the exhibition well.*

hastily organize sth (=very quickly) *Officials hastily organized new travel plans following the bombing.*

VERBS

help (to) organize sth *She was one of the people who helped organize the event.*

organized *adj*

arranged or organized in a particular way

ADVERBS

well organized *Keep your desk tidy and well organized.*

badly/poorly organized *The department does not have enough staff and is badly organized.*

highly organized *The crime was carried out by a highly organized group of criminals.*

properly organized *Make sure that your files are properly organized so that you can find things easily.*

carefully organized *The demonstrations were carefully organized.*

origin *n*
how or where something began to exist

> **Grammar**
> You can say **the origin of** something or **the origins of** something, with the same meaning.

VERBS + origin

have its origin(s) in sth (=begin to exist in a particular time or situation) *The ceremony has its origins in ancient times.*

find out/discover/trace the origin of sth *It is difficult to trace the origin of some words.*

O

origin + VERBS

sth's origins lie in sth (=used when saying how or where something first began) *The origins of the war lay in a quarrel between neighbouring princes.*

sth's origins go back to sth (=it began a long time ago) *The school's origins go back to the early 1800s.*

ADJECTIVES

sth's historical/geographical/political etc origin(s) *His research deals with the historical origins of the Christian faith.*

sth's precise/exact origin *The custom is an old one, though its precise origin is unknown.*

sth's true origin *Hardly anyone now remembers the true origin of the name.*

ancient origin(s) *Little remains of the town's ancient origins.*

sth's origins are unknown/obscure *The origins of this custom are unknown.*

PREPOSITIONS

in origin *This dish is Spanish in origin.*

PHRASES

sth's country/place of origin (=the country or place where something was made or produced) *The label shows the wine's country of origin.*

sth is of Italian/Indian etc origin *The game is of Italian origin.*

of unknown origin *Customers do not like buying meat of unknown origin.*

> **THESAURUS: origin**
> start, commencement, origin, the onset of sth, dawn, birth → **beginning (1)**

original *adj*
1 new and different

ADVERBS

highly original *Her work is highly original.*

truly/genuinely original *There is something truly original about their music.*

completely/entirely original *Very few artists are completely original.*

strikingly original (=in way that is very noticeable) *The building is of a strikingly original design.*

original + NOUNS

original ideas *She has no original ideas – she just copies other writers.*

original work *All competition entries must be your own original work.*

an original design/style *The dress is an original design by Valentino.*

original research *Your project must be based on original research.*

original material (=songs, ideas etc that someone has created themselves) *The band plays all original material.*

> **THESAURUS: original**
> recent, latest, original, fresh, novel, innovative, revolutionary, new-fangled → **new (1)**

2 how something was when it first started, or how it was before

NOUNS

the original plan/idea/intention *Our original plan was to take the train, but we changed our minds and decided to drive.*

sth's original position *We moved the sofa back to its original position next to the door.*

sth's original purpose *The building is still used for its original purpose.*

sth's original form *The church still survives in its original form.*

sth's original owner *Will the land be returned to its original owner?*

the original version *They have added some new scenes that were not in the original version of the movie.*

the original meaning *The original meaning of the word 'gay' was 'happy'.*

sth's original condition *Experts have been working to return the damaged painting to its original condition.*

original features (=parts that were there when a house was first built) *The kitchen still has many original features.*

orthodox *adj* THESAURUS **normal, religious (2)**

outbreak *n*
a period when something suddenly starts happening, for example fighting or a disease

ADJECTIVES

a recent outbreak *A recent outbreak of food poisoning at the school left 10 students in hospital.*

the latest outbreak *The latest outbreak of fighting began two weeks ago.*

a fresh outbreak *There has been a fresh outbreak of the disease.*

a further outbreak (=another one) *There was a further outbreak of strikes at the end of May.*

a serious/major/severe outbreak *An illness that affects just a few children can soon become a major outbreak.*

a sudden outbreak *There was a sudden outbreak of the disease in November.*

a prolonged outbreak (=lasting a long time) *We want to avoid a prolonged outbreak of violence.*

sporadic outbreaks (=that happen often, but not regularly) *There have been sporadic outbreaks of fighting in some parts of the country.*

VERBS

prevent an outbreak *How can we prevent a further outbreak of violence?*

cause/lead to an outbreak *A lack of clean drinking water led to an outbreak of the disease.*

an outbreak happens (*also* **an outbreak occurs** *formal*): *The first outbreak of trouble occurred in May.*

NOUNS + outbreak

a flu/measles etc outbreak *The hospitals are full because of a cholera outbreak.*

PREPOSITIONS

an outbreak of sth *During one outbreak of fighting, a police officer was killed.*

PHRASES

outbreaks of rain (=short periods of rain - used especially on weather reports) *There are likely to be outbreaks of rain later in the afternoon.*

outcome Ac *n* the final result of something

ADJECTIVES

the final/eventual/ultimate outcome *The final outcome of the investigation is still to be announced.*

a likely outcome *What is the likely outcome of the election?*

a possible outcome *We are prepared for any possible outcome.*

an inevitable outcome (=one that is certain to happen as a result of something) *The increase in crime was the inevitable outcome of the government's decision to cut funding for the police.*

a successful/satisfactory outcome *Our aim is to achieve a satisfactory outcome for everybody.*

a good/positive/favourable outcome *Everyone is hoping for a positive outcome to the talks.*

a bad/negative/unfavourable outcome *Stopping treatment too early may result in an unfavourable outcome.*

the desired outcome (=the one you want) *They failed to achieve the desired outcome.*

the same outcome *They repeated the experiment on three occasions, each time with the same outcome.*

a different outcome *Let's hope that this time there is a different outcome.*

VERBS

have a ... outcome *The meeting had a very satisfactory outcome.*

produce a ... outcome *How many of those measures produced the desired outcome?*

achieve a ... outcome *They are willing to work with us to achieve a successful outcome.*

affect/influence the outcome *Did media reports affect the outcome of the trial?*

decide/determine the outcome (=be the thing that causes the final result) *It is their votes that will determine the outcome of the election.*

predict the outcome *It is too early to predict the final outcome of the survey.*

await the outcome *They are awaiting the outcome of an appeal against the decision.*

PREPOSITIONS

the outcome of sth *The outcome of the election was announced the following day.*

outdated *adj* THESAURUS **old-fashioned**

outgoings *n* THESAURUS **spending**

outlay *n* THESAURUS **spending**

outline *n*

1 the main ideas or facts about something, without the details

ADJECTIVES

a broad/general outline *The report gives a broad outline of the company's plans.*

a basic outline *I remembered the basic outline of the story, but not how it ended.*

a brief outline *Each chapter begins with a brief outline of the topics covered.*

a rough outline (=not exact) *Thompson gave me a rough outline of what had happened at the previous meeting.*

the bare outline (=with no details at all) *The book gives readers only the bare outline of Milton's life.*

VERBS

give (sb) an outline *The leaflet gives you an outline of the Party's main policies.*

provide an outline *The first chapter provides an outline of the theory of evolution.*

PREPOSITIONS

an outline of sth *He begins with a brief outline of the aims of the research.*

2 the line around the edge of something that you can see

ADJECTIVES

a vague/dim outline (=difficult to see) *I could just see the vague outline of a house.*

a clear/sharp outline *From the air, the clear outlines of bombed buildings can be seen.*

outlook *n*

1 your general attitude to life and the world

ADJECTIVES

a positive outlook (=generally happy and hopeful) *Despite her health problems, she has a positive outlook.*

a negative outlook (=generally unhappy and not hopeful) *He seems to have rather a negative outlook on life.*

an optimistic outlook (=believing that good things will happen) *Jackie is maintaining an optimistic outlook for the future.*

a pessimistic outlook (=believing that bad things will happen) *This pessimistic outlook is characteristic of depressed people.*

a new/fresh outlook *New experiences can bring about a fresh outlook on life.*

a wider/broader outlook (=a greater knowledge or understanding of different things) *Education should give students a broader outlook.*

sb's mental outlook (=how you feel about the things in your life) *Exercise can help improve your mental outlook.*

sb's political outlook *They were very conservative in their political outlook.*

VERBS

have a ... outlook *He has quite a negative outlook on the future.*

give sb a ... outlook *June's new job gave her a fresh outlook.*

change sb's outlook *None of my arguments could change his outlook.*

sb's outlook changes *None of my arguments could change his outlook. | My outlook has changed since I left university.*

broaden sb's outlook (=make them know or accept more things) *Being at university broadened my outlook.*

PREPOSITIONS

sb's outlook on sth *Since then, I've changed my outlook on things.*

PHRASES

sb's outlook on life *Their marriage was happy because they had a similar outlook on life.*

2 what is expected to happen in the future

ADJECTIVES

the economic/financial outlook *There is concern over the global economic outlook.*

the general outlook *The general outlook remains gloomy.*

the long-term/short-term outlook *They believe the long-term outlook is good.*

the outlook is bleak/gloomy/grim (=things are likely to be bad) *With all these problems, the outlook for the company seemed bleak.*

the outlook is good *Everything has returned to normal and the outlook is good.*

the outlook is rosy/bright (=things are likely to be good) *He replied optimistically that the outlook was still bright.*

the outlook is encouraging (=things are fairly likely to be good) *He is still very sick, but on the whole the outlook is encouraging.*

the outlook is uncertain *The outlook for the store remains uncertain.*

VERBS

the outlook improves *The country's economic outlook is improving.*

the outlook worsens *The outlook for employment has worsened as a result of the recession.*

PREPOSITIONS

the outlook for sth/sb *The outlook for the farming industry is gloomy.*

out-of-date *adj* THESAURUS > old-fashioned

output *n*

the amount of goods or work produced

ADJECTIVES/NOUNS + output

total output *The company's total output of steel was 33. 95 million tons.*

annual output (=in a year) *The vineyard's annual output is around 30,000 bottles of wine.*

a high/large output *More efficient factories lead to higher outputs.*

a low/small output *The output at the coal mine is low compared to other mines.*

national/world output (=the total output in a country or the world) *National output has increased by 2%.*

industrial output *There has been a big fall in industrial output.*

manufacturing output *Manufacturing output fell by 4 per cent during 2012.*

economic output *How do you measure a country's economic output?*

agricultural output *Reduced agricultural output means that sales of fertilizer will also reduce.*

VERBS

output rises/grows *Grain output rose by 6%.*

output falls *Output has fallen sharply recently.*

affect output *The weather can affect agricultural output.*

expand/raise/increase output *The factory is looking at ways to expand output.*

reduce output *The strike reduced total coal output by a third.*

PREPOSITIONS

output of sth *The publishing company has an output of 850 books per year.*

PHRASES

a drop/fall in output *There was an immediate drop in output.*

a rise/increase/growth in output *There could be a fall in prices and a rise in output.*

a level of output *This has no effect on the level of output.*

outraged *adj* THESAURUS ▶ angry

outspoken *adj* THESAURUS ▶ honest

outstanding *adj* THESAURUS ▶ excellent

overcast *adj* THESAURUS ▶ cloudy

overcome *v*

to successfully deal with a problem

NOUNS

overcome a problem/difficulty *How did you overcome the problem of lack of space?*

overcome an obstacle/hurdle/barrier (=something that is preventing you from doing something) *Overcoming great obstacles, Mary got a degree.*

overcome a disadvantage *She was born poor and disabled, but overcame her disadvantages.*

overcome resistance/opposition *They had to overcome considerable resistance before starting the building project.*

overcome prejudice/discrimination *All his life, he struggled to overcome racial prejudice.*

overcome adversity (=deal with a very bad or difficult situation) *This is an inspiring story of how one man overcame adversity.*

overcome your fear *The course helps you overcome your fear of flying.*

overcome the urge to do sth (=not do something you have a strong desire to do) *She tried to overcome the urge to laugh.*

ADVERBS

overcome sth easily *This problem can be easily overcome.*

overcome sth quickly *He quickly overcame all resistance.*

overcome sth successfully *During her life she has successfully overcome many obstacles.*

partially overcome sth *The problem of itchy skin can be partially overcome by using a moisturising cream.*

finally/eventually overcome sth *How did you eventually overcome your fear of public speaking?*

VERBS

try/attempt to overcome sth *She tried to overcome the urge to scream.*

struggle to overcome sth *He was struggling to overcome his nerves.*

manage to overcome sth/succeed in overcoming sth *It's amazing how he has managed to overcome so many obstacles in his life.*

help to overcome sth *Yoga can help to overcome stress problems.*

overcrowded *adj* THESAURUS ▶ crowded

overestimate Ac *v*

to think that something is bigger, better, more important etc than it really is

ADVERBS

seriously overestimate sth (=by a large amount) *We seriously overestimated how much money we had available.*

massively/grossly/vastly etc overestimate sth (=by a very large amount) *Western countries massively overestimated the extent of the problem.*

consistently overestimate sth (=continue to overestimate something) *The US has consistently overestimated the military strength of its opponents.*

NOUNS

overestimate the size/number/extent etc of sth *The organizers of the games admitted that they had overestimated the number of visitors.*

overestimate the importance of sth/sb *It would be hard to overestimate her importance as an American writer.*

overestimate sb's ability *He said he initially overestimated his ability as a film maker.*

PHRASES

sth cannot be overestimated (*also* **sth can hardly be overestimated**) (=used when emphasizing that something is very important) *His influence on rock music cannot be overestimated.*

it is hard/difficult to overestimate sth (=used when emphasizing that something is very important) *It is hard to overestimate the effect the war has had on these children.*

it is easy to overestimate sth (=used when saying that something is not as important as some people think) *It is easy to overestimate the effect of prison on criminals.*

ANTONYMS **overestimate → underestimate**

overheads *n* THESAURUS ▶ spending

overjoyed *adj* THESAURUS ▶ happy

overseas *adj* THESAURUS ▶ foreign

overview *n*

a general description or idea of a subject or situation

ADJECTIVES

a brief/quick overview *It is useful to give a brief overview of the work done so far.*

O

a broad/general overview *This chapter gives a broad overview of accounting practices in the UK.*

a detailed overview (=with a lot of information) *A detailed overview of the research in this field has been published.*

a comprehensive/complete overview (=including all the important things) *She offers us the most comprehensive overview of Leibniz's work available today.*

a historical overview *The book gives a historical overview of the revolution.*

O

VERBS

give/provide/offer an overview *The report provides an overview of the recent policy changes.*

have an overview *Find someone who has an overview of the situation.*

get/gain an overview *I wanted to get an overview of the main environmental concerns.*

take an overview *In business, you take an overview of a problem and then try to come up with solutions.*

overweight

adj too heavy and fat

ADVERBS

slightly overweight/a little overweight (*also* **a bit overweight** *BrE*): *He had started going to the gym because he was slightly overweight.*

seriously/heavily overweight (=very overweight) *Being seriously overweight doubles the risk of heart disease.*

grossly overweight *disapproving* (=extremely overweight) *The vet said the dog was grossly overweight.*

PHRASES

5 kilos/20 pounds etc overweight *I'm about 15 pounds overweight.*

THESAURUS: overweight

overweight, big/large, obese, chubby, plump, flabby, portly → **fat**[1] **(1)**

owner

n someone who owns something

ADJECTIVES

the new owner *The new owners of the house want to add another bedroom.*

the present/current owner *The painting was sold to its present owner in 1984.*

a previous/former owner *The trees had been planted in the garden by a previous owner.*

the original owner *The bed was specially made for its original owner.*

the legal owner *You cannot sell the property because you are not the legal owner.*

the proud owner of sth *I am now the proud owner of a piano.*

the rightful owner *The stolen necklace will be returned to its rightful owner.*

joint owners *He and his wife are joint owners of the house.*

the sole owner (=the only owner) *She is the sole owner of the business.*

a private owner (=a person, not an organization, who owns something) *Not many of his paintings are still in the hands of private owners.*

NOUNS + owner

a car/home/dog etc owner *Dog owners should make sure that their pets are properly trained.*

PREPOSITIONS

the owner of sth *The owner of the land does not wish to sell it.*

PHRASES

the owner's permission/consent *He admitted taking the car without the owner's permission.*

ownership

n

if you have ownership of something, it officially belongs to you

ADJECTIVES/NOUNS + ownership

shared/joint ownership *The brothers have joint ownership of the farm.*

sole ownership (=not shared with anyone else) *The company will take over sole ownership of Inerox.*

full ownership (=complete ownership) *News Corp took full ownership of the TV station in March.*

private ownership (=not owned by the government) *The mine was returned to private ownership in 2010.*

public/state ownership (=owned by the government) *He opposed state ownership of major industries.*

foreign ownership *Workers at the factory worry that foreign ownership may put their jobs at risk.*

legal ownership *The family claimed legal ownership of the house.*

outright ownership (=complete ownership, so that you have all the legal rights to something) *In some countries, the law bans foreigners from outright ownership of residential property.*

home ownership (=when people own the place where they live, rather than rent it) *In the last 50 years, home ownership has increased.*

land ownership *The Native Americans had no concept of land ownership.*

VERBS

have ownership of sth *My wife and I have joint ownership of the house.*

take ownership of sth (*also* **assume ownership of sth** *formal*) (=start to own something) *Legal documents show that he took ownership of the land in 1995.*

retain ownership (of sth) (=continue to own something) *Hawkins retained ownership until 2006.*

claim ownership (of sth) (=say that you own

something) *Several different groups claim ownership of the land.*

transfer ownership (=legally give something you own to someone else) *In 2008, he transferred the ownership of his boat to his son.*

ownership passes to sb *Ownership will pass to you when the contract is signed.*

PREPOSITIONS

ownership of sth *There was a dispute over who had ownership of the property.*

under sb's ownership (=used when saying that something is owned by a particular person, company etc) *Nowadays the factory operates under the ownership of British Aerospace.*

PHRASES

a change of ownership *The hotel improved following a change of ownership.*

proof of ownership (=something that proves you own something) *You'll need a share certificate as proof of ownership.*

be under new ownership *Now under new ownership, the club offers even better facilities.*

Pp

pace *n*

the speed at which something happens or the speed at which someone moves

ADJECTIVES

a rapid/fast pace *Some people are finding it hard to cope with the rapid pace of change.*

a slow pace *The pace of life in the countryside is slower.*

a steady pace *The economy was growing at a slow but steady pace.*

a brisk pace (=a fast speed) *He set off for the station at a brisk pace.*

a frantic/hectic/furious pace (=a very fast speed) *We worked at a hectic pace.*

a leisurely/unhurried/gentle pace (=a slow speed) *The boy ran down the stairs, and John followed at a more leisurely pace.*

a glacial pace (=a very slow speed) *The country is indeed changing, but at a glacial pace.*

VERBS + pace

quicken/increase your pace (=go faster) *He quickened his pace, longing to be home.*

increase/accelerate/quicken the pace of sth (=make something happen more quickly) *The government seems committed to increasing the pace of reform.*

slacken/slow your pace (=go slower) *Rose, exhausted with running, slackened her pace a little.*

slow the pace of sth (=make something happen more slowly) *The agreement will do little to slow the pace of global warming.*

gather pace (=happen more quickly) *Support for the campaign is gathering pace.*

keep up/maintain the pace (=continue to do something as quickly as before) *Their society is changing but can it keep up the pace?*

set the pace (=go or do something faster, so that other people have to try to keep up with you) *The race leaders set a fast pace.*

PREPOSITIONS

the pace of sth *The pace of change accelerated dramatically in the early 1980s.*

at a ... pace *The race was run at a tremendous pace.*

PHRASES

the pace of life *I like the relaxed pace of life on the island.*

at a snail's pace (=very slowly) *Reform is proceeding at a snail's pace.*

at (a) breakneck pace (=extremely fast) *The country's economy grew at a breakneck pace.*

at your own pace (=at the pace that suits you) *Each child is able to learn at his or her own pace.*

⚠ Don't say 'in your own pace' or 'on your own pace'.

pack[1] *n*

1 a set of things that have been put together for someone to use or buy

NOUNS + pack

an information pack *Students receive an information pack at the start of the course.*

a training pack *The booklet is part of a training pack for teachers.*

a starter pack *This starter pack contains all the things you need to start making chocolates yourself.*

VERBS

a pack contains/includes sth *The pack includes workbooks and a poster.*

PREPOSITIONS

a pack of sth *I ordered a pack of six young geranium plants.*

PHRASES

in packs of three/four etc *The fruit juices are sold in packs of three.*

a six-pack/four-pack etc of beer *He bought a six-pack of beer.*

2 a small container made of paper or plastic that something is sold in

ADJECTIVES

a whole pack *He smoked a whole pack of cigarettes.*

an empty pack *Some people just throw the empty packs on the ground.*

PREPOSITIONS

a pack of sth *She went out to get a pack of chewing gum.*

This meaning of **pack** is more common in American English. In British English, people usually say **packet**.

3 a group - used about dogs, or about people who behave badly and in an uncontrolled way

PHRASES

a pack of wolves/dogs *He was attacked by a hungry pack of wolves.*

a pack of children *A pack of noisy children ran past us.*

a pack of reporters/photographers *The candidate was followed everywhere by a pack of reporters.*

a pack of thieves *He described the bankers as a pack of thieves.*

the leader of the pack *The leader of the pack is the strongest and most aggressive animal.*
hunt in packs *These wild dogs hunt in packs.*

pack² *v* THESAURUS **fill**

package *n*

something wrapped in paper or packed in a box, and then sent by mail or delivered

VERBS

send (sb) a package *I sent the package yesterday.*
post a package *BrE*, **mail a package** *AmE*: *I wanted to mail a package home to my family.*
deliver a package *The package was delivered to the wrong address.*
wrap a package *She gave me a little package wrapped in brown paper.*
get/receive a package *I got a package in the mail a few days ago.*
open a package *Eagerly, he opened the package.*
a package contains sth *The package contained a watch and a gold ring.*

ADJECTIVES

a small/little package *She handed over the small package.*
a large/bulky package *He wondered what was in the strange bulky package.*

In British English, people often say **parcel** instead of **package**.

packed *adj* THESAURUS **crowded, full (1)**

packet *n BrE*

a container made of paper, plastic, or cardboard that something is sold in

NOUNS + packet

a cereal/crisp/cigarette/seed packet *She read the list of ingredients on the cereal packet.*

ADJECTIVES

a small/big packet *Many mothers prefer to give children a small packet of raisins as a snack.*
an empty packet *He tossed the empty packet into the bin.*

VERBS

open a packet *He opened the packet of biscuits.*

PREPOSITIONS

a packet of sth *I lunched on a cheese roll and a packet of crisps.*
in a packet *He offered her the last sweet in the packet.*

This meaning of **packet** is used in British English. In American English, people say **pack** or **package**.

pact *n*

an agreement between groups, countries, or people to do something

ADJECTIVES/NOUNS + pact

a trade pact *The US and Canada agreed to a trade pact.*
a peace pact/non-aggression pact *The country has changed greatly since the peace pact was signed.*
a military pact *The two countries entered into a military pact.*
a defence/security pact *Six Gulf states signed their region's first defence pact.*
a suicide pact (=when two or more people decide to kill themselves together) *Kelly died with her lover in a suicide pact.*

VERBS

sign a pact *Britain and France signed a pact to build a new generation of nuclear power stations.*
make a pact *Jason and I made a pact that we wouldn't tell anyone about our secret.*
agree (to) a pact (*also* **enter (into) a pact** *formal*): *The management and the unions agreed a pact to end the dispute.*
break a pact *By resigning, he broke a pact which all ministers had signed.*

PREPOSITIONS

a pact with sb/sth *There is little support for a pact with the Republicans.*
a pact between sb/sth and sb/sth *About 50,000 troops are based in Japan under a security pact between Japan and the US.*
a pact on sth *The pact on climate change will do little to stop global warming.*
under a pact *Under the new pact, Australia and the Philippines could organize joint military exercises.*

PHRASES

the conditions/terms of a pact *The terms of the pact are still under negotiation.*

page *n*

one side of a piece of paper in a book, newspaper etc, or the sheet of paper itself

ADJECTIVES

the first/last page *The last page of the diary had been torn out.*
the next/previous page *The article is on the next page.*
the opposite/facing page *See the diagram on the opposite page.*
the left-hand/right-hand page *The answers are on the right-hand page.*
the front/back page (=of a newspaper) *Her picture was on the front page of every newspaper.*
the sports/arts/financial etc pages (=the part of a newspaper that deals with sport, art etc) *He only ever reads the sports pages.*

a blank page (=with nothing on it) *There were a couple of blank pages at the back of the book.*
a new/fresh page (=which has not yet been written on) *Start each section of your essay on a new page.*
a full page *There was a full page advertisement for the store in the 'New York Times'.*

VERBS

turn a page *I turned the page in order to find out what happened next.*
turn to a page *He got out his newspaper and turned to the letters page.*
flick/flip/leaf through the pages of sth (=turn them quickly) *She was flicking through the pages of a magazine.*
see page 22/45 etc *See page 12 for more details.*
sth jumps/leaps off the page (=is very noticeable) *One mistake jumped off the page.*

PREPOSITIONS

on a page *Look at the table on page 5.*
over the page (=on the back of the page you are reading) *The other winners are listed over the page.*

PHRASES

the top of the page *Write your name at the top of the page.*
the bottom/foot of the page *See the note at the bottom of page 38.*

pain *n*

the feeling you have when part of your body hurts

ADJECTIVES

great/considerable pain (*also* **a lot of pain**) *He was in great pain, but he managed to say a few words.*

⚠ Don't say 'big pain'.

a terrible/awful pain *I woke up with a terrible pain in my side.*
severe/intense pain (*also* **acute pain** *formal*): *Ever since the accident, Mike has suffered from severe back pain.*
excruciating pain (=very severe) *The pain was excruciating and I couldn't walk.*
bad pain *That night, the pain was really bad.*
constant pain (*also* **chronic pain** *formal*) (=continuing pain) *Many of the elderly patients suffer chronic pain.*
a slight pain *I just have a slight pain in my shoulder.*
a sharp pain (=short but severe) *She felt a sharp pain in the back of her throat.*
a dull pain (=a slight but continuous pain) *There had been a dull pain in his belly all day.*
a shooting pain (=a severe pain that goes from one part of your body to another) *I kept getting shooting pains all down my leg.*
a throbbing pain (=a pain that has a regular beat) *She woke with a throbbing pain in her head.*

NOUNS + pain

back/chest/stomach etc pain *Many people suffer from back pain.*
labour pains *BrE*, **labor pains** *AmE* (=when a woman is having a baby) *Becky was at work when labour pains began.*

VERBS + pain

have a pain *I have a terrible pain in my stomach.*
feel pain (*also* **experience pain** *formal*): *The dentist told me that I wouldn't feel any pain.*
suffer (from) pain *She suffers from pain in her legs.*
relieve/ease pain (*also* **alleviate pain** *formal*) (=make it less severe) *Exercise can help to relieve lower back pain.*
bear/endure pain *She couldn't bear the pain any longer.*
cause pain *The disease can cause severe pain.*
inflict pain (=deliberately hurt someone) *The guards enjoyed inflicting pain on the prisoners.*

pain + VERBS

the pain gets worse *If the pain gets any worse, see your doctor.*
the pain goes away (*also* **the pain subsides** *formal*) (=becomes less severe) *He lay still until the pain had subsided to a dull ache.*
the pain comes and goes (=keeps starting and stopping) *The pain comes and goes but it's never too severe.*

pain + NOUNS

pain relief (=a drug or treatment that makes pain less severe) *These drugs offer effective pain relief for the very sick.*
sb's pain threshold (=their ability to bear pain) *Everyone has a different pain threshold.*

PREPOSITIONS

a pain in your arm/side/chest etc *The pain in his arm grew worse.*
in pain *The woman lying on the ground was obviously in pain.*
with pain *He gasped with pain as the rock hit him.*

PHRASES

aches and pains *Everyone has a few aches and pains when they get older.*

painful *adj*

1 causing physical pain

ADVERBS

extremely/incredibly/terribly painful *Back problems can be incredibly painful.*
excruciatingly painful (=extremely painful – used for emphasis) *The sting of this insect is excruciatingly painful.*

VERBS

be/feel painful *His stomach felt painful and he was sweating a lot.*

2 unpleasant or making you feel upset

ADVERBS

extremely/intensely/terribly painful *It was an extremely painful decision to leave the house.*

unbearably painful *My last conversation with him was unbearably painful.*

NOUNS

a painful memory *The photograph brought back painful memories.*

a painful experience *Divorce is usually a painful experience.*

a painful process *It was just part of the painful process of growing up.*

a painful time/period *The country went through a painful period of adjustment.*

a painful decision *I made the painful decision to move far away from my family.*

a painful reminder *Everything in the house was a painful reminder of the past.*

a painful lesson *I learnt a painful lesson about investing money.*

PREPOSITIONS

painful for/to sb *The separation was painful for them.*

painless *adj*

1 not causing any pain

ADVERBS

relatively painless *People choose this operation because it is quick, relatively painless, and has reliable results.*

virtually painless (=almost painless) *The treatment is said to be virtually painless.*

completely painless *The whole procedure took 10-15 minutes and was completely painless.*

2 without any difficulties or problems – used especially when you expected something to be much worse

ADVERBS

relatively painless *The negotiations were relatively painless and swift.*

THESAURUS: painless

simple, straightforward, user-friendly, undemanding, mindless, painless, cushy → **easy**

painstaking *adj* THESAURUS **careful**

paint *n*

a coloured or white liquid that you put on a surface

ADJECTIVES/NOUNS + paint

wet paint *Careful – the paint is still wet.*

the paint is dry *Make sure the paint is completely dry.*

fresh paint (=paint that has just been put on something) *The place smelled of fresh paint and new carpets.*

peeling/flaking paint (=starting to come off a surface because it is old) *She lived in a gloomy old building with peeling paint on the walls.*

gloss paint (=paint that is shiny when it has dried)

matt paint (=paint that is not shiny when it has dried)

oil paint (=paint that contains oil)

VERBS + paint

put paint on (sth) (*also* **apply paint** *formal*): *Don't put the paint on too thickly.*

spray paint *Vandals had sprayed paint all over the walls.*

strip paint off sth (=remove all the paint from a surface) *We decided to strip the paint off the doors.*

paint + VERBS

paint dries *Wait for the paint to dry.*

paint peels/flakes (=pieces of paint come off) *The paint was starting to peel off the window frame.*

PHRASES

a can/tin/pot/tube of paint *He had spilt a can of paint on the floor.*

a coat of paint (=a layer of paint that is put on something) *Walls usually need at least two coats of paint.*

give sth a lick of paint *informal* (=quickly paint something to make it look more attractive) *All she needed to do to the kitchen was give it a lick of paint.*

painting *n* a painted picture

ADJECTIVES/NOUNS + painting

a famous painting *'The Night Watch' is one of Rembrandt's most famous paintings.*

an abstract painting *I like the shapes he uses in his abstract paintings.*

a modern/contemporary painting *The gallery has a collection of contemporary paintings.*

an oil painting (=one done using paints that contain oil) *Turner did some oil paintings, but he often worked with watercolours.*

VERBS + painting

do a painting *He did many paintings of the island.*

finish/complete a painting *The painting was completed by Van Gogh in July 1890.*

exhibit a painting *Her paintings have been exhibited all over the world.*

hang/display a painting *She plans to hang the painting in her dining room.*

painting + VERBS

a painting is of sb/sth *The painting is of an old man holding a guitar.*

a painting shows sb/sth (*also* **a painting depicts sb/sth** *formal*): *The painting shows a peaceful country scene.*

a painting hangs somewhere/is on show somewhere *The painting hangs in the Louvre in Paris.*

PREPOSITIONS

a painting of sb/sth *On the wall was a large painting of a ship.*

a painting by sb *We went to an exhibition of paintings by Jackson Pollock.*

in a painting *Who is the woman in the painting?*

palace *n*

the official home of a king, queen, or other person of very high rank

ADJECTIVES

a magnificent/great palace *We visited Louis XIV's magnificent palace at Versailles.*

a royal palace *Henry III built a royal palace here in 1237.*

an imperial palace (=for an emperor) *He will have a meeting with the Emperor Akihito at the Imperial Palace.*

a presidential palace (=for a president) *Thousands of protesters were marching toward the presidential palace.*

palace + NOUNS

the palace grounds (*also* **the grounds of the palace**) *A man was found hiding in the grounds of the palace.*

the palace gates *A crowd of people were waiting outside the palace gates.*

PREPOSITIONS

in a palace *The princess lived in a big palace.*

at the palace *There will be a garden party in his honour at the palace.*

pale *adj*

1 a pale colour is not bright

ADJECTIVES

pale blue/green/yellow etc *He has very pale blue eyes.*

THESAURUS: pale

faint, weak, pale, poor/bad, soft, low → **dim**

ANTONYMS **pale → dark (2)**

2 if your skin is pale, it is a much lighter colour than usual

VERBS

look pale *Her mother looked pale and tired.*

turn/go/grow pale (=become pale) *His face went pale when he heard the news.*

ADVERBS

deathly/ghostly pale *literary* (=extremely pale) *She looked older and thinner, and her skin was deathly pale.*

PHRASES

pale and drawn (=pale and with a thin face, because you are worried, ill, or tired) *She noticed how pale and drawn he looked. "Are you all right?" she asked.*

panel Ac *n*

a group of people who have been chosen to give advice or opinions on something

PHRASES

a panel of experts/judges/scientists *A distinguished panel of experts will give their opinions on the issue.*

a member of a panel (*also* **a panel member**) *I agree with the other members of the panel.*

the chairman/chair of a panel *The chairman of the panel is appointed by the government.*

ADJECTIVES/NOUNS + panel

an international panel *An international panel of scientists has warned that the drug may cause cancer.*

an independent panel *They were chosen for the award by an independent panel of judges.*

an advisory panel *He agreed with the advisory panel's conclusions.*

a selection panel *The team will be picked by a selection panel.*

VERBS + panel

set up a panel (=establish a panel) *The Market Research Society has set up a panel to investigate.*

appoint a panel *The government appointed a panel of food experts.*

sit on a panel (=be a member of a panel) *Professor Turner was invited to sit on the panel.*

chair/head a panel (=be in charge of a panel) *The advisory panel is chaired by Professor Michael Richards.*

panel + VERBS

a panel is made up of sb *The panel is made up of five independent legal experts.*

a panel meets *The panel meets once every two weeks.*

panel + NOUNS

a panel discussion *The talk will be followed by a panel discussion on modern families.*

PREPOSITIONS

on the panel *There are three people on the panel.*

panic *n*

a sudden strong feeling of fear or worry that makes you unable to think clearly or behave sensibly

ADJECTIVES

a big/huge panic *There was a big panic about the virus last year.*

widespread panic (=among many people) *The announcement caused widespread panic.*

growing/mounting/rising panic *She quickly packed a bag, trying all the time to control her mounting panic.*

total/sheer/blind panic (=used when emphasizing that someone is very worried) *A wave of total panic swept over her.*

sudden panic *Florrie exclaimed in sudden panic: "I've left my bag on the bus!"*

VERBS + panic

cause/create panic *The earthquake caused widespread panic.*

feel panic *When he got the phone call, he felt a sudden panic because he thought someone had died.*

get into a panic *There is no need to get into a panic.*

throw/send sb into a panic (=make someone feel very worried) *The question threw her into a panic.*

panic + VERBS

panic breaks out (=it starts among a group of people) *Suddenly, everything went dark and panic broke out.*

panic sets in (=it affects someone a lot) *It was one hour before the performance, and already panic was starting to set in.*

panic ensues *formal* (=it happens as a result of something) *Panic ensued as people ran out of the burning building.*

panic spreads (=it starts to affect more people) *Panic spread as news of the invasion reached Paris.*

panic subsides (=it becomes less strong) *Slowly, her panic subsided until she felt quite calm.*

panic + NOUNS

a panic attack (=a sudden unreasonable feeling of panic) *He had a panic attack in the street.*

PREPOSITIONS

a panic about/over sth *There was a panic about rising crime rates.*

in (a) panic *When the earth started shaking, people fled their homes in panic.*

PHRASES

in a state of panic *My mother called me in a state of panic.*

a sense/feeling of panic *She looked at him with a rising sense of panic.*

a wave/surge of panic (=a feeling of panic that you suddenly have) *A sudden wave of panic overcame him.*

paper *n*

1 material in the form of thin sheets that is used for writing on, wrapping things etc

ADJECTIVES/NOUNS + paper

writing paper *Can you fetch me a piece of writing paper and a pen?*

plain paper *The package was wrapped in plain brown paper.*

wrapping paper (=paper for wrapping presents) *He carefully removed the wrapping paper from his present.*

tissue paper (=very thin soft paper used for wrapping things) *All the clothes were wrapped in tissue paper.*

waste paper/wastepaper *About 25,000 tons of waste paper are collected each year.*

recycled paper (=paper made from waste paper) *The envelopes are made from 100 percent recycled paper.*

Notepaper is usually written as one word.

PHRASES

a piece of paper *Can I have another piece of paper?*

a sheet of paper *Each recipe was written down on a separate sheet of paper.*

a scrap/slip of paper (=a small piece) *He scribbled Pamela's address on a scrap of paper.*

pen and paper *Some writers still prefer to use pen and paper, not computers.*

put/get sth down on paper (=write it down) *He is putting a few thoughts down on paper.*

2 a newspaper

ADJECTIVES/NOUNS + paper

a local paper *You could try putting an advert in the local paper.*

a national paper *The story had been in all the national papers.*

a daily paper *Which of these daily papers do you usually read?*

a Sunday paper *I only get a Sunday paper if I've got lots of spare time.*

a tabloid paper (=one with small pages, especially one without much serious news) *Don't believe everything you read in the tabloid papers.*

PREPOSITIONS

in the paper *I read a review of the movie in the paper.*

Paper or newspaper?

In everyday English, **paper** is much more common than **newspaper**. In some cases, though, you can only use one of these words.

For example, you say a **paper boy/girl**, or a **paper shop**. (You do not use 'newspaper' in these phrases.)

P

You say a **newspaper article**, a **newspaper headline**, and a **newspaper editor**. (You do not use 'paper' in these phrases.)

3 a piece of writing or a talk on a particular subject by someone who has made a study of it

ADJECTIVES/NOUNS + paper

a scientific/academic paper *He has written six scientific papers on the topic of bird calls.*

a research paper *I am writing a research paper on German names.*

a joint paper (=by two or more people) *The result of their collaboration was a joint paper published in 1981.*

an influential/seminal paper (=one that is considered to be very important) *He published numerous influential papers on evolution.*

VERBS + paper

write a paper *He has written several papers on the subject.*

give/present a paper (=give a talk) *She gave a paper on Dickens's early works at a conference in Minneapolis.*

publish a paper *The paper was published in the journal 'Nature'.*

submit a paper (=ask an academic magazine to publish it) *We submitted our paper to three journals.*

paper + VERBS

a paper examines/explores/describes etc sth *This paper examines how attitudes to the environment have changed.*

PREPOSITIONS

a paper on sth *She is the author of a paper on the behaviour of bees.*

in a paper *He gives several examples in his paper.*

parade *n*

a celebration when people or vehicles move along while people watch

ADJECTIVES/NOUNS + parade

a grand/big parade *There will be a grand parade through the town.*

an annual parade *The city's annual Thanksgiving Day parade took place yesterday.*

a victory parade *The team are looking forward to their victory parade through the streets of London.*

a military parade *Soldiers from the Netherlands were expected to take part in the military parade.*

VERBS

have/hold a parade *An Easter parade will be held this weekend.*

march/take part in a parade *Another band was picked to march in the parade.*

watch a parade *Everyone else was still watching the parade.*

a parade takes place *The parade will take place under strict security.*

paradise *n*

a place or situation that is extremely pleasant, beautiful, or enjoyable

ADJECTIVES/NOUNS + paradise

a tropical paradise *We spent two weeks in that beautiful tropical paradise.*

an island paradise *Ischia is an island paradise in the Bay of Naples.*

an unspoiled paradise *The explorers discovered an unspoiled paradise.*

an earthly paradise *The people lived happily in a sort of earthly paradise.*

PHRASES

a paradise for children/walkers/divers etc *The area is a paradise for walkers and bird watchers.*

a shopper's/walker's etc paradise *New York is a shopper's paradise.*

sb's idea of paradise *A weekend spent reading is my idea of paradise.*

paradox *n*

a situation that seems strange because it involves two completely different ideas or features

ADJECTIVES

the great/central/ultimate paradox *The great paradox of the information age is that we have so many facts but very little useful knowledge.*

a strange/curious/interesting paradox *There is a curious paradox in his argument.*

an apparent/seeming paradox (=one that seems to exist) *How can we explain this apparent paradox?*

VERBS

present/pose a paradox *The figures present a paradox: the economy has improved but our international economic status has declined.*

create a paradox *This created the paradox that a rule designed to increase justice actually prevented people from accessing it.*

explain/resolve/solve a paradox *No one has so far managed to solve this paradox.*

PHRASES

be something of a paradox (=be rather a paradox) *It is something of a paradox that William Morris was concerned with helping the poor, but only very rich people could afford to buy his designs.*

paragraph Ac *n*

part of a piece of writing which starts on a new line and contains at least one sentence

ADJECTIVES

the first/opening paragraph *She glanced at the opening paragraph of the article.*

the last/final/closing paragraph *State your conclusion in the last paragraph of your essay.*
an introductory paragraph *Write an introductory paragraph saying how you will approach the question.*
the following/next paragraph *The issue of cost is discussed in the following paragraphs.*
the previous/preceding paragraph *All the places mentioned in the previous paragraph are open to the public.*
a new paragraph *I think you should start a new paragraph here.*
a short/long paragraph *Include a short paragraph explaining why you are applying for the job.*

VERBS

write a paragraph *Write a paragraph describing one of the characters in the story.*
read a paragraph *She had just read the last paragraph when the phone rang.*

PREPOSITIONS

a paragraph about sth *There was a paragraph about the incident in the local newspaper.*
in a paragraph *The figures quoted in this paragraph may not be entirely accurate.*

parallel *n*

if there is a parallel between two things, they seem similar in some way

ADJECTIVES

a close parallel *A close parallel exists between temperature patterns in east Canada and in Britain.*
an exact/direct parallel *He drew a direct parallel between the events happening in the two countries.*
a clear/obvious/striking parallel *There is a clear parallel between the two stories as both Jason and Theseus rely on help from a woman.*
an interesting/curious parallel *This article draws an interesting parallel between the banking industry of the past and the shipping industry of today.*
a historical parallel *He draws a historical parallel between the computer revolution and the invention of the printing press.*

VERBS

draw/make a parallel (=show that two things are similar in some way) *The writer attempts to draw a parallel between the human brain and a computer.*
there is a parallel *There is a parallel between the two films because they deal with similar themes.*
see/find a parallel *Can you see a parallel between what happens in the story and your own life?*

PREPOSITIONS

a parallel between sth and sth *Parallels exist between the situations in Northern Ireland and the Middle East.*
a parallel with sth *As I read the book, I found many parallels with my own experiences.*

parameters *n*

a set of fixed limits for doing something

VERBS

set/establish/determine/define the parameters (=decide what they are) *You need to define the parameters of your research.*
change the parameters *The software manual explains how to change the parameters of the game.*
narrow/broaden the parameters (=make them narrower or broader) *If you narrow the parameters of your search, the software will find what you want more quickly.*
choose the parameters *The program lets you choose the parameters that meet your needs.*

ADJECTIVES

certain parameters *The business has to operate within certain legal parameters.*
narrow/strict parameters *The research was done within a set of narrow parameters.*
the following parameters (=used when you are about to say what the parameters are) *The program allows the user to carry out a search using the following parameters.*

PREPOSITIONS

within the parameters of sth *We have to work within the parameters of time and budget.*
outside the parameters of sth *This topic falls outside the parameters of the current discussion.*

paramount *adj* THESAURUS **important (1)**

parasol *n* THESAURUS **umbrella**

parcel *n*

something that has been wrapped in paper, especially so that it can be sent by post

VERBS

send (sb) a parcel *Families are allowed to send prisoners parcels.*
post a parcel *BrE*, **mail a parcel** *AmE*: *I've got a parcel to post.*
wrap a parcel *Can you help me wrap this parcel?*
deliver a parcel *A parcel was delivered to his house on Christmas Eve.*
get/receive a parcel *I received an unexpected parcel in the post the other morning.*
open a parcel *When Katherine opened the parcel, she found a copy of 'War and Peace'.*
a parcel contains sth *The parcel contained clothing.*

NOUNS + parcel

a food parcel *At Christmas, toys and food parcels are delivered to deprived families.*
a brown paper parcel *A brown paper parcel arrived by special delivery.*

P

Parcel is used especially in British English. In American English, people usually say **package**.

pardon *n*

an official order allowing someone who has been found guilty of a crime to go free without being punished

VERBS

give sb a pardon (*also* **grant sb a pardon** *formal*): *Some of the prisoners were granted pardons.*

issue a pardon (=say officially that someone should have a pardon) *The president is under international pressure to issue a pardon.*

get/receive/obtain a pardon *The man was freed on Friday after receiving an unexpected pardon from the king.*

offer sb a pardon *A pardon was offered to the rebel soldiers, if they agreed to lay down their weapons.*

seek a pardon *One of the men convicted is seeking a pardon.*

ADJECTIVES

a full pardon (*also* **a free pardon** *BrE*): *She does not expect a full pardon, but hopes her sentence will be reduced.*

a royal/presidential pardon (=one given by a king, queen, or president) *Clinton gave him a presidential pardon.*

PREPOSITIONS

a pardon for sb/sth *They were promised a pardon for their past crimes.*

parent *n* someone's father or mother

ADJECTIVES/NOUNS + parent

a good/bad parent *Being a good parent is not about money, it is about caring and love.*

loving parents *He was born of poor but loving parents.*

a single parent (*also* **a lone parent** *BrE*) (=someone who has their children living with them, but no partner) *She is a single parent with two young sons.*

sb's biological/natural/birth parents (=who gave birth to a child) *Most children are reared by their natural parents.*

sb's real parents *She was raised by her aunt – she never met her real parents.*

adoptive parents (=people who legally become the parents of someone else's child) *Adoptive parents often have little practical preparation for parenthood.*

a foster parent (=someone who has other people's children living with them) *Teresa was removed from her mother's care and placed with foster parents.*

VERBS

become a parent *Are you looking forward to becoming a parent?*

respect your parents *I was brought up to respect my parents.*

blame the parents *Whenever a child gets in trouble, people always blame the parents.*

park *n*

1 a large open area with grass and trees, especially in a town, where people can walk, play games etc

ADJECTIVES/NOUNS + park

the local park *The boys from my school play football in the local park.*

a public park *The concert was held in a public park.*

a city park *The protesters gathered in the city park.*

VERBS

go to the park *Let's go to the park.*

park + NOUNS

a park bench *He sat on a park bench and read his newspaper.*

PREPOSITIONS

in the park *I went for a walk in the park.*

2 a large area of land in the country which has been kept in its natural state to protect the plants and animals there

ADJECTIVES/NOUNS + park

a national park *A survey has found just two white rhinoceroses in Hwange National Park, Zimbabwe.*

a country park *BrE*: *The country park has lots of beautiful walks.*

a state/county park *AmE*: *The state park is a popular spot for picnics and hikes.*

park + NOUNS

a park ranger (=someone whose job is to look after a park) *The park ranger found her wandering around and called the police.*

VERBS

visit a park *They want to increase the number of tourists visiting the Serengeti National Park.*

parliament *n*

the group of people who are elected to make a country's laws

VERBS

stand for parliament (=try to be elected) *Ms Jackson stood for Parliament as a Labour candidate.*

be elected to parliament (*also* **be returned to parliament** *BrE formal*): *She was elected to Parliament in 1997.*

enter/get into parliament (=be elected) *Tony Blair first entered Parliament in 1983.*

dissolve parliament *formal* (=officially end the

meeting of parliament before holding an election) *The prime minister will ask the Queen to dissolve Parliament and call an election.*

a bill goes through parliament (=it goes through the process of being made a law) *The bill is currently going through Parliament.*

parliament passes a bill/law *The bill was passed by Parliament last May.*

PHRASES

a member of parliament *He was the Conservative Member of Parliament for Edgbaston.*

an act of parliament (=a law that has been passed by parliament) *Their rights are guaranteed by Act of Parliament.*

a seat in parliament (=a position as member of parliament) *He resigned his seat in Parliament.*

a session of parliament (=when its members are working) *The Queen opened a new session of Parliament last week.*

> **Parliament** is usually written with a capital letter when referring to the British parliament.

parody *n*

a book, film, play, song etc that copies another more serious one, in order to make fun of it

ADJECTIVES

a brilliant/wonderful parody *Stella Gibbons' book was a brilliant parody of 19th-century romantic novels.*

a hilarious parody (=very funny) *The play is a hilarious parody of Shakespeare's 'Twelfth Night'.*

VERBS

do a parody *The group does parodies of classic rock songs.*

descend into parody *disapproving* (=change into a parody) *The movie frequently descends into parody.*

PREPOSITIONS

a parody of sb/sth *The film is a parody of those old Hollywood westerns.*

PHRASES

a subject for parody *Politicians are an obvious subject for parody.*

parole *n*

permission for someone to leave prison, on the condition that they promise to behave well

VERBS

apply for parole *The prisoners will be able to apply for parole after serving half their sentences.*

be considered for parole *The judge told him he would not be considered for parole.*

grant sb parole (=allow someone to leave prison) *He plans to return to his home town if he is granted parole.*

get parole (=be allowed to leave) *I feel like a prisoner who has just got parole.*

be denied/refused parole *He was considered dangerous and was denied parole.*

violate your parole (=do something that is not allowed while you are on parole) *He was arrested for violating his parole.*

parole + NOUNS

the parole board (=the group of people who make decisions about parole) *The parole board could consider him for release after six years.*

PREPOSITIONS

on parole *He had committed a burglary while on parole.*

PHRASES

be released on parole *He was released on parole after serving two years.*

be/become eligible for parole *She becomes eligible for parole in 2015.*

part *n*

one of the things, areas, or amounts that form something

ADJECTIVES

an important/vital/essential part *Fresh fruit is an important part of our diet.*

a large/big part (*also* **a good part**) (=much or most of something) *A large part of their work is funded by the government.*

a small/tiny part *Low wages are only a small part of the problem.*

all parts/every part of sth *He had access to all parts of the factory.*

a different part of sth *Public transport varied between different parts of the country.*

equal parts *I cut the orange into four equal parts.*

the best/worst part *The worst part was having to work even when it was raining.*

the upper/lower/central part *She suffered burns to the upper part of her body.*

the hard/easy part *Deciding what you're going to cook is the easy part.*

the northern/southern etc part *There could be snow in the northern part of the country.*

the early/first part *The school dates from the early part of the nineteenth century.*

the latter/later part (=the part towards the end) *The festival lasts for ten days during the latter part of May.*

the last/final part *We had reached the last part of our journey.*

the second/third etc part *The second part of the course takes beginners up to intermediate level.*

an integral part (=used to emphasize that a part is necessary or always there) *These workshops are an integral part of the course.*

VERBS

consist of two/three etc parts *The play consists of three parts.*

be composed of two/three etc parts *formal* (=consist of them) *The building is composed of two parts: an outer and an inner part.*
be divided/split into two/three etc parts *A few years later, the empire was divided into two parts, eastern and western.*
fall into two/three etc parts (=have two etc parts) *The proposals fall into two parts.*

PREPOSITIONS

a part of sth *The most interesting part of the story is the ending.*
in parts *The river has completely dried up in parts.*

PHRASES

part one/two/three etc *Part one of the survey asks for your personal details and part two for your comments on the course.*
a part of the world/country *There are wars going on in many parts of the world.*
a part of the body *The cancer may spread to other parts of the body.*

P

participant Ac *n*

someone who is taking part in an activity or event

ADJECTIVES

an active participant *They encourage all members of staff to be active participants in the decision-making process.*
a willing/enthusiastic participant *The producer said the teenagers were willing participants in the programme.*
an unwilling/reluctant participant (=persuaded or forced by other people) *The boy was a reluctant participant in the bullying.*
a full participant *Women could not be full participants in political life.*
a leading/prominent participant (=an important or well-known participant) *He was allegedly a leading participant in the 1989 coup attempt.*
a regular participant *She is a regular participant in television talk shows.*

VERBS

attract participants *The protest march attracted thousands of participants.*

NOUNS + participant

conference/workshop/course participants *All the conference participants wore name badges.*

PREPOSITIONS

a participant in sth *Half the participants in the study were interviewed again.*

participate Ac *v*

to do an activity together with other people

ADVERBS

participate fully *They participated fully in the life of the village.*
participate actively *Everyone in the class participates actively in discussions.*
participate freely *Women participated freely in every area of society.*

VERBS

agree to participate *A hundred people agreed to participate in the study.*
refuse to participate (*also* **decline to participate** *formal*): *The politician was invited to take part in a TV debate, but declined to participate.*

PREPOSITIONS

participate in sth *She was invited to participate in a poetry workshop.*

PHRASES

be free to participate *Anyone is free to participate.*
be unwilling to participate *Many small business owners are unwilling to participate in long legal battles.*

partner Ac *n*

1 a person, organization, or country who you do an activity with

ADJECTIVES/NOUNS + partner

a business partner *They were close friends as well as business partners.*
a trading partner (=a country that another country trades with) *The United States is Thailand's biggest trading partner.*
a dancing/dance partner *She was sad because she didn't have a dancing partner.*
an equal partner *Women should be equal partners with men in public life.*
a former partner *He bought his former partner's share of the business.*

VERBS

find a partner *He needs to find a partner for his new business.*
choose a partner *The teacher asked the students to choose a partner and then work in pairs.*

PREPOSITIONS

a partner in sth *The company's partners in the project include Japanese and Thai oil companies.*

2 one of two people who are married, or who have a sexual relationship

ADJECTIVES/NOUNS + partner

a new partner *She came to the wedding with her new partner.*
a potential partner (=someone who could be your partner) *The dating agency suggested several potential partners.*
a marriage partner (*also* **a marital partner** *formal*): *People often meet their marriage partner at work.*
a former partner *Her children still see her former partner at weekends.*

VERBS

find a partner *They got divorced, and both found new partners.*

choose a partner *When choosing a partner, you must trust your heart.*

PHRASES

sb's partner of 5/10 etc years *His partner of 18 years died last week.*

partnership Ac *n*

a relationship between two people, organizations, or countries, in which they do something together

ADJECTIVES/NOUNS + partnership

a close partnership *The two companies have built up a close partnership over the past four years.*

a strong partnership *We must build strong partnerships with countries such as South Korea and Japan.*

a successful/fruitful/productive partnership *The two musicians enjoyed a very successful partnership.*

an effective partnership *The agency tries to forge effective partnerships with communities and private businesses.*

a good partnership *A good partnership requires a lot of communication.*

an equal partnership *They regard marriage as an equal partnership.*

a working partnership *Theirs is one of the most fruitful working partnerships in modern science.*

a business partnership *He entered into a business partnership with his brother-in-law.*

VERBS

form/forge/establish a partnership (=start one) *He has forged a highly successful partnership with the singer Frances Black.*

go into partnership (*also* **enter into (a) partnership**) *I was keen to go into partnership with him.*

develop/build a partnership *The company plans to develop international partnerships.*

strengthen a partnership *This is an opportunity to strengthen existing partnerships.*

dissolve a partnership (=end it) *The partnership was dissolved, and Davis opened his own office.*

PREPOSITIONS

a partnership with sb *The company already has a partnership with a local research institute.*

a partnership between people/organizations etc *We want to strengthen the partnership between our two nations.*

in partnership *The parties are willing to share power and to work in partnership.*

party *n*

1 a social event when a lot of people meet together to enjoy themselves by eating, drinking, dancing etc

NOUNS + party

a birthday/Christmas/Halloween etc party *They met at her sister's 18th birthday party.*

a dinner party *Television is a favourite topic of conversation at dinner parties these days.*

a surprise party *His girlfriend has planned a surprise party for his birthday.*

a farewell/leaving party *Are you going to Michael's leaving party?*

a fancy-dress party *BrE*, **a costume party** *AmE* (=where people dress as famous people or characters, people with particular jobs etc) *I once went to a fancy-dress party dressed as a pirate.*

a cocktail party (=a fairly formal party, where alcoholic drinks are served) *I have to go to a cocktail party at the Spanish embassy.*

an office party *We usually have an office party at the end of the year.*

a street party *The neighbours organized a street party to celebrate the occasion.*

ADJECTIVES

a big/small party *I don't really like going to big parties.*

a lavish party (=where a lot of money has been spent) *He threw lavish parties for his celebrity friends.*

VERBS

have/hold a party *We're having a party on Saturday night. | The party was held at his flat.*

⚠ Don't say 'make a party'.

throw/give a party (=organize one) *Staff threw a party to celebrate the news.*

host a party (=give a large or formal party) *The party was hosted by the Danish ambassador.*

go to/come to a party (*also* **attend a party** *formal*): *Are you going to Tom's party?*

invite sb to a party *I've been invited to a birthday party next weekend.*

gatecrash a party (=go to it although you are not invited) *Some older boys tried to gatecrash the party.*

a party breaks up (=it ends and people go home) *The party broke up just after midnight.*

> **Have a party or hold a party?**
> **Hold a party** sounds more formal and is often used in the passive.

party + NOUNS

party games *The children had great fun playing party games.*

a party atmosphere (=the feeling of being at a

P

party) *There was a party atmosphere on board the ship.*

PREPOSITIONS

at a party *I met her at a party.*

PHRASES

there is a party going on *Somewhere near the hotel there was a party going on.*

a party is in full swing (=people at a party are having a good time talking, dancing etc) *At 3 a.m., the party was still in full swing.*

be in a party mood (=want to enjoy yourself at a party) *Kate wasn't really in a party mood, so she stayed home.*

2 a political organization, which you can vote for in elections

ADJECTIVES/NOUNS + party

a political party *The Labour Party and the Conservative Party are the two main political parties in Britain.*

the Labour/Republican etc Party *He is the leader of the Democratic Party.*

the ruling party (=the party that forms the government) *The ruling party's level of support grew throughout the year.*

an opposition party (=a party that does not form the government) *The tax increase was criticized by opposition parties.*

a right-wing/left-wing party *Support for the right-wing parties was strongest among young working-class men.*

the main/major parties *The changes were supported by all the major parties.*

VERBS

vote for a party *People will vote for the party that promises to make them better off.*

join a party *Bloomfield joined the Communist Party in 1946.*

form/found a party *The two politicians decided to form a new political party.*

lead a party *He resigned after leading the party for 13 years.*

a party wins/loses an election *Which party will win the election?*

party + NOUNS

the party leader *He met with opposition party leaders.*

a party candidate (=someone who represents a political party in an election) *The seat was won by the Socialist Party candidate with 68% of the vote.*

party supporters *She addressed a crowd of 5,000 party supporters.*

the party faithful (=strong supporters of a party) *His policies appeal to the party faithful.*

a party activist (=someone who works hard for a party) *Campaign literature is distributed by unpaid party activists.*

party politics (=activities concerned with getting support for one political party) *During the war, they agreed to put aside party politics and work together.*

party policy *There has been a change in party policy on education.*

a party conference *The minister will give a speech at the party conference.*

a party official *Senior party officials have denied the story.*

the party chairman *BrE*: *He resigned as Conservative Party chairman.*

PHRASES

a member of a party (*also* **a party member**) *I have been a member of the party for nearly 30 years.*

a party is in power (=it is in charge of the government of a country) *From 1945 until 1951 the Labour Party was in power in Britain.*

a party comes to power (=begins to be the government) *The ruling party came to power in May 2001.*

pass *v*

1 to be successful in a test

ADVERBS

pass sth easily *She should pass her driving test easily.*

just pass (=almost not pass) *You scored 51%, so you just passed.*

PHRASES

pass sth with flying colours *BrE*, **pass sth with flying colors** *AmE* (=do very well in a test) *Joe sat the test and passed with flying colours.*

pass sth with an A/with a distinction etc (=get a particular result when you pass a test) *She passed her physics exam with a grade B.*

ANTONYMS **pass → fail (2)**

2 to vote and agree to make a new law

ADVERBS

unanimously pass sth (=with all members voting yes) *Parliament unanimously passed the bill.*

PHRASES

pass sth by a large majority *The decision was passed by a large majority in the town council.*

THESAURUS: pass

pass, ratify, rubber-stamp → **approve (2)**

3 to give something to someone

THESAURUS: pass

donate, distribute, contribute, award, leave, lavish, confer, bestow, hand, pass, present → **give (1)**

passage *n*

a long narrow area with walls on either side which connects one room or place to another

ADJECTIVES

a narrow passage *A narrow passage led to a small room at the back of the house.*

a short/long passage *He found himself in a long passage with doors on either side.*

a dark passage *They went carefully along the dark passage.*

an underground/subterranean passage *The air in these underground passages is cold and damp.*

a secret passage *The bookcase moved to reveal a secret passage.*

VERBS

a passage leads to sth *Judy ran along the passage that led to the studio.*

PREPOSITIONS

along/down/through a passage *I led the way along the passage.*

PHRASES

the end of a passage *The dining room is at the end of the passage.*

a maze of passages (=many passages, in which it is easy to get lost) *We wandered through a maze of passages.*

passenger *n*

someone who is travelling in a vehicle, plane, boat etc, but is not driving it or working on it

passenger + VERBS

passengers get on/off a bus/plane/train *The bus stopped and half the passengers got off.*

passengers board a plane/train/ship etc *formal* (=get on it) *While he was asleep, two more passengers boarded the train.*

passengers travel *Most of the passengers who travel on these trains are satisfied with the service.*

passengers are stranded somewhere (=are unable to continue their journey) *At least 1,000 passengers were stranded at the airport because of the storm.*

VERBS + passenger

carry passengers *The plane was carrying over 500 passengers.*

pick up passengers (=let them get on) *The bus stopped to pick up some passengers.*

ADJECTIVES/NOUNS + passenger

rail/airline/bus passengers *Rail passengers will have to pay more for their tickets next year.*

first-class/second-class passengers *First-class passengers get large comfortable seats.*

foot passengers (=passengers on a boat, who are not in a car or other vehicle) *A queue of foot passengers was waiting to get on the ferry.*

passenger + NOUNS

the passenger seat (=the seat in the front of a vehicle next to the driver) *His wife was asleep in the passenger seat.*

a passenger train/plane/ship etc (=one that carries people not things) *No passenger train ever stops here.*

PREPOSITIONS

the passengers on/aboard a ship/plane etc *All 121 passengers aboard the plane survived the crash.*

passing *adj* THESAURUS ▶ **short (1)**, **temporary**

passion *n*

1 if you have a passion for something, you are very interested in it and like it a lot

ADJECTIVES

a great passion *Birds were my great passion.*

a consuming passion (=a very great passion) *The young Wordsworth had a consuming passion for poetry.*

a lifelong passion *His lifelong passion for natural history began in childhood.*

sb's real passion *His real passion was art.*

VERBS

have a passion for sth *She had a passion for music.*

develop a passion for sth *While at school, he developed a passion for acting.*

share a passion for sth *He and his wife share a passion for skiing.*

indulge your passion for sth (=do something that you enjoy doing very much) *The money enabled him to indulge his passion for horses.*

2 a very strong belief or feeling about something

ADJECTIVES

great passion *The orchestra played with great passion.*

strong/fierce passions *The issue has already stirred strong passions.*

VERBS

arouse/stir passions (=cause strong feelings in people) *The case aroused passions throughout the country.*

PREPOSITIONS

with passion *He speaks with passion about the suffering of children.*

PHRASES

passions run high (=people are very excited, angry, or upset) *The judge's decision is expected today and passions are running high.*

passionate *adj*

used when talking about someone who believes something very strongly or cares about something a lot

NOUNS

a passionate belief/conviction *We had a passionate belief in what we were doing.*

a passionate commitment to sth *There was no doubt about his passionate commitment to peace.*

a passionate concern for sth *She developed a passionate concern for human rights.*

a passionate supporter of sb/sth *President Johnson was a passionate supporter of the space programme.*

a passionate defender of sth *The actress is a passionate defender of women's rights.*

a passionate speech *Senator McCarthy delivered a powerful and passionate speech.*

PREPOSITIONS

passionate about sth *He is passionate about the environment.*

P

passport *n*

a small official document with details about yourself that you need in order to travel to another country

ADJECTIVES

a British/American etc passport *She was born in India but has a British passport.*

a false/fake/forged passport *He used a false passport to enter Kenya.*

VERBS

have a passport (*also* **hold a passport** *formal*): *I have a Canadian passport.*

apply for a passport *You can apply for an Italian passport if your parents are Italian.*

get a passport *I need to get a new passport.*

renew a passport (=get a new one) *I'd forgotten to renew my passport.*

travel on a passport *The men were convicted of travelling on a false passport.*

issue a passport *The passport was issued to him last year.*

check sb's passport *The official checked their passports and let them through.*

show your passport *You have to show your passport at the border.*

a passport expires (=the period of time when it can be used comes to an end) *My passport expires in January.*

passport + NOUNS

a passport photograph/photo *I hate my passport photo – it makes me look like a terrorist.*

a passport holder (=someone who has a passport) *British passport holders must obtain a visa before entering the country.*

password *n*

a secret group of letters or numbers that you type in so that you can use a computer, a program, a website etc

ADJECTIVES

a secret password *You need a secret password to log on.*

a correct/valid password *Only users who give the correct password can access the information.*

an incorrect/invalid password *I had accidentally typed an incorrect password.*

VERBS

enter/type (in) a password *Enter your user name and then your password.*

use a password *Someone else had logged on using his password.*

change your password *It is a good idea to change your password regularly.*

know the password *I'm the only person who knows the password.*

past *n*

the time that existed before the present

> **Grammar**
>
> In this meaning, you always say **the past**.

ADJECTIVES

the distant/remote past *Lions and tigers lived here long ago in the distant past.*

the recent past *In the recent past the country had a military government.*

the immediate past (=the very recent past) *Then they asked him about things that had happened in the immediate past, such as at school that day.*

VERBS

forget the past *We have to forget the past and look towards the future.*

be living in the past (=be behaving in a way which shows you do not realise that the situation has changed) *She needs to stop living in the past and find someone new.*

relive the past (=experience the same events that happened to you or another person a long time ago) *The band have no plans to play together again and say they have no wish to relive the past.*

PREPOSITIONS

in the past *In the past, most children didn't go to school at all.*

PHRASES

at some time in the past *The vase had clearly been repaired at some time in the past.*

in the dim and distant past (=a very long time ago) *In the dim and distant past, I used to sing in a band.*

be/become a thing of the past (=no longer exist) *We hope that war will become a thing of the past.*

a break with the past (=something that is done in a completely different way from before) *The new system is intended to be a break with the past.*

pastime *n*

something that someone enjoys doing

ADJECTIVES

sb's favourite pastime *BrE*, **sb's favorite pastime** *AmE*: *His favourite pastime was playing golf.*

a popular pastime *Criticizing the government seems to be a popular pastime these days.*

the national pastime (=a very popular pastime in a country) *Baseball is our national pastime.*

an expensive pastime *Horse-riding can be an expensive pastime.*

an enjoyable/pleasant pastime *Gardening is a very enjoyable pastime for people of all ages.*

VERBS

take up a pastime (=start doing it) *She took up a new pastime after she retired.*

enjoy a pastime (*also* **indulge in/pursue a pastime** *formal*) (=do something that you enjoy doing) *He was able to indulge in his favourite pastime of painting.*

patch *n*

a small area of something that is different from the area around it

ADJECTIVES

a small/large etc patch of sth *Some of the hills still had small patches of snow.*

a white/black/red etc patch *The bird has a large black patch on each side of its neck.*

a damp/wet patch *There were damp patches on the ceilings.*

a bald patch *He stroked the bald patch on the back of his head.*

a dark patch *She noticed two dark patches on the sleeve of his shirt.*

a clear patch *He had rubbed a clear patch on the steamy window.*

a bright patch *Wild flowers provided bright patches of colour along the road.*

icy patches *Some icy patches are likely on roads tonight.*

PREPOSITIONS

a patch of sth *There was a small patch of damp on the wall.*

in patches *The ground was dry in patches, but mostly it was still wet.*

path *n*

a track that people walk along

ADJECTIVES/NOUNS + path

a narrow/wide path *We walked along a narrow path beside a stream.*

a steep path *A steep path led down to the harbour.*

a rough path *The path now becomes very rough, so take care.*

a muddy path *The path was muddy after the rain.*

a rocky/stony path *Our guide went carefully down the rocky path.*

a winding path (=with many curves) *He climbed the winding path up the hill.*

a mountain/cliff path *Traveling along the mountain paths at night can be very dangerous.*

a cycle path (=for people riding bicycles) *They should put a cycle path along the edge of the road.*

VERBS + path

follow a path *We followed a path through the trees.*

take a path (=start going along it) *Take the path to the right.*

keep to the path *They kept carefully to the paths and did not go across the farmer's fields.*

path + VERBS

a path goes somewhere *The path goes through fields.*

a path leads to a place *There are many paths leading to the top of the mountain.*

a path winds somewhere (=it has many curves) *A narrow path wound down towards the beach.*

a path climbs/descends (=it goes up or down) *I could see the line of a path that climbed up from the bay.*

a path forks (=it divides into two paths going in slightly different directions) *We stopped where the path forked, wondering which way to go.*

pathetic *adj*

THESAURUS ▸ **sad (2)**, **weak (3)**

patience *n*

the ability to continue waiting, doing something, or accepting something without becoming angry or anxious

ADJECTIVES

great patience *Painting by this method requires great patience.*

infinite/endless/unlimited patience *She was lucky to have a maths teacher with infinite patience.*

VERBS + patience

have the patience to do sth *He didn't have the patience to wait until the weather improved.*

have no/little patience with sb *I have no patience with people who complain all the time.*

lose patience (with sb) *Eventually his family lost patience with him and his irresponsible behaviour.*

run out of patience (with sb) *She was wonderful with the children, and never ran out of patience.*

show patience *His employer has shown remarkable patience.*

take/need/require patience *It takes time and patience to build up a new business.*

P

try/test/tax sb's patience (=make it difficult for someone to continue to be patient) *The play was long, and tested the audience's patience.*

patience + VERBS

sb's patience is wearing thin (=they are becoming angry) *People's patience is wearing thin as the queues for visas get longer.*

sb's patience snaps (=they suddenly show their anger) *Celia's patience snapped when he dropped a second glass of wine on the carpet.*

sb's patience is rewarded (=they get what they were hoping and waiting to get) *After two hours, their patience was rewarded and they saw the bird.*

PHRASES

the patience of a saint (=very great patience) *Those children would try the patience of a saint.*

P

patient[1] *adj*

calm and not becoming annoyed because of someone's behaviour, or because something has not happened

ADVERBS

incredibly patient (=extremely patient) *My music teacher was incredibly patient with me.*

NOUNS

a patient man/woman *Romanov was not a patient man at the best of times.*

PREPOSITIONS

patient with sb *You need to be patient with her and wait for her to speak.*

PHRASES

be patient *Be patient. I'm sure they will contact you soon.*

ANTONYMS **patient → impatient**

patient[2] *n*

someone who is receiving medical treatment

ADJECTIVES/NOUNS + patient

a hospital patient *All hospital patients follow a daily routine.*

a cancer/AIDS etc patient *One in three cancer patients suffers no pain at all.*

a seriously/critically ill patient *Any seriously ill patients are sent to the state hospital.*

a private patient (=one who is paying for private treatment) *In the afternoon the doctor sees his private patients.*

VERBS + patient

treat a patient *The patient was being treated for depression.*

care for a patient *The hospital staff have the skills to care for these patients.*

see a patient *I waited while the doctor saw another patient.*

examine a patient *The patient was examined by a female doctor.*

patient + VERBS

a patient receives treatment/a drug *Twelve of these patients were receiving treatment with a new drug.*

a patient recovers *The treatment succeeded and the patient recovered rapidly.*

a patient is admitted (to hospital) (=comes into a hospital) *This examination should be done when the patient is admitted to hospital.*

a patient is discharged (from hospital) (=is allowed to leave a hospital) *The patient was discharged after eight days.*

patient + NOUNS

patient care *More money should be spent on patient care.*

PREPOSITIONS

a patient with cancer/AIDS etc *The drug is used to treat patients with breast cancer.*

patriotic *adj*

having or showing a great love of your country

ADVERBS

fiercely patriotic *He is fiercely patriotic towards his country.*

NOUNS

patriotic music/song *The soldiers were singing patriotic songs.*

a patriotic speech *On Independence Day, the president traditionally delivers a patriotic speech.*

sb's patriotic duty *He felt that it was his patriotic duty to join the army and fight for his country.*

patriotic fervour *BrE*, **patriotic fervor** *AmE* (=very strong feelings of patriotism) *Patriotic fervour gripped Spain as soccer fans celebrated their victory in the World Cup.*

patriotic sentiment *The prime minister's speech was full of patriotic sentiment.*

patriotic pride *The American flag is an important symbol of patriotic pride for the United States.*

a patriotic group/movement *She joined a patriotic group fighting for the country's independence.*

Patriotic or nationalistic?

If someone is **patriotic**, they love their country very much. If someone is **nationalistic**, they think their country is better than other countries. **Patriotic** is generally a positive word, but **nationalistic** is always used in a disapproving way.

patronizing *adj*

someone who is patronizing talks to you in a way that shows they think you are less intelligent or important than they are

NOUNS

a patronizing attitude *The head teacher was*

criticized for his patronizing attitude towards parents.

a patronizing tone *I did not like the patronizing tone of his letter.*

a patronizing smile *He gave the little girl a patronizing smile.*

a patronizing remark/comment *He made a rather patronizing remark about her paintings.*

a patronizing way/manner *She praised their efforts in a patronizing way.*

VERBS

sound patronizing *It may be hard to give advice without sounding patronizing.*

ADVERBS

rather/slightly patronizing *She was always rather patronizing towards her less well-off friends.*

so patronizing *Many women hate the label 'housewife' because it sounds so patronizing.*

PREPOSITIONS

patronizing towards sb *I wish you wouldn't be so patronizing towards me.*

pattern *n*

1 a regularly repeated arrangement of shapes, colours, or lines on a surface

ADJECTIVES

a complicated/complex/intricate pattern *She pretended to study the intricate pattern of the carpet.*

a simple pattern *Choose material with simple patterns such as checks and stripes.*

an abstract pattern *The vases are decorated with abstract patterns.*

a striped pattern *You can use different coloured paints to make a striped pattern.*

a geometric pattern (=involving straight lines or circles) *The carpet had a simple geometric pattern.*

a floral pattern (=a pattern of flowers) *She was wearing a silk dress with a floral pattern.*

a zigzag pattern *The layers of rock have been folded over millions of years into zigzag patterns.*

VERBS

form a pattern *The tiles are arranged to form a pattern.*

draw/paint/carve a pattern (on sth) *The children draw patterns on the eggs to decorate them.*

PREPOSITIONS

a pattern of dots/lines/flowers *The computer can recognize patterns of dots.*

2 the regular way in which something happens or is done

ADJECTIVES

the same/a similar pattern *Each of the murders has followed a similar pattern.*

a different pattern *There are different patterns of marriage and child-rearing in different societies.*

the basic pattern *The basic pattern of her working day rarely changed.*

the general pattern *Although there are small differences, the general pattern is clear.*

the normal/usual pattern *As soon as she could, she resumed the normal pattern of her life.*

a set/fixed pattern (=one that does not change) *These incidents followed a set pattern.*

VERBS

follow a pattern *Her headaches did not seem to follow any particular pattern.*

fit a pattern (*also* **conform to a pattern** *formal*) (=match a particular pattern) *Last week's bombing fits this pattern.*

establish a pattern *You should try to establish a pattern of working that suits you.*

a pattern emerges (=can be seen when something is studied) *When you look at all these cases, a pattern emerges.*

a pattern changes *Patterns of employment have changed since the 1950s.*

NOUNS + pattern

a weather pattern *Rising global temperatures are affecting weather patterns.*

a behaviour pattern *BrE*, **a behavior pattern** *AmE*: *He studied animal behaviour patterns.*

a spending pattern *The bank's computer can detect unusual spending patterns.*

PHRASES

a pattern of behaviour *BrE*, **a pattern of behavior** *AmE*: *It's easy to get stuck in the same old pattern of behaviour.*

a pattern of results *The scientists put forward an explanation for this pattern of results.*

a pattern of events *A research team in the Arctic observed a similar pattern of events.*

pause[1] *v*

to stop speaking or doing something for a short time before starting again

ADVERBS

pause briefly/momentarily *At the doorway she paused briefly.*

PREPOSITIONS

pause before doing sth *Sidney paused before answering.*

without pausing *Without pausing to think, he leaped across the gap.*

PHRASES

pause for a moment *He paused for a moment, seemingly overcome by emotion.*

pause for breath *She had to pause for breath after every two or three steps.*

pause for thought *"Of course," she replied, without pausing for thought.*

pause for effect (=in order to make people eager to hear what you are going to say) *"Now I know what to do," Brown said, pausing for effect.*

pause² *n*

a short time when someone or something stops before continuing

ADJECTIVES

a long pause *There was a long pause before anyone spoke.*

a brief/short/slight pause *"Well, that was a surprise," he said after a brief pause.*

a momentary pause (=very short) *There was a momentary pause during which Mr Hammond glanced at his wife.*

an awkward pause *After an awkward pause, Ray began to answer my question.*

a dramatic pause (=one that has a dramatic effect) *He left a dramatic pause before announcing the name of the winner.*

a pregnant pause (=one that is full of meaning or emotion) *There was a pregnant pause after she finished speaking.*

PREPOSITIONS

a pause in sth *He waited for a pause in the conversation.*

a pause between things *There are very few pauses between the jokes.*

a pause for sth *There will be pauses for discussion at appropriate points.*

without (a) pause *The bombing continued without pause.*

pay¹ *v*

1 to give someone money for something you buy or for a service

NOUNS

pay £10/$50 etc *I only paid ten pounds for it.*

pay a bill/invoice *He didn't have enough money to pay the electricity bill.*

pay rent *I can't afford to pay the rent on this apartment any more.*

ADVERBS

pay handsomely (=pay a lot of money) *Customers are willing to pay handsomely for anti-ageing creams.*

PREPOSITIONS

pay for sth *My parents paid for my trip.*

PHRASES

pay (in) cash *You have to pay in cash for the tickets.*

pay by cheque *BrE*, **pay by check** *AmE*: *I filled up with petrol and then paid by cheque.*

pay by credit card *Many websites charge more if you pay by credit card.*

pay in dollars/euros etc *American exporters want to be paid in dollars.*

2 to give someone money for the job they do

NOUNS

be paid wages/a salary *The workers are paid very low wages.*

pay sb money *Some people think footballers are paid too much money.*

pay sb £200 a week/$100 a day etc *The cleaners are paid £6 an hour.*

ADVERBS

well paid *Teachers here are well paid.*

highly paid *We don't need a highly paid expert to tell us what is wrong with the company.*

be paid weekly/monthly *Most of us get paid weekly or monthly.*

badly paid/poorly paid *Nurses are badly paid.*

PHRASES

be paid by the hour/day/week *I was working on a building site, being paid by the hour.*

> **Paid work and paid holiday**
> **Paid work** is work that you are paid to do. **Paid holiday** or **paid leave** is time when you are not working but are still paid.

pay² *n*

money that you are given for doing your job

ADJECTIVES/NOUNS + pay

low pay *They work long hours for low pay.*

good pay *The work was easy and the pay was pretty good.*

higher/better pay *Workers demanded higher pay.*

equal pay (=the same pay for the same type of work) *The women at the factory went on strike for equal pay.*

full pay *After the accusation was made, he was suspended on full pay.*

half pay *In 1822 he retired from the army as captain on half pay.*

sb's annual/monthly/weekly/hourly pay *His annual pay of over £100,000 was excessive.*

basic pay *BrE*, **base pay** *AmE* (=not including extra money such as overtime pay) *The basic pay is very low, so they work a lot of extra hours.*

take-home pay (=after tax etc has been taken away) *Their average take-home pay is just £120.*

overtime pay (=for extra hours that you work) *Police officers get a lot of overtime pay for working at weekends.*

holiday pay *BrE*, **vacation pay** *AmE* (=pay when you are on holiday) *People used not to get holiday pay.*

sick pay (=pay when you are ill) *As a self-employed person, you get no sick pay or benefits.*

maternity pay (=pay given to a woman who takes time off to have a baby) *If you have worked here a year, you are entitled to 3 months maternity pay.*

redundancy pay *BrE*, **severance pay** *AmE* (=a payment made to someone when there is no longer a job for them) *The former employees will receive 2 years' redundancy pay.*

pay + NOUNS

a pay increase *All staff will receive a 3% pay increase this year.*

a pay rise BrE, **a pay raise** AmE (=a pay increase) *If you get promoted, will you get a pay rise?*

a pay cut *Staff were asked to take a 10% pay cut.*

a pay freeze (=when no one's pay is increased) *Ministers have approved a public sector pay freeze.*

a pay dispute *Many flights were cancelled because of a pilots' pay dispute.*

VERBS

get/receive pay *His wife is also a doctor and receives similar pay.*

earn your pay (=deserve the money you get) *Every player earned his pay this week.*

increase/improve sb's pay *He thinks we should increase soldiers' pay.*

PREPOSITIONS

on low/full etc pay *Those on low pay do not have to pay for medical treatment.*

PHRASES

rate of pay/pay rate (=the amount paid every hour, week etc) *Many workers in the catering industry are on low rates of pay.*

pay and conditions *The unions are demanding better pay and conditions.*

THESAURUS: pay

pay, wages, income, earnings, the money → **salary**

payment *n*

an amount of money that is paid, or the act of paying for something

ADJECTIVES/NOUNS + payment

an annual/monthly/weekly payment *Home buyers have seen their monthly payments go up by more than 50 percent.*

late payment *A charge will be made for late payment of tax.*

prompt payment (=made immediately or at the right time) *Prompt payment of the fees would be very helpful.*

full/part payment *He never received full payment for his work.*

a down payment (=a small payment for something you are buying, when you will pay the rest later) *We were able to put a down payment on an apartment.*

an interest payment *Will you be able to keep up with the interest payments on the loan?*

a mortgage payment (=a payment towards a loan on your house) *Your mortgage payments could fall if interest rates drop.*

a bonus payment (=an additional payment because success has been achieved) *He received a bonus payment equivalent to 3 months' basic pay.*

VERBS

make (a) payment *The company agreed to make a further payment of $250,000.*

receive (a) payment *You will receive a cash payment on your 65th birthday.*

accept (a) payment *The judge had accepted illegal payments.*

meet/keep up the payments (on sth) (=be able to make regular payments) *He was having trouble meeting the mortgage payments.*

miss a payment *The borrower started missing interest payments.*

fall behind on/with the payments (=not make payments when you should) *I had big debts, and was beginning to fall behind with the payments.*

withhold payment (=not make a payment, often until something happens) *The buyer has the right to withhold payment until he or she is satisfied.*

PREPOSITIONS

payment for sth *She refused to accept payment for her advice.*

payment of sth formal: *Fees will be charged for late payment of bills.*

in payment *He had received £30,000 in payment for his services.*

PHRASES

payment in cash *He asked to receive payment in cash.*

payment in dollars/pounds etc *They would only accept payment in dollars.*

payment in full *She demanded immediate payment in full.*

a payment is due (=it should be made at a particular time) *The next payment is due on October 1st.*

payment in kind (=with things, not money) *They gave me some bottles of wine as payment in kind.*

peace *n*

1 a situation in which there is no war or fighting

ADJECTIVES/NOUNS + peace

world peace *The weapons pose a threat to world peace.*

a lasting/permanent peace *A lasting peace cannot be achieved by force.*

a fragile peace (=not likely to last) *UN peacekeepers are maintaining the fragile peace.*

an uneasy peace (=when people do not feel relaxed because they think the peace will not last) *An uneasy peace prevails in the region.*

VERBS

make peace (with sb) (=agree to stop fighting) *The English king wanted to make peace with France.*

P

bring peace to a place *She was praised for her efforts to bring peace to the region.*

achieve peace *Our goal is to achieve peace.*

negotiate peace *Many people have tried to negotiate peace in the Middle East.*

keep the peace/maintain (the) peace *Other countries have supplied troops to help keep the peace.*

promote peace (=help it to increase) *They believe the best way to promote peace is to promote democracy.*

threaten peace *The regime's aggression threatened peace and stability in the region.*

restore peace *The emperor's brother was able to restore peace in the troubled areas.*

peace + NOUNS

peace talks/negotiations *A fourth round of peace talks will begin on Monday.*

a peace conference *Will the US be sending a delegate to the Middle East peace conference?*

a peace treaty/agreement/accord *The formal signing of the peace agreement took place in Lisbon on May 31st.*

a peace settlement/deal *It is difficult to see how a peace settlement can be achieved.*

a peace plan *The leadership rejected the peace plan.*

the peace process *Britain is still committed to the peace process.*

a peace mission (=officials who are sent by their government to another country to discuss peace) *India's prime minister sent a peace mission to the Gulf.*

the peace movement (=people who work together to achieve peace) *As a young man, he was involved in the peace movement.*

a peace campaigner/protester/activist *Several peace campaigners were arrested at the demonstration.*

PREPOSITIONS

peace with a country *We want peace with our neighbours.*

peace between two countries/groups *There had been peace between the two countries for fifty years.*

PHRASES

be at peace (with sb) (=not be involved in a war) *Officially, England was at peace with Spain.*

live in peace (with sb) *I hope we can learn to live in peace.*

peace and security/stability/prosperity *The main purpose of the United Nations is to maintain peace and security.*

2 a very quiet and pleasant situation in which you are not interrupted

VERBS

leave sb in peace *Answer my question, and then I'll leave you in peace.*

disturb the peace (=end or spoil it) *Only church bells disturbed the peace.*

shatter the peace *literary* (=suddenly end it) *A sudden cry shattered the peace.*

peace reigns *literary* (=there is peace in a place) *Peace and tranquillity reign in the well-kept grounds.*

PREPOSITIONS

in peace *It was nice to be able to eat my lunch in peace.*

PHRASES

peace and quiet/tranquillity *We love the peace and quiet here.*

a haven of peace (=a very peaceful place) *Your home should be a haven of peace.*

peaceful *adj*

1 not involving war, fighting, or violence

NOUNS

a peaceful protest/demonstration *The students had planned to hold a peaceful protest.*

a peaceful solution/resolution/settlement *The authorities want a peaceful solution to the hostage crisis.*

a peaceful transition (=a peaceful change from one system to another) *They hope to achieve a peaceful transition to democracy.*

PHRASES

by/through peaceful means *We must redistribute power in this country by peaceful means.*

for peaceful purposes *They say their nuclear programme is for peaceful purposes.*

THESAURUS: peaceful

sleepy, peaceful, tranquil, calm, dead → **quiet (3)**

2 calm and quiet

NOUNS

a peaceful place *I was looking for a peaceful place where I could write my books.*

a peaceful atmosphere *The old town has a peaceful atmosphere.*

a peaceful scene *She looked at the peaceful scene outside her window.*

a peaceful life *He preferred the slow peaceful life of the Devon countryside to London.*

a peaceful day/morning/afternoon etc *You can have a peaceful day on your own, with no one bothering you.*

ADVERBS

largely/mostly peaceful *The day had been largely peaceful.*

strangely peaceful *The streets were strangely peaceful.*

peak *n*

1 the time when something or someone is best, greatest, highest, most successful etc

VERBS

reach a peak (*also* **hit a peak** *informal*): *The traffic reaches a peak between 5 and 6 p.m.*

fall from a peak *Visitor numbers have fallen from a peak of 1.8 million per year to under 1 million.*

PREPOSITIONS

at the peak of sth *He was then at the peak of his career.*

at its/your peak *The strawberry season is now at its peak.*

past its/your peak *By the next Olympics, she will be past her peak.*

PHRASES

peaks and troughs (=high points and low points) *The organization tries to be prepared for peaks and troughs in demand.*

2 the sharply pointed top of a mountain

ADJECTIVES/NOUNS + peak

a mountain peak *All around are the spectacular mountain peaks of the Jungfrau region.*

the highest peak *Mount McKinley is Alaska's highest peak.*

a snowy/snow-capped peak *The valley was ringed by mountains with snowy peaks.*

a jagged peak (=with several sharp points) *At first all I could see was the outline of a jagged peak.*

a rocky peak *The castle is situated on a rocky peak.*

a distant peak *The mist cleared to reveal distant peaks.*

a lofty/towering peak *literary* (=very high and impressive) *Its lofty peaks were almost hidden in cloud.*

THESAURUS: peak

summit, peak, crest → **top[1] (1)**

peel *v* THESAURUS cut[1] (1)

pen *n*

a thing you use for writing with, which contains ink

VERBS

use a pen *I always use this pen for signing my name.*

put your pen down *Kathy put her pen down and leaned back.*

a pen runs out (=the ink has all been used) *My pen has run out - can I borrow yours?*

PREPOSITIONS

in pen *Please fill out the form in pen.*

PHRASES

pen and ink (=used especially when comparing this with other ways of writing) *He still prefers to use pen and ink, rather than work on a computer.*

put pen to paper (=start writing something) *I decided to put pen to paper and describe my own experiences.*

(a) pen and paper *Sit down with a pen and paper and make a list.*

penalty *n*

a punishment for breaking a law, rule, or legal agreement

ADJECTIVES/NOUNS + penalty

a severe/stiff/heavy/tough/harsh penalty (=one in which someone is punished severely) *There were calls for stiffer penalties for killers of police officers.*

the maximum/minimum penalty *The maximum penalty for the offence is now three years' imprisonment.*

a financial penalty *Parents who fail to prevent their children committing crimes face heavy financial penalties.*

the death penalty (=the punishment of being killed) *If convicted, they could get the death penalty.*

VERBS

give/award sb a penalty *The judge gave him the death penalty.*

impose a penalty *formal* (=give someone a penalty) *Severe penalties are imposed for election fraud.*

get/receive a penalty *I think she should get a tougher penalty.*

pay a penalty *The company agreed to pay a penalty of $70,000.*

incur a penalty *formal* (=have to pay a penalty) *If they do not complete the work on time, they will incur financial penalties.*

face a penalty *He faces a possible penalty of 10 years' imprisonment.*

increase/reduce a penalty *They are proposing to increase the maximum penalty for helping prisoners to escape.*

a crime carries a penalty (=you will receive this penalty if you commit the crime) *Murder carries a minimum penalty of 15 years in prison.*

PREPOSITIONS

the penalty for (doing) sth *The penalty for dropping litter is a £50 fine.*

pencil *n*

a wooden stick with a black or coloured substance in the middle, used for writing or drawing

VERBS

draw/write/mark sth with a pencil *To make a circle on paper, draw around a plate with a pencil.*

use a pencil *I always use a soft pencil for drawing.*
sharpen a pencil *She sharpened her pencil and started writing.*

ADJECTIVES

a soft/hard pencil *It's better to use a hard pencil so that you get a clear line.*
a sharp pencil *Mark the edges with a sharp pencil.*
(a) blue/red etc pencil *Some of the names were underlined in red pencil.*
coloured pencils *BrE*, **colored pencils** *AmE*: *Elizabeth had given him a box of coloured pencils.*

pencil + NOUNS

a pencil drawing/sketch *I like her pencil drawings of animals.*
a pencil line/mark *He drew a pencil line on the wall to show where he wanted the shelf to go.*

PREPOSITIONS

in pencil *There's a note written in pencil on the back of the envelope.*

PHRASES

(a) pencil and paper *Get a pencil and paper, and I'll give you the details.*

penniless *adj* THESAURUS **poor (1)**

pension *n*

an amount of money paid regularly by the government or a company to someone who does not work any more

ADJECTIVES/NOUNS + pension

an old age pension (=a pension that is paid by the state to old people) *I will be able to get my old age pension when I'm 67.*
a retirement pension *Many workers lost their retirement pensions when the fund collapsed.*
a company pension/an occupational pension (=one that your employer pays) *He has a small occupational pension in addition to the state pension.*
a state pension *BrE*, **a public pension** *AmE* (=one that the government pays) *They argued that the state pension should rise in line with average earnings.*
a private/personal pension (=one that you arrange with a private pension company) *I decided to invest in a private pension.*
a good pension (=a large pension) *He can expect to draw a good pension.*
a disability pension (=for someone who is disabled, injured, or ill) *He was a war veteran and was living on a disability pension.*
a small/modest pension *Old people living on small fixed pensions were badly affected by inflation.*
a full pension (=the highest amount possible) *You have to work for the company for 30 years in order to receive a full pension.*

VERBS

get/receive a pension *They receive the basic state pension.*
have a pension *I have a pension of £360 a month from my former employers.*
draw your pension (=receive it) *He has got another ten years before he draws his pension.*
collect your pension (=receive it or go to get it) *She went to the post office every week to collect her pension.*
take out a pension (=make arrangements to have a pension later) *People were encouraged to take out private pensions.*
pay into a pension (=pay money regularly so that you will have a pension later) *When they were not working, they were unable to pay into a pension.*
live on a pension *She lives on a pension of $500 a month.*
retire on a pension *They can retire on a full pension at 55.*

pension + NOUNS

a pension plan (*also* **a pension scheme** *BrE*) (=an arrangement in which you pay money regularly so that you will have a pension later) *He contributes to a pension plan.*
pension contributions (=money that you pay into a pension) *You can make additional pension contributions.*
a pension fund (=a large amount of money that a company invests and uses to pay pensions) *The company wanted to take some money out of the pension fund.*

penultimate *determiner* THESAURUS **last[1] (1)**

percentage Ac *n*

an amount expressed as part of a total which is 100

ADJECTIVES

a high/large percentage *A high percentage of our students pass their driving test the first time.*
a small/low percentage *Only a small percentage of patients require surgery.*
a tiny percentage *Women make up only a tiny percentage of the company's workforce.*
a significant percentage *This country gets a significant percentage of its oil from Nigeria and Angola.*
the overall percentage (=including all things) *In England, the overall percentage of teachers from ethnic minorities is currently around 30%.*
the average percentage *Some stocks rose by more than the average percentage.*

VERBS

express sth as a percentage (=show an amount as a percentage rather than a number) *The figure is expressed as a percentage of total income.*

work out/calculate a percentage *We calculate the unemployment percentage from statistics produced by various government departments.*

measure the percentage *The tables measure the percentage of students leaving school with basic qualifications.*

percentage + NOUNS

a percentage point (=one percent) *The Tory party increased its share of the vote by almost 4 percentage points.*

a percentage increase/change *Crime figures published this week showed their largest percentage increase for five years.*

PREPOSITIONS

a percentage of sth *Only a relatively small percentage of young people are interested in politics.*

PHRASES

in percentage terms (=when calculated as a percentage) *The population in Wales is, in percentage terms, now rising more rapidly than that of England.*

perfect *adj*

not having any mistakes, faults, or damage

ADVERBS

absolutely perfect *His spoken English is absolutely perfect.*

almost/near perfect *Her performance was near perfect.*

PHRASES

far from perfect (=not at all perfect) *The weather conditions were far from perfect for flying.*

less than perfect (=not perfect) *Many great writers had less than perfect spelling.*

in a perfect world (=used to say how you would like life to be) *In a perfect world, we wouldn't need an army.*

perfection *n* the state of being perfect

ADJECTIVES

absolute perfection *If you insist on absolute perfection you will be disappointed.*

near perfection *Only one thing spoiled the near perfection of the landscape.*

physical perfection *She was considered a model of feminine physical perfection.*

technical perfection *The music examiner does not expect technical perfection.*

VERBS

strive for/seek perfection *We always strive for perfection.*

achieve perfection *With this work, he achieved perfection.*

reach perfection *The fruit reaches perfection in August.*

expect/demand perfection *She expected perfection from her staff.*

PHRASES

cooked/done/polished to perfection (=perfectly) *The beef was cooked to perfection.*

close to perfection (=almost perfect) *The climate here is close to perfection.*

bring sth to perfection (=make it perfect) *This type of poetry was brought to perfection by Alexander Pope.*

sb's search/quest for perfection *The motor industry is constantly improving designs in its search for perfection.*

the peak of perfection *They harvest each crop at the peak of perfection.*

perform *v*

to do something, especially something difficult or useful

ADVERBS

perform well *The class performed well on the test.*

perform effectively/efficiently *The engine will not perform very effectively in wet or cold conditions.*

perform successfully *China's economy has been performing successfully for many years.*

perform badly/poorly *The team has performed badly away from home this season.*

NOUNS

perform a task/job/duty *Do you need special skills to perform your job?*

perform a function/role (=have a particular purpose) *Software that performs this function can be downloaded from the internet.*

perform an experiment/study/test *Part of the chemistry exam involves performing an experiment.*

perform an operation (*also* **perform surgery**) *The surgeon who performed the operation said it had gone well.*

perform a ceremony (=do a set of official actions at an important religious or social event) *The opening ceremony was performed by the Queen.*

perform a service (=do something that is useful for other people) *Our troops are performing a remarkable service in very difficult conditions.*

perform miracles (=do things that seem impossible) *Liverpool's manager warned fans not to expect his young side to perform miracles.*

THESAURUS: perform

make, give, take, commit, carry out, conduct, perform, undertake, implement → do

P

performance *n*

1 an occasion when someone performs a play or a piece of music

ADJECTIVES/NOUNS + performance

a fine/good/great performance *There are fine performances by Kathy Bates and Daryl Hannah.*

a brilliant/magnificent/superb etc performance *Rogers gave a brilliant performance of Chopin's Piano Concerto No. 1.*

a memorable performance (=a good performance that you will remember for a long time) *There were memorable performances from Madonna and U2.*

a virtuoso performance (=showing great skill) *He delivered a virtuoso performance as the Phantom of the Opera.*

a live/public performance (=for people who are watching) *This is the band's first live performance since last year.*

a solo performance (=by a single musician, not a group) *Young's solo performances are often his most effective.*

a theatrical/stage performance *It was the first theatrical performance I had attended.*

VERBS

give/deliver/turn in a performance *Samuel L. Jackson gives a terrific performance in the film.*

go to a performance (*also* **attend a performance** *formal*): *We can go to the evening performance if you prefer.*

see/watch a performance *We went to see a performance of 'Hamlet' in London.*

put on/stage a performance (=organize and do a play or show) *They are planning to put on a performance of a new play by Tom Stoppard.*

2 how well or badly a person, company etc does something, especially their work

ADJECTIVES

a good/strong performance *England needs to produce another good performance against France.*

a poor performance *Why is his performance in school so poor?*

an outstanding performance (=very good) *He was rewarded for his outstanding performance.*

a solid performance (=good, but not excellent) *He started his running season with a solid performance in the London Marathon.*

a disappointing performance *The country's recent economic performance has been disappointing.*

a lacklustre performance *BrE*, **a lackluster performance** *AmE* (=not good or impressive) *The team must improve on Saturday's lacklustre performance.*

economic/financial performance *Britain's economic performance has not matched that of some other countries.*

academic performance *Problems at home can affect students' academic performance.*

VERBS

improve/boost/enhance sb's performance *The school has used technology to improve students' academic performance.*

affect sb's performance *Lack of sleep affects your performance at work.*

produce a good/poor etc performance (=do well etc) *Tiger Woods produced one of the best performances of his career.*

monitor sb's performance (=keep checking it) *The children's performance at school is continually monitored.*

performer *n*

an actor, musician etc who performs to entertain people

ADJECTIVES

a great/good/fine performer *She was a great performer and audiences loved her.*

a solo performer *He started out as a solo performer and then joined a band.*

a live performer (=who performs in front of an audience) *He is still a great live performer.*

an experienced/seasoned performer (=one who has been performing for a long time) *All the members of the cast are experienced performers.*

a legendary performer (=one who has been famous for a long time) *A new biography of the legendary performer has just been published.*

an amateur performer *Thousands of amateur performers entered the competition.*

a professional performer *He would not allow any of his children to become professional performers.*

NOUNS + performer

a circus performer *He decided that the life of a circus performer was not for him.*

a street performer *A crowd of people were watching the street performers.*

a stage performer *She became a stage performer at the age of six.*

perfume *n*

1 a liquid with a strong pleasant smell that women put on their skin or clothing to make themselves smell nice

ADJECTIVES

expensive/cheap perfume *He bought me a bottle of expensive French perfume for my birthday.*

strong perfume *That perfume you're wearing is very strong.*

an exotic perfume (=unusual and interesting because it seems foreign) *The dancers left a trail of exotic perfume in the air.*

VERBS

wear perfume *What's that perfume you are wearing?*

dab perfume on sth (=quickly put perfume on) *She dabbed some perfume on her neck.*

spray yourself with perfume *Jody sprayed herself with some of her mother's perfume.*

smell of perfume *Her coat smelled of cheap perfume.*

PHRASES

a bottle/jar of perfume *He gave me a bottle of my favourite perfume.*

the smell/scent of perfume *The smell of perfume filled the air.*

a whiff/hint of perfume (=a slight smell of perfume) *As she opened the letter, she noticed the faintest hint of perfume.*

2 a sweet or pleasant smell

ADJECTIVES

a sweet perfume *The sweet perfume from the roses came drifting through the window.*

a heady perfume (=strong and sweet) *In early summer, lilacs finally open and release their heady perfume.*

a faint perfume *She loved the faint perfume of a spring woodland.*

a delicate perfume *The flowers have a lovely delicate perfume.*

PREPOSITIONS

the perfume of sth *The room quickly filled with the perfume of freshly cut branches burning in the fire.*

peril *n*

great danger, or something that causes danger

PHRASES

be in peril *They didn't realise they were in peril until it was too late.*

sb's life is in peril *The passengers' lives were in peril when a fire broke out on board the aircraft.*

put sb/sth in peril *They put their own lives in peril to rescue their friends.*

be in peril of your life *You cannot shoot a burglar unless you can prove that you are in peril of your life.*

do sth at your own peril (=something bad could happen to you if you do something – used especially in warnings) *When you start playing with fire, you do so at your own peril.*

ADJECTIVES

in great/grave/serious/deadly peril *The ship was in grave peril and they all thought they were going to die.*

in immediate/imminent peril (=something bad could happen very soon) *The experts described the Earth as being in imminent peril due to the rise in sea levels.*

the hidden perils of sth *The article gives advice on avoiding the hidden perils of shopping on the internet.*

perilous *adj* THESAURUS ▸ **dangerous**

period Ac *n*

a particular length of time with a beginning and an end

ADJECTIVES/NOUNS + period

a long/lengthy period *The couple had to spend long periods apart.*

a short/brief period *He worked for a short period in Manchester.*

a prolonged period (=continuing for a long time) *If you experience the symptoms for a prolonged period, see your doctor.*

a limited period (=a fairly short length of time) *From May, the castle will be open to the public for a limited period.*

a fixed/set period (=one that will not be changed) *A tourist visa allows you to stay in the country for a fixed period.*

an indefinite period (=with no fixed end) *The painting had been loaned to the gallery for an indefinite period.*

a six-month/five-year etc period (*also* **a period of six months/five years etc**) *The drug was tested over a five-year period.*

a time period *The loan must be paid back over a certain time period.*

a trial period (=when you use someone or something for a short time, to find out if they are suitable) *The system was introduced for a trial period.*

PREPOSITIONS

a period of sth *There will be short periods of rain during the day.*

PHRASES

a period of time *His English has improved in a very short period of time.*

a period of the year *Christmas is a busy period of the year for us.*

periodical *n* THESAURUS ▸ **magazine**

permanent *adj*

continuing to exist for a long time or for all the time in the future

NOUNS

permanent damage/injury *Listening to loud music can cause permanent damage to your hearing.*

a permanent effect/impact/impression/mark *The accident had a permanent effect on him.*

a permanent change *The war led to a permanent change in the relationship between the two countries.*

a permanent job/permanent employment *Her son is still looking for a permanent job.*

a permanent home/address *There are now 180,000 single people without a permanent home.*

a permanent member *France is a permanent member of the UN Security Council.*

P

a permanent resident *She wants to become a permanent resident of the US.*

permanent staff *The Commission has a permanent staff of 24.*

a permanent exhibition *The museum has a permanent exhibition of his work.*

a permanent part/feature/fixture (=someone or something that is always there) *Stress is now a permanent feature of our lives.*

a permanent solution *What we need is a permanent solution.*

a permanent ban *They want a permanent ban on all nuclear weapons.*

VERBS

become permanent *The scheme was intended to last for three months, but it may become permanent.*

make sth permanent *The couple decided to make their relationship permanent and got married in the summer.*

PHRASES

on a permanent basis *Maybe you should come and work for me on a more permanent basis.*

on permanent display (=be shown permanently) *The statue is on permanent display at London's Barbican Centre.*

THESAURUS: permanent

lasting
effect | impact | influence | impression | solution | peace
continuing for a very long time:
The arrival of the railways had an important and lasting impact on the economy. | The experience left a lasting impression on him. | The negotiations are aimed at finding a fair and lasting solution to the dispute.

enduring
appeal | influence | memory | feature | legacy
continuing for a very long time:
Beatrix Potter's books have an enduring appeal for children. | His most enduring memory was of his time as an officer in the war. | The clock tower was an enduring feature and had been there for many years. | Darwin's theory of evolution is his enduring legacy (=something important that remains after someone dies).

perpetual
state | struggle | conflict | motion | diet
continuing all the time:
The people live in a perpetual state of fear. | There is a perpetual struggle for power. | Jennifer Nettles seems to live in a state of perpetual motion (=she is always moving around and doing things).

eternal
life | love | youth | gratitude | truth | optimist
continuing to exist forever:
Do you believe in eternal life? | The ring was meant to be a sign of his eternal love. | She thinks she may have found the secret of eternal youth (=a way to stay young forever).

everlasting
life | love | shame
continuing to exist forever:
Christ promised them everlasting life. | Gold is the symbol of everlasting love. | To my everlasting shame, I never told him how sorry I was for what happened.

ANTONYMS **permanent → temporary**

permission *n*

when someone is officially allowed to do something

VERBS

ask (for) permission (*also* **request permission** *formal*): *Tommy asked for permission to go to the bathroom. | Captain Miller requested permission to land.*

apply for permission (=ask for official written permission) *The company has applied for permission to drill for oil.*

seek permission (=try to get permission) *People wanting to visit the island have to seek permission from the authorities.*

have permission to do sth *They did not have permission to build on the land.*

get permission (*also* **obtain permission** *formal*): *We'll need to get permission to film inside the museum.*

get permission (*also* **receive permission** *formal*): *He has just received permission to build a huge swimming pool in the grounds of his mansion.*

give (sb) permission (*also* **grant (sb) permission** *formal*): *In 1961, he was granted permission to emigrate to Israel.*

refuse/deny (sb) permission *Betty's father refused her permission to attend the dance.*

need permission (*also* **require permission** *formal*): *You'll need written permission from your parents first.*

ADJECTIVES

special permission *The paintings cannot be taken out of Russia without special permission.*

official/formal permission *Mr Murphy was granted official permission to travel to North Korea.*

written permission *Doctors need written permission from the patient before they can operate.*

sb's express permission (=used when someone says clearly and definitely that something is allowed on this occasion) *He is not to leave without my express permission.*

planning permission (=official permission to build a new building or change an existing one) *Eventually, he was granted planning permission for the house.*

PREPOSITIONS

permission for sth *The organizers did not have permission for the protest march.*

permission from sb *We do not need permission from anyone to sell the land.*

without permission *Pages should not be copied without the permission of the publisher.*

with sb's permission *With your permission, I'd like to talk to your son alone.*

PHRASES

by kind permission of sb *formal* (=used when thanking someone for allowing something) *This photograph is reproduced by kind permission of the BBC.*

permit *n*

an official document giving you the right to do something

ADJECTIVES/NOUNS + permit

a work permit *She had problems getting a work permit.*

a parking permit *You need to have a parking permit in order to park here.*

a residence permit (*also* **a residency permit** *especially AmE*) (=one that allows you to live in a country) *Residence permits will be limited to five years.*

a travel permit *They have to obtain a travel permit to enter the city.*

a special permit (=that allows you to do a particular unusual thing) *You need to have a special permit to use this type of weapon.*

a building/construction permit *The number of applications for building permits has slowly increased over the last year.*

an export permit (=that allows a company to sell products or goods abroad) *An export permit is required for the export of nuclear material.*

VERBS

have a permit (*also* **hold a permit** *formal*): *Do you have a resident's parking permit?*

get a permit (*also* **obtain a permit** *formal*): *You have to get a special permit in order to visit the area.*

apply for a permit *Laboratories have to apply for a special permit to obtain the chemicals.*

give sb a permit (*also* **grant sb a permit** *formal*): *The immigration authorities refused to grant the men residency permits.*

issue a permit *Up to ten fishing permits are issued each day.*

need a permit (*also* **require a permit** *formal*): *EU citizens no longer need a permit to work in the UK.*

permit + NOUNS

a permit holder *Access to this car park is restricted to permit holders.*

a permit application *His work permit application is still being processed.*

PREPOSITIONS

a permit for sth *The authorities have denied a permit for the rally.*

perpetual *adj* THESAURUS ▸ **permanent**

persecution *n*

cruel or unfair treatment of someone over a period of time, especially because of their political or religious beliefs

ADJECTIVES

religious persecution *The Pilgrim Fathers went to America because they wanted to escape from religious persecution in Europe.*

political persecution *The organization helps people who face political persecution.*

VERBS

suffer (from) persecution *Some religious groups still suffer from persecution.*

face persecution/be subjected to persecution (=be persecuted) *The family faces persecution if they return to their own country.*

escape/flee from persecution *They went abroad in order to escape from persecution.*

persecution + NOUNS

a persecution complex (=a mental illness in which someone believes that other people are trying to harm them) *She had a persecution complex and was sure that everyone was trying to avoid her.*

PREPOSITIONS

the persecution of sb *The Nazis' persecution of the Jews resulted in the deaths of over 6 million people.*

PHRASES

victims of persecution *The men claimed they were victims of religious persecution.*

the fear of persecution *The fear of persecution discourages people from discussing politics openly.*

years/centuries of persecution *Gypsies have suffered centuries of persecution.*

persevere *v* THESAURUS ▸ **continue (1)**

persist *v* THESAURUS ▸ **continue (2)**

persistent *adj* THESAURUS ▸ **continuous, determined**

person *n*

a human being, especially considered as someone with their own particular character

ADJECTIVES/NOUNS + person

the average person *The average person is not interested in philosophy.*

an ordinary person *I'm just an ordinary person, living an ordinary life.*

an important person *Her son is the most important person in her life.*
the only person *My wife is the only person who really understands me.*
the best person *If you want some honest advice, the best person to ask is your mother.*
the right/wrong person *Voters are beginning to question whether he is the right person for the job of president.*
the first/last person *He was the first person to climb the mountain.*
a different person *Since losing all that weight, she looks like a different person.*
a morning/evening person (=someone who is more active in the morning or more active in the evening) *I'm not really a morning person, so getting up is the hardest part of my day.*

P

PREPOSITIONS

per person (=for each person) *The tickets cost $10 per person.*

PHRASES

sb is the sort/type/kind of person *Gary is not the sort of person who talks about his feelings.*

personal *adj*

1 belonging or relating to one particular person, rather than to other people or to people in general

NOUNS

sb's personal view/opinion *My personal opinion is that the project was too ambitious.*
sb's personal possessions/belongings/property (*also* **sb's personal effects** *formal*): *Your personal property should be clearly marked with your name and address.*
personal taste/preference *Music is very much a matter of personal taste.*
sb's personal qualities (=the good things about someone's character) *He got the job on the basis of his experience and his personal qualities.*
personal experience *I know from personal experience how hard it can be to raise a child.*
a personal relationship *She established good personal relationships with her co-workers.*
sb's personal interests (=things that benefit someone) *You should put your own personal interests to one side and think about other people for a change.*
a personal computer *Most young people have a personal computer or a laptop.*

PHRASES

take/have a personal interest in sth *The prime minister took a personal interest in the case.*
for (your) personal use *He bought a computer for his personal use.*
on a personal level (=used when giving your own opinion) *On a personal level, it's been a very positive experience.*

2 relating to the private parts of your life

NOUNS

sb's personal life *I won't answer questions about my personal life.*
personal details *Fill in your personal details, including your nationality, date of birth, and a current address.*
personal problems *These kids have a wide range of personal problems.*
a personal question *Can I ask you a personal question?*
a personal call (=a phone call that relates to private matters, not work) *We're not allowed to make personal calls from the office.*

ADVERBS

deeply/intensely personal (=very personal) *The content of the letter was deeply personal.*
rather personal (=very personal) *That's a rather personal question!*
strictly personal (=not related to business or work) *His visit to the country was on a strictly personal basis.*

PHRASES

for personal reasons *The company's chief executive has resigned for personal reasons.*

personality *n*

someone's character, especially the way they behave towards other people

ADJECTIVES

a strong personality *Mercer has a strong personality and always tells you his opinion.*
a forceful/powerful personality (=very strong) *The architect's forceful personality ensured that the work progressed rapidly.*
a dominant personality (=controlling other people) *He had a dominant personality and could be a bit of a bully.*
a warm personality (=friendly and kind to people) *Everyone who knew Roseanne will miss her warm personality.*
a magnetic/charismatic personality (=strong and attractive, so that people admire and respect you) *Clinton was a talented politician with a magnetic personality.*
a split personality (=used about someone who is mentally ill and has sudden extreme changes of behaviour) *The pop star had a split personality – he was obsessed with peace and quiet, but he was always shouting at people.*
an outgoing/extrovert personality (=liking to talk to people) *The job requires someone with an outgoing personality.*

personality + NOUNS

a personality type *The couple have very different personality types – he's very shy, but she likes being with people and going to parties.*
a personality trait *formal* (=a part of your personality) *She shares many of her mother's personality traits.*

a personality disorder (=a mental illness affecting someone's personality) *The hospital treats patients with severe personality disorders.*

a personality clash (=when people cannot work together because they are so different) *The band eventually split because of personality clashes.*

perspective Ac *n*

1 a way of thinking about something, especially one which is influenced by the type of person you are or by your experiences

ADJECTIVES/NOUNS + perspective

a new/different perspective *I like the programme because it gives you a different perspective on world news.*

a fresh perspective (=new and interesting or useful) *We need to approach this problem from a fresh perspective.*

an alternative perspective *The diaries and letters of ordinary people give an alternative perspective on the past.*

a wider/broader perspective *Exchange programmes help students get a wider perspective.*

a historical perspective *It is important to see the issue from a historical perspective.*

a global/international/local perspective *We need to look at environmental issues with a global perspective.*

a British/American/Russian etc perspective *From a French perspective, the war achieved nothing.*

a balanced perspective (=one that gives equal attention to all sides of an argument or situation) *It is impossible to get a balanced perspective when the only news agency is controlled by the state.*

a personal perspective *From a personal perspective, I learned a lot from the experience.*

a female/male perspective *Carson's lyrics are definitely written from a female perspective.*

VERBS

have a ... perspective *Everyone seems to have a different perspective on the issue.*

see/view sth from a ... perspective *A child can only see the world from his or her own perspective.*

give (sb) a ... perspective *Spending some time apart might give you both a better perspective on your relationship.*

provide/offer a ... perspective *Her novel provides a different perspective on the period.*

get/gain a ... perspective *When you reach my age, you get a more mature perspective.*

put a ... perspective on sth (=make you consider something in a particular way) *This new evidence put a whole new perspective on the case.*

PREPOSITIONS

a perspective on sth *His perspective on events may be completely different from yours.*

from the perspective of sb (*also* **from sb's perspective**) *The book is written from the perspective of a child.*

2 a sensible way of judging and comparing situations so that you do not imagine that something is more serious than it really is

VERBS

lose perspective *People sometimes lose perspective on what is really important in life.*

put sth into/in perspective (=consider something in a sensible way by comparing it with something else) *When I saw their suffering, it really put my own problems into perspective.*

get/see sth in perspective (=judge how important something is in relation to other things) *Discussing problems with friends can help get things in perspective.*

keep sth in perspective (=realize that something is not as important as other things) *I hope we can all keep this issue in perspective.*

PHRASES

a sense of perspective *Try to keep a sense of perspective about your job situation – at least you have a job!*

persuade *v*

to make someone decide to do something, especially by giving them reasons why they should do it, or asking them many times to do it

VERBS

try/attempt to persuade sb *If you say you're leaving, he'll try to persuade you to stay.*

manage to persuade sb (=succeed in persuading someone) *I finally managed to persuade her to go out for dinner with me.*

fail to persuade sb *He had failed to persuade voters to vote for him.*

ADVERBS

finally/eventually persuade sb *They eventually persuaded her to change her mind.*

gently persuade sb *See if you can gently persuade him to go to the doctor.*

be easily persuaded *They were easily persuaded to sell the land.*

PREPOSITIONS

persuade sb into (doing) sth *He managed to persuade her into getting in his car.*

PHRASES

an attempt to persuade sb *There was no attempt to persuade him to reconsider.*

let yourself be persuaded into doing sth *Don't let yourself be persuaded into buying things you don't want.*

persuasion *n*
the act of persuading someone to do something

ADJECTIVES

gentle persuasion *After a little gentle persuasion, Dad agreed to drive us to the mall.*

friendly persuasion *If friendly persuasion fails, what are you going to do then?*

VERBS

need persuasion *He didn't need much persuasion to accept the job offer.*

take persuasion *I don't think it will take much persuasion to get him to change his mind.*

use persuasion *We've tried using persuasion and it did not work.*

PHRASES

a method/means/form of persuasion *Economic sanctions will only be used if all other forms of persuasion have failed.*

the art of persuasion *As a former diplomat, she is skilled in the art of gentle persuasion.*

use all your powers of persuasion (=use all your skill at persuading people) *She had to use all of her powers of persuasion to stop him from going to the police.*

be open to persuasion (=be able to be persuaded to do something) *Although Mr Butler won't sell his shares, his partners might be open to persuasion.*

with a little persuasion *With a little persuasion from his mates, Robbie got up and sang.*

after some persuasion *After some persuasion, the nurse allowed me to see her for 5 minutes.*

pessimistic *adj*
expecting that bad things will happen in the future, or that someone cannot succeed

ADVERBS

very/extremely/deeply pessimistic *Experts are deeply pessimistic about the US economy.*

overly/unduly pessimistic (=too pessimistic) *Maybe I'm being overly pessimistic, but I don't think this target can be achieved.*

NOUNS

a pessimistic view/attitude/outlook *His ideas are based on a very pessimistic view of human nature.*

a pessimistic forecast/prediction *Their pessimistic predictions about supplies of oil have been proved wrong.*

VERBS

sound/seem/appear pessimistic *He sounded pessimistic about the chances of reaching an agreement.*

remain pessimistic *Many observers remain pessimistic about the political situation in the Middle East.*

PREPOSITIONS

pessimistic about sth *Workers are pessimistic about the chances of finding another job.*

ANTONYMS **pessimistic → optimistic**

pet *n*
an animal such as a cat or dog which you keep and care for at home

ADJECTIVES/NOUNS + pet

a family pet *These dogs make an ideal family pet.*

a domestic/household pet *Cats and other domestic pets give their owners a lot of pleasure.*

an exotic pet (=an unusual pet from a foreign country) *Often owners do not know how to care for exotic pets such as lizards.*

VERBS

have a pet *Do you have any pets?*

keep a pet (=have one in your home) *People who live in the building aren't allowed to keep pets.*

make good/ideal etc pets (=be good or very good as pets) *Rabbits make good pets.*

pet + NOUNS

a pet dog/cat/rabbit etc *I used to have a pet rabbit when I was young.*

a pet owner *The website has lots of useful information for pet owners.*

pet food *He bought two cans of pet food.*

petition *n*
a written request signed by a lot of people, asking someone in authority to do something or change something

ADJECTIVES/NOUNS + petition

an online petition *50,000 people signed an online petition protesting against the cuts.*

a protest petition *BrE: They presented a protest petition with 4,000 signatures to the government.*

VERBS

sign a petition *Most of the parents have signed the petition against the school closure.*

organize a petition *We organized a petition asking the government to repeal the law.*

hand in/present/deliver a petition *A group of pensioners went to Westminster to deliver the petition.*

a petition calls for/demands sth *A petition calling for an inquiry was signed by 15,000 people.*

a petition opposes sth *Local people signed a petition opposing the plans.*

PREPOSITIONS

a petition against sth *She asked me to sign a petition against building on local playing fields.*

a petition for sth *They collected over 20,000 signatures on a petition for a change in the law.*

petty *adj* THESAURUS **unimportant**

phase Ac *n*

one of the stages of a process of development or change

ADJECTIVES/NOUNS + phase

the first/second/third etc phase *The first phase of the police investigation is almost complete.*

the early/initial phase *In the early phase of the disease, the symptoms are relatively mild.*

the final/last phase *The civil war was entering its final phase.*

an important/critical/crucial phase *This was the most important phase of his political career.*

a pilot phase/an experimental phase (=one which is carried out as a test, to find out whether something will be successful) *It's better to find any faults at the pilot phase than when the product is in production.*

the development phase *In the development phase, we concentrated on the building's design and materials.*

distinct phases (=clearly separate phases) *The process went through three distinct phases.*

the acute/chronic phase (=the most serious stage of a disease or illness) *During the acute phase of the disease, patients must be watched very closely.*

a passing phase (=one that will soon change - used about someone's attitudes and behaviour) *Her parents hope her bad attitude is just a passing phase.*

VERBS

enter/begin/start a phase *Juan entered a new phase in his life when he got married.*

go through a phase *Like most teenagers, I went through a rebellious phase.*

reach a phase *The team must win tonight to reach the next phase of the competition.*

complete a phase *The first phase of the project will be completed in July.*

mark a phase (=show that a new phase is beginning) *The incident marks a new phase in the terrorist campaign.*

PREPOSITIONS

in a phase *The building work is still in its early phase.*

during a phase *During the cooling phase, the clay becomes hard again.*

PHRASES

phase one/two/three etc *Phase one of the project is expected to cost $4.6 million.*

phenomenon Ac *n*

something that happens or exists in society, nature etc

The plural of **phenomenon** is **phenomena**.

ADJECTIVES

a new phenomenon *The recent problems with the world economy are not a new phenomenon.*

a recent phenomenon *The demand for organic food is a fairly recent phenomenon.*

a common phenomenon *Blaming someone else for your mistakes is a common phenomenon.*

a growing phenomenon (=becoming more common) *Social networking websites are a growing phenomenon.*

a rare phenomenon *They were enjoying that rare phenomenon, a hot English summer.*

a unique phenomenon (=the only one of its kind) *A system of planets orbiting a sun is not a unique phenomenon.*

a strange phenomenon *This strange phenomenon has yet to be explained by scientists.*

a natural phenomenon (=one that happens in nature) *Natural phenomena, such as the appearance of comets, were seen as signs that something bad was going to happen.*

supernatural/paranormal phenomena (=ones that appear to be against the laws of nature) *Ghosts are one example of paranormal phenomena.*

a global/worldwide phenomenon (=in all parts of the world) *The book has become a global phenomenon.*

a universal phenomenon (=one that is found everywhere, or that always happens in every case) *Trade in slaves has been a universal phenomenon, affecting all primitive societies.*

VERBS

a phenomenon occurs/happens *This phenomenon occurs on average once in every 100 years.*

study/examine/investigate a phenomenon *The more we investigated these phenomena, the stranger they seemed.*

PREPOSITIONS

the phenomenon of sth *The phenomenon of global warming has been blamed for the disappearance of glaciers.*

philosophy Ac *n*

1 the study of ideas about existence and the meaning of life

ADJECTIVES

Western/Eastern philosophy *He became interested in Buddhism and Eastern philosophy while he was in Japan.*

Greek/Chinese/French etc philosophy *The writer is an expert on Greek philosophy.*

ancient/classical philosophy *The study of ancient philosophy focuses mainly on Plato and Aristotle.*

modern/contemporary philosophy *Her book tries to answer some of the questions raised by modern philosophy.*

VERBS

study philosophy *Laura is at university studying philosophy.*

teach philosophy *He now teaches philosophy at the University of Vermont.*

2 a set of ideas that someone believes in and follows

ADJECTIVES

sb's basic philosophy *My basic philosophy is simple: treat other people in the way that you want them to treat you.*

sb's personal philosophy *He has his own personal philosophy that he tries to live by.*

sb's guiding philosophy (=beliefs that help you when making difficult choices or decisions) *The company's guiding philosophy has been to focus on its core business.*

homespun philosophy (=simple ideas about life, rather than serious or complex ideas) *The book's charm lies in its mixture of humour and homespun philosophy.*

VERBS

follow a philosophy *The school follows a philosophy which basically says that learning should be fun.*

adopt a philosophy (=start to follow a philosophy) *He adopted a simple business philosophy, which he still believes in today.*

be based on a philosophy *These principles are based on the philosophy of freedom of choice.*

phone *n* a telephone

> **Phone** is the usual way of saying **telephone** in everyday English.

VERBS + phone

answer the phone (*also* **pick up the phone**) *When I called home, my dad answered the phone.*

use sb's phone *Do you mind if I use your phone?*

talk/speak to sb on the phone *Kate and I talk on the phone every day.*

call sb on the phone *I called her on the phone and invited her to Las Vegas.*

get on the phone to sb (=call them) *We got on the phone to the hospital straight away.*

get off the phone (=stop using the phone) *I'll tell her when she gets off the phone.*

put the phone down *I only remembered his name after I had put the phone down.*

slam the phone down (=put it down hard, because you are angry) *He was so mad he just slammed the phone down.*

come to the phone *I'm sorry, she can't come to the phone right now.*

be wanted on the phone (=someone has asked to speak to you on the phone) *Larry, tell Rosemary that she's wanted on the phone.*

phone + VERBS

the phone rings *The phone was ringing as she entered the room.*

phone + NOUNS

a phone call *I had a phone call from Sam yesterday.*

a phone conversation *The phone conversation with her mother had upset her.*

sb's phone number *Can I have your phone number?*

a phone line (=a telephone wire or connection) *The TV company's phone lines were jammed with angry viewers complaining about the programme.*

a phone book/directory (=a book containing the names, addresses, and phone numbers of the people in an area) *You'll find the number in the phone book.*

a phone bill (=a bill for phone calls) *Our last phone bill was huge.*

a phone company (=one that provides a telephone service) *Different phone companies offer different deals for making calls.*

ADJECTIVES/NOUNS + phone

a mobile phone *BrE*, **a cell phone** *AmE* (=a telephone that you can carry with you) *Most people have mobile phones now.*

a pay phone (=a public telephone) *Where's the nearest pay phone?*

PREPOSITIONS

by phone *He spoke to his lawyer by phone on Monday.*

on the phone (to sb) (=using the phone) *I was on the phone to my mother all morning.*

off the phone (=not using the phone or no longer using the phone) *I'll ask him when he gets off the phone.*

down the phone *BrE*: *Anna rang me, and she was crying down the phone.*

over the phone *You shouldn't give out personal details over the phone.*

PHRASES

the phone is busy (*also* **the phone is engaged** *BrE*) (=the person you are calling is already speaking to someone else) *I tried you earlier, but your phone was engaged.*

the phone goes/is dead (=the phone line stops working or is not working) *The phone suddenly went dead.*

take/leave the phone off the hook (=lift the part you speak into from its usual place so the phone cannot connect) *On Friday nights we just take the phone off the hook and relax.*

photocopy *v* THESAURUS copy[2] (1)

photograph *n*

a picture obtained by using a camera

ADJECTIVES/NOUNS + photograph

a wedding/graduation photograph *I kept all my wedding photographs in an album.*

a holiday photograph *They showed me their holiday photographs from their trip to Thailand.*

a colour photograph *BrE*, **a color photograph** *AmE*: *The book is illustrated with beautiful colour photographs.*

a black-and-white photograph *There are some old black-and-white photographs of your grandparents in that box.*

a digital photograph *If it's a digital photograph, you can email it to me.*

a framed photograph *On the desk was a framed photograph of her children.*

a signed photograph (=signed by the famous person shown in it) *He keeps a signed photograph of the singer in his office.*

an aerial photograph (=taken from above, usually from a plane) *Aerial photographs can be used to locate archaeological sites.*

a faded photograph *All her life she kept a faded photograph of Dad in his army uniform.*

a blurred/blurry photograph (=not clear or sharp) *Some of the photographs were rather blurred and it was difficult to see what was happening.*

a grainy photograph (=that looks unclear, as if the image is made of spots) *In one grainy old photograph, my grandfather is standing beside a Model T Ford.*

VERBS

take a photograph *Who took that photograph of you?*

get a photograph (=take one successfully) *I managed to get some great photographs of Manhattan.*

pose for a photograph (=sit or stand in a particular position when having your photograph taken) *The prime minister posed for photographs with other European leaders.*

print/publish a photograph *The newspaper printed photographs of him kissing another woman.*

blow up/enlarge a photograph (=make it bigger) *When the photograph was enlarged, it was possible to read the writing on the envelope.*

a photograph shows sb/sth *The photograph shows him with his younger brother.*

photograph + NOUNS

a photograph album (=a book in which you put photographs) *Mama kept a photograph album full of pictures of her family.*

PREPOSITIONS

a photograph of sb *Did you see that photograph of Leo in the newspaper?*

a photograph by sb *The gallery has a collection of photographs by Robert Mapplethorpe.*

in a photograph *Who's that man in the photograph?*

PHRASES

a photograph is out of focus (=it is not clear because the lens is not in the right position) *Some of the pictures were out of focus and it was difficult to see what was happening.*

a photograph is in focus (=it is clear because the lens is in the right position) *Before you press the shutter, make sure that the subject is in focus.*

In everyday English, people very often say **photo** instead of **photograph**. **Photo** can be used with all the same collocations as **photograph**.

phrase *n*

a number of words used together

ADJECTIVES

a famous/well-known phrase *I was reminded of Einstein's famous phrase: 'God does not play dice.'*

a memorable phrase *In that speech, Churchill used the memorable phrase 'an iron curtain'.*

a colourful phrase *BrE*, **a colorful phrase** *AmE* (=interesting or rude) *His conversation is full of colourful phrases.*

a well-turned phrase (=skilfully invented or chosen) *She creates lifelike characters with a few well-turned phrases.*

an empty phrase (=not sincere or not having any real effect) *The party's promises are just empty phrases.*

VERBS

use a phrase *Gauguin used the phrase 'working from memory' to describe his method.*

hear a phrase *We have all heard the phrase 'greenhouse gases', but do you know what it means?*

coin a phrase (=invent a phrase) *He was the man who coined the phrase 'desktop publishing'.*

borrow a phrase (=use a phrase that someone else invented or used) *Why is everyone – to borrow a phrase from Gore Vidal – 'stating the obvious with a very real sense of discovery'?*

turn a phrase (=say things in a good or interesting way) *This poet knows how to turn a phrase.*

PHRASES

a choice of phrase *It was an unfortunate choice of phrase.*

a turn of phrase (=a way of saying things or saying something) *She had an odd turn of phrase.*

THESAURUS: phrase

expression
a fixed phrase which is used in a language and has a particular meaning:
The teacher gave us a list of ***common*** *English* ***expressions*** *to learn.* | *Students often have difficulty understanding* ***colloquial expressions*** (=informal expressions used in everyday spoken language). | *'In the family way' is an* ***old-fashioned expression*** *which means pregnant.*

idiom
a group of words that has a special meaning which you cannot guess from the meanings of each separate word:
'Under the weather' is an idiom which means ill.

cliché
a phrase that is boring and no longer original because people use it a lot:
The phrase 'at the end of the day' has ***become a real cliché****. | There is some truth in the* ***old cliché*** *that time is a great healer.*

saying/proverb
a well-known phrase that gives advice about life:
There is an ***old*** *Chinese* ***proverb*** *which says 'A journey of a thousand miles starts with a single step'. | Do you know the saying 'A problem shared is a problem halved'?*

slogan
a short phrase that is easy to remember, especially one used in advertising or politics:
Protesters were ***shouting*** *anti-government* ***slogans****. | She started her career writing* ***advertising slogans****.*

motto
a phrase that expresses a person's or organization's beliefs and aims:
The ***school motto*** *was 'Truth and Honour'. | 'Don't do anything today, if you can leave it till tomorrow'* ***has always been my motto****.*

physical Ac *adj*

related to someone's body rather than their mind or emotions

NOUNS

physical activity/exercise *We all know about the health benefits of physical activity.*

physical fitness *You need to work on your physical fitness.*

physical education (=sport and physical exercise, taught as a subject at school) *On Friday afternoons we have physical education.*

physical strength *He had enormous physical strength.*

sb's physical appearance *In our culture we worry too much about physical appearance.*

physical harm (=injury or damage) *If we think a child is at risk of physical harm, we have a duty to tell the authorities.*

physical violence *We will not tolerate threats of physical violence.*

physical abuse (=beating or hurting someone's body) *He had suffered physical and mental abuse as a child.*

physical contact *If there is physical contact between players, there will inevitably be injuries.*

physical condition *The patient's physical condition is stable.*

physical pain *He was in great physical pain.*

physical health *Your grandmother is in good physical health for her age.*

a physical disability (=a condition that makes it difficult for someone to use a part of their body properly) *Her son was born with severe physical disabilities.*

picnic *n*

an occasion when people take food outdoors to eat it, or the food that you eat

VERBS

have a picnic *We decided to have a picnic down by the lake.*

go on/go for a picnic *If the weather's fine, we'll go for a picnic.*

take/bring a picnic (=used about the food itself) *We brought a picnic and a rug to sit on.*

picnic + NOUNS

a picnic lunch (=lunch that consists of a picnic) *It's a lovely day, so I thought we'd have a picnic lunch outside.*

a picnic area/site (=a special area with tables where people can have picnics) *There is a picnic area next to the car park.*

a picnic spot/place (=a place that is suitable for a picnic) *We found a lovely picnic spot by the river.*

a picnic basket/hamper (=a container in which you carry food for a picnic) *We took a picnic hamper with us full of sandwiches and bottles of beer.*

picture *n*

1 a painting, drawing, or photograph

VERBS + picture

draw/paint a picture *She drew a picture of a horse on the blackboard.*

do a picture of sb/sth (=draw or paint a picture) *We had to do a picture of a tree.*

take a picture (=take a photograph) *She took a picture of us standing on top of the mountain.*

print/publish a picture *The newspaper printed the picture on its front page.*

hang a picture (=put it on a wall) *I'm trying to decide where to hang this picture.*

picture + VERBS

a picture shows sth *The picture shows two women talking over a cup of tea.*

a picture hangs somewhere (=it is on the wall somewhere) *The picture hangs in the Museum of Modern Art.*

picture + NOUNS

a picture frame (=the wooden or metal structure surrounding a picture) *The picture frame needs to match the picture.*

PREPOSITIONS

a picture of sb/sth *On the walls of the cave, there are pictures of animals being hunted.*

a picture is of sb/sth (=used to talk about what a picture shows) *The picture is of a river with trees along its banks.*

2 a description or idea of what something is like

ADJECTIVES

a clear/good picture *He still didn't have a clear picture of what had happened.*

an accurate/true/realistic picture *Our aim is to build an accurate picture of the needs of disabled people.*

a detailed picture *We now have a more detailed picture of the bird's habits.*

a complete/full picture *When we have the full picture, then we will make our decision.*

an overall/general picture *The study is intended to provide an overall picture of voting habits.*

a vivid picture (=that gives a clear and strong impression) *Their diaries give us a vivid picture of their lives at the time.*

a distorted/misleading/false picture (=one that is not accurate) *These figures give a misleading picture of the company's financial state.*

a bleak/gloomy/depressing picture (=giving the impression that something is bad) *The article paints a rather bleak picture of the future of our planet.*

a positive picture (=one that makes it seem good) *The article gives a positive picture of the country's recent history.*

a rosy picture (=one that makes something seem better than it really is) *The figures contradict the rosy picture painted by the government.*

a balanced picture (=one that gives equal attention to all the arguments or issues) *Do you believe newspapers give you a balanced picture of events?*

VERBS

have a picture *After I talked to my client, I had a much better picture of what she wanted.*

get a picture *Scientists have been trying to get a better picture of how the drug works.*

a picture emerges (=becomes clear) *We are receiving reports of an earthquake, but as yet no clear picture is emerging.*

build up/form a picture (=gradually get an idea of what something is like) *Detectives are still trying to build up a picture of what happened.*

give/provide a picture *Her book gives us an interesting picture of life in early 19th-century Japan.*

present a picture *The media tends to present a rather grim picture of what's going on in the world.*

paint a picture (=create a particular idea or impression) *The latest survey paints a more positive picture.*

PREPOSITIONS

a picture of sb/sth *We have a good picture of what life was like in those days.*

PHRASES

have/keep a picture in your mind *I've never been there, but I have a picture in my mind of what it is like.*

picturesque *adj* THESAURUS ▸ beautiful

piece *n*

an amount of something that has been separated from the main part

ADJECTIVES

a small/little/tiny piece *The plate shattered into a thousand tiny pieces.*

a big/large/huge piece *We covered the hole with a large piece of wood.*

a long/short piece *I need a long piece of string and some scissors.*

another piece *Can I have another piece of cake?*

equal/equal-sized pieces *She cut the pie into four equal pieces.*

VERBS

cut sth into pieces *Cut the carrots into thin pieces.*

cut off a piece of sth *Cut off a piece of wood five centimetres in length.*

break sth into pieces *The sea was trying to break the ship into pieces.*

break off a piece of sth *He broke off a piece of bread and took a sip of beer.*

smash sth to pieces *The crowd knocked down the statue and smashed it to pieces.*

break/shatter into pieces *She dropped the mirror on the floor where it broke into many small pieces.*

tear sth to pieces *Oliver tore the meat to pieces with his teeth as if he were a wild animal.*

take sth to pieces (=remove a lot of parts from something, especially to repair it or find out how it works) *The mechanic had taken the motorcycle to pieces.*

PREPOSITIONS

a piece of sth *The lid was tied on with a piece of string.*

be in pieces *The map had been folded and unfolded so many times it was now in pieces.*

THESAURUS: piece

bit

of paper | of food | of wood | of metal | of rock | of stone | of glass | of cloth

a piece or part. **Bit** is more informal than **piece** and is often used about smaller pieces: *The notes were written on tiny bits of paper. | He threw a bit of wood onto the fire. | A bit of rock had got inside my shoe.*

P

lump
of sugar | of coal | of metal | of rock | of wood | of clay
a small piece of something solid or firm that does not have a regular shape:
He put seven lumps of sugar into his coffee. | A lump of rock just missed my head. | She picked up a big lump of clay and put it on the wheel.

scrap
of paper | of cloth | of material | of food | of wood
a small piece of something such as paper that is no longer needed:
I wrote the phone number on a scrap of paper. | They used the scraps of material to create the costumes for the play. | The dog was eating scraps of food off the floor.

strip
of paper | of cloth | of fabric | of plastic | of land | of grass | of beach
a long narrow piece of something:
Cut a strip of paper 12 centimetres wide. | Curtains can be held in position using strips of fabric or ribbons. | There was a narrow strip of land between the two houses. | The leather had been ***cut into strips****.*

sheet
of paper | of glass | of metal | of ice | of plastic | of card
a thin flat piece of paper or another material:
She was staring at a blank sheet of paper. | The lake was covered with a huge sheet of ice.

slice
of bread | of toast | of pizza | of cake | of cheese | of meat | of lemon | of tomato
a thin flat piece of bread or other food, cut from a larger piece:
Can I have another slice of bread? | Cut the tomatoes ***into thin slices****.*

chunk
of rock | of ice | of bread | of metal | of fruit
a piece of something solid that does not have a regular shape:
An enormous chunk of rock fell down the side of the mountain. | He wiped round his plate with a chunk of bread. | The fruit was ***cut into*** *large* ***chunks****.*

hunk
of bread | of cheese | of meat | of metal
a large piece with rough edges, which has been cut or has broken off a bigger piece:
Stan cut himself a big hunk of cheese. | A rough hunk of metal was stuck in my shoulder.

block
of ice | of wood | of stone | of marble | of concrete
a large piece of something solid, which has straight sides:
A young man opened the freezer and lifted out a big block of ice. | The statues are carved from solid blocks of wood. | The building was a big ugly block of concrete.

slab
of stone | of rock | of meat | of pie | of butter
a big thick flat piece of something:
The wall was made of long flat slabs of stone. | People wondered how the huge slabs of rock were transported across the island. | Her father was busy cutting slabs of meat into smaller pieces.

cube
of sugar | of ice
a piece that has six square sides:
I dropped five cubes of sugar into my coffee glass. | She put an ***ice cube*** *in her drink. |* ***Cut*** *the eggplant* ***into cubes****.*

wedge
of cheese | of lemon | of pie
a piece that has a thick end and a pointed end, and is shaped like a triangle:
The man in the store cut me a big wedge of cheese. | Serve the fish with a few wedges of lemon.

bar
of chocolate | of soap
a block of something such as chocolate or soap, which has straight sides:
He ate a whole bar of chocolate. | Go to the grocery store and buy yourself a ***candy bar****. | The gang stole* ***gold bars*** *worth more than £26 million.*

segment
one of the parts of an orange or grapefruit, after you have taken off the peel (=the hard outside part):
Divide *the oranges* ***into segments****.*

a very small piece

fragment
of rock | of bone | of glass | of metal
a small piece that has broken off something, especially something hard:
The archaeologists found tiny fragments of bone. | The window shattered, covering them with fragments of glass.

crumb
a very small piece of bread, cake etc:
There were just a few crumbs left on the plate.

> **Breadcrumb** is usually spelled as one word.

speck
of dust | of dirt
a piece of something such as dirt or dust which is so small you almost cannot see it:
She brushed the specks of dust from the table.

drop
of water | of rain | of blood | of moisture | of milk | of whisky
a very small amount of a liquid:
A drop of water fell on her bare arm. | There were tiny drops of blood on the floor.

pile *n*

a group of several things of the same type that are put on top of each other

ADJECTIVES

a neat pile *She picked up the books and put them in neat piles.*

a huge pile *His mother came in carrying a huge pile of ironing in her arms.*

PREPOSITIONS

a pile of sth *Flora looked through a pile of magazines.*

pill *n*

a small solid piece of medicine that you swallow whole

VERBS

take a pill *Have you taken your pills today?*

swallow a pill *She swallowed the pill with a few sips of water.*

a doctor prescribes pills (=tells someone to take them) *Her doctor prescribed some pills for her blood pressure.*

NOUNS + pill

a sleeping pill *I took a sleeping pill to help me sleep.*

vitamin pills *He was taking large quantities of vitamin pills to keep himself healthy.*

pipe *n*

a tube through which a liquid or gas flows

ADJECTIVES/NOUNS + pipe

a burst/broken pipe *Burst pipes can cause a lot of damage.*

a water/gas/fuel pipe *Insulating the hot water pipes will save you money on your heating bill.*

a waste pipe (=one for taking away used water from a sink, shower, washing machine etc) *The waste pipe must be blocked because the sink's still full of water.*

VERBS

a pipe leaks *One of the pipes in the bathroom is leaking.*

a pipe bursts *A pipe burst and flooded the kitchen.*

a pipe freezes *When the pipes froze last winter, we had no water.*

pipes lead somewhere *There are two pipes leading to the boiler, for hot and cold water.*

block a pipe *Something is blocking the waste pipe.*

lay a pipe (=put it carefully in place) *They were digging a trench to lay water pipes.*

pity *n*

sympathy for someone who is suffering or unhappy

PHRASES

be filled with/full of pity *His heart was filled with pity for the children who had survived the earthquake.*

take/have pity on sb (=feel sorry for someone and treat them with sympathy) *He was expecting a long prison sentence but the judge took pity on him.*

an object of pity (=someone who people feel sorry for) *He was a proud man and didn't want to be an object of pity.*

a feeling/sense of pity *Annie had a sudden feeling of pity for her aunt.*

a wave/surge of pity (=a sudden strong feeling of pity) *The woman looked so lost that a wave of pity washed over me.*

VERBS

feel pity *I felt pity for all those people who have lost their money.*

show pity *After they won the war, they showed no pity.*

ADJECTIVES

little/no pity *Meryl felt no pity for him, just contempt.*

some pity *"Have some pity!" begged Janet, almost in tears.*

PREPOSITIONS

pity for sb *I feel nothing but pity for him.*

with/without pity *He pushed her away without pity.*

out of pity (=because someone feels sorry for another person) *I think he only stayed with me out of pity.*

place *n*

1 a space or area, for example a particular point on a surface or in a room, building, town, city etc

ADJECTIVES/NOUNS + place

a nice/lovely/wonderful place *There are lots of nice places to eat.*

an interesting/fascinating place *I liked Morocco – it's a fascinating place.*

a good/great place (=suitable for something) *This is a good place for the children to play.*

a perfect place/the ideal place (=one that is extremely suitable for something) *Colorado is the perfect place for skiing.*

a safe place *Make sure you keep your passport in a safe place.*

the right/wrong place *These books are all in the wrong place.*

a meeting/gathering place *The club was a meeting place for young musicians.*

a hiding place *He watched them from his hiding place.*

place + NOUNS

a place name (=the name of a town, city etc) *A lot of the place names are Spanish in origin.*

PREPOSITIONS

in a place *Everything had been put back in a different place.*

a place for (doing) sth *The island is an ideal place for a holiday.*

in places (=in some places) *The wall was quite damp in places.*

PHRASES

sb's place of birth *formal: I need to know your date and place of birth.*

sth's place of origin *formal* (=the place where something came from) *The goods are clearly marked with their place of origin.*

places of interest (=places, such as areas of a city or museums, that are interesting to visit) *Jo pointed out the places of interest as we drove along.*

a place of worship *The Great Mosque has been a place of worship for Muslims for centuries.*

from place to place *I've spent the day dashing about from place to place.*

all over the place (=everywhere) *There were bags of rubbish lying all over the place.*

2 an opportunity to go to a university, go on a course, be a member of a team etc

VERBS

get a place *It's really hard to get a place on the course.*

have a place *She has a place at college starting in September.*

win a place *That year, he won a place at Oxford University.*

offer sb a place *The school called to offer him a place.*

lose your place *If you don't come to training you might lose your place on the team.*

refuse sb a place *She had been refused a place at her first-choice school.*

PREPOSITIONS

a place at a university/college/school etc *They were all competing for a place at the school.*

a place on a course/team/committee *There are still a few places left on the course.*

a place in a team/contest/nursing home *He beat 3,000 others to win a place in the national finals.*

plagiarize (*also* **plagiarise** *BrE*) *v*

THESAURUS **copy² (2)**, **steal**

plain¹ *adj*

1 very clear, and easy to understand or recognize

PHRASES

it is plain (that)... *It was plain that Giles was not going to agree.*

make it plain (=state something clearly) *I made it quite plain that I would never marry him.*

make yourself plain (=state something clearly, so that you cannot be misunderstood) *If you do that again you will be punished. Do I make myself plain?*

sth is plain to see (=easy to recognize or understand) *The advantages of living closer to work are plain to see.*

2 not beautiful or attractive

THESAURUS: plain

hideous, grotesque, revolting, repulsive, unattractive, unsightly, plain, homely → ugly (1)

3 simple and with no decoration, or using simple and clear words

THESAURUS: plain

plain, crude → **simple**

plain² *n* a large area of flat land

ADJECTIVES/NOUNS + plain

the vast/great plain(s) *Beyond the mountains lay the vast plains of the Central Valley.*

the open plain(s) *On the open plains of East Africa are zebras, antelopes, and gazelles.*

a flat plain *Here a group of small hills rises out of the flat plain.*

a grassy plain *The village is situated on the high grassy plains at the foot of the Sierra.*

a fertile plain (=good for growing crops) *The rains washed soil down to create fertile plains.*

a flood plain (=an area of flat land on either side of a river, which is sometimes covered in water) *The river's flood plain turns to hard sun-baked mud during the dry season.*

the Great Plains (=a large area of high flat land in the central United States and Canada) *It is estimated that there were more than 30 million buffalo on the Great Plains.*

plan¹ *n*

1 a set of actions for achieving something in the future, especially a set of actions that has been considered carefully and in detail

VERBS

have a plan *We have a plan for dealing with this type of situation.*

make a plan *Mary has been busy making plans for her wedding.*

come up with a plan (=think of a plan) *The chairman must come up with a plan to save the company $6 million.*

draw up a plan (=prepare a written plan) *The company has already drawn up plans to develop the site.*

devise/formulate/form a plan (=make a detailed plan) *He devised a daring plan of escape.*

carry out a plan (*also* **implement/execute a plan** *formal*) (=do what has been planned) *The bombers were arrested before they could carry out their plans.*

announce/unveil/reveal a plan (=officially tell people about it) *The minister unveiled the government's plans for modernising the health service.*

outline a plan (=describe it in a general way) *They listened carefully as he outlined his plan.*

approve/reject a plan (=officially say yes or no to it) *The plan was approved at a board meeting on 24 December.*

keep to/stick to a plan *We're sticking to our original plan.*

oppose a plan *Local residents are opposing plans to enlarge the airport.*

abandon/scrap/cancel a plan (=decide not to continue with it) *The plan had to be scrapped because it was too expensive.*

shelve a plan (=not continue with it, although you might continue with it later) *The plans will be shelved until the financial situation improves.*

ADJECTIVES/NOUNS + plan

a detailed plan *The generals drew up detailed plans for the invasion.*

a cunning/clever/ingenious plan *The gang devised a cunning plan to rob the bank.*

an ambitious plan *The plan was very ambitious, but it worked.*

sb's future/long-term plans *The prime minister outlined his long-term plans at the party conference.*

a five-year/ten-year etc plan *UNESCO has a 25-year plan to provide basic education to all.*

a business plan *The bank wants to look at the business plan before lending us any money.*

a peace plan *Both sides have agreed to implement the UN peace plan.*

a rescue/escape plan *The prisoners had a daring escape plan.*

a grand plan (=a plan that involves doing a lot of things in order to achieve something big) *The owners have grand plans for the business.*

a master plan (=a detailed plan for dealing with a complicated situation) *The governors came up with a master plan for saving the school.*

a contingency plan (=a plan for dealing with events, especially bad events, that might happen) *The hospital has drawn up contingency plans for coping with a large-scale emergency.*

PREPOSITIONS

a plan for (doing) sth *The government's plans for developing cleaner sources of energy will cost money.*

PHRASES

go according to plan (=happen in the way that was arranged) *If everything goes according to plan, we'll finish in January.*

a plan of action (*also* **an action plan**) (=a list of things that you must do to deal with something) *Ministers are discussing a plan of action to deal with the crisis.*

a plan of attack (=a plan to attack or achieve something) *The heads of the armed forces met to work on a coordinated plan of attack.*

2 something you intend to do

VERBS

have plans to do sth *I have no plans to retire yet.*

change your plans *We had to change our plans at the last minute.*

abandon/give up your plans *The school has abandoned its plans to enter the contest.*

cancel your plans *The weather got worse, and we cancelled our plans for a barbecue.*

ADJECTIVES

sb's immediate plans (=what they are going to do next) *So what are your immediate plans after graduation?*

a firm/definite plan *She had not made any firm plans for the summer.*

the best plan *BrE* (=the best thing to do) *I think the best plan is to take the train.*

PREPOSITIONS

plans for sth *Do you have any plans for the weekend?*

PHRASES

a change of plan *The day before my flight, my boss phoned and said there'd been a change of plan.*

plan[2] *v*

to think carefully about something you want to do, and decide how and when you will do it

ADVERBS

plan sth carefully *No matter how carefully you plan your lesson, something often goes wrong.*

plan sth meticulously (=extremely carefully) *The attack was meticulously planned to cause the maximum amount of damage.*

plan ahead *All businesses have to plan ahead for the next financial year.*

originally plan sth *The concert was originally planned for Saturday, but it had to be postponed.*

PREPOSITIONS

plan for sth (=make plans for something that you expect to happen) *You need to plan for your retirement.*

sth is planned for a date (=it is expected to happen then) *The concert was planned for June 30th.*

plan for a number of people (=make your preparations based on a number of people) *We had planned for over 100 guests at the party.*

PHRASES

go as planned (=happen the way it was

planned) *The trip didn't go as planned, and we missed our plane.*

plan for the future *You need to plan for the future and think about what you're going to do after university.*

plan sth in advance *We should plan our visit in advance because hotel rooms soon get fully booked.*

plan sth to the last detail *If you are cooking for a large number of people, you need to plan everything to the last detail.*

have sth (all) planned out (=you have planned everything that will happen) *He had his whole life planned out and was going to become a millionaire by the age of 30.*

P

plane *n*

a vehicle that flies in the air and has wings

plane + VERBS

a plane flies *Several planes flew overhead.*

a plane takes off (=goes into the air) *The plane took off from John F. Kennedy airport.*

a plane lands (=moves safely down onto the ground) *Because of the fog, our plane had to land at Luton.*

a plane touches down (=lands safely on the ground) *As soon as the plane touched down on the runway, I felt better.*

a plane leaves *My plane leaves in an hour.*

a plane taxies (=moves slowly along on the ground) *The plane taxied down the runway.*

a plane crashes *Their plane crashed shortly after take-off.*

a plane crash-lands (=lands in a sudden and dangerous way because of a problem) *Their small plane crash-landed on a busy road yesterday.*

a plane comes down (=lands or crashes) *The plane came down in the sea.*

a plane carries passengers *The plane can carry over 400 passengers.*

VERBS + plane

catch/take a plane *She caught the first plane back to New York.*

get on a plane (*also* **board a plane**) *We got on the plane and found our seats.*

get off a plane *Would he ever see her again after they got off the plane?*

step off a plane *As we stepped off the plane at Madrid airport, the heat hit us.*

fly/pilot a plane *I admire the guys who flew those planes.*

land a plane *The pilot managed to land the plane safely on the beach.*

shoot down a plane *The guerrillas shot down an Israeli fighter plane.*

hijack a plane (=take control of it using violence or threats) *The plane was hijacked by four terrorists.*

ADJECTIVES/NOUNS + plane

a private plane *He flew to Las Vegas in his private plane.*

a passenger plane *The airport is mainly used by passenger planes.*

a cargo plane (=for carrying goods) *cargo planes carrying emergency supplies for victims of the earthquake*

a military plane *Air Force jets intercepted two military planes that had entered the no-fly zone.*

a fighter plane (=a small fast military plane) *US fighter planes flew over the city.*

plane + NOUNS

a plane crash *Over 200 people died in the plane crash.*

a plane ticket *He said he would pay for her plane ticket.*

PREPOSITIONS

by plane *He arrived by plane three hours ago.*

on a plane *She slept on the plane.*

aboard/on board a plane *It is not clear how many passengers were aboard the plane.*

If you are talking about a small plane, use **in**, not **on**: *We flew over the jungle* ***in a small*** *plane.*

planet *n*

1 a very large round object in space that moves around the Sun or another star

planet + NOUNS

the planet Mars/Jupiter etc *There may be life on the planet Mars.*

ADJECTIVES

a distant planet (=far away) *One day we will be able to travel to distant planets.*

VERBS

orbit a planet (=go round a planet) *The spacecraft will orbit the planet Jupiter.*

PHRASES

a creature/alien from another planet *The film is about creatures from another planet who land on earth.*

the surface of the planet *Sunlight passes through the atmosphere to heat the surface of the planet.*

2 our world – used especially when talking about the environment

VERBS

save the planet *It may be too late to save the planet.*

live on a planet *There are billions of people living on our planet.*

destroy the planet *Man's activities are destroying the planet.*

ADJECTIVES

our planet *Oceans cover two-thirds of our planet's surface.*

the whole/entire planet *Global warming threatens the whole planet.*

planet + NOUNS

planet Earth *Scientists have various theories about how life began on planet Earth.*

plant *n*

1 a living thing that has leaves and roots and grows in earth

ADJECTIVES/NOUNS + plant

a common/rare plant *Bluebells are a common plant in woodland areas.*

a wild plant *Many wild plants are in danger of dying out.*

a garden plant *Butterflies feed on the flowers of several garden plants.*

a tomato/strawberry/banana/potato etc plant *Tomato plants are easy to grow in a greenhouse.*

an exotic/tropical plant (=one that grows in hot countries) *Exotic plants usually have to be grown in a greenhouse in this country.*

a potted plant (*also* **a pot plant** *BrE*) (=one that is grown in a container) *He leaves his house key under a potted plant on the porch.*

a house plant (=one that is grown in a pot in the house) *Rubber plants make excellent house plants.*

a climbing plant (=one that grows up a wall, tree etc) *The fence was covered with climbing plants.*

plant + VERBS

a plant grows *The plant grows to a height of about 20 cm.*

a plant flowers (=produces flowers) *Many plants start to flower in May.*

a plant thrives/flourishes (=it grows well) *A lot of plants thrive in partial shade.*

a plant dies *My house plants died from lack of water.*

a plant droops (=bends and looks weak) *The potted plant on his desk was drooping so I watered it.*

VERBS + plant

grow plants (*also* **cultivate plants** *formal*): *She grew most of these plants from seed.*

water a plant *He could see her watering the plants in her small garden.*

plant + NOUNS

a plant pot *The lemon tree needs a bigger plant pot.*

a plant species (*also* **a species of plant**) (=a type of plant) *Many plant species are becoming rare because of the use of chemicals for farming.*

plant life (=plants) *There is a lot of plant life near the river.*

PHRASES

a plant is in flower (=it produces flowers) *By May, most of the garden plants were in flower.*

2 a large factory, especially one where things such as energy, cars, or chemicals are produced

ADJECTIVES/NOUNS + plant

a car plant *Mazda plans to build a big new car plant in Thailand.*

a power plant (=where electricity is produced) *The old power plant will be shut down in November.*

a chemical plant *The air is filled with pollution from chemical plants.*

an assembly plant (=where different parts of a product, especially cars, are put together) *Production at the truck assembly plant is being increased to cope with demand.*

a manufacturing plant (=where products are produced or made) *The engines are produced at Rolls-Royce's manufacturing plant in Derby.*

an industrial plant (=where goods or substances such as gas or steel are produced in large quantities) *When industrial plants close in the US, jobs move overseas.*

a processing/treatment plant (=where materials are made cleaner, safer etc) *There are plans to build a water treatment plant to provide fresh drinking water for the islanders.*

a recycling plant (=where used materials are treated so that they can be used again) *The council has just opened a huge recycling plant to deal with the city's waste.*

VERBS

run/operate a plant *General Motors operates several plants in the country.*

a plant opens *The UK's biggest recycling plant has opened in Huddersfield.*

a plant closes (down)/shuts (down) *Plants are closing all over Europe as the recession deepens.*

a plant produces/makes/manufactures sth *The New Jersey plant produces 360,000 televisions a year.*

THESAURUS: plant

facility, plant, works, mill, refinery, foundry, assembly line/production line, sweatshop → factory

plate *n*

1 a flat and usually round dish that you eat from or serve food on

ADJECTIVES/NOUNS + plate

a clean/dirty plate *She put the clean plates away in one of the kitchen cupboards.*

an empty plate *After the meal, he cleared away the empty plates.*

P

a dinner plate (=a big plate used for the main course) *How many dinner plates will we need?*

a side plate (=a small plate used for bread, vegetables etc) *The vegetables were neatly arranged on a side plate.*

VERBS

wash/clean the plates *After dinner, I washed the plates and put them away.*

clear (away) the plates *The waiter began to clear away the plates.*

put the plates out (=put them on a table) *He put the plates out in preparation for the meal.*

PREPOSITIONS

a plate of sth *She prepared a plate of sandwiches.*

on a plate *He finished everything that was on his plate.*

2 a metal sign with words or numbers on it

NOUNS + plate

a number/licence/registration plate (=on a car) *The robbers used a car with a false number plate.*

a name plate *He had a name plate on his door.*

platform *n*

the place where you get on and off a train at a station

NOUNS + platform

a station platform *A public telephone is situated on the station platform.*

a railway platform *She was standing on the railway platform.*

VERBS

depart/leave from a platform *The next train to Cambridge will depart from Platform 3.*

arrive at a platform *Eventually the train arrived at the platform.*

wait/stand on a platform *A few passengers were already waiting on the platform.*

play[1] *v*

1 to take part in a game or sport

NOUNS

play tennis/badminton/golf etc *I usually play tennis once a week.*

play football/soccer/baseball/basketball etc *Like all boys, he loves playing soccer.*

play cards/chess/dominoes etc *Two old men were playing chess.*

play a game/match *Do you want to play another game?*

ADVERBS

play well/brilliantly/superbly *She played very well in the game last night.*

play badly/poorly *He played badly in the first match.*

PREPOSITIONS

play against sb *Manchester United will play against Chelsea in the final of the competition.*

play for a team *He used to play for the college football team.*

play in a competition *He played in the last World Cup.*

PHRASES

see/watch sb play *I sometimes watch Arsenal play.*

THESAURUS: play

go

swimming | jogging | running | skiing | bowling | sailing

to do a particular type of activity - used with verbs that end in **-ing**:

Do you want to go swimming on Saturday? | I go jogging about three times a week. | Going skiing can be very expensive.

do

judo | karate | aerobics

to play certain sports, especially sports that are not team sports:

I used to do judo at school. | She does aerobics twice a week.

2 to do things that you enjoy - used about children and pets

PHRASES

like/love to play *Our dog loves to play.*

let sb play *His mother doesn't let him play with other children.*

PREPOSITIONS

play with sth *She spent the afternoon playing with her dolls.*

play with sb *He should be outside playing with his friends.*

play in the street/park etc *When I was young, we could play in the street.*

3 to perform a piece of music on a musical instrument

ADVERBS

play sth well *He plays the piano very well.*

play sth beautifully *I thought she played the piece beautifully.*

play sth badly *I can play the violin very badly.*

play together *The band have been playing together for about three years.*

NOUNS

play the trumpet/piano/guitar etc *He's been playing the guitar for over 40 years.*

play a musical instrument *Can you play any musical instruments?*

play a song/tune/piece *At the concert she mainly played songs from her latest record.*

play music *The band started playing music together at school.*

play a concert *The singer will play a series of concerts in New York.*

PREPOSITIONS

play in a band/orchestra/group etc *My sister used to play in a jazz band.*

play with sb/sth *She plays with some friends from college.*

play sth on the piano/guitar etc *Hendrix played the song on the electric guitar.*

PHRASES

learn (how) to play *Joe is learning to play the trumpet.*

teach sb (how) to play *My dad taught me to play the piano.*

play² *n*

a story that is written to be performed by actors, especially in a theatre

NOUNS + play

a stage play (=a play in a theatre) *I occasionally write reviews of local stage plays.*

a TV/radio play (=a play written to be performed on TV or radio) *This horror story would make a good radio play.*

a school play *I got a small part in the school play.*

VERBS + play

write a play *Shakespeare wrote a play about King Henry V.*

go to (see) a play *While we were in New York, we went to a play.*

see a play *I've never seen the play.*

watch a play *Some of the audience were talking instead of watching the play.*

perform a play *The play was performed by Brighton Youth Theatre.*

act/perform/appear in a play *She acted in many plays on the London stage.*

do a play *spoken* (=organize it or perform in it) *Bob asked if I would do this play, and I agreed.*

put on/produce/stage a play (=organize it) *The school puts on a Nativity play every Christmas.*

⚠ Don't say 'give a play'. Say **put on a play**.

direct a play (=tell the actors what to do) *The play is directed by Paulette Randall.*

rehearse a play (=practise it) *We spent weeks rehearsing the play.*

play + VERBS

a play opens (=its performances start) *The play opens in San Francisco on Wednesday for a three-week run.*

a play runs (=it continues to be performed) *The play ran for five months.*

a play closes (=its performances stop) *The play closes on Sunday, so don't miss it!*

a play is set somewhere (=it takes place in a particular place or time) *The play is set in France in the 1930s.*

PREPOSITIONS

a play about sb/sth *It is a play about friendship.*

a play by sb *The opera is based on a play by Sophocles.*

in a play *It is one of the most important scenes in the play.*

player *n*

1 someone who takes part in a game or sport

ADJECTIVES

a good player *I like golf, but I'm not a very good player.*

a skilful/talented/gifted player *There are plenty of talented players on the team.*

a great/brilliant/outstanding player *Babe Ruth was one of the greatest baseball players of all time.*

a top player *Top players can earn huge amounts of money.*

the (world's) number one player *She has been the world's number one player for the last two years.*

the star player (=the best player) *He is the team's star player, and has scored over 20 goals this season.*

a professional/amateur player *Jeff wants to become a professional basketball player.*

an experienced player *She is the most experienced player on the team.*

a world-class player (=one of the world's best players) *The club has some world-class players.*

a promising young player (=someone who looks like they could become a good player) *The coach is always looking out for promising young players.*

an exciting player *Ronaldinho is one of the world's most exciting players.*

a terrible player (=one who plays very badly) *I used to be a terrible chess player.*

NOUNS + player

a basketball/tennis/rugby etc player *She's one of the college's best tennis players.*

a chess/bridge/card etc player *Chess players have to think several moves ahead.*

a Manchester United/Giants etc player *The Liverpool players were unhappy with the referee's decision.*

VERBS

buy/sell a player *The manager will have to sell one or two of his existing players.*

sign a player (=officially arrange for him or her to play on your team) *Each summer, football clubs try to sign players for the new season.*

a player is sent off (=is ordered to leave the game as a punishment) *United had one of their players sent off for arguing with the referee.*

P

the players come on/off *The players came off the field at half-time.*

2 someone who plays a musical instrument

NOUNS + player

a trumpet/guitar/saxophone etc player *He was one of the finest trumpet players of his generation.*

ADJECTIVES

an accomplished/gifted/talented player (=a very skilful player) *She is an accomplished violin player.*

plea *n*

1 an urgent request

ADJECTIVES

an urgent plea *The Red Cross sent out an urgent plea for water, food, and medicine.*

a desperate plea *The charity issued a desperate plea for more aid to help the homeless.*

an impassioned/passionate plea (=a request that is full of strong feeling) *His speech was an impassioned plea for an end to the fighting.*

a personal plea *The chairman made a personal plea, asking the workers not to strike.*

repeated pleas *Despite repeated pleas, nothing has been done about the situation.*

VERBS

make/issue a plea *The government made a plea to the terrorists to release the hostages.*

hear/listen to a plea *The council heard pleas from local people, urging them to stop the development.*

ignore/reject a plea *She said the neighbours had ignored her pleas to keep the noise down.*

accept a plea *He accepted her plea for forgiveness.*

PREPOSITIONS

a plea for sth *The prime minister made a plea for the release of the hostages.*

a plea to sb *Leading scientists issued a plea to politicians to take action on climate change.*

PHRASES

a plea for help *He ignored their pleas for help.*

2 a statement by someone in a court of law saying whether they are guilty or not

ADJECTIVES

a guilty/not guilty plea (*also* **a plea of guilty/not guilty**) *She served two years in prison after a guilty plea on tax charges.*

VERBS

make/enter a plea (=present a plea to a court of law) *His lawyer entered a not guilty plea on his behalf.*

accept a plea *The judge accepted a guilty plea on behalf of the businessman on charges of tax evasion.*

reject a plea *The court had rejected his plea.*

change a plea *She changed her plea from guilty to not guilty.*

pleased *adj* THESAURUS ▸ happy

pleasure *n*

the feeling of happiness, enjoyment, or satisfaction that you get from an experience

ADJECTIVES

great/enormous/immense pleasure *Her books have brought enormous pleasure to people.*

sheer/pure pleasure (=pleasure with no other emotion mixed with it) *He studied ancient languages for the sheer pleasure of learning.*

genuine/real pleasure *She smiled with genuine pleasure.*

obvious pleasure *He took obvious pleasure in my embarrassment.*

an unexpected pleasure *What an unexpected pleasure seeing you here.*

considerable pleasure *He derives considerable pleasure from writing.*

endless pleasure (=very great and lasting) *Children often get endless pleasure from playing with simple toys.*

VERBS

give (sb) pleasure *Over the years, working with young actors has given me a lot of pleasure.*

bring pleasure to sb (=give someone pleasure – more formal) *His singing has brought pleasure to millions.*

find pleasure in (doing) sth *I find great pleasure in reading.*

get pleasure from/out of sth (*also* **derive pleasure from sth** *formal*): *I derive great pleasure from seeing my grandchildren.*

take pleasure in (doing) sth (=enjoy doing something, especially because this makes someone else feel uncomfortable) *He took great pleasure in telling his boss that he was leaving.*

show/express pleasure *Mrs Dempsey showed no pleasure in seeing her daughter.*

feel/experience pleasure *He felt pleasure in his own ability.*

PREPOSITIONS

with pleasure *She sipped her drink with obvious pleasure.*

for pleasure *Is your trip for business or pleasure?*

PHRASES

sth is a source of pleasure *Her garden was a constant source of pleasure.*

pledge *n*

a serious promise or agreement

ADJECTIVES

a firm pledge *The minister gave a firm pledge to spend more money on schools.*

a solemn pledge (=serious and firm) *The*

manager has given us a solemn pledge that she will deal with the problem.

a personal pledge *He made a personal pledge to help us in whatever way he could.*

NOUNS + pledge

an election/campaign/manifesto pledge *The governor had kept her campaign pledge to reduce taxes.*

VERBS

make/give a pledge *Several European countries made similar pledges.*

take a pledge *literary* (=make one, especially formally) *He took a pledge never to drink alcohol again.*

honour/fulfil a pledge *formal* (*also* **keep a pledge**) (=do what you promised to do) *People want political parties to honour their pledges.*

abandon a pledge (*also* **renege on a pledge**) *formal* (=not keep it) *The government reneged on its electoral pledges.*

sign a pledge *The group is asking politicians to sign a pledge refusing to support the war.*

repeat a pledge *The party has repeated its pledge not to increase university fees.*

PHRASES

the pledge of allegiance (=a pledge which all US citizens have to make to obey the US Constitution) *Immigrants are sometimes asked to make a formal pledge of allegiance to their new country.*

pledge of support *We have received pledges of support from several leading companies.*

plenty *determiner* THESAURUS **enough**

plot *n*

1 a secret plan by a group of people to do something bad

NOUNS + plot

a murder plot *He was questioned about an attempted murder plot.*

an assassination plot *The story is about an assassination plot against the president.*

a terrorist plot *Police foiled a terrorist plot to attack a nuclear reactor.*

a bomb plot *She was arrested on suspicion of involvement in a bomb plot.*

VERBS

mastermind a plot (=be in charge of organizing it) *He is accused of masterminding a plot to bring down the government.*

uncover/discover a plot *Detectives uncovered a plot to blow up parliament.*

foil a plot (=prevent it from being successful) *The plot was foiled when he was stopped by US Customs agents.*

hatch a plot (=make one) *They have admitted hatching a plot to kill the president.*

PREPOSITIONS

a plot against sb/sth *He believed there was a plot against him.*

PHRASES

be involved in a plot *He was involved in a plot to kidnap the Pope.*

be part of a plot *He said that the accusations were part of a plot against him.*

be the victim of a plot *Some people say that the former prime minister was the victim of a plot by her political opponents.*

2 the events that form the story of a book, play, or film

ADJECTIVES

a complicated/complex plot *I found the plot rather complicated.*

a simple plot *The movie has a simple plot that children can easily follow.*

the basic/main plot *The film version follows the same basic plot as the book.*

VERBS

the plot develops/unfolds *We realize, as the plot develops, that the central character is not what she seems.*

a plot revolves around sth (=it is mainly about a particular person or thing) *The plot revolves around the mysterious disappearance of a young dancer.*

follow a plot (=understand what is happening) *There are a lot of different characters in the story and I found it hard to follow the plot.*

plot + NOUNS

a plot twist (*also* **a twist in the plot**) (=an unexpected event) *There is a clever plot twist at the end of the film.*

plump *adj* THESAURUS **fat[1] (1)**

poach *v* THESAURUS **cook[1]**, **steal**

pocket *n*

a small bag in clothes for carrying things in

ADJECTIVES/NOUNS + pocket

a back/front/side pocket *He took some money from his back pocket.*

an inside pocket (=on the inside of a coat, jacket etc) *The man pulled a photo from the inside pocket of his jacket.*

a jacket/trouser/shirt etc pocket (*also* **the pocket of your jacket/trousers/shirt etc**) *She slipped the map into her jacket pocket.*

a breast pocket (=on the chest) *There was a silk handkerchief in his breast pocket.*

VERBS

put sth in your pocket *I put the £5 note in my pocket.*

stuff/thrust sth in your pocket (=put it there quickly and carelessly) *He took off his cap and stuffed it in his pocket.*

take sth out of your pocket *She took a pair of dark glasses out of her pocket.*
check/search/go through sb's pockets *I checked my pockets for my train ticket but it wasn't there.*
reach into your pocket (*also* **feel/dig in your pocket**) (=put your hand into your pocket to find something) *"Do you want a cigarette?" he asked, reaching into his pocket.*
empty your pockets (*also* **turn out your pockets**) *His mother made him turn out his pockets.*

PHRASES
with your hands in your pockets *I saw him wandering along the beach with his hands in his pockets.*
sb's pockets are bulging (=they are very full) *His pockets were bulging with sweets he'd bought for his children.*

P

poem *n*
a piece of writing in short lines, often using words that rhyme

ADJECTIVES/NOUNS + poem
a famous poem *"I wandered lonely as a cloud" is the first line of a famous poem by William Wordsworth.*
a long/short poem *'Kaddish' is the title of a long poem by Allen Ginsberg.*
a love poem *We had to read Shakespeare's love poems when I was at school.*
an anonymous poem (=the name of the writer is not known) *The verse comes from an anonymous poem.*
a lyric/narrative/epic etc poem (=a poem in a particular style) *I was given a copy of the epic Greek poem, the 'Odyssey'.*

VERBS
write a poem (*also* **compose a poem** *formal*): *I've been writing short stories and poems for years.*
learn/memorize a poem *He had learned the whole poem by heart as a boy.*
read a poem *We had to read Shelley's poems for our English literature exam.*
recite a poem (=say it aloud without looking at it and reading it) *The little girl was standing up, reciting a poem.*

PHRASES
a book/volume/collection of poems *She has a new collection of poems coming out soon.*
an anthology of poems (=a book of poems by different people) *He gave me an anthology of poems for children.*
the opening/closing line of a poem *"A thing of beauty is a joy forever" is the opening line of a poem by Keats.*

poet *n* someone who writes poems

ADJECTIVES/NOUNS + poet
a good/great/fine poet *Pablo Neruda is one of Chile's greatest poets.*
a famous/well-known/distinguished poet *Lord Byron was probably the most famous poet in Europe at this time.*
a 19th-century/20th-century etc poet *Arthur Rimbaud was a well-known 19th-century French poet.*
a modern/contemporary poet (=living now) *He is one of this country's leading contemporary poets.*

poetry *n*
poems in general, or the art of writing them

ADJECTIVES
English/French/Greek etc poetry *He was a student of English poetry.*
modern/contemporary poetry *I find a lot of modern poetry difficult to understand.*

VERBS
write poetry *Lord Byron was famous for writing poetry.*
learn poetry *The teacher made us learn a lot of poetry by heart.*
recite poetry (=say it aloud from memory) *The children had to stand up and recite poetry.*

poetry + NOUNS
a poetry reading (=when poems are read to people, usually by the writer) *The festival consists of poetry readings and workshops.*
a poetry book *My grandfather loved reading poetry books.*

PHRASES
a book/volume of poetry *He has had two books of poetry published.*
an anthology of poetry (=a collection of poems by different writers) *She edited an anthology of poetry by the Liverpool poets.*
a line of poetry *She often quoted lines of poetry.*
a piece of poetry *For homework we had to memorize a piece of poetry.*

poignant *adj* THESAURUS **emotional (1)**

point *n*
1 a single fact, idea, or opinion that is part of an argument or discussion

ADJECTIVES
a good/excellent point *I think that's a very good point.*
an interesting point *He makes an interesting point in the next paragraph.*
an important point *Cost is an important point to bear in mind.*
a serious point *He's making a joke but there is a serious point to it.*

a valid point (=clearly true, fair, or important) *She raised a number of valid points in the speech.*

a general point *I'd like to make one further general point.*

a similar point/the same point *Other writers have made a similar point.*

the main/central point *The conclusion should summarize the main points of your essay.*

one final/last point *There is one final point I would like to make.*

VERBS

make a point *He makes the point that computers can also make mistakes.*

raise/bring up a point (=mention it) *I was hoping that someone would raise that point.*

illustrate/demonstrate a point *A simple example will illustrate the point.*

prove your/a point (=prove that what you say is right) *He was determined to prove his point.*

emphasize/underline a point *He showed some pictures of the damage, in order to underline his point.*

understand a point *I'm sorry, I don't understand your point.*

see/take/get sb's point (=understand or agree with it - often used when you want to add something else) *OK, I take your point, but there are still other problems to deal with.*

have a point (=used when saying that what someone says is right) *I hadn't thought of that, but maybe she has a point.*

labour the point *BrE*, **belabor the point** *AmE* (=keep repeating something too much) *I don't mean to labour the point, but why didn't you tell me sooner?*

clarify a point (=make it clearer) *Could you clarify a couple of points for me?*

press your point (=keep insisting that it is true) *Even though the others disagreed, he continued to press his point.*

PHRASES

put/get your point across (=make people understand it) *I think we got our point across to the audience.*

point taken (=used to say to someone that you accept what they say) *All right, point taken - I should have asked you first.*

2 the most important fact or idea

> **Grammar**
> In this meaning, you always say **the point**.

VERBS

get/come (straight) to the point (=talk about the most important thing immediately) *I haven't much time so let's get straight to the point.*

miss the point (=not understand it) *I think you're missing the point - the money does not belong to us.*

get the point (=understand it) *He didn't get the point at first.*

PHRASES

the point is (that)... *The point is that going by bus would be a lot cheaper.*

that's the (whole) point *That's the point. She didn't tell us what was going on.*

that's not the point *We'd earn a lot of money, but that's not the point.*

be beside the point (=be not the most important thing to consider) *He's the best person for the job so his age is beside the point.*

more to the point (=what is more important) *When did she leave, and, more to the point, why?*

3 an exact moment, time, or stage in the development of something

ADJECTIVES/NOUNS + point

a high point (=of success or happiness) *Winning the World Championship was the high point of my career.*

a low point (=of failure or unhappiness) *She helped me when I was at a low point in my life.*

a starting point *The following recipes are a good starting point for making your own bread.*

a turning point (=when an important change or improvement happens) *The elections were a turning point in the nation's history.*

crisis point (=when a situation becomes extremely serious) *The tensions within the country have reached crisis point.*

breaking point (=when someone or something can no longer deal with something) *Our resources are stretched to breaking point.*

bursting point (=when something is completely full) *The hospital was full to bursting point.*

saturation point (=when no more can be added to something) *Is the market for cellphones reaching saturation point?*

VERBS

reach a point (*also* **get to a point**) *Some couples reach a point where divorce is the only solution.*

mark a high/low/turning etc point (=be a particular time or event in the development of something) *The accident marked a turning point in his life.*

PHRASES

at one point (=at a time in the past) *At one point I was thinking of studying physics.*

at some point *Over half the population suffers from back pain at some point in their lives.*

at this/that point *I'm not prepared at this point to make any decision.*

at this/that point in time *formal* (=used especially in official speeches, announcements etc) *It would be wrong to comment at this point in time.*

to the point of sth (=until a stage is reached

or is near) *British industry was driven to the point of collapse.*

be on the point of (doing) sth (=be almost in a particular state, or almost do something) *I was on the point of leaving when she finally opened the door.*

there comes a point when... *There comes a point when you have to accept defeat.*

4 a particular quality or feature that something or someone has

ADJECTIVES

good points *The system is old, but it has its good points.*

bad points *We discussed the good and bad points of each candidate.*

sb's strong point *Mathematics was never my strong point* (=I was never good at it).

sb's weak point *Be honest about assessing your weak points.*

a positive/negative point *This design has a lot of positive points.*

a plus point *BrE* (=an advantage or good feature) *The airline's outstanding safety record is a major plus point.*

a selling point (=a quality or feature that makes people want to buy something) *The house's main selling point is its beautiful garden.*

5 a score in a game or sport

VERBS

score/win a point (*also* **get a point** *informal*): *The player who scores the most points wins.*

lose a point *If you get the answer wrong, you lose a point.*

give/award (sb) a point *The judges award points for technique and style.*

PHRASES

win/lose by 5/10 etc points *We only lost the match by two points.*

win/lose on points (=win or lose a fight because of the judges' decision) *He was knocked down twice, before losing on points.*

be level on points *BrE* (=have the same number of points) *The teams finished the season level on points.*

pointed *adj* THESAURUS ▸ **sharp (1)**

pointless *adj* THESAURUS ▸ **useless**

poison *n*

a substance that can cause death or serious illness

ADJECTIVES

deadly/lethal poison (=which can kill you) *The berries contain a deadly poison.*

a slow-acting/fast-acting poison (=which has a slow or quick effect) *Cyanide is a very strong fast-acting poison.*

VERBS

put poison in sth (*also* **lace sth with poison**) *She put poison in his wine.*

take/swallow poison *He committed suicide by taking poison.*

give sb poison (*also* **administer poison** *formal*): *Police are certain that her husband could not have administered the poison.*

PHRASES

traces of poison (=small amounts of poison in something) *Traces of the poison were found in her food.*

poisonous *adj*

containing or producing a substance that is likely to kill you, or make you very ill

NOUNS

poisonous gas/fumes *Car engines produce poisonous gases such as carbon monoxide.*

a poisonous snake/spider/insect/fish *If you have been bitten by a poisonous snake, you should seek medical help immediately.*

a poisonous mushroom/berry/plant *Some mushrooms are extremely poisonous.*

a poisonous substance/chemical *Many people do not like the idea of using poisonous chemicals in the garden.*

poisonous waste *The factory was dumping hundreds of tons of poisonous waste into the river.*

ADVERBS

highly/extremely poisonous *The tasty-looking berries are highly poisonous.*

deadly poisonous (=extremely poisonous and causing death) *This small spider has a deadly poisonous bite.*

PREPOSITIONS

poisonous to sb/sth *The leaves are poisonous to humans.*

THESAURUS: poisonous

toxic
waste | chemicals | substances | fumes | gases | metals
used about chemical substances that are harmful to people and the environment: *Toxic waste was being dumped in the ocean. | Crops are sprayed with* ***highly toxic*** *chemicals to prevent damage from insects. | Lead is* ***toxic to*** *humans.*

hazardous
waste | material | chemicals | substance
hazardous substances are likely to harm people, animals, or the environment if they are not dealt with or got rid of carefully:

Hazardous waste is stored deep under the ground in special containers. | There are strict regulations concerning the use of hazardous chemicals.

deadly
poison | snake | spider | gas | effect
extremely poisonous and likely to kill you:
He is seriously ill after swallowing a small amount of a deadly poison. | The red back spider is one of the most deadly spiders in Australia. | Nowadays people know much more about the deadly effects of radiation.

noxious *formal*
fumes | substance | gas | chemicals | substance | vapour
noxious gases and other substances are poisonous:
The firefighters were treated in hospital after breathing in noxious fumes. | The soil may be contaminated with noxious substances.

venomous *formal*
snake | reptile | creature | mammal | bite
a venomous snake or other animal uses poison to attack and kill other animals:
The black mamba is one of the most venomous snakes in the world.

police *n*

the people who make sure that everyone obeys the law

ADJECTIVES/NOUNS + police

armed police *Armed police surrounded the house.*

the secret police (=who work in secret, especially to investigate people's private lives and opinions) *He was arrested by the secret police after criticizing the government.*

riot police (=trained to control violent crowds) *Riot police moved in to disperse the crowd.*

traffic police *BrE: Traffic police closed the motorway after the accident.*

border police (=controlling people and things entering or leaving a country) *They were stopped by border police, who searched their vehicle.*

VERBS + police

call the police *Staff called the police when they noticed a broken window.*

contact/inform the police *If you see anything suspicious, contact the police.*

tell the police *Why didn't you tell the police?*

report sth to the police *Many crimes are not reported to the police.*

police + VERBS

the police investigate sth *Local police are investigating a break-in at the club.*

the police catch sb *The police are confident they will catch the killer.*

the police arrest sb (*also* **the police make an arrest**) *Police arrested him as he tried to leave the country.*

the police question/interview sb *Police are questioning two men about the incident.*

the police charge sb (=officially say that someone will be judged in a court for committing a crime) *The police have charged him with murder.*

the police hold sb (*also* **the police detain sb** *formal*) (=keep them at a police station) *The police can hold suspects for up to 24 hours without charge.*

the police release sb (=allow them to leave a police station) *The police released the woman after questioning.*

the police raid/storm a place (=enter it by surprise and by force) *The police raided his home and took his computer.*

the police appeal for sth *Police are appealing for witnesses to the attack.*

police + NOUNS

a police officer *The police officer asked to see his driving licence.*

a police spokesman *A police spokesman said officers are working hard on the case.*

a police station (=a building where the police work) *They took him to the police station for questioning.*

a police car *The men were being followed by an unmarked police car.*

a police dog *Police dogs were used to catch the thieves.*

a police investigation *Following a thorough police investigation, several arrests were made.*

the police force *Her son is in the police force.*

a police raid (=a surprise visit by the police to search for something illegal) *Six people were arrested in a police raid on the club.*

a police escort (=police officers who go with someone to guard or protect them) *The president drove through the city with a police escort.*

police brutality/harassment (=when the police hit or threaten people) *There were accusations of police brutality at the demonstration.*

police officer *n*

someone who is a member of the police force

ADJECTIVES/NOUNS + police officer

an armed/unarmed police officer *The house was surrounded by armed police officers.*

a plain-clothes police officer (=not wearing a uniform) *A plain-clothes police officer followed him across the street.*

an undercover police officer (=a police officer who works secretly in order to catch criminals) *She was arrested for trying to sell illegal drugs to an undercover police officer.*

an off-duty police officer (=a police officer at a time when he or she is not working) *The thief was arrested by an off-duty police officer who happened to be in the shop.*

a local police officer *The local police officers can ask for help from outside the region in an emergency.*

VERBS

a police officer arrests sb *Jones was arrested by a police officer for fighting in the street.*

a police officer stops sb *He was stopped by a police officer, who asked to see his papers.*

a police officer catches sb *The police officer caught the thief as he tried to climb over a wall.*

> **Police officer** or **policeman/policewoman?**
> In American English, people always use **police officer**. In British English, **police officer** is the preferred term. **Policeman** and **policewoman** are often also still used in everyday British English, but they are not considered politically correct. In official contexts, people always use **police officer**.

P

policy Ac *n*

someone's plans for dealing with a particular subject – especially ones that have been officially agreed by a government or organization

ADJECTIVES/NOUNS + policy

government policy *There has been a change in government policy on taxation.*

company/hospital/university etc policy *It is company policy to encourage more women to become senior managers.*

party policy *Party policy is to cut public spending.*

public policy (=government policies in general) *Big business is able to influence public policy by giving money to political parties.*

foreign policy (=towards other countries) *Support for human rights is a key element in our foreign policy.*

defence/education/housing/energy etc policy *Nuclear weapons still play an important role in Britain's defence policy.*

economic policy *I think that the government's economic policies have actually made the situation worse.*

a deliberate policy *Some companies have a deliberate policy of delaying payment.*

VERBS

have a policy of doing sth *The hotel said it had a policy of asking customers to provide credit card details.*

change your policy *The US government changed its policy towards China.*

reverse a policy (=change it back to how it was before) *The new government decided to reverse previous policies on immigration.*

pursue/follow a policy (=do something as part of your policy) *The company is pursuing a policy of cutting costs.*

make/formulate a policy (=decide what it will be) *Government advisers are heavily involved in making policy.*

implement a policy (=do what has been officially decided) *Local government is responsible for implementing central government policy.*

shape policy (=have an influence on it) *These terrorist acts will not be allowed to shape our foreign policy.*

adopt a policy (=decide to use one) *They adopted a policy of not speaking to reporters.*

policy + NOUNS

a policy decision *No policy decision can be made until the next meeting.*

a policy document (=suggesting a new policy) *The party has produced a 150-page policy document.*

a policy statement *The company's chief executive apologized if previous policy statements had been confusing.*

a policy maker (=someone who decides what the policy should be) *Government policy makers are always worried about the effect on voters.*

PREPOSITIONS

sb's policy on sth *There was discussion about the school's policy on student uniforms.*

sb's policy towards/toward sth *They want a change in US policy towards Cuba.*

a policy of (doing) sth *There was a policy of cutting taxes for very rich people.*

PHRASES

a change/shift in policy *This decision represented a major change in policy.*

a reversal of policy (=a change back to what it was before) *Strong opposition forced a rapid reversal of policy.*

polish *v* THESAURUS clean²

polite *adj*

behaving in a way that follows the rules of good behaviour and shows respect for other people, and often seems rather formal

ADVERBS

very/extremely/terribly polite *The man was very polite and asked us if we had had a pleasant journey.*

unfailingly polite (=always polite on every occasion) *The staff at our hotel were unfailingly polite and friendly.*

too polite to do sth *We were too polite to say what we really thought.*

VERBS

seem/sound polite *She wanted to leave the room, but it didn't seem polite.*

NOUNS

a polite voice *"I hope you have a pleasant stay," Judy said in a polite voice.*

a polite smile *The nurse looked at him with a polite smile.*

a polite letter *Some time later he got a polite letter saying that his application for the job had been unsuccessful.*

a polite way of doing sth *'Let's wait and see' is sometimes used as a polite way of saying 'no'.*

a polite request *There was a polite request to keep the noise down.*

a polite reminder (=a polite message telling someone that they should have done something) *The library sent me a polite reminder about the books.*

polite applause (=gentle clapping by people who are not very excited by a speaker or performance) *He received polite applause from a few people in the crowd.*

PREPOSITIONS

be polite to sb *The men shook hands and made an effort to be polite to each other.*

PHRASES

make polite conversation (with sb) (=talk about unimportant things such as the weather) *While they ate, she tried to make polite conversation.*

ANTONYMS **polite → rude**

political *adj*

relating to the government and public affairs of a country

NOUNS

a political party *I am not a member of any political party.*

a political system *He wants to see a parliamentary political system put in place.*

the political process *People choose not to vote because they have no faith in the political process.*

a political leader *The country needs a strong political leader.*

political power *Poor people seem to have little political power.*

political rights *Women had no political rights.*

sb's political career *He is facing the biggest decision of his political career.*

political life *At that time women were excluded from political life.*

a political issue *Health care has become a major political issue.*

a political solution *Leaders are eager for a political solution after years of war.*

the political agenda (=the list of things that are discussed in politics) *The subject of women's rights was suddenly very high on the political agenda.*

politician *n*

someone who works in politics, especially an elected member of the government

ADJECTIVES/NOUNS + politician

a senior politician *A number of senior politicians opposed the government's policy.*

a leading/prominent politician (=important and well known) *The scandal ruined the careers of several leading politicians.*

a Labour/Republican etc politician *Her mother was a Labour politician.*

a left-wing/right-wing politician *He had been under attack from right-wing politicians for some time.*

a local politician *The plan is strongly supported by local politicians.*

an opposition politician (=belonging to the party that is not in power) *Opposition politicians argued that there was not enough reason to go to war.*

an elected politician *Are the country's elected politicians trustworthy?*

a corrupt politician (=not honest) *Industry bosses had made quiet deals with corrupt politicians.*

a popular politician *He is the most popular politician in the country.*

an astute/shrewd politician (=clever and good at achieving the result that he or she wants) *He was a very astute politician and he knew how to deal with the media.*

a career politician (=one who is determined to be successful in politics and has no interest in anything else) *His opponents criticize him as a career politician with little regard for ordinary people.*

politics *n*

ideas and activities involved in running a country, city etc

ADJECTIVES/NOUNS + politics

international/world politics *I became interested in international politics when I was at university.*

domestic politics (=within a country) *The war had a major impact on the country's domestic politics.*

local politics *Ann is very active in local politics.*

national politics (=used when comparing this to local politics) *Mark had always wanted a career in national politics.*

party politics (=involving members of political parties, who are trying to defeat each other in arguments - often disapproving) *The health service is too important to be left to party politics.*

VERBS

go into/enter politics (=get involved in it as a job) *She went into politics because she wanted to help make society better.*

be involved in/take part in politics *He was involved in local politics for several years before he became a member of parliament.*

interfere/meddle in politics *He warned the army against interfering in politics.*

PHRASES

be active in politics (=be involved in it) *Women are becoming increasingly active in politics.*

poll *n*

1 an occasion when a large group of people are asked questions to find out their opinions

ADJECTIVES/NOUNS + poll

an opinion poll (=that measures what people think about something) *A recent opinion poll showed strong support for the government.*

a popularity poll (=measuring how popular someone is) *In most popularity polls, he is far behind his rivals.*

an exit poll (=when people are asked who they just voted for in an election) *The exit polls revealed that 46% of women had voted for Obama.*

a national poll *National polls show strong opposition to the plan.*

VERBS + poll

carry out/do a poll (*also* **conduct a poll** *formal*): *They carried out a poll to find out how many people supported the war.*

publish/release a poll *'The Times' has published a poll showing that most people were against increasing taxes.*

commission a poll (=ask an organization to carry out a poll) *The magazine commissioned a poll to discover what people spend on beauty products.*

poll + VERBS

a poll shows/indicates/suggests sth *Polls show that older voters are most concerned about economic issues.*

a poll finds sth *Our poll found that only 29 percent of people thought the president was doing a good job.*

poll + NOUNS

poll results/findings *The poll results are very encouraging for environmental campaigners.*

a poll rating (=showing how popular someone is) *His poll rating fell by several points following the scandal.*

PREPOSITIONS

in a poll *In a recent poll, consumers said they wanted more information on food labels.*

PHRASES

sb's lead in the polls *Labour soon regained its lead in the polls.*

sb's standing in the polls (=how popular a poll shows them to be) *The president's standing in the polls has fallen sharply.*

be ahead/leading in the polls *The good news is that we are ahead in the polls.*

be behind/trailing in the polls *At the moment the Democrats are trailing in the polls.*

2 political elections

> **Grammar**
> Always plural in this meaning.

VERBS

go to the polls (=vote in an election) *Will there be a change of government when the country goes to the polls next week?*

the polls open/close (=voting officially begins or ends) *The counting of votes begins as soon as the polls close.*

PREPOSITIONS

at the polls (=in an election) *Her party performed badly at the polls.*

polluted *adj* THESAURUS ▸ dirty

pollution *n*

damage caused to the environment, for example by chemicals from factories and vehicles

ADJECTIVES/NOUNS + pollution

the pollution is bad/severe *In some cities, the pollution is so bad that people have to wear masks.*

air pollution (*also* **atmospheric pollution** *formal*): *Air pollution can cause breathing problems for some people.*

water/river pollution *We tested the level of water pollution in local rivers and canals.*

environmental pollution *Most environmental pollution is produced by developed countries.*

industrial pollution (=from factories) *A study has linked ill health in the area with industrial pollution.*

noise/light pollution (=the bad effect of noise or artificial light in the environment) *Light pollution makes it harder to see the stars at night.*

marine pollution (=pollution of the sea) *Oil spills are a major cause of marine pollution.*

chemical pollution *Chemical pollution threatens the survival of these animals.*

VERBS

reduce/cut pollution *Tougher laws are needed to reduce pollution from cars.*

produce/cause/generate pollution *Battery-powered cars produce far less pollution.*

prevent pollution *Greenpeace wants to prevent pollution through better and more efficient design.*

control pollution *The report recommends the use of taxes to control pollution.*

tackle/combat pollution (=try to deal with it) *Governments have so far failed to tackle pollution.*

monitor pollution (=measure it) *Our job is to monitor pollution from industrial chimneys.*

pollution + NOUNS

pollution levels *The aim of the new regulations is to reduce pollution levels in the environment.*

PREPOSITIONS

pollution from sth *Pollution from factories is having a bad effect on people's health.*

PHRASES

a source/cause of pollution *Fumes from cars are a major cause of air pollution.*

pool *n*

1 a hole or container that has been specially made and filled with water so that people can swim or play in it

ADJECTIVES

a swimming pool *He dived into the swimming pool.*

an indoor pool *The indoor pool is used by swimmers practising for the Olympic Games.*

an outdoor/open-air pool *Our hotel had an outdoor pool.*

a heated pool *There is a heated swimming pool in the basement.*

a 25-metre/50-metre etc pool *The school has a 25-metre pool.*

an Olympic-sized pool *The stadium has an Olympic-sized swimming pool.*

a paddling pool *BrE* (=a small pool or plastic container of water for children to play in) *He set up the paddling pool in the back garden.*

VERBS

swim in a pool *We spent the afternoon swimming in the pool.*

dive/jump into a pool *The swimmers dived into the pool at the start of the race.*

lie beside a pool *She was lying beside the pool, trying to get a suntan.*

PREPOSITIONS

in/into the pool *We all jumped into the pool.*

out of the pool *She got out of the pool and went to get her towel.*

at the pool *"Where's Sue?" "She's at the pool."*

by the pool *We spent the holiday relaxing by the pool.*

PHRASES

the bottom of a pool *His feet were touching the bottom of the pool.*

the edge/side of a pool *She sat by the edge of the pool, chatting to one of her friends.*

2 a small area of liquid or light on a surface

PHRASES

a pool of blood/water *He was lying in a pool of blood.*

a pool of light *The pool of light from the torch shone down on her face.*

3 a small area of still water in a hollow place

ADJECTIVES

a deep/shallow pool *We came to a deep pool under some tall trees.*

NOUNS + pool

a rock pool *Crabs live in rock pools.*

a freshwater/saltwater pool *The insect is found near freshwater pools.*

poor *adj*

1 having very little money and not many possessions

NOUNS

a poor man/woman/person *Many poor people in the country are unable to read or write.*

a poor family *Children from poor families get free school meals.*

a poor country/nation *Nepal is one of the poorest countries in the world, but also one of the most beautiful.*

a poor area/region/neighbourhood etc *He was born in a poor neighbourhood and was raised by his grandparents.*

a poor part of sth *The school was in a poor part of London.*

a poor home/household/background *Students from poor backgrounds do not have to pay for their education.*

a poor farmer/worker/labourer *Her father was a poor farmer with a few acres of land.*

ADVERBS

desperately poor (=so poor that it causes great suffering) *Half the population remains desperately poor.*

dirt poor *informal* (=extremely poor) *The family was dirt poor and they couldn't afford to send their children to school.*

THESAURUS: poor

developing

country | **nation** | **world** | **economy**

a developing country is poor and has very little industry:

In developing countries, access to clean drinking water is often a problem. | *Nearly one million children die from the disease every year in the developing world.*

Developing is only used before a noun.

People also sometimes use **the Third World** to talk in general about poor countries. This use is not considered to be politically correct and it is better to say **the developing world**.

deprived

area | **neighbourhood** | **part** | **region** | **children** | **groups** | **families** | **background** | **childhood**

P

much poorer than other people or parts of a country, and not having the things that are necessary for a comfortable or happy life:
The fund gives extra money to schools in deprived areas. | It is well known that deprived children tend to do less well at school.

disadvantaged
groups | students | pupils | children | families | people | area | region | background
used about groups of people in society who have much less chance of being successful because they are poor:
Single-parent families are one of the fastest growing and most disadvantaged groups in society. | More money will be given to schools in disadvantaged areas.

needy
children | families | students
used about groups of people who have very little money, and therefore need help:
The group provides holidays for needy children. | More help should be given to needy families.

> **Needy** is often used as a noun: *The money goes to help **the needy**.*

destitute
people | family | refugees | country | nation
very poor and in a very bad situation, because you have no possessions and often nowhere to live:
*There are thousands of destitute people with serious mental problems on our streets. | Her family was **left destitute** after her father died. | The United Nations needs to do more to rebuild this destitute nation.*

impoverished *formal*
country | nation | people | families | children | workers
very poor, especially because something bad has happened to you:
This impoverished country has suffered from hundreds of years of colonial rule. | The money will be used to help the miners and their impoverished families.

poverty-stricken *formal*
people | family | country | nation | area
extremely poor, especially because something bad has happened to you:
*Medical supplies were sent to help the poverty-stricken people of Albania. | The family was **left poverty-stricken**. | In Somalia and many other poverty-stricken countries, thousands of people starved to death.*

> **Poverty-stricken or impoverished?**
> These words are very similar in meaning. **Poverty-stricken** sounds even poorer than **impoverished**.

penniless *especially literary*
student | artist | immigrant | widow
having no money:
*Epstein was a penniless student in Paris. | She **died penniless**. | Mary was **left penniless** and without any income.*

broke/hard up *informal*
having very little money, especially for a short period of time:
*We were so broke we couldn't afford to go out to the cinema. | Can I pay you back later? **I'm a bit hard up at the moment**.*

> **Broke** and **hard up** are not used before a noun.

ANTONYMS **poor → rich (1)**

2 bad

NOUNS

poor performance *The team's poor performance in the second half lost them the match.*

poor quality *The furniture was cheap and of poor quality.*

poor health *Some of the children are in very poor health.*

poor condition *Items in poor condition have a lower price.*

poor results *His parents were disappointed by his poor results in the exams.*

a poor record *The airline used to have quite a poor safety record.*

poor light (=not good enough for doing something) *Poor light stopped play.*

> **THESAURUS: poor**
> **poor, disappointing, unpleasant, negative, grim, undesirable, detrimental, unfavourable → bad (1)**

pop *n*

modern music that is popular with young people

pop + NOUNS

pop music *I like most kinds of pop music.*

a pop song *It is not easy to write a great three-minute pop song.*

a pop group/band *He thought the Beatles were the best pop group of all time.*

a pop singer *Do you need a good voice to be a pop singer?*

a pop star *She wanted to be a pop star or an actress.*

a pop concert *His mother said he was too young to go to a pop concert by himself.*

the pop charts (=the list of best-selling songs for a particular week) *The song reached number two in the pop charts.*

P

popular *adj*

1 liked by a lot of people

ADVERBS

highly popular *She was a highly popular student at college.*

immensely/hugely/enormously popular *His plays were immensely popular.*

wildly popular (=highly popular - used especially about something that excites people) *These bands are wildly popular in Cuba.*

increasingly popular *Business management courses are increasingly popular.*

universally popular (=liked by everyone) *Some foods are universally popular.*

enduringly/perennially popular *formal* (=always popular) *His most enduringly popular film is 'Singin' in the Rain'.*

genuinely popular *He became Russia's first genuinely popular politician in a long time.*

PREPOSITIONS

popular with/among people *The café is very popular with students.*

popular as sth *The island has become very popular as a holiday destination.*

ANTONYMS **popular → unpopular**

2 done or believed by a lot of people or by ordinary people

NOUNS

popular support *There was widespread popular support for the new law.*

by/due to popular demand (=because many people have said they want something to happen) *She will be performing here again next month, by popular demand.*

popular belief/opinion *Contrary to popular belief, spiders are not insects.*

the popular view *The popular view bears little relation to the known facts.*

a popular misconception (=a wrong idea that many people have) *There is a popular misconception that cats cannot swim.*

the popular image of sth/sb *The film star is very unlike the popular image of him in the press.*

popularity *n*

a situation in which something or someone is liked or supported by a lot of people

ADJECTIVES

great popularity *He has always enjoyed great popularity with British audiences.*

enormous/tremendous/immense popularity *Good advertising has maintained the enormous popularity of the drink.*

widespread/wide popularity (=with a lot of people, or in many places) *Astrology enjoyed widespread popularity.*

growing/increasing/rising popularity *How do we explain the increasing popularity of Scottish folk music?*

continuing/enduring popularity (=that lasts a long time) *Today, the novel enjoys enduring popularity and ranks among the USA's top-selling books.*

personal popularity *The president's personal popularity remained high.*

political popularity *Economic difficulties have seriously damaged the prime minister's political popularity.*

VERBS

enjoy popularity (=be popular) *The band enjoyed great popularity in the 1980s.*

achieve popularity (=become popular) *Her books achieved tremendous popularity on both sides of the Atlantic.*

gain/grow/increase in popularity *Extreme sports are growing in popularity.*

court popularity (=try to be popular by pleasing people) *It is tempting for politicians to court popularity.*

sb's popularity soars (=increases by a large amount) *Opinion polls showed that his popularity had soared to a record level.*

sth's popularity wanes/declines (=gradually decreases) *Every man once wore a hat but, as fashions changed, their popularity declined.*

popularity + NOUNS

a popularity contest (=a competition to find who the most popular person is) *The election should be about policies, not just a popularity contest.*

a popularity poll (=a survey to find how popular someone is) *In most popularity polls, he is in fourth or fifth place.*

sb's popularity rating (=how popular someone is according to a poll) *His popularity rating dropped dramatically after the events of last year.*

PREPOSITIONS

popularity among/with people *The band's popularity among older people has surprised music critics.*

population *n*

the people who live in a particular country or area

ADJECTIVES/NOUNS + population

a large/small population *California is a big state with a large population.*

a total population *The United Kingdom has a total population of over 60 million.*

the whole/entire population *The entire population will be celebrating.*

the world's population *A large proportion of the world's population is starving.*

the local population *The local population gave the sailors a friendly welcome at first.*

the general population *The mentally ill are no more violent than the general population.*
the British/French etc population *Around 10 per cent of the British population are left-handed.*
the urban population (=who live in towns) *The urban population will more than double in the next two decades.*
the rural population (=who live in the countryside) *Most of the rural population do not have access to the internet.*
the adult population *A third of the adult population pay no tax at all.*
an ageing population (=who are becoming old) *The rapidly ageing population is causing problems for the country's health care system.*
the indigenous population *formal* (=the people who have always lived in a place) *His new book assesses the impact of Spanish culture on the indigenous population of Mexico.*

P

VERBS

a place has a population of... *The city has a population of over 9 million.*
the population is/stands at... *The US population now stands at more than 300 million.*
the population grows/increases/rises *Between these years the population grew by 40%.*
the population falls/declines/decreases *The population in many rural areas has continued to fall.*
the population doubles (=it becomes twice as big) *The population of London doubled between 1580 and 1600.*
the population reaches... *It is predicted that the world's population will reach 10 billion by the year 2050.*

population + NOUNS

a population explosion (=a situation in which the population increases very quickly) *What will be the long-term effects of this population explosion?*
population growth/increase *India experienced rapid population growth.*
population size *There was no way that population size could be measured accurately.*

PREPOSITIONS

a population of 2 million/130,000 etc *The city has a population of 270,000.*
the population of a place *At that time, the population of Egypt was 6 million.*

pop up *v* THESAURUS appear (1)

port *n*

a place where ships can be loaded and unloaded

ADJECTIVES/NOUNS + port

a busy port *Hong Kong is one of the world's busiest ports.*
a major/important port *The city became a major port.*
a bustling port (=very busy) *Until the 1870s, Port Albert was a bustling port.*
a fishing port *The town is Iceland's biggest fishing port.*
a ferry port (=for boats carrying people, cars etc) *Dover is an important ferry port.*

VERBS

come into port *We stood on the quay and watched the ships come into port.*
leave port *Two fishing boats were preparing to leave port.*

PREPOSITIONS

the port of... *We arrived at the port of Southampton.*
a ship is in port *The island is much busier when a cruise ship is in port.*

> **Port of entry**
> This phrase is often used in official contexts, meaning the place where someone enters the country by ship, plane etc: *Dover is a major* **port of entry** *for the UK.*

portion Ac *n*

1 a part of something larger

ADJECTIVES

a large portion *Temperatures over a large portion of the country were well below normal.*
a significant/substantial/major/considerable portion *formal* (=very large and therefore important) *He owns a substantial portion of the company.*
a good portion (=large) *She spends a good portion of her salary on clothes and entertainment.*
a small portion *A small portion of the country remained under French control.*

2 an amount of food for one person

ADJECTIVES

a big/large portion (*also* **a generous portion** *formal*): *I was hungry so I asked for a large portion of fries.*
a small portion *One way of losing weight is to eat smaller portions.*
a double portion (=twice as large as a normal one) *I ordered a double portion of chicken.*

portion + NOUNS

portion size *If you are trying to eat less, pay attention to portion size.*

portrait *n* a picture of a person

ADJECTIVES/NOUNS + portrait

a self-portrait (=of yourself) *Rembrandt painted a self-portrait of himself as an old man.*
a group portrait *He painted a group portrait of the prince and his three sisters.*
a family portrait *The room is full of family portraits.*

an accurate portrait *Sketching the face before painting will result in a more accurate portrait.*

a flattering portrait (=which makes someone look better than they really are) *For a flattering portrait, usually soft light is the best.*

a full-length portrait (=including someone's whole body) *A full-length portrait of a pretty young girl in a red dress was hanging on the wall.*

a life-size portrait (=same size as in real life) *He keeps a life-size portrait of his father in the study.*

VERBS

paint/draw sb's portrait *He paints portraits of famous people.*

do a portrait of sb *Picasso did a portrait of her.*

pose/sit for a portrait *She sat for a portrait by Joshua Reynolds.*

commission a portrait (=officially ask someone to do a portrait for you) *He commissioned a portrait of his daughter from the painter.*

a portrait hangs somewhere (=it is on a wall there) *The portrait hangs in the Metropolitan Museum of Art.*

portrait + NOUNS

a portrait artist/painter/photographer *She is best known as a portrait artist.*

a portrait gallery *The National Portrait Gallery in London is worth a visit.*

a portrait studio *The most challenging part of a photographer's experience at a portrait studio is working with people.*

PREPOSITIONS

a portrait of sb *Whistler painted a famous portrait of his mother.*

a portrait by sb *There was a portrait by an unknown artist.*

position *n*

1 the place where something or someone is

ADJECTIVES

the correct/right position *Make sure the picture is in the right position before you knock the nail into the wall.*

the exact/precise position *The red dot marks the exact position of the ship.*

a prominent position (=one where something can easily be seen) *We want to display the trophy in a prominent position.*

VERBS

take up a position (=move to a position so that you are ready to do something) *She told the sales staff to take up their positions behind the counter.*

occupy a position (=be in a particular place) *Our house occupied a middle position in the street.*

change position *The photographer asked us to change position with each other.*

show/mark sth's position (*also* **indicate sth's position** *formal*): *They used this chart to mark the position of enemy aircraft.*

PREPOSITIONS

in/into position (=in or into the correct position) *Our troops were in position near the bridge.*

out of position (=not in the correct position) *The player had moved out of position, allowing his opponent to get past easily.*

2 the way someone is standing, sitting, or lying

ADJECTIVES

a comfortable position *She got herself into a comfortable position on the sofa.*

an awkward/uncomfortable position *My foot was in an awkward position.*

a sitting/kneeling/standing/crouching etc position *The priest rose from his kneeling position by the bed.*

VERBS

change/shift (your) position *He shifted his position to get a better view of the stage.*

hold a position (=stay in a position) *Pull in your tummy muscles and hold that position.*

3 the situation that someone is in

ADJECTIVES

the present/current position *The present position is that we do not have enough staff.*

the same position/a similar position *A lot of us are in the same position: we don't know if we'll still have a job next month.*

a strong/good/powerful position (=a situation in which you have an advantage) *A victory tonight will put the team in a strong position to win the championship.*

a difficult/awkward position *I was in the difficult position of having to choose between my wife and my daughter.*

an impossible position (=a very difficult situation) *I was angry with him for putting me in such an impossible position.*

a privileged position *The royal family has a very privileged position in society.*

an enviable position (=a situation that other people would like to be in) *He is in the enviable position of not needing to work.*

a weak position *Someone who is desperate to sell their house is in a weak position.*

a vulnerable position (=a situation in which you could easily be attacked or in trouble) *The country is in a vulnerable position because it depends entirely on imports of oil.*

a unique position *Their knowledge of the area places them in a unique position to advise you.*

sb's financial position *Has your financial position changed recently?*

VERBS

put/place sb in a position *I'm sorry if I put you in an uncomfortable position.*

find yourself in a position *Because of government opposition, aid organizations find themselves in a difficult position.*

reach a position *It has taken two years to reach the position where we can say we've succeeded.*

strengthen sb's position (=give someone a bigger advantage) *Political leaders were using the war to strengthen their own position.*

weaken/undermine sb's position (=give someone a bigger disadvantage) *The prime minister's position had been weakened by disagreements in his Cabinet.*

consider/review the position *We shall consider the position again in a few weeks' time.*

sb's position improves *By March, the Democrats' position had improved.*

P

PREPOSITIONS

be in a ... position *I'm in a rather unusual position because my boss is my wife.*

PHRASES

a position of strength (=a strong position) *The workers were negotiating from a position of strength.*

a position of power/authority/influence *Parents should not abuse their position of power over children.*

a position of trust *As a church leader, he was in a position of trust.*

4 an opinion or judgment on a particular subject

ADJECTIVES

sb's official position (=one that a government or organization says officially that it has) *This was the French government's official position.*

an extreme position *Few people hold this extreme position today.*

a middle position (=one that is between two extreme positions) *The party takes a middle position on government control of industry.*

a neutral position (=not supporting either side in an argument) *The country appeared to abandon its neutral position and give support to our enemies.*

an ideological/philosophical position (=based on political or philosophical beliefs) *Can such an ideological position be maintained in these difficult economic times?*

VERBS

take/hold a position (=have an opinion) *We take the position that these changes are to be welcomed.*

adopt a position (=start having an opinion) *This is the position the Church has adopted on the issue.*

change/shift your position *Since then, the party has changed its position.*

reconsider/rethink your position (=think again about it and perhaps change it) *We are urging the US government to reconsider its position.*

defend a position *The next speaker defended a different position.*

maintain a position *We maintain our position that job cuts are bad for the economy.*

PREPOSITIONS

sb's position on sth *What is the minister's position on gay marriage?*

5 a job - used especially about important jobs, or in formal situations

ADJECTIVES/NOUNS + position

a senior/junior position *David held a very senior position in the company.*

a key/important position *Hwang Jang Yop occupied a key position in the Party.*

a temporary position *They are offering a temporary position initially, for six months.*

a permanent position *I am hoping to find a permanent position when I leave university.*

a management position *She was one of the few women in a management position.*

an official position *People in official positions are not allowed to accept gifts.*

VERBS

hold/occupy a position (=have it) *She had previously held a more senior position in another school.*

apply for a position *I decided to apply for the position of marketing manager.*

take up a position (=start doing a job) *He took up a new position as managing director of a company in Belfast.*

leave a position *He left his position as Chief Conductor of the Moscow Radio Symphony Orchestra.*

resign from a position *She has resigned from her position as department secretary.*

offer sb a position *They offered me the position of store manager.*

fill a position (=find someone to do a job) *I'm afraid the position has already been filled.*

use your position *She tries to use her position to do some good.*

abuse your position (=use it wrongly) *He abused his position as a doctor.*

PREPOSITIONS

the position of sth *She currently holds the position of senior sales manager.*

a position as sth *He was hoping to find a position as a financial adviser.*

a position in/at sth *A position at the BBC would be her dream job.*

positive Ac *adj*

1 expecting or considering things to be good or hopeful

NOUNS

a positive attitude/outlook *Having a positive attitude makes life so much better.*

a positive approach *This is just the positive approach that the school needs.*

a positive view *He takes a fairly positive view of the future.*

positive thinking (*also* **positive thoughts**) *Many people believe that positive thinking can help your recovery from serious illnesses.*

a positive response *The suggestion got a very positive response from my colleagues.*

positive feedback *She received some pretty positive feedback from the teacher.*

VERBS

feel positive *Are you feeling positive about your chances of a medal?*

seem/sound positive *The minister didn't sound positive about the economy.*

stay positive *He's very sick, but we are trying to stay positive.*

PREPOSITIONS

positive about sth *I always try to be positive about students' work.*

PHRASES

think positive (=think positive thoughts) *Cheer up and think positive.*

ANTONYMS **positive → negative (1)**

2 good or useful

NOUNS

a positive effect/impact/influence *Exercise has a positive effect on health.*

a positive aspect *There are a lot of positive aspects to retirement.*

a positive thing *Did he mention any positive things about the experience?*

a positive image *It's important to promote a positive image of our industry to young people.*

a positive result/outcome *We hope there will be a positive outcome to the talks.*

a positive contribution *Most refugees are determined to make a positive contribution to their new country.*

a positive experience *Working here has been a very positive experience for me.*

a positive step *He welcomed the talks as a positive step towards peace.*

PHRASES

on the positive side (=used when saying what is good about something) *On the positive side, the club's financial position remains strong.*

see/present sth in a positive light (=see or show something in a way that makes it seem good) *The company tried to present the decision in a positive light.*

THESAURUS: positive

nice, fine, sound, attractive, desirable, favourable, positive, beneficial → **good (1)**

ANTONYMS **positive → negative (2)**

3 completely sure

ADVERBS

completely/absolutely/quite positive *Are you absolutely positive that you locked the door?*

fairly/almost positive *I'm almost positive that he is lying.*

VERBS

feel positive *He felt positive that this was the man he had seen.*

seem positive *She seems positive she'll get the job.*

PREPOSITIONS

positive about sth *It was after ten when the phone rang – I'm positive about that.*

positive of sth *You need to be positive of your facts before you publish the article.*

possession *n*

something that you have or you own

ADJECTIVES

personal possessions *The prisoners were allowed to keep a few personal possessions with them.*

sb's worldly possessions *literary* (=everything they own) *The bag contained all his worldly possessions.*

material possessions (=things you own, rather than personal qualities, relationships etc) *Love and family are far more important to me than material possessions.*

a precious possession (=one that is valuable or important to you) *She only had time to pack a few precious possessions before she had to leave.*

a prized/treasured/cherished possession (=one that is very important to you) *One of my most treasured possessions is a small book of prayers.*

possibility *n*

a situation in which something might happen or might be true

ADJECTIVES

a strong/good possibility (=something that is very likely) *There is a strong possibility that the treatment will fail.*

a real/distinct possibility (=something that is quite likely) *At this moment, job losses are a real possibility.*

a remote/faint possibility (=something that is

not very likely) *There's no point worrying about such a remote possibility.*

VERBS

a possibility exists *The possibility exists that he misunderstood my instructions.*

sth remains a possibility (=it could still happen) *War remains a possibility.*

consider/explore/examine a possibility *Police are considering the possibility that the death may be drugs-related.*

rule out/exclude a possibility (=say that something will definitely not happen or is definitely not true) *We can't rule out the possibility that the factory will close.*

PREPOSITIONS

the possibility of sth *Motor racing is a dangerous sport and there is always the possibility of accidents.*

PHRASES

there is a possibility that *There is a possibility that you could have lost all your work.*

P

possible *adj*

if something is possible, it can be done or achieved

PHRASES

it is possible to do sth *From the hilltop it was possible to see the sea.*

make it possible to do sth *Medical advances have made it possible to keep more patients alive.*

if possible (*also* **if at all possible**) *If possible, take light exercise first thing in the morning.*

where/wherever/whenever possible *Where possible, grill your meat rather than fry it.*

do everything possible *We must do everything possible to limit the damage we cause to the environment.*

in every way possible *We offered to help him in every way possible.*

as soon as possible *Please make a payment as soon as possible.*

as far as possible (=to the extent that is possible) *Remember that you should, as far as possible, avoid drinking the local water.*

VERBS

think/consider/believe sth possible *The new technology produces results that we didn't believe possible.*

prove possible *It proved possible to open the door without using the key.*

remain possible *Doctors are saying it remains possible that the patient's condition will worsen.*

ADVERBS

perfectly/quite possible (=definitely possible) *Combining a family with a career is perfectly possible.*

theoretically possible (=possible in theory, but difficult and unlikely) *It is theoretically possible for a student to get full marks.*

technically possible (=possible with the technology available) *It may be technically possible to make these vehicles go faster, but is it wise?*

humanly possible (=able to be done if someone tries hard enough) *It is not humanly possible to work for more than fifteen hours a day.*

reasonably possible *We need to keep the cost as low as is reasonably possible.*

THESAURUS: possible

feasible

solution | plan | idea | option | alternative

if something is feasible, it is possible and you can find a practical way of doing it:

Using specially trained staff, though expensive, is often the only feasible solution. | We need to find out first if the idea is ***technically feasible****. | It is not* ***feasible to*** *have security cameras in every part of the building. | Da Silva considered that* ***it was feasible that*** *uranium could be produced on an industrial scale.*

viable

alternative | solution | option | proposition

possible and likely to be successful, and therefore worth doing:

Some people argue that nuclear energy is the only viable alternative to coal or gas. | We have yet to find a viable solution to the problem. | Getting a loan was the only viable option (=the only thing that you could do). *| Plenty of people want to come to the city, so a new hotel seems like a viable proposition* (=something that could work). *| The company was no longer* ***financially viable*** (=it could not make enough money to be able to continue). *| The product needs to be* ***commercially viable*** (=it can make enough profit).

workable

solution | answer | system | plan | policy | framework | approach | arrangement | agreement | alternative

able to be done or used:

The engineers believe they have found a workable solution to the problem. | The banks are trying to come up with a workable system for preventing credit card fraud. | The plan sounds workable to me. | He urged both sides to reach a workable agreement as soon as possible. | There appeared to be no other workable alternative.

realistic

chance | prospect | target | goal | option | possibility | expectation | alternative

if something is realistic, it seems sensible to think that it can be done or achieved:

The team have a realistic chance of winning the game. | A five per cent increase in sales seems a realistic target. | His parents' expectations didn't seem very realistic.

achievable (*also* **attainable** *formal*)
goal | target
able to be achieved:
A 5% increase in output is an achievable goal. | A 15% cut in carbon emissions is achievable. | Perfect democracy is not attainable, nor is perfect freedom or perfect justice.

doable *informal*
if something is doable, you can do it because you have enough energy, skill, time etc:
Do you think the walk is doable? | Reducing gasoline consumption by 20% in ten years should be doable.

Doable is not used before a noun.

ANTONYMS **possible → impossible**

post *n*

1 the official system for carrying letters, packages etc from one place to another

VERBS

send sth by post *They sent me the contract by post.*

put sth in the post (=put it in a box to be collected) *I put it in the post on Friday, so it should have arrived today.*

get sth in the post (=receive it) *Did you get anything in the post today?*

sth comes/arrives in the post *This letter came in the post this morning.*

ADJECTIVES

first-class post *BrE* (=quicker and more expensive) *The package arrived by first-class post the next day.*

second-class post *BrE* (=slower and cheaper) *Items sent by second-class post can take up to five days to arrive.*

PREPOSITIONS

by post *You can vote by post if you register.*

in the post *The tickets are in the post, and you should receive them shortly.*

through the post *I got a leaflet about it through the post.*

PHRASES

sth gets lost in the post *I'm afraid the cheque must have got lost in the post.*

by return of post *BrE* (=almost immediately) *I received a reply by return of post.*

Post is used in British English. In American English, people usually say **mail** instead.

2 a job, especially in a large organization

ADJECTIVES/NOUNS + post

a senior/junior post *Senior posts in industry attract very high salaries.*

a permanent/temporary post *I have a two-year contract, not a permanent post.*

a full-time/part-time post *A part-time post as a university lecturer did not pay enough to feed his family.*

a teaching post *My first teaching post was in London.*

an academic post (=a teaching job at a university or college) *He left his job to take up an academic post in the US.*

a government post *I decided to apply for a local government post.*

VERBS

hold a post (=have a particular job) *He held the post of foreign minister in the last government.*

apply for a post *I am writing to apply for the post of Project Manager.*

take up a post (=start a new job) *She will take up her new post next month.*

leave a post *The previous sales director left his post in June.*

resign (from) your post (*also* **quit your post** *informal*) (=leave it) *Mr Sargent decided to resign his post as chairman.*

be dismissed from a post (*also* **be relieved of your post** *formal*) (=be told to leave) *As a result of the scandal, he was dismissed from his post.*

get a post *He managed to get a teaching post at a good school.*

offer sb a post *She was offered the post of ambassador to India.*

appoint sb to a post (=give someone a job officially) *Mrs Collingwood has been appointed to the post of head teacher.*

fill a post (=find someone to do a job) *I applied but was told the post had already been filled.*

PREPOSITIONS

sb's post as sth *After the election, he left his post as leader of the Social Democrat Party.*

the post of sth *The company has appointed Bill Anderton to the post of Chief Press Officer.*

poster *n*

a large printed notice, picture, or photograph, used to advertise something or as a decoration

ADJECTIVES/NOUNS + poster

a film/movie poster *He collects old movie posters.*

an election poster *There were election posters everywhere.*

an advertising poster *You often see her face on advertising posters.*

a full-colour poster *The magazine comes with a free full-colour poster of the band.*

VERBS + poster

have a poster on your wall *He has a poster of James Dean on his bedroom wall.*

put up/take down a poster *Students are allowed to put up posters in their rooms.*

design a poster *She designed the poster for the school concert.*

be covered with posters *The wall was covered with posters of pop stars.*

poster + VERBS

a poster shows sth *The poster shows Hendrix playing his guitar.*

a poster advertises sth *There was a big poster advertising his latest film outside the cinema.*

a poster appears/goes up *Posters for the concert started appearing all over town.*

poster + NOUNS

a poster campaign *The government used a poster campaign to discourage people from drinking and driving.*

PREPOSITIONS

a poster of sth/sb *There is a poster of the Swiss Alps in our local travel agency.*

a poster for sth *There are lots of posters for the exhibition.*

on a poster *He saw her face on a movie poster.*

postpone *v*

to change the date or time of a planned event or action to a later one

ADVERBS

postpone sth indefinitely (=no one knows when it will happen) *His trial has been postponed indefinitely.*

PREPOSITIONS

postpone sth until next week/next month etc *The match had to be postponed until next week.*

postpone sth from sth to sth *Elections were postponed from November to May.*

> **THESAURUS: postpone**
>
> call off, postpone, shelve, lift, repeal, annul → **cancel**

potential[1] Ac *adj*

likely to develop into a particular type of person or thing in the future

NOUNS

a potential customer/buyer/client *Advertisers want to reach as many potential customers as possible.*

a potential user *We asked potential users what they expected from this type of product.*

a potential candidate *We have put together a list of 10 potential candidates.*

a potential source of sth *A dirty kitchen is a potential source of infection.*

a potential benefit *The drug has many potential benefits.*

a potential problem *There is a potential problem with the new equipment.*

a potential danger/threat/risk/hazard *Tired drivers are a potential danger to other road users.*

potential[2] Ac *n*

a natural ability or quality that could develop into something good

ADJECTIVES/NOUNS + potential

great/enormous/vast potential *This is a team with great potential.*

considerable potential (=large enough to be noticed or important) *The technology has considerable potential in teaching.*

sb's full/maximum potential *We want every citizen to achieve his or her full potential.*

sb's true potential (=their full potential) *The team has at last begun to show its true potential.*

commercial/economic potential (=the potential to earn money) *They were quick to recognize the band's commercial potential.*

leadership potential *She always felt that I had leadership potential.*

VERBS

have potential *She has the potential to become a champion.*

show potential *The boy showed great potential as an actor.*

develop your potential (=make your skills or talents stronger) *A school aims to enable pupils to develop their potential.*

achieve/realize your potential (=be as good or successful as your ability allows) *A lot of athletes fail to achieve their full potential.*

see/recognize potential *She recognized the product's commercial potential.*

exploit potential *Until now, the island has not exploited its potential as a tourist destination.*

unlock/unleash sb's potential (=help someone to fully use their abilities) *Training is a way of unlocking employees' potential.*

harness sth's potential (=control and use it) *Businesses are competing to harness the full potential of the internet.*

PREPOSITIONS

with potential *This is a small company with great potential.*

sth's potential as sth *The study will examine the drug's potential as a cure for cancer.*

the potential for sth *Even as a young man, he showed the potential for success.*

poverty *n*

the situation or experience of being poor

ADJECTIVES/NOUNS + poverty

great/extreme poverty *They live in conditions of extreme poverty.*

abject poverty (=extremely severe) *He was shocked by the abject poverty that he saw.*

grinding poverty (=extremely severe and continuing to have a terrible effect on people's lives) *Families were living in grinding poverty behind the hotels where the rich tourists stayed.*

world poverty *The charity called for action to tackle the causes of world poverty.*

child poverty *Child poverty is becoming an increasing problem in this country.*

rural poverty (=in the countryside) *People come to the capital seeking to escape rural poverty.*

VERBS

live in poverty *Half the world is living in poverty.*

grow up in poverty *No child should grow up in poverty in the US in the 21st century.*

die in poverty *He gambled away all his money and died in poverty.*

fight/combat/tackle poverty (=take action to get rid of poverty) *The money should be spent on fighting poverty.*

alleviate poverty *formal* (=make the problem of poverty less severe) *What has the West done to alleviate poverty in the world?*

be reduced to poverty (=become very poor) *By the end of the war, millions of people had been reduced to poverty.*

poverty + NOUNS

the poverty line (*also* **the poverty level** *AmE*) (=the income below which people are officially considered to be poor) *Twenty percent of the population are living below the poverty line.*

the poverty trap (=a situation in which a poor person without a job cannot take a low-paying job because they would lose the money they receive from the government) *People will never escape the poverty trap while state benefits are high and wages are low.*

powder *n*

a dry substance in the form of very small grains

ADJECTIVES

a fine powder *Crush the peanuts into a fine powder.*

a white/blue etc powder *The drug comes in the form of a white powder.*

a dry powder *Simply add water to the dry powder.*

a loose powder (=not in a container) *The spice is usually sold as a loose powder.*

VERBS

grind/crush sth into a powder *The chillies are dried and then ground into a fine powder.*

PHRASES

in powder form *The drug is usually sold in powder form.*

power *n*

1 the ability or right to control people or events

ADJECTIVES

great/huge/enormous power *General Tong has enormous power.*

real power *The organization can make recommendations, but has no real power.*

limited power *Compared with other government departments, our power is limited.*

absolute power (=total power, with no limits) *Kings and queens had absolute power over their subjects.*

political/economic/military power *New buildings are being built everywhere, a sign of the country's growing economic power.*

VERBS

have power *People who have power never seem to use it to help others.*

get/gain power *Women were trying to gain power in a male-dominated world.*

use your power (*also* **exercise (your) power** *formal*): *Questions have been asked about the way the police exercised their power.*

wield power *formal* (=have and use a lot of power) *The Church still wields enormous power in the country.*

power lies with/rests with sb *The real power lies with the military.*

power + NOUNS

a power struggle (=a situation in which groups or leaders try to get control) *The country is caught in a power struggle between pro- and anti-democracy forces.*

sb's/sth's power base (=a group whose support makes a leader or party strong) *The Republican Party's power base is in the southern states.*

PREPOSITIONS

power over sth *People should have more power over decisions that affect their lives.*

the power of sth *The government was determined to break the power of the unions.*

PHRASES

the balance of power (=the way power is divided between people or groups) *There has been a change in the balance of power between the two countries.*

a position of power *Many of them were using their positions of power for personal advantage.*

an abuse of power *This cover-up was a shocking abuse of power.*

power is in sb's hands *Too much power is concentrated in the hands of one man.*

2 the position of having political control of a country or government

PHRASES

be in power *The law was passed when the Democrats were in power.*

sb's rise to power *The film examines Saddam Hussein's rise to power.*

sb's return to power *Supporters celebrated the party's return to power.*

VERBS

come to power (=start being in control) *Tony Blair came to power in 1997.*

take power (*also* **assume power** *formal*) (=start being in control, usually without an election) *Many people fled after the military took power last September.*

seize power (=take power by force) *His son seized power in a military coup.*

win power (=win an election) *Since winning power, the coalition has faced many problems.*

rise to power *The Roman emperor Vespasian rose to power through command of an army.*

return/be returned to power (=start being in control again, usually after an election) *The party was returned to power with an even larger majority.*

hold power (=be in power) *The economy prospered during the time that he held power.*

restore sb to power *In 2004, the army restored him to power.*

sweep to power (=win an election easily) *Reagan swept to power by promising economic reforms.*

cling (on) to power (=keep political control of a country, especially with difficulty) *The dictator clung to power for 27 years.*

3 energy that can be used to make a machine work or to make electricity

ADJECTIVES/NOUNS + power

nuclear power *The accident raised doubts about the safety of nuclear power.*

solar power (=energy produced by sunlight) *They use solar power for all their heating.*

wind power (=energy produced by the wind) *Is wind power the answer to the energy crisis?*

hydroelectric power (=energy produced by flowing water) *The factory is run on hydroelectric power.*

VERBS + power

run on solar/wind etc power (*also* **use solar/wind etc power**) *The lighting system runs on solar power.*

generate power *The river is used to generate power and to irrigate the land.*

power + NOUNS

a power source *We need to look for alternative power sources.*

a power plant/station *The river was affected by pollution from a local power station.*

power generation *Household waste can be used for power generation.*

PHRASES

a source of power *They rely on coal as their main source of power.*

under its own power (=without help from another machine) *The ship was able to leave port under its own power.*

4 a country that is strong and important, or has a lot of military strength

ADJECTIVES/NOUNS + power

a great power *Britain wanted to maintain her status as a great power.*

a major power *There will be representatives from all the world's major powers at the conference.*

a world/global power (=one with influence all over the world) *The United States had replaced Great Britain as the dominant world power.*

a military/naval power (=with a very strong army or navy) *Russia had become a naval power equal to Spain.*

a foreign power *He was charged with spying for a foreign power.*

an industrial power (=with many successful industries) *China is now a formidable industrial power.*

THESAURUS: power

nation, state, power, superpower, land → **country (1)**

5 the ability to do something – used about natural abilities, or special abilities that someone or something has

Grammar
Often plural in this meaning.

ADJECTIVES

mental powers (=the ability to think) *Holmes needed all his mental powers to solve the riddle.*

creative powers (=the ability to use your imagination and think of new things) *She was at the height of her creative powers when she wrote that novel.*

magical/supernatural/miraculous powers *Diamonds were once thought to have magical powers.*

healing powers (=the ability to make a sick person better) *The water was supposed to have healing powers.*

psychic powers (=mysterious powers, for example the ability to know what will happen in the future, or know what another person is thinking) *She claims to have psychic powers, but there's no proof.*

VERBS

have ... powers *Some plants are believed to have medicinal powers.*

lose the power to do sth *He was a brilliant speaker, who never lost the power to influence people.*

sb's powers are failing/waning (=becoming less good) *Mark felt that his creative powers were waning.*

PHRASES

the power of speech (=the ability to speak)

I was so surprised that I momentarily lost the power of speech.

the power of flight *Some birds have lost the power of flight.*

powers of observation *Sailors had to use their powers of observation to predict the weather.*

powers of concentration *As you get older, your powers of concentration may decrease.*

powers of persuasion *She used all her powers of persuasion to convince Tilly that the move was a good idea.*

be at the height of your powers (=be at the point in your life when your abilities are strongest) *Fonteyn was still at the height of her powers as a dancer.*

powerful *adj*

1 a powerful person, organization, country etc has a lot of power and is able to control or influence what happens

NOUNS

a powerful man/woman/leader *He was the second most powerful man in France after the king.*

a powerful nation/country *The United States is the richest and most powerful nation on earth.*

a powerful friend/ally *The senator has some powerful allies in Washington.*

a powerful organization/group/union/party *He is the leader of the powerful railway workers' union.*

a powerful family *Ford comes from a powerful political family.*

powerful (vested) interests (=big companies and other groups in society who have a lot of influence on government decisions) *Powerful interests will try to prevent any changes to the healthcare system.*

VERBS

become powerful *Parliament had become more powerful than the king.*

ADVERBS

extremely/enormously/incredibly powerful *She was the daughter of Henry Phipps, an enormously powerful steel multimillionaire.*

increasingly powerful/more and more powerful *The media is becoming increasingly powerful.*

THESAURUS: powerful

influential
person | figure | friend | member | thinker | writer | artist | book | report | newspaper | magazine | blog
having a lot of power to influence what happens, because people pay attention to what you say:
Tony Blair remains an influential figure in Washington today (=an influential person – a formal use). | *Coming from such an influential thinker as Fukuyama, this is an important statement.* | *Who was the most influential artist of the 20th century?* | *Keynes wrote a* ***highly influential*** *book called "The Economic Consequences of the Peace".* | *'The New Yorker' is an influential and well-respected magazine.*

dominant
position | role | force | group | class | religion | culture | ideology
more powerful than anyone or anything else:
The company has a dominant position in the market. | *He was the dominant force in tennis for many years.* | *Christianity became the dominant religion.*

strong
leader | leadership | government
a strong leader or government uses their power in a firm and determined way:
Thatcher was a strong leader who was admired by many people throughout the world. | *In a time of crisis, the country needs strong leadership.*

great
country | power | empire
a great country is very important and respected:
They were the kind of people who helped to make the US into a great country. | *There was a meeting of the world's great powers.* | *The Romans built the greatest empire the world had ever seen.*

2 a powerful machine, computer etc has a lot of power

NOUNS

a powerful engine/machine *The car's powerful V8 engine can take it to speeds of over 220 kilometres per hour.*

a powerful weapon *Today's nuclear weapons are hundreds of times more powerful than the one used at Hiroshima.*

a powerful computer/PC/chip *The information from the satellite is analysed using powerful computers.*

a powerful tool/device *The internet is a powerful tool for research.*

3 having a big effect on people's feelings or opinions

NOUNS

a powerful speech *The president gave a powerful speech in support of the bill.*

a powerful argument *One of the most powerful arguments against the death penalty is that it is possible that an innocent person could be executed.*

a powerful message *The protesters are hoping to send a powerful message to the government.*

a powerful film/movie/book/play *It is a powerful film about the horrors of war.*

P

4 causing a lot of damage

NOUNS

a powerful earthquake/storm *There was a powerful earthquake which measured 6.8 on the Richter scale.*

a powerful explosion *The building was destroyed by a powerful explosion.*

5 powerful feelings are very strong

> **THESAURUS: powerful**
> deep, powerful, intense → **strong (3)**

6 powerful arms, muscles etc are very strong

> **THESAURUS: powerful**
> powerful, muscular, well-built, hunky → **strong (1)**

P

practical *adj*

relating to real situations and events rather than ideas, emotions etc

practical + NOUNS

practical experience *You have to gain practical experience before you qualify as a doctor.*

practical work *The course includes a lot of hands-on experience and practical work.*

practical problems/difficulties *There are practical problems with running a large factory in the countryside.*

practical help/support (*also* **practical assistance** *formal*): *They provide financial and practical help for disabled students.*

practical advice *The booklet offers clear practical advice on running your business.*

practical use *The buttons are of no practical use as you can't undo them.*

practical matters *We should focus on practical matters, like where we are going to sleep tonight.*

practical considerations *There are a number of practical considerations that must be taken into account when choosing a car.*

practical skills *The course will give you the practical skills you need to become a carpenter.*

ADVERBS

purely/strictly practical (=completely and only) *My objections to the plan are purely practical: it will not work.*

PHRASES

in practical terms *In practical terms, the experiment is going to be difficult.*

practice *n*

1 the activity of doing something regularly, so that you can improve your skill at it

VERBS

sth takes/requires practice (=you can only learn to do it well by practising) *Learning to drive well takes a lot of practice.*

do some practice/do your practice *Have you done your piano practice?*

have had a lot of practice/have not had much practice *I'm not very good yet, but I haven't had much practice.*

get some practice/a lot of practice etc *You must get as much practice as possible before the competition.*

need more practice *She needs more practice if she's going to pass her driving test.*

NOUNS + practice

football/basketball etc practice *We have football practice on Thursdays.*

piano/cello etc practice *I've got to do my cello practice later.*

teaching practice *BrE*: *You have to do three months of teaching practice before you qualify.*

target practice (=practice shooting at something) *The area is used by the army for target practice.*

practice + NOUNS

a practice session *The team have regular practice sessions after school.*

a practice game *The girls have done well in practice games against players who are a lot older.*

PREPOSITIONS

with practice *You'll improve with practice, I'm sure.*

PHRASES

years/hours/months etc of practice *Learning to play like that takes years of practice.*

a lot/lots/plenty of practice *You'll get plenty of practice on the 5-day course.*

sb is out of practice (=they have not done something very much recently and are not as good as before) *I'm a bit out of practice so don't expect too much.*

2 the usual way of doing something

ADJECTIVES/NOUNS + practice

common/standard/normal practice (=the usual way that something is done) *Leaving a tip is standard practice in the US.*

best/good practice (=an example of a good way of doing something) *He illustrated his talk with examples of good practice in the classroom.*

bad practice *It's bad practice to leave your tools out overnight.*

accepted practice (=considered to be right) *It was accepted practice back then for women to stay at home and look after the children.*

established practice (=the way something has been done for a long time) *Over the years, this system has become established practice.*

working practices *Changes in working practices have improved efficiency.*

VERBS

adopt a practice (=start doing something in a

particular way) *The practice of using casual labour was adopted by many farms.*

follow a practice *Australia followed the British practice of driving on the left.*

introduce a practice *More flexible working practices were introduced last year.*

PREPOSITIONS

the practice of doing sth *The practice of using mercenaries to fight wars is not new.*

PHRASES

a code of practice *The company's code of practice on disciplinary procedures is set out in the Employee Handbook.*

changes in practice *Some changes in practice were introduced to conform with the new law.*

practise *BrE*, **practice** *AmE v*

to do an activity, often regularly, in order to improve your skill or to prepare for a test

ADVERBS

practise regularly *You need to practise regularly if you're going to be a good piano player.*

practise daily/every day *The best ballet dancers practise every day.*

practise hard *She has obviously been practising hard.*

PREPOSITIONS

practise for sth *He's practising for a singing competition.*

practise sth on sb *Everybody wants to practise their English on me.*

praise[1] *n*

words that you say or write to show that you admire and approve of someone or something

VERBS

give sb praise *Give your dog plenty of praise when it behaves well.*

heap/lavish praise on sb (*also* **shower sb with praise**) (=praise them a lot) *The media showered the young singer with praise.*

get/receive praise *His books did not get the praise they deserved.*

win/earn praise *The film has won praise from audiences and critics alike.*

deserve praise *She deserves praise for all the charity work she does.*

single sb/sth out for praise (=praise a particular person or thing) *One painting was singled out for special praise by the judges.*

ADJECTIVES

high praise (=praise that shows you think someone or something is very good) *He said she was the best young player he'd ever seen, which was high praise.*

special praise *The actress was given special praise for her achievements.*

lavish praise (=very high praise) *The critics heaped lavish praise on his performance.*

widespread praise (=from many people) *She has already won widespread praise for her leadership.*

PREPOSITIONS

praise for sth/sb *There was praise for the way he handled the affair.*

in praise of sb/sth (=praising them) *He wrote a poem in praise of his hero.*

PHRASES

be full of praise for sb/sth (=praise them a lot) *Her teacher was full of praise for her work.*

have nothing but praise for sb/sth (=praise them a lot because you admire what they have done) *Passengers had nothing but praise for the pilot.*

sing sb's praises (=tell other people that someone is good) *The boss has been singing your praises.*

words of praise *He had words of praise for the excellent nursing care provided.*

worthy of praise (=deserving praise) *There was only one design that was worthy of praise.*

praise[2] *v*

to say that you admire and approve of someone or something, especially publicly

ADVERBS

be highly praised (=be praised a lot) *The actor's performance was highly praised by the critics.*

be widely praised (=by many people) *Their efforts have been widely praised.*

PREPOSITIONS

praise sb for sth *The Mayor praised the rescue teams for their courage.*

prayer *n*

words that you say when praying to God or gods

VERBS

say a prayer *The children said their prayers and got into bed.*

kneel in prayer *A group of men were kneeling in prayer.*

offer a prayer (=say a prayer in a formal way, often in a group) *Special prayers were offered for the dead.*

recite prayers *formal* (=say the words of prayers aloud, usually with other people) *A stream of people reciting prayers followed the procession.*

perform your prayers (=kneel and pray at the same time each day - used especially about Muslims) *He went to a local mosque to perform his early morning prayers.*

answer sb's prayer (=God hears you and makes what you want happen) *I believe that one day my prayers will be answered.*

ADJECTIVES

daily prayers *Muslims face Mecca when they perform their daily prayers.*

a silent prayer *He said a silent prayer as he approached the house.*

prayer + NOUNS

a prayer service *There is usually a short prayer service in the morning.*

PREPOSITIONS

a prayer for sb *Prayers for the dead will be held during the evening service.*

a prayer to God *She offered a silent prayer to God.*

in/at prayer (=in the act of praying) *The monks spend most of their day in prayer.*

PHRASES

be in sb's prayers (=be prayed for) *You are always in my prayers.*

sb's prayers are/go with you *Our thoughts and prayers are with you at this sad time.*

remember sb in your prayers *Please remember them in your prayers and ask God to guide them.*

precaution *n*

something you do in order to prevent something dangerous or unpleasant from happening

ADJECTIVES/NOUNS + precaution

a sensible/wise precaution *Fitting window locks is a sensible precaution.*

a simple precaution *You can reduce the chance of anything going wrong by taking a few simple precautions.*

a necessary precaution *He knew the risks but failed to take the necessary precautions.*

a reasonable precaution *We take all reasonable precautions to safeguard the children.*

adequate/proper precautions *Companies have a legal responsibility to take adequate precautions against fire.*

basic/elementary precautions *You could get badly injured if you don't take some basic precautions.*

a safety precaution *Residents living near the gas leak were moved from their homes as a safety precaution.*

a security precaution *Security precautions have been increased at airports.*

elaborate precautions (=a lot of detailed precautions) *The police took elaborate precautions to prevent the demonstrators from reaching Parliament Square.*

VERBS

take precautions *Always take precautions and never reveal your password to anyone.*

take the precaution of doing sth *I took the precaution of insuring my camera.*

PREPOSITIONS

a precaution against sth *The pipes are insulated as a precaution against frost damage.*

as a precaution *After the gas leak the area was evacuated as a precaution.*

precedent Ac *n*

something similar that has been done or has happened before, which may be used as a reason for doing the same thing now

ADJECTIVES

a dangerous precedent (=one that could cause problems in the future) *They opposed the plan, saying it would create a dangerous precedent.*

an important precedent *By doing this, an important precedent was established.*

a legal precedent (=one that is important in law) *The case set a legal precedent.*

historical precedent (=a precedent in history) *My situation seemed to lack historical precedent.*

VERBS

set/establish a precedent *The decision could set a legal precedent for other similar cases.*

create a precedent *If we allow this once, it will create a precedent.*

follow a precedent *He is following a precedent set by other military leaders.*

break with precedent (=do something in a new way) *The king broke with precedent and allowed the ceremony to be filmed.*

use sth as a precedent *Other countries were afraid that the invasion would be used as a precedent.*

serve as a precedent (=be used as a precedent) *He hopes a ruling in his favor could serve as a precedent.*

cite (sth as) a precedent *formal* (=mention a precedent) *An established method of working can be cited as a precedent in disputes.*

PREPOSITIONS

sth is without precedent (=it has never happened before) *The team's achievement is superb and without precedent.*

a precedent for sth *There is a precedent for a team containing both boys and girls.*

precious *adj* very valuable or important

NOUNS

a precious metal/stone (=one that is worth a lot of money) *They used diamonds and other precious stones to make jewellery.*

a precious object (*also* **a precious artefact** *formal*): *The room was filled with carvings, sculptures, and other precious objects.*

a precious commodity *Water is a precious commodity.*

precious resources *The government has wasted the country's precious resources.*

precious time *My time is precious, and I don't want to waste it.*

precious seconds/moments/minutes/hours *We knew we only had a few more precious hours together.*

a precious asset *The organization's most precious asset is its staff.*

a precious gift *Her illness made her appreciate more the precious gift of life.*

THESAURUS: precious

precious, treasured, priceless, irreplaceable → **valuable (2)**

predict Ac *v*

to say that something will happen, before it happens

ADVERBS

accurately/precisely/correctly predict sth *They correctly predicted the result of the election.*

successfully/reliably predict sth *It is difficult to reliably predict when an earthquake will happen.*

wrongly predict sth *The weather forecasters wrongly predicted a long hot summer.*

be widely predicted (=by many people) *Usain Bolt is widely predicted to win a gold medal.*

VERBS

try/attempt to predict *Scientists are trying to predict how the Amazon will look in 20 years' time.*

PHRASES

sth is difficult/hard/impossible to predict *It is impossible to predict how she will react.*

predict sth with accuracy/certainty *No one can predict with any certainty what will happen with this type of investment.*

as predicted *As predicted, our team won.*

I can confidently predict that... (=used when you are sure that something will happen) *I can confidently predict that you will enjoy this book.*

predictable Ac *adj*

doing something or happening in exactly the way you would expect

ADVERBS

highly predictable *The movements of the planets are highly predictable.*

entirely/totally/utterly predictable *Moran's angry reaction was entirely predictable.*

fairly predictable *He began his speech in a fairly predictable way.*

boringly predictable *The results of the election were boringly predictable.*

NOUNS

a predictable pattern *Many of their arguments followed a predictable pattern.*

a predictable consequence/result/outcome *Poverty is a predictable consequence of rising unemployment.*

a predictable response/reaction *Logan's reaction was predictable.*

a predictable effect *The snow had a predictable effect on traffic.*

a predictable way/manner/fashion *Projects rarely develop in a totally predictable fashion.*

a predictable routine *He would have preferred a more predictable routine.*

PREPOSITIONS

predictable from sth *The child's reaction was predictable from a knowledge of his personality.*

prediction Ac *n*

a statement about what you think is going to happen

ADJECTIVES

an accurate prediction *For the first time people were able to make accurate predictions about the position of the stars.*

a prediction is correct/right *Jane's prediction later proved right.*

a prediction is wrong/incorrect *I'm hoping that their prediction of rain is wrong.*

a reliable prediction *We are not yet able to make reliable predictions about earthquakes.*

a dire/gloomy/pessimistic prediction (=saying that something bad will happen) *There have been some gloomy predictions about the economy recently.*

an optimistic prediction (=saying that something good will happen, often wrongly) *These estimates were based on optimistic predictions of growth.*

a confident prediction (=one that you think is probably right) *The situation is so uncertain that it is hard to make a confident prediction.*

VERBS

make a prediction *It is far too early to make predictions about what will happen in the election.*

confirm a prediction (=show that it was right) *They are now planning further tests to confirm their predictions.*

test a prediction *In order to test this prediction, Schultz carried out a number of experiments.*

sb's prediction proves right/accurate/wrong (=it is shown to be right, accurate, or wrong) *Their predictions of a long hot summer proved wrong.*

PREPOSITIONS

a prediction of/about sth *His predictions of success were accurate.*

predominant *adj* THESAURUS **main**

prefer *v*

to like someone or something more than someone or something else

P

ADVERBS

much prefer sb/sth *He much prefers his new job to his old one.*

greatly prefer sb/sth *Our family greatly prefers the way of life in Italy.*

strongly prefer sb/sth *The job advertisement said that previous experience was strongly preferred.*

really prefer sb/sth *I would really prefer to stay at home this evening.*

clearly/obviously prefer sb/sth *The little boy clearly preferred to be with his mother.*

generally/usually/on the whole prefer sth *People generally prefer to go on holiday in July or August.*

VERBS

would prefer sth *She would prefer to study in the US if she can.*

may/might prefer sth *I thought you might prefer to be alone.*

tend to prefer *People tend to prefer sweet foods.*

PREPOSITIONS

prefer sb/sth to sb/sth *I prefer this novel to her other ones.*

prefer sb/sth over sb/sth *In those days, employers preferred men over women.*

PHRASES

if you prefer *We can go by bus, but if you prefer, we can take a taxi.*

the preferred option *The cheaper plan was the preferred option.*

preference *n*

if you have a preference for something, you like it more than another thing and will choose it if you can

ADJECTIVES

a strong preference *There is a strong preference for fresh fruit and vegetables.*

a clear preference *The survey showed a clear preference for his style of leadership.*

a marked preference (=very noticeable) *Australians have a marked preference for separate houses surrounded by private space.*

a personal preference *My own personal preference is for darker colours.*

individual preferences *The company keeps details of its clients' individual preferences.*

VERBS

have a preference *Do you have a preference for any particular kind of tea?*

express a preference *He avoided expressing a preference for any of the candidates.*

show a preference *The girls showed a preference for being with other girls.*

suit sb's preferences *You can change things to suit your own preferences.*

PREPOSITIONS

a preference for sth *Babies have a preference for sweet foods.*

a preference as to/regarding sth *Parents can express a preference as to the school their child will attend.*

PHRASES

in order of preference *Please list your choice of colleges in order of preference.*

sth is a matter of personal preference (=it is something that you can choose, according to what you like) *Which phone you decide to buy is just a matter of personal preference.*

pregnant *adj*

if a woman or female animal is pregnant, she has a baby growing inside her body

VERBS

become pregnant (*also* **get pregnant** *informal*): *Sally became pregnant, and gave birth to a baby son.*

get sb pregnant *informal* (=make a woman pregnant, usually without planning to) *Her boyfriend didn't want to get her pregnant.*

ADVERBS

twelve weeks pregnant/two months pregnant etc *The doctor said that she was eight weeks pregnant.*

heavily pregnant (=almost ready to give birth) *I saw at once that the woman was heavily pregnant.*

PHRASES

be pregnant with twins/your first child etc *Her husband left her when she was pregnant with her second child.*

prejudice *n*

an unreasonable dislike and distrust of people who are different from you in some way

ADJECTIVES/NOUNS + prejudice

racial prejudice (=because of your race) *They found it difficult to get good jobs because of racial prejudice.*

class prejudice (=because of your social class) *There is no place for those old class prejudices in our modern society.*

anti-gay/anti-American/anti-Catholic etc prejudice (=against gay people, Americans etc) *There is still a lot of anti-American prejudice in this country.*

strong prejudice *Women managers often encounter strong prejudice from men.*

deep-seated prejudice (=very strong and difficult to change) *All these attitudes are based on deep-seated prejudice.*

blind prejudice (=prejudice that stops you from considering the facts) *They rejected his suggestion out of blind prejudice.*

VERBS

experience/encounter/face prejudice *Students with disabilities often encounter prejudice.*

overcome prejudice (=succeed in spite of prejudice) *He overcame poverty and prejudice to become a great athlete.*

fight (against) prejudice *All his life, he fought against prejudice.*

reinforce prejudice (=make it stronger) *The newspaper article will only have reinforced people's prejudices about gypsies.*

confirm sb's prejudices (=make someone think their prejudices are right) *His behaviour confirmed all my prejudices about the English.*

PREPOSITIONS

prejudice against sb *There is still a lot of prejudice against women in positions of authority.*

prejudice about sth/sb *We want to challenge prejudices about age.*

THESAURUS: prejudice

discrimination
the practice of treating one group of people differently from another in an unfair way:
There is ***widespread discrimination*** *against older people. | The government introduced new laws on* ***sex discrimination****.*

bigotry
a completely unreasonable hatred for people of a different race, religion etc, based on strong and fixed opinions:
His speeches were full of ***religious bigotry*** *and hate. | Hitler directed his* ***bigotry against*** *the Jews.*

intolerance
an unreasonable refusal to accept beliefs, customs, and ways of thinking that are different from your own:
Religious intolerance *is a problem in many parts of the world. | There is an atmosphere of intolerance in the media.*

racism/racial prejudice
unfair treatment of people because they belong to a different race:
Many black people have been the ***victims of racism*** *in Britain. | Some immigrant groups faced racism.*

sexism
the belief that one sex, especially women, is weaker, less intelligent etc than the other, especially when this results in someone being treated unfairly:
She accused the company of sexism because she didn't get a promotion.

ageism (*also* **agism** *AmE*)
unfair treatment of people because they are old:
The new law aims to stop ageism in the workplace.

homophobia
prejudice towards or hatred of gay people:
There is a lot of homophobia in the armed forces.

xenophobia
hatred and fear of foreigners:
Politicians sometimes try to stir up xenophobia and say that foreigners are taking all the jobs.

anti-Semitism
a strong feeling of hatred toward Jewish people:
Anti-Semitism is on the increase in some parts of Europe.

Islamophobia
hatred and fear of Muslims:
Many people are concerned about the rise of Islamophobia.

preliminary Ac *adj*

happening before the main part of something, especially in order to prepare for it

NOUNS

the preliminary results/findings *The preliminary results look very good.*

a preliminary report *The committee published their preliminary report.*

preliminary research/analysis/examination/study *Scientists have begun a preliminary analysis of the data.*

a preliminary investigation/inquiry *The preliminary investigation showed that the damage was caused by some kind of explosive.*

preliminary work *Preliminary work has begun on building the bridge.*

a preliminary stage/step *We are still in the preliminary stages of our work.*

the preliminary round (=the first part of a competition) *France beat Italy in the preliminary rounds of the competition.*

a preliminary meeting/discussion *They had a preliminary meeting before the conference took place.*

THESAURUS: preliminary

initial, preliminary, opening, introductory → **first[1]**

preparation *n*

1 the things that you do to get ready for something that is going to happen

Grammar
Always plural in this meaning.

VERBS

make preparations *He was making preparations for his retirement.*

P

begin preparations *The climbers rose at six and began their preparations.*

complete the preparations *All the preparations for the mission have now been completed.*

ADJECTIVES/NOUNS + preparation

final/last-minute preparations *Final preparations are being made for the president's visit tomorrow.*

(all) the necessary preparations *Will you have time to make all the necessary preparations?*

elaborate preparations *Elaborate preparations had been made for a meeting between the two kings.*

the wedding/Christmas/party etc preparations *Her mother helped with the wedding preparations.*

PREPOSITIONS

preparations for sth *She went to check on preparations for the party.*

PHRASES

preparations are underway (=they have started) *Preparations are underway for the anniversary celebrations.*

2 the process of getting ready, or making something ready

VERBS

do some/no etc preparation *She had obviously done no preparation for the meeting.*

need/require preparation *Important competitions need proper preparation.*

supervise the preparation of sth *Andrew was in the kitchen, supervising the preparation of the food.*

ADJECTIVES

careful preparation *Painting a wall requires careful preparation.*

thorough preparation (=very careful and detailed) *Thorough preparation is the best way to do well in an exam.*

meticulous preparation (=extremely careful not to miss any details) *The robbery took place after months of meticulous preparation.*

good/ideal preparation (=very useful) *This game was good preparation for our match next week.*

adequate/proper preparation *You cannot go on a dangerous trip like this without adequate preparation.*

poor/inadequate preparation (=not enough preparation) *He was defeated because of poor preparation.*

mental preparation *Mental preparation is as important as physical training.*

PREPOSITIONS

preparation for sth *Preparation for the interview is vital.*

in preparation for sth *He is practising every day, in preparation for the championship.*

the preparation of sth *Many people helped us in the preparation of this document.*

presence *n*

1 the fact that a substance, disease etc exists in something

VERBS

reveal/show the presence of sth *Tests revealed the presence of dangerous chemicals in the building.*

indicate/suggest the presence of sth *These plants indicate the presence of underground water.*

detect the presence of sth *The device is used for detecting the presence of alcohol.*

confirm the presence of sth *This test will confirm the presence of infection.*

explain the presence of sth *He couldn't explain the presence of the drugs at his home.*

PREPOSITIONS

the presence of sth *The test shows the presence of the disease.*

2 the fact that someone is there in a place, at an event etc

ADJECTIVES/NOUNS + presence

the constant presence of sb *There is always the constant presence of traffic.*

sb's continued presence *Many people are opposed to the continued presence of US troops.*

a permanent presence *Which Europeans were the first to establish a permanent presence in America?*

a strong presence (=the fact of being present in large numbers or in an active way) *The company has a strong presence in Asia.*

police/military presence (=the fact that police or soldiers are present) *What was the reason for the large police presence at the meeting?*

VERBS

notice sb's presence *He did not seem to have noticed my presence.*

sense/feel sb's presence (=be aware that someone is present without seeing them) *I sensed the presence of someone else in the room.*

acknowledge sb's presence (=speak to someone or make a sign to show that you know they are present) *He acknowledged my presence with a quick wave.*

request sb's presence *formal*: *Your presence is requested at the next meeting of the Council.*

PREPOSITIONS

in sb's presence *formal* (=while they are present) *Interviews were always held in the presence of a lawyer.*

PHRASES

be/become aware of sb's presence *It was only when I coughed that he became aware of my presence.*

present[1] *n*

something you give someone on a special occasion or to thank them for something

NOUNS + present

a birthday/Christmas/wedding etc present *The couple received hundreds of wedding presents.*

ADJECTIVES

an expensive present *I don't need expensive presents to prove you love me.*

a good/nice/lovely present *The best present I ever had from my dad was a guitar.*

an ideal/perfect present *This is the perfect present for a music-lover.*

a little present *Whenever he went away he brought her back a little present.*

a thank-you present (=given to thank someone) *I bought them some chocolates as a thank-you present.*

VERBS

give sb a present *She loved giving people presents.*

buy/get sb a present *He couldn't afford to buy her a present.*

get/receive a present *He got lots of presents from his friends.*

exchange presents (=give one another a present) *We exchange Christmas presents every year.*

wrap a present *She spent the afternoon wrapping birthday presents.*

open/unwrap a present *Can we open our presents now?*

PREPOSITIONS

a present for sb *She was looking for a present for her son.*

a present from sb *This ring was a present from my grandmother.*

as a present *I was given this book as a present.*

PHRASES

sth would make a nice/lovely/ideal etc present *I thought the bowl would make a nice present for someone.*

> In more formal English, people use **gift** instead of **present**.

present[2] *v*

1 to give something to someone, for example at a formal or official occasion

> **THESAURUS: present**
>
> donate, distribute, contribute, award, leave, lavish, confer, bestow, hand, pass, present → **give (1)**

2 to cause something to happen or exist

NOUNS

present a problem *These mountain roads present problems even to experienced drivers.*

present difficulties *Juggling work and family responsibilities presents difficulties for women.*

present an obstacle (=cause a problem that is difficult to deal with or solve) *Lack of money presented a huge obstacle.*

present a challenge *I'm enjoying my new job because it presents an interesting challenge.*

present a threat *The disease presents a serious threat to the farming industry.*

present a danger/risk *These dogs present a danger to the public.*

present an opportunity *The internet presents tremendous opportunities for businesses.*

PREPOSITIONS

present sb with sth *Freedom presents us with choices.*

present sth to sb *Short stories present a challenge to the writer.*

presentation *n*

1 a formal talk in which you describe or explain something to a group of people

VERBS

give a presentation *The chairman gave a presentation about the company's latest sales figures.*

do a presentation (=give a presentation - more informal) *I've been asked to do a presentation about my work.*

make/deliver a presentation (=give a presentation- more formal) *The course teaches you how to organize and deliver sales presentations.*

listen to/hear a presentation *We listened to a presentation about the management changes.*

attend a presentation (=go to it) *Over 100 people attended the presentation.*

prepare a presentation *She is busy preparing a presentation for tomorrow's meeting.*

ADJECTIVES/NOUNS + presentation

a short/brief presentation *The professor gave a brief presentation about her research.*

a 5-minute/10-minute/hour-long etc presentation *Each candidate has to give a 30-minute presentation about his or her previous work.*

a formal presentation *After the formal presentation, there will be an opportunity for people to ask questions.*

a sales presentation *The book has lots of useful tips on how to give an effective sales presentation.*

a video presentation

presentation + NOUNS

presentation skills *David's boss sent him on a course to improve his presentation skills.*

PREPOSITIONS

a presentation on/about sth *She has to give a presentation on her research.*

a presentation by sb *We attended a presentation by Professor Nordstrom.*

2 the act of giving something such as a prize or award to someone at a formal ceremony

ADJECTIVES/NOUNS + presentation

the official presentation *The official presentation of the trophy will take place immediately after the game.*

the annual presentation (=one that happens every year) *The annual presentation of diplomas will take place in July.*

an award presentation *The award presentation will be held on January 17th.*

presentation + NOUNS

a presentation ceremony *The presentation ceremony will be held at the University of Chicago.*

VERBS

make the presentation *The principal will make the presentation of the awards.*

PREPOSITIONS

the presentation of sth to sb *The evening ended with the presentation of the prizes to the winners.*

preserve *v*

1 to make something continue without changing

NOUNS

preserve the peace *It is the responsibility of the police to preserve the peace.*

preserve sb's freedom (=avoid being caught by the police etc) *He managed to preserve his freedom by fleeing abroad.*

preserve sth's independence *The country was able to preserve its independence by defeating Italian invaders in 1896.*

preserve the character of sth *The organization wants to preserve the character of the many historic neighborhoods throughout Houston.*

preserve a tradition *The museum was founded in order to preserve the traditions and culture of the region.*

preserve a memory *A wedding album is the ideal way of preserving memories of the most beautiful day in your life.*

preserve the status quo (=not make any changes) *The government is keen to preserve the status quo, and is unlikely to support any changes in the voting system.*

2 to save something or someone from being harmed or destroyed

NOUNS

preserve a town/village/building *They want to preserve the town so that it looks how it did three hundred years ago.*

preserve a forest/woodland *We must encourage the planting of new trees and preserve our existing woodlands.*

preserve the environment *Consumers can help preserve the environment by choosing recycled and eco-friendly products.*

ADVERBS

well/beautifully/perfectly preserved *The palace is beautifully preserved and looks just like it did when the king lived there.*

carefully preserved *The town's colonial architecture has been carefully preserved.*

lovingly preserved (=with a lot of care) *A two-year restoration has lovingly preserved the castle's original features.*

PHRASES

preserve sth for posterity/future generations (=so that people in the future can enjoy it) *Given its significance in the history of Western culture, this is a building that must be preserved for posterity.*

president *n*

1 the official leader of a country that does not have a king or queen

ADJECTIVES

the US/French/Russian etc president *The US president is having talks with the Japanese foreign minister.*

the vice president *The vice president will be in charge of the country while the president is away.*

a Democratic/Republican/Socialist etc president *Clinton became the first Democratic president for more than a decade.*

the former/previous president *The former president left the country in order to avoid arrest.*

a lame-duck president (=a president who has lost his or her power at an election) *He was a lame-duck president in the final weeks of office.*

VERBS

become president *Barack Obama became the 44th president of the United States.*

elect a president *He was elected president by a small majority.*

run for president (=try to be elected as president) *She is thinking of running for president next year.*

be sworn in as president (*also* **be inaugurated as president** *formal*) (=officially become president at a special ceremony) *He will be sworn in as president in January.*

serve as president (=have the job of president) *Nixon served as president from 1969 to 1974.*

impeach a president (=formally accuse a

president of a serious crime) *They threatened to impeach the president for lying to Congress.*

2 the person who has the highest position in a company or organization

ADJECTIVES/NOUNS + president

a company president *The company president announced his resignation.*

a university/college president *AmE: The article was written by the Princeton University president.*

a club president *Members will meet to choose a new club president.*

the vice/deputy president *She became vice president of the college debating society.*

the national president *Smith lost his job as national president of the Farmworkers' Union.*

VERBS

become president *He became president of the International College of Surgeons.*

appoint sb president (=give someone the job of president) *He was appointed president of the Hungarian National Bank.*

press[1] *v*

1 to push something such as a button or pedal with your finger or your foot

NOUNS

press a switch/button/buzzer *The man pressed a button and the gate opened.*

press the accelerator *especially BrE*, **press the gas pedal** *AmE: She pressed the accelerator and the car picked up speed.*

press your horn (=make a loud warning noise to other drivers) *The driver behind me kept pressing his horn.*

press a key (=on a keyboard, especially on a computer) *I must have pressed the wrong key.*

press Delete/Return/Save etc *When you've finished working on the file, press 'Save'.*

2 to push something against or into something

ADVERBS

press sth firmly *He pressed the cork firmly into the bottle.*

PREPOSITIONS

press sth against sth *She pressed her face against the window and tried to see what was happening.*

press sth to sth *I had to press the phone to my ear in order to hear her voice.*

press sth into sth *His grandfather pressed some money into his hand.*

press[2] *n*

newspapers and magazines, or the people who produce reports for them

> **Grammar**
> You usually say **the press**.

ADJECTIVES/NOUNS + press

the national/local press *There was very little about the incident in the national press.*

the British/American etc press *The British press loves stories about the royal family.*

the foreign press *African countries want the foreign press to report African affairs.*

a free press (=whose reports are not restricted by the government) *I am glad that we have a free press in this country.*

the tabloid/popular press (=popular newspapers with a lot of stories about famous people etc, rather than serious news) *He regularly appeared in the tabloid press alongside well-known actresses.*

the gutter press *BrE disapproving* (=newspapers that print shocking stories about people's private lives) *Details of the singer's sex life often appeared in the gutter press.*

VERBS

talk/speak to the press *He is reluctant to talk to the press.*

leak sth to the press (=give them secret information in an unofficial way) *The confidential report was leaked to the press.*

press + NOUNS

a press conference (=a meeting at which someone answers questions from reporters) *The police held a press conference to announce a new development in the case.*

press reports *According to press reports, he was suffering from exhaustion.*

press coverage (=articles about something in newspapers) *The event received a lot of press coverage.*

a press photographer *A group of press photographers was waiting for her outside.*

a press clipping (*also* **a press cutting** *BrE*) (=a short piece of writing cut out from a newspaper or magazine) *He showed me some old press cuttings about the case.*

PREPOSITIONS

in the press *The incident was not reported in the press.*

PHRASES

the freedom of the press (*also* **press freedom**) *These restrictions are an attack on the freedom of the press.*

get/have a bad/good press (=be criticized or praised in newspapers) *Bankers have had a bad press recently.*

pressure *n*

1 attempts to persuade or force someone to do something

ADJECTIVES

strong/intense pressure *There was strong pressure for a change of leadership.*

considerable/great/enormous etc pressure *The unions are under considerable pressure to accept the company's offer.*

increasing/mounting pressure *There was increasing pressure on the government to cut the tax on fuel.*

constant pressure *I am under constant pressure from my family to get married.*

public/popular pressure (=pressure from the public) *He faces mounting public pressure to resign.*

international pressure (=from many countries) *The country's leadership is sensitive to international pressure.*

political/diplomatic/economic pressure *The decision was changed because of political pressure from Washington.*

peer pressure (=pressure to behave in a certain way by people you know who are the same age as you) *Teenage boys often start drinking alcohol because of peer pressure.*

P

VERBS

put pressure on sb (*also* **exert pressure on sb** *formal*): *His family are putting pressure on him to get married.*

increase the pressure *The international community is increasing the pressure for a peaceful settlement.*

keep up/maintain the pressure *We must keep up the pressure until they change their minds.*

come under pressure (=be affected by pressure) *The new prime minister has already come under pressure to resign.*

feel pressure *I felt a lot of pressure to go to university, but I wanted to be an artist.*

resist pressure *He is resisting pressure to cancel the project.*

bow to/give in to pressure (=do what people want you to do) *Her father eventually gave in to pressure and agreed to lend them the money.*

respond to pressure (=do something as a result of pressure) *The government responded to public pressure and changed the law.*

PREPOSITIONS

pressure for sth *The government has been slow to respond to pressure for change.*

pressure on sb *There is a lot of pressure on girls to be slim.*

pressure from sb *The exam was changed as a result of pressure from schools.*

be under pressure to do sth *Apple growers are under pressure from the public to use fewer chemicals.*

PHRASES

put sb under pressure (=put a lot of pressure on them) *The men were put under pressure to sign the confessions.*

bring pressure to bear on sb (=put pressure on them) *Pressure must be brought to bear on the government to reform the system.*

2 things that make you feel worried, especially because you feel you have too many things to do

VERBS

cope with/handle the pressure (=deal with it successfully) *If you cannot handle the pressure, you shouldn't be a manager.*

increase the pressure *These tests will increase the pressure on students.*

ease/reduce the pressure *The deal would ease the financial pressure on both companies.*

PREPOSITIONS

the pressure on sb *He wants to ease the pressure on his players.*

PHRASES

be under a lot of/considerable etc pressure *The doctor made the mistake because he was under a lot of pressure.*

pressure(s) of work *He said he couldn't see her because of the pressure of work.*

the pressures of life *She found it hard to cope with the pressures of life.*

3 force when you press against something

ADJECTIVES

gentle/light/slight pressure *Apply gentle pressure when giving a massage.*

firm pressure *Firm pressure is needed so that the bandage sticks to the skin.*

VERBS

put pressure on sth *Put some pressure on the wound to help stop the bleeding.*

apply/exert pressure *Don't apply too much pressure or you'll damage the surface of the pot.*

feel the pressure of sth *She felt the gentle pressure of his hand on her back.*

4 the amount of force that a gas or liquid produces

ADJECTIVES/NOUNS + pressure

high/low pressure *The tank contains gas at high pressure.*

air pressure *The air pressure is lower in the mountains.*

blood pressure *His blood pressure was always high.*

atmospheric pressure *Just before a storm there is a drop in atmospheric pressure.*

VERBS

the pressure increases/builds up *Pressure builds up beneath the volcano.*

the pressure drops/falls *The engine pressure was dropping.*

prestige *n*

the respect or admiration that something has, especially a company or organization

ADJECTIVES

great/enormous/immense prestige *The professor used to enjoy enormous prestige within his profession.*

personal prestige *Winning the championship earned him personal prestige.*

social prestige *Being a doctor carries a lot of social prestige.*

international/national prestige *Hosting the Olympic Games would add to our country's international prestige.*

VERBS

have prestige *Cornell is one of the most famous universities in the US, and has considerable prestige.*

enjoy prestige (=have prestige - more formal) *He enjoys the prestige of being a very wealthy man.*

gain/win prestige *The firm gained a lot of prestige for its products.*

increase sth's prestige (*also* **enhance sth's prestige** *formal*): *The king wanted to enhance his prestige through war.*

THESAURUS: prestige

image, name, standing, prestige, stature → **reputation**

pretence *BrE*, pretense *AmE n*

a way of behaving which is intended to make people believe something that is not true

ADJECTIVES

an elaborate pretence (=carefully planned and carried out) *He made an elaborate pretence of yawning and said he was going to bed.*

an absurd pretence *Why do we keep up this absurd pretence?*

VERBS

make no pretence *I made no pretence of having any great musical knowledge.*

make a pretence *Steve made a vague pretence at being interested.*

keep up/maintain a pretence *She kept up the pretence that her husband had died in order to claim the insurance money.*

abandon/give up/drop a pretence *Maria had abandoned any pretence of believing what he said.*

PREPOSITIONS

a pretence of/at sth *No one was deceived by his pretence at being busy.*

PHRASES

under the pretence of doing sth *He stole her money under the pretence of helping her to invest it.*

pretend *v*

to deliberately behave as though something is true when it is not, either for fun or to deceive someone

ADVERBS

sb is just pretending *He's not asleep - he's just pretending.*

pretend otherwise (=pretend that something different is true) *I can't marry her and to pretend otherwise would be wrong.*

VERBS

pretend not to notice/hear/see *She pretended not to notice that he was standing next to her.*

let's pretend... *Let's pretend we're on the moon.*

stop pretending *Stop pretending you don't love him!*

sb can't go on pretending sth (=they cannot continue pretending) *We can't go on pretending that everything is OK.*

pretend + NOUNS

pretend ignorance (=pretend that you do not know) *To pretend ignorance of the situation would be irresponsible.*

pretty *adj* pleasant to look at

NOUNS

a pretty girl/woman *A pretty girl sat next to him on the bus.*

pretty face/eyes/mouth *Natalie has a pretty face and a lovely smile.*

pretty dress/shoes *I like your dress - it's really pretty.*

a pretty place/town/village/house *The village looks pretty in the summer, when all the flowers are out.*

pretty countryside *The countryside around Oxford is really pretty.*

a pretty picture *His paintings are more than just pretty pictures.*

VERBS

look pretty *The garden looked pretty in the morning sun.*

PHRASES

a pretty little... *There was a pretty little bird outside my bedroom window.*

sth is not a pretty sight *informal* (=it does not look good) *His stomach was not a pretty sight.*

THESAURUS: pretty

handsome, good-looking, pretty, attractive, cute, lovely, gorgeous, glorious, picturesque, magnificent, stunning, breathtaking/spectacular, exquisite → **beautiful**

prevalent *adj* THESAURUS **common (1)**

prevent *v*

to stop something from happening, or stop someone from doing something

P

NOUNS

prevent (a) disease *Taking regular exercise helps to prevent heart disease.*

prevent an accident/disaster *To prevent accidents, guns should not be loaded when being cleaned.*

prevent an attack *Four soldiers were killed while trying to prevent an attack on a government building.*

prevent violence *Police officers have been sent to the area to prevent possible violence.*

prevent damage *Wrap the china carefully to prevent damage.*

prevent loss *Buildings are insulated to prevent heat loss.*

prevent the spread of sth *Good hygiene is essential to prevent the spread of disease.*

prevent the development of sth *This treatment could prevent the development of diabetes.*

prevent the use of sth *These measures prevent the use of tobacco in public places.*

prevent a repeat/recurrence of sth *The club is hoping that extra security will prevent a repeat of last week's violent scenes.*

VERBS

try to prevent sth (*also* **attempt to prevent sth** *formal*): *She tried to prevent me from coming.*

fail to prevent sth *He braked, but failed to prevent a collision.*

be designed/intended to prevent sth *The law is designed to prevent fraud.*

help to prevent sth *Keeping a wound clean can help to prevent infections.*

take action to prevent sth *It is time for the government to take action to prevent crime.*

ADVERBS

successfully prevent sth *Protesters have successfully prevented the demolition team from starting their work.*

effectively prevent sth (=the effect is to prevent something) *The steep steps to the building effectively prevent wheelchair users from getting in.*

PREPOSITIONS

prevent sb/sth from doing sth *His back injury may prevent him from playing in tomorrow's game.*

prevention *n*

stopping something bad from happening

NOUNS + prevention

crime prevention *More money needs to be spent on crime prevention.*

fire prevention *The fire department can give you advice on fire prevention.*

accident prevention *Accident prevention is extremely important and people need to take it more seriously.*

disease prevention *There has been a lot of research into disease prevention.*

prevention + NOUNS

a prevention programme *BrE*, **a prevention program** *AmE*: *Huge amounts of money were spent on AIDS prevention programs.*

a prevention measure (=a way of preventing something) *People are advised to take crime prevention measures such as not leaving anything in their cars at night.*

ADJECTIVES

effective prevention *Effective flood prevention is needed urgently.*

PREPOSITIONS

the prevention of sth *New technology can be used in the prevention of crime.*

previous [Ac] *adj*

the previous person, thing, or time is the one before the one you are talking about

NOUNS

the previous year/day/month etc *When I spoke to her the previous day, she seemed fine.*

a previous occasion/time *She had been warned on four previous occasions about being late for work.*

the previous chapter/section/paragraph *As we saw in a previous chapter, a number of different factors are involved.*

the previous government/president/chairman etc *Previous governments have failed to deal with the problem of climate change.*

the previous owner *The furniture was left by the house's previous owner.*

sb's previous wife/husband etc *Diana asked him about his previous girlfriends.*

a previous marriage/relationship *She has two children from a previous marriage.*

a previous job/career *I had been very well paid in my previous job.*

previous experience *The interviewer asked him whether he had any previous experience.*

Previous, former, or old?

Former is more formal than **previous**. It is used to describe a person or thing that used to have a particular job or position: *George Bush is the* ***former*** *president of the United States.* | *her* ***former*** *husband* | *Krakow was the* ***former*** *capital of Poland* **Former** is also used about countries that used to exist: *the* ***former*** *Soviet Union.*

Old is more informal than **previous**. It is used about people you knew or things you had in the past : *my* ***old*** *boss* | *her* ***old*** *boyfriend* | *our* ***old*** *TV* | *my* ***old*** *school.* It is also used about things that existed in the past and have been replaced by a newer thing: *The new stadium is much bigger than the* ***old*** *one.*

price *n*

the amount of money you have to pay for something

ADJECTIVES/NOUNS + price

a high price *Fuel prices remain high.*

a low price *With such low prices, there are lots of eager buyers.*

a reasonable/fair price *The price was reasonable for such good food.*

a good price *Did you get a good price for your car?*

an affordable price (=not too high) *They sell quality furniture at affordable prices.*

an astronomical price (=extremely high) *Many fans paid astronomical prices for their tickets.*

an exorbitant/extortionate price (=much too high) *£10,000 seemed an exorbitant price for the rug.*

a competitive price (=lower than or similar to those of other companies) *The company wants to keep its prices competitive.*

half price *The bread was being sold off at half price.*

full price *I didn't pay full price for it – I got 20% off.*

the wholesale price (=the price that a business such as a shop pays for something) *Wholesale coffee prices have fallen.*

the retail price (=the price that people pay for something in a shop) *Tax is 40% of the retail price of a typical bottle of wine.*

⚠ Don't say 'a convenient price'. Say **a reasonable price** or **a fair price**.

NOUNS + price

food/energy/fuel etc prices *A poor harvest led to higher food prices.*

property/house prices *House prices have gone up again.*

ticket price *The usual ticket price at the museum is £10 for adults and £5 for children.*

a bargain price (*also* **a knockdown/giveaway price**) (=much lower than usual) *We sell quality cars at bargain prices.*

the asking price (=the amount of money that someone is asking for something, especially a house) *They offered less than the asking price.*

price + VERBS

a price goes up/rises/increases *When supplies go down, prices go up.*

a price goes down/falls/decreases *In real terms, the price of clothes has fallen over the last ten years.*

a price shoots up/soars/rockets (=increases quickly by a large amount) *The price of oil soared in the 1970s.*

prices fluctuate (=keep going up and down) *Gas prices have continued to fluctuate in recent months.*

prices start from £200/$300 etc *Ticket prices start from £39.*

prices range from £30 to £65 etc *Over 1,000 paintings will be shown with prices ranging from £50 to £5,000.*

VERBS + price

put up/increase/raise a price *Manufacturers have had to put their prices up.*

cut/lower/reduce a price *The company recently cut the price of its best-selling car.*

slash a price *informal* (=reduce it by a very large amount) *Many carpet stores have slashed prices to bring in customers.*

charge a price *Companies that charge very high prices will go out of business.*

pay a price *I paid a very reasonable price for my guitar.*

get a good/reasonable etc price *Farmers should get a decent price for their crops.*

set a price *He has not yet set a price on the land.*

agree on a price *I finally managed to agree on a price with the carpet salesman.*

sth fetches a good/high etc price *BrE*, **sth brings a good/high etc price** *AmE* (=it is sold for a lot of money) *I'm sure the painting would fetch a good price in London.*

negotiate a price *You can often negotiate a better price.*

price + NOUNS

a price cut/reduction *There are big price cuts on electrical goods.*

a price rise/increase *The price rises will affect everyone, but especially the poor.*

a price freeze (=when prices are kept at the same level by a company or by the government) *The company announced a price freeze on all its products.*

PREPOSITIONS

the price of sth *He asked the price of the book.*

a price for sth *They agreed a price for the land.*

PHRASES

a fall/drop in prices *Poor demand led to a sharp drop in prices.*

a rise in prices *The sharp rise in wholesale food prices will have to be passed on to customers.*

sth is in/outside sb's price range (=it has a price that someone can or cannot afford) *Unfortunately, there was nothing in our price range.*

THESAURUS: price

price, value, charge, fee, fare, rent, rate, toll → **cost[1] (1)**

priceless *adj* THESAURUS ▸ valuable (2)

pricey *adj* THESAURUS ▸ expensive

prickly *adj* THESAURUS ▸ sharp (1)

pride *n*

1 a feeling that you are proud of something that you or someone connected with you has achieved

ADJECTIVES

great/immense pride (=a lot of pride) *She remembers her achievement with great pride.*
justifiable pride (=that you are right to have) *He talks with justifiable pride of his father's actions during the war.*
national pride (=in your country) *A flag is a symbol of national pride.*
civic pride (=in your town or city) *The museum is a vital source of civic pride.*

VERBS

feel pride *I can't describe the pride I felt when he received his degree.*
take pride in sth (=feel proud of something) *She takes pride in her beautiful gardens.*
give sb pride *Being a member of this team gives me great pride.*
be bursting with pride (=feel very proud) *I could see that her mother was bursting with pride.*
swell with pride (=start to feel very proud) *He would swell with pride when he talked about his restaurant.*
glow with pride (=look very proud) *"I knew he could do it," she said, glowing with pride.*
express pride *The president expressed pride that his country had been chosen to host the games.*

PREPOSITIONS

pride in sth *His pride in his Italian heritage is obvious.*
with pride *He wore his medals with pride.*

PHRASES

a sense of pride *I still feel a sense of pride at having been a member of the regiment.*
sth is a source of pride (=it is a reason to feel proud) *The Chinese Olympic Games were a source of pride to the whole country.*
a glow of pride *literary* (=a feeling of pride) *As she thought about her children, she felt a glow of pride.*

2 a feeling that you respect yourself and deserve to be respected

ADJECTIVES/NOUNS + pride

personal pride *Winning the game was a matter of personal pride.*
professional pride *Professional pride demanded that she do the job properly.*
national/regional/local pride *The comedian had to apologize for his comments, which had wounded local pride.*
family pride *The people are concerned more with family pride than anything else.*

VERBS

hurt/wound/injure sb's pride *She had hurt his pride by rejecting him.*
restore some pride *A victory for the team would restore some national pride.*
salvage some pride (=not lose all your pride) *He managed to salvage some pride by winning one of the games.*

PHRASES

a matter of pride *They all felt they had to finish the race, as a matter of pride.*
a blow to sb's pride *He suffered a blow to his pride when he was made redundant.*
sb's pride is at stake (=they might lose it) *This is an important competition – there is local pride at stake.*

primary *adj* THESAURUS ▶ main

prime *adj* THESAURUS ▶ main

principal *adj* THESAURUS ▶ main

principle Ac *n*

1 a moral rule or belief about what is right and wrong that influences how you behave

> **Grammar**
> Usually plural in this meaning.

ADJECTIVES

high/strict principles (=that are of a very high standard) *He was a lawyer who was famous for his high principles.*
strong principles (=that someone believes in very strongly) *My father was a man of strong principles.*
moral principles *I don't eat meat – it is against my moral principles.*
religious/Christian etc principles *Doesn't working on Sunday conflict with your religious principles?*
political/socialist etc principles *Would he stick to his socialist principles after being elected prime minister?*

VERBS

have principles *I never cheat, because I have principles.*
stick to your principles (=follow them, even when this is difficult) *I respect him for sticking to his principles.*
betray/compromise your principles (=do something that is against your principles) *I knew I could lie to help him, but it would be betraying my principles.*
abandon your principles (=stop believing in them or trying to act by them) *He was accused of abandoning his political principles when he was in power.*

PREPOSITIONS

on principle (=because of a principle) *I am opposed to capital punishment on principle.*

sth is against sb's principles *It is against my principles to kill any living thing.*

PHRASES

as a matter of principle (=because of a principle) *As a matter of principle one should never give in to terrorists.*

a man/woman of principle (=someone with strong moral ideas) *He is the only candidate who has demonstrated that he is a man of principle.*

2 the basic idea that a plan or system is based on

ADJECTIVES

a general/broad principle *He explained the general principles of the constitution.*

an important/key principle *One important principle is that you should reward yourself for your success.*

a central/core principle *The party must not change its central principles.*

a basic/fundamental/underlying principle *Applicants should show that they understand the basic principles of marketing.*

a guiding principle (=a principle that helps you decide what to do) *Fairness is the guiding principle.*

first principles (=the most basic ideas that something is based on) *The researchers went back to first principles.*

VERBS

be based on a principle *The structure of the organization was based on the principle of equality.*

a principle applies *The same principle applies to all kinds of selling.*

a principle underlies sth *What are the principles underlying this form of treatment?*

establish a principle (=make it accepted) *Establish the principle that when your office door is shut you must not be disturbed.*

lay down a principle (=describe a principle and make it accepted) *The report lays down general principles for the teaching of English to speakers of other languages.*

apply/follow/use a principle *Follow the principles of cooking that have been laid down by great chefs.*

support a principle *They supported the principle of free health care.*

PREPOSITIONS

the principle behind sth *The basic principle behind all refrigerators is the same.*

priority Ac *n*

1 the thing that you think is most important and that needs attention before anything else

ADJECTIVES

a high priority (=very important) *Right now, the environment is a high priority.*

a low priority (=not very important) *At that time, architecture was a low priority.*

sb's top/main/number one priority *Controlling spending is his top priority.*

sb's first priority *The first priority for most unemployed people is obtaining a job.*

the overriding priority (=the most important one) *Reducing inflation must be the government's overriding priority.*

sb's immediate priority (=which must be dealt with immediately) *Their immediate priority was to find somewhere to sleep that night.*

an urgent priority *He sees these negotiations as an urgent priority.*

VERBS

make sth a priority *He promised to make education a priority.*

set priorities (=decide what the priorities are) *With any new project, it's important to set priorities.*

sort out your priorities (=decide which things are the most important as a way of dealing with a situation) *If you've got a lot of things to do, sort out your priorities.*

sb's priorities change *As you get older, your priorities may change.*

sth remains a priority *The issue of health care remains a priority.*

PHRASES

a list/set of priorities *Marriage isn't very high on my list of priorities.*

in order of priority (=with the most important first) *They asked voters to list issues in order of priority.*

get your priorities right (*also* **get your priorities straight** *AmE*) (=pay attention to what is most important) *Get your priorities right and don't spend time on unimportant things.*

2 the right to be given attention first and before other people or things

VERBS

have priority *Doctors have to choose which patients should have priority.*

get priority *Murder cases get priority.*

take priority (=be given most or earliest attention) *Winning the war took priority over everything else.*

give priority to sb/sth *The hospital always gives priority to emergency cases.*

PREPOSITIONS

priority over sth/sb *Boys' education was given priority over girls' education.*

If someone **has priority** on a road, other vehicles have to stop and let them go first: *Ambulances **have priority** over other vehicles.*

prison *n*

a building where people are kept as a punishment for a crime, or while they are waiting for their trial

VERBS

go to prison *She went to prison for murder.*

put sb in prison *I do not think mentally ill people should be put in prison.*

send sb to prison *I was afraid I might get sent to prison.*

throw sb in/into prison (=put someone in prison, often unfairly) *The men were arrested and thrown into prison.*

release sb from prison/let sb out of prison *He was released from prison six weeks ago.*

leave/come out of/get out of prison *He managed to find a job a month after he got out of prison.*

escape from prison *Blake escaped from a Missouri prison last year.*

prison + NOUNS

a prison sentence/term (=a period of time in prison as a punishment) *He is serving an eight-year prison sentence for armed robbery.*

the prison system (*also* **the prison service** *BrE*): *The prison system needs to be reformed.*

a prison cell (=a room where a prisoner lives) *Each prison cell can hold up to four prisoners.*

a prison guard (*also* **a prison officer/warder** *BrE*): *Last month, a prisoner attacked two prison officers with a knife.*

a prison inmate (=someone who is kept in prison) *Many of the other prison inmates claimed that they were innocent.*

ADJECTIVES/NOUNS + prison

an open prison *BrE* (=one where prisoners are given more freedom, usually because they have committed less serious crimes) *After two years, he was transferred to an open prison.*

a maximum security prison (=where prisoners are closely guarded) *He was sent to a maximum security prison where prisoners are kept in their cells almost 23 hours a day.*

PREPOSITIONS

in prison *No one knew she had been in prison.*

out of prison *He has been out of prison for three years now.*

PHRASES

spend/serve six months/two years etc in prison *He spent four years in prison for burglary.*

spend/serve time in prison *John had met Rick while serving time in prison.*

prisoner *n*

someone who is kept in a prison as a legal punishment for a crime or while they are waiting for their trial

ADJECTIVES

a political prisoner (=one who is in prison because of their political opinions) *We demand that the military government free all political prisoners.*

an escaped prisoner *Soldiers arrived, looking for escaped prisoners.*

VERBS + prisoner

release/free a prisoner *Hundreds of political prisoners were released.*

execute a prisoner *Many states use a lethal injection to execute prisoners.*

prisoner + VERBS

a prisoner escapes *No prisoner has ever escaped from this prison.*

a prisoner is held somewhere *Prisoners are being held in police stations because the prisons are all full.*

a prisoner serves a sentence (=spends a period of time in prison as a punishment) *The state decides whether a prisoner serving a life sentence can ever be released.*

PHRASES

a prisoner of conscience (=someone who is put in prison for their beliefs) *All eight men are prisoners of conscience, detained for peaceful protest.*

a prisoner of war (=a member of the armed forces kept as a prisoner by an enemy during a war) *He spent five years as a prisoner of war at the camp.*

pristine *adj* THESAURUS ▸ clean[1] (1)

privacy *n*

the state of being able to be alone, and not seen or heard by other people

ADJECTIVES

personal privacy *The bank's record on safeguarding personal privacy is not good.*

complete/total/absolute privacy *The house is surrounded by tall bushes, giving complete privacy.*

little privacy (=not enough privacy) *We had little privacy with seven kids growing up in such a small house.*

VERBS

want/need privacy *Everyone wants a little privacy from time to time.*

give sb privacy *We decided to put up a fence to give us more privacy.*

protect/safeguard sb's privacy *Names have been changed to protect the privacy of those involved.*

ensure privacy (=make certain that someone

has privacy) *He had locked the door to ensure privacy.*

respect sb's privacy *Show teenagers that you respect their privacy by knocking on their bedroom door.*

invade sb's privacy (=try to find out personal things about them, or disturb them when they want to be alone) *She complained that the magazine had invaded her privacy by printing the photos.*

violate sb's privacy (=hurt someone by not respecting their privacy) *The media is accused of violating the royal couple's privacy.*

PHRASES

an invasion of privacy *I think some of the questions on the form are an invasion of privacy.*

sb's right to privacy *Landlords should respect their tenants' right to privacy.*

a lack of privacy *The worst thing about being in prison was the total lack of privacy.*

private *adj*

1 if something is private, you do not want most people to know about it because it concerns your feelings, your relationships etc

NOUNS

sb's private life *I try to keep work and my private life separate.*

sb's private thoughts/feelings *She wrote down her most private thoughts in her diary.*

a private letter/email/phone call *Someone had been reading his private letters.*

a private conversation/meeting/discussion *After the meal, Stirling had a private conversation with the prime minister.*

sb's private business (=things that you do not want other people to talk about or be involved in) *What I do in my own home is my private business.*

ADVERBS

strictly private *The letter was marked 'Strictly Private'.*

THESAURUS: private

personal
life | feelings | thoughts | question
relating to your private life:
The singer has had a lot of problems in her personal life. | She talked about her own personal feelings. | They asked me a lot of personal questions. | I'd rather not talk about it – it's personal.

secret
thoughts | ambition | desire | wish | fear | worry | fantasies
used about feelings and thoughts that you do not tell anyone about:
I had the feeling he knew my most secret thoughts. | Her secret ambition was to become a pilot. | His secret fear was that Jenny would leave him.

intimate
details | secrets | conversation | moment
very private – used about things relating to your relationships and sexual feelings:
Many people share intimate details of their lives on the internet. | The couple appeared to be involved in an intimate conversation. | The film shows their most intimate moments together.

innermost
thoughts | feelings | emotions | desires
your innermost feelings, thoughts etc are your most private ones:
Patients are encouraged to talk about their innermost thoughts. | The painters' aim was to express their innermost desires.

In informal English, if something is private, and you do not think that someone should ask you about it, you say **it's none of your business** or **that's none of your business**: *It's none of your business how much I earn. | "Are you married?" "**That's none of your business.**"*

THESAURUS: private

confidential, private, clandestine, classified, sensitive, covert, undercover, underground, hush-hush → **secret[1]**

2 controlled by individual people or companies, not by the government

NOUNS

a private school/hospital *His parents sent him to an expensive private school.*

the private sector (=all businesses and organizations that are not controlled by the government) *People who work in the private sector get paid more than people who work in the public sector.*

private enterprise (=the activities of businesses that are not owned by the government, whose aim is to make profits) *The government wants to encourage private enterprise, and make people less dependent on the state.*

VERBS

go private (=become a privately owned business) *Britain's water companies went private in 1989.*

3 for one person or group to use, not for everyone

NOUNS

a private car park/swimming pool/garden etc *The hotel has its own private swimming pool.*

private property/land *There was a big sign which said 'Private Property. No Public Right of Way'.*

privilege *n*

a special advantage or lucky opportunity that few people have

ADJECTIVES

a special privilege *First-class passengers get special privileges including better food.*

a great/enormous privilege *It is a great privilege to play for your country.*

a rare privilege *The young reporter was given the rare privilege of an interview with the prime minister.*

a real privilege *It has been a real privilege to work with you.*

certain privileges *Club members enjoy certain privileges such as reduced ticket prices.*

P

VERBS

have a privilege *Managers have privileges which other workers do not have.*

enjoy/be entitled to/benefit from a privilege (=have a privilege) *Top party officials used to enjoy special privileges.*

get/receive a privilege *Foreigners in Egypt received considerable legal privileges.*

give/grant sb a privilege *Senior members of the government are given the privilege of having their own personal drivers.*

pay for the privilege *It is a private golf course so you have to pay for the privilege of playing on it.*

deny sb a privilege (=not let someone have it) *Men could join the golf club, but this privilege was denied to women.*

withdraw a privilege (=stop someone having it) *If a prisoner behaves badly, his privileges may be withdrawn.*

abuse a privilege *Website owners must not abuse the privilege of receiving confidential information.*

PREPOSITIONS

the privilege of sth *He has the privilege of sitting at the head of the table.*

sth is a privilege for sb *It was a great privilege for her to be invited to speak at the conference.*

privileged *adj*

having special advantages which other people don't have

NOUNS

a privileged position/status *Globally, boys still enjoy a privileged position in terms of access to education.*

a privileged few/minority/elite (=a small privileged group) *Only a privileged few can afford to send their children to private schools.*

a privileged background/upbringing *He comes from a privileged background.*

a privileged class/group *Professionals, such as doctors and lawyers, form a privileged class in society.*

a privileged life *Born into a wealthy family, she had always led a privileged life.*

ADVERBS

highly/enormously privileged *The country was ruled by a highly privileged upper class.*

THESAURUS: privileged

wealthy, affluent, prosperous, well-off, well-to-do, privileged, comfortably off → **rich (1)**

prize *n*

something that is given to someone who is successful in a competition, race, game of chance etc

ADJECTIVES/NOUNS + prize

first/second/third prize *She won first prize in a poetry competition.*

the top/star/grand prize *The film won the top prize at the Berlin Film Festival.*

a special prize *There will be a special prize for the best wildlife photograph.*

the booby prize *especially humorous* (=given to the person who comes last) *We teased her that her cake would win the booby prize.*

a consolation prize (=given to someone who has not won) *The runner-up will get a consolation prize of a camera.*

a runner-up prize *BrE* (=given to a person or team that comes second) *In addition to the star prize, there are 21 runner-up prizes to be won.*

a cash prize *You can win a holiday plus a cash prize of £500.*

VERBS

win a prize *In this month's competition you could win a prize worth $3,000.*

take a prize (=used when saying who or what won the prize) *Meryl Streep took the prize for best actress.*

get/receive a prize *The winner gets a £100 prize.*

share a prize *The two lucky winners will share the first prize of $500.*

give (sb) a prize *A prize will be given for the best-decorated egg.*

award (sb) a prize (=officially give someone a prize) *Four years later he was awarded the Nobel Prize for Medicine.*

collect a prize *I am afraid that Mr Newman cannot be here tonight to collect his prize.*

present a prize (*also* **present sb with a prize**) (=give a prize to someone, especially at a formal occasion) *The winner will be presented with their prize by the Lord Mayor.*

a prize goes to sb (=they get it) *The fiction prize goes to Carol Shields.*

prize + NOUNS

a prize winner *Congratulations to all the prize winners!*

prize money *The total prize money for the tournament is £30,000.*

a prize draw *BrE* (=a competition in which names or tickets are chosen by chance to win prizes) *He won the car in a prize draw.*

PREPOSITIONS

the prize for sth *The prize for best photograph has been won by a young Dutch artist.*

probability *n*

how likely something is to happen, exist, or be true, sometimes calculated in a mathematical way

ADJECTIVES

a high probability (=something is very likely) *This treatment has a high probability of success.*

a strong probability (=a high probability) *There is a strong probability that you are right.*

a low probability (=something is not very likely) *The probability of being struck by lightning is pretty low.*

an equal probability *There is an equal probability of the statement being true or false.*

the statistical probability *The statistical probability of a plane crash remains very low.*

a reasonable probability (=a fairly high probability) *Unless there is a reasonable probability of making a profit, you will find it hard to get investment.*

VERBS

increase the probability *Today's inflation figures increase the probability that interest rates will rise.*

reduce the probability *These health measures are aimed at reducing the probability of the virus spreading.*

calculate the probability *Using this data, we can calculate the probability of an event like this happening again.*

PREPOSITIONS

the probability of sth *The probability of winning the lottery is extremely low.*

PHRASES

in all probability (=very likely to happen or be the case) *In all probability, we will never know the full story.*

on the balance of probabilities *BrE* (=considering the probability of two or more events) *On the balance of probabilities, it is likely that the crash was caused by pilot error.*

probable *adj*

likely to exist, happen, or be true

ADVERBS

highly probable *It is highly probable that college fees will increase next year.*

quite probable (=very probable) *It is quite probable that you will lose all your money.*

most probable *What is the most probable explanation for the variation in the test results?*

equally probable *It is equally probable that they both could win.*

NOUNS

a probable cause *The probable cause of the accident was a mistake by the pilot.*

a probable result/consequence/outcome *The probable result of global warming is that sea levels will rise.*

a probable effect/impact *The article discusses the probable impact of climate change on the local bird population.*

a probable explanation/reason *The most probable explanation is that she forgot.*

VERBS

seem probable *It seems probable that a cure for the disease will eventually be found.*

problem *n*

1 a situation that causes difficulties

ADJECTIVES/NOUNS + problem

a big/major/serious/significant problem *The school's biggest problem is a shortage of cash.*

a huge/enormous problem *We faced huge problems.*

a little/small/minor/slight problem *Old cars often develop minor engine problems.*

the main/central problem *The main problem for the climbers was lack of sleep.*

a fundamental/basic problem *The government has done little to solve the fundamental problems of poverty and crime.*

a real problem *They quickly found that their real problem lay with marketing.*

a difficult problem *Does the team have the skills to tackle these difficult problems?*

a thorny/knotty problem (=difficult) *He still faced the thorny problem of finding a way out of the jungle.*

a pressing/urgent problem (=one that needs to be dealt with very soon) *Lack of clean drinking water is the most pressing problem facing the refugees.*

a long-term problem (=which will continue for a long time) *Lack of water looks like being a long-term problem.*

personal/family/relationship problems *My daughter found it hard to talk about her personal problems.*

a social problem *Domestic violence is a major social problem.*

financial/economic/money problems *Our financial problems are over.*

a technical/mechanical problem *The delay was caused by technical problems.*

an engine problem *The pilot reported engine problems.*

teething problems (=small problems at the start of something) *As with all new systems, there have been a few teething problems.*

a practical problem *Burying a pet can present practical problems.*

VERBS + problem

have a problem *We had a few problems at the beginning of the project.*

cause/create/lead to a problem *The building's lack of parking space could cause problems.*

present/pose a problem (=cause or be a problem) *A shortage of trained nurses is posing major problems.*

solve/resolve a problem (*also* **fix a problem** *informal*): *He solved his financial problems by selling his car.*

deal with/sort out a problem (=solve it or try to solve it) *The state has failed to deal with the problem of violence against women.*

tackle/handle a problem (*also* **address a problem**) (=try to solve it) *There is more than one way to tackle this problem.*

do something about a problem (=try to solve it) *Despite many complaints, nothing had been done about the problem.*

overcome a problem (=deal with it successfully) *We try to help families overcome housing problems.*

face/be faced with a problem *Other large organizations face similar problems.*

experience/encounter/run into a problem *You shouldn't encounter any further problems.*

be beset/plagued by problems (=experience a lot of problems) *The company has been beset by problems.*

be fraught with problems (=involve a lot of problems) *Filming in the Arctic is fraught with problems.*

exacerbate a problem *formal* (=make it worse) *The country's economic problems are exacerbated by the situation in Europe.*

raise a problem (=mention it, so that people can discuss it) *You should raise the problem with your local council.*

problem + VERBS

a problem arises/occurs (*also* **a problem comes up**) (=happens) *Problems may arise when the family wants to move house.*

a problem arises/results/stems from sth *The problem arises from unrealistic expectations.*

a problem faces sb *Terrorism is possibly the most important problem facing Western countries.*

the problem lies in/with sth (=relates to something) *The problem lies in the design of the rocket.*

PREPOSITIONS

the problem of sth *The government is addressing the problem of unemployment.*

a problem with sth *There was a problem with the computer link.*

a problem for sb *The snow is causing problems for drivers.*

PHRASES

a solution/answer to a problem *They are trying to find a solution to the problem.*

the root/heart of the problem (=the most important cause or part of a problem) *Poverty is the root of the problem.*

2 something wrong with your body or mind

ADJECTIVES/NOUNS + problem

a health/medical problem *Have you ever suffered from any of these health problems?*

a back/heart/kidney etc problem *He was born with heart problems.*

a hearing problem *There are special telephones for people with hearing problems.*

a weight problem (=the problem of being too fat) *Patients with weight problems were put on a strict diet.*

a drug/drink/alcohol problem (=the problem of being addicted to drugs or alcohol) *His drink problem caused the break-up of his marriage.*

psychological problems (*also* **mental health problems**) *She is being treated for psychological problems at a mental hospital in Oxford.*

emotional problems *He suffers from depression and other emotional problems.*

behavioural problems *Many of these children have behavioural problems.*

a serious/major problem *Lifting things carelessly can lead to serious back problems.*

a minor problem *She has had some minor medical problems.*

VERBS

have a problem *He's always had a weight problem.*

suffer (from) a problem *The patient began to suffer breathing problems.*

procedure Ac *n*

a way of doing something, especially the correct or usual way

ADJECTIVES/NOUNS + procedure

the correct/proper procedure *What is the correct procedure for applying for a loan?*

normal/standard/routine procedure *It is standard procedure to take photographs of the scene of the crime.*

a complex/complicated procedure *Buying and selling a house is quite a complex procedure.*

a simple procedure *Giving blood is a simple procedure.*

a legal procedure *He assured them that the case would be dealt with according to proper legal procedures.*

a safety procedure *On board, we were given a demonstration on the airline's safety procedures.*

a disciplinary procedure (=in which a group of people decide if a member of an organization should be punished) *The manager faces a disciplinary procedure for his actions.*

a complaints procedure *The standard complaints procedure takes 12 weeks.*

a selection procedure *An interview is an important part of our selection procedure.*

VERBS

follow a procedure *All schools have disciplinary procedures they must follow.*

use/employ a procedure *We used a tried and tested procedure for processing the information.*

establish a procedure *The bank is establishing a new procedure for dealing with complaints.*

go through a procedure (=follow all the steps in it) *We had to go through the whole procedure again.*

introduce a procedure *Introducing a complex new procedure at this stage would be a mistake.*

PREPOSITIONS

the procedure for sth *What's the procedure for getting a visa?*

under a procedure *Under normal procedures, the vote takes place in public.*

process Ac *n*

a series of actions or events that have a particular result

ADJECTIVES/NOUNS + process

a slow process *Collecting the data is a slow process.*

a gradual process *Forming relationships is a gradual process that takes time.*

a long/lengthy process *Recovery after surgery can be a long and painful process.*

a laborious process (=taking a lot of time and effort) *Making rugs by hand is a laborious process.*

a complex/complicated process *Getting a visa can be a complex process.*

a natural process *These changes are part of the natural process of evolution.*

the decision-making process *All staff should be involved in the decision-making process.*

the selection process *Candidates attend an interview as part of the company's selection process.*

the peace process *There was frustration with a lack of progress in the Middle East peace process.*

the creative process (=the process of producing new ideas or things) *As both writer and director, she is involved in the whole creative process of staging the play.*

VERBS

begin/start a process *After the hurricane, we began the slow process of rebuilding the town.*

go through a process (*also* **undergo a process** *formal*): *A lot of companies are going through a process of change.*

take part in a process (*also* **participate in a process** *formal*): *We want voters to actively participate in the political process.*

repeat a process *Stretch your left arm over the top of your head and then repeat the process with your right arm.*

speed up a process *In order to speed up the process, we submitted plans in advance.*

PREPOSITIONS

the process of doing sth *The process of finding, interviewing, and selecting new staff takes a long time.*

a process for doing sth *He invented a new process for making ice cream.*

PHRASES

be in the process of (doing) sth (=be in the middle of a process) *I am in the process of moving house.*

a part of a process *Listening is an important part of the learning process.*

a stage in a process *The next stage in the process is to send a planning application to the council.*

produce[1] *v* THESAURUS make (1)

produce[2] *n*

food or other things that have been grown or produced on a farm to be sold

ADJECTIVES/NOUNS + produce

fresh produce *It is important to use fresh produce when it is available.*

organic produce (=produced without artificial chemicals) *There is increased demand for organic produce.*

local produce *We use local produce as much as possible.*

dairy produce *BrE* (=milk, butter, cheese etc) *Vitamin A can also be obtained from dairy produce and eggs.*

agricultural/farm produce *The government bought surplus agricultural produce from farmers.*

VERBS

sell produce *Farmers use the market to sell their produce.*

buy produce (*also* **purchase produce** *formal*): *You can buy produce online these days.*

use produce *The restaurant prides itself on using fresh local produce.*

grow your own produce *We began growing our own produce about ten years ago.*

producer *n*

a person, company, or country that makes or grows goods, foods, or materials

ADJECTIVES

a large/major/leading producer *Brazil is the largest producer of coffee in the world.*

a small producer *Many small producers are going out of business.*

a local producer *Local producers find it difficult to compete with cheap imports.*

a domestic producer (=from your own country rather than abroad) *Domestic producers may face tough international competition.*

a foreign producer *They agreed to open their markets to foreign producers of timber.*

NOUNS + producer

a gas/oil producer *Russia is the largest oil producer in the world.*

a food producer *Food producers are constantly trying to bring new products on the market.*

a coffee/milk etc producer *The Kenya Coffee Producers Association is a national organization of coffee farmers.*

P

product *n*

something that is made and sold in large quantities

ADJECTIVES/NOUNS + product

food products *Why do most food products have so much packaging?*

agricultural products *The country exports a range of agricultural products, including wheat.*

dairy products (=that contain milk) *Some people are allergic to dairy products.*

meat products *Meat products must be kept in a refrigerator.*

household/cleaning products (=that you use for washing and cleaning the things in a house) *Do you know what chemicals are in household products such as washing powder?*

beauty/cosmetic products *She won't buy beauty products that have been tested on animals.*

a commercial product (=one that is bought for money) *This is free software, not a commercial product.*

a consumer product (=one that is bought by the public) *Demand for consumer products has increased in countries such as China.*

the finished product *The quality of the finished product is all-important.*

VERBS

make/produce/manufacture a product *Japanese car makers were able to manufacture their products more efficiently.*

create a product *We wanted to create a product that would appeal to different age groups.*

buy a product (*also* **purchase a product** *formal*): *We were able to purchase the product from another supplier.*

sell a product *It is illegal to sell tobacco products to anyone under the age of 18.*

use a product *Millions of people use the company's products.*

order a product *Customers can also order products online.*

design a product *We design products that we would like to own ourselves.*

supply a product *We supply a range of products to most supermarkets.*

product + NOUNS

product development *The profits are used to fund product development.*

a product line (=a type of things that a company makes and sells) *We are getting rid of unprofitable product lines.*

a product launch (=an event at which a company announces that it is selling a new product) *They are getting ready for a big product launch in the spring.*

PHRASES

a range of products *Consumers have a wide range of products that they can choose from.*

THESAURUS: product

goods
things that are produced in order to be sold, especially for use in the home:
They sell furniture and other ***household goods***. | ***electrical goods*** | ***white goods*** (=large electrical goods used in the home such as washing machines and refrigerators)

commodity *formal*
a type of product or raw material that can be bought and sold - used especially about basic food products, metals, and fuels:
The price of food and other ***basic commodities*** *has increased significantly.* | *All metal was a* ***valuable commodity*** *and was rarely wasted.*

merchandise *formal*
things that are being sold, especially in shops:
Sales of books, videos, and other merchandise have increased. | *Customers are not allowed to touch the merchandise.*

wares *written*
things that are offered for sale, especially in a market or on the street:
In the market, the traders began ***selling their wares***. | *Merchants brought their wares from all over the world.*

export
goods that are sent to a foreign country in order to be sold:
US exports rose to $11.5 billion. | *At the moment, oil is their* ***biggest export***.

import
goods that are brought from one country into another to be sold there:
The UK clothing industry cannot compete with ***foreign imports*** *on price.* | *They want to protect US famers from* ***cheap imports***.

production *n*

the process of making or growing things to be sold, especially in large quantities

ADJECTIVES

total production *New technology has helped the company to increase its total production by 25%.*

annual production (=the amount produced in a year) *The firm has doubled annual production to 750 bikes.*

mass production (=making products in large numbers with machines so that they can be sold cheaply) *Mass production allowed Henry Ford to lower the price of his Model T motor car.*

large-scale production (=making products in large quantities) *Large-scale production helps companies to keep costs down.*

industrial/agricultural production *Last year industrial production fell in the US.*

domestic production (=in your own country rather than abroad) *Oil imports began to decline as domestic production started to increase.*

global production (=production throughout the world) *Falling global production and rising demand drive prices higher.*

NOUNS + production

oil/coal/energy production *Nearly two-thirds of US oil production is used for transportation.*

car/steel etc production *It is expected that UK car production will fall in the next ten years.*

food/crop/milk etc production *The amount of land available for food production has decreased.*

VERBS + production

increase production *We had to increase production of olive oil to cope with demand.*

start/begin production *The company plans to start production before the end of the year.*

stop/halt production (*also* **cease/discontinue production** *formal*): *They ceased production of the car in 2008.*

move/switch production *The company switched production to Mexico.*

production + VERBS

production rises/increases *Industrial production rose by 8% last year.*

production falls/decreases *Sugar production fell to 129,920 tonnes.*

production + NOUNS

a production method/process *The company has spent several million pounds improving production methods.*

production costs *Production costs can make a considerable difference to the selling price.*

a production line (=a line of machines and workers in a factory, each doing one job in the process of making a product) *She works on the production line at the biscuit factory.*

production levels (*also* **the volume of production**) (=the amount of products that are made) *Firms are always looking for ways to increase production levels.*

production capacity (=the largest amount that can be made) *The country's oil production capacity is expected to increase from 4 million to 6 million barrels per day.*

PHRASES

a rise/increase in production *Kuwait is planning a rise in oil production to about half a million barrels a day.*

a fall in production *There has been a 25 percent fall in production in the first half of the year.*

be in production (=being made now) *The latest model is already in production.*

go into production (=start being made in a factory) *New products have to be carefully tested before they go into production.*

profession *n*

a job that needs a high level of education and training

ADJECTIVES/NOUNS + profession

the medical profession (=doctors, nurses etc) *Most people in the medical profession support the idea of free healthcare.*

the legal profession (=lawyers) *He followed his father into the legal profession.*

the teaching profession (=teachers) *I have the greatest respect for the teaching profession.*

the acting profession (=actors) *His career in the acting profession lasted 40 years.*

sb's chosen profession *He was really happy in his chosen profession.*

VERBS

enter/go into/join a profession *Hugh left college intending to enter the medical profession.*

work in a profession *You need specialized qualifications to work in professions such as architecture and law.*

choose a profession *He was beginning to think that he had chosen the wrong profession.*

belong to a profession *The committee is made up of people who belong to a variety of different professions.*

leave a profession *Why do you want to leave the profession?*

PREPOSITIONS

by profession (=used when saying what someone's job is) *Johnson was a lawyer by profession.*

PHRASES

a member of a profession *Some members of the legal profession support a change in the law.*

at the top of your profession *He was a very highly respected man at the top of his profession.*

professional Ac *adj*

1 relating to a job that needs special knowledge and training, or to the qualities needed to do such a job well

NOUNS

professional qualifications *What professional qualifications do you have?*

professional training *The teachers all have professional training.*
professional advice *You should seek professional advice before investing in the stock market.*
professional help/guidance *Sometimes parents may need professional help in dealing with their child.*
sb's professional career *He had a 25-year professional career as a scientist.*
sb's professional life *By resigning, she took the biggest risk of her professional life.*
a professional duty/responsibility *The doctor has a professional duty to act in the best interests of the patient.*
professional expertise/skills *She has exactly the kind of professional expertise we require.*
sb's professional judgment/opinion *Dr Mullins was guilty of a serious error of professional judgment in sending the patient home from hospital.*
professional standards *The Law Society's function is to maintain the highest professional standards.*
a professional body/association (=an organization for people who do a particular kind of work, for example doctors or lawyers) *Is your architect a member of a professional body?*

> You say that your relationship with someone you work with is **strictly professional** when you want to emphasize that you do not have a romantic relationship with them: *The coach said that the relationship between them was **strictly** professional.*

2 doing something with a high level of skill

ADVERBS

highly/extremely/thoroughly professional (=very professional) *The hospital staff were extremely professional at all times.*

profile *n*

1 someone or something's public image, and how much attention they receive

ADJECTIVES/NOUNS + profile

a high profile (=used when someone is well-known or receives a lot of attention) *The star has a high profile in the US, but he is less well known in Europe.*
a low profile (=used when someone is not well known or receives little attention) *The organization has chosen someone with a low profile for the job.*
sb's public profile *Her appearance in the film raised her public profile.*
sb's media profile (=how well known someone is through their appearances on television, in newspapers etc) *Over the past few years he has steadily built his media profile and has appeared on numerous TV channels.*

PHRASES

raise/increase sb's/sth's profile (=make people more aware of someone or something) *The advertising campaign aims to raise the company's profile.*
keep/maintain a low profile (=avoid doing things that will make people notice you) *The star has been keeping a low profile in recent months and has made few public appearances.*

2 a description of what someone or something is like

ADJECTIVES/NOUNS + profile

a detailed/comprehensive profile *This directory provides a detailed profile of US schools offering undergraduate engineering programs.*
a personal profile (=a description of what kind of person you are and the things you have done) *The advertisement asks you to send a personal profile and say why you would be suitable for the job.*
a customer profile *Many companies use customer profiles to help them identify people who would be interested in their products.*
sb's psychological profile *The police use psychological profiles of past killers to identify potential future killers.*
a DNA/genetic profile (=a person's unique set of genetic characteristics) *New research shows that certain genetic profiles increase the risk of heart attacks.*
a demographic profile (=a description of the kind of people who live somewhere or do something) *The company has done extensive market research to create a demographic profile of potential customers.*

VERBS

create/build up/construct a profile *Detectives are slowly building up a psychological profile of the killer.*
fit/match a profile *With her background and experience she matches the job profile perfectly.*

profit *n*

money that you gain by selling things or doing business, after your costs have been paid

ADJECTIVES

a big/huge/enormous profit *Drug companies make huge profits.*
a small/modest profit *The business produced a small profit last year.*
a quick profit (=happening quickly) *They were only interested in a quick profit.*
a good profit *There is a good profit to be made from selling cars.*
a substantial profit *The agent then sells the land for a substantial profit to someone else.*
a healthy/handsome/tidy profit (=a big profit) *By the second year, the restaurant began to make a healthy profit.*

a reasonable/decent profit (=good, or good enough) *He is entitled to make a reasonable profit on the deal.*
net profit (=after tax and costs are paid) *The company made a net profit of $10.5 million in the last financial year.*
gross profit (*also* **pre-tax profit**) (=before tax and costs are paid) *The hotel group made a gross profit of £51.9 million in 2011.*
trading/operating profit *Operating profits were lower than last year.*

VERBS + profit

make a profit *We are in business to make a profit.*
turn/earn a profit (=make a profit) *Without liquor sales, the store could not turn a profit.*
show a profit (=make a profit) *The business will not show any profit this year.*
report/post/announce a profit (=officially tell people about it) *The company reported net profits of $8.6 million for the year.*
generate/yield a profit (=produce a profit) *The oilfield generated huge profits for the company.*
reap a profit (=make a large profit) *The credit card industry reaps estimated profits of $6 billion a year.*
boost profits (=make them increase) *We aim to boost profits by cutting costs.*
maximize profits (=make them as big as possible) *Every company tries to maximize its profits.*

profit + VERBS

profits go up/down (*also* **profits are up/down**) *Pre-tax profits were up 21.5%.*
profits rise/increase/grow *Half of the firms surveyed expected profits to rise.*
profits soar/leap/surge (=increase by a large amount very quickly) *The supermarket's net profits soared by 32% to £148 million.*
profits fall/drop *The group saw profits fall from £24 million to £17.8 million.*
profits slump/plunge/plummet (=fall by a large amount very quickly) *The company's pre-tax profits slumped to £25.5 million.*

profit + NOUNS

the profit margin (=the difference between the cost of producing something and the price at which you sell it) *The profit margin was already tight before fuel prices began to go up.*

PREPOSITIONS

for profit/at a profit (=in a way that makes a profit) *They buy goods cheaply in large quantities and sell them for a profit.*
a profit on sth *Their profit on the deal was over £10 million.*
a profit from sth *You will have to pay tax on any profit from the sale.*

profitable *adj* making a profit

ADVERBS

highly/extremely profitable *The oil industry is a highly profitable business.*

NOUNS

a profitable business/company *She owns a highly profitable shoe company.*
a profitable investment *Rental properties can be a profitable investment.*
a profitable year *The company's most profitable year was 2012 when it made $7,246,667.*

profound *adj* THESAURUS ▶ **deep**

program *n*

a set of instructions given to a computer to make it perform an operation

NOUNS + program

a computer program *The images were generated by a special computer program.*
a software program *There are a number of software programs that you can use for keeping accounts.*

program + VERBS

write/create a program *We learned how to write our own programs on the course.*
design/develop a program *They developed a program that could read people's handwriting.*
run a program *You have to double-click on the icon to run the program.*
use a program *There is a video that shows you how to use the program.*
load/install a program (=put it on your computer) *Can you show me how to install the program on my computer?*
download a program (=copy it, especially from the internet, onto your computer) *You can download the program and use it free of charge for 90 days.*

program + VERBS

a program runs *The program won't run on my machine.*
a program crashes (=suddenly stops working) *I lost all my data when the program crashed.*

programme *BrE*, program *AmE n*

1 a series of actions which are designed to achieve something important

ADJECTIVES/NOUNS + programme

a major programme (=large and important) *A major programme of modernisation is transforming public transport in London.*
an ambitious programme *The institute plans an ambitious program of research.*
a radical programme (=involving very big changes) *He introduced a radical program of tax reform.*
a pilot/test programme (=a small one carried out to test whether an idea will be successful)

P

If the pilot programme goes well, the scheme will be introduced in other areas.

a reform programme *The reform programme is intended to make the country more democratic.*

an economic programme *The new president announced a radical economic program.*

a training programme *The company has cut its budget for training programmes.*

a spending programme *The government's spending programme has been widely criticized.*

an expansion programme (=involving opening new shops, factories etc) *The company's aggressive expansion program will double the size of the business in the next four years.*

a development programme *One thousand new houses will be built as part of the development program for the area.*

a screening programme (=testing a lot of people to find out if they have a disease) *The screening programme was introduced to detect cancer early.*

P

VERBS

set up/establish/introduce a programme *They are helping to set up a training programme for doctors in Romania.*

carry out a programme (*also* **implement a programme** *formal*) (=do what has been agreed) *Why have the government failed to implement the programme of reform?*

launch/embark on a programme (=start one) *The company launched a rapid expansion programme.*

finance/fund a programme (=pay for it) *The programme is financed by the European Union.*

plan a programme *The company is also planning a major investment program.*

PREPOSITIONS

a programme of sth *The government announced a programme of public spending cuts.*

2 something that you watch on television or listen to on the radio

ADJECTIVES/NOUNS + programme

a television/TV programme *There was an interesting television programme about China.*

a radio programme *I first heard about the company on a radio program.*

a cookery/wildlife/news/comedy etc programme *More and more people are watching cookery programmes on TV.*

sb's favourite programme *What's your favourite television program?*

a good programme *Are there any good programmes on the television this evening?*

VERBS

watch a programme *She was watching her favourite programme when the phone rang.*

see a programme *Did you see that program last night about crocodiles?*

listen to a programme *A lot of people listen to the program on the way to work.*

hear a programme *I heard an interesting programme on the radio yesterday.*

make a programme *The BBC makes wonderful wildlife programmes.*

present a programme *BrE*, **host a program** *AmE* (=introduce its different parts) *Emma Crosby presents the evening news programme on Channel 5.*

appear on a programme *I was invited to appear on the programme but decided not to.*

take part in a programme *He reluctantly agreed to take part in the programme.*

a programme is broadcast (=sent out) *The program is broadcast live from the studio every Thursday.*

PREPOSITIONS

a programme on/about sb/sth *I saw an interesting program on Islamic art.*

progress *n*

a process of improvement or achievement

ADJECTIVES

good/great progress *He is out of hospital and making good progress.*

significant/substantial/considerable progress *Significant progress has been made in reducing nuclear weapons.*

real progress *We have been looking for a house for months, but we still haven't made any real progress towards finding one.*

satisfactory progress *Doctors say the patient is now making satisfactory progress.*

steady progress *Steady progress has been made towards our objectives.*

rapid progress *The investigation is making rapid progress.*

slow progress *The task remains difficult and progress has been slow.*

little/limited/no progress *The builders have made little progress with the new office.*

further progress *The prospects of further progress are good.*

scientific/medical progress *Research is essential for medical progress.*

VERBS

make progress *The country has made significant economic progress.*

achieve progress *The talks ended with no real progress having been achieved.*

hinder sb's progress (=make it slower) *Language problems might hinder a child's progress at school.*

check (on) sb's progress *A social worker calls regularly to check on the children's progress.*

assess/evaluate sb's progress (=find out how good it is) *We evaluate each student's individual progress.*

follow/monitor/chart sb's progress (=keep checking it) *Throughout the night, doctors charted his progress.*

review sb's progress (=check it again) *We will review the progress of the project in March.*

PREPOSITIONS

progress towards/toward sth *Progress towards peace has been slow.*

progress with sth *She began to make progress with her research.*

progress on sth *Progress on a job should be constantly monitored.*

PHRASES

be pleased/satisfied/disappointed etc with sb's progress *Your parents must be pleased with your progress.*

a lack of progress *What is the reason for this lack of progress?*

the rate of progress *The rate of progress has been slower than we would have liked.*

prohibit Ac *v*

to say that an action is illegal or not allowed

> **Grammar**
> Often passive.

ADVERBS

sth is strictly prohibited *Smoking is strictly prohibited in the school.*

specifically/expressly prohibit sth (=in a clear and firm way) *The law expressly prohibits people from carrying loaded guns in a public place.*

PREPOSITIONS

prohibit sb from doing sth *Passengers are prohibited from drinking alcohol.*

project Ac *n*

a planned piece of work that will be done over a period of time

ADJECTIVES/NOUNS + project

a major project (=large and important) *The NHS is funding a major research project looking at the causes of addiction.*

an ambitious project *The aim of this ambitious project was to get young people to take more exercise.*

an exciting project *This is an enormously exciting project which will provide huge benefits for local people.*

a research project *The aim of this research project is to study modern eating habits.*

a joint project (=done by two or more people, organizations, or countries) *The fighter plane was conceived as a joint project by Germany, the UK, Italy, and Spain.*

a pilot project (=one that tests whether an idea will be successful) *The scheme was shelved after pilot projects showed poor results.*

a construction/building project *Spending on new construction projects has been cut dramatically.*

a development project (=that is intended to encourage economic growth somewhere) *The two countries have worked together on a range of economic development projects in recent years.*

a conservation project (=aimed at protecting animals or countryside from being harmed) *The World Wildlife Fund is currently sponsoring three major conservation projects in Africa.*

VERBS

set up a project (=organize it) *Jane was asked to help set up the project.*

work on a project *The team has been working on the project for three years.*

be involved in a project *I am involved in various projects at work.*

embark on a project (=start a new project) *The city is embarking on a major building project.*

undertake a project *formal* (=start work on a project) *He did not feel ready to undertake another project yet.*

manage/run a project *I had to manage the project on a very tight budget.*

fund/finance a project (=pay for it) *The project was funded by the Department of Education.*

complete/finish a project *The project is unlikely to be completed on time.*

project + NOUNS

a project manager/leader *The project manager is responsible for coordinating the entire team.*

project management (=the job of managing a project) *Candidates must have experience in project management.*

the project team *We have an excellent project team.*

PREPOSITIONS

on a project *She has been working on the project since last year.*

PHRASES

a phase/stage/part of a project *The first phase of the project must be completed by the end of July.*

the aim/objective of the project *We have succeeded in achieving the main aims of the project.*

prominent *adj* THESAURUS ▸ **important (2)**

promise[1] *n*

a statement that you will definitely do or provide something or that something will definitely happen

VERBS

make a promise *I made a promise to my mother that I'd look after Dad.*

P

give (sb) a promise *She hated keeping secrets, but she had given Mike her promise not to say anything.*

keep a promise (*also* **fulfil/honour a promise** *formal*) (=do what you promised to do) *She said she would come back, and she kept her promise.*

break a promise (=not do what you promised to do) *He would never break his promise to his wife.*

go back on your promise (=break it after it seemed that you would keep it) *Employees were angry that the company had gone back on its promise.*

renege on a promise *formal* (=break it – used especially about governments, political parties, companies etc) *The government reneged on its promise to hold free and fair elections.*

hold sb to their promise (=make them keep it) *The voters intend to hold the government to its promises.*

deliver on your promise (=do what you have promised) *He criticized the government for failing to deliver on its promises.*

ADJECTIVES/NOUNS + promise

a solemn promise (=a serious promise, which you must not break) *As governor, I made a solemn promise to defend the law.*

a firm promise (=a definite promise) *We have had several firm promises of help.*

a vague promise (=one that is not clear or definite) *Larry made a vague promise to visit soon.*

a false/empty/hollow promise (=one that you do not intend to keep) *He had deceived her with false promises of marriage.*

a broken promise (=one that someone did not keep) *The people are tired of broken promises from politicians.*

a campaign/election promise *The Chancellor was accused of breaking his campaign promise not to raise fuel tax.*

a binding promise (=one that must be obeyed) *The court ruled that his employer's promise was binding.*

PREPOSITIONS

a promise of sth *We received promises of support from several MPs.*

a promise to sb *If he breaks his promise to me again, we're finished.*

PHRASES

breach of promise *formal* (=failure to do what you have legally promised to do) *She sued her husband for breach of promise when he left her.*

promise² *v*

to tell someone that you will definitely do or provide something or that something will happen

> **Grammar**
> **Promise** is usually used with an infinitive: *She's promised to do all she can to help.* or with a **(that)** clause: *Hurry up – we promised we wouldn't be late.*

ADVERBS

faithfully promise (=with no intention of breaking your promise) *Ann faithfully promised never to reveal my secret.*

solemnly promise (=seriously) *Before her husband's death, she had solemnly promised never to marry again.*

PHRASES

as promised *He came back two hours later, as promised.*

promotion [Ac] *n*

a situation in which someone is given a more important job or position in a company or organization

VERBS

get a promotion *Mike got a promotion after working for two years at the company.*

gain promotion *formal* (=get a promotion) *He gained rapid promotion to Assistant Director.*

deserve (a) promotion *She deserves promotion after everything she has done for the firm.*

offer sb a promotion *The company offered him a promotion following the success of the project.*

be passed over for promotion (=not be promoted) *Helen was disappointed to be passed over for promotion yet again.*

ADJECTIVES

rapid promotion *Her energy and leadership qualities earned her rapid promotion.*

PHRASES

chance/opportunity for promotion *They are stuck in low-paying jobs with little chance for promotion.*

prospects for promotion (=the chances of being promoted) *The prospects for promotion in this company are very good.*

prompt *adj* THESAURUS ▸ **quick (1)**

pronunciation *n*

the way in which a language or a particular word is pronounced, or the way in which someone pronounces the words of a language

ADJECTIVES

the right/correct pronunciation *Don't be afraid to ask your teacher about the correct pronunciation of unfamiliar words.*

the wrong/incorrect pronunciation *I knew what the word meant, but I used the wrong pronunciation.*

the standard pronunciation *What is the standard pronunciation of 'bath' in English?*

English/French/Spanish etc pronunciation *This book will teach you the basic rules and patterns of French pronunciation.*

sb's pronunciation is good/perfect *Her English pronunciation is almost perfect.*

sb's pronunciation is bad/terrible *If your pronunciation is bad, people will not understand you.*

> **Received pronunciation** or **RP** is the name for the standard way of pronouncing British English.

VERBS

improve your pronunciation *Talking with native speakers helps improve your pronunciation.*

learn pronunciation *Try to learn the correct pronunciation of any new words you come across.*

practise pronunciation BrE, **practice pronunciation** AmE: *You can practise your pronunciation by recording yourself.*

correct sb's pronunciation *Please correct my pronunciation if I get any of your names wrong.*

pronunciation + NOUNS

a pronunciation problem *The difference between 'shi' and 'si' is one of the most common pronunciation problems for foreign students of English.*

a pronunciation exercise *These pronunciation exercises will help you speak clear and natural English.*

a pronunciation drill (=an exercise in which you have to repeat something many times) *The teacher made us do a pronunciation drill.*

(a) pronunciation practice *You will find the pronunciation practice at the end of each unit of your coursebook.*

PREPOSITIONS

the pronunciation of sth *The pronunciation of some of these names is very difficult.*

proof *n*

facts, information, documents etc that prove something is true

VERBS

have proof *The newspaper claimed it had proof that he had lied to the court.*

there is proof *There is no proof that he is who he says he is.*

find proof *We found no proof that he had stolen the money.*

provide/give/produce proof *You will be asked to provide proof of your identity.*

need proof *He needed proof to back up his allegations.*

want proof *If you want proof, check my bank statement.*

demand proof *He demanded proof that his son was still alive before paying the ransom.*

ADJECTIVES

scientific proof *They say they have scientific proof that the treatment works.*

clear proof *These figures are clear proof that the economy is heading out of recession.*

conclusive/irrefutable proof (=that definitely proves something must be true) *There is no conclusive proof that our client is guilty.*

tangible/concrete proof (=clear and definite, in a way that can be seen, touched etc) *The medal is tangible proof of his bravery.*

further proof (=additional proof) *He showed his driving licence as further proof of his identity.*

living proof (=someone whose existence or experience proves something) *She is living proof that staying active keeps you younger.*

PREPOSITIONS

proof of sth *There is no conclusive proof of life on other planets.*

without proof *Without proof, no one will believe us.*

PHRASES

proof of identity (=something that proves who you are) *Do you have any proof of identity, such as a passport?*

the burden of proof (=the duty to prove that you are right in a legal case) *The burden of proof is on the prosecution.*

proof positive (=definite proof that cannot be doubted) *This is proof positive that she lied.*

propaganda *n*

information which is false or which emphasizes just one part of a situation, used by a government or group to make people agree with them

ADJECTIVES/NOUNS + propaganda

government/official propaganda *According to the official propaganda, the country's economy was now more successful than ever.*

political propaganda *What we need are facts, not political propaganda.*

enemy propaganda *The radio was broadcasting enemy propaganda.*

party propaganda (=based on the opinions of a political party) *He accused the newspaper of printing party propaganda.*

right-wing/left-wing propaganda *These claims are nothing more than right-wing propaganda.*

British/American etc propaganda *He claimed the stories were untrue and that they were just American propaganda.*

VERBS

spread propaganda *The paper was accused of spreading anti-government propaganda.*

believe propaganda *He believed all the party's propaganda about helping the workers get better lives.*

propaganda + NOUNS

a propaganda campaign *The party mounted a massive propaganda campaign against their political opponents.*

a propaganda exercise (=something which is done as propaganda and has no useful purpose) *The meeting was just a propaganda exercise for the company.*

a propaganda film *She produced propaganda films for the Nazis.*

the propaganda machine (=people and systems producing official propaganda) *The government's propaganda machine presented the incident as a triumph.*

a propaganda weapon/tool (=something that can be used for propaganda) *Sporting success was used as a propaganda weapon by the government.*

a propaganda war/battle *They began a propaganda war for the hearts and minds of the people.*

PHRASES

a piece of propaganda *The film was a typical piece of wartime propaganda.*

a form of propaganda *More subtle forms of propaganda were used after the war.*

for propaganda purposes *Their problems have been exploited for propaganda purposes.*

property *n*

1 the thing or things that someone owns

> **Grammar**
> **Property** is uncountable in this meaning. Don't use it in the plural.

ADJECTIVES

sb's personal property (=things that a particular person owns) *My home insurance policy covers damage to personal property of up to £7,000.*

stolen property *Some of the stolen property was found in Mason's house.*

lost property (=bags or other things lost or left accidentally in a public place) *Luckily for me, someone had handed my wallet in at the lost property office.*

intellectual property (=something that someone has invented or has the right to make or sell, which cannot be legally copied) *There are laws governing the protection of intellectual property.*

NOUNS + property

school/company property *The boys were arrested and charged with damaging school property.*

2 a house, building, or an area of land or houses, buildings, or land in general

> **Grammar**
> In this meaning **property** can be countable: *She owns several **properties**.* or uncountable: *The company buys and sells **property**.*

ADJECTIVES/NOUNS + property

private property (=owned by a particular person, organization etc and not for other people to use) *The land on the other side of the gate is private property.*

commercial property (=buildings used by businesses) *Rents on commercial property are due to rise.*

residential property (=buildings for people to live in) *There is a big demand for residential property in the south of the country.*

VERBS

buy/sell (a) property *I bought the property in 2008. | She has been trying to sell the property since last July.*

own (a) property *She owns several properties in the area.*

rent/let (a) property *I decided to let the property I owned in London and buy a house in the country.*

view a property (=go and look around a house that you are interested in buying) *I made appointments to view several properties.*

property + NOUNS

property prices *Property prices are much lower here than in the capital.*

property values *Property values in this area have been rising.*

the property market *There are signs of an improvement in the property market.*

a property owner *Just now, it makes sense for property owners to extend their houses rather than move.*

a property developer (=a person or company who makes money by buying land and then building houses, factories etc on it) *The site was sold recently to a local property developer.*

3 a quality or feature that a substance, plant etc has

> **Grammar**
> This meaning of **property** is countable. It is often used in the plural.

ADJECTIVES

special properties *Carbon has special properties, which make it highly suitable for this type of use.*

similar properties *The virus shared similar properties with HIV.*

physical properties *The class were doing experiments to study the physical properties of water.*

chemical properties *The different substances are listed in groups according to their chemical properties.*
electrical properties *Each type of cell has distinct electrical properties.*
magnetic properties *We tested the magnetic properties of iron and nickel.*
healing/medicinal/health-giving properties *The old women know about the healing properties of local herbs.*
inherent properties (=a natural quality that something has) *Two of the inherent properties of aluminium are its lightness and strength.*

VERBS

have properties (*also* **possess properties** *formal*): *The root of the plant has medicinal properties.*
study sth's properties *Researchers began studying the biological properties of each cell.*

proportion Ac *n*

1 the amount of something, compared with the whole amount that exists

> **THESAURUS: proportion**
> quantity, volume, level, proportion, quota, yield → **amount**

2 used when talking about the size or importance of something

> **Grammar**
> Always plural in this meaning.

ADJECTIVES/NOUNS + proportion

enormous/massive/gigantic proportions *The oil spill in the Gulf of Mexico was an ecological disaster of enormous proportions.*
alarming proportions (=very worrying) *Credit card debt has reached alarming proportions in the UK.*
epic proportions (=extremely serious) *This was a public relations disaster of epic proportions.*
epidemic proportions (=used when saying that a problem affects a huge number of people) *The flu outbreak has reached epidemic proportions.*
historic proportions (=so serious that it will be remembered for a long time) *We were trapped for three days by a blizzard of historic proportions.*
manageable proportions (=not too big to deal with) *You need to keep your debts within manageable proportions.*

VERBS

reach alarming/serious/epidemic etc proportions *Shoplifting has reached epidemic proportions.*
grow to large/enormous etc proportions *The fish grows to gigantic proportions.*

PREPOSITIONS

of ... proportions *The volcanic eruption was of disastrous proportions.*

proposal *n* a formal plan or suggestion

VERBS

make a proposal *The report makes several proposals for improvement.*
put forward a proposal (=suggest one) *They put forward a proposal for a joint research project.*
submit a proposal (=officially make a proposal to an organization) *You will have to submit your proposal in writing.*
come up with a proposal (=think of one) *The group came up with a proposal to improve the local park.*
draw up a proposal (=write a proposal, after it has been officially discussed) *A committee of experts drew up proposals for a constitution.*
approve/accept a proposal *The proposal was approved by the committee.*
support/back a proposal *None of these groups support the government's proposals.*
reject a proposal *Councillors had twice rejected proposals for a new village school.*
consider a proposal *We shall consider their proposals carefully.*
discuss a proposal *He had discussed the proposal with the Egyptian president.*
vote on a proposal *Shareholders will vote on the proposal on 5 May.*

ADJECTIVES

a detailed proposal *They drew up a detailed proposal and submitted it to the planning committee.*
a specific/concrete proposal (=clear and definite) *The report will make specific proposals for further investigation.*
a controversial proposal (=one that people disagree about) *Ministers will vote on a controversial proposal to legalize the drug.*
a formal proposal *We have to submit a formal proposal to the shareholders.*

NOUNS + proposal

a government proposal *Thousands protested against government proposals to cut health budgets.*
a research proposal *Applicants should prepare a short research proposal on their chosen topic.*
a marriage proposal (*also* **a proposal of marriage**) (=the act of asking someone to marry you) *She had received several marriage proposals.*

PREPOSITIONS

a proposal for sth *Any proposals for change will have to win the support of local people.*
a proposal by sb *The proposal by city officials to increase parking fees has encountered opposition.*

under a proposal *Under the proposal, companies would be charged per tonne of waste disposed of.*

prospect Ac *n*

1 the possibility that something will happen – used especially when talking about how you feel about it

ADJECTIVES

an exciting prospect *Deana was facing the exciting prospect of a trip to Australia.*

an attractive/enticing prospect *A journey of that length was not an attractive prospect.*

a daunting prospect (=rather frightening) *Making a speech to 1,000 people is a pretty daunting prospect.*

a terrifying/frightening prospect *Change of any kind can be a frightening prospect.*

a gloomy/grim/bleak prospect *Many Britons face the grim prospect of losing their jobs.*

a realistic/real prospect (=something that could really happen) *There is no realistic prospect of success.*

an immediate prospect *The island faces the immediate prospect of more violence.*

little prospect of sth *These children had a poor education and little prospect of finding work.*

VERBS

face the prospect (of sth) *Greece faces the prospect of new general elections next month.*

raise/offer the prospect of sth (=make it a possibility that something might happen) *This discovery raises the prospect of a cure for the disease.*

relish the prospect (of sth) (=enjoy the thought of it very much) *She would have to speak to him. She didn't relish the prospect.*

welcome the prospect (of sth) *Ailsa welcomed the prospect of some company for the evening.*

dread the prospect (of sth) (=feel very worried about it) *I dread the prospect of staying here while you're away.*

consider the prospect (of sth) *He had never seriously considered the prospect of leaving his wife.*

discuss the prospect (of sth) *We are discussing the prospect of going to China next year.*

PREPOSITIONS

the prospect of (doing) sth *The prospect of marriage terrified Alice.*

PHRASES

be excited/thrilled/delighted etc at the prospect *I was excited at the prospect of going to Washington.*

be alarmed/appalled/upset etc at the prospect *She was secretly appalled at the prospect of staying at her aunt's.*

2 someone or something's prospects are their chances of future success

> **Grammar**
> Always plural in this meaning.

ADJECTIVES

future prospects *It can be difficult to predict the future prospects of a business.*

long-term/short-term prospects (=for a long time or a short time in the future) *She is very confident about her long-term prospects with the company.*

economic/political/commercial prospects *The study concluded that the economic prospects for the area are very poor.*

good/bright prospects *The family moved constantly, in search of better prospects.*

poor prospects (=not good) *Prospects for economic growth next year are poor.*

bleak prospects (=very bad, with the result that you do not have any hope for the future) *Job prospects are bleak for many teenagers in the city.*

NOUNS + prospect

job/career/employment prospects *She earned a higher salary, and had better career prospects than her husband.*

promotion prospects *Dan worried that this affair at work would affect his promotion prospects.*

VERBS

improve/enhance sb's/sth's prospects *The scheme aims to improve the employment prospects of young people.*

damage sb's/sth's prospects *Bad publicity will damage the company's prospects.*

prospects look good/bright/bleak etc *The country's economic prospects look brighter than they did last year.*

PREPOSITIONS

prospects for sth *Prospects for the climate treaty look less than promising.*

prosperous *adj* THESAURUS **rich (1)**

protect *v*

to keep someone or something safe from harm, damage, or illness

ADVERBS

protect sb/sth effectively/adequately *Some child car seats do not protect children adequately.*

protect sb/sth completely/fully *A strong bag protects your laptop fully from dust and dirt.*

be well protected *All the pipes are well protected against freezing temperatures.*

be poorly protected (=not well enough) *If your computer is poorly protected, it may get infected by viruses.*

be heavily protected (=by a lot of people, laws etc) *The soldiers live in a heavily protected military base.*

be legally protected (=by law) *After two years, their jobs are legally protected.*

VERBS

be designed to protect sb/sth from sth *The towers were designed to protect the country from invasion.*

help to protect against sth *Sunscreen helps to protect against sunburn.*

PREPOSITIONS

protect sb/sth against sb/sth *Physical exercise can protect you against heart disease.*

protect sb/sth from sth *Wear sunglasses to protect your eyes from the sun.*

protection *n*

when someone or something is protected

ADJECTIVES

good/effective protection *This lightweight jacket gives good protection from rain and wind.*

complete/full protection *No security system can ever give complete protection against a determined thief.*

greater/better protection *The law should give greater protection to victims.*

extra/added protection *The police were issued with body armour for extra protection.*

adequate/sufficient protection (=enough) *Car seats for children should provide adequate protection.*

inadequate protection (=not enough) *The design of the building provides inadequate protection against damp.*

legal protection (=protection given by laws) *This Act gives you legal protection if goods that you buy are faulty.*

NOUNS + protection

police protection (=protection by the police) *The witnesses were given police protection.*

consumer protection (=for people who buy goods) *The consumer protection regulations will include new online shopping rules.*

data protection (=protecting information from being stolen or wrongly used) *The company has a policy of strict data protection.*

VERBS

give/provide/offer protection *The drug provides protection against malaria.*

afford protection *formal* (=provide someone with protection) *They say they are afforded no protection by the security forces.*

have protection *When you are on the mountain you have no protection against the wind and rain.*

get/receive protection *The soldiers will get some protection from their gas masks.*

need/require protection *He seemed to think that she needed protection.*

seek protection *They were forced to seek the protection of the police.*

PREPOSITIONS

protection against sth *Vitamin C helps give protection against infection.*

protection for sb/sth *This law provides protection for threatened animals and plants.*

protection of sb/sth *The government must follow international standards for the protection of refugees.*

PHRASES

a degree/measure of protection (=some protection) *The shelter gave us a measure of protection against the bitter cold.*

the level of protection *Sun cream is classified according to the level of protection that it provides.*

protective *adj*

1 used for protection

NOUNS

protective clothing/suit *Firefighters wear special protective clothing.*

protective equipment *It is the employer's responsibility to supply workers with protective equipment such as safety glasses.*

a protective layer/cover/coating *The Earth has a protective layer known as the ozone layer.*

protective measures *Home-owners should take simple protective measures to protect their homes from thieves.*

PREPOSITIONS

be protective against sth (=prevent someone from getting a disease) *The drug is protective against the disease.*

2 wanting to protect someone or something from harm or danger

VERBS

feel protective towards sb/sth *She had always felt protective towards her younger brother.*

ADVERBS

fiercely protective *He is fiercely protective of his independence.*

highly protective *These dogs are ideal as guard dogs and are highly protective of their owners.*

too protective/overly protective *Parents should try not to be overly protective of their children.*

PREPOSITIONS

protective towards sb/sth (*also* **protective of sb/sth** *formal*): *I can't help feeling protective towards my kids.*

protest[1] *n*

1 public actions that are intended to show strong disagreement

ADJECTIVES/NOUNS + protest

political protest *Lee spent five years in prison for his involvement in political protest.*

P

a public/popular protest *The announcement led to widespread public protests.*

a peaceful protest *Around 5,000 students began a peaceful protest.*

a violent/angry protest *Three people died yesterday in violent protests against the government.*

a mass protest (=one involving a lot of people) *There were mass protests in the capital.*

a massive protest *They reacted to the king's forced abdication with massive public protests.*

widespread protests (=involving many people in many places) *Despite widespread protests, the government went ahead with the plan.*

a street protest *There was a ban on street protests.*

a student protest *Student protests were crushed by police.*

an anti-government/anti-war protest *Religious leaders continued to lead anti-government protests.*

VERBS

hold/stage/mount a protest *Opponents of the plan have staged several protests.*

take part in/join a protest *Hundreds of people joined the protest.*

lead to/spark (off)/provoke protests (=cause them) *The arrests sparked off violent street protests.*

organize a protest *Dissatisfied customers organized a protest outside the store.*

protest + NOUNS

a protest group/movement *Leaders of the protest movement have called for a general strike.*

a protest march *Students held a protest march against the war.*

a protest rally (=a large outdoor public meeting to protest about something) *A protest rally in the capital was attended by about 400 people.*

PREPOSITIONS

a protest against sth *Thousands of people took part in a protest against government cuts.*

a protest by sb *The announcement provoked widespread protests by students.*

in protest at sth *Employees came out on strike in protest at poor working conditions.*

PHRASES

a wave of protests (=several protests) *The incident resulted in a wave of protests.*

2 something you do or say to show that you do not like something or do not want to do something

ADJECTIVES

a loud protest *Judging by the loud protests, the children were not happy at having to do the test again.*

an angry protest *There were angry protests when the decision was first announced.*

a formal/official protest *The team has made a formal protest to the Football Association.*

a strong protest *Greece lodged a strong protest over the EU's decision.*

VERBS

make a protest (*also* **lodge a protest** *formal*): *He made a formal protest about the way he had been treated by the police.*

sth prompts/provokes/draws a protest (=causes a protest) *Her comments prompted protests from ministers.*

ignore a protest *He ignored their protests and continued with his criticism of their work.*

PREPOSITIONS

without protest *She drank the medicine without protest.*

a protest from sb *The comments drew protests from some community leaders.*

a protest against sth *The article was a clear protest against the way she had been treated.*

PHRASES

a storm of protest (=a lot of complaints) *There was a storm of protest when the programme was first broadcast.*

howls of protest (=loud or public complaints) *The announcement was met with howls of protest.*

a letter of protest *She wrote a letter of protest to the company.*

protest[2] *v*

to say that you disagree or do not want to do something, or to take action with a group of other people to show this

ADVERBS

protest strongly/vigorously *Human rights groups protested vigorously against the decision.*

protest loudly *She was protesting loudly because she did not want to go home.*

NOUNS

protest your innocence (=say repeatedly and publicly that you are innocent) *In jail he continued to protest his innocence.*

PREPOSITIONS

protest against sth *Thousands of people blocked the street, protesting against the new law.*

protest about/at sth *Parents have protested about the plan to close the school.*

> In British English, people usually say **protest against a decision/war etc**. In American English, people usually say **protest a war/decision etc**.

proud *adj*

feeling pleased about your achievements or possessions, or about the achievements of your family, your country etc

ADVERBS

very/really proud *Your family must be very proud of you.*

extremely/immensely/intensely proud *He said he was immensely proud to have been elected prime minister.*

fiercely proud (=extremely proud of something and reacting strongly if anyone criticizes them) *They are fiercely proud of their native land.*

rather proud *She was rather proud of herself for having the idea.*

justifiably/justly/rightly proud (=with good reason) *He is justifiably proud of what he and his father achieved.*

VERBS

feel proud *I felt very proud of my son when he got his master's degree.*

seem proud *She seems proud to be like her father.*

make sb proud *His success made his parents very proud.*

NOUNS

the proud owner (of sth) (*also* **the proud possessor of sth** *formal*): *She is now the proud owner of a new sports car.*

a proud mother/father/parent *Mark is the proud father of a three-week-old baby boy.*

PREPOSITIONS

proud of sb/sth *The company is justly proud of its achievements.*

proud of yourself *You should be proud of yourself – getting an A in English isn't easy.*

PHRASES

something to be proud of *His past achievements are certainly something to be proud of.*

have every/good reason to be proud (=it is right that someone is proud) *We have every reason to be proud of our country's health service.*

prove *v*

to show that something is true by providing facts, information etc

> **Grammar**
>
> In passives, you often say that something is or has been **proven**: *The drug has been proven to stop the spread of cancer.* You can also use the regular past participle **proved** in the same meaning.

PHRASES

prove sb guilty/innocent *The law states that you are innocent until proved guilty.*

prove sb wrong/right *They say I'm too old to do the job, but I'm going to prove them all wrong.*

prove sth beyond (any/all) doubt (*also* **prove sth beyond a shadow of a doubt**) *The analysis proves beyond all doubt that the painting is a fake.*

sth proves nothing (=it does not show that something is true at all) *These comments prove nothing.*

NOUNS

prove a theory *No evidence emerged to prove either theory.*

prove your case *The state had failed to prove its case.*

prove an allegation/claim *There is no evidence to prove the allegations that he was involved in the theft.*

prove sb's guilt/innocence *He claims the police destroyed records that could prove the officer's guilt.*

prove the existence of sth *These pictures do not prove the existence of water on Mars.*

prove your point (=show that you are right) *To prove her point, Dr Hurdal showed her audience a scan of a patient's brain.*

ADVERBS

prove sth conclusively (=without any doubt) *It is impossible to prove conclusively that the changes are a result of global warming.*

be scientifically proven *Smoking has been scientifically proven to cause serious damage to health.*

PREPOSITIONS

prove sth to sb *I knew he was lying, but there was no way I could prove it to the others.*

provisional *adj* THESAURUS ▶ **temporary**

psyche *n* THESAURUS ▶ **mind**

psychological Ac *adj*

relating to the way that your mind works and the way that this affects your behaviour

NOUNS

a psychological problem/disorder *About 10% of students seek help for emotional or psychological problems.*

psychological damage/harm/trauma *Constant criticism can inflict psychological damage on children.*

psychological stress *Living in poor conditions results in higher levels of psychological stress.*

psychological needs *Nurses should also take into account the patient's psychological needs.*

the psychological effects/impact of sth *There can be significant psychological effects of drug use.*

psychological health/well-being *Grief can have long-term effects on physical and psychological health.*

sb's psychological state *The report expressed deep concern about the psychological state of many of the prisoners.*

a psychological advantage *It gave me a psychological advantage to know that I had never lost a game against him.*

P

a psychological test *Psychological tests were used as part of the selection process for joining the army.*

a psychological theory *You may be familiar with some of the psychological theories of Sigmund Freud.*

psychological warfare (=methods in which you try to make people feel frightened, less confident etc so that you can win a war, sports game etc) *The terrorists are using a campaign of psychological warfare.*

ADVERBS

purely psychological *Some people react badly to food for purely psychological reasons.*

P

pub *n*

in Britain, a place where alcohol can be bought and drunk, and usually where meals are served

ADJECTIVES/NOUNS + pub

the local pub *He spends most evenings with his friends in the local pub.*

an old/traditional pub *We had a drink in a lovely old pub.*

a country pub *There's nothing nicer than a walk, followed by lunch in a country pub.*

a village pub *A lot of village pubs are closing down.*

VERBS

run a pub (=be in charge of a pub) *His parents run a pub in Essex.*

go to the pub (*also* **go down the pub** *informal*): *Shall we go to the pub tonight?*

meet in the pub *Let's meet in the pub for lunch.*

pub + NOUNS

a pub lunch *We could go for a walk, then have a pub lunch.*

a pub crawl *informal* (=an evening spent going to several pubs, one after another) *They went on a pub crawl to celebrate his birthday.*

a pub landlord/landlady (=a man or woman who is in charge of a pub) *The pub landlord was very friendly and welcoming.*

PREPOSITIONS

in the pub *I saw them last night in the pub.*

at the pub *Dan's probably at the pub.*

public[1] *adj*

1 relating to ordinary people in general

NOUNS

public opinion *Public opinion forced the government to change its unpopular policy.*

public health *The chemicals could be a risk to public health.*

public knowledge/awareness *We want to raise public awareness of the dangers of eating too much salt.*

public image/perception (=people's idea about someone or something) *He is very different from the public perception of him.*

public concern *There is widespread public concern about climate change.*

public confidence/support *The government seems to have lost public confidence.*

public attention/interest *The scandal attracted a lot of public attention.*

public pressure *The minister had to resign because of public pressure.*

PHRASES

be in the public interest (=be useful or important for ordinary people) *It is in the public interest for the government to publish the full details of the inquiry.*

in the public eye (=noticed or watched by people in general) *As a well-known actor he is always in the public eye.*

2 relating to things that are owned or provided by the government for everyone

NOUNS

public services (=services such as street cleaning, education, and health that are provided for everyone) *He argued that higher taxes were needed to improve public services.*

the public sector (=industries and services owned by the government) *The government will be forced to cut jobs in the public sector.*

public transport *BrE*, **public transportation** *AmE: Most people use public transport to get around London, rather than drive their own car.*

public spending/expenditure (=money spent by the government on public services) *He warned that it would be necessary to reduce public spending.*

public money/funds (=money paid in taxes to the government) *Should public money be spent on helping businesses in trouble?*

public ownership *In those days the railways were still in public ownership.*

a public building *The city has some magnificent public buildings, including a huge Victorian town hall.*

a public body *The Commission is a public body responsible for inspecting new buildings.*

public utilities *formal* (=services such as electricity, gas, or water, that are provided for everyone to use) *These people have no access to sanitation or public utilities.*

a public library *The book is available from any public library.*

a public servant/official (=someone who is paid by the government to serve the people) *Public servants should never accept gifts from companies or individuals.*

3 relating to things that can be seen, heard, or known about by many people, rather than being private or secret

NOUNS

a public debate/discussion *There needs to be a public debate about any changes to the voting system.*

a public inquiry/meeting *The plans for the new hospital will be discussed at a public meeting next week.*

a public place *Can we discuss this in a less public place?*

public access *There is currently no easy public access to this information.*

a public display *He did not like making public displays of emotion.*

PHRASES

in public (=when you are with other people and anyone can see or hear what you are doing) *In some countries, men and women are not allowed to show affection to each other in public.*

in the public domain (=available to be seen, used, or known about by anyone) *This information is all in the public domain and can be reprinted freely.*

public² *n*

ordinary people who do not work for the government or have any special position in society

You always say **the public**.

PHRASES

the general public *The meeting will be open to the general public.*

a member of the public (=an ordinary person) *Police warned members of the public not to approach the man, who may be armed.*

be open to the public *The castle is open to the public on payment of an admission charge.*

VERBS

inform/educate/warn the public *The aim of the campaign is to inform the public about safe food hygiene practices.*

protect the public *The police are there to serve and protect the public from crime.*

reassure the public (=stop them from worrying) *He reassured the public about the safety of the nation's water systems.*

serve the public *Parliament needs modernisation if it's to serve the public properly.*

deceive/mislead the public *He is deceiving the public by pretending to be something he is not.*

publication *n*

1 the process of printing a book, magazine etc, and offering it for sale

ADJECTIVES

electronic/online publication *A number of journals have moved entirely to electronic publication.*

VERBS

prepare/get sth ready for publication *Her latest book is currently being prepared for publication.*

submit sth for publication *Helen is thinking of submitting the paper for publication in a medical journal.*

accept sth for publication *Her article on Mexico has been accepted for publication.*

be selected for publication *His short story has been selected for publication in a literary journal.*

delay publication *Publication was delayed for technical reasons.*

prevent/stop publication *The government may seek to prevent publication of information it considers secret.*

cease publication *formal* (=stop being published) *The newspaper ceased publication at the end of last year.*

PREPOSITIONS

the publication of sth *Readers are eagerly awaiting the publication of his latest book.*

PHRASES

the date of publication (*also* **the publication date**) *The date of publication was 2012.*

2 something that has been published

ADJECTIVES

latest publication *The catalogue lists all the latest publications.*

sb's previous publications *Her previous publications have all been on similar subjects.*

sb's recent publication *Smith's recent publications include a series of detective stories.*

a scientific publication *His articles have appeared in scientific publications such as the British Medical Journal.*

an academic/scholarly publication *Below is a list of recent academic publications by staff members at the university.*

a forthcoming publication (=one that will be published soon) *His forthcoming publications include a study of Charles Darwin.*

a weekly/monthly/annual publication *The magazine is a monthly publication aimed at car enthusiasts.*

publicity *n*

the attention that someone or something gets from newspapers, television etc

ADJECTIVES

bad/negative/adverse publicity *The company is anxious to avoid any negative publicity.*

good publicity *The programme is a chance for him to get some good publicity for his new movie.*

free publicity *Giving away samples is one way of getting free publicity for your products.*

widespread/wide/extensive publicity (=in many places) *The scandal had received widespread publicity.*

massive/enormous publicity (=a lot of publicity) *His death got enormous publicity in the national media.*

considerable publicity (=quite a lot) *The opening of the trial generated considerable publicity.*

maximum publicity *They hoped to gain maximum publicity by inviting TV cameras to film them.*

national/international publicity *Candidates aim to get national publicity during election campaigns.*

unwelcome/unwanted publicity *The athlete's positive drugs test has attracted unwelcome publicity for the sport.*

VERBS

get/receive publicity *The concert is getting a lot of publicity – you see advertisements everywhere.*

attract publicity *Two recommendations in the report have attracted publicity.*

give publicity to sth *Much publicity was given to their allegations in the British press.*

generate publicity *The interview generated a huge amount of publicity for the film.*

avoid publicity *They wanted to settle the matter quietly in order to avoid bad publicity.*

seek publicity *He sought neither reward nor publicity for his work.*

the publicity surrounding sth *The publicity surrounding the case has encouraged more people to contact the police.*

publicity + NOUNS

a publicity campaign *The advertisement is part of a publicity campaign to promote their new product.*

a publicity stunt (=something that is only done to get publicity) *The singer denied that her marriage was just a publicity stunt.*

a publicity photo/shot *The band posed for publicity photos.*

publicity material (=information, advertisements etc for the press and public) *Publicity material relating to the programme is available in several languages.*

PREPOSITIONS

publicity for sb/sth *He wanted to get as much publicity for himself as he could.*

publicity about/over sth *The company had had some bad publicity over a defective product.*

PHRASES

the glare of publicity (=a lot of publicity, which can make you feel uncomfortable) *He carried on his life in the full glare of publicity.*

a blaze of publicity (=a lot of publicity) *His marriage broke up in a blaze of publicity.*

publish *v*

to arrange for something to be printed and sold or made available to the public

ADVERBS

first/originally published *The book was first published in 1982.*

recently/newly published *A recently published report claimed that many adults could not read simple instructions.*

pull *v*

to make something or someone move towards you or in a particular direction

PREPOSITIONS/ADVERBS

pull sb/sth hard *He pulled hard on the handle, but the door refused to open.*

pull sb/sth towards sb/sth *He pulled her towards him and kissed her.*

pull sth down/up *He pulled down his sweater.*

pull sth out *The man pulled something out of his briefcase.*

pull sth on/off *Sam was pulling on his socks.*

pull sth open *She pulled open the door and looked inside.*

pulse *n*

the regular beat that can be felt, for example at your wrist, as your heart pumps blood around your body

VERBS + pulse

take/check sb's pulse (=count the beats of their pulse) *Remember to take your pulse at intervals while you are exercising.*

feel for a pulse (=try to find and check someone's pulse) *I felt for a pulse, but I couldn't find one.*

find a pulse (=be able to feel a pulse, which shows that someone is alive) *To her relief, she found a pulse.*

pulse + VERBS

sb's pulse is beating *His pulse was beating with a fierce rhythm.*

sb's pulse races (=beats very quickly) *His fingers brushed hers, sending her pulse racing.*

sb's pulse quickens (=starts to beat faster) *He heard footsteps in the passage outside and felt his pulse quicken.*

ADJECTIVES

a weak/faint pulse *The boy's pulse was very weak.*

pulse + NOUNS

pulse rate (=how fast your pulse beats) *The doctor checked my weight and pulse rate.*

pulse beat *The rhythm was steady, as regular as a pulse beat.*

punch[1] *v*

to hit someone or something hard with your fist (=closed hand)

PHRASES

punch sb in the face/mouth/head/stomach *He punched Jack in the face.*

punch sb on the nose *Dan was punched on the nose.*

kick and punch/punch and kick *They were kicking and punching him as he lay on the ground.*

ADVERBS

punch sb/sth repeatedly *He was accused of repeatedly punching the man and knocking him to the ground.*

punch² *n*

a quick strong hit made with your fist (=closed hand)

VERBS

give sb a punch *The other boy gave him a punch on the nose.*

throw a punch (=try to hit someone) *Rob was so angry that he turned round and threw a punch at the man.*

land a punch (=succeed in hitting someone) *I managed to land a punch on his jaw.*

deliver a punch *formal* (=hit someone) *Lewis delivered the knockout punch.*

take a punch (=be hit, or deal well with being hit) *The other fighter took a lot of punches in the final round.*

trade/exchange punches (=hit each other) *The two men traded punches after an argument got out of control.*

ADJECTIVES/NOUNS + punch

a hard/powerful punch *My stomach took a couple of hard punches.*

a good punch *Tyson landed one good punch but it wasn't enough.*

a knockout punch (=one that knocks someone down so that they cannot get up again) *In the fourth round, Lewis produced a knockout punch that ended the fight.*

PREPOSITIONS

a punch on the nose/jaw/arm *Then he gave me a smile and a playful punch on the arm.*

a punch in the face/mouth/stomach *He needs a punch in the mouth.*

a punch to the face/head/jaw/stomach/chest etc (=used especially in reports about attacks on people) *A punch to the stomach can cause severe internal bleeding.*

punish *v*

to do something unpleasant to someone because they have done something wrong or broken the law

ADVERBS

punish sb severely *Her father punished her severely for telling lies.*

PREPOSITIONS

punish sb for sth *When the children behave badly, no one punishes them for it.*

punish sb by doing sth *They punished him by not letting him go out in the evening.*

PHRASES

sb/sth deserves to be punished *The company deserves to be punished for putting passengers at risk.*

punishment *n*

the act of punishing someone

ADJECTIVES

a harsh/severe punishment *Drug smugglers are given severe punishments.*

a just/fitting punishment (=suitable and fair) *Death would be a just punishment.*

capital punishment (=the system of killing people as a punishment for serious crimes) *Do you agree with capital punishment?*

corporal punishment (=punishing a child by hitting them, especially when this is an accepted system) *Corporal punishment is banned in state schools.*

a maximum punishment *The charge against him carries a maximum punishment of a year in jail.*

a light punishment (=not severe) *It seems a very light punishment for such a serious offence.*

VERBS

give sb a punishment (*also* **impose a punishment** *formal*): *He was given a punishment of two weeks without video games.*

get/receive a punishment *He received the maximum punishment.*

escape/avoid punishment *The thieves managed to escape punishment.*

hand out punishments (*also* **mete out punishments** *formal*) (=give people punishments) *The courts are handing out harsher punishments to careless drivers.*

inflict a punishment (on sb) (=punish someone, especially physically) *Harsh punishments were inflicted on those who disobeyed the rules.*

face a punishment (=be going to get one) *She now faces a punishment of up to five years in jail.*

deserve a punishment *He didn't deserve the punishment because he hadn't done anything wrong.*

carry a punishment (=used when saying what the punishment for something is) *The offence carries a punishment of up to 10 years in prison.*

PREPOSITIONS

a punishment for sth *What is a suitable punishment for handing in work late?*

as a punishment *I was sent to bed as a punishment.*

PHRASES

the punishment should fit the crime (=it should be appropriate) *In law, it is important that the punishment should fit the crime.*

puny *adj*

THESAURUS **weak (1)**

pure *adj*

1 a pure substance or material is not mixed with anything else

NOUNS

pure gold/silver *The necklace is made of pure gold.*

pure cotton/wool/silk/linen *Ella was wearing a dress made from pure silk.*

pure orange juice/grapefruit juice etc *He asked for a glass of pure orange juice.*

the air/water is pure *The air is very pure in the mountains.*

pure olive oil/coconut oil etc *Pure lavender oil smells lovely.*

ADVERBS

completely/absolutely pure *The water is tested to make sure that it is absolutely pure.*

100%/80% etc pure *This type of gold is 75% pure.*

P

2 used when you want to emphasize that something was the only reason, feeling etc

> **Grammar**
> **Pure** is only used before a noun in this meaning.

NOUNS

pure chance/luck *He had discovered the truth by pure chance.*

pure coincidence (=used when the same thing happens twice, completely by chance) *It was pure coincidence that we both arrived on the same plane.*

pure joy/pleasure/delight *She looked at him with pure joy.*

pure hatred/jealousy/evil *She remembered the look of pure hatred in his eyes.*

pure speculation (=just guesses, not things that you know are facts) *Most of what you hear is pure speculation.*

pure fantasy/fiction (=something that is not true at all) *He dismissed the allegations as 'pure fantasy'.*

pure genius *His second goal was pure genius.*

pure hell (=an extremely bad experience) *He has described his time in jail as 'pure hell'.*

purple *adj, n*

a colour that is a mixture of red and blue

TYPES OF PURPLE

dark/deep purple *There was a deep purple bruise on his arm.*

pale/light purple *The plant has pale purple flowers.*

bright purple *He wore a bright purple shirt.*

> You can also use **mauve**, **lavender**, or **lilac** to describe something that is pale purple.

PREPOSITIONS

in purple (=in purple clothes or purple ink) *The emperor was dressed in purple.*

PHRASES

a shade of purple *The flowers were a beautiful shade of purple.*

purple with rage/fury (=used to describe someone's face) *His neighbour was purple with rage.*

purpose *n*

the reason you do something, and the thing you want to achieve when you do it

ADJECTIVES

the main purpose *The main purpose of our trip was to visit my family.*

the chief/primary/principal purpose (=main purpose - more formal) *Their primary purpose is to report the news.*

a useful purpose *Nuclear weapons have no useful purpose.*

sth's original purpose *The building is no longer needed for its original purpose.*

the real purpose *What was the real purpose of his question?*

the whole purpose (=used when you want to emphasize that something is the only important purpose) *The whole purpose of running a business is to make money.*

sole purpose (=only purpose) *I used to bake cakes for the sole purpose of giving them away.*

a practical purpose *It is a beautiful object, but it does not really have any practical purpose.*

a dual purpose (=two purposes) *A dog can fulfil a dual purpose by providing both company and security.*

a common purpose (=one that people share) *We were united by a common purpose and a determination to improve things.*

a specific/particular purpose *What is the specific purpose of your visit to England?*

VERBS

have a purpose *A meeting should have a clear purpose.*

serve/fulfil a purpose (=be used for a particular reason) *The building must have served a religious purpose.*

achieve your purpose (=achieve what you wanted to achieve) *She had achieved her purpose, at least in part.*

defeat the purpose (of sth) (=stop something from achieving what it is intended to do) *You're defeating the purpose of a low-fat dessert if you pour lots of cream on it.*

PREPOSITIONS

the purpose of sth *The purpose of this meeting is to elect a new chairman.*

sb's purpose in doing sth *Her purpose in writing the book was to tell the stories of the victims of war.*

for a purpose *The gun was there for a purpose.*

PHRASES

for political/military/educational/medicinal etc purposes *This technology could be used for military purposes.*

for business/research etc purposes *About one in five of all trips is made for business purposes.*

for/with the purpose of doing sth *Troops were sent solely with the purpose of assisting refugees.*

with/for the express purpose of doing sth (=used to emphasize that someone had one particular purpose) *They had travelled to Paris with the express purpose of visiting the Louvre.*

THESAURUS: purpose

aim
what you want to achieve when you do something:
The ***main aims*** *of the project are as follows. | Their* ***ultimate aim*** *is to find a cure for cancer.*

goal
something that you hope to achieve in the future, even though this may take a long time:
It took Mandela over forty years to ***achieve*** *his* ***goal*** *of a democratic South Africa. | the* ***goal of*** *ending child poverty*

objective
something that you are working hard to achieve, especially in business or politics:
The bank ***achieved*** *its* ***objective*** *of increasing its share of the market. | The government's* ***long-term objective*** *is to cut carbon emissions by 50%.*

the object of sth *formal*
the specific purpose of an activity:
The object of *the game is to get as many points as possible. | The students will benefit, and that must be* ***the object of the exercise*** (=the main thing that you are trying to do).

the point
the purpose of doing something and the reason why it is right or necessary:
At fourteen, I couldn't ***see the point*** *of going to school. |* ***What's the point*** *in waiting?* (=I don't think it is useful or necessary)

intention
the purpose that you have in your mind when you do something:
He kept his ***real intentions*** *well hidden. | Although we made a lot of money, this wasn't our* ***original intention****.*

ends
the result that someone is trying to achieve - used especially when you disapprove of what someone is doing:
They are using religion ***for political ends****. |* ***The ends do not justify the means*** (=you should not use violence, cruelty, dishonest behaviour etc to achieve your aims).

pursue Ac *v*

to continue doing an activity or trying to achieve something over a long period of time

NOUNS

pursue a goal/aim/objective *She was known to be ruthless in pursuing her goals.*

pursue a policy/strategy *The organization is pursuing a policy of cost cutting.*

pursue a career *She plans to pursue a career in politics.*

pursue your interest *Always encourage children to pursue their interests.*

pursue your ambition *David left the company to pursue his political ambitions.*

pursue a dream (=try to achieve something you have wanted very much for a long time) *He decided to pursue his childhood dream of being an actor.*

pursue your studies *After the war, he went to Heidelberg University to pursue his studies.*

ADVERBS

actively pursue sth *She is actively pursuing her music career, and has already made some recordings.*

vigorously pursue sth (=in a determined and energetic way) *The government will vigorously pursue its policies in fighting crime.*

doggedly pursue sth (=in a determined way) *He was still doggedly pursuing his studies.*

aggressively pursue sth (=in a very determined way) *The organization has aggressively pursued a policy of non-discrimination.*

relentlessly pursue sth (=continuing for a long time without giving up) *For the next 12 years, he relentlessly pursued his goal.*

pursuit *n*

1 the act of chasing or following someone

Grammar
This meaning of **pursuit** is uncountable, and is most commonly used in the phrase **in pursuit**.

PHRASES

in pursuit (of sb) *There were four police cars in pursuit of the stolen vehicle.*

set off in pursuit (of sb) *They set off in pursuit of the enemy.*

in hot/close pursuit (=following someone

P

closely in order to try to catch them) *Three policemen set off in hot pursuit of the thief.*

VERBS

give pursuit (=try to catch someone) *When the car drove away, two of the officers gave pursuit and stopped the vehicle.*

2 the act of trying to get or achieve something

> **Grammar**
> You usually say **the pursuit of sth**. This meaning of **pursuit** is uncountable.

PHRASES

the pursuit of power *Stalin was completely ruthless in his pursuit of power.*

the pursuit of happiness/pleasure *The pursuit of pleasure was his main goal in life.*

the pursuit of knowledge/wisdom/truth *She devoted her life to the pursuit of scientific knowledge.*

the pursuit of justice *The pursuit of justice for the victims has been a slow and difficult process.*

the pursuit of excellence *The pursuit of excellence is the driving force behind the company.*

the pursuit of a goal/objective/aim *The two teams of researchers are assisting each other in the pursuit of this goal.*

the pursuit of profit/wealth *The firm was criticized for its pursuit of profit regardless of workers' safety.*

ADJECTIVES

relentless pursuit (=without ever stopping) *He is known for his relentless pursuit of perfection.*

single-minded pursuit (=having a clear aim and working hard to achieve it) *Her career was driven by a single-minded pursuit of success.*

PREPOSITIONS

in (the) pursuit of sth *People are having to move to other areas in pursuit of work.*

3 something such as a hobby that you spend time doing

> **Grammar**
> **Pursuit** is countable in this meaning.

ADJECTIVES

sb's favourite pursuit *BrE*, **sb's favorite pursuit** *AmE*: *Her favourite pursuit was riding her horse.*

a leisure pursuit *Walking is a popular leisure pursuit in Madeira.*

outdoor pursuits *The town offers a unique setting for many outdoor pursuits including walking, cycling, and horse-riding.*

an academic/intellectual pursuit *He was persuaded by his father to change his academic pursuits to law.*

cultural pursuits *She enjoys a number of cultural pursuits such as visiting art galleries.*

a solitary pursuit (=which you do on your own) *Running is generally a solitary pursuit.*

VERBS

follow a pursuit (=do it) *He has continued to follow his musical pursuits.*

push *v*

to make someone or something move by pressing them with your hands, arms etc

PREPOSITIONS/ADVERBS

push sb/sth hard *The door didn't move, so she pushed harder.*

push sb/sth away *She pushed him away.*

push sb/sth back *Maria pushed her hair back from her forehead.*

push sb/sth towards sb/sth *Philip pushed him towards the door.*

push sth open *I slowly pushed the window open.*

put *v*

1 to move something to a particular place or position, especially using your hands

PREPOSITIONS/ADVERBS

put sth somewhere carefully *Mary folded the letter and put it carefully in the drawer.*

put sth somewhere gently *She put the baby down gently, so as not to wake him.*

put sth in/into/inside sth *He put the gun in his pocket.*

put sth on sth *Can you put the plates on the table?*

put sth down *She put down her shopping bags.*

put sth out/outside *We put out the rubbish on Fridays.*

put sth back *Watson put the book back on the shelf.*

2 to say something

NOUNS

put a question (to sb) *I will be putting that question to her when I meet her tomorrow.*

put a proposal/proposition to sb (=suggest an idea to someone) *I have a proposition to put to you.*

put a point to sb *You should put that point to the Chancellor.*

put your case (to sb) (=explain your reasons to someone) *He wanted to see the committee to put his case.*

ADVERBS

put sth well *Sorry, I'm not putting it very well.*

put sth carefully/gently/tactfully (=trying not to offend or upset someone) *He hesitated, uncertain how to put the question tactfully.*

put sth bluntly/crudely/plainly (=in a direct way that may offend) *She's fat, as John bluntly put it.*

PHRASES

to put it another way *The dress was too small*

for me, or, to put it another way, I was too big for it.

to put it mildly (=used for saying that you could have expressed something in a more extreme way) *His theory is controversial, to put it mildly.*

put sth into words (=say what you are feeling or thinking) *She couldn't put her feelings into words.*

to put it simply/put simply *Put simply, our aim is to create art.*

put it to sb that *I put it to him that what we needed was some independent advice.*

3 to write something

THESAURUS: put

put, enter, type in/key in, take, sign, fill out/in, transcribe, jot down, scribble, scrawl, dash off → write (1)

puzzle *n*

1 a game in which you have to solve a problem, answer a set of questions, or fit pieces of a picture together

NOUNS + puzzle

a jigsaw puzzle (=one where you fit pieces of a picture together) *Some jigsaw puzzles have thousands of pieces.*

a word puzzle *We did a type of word puzzle where the first letters of the answers form another word.*

a crossword puzzle (=one where you answer questions to fit words in numbered squares) *Dad was doing the crossword puzzle on the back page of his newspaper.*

VERBS

do a puzzle *I like doing crossword puzzles.*

solve a puzzle *When you think you've solved the puzzle, you can check your answers at the back of the book.*

puzzle + NOUNS

a puzzle book *She took a puzzle book on the train to pass the time.*

2 something that is difficult to understand or explain

ADJECTIVES

a real puzzle *It's a real puzzle how these animals manage to survive the winter.*

a great puzzle *His comments were a great puzzle to me.*

VERBS

solve a puzzle *I think I've solved the puzzle of what happened to the money.*

piece together a puzzle (=solve it by putting together different pieces of information) *Detectives desperately tried to piece together the puzzle of his disappearance.*

pose/present a puzzle (=be a puzzle for someone) *How the disease is passed on poses a puzzle for scientists.*

remain a puzzle *The true identity of this mystery woman remains a puzzle.*

PREPOSITIONS

sth is a puzzle to sb *I don't know how he got the job – it's always been a puzzle to me.*

PHRASES

a piece of the puzzle (=a piece of information that will help solve a puzzle) *Police want to find this car, which they think is an important piece of the puzzle.*

the solution to a puzzle *A Cambridge scientist was the first to see the solution to this puzzle.*

the key to the puzzle (=the thing that will help you find the solution) *Professor Jones thinks that he may have found the key to the puzzle.*

puzzling *adj*

THESAURUS **confusing, mysterious**

Qq

qualification *n*

something that shows you have successfully finished a course of study

ADJECTIVES/NOUNS + qualification

educational qualifications *Too many children leave school without any educational qualifications.*

academic qualifications *Eva had excellent academic qualifications and had studied at Oxford University.*

a teaching/medical/legal etc qualification *BrE: All teachers must have a teaching qualification.*

a professional qualification *BrE* (=one relating to a professional job, such as a teacher, lawyer etc) *A professional qualification in accountancy would be an advantage.*

good/excellent qualifications *Good qualifications are very important.*

formal/paper qualifications (=official qualifications rather than experience) *He had no formal qualifications for the job.*

the necessary qualifications *She didn't have the necessary qualifications to become a nurse.*

the minimum qualification *The minimum qualification for the course is a diploma in graphic design.*

a vocational qualification *BrE* (=one relating to a skilled job, such as a nurse or a builder) *The college offers vocational qualifications in the tourism industry.*

VERBS

have a qualification (*also* **hold a qualification** *formal*): *You must have a teaching qualification to work at this school.*

get a qualification *She wants to go to college to get some qualifications.*

need a qualification *You don't need any qualifications for this job.*

recognize a qualification (=accept it) *Some British qualifications are not recognized in other EU countries.*

PREPOSITIONS

a qualification in sth *Do you have a qualification in maths or science?*

with no qualifications/without any qualifications *She left school without any qualifications.*

qualified *adj*

someone who is qualified to do something has passed a professional examination

ADVERBS

highly qualified *The pilots who fly these planes are highly qualified.*

fully qualified *He was a fully qualified engineer.*

suitably/properly qualified *Make sure that the therapist is properly qualified.*

professionally qualified *All our staff are professionally qualified.*

newly qualified *A newly qualified nurse gets paid about £20,000 a year.*

NOUNS

a qualified doctor/teacher/accountant etc *After seven years of training, she is now a qualified doctor.*

qualified staff *Qualified staff earn more than non-qualified staff.*

a qualified instructor *There are qualified instructors who can advise you about the right exercise programme for you.*

PREPOSITIONS

qualified as sth *Matthew is already qualified as a vet.*

quality *n*

1 how good or bad something is

ADJECTIVES

good/high quality *The quality of their products is very good.*

poor/low quality *Low quality paper can get stuck in the printer.*

excellent/outstanding quality *The T-shirts are only $10 and the quality is excellent.*

superior quality *formal* (=good or better quality) *These speakers offer superior quality sound.*

top quality *Our chef uses only top quality ingredients.*

NOUNS + quality

water/air quality *Scientists took samples to test the water quality.*

sound quality *I apologise for the poor sound quality of this recording.*

picture/image quality *Does this type of TV set have a better picture quality?*

VERBS

improve the quality (*also* **enhance the quality** *formal*): *Use a filter to improve the quality of your tap water.*

affect the quality *Lack of sleep started to affect the quality of his work.*

test/check/monitor the quality *The equipment is used to monitor the city's air quality.*

maintain the quality *It is important to maintain the quality of your work.*

sacrifice the quality (=make the quality worse in order to make something else better) *We need to reduce costs without sacrificing the quality of the product.*

the quality goes up/down *I think the quality has gone down over the years.*

the quality suffers (=it is badly affected by something) *The picture quality suffers if the signal isn't digital.*

PREPOSITIONS

the quality of sth *The quality of the soil is very poor.*

of high/poor/excellent etc quality *The accommodation is of a high quality.*

PHRASES

sb's quality of life *We moved to the country to improve our quality of life.*

⚠ Don't say 'living quality' or 'life quality'.

quality + NOUNS

quality standards *All products have to meet the European Union's strict quality standards.*

quality control (=the process of checking the quality of goods as they are produced) *In those days, there was no proper quality control.*

2 a part of the character of someone or something

ADJECTIVES

personal qualities *A teacher's personal qualities are very important.*

a good/positive quality *For most people, confidence is a good quality.*

a bad/negative quality *We all have our negative qualities – mine is that I am lazy.*

sb's best/worst quality *Her jealousy is one of her worst qualities.*

an essential quality *The essential quality of a good parent is patience.*

a unique quality *The wine possesses a unique quality.*

a redeeming quality (=that stops something being completely bad) *The hotel had one redeeming quality – it was cheap.*

a timeless quality (=never old-fashioned) *His paintings have a timeless quality to them.*

a magical quality *These descriptions give the story a magical quality, almost like a fairy tale.*

a dream-like quality *I like the dream-like quality of the film.*

NOUNS + quality

leadership qualities *She has great faith in her own leadership qualities.*

star quality (=a special quality that could make someone famous) *We're looking for a singer with star quality.*

VERBS

have a quality (*also* **possess a quality** *formal*): *Her voice has a unique quality.*

show a quality *He showed leadership qualities from a young age.*

give sth a quality *The snow gave the forest a magical quality.*

quantity *n* an amount of something

ADJECTIVES

a large quantity *A large quantity of clothing was stolen from the shop.*

a great quantity *The mine produced great quantities of lead and silver.*

a vast/huge/enormous quantity *Computers can handle vast quantities of data.*

a considerable/substantial quantity (=fairly large) *We will need considerable quantities of cement.*

a sufficient quantity (=enough) *How did they obtain sufficient quantities of food to survive?*

a small/tiny quantity *You only need a small quantity of butter.*

a minute quantity (=extremely small) *The rock contains minute quantities of copper.*

an unlimited/limited quantity *Beer was available in unlimited quantities at every meal.*

an equal quantity *He poured equal quantities of sugar and flour into a cup.*

PREPOSITIONS

quantity of sth *The police also found a large quantity of drugs in the apartment.*

in large/small etc quantities *Buy vegetables in small quantities so you can eat them when they are fresh.*

THESAURUS: quantity

quantity, volume, level, proportion, quota, yield → amount

quarrel *n especially BrE* an argument

ADJECTIVES

a bitter quarrel (=involving strong feelings of anger or hatred) *The two men had a bitter quarrel, which nearly ended in violence.*

a violent quarrel *That morning, after a violent quarrel, she threatened him with a kitchen knife.*

a serious quarrel *Soon afterwards, they had their first serious quarrel.*

NOUNS + quarrel

a family quarrel *Your family quarrels are none of my concern.*

a lovers' quarrel *Outside, two teenagers were having a lovers' quarrel.*

VERBS

have a quarrel *We had a terrible quarrel last night.*

start a quarrel *Olsen started the quarrel by complaining that he wasn't getting paid enough.*

pick a quarrel with sb (=deliberately start a quarrel with someone) *She made the mistake of picking a quarrel with Sue.*

patch up a quarrel *BrE* (=end it) *The brothers eventually patched up their quarrel.*

Q

a quarrel breaks out (=starts to happen) *A fresh quarrel broke out between the players.*

PREPOSITIONS

a quarrel with sb *Jacob left after a quarrel with his wife.*

a quarrel between sb and sb *I overheard a quarrel between Emma and her mother.*

a quarrel about/over sth *They had a quarrel about some girl.*

queen *n*

the female ruler of a country, or the wife of a king

VERBS

become queen *Mary Tudor became queen in 1553.*

make sb queen *The king wanted to marry her and make her his queen.*

crown sb queen (=officially make someone queen) *The next day she was crowned Queen of England.*

proclaim sb queen (=say that she is now officially the queen) *When her father died, she was proclaimed queen.*

a queen rules/reigns (=is in charge of a country) *Queen Victoria reigned for over 60 years.*

a queen abdicates (=gives up the position of being queen) *The Queen is unlikely to abdicate.*

ADJECTIVES

the rightful queen (=the woman who should be the ruler) *She still regarded herself as the rightful queen of Scotland.*

the future queen *We visited the palace where the future queen spent her childhood.*

PREPOSITIONS

under Queen Elizabeth/Victoria etc (=while she is queen) *The British Empire flourished under Queen Victoria.*

PHRASES

the reign of Queen Elizabeth/Victoria etc (=when she is queen) *She was born in the reign of Queen Victoria.*

Her Majesty the Queen (=used when talking about a queen) *Her Majesty the Queen will be visiting Australia in July.*

a queen's subjects (=the people she rules over) *Many of the queen's subjects did not approve of her choice of husband.*

swear allegiance to a queen (=promise to be loyal to her) *Members of the armed forces have to swear allegiance to the Queen.*

query *n*

a question that you ask to get information, or to check that something is true or correct

ADJECTIVES

a small/little/minor query *I just have one small query: how do I save the file?*

a particular/specific query *If you have a specific query about any of our products, please call this number.*

NOUNS + query

a customer query *My job is to answer the phone and deal with customer queries.*

VERBS

have a query *You're welcome to call me if you have any queries.*

answer a query *Staff are always available to answer your queries.*

reply to a query (*also* **respond to a query** *formal*): *The company was slow to respond to our query.*

deal with/handle a query *Someone will deal with your query as soon as possible.*

PREPOSITIONS

a query about/on sth *I have a couple of queries about the course.*

a query regarding sth *formal* (=about something) *I have received your query regarding your tax payment.*

question[1] *n*

1 a sentence that asks for information

ADJECTIVES

a difficult/hard/tough/tricky question *Some of the questions in the last section were very difficult.*

an easy/simple question *These questions should be easy for you.*

a good question (= used especially about a question that is difficult to answer) *"How much will it all cost?" "That's a good question."*

a serious question *Don't laugh – it's a serious question.*

a stupid/silly question (=one whose answer is obvious) *Are you happy you won, or is that a stupid question?*

a personal question (=about someone's private life) *Can I ask you a personal question?*

an embarrassing/awkward question *Children sometimes ask awkward questions.*

a direct question (=one that asks for information in a very direct way) *She was surprised by such a direct question.*

a relevant/irrelevant question (=which is connected or not connected with what you are talking about) *She kept asking irrelevant questions.*

a searching/probing question (=one designed to find things out) *The policeman asked me some searching questions.*

an impertinent question (=one which you have no right to ask) *How dare she ask such an impertinent question!*

a rhetorical question (=a question you ask without expecting an answer) *When I said "Will anyone notice?" it was a rhetorical question.*

the burning question (=the one that people very much want to know the answer to) *The burning question is this - will the baby be another boy?*

VERBS

ask (sb) a question (*also* **pose a question** *formal*): *Don't be afraid to ask questions.*

put a question to sb (=ask a question in a formal situation) *I recently put some of these questions to a psychologist.*

answer a question *You haven't answered my question.*

have a question (=want to ask a question) *Does anyone have any questions?*

avoid/evade/dodge a question (=not give a direct answer) *He had skilfully evaded Margie's questions.*

set a question (=invent a question for a test) *He used to set the questions for a TV quiz show.*

do a question (=answer a question in a test) *I couldn't do all the questions.*

rephrase a question (=ask it in a different way) *He didn't answer, so I rephrased my question.*

bombard sb with questions (=ask someone a lot of questions) *The reporters bombarded him with questions about the case.*

field questions (=answer a lot of questions, usually at a public meeting) *He fielded questions from reporters about the announcement.*

NOUNS + question

a test/exam/essay question *You have to answer 20 exam questions.*

a multiple choice question (=which asks you to choose between a set of possible answers in a test) *Students are given a series of multiple choice questions.*

PREPOSITIONS

a question about sth *They asked me questions about my previous experience of this type of work.*

a question on sth *The test includes questions on a range of different subjects.*

PHRASES

an answer to a question *Can anyone give me an answer to my question?*

in answer to sb's question *In answer to your last question, "Yes".*

2 an issue

ADJECTIVES

an important question *The role of the army is an important question.*

a big question (=important) *What are the big questions facing the country today?*

a basic/fundamental question *Their experiences have highlighted fundamental questions of human rights.*

serious questions *The incident has raised serious questions about police conduct.*

a vexed/thorny question (=difficult to deal with) *Finally, there's the thorny question of money.*

a moral/ethical question (=relating to principles of what is right and wrong) *This area of medical research poses serious ethical questions.*

VERBS

bring up/raise/pose a question (=bring it to people's attention) *This study raises several important questions.*

consider a question *We must also consider the question of what the price should be.*

discuss a question *They discussed the question of who should replace her.*

deal with a question *This question will be dealt with in Chapter 4.*

tackle a question (=try to deal with a difficult question) *Who has the ability to tackle the tough questions facing the nation?*

address a question (=start trying to deal with it) *Two questions need to be addressed.*

resolve/settle a question (=deal with it in a satisfactory way) *We will proceed just as soon as we can resolve the question of the fee.*

a question arises (=it starts to exist) *A number of questions arise from this unhappy situation.*

PREPOSITIONS

the question of sth *We discussed the question of confidentiality.*

3 doubt about something

PHRASES

sth is open to question (=it is not certain or definitely true) *The exact cause of death is still open to question.*

call/bring/throw sth into question (=make people doubt it) *The scandal brought into question all the principles on which the financial system was based.*

come into question (=start to be doubted) *Freedom of the press has come into question in recent years.*

there's no question (=it is certain) *There's no question that they have done an excellent job.*

PREPOSITIONS

question(s) about/over sth (*also* **question(s) as to sth** *formal*): *There are questions about the player's fitness.*

sth is in question (=used when saying that people have doubts about something) *His honesty is now in question.*

sth is beyond question (=used when saying that you have no doubts at all about something) *Her loyalty is beyond question.*

without question (=used when saying that you are completely sure about something) *The price is, without question, too high.*

question² *v*

1 to ask someone questions in order to get information about something, especially when you think they have done something wrong

ADVERBS

question sb closely (=in a very detailed way) *They questioned him closely about his train journeys through Turkey and Iran.*

PREPOSITIONS

question sb about sth *She hates being questioned about her past.*

PHRASES

question sb at length (=for a long time, asking a lot of questions) *The interviewers questioned me at length about why I left my last job.*

2 to say that you doubt that something is right or true

ADVERBS

openly/publicly question sth *Many scientists have publicly questioned the theory.*

seriously question sth *Sometimes, I seriously question your intelligence.*

rightly question sth *They rightly questioned the need to do the survey every year.*

rarely question sth *People rarely question their doctor's ability.*

VERBS

begin to question sth *For the first time, he began to question whether there was a God.*

questionnaire *n*

a written set of questions which you give to a large number of people in order to collect information

VERBS

fill in/fill out/complete a questionnaire (=answer all the questions in it) *The students were asked to complete a questionnaire.*

answer/respond to a questionnaire *The majority of the staff have responded to the questionnaire.*

give sb a questionnaire *They were given a questionnaire on their shopping habits.*

send (out) a questionnaire *The society sent a questionnaire to all its members.*

return/send back a questionnaire *Return the completed questionnaire to this address.*

a questionnaire asks sth *Participants fill in a questionnaire that asks them to rate their own abilities.*

ADJECTIVES

a short/simple questionnaire *We'd like everyone to complete a short questionnaire at the end of the meeting.*

a detailed/lengthy questionnaire *The women were given a detailed questionnaire about their health.*

a ten-page/20-page etc questionnaire *Before I could join the gym, I had to fill out a ten-page questionnaire.*

PREPOSITIONS

a questionnaire about/on sth *Employees were given a questionnaire on their feelings about the changes.*

queue *n BrE*

a line of people waiting to do something, or a line of vehicles waiting to move

VERBS + queue

stand/wait in a queue *She stood in the queue at the checkout.*

form a queue *Other passengers for the train were forming a queue.*

join a queue *He went back inside to join the queue for the toilets.*

jump the queue (=go to the front rather than joining the end of a queue) *An argument developed when she tried to jump the queue.*

queue + VERBS

a queue forms *A queue had formed outside the shop.*

a queue builds up (=becomes bigger) *In the summer, huge queues build up on the roads.*

a queue stretches somewhere *The queue stretched all the way to the end of the street.*

ADJECTIVES

a long/big/huge queue *Already a long queue had formed outside the concert hall.*

an endless queue (=very long) *People waited in endless queues for food.*

NOUNS + queue

a bus queue *Why stand in a bus queue or sit in a traffic jam when you can walk?*

PREPOSITIONS

a queue of sb *I saw a queue of people waiting for the bus.*

a queue for sth *There are very long queues for rides at the park.*

in a queue *We had already been in the queue for 15 minutes.*

PHRASES

a queue of people/cars/traffic etc *The queue of traffic on the motorway stretched for miles.*

the front/head of the queue *He pushed his way to the front of the queue.*

the back of the queue *I told him to get to the back of the queue.*

be first in the queue *I wanted to be first in the queue when the doors opened.*

take your place in a queue (=join it) *I walked to the bus stop and took my place in the queue.*

form an orderly queue (= stand quietly in a neat line) *She told the children to form an orderly queue.*

Queue is used in British English. In American English, people say **line**.

quick *adj*

1 taking only a short time to do something

NOUNS

a quick look/glance/check *He took a quick look at my passport and waved me on.*

a quick wash/shower/bath *Do I have time for a quick shower before we go out?*

a quick meal/drink/lunch *They stopped off for a quick drink.*

a quick visit/journey/trip *This is just a quick visit – we won't be staying long.*

a quick kiss/hug *He gave her a quick kiss outside the station.*

a quick response/reaction/answer *Aid workers were praised for their quick response to the disaster.*

a quick decision *It was getting late and I had to make a quick decision.*

a quick way/method *What's the quickest way to the airport?*

quick action *Their quick action saved his life.*

a quick profit *Firms only want to make a quick profit.*

a quick recovery *Her son made a quick recovery from his illness.*

ADVERBS

remarkably/surprisingly/amazingly/incredibly quick *Their delivery service is amazingly quick.*

PHRASES

That was quick! (=used when someone has done something surprisingly quickly) *That was quick! I thought you'd be another hour.*

in quick succession (=quickly, one after the other) *Three bombs went off in quick succession.*

have a quick word with sb (=talk to someone for a short time about something) *Can I have a quick word with you about tomorrow?*

make a quick exit (=leave quickly) *The police arrived and we had to make a quick exit.*

THESAURUS: quick

fast
way | rate | response | learner
taking only a short time to do something:
The fastest way to learn a foreign language is to live in the country where it is spoken. | We are using up the world's resources at an incredibly fast rate. | Fast response times are needed in an emergency. | Richard is a fast learner and was playing the game in no time.

Fast or quick?
When talking about doing something in a short time, you usually use **quick**. You usually use **fast** when talking about speed of movement. With **way**, **rate**, or **response** you can use **fast** or **quick**.

rapid
growth | expansion | spread | increase | rise | change | development | progress | rate | decrease | improvement | decline
used when something is changing quickly:
The Chinese economy is experiencing rapid growth. | There has been a rapid increase in crime. | The population is growing at a rapid rate.

speedy
recovery | end | conclusion | resolution | settlement | return | response | progress | action
happening quickly, especially so that you get the result that you want:
She sent him a letter wishing him a speedy recovery from his illness. | The war was brought to a speedy conclusion. | They want a speedy return to democracy. | The bill has made speedy progress through Parliament.

prompt
action | payment | response | reply | answer | delivery
done without any delay:
The building was saved because of the prompt action by the firefighters. | There is a discount for prompt payment. | Thank you for your prompt reply.

Prompt is usually used before a noun.

hasty
decision | departure | retreat | conclusion | reaction | exit | meal | words
deciding or doing something very quickly, especially when this has bad results:
*It was a hasty decision, which he later regretted. | The guests **beat a hasty retreat** back into the house when it started to rain* (=they went back there quickly). *| You shouldn't **jump to hasty conclusions*** (=decide too quickly that something is true, when you do not know all the facts). *| Perhaps I was too **hasty in** rejecting the idea.*

cursory *formal*
glance | look | search | inspection | attention | reading | manner | treatment | discussion
looking at or considering something very quickly, without much attention to detail:
Even a cursory glance at these figures shows that there is a problem. | The officer made a cursory inspection of the truck. | There is only a cursory discussion of the role of women.

Cursory is usually used before a noun.

THESAURUS: quick

brief, quick, temporary, short-lived, short-term, fleeting, momentary, passing, ephemeral → **short (1)**

2 moving quickly

THESAURUS: quick

quick, high-speed → **fast¹ (2)**

quiet *adj*

1 making very little noise. Also used to describe a place where there is very little noise

NOUNS

a quiet car/plane/engine *Battery-powered cars are much quieter than ordinary cars.*

a quiet voice *"It's time to go," she said in a quiet voice.*

a quiet room/place/area/spot *They found a quiet room where they could talk without being disturbed.*

VERBS

become/go quiet *The room suddenly went quiet.*

be/keep quiet *Ssh! Be quiet! You'll wake the baby.*

keep sb quiet *I let the kids play on their computer to keep them quiet.*

ADVERBS

so quiet *It's so quiet now she's gone.*

deathly quiet (=extremely quiet) *Inside the house it was deathly quiet, except for the buzzing of a fly.*

eerily quiet (=very quiet, in a strange and frightening way) *The forest was eerily quiet at night.*

PHRASES

nice and quiet *It's nice and quiet in here.*

somewhere quiet *I need somewhere quiet to work.*

THESAURUS: quiet

low
voice | volume
not very loud, especially because you do not want other people to hear:
Doug was on the phone, speaking in a low voice. | I turned the radio down to low volume.

soft
voice | music
quiet and pleasant to listen to:
Her voice was soft and gentle. | Soft music was playing in the background.

silent
completely quiet and not making any sound at all, or not saying anything at all:
*The man **remained silent** and refused to answer any questions. | The room suddenly **went silent*** (=became silent). | *For a moment, the two men **fell silent*** (=became silent - a formal use).

Silent is much less common before a noun. You use it in certain fixed phrases: *a **silent film/movie*** (=an old film without any sound) | *a **silent prayer*** (=when you pray without saying the words aloud)

hushed
voice | tones | silence | whisper | conversation
very quiet, especially because you do not want other people to hear:
I could hear hushed voices in the next room. | The doctors were talking in hushed tones. | A hushed silence fell on the room (=people suddenly became silent).

faint
sound | voice | cry | whisper | echo
a faint sound is quiet and difficult to hear, especially because it comes from a long way away:
Jean heard the faint sound of the bells in the distance. | She began to cry out in a faint voice: "Help me!"

muffled
voice | sound | cry | shout | explosion | roar
a muffled sound is difficult to hear clearly, because something such as a wall or cover prevents the sound from reaching you:
Muffled voices were coming from one of the rooms downstairs. | There was a muffled explosion somewhere inside the building.

dull
thud | rumble | roar | crack | sound
a dull sound is not loud or clear:
His body hit the ground with a dull thud. | There was a dull crack as the chair began to break.

inaudible *formal*
sound | voice | whisper | sigh
too quiet to hear:
*Dogs are able to hear sounds that are **inaudible to the human ear*** (=that humans cannot hear). | *Joseph kept walking until his father's voice became inaudible.*

You can also say that a sound is **barely audible** (=you can only just hear it): *His voice was **barely audible** above the noise of the traffic.*

ANTONYMS **quiet → loud**

2 a quiet person does not say very much, especially because they are shy

NOUNS

a quiet man/woman/boy/girl/child *He is a quiet boy who loves reading.*

quiet authority (=used when someone does not say very much, but you respect them because they seem to know a lot) *When he spoke, he had an air of quiet authority.*

PHRASES

sb is as quiet as a (church) mouse (=he or she is a shy quiet person who does not disturb anyone) *Her neighbour was as quiet as a mouse and Ruth hardly knew she was there.*

THESAURUS: quiet

reserved *formal*
not wanting to talk about your feelings or show them:
Flora was a ***reserved woman****, who was astonished when reviewers praised her work. | The English have a reputation for being* ***rather reserved****.*

reticent *formal*
not wanting to tell people about something:
She's always been ***reticent about*** *her past.*

> **Reticent** is not used before a noun.

taciturn *formal*
not saying very much, especially in a way that seems rather unfriendly or bad-tempered:
Her father was a ***taciturn man*** *who spent most of his time locked in his study. | She found Vaughn a taciturn and rather difficult person.*

silent
not saying very much:
She usually goes for ***the strong silent type*** (=she likes strong men who do not say very much).

> You can also say that someone is **a man/woman of few words**: *Like many great scientists, he was* ***a man of few words*** (=he did not say very much, and only spoke when there was something important to say).

3 a quiet place or time is one in which there is little activity

NOUNS

a quiet town/village *She left her small quiet town in Mexico on her 16th birthday.*

a quiet place/area/street *The streets are quiet after ten o'clock.*

a quiet restaurant/bar *Later they found a quiet restaurant on the edge of town.*

a quiet time *January is normally a quiet time of year and many of the stores are closed.*

a quiet life (=one in which not much exciting happens, or people do not keep bothering you) *All I want is a nice quiet life.*

VERBS

go quiet *Business has gone quiet because of the recession* (=there is less business activity and fewer things are being sold).

PHRASES

things are quiet *Things were quiet in the pub on weekdays.*

THESAURUS: quiet

sleepy
town | village | suburb | place | backwater
used about a place where very little happens:
Formby grew from a sleepy little village of 7,000 people into a large town. | After the oil industry disappeared, the town returned to being a sleepy backwater (=a place where nothing exciting happens, especially one that is far from the busiest parts of a country or area).

peaceful
place | village | town | scene | surroundings | setting | atmosphere | life | existence
quiet in a pleasant and relaxing way:
The monastery was a peaceful place. | The hotel is set in peaceful surroundings in the middle of the countryside. | He was hoping for a peaceful life when he retired six years ago.

tranquil *literary*
village | town | place | scene | surroundings | setting | atmosphere | beauty | life | existence
quiet in a pleasant and relaxing way:
The tranquil village of Catton lies just 20 minutes from York. | You can go for long walks in the tranquil surroundings of the lake. | Their tranquil existence is threatened by plans to build a new railway line.

> **Tranquil or peaceful?**
> **Tranquil** means the same as **peaceful** and is used with the same collocations. It is mainly used in literature.

calm
weather | day | sea | city | atmosphere
if the weather is calm, there is no strong wind. If the sea is calm, there are no waves. If a place is calm, there is no violence, fighting, or strong emotions:
It was a cold calm day with no wind. | The next morning the weather was fine and the sea was calm. | The city is calm now after the riots.

dead *informal*
used about a place that is boring because nothing exciting happens:
This place is dead at weekends and there is nothing for young people to do.

> **Dead** is not used before a noun in this meaning.

quiz *n*
a competition or game in which people have to answer questions

VERBS

take part in a quiz *Four teams took part in the quiz.*

enter a quiz *Would you like to enter our literary quiz?*

win a quiz *The person who wins the quiz will receive £50.*

have/hold a quiz *The club will be holding its annual quiz next month.*

NOUNS + quiz

a general knowledge quiz *You need a wide range of knowledge to win a general knowledge quiz.*

a music/gardening/sports etc quiz *There was a music quiz about songs from the 1980s.*

a trivia quiz (=a quiz with questions about little-known facts) *He's very good at trivia quizzes.*

Q

quiz + NOUNS

a quiz question *I knew the answers to a lot of the quiz questions.*

a quiz show *especially BrE: She presents a TV quiz show.*

a quiz night *BrE: The club organized a quiz night.*

quota *n*
the largest or smallest amount of something that is allowed, or a rule about this

ADJECTIVES/NOUNS + quota

a strict quota *The government is planning to introduce strict quotas on the number of people who can enter the country.*

an annual/monthly/weekly/daily quota *The US immigration laws imposed a strict annual quota for each country of origin.*

the full quota *He had never taken his full quota of holiday.*

import/export quotas *British industry was protected from foreign competition by import quotas.*

a sales quota *The department had failed to meet its sales quota.*

production quotas *Production quotas were imposed on dairy farmers.*

fishing quotas *The fishing quotas are strictly enforced.*

VERBS

impose/introduce a quota (=officially start having one) *In 1993 the European Union imposed quotas on banana imports.*

set a quota (=say how much it is) *They have the right to set fishing quotas.*

meet/make/achieve a quota (=do or get as much as is required) *Some workers had difficulty meeting their quotas.*

enforce a quota (=make sure that it is obeyed) *It is not possible to enforce the quota.*

lift/scrap a quota (=end it) *The minister for trade lifted all quotas on imports and exports.*

fill a quota (=do or get as much as is required) *They had already filled their quota, so they didn't need to recruit any more people.*

exceed a quota *The fishermen were accused of exceeding their quotas.*

THESAURUS: quota

quantity, volume, level, proportion, quota, yield
→ **amount**

quotation Ac *n*
a sentence or phrase taken from a book, speech etc

VERBS

a quotation is taken from sth *The quotation is taken from 'Nineteen Eighty-Four', by George Orwell.*

a quotation comes from sth *The following quotation comes from a letter he wrote in 1918.*

use a quotation *President Obama used a quotation from Abraham Lincoln in his speech.*

ADJECTIVES

a famous quotation *The incident brings to mind a famous quotation from the Bible: "Put not your trust in princes".*

a long/short quotation *He included long quotations from the play in his essay.*

a direct quotation *That is a direct quotation from a speech he made last year.*

PREPOSITIONS

a quotation from sth/sb *At the beginning of the chapter is a quotation from a Chinese philosopher.*

In more informal English, people say **quote**: *This is a* ***quote*** *from his diary.*

quote Ac *v*
to repeat exactly what someone else has said or written

ADVERBS

quote directly *I am quoting directly from their report.*

much/frequently quoted (=often quoted) *His complaints about the way the competition was organized have been much quoted.*

NOUNS

quote a line/verse/phrase *My uncle often used to quote these lines of poetry.*

quote a writer/author *Kerry quoted the French writer André Gide: "Do not try to understand me too quickly."*

quote a passage *He quoted a passage from a speech by President Lincoln.*

quote a remark *Rollins quoted a remark by James Joyce.*

PREPOSITIONS

quote from sb/sth *He quotes from the work of other writers.*

PHRASES

quote sth in full (=quote all the words) *Her reply is worth quoting in full.*

quote at length from sb/sth (=quote a lot from something) *He quotes at length from Stephen Bloom's account of his childhood.*

quote sb as saying sth *A military spokesman was quoted as saying that the border area is now safe.*

don't quote me on that *spoken: I think he's going to lose, but don't quote me on that.*

race *n*

1 a competition in which people or animals try to get to the end of a course fastest

VERBS

win/lose a race *He did not win another race that season.*

come first/last etc in a race (*also* **finish first/last etc in a race**) *She came third in the 200-metre race.*

compete in a race *Bolt should be fit enough to compete in the race.*

take part in a race *Runners from all over the world will take part in the race.*

enter a race *He entered the London to Manchester Air Race.*

enter sth in/for a race *The horse is entered in a race at Worcester the day after tomorrow.*

have a race *We decided to have a race and I won.*

hold a race *The next race will be held on 25th February.*

lead the race (=be ahead of everyone else) *She led the race from start to finish.*

finish the race *Paul hopes to finish the race in under three hours.*

run a race *I thought I ran a good race.*

dominate a race (=be leading at most times in a race, or usually win this race) *African runners have dominated this race for a decade.*

withdraw from a race *Three other yachts were also forced to withdraw from the race.*

ADJECTIVES

a tough/hard race *He knows it will be a tough race.*

the big race (=an important race) *There are only three days to go until the big race.*

NOUNS + race

a horse/boat/bike etc race *It is legal to gamble on horse races.*

a road race (=when people run, cycle etc on ordinary roads) *She regularly competes in 10-kilometre road races.*

a 2-lap/50-lap etc race (=two times, 50 times etc round a course) *The drivers had completed lap four of a 25-lap race when the collision occurred.*

2 one of the main groups that humans can be divided into according to the colour of their skin and other physical features

PHRASES

people of all races/people of different races *People of all races attended the church.*

race + NOUNS

race relations (=the relationships between people of different races who live in the same country) *Race relations in the city are generally very good.*

race riots (=fighting between people of different races who live in the same country) *The killing of a black protester led to race riots.*

VERBS

belong to a race *We all belong to the same race - the human race.*

ADJECTIVES

mixed race (=having parents from different races) *One in five pre-school children is of mixed race.*

racial *adj*

relating to the relationships between different races of people who live in the same country

NOUNS

racial equality (=when people of all races have the same rights and treatment) *We are firmly committed to achieving racial equality.*

racial harmony (=when people of different races live or work together without problems) *Dr King's dream of racial harmony has never been fully realized.*

racial discrimination (=unfair treatment because of someone's race) *They found no evidence of racial discrimination.*

racial prejudice/hatred *He claimed that his opponents were motivated by racial prejudice.*

racial harassment (=threatening behaviour towards someone because of their race) *The court case increased public awareness of racial harassment at work.*

racial abuse (=insulting remarks based on someone's race) *Their children faced racial abuse on the streets and in school.*

racial tension (=bad feelings between people of different races, which could develop into violence) *His arrest is likely to heighten racial tensions.*

racial violence *Combating racial violence is a priority for the police.*

a racial attack *He was the victim of a racial attack.*

racial segregation (=when people of different races are forced to live, work etc separately) *The 1964 Civil Rights Act prohibited racial segregation in public buildings.*

racism *n*

unfair treatment of people, or violence against them, because they belong to a different race from your own

PHRASES

accusations/allegations/charges of racism *His comments have led to accusations of racism.*

a victim of racism *The defeated candidate said he was a victim of racism.*

the problem/issue of racism *We must address the problem of racism.*

a form/kind of racism *Blatant discrimination has been replaced by subtler forms of racism.*

the fight/struggle against racism *We have not won the struggle against racism.*

VERBS

accuse sb of racism *He was accused of racism by one of his employees.*

experience/encounter racism *I didn't experience any racism at school.*

combat/fight/tackle racism *We are committed to combating racism.*

stamp out/eradicate racism (=completely end it) *He wants to stamp out racism in his party.*

racism exists *The university admits that racism exists on campus.*

ADJECTIVES

overt/blatant racism (=very obvious racism) *It was my first encounter with blatant racism.*

institutional racism (=racism that has become normal in a group) *The report claimed there was institutional racism in the police force.*

PREPOSITIONS

racism against sb *They are guilty of racism against Asians.*

racism among sb *There were allegations of racism among the jurors.*

THESAURUS: racism

discrimination, bigotry, intolerance, racism/racial prejudice, sexism, ageism, homophobia, xenophobia, anti-Semitism, Islamophobia → prejudice

radical Ac *adj*

very different from what happened before or to what is usual

NOUNS

a radical change *The move to the country would mean a radical change in lifestyle.*

a radical transformation (=a complete change in appearance) *The city has undergone a radical transformation.*

a radical departure from sth (=something very different) *The design of the building is a radical departure from tradition.*

radical reform *He said the institution was in need of radical reform.*

a radical overhaul (=big changes in order to improve something) *The government is planning a radical overhaul of the health care system.*

radical measures (=extreme actions) *Instead of retreating, he suggested even more radical measures.*

a radical idea/view *His ideas on education were too radical for most people to accept.*

a radical solution *One scientist proposed a radical solution to the problem.*

a radical approach *A more radical approach is needed.*

a radical rethink (=when you think about a plan or idea again in a very different way) *The Conservative Party leader called for a radical rethink of economic policy.*

radio *n*

a piece of equipment which you use to listen to programmes that are broadcast, or the programmes themselves

ADJECTIVES/NOUNS + radio

national/local radio *I heard the game on the local radio.*

state radio (=controlled by the government of a country) *In a message read on state radio and television, the president called for calm.*

commercial radio *He has worked for the BBC and in commercial radio.*

internet radio *There are dozens of internet radio stations.*

VERBS

listen to the radio *She was sitting up in bed, listening to the radio.*

hear sth on the radio *I heard on the radio that the weather was going to get warmer.*

turn/switch the radio on *Dad switched on the radio for the eight-thirty news.*

turn/switch the radio off *She turned the radio off and went to bed.*

turn the radio down/up (=make it quieter or louder) *I asked them to turn the radio down.*

tune a radio to a station (=make it receive broadcasts from a particular station) *The radio was tuned to a country music station.*

radio + NOUNS

a radio programme/show *It's my favourite radio programme.*

a radio broadcast *All radio broadcasts continue to be closely monitored by the government.*

a radio interview *He said in a radio interview that he was looking forward to the match.*

a radio station (=an organization that broadcasts radio programmes) *There are currently nearly 50 commercial radio stations.*

a radio announcer (=someone who reads news or information on the radio) *The radio announcer said the next program would be the six o'clock news.*

PREPOSITIONS

on the radio *It wasn't easy to get their record played on the radio.*

rage *n*
a very strong feeling of anger

PHRASES

sb is filled with rage *Afterwards, he was filled with rage and he felt like leaving his job.*
be speechless with rage (=be so angry that you cannot speak) *Speechless with rage, she threw the letter in the fire.*
be beside yourself with rage (=be so angry that you cannot control yourself) *They had been publicly humiliated and were beside themselves with rage.*
be white with rage *He went white with rage when he realised what they had done.*
sb's face is dark/red/purple with rage *His face was dark with rage and his eyes blazed furiously.*
in a fit of rage (=because you suddenly feel very angry) *In a fit of rage, he seized the poor man by the shoulders and shouted at him.*
sb's face is twisted/contorted with rage *Mike's usually calm face was contorted with rage.*

ADJECTIVES

a jealous rage *He killed his wife in a jealous rage.*
a drunken rage *He smashed up his guitar in a drunken rage.*
a terrible/towering rage (=extreme anger) *She called her lawyer in a towering rage.*
blind/uncontrollable rage (=extreme uncontrolled anger that makes someone violent) *His fear turned to blind rage.*

VERBS

feel rage *I had never felt such rage before.*
seethe with rage (=feel extremely angry) *The injustice of it made Melissa seethe with rage.*
shake/tremble with rage *When he put down the phone, he was shaking with rage.*
cry with rage *I was crying with rage and frustration.*
fly into a rage/explode with rage (=suddenly become very angry) *She knew her father would explode with rage if he found out.*

PREPOSITIONS

in a rage *Moran was always in a rage about something.*
rage at sb/sth *They were filled with rage at the prejudice they had experienced.*

raid *n*
a short military attack on a place, in order to cause damage

NOUNS + raid

an air raid (=when bombs are dropped from planes) *His parents were killed in an air raid.*
a bombing raid *Bombing raids had destroyed most of the country's oil refineries.*
a commando raid (=by specially trained soldiers) *They were planning a commando raid to rescue the hostages.*
a guerrilla raid (=a raid by a small unofficial military group) *From their base in the rainforest they staged guerrilla raids on Nicaragua.*

ADJECTIVES

a heavy raid (=when lot of bombs are dropped on a place) *There were heavy raids on London that night.*
a daring raid *The rebels carried out several daring raids on government buildings.*

VERBS

carry out/make a raid (*also* **conduct/stage/mount a raid** *formal*): *The pirates carried out raids on English ships.*
launch a raid (=start a raid) *Rebel forces launched raids from across the border.*
take part in a raid *They took part in various raids, including the bombing of Cologne in 1942.*
lead a raid *He was awarded a medal for leading a successful raid.*

PREPOSITIONS

a raid on/against sth *During the raid on Pearl Harbor the Japanese lost 29 aeroplanes.*
a raid into an area *There were frequent Turkish raids into Croatia.*

railroad *n AmE*
a system of tracks along which trains run, or a system of trains

railroad + NOUNS

a railroad station *I offered to drive him to the nearest railroad station.*
a railroad track *The city plans to build 120 miles of railroad track.*
the railroad system *The railroad system is suffering from a lack of investment.*
a railroad company *The land near the station was owned by the railroad company.*
railroad workers *The railroad workers went on strike.*
a railroad car (=one of the parts of a train) *We all got into the railroad car.*
a railroad accident *His father was badly injured in a railroad accident.*
a railroad crossing (=a place where vehicles and people can cross the railroad track) *The truck failed to stop at a railroad crossing.*

VERBS

build a railroad *The railroad was built over 100 years ago.*
run a railroad *In France, the government runs the railroad.*

PREPOSITIONS

on the railroad *He worked on the railroad for 30 years.*

railway *n BrE*
a system of tracks along which trains run, or a system of trains

railway + NOUNS

a railway station *I'll meet you at the railway station.*

a railway line/track *The first railway line between Yokohama and Tokyo opened in 1872.*

a railway journey *The children enjoyed the railway journey to the seaside.*

the railway system/network *The railway system expanded rapidly.*

a railway company *The railway company has a duty to ensure passengers' safety.*

railway workers/staff *Railway workers threatened to go on strike.*

the railway timetable *She checked the railway timetable to see what time the next train would arrive.*

a railway carriage *A group of teenagers entered the railway carriage.*

a railway accident *Her uncle died in a railway accident.*

a railway bridge *A railway bridge crosses the canal at this point.*

VERBS

build a railway *The railway was built to connect the quarries with the port.*

run a railway *How can the railways be run more efficiently?*

ADJECTIVES

a mainline railway (=joining large towns or cities) *A mainline railway runs through here.*

a high-speed railway *The airport will be linked to Hong Kong by a high-speed railway.*

a steam railway *He can still remember the days of steam railways.*

PREPOSITIONS

on the railway(s) *My father worked on the railway.*

rain[1] *n*

water that falls in small drops from clouds in the sky

ADJECTIVES

heavy rain (=a lot of rain comes down) *There was heavy rain all night.*

pouring rain (=very heavy) *She left us standing in the pouring rain.*

torrential rain (=extremely heavy) *I woke to the sound of torrential rain.*

driving rain (=heavy rain that is being blown by the wind) *They struggled to walk against driving rain.*

light/fine rain (=consisting of small drops of water) *A light rain began to fall.*

soft/gentle rain (=light rain – used when this seems pleasant) *She felt the soft rain on her face.*

steady/persistent rain (=continuous rain) *The match was played in persistent rain.*

incessant rain (=continuing for a long time without stopping, in a way that is annoying or causes problems) *The incessant rain made the rescuers' work more difficult.*

VERBS

the rain falls/comes down *The rain was still falling in the afternoon.*

the rain pours down (=a lot of rain comes down) *The rain was pouring down and I was quickly soaked.*

the rain beats down/lashes down (*also* **the rain beats/lashes (against) sth**) (=it falls on something with a lot of force) *The rain lashed against the windows of the car.*

the rain eases off/lets up (=it starts to rain less) *The rain should ease off in a minute.*

the rain holds off (=it does not start, when people are expecting it to start) *Fortunately, the rain held off until we got back.*

the rain stops *They went into a café and waited for the rain to stop.*

rain + NOUNS

a rain cloud *There were thick black rain clouds in the sky.*

a rain shower (*also* **a shower of rain** *BrE*) (=a short period of rain) *A sudden rain shower made everyone run for cover.*

> **Raindrop**, **rainwater**, **rainstorm**, and **rainfall** are written as one word.

PREPOSITIONS

in the rain *He walked home in the rain.*

out of the rain *She opened the door and said, "Come in out of the rain."*

PHRASES

it is pouring with rain *BrE*, **it is pouring rain** *AmE* (=a lot of rain is falling) *It was pouring with rain so I decided to drive, not walk.*

it looks like rain (=rain appears likely because there are dark clouds in the sky) *We ate indoors because it looked like rain.*

get caught in the rain (=be outside when it starts raining) *I got caught in the rain and I didn't have an umbrella.*

a drop of rain *Robert felt a drop of rain on his face.*

sheets of rain *He drove home slowly, through sheets of rain.*

an inch/25 millimetres etc of rain *Two inches of rain fell in twelve hours.*

outbreaks of rain (=short periods of rain – used in weather forecasts) *Outbreaks of rain will spread across northern parts.*

rain[2] *v*

when it rains, drops of water fall from clouds in the sky

> **Grammar**
> You always say **it rains/it is raining**.

ADVERBS

it is raining heavily/hard (=a lot of water comes down) *It was raining heavily when we arrived in New York.*

⚠ Don't say 'It rained very much.' Say **It rained heavily.**

it is raining slightly/lightly/a little (=a little water comes down) *It's raining slightly, but we can still go out.*

it rained non-stop/solidly/steadily (=without stopping) *It rained solidly all day.*

VERBS

it starts/begins to rain *It started to rain, so we went inside.*

it stops raining *I wish it would stop raining.*

If it rains heavily, you can say **it is pouring down** (in British English) or **it is pouring rain** (in American English): *It's been pouring down/pouring rain all morning.*
People sometimes say **it's raining cats and dogs** in this meaning, but this phrase now sounds a little old-fashioned.

R

rainfall *n*

the amount of rain that falls on an area in a particular period of time

ADJECTIVES/NOUNS + rainfall

heavy rainfall *Heavy rainfall also affected Mexico, causing flooding in the state of Veracruz.*

high/low rainfall (=a lot or a little) *Low rainfall can seriously affect agricultural production.*

the average rainfall *About 70 percent of the average rainfall in the country falls between November and March.*

the annual rainfall (=the total amount in a year) *The annual rainfall averages only 45 inches.*

VERBS

measure the rainfall *The students will measure the rainfall every day and record their observations.*

rainfall + NOUNS

rainfall patterns *Global warming is already affecting the world's rainfall patterns.*

rainfall levels *The Tully region has one of the highest rainfall levels in Australia.*

PHRASES

5 inches/30 millimetres etc of rainfall *The Bristol area had over two inches of rainfall in two days.*

the amount of rainfall *October has the highest amount of rainfall during the year.*

rainforest *n*

a tropical forest with tall trees in an area where it rains a lot

ADJECTIVES

tropical rainforest *The tropical rainforests of Ecuador contain thousands of species of plants.*

virgin rainforest (=not damaged by humans) *Ghana has lost 90% of its virgin rainforest in the past 50 years.*

dense rainforest (=with a lot of trees growing closely together) *The island is covered in dense rainforest.*

the Amazonian/Brazilian/African etc rainforest *Huge areas of Brazilian rainforest are being cleared to create agricultural land.*

VERBS

save the rainforest *The best way to save the rainforest is to stop cutting down the trees and vegetation.*

protect the rainforest *If we want local people to protect the rainforest and its wildlife, then we must support them.*

destroy the rainforest *Why are multinational companies helping to destroy the rainforest?*

threaten the rainforest *Logging is threatening the rainforest.*

rainforest + NOUNS

rainforest conservation *Rainforest conservation is crucial to limiting the greenhouse effect.*

a rainforest campaigner *Rainforest campaigners are warning that biofuels could become the main reason for rainforest destruction worldwide.*

a rainforest region/area *Brazil has the world's largest rainforest areas.*

rainforest trees/plants *About a quarter of all the medicines we use come from rainforest plants.*

PHRASES

the destruction of the rainforest *The rate of destruction of the Amazon rainforest has increased over the last five years.*

rainy *adj*

if the weather is rainy, it rains a lot

NOUNS

a rainy day/night/morning etc *It was a cold rainy day in November.*

rainy weather *We didn't let the rainy weather spoil our holiday.*

the rainy season (=the period when it rains a lot each year) *The rainy season arrived early this year and there were lots of big storms.*

a rainy sky *Cloudy rainy skies turned bright and sunny.*

THESAURUS: rainy

wet
weather | day | night | morning | afternoon | weekend | summer | season | conditions
rainy:
The wet weather is expected to continue. | I think it's going to be another wet day. | They

say it will be a wet summer. | *Travel is extremely difficult during the wet season.* | *It's been wet all week.*

Wet or rainy?
These words mean the same and are used with many of the same collocations - you can say **wet weather** or **rainy weather**, a **wet day** or a **rainy day**.
There are some small differences of collocation. You usually say **rainy skies** (not 'wet'). Some countries such as Japan have a **rainy season**. Other countries have a **wet season**.

damp
day | **morning** | **evening** | **weather** | **climate**
if the air feels damp, there is a lot of moisture in the air and it may be raining slightly:
It was a damp and rather miserable day. | *a damp November morning* | *In November the weather turns cold and damp.*

showery
weather | **day** | **night** | **morning** | **afternoon** | **outbreaks**
raining for short periods:
The weather will be showery, with some sunny intervals. | *It will be a cool dull day with some showery outbreaks of rain* (=sudden short periods of rain).

drizzly
day | **morning** | **afternoon** | **weather**
if it is drizzly, little drops of rain are falling:
The morning was grey and drizzly. | *a drizzly afternoon in October*

grey *BrE*, **gray** *AmE*
sky | **day** | **morning** | **weather**
if the sky is grey, there are a lot of clouds, and it looks like it will rain:
The next morning, the sky was grey. | *It's such a grey day.*

raise *v*

THESAURUS lift[1] (1)

random Ac *adj*

happening or chosen without any definite plan or pattern

ADVERBS

completely/entirely random *The atomic particles seem to move in completely random directions.*

apparently/seemingly random *There had been a wave of apparently random attacks.*

purely/truly random *How can we be sure that the selection is truly random?*

NOUNS

a random number *The computer picks a random number.*

a random selection *He looked at a random selection of the files.*

a random sample *A test was carried out on a random sample of the cattle.*

a random sequence *They were asked to memorize a random sequence of numbers.*

random checks/tests *There are random drug tests at the prison.*

a random attack *The police believe this was not a random attack.*

PHRASES

at random *One of the students was chosen at random for the experiment.*

in random order *The names are in random order.*

range Ac *n*

a number of different people or things of the same general type

ADJECTIVES

a wide/broad range *The college offers a wide range of courses.*

a narrow/limited range *They only had a very limited range of products available.*

a large/great/huge/vast range *A vast range of plants are used in medicines.*

an extensive/comprehensive range (=a range that includes every type of goods, services etc) *The restaurant has an extensive range of wines.*

a good range *The shop sells a good range of books.*

an impressive range *The camera has an impressive range of features.*

a diverse range (=a number of very different things) *During his career he has run a diverse range of businesses.*

a complete/full range *There is a complete range of property available in the area.*

a whole range (=a very wide range of different things) *They discussed a whole range of different issues.*

NOUNS + range

age range *The book is suitable for children in the 7–11 age range.*

ability range *The programme helps students at the lower level of the ability range.*

price range (=the range of prices that exist, or that someone can afford) *Students have difficulty finding housing within their price range.*

temperature range *This aquarium plant needs a temperature range of 75°–78°F.*

VERBS

extend/expand/broaden your range *The store is expanding its furniture range.*

rank *n*

the position that someone has in an organization with different levels, such as the army

ADJECTIVES

high/low/middle rank *Her father had been an army officer of fairly high rank.*

senior/junior rank *He held a junior rank in the army.*

VERBS

hold a rank *From 1 December 1914 to 31 October 1915 he held the rank of captain.*

rise to/achieve/reach a rank (*also* **attain a rank** *formal*): *She rose to the rank of colonel.*

be promoted to a rank *For this service, he was promoted to the rank of major.*

be stripped of your rank (=have it taken from you as a punishment) *The officer was stripped of his rank for his part in the affair.*

ransack *v* THESAURUS ▸ steal

rapid *adj*

happening or done very quickly and in a very short time

NOUNS

rapid growth/expansion/development *The industry is experiencing rapid growth.*

a rapid increase/rise *The country cannot cope with a rapid increase in population.*

rapid change *The 1980s were a period of rapid change.*

the rapid spread of sth *Close contact between people resulted in the rapid spread of the disease.*

a rapid decline/deterioration *There was a rapid decline in the health of the fish.*

rapid progress *The students had made rapid progress under his guidance.*

a rapid response *He praised state health authorities for their rapid response to the crisis.*

PHRASES

at a rapid rate/pace *The world is changing at a rapid rate.*

in rapid succession (=quickly, one after the other) *He fired three times in rapid succession.*

THESAURUS: rapid

fast, rapid, speedy, prompt, hasty, cursory → **quick (1)**

rare *adj*

not seen or found very often, or not happening very often

NOUNS

a rare bird/plant/animal *The orchid is one of the rarest plants in Britain.*

a rare species/breed *The island is home to several rare species of bird.*

a rare disease/illness/disorder/condition *Meningitis is quite a rare disease but it can be very serious.*

a rare form of sth *His mother suffers from a rare form of cancer.*

a rare sight (=something that you do not see very often) *Mountain lions were once a rare sight.*

a rare occasion/instance *He never cried, except on a few rare occasions.*

a rare event/occurrence (=something that does not happen very often) *Murder is a rare event in this part of the country.*

a rare opportunity/chance *This is a rare opportunity to see his early paintings.*

a rare visit *She met the singer on one of his rare visits to Europe.*

a rare treat (=something that is unusually good and enjoyable, that you do not get very often) *Her latest novel is a rare treat.*

a rare delicacy (=a type of food that is hard to get and is often very expensive) *In those days, fresh pineapple was a rare delicacy.*

ADVERBS

extremely rare *Shark attacks are extremely rare.*

comparatively/relatively rare (*also* **quite rare** *BrE*) (=rather rare) *Crime on the island is comparatively rare.*

increasingly rare *These beautiful birds are becoming increasingly rare.*

VERBS

sth is considered (to be) rare *The disease used to be considered rather rare.*

THESAURUS: rare

scarce

if something is scarce, there is not enough of it available:

After the war, food and clothing were scarce. | *Building land is extremely scarce and prices are high.*

> **Scarce** is much less common before a noun, except in the phrase **scarce resources**: *People are having to compete for scarce resources.*

uncommon

not happening often, or not existing in large numbers:

It is fairly **uncommon for** *adult relatives to share households today.* | *In Western countries, the disease is* **relatively uncommon**.

> **Uncommon** is used especially in the phrase **not uncommon**, when saying that something happens often: *Volcanic eruptions are* **not uncommon**. **Uncommon** is not usually used before a noun.

infrequent *formal*

visits | trips | use | occurrence | occasions | visitor

not happening often:

As time went on, her visits became more and more infrequent. | *Cattle stealing was a relatively infrequent* occurrence (=it did not happen very often). | *The bird is an infrequent visitor to this country.*

If there are very few of a type of person or thing, you can say that they are **something of a rarity**: *Women are still* ***something of a rarity*** *in senior management positions.* You can also say that they are **few and far between**: *Luckily, accidents such as these are* ***few and far between****.*

THESAURUS: rare

rare, exotic, exceptional, out of the ordinary, freak, unprecedented, unheard of, eccentric, unconventional, unorthodox → **unusual**

ANTONYMS **rare** → **common (1)**

rash *adj*

deciding to do something too quickly, without thinking carefully about whether it is sensible or not

NOUNS

a rash decision *Think about it first – don't go making any rash decisions!*

a rash action/move (=something that you decide to do too quickly) *Getting married was a rash move which she later regretted.*

a rash statement/promise/claim *The minister was forced to apologize for his earlier rash statement.*

a rash assumption (=you think something must be true, when in fact it is not) *He's making very rash assumptions based on little evidence.*

ADVERBS

extremely rash *It would be extremely rash to come to any fixed conclusions at this early stage of the research.*

too rash (*also* **a bit rash** *BrE informal*): *Maybe I was a bit rash, but I really wanted the car.*

rate *n*

1 the number of times something happens

ADJECTIVES

a high/low rate *The city has one of the highest rates of violent crime.*

a rising/falling rate *The rising rate of unemployment is causing concern.*

NOUNS + rate

the crime rate *Police in the area have managed to bring crime rates down.*

the birth rate *In many developing countries, birth rates are falling.*

the death/mortality rate *The death rate among homeless people is three times higher than for the rest of the population.*

the divorce rate *The UK has one of the highest divorce rates in Europe.*

the unemployment rate *The economy is doing well and the unemployment rate has fallen.*

the success/failure rate *The operation has a high success rate.*

the survival rate *The survival rate of people with cancer has increased in recent years.*

VERBS

the rate rises/goes up/increases *The crime rate just keeps going up.*

the rate falls/goes down *We are expecting unemployment rates to fall.*

PREPOSITIONS

at a rate of sth *Restaurants in the area are closing at a rate of almost one a week.*

2 the speed at which something happens

ADJECTIVES

a rapid/fast rate *The rapid rate of industrial development has caused some problems.*

a slow rate *People are frustrated at the slow rate of progress.*

an alarming rate *The pollution levels have been increasing at an alarming rate.*

a tremendous/phenomenal rate (=extremely fast) *He started to produce movies at a tremendous rate.*

an unprecedented rate (=faster than ever before) *Species are disappearing from the Earth at an unprecedented rate.*

a constant/steady rate *The process happens at a constant rate.*

NOUNS + rate

the growth rate *Britain's growth rate was the highest in Europe.*

sb's heart/pulse rate *Exercise increases your heart rate.*

VERBS

a rate increases *When you are stressed, your heart rate increases.*

a rate slows (down) *The rate of progress is slowing down.*

PREPOSITIONS

at a rate of sth *The population is growing at a rate of 12% a year.*

3 a charge or payment that is set by someone

ADJECTIVES

a high/low rate *I wanted an account that paid a high rate of interest.*

the minimum/maximum rate *The minimum rate of pay is just under £5 an hour.*

the hourly/weekly rate *Women have lower hourly rates of pay than men.*

a special/reduced rate (=a lower charge) *Reduced rates are available for groups of 10 or more visitors.*

a flat/fixed rate (=one that does not change) *Profits were taxed at a flat rate of 45%.*

the going rate (=the usual amount that people pay for something) *She paid her cleaner more than the going rate.*

NOUNS + rate

the exchange rate (=the value of the money of one country compared to the money of another country) *The exchange rate between the dollar and the euro remains stable.*

the tax rate *Ireland has lower tax rates than most other European countries.*

the interest rate (=the amount of interest charged on a loan or paid on savings) *Interest rates have remained high.*

VERBS

raise/put up a rate *If the banks raise interest rates, this will reduce the demand for credit.*

cut/reduce/lower a rate *The building society is to cut its mortgage rate by 0.7%.*

PREPOSITIONS

the rate of interest/pay/tax etc *The government may have to raise the basic rate of tax.*

at a rate of sth *Some customers are paying interest at a rate of over 15%.*

the rate for sth *They should be paid the normal rate for the job.*

THESAURUS: rate

price, value, charge, fee, fare, rent, rate, toll → cost[1] (1)

ratify *v* THESAURUS approve (2)

ratio *n*

the relationship between two amounts or numbers

ADJECTIVES

a high ratio *The college has a high ratio of teachers to students.*

a low ratio *A low teacher-to-student ratio is better for the students.*

an inverse ratio (=one thing increases while another decreases) *They found an inverse ratio between the number of different animals and their size.*

the optimum ratio (=the best one) *According to her diet plan, the optimum ratio is one part of protein to seven parts of carbohydrate.*

NOUNS + ratio

the male-to-female ratio (*also* **the sex ratio**) (=between males and females) *The male-to-female ratio is 100:115.*

the staff-to-student ratio/the staffing ratio *The staff-to-student ratio at the college is approximately 1:10.*

VERBS + ratio

calculate the ratio *How do you calculate the ratio between two numbers?*

increase/decrease the ratio *Telecommunication systems try to increase the ratio of signal level to noise level in order to effectively transmit data.*

ratio + VERBS

the ratio increases *The ratio of females to males studying engineering is slowly increasing.*

the ratio decreases/falls/drops *The ratio of managers to workers has decreased in recent years.*

PREPOSITIONS

the ratio between sth *To calculate the ratio between two numbers we need to divide them by each other.*

the ratio of sth to sth *The ratio of nursing staff to doctors is 2:1.*

rational Ac *adj*

using or based on reasons rather than emotions

NOUNS

a rational explanation *There must be some simple rational explanation.*

a rational decision/choice *The patient was incapable of making a rational decision.*

a rational approach *Her approach to the problem was rational and objective.*

a rational analysis *Emotions are running so high that any rational analysis of the situation is difficult.*

rational thought/thinking *Babies were thought to be incapable of rational thought.*

rational argument/debate *It can be difficult to have a rational argument on the subject of religion.*

a rational conversation/discussion *It's impossible to have a rational conversation with him.*

a rational response *The decision was not alarmist, but was a rational response to a real risk.*

a rational person/man/woman *Any rational person would agree with you.*

ADVERBS

perfectly/entirely rational *"I'm being perfectly rational," she insisted.*

ANTONYMS **rational → irrational**

raw *adj* not cooked

NOUNS

raw food *Wash chopping boards and knives after preparing raw food.*

raw meat/beef/chicken etc *You shouldn't eat raw chicken.*

raw fish *Japanese people often eat raw fish.*

raw vegetables/carrot/celery etc *He nibbled a piece of raw carrot.*

(a) raw egg *Someone threw a raw egg at him.*

ADVERBS

completely raw *The chicken was completely raw in the middle.*

PHRASES

eat sth raw *Cabbage can be eaten raw.*

reach *v*

1 to get to a particular level, point, or stage

NOUNS

reach a point/stage/level *I've reached the point in my life where I need a new challenge.*

reach a height/length/speed *The car reached a speed of 130 miles per hour.*

reach an age *The payments will be made until the child reaches college age.*

reach the end *Some of these power stations are reaching the end of their useful life.*

reach the final/quarter-final etc (=in a competition) *Chelsea could reach the final of the European Cup.*

reach your peak (=be the best or most successful that you will ever be) *Most players don't reach their peak until their late twenties.*

reach adulthood *The country's death rates are high and many children never reach adulthood.*

reach maturity (=become fully grown or developed) *It takes ten years for the fish to reach maturity.*

THESAURUS: reach

accomplish, attain, reach, realize → **achieve**

2 to agree on something or decide something after a lot of discussion or thought

NOUNS

reach a decision *It took several hours for the committee to reach a decision.*

reach a conclusion *Cathy had reached the conclusion that she didn't like the job very much.*

reach a verdict *The jury failed to reach a verdict.*

reach a solution *Efforts to reach a solution to the political crisis have not succeeded.*

reach an agreement/compromise/settlement/deal (=decide on an arrangement that is acceptable to both groups) *Progress was made toward reaching an agreement.*

reach agreement/consensus (=agree about something) *The experts seem unable to reach consensus on this point.*

3 to arrive somewhere

THESAURUS: reach

get, come, reach, show up, get in, land, pull in, dock → **arrive**

react Ac *v*

to behave in a particular way or show a particular emotion because of something that has happened or been said

ADVERBS

react angrily/furiously *She reacted angrily to the suggestion that she had lied.*

react violently *He reacted violently and started punching the man.*

react badly (=become annoyed or upset) *Do you react badly to criticism?*

react strongly (=show strong emotion, especially anger) *Scott reacted strongly when he felt his treatment was unfair.*

react quickly/swiftly *The goalkeeper had to react quickly.*

react positively/negatively (=with positive or negative emotions or opinions) *We want versatile people who react positively to change.*

react cautiously (=carefully, so that you avoid danger or risk) *The United States has reacted cautiously to the offer.*

react instinctively (=without thinking or needing to think) *She reacted instinctively and reached for a weapon.*

react accordingly (=in a way that is suitable or based on what someone has said or done) *They realized they were in danger and reacted accordingly.*

react differently *People react differently to stress.*

PREPOSITIONS

react to sth *How did Wilson react to your idea?*

react by doing sth *The government reacted by imposing a ban on imports.*

react with anger/shock/joy etc *She reacted with anger to the accusation.*

reaction Ac *n*

something that you feel or do because of something that has happened or been said

ADJECTIVES/NOUNS + reaction

sb's first/initial/immediate reaction *His first reaction was to laugh.*

a natural reaction *Anger is a natural reaction when you feel you have been treated unfairly.*

an emotional reaction (=showing strong emotion, especially by crying) *I was surprised by her emotional reaction to the news.*

a positive/favourable reaction (=showing that someone agrees or likes something) *There has been a positive reaction to the campaign.*

a negative reaction (=showing that someone disagrees or dislikes something) *I wasn't expecting such a negative reaction to my suggestion.*

mixed reactions (=some positive and some negative reactions) *The book met with mixed reactions.*

a violent/angry/hostile reaction *There was an angry reaction from the crowd and some people started throwing stones at the police.*

a strong reaction *There was a strong reaction from the union against the changes.*

the public reaction *The public reaction to the film was mainly positive.*

a delayed reaction (=one that comes some time after an event) *You're suffering a delayed reaction to the accident.*

sb's gut reaction *informal* (=what they feel or decide immediately, before thinking) *My gut reaction is that it sounds like a good idea.*

sb's instinctive reaction (=what they do immediately, before thinking) *Often your instinctive reaction is to blame someone else.*

a knee-jerk reaction (=an immediate one that happens without sensible thinking) *There's often a knee-jerk reaction when changes are announced.*

VERBS

provoke/produce/bring a reaction (=make someone have a reaction) *The decision provoked an angry reaction from the local tourist industry.*

get a reaction *We didn't know what kind of reaction we would get.*

meet with/draw a reaction *formal* (=get a reaction) *The article drew a furious reaction from ministers.*

gauge sb's reaction (=judge or find out someone's reaction) *He watched Jane's face, trying to gauge her reaction.*

PREPOSITIONS

sb's reaction to sth *His reaction to the news had been predictable.*

the reaction from/of sb *I can understand the reaction of the fans, and why they were so upset.*

in reaction to sth *An emergency fund was set up in reaction to the famine.*

PHRASES

judging by sb's reactions *Judging by the audience's reactions, the show will be a great success.*

read *v*

to look at written words, in order to find information or for enjoyment

ADVERBS

read sth carefully *Always read the manufacturer's instructions carefully.*

read sth aloud/out loud (=say the words of something as you read it, so that people can hear them) *The teacher read the story aloud to the class.*

read sth out (=say the words of something, especially a series or list of things) *The judge read out the charges against him.*

be widely read (=read by many people) *His novels are widely read in the US.*

PREPOSITIONS

read about sb/sth *Everything you read about her is true.*

read of sth (=read that something has happened or exists) *We were saddened when we read of his death.*

read (sth) in a newspaper/book *I read in the newspaper that the couple were getting divorced.*

⚠ Don't say 'I read (sth) on the newspaper.'

read (sth) to sb *The teacher began the lesson by reading a poem to the students.*

read from sth *The mayor was reading from notes when he made his statement.*

read through sth *She read through her essay, looking for spelling mistakes.*

PHRASES

read and write *Too many children leave school unable to read and write.*

read sth from cover to cover (=read all of something, because you are very interested) *She read the book from cover to cover.*

read sth with interest *I always read his articles with great interest.*

read (sth) for pleasure *Students should be encouraged to read for pleasure, not just for exams.*

reader *n*

someone who reads books, or who reads in a particular way

ADJECTIVES

a slow/fast reader *Her son was quite a slow reader.*

a great reader (=someone who reads a lot) *My father was a great reader.*

an avid/voracious reader (=someone who reads a lot – more formal) *She was an avid reader of historical novels.*

reading *n*

the activity of reading, or things that you read

PHRASES

do some reading/a lot of reading etc *I've done some reading on the subject.*

do some background reading (=read about something in order to get basic information about it) *It is important to do some background reading before buying a pet.*

sth makes interesting/uncomfortable etc reading (=it is interesting, uncomfortable etc to read) *The report makes interesting reading.*

sth is essential reading (=you must read it) *This book is essential reading for every voter.*

sth is recommended reading (=you should read it) *The book is recommended reading for all gardeners.*

sb has a reading age of 8/11/15 etc (=he or she has the same reading ability as an average child of 8, 11 etc) *Thirty seven per cent of the prison population have a reading age of under 11.*

reading + NOUNS

reading ability *The test is designed to measure children's reading ability.*

reading skills *She has poor reading skills.*
reading glasses *He put on his reading glasses and looked at the letter.*
reading material/matter (=things to read) *You will find magazines and other reading matter in the waiting room.*
a reading list (=a list of things that you need to read, especially for a course) *Their teacher has given them a reading list.*

ADJECTIVES

light reading (=something that is easy and enjoyable to read) *I took some light reading on holiday with me.*
extensive reading (=reading a lot of books, so that you have a lot of knowledge) *Because of his extensive reading, he knew a lot about the topic.*
further reading (=other related things you can read) *The book contains plenty of suggestions for further reading.*

NOUNS + reading

bedtime reading *This story is too scary to make good bedtime reading.*
holiday reading *My holiday reading tends to be biographies.*

ready *adj*

1 if you are ready, you are prepared for what you are going to do

ADVERBS

completely/all ready *Let me know when you're completely ready.*
almost/nearly ready *We're almost ready – we'll be with you in a second.*
ready yet *Can you wait a minute? I'm not ready yet.*

VERBS

get ready *Why does it take you so long to get ready to go out?*
make ready *formal* (=get ready) *The crew started making ready for the journey home.*
get sb/sth ready *I need to get the children ready for school.*

PREPOSITIONS

ready for sb/sth *Are you ready for your trip?*

PHRASES

ready to leave/go/start etc *Everything's packed, and we're ready to leave.*
ready and waiting *When the doorbell rang he was ready and waiting.*
ready for anything *I felt strong, fit, and ready for anything.*

2 willing to do something

ADVERBS

always ready *His father was always ready to give advice.*
more than ready/only too ready (=very willing) *The local people were more than ready to help us.*

PHRASES

ready and willing *His boss said he was ready and willing to consider any suggestions.*

real *adj*

1 not false or artificial, or not imagined or pretended

NOUNS

real wood/leather/gold/diamonds *The statue is made of real gold.*
sb's real name *The singer Bono's real name is Paul Hewson.*
a real person/place/event *I used to think that Santa Claus was a real person.*
real life *The pictures make him look older than he does in real life.*
the real world *Politicians are totally unaware of what is happening in the real world.*
the real story *We now know the real story about what happened in Stalin's Russia.*
the real situation *No one actually knows what the real situation is.*
the real reason/purpose/cause *They found out the real reason for her decision later.*
the real thing *The watch looks like the real thing.*
the real America/Japan etc *I wanted to see the real China, not just the usual tourist spots.*
a real sense of sth *There is a real sense of community here, and our neighbours will do anything to help us.*

VERBS

look/seem real *In wrestling, the fights are made to look real, but no one gets hurt.*

PHRASES

sth is for real (=something is really happening or really true) *This isn't a computer game. This is for real.*
sb/sth is the real deal/the real McCoy *informal* (=they really are that person or thing – used especially about a very impressive or valuable person or thing) *This guy is the real deal, I thought to myself.*

THESAURUS: real

genuine
concern | interest | desire | love | surprise | belief | attempt | mistake | document | letter | painting | refugee
used when someone's feelings are sincere, or something or someone really is what they seem to be:
She seemed to have a genuine concern for our safety. | There is a genuine desire to reach an agreement. | There was a genuine attempt to

R

improve living conditions for the working classes. | *Experts believe that the painting is genuine.*

authentic
food | cooking | dish | music | instrument | atmosphere | experience | design
authentic food, music, designs etc are correct for the place or the period in history that they are supposed to be from:
The restaurant serves authentic Mexican dishes. | *The band plays authentic Jamaican music.* | *The dancers wore authentic American Indian designs.*

true
feelings | identity | nature | extent | value | cost | happiness | love | friend
real – used when someone or something is different from how they seem, or when saying that someone or something is how they should be:
Helen tried to hide her true feelings from her family. | *He was worried that someone would discover his true identity.* | *People did not realise the true nature of the crisis.* | *The true cost of the repairs is closer to $600 million.* | *Money doesn't give you true happiness.* | *A true friend will always help you when you are in trouble.*

bona fide/bonafide
member | guest | employee | candidate | purchaser | reason | claim | expenses | qualification
bona fide people or things are really what they say they are, especially when this can be checked by looking at official documents:
The club is only open to bona fide members. | *The company says the decision was made for bonafide commercial reasons.*

hard
evidence | facts
hard evidence or facts can definitely be shown to be true:
There is no hard evidence to support his theory. | *He said he had no hard facts to support the rumours.*

ANTONYMS **real → false**

ANTONYMS **real → artificial**

2 used when saying that something is serious or important

NOUNS

a real problem/issue/challenge *Traffic noise is becoming a real problem.*

a real danger/emergency *There is a real danger that the forest will disappear altogether.*

a real worry *The only real worry is that terrorists could try to cause an explosion.*

the real question *The real question is whether governments are actually going to do something about global warming.*

PHRASES

sth is all too real (=used when emphasizing that something really exists and is really serious) *The threat of war is now all too real.*

realistic *adj*

1 based on a situation as it really is

NOUNS

a realistic chance/prospect *We felt we had a realistic chance of beating England.*

a realistic alternative/option *We do not believe there is any realistic alternative.*

a realistic solution *Compromise is the only realistic solution.*

a realistic goal/target *Make sure that you set yourself a realistic target.*

a realistic hope *This discovery offers a realistic hope of finding a cure for the disease.*

a realistic figure/price *A more realistic figure for energy saving would be 20%.*

a realistic assessment/appraisal (=judgment) *We need time to make a calm and realistic appraisal of our needs.*

2 looking or sounding like something in real life

VERBS

look/sound realistic *To make the injuries look more realistic, she used fake blood.*

NOUNS

a realistic picture/model *By the age of 10, he was building highly realistic models of trains.*

a realistic portrayal *The movie is a realistic portrayal of life with an alcoholic.*

ADVERBS

highly realistic *Computer-generated images are now highly realistic.*

perfectly realistic *She produced a perfectly realistic representation of the building.*

reality *n*

what actually happens or is true, not what is imagined or thought

ADJECTIVES

the harsh/grim/stark/hard reality (=a situation that is very bad or unpleasant) *Millions of people have to live with the harsh realities of unemployment.*

the sad reality *The sad reality is that many children grow up never seeing their fathers.*

the political/social/economic realities *People forget the economic realities and think the government can spend as much as it wants.*

the reality is different *Everyone thought the couple were happily married, but the reality was very different.*

VERBS

face (up to)/accept reality *It's painful, but you have to face reality.*

wake up to reality (=realize what is happening

or real) *People are beginning to wake up to reality about climate change.*

ignore the reality *Voters are ignoring the reality of American politics.*

escape from reality *His films helped people to escape from reality.*

become a reality *The paperless office may one day become a reality.*

reflect reality (=match or show what is really happening or true) *Do these novels accurately reflect the reality of the time?*

be divorced from reality (=not connected in any way to what is really happening) *His ideas are completely divorced from reality.*

PREPOSITIONS

the reality of sth *The reality of the situation is that no one really wants to work – we just want the money.*

PHRASES

bear no relation to reality (=not match what is really happening or true) *His idea of recent history bears no relation to reality.*

lose touch with reality (*also* **lose your grasp/grip on reality**) (=stop realizing what the real situation is like) *As he got older, he began to lose his grasp on reality.*

bring sb back to reality (=make them realize what is happening around them or true) *She was brought back to reality by the pain in her chest.*

(get) back to reality *After three weeks' holiday, it was time to get back to reality.*

be confronted with the reality of sth (=experience what a bad situation is really like) *Nurses are directly confronted with the reality of suffering every day.*

an escape from reality *People use alcohol as an escape from reality.*

realize (*also* realise *BrE*) *v*

1 to begin to understand, notice, or know something that you did not understand etc before

ADVERBS

suddenly realize *I suddenly realized I was late for work.*

soon/quickly realize *You will quickly realize that skiing is not as easy as it looks.*

immediately/instantly realize *She immediately realized the old lady was blind.*

gradually/slowly realize *People are gradually realizing that disabled people are just like everyone else.*

finally/eventually realize *He had finally realized that there was no chance of returning home.*

first realize *When did you first realize there was something wrong?*

fully realize *They don't fully realize how serious the situation is.*

NOUNS

realize the importance/significance of sth *We didn't realize the importance of these events at the time.*

realize the extent/seriousness of sth *At first the doctors hadn't realized the extent of his injuries.*

realize your mistake/error *I only realized my mistake afterwards.*

realize the truth *Her parents didn't realize the truth about what had happened to her.*

realize the danger of sth *People are beginning to realize the dangers of eating a high-fat diet.*

realize the benefits of sth *It took me a while to realize the benefits of riding my bicycle to work.*

PHRASES

I wish I had realized earlier *I wish I had realized earlier how unhappy she was.*

2 to achieve what you wanted

THESAURUS: realize

accomplish, attain, reach, realize → **achieve**

reason *n*

why something happens, or why someone does something

ADJECTIVES

a good reason *There is usually a good reason why the price is so low.*

the main reason *The main reason for his success was the support of his family.*

a major reason (*also* **a big reason** *informal*): *A major reason for the decrease in smoking is the ban on cigarette advertising.*

the only/sole reason *The only reason he's coming tonight is that I said you'd be here.*

the real reason *What do you think was the real reason for their decision?*

a strong/compelling reason *There are compelling reasons to believe that this is true.*

an important reason *A more important reason for losing weight is to improve health.*

an underlying reason (=basic or important but not obvious) *There are often underlying reasons for a child's bad behaviour.*

a valid/legitimate reason (=good and acceptable) *An employer can't fire someone without a valid reason.*

a simple reason *Sales are down by 10% and the reason is simple.*

a logical reason *People don't always have logical reasons for the things they do.*

VERBS

have a reason *We had many reasons to celebrate.*

give/offer a reason *No reason was given for the change.*

think of a reason/see a reason *I can't think of any reason why she would lie.*

explain the reasons for sth *Explain the reasons for your choice.*

know/understand the reason *The children were too young to understand the reason why their mother left.*

PREPOSITIONS

a reason for (doing) sth *What was the reason for the delay?*

the reason behind sth *He explained the reasons behind the decision.*

PHRASES

for this/that reason *For that reason, I didn't want to go back there ever again.*

for some (unknown) reason (=for a reason that you do not know) *For some reason she felt like crying.*

for legal/political/medical reasons *The boy cannot be named for legal reasons.*

for health/family reasons *I don't eat meat for health reasons.*

for safety/security reasons *The road will be closed for safety reasons.*

for personal reasons *He resigned for personal reasons.*

for sentimental reasons (=because you like something or someone very much) *The ring was important to me for sentimental reasons.*

for the right/wrong reasons *She got married for all the wrong reasons.*

for obvious reasons *This arrangement must be kept secret, for obvious reasons.*

for no apparent reason (=for no reason that you can see) *The man attacked him for no apparent reason.*

R

reasonable *adj*

1 fair and sensible

ADVERBS

perfectly/entirely reasonable (*also* **eminently reasonable** *formal*) (=completely reasonable) *The proposal sounds perfectly reasonable.*

reasonable enough (=fairly reasonable) *It was a reasonable enough question.*

NOUNS

a reasonable explanation/excuse *He gave what seemed a reasonable excuse for his lateness.*

a reasonable question/request *I asked who was paying for it, which I thought was a reasonable question.*

a reasonable assumption *They made a quite reasonable assumption about what had happened.*

a reasonable argument *There is a reasonable argument that students who are interested will achieve more.*

a reasonable offer *He will accept any reasonable offer for the car.*

reasonable grounds (=good reasons) *She must show that she had reasonable grounds for her decision.*

reasonable precautions/care *All reasonable precautions are taken to ensure that information given is accurate.*

a reasonable person *No reasonable person would object to this decision.*

VERBS

seem reasonable *It seems reasonable to assume that the situation has changed since then.*

sound reasonable *The request sounds perfectly reasonable to me.*

PHRASES

fair and reasonable *We need to set targets that are fair and reasonable.*

THESAURUS: reasonable

reasonable, just, impartial, balanced, even-handed, equitable → **fair**

2 not too expensive

THESAURUS: reasonable

inexpensive, low, reasonable, economical, affordable, competitive, budget → **cheap**

3 fairly good or big

NOUNS

a reasonable amount/number *They wanted to buy a farm with a reasonable amount of land.*

a reasonable chance/prospect *The team has a reasonable chance of winning.*

a reasonable level/standard/degree *Any goods that you buy should be of a reasonable standard.*

a reasonable size/distance *The rooms are of a reasonable size and there is enough space for all our furniture.*

a reasonable job *The builders did a reasonable job, but not a brilliant one.*

rebellion *n*

1 an organized attempt to change the government or leader of a country, using violence

ADJECTIVES

armed rebellion *There was the threat of armed rebellion.*

open rebellion (=clear and not hidden) *Algiers was in open rebellion.*

VERBS

a rebellion breaks out (=starts) *While he was away, a rebellion broke out in Aquitaine.*

lead a rebellion *He led a peasant rebellion against Catherine the Great.*

suppress/crush/put down a rebellion (=end it by force) *Troops moved in to suppress the rebellion.*

stage/launch a rebellion (=organize it) *Farmers staged a rebellion that forced the government to back down.*

PREPOSITIONS

a rebellion against sb/sth *In 1641, there was a Catholic rebellion against the Protestants of Ulster.*

2 refusal to obey someone in authority or the accepted ways of doing things

ADJECTIVES/NOUNS + rebellion

teenage/adolescent rebellion *His behaviour is just normal teenage rebellion.*

PREPOSITIONS

rebellion against sb/sth *This behaviour was part of Vincent's growing rebellion against his parents.*

PHRASES

an act of rebellion *In an act of rebellion, the minister voted against his own party.*

rebellious *adj* THESAURUS ▸ naughty

receive *v*

1 to be given something

NOUNS

receive a prize/award/medal *The photo shows the winner receiving her prize.*

receive a present/gift *Martha received a special present from her parents.*

receive money/a payment/a fee etc *He did not receive any payment for his work.*

receive attention/publicity *The case has received much attention in the media.*

receive support/help *The plan has received widespread international support.*

receive votes *He received twice as many votes as the other candidate.*

receive education/training *She had received a good education.*

receive a sentence *He was found guilty and received a five-year sentence.*

receive treatment *The victims are currently receiving medical treatment at a local hospital.*

PREPOSITIONS

receive sth from sb *Did you receive any money from him?*

> **THESAURUS: receive**
>
> receive, obtain, acquire, gain, win, earn, inherit, get hold of sth → **get (1)**

2 to get something that someone has sent you, or get an answer, invitation, complaint etc

NOUNS

receive a letter/message/email *Perhaps they have not received your letter yet.*

receive a (phone) call *One morning, I received a call from my mother in California.*

receive an answer/reply/reaction *I have not yet received a reply to my email.*

receive an invitation/offer *A year later, I received an invitation to their wedding.*

receive a complaint *The company has received a number of complaints from customers.*

receive a request *They have received a request for assistance from the French police.*

receive an apology *They received a public apology from the president.*

receive information/news *I have received some new information.*

receive a copy *Everyone on the committee will receive a copy of the report.*

PREPOSITIONS

receive sth from sb *I received an email from an old friend yesterday.*

3 to react in a particular way to a suggestion, idea, performance etc

ADVERBS

be well received (*also* **be favourably/enthusiastically received**) (=used when people like something and think it is good) *The band's next album was well received by the critics.*

be warmly received (=used especially when people show that they like someone's speech or idea) *Her speech was warmly received by the audience.*

be badly received (=used when people do not like something) *His first film had been badly received.*

sth will be gratefully received (=used when asking people to suggest or give something) *Any contributions will be gratefully received.*

NOUNS

receive the news *Her father received the news without surprise.*

PHRASES

be received with enthusiasm/scepticism/hostility etc *The claim was received with skepticism by the public* (=they doubted whether it was true).

recent *adj* THESAURUS ▸ new (1)

reception *n*

1 a particular type of welcome for someone, or a particular type of reaction to their ideas, work etc

ADJECTIVES

a warm reception (=friendly or approving) *The prince was given a warm reception when he visited Birmingham.*

an enthusiastic/rapturous/rousing reception (=in which people show a lot of approval in a noisy way) *She received an enthusiastic reception.*

a hostile reception (=unfriendly or angry) *When reporters arrived at the house, they got a hostile reception.*

a cool/chilly/frosty reception (=not friendly or approving) *His idea got a cool reception from his colleagues.*

a lukewarm reception (=not enthusiastic) *The band's latest album is getting a lukewarm reception.*

a mixed reception (=when some people like something and some do not) *His first novel received a mixed reception.*

a positive/favourable reception (=people like someone or something) *The movie had a favourable reception from audiences and critics alike.*

VERBS

get/receive/have a ... reception *As he came on stage, Rocky got a great reception from the crowd.*

meet with a ... reception *formal* (=be given a reception) *They met with a chilly reception from my mother.*

give sb/sth a ... reception *Opposition parties gave the proposals a lukewarm reception.*

PREPOSITIONS

reception from/by sb *He is sure to get an enthusiastic reception from fans.*

2 a large formal party to celebrate an event or to welcome someone

ADJECTIVES/NOUNS + reception

a wedding reception *There were over 200 guests at our wedding reception.*

a civic reception (=one given by the authorities of a city) *The plaque was unveiled during a civic reception held at Glasgow City Chambers.*

an official reception *After an official reception at the Embassy, they visited the White House.*

a formal reception *There will be a formal reception in honour of his life and work.*

VERBS

have/hold a reception *The wedding reception will be held at The Grand Hotel.*

go to/attend a reception *A few hundred guests attended the reception at the White House.*

host a reception *The mayor will host a reception in honour of Chinese officials visiting the city.*

PREPOSITIONS

a reception for sb *The president is hosting a reception for diplomats.*

at a reception *There were over 500 people at the reception.*

recession *n*

a time of difficulty in a country's economy, when there is less trade, business activity etc than usual

ADJECTIVES/NOUNS + recession

an economic recession *Britain was in the middle of an economic recession.*

a world/global/worldwide recession *America's airlines have been badly hit by the global recession.*

a deep/severe recession *We are in the middle of a severe recession.*

a deepening recession (=becoming worse) *The deepening recession led to a fall in demand for luxury goods.*

worst recession *Colombia was going through its worst recession in decades.*

VERBS

suffer/experience a recession *The country was suffering a deep recession.*

go/slide/slip into recession (=start to experience a recession) *Most analysts don't believe the economy will slide into recession.*

plunge into recession (=start to experience a deep recession) *The US is about to plunge into recession.*

be hit by a recession (=be badly affected by it) *Rural areas have been hardest hit by the recession.*

come out of a recession *It could take a long time for the country to come out of the recession.*

survive/weather a recession (=continue to exist during one) *Many small businesses will not survive the recession.*

cause/trigger a recession *Rising oil prices help to fuel inflation and cause a recession.*

pull a country/economy out of recession *The budget is intended to pull Britain out of recession.*

PHRASES

be in the middle/midst of a recession *We are in the midst of a world recession.*

be in the depths of recession (=be badly affected by a recession) *The country is in the depths of recession.*

the beginning/end of the recession *The Chancellor is confident that we will see the end of the recession in the next few months.*

recipe *n*

a set of instructions for cooking a particular type of food

ADJECTIVES

an old/classic/traditional recipe *The dish is based on a traditional French recipe.*

a delicious/tasty recipe *The book is packed with delicious recipes.*

a good recipe *Do you know a good recipe for fish pie?*

a family recipe *This is an old family recipe.*

a secret recipe *The company uses a secret recipe to make its cookies.*

VERBS

follow a recipe *She followed the recipe exactly.*

use a recipe *I always use the same recipe.*

invent/devise/come up with a recipe *The recipe was invented by a French chef.*

adapt a recipe *Vegetarians can adapt this recipe by omitting the bacon and adding cheese.*

be made to/from a recipe *The sauce is made to an old recipe.*

the recipe says *The recipe says bake for 25 minutes.*

NOUNS + recipe

a cake/soup/sauce etc recipe *What is your favourite cake recipe?*

recipe + NOUNS

a recipe book *This recipe book contains lots of ideas for desserts.*

PREPOSITIONS

a recipe for sth *She promised to give me a recipe for the cake.*

reckless *adj* THESAURUS careless

recognize (*also* recognise *BrE*) *v*

1 to know who someone is or what something is, especially because you have seen or heard them before

> **Grammar**
> This meaning of **recognize** is not used in the progressive. Don't say 'I am recognizing him.' Say **I recognize him.**

ADVERBS

recognize sb/sth immediately/instantly *I hadn't seen her for ten years, but I recognized her immediately.*

PHRASES

recognize sb from sb's description (=know who someone is because someone else has told you what they look like) *A police officer recognized the man from the victim's description, and arrested him.*

I didn't recognize sb in sth *Rachel, I didn't recognize you in your nurse's uniform.*

2 to accept that something is true, important, or of a high standard

ADVERBS

be widely/generally recognized (=by many people) *It is now widely recognized that eating a lot of salt is bad for your health.*

be internationally/nationally recognized *Professor Thamer is internationally recognized as an expert in the field of oceanography.*

be universally recognized (=everywhere) *Monitoring changes in the environment is universally recognized as being of great importance.*

be fully recognized *The problem of child neglect is only now being fully recognized.*

recommend *v*

1 to say that something or someone is good, or suggest them for a particular purpose or job

ADVERBS

highly recommend sth/sb *It's a great book – I highly recommend it.*

definitely/certainly recommend sth/sb *We would definitely recommend visiting the Golden Temple.*

thoroughly recommend sth/sb *Overall I can thoroughly recommend this film to anyone with an interest in space travel.*

personally recommend sth/sb (=from your own personal experience) *Are there any hair-colouring products you can personally recommend?*

heartily recommend sth/sb (=strongly and enthusiastically – a rather formal use) *This is a book I heartily recommend to all hillwalkers.*

PREPOSITIONS

recommend sb/sth to sb *One of my friends recommended the place to me.*

recommend sb/sth for a job/position *I have decided to recommend you for the position of senior tutor.*

PHRASES

I can recommend sb/sth *I can recommend the mixed vegetable curry – it's really good.*

sb/sth comes highly recommended (=someone or something has been recommended to you) *His nurse was an efficient woman who came highly recommended.*

2 to advise someone to do something, especially because you have special knowledge of a situation or subject

> **Grammar**
> This meaning of **recommend** is used with **(that)**: *The doctor* ***recommended that*** *he should lose some weight.*

ADVERBS

strongly/highly recommend sth *We strongly recommend that you get legal advice.*

recommendation *n*

1 official advice given to someone about what to do

ADJECTIVES

the main/key recommendation *One of the main recommendations in the report is more parental involvement in education.*

specific/detailed recommendations *We made a number of specific recommendations for improving women's health.*

R

VERBS

make a recommendation *The inspectors will make their recommendations to the Environment Secretary.*

accept/approve/adopt a recommendation *The president accepted the report's recommendations.*

reject/ignore a recommendation *Officers rejected a recommendation that cameras be installed in the building.*

implement recommendations *We will implement the recommendations of the Woolf Report to improve prison conditions.*

PREPOSITIONS

recommendations for sth *The committee made several recommendations for change.*

recommendations on sth *The doctor had given him some recommendations on diet.*

on sb's recommendation *The decision was made on the recommendation of the panel.*

2 a suggestion to someone that they should choose a particular person or thing that you think is very good

ADJECTIVES

a glowing recommendation (=one saying that someone or something is very good) *She hadn't expected to be given such a glowing recommendation.*

a personal recommendation *Many people rely on personal recommendations when looking for a plumber.*

VERBS

give sb a recommendation *He gave me some recommendations on the best places to eat.*

have any recommendations (=have something or someone that you recommend) *I'm looking for somewhere exciting to go on holiday – do you have any recommendations?*

PREPOSITIONS

at/on sb's recommendation *On John's recommendation, we stayed at the Grange Hotel.*

record[1] *n*

1 a song, a set of songs, or a piece of music by someone, which is made available for people to buy

ADJECTIVES/NOUNS + record

a pop/jazz/blues etc record *Dylan wrote some of the greatest pop records of all time.*

sb's favourite record *BrE*, **sb's favorite record** *AmE*: *My favourite Beatles record is 'Strawberry Fields Forever'.*

sb's latest record *Have you heard Adele's latest record?*

sb's best record *Amy Winehouse's best record was 'Back to Black'.*

a hit record (=one that is very popular and sells a lot) *The Rolling Stones had dozens of hit records in the 1960s and 70s.*

a number one record (=the most popular record) *The number one record in the charts this week is by a young Irish band.*

a solo record (=by one person) *Gallagher left the band and released his own solo record.*

VERBS

make a record *The singer made over 40 records in his lifetime.*

produce a record (=be in charge of making it and deciding how it sounds) *Her latest record was produced by Mark Ronson.*

release/put out a record (=make it available for people to buy) *The record has sold more than a million copies since it was released.*

sell a record *The Velvet Underground didn't sell a lot of records, but they had a big influence on other groups.*

listen to/hear a record *Whenever I listen to his records, they always make me feel good.*

record + NOUNS

a record collection *He has an amazing record collection.*

a record company/label *The band signed a deal with an American record label.*

2 information about something that is written down, stored on computer etc, so that it can be looked at in the future

ADJECTIVES

a detailed record *He kept a detailed record of his experiments.*

official records *This has been the wettest winter since official records began.*

a written record *The earliest written record of diamond cutting comes from Antwerp in 1550.*

an accurate record *It's important to keep an accurate record of the amount of money you have spent.*

a permanent record *You will have a permanent record of your work.*

confidential records *The file contained confidential student records.*

historical records *The town is mentioned in historical records as far back as 1128.*

medical/health records *I don't want other people looking at my medical records.*

financial records *The company's financial records show that it made a small profit last year.*

public records (=records of births, deaths etc, that the public are allowed to look at) *He found the information while examining public records.*

NOUNS + record

hospital/school/court records *School records show that he was often late.*

patient/student records *Patient records are kept on computer.*

police records *There was no evidence to link him with the crime, according to police records.*

VERBS

keep a record (*also* **maintain a record** *formal*): *Teachers keep a record of students' progress.*

make/compile a record *He started compiling a record of all cadets who had taken part in the training.*

place/put sth on record (=officially say something or write it down) *I wish to put on record my objection to the scheme.*

examine records *Researchers examined the clinical records of patients with lung cancer.*

records show/indicate sth *Official records show that 44 businesses have stopped trading in the last 12 months.*

PREPOSITIONS

according to records *According to official records, five people were killed last year near that road junction.*

a record of sth *Keep a record of the money you spend.*

PHRASES

the biggest/highest etc on record *Last summer was one of the hottest on record.*

sth is a matter of public record *formal* (=something that has been written down so that anyone can know it) *His salary is a matter of public record.*

have access to records (=be able to look at them) *Every citizen has the right to access their medical records.*

3 the facts about how good, bad etc someone or something has been in the past

ADJECTIVES

a good/excellent record *He had a good record as a soldier.*

a poor/bad/appalling record *Some countries have a poor record on human rights.*

an impressive record *She had an impressive record of achievements as a tennis player.*

an unblemished record (=with no bad parts) *Bates had an unblemished record during forty years of service.*

a proven record (=shown to be true) *This management method has a proven record of success.*

a long record of sth *He had a long record of gambling and crime.*

> If someone has a **criminal record**, they have been guilty of committing crimes in the past.

NOUNS + record

a safety record *The safety record of today's aircraft is excellent.*

an attendance record *Some students at the school have a poor attendance record.*

VERBS

have a good/bad etc record *The drug has an excellent safety record.*

PREPOSITIONS

sb's record on sth *She criticized the government's record on the environment.*

a record of (doing) sth *Spencer had a record of violence and drugs offences.*

a record in sth *He has a long record in football management.*

sb's/sth's record as sth *His record as prime minister has not been that impressive.*

4 the fastest speed, longest distance, the highest or lowest amount etc that has ever been achieved or reached, especially in sport

ADJECTIVES/NOUNS + record

a world record *The team set a new world record in the 400 metre relay.*

an Olympic record *He won a gold medal and broke the Olympic record by 44 seconds.*

a British/American etc record *Jones finished the race in 9.93 seconds, a new British record.*

an all-time record (=the best or highest ever) *The price of oil has hit an all-time record.*

an unbeaten record (=one in which you have never been defeated) *Hodgson is hoping to maintain his unbeaten record.*

VERBS

hold a record (=have it) *Davies holds the record for most points in a season.*

set a record (=achieve it for the first time) *The twenty-year-old set a new British record of 44.47 seconds.*

break/beat a record (=do better or be greater than an existing record) *He broke the world record twice.*

smash/shatter a record (=beat it easily) *She smashed the record by a massive 28 seconds.*

equal a record (*also* **tie a record** *AmE*) (=do as well as the record) *Woods equalled the course record and finished well ahead of all the other players.*

maintain/retain a record *The athlete maintained his record in the 100 metres with an excellent race on Saturday.*

a record stands (=is not beaten) *His record stood for 42 years.*

record + NOUNS

the record holder *The Jamaican athlete is the world record holder in the 100 metres.*

a record attempt (=an attempt to break a record) *The runner is planning to make another record attempt next month.*

the record books (=used in phrases meaning that someone or something holds the record for something) *The gallery is in the record books for paying the highest price for a painting.*

PREPOSITIONS

a record for (doing) sth *The museum set a new record for visitor numbers last year.*

record² v

1 to put information on paper or store it in a computer so that it can be looked at in the future

ADVERBS

record sth daily/monthly etc *The patients' symptoms were recorded daily.*

record sth carefully *He carefully recorded everything he observed.*

record sth accurately *The weights must be recorded accurately.*

record sth meticulously (=very carefully and accurately) *He kept a journal in which he meticulously recorded every detail of his daily life.*

record sth faithfully (=accurately, not changing anything) *I faithfully recorded his words in my notes.*

2 to store sounds or moving images

ADVERBS

record sth secretly *FBI agents had secretly recorded their conversation.*

PREPOSITIONS

record sth on tape/video/film etc *All telephone calls were recorded on tape.*

record³ adj

better, greater, lower, worse etc than ever before

record + NOUNS

a record number/level/time etc *Pollution in the lake has reached record levels.*

a record high/low *The stock market reached a record high on August 21st.*

a record year *Last year was a record year for the company.*

record profits/sales *Many airlines have enjoyed record profits this year.*

a record crowd *The event attracted record crowds.*

recover Ac v

to get better after an illness, accident, shock etc

ADVERBS

completely/fully recover *He has still not fully recovered from his injuries.*

slowly/gradually recover *Maria is slowly recovering from the shock of discovering that she has a brother she has never met.*

soon recover *She soon recovered and was able to leave hospital.*

never recover *They never recovered from the death of their child.*

recover enough/sufficiently *By April, I had recovered sufficiently to return to work.*

PREPOSITIONS

recover from sth *He's in hospital, recovering from a heart attack.*

recovery Ac n

1 the process of getting better after an illness, injury, or medical operation

ADJECTIVES

a full/complete recovery *She was severely injured but made a full recovery.*

a good/satisfactory recovery *He is making a good recovery from a knee injury.*

a remarkable/amazing/miraculous recovery *Doctors have been amazed at her remarkable recovery.*

a speedy/quick/swift recovery *We wish him a speedy recovery.*

a slow recovery *His recovery was slow, but eventually he was able to walk again.*

VERBS

make a recovery *Doctors expect him to make a full recovery.*

speed (up) sb's recovery (=make them recover more quickly) *She believes that a holiday would speed my recovery.*

aid (sb's) recovery (=help someone to recover) *Gentle exercise can aid recovery.*

PREPOSITIONS

recovery from sth *Rossi made an amazing recovery from injury.*

PHRASES

a sign of recovery *The first sign of recovery came when he opened his eyes.*

2 the process of returning to a normal condition after a period of difficulty, especially financial or economic difficulty

ADJECTIVES

economic recovery *Europe is showing signs of economic recovery.*

a slow recovery *A slow recovery in the hotel market is likely to hold back the company's profits.*

VERBS

make/stage a recovery *The Turkish economy has staged a spectacular recovery.*

PHRASES

a sign of recovery *The US economy was showing signs of recovery.*

recycle v

to put used objects or materials through a special process so that they can be used again

NOUNS

recycle glass/plastic/paper *New techniques for recycling plastics are being introduced.*

recycle bottles/cans *We take all our bottles to be recycled.*

recycle rubbish/waste *The government is launching a campaign to encourage people to recycle their household waste.*

PHRASES

recycle more *We need to encourage people recycle more.*

recycling facilities (=places where you can leave things to be recycled) *Are there enough recycling facilities in your city?*

a recycling plant *The company has two advanced fridge recycling plants, capable of recycling one million refrigerators each year.*

> If something can be recycled, you say that it is **recyclable**: *The bags are made from **recyclable** plastic.* If it cannot be recycled, you say that is **non-recyclable**: *Firms are being encouraged to reduce the amount of **non-recyclable** packaging.*

red *adj, n*

1 the colour of blood

TYPES OF RED

bright red *She was wearing bright red lipstick.*

dark/deep red *He gave her a single deep red rose.*

rich red (=a dark strong red) *The study walls are a rich red.*

fiery/flaming red (=a strong bright red) *The leaves turn fiery red in autumn.*

brilliant/vivid red *Brilliant red geraniums stood in pots outside the house.*

blood red *In winter there were blood red berries on the holly bushes.*

cherry red *He bought a cherry red guitar.*

> You can also use **crimson** to describe something that is deep red, or **scarlet** to describe something that is bright red.

PREPOSITIONS

in red (=in red clothes or red ink) *You look good in red.* | *The word 'Urgent' was underlined in red.*

PHRASES

a shade of red *The carpet was a lovely shade of red.*

2 if you go red, your face becomes bright pink, especially because you are embarrassed or angry

TYPES OF RED

deep/bright red *When he said she looked nice, she went bright red.*

(as) red as a beetroot *BrE*, **red as a beet** *AmE* (=a very deep red colour) *The boy's face was as red as a beetroot.*

VERBS

go/turn red (=become red) *He went red when he realized what he'd said.*

PHRASES

red with embarrassment/anger etc *His face was red with anger.*

reduce *v*

to make something smaller or less in size, amount, or price

NOUNS

reduce the number/amount/level of sth *They have reduced the number of accidents by half.*

reduce the size of sth *There are plans to reduce the size of the army.*

reduce costs/prices *To reduce costs, libraries will open for fewer hours.*

reduce the risk of sth *There is evidence that eating less red meat can reduce the risk of a heart attack.*

reduce the chances/likelihood of sth (=make something less likely to happen) *Smoking during pregnancy reduces the chances of having a healthy baby.*

reduce the need for sth/to do sth *We are hoping that the new public transport policy will reduce the need to use cars.*

reduce the time (it takes to do sth) *The airline has reduced the time it takes to travel to Europe.*

reduce demand *The economic crisis has reduced demand for oil.*

reduce emissions/pollution *Governments need to act to reduce emissions of greenhouse gases.*

reduce crime/unemployment/poverty *To reduce crime, we need to address the root cause.*

reduce stress/tension/pain *The plant can help to reduce stress and anxiety.*

ADVERBS

greatly/substantially/considerably reduce sth (=by a large amount) *It is hoped that the new road will substantially reduce traffic congestion in the town.*

significantly reduce sth *Taking exercise significantly reduces your risk of developing heart disease.*

dramatically/drastically reduce sth (=suddenly and by a very large amount) *They are committed to drastically reducing the size and cost of government.*

sharply reduce sth (=by a very large amount) *Medical progress has sharply reduced death rates.*

gradually reduce sth *The aim is to gradually reduce the number of troops in the area.*

PREPOSITIONS

reduce sth from sth to sth *The new bridge should reduce travelling time from 50 minutes to 15 minutes.*

reduce sth to sth *All the shirts were reduced to £10.*

reduce sth by half/50%/25 points etc *The workforce has been reduced by half.*

THESAURUS: reduce

cut
cost | **price** | **time** | **jobs** | **wages** | **taxes** | **spending** | **pollution** | **emissions** | **the budget** | **the deficit** | **the number of sth** | **the amount of sth**
to reduce something, especially by a large amount. **Cut** sounds more informal than **reduce**:
Companies are always looking for ways to cut costs. | *The airline says it has cut the price of tickets by 20%.* | *The new service will cut the journey time to under 2 hours.* | *We need to cut carbon emissions by 50%.* | *The new buses will cut the amount of air pollution.*

lower
price | **risk** | **value** | **temperature** | **taxes** | **limit** | **age**
to reduce something. **Lower** sounds rather formal:
Stopping smoking helps to lower the risk of heart disease. | *The speed limit was lowered to 20 miles per hour.* | *The voting age was lowered to 18.*

R

bring sth down
inflation | **unemployment** | **interest rates** | **cost** | **wages** | **price** | **the number of sth** | **the level of sth**
to reduce something. **Bring sth down** is less formal than **lower**:
The government wants to bring down inflation. | *The company is trying to bring its costs down.* | *Greater competition will help to bring down electricity prices.*

slash *informal*
price | **cost** | **taxes** | **spending** | **budget** | **interest rates** | **the number of sth**
to reduce an amount or price by a very large amount – used especially in newspapers and advertisements:
Prices slashed for one week only! | *California was slashing its budget for libraries and parks to save money.*

cut sth back
budget | **production** | **spending**
to reduce the amount of something – used especially about people deciding to spend less, do less, or use less of something:
The education budget has been cut back again. | *They **cut back** production **drastically** because sales were falling* (=reduced by a very large amount). | *He wants Congress to cut back defense spending.* | *I need to **cut back on** my workload.*

downsize
company | **government** | **workforce** | **operations**
to reduce the number of people employed in order to reduce costs:
He downsized his company and made it more profitable. | *The company is planning to downsize its European operations.*

relieve/ease
pain | **suffering** | **pressure** | **stress** | **tension** | **boredom** | **monotony**
to make pain or feelings less unpleasant:
The drug is used to relieve pain. | *They hired new staff in order to relieve the pressure on their employees.* | *A joke can help to ease the tension.*

alleviate *formal*
pain | **poverty** | **suffering** | **problem** | **situation** | **symptoms**
to reduce pain or suffering, or make a problem less serious:
She was given morphine to alleviate the pain. | *The programme is aimed at alleviating poverty.* | *The new road was supposed to alleviate the traffic problem.*

ANTONYMS **reduce → increase[1] (2)**

reduction *n*

a decrease in the size, price, or amount of something, or the act of decreasing something

ADJECTIVES

a significant reduction (=large and noticeable) *There has been a significant reduction in the number of accidents.*

a substantial/considerable reduction (=large enough to have an effect or be important) *Some people want a substantial reduction in taxes, because it will help to stimulate the economy.*

a big/large reduction *Changing from cars to public transport will lead to a large reduction in air pollution.*

a massive/huge reduction (=very large) *New technology has led to a massive reduction in the number of staff needed.*

a dramatic/drastic reduction (=surprisingly large) *There was a dramatic reduction in crime.*

a sharp reduction (=large and quick) *The company reported a sharp reduction in sales.*

a small/slight reduction *You can get a small reduction in price if you buy more than ten tickets.*

a gradual reduction *There has been a gradual reduction in the number of new cases of the disease.*

a 10%/40% etc reduction *The new speed limit led to a 50 percent reduction in deaths in the area.*

VERBS

make a reduction *Significant reductions are being made in the defense budget.*

achieve a reduction *A combination of diet and exercise can help you achieve a substantial reduction in weight.*

see/experience a reduction *Some police forces have seen a 40% reduction in crime.*

offer a reduction (=sell something for less

than the usual price) *The hotel is offering a reduction on stays of three nights or more.*

get a reduction (=buy something for less than the usual price) *You get a 10% reduction if you buy four or more tickets.*

NOUNS + reduction

a price/cost reduction *Stores are advertising big price reductions to attract customers away from their competitors.*

debt reduction *The government wants to focus on debt reduction.*

crime/poverty reduction *It is too early to say if efforts at crime reduction have been successful.*

PREPOSITIONS

a reduction in sth *There has been a reduction in the number of deaths due to drink-driving.*

a reduction on sth (=a reduction in the cost of something you buy) *The restaurant is offering a 20% reduction on all meals.*

a reduction of 10%/$5 etc *The sale is now on with reductions of 50% on all winter clothes.*

THESAURUS: reduction

fall/drop, decline, reduction, cut → **decrease**[1]

redundant *adj BrE*

if someone is made redundant, they lose their job

VERBS

make sb redundant (from a company/job) *The company made a quarter of its staff redundant. | He was made redundant from his last job.*

become redundant *I was quite well-off before I became redundant.*

NOUNS

redundant workers/employees/staff *Some redundant workers are planning to retrain.*

re-elect *v* THESAURUS ▸ **vote**[1]

reference *n*

part of something you say or write in which you mention a person or thing

ADJECTIVES

frequent/constant/repeated references *He makes frequent references to Abraham Lincoln in his speeches.*

an occasional reference *There are occasional references to the situation in Europe at the time the book was written.*

a direct/explicit/specific reference *The title of the film is a direct reference to Shakespeare.*

a brief reference *There is a brief reference to him in the introduction.*

a clear reference *These comments were a clear reference to the war.*

a veiled/oblique reference (=one that is not direct, often when you are criticizing someone) *He added, in an oblique reference to the US, that "some countries could do more to help".*

an apparent reference (=used when saying who or what you think someone is referring to) *Her remarks were an apparent reference to a famous murder case.*

a passing reference (=a quick reference that you make while you are talking about something else) *The other scientists' work received no more than a passing reference in his talk.*

VERBS

make reference to sth *Official reports made no reference to the incident.*

PREPOSITIONS

a reference to sth *There are a lot of references to nature in Hughes's poems.*

in a reference to sb/sth *In a reference to recent events, the president said that the US was ready to deal with any terrorist threat.*

referendum *n*

a vote by all the people who live somewhere, in order to decide something

ADJECTIVES

a national referendum *The future of the monarchy should be determined in a national referendum.*

VERBS

hold a referendum *They want to hold a referendum on independence as soon as possible.*

vote in a referendum *Only 28 percent of the people voted in the referendum.*

win/lose a referendum *The prime minister is confident of winning the referendum.*

put/submit sth to a referendum (=ask people to vote to decide something) *The proposals will be put to a referendum.*

call for a referendum (=say that there should be one) *He called for a referendum to decide the future of the island.*

referendum + NOUNS

a referendum campaign *The referendum campaign had been fiercely fought by both sides.*

PREPOSITIONS

a referendum on sth *I think there should be a referendum on the death penalty.*

by (a) referendum *A new constitution was approved by referendum in December 1979.*

in a referendum *The reforms were rejected in a referendum.*

refinery *n* THESAURUS ▸ **factory**

R

reflection *n*

1 an image that you can see in a mirror, a glass, or water

VERBS

see sb's/sth's reflection *You could see the reflection of the moon in the lake.*

look at your reflection *I looked at my reflection in the mirror.*

examine/study your reflection *She stopped to examine her reflection.*

admire your reflection (=look at it and think you look good) *He admired his reflection in a shop window as he passed.*

PREPOSITIONS

a reflection in sth *He could see his reflection in the water.*

2 something that shows what something else is like, or that is a sign of a particular situation

ADJECTIVES

an accurate/true reflection *These reports were not an accurate reflection of people's attitudes.*

a fair reflection (=reasonable and right) *The score was 4–1, which was a fair reflection of the difference between the teams.*

a direct reflection *This child's behaviour is a direct reflection of its parents' behaviour.*

a sad reflection *The fact that nobody stopped to help her is a sad reflection on society.*

PREPOSITIONS

a reflection of sth *His speech was an accurate reflection of the public mood.*

a reflection on sb/sth *A student's grades are not always a reflection on the teacher.*

reform[1] *n*

a change or changes made to a system or organization in order to improve it

> **Grammar**
> **Reform** can be used as a countable noun: *a program of political **reforms***, or an uncountable noun: *the need for political **reform***.

ADJECTIVES

political/economic/social/legal reform *The prime minister has promised to push ahead with economic reform.*

a major reform *He called for a major reform of the drug laws.*

radical reform (=very big and important changes) *The government adopted a policy of radical reform.*

fundamental reform (=changes to the most basic and important parts of something) *Ministers are demanding fundamental reform of the EU's agricultural policy.*

far-reaching/sweeping/wide-ranging reforms (=that affect many things or have a great effect) *The new government began a series of far-reaching reforms.*

a proposed reform *Local councillors are angry about the proposed reforms.*

democratic/constitutional reform *He stressed that democratic reform could not be achieved overnight.*

electoral reform (=of the voting system) *The new government promised to look at electoral reform.*

NOUNS + reform

tax reform *The proposals for tax reform met strong resistance.*

education/healthcare/welfare reform *Teachers say the government's education reforms are being pushed through too quickly.*

prison reform *Elizabeth Fry campaigned in the 1800s for prison reform.*

VERBS

make/carry out reforms *Reforms were made to the healthcare system.*

introduce reforms *The new government plans to introduce political reforms.*

push through reforms (=make them happen as soon as you can) *He has failed to push through much-needed economic reforms.*

implement reforms (=carry out planned reforms) *Much will depend on how local managers implement the reforms.*

call for/demand reform *Citizens demanded reform of the country's police force.*

announce reforms *Ms Howard announced sweeping reforms of the tax system.*

support reform *Most voters support the reforms.*

oppose reform *The armed forces will oppose any reforms to the constitution.*

reform + NOUNS

a reform programme *BrE*, **a reform program** *AmE*: *The reform programme will cut the rail workforce by 15%.*

PREPOSITIONS

reform of sth *A reform of the legal system is much needed.*

PHRASES

a package/programme of reforms *A package of reforms was approved by the National Assembly on 12 April.*

sth is in need of reform *The criminal justice system is in need of reform.*

> **THESAURUS: reform**
> alteration, reform, shift, swing, fluctuation, transformation, revolution, shake-up, U-turn → **change[2]**

reform[2] *v*

to change something in order to improve it, especially a law or system

R

ADVERBS

completely/totally reform sth *The health care system needs to be completely reformed.*

radically reform sth (=involving big and important changes) *The Dutch government intends to radically reform the country's existing system of road tax.*

drastically reform sth (=in an extreme and sudden way) *This law was designed to drastically reform the credit card industry and to protect consumers.*

fundamentally reform sth (=involving the most basic and important parts of something) *Parliament must be fundamentally reformed.*

PHRASES

attempts to reform sth *This chapter deals with the social security system and attempts to reform it.*

the need to reform sth *Recent political debate has focussed on the need to reform the civil service.*

THESAURUS: reform

alter, adapt, adjust, turn sth up/down, reform, revise, restructure, transform, revolutionize, distort, twist, misrepresent → **change[1] (2)**

refugee *n*

someone who has been forced to leave their country, especially during a war, or for political or religious reasons

ADJECTIVES

a political refugee *He is a political refugee who has reason to fear persecution.*

a genuine refugee *They were accepted as genuine refugees and granted permission to stay.*

VERBS

refugees flee sth/somewhere *More than 7,000 refugees have fled the fighting. | Thousands of refugees fled south.*

refugees pour/flood/stream somewhere (=go there in large numbers) *Refugees began pouring across the border.*

refugees arrive *Refugees were arriving in Kenya at the rate of 2,800 a day.*

accept/take in refugees *The government has said it will accept around 4,000 refugees.*

refugee + NOUNS

a refugee camp *The family are now living in a refugee camp in Pakistan.*

a refugee problem/crisis *The civil war has created an enormous refugee crisis on the border.*

refugee children *Many British families took in refugee children.*

refugee status *They did not qualify for refugee status.*

PREPOSITIONS

a refugee from sth *Her father was a refugee from the war in Afghanistan.*

PHRASES

a flood/influx of refugees (=the sudden arrival of a large number of refugees) *The flood of refugees is creating problems for neighbouring countries.*

refund *n*

an amount of money you have paid that is given back to you

ADJECTIVES

a full refund *If the show is cancelled, you will get a full refund.*

a partial refund (=of part of your money) *Since the train was an hour late, you are entitled to a partial refund.*

VERBS

ask for a refund/claim a refund (*also* **request a refund** *formal*): *Fill in this form to claim a refund.*

demand a refund *The customer was furious and demanded a refund.*

give sb a refund *The company agreed to give him a refund of $20.*

make a refund *They agreed to make refunds to customers whose internet service had been interrupted.*

offer sb a refund *You should have been offered a refund.*

get/receive/obtain a refund *Customers who return faulty shoes will get a refund.*

be entitled to a refund (=you have a right to ask for one) *If the goods are faulty, you are entitled to a refund.*

NOUNS + refund

a cash refund *I was given a voucher, not a cash refund.*

a tax refund *They will get a tax refund of $1,600 this year.*

PREPOSITIONS

a refund for sth *Does the airline offer refunds for canceled flights?*

a refund on sth *I tried to get a refund on the ticket.*

a refund of sth *You are entitled to a full refund of your money.*

refusal *n*

the act of saying firmly that you will not do, give, or accept something

ADJECTIVES

a stubborn/obstinate/wilful refusal (=one that other people think is unreasonable) *Her stubborn refusal to admit the truth made him angry.*

a blunt refusal (=honest and direct but likely

R

to upset someone) *They were offended by his blunt refusal to help.*
a polite refusal *My request was met with a polite refusal.*
a flat/outright/point-blank refusal (=definite, direct, and without giving a reason) *We were met with a point-blank refusal to discuss the issue.*
a steadfast refusal (=continuing refusal, even though other people try to persuade you) *The company's steadfast refusal to apologize shocked many people.*
continued/persistent/repeated refusal *The government's continued refusal to hold an inquiry raises suspicions.*

VERBS

meet with a refusal (=be refused) *Her request for help met with a refusal.*

PREPOSITIONS

refusal of sth *Her friends couldn't understand her refusal of their offer.*

refuse *v*

to say that you will not do, accept, or give something

Grammar
Refuse is usually followed by an infinitive: *She **refused to leave** without him.*

ADVERBS

stubbornly refuse *He stubbornly refused to pay the fine.*
politely refuse *He politely refused their invitation to lunch.*
adamantly refuse *formal* (=in a determined way) *They are still adamantly refusing to release the data to the general public.*
steadfastly refuse (=continue to refuse to do something, even though people try to persuade you) *She steadfastly refused to comment on the situation.*
consistently/repeatedly refuse (=many times) *Politicians have consistently refused to listen to us.*
flatly/categorically refuse (=in a firm and definite way) *He flatly refused to tell me anything.*
refuse point-blank (=directly and without explanation) *I refused point-blank to let him in.*
simply refuse (=used especially when you are shocked by someone's behaviour) *Some children simply refuse to do what they're told.*

NOUNS

refuse sb permission *He was refused permission to build an extension to his house.*
refuse a request/demand *His boss refused his request for some time off work.*
refuse an offer *How could you refuse the offer of a free drink?*
refuse an invitation *He was very shy and refused all invitations to go out.*
refuse an application *Their application to build a house on the site was refused.*
refuse sb entry/access/admission *Dobrovsky was refused entry because his visa had expired.*
refuse treatment/food *She later died after refusing medical treatment.*

PHRASES

sb can hardly refuse (=it would be unreasonable or very difficult to refuse) *The company offered me $100,000 a year, and I felt that I could hardly refuse.*

regard *n*

1 respect and admiration for someone or something

ADJECTIVES

high/great/considerable regard (=you think someone or something is good) *The players have a considerable regard for their manager.*
low regard (=you do not think someone or something is good) *He has a very low regard for his opponent.*
mutual regard (=which people feel for each other) *There seems to have been a genuine mutual regard between the two leaders.*

VERBS

have a high/low etc regard for sb/sth (=you think they are very good, bad etc) *I have the highest regard for my colleagues.*
hold sb/sth in high/low etc regard (=you think they are very good, bad etc) *His work is held in high regard by many scientists.*

PREPOSITIONS

regard for sb/sth *She had a particular regard for Eliot because of his expertise.*

2 attention or consideration that is shown towards someone or something

ADJECTIVES

due/proper regard *formal* (=giving proper attention to something) *The aim is to get the job done as cheaply as possible, with due regard to high standards.*
little regard (=not enough regard) *He worked too hard, and had too little regard for his own health.*
scant regard (=very little regard) *Should we sell arms to countries who show scant regard for human rights?*
no regard *The decision was made with no regard for the families still living on the estate.*

VERBS

have no/little regard for sth *Some drivers have no regard for other road users.*
show regard for sth *She showed no regard for her mother's feelings.*

pay regard to sth *The architect who designed the building paid too little regard to its function.*

have regard to sth *formal: The court must have particular regard to the needs of the child.*

PREPOSITIONS

without regard to sth *All students must have access to quality education without regard to wealth or social class.*

region Ac *n*

a large area of a country or of the world

ADJECTIVES

the whole/entire region *There was heavy snow throughout the entire region.*

the northern/southern etc region *The animal lives mainly in the northern region of the country.*

surrounding regions *There was also some flooding in surrounding regions.*

a neighbouring region *BrE*, **a neighboring region** *AmE* (=next to a country) *The war might spread to neighbouring regions.*

the central region *They live in the mountainous central region of Italy.*

coastal regions *The storm caused most damage in coastal regions.*

a remote region (=far away) *The family lives in a remote region of China.*

NOUNS + region

a border region *Enemy troops continued to occupy the border region.*

a desert region *These plants grow in the desert regions of North America.*

PREPOSITIONS

in a region *These conditions are found particularly in the southern regions of the country.*

across/throughout a region *The problem is affecting farms throughout the entire region.*

VERBS

live in a region (*also* **inhabit a region** *formal*): *The film is about the wildlife that inhabits the region.*

THESAURUS: region

region, zone, district, neighbourhood, suburb, quarter, slum, ghetto → **area (1)**

register[1] *n* an official list or record

ADJECTIVES

a national register *The building is listed on the National Register of Historic Places.*

a public register *If you are worried about your name appearing on the public register, you should contact your local council.*

an official register *There is no official register of ancient trees in the UK.*

a central register *The central register of births, deaths, and marriages was begun on 1st July 1837.*

the electoral register (=the list of people who can vote) *His name was missing from the electoral register.*

VERBS

keep/maintain a register *Every company must keep a register of its directors.*

compile/create a register *We have compiled a register of the data we have received.*

set up a register *The council is setting up a register of people who are willing to give dogs a home.*

remove sb/sth from a register *Her name was removed from the register.*

strike sb off the register (=take someone's name off the list of people who are allowed to do a job) *The number of nurses struck off the register for professional misconduct rose by 50% last year.*

call the register *BrE* (=read out the list of the students in a class, to check if they are there) *The teacher always calls the register at the beginning of the day.*

PREPOSITIONS

a register of sb/sth *The hospital keeps a register of patients.*

on a register *The bank has more than two million private shareholders on its register.*

register[2] Ac *v*

to put your name or other information on an official list

ADVERBS

officially/formally register sth *The number of officially registered cases of the disease has gone down.*

PREPOSITIONS

register for sth *Students spend the first few days registering for courses.*

register with sb *Have you registered with a dentist yet?*

be registered as sth *The club is registered as a charity.*

register at sth *He attempted to register at the university but was turned away.*

registration Ac *n*

the act of putting your name or other details on an official list

ADJECTIVES/NOUNS + registration

online registration *Online registration has made the process much faster.*

voter registration *The aim is to increase voter registration.*

student registration *There's a new system of student registration by phone.*

registration + NOUNS

a registration form *In order to join the course, you need to fill out a registration form.*

registration documents *He didn't have all the necessary registration documents.*

registration requirements *People need clear information on registration requirements.*

a registration fee *There is a small registration fee for students.*

the registration process *The lengthy registration process is very frustrating.*

the registration deadline (=the time when you must have registered) *They've set a registration deadline of March 29th.*

VERBS

complete sb's registration *You receive the card when you complete registration.*

process sb's registration *The council failed to process my registration properly.*

apply for registration *To apply for registration, you must first complete the form.*

PREPOSITIONS

registration for sth *An official refused to accept my registration for the race.*

regret[1] *v*

to feel sorry that something has happened, especially something that you have said or done

ADVERBS

deeply/greatly regret sth *I deeply regretted what had happened.*

bitterly regret sth (=with a feeling of great sadness) *I bitterly regret my decision to leave.*

sincerely regret sth *The airline sincerely regrets any delays to passengers.*

very much regret sth *We very much regret that there will be job losses.*

instantly/immediately regret sth *I agreed to go, then instantly regretted it.*

soon regret sth *Lear soon regretted his decision.*

later regret sth *Don't rush into a decision that you may later regret.*

PHRASES

live to regret sth (=regret it in the future) *If you don't go, you may live to regret it.*

regret the fact that *The old man regretted the fact that he hadn't travelled much when he was younger.*

begin to regret sth *Ella was beginning to regret having been so rude to Carla.*

regret[2] *n*

sadness that you feel about something, especially because you wish it had not happened

ADJECTIVES

great/deep regret *I accepted his resignation with great regret.*

bitter regret (=in which you feel very unhappy) *After she left, I was filled with bitter regret.*

sb's biggest/greatest regret *Her biggest regret was not having children.*

sb's only regret *My only regret is that my parents did not live to see this day.*

sincere/genuine regret *I'd like to express my sincere regret to the staff who have lost their jobs.*

VERBS

have regrets *I have absolutely no regrets about leaving.*

express regret *The president expressed his regret at the deaths.*

PREPOSITIONS

regret at/about/over sth *I have no regrets about the decision I made.*

regret for sth *He expressed regret for the pain he had caused his wife and family.*

to sb's regret (=with the result that someone feels sad) *I lost touch with her, much to my regret.*

with/without regret *With regret, the prince and princess have decided to separate.*

PHRASES

a sense of regret *There is a sense of regret when he talks about his life.*

no regrets (at all/whatsoever) *No regrets. I made a lot of money, and it's time to find something else to do with my life.*

regular *adj*

happening every hour, every week, every month etc, usually with the same amount of time in between

NOUNS

a regular meeting/session *The company holds regular meetings with employees.*

regular exercise *It is important to take regular exercise.*

a regular visitor/visit *Father Poole had been a regular visitor every Sunday evening.*

a regular job (=not part-time or temporary) *It's time he got a regular job.*

PHRASES

at regular intervals (=every few minutes, every hour, every month etc) *Trains will run at regular intervals from 11 a.m. to 4 p.m.*

on a regular basis *We hear from him on a regular basis.*

regular as clockwork (=always at the same time) *He phones us every Sunday at six, regular as clockwork.*

sth is a regular feature of sth (=it often happens) *Wildfires are a regular feature of Australia's hot summers.*

sth is in regular use (=it is used often) *The hall is still in regular use.*

be in regular contact with sb (=you often speak or write to someone) *She says she is in regular contact with Captain Bacci.*

slow and regular *His breathing was slow and regular.*

regulation Ac *n* an official rule or order

Grammar
Often plural.

ADJECTIVES/NOUNS + regulation

strict/tough/tight regulations *The regulations surrounding the handling of nuclear waste are very strict.*

government/federal regulations *Small businesses are fed up with government regulations.*

current/existing regulations (=existing now) *Under current regulations, baby food products cannot contain salt.*

statutory regulations (=that are fixed or controlled by law) *All government agencies must meet statutory regulations on race and sex discrimination.*

safety regulations *According to the safety regulations, a qualified electrician should install the lighting.*

fire regulations (=to prevent fires) *Furniture in public buildings must comply with fire regulations.*

hygiene regulations (=to keep places clean and free from disease) *The restaurant was closed down after it failed to meet the hygiene regulations.*

planning regulations (=relating to what buildings can be built in an area) *All new houses must conform to planning regulations.*

building regulations *The height of the building is controlled by the building regulations.*

VERBS + regulation

meet/comply with/conform to a regulation (=obey it) *Hotel kitchens must comply with these regulations.*

break a regulation (*also* **violate/breach a regulation** *formal*) (=not obey it) *The penalties for breaking the regulations were severe.*

introduce/impose a regulation *The local authority is introducing new planning regulations.*

make a regulation *The agency has the power to make regulations.*

enforce a regulation (=make people obey it) *Local councils should do more to enforce existing regulations on pollution.*

change a regulation *There are plans to change the regulation because people think it is unfair.*

tighten a regulation (=make it stricter) *The president is expected to announce new efforts to tighten gun-control regulations.*

relax a regulation (=make it less strict) *He has voted in favor of relaxing environmental regulations.*

regulation + VERBS

a regulation says sth *The regulations say that the carrots should be more than 2 cm wide.*

a regulation stipulates sth (=says what must be done) *The hospital regulations stipulate minimum staffing levels.*

a regulation prevents/prohibits sth *Regulations prohibit train crews from working more than 12 hours at a time.*

a regulations applies to sth *The regulations apply to all new buildings.*

the regulations governing sth (=which control it) *There are regulations governing the safety of toys.*

PREPOSITIONS

regulations on sth *New regulations on imports were introduced.*

a regulation about/concerning sth *A regulation controlling the flow of personal information over telephones and the internet will start in February.*

a regulation against sth *I'm not sure you're allowed to make cheese without a license - there's a regulation against it.*

under regulations *Under the new regulations, all staff must have safety training.*

PHRASES

rules and regulations *She felt that the club had too many rules and regulations.*

in accordance with the regulations *formal* (=in a way that meets regulations) *Such claims will be processed in accordance with the regulations.*

reject Ac *v*

to refuse to accept, believe in, or agree with something

ADVERBS

reject sth outright (=completely) *He has not rejected the idea outright.*

totally reject sth *My client totally rejects the accusations.*

categorically/unequivocally reject sth (=in a definite way, leaving no doubt) *We categorically reject the claims made in the press.*

firmly reject sth *The British proposals were firmly rejected by other EU countries.*

flatly reject sth (=in a firm and definite way) *Ministers have flatly rejected the rebels' demands.*

unanimously reject sth (=when all members of a group reject something) *The board unanimously rejected the proposal.*

repeatedly reject sth (=reject it several times) *The government has repeatedly rejected calls for lower taxes.*

PREPOSITIONS

reject sth as... *The site has been rejected as unsuitable for a large sporting competition.*

R

related *adj*

1 things that are related are connected in some way

ADVERBS

closely related *I want to focus on a small number of closely related questions.*

strongly related *People's occupations are strongly related to their level of education.*

intimately related (=very closely related) *Learning to read and learning to write are intimately related.*

directly/indirectly related *A number of illnesses are directly related to poverty.*

loosely related (=not closely related) *The article is simply a series of loosely related ideas.*

PREPOSITIONS

related to sth *Hard work is not always related to high income.*

2 people who are related belong to the same family

ADVERBS

closely related (=brother and sister, father and son, mother and daughter etc) *Even people who are closely related can have very different tastes.*

distantly related (=not closely related, but having the same grandparents, great grandparents etc) *She is distantly related to the prime minister.*

related biologically *She calls him her father, although they are not related biologically.*

PREPOSITIONS

related to sb *I discovered that I was distantly related to Jane Austen.*

PHRASES

related by marriage *He is my brother-in-law, so we are only related by marriage.*

related by birth *People who are related by birth usually look like each other at least a little.*

relation *n*

1 the relationship between people, organizations, and countries

> **Grammar**
> Always plural in this meaning.

ADJECTIVES/NOUNS + relation

close relations *The university has close relations with local companies.*

good/friendly relations *He had begun to establish friendly relations with the other workers.*

strained relations (=not good) *The strained relations between Russia and Japan became even worse.*

race relations (=between people of different races) *Race relations are good in this area.*

industrial relations (*also* **labour relations** *BrE*, **labor relations** *AmE*) (=between managers and workers) *Industrial relations have improved, and there have been no more strikes.*

diplomatic/international/foreign relations (=between countries) *The president's visit will be good for international relations.*

community relations (=between different groups in society) *Two police officers are responsible for community relations in the area.*

customer relations (=between a company and its customers) *All staff have training in customer relations.*

public relations (=between an organization and the public) *The affair was disastrous in terms of public relations.*

VERBS

have ... relations *Britain and the US have had friendly relations for a very long time.*

enjoy good/close etc relations (=have good, close etc relations) *For years, the company enjoyed good relations with its workers.*

break off/sever relations (=end them) *The US broke off all relations with Cuba.*

establish/develop relations *The company has tried to establish relations with several universities.*

maintain relations *The Indian government wants to maintain good relations with China.*

restore/resume relations (=begin them again after they were stopped or interrupted) *Britain agreed to restore full diplomatic relations with Libya.*

improve relations *In his speech, he emphasized the need to improve relations with neighbouring countries.*

strain/sour relations (=make them less friendly) *The dispute has soured relations between the two countries.*

relations improve *Relations between us have improved significantly.*

relations deteriorate (=they get worse) *Relations deteriorated and they refused to speak to each other.*

PREPOSITIONS

relations with sb *His relations with his family were never very good.*

relations between sb (and sb) *Relations between the two countries have improved recently.*

relations among sb *There are excellent relations among the workers.*

2 a member of your family

ADJECTIVES/NOUNS + relation

a close relation (=a brother, parent, aunt etc) *Her son is her only close relation who is still alive.*

a distant relation (=one who is not close) *He was some distant relation of the King of Spain.*

a blood relation (=one related by birth not marriage) *Harry and I are not blood relations – I'm married to his brother.*

PREPOSITIONS

a relation to sb *What relation are you to Jessica?*

PHRASES

no relation (=used for saying someone is not related to another person) *Mark Knight works for Sharon Knight (no relation).*

a relation by marriage *She's a relation by marriage because she married my cousin.*

friends and relations *We miss our friends and relations in the UK.*

3 a connection between things

ADJECTIVES

a close relation *Business and technology have a close relation with each other.*

a direct relation *There is no longer a direct relation between the cost of a product and its quality.*

a possible relation *He wrote about smoking and its possible relation with lung cancer.*

a causal relation *formal* (=between one thing and the thing that causes it) *Is there a causal relation between exercise and sleep?*

PREPOSITIONS

sth's relation to sth *It's an article on emotional well-being and its relation to health.*

the relation between sth (and sth) *The relation between mind and body is important in philosophy.*

in relation to sth *formal* (=when compared with something) *Women's earnings are still low in relation to men's.*

PHRASES

have/bear no relation to sth (=not be connected to something) *These theories bear no relation to what children are really like.*

have/bear little relation to sth *The story bears little relation to historical fact.*

relationship *n*

1 the way in which people behave towards each other

ADJECTIVES/NOUNS + relationship

a good/great relationship *Over the years, we've developed a good relationship.*

a close relationship *Laura had a very close relationship with her grandmother.*

a friendly relationship (*also* **a harmonious relationship** *formal*): *My friendly relationship with Scott's family continued after his death.*

a strong relationship *Our relationship is strong enough to survive anything.*

a special relationship (=a particularly close relationship) *I did not want to risk losing this special relationship we shared.*

a supportive relationship *People who lack supportive relationships may be at risk of depression.*

a love-hate relationship (=when someone both likes and dislikes someone else) *The local people have a love-hate relationship with tourists.*

family relationships *Travelling a lot for business can strain family relationships.*

human relationships *Human relationships fascinate me.*

a personal relationship *Drinking affects personal relationships.*

a working relationship (=a relationship appropriate for people who work together) *She's a fine actress and we developed a great working relationship.*

a social relationship *He is not very good at forming social relationships.*

a business/professional relationship *Both companies want to continue their business relationship into the future.*

VERBS

have/enjoy a relationship *We've always had a good relationship with our neighbours.*

develop/form/build a relationship *By that age, children start developing relationships outside the family.*

make relationships *I found it hard to make new relationships.*

establish a relationship *A shopkeeper needs to establish a friendly relationship with his customers.*

forge a relationship (=develop a strong relationship) *We want to forge closer relationships with our allies.*

maintain a relationship *The US government is keen to maintain good relationships with all countries in the region.*

cement a relationship (=make it firm and strong) *We want to cement relationships with other clubs in the area.*

damage/undermine a relationship *We don't want to risk undermining the good relationship between different faith communities here.*

PREPOSITIONS

a relationship between sb (and sb) *The relationships between pupils and teachers are excellent.*

a relationship with sb *The company has always had a good relationship with the media.*

a relationship of trust/confidence/respect etc *It's important that a relationship of trust exists between workers and managers.*

2 the way in which things are connected and affect each other

ADJECTIVES

a close relationship *There is a close relationship between drugs and crime.*

a strong/significant relationship *Studies show a significant relationship between smoking and heart disease.*

a direct relationship *There is a direct relationship between the demand for a particular product and its price.*
an inverse relationship *formal* (= when one is great, the other is small) *There seems to be an inverse relationship between the amount of advice that a parent gives and a child's willingness to listen.*
a causal relationship *formal* (=when one thing causes another) *There is no causal relationship between the age of the mother and these birth defects.*

VERBS

have/bear a relationship (to sth) *The allegations bore no relationship to the facts.*
establish/discover a relationship (=prove that it exists) *The book tries to establish a relationship between the war and social conditions in Europe.*
explore/examine/investigate a relationship (=consider or discuss it) *The next chapter explores the relationship between China's history and its current economic success.*
there is a relationship/a relationship exists *No relationship exists between the size of the prison population and the level of crime.*
a relationship emerges (=people realize that it exists) *If we look at these figures, a close relationship emerges between work done and profit earned.*

PREPOSITIONS

a relationship to sth *I considered students' patterns of study and their relationship to exam performance.*
a relationship between sth (and sth) *In this programme, we look at the relationship between food and health.*

3 a friendship between people who love or like each other very much

ADJECTIVES

a serious/steady/long-term relationship (=one that lasts a long time) *It was her first serious relationship.*
a sexual relationship *He admitted having a sexual relationship with a patient.*
a stormy/turbulent relationship (=one that involves many arguments) *The singer had a stormy relationship with her boyfriend and they split up several times.*
a loving relationship (=in which people love each other) *They had a warm loving relationship.*

VERBS

end a relationship (*also* **break off a relationship**) *She was very upset when he ended their relationship.*
start/begin a relationship *I'm in no hurry to start another relationship.*
a relationship ends/fails (*also* **a relationship breaks up/down**) *She moved to a different city and the relationship ended soon after.*

PREPOSITIONS

a relationship with sb *She's the actress who had a relationship with the president.*
be in a relationship (=have a relationship with each other) *Even their closest friends didn't know they were in a relationship.*

relative *n* a member of your family

ADJECTIVES/NOUNS + relative

a close relative (=a brother, parent, aunt etc) *He lost several close relatives in the war.*
a distant relative *She claims to be a distant relative of the Queen.*
a blood relative (=one related by birth, not marriage) *The doctors need cells from a blood relative of the patient.*
a living/surviving relative *She has no living relatives.*
an elderly relative *He spends Sundays visiting elderly relatives.*

PHRASES

a relative by marriage *My uncle's wife is a relative by marriage.*
friends and relatives *About 35 close friends and relatives attended the wedding.*

relaxation Ac *n*

a way of resting and enjoying yourself

ADJECTIVES

total/complete relaxation *This quiet beach is the perfect place for total relaxation.*
deep relaxation *You can achieve deep relaxation by closing your eyes and listening to some gentle music.*

relaxation + NOUNS

a relaxation exercise *Relaxation exercises can help if you suffer from stress.*

VERBS

aid/promote relaxation (=help you to relax) *Many people do yoga to aid relaxation.*

PREPOSITIONS

for relaxation *I play the piano for relaxation.*

PHRASES

a state of relaxation *Meditation aims to put you into a state of relaxation.*

relaxed *adj*

feeling calm, comfortable, and not worried or annoyed

ADVERBS

totally relaxed *Yoga helps you feel totally relaxed.*
fairly/pretty relaxed *The atmosphere was fairly relaxed and everyone was in a good mood.*

VERBS

feel relaxed *I felt more relaxed after my holiday.*
appear/seem/look relaxed *At the start of the meeting she appeared confident and relaxed.*

R

NOUNS

a relaxed atmosphere/mood *The hotel has a friendly relaxed atmosphere.*

a relaxed attitude/manner/approach *The local people have a relaxed attitude to life.*

PREPOSITIONS

relaxed about sth *I think I'm more relaxed about the idea of going on stage.*

relaxing *adj* making you feel relaxed

NOUNS

a relaxing drink *They were enjoying a relaxing drink on the terrace.*

a relaxing break (*also* **a relaxing holiday** BrE, **a relaxing vacation** AmE): *The hotel is perfect for a relaxing break.*

a relaxing atmosphere *All our treatment rooms have been designed to provide a relaxing atmosphere.*

a relaxing evening/weekend *I was looking forward to a relaxing evening at home.*

a relaxing experience *Eating in a restaurant with young children is not usually a relaxing experience.*

a relaxing massage/bath *The pain can be soothed by a relaxing massage.*

a relaxing hobby *Betty finds knitting a very relaxing hobby.*

release[1] Ac *v*

1 to let someone go free, after having kept them somewhere

NOUNS

release a prisoner/hostage/captive *All the prisoners have been released.*

PREPOSITIONS

be released from sth *He was released from jail yesterday.*

PHRASES

be released on bail (=be allowed to leave prison until a legal trial, if you pay money) *He spent three months in custody before being released on bail.*

be released on parole (=be allowed to leave prison on the condition that you behave well) *She was released on parole after serving two years in jail.*

release sb unharmed *The hostages have been released unharmed.*

be released without charge (=be allowed to leave a police station without being accused of any crime) *The man was interviewed by the police but was released without charge.*

2 to make something available to the public

ADVERBS

officially/publicly release sth *I can't tell you any more until the details have been officially released.*

a newly released report/document etc *Newly released documents reveal what really happened at the meeting.*

NOUNS

release information *Police did not release any information about the man's injuries.*

release details *The company has released details of its new product range.*

release results *The results released yesterday were worse than expected.*

release figures/statistics *New figures released today show that unemployment has risen by two per cent.*

release a statement *The group released a statement denying that they were responsible for the attack.*

release a report/document *Federal investigators released a report blaming the pilot for the fatal air crash.*

release an album/DVD/movie etc *Her last hit movie was released in 2009.*

release[2] Ac *n*

the act of allowing someone to leave somewhere and be free, after being kept in a place such as a prison

ADJECTIVES

immediate release *They are demanding the immediate release of the hostages.*

early release *He may be able to apply for early release.*

unconditional release (=not limited by any demands) *The president succeeded in obtaining the unconditional release of the soldiers.*

VERBS

call for/demand sb's release *Human rights groups are calling for her release.*

order sb's release *The judge ordered the release of the two men.*

obtain/secure sb's release (=succeed in getting it) *The government attempted to secure the release of the journalist who had been put in prison.*

negotiate sb's release (=discuss it in order to reach an agreement) *He has been trying to negotiate the release of a captured soldier.*

release + NOUNS

a release date *The prisoner hasn't been given a release date yet.*

PREPOSITIONS

release from sth *After his release from prison, he went to live with his mother.*

PHRASES

be/become eligible for release (=be allowed to go free) *He will become eligible for release next year.*

relevance *n*
if something has relevance, it is directly related to what you are discussing, to your situation, or to the things that you are interested in

ADJECTIVES

great/considerable relevance *His books still have great relevance to people living today.*

special/particular relevance *They discussed issues that were of particular relevance to women.*

direct relevance *His evidence is of direct relevance to this case.*

immediate relevance (=relevance to what you are dealing with now) *In your essay you should stick to subjects that are of immediate relevance.*

little/no relevance *Young people feel that politics has little relevance to them.*

limited relevance *Her past experience only has limited relevance to her new job.*

VERBS

have relevance *These ancient stories still have relevance today.*

lose its relevance *Is religion losing its relevance to modern society?*

doubt/question the relevance of sth *People often question the relevance of studying subjects such as Latin and ancient Greek.*

PREPOSITIONS

the relevance of sth *I was not sure about the relevance of his question.*

sth's relevance to/for sb *His writings still have relevance to people who live now.*

be of relevance to sb/sth *I think this information may be of relevance to you.*

PHRASES

in order of relevance (=with the most relevant one listed first) *The websites are listed in order of relevance.*

relevant Ac *adj*
directly relating to the subject or problem being discussed or considered

ADVERBS

very/highly relevant *The lawyer argued in court that the evidence was highly relevant to the case.*

particularly/especially relevant *Protecting the environment seems particularly relevant today, when everyone is worried about global warming.*

directly relevant *She has a lot of experience which is directly relevant to her new job.*

still relevant *His words are still relevant for people living in the modern world.*

no longer relevant *Some people think that the church's teachings are no longer relevant.*

NOUNS

relevant experience *For this job you need a degree and some relevant experience.*

relevant information/facts/data/material *We have received all the relevant information.*

a relevant question *I'm not sure if that is a relevant question.*

a relevant factor *Age is a relevant factor to consider when choosing a party leader.*

the relevant authorities/body/department *You must send a copy of this document to the relevant authorities.*

PREPOSITIONS

relevant to sth *Amir has a lot of experience that is relevant to this job.*

relevant for sb *This information is particularly relevant for older people.*

THESAURUS: relevant

pertinent *formal*
directly relating to a subject or situation and important when considering it:
The court should consider ***pertinent information*** *contained in the report.* | *He asked me several very* ***pertinent questions****.* | *This issue seems* ***highly pertinent****.*

to the point
if something you say or write is to the point, it is directly connected to what is being discussed:
Your notes should be ***brief and to the point****.* | *The treatment is expensive and,* ***more to the point****, potentially dangerous.*

applicable
if something is applicable to a particular person, group, or situation, it affects them or relates to them:
These rules are ***applicable to*** *all students.*

ANTONYMS **relevant → irrelevant**

reliable Ac *adj*
someone or something that is reliable can be trusted or depended on

ADVERBS

completely/totally reliable *This method is not always completely reliable.*

very/highly/extremely reliable *The pregnancy test is highly reliable.*

fairly/reasonably reliable *The estimate is probably fairly reliable.*

sufficiently reliable (=reliable enough) *We do not have sufficiently reliable data.*

NOUNS

reliable information/data/figures etc *Patients need reliable information about the different types of treatment available.*

reliable evidence *There is no reliable evidence to support these claims.*

a reliable method/means/way/system *Schools need a reliable way of measuring students' progress.*

a reliable indicator/guide *Heart rate is the most reliable indicator of how hard your body is working.*

a reliable witness *The judge said Bates wasn't a reliable witness.*

a reliable source *The information had come from a reliable source.*

reliance Ac *n*

when someone or something is dependent on someone or something else

ADJECTIVES

great/heavy reliance *Our heavy reliance on oil is damaging the environment.*

increasing/growing reliance *Increasing reliance on convenience food means that many people do not know how to cook.*

total/exclusive/sole reliance *The child is still at the stage of total reliance on the mother.*

VERBS

place reliance on sth *You should not place too much reliance on these figures.*

increase/reduce reliance on sth *We need to reduce our reliance on carbon fuels.*

PREPOSITIONS

reliance on sb/sth *The country's reliance on foreign imports has increased.*

reliant Ac *adj*

depending a lot on someone or something for the things you need

ADVERBS

very/heavily/hugely reliant *Japan is heavily reliant on foreign energy and imports nearly all of its oil.*

totally/completely/entirely reliant *She had no money, and was totally reliant on her parents.*

overly/excessively reliant (=too reliant) *Students may become overly reliant on the internet and not use other resources.*

increasingly reliant *She became increasingly reliant on her husband.*

VERBS

become reliant *We have become very reliant on our cars.*

remain reliant *The country remains heavily reliant on tourism.*

PREPOSITIONS

reliant on sb/sth *The global economy is increasingly reliant on electronic communications and information.*

relief *n*

a feeling of comfort when something frightening, worrying, or painful has ended or has not happened

ADJECTIVES

a great/enormous/tremendous relief *It was a great relief when she returned safely.*

a welcome relief *The holiday was a welcome relief from the pressure of work.*

VERBS

come as a relief *The court's decision came as a huge relief.*

feel/experience relief *I felt nothing but relief when the exams were over.*

give/bring sb relief *It's a painful injury, but the treatment has brought me some relief.*

provide/offer (sb) relief *The cool house offered welcome relief from the blazing African sun.*

find/get relief *The illness gives her constant pain but she can get some relief by taking a warm bath.*

relief floods through sb *literary*: *When she heard he was still alive, relief flooded through her.*

NOUNS + relief

pain relief (=medical treatment that reduces pain) *She made a decision to refuse all pain relief during childbirth.*

PREPOSITIONS

a relief to sb *It was a great relief to him to see her looking so healthy.*

relief from sth *Is there any treatment that can give him relief from the pain?*

PHRASES

breathe/heave a sigh of relief *United fans breathed a huge sigh of relief as the shot went wide of the goal.*

a sense/feeling of relief *She was filled with an overwhelming sense of relief.*

what a relief *What a relief to be able to say what I really feel!*

such a relief *It's such a relief that my exams are over!*

to my relief (=used when something gives you a feeling of relief) *We arrived at the hotel, which, to my relief, was actually clean and comfortable.*

relieve *v*

to reduce someone's pain or unpleasant feelings

NOUNS

relieve pain *What's the best way of relieving back pain?*

relieve stress/tension/anxiety *They all laughed and it helped to relieve the tension.*

relieve the pressure on sb/sth *The company hired more staff to relieve the pressure on their employees.*

relieve the boredom/monotony *Listening to music can help relieve the boredom of a long flight.*

relieve the symptoms *Drinking plenty of water should help to relieve the symptoms.*

ADVERBS

relieve sth temporarily *A mild painkiller will relieve the symptoms temporarily.*

PHRASES

help (to) relieve sth *Some gentle stretching can help relieve pain in the joints.*

be designed/intended to relieve sth *These exercises are designed to relieve stiffness in the legs.*

THESAURUS: relieve

cut, lower, bring sth down, slash, cut sth back, downsize, relieve/ease, alleviate → **reduce**

relieved *adj*

feeling happy because you are no longer worried about something

ADVERBS

greatly/hugely relieved *I was greatly relieved when he agreed to lend us the money.*

extremely/immensely relieved *We were all immensely relieved when the exams were over.*

somewhat/rather relieved (=fairly relieved - often used when someone is actually very relieved) *I was somewhat relieved to hear the wine was actually £10 a bottle, not £100.*

obviously/clearly/visibly relieved *She was obviously relieved to have passed the test.*

mightily relieved (=greatly relieved) *He was mightily relieved to hear that he was not losing his job.*

VERBS

feel relieved *She was tired, and felt relieved when they all decided to go.*

sound/look relieved *When we told her the good news, she looked relieved.*

PREPOSITIONS

relieved at sth *We are relieved at the news that the arts centre is to remain open.*

religion *n*

a set of beliefs about God, and the ceremonies and customs that go with these beliefs. Also used when talking about all religions in general

ADJECTIVES/NOUNS + religion

the Christian/Jewish/Hindu etc religion *Some European philosophers rejected the Christian religion.*

a great religion *Islam is one of the world's great religions.*

the established religion *In those days, most people followed the teachings of the established religion without question.*

the dominant religion (=the one that most people belong to) *The dominant religion in the country is Buddhism.*

organized religion (=religion in which people follow the accepted beliefs and practices of the main world religions) *People began turning away from organized religion.*

orthodox religion (=which is based on the traditional beliefs and rules of a religion) *The priests want everyone to follow the teachings of orthodox religion.*

VERBS

belong to a religion *Everyone should be able to study here, no matter what religion they belong to.*

change your religion *She told her parents that she was thinking of changing her religion.*

practise your religion *BrE*, **practice your religion** *AmE* (=pray and take part in the ceremonies of your religion) *In some countries, Christians are forbidden from practising their religion.*

spread a religion *He feels his purpose in life is to spread the Christian religion.*

find religion (=start believing very strongly in a religion) *While in jail, Belmontes found religion and his attitude changed completely.*

PHRASES

freedom of religion *The US Constitution promises freedom of religion.*

followers of a religion (=people who believe in it) *We should show respect towards followers of other religions.*

religious *adj*

1 relating to religion

NOUNS

religious belief/faith *It is important to respect other people's religious beliefs.*

a religious leader *Religious leaders called for the book to be banned.*

a religious group/minority *The constitution guarantees the rights of religious minorities.*

a religious experience *He claimed that he had some kind of religious experience.*

religious education *Children receive classes in religious education at school.*

a religious ceremony *The building was used for religious ceremonies.*

religious freedom *The country has a very poor record on religious freedom and human rights.*

religious persecution/discrimination (=unkind or unfair treatment of people because of their religion) *Many people moved to America in order to escape religious persecution.*

religious bigotry (=strong and unreasonable beliefs which cause someone to hate people who belong to a different religion) *Religious bigotry has no place in the modern world.*

PHRASES

for religious reasons *They don't eat pork for religious reasons.*

2 believing strongly in a religion and obeying its rules

ADVERBS

deeply/devoutly religious (=very religious) *My father was a deeply religious man.*

NOUNS

a religious man/woman/person/family *Ted comes from a very religious family.*

THESAURUS: religious

devout
having a very strong belief in a religion:
Her mother was a ***devout Catholic*** *and she did not want her to get divorced. |* ***Devout Muslims*** *pray five times a day. | They are* ***deeply devout*** *and they always go to church every Sunday.*

orthodox
believing in the traditional beliefs, laws, and practices of a religion:
He came from a family of ***orthodox Jews****. | In the 1960s, many people started to turn away from* ***orthodox religion****.*

fundamentalist *disapproving*
having extreme traditional beliefs:
Fundamentalist groups *support suicide attacks on foreigners. | Some* ***fundamentalist Christians*** *object to stories such as 'The Wizard of Oz'.*

Ways of saying that someone is not religious
An **atheist** is someone who does not believe there is a God. An **agnostic** is someone who believes that people cannot know if God exists or not.

relish *v* THESAURUS **enjoy (1)**

reluctance Ac *n*

the feeling of not wanting to do something

ADJECTIVES

great/deep/extreme reluctance *I loved living in Japan and I left with great reluctance.*

considerable reluctance *There was considerable reluctance to question the chairman's judgment.*

obvious reluctance *He accepted my decision, but with obvious reluctance.*

understandable/natural reluctance *There is an understandable reluctance to talk about such terrible events.*

initial reluctance (=reluctance at the beginning, which goes away later) *Despite some initial reluctance, the committee approved the plan.*

growing reluctance *There is a growing reluctance among banks to lend money to businesses.*

VERBS

overcome sb's reluctance (=make yourself or another person do something, which you or they did not originally want to do) *I worked hard to overcome the students' reluctance to speak in class.*

show reluctance *The government has shown great reluctance to deal with the problem.*

express reluctance *The prime minister expressed his reluctance to take the country into another war.*

understand sb's reluctance *I can understand her reluctance to discuss such a private matter.*

PREPOSITIONS

with reluctance *He agreed to come, but with great reluctance.*

reluctance among/by sb (*also* **reluctance on the part of sb**) *There is reluctance on the part of teenagers to listen to any advice from an adult.*

reluctant *adj* not wanting to do something

ADVERBS

highly/extremely reluctant *His mother is extremely reluctant to lend him the money.*

initially reluctant/reluctant at first *Kennedy was initially reluctant to support the proposal.*

understandably reluctant *The old man is understandably reluctant to agree to sell the house he has lived in for 50 years.*

strangely/curiously reluctant *The local people seemed strangely reluctant to help us.*

VERBS

seem/appear reluctant *The politician appeared reluctant to answer any of the interviewer's questions.*

feel reluctant *Helen felt reluctant to criticize her parents.*

NOUNS

reluctant acceptance/agreement *She nodded her head in reluctant acceptance of the situation.*

reluctant admiration *John could not help noticing, with reluctant admiration, that his opponent seemed much less frightened than he was.*

a reluctant participant *He was a reluctant participant in the contest and had only agreed to take part at the last moment.*

a reluctant hero *Ford play's the part of the film's reluctant hero.*

PHRASES

come to the reluctant conclusion that... *They came to the reluctant conclusion that some workers would have to be made redundant.*

THESAURUS: reluctant

reluctant, grudging → **unwilling**

rely on *v*

1 to need someone or something in order to do something

ADVERBS

rely heavily on sb/sth (=a lot) *The country's economy continued to rely heavily on tourism.*

rely completely/entirely on sb/sth *He relies on his wife completely.*

R

rely solely/exclusively on sb/sth (=only on someone or something) *There are a lot of people who rely solely on money from the government in order to live.*

VERBS

be forced to rely on sb/sth *We were forced to rely on other people to take us everywhere.*
tend to rely on sb/sth *People tend to rely a lot on their cars when they live in the country.*

PREPOSITIONS

rely on sb/sth for sth *The villagers have to rely on the river for their water.*

2 to trust someone or something

ADVERBS

rely on sb/sth completely *It's always good to know that there's someone who you can rely on completely.*
you can safely rely on sb *You can safely rely on him if you ever get into trouble.*

PHRASES

sb can rely on sb/sth *I knew I could rely on him.*
sb shouldn't rely on sb/sth *You shouldn't rely on everything you read in the newspapers.*

R

remains *n*

the parts of something that are left after the rest has been destroyed or has disappeared

Grammar
Always plural.

ADJECTIVES/NOUNS + remains

ancient/prehistoric remains (=of things that existed hundreds or thousands of years ago) *The Natural History Museum has one of the finest collections of prehistoric remains in the country.*
archaeological remains (=of things that existed a very long time ago, which are used to study how people lived then) *Archaeological remains were discovered during the digging of subways.*
Roman/Greek remains *The Roman remains included some old coins and some jewellery.*
human remains *Police said they found human remains in the forest.*
fossilized/fossil remains (=where the bones of an animal have become part of the rock or the ground, over millions of years) *In the rocks were the fossilized remains of a huge dinosaur.*
the burnt-out/charred remains (=left after someone or something has been burned) *He was looking at the charred remains of the house.*

VERBS

discover/find/uncover remains *They found the remains of an ancient temple.*

PREPOSITIONS

the remains of sth *You can see the remains of an old house.*

remark *n* something that you say

ADJECTIVES

a rude remark *The children kept interrupting and making rude remarks.*
a sarcastic remark (=that has the opposite meaning of what you want to say, especially in order to criticize someone) *She was tired of his sarcastic remarks about her work.*
a witty remark (=clever and amusing) *Stephen is good at making witty remarks.*
a personal remark (=about someone's appearance or behaviour, especially in an unkind way) *He kept making personal remarks about her clothes.*
a racist remark (=an offensive remark about someone's race) *When I first arrived in this country, I often heard people making racist remarks.*
a sexist remark (=a remark that is offensive to women, or in rarer cases, to men) *Women had to put up with sexist remarks from male colleagues.*
a disparaging remark *formal* (=that shows you do not think someone or something is very good) *My aunt always makes disparaging remarks about my appearance.*
a snide remark (=that criticizes in an indirect way, especially unfairly) *Will you stop making snide remarks about my mother!*
a casual/throwaway remark (=that you do not think about carefully) *These days a casual remark can get you into trouble.*
a kind remark *Thank you for your kind remarks.*
opening/introductory remarks (=at the beginning of a talk, book etc) *In his introductory remarks, Kershaw sets out the aims of the book.*
closing/concluding remarks (=at the end of a talk, book etc) *In her closing remarks, she said there was still a lot more research to be done.*

VERBS

make a remark *People often make rude remarks about his hairstyle.*
ignore a remark *He ignored my remark and carried on working.*
address your remarks to sb (=make your remarks to someone) *He addressed all his remarks to her husband.*
withdraw a remark (=say that you do not mean it) *She refused to withdraw the remark and apologize.*

PREPOSITIONS

a remark about sth *Her remark about the school surprised me.*

remedy *n*

1 a way of dealing with a problem

ADJECTIVES

a simple/easy remedy *There is no simple remedy for lack of confidence.*

a possible remedy *There are a number of possible remedies to this problem.*

VERBS

find a remedy *Our job is to identify problems with the system and find remedies for them.*

provide a remedy *We are hoping that the government will be able to provide some sort of remedy to the problem.*

exhaust all (the) other remedies (=try all possible remedies) *Before calling the police, she wanted to exhaust all other remedies first.*

PREPOSITIONS

a remedy for/to sth *Governments seem unable to find long-term remedies for poverty.*

a remedy against sth *The new law gives employers remedies against workers who go on strike.*

2 a medicine to cure an illness or pain that is not very serious

ADJECTIVES

a natural remedy *She prefers natural remedies to the pills the doctor offers her.*

a herbal remedy (=made from plants) *He makes his own herbal remedy for hay fever.*

an effective remedy *Peppermint tea can be an effective remedy against stomach ache.*

a traditional/folk remedy (=one that people in a place have been using for a long time, but is not one that doctors use) *Fish oil has been used as a folk remedy since the 18th century.*

over-the-counter remedies (=which people can buy in shops) *The report claims that most over-the-counter remedies are useless.*

NOUNS + remedy

a cold/cough/flu remedy *Most cold remedies have little effect.*

a home remedy (=one that you make at home) *Home remedies for colds include honey and lemon.*

VERBS

take a remedy *Have you tried taking herbal remedies?*

PREPOSITIONS

a remedy for sth *There is no effective remedy for flu.*

remember *v*

to think about things from the past

ADVERBS

remember sth/sb well (=thoroughly and completely) *I remember so well my first day at school.*

remember sth/sb clearly/vividly/distinctly (=well, with a lot of detail) *She remembers clearly how scared she was to see soldiers in the streets.*

vaguely/dimly remember sth/sb (=not well) *He can only vaguely remember his mother's face.*

fondly remember sth/sb (=with feelings of liking them a lot, especially a long time ago) *The old hotel is fondly remembered by people who stayed there.*

hardly/barely remember sth/sb (=almost not at all) *He died such a long time ago that I can hardly remember him.*

always remember sb/sth (*also* **remember sb/sth forever**) *I will always remember those happy days we spent together.*

PREPOSITIONS

remember sb/sth for sth *She is remembered by fans for her beautiful singing voice.*

remember sb/sth as sth *She remembers her schooldays as a very happy time.*

PHRASES

as far as I can remember (*also* **if I remember rightly**) (=used when saying that your memory of something might not be correct) *If I remember rightly, his family lived in the house on the corner.*

for as long as I can remember (=for a very long time) *The shop has been here for as long as I can remember.*

ANTONYMS **remember → forget**

remind *v*

1 to make someone remember something that they must do or something that they should know

ADVERBS

constantly/continually remind sb *The teacher is constantly reminding students to hand their homework in on time.*

gently remind sb *He gently reminded me that we needed to leave soon.*

politely/respectfully remind sb *The security officer politely reminded us that dogs were not allowed in the building.*

VERBS

serve to remind sb *formal* (=have the effect of reminding someone) *The attack served to remind people of the need for greater airport security.*

PREPOSITIONS

remind sb about sth *I sent him an email to remind him about the meeting.*

PHRASES

keep reminding sb *I had to keep reminding myself that it was only a film.*

2 to seem similar to another person or thing in some way

ADVERBS

remind sb strongly/sharply *The view of the mountains strongly reminded me of Switzerland.*

remind sb vividly (=in such a clear way that something seems real) *Smells can vividly remind you of a particular event or time.*

remind sb instantly (=immediately) *When I saw the building, I was instantly reminded of my old school.*

remind sb vaguely (=in a not very clear or exact way) *He reminds me vaguely of my uncle.*

PREPOSITIONS

remind sb of sb/sth *He reminds me of his brother.*

reminder *n*

something that makes you notice, remember, or think about something

ADJECTIVES

a constant/permanent reminder (=that makes you think about something all the time) *His picture on the wall is a constant reminder of our happy times together.*

a timely reminder (=a useful and important one that comes at the right time) *This a timely reminder of the risks of sunbathing.*

a stark/sharp reminder (=strong or unpleasant) *This incident is a stark reminder of the dangers police officers face.*

a helpful/useful reminder *The list will be a useful reminder of the topics covered in the course.*

a gentle reminder *It was meant to be a gentle reminder rather than a criticism.*

a friendly reminder *If you don't pay the bill on time, the credit card company sends you a friendly reminder.*

a painful/uncomfortable reminder *This attack is a painful reminder that peace is still a long way away.*

a powerful/potent reminder *The soldiers' deaths are a powerful reminder of the price we pay for freedom.*

a vivid reminder (=very clear) *Their performance was a vivid reminder of just why this band has remained so successful.*

a salutary reminder *formal* (=one that teaches you something) *The earthquake is a salutary reminder of the power of nature.*

a poignant reminder (=making you feel sad) *The empty seats were a poignant reminder of all the people who were no longer with the company.*

a grim/sobering/chilling reminder (=making you feel serious and worried or frightened) *The presence of soldiers on the streets is a grim reminder of the threat of terrorism.*

VERBS

serve/act as a reminder (=be a reminder) *The photograph will serve as a lovely reminder of your visit.*

provide/offer a reminder *The case has provided a chilling reminder of what domestic violence really means.*

get/receive a reminder *If you fail to return your books, you will receive a reminder from the library.*

send sb a reminder *The university will send you a reminder when it's time to pay your fees.*

need a reminder *Sometimes we all need a reminder of what is really important in life.*

PREPOSITIONS

a reminder of sth *The attack is a reminder of the political tensions in the region.*

a reminder to sb *The film is a reminder to our generation of our grandparents' sacrifices.*

remote *adj, adv* THESAURUS ▶ **far**

remove Ac *v*

to get rid of something, or take it out or away

ADVERBS

remove sth completely/entirely/altogether *The tumor has been completely removed.*

remove sth carefully/slowly *Carefully remove all the dust before you start painting.*

safely remove sth *The truck remained on the road for six hours until fire crews could safely remove it.*

surgically remove sth (=in a medical operation) *The lump had to be surgically removed.*

PREPOSITIONS

remove sth from sth *They removed all the dirt from the carpet.*

PHRASES

sth can easily be removed *Most stains can easily be removed by rubbing with a damp cloth.*

sth is difficult to remove *Some viruses on your computer can be difficult to remove without special software tools.*

renewable *adj* THESAURUS ▶ **environmentally friendly**

renovate *v* THESAURUS ▶ **repair[1]**

renowned *adj* THESAURUS ▶ **famous**

rent *n*

the money that someone pays regularly to use a room, house etc that belongs to someone else

ADJECTIVES/NOUNS + rent

high rent *Rents in the city centre are very high.*

low/cheap rent *Government workers get low rents and other benefits.*

the annual/monthly/weekly rent *Our annual rent is just over $15,000.*

affordable rent (=which people can easily pay) *The city plans to provide more homes at affordable rents.*

exorbitant rent (=much too high) *Some landlords charge exorbitant rents.*

ground rent *BrE* (=rent paid to the owner of the land that a house, office etc is built on) *There is an additional ground rent of £30 per month.*

VERBS

pay rent *She couldn't afford to pay the rent.*

increase/raise/put up the rent *The landlord wants to put up our rent.*

owe rent *We haven't paid the electricity bill for months and we still owe rent of around £1,000.*

collect the rent *His job is to collect the rents from the tenants.*

the rent increases/goes up *The rent has gone up by over 50% in the last two years.*

rent + NOUNS

a rent increase *How can they justify such big rent increases?*

rent arrears *BrE* (=money that you owe because you have not paid your rent) *The most common debts were rent arrears.*

PREPOSITIONS

the rent on sth *The rent on a small apartment can be as much as $1,000 a month.*

PHRASES

the rent is due *The rent is due at the beginning of the week.*

fall/get behind with the rent (=fail to pay your rent on time) *You could lose the flat if you fall behind with the rent.*

THESAURUS: rent

price, value, charge, fee, fare, rent, rate, toll → **cost[1] (1)**

repair[1] *v*

to make something be in good condition or work properly again, when it has been damaged or stopped working

NOUNS

repair a car/truck/plane *The cost of repairing the car is more than its value.*

repair a house/building/church *The school buildings urgently need to be repaired.*

repair a roof/ceiling/wall/fence *The builders are coming to repair the roof.*

repair a road/bridge/tunnel *It could take up to three months to repair the road.*

repair a machine/computer/television/watch *The washing machine needs repairing.*

repair shoes/clothes *Where can I get my shoes repaired?*

repair the damage *Engineers are working to repair the damage caused by the storms.*

repair a hole *He had surgery to repair a hole in his stomach.*

VERBS

have/get sth repaired (=pay for someone to repair it for you) *I get my computer repaired by a man who lives locally.*

sth needs repairing/needs to be repaired *The dishwasher needs repairing – it keeps making a funny noise.*

pay for sth to be repaired *The driver offered to pay for my bike to be repaired.*

Repair, fix, or mend?

Repair is the usual word to use, but it can sound a little formal. In spoken English, people often use **fix** or **mend**.

British people use **fix**, especially about machines and mechanical problems. British people use **mend** about repairing clothes, roofs, roads etc.

American people use **fix** about all types of repairs, and **mend** is much less common in American English.

THESAURUS: repair

fix
car | computer | machine | boiler | roof | door | damage
to repair something. **Fix** is more informal than **repair** and is very common in spoken English:
Most kids help their dad fix the car. | Richard is still fixing the flood damage to his house.

mend *especially BrE*
roof | fence | road | car | boat | clothes | shoes | net | boiler | damage | hole
to repair something that is damaged, torn, or not working:
My first job was to mend the roof and stop the rain from getting in. | The workmen are mending the road. | The carpenters are mending the damage to the ship.

service
car | plane | boiler | machine | computer
to check a vehicle or machine and repair it if necessary, especially regularly:
You should have your car serviced every six months. | The boiler has only just been serviced, so there shouldn't be anything wrong with it.

renovate
building | house | home | church | hotel
to repair an old building so that it looks in good condition again:
They spent thousands of pounds renovating the house. | They need to raise $450,000 to renovate the church.

restore
building | house | church | hotel | palace | city | painting | picture | furniture | car | train
to repair something old and valuable, so that it looks the same as it did originally:
The church has now been ***fully restored*** (=completely restored). | *The workmen are* ***restoring*** *the palace* ***to its former splendour*** (=repairing it so that it looks as impressive as it did before). | *The painting has been* ***restored to its original condition.***

do up *BrE informal*, **fix up** *AmE informal*
house | place | car | room
to repair an old building or vehicle, so that it looks in good condition again:
*Laura loves buying old houses and doing them up. | He's been there a year **fixing up** the place.*

patch up
hole | damage | crack | wound | ship
to quickly repair something that has a hole in it, usually by putting a piece of material on it. **Patch up** is rather informal and is used about temporary repairs:
I used a bit of wood to patch up the hole in our roof. | The wound was patched up and he was ready to play again.

You can also **patch up** your relationship with someone after an argument: *He tried to **patch things up** by buying her a gold bracelet* (=he tried to repair the damage to their relationship).

darn
socks | stockings
to repair holes in clothes:
Are you any good at darning socks?

R

repair² *n*

something that you do to fix a thing that is damaged or not working

Grammar
Usually plural, except when used before another noun.

ADJECTIVES

minor repairs *We had to carry out some minor repairs to the boat.*
major repairs *Luckily, no major repairs were needed to the car.*
necessary/essential repairs *The council has agreed to undertake essential repairs to the fencing.*
urgent repairs *More than £40,000 is needed for urgent repairs to the building.*
extensive repairs (=a lot of repair work) *The boat needed extensive repairs.*
structural repairs (=to the main parts of a building or other structure) *Significant structural repairs to the bridge are planned.*

VERBS

do/make/carry out repairs *The builders are doing some repairs to the roof.*
undertake repairs *formal* (=do them) *The road will be closed tonight while workmen undertake essential repairs.*
undergo repair *formal* (=have repairs done on it) *Several of the ships are undergoing repair.*

repair + NOUNS

the repair bill *The repair bill will be hundreds of thousands of pounds.*
repair costs *The insurance company has agreed to pay all repair costs.*
repair work *The repair work is being done by a local firm.*
a repair kit (=a set of tools or equipment that you use to repair something) *Always carry a repair kit with you when you go cycling.*

PHRASES

be under repair (=be being repaired) *A large section of the road was under repair.*
be in need of repair *Many of the cottages were badly in need of repair.*
be beyond repair/be damaged beyond repair (=be so badly damaged that it cannot be repaired) *Unfortunately the engine is beyond repair.*
be in a good/poor state of repair (*also* **be in good/poor repair**) (=be in good or bad condition) *The house was old and in a poor state of repair.*
be closed for repairs *The bridge will be closed for repairs for two months.*

repeal *v* THESAURUS cancel

repeat *v*

1 to say or write something again

NOUNS

repeat a question *Ellie repeated her question since her father had ignored it the first time.*
repeat a name/word/phrase *Could you repeat your name, please?*
repeat a request/call for sth *He repeated his request for a meeting.*
repeat a warning *After the latest attack, police repeated their warning to people living in the area.*
repeat a story *I asked my mother to repeat the story of how she had met my father.*
repeat a claim/assertion *Republicans repeated their assertion that Democrats would raise taxes.*

ADVERBS

repeat sth again *Sorry, I didn't hear you. Can you repeat that again?*
endlessly/constantly repeat sth *The newspapers have endlessly repeated the same story.*
only/merely/simply repeat sth *I'm merely repeating what she said.*
repeat sth verbatim (=using exactly the same words) *He repeated verbatim what he had been told.*

VERBS

keep repeating sth *She kept repeating the word over and over again like a robot.*

PHRASES

repeat yourself (=say the same thing again)

All I can do is keep repeating myself and hope he eventually listens.

2 to do something again

NOUNS

repeat an experiment *The experiment was repeated at various temperatures.*

repeat an exercise *Repeat the exercise, this time kneeling on your right knee.*

repeat a procedure/process *This process is repeated for each column of data.*

repeat a mistake *We want to avoid repeating the mistakes of the previous government.*

repeat an experience *I had no wish to repeat the experience.*

repeat a year/class/grade (=do the same class at school again) *She failed her exams and had to repeat the year.*

ADVERBS

repeat sth again *Repeat the movement again, this time more slowly.*

PHRASES

history repeats itself (=used for saying that things often happen in the same way as before) *Sadly history repeated itself, and the team lost again.*

replacement *n*

someone or something that replaces another person or thing

ADJECTIVES

a possible replacement *Can you suggest anyone as a possible replacement when Jane retires?*

a suitable replacement *We are looking for a suitable replacement for our old car.*

a permanent replacement *He will act as chairman until a permanent replacement can be found.*

a temporary replacement *The garage gave me this car as a temporary replacement until mine is fixed.*

a late/last-minute replacement *Ralf was a last-minute replacement for Andrew who was unwell.*

a direct replacement (=replacing someone or something exactly) *She was hired as a direct replacement for Tom.*

VERBS

find a replacement *It can be hard to find a replacement for a part on an old machine.*

look for a replacement (*also* **seek a replacement** *formal*): *We are still seeking a replacement for our goalkeeper.*

buy/get a replacement *If a tile gets damaged, you can buy a replacement.*

provide a replacement *Please return goods if they are faulty, and we will provide a replacement.*

appoint a replacement (=give a job to another person) *They wanted to sack him and appoint a replacement.*

NOUNS + replacement

a joint/hip/knee replacement (=an artificial knee, hip etc that replaces your own) *Many people are waiting for hip replacements.*

replacement + NOUNS

a replacement window *They were planning to install replacement windows.*

a replacement part *Where can I get a replacement part for my washing machine?*

PREPOSITIONS

a replacement for sb/sth *Byfield is a replacement for the injured David Noble.*

as a replacement *We need to consider the contribution of nuclear energy as a replacement for fossil fuels.*

replenish *v* THESAURUS ▸ **fill**

reply[1] *v*

to answer someone by saying, writing, or doing something

ADVERBS

reply personally (=write or speak to someone directly yourself) *The manager always replies personally to any customer complaints.*

reply quickly/immediately/at once *He sent a text to his wife, and she replied immediately.*

reply firmly *"Certainly not," Maggie replied firmly.*

reply angrily (*also* **reply crossly** *BrE*): *"That's a lie!" he replied angrily.*

reply tersely/curtly *especially literary* (=using few words, usually because you are angry) *"I'm fine," Phil replied tersely.*

reply quietly/calmly/coolly *She replied calmly that she was sure there was an explanation.*

reply politely *"No, thank you," the child replied politely.*

PREPOSITIONS

reply to sb *The company replied to Mrs Clark in a letter a few days later.*

reply to a letter/email/question etc *I asked her, but she hasn't replied to my email yet.*

reply by doing sth *The speaker replied by inviting him to come up onto the stage.*

reply with sth *He replied with a nod.*

> **Reply** is often used in written descriptions, when reporting exactly what someone said: *"No thanks," she **replied** quickly.*

reply[2] *n*

something that is said, written, or done as a way of replying

ADJECTIVES

a written reply *I received a written reply from the company, saying they had received my application.*

R

an immediate reply *"Yes, I'd love to come!" was his immediate reply.*

a prompt/early reply (=a reply that comes soon) *I would be grateful for a prompt reply to my query.*

a positive/negative reply (=a reply which says yes or no) *He had asked for more time and received a positive reply.*

a satisfactory/suitable reply *She could not think of a suitable reply.*

a brief/short/curt reply *"Not now," was the brief reply.*

a long/lengthy reply *He wrote to all the newspapers with a lengthy reply.*

a standard reply *The standard reply to this question is to quote health and safety reasons.*

VERBS

get/receive a reply *He knocked, then, getting no reply, pushed open the door.*

give/make a reply *She was tempted to give a rude reply.*

send a reply *Josh has sent a reply to my email.*

hear sb's reply *I asked her name, but didn't hear the reply.*

wait for a reply (*also* **await sb's reply** *formal*): *I'm still waiting for a reply to my question.*

expect a reply *She wrote to the president, but didn't really expect a reply.*

PREPOSITIONS

a reply to a question *The best reply to such a question would be "None of your business".*

a reply to a letter/email/message etc *I still haven't had a reply to my email.*

a reply to an argument/criticism etc *The obvious reply to this argument is that the public have a right to know.*

a reply from sb *She asked again, and again there was no reply from Violet.*

in reply (=as a reply) *Her friend only giggled in reply.*

PHRASES

there was no reply/sb made no reply *I phoned him just now, but there was no reply.*

report[1] *n*

1 an official document or talk which provides information about something

ADJECTIVES/NOUNS + report

an official report *The economic situation is improving, according to an official report.*

a government report *A government report said that there needed to be more training for young people.*

a written report *The manager asked me to send him a written report about my visit.*

a formal report *At the end of each year, your supervisor will complete a formal report on your performance.*

a full/detailed/in-depth report (=containing all the information about something) *A full report will be prepared for the next committee meeting.*

a confidential report (=one that only a few people are allowed to see) *He made a confidential report to UN headquarters in New York.*

an annual report (=every year) *Our annual report shows that the company is making good profits.*

a monthly/weekly report *Each member of the sales force has to write a weekly report.*

a scientific/medical/financial etc report *Only patients themselves have access to their medical reports.*

a school report (=about how well a student is doing at school) *Her last school report was very good and she got As in all her subjects.*

a glowing report (=praising someone or something a lot) *Paul received a glowing report from his previous employers.*

VERBS + report

write a report *She has been asked to write a report about her research.*

make a report *We make regular progress reports to our manager.*

give a report (*also* **deliver a report** *formal*) (=make a report, usually a spoken one) *He came to the office to give his report in person.*

publish/release a report *The Ministry of Defence will publish its report into the accident next week.*

submit a report *formal* (=give a written report to someone) *Doctors will have to submit weekly reports.*

draft a report (=prepare a report) *The data protection officers have been drafting their report since September.*

commission/order a report (=ask someone to write a report) *The government has commissioned an independent report into the affair.*

report + VERBS

a report says/states (that)... *The report says that it will cost another £250 million to repair the damage.*

a report finds (that)... *The report found that carbon monoxide emissions had risen by 30%.*

a report reveals/shows sth *A recent report reveals an increase in the number of people suffering from the disease.*

a report examines/looks into sth *The report will examine the events leading up to the war.*

a report recommends sth *The report recommended that teachers' pay should be increased.*

a report highlights/emphasizes sth (=says that it is particularly important) *The report emphasizes the need for better safety checks.*

PREPOSITIONS

a report on sth *The government published a report on the country's energy needs.*

a report into sth (=on something, especially the causes and reasons for something) *The official report into the accident says it was caused by human error.*

a report by/from sb *A new report from the Health Department recommends changes.*

according to a report *The school is improving, according to a recent government report.*

2 a description of an event or situation, especially on the news

ADJECTIVES/NOUNS + report

a news report *According to one news report, over a hundred people have been killed.*

a television/radio report *A television report showed pictures of the town after the earthquake.*

an eyewitness/first-hand report (=from someone who saw what happened) *He was able to give an eyewitness report of what happened when the city was attacked.*

an accurate report *We still don't know if this a fair and accurate report of what happened.*

a reliable/credible report (=which you can trust to be accurate) *We received reliable reports that there were whales in the area.*

an unconfirmed report (=not yet supported by official information) *There are unconfirmed reports that up to 2,000 people have been killed.*

an unofficial report *According to unofficial reports, the president had talks with rebel leaders.*

conflicting reports (=reports saying very different things) *Conflicting reports of the attacks continued to emerge from the area.*

a misleading report (=likely to make you believe something that is not true) *There were misleading reports of the causes of the violence.*

an initial/early report *Initial reports claimed that nobody was injured in the attack.*

VERBS

get/receive a report *We have received several reports of the mistreatment of prisoners.*

have had reports of sth *The police say they have had reports of a gang shooting in East London.*

confirm a report (=say that it is true) *The report has never been confirmed by authorities.*

deny a report (=say that it is not true) *Government officials have denied reports that the minister is planning to resign.*

PREPOSITIONS

a report on sth *We watched the TV reports on the war.*

amid reports (=while people are saying that a particular thing is happening) *The manager resigned amid reports that the players had lost confidence in him.*

report² *v*

1 to tell people about something that has happened by writing about it in a newspaper, showing film of it on the television etc: *The BBC reported that a man had been arrested.*

PREPOSITIONS

report on sth *The Wall Street Journal reported on the company's decision.*

sth is reported in a newspaper *The incident was reported in the London Evening Standard.*

2 to tell someone in authority that something has happened, especially something bad

NOUNS

report a crime *If your car is broken into, you should report the crime as soon as possible.*

report an incident (=report an event, especially a crime) *He reported the incident to the local police.*

report an accident *Failing to report an accident is a criminal offence.*

report a problem/fault *I've reported the fault to the telephone company.*

PREPOSITIONS

report sth to sb *He reported the problem to his manager.*

PHRASES

be reported missing *The boy was reported missing when he failed to return home from school.*

3 to officially tell people about the information you have found

NOUNS

report findings/results *The committee will report its findings in March.*

report an increase/an improvement *Doctors have reported a 13% increase in cases of breast cancer.*

report a change *They reported a change in the students' behaviour.*

report sales *The company has reported disappointing sales.*

PREPOSITIONS

report on sth *The scientists will report on the findings of their research.*

reporter *n*

someone whose job is to write or speak about news events

ADJECTIVES/NOUNS + reporter

a newspaper reporter *The case attracted newspaper reporters from all over the world.*

a television/radio reporter *He told television reporters that he had no plans to resign.*

a news reporter *He started as a news reporter on Radio 1.*

a sports reporter *She worked as a sports reporter for a local newspaper.*

a political reporter *Pinchetti became the magazine's top political reporter.*
an investigative reporter (=one that tries to find out the truth about something important) *Two investigative reporters wrote an article linking the CIA to drug crime in Los Angeles.*
a junior/cub reporter (=a young one without much experience) *In the film, she plays a cub reporter with the 'New York Times'.*
a roving reporter (=who travels to different places to find news) *He was the BBC's top roving reporter.*

VERBS

tell reporters *He told reporters that he was happy with the decision.*
brief reporters (=give them information) *The minister will brief reporters on his meeting with European leaders.*

PREPOSITIONS

a reporter on/for sth *She is a reporter on the 'Washington Post'.*

represent *v*

1 to speak or do something on behalf of another person, organization, country etc

NOUNS

represent sb's interests *A lawyer's job is to represent the best interests of his or her client.*
represent your country/city/school etc *Anna has been chosen to represent her country at the next Olympic Games.*
represent a constituency (=be elected to speak in parliament on behalf of the people who live in an area) *Skinner has represented the same constituency for over 25 years.*
represent your members *The union is there to represent its members and make sure that they get good pay and conditions.*

2 used when saying how many of a particular type of person or thing there are in a group

> **Grammar**
> In this meaning, **represent** is always passive.

ADVERBS

be well/strongly represented (=there are a lot) *Doctors were well represented at the conference.*
be adequately/properly/fully represented (=there are enough) *Women are still not adequately represented in senior jobs.*
be poorly represented/under-represented (=there are not many or not enough) *Until this time, his paintings had been poorly represented in national collections.*
be disproportionately represented (=there are too many or too few in relation to something or someone else) *Young black men are disproportionately represented in UK prison populations.*

3 to be something – used especially in formal contexts

NOUNS

represent a change/shift in sth *The announcement represents a major change in government policy.*
represent an improvement/advance *The new hospital will represent a significant improvement on the old one.*
represent an increase *These figures represent a 22% increase on last year's figures.*
represent an achievement/breakthrough *Building the tunnel represented a great technical achievement.*
represent a problem *Skin cancer represents a significant health problem in this country.*
represent a threat/danger/risk *The escaped prisoner is dangerous and represents a threat to public safety.*

representation *n*

1 a description, sign, painting etc that shows something

ADJECTIVES

an accurate representation *The painting is an accurate representation of the city as it really was at that time.*
a visual representation *This picture is a visual representation of the artist's thoughts about the horrors of war.*
a symbolic representation (=one that represents a particular idea or quality) *The eagle is a symbolic representation of the United States.*

VERBS

create/produce a representation *The program creates a computerized representation of the room.*
offer/present a representation *The screen display offers a 3-D representation of the city.*

2 the activity of speaking, voting, or making decisions on behalf of another person or group

ADJECTIVES

legal representation *Everyone has a right to legal representation if they are arrested.*
political/parliamentary representation *In some countries, women do not have any political representation.*
equal representation *The companies will have equal representation on the committee.*

VERBS

have any/no representation *The party doesn't have any representation in parliament.*
be entitled to representation (=be officially allowed representation) *Workers are entitled to union representation.*
provide/give representation *The law firm provides representation on behalf of its clients.*

NOUNS + representation

union representation *A large number of workers have no union representation.*

representative[1] *n*

someone who has been chosen to speak, vote, or make decisions for someone else

ADJECTIVES

an official representative *Official representatives of the Catholic Church attended the meeting.*

an elected representative *The school council is made up of elected representatives.*

a legal representative *A legal representative for the company has advised against the action.*

a senior representative *The president met with senior representatives of the company.*

a local/regional representative *She is the local representative of Ice Hockey UK.*

a special representative *Jones was appointed as the UN's special representative in the area.*

an authorized representative (=one who has official permission) *The drugs must be collected by the patient or an authorized representative.*

a personal representative *The president sent his personal representative.*

VERBS

elect a representative *They voted to elect a representative.*

appoint a representative (=give someone the job of being a representative) *He appointed a legal representative.*

send a representative *Most European countries sent representatives to the meeting.*

NOUNS + representative

a sales representative *Alex is a sales representative for an insurance company.*

a union representative *Union representatives claim that jobs will be lost.*

a company representative *Company representatives denied that the company was responsible for the accident.*

PREPOSITIONS

a representative of sth *Representatives of EU governments met in Brussels.*

a representative for sb/sth *She became a union representative for the school.*

a representative from sth *The committee is made up of representatives from each region.*

representative[2] *adj*

typical of a kind of person or thing

ADVERBS

truly/genuinely representative *The country has the opportunity to create for itself a truly representative form of government.*

highly representative (=very representative) *These paintings are highly representative of the artist's style.*

broadly representative (=of most people or things in a group) *Ideally, members of parliament should be broadly representative of the whole of British society.*

statistically representative *The group of people surveyed is not statistically representative of the total population.*

NOUNS

a representative sample/selection *A representative sample of people living in New York were asked for their opinions.*

a representative cross-section (=a group of people or things that is typical of a much larger group) *A representative cross-section of the student population took part in the survey.*

a representative view *Is the sample large enough to provide a representative view of consumer opinion as a whole?*

PREPOSITIONS

be representative of sb/sth *This latest incident is representative of a wider trend.*

reprimand *v*

to tell someone officially that something they have done is very wrong

ADVERBS

severely reprimand sb *The player was severely reprimanded for his behaviour in the game.*

officially/formally/publicly reprimand sb *The police officers will be officially reprimanded for their behaviour.*

PREPOSITIONS

reprimand sb for sth *The military court reprimanded the captain for failing to do his duty.*

reproduce *v* THESAURUS copy[2] (1)

repulsive *adj* THESAURUS ugly (1)

reputable *adj*

respected for being honest or for doing work that is of good quality

NOUNS

a reputable company/firm/organization *We chose that company because we thought they were reputable.*

a reputable source *Always make sure that you buy from a reputable source.*

a reputable shop/store *Can someone please recommend a reputable shop where I can take my coffee machine to be serviced?*

a reputable dealer/supplier/lender *Buying from a reputable dealer is the safest way to purchase a secondhand car.*

a reputable journal/publication *The paper was published in a reputable journal.*

ADVERBS

highly reputable *This is a great opportunity to join a highly reputable organization with over 15 years in the business.*

reputation *n*

people's opinion of someone or something

ADJECTIVES

a good/excellent reputation *The university has a very good reputation.*

a bad/poor reputation *The city doesn't deserve its bad reputation.*

an international/worldwide reputation *The department has a worldwide reputation for its research.*

a formidable reputation (=very good, so that people have a lot of respect for you or are afraid of you) *After the meeting, I understood why he had such a formidable reputation.*

an enviable reputation (=a good one that others would like to have) *The company has established an enviable reputation for quality.*

a well-deserved/well-earned reputation (=that someone deserves to have) *France has a well-deserved reputation for good food.*

sb's professional reputation *The scandal damaged his professional reputation.*

VERBS

have a good/bad etc reputation *The law firm has an excellent reputation.*

get a reputation (*also* **gain/acquire a reputation** *formal*): *He didn't want to get a reputation as a troublemaker.*

earn/win a reputation *As a young publisher, she earned a reputation for toughness.*

enjoy a reputation (=have a reputation) *The hotel enjoys a good reputation.*

deserve a reputation (=have earned it) *The restaurant deserves its reputation for good food.*

live up to its reputation (=be the same as people say it is) *New York certainly lived up to its reputation as an exciting city.*

establish a reputation (=make people accept that you are good at doing something) *By then Picasso was already establishing his reputation as an artist.*

build/develop a reputation *Our business has built a reputation for reliable service.*

improve sb's reputation (*also* **enhance sb's reputation** *formal*): *The performance greatly enhanced the actor's reputation.*

damage sb's reputation (*also* **tarnish sb's reputation** *formal*): *She wouldn't do anything to damage her family's reputation.*

destroy/ruin sb's reputation *If the story gets out, it could ruin your reputation.*

PREPOSITIONS

a reputation for sth *Judge Kelso has a reputation for being strict but fair.*

a reputation as sth *She gained a reputation as a hard worker.*

by reputation *He is, by reputation, a rude and difficult man.*

R

THESAURUS: reputation

image
the idea that people have about what something is like, especially when this is created through newspaper stories, advertising etc:
*A PR campaign was launched in an effort to improve the company's image. | Boxing has rather a **negative image**. | The princess tried to **project** an **image** of herself as serious and hard-working* (=she tried to give people the idea that she was serious and hard-working).

name
the reputation that a person, organization etc has - used especially in the following phrases:
*The company is anxious to protect its **good name**. | Cyclists who ignore traffic rules give other cyclists **a bad name**. | He went to court in order to try to **clear his name*** (=prove that he is innocent).

standing
someone's reputation and position compared to other people in a group or society, based on other people's opinion of them:
*The class system in the UK encourages people to be very aware of their **social standing**. | He needs to improve his standing among female voters. | Jacques Tati was a man of international standing in the world of screen comedy.*

prestige
the good reputation that a company, organization, group etc has, which makes people respect and admire them:
*Rolls-Royce **enjoys great prestige** as a maker of luxury cars. | Does Stanford University **carry** the same **prestige** as Harvard or Yale? | Hosting the Olympic Games would **enhance** our country's international **prestige*** (=give it more prestige). | *The profession has **lost** the **prestige** it had in the past.*

stature *formal*
the importance and respect that a person or organization has, because of their achievements or their influence:
*As he got older, Picasso's stature as an artist increased. | Their work is **equal in stature**. | an actor **of international stature** | The party's stature has increased in recent years.*

request *n*

the action of asking for something, especially officially

ADJECTIVES

a formal/official request *The country made a formal request for food aid.*

a written request *You have to make a written request for a visa.*

a special request *Please let the restaurant know in advance if you have any special requests.*

an urgent request *The family made an urgent request for help in finding their daughter.*

repeated requests *The company would not reveal its secret recipe, despite repeated requests from customers.*

a reasonable request *It sounded like a perfectly reasonable request.*

a strange/unusual request *The actor occasionally receives strange requests from female fans.*

VERBS

make a request *The pilot made a request for assistance.*

submit a request/put in a request (=make a formal request) *He put in a request for two weeks' holiday.*

agree to a request (*also* **grant sb's request** *formal*): *The council has agreed to our request to demolish the wall.*

turn down/refuse/reject a request *The manager has turned down their request for a meeting.*

receive a request *The army received an urgent request for assistance.*

consider a request *After carefully considering this request, the council rejected it.*

respond to a request *Thank you to those who responded to our request for information last month.*

ignore a request *The family ignored repeated requests to leave the property.*

PREPOSITIONS

a request for sth *Every year, the coastguard receives hundreds of requests for help from ships in trouble.*

a request from/by sb *The boys received several requests from neighbours to turn their music down.*

on/upon request (=when someone asks for it) *A full financial statement is available to shareholders on request.*

at sb's request (=because someone has asked for it) *We have reduced the amount of packaging we use, at the request of our customers.*

PHRASES

sth is available on request *A comprehensive list of the company's services is available on request.*

by popular request (=because many people have asked for it) *The well-loved TV series is to be repeated in the spring, by popular request.*

requirement Ac *n*

something that someone needs or asks for

ADJECTIVES/NOUNS + requirement

a legal/statutory requirement (=something the law says you must do) *There is no legal requirement to carry identity papers.*

a basic requirement *Water is a basic requirement of life.*

an essential requirement *Confidence is an essential requirement for success.*

a minimum requirement *This qualification is a minimum requirement for entry to music college.*

a special requirement *He modified the car to suit his own special requirements.*

entry requirements (=the skills, qualifications etc you must have in order to enter a school, university, or country) *Applicants must satisfy the normal entry requirements for the course.*

safety requirements *All companies must comply with health and safety requirements.*

VERBS

meet/match a requirement (=have or do what is needed) *We finally found a house that met all of our requirements.*

satisfy/fulfil a requirement (=meet it) *Our aim is to satisfy our customers' requirements.*

comply with requirements *formal* (=meet the requirements of a law or rule) *Failure to comply with these requirements is a criminal offence.*

impose requirements (=state that something has to be done) *The regulations impose new and costly requirements on small businesses.*

lay down/set out requirements (=say what they are) *The document sets out the legal requirements that apply to financial organizations.*

suit sb's requirements (=be suitable for someone in a particular situation) *You could design and build a house to suit your requirements.*

waive a requirement (=say that it is not necessary) *In special circumstances, the council may waive this requirement.*

go beyond/exceed requirements (=be better than what is asked for) *The new factory will go beyond environmental requirements set out under EU law.*

PHRASES

be surplus to requirements *BrE* (=be no longer needed) *The old school building is now surplus to requirements.*

rescue *n*

the act of saving someone or something from a dangerous or difficult situation

PHRASES

come/go/rush to sb's rescue (=come or go to help someone) *We saw the car hit the tree and we rushed to the driver's rescue.*

ADJECTIVES/NOUNS + rescue

a dramatic rescue *A woman is in hospital following a dramatic rescue from her blazing flat.*

a daring rescue *The hostages were freed in a daring rescue by US special forces.*

an emergency rescue *The ship's crew had to carry out an emergency rescue after a man fell overboard.*

a mountain/sea rescue *Climbers carry flares for use in a mountain rescue.*

VERBS

carry out a rescue *He was held hostage for 15 days before commandos carried out a dramatic rescue.*

attempt/mount a rescue (=try to rescue someone) *The stormy conditions made it impossible to mount a rescue.*

rescue + NOUNS

a rescue attempt/effort *One firefighter was severely burned in the rescue attempt.*

a rescue operation/mission *A major rescue operation was launched yesterday after two divers were reported missing.*

a rescue worker *Rescue workers are searching through the rubble for survivors.*

a rescue team *He was still conscious when the rescue team arrived.*

a rescue helicopter/plane/ship etc *A rescue helicopter is on its way.*

research Ac *n*

serious study to discover new facts or test new ideas

ADJECTIVES/NOUNS + research

scientific/medical research *The university is an important centre for scientific research.*

cancer/AIDS etc research *She is raising money for cancer research.*

the latest research (=the most recent research) *The latest research is published in this month's 'Nature' magazine.*

pioneering/groundbreaking research (=producing completely new information) *Watson and Crick did pioneering research into DNA.*

basic research *He wants to conduct basic research into the nature of human cells.*

historical research *This is a fascinating piece of historical research.*

extensive research (=examining a lot of information and details) *The paper was the result of years of extensive research.*

painstaking research (=very careful and thorough) *She spent years carrying out painstaking historical research.*

VERBS

do research/carry out research (*also* **conduct research** *formal*): *The research was carried out by a team of scientists at Tokyo University.*

⚠ Don't say 'make research'.

undertake research *formal* (=do research, or start doing research, especially into a complicated subject) *They are planning to undertake research into the genetic causes of the disease.*

publish research *His research was published in the 'New England Journal of Medicine'.*

present research (=tell people the results of your research) *We will present our research at the conference.*

be based on research *The book is based on research carried out over a number of years.*

research shows/suggests/indicates sth *All the research suggests that the Earth's climate is getting warmer.*

research + NOUNS

a research project/programme/study *We are starting an exciting new research project.*

research results/findings (=what is discovered by research) *He will present his research findings at the conference.*

research work *The original research work was done in the 1960s.*

research methods *The scientists repeated the experiment using the same research methods.*

a research team *A research team in Edinburgh are investigating the causes of the disease.*

a research student *He supervises the work of research students at the university.*

a research paper *The research paper will be published in an international journal.*

PREPOSITIONS

research into sth *They are carrying out research into the causes of global warming.*

research on sth *Pavlov was famous for his research on dogs.*

PHRASES

an area/field of research *Genetics is a very exciting area of research.*

a piece of research *This is an interesting piece of research.*

a body of research (=results from several pieces of research) *There is a large body of research which indicates that passive smoking causes cancer.*

THESAURUS: research

work
the studies that have been done on a particular subject:
A lot of ***work*** *has been* ***done on*** *hydrogen-powered cars. | Faraday is famous for his* ***work on*** *electricity. | Their* ***groundbreaking work*** *had an enormous influence on the study of genetics* (=very important and discovering things that are completely new).

study
a piece of work in which someone examines a particular subject in order to find out more about it, and writes about what they have found:
The ***study showed*** *that 25 percent of adults do not eat breakfast at all, compared with 14 percent in 1961. |* ***Recent studies suggest*** *that*

our sense of smell is closely linked with the part of the brain that deals with memory. | *The* ***study*** *was* ***carried out*** *under laboratory conditions.*

experiment
a scientific test in order to find out what happens when you do something:
They ***carried out*** *a series of* ***scientific experiments*** *in order to try to prove their theory* (=they did a series of experiments). | ***Experiments*** *have* ***shown*** *that there is an increased risk of some forms of cancer.*

resemblance *n*

a situation in which two people or things are similar, especially in the way they look

ADJECTIVES/NOUNS + resemblance

a close/strong resemblance *This photograph shows that she bears a close resemblance to her mother as a young woman.*

a striking resemblance (=very strong and noticeable) *There's a striking resemblance between the brothers.*

a remarkable resemblance (=unusual or surprising) *Everyone notices the remarkable resemblance between her and her friend.*

an uncanny resemblance (=so strong that you almost cannot believe it) *He bears an uncanny resemblance to the Hollywood star.*

a slight/faint/passing resemblance (=not strong) *Don't you think she has a slight resemblance to that blonde singer in Abba?*

a superficial resemblance (=when something seems like something else, but is in fact quite different) *The animal's spines give it a superficial resemblance to a hedgehog.*

sb's physical resemblance to sb *People often commented on his physical resemblance to his father.*

a family resemblance (=between members of the same family) *Although they were brothers, there was no family resemblance between them.*

VERBS

there is a resemblance between sb/sth *There is definitely a resemblance between the two girls.*

bear/have a resemblance to sb/sth (=seem similar) *People said he bore a striking resemblance to the president.*

bear little/no resemblance to sb/sth (=seem very different) *The film bears little resemblance to the book.*

see a resemblance *I don't see any resemblance between your job and mine.*

PREPOSITIONS

a resemblance to sb/sth *Did you notice his resemblance to his father?*

a resemblance between people/things *The resemblance between the two paintings was striking.*

resemble *v*

to look like, or be similar to, someone or something

ADVERBS

closely/strongly/greatly resemble sth *The painting closely resembles one of his earlier pictures.*

vaguely resemble sth (=slightly) *I heard a weird sound vaguely resembling the bark of a dog.*

PREPOSITIONS

resemble sth in shape/size/taste etc *The building resembles a church in its tall narrow outline.*

PHRASES

nothing remotely resembling sth (=nothing at all like something or as good as something) *Nothing remotely resembling a cure has been found.*

in no way resemble sth (=not resemble it at all) *In no way does she resemble her mother, who was a horrible person.*

resentment *n*

a feeling of anger because something has happened that you think is unfair

ADJECTIVES

deep resentment *The new tax caused deep resentment among voters.*

widespread resentment (=among many people) *The actions of the police during the strike caused widespread resentment.*

bitter resentment (=very strong) *There was bitter resentment among people who had lost their land.*

great/considerable resentment *The decision to cut wages led to great resentment among the workforce.*

growing/increasing resentment *Food shortages caused growing resentment against the government.*

simmering/smouldering resentment (=felt for a long time but not expressed) *His smouldering resentment against his neighbour erupted into violence.*

VERBS

cause/create resentment (*also* **lead to resentment**) *Giving some students special privileges will cause resentment among the other students.*

feel resentment *He felt a lot of resentment because of the way he had been treated by the government.*

harbour resentment *BrE*, **harbor resentment** *AmE* (=continue to feel it) *You obviously harbour some resentment against your ex-boyfriend.*

breed/provoke resentment (=cause it) *These misunderstandings had bred resentment.*

arouse resentment (=make people feel it) *The*

terms of his contract aroused deep resentment among the other players.

fuel resentment (=make it stronger) *Any further sign of unfair treatment would fuel the resentment that workers already felt.*

PREPOSITIONS

resentment at/over/about sth *There was resentment at the way some people were able to avoid paying any tax.*

resentment against/towards sb *There is a lot of resentment against the police.*

PHRASES

a cause/source of resentment *Her husband's failure to do any housework was a major source of resentment.*

a sense/feeling of resentment *There is a strong sense of resentment among workers when they hear that bosses are getting huge bonuses.*

reservation *n*

1 an arrangement to use a place in a hotel, restaurant, plane etc at a particular time in the future

VERBS

make a reservation *I made a reservation at our favourite hotel.*

have a reservation *The waiter asked if we had a reservation.*

confirm a reservation *We will send you an email to confirm your reservation.*

cancel a reservation *She called the restaurant and cancelled the reservation.*

NOUNS + reservation

a dinner/lunch reservation *Dozens of people called the new restaurant to make dinner reservations.*

a hotel reservation *I cancelled my hotel reservation.*

an airline reservation *Make sure you have an airline reservation before booking the hotel.*

a seat reservation *Seat reservations must be made in advance for all peak time trains.*

reservation + NOUNS

a reservation fee *There is a reservation fee if you book over the phone.*

a reservation service *Rooms at these hotels are booked through a central reservations service.*

reservations staff *Our reservations staff are waiting to take your call.*

PREPOSITIONS

a reservation for sth/sb *I made a reservation for lunch for eight people.*

a reservation for 7.30/8 o'clock/tonight etc *We have a reservation for eight o'clock.*

a reservation at sth *She had made a reservation at a hotel nearby.*

2 a feeling of doubt about whether something is good or right

> **Grammar**
> Usually plural in this meaning.

VERBS

have reservations *I have my reservations about his work.* | *I had no reservations about her abilities as a manager.*

harbour reservations *BrE formal*, **harbor reservations** *AmE formal* (=have them, especially for some time) *We agreed to the change, although we still harboured some reservations.*

express/voice reservations (=say that you have reservations) *He expressed reservations about the practicality of the idea.*

ADJECTIVES

some/certain reservations *Despite some reservations, I recommend this book.*

serious/grave reservations *They had serious reservations about the plan.*

strong reservations *Five of the committee members expressed strong reservations about the product's safety.*

considerable reservations *We have considerable reservations about the government's economic proposals.*

a minor/slight reservation (=not serious or important) *I voted 'yes', although I had a few minor reservations*

a major reservation (=serious or important) *We have major reservations about his ability to do the job.*

PREPOSITIONS

reservations about/over/concerning sth (*also* **reservations as to sth**) *We had a few reservations concerning the car's design.*

PHRASES

without reservation *I can say without reservation that he would be an excellent team coach.*

reserve[1] *v*

to arrange for a place in a hotel, restaurant, plane etc to be kept for you to use at a particular time in the future

NOUNS

reserve a seat *It's a good idea to reserve seats on the train.*

reserve a table (=at a restaurant) *I'd like to reserve a table for two.*

reserve a place *Pay a deposit of £10, and we will reserve a place for your child on the course.*

reserve a room *When visiting Korea on business, it is best to reserve your room well in advance.*

reserve a ticket *Call the box office now to reserve your tickets.*

PREPOSITIONS

reserve sth for sb/sth *We've reserved a table for you.*

reserve² *n*

1 a supply of something which you can use later

ADJECTIVES

a large/vast/huge reserve *Iraq has vast oil reserves.*

a small reserve *They kept a small reserve of money for use in emergencies.*

a dwindling reserve (=one that is becoming smaller) *The company has dwindling cash reserves.*

VERBS

have/hold a reserve *The country has the largest oil reserves in the world.*

build up/accumulate a reserve (=get a lot of something so that you have a reserve) *Birds need extra food to build up their fat reserves for winter.*

use/draw on a reserve *The team will have to draw on their reserves of strength.*

dip into a reserve (=use some of a supply of money) *Mexico was forced to dip into reserves to support the peso.*

deplete a reserve (=make it much smaller) *A long period without rain had depleted water reserves.*

replenish a reserve (=make it bigger again) *Sleep helps to replenish energy reserves.*

exhaust a reserve (=use all of it) *We will need other forms of power when coal reserves have been exhausted.*

NOUNS + reserve

a cash reserve *Building up a cash reserve for the future makes good sense.*

gas/coal/oil/gold reserves *The bank sold one fifth of its gold reserves last year.*

energy/fuel reserves *The plane had already used most of its fuel reserves.*

PREPOSITIONS

a reserve of sth *Russia holds large reserves of gas.*

PHRASES

keep/hold sth in reserve (=keep it so that it is ready to be used if needed) *The money should be kept in reserve until needed.*

THESAURUS: reserve

stock, supply, reserves → **store (2)**

2 *BrE* a place where wild animals and plants are protected

ADJECTIVES/NOUNS + reserve

a wildlife/nature reserve *They visited a wildlife reserve in Borneo.*

a game reserve *The Masai Mara game reserve in Kenya is very popular with tourists.*

a bird/tiger etc reserve *The area has a coastal bird reserve.*

a marine reserve (=one for sea animals) *Marine reserves have a role in boosting fish stocks.*

a forest reserve *The government wants to establish national forest reserves.*

VERBS

visit a reserve *Hundreds of people have visited the reserve to see the birds.*

create/establish a reserve *The Wildlife Trust has created a nature reserve.*

manage a reserve *The organization manages ten reserves.*

reserved *adj* THESAURUS ▸ **quiet (2)**

residence Ac *n formal*

1 someone's house - used especially about a large house where an important person lives

ADJECTIVES/NOUNS + residence

sb's official residence *The prime minister's official residence is 10 Downing Street.*

a private residence *The hotel was formerly a private residence.*

the royal residence (=where the king or queen lives) *Balmoral is the Queen's royal residence in Scotland.*

the presidential residence (=where the president lives) *Villa Somalia is the presidential residence.*

sb's main/principal/primary residence *The house is his main residence, but he also has a cottage in the country.*

a desirable residence *The old house was completely rebuilt and is now a very desirable residence.*

a summer residence *Castel Gandolfo is the Pope's summer residence.*

2 if someone is in residence somewhere, they are living there. **Residence** is used mainly in official contexts, or in formal writing

PHRASES

sb's place/country of residence (=the place where someone lives) *The form asks you to give your country of residence.*

sb is in residence (=they are staying in a place) *The flag flies above the palace when the Queen is in residence.*

VERBS

take up residence *formal* (=start living somewhere) *Some bees have taken up residence in the wall.*

apply for residence (=ask for the legal right to live in a country) *He applied for permanent residence in Canada.*

grant sb residence (=give official permission to live in a country) *She was granted residence in the UK in 2006.*

ADJECTIVES

permanent/temporary residence *formal*: *The birds seem to have taken up permanent residence near the lake.*

residence + NOUNS

a residence permit (=an official document allowing you to live in a country) *He had applied for a residence permit.*

resign *v*

to officially say that you will leave your job or position

VERBS

be forced to resign *The manager was forced to resign after another terrible season for the club.*

be asked to resign *There are rumours that the chief executive has been asked to resign.*

call on sb to resign (=say publicly that you think they should resign) *Some politicians are calling on the prime minister to resign.*

decide to resign *He decided to resign because of ill health.*

threaten to resign *She threatened to resign if changes were not made immediately.*

refuse to resign *Although he is deeply unpopular, he is refusing to resign as president.*

NOUNS

resign your post/position/office *She later resigned her post as minister of energy.*

resign your seat (=resign as member of Parliament, Congress, a committee etc) *A majority of voters think he should resign his seat in Congress.*

resign your membership *He recently resigned his membership of the National Rifle Association.*

ADVERBS

resign immediately *We call on the company chairman to resign immediately.*

resign voluntarily (=without being forced to do so) *There is little chance that she will resign voluntarily.*

PREPOSITIONS

resign from sth *She resigned from the government last week.*

resign as sth *He resigned as Governor in August.*

resign over sth (=because of it) *I don't think any minister will be asked to resign over this issue.*

resignation *n*

an occasion when you tell someone you are leaving your job

VERBS

hand in your resignation (*also* **tender/submit your resignation** *formal*) (=say that you are going to leave an organization) *I'm thinking of handing in my resignation.*

announce your resignation (=tell people you have resigned) *No one was surprised when she announced her resignation.*

accept sb's resignation *The prime minister reluctantly accepted her resignation.*

demand/call for sb's resignation (=ask for it publicly) *His political opponents demanded his resignation.*

offer your resignation *Claire apologized and offered her resignation.*

withdraw your resignation (=say that you will not leave, after having said you would) *The president persuaded him to withdraw his resignation.*

force sb's resignation (=make them have to resign) *Illness forced his resignation.*

ADJECTIVES/NOUNS + resignation

sb's immediate resignation *They called for his immediate resignation.*

sb's sudden resignation *Her sudden resignation shocked everyone.*

a surprise/shock resignation *They had to find a new coach after the shock resignation of Kenny Dalglish.*

mass resignations (=by a lot of people) *The dispute led to mass resignations.*

PREPOSITIONS

sb's resignation as sth *He announced his resignation as party secretary.*

sb's resignation from sth *No one knows the reasons for her resignation from the government.*

PHRASES

a letter of resignation *I'm thinking of writing a letter of resignation.*

a call for sb's resignation *Despite calls for his resignation, he is continuing in the job.*

resist *v*

1 to try to prevent something from happening

ADVERBS

strongly/vigorously/strenuously resist sth *They strongly resisted any attempt to change the law.*

fiercely resist sth *The proposed change has been fiercely resisted by car companies.*

stubbornly resist sth (=in a very determined way) *Workers stubbornly resisted all attempts to modernize the factory.*

successfully resist sth *He successfully resisted a challenge to his leadership.*

actively resist sth (=by taking action) *Opposition politicians say they will actively resist proposals to change the voting system.*

repeatedly resist sth *They have repeatedly resisted attempts by foreign troops to take control of the island.*

NOUNS

resist pressure *The government resisted pressure to cut taxes.*

resist an attempt to do sth (*also* **resist efforts to do sth**) *Club members resisted the chairman's attempts to change the rules.*

resist change *People resist change because they fear the unknown.*

resist demands/calls for sth *She has so far resisted calls for her resignation.*

resist arrest (=fight with police officers who are trying to arrest you) *Police said the suspect was injured while resisting arrest.*

2 to stop yourself from having what you want, or doing something that you want to do

PHRASES

cannot resist (doing) sth *I can't resist chocolate.*

be unable/powerless to resist sth *He was unable to resist the temptation to smoke.*

be hard/difficult to resist *The urge to follow them was hard to resist.*

be impossible to resist *The impulse to give him a hug was almost impossible to resist.*

NOUNS

resist the temptation to do sth *He resisted the temptation to look back.*

resist the urge/impulse to do sth *She resisted the urge to touch his hand.*

resist the lure/pull of sth (=resist its attractive quality) *Bond could never resist the lure of a beautiful woman.*

sb cannot resist a challenge *He is a man who cannot resist a challenge.*

resist an invitation *It's hard to resist an invitation like that.*

ADVERBS

resist sth strongly/firmly *She strongly resisted the temptation to tell him her news.*

resist sth successfully *I had successfully resisted the urge to open another bottle of wine.*

resistance *n*

1 a refusal to accept new ideas or changes

ADJECTIVES

strong/fierce/stiff resistance *There was strong resistance to the changes among the staff.*

considerable resistance *The suggestion met with considerable resistance from his colleagues.*

stubborn resistance (=very determined and refusing to change) *The workers' stubborn resistance to the new system is frustrating for managers.*

token resistance (=only a small amount of resistance, because you know you cannot stop something from happening) *His parents put up only a token resistance to his plans.*

VERBS

put up/offer resistance (=resist someone or something) *If the rest of us are agreed, I don't think he'll put up much resistance.*

meet (with) resistance (*also* **encounter resistance** *formal*) (=be resisted) *Attempts to change the education system have met with strong resistance in many colleges.*

overcome resistance (=fight and win against it) *The president will have to overcome resistance to the reforms in Congress.*

PREPOSITIONS

resistance to sth *Has there been much resistance to that idea?*

resistance from sb *The plans to build the airport met with a lot of resistance from people living in the local area.*

2 fighting against someone who is attacking you

ADJECTIVES

armed resistance *The soldiers met with little armed resistance and they quickly took control of the city.*

fierce/strong resistance *Government troops met with fierce resistance from rebel forces.*

violent resistance *Three days of violent resistance left over a thousand people dead.*

heroic resistance *The people of Stalingrad put up a heroic resistance against the invading German army.*

little/no resistance *The army met with little resistance and soon took the capital city.*

passive resistance (=a way of protesting or opposing a government without using violence) *Women struggling for equal rights fought a campaign of passive resistance.*

VERBS

put up/offer resistance (=resist someone or something) *The invading army did not expect the local population to put up so much resistance.*

meet (with) resistance (*also* **encounter resistance** *formal*) (=be resisted) *The troops advanced swiftly, encountering only minor resistance.*

crush resistance (=end it by force) *The dictator warned that any resistance would be crushed.*

resistance collapses *Troops crossed the river with ease, as local resistance seemed to have collapsed.*

resistance + NOUNS

the resistance movement (=people who work together to resist forces controlling their country) *Members of the resistance movement were arrested and shot.*

PREPOSITIONS

resistance from sb *They met with strong resistance from local people.*

resistance against sb *He fought in the resistance against the occupying forces.*

resolute *adj* THESAURUS ▶ **determined**

resolve Ac *v*

to find a satisfactory way of dealing with a problem or difficulty

R

ADVERBS

resolve sth fully/completely *The problem has not yet been fully resolved.*

resolve sth satisfactorily *We are hoping that the dispute can be satisfactorily resolved.*

resolve sth peacefully *The police say they want to resolve the situation peacefully, without using force.*

resolve sth amicably (=in a friendly way) *We will always do our best to resolve complaints amicably.*

resolve sth quickly/promptly/swiftly *The matter was resolved fairly quickly.*

resolve sth diplomatically (=by political discussions, not military force) *We hope that the two sides can resolve the dispute diplomatically.*

NOUNS

resolve a problem/crisis/situation *Action is being taken to resolve the problem.*

resolve a dispute/conflict *Open discussion is the only way to resolve a dispute.*

resolve an issue/matter/question *Unless this issue is resolved, there is no chance of reaching an agreement.*

resolve your differences (=stop arguing with each other) *She had finally resolved her differences with her mother.*

PREPOSITIONS

resolve sth by/through sth *Most problems are best resolved through discussion.*

resort *n*

a place where a lot of people go for holidays

ADJECTIVES/NOUNS + resort

a tourist resort *Sharm el-Sheikh is a well-known tourist resort in Egypt, on the Red Sea.*

a holiday resort *BrE*: *The south coast of the island is full of crowded holiday resorts.*

a popular resort *The popular resort of Brighton is only 50 minutes away from London.*

a fashionable resort *They ski at the fashionable resort of Aspen, Colorado.*

a beach resort *We stayed at a relaxing beach resort on the east coast.*

a coastal resort *The coastal resort of Phuket in Thailand is very popular with Western tourists.*

a seaside resort *BrE* (=next to the sea) *Newquay is a popular seaside resort in Cornwall.*

a ski resort/winter resort *The lack of snow is causing problems for ski resorts.*

a mountain resort *The royal couple are having a two-week holiday in the exclusive Swiss mountain resort of Klosters.*

a health resort (=a place where people go for health treatments) *Bath was famous as a health resort in the 18th century.*

a lively resort *Pattaya is a lively resort with plenty of bars and cafés.*

PREPOSITIONS

at/in a resort *They had a two-week holiday in the resort of Orlando.*

resource Ac *n*

1 something such as land or oil that exists in a country and can be used to increase its wealth

> **Grammar**
> Often plural in this meaning.

ADJECTIVES/NOUNS + resource

natural resources *The country has always relied on coal and other natural resources.*

mineral resources *This area is rich in mineral resources.*

energy resources *This small nation has few energy resources of its own.*

a renewable resource (=one that replaces itself naturally, or is easily replaced) *Trees are a renewable resource.*

a non-renewable resource *We should reduce our use of non-renewable resources.*

a finite resource (=one which is limited in amount, so that it will no longer exist if people continue to use it) *Crude oil is a finite resource.*

dwindling resources (=becoming smaller and smaller, so that there is very little left) *We need to change the way we manage the Earth's dwindling resources.*

water/oil resources *The discovery of oil resources in the North Sea was good for Britain's economy.*

a national resource *High-quality agricultural land is a valuable national resource.*

VERBS

use resources *Modern products use fewer natural resources.*

exploit resources (=get them out of the ground and use them to make or do things) *Russia still has huge resources waiting to be exploited.*

tap resources (=get them from a place) *Several nations are eager to tap the mineral resources in Antarctica.*

PHRASES

be rich in resources (=have a lot of them) *Swaziland is rich in natural resources.*

2 something such as money, workers, or materials that is available to use

> **Grammar**
> Often plural in this meaning.

ADJECTIVES

available resources *We will need to use all our available resources.*

limited/scarce resources *The charity does a great job with very limited resources.*

meagre resources *BrE*, **meager resources** *AmE* (=very small in amount) *The family would have to manage on very meagre resources.*

additional/extra resources *The hospital would need extra resources if there was a major disaster.*

a valuable/precious resource *Summer workers are a valuable resource for the farming industry.*

an untapped resource (=which exists but is not used) *Women workers were a great untapped resource.*

financial/economic resources *Lack of financial resources should not be a barrier to education.*

material resources (=money, equipment, and other things that people have) *Material resources are not the only things that matter – you can have all these things and still be unhappy.*

human resources *formal* (=the workers in a company, or the department responsible for hiring and managing them) *She's head of human resources for a major chemical company.*

VERBS

have resources *Do the police have all the resources they need?*

use resources (*also* **make use of resources**) *We must use our resources efficiently.*

allocate resources (=give them to a particular person, group etc) *I spoke to the official who was in charge of allocating the resources.*

target resources (=decide to use them for a particular purpose) *Limited resources need to be targeted at the most urgent projects.*

pool your resources (=put together the resources that each of you have) *The three families pooled their resources to buy a business.*

waste resources *We cannot afford to waste our resources on fighting each other.*

resource + NOUNS

a resource centre *BrE*, **a resource center** *AmE* (=a place where books and other materials are available for people to use) *The building has a resource centre for unemployed people.*

respect[1] *v*

1 to admire someone because you think they are very good, fair etc

ADVERBS

respect sb greatly *I admire her and respect her greatly.*

highly respected *The author is a highly respected historian.*

widely respected (=by many people) *The general is widely respected in the army.*

well respected *She was well respected by her colleagues.*

much respected *David was a much respected member of the staff.*

widely respected (=by many people in many places) *Johnson was widely respected as a critic.*

internationally respected *The former US president is an internationally respected figure.*

universally respected (=respected by everyone) *Pele is one of the most universally respected footballers of all time.*

PHRASES

a respected member *Her father was a greatly respected member of the community.*

a respected figure (=person) *We were lucky to have such a respected figure as a teacher.*

a respected journalist/historian/writer etc *The programme's presenter is a respected historian.*

PREPOSITIONS

respect sb for sth *She respected him for his honesty.*

2 to treat something as being very important and not do anything against it

NOUNS

respect sb's wishes *The council should respect the wishes of local people.*

respect sb's views *I respect your views even if I don't agree with them.*

respect sb's decision/choice *I had to respect my son's decision.*

respect the law/a rule *She had been brought up to respect the law.*

respect sb's right(s) *Governments must respect human rights.*

respect sb's privacy *We respect the privacy of our customers, and never pass personal information on to anybody else.*

respect confidentiality (=respect the right to keep something secret) *Doctors must respect the confidentiality of patients.*

respect a need *Please respect the needs of others by keeping noise to a minimum.*

respect differences/diversity *We should respect differences between ourselves and other people and their cultures.*

THESAURUS: respect

follow, abide by, comply with, respect → **obey**

respect[2] *n*

1 the feeling you have when you think someone is good or the standard of their work is good

ADJECTIVES

great respect *He liked Bill and had great respect for his ability as chairman.*

the utmost respect (=a lot of respect) *I have the utmost respect for the prime minister.*

mutual respect (=when two people respect each other) *Their relationship is based on mutual respect.*

grudging respect (=respect, after at first feeling uncertain or unwilling about this) *For the first time in his life, he felt a grudging respect for Ryan.*

R

VERBS

have/feel respect for sb/sth *I have great respect for his work.*

win/earn/gain respect (=start to be respected) *The new coach quickly earned the respect of his players.*

command respect (=be respected) *Lady Thatcher commanded huge respect from everyone she worked with.*

deserve respect *Nurses deserve our respect and admiration.*

lose respect for sb (=no longer respect them) *She had lost all respect for him.*

lose sb's respect (=no longer be respected by them) *Once a child knows you have lied, you will lose their respect.*

PREPOSITIONS

respect for sb/sth *I have a lot of respect for people like Jane.*

2 behaviour in which you treat other people politely, or treat something as being important

VERBS

show respect *Students should show respect for their teachers.*

treat sb/sth with respect *When we were young, we treated our parents with respect.*

have respect for sb/sth *That boy has no respect for authority.*

get respect (=be treated with respect) *You get more respect if you dress smartly.*

ADJECTIVES

proper respect (=suitable) *A guest should be treated with proper respect.*

deep respect *The islanders have a deep respect for the ocean.*

PHRASES

respect for sb/sth *They have no respect for human rights.*

out of respect (for sb/sth) (=because you respect someone or something) *Alcohol will not be served, out of respect for our Muslim visitors.*

PHRASES

a lack of respect *The boys showed a complete lack of respect for authority.*

as a mark of respect (=as a sign of respect, especially for someone who has just died) *As a mark of respect for the victims, they held a minute's silence.*

with (all) due respect *formal* (=used when you disagree with someone or criticize them in a polite way) *With all due respect, I think you're wrong.*

3 an aspect of something

PHRASES

in some/certain respects *In some respects, this is true.*

in this/that respect *Her mother is very beautiful, and Kim takes after her in that respect.*

in one respect *In one respect, he improved the system.*

in every respect/in all respects *The hotel was good in every respect.*

respectable *adj* THESAURUS > **good (3)**

respond [Ac] *v*

to do something as a reaction to something that has been said or done

ADVERBS

respond immediately *The US government responded immediately to their request for help.*

respond quickly/rapidly/promptly *You need to respond quickly in an emergency.*

respond positively/favourably (=in a way that shows you like something) *People responded favourably to the changes.*

respond appropriately/effectively *Businesses must respond appropriately to changing markets.*

respond accordingly (=in a way that is suitable or based on what has happened) *Inform us of any problem and we will respond accordingly.*

respond angrily *He responded angrily to claims that he had cheated.*

respond enthusiastically *Eugenie responded enthusiastically to this news.*

PREPOSITIONS

respond to sth *We aim to respond to complaints quickly.*

respond by doing sth *Her father responded by sending her some more money.*

respond with sth *Villagers responded with offers of help.*

PHRASES

fail to respond *The pilot failed to respond quickly enough to the situation, and the plane crashed.*

response [Ac] *n*

something that is done as a reaction to something that has happened or been said

ADJECTIVES

a positive/favourable response (=which shows you like something) *The measures were greeted with a positive response from most business leaders.*

a negative response (=which shows you do not like something) *I didn't understand the negative response to the book.*

a good/encouraging response (=when people like something or show interest) *We've had a good response from the students to our questionnaire.*

a poor response (=not many people have responded) *So far there has been a poor response to our appeals for information.*

an enthusiastic response *There has been an enthusiastic response to the UN's proposals.*

R

a lukewarm response (=not showing much interest or excitement) *His suggestion got only a lukewarm response.*

a mixed response (=when some people like or agree with something but others do not) *Despite a mixed response from critics, the film has done well at the box office.*

sb's immediate response *When he heard the news, his immediate response was disbelief.*

a direct response (=with no other factors involved) *Her resignation was a direct response to the party's poor results in the elections.*

an appropriate response *She laughed, which didn't really seem an appropriate response.*

an angry response *The decision provoked an angry response from residents.*

VERBS

get/receive a response *She got an enthusiastic response to her suggestion.*

meet with a response (=get it) *The changes met with a mixed response from employees.*

provoke a response (=cause a quick or sudden response) *The report provoked a strong response from senior police officers.*

bring a response *His cries for help brought no response.*

draw/produce a response *His comments drew an angry response from other EU leaders.*

elicit/evoke a response *formal* (=get someone to respond) *So far I have failed to elicit any response to my inquiry.*

response + NOUNS

the response time (=how long someone or something takes to respond, especially the emergency services) *The average response time to 999 calls is 4 minutes.*

PREPOSITIONS

sb's response to sth *We have been overwhelmed by the public's response to our appeal for help.*

a response from sb *His first novel received a favourable response from the critics.*

in response to sth (=because something has happened or someone has said or done something) *The law was passed in response to public pressure.*

PHRASES

a lack of response *She was disappointed by the lack of response to her request.*

responsibility *n*

1 a duty to be in charge of something

ADJECTIVES

my/your/her etc responsibility *It's my responsibility to make sure that the work is done on time.*

personal responsibility *Workers have personal responsibility for the quality of the products they produce.*

direct/total responsibility *He has taken over direct responsibility for the running of the company.*

sole responsibility (=not shared with others) *The financial director has sole responsibility for financial matters.*

overall responsibility (=for all of something) *The Department for Education has overall responsibility for schools and universities.*

collective responsibility (=shared equally by a group of people) *Head teachers should encourage a sense of collective responsibility among teachers.*

primary responsibility (=you are the person who has the main responsibility) *I have primary responsibility for the children.*

ultimate responsibility (=responsibility for making a final decision) *Ultimate responsibility for the company lies with its directors.*

VERBS

be sb's responsibility *It's the project manager's responsibility to make sure that we don't spend too much money.*

have responsibility for (doing) sth *The prime minister has responsibility for running the government.*

take responsibility for (doing) sth *Who do you trust to take responsibility for our country's defence?*

take on responsibility (*also* **assume responsibility** *formal*) (=start to have responsibility for something) *Men are taking on more responsibility at home.*

shoulder responsibility (=agree to start having a difficult or unpleasant duty) *Should children shoulder responsibility for caring for their elderly parents?*

exercise responsibility *formal* (=take action because you have responsibility for something) *Governments must exercise their responsibility to protect their people.*

shirk responsibility (=not accept a duty you should accept) *He doesn't shirk responsibility.*

abdicate responsibility *formal* (=refuse to have responsibility for something any longer) *The state should not allow parents to abdicate responsibility for their children.*

the responsibility lies/rests with sb (=they are responsible for it) *The responsibility for learning lies with the student.*

PREPOSITIONS

responsibility for sth *He is a manager with responsibility for over 100 staff.*

PHRASES

a position of responsibility (=a job in which you have a lot of responsibility) *People in positions of responsibility should not behave like this.*

a sense of responsibility (=a feeling that you are responsible) *She felt an enormous sense of responsibility towards the rest of the band.*

a burden of responsibility (=a lot of responsibility, that worries you) *Being the only wage earner put a great burden of responsibility on my father.*

2 blame for something bad that has happened

ADJECTIVES

full responsibility *The airline accepted full responsibility for the crash.*

personal responsibility *I take personal responsibility for what went wrong.*

VERBS

accept/take responsibility for sth *The doctor admitted full responsibility for the error that led to her death.*

claim/admit responsibility (for sth) (=say that you are responsible for something bad) *No group has yet claimed responsibility for the bombings.*

deny responsibility for sth *He denied responsibility, blaming the other driver for the accident.*

bear responsibility for sth (=be responsible for something bad) *Developed countries must bear much of the responsibility for environmental problems.*

PREPOSITIONS

responsibility for sth *The firm is denying all responsibility for the mistake.*

3 something you have to do or ought to do

ADJECTIVES

a big/major responsibility (=involving a lot of work) *Running a farm is a big responsibility.*

a heavy responsibility (=serious and important) *You take on a heavy responsibility when you adopt a child.*

daily/day-to-day responsibilities *Her day-to-day responsibilities involve answering the phone and typing letters.*

a moral responsibility (=that you do because it is the right thing to do, rather than because you have to do it) *We have a moral responsibility to help people in developing countries.*

a social responsibility (=towards society) *Companies have social responsibilities – it's not just about making as much profit as possible.*

NOUNS + responsibility

family/work responsibilities *I can't stay late in the evenings because of family responsibilities.*

VERBS

have a responsibility to do sth *We all have a responsibility to protect the environment.*

take on a responsibility (=start doing something someone has asked you to do) *She was happy to take on the extra responsibilities.*

carry out/meet your responsibilities (=do what you should do) *He was too ill to carry out his responsibilities as governor.*

face your responsibilities (=start doing what you should be doing) *It's time you faced your responsibilities and started thinking about your kids.*

shirk your responsibilities (=not do what you should be doing) *She was always trying to shirk her responsibilities.*

PREPOSITIONS

sb's responsibility is to sb/sth *A doctor's first responsibility is to his patients.*

responsible *adj*

1 used for saying that a person or thing did something or caused a situation

ADVERBS

directly responsible *He has been blamed for the failure of the company but he is not directly responsible.*

indirectly responsible *The parents are indirectly responsible for the problems their son has caused.*

partly responsible *They were both partly responsible for the breakup of their marriage.*

largely responsible *Exports are largely responsible for their impressive economic performance.*

personally responsible (=the one person who is responsible) *I will hold you personally responsible if anything goes wrong.*

VERBS

hold sb responsible (=consider someone to be responsible) *If these keys get lost, I will hold you responsible.*

feel responsible *I would feel responsible if anything went wrong.*

be thought/believed to be responsible *Local youths are thought to be responsible for the fire.*

find sb responsible *If the courts find him responsible, he will have to pay a fine.*

PREPOSITIONS

responsible for sth *The person responsible for the accident should pay for any damage.*

PHRASES

those responsible (=the people who are responsible) *Those responsible for this terrible crime will be severely punished.*

2 if you are responsible for someone or something, it is your duty to be in charge of them

ADVERBS

legally responsible *Your parents are legally responsible for you until the age of 18.*

solely responsible *One person can't be solely responsible for all this work.*

jointly responsible *John and Alan are jointly responsible for paying the rent.*

collectively responsible *All members of the team are collectively responsible for decisions.*

R

primarily/mainly responsible *In most homes, women are still primarily responsible for buying food.*

responsible + NOUNS

a responsible position/job (=one that is important because you are in charge of someone or something) *Judges have a very responsible position in society.*

PREPOSITIONS

responsible for sth *Linda is responsible for a large sales team.*

rest *n*

a period of time when you are relaxing or sleeping

VERBS

have/take a rest *I'm going upstairs to have a rest.*

need a rest (*also* **be in need of a rest**) *He'd been gardening all day and needed a rest.*

get some rest *You'd better get some rest if you're driving back tonight.*

deserve a rest *I think we deserve a rest after all that hard work.*

give sth a rest (=stop using a part of your body for a while) *Try and give your ankle a rest so it can heal.*

ADJECTIVES

a well-earned/well-deserved rest (=a rest after working hard) *Our players are taking a well-earned rest before the start of the new season.*

a complete rest *The doctor had advised a complete rest for a fortnight.*

a little/short rest *He decided to stop and take a short rest.*

a long rest *What I need is a nice long rest.*

a good rest (=a complete rest that relaxes you) *After a good rest, he felt a lot better.*

enough rest (*also* **adequate rest** *formal*): *Make sure you get adequate rest.*

rest + NOUNS

a rest day/period *The players will get a rest day on Monday.*

PREPOSITIONS

a rest from sth *She decided that she needed a rest from her job and booked a vacation.*

restaurant *n*

a place where you can buy and eat a meal

ADJECTIVES/NOUNS + restaurant

a Chinese/Italian etc restaurant *I booked a table at a local Italian restaurant.*

an expensive restaurant *He took her out to an expensive restaurant.*

a trendy/fashionable restaurant *The hotel is surrounded by elegant boutiques and trendy restaurants.*

a fancy restaurant *informal* (=expensive and fashionable) *We went out to a fancy restaurant for our anniversary.*

a posh restaurant *informal* (=expensive and formal) *I can't afford to eat at posh restaurants on my salary.*

a fast-food restaurant *The High Street is full of fast-food restaurants.*

a self-service restaurant (=one where you collect the food yourself) *You need to go up to the counter to get your food – it's a self-service restaurant.*

a fish/seafood restaurant *I went to a seafood restaurant by the harbour for lunch.*

a hotel restaurant *We went downstairs for a meal in the hotel restaurant.*

VERBS + restaurant

go to a restaurant *We went to a little Italian restaurant near Covent Garden.*

take sb to a restaurant *He's taking me to a Japanese restaurant in town.*

eat at/in a restaurant (*also* **dine at/in a restaurant** *formal*): *Have you eaten in this restaurant before?*

manage/run/operate a restaurant *My husband and I ran a restaurant together.*

own a restaurant *Her family owns a restaurant which she manages.*

open a restaurant (=start operating a new restaurant) *He plans to open a chain of restaurants in the Midwest.*

restaurant + VERBS

a restaurant serves sth *The restaurant serves lunch from midday until 2.30.*

a restaurant specializes in sth *Restaurants near the waterfront tend to specialize in seafood.*

restaurant + NOUNS

a restaurant manager *I asked to speak to the restaurant manager.*

PHRASES

a chain of restaurants *The company owns a chain of restaurants.*

restore *v* THESAURUS ▶ **repair**[1]

restriction Ac *n*

a rule or law that limits or controls what people can do

> **Grammar**
> Usually plural.

ADJECTIVES/NOUNS + restriction

severe/strict restrictions *The government put severe restrictions on the media.*

tough/tight restrictions *Many voters want to see tighter restrictions on gun ownership.*

petty restrictions (=that seem unreasonable and unnecessary) *The removal of petty restrictions has made it much easier to do business.*

R

financial restrictions *The financial restrictions imposed on the country are finally being lifted.*
legal restrictions *Legal restrictions prevented him from talking to news reporters.*
speed restrictions *Drivers are ignoring speed restrictions.*
age restrictions *There are no age restrictions for taking part in the competition.*
trade restrictions (=on the sale of goods between countries) *Trade restrictions between the islands were removed.*
import/export restrictions *Import restrictions on manufactured goods have been lifted.*
travel restrictions *The government placed travel restrictions on people who were suspected of being terrorists.*
planning restrictions (=controlling what buildings can be built somewhere) *There are planning restrictions on what kind of houses can be built in this area.*
parking restrictions *Are there parking restrictions in the city centre?*

VERBS

put/place restrictions on sth *The authorities placed strict restrictions on diamond exports.*
impose restrictions *formal* (=put restrictions on something) *Some countries have imposed restrictions on advertising aimed at children.*
introduce restrictions *Other cities now plan to introduce similar traffic restrictions.*
lift/remove restrictions (=end them) *He promised to lift restrictions on press freedom.*
abolish restrictions (=officially end them completely) *We want to abolish age restrictions on recruitment.*
tighten restrictions (=make them stricter) *The government recently tightened restrictions on immigration.*
enforce restrictions (=make people obey them) *Bar owners will have to enforce restrictions on smoking.*
relax/ease restrictions (=make them less strict) *The EU relaxed restrictions on UK beef.*
a restriction applies to sb/sth *These restrictions will apply to everyone who lives in the area.*

PREPOSITIONS

restrictions on sth *There are restrictions on travel to Cuba by US citizens.*
without restriction(s) *We could travel wherever we wanted, without restriction.*
the restriction of sth *The restriction of competition will hurt the economy.*

PHRASES

there is no restriction on sth *There is no restriction on the amount of money you can take out of your bank account.*

be subject to a restriction (=be affected by it) *Court cases are subject to reporting restrictions.*

restructure *v* THESAURUS change[1] (2)

result *n*

1 something that happens because of another thing, or because of someone's actions

ADJECTIVES/NOUNS + result

a direct result *The country's economic problems are a direct result of the situation in the US.*
an indirect result (=not directly caused by something, but related to it in some way) *The job losses were the indirect result of lower-cost imports.*
the final/end result *No one knows what the final result of all these changes will be.*
good/positive/satisfactory/excellent results *The new approach is starting to have some positive results.*
disappointing results (=not as good as you had hoped) *The results of the campaign have been disappointing.*
disastrous/catastrophic results (=extremely bad) *The government decided to increase taxes, with disastrous results for the economy.*
the overall/net result (=after everything has been considered) *The net result was a decrease in the overall amount of crime.*
the immediate result *The immediate result of the treatment was a sudden change in his behaviour.*
an inevitable result (=one that is impossible to avoid) *If oil prices increase, the inevitable result is that other prices will also increase.*
the desired result (=the result you want) *We use tried and tested materials because we know they will produce the desired result.*

VERBS

have a result *The reforms had some unintended results.*
achieve/obtain a result *The artist achieved the result he wanted.*
produce a result (*also* **yield a result** *formal*): *This method of growing crops can produce some excellent results.*

PREPOSITIONS

sth is a result of sth *High unemployment is a direct result of the recession.*
as a result of sth (=because of it) *As a result of the pilots' strike, all flights have had to be cancelled.*
with the result (that)... *Sara was ill last week, with the result that she missed an important test.*
with ... results *His parachute failed to open properly, with disastrous results.*

2 the information produced by a scientific test or from research

ADJECTIVES

the results are positive/negative (=they show something is or is not present) *When they tested him for the disease, the results were negative.*

the first/initial/preliminary results (=the results that you get at the beginning) *The initial results of the research look good.*

a promising result (=showing something is likely to be successful or good in the future) *We have had promising results with this drug in treating patients.*

NOUNS + result

the test results *The blood test results came back normal.*

the laboratory results *We are still waiting for the laboratory results.*

result + VERBS

results show/reveal sth *The results of their tests showed that there was a high level of pollution in the area.*

results suggest/indicate sth (=show that something is likely) *Our results suggest that boys benefit from this kind of teaching.*

results confirm sth *These results confirm our earlier findings.*

results demonstrate sth (=show that it is definitely true) *The results of the clinical trial clearly demonstrate the effectiveness of the drug.*

VERBS + result

analyze/examine/evaluate the results *When we analyzed the results more closely, we found traces of lead in the paint.*

wait for the results *The doctors are still waiting for the results to come back from the laboratory.*

get/see/obtain the results *We won't know anything for certain until we get the results of the X-ray.*

reproduce the results (=produce the same results) *Other studies have not been able to reproduce these results.*

publish your results *They published the results of their research in the 'New England Journal of Medicine'.*

PREPOSITIONS

the results of sth *Professor Jones will give a talk about the results of his research.*

3 the final number of goals, points, or votes at the end of a game, competition, or election

NOUNS + result

an election result *The election result surprised everyone.*

the football results *BrE: He switched on the radio to hear the football results.*

VERBS

the result is announced *The result will be announced by election officials today.*

read out the results (=say them on radio or television) *They read out the football results on the news.*

PREPOSITIONS

the result of sth *The result of the election was never really in doubt.*

result in sth *v* THESAURUS ▸ **cause**[2]

resume *v* THESAURUS ▸ **start**[1] **(1)**, **(2)**

résumé *n*

1 *AmE* a document giving details of your qualifications and work experience, which you send to companies when applying for a job

ADJECTIVES

a full résumé *They asked me to send a full résumé with my application form.*

an impressive résumé *His résumé looks very impressive and he has a lot of experience.*

VERBS

send a résumé *Please send your résumé to the following address.*

enclose a résumé (=include it in your letter) *I am interested in applying for the post of sales manager and I enclose my résumé.*

write a résumé *When you write your résumé, you list your academic qualifications and the companies you have worked for.*

update a résumé (=change it to include the latest information) *The last time I applied for a job was three years ago and my résumé needs updating.*

British people say **CV**.

2 *formal* a short account of something, giving the main details

ADJECTIVES

a brief/quick résumé *Here is a brief résumé of the day's events.*

VERBS

give (sb) a résumé *His report gave a résumé of the year's business.*

present a résumé *We were asked to present a brief résumé of our work.*

PREPOSITIONS

a résumé of sth *The article is a résumé of previous writings on the subject.*

reticent *adj* THESAURUS ▸ **quiet (2)**

retire *v*

to stop working at the end of your career

ADVERBS

retire early *He became ill and retired early.*

retire prematurely (=earlier than you wanted or intended) *She was forced to retire prematurely.*

officially retire *Although he has officially retired, he still does a lot of work for the church.*

newly/recently retired *Newly retired people sometimes find it difficult to adjust to their new life.*

VERBS

be due to retire *Mike is due to retire next year.*
be forced to retire *He was forced to retire early because of poor health.*
have to retire *You don't have to retire yet.*
plan to retire *I'm planning to retire when I'm 55.*
can/can't afford to retire *Many people would like to stop working, but can't afford to retire.*

PREPOSITIONS

retire from sth *Sue retired from teaching three years ago.*
retire as sth *He retired as a doctor last year.*
retire through sth (=because of something) *He worked at the factory for 30 years, before retiring through ill health.*
retire at 60/65/70 (=at a particular age) *Most people expect to retire at 65.*

retirement *n*

the time when people stop working or playing a professional sport, usually because of their age

ADJECTIVES

early retirement (=before the usual or expected time) *She applied for early retirement when she was 58.*
premature retirement (=before the natural or proper time) *The injury forced him into premature retirement.*

VERBS

announce your retirement *Shortly after the election defeat, he announced his retirement from politics.*
approach/near retirement *He's 64 this year and nearing retirement.*
consider/contemplate retirement (=think about retiring) *I asked Sir Alan if he had ever seriously considered retirement.*
come out of retirement (=start working or playing a professional sport again) *The former world champion came out of retirement for one last fight.*

retirement + NOUNS

retirement age *Sixty-five was the normal retirement age for men.*
retirement benefits (=money that you receive from a pension scheme) *Part-time workers at the company get health and retirement benefits.*
retirement date *My retirement date is July 10th next year.*

PREPOSITIONS

sb's retirement as sth *In April, Ms Fielding announced her retirement as director of the company.*
sb's retirement from sth *After his retirement from the army, he became a teacher.*

PHRASES

take early retirement (=retire earlier than usual) *He took early retirement after working as a firefighter for 25 years.*

return[1] *v*

1 to go or come back to a place where you were before

ADVERBS

return home *Her husband returned home late that evening.*
return safely *The space shuttle returned safely to earth.*
return immediately/as soon as possible *Passengers must return to the bus immediately.*
sb has recently/just returned from somewhere *He has recently returned from New York.*

VERBS

plan/hope/wish to return *The singer is planning to return to Europe this summer.*
fail to return *Three of our aircraft failed to return.*

PREPOSITIONS

return to somewhere *Joey plans to return to school in the fall.*
return from somewhere *She had just returned from a visit to India.*

PHRASES

be due to return/be expected to return *He is due to return home in the next few days.*

> **Return or go back?**
> **Return** is more formal and is used especially in written English. In spoken English, people usually say **go back**.
> In spoken English, you also often say that someone **will be back**: *She'll* **be back** *soon.*

2 to do something to someone because they have done the same thing to you

NOUNS

return sb's call (=phone someone who phoned you) *I left a message but he hasn't returned my call.*
return sb's smile *Mark returned her smile.*
return sb's gaze/stare *She kept her eyes fixed on the floor, refusing to return his gaze.*
return sb's love/feelings (=love someone who loves you) *Sadly, she could never return his love.*
return the favour BrE, **return the favor** AmE (=help someone who helped you) *Thanks a lot. I hope I'll be able to return the favour.*
return fire (=shoot back at someone) *One plane opened fire on the American aircraft, which immediately returned fire.*

3 to give, take, or send something back

NOUNS

return a book *All library books must be returned by the end of term.*

return a letter/package/parcel *She returned his letters unopened, and threw away his presents.*

return goods/a product *You can return the product within 30 days if you are not satisfied with it.*

4 to change and be the same as before

PHRASES

return to normal *It will take a few days for the situation to return to normal.*

return² *n*

1 the act of returning from somewhere

ADJECTIVES

sb's safe return *His friends prayed for his safe return.*

an emotional return (=one which makes someone have strong feelings) *After twelve years away, he made an emotional return home.*

VERBS

celebrate sb's return *I bought a bottle of champagne to celebrate your return.*

look forward to sb's return *The whole family is looking forward to her return.*

delay your return *Daniel decided to delay his return for a few days.*

ADVERBS

sb's return home *Soon after his return home he had to go away again.*

return + NOUNS

the return journey/trip (=the journey back to the place where you started) *The return journey took much longer in the rush-hour traffic.*

a return flight (=a flight from one place to another and back again, or the flight itself) *It cost me €215 for a return flight to Paris.*

a return visit (=when you go back to a place you have been to before) *She made a return visit to Northern Ireland in 2009.*

a return ticket *BrE* (=which includes going somewhere and coming back) *It is usually cheaper to buy a return ticket.*

a return fare (=the cost of travelling from one place to another and back again) *The standard return fare is over $1,000.*

PREPOSITIONS

on sb's return *On his return to Canada, he joined the army.*

sb's return from somewhere *He visited her a few days after his return from France.*

sb's return to somewhere *The emperor was greeted enthusiastically on his return to Rome.*

⚠ You say someone's **return home**: *I will see you on my return home.* Don't say 'return to home'. You do not use the preposition **to** with **home**.

2 a change back to a previous state or situation

ADJECTIVES

a successful return *He hopes to make a successful return to cycling after the operation.*

a triumphant/triumphal return (=very successful) *The play marks her triumphant return to the stage.*

a speedy/swift return (=happening quickly) *I wished him a speedy return to good health.*

VERBS

make a return *Liverpool's goalkeeper makes his return from injury in today's match.*

mark a return (=show that something is returning) *The elections mark a return to democracy after 20 years of military rule.*

signal/herald a return *formal* (=be a sign of something returning) *The flowers herald the return of spring.*

PREPOSITIONS

sb's return to sth *The last election brought about the Democrats' return to power.*

sb's return from sth *Barcelona's captain marked his return from injury with a stunning goal.*

revenge *n*

something you do in order to punish someone who has harmed or offended you

VERBS

take revenge *He swore to take revenge on his father's killers.*

get (your) revenge *Louise eventually got her revenge by reporting him to the authorities.*

have your revenge *One day I'll have my revenge.*

seek revenge (=try to get revenge) *I play the role of a woman who seeks revenge on her former partner.*

want revenge *You broke her heart and now she wants revenge.*

exact/wreak revenge *formal* (=take revenge) *By planting the bomb, he was exacting revenge on society.*

vow/swear revenge (=promise to take revenge) *His supporters vowed revenge for his death.*

be looking for revenge (=actively seeking revenge) *He knew that Miguel's brothers would be looking for revenge, so he moved to another city.*

ADJECTIVES

a terrible/awful revenge *The king exacted a terrible revenge on the men who had plotted against him.*

revenge + NOUNS

a revenge attack *The camp was burned down, apparently in a revenge attack.*

a revenge killing *Her death was followed by a series of revenge killings.*

PREPOSITIONS

revenge for sth *She decided to get her revenge for what they had done to her.*

revenge on sb *This was his best chance for revenge on his enemies.*

revenge against sb/sth *He vowed revenge against everyone who had made his life such a misery.*

in revenge for sth *She claimed that she killed her husband in revenge for all that he had done to her.*

PHRASES

an act of revenge *The men were shot dead in an act of revenge for Khan's assassination.*

revenge is sweet (=said when someone feels good because they have got revenge) *It took me a long time, but revenge is sweet.*

revenue *n*

money that an organization receives or earns

ADJECTIVES

total revenue *One third of our total revenue comes from sales of this product.*

annual revenue *The company's annual revenue is over a million dollars.*

additional/extra revenue *Extra revenue will be raised through a new tax.*

lost revenue (=money that could have been earned, but was not) *Strikes have cost $20 million in lost revenue.*

R

VERBS

bring in/earn/raise revenue (=get revenue) *The charges are an efficient way of raising revenue.*

provide/generate/produce revenue *The railways were costing the government money, not providing revenue for it.*

increase/boost revenue (=get more revenue) *Football clubs can boost revenue by playing more matches.*

lose revenue *We cannot continue to lose revenue.*

revenue goes up/increases/rises *Revenue rose slightly this year.*

revenue goes down/falls *Revenue from ticket sales has fallen by 20%.*

NOUNS + revenue

sales revenue *Sales revenue has fallen by 5%.*

export revenue *Cotton accounts for 60% of the country's export revenue.*

advertising revenue (=money paid by companies to be allowed to advertise) *Most TV companies rely on advertising revenue.*

tax revenue *Tax revenue is necessary to pay for government spending.*

government revenue *Thirty percent of government revenue comes from oil.*

revenue + NOUNS

a revenue source *Government contracts are our most important revenue source.*

a revenue stream (=something that provides revenue continuously) *The new college already has a revenue stream from its courses.*

PREPOSITIONS

revenue from sth *Revenue from product sales is invested in research.*

PHRASES

a source of revenue *The island's main source of revenue is tourism.*

a loss of revenue *No planes could fly for a week, causing huge loss of revenue for airlines.*

an increase/rise in revenue *The firm reported a 17% increase in revenue.*

a decrease/fall/drop in revenue *We expect a fall in revenue due to the recession.*

review *n*

1 a careful examination of a situation or process, usually to see if changes are needed

ADJECTIVES/NOUNS + review

a major review *We are conducting a major review of our procedures.*

a thorough/comprehensive/full review *Their conclusion is based on a comprehensive review of previous studies.*

an extensive/wide-ranging review (=one that examines a lot of different aspects of something) *The Chancellor is currently conducting a wide-ranging review of public spending.*

a fundamental review (=one that examines the most basic and important parts of something) *There have been calls for a fundamental review of our voting system.*

a complete/full-scale review *He turned down demands for a full-scale review of the law.*

an annual review *There will be an annual review of your salary.*

an independent review *Their findings have been confirmed by a recent independent review.*

a policy review *The policy review proposed radical changes to the law.*

peer review (=in scientific and other studies, the examination of someone's work by other scientists, researchers etc) *There is a tradition of validating academic research by peer review.*

VERBS

carry out a review (*also* **conduct a review** *formal*): *No one has yet carried out a full review of the system.*

undertake a review (=start doing it) *The department plans to undertake a thorough spending review.*

call for/ask for a review *Police chiefs have called for a review of security procedures.*

seek a review (=try to get a review) *We oppose the decision and will go to the High Court to seek a judicial review.*

order a review (=officially say that there must

be one) *The Home Secretary ordered a full review of the case.*

review + NOUNS

a review body/committee/panel/board *We will set up a pay review body for all staff.*

a review process *We cannot comment until the review process is over.*

PREPOSITIONS

under review (=being reviewed) *During the period under review, wages increased by 8 per cent in total.*

for review *The bill will be sent to a parliamentary committee for review.*

a review of sth *The committee announced a review of all health and safety legislation.*

PHRASES

keep sth under review (=continue to review something) *He recommended that the matter should be kept under review.*

come up for review (=be reviewed after a particular period of time has ended) *His contract is coming up for review in April.*

be subject to review *formal* (=something may be reviewed or changed) *These prices are subject to review.*

2 an article that gives an opinion about a book, film, play, CD etc

ADJECTIVES

a good/bad review *The book received good reviews when it was published.*

a rave review *informal* (=that has a lot of praise) *The album got rave reviews from the music press.*

a glowing review (=that is full of praise) *'The Times' gave the play glowing reviews.*

mixed reviews (=some good and some bad) *The film has had mixed reviews.*

NOUNS + review

a film/movie review *I often disagree with his film reviews.*

a book/record etc review *Our English assignment was to write a book review.*

a restaurant/hotel review *These days you can see the restaurant reviews on the internet.*

VERBS

write a review *He now writes book reviews for the 'Chicago Sun-Times'.*

read a review *I decided to see the movie after reading the review.*

get/receive a review *The exhibition got great reviews in the American press.*

a review appears in sth *His restaurant reviews appear every week in the 'Sunday Times'.*

revise *v* THESAURUS change[1] (2)

revolting *adj* THESAURUS ugly (1)

revolution Ac *n*

1 a complete change in ways of thinking, methods of working etc

ADJECTIVES/NOUNS + revolution

a major revolution *There has been a major revolution in the study of genetics.*

a quiet revolution (=one that has been difficult to notice) *Over the last half-dozen years there has been a quiet revolution in the water industry.*

a technological/digital revolution *We are living through a technological revolution, with 40 new drugs for cancer becoming available in the next five years.*

the scientific revolution (=when modern science first developed) *Newton was one of the fathers of the scientific revolution.*

the Industrial Revolution (=when modern methods of making goods in factories were first used) *In the Industrial Revolution, Birmingham became the workshop of the world.*

the internet/information revolution *Around the world, the internet revolution is giving ordinary people a voice.*

a social revolution (=big changes in society) *The 1960s was the biggest social revolution we have had in this country.*

a green revolution (=a revolution in farming methods) *They are hoping that the technology can create a green revolution that will help farmers grow food more productively.*

VERBS

bring about a revolution *Keynes's work brought about a revolution in the study of economics.*

experience/undergo a revolution (=be affected by one) *We've experienced a revolution in healthcare over the past few years.*

herald a revolution *formal* (= be a sign that something is going to happen) *The opening of the store heralded a revolution in fashion design.*

PREPOSITIONS

a revolution in sth *In the last ten years there has been a revolution in education.*

THESAURUS: revolution

alteration, reform, shift, swing, fluctuation, transformation, revolution, shake-up, U-turn → **change[2]**

2 a situation in which the people change the government and the way in which a country is ruled

ADJECTIVES/NOUNS + revolution

the French/Russian/Arab etc revolution *We had to write an essay about the causes of the French Revolution.*

a socialist revolution *The Marxists claim that a socialist revolution will lead to a classless society.*

R

a violent/bloody revolution *England has never experienced a violent revolution.*

a peaceful revolution *The revolution in Tunisia was mainly peaceful.*

a permanent revolution *Trotsky wanted there to be a permanent revolution.*

a world revolution *They hoped to bring about a world revolution.*

VERBS

lead the revolution *Lenin led the revolution in Russia.*

call for a revolution *He called for a revolution against the government.*

stage/carry out/mount a revolution (=make one happen) *There was an attempt to stage a socialist revolution in 1905.*

a revolution overthrows a government/king etc (=it removes them from power) *He participated in the democratic revolution that overthrew the Tsar.*

PREPOSITIONS

a revolution against sb/sth *There was a revolution against the government of President Mubarak.*

> **Revolution** or **rebellion?**
> A **revolution** is often successful and results in a complete change to the old political system in a country. A **rebellion** is often unsuccessful and does not have such a big effect.

R

revolutionary *adj* THESAURUS ▸ **new (1)**

revolutionize (*also* **revolutionise** *BrE*) *v* THESAURUS ▸ **change[1] (2)**

reward *n*

1 something that you get because you have done something good or helpful or have worked hard

> **Grammar**
> In this meaning **reward** is used as a countable noun: *great rewards | a just reward*, or as an uncountable noun: *little reward.*

ADJECTIVES

great/big/high rewards *His new job brought greater responsibility and greater rewards.*

rich rewards (=great rewards) *Top athletes can expect rich rewards if they win.*

little reward *They have to work very hard for very little reward.*

financial rewards (*also* **monetary rewards** *formal*): *It's a difficult job, but the financial rewards are considerable.*

material rewards (=money or possessions that you get) *They think material rewards are more important than quality of life.*

tangible reward(s) (=things that are clearly valuable) *The war brought little tangible reward for either side.*

a just/fitting reward (=one that someone deserves) *Winning the championship would be a just reward for all their hard work.*

the potential reward(s) *The risk is high but the potential rewards are enormous.*

VERBS

get/receive your reward *They have worked hard and they have got their reward.*

reap the rewards of sth (=get the rewards from what you have done) *She is now reaping the rewards of all her effort.*

give (sb) a reward *If you have done all the jobs on your list, give yourself a reward.*

deserve a reward *They deserve some reward for their work.*

bring rewards (=cause someone to get rewards) *Winning the title brings huge financial rewards.*

PREPOSITIONS

a reward for (doing) sth *The trip was a reward for good behaviour.*

as a reward *The king gave him the castle as a reward for his loyalty.*

2 money that is offered to people for helping find someone or something, especially for helping the police

> **Grammar**
> In this meaning **reward** is usually used as a singular noun.

ADJECTIVES

a large/substantial reward *Despite a substantial reward being offered, the painting has never been found.*

a £10,000/$500 etc reward *A $100,000 reward was offered by her family after her disappearance.*

VERBS

offer a reward/put up a reward *The store has offered a £500 reward for information leading to a conviction.*

claim a reward *He handed them over to the police and claimed his reward.*

collect a reward *She said she had come to collect the reward.*

reward + NOUNS

reward money *He contacted the police, hoping to claim the reward money offered by the bank.*

PREPOSITIONS

a reward for sth *He is offering a reward for the return of the stolen jewellery.*

a reward of £10,000/$500 etc *The newspaper offered a reward of £7,000 for information leading to the arrest of her killer.*

rewarding *adj*

making you feel happy and satisfied or giving you some kind of benefit

ADVERBS

extremely/highly rewarding *Taking part in the competition was extremely rewarding for the students.*

hugely/incredibly/immensely rewarding *I find my job hugely rewarding.*

richly rewarding *Participation in sport at any level can be a richly rewarding experience.*

particularly/especially rewarding *Fishing at night can be especially rewarding because fish are more active and easier to catch.*

financially rewarding *As a banker, he enjoyed the benefits of a financially rewarding career.*

NOUNS

a rewarding job/career *Nursing is a very rewarding career.*

a rewarding experience *Doing voluntary work for a charity can be a rewarding experience on many levels.*

rewarding work *It takes extensive schooling to become a doctor, but it is rewarding work.*

a rewarding hobby/pastime *Collecting antiques is a rewarding hobby because each antique is a piece of history.*

a rewarding time/day/afternoon etc *She spent a rewarding afternoon in the city's art museum.*

a rewarding aspect of sth *One of the most rewarding aspects of the job is seeing students make progress.*

VERBS

find sth rewarding *He found it rewarding to see his students succeed in life.*

prove rewarding (=be rewarding) *The course proved rewarding and she learnt lots of new things.*

PREPOSITIONS

rewarding for sb *The experience of living and working in Africa was especially rewarding for her.*

THESAURUS: rewarding

agreeable, rewarding, entertaining, fun → **enjoyable**

rhythm *n*

a regular repeated pattern of sounds

ADJECTIVES

a regular rhythm *She listened to the regular rhythm of the train on the track.*

a steady/constant rhythm *I could hear the steady rhythm of her heart beat.*

a strong rhythm *Music with a strong rhythm is best for an exercise class.*

a slow rhythm *The guitar was playing in a slow rhythm.*

VERBS

beat a rhythm (=hit something in a rhythm) *The rain beat a dull rhythm on the roof.*

make a rhythm *I listened to my feet making a steady rhythm on the ground.*

keep a rhythm (=play or beat a rhythm) *A drummer must be able to keep a rhythm.*

tap out a rhythm (=make or copy a rhythm by hitting something gently) *He tapped out the rhythm with his fingers on the table.*

PREPOSITIONS

in rhythm *When he sang, she snapped her fingers in rhythm.*

PHRASES

dance/move to the rhythm of sth *They danced to the rhythm of the music.*

a sense of rhythm (=the ability to move well to a music's rhythm) *You don't have to be a trained dancer – you just need a sense of rhythm.*

rich *adj*

1 someone who is rich has a lot of money and valuable possessions

NOUNS

a rich man/woman/person *She is one of the richest women in America.*

a rich husband/wife/widow etc *Jane found herself a rich husband.*

a rich family *He came from a rich family.*

a rich friend *A rich friend helped him buy the house.*

a rich country/nation *Saudi Arabia is one of the richest nations in the world.*

a rich city/area/neighbourhood *Sao Paulo is Brazil's richest city.*

a rich company *It has now become a hugely powerful, rich company.*

VERBS

become rich *Once a country becomes rich, it tends to stay rich.*

get rich (=become rich, especially quickly) *He thought he had found a way to get rich.*

grow rich (=become rich, especially over a long period) *Some companies have grown incredibly rich.*

make sb rich *His investments had made him rich.*

ADVERBS

fabulously rich (=extremely rich) *She was both beautiful and fabulously rich.*

incredibly/immensely rich (=extremely rich) *He was immensely rich and owned his own oil company.*

stinking/filthy rich *disapproving informal* (=extremely rich) *The bankers are all stinking rich, but they still want more money.*

PHRASES

rich beyond your wildest dreams (=extremely rich) *Their manager promised he would make them rich beyond their wildest dreams.*

as rich as Croesus *literary* (=extremely rich) *Her grandfather was as rich as Croesus.*

Rich is often used as a noun: *The* ***rich*** *are getting richer.*

THESAURUS: rich

wealthy
man | woman | people | family | businessman | businesswoman | landowner | farmer | merchant | country | area | suburb
rich - used about people and places, especially when they have been rich for a long time:
She was from a wealthy family and did not need to work. | His father was a wealthy businessman who owned coffee plantations in Brazil. | They live in a wealthy suburb of Los Angeles.

Wealthy is often used as a noun: *the homes of* ***the wealthy****.*

affluent
society | area | suburb | neighbourhood | city | country | nation | family | parents | lifestyle
rich and having a lot of expensive possessions, nice houses etc:
In today's affluent society, people don't bother to repair things, they just buy new ones. | Her hotel was in an affluent suburb, surrounded by elegant boutiques. | Sweden is one of Europe's more affluent nations.

prosperous
area | region | country | town | city | merchant | future | times
rich - used especially when people's money is related to success in business:
This is a ***relatively prosperous*** *area, attracting around 30 million tourists a year. | The town became prosperous because of the cotton trade. | We want to create a prosperous future for all our citizens.*

well-off
family | people
fairly rich compared to other people, so that you can live very comfortably:
Children from well-off families usually went to private schools. | Well-off people can afford to pay more tax. | They're ***fairly well-off*** *and they have a big house.*

Well-off is often used as a noun: *Health care was a luxury available only to* ***the*** *well-off.*

well-to-do
family | people | farmer | houses
rich - used especially in the past about families and people who had a fairly high position in society:
Only well-to-do families could afford to live there. | The Westons were well-to-do and there was no necessity for work.

privileged
background | upbringing | childhood | class | group | minority | elite | few
having special advantages because your family have a lot of money and a high position in society:
All the top jobs were taken by people from privileged backgrounds. | The French president had a privileged upbringing in an affluent Paris suburb. | The sport was only played by ***a privileged few*** (=a small group of rich people).

comfortably off
having enough money to have a nice life without having to worry about money:
I wouldn't say that we were rich - just comfortably off.

ANTONYMS **rich → poor (1)**

2 having a strong dark colour

THESAURUS: rich

deep, rich → **dark (2)**

ride¹ *v*

to move along on a horse, bicycle, or motorcycle

NOUNS

ride (on) a horse/bicycle/motorcycle etc *I had never ridden a bike before.*

ADVERBS

ride safely *We teach motorcyclists how to ride safely.*
ride slowly/fast *He rode slowly down the path.*
ride well *She loves horses and rides very well.*
ride side-saddle (=with your legs on one side of a horse) *Women used to ride side-saddle.*

PREPOSITIONS

ride on sth *A boy was riding on his bike down the street.*

PHRASES

learn to ride *She learned to ride when she was seven.*
teach sb (how) to ride *My grandfather taught me to ride on his farm.*

ride² *n*

a journey in a vehicle, when you are not driving

VERBS

take/have a ride *Visitors can take a ride on a steam train.*
go for a ride *He went for a ride in a private plane piloted by a friend.*
give sb a ride *Ellie gave us a ride to school.*
get a ride *AmE: I left the farm, and got a ride into town.*
hitch a ride (=get a free ride from a passing vehicle) *He hitched a ride to Denver on a truck.*

take sb for a ride *Hugh took me for a ride in his new car.*

ADJECTIVES/NOUNS + ride

a car/bus/train etc ride *The resort is a short bus ride away from the hotel.*

a short/long ride *I climbed slowly aboard the bus for the long ride to Glasgow.*

a smooth/comfortable ride *It wasn't a very comfortable ride, but the fare was only 5 cents.*

a bumpy ride *After a bumpy ride down a rough track, we reached the farm.*

ridiculous *adj* very silly or unreasonable

ADVERBS

absolutely/totally/utterly ridiculous *The suggestion that the painting is a fake is absolutely ridiculous.*

quite ridiculous (=totally ridiculous) *I thought his behaviour was quite ridiculous.*

slightly/faintly ridiculous *Andrew felt slightly ridiculous carrying the dog.*

patently ridiculous (=obviously ridiculous) *Her excuse was patently ridiculous.*

NOUNS

a ridiculous idea *She told herself it was a ridiculous idea.*

a ridiculous question *That is the most ridiculous question I ever heard.*

a ridiculous thing to do/say etc *What a ridiculous thing to say!*

a ridiculous story/excuse *None of us believed his ridiculous story.*

a ridiculous situation *How had she got herself into such a ridiculous situation?*

a ridiculous amount/price *They paid me a ridiculous amount of money for it.*

a ridiculous waste of time/money *He didn't buy bottled water because he thought it was a ridiculous waste of money.*

VERBS

look/sound/seem ridiculous *I must have looked ridiculous in that silly costume.*

riding *n*

the sport or activity of riding horses

VERBS

go riding *Shall we go riding on Saturday?*

NOUNS + riding

horse riding *BrE*, **horseback riding** *AmE*: *She enjoys walking and horse riding.*

riding + NOUNS

a riding lesson *I don't own a horse, but I do have riding lessons.*

a riding accident *He hurt his back in a riding accident.*

a riding school *Paula is learning to ride at a local riding school.*

riding stables *She keeps her pony at the riding stables down the road.*

riding hat/boots *Always wear a riding hat to protect your head when riding a horse.*

rife *adj* THESAURUS **common (1)**

right[1] *adj*

1 if what someone says or thinks is right, it is correct

ADVERBS

quite/absolutely right (=completely right) *She is quite right - it's better to wait a few days.*

dead right *informal* (=completely right) *You were dead right not to trust him.*

exactly right *My figures may not be exactly right.*

about/roughly/approximately right *His calculations should be roughly right.*

nearly right *You're nearly right - the correct answer is a little higher than that.*

half/partly right (=correct to some degree, but not completely) *His theory may still be partly right.*

VERBS

sound/seem/look right *Fifty dollars sounds about right to me.*

get sth right *For once, he got my name right.*

be proved right *We warned that it would not work, and we have been proved right.*

NOUNS

the right answer *I'm sure that's the right answer.*

PREPOSITIONS

right about sth/sb *He was right about the deaths being linked.*

PHRASES

be right in saying/thinking that... *I think I am right in saying that they once employed 2,000 people.*

> **Right** or **correct?**
> **Correct** is more formal than **right** and is the usual word to use in official contexts and in academic writing.

ANTONYMS **right → wrong (1)**

2 suitable for something or someone

> **Grammar**
> In this meaning, you usually say **the right**...

NOUNS

the right way *He showed me the right way to hold the baseball bat.*

the right time/moment *Now is the right time for planting tomatoes.*

the right place *If you want sunshine, you've come to the right place.*

R

the right kind/sort of sth *I wasn't sure if it was the right kind of book for a child.*

the right way/direction *We are going in the right direction and are close to reaching an agreement.*

ANTONYMS **right → wrong (2)**

right² *n*

something that you are morally, legally, or officially allowed to do or have

ADJECTIVES/NOUNS + right

human rights (=the rights that everyone should have) *The country has been accused of human rights abuses.*

civil rights (=the rights that every person in a society should have) *As a young man, he was involved in the struggle for civil rights.*

equal rights *Women demanded equal rights.*

a democratic right *The students are exercising their democratic right to protest.*

a legal/statutory/constitutional right *Banks have the legal right to recover their money.*

political rights *Slaves had no political rights.*

a fundamental/basic right *The law recognises a person's fundamental right to defend his home and his property.*

a moral right *They thought they had a moral right to break the law.*

women's rights *New laws have been passed to protect women's rights.*

workers' rights *The company's actions are a violation of workers' rights.*

animal rights (=the rights of animals) *Animal rights campaigners want hunting to be banned.*

VERBS

have a right to do sth *The public has a right to know what is going on.*

enjoy a right *formal* (=have a right, especially over a long period of time) *These people have traditionally enjoyed hunting rights in the area.*

demand a right *We demand the same rights that other European workers enjoy.*

exercise a right *formal* (=do what you have a right to do) *The insurance company decided not to exercise its right of appeal.*

violate/infringe sb's rights *formal* (=stop them doing something they have a right to do) *Imprisoning the men without trial violated their rights.*

deny sb a right (=not allow someone to do something they have the right to do) *Women were denied the right to vote.*

respect a right (=not do anything to stop people having a right) *The new leader promised to respect human rights.*

defend/protect a right *We should defend our right to demonstrate.*

stand up for your rights (=defend them) *He was not afraid to stand up for his rights.*

uphold sb's rights (=make sure that people's rights are respected, usually in the courts) *The new government has promised that it will uphold human rights.*

waive a right *formal* (=choose not to do what you have a right to do) *She waived her right to be present during the trial.*

forfeit a right (=do something that means you should no longer have it) *He argued that a murderer forfeits his right to life.*

PREPOSITIONS

a right to sth *The children are being denied their right to education.*

by right (=because you have a right to have something) *The land is theirs by right.*

be within your rights (to do sth) (=have the right to do something) *In that situation, you are within your rights to ask for your money back.*

PHRASES

a right of appeal (=the right to ask for an official decision to be changed) *When the High Court has reached its final verdict, there is no right of appeal.*

a right of access (=the right to enter a place, or to see something or someone) *You have rights of access to data held about you.*

a right of reply (*also* **the right to reply**) (=the right to say or write something in answer to a criticism) *People should have the right of reply when a magazine has published letters criticizing them.*

rights and responsibilities *Parents have certain rights and responsibilities.*

rigid *adj* THESAURUS ▸ **hard (1)**

ring *n*

a piece of jewellery that you wear on your finger

ADJECTIVES/NOUNS + ring

a gold/silver/diamond etc ring *He had a gold ring on his little finger.*

a wedding ring *He never took his wedding ring off.*

an engagement ring (=which shows you intend to marry someone) *I noticed that she had an engagement ring on her finger.*

an eternity ring (=a ring given as a sign of lasting love, especially one with stones all round it)

a plain ring *She wore a plain gold ring.*

a heavy ring (=thick) *Her fingers were covered in heavy rings.*

VERBS

wear a ring *He wore a gold ring on his right hand.*

have a ring (on) (=be wearing a ring) *They saw I didn't have a wedding ring on.*

rinse *v* THESAURUS ▸ **clean², wash¹**

riot *n*

a situation in which a large crowd of people are behaving in a violent and uncontrolled way

ADJECTIVES/NOUNS + riot

a serious/major riot *The jail was the scene of a serious riot last year.*

a full-scale riot (=involving a lot of people, violence, and damage) *The disturbance turned into a full-scale riot.*

a violent/bloody riot *The shooting sparked a violent riot that claimed several lives.*

a street riot *Seven people died in street riots the same day.*

a prison riot *The prison riots were caused by bad physical conditions and poor security.*

race riots (=caused by a problem between different races) *In 1967, there were race riots in a number of major American cities.*

VERBS

cause/provoke a riot *When the election results were announced, it caused riots in the capital.*

start a riot *They accused him of trying to start a riot.*

spark/trigger a riot (=make it start) *The incident sparked a riot which lasted for three days.*

quell/suppress a riot (=use force to stop it) *The police marched in to quell the riots.*

a riot begins/breaks out/erupts *Riots broke out all over the country.*

riot + NOUNS

the riot police *The authorities brought in the riot police to deal with the demonstration.*

the riot squad (=a group of police who deal with riots) *Someone called the riot squad.*

riot control *All officers are trained in riot control.*

riot gear (=special clothing worn by police dealing with a riot) *Almost 1,000 officers, many in riot gear, were needed to restore order.*

a riot shield (=a plastic shield used by a police officer) *The police moved in on the demonstration using riot shields and tear gas.*

rise¹ *v*

to increase in number, amount, or value

ADVERBS

rise sharply/steeply/dramatically (=a lot in a short time) *The value of the painting has risen sharply in recent years.*

rise rapidly/quickly/fast *House prices rose rapidly last year.*

rise slowly/gradually *Wages have risen more slowly than prices.*

rise substantially/significantly *University fees have risen substantially, causing problems for poorer students.*

rise steadily *My salary had risen steadily each year.*

rise slightly *They found that the water temperature had risen slightly.*

PREPOSITIONS

rise by 10%/40% etc *The cost of living is expected to rise by 3% next year.*

rise (from sth) to sth *Between 1831 and 1870, the number of inhabitants rose from 833,000 to 2 million.*

rise above sth *Temperatures there rarely rise above freezing.*

rise² *n*

1 an increase in number, amount, or value

ADJECTIVES

a sharp/steep/dramatic rise (=great and sudden) *Cold weather can cause a sharp rise in energy prices.*

a big/large/huge etc rise *There has been a big rise in violent crime.*

a substantial/significant rise *Wealthy Americans face a significant rise in their income tax rate.*

a small/slight/modest rise *The company expects only a small rise in profits this year.*

a rapid rise *The post-war years saw a rapid rise in prosperity.*

a sudden rise *These problems were caused by the sudden rise in the price of oil.*

a steady rise *They have experienced a steady rise in their standard of living.*

an alarming rise *There has been an alarming rise in the number of overweight children.*

a 10%/40% etc rise *The company reported an 81% rise in profits.*

VERBS

experience a rise *Since 1969, American workers have experienced a substantial rise in hours of work.*

see a rise (=used to say where or when a rise occurs) *These years saw a rapid rise in living standards.*

lead to/cause a rise *The thinning ozone layer may be leading to a rise in skin cancer.*

NOUNS + rise

a price rise *Delays in deliveries of food led to price rises.*

a pay rise *BrE: The workers are demanding a pay rise.*

a rent rise *BrE: Tenants face huge rent rises.*

a temperature rise *They predicted a global temperature rise of 2.5 degrees by the end of the century.*

PREPOSITIONS

a rise in sth *The rise in unemployment was greater than expected.*

a rise of 10%/40% etc *That represents a rise of 1.1 per cent in the size of the labour force.*

PHRASES

a rise in the number of sth *There has been a rise in the number of arrests for drug offences.*

2 the achievement of importance, success, or power

ADJECTIVES

sb's rapid/swift rise *Her rapid rise to the top is well deserved.*

sb's spectacular rise *The spectacular rise of his far-right party has astonished everyone.*

sb's meteoric rise (=very great and quick) *What can explain his meteoric rise in politics?*

sb's inexorable rise *formal* (=impossible to stop) *The country is continuing its seemingly inexorable rise as a global power.*

PREPOSITIONS

sb's rise from sth to sth *Her rise from waitress to film star was complete.*

PHRASES

sb's rise to power *They were alarmed by Hitler's rise to power.*

sb's rise to fame/stardom *Her success in the film ensured a rapid rise to fame.*

sb's rise to the top *Blair's rise to the top of his party seemed effortless.*

the rise and fall of sb/sth *The exhibition tells the story of the rise and fall of Roman civilization.*

R

rising *adj* THESAURUS ▶ **high (2)**

risk[1] *n*

the possibility that something bad, unpleasant, or dangerous may happen

ADJECTIVES

a high risk *There is a high risk of failure.*

a big/great/considerable/huge risk *There is a great risk that the audience will become bored.*

a serious/grave risk (=real and big) *There is a serious risk of flooding.*

a real risk *There is a real risk that there could be another war.*

an increased/reduced risk *Those who smoke have an increased risk of heart disease.*

a low risk *The risk to public health remains low.*

a small/slight risk *There is only a small risk of infection.*

little risk *People will cheat if there is little risk of being caught.*

the risk is negligible/minimal (=extremely small) *He stressed that the risk to patients was negligible.*

an unnecessary risk *There is no point in taking unnecessary risks.*

a calculated risk (=a risk you take because you think a good result is likely) *The police took a calculated risk and released the suspect.*

an unacceptable risk *This measure would expose our economy to unacceptable risks.*

a potential risk *The potential risks associated with this operation should not be ignored.*

attendant risks *formal* (=risks involved in something) *People working with chemicals are generally aware of the attendant risks.*

a financial risk *There is relatively little financial risk for the company.*

a political risk *The political risks for the president are great.*

VERBS

carry/involve a risk (*also* **entail a risk** *formal*) (=might be dangerous) *Most medical operations carry some risk.*

take a risk (=do something that may result in something bad happening) *A good businessman is willing to take risks.*

pose/present a risk (to sb/sth) (=might be dangerous) *Climate change poses serious risks to the environment.*

run a risk (=be in a situation where there is a risk of something happening) *Those who tried to escape ran the risk of being shot.*

have a risk of sth *Older men have a higher risk of developing this disease.*

face a risk *Miners face great risks.*

avoid a risk *They are anxious to avoid any risk of criticism.*

reduce/minimize a risk *This diet could reduce your risk of certain cancers.*

increase a risk *Smoking increases the risk of heart disease.*

eliminate risk (=remove risk completely) *You can't eliminate risk in your life completely.*

assess the risk *The company needs to assess the risk before making a decision.*

risk + NOUNS

a risk factor (=something that increases a risk) *High blood pressure is a risk factor for heart disease.*

risk assessment (=a calculation of how much risk is involved in something) *The organizers of the event carried out a risk assessment.*

PREPOSITIONS

the risk of sth *The risk of serious injury is small.*

a risk to sb/sth *They reassured the public that there was no risk to health.*

at risk (=in a situation where you may be harmed) *They are at risk of losing their jobs.*

PHRASES

an element/degree of risk (=some risk) *There is always an element of risk in flying.*

the risks involved/the risks associated with sth *The soldiers were well aware of the risks involved.*

sth is worth the risk *It could have gone horribly wrong, but I thought it was worth the risk.*

the benefits outweigh the risks (=they are more important than the possible risks) *The benefits to patients who are taking the drug far outweigh the risks.*

at great risk to yourself (*also* **at great personal risk**) *At great risk to himself, he helped them escape.*

risk² *v*

1 to get into a situation where something unpleasant might happen to you

NOUNS

risk death *He risked death to save her from the fire.*

risk injury *Workers are risking injury by not using the proper safety equipment.*

risk arrest/imprisonment *Anyone who criticizes the government risks arrest.*

2 to put something in a situation in which it could be lost, destroyed, or harmed

NOUNS

risk your life *People risked their lives helping others to escape.*

risk your health *If you smoke, you are risking your health.*

risk your job/career *He risked his job by reporting his employer's actions.*

risk your reputation *She risked her reputation to defend him.*

risk money *No-one wants to risk their own money on the project.*

risk everything *They risked everything to try to save the company.*

PREPOSITIONS

risk sth on sth *He risked a lot of money on the investment.*

risk sth for sb/sth *These soldiers are risking their lives for their country every day.*

risky *adj* THESAURUS **dangerous**

rival *n*

a person, group, or organization that you compete with in sport, business, politics etc

ADJECTIVES

sb's main/chief rival *Who is the champion's main rival?*

sb's nearest/closest rival (=the one that is closest to beating them) *She finished 7.1 seconds ahead of her nearest rival.*

a serious/dangerous rival (=one that might beat you) *He knows that he has no serious rival for the job.*

a formidable rival (=one it will be hard to beat) *He faced formidable rivals for the position.*

a great/big rival (=an important rival for a long time) *Oxford University and Cambridge University have always been great rivals.*

a bitter/deadly rival (=one that hates you) *The two brothers had become bitter rivals.*

a fierce rival (=one that wants very much to beat you) *They used to be fierce rivals but are now campaigning together.*

sb's arch-rival (=their main or strongest rival) *The company is now doing better than its arch-rival.*

an old/long-time rival *The team had a convincing victory over their old rivals.*

a potential rival *We see their business as a potential rival.*

a political rival *The two men were great political rivals.*

VERBS

have/face a rival *She faces several dangerous rivals.*

beat/defeat a rival *He defeated his rival by one vote.*

outdo your rival (=do better than them) *Each company tried to outdo its rivals.*

rival + NOUNS

a rival company/firm *She left her job and went to work for a rival company.*

a rival team *The rival team's fans were at the other end of the ground.*

a rival gang *He was attacked by members of a rival gang.*

rival fans/supporters *There were fights between rival fans after the match.*

rival factions/groups *My task is to unite the rival factions within the party.*

a rival candidate *He spread damaging rumours about a rival candidate.*

PREPOSITIONS

a rival for sth *He saw Wilson as his main rival for the position.*

a rival to sb/sth *The city was a rival to Athens until 506 BC.*

rivalry *n*

a situation in which people, teams, or groups try to show that they are better than each other

ADJECTIVES/NOUNS + rivalry

great rivalry *There is a great rivalry between the two tennis stars.*

bitter rivalry *A bitter rivalry exists between supporters of Manchester United and Liverpool.*

fierce/intense rivalry *There has always been intense rivalry between New Zealand and Australia.*

friendly rivalry *The two players have developed a friendly rivalry.*

long-standing/long-running rivalry *The Philadelphia Eagles and the Dallas Cowboys have a long-standing rivalry.*

age-old rivalry *The age-old rivalry between Oxford and Cambridge universities continues in the form of an annual boat race.*

personal rivalry *She denied rumours that there was any personal rivalry between her and the other two actresses in the TV show.*

healthy rivalry (=a good type of rivalry) *He is looking forward to another year of healthy rivalry with his team-mate Sebastian Vettel.*

sibling rivalry (=between brothers and sisters)

She had never overcome her feelings of sibling rivalry to her brother.

PREPOSITIONS

rivalry between two people/groups etc *The rivalry between Craig Gordon and Allan McGregor goes back to their schooldays.*

rivalry among several people/groups etc *The book describes the bitter rivalry among the three political leaders.*

rivalry with another person/group etc *The racing driver has spoken out about his relationship and rivalry with the late Ayrton Senna.*

rivalry for/over sth *They hated each other because of rivalry over a woman.*

river *n*

a flow of water across land into the sea

ADJECTIVES

a wide/broad river *A wide river stretched out into the distance.*

a long river *The Severn is the longest river in Britain.*

a swollen river (=containing much more water than usual) *The swollen river finally burst its banks.*

a fast-flowing river (*also* **a raging river** *literary*): *He was swept downstream by the fast-flowing river.*

a polluted river (=dirty, especially because of chemicals from factories) *The river is too polluted to swim in.*

a mighty river (=very big and impressive) *Cairo sits at the mouth of the mighty River Nile.*

a river is navigable (=people are able to travel along it in a boat) *The river is navigable in the winter months.*

> **Names of rivers**
> Two styles are used. With some rivers you say **the River Thames/Seine/Ganges/Amazon etc**. With other rivers you say **the Mississippi/Colorado/Hudson River etc**. British speakers tend to use the first style, and American speakers tend to use the second style, but the names for the rivers in Britain and the US are fixed.

VERBS

a river flows *I could hear the river flowing past our house.*

a river runs (=it flows in a particular direction) *This is the place where the river runs into the sea.*

a river winds (=it turns and curves, rather than going in a straight line) *He could see the river winding across the plain.*

a river floods *There are fears that the river could flood.*

a river dries up *Further downstream the river has dried up completely.*

a river narrows/widens (=it becomes narrower or wider) *The river narrows at this point.*

a river rises somewhere *formal* (=it starts there) *The River Euphrates rises in Turkey and flows through Syria.*

cross a river *Cross the river by the road bridge and then turn right.*

ford a river (=cross it on foot, in a vehicle, or on a horse, without using a bridge) *The water was shallow enough for us to be able to ford the river.*

navigate a river (=travel along it in a boat) *The narrow cliffs once made the river dangerous to navigate.*

river + NOUNS

a river bank *Crowds lined the river banks to watch the boat race.*

a river bed (=the bottom of a river) *They walked along a dry river bed.*

a river basin (=an area from which all the water flows into the same river) *There are a lot of farms in the river basin.*

a river delta (=an area where a big river divides into smaller rivers and them joins the sea) *We saw the huge Mississippi Delta from the plane.*

> **Riverside** (=the land next to a river) is written as one word.

PREPOSITIONS

on a river *There were several boats on the river.*

in a river *You can swim in the river here.*

along a river *We went for a walk along the river.*

down a river *The boat drifted slowly down the river.*

across a river *There's a bridge that goes across the river.*

PHRASES

the banks of a river (=the land near a river) *He bought a house on the banks of the River Wye.*

the mouth of a river (=where it joins the sea) *The Statue of Liberty stands at the mouth of the Hudson River.*

the source of a river (=the place where it starts) *Where exactly is the source of the River Ganges?*

a bend in a river *They rounded a bend in the river and saw the city ahead of them.*

the upper/lower reaches of a river (=the upper, lower etc parts) *We sailed down the lower reaches of the river.*

a river bursts its banks (=it floods) *The River Ouse burst its banks and flooded the town.*

a river is in spate *BrE* (=it is very full and the water is flowing very quickly) *The snow had just melted and the rivers were in spate.*

road *n* a hard surface for vehicles

ADJECTIVES/NOUNS + road

a busy road (=with a lot of traffic) *We have to cross a busy road to get to school.*

a quiet road (=with little traffic) *At that time of night, the roads were quiet.*

a clear road (=with no traffic or nothing blocking it) *Before you overtake, make sure the road is clear.*

a main road (=an important road that is used a lot) *The hotel is on the main road to the airport.*

a minor road (=a less important road that is not used a lot) *France has a huge network of minor roads.*

a side/back road (=a small road that is not used much) *He drove into a quiet side road and stopped the car.*

a country/mountain/coast road *These country roads are very narrow.*

a dirt road (=made of hard earth) *We were bumping along a dirt road when the storm started.*

a winding road (=with a lot of smooth bends) *The route is all winding roads and steep hills.*

the open road (=without much traffic or anything to stop you getting somewhere) *This car is at its best on the open road.*

> **Road** is used in the names of roads and streets: *She lives on* ***Victoria Road****.* In addresses, you can use the abbreviation **Rd.**: *58* ***Chesterwood Rd****.*

VERBS + road

cross a road *Look both ways before crossing the road.*

go down a road *I heard the sound of her car going down the road.*

follow a road (=continue along it) *I followed the main road into the town centre.*

turn onto a road (*also* **turn into a road** *BrE*): *We turned onto a quiet road.*

pull off a road (=leave it when you are driving) *If you feel tired, pull off the road and have a rest.*

run (out) into a road *A child ran out into the road and was almost hit by a car.*

live on a road *Chris lives on Mount Vernon Road.*

road + VERBS

a road leads/goes/runs somewhere *We turned into the road leading to the village.*

a road winds (=it turns and curves, rather than going in a straight line) *A long road wound through the park.*

a road forks (=starts going ahead in two different directions) *At Salen, the road forks right and left.*

a road narrows/widens (=it becomes narrower or wider) *After a couple of miles, the road narrows.*

a road is blocked *The main road was blocked for an hour while police cleared the accident.*

road + NOUNS

a road accident *Her husband was killed in a road accident.*

road safety *It's important to teach children about road safety.*

road sense (=knowledge of how to behave safely near traffic) *Young children don't have any road sense.*

a road junction (=a place where two or more roads meet) *The accident happened at a busy road junction.*

a road network (=a system of roads that cross or are connected to each other) *The road network in Amsterdam is quite complicated.*

a road sign *What does that road sign mean?*

a road map *I'm lost. Did we bring a road map?*

PREPOSITIONS

on the road *There were a lot of cars parked on the road.*

along a road *She was seen walking along the road on her own.*

up/down the road (=along a road - used especially in spoken English) *I ran down the road to see what had happened.*

in the road *Someone was standing in the road, blocking the traffic.*

across the road *She lives across the road.*

by road *The volcano cannot be reached by road.*

> **Up/down the road**
> People often use **up/down the road**, when saying that someone or something is near you: *He lives* ***up the road*** *from me.*

PHRASES

the side of the road *We stopped and had something to eat by the side of the road.*

the middle of the road *A police officer was standing in the middle of the road, directing traffic.*

the road ahead (=in front of you) *The road ahead was completely flooded.*

a fork in the road (=a place where a road goes in two different directions) *We had to ask for directions each time we got to a fork in the road.*

a stretch of road (=a length of road) *Several people have been killed on this stretch of road.*

THESAURUS: road

street
a road in a town or city, with houses or shops on each side:
She lives on our street. | *We walked along the streets of the old town.* | *Oxford Street is one of Europe's busiest shopping areas.* | *He was stopped by the police, driving the wrong way down a* ***one-way street****.* | *Turn left on* ***Main Street*** (=the street in the middle of a town, where most of the shops are - used in American English). | *These days the same*

R

shops are on every ***high street*** (=the street in the middle of a town, where most of the shops are – used in British English).

avenue
a road in a town or city, often with trees on each side:
the busy avenue in front of the cathedral | He lived on Park Avenue.

boulevard
a wide road in a city – used especially in street names in the US, France etc. In the UK, streets are usually called **avenue** rather than **boulevard**:
We visited the world-famous Sunset Boulevard in Los Angeles.

lane
a narrow road in the country:
I was cycling along a winding ***country lane****, with very little traffic.*

cul-de-sac
a short street which is closed at one end:
The house is situated in a ***quiet cul-de-sac*** *in North Oxford.*

track *especially BrE*, **dirt road** *AmE*
a narrow road in the country, usually without a hard surface:
The farm was down a ***bumpy track****.*

ring road *BrE*, **beltway** *AmE*
a road that goes around a town or city:
The airport is on the ring road just outside the city.

bypass *BrE*
a road that goes past a town or city, allowing traffic to avoid the centre:
The bypass would take heavy traffic out of the old city centre.

dual carriageway *BrE*, **divided highway** *AmE*
a road with a barrier or strip of land in the middle that has lines of traffic travelling in each direction:
I waited until we were on the dual carriageway before I overtook him.

freeway/expressway *AmE*
a very wide road in a city or between cities, on which cars can travel very fast without stopping:
Take the Hollywood Freeway (101) south, exit at Vine Street, and drive east on Franklin Avenue. | Over on the side of the expressway, he saw an enormous sedan, up against a stone wall.

motorway *BrE*, **highway** *AmE*
a very wide road for travelling fast over long distances:
The speed limit on the motorway is 70 miles an hour. | the Pacific Coast Highway

interstate *AmE*
a road for fast traffic that goes between states:
The accident happened on Interstate 84, about 10 miles east of Hartford.

toll road
a road that you pay to use:
The government is planning to introduce toll roads, in an effort to cut traffic congestion.

turnpike *AmE*
a large road for fast traffic that you pay to use:
He dropped her off at an entrance to the New Jersey Turnpike.

roast *v* THESAURUS ▶ **cook**[1]

rob *v* THESAURUS ▶ **steal**

robbery *n*

the crime of stealing money or things from a bank, shop etc, especially using violence

ADJECTIVES/NOUNS + robbery

a bank robbery *Police are investigating a series of bank robberies in the area.*

a street robbery *These phones are a common target in street robberies.*

armed robbery *He received a 10-year prison sentence for armed robbery.*

attempted robbery *He was charged with attempted robbery.*

a daring robbery *They carried out a daring robbery and escaped with millions of dollars.*

a failed robbery *He was arrested during a failed robbery.*

VERBS

commit/carry out a robbery *The robbery was carried out by an armed gang.*

take part in a robbery *He was one of the men who took part in a robbery on a post office.*

foil a robbery (=prevent it from being successful) *The police were able to foil the robbery.*

PHRASES

a string of robberies (=several robberies) *They were responsible for a string of robberies.*

robbery with violence *Her son is in prison for robbery with violence.*

rock *n*

1 the hard substance that forms the main surface of the Earth, or a piece of this

ADJECTIVES

solid rock *Steps had been carved out of the solid rock.*

bare rock (=not covered by soil) *Here there was no grass, only bare rock.*

volcanic rock *The fossils were found between two layers of volcanic rock.*

molten rock (=rock that is so hot it is liquid) *Molten rock flowed into these cracks.*

a jagged rock (=with sharp points and edges) *The fishermen take care to avoid the jagged rocks beneath the waves.*

a smooth rock *The water flowed over the smooth rocks.*

VERBS

rock forms/is formed *These rocks were formed at the bottom of an ancient ocean.*

sth erodes the rock (=gradually removes the surface) *The river has eroded the rock.*

the rock erodes (away) (=its surface is gradually removed by water, wind etc) *The rocks had eroded away over the years.*

rock + NOUNS

a rock formation (=a shape formed naturally from rock) *The island is known for its amazing rock formations.*

a rock face (=a very steep surface of rock on the side of a mountain) *They climbed slowly down the rock face.*

PHRASES

a lump/piece of rock *His leg was trapped under a large lump of rock.*

a layer of rock *You can see six layers of rock in the cliff.*

an outcrop of rock (=a mass of rock that sticks up above the ground) *The birds nested on an outcrop of rock.*

2 a type of loud pop music with a strong beat, played using guitars and drums

rock + NOUNS

rock music *He used to play loud rock music late at night.*

a rock band/group *I had always wanted to be in a rock band.*

a rock singer/musician/guitarist *Many famous rock singers have died young.*

a rock star *He is one of the world's biggest rock stars.*

a rock concert *Thousands of people attended the rock concert at the stadium.*

a rock fan *Their songs are familiar to rock fans.*

role Ac *n*

1 the way someone or something is involved in something

ADJECTIVES

an important role *She played an important role in her husband's political career.*

a major/significant/prominent role (=important) *Technology is already playing a significant role in classroom teaching.*

a key/central/leading role (=the most important) *The report recognized the key role of teachers.*

a vital/crucial/essential role (=very important) *Every member of the team has a vital role to play.*

a minor/limited role *Dirty needles play only a minor role in spreading AIDS in Africa.*

an active role (=doing practical things to achieve particular aims) *She took an active role in the community.*

a dual role (=two roles) *People have dual roles in society as producers and consumers.*

sb's traditional role *Some women are happy with their traditional role as carers.*

VERBS

play/have a role (*also* **fulfil a role** *formal*): *The internet plays an important role in people's daily lives.*

take a role (=start being involved in something) *Charlie began to take a more active role on the farm.*

take on a role (*also* **assume a role** *formal*) (=start having a particular job or function) *Mr Jones took on the role of spokesperson for the organization.*

give sb a role *He was given a key role in the election campaign.*

cast sb in a role (=give someone a role, especially one they do not want) *He found himself cast in the role of guide and translator.*

switch/reverse roles (=start doing what someone else did, while they start doing what you did) *Sometimes we reverse roles, and I drive while he map-reads.*

PREPOSITIONS

a role in sth *Women's role in society has changed.*

a role as sth *She gets a lot of satisfaction from her role as a mother.*

the role of sth *They studied the role of diet in the prevention of disease.*

in a role *It was the first time I had seen him in that role.*

2 the character played by an actor

ADJECTIVES/NOUNS + role

a major/big role *It was his first major role.*

a minor/small role *She has had small roles in several other films.*

the lead/leading role (=the most important role) *He had already cast Tom Hanks in the lead role.*

a starring role (=one of the most important roles) *She had to turn down a starring role in a film to continue with the play.*

the title role (=the role of the character whose name is the title of the film or play) *She will play the title role in 'Emma' later this year.*

a supporting role (=not one of the main roles) *She has a supporting role as the wife of the hero.*

a comic role *She admits she is attracted to comic roles.*

VERBS

play a role *John will play the role of Hamlet.*

have a role *His son has a small role in the series.*

take a role *In the end, I decided not to take the role.*

give sb a role (*also* **cast sb in a role**) *Television producers would not cast her in lead roles.*

land a role (=be given a role) *He landed a role in a famous Broadway musical.*

turn down a role (=say that you will not play it) *I got the part after another actress turned down the role.*

PREPOSITIONS

in a role *I would like to see a French actor in this role.*

the role of sb *Who wants to play the role of Joseph?*

roll *v*

if something rolls, or if you roll it, it moves along a surface by turning over and over

PREPOSITIONS/ADVERBS

roll down (sth) *The coin slipped from her hand and rolled down the hill.*

roll off (sth) *One of the eggs rolled off the counter.*

roll around (sth) *An apple was rolling around on the floor of the car.*

roll into sth *The ball rolled into the street.*

roll sth in sth *Roll the chicken breasts in flour.*

NOUNS

roll a ball *Bruce rolled the ball back to him.*

roll the dice (=throw it to see which number it lands on) *Each player takes their turn to roll the dice.*

romantic *adj*

1 relating to being or falling in love

NOUNS

romantic love (=as opposed to other kinds, such as a parent's love for a child) *Kissing is a gesture of romantic love.*

a romantic relationship *They said they were just friends, and there was no romantic relationship.*

a romantic gesture *Neil bought her some flowers as a romantic gesture.*

a romantic setting/place *The castle is a romantic setting for a wedding.*

a romantic evening/weekend *What would be your ideal romantic evening?*

a romantic dinner/meal *My boyfriend took me out for a romantic meal.*

a romantic film/movie *It's a very romantic film, perfect for a date.*

ADVERBS

highly/intensely romantic *It is a highly romantic love story.*

wonderfully romantic *They spent a wonderfully romantic weekend together.*

2 not practical, or not based on reality

NOUNS

a romantic idea/notion *Many people have romantic notions about living in the countryside.*

a romantic view *He has a very romantic view of travel.*

a romantic vision *I had romantic visions of myself as a poet.*

a romantic image *TV detective series can give an overly romantic image of police work.*

a romantic ideal *A little cottage in the country is a romantic ideal.*

roof *n*

the structure that forms the top of a building or vehicle

ADJECTIVES/NOUNS + roof

a flat roof *The houses all have flat roofs.*

a leaky/leaking roof (=one that lets rain in) *We needed to fix the leaky roof.*

a sloping roof *The path led to a log cabin with a sloping roof.*

a thatched roof (=made of dried straw) *She lived in a pretty country cottage with a thatched roof.*

roof + NOUNS

roof tiles (=flat hard objects used for covering a roof) *A few roof tiles had blown off in the storm.*

a roof garden/terrace *The restaurant has a roof garden.*

PREPOSITIONS

on the roof *Birds were perching on the roof of the farmhouse.*

through the roof *Rain was coming in through the roof.*

room *n*

1 a part of the inside of a building that has its own walls, floor, and ceiling

ADJECTIVES

a small/tiny room *Each apartment consists of three small rooms.*

a large/spacious/big room *The house has a spacious living room.*

a bright/airy/light room *The bright living room opens onto a patio.*

a comfortable/cosy/warm room *The hotel offers comfortable rooms.*

a crowded room (=with a lot of people in) *She looked around the crowded room for her friend.*

a spare room (=a bedroom in your house for guests) *We have a spare room you could stay in.*

the next room (=the one beside the room you are in) *Someone was laughing in the next room.*

a single room (=a bedroom for one person with one bed) *A single room is $36. 50 a night.*

a double room (=a bedroom for two people with one large bed) *I'd like to book a double room for two nights.*

a twin room (=a bedroom for two people with two separate beds) *Accommodation is available from £26 a night per person, sharing a twin room.*

the front room (=a room used for sitting in at the front of a house) *She sat in the front room watching television.*

NOUNS + room

a hotel room (=a bedroom in a hotel) *I went back to my hotel room to have a rest.*

a living/dining/sitting room *The house has a large dining room.*

a waiting/changing/dressing room *I read a magazine in the doctor's waiting room.*

a conference/meeting/lecture room *The hotel has a large conference room available for hire.*

a reception room *BrE* (=a room for relaxing or eating in - used to describe a house when selling it) *The house has three reception rooms.*

a games room (=with equipment for playing games) *There is a games room with a full-sized snooker table.*

a guest room (=a hotel bedroom, or a bedroom for visitors in a house) *You will be staying in the guest room.*

a shower room *There is a shower room on the first floor.*

> **Bathroom** (= the toilet) and **cloakroom** (= the room where you can hang your coat) are always written as one word.
> **Staffroom** (= a room for teachers when they are not teaching) is usually written as one word.

VERBS

come into/go into/enter a room *Billy knocked, and entered the room.*

go out of/come out of/leave a room *She left the room and went upstairs.*

burst into a room (=enter very suddenly) *He burst into the room and rushed towards me.*

storm out of a room (=leave suddenly because you are angry) *Janette started arguing and then stormed out of the room.*

sb/sth fills a room *Talking and laughter filled the room.*

a room contains sth *The room contained a double bed and a desk.*

PREPOSITIONS

in a room *There was a lot of furniture in the room.*

2 space or enough space

ADJECTIVES

enough room (*also* **sufficient room** *formal*): *There isn't enough room for a desk.*

ample room (=more than enough) *The terrace is large, with ample room for relaxing.*

VERBS

have room *Do you have room in your car for me?*

make room *He moved to make room for Ann on the sofa.*

leave room *Make sure you leave room for dessert.*

find room *I'm sure we can find room for this table.*

PREPOSITIONS

room for sth/sb *Is there room for a washing machine?*

rope *n*

very strong thick string, made by twisting together many thinner strings

ADJECTIVES

a strong rope *We will need some strong rope to pull the car back onto the road.*

a thick rope *The boat was tied to the post with a thick rope.*

a rope is tight *Make sure the rope is tight.*

> A **tightrope** is a high strong wire that a performer walks across as a circus act.

VERBS

tie/attach/fix a rope somewhere (*also* **secure a rope** *formal*): *They tied a rope around my waist and pulled me up.*

untie a rope *He untied the ropes and pushed the boat out.*

climb a rope *He started to climb the rope.*

pull (on) a rope *Pull this rope to ring the bell.*

throw a rope *She threw a rope to the man in the water.*

coil a rope (=wind it into several rings) *The man was coiling a length of rope.*

NOUNS + rope

a skipping rope *BrE*, **a jump rope** *AmE* (=for playing a game in which you jump over a rope which moves up and down) *The girls took skipping ropes to school.*

a safety rope (=used to stop someone from falling) *They put a safety rope around my waist.*

a climbing rope *We always take climbing rope with us when we are in the mountains.*

a tow rope (=for pulling a car, boat etc behind another vehicle) *The car was being pulled by a tow rope.*

PHRASES

a length/piece of rope *He tied a length of rope to the boat.*

a coil of rope (=rope that has been wound

into rings) *There was a large coil of rope lying on the deck.*

rough *adj*

1 not smooth or flat – used about the surface of the ground, or the surface of something you touch

NOUNS

rough ground (*also* **rough terrain** *formal*): *The car had big thick tyres for driving over rough ground.*

rough sea/water (=with a lot of waves) *The sea was too rough for swimming.*

a rough track/path/road *A rough track leads up to the farmhouse.*

a rough surface *The stones have a rough surface, which stops you from slipping on them.*

a rough texture *Woollen cloth has a rough texture.*

rough hands/skin *His big rough hands were covered in dirt.*

rough cloth/material *The coat was made of rough dark material.*

THESAURUS: rough

uneven
floor | ground | surface | steps | wall
an uneven surface has areas that are not flat or not all at the same level:
The floor was uneven and the table kept wobbling. | Motorists reported damage to their vehicles caused by the uneven road surface.

bumpy
road | track | lane | field | ground | journey | ride | landing | flight
a bumpy road or area of land has a lot of bumps (=raised parts) and holes in it. You also use **bumpy** about journeys in which the vehicle keeps moving up and down:
We turned off the highway, onto a bumpy track. | The pilot warned us that this was likely to be a bumpy flight.

coarse
cloth | material | wool | linen | hair | grass
a coarse material feels rough when you touch it:
The blanket was made of coarse cloth.

rugged
terrain | landscape | mountains | coast | coastline
not flat and having a lot of hills, mountains, or bumps:
The best way to explore the rugged terrain is on horseback (=used about ground that is not flat). | There are superb views of the wild rugged landscape. | The road follows California's rugged coastline.

ANTONYMS **rough → smooth (1)**

2 not exact

NOUNS

a rough estimate/guess/approximation *At a rough estimate, 50 percent of the children can write a few words.*

a rough calculation *I quickly did a rough calculation and decided we could afford it.*

a rough idea/indication *He gave me a rough idea of what the job involved.*

a rough guide *This chart is only a rough guide to your ideal weight.*

a rough translation *I knew enough French to make a rough translation of the poem.*

a rough sketch/drawing/map *He drew a rough sketch on the back of an envelope.*

a rough draft/outline (=a piece of writing that is not in its finished form) *She has finished the rough draft of her new novel.*

ANTONYMS **rough → exact**

round *adj* shaped like a circle

NOUNS

a round hole *There was a small round hole in the top of the box.*

a round shape *He drew round shapes for the wheels.*

a round table *They sat at a round table.*

a round face/head *Pat had a red round face.*

round eyes *He watched her with big round eyes.*

ADVERBS

perfectly round *The Earth isn't perfectly round.*

THESAURUS: round

circular
motion | movement | route | walk | hole | table | area
shaped like a circle. **Circular** is slightly more formal than **round**, and can also be used about movements:
She rubbed her stomach in a circular motion. | Brush your teeth using small circular movements. | The bus ran a circular route. | This is a pleasant five-mile circular walk. | There was a circular hole in the floor. | They were seated around a circular table. | In the middle is a circular area with benches and a fountain.

spherical
shape | object
shaped like a ball. **Spherical** is usually used in technical English:
Most moons and planets have a spherical shape. | People reported seeing an orange spherical object move through the sky.

curved
surface | line | shape | edge | path | roof | wall
not straight, but not completely round:

R

There was a crack in the curved surface of the cup. | She drew a curved line. | I arranged the candles in a curved shape. | The table's curved edge is to stop small children from banging their heads. | A curved path leads through the garden. | The stadium has a curved roof. | The building had curved walls and round windows.

route Ac *n*

a way from one place to another

ADJECTIVES

a direct route *This road is the most direct route.*

the best route *I had a look at the map and worked out the best route.*

the quickest/shortest/fastest route *They took the shortest route back to the hotel.*

a roundabout route (*also* **a circuitous route** *formal*) (=one that is not at all direct) *We were late because we had taken a rather circuitous route.*

the scenic route (=a route that is not direct but goes through a beautiful or interesting area) *I had lots of time, so I decided to take the scenic route.*

a northerly/southerly etc route *She followed the northerly route across Spain to Bilbao.*

the same route/a different route *He had intended to return by the same route.*

an alternative route (=one that you can use instead) *Because of the floods, they had to find an alternative route.*

the usual/normal route *I went home by my usual route.*

an easy route *The other group had reached the top of the mountain by an easier route.*

a busy route *This is one of the region's busiest traffic routes.*

VERBS

follow a route *They both followed the same route.*

take a route *They had been forced to take a longer route.*

use a route *We planned to use the north-south route through the desert.*

travel a route *I travel this route at least once a week.*

plan/work out your route *We studied the map and planned our route.*

trace a route (=move your finger along it on a map) *She traced his probable route on the map.*

block a route *The police blocked the planned route of the protest march.*

a route takes sb somewhere *Her route took her along Wellingborough Road.*

NOUNS + route

an escape route (=a way of leaving a place in an emergency such as a fire) *Check that your escape route is clear.*

a trade route (=used for transporting goods between countries) *The trade route between Europe and Central Asia came under Russian control.*

a bus route *Our house was on a bus route, so it was easy to get into town.*

a shipping route (=used by many ships) *This is one of the busiest shipping routes in the world.*

a sea route (=using the sea) *Columbus wanted to find a western sea route to China.*

an air route *The North Atlantic is a very popular air route.*

PREPOSITIONS

a route to/from a place *What is the quickest route from the airport to Manhattan?*

by a route *They walked back by a different route.*

on a route *The town lay on the route to Rome.*

routine[1] *n*

the usual order in which you do things, or the things you regularly do

ADJECTIVES/NOUNS + routine

sb's daily routine *Make exercise part of your daily routine.*

sb's normal/usual/regular routine *Although he had gone, I continued with my normal routine.*

sb's morning routine *His morning routine started with a cup of tea followed by a shower.*

the old routine *I get sick of the same old routine day after day.*

a familiar routine *Dogs like a familiar routine.*

VERBS

get (sb) into a routine (=develop a fixed order of doing things, or make someone do this) *Try to get your baby into a routine of feeding and sleeping.*

slip/fall/settle into a routine (=get into a routine without making an effort) *The team slipped quickly into a routine.*

break a routine (=do something different) *Bella didn't break her routine for anyone.*

disrupt/upset sb's routine *She disliked things that disrupted her routine.*

PHRASES

a matter of routine *Checks were carried out on patients as a matter of routine.*

a break from routine (=a change) *I needed a break from routine.*

routine[2] *adj*

happening as a normal part of a job or process

NOUNS

routine work *We need more junior staff to help out with the routine work.*

routine maintenance *The system will be shut down overnight for routine maintenance.*

routine questions/inquiries *The nurse went through the list of routine questions.*

a routine check/inspection *Police stopped the vehicle for a routine check.*

routine monitoring/screening *They introduced routine screening for breast cancer for all women over 50.*

a routine operation/procedure (=a medical operation that is fairly common and not serious) *She went into hospital for a routine operation.*

row[1] *n* a line of things or people

ADJECTIVES

the front/back/middle row *I managed to get a seat in the front row.*

the top/bottom row *The optician asked her if she could read the bottom row of letters.*

the first/second etc row *Make sure the first row of tiles is straight.*

a neat/orderly row *The children sat in neat rows.*

a straight row *They plant the trees in nice straight rows.*

a long row *Near their house was a long row of shops.*

a horizontal/vertical row *The figures are displayed in a horizontal row.*

PREPOSITIONS

in a row *The chairs were arranged in rows.*

PHRASES

row upon row (=many rows) *His vast library contained row upon row of books.*

row[2] *n BrE*

an angry argument, especially between people who know each other well or between people in public life

> **Pronunciation**
> This meaning of **row** is pronounced like 'cow'.

ADJECTIVES/NOUNS + row

a huge/big/terrible row *I heard them having a huge row.*

a major row (=a big row, especially between politicians, countries etc) *There was a major row between the Ministry of Agriculture and the Department of the Environment.*

a heated/fierce/bitter row (=an angry row) *The discussion developed into a heated row.*

a furious/blazing/flaming row (=a very angry row) *She left after a furious row with her boyfriend.*

a stand-up row (=a very angry row) *One player had a stand-up row with his own captain.*

an unholy/almighty row *informal* (=a very angry row) *An unholy row broke out between two of the men drinking in the bar.*

a family row *When he turned up late, there was a family row.*

a drunken row *He hit her during a drunken row.*

a political row *The MP is at the centre of a political row.*

a diplomatic row (=between countries) *The incident caused a diplomatic row between North and South Korea.*

VERBS + row

have a row *He had had a row with his wife.*

get into a row (=become involved in a row) *I don't want to get into a row over this.*

spark/cause a row (=make it start) *The arrests sparked a diplomatic row.*

end a row *They are holding talks in an effort to end the row.*

defuse a row (=end it or make the people involved less angry) *The government is trying to defuse the growing row over education cuts.*

row + VERBS

a row breaks out/erupts/blows up (=it starts) *A row broke out over the plans.*

a row escalates (=it becomes more serious) *They are hoping the row between the two countries does not escalate.*

a row is brewing (=it is likely to start soon) *A row is brewing among scientists about the new treatment.*

PREPOSITIONS

a row with sb *She had left home after a row with her parents.*

a row between sb and sb *The disagreement led to a row between the president and the prime minister.*

a row about/over sth *Couples often have rows about money.*

rowdy *adj* THESAURUS loud

royal *adj*

relating to or belonging to a king or queen

NOUNS

the royal family *Prince Harry is a member of the British royal family.*

the royal couple *The royal couple toured the hospital.*

a royal palace/residence/castle *Sandringham House is a royal residence in Norfolk.*

the royal court (=place where a king or queen lives and works) *He was a frequent visitor to the royal court.*

the royal household (=the royal family and all the people who work for them) *The aide was adviser to the royal household.*

a royal visit/visitor *The royal visit to Dublin was a great success.*

rubbish *n especially BrE*

1 food, paper etc that is no longer needed and has been thrown away

rubbish + NOUNS

a rubbish bin/bag *She put the plastic wrapper in the rubbish bin.*

a rubbish tip/dump (=a place where people take their rubbish, or where rubbish is buried in the ground) *We took the old toys to the rubbish tip.*

rubbish collection *They reduced rubbish collections to once a fortnight.*

VERBS

dump rubbish (=put large quantities of rubbish in a place where it should not be) *People have spoiled the woods by dumping rubbish there.*

put sth in/with the rubbish *We don't need the bags anymore - you can put them in the rubbish.*

put the rubbish out (=put it where it can be collected) *When putting out the rubbish, make sure that you wrap broken glass in newspaper.*

collect rubbish *They complained that their rubbish had not been collected for two weeks.*

dispose of rubbish *formal* (=get rid of it) *We can dispose of rubbish by burning it or burying it.*

recycle your rubbish (=do something to it so it can be used again) *People are being encouraged to recycle their rubbish.*

be littered/strewn with rubbish (=have a lot of rubbish on it) *The streets are littered with rubbish.*

ADJECTIVES/NOUNS + rubbish

household/domestic rubbish *Over a third of British household rubbish is made up of packaging.*

PHRASES

a pile of rubbish *There were piles of rubbish on the streets.*

> **Rubbish** is used especially in British English. American speakers say **trash** or **garbage**.

2 *informal* something that seems very silly or wrong

ADJECTIVES

absolute/utter/complete rubbish *What they are saying is absolute rubbish.*

old rubbish (=used when emphasizing how bad something is) *They think that people will buy any old rubbish.*

such rubbish *I've never heard such rubbish in my life.*

VERBS

talk rubbish *People who say he will lose the election are talking rubbish.*

PHRASES

a load of (old) rubbish (=used when saying that something is very bad or silly) *The show was a load of rubbish.*

rude *adj*

speaking or behaving in a way that is not polite and is likely to offend or annoy people

ADVERBS

extremely/incredibly rude *The woman at the hotel desk was incredibly rude.*

downright/plain rude (=extremely rude in a shocking way) *Mahoney had changed from being helpful to being downright rude.*

rather/somewhat/a little rude *Sorry if I was a little rude to you the other day.*

NOUNS

a rude remark/comment *They kept making rude remarks about his stomach.*

rude behaviour *BrE*, **rude behavior** *AmE*: *He wanted to apologize for his rude behaviour.*

a rude man/boy/woman etc *He's the rudest man I've ever met.*

VERBS

seem/sound/appear rude *It seems rude not to ask her to the party.*

sth is considered rude *It is considered rather rude to talk and eat at the same time.*

PREPOSITIONS

rude to sb *Why are you so rude to her?*

PHRASES

it is rude to do sth *It's rude to stare at people.*

not mean to be rude/not wish to appear rude *I didn't mean to be rude, but I had to leave early.*

ANTONYMS **rude → polite**

rudimentary *adj* THESAURUS **simple**

rugged *adj* THESAURUS **rough (1)**

ruin[1] *v*

to spoil or destroy something completely

ADVERBS

completely/totally/utterly ruin sth *Look at the carpet! It's completely ruined!*

almost/nearly ruin sth *The singer's career was almost ruined by alcohol and drugs.*

permanently ruin sth/ruin sth forever *If the wind farm is built, it will ruin the countryside forever.*

NOUNS

ruin sb's career *The scandal ruined his career as a politician.*

ruin sb's life *That man has completely ruined her life.*

ruin sb's holiday/day *Their first skiing holiday was ruined by the press, who followed them everywhere.*

ruin sb's plans *I didn't want the bad weather to ruin all our plans.*

ruin sb's marriage/relationship *He said the court case ruined his marriage.*

ruin sb's clothes/dress etc *Her dress was accidentally ruined by the dry cleaners.*

ruin sb's chances of sth *The defeat ruined the team's chances of winning the league.*

R

ruin sb's name/reputation/credibility *The affair ruined his reputation.*

ruin sb's enjoyment *My enjoyment of the film was ruined by other people in the audience talking and eating noisily.*

ruin² *n*

the parts of a building that are left after the rest has been destroyed

> **Grammar**
> Usually plural in this meaning.

ADJECTIVES

old/ancient ruins *Tourists come to see the town's ancient ruins.*

crumbling ruins (=with small pieces breaking off) *High on the hill sit the crumbling ruins of an old cottage.*

smoking ruins (=with smoke coming from them, after a fire or explosion) *Firefighters were bringing people out of the smoking ruins.*

charred ruins (=burned by fire) *All that remained of the village was charred ruins.*

Roman/Greek etc ruins *They toured Italy looking at Roman ruins.*

NOUNS + ruin

the castle/church/temple etc ruins *There is a path down to the castle ruins.*

PREPOSITIONS

the ruins of sth *We visited the ruins of an old castle.*

in the ruins *He hid in the ruins, hoping no one would find him.*

among the ruins *They found some old photographs among the ruins of the house.*

PHRASES

be/lie in ruins (=be almost completely destroyed) *By the end of the war, the whole town lay in ruins.*

fall into/go to ruin (=become damaged or destroyed) *How could such a beautiful building be allowed to go to ruin?*

leave sth in ruins (=almost completely destroy it) *A car bomb left part of the town centre in ruins.*

rule¹ *n*

a statement about what is allowed or what you should do

ADJECTIVES

strict rules *There are strict rules about what clothes you can wear.*

simple rules *The rules of the game are simple.*

basic rules *One of the basic rules of survival is never get separated from the rest of your group.*

petty rules (=unreasonable rules about unimportant things) *One reason I left the army was that I was fed up with all the petty rules.*

an unwritten rule (=a rule of behaviour that everyone in a group understands, but that is not usually mentioned) *There's an unwritten rule that you never call an actor before 10 a.m.*

hard and fast rules (=clear, definite rules about what to do) *It is impossible to give hard and fast rules, but here are some points to consider.*

grammatical rules *She doesn't understand the basic grammatical rules of English.*

NOUNS + rule

a school/prison/club etc rule *He had broken one of the school rules.*

ground rules (=basic rules about how someone should behave or what they should do) *I started the first class by giving the students some ground rules.*

VERBS + rule

obey/follow a rule *We all have to obey the rules.*

observe/comply with/abide by a rule *formal* (=obey it) *Members must comply with the rules of the organization.*

stick to/go by the rules *informal* (=obey them carefully) *We all have to stick to the rules.*

break a rule (*also* **violate a rule** *formal*) (=not obey it) *Anyone who breaks this rule will be punished.*

flout a rule (=break it, without trying to hide what you are doing) *The party continues to flout its own rules.*

make the rules *I'm only an assistant manager – I don't make the rules.*

play by the rules (=do what is expected and agreed) *The system works well enough – as long as everyone plays by the rules.*

bend/stretch the rules (=allow someone to do something that is not normally allowed) *Couldn't you bend the rules on this occasion?*

relax the rules (=make them less strict) *Britain relaxed its immigration rules.*

tighten (up) the rules (=make them stricter) *The EU has tightened the rules on the quality of drinking water.*

enforce a rule (=make sure that it is obeyed) *Unfortunately, they have no power to enforce these rules.*

be bound by rules (=have to obey them) *We are bound by strict rules that prevent us from giving any information to the public.*

rule + VERBS

the rule says (that)... (*also* **the rule stipulates (that)...** *formal*): *The rule says that you must be standing inside the line.*

the rule prohibits/forbids sth (=does not allow it) *The rule forbids women from becoming members of the club.*

the rule requires... *formal* (=says that people must do something) *School rules required all girls to tie back their hair.*

the rule applies to sb/sth (=it affects someone or something) *Everyone thinks that the rule doesn't apply to them.*

PREPOSITIONS

the rules of sth *He tried to teach me the rules of chess.*

the rules about/concerning sth *There are no rules about how much you can earn.*

the rules relating to/governing sth *The leaflet explains the rules governing food labeling.*

be against the rules (=something is not allowed) *It was against the rules to talk in class.*

under the rules (=according to the rules) *Under the rules, the company must publish its annual accounts.*

PHRASES

a change in the rules *I didn't realise that there had been a change in the rules.*

a breach of the rules *formal* (=something that is against the rules) *There has been a serious breach of the rules.*

rules and regulations *The government keeps introducing more and more rules and regulations.*

rules are rules *spoken* (=a rule must be obeyed) *Rules are rules and you have to obey them.*

rule[2] *v* THESAURUS **control[1] (1)**

rumour *BrE*, rumor *AmE n*

information passed from one person to another, which may or may not be true

VERBS + rumour

hear a rumour *I heard a rumour that she was leaving.*

spread rumours *Someone has been spreading rumours about us.*

believe a rumour *I don't believe all the rumours about him – he seems fine.*

deny a rumour *The star is denying rumors that he plans to get married.*

confirm a rumour (=say that it is true) *The actor's agent would not confirm the rumour.*

rumour + VERBS

a rumour spreads *A rumour spread that he had been killed.*

a rumour goes around (=it is passed among people) *There are rumors going around that they're going to sell the company.*

rumours fly around (=they are passed around among a lot of people very quickly) *There were wild rumours flying around the office on Wednesday.*

ADJECTIVES

a false/unfounded rumour (=containing false information) *The rumours are completely unfounded.*

wild rumours (=ones that are extremely unlikely to be true) *Wild rumours caused panic on the stock markets.*

a malicious rumour (=a false one that someone spreads to make trouble) *The claims were dismissed by the government as 'malicious rumours'.*

a scurrilous rumour *formal* (=damaging and false) *Journalists spread scurrilous rumours about the school.*

a widespread rumour (=that many people hear about) *The arrests followed widespread rumours of police corruption.*

a persistent rumour (=that keeps being repeated for a long time) *Despite persistent rumours of an affair, his wife stood by him.*

a strong rumour (=that is likely to be true) *There is a strong rumour that the government is planning to raise taxes.*

an unsubstantiated rumour (=not proved to be true) *These are only unsubstantiated rumours.*

an ugly/nasty rumour (=about something bad) *Ugly rumours persisted that someone had lied to the police.*

PREPOSITIONS

a rumour about sth *We've been hearing rumours about her health.*

rumours of sth *Rumours of his arrest spread quickly.*

PHRASES

rumour has it (that)... (=it is being said) *Rumour has it that they plan to get married.*

rumours are rife (that)... (=are talked about by a lot of people) *Rumours were rife that the band were splitting up.*

run *v*

1 to move very quickly, by moving your legs more quickly than when you walk

ADVERBS

run quickly/fast *I ran out of the house as fast as I could.*

run downstairs/upstairs *I'll run upstairs and get a hairbrush.*

run away/off *The boys ran off into the crowd.*

PHRASES

run for your life (=run as quickly as possible because you are frightened) *She struggled free and ran for her life.*

run for it *informal* (=run as quickly as possible) *We had better run for it or we'll miss the train.*

come running *The children came running out of school.*

2 to be in charge of an organization or event

ADVERBS

run sth efficiently *Savings can be made by running the business more efficiently.*

be well run *The Duomo is a hotel which is well run and has a friendly atmosphere.*

be badly/poorly run *The hospital is poorly run and faces possible closure.*

be privately run (=not by the government) *Many schools in the country are privately run.*
be independently run (=by a person or family and not a large company) *It is a small arts cinema which is independently run.*
be jointly run (=with another person or organization) *The health program is jointly run by the main federal agencies responsible for public health.*

PREPOSITIONS

run sth for sb *We're running a course on grammar for intermediate students.*

> **THESAURUS: run**
>
> be in charge, be in power, run, manage, rule, supervise → **control¹ (1)**

runner *n*

someone who runs for sport or pleasure

ADJECTIVES/NOUNS + runner

a good/fast runner *Charlie is a very good runner.*
a top runner (=one of the best) *He is one of Japan's top runners.*
a marathon runner *Tom is also a keen marathon runner.*
a distance/long-distance runner *East Africa has produced many of the world's greatest distance runners.*
a middle-distance runner (=who runs 800 or 1500 metres) *Strang was a middle-distance runner who won the silver medal.*

> Someone who runs short distances, such as 100 metres or 200 metres, is called a **sprinter**.

rural *adj*

happening in or relating to the countryside, not the city

ADVERBS

mainly/largely/predominantly rural *The region is predominantly rural.*

NOUNS

a rural area/district/village *Many schools in rural areas have closed.*
a rural community *This service will benefit the rural communities of the Highlands.*
rural life *She didn't enjoy rural life, and returned to the city.*
the rural economy *Changes in farming methods have an effect on the rural economy.*
rural poverty *The government has done little to tackle the problem of rural poverty.*
a rural idyll (=a place in the countryside that seems perfect and happy) *I always dreamed of moving to some rural idyll.*

ANTONYMS **rural → urban**

rush¹ *v*

to move very quickly, especially because you need to be somewhere very soon

PREPOSITIONS/ADVERBS

rush into sth *Tom rushed into the principal's office.*
rush out of sth *The boys rushed out of the house.*
rush past sb/sth *A small girl rushed past her.*
rush downstairs/upstairs *She rushed downstairs to answer the door.*
rush off (=leave quickly) *I can't stay – I have to rush off for a meeting.*
rush headlong into sb/sth (=with a lot of force) *He rushed headlong into someone who was walking in the opposite direction.*

rush² *n*

a busy time when a lot of people do something or when you do something in a hurry

ADJECTIVES

a big/great rush *There was a big rush to vote in the elections.*
a mad/frantic rush *At five past twelve there was a mad rush to the dinner hall.*
a headlong rush (=something done very quickly without stopping) *The country's headlong rush into democracy shows no signs of stopping.*
a sudden rush *There was a sudden rush to get to the bar.*
a last-minute rush (=as late as possible before something happens or ends) *A last-minute rush by Christmas shoppers boosted sales.*

NOUNS + rush

the morning/evening rush *The evening rush was just starting.*
the Christmas rush *Buy your presents now and avoid the Christmas rush.*

rush + NOUNS

the rush hour (=the time when many people are travelling to or from work) *Traffic is always heavy during the rush hour.*

VERBS

avoid/beat the rush *Get the earlier bus and avoid the rush.*

PREPOSITIONS

a rush for sth *There was a rush for tickets.*

PHRASES

be in a rush (=in a situation in which you must hurry) *I was in a rush and didn't have time to brush my teeth.*
do sth in a rush (=do something quickly because you need to hurry) *I did my homework in a rush and I knew it wasn't very good.*
there's no (great/big) rush (=you do not need to hurry) *Give it back when you've finished – there's no rush.*

ruthless *adj* THESAURUS **determined**

Ss

sacred *adj*

if something is sacred, it is treated with special respect, especially because it is connected with God or religion

NOUNS

a sacred place/site *The shrine is one of the most sacred places in Japan.*

sacred ground/land *They regard the cave as sacred ground.*

a sacred animal *The cow is considered to be a sacred animal.*

a sacred tree/river/mountain *The Ganges is the sacred river of the Hindus.*

a sacred text/book *The Qur'an is the sacred text of Islam.*

sacred writings/scripture *God speaks to us in the Bible and other sacred scriptures.*

sacred music *The choir will sing a selection of sacred music.*

sacred relic (=a sacred object, especially one that is very old) *The church has many sacred relics.*

a sacred fire/flame *The sacred flame is kept burning in the temple.*

a sacred ritual *The lady of the house performs the sacred ritual of lighting two candles.*

VERBS

be considered sacred/be regarded as sacred *Certain animals were considered sacred.*

PREPOSITIONS

sacred to sb *The land is sacred to Native Americans.*

> **Sacred** or **holy?**
>
> These words mean the same and have many of the same collocations. You can say a **sacred place/city/mountain/relic** or a **holy place/city/mountain/relic**.
>
> There are some differences. You say a **holy man** and a **holy war** (not a 'sacred' one). It is more common to say a **sacred text** than a 'holy' text.

sad *adj*

1 not happy, especially because something unpleasant has happened

VERBS

be/feel sad *I feel sad that she's not here any more.*

look sad *You look sad. What's the matter?*

seem sad (*also* **appear sad** *formal*): *She always seems so sad.*

make sb sad *It makes me sad to think that he can't be here with us.*

NOUNS

a sad look/expression *There was a sad look in her eyes.*

a sad face *Why the sad face?*

sad eyes *He was smiling, but his eyes were sad.*

a sad smile *She gave a slight sad smile.*

a sad voice *"I'm always alone on Christmas Day," he said in a sad voice.*

a sad day/time/moment *When my parents divorced, it was a very sad time for the whole family.*

a sad occasion *Henry's funeral was a very sad occasion.*

a sad life *She married a horrible man, and had a very sad life.*

ADVERBS

terribly/desperately/unbearably sad (=very sad) *Emma was desperately sad when her father died.*

deeply sad (=used when you wish something had not happened) *I feel deeply sad for the families who have been affected by the disaster.*

strangely sad (=sad when this is surprising) *I'd won the argument, but felt strangely sad.*

PREPOSITIONS

sad about sth *Tom felt sad about leaving home.*

sad for sb *I feel sad for the children.*

> **THESAURUS: sad**
>
> **unhappy**
>
> **marriage | childhood | man | woman | person**
>
> sad – used especially when this feeling continues for a long time. You can use **unhappy** about people and periods of time: *Mrs Robinson feels trapped in an unhappy marriage. | Sam had an unhappy childhood and his mother was an alcoholic. | I was* ***deeply unhappy*** *at school. | She* ***feels unhappy about*** *her weight and desperately wants to get slim.*
>
> > **Sad** or **unhappy?**
> >
> > You use **unhappy** about a long period of time. You say an **unhappy childhood/marriage** (not a 'sad' one). You usually use **sad** about a short period – you say a **sad moment/occasion/day** (not an 'unhappy' one).
> >
> > You often use **sad** when something has just happened, which you did not want: *I'm* ***sad*** *that the holiday's over.* You often use **unhappy** about a feeling that continues for a long time. You say *He is* ***unhappy*** *in his job* (not 'he is sad').

homesick
sad because you are away from your home, family, and friends:
My sister was very homesick when she first went to college.

Homesick is not usually used before a noun.

gloomy
mood | atmosphere | expression | thoughts
looking or sounding sad and without hope:
There was a gloomy mood in the office that day. | He always has a rather gloomy expression on his face.

dejected/downcast
expression
looking sad and disappointed because something you hoped for did not happen:
His expression was downcast and he said "I wish you could stay longer." | "I didn't pass," she said, looking dejected.

mournful *literary*
sound | eyes | expression | face | cry
looking or sounding sad:
They heard the mournful sound of the church bell. | The dog looked at her with his big mournful eyes.

wistful *literary*
smile | expression | look | glance | longing
looking a little sad and thoughtful, because you wish that the situation was different:
She looked at the young couple with a wistful smile. | In England there is always a wistful longing for the past.

very sad

miserable
time | life
very sad, especially because you are lonely, cold, ill, or upset – used about people and periods of time:
I had a miserable time at college. | Why is my life so miserable? | He sat all alone in his room, feeling ***thoroughly miserable*** (=completely miserable).

depressed
very sad and without hope for a long time, because things are wrong in your life or because of a medical condition:
After his wife left him, he ***became depressed*** *and refused to talk to anyone.*

Depressed is much less common before a noun.

heartbroken
extremely sad because a relationship has ended or someone has died:
When Gary left her, she was heartbroken.

Heartbroken is not used before a noun.

devastated
extremely sad and shocked, because something very bad has happened:
The whole town was devastated by the tragedy.

Devastated is not used before a noun.

ANTONYMS **sad** → **happy**

2 making you feel sad

NOUNS

a sad story/song/film *He listened to her sad story about her awful life.*

a sad ending *The book has a very sad ending.*

sad news *I have some sad news to tell you.*

a sad case *It was a sad case – the boy ended up in prison.*

a sad loss (=after someone dies or leaves) *Mr Hay will be a sad loss to the English department.*

sad memories *It brought back some sad memories.*

a sad sight *All these empty seats are a sad sight.*

the sad truth *The sad truth is that this was not an isolated incident.*

ADVERBS

terribly/desperately/unbearably sad (=very sad) *That is such an unbearably sad story.*

PHRASES

it is sad *It's always sad when people split up.*

find it sad (that)... (=think it is sad that) *I find it sad that he can't even remember his own name.*

the sad thing is... *The sad thing is that it's too late to do anything.*

it is a sad fact (that)... (=used for saying you are sad that something is true) *It is a sad fact that a lot of crime is committed by young people.*

a sad state of affairs (=a bad situation) *This sad state of affairs must not be allowed to continue.*

be a sad reflection on sth (=show something unpleasant about something) *It is a sad reflection on life that it takes suffering to bring people closer together.*

THESAURUS: sad

depressing
experience | place | news | thought | sight | prospect | outlook | situation
making you feel that there is nothing to be happy about and not much hope for the future:
Walking past the rows of empty shops is a depressing experience. | The news is all very depressing. | The latest sales figures ***make for depressing reading*** (=they look depressing).

dismal
weather | place | day | morning | afternoon | state
making you feel unhappy and not at all

S

hopeful. **Dismal** sounds stronger than **depressing** and is often used about the weather:
She was fed up with the dismal English weather. | The world seemed a sad and dismal place. | The oil companies have left the area in a dismal state.

tragic
death | accident | events | circumstances | consequences | story | case | loss | history | hero | heroine
very sad, and often involving someone's death:
The princess died in a tragic accident. | The book tells the tragic story of black slaves torn from their roots in Africa. | Antigone is the play's tragic heroine.

heartbreaking
story | tale | tragedy | news | images | sight | decision
making you feel very sad and having a very strong effect on you:
The film is a heartbreaking story about a man who loses everything. | It was ***heartbreaking to see*** *him wasting his life away on drugs.*

pathetic
sight | figure | creature
making you feel sadness and sympathy:
He was a pathetic sight and his clothes were covered in mud. | She looked at him now, a pathetic and solitary figure.

Pathetic is usually used before a noun in this meaning. If you say *I think you're* ***pathetic***, that has a very different meaning – it means "I have no respect for you at all".

ANTONYMS **sad → happy**

sadistic *adj* **THESAURUS** **cruel (1)**

sadness *n* the state of feeling sad

ADJECTIVES

great/deep sadness *It was with great sadness that we learned of his death.*

overwhelming sadness (=so great that you cannot think about or do anything else) *Claudia felt an overwhelming sadness – she could not bear the thought of losing him.*

VERBS

feel sadness *I remember the sadness I felt when I realised she was not there anymore.*

PHRASES

a sense/feeling/air of sadness *She was left with a deep sense of sadness and sorrow.*

a touch/hint of sadness (=a little sadness) *There was a touch of sadness in her voice.*

be tinged with sadness (=have some sadness as well as joy) *His pleasure at winning the award is tinged with sadness because his mother, Joanna, isn't there to see him.*

be full of sadness/be filled with sadness *Yesterday my heart was full of sadness.*

safe *adj*

1 not in danger, or not harmed or stolen

ADVERBS

completely/totally/perfectly/absolutely safe *You will be completely safe if you stay in your car.*

VERBS

feel safe *I feel safer in Tokyo than I do in London.*

keep sb/sth safe *Make sure that you keep these documents safe.*

make sth safe *Boxing is dangerous, and it will never be possible to make the sport completely safe.*

NOUNS

a safe place (=where something is not likely to be stolen, or someone is not likely to be harmed) *Keep your passport in a safe place.*

a safe environment (=where someone can do what they like without being harmed) *Children need to feel that they are in a safe environment.*

a safe journey/trip *I wished them a safe journey.*

a safe return (=someone or something comes back safely) *The owner of a missing cat made an appeal for its safe return.*

safe passage (=the right to go somewhere without being arrested) *The terrorists have demanded safe passage out of the country.*

PREPOSITIONS

safe from sb/sth *The ants live in underground nests where they are safe from birds and lizards.*

safe with sb *Your luggage will be safe with us.*

PHRASES

from/at a safe distance *We watched the fireworks from a safe distance.*

safe and sound (=safe and unharmed after being in danger, when other people were worried about you) *I'm sure she will come back safe and sound.*

your secret is safe with me/will remain safe with me (=you will not tell other people about it) *Don't worry – your secret will remain safe with me.*

(as) safe as houses *BrE informal* (=completely safe) *Your money should be as safe as houses if you put it in a bank.*

2 not likely to cause harm

ADVERBS

completely/totally/perfectly/absolutely safe *Do you think that nuclear energy is completely safe?*

NOUNS

a safe driver *She's a very safe driver and she's never had an accident.*

the safe handling/disposal of sth *The two countries signed an agreement about the safe disposal of nuclear weapons.*

VERBS

make sth safe *Engineers are working to make the building safe after the earthquake.*

declare sth safe *The milk was declared safe after tests by government scientists.*

PREPOSITIONS

safe for sb *We want the streets to be safe for our children.*

PHRASES

it is safe to do sth *We waited until it was safe to go outside.*

safe to use *The government says that the vaccine is safe to use.*

safe to drink/eat *The water is safe to drink – it comes straight from a mountain spring.*

ANTONYMS **safe → dangerous**

safeguard *n*

a rule, agreement etc that is intended to protect someone or something from possible dangers or problems

ADJECTIVES

an additional/further/extra safeguard *He suggested additional safeguards for preventing fraud.*

a necessary/important safeguard *This is an important safeguard for the consumer.*

an effective safeguard *We need effective safeguards to stop people from being charged too much for loans.*

a proper/adequate/sufficient/appropriate safeguard *The company failed to provide adequate safeguards to protect investors.*

a strong/strict/stringent/tough safeguard *He has called for tougher safeguards to protect workers.*

a built-in safeguard (=one that is part of something) *There are built-in safeguards to prevent people from abusing the system.*

VERBS

provide a safeguard *Schools must provide proper safeguards to protect children.*

introduce/put in place a safeguard *The hospital has introduced new safeguards for patients.*

implement a safeguard (=introduce a safeguard that has been agreed) *Many of the safeguards that were suggested in the report still haven't been implemented.*

build a safeguard into sth (=include a safeguard as part of something) *Further safeguards have been built into the project.*

strengthen/improve a safeguard *This new rule is intended to strengthen the safeguards against discrimination.*

need/require a safeguard *Safeguards are needed to ensure the quality of food products.*

safeguard + NOUNS

a safeguard measure *Safeguard measures were introduced.*

PREPOSITIONS

a safeguard against sth *We need safeguards against the exploitation of children.*

a safeguard for sb/sth (=to protect them) *Unions want safeguards for their members' rights.*

safety *n*

a situation in which someone or something is safe from danger or harm

ADJECTIVES/NOUNS + safety

sb's own/personal safety *She jumped in the river with no thought for her own safety.*

public safety (=of ordinary people) *The police stopped the demonstration because of fears about public safety.*

road/air safety *After the plane crash, people became more concerned about air safety.*

fire safety *Fire safety regulations state that exits must be clearly marked.*

food safety *Food safety is important and you should always wash your hands before cooking.*

nuclear safety *Nuclear safety has improved, but there are always risks involved.*

in complete/perfect safety *We can watch the animals close up and in complete safety.*

in relative/comparative safety (=fairly safely) *The refugees can now return to their homes in relative safety.*

VERBS

be worried/concerned about sb's safety (*also* **fear for sb's safety**) *They fear for the safety of relatives they have left behind.*

ensure/guarantee sb's safety (=make sure they are safe) *The lifeguard's job is to ensure the safety of people using the swimming pool.*

improve safety *New plans have been announced to improve safety on the railways.*

endanger/threaten safety (=make something less safe) *Organisers of the event were accused of endangering public safety by selling too many tickets.*

get to/reach safety (=arrive in a safe place) *The men walked for days before finally reaching safety.*

get/lead/carry sb to safety (=take them to a safe place) *The firefighters carried the children to safety.*

safety + NOUNS

(as) a safety precaution/measure (=something you do in order to prevent accidents) *A fence was put around the lake as a safety precaution.*

safety standards/requirements *Some restaurants do not have high enough food safety standards.*

safety regulations (=rules) *There are strict safety regulations about what you can carry on a plane.*

safety instructions *Safety instructions should be supplied with all equipment.*

safety equipment *Your employer should provide the necessary safety equipment.*

a safety device/mechanism (=part of a piece of equipment that makes it safe) *A safety device cuts off the gas supply if the tap is accidentally left open.*

a safety hazard (=something that could be dangerous) *The wires on the floor are a safety hazard, because someone could fall over them.*

a safety inspection (=an official check to make sure that something is safe) *A safety inspection was carried out on the boiler system.*

a safety belt (=a belt that protects you in an accident in a car, plane etc) *Fasten your safety belts.*

PREPOSITIONS

in safety *New lighting has been installed, so that people can walk in safety.*

for sb's safety *The school was closed for the safety of the students, while the damage was being repaired.*

PHRASES

for your own safety *He is being kept at the police station for his own safety.*

for safety reasons/on safety grounds (*also* **for safety's sake** *spoken*) (=in order to make something safe) *For safety reasons, you must wear a helmet on the building site.*

for added/extra safety *For added safety, take a torch and spare batteries.*

a place of safety *They finally reached a place of safety, away from the floods.*

be safety conscious (=be always thinking about safety) *She is very safety conscious and would never let her children play with scissors.*

have a good safety record (=have had few accidents in the past) *The aircraft has a good safety record.*

have a poor safety record (=have had a lot of accidents in the past) *The mine has a poor safety record and several miners have died in the past three years.*

health and safety (=used about an area of government or law) *New health and safety regulations were introduced to protect workers.*

safety first (=safety is the most important thing - used when warning people to be careful) *Always remember, safety first! Fasten your seat belt before you start the car.*

sail *v*

to travel across an area of water in a boat

PREPOSITIONS/ADVERBS

sail to/from sth *We sailed from Southampton to New York.*

sail across sth *They were the first Europeans to sail across the Atlantic.*

sail around sth *She always wanted to sail around the world.*

sail for sth (=sail towards a place) *The boat sailed for Algiers in 1943.*

sail away/off *He got into the boat and sailed away.*

sail north/south/east/west *They sailed south to Easter Island.*

sail solo/single-handed *She was the first woman to sail solo around the world.*

NOUNS

sail a boat/ship/yacht/dinghy *Do you need a licence to sail a boat?*

sail the sea/ocean *She dreamt of sailing the sea.*

sail the Atlantic/Pacific etc *He took time off work to sail the Atlantic.*

a ship/boat/vessel/ferry sails *The ship sailed from New York on November 12th.*

salary *n*

money that you receive as payment from the organization you work for, usually paid to you every month

ADJECTIVES

a high salary *I wanted a job with a higher salary.*

a low salary *It sounds an interesting job, but the salary is too low.*

a big/large/huge/enormous salary *Some bankers are on huge salaries.*

a good salary *Doctors get good salaries.*

an attractive salary *The company are offering a very attractive salary.*

a modest salary (=not very big) *My salary is comparatively modest compared to his.*

a six-figure salary (=one over £100,000 or $100,000) *He's now a top executive with a six-figure salary.*

sb's annual salary *His annual salary is $200,000.*

sb's monthly salary *The tax is taken from your monthly salary.*

sb's current salary *His current salary is just over £30,000 a year.*

the average salary *The average salary for a teacher is $40,000 a year.*

the gross salary (=before tax is taken off) *40% of his gross annual salary is taken in tax.*

the basic/base salary (=the basic amount that someone is paid) *The basic salary is $50,000 a year, plus other benefits including a company car.*

the starting salary (=the salary someone gets when they start a job) *The starting salary for a hotel manager is $26,400.*

VERBS

earn/get/receive a salary *His father earns a good salary.*

be on a salary *BrE* (=be earning a particular amount of money) *She's on a salary of £20,000 a year.*
command a salary *formal* (=be able to get a salary, usually a high salary) *Managing directors can command high salaries.*
pay sb a salary *Large companies often pay better salaries.*
offer sb a salary *They offered her a starting salary of $70,000 a year.*
increase sb's salary *His annual salary was increased to £300,000.*
cut sb's salary (=reduce someone's salary) *The company plans to cut salaries by as much as 20%.*
cap sb's salary (=say officially that someone's salary must not be higher than a particular amount) *Government officials are having their salaries capped.*
live on a salary (=use it to buy the things you need to live) *Most people would find it hard to live on a salary of £12,000 a year.*

salary + NOUNS

a salary increase *He was given a huge salary increase.*
a salary cut (=a decrease in someone's salary) *The workforce agreed to take salary cuts.*
the salary scale/structure (=the list of increasing salaries that someone in a job can earn) *He is almost at the top of his salary scale.*
a salary package (=salary and other things such as a pension or shares, which a company offers for a job) *They are offering an excellent salary package.*

PHRASES

a drop/cut in salary (=a reduction in salary) *He couldn't afford to take a drop in salary.*
an increase/rise in salary *They were offered a 10% increase in salary.*

THESAURUS: salary

pay
the money you receive for doing a job:
*The **pay is good** but you have to work long hours. | Teachers are asking for **higher pay**. | They work long hours for **low pay**. | The **hourly pay** went up by £2. | The **take-home pay** is around £250 a week* (=the pay you get after tax and other things have been taken off).

wages (*also* **wage**)
the money that someone is paid every week by their employer, especially someone who works in a shop or factory:
*In those days, miners could **earn good wages**. | Many restaurant staff **are on low wages**. | The **average weekly wage** is $12. | The workers are asking for a **wage increase**.*

income
the money that you receive regularly for doing your job, and from things such as a business or investments:
*The amount of tax you have to pay depends on your income. | The government wants to help families **on low incomes**. | Single men often have high **disposable incomes*** (=a lot of money after paying taxes, bills etc, that you can spend on buying things).

earnings
the total amount of money you earn from any job you do – used especially when talking in general about people's salaries:
*The **average earnings** are much higher in Western countries. | The new tax is aimed at people with earnings of over £150,000 a year.*

the money *informal*
the amount of money that someone is paid for their work – used especially when saying if this seems a lot or a little:
*Firefighters **earn good money**. | I like my job, but **the money is not very good**. | "What's the money like?" "I'd say it's about average."*

sale *n*

1 sales of a product are the total number that are sold during a particular period of time

Grammar
Always plural in this meaning.

ADJECTIVES/NOUNS + sale

annual sales *The company has annual sales of over $300 million.*
worldwide sales *His last album achieved worldwide sales of over two million.*
sales are up/down (=they have increased or decreased) *Sales are up by 15% over last year.*
strong sales (=a lot of products are sold) *The company reported particularly strong sales of personal computers.*
record sales (=better than ever before) *The store achieved record sales in the final weeks before Christmas.*
better sales *If the price was lower, we could have achieved better sales.*
poor/disappointing sales *The product was taken off the market, after disappointing sales.*
car/ticket/book etc sales *There has been a big increase in ticket sales.*
retail sales (=sales of things to the public in shops and on the internet) *Retail sales have increased by 3%.*
online sales (=on the internet) *Online sales will soon overtake sales of goods sold in high street stores.*
export sales *Export sales are down.*

VERBS

sales increase/rise/grow/go up *Sales are expected to rise by 50%.*

sales soar/shoot up/rocket (=increase quickly and by a large amount) *Sales soared as prices continued to come down.*

sales improve *Sales seem to be improving slowly.*

sales fall/drop/go down (=become lower) *European sales have fallen by 12%.*

sales slump (=decrease quickly and by a large amount) *Meat sales have slumped following a recent health scare.*

sale + NOUNS

sales figures *The company said its sales figures continued to show growth.*

a sales target *Companies have had to lower their sales targets.*

a sales force (=the people who sell a company's products) *The sales force had grown from 40 to 270.*

sales performance (=how much a company sells) *This year's sales performance was rather disappointing.*

the sales forecast (=how much a company expects to sell) *The sales forecast was for 10,000 copies of the book to be sold in the first year.*

a sales pitch (=a talk for persuading someone to buy something) *They invited him to their office to hear his sales pitch.*

PHRASES

an increase/growth in sales *They are expecting a 20% increase in sales next year.*

a fall/drop/slump in sales *Some jobs may be cut following a big drop in sales.*

the volume of sales (=the amount of goods a company sells) *Because of its high volume of sales, the company can keep prices low.*

2 the act of selling something

ADJECTIVES

a quick sale *He wants a quick sale, so he might reduce the price.*

the sale of sth is illegal *The sale of alcohol is illegal in some countries.*

VERBS

make a sale (=sell something as part of your job) *The salesman's job is to make a sale.*

lose a sale (=fail to sell something) *I called the customer back because I didn't want to lose the sale.*

close a sale (=complete it) *He had to lower the price to close the sale.*

ban/prohibit/forbid the sale of sth (=order that it should not be sold) *Sales of the book were banned.*

a sale falls through (=it does not happen) *The sale fell through because the buyers suddenly changed their minds.*

a sale goes ahead (=it happens successfully) *If the sale goes ahead, it will be the highest price ever paid for a painting.*

sale + NOUNS

the sale price *The sale price was one million dollars.*

PHRASES

be (up) for sale (=be available to be bought) *How long has the house been for sale?*

be on sale (=being sold) *Their new album is on sale now.*

3 an event at which things are sold

ADJECTIVES/NOUNS + sale

an art/food/clothes etc sale *The event is one of the biggest art sales in the country.*

a (car) boot sale *BrE* (=an outdoor sale where people sell things from the back of cars) *She got the picture frame for 50p at a car boot sale.*

a jumble sale *BrE*, **a rummage sale** *AmE* (=a sale of used clothes, books etc, in order to collect money for a church, school etc) *I'll give the jacket to a jumble sale.*

a garage/yard sale *AmE* (=a sale of someone's possessions in their garage/yard) *Our neighbors are having a garage sale.*

a bring-and-buy sale (=a sale where people bring cheap things for people to buy, usually to collect money) *We're having a bring-and-buy sale at our local church.*

VERBS + sale

have a sale *They're having a book sale in the school hall.*

hold a sale (=have one) *We are holding a cake sale to raise money for charity.*

4 an event at which a shop sells goods at a reduced price

ADJECTIVES/NOUNS + sale

the January/New Year/summer etc sales *There are hundreds of bargains in the January sales.*

a big sale *The store is having a big sale.*

VERBS

buy/get sth in a sale *I bought the jacket in a sale – it was half price.*

have a sale *They usually have a sale in the autumn.*

same *adj, pronoun* not different

⚠ You always say **the same**. For example, you say **We are the same height** (not 'We are same height.')

ADVERBS

exactly the same *The two paintings look exactly the same.*

roughly/about the same *The students are all roughly the same age.*

S

almost/practically/virtually the same *The two poems both contain almost the same number of lines.*

just the same *She treats him just the same as the other children.*

much the same (=used when saying that something has not changed) *The town is much the same as it was 100 years ago.*

VERBS

look/sound/feel/taste the same *The words 'eight' and 'ate' sound the same.*

stay/remain the same *The price has stayed the same for the last three years.*

PREPOSITIONS

the same as *His car is the same as mine.*

PHRASES

the same old... *especially spoken* (=used when something does not change) *They always ask the same old questions.*

sb/sth are all the same *Politicians are all the same – they never keep their promises.*

ANTONYMS **same → different**

sample *n*

1 a small part or amount of something, that shows what the rest is like

NOUNS + sample

a blood/urine/tissue sample *The doctor took a blood sample and sent it off for analysis.*

a water/soil sample *They collected water samples from the river.*

a DNA sample (=a sample that contains a particular person's genes) *Police can use DNA samples to prove that someone committed a crime.*

a control sample (=for comparing other samples to) *A control sample and a sample of flour to be tested are placed side by side.*

VERBS

take/collect a sample *The study used blood samples taken from workers at four nuclear plants.*

give/provide a sample *Patients were asked to give a sample of their saliva.*

analyse/test a sample *All the samples were tested for bacteria.*

contaminate a sample (=get into it and spoil it) *The sample had been contaminated with iron.*

samples match (=they are the same) *His blood sample and the one found at the murder scene matched.*

PREPOSITIONS

a sample of sth *The gallery owner asked to see some samples of his work.*

a sample from sth *We've got some small samples from the tyres.*

2 a group of people in a survey

ADJECTIVES

a small/big sample *The findings of the research were only based on a small sample.*

a random sample (=not deliberately chosen) *We interviewed a random sample of people in the street.*

a representative sample (=including a typical range of people) *They asked a representative sample of students for their opinion.*

VERBS

choose a sample (*also* **select a sample** *formal*): *First, they selected a sample of 800 teachers.*

study/examine a sample *We studied a sample of 200 heart patients.*

interview a sample *You could interview a sample of library users or ask them to fill in questionnaires.*

a sample consists of/comprises sth (=it is formed from something) *The sample comprised both single and married women.*

sample + NOUNS

the sample size (*also* **the size of the sample**) *The sample size was too small to draw definite conclusions.*

a sample group *The sample group were all students at the university.*

PREPOSITIONS

a sample from sth *This is just a small sample from the whole population.*

a sample of sb *A sample of children between the ages of three and five were studied.*

sanctions *n*

official orders stopping trade or communication with another country

ADJECTIVES/NOUNS + sanctions

economic/trade sanctions *The United Nations is considering new economic sanctions.*

international sanctions *International sanctions were imposed on Iraq after it invaded Kuwait.*

tough/strict sanctions *Due to strict sanctions, the country is unable to import the medicines it needs.*

VERBS

impose sanctions (=start using them) *The US imposed economic sanctions on Cuba.*

lift sanctions (=stop using them) *Sanctions against South Africa were lifted when the apartheid system ended.*

ease/relax sanctions (=make them less strict) *They want to ease sanctions, and allow supplies of food and medicine into the country.*

tighten sanctions (=make them more strict) *There has been a proposal to tighten the sanctions.*

enforce sanctions (=make sure they are

obeyed) *The UN will have the job of enforcing the sanctions.*

break sanctions (*also* **violate sanctions** *formal*) (=send goods to another country when this is not allowed) *Several companies broke trade sanctions by continuing to export weapons.*

call for sanctions (=say you want them to be used) *The Council of Europe called for sanctions against Serbia.*

threaten sanctions *The European Union threatened economic sanctions.*

support/oppose sanctions *I oppose sanctions because they only increase the suffering of ordinary people.*

PREPOSITIONS

sanctions against sb *The sanctions against Italy were lifted.*

sanctions on sb *There should be sanctions on countries that use chemical weapons.*

PHRASES

the threat of sanctions *The UN should use the threat of sanctions to make the government stop the killing.*

the imposition of sanctions *formal* (=starting to use them) *Some countries called for the imposition of sanctions.*

sanctuary *n*

1 a peaceful place where someone can be safe

VERBS

find sanctuary *She ran away from him and found sanctuary at her friend's house.*

seek sanctuary *The man was seeking sanctuary from the secret police.*

give/offer (sb) sanctuary *Britain has a tradition of giving sanctuary to people who cannot live safely in their own countries.*

leave the sanctuary of sth *He did not want to leave the sanctuary of his home.*

PREPOSITIONS

a sanctuary for sb/sth *The shelter is a sanctuary for homeless people.*

the sanctuary of sth *From the busy street, he entered the sanctuary of the library.*

a sanctuary (away) from sth *The hotel provided a sanctuary from his stressful life.*

2 an area for birds or animals where they are protected and cannot be hunted

NOUNS + sanctuary

an animal sanctuary *The animal sanctuary is currently looking after around 150 animals.*

a bird sanctuary *The island in the middle of the lake is a bird sanctuary.*

a wildlife sanctuary *We visited a local wildlife sanctuary.*

a donkey/tiger etc sanctuary *The donkey sanctuary takes care of donkeys that have been badly treated.*

PREPOSITIONS

a sanctuary for sth *She set up a sanctuary for injured and sick birds.*

sarcasm *n*

a way of speaking or writing that involves saying the opposite of what you really mean, especially in order to make an unkind joke or to show that you are annoyed

ADJECTIVES

heavy sarcasm (=very obvious sarcasm) *"That's so very kind of you," he said with heavy sarcasm.*

bitter sarcasm *The article is full of bitter sarcasm and the writer obviously feels that he was treated very unfairly.*

PHRASES

be dripping (with) sarcasm (=be full of sarcasm) *Her voice was dripping with sarcasm.*

a hint/note/touch of sarcasm (=a little sarcasm) *He detected a note of sarcasm in her voice.*

sarcastic *adj*

saying things that are the opposite of what you mean, especially in order to make an unkind joke or to show that you are annoyed

NOUNS

a sarcastic comment/remark *Her husband was always making sarcastic comments about her clothes.*

a sarcastic tone/voice *I didn't like the sarcastic tone of her remarks.*

VERBS

sb is being sarcastic *Maybe she was just being sarcastic.*

satire *n*

the use of humour to criticize something by making it seem stupid, or a play, book, film etc that uses this type of humour

ADJECTIVES

political satire *Her new TV show will include a lot of political satire.*

social satire *The book is a social satire of the English class system.*

savage/biting/scathing satire (=which has very strong or angry criticism) *His next film was a biting satire of American politics.*

gentle satire *'Welcome To LA' was a gentle satire of life in Southern California.*

VERBS

use satire *In his book, Voltaire uses satire to show the weaknesses in Leibniz's argument.*

write a satire *Achebe wrote a satire on corruption in Africa.*

PREPOSITIONS

a satire on/about sth *The book is a satire on fashionable London society.*

S

satisfaction *n*

a feeling of happiness or pleasure because you have achieved something or got what you wanted

ADJECTIVES

great/deep satisfaction *It was hard work, but it gave her great satisfaction.*

immense/enormous satisfaction (=very great) *Dancing gives her immense satisfaction.*

a lot of satisfaction *He gets a lot of satisfaction from his job.*

little satisfaction *There's very little satisfaction in cleaning all day.*

complete satisfaction *They expressed complete satisfaction with the agreement.*

real satisfaction *She gets real satisfaction from helping other people to overcome their problems.*

personal satisfaction (=with your own life or achievements) *There is enormous personal satisfaction when you finish writing a book.*

quiet satisfaction *She looked at the painting with quiet satisfaction.*

grim satisfaction (=when you are proved right about something bad) *He listened to the news with a look of grim satisfaction on his face.*

smug satisfaction *disapproving* (=when you are too satisfied with your own cleverness or success) *He spoke with an air of smug satisfaction that made her want to hit him.*

NOUNS + satisfaction

job satisfaction (=pleasure from your job) *Job satisfaction is more important than the amount of money you get paid.*

customer/patient/voter etc satisfaction (=among customers, patients, voters etc) *Customer satisfaction with the airline remains very high.*

VERBS

get satisfaction from sth (*also* **gain/derive satisfaction from sth** *formal*): *I get a lot of satisfaction from helping other people.*

find satisfaction *The book is supposed to help you find satisfaction in life.*

take satisfaction in/from sth *He took great satisfaction in doing his job well.*

have the satisfaction of sth *At least I had the satisfaction of knowing that I was right.*

sth gives/brings satisfaction *Saving people's lives gives enormous satisfaction.*

feel satisfaction *As she looked at what she had created, she felt a quiet satisfaction.*

express satisfaction *He expressed satisfaction with the way the meeting had gone.*

guarantee/ensure satisfaction (=make certain that someone gets it) *The builder's ad promised 'satisfaction guaranteed'.*

PREPOSITIONS

with satisfaction *She finished her letter and read it through with satisfaction.*

in satisfaction *Harry watched in satisfaction as his team scored the winning goal.*

to sb's satisfaction (=with the result that someone is satisfied) *When the job is done to my satisfaction, I will pay you.*

satisfaction with sth *How would you rate your satisfaction with your work?*

PHRASES

a sense/feeling of satisfaction *I get a great sense of satisfaction from learning new things.*

a smile/sigh/look of satisfaction *A look of satisfaction crossed his face.*

the level of satisfaction (=the number of people who feel satisfied) *There is a high level of satisfaction with the company's products.*

a source of satisfaction (=something that gives you satisfaction) *Work can be an enormous source of satisfaction.*

THESAURUS: satisfaction

contentment *formal*
a feeling of happiness with your life, because things are how you want them to be:
*He sat back with **a look of deep contentment** on his face. | Few people **find contentment** from having lots of money. | Laura **sighed with contentment** as she looked at the beautiful view from her window.*

fulfilment *BrE*, **fulfillment** *AmE*
the feeling that you have achieved the things that you wanted to achieve in your life:
*Some women **find fulfillment** in being a mother, but this is not true for all women. | We all **seek fulfilment** in our lives, but how many people actually achieve it? | He enjoyed his job – it gave him **a sense of fulfilment** and achievement.*

satisfactory *adj*

good enough for you, or good enough for a particular situation or purpose

ADVERBS

very/highly/most satisfactory *She has made a very satisfactory recovery from her illness.*

perfectly/quite satisfactory (=used when emphasizing that something is satisfactory) *If you don't have olive oil, sunflower oil is perfectly satisfactory.*

entirely/wholly/completely satisfactory *Neither system was wholly satisfactory.*

broadly/generally satisfactory (=mostly satisfactory) *Although his work is broadly satisfactory, there are things that can be improved.*

far from/less than satisfactory (=not satisfactory) *His behaviour has been far from satisfactory this year.*

barely/hardly satisfactory (=not really satisfactory) *The food was very expensive, and the service was barely satisfactory.*

NOUNS

a satisfactory explanation *There seems to be no satisfactory explanation.*

a satisfactory answer *No-one could give Donna a satisfactory answer to her question.*

a satisfactory arrangement *Having your brother living with us is not a satisfactory arrangement.*

a satisfactory result/outcome *Our main aim is to achieve a satisfactory outcome for both sides.*

a satisfactory solution *We will not rest until a satisfactory solution is found.*

satisfactory progress *His progress this term has been satisfactory.*

satisfactory work *You won't get paid unless your work is satisfactory.*

a satisfactory performance *The team's performance was far from satisfactory.*

a satisfactory recovery *The patient has made a satisfactory recovery.*

PREPOSITIONS

satisfactory to sb *We want an arrangement that is satisfactory to both sides.*

satisfied *adj*

feeling that someone or something is as good as they should be, or that something has happened in the way that you want

ADVERBS

completely/totally/entirely/fully satisfied *Most people said that they were completely satisfied with their lives.*

perfectly satisfied (=used when saying that someone thinks that there is nothing wrong with something, and does not want to complain or change anything) *She seemed perfectly satisfied with his explanation.*

reasonably satisfied *All the equipment is checked regularly, and you can be reasonably satisfied that it is safe.*

never satisfied *Good players are never satisfied – they always want to improve their game.*

NOUNS

a satisfied customer *The hotel has dozens of emails from satisfied customers on its website.*

a satisfied smile/grin/expression/look *Sarah watched the children with a satisfied expression on her face.*

VERBS

feel satisfied *Do you feel satisfied with your life, or is there something you would like to change?*

look/seem/appear satisfied *Members seem satisfied that they are receiving good value for money.*

keep sb satisfied *It is always important to keep the customer satisfied.*

PREPOSITIONS

satisfied with sth *If you are not satisfied with our service, please let us know.*

PHRASES

more than satisfied (=extremely satisfied) *The coach says that he is more than satisfied with the team's performance.*

far from satisfied (=not at all satisfied) *We are far from satisfied with the security arrangements.*

satisfy *v*

1 if you satisfy someone's needs, demands etc, you provide what they need or want

NOUNS

satisfy a need *Babies rely on adults to satisfy their needs.*

satisfy demand *The company was unable to satisfy demand for the product.*

satisfy sb's hunger/appetite (=stop them being hungry) *The soup was nice, but it didn't really satisfy my hunger.*

satisfy a desire *He needs a job that satisfies his desire for power.*

satisfy an urge *Her urge to travel had never been fully satisfied.*

satisfy sb's curiosity (=let them know something they want to know) *Just to satisfy my curiosity, how much did it cost?*

2 to be good enough for a particular purpose, standard etc

NOUNS

satisfy a requirement *All new products must satisfy safety requirements.*

satisfy a condition *They did not satisfy the conditions for financial assistance.*

satisfy a criterion (=satisfy a standard used to judge something) *To join this group you must satisfy certain criteria.*

satisfying *adj*

making you feel pleased and happy, especially because you have got what you wanted

ADVERBS

deeply/highly satisfying (=very satisfying) *There is something deeply satisfying about making your own bread.*

extremely/immensely satisfying *Teaching can be immensely satisfying.*

particularly/especially satisfying *It is particularly satisfying when people say that they have enjoyed the show.*

personally satisfying *I'm not just interested in money, I want to find a job that is personally satisfying.*

NOUNS

a satisfying experience/feeling *Decorating your home can be an enjoyable and satisfying experience.*

a satisfying hobby *Gardening is a very satisfying hobby for many people.*

VERBS

find sth satisfying *He finds his work incredibly satisfying.*

saving *n*

1 your savings are all the money that you have saved, especially in a bank

Grammar
Always plural in this meaning.

ADJECTIVES/NOUNS + saving

life savings (=the money you have saved during your life) *The couple spent their life savings on a villa in Spain.*

personal/private savings *Many small business owners use their personal savings to start their businesses.*

retirement savings *You can get tax back on retirement savings.*

VERBS

spend your savings *He spent all his savings on a sports car.*

invest your savings *They have to decide how best to invest their savings.*

saving + NOUNS

a savings account (=a bank account for keeping savings for some time, which pays a higher rate of interest) *I'm going to leave the money in my savings account.*

a savings bank (=a bank where people can save small amounts of money and receive interest on it) *The best thing you can do is to put the money in a savings bank.*

a savings plan/scheme (=an arrangement to save amounts of money regularly) *He pays £100 a month into a savings plan.*

2 an amount of money that you have not spent, or an amount of something that you have not used

ADJECTIVES

a big/large/great saving *Small price differences between stores can add up to large savings on your weekly shopping.*

a considerable/significant/substantial saving *By buying in large quantities you can make a considerable saving.*

a total saving *You could make a total saving of up to a quarter on your heating bills.*

a potential saving (=one you could make) *There are lots of potential savings from changing to solar power.*

an annual saving (=the amount saved each year) *The dishwasher uses half as much water as washing by hand, an annual saving of 8,760 litres.*

VERBS

make a saving (*also* **achieve a saving** *formal*): *You can make quite a large saving by booking holiday flights early.*

produce a saving *Reducing the number of people invited by half would produce a saving of over £1,500.*

result in a saving *Improved energy efficiency has resulted in a saving of £20,000 per year.*

NOUNS + saving

cost saving *The employment of part-time workers results in wage cost savings.*

energy/fuel saving *Energy saving is an important issue for all businesses.*

time saving *The website suggests lots of time-saving ideas.*

tax saving (=an amount of tax you can save) *This would give a tax saving of almost £2,000 for the average tax payer.*

PREPOSITIONS

a saving of sth *We offer savings of up to 40% off manufacturers' recommended prices.*

a saving on sth *Companies are always looking for ways of making savings on staff costs.*

saw *v* THESAURUS cut[1] (1)

say *v*

to express an idea, feeling, thought etc using words

ADVERBS

say sth angrily/calmly/cheerfully etc *"That's not true," he said angrily.*

say sth quietly/softly/loudly *"He's asleep," she said quietly.*

say sth aloud/out loud (=say something so that other people can hear, not just think about it) *She would never say these things out loud.*

say sth publicly/openly *No one wants to say it publicly, but his career is over.*

say sth privately/in private *She said privately that she was thinking of resigning.*

say sth categorically (=in a definite way because you are certain about it) *They could not say categorically that his illness was cured.*

sb rightly/correctly says *As Gandhi rightly said, if you want to see the real India, go to the villages.*

PREPOSITIONS

say sth to sb *We said goodbye to the children.*

say sth about sth *Did he say anything about his trip?*

say sth with a smile/sigh/frown etc *"Keep them," she said with a smile.*

PHRASES

say hello/goodbye *I came to say goodbye.*

say thank you *I just wanted to say thank you for all your help.*

say sorry/say that you're sorry *It was too late to say sorry.*

say yes/no *Some parents are unable to say no to their children.*

say so (=say that something is true) *"Are they getting married?" "Everyone says so."*

say something/anything/nothing *He looked as if he was going to say something.*

have something/anything/nothing to say *He usually has something to say about just about everything.*

not say *"Why did she leave?" "She didn't say."*

a terrible/stupid/odd etc thing to say *I know it's a terrible thing to say, but I wish he wasn't here.*

say a few words (=make a short speech) *I'd like to say a few words about Jean.*

say sth under your breath (=very quietly so that no-one can hear) *"What nonsense," she said, under her breath.*

I can honestly/truthfully say *I can honestly say it was the best film I have ever seen.*

I can safely say (=used when saying that something is definitely true) *I can safely say that I will not be inviting him to my house again.*

What makes you say that? (=why do you think that?) *"She's not happy." "What makes you say that?"*

saying *n*

a well-known short statement that expresses an idea most people believe is true and wise

ADJECTIVES

an old saying *You know the old saying: "Don't judge a book by its cover."*

a famous/well-known saying *There is a famous saying: "Life begins at 40."*

a favourite saying *BrE*, **a favorite saying** *AmE*: *One of his favourite sayings is: "If a thing's worth doing, it's worth doing well."*

a wise saying *His books are full of wise sayings.*

PHRASES

as the saying goes (=used when mentioning the words of a saying) *As the saying goes, you can't please all the people all the time.*

THESAURUS: saying

expression, idiom, cliché, saying/proverb, slogan, motto → **phrase**

scale *n*

1 the size or level of something, or the amount that something is happening

Grammar

Scale is often used in the phrase **on a ... scale**, for example: *on a large/massive/modest/unprecedented etc* **scale**.

ADJECTIVES

a large/huge/massive scale *The crops are grown on a massive scale.*

a grand scale (=very large and impressive) *I was impressed by the grand scale of her ambitions.*

a small scale *Because of the small scale of the operation, we didn't need many staff.*

the full scale of sth (=how big or bad something is) *The full scale of the problem is not known.*

the sheer scale of sth (=the fact that it is very big or great) *He was shocked by the sheer scale of the destruction.*

a modest scale (=small and not very impressive) *My apartment was similar, but on a more modest scale.*

an unprecedented scale (=more than ever before) *The floods are a disaster on an unprecedented scale.*

a human scale (=small enough for people to understand and be happy with) *The architect aims to give the building a more human scale.*

a commercial scale (=enough for buying and selling to make a profit) *If they find enough oil, production on a commercial scale will begin in five years.*

a national/international scale *This is a disaster on a national scale.*

a global/world scale (=involving the whole world) *Pollution could cause changes to weather patterns on a global scale.*

VERBS

show/reveal the scale of sth *Inspections aim to reveal the scale of the country's nuclear program.*

assess/determine the scale of sth *First, try to assess the scale of the damage.*

increase/reduce the scale of sth *We need to increase the scale of this work.*

understand/realize the scale of sth *The police began to understand the scale of his terrible crimes.*

underestimate the scale of sth (=think it is smaller, less serious etc than it really is) *We had underestimated the scale of the problem.*

PREPOSITIONS

on a ... scale *The village had a market, but on a very limited scale.*

the scale of sth *The scale of the disaster was immediately obvious.*

large/small etc in scale *The temple is smaller in scale than others in the region.*

PHRASES

economies of scale (=savings from buying or doing things in large quantities) *Large firms benefit from economies of scale.*

2 a whole range of different types of people or things, from the lowest level to the highest

ADJECTIVES/NOUNS + scale

a pay/salary scale *As a senior teacher, she has reached the top of her pay scale.*

the social scale (=from the poorest, least powerful people to the richest and most important in a society) *She gradually made her way up the social scale.*

the evolutionary scale (=from the least to the most intelligent animals) *Birds are much lower on the evolutionary scale than dogs.*
a sliding scale (=changing according to certain conditions) *Fees are calculated on a sliding scale.*
a fixed scale (=not changing) *Their pay increases every year, according to a fixed scale.*
a four-point/seven-point/ten-point etc scale (=with four, seven etc levels) *Each incident is rated on a five-point scale of seriousness.*

VERBS

move up/down a scale *They want to go to university because they think it will help them to move up the social scale.*

PHRASES

the top/bottom of a scale *He started at the bottom of the pay scale.*
the end of a scale (=the top or bottom) *At the other end of the scale, the youngest competitor was just 16 years old.*
further/higher up a scale *She wanted to get married to someone who was higher up the social scale.*
further/lower down a scale *Bonuses are not paid to people lower down the salary scale.*

scandal *n*

an event in which someone, especially someone important, behaves in a bad way that shocks people

ADJECTIVES/NOUNS + scandal

a big/major scandal *South Korea's environment minister has been sacked following a major scandal.*
a minor scandal (=a small one) *His image has been spoiled by a series of minor scandals.*
the worst scandal *It was the worst financial scandal the world had ever seen.*
a public scandal *The award was soon the centre of a public scandal.*
a financial scandal *He was suspected of involvement in a major financial scandal.*
a political scandal *Christine Keeler was famous for her role in the political scandal which led to the resignation of John Profumo.*
a corruption scandal (=involving illegal payments) *They are investigating a major police corruption scandal.*

VERBS + scandal

cause a scandal *It caused quite a scandal when he left his wife.*
be involved in a scandal *A number of leading politicians were involved in the scandal.*
be implicated in a scandal (=be suspected of being involved) *One of the ministers implicated in the scandal resigned.*
uncover/expose a scandal (=make it known) *The scandal was uncovered by a journalist.*
cover up a scandal (=keep it secret) *The government tried to cover up the scandal.*
avoid/prevent a scandal *The company is anxious to avoid a scandal.*

scandal + VERBS

a scandal rocks/shakes sth (=makes people very shocked) *The scandal has rocked the art world.*
a scandal breaks (=becomes known) *He had already announced his resignation when the scandal broke.*
a scandal erupts (=becomes known with serious effects) *A major scandal erupted in Washington last year.*
the scandal surrounding sb/sth *They knew about the scandal surrounding the actor, but they still chose to hire him.*

PREPOSITIONS

a scandal over sth *The newspaper reported the scandal over illegal arms sales.*
the scandal of sth *He survived the scandal of his affair with a young model.*

PHRASES

be at the centre of a scandal *BrE*, **be at the center of a scandal** *AmE*: *The banker at the centre of the scandal has disappeared.*
a series/succession of scandals (=several, one after the other) *A series of scandals forced the departure of the Chairman.*

scar *n*

1 a mark that is left on your skin after you have had a cut or wound

ADJECTIVES

a big/long/deep scar *The man had a long scar down his right cheek.*
a small/faint scar *Spots can leave small scars.*
a permanent scar *The cut left a permanent scar.*

VERBS

have a scar *He had a small white scar under his left eye.*
leave a scar *The cut is deep and will leave quite a scar.*
a scar runs somewhere *The scar ran down his leg.*
a scar heals (=it gradually disappears) *Don't worry – the scars will soon heal.*

2 permanent damage caused by something

ADJECTIVES

a deep scar *The war left deep scars on the local community.*
a permanent scar *Some permanent scars still remain.*
the psychological/mental/emotional scars (=a feeling of sadness or fear that remains after an unpleasant experience) *He is still dealing with the mental scars left by the accident.*

VERBS

leave a scar *The trial left a deep scar on our family.*

S

bear/carry the scars (=be affected by them) *Haiti still bears the scars of centuries of violence, poverty, and corruption.*

a scar heals (=it gradually disappears) *The mental scars will eventually heal.*

scarce *adj*

if something is scarce, there is not very much of it available

ADVERBS

increasingly scarce *Clean drinking water has become increasingly scarce in some parts of the country.*

relatively scarce *These birds are relatively scarce in the UK.*

NOUNS

scarce resources *Many of the Earth's natural resources are becoming increasingly scarce.*

a scarce commodity (=a useful substance or quality that is scarce) *Water is a scarce commodity in the desert.*

food is scarce *Food is scarce in winter.*

THESAURUS: scarce

scarce, uncommon, infrequent → **rare**

scared *adj*

frightened or worried that something bad may happen

VERBS

be/feel scared *It was getting late and she was beginning to feel scared.*

look scared *What's the matter? You look scared.*

sound scared *Don't sound so scared – everything will be fine.*

get scared (=start to feel scared) *It was now completely dark and I was getting scared.*

make sb scared *The bullies made me scared to go to school.*

PREPOSITIONS

scared of sth *She's always been scared of dogs.*

scared about sth *Everyone's scared about losing their jobs.*

scared at sth *I was scared stiff at the thought of making a speech.*

PHRASES

scared stiff/to death *informal* (=extremely scared) *He looked scared to death.*

scared witless/out of your wits *informal* (=extremely scared) *She admitted she was scared witless.*

be running scared (=be scared, especially because another person, team, company etc is likely to defeat you) *Their new software has the other companies running scared.*

scary *adj* THESAURUS **frightening**

scenario Ac *n*

a situation that could possibly happen

ADJECTIVES/NOUNS + scenario

a possible scenario *We need to consider every possible scenario.*

a likely scenario *The most likely scenario is that world population will continue to increase.*

a plausible scenario (=one that you believe could happen) *War between the two countries is a perfectly plausible scenario.*

an unlikely scenario *Only massive investment from outside could save the business, and this is an unlikely scenario.*

the worst-case/worst scenario (=the worst thing that might happen) *The worst-case scenario is that we might have to sell the house.*

the best-case scenario (=the best thing that might happen) *In the best-case scenario, the project will be finished by July.*

a nightmare scenario (=a very bad thing that might happen) *The nightmare scenario would be a number of simultaneous terrorist attacks.*

a doomsday scenario (=a great disaster that might happen) *The doomsday scenario is that mankind will die out as a result of global warming.*

the ideal scenario *In an ideal scenario, changes would have the support of everyone in the company.*

an alternative/different scenario *It can be helpful to imagine alternative scenarios so you are ready for any challenge.*

VERBS

consider a scenario (=think about what might happen) *The government has considered various possible scenarios.*

imagine a scenario *It is difficult to imagine a scenario in which this could happen.*

PREPOSITIONS

in a scenario *In this scenario, the company would have to spend another $3 billion.*

under a scenario *These people would not vote for her under any scenario.*

scene *n*

1 a part of a play or film

PHRASES

scene one/two etc *At the end of scene one, a ship magically appears on the stage.*

ADJECTIVES/NOUNS + scene

the first/opening scene *The opening scene of the play is set in a forest.*

the final/last/closing scene *We do not know who killed her until the final scene.*

a funny/sad/violent etc scene *Some of the scenes are very violent.*

a love/fight/death etc scene *She said she ate garlic before doing love scenes.*

a bedroom/courtroom scene *The courtroom scene is at the centre of the film.*

S

a nude scene (=in which an actor wears no clothes) *Some actors refuse to do nude scenes.*

VERBS

a scene takes place somewhere/is set somewhere *The scene takes place in a bar.*

act/play/do a scene *The director tells you how to play your scenes. | He's good at doing funny scenes.*

film/shoot a scene *It took 20 attempts to shoot that scene.*

rehearse a scene/run through a scene (=practise it) *First, we run through our scenes, then filming begins.*

cut/delete a scene *They had to cut some scenes because they were too violent.*

PREPOSITIONS

a scene from sth *We rehearsed a scene from 'Romeo and Juliet'.*

a scene between sb and sb *The scenes between Kate and her daughter were particularly sad.*

in a scene *He is killed in the final scene.*

2 a type of activity that people are involved in

ADJECTIVES/NOUNS + scene

a lively/vibrant scene (=interesting and exciting) *Berlin has a lively arts scene.*

a thriving/flourishing scene (=with a lot of interesting things happening) *The UK has a thriving music scene.*

the national/international/world scene *He is a major figure on the international political scene.*

the political/cultural/literary scene *Anthony Burgess had a huge influence on the literary scene.*

the music/theatre/arts scene *Do you know anything about the New York arts scene?*

the jazz/pop/rap etc scene *She is the best singer on the jazz scene today.*

the social scene (=parties etc that people go to, to enjoy themselves) *She loved the city, and really enjoyed the social scene.*

the club scene (=going to nightclubs) *He knows everything about the local club scene.*

VERBS

be part of a scene *These parties were an important part of the social scene.*

be involved in a scene *I knew that he was involved in the music scene.*

appear/arrive on the scene (=become known) *She first appeared on the arts scene in 2010.*

burst/explode onto the scene (=suddenly become very well known) *He burst onto the film scene in 2008.*

dominate a scene (=have a very big effect on it) *The issue continues to dominate the political scene.*

disappear/vanish from the scene *Many great players have now disappeared from the scene.*

3 the place where an accident, crime etc happened

NOUNS + scene

a crime/murder scene *Detectives are already at the crime scene.*

an accident/crash scene *Keep away from accident scenes unless you are there to help.*

VERBS

be called to the scene *Armed police were called to the scene.*

arrive at/on the scene *By the time I arrived on the scene it was too late.*

reach the scene *Rescuers are still trying to reach the crash scene.*

go/rush/run to the scene *He went to the scene and was shocked at what he saw.*

leave the scene (*also* **depart from the scene** *formal*): *Do not allow anyone to leave the scene.*

run/flee from the scene *The murderer then fled the scene.*

PREPOSITIONS

at the scene *Investigators are now at the scene.*

on the scene *Journalists were on the scene within minutes.*

the scene of sth *The police soon arrived at the scene of the crime.*

scenery *n*

the natural features of an area, such as mountains, forests, lakes etc

ADJECTIVES/NOUNS + scenery

beautiful scenery *The scenery was beautiful and the people were really friendly.*

magnificent/spectacular/dramatic scenery (=very impressive) *Tourists come for the winter sports and the spectacular scenery.*

stunning/breathtaking/wonderful scenery (=very impressive) *We drove through some stunning scenery.*

mountain scenery *This fascinating village is surrounded by magnificent mountain scenery.*

alpine scenery (=mountains, especially those in the Alps) *The pictures showed views of snow-capped mountains and alpine scenery.*

VERBS

look at/admire the scenery *We stopped the car and got out to look at the scenery.*

enjoy the scenery *There is a beautiful lake, where you can swim, picnic, or just enjoy the scenery.*

take in the scenery (=enjoy it – used when there is a lot to see) *Relax with a glass of local wine while you take in the beautiful scenery.*

scent *n* THESAURUS ▸ smell[1]

schedule Ac *n*

a plan of what someone is going to do and when they are going to do it

ADJECTIVES

a busy schedule (=you have arranged to do a lot of things) *The president has a busy schedule that includes meetings with law-makers and church leaders.*

a hectic schedule (=very busy) *He has a hectic schedule for today, with stops in Tucson, Sierra Vista, Casa Grande, Tombstone, Globe, and Safford.*

a full schedule (=busy, so that you do not have time for other things) *Like most finance directors, she has a very full schedule with engagements on most evenings.*

a tight schedule (=busy because you have to do a lot of things in a short time) *We're going to be working to a very tight schedule.*

a gruelling schedule *BrE*, **a grueling schedule** *AmE* (=very tiring) *The band has a gruelling schedule of ten concerts in eight days.*

a light schedule (=you do not have many things to do) *I wanted to keep my schedule as light as possible.*

daily schedule *You should try to make exercise part of your daily schedule.*

VERBS

have a schedule *We have an attractive schedule of events for this afternoon.*

keep to/stick to a schedule *I think it's best if we stick to the original schedule.*

rearrange/juggle your schedule (=change it so that you can do something) *I had to juggle my schedule so that I could find time to meet him.*

fall behind schedule (=be done later than planned) *The production of the movie fell behind schedule.*

work out your schedule (=decide what it is) *I haven't worked out my schedule yet.*

PREPOSITIONS

schedule for sth *What's your schedule for tomorrow?*

on schedule (=at the agreed time) *The work was completed on schedule.*

ahead of schedule (=doing things earlier than the agreed time) *Meg's new book is still well ahead of schedule.*

behind schedule (=doing things later than the agreed time) *The construction work is three months behind schedule.*

scheme Ac *n BrE*

an official plan to help people in some way, for example by providing education or training

ADJECTIVES

a new scheme *The new scheme aims to reduce street crime by 30%.*

a major scheme *The government is introducing a major road-building scheme.*

a controversial scheme (=causing a lot of disagreement) *The scheme was controversial and many people thought it wouldn't work.*

an innovative/pioneering scheme (=using new ideas) *Local authorities are using an innovative scheme to help the unemployed get back to work.*

a grand/ambitious scheme (=trying to achieve a lot) *In the end, their grand scheme came to nothing.*

a successful scheme *If successful, the scheme could be introduced throughout the country.*

a voluntary scheme (=which you can take part in if you want) *There is a voluntary scheme which asks companies to show how much salt their products contain.*

NOUNS + scheme

a training scheme *We have a training scheme for new employees.*

a pension/insurance scheme *Does your company offer a pension scheme?*

a compensation scheme (=that gives money to people who suffer injury or loss) *There is a new compensation scheme for accident victims.*

an incentive scheme (=that encourages people to do something by giving them money if they do) *There is a generous incentive scheme for the sales force.*

a bonus scheme (=that gives extra money as a reward) *They've started a bonus scheme for people who ride a bike to work.*

a pilot scheme (=in which you do something to find out if it works, usually with a small group of people) *The pilot scheme was a great success.*

a government scheme *A new government scheme aims to help the homeless.*

VERBS

introduce/bring in/launch a scheme *The scheme was launched last year.*

run/operate a scheme *Parents are helping to run the scheme, which is intended to improve children's reading ability.*

devise/come up with a scheme (=think of a scheme) *The government needs to come up with a scheme to deal with the problem.*

set up a scheme (=organize it) *They have set up a scheme to help families of sick children.*

start a scheme *The council started a scheme which encourages people to grow their own vegetables.*

join a scheme *Many more companies have now joined the scheme.*

take part in a scheme (*also* **participate in a scheme** *formal*): *She is taking part in a training scheme for young unemployed people.*

be covered by a scheme (=be able to benefit from a scheme) *Workers are covered by a private health insurance scheme.*

PREPOSITIONS

in a scheme *Can anyone be in the scheme?*

under a scheme *Under the scheme, anyone over 60 can travel by bus for free.*

a scheme for sth *The government announced a scheme for students, which allows them to pay back their loans over a period of 30 years.*

school *n*

a place where children are taught

ADJECTIVES/NOUNS + school

a secondary school (=for children from 11 to 16 or 18) *She teaches in a secondary school.*

a high school *AmE* (=a school for students aged 14 to 18) *We studied chemistry and biology in high school.*

a primary school *BrE*, **an elementary school** *AmE* (=for children up to 11) *I learned to read when I was in elementary school.*

an infant school *BrE* (=for children aged 5 to 7) *Aileen was my best friend in the first year at infant school.*

a nursery school (=for children under 5) *At the age of four I went to a nursery school a few doors away from our house.*

a state school *BrE*, **a public school** *AmE* (=which is free for students to go to, and gets its money from the government) *More students from state schools are going to university.*

a private school (*also* **a public school** *BrE*) (=where students pay to study) *He was educated at a private school.*

a comprehensive school *BrE* (=a secondary school for children of all abilities) *Nine out of ten children are in comprehensive schools.*

a grammar school *BrE* (=for children who have passed an exam when they are 11) *Bill was educated at the Royal Grammar School, Lancaster, and the University of Manchester.*

a single-sex/all-boys/all-girls school (=which has only boys, or only girls) *Girls do better at single-sex schools.*

a boarding school (=where children also live and sleep) *Her parents sent her away to boarding school when she was 11.*

sb's old school (=the school someone went to when they were young) *He went back to his old school to give a talk to the children.*

a local school (=a school near where someone lives) *They sent their kids to the local school.*

an inner-city school (=in a poor area near the centre of a big city) *In inner-city schools, the students' first language is often not English.*

VERBS

go to school (*also* **attend (a) school** *formal*): *Where do you go to school?*

start school *Children in Britain start school when they are five.*

leave school *He left school when he was 16.*

come home from school *When you come home from school, do your homework.*

be off school *BrE* (=not be at school, for example because you are ill) *I was off school, so I missed that lesson.*

send sb to (a) school *His parents sent him to a private school.*

pick sb up from school (=go there to bring them home) *His mother always used to pick him up from school.*

be expelled from school (*also* **be kicked out of school** *informal*) (=not be allowed to go to a school any more because of bad behaviour) *He was expelled from school for fighting.*

drop out of school (=leave school before the end of your studies) *After dropping out of school, she had a baby.*

school + NOUNS

a school teacher/schoolteacher *My dad is a school teacher.*

school children/schoolchildren *The play was performed by local school children.*

a school friend/schoolfriend *She met some old school friends.*

the school holidays *BrE*: *I'm looking forward to the school holidays.*

a school trip *They are going on a school trip to Paris.*

the school day *Children are often tired at the end of the school day.*

the school playground/library/bus etc *We used to play football in the school playground.*

the school curriculum (=the range of different subjects that must be taught in a school) *Head teachers were asked to include road safety education in the school curriculum.*

the school system *The school system in England is different from the rest of Europe.*

a school uniform/tie *He was still wearing his school uniform.*

school meals/lunches (*also* **school dinners** *BrE*): *Children from poor families can get free school meals.*

the school run *BrE* (=the journey taking children to and from school each day) *She had to be back in time for the school run.*

a school leaver (=someone who has just finished school) *Many school leavers have difficulty finding a job.*

Schoolboy, **schoolgirl**, and **schoolbag** are usually written as one word.

PREPOSITIONS

at school *BrE*, **in school** *AmE*: *"Where's Katie?" "She's at school."*

in a school/in sb's school *In our school, the teachers are very strict.*

before/after school *My parents usually pick me up after school.*

science *n*

the study of the world, especially based on examining, testing, and proving facts, and knowledge based on this study

ADJECTIVES/NOUNS + science

medical science *Advances in medical science have saved millions of lives.*

computer science *She has a degree in computer science from the University of Leeds.*

natural science/the natural sciences (=the study of the physical world, especially biology, chemistry, or physics) *We studied the natural sciences, including the theory of evolution.*

physical science/the physical sciences (=the study of things that are not living, especially chemistry and physics) *Richter won the Nobel Prize for physics and was professor of physical sciences at Stanford University.*

life science/the life sciences (=the study of humans, plants, and animals) *They want to use biotechnology and life sciences to build better lives for people around the world.*

social science/the social sciences (=the scientific study of people in society) *More students are taking social science subjects such as psychology.*

the earth sciences (=the study of the Earth, especially geography or geology) *Earthquakes provided important evidence for research into the earth sciences.*

modern science *The increase in life expectancy is one of the great achievements of modern science.*

pure science (=the study of scientific theory, rather than using science for commercial purposes) *These days it is difficult to get funding for research into pure science.*

applied science (=scientific work that is used for practical purposes) *Rutledge is chair of the Department of Engineering and Applied Science at the California Institute of Technology.*

popular science (=which explains scientific ideas in a way that ordinary people can understand) *There are many popular science books which set out to explain new theories or discoveries.*

VERBS

study science *There has been an increase in the number of women choosing to study physical science and engineering.*

teach science *The report emphasizes the importance of teaching science at all levels of education.*

science + NOUNS

a science course/class/degree *The candidate must have a good computer science degree.*

a science teacher *There is a shortage of science teachers in schools.*

a science museum *The clock is now in the Science Museum in London.*

PHRASES

the laws of science *Some events cannot be explained using the current laws of science.*

blind sb with science (=confuse someone by talking about complicated technical things) *There is a technical difference, but I don't want to blind you with science.*

scientific *adj*

about or related to science, or using its methods

NOUNS

scientific research/study *Scientific research shows that women are more sensitive to smell than men.*

scientific evidence *Scientific evidence suggests that sea levels here will rise by at least 30 centimetres by 2030.*

scientific knowledge *Scientific knowledge is changing all the time and new discoveries are constantly being made.*

a scientific theory *Psychology tries to produce a scientific theory of the mind.*

a scientific experiment *Do you think it is right to use animals in scientific experiments?*

a scientific discovery/advance *Genetics has been the subject of some of the most important scientific discoveries of the past century.*

scientific progress/advances *Recent scientific advances have given doctors a better understanding of the illness.*

a scientific journal (=a magazine containing reports of scientific research) *His research was published in a scientific journal.*

the scientific community (=scientists considered as a group) *The professor's latest book has caused a lot of discussion within the scientific community.*

the scientific method (=the scientific approach) *Weber argued that the scientific method is useful for describing and categorizing society.*

PHRASES

sth is of scientific interest *The lake is of great scientific interest because it contains an ancient type of fish.*

scientist *n*

someone who works or is trained in science

ADJECTIVES/NOUNS + scientist

a great/brilliant scientist *Einstein was one of the greatest scientists in history.*

a leading/top scientist *Leading scientists agree that climate change is caused by greenhouse gas emissions from industry, especially carbon dioxide.*

an eminent/distinguished scientist (=greatly respected) *Several eminent scientists have been invited to speak at the conference.*

a research scientist *She is a research scientist at the University of California.*

a nuclear scientist *Nuclear scientists are working on ways to meet the increasing demand for electricity.*

a mad scientist (=one who has strange ideas)

The film is about a mad scientist who wants to destroy the world.

VERBS

a scientist studies/researches/investigates sth *Scientists have been studying how whales communicate with each other.*

a scientist works on sth *Scientists are working on a new treatment for cancer.*

a scientist discovers/finds/invents sth *The particle was named after the scientist who first discovered it.*

scientists believe (that)... *Scientists believe that the earth is 4.5 billion years old.*

scope Ac *n*

1 the range of things that a subject, activity, book etc deals with

ADJECTIVES

a broad/wide scope *The investigation will have a very broad scope.*

a limited/narrow scope *The scope of the research was quite limited.*

global/international scope (=in many countries) *We need to understand the global scope of this type of crime.*

the sheer scope of sth (=used when emphasizing that something deals with many different things) *The sheer scope of her work is incredible.*

VERBS

have a ... scope *This book has quite a narrow scope.*

widen/broaden the scope of sth *The police are widening the scope of their investigation.*

extend/expand the scope of sth *They may extend the scope of the study to examine more factors.*

narrow/limit/restrict the scope of sth *These measures are aimed at limiting the scope of criminals' activities.*

define the scope of sth *The group's first task was to define the scope of the inquiry.*

PREPOSITIONS

beyond/outside the scope of sth (=not included in it) *A full discussion of that issue is beyond the scope of this book.*

within the scope of sth (=included in it) *Banks fall within the scope of the new legislation.*

broad/narrow/limited etc in scope *Our study was quite narrow in scope.*

2 the opportunity to do something, or to change and develop

ADJECTIVES

great/considerable scope *There is considerable scope for further economic growth.*

limited/little/not much scope *My old job offered little scope for personal development.*

plenty of scope/ample scope *There's plenty of scope for improvement in the team.*

endless scope (=a lot of scope) *There was endless scope for arguments.*

VERBS

there is scope for sth *There is always scope for change.*

offer/allow scope *He wanted a job that offered more scope for creativity.*

give sb scope/provide sb with scope *A good oven gives you lots of scope for cooking different dishes.*

PREPOSITIONS

scope for sth *There was no scope for progression in the company.*

scorch *v* THESAURUS ▸ **burn[1] (2)**

score[1] *v*

to win a point in a sport, game, competition, or test

NOUNS

score a point *You score two points for every question you get right.*

score a goal *Ronaldo scored the winning goal in the final minutes of the game.*

score a touchdown (=score by taking the ball across the opposing team's goal line in American football) *The New York Giants scored a touchdown in the third quarter.*

score runs (=score points in cricket) *The team found it difficult to score runs against the Australians.*

score a hat trick (=one player scores three goals in one game) *Geoff Hurst scored a hat trick for England in the 1966 Word Cup final.*

score[2] *n*

the number of points that someone gets in a game, competition, or test

ADJECTIVES

a good/high/big score *She finished the game with an impressively high score.*

a poor/low score *I only got a very low score on the test.*

a total/overall score (=including all the points you have scored) *We add together your six best scores to give your overall score.*

an average score *The students' average score on the test was 65%.*

the final score (=at the end of a game) *The final score was 3–2 to Arsenal.*

VERBS

keep the score (=make a record of the score) *Jim kept the score when his friends played tennis.*

level the score *BrE*, **tie the score** *AmE* (=make both players or teams have the same number of points) *Terry put the ball in the net to level the score at 2–2.*

NOUNS + score

a test score *His test scores were very good.*

PREPOSITIONS

a score in a game *The final score in this game was 4–0 to United.*

a score in/on a test *What was your score on the spelling test?*

scorn *n*

the feeling that someone or something is stupid and does not deserve respect

VERBS

look at sb/sth with scorn *When she said she didn't know the answer, they looked at her with scorn.*

treat sb/sth with scorn *My boss treated my attempts to explain with scorn.*

meet sth with scorn (=treat something with scorn) *His theories were met with scorn from his fellow scientists.*

heap/pour scorn on sb/sth (=treat someone or something with a lot of scorn) *They heaped scorn on her suggestion, saying it was completely unrealistic.*

be filled with scorn *"Is that all?" Her voice was filled with scorn.*

PHRASES

an object of scorn (=someone or something people feel scorn for) *As a result of the scandal he became an object of scorn in the national newspapers.*

scowl[1] *v*

to look at someone in an angry way

ADVERBS

scowl angrily *"You're late," she said, scowling angrily.*

scowl fiercely (=in an angry and frightening way) *The tennis player scowled fiercely at his opponent.*

scowl darkly (=in an angry or threatening way) *She scowled darkly at him in disapproval.*

scowl back *I waved to Dan, but he just scowled back.*

PREPOSITIONS

scowl at sb/sth *He scowled at me when I interrupted.*

scowl[2] *n*

an angry or disapproving expression on someone's face

ADJECTIVES

an angry scowl *He looked at her with an angry scowl.*

a dark/black/furious scowl (=expressing a lot of anger) *He sat alone, his face set in a dark scowl.*

a permanent scowl *He is a bad-tempered man with a permanent scowl on his face.*

VERBS

give (sb) a scowl *The teacher gave me a scowl when I arrived late for class.*

sb's scowl deepens (=they frown more angrily) *His scowl deepened when he realized everybody was laughing at him.*

PREPOSITIONS

with a scowl *"It's your fault," she said with a scowl.*

PHRASES

have a scowl on your face *He had a furious scowl on his face when he came back.*

scramble *v* THESAURUS ▸ climb

scrap *n* THESAURUS ▸ piece

scratch *n*

a small cut on someone's skin or on an object

ADJECTIVES

a tiny/little scratch *There are tiny scratches on the surface of the glass.*

a slight/minor scratch *She has a slight scratch on her neck.*

a big scratch *There was a big scratch down the side of his car.*

a deep scratch *The path was marked out by deep scratches in the rock.*

a shallow scratch *Make a shallow scratch along the tile and then break it in two.*

a long scratch *A long scratch ran from his eyebrow to his ear.*

VERBS

leave a scratch *Some cleaning products can leave scratches on glass.*

be covered in scratches *When she had finished the gardening her hands were covered in scratches.*

scratch + NOUNS

scratch marks *The prisoners made scratch marks on the wall to count the days.*

PREPOSITIONS

a scratch on sth *The cat has a little scratch on the end of her nose.*

a scratch in sth *There was a large dent in the car door and a scratch in the paint.*

without a scratch (=used to say that someone is not injured at all) *Amazingly, the driver walked away from the crash without a scratch.*

PHRASES

it's just/only a scratch *It's just a scratch – nothing serious.*

cuts and scratches (=injuries that are not serious) *She was fine apart from a few cuts and scratches.*

scrawl *v* THESAURUS ▸ write (1)

S

scream[1] *v*

to make a loud high noise with your voice because you are hurt, frightened, excited etc

ADVERBS

scream loudly *I saw someone on the stairs and screamed as loudly as I could.*

scream wildly (=in a loud uncontrolled way) *George, screaming wildly, was carried upstairs by his father.*

scream hysterically (=in a completely uncontrolled way) *Some of the girls started screaming hysterically.*

VERBS

start screaming/start to scream *There was a loud bang, and people started screaming.*

stop screaming *"Stop screaming!" she shouted furiously.*

hear sb scream *No-one could hear her scream.*

want to scream/feel like screaming *I was so frustrated I wanted to scream.*

PREPOSITIONS

scream at sb *Sam screamed at me to stay back.*

PHRASES

scream in pain/terror/fear *We could hear her screaming in pain.*

scream with laughter/delight/excitement etc *They screamed with laughter at his jokes.*

scream for help/mercy/attention *He opened his mouth to scream for help, but no sound came out.*

scream your head off *informal* (=a lot) *They took him away screaming his head off.*

scream blue murder *informal* (=very loudly because of fear or anger) *She flew into a rage and screamed blue murder at him.*

run screaming somewhere *A mother ran screaming into the building trying to find her children.*

drag sb kicking and screaming *He was dragged kicking and screaming into a police van.*

scream abuse (=shout unpleasant things) *You don't expect strangers to scream abuse at you.*

scream obscenities (=shout rude things) *The crowd were screaming obscenities at the referee.*

scream and shout *Small children often scream and shout if they don't get what they want.*

scream[2] *n*

a loud high sound that you make with your voice because you are hurt, frightened, excited etc

ADJECTIVES

a loud scream *Suddenly I heard a loud scream.*

a high-pitched scream (=with a high sound) *The baby's high-pitched scream told me something was wrong.*

a piercing/shrill scream (=with a high unpleasant sound) *The sound of gunfire was mixed with the piercing screams of the injured.*

a bloodcurdling scream (=very frightening) *With bloodcurdling screams, the enemy soldiers began running towards us.*

a terrified scream (=by someone who is terrified) *The boy let out a terrified scream and ran away.*

a terrible scream (=by someone suffering great pain or fear) *We were woken by the most terrible screams.*

a little scream (=a short quiet one) *She gave a little scream when she saw the mouse.*

a muffled/stifled scream (=quiet, for example because someone's hand is over your mouth) *There were muffled screams coming from the trunk of the car.*

VERBS

let out/give a scream (=scream) *She saw the knife and let out a scream.*

hear a scream *A man heard my screams and ran to help.*

a scream comes from somewhere *There were screams coming from the back of the house.*

PREPOSITIONS

with a scream *She jumped off the high diving board with a scream.*

PHRASES

a scream of laughter/pain/terror etc *We could hear the children's screams of laughter.*

screen *n*

the part of a television or computer where the picture or information appears

ADJECTIVES/NOUNS + screen

a television screen *The actor is a familiar sight on our television screens.*

a computer screen *He was staring at his computer screen.*

a cinema/movie screen *The film was shown on a 20-foot high cinema screen.*

a big/small/giant screen *We watched the football game on a giant screen outside the stadium.*

a flat screen *A TV with a flat screen can be hung on a wall like a picture.*

a blank screen *She turned off the computer and stared at the blank screen.*

a touch screen (=one that you touch to move or choose information) *The phone has a touch screen.*

full screen (=the whole of a screen) *You can make photos full screen size if you like.*

VERBS

appear/come up on a screen *A warning message came up on my screen.*

be displayed/shown on a screen *The icons displayed on the screen can be used to open programs.*

disappear from the screen *All of a sudden, the picture disappeared from the screen.*

flash across the screen *Coloured images flashed across the screen.*

fill the screen *How can I make my document fill the whole screen?*

stare at/watch the screen *He went on staring at the TV screen.*

be glued to the screen (=watch it very closely with great interest) *Mrs Quigley was sitting on the sofa, her eyes glued to the screen.*

work on screen (=work using a computer) *If you work on screen, you need to make sure that you take enough breaks.*

a screen flickers (=the images or words on the screen make sudden small movements) *I think there's something wrong with my computer - the screen keeps flickering.*

the screen goes blank (=everything disappears and there is nothing on it) *Suddenly, the screen went blank.*

screen + NOUNS

screen resolution (=a measure of how clear the picture on a screen is) *Try viewing the file using a higher screen resolution.*

a screen saver (=a moving image that appears on a computer screen when it is not being used) *She has a picture of her dog on her screen saver.*

PREPOSITIONS

on (the) screen *Check the text on screen before you print it.*

> **The big/small screen**
> **The small screen** is used to refer to television and **the big screen** to cinema: *We have seen him many times on* ***the big screen****.*

scribble *v* THESAURUS write (1)

scrub *v* THESAURUS clean²

scrutiny *n*

careful and thorough examination of someone or something

ADJECTIVES

careful scrutiny *The figures need careful scrutiny.*

close/intense/rigorous scrutiny (=very careful scrutiny) *These areas of law have come under close scrutiny by the courts.*

detailed scrutiny *The wreckage of the plane will now be subjected to detailed scrutiny.*

constant scrutiny (=all the time) *He is under constant scrutiny in his job.*

critical scrutiny *Marxist theory has been subjected to intense critical scrutiny.*

public scrutiny (=by ordinary people) *Much of the work that we do is open to public scrutiny.*

VERBS

come under/face scrutiny (=be examined) *Their activities have come under police scrutiny.*

stand up to/bear scrutiny (=be found to have no faults when examined) *Such arguments do not stand up to scrutiny.*

deserve/warrant scrutiny (=need to be examined) *Their claims deserve closer scrutiny.*

require scrutiny (=need to be examined, or say that something must be examined) *The regulations require close scrutiny of imported waste.*

avoid/escape scrutiny *Some organizations manage to avoid scrutiny almost entirely.*

PREPOSITIONS

under scrutiny (=being examined) *His behaviour is constantly under scrutiny.*

scrutiny by sb *New drugs require years of scrutiny by medical experts.*

PHRASES

be the subject of scrutiny (*also* **be subjected to scrutiny**) (=be examined) *The way in which banks award bonuses has been the subject of scrutiny recently.*

be subject to scrutiny (=be able to be examined) *All the accounts are subject to scrutiny by auditors.*

open to scrutiny (=be able to be examined easily) *Government actions should be more open to public scrutiny.*

sculpture *n*

an object made out of stone, wood, clay etc by an artist

ADJECTIVES/NOUNS + sculpture

a stone/marble/bronze etc sculpture *The picture shows a bronze sculpture of the Greek goddess Athena.*

a life-size sculpture (=the same size as the real thing) *In the courtyard was a life-size sculpture of a horse.*

an abstract sculpture (=not like a real person or thing) *Henry Moore is famous for his abstract sculptures, which often consist of large pieces of stone with a hole in the middle.*

a modern/contemporary sculpture *We went to see an exhibition of modern sculpture.*

a classical sculpture (=from ancient Greece or Rome) *Michelangelo's statue of David is a famous classical sculpture.*

VERBS

make/create/produce a sculpture *The artist will be making a new sculpture for the exhibition.*

exhibit/display a sculpture (=show it) *The sculpture is exhibited in the main entrance hall of the museum.*

PREPOSITIONS

a sculpture of sth *I made a sculpture of an elephant.*

a sculpture by sb *There is a sculpture by Picasso.*

PHRASES

a piece of sculpture *This is a magnificent piece of sculpture.*

sea *n*

the large area of salty water that covers much of the Earth's surface

ADJECTIVES

blue sea *The coast is beautiful, with golden sand and blue sea.*

calm sea *The sea was perfectly calm.*

rough sea (=with big waves) *The sea was too rough to swim in.*

choppy sea (=with a lot of small waves) *There was a strong wind and the sea was choppy.*

heavy seas (=a rough sea) *Heavy seas made the rescue effort more difficult.*

a stormy sea *A picture of a ship in a stormy sea hung on the wall.*

the open sea (=the part of the sea that is far away from land) *They are trying to get the whales back out into the open sea.*

the deep sea (=the water deep under the surface of the sea) *The deep sea is the most unexplored area left on the planet.*

VERBS

cross the sea *They left England and crossed the sea to France.*

go to sea (=go to work on a ship) *He went to sea when he was 18.*

put to sea (=sail a boat away from land) *The fishermen put to sea early in the morning.*

be lost at sea *formal* (=be drowned in the sea) *His father had been lost at sea three months before.*

be swept out to sea (=be taken far away from land by the sea) *If you fall off the rocks you could be swept out to sea.*

look out to sea (=look at the sea far away from the land) *He stood at the window looking out to sea.*

the sea laps/washes somewhere (=it touches or moves there gently) *She felt the sea lap around her ankles.*

the sea batters/pounds sth (=it hits something with a lot of force) *The rough sea battered the coastline.*

sea + NOUNS

sea creatures (=animals that live in the sea) *The area is home to dolphins, whales, and other sea creatures.*

sea water *Removing salt from sea water is an expensive process.*

a sea view *All the bedrooms have a sea view.*

sea level *Sea levels are rising.*

the sea air (=the air close to the sea) *He breathed in the fresh sea air.*

a sea breeze (=a light wind that blows from the sea onto the land) *It feels cooler on the beach because of the sea breeze.*

the sea bed/floor/bottom (=the land at the bottom of the sea) *The starfish live on the sea bed.*

PREPOSITIONS

in the sea *It's too cold to swim in the sea.*

on the sea *I love sailing, especially on the sea.*

across the sea *The land across the sea is Greece.*

by the sea (=next to the sea) *We stayed in a little house by the sea.*

by sea (=using boats that travel on the sea) *They deliver the goods by sea.*

at sea (=on a journey in a boat on the sea) *Charles was in the Navy and spent much of his time at sea.*

seal *v* THESAURUS **close[1] (1)**

search[1] *n*

1 an attempt to find someone or something

ADJECTIVES/NOUNS + search

a thorough/careful search *We conducted a thorough search of the building.*

a painstaking search (=very careful) *Experts are carrying out a painstaking search of the wreckage to see what caused the crash.*

a systematic search (=done in an organized way) *They set about a systematic search of the ship.*

a desperate/frantic search *After the war, many people returned to rural areas in a desperate search for food.*

a fruitless search (=unsuccessful) *I spent many hours in a fruitless search for accommodation.*

a nationwide search (=in every part of a country) *Kim was missing for two months, prompting a nationwide search.*

a police search *Her disappearance sparked a massive police search.*

a house-to-house search (=of every house or building in an area) *Police officers are conducting house-to-house searches in the area where the girl disappeared.*

VERBS

carry out/do a search (*also* **conduct a search** *formal*): *Police have carried out a search of his home.*

launch/mount a search (=start one) *A massive search was launched for the former soldier.*

call off/abandon a search (=stop it) *They called off the search when it got dark.*

resume a search (=start it again) *We will resume the search in the morning.*

spark/prompt a search (=make it happen) *The discovery sparked a search by more than 50 police officers.*

widen a search (=look in a bigger area or

amongst a bigger group) *Police have widened their search because they believe the man may have moved out of the area.*

search + NOUNS

a search party (=a group of people who search for someone who is missing or lost) *A search party was out looking for him.*

a search warrant (=a document that allows police to search a building) *They can't enter the house without a search warrant.*

the search area *The search area has now been widened.*

PREPOSITIONS

the search for sth *The search for survivors continues.*

a search of sth *Two more bodies were found after a search of the woods.*

PHRASES

the search is on (=people are trying to find someone or something) *The search is on for someone with the same blood type.*

a search is under way/underway (=it has started) *A search is underway for two walkers in the Cairngorm mountains.*

2 an occasion when you look for something on the internet

ADJECTIVES/NOUNS + search

an internet/online search *She did an online search for good hotels in the area.*

VERBS

do a search (on the internet) *I did a search on the internet and found an article about the history of the town.*

search + NOUNS

a search engine (=a computer program that helps you find information on the internet) *I tried looking for the information again, using a different search engine.*

search results (=the information you get from an internet search) *The search results are displayed at the top of the screen.*

a search string (=a series of words that you search for) *I tried again, using a different search string.*

search[2] *v*

to look carefully for someone or something

ADVERBS

search carefully/thoroughly *Police searched the building carefully, but didn't find a weapon.*

search frantically/desperately (=in a hurried way, because you feel very worried) *Parents frantically searched for their children.*

search everywhere *They searched everywhere but there was no sign of Henry.*

search around (=in many places) *They searched around until they found the keys.*

search far and wide (=over a large area) *We had to search far and wide to find a shop that stocked this product.*

search sth from top to bottom (=search all the rooms in a building) *They searched the house from top to bottom.*

search high and low (=search in every place you can think of – used especially when you have been unsuccessful) *I've searched high and low for my glasses.*

PREPOSITIONS

search for sb/sth *Detectives continue to search for clues.*

search through sth *She searched through all his clothes.*

search under/in etc sth *Katie searched under the bed for her shoes.*

PHRASES

search in vain (=without success) *He searched in vain for a means of escape.*

season *n*

1 a period of time in a year during which a particular activity takes place, or during which something usually happens

ADJECTIVES

a good/successful season *The baseball team has had another successful season.*

a poor/disappointing season *It's been a disappointing season for Arsenal.*

(the) high/peak season (=when most people visit a place, and prices are highest) *Hotel rooms cost from $200 a night in high season.*

(the) low season (=when fewest people visit a place, and prices are lowest) *Many retired people go on holiday in low season.*

the busy season *We are just entering our busy season, preparing for our end-of-year results.*

the festive season *BrE* (=the Christmas period) *More people are choosing to go abroad for the festive season.*

NOUNS + season

the football/cricket/racing etc season *The racing season starts in June.*

the hunting/shooting/fishing season *Some footpaths are closed during the shooting season.*

the breeding/mating season (=when animals produce young animals) *In the mating season finding a partner is the bird's main aim.*

the growing/planting season (=for growing or planting crops) *The planting season is in late spring.*

the holiday season *BrE*, **the vacation season** *AmE* (=when most people go on holiday) *The roads are always busy during the holiday season.*

the tourist season (=when a lot of tourists visit an area) *It's almost impossible to get a hotel room in the tourist season.*

PREPOSITIONS

the season for sth (=when something is

usually available or usually happens) *The season for strawberries usually starts in early June.*

in season (=available because it is the right time - used of fruit, vegetables etc) *I love this time of year, when peas are in season.*

PHRASES

the beginning/end of the season *She'll be glad when it's the end of the football season.*

the height of the season (=in the middle, when it is busiest) *In the height of the season, the island is full of visitors.*

2 one of the parts which the year is usually divided into, based on the weather

ADJECTIVES

sb's favourite season *BrE*, **sb's favorite season** *AmE*: *My favourite season is autumn - I love the colours of the trees.*

the best season *Many people think that spring is the best season, when all the flowers are starting to come out.*

the rainy/wet/dry season (=when the weather is rainy or dry) *In the rainy season, roads became impossible to drive on.*

NOUNS + season

the summer/winter season *The resort will remain open to visitors throughout the winter season.*

the monsoon season (=when it rains a lot in South Asia) *The monsoon season is now over.*

the hurricane season (=when some parts of the world get very strong fast winds) *He wanted to sail south before the hurricane season.*

PREPOSITIONS

during a season *The river turns to hard mud during this season.*

throughout the seasons *Supermarkets are able to provide fresh food throughout the seasons.*

with the seasons (=according to the seasons) *Prices vary with the seasons of the year.*

seat *n*

1 a place where you can sit

ADJECTIVES/NOUNS + seat

an empty/free seat (*also* **a vacant seat** *formal*): *Excuse me, is this seat free?*

the front seat (=of a car) *Children under four should not travel in the front seat.*

the back/rear seat (=of a car) *My bag was on the back seat of the car.*

the driver's seat *He climbed into the driver's seat.*

the passenger seat (=the seat next to the driver) *The man in the passenger seat was unhurt.*

a window seat (=next to the window in a plane or restaurant) *I'd prefer a window seat, please.*

a good seat (=one from which you can see well) *The good seats are very expensive.*

a comfortable seat *The seats in the cinema weren't very comfortable and I couldn't sit still.*

a front-row seat (=one at the front of a theatre, sports ground etc) *We had front-row seats.*

a ringside seat (=one in the front row at a sports event, especially a boxing match) *We managed to get ringside seats, so we had a great view of the fight.*

VERBS

sit on/in a seat (*also* **occupy a seat** *formal*): *Someone's sitting in my seat.*

have/take a seat (=sit down) *Take a seat, please.*

book/reserve a seat *You can book seats online.*

show sb to their seat *A flight attendant showed them to their seats.*

go back to/return to your seat (*also* **resume your seat** *formal*): *The audience clapped as he returned to his seat.*

save sb a seat *I'll save you a seat next to me.*

give up your seat (=let someone sit on it) *I gave up my seat for an old lady.*

raise/lower a seat *How do you raise the seat on a bicycle?*

a seat goes back (*also* **a seat reclines** *formal*) (=you can make it move back down so that you can sleep) *Do you know that these seats recline?*

PREPOSITIONS

in a seat *Paul was in the driver's seat.*

on a seat *I sat down on the nearest empty seat.*

2 a position in a parliament, congress, or another official group

ADJECTIVES/NOUNS + seat

a parliamentary seat (=in Parliament) *She was the first woman to win a parliamentary seat.*

a congressional seat (=in Congress) *He plans to retire from his congressional seat.*

a Senate seat *Who holds the Senate seat for Illinois?*

a Labour/Republican etc seat (=one that a particular party usually wins) *Newbury was traditionally a Conservative seat.*

a safe seat *BrE* (=one that a party is unlikely to lose) *Maidstone is considered a safe seat for the Conservatives.*

a marginal seat *BrE* (=one that a party might easily lose) *Devlin admits he could lose his marginal seat.*

VERBS

have/hold a seat *The Labour Party now has 292 seats in Parliament.*

win a seat *He won the seat by 70 votes.*

get/gain a seat *At the next election the Republicans gained 12 seats in the Senate.*

take a seat from sb *Labour took over 50 seats from the Conservatives.*

lose a seat *She lost her seat at the last election.*

keep/hold onto a seat (*also* **retain a seat** *formal*) (=not lose it in an election) *He is unlikely to retain his seat after next year's election.*

run for/contest a seat (=try to win it in an election) *Twenty-four candidates contested the five seats.*

defend a seat (=try not to lose it in an election) *Mr Cummings is defending his seat for Labour.*

PREPOSITIONS

a seat in sth *He has a seat in the National Assembly.*

a seat on sth *Promotion would mean a seat on the board of directors.*

second *n*

1 a unit for measuring time. There are 60 seconds in a minute

ADJECTIVES

the final/last seconds *France scored in the final seconds of the game.*

VERBS

take five/ten etc seconds *It only takes ten seconds to activate the system.*

last (for) five/ten etc seconds *The injection is painful, but it only lasts a few seconds.*

count the seconds *I was counting the seconds until I could go home.*

seconds go by/pass *Another 30 seconds went by in silence.*

seconds tick away/by (=time passes, especially when someone is trying to do something) *Henry sat in his chair as the seconds ticked away.*

PREPOSITIONS

for five/ten etc seconds *Hold the button down for two or three seconds.*

PHRASES

half a second *The flash only lasted for half a second.*

metres/steps/miles etc per second *Ultrasonic waves travel at around 300 metres per second.*

every five/ten etc seconds *A plane arrives at or departs from the airport every 30 seconds.*

with each/every passing second *She grew more annoyed with each passing second.*

2 a very short time

ADJECTIVES

a split second (=an extremely short time) *He only had a split second to decide what to do.*

VERBS

wait a second/hang on a second *Wait a second! I'll be with you very soon.*

take a second *It won't take a second to put a new battery in.*

have a second *I need to talk about something – do you have a second?*

PREPOSITIONS

in a second *I'll be with you in a second.*

in/within seconds *In seconds his boots were full of water.*

for a second *For a second I thought I'd forgotten my passport.*

seconds before/after sth *The pictures were taken seconds before the plane crashed.*

PHRASES

a fraction of a second *He hesitated for a fraction of a second.*

in a matter of seconds (=in a very short time) *It was all over in a matter of seconds.*

seconds later (=a short time later) *Seconds later she was gone.*

secondary *adj* THESAURUS ▸ **unimportant**

secret[1] *adj*

if something is secret, you do not tell other people about it

NOUNS

a secret place/location *She keeps her money in a secret hiding place.*

a secret drawer/compartment/passage *The drugs were hidden in a secret compartment in the bottom of the suitcase.*

a secret meeting/rendezvous *US officials had secret meetings with the terrorists.*

secret talks/negotiations *The two companies are holding secret talks to discuss a merger.*

secret information/documents/files *He passed on secret information to the enemy.*

secret thoughts/fears *I had told her about my most secret thoughts.*

the secret police/the secret service/a secret agent *The spies were working for the secret police.*

a secret organization/society *He belongs to a secret government organization.*

a secret mission *The agents were on a secret mission behind enemy lines.*

a secret plan/recipe *She has her own secret recipe for making Christmas pudding.*

a secret life *My father had a secret life, which the rest of the family knew nothing about.*

a secret world *The programme is about the secret world of the giant panda.*

a secret weapon (=something you think will help you be successful) *The team have a new secret weapon – a talented young player who they hope will score lots of goals.*

VERBS

keep sth secret *They kept their relationship secret from their parents.*

remain secret *The details of the proposal must remain secret.*

ADVERBS

top secret (=containing very important secret information, especially about the government) *The files were marked 'top secret'.*

highly secret *A highly secret meeting was held at the company headquarters.*

THESAURUS: secret

confidential
information | **details** | **report** | **document** | **file** | **letter** | **material** | **advice** | **nature**
if something is confidential, it must not be shown or mentioned to anyone else, because it contains personal details or information that an organization needs to keep secret:
Information about patients' records is ***strictly confidential****.* | *The report is* ***highly confidential*** *and only a few people have seen it.* | *You can ring our helpline for free confidential advice.*

private
life | **affairs** | **thoughts** | **letter** | **call**
if something is private, it concerns your personal life and you do not want other people to know about it:
Details of his private life appeared in a national newspaper. | *Please do not discuss my private affairs in public.* | *I can't tell you what he said –* ***it's private****.*

clandestine
meeting | **affair** | **relationship** | **organization** | **movement** | **network** | **operation** | **mission** | **talks** | **war** | **shipment**
clandestine meetings and organizations are secret, because you do not want other people to know what you are doing. **Clandestine** is more formal than **secret** and is used about secret love affairs and secret political activities:
The couple had clandestine meetings in the park. | *He belongs to a clandestine organization whose aim is to overthrow the government.* | *The CIA was involved in a clandestine operation to kill Fidel Castro.*

classified
information | **document** | **report** | **material**
if information is classified, the government has ordered that it must be kept secret:
He was accused of passing on classified information to the Russians in the 1950s. | *The file contains* ***highly classified*** *material about nuclear weapons technology.*

sensitive
information | **documents** | **material**
sensitive information must be kept secret because there would be problems if people outside a government or company knew about it:
The document contains ***commercially sensitive*** *information.* | *Some of the material in these files is* ***highly sensitive*** *and could cause huge embarrassment for the US government.*

covert
operation | **activities** | **involvement** | **surveillance** | **filming**
covert activities are done secretly on behalf of the government, the army, or another official organization:
The planes are used by British Intelligence for covert operations. | *The security police carried out covert surveillance of the activities of opposition politicians.*

You also use **covert** when people are secretly treated unfairly: *There is* ***covert discrimination*** *against women.*

undercover
agent | **operation** | **officer** | **police** | **detective** | **reporter** | **journalist** | **investigator**
working secretly to find out information, especially about criminal activities:
The man tried to buy explosives from an undercover agent. | *Detectives arrested the suspect after a five-day undercover operation.*

underground
newspaper | **press** | **organization** | **movement** | **network**
an underground newspaper or organization works secretly to oppose the government:
He started his own underground newspaper at college. | *Her father was a member of the underground resistance movement in the war.* | *The magazine* ***went underground*** *after police raided its offices* (=it started operating secretly).

hush-hush *informal*
project
if something is hush-hush, it has been officially decided that it must be kept secret:
The strange things in the sky were part of some kind of hush-hush military project. | *I've no idea what he does –* ***it's all very hush-hush****.*

Saying that something is very secret
You say that something is **top secret** or **highly secret** | **highly confidential** or **strictly confidential** | **highly sensitive** or **extremely sensitive**.

secret² *n*

1 something that is kept hidden from people

ADJECTIVES/NOUNS + secret

a big secret (=an important secret or one that very few people know) *No one knows what they're planning – it's all a big secret.*

a little secret (=a personal secret that very

few people know) *You must promise me that this will be our little secret.*

a closely guarded/well-kept secret (=that few people are allowed to know) *The recipe is a closely guarded secret.*

an open secret (=that a lot of people know, but do not talk about because it is supposed to be a secret) *It was an open secret that he was having an affair.*

a dark/terrible secret (=about something bad) *I'm sure every family has a few dark secrets.*

a dirty secret (=about something immoral) *The exclusion of black people from the film industry is one of Hollywood's dirty little secrets.*

a guilty secret (=that someone feels guilty about) *He had finally discovered Jo's guilty secret.*

sb's innermost secrets (=very private or personal secrets) *They shared their innermost secrets with each other.*

a family secret *Their affair was a closely guarded family secret.*

a state/official secret (=a government secret) *He was accused of passing on state secrets to a foreign government.*

a trade secret (=a company or business secret) *An employee must not betray his or her employer's trust, for instance by giving away trade secrets.*

military secrets *Norman was sent to prison for five years in 1933 for selling military secrets to Germany.*

VERBS

remain a secret *Until now, his past had remained a secret.*

have a secret *We have no secrets from each other.*

know a secret (=about someone else) *You can tell Tom that I know his secret.*

keep a secret (=not tell it to anyone) *Can you keep a secret?*

tell sb a secret *Shall I tell you a secret?*

⚠ Don't say 'say a secret'.

let sb in on a secret (=tell them a secret, especially one that several other people know about) *Frank let me in on the secret.*

reveal a secret (*also* **divulge a secret** *formal*): *He was accused of revealing state secrets.*

give away a secret (=tell it to someone carelessly or by mistake) *I had to be careful not to give away any secrets.*

share a secret (=tell it to someone because you trust them) *I trusted Alex, so I decided to share my secret with him.*

discover/find out a secret *He was afraid that someone would discover his secret.*

a secret comes out/gets out (=people start to know about it) *We mustn't let this secret get out.*

PHRASES

it's a secret *I can't tell you – it's a secret.*

it is no secret that... (=everyone knows that...) *It's no secret that she is looking for a new job.*

make no secret of sth/not make a secret of sth (=not try to hide something) *He made no secret of his hatred for his boss.*

your secret is safe with me (=I won't tell anyone about it) *Don't worry – your secret is safe with me.*

PREPOSITIONS

in secret (=without anyone knowing) *Their meetings were held in secret.*

a secret about sth *He knew a secret about her that he could not share.*

a secret from sb *I have no secrets from anyone.*

2 the way to achieve something good

> **Grammar**
> In this meaning, you usually say **the secret** or **his/her/my etc secret**.

VERBS

discover/find the secret *He thinks he has discovered the secret of true happiness.*

know the secret *They all wanted to know the secret of Ellen's coffee.*

reveal the secret/let sb know the secret *The coach revealed the secret behind the team's success.*

tell sb your secret *In the book, he tells us his secret to the perfect loaf of bread.*

hold the secret *Science may hold the secret to a better golf swing.*

PREPOSITIONS

the secret to (doing) sth *The secret to making good pastry is to use very cold water.*

the secret of sth *What is the secret of a long and happy life?*

the secret behind sth *He says the secret behind his 20-year football career is never being satisfied with what he has won.*

PHRASES

the secret is to do sth *The secret is to use lots of butter.*

what the secret is *I wish I knew what the secret was to a good relationship.*

the secret of sb's success *The secret of his success is a lot of hard work.*

section *n*

1 one of the parts that a piece of writing is divided into

ADJECTIVES

the next/following section *The results of the survey are given in the next section.*

the previous/last section *This subject was dealt with in the previous section.*

the preceding sections (=the ones before the one you are talking about) *The proposals were set out in the preceding sections.*

the first/opening/introductory section *In the opening section of the book, we are introduced to the two main characters.*

the final/concluding/last section *The final section of the chapter discusses possible future developments.*

a short/long section *There is a short section about business strategy.*

a separate section *The book has a separate section on growing fruit.*

the main section *The main section of the report has over 400 pages.*

VERBS

be divided into sections *The book is divided into four sections.*

add a section *She read my essay and suggested I add a section about my research methods.*

NOUNS + section

the sports/business/travel section (=part of a newspaper) *There's an article about Fiji in the travel section.*

PHRASES

a section of a book/report/essay/form etc *This is the most interesting section of the book.*

2 a part of something

ADJECTIVES

the main section *In 1959, the main section of the road was opened.*

the opening/closing section (=the first or last section of a film, play, speech etc) *The city appears in the opening section of the film.*

the top/front/rear/side section *There is a big hole in the front section of the plane.*

VERBS

be divided into sections *The building is divided into three sections.*

NOUNS + section

the brass/string/rhythm section (=part of an orchestra or band) *The brass section consists of trumpets, French horns, and trombones.*

the toy/menswear/sports section (=part of a shop) *Dolls are in the toy section.*

PHRASES

a section of road/track *A long section of the road is closed.*

a section of society/the population/the community *People from all sections of society suffer from depression.*

a section of an audience/crowd *There was booing from one section of the audience.*

sector Ac *n*

a part of a country's business activity

ADJECTIVES/NOUNS + sector

an economic sector *The money will be needed for other economic sectors such as transport.*

an important/key sector *The oil industry has become an important sector of the economy.*

a growing sector *Internet shopping is a growing sector of the economy.*

a growth sector (=one that is growing) *Clothing appeared to be the biggest growth sector.*

the public sector (=which is controlled by the government) *The government has been holding down pay in the public sector.*

the private sector (=which is not controlled by the government) *Generally speaking, employees in the private sector are well rewarded.*

the manufacturing/industrial sector (=producing goods in factories) *As the industrial sector grew, more and more people moved to the cities.*

the financial/banking sector *The banking sector is in trouble.*

the retail sector (=shops) *The retail sector is doing well.*

the service sector (=providing services, such as banking or tourism) *The proportion of service sector jobs within the economy has grown.*

the agricultural sector (=farming) *Drought has caused many problems in the agricultural sector.*

the voluntary sector (=charities and unpaid workers) *The voluntary sector has an important role in tackling homelessness.*

PREPOSITIONS

a sector of sth *Agriculture remains the largest sector of the economy here.*

security Ac *n*

1 things done to keep people, places, or things safe

ADJECTIVES/NOUNS + security

tight/strict/heavy security (=there are a lot of people protecting someone or something) *The president arrived surrounded by tight security.*

lax security (=there is not enough security) *Passengers complained of lax security at airline check-in desks.*

heightened security (=more than usual, especially because people are expecting an attack) *There is heightened security in the capital following bomb threats.*

national/state security (=the security of a country) *The men were arrested because they were believed to be a threat to national security.*

personal security (=of an individual person) *It's not just a question of your own personal security, but also that of your family.*

internet security *We advise companies on internet security.*

high-security/low-security *The prisoners are being held in a high-security prison.*

maximum-security/top-security *He was sent to a maximum-security jail.*

VERBS

improve/tighten security (=make it better) *Mexico has tightened security along its southern border.*

provide security *Security was provided by a private firm.*

ensure/guarantee security (=keep something safe) *Nuclear weapons do not guarantee national security.*

threaten/compromise security (=make something less safe) *They were found guilty of threatening the security of the state.*

security + NOUNS

a security guard *There are armed security guards outside the palace.*

the security services/forces (=the police, army etc) *The security forces opened fire, killing two people.*

a security check *There are security checks at the entrance to the courtrooms.*

security measures/arrangements (=things that are done to protect someone or something) *A large number of homes lack adequate security measures.*

a security system (=a system of cameras, alarms etc to provide security) *We've installed a new electronic security system.*

a security camera *The thief was caught on a security camera.*

a security risk/threat *His presence in the area posed a significant security risk.*

the security situation (=how safe a place is) *Until the security situation improves, it is too dangerous to travel there.*

security clearance (=permission to do something after being checked and found to be safe) *You need security clearance before you can be hired for a government job.*

a security firm *Computer security firms have issued a warning about the virus.*

PREPOSITIONS

under tight/strict/heavy security *The trial was held under tight security.*

for security *We all carry ID passes for security.*

PHRASES

be security conscious (=be always careful about security) *Most airports are extremely security conscious.*

for security reasons *You can't take your bag into the building for security reasons.*

a breach of security (=when something happens that security should not have allowed) *There was a serious breach of security at the prison last Friday.*

a threat to security (=something that stops something being safe) *He was considered a threat to national security, and ordered to leave the country.*

2 protection from bad things that could happen to you

ADJECTIVES

financial/economic security *The insurance plan offers your family financial security in the event of your death.*

emotional/psychological security *She was given no emotional security when she was a baby.*

NOUNS + security

job security (=not being in danger of losing your job) *Workers want greater job security.*

food security (=there is enough food to feed everyone) *There are fears about global food security as the world's population continues to expand.*

VERBS

provide sb with security/give sb security *By working, she provides her family with financial security.*

PHRASES

a feeling of security *Living close to her family gives her a feeling of security.*

a sense of security (=a feeling of security) *Children need to have a sense of security.*

lull sb into a false sense of security (=make someone feel safe when in fact they are not) *He lulled his victims into a false sense of security and then stole all their money.*

see *v*

to notice something with your eyes, usually without planning to

VERBS

can/can't see sth *I could see a small mark on the wall.*

ADVERBS

can clearly see sth *The bullet holes can still clearly be seen.*

can just see sth *You can just see the islands on the horizon.*

can hardly see sth *I can hardly see anything without my glasses.*

PHRASES

as you can see *As you can see, the house needs some work doing on it.*

as soon as sb saw sth/the moment sb saw sth *The moment we saw the house, we knew we wanted to buy it.*

seed *n*

a very small thing that plants produce, which a new plant grows from

NOUNS + seed

flower/sunflower/tomato etc seeds *I bought a packet of poppy seeds.*

VERBS

plant/sow seeds (=put them in the soil) *Sow the seeds in trays or pots.*

grow sth from seed (=rather than buying it as a small plant) *You can grow most vegetables from seed.*

produce seeds *Under these conditions, the plant will grow well and be able to produce seeds.*

seeds germinate (=start to grow) *The seeds should start to germinate after a few days.*

seed + NOUNS

a seed pod (=long narrow part of some plants that contains seeds) *Seed must be gathered from freshly ripened seed pods.*

PHRASES

a packet of seeds *He picked up the packet of seeds and read the planting instructions.*

seek Ac *v*

to try to achieve or get something

NOUNS

seek help/assistance *He sought help from the police.*

seek advice/information/guidance *If in any doubt, seek the advice of a lawyer.*

seek work/employment *People come to the city seeking work.*

seek permission *They are seeking permission to build 200 new houses.*

seek refuge/sanctuary/asylum (=try to find somewhere safe) *We sought refuge inside the castle.*

seek revenge *Dafoe plays a computer mastermind who seeks revenge on his former employer.*

seek compensation/damages (=ask for money because of something bad you have suffered) *He is seeking compensation for wrongful imprisonment.*

seek an answer/solution to sth *People have been seeking an answer to the problem for a long time.*

seek your fortune (=try to find a way of making a lot of money) *He made his way to London to seek his fortune.*

ADVERBS

actively seek sth (=make strong efforts to get something) *Other companies are actively seeking to become involved in the research.*

desperately/urgently seek sth *They ran in all directions, desperately seeking a way out.*

constantly/continually seek sth *We are continually seeking an answer to this problem.*

seem *v*

to have a particular appearance or qualities, which make you think that something is true about someone or something

> **Grammar**
>
> **Seem** is often used with an adjective: *He* **seems** *older than he really is.* | *The weather* **seems** *unusually cold.*
>
> You can use **seem** with the verb **to be**: *The car* **seems to be** *OK.* You can also use **seem** with **like**: *Teri* **seems like** *a nice girl.*

PHRASES

it seems that... *It seemed that no one knew anything about the murder.*

it seems like.../as if... *It seemed as if their world had ended.*

or so it seems *She had lived there all her life – or so it seemed.*

it seemed like a good idea at the time *"Why did you want to play in a band?" "Well, it seemed like a good idea at the time."*

sth seems like hours *especially spoken* (=it seems a very long time) *The film went on for what seemed like hours.*

seemingly *adv*

appearing to have a particular quality, when this may or may not be true

ADJECTIVES

seemingly endless/limitless *We looked out over seemingly endless pine forests.*

seemingly impossible *He was faced with a seemingly impossible task.*

seemingly intractable (=seeming impossible to deal with) *Unemployment remained a serious and seemingly intractable problem.*

seemingly harmless *This seemingly harmless creature is in fact very poisonous.*

seemingly innocuous/innocent (=seeming unlikely to cause any problems) *Even seemingly innocuous questions can get an employer into trouble.*

seemingly trivial (=not seeming important) *Seemingly trivial symptoms can turn out to be of crucial importance.*

seemingly unrelated *He gave me a few seemingly unrelated bits of information.*

seemingly unaware/oblivious (=seeming not to notice something) *She was seemingly unaware of all the activity around her.*

see-through *adj* THESAURUS › **clear[1] (4)**

segment *n* THESAURUS › **piece**

selection Ac *n*

1 a group of things of a particular type

ADJECTIVES

a wide/large/big selection *The library has a wide selection of books.*

a good/excellent/superb selection *There is a good selection of bars and cafés nearby.*

a varied selection (=consisting of a lot of different things) *The supermarket has a varied selection of fruit juice drinks especially for children.*

a small/limited selection *They have only a limited selection of colours to choose from.*

a random selection (=chosen by chance, without any reason or order) *They took a random selection of children and tested them.*

S

a representative selection (=specially chosen to be typical of a group) *The report included a representative selection of people's opinions.*

VERBS

have a selection *Good gyms will have a large selection of exercise machines.*

offer a selection *Both ships offer a superb selection of restaurants.*

contain/include a selection *The book contains a large selection of Caribbean recipes.*

feature a selection (=include a selection – used especially when you think this is a good thing) *He was asked to contribute to an album featuring a selection of Elvis Presley songs.*

choose from a selection *Customers can choose from a wide selection of knitwear.*

PREPOSITIONS

a selection of sth *Here is a selection of the photographs I took.*

2 the process of choosing someone or something from a group

ADJECTIVES

final selection *Think carefully before making your final selection.*

random selection (=chosen by chance, not because of any reason) *The choice of people for the survey is based on random selection.*

careful selection *The study is based on a careful selection of all the relevant information.*

initial selection (=the first selection) *After the initial selection has been made, the candidates are asked to come in for an interview.*

VERBS

make a selection *The judges have made their final selection.*

selection is based on sth *Selection is based on written tests.*

selection + NOUNS

the selection process/procedure *The interview is an important part of the selection procedure.*

the selection criteria (=reasons used for choosing something) *What are your selection criteria?*

a selection committee (=a group of people responsible for choosing something) *All the novels have been carefully chosen by a very experienced selection committee.*

PREPOSITIONS

the selection of sb/sth *The selection of a new leader can take months.*

selection for sth *He narrowly missed selection for the team.*

selection as sth *Her selection as president of the association showed how much people respected her.*

selfish *adj*

caring only about yourself and not about other people

ADVERBS

totally/extremely selfish *Some people are totally selfish and don't really think about anyone else.*

purely selfish *Making money and owning things are purely selfish activities.*

NOUNS

selfish reasons/motives *He went there for selfish reasons.*

semester *n especially AmE*

one of two periods in a high school or university year

ADJECTIVES/NOUNS + semester

fall semester *Some colleges start their fall semester in August.*

spring semester *When does spring semester end?*

first/second semester *All students have exams at the end of their second semester.*

last/next semester *Mr Wright will be teaching us next semester.*

the following/previous semester *She had not kept her lecture notes from the previous semester.*

VERBS

spend a semester somewhere *I spent a semester at Yale University.*

complete/finish a semester *If I get sick, can I still complete the semester?*

semester + NOUNS

a semester system *Their academic year is based on a semester system.*

a semester exam (=at the end of a semester) *They have semester exams next week.*

semester break (=a period without classes in the middle of a semester) *I went home to visit my parents in the semester break.*

> **Semester** is used mainly in the US. In Britain, the school or university year is divided into three **terms**.

send *v*

to arrange for something or someone to go or be taken to another place

NOUNS

send (sb) a message/letter/email *Tom sent a message saying that he would be late.*

send (sb) a card/postcard *Have a nice time in Barcelona – send me a postcard!*

send (sb) an invitation *Have you sent the wedding invitations yet?*

send (sb) a bill/invoice *They sent us a bill for the costs of cleaning the house after we stayed.*

send (sb) a copy (of sth) *Tony sent her a copy of the article.*

send (sb) details/information *Please could you send me more information about the course?*

S

send (sb) flowers *We sent Mom flowers for Mother's Day.*
send troops *The president pledged to send more troops to Afghanistan.*
send aid/money/donations *My parents sent me some money.*

PREPOSITIONS/ADVERBS

send sth to sb *I'm going to send an email to Chris.*
send sb to prison/school/Iraq etc *He was sent to prison for attacking another man.*
send sth by post/email etc *Don't send valuable items by post.*
send sth back/up etc *She arranged for some coffee to be sent up for our meeting.*

senior *adj*

having a higher position, level, or rank

NOUNS

a senior manager/executive *She's now a senior manager for a large toy company.*
senior management *Senior management have approved her proposal.*
senior staff *Some senior staff criticized the head teacher's decision.*
a senior official *A meeting of senior government officials was called.*
a senior officer *Inspector Wild is the senior officer in charge of the investigation.*
a senior member *A senior member of the government has resigned.*
a senior level/position/rank *A new appointment has been made at a senior level.*

S

PREPOSITIONS

senior to sb *He is senior to me in the company.*

sensation *n*

a feeling that you get, especially a physical one

ADJECTIVES

a pleasant sensation *She was enjoying the pleasant sensation of being in the warm water.*
an unpleasant sensation *I felt a rather unpleasant sensation in my chest.*
a painful sensation *While he was running he had an extremely painful sensation in his knee.*
a strange/odd/curious sensation *As we looked at each other I had a strange sensation.*
a physical sensation *Babies soon learn to recognize the physical sensation of hunger.*
a burning sensation *These chemicals can cause a burning sensation.*
a tingling/prickling sensation (=little sharp feelings on your skin) *She felt a tingling sensation, like a mild electric shock.*

VERBS

feel/have/experience a sensation *He felt a tingling sensation down his left side.*
enjoy a sensation *Some people eat a lot because they enjoy the sensation of eating.*
cause/produce a sensation *The drug can produce strange sensations in some patients.*

PREPOSITIONS

the sensation of sth *He likes the sensation of speed.*

sense *n*

1 one of the five physical ways of finding out about things

ADJECTIVES

a good/keen/acute sense of sth *Pigs have a keen sense of smell.*
a poor sense of sth *Owls have acute hearing, although they have a poor sense of smell.*

VERBS

have a sense of sth *You have to have a good sense of hearing to play the violin.*
lose your sense of sth *I think I'm losing my sense of smell.*
use your sense of sth *These animals use their sense of smell to find their prey.*
sharpen/heighten your senses (=make them better) *She felt that her close encounter with death had sharpened her senses.*
dull your senses (=make them less good) *The drug dulls the senses.*

PHRASES

sense of smell/taste/touch/hearing/sight *My sense of taste came back when I stopped smoking.*
the five senses (=sight, taste, smell, hearing, and touch) *We use all five senses to explore the world around us.*

2 a natural ability or feeling about something

ADJECTIVES

a good/great sense of sth *He is a popular boy with a good sense of humour.*
a strong/keen/deep sense of sth *He had a strong sense of responsibility.*
an overwhelming/tremendous sense of sth (=very strong) *She was filled with an overwhelming sense of loss.*
a natural sense of sth *She did not have a natural sense of direction.*
a growing sense of sth *She looked around with a growing sense of unease.*
a renewed sense of sth (=now strong again) *He returned to Washington with a renewed sense of purpose.*

NOUNS + sense

dress/clothes sense (=an ability to choose clothes well) *Her dress sense was faultless.*
business sense (=an ability to make good decisions in business) *Few young people have much business sense.*

VERBS

have a sense of sth *These people have a great sense of community.*

feel/experience a sense of sth *I felt a deep sense of pride.*

give sb a sense of sth *The job gave her a sense of control over her life.*

gain a sense of sth *She helped me gain some sense of proportion about my problems.*

lose your sense of sth *He is in pain but has not lost his sense of humour.*

lose all sense of time/direction/proportion (=no longer know how much time has passed, which direction you are going etc) *When I was in hospital, I lost all sense of time.*

keep a sense of sth (*also* **retain a sense of sth** *formal*): *Throughout it all she retained her sense of fun.*

PHRASES

a sense of humour *BrE*, **a sense of humor** *AmE* (=the ability to recognize and enjoy things that are funny) *A good teacher needs a sense of humour.*

a sense of direction (=the ability to judge which way you should be going) *He has an excellent sense of direction.*

a sense of timing (=the ability to choose the right moment to do or say something) *Actors need to have a good sense of timing.*

a sense of purpose (=a feeling that you know what you are trying to achieve) *Becoming a mother had given her a new sense of purpose.*

a sense of achievement/satisfaction *Even a small success gives a sense of achievement.*

a sense of justice/fairness *Anyone with a sense of justice can see this is not fair.*

a sense of proportion/perspective (=the ability to judge how important something is) *It's important to keep a sense of proportion.*

a sense of identity (=a feeling of confidence about who you are) *Change can threaten our fragile sense of identity.*

a sense of occasion (=a feeling that an event is special or important) *The live music added to the sense of occasion.*

a sense of responsibility/duty/loyalty *Parents try to give their children a sense of responsibility.*

a sense of urgency (=a feeling that something is urgent) *The rescuers felt a real sense of urgency now.*

a sense of relief/panic/guilt/unease etc (=a particular feeling) *We reached the medical centre with a sense of relief.*

a sense of loss *Many women experience a sense of loss when their children leave home.*

a sense of security (=feeling safe) *They were lulled into a false sense of security.*

a sense of belonging/community (=the feeling of belonging to a group) *There is a real sense of community at the school.*

3 a meaning, or a way in which something can be true

PHRASES

in one sense/in a sense *In one sense, you are right.*

in every sense *He is lucky in every sense.*

in no sense (=not at all) *This is in no sense a criticism.*

in the true sense of the word *He was a hero in the true sense of the word.*

in a general/broad sense *I was using the word in its broadest sense.*

in a narrow/limited sense *He didn't mean art in the narrow sense of drawing, painting, or sculpture.*

in the ordinary/usual/conventional sense *These snakes do not hear in the ordinary sense, as they have no ears.*

in the strict sense *Tomatoes are not vegetables in the strict sense of the word.*

in a literal sense (=according to the most basic meaning of words) *He was using the word 'challenge' in its literal sense.*

in the technical/legal sense *I was using the word 'compound' in its technical sense.*

sensible *adj* showing good judgment

NOUNS

sensible advice *She is always full of sensible advice.*

a sensible decision *Everyone agreed that it was a sensible decision.*

a sensible idea/suggestion *I will only listen to sensible suggestions.*

the sensible thing to do *Moving house seemed like the sensible thing to do.*

a sensible approach *He has a very sensible approach to his work.*

a sensible way of doing sth *Missing meals is not a sensible way of losing weight.*

a sensible precaution (=something you do in case of trouble) *It's a sensible precaution to take a blanket when driving in winter.*

a sensible person/boy/girl etc *Sarah is a very sensible girl.*

a sensible diet (=eating healthy food) *Eat a sensible diet with plenty of fruit and vegetables.*

sensible shoes (=that are easy to walk in and do not hurt your feet) *Make sure you wear sensible shoes when you have to walk a long way.*

PREPOSITIONS

sensible about (doing) sth *I wish he would be sensible about this.*

sensitive *adj*

1 easily upset or offended

NOUNS

a sensitive child *Ben is a very sensitive child, and doesn't like it if people laugh at him.*

a sensitive soul *BrE* (=a sensitive person) *She really is quite a sensitive soul.*

PREPOSITIONS

sensitive about sth *Laura is sensitive about her weight.*

sensitive to sth *He is very sensitive to criticism.*

2 needing careful treatment, because it is private or causes disagreement

NOUNS

a sensitive issue/subject/matter *Abortion is a very sensitive issue.*

a sensitive area (=a sensitive subject) *AIDS is a sensitive area which many schools are unsure how to tackle.*

sensitive information *She was accused of passing sensitive information to the enemy.*

sensitive documents *He lost his job after he left sensitive documents on a train.*

the sensitive nature of sth *Because of the sensitive nature of the issue, the discussions were not made public.*

ADVERBS

highly sensitive *Details of the highly sensitive information have not been made public.*

politically sensitive *The subject of population control is politically sensitive.*

commercially/environmentally sensitive *How can we protect commercially sensitive information?*

S

THESAURUS: sensitive

confidential, private, clandestine, classified, sensitive, covert, undercover, underground, hush-hush → **secret[1]**

sentence *n*

1 a group of words, which begins with a capital letter and ends with a full stop, and usually contains a verb

ADJECTIVES

a long/short sentence *James uses long sentences in his novels, which can make them difficult to understand.*

a full/complete/whole sentence *Answer the questions in complete sentences – do not give one-word answers.*

a simple sentence *Use simple sentences when talking to young children.*

a complex sentence *As students learn more of a language, they should write longer and more complex sentences.*

a grammatical/ungrammatical sentence (=correct/not correct according to the rules of grammar) *Is this sentence grammatical?*

the opening/closing sentence (=the first or last sentence in a book, report, talk etc) *"It was a bright cold day in April, and the clocks were striking thirteen." is the opening sentence of George Orwell's 'Nineteen Eighty-Four'.*

a single sentence (=one sentence) *He didn't say a single sentence.*

VERBS

write a sentence *Write a few sentences about yourself.*

read a sentence *I can't read the last sentence.*

say a sentence *He can say a few sentences in German.*

begin/end a sentence *Always begin a new sentence with a capital letter.*

form/construct a sentence *The aim is to construct sentences so that the exact meaning is given in the fewest possible words.*

string together a sentence (=form a sentence – used especially when someone has difficulty doing this) *She couldn't even string a sentence together.*

finish sb's sentence (=complete a sentence that someone else started saying) *His wife is always interrupting and finishing his sentences for him.*

sentence + NOUNS

sentence structure *Two types of sentence structure were used.*

PREPOSITIONS

in a sentence *Describe in a short sentence what is meant by each word on the list.*

PHRASES

the beginning/end of a sentence *His voice dropped at the end of the sentence.*

2 a punishment given by a judge

ADJECTIVES/NOUNS + sentence

a prison/jail sentence *If found guilty, he faces a long jail sentence.*

a five-year/eight-year etc sentence (=five, eight etc years in prison) *He was serving an eight-year sentence for burglary.*

the maximum/minimum sentence *The maximum sentence for this offence is five years.*

a severe/tough/harsh/stiff sentence *Police officers are demanding tougher sentences for people who carry knives.*

a light/short sentence (=a short time in prison) *People who have not broken the law before often get lighter sentences.*

a long sentence *The gang all received long sentences.*

a life sentence (=prison for the rest of your life, or a very long time) *In 1978 he was given a life sentence for attacking an old woman.*

a death sentence (=a punishment of death) *They are demanding the death sentence.*

a suspended sentence (=one which someone will serve only if they commit another crime) *Her attacker got a two-year suspended sentence.*

a custodial sentence *BrE formal* (=a period in prison, not a fine or other punishment) *The judge warned him that he should expect a custodial sentence.*

a non-custodial sentence *BrE formal* (=not in prison) *The judge said the offence was too serious for a non-custodial sentence.*

VERBS

get/receive a sentence (*also* **be given a sentence**) *She was given a three-year prison sentence.*

face a sentence (=be likely to receive a sentence) *He faces a long prison sentence if he is found guilty.*

serve a sentence (=spend time in prison) *Her husband is serving a two-year sentence for gun crime.*

complete a sentence *She will complete the rest of her sentence in a low-security prison.*

a crime carries a sentence (=that is the punishment for that crime) *Rape should carry an automatic life sentence.*

impose/hand down a sentence (=officially give someone a sentence) *The judge imposed a three-year sentence.*

pass sentence *formal* (=officially say what someone's punishment will be) *It is now my duty to pass sentence.*

overturn a sentence (=officially say that someone does not have to serve it) *The next year his sentence was overturned.*

PREPOSITIONS

a sentence for sth *He has just begun a life sentence for murder.*

PHRASES

a sentence of three years/six months etc *He now faces a sentence of 15–20 years.*

under sentence of death (=having received a death sentence) *She visited him in prison when he was under sentence of death.*

sentimental *adj* THESAURUS

emotional (1)

separate *adj*

if two things are separate, they are different and not the same

VERBS

keep sth separate *I try to keep my work and my home life separate.*

remain separate *He believed that religion and politics should remain separate.*

be regarded/considered/treated as separate *The two cases can be regarded as entirely separate.*

ADVERBS

entirely/completely/totally separate (*also* **quite separate** *BrE*): *These are totally separate issues.*

PREPOSITIONS

separate from sth *This event should be viewed as separate from the others.*

series Ac *n*

1 several events or actions of a similar type that happen or are planned to happen one after the other

> **Grammar**
> This meaning of **series** is usually used in the phrase **a series of sth**.

NOUNS

a series of events *They are holding a series of events to mark the anniversary.*

a series of cases *There has been a series of cases of theft at the school.*

a series of books/articles/films *She wrote a series of articles on education.*

a series of meetings/lectures/workshops *We have planned a series of workshops.*

a series of tests/experiments *She underwent a series of tests to find out what was wrong.*

a series of questions *I had to answer a series of questions.*

a series of proposals/suggestions *We have come up with a detailed series of proposals.*

a series of protests/demonstrations/strikes *Price increases caused a series of protests.*

a series of attacks/bombings *The city suffered a series of bombings.*

ADJECTIVES

a whole/entire series (=used to emphasize how many there are) *We faced a whole series of problems.*

a long/short series *There has been a long series of delays.*

PREPOSITIONS

a series of sth *The police are investigating a series of attacks in the area.*

in a series *The second lecture in the series was held in Mexico.*

PHRASES

the latest in a series (=the most recent) *This was the latest in a series of changes.*

the first/second/last etc in a series *This meeting will be the first in a series.*

THESAURUS: series

a sequence of sth

events | actions | stages | steps | instructions | commands | operations | activities | numbers | letters | images

a series of things, especially things that happen or are done in a particular order, and are connected to each other in some way:

In Lithuania, a similar sequence of events occurred. | We follow a particular sequence of steps when planning a project. | Your password will be a sequence of numbers and letters. | The two poems are intended to be read **in sequence** (=they should be read one after the other in a particular order).

a succession of sth
jobs | owners | governments | changes | visitors | boyfriends | girlfriends
a series of things or people – used to emphasize that they keep changing without any break:
Karl moved aimlessly through a succession of jobs. | The programme has survived an endless succession of changes. | Pauline was busy all morning with a succession of visitors. | He won the competition three years **in succession** (=one after another without a break).

a set of sth
rules | ideas | principles | values | questions | guidelines | criteria | figures | circumstances
a series of things, especially things that are used or done together:
The school has developed a new set of rules. | We need to use a different set of criteria (=use different standards for judging something). | *The latest set of figures shows that crime has increased. | We were faced with a new set of circumstances.*

a string of sth
attacks | bombings | scandals | successes | awards | hits | defeats | failures | boyfriends | girlfriends
a series of things or people – used to emphasize that there are a lot, often of bad things:
The bombing was the latest in a string of attacks. | The singer has enjoyed a string of successes. | The team has suffered a string of defeats. | Ella had a string of boyfriends.

a chain of sth
events | reactions | islands | mountains
a series of connected things or places:
This decision set in motion a chain of events. | The Antilles are a chain of islands in the Caribbean Sea.

a catalogue of sth *BrE*, **a catalog of sth** *AmE*
errors | failures | disasters | problems | complaints | injuries | crimes
a series of bad things – used when you want to emphasize that there are a lot of them:
A catalogue of errors led to last year's train crash. | The trip was a catalogue of disasters which began when we missed the flight. | He has suffered a catalogue of injuries since the World Cup final.

2 a set of television or radio programmes that have the same characters or deal with the same subject

NOUNS + series

a television/TV/radio series *'ER' was a television series set in a hospital emergency room.*

a drama/comedy series *Armstrong will star in a new TV comedy series.*

a cartoon series *'The Simpsons' is a popular cartoon series.*

a police/crime series *I enjoy watching crime series.*

a documentary series (=giving information about a particular subject) *They are showing a new documentary series about China.*

a three-part/six-part etc series *He will present a new six-part series 'How to Save the Earth'.*

a reality series (=in which ordinary people are filmed in real situations) *He had appeared in the reality series 'Big Brother'.*

ADJECTIVES

a popular/successful/hit series (=watched by a lot of people) *She starred in the hit series 'The Gentle Touch'.*

a long-running series (=continuing over many years) *This was the last episode of ITV's long-running police series.*

the first/second/last etc series *I missed the first series.*

VERBS

watch a series *I watched the last series on DVD.*

write a series *The series was written by Kay Mellor.*

make/produce a series *He produced a TV series in the 1990s.*

commission a series (=officially ask someone to make a series) *The BBC commissioned a third series.*

broadcast/screen/show a series *The series was first broadcast in 2005.*

present a series *He currently presents two series for the Discovery Health channel.*

appear in/star in a series (=be an actor in a series) *The actor has appeared in many TV series, including 'Doctor Who'.*

serious *adj*

1 a serious situation, problem, accident etc is extremely bad or dangerous

NOUNS

a serious problem *Car crime is a serious problem in the area.*

a serious injury/illness/disease *The driver was taken to hospital with serious injuries.*

a serious accident *He is recovering from a serious accident.*

serious damage/harm *The fire caused serious damage to their apartment.*

a serious threat *The oil slick posed a serious threat to wildlife.*

serious danger *The trapped miners were never in serious danger.*

a serious crime/offence *Kidnapping is a serious crime.*

a serious mistake *She admitted she had made a serious mistake.*

serious trouble *The economy was in serious trouble.*

serious consequences *Missing school can have serious consequences.*

a serious situation *The situation there is extremely serious.*

THESAURUS: serious

serious, severe, grave, desperate, acute → **bad (2)**

2 not joking or laughing, or not pretending

NOUNS

a serious expression/face/look *The man had a serious expression on his face.*

a serious voice/tone *"Are you quite sure about this?" he asked in a very slow and serious voice.*

a serious matter (=something that you should not joke about) *Pay attention. This is a serious matter.*

VERBS

sound/look/seem serious *Her voice sounded serious on the phone.*

PREPOSITIONS

serious about sth *They seem to be serious about their relationship.*

seriously *adv*

in a way that has a very bad effect on someone or something

ADJECTIVES

seriously ill *Her mother is seriously ill in hospital.*

seriously injured/hurt/wounded *He was seriously injured in a car accident.*

seriously damaged *His reputation had been seriously damaged.*

seriously affected *The area was seriously affected by flooding last year.*

seriously worried/concerned *It was late, and her parents were now seriously worried.*

seriously wrong *I was worried there was something seriously wrong with me.*

seriously flawed (=having a bad weakness or fault) *The design is seriously flawed.*

servant *n*

someone, especially in the past, who was paid to clean someone's house, cook for them, answer the door etc, and who often lived in the house

ADJECTIVES/NOUNS + servant

a domestic/household servant (=working in a house, usually as a cleaner) *Many young girls became domestic servants.*

a faithful/loyal servant *Williams was a faithful servant and told no one of his master's secret.*

a trusted servant *Paulus was a trusted servant of the emperor.*

a royal servant *Dudley was a trusted royal servant.*

Your humble servant is an old-fashioned respectful way of ending a letter or introducing yourself to someone: *Your **humble servant**, Philip Miller.*

VERBS

have a servant *In those days, many families had servants.*

hire/employ a servant *They were wealthy enough to employ servants.*

become a servant *His daughter became a servant in the royal household.*

servant + NOUNS

a servant girl/boy *A servant girl brought us some water.*

service[1] *n*

1 something that is provided for people to use by a company, an organization, or by the government

ADJECTIVES

a free service *We offer a free advice service to our members.*

an online service (=using the internet) *Next time, why don't you use our online service?*

a 24-hour service (=available at any time) *The ticket office has a 24-hour service.*

a vital/essential service (=very important and necessary) *For many old people, the local post office is a vital service.*

a comprehensive service (=which includes everything) *We provide a comprehensive service to all our clients.*

financial/legal services *The cost of legal services deters many people from consulting a lawyer.*

medical services *The health system in Britain gives people free access to medical services.*

public services (=provided by the government for people in general) *Many people in the world live without public services such as clean water.*

local services (=services such as public transport and waste collection) *Local services are being cut back to save money.*

the postal service *The postal service is usually good.*

NOUNS + service

the emergency services (=police, fire, and ambulance services) *To call the emergency services in Britain, you dial 999.*

the fire/police/ambulance service *Calls to the ambulance service increase during the winter months.*

the health/education service *We are proud of our country's health service.*

a delivery service *They offer a free delivery service on all orders over $30.*

an advice/counselling service *The university offers a counselling service for students.*

an information/news service *The information service provides busy managers with all the information they need.*

a support service *We provide support services for disabled people.*

the library service *The library service in schools is being cut.*

a telephone/broadband service *The company offers a mobile broadband service.*

VERBS

offer/provide a service *The organization provides a customer advice service.*

deliver a service *Our aim is to deliver a high-quality support service.*

use a service *Many elderly people use this service.*

access a service (=be able to use it) *A growing range of services can now be accessed online.*

launch/introduce a service *The company has launched a new online booking service.*

develop a service *We plan to develop new services in the future.*

expand/extend a service *They have plans to expand the service to other areas.*

cut/axe a service (=stop providing it) *The council will be forced to cut this service unless more funding can be found.*

improve a service *We need extra funding to improve library services.*

service + NOUNS

a service provider *Who is your internet service provider?*

2 the work of dealing with customers in a shop, business, hotel etc

ADJECTIVES

good/great/excellent service *You expect good service if you're paying so much.*

poor/bad/terrible service *I always complain when I receive poor service.*

personal service *Everyone who comes into our store gets friendly and personal service.*

slow service *The food was good, but the service was very slow.*

quick/prompt/swift service *We promise you quick service, even at busy times.*

efficient service *The service in the store is extremely efficient.*

friendly service *It's a hotel with a reputation for friendly service.*

NOUNS + service

customer service *The company offers excellent customer service.*

after-sales service (=advice and help with a product after buying it) *Good after-sales service is important when you are buying a car.*

VERBS

receive good/poor etc service *If you have received poor service, let us know.*

offer/provide service *We are committed to providing excellent service.*

improve service *They need to improve the service in the hotel.*

PHRASES

the standard/quality of service *They have improved the standard of service.*

3 *BrE* a regular system of buses, trains, planes, or boats to and from a particular place

ADJECTIVES

a direct service *There's a direct service to London.*

a daily/hourly etc service *There's an hourly bus service into the city centre.*

a frequent service *There is a frequent service into the centre of Paris.*

a reliable/efficient service *The town has a very reliable bus service.*

a limited/reduced service *They operate a reduced service at weekends.*

a full service *A full service will operate during July and August.*

a scheduled service *Pan Am operated the first scheduled service across the Atlantic.*

NOUNS + service

a rail/train service *The company runs train services between London and Edinburgh.*

a bus/coach service *There is a regular bus service to the village.*

a ferry service *A ferry service runs from Portsmouth to Bilbao.*

a transport service *Passengers want a reliable transport service.*

a shuttle service (=one that covers a short distance several times a day) *A shuttle service takes you from the airport car park to the terminal building.*

a passenger service *The first passenger service on this route was in 1961.*

VERBS

use a service *Many people use the 7.40 service.*

lay on/provide a service *At Christmas, the rail company will lay on extra services to cope with demand.*

launch a service *The airline is launching two new services to Tenerife.*

run/operate a service *P&O operate ferry services to Zeebrugge.*

a service runs/operates *The service operates seven days a week.*

cut/axe a service *The Sunday service has been axed.*

4 a religious ceremony

ADJECTIVES/NOUNS + service

a church service *He attended the church service on Christmas Day.*

a religious service *She had been to a Jewish religious service.*

a funeral service (=one held for burying or cremating someone who has died) *Over 350 people attended her funeral service.*

a memorial service (=one to remind people of someone who has died) *A memorial service for the victims of the bombing will be held next week.*

a wedding/marriage service *She wanted a traditional wedding service in a church.*

VERBS

conduct a service *The service was conducted by Reverend Salters.*

attend a service *Over 1,000 people attended the service in the cathedral.*

hold a service *The memorial service will be held on 26 September.*

service² *v* THESAURUS repair¹

session *n*

a planned period of time when people do something

ADJECTIVES/NOUNS + session

a training session *One player failed to turn up for the training session.*

a practice session *He crashed during a practice session before the Belgian Grand Prix.*

a weekly/monthly session *Weekly advice sessions are provided for people who are starting their own business.*

a one-hour/two-hour etc session *We have a two-hour session every Monday morning.*

a group session *The group sessions were led by a psychiatrist.*

an individual/one-to-one session (=when one person is taught or helped by someone) *She may benefit from individual counselling sessions.*

an exercise session *An exercise session shouldn't leave you feeling exhausted.*

a brainstorming session (=when people think up new ideas) *I think we should just get together and have a brainstorming session.*

a question-and-answer session (=when people ask a speaker questions) *His talk was followed by a question-and-answer session.*

a recording session (=when music is recorded) *It was the band's first recording session.*

a photo session (=when someone is photographed for a magazine etc) *I normally have two or three photo sessions a week.*

a therapy/counselling session (=time to talk about personal problems with someone who can give advice) *At one point his parents joined him for a family therapy session.*

VERBS

have a session *I started having exercise sessions with a personal trainer.*

hold/run/conduct a session *They are planning to hold a special training session for new employees.*

take part in/attend a session *Most of the students who took part in the sessions said they found them useful.*

do a session *informal*: *We're doing a photo session tomorrow.*

lead a session *Each session will be led by a media expert.*

miss a session *He never missed a training session.*

PREPOSITIONS

a session of sth *The two sides agreed to a further session of talks.*

set¹ *v*

1 to decide and state when something will happen, how much something should cost, what should be done etc

NOUNS

set a date/time *No date has been set for the election.*

set a price *We set the price at £30.*

set standards/guidelines (=decide on standards, rules etc) *The government has set new food quality standards for all school canteens.*

set limits/boundaries *Set strict limits on your spending.*

2 to establish a way of doing something that is then copied or followed

NOUNS

set an example (=behave well in a way that other people can copy) *Parents should try to set a good example to their children.*

set a precedent (=do something that later actions or decisions may be based on) *To ignore the law in this case would set a dangerous precedent.*

set the pattern/trend (=do something in a way that is later repeated) *That first day seemed to set the pattern for the following weeks.*

set the tone (=establish a general mood or feeling) *The gloomy first chapter sets the tone for the rest of the novel.*

set the standard (=be very good, and so show how good other people or things should be) *They wanted to set the standard for online shopping.*

set the agenda (=say what should be done or discussed) *One country cannot set the agenda for the entire conference.*

set the pace (=move or change quickly, so that others try to do the same) *Britain set the pace for industrialization in the early 1800s.*

3 to make something ready to operate

NOUNS

set the alarm *Don't forget to set the alarm before you leave the house.*

set a watch/clock *We set our watches to the local time.*

set² *n*

a group of similar things that belong together or are related in some way

ADJECTIVES

a complete/full set *You need to have a full set of tools.*

a new/different set *This time they were faced with a completely different set of problems.*

a complex/complicated set *The system works according to a complicated set of rules.*

PHRASES

a set of rules/instructions/conditions/guidelines *Grammar is the set of rules which determines how people use a language.*

a set of problems/questions/issues *At the end of the text there is a set of questions.*

a set of criteria/principles/values *The judges use a strict set of criteria when judging the paintings.*

a set of data *The scientists compared the two sets of data.*

setback *n*

an event that delays or prevents progress, or makes things worse

ADJECTIVES

a major/big setback *The defeat was a major setback.*

a serious/severe/significant setback *He said the attack was a serious setback for the peace process.*

a minor setback *After a few minor setbacks, the project went really well.*

a temporary setback *Try not to be discouraged by temporary setbacks.*

an early/initial setback *The policy has been successful, despite some early setbacks.*

a political/military/economic setback *The defeat represented a major political setback for the party.*

VERBS

suffer/receive/have a setback *The team suffered a serious setback when their goalkeeper was injured.*

overcome a setback (=deal with it) *I think we can overcome this setback.*

represent a setback (=be a setback) *The decision represented a setback for chemical companies.*

PREPOSITIONS

a setback for sb *These election results were a setback for the Social Democratic Party.*

a setback to sth/sb *There has been a serious setback to our efforts to control the disease.*

setting *n*

the place where something is or where something happens

ADJECTIVES

a beautiful/lovely/magnificent setting *The event takes place in the magnificent setting of Bramham Park.*

a perfect/ideal setting *The castle was a perfect setting for the wedding.*

a peaceful/tranquil setting *The gardens are a peaceful setting for a walk.*

an idyllic setting (=a very beautiful and peaceful place) *This idyllic setting is just the place to relax.*

a rural setting (=in the countryside) *Some customers are amazed to find this high-tech business in such a rural setting.*

an urban setting (=in the city) *What kind of garden is best in an urban setting?*

a natural setting *They were able to study the animals in their natural setting.*

an unlikely setting *This quiet village may seem an unlikely setting for a top restaurant.*

PREPOSITIONS

a setting for sth *The building will be the setting for two special events this year.*

VERBS

provide a setting *The hotel provides an ideal setting for conferences.*

settle *v*

to end an argument or solve a disagreement

NOUNS

settle a dispute/argument/conflict *Every effort was made to settle the dispute.*

settle a lawsuit/case *The city will pay $875,000 to settle the lawsuit.*

settle a matter/issue/question *It is important that the matter is settled quickly.*

settle your differences (=agree to stop arguing) *The two recently met to settle their differences.*

ADVERBS

finally/eventually settle sth *The issue was finally settled many years later.*

settle sth amicably (=in a friendly way, without using a court of law) *The dispute was settled amicably.*

PREPOSITIONS

settle with sb *He said he hoped the company would settle with the victims' families.*

PHRASES

settle out of court (=come to an agreement without going to a court of law) *She talked to a* *lawyer and settled out of court with her former employer.*

settlement *n*

an official agreement or decision that ends an argument, a court case, or a fight

ADJECTIVES/NOUNS + settlement

a peace settlement (=one that ends a war) *Hopes of a peace settlement receded.*

a political settlement (=one that is reached by political discussion, not fighting) *The British government favours a political settlement in the Middle East.*

a peaceful settlement (=without fighting) *Both sides are working towards a peaceful settlement.*

a lasting settlement *Only a political solution can provide a lasting settlement.*

an amicable settlement (=when people agree in a friendly way) *The village council attempted to bring about an amicable settlement.*

a divorce settlement (=an agreement about money and property at the end of a marriage) *She gained ownership of the building in her divorce settlement.*

an out-of-court settlement (=an agreement made to avoid a court case) *They paid the government $470 million as part of an out-of-court settlement.*

VERBS

reach a settlement *The companies reached a settlement in March.*

agree (to) a settlement *The French king had agreed to a settlement.*

achieve/bring about a settlement *The government was determined to achieve a settlement in Northern Ireland.*

negotiate a settlement (=have discussions to try to reach a settlement) *His lawyers are understood to be negotiating a settlement.*

seek a settlement *I went to present my case and to seek a reasonable settlement.*

PREPOSITIONS

under a settlement *Under the settlement, the workers will be paid compensation.*

PHRASES

the terms of a settlement *They have agreed on the terms of the settlement.*

set up *v* THESAURUS ▶ start[1] (3)

severe *adj*

severe problems, injuries, illnesses etc are very bad or very serious

NOUNS

severe damage *The blast caused severe damage to the surrounding buildings.*

severe problems/difficulties *The clothing industry has experienced severe problems in recent years.*

a severe injury/illness *She had suffered severe head injuries.*

severe pain *He was in severe pain and unable to call for help.*

severe depression *He suffered from severe depression when he was younger.*

a severe case (=of a medical condition) *Hospitalization is necessary in severe cases.*

a severe blow (=an event that has a very bad effect) *The closure of the mine was a severe blow to the country's economy.*

THESAURUS: severe

serious, severe, grave, desperate, acute → **bad (2)**

severely *adv*

very badly or to a great degree

ADJECTIVES

severely damaged *The hotel was severely damaged by fire last November.*

severely disabled/injured/wounded *The accident left him severely disabled.*

severely affected *The town is severely affected by aircraft noise.*

severely disrupted *The bad weather means that rail services will be severely disrupted.*

severely tested (=put under a lot of pressure and almost destroyed) *Her trust in him was severely tested by his behaviour.*

VERBS

severely limit/restrict sth *Lack of funds severely limits what we are able to achieve.*

punish sb severely *Organizations that break the rules will be severely punished.*

deal with sb severely *formal* (=give someone a harsh punishment) *The courts should deal with violent criminals most severely.*

criticize sb/sth severely *The government has been severely criticized for not dealing with the problem sooner.*

shade *n*

1 slight darkness or shelter from the direct light of the sun, made by something blocking it

ADJECTIVES

deep shade *The plant will even grow in deep shade.*

partial shade *These plants do well in sun or partial shade.*

cool shade *I was looking forward to being back in the cool shade of our house.*

dappled shade (=with spots of light and shade) *The cherry tree cast a dappled shade.*

VERBS

provide/offer/create shade *Olive trees provided shade.*

cast shade (=make shade appear) *The forest cast a deep shade.*

seek shade *In mid-summer, you should seek shade in the middle of the day.*

find shade *We found some shade under a tree.*

PREPOSITIONS

in the shade (=in a place which is out of direct sunlight) *The temperature was over 90 degrees in the shade.*

under the shade of sth (=using something to protect you from the light of the sun) *She was sitting under the shade of a large oak tree.*

PHRASES

light and shade *She was looking at the patterns of light and shade created by the sunlight.*

2 a particular type of a colour

ADJECTIVES

a pale/pastel shade *The walls were painted in pastel shades.*

a deep/dark shade *She had dyed her hair a dark shade of red.*

a bright/vivid shade *The sky was a vivid shade of blue.*

a rich shade (=a strong and attractive one) *The carpet was a rich shade of brown.*

a subtle/delicate/soft shade (*also* **a muted shade** *formal*): *The flowers were a subtle shade of pink.*

a natural shade *I let my hair go back to its natural shade.*

a neutral shade (=one such as cream, light brown, or grey) *The house had been furnished in neutral shades.*

different/various shades *The dress is available in various shades.*

PREPOSITIONS

a shade of blue/red etc *There were fabrics in every shade of red.*

shadow *n*

the dark shape that forms on a surface when something is between that surface and the light

ADJECTIVES

a dark/black shadow *She saw the dark shadow of a man in the doorway.*

a long shadow *Long shadows stretched across the grass from the apple trees.*

flickering shadows (=shadows that move about quickly) *Candles cast strange flickering shadows on the walls.*

VERBS

cast/throw a shadow (=make it appear) *The old machines cast shadows on the floor.*

a shadow falls somewhere (=appears on something) *The footsteps came closer, and a shadow fell across the table.*

the shadows lengthen (=get longer, as it gets later in the day) *Already the shadows were lengthening.*

move/step out of the shadows (*also* **emerge from the shadows** *formal*): *She was walking home late at night when someone emerged from the shadows and attacked her.*

PREPOSITIONS

among the shadows *The dark animals were difficult to see among the shadows.*

in the shadows *He waited in the shadows until it was safe to come out.*

in the shadow of sth (=where the shadow of something is) *It was hot and we decided to walk in the shadow of the wall.*

shady *adj*

protected from the sun, or producing shade

NOUNS

a shady place/spot *They found a shady spot for a picnic.*

a shady garden *The hotel has a shady garden where you can stroll.*

a shady corner *The plant brightens up a shady corner of the garden.*

a shady tree *The cows were lying under a big shady tree.*

the shady side of sth *We kept on the shady side of the street.*

PHRASES

cool and shady/nice and shady *She sat down somewhere cool and shady.*

THESAURUS: shady

gloomy, shady, murky, dimly lit, unlit, darkened, pitch-dark/pitch-black → **dark (1)**

shake *v*

to make small quick movements from side to side or up and down

ADVERBS

shake violently *The building shook violently for over a minute.*

shake uncontrollably *His body was shaking uncontrollably.*

shake slightly *Adam opened the envelope, his hand shaking slightly.*

be visibly shaking (=in a way that other people can easily see) *He was visibly shaking with anger.*

PHRASES

shake with laughter/anger/fear etc *Both women shook with laughter.*

be shaking all over (=your whole body is shaking) *She was shaking all over, partly from cold, partly from shock.*

be shaking like a leaf (=be shaking a lot because you are nervous or frightened) *I was*

S

shaking like a leaf as I stood up to make the speech.

shake-up *n* THESAURUS change[2]

shaky *adj* THESAURUS weak (1)

shallow *adj* not deep

NOUNS

shallow water *I dipped my hand into the shallow water of the stream.*

a shallow pool *The statue was surrounded by a shallow pool of water.*

a shallow river/lake *The crocodiles live in shallow rivers.*

a shallow hole *The turtle digs a shallow hole in which to lay its eggs.*

a shallow grave *The body was found buried in a shallow grave in the forest.*

a shallow bowl/dish/container *Arrange the vegetables in a shallow dish.*

the shallow end (=of a swimming pool) *He stepped into the pool at the shallow end.*

ANTONYMS **shallow → deep (1)**

shame *n*

1 used when you wish a situation was different, and you feel sad or disappointed

> **Grammar**
> In this meaning, **shame** is usually used in the phrases **it is a shame** and **what a shame**.

PHRASES

it is a shame *It's a shame that you have to leave so soon.*

it is a great/terrible/awful shame *It's a great shame she can't be here with us.*

it is such a shame *It's such a shame to cover this beautiful table with a tablecloth.*

it is a bit of a shame *especially BrE: It's a bit of a shame about the weather.*

it seems a shame/it would be a shame *It seems a shame not to tell her.*

what a shame/that's a shame *"She's failed her test again." "What a shame!"*

it is a crying shame (=it is a very great shame and it should not be allowed to happen) *It would be a crying shame if the trees were cut down.*

PREPOSITIONS

(it's a) shame about sth *It's a lovely place – shame about the weather.*

2 the feeling you have when you feel guilty and embarrassed because you have done something wrong, or someone close to you has done something wrong

ADJECTIVES

deep shame *Afterwards, I was filled with deep shame.*

no shame *There is no shame in admitting you're wrong – people will respect you for it.*

VERBS

feel shame *I feel a lot of shame for what I did.*

be filled with shame *His face was filled with shame.*

bring shame on sb *Leaving her husband would bring shame on the whole family.*

die of shame (=feel very ashamed) *If my parents ever find out about this, I will die of shame.*

PREPOSITIONS

in/with shame (=because you feel ashamed) *Her face turned bright red in shame.*

the shame of sth *He did not want to suffer the shame of defeat.*

sb's shame at sth *The father expressed shame at his son's activities.*

PHRASES

a sense/feeling of shame *There is a growing sense of shame for what happened during the war.*

hang/bow your head in shame (=show by your behaviour that you are very ashamed) *The people who did this should hang their heads in shame.*

a shame attached to sth *In those days there was a lot of shame attached to divorce.*

shape *n*

the form that something has, for example round, square, triangular etc

ADJECTIVES/NOUNS + shape

a square/rectangular/triangular etc shape *The room was a narrow rectangular shape.*

a round/rounded shape *The pills' small rounded shape makes them easy to swallow.*

a heart/diamond/egg etc shape (=like a heart, diamond, egg etc) *The paper had been cut into a diamond shape.*

a V/L etc shape *He cut a little V shape in the paper.*

sb's face/head/body shape *The haircut really suits her face shape.*

an irregular shape *Some of the pots have a very irregular shape.*

a symmetrical shape (=one that is the same on each side) *Her face had a perfectly symmetrical shape.*

a distinctive shape (=one that is easy to recognize) *I recognized him by the distinctive shape of his hat.*

a geometric/geometrical shape (=simple and regular) *The design included simple geometric shapes such as squares and circles.*

VERBS

have a ... shape *The cup had an unusual shape.*

make/create/form a ... shape *Roll out the pastry and trim to form a heart shape.*
sth loses its shape *The T-shirt had stretched and lost its shape.*
sth keeps/holds/retains its shape *The rice retains its shape when cooked.*

PREPOSITIONS

the shape of sth *You can recognize a tree by the shape of its leaves.*
in the shape of sth *There was a lamp in the shape of a bird.*
out of shape (=no longer in the right shape) *The wheel had been bent out of shape.*

PHRASES

be square/rectangular etc in shape *The shield was triangular in shape.*
all shapes and sizes (*also* **every shape and size**) *Pasta comes in all shapes and sizes.*

share[1] *v*

1 to have the same opinion, feeling, or quality as someone else

NOUNS

share a belief/opinion *It was clear that Jim shared her opinion.*
share a view *He shared my view of what had been going on.*
share a feeling (*also* **share a sentiment** *formal*): *I know that many people do not share my feelings.*
share sb's values (=have the same ideas about what is right and wrong) *The only way to change things is to elect politicians who share our values.*
share sb's concern/enthusiasm etc (=feel the same concern, enthusiasm etc as someone else) *I share the concern of parents about the content of some of these computer games.*
share an interest *He shared her passionate interest in Indian culture.*
share a characteristic/trait *Determination was a characteristic he shared with his mother.*

ADVERBS

be widely shared (=shared by a lot of people) *This view is now widely shared.*

PREPOSITIONS

share sth with sb *Art is an interest which I share with my father.*

2 to use or have something with someone else

NOUNS

share a room/bedroom *My brother and I share a bedroom.*
share a house/apartment *At the time, he was sharing a house with two friends.*
share a bed *I'd rather sleep on the floor than share a bed with him.*
share a taxi *Several of us shared taxis back to the hotel.*
share a stage (=act or perform with someone) *For a year, he shared the stage with one of the country's finest actors.*

PREPOSITIONS

share sth with sb *On the school trip, I shared a room with Chloe and Georgia.*

3 to tell other people about your ideas, experiences etc

NOUNS

share your experience *There will be an opportunity for students to share their experiences.*
share information/knowledge *Companies share information about customers.*
share expertise *Teachers should be willing to share their expertise.*
share your thoughts/feelings/ideas *I'd like to share my thoughts with you about this issue.*
share a joke *Would you like to share the joke with the rest of the class?*
share a secret *He desperately wanted to share his secret with her.*

PREPOSITIONS

share sth with sb *Ben didn't feel able to share his feelings with his mother.*

PHRASES

be willing/unwilling to share sth *Our staff are willing to share their knowledge and expertise.*
be reluctant to share sth *All governments are reluctant to share military intelligence.*

share[2] *n*

1 one of the equal parts into which the ownership of a company is divided

VERBS

have/hold/own shares *A lot of the employees own shares in the company.*
invest in/buy shares *The government wanted to encourage people to invest in shares.*
sell shares *This isn't a good time to sell shares.*
trade in/deal in shares (=buy and sell shares as a business) *They make their money by trading in stocks and shares.*
issue shares (=make them available for sale) *A firm can issue shares to raise money.*
shares rise/go up (=their value increases) *The company's shares rose 5.5p to 103p.*
shares fall/go down (=their value decreases) *Shares fell sharply on the London Stock Market yesterday.*

share + NOUNS

share price/value *The company's share price has continued to go down.*
share ownership *There has been an increase in share ownership by employees.*
share dealing (=buying and selling shares as a business) *He was convicted of illegal share dealing.*

a share issue (=an occasion when a company makes new shares available for people to buy) *Most of the money would be raised by a share issue.*

the share index (=the official public list of share prices) *The FTSE 100 share index rose by 150 points.*

PREPOSITIONS

shares in sth *He has shares in several companies.*

PHRASES

stocks and shares *BrE: Do you have any investments such as stocks and shares?*

2 a part of something, especially the part that someone has or gets when it is divided between several people

ADJECTIVES/NOUNS + share

an equal share *Make sure each child gets an equal share of the cake.*

a large/significant/substantial share *They must accept a large share of the responsibility.*

a small share (*also* **a modest share** *formal*): *The company only has a small share of the market in mobile phones.*

a 60%/two-thirds etc share *The deal would give British Airways a 15% share in United Airlines.*

a fair share (=that someone deserves to have) *Everyone will get their fair share of the profits.*

market share (=the percentage of sales in a market that a company or product has) *The company's aim is to increase market share.*

VERBS

get/receive a share *Don't worry, you'll get your share of the money.*

give sb a share *I gave them my share of the bill and left.*

have a share *They gave employees the chance to have a share in the profits.*

increase your share *They have increased their share of the market by 20%.*

do your share (=do part of something) *I do my share of the housework.*

account for a share (=form it) *Sports shoes account for a large share of the footwear market.*

be entitled to a share (=you should be allowed to have it) *You may be entitled to a share of your ex-husband's pension.*

PREPOSITIONS

a share in sth *Anna's share in her grandfather's will was £10,000.*

a share of sth *He couldn't pay his share of the rent.*

PHRASES

the lion's share (=most of something) *The youngest child always gets the lion's share of its mother's attention.*

sharp *adj*

1 having a very thin edge or point

NOUNS

a sharp knife *Remove the peel from an orange using a sharp knife.*

a sharp blade *The blade was so sharp it could cut through bone.*

sharp teeth *This dinosaur had big sharp teeth.*

a sharp spike/spine *The turtle has sharp spikes around the edge of its shell.*

a sharp edge *Crystals have sharp edges.*

a sharp point *He drew a line in the sand with the sharp point of his spear.*

a sharp pencil *He drew the details on the map with a sharp pencil.*

a sharp tool *Early men made sharp tools out of rocks.*

a sharp rock *There are sharp rocks just under the water.*

THESAURUS: sharp

razor-sharp
teeth | blade | edge
extremely sharp:
Sharks have razor-sharp teeth.

pointed
teeth | chin | hat | shoes | stick
ending in a point:
Mice have small pointed teeth. | Witches are usually drawn wearing pointed hats. | They dig using pointed sticks.

jagged
edge | hole | piece | rock | peak | mountain
having an irregular edge with a lot of sharp points:
He cut his finger on the jagged edge of a piece of metal. | The floor was covered with jagged pieces of glass.

spiky
leaves | plant | hair
having a lot of sharp points, or ending in a sharp point:
The plant has spiky leaves. | She had pink spiky hair and wore crazy clothes.

prickly
bush | plant | leaves
covered in a lot of small sharp points. **Prickly** is used mainly about plants:
She fell off her bicycle and landed in a prickly bush. | Most types of holly have prickly leaves.

serrated
edge | blade | knife
a serrated edge on a saw or knife has a lot of sharp points on it:
It's best to use a knife with a serrated edge.

Ways of saying that something is not sharp

You use **blunt** when saying that a knife,

pencil, or tool is not sharp: *She tried to cut the rope, but the **knife** was **blunt**.* **Blunt** is also used in the phrase **a blunt instrument** (= a heavy object that is not sharp, especially one that is used as a weapon): *The man was attacked with a **blunt instrument**.*

You use **dull** about a knife or blade which is not sharp: *The **blade** was **dull** – she would have to sharpen it.*

2 sudden and great

NOUNS

a sharp increase/rise *There has been a sharp increase in crime.*

a sharp drop/fall/decline *There was a sharp fall in the birth rate during the First World War.*

a sharp pain *She felt a sharp pain in her leg.*

a sharp bend/turn/angle *He slowed down before the sharp bend.*

a sharp crack *I heard a sharp crack as the wind tore a branch from a tree.*

sharply *adv*

1 suddenly and by a large amount

VERBS

rise/increase sharply *The value of your investments has risen sharply in recent years.*

fall/drop sharply (*also* **decline sharply** *formal*): *Oil prices fell sharply.*

sharply reduce/cut sth *The new measures could sharply reduce pollution from road traffic.*

deteriorate sharply (=quickly get much worse) *The quality of these services has deteriorated sharply in recent years.*

2 in a way that makes differences very easy to notice

VERBS

contrast sharply (=very much) *Our rail system contrasts sharply with the efficient and affordable systems found in northern Europe.*

differ sharply *Opinions on the importance of sport differ sharply between men and women.*

ADJECTIVES

sharply divided *Opinion is sharply divided on the issue of private education.*

shatter *v*

1 to completely ruin something such as someone's beliefs or life

ADVERBS

completely/totally shatter sth *The news has completely shattered his hopes of competing internationally.*

rudely/abruptly shatter sth (=in a sudden and shocking way) *This book rudely shatters the image of the honourable soldier.*

brutally shatter sth (=in a cruel way) *The attacks brutally shattered America's belief in its ability to defend itself.*

shatter sth irrevocably/irretrievably (=so badly that it can never exist again) *He knew the injury had shattered his career irrevocably.*

NOUNS

shatter sb's hopes *Their hopes for the future had been shattered by the war.*

shatter sb's confidence *Public confidence in the government has been shattered.*

shatter a dream (=make it impossible for someone to achieve or get something they want) *An injury shattered his dream of taking part in the Olympics.*

shatter sb's illusions (=make someone realize that their beliefs are wrong) *I hate to shatter your illusions, but he lied to you.*

shatter an image (=make people realize that the idea they have about something is wrong) *The book shattered the image of the contented American housewife.*

shatter a myth (=show that an idea was completely wrong) *Her research shattered many myths about the differences between men and women.*

shatter the calm/peace of sth *The explosion shattered the calm of a Sunday afternoon in the village.*

2 to break into a lot of pieces, or to make something do this

PHRASES

shatter into pieces *The mirror shattered into a thousand pieces.*

ADVERBS

completely shatter *The car windscreen completely shattered.*

THESAURUS: shatter

smash, shatter, crumble, split, snap, crack, fracture, tear, burst → **break[1] (1)**

shave *v*

to cut off hair very close to the skin, especially from the face, using a razor

NOUNS

shave yourself *He shaved himself in front of the mirror.*

shave your beard/moustache *He shaved his beard and cut his hair.*

shave your head *Karl had shaved his head.*

shave your legs *She showered and shaved her legs.*

PREPOSITIONS/ADVERBS

shave sth off *He had shaved off his beard.*

PHRASES

cut yourself shaving *Brian had cut himself shaving.*

THESAURUS: shave

saw, chop, slice, carve, snip, slit, slash, dice, grate, peel, trim, shave, mow → **cut[1] (1)**

sheet *n*

1 a piece of something flat

ADJECTIVES

a blank/clean sheet (=paper with nothing on it) *He stared at the blank sheet of paper in front of him.*

a folded sheet *She pulled a folded sheet of paper from her pocket.*

a thin/thick sheet *The container is reinforced with thick sheets of metal.*

PHRASES

a sheet of paper/newspaper/card *Have you got a sheet of paper I can use?*

a sheet of glass/plastic/metal etc *A sheet of glass had been placed over the case.*

THESAURUS: sheet

bit, lump, scrap, strip, sheet, slice, chunk, hunk, block, slab, cube, wedge, bar, segment, rasher, fragment, crumb, speck, drop → **piece**

2 a large piece of thin cloth that you put on a bed to lie on or lie under

ADJECTIVES

fresh/clean sheets *He put clean sheets on the spare bed.*

crisp sheets (=clean, fresh, and new) *The bed was made up with crisp white sheets.*

a crumpled sheet *The sheets were crumpled as if someone had slept in them.*

a cotton/silk/satin sheet *There were white cotton sheets on the bed.*

VERBS

change the sheets (=take dirty sheets off a bed and put clean ones on) *I change the sheets every week.*

tuck in a sheet (=push a sheet under the edge of the bed) *Grandma always tucks the sheets in really tightly.*

put a sheet on the bed *I've put some fresh sheets on the bed.*

NOUNS + sheet

a bed sheet *The curtains matched the bed sheets.*

PREPOSITIONS

between the sheets (=in bed) *She lay between the sheets unable to sleep.*

shelf *n*

a long flat piece of wood or other material fastened to a wall or frame, that you put things on

ADJECTIVES/NOUNS + shelf

the top/bottom/middle shelf *There was a photograph of her graduation on the top shelf of the bookcase.*

a glass/wooden shelf *I put my watch on the glass shelf above the sink.*

VERBS

put sth on a shelf/take sth off a shelf *I put the book back on the shelf.*

sit on a shelf (=be on a shelf) *The bottle has been sitting on my shelf for weeks.*

put up/build shelves *I'm going to put up some new shelves in the kitchen.*

stack shelves (=put food products on a shelf in a store) *He works in a supermarket stacking shelves.*

the shelves are filled with sth *The shelves in his office are filled with books.*

line the shelves (=be in a neat row on a shelf) *Jars containing herbs and spices lined the kitchen shelves.*

shelf + NOUNS

shelf space (=the amount of room on a shelf) *I got rid of those old magazines because I needed more shelf space.*

PREPOSITIONS

on a shelf *The glasses are on the top shelf.*

shell *n*

the hard outer part that covers and protects an egg, nut, or the body of some creatures

ADJECTIVES

a hard/soft shell *The nuts have a hard shiny shell.*

a thick/thin shell *The bird's eggs have a thick shell.*

an outer shell *He cracked open the walnut's outer shell.*

a protective shell *Most insects cannot get inside the nut's thick protective shell.*

VERBS

break open/crack open a shell *The monkeys learnt how to break open palm nut shells with a rock.*

NOUNS + shell

a coconut/peanut etc shell *The floor of the bar was littered with peanut shells.*

Seashell and **eggshell** are usually written as one word.

shelter *n*

1 protection from danger or from weather

VERBS

take shelter (=go into a place where you are protected from something) *When it started raining, they took shelter in a cave.*

find shelter *He slept wherever he could find shelter.*

seek shelter *formal* (=try to find shelter) *They sought shelter under the trees.*

run for shelter *The residents were running for shelter from the bombing.*

S

give/provide shelter (*also* **afford shelter** *formal*): *The trees gave shelter from the wind.*

PREPOSITIONS

shelter from sth *Animals were trying to find shelter from the storm.*

the shelter of sth *We were grateful for the shelter of a small cave.*

2 a building or other structure that gives protection from danger or weather

ADJECTIVES/NOUNS + shelter

a temporary shelter *The huts were used by climbers as a temporary shelter from bad weather.*

a makeshift shelter (=made from any materials that are available) *Old pieces of wood had been used to build a makeshift shelter.*

a crude/rough shelter (=built quickly and without skill) *Someone had made a crude shelter against the wall.*

a bomb shelter/air-raid shelter (=protecting people from bombs dropped by planes) *There's a large bomb shelter beneath the apartment building.*

VERBS

build/make/construct a shelter *We can cut off a few branches to make a rough shelter.*

shelve *v* THESAURUS **cancel**

shift Ac *n*

1 a change in the way people think about something, in the way something is done etc

ADJECTIVES

a big/major shift *There has been a big shift in people's attitudes to marriage.*

a significant/marked shift (=big and noticeable) *There was a significant shift in government policy on education.*

a fundamental shift (=a complete change) *The 1960s saw a fundamental shift in attitudes to sex.*

a sudden shift *She hated his sudden shifts of mood.*

a dramatic shift (=a big and sudden change) *There needs to be a dramatic shift in behaviour if we are to tackle climate change.*

a small/slight/subtle shift *The opinion polls showed a slight shift in people's views about the president.*

a gradual shift *There has been a gradual shift of power.*

VERBS

mark/represent a shift *The idea represents a dramatic shift in healthcare policy.*

cause/produce a shift (*also* **bring about a shift**) *The recession brought about a shift in people's views on the environment.*

see/detect/notice a shift *Some commentators detect a shift in the government's attitude.*

PREPOSITIONS

a shift in sth *Has there been a shift in American attitudes towards Russia?*

a shift towards/toward sth *We're seeing a shift towards buying goods online.*

a shift away from sth *There has been a huge shift away from the postal system as our main means of communication.*

THESAURUS: shift

alteration, reform, shift, swing, fluctuation, transformation, revolution, shake-up, U-turn → **change²**

2 a part of a working day in a factory, hospital etc

ADJECTIVES/NOUNS + shift

the night/day shift *She worked on the night shift in a busy hospital.*

the morning/afternoon/evening shift *All the machines are cleaned at the end of every afternoon shift.*

the early/late shift *Nobody wants to do the late shift.*

a 10-hour/12-hour etc shift *The nurses are sometimes asked to work 12-hour shifts.*

VERBS

work/do a shift *Some doctors work very long shifts.*

finish a shift *I had just finished a 10-hour shift and was exhausted.*

change shifts (=when one person's shift finishes as another person's starts) *The only time the factory is busy is when workers are changing shifts.*

shift + NOUNS

shift work/working (=working shifts) *Many healthcare jobs involve shift work.*

shine *v* to produce bright light

ADVERBS

shine brightly *The sun shone brightly in the sky.*

PHRASES

shine in sb's eyes (=shine in a way that makes it difficult for someone to see things) *That lamp's shining in my eyes.*

shiny *adj*

having a smooth bright surface

NOUNS

shiny shoes/boots *The boy was wearing shiny new shoes.*

shiny hair/fur *Her hair was long and shiny.*

shiny teeth/lips/eyes *When he smiled you could see his shiny gold teeth.*

shiny skin/face/nose/forehead *His face was shiny with sweat.*

shiny paper/plastic/metal/leather *The plane's wings were made of shiny metal.*

a shiny suit *The salesman was wearing a shiny silk suit.*

a shiny car *The man got out of a shiny red sports car.*

a shiny surface *I looked at my reflection in the shiny surface of the table.*

a shiny object *Crows like picking up shiny objects.*

shiny leaves *The plant has big shiny leaves.*

a shiny apple *He picked a shiny red apple off the tree.*

PHRASES

all shiny and new *The floor was all shiny and new.*

THESAURUS: shiny

glossy
hair | fur | leaves | magazine | brochure | advertisement | pages | photograph | cover | paper | surface
glossy hair, fur, or leaves look shiny and healthy. **Glossy** magazines and books use expensive shiny paper:
The shampoo is supposed to make your hair glossy. | The dog's fur was all glossy. | She was looking at the pictures in a glossy magazine. | The printer uses special paper which has a glossy surface on one side.

sleek
fur | body | shape | lines | curves | car | plane
shiny and smooth in a way that looks very attractive:
He stroked the cat's sleek fur. | The picture emphasizes the building's sleek modern lines (=its smooth shiny shape). | *She arrived in a sleek white sports car.*

silky
fabric | material | texture | dress | hair | skin
very soft and smooth to touch, like silk:
Her jacket was made of a smooth silky fabric. | Fernando stroked her long silky hair.

gleaming
teeth | smile | eyes | hair | car | motorcycle | building | floor | walls | glass | wood | sand | gold | silver | paintwork
very shiny and clean – used especially about something that has just been cleaned or polished, or when someone looks happy or excited:
I could see his gleaming white teeth. | Her eyes were gleaming with amusement. | The capital is full of gleaming new office buildings. | The tourist brochures show mile after mile of gleaming white sand.

Collocations with words meaning shiny
With all these words, often the next word is a colour: *shiny* ***black*** *shoes | glossy* ***brown*** *hair | a sleek* ***white*** *sports car | gleaming* ***white*** *teeth*

glistening *literary*
skin | hair | eyes | body | drop
something that is glistening is shiny, especially because it is wet:
A glistening drop of water fell off the branch. | His shoulders were ***glistening with sweat****. | Her eyes were* ***glistening with tears****.*

lustrous *literary*
hair | eyes | lips | pearls | sheen | surface
shining in a soft gentle way which looks very attractive:
She pushed back her lustrous dark brown hair. | His eyes were dark and lustrous. | The fabric has a smooth lustrous surface.

dull
eyes | surface
not shiny or bright – used about things that should be shiny:
They stared at him with dull eyes. | The oil helps restore the shine to a dull surface.

matt/matte
paint | paper | surface | finish
matt paint and paper is specially designed not to be shiny:
Some people think matt paint looks better. | I printed the photos on matte paper.

ship *n*

a large boat used for carrying people or goods across the sea

NOUNS + ship

a passenger ship (=one that carries people) *The 'Titanic' was the world's biggest and most expensive passenger ship.*

a cruise ship (=a large ship that people have holidays on) *Visit the ancient temples and the tombs of the Pharaohs as your cruise ship sails down the Nile to Luxor.*

a cargo ship/merchant ship (=one that carries goods) *A cargo ship carrying nuclear waste was refused permission to dock.*

a container ship (=one that carries goods in special containers which can be put on trucks) *The goods are brought from China on massive container ships.*

Battleship and **warship** are written as one word.

ship + VERBS

a ship sails somewhere *A big ship sailed into the harbour.*

a ship carries sth *The ship was carrying over a thousand tons of oil.*
a ship arrives/docks somewhere (=it stops at a port) *The ship docked at Southampton.*
a ship takes on sb/sth *The ship took on more passengers at the next port.*
a ship unloads its cargo *I went down to the harbour to see the ships unloading their cargo.*
a ship sinks/goes down *The ship sank when it hit an iceberg.*

VERBS + ship

sail the ship *He sailed the ship around the world.*
steer a ship (=control the direction of a ship) *I steered the ship out into the ocean.*
anchor/moor a ship (=tie it somewhere so that it does not move) *We anchored the ship a few hundred yards from the shore.*
name a ship *They named the ship the 'Queen Mary'.*
abandon ship (=leave the ship, because you are in a dangerous situation) *The captain gave the order to abandon ship.*

PREPOSITIONS

by ship *Most of the wine is sent by ship.*

PHRASES

a ship sets sail/puts to sea (=it starts a journey) *The ship set sail for the New World.*
a ship runs/goes aground (=it gets stuck in shallow water) *The ship ran aground off the coast of Italy.*
go on board/go aboard a ship (=get on it) *We waited to go on board the ship.*

S

shirt *n*

a piece of clothing that covers the upper part of your body and your arms, usually has a collar, and is fastened at the front by buttons

ADJECTIVES/NOUNS + shirt

a clean shirt *Comb your hair and put on a clean shirt.*
an open-necked shirt (=a shirt with the top button unfastened) *It's quite common now for men to wear an open-necked shirt with a suit.*
a check/checked shirt (*also* **a plaid shirt** *AmE*) (=with a pattern of squares and crossed lines) *I think I'll wear my short-sleeve check shirt.*
a striped shirt *The men wore business suits and striped shirts.*
a long-sleeved/long-sleeve shirt *He put on a long-sleeved shirt to protect his arms from the sun.*
a short-sleeved/short-sleeve shirt *I usually wear short-sleeved shirts in the summertime.*

VERBS

wear a shirt *He wore a checked shirt and jeans.*
put on a shirt *I put on a clean shirt and went out.*
wash a shirt *Thanks for washing my shirt, Mum.*
iron a shirt *I need to iron my shirt.*
button up/do up your shirt *He stood in front of the mirror, buttoning up his shirt.*
unbutton/undo your shirt *I took off my tie and unbuttoned my shirt.*

shirt + NOUNS

sb's shirt pocket *He put the ticket in his shirt pocket.*
sb's shirt collar *His suit looked old and his shirt collar was worn.*
sb's shirt sleeves *He rolled up his shirt sleeves.*

PHRASES

a shirt and tie *I have to wear a shirt and tie to work.*
be in shirt sleeves (=not wearing a jacket) *The mayor was dressed informally in shirt sleeves.*

shock[1] *n*

1 a strong feeling of surprise, especially because of something unpleasant

ADJECTIVES

a big/great shock *It was a big shock when he lost his job.*
a terrible/awful shock *Her death was a terrible shock to everyone.*
a complete/total shock *No one expected the factory to close – it was a complete shock.*
a nasty shock *especially BrE* (=very unpleasant and upsetting) *Come and sit down. You've had a nasty shock.*
the initial shock (=the shock when something first happens) *After the initial shock when she discovered she was pregnant, she soon got used to the idea.*

NOUNS + shock

culture shock (=the feeling of being confused or anxious when you visit a place that is very different from what you are used to) *Moving to London was a bit of a culture shock after ten years of living in the country.*

VERBS

get/have a shock *I got a shock when I saw how thin he had become.*
give sb a shock *Oh! You gave me quite a shock.*
get over/recover from a shock *He hasn't got over the shock of losing his job yet.*
lessen a shock (=make it less strong) *Knowing that someone is going to die does not lessen the shock when it happens.*

shock + NOUNS

shock tactics (=ways of attracting people's attention by shocking them) *The latest advertisement uses shock tactics to get people to drive more safely.*
shock value (=an interesting quality that something has because it is shocking) *A lot of the things he did were for shock value.*
a shock decision/announcement/defeat etc (=one that was not expected) *His shock resignation surprised everyone.*

PREPOSITIONS

shock at sth *Neighbours expressed their shock at the murder.*

the shock of sth *The shock of the burglary could have caused her death.*

in shock (=shocked) *I'm in shock - I can't believe this has happened.*

with a shock *She realized with a shock that he was dead.*

PHRASES

a feeling/sense of shock *He realized with a sense of shock that he had been shot.*

come as a shock (*also* **be a bit of a shock** *BrE especially spoken*) (=be very unexpected) *The collapse of the company came as a shock to us all.*

be a shock to the system (=be strange because you are not used to something) *Having to work full-time again was quite a shock to the system.*

be in for a shock (=be likely to have a shock) *Anyone who thinks that bringing up children is easy is in for a shock.*

be in a state of shock (*also* **be in deep shock**) (=be very shocked and upset) *Eva left the room in a state of shock.*

get the shock of your life (=get a very big shock) *He got the shock of his life when he found out who I was.*

nearly die of shock *informal* (=be very surprised) *I nearly died of shock when I saw Helen at the door.*

2 a medical condition you get after a bad or frightening experience

ADJECTIVES

severe shock (=serious) *Many of the victims were suffering from severe shock.*

mild shock (=not very serious) *She was taken to the hospital with symptoms of mild shock.*

delayed shock (=not immediately after a shocking event) *Delayed shock can affect people in many different ways.*

NOUNS + shock

shell shock (=mental illness caused by terrible experiences fighting a war) *Many of the soldiers who returned from the war were suffering from shell shock.*

VERBS

be in/be suffering from shock *He was bleeding from the head and suffering from shock.*

go into shock *A person can go into shock for many different reasons.*

treat sb for shock *The driver was treated for shock and later released from hospital.*

shock[2] *v*

to make someone feel very surprised and upset, and unable to believe what has happened

ADVERBS

shock sb deeply *The news had shocked him deeply.*

be easily shocked *Don't go see this movie if you are easily shocked.*

PHRASES

be shocked to hear/see sth *I was shocked to hear that Pete had died.*

be shocked to find/discover/learn sth *We arrived at the hotel, and were shocked to find that our reservation had been cancelled.*

have/lose the power to shock (sb) *These old photographs still have the power to shock.*

shocked *adj*

feeling surprised and upset by something very unexpected and unpleasant

ADVERBS

deeply shocked *We are all deeply shocked by what's happened.*

badly shocked *She arrived home badly shocked but unharmed.*

genuinely shocked *He sounded genuinely shocked when I told him the news.*

visibly shocked (=in a way that is easy for others to see) *She was visibly shocked by the conditions she witnessed in the camps.*

NOUNS

shocked silence *There was a moment of shocked silence in the room.*

shocked surprise/amazement *He smiled at her expression of shocked surprise.*

sb's shocked expression/face *I could see shocked expressions in the audience.*

sb's shocked reaction *We did not expect such a shocked reaction to the film.*

shocked onlookers (=people who see something happen and are shocked by it) *The camera captured the faces of shocked onlookers.*

VERBS

seem/look/appear shocked *Bad news had been expected but people still looked shocked.*

sound shocked *"Of course not!" he exclaimed, sounding shocked.*

PREPOSITIONS

shocked at/by sth *They were shocked at the news.*

shocking *adj*

making you feel very surprised or upset

ADVERBS

very/deeply/profoundly shocking *The news was deeply shocking for his family.*

absolutely shocking *The photographs of the car after the accident were absolutely shocking.*

truly shocking *This is a truly shocking situation and something needs to be done about it.*

particularly shocking *His death was particularly*

S

shocking since the government were obviously involved in some way.

VERBS

find sth shocking *I found the case really shocking.*

NOUNS

shocking news *Anne heard the shocking news that Cormac O'Neill had hanged himself.*

a shocking waste of sth *The scheme was a shocking waste of money.*

in a shocking state *When we first arrived, the house was in a shocking state.*

the shocking truth about sth *The media reported the shocking truth about the camps.*

shoe *n*

something that you wear to cover your feet, made of leather or some other strong material

ADJECTIVES/NOUNS + shoe

leather/suede etc shoes *He was wearing an old pair of leather shoes.*

running/jogging/training/tennis shoes *Get yourself a good pair of running shoes if you want to take up running.*

school/work shoes *The children all need new school shoes.*

high-heeled shoes *You can't walk round town all day in high-heeled shoes!*

flat shoes (=with no high heel) *Flat shoes are much more comfortable for walking in.*

sensible shoes (=that are easy to walk in and do not hurt your feet) *They were the kind of sensible shoes my mother used to make me wear.*

VERBS

wear shoes *He was wearing smart black shoes.*

put your shoes on *Put your shoes on and get your coat.*

take your shoes off *They took off their shoes in the hallway.*

⚠ Don't say 'put off your shoes'.

tie your shoes (*also* **lace up your shoes**) *He bent over to tie his shoes.*

slip your shoes on/off (=put them on or take them off quickly or gently) *She slipped off her shoes and lay on the couch.*

kick your shoes off (=take them off using your feet, not your hands) *Maria kicked off her shoes and sat down.*

clean/polish your shoes *We used to clean our shoes every evening before we went to bed.*

shoe + NOUNS

a shoe shop *BrE*, **a shoe store** *AmE*: *There's a shoe shop on the next corner.*

shoe size *My son has the same shoe size as me.*

shoe polish *Do you have any brown shoe polish?*

Shoelaces (=things like strings that you use for tying your shoes) are usually written as one word.

PHRASES

a pair of shoes *I need a new pair of shoes.*

shoes and socks *He walks around without his shoes and socks on.*

shoot *v*

to use a gun to fire bullets, or to kill or injure someone using a gun

PHRASES

shoot yourself *Smith killed his boss and then shot himself.*

shoot sb dead *The man was shot dead in an attempted robbery.*

shoot sb in the leg/arm/back etc *The victims had been shot in the back.*

shoot to kill (=shoot with the intention of killing someone) *The next time they said they would shoot to kill.*

shoot sb on sight (=as soon as you see someone) *The guards have orders to shoot on sight anyone who tries to escape.*

shop *n*

a building or part of a building where you can buy things

ADJECTIVES/NOUNS + shop

a shop is closed/shut *The shops are all closed on Sunday evening.*

a shop is open *The shops are open till late on Fridays.*

a food/clothes/flower/shoe etc shop *You can buy them in any good health food shop.*

high street shops *BrE*: *Many high street shops are having difficulties because of the recession.*

a local shop *We get most of our things from the local shop.*

a corner shop (=a small local shop on the corner of a street in a town) *The corner shop sells newspapers and cigarettes.*

a village shop *The village shop is the centre of life in the village.*

Bookshop is usually written as one word.

VERBS + shop

buy sth in/from a shop *I bought the dress in a shop on Kensington High Street.*

go to the shops (=go shopping) *She has gone to the shops to get some milk.*

wander around/look around the shops *I spent a happy afternoon wandering around the shops.*

own a shop *The shop is owned by my father.*

run a shop *His uncle runs a fruit shop.*

establish/set up a shop *The shop was established in 1922.*

take sth back to the shop *I took the bike back to the shop because there was something wrong with the brakes.*

shop + VERBS

a shop opens *The shops open at 9.30.*

a shop closes/shuts *The shops all close early today.*

a shop sells sth *Do you know a shop that sells watch batteries?*

shop + NOUNS

a shop window *Shirley saw the doll in the shop window.*

PREPOSITIONS

in the shops *New potatoes are in the shops now.*

PHRASES

the man/woman in the shop (=the person who sells you something in a shop) *The man in the shop said that the battery would last for at least three years.*

Shop is used especially in British English. American speakers usually say **store**.

shopping *n*

the activity of going to shops or using websites to buy things

VERBS

go shopping *We went shopping and I bought a new skirt.*

do the shopping/do some shopping etc *I need to do some shopping tomorrow.*

ADJECTIVES/NOUNS + shopping

weekly shopping *She does her weekly shopping in the supermarket.*

grocery/food shopping *I do my grocery shopping online.*

clothes shopping *My husband doesn't enjoy clothes shopping.*

Christmas shopping *Have you done all your Christmas shopping?*

internet/online shopping *The growth of internet shopping has affected many high street stores.*

window shopping (=when you look at goods in shop windows but do not intend to buy anything) *It was just window shopping – I couldn't really afford to buy anything.*

shopping + NOUNS

a shopping list (=a list of what you need to buy, especially of food) *Always take a shopping list so you are not tempted to buy things you do not need.*

a shopping mall (*also* **a shopping centre** *BrE*) (=building with many shops in it) *We drove to a big out-of-town shopping mall.*

a shopping expedition/trip *I took him on a shopping trip for his birthday.*

a shopping spree (=when you buy a lot of things) *She went on a shopping spree with her parents' credit card.*

short *adj*

1 not continuing for a long time

NOUNS

a short time *I lived in Canada for a short time.*

a short period (of time) *She returned to work after a short period of time.*

a short holiday/vacation/visit *The family are in Florida for a short vacation.*

a short journey/trip *Cycling is good for short journeys in city areas.*

a short walk/drive/flight *It's only a short walk to the beach.*

a short break/pause/delay *Let's take a short break for lunch.*

a short course *The college offers short courses in design.*

a short life/career *In his short life, he published eleven volumes of poetry.*

the shortest route/way *We went by the shortest possible route.*

VERBS

get shorter *Winter is coming and the days are getting shorter.*

keep sth short *There's not much time, so I'll keep it short.*

ADVERBS

relatively/comparatively short (=rather short) *The city's population rose from 100,000 to 1 million in a relatively short period.*

PHRASES

in/after a short while *especially spoken* (=in or after a short period of time) *He will be back in a short while.*

in a short space of time (=used when a lot happens or someone does a lot in a short period of time) *Students have to learn a vast amount of information in a short space of time.*

in the short term (=in the near future) *The situation is unlikely to improve in the short term.*

in a few short weeks/months/years (=used when saying that something seems to happen very quickly) *In a few short years the children will all have grown up.*

at short notice (=you are only told about something a short time before it happens) *The meeting was cancelled at short notice.*

short and sweet *especially spoken* (=short in a way that is good) *She was feeling tired, so we kept our visit short and sweet.*

THESAURUS: short

brief

period | **moment** | **instant** | **look** | **glimpse** | **visit** | **stay** | **appearance** | **pause** | **silence** | **smile**

lasting only for a short time. **Brief** is more formal than **short**:
There was a brief period of calm. | Fans caught a brief glimpse of the singer as he came out of his hotel (=they saw him for a short time). *| She makes a brief appearance in the film.*

Brief or short?
Brief is more formal, and is often used about things that are very short. With some words, **brief** is more common than **short**. You usually say a **brief moment/ glimpse/appearance**. You always say a **brief instant** (not a 'short' one).

quick
look | glance | check | wash | shower | bath | visit | meal | drink | response | way
taking only a short time to do something:
I had a quick glance at my watch. | Is there time for a quick shower? | We can have a quick meal at the airport. | The quickest way is by bus.

temporary
accommodation | home | shelter | job | work | employment | solution | measure
only expected to continue for a short time and not permanent:
The family are living in temporary accommodation until the work is completed. | Ben found a temporary job for the summer.

short-lived
success | triumph | victory | glory | joy | interest | romance | marriage | optimism | ceasefire
lasting only for a short time, especially shorter than you wanted:
Unfortunately, the team's success was short-lived and they lost the next game. | She shocked the world with her short-lived marriage to Frank Sinatra.

short-term
profits | gains | effect | benefit | solution | contract | loan
used about something that is only expected to continue for a short time in the future:
Some companies were only interested in short-term profits, and didn't care about the long-term effects on the environment. | Scientists studied the short-term effects of reduced sleep on the brain. | Borrowing more money is only a short-term solution to the country's economic problems.

fleeting
moment | instant | second | glimpse | glance | visit | appearance | smile | expression | thought | impression
lasting only for an extremely short time:
For a fleeting moment I saw his face in the mirror. | It was cloudy most of the time and we only had a fleeting glimpse of the sun.

momentary
pause | silence | lapse | hesitation | panic | confusion | pleasure | desire | relief
lasting for a very short time - used especially about feelings or pauses:
The accident was caused by a momentary lapse in concentration by one of the drivers (=they stopped paying attention for a very short time). *| There was a momentary panic when I thought I'd lost my wallet.*

passing
phase | fashion | fad | mention | reference | interest | thought
lasting only for a short time - used especially when someone is only interested in something for a short time, or only mentions something very quickly:
Some children won't eat vegetables, but usually this is just a passing phase. | He made only a passing reference to the other members of the team.

Passing is always used before a noun.

ephemeral *formal*
beauty | nature | world
lasting only for a short time, and ending quickly like everything else in this world:
Snow has a kind of ephemeral beauty. | In the ephemeral world of popular culture, people suddenly become famous and then are never heard of again.

ANTONYMS **short → long (2)**

2 not long in length or distance

NOUNS

a short distance/way *She lived a short distance from the school.*

a short piece of sth *The papers were tied together with a short piece of string.*

short hair/fur *Her hair was cut short, like a man's.*

short fingers/arms/legs/body *My arms are too short for this jacket.*

a short skirt/dress/jacket/coat *The school did not allow girls to wear short skirts.*

short sleeves *Short sleeves are cooler in summer.*

ANTONYMS **short → long (1)**

3 consisting of only a few pages, words, or letters

NOUNS

a short book/article/report/essay *His short book, 'The Problems of Philosophy', is an excellent introduction to the subject.*

a short speech/talk/statement *The company issued a short statement apologizing for any inconvenience.*

a short word/phrase/name/title *His films usually have short titles.*

S

a short description *Write a short description of the main character in the story.*

a short answer *The short answer is 'no'.*

a shorter version of sth *A shorter version of this article appeared in the 'Chicago Tribune' on 27 September.*

a short piece (of writing) *They have asked me to write a short piece for the school magazine.*

VERBS

keep sth short *It's usually best to keep your sentences short.*

THESAURUS: short

brief
description | statement | mention | account | introduction | explanation | outline | summary | overview | history | survey
using only a few words and not giving a lot of details:
*There is a brief description of the hotel in the brochure. | The subject only receives a brief mention in his book. | Austen offers us a brief account of Emma's past and present situation. | Can you **be brief**? We don't have a lot of time.*

Brief or short?
Brief is often used when you do not give many details. **Short** just means "not long".
Brief is more common than **short** with **description**, **statement**, **account**, **introduction**, **explanation**, **outline**, and **summary**.
You say **be brief,** (not 'be short'). You give something a **brief mention**, (not a 'short' one).

concise
description | account | analysis | statement | summary | overview | instructions | style | way
short and clear, and with no unnecessary words or information:
*The author provides a concise analysis of the country's recent history. | She writes in a very **clear and concise** style.*

succinct
comment | answer | reply | statement | language | explanation
using only very few words, so that the meaning of what you are saying is very clear:
Prescott's comments on articles about him are succinct: "I don't read them. I never see them." | I will try to keep my answers as succinct as possible.

Concise or succinct?
Concise is often used about longer pieces of text, for example in a book. **Succinct** is often used about short answers and comments that someone makes.

pithy
description | comment | observation | phrase | saying | slogan | quote
using only a few words, in a way that expresses something cleverly and well:
His poems are full of sharp pithy descriptions. | It is sometimes difficult to put all your ideas into one pithy phrase.

ANTONYMS **short → long (3)**

4 not tall

NOUNS

a short man/woman/boy/girl *He was a short man of about 55.*

short grass *The grass is kept short by the sheep.*

Short sounds very direct and not very polite. It sounds gentler and more polite to say that someone is **not very tall**: *She wasn't very tall – maybe about 1.60 metres.*

THESAURUS: short

small
man | woman | boy | girl | child | tree | plant | flower | animal | dog | horse
used about someone who is short and has a small body. You also use **small** about plants, trees, and animals that are not big in size:
*He was a small man, about five feet in height. | The girl was quite **small for her age*** (=smaller than other girls of the same age). | *Small dogs often make a lot of noise.*

low
hill | building | table | chair | wall | ceiling | bridge | tree
used about things that are not high:
The city is surrounded by low hills. | They sat on the floor around a low table. | The bird builds its nests in low trees.

petite
woman
used about a woman who is short and thin in an attractive way:
Catherine was a petite woman with long blonde hair. | She is slim, petite, and very feminine.

dumpy
woman | girl | figure | body
used about a short woman or girl who does not look attractive because she is rather fat:
His wife was a short dumpy woman with glasses. | Agnes thought that a dumpy girl should not wear a tall hat.

stocky
man | boy | child | build | figure
rather short, with a strong heavy-looking body – used especially about men and boys:
The referee was a stocky man with a whistle round his neck. | The police say he is of stocky

S

build (=he has a short heavy body). | *A stocky figure with powerful forearms stood next to the bar.*

diminutive *formal*
figure | size | stature | body | star
short and with a small body – used especially in descriptions in novels:
A diminutive figure dressed in black entered the room. | *With his diminutive stature and mild voice, it was hard to imagine him threatening anyone* (=short height).

stunted
trees | growth | development
if something is stunted, it is short because it has been damaged or has not grown properly:
All that remained of the forest was a few stunted trees. | *Lack of calcium can result in stunted growth* (=stop someone's body from growing and developing).

ANTONYMS **short → tall**

shortage *n*

a situation in which there is not enough of something that people need

ADJECTIVES

a severe/serious shortage *There is a serious shortage of food.*
an acute shortage (=very bad) *Hospitals are suffering from an acute shortage of trained medical staff.*
a desperate/dire shortage (=very serious and worrying) *There is a desperate shortage of fresh drinking water.*
a chronic shortage (=very bad and existing for a long time) *There is a chronic shortage of housing in rural areas.*
a growing shortage (=increasing) *The country is facing a growing shortage of skilled workers.*
a general shortage (=a shortage of lots of different kinds of things or people) *There was a general shortage of all types of goods.*
a national/nationwide shortage (=throughout a country) *The education authority says there is a national shortage of teachers.*

NOUNS + shortage

a water/food/housing etc shortage *The water shortage was reaching crisis proportions.*
a labour/manpower shortage (=a shortage of people to do work) *During the war, there was a severe labour shortage, so women began doing jobs they had never done before.*
a staff shortage (=a shortage of people to work at a particular business) *The company blamed staff shortages for the delays.*
a world shortage (=a shortage all over the world) *There is likely to be a world shortage of oil in the future.*

VERBS

there is a shortage of sth *Everyone knows there is a shortage of doctors.*
create/cause a shortage *Poor harvests could cause food shortages in the winter.*
lead to/result in a shortage *The strike led to serious shortages of fuel in some areas.*
face a shortage (=be likely to suffer a shortage) *The refugees face desperate shortages of food and water.*
ease a shortage (=make it less serious) *Heavy rain has helped ease the water shortages of previous years.*
worsen a shortage (*also* **exacerbate a shortage** *formal*) (=make it more serious) *The low status of manufacturing has exacerbated the shortage of engineers.*

PREPOSITIONS

a shortage of sth *The shortage of drugs means that people are dying unnecessarily.*

short-term *adj* THESAURUS **short (1)**

shot *n*

1 an act of firing a gun

VERBS + shot

fire a shot *The man fired three shots into the car.*
take a shot at sb (=fire a shot trying to hit someone) *Someone took a shot at her, but missed.*
hear a shot *Where were you when you heard the shot?*

shot + VERBS

a shot hits sb/sth *The shot hit Paul in the chest.*
a shot kills sb *It was the second shot that killed him.*
a shot misses sb/sth (=doesn't hit them) *The first shot missed my head by inches.*
a shot rings out (=is heard) *Suddenly, two shots rang out.*

ADJECTIVES

a single shot (=just one shot) *He died from a single shot to his heart.*
the fatal shot (=the shot that killed someone) *It wasn't clear who had fired the fatal shot.*
a good shot *It was difficult to get a good shot in the dense forest.*

NOUNS + shot

a pistol/rifle shot (=from a particular type of gun) *It sounded like a pistol shot.*
a warning shot (=one fired as a warning to someone) *Police fired warning shots into the air.*

Gunshot (= an occasion when a gun is fired) is written as one word.

PREPOSITIONS

a shot from sth *We heard two shots from a gun.*

a shot to sth *He was killed by a shot to the back of the head.*

PHRASES

take a pot shot at sb/sth (=shoot at them without aiming carefully) *The boy took a pot shot at one of the passing cars.*

a volley of shots (=a number of shots fired quickly) *He fired off a volley of shots from his rifle.*

2 an act of kicking, throwing, or hitting a ball

VERBS + shot

take a shot *He took a shot and scored.*

hit a shot *The player hit a low shot into the far corner of the goal.*

miss a shot *How could she miss such an easy shot?*

save a shot *The goalkeeper saved an excellent shot from Torres.*

block a shot *The shot was blocked by one of the defenders.*

shot + VERBS

a shot misses *The shot missed the goal.*

a shot goes in *The crowd went wild when Woods's shot went in.*

a shot goes wide (=it misses the goal and goes to the side of it) *He struck the ball but his shot went wide.*

ADJECTIVES

a great/excellent/fine shot *Lee Fagan scored with a great shot in the final moments of the game.*

a bad/poor/terrible shot *I hit some terrible shots today.*

an easy shot (=one that someone should score) *It should have been an easy shot for a tall girl like Rose.*

a long/straight/low etc shot *He kicked a long shot into the back of the net.*

3 used when saying how good someone is at shooting, throwing, kicking etc something at a target

ADJECTIVES

a good/great/bad/terrible etc shot *After all the practice, he was becoming a very good shot.*

4 a photograph

VERBS

take a shot *First, he took some shots of the beach.*

get a shot *You'll get a better shot from over here.*

ADJECTIVES

a good shot *I managed to get some good shots of the runners.*

NOUNS + shot

a close-up shot (=which shows someone or something from very close) *I want a close-up shot of your face.*

an action shot (=taken of someone while they are moving) *She showed me some action shots of the players.*

a publicity shot (=for advertising something) *We hired a photographer to take some publicity shots.*

> **Snapshot** (= a photograph that you take quickly of someone or something, for example when you are on holiday) is written as one word.

PREPOSITIONS

a shot of sth *I wanted to get a shot of our hotel.*

shoulder *n*

one of the two parts of the body at each side of the neck where the arm is connected

ADJECTIVES

broad/wide shoulders *He was of medium height, with broad shoulders.*

strong/powerful shoulders *He had powerful shoulders and a thick neck.*

massive/huge shoulders *He pushed the door open with his massive shoulders.*

narrow/slim shoulders *Her dark hair spilled over her narrow shoulders.*

thin/bony shoulders *She put her arm around the girl's thin shoulders.*

a dislocated shoulder (=one in which the bone has moved out of its correct position) *He's in a lot of pain with his dislocated shoulder.*

VERBS

shrug your shoulders (=raise them to show that you do not know or care about something) *Susan just shrugged her shoulders and said nothing.*

hunch your shoulders (=raise your shoulders and bend them forwards slightly) *He hunched his shoulders against the rain.*

look/glance over your shoulder (=look behind you) *He glanced over his shoulder to see if she was following him.*

dislocate your shoulder (=injure it by the bone moving out of its correct place) *George has dislocated his shoulder and won't play in Saturday's game.*

shout[1] *v* to say something very loudly

ADVERBS

shout angrily *"Don't touch me!" he shouted angrily.*

shout loudly *He hears the voice of his downstairs neighbor shouting loudly.*

shout back *"I'm coming!" she shouted back.*

shout up/down *I was in my room when my dad shouted up that dinner was ready.*

PREPOSITIONS

shout at sb *I try not to shout at the children.*

shout sth to sb *"He's down here!" she shouted to me.*

shout for help/attention/a doctor etc *I opened my mouth to shout for help.*

PHRASES

shout at the top of your voice (=shout as loudly as possible) *"Watch out!" he shouted at the top of his voice.*

screaming and shouting *You don't persuade people to do what you want by screaming and shouting.*

shout² *n*

a loud call expressing anger, pain, excitement etc

ADJECTIVES/NOUNS + shout

a loud shout *I could hear loud shouts coming from downstairs.*

a great/mighty shout (=a very loud shout) *With a great shout the soldiers ran towards the enemy lines.*

an angry shout *There were angry shouts from the audience when the show suddenly ended early.*

a muffled shout (=one that cannot be heard clearly) *Someone heard his muffled shouts for help coming from behind the wall.*

a warning shout *He failed to hear the warning shouts, and was swept away by the water.*

VERBS

give a shout *Dad gave a loud shout, pointing to thick smoke coming from the car.*

let out a shout *Sam let out a shout and started to run.*

hear a shout *I could hear faint shouts coming from next door.*

a shout goes up (=a group of people start shouting) *As the band came on stage, a great shout went up from the crowd.*

PHRASES

a shout of encouragement/laughter/anger etc *There were shouts of encouragement from his family and friends.*

show¹ *v*

to prove that something is true

ADVERBS

show sth clearly *The evidence shows clearly that he is innocent.*

show sth conclusively (=so that there can be no doubt at all) *Dozens of studies have shown conclusively that there is a link between smoking and cancer.*

VERBS

appear/seem to show sth *These figures appear to show that the crime rate has gone down.*

try to show sth *In this article I have tried to show that these two ideas are linked.*

be expected to show sth *The statistics are expected to show that the economy is getting better.*

PHRASES

show sth beyond reasonable doubt (=so that there can be no doubt - used about crimes) *The prosecution has to show beyond reasonable doubt that the accused person is guilty.*

show² *n*

1 a television or radio programme

ADJECTIVES/NOUNS + show

a TV/television/radio show *What's your favourite TV show?*

a comedy/news/quiz show *We always watch the morning news show.*

a game show (=in which people play games or answer questions to win prizes) *It's a popular game show in which you can win a million dollars.*

a chat show *BrE*, **a talk show** *AmE* (=in which famous or interesting people talk to someone about themselves) *She was on the chat show to talk about her new movie.*

a reality (TV) show (=showing ordinary people doing real things) *'The Hotel' is a reality TV show about a hotel on the south coast of England.*

a hit show (=very successful and popular) *'Hawaii Five-O' was a hit show in the 1980s.*

a daytime/lunchtime/late-night show *He plays some great music on his late-night show.*

the breakfast show (=broadcast in the early part of the morning) *She presents the breakfast show on morning TV.*

a live show (=broadcast on TV or radio as it is happening) *It's a live show recorded in front of a studio audience.*

a family show (=suitable for families and children to watch) *It's a real family show, with something for everyone.*

VERBS

watch a show *People of all ages watch the show.*

see a show *I've never actually seen the show.*

appear on/take part in a show (=be a guest on it) *A lot of famous people have appeared on the show.*

host a show (*also* **present a show** *BrE*) (=be the person who introduces the different parts of it, or who talks to guests) *He presents his own talk show on Saturday evenings.*

a show stars sb (=has someone as a main character) *The show stars Lucille Ball.*

PREPOSITIONS

be on a show *Madonna will be on the show tomorrow.*

PHRASES

the star of the show *Very quickly, Williams became the star of the show.*

S

2 a performance on a stage

ADJECTIVES/NOUNS + show

a comedy show *Would you like to go and see a comedy show?*

a talent show (=in which ordinary people sing, dance, do magic etc) *There's a talent show every Thursday night.*

a school show *I'm hoping to get a part in the school show.*

a travelling show *BrE*, **a traveling show** *AmE* (=that moves from place to place) *The actors are part of a travelling show that has been all over Europe.*

a one-man show (=with only one performer) *The comedian has his own one-man show.*

a stage show (=a performance on stage, rather than in a movie) *The stage show and the movie are very different.*

a Broadway/West End show (=on Broadway in New York, or in the West End of London, where there are many theatres) *'Priscilla' is my favourite West End show.*

VERBS

go to a show *I'd like to go to a show while we're in London.*

see a show *You can win two free tickets to see the show.*

watch a show *The theatre was full of people watching the show.*

put on a show (=organize and perform a show) *The kids love putting on shows in the garage.*

appear in a show *She's appearing in her first Broadway show.*

a show sells out (=all the tickets for it are sold) *The show sold out in the first week.*

PREPOSITIONS

in a show *There's a lot of singing in this show.*

3 an exhibition or display

ADJECTIVES/NOUNS + show

an art show *The college has an art show at the end of the year.*

a fashion show *They're organizing a fashion show for charity.*

a flower/boat/dog etc show *Crufts is the name of a famous dog show in London.*

a spring/summer etc show *At the summer show you can see cows, sheep, horses, and other animals.*

an annual show *The Association of Art Dealers is holding its fifth annual show.*

a trade show (=where businesses display their products) *The Frankfurt Book Fair is a trade show for publishing companies.*

VERBS

have a show *The Royal Academy has a show of paintings and drawings every summer.*

hold a show *The show is held once a year.*

organize a show *The students are organizing a show of their work.*

go to a show (*also* **attend a show** *formal*): *Thousands of people are expected to attend the show.*

put/enter sth in a show *Your pictures are very good – you should put them in a show.*

PREPOSITIONS

a show of sth *There will be a show of his work at a gallery in New York.*

at a show *I bought some paintings at the show.*

shower *n*

1 a piece of equipment that you stand under to wash your body, or the activity of washing your body in a shower

ADJECTIVES

a hot/cold shower *You'll feel better when you've had a nice hot shower.*

a quick shower *After breakfast and a quick shower, she set off.*

a long shower *I took off my wet clothes and had a long hot shower.*

a refreshing shower *He enjoyed a refreshing shower after his run.*

an electric shower *Pull the cord to switch on the electric shower.*

a private/en-suite shower (=attached to the bedroom) *Most of the hotel rooms have a private shower and a balcony.*

VERBS

have a shower *especially BrE*, **take a shower** *especially AmE*: *I took a quick shower, dressed and left for work.*

use the shower *Is it OK if I use the shower?*

grab a shower *informal* (=take a quick shower) *I barely had time to grab a shower before Pat's family arrived.*

turn the shower on/off *He turned on the shower and waited for the hot water to flow through.*

stand under the shower *She stood under the shower for a long time.*

step into/out of the shower *Mom slipped on some soap when she was stepping out of the shower.*

NOUNS

a shower curtain *She pulled back the shower curtain and stepped into the tub.*

a shower cubicle/enclosure (=an enclosed area containing a shower) *The bathroom has a separate shower cubicle.*

a shower room *Steam was coming from the shower room.*

shower gel (=liquid soap)

PHRASES

in the shower *I told him that you were in the shower and would call him back.*

2 a short period of rain or snow

ADJECTIVES

a heavy shower *More heavy showers are expected tomorrow.*

a light shower *There were a few light showers, but generally the weather was good.*

scattered showers (=a few showers spread over a wide area) *It will be mainly bright with just a few scattered showers in the afternoon.*

the occasional/odd shower *I think we could have the odd shower later in the day.*

frequent showers *The weather was generally cold and damp with frequent showers.*

a wintry shower (=with a little snow) *The cold northerly wind brought heavy wintry showers.*

thundery showers *We've had a lot of thundery showers this summer.*

squally showers (=with strong winds) *The occasional squally showers will be heavy, especially near the coast.*

NOUNS + shower

a rain/snow shower *There was some warm sunshine between the rain showers.*

an April shower (=light rain falling in April, which is considered typical of that month in England) *It started to rain, but it looked like it would only be an April shower.*

VERBS

showers fall *Snow showers began falling over high ground.*

showers are forecast/expected *Heavy showers are forecast for today.*

S

shrink *v* to become smaller

ADVERBS

shrink considerably *The number of people using the service shrank considerably when the price doubled.*

shrink slightly/a little *My shirt had shrunk slightly in the wash.*

shrink rapidly/quickly *The forest is shrinking rapidly, with more than 1,800 acres destroyed last year.*

shrink dramatically (=in a great or sudden way) *The coal industry in Britain shrank dramatically during the 20th century.*

shrink drastically (=in an extreme and sudden way) *Following this treatment, the patient's tumour shrank drastically.*

PREPOSITIONS

shrink by sth *The mass of ice at the North Pole has shrunk by over 30% in the past 50 years.*

shrink from sth *The army shrank from 2.7 million to 1.2 million troops.*

shrink to sth *During the summer months the lake will shrink to half its normal size.*

PHRASES

shrink in size/value *Mobile phones have been shrinking in size ever since they first appeared.*

shut[1] *v*

1 to close something, or to become closed

shut + NOUNS

shut a door/window/gate *It was getting cold so I shut the window.*

shut your eyes *He shut his eyes and nodded.*

shut a book *Stephen finished reading the story and shut the book.*

shut a box/case/suitcase *He shut the box and locked it.*

shut a drawer *She shut the drawer and turned the key.*

shut the lid *He put the toys back in the box and shut the lid.*

NOUNS + shut

a door/gate shuts *I heard his bedroom door shut.*

> If you cannot shut something, you say that it **won't shut**: *The car door* ***won't shut****.*

ADVERBS

shut sth firmly *Louise marched down the corridor into her office, shutting the door firmly behind her.*

shut sth tightly/tight (=used especially about your eyes) *He shut his eyes tight while the nurse put the needle in his arm.*

PREPOSITIONS

shut (sth) behind you *Ella walked in and shut the door behind her.*

shut sth/sb in a place (=put them in there and shut the door, lid etc) *She shut the dogs in their kennels for the night.*

> **THESAURUS: shut**
>
> shut, slam, draw, lock, seal → **close[1] (1)**

2 if a store, bank, museum etc shuts, it stops being open for people to go there

PREPOSITIONS

shut at 5.30/6 p.m. etc *The bank shuts at 3.30.*

shut for lunch/for the holidays etc *The college office shut for lunch at one o'clock.*

> **Shut or close?**
>
> Both **shut** and **close** are used in the same meaning. **Shut** sounds a little more informal, and is used especially in spoken English.

shut[2] *adj*

1 not open

> **Grammar**
>
> **Shut** is not used before a noun.

ADVERBS

tightly/tight shut *He kept his eyes tightly shut.*

firmly shut *The door remained firmly shut.*

properly shut *She made sure that the door was properly shut.*

VERBS

keep sth shut *When it's so hot, we keep the windows shut and put on the air conditioner.*

stay/remain shut *The door won't stay shut.*

sth slams/bangs shut *The front door slammed shut.*

sth swings shut *The gate swung shut behind her.*

pull/kick/slam sth shut *He pulled the trapdoor shut over his head.*

screw/squeeze your eyes shut (=shut your eyes tight) *Martina squeezed her eyes shut, afraid to watch what he was doing.*

2 if a store, bank, museum etc is shut, it is not open and people cannot enter or use it

PREPOSITIONS

be shut on Mondays/Saturdays etc *The post office is shut on Sundays.*

> **Shut** or **closed?**
> **Shut** means the same as **closed**. **Shut** is mainly used in spoken English. Signs on buildings say **closed**, not 'shut'. You usually say **temporarily/permanently closed**, not 'temporarily/permanently shut'.

shy *adj*

nervous and embarrassed about meeting and speaking to other people, especially people you do not know

ADVERBS

extremely/incredibly/painfully shy *As a teenager he was painfully shy.*

NOUNS

a shy man/girl/child/person etc *I'm really a shy person and I don't feel confident when I'm with people.*

a shy smile/grin *She said nothing, but just gave a shy smile.*

PREPOSITIONS

shy with sb *Anthony was shy with strangers and afraid of showing his feelings.*

> **Shy** or **timid?**
> A **shy** person lacks confidence when he or she is with other people. A **timid** person or animal is easily frightened: *I always thought that sheep were **timid** creatures.*

sick *adj*

1 suffering from a disease or illness

NOUNS

a sick child/son/relative etc *She had a sick child to take care of.*

a sick animal/dog/horse etc *Antibiotic drugs are used to treat sick animals.*

sick leave (=time that you can stay away from work because you are ill) *He returned to duty after two months' sick leave.*

sick pay (=money paid to an employee who is too ill to work) *Only full-time employees got sick pay.*

sick days (=days when you do not go to work or school because you are ill) *Employees took more sick days last year than in previous years.*

sb's sick bed (=the bed where a sick person is lying) *He left his sick bed to play in the game.*

the sick room (=a special room for people who are sick) *I went to the sick room to lie down.*

the sick bay (=a room where there are beds for people who are sick, for example on a ship or in a school) *I was confined to the ship's sick bay until we arrived back in Liverpool.*

VERBS

call/phone/ring in sick (=phone to say you are not coming in to work because you are ill) *I could have called in sick, but I knew you needed this report.*

get sick *AmE* (=become ill) *At the last minute, I got sick and couldn't go.*

fall/take sick *AmE formal* (=become ill, especially with something serious or that will last a long time) *He fell sick and died within a matter of weeks.*

PREPOSITIONS

sick with sth *I have been sick with flu.*

PHRASES

be off sick *BrE*, **be out sick** *AmE* (=be away from work or school because you are ill) *Half the staff were off sick.*

> In American English, **sick** is the usual word to use for someone who has an illness. In British English, **sick** is usually used when talking about absence from work or school, but in other situations, people usually say **ill**.

2 if you are or feel sick, the food in your stomach comes up through your mouth, or you feel like it is going to happen

VERBS

feel sick *I had stomach ache and felt sick.*

get sick *I get sick on boats.*

make yourself/sb sick *You'll make yourself sick if you eat all that chocolate.*

ADVERBS

physically sick *When he read the message he felt physically sick.*

violently sick (=suddenly and forcefully) *I woke up and was violently sick all over the bed.*

3 *informal* feeling very annoyed by or bored with someone or something

> **Grammar**
> In this meaning, you always say **sick of** someone or something.

PHRASES

sick and tired of sb/sth (=used to emphasize how annoyed or bored you are) *He was getting sick and tired of waiting.*

sick to death of sb/sth (=extremely annoyed or bored with them) *Most people are sick to death of this government and its lies.*

ADVERBS

heartily/thoroughly sick of sb/sth (=completely) *I had only been there an hour, and I was heartily sick of him already.*

PREPOSITIONS

sick of sb/sth *I am sick of your excuses, Carl! Just get on with your work.*

side *n*

1 one of the two areas that are on the left or the right of an imaginary line, or on the left or the right of a border, wall, river etc

ADJECTIVES

one side *A path leads down one side of the garden to a gate.*

the other/opposite side *On the other side of the river are some low hills.*

either side (=both sides) *There were tall hedges on either side of the lawn.*

the far side (=the other side, quite a long way away) *Nicolo was standing on the far side of the room.*

the left/right side *He received a deep cut on the right side of his face.*

the left-hand/right-hand side *In Sri Lanka they drive on the left-hand side of the road.*

the east/west etc side *The south side of town is poorer.*

PREPOSITIONS

a side of sth *Which side of the road is the library on?*

on the ... side *Fuel is cheaper on the French side of the border.*

to the side/to one side *She tilted her head to the side.*

2 one part or feature of something

ADJECTIVES

the business/financial side *Geller handles the business side of things.*

the technical side *Gregory works on the technical side, with the sound and lighting people.*

the social side *The social side of school is very important.*

the physical side *He missed the physical side of their relationship.*

the funny/serious side *Luckily, when I explained the situation, he saw the funny side of it.*

the positive/negative side *The business was a failure but on the positive side, we learned a lot from this experience.*

the dark side (=bad things relating to something) *The book is an examination of the dark side of genius.*

sb's creative/caring/feminine etc side *The art program is meant to bring out children's creative side.*

VERBS

see a side *I saw a side of him which I hadn't seen before.*

show/reveal a side *This generous act showed a much softer side of his character.*

bring out a side *The summer weather had brought out his sporty side.*

explore a side *The writer explored the darker side of life on the island.*

PHRASES

on the bright side (=considering or emphasizing what is good about a situation) *She's an optimist, who always tries to look on the bright side.*

siege *n*

a situation in which an army or the police surround a place and try to gain control of it or force someone to come out of it

PHRASES

be under siege (=be surrounded by an enemy) *The troops, who had been under siege for three months, finally surrendered.*

lay siege to sth (=try to get control of a place by surrounding it) *Armed police laid siege to the flat for two days.*

be in a state of siege *The capital was in a state of siege, with road blocks on all the surrounding roads.*

ADJECTIVES

a long siege *The bank robbers surrendered after a long siege.*

a 30-day/3-month etc siege *The city was finally captured in November, at the end of a three-month siege.*

VERBS

a siege begins/starts *Food has not been allowed into the town since the siege began.*

a siege ends *The siege ended when the men gave themselves up to police.*

lift/raise a siege (=end it) *The UN has repeated its call to lift the siege and end the suffering.*

break a siege (=stop it from continuing) *He predicted that any attempt to break the siege would fail.*

withstand a siege (=be strong enough not to be captured by a siege) *The castle was built to withstand a siege.*

a siege lasts two days/three weeks etc *Police officers arrested the suspect after a siege that lasted ten hours.*

sigh[1] *v*

to breathe out with a long sound, especially because you are bored, disappointed, tired, or pleased about something

ADVERBS

sigh deeply/heavily *Frankie stared out of the window and sighed deeply.*

sigh loudly *He showed his disappointment by sighing loudly.*

sigh softly *Dougal heard him sigh softly with relief.*

sigh wearily (=in way that shows you are tired) *Donna sighed wearily and continued her work.*

sigh audibly (=in a way that people can hear) *His mother sighed audibly but said nothing.*

sigh inwardly (=in your own mind but not in a way that other people can hear) *I sighed inwardly when he said the talk would last another 20 minutes.*

PHRASES

sigh with relief/frustration/despair etc *Marcus sighed with relief when he saw her.*

sigh[2] *n*

the act of breathing out with a long sound, because you are bored, disappointed, tired, or pleased about something

ADJECTIVES

a deep sigh *Paul gave a deep sigh of relief when he heard that the children were safe.*

a long sigh *With a long sigh, he turned and pulled the door shut.*

a huge/great/big sigh *She heaved a great sigh as she put her bags down.*

a heavy sigh (=a big sad sigh) *Finally, she turned away from the mirror with a heavy sigh.*

a little/small sigh *Quinn let out a little sigh and closed the book.*

a weary sigh (=which shows you are tired) *With a weary sigh, he rubbed a hand over his eyes.*

an audible sigh (=that people can hear) *There was an audible sigh from the teacher when I gave my answer.*

a collective sigh (=one that many people give at the same time) *She heard a collective sigh of relief as she announced her decision.*

VERBS

let out/give a sigh *She let out a sigh of disappointment.*

heave a sigh (=sigh loudly and deeply) *Uncle Walter heaved a sigh and slumped back in his chair.*

PREPOSITIONS

a sigh of relief/exasperation/satisfaction etc *At last the girl stopped eating and sat back with a sigh of satisfaction.*

PHRASES

breathe a sigh of relief (=stop feeling worried or frightened, especially when you also sigh) *When he had left, Miranda breathed a sigh of relief.*

sight *n*

1 something or someone that you see

ADJECTIVES

a familiar/common sight (=one that you often see) *Horses were once a familiar sight on the city's streets.*

a rare sight *Mountain lions are a rare sight in this area.*

a welcome sight (=one that you have been wanting to see) *The rising of the sun was a welcome sight.*

an amazing/impressive/wonderful/magnificent sight *The city was a magnificent sight.*

a beautiful sight *It must have looked a beautiful sight!*

a sad/pitiful sight (=used when you feel sorry for someone or something) *She was a pitiful sight in her dirty torn clothes.*

a strange sight *The boat stuck on top of the house must have been a very strange sight.*

sb/sth is not a pretty sight (=it is very unpleasant to see) *I've seen animals suffering from this disease and it is not a pretty sight.*

VERBS

see/witness a sight *Very few people have ever witnessed this sight.*

a sight greets/confronts/meets sb (=you see it when you arrive somewhere) *When you arrive at the airport, you will be greeted by the sight of armed police.*

PREPOSITIONS

the sight of sb/sth *The sight of blood made her feel sick.*

at the sight of sth *Even Charles cheered up at the sight of the food.*

2 the ability to see

ADJECTIVES

good sight *My grandmother still has good sight.*

poor sight *His sight was quite poor.*

failing sight (=becoming worse) *He ran the business until failing sight forced him to retire.*

VERBS

have poor/good etc sight *Mary has very little sight in her right eye.*

lose your sight *As the result of a severe illness, she lost her sight at the age of 12.*

save sb's sight *Surgeons believe they can save her sight.*

restore sb's sight (=make someone able to see again) *His sight was restored and he was able to see his children for the first time in years.*

sb's sight fails (=gets much worse) *Graham was in his seventies when his sight began to fail.*

sight + NOUNS

sight loss *The illness can cause sight loss.*

a sight problem *It is estimated that 25% of children will have a sight problem that needs attention.*

3 the area that you can see

VERBS

come into sight *As we went round the bend, a farmhouse came into sight.*

disappear/vanish from sight *Within a few seconds, he had disappeared from sight.*

be hidden from sight *The house was hidden from sight by a row of tall trees.*

PREPOSITIONS

in/within sight *The house was now within sight.*

out of sight *They waited until the police car was out of sight.*

PHRASES

every ... in sight *Billy was very hungry and ate everything in sight. | Rioters burned every car in sight.*

be nowhere in sight (=you cannot see someone or something, especially when you are looking for them) *It was nearly time for the performance, but the band leader was nowhere in sight.*

sb's line of sight (=the area that someone can see) *A young woman moved into Luke's line of sight.*

in full sight of sb (=where other people can see you clearly, especially when you are doing something surprising or shocking) *He took his clothes off in full sight of the party guests.*

not let sb out of your sight (=watch someone very carefully) *In the park she didn't let the children out of her sight.*

S

sign[1] *n*

1 a piece of paper, metal, or wood with words or a picture that gives people information, warnings, or instructions

ADJECTIVES/NOUNS + sign

a street/road/traffic sign *The street signs are written in Arabic.*

a stop sign (=which tells drivers to stop at a junction) *He failed to slow down for a stop sign.*

a speed limit sign *New Hampshire has plenty of speed limit signs on its highways.*

a no-smoking sign *There are no-smoking signs in the bar.*

an advertising sign *The road is lined with advertising signs.*

a warning sign *There are warning signs about thieves.*

a neon sign (=a sign made from glass tubes which contain a special gas, often used for advertisements) *Tokyo is full of bright neon signs.*

VERBS + sign

see a sign *I saw a sign which said 'Turn right'.*

read a sign *She stopped the car to read the sign.*

put up a sign (*also* **erect a sign** *formal*): *The owner had put up a big sign outside the shop.*

take down a sign *They took down the 'rooms to let' sign.*

follow the sign *We followed the signs for the city centre.*

ignore a sign *Don't ignore the fog warning signs.*

sign + VERBS

a sign says sth *The sign said 'No through road'.*

a sign points somewhere *I could see a sign pointing to Carnaby Street.*

2 something that shows that a particular thing is true, exists, or is happening

> **Grammar**
> **Sign** is often used in the phrases a **sign of** something, or a **sign that** something is true.

ADJECTIVES/NOUNS + sign

a clear/obvious/unmistakable sign *There are clear signs of a slowdown in economic growth.*

a sure sign (=a very clear sign) *He was walking up and down, a sure sign that he was worried.*

a good/positive/encouraging/hopeful sign (=a sign of something good) *If she can move her legs, that's a good sign.*

a bad/ominous sign (=a sign of something bad) *The jury was taking ages to make up its mind, which he felt was probably a bad sign.*

a warning/danger sign (=one that shows something bad might be happening) *In this case, social workers missed the warning signs and failed to protect the children.*

an outward/visible sign (=one that people can see clearly) *Kim received the news without showing any visible sign of emotion.*

a telltale/tell-tale sign (=signs that clearly show something bad) *She would not look at me directly, a tell-tale sign that she was embarrassed.*

the first sign of sth *They ran away at the first sign of trouble.*

an early sign (=which shows that something is starting) *The tree's blossoms are an early sign of spring.*

no sign of sth *The curtains were still drawn and there was no sign of activity.*

VERBS

there are signs *There are now signs of an improvement in the economy.*

see/detect signs *I could see some signs that her health was getting better.*

show signs of sth *Did she show any signs of distress?*

bear signs of sth *formal* (=have signs which

show something) *The bed was neatly made and bore no signs of having been slept in.*

have (all) the signs of sth (=you can see clearly that something is true) *It had all the signs of a crime of passion.*

PREPOSITIONS

a sign of sth *Some men see going to a doctor as a sign of weakness.*

PHRASES

sth is a sign of the times (=it shows you what the situation is in a country at a particular time, especially when there is a bad situation) *The job losses are a sign of the times.*

sign² *v* THESAURUS write (1)

signal *n*

1 an event or action that tells you something about a situation

ADJECTIVES/NOUNS + signal

a clear/strong signal *My body was giving me a clear signal that something was wrong.*

a warning/danger/alarm signal (=showing that there is danger) *Everyone should know the danger signals of a heart attack.*

the wrong signal (=one that gives someone the wrong idea about a situation) *Wearing jeans to work sends out the wrong signal to other people.*

mixed signals (=confusing because they seem to show two different things) *It is important not to give children mixed signals about how you expect them to behave.*

VERBS

give/send (sb) a signal *He doesn't want to give her the wrong signals.*

send out/give out a signal *The public protests sent out a clear signal to the government that people were dissatisfied.*

read the signals (=understand them correctly) *President Nixon read the signals and decided it was time to resign.*

act as a signal (=be a signal) *A baby's crying acts as a signal to its mother.*

take sth as a signal (=consider it to be a signal) *He paused, and that was taken as a signal for cheers and shouts.*

respond to a signal *Managers did not respond to market signals early enough.*

PREPOSITIONS

a signal from sb/sth *He may be waiting for a signal from you before he asks you out.*

a signal to sb/sth *This should be a signal to the world to take action.*

a signal for sb to do sth *That was the signal for us to leave.*

a signal of sth *As a signal of goodwill, we will refund your money.*

2 an action or sound that is made to give information or tell someone to do something

VERBS

give (sb) a signal *Don't do it yet - wait until I give the signal.*

wait for a signal *The soldiers were waiting for a signal to start firing.*

NOUNS + signal

a hand signal *The cyclist used a hand signal to show he was going to turn right.*

PREPOSITIONS

a signal for sb to do sth *When I nod my head, that's the signal for you to start playing.*

at/on a signal (=when a signal is given) *At my signal, you will start singing.*

3 a light or set of lights that tells drivers what to do

NOUNS + signal

traffic signals *Turn left after the traffic signals.*

railway signals *BrE*, **railroad signals** *AmE*: *The purpose of railway signals is to give train drivers enough warning to stop.*

a stop signal *He completely ignored the stop signal.*

VERBS

a signal changes (=from one colour to another) *Get ready to go as soon as the signal changes.*

a signal turns red/green *We just sat there, waiting for the signal to turn green.*

signal + NOUNS

signal failure (=when a set of signals does not work properly) *The train crash was caused by signal failure.*

4 a series of light or sound waves that carry an image or sound

ADJECTIVES/NOUNS + signal

a strong signal *I can't use my phone because the signal isn't strong enough here.*

a weak/faint signal *The signals were too weak for the receiver to pick up.*

a digital/electrical signal *Digital signals can be compressed to take up less space.*

a radio/radar/television signal *The first television signals were sent by John Logie Baird in 1929.*

VERBS

get/receive a signal *It is difficult to get a signal in some areas of the country.*

pick up a signal (=receive it - used about a piece of equipment) *The antenna that will pick up the signals is a 12-metre satellite dish.*

send a signal (*also* **transmit a signal** *formal*): *The signals are transmitted via satellites.*

send out a signal (*also* **emit a signal** *formal*): *The device emits a signal which can be picked up by a submarine.*

carry a signal (=allow it to travel along or through something) *Copper wires carry the electrical signals.*

PREPOSITIONS

a signal from sth *There was no signal from the microphone.*

signature *n*

your name written on a cheque, letter etc in the way you usually write it, to show that you have written it

VERBS

put/write your signature somewhere *Just put your signature here.*

add your signature to sth *The prime minister added his signature to the treaty.*

gather/collect signatures *We collected hundreds of signatures from parents, calling for the school to stay open.*

sth requires sb's signature *formal* (=they need to sign it) *The marriage certificate requires the signatures of two witnesses.*

sth bears/carries sb's signature *formal* (=it has someone's signature on it) *The painting bore the signature of a famous local artist.*

forge sb's signature (=make a false copy of someone's signature, in order to deceive people) *He forged his boss's signature on the cheque.*

get sb's signature (*also* **obtain sb's signature** *formal*): *To go on the trip, each child must obtain their parents' signature on the consent form.*

witness sb's signature (=sign to say that you saw someone sign an official document) *You must get someone to witness your signature on a passport application.*

ADJECTIVES

a forged signature (=written by someone else in order to deceive people) *Mr Adams, whose forged signature is on the form, can prove that he was out of the country on that date.*

significance *n*

the importance of an event, action etc, especially because of the effects or influence it will have in the future

ADJECTIVES

great/considerable significance *The judge said the new evidence was of great significance.*

deep/profound significance *Jerusalem has a deep religious significance for Jews, Christians, and Muslims.*

little significance *This information on its own is of little significance.*

wider significance *The research dealt with one small group, but their conclusions are of much wider significance.*

special/particular significance *Japan has a special significance for me because it is where I met my wife.*

political/social/historical significance *The political significance of this change is enormous.*

new significance *Old problems have taken on a new significance.*

VERBS

understand/realize/appreciate/grasp the significance of sth (=realize that something is significant) *People were slow to grasp the significance of what had happened.*

have/hold significance *This day has a special significance for French people.*

take on a new/special etc significance (=become important) *Religious differences have taken on a new significance.*

attach significance to sth (=give something importance) *He thought her comment was odd, but he didn't attach any significance to it.*

acquire/assume significance (=begin to have it) *The town acquired a special significance in the history of Ireland.*

assess the significance of sth (=decide how important something is) *It is too soon to assess the significance of these events.*

downplay the significance of sth (=try to make something seem less important) *The president downplayed the significance of the opinion poll.*

underestimate the significance of sth (=not realize how important something is) *People have tended to underestimate the significance of this victory.*

exaggerate the significance of sth *The article falsely raised people's hopes of a cure, by exaggerating the significance of these findings.*

sb's/sth's significance lies in sth (=the reason why something is significant is...) *The book's significance lies in its ideas about the nature of political power.*

PREPOSITIONS

the significance of sth *The significance of this event was not appreciated at the time.*

significance for/to sb/sth *This date has special significance for Tibetans.*

PHRASES

of little/great/no etc significance *The station was built on a site of particular significance in the history of Mumbai.*

significant *adj* THESAURUS ▸ **important (1)**

silence *n*

1 complete absence of sound or noise

ADJECTIVES

complete/total/absolute/utter silence *The students have to work in complete silence.*

dead silence (=complete silence) *We all sat in dead silence waiting for him to speak.*

a long silence *There was a long silence and then people suddenly started shouting.*

S

a short/brief silence *After a brief silence, Katherine nodded.*

a sudden silence *At the mention of his name, a sudden silence fell on the room.*

an awkward/uncomfortable/embarrassed silence *"Fred tells me you like books," Steve said, after an awkward silence.*

a stunned/shocked silence *There was a stunned silence at the other end of the phone.*

a tense silence *There was a tense silence as we waited.*

an eerie silence (=one that is strange and rather frightening) *There was an eerie silence after the bomb exploded.*

an ominous silence (=one that makes you feel that something bad is going to happen) *Their only reply to my question was an ominous silence.*

stony silence (=unfriendly silence) *My joke was greeted by a stony silence.*

VERBS + silence

break/shatter the silence (=suddenly end it) *The silence was shattered by the sound of gunfire.*

disturb the silence (=end it by making a sound) *Here, there was nothing to disturb the silence but birdsong.*

lapse into silence (=stop talking and be quiet) *After a brief conversation about the weather, we lapsed into silence again.*

fill the silence (=say something to avoid silence) *"Have you been here before?" Daniel asked to fill the silence.*

silence + VERBS

silence falls/descends (=it begins) *A sudden silence fell over the audience.*

silence reigns (=there is silence) *In the waiting room, tense silence reigned.*

a silence follows/ensues *A long silence followed.*

PREPOSITIONS

in silence *The two men sat in silence.*

2 a situation in which people refuse to talk about something

ADJECTIVES

complete/absolute/total silence *There has been a complete silence over what happened to these prisoners.*

a deafening silence (=very noticeable) *These allegations have prompted only a deafening silence from the company.*

a dignified silence *His wife has maintained a dignified silence on the affair.*

VERBS

keep/maintain (a) silence *The singer has maintained absolute silence about his relationships.*

meet with silence *Enquiries from journalists have met with silence.*

PREPOSITIONS

silence on/over sth *The government's silence on this issue is surprising.*

PHRASES

a wall of silence (=when no one will speak about something) *Detectives investigating his murder have met a wall of silence.*

a conspiracy of silence (=when people agree not to talk about something that should not be kept secret) *There's often a conspiracy of silence surrounding bullying in schools.*

a vow of silence (=a promise not to talk about something) *Anger led him to break his vow of silence.*

silent *adj* THESAURUS **quiet (1)**, **(2)**

silky *adj* THESAURUS **shiny**

silly *adj* not sensible

NOUNS

a silly question *The reporters kept asking silly questions.*

a silly idea *At first, Howard thought the book was a silly idea.*

a silly mistake *He made one silly mistake, which lost him the game.*

a silly fool/idiot/person *The silly idiot thought that I was talking about him.*

a silly thing *I said some silly things, and I'm sorry.*

> You can also use **silly thing** about people, especially when you are talking in a gentle friendly way: *Don't worry, you **silly thing**!*

VERBS

seem/sound/look silly *It sounds silly now, but at the time I was really frightened.*

PHRASES

it was silly of sb to do sth *It was silly of me to ask the question, when I already knew the answer.*

silly old *Don't listen to him – he's just a silly old fool.*

silly little *We always argue about silly little things.*

silver *n* a valuable light grey metal

ADJECTIVES

solid/pure silver (=containing only silver and no other metal) *The winner receives a solid silver trophy.*

sterling silver (=silver that is at least 92% pure) *The cup is made of sterling silver and weighs over 20 lbs.*

silver + NOUNS

a silver coin *The bag, which had been buried under a wall, was full of old silver coins.*

S

a silver medal (=a prize for second place) *She took the silver medal in the 400 meters and bronze in the 1,500 meters.*

silver jewellery *BrE*, **silver jewelry** *AmE*: *I prefer silver jewellery to gold.*

> **Silver-plated**
> You use **silver-plated** about something that is covered in a thin layer of **silver**: *a silver-plated candlestick*

similar Ac *adj* almost the same

ADVERBS

very similar *I was in a very similar situation.*

broadly/roughly similar (=in many ways) *Her new job will be broadly similar to her old one.*

quite/fairly/somewhat similar (=rather similar) *The two birds are quite similar.*

remarkably/strikingly/startlingly similar *Studies done all over the world have had remarkably similar results.*

uncannily/eerily similar (=very similar, especially when this seems strange) *Her death is uncannily similar to that of another young woman in the area 30 years ago.*

VERBS

look/sound/taste/feel similar *The two products look quite similar.*

PREPOSITIONS

similar to sth *His speech was strikingly similar to one given by the American president earlier this year.*

similar in sth *The birds are both a brownish colour and similar in size.*

similarity Ac *n*

if there is a similarity between two things or people, they are similar in some way

ADJECTIVES

a close/great/strong similarity *There are close similarities between the two paintings.*

a remarkable/striking/marked similarity (=one that is very noticeable) *Chimpanzees' facial expressions show remarkable similarities to those of humans.*

a certain similarity (=a particular similarity) *There are certain similarities between us.*

a superficial similarity (=in which an obvious feature is similar, but other features are not) *There is a superficial similarity between the two songs, but they are really very different.*

an apparent similarity (=one that seems similar but really is not) *Many apparent similarities between the two politicians disappear on closer examination.*

an uncanny similarity (=a close similarity, especially when this seems strange) *His drawings have an uncanny similarity to the work of William Blake.*

a physical/cultural/structural etc similarity *There are some cultural similarities between the two countries.*

VERBS

there is a similarity/there are some similarities *There is a similarity between a movie director and a conductor.*

bear a/some similarity to sth (=be similar) *The attack bore a striking similarity to another 25 miles away.*

have similarities (=be similar) *The two towns have many similarities.*

show similarities *Twins who are raised apart still show similarities in their behaviour.*

be struck by a similarity (=notice it) *I was struck by the similarities in their opinions.*

the similarity ends there (*also* **there the similarity ends**) (=there are no other similarities) *Both women are blonde, but there the similarity ends.*

PREPOSITIONS

similarity between sth/sb and sth/sb *There are lots of similarities between the two bikes.*

a similarity with sb/sth *Yiddish is a distinct language, although there are similarities with German.*

a similarity in sth *The cheeses have some similarities in flavour.*

simple *adj*

not complicated, and easy to do, use, or understand

NOUNS

a simple question *It's a simple question requiring a yes or no answer.*

a simple answer/explanation *People always want a simple answer.*

a simple solution *Fortunately, there is a simple solution to this problem.*

a simple way/method/technique *One simple way of making a room look bigger is by using mirrors.*

a simple process *Creating a new document is a fairly simple process.*

a simple idea *Do you have any simple ideas for decorating a child's birthday cake?*

a simple task *Thanks to technology, washing clothes is now a simple task.*

a simple message *The article contains a simple message.*

a simple test *A simple test can determine whether you are suffering from diabetes.*

simple rules *There are a few simple rules which can help you be successful at a job interview.*

ADVERBS

very/extremely/incredibly/remarkably simple *I came up with a very simple answer to this problem.*

S

perfectly simple (=very simple) *I'm sure there's a perfectly simple explanation.*

relatively/fairly/quite simple *The rules are quite simple.*

simple enough (=quite simple) *The essence of his argument is simple enough.*

deceptively/seemingly simple (=seeming simple, but in fact complicated or difficult) *It's a deceptively simple exercise, but it requires a lot of concentration.*

surprisingly simple *The rules are surprisingly simple.*

VERBS

seem simple *It seemed simpler not to say anything.*

look/sound simple *It's a game that sounds simple but isn't.*

keep sth simple *Keep your explanation as simple as possible.*

make sth simple *The government has tried to make the tax system simpler.*

PHRASES

simple to use/make/operate etc *The machine is very simple to use.*

simple but effective *Any child's behaviour can be improved by this simple but effective technique.*

in simple terms *In simple terms, the company needs to sell more products at higher prices to improve profits.*

it's as simple as that *We can't afford to pay you any more – I'm afraid it's as simple as that.*

clear and simple *The adverts have a clear and simple message.*

simple and straightforward *Installation of software should be simple and straightforward.*

THESAURUS: simple

plain

furniture | shirt | curtains | language | English

things that are plain have no decoration or no other things added. Plain language uses simple and clear words, so that you cannot misunderstand the meaning:

I prefer plain wooden furniture. | He was wearing a dark jacket and a plain white shirt. | The poem uses plain language which anyone can understand. | She explained what the document meant in plain English.

crude

method | attempt | form | shelter | sketch | drawing

doing something in a very simple way, which is not very accurate or effective:

The researchers used a rather crude method of measuring productivity. | They made a crude shelter out of a few branches and some leaves. | He drew a crude pencil sketch on a napkin.

THESAURUS: simple

simple, straightforward, user-friendly, undemanding, mindless, painless, cushy → easy

ANTONYMS **simple → complicated**

simulated *adj* THESAURUS ▸ **artificial**

sin *n*

an action that is against religious rules, or that is considered a very bad thing to do. **Sin** was originally used about religion, but is now used in a much more general way

VERBS

it is a sin to do sth *They believe it is a sin to have sex outside marriage. | It would be a sin to waste all that good food.*

commit a sin (=do something that is a sin) *He knew that he had committed a grave sin.*

confess your sins (=admit them) *He knelt and confessed his sins to God.*

forgive sins *God will forgive your sins if you repent.*

repent (of) your sins *formal* (=be sorry you committed them) *I sincerely repent of my sins.*

ADJECTIVES

a great/grave sin *Divorce was considered to be a great sin.*

an unforgivable sin *Luke O'Malley had committed the unforgivable sin – he had spoken to the police about his neighbours.*

sth is no sin/not a sin *Being in love is not a sin!*

PREPOSITIONS

a sin against sb *Sin against others is seen as a sin against God.*

PHRASES

the seven deadly sins (=seven bad feelings or desires, in the Christian religion, for example greed or too much pride) *I think I've committed all the seven deadly sins.*

sincere *adj*

honestly feeling or believing something, or honestly meaning what you say

VERBS

sound sincere *His apology sounded sincere, so I forgave him.*

seem sincere *She seemed perfectly sincere when she praised the painting.*

look/appear sincere *Joe tried his best to look sincere but no one believed him.*

ADVERBS

completely/totally/utterly sincere *He was completely sincere about loving the work.*

not entirely sincere *Somehow her smile did not seem entirely sincere.*

S

perfectly sincere (*also* **quite sincere** *BrE*): *I was being perfectly sincere when I said you deserved to win.*

most sincere *formal*: *Please accept our most sincere apologies for what has happened.*

apparently/seemingly sincere *When we get information from a seemingly sincere source, we have to follow it up.*

NOUNS

sincere apology/apologies *I want to offer my sincere apologies to passengers who suffered delays.*

sincere belief *We published the letter in the sincere belief that it was genuine.*

sincere thanks (*also* **a sincere thank you**) *Our sincere thanks go to everyone who helped make this day such a success.*

a sincere desire *She showed a sincere desire to help.*

sincere condolences (=sympathy after someone has died) *I'd like to express my sincere condolences to Mr Smith's family.*

sincere hope *It is my sincere hope that I will be able to return to England some day.*

PREPOSITIONS

sincere in/about sth *I think he is sincere in his views.*

THESAURUS: sincere

truthful, sincere, frank, straight, open, candid, direct, blunt, forthright, outspoken, upfront → **honest**

S

sing *v*

to produce a musical sound with your voice

ADVERBS

sing softly/quietly/gently *He was singing quietly to himself as he worked.*

sing loudly *Inside the stadium, both sets of supporters were singing really loudly.*

sing well/badly *I never knew you could sing so well.*

sing beautifully *I think she sings beautifully, don't you?*

sing along (=with someone else who is already singing) *Mary sang along to the radio while she did the cleaning.*

sing live (=in front of an audience) *This is the first time I've heard him sing live on stage.*

sing professionally (=as a paid job rather than for fun) *Amy began singing professionally when she was 18.*

sing + NOUNS

sing a song *My fans prefer me to sing love songs.*

sing a hymn/carol *The choir sang a lovely hymn.*

sing the national anthem (=a country's national song) *Every morning, US schoolchildren sing the national anthem.*

sing Happy Birthday *We gathered around the table and everyone sang Happy Birthday to Grandad.*

PREPOSITIONS

sing to sb *She sang to the baby while she bathed him.*

PHRASES

sing in tune/out of tune (=sing the correct notes or the incorrect notes) *The teacher told her she was singing out of tune.*

sing sb to sleep (=sing to someone until they fall asleep) *She held the baby in her arms and gently sang him to sleep.*

sing at the top of your voice/lungs (=sing as loudly as you possibly can) *Joe was in the bath, singing at the top of his voice.*

singer *n* someone who sings

ADJECTIVES/NOUNS + singer

a pop/folk/opera etc singer *She always wanted to become a pop singer.*

a fine/good/great singer *The members of the choir are all fine singers.*

a talented singer *He's a talented singer with a great future ahead of him.*

sb's favourite singer *BrE*, **sb's favorite singer** *AmE*: *My favourite singer is Robbie Williams – he has a great voice.*

a famous/well-known singer *Pavarotti was a famous Italian opera singer.*

a legendary singer (=one who is very famous for a long time) *He played with many legendary singers, including Billie Holiday and Bessie Smith.*

a popular singer *She became one of the most popular singers in Britain.*

a professional singer (=done as a job rather than for fun) *His voice isn't bad, but he'll never make it as a professional singer.*

the lead singer (=the main singer) *She's the lead singer in a rock band.*

a backing singer (*also* **a back-up singer**) (=someone who sings with the lead singer) *The backing singers sang the chorus.*

a cabaret/nightclub singer *She plays the role of a cabaret singer whose career is going downhill.*

a female/male singer *She was voted best female singer of the year by the magazine's readers.*

VERBS

a singer sings *They always have a famous singer singing the national anthem before the game.*

a singer performs *The singers performed a duet together.*

single *adj*

1 not married or not in a romantic relationship with anyone

NOUNS

a single man/woman *She wondered where she could meet nice single men.*

a single mother/father *Single mothers are more likely to be living in poverty.*

a single parent *I am a single parent with two children.*

VERBS

stay single *Take my advice and stay single.*

2 for only one person

NOUNS

a single room (=for one person to sleep in) *Single rooms are available at the hotel.*

a single bed *The room had two single beds and a table in it.*

a single mattress *There was a single mattress on the floor.*

a single duvet/sheet (=for a bed that one person sleeps in) *A single duvet cost £20.*

sink *v*

to go down below the surface of something

ADVERBS

sink slowly *Their feet slowly sank in the mud.*

sink deep into sth *He sank deep into the chair.*

PREPOSITIONS

sink below/beneath sth *The ship sank beneath the waves.*

sink into sth *Our chairs sank into the soft ground.*

PHRASES

sink to the bottom of sth *A boat carrying four men turned over and sank to the bottom of the lake.*

sink without trace (=without leaving any sign) *The plane crashed into the sea and sank without trace.*

sink like a stone (=quickly and immediately) *The submarine was hit by a torpedo and sank like a stone.*

sister *n*

a girl or woman who has the same parents as you

ADJECTIVES/NOUNS + sister

an older/elder sister *He had two older sisters, Karen and Jane.*

a big sister (=older sister – more informal) *She misses her big sister a lot.*

a younger sister *Mary was often aggressive towards her younger sister.*

a little sister/kid sister (=younger sister – more informal) *He was very fond of his little sister.*

a baby sister (=one who is a baby, or who is much younger) *She wanted a baby sister.*

a twin sister *He is devoted to his twin sister.*

a half-sister (=a sister with only one parent the same as yours) *She doesn't see her half-sister very often.*

sit *v*

to be resting your weight on your bottom somewhere, or to move into this position

ADVERBS

sit down (=stop standing and change to a sitting position) *She sat down on the sofa.*

sit still (=without moving) *Young children find it almost impossible to sit still.*

sit quietly (=without talking) *Mac sat quietly in the back of the car.*

sit patiently *He sat patiently waiting for them to finish.*

be sitting comfortably *She was sitting comfortably on the sofa.*

sit up straight/sit upright (=with your back straight) *Sit up straight at the table, children.*

sit bolt upright (=suddenly sit up very straight, for example because you hear something) *Suddenly she sat bolt upright and said: "What was that?"*

sit cross-legged (=with your legs bent and crossed over in front of you) *Farooq was sitting cross-legged on the grass.*

PREPOSITIONS

sit at a table/desk etc *Jean sat at the table writing a letter.*

sit in a chair/armchair/seat *Her uncle was sitting in a huge leather armchair.*

sit on a chair/sofa/stool etc *She sat on a stool at the bar.*

sit next to/beside sb/sth *He came over and sat beside her.*

sit opposite sb/sth *The man sitting opposite her had a moustache.*

PHRASES

sit and watch/listen *It's a good place to sit and watch the sun go down.*

sit and stare *He sat and stared at the desk in front of him.*

sit and wait *They sat and waited in silence.*

sit and talk *They would sit and talk for hours.*

a place to sit (*also* **somewhere to sit**) *Let's look for a quiet place to sit.*

site Ac *n*

1 a place that is used for something or where something important or interesting happened

ADJECTIVES/NOUNS + site

a building/construction site *The field is now a building site.*

a historic site *There are numerous historic sites to visit.*

an ancient site *The organization maintains and restores ancient sites, castles, monuments etc.*

an archaeological site *BrE*, **an archeological site** *AmE* (=containing remains from people who lived long ago) *Archaeological sites are often discovered by accident.*

a burial site (=the place where someone is buried) *They believe that the abbey is the burial site of King Arthur.*

the crash site (=where a plane etc crashed) *Wreckage was seen 200 metres away from the crash site.*

a sacred site *Ayers Rock is the most sacred site of the Aborigines.*

a brownfield site *BrE* (=a piece of land that has been built on before) *The majority of the houses will be built on brownfield sites.*

a bomb site (=where a bomb has exploded) *Her room looked like a bomb site.*

Campsite is usually written as one word.

VERBS

be the site of sth *Chernobyl was the site of the world's worst nuclear accident.*

visit a site *He had visited many of the historic sites in Egypt.*

occupy a site *A gallery now occupies the site where the church once stood.*

develop a site *The council plans to develop the site and build a new concert hall.*

PREPOSITIONS

on a site *There has been a paper mill on this site for over 200 years.*

the site of sth *The house is built near the site of a medieval prison.*

2 a website See → **website**

situation *n*

a set of things that are happening

ADJECTIVES/NOUNS + situation

a difficult/tricky situation *I found myself in a difficult situation.*

an impossible situation *He was in an impossible situation.*

a dangerous situation *The situation was becoming increasingly dangerous.*

a stressful situation *She doesn't cope very well with stressful situations.*

the present/current situation *The present situation in Afghanistan is very worrying.*

the economic/political situation *The country's economic situation continued to deteriorate.*

the security situation (=how safe a place is) *Until the security situation improves, it is far too dangerous for staff to work there.*

sb's financial situation (=how much money someone has) *What is your current financial situation?*

a social situation (=a situation in which someone is with other people) *He felt uncomfortable in social situations.*

a work situation (=a situation at work) *These problems often arise in work situations.*

a no-win situation (=one in which there will be a bad result whatever happens) *We're in a no-win situation – either way, we're going to be criticized.*

a win-win situation (=one in which everyone gets what they want) *Shorter work weeks are a win-win situation for both the employee and employer.*

VERBS + situation

be in a situation *I've never been in this kind of situation before.*

put sb in a situation *That puts me in a very difficult situation.*

deal with a situation *He had no idea how to deal with the situation.*

create a situation *We don't want to create a situation where no-one trusts us.*

assess/review a situation (=examine it to see what it is like) *Take time to review the situation before making a decision.*

monitor a situation (=watch to see how it develops) *The bank is monitoring the situation closely.*

explain a situation *Maria explained the situation to everyone.*

accept a situation *I just cannot accept this situation.*

improve a situation *They are doing what they can to improve the situation.*

remedy a situation (=make it good again) *What can be done to remedy this situation?*

defuse a situation (=make people less angry) *She'd just been trying to calm Gerry down and defuse the situation.*

exacerbate a situation *formal* (=make it worse) *Such action will only exacerbate the situation.*

situation + VERBS

a situation happens/comes about (*also* **a situation arises** *formal*): *I don't know how this situation has come about.*

a situation continues (*also* **a situation persists** *formal*): *If this situation persists we will need to employ more staff.*

a situation changes *I'll let you know if the situation changes.*

a situation improves *The situation has improved over the last decade.*

a situation gets worse (*also* **a situation deteriorates** *formal*): *If the situation gets any worse, we will have to take action.*

PREPOSITIONS

in a situation *She coped well in a difficult situation.*

PHRASES

take advantage of a situation (=use it to get what you want) *Anyone who didn't take advantage of a situation like this was a fool.*

take control of a situation *The police arrived and took control of the situation.*

lose control of a situation *I feel as if I've lost control of the situation.*

be aware of a situation *Are her parents aware of the situation?*

the seriousness/gravity of a situation (=how serious it is) *She immediately realized the gravity of the situation.*

size *n*

1 how big or small something is

ADJECTIVES

the same size *The animal was about the same size as a rat.*

a different size *Six towns of different sizes were selected for the research.*

a good/fair size (=fairly big) *The garden is a good size.*

the small size of sth *One problem was the very small size of the department.*

the large size of sth *They are not aggressive animals, despite their large size.*

the sheer size of sth (=used to emphasize that something is large) *The sheer size of some dinosaurs is amazing.*

sth's original size *The lake has already shrunk to half its original size.*

full size (=the largest size) *He's quite a big dog, but he's still not full size yet.*

an average size *The rooms are of average size.*

the maximum/minimum size *The maximum class size in the school is 30 children.*

NOUNS + size

class size *The government has promised to reduce class sizes in schools.*

body size *People are often worried about their body size.*

family size *The average family size has gone down.*

VERBS

increase the size of sth *They increased the size of the house by building an extension.*

reduce the size of sth *He had an operation to reduce the size of his nose.*

double the size of sth *Ethiopia doubled the size of its army to 200,000.*

limit the size of sth *We limit the size of the group to just 20 students.*

measure the size of sth *She measured the size of the sofa to make sure it would fit in the room.*

estimate the size of sth *It is difficult to estimate the size of the market.*

reach a size *Once the animal reaches a certain size, it is returned to the wild.*

PREPOSITIONS

in size *The apartment is roughly 360 square feet in size.*

the size of sth *The firm underestimated the size of the market for their new product.*

PHRASES

be twice the size of sth *The creature was about twice the size of a small dog.*

be half the size of sth *Kosovo is about half the size of Wales.*

(of) this/that size *In a class this size, there are bound to be a few troublemakers.*

in all/various shapes and sizes *These phones come in all shapes and sizes.*

the size of sth (=the same size as) *I saw a spider the size of my hand in the backyard.*

2 one of a set of standard measures to which clothes and other products are made and sold

ADJECTIVES/NOUNS + size

a small/medium/large size *The rugs cost just £25 for the medium size.*

shoe/bra/collar size *British shoe sizes are different from those in the rest of Europe.*

waist/chest/bust size *I found a child's jumper, chest size 26 inches.*

dress size (=size used for women's clothes) *Most women are a dress size 14 or over.*

a size 8/12 etc (=used when talking about clothes sizes) *My sister is a size 16.*

VERBS

take/wear a size *What size shoes do you take?*

PREPOSITIONS

in a size *Do you have this shirt in a bigger size?*

> When talking about the size of a piece of clothing, a drink etc, you usually say **a medium**, **a large** etc: *Do you have this sweater in **a medium**?*

ski *n*

1 one of a pair of long thin narrow pieces of wood or plastic that you fasten to your boots and use for moving on snow

VERBS

wear skis *Never wear skis that are too big or too small for you.*

put on/take off skis *She is putting on her skis.*

rent skis (*also* **hire skis** *BrE*): *I wanted to hire some skis for the weekend.*

PHRASES

a pair of skis *He was carrying a pair of skis.*

2 relating to the sport of skiing

ski + NOUNS

a ski resort (=a place where people can go skiing) *St Moritz is a famous ski resort in Switzerland.*

a ski slope (=a piece of ground for skiing) *The ski slopes were covered in ice.*

a ski trip *The school is organizing a ski trip to Austria.*

a ski instructor *He works as a ski instructor during the winter.*

a ski lift (=which carries you up to the ski slopes) *You can buy a pass to use on the ski lifts.*

ski jacket/boots/poles/goggles *Dooley was wearing sweatpants and a ski jacket.*

> **Ski or skiing?**
> Both these words are used about things that relate to the sport of skiing, but they have different collocations. You say a **ski resort/slope/instructor/lift/jacket**. You say a **skiing holiday/vacation** and **skiing conditions**. You **go skiing** (not 'go ski').

skiing *n*

a sport in which you move over snow on skis

VERBS

go skiing *I'm going skiing next month for the first time.*

skiing + NOUNS

a skiing holiday/vacation/trip *He's away on a skiing holiday catching the last of the snow.*

a skiing accident *Klaus damaged his foot in a skiing accident.*

skiing conditions *Two days of heavy snow made skiing conditions almost perfect.*

S

skilful *BrE*, skillful *AmE adj*

good at doing something, especially something that needs special ability or training

NOUNS

a skilful player/driver *He is one of the team's most skilful players.*

a skilful politician/diplomat *She has the reputation of being a skillful politician.*

skilful use of sth *I like the skilful use of colour in his paintings.*

PREPOSITIONS

skilful at (doing) sth *Delamotte became skilful at drawing.*

THESAURUS: skilful

skilled
worker | labour | workforce | staff | craftsman | professional | job | work | hands
able to do a job well, because you have had a lot of experience and training:
*Skilled workers can earn a lot of money. | The key to a successful modern economy is a well-educated and **highly skilled** workforce. | Cutting glass is a skilled job. | In her skilled hands a snake of clay is shaped into a large jar. | Prison officers are **skilled at** handling prisoners.*

> **Skilled or skilful?**
> These words are similar in meaning. **Skilful** means "good at doing something". **Skilled** means "good at doing something because you have a lot of experience and training". You also use **skilled** about jobs and work that need a lot of skill and experience.
> You say a **skilled worker/workforce** (not 'a skilful one'). You say a **skilled job** or **skilled work** (not 'skilful').

talented
player | musician | writer | artist | student
having a natural ability to do something well:
*The team has some **exceptionally talented** young players. | His father was a **highly talented** musician, who dreamed of a career as a pianist.*

gifted
child | player | teacher | writer | student | musician
having a great natural ability, which few people have:
Her son goes to a special school for gifted children. | Williams described him as "a gifted writer who will be sadly missed".

expert
swimmer | skier | sailor | cook | horseman | horsewoman | staff
extremely skilful because you have a lot of experience and knowledge about doing something:
*The people who live on the islands are expert swimmers. | My mother was an expert cook and she served the most delicious meals. | Politicians are **expert at** avoiding difficult questions.*

accomplished
artist | musician | pianist | singer | liar | writer | player | performer | actor
very skilful because you have had a lot of experience of doing something:
*Bechard was an accomplished musician, who played trumpet professionally in a jazz band. | He was an accomplished liar and I knew that I couldn't trust anything he said. | Her first detective novel was a **highly accomplished** piece of work.*

virtuoso
performance | display | guitarist | violinist | pianist | performer
extremely skilful and impressive:
Dustin Hoffman gives a virtuoso performance in the film. | Atkins was a virtuoso guitarist who played with Elvis Presley.

> **Virtuoso** (adjective) is only used before a noun.

skill *n*

an ability to do something well, especially because you have learned and practised it

ADJECTIVES/NOUNS + skill

great/considerable skill (=a lot of skill) *He plays chess with great skill.*

good skills *We need someone with good computer skills.*

basic skills *The basic skills can be acquired very quickly.*

practical skills *Students will have the opportunity to learn a lot of practical skills.*

technical skills *Good technical skills are not enough.*

management skills *She needs to develop her management skills.*

computer/IT skills *We're looking for someone with good IT skills.*

reading/writing skills *Their reading skills are poor.*

communication skills (=the ability to communicate well with people) *The nurse must use her communication skills to help the patient feel at ease.*

social skills (=the ability to get on well with people) *She has no social skills and finds it difficult to make friends.*

people skills (*also* **interpersonal skills** *formal*) (=the ability to deal with people) *He wasn't a good communicator and had no people skills at all.*

language skills (=the ability to use a language) *We need to hire people with useful language skills.*

VERBS

have a skill *He didn't have the right skills for the job.*

learn a skill (*also* **acquire/master a skill** *formal*): *It's important to keep learning new skills.*

develop a skill (=improve it) *We will give you the opportunity to develop your skills.*

hone a skill (=improve it, especially when it is already very good) *The course will help you hone your writing skills.*

use a skill *I am sure you can use your communication skills to get your message across.*

take skill (*also* **require skill** *formal*) (=need skill) *It's a difficult task, which requires skill and experience.*

lack a skill (=not have it) *He lacked the skills to do the job.*

PREPOSITIONS

skill in (doing) sth *Skill in reading and writing is not important in some jobs.*

skill at (doing) sth *He was impressed with her skill at tennis.*

with skill *The team played with skill and determination.*

skilled *adj*

a skilled worker has the training and experience needed to do something well. A skilled job needs training and experience to do it well

NOUNS

a skilled worker *There is a shortage of skilled workers.*

a skilled craftsman (=skilled at making things with their hands) *The furniture factory employs skilled craftsmen.*

a skilled workforce (=group of workers) *The firm is proud of its highly skilled workforce.*

skilled labour *BrE*, **skilled labor** *AmE* (=all the skilled workers in a company, country etc) *There is a big demand for skilled labour.*

skilled people/staff *A team of skilled staff is available each weekday to provide advice.*

a skilled job/skilled work *Cutting these sections is a skilled job.*

a skilled negotiator *The government team is led by Schwartz, who is a tough and skilled negotiator.*

sb's skilled hands *In his skilled hands, an old piece of metal quickly becomes a beautiful sculpture.*

ADVERBS

highly skilled *We are fortunate to have a highly skilled and dedicated workforce.*

PREPOSITIONS

skilled at (doing) sth *She became skilled at interviewing candidates.*

skilled in sth *He was skilled in the art of clock-making.*

THESAURUS: skilled

skilled, talented, gifted, expert, accomplished, virtuoso → **skilful**

skin *n*

the natural outer layer of a person's or animal's body

ADJECTIVES

fair/pale skin (=light in colour) *I have fair skin that burns very easily.*

dark skin *The model had beautiful dark skin.*

brown/black/white skin *This make-up is especially for black skin.*

olive skin (=the colour typical of people from Greece, Italy etc) *She is Spanish, with olive skin and dark hair.*

smooth/soft skin *Her skin was smooth and pale.*

rough skin (=not smooth or soft) *The skin on his hands was rough from working in the fields.*

good/healthy/clear skin (=smooth and without any red spots) *Vitamin E helps keep your skin healthy.*

bad/terrible skin (=with many spots or marks) *I had terrible skin when I was a teenager.*
flawless skin (=perfect, with no spots or marks) *The girls all had perfect features and flawless skin.*
dry skin *My skin gets very dry in the winter.*
oily/greasy skin *My skin has a tendency to be oily.*
sensitive skin (=becoming red or sore easily) *Special products are available for those with sensitive skin.*
wrinkled skin (=covered in lines because of age) *Her skin was becoming wrinkled around her eyes.*
tanned skin (=brown from the sun) *His skin was slightly tanned.*
leathery skin (=thick and with a surface like leather - used especially about old people) *The old man had leathery skin.*
itchy skin (=making you want to scratch) *The cream made my skin feel itchy.*

VERBS + skin

damage your skin *Strong sunlight can damage your skin.*
burn your skin *The hot coffee spilt on his legs, burning his skin.*
protect your skin *It's important to use sunscreen to protect your skin.*
break the skin (=make a hole in it) *The little boy bit her so hard it broke the skin.*
irritate your skin (=make it red or sore) *Some types of make-up can irritate your skin.*

skin + VERBS

sb's skin glows/shines (=it looks healthy) *Her skin glowed after she had had her shower.*
sb's skin peels (=the top layer comes off after you have had a sun tan) *Using lots of moisturizer may stop your skin from peeling. | A week after I came back from holiday, my skin started to peel.*
sb's skin sags (=it hangs down in loose folds, because you are old) *The skin on her arms was already starting to sag.*

skin + NOUNS

skin colour *BrE*, **skin color** *AmE* (*also* **the colour of sb's skin**) *Everyone should be treated the same, whatever their skin colour.*
skin tone (=how light or dark someone's skin is) *Is your skin tone fair or dark?*
a skin condition/complaint (=a medical problem with your skin) *She suffers from a nasty skin condition.*
skin irritation (=when your skin is sore or uncomfortable) *A lot of chemicals can cause skin irritation.*
a skin rash (=an area of red or spotty skin) *Skin rashes are common among children.*
skin cancer *Everyone is worried about getting skin cancer.*

skinny *adj* THESAURUS ▸ thin (1)

skirt *n*

a piece of clothing worn by women and girls, which hangs down from the waist

ADJECTIVES/NOUNS + skirt

a short/long skirt *Short skirts are back in fashion this year.*
a knee-length/ankle-length skirt *These boots would go well with a knee-length skirt.*
a tight skirt *I must have put on weight - this skirt is too tight.*
a matching skirt (=one that has the same colour as another piece of clothing) *The woman was dressed in a blue blouse and a matching skirt.*
a pleated skirt (=one with a lot of narrow folds) *Helen wore a jacket with a neat pleated skirt.*
a pencil skirt (=a long narrow straight skirt) *She often wears a grey pencil skirt when she's in the office.*

VERBS

wear a skirt *Today she's wearing a blue skirt.*
put on/take off a skirt *I put on a white blouse and a red skirt for the interview.*
smooth (down) a skirt (=make a skirt flat by moving your hands across it) *She sat down and smoothed her skirt.*

skirt + NOUNS

a skirt pocket *She reached into her skirt pocket and took out some money.*

sky *n*

the space above the earth where clouds, the sun, and stars appear

ADJECTIVES/NOUNS + sky

blue sky *The sky was blue and the sun was shining.*
grey sky *BrE*, **gray sky** *AmE*: *Grey skies often mean it's going to rain.*
dark/black sky *Fireworks burst up into the dark sky.*
bright/clear/cloudless sky (=without clouds) *The sun rose higher in the cloudless sky.*
cloudy/dull/overcast sky (=with clouds) *Cloudy skies were forecast.*
a starry sky (=with a lot of stars) *We had dinner on the terrace under a beautiful starry sky.*
azure sky *literary* (=bright blue) *The sun shone out of a clear azure sky.*
leaden sky *literary* (=with a lot of grey cloud) *The leaden skies cleared and the sun came out.*
the night/evening/morning sky *The moon is the brightest object visible in the night sky.*
the summer/winter sky *Her eyes were as blue as the summer sky.*

S

the open sky (=a large area of sky) *They lay on the ground under the open sky.*

a big sky (=a sky that looks large) *Montana is still a land of big skies.*

VERBS

the sky clouds over (=clouds appear) *The sky was beginning to cloud over.*

the sky clears (=clouds disappear) *By dawn the sky had cleared.*

the sky darkens *The bright sky darkened to grey.*

light up the sky (*also* **illuminate the sky** *formal*): *A flash of lightning illuminated the sky.*

PREPOSITIONS

in/into the sky *We watched the plane go up into the sky.*

out of/from the sky *Ice crystals fall from the sky as snowflakes.*

across the sky *A soft golden light spread across the sky.*

under/beneath a sky *He hurried home under a sky full of stars.*

the sky above/over sth *The sky above the red roofs was a clear blue.*

PHRASES

the sky grew dark *The evening sky was growing dark.*

there wasn't a cloud in the sky *It was a beautiful summer's day and there wasn't a cloud in the sky.*

slab *n* THESAURUS **piece**

slam *v* THESAURUS **close[1] (1)**

slang *n*

very informal language that is used especially by people who belong to a particular group

VERBS

use slang *You should not use slang in your school essays.*

talk/speak (in) slang *The kids all talk in slang and it can be difficult to understand what they are saying.*

slang + NOUNS

a slang word (*also* **a slang term** *formal*): *'Bad' is sometimes used as a slang word meaning 'good'.*

ADJECTIVES/NOUNS + slang

prison/street/army slang *'Click' was army slang for a kilometre.*

American/Australian etc slang *A 'Pom' is an English person in Australian slang.*

Cockney rhyming slang *BrE* (=slang based on words that end with the same sound, used in London) *'Apples and pears' is Cockney rhyming slang for 'stairs'.*

PREPOSITIONS

slang for sth *'Bread' or 'dough' is slang for 'money'.*

slaughter *v* THESAURUS **kill**

slave *n*

someone who is owned by another person and has to work for them for no money

VERBS

keep/own a slave *The king kept many slaves in his palace.*

buy/sell a slave *Slaves were bought by landowners and made to work in the cotton fields.*

free a slave *Wilberforce successfully campaigned to free the slaves.*

ADJECTIVES

a former slave *The university was established in the mid-nineteenth century to educate former slaves.*

a freed slave *The children of freed slaves were allowed to become Roman citizens.*

a runaway slave (=who has escaped from his or her master) *Their ancestors were runaway slaves.*

slave + NOUNS

the slave trade (=the buying and selling of slaves) *Millions of Africans lost their lives as a result of the slave trade.*

slave labour *BrE*, **slave labor** *AmE* (=work done by slaves, or the people who do this work) *The temple was built by slave labour.*

a slave owner *Some slave owners treated their slaves worse than farm animals.*

a slave ship (=a ship that was used for transporting slaves, especially from Africa across the Atlantic) *Conditions on board the slave ships were truly terrible.*

a slave boy/girl *The princess had several slave girls to serve her.*

a slave revolt *The first successful slave revolt in the Caribbean took place in Haiti.*

a slave market (=a place where slaves were bought and sold) *Two slave markets operated in New Orleans before the Civil War.*

PHRASES

treat sb like a slave (=treat them very cruelly) *He treated his wife like a slave.*

slavery *n*

the system of having slaves, or the condition of being a slave

VERBS

abolish slavery (=officially end it) *Slavery was abolished in the British Empire in 1833.*

sell sb into slavery *His wife and children were sold into slavery.*

free sb from slavery *It was a long time before many African Americans were freed from slavery.*

PHRASES

the abolition of slavery (=the official ending of slavery) *The abolition of slavery in Brazil took place in 1888.*

the campaign against slavery *Wilberforce led the campaign against slavery.*

sleek *adj* THESAURUS ▶ **shiny**

sleep[1] *v*

to rest your mind and body, usually in bed

ADVERBS

sleep well *Did you sleep well?*

sleep badly *Eleanor slept badly that night.*

sleep soundly/deeply (=not likely to wake up) *Within seconds, Maggie was sleeping soundly.*

sleep peacefully *Celia slept peacefully beside him.*

sleep uneasily (=not sleep well, because you are worried) *That night I slept uneasily, anxious about the meeting the next day.*

sleep fitfully *literary* (=sleep badly, waking up after short periods) *She slept fitfully, her mind filled with images of Jack's face.*

barely/hardly sleep (=not sleep much) *I hardly slept the night before the wedding.*

sleep late (=wake up late) *She had slept late; it was already 11.*

sleep in (=wake up late) *I usually sleep in on Saturdays.*

sleep rough *BrE* (=sleep on the streets, because you have no home) *He'd been sleeping rough since his parents threw him out.*

VERBS

can't/couldn't sleep (*also* **be unable to sleep** *formal*): *I went to bed, but I couldn't sleep.*

try to sleep *Be quiet – I'm trying to sleep!*

let sb sleep *He was very tired, so we let him sleep.*

sleep + NOUNS

the sleeping arrangements *What will be the sleeping arrangements when you all go on holiday together?*

a sleeping pill *I took a sleeping pill and tried to go back to sleep.*

a sleeping bag (=a large warm bag that you sleep in, especially when camping) *You'll need a warm sleeping bag in the mountains.*

PREPOSITIONS

sleep for eight hours/two days etc *I usually sleep for six hours.*

sleep through sth (=not be woken by it) *She was so tired she slept through all the noise.*

sleep in a bed *I'm looking forward to sleeping in my own bed.*

sleep on the floor/sofa etc *There weren't enough beds, so some people had to sleep on the floor.*

PHRASES

sleep like a log (*also* **sleep like a baby**) *informal* (=sleep very well) *I was exhausted and slept like a log.*

have trouble sleeping (=not sleep well) *Fortunately, I never have any trouble sleeping.*

not sleep a wink *informal* (=not sleep at all) *I didn't sleep a wink last night.*

sleep on your back/front/side *Some people are more comfortable sleeping on their fronts.*

somewhere to sleep *I need to find somewhere to sleep tonight.*

Sleep or be asleep?

You use **be asleep** when saying that someone is not awake: *Is the baby* ***asleep****? | Don't wake him – he's* ***fast asleep*** (=completely asleep).

You usually use **sleep** when talking about how well, how long, or where someone sleeps: *I* ***slept*** *well last night. | You can* ***sleep*** *in the spare bedroom.*

sleep[2] *n*

the natural state of resting your mind and body, usually at night

ADJECTIVES

a long sleep *After a long sleep he felt much better.*

a little/short sleep *I always have a little sleep in the afternoon.*

a deep/sound/heavy sleep (=from which you cannot easily be woken) *He was in such a deep sleep he didn't hear the alarm.*

a light sleep (=from which you can easily be woken) *I woke up from a light sleep.*

an exhausted sleep (=because you were very tired) *He fell immediately into an exhausted sleep.*

a fitful/restless/uneasy sleep (=in which you keep moving or waking) *My alarm woke me from a fitful sleep.*

VERBS

go to sleep (=start sleeping) *He turned over and went to sleep.*

⚠ Don't say 'go sleep'.

get to sleep (=succeed in starting to sleep) *Last night I couldn't get to sleep.*

go back/get back to sleep (=sleep again after waking up) *He shut his eyes and went back to sleep.*

drift off/drop off to sleep (=start sleeping, especially without meaning to) *I felt myself drifting off to sleep.*

send sb to sleep (=make someone start sleeping) *She hoped the music would send her to sleep.*

have a sleep *BrE* (=sleep for a short time) *The baby usually has a sleep after lunch.*

sing/rock etc sb to sleep (=make someone sleep by singing, rocking them etc) *She was usually able to rock the baby back to sleep quite quickly.*
need sleep *Some people don't seem to need much sleep.*
disturb sb's sleep (=make it difficult for someone to sleep well) *Drinking too much coffee in the evening can disturb your sleep.*
sleep overcomes sb (=they start sleeping because they are tired) *She lay worrying for about an hour before sleep overcame her.*

sleep + NOUNS
sleep deprivation (=a situation in which someone does not get enough sleep) *Sleep deprivation can result in mental disorders.*
sleep patterns (=the times when you are asleep) *Disturbed sleep patterns are one symptom of depression.*

PREPOSITIONS
in your sleep (=while you are asleep) *She died peacefully in her sleep.*

PHRASES
a good night's sleep (=when you sleep well) *I woke up refreshed after a good night's sleep.*
five/eight etc hours' sleep *Two hours' sleep is not enough for anyone.*
lack of sleep *Lack of sleep can affect your ability to do your job properly.*
fall into a deep/long etc sleep (=start sleeping deeply, for a long time etc) *He lay down on his bed and fell into a deep sleep.*
not get a wink of sleep (=not sleep at all) *They were making so much noise that I didn't get a wink of sleep.*
cry yourself to sleep (=cry until you fall asleep) *I used to cry myself to sleep every night.*
get some sleep *You'd better get some sleep.*
not get much/any sleep *I didn't get much sleep last night.*
wake/be woken from a deep/long etc sleep *A very long time later I woke from a deep sleep.*
drift in and out of sleep (=keep waking up and then going back to sleep) *I lay in the garden, drifting in and out of sleep.*
catch up on some sleep (=sleep after not having enough sleep) *I suggest you try and catch up on some sleep.*

sleepy *adj* tired and ready to sleep

VERBS
feel sleepy *It was getting late and I was beginning to feel sleepy.*
become/get sleepy *The children get sleepy on long car trips.*
make sb sleepy *The warm air in the room was making her sleepy.*
look/sound sleepy *You look sleepy. Have you just got up?*

NOUNS
sleepy eyes *She woke up and looked at him with sleepy eyes.*
a sleepy voice *"What time is it?" he asked in a sleepy voice.*
a sleepy child *The sleepy child rubbed her eyes and yawned.*
sleepy head *informal* (=used when talking to someone who is sleepy and has just woken up) *"Wake up, sleepy head!" she called.*

THESAURUS: sleepy
sleepy, peaceful, tranquil, calm, dead → **quiet (3)**

sleeve *n*
the part of a piece of clothing that covers all or part of your arm

ADJECTIVES/NOUNS + sleeve
short/long sleeves *Her blouse has short sleeves.*
a shirt/jacket/coat sleeve *His watch was under his shirt sleeve.*
wide/full sleeves *A kimono is a traditional piece of Japanese clothing, like a long coat with wide sleeves.*

VERBS
roll up/down your sleeves *He rolled up his shirt sleeves and got to work.*
pull up/down your sleeve *He pulled up his sleeve to show her his tattoo.*
tug at sb's sleeve (=pull it many times) *The kids kept tugging at my sleeve, asking to go home.*

slender *adj* THESAURUS **thin (1), (2)**

slice[1] *n*
a thin flat piece of food cut from a larger piece

ADJECTIVES
a thin slice *Serve the soup with thin slices of bread and butter.*
a thick slice *Cut the pineapple into thick slices.*
a large/big slice *He was eating a large slice of chocolate cake.*
a small slice *She politely accepted a small slice of pie.*
a generous slice (=thick or big) *He cut himself a generous slice of cheese.*

VERBS
cut a slice *She cut another slice of bread.*
cut sth into slices *Cut the orange into thin slices.*

PREPOSITIONS
a slice of sth *Would you like another slice of pizza?*
in slices *Serve the tart cold, in slices.*

THESAURUS: slice

bit, lump, scrap, strip, sheet, slice, chunk, hunk, block, slab, cube, wedge, bar, segment, rasher, fragment, crumb, speck, drop → **piece**

slice² *v* THESAURUS **cut¹ (1)**

slight *adj* small and often not important

NOUNS

a slight increase/rise *The figures show a slight increase in the number of accidents.*

a slight decrease/decline/fall *There has been a slight decline in the number of students studying science at university.*

a slight improvement *Her spelling has started to show a slight improvement.*

a slight change *There has been a slight change of plan.*

a slight difference *There's a slight difference in height, but it's only a couple of centimetres.*

a slight problem *Unfortunately, there is a slight problem with your licence – it's out of date.*

a slight delay *There was a slight delay due to roadworks, but nothing serious.*

a slight pause *After a slight pause, he continued speaking.*

ADVERBS

comparatively/relatively slight (=when compared to something else) *The damage seemed comparatively slight considering the strength of the storm.*

only slight (=used to emphasize that something is very small) *The only slight criticism I have is that the pool wasn't heated.*

so slight *The risk seemed so slight I was prepared to take it.*

however slight (=used to say that a small difference can still have an effect) *An injury, however slight, can affect an athlete's performance.*

PHRASES

not the slightest doubt *Their coach does not have the slightest doubt that the team can win the title.*

Slight is often used when speaking ironically (=using words that have the opposite meaning): *There is a* ***slight*** *problem – we don't have any money* (=there is a big problem).

THESAURUS: slight

little, low, minor, slight, modest, compact, cramped → **small (1)**

slim *adj* THESAURUS **thin (1)**, **(2)**

slit *v* THESAURUS **cut¹ (1)**

slogan *n*
a short phrase used in advertisements, or by politicians, organizations, protesters etc

ADJECTIVES/NOUNS + slogan

a campaign/election slogan *His campaign slogan was 'Peace, stability, and prosperity'.*

a political slogan *The walls had political slogans painted on them.*

an advertising/marketing slogan *Their advertising slogan was 'A Mars a day helps you work, rest, and play'.*

a catchy slogan (=one that is easily remembered) *The Liberal Democrats were searching for a more catchy slogan.*

a snappy slogan (=one that is short and effective) *They've come up with a good snappy slogan for the product.*

an empty/hollow slogan (=a slogan making a promise that is not kept) *We want real progress, not just empty slogans.*

an anti-government slogan *Protesters carried banners bearing anti-government slogans.*

an anti-war slogan *Demonstrators lined the streets and chanted anti-war slogans.*

VERBS

shout slogans *Five youths were arrested after shouting anti-government slogans.*

chant slogans (=keep shouting them together in a regular way) *Dozens of demonstrators waved banners and chanted slogans.*

bear/carry a slogan (=have a slogan printed on it) *There was a stall selling badges bearing campaign slogans.*

coin a slogan (*also* **come up with a slogan**) (=invent it) *He was the man who coined the slogan 'Small is beautiful'.*

PREPOSITIONS

under a slogan *The party campaigned under the slogan 'back to basics'.*

the slogan of sb/sth *The Beatles song 'All You Need is Love' became a slogan of the hippy movement.*

THESAURUS: slogan

expression, idiom, cliché, saying/proverb, slogan, motto → **phrase**

slope *n*
a piece of ground or a surface that is higher at one end than the other

ADJECTIVES

a steep slope *We struggled to get up the steep slope.*

a gentle slope (=not steep) *These are gentle slopes which beginners should be able to ski down.*

a long slope *The fence is at the bottom of a long slope.*

a downward/downhill slope *The garden has a slight downhill slope.*

an uphill slope *It is hard to land on an uphill slope.*

a grassy slope *The children had fun rolling down a grassy slope.*

a wooded slope (=with a lot of trees) *We looked down on the wooded slopes of the valley.*

a rocky slope *The castle is perched high up on a rocky slope.*

the lower/upper slopes of sth *Only the lower slopes of the mountain could be seen through the mist.*

the eastern/northern etc slopes of sth *Vines are grown on the eastern slopes of the hill.*

NOUNS + slope

a mountain slope *Snow was falling on the mountain slopes.*

a ski slope *The most experienced skiers race down the steepest ski slopes.*

VERBS

climb up/down a slope (*also* **ascend/descend a slope** *formal*): *We climbed down the southern slope of the mountain.*

PHRASES

at the bottom/foot of a slope *The house sits at the foot of a grassy slope.*

the top of a slope *The skiers get a chairlift back to the top of the slope.*

be perched on a slope (=used when emphasizing that something is high up on a steep slope) *The house is perched on the sunny southern slope.*

sloppy *adj* THESAURUS **careless**

slow *adj*

not happening quickly, or not moving or doing something quickly

NOUNS

slow growth/development *The slow growth in sales is causing concern.*

a slow rate/pace *The economy grew at a slow rate.*

a slow speed *The car was travelling at a very slow speed.*

a slow process *Finding the right person can be a slow process.*

slow progress/improvement *It was a difficult climb and progress was slow.*

a slow start (=it began very slowly) *The work got off to a very slow start.*

a slow reader/learner/walker/swimmer *I was a slow learner and I couldn't read till I was 14.*

the slow lane (=the part of a road for vehicles that can only drive slowly) *The bus pulled into the slow lane.*

the slow train (=one that stops at a lot of stations) *We missed the express and we had to take the slow train.*

slow breaths *Take a few deep slow breaths and relax.*

ADVERBS

extremely/incredibly slow *The old machines were incredibly slow.*

painfully slow (=extremely slow, especially when this is annoying) *Downloading files can be a painfully slow process.*

frustratingly/agonizingly slow (=very slow in a way that makes you feel impatient) *If your progress seems agonizingly slow at first, don't worry.*

a little slow *The server is a little slow at the moment.*

THESAURUS: slow

gradual
process | increase | rise | improvement | change | reduction | deterioration | decline | shift
happening slowly over a long period of time:
Establishing a democracy is a gradual process. | There was a gradual increase in temperature. | There has been a gradual shift in people's attitudes to divorce (=a change from one attitude to a different one).

leisurely
pace | lunch | breakfast | meal | walk | stroll | drive
moving or doing something slowly, especially because you are enjoying what you are doing and do not have to hurry:
The couple walked home at a leisurely pace. | After a leisurely breakfast we went for a swim in the hotel pool. | He walked down to the beach ***in a leisurely fashion*** (=in a slow relaxed way).

unhurried
manner | way | pace
moving or doing something in a slow and calm way, without rushing:
The doctor explained the treatment in a calm unhurried manner. | She continued to listen, seeming relaxed and unhurried.

measured
approach | way | response | tone | fashion
doing something or speaking in a slow and careful way:
The committee insisted on taking a measured approach to the problem. | Reno gave a measured response to the reporter's questions. | He used a more measured tone in a statement last night.

sluggish
economy | growth | sales | demand | performance | start
used about a person who is slow and lacks energy. Also used when business is slow and not many goods are sold:

The US economy was sluggish in the early part of the year. | Sales of the new phone have been sluggish. | Alexandra woke up late, feeling tired and sluggish.

lethargic
moving slowly, because you feel as if you have no energy and no interest in doing anything:
His son became depressed and lethargic and lost interest in his schoolwork. | If I sit in front of the computer all day long I often feel lethargic.

Lethargic is not usually used before a noun.

languid *literary*
hand | **gesture** | **movement** | **wave** | **smile** | **indifference** | **grace** | **afternoon** | **summer**
a languid movement is slow, elegant, and uses very little effort. You also use **languid** about times when people do things slowly, especially because it is very hot:
She lifted a languid hand to push back her long blonde hair. | He remembered long languid afternoons by the river in August.

If something moves or happens very slowly, you say that it moves or happens **at a snail's pace**: *The game began **at a snail's pace**.*
In more informal contexts, if something seems to happen very slowly, you can say that it **goes on forever**: *The meeting seemed to **go on forever**.*

ANTONYMS **slow** → **fast**[1]

slum *n* THESAURUS > **area (1)**

sly *adj* THESAURUS > **dishonest**

small *adj*

1 not large in size or amount, or not serious

NOUNS

a small town/country/place *Exmouth is a small town of about 2,500 people.*

a small man/woman/boy/animal etc *Our guide was a small man with a moustache.*

a small car/plane/boat etc *Small cars use less gas.*

a small company/business *He owns a small business which employs eight people.*

a small amount/quantity/proportion *The family was able to save a small amount each month.*

a small number *The hotel only has room for a small number of guests.*

a small piece/part *She ate a small piece of cake.*

a small group *The students are taught in small groups.*

a small minority *The trouble is caused by a small minority of young people.*

a small change/increase/decrease *There has been a small increase in the number of people who are looking for work.*

a small problem *There are some small problems that still exist.*

a small difference *There are one or two small differences between them.*

ADVERBS

relatively/comparatively small (=rather small, especially compared to other things) *The number of people who die from the disease is relatively small.*

rather/quite/fairly small (*also* **pretty small** *informal*): *Luckily the hole was fairly small.*

PHRASES

small but perfectly formed *humorous* (=small but nice) *This new Italian restaurant is small but perfectly formed.*

THESAURUS: small

little
little means the same as **small**. It is often used when saying how you feel about someone or something, for example when saying that you like them or feel sorry for them:
It's a good little car. | The cake was decorated with pretty little flowers. | They had a few little problems.

Little or small?
If you say *a **small** boy*, you just mean he is not very big. If you say *a **little** boy*, you mean he is small and young and you feel sorry for him, think he is cute etc.
You say *a **small** number*, not 'a little number'. It is much more common to say *a **small** quantity/amount* than 'a little quantity/amount'.
Little is used with uncountable nouns, when saying there is not very much of something: *They made **little** progress. | You can grow your own vegetables, at very **little** cost.*
Little is also used when talking about people in your family who are younger than you: *He's my **little** brother* (=my younger brother).

low
price | **cost** | **wages** | **income** | **rent** | **level** | **rate** | **risk**
not large in amount:
The restaurant offers good food at low prices. | The workers' wages are very low. | I chose the apartment because the rent was low. | The crime rate is low in this area. | There is a low risk of side effects.

S

minor
injuries | damage | problem | changes | alteration | role | offence | detail | differences | repairs | adjustment
small and not important or not serious. **Minor** sounds rather formal:
The children were treated for minor injuries. | There were other minor problems which I will not bore you with. | For minor offences, the police often just give a warning. | The maps are the same, apart from one or two minor differences.

slight
increase | decrease | reduction | improvement | change | difference | problem | pause | delay | movement
very small and not very important or not very noticeable:
There was a slight increase in sales in November. | He noticed a slight improvement in his health. | There's just one slight problem – I've forgotten to bring my wallet.

modest
amount | increase | improvement | reduction | effect | success | profit | price | fee | sum | income | salary
rather small:
She was able to earn a modest amount of money as a nurse. | There has been a modest increase in sales. | Some studies show that the drug has a modest effect. | He achieved modest success as an actor. | Last year, the company recorded a modest profit of £1.4 million.

compact
camera | car | version | city | apartment | kitchen
used about things that are specially designed to be small, or places that are small but easy to get around:
A compact camera will fit in your shirt pocket. | Amsterdam is a very pleasant and compact city.

cramped *disapproving*
conditions | room | apartment | office | car
too small because people do not have enough room to move around:
The people work in very cramped conditions. | They all lived together in a cramped apartment. | The office feels very cramped with all this furniture.

ANTONYMS **small → big**

2 not tall

THESAURUS: small
small, low, petite, dumpy, stocky, diminutive, stunted → **short (4)**

3 very young

THESAURUS: small
small/little, teenage, adolescent, juvenile, youthful, junior → **young**

4 not important

THESAURUS: small
minor, small, trivial, insignificant, negligible, petty, secondary → **unimportant**

smart *adj* **THESAURUS** **intelligent**

smash *v* **THESAURUS** **break[1] (1)**

smell[1] *n*

the quality that people and animals recognize by using their nose

ADJECTIVES

a strong smell *Vinegar has rather a strong smell.*
a faint smell (=not strong) *I noticed a faint smell of perfume.*
a pungent smell (=very strong) *A pungent smell of garlic filled the air.*
an overpowering smell (=extremely strong) *The smell of dead bodies was overpowering.*
a nice/pleasant/lovely smell *There was a lovely smell of fresh coffee.*
a delicious smell (=a pleasant smell of food) *There were delicious smells coming from the kitchen.*
a bad/unpleasant/horrible smell *What's that horrible smell?*
a strange/funny/odd smell *There was a funny smell coming from her bedroom.*
a sweet smell *She liked the sweet smell of hay in the barn.*
a sickly smell (=sweet and unpleasant) *He hadn't washed for days and his clothes had a sickly smell.*
an acrid smell (=strong and bitter) *The acrid smell of smoke was everywhere.*
a musty/stale/sour smell (=old and not fresh) *The clothes in the wardrobe had a damp musty smell.*
a distinctive smell (=easy to recognize) *The flowers have a distinctive smell.*

VERBS

have a strong/sweet etc smell *This perfume has a nice smell.*
be filled with a smell *The house was filled with the smell of baking bread.*
give off a smell (=produce it) *Rubber gives off a strong smell when it is burned.*
notice/smell a smell (*also* **detect a smell** *formal*): *He detected a faint smell of blood.*
mask a smell (=hide it) *Air fresheners are used to mask unpleasant smells.*

a smell comes from sth (*also* **a smell emanates from sth** *formal*): *He was getting complaints about the smell emanating from his shop.*

a smell wafts somewhere (=moves there through the air) *The smells wafting up the stairs from the kitchen were making her feel hungry.*

PREPOSITIONS

the smell of sth *The air was filled with the smell of flowers.*

THESAURUS: smell

scent
a smell - used especially about the pleasant smell from flowers, plants, or fruit. Also used about the smell left by an animal:
The flowers had a ***beautiful scent****.* | *Cats* ***use their scent*** *to mark their territory.* | *The air was filled with the* ***heady scent*** *of the roses* (=strong scent).

fragrance/perfume
a pleasant smell, especially from flowers, plants, or fruit. **Fragrance** and **perfume** are more formal than **scent**:
The air is filled with the ***sweet perfume*** *of the orange blossoms.* | *Each mango has its own* ***special fragrance****.*

aroma *formal*
a pleasant smell from food, coffee etc:
The ***aroma*** *of fresh coffee* ***wafted across*** *the street* (=moved through the air). | *Each wine has its own* ***distinctive aroma*** (=a special aroma that makes it different from others). | *The bread has a* ***wonderful aroma*** *when it comes out of the oven.*

whiff
something that you smell for a short time:
He ***caught a whiff*** *of her perfume.* | *There was a* ***faint whiff*** *of jasmine.* | *There was a* ***distinct whiff*** *of tobacco smoke* (=easy to notice).

odour *BrE*, **odor** *AmE formal*
an unpleasant smell:
An ***unpleasant odour*** *was coming from the dustbins.* | *The room was filled with the odor of stale sweat.*

pong *BrE informal*
an unpleasant smell:
What's that ***horrible pong****?*

stink/stench
a very strong and unpleasant smell:
I couldn't get rid of the stink of sweat. | *The toilet gave off a* ***terrible stench****.*

smell[2] *v* to have a particular smell

ADJECTIVES

smell good/nice etc *The food smelled good.*
smell delicious *That soup smells delicious.*
smell fresh *Rub your chopping board with lemon to keep it smelling fresh.*
smell sweet *A ripe melon will smell sweet.*
smell bad/awful/terrible/disgusting etc *Cigarettes make your clothes smell awful.*
smell funny/strange *This place smells funny sometimes.*

ADVERBS

smell strongly of sth *The man smelled strongly of alcohol.*
smell faintly/slightly/vaguely of sth *His suit smelled faintly of tobacco.*

PREPOSITIONS

smell of sth *The kitchen always smells of fried food.*
smell like sth *This wine smells like grass.*

smile[1] *v*

to make your mouth curve upwards, in order to be friendly or because you are happy or amused

ADVERBS

smile politely *I shook his hand and smiled politely.*
smile sweetly (=in a friendly way, but often not sincerely) *He sat there smiling sweetly as if he knew nothing about it.*
smile warmly (=in a friendly way) *She welcomed them at the door, smiling warmly.*
smile broadly (=very happily, with a wide smile) *He sat there smiling broadly.*
smile faintly/slightly (=a little) *She smiled faintly back at him.*
smile weakly *literary*: *His aunt smiled weakly and asked for another glass of water.*
smile grimly *literary* (=smile in an unpleasant situation) *The guard smiled grimly.*
smile ruefully *literary* (=in a slightly sad way, because you wish something had not happened) *"I'm sorry," she said, and smiled ruefully.*
smile wryly *literary* (=when a situation is bad but also amusing) *"I suppose we'd better have another drink," he said smiling wryly to himself.*

VERBS

make sb smile *His comment made her smile.*
try to smile *"I'm fine," I said, trying to smile.*
manage to smile (=succeed in smiling, even though you have been unhappy or in a difficult situation) *She managed to smile through her tears.*

PREPOSITIONS

smile at sb/sth *The girl in the next seat was smiling at me.*

PHRASES

smile to yourself *Maggie looked at the photo and smiled to herself.*

S

have something/nothing etc to smile about *These poor people do not have much to smile about.*

smile² *n*

a happy expression made using your mouth

ADJECTIVES

a big/broad/wide smile *She came out of the interview with a big smile on her face.*

a warm/friendly smile *The waitress gave them a warm smile.*

a sweet smile (=a nice smile) *You have a really sweet smile, very charming.*

a gentle/reassuring smile *"You'll be alright," she said with a reassuring smile.*

a dazzling smile (=a big smile which shows someone's white teeth) *Diana gave a dazzling smile for the photographers.*

a bright/beaming/radiant smile (=which shows that you are very happy) *"I'm so pleased," he told her with a beaming smile.*

a little/faint/slight smile *A faint smile spread across his lips.*

a quick smile *"Thank you for your help," Sabrina said with a quick smile.*

a wry smile *literary* (=when you think a bad situation is slightly amusing) *"I'm afraid it's a little crowded in here," he said with a wry smile.*

a rueful smile *literary* (=when you wish you had not done something) *"I've been pretty stupid, haven't I?" Harry said with a rueful smile.*

VERBS + smile

give (sb) a smile *His mother gave him a big smile and told him not to worry.*

break into a smile (=suddenly start to smile) *Anna's face broke into a smile when she saw her mother.*

return sb's smile (=smile at someone after they have smiled at you) *"Nice to meet you too," she said, returning his smile.*

flash (sb) a smile (=give a quick smile) *She went out, flashing him a smile, and closing the door behind her.*

force/manage a smile (=smile when you do not really feel happy or friendly) *He forced a smile, but she could see disappointment on his face.*

smile + VERBS

a smile spreads across sb's face (=someone starts to smile) *As she heard the news, a faint smile spread across her face.*

sb's smile broadens (=it gets bigger) *His smile broadened when Sarah walked in.*

sb's smile fades/vanishes (=they stop smiling) *Her smile faded and she began to panic.*

PREPOSITIONS

with a smile *"I'm fine," Anna replied with a smile.*

PHRASES

have a smile on your face/lips *Rosie always has a smile on her face.*

a smile of satisfaction/relief/triumph etc *There was a smile of satisfaction on his face.*

sb is all smiles *informal* (=someone smiles a lot and is friendly or happy) *One moment he's all smiles, the next moment he shouts at me.*

smoke¹ *n*

white, grey, or black gas produced by something that is burning

ADJECTIVES

black/blue/white/grey smoke *Black smoke was pouring out of the engine.*

thick/dense smoke *Thick smoke spread through the building.*

acrid smoke (=smelling bad and making you cough) *The bar was full of acrid smoke.*

secondhand smoke (=that you breathe in from other people smoking cigarettes) *We are becoming more aware of the dangers of secondhand smoke.*

NOUNS + smoke

cigarette/cigar/tobacco smoke *The air was thick with cigarette smoke.*

wood smoke *I love the smell of wood smoke.*

VERBS

smoke is coming out of/from sth *Smoke was coming out of the kitchen.*

smoke is pouring out of/from sth *Smoke was pouring out of the back of the car.*

smoke rises *Smoke was rising from the top of the tower.*

smoke billows (=large clouds of smoke come from a fire) *She noticed smoke billowing out of one of the bedrooms.*

smoke drifts *The cigarette smoke drifted away on the breeze.*

smoke curls *On the campsite, smoke curled round the tents from nearby fires.*

smoke clears (=disappears) *The kitchen door was still open, and inside the smoke was clearing.*

belch (out) smoke (=send out large amounts of smoke) *The town is full of factories belching out smoke.*

smoke + NOUNS

a smoke detector/alarm (=a piece of equipment that makes a noise if there is a fire inside a building) *Make sure that every room is fitted with a smoke alarm.*

smoke inhalation (=when you breathe in a lot of smoke from a fire inside a building) *Several people were taken to hospital, suffering from smoke inhalation.*

PHRASES

a cloud of smoke (=a large amount) *He lit a cigarette and blew out a cloud of smoke.*

billows of smoke (=large clouds of smoke

coming out from a fire etc) *The green fresh leaves will burn slowly, with billows of smoke.*
a pall of smoke (=a thick cloud of smoke hanging over something) *A thick pall of smoke hung over the city.*
a column/plume of smoke (=a line rising up) *He could see a thin black column of smoke rising vertically into the sky.*
a puff of smoke (=a small amount that comes quickly from something) *There was a puff of white smoke from the man's gun.*
a wisp of smoke (=a thin line of smoke) *The fire was out, with only a few wisps of smoke rising here and there.*

smoke² *v*

to suck or breathe in smoke from a cigarette, pipe etc

ADVERBS

smoke heavily *The risk of heart disease increases if you smoke heavily.*
smoke too much *He's very unhealthy – he smokes too much and he is overweight.*

smoke + NOUNS

smoke a cigarette/cigar/pipe etc *Her father always smoked a cigar after dinner.*

VERBS

be allowed to smoke *You are not allowed to smoke in any public building in the UK.*

PHRASES

smoke like a chimney (=smoke a lot of cigarettes) *They both smoke like chimneys and the house stinks of cigarettes.*

S

smoker *n* someone who smokes

ADJECTIVES

a heavy smoker (=someone who smokes a lot) *My father was a heavy smoker and he died of lung cancer.*
a regular smoker *I used to be a regular smoker.*
a social smoker (=someone who smokes only when they are meeting other people, for example at a party) *He says he is a social smoker and he never buys his own cigarettes.*

NOUNS + smoker

a chain smoker (=someone who smokes one cigarette after another without stopping) *His wife was a chain smoker and always had a cigarette in her mouth.*
a cigarette/cigar/pipe smoker *Cigarette smokers know that they are taking a risk with their health.*

PHRASES

a smoker's cough *I'm not ill – it's just a smoker's cough.*

smoking *n*

the activity of breathing in tobacco smoke from a cigarette, pipe etc

ADJECTIVES

heavy smoking (=smoking a lot) *After a lifetime of heavy smoking, he is in poor health.*
passive smoking (=breathing in smoke from other people's cigarettes) *We all know about the dangers of passive smoking.*

smoking + NOUNS

a smoking habit (=a strong physical need to keep smoking) *He died of lung cancer, the result of a 40-a-day smoking habit.*
a smoking ban (*also* **a ban on smoking**) *The smoking ban led to a fall in cigarette sales.*

VERBS

give up/quit/stop smoking *I've been trying to give up smoking for years.*
start/begin smoking *How old were you when you started smoking?*
cut down on smoking *You should cut down on smoking and try to lose some weight.*
smoking causes sth *Smoking causes lung cancer.*

PHRASES

no smoking *The sign says 'No Smoking'.*
anti-smoking *The government launched an anti-smoking campaign.*
the dangers/risks of smoking *Cigarette packets carry strong warnings about the dangers of smoking.*

smooth *adj*

1 without lumps, bumps, or rough parts

NOUNS

smooth skin *His beard felt rough against her smooth skin.*
a smooth surface *The leaves of the plant have a smooth shiny surface.*
a smooth paste *Mix the ingredients together until you have a smooth paste.*
a smooth finish (=a smooth surface that has been painted or treated in some way) *The varnish gives a nice smooth finish.*
a smooth landing *The plane made a smooth landing at Heathrow airport.*

VERBS

feel smooth *After using the cream for a week, her skin felt smooth.*
be worn smooth *The stones on the beach had been worn smooth by the sea.*

PHRASES

(as) smooth as silk/glass *Her skin was as smooth as silk.*
silky smooth *The conditioner leaves your hair feeling silky smooth.*

THESAURUS: smooth

level, even, smooth, horizontal → **flat¹**

ANTONYMS **smooth → rough (1)**

2 without problems

NOUNS

the smooth operation/running of sth *Good communications are vital to the smooth operation of the company.*

a smooth transition (=change from one state to another) *We hoped the country would have a smooth transition to democracy.*

a smooth passage (=movement to another stage in something) *The team had a smooth passage through to the next round of the competition.*

a smooth ride/flight/crossing (=a comfortable journey without any sudden movements or problems) *We arrived on time after a very smooth flight.*

PHRASES

sth is smooth sailing (=you do not have any problems) *With so many enemies, her presidency would not be all smooth sailing.*

THESAURUS: smooth

comfy, cosy, snug, smooth → **comfortable**

snack *n*

a small amount of food that is eaten between main meals or instead of a meal

ADJECTIVES/NOUNS + snack

a light/small snack *I fixed myself a light snack and watched TV.*

a quick snack *She grabbed a quick snack on her way to the gym.*

a mid-morning/afternoon/evening snack *I usually have a mid-morning snack about 11 o'clock.*

a midnight/bedtime snack *Do you ever come downstairs in the night for a midnight snack?*

a tasty snack *You will find a range of tasty snacks at the bar.*

a healthy snack *Try to give your kids fruit and healthy snacks instead of candy.*

VERBS

have/eat a snack *He usually has a snack when he comes home from school.*

serve snacks *The pool serves snacks and drinks throughout the day.*

make (sb) a snack (*also* **fix (sb) a snack** *AmE*): *I'll make you a snack if you're hungry.*

cook/prepare a snack *I prepared some snacks for the kids to take with them.*

grab a snack (=eat one quickly because you are busy) *I only had time to grab a snack for lunch.*

NOUNS

snack foods *Many snack foods, like crisps and peanuts, contain quite a lot of salt.*

a snack bar (=a small café or counter selling snacks) *There is quite a long queue at the snack bar.*

snake *n*

an animal with a long thin body and no legs, that often has a poisonous bite

ADJECTIVES/NOUNS + snake

a poisonous snake (*also* **a venomous snake** *formal*): *He warned me there were poisonous snakes in the area.*

a deadly snake (=which can kill you) *This is one of the most deadly snakes in the world.*

a tree/sea/water etc snake *The fishermen regularly catch sea snakes.*

VERBS

a snake bites sb *The man had been bitten by a snake.*

a snake hisses (=it makes a noise which sounds like 'ssss') *The snake hissed at him and opened its mouth.*

a snake slithers somewhere (=it moves there) *A green snake slithered silently across the path.*

a snake coils itself around sth (=moves its body around it) *The snake coiled itself around the branch.*

snake + NOUNS

a snake bite/snakebite *The leaves are used as a treatment for snake bites.*

a snake charmer (=someone who plays music to make a snake move for public entertainment) *A group of people had gathered around a snake charmer sitting on the pavement.*

snake venom (=poison produced by a snake) *The snake venom is extremely poisonous.*

snap *v* THESAURUS → **break[1] (1)**

sneaky *adj* THESAURUS → **dishonest**

snip *v* THESAURUS → **cut[1] (1)**

snob *n*

someone who thinks they are better than people from a lower social class – used to show disapproval

ADJECTIVES/NOUNS + snob

a terrible/dreadful/awful snob *She was a terrible snob and refused to use public transport.*

an intellectual snob *Her boyfriend is an intellectual snob who thinks anyone who hasn't been to university is stupid.*

a wine/music etc snob (=who knows a lot about something and only likes what they think is the highest quality kind) *Music snobs automatically dismiss local bands as second rate.*

snob + NOUNS

snob value/appeal (=used about something that is liked by snobs) *The real snob value of a car like this is that normal people can't afford one.*

S

snow[1] *n*

soft white pieces of frozen water that fall from the sky in cold weather

ADJECTIVES

deep snow *The snow was quite deep in places.*
heavy snow (=a lot of snow falling) *Heavy snow is forecast for next week.*
light snow (=a small amount of snow falling) *A light snow had begun to fall.*
fresh snow (=recently fallen) *The tracks I'd made were now covered with fresh snow.*
powdery snow (=soft and light) *The snow is powdery and good for skiing.*
driving snow (=falling fast) *We walked home through driving snow.*
swirling snow (=blowing around as it falls) *It was difficult to see in the swirling snow.*
artificial snow (=not real) *The ski slope has artificial snow, so you can ski all year round.*

VERBS

snow comes down/falls *We sat at the window watching the snow falling outside.*
snow settles (=stays on the ground) *The snow was beginning to settle.*
snow drifts (=is blown into deep piles) *The snow had drifted up against the wall.*
snow covers sth (*also* **snow blankets sth** *literary*): *The ground was covered with snow.*
snow melts/thaws (=turns to water) *The snow has melted and the ground is bare once more.*
clear snow *He spent an hour clearing snow from his driveway.*

snow + NOUNS

snow chains (=chains that go around a car's tyres to stop it sliding in the snow) *The cars all have snow chains.*
snow tyres *BrE*, **snow tires** *AmE*: *You can't drive up there without snow tires.*

> **Snowflake**, **snowfall**, **snowball**, **snowman**, **snowboarding**, and **snowdrift** are written as one word.

PREPOSITIONS

in the snow *There were footprints in the snow.*
under snow *The mountain tops were under deep snow.*

PHRASES

centimetres/inches/feet etc of snow *More than 20 cm of snow fell in 48 hours.*
a blanket/carpet of snow (=a layer of snow that covers everything) *Within an hour, the town was buried under a blanket of snow.*
flakes of snow/snowflakes (=individual pieces of snow) *A few flakes of snow started to fall.*
a flurry of snow/a snow flurry (=a small amount of snow blown around in the wind) *The day was cold, with a few flurries of snow.*
a fall of snow/a snowfall (=an occasion when it snows) *We had our first fall of snow in mid-November.*

> **Snow-capped** mountains have snow on the top: *All around the city are* ***snow-capped*** *mountains.*

snow[2] *v*

if it snows, snow falls from the sky

PHRASES

it snows/snowed *It might snow tomorrow.*
it is/was snowing *When we woke up in the morning it was snowing.*

ADVERBS

snow heavily/hard *It has been snowing heavily for the last two days.*
snow lightly *It was still snowing lightly when I walked back to my car.*
snow steadily *It snowed steadily all night.*

VERBS

start/begin to snow *As we arrived, it was just starting to snow.*
stop snowing *I'll wait until it stops snowing before I go out.*

soap *n*

the substance that you use to wash your body

PHRASES

a bar of soap *A new bar of soap was lying in the dish.*
soap and water *She only uses soap and water on her face.*
wash sth with soap *Make sure you wash your hands with soap.*

soap + NOUNS

a soap bubble *The sink was filled with soap bubbles.*
soap suds (=a lot of soap bubbles) *She was washing clothes by hand, and her arms were covered in soap suds.*
a soap dish (=a container for a bar of soap) *There was also a small nailbrush in the soap dish.*

ADJECTIVES

scented/perfumed soap *His hands smelled of perfumed soap.*

VERBS

soap lathers (=it produces bubbles when made wet) *Soap will not lather in hard water.*

soccer *n*

a sport played by two teams of 11 players, who try to kick a round ball into the other team's goal

ADJECTIVES/NOUNS + soccer

professional soccer *Wayne's ambition was to play professional soccer.*
international soccer (=played by teams

representing their country) *He will retire from international soccer after the World Cup.*

VERBS

play soccer *The kids were playing soccer.*

watch soccer *The men were watching soccer on TV.*

soccer + NOUNS

a soccer team/club *Jean played for the French soccer team.*

a soccer player/star *His uncle was a talented soccer player.*

a soccer fan (=someone who likes soccer a lot) *I'm not really a soccer fan.*

a soccer match/game *We're going to a soccer match on Saturday.*

a soccer field (*also* **a soccer pitch** *BrE*) (=an area of grass where soccer is played) *She ran up and down the soccer field.*

a soccer stadium (*also* **a soccer ground** *BrE*) (=a place where soccer is played) *They plan to build a 70,000-seat soccer stadium.*

a soccer tournament *They won the Asia Cup soccer tournament last July.*

the soccer season (=the period in a year when soccer is played) *It was an exciting end to the soccer season.*

a soccer league (=a group of soccer teams who play against each other) *She helps organize a local youth soccer league.*

a soccer ball *The boys were kicking a soccer ball around the field.*

a soccer manager/coach *Charles is the men's soccer coach at Portland University.*

a soccer referee (=the person who makes sure that the rules are followed during the game) *He is a qualified soccer referee.*

a soccer hooligan (=someone who behaves in a violent way at a soccer match) *The police tried to control the soccer hooligans.*

Soccer is used especially in American English. In British English, people usually say **football**.

social *adj*

1 relating to society or to people in general

NOUNS

a social class/group *People from different social classes began to meet each other.*

social status (=low or high position within society) *Marriage to a rich woman could improve a young man's social status.*

social change/reform *During that time, the country experienced major social change.*

social history (=dealing with people's lives, not with politics or wars) *She called for more social history to be taught in schools.*

social problems/issues *The government must address social problems such as poor housing.*

social conditions *The social conditions at the time created an atmosphere of revolution.*

social justice (=when all social groups are treated fairly) *People in the upper classes had little concern for social justice.*

social equality (=when all people are treated as equal) *The book argues that social equality is not necessarily a good thing.*

social deprivation (=very bad living conditions) *In the richest countries, there are still areas of incredible social deprivation.*

2 relating to meeting people, forming relationships with them, and spending time with them

NOUNS

social life (=activities that involve being with other people for pleasure) *He has an active social life and has many friends.*

social skills (=the ability to deal with people easily) *In school, the children also learn social skills.*

social graces (=good and polite behaviour towards other people) *He lacked social graces, but he was kind-hearted.*

social contact/interaction *Work provides social contact.*

a social call (=a visit because you want to have a friendly talk or meeting, not for business) *This is purely a social call – I just came to say hello.*

ADVERBS

purely social (=just for meeting or talking to someone, not for business) *The invitation is nothing to do with work – my reason for asking you is purely social.*

society *n*

a particular large group of people who share laws, organizations, customs etc

ADJECTIVES

a modern society *Electricity services are an essential feature of modern society.*

an advanced society *Japan is one of the most advanced societies in the world.*

a democratic society *Education is important in a democratic society.*

a free society (=one where you can do what you want) *We all think that we are living in a free society.*

a civilized society *A civilized society should treat its elderly members well.*

a multicultural/multiracial society *We live in a multicultural society.*

Western society *The values of Western society are not shared by some communities.*

an industrial society *Industrial societies place a high importance on economic growth.*

a classless society (*also* **an egalitarian society** *formal*) (=one in which people are not divided into different social classes) *Do you think that there is such a thing as a classless society?*

larger/wider society (=used when comparing a small group of people to society as a whole) *The poorest people must be made to feel part of the wider society.*

a primitive society *In almost all primitive societies, volcanoes have been regarded with fear.*

(a) civil society *formal* (=a society based on laws that everyone accepts) *The protection of human rights is essential for civil society.*

a just society (=one in which all the people are treated fairly) *He had a vision of a better and more just society.*

a divided society *British society is deeply divided by class.*

VERBS + society

build/create a society *The purpose of politics should be to build a better society.*

shape/change/transform (a) society *The French Revolution was important in shaping modern European society.*

PREPOSITIONS

in (a) society *We have to accept that some groups in society need support.*

PHRASES

a member of society *The law needs to protect the least powerful members of society.*

a section/sector of society *The desire for more luxury exists in every sector of society.*

sb's place in society *Indian citizens are very aware of their relative place in society.*

society at large/in general (=ordinary people, not people such as political leaders) *The views of high court judges often have nothing in common with those of society at large.*

a cross-section of society (=a group that includes many different types of people) *The survey attempted to include a cross-section of society.*

sock *n*

a soft piece of clothing that you wear on your foot inside your shoe

PHRASES

a pair of socks *He had a spare pair of socks in his gym bag.*

shoes and socks *We took off our shoes and socks and waded in the stream.*

VERBS

wear socks *He always wore red socks.*

put/pull your socks on *He quickly pulled on his socks and his shoes.*

take your socks off *My feet got so hot and sweaty I took my trainers and socks off.*

ADJECTIVES/NOUNS + sock

thick socks *Wear thick socks and boots.*

cotton/nylon/wool socks *Cotton socks are better for your feet.*

odd socks (=socks that are not a pair) *He was wearing odd socks – one blue one and one black one.*

ankle socks (=short socks that reach only up to the ankles) *The girls wore navy dresses and white ankle socks.*

soft *adj*

1 not hard, firm, or stiff, but easy to press

NOUNS

soft skin/hair/fur *The baby's skin was lovely and soft.*

soft ground/earth/grass/sand *My feet sank into the soft ground.*

soft material/fabric/leather *The shoes were made of soft brown leather.*

soft food/fruit/cheese/bread *Soft sugary foods are bad for your teeth.*

a soft texture/feel *The bread has a pleasantly soft texture.*

VERBS

go soft *The ice cream will go soft if you leave it outside the freezer.*

keep sth soft *The cream helps to keep your skin soft.*

stay/remain soft *The chocolate will stay soft for hours after baking.*

ADVERBS

beautifully/wonderfully soft *The fabric has a beautifully soft texture.*

PHRASES

as soft as silk *Her face was as soft as silk.*

soft to the touch *The leaves were soft to the touch and covered in tiny hairs.*

THESAURUS: soft

tender
meat | beef | steak | chicken | pork | flesh | vegetables | carrots | potatoes
used about meat or vegetables that are soft and easy to cut, especially because they have been well cooked:
The beef was lovely and tender. | Cook the carrots until tender.

soggy
bread | vegetables | cabbage | rice | pastry | sandwich | ground | field | paper | mess
if something is soggy, it is too soft because it contains a lot of liquid, especially in a way that seems unpleasant:
English food used to consist of soggy boiled vegetables and overcooked meat. | His feet sank into the soggy ground. | The plants were a soggy mess after the rain.

squishy (*also* **squashy** *BrE*)
tomato | sofa | armchair | toy | leaves
very soft and easy to press:

The tomatoes have gone all squishy - I think I'll throw them out. | I sat down on a big squashy sofa. | The leaves were squishy under our feet.

The word **squishy** shows the sound that something soft makes when you press it.

spongy
texture | foam | ground | soil | earth
soft and full of holes that contain air or liquid like a sponge:
The bread has a soft spongy texture. | The shoes have spongy foam in the soles. | His boots sank into the spongy soil.

springy
turf | mattress | surface | texture | hair
used about a surface that comes back to its normal shape after being pressed or walked on:
The turf was springy beneath her feet (=the grass was springy). *| Her hair felt lovely and springy.*

mushy
very soft and becoming like a liquid - used especially about food that has been cooked for too long or is no longer fresh:
Cook the fruit until it is soft but not mushy. | The sprouts were mushy and the gravy was lumpy.

pliable
able to be bent or pressed without breaking or cracking:
The clay was still pliable and not too dry. | Soak the dried mushrooms in water until soft and pliable.

ANTONYMS **soft → hard (1)**

2 gentle

NOUNS

a soft voice/sound *Her voice was soft and calming.*

soft light/lighting/glow *The soft lighting makes the room feel nice and cosy.*

soft eyes/face/smile *The horse had big soft brown eyes.*

THESAURUS: soft

low, soft, silent, hushed, faint, muffled, dull, inaudible → **quiet (1)**

faint, weak, pale, poor/bad, soft, low → **dim**

software *n*

a computer program or set of programs

ADJECTIVES/NOUNS + software

computer software *He works for a computer software company.*

anti-virus software (=which protects against viruses) *It's important to have good anti-virus software installed.*

VERBS

use software *Several companies have already begun using the software.*

run software *To run the software, you will need the latest version of Windows.*

download software *Users can download the software for free.*

load/install software *It only takes a few minutes to install the software.*

write/design/develop software *He designs software for an Atlanta-based company.*

upgrade/update software (=get a better or more modern version) *Make sure you regularly update your anti-virus software.*

software + NOUNS

a software developer/engineer/designer *She got a job in California as a software developer.*

a software company *He owns a small software company.*

the software industry *The software industry employs millions of people.*

software products *She developed a range of software products for use in cellphones.*

a software package/suite/bundle (=a set of programs) *Select a software package which suits your requirements.*

PHRASES

a piece of software *This excellent piece of software is compatible with both PCs and Macs.*

soggy *adj* THESAURUS **soft (1)**, **wet[1] (1)**

soil *n*

the top layer of the earth in which plants grow

ADJECTIVES

good/rich/fertile soil (=good for growing plants) *The soil is very fertile and good for growing crops.*

poor soil (=not good for growing plants) *If the soil is poor, add manure or compost.*

deep soil *Parsnips need deep soil.*

thin soil (=not deep) *The thin soil is easily washed away.*

moist/dry soil *Keep the soil moist.*

light/sandy soil (=containing a lot of sand) *Some plants prefer sandy soils.*

heavy/clay soil (=containing a lot of clay) *The soil was too heavy for growing carrots.*

well-drained soil (*also* **free-draining soil**) (=letting water pass through easily) *Tomatoes prefer a well-drained soil.*

acid/alkaline soil *Blueberries need acid soil.*

VERBS

improve the soil *Adding manure helps to improve the soil.*

weed the soil (=remove the weeds) *The soil needs weeding every couple of weeks.*

till the soil (=prepare it to grow crops, especially using a special tool such as a hoe or a plough) *Their time is spent in constantly tilling the soil.*

soil + NOUNS

soil erosion (=when water or wind removes soil) *Planting these grasses helps to prevent soil erosion on slopes.*

soiled *adj* THESAURUS ▸ dirty

soldier *n*

a member of the army of a country, especially someone who is not an officer

ADJECTIVES

a British/US/Pakistani etc soldier *Two British soldiers were killed yesterday.*

a brave soldier *One brave soldier carried his injured comrade to safety.*

a wounded soldier *The television report showed wounded soldiers returning from the war.*

a young soldier *Here is a picture of my father as a young soldier.*

an old soldier (=someone who was a soldier in the past) *Like many old soldiers, he liked to spend time alone.*

a regular/professional soldier (=someone whose job is being a soldier) *Members of the volunteer army fought alongside regular soldiers.*

NOUNS

an enemy soldier *We saw a line of enemy soldiers advancing towards our position.*

a foot soldier (=who travels by walking, not on a horse or in a vehicle) *He sent 1,000 cavalry and 15,000 foot soldiers to the region.*

a rebel soldier (=fighting against a government) *The outskirts of the city have been attacked by rebel soldiers.*

a child soldier *The African leader's army used child soldiers.*

VERBS

a soldier dies/is killed *A British soldier died after his vehicle was hit by a roadside bomb.*

a soldier is wounded *Five soldiers were wounded, one seriously.*

a soldier fights *He was a brave soldier who fought for his country.*

a soldier returns from a war/battle etc *The film shows hundreds of soldiers returning from the battlefields of northern France.*

a soldier is stationed somewhere (=sent to live and work somewhere) *These soldiers have been stationed in the Helmand province of Afghanistan for six months.*

play soldiers (=pretend to be soldiers - used about children) *In the garden, two young boys were playing soldiers.*

PHRASES

send soldiers into battle *The prime minister understands the responsibility of sending soldiers into battle.*

lead soldiers into battle *I imagine the general leading his soldiers into battle with his sword outstretched.*

soldiers in the field (*also* **soldiers on the ground**) (=in the area where a war is taking place) *We need more soldiers on the ground to do the job properly.*

solemn *adj*

1 serious, especially because something sad has happened

NOUNS

a solemn face/expression *I knew from their solemn faces that something bad had happened.*

a solemn voice/solemn tones *"This is a very serious matter," he said in solemn tones.*

solemn words *The crowd listened to these solemn words in silence.*

a solemn occasion *I had no clothes suitable for a solemn occasion such as a funeral.*

a solemn moment *Both men signed the treaty. It was a solemn moment.*

a solemn ceremony *At a solemn ceremony, the president read out a list of those who had died.*

a solemn procession *Her body was carried in a solemn procession to the church.*

solemn music *When he died, the state radio station played solemn music all day.*

VERBS

look solemn *He was looking very solemn. "What's the matter?" she asked.*

sb's face grows solemn *As she read the letter, her face grew solemn.*

2 a solemn promise, warning, or duty is one that you are very serious about

NOUNS

a solemn promise/pledge/undertaking *How could she break her solemn promise?*

a solemn vow/oath *I made a solemn vow not to smoke another cigarette.*

sb's solemn word (=a solemn promise) *I give you my solemn word that nothing bad will happen to you.*

a solemn declaration *They each make a solemn declaration that they will judge the case fairly.*

a solemn warning *She was given a solemn warning about what would happen if she disobeyed.*

a solemn duty/responsibility *I had a solemn duty to warn them.*

solid *adj*

1 consisting of a thick hard material and not hollow or liquid

NOUNS

solid rock *They were drilling into solid rock.*

a solid block of sth *The water had frozen into a solid block of ice.*

a solid mass of sth *My way was blocked by a solid mass of people.*

a solid object *Sound waves travel more easily through solid objects than through the air.*
solid food (=food that is not a liquid) *She was too ill to eat solid food.*
solid gold/silver/wood/marble etc (=made only of gold, silver etc) *He gave her a solid gold bracelet.*
solid matter/material *Solid matter is carried along by the water.*
solid ground *She was glad to be back on solid ground.*
a solid form *This substance is not dangerous in its solid form.*
solid waste *The solid waste is buried or burned.*
solid fuel (=fuel that is not a liquid or a gas) *The heater burns solid fuel.*

VERBS

freeze solid *The stream had frozen solid.*

THESAURUS: solid

firm, stiff, solid, rigid, crispy, crunchy, tough, rubbery, brittle → **hard (1)**

2 good or able to be depended on

NOUNS

solid evidence *The investigators could not find any solid evidence of a crime.*
a solid performance *The goalkeeper gave a solid performance.*
solid achievement/work *We can look back on 2010 as a year of solid achievement.*
a solid reputation *The company has a solid reputation for excellent service.*
solid support *The president has solid support in most parts of the country.*
a solid foundation/base/basis *This is a solid foundation for the future growth of their business.*
a solid background/grounding *He has a solid background in the law.*
a solid relationship *They appeared to have a solid working relationship.*
a solid guarantee *I want a solid guarantee that I will not lose any money.*

PHRASES

rock solid (*also* **as solid as a rock**) *Their marriage remains rock solid.*

solution *n*

1 a way of solving a problem or dealing with a difficult situation

ADJECTIVES/NOUNS + solution

a good/effective solution *I hope someone can think of a good solution.*
the best/perfect/ideal solution *Locking people in prison is not necessarily the ideal solution.*
a satisfactory solution (=good enough) *We will not rest until a satisfactory solution is found.*
a neat solution (=simple and clever) *This sounded like a neat solution to the problem.*
the real solution (=the only good solution) *The real solution to the waste problem is to produce much less waste.*
a possible solution *There are three possible solutions to this problem.*
an alternative solution *We need to look for alternative solutions.*
a simple/easy solution *There is no easy solution to the problem.*
a quick solution *We need to find a quick solution.*
a practical/workable solution (=one that is really possible) *They've had to find practical solutions to practical problems.*
a long-term solution (=that will be effective for a long time) *A long-term solution to the problem will not be possible until that conflict is resolved.*
a quick-fix solution (=that solves a problem for a short time only) *He has accused the government of looking for quick-fix solutions.*
a peaceful solution (=one that does not involve fighting) *Everyone is hoping for a peaceful solution to the crisis.*
a compromise solution (=in which each side has to accept a little less than what they wanted) *They will never agree to any compromise solution.*

VERBS

come up with/find a solution *We are working together to find the best solution we can.*
look for a solution (*also* **seek a solution** *formal*): *The company is still seeking a solution to its financial problems.*
provide/offer a solution *I don't think that tourism will provide a long-term solution to employment problems.*
suggest a solution *Can anyone suggest a solution?*
put forward a solution (=suggest one) *The chairman put forward a possible solution.*
have a solution *Every problem has a solution.*

PREPOSITIONS

a solution to sth *There is no simple solution to this problem.*
a solution for sth *Nature has a solution for everything.*

2 a liquid in which a solid or gas has been mixed

ADJECTIVES/NOUNS + solution

a weak/dilute solution (=containing a small percentage of a solid or gas) *Use only a very weak solution.*
a strong/concentrated solution (=containing a high percentage of a solid or gas) *Drop the egg shells into a strong solution of water and food colouring.*

a sugar solution *The water passes into the sugar solution.*

a saline solution (=containing salt) *They cleaned the wound with a saline solution.*

PREPOSITIONS

a solution of sth *Wash the wool in a solution of water and soap.*

solve *v*

1 to find or provide a way of dealing with a problem

NOUNS

solve a problem *He solved the problem by buying a better computer.*

solve a crisis *Congress had not been able to solve the financial crisis.*

solve a dispute/conflict *The two sides have agreed to solve their dispute by peaceful means.*

solve a dilemma *How do you solve the dilemma of giving rights to people who do not want them?*

solve sb's difficulties *You can't solve your difficulties by running away.*

solve a question/issue *People have been trying to solve the Israel/Palestine issue for decades.*

ADVERBS

solve sth peacefully *There is a real chance to solve this crisis peacefully.*

solve sth diplomatically (=by having political discussions, not wars) *We are hopeful that the two nations can solve their differences diplomatically.*

solve sth overnight (=quickly and easily) *The issue of how to improve healthcare cannot be solved overnight.*

VERBS

help (to) solve sth *We offer a counselling service to help couples solve their difficulties.*

try/attempt to solve sth *The engineers are still trying to solve the problem.*

2 to find an explanation for something, or find the answer to a question

NOUNS

solve a crime/case *The crime was never solved.*

solve a murder *Police have called for witnesses to help them solve the murder.*

solve a mystery *Staff in the shop think they have solved the mystery of the missing money.*

solve a puzzle *You progress through the game by solving puzzles.*

solve a riddle *Experts still haven't really solved the riddle of how the pyramids were built.*

solve an equation *At the age of six, he could solve complicated mathematical equations.*

someone, somebody *pronoun*

used to mean a person, when you do not know or say who the person is

ADJECTIVES

someone important/famous *She knew the phone call must be from someone important.*

someone new/different *I feel shy when I'm talking to someone new.*

someone else *Ask someone else to check your work.*

someone special *Do you have someone special in your life?*

someone close to sb *It was the first time that someone close to me had died.*

someone nice *I hope she meets someone nice.*

someone willing to do sth *They had difficulty finding someone willing to take on the job.*

someone younger/older *She didn't get the part because the director wanted someone younger.*

PREPOSITIONS

someone like sb *I would never marry someone like him.*

someone with sth *We need someone with experience.*

PHRASES

someone to talk to/love/blame etc *She just needed someone to talk to.*

something *pronoun*

used to mean a particular thing, when you do not know or say exactly what it is

ADJECTIVES

something important *I have something important to tell you.*

something special *We must do something special for her birthday.*

something strange/odd/funny *Then I noticed something odd.*

something new/different *She was learning something new every day.*

something similar *Try to stop the bleeding with a clean handkerchief or something similar.*

something else *If that doesn't work, we'll have to try something else.*

something bad/terrible *I was afraid that something terrible was going to happen.*

something good/nice/wonderful *I'll buy you something nice.*

something suitable *She looked through her clothes for something suitable to wear.*

PREPOSITIONS

something about sb/sth *There was something about my old school in the newspaper yesterday.*

something like sth (*also* **something akin to sth** *formal*): *She looked at me with something like hatred.*

VERBS

say something *The man said something in French.*

do something *She knew she had done something terrible.*

something happens *Something extraordinary is happening.*

PHRASES

something to eat/read/do etc *We stopped to get something to eat.*

there's something wrong/something the matter (with sth) *There's something wrong with his heart.*

there's something strange/special etc about sb/sth *There was something strange about him.*

have something to do with sth (=be connected with something in some way) *She thought the pains had something to do with her pregnancy.*

somewhere *adv*

used to mean in or to a place, when you do not know or say exactly where

ADJECTIVES

somewhere safe *Put the money somewhere safe.*

somewhere nice *He said he would take her somewhere nice for dinner.*

somewhere quiet *He wanted somewhere quiet to work.*

somewhere warm/hot *Let's go somewhere warm this winter.*

somewhere different/new *Do you use a map when going somewhere new in a car?*

somewhere else *She wished she were somewhere else.*

VERBS

go somewhere *Let's go somewhere quieter.*

live somewhere *I think she lives somewhere near Edinburgh.*

find somewhere *Eventually, they found somewhere to sit and talk.*

PREPOSITIONS

somewhere in Florida/China etc *He is believed to be living somewhere in Florida.*

PHRASES

somewhere to live/sit/hide/eat etc *He is looking for somewhere to live.*

son *n* someone's male child

ADJECTIVES

eldest/oldest son *Their eldest son inherited the house.*

youngest son *Nigel was the youngest son.*

elder/older son (=used when someone has two sons) *William is Charles's elder son.*

younger son (=used when someone has two sons) *His younger son is called Harry.*

second/third etc son *Soon after their second son Bill was born, they moved to America.*

middle son *He is the middle son of three.*

only son *She fussed over her only son.*

5-year-old/14-year-old etc son *They have a two-year-old son.*

young/little/small son *He left a widow and four young sons.*

teenage son *He is divorced with two teenage sons.*

baby son *She was carrying her baby son in her arms.*

grown-up/adult son *He has two grown-up sons from his previous marriage.*

adopted son (=who has legally become their child after being born to other parents) *Augustus was the adopted son of Julius Caesar.*

a good/dutiful son (=one who behaves towards his parents as he should) *He had always been a dutiful son.*

VERBS

have a son *They have three sons.*

bring up/raise your son *She left work to bring up her son.*

sb's son is born *Our son was born 14 weeks early.*

PHRASES

give birth to a son *In 1995 she gave birth to a son, David.*

sons and daughters *I am proud of all my sons and daughters.*

song *n*

a piece of music with words that you sing

ADJECTIVES/NOUNS + song

a good/great song *The band wrote some great songs.*

a new/old song *People always want to hear their old songs.*

sb's favourite song *BrE*, **sb's favorite song** *AmE*: *David Bowie's 'Heroes' is one of my favourite songs of all time.*

a catchy song (=easy to remember) *It's such a catchy song that we knew people would like it.*

a hit song (=very successful) *Elvis's first hit song was 'Heartbreak Hotel'.*

a pop song (=a modern song popular with young people, usually with a simple tune and a strong beat) *I love all those 80s pop songs.*

a folk song (=a traditional song from a particular area) *It's a traditional Spanish folk song.*

a love song *He is releasing an album of love songs for Valentine's Day.*

a protest song *They were singing old protest songs from the 1960s.*

a Beatles/Bob Dylan etc song *She sang an old Amy Winehouse song.*

the theme song (=that is sung at the beginning of a TV show, film etc) *Who sang the theme song for the last James Bond movie?*

VERBS

sing a song *They sat round with guitars, singing songs.*

play a song *The band played a lot of their old songs.*

perform a song (=play it in front of an audience) *He doesn't like performing his songs live.*

write/compose a song *Do they write their own songs?*

record a song *The song was first recorded in 1982.*

listen to a song *I spent the afternoon listening to some of my favourite songs.*

burst/break into song (=start singing) *The crowd suddenly burst into song.*

song + NOUNS

a song title *We were trying to think of song titles about rain.*

song lyrics (=the words of a song) *The song lyrics are printed on the back of the album.*

> **Songwriter**, **songbook**, and **birdsong** are usually written as one word.

PREPOSITIONS

a song about sth *She was singing a song about lost love.*

in a song *There's a lot of emotion in this song.*

soon *adv*

in a short time from now, or a short time after something else happens

PHRASES

soon after/afterwards *Paula became pregnant soon after they were married.*

sooner than sb expected/thought *David arrived sooner than I expected.*

soon enough (=used when telling someone that something will happen soon) *You'll find out who the winner is soon enough.*

sooner or later (=at some time in the future, although you do not know exactly when) *The weather must get better sooner or later.*

See you soon! *spoken: Thanks for a lovely evening – see you soon!*

So soon? *spoken* (=used especially when saying that you are disappointed that something has ended so quickly) *"We have to go now." "So soon?"*

sophisticated *adj*

a sophisticated machine, system, method etc is very advanced, and often complicated

NOUNS

sophisticated equipment/technology *Sophisticated equipment is now used to keep patients alive.*

a sophisticated system *The police have a sophisticated computer system.*

a sophisticated form/version of sth *These ancient people practised a very sophisticated form of agriculture.*

a sophisticated technique/method *She introduced sophisticated marketing techniques into the organization.*

sophisticated weapons *Where did the terrorists get such sophisticated weapons?*

sophisticated software *They used very sophisticated computer software.*

ADVERBS

highly sophisticated *The plane was equipped with a highly sophisticated navigation system.*

increasingly sophisticated *Car security systems are becoming increasingly sophisticated.*

> **THESAURUS: sophisticated**
>
> sophisticated, highly developed, high-tech/hi-tech, state-of-the-art, cutting-edge → **advanced (1)**

sorrow *n*

a feeling of great sadness because something very bad has happened, especially when someone has died

ADJECTIVES

great/deep/profound sorrow *They helped me in a time of great sorrow.*

overwhelming/unbearable sorrow (=very great sorrow) *She was filled with overwhelming sorrow after the death of her husband.*

VERBS

feel sorrow *When he died, I felt no sorrow.*

fill sb with sorrow *Her suffering filled them with sorrow.*

express your sorrow *They expressed their sorrow at the news.*

cause/bring (sb) sorrow *I regret the sorrow I have caused you.*

share sb's sorrow *The president said that he shared their sorrow.*

PREPOSITIONS

sorrow at sth *His colleagues expressed their sorrow at his death.*

sorrow for sb/sth *She felt a deep sorrow for him.*

in sorrow *Their heads were bent in sorrow.*

to sb's sorrow *To his great sorrow, he had no memory of his mother's face.*

PHRASES

a feeling/sense of sorrow *Someone who has lost their job may have feelings of sorrow and anger.*

tears of sorrow *As he walked along he wept tears of sorrow and regret.*

sorry *adj*

1 feeling regret, shame, or sadness

ADVERBS

really/terribly/awfully sorry *I'm really sorry about forgetting your birthday.*

deeply/truly sorry *formal* (=very sorry) *I am deeply sorry if I upset you.*

so sorry *I was so sorry to hear about your accident.*

genuinely/sincerely sorry (=really feeling sorry, not just saying sorry in order to be polite) *He seemed genuinely sorry to learn that I'd failed my test.*

PREPOSITIONS

sorry about sth/sb *I'm sorry about the delay.*

sorry for (doing) sth *She's sorry for shouting at you.*

PHRASES

sorry to hear/learn sth *I was sorry to hear you didn't get the job.*

sorry to see sth *We all liked her and were sorry to see her leave.*

sorry to say sth (*also* **sorry to tell sb sth**) *I'm sorry to say that I was too shy to ask.*

sorry to report *formal*: *We are sorry to report that his health is failing.*

sorry to interrupt/bother/disturb you *I'm sorry to bother you, but I need to ask you a question.*

sorry to disappoint you *I'm sorry to disappoint you, but your plan has failed.*

sorry to keep you waiting *I'm sorry to keep you waiting. Can I help you?*

2 feeling pity or sympathy for someone

> This meaning of **sorry** is always used in the phrase **feel sorry for** someone.

VERBS

feel sorry for sb *We felt sorry for the little girl, sitting all alone.*

feel sorry for yourself *You shouldn't stay at home feeling sorry for yourself.*

ADVERBS

feel so sorry for sb *I felt so sorry for him that I invited him to join us.*

feel really sorry *He's a horrible man. I feel really sorry for his wife.*

feel rather sorry (*also* **feel a bit sorry** *informal*): *I feel a bit sorry for her, actually.*

sort *n* a type of person or thing

ADJECTIVES

this/that sort *We must make sure that this sort of thing does not happen again.*

some sort *There has been some sort of error.*

the same sort *Both boys had the same sort of family background.*

a similar sort *Yours is a similar sort of house to ours.*

a different sort *She's trying to create a different sort of life for herself.*

the right sort *Climbers know that wearing the right sort of clothing could save their life.*

other sorts *What other sorts of books do you like?*

all sorts (=many different sorts) *He collects all sorts of musical instruments.*

PREPOSITIONS

a sort of sth *She likes to watch different sorts of films.*

PHRASES

of one sort or another (=of various sorts) *Every passenger suffered an injury of one sort or another.*

soul *n*

the part of a person that is not physical, which some people believe continues after death

ADJECTIVES

the human soul *He has no understanding of the human soul.*

an immortal/eternal soul *Does an animal such as a dog have an immortal soul?*

VERBS

pray for sb's soul *When I am dead, pray for my soul.*

save sb's soul *"Jesus died to save our souls," said the priest.*

PHRASES

the souls of the dead *They believe the souls of the dead return to earth.*

the depths of sb's soul *It seemed as if he could see into the depths of her soul.*

have mercy on sb's soul *May God have mercy on her soul.*

body and soul *I was tired in body and soul.*

heart and soul *She loved him with all her heart and soul.*

sound[1] *n* something that can be heard

ADJECTIVES

a loud sound *There was a loud sound and the branch suddenly snapped.*

⚠ Don't say 'a strong sound'.

a faint/soft sound (=not loud) *The sound was so faint I wasn't sure what it was at first.*

a deafening sound (=very loud) *The sound of the waterfall was deafening.*

a strange sound *I heard a strange sound coming from outside.*

a familiar sound *She heard the familiar sound of the key being turned in the front door.*

a distinctive/unmistakable sound (=easy to recognize) *Suddenly from below came the unmistakable sound of gunfire.*

a distant sound (=far away) *All seemed quiet, except for the distant sound of police sirens.*

a muffled sound (=not clear) *There were muffled sounds of movement in the next room.*

a banging/tearing/hissing etc sound *The explosion left her with an odd buzzing sound in her ears.*

S

a deep/low sound *The biggest drums make the deepest sounds.*

a high-pitched sound (=very high) *Bats make high-pitched sounds which humans cannot hear.*

VERBS + sound

hear a sound *She heard the sound of a car starting.*

make a sound *The machine made a strange hissing sound.*

sound + VERBS

a sound comes from somewhere *The sounds seemed to be coming from the garden next door.*

sound travels *Sound travels at a slower speed than light.*

sound carries (=can be heard some distance away) *The sound of these horns carries for miles across the mountains.*

a sound rings out (=can be heard very clearly and loudly) *The sound of a gunshot rang out across the town.*

a sound fills a place *The sound of laughter filled the theatre.*

a sound stops *The sound of the rain suddenly stopped.*

a sound dies away (=stops gradually) *The storm passed and the sound of thunder died away.*

PREPOSITIONS

the sound of sth *Then I heard the sound of a child crying.*

without a sound (=silently) *When everyone was asleep, she slipped out of the house without a sound.*

PHRASES

not make a sound (=be completely quiet) *He lay still and didn't make a sound.*

sound² *adj*

1 sensible and likely to produce good results

ADVERBS

basically/fundamentally sound *His argument is fundamentally sound.*

perfectly/entirely sound *Her reasons for taking the job are perfectly sound.*

generally sound *Their management of the company has been generally sound.*

apparently sound *The decision was taken for apparently sound reasons.*

environmentally/ecologically sound *The government encourages environmentally sound management of the countryside.*

NOUNS

sound advice *She received sound advice on choosing a career.*

sound judgment *We admired her sound judgment under pressure.*

a sound reason *Customers do not always have sound reasons for choosing the things they buy.*

a sound basis/footing *Friendship is a sound basis for a good marriage.*

a sound investment *Property is usually a sound investment.*

a sound policy *The problems of industry will only be solved by sound economic policies.*

sound principles *The business needs to be organized on sound financial principles.*

THESAURUS: sound

nice, fine, sound, attractive, desirable, favourable, positive, beneficial → **good (1)**

2 in good condition

ADVERBS

structurally sound *The building was old but structurally sound.*

perfectly/entirely sound *The doctors say her hearing is perfectly sound.*

apparently sound *We even replaced the wood that was apparently sound.*

generally sound *His teeth were rather yellow but generally sound.*

financially sound *Our examination of the accounts showed that the company was financially sound.*

PHRASES

safe and sound (=unharmed) *It was a long and tiring journey but we arrived safe and sound.*

source Ac *n*

1 a thing that provides something

ADJECTIVES

a good/excellent/rich source (=a source that provides a lot of something) *Milk is a good source of calcium.*

a useful source *The internet is an extremely useful source of information.*

a major/important source *The mines were once a major source of employment for people here.*

a great source *In times of stress, food can be a great source of comfort.*

the main/primary source *It started as a hobby, but now it is his main source of income.*

an alternative source (=that can be used instead of another) *The museum is trying to find alternative sources of funding.*

a constant source *My wife has been a constant source of support to me.*

a potential source *The issue of land is a potential source of conflict between the two countries.*

an untapped source (=which exists but has not yet been used) *Colleges are realizing that local businesses are a large untapped source of sponsorship.*

NOUNS + source

an energy source *We hope to see increased use of renewable energy sources.*

a food source *Leaves from crops are an important food source for these insects.*

a power source (=something that produces power) *Batteries are the main power source for portable electronic devices.*

a light source (=something that produces light) *The statue is illuminated by a hidden light source.*

VERBS

use/exploit a source *We plan to exploit the huge source of mineral wealth in the region.*

provide a source (=be a source) *Beans provide an important source of protein.*

PREPOSITIONS

a source of sth *Her friendship is a great source of comfort to me.*

2 a book or other publication providing information

ADJECTIVES

a primary source (=one written by people directly involved in something) *It is important to look at primary sources for the facts.*

a secondary source (=one that comments on things written, done etc by other people) *The research is mostly based on secondary sources.*

an authoritative source (=which people believe gives good information) *The magazine is one of the UK's most authoritative sources of scientific information.*

VERBS

use a source *For any essay, use as wide a range of sources as possible.*

cite/quote a source (=mention something that another person has said or written) *She quotes several reliable sources in the article.*

acknowledge a source (=say in your writing that you have used it) *It is good practice to acknowledge all your sources.*

check a source *I read the article and decided to check a few of its sources.*

3 a person who gives information to other people, for example to news reporters

ADJECTIVES/NOUNS + source

a reliable/credible/trusted source *He was regarded by the press as a reliable source.*

an unnamed/anonymous source *The information comes from an unnamed source.*

a government source *There are no plans to change this policy, a government source has stated.*

diplomatic sources *Diplomatic sources said that there has been little progress in the trade talks.*

VERBS

protect a source (=not tell other people who the source is) *A good journalist will always protect his or her sources.*

reveal/disclose/identify a source (=tell other people who the source is) *She refused to identify her source.*

PHRASES

sources close to sb *Sources close to the minister have denied the rumour.*

according to a source *According to White House sources, the president is unlikely to change his mind.*

south *adj, adv, n*

the direction that is at the bottom of a map of the world, or the part of a place that is in this direction

south + NOUNS

the south side/end *We sailed to the south end of the lake.*

the south coast *They're going down to the south coast.*

the south bank *The site is on the south bank of the River Thames.*

the South Pole *He died on an expedition to the South Pole.*

a south wind (=a wind from the south) *They were waiting for a south wind.*

ADJECTIVES

the far south *The following morning we flew to Tacna in the far south of Peru.*

the Deep South (=the states of Alabama, Mississippi, Louisiana, South Carolina, and Georgia, in the southeast of the US) *He was born in the Deep South.*

ADVERBS

further south *They are not as friendly as the people further south.*

due south (=directly south) *He rode due south.*

VERBS

go/travel/head south *We decided to go south.*

face south *My bedroom faces south.*

PREPOSITIONS

in the south *I grew up in the south.*

to/towards the south *Two miles to the south is the university.*

from the south *The army was approaching from the south.*

the south of a place *He's on holiday in the south of France.*

souvenir *n*

an object that you buy or keep to remind yourself of a special occasion or a place you have visited

ADJECTIVES

a cheap souvenir *The vase wasn't worth anything – it was just a cheap souvenir.*

a little souvenir *I've brought you a little souvenir.*

VERBS

buy a souvenir *I'm going to buy a few souvenirs to take back home.*

sell souvenirs *The shop sells postcards and souvenirs.*

bring sb (back) a souvenir *He had brought back souvenirs for his children.*

keep sth as a souvenir *We kept the wine bottle as a souvenir.*

souvenir + NOUNS

a souvenir shop/store/stall *Tourists spend many happy hours visiting the souvenir shops.*

a souvenir programme/mug/T-shirt etc *He had a 1966 World Cup souvenir programme.*

PREPOSITIONS

a souvenir of sth *Their house is full of souvenirs of their travels.*

a souvenir from a place *This bowl is a souvenir from Rome.*

space *n*

1 an empty place

ADJECTIVES

a small space *There was only a small space between the car and the wall.*

a narrow space *Rats can squeeze through very narrow spaces.*

an empty space *There was an empty space where the TV used to be.*

a blank space (=on a page, wall etc) *Write your name in the blank space below.*

VERBS

clear/make a space *Jack cleared a space for his newspaper on the table.*

leave a space *Leave a space for the title at the top of the page.*

PREPOSITIONS

a space between sth and sth *There was a big space between her two front teeth.*

2 an area that is available to use

ADJECTIVES/NOUNS + space

enough space *There is enough space for three people in the back of the car.*

ample space/plenty of space (=more than enough) *There is ample space for a large breakfast table.*

limited space *They live in a small apartment and space is limited.*

a confined/enclosed space (=small and enclosed) *He dislikes being in confined spaces such as lifts.*

storage space (=for storing things) *Our house has very little storage space.*

living space (=areas such as rooms, for living in) *We had two children and we needed more living space.*

floor space *I need a desk that takes up less floor space.*

office space *The building offers plenty of office space.*

disk space (=available memory on a computer disk) *I'm running out of disk space on the c drive.*

a parking space (=a place where you can park your car) *I managed to find a parking space near the entrance.*

a public space (=an outdoor area such as a public park) *It is a beautiful city with very attractive public spaces.*

VERBS

save space (=provide extra space) *You could save space by storing things under the bed.*

waste space *By having a circular table, we're wasting a lot of space.*

take up space (*also* **fill/occupy space**) (=use it by being in it) *The bed takes up most of the space in the room.*

lack space (*also* **be short of space**) *A bigger desk would be nice but I'm very short of space.*

fit in/into a space *Decide what kind of furniture will fit best into the space.*

squeeze sth into a space (=fit it into a small space) *They've managed to squeeze a lot of furniture into the space.*

3 the area beyond the Earth where the stars and planets are

ADJECTIVES

outer space (=areas a long way from the Earth) *Our planet is struck regularly by objects from outer space.*

deep space (=areas a very long way from the Earth) *The rocket will continue its journey into deep space.*

space + NOUNS

space travel *What will space travel be like in the future?*

space exploration *They are developing robots that can be used for space exploration.*

space research *The institute is a world leader in space research.*

space flight *One day there will be commercial space flights to the moon.*

a space programme *BrE*, **a space program** *AmE*: *This technology was originally developed by the US space program.*

a space station (=a place in space where people can live and work) *The research lab will form part of a space station.*

a space shuttle (=a vehicle that goes into space and then comes back to land on Earth like an aeroplane) *He was the captain of the first NASA space shuttle.*

> **Spaceman**, **spacewoman**, **spacecraft**, **spaceship**, and **spacesuit** are usually written as one word.

S

PREPOSITIONS

in space *A Russian man was the first person in space.*

into space *NASA has sent dozens of people into space.*

PHRASES

the far/furthest reaches of space (=the areas of space that are very far from the Earth) *Light takes time to travel from the far reaches of space.*

the vast reaches of space (=the very large areas that exist in space) *They are designing vehicles that will be able to explore the vast reaches of space.*

spare *adj*

1 available to be used in addition to the one that is normally used

NOUNS

a spare key/battery/wheel etc *She keeps a spare key under a flower pot by the front door.*

spare clothes *Take some spare clothes in case you get wet.*

a spare room/bedroom *You can sleep in the spare room.*

a spare bed *He offered me his spare bed for the night.*

a spare pair/set of sth *He always carried a spare pair of glasses.*

a spare part (=a part for a machine or vehicle that is used to replace a damaged one) *They sell spare parts for washing machines.*

2 not being used for anything else or by anyone else

NOUNS

spare time *He spends most of his spare time playing golf.*

a spare moment/minute/hour *If you have a spare moment, give me a call.*

spare money/cash/change *Don't leave spare cash lying around your house.*

a spare copy of sth *There are some spare copies of the report on my desk.*

sparkle *v*

to shine in small bright flashes

PHRASES

sparkle in the sun *The water in the pool sparkled in the midday sun.*

sparkle like diamonds *Her eyes sparkled like diamonds.*

sb's eyes sparkle with excitement/joy/enthusiasm *The children's eyes sparkled with excitement.*

speak *v*

1 to be able to talk in a particular language

NOUNS

speak French/German/Spanish etc *Does your friend speak Italian?*

speak a language *She can speak six different languages.*

VERBS

can speak sth *Can you speak Portuguese?*

learn to speak sth *She is learning to speak Japanese at evening classes.*

ADVERBS

speak sth fluently (=very well, like a native speaker) *He lived in Seoul for years and speaks Korean fluently.*

speak sth a little *She says she can speak French a little.*

PREPOSITIONS

speak in French/German/Spanish etc *Is it OK if we speak in English?*

PHRASES

sb can speak a little French/some Italian etc *I can speak a little Chinese.*

sb can speak a few words of French/Italian etc *I can speak a few words of Greek, but that's all.*

sb speaks with an English/French etc accent *The man spoke with a strong German accent.*

> If someone **speaks** a language very well, like a native speaker, you say that they **are fluent in** it: *The ambassador **is fluent in** Russian and Polish.*

2 to talk to someone about something

ADVERBS

speak at length (=have a long conversation) *I have spoken to her at length about the problems.*

speak briefly (=have a short conversation) *The president spoke briefly to reporters before boarding the plane.*

PREPOSITIONS

speak to sb (*also* **speak with sb** *AmE*): *A customer asked to speak to the manager.*

speak about sth (*also* **speak of sth** *formal*): *I have never spoken about this to anyone before.*

PHRASES

can I speak to.../I'd like to speak to... *Can I speak to you in private?*

(this is ...) speaking (=used on the phone, when saying that you are the person that someone wants to talk to) *"Hello. I'd like to speak to Mrs Jones." "Speaking."*

3 to say something that expresses your ideas or opinions

PHRASES

generally speaking (=used when saying that something is true in most cases) *Generally speaking, the results have been good.*

speaking personally (=used when emphasizing that you are giving a personal opinion) *Speaking personally, yes, I am worried about him.*

S

strictly speaking (=used when emphasizing that your statement is correct, although many people do not realize it) *Strictly speaking, the tomato is a fruit.*

roughly/broadly speaking (=used when giving an approximate description, amount etc) *The differences between men and women are, roughly speaking, what this book is about.*

relatively speaking (=in comparison with some other things) *Property here is cheap, relatively speaking.*

speaking as a parent/teacher/doctor etc *Speaking as a parent, I wouldn't want my children outside after ten o'clock in the evening.*

ADVERBS

speak highly/well of sb/sth (=say that you think they are good) *He always spoke very highly of his staff.*

speak warmly/fondly of sb/sth (=speak in a way that shows you like them very much) *She speaks very fondly of her time in Paris.*

speak ill of sb *formal* (=say bad things about them) *She never speaks ill of her ex-husband.*

speak frankly/candidly/plainly (=give an honest opinion, even if it upsets people) *The Hollywood star spoke candidly about her health problems.*

speak freely/openly (=speak without hiding anything, or without worrying that you will be criticized or punished) *We are all friends here, so please speak freely.*

speak movingly/powerfully (=in a way that makes the listener feel strong emotions) *He speaks very movingly of the effects of the war on young children.*

S

speaker *n*

1 a person who speaks a particular language

ADJECTIVES/NOUNS + speaker

a native speaker (=who speaks a language as their first language) *She's an American citizen and a native speaker of Korean.*

a non-native speaker (*also* **a foreign speaker**) (=who has learnt a language as a foreign language) *The dictionary is designed for non-native speakers of English.*

a fluent speaker (=who speaks a language well and confidently) *We expect the successful candidate to be a fluent speaker of Spanish.*

a French/Italian/Spanish etc speaker *Only a French speaker would understand that phrase.*

PREPOSITIONS

a speaker of... *She's a fluent speaker of Portuguese.*

2 someone who makes a formal speech to a group of people

ADJECTIVES/NOUNS + speaker

a public speaker *A politician needs to be a good public speaker.*

an after-dinner speaker (=who makes a speech after a formal meal) *After retiring from sport he became an after-dinner speaker.*

the guest speaker *The guest speaker at the ceremony will be Professor Brian Cox.*

the keynote/main speaker (=the most important speaker at a conference) *The keynote speaker is Olympic champion Sir Steve Redgrave.*

an inspirational speaker (=whose speeches make people very interested and feel they want to do something) *Many people voted for Obama because they thought he was an inspirational speaker.*

special *adj*

not ordinary or usual, but different in some way and often better or more important

NOUNS

a special occasion *He only wears this suit on special occasions.*

a special case (=a situation in which normal rules or methods cannot be used) *Students are not usually allowed to miss classes, but this is a special case.*

special circumstances (=a situation which is different from usual) *The court decided that there were special circumstances and that he should not be sent to prison.*

special treatment *Although he was a senior officer, he insisted that he should not receive any special treatment.*

special attention *The last paragraph deserves special attention.*

special care *The designers have taken special care over the shape of the seats.*

special arrangements *They are making special arrangements for the prince's visit.*

special privileges *As the president's husband, he has special privileges.*

a special relationship *We want to preserve the special relationship between our two countries.*

a special offer/rate (=when people can buy something at a lower price than usual) *They are having a special offer - you can stay for three nights for the price of two.*

PHRASES

anything special *Are you doing anything special this weekend?*

nothing special *The theatre was very impressive but the play was nothing special.*

specialist *n, adj*

someone who knows a lot about a particular subject

ADJECTIVES

a leading/top specialist (=best and most well known) *They asked one of Britain's leading cancer specialists for his opinion.*

a medical/technical/financial specialist *The work is done by a small number of technical specialists.*

NOUNS + specialist

a cancer/heart/eye etc specialist *She went to see a heart specialist at the hospital.*

a computer/marketing/communications etc specialist *Computer specialists are analyzing more than 600 files found on a personal computer.*

VERBS

see/consult a specialist *The pain got worse so I decided to see a specialist.*

refer sb to a specialist (=send someone to see a medical specialist) *My doctor referred me to a specialist.*

specialist + NOUNS

specialist knowledge/skills/training *Repairing this kind of equipment requires specialist knowledge.*

specialist advice/help *I decided to get some specialist advice.*

PREPOSITIONS

a specialist in/on sth *He is a specialist in Russian history and politics.*

species *n*

a group of animals or plants whose members can breed with each other

ADJECTIVES

a rare species *The area contains many rare species of plants.*

a common species *Here you will see most of the common species of African wildlife.*

a new species (=not known about before, or not existing before) *A new species of spider has been discovered in a field in Cambridgeshire.*

different species *Thirty-six different species of birds were recorded.*

several species *Mexico is a major nesting area for several species of sea turtles.*

a native/indigenous species (=one that has always lived or grown in a particular country) *We prefer to grow native species of trees in these forests.*

a foreign/non-native species (=from a foreign country) *The grey squirrel is a non-native species which was introduced into the UK in the 19th century.*

a protected species (=protected by law) *Elephants are a protected species.*

an endangered/threatened species (=in danger of no longer existing because there are very few still alive) *The park is a sanctuary for endangered species.*

an extinct species (=that no longer exists) *About a hundred species are becoming extinct every day.*

NOUNS + species

a bird/animal/plant species (*also* **a species of bird/animal/plant**) *You can see many different bird species on the canal.*

species + VERBS

a species is found somewhere *This species is found only in the Southern Hemisphere.*

a species lives somewhere *Many rainforest species cannot live anywhere else.*

a species grows somewhere *The species grows wild in Europe.*

PREPOSITIONS

a species of sth *He has photographed several rare species of insect.*

specific *adj*

relating to one particular thing or situation

NOUNS

a specific area/aspect *Students are asked to focus on a specific area of study.*

a specific type/group *This approach can be used to solve a specific type of problem.*

a specific case/example/instance *I don't want to discuss details of specific cases.*

a specific problem/issue *Every country has their own specific problems.*

a specific aim/goal/purpose/target *Our specific aim is talk to as many people as possible.*

specific needs/requirements *The product can be adapted to meet the specific needs of each customer.*

a specific point *We shall come back to this specific point later.*

a specific job/role *Each person was given a specific job to do.*

a specific time/date *The chart shows temperatures at a specific time.*

a specific question *The experiment was designed to answer a specific question.*

specific information *The police had specific information that a terrorist attack was being planned.*

a specific detail *I'm sure about the specific details of the case.*

ANTONYMS **specific → general**

speck *n* THESAURUS **piece**

spectacular *adj*

very impressive or very surprising

ADVERBS

absolutely spectacular *The view from the top of the mountain is absolutely spectacular.*

truly spectacular *In Scotland there are dozens of truly spectacular castles.*

⚠ Don't say 'very spectacular'.

Nothing spectacular
You use this phrase when saying that something was not very good: *Last year's results were OK, but* ***nothing spectacular****.*

S

THESAURUS: spectacular

spectacular, majestic, imposing, breathtaking, awe-inspiring, dazzling, glittering → **impressive**

speculation *n*

guesses about something without knowing all the facts

ADJECTIVES

growing/increasing speculation *There is growing speculation in the press that the player may move to Barcelona.*

widespread/much speculation (=a lot of speculation) *There was widespread speculation about his political future.*

pure/mere speculation (=just guessing, not based on any knowledge) *A government official yesterday dismissed the reports as "pure speculation".*

wild/idle speculation (=unlikely to be true) *Experts' fears about the environment are not wild speculation.*

intense speculation (=in which people try hard to guess what has happened) *The reason for his resignation was the subject of intense speculation.*

renewed speculation (=which has started again) *The speech has led to renewed speculation that an election will be held in April.*

S

NOUNS + speculation

press/media speculation (=in news reports) *She appealed for an end to press speculation about her marriage.*

VERBS

lead to/give rise to speculation (=result in it) *This development led to speculation that she was about to resign.*

prompt/provoke speculation (=cause it) *The speech has prompted speculation that she will soon retire.*

fuel speculation (=make it increase) *The announcement has fueled speculation that the company will be sold.*

dismiss speculation (=say that it is not true) *The governor dismissed speculation that he might run for president.*

end speculation *Smith has ended speculation by signing a new contract.*

speculation grows/mounts *Speculation is growing at the club about the manager's future.*

speculation surrounds sb/sth *There seems to be no end to the speculation surrounding his private life.*

PREPOSITIONS

speculation about/on/over sth *There has been further speculation about the British army's role in the affair.*

speculation concerning/regarding sb/sth (=about - more formal) *She wanted to put an end to speculation concerning her career.*

speculation as to sth *There is still a lot of speculation as to her reasons for leaving the government.*

speculation among sb *The news has prompted speculation among some commentators that Obama may change his policy.*

amid speculation (=used when saying that there is speculation at a time when something else happens) *He resigned amid speculation that he had an affair.*

PHRASES

there is speculation that... *There has been speculation in the media that the star is about to marry.*

sth is a matter for/of speculation *The exact details of the deal are a matter for speculation.*

sth is the subject of speculation *His role in the affair has been the subject of speculation in the press.*

a flurry/frenzy of speculation (=a lot of sudden speculation) *A flurry of speculation followed the news that the club was about to be sold.*

speech *n*

1 a talk, especially a formal one about a particular subject, given to a group of people

ADJECTIVES

a long speech *He gave a long speech about the economy.*

a short/brief speech *The chairman opened the meeting with a brief speech.*

a major speech (=an important one) *This was her first major speech as party leader.*

a political speech *She began writing political speeches for local politicians.*

a powerful/moving speech (=having a strong effect on people's emotions) *In a moving speech, Butts declared that America had lost its sense of values.*

a passionate/impassioned speech (=full of strong feeling) *She made an impassioned speech on the need to respect human rights.*

an emotional speech (=showing emotions, especially by crying) *On retiring, he delivered an emotional farewell speech.*

a rousing/stirring speech (=making people feel excited and eager to do something) *Thousands of people were inspired by his stirring speeches.*

an opening/closing speech (=which begins or ends an event) *The head of the Olympic Association made a long opening speech.*

an after-dinner speech (=after a formal dinner) *He gets paid a lot for making after-dinner speeches.*

a televised speech (=shown on television) *In a*

televised speech last night, the president appealed for an end to the violence.

sb's inaugural speech (=someone's first speech as president, mayor, or in another important political job) *In his inaugural speech, Kennedy famously said: "Ask not what your country can do for you, ask what you can do for your country."*

sb's maiden speech (=someone's first speech, especially in parliament or in an important political job) *In his maiden speech in Parliament, Jones spoke about the living conditions he grew up in.*

NOUNS + speech

a campaign speech (=given during a political campaign) *Obama used the phrase "Yes we can" a lot in his campaign speeches.*

a farewell speech (=by someone who is leaving) *We all noticed that he didn't mention the boss in his farewell speech.*

a keynote speech (=the most important one at an event) *The prime minister will make his keynote speech at the party conference today.*

sb's acceptance speech (=when someone accepts a job, prize, or award) *In her acceptance speech, she thanked her husband and family for their support.*

VERBS

give/make a speech *I've been asked to give a speech at the wedding. | He made a speech about the need for a return to traditional family values.*

deliver a speech *formal* (=give an important speech) *The president delivered a major speech to Congress yesterday.*

write/draft/prepare a speech *She's in her office preparing her speech.*

rehearse a speech (=practise making it) *It's important to rehearse the speech to get the timing right.*

PREPOSITIONS

a speech on/about sth *She gave an interesting speech on women's rights.*

a speech to sb *The health minister will make a speech to the nurses' union today.*

in a speech *In her speech, she proposed major changes to the welfare system.*

PHRASES

a transcript of a speech (=a written record of exactly what is said) *The books contain transcripts of all speeches made in Parliament.*

an extract/passage from a speech (=a part of a speech) *The following is an extract from one of Churchill's most famous speeches.*

2 spoken language

ADJECTIVES

direct speech (=the actual words that someone says) *The writer uses a lot of direct speech and there are long dialogues between the characters.*

indirect/reported speech *In indirect speech, the tense of the verb often changes, so "I will be late" becomes "She said that she would be late".*

speech + NOUNS

speech recognition (=a program that allows you to speak instructions to a computer or other device) *The phone uses speech recognition technology so that you can ask it questions.*

speech patterns *She studied the speech patterns of people in different regions of America.*

speech marks (=punctuation marks used in writing to mark the words that someone says) *Always remember to put quotations in speech marks.*

3 the ability to speak, or to say what you want

ADJECTIVES

free speech (=the ability to say anything you like publicly) *Free speech is an important part of any democracy.*

speech + NOUNS

a speech impediment (=a physical or nervous problem that affects speech) *He was embarrassed about speaking because of his speech impediment.*

speech therapy (=treatment for a speech impediment) *The boy had been receiving speech therapy since he was eight.*

a speech therapist (=someone who gives speech therapy) *The speech therapist gave her some exercises to do.*

PHRASES

freedom of speech *The new government passed laws limiting people's freedom of speech.*

speed *n*

the rate at which something moves or travels

PHRASES

at a speed of 50 miles/100 kilometres per hour etc *The truck was travelling at a speed of 50 miles per hour.*

at high/great speed *The train was moving at high speed.*

at low/slow speed *Even at low speed, an accident could mean serious injury for a child.*

at full speed (=as fast as possible) *He ran past us at full speed.*

at/with lightning speed (=very quickly) *The player moved with his usual lightning speed.*

at breakneck speed (=very quickly) *The car drove away at breakneck speed.*

at the speed of light/sound (=at the same speed as light or sound waves) *These particles travel at the speed of light.*

a burst of speed (=a short period when someone or something suddenly goes fast) *The train continued north with an occasional burst of speed.*

ADJECTIVES

an average speed *Our average speed was 70 miles per hour.*

a constant/steady speed (=not changing much) *The disc revolves at a constant speed.*

a top/maximum speed (=the highest possible) *The car has a top speed of 220 kilometres per hour.*

excess/excessive speed (=going too fast) *In most road accidents, excessive speed is to blame.*

NOUNS + speed

wind speed (=the speed of the wind) *The average wind speed will be about 20 miles an hour.*

air speed (=the speed of a plane in relation to the air around it) *The plane went on to set a world air speed record.*

VERBS

increase your speed *She increased her speed until she was running as fast as she could.*

pick up/gain/gather speed (=go faster) *The Mercedes was gradually picking up speed.*

reach a speed *The trains will reach speeds of 240 miles per hour.*

maintain a speed (=keep the same speed) *The aircraft is designed to maintain a steady speed.*

reduce speed (=slow down deliberately) *She reduced speed as she approached the village.*

lose speed (=slow down without wanting to) *The engine made a strange sound and we lost speed.*

speed + NOUNS

a speed limit *Breaking the speed limit can be dangerous.*

a speed restriction *New speed restrictions have been introduced.*

a speed camera (=a camera that photographs vehicles going too fast) *The car was caught on speed camera doing over 180 kilometres an hour.*

speedy *adj* THESAURUS quick (1)

spell[1] *v*

to form a word by writing or naming the letters in order

ADVERBS

spell sth correctly/right *Make sure you have spelled everyone's name correctly.*

spell sth wrong/wrongly *You've spelled 'Wednesday' wrong.*

be spelled differently/the same *'Here' and 'hear' are pronounced the same but spelled differently.*

spell sth backwards *'Evil' is 'live' spelled backwards.*

NOUNS

spell a word *Can you tell me how to spell this word?*

spell sb's name/surname *I didn't know how to spell his name.*

PREPOSITIONS

spell sth with a C/G/Y etc *In British English, the word 'tyre' is spelled with a Y.*

spell sth as sth *Some of the students spelled Freud as Frued.*

PHRASES

how do you spell...? *How do you spell 'deceive'?*

be hard/difficult/easy to spell *'Mississippi' is hard to spell.*

spell[2] *n*

1 a period of time when something happens

ADJECTIVES

a brief/short spell *After a brief spell working in a flower shop, she became a hairdresser.*

a long/prolonged spell *He had a long spell off work due to illness.*

a dry/wet spell (=when it does not rain, or when it rains a lot) *Don't forget to water your plants during dry spells.*

a cold/warm/hot spell (=a period of particular weather) *There was a very cold spell in late November.*

sunny spells *Tuesday will be dry with sunny spells.*

a dizzy/fainting spell (=when you feel unable to stand steadily or stay conscious) *She must have had a dizzy spell and fallen.*

a good/bad spell *The team had some good spells during the match.*

a quiet spell (=when not much is happening) *We're having a quiet spell at work at the moment.*

VERBS

go through a ... spell (=experience a spell) *The company has been going through a difficult spell in recent years.*

enjoy a ... spell (=experience a spell - used about good things) *He's been enjoying a very successful spell in a Broadway show.*

PREPOSITIONS

a spell of sth *It's good to see some sunshine after that spell of grey weather.*

a spell as sth *She enjoyed a brief spell as a managing editor.*

2 something that seems to have an effect like magic on someone

VERBS

cast a spell (on/over sb) (=have an effect like magic on someone) *The singer cast a spell over her audience from the very first song.*

weave a spell on/over sb/sth (=have an effect like magic on someone, especially gradually) *Cohen's soft sad voice seemed to weave a spell over the room.*

break a spell (=end the effect) *The spell was broken by the sound of someone firing a gun.*

fall/come under sb's spell (=become affected by someone or something) *She was dangerous to those who fell under her spell.*

PREPOSITIONS

be under a spell *The whole country seems to be under the spell of the past.*

3 a set of words or actions, used to make magic things happen – used especially in stories

ADJECTIVES

a magic spell *She found an ancient book of magic spells.*

an evil spell *These people believe in evil spells.*

VERBS

put a spell on sb/cast a spell (on sb) (=make magic affect someone, using special words or actions) *The fairy put a terrible spell on the princess.*

weave a spell on sb (=put a spell on someone, usually over a period of time) *Diana wove a spell over him, so that he slept forever and never grew old.*

break a spell (=end the effect of some magic) *No one knew how to break the spell.*

PREPOSITIONS

be under a spell *In the story, she sleeps for a hundred years, under the spell of an evil witch.*

spelling *n*

1 the act of spelling words correctly, or the ability to do this

ADJECTIVES

bad/good spelling *Your writing is neat and your spelling is good.*

English/German/French etc spelling *English spelling causes problems for English people as well as foreign learners.*

VERBS

check sb's spelling *When I've written the letter, could you check my spelling?*

correct sb's spelling *The teacher corrected my spelling.*

sb's spelling improves *Her spelling has improved.*

spelling + NOUNS

a spelling mistake/error *The article contains several spelling mistakes.*

spelling rules *Learn these basic spelling rules.*

a spelling test *The children have a weekly spelling test.*

a spelling bee (=a spelling competition) *She won the school spelling bee.*

2 the way in which a word is spelled

ADJECTIVES

the correct/right spelling *Is that the correct spelling?*

an incorrect spelling *You lose one point for each incorrect spelling.*

the British/American spelling *'Favourite' is the British spelling; 'favorite' is the American spelling.*

a different spelling *The words have the same pronunciation but different spellings.*

an alternative spelling *'Connection' has an alternative spelling: 'connexion'.*

an acceptable spelling *Both 'yoghurt' and 'yogurt' are acceptable spellings.*

VERBS

use a spelling *You can use either spelling.*

PREPOSITIONS

the spelling of sth *Students are encouraged to check the spelling of difficult words in a dictionary.*

PHRASES

get the spelling right/wrong *Have I got the spelling right?*

spend *v*

1 to use your money to pay for things

NOUNS

spend money/£50/$100 etc on sth *Companies spend millions of dollars on advertising each year.*

spend a fortune (on sth) *informal* (=spend a lot of money) *We spend a fortune on electricity.*

ADVERBS

spend sth wisely/carefully *Make sure that you spend the money wisely.*

PREPOSITIONS

spend money on sth *She spends all her money on clothes.*

PHRASES

sth is money well spent (=although something costs a lot of money, it is worth it) *A good bike can cost up to £1,000, but it is money well spent.*

2 to use time doing something

NOUNS

spend time (doing sth) *I spent too much time studying and not enough time enjoying myself.*

spend the day/morning/afternoon etc *He spent the morning looking round Edinburgh.*

spending *n*

the amount of money that someone spends – used especially about the government, or about people in general

ADJECTIVES/NOUNS + spending

total spending *Total spending on healthcare increased by over 10%.*

annual spending *The government needs to reduce annual spending on defence.*

additional/extra spending *The council has plans for additional spending on roads.*

public/government/state spending *The government is determined to keep public spending under control.*

consumer spending (=spending by members of the public) *There are some signs that consumer spending is increasing.*

defence/welfare/education etc spending (=spending on defence etc) *Further cuts in defence spending are being considered.*

federal spending (=by a national government, especially in the US) *Republicans want major reductions in federal spending.*

VERBS

increase/raise spending *The socialists want to increase public spending and raise taxes.*

cut/reduce spending *The alternative to earning more money is to cut spending.*

control/cap spending *The minister emphasized the need to cap public spending.*

spending + NOUNS

a spending cut *The government announced big spending cuts.*

a spending increase *There is not likely to be a public spending increase for several years.*

spending habits/patterns *Supermarkets collect information on the spending habits of their customers.*

PREPOSITIONS

spending on sth *It seems likely that spending on welfare will be cut.*

PHRASES

an increase/rise in spending *She called for an increase in spending on hospitals.*

a cut in spending *How can schools improve if there are more cuts in education spending?*

a decline/drop/slowdown in spending *Shops are seeing a decline in spending on luxury items.*

THESAURUS: spending

expenditure *formal*
the amount of money that a government, organization, or person spends during a particular period of time - used especially in official documents or reports:
*Government **expenditure** on healthcare was consistently high during this period.* | *They want to increase **military expenditure**.* | ***Expenditure on** advertising has gone down.*

costs
the money that a person or organization has to spend on heating, rent, wages etc:
*Falling sales have forced companies to **cut costs**.* | *What are your annual **fuel costs**?* | *Increased oil prices will put up **food costs*** (=make them increase). | *Companies are always looking at ways to keep down **plant costs*** (=the cost of the staff, buildings, equipment etc needed to produce goods).

expenses
the money that you spend on things that you need, for example on food, rent, and travel:
***Living expenses** are much higher in New York.* | *I kept a record of all my **travel expenses** so that I could claim them back.*

outgoings
the money that someone has to spend regularly on rent, bills, food etc for their home or business:
*The **monthly outgoings on** a house this size are very high.* | *I don't have a record of our **total outgoings**.*

outlay
the amount of money that someone must spend when they first start a new business or activity:
*The **initial outlay** on machinery was quite high.* | *We have got back our **original capital outlay*** (=the money you spent).

overhead (*also* **overhead** *BrE*)
the money that a business spends regularly on rent, insurance, and other things that are needed to keep the business operating:
*In London, small businesses often have **high overheads**.*

spicy *adj*

food that is spicy has a pleasantly strong taste, and gives you a pleasant burning feeling in your mouth

ADVERBS

too spicy *Some of the dishes were too spicy for me.*

mildly/lightly spicy *This curry is mildly spicy.*

deliciously spicy *The sauce is rich and deliciously spicy.*

very/really spicy *The lamb dish was really spicy.*

NOUNS

a spicy flavour/taste *The soup has a rather spicy flavour.*

spicy food *All my family love spicy food.*

a spicy sauce *They served us chicken in a spicy sauce.*

a spicy dish *He chose the spiciest dish on the menu.*

Instead of saying that something is **spicy**, you often say that it is **hot**: *This curry is really **hot**.*

spider *n*

a small creature with eight legs, which catches insects using a fine network of sticky threads

PHRASES

a spider's web (=the network of threads a spider makes) *The insect was trapped in a spider's web.*

S

ADJECTIVES

a poisonous spider *You find more poisonous spiders in warmer climates.*

a deadly spider (=one that can kill you) *She recognized it as the deadly Australian spider.*

a giant/huge spider *He had to get a giant spider out of the bath.*

VERBS

a spider spins/weaves a web (=makes a network of threads) *We watched a spider spinning a web on the leaf.*

a spider climbs somewhere *There's a spider climbing up your leg.*

a spider crawls somewhere *A huge spider just crawled under that chair.*

spiky *adj* THESAURUS **sharp (1)**

spill *v*

if you spill a liquid, or if it spills, it accidentally flows over the edge of a container

ADVERBS

accidentally spill sth *She accidentally spilt her drink.*

almost/nearly spill sth *Jenna jumped up, almost spilling her coffee.*

NOUNS

spill coffee/beer/water etc *Someone spilled water on the keyboard, and it doesn't work anymore.*

spill a drink *I spilled a hot drink on my leg.*

spill the contents (of sth) *He knocked a vase, spilling the contents.*

oil/water/blood spills somewhere *Several gallons of oil have spilled into the river.*

PREPOSITIONS/ADVERBS

spill sth on sth *I accidentally spilled some paint on the carpet.*

spill sth down sth *Oh no! I've spilt soup down my shirt!*

spill sth over sth *He had spilled wine over the letter.*

sth spills over (sth) *Water was spilling over the edge of the bath.*

sth spills into sth *Oil had spilled into the ocean.*

PHRASES

without spilling a drop (=used to emphasize that someone does not spill anything) *She poured it back into the bottle without spilling a drop.*

spirit *n*

1 your spirits are how happy, hopeful, or confident you feel

> **Grammar**
> Always plural in this meaning.

ADJECTIVES

high/good spirits (=when someone is happy and excited) *The players were all in high spirits.*

low/flagging spirits (=when someone is sad) *She was tired and her spirits were low.*

VERBS

lift/raise/revive sb's spirits (=make someone feel happier) *A brisk walk helped to lift my spirits.*

dampen sb's spirits (=make someone feel less happy) *They refused to let the rain dampen their spirits.*

sb's spirits rise/lift/soar (=someone starts feeling happier) *Her spirits rose as they left the ugliness of London behind.*

sb's spirits sink (=someone starts feeling less happy) *His spirits sank at the thought of spending a weekend in a tent.*

PHRASES

in high/good/low etc spirits *The next day she seemed to be in better spirits.*

keep sb's spirits up (=keep someone feeling happy) *She sang to herself softly to keep her spirits up.*

2 someone's attitude to life, to other people, or to an activity

ADJECTIVES

fighting spirit (= in which you keep trying hard to win or to do something) *He survived his injuries due to his incredible fighting spirit.*

indomitable spirit (=in which you never give up, even in very difficult situations) *Alice Fernie was a woman of indomitable spirit and she was determined to succeed.*

generous spirit (=that shows a willingness to behave in a fair or kind way) *The local people are known for their generous spirit.*

pioneering spirit (=willing to be the first to do new things) *He admired the pioneering spirit of those early explorers.*

entrepreneurial spirit (=people are good at making money from business) *Britain became rich thanks to the entrepreneurial spirit of its people.*

a strong spirit of sth *There is a very strong spirit of independence on the island.*

NOUNS + spirit

team spirit *The coach has created an excellent team spirit.*

community spirit *There is a strong community spirit in the town.*

VERBS

show/display/demonstrate a spirit *We need to show a spirit of toleration.*

capture/reflect the spirit (=describe or show it accurately) *The film captures the spirit of the time.*

embody a spirit *formal* (=always behave in a

S

way that is typical of a particular attitude) *He is a competitor who embodies the Olympic spirit.*

PREPOSITIONS

a spirit of sth *There was a spirit of friendship and cooperation, which seems lacking these days.*

in a spirit of sth *Athletes make a promise to compete in a spirit of fairness.*

PHRASES

the spirit of the age/time *Scott Fitzgerald's books reflect the spirit of the age.*

in the right spirit *To enjoy the game, you must play it in the right spirit.*

3 determination and energy

NOUNS

great spirit/a lot of spirit/plenty of spirit *The Arsenal team showed plenty of spirit and fought back to win the game 4–3.*

VERBS

have (a lot of) spirit *Morgan had spirit and intelligence as well as beauty.*

spiteful *adj* THESAURUS ▸ **unkind**

split *v* THESAURUS ▸ **break¹ (1)**

spoil *v*

to have a bad effect on something so that it is no longer attractive, enjoyable, useful etc

ADVERBS

completely spoil sth *Having our money stolen completely spoilt the holiday.*

rather spoil sth *The wintry weather rather spoiled the celebrations.*

NOUNS

spoil sb's day/evening/holiday etc *Bad news can spoil your day.*

spoil sb's fun *I don't want to spoil your fun.*

spoil sb's plans *Bad weather spoiled their plans for a picnic.*

spoil the view *Local people complained that the new office building would spoil the view of the cathedral.*

spoil everything *Why do you always have to spoil everything?*

spoken *adj*

spoken language is said by one person to another, rather than written down

NOUNS

spoken language *Spoken language contains many incomplete sentences.*

spoken English/French/Arabic etc *His spoken English is much better than his written English.*

the spoken word (=things that people say, rather than things people write) *There was no written language in those days, so all communication was through the spoken word.*

THESAURUS: spoken

oral
test | exam | culture | tradition | history
using spoken language:
I didn't do very well in the oral test. | We had a 15-minute oral exam in German. | Anglo-Saxon stories and poems were part of a mainly oral culture.

verbal
agreement | contract | consent | abuse | attack | battle | warning | report | message | response
using spoken language:
We had a verbal agreement but no written contract. | The women have suffered emotional and verbal abuse from their husbands. | He received a verbal warning from his superior officer (=he was told that he must not do something again).

You can also say that you hear or find out about something **by/through word of mouth** (=someone tells you about it): *He found out about the job* ***by word of mouth.***

ANTONYMS **spoken → written**

spongy *adj* THESAURUS ▸ **soft (1)**

sponsor *n*

a person or company that supports an event, sports team, show etc by giving money

ADJECTIVES

main/chief/principal sponsor *The bank is the main sponsor of the competition.*

a major/leading sponsor *The Wolfson Foundation is one of Britain's leading sponsors of university research.*

an official sponsor *Adidas was the official sponsor of the event.*

a corporate/commercial sponsor (=a company that gives money) *The exhibition attracted $100,000 from corporate sponsors.*

a private sponsor (=companies or people, not the government) *The colleges will be funded by private sponsors.*

a potential sponsor (=someone who might be a sponsor) *We are having discussions with potential sponsors.*

VERBS

look for/seek a sponsor *They are still seeking a sponsor for the event.*

find/get a sponsor *They have finally found a sponsor for the team.*

attract a sponsor *It is becoming harder for museums to attract sponsors.*

PREPOSITIONS

a sponsor of/for sth *The company has been a*

sponsor of the Scottish Golf Championship for the past three years.

sponsorship *n*

financial support for an activity or event

ADJECTIVES

corporate/commercial/business sponsorship (=from companies) *There has been a reduction in corporate sponsorship of the arts.*

private sponsorship (=from companies or people, not the government) *The school will need to find private sponsorship for this project.*

generous sponsorship *This exhibition could not have happened without the generous sponsorship of local businesses.*

NOUNS + sponsorship

sports/arts sponsorship *Sports sponsorship by cigarette companies was banned.*

VERBS

get/receive sponsorship *The college receives sponsorship from several companies.*

look for/seek sponsorship *The team is looking for sponsorship from one of the major banks.*

win/find sponsorship (*also* **secure sponsorship** *formal*): *We contacted several businesses in an attempt to secure sponsorship.*

raise sponsorship *We are trying to raise sponsorship for the exhibition.*

attract sponsorship *The competition needs to attract sponsorship.*

offer sponsorship *Several major companies have offered sponsorship.*

withdraw your sponsorship (=stop offering it) *The future of the event is in doubt after the bank withdrew its sponsorship.*

sponsorship + NOUNS

a sponsorship deal/agreement/contract *The player signed a sponsorship deal with a German company.*

PREPOSITIONS

sponsorship for sth *Failure to attract sponsorship for the event has left organizers with a problem.*

sponsorship of sth *We are grateful to IBM for its sponsorship of the programme.*

sponsorship from sb *They received generous sponsorship from two Japanese companies.*

spooky *adj* THESAURUS **frightening**

sport *n*

a physical activity in which people compete against each other

> **Grammar**
> When talking about sport in general, British speakers say **sport**: *I like watching* **sport** *on TV.* American speakers say **sports**: *I like watching* **sports** *on TV.*

VERBS

play (a) sport *What sports do you play?*

take part in (a) sport *Students are encouraged to take part in a sport of some kind.*

do sport *BrE*, **do sports** *AmE*: *I did a lot of sport at school.*

take up a sport (=start doing it) *She only took up the sport three years ago.*

compete in a sport (=do that sport in competitions) *She competed in various sports when she was young.*

be involved in sport(s) *Kids who are involved in sport tend to do better at school.*

> ⚠ Don't say 'make a sport'. Say **play a sport**.

ADJECTIVES/NOUNS + sport

professional sport(s) (=which people are paid to do) *There is a lot of cheating in professional sport.*

amateur sport(s) (=which people are not paid to do) *He began his career in amateur sport.*

competitive sport(s) (=in which people compete and try to win) *Competitive sport teaches valuable lessons which last for life.*

winter sports (=skiing, ice skating etc) *More and more people are taking up winter sports.*

water sports (=sports that you play in water) *He enjoys water sports, especially windsurfing.*

an extreme sport (=a dangerous sport such as rock climbing) *Many teenagers are attracted to extreme sports such as snowboarding.*

a team sport (=that you play in a team) *I like team sports such as football and rugby.*

an individual sport (=that you play on your own) *You have to be mentally tough to compete in individual sports.*

a spectator sport (=one that people enjoy watching) *Football is the most popular spectator sport.*

a contact sport (=in which players have physical contact with each other) *People get hurt in contact sports, but they also have fun.*

a minority sport (=one that very few people do) *Minority sports rarely feature on TV.*

sport + NOUNS

a sports team *A lot of schools have their own sports teams.*

a sports club *She joined her local sports club.*

a sports field/ground *The village has its own sports field.*

a sports event *Is this country able to stage a major sports event?*

a sports fan (=someone who enjoys watching sport) *He was a big sports fan.*

sports facilities *All our holiday camps have wonderful sports facilities.*

sports equipment *We sell all kinds of sports equipment.*

sports clothes/shoes/bag etc *Don't forget your sports clothes.*

a sports injury *The clinic specializes in treating sports injuries.*

a sports personality (=someone who is famous for playing sport) *The event will be opened by a well-known sports personality.*

PREPOSITIONS

in sport(s) *What are your views on drugs in sport?*

the sport of sth *Many famous people from the sport of football attended his funeral.*

spot *n*

1 a particular place or area, especially a pleasant place where you spend time

ADJECTIVES

the exact spot *This is the exact spot where the crash happened.*

a quiet spot *The hotel is in a quiet spot on the edge of town.*

a remote/isolated spot (=a long way from places where people live) *The accident happened in a remote spot.*

a secluded spot (=where it is quiet and people cannot see you) *The lovers drove to a secluded spot.*

a sheltered spot (=protected from wind, rain etc) *I found a sheltered spot on the deck of the ship.*

a shady spot (=away from the sun) *She parked the car in a shady spot under a tree.*

a sunny spot *The plant grows best in a sunny spot.*

an idyllic spot (=used to emphasize that it is beautiful) *This is an idyllic spot for a romantic holiday.*

a perfect/ideal spot *The bar is an ideal spot by the lake to enjoy a relaxing drink.*

a popular spot (*also* **a favourite spot** *BrE*, **a favorite spot** *AmE*): *This is a popular spot for picnics.*

VERBS

find a spot *We found a spot where we could sit quietly.*

pick/choose a spot *I chose a pleasant spot under some trees for our picnic.*

mark a spot *They planted a tree to mark the spot where the dog had been buried.*

occupy a spot *formal* (=be situated somewhere) *The cottage occupies a lovely spot on the banks of the river.*

reach a spot *By the time we reached the spot, they had gone.*

visit a spot *Thousands of fans visited the spot where he died.*

be rooted to the spot (=unable to move because you are so frightened, interested etc) *When I saw the snake I just stood there, rooted to the spot.*

NOUNS + spot

a parking spot *He drove around looking for a parking spot.*

a holiday spot *BrE*, **a vacation spot** *AmE*: *Wengen is one of Switzerland's most popular holiday spots.*

a tourist spot *Long Beach is a tourist spot with a boardwalk and beautiful beaches.*

a beauty spot (=a place that is beautiful) *Guests can enjoy trips to local beauty spots.*

a picnic spot *The area has plenty of beautiful picnic spots.*

a trouble spot (=a place where there are problems, especially fighting) *This part of town is a well-known trouble spot.*

PREPOSITIONS

in a spot *He lay down in a shady spot.*

on a spot *Why do they want to build a house on this particular spot?*

a spot for sth *It was an ideal spot for a picnic.*

2 a small mark on someone's skin, especially on their face

VERBS

be covered in spots *Her face was covered in spots.*

break out/come out in spots (=a lot of spots appear) *The illness had made him come out in spots.*

a spot appears *A large spot had appeared on the end of his nose.*

spot + NOUNS

spot cream/remover (=a substance for treating spots) *I need to get some spot cream from the chemist's.*

PREPOSITIONS

a spot on sth *I can't go out with all these spots on my face!*

spotless *adj* THESAURUS **clean[1] (1)**

spread *v*

if something spreads, or someone spreads it, it starts to affect more people or a larger area

ADVERBS

spread rapidly/quickly *The fire spread rapidly, destroying many buildings.*

NOUNS + spread

a disease spreads (=among a group of people) *In hot conditions, the disease will spread rapidly.*

a cancer/infection spreads (=in someone's body) *The cancer had spread to his brain.*

news/word spreads (=people hear that something has happened) *As news of their leader's death spread, soldiers started to lose confidence.*

a story spreads (*also* **a rumour spreads** *BrE*), **a rumor spreads** *AmE*: *It was the sort of sensational story that would spread rapidly.*

fire spreads (*also* **flames spread**) *The fire quickly spread to a nearby shed.*

violence/fighting spreads *The violence is likely to spread to neighbouring countries.*

sb's fame/reputation spreads *Their musical fame has spread far beyond their native country.*

spread + NOUNS

spread disease/infection *Wash your hands carefully to avoid spreading infection.*

spread the news *We should be spreading the news about these great British successes.*

spread a story (*also* **spread a rumour** *BrE*), **spread a rumor** *AmE*: *Her former lover had spread stories about her private life.*

spread disinformation/misinformation (=deliberately give people false information) *He accused his rival candidate of spreading misinformation during the election campaign.*

spread lies/gossip *How dare you spread such vicious lies!*

spread terror/panic *The murders were clearly intended to spread terror throughout the city.*

PREPOSITIONS

spread to sth *The disease soon spread to smaller towns and villages.*

spread through/throughout sth *Within hours, the rumor had spread throughout the entire school.*

spread across sth *A smile slowly spread across his face.*

PHRASES

spread like wildfire (=spread extremely quickly) *The news spread like wildfire through the town.*

spread the word (=give people information encouraging them to do something) *The government needs to do more to spread the word about healthy eating.*

spring *n*

the season between winter and summer, when leaves and flowers appear

ADJECTIVES

early spring *It was a cold sunny day in early spring.*

late spring *The tourist season is from late spring until the end of the summer.*

next spring *The building will be completed next spring.*

last spring *Last spring I was in Morocco.*

the previous spring *She had met him in New York the previous spring.*

the following spring *The following spring he moved to Hong Kong.*

VERBS

spring comes/arrives *Spring came late this year.*

spring + NOUNS

a spring morning/day/evening *It was a bright spring morning.*

spring sunshine *It was warm in the spring sunshine.*

spring weather *We had two days of fine spring weather.*

spring flowers *She was carrying a basket of spring flowers.*

a spring break (=time in spring when you do not have to work or study or when you go away) *He spent the spring break in Florida.*

the spring term *BrE*, **the spring semester** *AmE* (=the time between January and Easter at a school, college, or university) *Do you have any exams during the spring term?*

PREPOSITIONS

in (the) spring *The store will open in the spring.*

during (the) spring *During the spring the field is full of flowers.*

the spring of 1987/2010 etc *The election was held in the spring of 2008.*

PHRASES

the first sign of spring (=something that shows that spring is starting) *The flowers are the first sign of spring.*

spurious *adj* THESAURUS › **false**

spy *n*

someone whose job is to find out secret information about another country, organization, or group

ADJECTIVES/NOUNS + spy

a British/Russian/American etc spy *They suspected that he was an American spy.*

a foreign spy/enemy spy *He gave information to foreign spies.*

a government spy *The men thought I was a government spy.*

a former spy (=someone who used to be a spy) *Police are investigating the death of a former Russian spy.*

VERBS

work as a spy *She worked as a spy for the Americans.*

spy + NOUNS

a spy story/novel/movie/thriller etc *The film is based on a spy story by John Le Carré.*

a spy ring/network (=a group of spies) *Burgess and Maclean were members of a Soviet spy ring.*

a spy satellite/plane *The information was obtained using a spy satellite.*

a spy chief (*also* **a spymaster**) *She was Britain's first woman spy chief.*

squad *n*

1 a group of players from which a team will be chosen for a particular sports event

ADJECTIVES/NOUNS + squad

a soccer/hockey etc squad *Tom was left out of the hockey squad because of injury.*

a national/international squad (=a team that represents their country) *She was in Canada's national squad.*

the England/Germany etc squad (*also* **the English/German etc squad** *formal*): *He has been included in the Ireland squad for the World Cup.*

the World Cup/Olympic etc squad *She is competing for a place in Japan's Olympic squad.*

a strong squad *We have a strong squad for this competition.*

the senior/junior squad *He has been training with the senior squad.*

a full squad (=including all the best players) *The manager will have a full squad to choose from.*

VERBS

pick/choose a squad (*also* **select a squad** *formal*): *The coach has to pick a squad for next week's game.*

name/announce a squad (=say which players will be in it) *The manager has named his squad for the World Cup.*

be left out of/be dropped from a squad (=not be included) *Kenny has been left out of the squad due to illness.*

join a squad *The player joined the national squad last year.*

make the squad (=succeed in achieving a place in a squad) *Patterson failed to make the squad due to injury.*

lead a squad *Kuerten will be leading the Brazilian squad in the world championship.*

field a squad (=use a squad) *He is fielding a much younger squad this season.*

withdraw from a squad (=say you do not want to be in it) *Jenas withdrew from the England squad.*

a squad includes sb *Their squad includes some of the best players in the world.*

squad + NOUNS

a squad member *He is the youngest England squad member.*

PREPOSITIONS

in a squad *BrE*, **on a squad** *AmE*: *There are some good players in the squad.*

2 a group of police officers or soldiers who have a particular job

ADJECTIVES/NOUNS + squad

the bomb squad *The bomb squad was called to examine the suspicious package.*

the riot squad (=special police trained to deal with violent crowds of people) *The riot squad were called in to deal with fighting on the streets.*

the drug/fraud/murder/anti-terrorist etc squad *The house was raided by the drug squad.*

squalid *adj* THESAURUS ▸ **dirty**

squeaky *adj* THESAURUS ▸ **high (3)**

squeeze *v*

to press something together with your fingers or hand

ADVERBS

squeeze (sth) gently *He squeezed her hand gently in his.*

squeeze (sth) hard *She pointed the gun and squeezed the trigger hard.*

squeeze (sth) tightly *She was squeezing so tightly that her knuckles were white.*

PREPOSITIONS

squeeze sth out of sth (=remove it by squeezing) *I tried to squeeze a little toothpaste out of the tube.*

squeeze sth together *Squeeze your legs together for ten seconds.*

stability Ac *n*

the condition of being steady and not changing

ADJECTIVES

political/social stability *The new government promised a return to political stability.*

financial/economic stability *There were concerns about the company's financial stability.*

greater/increased stability *The last decade was a period of greater stability.*

relative stability (=more stability than at other times) *The fighting followed a period of relative stability.*

long-term stability *This policy will be disastrous for the country's long-term stability.*

future stability *The future stability of the company is in doubt.*

global/international stability *Climate change is possibly the greatest threat to global stability.*

regional stability (=stability of a region) *A divided country would also threaten regional stability.*

NOUNS + stability

price stability *One of the economic aims was to achieve price stability.*

VERBS

bring/provide/create stability *The country needs a strong leader who can bring stability.*

maintain stability *Troops were sent to the area to maintain stability.*

ensure/guarantee stability *The problem is how to ensure the future stability of the region.*

achieve stability *Achieving stability will not be easy.*

S

restore stability *The policy was an attempt to restore stability to the financial markets.*

threaten/undermine stability (=harm stability) *This dispute threatens the stability of the government.*

promote/improve/increase stability *All sides should work to promote stability in the area.*

PHRASES

peace and stability *It could threaten the peace and stability of the region.*

a degree of stability *The country has maintained a degree of stability.*

a threat to stability *Terrorism will remain a threat to stability in the region.*

a period of stability *The team now needs a period of stability.*

stable Ac *adj*

steady and not likely to change

ADVERBS

politically stable *Iceland is a politically stable democracy.*

financially/economically stable *The company is more financially stable and it has paid off its debts.*

emotionally stable *He seemed calm and emotionally stable.*

reasonably/fairly/relatively stable *The situation appears to be reasonably stable.*

remarkably stable (=in a way that is unusual or surprising) *Prices have remained remarkably stable.*

NOUNS

a stable environment *Children like a stable environment.*

a stable relationship *He isn't married but he's in a stable relationship.*

a stable home *We felt we could offer a stable home to the children.*

a stable government *The nation needs a strong and stable government.*

a stable democracy/country *The country has still not become a stable democracy.*

stable prices *Oil prices remained stable.*

a stable economy *Germany is known for having a stable economy.*

a stable currency *Switzerland has a stable currency and very little debt.*

VERBS

remain stable *His body temperature remained stable.*

PHRASES

be in a stable condition (=used about someone in a hospital who is ill but not getting worse) *She is in a stable condition following the accident.*

stadium *n*

a building for public events, especially sports and large rock music concerts, consisting of a playing field surrounded by rows of seats

ADJECTIVES

a national stadium *The game will be played at the national stadium.*

the Olympic stadium *We visited the Olympic stadium in Seoul.*

a packed stadium (=full of people) *The band has been playing to packed stadiums around America.*

an all-seater stadium (=with seats only, and no areas where the audience stands) *A new all-seater stadium was built with a 60,000 capacity.*

NOUNS + stadium

a sports stadium *They built a big new sports stadium for the Olympic games.*

a football/baseball etc stadium *They live near the Durham Bulls baseball stadium.*

VERBS

build a stadium *The new stadium will be built on a site near the river.*

play at a stadium (=play in a sports match there) *It was the first time he had played at the national stadium.*

PREPOSITIONS

at a stadium *They played their last game at the stadium in 1992.*

inside a stadium *The atmosphere inside the stadium is electric.*

staff *n*

the people who work for an organization

ADJECTIVES/NOUNS + staff

full-time/part-time staff *The hotel has more than 50 full-time staff.*

permanent/temporary staff *Much of the work is done by temporary staff.*

senior/junior staff *I have listened to the comments of my senior staff.*

medical/academic/technical etc staff *We would like to thank all the medical staff at Broadgreen Hospital.*

hospital/library/office etc staff *He had responsibility for training library staff.*

support staff (=office staff, technical staff etc who support the main work of an organization) *A school needs good support staff.*

trained/qualified staff *We simply do not have enough trained staff to do the job properly.*

staff + NOUNS

a staff member (*also* **a member of staff** *BrE*): *If you don't know where your appointment is, please ask a staff member to help you.*

a staff meeting *On Wednesdays there's our weekly staff meeting.*

staff training/development *The company has made a massive investment in staff training.*

the staff room *BrE* (=a room for teachers in a

school) *I usually have a coffee in the staff room before school starts.*

staff morale (=how happy and confident the staff feel) *Staff morale has been badly affected by the reorganization.*

a staff shortage (=when there are not enough workers) *The rail service has suffered from severe staff shortages.*

staff turnover (=how often workers leave an organization and new workers arrive) *A high staff turnover suggests problems in the company.*

a staff discount (=a special low price for goods or services, available to workers) *The great thing about working at the shoe store is the staff discount.*

the staff canteen (=a restaurant at an office, factory etc, where staff can have lunch) *She usually has lunch in the staff canteen.*

VERBS

have/employ staff *The hotel employs over 100 staff.*

join the staff *She has joined the staff of a major newspaper as editor-in-chief.*

train staff *The company spends thousands of pounds a year training its staff.*

recruit/hire staff (*also* **take on staff** *BrE*) (=start to employ them) *We recruit a lot of our staff straight from college.*

retain staff (=make them want to stay in an organization) *The association seems to have difficulty retaining staff.*

PREPOSITIONS

a staff of *Our department has a staff of seven.*

staff at/in sth *Staff at the hospital have been told not to speak to journalists.*

be on the staff *BrE*, **be on staff** *AmE*: *David Taylor is no longer on the staff.*

stage *n*

1 a particular time or state in a process

ADJECTIVES

the early/initial stages *We had a few problems in the early stages of the project.*

the later/final/closing stages *The team are in the final stages of the competition.*

the halfway stage *He was in the lead at the halfway stage of the race.*

an advanced stage *Negotiations have reached an advanced stage.*

a new stage *The job marked the beginning of a new stage in my life.*

a critical/crucial stage (=very important because it affects future success) *The football season is reaching a crucial stage.*

a formative stage (=when someone or something is developing) *This plan is still in its formative stages.*

a difficult/awkward stage *He was 13 and going through an awkward stage.*

a delicate/vulnerable stage (=when complete failure is possible) *The discussions are at a very delicate stage.*

VERBS

enter a stage *He is entering a new stage of his career.*

reach a stage (*also* **get to a stage**) *We have reached the stage where no-one is safe to walk our streets at night.*

go/pass through a stage *Most young people go through a rebellious stage.*

mark a stage (=be a particular point in the development of something) *The election marks an important stage in the rebuilding of the country.*

approach/near a stage *The situation is so bad that we are nearing the stage when the police may be called.*

PREPOSITIONS

a stage of sth *The next stage of the journey is from Paris to Berlin.*

a stage in sth *At this stage in the game, either team could win.*

at a stage *The baby is at the stage where he is just starting to walk.*

PHRASES

at this/that stage *At this stage his wife did not realize he was ill.*

at one stage (=at a time in the past) *At one stage I had to tell him to calm down.*

at some stage *Four out of ten people are likely to contract cancer at some stage in their lives.*

at an early/late stage *I can't change my plans at this late stage.*

at a later stage *These points will be dealt with at a later stage.*

a stage of development *We have several new products in various stages of development.*

take sth a stage further (=develop it) *We then took the experiment a stage further.*

2 the raised area in a theatre where the performance happens

VERBS

be on stage *He was on stage for most of the first act.*

appear on stage *Recently she has appeared on stage in 'Private Lives'.*

go/come on stage *I'm always nervous before going on stage.*

walk on stage (*also* **walk onto the stage**) *The audience broke into applause as soon as he walked on stage.*

take the stage (=go on stage) *The band took the stage shortly after ten o'clock.*

leave the stage (*also* **come off stage**) *Everyone except the main character gradually leaves the stage.*

walk off the stage (=leave the stage before

the performance has ended) *The pianist walked off the stage after playing only a few notes.*

share the stage with sb (=perform with them) *She once shared a stage with Barbra Streisand.*

stage + NOUNS

a stage play/production (=performed in a theatre, not on television) *The film was adapted from a very successful stage play.*

a stage set (=the furniture and painted backgrounds used on a theatre stage) *The room had the slightly unreal look of a stage set.*

stage props (=furniture and other objects used in a play) *The gun was one of the many stage props kept in this cupboard.*

stage directions (=written instructions telling actors where to stand etc) *The playwright gives the actors only the most basic stage directions.*

stage lighting *Clever use of stage lighting can transform the set.*

stain *n*

a mark that is difficult to remove, especially one made by a liquid such as blood, coffee, or ink

ADJECTIVES/NOUNS + stain

a coffee/blood/wine etc stain *There is a coffee stain on my shirt.*

a dark stain *I noticed a dark stain on the ceiling.*

a faint stain *The wine had left a faint stain on the carpet.*

a stubborn stain (=one that is hard to remove) *Bleach is good for getting rid of stubborn stains.*

VERBS

remove/get rid of a stain *He was trying to remove a stain from his jacket.*

get a stain out (=remove it) *You'll never get that stain out.*

sth leaves a stain *The soup left a stain on his tie.*

stairs *n*

a set of steps built for going from one level of a building to another

ADJECTIVES

the main stairs *The main stairs of the hotel were made of marble.*

the back/front stairs (=at the back or front of a building) *Her room was up the front stairs.*

steep stairs *I nearly fell down the steep stairs.*

narrow/wide stairs *Sarah followed him up the narrow stairs.*

wooden/stone/marble etc stairs *He could hear his mother's footsteps on the wooden stairs.*

spiral/winding stairs (=ones that go round and round) *She climbed the winding stairs to the top of the tower.*

VERBS

go up/climb the stairs (*also* **mount the stairs** *formal*): *Sylvie went quietly up the stairs.*

go down/come down the stairs (*also* **descend the stairs** *formal*): *We went down the stairs into the kitchen.*

fall down the stairs *Yoshie fell down the stairs and broke her leg.*

run up/down the stairs (*also* **race up/down the stairs**) (=go up or down them as quickly as you can) *He raced down the stairs to find out what was happening.*

bound up/down the stairs (=run fast because you are happy, excited, frightened etc) *She turned and bounded up the stairs.*

creep up/down the stairs (=go quietly) *Emma crept down the stairs hoping no one would hear her.*

use/take the stairs *I don't like elevators so I always take the stairs.*

the stairs lead (down/up) to sth *The stairs led down to the basement.*

PREPOSITIONS

up/down the stairs *She ran up the stairs to get her bag.*

on the stairs *I passed him on the stairs.*

under the stairs *There was a cupboard under the stairs.*

PHRASES

a flight of stairs (=a set of stairs) *We walked up four flights of stairs.*

the bottom/foot of the stairs *"I'm home," he called from the foot of the stairs.*

the top of the stairs *Maria stood at the top of the stairs.*

stalemate *n*

a situation in which it seems impossible to settle an argument or disagreement, and neither side can get an advantage

VERBS

reach a stalemate *It seems that negotiations have reached a stalemate.*

end/result in a stalemate *The dispute between them ended in a stalemate.*

be locked in a stalemate *The two sides have been locked in a stalemate for months.*

break/end a stalemate (*also* **resolve a stalemate** *formal*): *More talks are planned to help resolve the stalemate.*

a stalemate continues/persists *While the stalemate continues, no political development is possible in the country.*

ADJECTIVES/NOUNS + stalemate

a military/political stalemate *A new leader may bring an end to the political stalemate between the two nations.*

PREPOSITIONS

a stalemate in sth *There is still a depressing stalemate in the dispute.*

a stalemate over sth *It will be difficult to resolve the stalemate over pay.*

a stalemate between people/countries/groups *There was an uneasy stalemate between the two superpowers.*

stamina *n*

the ability to do something for a long time without getting tired

ADJECTIVES

physical/mental stamina *The job needs a lot of physical stamina.*

great/considerable stamina *He was a man of considerable stamina.*

VERBS

need/require stamina *The race requires great stamina.*

have stamina *I certainly don't have the stamina to keep up with my daughter.*

run out of stamina *I was worried that I was running out of stamina.*

lack stamina *People thought that the women lacked the physical stamina of the men.*

improve/increase/build up your stamina *He hopes the training will improve his stamina.*

PHRASES

sth is a test of stamina (=it is long and tiring) *The 30 kilometre walk is a test of stamina.*

stand *v*

to be on your feet in an upright position

ADVERBS

stand still *He stood still and listened but he couldn't hear anything.*

stand silently *Hundreds of people stood silently to remember the victims of the war.*

stand upright/stand up straight (=stand so that your back is very straight) *"Stand up straight, and walk properly!" the teacher called after him.*

stand transfixed (=stand still because you are very surprised, shocked etc) *For a moment she stood transfixed in shock and disbelief.*

PREPOSITIONS

stand next to/beside sb/sth *Julia went to stand beside him on the balcony.*

stand behind/in front of sb/sth *Mrs Hayes was standing behind her desk.*

PHRASES

stand on tiptoe (=stand on your toes to make yourself taller) *If he stood on tiptoe, he could reach the shelf.*

stand with your back to sth *Pedro was standing with his back to the fire.*

standard[1] *n*

the level that is considered to be acceptable, or the level that someone or something has achieved

ADJECTIVES/NOUNS + standard

a high/good standard *Her work is of a very high standard.*

a low/poor standard *The report says the standard of children's diet in Britain is poor.*

an acceptable standard *Their behaviour often falls below acceptable standards.*

the required standard *He couldn't be a pilot because his eyesight was not up to the required standard.*

stringent/strict/rigorous/tough standards (=high standards that are difficult to reach) *Our rigorous standards mean that we have only the best people working for us.*

international standards *There should be international standards for food safety.*

safety/hygiene/quality etc standards *All our products meet the current safety standards.*

academic/educational standards *They need to raise academic standards within the school.*

environmental standards (=for protecting the environment) *They called on the Indian government to apply stricter environmental standards.*

professional standards (=in a particular profession) *The new rules were aimed at improving professional standards in the financial services sector.*

moral standards (=relating to right or wrong behaviour) *She was very strict and had high moral standards.*

living standards (*also* **standard of living**) (=the level of comfort and the amount of money people have) *Living standards at all income levels improved over that period.*

VERBS

meet/reach/achieve a standard *Students have to reach a certain standard or they won't pass.*

lay down/set a standard (=say what it should be) *The government sets standards that all hospitals must reach.*

raise/improve standards *We are determined to raise standards in our schools.*

lower standards *He refused to lower his standards.*

maintain standards (=keep them at a good level) *Managers should maintain standards of work and behaviour.*

assess the standard of sth (=see how good it is) *This task will help us assess the standard of your written English.*

standards improve *The standard of this festival improves every year.*

standards fall/slip/decline (=get worse) *School inspectors say that educational standards have fallen.*

PREPOSITIONS

the standard of sth *The standard of care in this hospital is very good.*

standards in sth *The government has promised higher standards in education.*

to a standard *She plays piano to a very high standard.*

below/above a standard *Your driving is below the required standard.*

below standard (=not good enough) *His performance yesterday was below standard.*

PHRASES

an improvement/rise in standards *There has been a big improvement in standards recently.*

a decline/drop in standards *What is the cause of the decline in standards of literacy?*

have good/strict/poor etc standards *The airline has rigorous safety standards.*

be/come up to standard (=be good enough) *Her work was not up to standard.*

bring sth up to standard (=make it good enough) *With just a few changes, we can bring this department up to standard.*

by sb's standards (=judging by what someone is used to) *Class sizes are small by British standards.*

by modern/today's standards *The technology was basic by modern standards.*

standard² *adj*

accepted or given as normal or usual, not special or extra

NOUNS

standard practice/procedure (=what is usually done in situations like this) *It's standard procedure for a police officer to take your name and address.*

the standard method *This is the standard method for treating the disease.*

the standard rate/fee *She expects to be paid the standard hourly rate.*

the standard size *The standard size of a bath is 1700 x 700mm.*

PHRASES

come as standard/be fitted as standard (=be included as a usual part of something when you buy it) *On all our cars, airbags come as standard.*

standing *n* THESAURUS **reputation**

star *n*

1 a large ball of burning gas in space that can be seen at night as a point of light in the sky

ADJECTIVES

a bright star *Sirius is the brightest star in the night sky.*

a distant star (=very far away) *She stared up towards the distant stars.*

> A **shooting star** is a ball of rock and burning gas that makes a line in the sky as it falls through the atmosphere.

VERBS

a star shines *I looked up and saw hundreds of stars shining in the sky.*

a star twinkles (=shines with an unsteady light) *Stars began to twinkle in the darkening night sky.*

the stars appear/come out (=appear in the sky) *We arrived home just as the stars were coming out.*

the stars are out (=they are shining) *There was a full moon, and the stars were out.*

look up at the stars *I had spent a lot of time looking up at the stars as a kid.*

sleep under the stars (=in a place with no roof) *In the desert, they slept out under the stars.*

PHRASES

a cluster of stars (=a small group of stars close together in the sky) *He fixed his telescope on a tiny cluster of stars in the constellation of Taurus.*

2 a famous and successful actor, musician, or sports player

ADJECTIVES

a big star (=a very famous and successful star) *He has worked with some of the world's biggest stars.*

an international star *His performance in 'Titanic' made him an international star.*

a rising star (=someone who is becoming famous and successful) *She is one of Hollywood's rising stars.*

NOUNS + star

a movie/film/Hollywood star *He looked like a movie star.*

a pop/rock star *Who's your favourite pop star?*

a TV star *The magazine is full of pictures of famous TV stars.*

a soap star (=a star in a television soap opera (=a programme about the lives of an imaginary group of ordinary people) *She was known as a soap star before she took up singing.*

a sports/football/basketball etc star *Sam was a football star in college.*

a child star (=a child who is a famous performer) *The production team say they have been careful to look after all their child stars.*

star + NOUNS

star quality (=a special quality that could make someone a star) *She radiates genuine star quality.*

star status (=the position of being a star) *Pfeiffer struggled for ten years to achieve star status.*

star treatment (=special treatment that a star gets) *Winners get star treatment from the media.*

a star vehicle (=a film or television programme that is intended to show the abilities of one particular star) *He denied that the movie was just a star vehicle for Tom Hanks.*

PREPOSITIONS

the star of sth *Elizabeth Taylor was the star of 57 films.*

PHRASES

a star of stage and screen (=a star who has been in plays and films) *Now this much-loved star of stage and screen has been made a Dame.*

3 used about the best or most important actor, performer, player etc

star + NOUNS

star player/performer *The team will be without their star player.*

star guest *And now for our star guest, Mr Robbie Williams.*

PHRASES

sb is the star of the show *George Michael was definitely the star of the show.*

stare[1] *v*

to look at someone or something for a long time

ADVERBS

stare hard/intently (=very steadily, with a lot of attention) *She stared hard at him, as if she couldn't believe he was there.*

stare fixedly (=without moving your head or eyes) *He refused to look at me, staring fixedly out of the window.*

stare blankly (=without emotion, understanding, or interest) *The child stared blankly at the teacher.*

stare unseeingly/blindly *literary* (=not noticing anything, although your eyes are open) *She sat on the bed, staring unseeingly at the wall.*

stare vacantly (=seeming not to notice or be thinking anything) *The man was staring vacantly at the fire.*

stare moodily (=rather unhappily) *One customer was staring moodily into his glass.*

PREPOSITIONS

stare at sth/sb *She didn't say anything; she simply stared at me with her mouth open.*

PHRASES

stare in disbelief/horror/amazement etc *He stared in disbelief at the newspaper headline.*

stare into space (=look for a long time at nothing) *The kids just lie on the sofa staring into space.*

stand and stare *People just stood and stared as the building collapsed before their eyes.*

stare[2] *n*

a long steady look at someone or something

VERBS

give sb a stare *The detective gave her a long stare.*

fix sb with a stare *literary* (=stare at someone) *He fixed her with a cool stare.*

return sb's stare (=stare back at them) *I returned his stare and he looked away.*

meet sb's stare (=look back at them) *She met his angry stare calmly.*

ADJECTIVES

a hard stare (=very steady, with a lot of attention) *As he passed, he gave us a hard stare.*

a long stare *The man fixed him with a long deliberate stare.*

a blank stare (=showing no emotion, understanding, or interest) *Mention his name and you get mostly blank stares.*

a vacant stare (=seeming not to notice or be thinking anything) *She was gazing out of the window with a vacant stare.*

a fixed/unwavering/unblinking stare (=with your eyes not moving at all) *His unwavering stare was making me feel uneasy.*

a cold/stony/hostile stare (=unfriendly) *I smiled and said "hello" but only got a cold stare.*

a curious/inquisitive stare (=showing that you want to find out information) *As a new arrival in the village, you will probably receive a few curious stares.*

start[1] *v*

1 to begin to do something

> **Grammar**
> **Start** can be followed by an infinitive or a participle in this meaning. You can say *I* ***started to*** *run.* Or you can say *I* ***started*** *runn****ing****.*

NOUNS

start work *Members of the TV crew are expected to start work at 6 a.m.*

start a job/career *I've recently started a job as a drama teacher.*

start a conversation/discussion/argument *Jane tried to start a conversation with him.*

start a book/letter/speech *He starts the letter with "Dear Ms Jones".*

start a fire *The fire was started by someone carelessly throwing a cigarette on the ground.*

start a journey *It's best to check the weather before starting your journey.*

start a war *Russia has no intention of starting a war with Georgia.*

start a new life *She was going to California to start a new life.*

ADVERBS

start immediately/straightaway *They say they are ready to start work immediately.*

PREPOSITIONS

start by doing sth *The artist starts by doing a quick pencil drawing.*

start with sth *He starts with a brief introduction to the subject.*

start at/from sth *Let's start at the beginning.*

PHRASES

get started *We had better get started soon.*

start (sth) from scratch (=start from the beginning, doing everything yourself) *No one had done this kind of research before, and we had to start from scratch.*

THESAURUS: start

begin
to start to do something. **Begin** is more formal than **start**, and is used especially in written English:
He began to speak. | The orchestra began playing. | The company wants to begin work on the project next summer. | They began their research in 2010.

Start or **begin?**
Start and **begin** are both used in the same meaning with many nouns. You can **start work** or **begin work**. You can **start a conversation** or **begin a conversation**. The only difference is that **begin** is more formal than **start**.
With some words, you can only use **start**. You **start an argument/war/fire**. You do not use 'begin' with these words.

commence *formal*
to start to do something:
The company will commence drilling next week. | Mozart commenced work on the opera while he was still in Salzburg.

Commence is usually used with a participle, or with the word **work**.

set off
to start a journey:
What time do you have to set off in the morning? | I usually **set off for** *school at about 8.30.*

set out
to start a long journey:
The ship **set out from** *Portsmouth on July 12th. | They* **set out for** *India.*

get down to
work | business
to finally start doing something, especially your work:
It was 11 o'clock by the time we got down to some work. | Let's get down to business. What experience do you have of this job? (=start talking about the main subject, or start doing the main thing that you need to do)

take up
painting | writing | smoking | game | golf | photography | gardening
to start doing something, especially for enjoyment:
What inspired you to take up painting? | Children often take up smoking because their friends smoke. | More and more women are taking up the game.

resume
duties | work | service | journey | talks | negotiations | trade
to start doing something again after a break:
We hope that he gets well soon and is able to resume his duties. | She plans to go back to New York and resume her work with the homeless. | Normal service will be resumed as soon as possible. | We got back in the car and resumed our journey. | Trade was resumed after the end of the war.

launch
campaign | investigation | inquiry | programme | attack | offensive | appeal
to start doing something:
Local people launched a campaign to save the forest. | The company has launched an internal investigation into the allegations. | They launched a series of attacks on the enemy.

open
investigation | inquiry | negotiations | talks | dialogue
to start doing something, especially an investigation or negotiations:
He called for the military police to open an investigation into the incident. | The two governments agreed to open negotiations.

enter into
talks | negotiations | discussion | dialogue | debate
to start talking about something with another person or group. **Enter into** sounds rather formal:
They refused to enter into negotiations with the terrorists. | This is not the place to enter into a detailed discussion of the issue. | The author has refused to enter into a public debate about the book.

embark on
career | programme | adventure | project | campaign | journey | tour | mission
to start doing something, especially something new, difficult, or exciting:
He is thinking of embarking on a career as a surgeon. | The government embarked on a major programme of economic reform. | The two boys embark on a series of adventures.

2 to begin to happen

NOUNS

a story/show/film/play starts *Doors open at noon and the show starts at 2 p.m.*

an event/performance starts *The event starts on Saturday at the Los Angeles Convention Center.*

a meeting/party/class starts *I found this out ten minutes before the meeting started.*

a game/competition starts *Once the game starts, I forget about everything else.*

work starts *Work had already started on the bridge when the error was spotted.*

a problem/the trouble starts *Many health problems start in early life.*

a war/battle/fighting starts *He was only 19 when the war started.*

the day/season/year etc starts *The day starts with the great American breakfast – eggs, bacon, toast, and unlimited coffee.*

a course starts/school starts *The course starts with an introduction to web page design.*

ADVERBS

start well/badly *The season started well for the team.*

PHRASES

be due/scheduled to start (=be expected to start) *The trial had been due to start on Monday.*

start on time/start late *The class will start on time.*

start with a bang *informal* (=in a very exciting way) *The novel starts with a bang.*

THESAURUS: start

begin
to start. **Begin** is more formal than **start** and is used especially in written English:
The course begins in September. | Work on the tunnel will begin early next year.

commence *formal*
to start:
The work is scheduled to commence in April. | Detailed planning has already commenced. | The results will be announced in **the week commencing** *June 18th.*

Start, begin, or **commence?**
Start and **begin** mean the same and are used with the same collocations. **Start** is more common in spoken English, and **begin** is more common in written English.
Commence means the same as the other words, but is much more formal. It is used especially about things that have been officially arranged to start at a particular time. You do not use **commence** about informal events such as parties, or about problems and difficulties.

resume
talks | discussions | negotiations | meeting | trial
to start again after a break:
The peace talks will resume next week. | The trial resumes on Monday.

open
show | exhibition | film | movie | play | musical | trial | talks
to start – used especially when something starts being shown to the public:
The show will open to the public later this week. | The movie got very good reviews when it opened in the US. | The trial opened in February last year.

You can also use **open** when saying that a shop, bank, office, museum etc starts being available for people to use: *The bank opens at nine o'clock.*

break out
fire | blaze | fight | fighting | scuffles | violence | argument | war | disease
to start – used especially about fires, fights, and diseases:
A fire broke out in a chemical factory. | A fight breaks out and one man is hurt. | Scuffles broke out when riot police stopped a group of the protesters (=small fights started). *| An argument broke out and people started shouting at each other. | He was in the army when war broke out.*

kick off *informal*
match | game | campaign | festival | celebration
to start:
The match kicks off at three o'clock. | The election campaign kicked off in July. | The theater festival kicks off next week. | The celebration kicks off at 7.30.

The original meaning of **kick off** is to start a game in which you **kick** a ball. In informal English, this has spread to other situations in which you start doing something.

get under way
work | construction | trial | campaign | voting | conference | season | preparations
to start happening – used when something is likely to last for a long time, or you have been waiting a long time for something to start:
Work will get under way on the new high-speed railway line. | The trial is expected to get under way some time next year. | Voting got under way Sunday morning in Venezuela.

3 to make an organization start to exist

NOUNS

start a company/business *Zuckerberg started the company when he was only 19.*

start a shop/store/bank *The store was started more than 50 years ago by his parents.*

THESAURUS: start

open
shop | **store** | **restaurant** | **hotel**
to start a business such as a shop or a restaurant, which provides services to the public:
The company plans to open a big new store in Shanghai. | *McDonald's opened their first restaurant in 1955.*

establish
company | **business** | **firm** | **society** | **organization** | **committee** | **commission** | **club** | **party** | **school** | **college**
to start an organization or an official group, especially one that is intended to be permanent or last a long time:
The business was established over 50 years ago. | *The government established a commission to examine the problem of corruption.* | *The school was established in the late 19th century.*

Establish is often used in the passive.

found
company | **firm** | **bank** | **society** | **club** | **party** | **university** | **college** | **school** | **museum** | **church**
to start an organization – used especially about an important organization that was started a long time ago. The person who **founds** the organization usually provides the money for it:
The Bank of New York was founded in 1784. | *St Andrews is Scotland's oldest university and was founded in 1413.* | *The church was founded by Wenceslas II in 1285.*

Found is often used in the passive.

set up
company | **business** | **firm** | **committee** | **commission**
to start an organization or an official group. **Set up** is more informal than **establish** or **found**:
Barker set up the company only a year ago. | *She plans to set up her own clothing business.* | *The government set up a committee to look into ways of reforming the system.*

form
group | **band** | **alliance** | **partnership** | **coalition** | **government** | **administration** | **party** | **company**
to start a group or organization, by working together with other people, groups, or countries:
Mick and Keith formed the band in the early 1960s. | *Nasser formed a military alliance with Saudi Arabia, Syria, and Yemen.* | *Tomorrow morning we will know which party will form the next government.*

start² *n*

the way or time that something begins

ADJECTIVES

a good/great etc start *We had a nice breakfast, which was a good start to the day.*

a bad/poor/disastrous/terrible etc start *The meeting got off to a bad start when two people turned up late.*

a slow start *Work got off to a very slow start because of bad weather.*

an early/late start *It was a long trip so we planned an early start.*

a promising start (=a good start that makes success seem likely) *Her teacher says she's made a promising start in learning Spanish.*

a flying start (=a very good start) *Our season got off to a flying start with victories in our first three games.*

a disappointing start *He accepted full responsibility for the club's disappointing start to the season.*

a shaky start *informal* (=a rather bad start) *After a shaky start when she seemed to forget her lines, she performed really well.*

a fresh start (=a completely new start in your life, your marriage etc, especially after you had problems in the past) *He's determined to make a fresh start when he comes out of prison.*

VERBS

make a good/bad etc start *The team has made an excellent start to the season.*

get off to a good/bad etc start (=make a good, bad etc start) *On your first day at work, you want to get off to a good start.*

have a good/bad start *Hamilton had a bad start to the race, when he crashed into another car.*

start + NOUNS

start date/time *We're nearly ready to begin the project, so we're looking at a start date in early May.*

PHRASES

at the start *He seemed unsure of himself at the start, but soon became more confident.*

from the start *She was the best player from the start, and won the match easily.*

PHRASES

from start to finish (=throughout an event, process etc) *The minister's involvement in the scandal affected his re-election campaign from start to finish.*

THESAURUS: start

start, commencement, origin, the onset of sth, dawn, birth → **beginning (1)**

S

starvation *n*

suffering caused by lack of food

VERBS

die of/from starvation *Millions of children die of starvation each year.*

be suffering from starvation *Many of the refugees are suffering from starvation.*

face starvation *Thousands of people faced starvation following a 75% fall in food production.*

PHRASES

be on the verge/brink/edge of starvation (=be almost dying of hunger) *The country was on the verge of starvation.*

state[1] *n*

1 the condition that someone or something is in

ADJECTIVES

a bad/poor state *The report commented on the poor state of the roads.*

a terrible state *His apartment was in a terrible state.*

a sorry state *BrE* (=a very bad state) *His clothes were in a sorry state.*

a parlous state *formal* (=very bad, so that something is in great danger) *The previous government left the economy in a parlous state.*

a healthy state (=a good state) *Student numbers at the college are in a healthy state.*

sb's mental/emotional state *Whenever Ben stops his medication, his mental state deteriorates.*

sb's physical state *Our emotions can have an effect on our physical state.*

sth's natural state *There's a plan to return large areas of farmland to their natural state.*

sth's present/current state (=how it is now) *We can deduce how the planet evolved from its beginnings to its present state.*

a constant/permanent/perpetual state (=continuing all the time) *They lived in a constant state of fear.*

VERBS

get into a state (=used about a bad state, such as being untidy or upset) *She had let the house get into a terrible state.*

go into a state (=used about a person's physical state or reaction, such as shock) *The patient has gone into a state similar to a deep sleep.*

reach a state *The political system had reached a state where less than half the people bothered to vote.*

live/exist in a state of sth *She's living in a constant state of worry.*

reflect the state of sth (=show what something is like) *These figures reflect the terrible state of European economies in general.*

PHRASES

sb's state of mind *What was his state of mind at the time of the attack?*

sb's state of health *The doctor said my general state of health was good.*

sth's state of repair/preservation *School buildings should be kept in a good state of repair.*

a state of shock/confusion/panic etc *Howard, still in a state of shock, stared at Newman.*

a state of collapse (=the state of being very ill or weak) *The economy was in a state of collapse.*

a state of war *Syria was still in a state of war with Israel.*

an advanced state of decay/decomposition *The dead bird was in an advanced state of decay.*

the present/current state of knowledge *That is the best advice we can offer, given our current state of knowledge about the disease.*

be in no fit state to do sth (=be unable to do something, for example because of illness, strong emotion etc) *He had been drinking for some time and was clearly in no fit state to drive.*

look at the state of sth/sb *spoken* (=used for saying that something or someone is in a bad state) *Look at the state of the kitchen! It's a terrible mess.*

2 a country considered as a political organization

ADJECTIVES

an independent state (*also* **a sovereign state** *formal*): *Croatia became an independent state in 1991.*

a democratic state *They want to transform the country into a modern democratic state.*

a totalitarian state (=where there is no democracy) *In a totalitarian state, free speech is not allowed.*

a communist/socialist state *The former communist states began opening up their markets to foreign investment.*

a fascist state *At that time, Italy was a fascist state.*

a one-party state (=where only one party is allowed to have control) *Until recently, the country was a one-party state.*

warring states (=countries that are fighting each other) *Europe should not use force to bring about peace between these warring states.*

NOUNS + state

a nation state (=a politically independent country) *The party is convinced that Scotland could be a successful nation state.*

a member state (=a country that belongs to an organization of countries) *The statement said that NATO would respond to any attack against a member state.*

a police state (=where the government strictly controls what people can say or do) *I want the police to be able to stop terrorists, but I don't want this country to become a police state.*

VERBS

become a state *The General's forces won and the country became a fascist state.*

create a state *There has been some progress in efforts to create a Palestinian state.*

state + NOUNS

state secrets (=information that a government keeps secret) *She was arrested on suspicion of selling state secrets.*

THESAURUS: state

nation, state, power, superpower, land → **country (1)**

state² *v formal* to say or write something

state + NOUNS

state the facts *Often newspaper reports fail to state the facts completely.*

state your aim/intention/purpose *The researchers state the aims of the study in the introduction.*

state your opinion/view *You have stated your opinion very clearly.*

state your case/position *He must be allowed to state his case.*

state the obvious (=say things that are obvious, especially in a way that is annoying) *When you are writing an essay, there is a tendency to state the obvious.*

NOUNS + state

a law/rule/agreement states sth *The law states that all motorcyclists must wear helmets.*

a report states sth *The report states that there has been an increase in poverty in some areas.*

ADVERBS

state sth clearly/plainly *The agreement clearly states the responsibilities of both companies.*

state sth officially/formally/publicly *This is part of the government's officially stated policy.*

state sth firmly/emphatically *"We don't have enough money," she stated firmly.*

state sth bluntly (=in a very direct way, even though you know some people may not like what you are saying) *The doctor stated bluntly that my eyes could be permanently damaged.*

state sth openly (=without trying to hide anything) *She was annoyed with herself for not stating openly what was really worrying her.*

state sth briefly/concisely *State your reasons briefly.*

PHRASES

fail to state sth *The company failed to state the risks of taking the drug.*

sth is stated above/below *The conditions of the agreement are stated below.*

unless otherwise stated *Unless otherwise stated, prices do not include tax.*

statement *n*

something you say or write, especially publicly or officially

ADJECTIVES

an official/formal statement *The company is expected to make an official statement tomorrow.*

a public statement *We will be making no further public statements about the matter.*

a written statement *One neighbour said in a written statement that she often heard a baby "crying for help".*

a short/brief statement *Police last night issued a brief statement about the incident.*

a full/detailed statement *You will be taken to the police station where you will be asked to make a full statement.*

a clear/strong statement (=giving an opinion clearly) *The article was a clear statement of his beliefs.*

a false/misleading statement (=one that is not true) *She is accused of making false statements to obtain a passport.*

a sweeping statement (=one that is too general and is not true about every person or thing) *To say that all women are better drivers is a bit of a sweeping statement.*

a joint statement (=one made by two people or groups) *The two leaders issued a joint statement.*

a prepared statement (=one that is prepared and then read out) *His solicitor read a prepared statement on his behalf.*

a sworn statement (=one that you officially promise is true) *The reports were based on sworn statements of graduates of the terrorist training camp.*

VERBS

make a statement *The minister will make a statement on the matter tomorrow.*

give a statement (=make a statement, especially to the police) *He gave a statement to the police.*

issue/release/put out a statement (=give a written statement to newspapers, TV etc) *The Russian Foreign Ministry issued a short statement saying the meeting was "useful".*

take/get a statement from sb (=officially write down what someone says) *The police are taking statements from witnesses.*

withdraw your statement (=say that a statement you gave is not true) *She was later forced to withdraw her statement.*

NOUNS + statement

a government statement *A government statement said that unemployment was rising.*

a police statement (=one made by or to police) *Eleven students were arrested, according to a police statement.*

a witness statement (=one from someone who has seen a crime happen) *The witness statement was read out in court.*

a policy statement (=one that explains what an organization plans to do) *The government issued a policy statement on tax reform.*

a mission statement (=one in which an organization states its aims) *Disneyland has gotten its mission statement down to just three words: "We create happiness".*

PREPOSITIONS

in a statement *In an official statement, she formally announced her resignation.*

a statement on/about sth *The minister will make a statement on the issue tomorrow.*

a statement from/by sb *A statement from the chief executive was read out this morning.*

a statement to sb *The woman made a statement to police.*

a statement of sth *The document includes a detailed statement of the company's financial affairs.*

according to a statement *According to an official government statement, over 300 people were hurt.*

state-of-the-art *adj* THESAURUS

advanced (1), modern (2)

station *n*

a place where trains or buses regularly stop so that passengers can get on and off, goods can be loaded etc, or the buildings at such a place

ADJECTIVES

the main station *The hotel is in front of the city's main station.*

the next/previous station *You need to get off at the next station.*

the first/last etc station *Cambridge is the last station on the line.*

every station *This train stops at every station.*

my/your etc station *This is my station. I'll see you tomorrow.*

NOUNS + station

a train/railway/railroad station *She took a taxi to the railway station.*

the bus/coach station *I'll call you when I arrive at the bus station.*

an underground/tube station *BrE*, **a subway station** *AmE: The next tube station is Oxford Circus.*

VERBS

arrive/get to a station *The train gets to the station at 4.30.*

leave from/go from a station (*also* **depart from a station** *formal*): *What time does the last train leave the station?*

a train pulls into/out of a station (=used when describing a train moving as it arrives at or leaves a station) *The guard blew his whistle and the train pulled out of the station.*

statistic Ac *n*

a set of numbers which represent facts or measurements

> **Grammar**
> Usually plural.

ADJECTIVES

official statistics *Official statistics indicate that educational standards are improving.*

national statistics *Experts claim that national statistics on drug misuse underestimate the problem.*

economic statistics *Recent economic statistics show just how weak the economy really is.*

the latest statistics *The latest statistics show a rise in the population of about 2% in the last year.*

misleading statistics (=that give a wrong impression) *Doctors are advising patients not to be worried by these misleading statistics.*

a shocking/alarming/disturbing statistic *The rat population in England increased by 20% last year. This is an alarming statistic.*

a telling statistic (=that reveals an important piece of information) *The most telling statistic is that only 3% of university students come from poor backgrounds.*

NOUNS + statistic

government statistics *According to government statistics, unemployment is falling.*

crime/accident/unemployment etc statistics *Crime statistics are produced by the police and the courts.*

VERBS

statistics show/indicate sth *Statistics show that smokers have an increased risk of heart disease.*

statistics suggest sth *Housing conditions are far worse than the statistics suggest.*

compile/collect/gather statistics (=prepare a list of them) *The government says it has not yet compiled statistics for this year.*

publish/release statistics *The Department of Health will publish these statistics next week.*

keep statistics *We were shocked to discover that the police do not keep statistics on such attacks.*

PREPOSITIONS

according to statistics *Women prefer dogs to cats, according to statistics published in a national newspaper.*

statistics on sth *This website lists statistics on countries that trade with the US.*

statue *n*

a solid image of a person made of stone or metal, usually in a public place

ADJECTIVES/NOUNS + statue

a marble/stone/bronze etc statue *Outside the palace is a magnificent marble statue of Frederick the Great.*

a huge/giant statue (*also* **a colossal statue** *formal*) (=very large) *The north side of the*

S

building is dominated by a colossal statue of Bishop Gregory.

a life-size statue (=the same size as the person or animal it shows) *There is a life-size bronze statue of the athlete outside the stadium.*

VERBS

put up a statue (*also* **erect a statue** *formal*) (=put it in a public place) *They put up a statue of him in the main square.*

a statue stands somewhere *His statue now stands in the courtyard.*

a statue commemorates sth *In front of the university is a large statue commemorating the protests of 1968.*

unveil a statue (=show a new statue to the public in a formal ceremony) *A statue of the former prime minister was unveiled in 1972.*

carve/sculpt a statue (=make it using special tools) *The statues were carved thousands of years ago.*

PREPOSITIONS

a statue of sb *The mountain has a huge statue of Jesus Christ on it.*

stature *n* THESAURUS **reputation**

status Ac *n*

your position or rank in relation to other people in society or in a profession, group etc

ADJECTIVES

high status *They were men of high status and great influence.*

low status *Why does childcare have such a low status in our society?*

equal status *Women should have equal status to men.*

higher/superior status *Landowners had superior status.*

lower/inferior status *Black people had inferior status.*

social status *Doctors enjoy a high social status.*

socioeconomic status *formal* (=relating to your social rank and money) *Farm workers have a low socioeconomic status.*

professional status *He was proud of his professional status as a teacher.*

marital status (=whether someone is married or not) *Give your name, age, and marital status.*

NOUNS + status

employment status (=whether someone has a job, or whether they work full-time, part-time etc) *In the box headed 'employment status', write 'employed' or 'self-employed'.*

refugee status (=the legal position of needing protection by a foreign country for political reasons) *Over 40,000 people applied for refugee status in Britain last year.*

VERBS

have status (*also* **enjoy status** *formal*): *Here, old people are respected and have high social status.*

give sb status (=make someone have a high status) *Owning a lot of cattle gives a man status in the village.*

achieve/acquire/attain a status *The institution achieved the status of a university in 1929.*

PREPOSITIONS

sb's status as sth *Her status as a government minister earned her immediate respect.*

statutory *adj* THESAURUS **legal (2)**

stay[1] *v*

to not leave a place, or to be in a place for a particular period of time

ADVERBS

stay late *She stayed late to finish the report.*

stay home *Thousands of schoolchildren were told to stay home yesterday because of the storm.*

stay out (=remain away from home during the evening or night) *She went to a party and stayed out all night.*

PREPOSITIONS AND PHRASES

stay for two hours/ten days etc *I went to see John, and stayed for a couple of hours.*

stay in/at a place *Stay in bed if you don't feel well.*

stay after class/school *Some of the students stayed after class to talk.*

stay for a meal/for dinner etc *Why don't you stay for dinner?*

stay[2] *n*

a limited time during which you live in a place

ADJECTIVES

a long stay (*also* **a lengthy/extended stay** *formal*): *During his long stay in the south, he painted only one portrait.*

a short/brief stay *No visa is required for short stays.*

an overnight stay *Business trips may involve an overnight stay.*

a pleasant/enjoyable stay *Our driver said goodbye and wished us a pleasant stay.*

PREPOSITIONS

during a stay *They visited several palaces during their week-long stay.*

throughout sb's stay *She had been a great friend to me throughout my stay in France.*

a stay in/at a place *The couple had an overnight stay at a fashionable New York hotel.*

PHRASES

have a nice/pleasant/good etc stay (=used when saying that you hope someone enjoys their stay) *We hope you have a pleasant stay.*

extend/prolong your stay (=stay longer) *He could not be persuaded to extend his stay.*
enjoy your stay *We hope you have enjoyed your stay at our hotel.*
cut your stay short (=leave before the planned time) *He had to cut short his stay because his wife was taken ill.*

steady *adj*

continuing in a regular way or developing gradually

NOUNS

steady progress *We're making steady progress in reducing unemployment.*
steady growth *During the 1960s most of the Western world enjoyed steady economic growth.*
a steady increase/rise *The university has had a steady increase in student numbers.*
a steady decline *Higher charges have caused a steady decline in membership.*
a steady stream/flow/trickle *The restaurant usually has a steady stream of customers all day long.*
a steady supply *The economy needs a steady supply of skilled workers.*
a steady rate/pace *The industry is developing at a steady pace.*

VERBS

hold/remain steady (=continue to be steady) *A recent survey shows that the president's popularity is holding steady.*

PHRASES

slow but/and steady *She is making a slow but steady recovery after the accident.*

S

steal *v*

to illegally take something that belongs to someone else

NOUNS

steal some money/jewellery etc *She accused him of stealing money from her.*
steal sb's wallet/purse/credit card/phone etc *Someone stole my wallet.*
steal a car/computer/painting etc *The car was stolen from outside their house in the early hours of the morning.*
steal sb's land *The local people say that the settlers stole their land, and now they want it back.*
steal sb's idea *Another firm stole his idea and made a lot of money.*
steal sb's identity *Every year, thousands of people have their identity stolen by criminals on the internet.*
stolen goods *Police found hundreds of pounds worth of stolen goods.*

PREPOSITIONS

steal sth from sb *He stole money from his parents in order to buy drugs.*

THESAURUS: steal

take
to remove something that belongs to someone else, without asking permission:
The thieves took all her money. | They didn't take much – just a few items of jewellery.

Take or steal?
Take is often used about money and other things that can easily be carried away. You can **take** something by accident, without realizing that it belongs to another person: *Sorry, have I* ***taken*** *your chair?*
Steal sounds stronger and more disapproving than **take**.

nick *BrE informal*
to steal something:
Someone's nicked my wallet! | Things are always getting nicked at school.

Nick is very informal. Don't use it in writing.

rob
bank | **shop** | **store** | **post office**
to steal money or other things from a bank, shop, or person:
Tempton was arrested after robbing a bank in Texas. | He used the gun to rob a convenience store. | An elderly man was attacked and ***robbed of*** *all his money by a gang of youths.*

mug
to attack someone in the street in order to steal something from them:
People in this area are frightened of being mugged when they go out. | Someone tried to mug me outside the station.

burgle *BrE*, **burglarize** *AmE*
house | **apartment** | **flat**
to go into someone's home and steal things, especially when the owners are not there:
Their house was burgled while they were away on holiday. | We've been burgled three times.

hold up
bank | **post office** | **shop** | **store** | **driver**
to steal from a place or person, by threatening to use a gun or other weapon:
The couple went around the US holding up banks. | The movie is about a gang of robbers who hold up a jewelry store. | He ***held*** *me* ***up at gunpoint*** *and stole my Porsche* (=he threatened to shoot me if I didn't give him what he wanted).

loot
shops | **stores** | **businesses** | **houses** | **museum** | **tomb** | **city** | **country** | **gold** | **art**
to steal things from shops and other buildings, especially during a war, a protest,

or a natural disaster, when the police or the army do not have control of an area:
Angry crowds looted local shops. | The city was looted by enemy soldiers. | The gold was looted by the Nazis.

ransack
home | house | shop | place | building | church | town | city
to go through a place stealing things and causing damage:
Masked robbers tied her up and ransacked her home. | After beating him, they ransacked the house, looking for anything valuable. | The town was ransacked by rebel soldiers.

defraud
government | company | employer | investors | people
to get money from an organization or group of people in a dishonest way:
The men face long prison sentences for attempting to defraud the US government. | Xu and others are accused of ***defrauding*** *people* ***of*** *32 million yuan ($4 million).*

embezzle
money
to steal money from the organization you work for, especially money that you are responsible for:
The governor and his wife were convicted of embezzling public money. | Government officials ***embezzled*** *more than $2.5 million* ***from*** *the department.*

poach
staff | customers | clients | passengers | players
to secretly get workers or customers from another company:
They ***poached*** *staff* ***from*** *IBM, in order to set up their own company. | Someone has been poaching our customers by offering them cheap deals.*

Poach was originally used about secretly hunting animals on someone else's land.

plagiarize (*also* **plagiarise** *BrE*)
work | book | essay | speech | ideas | words
to take another person's work or ideas and pretend that you wrote them yourself:
If they find out you've been plagiarizing other students' work, you could be in serious trouble. | He accused Obama of plagiarizing his speeches.

The crime of stealing things from shops is called **shoplifting**: ***Shoplifting*** *costs stores millions of pounds every year.*

steam *v* THESAURUS ➤ **cook**[1]

steep *adj*

1 a road, hill etc that is steep slopes at a high angle

NOUNS

a steep hill *The house was at the top of a steep hill.*

a steep slope *The steep slopes are cut into terraces for growing coffee.*

a steep bank *He scrambled down the steep bank.*

a steep path/road *A steep path leads down to the beach.*

steep stairs *She's getting too old to climb these steep stairs.*

the steep sides of sth *The steep sides of the valley were covered in trees.*

a steep gradient *formal* (=a steep slope - used especially of a road or railway track) *The Snowdon Mountain Railway has the steepest gradient of any track in Britain.*

a steep climb *A steep climb brought us to the top of the waterfall.*

a steep descent (=a steep journey, slope, or path downwards) *The group made the steep descent into the valley.*

ADVERBS

fairly/pretty/rather steep *It's a fairly steep climb from the beach to the nearby road.*

particularly steep *The northern slope of the hill is particularly steep.*

incredibly steep *On one side, the vineyard is incredibly steep.*

dangerously steep *The path down to the river seems dangerously steep.*

2 sudden and very large in extent

NOUNS

a steep decline/drop/fall *Following the TV campaign, there was a steep decline in the number of drink-driving cases.*

a steep rise/increase (*also* **a steep hike** *informal*): *The energy industry is warning of a steep hike in prices.*

step *n*

1 one of a series of things that you do in order to deal with a problem or to succeed

ADJECTIVES

the first step *The first step is to decide which subject you want to study.*

the next step *The next step is to apply to a college.*

the final step *The final step is usually an interview.*

an important/major/big step *The new law is seen as a major step towards a fairer tax system.*

a small step *These minor changes to the system are a small step in the right direction.*

S

an initial/preliminary step (=done at the beginning of a process) *As an initial step, I've written to the head teacher asking for permission.*

a positive step (=an action that will have a good effect) *By exercising a little every day, you are taking a positive step.*

a backward/retrograde step (=which makes a situation worse) *We feel that introducing higher fees would be a retrograde step.*

an unusual step *Police took the unusual step of releasing a photograph of the crime scene.*

an unprecedented step (=something that has never been done before) *The company took the unprecedented step of firing all its senior managers.*

a bold step (=a daring one) *He made bold steps to expand his business.*

a drastic step (=an extreme one) *Avoid any drastic steps that you might regret.*

a tentative step (=a small step, because you hope it will help you to achieve something later) *She has taken a tentative step towards changing her career.*

a logical step *For someone interested in acting, the first logical step would be to join a drama group.*

VERBS

take a step *The local council will take steps to provide you with suitable housing.*

ADVERBS

a step forward (=an action that makes things better) *The deal is a big step forward for the company.*

a step backward (=that makes things worse or reverses progress) *The president called it a step backward in international relations.*

PREPOSITIONS

a step towards/toward sth *The election is a major step towards democracy in the region.*

a step in doing sth *The book is a good first step in making the problem more widely known.*

PHRASES

step by step/one step at a time (=doing something in stages and going from one stage to another) *The book teaches you step by step how to bake your own bread.*

a step in the right direction (=an action that helps to improve things) *Environmentalists said the law was a step in the right direction.*

a number/series of steps *We are taking a number of steps to improve our service to customers.*

take immediate steps to do sth *We believe the government should take immediate steps to create jobs.*

take (all) the necessary steps to do sth *The government is taking all the necessary steps to prevent the disease from spreading.*

take reasonable steps to do sth (=try as hard as you can to make sure that something happens) *Organizations must take reasonable steps to ensure that the information they publish is accurate.*

(if you take) one false step (=if you do one thing wrong or badly, something very bad could happen) *If we take one false step now, the whole project could fail.*

2 a movement of the foot when you are walking

VERBS

take a step *She took a step towards the door.*

go a few steps/another step *She had only gone a few steps when she realized she had forgotten her passport.*

hear steps *She heard steps behind her and turned around.*

retrace your steps (=go back the same way you came) *I retraced my steps along the path, looking for the keys.*

PREPOSITIONS

a step towards sth/sb *The man took a step towards me, his gun raised.*

a step away from sth/sb *They moved a few steps away from the dog.*

ADVERBS

a step forward *He took a step forward and reached for her arm.*

a step back/backward(s) *I took a step backwards and fell over a low wall.*

3 steps are things that you walk up or down to go from one level to another

ADJECTIVES

steep steps *There were some steep steps down to the beach.*

narrow/wide steps *He hurried up the narrow steps onto the roof.*

stone/wooden etc steps *I descended the stone steps to the street.*

VERBS

go up/climb the steps *He parked his car and climbed the three steps up to the front door.*

go down the steps (*also* **descend the steps** *formal*): *I went down the steps into the pool.*

fall down the steps *He was taken to hospital after falling down some steps in the New York subway.*

run up/down the steps (*also* **race up/down the steps**) (=go up or down them as quickly as you can) *He ran up the steps and knocked, but no one answered.*

steps lead (down/up) to sth *There were some steps leading down to the back garden.*

PHRASES

a flight of steps (=a set of steps) *On the mountain stood a golden castle with a flight of steps leading to it.*

the bottom/foot of the steps *He stood at the bottom of the steps and looked up at her.*

S

the top of the steps *The children waited at the top of the church steps.*

stereotype *n*

a belief, especially unfair or untrue, about what a particular type of person or thing is like

ADJECTIVES/NOUNS + stereotype

the old/traditional stereotype *He clearly believes the old stereotype about Scottish people being mean with money.*

racial/racist stereotypes *The film is full of racial stereotypes.*

cultural/national stereotypes *His jokes often depend on national stereotypes.*

sexual/gender stereotypes *Women are right to object to these sexual stereotypes.*

a popular/common stereotype *There is a popular stereotype about old people not being very good with computers.*

a negative stereotype *We should avoid negative stereotypes about teenagers.*

VERBS

reinforce a stereotype (=make it stronger by showing or describing someone in the usual way) *Organizations aimed at helping older people must be careful not to reinforce negative stereotypes.*

perpetuate a stereotype *formal* (=make people continue to believe it) *The article perpetuates the stereotype that men are not caring parents.*

fit a stereotype (*also* **conform to a stereotype** *formal*) (=be like the usual idea of something) *He doesn't fit the stereotype of a university student.*

challenge a stereotype (=be different from the usual idea of something) *These young women want to challenge gender stereotypes.*

break down a stereotype (*also* **subvert/overturn a stereotype** *formal*) (=make people stop believing it) *Her films aim to break down stereotypes about Asian women.*

PREPOSITIONS

a stereotype of sb/sth *He looked just like the stereotype of an English person, with his umbrella and his bowler hat.*

sterile *adj* THESAURUS ▸ clean[1] (1)

sterilize (*also* sterilise *BrE*) *v* THESAURUS ▸ clean[2]

stern *adj* THESAURUS ▸ strict (1)

stiff *adj*

1 difficult to bend

THESAURUS: stiff

firm, stiff, solid, rigid, crispy, crunchy, tough, rubbery, brittle → **hard (1)**

2 severe or strong

NOUNS

stiff competition *The players expect some stiff competition in the later rounds of the competition.*

stiff opposition/resistance *There is likely to be stiff opposition to the government's proposals.*

a stiff challenge/test *Climbing the mountain in a single day is a stiff challenge.*

a stiff fine/penalty/sentence *People who are caught stealing face very stiff penalties.*

stigma *n*

the feeling of being embarrassed or ashamed because other people disapprove of you or what you have done

ADJECTIVES

a social stigma *There is a social stigma about mental illness.*

a terrible/enormous stigma *The disease had a terrible stigma in those days.*

VERBS

carry a stigma (*also* **bear a stigma** *formal*): *He carries the stigma of having worked for the enemy.*

a stigma is attached to sth/associated with sth *There is a stigma attached to smoking now.*

a stigma surrounds sth *There is a lot of stigma and confusion surrounding AIDS.*

remove/eradicate/get rid of the stigma *We need to remove the stigma from mental health problems.*

overcome the stigma (=deal with it so that it is not a problem) *It is difficult to overcome the stigma in people's minds.*

reduce the stigma *The campaign aims to reduce the stigma attached to this condition.*

PREPOSITIONS

there is a stigma against sb/sth *There is a social stigma against fat people that causes the psychological problems.*

there is a stigma about sth *There is a social stigma about suicide and no one wants to discuss it.*

stimulating *adj* THESAURUS ▸ interesting

stimulus *n*

something that has the effect of encouraging another thing to happen

ADJECTIVES

a major/powerful stimulus *Cheap energy provided a major stimulus to economic development in Western Europe and Japan.*

an economic stimulus (*also* **a fiscal stimulus** *formal*): *The government hopes that this economic stimulus will encourage growth.*

a visual stimulus *The picture acts as a visual stimulus that can help children begin to imagine a character's personality.*

external stimuli *technical* (=things outside someone or something that have an effect on

S

them) *They tested his reaction to external stimuli such as light and changes of temperature.*

VERBS

provide/give a stimulus *Tax cuts provided the stimulus which the economy needed.*

act as a stimulus *The change in the weather acts as a stimulus for the birds to migrate abroad.*

use sth as a stimulus *The teacher used the video clip as a stimulus to encourage discussion among the students.*

respond to a stimulus *The aim of the experiment was to see how men's and women's brains respond to different stimuli.*

PREPOSITIONS

a stimulus for sth *This remarkable study provided the stimulus for several other research projects on the same subject.*

PHRASES

stimulus and response *In classic stimulus and response fashion, the dog became excited as soon as he smelt the meat.*

stink *n* THESAURUS smell[1]

stock *n*

a supply of something that an organization, store, or person has available

ADJECTIVES

a large/huge stock *We have a huge stock of carpets on sale.*

a small stock *I keep a small stock of tinned food for emergencies.*

new/old stock *The bookseller was unpacking his new stock.*

existing stock (=that you have now) *The two countries agreed to get rid of two-thirds of their existing stock of nuclear weapons.*

surplus stock (=which you do not need because you have too much) *Stores often sell off their surplus stock at a discount.*

a decreasing/diminishing stock *Because of diminishing stocks of fossil fuels, more countries are turning to nuclear power.*

an adequate stock (=a big enough supply of something) *We have an adequate stock of wood for the winter.*

VERBS

have/keep a stock *She keeps a stock of envelopes in her desk.*

build up a stock *We are trying to build up the stock of books at our school.*

stocks are depleted *formal* (=they have been used so that there is very little or none left) *Our food stocks were almost depleted.*

replenish a stock (=add more so there is the same amount as before) *We need more of the vaccine to replenish our stocks.*

stocks decline/dwindle *formal* (=get smaller) *Housing stocks are dwindling at the rate of 10% a year.*

NOUNS + stock

food/weapons stocks *The government agreed to destroy its chemical weapons stocks.*

housing stock (=places available for people to live in an area) *Much of the city's housing stock is in a bad condition.*

fish stocks (=the number of fish in the sea) *There are concerns about diminishing fish stocks.*

PREPOSITIONS

a stock of sth *I always keep a stock of ready-made meals in the freezer.*

in stock (=available to buy in a shop) *Do you have the computer in stock, or do I have to order it?*

out of stock (=a shop does not have any more of something left) *The dress is out of stock in your size.*

PHRASES

stocks run low (=reach a point where there is not much left of something) *By January, food stocks had run dangerously low.*

while stocks last (=until all the stock has been sold - used in shop advertisements) *50% off while stocks last!*

THESAURUS: stock

stock, supply, reserves → **store (2)**

stomach *n*

the organ inside your body where food begins to be digested

ADJECTIVES

an upset stomach (=used when you have stomach problems after eating something, or because of illness) *Debbie was at home because she had an upset stomach.*

an empty stomach (=one that has no food in it) *The tablets shouldn't be taken on an empty stomach.*

a full stomach (=one that is full of food) *I'd had a meal and my stomach was comfortably full.*

stomach + NOUNS

(a) stomach ache *I had terrible stomach ache last night.*

stomach pains/cramps *He complained of acute stomach pains.*

a stomach bug (=an illness you have caught that affects your stomach) *He's off work with a stomach bug.*

stomach flu *AmE* (=an illness you have caught that affects your stomach) *She missed Saturday's game because of stomach flu.*

a stomach upset (=when your stomach is affected by illness or because of eating something) *The boy had a stomach upset after eating berries from the garden.*

VERBS

sb's stomach rumbles (=it makes a noise

because they are hungry) *She felt her stomach rumble.*

sb's stomach churns (=they feel sick because they are nervous or frightened) *John's stomach was churning with anxiety.*

sb's stomach lurches/tightens (=it suddenly feels tight because they are frightened) *Her stomach lurched at the thought of leaving Millfield.*

settle sb's stomach (=stop it feeling uncomfortable) *The doctor gave me some tablets to settle my stomach.*

PREPOSITIONS

in your stomach *He had a pain in his stomach.*

PHRASES

in the pit of your stomach (=used when you have a strong feeling such as fear or anxiety which makes your stomach feel strange) *I had a horrible feeling in the pit of my stomach.*

feel sick to the stomach *AmE* (=feel as if you are going to vomit) *Spinning round made me a little sick to the stomach.*

you need a strong stomach (=used when saying that something is very violent or upsetting) *You need a strong stomach to watch some of these videos.*

stop[1] *v*

1 to not continue doing something

> **Grammar**
> **Stop** is often followed by a participle in this meaning: *They* ***stopped*** *work****ing*** *at five o'clock. | It's so hard to* ***stop*** *smok****ing****. | I wish he would* ***stop talking****.* Don't say 'They stopped to work.'
> You use **stop to do sth** when you stop doing something, in order to do something else: *We* ***stopped to*** *have lunch.* **Stop to do sth** is short for **stop in order to do sth**.

PHRASES

stop for a minute/second/moment etc *Can we stop for a minute? I need a break.*

stop for lunch/coffee/a rest etc *They decided to stop for lunch.*

NOUNS

stop work *She stopped work and went outside for a breath of fresh air.*

stop production *The country has stopped production of nuclear weapons.*

THESAURUS: stop

cease *formal*
production | operation | publication | trading
to stop doing or producing something:
The company announced it intends to cease production of sports cars. | The mine has ceased operation. | The firm has ceased trading, with the loss of over a hundred jobs.

give up
smoking | drinking | trying | job | work | career | game
to stop doing something, especially something that you have been doing for a long time:
Her husband promised he would give up drinking. | I've given up trying to tell my son to clean his room. | John gave up his job to take care of his elderly mother. | He was forced to give up the game because of injury.

quit *informal*
smoking | drinking | job
to stop doing something:
The campaign is intended to encourage people to quit smoking. | She quit her job and went travelling. | It's too late for us to quit now.

pull out of sth
competition | tournament | race | talks | negotiations
to stop taking part in something:
Murray pulled out of the competition on Friday with a leg injury. | The unions have pulled out of the negotiations.

have/take a break
to stop doing something for a short time, in order to rest:
Okay, everyone. Let's take a ten-minute break.

2 if something stops, it does not continue any longer

NOUNS

the rain/wind/snow stops *The rain stopped and the sun came out.*

the fighting/shooting/killing stops *They just want the fighting to stop.*

the music/noise/sound stops *The music stopped and the people stopped dancing.*

a clock/watch stops *Her watch had stopped and she wasn't sure exactly what time it was.*

> Instead of saying **the rain/snow stopped**, you often stay **it stopped raining/snowing**.

THESAURUS: stop

cease *formal*
rain | fighting | firing | noise | sound
to stop:
The sky cleared and the rain ceased. | The fighting has almost ceased.

wear off
pain | feeling | excitement | shock | effect | anaesthetic
if a feeling wears off, it gradually stops:
If you take some aspirin, the pain will soon wear off. | By the end of the second day the excitement had worn off. | The effects of the drug are starting to wear off. | ***The novelty had***

S

worn off and the kids started to get bored (=something no longer seemed new and exciting, so they started to get bored).

go away
pain | problem | issue
if something bad goes away, it stops causing problems for you. **Go away** sounds rather informal:
I waited for the pain to go away. | If we do nothing, the problem won't just go away on its own.

peter out
road | path | trail | voice | conversation
to gradually become smaller or weaker and then stop:
The road peters out and becomes a muddy track. | Her voice petered out and she started to cry.

subside
wind | storm | flood | pain | anger | laughter | violence | panic | controversy
to become much less loud, strong, or active:
The skies cleared and the wind subsided. | When the floods subsided, the streets were covered in mud. | Her anger subsided and she apologized for what she had said.

die down
wind | storm | noise | traffic | fire | flames | laughter | excitement | controversy
to become much less loud, strong, or active. **Die down** means the same as **subside**, but is more informal:
The wind died down and the sun came out. | The speaker waited for the laughter to die down. | The government is hoping that the controversy will die down and people will forget about it.

3 to make something stop happening

NOUNS

stop a game/competition *The referee stopped the game.*
stop a meeting/trial *The trial had to be stopped because the defendant was very ill.*
stop the war/fighting/violence *The protesters want the government to stop the war.*
stop the destruction of sth *If we don't stop the destruction of the rainforest soon, our planet will be in big trouble.*
stop the spread of sth *Doctors are trying to stop the spread of the disease.*
stop the flow of sth *They are unable to stop the flow of illegal drugs into the US.*
stop the blood/bleeding *He put a bandage around his arm to stop the bleeding.*

PREPOSITIONS

stop sb/sth from doing sth *Firefighters tried to stop the fire from spreading.*

THESAURUS: stop

suspend
talks | negotiations | aid | strike | trial | work | operations | flights | constitution
to officially order that something should be stopped for a period of time, especially when you intend to let it start later:
The talks were suspended after India blamed Pakistan for the bombings. | The constitution was suspended in 1973, when the army took control.

abort
mission | flight | landing | plan
to stop doing something because it is too dangerous to continue, especially when it has already started:
The mission was aborted after an Ariane 5 rocket exploded. | The pilot had to abort the landing due to the severe winds.

halt
progress | spread | flow | violence | attacks | killings | conflict | exports | sale
to stop something from continuing, spreading, or developing:
His enemies are eager to halt his progress. | The authorities are trying to halt the spread of the disease. | UN soldiers have failed to halt the violence in the region.

stem
flow | flood | tide | decline | bleeding
to stop something from continuing or getting worse:
Western countries are trying to stem the flow of illegal diamonds from Africa. | Efforts were made to stem the tide of road accidents (=stop them from increasing). *| The ice helps to stem the bleeding.*

curb
violence | inflation | pollution | greenhouse gases | corruption | immigration | spending
to stop something from increasing, especially something harmful, and try to control it and reduce it. **Curb** sounds rather formal:
We will do everything in our power to curb the violence. | The president has not done enough to curb public spending.

clamp down on sth
crime | drugs | tax evasion | vandalism | bullying | spending
to take firm action to try to stop or reduce something, especially because it is illegal or harmful:
The police are clamping down on knife crime. | The authorities are clamping down on hard drugs.

put a stop to sth
to stop someone from doing something, because you think they should not do it. **Put a stop to sth** sounds rather informal:
He spent every evening gambling on the internet, until his father ***put a stop to it***. | *People were climbing over the fence to get into the concert, but they soon* ***put a stop to that***.

4 to stop moving

NOUNS

sb stops *They stopped to admire the view.*

a car/bus/taxi/truck stops *The car stopped at a red light.*

a plane/train/boat stops *The plane stopped to refuel in Dubai.*

THESAURUS: stop

pull up
car | taxi | truck
to stop close to something:
The taxi pulled up outside her house. | *He pulled up next to our car.*

pull over
car | truck | bus | vehicle
to move to the side of the road and stop:
The car pulled over to the side of the road, with smoke coming out of its engine. | *The police officer was waving at him to pull over.*

come to a halt *especially written*
train | car | truck | bus | vehicle | plane
to move more slowly and then stop:
The train came to a halt just outside the station.

come to a standstill
traffic | cars
to go slower and then stop moving completely – used especially about traffic:
The road was blocked by an accident, and the traffic quickly came to a standstill.

stop² *n*

1 if a vehicle comes to a stop, it stops moving

PHRASES

come to a stop *The truck came to a stop right outside our house.*

jerk/shudder to a stop (=suddenly stop) *Some passengers fell forward as the bus suddenly jerked to a stop.*

ADJECTIVES/NOUNS + stop

a dead stop (=no longer moving at all) *The vehicle gave a sudden lurch and came to a dead stop.*

an abrupt/sharp stop (=very sudden) *There was a loud clanking noise and the tractor shuddered to an abrupt stop.*

an emergency stop (=when a vehicle has to stop very suddenly to avoid an accident) *She had to make an emergency stop when a dog ran in front of her car.*

2 a time or place when you stop for a short time during a journey

VERBS

make a stop *The coach will be making a brief stop at Carlisle.*

have a stop *I was hoping we could have a stop soon.*

ADJECTIVES

a brief/short stop *The president will make a brief stop at a local elementary school.*

an overnight stop (=you stay the night somewhere during your journey) *We had an overnight stop in Paris.*

a scheduled/unscheduled stop (=that you had planned or not planned to make) *Security officers don't like the prince making unscheduled stops to speak to the public.*

PREPOSITIONS

a stop at a place *The train makes a stop at York.*

a stop for sth *After a half-hour stop for lunch, we continued the long drive north.*

store *n*

1 a place where goods are sold to the public

ADJECTIVES/NOUNS + store

a local store *She prefers to do her shopping at her local store, rather than going to a big supermarket.*

a food/furniture/toy etc store *We ordered a new sofa from the furniture store.*

an electrical store (=selling televisions, computers etc) *Electrical stores are suffering as more and more people buy their computers and televisions online.*

an online store (=on the internet) *Apple introduced an online store in addition to its retail stores.*

a department store (=a large store with different departments for clothes, cosmetics, toys, electrical goods etc) *Macy's is a big department store in New York.*

a high street store *BrE* (=on one of the main streets of a city or town) *Most people buy their clothes from high street stores.*

a chain store (=with branches in many different places) *You can buy less expensive versions of designer dresses in chain stores.*

a convenience/corner store (=a small store on a street where people live, selling many different things they need to buy often) *He's gone to the convenience store to get milk.*

a general store (=selling many different goods) *There is a post office and a general store in the village.*

a flagship store (=the best or most important one a company owns) *Selfridges' flagship store is on Oxford Street.*

a discount store (=one that sells goods at low prices) *In discount stores, goods are often sold from the boxes they come in.*

a dime store *AmE* (=one that sells many different kinds of cheap goods, especially for the house) *It was a cheap plastic toy from a dime store.*

a DIY store *BrE* (=one that sells things for decorating and repairing your house) *You can buy paint from your local DIY store.*

a liquor store *AmE* (=one that sells alcohol) *He bought a bottle of brandy from the liquor store.*

Bookstore is usually written as one word.

VERBS

a store closes/opens *The store opens at 8.30 a.m.*

a store sells sth *Many stores sell recycled products.*

run a store *Mr and Mrs Johnson run our local store.*

go to the store *AmE*: *I need to go to the store for some bread.*

store + NOUNS

a store manager/owner *The store manager is interviewing for new staff on Saturday.*

a store detective (=someone who stops customers stealing from a store) *A store detective noticed him putting a pair of expensive sunglasses in his pocket.*

a store window *The dress looked great in the store window.*

a store card *BrE* (=used for buying goods from a particular store and paying for them later) *She paid for the jeans using her store card.*

PREPOSITIONS

in a store *She works in a big store on Oxford Street.*

sb is at the store *AmE* (=they are buying things in a store) *Someone called while you were at the store.*

Store is the usual word in American English.
In British English, people usually say **shop**. A **store** is used especially about a large shop, or in advertisements for shops.

2 an amount of something that is available to be used

ADJECTIVES/NOUNS + store

a large/great store (*also* **a vast store** *formal*): *Over the years, he has gained a vast store of knowledge.*

a rich store (=a large store of history, knowledge, information etc) *The city has a rich store of history.*

a secret store *She got a bar of chocolate from her secret store.*

fat/energy stores *If we do not eat enough, the body starts breaking down its fat stores.*

store + NOUNS

a store cupboard *BrE*: *He took a packet of sugar from the store cupboard.*

Storeroom (=a room where you store things) is written as one word.

VERBS

have a store of sth *John has a store of jokes for every occasion.*

keep a store of sth *We keep a store of medicines in case anyone gets ill.*

PREPOSITIONS

a store of sth *I always keep a store of bottled water.*

PHRASES

a store of information/knowledge/wisdom/experience *Readers have access to a huge store of scientific information.*

a store of energy *The animals have to build up enough stores of energy to last them through the winter.*

a store of food/water *The land sits on top of one of the world's greatest underground stores of water.*

THESAURUS: store

stock
a store of products to be sold in a shop, or of resources that are available to be used if necessary:
We have a ***large stock of*** *children's clothing.* | *Our* ***stock of*** *fossil fuels is running low.*

supply
an amount of something that is needed continuously:
They won a year's ***supply of*** *baby food.* | *The steel industry depends on a* ***regular supply of*** *raw materials.*

reserves
a supply of money or natural resources that a country or organization has available to use if they are needed:
Norway's ***gas reserves*** *are greater than its* ***oil reserves****.* | *The government has large* ***reserves of*** *foreign currency.*

storm *n*

1 a period of very bad weather when there is a lot of rain or snow, strong winds, and often lightning

ADJECTIVES/NOUNS + storm

a big storm *There was a big storm which caused a lot of damage.*

a bad/terrible storm *It was the worst storm for 50 years.*

S

a severe/violent/fierce storm *Violent storms swept across the country.*

a great storm (=a very severe one) *Many buildings were damaged in the great storm of 1987.*

a tropical storm *The tropical storm smashed through the Bahamas.*

a dust storm (=one in which a lot of dust is blown around) *Dust storms are relatively common in the Sahara.*

an electrical storm (=one with lightning) *Power supplies have been affected by severe electrical storms in some parts of the country.*

a winter/summer storm *People fear there may be more flooding when the winter storms hit.*

a freak storm (=an unexpected and unusually violent one) *The ship sank in a freak storm.*

Rainstorm, **snowstorm**, and **thunderstorm** are usually spelled as one word.

⚠ Don't say a 'strong storm' or a 'hard storm'. Say a **big storm**, a **bad storm**, or a **violent storm**.

VERBS

a storm blows up (=it starts) *That night, a storm blew up.*

a storm breaks (=it starts suddenly, after there has been a lot of cloud in the sky) *The storm broke at five o'clock.*

a storm is brewing (=it is likely to start soon) *He could feel that a storm was brewing.*

a storm rages (=a violent storm is happening) *By the time we reached the airfield, a tropical storm was raging.*

a storm hits/strikes a place *The storm hit the island in the early hours of the morning.*

a storm lashes/batters a place (=the wind and rain blow against a place) *Fierce storms lashed the coastline.*

a storm passes (*also* **a storm abates** *formal*): *We sat and waited for the storm to pass.*

a storm blows itself out (=it finally ends) *The storm finally blew itself out.*

ride out the storm (=survive it without being damaged - used especially about ships) *The Greek fleet had ridden out the storm near the coast of Euboia.*

storm + NOUNS

storm clouds *We could see storm clouds in the distance.*

storm damage *A lot of buildings suffered storm damage.*

PHRASES

the eye of the storm (=the calm part in the centre of the storm) *The eye of the storm must be passing over us.*

there is a storm coming *The weather forecast says that there is a storm coming.*

2 a situation in which people suddenly express very strong feelings about something that someone has said or done, especially when this is reported in the news

ADJECTIVES/NOUNS + storm

a political storm *The company became the centre of a political storm.*

a diplomatic storm (=between the governments of two or more countries) *There was a diplomatic storm between Russia and the US after the men were accused of spying.*

a media storm (=in the newspapers, on the television etc) *The star found herself at the centre of a media storm.*

VERBS

cause/create a storm *The minister caused a storm by criticizing doctors.*

provoke/spark/raise a storm (=make it start) *This decision provoked a storm of protest from civil rights organizations.*

a storm blows up (=starts) *A diplomatic storm blew up between the two countries.*

a storm blows over (=ends) *The president is just hoping that the storm will blow over quickly.*

ride out/weather a storm (=survive a storm) *The company has weathered a storm of negative publicity in the last month.*

PHRASES

a storm of protest *Government plans for hospital closures provoked a storm of protest.*

a storm of controversy *His book raised a storm of controversy.*

a storm of criticism *A storm of criticism forced the government to withdraw the proposal.*

be at the centre of a storm (=be the person or thing that is causing strong protest, criticism etc) *He has been at the centre of a storm over plans to cut the education budget.*

stormy *adj* THESAURUS ▸ **windy**

story *n*

1 a description of events, told to entertain people

ADJECTIVES

a true story *'Schindler's List' is the true story of a man who saved the lives of hundreds of people during the war.*

a classic story (=old and known or admired by many) *It is the classic story about a little girl who falls down a rabbit hole.*

a remarkable/amazing/incredible story *The film tells the remarkable story of his life.*

a fascinating/intriguing/curious story *The book is the fascinating story of Mary Shelley, the woman who wrote 'Frankenstein'.*

a heartwarming story (=one that affects your emotions, especially one in which people are very kind) *There is a heartwarming story of a lonely little boy and his search for his sister.*

S

a short story *He has published two collections of short stories.*

NOUNS + story

a children's story *Enid Blyton is famous for writing children's stories.*

a love story *'Romeo and Juliet' is a classic love story.*

a fairy story (=a children's story in which magical things happen) *She looked like a princess in a fairy story.*

an adventure story *He writes exciting adventure stories for children.*

a detective story *Most detective stories are about a murder.*

a ghost/horror story *She likes reading horror stories.*

a bedtime story (=one read or told to a child before they go to sleep) *He remembered his mother reading him a bedtime story.*

VERBS

tell (sb) a story *Would you like me to tell you a story?*

⚠ Don't say 'say someone a story'.

read (sb) a story *She reads a lot of detective stories.*

write a story *The story was written by Lewis Carroll.*

PREPOSITIONS

a story about sth *Martinez wrote a story about a girl who wanted desperately to be a model.*

S

2 a report about something in a newspaper or on a news programme

ADJECTIVES

a big story (=a report about something important) *Today's big story is the fall in share prices.*

the lead/top story (=the most important story in a newspaper or news programme) *The floods were the lead story on the news that evening.*

NOUNS + story

a newspaper story *I read a newspaper story about a family who had 20 children.*

a front-page story *'The Times' published a front-page story about the scandal.*

a cover story (=the main story in a magazine, mentioned on the cover) *The magazine did a cover story on her wedding.*

VERBS

print/publish a story *The editor decided not to print the story.*

do a story (=write a report or make a news film about it) *He went to Afghanistan to do a story on the war.*

run/carry a story (=print it or broadcast it) *There wasn't enough definite information to run the story.*

cover a story (=report on it) *Her family complained about the way that journalists had covered the story.*

break a story (=report on it for the first time) *The 'Daily Mail' was the paper which broke the story.*

leak a story (=secretly tell a reporter about it) *We may never know who leaked the story to the press.*

follow a story (=continue to report on it) *The 'Today' programme has been following the story for several weeks.*

a story breaks (=it is reported for the first time) *I still remember the shock when that story broke.*

3 an account of something that has happened, especially one that people tell each other

NOUNS + story

the full/whole story *Wait until you know the full story before making a judgment.*

a plausible/convincing story (=one that people are likely to believe) *She tried to think up a convincing story to tell her parents.*

an apocryphal story *formal* (=one that is well known but probably not true) *There are many apocryphal stories about him.*

the inside story (=including facts that are known only to people involved) *Though I'd seen the official report, I wanted the inside story.*

a strange/bizarre story *She told us a bizarre story about finding a snake in the toilet.*

a success story *His career is a remarkable success story.*

a hard-luck story (=about something bad that happens in someone's life, especially told in order to get sympathy) *There was the usual hard-luck story, then he asked me for money.*

VERBS + story

tell (sb) a story (*also* **recount/relate a story** *formal*): *I'd better tell you the whole story from the beginning.*

give sb a story *I had the feeling that she wasn't giving me the full story.*

hear a story (*also* **listen to a story**) *I've heard that story a hundred times.*

make up/invent a story *She confessed to making up the story of her bag being stolen.*

stick to your story (=keep saying it is true) *He didn't believe her at first, but she stuck to her story.*

change your story *During police interviews, Harper changed his story several times.*

believe a story *The jury did not believe Evans's story.*

swap stories (=tell each other stories) *They swapped stories and shared their experiences.*

story + VERBS

the story goes (=this is what people say

happened) *The story goes that he drowned, but not everyone believes it.*

a story goes around (=people tell it to each other) *A story went around that she had been having an affair.*

a story emerges (=people start to say something has happened) *The story was emerging that the president had been shot.*

PHRASES

that's another story *spoken* (=I will tell you about that at some future time) *And then there was a problem with the car, but that's another story.*

sb's side of the story (=someone's account of what happened, which may be different from someone else's) *I would like to give my side of the story.*

it's a long story *spoken* (=used when saying that a lot of things happened) *"How did you come to be arrested?" "Well, it's a long story."*

to cut a long story short *spoken* (=used when going straight to the most important part of your story) *There were problems in their marriage and, to cut a long story short, they got divorced.*

straight *adj*

1 something that is straight does not bend or curve

ADVERBS

completely/absolutely/perfectly straight (*also* **dead straight** *BrE informal*): *The road is absolutely straight for the next five miles.*

fairly/relatively straight *The line was fairly straight.*

NOUNS

a straight line *Use a ruler to draw a straight line.*

straight hair *She's the tall woman with straight black hair.*

a straight edge *A rectangle has four straight edges.*

a straight road/path *The field is crossed by a narrow, perfectly straight road.*

a straight road (=going directly to a place, with no possibility for getting lost) *Once you're through the village, it's a straight road to the hotel - you can't miss it.*

PHRASES

in a straight line *First of all, arrange the tiles in a straight line.*

2 level or upright, not leaning to one side

ADVERBS

completely/absolutely/perfectly straight (*also* **dead straight** *BrE informal*): *Make sure the door frame is perfectly straight.*

nearly straight (*also* **more or less straight**) *The picture is more or less straight.*

VERBS

look straight *The fence did not look completely straight.*

stand straight *He stood perfectly straight, looking ahead.*

hang straight *If you put small weights in the curtains, they hang straight.*

hang sth straight *Make sure you hang the paintings straight.*

3 honest and direct

NOUNS

straight talk/talking *There is not enough straight talking in politics.*

a straight answer *I want a straight answer: yes or no.*

ADVERBS

totally/completely/absolutely straight *We have been totally straight with you from the beginning.*

fairly straight (*also* **pretty straight** *informal*): *He seemed like a pretty straight kind of guy.*

PREPOSITIONS

straight with sb *I'm confident that she's been completely straight with me.*

straight about sth *He was not really straight about his lack of experience.*

> **THESAURUS: straight**
>
> truthful, sincere, frank, straight, open, candid, direct, blunt, forthright, outspoken, upfront → **honest**

straightforward *adj* THESAURUS ▸ **easy**

strain *n*

pressure or worry caused by having to deal with a difficult situation

ADJECTIVES

great/considerable/severe strain *He has been under great strain at work recently.*

a terrible strain *The weeks following the accident were a terrible strain for the family.*

an intolerable strain (=too great to bear) *The cost of the war put an intolerable strain on the economy.*

emotional strain *She has been suffering from considerable emotional strain.*

financial strain *The government wants to ease the financial strain on families with young children.*

undue strain (=too much strain) *We cannot start any new projects that might put undue strain on the company's finances.*

VERBS

ease/relieve/lessen the strain (=make it less) *The company are taking on more staff to help to ease the strain.*

S

stand/take the strain (=continue in spite of it) *I don't know if I can stand the strain of another divorce.*

cope with/deal with the strain *Staying fit helps her cope with the strain of her husband's illness.*

feel the strain (=start to find a situation very difficult to deal with) *The school is short of teachers, and everyone is feeling the strain.*

PHRASES

be under (a) strain *Doctors are under considerable strain.*

put/place (a) strain on sb/sth *Living so far apart put quite a strain on our marriage.*

collapse under the strain (=become unable to continue normally because of the strain) *If more prisons are not built soon, the system might collapse under the strain.*

stresses and strains *Holidays help people to cope with the stresses and strains of life.*

signs of strain *She is getting very little sleep and she is starting to show signs of strain.*

strange *adj*

unusual or surprising, especially in a way that is difficult to explain or understand

NOUNS

a strange thing *They were walking through the forest when a strange thing happened.*

a strange feeling/sensation/experience *David had the strange feeling that he had seen her somewhere before.*

a strange place/land/world *The desert was a strange place at night.*

a strange way *Your memory sometimes works in a strange way.*

a strange man/woman/person *You meet all kinds of strange people when you're travelling.*

strange behaviour *BrE*, **strange behavior** *AmE*: *His friends couldn't understand his strange behaviour.*

a strange noise/sound *There was a strange noise coming from the other room.*

VERBS

seem/sound/look strange *It seems strange that he didn't say where he was going.*

find sth strange *They found it strange that their son was so interested in ballet.*

PREPOSITIONS

strange to sb *His voice sounded strange to her.*

PHRASES

something strange (about sb/sth) *There is something strange about Mr Hyde, something evil.*

for some strange reason *For some strange reason, she seems to like you.*

that's strange/how strange *spoken* (=used when something strange has happened) *That's strange – all my work has just disappeared.*

S

stranger *n* someone that you do not know

ADJECTIVES

a complete/perfect/total stranger (=used to emphasize that you do not know the person) *Sometimes it's easier to talk about personal problems to a complete stranger.*

a virtual/relative/comparative stranger (=someone you hardly know) *I hadn't seen him for so long that he seemed like a virtual stranger.*

a passing stranger (=one you pass in the street) *They asked a passing stranger to take their photograph.*

a mysterious stranger *She never knew who the mysterious stranger was who had helped her that night.*

PREPOSITIONS

a stranger to sth/sb *I had never seen the man before – he was a complete stranger to me.*

PHRASES

I'm a stranger here (myself) (*also* **I'm a stranger to/in these parts**) *I'm afraid I don't know the way – I'm a stranger here myself.*

speak/talk to strangers *Parents teach their children not to speak to strangers.*

strategy Ac *n*

a planned series of actions for achieving something

ADJECTIVES

a new/different/alternative strategy *They decided to try again using a different strategy.*

a similar strategy *Several kinds of insects adopt a similar strategy.*

a successful/effective strategy *The most successful strategy is often the simplest one.*

an ambitious strategy *Union leaders are calling for an ambitious strategy to create half a million jobs.*

a risky/high-risk strategy *This is a high-risk strategy which could easily fail.*

a clear strategy (*also* **a coherent strategy** *formal*): *It is important that the company has a clear marketing strategy.*

an economic/political strategy *The government has changed its economic strategy.*

a national/global strategy *We need a national strategy for dealing with this problem.*

a comprehensive strategy (=one that deals with every part of something) *This plan provides a comprehensive strategy for the prevention and control of infectious diseases.*

a joint/common strategy (=involving two or more groups, countries etc) *The leaders of the islands discussed a joint strategy on climate change.*

a long-term strategy *The closure of these factories is part of the company's long-term strategy.*

NOUNS + strategy

a business/investment/marketing etc strategy *This is a high-risk business strategy.*

a coping/survival strategy (=for dealing with personal stress and difficult situations) *A psychologist can teach victims a range of coping strategies.*

an exit strategy (=for escaping from a difficult situation if things go wrong) *The country went into the war without an exit strategy.*

VERBS + strategy

think of/come up with/work out a strategy *We need to think of a strategy to deal with the problem.*

devise/formulate a strategy *formal* (=think of one) *They were asked to devise a strategy for saving money.*

use a strategy (*also* **employ a strategy** *formal*): *What strategies do you use to deal with difficult customers?*

adopt a strategy (=start to use it) *Both players adopted the same strategy.*

follow/pursue a strategy (=do a particular planned series of actions) *The government has been pursuing an energy strategy based on fossil fuels.*

implement a strategy *formal* (=do what has been agreed) *The company needs to implement this new strategy as soon as possible.*

develop a strategy *Experts were called in to help the company develop new marketing strategies.*

rethink a strategy (=consider changing it) *If a particular economic strategy isn't working, the government needs to rethink it.*

evolve a strategy (=develop it, especially through a process of natural change) *The creatures which live in the river have evolved strategies for surviving sudden floods.*

suggest/propose a strategy *A good business adviser can suggest alternative strategies for a failing company.*

strategy + VERBS

a strategy works *The government's economic strategy was not working.*

a strategy fails *If this strategy fails, then we will have to think of something else.*

a strategy backfires (=it has the opposite effect of what you want) *The coach's strategy backfired and the team lost 48-7.*

a strategy is aimed at doing sth/is designed to do sth *This latest strategy is aimed at involving more young people in politics.*

PREPOSITIONS

a strategy for doing sth *They need a strategy for improving customer service.*

stream *n*

1 a small river

ADJECTIVES/NOUNS + stream

a mountain stream *They went swimming in a mountain stream.*

an underground stream *The water comes from an underground stream.*

VERBS

a stream runs/flows somewhere *The stream flowed gently under the bridge.*

2 a continuous flow of something

ADJECTIVES

a steady/constant/unbroken stream *The museum attracts a steady stream of visitors.*

an endless/never-ending stream *She had an endless stream of admirers.*

NOUNS + stream

a revenue/income stream (=a continuous supply of money from selling or doing something) *We need to have a regular revenue stream.*

PHRASES

a stream of traffic/cars *A steady stream of traffic made it difficult to cross the road on foot.*

a stream of visitors/customers/people *There was a constant stream of customers all day long.*

a stream of abuse *He shouted a stream of abuse at the other driver.*

a stream of consciousness (=the expression of thoughts and feelings in writing exactly as they pass through your mind) *The novel is written in the form of a stream of consciousness.*

S

street *n*

a road in a city or town that has houses, shops etc on one or both sides

ADJECTIVES

a busy street (=with a lot of traffic or people) *The house faces onto a busy street.*

a crowded street (=with a lot of people) *The streets get very crowded at weekends.*

a quiet street (=with very few people) *It was late and the streets were quiet.*

an empty/deserted street (=with no people) *As he walked home, the street was deserted.*

a narrow street *Riva's narrow streets and elegant cafés are a delight.*

the main street (=the biggest street in a town or village) *They drove slowly along the main street.*

the high street *BrE* (=the main street with shops) *I bought this coat at a shop on the high street.*

a shopping street *BrE* (=with a lot of shops) *This is one of Europe's most elegant shopping streets.*

a residential street (=with houses, not shops) *The house is on a quiet residential street.*

a one-way street (=in which you can only drive in one direction) *He was caught driving the wrong way down a one-way street.*

a side/back street (=a small quiet street near the main street) *The restaurant is tucked away in a side street.*

winding streets (=streets that turn in many directions) *We spent hours exploring the town's winding streets.*

VERBS

cross the street (=walk to the other side) *She crossed the street and walked into the bank.*

walk the streets *I didn't feel safe walking the streets after dark.*

live on the street(s) (=not have a home) *He lost his job and was forced to live on the streets.*

roam/wander the streets (=walk along streets without any clear purpose or direction) *Dogs roam the city's streets.*

people line the street (=they form rows along the side of a street) *Crowds lined the street, hoping to see the princess.*

street + NOUNS

a street corner (=a place where streets meet) *Youths were standing around on street corners.*

a street light/lamp *It was getting dark, and the street lamps were already on.*

a street vendor (=someone who sells things on a street) *He bought a bunch of flowers from a street vendor.*

a street musician/performer/entertainer *Amy liked listening to the street musicians who played outside the market.*

street crime/violence (=when people are attacked in the street) *Young men are most likely to be victims of street crime.*

a street protest/demonstration *There were mass street protests against the government.*

a street battle *A street battle between local youths and police broke out.*

street clothes (=ordinary clothes, not a special uniform or costume) *She changed into her street clothes and left the theatre.*

street people/children (=people without a home who live on the streets) *The charity aims to help street children.*

a street gang (=a group of people who commit crimes in the street) *He was shot by members of a street gang.*

PREPOSITIONS

on/in a street *There is a new café on our street.*

in the street *Children played in the street.*

down/along the street *A man was walking down the street.*

across the street *Someone just moved in across the street.*

PHRASES

on the other side of the street *There was a car parked on the other side of the street.*

the streets are full of sb *On Saturday morning, the streets are full of shoppers.*

THESAURUS: street

street, avenue, boulevard, lane, cul-de-sac, track, ring road, bypass, dual carriageway, freeway/expressway, motorway, interstate, toll road, turnpike → **road**

strength *n*

1 the physical power and energy that makes someone strong

ADJECTIVES

great/enormous strength *Hercules was famous for his great strength.*

physical strength *Some of the tasks required considerable physical strength.*

superhuman strength (=much greater than ordinary strength) *The drug is supposed to give you superhuman strength.*

superior strength (=greater than someone else's) *Using his superior strength, he managed to keep his opponent on the ground.*

brute strength (=physical strength rather than intelligence or careful thinking) *There is more to wrestling than just brute strength.*

full strength *It takes time to get your full strength back after you have been ill.*

VERBS

have the strength to do sth (=used especially in negative sentences) *He didn't even have the strength to sit up.*

use your strength *He used all his strength to hold the door shut.*

find the strength to do sth *She found the strength to climb up onto the upturned boat.*

build up your strength (=make yourself stronger) *You need to build up your strength before you can return to work.*

gather/muster/summon your strength (=get enough strength to do something) *He sat for a couple of minutes, gathering his strength.*

gain strength *After the operation, he spent several weeks relaxing and gaining strength.*

recover/regain your strength (*also* **get your strength back**) (=become strong again after being weak) *After such a serious illness, it may be some time before you regain your strength completely.*

sap/exhaust your strength (=use all of it) *The long walk had sapped her strength.*

sb's strength returns *After a rest and some food, she knew her strength would soon return.*

sb's strength ebbs (away) (*also* **sb's strength drains (away)**) (=it disappears) *She was getting tired and she could feel her strength ebbing away.*

S

PHRASES

with all your strength *He pulled on the rope with all his strength.*

2 determination

ADJECTIVES

great strength *She showed great strength in dealing with her problems.*

inner strength *He had an inner strength which got him through the tough times.*

mental strength *He's a player who has the skill and the mental strength to win.*

VERBS

show strength *The decision to continue shows incredible strength and courage.*

have the strength to do sth *He knows he has the strength to cope with such a high-powered job.*

find the strength to do sth *She had found the strength to escape from an abusive marriage.*

gain/draw strength from sb/sth *He gained strength from being with the people he loved.*

PHRASES

strength of character (=strong ability to deal with difficult situations) *The victims' families have shown amazing strength of character.*

strength of purpose/mind (=determination to do something) *In pursuing his ambition, he showed remarkable strength of purpose.*

a tower of strength (=someone whose brave and determined attitude helps others) *Her friends know her as a tower of strength in difficult times.*

a source of strength (=a person or thing that makes you brave or determined) *Her religious faith has always been a source of strength for her.*

3 a particular quality or ability that gives someone or something an advantage

ADJECTIVES

a great strength *The richness of its culture is one of India's greatest strengths.*

a real strength *The play's real strength is the way it explores relationships.*

a main/key strength *His ability to communicate with ordinary people is one of his main strengths.*

sb's own/individual/particular strengths *Think about how you can use your own strengths to help the team.*

VERBS

sb's/sth's strength lies in sth *The show's strength lies in the fact that it appeals to all ages.*

know sb's strengths *It's important to know your strengths as well as your weaknesses.*

identify sb's strengths *The teacher can identify each child's strengths.*

build on/capitalize on a strength (=use it as a basis for further achievement) *The organization must move forward and capitalize on its strengths.*

play to your strengths (=use the skills you have in the best way in order to achieve something) *If we play to our strengths, we have a good chance of winning.*

PREPOSITIONS

the strength of sth *The strength of the system is its flexibility.*

PHRASES

strengths and weaknesses *We all have our different strengths and weaknesses.*

strengthen *v*

to make something stronger, more effective, or more powerful

ADVERBS

strengthen sth considerably/greatly/ significantly *Security has been strengthened considerably.*

further strengthen sth *The trade agreement will further strengthen the relationship between the two countries.*

NOUNS

strengthen sb's position *Recent successes in elections have strengthened the party's position in the north.*

strengthen sb's hand (=make them more powerful) *Her involvement in the scandal has strengthened the hand of her critics.*

strengthen sb's resolve (=make them more determined) *Other people's doubts only strengthened my resolve to start my own business.*

strengthen ties/bonds/links *He wants to strengthen ties with the West.*

strengthen a relationship *Speaking to a marriage expert could strengthen your relationship.*

strengthen sb's role *We want to strengthen the role of parents in the running of the school.*

stress[1] Ac *n*

1 continuous feelings of worry about your work or personal life, that prevent you from relaxing

ADJECTIVES

great/considerable/enormous stress *I was under considerable stress at work.*

mental/emotional stress *The situation caused him severe emotional stress.*

VERBS

suffer from stress *If you are suffering from stress, you are more likely to become ill.*

cause stress *Moving house often causes stress.*

cope with/deal with stress *People find different ways of dealing with stress.*

reduce/relieve/alleviate stress *Exercise helps to relieve stress.*

stress + NOUNS

sb's stress level (*also* **sb's level of stress**) *Stress levels often rise before an exam.*

stress management *Some patients may benefit from being taught stress management skills.*

S

PREPOSITIONS

be under stress *She has been under a lot of stress lately.*

PHRASES

a cause/source of stress *Balancing work and family is the main cause of stress for many people.*

signs/symptoms/effects of stress *Headaches and sudden mood changes are all signs of stress.*

stresses and strains (=a lot of different worries that are caused by something) *If you are fit, you will find it easier to cope with the stresses and strains of everyday life.*

stress-related *A lot of illnesses are stress-related.*

2 special attention or importance given to something

ADJECTIVES

great stress *Government policy put great stress on education and training.*

VERBS

put/lay/place stress on sth *The company lays particular stress on providing good customer service.*

PREPOSITIONS

stress on sth *The cookbook's stress on quick but healthy meals makes it a pleasure to use.*

stress[2] Ac *v*

to emphasize a statement, fact, or idea

ADVERBS

repeatedly stress sth *The government has repeatedly stressed the need for a fairer tax system.*

constantly/continually stress sth *Doctors are continually stressing the importance of regular exercise.*

rightly stress sth *Dr Stuart rightly stresses the lack of research into this subject.*

NOUNS

stress the importance of sth *He stresses the importance of a regular diet.*

stress the need for sth *The president stressed the need for calm.*

stress a point *This point needs to be stressed as much as possible.*

stress a fact *The doctor stressed the fact that I must not take more than the stated dose of the medicine.*

stress the role of sb/sth *In her speech, she stressed the role of parents in preventing youth crime.*

stress your commitment to (doing) sth *The president stressed his commitment to tackling world poverty.*

PHRASES

it is important to stress sth *We think it is important to stress that we are opposed to the war.*

sb is keen to stress sth (*also* **sb is at pains to stress sth**) *He was keen to stress that he did not want to leave the company.*

it must be stressed that... *It must be stressed that the government made no attempt to conceal this information.*

it is worth stressing sth *It is worth stressing the value of the library to the local community.*

I cannot stress sth enough (*also* **sth cannot be stressed enough**) *The importance of honesty and openness cannot be stressed enough.*

stressed (*also* stressed out) *adj informal*

so worried and tired that you cannot relax

VERBS

feel stressed *I always eat when I'm feeling stressed.*

look stressed *She was shouting at the kids and looking very stressed.*

get/become stressed *If you don't plan ahead, you'll get stressed.*

make sb stressed *Stop hurrying me – you're making me stressed!*

PREPOSITIONS

stressed about sth *He's stressed about work.*

stressed over sth *She sometimes gets stressed over nothing.*

stressful Ac *adj*

making you worried and unable to relax

NOUNS

a stressful experience *Moving to a new house can be a very stressful experience.*

a stressful situation/event *I try to avoid stressful situations.*

stressful conditions *Police officers may be working in stressful conditions.*

a stressful lifestyle/life *A stressful lifestyle may lead to a number of medical problems.*

a stressful job *She's tired because she has a very stressful job.*

a stressful day/week/time *He's having a stressful day.*

ADVERBS

highly stressful (=very stressful) *Clare's work is highly stressful.*

emotionally stressful *Some people find these meetings emotionally stressful.*

VERBS

find sth stressful *Many people find looking after young children stressful.*

make sth stressful *Having little or no support makes life more stressful.*

sth can be stressful *Driving on busy roads can be stressful.*

strict *adj*

1 expecting people to obey rules or to do what you say – used especially about parents, teachers, or organizations

NOUNS

a strict teacher *The teachers in our school were very strict and we weren't allowed to talk in class.*

a strict parent/father/mother etc *She escaped her strict father by marrying her cousin.*

a strict disciplinarian (=someone who is very strict and often punishes people) *As well as being a strict disciplinarian, Captain Burrows was a good administrator.*

ADVERBS

too strict/overly strict *You must not be too strict with her – she's only a child.*

fairly/relatively/quite strict *I remember him as a fairly strict parent.*

PREPOSITIONS

strict about/on sth *The school is very strict about the way students dress.*

strict with sb *My parents were very strict with me.*

THESAURUS: strict

firm
voice | control
showing that you are in control of the situation and will not change your opinion, especially when you are telling someone what to do:
He issued his instructions in a firm voice. | Parents should keep a firm control over their children. | I'll be ***firm with*** *him and tell him he can't have any more money.*

tough
determined that your orders or decisions will be obeyed – used especially when you think that someone is right to be strict:
We need a government that is ***tough on*** *crime. | She can be quite* ***tough with*** *her students, but they respect her for it. | He knows he needs to be tough and keep government spending down.*

harsh
punishing or criticizing someone in a way that seems very severe, often too severe:
Don't be too ***harsh on*** *her – she's only a child. | It may* ***seem rather harsh*** *to punish him, but he has to learn that this kind of behaviour is unacceptable. | Her reaction to the child's bad behaviour was* ***unnecessarily harsh****.*

stern
look | expression | man | woman
strict in a serious, disapproving, and rather unfriendly way:
Her mother gave her a stern look. | He was very much aware too, of the stern expression on Christopher's face. | Her grandfather was a stern man who rarely smiled. | Sheila walked into the museum, ***under the stern gaze of*** *the curator* (=while someone looked at her in a strict way to make sure that she was not doing anything wrong).

authoritarian *disapproving*
regime | government | state | system | father | parents | methods | manner
very strict about forcing people to obey rules or laws, and punishing them very severely if they fail to do this:
The country is governed by an authoritarian military regime which has no regard for human rights (=a government, especially one that you disapprove of). *| Under the authoritarian system of the past, there was no freedom of the press. | The government's response was to use even more authoritarian methods.*

2 a strict order or rule is one that must be obeyed

NOUNS

strict orders/instructions *He left strict instructions not to be disturbed.*

strict rules/regulations/guidelines *There are strict rules regarding doctors' behaviour towards patients.*

strict limits *Many airlines impose strict limits on the weight of baggage.*

a strict interpretation of the law/rules *There is a strict interpretation of Islamic law, and women are not allowed to drive or vote.*

strict control *He called for stricter control of government spending.*

strict discipline (=rules of behaviour) *The head teacher insists on strict discipline throughout the school.*

strict requirements *Landlords must follow strict safety requirements.*

strict criteria (=standards used for judging someone or something) *The supermarket's suppliers must meet strict criteria.*

a strict code (=set of rules) *The club has a strict dress code.*

a strict diet *He went on a strict diet and lost a lot of weight.*

a strict deadline (=a time by which something must be done) *The work was completed to very strict deadlines.*

PHRASES

in strict confidence (*also* **in the strictest confidence**) (=kept completely secret) *Any information you give will be treated in the strictest confidence.*

THESAURUS: strict

tight
controls | restrictions | regulations | rules | limits | security
very strict, especially about what is allowed and what is not allowed:

S

The report recommends tighter controls on the advertising of alcohol. | There are tight limits on the use of nitrogen fertilizer and pesticides. | Tight security was in force at the airport for the Pope's visit. | The new government says it will **keep a tight rein on** *spending* (=it will carefully control how much money is spent).

tough
rules | laws | legislation | measures
tough laws or rules are very strict:
The federal government is introducing tough new rules on immigration. | They want tougher laws against drinking and driving. | The president was urged to take extremely tough measures on terrorism (=tough laws or actions to deal with something).

harsh
treatment | measures | penalty | punishment
very severe, often too severe:
Domestic workers often complain of harsh treatment by their employers. | The government has brought in harsh measures to stop the rioting (=laws or ways of dealing with something). *| There are harsh penalties for drug smugglers. | They may be forced to sell the company. This would be a harsh punishment.*

stringent
criteria | conditions | requirements | controls | checks | tests | regulations | rules | restrictions
very strict, and often based on very high standards:
New products have to meet stringent criteria. | Stringent controls were placed upon banks. | The government introduced stringent new food safety regulations.

strike *n*

1 a period of time when a group of workers deliberately stop working because of a disagreement about pay, working conditions etc

ADJECTIVES/NOUNS + strike

a national/nationwide strike (=all over the country) *In April 1984 the National Union of Mineworkers called a national strike.*

a general strike (=when workers from most industries strike) *The workers threatened to call for a general strike.*

a one-day/two-week etc strike *A three-day strike is planned for next week.*

teachers'/pilots'/miners' etc strike (=by teachers, pilots etc) *The transport workers' strike inflicted serious damage on the economy.*

a rail strike (=by railway workers) *A rail strike would cause enormous public inconvenience.*

an indefinite strike (=with no end planned) *Workers at the processing plant have begun an indefinite strike.*

an all-out strike *BrE* (=when all the workers in a factory, industry etc strike) *The dockers voted for an all-out strike.*

an unofficial strike (=not organized by a trade union) *Some workers had been sacked for taking part in unofficial strikes.*

a wildcat strike (=unofficial and without any warning) *Legislation to curb wildcat strikes will be introduced during the coming parliamentary session.*

VERBS

be (out) on strike *Teachers are on strike again this week.*

go on strike/come out on strike (=start a strike) *An estimated 70,000 public sector workers went on strike.*

⚠ Don't say 'go on a strike'. Say **go on strike**.

begin a strike *Dock workers began a 24-hour strike last night.*

call a strike (=ask people to strike) *The union threatened to call a strike.*

stage a strike (=organize a short strike) *Health workers will stage a two-day strike next week.*

end/call off a strike (=decide not to continue with it) *The strike was called off two days later.*

break a strike (=force workers to end it) *Attempts to break the strike failed.*

avoid/avert a strike (=prevent it from happening) *Managers are in talks with the union in an attempt to avert a strike.*

strike + NOUNS

strike action (=a strike) *Hospital workers have voted in favour of strike action.*

a strike call (=when a group asks people to strike) *The ANC estimated that more than 4,000,000 people heeded its strike call.*

a strike ballot *BrE* (=when workers vote on whether to strike) *The union is going to hold a strike ballot.*

PREPOSITIONS

a strike over sth *A two-week strike over pay has ended.*

a strike against sth *Prison workers went on a one-day strike against the privatisation of prisons.*

a strike by sb *The strike by teachers meant that many schools were closed yesterday.*

2 a military attack, especially by planes dropping bombs

VERBS

launch a strike *Britain and the US launched air strikes against Iraq.*

ADJECTIVES/NOUNS + strike

an air strike *The building had been destroyed in an air strike.*

a military strike *An Israeli official refused to rule out a military strike.*

a missile strike *Eighty people were killed in a missile strike against the town.*

a pre-emptive strike (=done to prevent someone attacking you) *Their only chance of victory was to launch a pre-emptive strike against the US.*

a retaliatory strike (=done because someone has attacked you) *There are fears that the attack could trigger retaliatory strikes.*

PREPOSITIONS

a strike against/on sth *The aircraft were used to launch a strike against Dutch Harbor.*

stringent *adj* THESAURUS ▸ strict (2)

strip *n* THESAURUS ▸ piece

strong *adj*

1 having a lot of physical power so that you can lift heavy things, do hard physical work etc

NOUNS

a strong man/woman *It took four strong men to lift the boat out of the water.*

strong arms/hands/shoulders/legs *He held the baby in his big strong arms.*

strong body/physique *They were admiring his tall strong body.*

strong muscles *People who do yoga often have strong muscles.*

a strong swimmer *She won't drown. She's a strong swimmer.*

ADVERBS

incredibly strong *His hands were incredibly strong.*

strong enough *I'm not strong enough to lift the case on my own.*

PHRASES

big and strong *He'll grow up big and strong like his father.*

as strong as an ox (=very strong and healthy) *The old man was as strong as an ox.*

THESAURUS: strong

powerful
body | arms | hands | shoulders | legs | physique
very strong:
A pair of powerful arms seized me from behind. | Kangaroos have ***incredibly powerful*** *legs.*

muscular
body | arms | legs | man
having big muscles and looking strong and attractive:
He had a firm muscular body. | She liked men who were big and muscular.

well-built
man | woman | lady
a well-built man or woman has a big strong body:
Police say the man they are looking for is 36 years old, six feet tall, and well built. | The door was opened by a well-built lady in her early fifties.

hunky *informal*
guy | men | boyfriend | star | looks
strong and attractive – used about young men:
The advertisements showed hunky men on surfboards. | She married hunky Hollywood star Brad Pitt.

2 not easily broken or damaged

NOUNS

strong plastic/cotton/material *The case is made of strong plastic.*

strong shoes *You will need a pair of good strong shoes.*

strong walls/door *The castle had strong stone walls.*

ADVERBS

incredibly strong *The columns which hold up the roof need to be incredibly strong.*

strong enough *The branch was strong enough to support his weight.*

3 used about feelings that affect you deeply, or opinions that you care a lot about

NOUNS

strong feeling/emotion/passions *People have strong feelings on this issue.*

strong views/opinions/beliefs *My grandfather had strong views about politics.*

a strong taste/smell *The coffee had a very strong taste.*

a strong sense of sth *There is a strong sense of duty in Japan.*

strong support/opposition *The party has strong support in rural areas.*

a strong interest in sth *Paul had always taken a strong interest in his students.*

a strong desire/temptation/urge *As a young man he had a strong desire to visit the United States.*

a strong influence/impression *The war left a strong impression on him.*

strong commitment/loyalty *She had a strong commitment to women's rights.*

You can also say that someone is a **strong believer** in something, or a **strong supporter/advocate** of something: *He is a* ***strong believer*** *in reform.*

THESAURUS: strong

deep
feeling | emotion | love | affection | desire | hatred | sympathy | sorrow | disappointment
very strong:

S

Parents often suffer deep feelings of guilt if their children fail to succeed. | *Morris's designs show his deep love of nature.* | *Please accept my deepest sympathies* (=used when someone has died).

powerful
emotion | **feeling**
extremely strong and having a great effect on someone:
Fear is a powerful emotion. | *There are powerful feelings of guilt about racism in this country.*

intense
feeling | **emotion** | **interest** | **fascination** | **desire** | **pleasure** | **dislike** | **irritation** | **pressure**
extremely strong and having a great effect on someone:
She was filled with an intense feeling of sadness. | *There was intense interest about the affair in the media.* | *She developed an intense dislike of her boss.* | *The president was **under intense pressure** to resign* (=people were trying very hard to persuade him to resign).

4 having a lot of power or influence, or successful in what you do

NOUNS

a strong leader/ruler/king/government (=one who uses their power in a firm and determined way) *We need a strong leader who can get us out of this mess.*

a strong economy *Germany has a very strong economy which is based on exports.*

sb's/sth's strong point (=the thing which makes someone or something likely to succeed) *When you are in an interview, it's best to focus on your strong points.*

ADVERBS

financially/economically/politically/militarily strong *Although the country was economically strong, there was no democratically elected government.*

PHRASES

in a strong position *If they win the game, the team will be in a strong position to take the championship.*

THESAURUS: strong

influential, dominant, strong, great → **powerful (1)**

ANTONYMS **strong → weak (2)**

5 very bright

THESAURUS: strong

strong, brilliant, dazzling, blinding, harsh, light, well-lit → **bright (1)**

structure Ac *n*

the way in which the parts of something are arranged or organized

ADJECTIVES

the basic structure *The students are learning about the basic structure of cells.*

a complex/complicated structure *These molecules have a complex structure.*

a simple structure *The chair's simple structure makes it easy to produce.*

a rigid structure (=very fixed) *Japanese society in those days had a very rigid structure.*

the social/political/economic structure *Many changes had taken place in the social and political structure of the island.*

the internal structure *There are problems with the internal structure of the company.*

a hierarchical structure (=organization into junior and senior levels) *All military organizations have a hierarchical structure.*

the molecular structure *They discovered the molecular structure of DNA.*

NOUNS + structure

class structure (=the way society is organized according to education, jobs, income etc) *Britain had a very rigid class structure at that time.*

power structure (=the way in which the group of people who control a country or organization are organized) *He was a critic of the country's political power structure.*

management structure *Reform of the management structure was needed.*

career structure (=the way a profession is organized which allows progress to better jobs) *Teachers now have a proper career structure.*

VERBS

create/establish/devise a structure *We have devised a management structure that shares responsibilities equally between workers.*

change/alter the structure of sth *It was agreed that the company would change its financial structure.*

PREPOSITIONS

the structure of sth *The war brought a major change in the structure of the economy.*

within a structure *Town councils operate within this structure.*

struggle *n*

1 a situation in which someone tries hard to achieve something or defeat someone

ADJECTIVES

a long struggle *The prisoners finally won their long struggle for freedom.*

a constant struggle *Her life has been a constant struggle against illness.*

an uphill struggle (=one in which you have to

try hard for a long time) *It has been an uphill struggle to keep the business going.*

a heroic struggle *Mandela is famous for his heroic struggle against the apartheid system.*

a bitter struggle *There was a bitter struggle for power.*

a desperate struggle/a life-and-death struggle *Millions of people are facing a desperate struggle to survive.*

a political struggle *The two men were locked in a political struggle.*

the armed struggle (=the use of weapons and violence to get freedom) *The organization agreed to give up the armed struggle and take part in democratic elections.*

an internal struggle (=between members of a government or a political party) *The party was torn apart by internal struggles.*

the final struggle *Gandhi led India's final struggle for freedom from the British.*

NOUNS + struggle

a power struggle (=a struggle to get power) *There was a power struggle between the church and the state.*

a class struggle (=between the rich and the poor classes) *The class struggle in France eventually led to the Revolution.*

a liberation struggle (=a struggle to get freedom for a country) *Her father had fought in the liberation struggle.*

VERBS

be involved/engaged in a struggle *A large number of women became involved in the struggle for women's rights.*

be locked in a struggle *The two companies are locked in a struggle over which of them will control most of the world's internet traffic.*

wage a struggle (=be involved in a struggle against someone or something) *They believe they are waging a struggle against an oppressive government.*

give up/abandon/renounce a struggle *The workers never abandoned the struggle for better conditions.*

face a struggle *The company is facing a struggle to remain profitable.*

a struggle ensues (=it happens after something) *After independence in 1975, a power struggle ensued in Angola.*

PREPOSITIONS

a struggle for sth *He led the people in their struggle for independence.*

a struggle against sth *The struggle against racism has not ended.*

a struggle between sb/sth *There was a power struggle between Mrs Thatcher and the unions.*

PHRASES

a struggle for power/control *When the king died, there was a struggle for power between his two sons.*

a struggle for independence/freedom/democracy *She has never abandoned her commitment to a non-violent struggle for democracy.*

a struggle for survival/existence *Polar bears face a struggle for survival as the Arctic climate changes.*

> If you say that something **is a real struggle** or **is a bit of a struggle**, you mean that it is difficult for you to do: *It's a **real struggle** getting the children to bed.*

2 a fight between people in which they try to hurt each other

ADJECTIVES

a violent struggle *There was a violent struggle and someone fired a gun.*

VERBS

a struggle breaks out (=it starts) *Three people were injured after a struggle broke out in a bar.*

PREPOSITIONS

a struggle between sb *There was a struggle between the two boys in the playground.*

without a struggle *The police managed to arrest him without a struggle.*

PHRASES

signs of a struggle *Detectives found signs of a struggle at the scene of the murder.*

stubborn *adj*

determined not to change your mind, even when people think you are being unreasonable

NOUNS

a stubborn streak (=a tendency to behave in a stubborn way) *Nancy has a stubborn streak and she doesn't like being rushed.*

stubborn refusal *There was a stubborn refusal to accept reality.*

stubborn determination *When he started, all he had was talent and stubborn determination.*

stubborn resistance *The other team put up stubborn resistance.*

PHRASES

sb is as stubborn as a mule *spoken* (=extremely stubborn) *I tried to make him change his mind, but he's as stubborn as a mule.*

> You often use **stubborn** when you think someone is behaving in an annoying and unreasonable way: *I wish you would stop being so **stubborn**!* You also use it when you admire someone, because they refuse to give up trying to do something: *He succeeded through hard work and a **stubborn refusal** to accept defeat.*

S

THESAURUS: stubborn

stubborn, single-minded, tough, firm, resolute, tenacious, dogged, persistent, ruthless, feisty, strong-willed, headstrong → **determined**

student *n*

someone who is studying at a university, school etc

ADJECTIVES

a good student *She was the best student in her class.*

a bright student (=intelligent) *The course is aimed at bright students who have a deep interest in the subject.*

an outstanding/gifted student (=extremely good) *Correa was always an outstanding student at every level of his education.*

a promising student (=likely to be successful) *The prize is given to the most promising student.*

a weak/poor student *In mathematics, he was one of the weaker students.*

an A/B/C student *AmE* (=one who usually gets an A, B, or C for their work) *He was an A student all the way through high school.*

a mature student *especially BrE* (=a student who is over 25 years old) *He took a degree as a mature student at Birmingham University.*

a foreign/overseas student *The university welcomes applications from overseas students.*

a full-time/part-time student *He became a part-time student at Sir John Cass School of Art in London, studying there two days a week.*

a first-year/second-year etc student (=in their first year, second year etc at college or university) *First-year students have an exam at the end of term.*

an undergraduate student (=one who is studying for a first degree) *Chester College currently has 2,000 full-time undergraduate students.*

a postgraduate student *BrE*, **a graduate student** *AmE* (=one who has already done a first degree) *Postgraduate students usually have to write a dissertation on their chosen subject.*

NOUNS + student

a law/medical/chemistry/art etc student *Approximately 40% of law students are women.*

a university/college student *We met when we were university students.*

a high school/elementary school student *AmE*: *Her son is a high school student.*

a research student (=doing research in a university) *The original work was carried out by research students at MIT.*

a BA/MA/PhD etc student *He registered as a PhD student at King's College, London, studying philosophy and psychology.*

student + NOUNS

a student loan/grant (=money that is lent or given to a student) *Some of them are still paying off student loans.*

student life (=the way of life of university and college students) *Parties are an important part of student life.*

a student teacher/doctor/nurse (=someone who is learning to be a teacher, doctor, or nurse) *Student teachers work alongside qualified teachers to gain classroom experience.*

PHRASES

students with learning difficulties/special needs (=students who are born with mental or physical problems) *Most schools have special classes for students with learning difficulties.*

studio *n*

a place where films and TV and radio programmes are made or where music is recorded

ADJECTIVES

a big/major studio *Every major studio wanted to make the film.*

a recording studio (=where music is recorded) *The band have spent months in the recording studio.*

NOUNS + studio

a television/TV studio *The show is broadcast live from the television studio.*

a film studio *These amazing effects were created in a film studio.*

a radio studio *He arrived at the radio studio to give an interview.*

a sound studio (=where sounds, radio programmes, music etc are recorded) *Radio commercials are usually made by outside sound studios.*

studio + NOUNS

a studio audience *The show is broadcast in front of a studio audience.*

the studio floor *Down on the studio floor, the cameramen were ready to start the show.*

a studio album *The band have released both a studio album and a live album.*

study[1] *v*

1 to learn about a subject at school, university etc

ADVERBS

study hard *If you study hard, I'm sure you'll pass your test.*

PREPOSITIONS

study (sth) at school/university *Stephen is currently studying at Exeter University.*

study for a test/exam *I've only got three weeks left to study for my exams.*

study under/with sb (=have someone as your teacher, especially a famous person) *He studied under the psychologist Carl Jung in Zurich.*

2 to look at or examine something or someone carefully

ADVERBS

study sth/sb carefully/closely/intently (=look at something or someone carefully) *She studied him closely. It was hard to tell when he was joking.*

study sth extensively (=used when many people have examined every part of something as part of their research) *This theory has been studied extensively.*

PHRASES

study sth in detail/in depth (=study all the details of something) *We'll make a decision after we have studied the plans in detail.*

study² *n*

a piece of work done to find out information

ADJECTIVES

a detailed/in-depth study *Scientists carried out a detailed study of the disease in farm animals.*

a huge/massive study *The journal published the results of a massive study of 87,000 women.*

a previous/earlier study *The report is a summary of work done in earlier studies.*

a preliminary study (=the first one, after which there will be others) *Preliminary studies indicate that giving the police guns would increase the level of gun crime.*

NOUNS + study

a research study *Research studies have found that young people are doing less physical exercise.*

a two-year/three-month etc study *They commissioned a five-year study into the effects of calcium on bone health.*

a pilot study (=one done to find out if something will be successful) *The government has just completed a pilot study, with some encouraging results.*

a feasibility study (=one done to find out if something is possible or practical) *The company commissioned a feasibility study into re-opening the old railway line.*

VERBS + study

do a study (*also* **carry out/conduct a study** *more formal*): *Scientists are carrying out various studies into the effects of global warming.*

publish a study *The study was published in the 'British Medical Journal'.*

fund a study (=pay for it) *The study was funded by a major US drugs company.*

commission a study (=ask someone to carry out a study) *The government has commissioned a study into the health of residents living near the power station.*

study + VERBS

a study finds sth *The study found that male drivers are more likely to take risks.*

a study shows sth *Studies have shown that the drug works.*

a study suggests/indicates sth *A British study suggests that older people are more reliable workers.*

a study reveals sth (=shows something, especially something surprising) *A recent study revealed that 74% of people choose to buy food because of its packaging.*

a study confirms sth (=shows that something is true) *The study confirms that smoking is also bad for the people around you.*

a study highlights sth (=shows that something is particularly important) *A recent study highlights the need for more qualified teachers.*

a study looks at sth *They did an in-depth study looking at women's health during pregnancy.*

a study aims to do sth *The study aimed to identify the housing needs of local people.*

PREPOSITIONS

a study of sth *A recent study of teenage mothers shows that many are living in very poor conditions.*

a study into sth *She carried out a study into the breeding habits of these birds.*

PHRASES

the aims of a study *The aims of this study are to examine people's spending habits.*

the results/findings of a study *The results of this study suggest that the drug is effective in over 80% of cases.*

THESAURUS: study

work, study, experiment → **research¹**

stunning *adj* THESAURUS ▸ **beautiful**

stunted *adj* THESAURUS ▸ **short (4)**

stupid *adj*

showing a lack of good sense or good judgment – used especially when you are annoyed with someone

NOUNS

a stupid thing *She kept telling herself that this was a really stupid thing to do.*

a stupid question *Don't waste my time asking stupid questions!*

a stupid mistake *I promised never to make the same stupid mistake again.*

a stupid idea *Her friends all thought it was a stupid idea.*

a stupid idiot/fool/person *You're hurting me, you stupid idiot!*

VERBS

seem/sound/look stupid *I know it sounds stupid, but it's true.*

S

ADVERBS

completely/totally stupid *The government must think people are totally stupid.*

just plain stupid informal (=completely stupid) *Are you crazy or just plain stupid?*

PHRASES

it was stupid of sb to do sth *It was stupid of me to lose my temper.*

> **Stupid** or **silly?**
> **Stupid** sounds much stronger than **silly**, and is often used when you are criticizing someone: *The* ***stupid*** *fool left his car unlocked.*
> **Silly** sounds much gentler and less serious than **stupid** and sounds more friendly: *We all make* ***silly mistakes****.*

stupidity *n*

stupid behaviour or lack of intelligence

ADJECTIVES

sheer stupidity (=used when you are surprised by someone's stupidity) *I can't believe the sheer stupidity of some people.*

incredible stupidity *In an act of incredible stupidity, he lit up a cigarette at a petrol station.*

crass stupidity (=very shocking stupidity) *The decision is yet another example of the government's crass stupidity.*

sb's own stupidity *He has only his own stupidity to blame for the mistake.*

PREPOSITIONS

the stupidity of sb/sth *She was disgusted by the stupidity of it all.*

through stupidity *Through stupidity he managed to lock himself out of his own house.*

PHRASES

an act of stupidity *In court today the judge said throwing the concrete block off the bridge was an act of breathtaking stupidity.*

style *n*

1 a particular way of doing, designing, or producing something

ADJECTIVES

a new style *Picasso and Braque invented a completely new style of painting.*

a different style *People use different styles of writing for different purposes.*

the same style *My hair has always been in the same style – long and blonde.*

sb's own/personal style *Teachers are encouraged to develop their personal style of teaching.*

a distinctive/unique style (=different from everyone else's style) *She has a very distinctive style of singing.*

a modern style *The rooms are decorated in a modern style.*

a traditional style *I prefer the more traditional style of garden.*

a simple style *She dressed in a simple style that had mostly gone out of fashion in New York.*

a formal/informal style *People like his informal management style.*

French/American etc style *The house is in a typical Spanish style.*

an architectural style (=a way of designing buildings) *The building is typical of the architectural style of the region.*

NOUNS + style

a leadership/management style *He has changed his leadership style.*

a writing style *How can you develop a good writing style?*

> **Lifestyle** and **hairstyle** are usually written as one word.

VERBS

use a style *The two artists use the same style of drawing.*

adopt a style (=start using it) *He decided to adopt a more informal style of doing business.*

change/alter a style *Should I change my style of dress?*

create/develop a style *By the age of 11, most children will have developed their own handwriting style.*

suit sb's style *Choose a racket that suits your style of play.*

PREPOSITIONS

a style of sth *She's very good at this style of dance.*

PHRASES

in the style of sth *They performed the play in the style of a Greek tragedy.*

in great/grand/fine style *You can dine in fine style in the formal dining room.*

it's not sb's style (=not the way someone usually behaves) *It's not her style to be critical.*

a range/variety of styles *The studio has produced films in a range of styles.*

2 a way of doing something which you admire

ADJECTIVES

great style *She dresses with great style.*

a certain style *The French have a certain style when it comes to food.*

VERBS

have style *He definitely had style and he knew how to enjoy life.*

PREPOSITIONS

with style *Lesley Ann Warren plays the role with a lot of style.*

subconscious *n* THESAURUS ▸ **mind**

subject *n*

1 the thing you are talking about or considering in a conversation, discussion, book, film etc

ADJECTIVES

an interesting/fascinating subject *Animal behaviour is a fascinating subject.*

a difficult/complex subject (=very complicated) *This aspect of the law is a complex subject.*

a controversial subject (=one that people do not agree on) *Gun control is a controversial subject in the US.*

a sensitive/touchy subject (=one that people may get upset about) *Race and religion can be sensitive subjects.*

a delicate subject (=one that may be embarrassing) *She carefully avoided discussing the delicate subject of money.*

a taboo subject (=one that it is not acceptable to mention) *These days, death is a taboo subject.*

VERBS

discuss/talk about a subject *She refused to discuss the subject of her marriage.*

deal with/cover a subject (=speak or write about it) *The subject is dealt with in great detail in his previous book.*

change the subject (=start talking about something different) *Kate tried to change the subject.*

mention a subject *The subject was not mentioned again.*

bring up/raise a subject (=start talking about it) *You brought the subject up, not me.*

broach a subject (=start talking about a sensitive subject) *She hesitated, wondering exactly how to broach the subject of their sleeping arrangements.*

touch on a subject (=say or write a little about it) *In his speech, he touched on the subject of tax reform.*

get onto a subject (=start talking about it after talking about something else) *We somehow got onto the subject of detective stories.*

get back to a subject *Somehow I just knew in the end we would get back to the subject of money.*

drop a subject (=stop talking about it) *To her relief, Julius dropped the subject.*

avoid/keep off/stay off a subject (=not talk about it) *She hoped that Anna would keep off the subject of Luke for the next few hours.*

a subject comes up (=people start talking about it) *The subject of payment never came up.*

subject + NOUNS

a subject area (=a group of related subjects) *He has written a lot in this subject area.*

the subject matter (=what is being talked about or written about) *Love is the subject matter of many poems.*

PREPOSITIONS

on a subject *While we're on the subject of money, do you have the $10 you owe me?*

the subject of sth *Truffaut's childhood memories were the subject of his first film.*

PHRASES

a subject of/for discussion *TV is a favourite subject for discussion.*

a subject of conversation *She searched for a new subject of conversation.*

a subject of/for debate (=a subject people discuss and disagree about) *The reason for the increased risk of cancer is a subject of debate.*

a range of subjects *The book covers a range of subjects.*

2 something that you study at school, college, or university

ADJECTIVES

sb's favourite subject *BrE*, **sb's favorite subject** *AmE*: *My favourite subject is art.*

an academic subject *I was good at sports but not at academic subjects.*

a vocational subject (=one relating to skills needed for a particular job) *The college offers vocational subjects such as accountancy and medicine.*

a compulsory subject (=one that you must study) *Religious education was a compulsory subject in many schools.*

an optional subject (=one that you can choose to study) *From year nine onwards, music is an optional subject.*

NOUNS + subject

an arts/science subject *We want to encourage more girls to take science subjects.*

VERBS

study/take/do a subject (=study a course in a subject) *We have to take eight subjects including English and maths.*

teach a subject *"Which subject does she teach?" "History."*

choose a subject *I wasn't sure which subjects to choose.*

PHRASES

a range of subjects *Most colleges offer a range of subjects.*

subjective *adj*

based on your own personal ideas or opinions

ADVERBS

highly subjective *Art criticism is highly subjective and it is difficult to agree on what makes a good work of art.*

purely subjective *These opinions are, of course, purely subjective.*

subside *v*

to gradually become less and then stop

S

ADVERBS

slowly/gradually subside *The wind gradually subsided.*

subside quickly *The floodwaters are expected to subside quickly.*

subside completely *It took seven days for the swelling to completely subside.*

subside spontaneously (=with no-one doing anything) *No treatment was given and her symptoms subsided spontaneously.*

VERBS

begin/start to subside *At last the feeling of nausea began to subside.*

> **THESAURUS: subside**
>
> cease, wear off, go away, peter out, subside, die down → **stop[1] (2)**

subsidy Ac *n*

money that is paid by the government towards the cost of something

ADJECTIVES/NOUNS + subsidy

a government/public/state subsidy (*also* **a federal subsidy** *AmE*): *Without state subsidies, the railways could not survive.*

a heavy/high/generous subsidy (=a large one) *Japanese farmers receive heavy subsidies from the government.*

price/tax subsidies *Price subsidies on many basic goods were removed.*

a trade/export subsidy *There was an international disagreement over trade subsidies.*

a food/housing subsidy *The country operates huge food subsidies.*

an agricultural/farm subsidy *Farmers are struggling to cope with reduced agricultural subsidies.*

a direct/indirect subsidy (=money given directly, or financial help given in an indirect way) *Houses could not be built fast enough without a direct subsidy from the taxpayer.*

VERBS

get/receive a subsidy *Public art galleries receive subsidies from local government.*

offer a subsidy *The government offers subsidies to businesses who set up in certain areas.*

grant/provide/pay a subsidy *The government could no longer continue to pay subsidies to keep prices artificially low.*

increase a subsidy *We should increase subsidies to renewable energy producers.*

cut/reduce a subsidy *Congress may cut some subsidies to farmers.*

end/remove/abolish a subsidy *Subsidies for state enterprises are being abolished.*

PREPOSITIONS

a subsidy on sth *The subsidy on exports will be removed.*

a subsidy to/for sb *The government is giving subsidies to farmers to encourage them to grow more rice.*

substance *n*

1 a particular type of solid, liquid, or gas

ADJECTIVES

a dangerous/hazardous/harmful substance *Using hazardous substances at work can put people's health at risk.*

a poisonous substance (*also* **a noxious substance** *formal*) (=harmful to people) *Cigarette smoke contains several poisonous substances.*

a toxic substance (=harmful to people and the environment) *All toxic substances should be labelled and carefully stored.*

a radioactive substance (=releasing a form of energy that can harm people) *People who work with radioactive substances are subject to strict regulations.*

an illegal/banned/prohibited substance (=used mainly to refer to illegal drugs) *Any athlete found guilty of using banned substances would have their medal taken away.*

a controlled substance *formal* (=an illegal drug) *He was charged with possessing a controlled substance.*

an organic substance (=from a living thing) *Despite being an organic substance, ivory is remarkably durable.*

a chemical substance *Vehicle engines produce a wide range of chemical substances.*

2 important ideas, which make something good, interesting, or useful

ADJECTIVES

real substance *It is an entertaining book but it has no real substance.*

added substance *You need some quotations and statistics to give the article added substance.*

VERBS

have substance *None of her movies really has any substance.*

lack substance *Most critics think the play lacks substance.*

give sth substance (*also* **lend sth substance** *formal*): *They brought in a university professor to lend the event some substance.*

PREPOSITIONS

the substance of sth *What is the substance of the committee's argument?*

PHRASES

in substance (=used for saying what the important ideas are) *Her argument is, in substance, that women and men should be regarded as equal.*

anything/nothing of substance (=anything or nothing that is important) *I don't see anything of substance in the article at all.*

substantial *adj* THESAURUS ▸ big (3)

substitute Ac *n*

someone or something that replaces another person or thing

ADJECTIVES

a good substitute *If you don't have any sugar, honey is a good substitute.*

a poor substitute *Their local bus service was a poor substitute for their own car.*

a cheap substitute *The material used to be used as a cheap substitute for steel.*

an adequate/inadequate substitute *I find soy milk an adequate substitute for cow's milk.*

a perfect substitute (=something that can replace something else with no difference) *Tofu is the perfect substitute for meat in many dishes.*

VERBS

use sth as a substitute *Machines started to be used as a substitute for workers.*

act as/serve as a substitute *The videos will serve as a substitute to anyone who missed the programmes.*

bring on a substitute (=replace a player on the field with a different one) *The coach decided to bring on a substitute.*

substitute + NOUNS

a substitute product *If we do not have your item in stock, we will supply a substitute product.*

a substitute player/striker/goalkeeper *At half-time, they brought on their substitute goalkeeper.*

a substitute teacher *AmE: Miss French was sick, so a substitute teacher took the class.*

PREPOSITIONS

a substitute for sth/sb *The team has to find a substitute for Tim.*

subtle *adj*

not easy to notice or understand unless you pay careful attention

ADJECTIVES

a subtle change/shift *There had been a subtle change in her attitude towards him.*

a subtle difference/variation *There are subtle differences between the two versions of the song.*

a subtle nuance/distinction (=a difference that is very small and hard to notice) *It is quite hard to explain these subtle nuances of meaning.*

a subtle hint *The look she gave me was a subtle hint that I should stop talking.*

subtle colours *BrE*, **subtle colors** *AmE* (*also* **subtle shades**) *The room was painted in subtle shades of green.*

a subtle flavour *BrE*, **a subtle flavor** *AmE* (*also* **a subtle taste**) *The soup has a subtle flavour of cinnamon.*

PHRASES

a subtle way of doing sth *Yawning was her subtle way of telling me she wanted to go home.*

a subtle form of sth *Saying nothing can be a subtle form of criticism.*

suburb *n*

an area away from the centre of a town or city, where a lot of people live

ADJECTIVES

a wealthy/rich/affluent/prosperous suburb (=one where the people have a lot of money) *He lives in Lexington, an affluent suburb of Boston.*

the outer/outlying suburbs *As you reach the outer suburbs, the houses get bigger.*

sprawling suburbs (=spreading over a long distance) *The city's sprawling suburbs seemed to go on forever.*

a leafy suburb (=pleasant, with a lot of trees) *I took the train to Motspur Park, a leafy suburb of south-west London.*

an exclusive suburb (=very expensive, so few people can afford to live there) *The estate is located in one of Philadelphia's most exclusive suburbs, about 13 miles west of downtown.*

PREPOSITIONS

a suburb of sth *I was born in a suburb of Birmingham.*

in the suburbs *Don't you get bored living out here in the suburbs?*

THESAURUS: suburb

region, zone, district, neighbourhood, suburb, quarter, slum, ghetto → area (1)

subway *n AmE*

a railway system that runs under the ground below a big city

VERBS

take the subway *We took the subway to the Museum of Modern Art.*

subway + NOUNS

a subway train *The incident happened on a crowded subway train.*

a subway station *I got off at the next subway station.*

a subway system *Boston has the oldest subway system in the US.*

a subway line *She got on the wrong subway line and ended up in Brooklyn.*

Subway is used mainly in American English. British people usually say **the underground**, or in London **the tube**.

S

succeed *v* to do what you wanted to do

ADVERBS

finally/eventually/ultimately succeed *I finally succeeded in making contact with him in Rome.*

almost succeed *They planned to destroy the Takeda family, and they almost succeeded.*

sb/sth has largely succeeded (=mostly succeeded) *The police largely succeeded in preventing any more violence.*

partially/partly succeed *The book only partially succeeds in explaining what happened.*

NOUNS

a plan succeeds *The plan succeeded and they were able to get the money.*

talks/negotiations succeed *Unless the talks succeed, there is a serious risk of war.*

an experiment succeeds *They kept trying until finally the experiment succeeded.*

PREPOSITIONS

succeed in (doing) sth *The climbers succeeded in reaching the top of the mountain.*

⚠ Don't say that someone 'succeeds to do sth'.

PHRASES

succeed in your aim/goal/objective/ambition *They have succeeded in their goal of reducing the amount of waste.*

succeed in your attempt to do sth *He succeeded in his attempt to become the city's first black mayor.*

succeed in business/life/your career *The course helps you to develop the skills needed to succeed in business.*

succeed at school/university/work *Do you think that physically attractive people are more likely to succeed at work?*

be determined to succeed *It doesn't bother me. It just makes me more determined to succeed.*

succeed against the odds (=succeed, even though it seems likely that you will fail) *Some students from poor families succeed against the odds, but they are in a minority.*

succeed beyond all (sb's) expectations (=be much more successful than you expected) *Joanna's plan succeeded beyond all expectations.*

succeed beyond your wildest dreams (=be extremely successful) *If he wanted to cause trouble, he has succeeded beyond his wildest dreams.*

THESAURUS: succeed

manage
to succeed in doing something, especially something that needs effort. **Manage** is often used in everyday English instead of **succeed**:
*He finally **managed to** find an apartment near his office. | Don't worry – I'm sure we **can manage** somehow.*

pass
test | exam | examination | interview
to be successful in a test or interview:
*She is hoping to pass her driving test on her third attempt. | He **passed** his exams **with flying colours*** (=he got a very good grade in them). *| Diana passed her interview and began teaching at the Vacani dance studio.*

work
plan | idea | drug | treatment | method | system
if something works, it succeeds or is effective:
*Branson is sure that his plan will work. | The study concluded that the treatment works in over 60% of cases. | Lindner believes that he has found a method that works. | Try using hot water – **that sometimes works**.*

If someone is successful in their career, or succeeds in doing something difficult, you can say that they **make it**: *When I saw my name above the door, I knew I had **made it**. | They **made it** to the top of the mountain.*
If someone achieves something after a lot of effort, you can say that they **get there**: *Don't worry, you'll **get there** in the end.*

ANTONYMS **succeed → fail (1)**

success *n*

a situation in which you achieve what you wanted, get good results, or make a lot of money

ADJECTIVES

a great/big/huge/major success *Everyone agreed that the party was a great success.*

a resounding/outstanding/spectacular success (=very great success) *Financially, the event was a resounding success.*

a runaway success (=something that is a success because it quickly makes a lot of money) *The movie has been a runaway success.*

an unqualified success (=a complete success) *The competition was an unqualified success for Germany.*

considerable success *She achieved considerable success as an artist.*

some success *I had some success in the first game and that gave me confidence that I could play.*

little/no success *Attempts to resolve the dispute met with little success.*

limited/modest success (=not very much success) *These methods were used with limited success.*

(a) commercial/economic/financial success (=when something is successful and makes money) *None of his ideas had any commercial success.*

academic success (=success in education)

There is no evidence that early teaching of reading leads to academic success.

military success *This military success was achieved at a cost.*

VERBS

have/achieve success *Good planning is necessary to achieve success.*

⚠ Don't say 'make success'.

make a success of sth (=be successful in something) *They believe that a good education is essential if they are to make a success of life.*

enjoy success *formal* (=have success) *The company enjoyed great success in Japan.*

meet with success *formal* (=be successful) *We are disappointed that the negotiations have not met with success.*

put your success down to sth (=say that your success was the result of it) *They put their success down to their excellent teamwork.*

guarantee/ensure success (=make sure that someone is successful) *His presence will help to ensure the success of the event.*

repeat the success of sth (=achieve something good again) *The team is hoping to repeat the success of last season.*

prove a success (=be successful) *The scheme has already proved a big success.*

success comes *Brabham's first Grand Prix success came in 1959.*

success depends on sth *The plan's success depends on the support of doctors.*

success + NOUNS

the success rate (=what percentage of actions are successful) *The success rate of this treatment is very high.*

a success story (=someone or something that is successful) *Stuart is a success story who overcame drug addiction and started his own business.*

PREPOSITIONS

without success *I tried to contact him, but without success.*

with great/some etc success *Many zoos have tried to breed pandas, with little success.*

success in (doing) sth *He hasn't had any success in finding a job.*

success as sth *Her success as team manager is due to determination and hard work.*

success with sth/sb *Rob hadn't had much success with women.*

PHRASES

a chance of success *The book has a good chance of success.*

the secret of sb's success (=what makes them successful) *A visitor asked Connie the secret of her success with growing roses.*

the key to success (=the main thing that makes someone or something successful) *The key to success is confidence.*

a degree/measure of success (=an amount of success) *As a player, he had achieved a considerable measure of success.*

be confident of success (=believe that you will be successful) *We have a good team and we're confident of success.*

be no guarantee of success *Spending a lot of money on a project is no guarantee of success.*

ANTONYMS **success → failure**

successful *adj*

1 if you are successful, you achieve the result that you wanted

NOUNS

a successful attempt/bid *His second attempt to climb the mountain was successful.*

successful efforts *We hope their efforts to find a solution will be successful.*

a successful application/appeal *Her application was successful and she got the job.*

a successful operation *The operation was successful and he is well enough to go back to work.*

a successful conclusion/outcome *The negotiators are hoping to bring the talks to a successful conclusion.*

a successful campaign/scheme *Local people organized a successful campaign against the development.*

a successful meeting/trip/visit *Everyone agreed that it had been a highly successful meeting.*

successful talks/negotiations *Both sides want the talks to be successful.*

a successful day/evening/morning *I hope you have a more successful day tomorrow.*

successful treatment *The treatment was successful and she is now completely cured.*

ADVERBS

highly successful *It was a highly successful and very enjoyable evening.*

completely/totally successful *The operation was completely successful and all the hostages were released unharmed.*

phenomenally/hugely/enormously/ tremendously successful (=used when you want to emphasize how successful something is) *The scheme, now in its second year, has been hugely successful.*

partially successful (=not completely) *The treatment was only partially successful and he had to go back for another operation.*

moderately successful (=not very) *The authorities have been moderately successful in reducing water pollution.*

VERBS

prove successful *formal* (=be shown to be

S

successful) *Similar schemes have proved successful elsewhere.*

PREPOSITIONS

be successful in doing sth *The government has been successful in reducing inflation.*

THESAURUS: successful

effective
way | method | means | system | strategy | treatment | remedy | action | solution | approach | drug
if something is effective, it works and does what you want:
Regular exercise is a ***highly effective*** *way of losing weight. | The treatment is effective in more than 80 per cent of cases. | The drug has been shown to be* ***effective against*** *cancer.*

fruitful *formal*
area | source | meeting | discussion | dialogue | relationship | partnership | period
producing good results:
This appears to be a very fruitful area for future research. | They described the meeting as fruitful and very useful. | This was the beginning of a long and fruitful relationship between the two artists.

ANTONYMS **successful → unsuccessful**

2 winning a competition, election etc, passing a test, interview etc, or doing well in your job

NOUNS

a successful team/player/competitor *Brazil has one of the world's most successful soccer teams.*

a successful candidate *The name of the successful candidate will be announced tomorrow.*

a successful career *He enjoyed a long and successful career in politics.*

a successful year/season *The team have had their most successful season ever.*

ADVERBS

highly successful *Her husband is a highly successful racehorse owner.*

THESAURUS: successful

victorious
army | team
successful as a result of winning in a game, election, or war:
Crowds of people lined the streets to welcome the victorious army home. | She ***emerged victorious*** *in the second round of voting* (=she was the winner – a formal use).

winning
team | side | entry | numbers | party | candidate
used about the person or team that wins a competition, game, race etc:
Drogba played well and he deserved to be on the ***winning side*** *(=the winning team). | The winning entry will receive a $1,000 prize.*

Winning is always used before a noun.

promising
player | career | future | start
likely to be very successful in the future, used especially about someone who is good at a job, a sport, art etc:
Chicago has a lot of promising young players. | Sadly his promising career was cut short by a car accident. | The team has a promising future.

ANTONYMS **successful → unsuccessful**

3 making a lot of money

NOUNS

a successful business/company/firm *They started a successful software business.*

a successful businessman/businesswoman/ entrepreneur *Revson went on to become one of the most successful entrepreneurs in the US* (=someone who starts companies and does business deals in order to make money).

a successful product/model *Companies are always looking for new and successful products.*

a successful film/book/record etc *James Cameron's 'Avatar' is the most successful film ever.*

a successful economy/industry *Germany has one of the world's most successful economies.*

ADVERBS

highly successful *Branson is now a highly successful businessman.*

phenomenally/hugely/enormously/ tremendously successful (=used when you want to emphasize how successful something is) *Las Vegas has a phenomenally successful tourist industry.*

moderately successful (=not very) *She was only moderately successful as a writer.*

THESAURUS: successful

hit
song | record | single | movie | film | show | series | musical
a hit song, show, movie etc is very successful:
Stevie Wonder has written many hit songs, including 'I Just Called To Say I Love You'. | Spielberg directed the hit movie 'Jurassic Park'.

best-selling
book | novel | album | author | novelist | product
a best-selling book or record is bought by many people:
The film is based on Alice Walker's best-selling book. | Michael Jackson's 'Thriller' is the

best-selling album of all time. | *Krentz is a best-selling author whose novels have sold over 23 million copies.*

Best-selling is always used before a noun.

thriving
business | **company** | **economy** | **industry** | **trade** | **market** | **town** | **city** | **port**
a thriving business, industry, or place is very successful and people are earning a lot of money:
The brothers have built up a thriving business and now own more than 30 restaurants. | *The town once had a thriving textile industry.* | *At that time, Georgetown was a thriving town of 5,000 people.*

Thriving can either be used as an adjective: *a* ***thriving*** *business*, or as a verb: *The business is* ***thriving***.

booming
economy | **industry** | **business** | **sales** | **demand** | **market**
a booming economy, industry etc is extremely successful and the amount of business is increasing quickly:
China has a booming economy. | *Weddings are now a booming business.* | *The company has reported booming sales of its products for the first quarter of this year.*

Booming can either be used as an adjective: *a* ***booming*** *economy*, or as a verb: *The economy is* ***booming***.

Instead of saying that something was **successful**, you can say that it was **a success**: *The show was very* ***successful***. | *The show was* ***a*** *big* ***success***.
Instead of saying a **hit** record, show etc, you can say that a record, show etc is **a hit**: *Here is the band's latest* ***hit*** *record.* | *Here is the band's latest* ***hit***.
Instead of saying a **best-selling** book or novel, you can say a **best-seller**: *He wrote several* ***best-selling*** *novels.* | *He wrote several* ***best-sellers***.

ANTONYMS **successful → unsuccessful**

successor Ac *n*

someone who takes a job or position after someone else

ADJECTIVES

a possible/potential successor *She is regarded as a possible successor to the president.*
a likely successor *Who is his most likely successor as director of the company?*
a worthy successor (=someone who is good and deserves to be someone's successor) *He is proving to be a worthy successor to his father in the business.*
a natural/logical successor (=someone who you expect to be another person's successor) *Stalin was seen as the natural successor to Lenin.*
an obvious successor *She doesn't have an obvious successor as leader.*
sb's immediate successor (=the next person to have someone's job or position) *The emperor's immediate successor was killed in the year 455.*
a would-be successor (=someone who would like to have a job or position after another person) *He spent too many years as the would-be successor to Tony Blair.*
sb's chosen successor (*also* **sb's designated successor** *formal*): *Her chosen successor as principal is a young man from Oxford.*

VERBS

choose/appoint a successor *The Board met to choose his successor.*
find a successor *He will act as chairman until a permanent successor is found.*
elect a successor *The people of Ghana will elect their president's successor later this week.*
name a successor (=tell people who the successor will be) *The company is expected to name a successor to Corbett in May.*
hand over to a successor (=stop doing a job that is then given to someone else) *She will hand over to her successor at the close of this year's Festival.*
be tipped as sb's successor (=be said to be a possible or likely successor) *She was about to retire, and her deputy was widely tipped as her successor.*
a successor takes over (=start doing someone's job instead of him or her) *His successor will take over in May.*

PHRASES

the appointment of a successor *She will stay on as Managing Director until the appointment of a successor has been finalized.*

succinct *adj* THESAURUS **short (3)**

suffer *v*

1 to have an illness or medical problem, often over a long time

Grammar
This meaning of **suffer** is always used with **from**.

PHRASES

suffer from a disease/illness *Many people suffer from this disease.*
suffer from cancer *He suffers from a rare form of cancer.*
suffer from depression/stress *Helen suffered from depression after her baby was born.*

S

suffer from headaches/stomach pains etc *She told the doctor she had been suffering from severe headaches.*

suffer from health problems *Local people are still suffering from health problems caused by the nuclear accident.*

2 to experience something unpleasant

NOUNS

suffer an injury *Ten people suffered minor injuries in the crash.*

suffer a heart attack/a stroke *He died after suffering a massive heart attack.*

suffer damage *The US ship suffered no damage.*

suffer a defeat *The team has now suffered five successive defeats.*

suffer hardship (=experience very poor living conditions) *Many of these families are suffering incredible hardship.*

suffer a setback/blow (=experience a situation or event that causes difficulty or sadness) *Her plans suffered a setback when she injured her leg during training.*

suffer a loss *Both companies have suffered heavy financial losses.*

ADVERBS

suffer badly *The town had suffered badly in the war.*

suffer greatly/enormously *Her confidence has suffered enormously as a result of recent failures.*

suffer horribly/terribly *Some of the prisoners had suffered horribly.*

suffer needlessly/unnecessarily *Our aim is to prevent children from suffering needlessly.*

suffer disproportionately *formal* (=far too much) *The government should make sure that small businesses do not suffer disproportionately.*

suffer financially *The museum suffered financially under his administration.*

suffer mentally/emotionally *Some of the soldiers had suffered mentally as a result of their experiences.*

suffer physically *They were beginning to suffer physically from lack of food.*

suffering *n*

serious physical or mental pain

ADJECTIVES

great/terrible/enormous/huge suffering *The city went through great suffering in the war.*

unimaginable suffering (=extremely bad) *The earthquake has led to unimaginable suffering.*

human suffering *A great deal of human suffering was caused by the floods.*

mental/physical suffering *She was found guilty of inflicting mental suffering on a child.*

widespread suffering (=among many people in many places) *The invasion caused widespread suffering in Iraq.*

unnecessary/needless suffering *He did not want to cause any unnecessary suffering to the animal.*

VERBS

cause suffering *Knee injuries can cause a lot of suffering.*

relieve/ease/alleviate suffering (=make it less severe) *Advances in medical science save lives and ease suffering.*

prevent suffering *The vaccine will prevent needless suffering.*

endure suffering *Haiti is a country that has long endured considerable suffering.*

PREPOSITIONS

the suffering of sb *He cared deeply about the suffering of others.*

PHRASES

pain and suffering *Her face showed the pain and suffering she had experienced in her life.*

sufficient Ac *adj formal*

as much as is needed

ADVERBS

quite sufficient (=used to emphasize that something is enough) *£50 should be quite sufficient.*

NOUNS

sufficient time *Allow sufficient time to get to the airport.*

sufficient evidence/proof *We can only prosecute if there is sufficient evidence.*

sufficient information/detail *The document did not give sufficient detail.*

sufficient funds/money/resources *The money is not sufficient to cover everything that needs doing.*

a sufficient number/quantity *We need to be sure that a sufficient number of people will see the advert.*

sufficient space *Make sure you have sufficient space on the disk.*

sufficient reason/cause/grounds *Lateness is not sufficient reason to dismiss someone.*

sufficient understanding/knowledge *At that age, a child does not have sufficient understanding to distinguish right and wrong.*

sufficient support *The party had been unable to get sufficient support from the public for their plans.*

sufficient food *In winter it can be difficult for the birds to find sufficient food.*

PREPOSITIONS

sufficient for sb/sth *The recipe is sufficient for six people.*

THESAURUS: sufficient

sufficient, adequate, ample, plenty → **enough**

suggestion *n*

1 an idea or plan that someone mentions

ADJECTIVES

a good/excellent suggestion *I think that's an excellent suggestion.*

a helpful/useful/valuable suggestion *Matthew thanked them for their helpful suggestions.*

a sensible suggestion *This was the first sensible suggestion she had heard from him.*

a constructive/positive suggestion (=involving helpful ideas, not criticism) *John made some constructive suggestions for improvement.*

a stupid/ridiculous/ludicrous suggestion *It seemed a ridiculous suggestion.*

a practical suggestion (=based on real situations, not just ideas) *What practical suggestions can you offer to teachers of children with learning difficulties?*

a further suggestion (=another suggestion) *May I make a further suggestion?*

VERBS

make a suggestion *Can I make a suggestion?*

put forward/offer a suggestion (=make a suggestion) *A few suggestions were put forward.*

have a suggestion *I have a suggestion for you.*

come up with a suggestion (=think of something to suggest) *We've come up with five suggestions.*

consider a suggestion *I hope that they will consider all the suggestions that have been made.*

accept/adopt a suggestion (=do what is suggested) *The issue was finally settled when Amelia's suggestion was adopted.*

reject a suggestion (=not do what is suggested) *The government rejected the suggestion of a referendum.*

ignore sb's suggestion (=not take any notice of it) *Dr Ayles accepts that many people tend to ignore suggestions to change diet.*

welcome suggestions (=want people to make suggestions) *We welcome your comments and suggestions.*

suggestion + NOUNS

a suggestion book/box (=a book or box in a school, store etc where people can put suggestions) *We welcome comments and ideas from customers, and there's a suggestion box in all our stores.*

PREPOSITIONS

a suggestion for sth *Here are some suggestions for further activities.*

a suggestion about sth *My suggestion about menus was ignored.*

a suggestion as to sth *Do you have any suggestions as to how we can deal with the problem?*

a suggestion from/by sb *Comments and suggestions from readers are very welcome.*

at sb's suggestion (=after someone suggested something) *At Jan's suggestion, they went out for a coffee.*

PHRASES

be open to suggestions (=be willing to listen to suggestions) *We don't have a firm plan yet, so we're open to suggestions.*

2 a possibility or sign that something is true or that something exists

ADJECTIVES

a strong suggestion *There are very strong suggestions that the accident was caused by mechanical failure.*

a faint suggestion *There was a faint suggestion of alarm in his voice.*

VERBS

reject/dismiss/deny/refute a suggestion *Friends dismissed any suggestion that he was involved in the crime.*

support a suggestion *There is plenty of evidence to support the suggestion that drinking alcohol in pregnancy can harm the baby.*

PREPOSITIONS

suggestion of sth *The minister denied any suggestion of wrongdoing.*

suicide *n* the act of killing yourself

VERBS

commit suicide (=kill yourself) *Most people who commit suicide have had depressive illnesses.*

attempt suicide *She had attempted suicide twice.*

contemplate suicide (=think that you might try to kill yourself) *I contemplated suicide on several occasions after my daughter died.*

threaten suicide *Her husband threatened suicide when she said she was leaving.*

ADJECTIVES

mass suicide (=when many people commit suicide together) *He ordered his followers to commit mass suicide.*

assisted suicide (=when someone such as a doctor helps a very ill person commit suicide) *Thirty-four other states have adopted similar laws banning assisted suicide.*

suicide + NOUNS

a suicide attempt/bid *He overdosed on pills in a failed suicide attempt.*

the suicide rate (=the number of people who kill themselves) *The suicide rate among former soldiers is high.*

a suicide note (=a letter in which someone explains their reasons for killing themselves) *They found a suicide note by his body.*

a suicide pact (=an agreement between people to kill themselves at the same time)

She shot her husband and herself in an apparent suicide pact.

a suicide threat *Depression may sometimes lead to suicide threats.*

a suicide attack (=in which someone kills himself or herself as a way of also killing others) *A suicide attack on a packed train killed over 50 people.*

a suicide bomb/bomber *Suicide bombers believe that they have the right to kill innocent people.*

suit *v*

to be acceptable, suitable, or convenient

ADVERBS

suit sb well *Our new house suits us very well.*

suit sb perfectly *The arrangement suited me perfectly.*

suit sb fine *spoken*: *Either Monday or Tuesday would suit me fine for our meeting.*

PHRASES

suit sb down to the ground *informal* (=suit someone very well) *Country life suits him down to the ground.*

be tailored to suit sb (=be designed to suit someone exactly) *The courses can be tailored to suit an individual student's needs.*

be adapted/modified to suit sb *Several rooms have been adapted to suit disabled guests.*

S

suitable *adj*

having the right qualities for a particular person, purpose, or situation

ADVERBS

very/highly suitable (*also* **eminently suitable** *formal*): *The animal's long legs are highly suitable for running.*

particularly/especially suitable *The hotel is particularly suitable for families.*

equally suitable *The bike is equally suitable for riding in the city and in the countryside.*

perfectly suitable (=completely suitable) *The programme is perfectly suitable for children of all ages.*

hardly suitable (=not very suitable) *Those shoes are hardly suitable for a walk in the country.*

NOUNS

a suitable time *Please call me to arrange a suitable time for an interview.*

a suitable place/location *We finally found a suitable place for a picnic.*

a suitable person/candidate/husband/wife *They don't consider him a suitable husband for their daughter.*

a suitable replacement *I'm having to use the old drill until I can find a suitable replacement.*

a suitable reply/answer *Maggie couldn't think of a suitable reply and decided not to say anything.*

VERBS

consider sth (to be) suitable (*also* **deem sth suitable** *formal*): *I don't understand how a film like this could be deemed suitable for children.*

PREPOSITIONS

suitable for sth *The game is suitable for children over the age of six.*

suitable as sth *Not all animals are suitable as pets.*

suitable to sth/sb *Begin and end the letter in a way that is suitable to the person you are writing to.*

ANTONYMS **suitable → unsuitable**

suitcase *n*

a large case with a handle, used for carrying clothes when you travel

ADJECTIVES

a heavy suitcase *Henry lifted the heavy suitcase into the taxi.*

an empty suitcase *An empty suitcase lay open on the bed.*

a battered suitcase (=old and in bad condition) *All his possessions were in one battered suitcase.*

VERBS + suitcase

pack/unpack your suitcase *I got home last night, and I still haven't had time to unpack my suitcase.*

open/close a suitcase *The customs officer asked him to open his suitcase.*

carry a suitcase *Let me carry your suitcase out to the car.*

lift a suitcase *I couldn't even lift my suitcase.*

pick up your suitcase *He picked up his suitcase and headed for the exit.*

fill a suitcase *She brought enough clothes to fill two suitcases.*

PHRASES

live out of a suitcase (=travel around a lot, with no permanent place to stay) *It feels like I've been living out of a suitcase for months.*

a suitcase full of sth *Police found a suitcase full of money in the car.*

sum Ac *n* an amount of money

ADJECTIVES/NOUNS + sum

a large/considerable/substantial sum *He lost a substantial sum of money on the deal.*

a huge/enormous/vast sum *The company has invested huge sums in research.*

a five-figure/six-figure/seven-figure etc sum (=an amount in the ten thousands, hundred thousands etc) *The newspaper paid a six-figure sum for the photograph of the princess.*

a small sum *Guests in the hotel pay a small sum for the use of the gym.*

a modest sum (=not a very big amount of

money) *She paid a surprisingly modest sum for the paintings.*

a lump sum (=paid as a single amount) *You can have the money in monthly instalments or as a lump sum.*

a cash sum *The first prize is a substantial cash sum.*

an undisclosed sum (=an amount that is being kept secret) *He sold the company for an undisclosed sum.*

the total sum *The total sum lost is believed to be around £2 million.*

the princely sum of... (=a large amount - often used humorously to mean a small amount) *They paid me the princely sum of £50 a week.*

a tidy sum *informal* (=a large amount of money) *I had managed to save a tidy sum.*

a paltry/trifling sum (=extremely small) *Let's not argue about such a trifling sum.*

a derisory sum (=so small that it is unfair) *They offered her the derisory sum of £2 per hour.*

VERBS

charge a sum *Some lawyers charge enormous sums for their advice.*

earn a sum *She can earn a substantial sum from her work.*

borrow a sum *People are borrowing enormous sums just to pay their regular bills.*

pay a sum *Companies pay quite small sums for this kind of work.*

agree (on) a sum *We agreed a total sum of £2,000 for the articles she will write.*

PREPOSITIONS

a/the sum of £5/$50 etc *A small item of jewellery can be bought for the sum of a few pounds.*

PHRASES

a sum of money *The police are urging people not to keep large sums of money in their houses.*

summarize Ac (*also* **summarise** *BrE*) *v*

to give or show only the main information and not the details

ADVERBS

briefly summarize sth *The report's recommendations are summarized briefly in the introduction.*

succinctly summarize sth (=very clearly and using only a few words) *His article succinctly summarises the situation.*

neatly summarize sth (=in a simple but effective way) *This incident neatly summarizes the city's problems.*

NOUNS

summarize findings *In Chapter 5, Vaughan summarizes her findings.*

summarize results *The results are summarized in table 6.11.*

summarize information *Could you just summarize the information for me, please?*

summarize evidence *The lawyer stood up to summarize the evidence.*

summarize arguments *The newspaper summarized the arguments for and against changing the voting system.*

summarize points *She always gives students handouts summarizing the main points.*

summarize conclusions *It may be useful to summarise the conclusions we have reached so far.*

summarize the situation *The writer summarizes the situation very succinctly in her article.*

PHRASES

to summarize (=used as a way of introducing a short statement giving the main information) *To summarize, most schools were achieving the required standards.*

summary Ac *n*

a short statement that gives the main information about something, without giving all the details

ADJECTIVES

a brief/short/quick summary *You can find a brief summary of today's events on the BBC news website.*

a concise summary (=short, with no unnecessary words or information) *The book is useful for its concise summary of his work.*

a detailed summary *For a more detailed summary of the rules, see the appendix on page 25.*

a full/complete/comprehensive summary (=one that includes all the important details or facts) *The team published a comprehensive summary of their findings in the 'British Medical Journal'.*

a general/overall summary (=one that describes the main features, not the details) *I asked Michelle to read the report and send us a general summary of its contents.*

a fair/reasonable summary *I think you have given a fair summary of the issues we face.*

a useful/helpful summary *You can find an overview of the events in the useful summary supplied by the author.*

a good/excellent summary *The article gives a good summary of all the latest research.*

VERBS + summary

provide/give a summary *This chapter provides an overall summary of the process.*

make a summary *I started by making a brief summary of the data published in previous articles.*

include/contain a summary *Your essay should include a summary of the novel's plot.*

produce/write/compile a summary *I have to produce a summary of the speech for the college magazine.*

PREPOSITIONS

a summary of sth *The scientists produce a monthly summary of their research.*

in summary (=used to introduce your general conclusion) *In summary, although house prices have gone down recently, property remains a good investment.*

summer *n*

the season after spring and before autumn, when the sun is hottest and the days are longest

ADJECTIVES

this/last/next summer *We're going to Italy next summer.*

the previous/following summer *They had married the previous summer.*

early summer *The building work will take place during the spring and early summer.*

late summer *In the late summer of 1931, Joe returned to Oxford.*

high summer (=the middle of summer) *Parts of Spain are extremely hot in high summer.*

a hot summer *It had been the hottest summer for 20 years.*

a dry/wet summer *We've had a very dry summer.*

an Indian summer (=a period of warm weather in autumn) *The south of England has been enjoying an Indian summer.*

VERBS

summer comes/arrives *When summer came, they went on picnics.*

summer + NOUNS

a summer day/morning/evening/afternoon (*also* **a summer's day/evening etc**) *It was a beautiful summer evening.*

the summer months *The garden is open daily in the summer months.*

the summer term *BrE*, **the summer semester** *AmE* (=the time between April and July at a school, college, or university) *I had just completed the summer semester at university.*

a summer holiday *BrE*, **a summer vacation** *AmE: Where are you going for your summer holiday?*

summer weather *Poor summer weather has affected the tourist industry.*

the summer season (=the time in the summer when hotels etc are usually busy) *The resort was crammed with holidaymakers for the whole of the summer season.*

the summer heat *The players were all struggling in the summer heat.*

the summer sun *They lay on the beach, soaking up the summer sun.*

a summer dress (=designed to be worn in summer) *We watched women walk by in their summer dresses.*

summer school (=courses you can take in the summer at a school, university, or college) *We will run summer schools for students who need to resit exams.*

summer camp (=a place where children can stay in the summer and do activities) *In August the kids usually go to summer camp.*

PREPOSITIONS

in (the) summer *It's usually hot here in summer.*

during (the) summer *The children play on the beach during the summer.*

the summer of 2010/1977 etc *We moved to Montana in the summer of 1998.*

PHRASES

in/at the height of summer (=in the middle of summer) *Even in the height of summer, it's cool in here.*

summit *n* the top of a mountain

VERBS

get to/reach the summit *On the third day of climbing they reached the summit.*

climb to the summit *His goal was to climb to the summit of Mount McKinley.*

summit + NOUNS

a summit attempt/bid (=an attempt to reach the summit) *The weather improved, so they decided to make their summit attempt.*

PREPOSITIONS

the summit of sth *From there we continued to the summit of Ben Nevis.*

at the summit *He took this photograph at the summit of Mount Everest.*

on the summit *Even in summer, there was snow on the summit.*

from the summit *We had an amazing view from the summit.*

THESAURUS: summit

summit, peak, crest → **top[1] (1)**

sun *n*

the large bright object in the sky that gives us light and heat, and around which the Earth moves

VERBS

the sun shines *The sky was blue and the sun was shining.*

the sun rises/comes up (=appears at the beginning of the day) *The sun rose at 6.09 a.m.*

the sun sets/goes down (=disappears at the end of the day) *It is a good place to sit and watch the sun go down.*

the sun comes out (=appears when cloud moves away) *The rain stopped and the sun came out.*

the sun sinks (=gradually disappears at the end of the day) *The sun sank lower and the breeze grew cool.*

the sun beats down/blazes down (=shines with a lot of light and heat) *The sun beat down on her head.*

the sun streams through/into etc sth (=light from the sun shines through, into etc something) *The sun was streaming through my bedroom window.*

ADJECTIVES

the hot/warm sun *I lay on the beach in the warm sun.*

the blazing/burning sun (=very hot) *We walked across the square in the blazing sun.*

a bright sun *It was a warm day with a bright sun overhead.*

the fierce sun *literary* (=very hot) *She raised a hand to shade her eyes against the fierce sun.*

the setting sun (=the sun as it goes down and disappears from the sky) *The fields were filled with light from the setting sun.*

the rising sun (=the sun as it comes up and appears in the sky) *We watched the first rays of the rising sun come up over the horizon.*

NOUNS + sun

the morning/afternoon/evening sun *We ate breakfast outside in the gentle morning sun.*

the midday/noonday sun *They tried to find some shade from the blazing midday sun.*

the summer/winter sun *We walked up the hill, the summer sun warming our backs.*

the desert sun *A tent had been set up to provide shade from the desert sun.*

sun + NOUNS

the sun's rays *This cream will protect your skin from the sun's rays.*

PREPOSITIONS

in the sun (=in the heat or light from the sun) *We sat in the sun.*

PHRASES

the sun is high/low in the sky *They walked until the sun was low in the sky.*

sunlight *n*

natural light that comes from the sun

ADJECTIVES

bright sunlight *She shaded her eyes against the bright sunlight.*

strong sunlight *Don't expose babies under six months to strong sunlight.*

direct sunlight *This plant prefers to be kept out of direct sunlight.*

dappled sunlight (=when sunlight comes through trees) *They sat in the dappled sunlight of the forest.*

the fading sunlight (=at the end of the day) *The hills looked beautiful in the fading sunlight.*

NOUNS + sunlight

the morning/afternoon/evening sunlight *Mr Berkley blinked in the morning sunlight.*

VERBS

sunlight streams/pours/floods somewhere (=a lot comes in) *I pulled back the curtains and sunlight streamed in.*

sunlight falls somewhere *The door was open and warm sunlight fell on the tiled floor.*

sunlight filters somewhere (=a little comes in) *The tree allows some sunlight to filter through to the bottom of the garden.*

sunlight fills a place *Bright summer sunlight filled the dining room.*

be exposed to sunlight *Your skin should not be exposed to strong sunlight for longer than an hour.*

PHRASES

sth shines/sparkles/glitters in the sunlight *His newly polished buttons glittered in the sunlight.*

a shaft/ray/beam of sunlight (=a line of sunlight) *A shaft of sunlight lit up the left side of his face.*

sunny *adj*

if it is sunny, the sun is shining

NOUNS

sunny weather *I was enjoying the hot sunny weather.*

a sunny day/morning/afternoon *It was a lovely sunny afternoon, so I went for a walk.*

sunny periods/spells/intervals (=periods in a day when it is sunny - used in weather forecasts) *Elsewhere, it will be a day of sunny spells and scattered showers.*

a sunny spot (=a small area that gets a lot of sunshine) *This plant needs a sunny spot.*

ADVERBS

brilliantly/gloriously sunny *The month of May might be wet and grey one year and gloriously sunny the next.*

mostly sunny *The weather was mostly sunny but at times it was cold.*

> You can describe a room as **sunny** if a lot of sunlight comes into it: *The kitchen is a nice sunny room.*

THESAURUS: sunny

good
weather
if the weather is good, it is sunny and warm:
We hope the weather will be good on Sunday.

fine *especially BrE*
weather | day | morning | afternoon | night
if the weather is fine, it is not raining and not cloudy:
We prayed for fine weather. | On a fine day, you can see across to the islands.

nice (*also* **lovely** *especially BrE*)
weather | day | morning | afternoon
if the weather is nice, it is pleasantly warm

S

and sunny. **Nice** and **lovely** are used especially in spoken English:
When the weather is nice, we eat in the garden. | It's a lovely day – why don't we go for a walk?

bright
day | morning | afternoon | sunshine | sunlight | sky | weather
if it is a bright day, the sun is shining and there is plenty of light:
It was a bright spring morning. | They walked out of the dark cave into the bright sunshine.

beautiful/glorious
weather | day | morning | afternoon | sunshine
if the weather is beautiful or glorious, it is very good and there is a lot of sunshine:
We had beautiful weather, and the hotel was excellent. | What a beautiful day! | They woke to blue skies and glorious sunshine.

clear
weather | day | morning | night | sky
with no clouds or mist:
It's best to go walking in clear weather. | On a clear day, you can see seven lakes from here. | It was a clear night, with a full moon.

cloudless *literary*
sky | day | morning | afternoon | night
with no clouds:
The sun shone from a cloudless sky. | It was a beautiful cloudless morning.

dry
weather | day | night | spell | period | season | conditions
with no rain:
Remember to water young plants in dry weather. | The dry spell (=a period of dry weather) *was followed by exceptionally wet weather. | There are water shortages during the dry season.*

S

sunshine *n*

light and heat from the sun when there is no cloud

ADJECTIVES

bright/brilliant/blazing/dazzling sunshine *We stepped out of the plane into the bright sunshine.*

glorious sunshine (=very bright – used when you are pleased about this) *They woke to blue skies and glorious sunshine.*

warm/hot sunshine *Don't spend too long in hot sunshine without a hat.*

pale sunshine (=not strong or hot) *It was early spring, and pale sunshine shone on the fields.*

hazy sunshine (=sunshine with air that is not clear because of mist etc) *Tomorrow morning will be dry with hazy sunshine.*

NOUNS + sunshine

the spring/summer/autumn/winter sunshine *She was sitting in the garden, enjoying the spring sunshine.*

the morning/afternoon/evening sunshine *The morning sunshine brightened the room.*

PREPOSITIONS

in the sunshine *Let's eat outside in the sunshine.*

PHRASES

a ray of sunshine (=a line of sunshine) *A ray of sunshine filtered through the dirty window.*

bask in the sunshine (*also* **soak up the sunshine**) (=enjoy sitting or lying in a sunny place) *They lay in the garden, basking in the sunshine.*

superb *adj* THESAURUS ▸ **excellent**

superior *adj*

better, more powerful, more effective etc than someone or something else

ADVERBS

far/vastly/greatly superior (=much better) *The opposing team's players were far superior to our own.*

infinitely superior (=very much better) *The food at the second hotel was infinitely superior.*

marginally superior (=slightly superior) *This wine is much more expensive, but only marginally superior.*

inherently superior (=better because of its nature) *He saw the theatre as inherently superior to the cinema.*

morally superior *They accuse Christians of considering themselves to be morally superior.*

technically superior *We must persuade consumers that our product is technically superior to its competitors.*

numerically superior *formal* (=there are more people or things) *The Scots defeated the numerically superior English army.*

VERBS

feel (yourself) superior *It was clear from her attitude that she felt herself superior to the rest of us.*

be considered superior (*also* **be regarded as superior**) *Champagne is considered superior to all other sparkling wines.*

NOUNS

superior quality *Digital radios offer a superior quality of sound.*

superior performance *Most motoring critics agree that the older model had superior performance.*

superior knowledge/intelligence *She was always showing off her superior knowledge.*

superior strength/power *He used his superior strength to wrestle his opponent to the ground.*

PREPOSITIONS

superior to sb/sth *She was superior to her opponent in every aspect of the game.*

supermarket *n*

a very large shop that sells food and things that people need regularly in their homes

ADJECTIVES

the local supermarket *Is the local supermarket open on Sundays?*

VERBS

go to the supermarket *He went to the supermarket to get something to cook for dinner.*

buy sth at/from the supermarket *You can even buy a television at the supermarket these days.*

shop in/at a supermarket (=buy things there) *Do you usually shop at the supermarket?*

a supermarket sells sth *Supermarkets sell a wide range of fruit and vegetables.*

supermarket + NOUNS

a supermarket chain (=a large company that owns a number of stores in different towns or cities) *The UK's largest supermarket chain is planning to open more high street stores.*

a supermarket checkout (=the place in a supermarket where you pay for goods) *There were long lines at all the supermarket checkouts.*

a supermarket trolley *BrE* (=a large basket on wheels, used for carrying the things you are buying) *The canal is full of supermarket trolleys and rubbish.*

PHRASES

available in/at supermarkets *Goats' milk is now available in many supermarkets.*

superpower *n* THESAURUS **country (1)**

supersonic *adj* THESAURUS **fast[1] (1)**

superstition *n*

a belief that some objects or actions are lucky and some are unlucky, which is usually based on old ideas or magic

ADJECTIVES

an old superstition *Have you heard the old superstition that seagulls are the souls of dead sailors?*

an ancient/primitive superstition (=from a very long time ago) *Many of these primitive superstitions still exist today in parts of the country.*

a popular/common superstition *The belief that touching wood brings luck is a popular superstition, but where does it come from?*

a local superstition *There's a local superstition that garlic keeps you safe from evil spirits.*

VERBS

have a superstition *Most cultures have their own superstitions.*

be based on superstition *His fears are based solely on superstition, not reason.*

PREPOSITIONS

a superstition about sth *There are a lot of superstitions about the disease.*

PHRASES

ignorance and superstition *People's beliefs were full of ignorance and superstition.*

supervise *v* THESAURUS **control[1] (1)**

supper *n*

the meal that you have in the evening

ADJECTIVES/NOUNS + supper

an early/late supper *They went for a late supper after the show.*

a light supper *We had a light supper and went to bed early.*

a buffet supper (=different foods on large plates, from which you serve yourself) *The invitation says that drinks and a buffet supper will be served from 7 p.m.*

VERBS

have/eat supper *What time do you usually eat supper?*

have/eat your supper *The kids are allowed to have their supper in front of the TV.*

make/cook supper (*also* **prepare supper** *formal*): *She started making supper as soon as she got home from work.*

come (over) for supper *Why don't you come over for supper on Friday?*

stay for supper *Would you like to stay for supper?*

invite/ask sb to supper *We've invited our neighbors to supper tonight.*

serve supper (=start giving people food) *I'm going to serve supper about eight.*

sit down to supper *It's great to sit down to supper with the whole family.*

supper + NOUNS

the supper table *We sat down at the supper table and had a glass of wine.*

supper time *I have to be home by supper time.*

PREPOSITIONS

for supper *We weren't very hungry, so we just had sandwiches for supper. | What's for supper, Dad?*

> The meal you eat in the evening can also be called **dinner** or, especially in some parts of Britain, **tea**. In British English, some people use **supper** only to refer to a small meal you eat late in the evening, rather than a main meal.

supplement *n* THESAURUS **magazine**

S

supply *n*

an amount of something that is available to be used

ADJECTIVES

an adequate supply (=enough) *Does the hospital have an adequate supply of medicine?*

a plentiful/abundant supply (=more than enough) *There was a plentiful supply of books and magazines to read.*

a good supply *In hot countries, always carry a good supply of water.*

a small/limited supply *There is a limited supply of land for building.*

a dwindling supply (=one that is getting smaller) *We cannot rely on the dwindling supplies of crude oil and natural gas.*

a constant/steady/regular supply *Farmers need a constant supply of grass to feed their animals.*

an endless/inexhaustible supply (=one that does not end, or seems not to end) *He has an endless supply of jokes.*

a ready supply (=one that is easily available) *Any restaurant in a hotel has a ready supply of customers.*

a fresh supply *As soon as the vegetables ran out, fresh supplies were delivered from the farm.*

NOUNS + supply

electricity/gas/energy supply *The electricity supply is not very reliable.*

food/water supply *The army has to make sure there is a steady food supply to the soldiers fighting on the front.*

VERBS

use up/exhaust a supply (=use all of it) *The diver had nearly used up his supply of oxygen.*

replenish a supply (=get more of something to replace what you have used) *We went to the supermarket to replenish our food supply.*

increase a supply *They asked Saudi Arabia to increase the supply of oil to European countries.*

control a supply *By controlling the supply of water, we would be able to stay alive for longer.*

cut off a supply (=stop it being available) *A twist in the tube had cut off the oxygen supply.*

disrupt/interrupt a supply (=stop it being available for a short time) *The bombing caused damage that disrupted the gas supply.*

restore a supply (=make it available again) *Only three days after the storm, we have restored electricity supplies to the entire region.*

a supply runs out (=all of it is used) *They knew their food supply would run out in another few days.*

supply + NOUNS

a supply chain (=the set of organizations or systems used to supply something) *We made sure that every part of the supply chain was running efficiently.*

a supply depot (=a place from which goods are sent out to people) *I discovered that the package had still not left the supply depot.*

PREPOSITIONS

a supply of sth *They had only a limited supply of medicine.*

PHRASES

sth is in short supply (=there is not enough of it) *In some of these families, love is in short supply.*

THESAURUS: supply

stock, supply, reserves → **store (2)**

support[1] *v*

1 to agree with someone or something and say this publicly

ADVERBS

strongly support *We strongly support the peace process.*

wholeheartedly support (=strongly support – more formal) *I wholeheartedly support the views of my colleague.*

fully support *He fully supported the action taken by the police.*

enthusiastically support *It was an idea which had been enthusiastically supported by the government.*

2 to give someone help and encouragement so that they can do something

ADVERBS

loyally/steadfastly support *Mr Hawke was loyally supported by his wife.*

actively support *He denied that his government was actively supporting the terrorists.*

VERBS

agree to support sb/sth *His parents have agreed to support him while he is at university.*

3 *BrE* to like a particular team and want them to win

NOUNS

support a team/Manchester United/England etc *"Which team do you support?" "Arsenal."*

4 to hold the weight of something and stop it from falling

NOUNS

support sb's weight *The branch was too weak to support his weight.*

PREPOSITIONS

be supported by sth *The ceiling was supported by huge stone columns.*

support[2] *n*

approval, encouragement, and help

ADJECTIVES

public/popular support (=from the people

S

who live in a country) *There seemed to be no popular support for war.*

widespread/wide/general support (=by many people) *There is widespread support for the changes.*

massive support (=a lot of support) *The party enjoys massive public support.*

strong support *A survey found strong support for the project among hospital staff.*

wholehearted support (=strong support - more formal) *I want you to know that you have my wholehearted support.*

enthusiastic support *The plan received enthusiastic support from environmental groups.*

sb's full support *That view deserves the full support of all farmers.*

active support (=approval and help) *She managed, with the active support of her husband, to run 100 miles in two days.*

unanimous support (=all members of a group support something) *There was nearly unanimous support for the proposal.*

unfailing support (=continuing for a long time, in spite of difficulties) *She thanked her family for their unfailing support.*

VERBS

have support (*also* **enjoy support** *formal*): *The extreme right-wing parties don't have much popular support.*

give (your) support (*also* **lend (your) support** *formal*): *The American people gave him their enthusiastic support.*

show (your) support *Several of her colleagues have shown their support for her at this difficult time.*

voice your support (=say that you support something or someone) *A number of newspapers have voiced their support for the government's proposals.*

pledge/offer (your) support (=say that you will support something or someone) *Both the opposition parties pledged full support for the new administration.*

get/draw support *The plan drew wide support from parents.*

win/gain/attract support *Try to win the support of local shopkeepers.*

enjoy/command support *formal* (=have support) *His views were too extreme to command general support.*

drum up/rally support (=get people's support by making an effort) *Both sides have been drumming up support through the internet.*

enlist sb's support *formal* (=ask for and get their support) *He wrote to the prime minister in an attempt to enlist his support.*

mobilize support (=get people to support something in an active way) *Their aim was to mobilize popular support for their leader.*

build (up) support (=increase it) *Now he needs to build his support by explaining his political beliefs.*

withdraw your support (=no longer support someone or something) *He's decided to withdraw his support for the project.*

PREPOSITIONS

in support of sb/sth *He gave a speech in support of the war.*

support of sb/sth *I would like to thank fans for their unfailing support of the team during these difficult years.*

support for sb/sth *Is there much support for the elderly president?*

support among people *The plan has won a lot of support among people aged 18–25.*

support from sb *Support from older members would be particularly valuable.*

supporter *n*

someone who supports a particular person, team, political idea etc

ADJECTIVES

a strong supporter *He was a strong supporter of the prime minister.*

a loyal/faithful supporter *The football club has many loyal supporters.*

a staunch supporter (=a strong and loyal supporter) *Even his staunchest supporters admit that he is unlikely to win the election.*

an enthusiastic/keen supporter *Even her most enthusiastic supporters will admit that she sometimes made mistakes.*

an ardent/fervent supporter (=very enthusiastic) *He is an ardent supporter of women's rights.*

a vocal/outspoken/vociferous supporter (=who speaks very openly about their support for something or someone) *The actor is one of the party's most vocal supporters.*

a lifelong supporter (=who has supported someone or something all their life) *Her husband is a lifelong Manchester United supporter.*

an active supporter *She remained an active supporter of several environmental groups.*

a leading supporter *Many of the dictator's leading supporters had left the country.*

a political supporter *He is one of the governor's key political supporters.*

Labour/Republican etc supporters *Most of the newspaper's readers were Labour supporters.*

NOUNS + supporter

football/rugby/cricket etc supporters *BrE* (=who support a particular sports team) *A noisy crowd of rugby supporters was in the pub.*

human rights/gay rights etc supporters *There will be a march through the streets by gay rights supporters.*

VERBS

attract supporters *The plan has attracted supporters from every political party.*

alienate supporters (=make them want to stop supporting you) *Her recent comments on TV alienated many of her supporters.*

mobilize supporters (=encourage them to take action) *Anti-war groups are mobilizing their supporters for this weekend's protest march.*

PREPOSITIONS

a supporter of sb/sth *Supporters of the president are urging the public to be patient.*

THESAURUS: supporter

admirer, lover, supporter, buff, addict, enthusiast → **fan**

sure *adj*

confident that you know something or that something is true or correct

ADVERBS

absolutely sure (*also* **quite sure** *formal*): *Are you quite sure you have all the information you require?*

pretty sure (=almost sure) *I'm pretty sure it was the same woman who called the office last week.*

not quite/entirely sure (*also* **not altogether sure** *formal*): *"What are these little objects?" "I'm not entirely sure."*

not exactly sure *I'm not exactly sure when the meeting is.*

not very/too sure *Make a list of any words or phrases whose meaning you are not too sure about.*

not at all sure *By now, we were not at all sure where we were.*

VERBS

feel sure *I felt sure I'd seen her before.*

seem/appear sure *She seemed very sure that her information was correct.*

look/sound sure *Was it really ten o'clock when you left? You don't sound very sure.*

PREPOSITIONS

sure about sth *I can't be sure about the time he arrived.*

sure of sth *His wife was angry about something – he was sure of that.*

PHRASES

make sure (=to check that something is true or something has been done) *I think I locked the door but I'd better make sure.*

I'm not sure *"What time does the show start?" "I'm not sure."*

sure enough *spoken* (=used for saying that you expected something to happen) *I didn't think he'd miss a party like this and, sure enough, there he was.*

surface *n*

the outside or top layer of something

ADJECTIVES

a flat surface *Put the compass on a flat surface.*

a hard surface *The path has a hard surface suitable for wheelchairs.*

a smooth surface *Marble provides a cool smooth surface.*

a shiny surface *This type of cloth has a shiny surface on one side.*

a rough surface *I touched the rough surface of the stone wall.*

a textured surface (=not smooth, because of its design) *Many floor tiles have a textured surface to make them less slippery.*

a slippery surface (=one that could cause someone to slide and fall over) *The sign read: 'Beware: slippery surface.'*

the upper/top surface *The upper surface of the leaf is dull green.*

the outer/inner surface *There are lines on the outer surface of the shell.*

surface + NOUNS

the surface temperature *The surface temperature of the water is a few degrees higher.*

the surface layer *The surface layer of the soil is only a few centimetres thick.*

VERBS

break the surface (=go through the surface) *From our boat, we watched as this enormous whale broke the surface of the water.*

PREPOSITIONS

the surface of sth *Sunlight reflected off the surface of the water.*

on the surface *Litter was floating on the surface of the lake.*

below/beneath/under the surface *These divers can stay below the surface for more than ten minutes.*

surgery *n*

medical treatment in which a surgeon cuts open your body to repair or remove something inside

ADJECTIVES

major/minor surgery *He will require major surgery to remove the lump.*

cosmetic/plastic surgery (=to improve someone's appearance) *More and more people are choosing to have plastic surgery.*

NOUNS + surgery

heart/knee/brain etc surgery *She is now fit again after knee surgery.*

emergency surgery (=done quickly, in an emergency) *The teenager underwent emergency surgery after a bullet pierced her lung.*

laser surgery (=done using a laser) *The doctor suggested laser surgery to improve her eyesight.*

keyhole surgery (=done through a very small

hole in the skin) *The operation can be done using keyhole surgery.*

VERBS

have surgery (*also* **undergo surgery** *formal*): *She had surgery on her hip last year.*

carry out/do surgery (*also* **perform surgery** *formal*): *The patient has a chance to meet the doctor who will carry out the surgery.*

⚠ Don't say 'make surgery'.

need surgery (*also* **require surgery** *formal*): *He is likely to need surgery in the near future.*

await surgery *formal* (=be waiting to have surgery) *This is a ward for patients awaiting surgery.*

PREPOSITIONS

surgery on sth *It is likely she will need surgery on her knee.*

surgery for sth *He needed emergency surgery for a gunshot wound.*

in surgery (=having surgery) *The patient was still in surgery.*

surprise *n*

1 an unexpected or unusual event

ADJECTIVES

a big/great surprise *The results were a big surprise.*

a complete/total surprise *The news came as a complete surprise.*

a nice/pleasant/lovely surprise *It's a lovely surprise to see you.*

an unpleasant/nasty surprise *We don't want any unpleasant surprises.*

a real surprise *It was a real surprise to see his name appear on my computer screen.*

a welcome surprise (=one that you are pleased to get) *Her last-minute help was a welcome surprise.*

an unwelcome surprise (=one that you did not want) *Finding personal information about himself on the internet was an unwelcome surprise.*

VERBS

get/have/receive a surprise *We got a surprise when we arrived home and found him waiting for us.*

come as a surprise (=be surprising) *The announcement came as a surprise to most people.*

give sb a surprise *He bought the ring because he wanted to give her a surprise.*

have a surprise for sb (=be planning to give someone a surprise) *I think Jenny might have a surprise for you.*

spring a surprise (on sb) (=give someone a surprise) *The chairman sprang a surprise this week by announcing his intention to quit.*

surprise + NOUNS

a surprise visit *Environmental health inspectors made a surprise visit to the restaurant.*

a surprise party *His friends had planned a surprise party for him.*

a surprise announcement *In a surprise announcement, the company said they were withdrawing their planning application.*

a surprise victory *She came to power in 1977, after a surprise victory in the general election.*

a surprise attack *Instead they launched a successful surprise attack on the castle.*

a surprise move (=an unexpected action) *In a surprise move, the government lifted the ban on arms exports to the country.*

PREPOSITIONS

a surprise to sb *The results were a surprise to many people.*

a surprise for sb *Her visit was a lovely surprise for everyone.*

PHRASES

come as no/little surprise (=not be surprising) *It came as no surprise when Lester got the job.*

be in for a surprise (=be going to have a surprise) *Compare our prices. You'll be in for a pleasant surprise.*

there's a surprise in store (for sb) (=something unexpected is going to happen) *There were plenty more surprises in store for him.*

an element of surprise (=a part of something that is a surprise) *He ruined the element of surprise by telling Jane about the party.*

2 the feeling you have when something happens which you did not expect

PHRASES

to sb's surprise (=used when saying that someone is surprised by something) *To everyone's surprise, they announced that they were getting married.*

ADJECTIVES

great surprise *The news will not cause any great surprise.*

mild surprise *She looked at him in mild surprise.*

complete/utter surprise *To my utter surprise, I won first prize for my essay.*

genuine surprise *There was genuine surprise in his voice.*

VERBS

cause surprise *The decision caused surprise among government officials.*

express surprise *She expressed surprise when I said that I was coming with her.*

take/catch sb by surprise (=make someone feel very surprised) *His sudden departure took Anna by surprise.*

hide your surprise *"Of course I knew about it," I said, trying to hide my surprise.*

feign surprise (=pretend that you are surprised) *"Are the diamonds fake?" she asked, feigning surprise.*

PREPOSITIONS

surprise at sth *Palmerston's surprise at the announcement seems genuine.*

in/with surprise *Shelley looked at him with surprise.*

surprised *adj* having a feeling of surprise

ADVERBS

really surprised *I was really surprised when he said he was leaving the company.*

greatly surprised (=very surprised) *No-one was greatly surprised to hear they were getting divorced.*

pleasantly/agreeably surprised (=surprised and pleased) *You will probably be pleasantly surprised at how easy the job is.*

a little surprised *They were a little surprised by the study's findings.*

mildly surprised (=slightly surprised) *He looked mildly surprised by the question.*

genuinely surprised *She seemed genuinely surprised to have won.*

not exactly surprised *spoken* (=not surprised at all, because you expected something to happen) *To be honest, I'm not exactly surprised we lost.*

NOUNS

a surprised look/expression *We were amused by the surprised look on her face.*

PREPOSITIONS

surprised by sth *We were surprised by people's angry reaction to the proposal.*

surprised at sth *They were surprised at how expensive the meal was.*

PHRASES

surprised to find/learn/hear *I was surprised to learn that this very English-looking woman is actually French.*

surprised to see *We were surprised to see him back at work so soon after his illness.*

I wouldn't be surprised *spoken* (=used for saying that you expect something to happen) *I wouldn't be surprised if she never spoke to you again after the way you treated her.*

don't be surprised if... *spoken* (=used for warning someone that something might happen) *Don't be surprised if you don't get a reply straight away.*

surprising *adj*

if something is surprising, you do not expect it to happen

ADVERBS

rather/somewhat surprising *The results of the survey were somewhat surprising.*

a little surprising *It was a little surprising the group did so well last year.*

hardly/scarcely surprising (*also* **not altogether surprising**) (=not surprising - used when saying that you expected something to happen) *It's hardly surprising that the government is so unpopular.*

VERBS

seem surprising *It seems surprising that he's not married.*

find sth surprising *Some people may find the book rather surprising.*

NOUNS

a surprising number/amount of sth *A surprising number of books have been written about the subject.*

a surprising lack *There is a surprising lack of research into the disease.*

a surprising twist (=a surprising part of a story) *There is a surprising twist at the end of the film.*

a surprising omission (=something you are surprised has not been included) *There are one or two surprising omissions from the list.*

PREPOSITIONS

surprising to sb *It is not surprising to me that the jury found him guilty.*

surrender *v*

to say officially that you want to stop fighting, because you realize that you cannot win

ADVERBS

surrender unconditionally (=completely, without asking for any special conditions) *Japan surrendered unconditionally, after the US dropped atomic bombs on Hiroshima and Nagasaki.*

formally surrender *The rebels formally surrendered and the war ended.*

PREPOSITIONS

surrender to sb *The hijackers surrendered to the authorities.*

surrounding *adj* THESAURUS near

surroundings *n*

the objects, buildings, or natural things that are around you in the place where you are

ADJECTIVES

familiar surroundings (=a place that you know well) *He was relieved to be back in familiar surroundings after travelling for so long.*

unfamiliar/strange surroundings *If a baby wakes up in unfamiliar surroundings, it may cry.*

sth's immediate surroundings (=the area near to a place) *The police began a search of the farm and its immediate surroundings.*

sb's new surroundings *It took me a while to settle in to my new surroundings and get to know people.*

S

sth's natural surroundings (=where an animal normally lives) *We came here to study the creature in its natural surroundings.*

beautiful/pleasant surroundings (=used especially about beautiful countryside) *We are very fortunate to live in such beautiful surroundings.*

idyllic surroundings (=so beautiful as to seem perfect) *They held a wedding reception for 200 guests in idyllic surroundings.*

comfortable surroundings (=used about a room or building, especially a hotel) *It's the ideal place to spend a relaxing holiday in comfortable surroundings.*

elegant/stylish surroundings (=used about expensive or fashionable hotels or houses) *Guests at the hotel dine in elegant surroundings.*

luxurious/magnificent/sumptuous/opulent surroundings (=very expensive and comfortable) *He felt out of place in the opulent surroundings of the palace.*

VERBS

blend/fit in with the surroundings (=look like the surroundings) *He wants the building to blend in with its surroundings.*

survey/examine/explore your surroundings (=look at them) *He switched on the light and examined his surroundings.*

adapt to your surroundings (=change and be successful there) *The troops had to adapt to their new surroundings quickly.*

PREPOSITIONS

in ... surroundings *The same piece of furniture can look completely different in different surroundings.*

surveillance *n*

when the police, army etc watch a person or place carefully because they may be connected with criminal activities

> **Grammar**
> **Surveillance** is often used in the phrase **under surveillance**.

ADJECTIVES/NOUNS + surveillance

constant surveillance *Prisoners were under constant surveillance.*

close surveillance *He was not immediately arrested but was kept under close surveillance.*

electronic surveillance *Information from electronic surveillance showed that the man was involved in selling drugs.*

covert surveillance (=done secretly) *The evidence had been obtained by covert surveillance.*

video/camera/satellite surveillance *More and more public areas are kept under video surveillance.*

police/government surveillance *The man had been under police surveillance for some time.*

VERBS

keep/place sb/sth under surveillance (=watch them) *The suspects were kept under surveillance.*

carry out surveillance (*also* **conduct surveillance** *formal*): *The man was disturbed by guards who were carrying out surveillance on the base.*

surveillance + NOUNS

a surveillance operation *A police surveillance operation had been taking place at the house.*

a surveillance system *A new video surveillance system has been installed.*

a surveillance camera *Surveillance cameras in the restaurant showed the two men talking.*

surveillance equipment *Using sophisticated surveillance equipment, they are able to monitor the movements of suspected terrorists.*

a surveillance plane/aircraft *Australian surveillance aircraft may soon assist in spotting pirate ships entering the waters.*

a surveillance flight *The US has increased surveillance flights along the border.*

PREPOSITIONS

under surveillance *The group had been under surveillance by the security services.*

surveillance of sb/sth *Police conducting surveillance of a stolen car saw two men getting into it.*

surveillance by sb *The suspect disappeared despite surveillance by the police.*

survey Ac *n*

a set of questions that you ask a large number of people in order to find out about their opinions or behaviour

ADJECTIVES

a recent/new survey *According to a recent survey, students buy an average of 11 books a year for their courses.*

an annual survey *Every council will be required to conduct an annual survey of residents.*

a national/nationwide survey *A national survey revealed that one in four 15-year-olds smokes regularly.*

a full/comprehensive/extensive survey *We conducted an extensive survey asking patients to suggest ways in which the service could be improved.*

a detailed survey *The author carried out a detailed survey of 32 organizations in Japan and Korea.*

a quick/brief survey *They did a quick survey of visitors to the museum.*

a preliminary survey (=it happens before something more important) *A preliminary survey revealed that most fans were in favour of the club moving to a bigger stadium.*

NOUNS + survey

an opinion survey *Opinion surveys showed*

consistently that unemployment remained a matter of concern.

a customer survey *They have begun to listen carefully to their customers through customer surveys.*

VERBS

carry out/do a survey (*also* **conduct a survey** *formal*): *The survey was carried out by Warwick University.*

take part in/participate in a survey *Over 2,000 participants took part in the survey.*

complete a survey *The survey only takes about ten minutes to complete.*

publish a survey *The survey will be published in the 'British Medical Journal'.*

a survey shows/reveals sth *Our survey showed that many women are afraid to go out alone at night.*

a survey finds sth *A survey found that 37% of students were born outside the country.*

a survey suggests sth *The survey suggests that young men today spend more time thinking about their careers.*

PREPOSITIONS

a survey of sth *According to a survey of city residents, garbage collection was the city service people liked most.*

in a survey *In a recent survey, orchids were voted the nation's most popular houseplant.*

PHRASES

based on/according to a survey *According to a survey, house prices have risen by 1.5% in the last three months.*

the results/findings of a survey *The results of the survey have not yet been analysed.*

a survey of the literature *Near the beginning of your thesis you should include a survey of the literature published on the subject.*

survival Ac *n*

a situation in which someone or something continues to live or exist

ADJECTIVES

long-term survival (=someone's or something's ability to continue to exist for a long time) *The long-term survival of the organization is at risk.*

economic survival *The country depends on tourism for its economic survival.*

political survival *The prime minister is fighting for his political survival.*

continued survival *The continued survival of this species of dolphin seems uncertain.*

survival + NOUNS

the survival rate *The survival rate of these animals when they are returned to the wild is low.*

sb's survival instinct (=a natural ability to know how to survive) *My survival instinct told me to run.*

survival skills *They learned survival skills from the local Indian tribe.*

a survival strategy *What's the best survival strategy for small businesses in a recession?*

a survival kit (=a set of equipment that will keep you alive in dangerous conditions) *Nobody should go into this desert without a survival kit and plenty of water.*

VERBS

fight/struggle for survival *Many construction companies are fighting for survival.*

ensure the survival of sth/sb (=make sure they survive) *Controlling land development would ensure the survival of many types of wildlife.*

owe your survival to sb/sth *The frogs owe their survival to a conservation programme.*

PREPOSITIONS

the survival of sth/sb *The new laws are designed to ensure the survival of these tigers.*

PHRASES

sb's chance(s) of survival (*also* **sb's survival chances**) *He knew that his chances of survival were small.*

sb's fight/struggle/battle for survival *Their lives had been one long struggle for survival.*

the survival of the fittest (=the strongest will survive - first used by Charles Darwin) *Evolution is all about the survival of the fittest.*

survive Ac *v*

to continue to live or exist, especially after something bad has happened

PHRASES

be lucky to survive (sth) *He was lucky to survive the crash.*

be likely/unlikely to survive (sth) *We were told that the baby would be unlikely to survive.*

manage to survive *Despite economic recession, most companies have managed to survive.*

struggle to survive *People are struggling to survive in freezing conditions.*

ADJECTIVES

survive unscathed (=without being hurt - used about people) *He was grateful to survive unscathed.*

survive intact (=without being damaged - used about things) *Unfortunately, few of the manuscripts have survived intact.*

ADVERBS

sth still survives *This fifteenth-century building still survives.*

miraculously survive (sth) (=in a way that is lucky and very unexpected) *One victim miraculously survived despite being shot 18 times.*

barely survive (sth) *Many of the towns barely survived the air raids.*

somehow survive (sth) (=in a way that you cannot explain) *The glass bottle had somehow survived the journey intact.*

suspect[1] *v*

to think that something is probably true, especially something bad

ADVERBS

strongly suspect sth *I strongly suspect the rumour may be true.*

never suspect sth *Her parents never suspected she was pregnant.*

be widely suspected (=by many people) *He is widely suspected of ordering the massacre.*

have always suspected sth (*also* **have suspected sth all along**) (=all the time) *Police had suspected all along that the husband was the murderer.*

have long suspected sth (=for a long time) *People have long suspected that he was involved in the princess's death.*

PREPOSITIONS

suspect sb of sth *They suspected her of being a spy.*

PHRASES

begin to suspect sth *I was beginning to suspect that she didn't love me at all.*

have reason to suspect sth *Do you have any reason to suspect that he is not telling the truth?*

suspect[2] *n*

someone who is thought to be guilty of a crime

ADJECTIVES

the main/chief/prime suspect *She was the prime suspect in a murder case.*

the number one suspect (=the main suspect) *The person who finds the body is often the number one suspect.*

a possible/potential suspect *The police have drawn up a list of possible suspects.*

a likely suspect *For a shooting like this, the Mafia were always the likely suspects.*

NOUNS + suspect

a murder/burglary/terror etc suspect *The murder suspect is a man in his early 20s.*

VERBS

arrest a suspect *Detectives arrested the suspect after a five-day operation.*

detain a suspect (=keep them under arrest at a police station etc) *Two suspects were detained for further questioning.*

name sb as a suspect *A British man was yesterday named as a suspect in the bombings.*

question/interrogate/interview a suspect *Police confirmed that six suspects are being questioned.*

PREPOSITIONS

a suspect in sth *The 24-year-old man is the chief suspect in a recent bomb attack.*

suspend *v* THESAURUS **stop[1] (3)**

suspicion *n*

1 a feeling that someone is probably guilty of doing something wrong or dishonest

VERBS

have your suspicions *Many of us had our suspicions about him, but we couldn't prove anything.*

harbour a suspicion *BrE formal*, **harbor a suspicion** *AmE formal* (=have a suspicion) *He began harbouring suspicions about his wife's male colleagues.*

confirm sb's suspicions (=show that someone's suspicions were right) *The letter confirmed my suspicions that she had lied.*

arouse suspicion (*also* **raise suspicions**) (=make people think that someone has done something wrong) *How was he able to kill his victims without arousing suspicion?*

allay/dispel suspicion *formal* (=make people stop having suspicions) *A public statement will help to allay people's suspicions.*

divert suspicion (=make people have suspicions about someone else) *He started the rumour to divert suspicion from himself.*

regard sb with suspicion *His activities were regarded with suspicion by detectives.*

suspicion falls on sb *Suspicion fell on a young man who had been seen near the scene of the crime.*

PHRASES

be/come under suspicion (=be thought to have probably done something wrong) *He was still under suspicion of fraud.*

grounds for suspicion (=reasons for suspicion) *Police can stop and search you if they have grounds for suspicion.*

above/beyond suspicion (=so honest that you are never thought to have done something wrong) *He regarded his old friend as above suspicion.*

on suspicion of sth (=because the police think you have committed a crime) *He was arrested on suspicion of involvement in the robbery.*

the finger of suspicion points to sb (=used for saying who you are suspicious of) *At first, the finger of suspicion pointed very clearly to the dead man's wife.*

2 a feeling you have that something is true, especially something bad

ADJECTIVES

a strong suspicion *She had a strong suspicion he was lying.*

a sneaking suspicion (=used when you think something is probably true) *We have a sneaking suspicion they're trying to put together a deal without us.*

a nasty/awful suspicion *I had a nasty suspicion that she was right.*

not have the slightest suspicion (=someone did not know about something at all) *He never* *had the slightest suspicion that she was in love with him.*

a vague suspicion (=very slight) *I had the vague suspicion that she was enjoying my embarrassment.*

a nagging suspicion (=one that you have all the time) *I had a nagging suspicion that he wasn't telling me the whole truth.*

VERBS

have a suspicion *I have a suspicion that he forgot to post the letter.*

suspicion grows *Suspicion grew that we were going to lose our jobs.*

suspicious *adj*

1 thinking that someone might be guilty of doing something wrong or dishonest

ADVERBS

deeply/highly suspicious (=extremely suspicious) *People are deeply suspicious of politicians.*

increasingly suspicious (=more and more suspicious) *She had grown increasingly suspicious about Deng's relationship with her husband.*

a little suspicious (*also* **a bit suspicious** *informal*): *The singer is a little suspicious of journalists.*

VERBS

become suspicious *The driver became suspicious when the man refused to say where he wanted to go.*

make sb suspicious *His quiet life made the police suspicious.*

NOUNS

a suspicious look/expression/glance *She gave me a suspicious glance.*

a suspicious mind *I'm not interested in his money - you've got a very suspicious mind!*

PREPOSITIONS

suspicious of sb/sth *I was suspicious of her motives.*

suspicious about sth *His colleagues became suspicious about his behaviour.*

2 if someone or something seems suspicious, they make you think that something dishonest or illegal is happening

ADVERBS

deeply/highly suspicious (=extremely suspicious) *The two men were behaving in a highly suspicious manner.*

a little suspicious (*also* **a bit suspicious** *informal*): *It may look a little suspicious if we ask him about the money.*

NOUNS

a suspicious character *There were some suspicious characters standing outside the house.*

suspicious behaviour/activities *Keep a close watch for any suspicious behaviour.*

a suspicious package/object (=one that might contain a bomb) *If you see a suspicious package, contact the police immediately.*

a suspicious death (=in which someone may have been murdered) *The authorities are questioning a man over the suspicious death of a woman in Strabane.*

VERBS

seem/look suspicious *This guy looked suspicious, with his crazy clothing and his long hair.*

treat sth as suspicious *The police are treating the boy's death as suspicious.*

PHRASES

in suspicious circumstances *The man disappeared in suspicious circumstances.*

something/anything suspicious *Did you notice anything suspicious about him?*

sustainable Ac *adj*

able to continue without using up resources and causing damage to the environment

ADVERBS

environmentally/ecologically sustainable *We must find methods of intensive farming that are environmentally sustainable.*

NOUNS

sustainable development *The UN wants to encourage sustainable development in Africa.*

sustainable agriculture/farming/forestry *The government should do more to promote sustainable agriculture.*

sustainable energy *We need to move towards greener, more sustainable energy.*

sustainable tourism *A policy of sustainable tourism would be welcomed in the Himalayas.*

sustainable transport *Sustrans is a cycling charity which campaigns for sustainable transport in cities.*

a sustainable future *He believes that this type of fuel offers the most sustainable future for the planet.*

a sustainable source *Make sure you buy wood that has come from sustainable sources.*

a sustainable lifestyle *Many people are interested in living a more sustainable lifestyle.*

sustainable living *The group is calling for a strategy for sustainable living.*

THESAURUS: sustainable

eco-friendly, green, clean, renewable, sustainable, carbon-neutral, low-carbon, low-energy → **environmentally friendly**

sweat[1] *n*

salty liquid that comes out through your skin when you are hot etc

VERBS + sweat

be dripping with sweat *After two hours' climbing, their bodies were dripping with sweat.*

wipe the sweat from your brow/forehead *He wiped the sweat from his brow and carried on digging.*

be drenched/soaked with sweat (=covered in a lot of sweat) *His shirt was drenched with sweat.*

wake (up) in a sweat (=used when saying that someone is sweating when they wake up) *I woke in a sweat at five o'clock.*

break (into) a sweat (=begin to sweat when you are doing exercise or work) *He can run five miles without even breaking into a sweat.*

glisten with sweat (=be wet and shiny with sweat) *His chest glistened with sweat.*

sweat + VERBS

sweat runs/pours somewhere *My hand was shaking and sweat was pouring off my forehead.*

sweat trickles somewhere (=flows slowly) *I could feel the sweat trickling down my back.*

sweat stands out on sb's forehead (=there are drops of sweat on someone's forehead) *He looked exhausted and sweat stood out on his forehead.*

ADJECTIVES

stale sweat (=old and smelling bad) *The men's changing room smelt of stale sweat.*

PHRASES

be wet/damp with sweat *She had been exercising and her hair was damp with sweat.*

beads of sweat (=small round drops of sweat) *There were beads of sweat on his forehead.*

a trickle of sweat (=sweat that is flowing somewhere) *A trickle of sweat ran down my neck.*

sweat[2] *v*

to have drops of salty liquid coming out through your skin because you are hot, ill, frightened, or doing exercise

ADVERBS

sweat a lot *I sweat a lot when I'm exercising.*

sweat heavily (*also* **sweat profusely** *formal*) (=a lot) *By the time I reached the station, I was sweating profusely.*

sweat slightly *The palms of his hands were sweating slightly.*

VERBS + sweat

begin/start to sweat (*also* **begin/start sweating**) *I started sweating as soon as I walked out of the air-conditioned building.*

make sb sweat *Running up the hill had made him sweat.*

wake up sweating *Alix had a bad dream and woke up sweating.*

NOUNS + sweat

sb's palms/hands are sweating *Her palms started sweating and her heart started thumping.*

PHRASES

sweat with fear/anxiety/effort *She hid behind the door, sweating with fear.*

sweat blood (=work very hard to achieve something) *He sweated blood trying to build up the business.*

swift *adj* **THESAURUS** ▶ **fast[1] (1)**

swim *v*

to move yourself through water using your arms and legs

PHRASES

go swimming *Let's go swimming tomorrow.*

swim against the current/tide *She had to swim against a strong current to reach the rocks.*

VERBS

can swim *Can you swim?*

learn (how) to swim *I learned to swim when I was young.*

teach sb (how) to swim *That summer, Fabio taught her how to swim.*

know how to swim *The kids know how to swim, but they're not strong swimmers.*

be able to swim *It was fortunate that you were able to swim.*

PREPOSITIONS/ADVERBS

swim in sth *That afternoon, we swam in the pool.*

swim across sth *He swam across the lake to the island.*

swim ashore (=to the shore of the sea, lake, or river) *Luckily, she managed to swim ashore.*

swim away *The seals swam away as the boat approached.*

> Instead of saying **go swimming**, you can also say **go for a swim**: *Do you want to **go for a swim** tomorrow?*

swing[1] *v*

to move forwards and backwards or from one side to another from a particular point, or to make something do this

ADVERBS

swing (sth) back and forth *He was swinging his bag back and forth.*

swing (sth) from side to side *She swung her legs from side to side.*

swing wildly *He swung wildly on the rope, reaching out desperately with his feet.*

swing freely *He walked along, his arms swinging freely.*

NOUNS

sb's arms/legs/feet swing *Let your arms swing as you walk.*

swing your arms/legs/feet *The girls sat on stools swinging their feet.*

PREPOSITIONS

swing sth by sth *She was swinging her schoolbag by its strap.*

swing² *n* THESAURUS ▶ change²

switch¹ *n*

a piece of equipment that starts or stops the flow of electricity to a machine, light etc when you push it

NOUNS + switch

a light switch *He reached for the light switch.*

an on-off switch *I couldn't find the on-off switch.*

the power switch *The power switch is on the side of the computer.*

VERBS

press a switch *He pressed a switch on the wall and the door opened.*

flick/flip a switch (=move it so something starts or stops) *You start the fan by flipping this switch.*

throw a switch (=move it so something starts or stops, especially something big) *Could a nuclear war really be started by someone just throwing a switch?*

turn on/off a switch *I turned off the switch and the whole room went dark.*

PREPOSITIONS

the switch for sth *Where's the switch for the air conditioning?*

PHRASES

at the flick/touch of a switch (=very quickly and easily, with a switch) *On sunny days, the car roof folds back at the flick of a switch.*

switch² *v*

1 to make something start or stop working, by pressing something

PREPOSITIONS/ADVERBS

switch sth on *Can you switch the television on?*

switch sth off *Don't forget to switch off the computer.*

switch out the light *Wycliffe opened the door and waited for her to switch out the lights.*

2 to change from doing or using one thing to doing or using another

ADVERBS

switch easily/simply *Customers can easily switch from one supplier to another.*

switch back and forth (=repeatedly from one thing to another then back) *The actor seems uncertain of his accent, switching back and forth between Scottish and Irish.*

switch seamlessly (=so that the change is not noticed) *The film switches suddenly and seamlessly from comedy to drama.*

NOUNS

switch sides (=start supporting someone or something else) *Three senators switched sides and voted against the president.*

switch (your) allegiance (=start supporting someone else) *Most of his supporters had switched their allegiance to his rival.*

switch channels (=start watching a different TV channel) *He quickly switched channels to avoid seeing the result of the game.*

switch tactics *If the party loses a lot of popular support, they may have to switch tactics.*

switch your attention/focus to sth *After studying French for years, he has now switched his attention to Spanish.*

switch brands *Many consumers will switch brands to support companies they see as socially responsible.*

PREPOSITIONS

switch to sth *She has switched to tennis as her main sport.*

switch from sth *Tourists are now using cash machines abroad, switching from traveller's cheques.*

switch between sth and sth *He switches easily between English and Korean.*

sword *n*

a weapon with a long pointed blade and a handle

VERBS

be armed with a sword *He was attacked by two men armed with swords.*

carry a sword (=have one with you) *The pirates all carried swords.*

draw your sword (=take it out of its container) *Hearing the noise, the guards drew their swords.*

raise your sword (=lift it up) *He raised his sword as if to strike.*

wield a sword (=hold it ready to attack someone) *The picture shows a knight wielding a huge sword.*

swing your sword (=move it in order to attack someone) *He swung his sword and wounded his opponent.*

sword + NOUNS

a sword fight *If Arthur got into a sword fight with this man, he knew he would be killed.*

syllabus *n*

a plan that says exactly what students at a school or college should learn in a subject

ADJECTIVES

the national syllabus *The national syllabus is used in schools all over the country.*

the official syllabus *Classes at the School of Dance follow the official syllabus of the British Ballet Association.*

NOUNS + syllabus

an examination syllabus *The course is designed to guide students through the examination syllabus.*

the school syllabus *The school syllabus is approved by the Ministry of Education.*

the history/biology/geography etc syllabus *The history syllabus offers students the opportunity to study the major international events of the 20th century.*

the course syllabus *The course syllabus includes extensive examination preparation.*

VERBS

include sth on a syllabus *Grammar exercises are included on the syllabus.*

take sth off a syllabus *Following complaints from parents, the book was taken off the syllabus.*

write a syllabus *He wrote the syllabus and selected the course materials.*

teach a syllabus *Most schools teach the syllabus designed by the state government.*

follow a syllabus *All teachers are obliged to follow the syllabus.*

a syllabus includes/covers sth *The syllabus covers all areas of accounting.*

syllabus + NOUNS

syllabus design *Teachers learn about syllabus design as part of their training.*

PREPOSITIONS

be on a syllabus *Two Shakespeare plays are on the English Literature syllabus this year.*

a syllabus for sth *The syllabus for mathematics consists of four sections.*

symbol Ac *n*

1 a letter, number, or sign that represents something such as a sound, an amount, or a chemical substance

ADJECTIVES

a chemical symbol *C is the chemical symbol for carbon.*

a mathematical symbol *The Greek letter Pi is used as a mathematical symbol.*

a special symbol *We use a system of special symbols to identify different products.*

a phonetic symbol (=one that represents a sound) *This phonetic symbol represents the vowel sound used in 'cup' and 'cuddle'.*

VERBS

a symbol stands for/represents sth *In chemistry the symbol H represents hydrogen.*

a symbol means sth *What does this symbol mean?*

PREPOSITIONS

a symbol for sth *A list of the symbols for the different sounds in English can be found at the front of the book.*

2 someone or something that represents a particular meaning, quality, or idea

ADJECTIVES/NOUNS + symbol

a national symbol *The eagle is the national symbol of the USA.*

a powerful/potent symbol (=one that has a strong effect) *This shocking photograph became a powerful symbol of the horrors of war.*

a religious/political symbol *The cross is an important religious symbol for Christians.*

a traditional symbol *Red roses are the traditional symbol for love and romance.*

a universal symbol (=one that is understood by everyone) *The universal symbol of the Christian Church is the cross.*

a visual symbol (=one that you can see) *You can use visual symbols to help the child understand what you mean.*

a sex symbol (=a well-known person who is considered very sexually attractive) *She has dated sex symbols such as George Clooney.*

PREPOSITIONS

a symbol of sth *The dove is a symbol of peace.*

symbolic Ac *adj*

if something is symbolic, it is important because of what it represents

NOUNS

a symbolic gesture/act (=something you do that acts as a symbol) *The meeting between the two leaders is a symbolic gesture of cooperation.*

symbolic importance/significance/value *This place has great symbolic importance for Jews, Muslims, and Christians.*

ADVERBS

largely symbolic *The vote was largely symbolic.*

purely symbolic *Our protest was meant to be purely symbolic.*

highly/deeply symbolic *The bishops kiss the Pope's ring in a gesture that is deeply symbolic.*

PREPOSITIONS

symbolic of sth *The design of the palace is symbolic of the wealth and power of the princes.*

sympathetic *adj*

showing that you feel sorry for someone who has problems

ADVERBS

deeply sympathetic *The other officers remembered him as a patient and deeply sympathetic man.*

NOUNS

a sympathetic listener *Jill was a very sympathetic listener.*

a sympathetic ear (=someone who will listen to another person talking about their problems and show that they feel sorry for that person) *He needs a sympathetic ear.*

THESAURUS: sympathetic

generous, considerate, thoughtful, caring, sympathetic, compassionate, warm-hearted/kind-hearted, benevolent, benign, nice, good, sweet → **kind²**

sympathy *n*

1 the feeling of being sorry for someone who is in a bad situation

ADJECTIVES

great sympathy *I have great sympathy for the people affected by the earthquake.*

deep/deepest sympathy *We'd like to offer our deepest sympathy to Hilda and her family.*

heartfelt sympathy (=deep and sincere) *Heartfelt sympathy to our dear friend Sadie on the death of her mother.*

some/little/no sympathy *I don't like him much but I do have some sympathy for him.*

public sympathy *There was much public sympathy for the refugees.*

Deep sympathy and **deepest sympathy** are often used when someone has died.

VERBS

have/feel sympathy for sb *It's hard not to feel sympathy for the losing team.*

express/offer (your) sympathy *Everyone there expressed their sympathy.*

show (sb) sympathy *Critics showed little sympathy for him.*

get sympathy from sb *She didn't get much sympathy from her parents.*

win sympathy (=get it) *The woman claimed that she was seriously ill in an attempt to win sympathy.*

deserve sympathy *He doesn't deserve any sympathy – it's his own fault.*

play on sb's sympathy (=make someone feel sorry for you in order to get an advantage for yourself) *If that doesn't work, she knows how to play on his sympathy.*

expect sympathy *I know I can't expect any sympathy from her!*

attract sympathy *Rich people don't attract much public sympathy when things go wrong.*

lose sb's sympathy *He lost the sympathy of colleagues with his constant complaints.*

PREPOSITIONS

sympathy for sb *The attacker didn't show the slightest sympathy for his victims.*

sympathy from sb *She has attracted a lot of sympathy from many people.*

PHRASES

a message/letter of sympathy *We are grateful for all the messages of sympathy we have received.*

an expression of sympathy *I murmured an expression of sympathy.*

an outpouring of sympathy (=when a lot of people express sympathy) *The princess's death led to an outpouring of sympathy.*

have every sympathy for sb (=feel very sorry for someone – often used when you have had a similar experience yourself) *I have every sympathy for people who find it hard to give up smoking.*

you have my sympathy (=used when saying that you feel sorry for someone) *It must be difficult – you have my sympathy.*

extend your sympathy to sb *formal* (=express sympathy) *I'd like to extend my deepest sympathy to the victim's family.*

my/our sympathy goes out to sb *formal* (=used to formally express sympathy) *Our sympathy goes out to Peggy in her great loss.*

my/our sympathies are with sb *Our sympathies are with the families of the victims.*

2 belief in or support for something, especially in politics

ADJECTIVES

political sympathies *Officers should not be appointed on the basis of their political sympathies.*

liberal/left-wing/communist etc sympathies *It is a group with left-wing sympathies.*

VERBS

sb's sympathies lie with sb/sth *Anne's sympathies lay strongly with the Conservative Party.*

PREPOSITIONS

sympathy with sb/sth *I have some sympathy with the organization's aims.*

in sympathy with sth *The only person not in sympathy with this plan was my father.*

symptom *n*

something wrong with your body or mind which shows that you have a particular illness

ADJECTIVES

physical symptoms *Depressed people often complain of physical symptoms such as headaches.*

severe symptoms *If the baby develops severe symptoms, call an ambulance.*

mild symptoms *The disease can be serious even where there are only mild symptoms.*

a common symptom *By far the most common symptom of the disease is a sore throat.*

a classic symptom (=a very typical symptom) *These are all classic symptoms of hay fever.*

withdrawal symptoms (=symptoms you get when you stop taking a substance) *People who try to give up smoking usually get withdrawal symptoms.*

S

VERBS

have symptoms *We both had the same symptoms.*

experience/suffer symptoms *I had suffered mild symptoms of asthma as a child.*

show symptoms *The patient is showing symptoms of a fever.*

display/exhibit symptoms *formal* (=show symptoms) *She was displaying symptoms of stress.*

cause symptoms *Make a note of which foods cause the symptoms.*

relieve/alleviate symptoms *formal* (=make them less severe) *Take aspirin to relieve the symptoms.*

exacerbate/aggravate symptoms *formal* (=make them worse) *Hot weather seems to exacerbate the symptoms.*

recognize symptoms *Luckily, the nurse recognized the symptoms and took action.*

symptoms persist *formal* (=they do not stop) *If the symptoms persist, see your doctor.*

symptoms disappear *The symptoms usually disappear after a few days.*

PREPOSITIONS

a symptom of sth *These marks on the skin are a common symptom of the illness.*

syndrome *n*

an illness or medical condition which consists of a particular set of physical or mental problems

VERBS

suffer from a syndrome *The doctor has treated many people suffering from this syndrome.*

diagnose sb with a syndrome (=find out that someone has a syndrome) *She was diagnosed with the syndrome when she was a child.*

cause a syndrome *Some syndromes are caused by the lack of a particular chemical in the body.*

a syndrome affects sb/sth *This syndrome affects both men and women.*

> **Syndrome** is often used in the names of specific diseases or medical conditions, for example **Down's syndrome**.

synthetic *adj* THESAURUS **artificial**

system *n*

1 a group of related parts that work together

ADJECTIVES/NOUNS + system

a heating system (=in a building) *We're waiting for the heating system to be repaired.*

an alarm/security system *A new alarm system has been installed.*

an air-conditioning system *The building hasn't got an air-conditioning system.*

the rail/road system (=all the roads or railways in a country) *Traffic problems are made worse by the country's inadequate road system.*

the transport system *The snow brought the transport system to a halt.*

sb's digestive/reproductive/nervous system (=in someone's body) *These vitamins are essential for a healthy nervous system.*

sb's immune system (=that keeps your body healthy) *You are more likely to get the infection if your immune system is weak.*

an operating system (=that makes all a computer's programs work together) *At the time, we were using the Windows XP operating system.*

VERBS

install a system (=put it into a building) *Our security system is simple to install.*

build/design/develop a system *The city has built a system to treat and reuse water.*

a system works *The alarm system wasn't working.*

a system fails/breaks down *If the air-conditioning system breaks down, staff will have to be sent home.*

2 a way of organizing or doing things

ADJECTIVES/NOUNS + system

an effective/efficient system *Schools must develop an effective system for dealing with bullying.*

an inefficient system *He described the tax system as inefficient and unfair.*

a complex/complicated system *The Australian health care system is extremely complex.*

an elaborate system (=carefully planned and with many details) *The proposal has to get through an elaborate system of committees.*

the current/existing system *The current system of staff reporting is too complicated.*

the political system *Britain's political system is different from that of the US.*

the legal/justice system *The country is rightly proud of its legal system.*

the electoral/voting system *He campaigned to change the voting system.*

the educational/education/school system *England's education system requires children to be in school by the age of five.*

the economic/banking/tax system *There are fears that the whole banking system could collapse.*

the health care system *The West should be helping developing countries to modernize health care systems.*

VERBS

have a system *Birds have a complicated system of courtship.*

use/run/operate a system *We operate a computerized booking system.*

develop a system (=create a new one) *The Environment Agency has developed a new national flood warning system.*

introduce a system (=start to use it) *The government has introduced a system of student loans.*

adopt a system (=decide to use it) *They decided to adopt the electoral system used in Britain.*

a system operates/works (=exists and is used) *He tried to explain how the planning system operates.*

a system works (=is successful) *The current complaints system does not work.*

a system breaks down/fails *Our communication systems seem to have broken down.*

a system collapses (=fails completely) *The European Exchange Rate system collapsed in the 1970s.*

modernize/reform a system *We need to reform the electoral system.*

PREPOSITIONS

a system for doing sth *We've got a good system for dealing with customer orders.*

under a system *Under the present system, there is no flexibility.*

PHRASES

a system of government/education/justice etc *She favoured a presidential system of government.*

systematic *adj* THESAURUS **careful**

S

Tt

table *n*

1 a piece of furniture with a flat top supported by legs

ADJECTIVES/NOUNS + table

a kitchen/dining-room/bedside table *They were chatting around the kitchen table.*

the dinner/breakfast table *Will you clear the breakfast table?*

a coffee table (=a low table that you put cups, newspapers etc on) *Dale put her glass down on the coffee table.*

a side table (=a small table, especially one that you put next to a wall) *Darius noticed a china vase on the side table.*

a picnic table *There are some wooden picnic tables in the park.*

the top table *BrE*, **the head table** *AmE* (=the table where the most important people sit at a formal meal, for example at a wedding) *The wedding couple and their parents usually sit at the top table.*

VERBS

set/lay the table (=put knives, forks etc on a table before a meal) *Mom asked me to set the table.*

clear the table (=take plates etc off) *Do you want me to clear the table?*

sit at a table *He was sitting at a corner table.*

sit around a table *We sat around the table and talked.*

get up from/leave the table *She stood up from her chair and left the table.*

book/reserve a table (=in a restaurant) *I've booked a table for four at a local restaurant.*

a table is groaning with sth (=there is a lot of food on it) *The tables were groaning with cakes and desserts.*

PREPOSITIONS

on a table *Amy put the newspaper on the table.*

at a table (=used when people are sitting at a table) *The talk at the table was mainly about horses.*

under the table *A dog lay under the table, asleep.*

PHRASES

at the head of the table (=in the place where the most important person sits) *My father always sat at the head of the table.*

2 a list of facts, numbers, or information arranged in rows across and down a page

VERBS

a table shows sth *The table shows the temperatures in each country during 2010.*

compile/produce a table *Compile a table comparing the data from both countries.*

publish a table *They published a table showing the best schools in Britain.*

PHRASES

the table of contents (=the list at the front of a book, report, document etc that shows what is in it) *The table of contents should be on a separate page at the beginning.*

tablet *n*

a small round hard piece of medicine which you swallow

ADJECTIVES/NOUNS + tablet

a sleeping tablet (=one that helps you sleep) *Sleeping tablets can be addictive.*

a headache/indigestion/malaria etc tablet (=one used to treat or prevent a condition) *I've got a bad stomach and I need to get some indigestion tablets.*

a vitamin tablet *Some people think that taking vitamin tablets stops you from getting colds and flu.*

VERBS

take a tablet *You need to take the tablets 3 times a day, after meals.*

prescribe tablets (=a doctor says that someone should take the tablets and writes a note so that the person can get them) *The doctor prescribed some tablets to help reduce the pain.*

PREPOSITIONS

tablets for sth *I have to take tablets for my blood pressure.*

be on tablets *spoken* (=be taking tablets) *He's on tablets for his heart.*

PHRASES

in tablet form *Although this drug is available in tablet form it is often prescribed as a powder.*

taboo *n*

a custom that says you must avoid a particular activity or subject, either because it is considered offensive or because your religion does not allow it

ADJECTIVES

a social/cultural/religious taboo *There is a social taboo about asking a woman her age.*

an ancient taboo *The custom is based on an ancient taboo.*

the ultimate taboo (=most serious) *To lose the respect of colleagues is the ultimate taboo in Chinese society.*

VERBS

break a taboo (*also* **violate a taboo** *formal*): *He was a daring artist who broke many taboos.*

observe a taboo (=not do something that is considered offensive or unacceptable) *The family still observe the old taboo against eating meat on Fridays.*

consider sth (a) taboo *Asking someone how much they earn is considered a taboo in our culture.*

PREPOSITIONS

the taboo against/on sth *We were careful to observe the taboo against holding hands in public.*

the taboo surrounding sth (=relating to something) *The princess's visit did much to remove the taboo surrounding the disease.*

tackle *v*

to try to deal with a difficult problem

ADVERBS

tackle sth head-on (=in a direct and determined way) *The issue of cost must be tackled head-on.*

tackle sth directly *We cannot improve people's lives without directly tackling the causes of poverty.*

tackle sth effectively *They need to work together to tackle the problem effectively.*

tackle sth successfully *The school has tackled the issue of bullying very successfully.*

tackle sth properly *Western nations are only now beginning to tackle terrorism properly.*

tackle sth seriously *Until the council tackles this question seriously, no progress will be made.*

tact *n*

care not to upset other people

ADJECTIVES

great/considerable tact *The manager dealt with the situation with great tact.*

the utmost tact (=very great tact) *She behaved with the utmost tact.*

VERBS

use tact (*also* **exercise tact** *formal*): *You need to use tact when you have to tell someone the truth about themselves.*

need tact (*also* **require tact** *formal*): *Helping people with marriage problems requires a great deal of tact and patience.*

handle sth with tact/deal with sth with tact *She handled the matter with a great deal of tact.*

lack tact *He often lacked tact in expressing his views.*

PHRASES

with your usual tact *She answered the question with her usual tact and sensitivity.*

tact and diplomacy *It was a delicate situation that required tact and diplomacy.*

tactic *n*

a method that you use to achieve something

ADJECTIVES/NOUNS + tactic

a delaying tactic (=an action which gives you more time) *His question about the rules was just another delaying tactic.*

scare tactics (=in which you say that something very bad will happen if someone does not do what you want) *The prime minister accused his opponents of scare tactics.*

shock tactics (=in which you deliberately try to shock people) *The charity resorted to shock tactics to try to get its message across.*

strong-arm tactics/bullying tactics (=the use of force, violence, or threats) *The government used strong-arm tactics to make people vote for them.*

underhand/unfair tactics (=actions which are not fair or honest) *The other company used underhand tactics to get the contract.*

a diversionary tactic (=an action which draws attention away from something) *Before the attack, nearby areas were bombed as a diversionary tactic.*

a sales tactic *When he offered to lower the price, I thought this was a sales tactic.*

defence tactics *Military officers are busy studying the defence tactics used during the Second World War.*

VERBS

use a tactic *We used various tactics to get their support.*

employ/adopt a tactic *formal* (=use a tactic) *Lizards and insects employ similar tactics to defend themselves, for example by changing colour to match their surroundings.*

change/switch tactics *The England team switched tactics in the second half.*

resort to a tactic (=use it after trying other methods) *He would never resort to such violent tactics.*

a tactic works (=is successful) *The tactic worked and he agreed to marry her.*

PREPOSITIONS

a tactic of doing sth *This tactic of not speaking to the media has made her very unpopular.*

a tactic for doing sth *Our tactic for keeping customers happy is simply to provide an excellent service.*

PHRASES

a change of tactics *They were losing 2–1 at half-time, but a change of tactics brought a 3–2 win.*

tactless *adj* THESAURUS **careless**

tag *n*

a small piece of paper, plastic etc attached to something to show what it is, who owns it, what it costs etc

NOUNS + tag

a price tag *The price tag said $49.*

a name tag (*also* **an identity/ID tag**) *Every baby in the hospital has a name tag on his or her wrist.*

a security tag (=to prevent something being stolen) *Expensive items have security tags which have to be removed at the checkout.*

a gift tag (=a tag attached to a gift that says who it is from) *I need to buy wrapping paper and gift tags.*

a luggage tag *BrE*, **a baggage tag** *AmE*: *The travel company sent the plane tickets and luggage tags.*

ADJECTIVES

an electronic tag (=which contains or sends information in electronic form) *All the animals are fitted with an electronic tag so we can track their location.*

PHRASES

put a tag on sth/attach a tag to sth *Staff at the airport check your ticket, your passport, and put a tag on your luggage.*

tail *n*

the part that sticks out at the back of an animal's body, which it can move

ADJECTIVES

a long/short tail *The bird has a yellow beak and a long black tail.*

a bushy tail (=with long thick fur) *My cat has a soft bushy tail.*

a prehensile tail *formal* (=able to hold things) *Many monkeys have prehensile tails.*

VERBS

a dog wags its tail (=quickly moves it from side to side) *The dog looked up at him and wagged its tail.*

a cow swishes its tail (=quickly moves it from side to side) *The cow wandered off, swishing her tail.*

tail + NOUNS

tail feathers *The bird's wings and tail feathers were a beautiful purple colour.*

take *v*

1 to move someone or something from one place to another, or have something with you when you go somewhere

PREPOSITIONS/ADVERBS

take sb/sth to a place *I took my coat to the cleaner's.*

take sb/sth with you *His wife went to Australia, taking the children with her. | Don't forget to take your passport with you.*

take sb/sth home *Would you mind taking Susie home?*

take sth back *I took the books back to the library.*

2 to react in a particular way when you are told about something, or when something happens

ADVERBS

take sth badly *"How did she take the news?" "She took it pretty badly - she was very upset."*

take sth well *The children took the news better than I expected.*

3 to do something - used about tests and everyday actions such as going for a walk or having a shower

THESAURUS: take

make, give, take, commit, carry out, conduct, perform, undertake, implement → do

4 to steal something

THESAURUS: take

take, nick, rob, mug, burgle, hold up, loot, ransack, defraud, embezzle, poach, plagiarize → steal

5 to write something

THESAURUS: take

put, enter, type in/key in, take, sign, fill out/in, transcribe, jot down, scribble, scrawl, dash off → write (1)

takeover *n*

when one company takes control of another by buying more than half its shares

ADJECTIVES

a hostile takeover (=one that is not wanted by the company being bought) *The company is fighting a hostile takeover by another airline.*

a corporate takeover (=of a large company) *Corporate takeovers often result in the loss of hundreds of jobs.*

a proposed takeover (=one that has been formally suggested) *The European Commission stopped the proposed takeover.*

a major takeover *It was the second major takeover this week.*

VERBS

launch a takeover (=start it) *The company has just launched a takeover of another firm.*

complete a takeover *Chase Manhattan completed a takeover of J.P. Morgan to become J.P. Morgan Chase.*

prevent/fight/resist a takeover *The managers are doing everything they can to prevent the takeover.*

announce a takeover *Harbinger announced the takeover of Applica on October 19th.*

takeover + NOUNS

a takeover bid/offer *The company may become*

the target of a takeover bid as a result of recent business problems.

a takeover attempt *The firm fought off a £1.8 billion takeover attempt.*

a takeover battle (=in which someone tries to prevent a takeover) *Nestlé and Suchard had been involved in a takeover battle for the ownership of a Belgian chocolate company.*

PREPOSITIONS

a takeover of sth *Polygram has announced the takeover of A&M Records.*

a takeover by sth *The company is facing a takeover by General Motors.*

tale *n*

a story, especially about exciting imaginary events

ADJECTIVES/NOUNS + tale

a fairy tale (=a traditional children's story) *It looked like a castle from a fairy tale.*

a folk tale (=a traditional story) *The story is from a book of Scottish folk tales.*

a cautionary tale (=one that is told to warn someone about the dangers of something) *This cautionary tale shows the dangers of trying to make quick profits.*

a tall tale (=one that is difficult to believe and unlikely to be true) *She enjoyed making up tall tales to tell the children.*

a morality tale (=giving advice on how to behave) *The movie is clearly intended as a modern morality tale.*

VERBS

tell a tale (*also* **recount a tale** *formal*): *He liked telling tales of his adventures in the wilderness.*

weave/spin a tale *formal* (=tell or write it) *As a writer, she has a talent for weaving a good tale.*

PREPOSITIONS

a tale of sth *These short stories are tales of greed and selfishness.*

a tale about sth *It is a Japanese tale about a tiny boy who lives in a teacup.*

talent *n*

a natural ability to do something well

ADJECTIVES

great/considerable/immense talent *He had a great talent for making money.*

exceptional talent (=unusually good talent) *Pamuk is a writer of exceptional talent.*

real talent *She has real talent and could become a top international player.*

natural talent *Dahl had a natural talent for seeing a story from a child's point of view.*

raw talent (=natural ability without much training) *He's got lots of raw talent but he needs a good coach.*

homegrown talent (=of people from within your own club, town, country etc) *There isn't enough homegrown talent in English Premier League soccer.*

untapped talent (=talented people whom the public does not know about) *There's a huge amount of untapped acting talent within local theatre groups.*

a hidden talent (=one that other people do not know about) *He has lots of hidden talents!*

precocious talent (=a lot of talent in a young person) *From an early age he displayed a precocious talent for computing.*

musical/artistic/creative etc talent *It was at school that her musical talents were spotted.*

VERBS

have talent (*also* **possess talent** *formal*): *Your son has a real talent for drawing.*

show talent *A few of the young players showed natural talent.*

use your talents *The students have been using their artistic talents to brighten up the school.*

develop your talent *A good teacher allows students to develop their talent to the full.*

waste your talents (*also* **squander your talents** *formal*): *She was an impressive player who was clearly wasting her talents at this club.*

spot/discover talent *He visits football grounds around the country in order to spot new talent.*

showcase talent (=give people the chance to show their talent publicly) *The competition is a way to showcase top UK talent in dance.*

foster/nurture talent (=encourage and develop people's talent) *The aim of these classes is to nurture talent.*

sb's talents flourish (=develop successfully) *The school created an atmosphere in which talent could flourish.*

sb's talent lies in sth (=used for saying what someone is good at) *His real talent lies in organizing parties.*

talent + NOUNS

a talent contest/show/competition *Winning a major talent contest can be the start of a career.*

a talent scout/spotter (=whose job is to find people with talent) *He worked as a talent scout for a top football club.*

PREPOSITIONS

a talent for (doing) sth *She realized that she had a talent for making people laugh.*

with/of talent (=who has talent) *There are plenty of players with talent, but you need more than that to succeed.*

without talent *He is young and handsome but, I'm afraid, completely without talent.*

PHRASES

a wealth of talent (=a large amount of talent) *There's a wealth of musical talent in our school.*

a pool of talent (=lots of talented people) *Employers can draw on an enormous pool of talent in this city.*

a man/woman of many talents *often humorous*: *He plays the violin and he bakes bread – a man of many talents!*

talented *adj*

having a natural ability to do something well

ADVERBS

highly talented *Brian Jones was a highly talented musician who could play several instruments.*

extremely/incredibly/hugely/enormously talented *The Canadian team are incredibly talented and very quick.*

exceptionally talented (=having an unusual amount of talent) *Drogba is an exceptionally talented player.*

> **THESAURUS: talented**
>
> skilled, talented, gifted, expert, accomplished, virtuoso → **skilful**

talk[1] *v*

to use words to communicate with someone about something

ADVERBS

talk loudly/quietly *Two men were talking loudly to each other outside the bar.*

talk openly/freely/candidly (=in an honest way and without hiding your feelings) *She talked openly about her divorce.*

talk freely (=without worrying if someone will hear you or disapprove of what you say) *We can talk freely without fear of being overheard.*

talk at length (=talk a lot about something, giving a lot of details) *In the interview he talks at length about his battle with alcohol.*

talk nonstop (=without any pauses) *While she was driving, Karen talked nonstop about her childhood and her family.*

talk endlessly (=for a long time, especially when this is boring or annoying) *The other women talked endlessly about their boyfriends.*

talk enthusiastically/excitedly/animatedly *She talks enthusiastically about her role in the movie.*

talk sensibly *Maybe we can talk about this more sensibly when you are not so tired.*

talk vaguely (=without exact details or plans) *They had talked vaguely about having a second child.*

talk directly *The comedian moved to the front of the stage so that he could talk directly to the audience.*

PREPOSITIONS

talk about sth *English people love to talk about the weather.*

talk of sth (=talk about something, often about future plans) *Hartigan talked of cutting taxes and running government like a business.*

talk to sb *Talk to your teacher if you're worried.*

talk about sth with sb *I didn't feel comfortable talking about it with my parents.*

PHRASES

be easy to talk to *Abbas was friendly and easy to talk to.*

be talking rubbish *BrE informal* (=be saying something that is silly or not true) *Don't believe a word he says – he's talking rubbish.*

talk with your mouth full (=talk and eat at the same time) *It's rude to talk with your mouth full.*

talk all the time about sth *He and I used to talk all the time about football.*

talk[2] *n*

1 an occasion when someone talks about something to a group of people

ADJECTIVES/NOUNS + talk

a brief/short talk *All visitors receive a brief talk on safety.*

an interesting/informative talk *Thank you for an interesting talk.*

an entertaining talk *The actor gave us a very entertaining talk on life in Hollywood.*

an introductory talk (=giving basic information about a subject) *The course begins with an introductory talk on the study of history.*

a pep talk (=intended to make someone feel confident and enthusiastic) *The director always had to give me a little pep talk before I went on stage.*

a pre-match talk (=by a coach to a player or team before a sports match) *I'd love to be in the dressing room for the pre-match talk.*

VERBS

give a talk (*also* **deliver/present a talk** *formal*): *The professor will give a talk on the history of the island.*

go to a talk (*also* **attend a talk** *formal*): *New students are invited to attend an informal talk in the main hall.*

hear a talk *The group heard a fascinating talk on the history of the region.*

PREPOSITIONS

a talk on/about sth *There will be a short talk on local wildlife before visitors are taken out into the park.*

a talk to sb *He's giving a talk to students at his old school.*

2 a conversation about something

ADJECTIVES

a long talk *I had a long talk with my parents.*

a little talk *I'm glad we've had this little talk.*

a serious talk *I need a serious talk with her before she goes to college.*

a quiet/private talk *Could we have a quiet talk when you're free?*

a good talk (=a long talk about important or

interesting things) *She was upset, but we've had a good talk and things are okay now.*

a nice talk *We all had lunch together and a nice talk.*

VERBS

have a talk *I must have a talk with Dad before I leave.*

PREPOSITIONS

a talk with sb *If there are any problems, have a talk with your teacher.*

a talk about sth *We must have a talk about holidays soon.*

3 formal discussions between governments, organizations etc

> **Grammar**
> Always plural in this meaning.

ADJECTIVES

direct talks *The government wants to have direct talks with the rebels.*

high-level talks (=involving very important people) *The announcement came after a morning of high-level talks.*

bilateral talks (=involving two groups or countries) *China and the US held bilateral talks.*

multilateral talks (=involving several groups or countries) *It is hoped that these multilateral talks will produce an agreement.*

round-table talks (=in which everyone involved can discuss things in an equal way) *The new rules were agreed after round-table talks between the company and the union.*

urgent talks *He flew to Washington for urgent talks with the president.*

NOUNS + talk

peace talks *A new round of peace talks will begin next month.*

trade talks *Trade talks between the EU and the US have once again collapsed.*

crisis talks (=talks to stop a situation getting worse or more dangerous) *The unions will hold crisis talks with the company in an attempt to save jobs.*

VERBS + talk

have/hold talks (*also* **conduct talks** *formal*): *The government is holding talks with the rebels to try to end the fighting.*

enter into talks (=start having talks) *The ambassador said that France was prepared to enter into talks on the issue.*

start/begin talks *China and the US have begun trade talks.*

initiate talks *formal* (=be the person or group that organizes or begins talks) *The president initiated talks with opposition forces.*

walk/pull out of talks (=leave before talks have finished) *The management walked out of talks with the union this morning.*

abandon talks *The talks were abandoned due to lack of progress.*

talk + VERBS

talks begin *Talks began in October and an agreement was signed two months later.*

talks continue *Talks will continue through the weekend.*

talks break down/collapse (=stop because of disagreement) *Talks broke down today between the Russian and Japanese delegations.*

talks resume (=begin again after stopping for a short period of time) *Talks resumed in Geneva after a month's break.*

talks end *The talks ended without a settlement being reached.*

talks fail *Talks on this issue have failed before.*

PREPOSITIONS

talks with sb *The organization has had talks with various community groups.*

talks between sb and sb *Trade talks between these major European nations will continue into next week.*

talks on/about sth *There must be further talks on pay and working conditions.*

PHRASES

a round of talks (=a series of talks that is part of a longer process) *A third round of talks was held in May.*

the breakdown/collapse of talks *The collapse of peace talks is a worrying development.*

be in talks with sb (=be involved in talks) *We're in talks with consumer groups about ways to improve our service.*

talks are under way *European leaders arrived last night and talks are now under way.*

tall *adj* THESAURUS high (1)

tank *n*

a large container for storing things such as liquid or gas

NOUNS

a petrol tank *BrE*, **gas tank** *AmE*: *He stopped to fill up the gas tank.*

a fuel tank *The plane's fuel tank caught fire.*

a water/oil tank *The hot water tank holds 25 gallons of water.*

an oxygen tank (=used to help you breathe) *The divers had oxygen tanks attached to their backs.*

a storage tank *The oil is kept in a big storage tank.*

ADJECTIVES

an empty tank *The gas tank was nearly empty.*

a full tank *We began our journey with a full tank of petrol.*

VERBS

fill (up) a tank *I went to the gas station to fill up the tank.*

refill a tank *The cars usually have to stop at least once during the race to have their fuel tanks refilled.*

empty a tank *She emptied the tank and filled it with fresh water.*

a tank contains sth *The tank contained radioactive waste.*

tantrum *n*

a sudden short period when someone, especially a child, behaves very angrily and unreasonably

VERBS

have/throw a tantrum *The little boy threw a tantrum when he wasn't allowed to watch TV.*

fly into a tantrum (=suddenly have a tantrum) *When she can't get what she wants, she flies into a tantrum.*

NOUNS

a temper tantrum (=a tantrum in which a child suddenly gets very angry) *All young children have temper tantrums from time to time.*

PREPOSITIONS

in a tantrum (=having a tantrum) *It is difficult trying to control a small child in a tantrum.*

tap *n*

1 *especially BrE* a piece of equipment for controlling the flow of water, gas etc from a pipe or container

ADJECTIVES/NOUNS + tap

the cold/hot tap *She scrubbed her hands under the cold tap.*

the kitchen/bath/garden tap *The water coming out of the kitchen tap looked cloudy.*

a mixer tap *BrE* (=one through which cold and hot water can run together) *He fitted a mixer tap to the bath.*

a dripping tap *I could hear a dripping tap.*

a running tap *If you burn your finger, hold it under a running tap.*

a leaking/leaky tap (=with drops of water coming from the end) *There were stains on the wall and the taps were leaky.*

VERBS

turn on a tap *Run some cold water into the bath before turning on the hot tap.*

turn off a tap *I forgot to turn the tap off.*

run a tap (=make water flow out of it) *She stood at the sink, running the tap to get a glass of cold water.*

a tap is running (=water is flowing out of it) *I think you must have left the tap running.*

a tap is dripping (=drops of water are coming out of it) *The noise of the tap dripping kept me awake.*

tap + NOUNS

tap water (=water that comes out of a tap) *I prefer drinking tap water, not bottled water.*

PREPOSITIONS

under a tap (=in the water flowing from a tap) *Rinse your hands under the hot tap.*

> **Tap** is used by British speakers. American speakers say **faucet**.

2 an act of hitting something lightly, for example to get someone's attention

ADJECTIVES

a gentle/little/soft tap *There was a gentle tap on the door.*

a sharp tap (=quite hard and loud) *Give the nail a few sharp taps with a hammer.*

VERBS

give sth/sb a tap *The woman gave the dog a gentle tap with her umbrella.*

hear a tap *He heard a light tap on the window.*

feel a tap *I felt a little tap on my arm.*

PREPOSITIONS

a tap at sth *There was a tap at the door.*

a tap on sth *She gave him a quick tap on his shoulder.*

tape Ac *n*

1 a long thin band of plastic with a sticky substance on it, used for fastening things together

ADJECTIVES

sticky tape *She attached the poster to the wall with some sticky tape.*

VERBS

hold sth together with tape *His glasses were held together with bits of tape.*

seal sth with tape *The box was firmly sealed with tape.*

2 narrow plastic material covered with a special magnetic substance, on which you can record sounds, pictures, or computer information

ADJECTIVES/NOUNS + tape

video tape *A video tape of the crime was used as evidence in court.*

audio tape *The interview was recorded on audio tape.*

a blank tape (=with nothing recorded on it) *The video camera wasn't working and the tape was blank.*

VERBS

play a tape *He played me a tape of a song he'd recorded from the radio.*

listen to/watch a tape *Police listened to a tape of the phone call.*

make a tape *The band made a tape of their music and sent it to the radio station.*

tape + NOUNS

a tape recorder/machine *A tape recorder is an essential piece of equipment for a journalist.*

a tape recording *Someone made a secret tape recording of the men discussing the robbery.*

PREPOSITIONS

a tape of sth *We watched a video tape of an old horror film.*

on tape *The newspaper says it has the entire interview on tape.*

target Ac *n*

1 something that you are trying to achieve

ADJECTIVES/NOUNS + target

an ambitious/high target *A 50% increase in sales seems a very ambitious target.*

a modest target (=not very high) *The agreement set fairly modest targets for reducing pollution.*

an achievable/realistic target *The target is achievable, but only by hard work.*

a financial target *Both businesses exceeded their financial targets.*

a sales/growth target *I'm confident we will meet our sales target by the end of the year.*

a spending/recycling target *Several departments have reduced their spending targets by over 20%.*

VERBS

meet/reach/achieve a target (=achieve what you want to achieve) *The government is unlikely to meet its target of building three million new homes in the next five years.*

set a target *The company has set ambitious targets.*

exceed a target (=achieve more than you wanted to) *We have exceeded our sales target of £200,000.*

chase a target (=try to achieve it) *The club is chasing a target of 50 points by the end of the season.*

target + NOUNS

a target date *The target date for completion of the building is next October.*

a target figure *The government has set a target figure for economic growth of 2%.*

a target audience (*also* **a target demographic** *formal*) (=the type of people that an organization wants as customers, readers, viewers etc) *That kind of music does not appeal to our target demographic.*

a target market (=the people or places that a company wants to do business with or in) *Our target market is young wealthy individuals in the 25-35 age range.*

PREPOSITIONS

on target (=it is likely you will achieve a target) *After today's win, Arsenal is still on target to win the championship.*

off target (=it is unlikely you will achieve a target) *Our current level of spending is way off target.*

a target of sth *We have set ourselves a savings target of £500 a month.*

a target for sth *My target for weight loss is five pounds per month.*

PHRASES

fall short of a target (=achieve less than you wanted to) *Car production at the plant has fallen short of its target by 5%.*

stay on/within target (=remain at a level that makes it likely you will achieve a target) *His job is to make sure the progress of the work stays on target.*

THESAURUS: target

goal, target, objective, ambition → **aim**

2 an object, person, or place that is deliberately chosen to be attacked

ADJECTIVES

a prime/obvious target (=the most suitable or most likely to be chosen) *Sporting events could become a prime target for terrorists.*

the main target *The rebel-held town is one of the main targets for US troops.*

an easy/soft target *Some thieves now regard schools as easy targets.*

a sitting target (=someone who is easy to attack) *In the open, the soldiers are sitting targets.*

a potential target (=which might be attacked) *Any area that attracts Western tourists is now a potential target.*

sb's intended target *The gunman missed his intended target.*

a military/civilian target *The group insists that its bombs were directed only against military targets.*

a legitimate target (=one that it is fair to attack) *The rebels consider trains carrying soldiers to be a legitimate target.*

VERBS

attack a target *They have attacked military targets such as army camps and airfields.*

hit a target *Not every bomb hits its target.*

miss a target *All of the missiles missed their target and no-one was killed.*

PREPOSITIONS

a target for sb/sth *Her public statements made her a target for terrorists.*

task *n*

a piece of work that must be done

ADJECTIVES

a difficult task *The task of selecting just five candidates is a difficult one.*

T

an impossible task *Finishing the job by five o'clock was an impossible task.*

a simple task *The children help with simple tasks like carrying water.*

sb's first/main task *Their first task was to rebuild the wall.*

a formidable/daunting task *formal* (=very difficult) *Achieving these targets will be a formidable task.*

an arduous task *formal* (=needing a lot of effort and hard work) *We began the arduous task of carrying the furniture to the top floor.*

an unenviable task (=very unpleasant or difficult) *He has the unenviable task of telling hungry people that there is no food.*

a thankless task (=a difficult but necessary job) *Driving a bus in London must be a pretty thankless task.*

VERBS

carry out/do a task (*also* **perform a task** *formal*): *We don't have enough staff to carry out this task.*

set/give sb a task (*also* **assign sb a task** *formal*): *I was given the task of writing his speech.*

take on a task (*also* **undertake a task** *formal*): *No-one else is willing to take on this difficult task.*

complete/finish a task *Your task must be completed by the end of the month.*

handle/tackle a task (=do it) *We needed someone more experienced to handle this task.*

a task faces sb *The task facing us is too difficult to finish in just a few weeks.*

PREPOSITIONS

the task of doing sth *He had the task of judging the competition.*

PHRASES

sth is not an easy task (*also* **sth is no easy task**) (=it is difficult) *Finding experienced staff is no easy task.*

sb's task is to do sth (*also* **the task of sb is to do sth**) *The manager's task is to get all the players working together as a team.*

the task ahead (=the thing that needs to be done) *We have to forget these recent disappointments and concentrate on the task ahead.*

taste[1] *n*

1 the feeling that is produced by a particular food or drink when you put it in your mouth

ADJECTIVES

a delicious/nice/pleasant taste *The taste was absolutely delicious.*

a nasty/unpleasant taste *The egg had a nasty taste.*

a strange/odd/peculiar/funny taste *The sweets have a rather peculiar taste.*

a strong taste *Some French cheeses have a very strong taste.*

a mild taste *The taste of the leaves is milder than the root.*

a sweet taste *The fruits have an excellent sweet taste.*

a bitter taste *I thought that the medicine had a slightly bitter taste.*

a sour taste *Lemons have a sour taste and it's usually best to add some sugar.*

a sharp taste (=very sour) *I used too much vinegar in the dressing and it had a sharp taste.*

a salty taste *Anchovies have rather a salty taste.*

a spicy taste *Add a little curry powder to give the soup a spicy taste.*

a creamy/buttery/fruity/nutty etc taste (=tasting of cream, butter etc) *The cookies had a very buttery taste.*

a bland taste (=not strong or interesting) *Some people find the taste of rice too bland.*

a distinctive/characteristic taste (=a taste which makes something different from other things) *The hop plant gives beer its distinctive bitter taste.*

an authentic taste (=like the real food of a country or area) *The food in the restaurant has that authentic French taste.*

VERBS

have a sweet/strange etc taste *The soup had a funny taste.*

give sth a taste *The spices gave the bread a rather interesting taste.*

like the taste *I don't like the taste of meat.*

enjoy the taste *He was enjoying the taste of the wine.*

improve/enhance the taste *A little salt helps to improve the taste of bread.*

spoil/ruin the taste *Don't add too much ketchup – it will ruin the taste.*

take away the taste (=make it go away) *I need something to take away the taste of the curry.*

leave a taste (in your mouth) *The coffee leaves a rather bitter taste in your mouth.*

PHRASES

sense of taste *Some birds have a highly developed sense of taste.*

2 the kind of things that someone likes: *He asked about my taste in music.* | *While she was in France she developed a taste for fine wines.*

ADJECTIVES/NOUNS + taste

similar tastes/the same taste *We have similar musical tastes.*

different tastes *Their tastes in movies were very different.*

expensive tastes *He was a man of expensive tastes.*

sophisticated tastes (=which show a lot of knowledge about something) *Amelia had developed quite sophisticated tastes in music – she liked the German composers, particularly Wagner.*

simple tastes (=you like simple things) *He was a man of simple tastes.*

strange/odd/eccentric tastes *She had strange tastes in colour.*

eclectic tastes (=liking a wide variety of different things) *My tastes in art are very eclectic.*

musical/literary/artistic taste *His musical tastes changed radically.*

your personal taste *Which one you choose is a question of personal taste.*

public/popular taste *The shop created a unique style of goods that appealed to the popular taste.*

an acquired taste (=something that people do not like at first) *This kind of tea is an acquired taste, but very refreshing.*

consumer tastes *Stores are always watching out for changes in consumer tastes.*

VERBS

have ... tastes *Josh and I have the same tastes.*

have a taste for sth (=like something) *She certainly has a taste for adventure.*

get/develop a taste for sth (*also* **acquire a taste for sth** *formal*) (=start to like something) *At university she developed a taste for performing.*

share a taste (=have the same taste as someone else) *You obviously share her taste in literature.*

appeal to/suit sb's tastes (=be the kind of thing that someone likes) *We have music to suit every taste.*

PREPOSITIONS

taste in sth *I'm not sure about his taste in furniture.*

PHRASES

be to sb's taste (=be something that someone likes) *If her books are not to your taste, there are plenty of books by other writers.*

be too bright/modern etc for sb's taste *The building was too modern for my taste.*

in the worst/best possible taste *The house was decorated in the worst possible taste.*

sth is a matter of taste (=different people have different opinions about what is good or right) *The choice of wood is largely a matter of taste.*

there's no accounting for taste (=used humorously to say that you do not understand why someone likes something) *I think his films are awful, but I suppose there is no accounting for taste.*

sth caters for/to all tastes (=it has things that everyone likes) *The magazine caters to all tastes.*

3 if you have a taste of something, you eat a little to find out what it is like

VERBS

have/try a taste *This cheesecake is delicious. You must have a taste!*

ADJECTIVES

a little taste *Can I try a little taste of your soup?*

taste² *v*

to have a particular kind of taste

ADJECTIVES

taste good/nice/delicious/great *The apples weren't very big but they tasted good.*

taste horrible/awful/disgusting/foul *The tea tasted absolutely disgusting.*

taste funny/odd/strange *These fruit drinks taste a bit funny at first.*

taste sweet/bitter/sour/salty *The coffee tasted too sweet.*

ADVERBS

taste strongly of sth *The water in the pool tasted strongly of chlorine.*

taste faintly/slightly/vaguely... *The sauce tasted slightly burned.*

PREPOSITIONS

taste of sth *The soup tastes of garlic.*

taste like sth *He makes a carrot wine that tastes like whisky.*

PHRASES

sweet-tasting/strong-tasting etc *They produce a range of sweet-tasting drinks aimed at children.*

tasty *adj* THESAURUS ▶ **delicious**

tax *n*

an amount of money that you must pay to the government according to your income, property, goods etc, and that is used to pay for public services

ADJECTIVES/NOUNS + tax

high taxes *Most people do not want to pay higher taxes.*

low taxes *The government promised lower taxes.*

income tax (=tax on money that you earn) *The rich should pay more income tax.*

sales tax (=tax on things you buy) *We have to pay 15% sales tax on everything we buy.*

a direct tax (=a tax on income) *The government's revenue comes mainly from direct taxes.*

an indirect tax (=a tax on things you buy) *The effect of indirect taxes is to raise the prices of goods.*

green taxes (=taxes to protect the environment) *The British government is considering new green taxes on cheap airline flights.*

inheritance tax (=tax on money, property etc that you have received from someone who has died) *We had to sell the house to pay the inheritance tax.*

corporation/corporate tax (=tax that businesses must pay on profits) *The rate of corporation tax was reduced.*

a flat (rate) tax (=a tax that is the same for different people or things) *Some people want to replace income tax with a flat rate tax.*

VERBS

pay tax *Many people feel they are paying too much tax.*

raise/increase taxes (*also* **put up taxes** *BrE*): *The government keeps putting up taxes on fuel.*

lower/cut/reduce taxes *Both parties have promised to cut taxes.*

impose/levy a tax on sb/sth (=officially say that someone must pay a tax) *They had the power to levy a tax on ships entering the port.*

introduce a tax *He wants to introduce a 10% tax on all goods and services.*

collect a tax *The tax collected on each packet of cigarettes in this state is 70% of the total price.*

tax + NOUNS

the tax rate (*also* **the rate of tax**) *The government reduced the basic rate of tax to 25p in the pound.*

tax cuts *He believes that big tax cuts will encourage economic growth.*

tax increases *He accused the president of planning the biggest tax increases in US history.*

tax incentives (=lower taxes that encourage people to do something) *We have introduced new tax incentives for businesses.*

a tax break (=a special reduction in tax) *The government will offer new tax breaks for families.*

a tax allowance (=the amount you can earn without paying tax on it) *The personal tax allowance is just under $10,000.*

tax relief *BrE* (=when you do not have to pay tax on part of what you earn, especially because you use it for a particular purpose) *You can get tax relief on private health insurance.*

the tax burden (=the amount of tax paid) *The total tax burden has risen only slightly.*

the tax year (=a period of 12 months used for calculating taxes) *In Britain, the tax year starts on April 6th.*

tax evasion (=the crime of not paying enough tax) *He was jailed for tax evasion.*

a tax return (=an official document on which you write information so that the tax you owe can be calculated) *Have you completed your tax return yet?*

PREPOSITIONS

a tax on sth *The government increased taxes on cigarettes and alcohol.*

PHRASES

for tax purposes *They are considered to be UK residents for tax purposes.*

sth is tax exempt/exempt from tax (=you do not have to pay tax on something) *This type of income is tax exempt.*

taxation *n formal*

the system of charging taxes

ADJECTIVES

high/heavy taxation *High taxation is bad for business.*

low taxation *The party has traditionally supported low taxation.*

increased taxation *Increased taxation on oil companies could bring in €31,000 million.*

corporate taxation (=taxes paid by companies) *Business leaders want the government to cut corporate taxation.*

personal taxation (=taxes paid by individual people rather than businesses) *Personal taxation has increased considerably under the present government.*

direct taxation (=taxes paid directly to the government rather than on goods, services etc) *Direct taxation will not be increased for people on average incomes.*

indirect taxation (=taxes on goods and services) *Indirect taxation is unfair because rich people pay the same as poorer people.*

general taxation (=taxes paid by everyone to the government) *Britain's national system of health care is largely funded from general taxation.*

local taxation (=taxes paid to local government) *Under the current system of local taxation, people pay tax according to the value of their home.*

VERBS

increase/raise taxation *The government is going to increase taxation on cigarettes.*

reduce/cut taxation *The party has promised to reduce taxation.*

introduce taxation *Motor vehicle taxation was introduced in 1909.*

taxation + NOUNS

a taxation rate *The country has one of the highest taxation rates in the EU.*

a taxation system *The taxation system is extremely complicated.*

PREPOSITIONS

before/after taxation *What was the company's profit after taxation?*

taxation on sb/sth *Should the government raise the level of taxation on the rich?*

PHRASES

an increase/reduction in taxation *There is likely to be a small increase in taxation.*

a level of taxation *The president may have to increase levels of taxation to pay off the US's huge debts.*

the burden of taxation (=the amount of tax you have to pay compared to other people) *The burden of taxation must not be increased on the poorer members of society.*

taxi *n*

a car and driver that you pay to take you somewhere

VERBS

take/get a taxi *We took a taxi to the hotel.*

go/come/arrive by taxi *I went home by taxi.*

hail a taxi (=wave or call to a taxi to stop for you to get in) *I rushed outside and hailed a taxi.*

call/phone for/order a taxi (=telephone for a taxi to come) *You call a taxi and I'll get our coats.*

call sb a taxi (=telephone for a taxi to come for someone else) *Call me a taxi, would you?*

get into/in/out of a taxi *He got into a taxi outside the station.*

⚠ Don't say 'get on a taxi'. Say **get in a taxi**.

taxi + NOUNS

a taxi ride *The centre of town is a five-minute taxi ride away.*

a taxi fare *She couldn't afford the £18 taxi fare.*

a taxi driver *He paid the taxi driver and got out.*

a taxi service *We operate a taxi service to and from the airport.*

a taxi rank *BrE*, **a taxi stand** *AmE* (=a place where taxis wait for customers) *There's a taxi rank just outside the hotel.*

tea *n*

a drink made by pouring boiling water onto dried leaves

ADJECTIVES/NOUNS + tea

hot tea *What I need is a nice cup of hot tea.*

iced tea/ice tea *I love drinking iced tea in the summer.*

sweet tea *I poured her a mug of sweet tea.*

strong/weak tea *You've made the tea too strong.*

black/white tea (=without milk or with milk) *I ordered black tea and toast.*

milky tea (=with a lot of milk) *We give the grandchildren milky tea.*

VERBS

drink tea *I usually drink tea with my breakfast.*

pour tea *She poured the tea and handed me a cup.*

tea + NOUNS

a tea break (=a short rest from work) *Let's have a ten-minute tea break.*

a tea shop/tea room (*also* **a teashop/tearoom**) (=a small restaurant where hot drinks and snacks are served) *We always go to a little tea shop in the high street.*

> **Teacup** and **teapot** are usually written as one word.

PHRASES

a cup/mug of tea *Would you like another cup of tea?*

a pot of tea *Shall I make a pot of tea?*

take your tea with milk/sugar (*also* **take milk/sugar in your tea**) *Do you take your tea with milk?*

tea and coffee *There's a stand serving tea and coffee and cakes.*

> Some British speakers also use **tea** instead of saying **dinner**, when talking about their evening meal.
> In the UK, **afternoon tea** is a small afternoon meal that consists of tea and sandwiches. A **cream tea** is a small afternoon meal that consists of scones (= a type of small cake) with cream and jam.

teach *v*

to give lessons in a school, college, or university, or to help someone learn about something by giving them information

PREPOSITIONS

teach at a school/college/university *He teaches physics at Cambridge University.*

teach sth to sb *I'm teaching English to Italian students.*

teach sb about sth *We were never taught anything about other religions.*

ADVERBS

well/badly taught *She was well taught by good teachers.*

widely taught (=in many places) *English is widely taught in schools in Korea.*

PHRASES

teach sb how to do sth *My dad is teaching me how to drive.*

qualified to teach *I'm qualified to teach in a secondary school.*

teacher *n*

someone whose job is to teach, especially in a school

ADJECTIVES/NOUNS + teacher

a good/great/excellent teacher *I had a really good teacher.*

a bad/terrible/incompetent teacher *He's a good cook, but unfortunately he is a terrible teacher*

sb's favourite teacher *BrE*, **sb's favorite teacher** *AmE*: *I like her – she's my favourite teacher.*

a science/French etc teacher *Mrs Gonzales was our Spanish teacher.*

a piano/dance/art teacher *Harry has a lesson with his piano teacher on Saturday mornings.*

a school teacher (*also* **a schoolteacher**) *School teachers should be paid more money.*

an elementary school/high school etc teacher *I always wanted to be a high school teacher.*

a classroom teacher (=one who works in a classroom) *Some classroom teachers spend half*

T

their time trying to keep the students under control.

the head teacher *BrE* (=the person in charge of a school) *Judith is head teacher of a primary school in Salford.*

a full-time/part-time teacher *Helen got a job as a part-time teacher.*

a qualified teacher *Schools are only allowed to employ qualified teachers.*

a first-grade/second-grade teacher *AmE: She worked as a sixth-grade teacher.*

a woman teacher *There are more women teachers in elementary schools.*

a substitute teacher (=one who replaces the usual teacher) *Mrs Jones was ill, so we had a substitute teacher.*

a supply teacher *BrE* (=one who does temporary work in schools) *The school has to rely on supply teachers.*

teacher + NOUNS

teacher training *I want to do a teacher training course.*

teaching *n*

the work or profession of a teacher

NOUNS + teaching

language/science/French etc teaching *She has considerable experience of English language teaching.*

high school/university etc teaching *He's thinking about secondary school teaching as a new career.*

mixed-ability teaching (=in classes with students who have various levels of ability) *If there are fewer teachers, that means more mixed-ability teaching.*

one-to-one teaching (=in which a teacher teaches a single student) *In some subjects, one-to-one teaching is available.*

VERBS

go into teaching (=become a teacher) *20% of our graduates go into teaching.*

teaching + NOUNS

the teaching profession (=teachers, or the career of teaching) *More and more people are choosing to go into the teaching profession.*

the teaching staff (=the teachers at a school, college etc) *She attended a girls' school where all the teaching staff were women.*

teaching methods *Our teaching methods are quite traditional.*

teaching materials *New teachers need time to prepare their own teaching materials.*

a teaching aid (=something that a teacher uses in the classroom) *The school is equipped with modern teaching aids, including interactive whiteboards.*

teaching practice *BrE*, **student teaching** *AmE* (=a period of teaching done by someone who is training to be a teacher) *Trainee teachers do over 90 hours of teaching practice.*

a teaching job/post *He took up his first teaching post in 2005.*

a teaching career *She began her teaching career at a school in inner London.*

team Ac *n*

1 a group of people who play a game or sport together against another group

ADJECTIVES/NOUNS + team

a good/strong team *The game will be tough for us because Barcelona has a very strong team.*

the winning/losing team *Everyone on the winning team will get a medal.*

a soccer/basketball etc team *China's basketball team is preparing for the Olympic Games.*

the school team *I played for the school cricket team.*

the national team *He coached the Italian national team.*

the home team (=the team whose sports field a game is being played on) *Hayward then increased the home team's lead.*

the visiting team (=the team who have travelled to their opponents' sports field) *The visiting team failed to score.*

the opposing team *A member of the opposing team grabbed hold of his shirt.*

the women's/men's team *Gunnell was captain of the British women's team.*

the first team *BrE* (=the team with the best players in a school, club etc) *He has played several times for the first team.*

the second team (=the team with players who are not as good as those in the first team) *He stepped up from the second team when Roberts was injured.*

VERBS + team

play for a team *He wants to play for a better team.*

support a team *"Which team do you support?" "Chelsea."*

beat a team *We beat one of the best teams in the league.*

captain a team (=be the captain of a team) *James captained his school basketball team.*

coach a team (=teach skills to a team) *Cheung had coached the team since 2005.*

make the team (=be chosen as a member of a team) *He was never good enough to make the team.*

drop sb from a team (=decide that someone should not play for a team) *He has been dropped from the team because of injury.*

pick a team (=choose who will be in it) *Capello will be picking the team for Wednesday's game.*

field a team (=have a team that plays)

Hungary fielded a strong team in the game last night.

team + VERBS

a team plays *The team played well today.*

a team wins (sth) *His team won the first game 3–2.*

a team loses (sth) *The team has lost the last three games.*

team + NOUNS

the team captain *The cup was presented to the team captain.*

a team member (*also* **a member of a team**) *He's the eldest team member.*

the team manager/coach *Who do you think will be the next England team manager?*

a team game/sport (=one that is played by teams) *She enjoys team sports such as basketball and hockey.*

PREPOSITIONS

in a team *BrE*, **on a team** *AmE*: *Bobby Charlton was in the team that won the World Cup.*

PHRASES

play as a team (=work well with other people in the team) *One reason for the 49ers' success is that they play as a team.*

> **Grammar**
> **Team** is usually followed by a singular verb: *Our* ***team is*** *winning.* In British English, **team** can also be followed by a plural verb: *Our* ***team are*** *winning.*

2 a group of people who have been chosen to work together to do a particular job

ADJECTIVES/NOUNS + team

a management/research/sales etc team *The design team has come up with a few ideas.*

a rescue team *He was in the water for two hours before a rescue team arrived.*

a legal/medical/surgical team *Bamber's legal team argued that the new evidence should be taken into account.*

a good/strong team *We have a very strong sales team.*

a three-man/four-man etc team (=one with three, four etc people) *About a month ago he hired a four-man team of personal trainers.*

a 10-strong/14-strong etc team (=one with 10, 14 etc people) *A six-strong team from the Transport Research Laboratory is at the crash scene.*

team + NOUNS

a team member (*also* **a member of a team**) *Team members meet on a regular basis.*

a team leader *The team leader will coordinate the work.*

a team effort (=when members of a team achieve something together) *It was a great team effort and all the crew did a magnificent job.*

a team meeting *Hold team meetings to discuss problems.*

team spirit (=willingness to work together to achieve something) *There was great team spirit on this project.*

team building (=the activity of forming a team and making people work well together) *The course will focus on team building.*

a team player (=someone who works well as part of a team) *Betsy's not a team player and is better working on her own.*

VERBS

lead/head a team *Giles led the team of surgeons who saved the singer's life.*

join a team *He will join the team of officials who are overseeing the negotiations.*

put together/assemble/build a team *They have assembled a team of lawyers to look through the evidence.*

PREPOSITIONS

a team of sth *The committee consists of a team of experts.*

PHRASES

work as a team (=work well with other people in the team) *Our success lies in working together as a team.*

make a good team (=work well together as a team) *You and I make a good team.*

tear[1] *n*

a drop of liquid that comes out of your eye when you are crying

> **Grammar**
> Usually plural.

PHRASES

in tears (=crying) *When she put the phone down, she was in tears.*

in floods of tears *BrE* (=crying a lot) *I arrived to find him in floods of tears.*

close to tears (*also* **on the verge of tears**) (=almost crying) *He could see that she was close to tears.*

moved to tears (=so upset that you cry) *Members of the audience were moved to tears by her singing.*

bring tears to sb's eyes (=make someone cry) *This unexpected kindness brought tears to my eyes.*

reduce sb to tears (=make someone cry) *Her insults had reduced him to tears.*

sb's eyes fill with tears *His eyes filled with tears as he remembered his mother.*

there are tears in sb's eyes *As she watched, there were tears of joy in her eyes.*

tears well up in sb's eyes (=tears come into their eyes) *Listening to his story, I could feel the tears welling up in my eyes.*

tears run/roll/stream down sb's face *She laughed until tears ran down her face.*

VERBS

burst into tears (*also* **break down in tears**) (=suddenly start crying) *She burst into tears and begged me to stay.*

weep bitter/angry etc tears *I wept tears of joy when I saw him again.*

hold back tears (=not cry, even though you feel like crying) *She told her story, often struggling to hold back tears.*

fight/choke/blink back tears (=try not to cry) *He fought back tears as he argued.*

> **Shed tears**
> This phrase literally means "to cry about something". It is often used in negative sentences, when saying that someone was not sad when something happened. *Nobody* ***shed*** *any* ***tears*** *when he left.*

ADJECTIVES

bitter tears (=expressing painful emotions) *She wept bitter tears, knowing she was leaving her family behind.*

angry tears *There were angry tears when the children heard the trip was cancelled.*

silent tears *He sat in his office, weeping silent tears of frustration.*

hot tears *I felt the hot tears running down my face.*

PREPOSITIONS

tears of joy/frustration/rage etc *The tears were tears of joy.*

tear[2] *v*

to damage something such as paper or cloth by pulling it hard, either deliberately or accidentally

PHRASES

tear sth in two/half *He angrily tore the letter in two and threw it in the fire.*

tear sth to pieces/shreds *The dogs tore the meat to pieces.*

NOUNS

tear a hole in sth *She caught her jumper on a nail and tore a hole in it.*

tear a muscle (=injure yourself by damaging your muscle) *The player tore a muscle in his right knee.*

PREPOSITIONS/ADVERBS

tear sth up (=into many pieces) *She tore up the photograph and put it in the wastepaper basket.*

tear sth open *Alan tore open the envelope and quickly read the letter.*

tear (sth) off sth *He tore off a piece of paper and wrote down his phone number.*

tear sth on sth *I tore my jacket on a piece of sharp wire.*

> **THESAURUS: tear**
> smash, shatter, crumble, split, snap, crack, fracture, tear, burst → **break[1] (1)**

tease *v*

to laugh at someone and make jokes in order to have fun by embarrassing them, either in a friendly way or in an unkind way

ADVERBS

tease sb gently *Sometimes, Amelia would tease him gently and pretend that she was angry with him.*

tease sb mercilessly (=tease someone a lot) *Her friends used to tease her mercilessly about her hair.*

be always teasing sb (=tease someone often) *His wife was always teasing him because he was terrible at spelling.*

be only teasing *Don't get upset. I was only teasing.*

PREPOSITIONS

tease sb about sth *My sister used to tease me about my weight.*

technical Ac *adj*

1 relating to machines and systems

NOUNS

a technical problem/difficulty/fault *The flight was cancelled because of a technical problem with one of the plane's engines.*

technical staff *The technical staff are responsible for maintaining the classroom equipment.*

a technical expert *He is one the country's leading technical experts on this type of system.*

2 relating to detailed knowledge or special skills

NOUNS

technical help/advice/support/assistance *The company provides technical support for customers.*

technical knowledge/expertise/skills *The job requires a lot of technical knowledge.*

technical details *I asked him to explain the technical details.*

technical language/jargon *This book contains a lot of technical language, which is difficult for ordinary people to understand.*

a technical term *URL is the technical term for what is often called a 'web address'.*

ADVERBS

highly technical *The manufacturing process is highly technical.*

technique Ac *n*

a special way of doing something

ADJECTIVES

basic techniques *Students are taught the basic techniques of jewellery making.*

modern techniques *Modern techniques give much more accurate results.*

a simple technique *It is amazing what a difference this simple technique can make.*

an effective technique *This is an effective technique for removing grease stains.*

a standard technique *She uses the standard technique for checking blood pressure.*

surgical techniques *Surgical techniques have improved considerably in the last 20 years.*

NOUNS + technique

relaxation techniques *Patients are taught relaxation techniques to use at home.*

management techniques *Head teachers are bringing new management techniques into schools.*

problem-solving techniques *Students are trained in a range of problem-solving techniques.*

VERBS

use a technique (*also* **employ a technique** *formal*): *By using this simple technique, you can read much more quickly.*

develop/devise a technique *Researchers hope to develop more accurate techniques for testing students.*

learn a technique *We started by learning some basic techniques.*

teach a technique *We teach a number of techniques for improving concentration.*

practise a technique *BrE*, **practice a technique** *AmE*: *He likes to practice his technique before the game.*

technology Ac *n*

new equipment and methods that are based on modern scientific knowledge

ADJECTIVES/NOUNS + technology

modern technology *With the help of modern technology, we can now see deep into space.*

new technology *Some people are suspicious of new technology.*

information technology (=computers and similar communication equipment) *Countries that invest in information technology see economic benefits.*

computer technology *Computer technology developed rapidly in the 1950s and 1960s.*

digital technology *Digital technology is completely changing the way we communicate.*

the latest technology (=the most modern technology) *The plane is equipped with the latest technology.*

the existing technology (=that is available now) *The research was based on existing technology.*

advanced technology *The researchers use advanced technology to study cells.*

cutting-edge technology (=extremely advanced) *The plane uses cutting-edge technology which makes it invisible to radar.*

medical technology *The advance of medical technology has meant that more patients survive.*

military technology *Military technology makes huge advances during wartime.*

VERBS

use technology (*also* **employ technology** *formal*): *We should be using technology to make our lives easier.*

introduce technology (=start using it) *They plan to introduce the new technology in all their factories.*

invest in technology *Companies are investing heavily in technology.*

embrace technology (=use it with enthusiasm) *You have to be willing to embrace new technology at work.*

technology advances/evolves (=it develops and gets better) *Medical technology has advanced in recent years.*

PHRASES

advances/developments in technology *Developments in technology have made these phones incredibly powerful.*

science and technology *There is less interest in the arts, and more in science and technology.*

tedious *adj* THESAURUS ▸ **boring**

teenage *adj* THESAURUS ▸ **young**

teenager *n*

someone who is between 13 and 19 years old

ADJECTIVES

a young teenager *The book was written for young teenagers.*

an older teenager *The film is likely to appeal to older teenagers.*

a local teenager *Local teenagers like to gather in the park.*

a rebellious teenager (=one who deliberately does not obey people in authority) *He was a rebellious teenager who was always getting into trouble.*

PHRASES

as a teenager (=when someone is a teenager) *As a teenager, he played in several rock bands.*

telephone *n*

the system or piece of equipment that you use to have a conversation with someone in another place

VERBS

the telephone rings *The telephone rang, but Tom didn't answer it.*

answer the telephone *When I called, Mike answered the telephone.*

use the telephone *May I use your telephone?*

talk on the telephone *He was talking on the telephone when the doorbell rang.*

pick up the telephone *As soon as she got home, she picked up the telephone and dialled his number.*

put down the telephone *Before he could answer, she put down the telephone.*

call sb on the telephone *Her son doesn't even call her on the telephone.*

telephone + NOUNS

a telephone call *She got a telephone call from Joe last night.*

a telephone conversation *We had a long telephone conversation.*

a telephone interview (=when a journalist asks someone questions using a telephone) *In a telephone interview, he said that at least 200 people had been killed.*

a telephone line *They didn't even have a telephone line.*

sb's telephone number *He gave me his address and telephone number.*

a telephone bill *I need to pay my telephone bill.*

the telephone system/service/network *The country is planning to modernize its telephone system.*

a telephone company *Complaints against telephone companies have increased.*

a telephone message *When she got home, there was a telephone message for her to call George.*

a telephone helpline/hotline (=a number that you can phone for information or help) *The government has set up a telephone helpline for people who are concerned about relatives in the earthquake area.*

⚠ Don't say 'I had a telephone from him'. Say **I had a telephone call from him**.

PREPOSITIONS

by telephone *Reservations can be made by telephone.*

on the telephone (=talking to someone using a telephone) *She's been on the telephone all evening.*

down the telephone *BrE: He shouted at me down the telephone.*

over the telephone *I read the names out to him over the telephone.*

> **Telephone or phone?**
> **Telephone** sounds formal. In everyday English, people usually say **phone**.

television *n*

a piece of electronic equipment with a screen, on which you can watch programmes, or the programmes that you can watch

VERBS

watch television *The kids were watching television upstairs.*

see/watch sth on television *She saw the game on television.*

turn/switch the television on *Lucy turned the television on to watch the news.*

turn/switch the television off *I switched off the television and went to bed.*

turn the television up/down (=make it louder or quieter) *Rory had turned the television up so loud that the people next door complained.*

⚠ Don't say 'see/watch sth in television'. Say **see/watch sth on television**.

television + NOUNS

a television show *The singer now has his own television show.*

a television programme *BrE*, **a television program** *AmE: Her favourite television programme was just starting.*

a television series (=a set of programmes with the same characters or subject, broadcast every day or every week) *He starred in the popular television series 'Friends'.*

a television station/channel (=an organization that makes television programmes) *The man told Brazil's RBS television station that he was worried about his daughter's disappearance.*

the television news *She was interviewed by Channel 4 television news.*

a television documentary/drama/advertisement/interview etc *We watched a television documentary about China.*

a television adaptation (=a programme based on a book, film, or play) *The programme is a television adaptation of Dickens' famous book.*

television coverage (=reporting about something on television) *There has been extensive television coverage of the election campaign.*

a television presenter *BrE: Ross is a well-known television presenter.*

a television reporter/journalist *Grant was interviewed by a BBC television journalist.*

a television producer/director (=someone who makes television programmes) *A television producer asked her if she would like to appear in the series.*

television audience/viewers *The programme was seen by millions of television viewers.*

a television (film) crew (=a group of people who produce and film television programmes) *A television crew were allowed to film the meeting.*

a television screen *Bella's eyes were fixed on the television screen.*

a television set (=a television) *Most people in Britain have at least one television set.*

ADJECTIVES/NOUNS + television

live television *The game was shown on live television.*

national television *The president went on national television to appeal for calm.*

satellite/cable television *They have a dish for satellite television.*

digital television *The switchover to digital television has begun.*

terrestrial television *BrE* (=television that is not broadcast using a satellite or cable) *Many of these games are not available on terrestrial television.*

high definition/HD television *They plan to introduce a new high definition television channel.*

3D television (=which makes people and objects seem more real) *For 3D television, you have to wear special glasses.*

a widescreen television (=a television with a wide screen) *Widescreen televisions are getting more popular, especially in home cinema systems.*

a plasma/LCD television *Each hotel room has a minibar and plasma television.*

a flatscreen television *We offer a buyer's guide to the latest flatscreen televisions.*

PREPOSITIONS

on television *Is there anything good on television tonight?*

in front of the television (=facing the television) *We ate our meal in front of the television.*

> **Television or TV?**
> In everyday spoken English, **TV** is more common.
> In informal British English, people also say **the telly**. In informal American English, people also say **the tube**.

T

tell *v*

to give someone information by speaking or writing to them

NOUNS

tell a story/tale *He told the story of how he and his wife met.*

tell a joke *They sat around laughing and telling jokes.*

tell sb a secret *I offered to tell her my secret if she didn't tell anyone else.*

tell a lie *The newspaper told lies about us.*

tell the truth *"I'm telling you the truth," she insisted.*

ADVERBS

tell sb firmly *"Calm down, Laura," he told her firmly.*

tell sb bluntly/frankly/flatly (=in a very direct way, which may upset someone) *The teacher told him bluntly that if he didn't improve, he would lose his place on the course.*

tell sb gently *I tried to tell her as gently as possible, so as not to hurt her feelings.*

tell sb truthfully *She told him truthfully that she did not have the keys.*

PREPOSITIONS

tell sb about sth *Mark was telling us about his new job.*

tell sb of sth *formal* (=tell someone about something) *She told us of her pride at seeing her son graduate.*

tell sth to sb *We advised him not to tell this story to reporters.*

PHRASES

tell sb all about sth *"Have you heard about Sarah and Jeff?" "Yes, Mike told me all about it."*

you must not tell anyone *It's a secret - you mustn't tell anyone.*

I hate to tell you, but... *spoken* (=used for introducing unpleasant news) *I hate to tell you, but it looks like someone's stolen your car.*

temper *n*

if someone has a temper, they become angry suddenly or easily

ADJECTIVES

a quick/short temper (=likely to get angry easily) *He's got a quick temper which often gets him into trouble.*

a bad/terrible/nasty temper *Dan arrived home in a terrible temper.*

a fiery/violent/explosive temper (=likely to get very angry very quickly) *Mary has learned to control her fiery temper.*

VERBS

lose your temper (=become angry) *It was hot and I was beginning to lose my temper.*

have a temper *Grandad had quite a temper, so we kept out of his way.*

control/keep your temper *She tried to speak calmly and control her temper.*

tempers flare/rise (=people become angry) *Tempers flared and people said some hurtful things.*

tempers cool (=people stop being angry) *We decided to break off discussions to allow tempers to cool.*

PHRASES

a temper tantrum (=when someone, especially a child, behaves very angrily and unreasonably) *Young children sometimes have temper tantrums if they don't get what they want.*

a fit/flash/burst of temper (=when you are very angry for a short time) *He had smashed the picture in a fit of temper.*

in a temper *Sarah banged doors and screamed at her mother when she was in a temper.*

fly into a temper (=suddenly become very angry) *He flew into a temper at the slightest thing.*

tempers get/become frayed BrE (=people become annoyed) *People were pushing each other, and tempers were becoming frayed.*

temperature *n*

a measure of how hot or cold a place or thing is

ADJECTIVES

a high temperature *The metal is heated to a high temperature.*

a low temperature *Temperatures were so low that most plants could not survive.*

a constant temperature *The temperature of the laboratory is kept constant.*

extreme temperatures *The material has to be able to withstand extreme temperatures.*

sub-zero/freezing temperatures *They spent six hours on the mountain in sub-zero temperatures.*

the average temperature *The average temperature in the city during 2009 was 11.2°C.*

maximum/minimum temperature *The water in the pool is kept at a minimum temperature of 20°C.*

NOUNS + temperature

the air/water temperature *The water temperature should be between 60 and 65°F.*

sb's body temperature *His body temperature is normal.*

temperature + VERBS

the temperature rises/goes up *The temperature rose steadily throughout the morning.*

the temperature soars (=rises quickly to a high level) *In summer the temperature can soar to over 40°C (104°F).*

the temperature falls/drops/goes down *Last winter, the temperature fell below freezing on only five days.*

the temperature plummets (=goes down quickly to a very low level) *The temperature plummeted to -50°.*

VERBS + temperature

take/check sb's temperature (=measure it) *The nurse took his temperature.*

measure the temperature of sth *The scientists measured the Earth's average temperature.*

raise the temperature *The thermostat allows you to raise the temperature.*

lower the temperature *Paracetamol lowers your body temperature.*

temperature + NOUNS

a temperature range *The plant grows best within a temperature range of 20–25°C.*

temperature control *Temperature control is very important when storing food.*

PREPOSITIONS

the temperature of sth *The temperature of the water was just right for swimming.*

at a temperature *The clothes were washed at a high temperature.*

PHRASES

a rise in temperature (*also* **a temperature rise**) *The result was a rise in the Earth's temperature.*

a drop/fall in temperature *At night there is a dramatic drop in temperature.*

a change in temperature (*also* **a temperature change**) *The oil is affected by changes in temperature.*

at room temperature *Store the wine at room temperature.*

temple *n*

a building where people go to worship in some religions

ADJECTIVES

an ancient temple *The ancient temples of Egypt attract many tourists.*

a Buddhist/Hindu etc temple *Wat Pho is the oldest Buddhist temple in Bangkok.*

a Roman/Greek etc temple (=from ancient Rome or Greece) *The Temple of Zeus was a magnificent Greek temple in the city of Olympia.*

a classical temple (=from ancient Roman or Greek times) *The front of the museum is made to look like a classical temple.*

VERBS

build a temple *The temple was built thousands of years ago.*

visit a temple *When we were in Thailand we visited lots of temples.*

worship at a temple (=pray or sing in order to show respect and love for a god) *It is traditional for people to worship at the temple on New Year's Day.*

temporary Ac *adj*

continuing for only a limited period of time

NOUNS

temporary work *Students are usually able to find temporary work during the summer.*

a temporary job/position/appointment *I've been offered a temporary job in a department store.*

temporary workers/staff/employees *It is cheaper for employers to use temporary workers than permanent staff.*

temporary accommodation *The family will live in temporary accommodation until the work on their house is completed.*

a temporary office/classroom/bed/shelter *He was speaking from the tent which is now his temporary office.*

a temporary arrangement/solution *This is just a temporary arrangement, until we can find a permanent solution.*

a temporary measure (=a temporary way of dealing with a problem) *Staff have moved into a different office as a temporary measure.*

temporary relief (=a temporary way of making

someone feel less pain or a problem less serious) *The treatment should provide some temporary relief from the pain.*

a temporary replacement *He is just a temporary replacement while they find a new manager.*

the temporary closure of sth *The demonstrations led to the temporary closure of several main roads.*

ADVERBS

only/just temporary *Don't worry – the effects are only temporary.*

PHRASES

on a temporary basis *She's working in the library on a temporary basis.*

THESAURUS: temporary

provisional
government | licence | figures | results | date | agreement | arrangement | booking
only arranged to last for a short time. You also use **provisional** about information that is likely to change after a short time:
The two parties announced that they had formed a provisional government. | Provisional figures showed that inflation was running at 8%. | The provisional date for the meeting is Sunday, September 17th.

stopgap
measure | solution
temporary – used about a way of dealing with a problem that you use for a short time, until you can find something better:
As a stopgap measure, the school has moved into a nearby church hall (=a temporary way of dealing with a problem). | *The loan from the European Central bank is intended to be a stopgap solution.*

Stopgap is only used before a noun.

passing
phase | fad
used about something that people are only interested in for a short time and is not serious or important:
Children sometimes refuse to eat certain foods, but this is normally just a passing phase. | Some people think that organic food is just a passing fad (=something that is fashionable for a short time).

Passing is only used before a noun.

ephemeral *formal*
nature | beauty
existing for only a very short time and then disappearing completely – used especially when making serious statements about life and the world:
For Japanese people, cherry blossoms are a symbol of the ephemeral nature of life. | Snow has an ephemeral beauty – you know that it won't be there forever. | Fame is ephemeral.

transient *formal*
phenomenon | condition | change | nature | population
existing or staying somewhere only for a short time – used when a situation is always changing:
Far from being a transient phenomenon, high unemployment has become a long-term feature of the economy. | Arizona has a highly transient population.

ANTONYMS **temporary → permanent**

temptation *n*

a strong desire to have or do something even though you know you should not

ADJECTIVES

a great/strong temptation *There is a strong temptation to ignore these problems.*

an overwhelming temptation (=extremely strong) *He felt an overwhelming temptation to kiss her.*

a constant temptation *Working at night, he has to fight the constant temptation to sleep.*

a natural temptation *When a player is performing badly, there is a natural temptation to look for excuses.*

an irresistible temptation (=which you cannot control) *If the money is there, he feels an irresistible temptation to spend it.*

VERBS

resist the temptation to do sth *Resist the temptation to eat unhealthy snacks when you're hungry.*

give in to temptation (*also* **succumb to/yield to temptation** *formal*) (=do what you feel you want to do, even though you know you should not do it) *Be strong – don't give in to temptation.*

avoid the temptation to do sth *Avoid the temptation to cheat.*

PHRASES

there is (always) a temptation to do sth *There is always the temptation to start drinking again.*

out of temptation's way (=in a place where you will not be tempted to have or do something) *I put the chocolates in the cupboard, out of temptation's way.*

tenacious *adj* THESAURUS ▸ determined

tendency *n*

when someone usually does something, or when something usually happens

ADJECTIVES

a strong tendency *There is a strong tendency to give patients far more drugs than is necessary.*

a natural tendency (*also* **an inherent/innate tendency** *formal*) (=one you are born with) *His recent experiences had reinforced a strong natural tendency towards caution.*

a common tendency (=among many people) *There is a common tendency to drive too close to the vehicle in front.*

a marked tendency (=noticeable) *There is a marked tendency for Hollywood marriages to end in divorce.*

an increasing/growing tendency *We are disturbed by the growing tendency among young people to smoke.*

aggressive/violent tendencies *Some breeds of dog have aggressive tendencies.*

criminal tendencies *How should we deal with young people who have criminal tendencies?*

artistic tendencies *As a young man, he displayed artistic tendencies.*

suicidal tendencies *Doctors failed to inform the prison authorities of the man's suicidal tendencies.*

VERBS

have a tendency *He has a tendency to argue with people when he's drunk.*

show a tendency (*also* **reveal/display a tendency** *formal*): *Students in warmer classrooms showed a tendency to fall asleep.*

resist/overcome a tendency (=control it) *She tried to resist her tendency to criticize.*

counter/counteract a tendency (=make it less likely) *Is there anything we can do to counteract this tendency?*

reinforce a tendency (=make it more likely) *The culture he grew up in reinforced his natural tendency to be aggressive.*

PREPOSITIONS

a tendency for sth *There is a tendency for people to pretend that the problem doesn't exist.*

a tendency to/towards sth *There is a marked tendency towards crime in these neighbourhoods.*

a tendency among people *There was a tendency among younger candidates to exaggerate their success.*

PHRASES

a tendency to do sth *She has a tendency to become irritated with people.*

a tendency on the part of sb *There's a tendency on the part of some newspapers to blame the victim.*

tender *adj* THESAURUS **soft (1)**

tennis *n*

a game for two people or two pairs of people who use rackets to hit a small soft ball backwards and forwards over a net

VERBS

play tennis *I enjoyed playing tennis at the weekend.*

watch tennis *She enjoys watching tennis on television.*

ADJECTIVES/NOUNS + tennis

professional tennis *The best players in professional tennis can earn a lot of money.*

men's/women's tennis *She is this year's women's tennis champion.*

lawn tennis (=played on grass) *Wimbledon is the most famous lawn tennis championship in the world.*

indoor tennis *He won the indoor tennis tournament.*

tennis + NOUNS

a tennis player *She is a very good tennis player.*

a tennis racket/racquet (=the wooden or metal thing you use to hit a tennis ball) *I've broken some of the strings on my tennis racquet.*

a tennis ball *The children were throwing a tennis ball to each other.*

a tennis court (=a four-sided area that you play tennis on) *Our hotel had two tennis courts and a swimming pool.*

a tennis match *He's watching a tennis match on TV.*

a tennis club *I've decided to join the local tennis club.*

a tennis champion/star *One day he hopes to become a tennis champion.*

a tennis championship/tournament/competition *My sister recently won a tennis tournament.*

a tennis coach (=someone who helps people to improve their tennis skills) *Darren works as a tennis coach at the sports centre.*

a tennis lesson *I've got a tennis lesson this afternoon.*

PHRASES

a game of tennis *We decided to play a game of tennis.*

tense Ac *adj*

anxious and worried because of something bad that might happen, or making you feel like this

VERBS

feel tense *I always feel tense before an exam.*

look/sound tense *Her voice sounded tense on the telephone.*

NOUNS

a tense situation *She tried to calm the tense situation as the two men faced each other.*

a tense atmosphere *There was a tense atmosphere in the stadium before the game.*

a tense time/period *It was a tense time for everyone when Dad was ill.*

a tense moment *There was a tense moment when one of the riders fell off her horse.*

a tense silence *There was a tense silence in the room.*

a tense expression *She had a tense expression on her face.*

tense relations/a tense relationship *Tense relations have existed between the two countries for many years.*

tense negotiations/a tense discussion *After tense negotiations, the army left peacefully.*

tension Ac *n*

1 a nervous worried feeling that makes it impossible for you to relax

ADJECTIVES

nervous tension *The night before the wedding my mother was in a state of nervous tension.*

unbearable tension (=you feel the tension so strongly that you cannot think about anything else) *The tension as we waited for the announcement was almost unbearable.*

palpable tension *formal* (=very strong) *There was a moment of palpable tension as she opened the envelope.*

pent-up tension (=not expressed) *His body was stiff with pent-up tension.*

VERBS

reduce/ease/relieve tension *Breathing deeply helps to clear the mind and reduce tension.*

feel/sense the tension *She could sense the tension in the room.*

PREPOSITIONS

tension in sth *I could see the tension in his face.*

PHRASES

a state of tension *Marie lived in a constant state of tension waiting for his phone calls.*

an atmosphere of tension *Voting took place in an atmosphere of tension.*

T

2 the feeling that exists when people or countries do not trust each other and may suddenly attack each other or start arguing

ADJECTIVES

increasing/growing/mounting/rising tension *There are reports of increasing tension along the border.*

tensions are/remain high *Tensions are high and fighting could start at any minute.*

heightened tension (=greater than before) *This is a time of heightened tension between the two countries.*

racial/ethnic tension *Martin Luther King had an important role in calming the racial tensions of America in the 1960s.*

social/political tension *The economic crisis was accompanied by mounting social tension.*

sectarian/religious tension (=between different religious groups) *Police are concerned about the possibility of sectarian tension at the event.*

VERBS

defuse the tension (=make a situation more friendly) *His statement was intended to defuse the tension.*

create/cause tension *Politicians need to realize that an angry speech can create a lot of tension.*

raise/increase tension *The arrests only served to raise tension among local people.*

stir up/fuel tension (=make it worse) *The terrorist attack was designed to fuel tension between the religious communities.*

heighten/ratchet up the tension (=make it reach a very high level) *The sound of distant gunfire ratcheted up the tension in the city today.*

tension rises/mounts (*also* **tension escalates** *formal*): *Tension in the region is mounting following the disputed election.*

tension flares up/boils over (*also* **tension erupts**) (=there is sudden violence) *If people see the government taking no action, tension may well flare up again.*

PREPOSITIONS

tension between people *The statement caused tension between Christians and Muslims.*

tension among people *This statement was designed to reduce tension among party members.*

tension over sth *There is still a lot of tension over the ownership of the land.*

PHRASES

a source of tension *This agreement should remove a major source of tension among America's allies.*

the tensions are beneath the surface (=they are hidden and you do not notice them immediately) *The old tensions were still there beneath the surface.*

3 an exciting quality in a film, book etc that exists when you are expecting something to happen

ADJECTIVES/NOUNS + tension

increasing/mounting tension *There is mounting tension in the second part of the film as we wait for the bomb to explode.*

dramatic tension *It is a scene full of dramatic tension.*

sexual tension (=between people who are sexually attracted to each other) *Audiences loved the sexual tension between the two main characters.*

VERBS

keep up the tension (*also* **maintain the tension** *formal*): *Unfortunately, the author fails to maintain this tension in the second half of the book.*

heighten the tension (=make it stronger) *The sound of a clock ticking serves to heighten the tension.*

lack tension *Once this secret has been revealed, the film seems to lack dramatic tension.*

tent *n*

a shelter consisting of a sheet of cloth supported by poles and ropes, used especially for camping

VERBS

pitch/set up/put up a tent (*also* **erect a tent** *formal*): *We looked for a flat area where we could pitch our tent.*

take down a tent *In the morning we took down our tents.*

pack up a tent (=take it down and put it in a bag) *We packed up the tent and set off up the mountain.*

sleep in a tent *Many homes have been destroyed, and people are being forced to sleep in tents.*

NOUNS + tent

a two-person/five-person etc tent *They bought a large six-person tent for family camping.*

a circus tent (=a large tent in which a circus performs) *The large striped circus tent will seat an audience of 500.*

a mess tent (=a large tent used by soldiers to eat in) *A group of soldiers were eating breakfast in the mess tent.*

a hospitality/beer/lunch etc tent (=a large tent used for providing drinks or food) *Ron headed straight for the beer tent.*

tent + NOUNS

a tent peg (=a small stick that holds the tent to the ground) *It was hard to hammer the tent pegs into the rocky ground.*

term *n*

1 a word or expression with a particular meaning, especially one that is used for a specific subject or type of language

ADJECTIVES/NOUNS + term

a legal/medical term *The website provides a list of legal terms.*

a technical term *'Gender' is a technical term in grammar.*

a slang term *'The Old Bill' is a slang term for the police.*

a derogatory/pejorative term (=one that is insulting or disapproving) *'Pinko' is a derogatory term for someone with socialist ideas.*

VERBS

use a term *'IED' is a term used by the military to describe a homemade bomb.*

coin a term (=invent it) *Funk coined the term 'vitamin' in 1912.*

define a term (=explain what it means) *Question three asks you to define the term 'relative atomic mass'.*

be couched in ... terms *formal* (=be expressed in a particular way) *Their demands were couched in polite terms.*

a term means sth *The term 'reasonable force' means different things to different people.*

a term refers to/describes sth *'Domicile' is a term that refers to the place where you live.*

PREPOSITIONS

a term for sth *'Multimedia' is the term for any technique combining sounds and images.*

PHRASES

a term of abuse (=a word that is offensive or deliberately rude) *'Fruitcake' is used as a term of abuse, when you think someone is crazy.*

a term of endearment (=a word that expresses your love for someone) *Many people use terms of endearment like 'love', 'dear', and 'honey'.*

in layman's terms (=using ordinary words, not technical words) *I want something that will explain in layman's terms how my computer works.*

in glowing terms (=praising someone or something highly) *Friends and relatives speak of him in glowing terms.*

in strong terms *The Pope condemned both Nazism and Communism in strong terms.*

2 used when describing or considering something in a particular way

Grammar
Always plural in this meaning.

ADJECTIVES

in general/broad terms *They have talked in general terms about making some changes.*

in simple terms *In simple terms, the company needs to sell more products at higher prices.*

in real/absolute terms (=calculated by including the general decrease in the value of money over a period of time) *Spending on education has increased by 5% in real terms.*

in practical terms *In practical terms, what will the tax increase mean for families?*

in relative terms (=when compared with other things or people) *In relative terms, the building wasn't too badly damaged.*

in human terms *The cost of going to war, in human terms, has been huge.*

in economic/financial/military etc terms *The two countries are comparable in economic terms.*

PREPOSITIONS

in terms of sth *It's the largest company in terms of employees.*

PHRASES

describe/express/define sth in terms of sth *Femininity is still defined in terms of beauty.*

talk/speak in terms of sth *He's absolutely genuine when he talks in terms of his beliefs and ambitions.*

measure/evaluate sth in terms of sth *A company's success is often measured in terms of how much profit it makes.*

think of sth in terms of sth *It's a mistake to think of Florida only in terms of its tourist attractions.*

3 a fixed period of time during which someone does something or something happens

ADJECTIVES/NOUNS + term

a prison/jail term *He faced a maximum prison term of 25 years.*

a five-year/ten-year etc term *The president is elected for a five-year term.*

a fixed term *The contract was for a fixed term of three years.*

a maximum/minimum term *The maximum term was life imprisonment.*

VERBS

serve a term *She served a term as chairwoman of the council.*

PREPOSITIONS

a term as sth *Gilbert is now serving his second term as mayor.*

a term of five years/ten years etc *The lease runs for a term of 99 years.*

PHRASES

a term of/in office *The Governor ends his term of office in September.*

a term of imprisonment/detention *She was sentenced to a long term of imprisonment.*

4 one of the periods of time that the school or university year is divided into. In Britain, there are usually three terms in a year

ADJECTIVES

this term *This term we're studying Shakespeare's Midsummer Night's Dream.*

next term *I have my exams next term.*

last term *We studied American history last term.*

the new term *Are you looking forward to the new term?*

NOUNS + term

the school/university term *The school term was about to start.*

the spring/summer/autumn etc term *Mrs Collins will be leaving us at the end of the summer term.*

PHRASES

the beginning/start of term *The beginning of term was only two days away.*

the end of term *We had a party at the end of term.*

the first/last day of term *On the last day of term we went home early.*

in/during term-time (=when students are at school or college) *Parents need permission to take their children out of school during term-time.*

US speakers usually say **semester**.

5 the terms of an agreement, contract, arrangement etc are the conditions that have been decided for it

Grammar
Always plural in this meaning.

VERBS

agree terms *The two sides failed to agree terms, and the deal was cancelled.*

negotiate terms *Farmers are trying to negotiate better terms from supermarkets for their products.*

accept the terms of sth *Japan accepted the terms of the treaty.*

set terms (=decide what they will be) *Under the terms set by the European Commission, airlines are able to offer a range of prices for air tickets.*

set out terms (=explain them in writing) *The document sets out the terms of insurance for the insured property.*

secure terms (=obtain them) *The big energy companies were able to secure highly favourable terms from the government.*

dictate terms (=control or influence them) *If there is a lot of demand for a product, the seller can dictate terms.*

break the terms of sth (*also* **violate/breach the terms of sth** *formal*): *He was arrested for violating the terms of his parole.*

comply with the terms of sth (=do what the terms say) *Failure to comply with the terms of the contract will result in a fine.*

ADJECTIVES

favourable terms (=good and giving you an advantage) *The company was able to arrange a loan on very favourable terms.*

unfavourable terms (=bad and giving you a disadvantage) *Poorer countries often find that the unfavourable terms of trade are an obstacle to development.*

attractive terms (=ones that seem good) *There are attractive terms for private investors.*

PREPOSITIONS

the terms of sth *The contract sets out the terms of the sale.*

under the terms of sth *Under the terms of the deal, the two companies will have an equal share in the new business.*

PHRASES

the terms and conditions *Read all the terms and conditions before signing the contract.*

terminate Ac *v*

if something terminates, or if you terminate it, it ends

NOUNS

terminate a contract/agreement *The court ruled that the contract must be terminated.*

T

terminate sb's employment *The company terminated his employment after he admitted to theft.*

terminate a relationship *She had recently terminated her relationship with her boyfriend of six years.*

terrible *adj* extremely bad or severe

NOUNS

a terrible mistake *The decision was a terrible mistake.*

a terrible accident *A terrible accident left her unable to walk.*

a terrible injury/pain/disease *I had a terrible pain in my chest.*

a terrible shock/blow *Finding him dead was a terrible shock.*

a terrible experience/ordeal/time *She's been through a terrible ordeal and needs time to recover.*

a terrible event/tragedy *The world will never forget the terrible events of 9/11.*

terrible weather/rain/storm *The weather's terrible here and I'd like to move abroad!*

terrible food *The prison food was terrible.*

a terrible sight/smell/sound *He looked a terrible sight after the accident.*

terrible news *I've just had some terrible news about my brother.*

terrible trouble/danger *They were in terrible danger as water started to fill the car.*

a terrible mess *He left the bathroom in a terrible mess, with clothes all over the floor.*

a terrible waste *The war was a terrible waste of human life.*

VERBS

look/feel/sound terrible *David felt terrible when he woke up the next morning.*

ADVERBS

absolutely terrible *It must be absolutely terrible for his parents.*

⚠ Don't say 'very terrible'.

PHRASES

be in a terrible state *She hadn't eaten for several days and was in a terrible state.*

something terrible *James was worried that something terrible had happened to her.*

THESAURUS: terrible

awful *especially spoken* (*also* **dreadful** *BrE*)
mess | mistake | moment | day | weather | place | feeling | shock | pain | job | smell
terrible:
The whole situation is an awful mess. | For a dreadful moment, I thought Anne was going to collapse. | I've had an awful day. | He hadn't slept and he ***looked dreadful****.*

appalling/atrocious/horrendous
conditions | state | situation | record | crime | act | tragedy | injury | weather
terrible and shocking:
The refugees are living in appalling conditions. | The country has an appalling record on human rights. | The weather was atrocious so we didn't go sailing.

horrible
feeling | thought | experience | place | person | smell | sight | mistake | death | crime
very bad and unpleasant – used especially when something has a strong effect on you and you feel shocked, annoyed, or sick:
I had a horrible feeling that someone was watching me all the time. | Being in prison is a horrible experience. | There was a horrible smell of vomit. | This soup ***tastes horrible****.*

horrific
accident | crash | injuries | burns | crime | murder | attack | death | event | incident | scene
terrible in a way that is frightening, shocking, or upsetting. **Horrific** is usually used when people suffer injuries or die:
Eva lost both legs in a horrific accident. | She suffered horrific injuries in the explosion. | The attack was ***absolutely horrific****.*

hideous
creature | monster | face | sight | building | crime
used when something looks terrible, or seems shocking:
They looked like hideous creatures from another universe. | The town centre is full of hideous modern buildings. | He used his position as a doctor to commit hideous crimes.

disgusting
food | taste | smell | behaviour | habit | act | language | person
having a very unpleasant taste or smell. You also use **disgusting** about other things that people say or do that are very shocking:
The food was so disgusting that he couldn't eat it. | The smell was absolutely disgusting and I had to go out. | He has a disgusting habit of spitting all the time.

dire
consequences | effects | situation | conditions | circumstances | need | poverty
extremely severe or terrible – used especially when someone could suffer or die:
Misuse of this drug can have dire consequences. | The report describes the dire conditions in the city's prison. | The building is ***in dire need of*** *repair.*

In spoken English, you also use **dire** when saying strongly that you do not like something. It is not usually used before a noun in this meaning: *His last record was absolutely* ***dire****.*

T

lousy *informal*
job | day | place | service | weather | idea | writer | book | film | programme
terrible – used especially when you are annoyed because something is so bad:
The government is doing a lousy job. | I'm having such a lousy day. | The service in the restaurant was lousy. | I thought it was a lousy film.

ghastly *BrE informal*
mistake | sight | image | thought | mess | experience | crime | news
terrible – used especially when something upsets or shocks you:
There must have been some kind of a ghastly mistake. | Blood was pouring down his face and he looked a ghastly sight. | I might have been on the train that hit him! What a ghastly thought!

vile *informal*
smell | food | weather | conditions | man | woman
terrible and unpleasant:
There was a vile smell coming from the pipe. | The vile weather meant that many people had stayed at home.

diabolical *BrE informal*
situation | mess | performance | weather | service | film
terrible – used to express great disapproval:
She didn't know how to get out of this diabolical situation. | The team gave a diabolical performance on Saturday.

abysmal
performance | record | conditions | state | quality | job | service | start | lack
terrible and of a much lower standard than you expect:
The team's performance was abysmal. | The country has an abysmal record on democracy. | He has shown his abysmal lack of knowledge about the subject.

Collocations with words meaning terrible
You don't use **very** with any of these words. You can use **absolutely** or **really** instead *The weather was* ***absolutely awful****. | The conditions are* ***really appalling****. | This tastes* ***absolutely disgusting****.*

terrifying *adj* THESAURUS ▸ **frightening**

territory *n*

1 land that is owned or controlled by a particular country, ruler, or military force

ADJECTIVES/NOUNS + territory

enemy/hostile territory *They were flying deep into enemy territory.*

occupied territory (=land controlled by a foreign country or its army) *Much of the country is now occupied territory.*

disputed territory (=land that two or more countries claim control of) *Talks over the disputed territory begin next week.*

neutral territory (=that is not controlled by any of the groups or countries involved in a war) *After crossing the frontier, he would be safe in neutral territory.*

Chinese/German etc territory *The Russians gave Poland a large area of German territory.*

VERBS

defend/protect territory *They did not have sufficient forces to protect the southern territories.*

seize/capture territory *The government's forces seized territory previously held by the rebels.*

invade territory *Soon after signing the agreement, Hitler ordered his armies to invade Polish territory.*

recapture/regain territory *Our troops are trying to regain territory to the east.*

hold territory (=continue to control it) *They were managing to hold the territory north of the river.*

lose territory *We knew we could not afford to lose any more territory.*

PREPOSITIONS

on US/British/Spanish etc territory *The incident happened on British territory, so the trial should be held in a British court.*

2 a particular area of experience, knowledge, or discussion

ADJECTIVES

familiar territory *Much of the course will be familiar territory for students of English literature.*

uncharted/unexplored territory (=not familiar) *A relationship with a younger man was uncharted territory for her.*

forbidden territory *We never discussed the past – it was forbidden territory.*

VERBS

cover territory *The story covers territory that will be very familiar to fans of his earlier films.*

stray into/wander into ... territory (*also* **enter ... territory**) *The discussion was in danger of straying into controversial territory.*

terror *n*

1 a feeling of extreme fear

ADJECTIVES

sheer/pure terror (=complete and total terror) *The horse heard the noise and galloped off in sheer terror.*

absolute/stark terror (=extreme terror) *On his face was an expression of absolute terror.*

mortal terror *literary* (=very great terror) *The crew was in mortal terror of drowning.*

VERBS

inspire terror *The main aim of suicide bombers is to inspire terror in the population.*

instil terror in sb *BrE*, **instill terror in sb** *AmE* (=make them feel it) *He was a cold-blooded killer who instilled terror in his victims.*

PREPOSITIONS

in terror of sb/sth (=terrified of them) *It's a country where everyone lives in terror of the police.*

PHRASES

strike terror into sb's heart *literary: His fearsome appearance strikes terror into the hearts of his enemies.*

flee in terror *The children fled in terror as the fire spread.*

scream/shriek in terror *She jumped to her feet, screaming in terror.*

2 the organized use of violence to achieve a political aim

terror + NOUNS

a terror attack *She was killed in the 9/11 terror attack.*

a terror suspect *Police have the right to question terror suspects for longer.*

a terror group/organization *They received threatening letters from a terror group.*

a terror threat *We believe there is a very real terror threat to people in the city.*

a terror plot *Police believe they have uncovered a major terror plot.*

a terror campaign *There were hundreds of victims of the group's ten-year terror campaign.*

terror laws (=laws against terrorism) *Some politicians are arguing for tougher terror laws.*

VERBS

fight/combat terror *Computer technology is one of many weapons used to combat terror.*

use terror *We have no respect for people who would use terror to achieve their goals.*

resort to terror *They refuse to have talks with any group that resorts to terror.*

PHRASES

the war on/against terror (=actions that governments take to stop it) *Our nations are united in the war on terror.*

an act of terror *We consider the attack to be an act of terror.*

terrorism *n*

the use of violence against non-military targets to achieve a political aim

ADJECTIVES

international/global terrorism *The attacks made Americans very concerned about international terrorism.*

political terrorism *He openly supported political terrorism in his youth.*

VERBS

fight/combat terrorism *The government needs to provide more money to combat terrorism.*

defeat terrorism *We remain committed to the aim of defeating terrorism.*

give in to terrorism (=do what terrorists are demanding) *She said that paying a ransom for the hostages would be giving in to terrorism.*

sponsor terrorism (=give money or other help to terrorists) *He denied that his government in any way sponsored terrorism.*

renounce terrorism (=officially say you will stop using it) *The group will have to renounce terrorism before talks can take place.*

terrorism + NOUNS

a terrorism suspect *They were accused of using torture when questioning terrorism suspects.*

terrorism charges *Three men are being held by police on terrorism charges.*

PHRASES

an act of terrorism *The men are suspected of involvement in acts of terrorism.*

the fight against terrorism (*also* **the war on/against terrorism**) *We must never give up the fight against terrorism.*

the threat of terrorism *Security has been tightened because of the increased threat of terrorism.*

terrorist *n, adj*

someone who uses violence against non-military targets to achieve a political aim

ADJECTIVES

an international terrorist *The kidnap was carried out by a group of international terrorists.*

a suspected terrorist *Police arrested six suspected terrorists.*

an armed terrorist *They were gunned down by armed terrorists outside their hotel.*

a convicted terrorist (=someone who a court has decided is guilty of terrorism) *Convicted terrorists should never be released from prison.*

terrorist + NOUNS

a terrorist attack/bombing/act (*also* **a terrorist incident** *formal*): *More than 50 people were injured in the latest terrorist attack.*

a terrorist group/organization *No terrorist group has yet claimed responsibility for the bombing.*

terrorist activity *The Foreign Office has issued a warning to tourists about terrorist activity in the country.*

terrorist violence *The organization is continuing its campaign of terrorist violence in the region.*

the terrorist threat *The terrorist threat has caused a major increase in airport security.*

a terrorist cell (=a small secret group of terrorists) *Detectives believe they have uncovered a terrorist cell in the heart of the capital.*

a terrorist suspect *The police have been given new powers to question terrorist suspects.*
a terrorist target *It is feared that holiday resorts may become terrorist targets.*
a terrorist training camp *He studied bomb-making in a terrorist training camp in Afghanistan.*

PHRASES

a gang of terrorists *Waite was kidnapped by a gang of terrorists.*

test[1] *n*

1 a set of questions or practical activities, which are intended to find out how much someone knows about a subject or skill

ADJECTIVES/NOUNS + test

a biology/history etc test *On Monday we had a French test.*
a spelling/reading/listening test *I didn't do very well in the listening test.*
a driving test *A driving test can be a nerve-racking experience.*
a written test *Selection was based on written tests in English and mathematics.*
an oral test (=a spoken one) *The oral test will consist of a conversation of about ten minutes in German.*
a multiple-choice test (=in which each question has a list of answers to choose from) *There is some debate about whether multiple-choice tests are a good way of assessing students' knowledge.*
an aptitude test (=one that measures your natural abilities) *All candidates for the job are given an aptitude test.*
an intelligence/IQ test *She did very well on the IQ test.*

VERBS

take a test (*also* **do/sit a test** *BrE*): *All candidates have to take a test.*
⚠ Don't say 'make a test'.
pass a test (=succeed in it) *She passed her driving test first time.*
fail a test (*also* **flunk a test** *AmE informal*): *He failed the test and had to take it again.*
do well/badly in a test *BrE*, **do well/badly on a test** *AmE*: *I didn't do very well in the first part of the test.*
give sb a test *The students were given a reading test.*
mark a test *BrE*, **grade a test** *AmE*: *I spent the day marking tests.*
study for a test (*also* **revise for a test** *BrE*): *I've been revising for the English test.*

test + NOUNS

a test paper *The teacher began handing out the test papers.*
a test result/score *The test results are out on Friday.*
a test question *Some of the test questions were really difficult.*

PREPOSITIONS

a test on sth *We have a test on irregular verbs tomorrow.*
in a test *BrE*, **on a test** *AmE*: *Did you get a good mark in the test?*

2 an examination of something to find out information

NOUNS + test

a blood test *A blood test revealed his alcohol level was above the legal limit.*
an eye/sight test *All children starting school are given a sight test.*
a hearing test *I went for a hearing test last week.*
a fitness test *Walcott will have a fitness test this morning to decide whether he can play.*
a pregnancy test (=to find out if someone is pregnant) *The pregnancy test was positive.*
a drug test (=to find out if someone has taken drugs) *Two athletes were banned from competing after failing drug tests.*
a breath test (=to find out if someone has drunk alcohol) *Some people think the police should be able to carry out random breath tests.*
a DNA test (=one giving genetic information about a particular person) *The results of the DNA test proved that Simmons was the rapist.*
laboratory tests *Independent laboratory tests have confirmed that the product works very successfully.*
a safety test *All toys undergo rigorous safety tests.*

VERBS

carry out/do a test (*also* **perform/conduct a test** *formal*): *Your doctor will need to carry out some tests.*
have a test (*also* **undergo a test** *formal*) (=be tested) *She had to have a blood test.*
go for a test *I'm going for an eye test next week.*
a test shows/reveals sth *The test showed that he was immune to the disease.*
a test proves/confirms sth *DNA tests confirmed that Stuart is the baby's father.*

ADJECTIVES

a medical/scientific/genetic test *Medical tests are continuing today to establish the cause of her death.*
a simple test *Your doctor can give you a simple blood test to check for anaemia.*
a routine test *Hospitals conduct routine tests on blood products.*
a positive test (=showing that someone has a condition) *My first pregnancy test was positive.*
a rigorous/stringent test (=one that is very thorough) *All our products have passed stringent safety tests.*

T

a negative test (=showing that someone does not have a condition) *All the tests came back negative.*

a diagnostic test (=to find out what disease someone has or what is wrong with a machine, engine etc) *There are now new diagnostic tests for the disease.*

a forensic test (=for finding out information about a crime) *Forensic tests showed that the fingerprints in the car were his.*

a nuclear test *The country was planning to conduct nuclear tests.*

test + NOUNS

test results *The test results showed that she had meningitis.*

a test site (=a place where something can be tested) *A nuclear device was detonated at the Trinity test site in New Mexico, on July 16th 1945.*

a test kit *A test kit can be used to check the water for pollution.*

PREPOSITIONS

a test on sb/sth *Tests on the drug showed that it was not safe for human use.*

a test for sth *Doctors are hoping to develop an early test for lung cancer.*

3 a difficult situation which shows someone's qualities and ability

ADJECTIVES

a tough/stern/stiff test *The Olympics will be his sternest test so far.*

an important test *This crisis will be an important test of his leadership.*

a crucial test (=very important) *The political debates will be a crucial test of McCain's confidence.*

VERBS

face a test *Mr Cameron will face the toughest test of his career tomorrow.*

survive a test *Federer survived a test of nerves in an exciting game.*

PHRASES

a test of courage/strength/endurance/character etc *Taking part in such a risky event is a real test of courage.*

test[2] *v*

to check or use something to see what it is like or how good it is

NOUNS

test sb's ability/skill/understanding *The exam tests your ability to think logically.*

test a drug/medicine/vaccine *Scientists want to start testing a new cancer drug.*

test a product/car/device etc *The device has been tested and its design improved.*

test a theory/hypothesis *Research will test her hypothesis.*

test sb's eyes/hearing *The machine will help test babies' hearing.*

test sb's blood/urine *They regularly have their blood tested for HIV.*

test a sample *Soil samples are being tested for bacteria.*

test the validity/accuracy of sth *How can we test the validity of this theory?*

test the effectiveness of sth *Harrison carried out an experiment to test the effectiveness of this technique.*

ADVERBS

be fully/thoroughly/rigorously tested *The new system will be fully tested before being installed on the company's computers.*

be properly/adequately tested *The equipment had not been properly tested.*

be extensively tested *The product was extensively tested before being launched.*

be successfully tested *No American rocket of that type had yet been successfully tested.*

PREPOSITIONS

test sb/sth for sth *They tested her for diabetes.*

test sth on sb/sth *I don't use cosmetics which have been tested on animals.*

PHRASES

have/get sth tested *You should get your eyes tested at least once every two years.*

test positive for sth (=be found to have a condition or to have a substance in your body) *The athlete tested positive for drugs and was banned.*

test negative for sth (=be found not to have a condition or not to have a substance in your body) *She tested negative for the virus.*

text Ac *n*

the words that form a piece of writing

ADJECTIVES

the original text *The error did not appear in the original text of the article.*

the final text *She is working on the final text of her novel.*

the full text *The full text of his lecture is available from the Law Faculty office.*

the main text *This incident is mentioned at the bottom of the page, not in the main text.*

printed text *Handwriting is usually harder to read than printed text.*

VERBS

edit text *The text should have been edited more carefully.*

copy text *You can easily copy text on a computer.*

delete text *What should you do if you have accidentally deleted some text?*

highlight/select text *Highlight the text you want to move.*

store text *Large amounts of text can be stored on the disk.*

PHRASES

a line of text *Leave space for three lines of text.*

a page of text *This publication has only 30 pages of text.*

a piece/block/section of text *You can move blocks of text around.*

texture *n*

the way a substance feels when you touch it or eat it

ADJECTIVES/NOUNS + texture

a soft texture *The texture of the cheese is soft and creamy.*

a firm texture *He prefers bread with a firmer texture.*

a smooth texture *The dessert has a good flavour and a smooth texture.*

a silky texture (=soft, smooth, and shiny) *Your omelette should have a silky texture.*

a velvety texture (=smooth and soft) *The cream gave my skin a velvety texture.*

a rough texture *She felt the rough texture of his beard against her cheek.*

a creamy texture (=tasting thick and smooth) *The soup looked beautiful and the texture was really creamy.*

a crunchy texture (=tasting firm and making a noise when bitten) *The salad has a lovely crunchy texture.*

surface texture *The walls have rather a rough surface texture.*

skin texture *She uses a wheat-based cream to improve her skin texture.*

VERBS

have a ... texture *The shirt has a very rough texture.*

give sth a ... texture *Add cream to give the sauce a smoother texture.*

PREPOSITIONS

in texture *The first cheese was smoother in texture.*

thank *v*

to tell someone that you are pleased and grateful for something they have given you or done for you

ADVERBS

thank sb personally *Alan wants to meet you and thank you personally.*

thank sb publicly *I wish to thank him publicly for his long service and commitment to the University of Colorado.*

thank sb profusely *formal* (=very much) *Mr Barker thanked her profusely for coming.*

thank sb politely *He thanked the driver politely for the ride.*

PREPOSITIONS

thank sb for sth *She thanked them for the presents.*

PHRASES

I would like to thank sb for sth *I would like to thank everyone for all their hard work on this project.*

thanks *interjection, n*

1 a short way of saying **thank you**. **Thanks** is more common than **thank you** in everyday spoken English and is more informal

ADJECTIVES

thanks very much/thanks a lot *"Here's your meal." "Thanks very much."*

many thanks for sth (=thanks very much - more formal) *Many thanks for all the lovely presents.*

no thanks *"More coffee?" "No thanks."*

PREPOSITIONS

thanks for sth *Thanks for your help.*

2 the things you say or do to show that you are grateful to someone

ADJECTIVES

grateful thanks *I wanted to offer our grateful thanks to everyone who helped to organize the event.*

sincere/heartfelt thanks (=used when saying that you really feel grateful for something) *Please accept my most sincere thanks for all your help.*

special thanks *Special thanks to my coach for all his work with me over the years.*

VERBS

give thanks *Let us give thanks to God.*

express your thanks (=say that you are grateful) *I would like to express my thanks to you for all your support.*

offer/extend your thanks *formal* (=thank someone publicly) *We would like to extend our heartfelt thanks to the doctors and nurses at the hospital.*

pass on your thanks (*also* **send your thanks**) (=give a message of thanks) *Please pass on our thanks to all your staff.*

get no thanks/not get any thanks *You won't get any thanks from him.*

PHRASES

my/our thanks go to sb (=used when thanking someone in public) *Above all, my thanks go to the staff who worked so hard to put on the show.*

without a word of thanks (=without saying thank you) *He ate and drank, then left without a word of thanks.*

thank you *interjection, n*

used to tell someone that you are grateful for something they have given you or done for you

ADVERBS

thank you very much (indeed) *It's lovely - thank you very much.*

T

thank you so much *Thank you so much for helping me.*

thank you again *Thank you again for inviting me.*

⚠ Don't say 'thank you a lot'. Say **thank you very much** or, informally, **thanks a lot**.

VERBS

say thank you *I must find Susan and say thank you to her before we leave.*

ADJECTIVES

a big thank you *Once again, a big thank you to everyone who helped organize the party.*

a special thank you *I'd like to say a special thank you to the nurses.*

PREPOSITIONS

thank you for (doing) sth *Thank you for the flowers. | Thank you for coming.*

a thank you to sb *I took a cake into the office as a thank you to my team.*

Spelling

Thank you is normally written as two separate words. It is written with a hyphen **thank-you** when it is used as an adjective, for example in **thank-you letter/note/card/present**.

theatre *BrE*, theater *AmE n*

a place with a stage where plays and shows are performed, or the activity of performing plays

ADJECTIVES/NOUNS + theatre

a 300-seat/1,000-seat theatre *There are plans to build a new 2,000-seat theatre.*

a crowded/packed theatre (=full of people) *On the first night of the play, the theatre was completely packed.*

an open-air theatre (=one that is outside) *The Globe is an open-air theatre and there is no roof.*

theatre + NOUNS

a theatre company (=a group of actors that perform plays) *The local theatre company is putting on a production of 'The Merchant of Venice'.*

a theatre producer *A theatre producer on Broadway wanted him to appear in the show.*

a theatre critic *The theatre critics all loved the play.*

theft *n* the crime of stealing

ADJECTIVES

attempted theft *He was charged with attempted theft.*

petty theft (=the stealing of something that is not very valuable) *There had been a series of petty thefts at the school.*

NOUNS + theft

car theft *BrE*, **auto theft** *AmE*: *The region has one of the highest levels of car theft in Europe.*

identity theft (=when someone steals your personal information and uses it to obtain goods or money) *It seems she has become the victim of identity theft.*

art theft *Robbers stole paintings worth £25 million in France's biggest art theft.*

VERBS

commit a theft *Detectives took us to the place where the theft had been committed.*

report a theft *You must report the theft to the police as quickly as possible.*

theft + NOUNS

theft charges *Her son was arrested on theft charges.*

theft offences *Police arrested over 30 people at the festival for theft offences.*

PREPOSITIONS

the theft of sth *He reported the theft of a watch from his hotel room.*

PHRASES

a spate/string/series of thefts (=several thefts happening during a short period of time) *There has been a spate of thefts from garden sheds in the area.*

theme Ac *n*

the main subject or idea in a speech, film, piece of writing etc

ADJECTIVES

the main/central/dominant theme *The main theme of the book is the importance of honesty.*

a major theme *Cultural change is a major theme of his work.*

a common theme *Death and rebirth is a common theme in Eliot's poetry.*

a constant/perennial theme (=one that is always there) *The loneliness of the individual is a perennial theme in crime writing.*

a recurrent/recurring theme (=one that appears several times) *Childhood is a recurrent theme in her work.*

an underlying theme (=one that is important but not always very noticeable) *One of the book's underlying themes is the struggle for human rights.*

a universal theme (=one that affects people everywhere) *Readers everywhere can relate to the universal themes in his work.*

VERBS

deal with a theme (*also* **address/explore a theme** *formal*): *The first part of the play deals with the theme of personal loss.*

develop/pursue a theme *How well does the writer develop this theme in later chapters?*

a theme emerges (=becomes noticeable) *This tragic theme does not emerge until the second act.*

a theme runs through sth (=exists in all parts of it) *The theme of human evil runs through all his paintings.*

PREPOSITIONS

the theme of sth *Students are invited to discuss the main theme of the poem.*

PHRASES

variations on a theme (=things with a similar basic subject, style etc) *Most of her short stories are variations on the theme of betrayal.*

theory Ac *n*

an idea or set of ideas that is intended to explain something

ADJECTIVES/NOUNS + theory

a scientific/political/economic etc theory *Scientific theories can be tested experimentally.*

a conspiracy theory (=a theory that an event was the result of secret plan made by several people) *There are dozens of conspiracy theories about President Kennedy's assassination.*

a pet theory (=a personal theory that you strongly believe) *Each of these historians has his pet theory on what caused the revolution.*

literary/critical theory (=ways of thinking about literature and art) *Students will study critical theory as well as reading literature.*

VERBS + theory

have a theory (*also* **hold a theory** *formal*): *She has a theory that there are fewer differences between girls and boys than we think.*

put forward a theory (*also* **advance a theory** *formal*) (=suggest it) *The article puts forward the theory that Americans dislike their economic power.*

come up with a theory (*also* **develop a theory**) *These birds helped Darwin develop his theory of natural selection.*

test a theory *Researchers gave workers a questionnaire to test their theory.*

prove a theory *No evidence exists to prove his theory.*

support a theory *Modern research strongly supports a different theory.*

disprove a theory (*also* **refute a theory** *formal*) (=show that it is wrong) *Later experiments seemed to disprove the theory.*

discredit a theory (=make people stop believing it) *These latest findings discredit his entire theory.*

theory + VERBS

a theory states/holds that... *His main political theory states that all societies need a class system.*

a theory assumes that... *This theory assumes that everybody wants to be a winner.*

theories abound (=there are many of them) *Of course, theories abound as to why people love their pets.*

PREPOSITIONS

a theory about sth *There are numerous theories about why dinosaurs died out.*

the theory of evolution/natural selection/relativity *According to the theory of relativity, nothing can travel faster than light.*

PHRASES

in theory (=used for saying what is supposed to be true but may not really be true) *Higher wages will, in theory, lead to more spending.*

therapy *n*

treatment for an emotional problem, an illness, or an injury

VERBS

have therapy (*also* **undergo therapy** *formal*): *He underwent months of therapy after the accident.*

receive therapy *She is receiving therapy for her depression.*

need therapy *He needed therapy to help him overcome various psychological problems.*

treat sb/sth with therapy *Back pain should be treated with medicine or therapy.*

ADJECTIVES

occupational therapy (=activities that are intended to help people get better after an illness) *Occupational therapy can help to solve practical problems you may have in carrying out everyday activities.*

physical therapy *AmE*: *Your doctor will likely recommend physical therapy to speed recovery of a broken ankle.*

behavioural therapy *BrE*, **behavioral therapy** *AmE*: *Phobias can be treated with behavioural therapy.*

alternative/complementary therapy *This article reviews the different popular alternative cancer therapies practiced in India.*

NOUNS + therapy

speech therapy *The centre provides speech therapy for both adults and children.*

drug therapy *Treatment for the disease usually involves drug therapy.*

gene therapy (=treatment of diseases by changing the genetic structure of something) *Gene therapy could be used to treat a range of different medical conditions.*

cancer/HIV etc therapy *Improved cancer therapies have led to an increase in survival rates among patients.*

therapy + NOUNS

a therapy session *He booked a therapy session with a psychiatrist.*

PHRASES

be in therapy (=be receiving treatment for emotional problems, in which you talk to someone who is trained to help you) *She was in therapy for several years.*

T

a course of therapy *Patients must complete a course of therapy for this disease.*

thesis *n*

1 a long piece of writing about a particular subject that you do as part of an advanced university degree

ADJECTIVES/NOUNS + thesis

MA/master's thesis *He began working on his MA thesis during the summer.*

PhD/doctoral thesis *She wrote an excellent PhD thesis on the genetics of fruit flies.*

VERBS

write/do a thesis *You have to write a thesis if you are doing a PhD.*

read a thesis *Have you read his thesis on German cinema?*

submit a thesis (=hand it in) *You submit your thesis before the end of the academic year.*

mark a thesis *BrE*, **grade a thesis** *AmE*: *The thesis will be marked by two examiners.*

publish a thesis *You should consider publishing your thesis as a book.*

supervise sb's thesis *Professor Eggers supervised his thesis.*

thesis + NOUNS

a thesis topic *Choose a thesis topic that interests you.*

PREPOSITIONS

a thesis on sth *She wrote her thesis on the French poet Guillaume Apollinaire.*

PHRASES

the title of sb's thesis *The title of his thesis was 'The Nature of Religious Belief in Contemporary Britain'.*

2 an idea or opinion about something that you discuss in a formal way and give examples for

ADJECTIVES

the central/main thesis *The central thesis of his argument is that the Earth is like a single organism.*

the basic/fundamental thesis *Their basic thesis was that the rise in earnings was due to improvements in education.*

VERBS

put forward/propose a thesis *He put forward the thesis that the explorer Marco Polo never got as far as China.*

disprove a thesis (*also* **refute a thesis** *formal*): *He attempts to disprove the thesis that the illness is caused by a lack of iron.*

challenge a thesis *The article challenges the thesis that more people in prison means less crime on the streets.*

support a thesis *The research supports the thesis that health problems are strongly correlated with lack of regular exercise.*

PREPOSITIONS

a thesis about sth *She put forward a thesis about the spread of the disease.*

thick *adj*

1 if something is thick, there is a large distance between its two opposite surfaces or sides

NOUNS

a thick slice/piece *The boy cut himself a thick slice of bread.*

a thick coat/sweater/scarf etc *She wore a thick coat with a fur collar.*

a thick carpet/blanket/curtain/towel *She padded across the thick bedroom carpet.*

thick paper/glass/material *The bag was made of thick strong paper.*

a thick wall/door *The castle has immensely thick walls.*

a thick book/volume *She opened a thick book lying on the table.*

a thick envelope *He took a thick envelope from his coat pocket and handed it to me.*

a thick layer *The town was covered by a thick layer of ash.*

thick glasses/lenses *An elderly man wearing thick glasses came into the room.*

thick soles *He moved along soundlessly on his thick rubber soles.*

a thick neck *He had broad powerful shoulders and a thick neck.*

thick lips/fingers/ankles *He had thick fingers, like sausages.*

PHRASES

12 centimetres/3 feet/20 metres etc thick *The walls of the tower are ten feet thick.*

THESAURUS: thick

fat
wallet | envelope | book | cigar
thick, usually because of being full of something:
The well-dressed man took a twenty pound note out of his fat wallet. | The fat envelope contained the manuscript of her latest book. | I hoped I would have time to read a couple of fat books on holiday. | He was smoking a big fat cigar.

Fat sounds rather informal. It is often used after **big**.

chunky
necklace | ring | earrings | jewellery | sweater
thick, solid, and heavy:
Chunky gold earrings swung from her pierced ears. | His mother gave him chunky handknitted sweaters for Christmas.

heavy
coat | overcoat | sweater | curtain | cloth | fabric

heavy clothing or cloth is thick and usually warm:
People stood around in heavy winter coats, stamping their feet to keep warm. | She pulled back the heavy red velvet curtain. | The men all wore trousers and jackets made of a heavy woollen fabric.

THESAURUS: thick

broad, thick → **wide (1)**

2 very dense or growing very closely together

NOUNS

thick forest/jungle *Not much light penetrates into the thick jungle.*
thick undergrowth/vegetation *They moved slowly through the thick undergrowth.*
thick smoke *They saw thick black smoke pouring out of the factory.*
thick fog/mist *The fog was so thick I could not see the end of the street.*
thick cloud *We were flying through thick cloud.*
thick hair *The old man had thick white hair.*
a thick beard *He had a thick beard that covered half of his face.*
thick grass *We had to trudge through thick grass.*

thief *n*

someone who steals things from another person or place

ADJECTIVES/NOUNS + thief

a petty thief (=one who steals small things) *He was a petty thief who stole goods from shops to pay for drugs.*
a common thief (=a thief – used when saying that someone does not deserve any respect) *The mayor was taken away and put in prison like a common thief.*
a car thief *Car thieves are operating in this area.*

VERBS

catch a thief *Police caught the thieves outside the store.*
a thief steals/takes sth *The thieves took all her credit cards.*
a thief breaks into sth *Thieves broke into the offices and stole $100,000 of computer equipment.*
a thief grabs/snatches sth *The thief grabbed her handbag and ran off down the street.*
a thief gets away with sth *The thieves got away with paintings worth millions of dollars.*

PHRASES

a gang of thieves *A gang of thieves broke into the house and stole all their money.*

thin *adj*

1 a thin person has little fat on his or her body

NOUNS

a thin man/woman/boy/girl *The clerk was a small thin man with yellow teeth.*
a thin face *She had a long thin face.*
thin lips *There was a faint smile on his thin lips.*
thin legs *Her long cotton dress flapped against her thin legs.*
thin arms/wrists/fingers *His thin arms trembled in the cold.*
a thin body *She put her arms around his poor thin body.*

VERBS

look thin *He looks thinner than the last time I saw him.*
get/become thin *You need to eat more – you're getting very thin.*
stay thin *I wonder how she manages to stay so thin.*

ADVERBS

extremely/incredibly thin *Some fashion models are incredibly thin.*
painfully thin (=much too thin – used when you feel sorry for someone) *The dogs were painfully thin and many were diseased.*

PHRASES

as thin as a rake (=very thin) *When he came out of prison, he was as thin as a rake.*

THESAURUS: thin

narrow
waist | hips | shoulders | chest | face | feet
not wide – used about parts of someone's body:
Women had very narrow waists in those days. | His hips were narrow, like those of a young boy. | He has a narrow face and a long thin nose.

slim
woman | man | build | figure | body | waist | legs | hips
thin in an attractive way:
She was a slim young woman with curly hair. | He had the slim build of an athlete. | We were all envious of her slim figure.

slender *literary*
body | figure | woman | legs | fingers | neck
thin in an attractive and graceful way:
A towel was wrapped around her slender body. | The dress showed off her long slender legs. | Her long slender fingers paused over the keyboard.

skinny *informal*
legs | arms | body | boy | kid | man | woman | model
very thin, especially in a way that is not attractive:

T

Her skinny legs were shaking because of the cold. | *I was just a skinny kid and I wasn't going to fight.*

lean
body | **figure** | **face** | **frame**
looking healthy and fit, without any fat at all:
I could see his strong lean body under his shirt. | *The tight suit emphasized his lean frame.*

gaunt *literary*
face | **features** | **figure** | **woman** | **man**
very thin and pale, especially because you are tired, worried, or ill:
The old man's gaunt face broke into a smile. | *The photograph showed a gaunt figure lying in a hospital bed.*

underweight
below the usual weight for someone of your height, and therefore too thin:
The doctor says I'm underweight and has put me on a special diet. | *She gave birth to an* ***underweight baby***.

anorexic
extremely thin because of a mental illness that makes you want to stop eating:
Her daughter is anorexic.

size zero
model
the smallest size of women's clothing in the US - used to describe models and women who are very thin:
The use of size zero models in advertising creates an unrealistic image of women's bodies.

ANTONYMS **thin → fat[1] (1)**

2 if something is thin, there is only a small distance between its two opposite sides or surfaces

NOUNS

a thin slice *He cut himself a thin slice of bread.*

a thin strip *Cut the bacon into thin strips.*

a thin layer/film/sheet *The furniture was covered in a thin layer of dust.*

a thin line *She noticed a thin line of sweat on his upper lip.*

thin material/fabric/cotton/silk etc *She was wearing a thin cotton dress.*

a thin jacket/shirt/pullover etc *The wind cut through his thin shirt like a knife.*

a thin chain/wire/string *A thin gold chain hung from her neck.*

a thin wall *He could hear the neighbours arguing through the thin wall.*

thin ice *The lake was covered in thin ice.*

ADVERBS

extremely/incredibly thin *Television screens are incredibly thin nowadays.*

THESAURUS: thin

slim
volume | **book** | **paperback** | **box** | **watch**
slim books are short and thin. **Slim** is also used about other objects which are thin and attractive:
He began reading from a slim volume of poetry (=a thin book of poetry). | *She glanced at the slim gold watch on her wrist.*

slender *literary*
tree | **stem** | **thread** | **column** | **vase** | **book**
tall and thin or long and thin, in a way that looks attractive but is often not very strong:
The slender trees had lost all their leaves. | *The spider was hanging by a slender thread.* | *The roof was supported by four slender columns.*

paper-thin/wafer-thin
wall | **slice** | **sheet** | **scrap** | **petal**
extremely thin, like paper. **Wafer-thin** is even thinner than **paper-thin**:
The walls of the apartment were paper-thin. | *He cut the cheese into wafer-thin slices.*

fine
hair | **thread** | **wire** | **needle** | **tip**
extremely narrow - used especially about hair, thread etc:
Polly felt the fine hairs on her arm rise. | *The cotton is spun to a fine thread.* | *The cloth is richly decorated with fine gold wire.* | *The plant's broad leaves curve to a fine tip.*

ANTONYMS **thin → thick (1)**

thing *n*

1 an idea, action, feeling, or fact

ADJECTIVES

a good/bad thing *The bad thing about the house is how cold it is in winter.*

the right thing (=what is fair, reasonable, or morally correct) *I was confident that he would do the right thing.*

the important thing *The important thing to remember is that it's your choice.*

the best thing *The best thing to do is discuss the problem with a friend.*

a strange/curious/odd/funny thing *There were some funny things about him.*

the last thing (=something that you did not want or intend to do at all) *Upsetting her is the last thing I intended.*

PHRASES

a ... thing to do/say *It wasn't a very nice thing to say to your friend.*

it's no bad thing (=it is a good thing) *If we arrive a little later, it's no bad thing.*

I did/said no such thing (=used when denying that you said or did something) *She says I insulted her, but I did no such thing.*

teach sb/know a thing or two (=teach or know a lot of things) *She's taught me a thing or two about relationships.*
say/do a thing like that (=say or do something as bad, unfair, harmful etc as that) *How can you say a thing like that after all the help I've given you!*
do/say/think etc such a thing (=do, say, think etc a thing like that) *I would never say such a thing!*

2 used when talking in general about a situation

> **Grammar**
> This meaning is always plural.

VERBS
things change *Things have changed dramatically over the last few years.*
things improve *Things at school appear to be improving.*

PHRASES
things go well/badly/smoothly *If things went well, we would double our money in five years.*
things get worse *After I lost my job, things got worse at home.*
make things worse/easier/difficult *The new traffic system has actually made things worse.*
as things stand (=at present) *As things stand, I can hardly afford to pay the rent.*
things look good/bright/promising (=the future situation is likely to be good) *Things look good for the retail industry as sales continue to rise.*
things look bleak/grim (=the future situation is likely to be bad) *With only three wins all season, things are looking bleak for the team.*
as things turned out (=used to say what happened or was discovered in the end) *As things turned out, I was completely wrong about this.*
the way things are (=the present situation) *If you're not happy with the way things are, make a change.*
things get out of control (*also* **things get out of hand**) *Things got out of control and we had to fire him.*

3 clothes, equipment, or general possessions

> **Grammar**
> This meaning is always plural: *I haven't packed my* ***things*** *yet.*

VERBS
pack/unpack your things *I'm going to unpack my things then have a shower.*
bring/take your things *I'll bring my night things, then I can sleep over.*

NOUNS + thing
football/tennis/swimming etc things *Don't forget to take your swimming things to school.*
breakfast/lunch etc things *It's your turn to wash the breakfast things.*

PHRASES
put/clear/tidy things away *Tidy your school things away before you put the TV on.*
get things together *He was still getting his fishing things together when his friends arrived.*
put things on *She's putting her gardening things on.*
take things off *Take those wet things off.*

think *v*

1 to use your mind to consider, decide, or imagine something

ADVERBS
think carefully *Think carefully before you spend such a lot of money.*
think hard (=with a lot of mental effort) *I thought really hard before making this decision.*
think deeply *I should have thought more deeply before I agreed.*
think seriously *I thought seriously about my doctor's advice.*
think clearly *She was simply too tired to think clearly.*
think fast *There was only five minutes left. I would have to think fast.*
think twice (=consider something carefully) *You should think twice before making such a big change in your life.*
think big *informal* (=to have ambitious plans) *You have to think big to be successful in professional sport.*

PREPOSITIONS
think about sth/sb (*also* **think of sth/sb**) *I often think about the great times we had together.*

PHRASES
think long and hard (=think for a long time before making a decision) *I thought long and hard about taking the job.*
I hate/dread/shudder to think (=I do not want to think about something bad) *I dread to think what might have happened if we hadn't found her.*
think in terms of... (=think that you should do something) *We should be thinking in terms of expanding the company.*

2 to have a particular opinion or belief

> **Grammar**
> **Think** is usually followed by **(that)** in this meaning: *I* ***think (that)*** *you're right.* | *She didn't* ***think (that)*** *the film was very good.*

T

ADVERBS

honestly/seriously think sth *I honestly think you should see a doctor.*

personally think sth *I personally think he has done nothing wrong.*

think otherwise/differently (=have a different opinion) *I thought it was unfair, but Dad thought otherwise.*

think highly/well of sb/sth (=have a good opinion of them) *All his teachers think very well of him.*

PHRASES

what do you think of/about...? (=used when asking someone's opinion) *What did the kids think of the film?*

think it best/wise/appropriate etc *He thinks it best if he stays at home.*

I can't help thinking... (*also* **I am inclined to think...**) *spoken* (=used for giving an honest opinion after considering something) *She keeps ignoring me, so I can't help thinking I've done something to offend her.*

not think much of sb/sth (=have a low opinion of them) *I didn't think much of his cooking.*

am I right in thinking...? *spoken* (=used for asking someone if your opinion or belief is correct) *Am I right in thinking that the tall lady is his wife?*

> **Think** or **believe?**
>
> You use **believe** about serious or important subjects: *I* ***believe*** *that everyone has the right to free speech. | Many* ***people*** *believe that standards of English are falling.*
>
> You can use **think** about any opinion: *I* ***think*** *blue looks good on you. | Do you* ***think*** *that the death penalty should be abolished?*

thinking *n*

1 the act of using your mind to produce ideas or thoughts

ADJECTIVES

quick thinking *He was only saved by the quick thinking of two doctors.*

hard thinking *Over the next two days a lot of hard thinking went into the campaign.*

serious thinking *Your mother and I have been doing some serious thinking.*

clear/logical thinking *Above 24,000 feet, the lack of oxygen makes clear thinking almost impossible.*

critical thinking (=when you make careful judgments about how good or bad something is) *The course gives students the chance to practise critical thinking.*

creative thinking (=when you use your imagination to produce new ideas or things) *Her solution to the problem was an example of good creative thinking.*

positive thinking (=thinking in which you feel sure that good things will happen, which helps you to be successful) *What we need is positive thinking.*

joined-up thinking *BrE* (=when all the different parts of a plan or situation are considered together, with better results) *The media has criticized the lack of joined-up thinking in the government's plan.*

PHRASES

do some/a lot of/a little thinking *I've had a chance to do some thinking.*

2 an opinion or idea

ADJECTIVES

new/fresh thinking *There is a need for fresh thinking to solve these problems.*

current thinking (*also* **contemporary thinking** *formal*): *What is the current thinking on the use of these drugs?*

the latest thinking *The latest thinking is that the mother's own milk is best for a baby.*

good thinking (=used for saying that an idea is good) *"We'd better lock the door." "Good thinking."*

original thinking *The best students demonstrate original thinking on the subject.*

philosophical/political etc thinking *Modern political thinking sees the issue differently.*

VERBS

explain/outline your thinking *The article explains our thinking on this issue.*

clarify your thinking *Would the minister clarify her thinking on the question of arms sales?*

PREPOSITIONS

thinking on/about sth *This is the latest government thinking on student fees.*

the thinking behind sth *I don't understand the thinking behind this decision.*

thirst *n*

1 the state of wanting or needing a drink

ADJECTIVES

a powerful thirst (=a strong feeling of thirst) *Joe had a powerful thirst and drank the whole bottle in seconds.*

a raging/terrible thirst (=a very strong feeling of thirst) *After the party, he woke up with a headache and a raging thirst.*

VERBS

quench your thirst (=drink to get rid of it) *He brought them water to quench their thirst.*

slake your thirst *literary* (=quench it) *Animals come to slake their thirst at the pool.*

suffer from thirst *They marched on, suffering terribly from thirst.*

die of thirst *Their companions had died of thirst.*

⚠ Don't say 'I have thirst'. Say **I'm thirsty**.

2 *literary* a strong desire for something

ADJECTIVES

a great/tremendous thirst *In today's world, there is a tremendous thirst for information.*

an insatiable/unquenchable thirst (=a strong desire that cannot be stopped) *He had an unquenchable thirst for hard work and did all the organizing.*

VERBS

have a thirst for sth *She had a thirst for facts.*

satisfy sb's thirst for sth *His job as a ski instructor failed to satisfy his thirst for adventure.*

PREPOSITIONS

a thirst for sth *He was delighted by his students' thirst for knowledge.*

thirsty *adj*

feeling that you want or need a drink

VERBS

be/feel thirsty *Can I have a glass of water? I'm really thirsty.*

make sb (feel) thirsty *The heat makes you thirsty.*

PHRASES

sth is thirsty work (=it makes you feel thirsty) *All this digging is thirsty work*

hot and thirsty *He had been working in the garden and was feeling hot and thirsty.*

thorough *adj*

including every possible detail

ADVERBS

very/extremely thorough *He promised an extremely thorough investigation.*

admirably thorough (=used when you admire someone's work because it is very thorough) *Her research for the book was admirably thorough.*

THESAURUS: thorough

cautious, thorough, methodical, systematic, meticulous, painstaking → **careful**

thought *n*

1 something that you think of, remember, or realize

ADJECTIVES

sb's first thought *My first thought was that he must have forgotten our meeting.*

a pleasant/nice thought *Maybe she was getting old. It was not a pleasant thought.*

a strange/funny thought *A strange thought crossed his mind.*

a comforting thought *I miss my daughter, but knowing that she's happy is a comforting thought.*

a frightening/chilling/horrible/disturbing/ thought *A horrible thought struck her: could he be having an affair?*

a depressing thought *"The holiday is almost over." "What a depressing thought!"*

a sobering thought (=one that makes you feel serious) *We have the power to destroy the world, which is a sobering thought.*

a passing/fleeting thought (=a quick, not very serious thought) *He never gives his appearance more than a passing thought.*

a sudden thought *At first she couldn't think what to do, but then she had a sudden thought.*

negative/positive thoughts *Try to clear your mind of negative thoughts.*

sb's innermost thoughts (=personal and secret ones) *He would never share his innermost thoughts with anyone.*

VERBS + thought

have a thought *I just had a funny thought.*

express your thoughts (=say what they are or tell other people about them) *He was finding it difficult to express his thoughts.*

share your thoughts (=tell them to other people) *It's good to have someone to share your thoughts with.*

can't bear the thought of sth (*also* **hate the thought of sth**) *I can't bear the thought of you being hurt.*

dismiss a thought (=refuse to consider it) *Was her husband involved in the crime? She dismissed the thought instantly.*

thought + VERBS

a thought occurs to/comes to/strikes sb (=someone suddenly has a thought) *The thought occurred to him that she might be lying.*

a thought crosses sb's mind (=someone has a thought) *The thought never crossed my mind that I could be wrong.*

sb's thoughts turn to sth (=they start thinking about something) *As summer approaches, people's thoughts turn to holidays.*

sb's thoughts drift (back) to sth (=they stop thinking about something and start thinking about something else) *My thoughts drifted back to last night.*

PREPOSITIONS

the thought of (doing) sth *I didn't like the thought of going back there again.*

thoughts about sth *He kept having thoughts about death.*

PHRASES

the very thought (=even the idea of doing something) *The very thought of going on stage made her feel ill.*

spare a thought for sb *BrE* (=used for telling someone that they should think about someone in a worse situation than they are) *Spare a thought for those who have to work while you're out enjoying yourself.*

on second thoughts (=used when saying that you have changed your decision, because you have thought of something else) *On second thoughts, can we have the meeting next week? I'm busy all this week.*

2 the act or process of thinking about something

ADJECTIVES

serious/careful thought *He had foolishly made this promise without any serious thought.*

deep thought *Holmes stood still, apparently in deep thought.*

some/little/a great deal of/much thought *Karen had been giving the matter a great deal of thought over the last few weeks.*

conscious thought *Without conscious thought, she placed her hand on his arm.*

rational thought *Mental illness can interfere with rational thought.*

VERBS

give some/careful etc thought to sth (=think about something) *Carmel gave some thought to what he had said.*

thought goes into sth *A lot of thought had gone into planning the event.*

thought + NOUNS

thought process *Most of our thought processes are unconscious.*

a thought pattern (=a way that someone regularly thinks) *People who suffer from depression tend to have negative thought patterns.*

PREPOSITIONS

without thought *What they did, they did carelessly, without thought.*

PHRASES

be deep/lost in thought *Rae walked on, lost in thought.*

with no thought for sth *He dived in to rescue the child, with no thought for his own safety.*

a train/line of thought (=a series of related thoughts that are developing in your mind) *The loud noise interrupted her train of thought.*

freedom of thought (=when people are allowed to think whatever they want) *Everyone has the right to freedom of thought.*

food for thought (=something that makes you think carefully) *The workshop and discussion should provide us with plenty of food for thought.*

thoughtful *adj*

1 serious and quiet because you are thinking a lot

VERBS

look thoughtful *He looked thoughtful for a moment.*

NOUNS

a thoughtful look/expression *He had a thoughtful expression on his face.*

a thoughtful mood *She was in a thoughtful mood.*

a thoughtful silence/pause *There was a thoughtful pause before the conversation started up again.*

ADVERBS

deeply thoughtful *As we walked home, Lisa was silent and deeply thoughtful.*

2 showing that you have thought carefully about how to do something

NOUNS

a thoughtful approach/manner/way *A more thoughtful approach to fighting violent crime is required.*

a thoughtful analysis *The article provides a thoughtful analysis of some key issues.*

3 thinking about other people's feelings

PHRASES

it was thoughtful of sb to do sth *It was thoughtful of them to leave the room so that we could talk in private.*

a thoughtful thing to do *Offering to carry her bags was a thoughtful thing to do.*

How thoughtful (of you)! *"I've brought some of your favourite chocolates." "How thoughtful of you!"*

THESAURUS: thoughtful

generous, considerate, thoughtful, caring, sympathetic, compassionate, warm-hearted/kind-hearted, benevolent, benign, nice, good, sweet → **kind**[2]

thoughtless *adj* THESAURUS ▸ careless

thread *n*

a long thin string of cotton, silk etc used, for example, in sewing

ADJECTIVES/NOUNS + thread

cotton/silk/nylon etc thread *The hole had been sewn up with nylon thread.*

gold/silver thread *The robe was richly embroidered with gold thread.*

sewing thread *You will need some strong sewing thread.*

fine thread (=thin thread) *Use fine thread when you are sewing a delicate fabric such as silk.*

strong thread *Polyester thread is very strong.*

VERBS

spin thread (=make thread by twisting wool, cotton etc) *Women would spin thread and make cloth.*

PHRASES

a piece/length of thread *He bit off a piece of thread.*

a spool/reel of thread (=a small object that thread is wound around) *I bought a spool of white thread.*

(a) needle and thread *She was an expert with needle and thread.*

threat *n*

1 a statement in which you tell someone that you will cause them harm or trouble if they do not do what you want

VERBS

make/issue a threat *Neighbours say that they heard the man make threats against his wife.*

carry out a threat (=do what you threatened to do) *She should have carried out her threat to tell the police.*

receive a threat *He has received many threats against his life.*

lift/withdraw a threat (=say that it is no longer true) *The group has lifted its earlier threat of armed attack.*

give in to a threat (=do what someone wants you to do after they threaten you) *The government is not going to give in to terrorist threats.*

ADJECTIVES/NOUNS + threat

a death threat (=a threat to kill someone) *Scientists involved in the research have received death threats.*

a bomb threat *The station was closed because of a bomb threat.*

an empty/idle threat (=that someone does not intend to carry out) *I knew she was not making idle threats.*

a veiled threat (=one that is not made directly) *The emails contained veiled threats of harm.*

PREPOSITIONS

the threat of sth *Government uses the threat of withdrawing funding to control organizations.*

a threat against sth/sb *The terrorists have made threats against police officers.*

the threat from sb *Experts believe the threat from these paramilitary groups is very real.*

2 something or someone that could cause harm or problems

ADJECTIVES/NOUNS + threat

a serious/major/grave threat *Pollution poses a serious threat to public health.*

the greatest/biggest threat *The greatest threat to our planet is climate change.*

a real threat *Competition from abroad poses a real threat to the car industry.*

a potential threat *He see me as a potential threat to his position as manager.*

a perceived threat (=which people believe exists) *People are very worried about the perceived threat of violent crime.*

an apparent threat (=which seems to exist) *There seemed no apparent threat of the school being closed.*

an immediate/imminent threat (=the possibility that something bad will happen very soon) *There is no immediate threat to nearby towns from the volcano.*

a long-term/short-term threat *The banking crisis could be a long-term threat to the economy.*

a direct threat *Workers saw the new technology as a direct threat to their jobs.*

an ever-present threat (*also* **a constant threat**) *There is an ever-present threat of attack from terrorist groups.*

a military threat *Each country regarded the other as a major military threat.*

a terrorist threat *US officials underestimated the terrorist threat before the 25th June bombing.*

a security threat *If this technology became available to terrorist groups, it would pose a serious security threat.*

VERBS

pose/present a threat (=be a threat) *The rebels pose no immediate threat to the government.*

represent a threat *He is not worried, because you represent no threat to him.*

counter/combat a threat *We must work together to counter the threat of terrorism.*

face a threat (=be likely to be affected by something) *The factory is facing the threat of closure.*

meet a threat (=deal with it) *Our armed forces have to evolve to meet new threats.*

eliminate a threat (=get rid of it) *The new law does not eliminate the threat posed by these drugs.*

PREPOSITIONS

a threat of sth *The nuclear industry does not accept that there is a constant threat of disaster.*

a threat to sb/sth *Is there any real threat to public safety?*

the threat from sb/sth *The threat to health from alcohol abuse is still not fully recognized.*

be under threat (=something could stop existing or be destroyed because of something) *The hospital is still under threat of closure. | Many species of animals are under threat because of global warming.*

threaten *v*

1 to say that you will cause someone harm or trouble if they do not do what you want

> **Grammar**
> **Threaten** is usually used with an infinitive in this meaning: *They threatened **to kill** the hostages.*

T

PHRASES

threaten sb with a knife/gun etc *He was threatened with a knife during the robbery.*

threaten sb with violence *Nobody deserves to be threatened with violence for doing their job.*

ADVERBS

repeatedly threaten to do sth *He had repeatedly threatened to leave.*

2 to be likely to harm or destroy something

ADVERBS

seriously threaten sth *The strikes could seriously threaten the economy.*

NOUNS

threaten the security/stability of sth *The court deals with matters which threaten national security.*

threaten the existence of sth *This policy is threatening the existence of smaller companies.*

threaten the survival of sth *Pollution could threaten the survival of these whales.*

threaten sb's livelihood (=be likely to harm their ability to earn money to live) *The government's agricultural policy is threatening the livelihood of farmers.*

threaten sb's life *The operation is to remove a blood clot which is threatening his life.*

threaten the future of sth *It was a bitter political row which threatened the future of the European Union.*

PHRASES

be threatened with closure *Rural schools were threatened with closure.*

be threatened with extinction *Many rare and beautiful plants are threatened with extinction.*

be threatened with demolition/destruction *The building is threatened with demolition to make way for a new road.*

threshold *n*

the level at which something starts to happen or have an effect

ADJECTIVES

a high/low threshold *Young children have very low boredom threshold.*

NOUNS + threshold

sb's pain threshold (=your ability or inability to deal with pain) *A woman's experience of childbirth can depend on her pain threshold.*

sb's boredom threshold (=whether you do or do not get bored easily) *She has a low boredom threshold, so she loves new challenges.*

the tax threshold (=the level at which you start paying tax on the money you have earned) *The government promised to help the lower paid by raising the tax threshold.*

VERBS

exceed a threshold (=be more than the threshold) *The value of many family homes far exceeds the threshold for paying inheritance tax.*

lower a threshold *Lack of sleep can lower your pain threshold.*

raise a threshold *The government is considering raising the tax threshold to £50,000.*

cross the threshold *With this lie he crossed the threshold from dishonesty into crime.*

set/fix/establish a threshold *If the government set a lower threshold, more people would pay the tax.*

PREPOSITIONS

the threshold for sth *What is the current threshold for paying income tax?*

above/below a threshold *Her earnings are now above the 40% tax threshold.*

thrill *n*

a sudden strong feeling of excitement and pleasure, or the thing that makes you feel this

ADJECTIVES

a big/great/tremendous thrill *It was a great thrill for me to beat the champion.*

a real thrill *Driving a race car is a real thrill for me.*

a cheap thrill *disapproving* (=excitement that you can get easily from something silly or bad) *Young people go to the big city in search of cheap thrills.*

a vicarious thrill (=that you get from watching or hearing about someone else doing something exciting) *Many of us enjoy the vicarious thrill of a murder investigation on TV.*

a special thrill *For any performer, appearing in this wonderful theatre is a special thrill.*

VERBS

get a thrill *Some people get a thrill out of skydiving.*

feel/experience a thrill *I felt a thrill of anticipation as I waited for her train to arrive.*

give sb a thrill *It gave her a big thrill to meet a real movie star.*

PHRASES

a thrill of excitement/anticipation/pleasure *As the plane took off, he felt a thrill of excitement.*

thrilled *adj* THESAURUS ▸ **happy**

thriving *adj* THESAURUS ▸ **successful (3)**

throat *n*

the passage that goes from the back of your mouth down inside your neck

ADJECTIVES

a sore throat (*also* **a bad throat** *BrE*) (=one that feels painful) *I had a sore throat and a bit of a cough.*

a dry throat *Her throat was dry with nerves.*

T

VERBS

clear your throat (=cough a little before speaking) *He cleared his throat as if he was about to say something.*

burn sb's throat (=make it hurt and feel hot) *The whisky burned his throat.*

sb's throat hurts *I had to shout so loud my throat hurt.*

sb's throat tightens *My throat tightened with fear.*

throat + NOUNS

a throat infection *He has a severe throat infection.*

PREPOSITIONS

down sb's throat *He poured the drink down his throat.*

PHRASES

have sth stuck in your throat *I had a fishbone stuck in my throat.*

have a lump in your throat (=feel that you want to cry) *When I said goodbye to them, I had a lump in my throat.*

have a frog in your throat (=need to clear your throat) *She started to explain, but she had a frog in her throat.*

thunder *n*

the loud noise that you hear during a storm, usually after a flash of lightning

PHRASES

a clap/crash/crack of thunder (=one extremely loud sound) *Lightning flashed, followed seconds later by a loud crack of thunder.*

a rumble/roll of thunder (=one of a series of deep sounds) *We could hear the rumble of thunder in the distance.*

thunder and lightning *The children were frightened by the thunder and lightning.*

VERBS

thunder crashes/booms (=it makes a sudden loud sound) *Thunder crashed overhead, waking the baby.*

thunder rumbles/rolls (=it makes a continuous deep sound) *Thunder rumbled over the hills.*

ADJECTIVES

distant thunder *We heard the rumble of distant thunder in the night.*

thunderous *adj* THESAURUS ▸ loud

thunderstorm *n*

a storm with thunder and lightning

ADJECTIVES

a violent thunderstorm *There was a violent thunderstorm last night.*

a heavy/severe thunderstorm *Severe thunderstorms are expected in Georgia.*

a big/massive thunderstorm *A massive thunderstorm is about to hit Melbourne.*

ticket *n*

a printed piece of paper which shows that you have paid to do something such as travel on a train, go to a concert, enter a competition etc

ADJECTIVES/NOUNS + ticket

a train/bus/coach ticket *I've lost my train ticket.*

an airline/plane/air ticket *You can pick up your airline tickets at the check-in desk.*

a theatre/concert ticket *The special rate includes theatre tickets and transport from the hotel to the theatre.*

a lottery/raffle ticket *Eva bought a lottery ticket in the hope of winning some money.*

a one-way ticket (*also* **a single ticket** *BrE*) (=a ticket to a place but not back again) *I bought a one-way ticket to London.*

a return ticket *BrE*, **a round-trip ticket** *AmE* (=a ticket to a place and back) *How much is a round-trip ticket to Boston?*

a season ticket (=one that allows you to make a journey or go to a sports stadium, theatre etc as often as you like during a fixed time period) *He has a season ticket for Manchester United.*

a valid ticket (=one that is legally or officially acceptable) *You cannot travel without a valid ticket.*

a free ticket (*also* **a complimentary ticket** *formal*): *We were given some free tickets for the event.*

VERBS

book/reserve a ticket *We booked our tickets well in advance.*

buy a ticket (*also* **purchase a ticket** *formal*): *Sheila bought a ticket for the next flight home.*

ticket + NOUNS

a ticket holder (=someone who has a ticket) *The event is open to ticket holders only.*

a ticket office/booth/counter (=a place where you can buy tickets) *There was a long queue at the ticket office.*

a ticket machine *The ticket machine wasn't working.*

the ticket barrier *BrE* (=a gate or other barrier at a station that you need a ticket to get through) *John insisted on carrying my case as far as the ticket barrier.*

a ticket agency (=a company that sells tickets for concerts, sporting events etc) *Book your tickets online from one of the many ticket agencies.*

a ticket price *Ticket prices for the show range from £15 to £45.*

ticket sales *The concert was cancelled because of poor ticket sales.*

a ticket collector/inspector (=someone who checks tickets on a train or at a station) *The*

T

boy had been challenged by the ticket collector for not having a ticket.

a ticket tout *BrE* (=someone who sells tickets at a high price outside a theatre, sports ground etc because there are not many tickets available) *Ticket touts were standing outside the football stadium.*

PREPOSITIONS

a ticket for sth *How much are tickets for the concert?*

a ticket to somewhere *I'd like a return ticket to London, please.*

tide *n*

the regular rising and falling of the level of the sea

PHRASES

the tide is in (=the sea covers the shore) *You can't walk on the beach when the tide is in.*

the tide is out (=the sea has stopped covering the shore) *Let's go for a walk along the beach while the tide is out.*

ADJECTIVES

high tide (=when the sea reaches its highest point) *At high tide the island is completely cut off.*

low tide (=when the sea reaches its lowest point) *The sands are exposed at low tide.*

the incoming tide (=the tide coming onto the shore) *Be careful that you don't get caught by the incoming tide.*

the rising tide *The rising tide had begun to fill up the channel.*

an ebb tide (=the flow of the sea away from the shore) *We sailed out to sea on the ebb tide.*

VERBS

the tide comes in (=the sea comes nearer) *Once the tide comes in, the cove is cut off.*

the tide goes out *They sat on the beach watching the tide going out.*

the tide turns (=starts coming in or going out) *Soon, the tide would turn and the waves would begin to creep inshore again.*

be cut off by the tide (=become trapped as the sea rises) *Two anglers had to be rescued after getting cut off by the tide.*

tidy *adj especially BrE*

a room, house, desk etc that is tidy is neatly arranged with everything in the right place

VERBS

keep sth tidy *I try to keep my desk tidy.*

PHRASES

neat and tidy/clean and tidy *Ellen's room is always neat and tidy.*

ANTONYMS **tidy → untidy**

tie[1] *v*

1 to fasten or hold things in position using a piece of string, rope etc

ADVERBS

tie sth back *She ties her hair back when she's running.*

tie things together *Use this knot to tie together ropes of different thicknesses.*

tie sth up (=tie it firmly together) *He tied all the old newspapers up in a bundle.*

tie sth down (=firmly to the floor or the ground) *Boxes must be tied down before the plane takes off.*

tie sth firmly/strongly *Tie the rope firmly around the horse's middle.*

NOUNS

tie a knot/bow *Tie a knot round the end of the rope to stop it slipping through the hole.*

tie a rope/string/shoelace etc *Find a tree or rock to tie the rope to.*

PREPOSITIONS

tie sth to sth *Tie this label to your suitcase.*

tie sth round/around sth *He tied a scarf around his head.*

tie sth with sth *I kept all his letters tied together with a ribbon.*

2 to relate or connect one thing to another

> **Grammar**
> **Tie** is usually passive in this meaning.

ADVERBS

be inextricably tied to sth (=so closely that it cannot be separated) *The wealth of the region is inextricably tied to the global economy.*

be intimately tied to sth (=very closely) *The story of the railways is intimately tied to the spread of industry in Europe.*

be closely tied to sth *The future of Austria was closely tied to that of Germany.*

be necessarily tied to sth *For people living in these conditions, health is necessarily tied to poverty.*

PREPOSITIONS

be tied to sth *Your chances of employment are tied to experience and qualifications.*

be tied up with sth *The future of the project is all tied up with the company's budgets.*

tie[2] *n*

1 a strong relationship between people, groups, or countries

> **Grammar**
> Usually plural in this meaning.

ADJECTIVES/NOUNS + tie

close/strong ties *Britain and the US have close ties with each other.*

family/blood ties *Family ties have been weakened by people moving away from their parents.*

personal ties *I have strong personal ties connecting me to this area.*

emotional ties *He was a loner who failed to develop emotional ties with others.*

social ties *Besides marriage, other social ties drew people together.*

economic/diplomatic ties *Japan and South Korea have strong economic ties.*

VERBS

have ties *We have close political ties with several countries in the region.*

develop/establish/forge ties *They are developing business ties with a major Indian company.*

strengthen ties *We are strengthening ties with our European partners.*

sever/cut ties (=stop having them) *They have severed all diplomatic ties with Libya.*

maintain ties *The university is committed to maintaining close ties with industry.*

PREPOSITIONS

ties with sth *They have established ties with researchers in Finland.*

ties to sth *She questioned the minister's close ties to the company.*

ties between sth and sth *There are strong emotional ties between the two families.*

PHRASES

ties of marriage/friendship/blood etc *We should not forget the ties of friendship that unite the two countries.*

2 *especially BrE* a thing that a man wears around his neck under the collar of his shirt

VERBS

wear a tie *I have to wear a tie for work.*

put on/take off your tie *Dan took off his tie and sat down.*

adjust your tie (=slightly change the position) *He was adjusting his tie in front of the mirror.*

do up your tie/knot your tie (=make a knot in it) *His mother showed him how to knot his tie.*

loosen your tie (=make it less tight) *It was very hot and I wanted to loosen my tie.*

ADJECTIVES/NOUNS + tie

sb's tie is undone (=it is not pulled in a tight knot) *His tie was undone and his hair was a mess.*

a school tie *The boys were all wearing their school ties.*

T

The old school tie
This phrase is used when talking about the British class system, in which a small number of people help each other to get the best jobs, because they went to the same expensive schools: *The age of **the old school tie** is far from over.*

tight[1] *adj*

1 fitting very closely

NOUNS

tight clothing *Don't wear tight clothing for hiking.*

tight jeans *He was wearing tight black jeans and a leather jacket.*

tight shoes/boots *My boots were too tight and hurt my feet.*

a tight skirt/dress/top etc *She wore a short skirt and a tight top.*

ADVERBS

too tight *Those shorts are much too tight.*

Skin-tight clothes fit very tightly: *She was wearing a **skin-tight** dress.*

VERBS

feel tight *I've put on weight – my skirt feels very tight.*

PREPOSITIONS

tight for sb *I borrowed his boots, which were a bit tight for me.*

ANTONYMS **tight → loose**

2 used to say that someone is holding something very firmly

NOUNS

a tight hold/grip *She kept a tight hold on her bag.*

3 strict, or not allowing you to do much

NOUNS

tight control *He keeps tight control of his business empire.*

tight restrictions *There are very tight restrictions on the way we can spend our money.*

tight security (=very thorough) *Security was tight around the parliament building.*

a tight schedule (=you have arranged to do a lot of things in a short time) *He said he would try to fit the event into his tight schedule.*

a tight deadline (=you must finish something in a very short time) *They are working hard to meet the tight deadline.*

a tight budget (=you only have a very limited amount of money to spend) *You can buy a good computer even if you are on a tight budget.*

ADVERBS

extremely tight *We are working to an extremely tight budget.*

incredibly tight *Security was incredibly tight at the airport.*

PHRASES

keep a tight grip/hold/rein on sth (=control it firmly) *It is essential to keep a tight rein on public spending.*

THESAURUS: tight

tight, tough, harsh, stringent → **strict (2)**

tight² *adv* very firmly or closely

VERBS

hold (on) tight *I held on tight to the rope.*

hold sb/sth tight *We held each other tight and kissed each other.*

shut/close sth tight *She shut her eyes tight.*

squeeze sth tight *He put his arms around me and squeezed me tight.*

tie sth tight *I hadn't tied the ropes tight enough.*

pull/draw sth tight *Make sure you pull the knot tight.*

screw sth on tight *Screw the lid back on tight.*

time *n*

1 the thing that is measured in minutes, hours etc using clocks

ADJECTIVES/NOUNS + time

a long time *I haven't seen him for a long time.*

a short time *A short time later, she heard him drive away.*

⚠ Don't say 'a small time'.

some time (=quite a long period of time) *I've known the truth for some time.*

a limited time (=a short period of time) *The offer is available for a limited time only.*

free/spare time *He spends all his free time watching television.*

precious/valuable time *I'm sorry if I'm taking up your valuable time.*

the journey time (=the time it takes to travel somewhere) *By train, the journey time to London is about two hours.*

VERBS

spend time *I'm going to spend some time with my family.*

have time (*also* **have got time** *BrE*) (=have enough time to do something) *I didn't do it because I didn't have time.*

save time *I used a ready-made sauce in order to save time.*

waste time *You are wasting your time arguing with him.*

take time (=you need a long time to do something) *Learning a new skill takes time.*

take some/a little/more etc time (=used when saying how much time you need to do something) *Making this cake hardly takes any time.*

get time *spoken* (=have time free) *Will you read this for me if you get time?*

pass the time (=spend a period of time doing something) *The prisoners pass the time reading, or writing letters.*

kill time (=spend time doing something unimportant while waiting for something) *He went for a walk to kill time before his appointment.*

time passes (*also* **time goes by**) *As time passed, their love grew stronger.*

PREPOSITIONS

time for sth *I don't have time for a long chat now.*

PHRASES

a period of time *All this happened over a long period of time.*

an amount/length of time *Customers only have a limited amount of time to inspect the goods.*

there is time to do sth (=there is enough time to do it) *There was no time to discuss it.*

it takes time to do sth *It took them a long time to struggle through the crowds.*

in five/ten etc minutes' time (=after five, ten etc minutes have passed) *I have an urgent meeting in 15 minutes' time.*

as time goes by/on (=as time passes - used when something happens gradually) *I understood him better as time went on.*

time is running out (=there is not much time left to do something) *Time is running out to do something about climate change.*

time's up *spoken* (=the time allowed for something has finished) *Time's up, class; put your pens down.*

have time to kill (=have time to do something unimportant while waiting for something) *We had some time to kill before our flight, so we decided to do some shopping.*

make/find time to do sth (=do something, even though you are busy) *You need to make time to do things you enjoy.*

in plenty of time (*also* **in good time**) (=well before the necessary time for something) *Make sure you arrive at the airport in plenty of time.*

2 an occasion when you do something or when something happens

ADJECTIVES

many times/lots of times/countless times *He had been to Paris many times before.*

a few times/a couple of times *I saw her a few times during the summer.*

a good/suitable/appropriate time *Is this a good time to ask about money?*

a bad time *It might be a bad time to mention her ex-husband.*

the right/wrong time (=a time that is suitable or not suitable) *That was the wrong time to make a joke.*

VERBS

remember a time *Do you remember the time when the children camped in the garden?*

the time comes *Do you think the time will ever come when people live on the moon?*

PHRASES

for the last time *I knew I was saying goodbye to her for the last time.*

the time is ripe (=this is a suitable time for something which perhaps should have happened sooner) *People are saying that the time is ripe for a change of government.*

3 a particular period in history, or in someone's life

PHRASES

at that time *At that time very few people had computers.*

at the present time (=now - used when the situation is likely to change) *At the present time there is no treatment for the disease.*

ADJECTIVES

modern/recent times *This is the worst economic crisis in modern times.*

ancient times *People have lived here since ancient times.*

prehistoric times (=tens of thousands of years ago) *The area was used as a burial ground in prehistoric times.*

a happy time *School days are supposed to be the happiest time of your life.*

a sad time *It was a very sad time when he died.*

a difficult/hard time *Many people are having a hard time because of the recession.*

timetable *n*

a list of times when things are planned to happen

NOUNS + timetable

a bus/train timetable *BrE* (=when buses and trains arrive and leave) *Have you got the new bus timetable for this year?*

the school timetable *BrE* (=the list of classes that are taught in a school) *There are no sports classes in the afternoons on the school timetable.*

ADJECTIVES

a tight/strict/rigid timetable *The bus drivers have to keep to a strict timetable.*

a provisional timetable (=likely to be changed in the future) *A provisional timetable for the conference is now available.*

VERBS

the timetable says/it says on the timetable *The timetable said there was another train at 6.15.*

keep to the timetable *Increasing city traffic has made it harder for buses to keep to a timetable.*

set a timetable *No deal has been reached, nor has a timetable been set to complete the talks.*

PREPOSITIONS

the timetable for sth *He gave no indication of a timetable for the introduction of the changes.*

on the timetable *Morning examinations start at 09.30 a.m. unless otherwise stated on the timetable.*

according to the timetable *According to the timetable, the next train leaves in half an hour.*

Timetable is used in British English when talking about the list of bus and train times, or the list of classes at a school. American speakers say **schedule**.

timing *n*

1 someone's skill at choosing the right time to do something

ADJECTIVES

good/bad timing *Success in business usually depends on good timing.*

perfect timing (=used when someone's timing is exactly right) *We arrived just as the train was coming into the station. Perfect timing!*

comic timing (=the ability to know when to do something so that it is funny) *Hardy is a skilled comedian with expert comic timing.*

split-second timing (=very accurate timing) *This technique requires split-second timing.*

sb's timing is spot on *informal* (=exactly right) *In tennis, your timing has to be spot on in order to hit the ball accurately.*

PHRASES

sb's sense of timing *Once again, it seemed that his sense of timing had been just right.*

2 the time when something happens

ADJECTIVES

the exact/precise timing *The exact timing of the event has not yet been decided.*

VERBS

change/alter the timing *The timing of the meeting had to be changed because several people were away on holiday.*

affect/influence the timing *The election may have influenced the timing of his decision.*

determine/dictate the timing (=make someone decide to do something at a particular time) *The patient's condition determines the timing of the surgery.*

PREPOSITIONS

the timing of sth *The timing of the festival varies from year to year.*

tiny *adj* extremely small

NOUNS

a tiny room/house *His room is tiny compared to mine.*

a tiny village/island/country *They live in a tiny village where the local school has ten students.*

a tiny piece/part/particle *Electricity is the motion of tiny particles called electrons.*

a tiny proportion/fraction/number *Organic farmers produce only a tiny proportion of the country's vegetables.*

a tiny amount *You only need to use a tiny amount of oil when you cook.*

a tiny baby *She held the tiny baby in her arms.*

tiny hands/fingers/feet/waist *In those days women had tiny waists.*

ADVERBS

very tiny *There was a very tiny hole in the curtain.*

incredibly tiny *The words were written in incredibly tiny letters.*

PHRASES

tiny little *The baby has tiny little fingers.*

THESAURUS: tiny

minute
amount | quantity | traces | particle | differences
extremely small and extremely difficult to see or notice:
The soil contains minute quantities of uranium. | They found minute traces of poison in his body (=very small amounts that remain). | *There are minute particles of dust in the air we breathe.*

miniature
camera | transmitter | railway | submarine | version | horse | poodle
made in an extremely small size, or bred to be a very small size:
The spy used a miniature camera.

microscopic
particle | organism | cell
extremely small and impossible to see without special equipment:
Diesel fumes contain microscopic particles of sticky carbon. | The disease is caused by microscopic organisms in the water.

A **microscope** is a scientific instrument used for looking at very small objects.

minuscule
amount | budget | number | fraction | handwriting
extremely small – used when this is surprising:
His first film was made on a minuscule budget of $500. | The number of women in management positions was minuscule. | The threat from terrorism is minuscule compared to the danger of being killed in a road accident.

Be careful with spelling. Don't write 'miniscule'.

tip *n*

1 a helpful piece of advice

ADJECTIVES/NOUNS + tip

a good/useful/helpful/handy tip *Go to their website to find useful tips on buying and selling a home.*

a simple tip *He has some simple tips for saving money when you're at the supermarket.*

cooking/gardening tips *Most recipes come with added cooking tips.*

beauty/safety tips *The article contains some useful beauty tips.*

VERBS

give sb a tip *He gave me some tips on how to improve my game.*

pass on a tip (=give someone a tip you have learned from someone or from doing something) *The writer passes on many tips from his travels.*

follow a tip (=do what someone suggests) *To keep your bike in good condition, follow these simple tips.*

pick up a tip (=learn a tip) *If you listen to the show, you'll pick up some really useful gardening tips.*

PREPOSITIONS

a tip on doing sth *The article gives some handy tips on decorating a small flat.*

a tip for sb *Do you have any tips for new writers?*

PHRASES

take my tip/take a tip from me (=used when giving someone a tip) *Take a tip from me and repair your roof before the winter.*

2 a small amount of extra money that you give to someone such as a waiter or a taxi driver

ADJECTIVES

a big/large/generous tip *The service was great and we left a large tip.*

a small tip *If the tip is too small, it can seem insulting.*

a 5%/10% etc tip *A 15% tip is usual in restaurants.*

a £2/$5 tip *He gave the waitress a $10 tip.*

VERBS

leave a tip *Aren't you going to leave the waiter a tip?*

give sb a tip *Kim gave the driver a tip.*

get a tip *The waiters get more tips in the evenings.*

3 the end of something long and thin

ADJECTIVES

a pointed tip *The leaves have sharply pointed tips.*

the southern/northern tip (=of an island or area of land) *It's a small village on the southern tip of the island.*

PREPOSITIONS

the tip of sth *She can touch her nose with the tip of her tongue.*

at the tip (of sth) *There is a white line at the tip of the fish's tail.*

tired *adj*

1 feeling that you want to sleep or rest

VERBS

be/feel tired *They felt tired after the long journey.*

get/become tired *If you get tired, we can take a break.*

look/sound tired *You look tired – you should go home and get some rest.*

make sb tired *Looking after the baby at night was making her feel tired during the daytime.*

ADVERBS

physically/mentally/emotionally tired *Although I was physically tired I knew that my brain wasn't ready for sleep.*

tired out (=extremely tired) *When he comes home from school he's tired out.*

NOUNS

a tired voice *"I think we've waited long enough," she said in a tired voice.*

tired face/eyes *Helen studied her mother's tired face, which seemed older than her 52 years.*

a tired smile/sigh/look *She looked into his eyes with a tired smile.*

sb's arms/legs/hands are tired *Can I put the box down? My arms are tired.*

PREPOSITIONS

tired from/after sth (=tired because of doing something) *You must be tired from your long drive.*

PHRASES

tired and drawn (=having a tired-looking face, especially because you are ill or have been worrying a lot) *Taylor came into the doctor's office looking tired and drawn.*

2 bored or annoyed with someone or something – used especially when someone has done something too much or a situation has continued for too long

Grammar
You always say **tired of sb/sth** in this meaning.

VERBS

be/feel tired of sb/sth *He was tired of living in hotels.*

get/become tired (*also* **grow tired** more formal): *Her friends had grown tired of waiting for her to call.*

PREPOSITIONS

tired of (doing) sth *I'm tired of listening to their excuses.*

tired of sb (doing sth) *Farmers are tired of politicians telling them what to do.*

PHRASES

sick and tired of sb/sth (=said when you are very annoyed) *I'm sick and tired of his stubbornness.*

tireless *adj* THESAURUS **energetic**

tiresome *adj* THESAURUS **annoying**

tiring *adj*

making you feel that you want to sleep or rest

NOUNS

a tiring day/morning/week *I've had a tiring day and I want to have a rest.*

a tiring job/tiring work *It was tiring work pulling the sails up and down.*

a tiring journey/drive *They reached Las Vegas after a long and tiring journey.*

VERBS

get tiring *I like shopping but it gets tiring after a while.*

find sth tiring *Many people find it tiring to have to speak in a foreign language all day.*

PREPOSITIONS

sth is tiring for sb *One-to-one teaching is tiring for both the learner and the teacher.*

THESAURUS: tiring

exhausting
day | experience | work | task | process | journey | tour | schedule
extremely tiring:
*It had been a long and exhausting day. | He and Diana had just returned from an exhausting tour of America. | I had to drive nine hours without a break – **it was exhausting**.*

hard
day | job | work | journey | drive | game | race | life
very tiring and difficult:
*She came home after a hard day at the office. | Bringing up a child is hard work. | It's a hard life being a farmer. | **It's hard** getting up at 5 a.m. every day. | He **found** the training really **hard**.*

gruelling *BrE*, **grueling** *AmE*
journey | flight | tour | schedule | season | race | campaign | climb | ordeal

T

very tiring and needing a lot of effort over a long period of time:
Steinbeck's novel is about a family's grueling journey across America in search of work. | The marathon is a particularly gruelling race. | The two candidates have just finished a gruelling five-week election campaign.

punishing
schedule | regime
very tiring and needing a lot of effort over a long period of time:
He has a punishing schedule of conferences, talks, and lectures. | The new soldiers go through a punishing physical regime (=a very tiring set of things that you have to do each day).

Punishing or **gruelling?**
These words mean the same. **Punishing** is usually used about **schedules**.

backbreaking
work
backbreaking work is extremely tiring and needs a lot of physical effort:
Clearing the land was slow backbreaking work.

wearing
tiring and often boring or annoying, because the same thing happens many times:
*He **found** her constant questions rather **wearing**. | It **gets wearing** being on stage every night.*

Wearing is not used before a noun.

title *n*

1 the name given to a particular book, painting, play etc

ADJECTIVES

the full title *The book's full title is 'Alice's Adventures in Wonderland'.*

the original title *The film's original title was 'The King of Kong', but they later changed it to 'King Kong'.*

VERBS

choose a title/think of a title *I can see why you chose that title for the book.*

give sth a title *They decided to give the record the title 'Dark Side of the Moon'.*

title + NOUNS

the title page *The title page gave the names of the author and the translator.*

the title role (=the role of the person who is in the title of a film, book, or play) *Meryl Streep plays the title role in the film.*

the title character (=who is referred to in the title of a book, film etc) *Huckleberry Finn is the title character of the book.*

the title track (=a song with the same name as the title of an album) *The CD's title track was a massive hit.*

PREPOSITIONS

the title of sth *The title of the film is very long.*

a title for sth *We need to think of a title for the book.*

under a title (=using a title) *The book was originally published under the title 'A Country Childhood'.*

2 the position of being the winner of an important sports competition

ADJECTIVES/NOUNS + title

the world title *He believes that he can win the world title.*

the national title *The teams are competing for the national title.*

a major title *She has just won her first major title.*

the cup/league etc title (=the position of winner of a particular cup, league etc) *Chelsea won the cup title last year.*

VERBS

win a title *They won the British title the following year.*

take a title (=win it) *He knocked out the champion and went on to take the title.*

clinch a title (=succeed in winning it) *The Braves clinched the division title with a win over the Astros.*

hold a title *He briefly held the world title.*

compete for a title *Sixteen teams will be competing for the title.*

defend a title (=try to win it again the year after winning it) *Lewis was defending his heavyweight title against Tucker.*

retain a title (=keep it) *He is convinced Chelsea can retain their league title.*

be stripped of your title (=have it officially taken from you because you have done something wrong) *He was stripped of his title after failing a drugs test.*

title + NOUNS

the title holder *Alison White is the current title holder.*

a title fight (=a boxing match to win a particular title) *He was knocked out in his title fight at Wembley.*

toe *n*

one of the five movable parts at the end of your foot

ADJECTIVES

sb's big toe (=the widest toe on each foot) *The shoes hurt my big toes.*

sb's little toe (=the smallest toe on each foot) *He broke his little toe.*

bare toes *The broken glass had cut her bare toes.*

VERBS

stand on your toes (*also* **stand on tiptoe**) *She had to stand on her toes to reach the top shelf.*

step/tread on sb's toe *The man in front of me moved and trod on my toe.*

tap your toes (=keep hitting the floor gently with your toes) *The music started and everyone began tapping their toes.*

wiggle/wriggle your toes (=move them up and down) *She took off her shoes and wriggled her toes.*

stub your toe (=hurt it by hitting it against something) *He stubbed his toe on a rock and yelled with pain.*

point your toes *Point your toes as you dance.*

PHRASES

fingers and toes *My fingers and toes were really cold.*

from head to toe/from top to toe *He was dressed from head to toe in black.*

toilet *n*

the place where you go to get rid of waste from your body, or the thing that you use for this

ADJECTIVES/NOUNS + toilet

a public toilet *He set off across the square in search of a public toilet.*

the ladies' toilets (=for women in a public building) *There was a long queue for the ladies' toilets.*

the gents' toilets (=for men in a public building) *The gents' toilets are through this door.*

a disabled toilet (=for disabled people) *Is there a disabled toilet in the theatre?*

an outside/outdoor toilet (=one that is outside a house, not in it) *The house was small, with no hot water and an outside toilet.*

an indoor toilet (=one that is inside a house) *Many cottages lacked a bathroom or indoor toilet.*

VERBS

go to the toilet (*also* **use the toilet** *especially BrE*): *He got up to go to the toilet in the middle of the night.*

need the toilet *BrE* (=need to use the toilet) *Does anyone need the toilet before we set off?*

flush the toilet (=make water go through it to clean it) *I heard someone flush the toilet.*

be desperate for the toilet *BrE* (=need to use the toilet very soon) *I was desperate for the toilet so I stopped the car.*

> ⚠ Don't say 'go to toilet'. Say **go to the toilet**.

toilet + NOUNS

toilet facilities *Toilet facilities are available at the bus station.*

toilet paper (*also* **toilet roll** *BrE*): *It looks like we've run out of toilet paper.*

> **Toilet** is used in British English to mean a room. In American English, people usually say **bathroom**.

tolerance *n*

1 willingness to allow people to do, say, or believe what they want, or to accept people who are different from you

ADJECTIVES

religious tolerance *The country has a tradition of religious tolerance.*

racial tolerance *Malaysia is proud of its racial tolerance.*

great tolerance *There is a need for greater tolerance and understanding.*

little tolerance *She has very little tolerance for noise when she is trying to work.*

zero tolerance (=used to say that no crime or bad behaviour will be accepted, even if it is very minor) *The company has a policy of zero tolerance of drug use by employees.*

mutual tolerance (=all accepting each other) *There was mutual tolerance between different communities.*

VERBS

have tolerance *My boss did not have much tolerance for mistakes.*

show tolerance *Perhaps we should try showing a little tolerance towards each other.*

promote tolerance *They have taken the lead in promoting tolerance between Catholics and Protestants.*

teach (sb) tolerance *Being with people of different cultures has taught me tolerance.*

learn tolerance *These role-playing sessions are intended to help people learn tolerance.*

PREPOSITIONS

tolerance of/for sth *I believe in tolerance of other religions.*

tolerance towards sb *There was a general atmosphere of tolerance towards gay people.*

2 the degree to which a living thing can experience something without being harmed, affected, or upset by it

ADJECTIVES

a high/low tolerance *She had a very low tolerance for boredom.*

VERBS

tolerance increases/decreases *Remember that tolerance for alcohol decreases with age.*

tolerance + NOUNS

a tolerance level (*also* **a level of tolerance**) *People have different tolerance levels for cold.*

PREPOSITIONS

tolerance of/for/to sth *These plants are known for their tolerance of shade.*

toll *n* THESAURUS **cost[1] (1)**

tone *n*

1 the way you say something or write a message, which shows how you are feeling or what you mean

ADJECTIVES

a friendly/gentle tone *His voice had a friendly tone.*

an aggressive/angry tone *There is no need for such an aggressive tone.*

hushed tones (*also* **low/quiet tones**) (=speaking very quietly) *They sat at the far end of the carriage, talking in hushed tones.*

a matter-of-fact tone (=showing no emotion when what you are saying is exciting, frightening, upsetting etc) *His tone was matter-of-fact, but she noticed he was shaking.*

a measured tone (=very carefully controlled) *He spoke slowly, in a calm and measured tone.*

a conciliatory tone (=showing that you do not want to upset someone or have an argument with them) *In her second email she used a more conciliatory tone.*

PREPOSITIONS

in a ... tone *She answered in rather an aggressive tone.*

PHRASES

a tone of voice *Try talking to the child in a firm tone of voice.*

2 the general feeling or attitude expressed in something, e.g. a film or a piece of writing

ADJECTIVES

the general/overall tone *How would you describe the overall tone of these paintings?*

a positive/negative tone *The audience responded well to the positive tone of her speech.*

a serious tone *The slow sad music matches the serious tone of the film.*

a light/light-hearted tone (=not serious) *Was such a light-hearted tone appropriate for this sad topic?*

VERBS

set/establish the tone *Opening remarks are important because they set the tone of the speech.*

give sth a ... tone *The music gives the film a lovely light tone.*

have a tone *The occasion had a very solemn tone.*

maintain a tone *The writer maintains this humorous tone throughout the piece.*

change the tone *The murder at the end of Act One changes the tone of the play completely.*

lighten the tone (=make it less serious) *We needed a few jokes to lighten the tone of the evening.*

lower the tone (=make something less pleasant, less impressive, or less socially acceptable) *He arrived drunk and immediately lowered the tone of the evening.*

PREPOSITIONS

the tone of sth *The tone of these later poems is quite different.*

in tone *I was hoping for a programme that was far more serious in tone.*

PHRASES

a change/shift of tone *With the leadership change, we noticed an interesting change of tone in party policy.*

tongue *n*

the soft part inside your mouth that you can move about

VERBS

stick your tongue out (=especially to be rude to someone) *The boy stuck his tongue out at me and ran off.*

run your tongue over sth *She ran her tongue nervously over her lips.*

flick your tongue *The snake flicked its tongue a couple of times.*

click your tongue (=make a sharp noise with your tongue, especially to show that you are annoyed) *His mother clicked her tongue at the swear word.*

ADJECTIVES

a long tongue *An anteater has a long sticky tongue.*

a pink/red tongue *The cats were licking the plates with their small pink tongues.*

a forked tongue (=with the end divided in two) *Snakes have forked tongues.*

PHRASES

the tip of your tongue *She moistened her lips with the tip of her tongue.*

tool *n*

1 something that you hold in your hand and use to do a particular job

ADJECTIVES/NOUNS + tool

a simple/basic tool *Carving can be done with quite simple tools.*

a sharp tool *Make a hole in the bottle with a sharp tool such as a knife.*

traditional tools *These craftsmen use traditional tools and techniques.*

garden tools *We have a shed for storing garden tools.*

agricultural/farm tools *Gradually, agricultural tools improved and farming became more efficient.*

power tools (=that use electricity) *Always be careful when using power tools.*

hand tools (=that do not use electricity) *In those days, they only had hand tools.*

VERBS

use a tool *Early humans used stone tools.*

PREPOSITIONS

a tool for doing sth *I need some kind of tool for making holes.*

Toolkit and **toolbox** are usually written as one word.

THESAURUS: tool

implement *formal*
kitchen | agricultural | farm | writing
a tool:
She took a wooden spoon from a drawer full of kitchen implements. | The blade probably came from an agricultural implement. | The prisoners were not allowed to have writing implements.

instrument
scientific | surgical | medical | writing
a small tool used in work such as science or medicine:
He collects early scientific instruments such as microscopes. | All surgical instruments must be completely clean. | The company makes high-quality writing instruments.

utensil *formal*
cooking | kitchen | eating
a tool or piece of equipment, usually one used for preparing or eating food:
Wash your hands and all cooking utensils after preparing raw meat. | The patient may have difficulty holding eating utensils.

gadget
kitchen | household
a small tool or piece of equipment that has been cleverly designed to help you do something more easily:
She demonstrates new kitchen gadgets on TV. | He has all ***the latest*** *household* ***gadgets****. | They have designed an* ***electronic gadget*** *that can print labels. | It's a* ***clever little gadget*** *for getting the stones out of cherries.*

2 something that you can use to achieve something

ADJECTIVES/NOUNS + tool

an important/essential tool *The internet has become an essential tool for research.*

a useful/valuable tool *The test could be a useful tool in schools.*

a powerful tool *Advertising is a powerful tool for influencing people's buying habits.*

a teaching/educational/learning tool *The book can be used as a teaching tool.*

a research tool *The database is a powerful research tool.*

PREPOSITIONS

a tool for (doing) sth *A survey is a tool for gathering information.*

a tool for students/designers/architects etc *This program is a good tool for architects.*

tooth *n*

one of the hard white objects in your mouth that you use to bite and eat food

ADJECTIVES/NOUNS + tooth

sb's front/back teeth *Some of his front teeth were missing.*

white/yellow teeth *Her teeth were beautifully white.*

sharp teeth *The fish has small but very sharp teeth.*

good/perfect teeth *She smiled, showing a mouthful of perfect teeth.*

a bad/rotten tooth *She felt ashamed of her bad teeth and rarely smiled.*

even teeth (=all of the same height) *Models need to have even teeth*

crooked teeth (=not straight) *The old man had crooked teeth.*

a loose tooth *The little boy was wobbling his loose tooth.*

a broken/chipped tooth *Ali then punched Dan, causing a swollen lip and broken tooth.*

a wisdom tooth (=one of the four teeth at the furthest sides of your mouth) *You don't usually get your wisdom teeth until you're an adult.*

a false tooth *He removed his false teeth before getting into bed.*

VERBS

brush your teeth (*also* **clean your teeth** *BrE*): *I brush my teeth twice a day.*

floss your teeth (=clean between your teeth using dental floss) *My dentist said I should floss my teeth more.*

have a tooth out *BrE*, **have a tooth pulled** *AmE* (=have a tooth removed) *He's gone to the dentist to have a tooth out.*

extract a tooth (=take it out) *The dentist announced that she would have to extract two teeth.*

lose a tooth (=no longer have it) *Many of the men had lost all their teeth by the age of 40.*

break/chip a tooth *She had broken a tooth on some candy.*

bare your teeth (=show them, especially in an angry or threatening way) *The dog bared its teeth and snarled.*

grit/clench your teeth (=put them firmly together, especially in a way that shows you are determined, annoyed etc) *He was gritting his teeth against the pain.*

grind your teeth (=move them against each other, sometimes because you are angry)

Many people grind their teeth when they are asleep.

sink your teeth into sth (=put your teeth into someone's flesh, into food etc) *The dog sank its teeth into the boy's hand.*

sb's teeth chatter (=hit together quickly because someone is cold or afraid) *My teeth began to chatter, and I regretted leaving my jacket behind.*

⚠ Don't say 'wash your teeth'. Say **brush your teeth** or **clean your teeth**.

tooth + NOUNS

tooth decay *Brushing regularly helps prevent tooth decay.*

the tooth fairy (=an imaginary person that children believe gives them money when a tooth falls out) *Did you get some money from the tooth fairy?*

tooth/teeth marks *I had tooth marks on my arm where the boy had bitten me.*

Toothache and **toothpaste** are written as one word.

PHRASES

a set of teeth *He still has a good set of teeth.*

through clenched teeth (=with your teeth firmly together because you are angry, in pain etc) *"Why are you doing this?" Donna said through clenched teeth.*

top[1] *n*

1 the highest part of something

ADJECTIVES

the very top (=the highest part – used for emphasis) *They live at the very top of the hill.*

VERBS

reach/get to the top *It was getting dark when we reached the top of the mountain.*

climb to the top *She climbed to the top of the tree.*

PREPOSITIONS

the top of sth *He kissed the top of her head.*

at the top *Your name was at the top of our list.*

to the top *I took her to the top of the tower.*

on (the) top *Melt the butter in a pan on top of the stove.*

PHRASES

right at/to the top (=at or to the highest part – used for emphasis) *The bathroom is right at the top of the house.*

Hilltop, **mountaintop**, **clifftop**, **treetop**, and **rooftop** are written as one word.

THESAURUS: top

summit
the top of a high mountain:
*They had **reached the summit** of the world's highest mountain. | You get a really good view from the summit of Mount Fuji.*

peak
the sharply pointed top of a mountain, especially one that you can see in the distance:
*All around are the spectacular **mountain peaks** of the Alps. | The mountain's **jagged peaks** poked through the clouds* (=peaks with a very rough and uneven shape).

crest
the top of a hill or wave:
*The little boat rode **the crest of** each **wave**. | When I **reached the crest of** the hill I turned to look back.*

ANTONYMS **top → bottom[1] (1)**

2 the best, most successful, or most important position in an organization or group

ADJECTIVES

the very top (=the highest position – used for emphasis) *To reach the very top in sport, you must have tremendous dedication.*

VERBS

reach/get to the top *It takes hard work to reach the top in this sport.*

make it to the top (=succeed in getting to the top) *She was determined she was going to make it to the top.*

rise to the top *He came from a poor family and rose to the top through hard work.*

PREPOSITIONS

the top of sth *He was a highly respected man at the top of his profession.*

at the top *His career at the top of British politics was at an end.*

to the top *Her rapid rise to the top is well deserved.*

PHRASES

right at/to the top (=at or to the highest position – used for emphasis) *Her talent will take her right to the top.*

ANTONYMS **top → bottom[1] (2)**

3 a cover for the top of something such as a bottle, tube, or pen

VERBS

take/get the top off sth *It's difficult to get the top off the jar.*

unscrew the top (=take it off by turning) *Can you unscrew the top for me?*

put the top (back) on sth *He never puts the top back on the toothpaste.*

top² *adj*

1 at a higher level than the other one or other ones

NOUNS

the top drawer/shelf *The scissors are in the top drawer.*

the top floor *Her office was on the top floor.*

the top layer/row *Every month the top layer of your skin is replaced by a new one.*

the top step *He stopped on the top step to look down at her.*

the top half/part *There was glass in the top half of the door.*

the top left-hand/right-hand corner *Write your name in the top left-hand corner.*

the top button *He had undone the top button of his shirt.*

sb's top lip *There was sweat on his top lip.*

ANTONYMS **top → bottom²**

2 best, highest, or most important

NOUNS

a top scientist/sportsman/executive etc *Hundreds of the country's top scientists attended the conference.*

a top company *It is one of the world's top IT companies.*

a top job *There is fierce competition for the top jobs.*

top marks/the top score/the top grade *He got top marks in all his exams.*

top speed *The car has a top speed of 160 miles per hour.*

top quality *All the meat they use is top quality.*

the top level *Does he have the skills needed to compete at the top level?*

a top priority *Reducing violent crime is their top priority.*

> **THESAURUS: top**
>
> top, key, leading, influential, prominent, valued **→ important (2)**

topic [Ac] *n*

a subject that people talk or write about

ADJECTIVES

the main topic *The main topic of this chapter is the relation between language and culture.*

an important topic *The ministers will discuss a number of important topics.*

a hot topic *informal* (=one that people are talking about a lot now) *Gang crime is a hot topic at the moment.*

a controversial/contentious topic (=one that causes a lot of disagreement and strong feelings) *Abortion is a very controversial topic.*

a sensitive topic (=one that must be dealt with carefully, because it may offend people) *It's best to stay away from sensitive topics such as religion.*

an emotive topic (=one that people have very strong opinions about) *Hunting animals for sport can be a very emotive topic.*

an interesting/fascinating topic *Early English history is a fascinating topic.*

a related/relevant topic *The report deals with protecting the environment and other related topics.*

VERBS

discuss a topic *We discussed a wide range of different topics.*

deal with/address a topic *I think we've already dealt with that topic.*

cover/include a topic *The book covers topics such as business strategy and marketing.*

bring up/raise/mention a topic (=start talking about it) *I was hoping someone would bring up that topic.*

change the topic (=talk about something else) *I'm bored. Can we change the topic?*

leave a topic (=stop talking about it) *Before we leave this topic, may I add one more thing?*

topic + NOUNS

a topic area *Below is a list of the main topic areas covered by the course.*

PREPOSITIONS

the topic of sth *He will speak on the topic of violence in schools.*

PHRASES

a topic of conversation *Her favourite topic of conversation is herself.*

a topic of discussion/debate (*also* **a topic for discussion/debate**) *The main topic of discussion was dealing with the financial crisis.*

a range of topics *We discussed a range of topics.*

tornado *n* THESAURUS **wind**

tortuous *adj* THESAURUS **complicated**

total *n*

the final number or amount of things, people etc when everything has been counted

ADJECTIVES/NOUNS + total

the final total *The final total was over $800.*

a combined/overall/grand total (=the sum of two or more amounts added together) *The Jones family has a combined total of 140 years' experience of farming.*

an annual/monthly/weekly/daily total *The city produces an annual total of 13 million tons of waste.*

a huge total *Her various jobs have earned her over £110,000 this year, which is a huge total.*

a staggering total (=extremely high) *More than 600 people wrote letters of support, a staggering total.*

NOUNS + total

the sum total (=the whole of an amount, when everything is added together) *This was the sum total of her grandfather's possessions.*

VERBS + total

make/give a total *Staff raised £1,750 and the company matched it, making a total of £3,500.*

exceed a total (=be more than it) *The number of accidents this year seems likely to exceed last year's total.*

bring the total to 100/2,000 etc *Police arrested more than 200 protesters yesterday, bringing the total detained to nearly 500.*

add to a total *He wants to add to his total of three Olympic gold medals.*

total + VERBS

a total reaches sth *Sales are strong, with the total for this month likely to reach $5,000.*

a total comes to sth (=it is a particular number or amount when added together) *The total for the meal came to just under $50.*

a total stands at sth (=it is a particular number or amount - used when it may increase) *Our total this season stands at 56 points.*

PREPOSITIONS

a total of sth *To reach the top of the tower we had to climb a total of 250 steps.*

in total (=used when saying what the total is) *In total, over 50,000 people visited the museum last year.*

out of a total of sth (*also* **from a total of sth**) *Only 300 of the students were Asian, out of a total of nearly 10,000.*

touch[1] *v*

to put your fingers or hand onto someone or something for a very short time

ADVERBS

gently/lightly touch sb/sth *He reached out and touched her face gently.*

accidentally touch sb/sth *If you accidentally touch something hot, the pain makes you take your hand away.*

briefly touch sb/sth *She put a hand out and briefly touched my arm.*

touch[2] *n*

1 the act of touching someone or something

ADJECTIVES

gentle/delicate/soft touch *She felt the gentle touch of his hand on her cheek.*

PHRASES

be smooth/soft/hard etc to the touch (=feel smooth, soft etc when you touch it) *The baby's skin was soft to the touch.*

2 a small amount of a feeling or quality

PHRASES

a touch of class/glamour/sophistication etc *He looked good in his new suit - it gave him a touch of class.*

a touch of sadness/humour *There was a touch of sadness in her voice.*

3 a special ability to do something well

ADJECTIVES

the magic touch *Lennon and McCartney seemed to have the magic touch and they wrote a string of classic songs.*

the common touch (=the ability to understand ordinary people and make them like you) *Some people say that the president lacks the common touch.*

VERBS

lose/find your touch *I was beginning to worry that I had lost my touch.*

tough *adj*

1 difficult to do or deal with

NOUNS

a tough decision/choice *Picking the best candidate for the job was a very tough decision.*

a tough fight/battle *Local people face a tough fight to try to stop the airport being built.*

a tough game/match/race *The opposition are good, so it's going to be a tough game.*

a tough job/task *The judges have a tough job.*

a tough question *The senator is going to have to answer some pretty tough questions.*

a tough time/year/life *He is having a tough time at the moment because business is bad.*

a tough challenge *She has dealt with some tough challenges in her life.*

tough competition *British car makers faced tough competition from other European manufacturers.*

VERBS

find sth/it tough *Scott found it tough to talk about his feelings.*

PREPOSITIONS

tough on sb *My husband and I got divorced, and it's been tough on the kids.*

PHRASES

things get tough *We all need help sometimes when things get tough.*

be tough to beat/find/handle etc *She is a great player, and she will be tough to beat.*

tough going (=difficult to continue with) *I found the diet tough going.*

THESAURUS: tough

hard, tough, demanding, challenging, daunting, awkward, tricky, delicate → **difficult**

2 very strict or firm

NOUNS

tough action/measures *The authorities seem unable or unwilling to take tough action.*

a tough law/restriction *The government brought in tough anti-terrorist laws.*

a tough penalty *There will be tough penalties for industries which cause water pollution.*

tough standards *Tough new environmental standards have recently been introduced.*

a tough line/stance (=a tough attitude or way of dealing with something) *He wants to take a tough line on drugs.*

VERBS

get tough (=start dealing with someone very strictly or firmly) *We are going to get tough with people who don't pay their bills on time.*

PREPOSITIONS

tough on sb/sth *Politicians want to appear tough on crime.*

tough with sb *You need to be tough with him and show him who is the boss.*

> **THESAURUS: tough**
>
> firm, tough, harsh, stern, authoritarian → **strict (1)**
>
> tight, tough, harsh, stringent → **strict (2)**

3 having a strong character and determined to succeed, even in difficult situations

> **THESAURUS: tough**
>
> stubborn, single-minded, tough, firm, resolute, tenacious, dogged, persistent, ruthless, feisty, strong-willed, headstrong → **determined**

4 hard and difficult to chew or cut

> **THESAURUS: tough**
>
> firm, stiff, solid, rigid, crispy, crunchy, tough, rubbery, brittle → **hard (1)**

tour *n*

1 a journey in which you visit several different places

ADJECTIVES/NOUNS + tour

a ten-day/two-month etc tour *The family are on a ten-day tour of Europe.*

a walking/cycling tour *He and a friend are planning a cycling tour this summer.*

a bus/coach tour *As neither of us drives, we are thinking of going on a coach tour.*

a concert tour *The band has just begun a 15-month concert tour.*

a lecture/speaking tour *He made a highly successful lecture tour of the US in 2010.*

a national/nationwide tour *The event is part of a national tour to promote her book.*

a world/European/North American etc tour *The singer arrived in Singapore for the next stage of his world tour.*

a short tour *The guitarist arrives in Ireland for a short tour later this month.*

an extensive/extended tour (=a long tour) *The band have announced details of their most extensive tour yet.*

a whistlestop/whirlwind tour (=a very quick tour) *The president then made a whirlwind tour of military bases in the north of the country.*

a package tour (=with the travel and accommodation arranged by one company) *Package tours are usually cheaper than booking everything yourself.*

a promotional/publicity tour (=one in which you go to a lot of places to advertise a book, film etc) *The director is on a promotional tour for his new film.*

VERBS

go on (a) tour *It would be nice to go on a tour of the islands.*

make/take/do a tour of sth *The president made a tour of ten Latin American countries.*

lead a tour *The tour will be led by a local guide.*

a tour includes sth *The tour includes boat trips along the Kok and Mekong Rivers.*

tour + NOUNS

a tour guide (=someone who leads a tour) *A tour guide was showing a group around the cathedral.*

a tour company (*also* **a tour operator** *BrE*): *This tour company specialises in holidays to China.*

a tour bus *We got back on the tour bus and returned to our hotel.*

PREPOSITIONS

a tour of sth *The Indian team performed well on its tour of South Africa.*

a tour around/round sth *He went on a publicity tour around the States.*

on tour (=used about a team, band, singer etc) *The band are currently on tour in Europe.*

PHRASES

a leg/stage of a tour (=a part of a tour) *They are preparing for the second leg of their tour.*

2 a short trip around a place to see it

ADJECTIVES

a guided tour *There is a guided tour of the museum every afternoon.*

a quick/short tour *Come and have a quick tour of the house.*

a sightseeing tour (=in which you visit famous or interesting places in an area) *On Saturday, we went on a sightseeing tour of London.*

an interactive/virtual tour (=in which you see pictures of something on a computer) *You can* *take a virtual tour of the art gallery and see all the paintings.*

VERBS

go on a tour of sth *We went on a tour of the town.*

do/have a tour of sth *We'd love to do a tour of the gardens.*

give sb a tour (=show someone around a place) *I called on them in their new house and they gave me a tour.*

take sb on a tour of sth *Joe took me on a tour of the offices.*

PREPOSITIONS

a tour of sth *Would you like a tour of the school?*

a tour around/round sth *I'm looking forward to our tour round the chocolate factory next Wednesday.*

tourism *n*

the business of providing things for people while they are on holiday

VERBS

rely on/depend on tourism (*also* **be dependent on tourism**) *New Orleans depends heavily on tourism.*

boost tourism (=increase it) *The movie has boosted tourism in the city by almost 50 percent.*

promote tourism (=encourage it) *The event was organized to promote tourism to the region.*

develop tourism *The state has actively sought to develop tourism.*

ADJECTIVES

mass tourism (=by large numbers of people) *Morocco's countryside is still unspoilt by mass tourism.*

international tourism *The country has been opened up to international tourism.*

domestic tourism *The air travel difficulties resulted in increased domestic tourism.*

sustainable/green tourism (*also* **ecotourism**) (=tourism that does not damage the environment) *Cycling is the ideal form of green tourism.*

tourism + NOUNS

the tourism industry *Thousands of people are employed in the tourism industry.*

PHRASES

an increase in tourism *The building of the new airport resulted in an increase in tourism.*

the growth of tourism *The growth of tourism has affected the environment.*

a drop/decline in tourism *There has been a drop in tourism because of the fighting.*

the impact of tourism *The environmental impact of tourism is a subject of growing concern.*

tourist *n*

someone who is visiting a place for pleasure on holiday

ADJECTIVES

foreign tourists *Millions of foreign tourists visit the capital every year.*

an American/Japanese etc tourist *A crowd of Japanese tourists stood outside the cathedral.*

VERBS

tourists visit sth *About six million tourists visit the country each year.*

tourists flock to sth (=visit it in large numbers) *Tourists have flocked to the area ever since the TV series was filmed there.*

attract tourists (*also* **pull in/bring in tourists** *informal*): *They hope to change the image of the city and attract more tourists.*

tourist + NOUNS

a tourist attraction (=something interesting for tourists to see or do) *Yellowstone National Park is a major tourist attraction.*

a tourist information office/centre *There was a tourist information centre near the hotel.*

a tourist destination *Egypt became a popular tourist destination in the nineteenth century.*

the tourist industry *The tourist industry is extremely important to the island.*

the tourist season (=the period in a year when large numbers of tourists visit a place) *Even in the tourist season the beaches don't get too full.*

a tourist resort *The island is one of the region's most popular tourist resorts.*

a tourist guide (= a person who shows tourists around a place, or a book that gives information about it) *Some students work as tourist guides in the summer. | The hotel is mentioned in the tourist guide.*

the tourist trail/route (=the places in an area that tourists usually visit) *Although the village is a long way off the tourist trail, it is well worth a visit.*

PHRASES

a group/party of tourists *The guide was talking to a party of tourists.*

a busload/coachload of tourists *The café was quiet until a coachload of tourists arrived.*

be crowded with tourists (*also* **be full of tourists**) *The town is crowded with tourists in the summer months.*

be a magnet for tourists (=many tourists visit it) *With its fantastic castles and pretty villages, the area is a magnet for tourists.*

towel *n*

a piece of cloth that you use for drying your body or for drying things such as dishes

ADJECTIVES

a clean/fresh towel *There are clean towels in the bathroom.*

a wet/damp towel *I wish you wouldn't throw your wet towel on the bathroom floor.*

a dry towel *Let me get you a dry towel.*

a soft/fluffy towel *His mother dried him with a soft white towel.*

a thick towel *The hotel bedroom was supplied with thick white towels.*

VERBS

dry sth with a towel *Hal came in, drying his face with a towel.*

wipe/dry sth on a towel *He wiped his hands on a towel.*

rub sth with a towel *She washed her hair and rubbed it with a towel.*

wrap sb/yourself in a towel *Flora got out of the bath and wrapped herself in a towel.*

hang/drape a towel around/over sth *He draped the towel around his shoulders.*

NOUNS + towel

a bath towel (=a large towel to dry your body after a bath or shower) *She was wearing nothing but a bath towel.*

a beach towel (=a large towel for the beach) *He was lying in the sun on a beach towel.*

a hand towel (=a small towel for drying your hands) *She put a clean hand towel next to the washbasin.*

a tea towel *BrE*, **a dish towel** *AmE* (=for drying dishes, plates etc) *She handed me a tea towel and said: "I'll wash up, if you dry."*

towel + NOUNS

a towel rail/rack (=a bar or frame for hanging towels on) *There should be a clean towel on the towel rail.*

tower *n*

a tall narrow building, part of a building, or structure

ADJECTIVES

a tall/high tower *The church has a tall tower.*

a great/huge/massive tower *He looked up at the great tower soaring above him.*

a 90-foot-high/40-metre-high etc tower *There are wonderful views from the 90-foot high tower of Orford Castle.*

VERBS

climb (up) a tower *Visitors can climb the tower to enjoy the views.*

NOUNS + tower

a church tower *Peter saw a church tower in the distance.*

a clock/bell tower *The bell tower of Pavia cathedral collapsed in 1989.*

PHRASES

the top of the tower *She had climbed the 79 steps to the top of the tower.*

town *n*

a large area with houses, shops, offices etc where people live and work, that is smaller than a city and larger than a village

ADJECTIVES/NOUNS + town

a big/large/major town *The nearest big town is 20 miles away.*

a small/little town *He was born in Cottonwood, a small town in Idaho County.*

a busy/bustling town *The town was busy even in November.*

a quiet town *Cannigione is a quiet little town with a few shops, restaurants, and cafés.*

a sleepy town (=very quiet, with not much happening) *Johnson grew up in the sleepy retirement town of Asheville.*

a ghost town (=one that used to have a lot of people living and working there but now has very few) *The town is in danger of becoming a ghost town if local businesses and factories close.*

sb's home town/hometown (=the town where someone was born) *He was buried in his home town of Keene.*

a historic/ancient town *Visitors can go on a tour of this historic town.*

an industrial town *Thousands moved to the new industrial towns to work in the mills.*

a coastal town *The company is based in the English coastal town of Workington.*

a seaside town (=one on the coast, especially one where people go for holidays) *Many young people look for seasonal work in seaside towns.*

a provincial town (=one that is not near the capital) *His family moved to the provincial town of San Miguel.*

a market town (=a town in Britain where there is a regular outdoor market) *The pretty market town of Ashbourne is only nine miles away.*

a university town *You will have a chance to visit the ancient university town of St Andrew's.*

a border town *He was attacked in his home in the Irish border town of Dundalk.*

a new town (=one of several towns built in Britain since 1946) *The design of Milton Keynes and other new towns proved unpopular.*

town + NOUNS

the town centre *BrE*, **the town center** *AmE*: *The hotel was right in the town center.*

town planning/planner *The approach to town planning changed in the 1950s.*

PREPOSITIONS

the town of sth *The Swiss town of Montreux hosts an international jazz festival every year.*

in town (=visiting a town or city) *You must come and stay with us when you're next in town.*

out-of-town (=outside the centre of a town) *They are planning to build a huge out-of-town development with shops and apartments.*

PHRASES

the outskirts of a town (=the part near the edge) *It was six o'clock when she reached the outskirts of the town.*

T

towns and cities/towns and villages *In towns and cities across Britain, there has been an increase in the number of homeless people.*

toxic *adj* THESAURUS ▸ **poisonous**

toy *n*

an object for children to play with

ADJECTIVES/NOUNS + toy

a little toy *Aunt Maria used to bring us sweets and little toys.*

a child's toy *The carved wooden figure could be a child's toy.*

plastic/wooden toys *Brightly coloured plastic toys were scattered over the carpet.*

a stuffed toy (*also* **a soft/cuddly toy** *BrE*) (=one that looks like an animal, made of cloth and filled with soft material) *Her bed is covered with stuffed toys.*

VERBS

play with a toy *The children were playing with toys on the floor.*

toy + NOUNS

a toy car/gun/telephone etc (=one that is a toy) *The little boy was pushing a toy car along the table.*

a toy box/chest/cupboard (=where toys are kept) *Put everything back in the toy box.*

trace Ac *n*

a small sign that shows someone or something was there, or a small amount of something

ADJECTIVES

a faint/slight trace (=very small) *There were faint traces of blood on the floor. | She spoke good English with only a slight trace of an accent.*

the last trace(s) of sth *The last trace of cloud had disappeared from the sky.*

all trace(s) of sth *Make sure that your skin is free of all traces of make-up.*

no trace/not a trace of sth *There was not a trace of cancer in his body.*

VERBS

contain a trace of sth *The water contains traces of metal.*

leave a trace *The murderer had been careful to leave no traces.*

show/bear traces of sth *The walls of the buildings show traces of battle.*

find a trace *The police had found no trace of him.*

detect a trace of sth (=notice something by looking carefully) *Kelly thought she detected a trace of bitterness in his voice.*

remove traces *Wash fruit and vegetables thoroughly to remove all traces of soil.*

obliterate/erase traces (=destroy them completely) *These changes have obliterated most traces of the ancient landscape.*

traces remain *Very few traces of the gardens remain.*

PHRASES

disappear/vanish/sink without (a) trace (=disappear completely, in a mysterious way) *In 1941, the aircraft she was flying disappeared without trace.*

track *n*

1 a narrow path or road, especially one with a rough surface

ADJECTIVES

a narrow/wide track *He turned down a narrow track that led to the ocean.*

a steep track *The house was up a steep track.*

a winding track (=with many curves) *We followed winding country tracks.*

a rough/bumpy track *The car bumped along the rough track.*

a muddy/dusty/grassy/stony track *The farm lay at the end of a muddy track.*

NOUNS + track

a dirt track *There was a dirt track leading off into the hills.*

a forest/mountain track *I came across a deer on a forest track.*

a farm track *She left the road and took a farm track across a field.*

VERBS

take a track (=start going along a track) *After 300 yards, take the track on the left.*

follow a track *Follow the track back to the car park.*

a track leads somewhere *I began walking along the track leading towards the village.*

PREPOSITIONS

along a track *He strode along the track.*

down/up a track *A car was coming up the track towards the farm.*

THESAURUS: track

street, avenue, boulevard, lane, cul-de-sac, track, ring road, bypass, dual carriageway, freeway/expressway, motorway, interstate, toll road, turnpike → **road**

2 tracks are marks left on the ground by a moving person, animal, or vehicle

ADJECTIVES

fresh tracks (=made a short time ago) *Each morning there were fresh fox tracks around the hen huts.*

deep tracks *There were deep tracks, evidently made by a tractor.*

clear tracks *Their feet left clear tracks in the grass.*

NOUNS + track

tyre tracks *BrE*, **tire tracks** *AmE*: *There were two sets of tyre tracks.*

car tracks *The police are studying car tracks found in the mud.*

animal tracks *He knew how to identify animal tracks.*

VERBS

leave/make tracks *Several animals had left tracks in the snow.*

find tracks *We found fresh coyote tracks.*

follow tracks *We followed the tracks of a deer to the river.*

trade *n*

the activity of buying or selling goods or services

ADJECTIVES/NOUNS + trade

international/foreign trade *International trade is essential for long-term economic growth.*

global/world trade *We want the poorer nations to benefit from increased global trade.*

free trade (=taking place without strict rules or other controls) *The government remains committed to the principle of free trade.*

the arms/drugs/slave/sex trade *The police have difficulty controlling the country's drugs trade.*

the tourist trade *The wildlife and scenery have helped to make the tourist trade Alaska's second industry.*

the retail trade (=businesses which sell goods in shops to customers) *Thousands of people work in the retail trade.*

VERBS

encourage/stimulate/promote trade *The agreement will help to encourage international trade.*

boost trade (=make it increase a lot) *The trip has been organized in order to boost trade with China.*

restrict trade *There is a risk that new regulations could restrict trade.*

control/regulate trade *One of the department's jobs is to regulate trade between the two countries.*

trade + NOUNS

trade barriers (*also* **barriers to trade** *formal*) (=things that make trade between two countries more difficult or expensive, such as taxes on imports) *The removal of trade barriers will help our trading partnership.*

a trade agreement/deal/pact *In April, a new trade agreement between Romania and the US was signed.*

a trade embargo (=an official order to stop trade with another country) *Delegates urged the US government to lift its trade embargo against Cuba.*

trade talks/negotiations *A further round of trade talks begins this week in Geneva.*

a trade deficit (=the amount by which the total goods one country sells to others is less than the amount it buys from them) *The foreign trade deficit grew by 42% compared with the previous year.*

a trade surplus (=the amount by which the total goods one country sells to others is more than the amount it buys from them) *China has a huge trade surplus with the US.*

a trade fair (=an event at which companies advertise their services or goods to possible customers and partners) *The hall is used for trade fairs.*

a trade dispute *The two leaders are anxious to avoid a trade dispute between their countries.*

PREPOSITIONS

trade in sth *Trade in ivory has been banned since 1990.*

trade between sb and sb *Trade between China and Africa amounted to 39.7 billion dollars.*

trade with sb *There has been a big increase in trade with India.*

THESAURUS: trade

trade, commerce, e-commerce → **business (1)**

tradition *n*

a custom, belief, or story that has existed for a very long time

ADJECTIVES/NOUNS + tradition

an old/ancient tradition *The ceremony is part of an ancient tradition.*

a local tradition *The villagers are all keen to preserve local traditions.*

a long tradition/long-standing tradition *Britain has a long tradition of accepting political refugees.*

an age-old tradition (=one that has existed for a long time and still continues now) *In most African countries, open-air markets are an age-old tradition.*

a proud tradition *Liverpool has a proud tradition of producing talented comedians.*

a strong tradition *There is a strong tradition of sport at the school.*

a family tradition *According to family tradition, he must sing at his own wedding.*

a cultural/religious tradition *The country has cultural traditions that date back many generations.*

American/British/southern etc tradition *The festival is a part of Scottish tradition which is worth preserving.*

VERBS

follow a tradition (=do what has been done before) *He followed the family tradition and became a doctor.*

maintain/carry on/continue/uphold a tradition (=make it continue in the same way as before) *We maintain a tradition of*

T

cheese-making which dates back for hundreds of years.

break with tradition (=not follow a tradition) *They decided to break with tradition and have fish instead of turkey for Christmas lunch.*

establish a tradition *They are continuing a tradition which was established over a hundred years ago.*

be steeped in tradition (=have many traditions and a long history) *Glastonbury is a town which is steeped in tradition.*

tradition dictates sth (=says that something must be done in a particular way) *As tradition dictates, she went to live with her husband's family after she got married.*

a tradition goes back/dates back to sth *The tradition goes back to the tenth century.*

PREPOSITIONS

by tradition (*also* **according to tradition**) *By tradition, it's the bride's parents who pay for the wedding.*

a tradition of (doing) sth *It's a religious group with a tradition of silence.*

PHRASES

in keeping with tradition (=as part of a tradition) *In keeping with tradition, everyone wore black.*

keep a tradition alive (=make it continue) *The family has played a large part in keeping this tradition alive.*

in time-honoured tradition *BrE*, **in time-honored tradition** *AmE* (=based on a tradition that has existed for a very long time) *In time-honoured tradition, they have a drink in every pub along the high street.*

traditional Ac *adj*

existing or done in a way that has been used and accepted for a long time

NOUNS

a traditional method/way/approach *She believes in traditional teaching methods.*

traditional values (=ideas about morality) *He called for a return to traditional values.*

traditional beliefs *Traditional beliefs can be difficult to change.*

a traditional form of sth *Traditional forms of industry have been replaced by high-technology jobs.*

a traditional style *The houses were built in a traditional style.*

the traditional view *The traditional view is that young children are best cared for by their mothers.*

sb's traditional role *The government promoted women's traditional role as wives and mothers.*

traditional cooking/cuisine/dishes *She prepared traditional Peruvian dishes for her family.*

traditional music/song *The festival presents traditional music from around the world.*

traditional culture *They want to preserve the island's traditional culture.*

traditional medicine *This plant is used in Chinese traditional medicine.*

traffic *n*

the vehicles moving along a road or street

ADJECTIVES/NOUNS + traffic

heavy traffic (=a lot of cars on the road) *We got stuck in heavy traffic near the airport.*

light traffic (=not many cars on the road) *The traffic is fairly light at this time of day.*

bad/terrible traffic *The traffic was terrible this morning.*

slow/slow-moving traffic *Traffic's very slow going out of New York.*

stationary traffic (=traffic that is not moving) *The truck ploughed into a line of stationary traffic on the motorway.*

rush-hour traffic *I left early to try to miss the rush-hour traffic.*

local traffic *There is quite a lot of local traffic.*

motorway traffic *BrE*, **freeway traffic** *AmE*: *As motorway traffic worsens, commuters may have to find other ways of getting to and from work.*

oncoming traffic (=traffic coming towards you) *The driver, too busy watching oncoming traffic, doesn't notice the pedestrian ahead.*

VERBS

be stuck/caught/held up in traffic *Sorry I'm late – I was stuck in traffic.*

avoid/miss the traffic (=avoid driving when there are a lot of vehicles) *I left early, hoping to miss the traffic.*

cut/reduce traffic *The congestion charge did cut traffic in central London.*

increase traffic *New housing will increase traffic in the area.*

traffic moves/flows *At last the traffic was moving again.*

traffic is diverted (=made to go in another direction) *Traffic was diverted onto the A166 as emergency services cleared the wreckage.*

direct traffic (=show vehicles where to go) *Police were on duty directing traffic.*

disrupt traffic (=stop it from moving freely) *The roadworks are likely to disrupt traffic.*

traffic + NOUNS

a traffic jam (=a line of cars that have stopped, or are moving very slowly) *She spent two hours sitting in a traffic jam.*

traffic congestion (=when the roads are full of traffic) *There have been efforts to cut traffic congestion in Britain's cities.*

traffic problems *A new road won't solve the city's traffic problems.*

traffic delays/disruption *The accident caused serious traffic delays.*

traffic flow (=the steady movement of traffic)

The road widening should help to improve traffic flow.

a traffic accident *formal: He's been involved in a traffic accident.*

the traffic police (=police dealing with traffic problems and illegal driving) *The teenagers got stopped by the local traffic police.*

traffic noise *You get a lot of traffic noise living here.*

traffic fumes *Traffic fumes are the biggest cause of air pollution in most cities.*

traffic calming (=things that are done to make people drive more slowly) *We plan to extend traffic calming measures in residential streets.*

PHRASES

the volume of traffic *The new ring road will reduce the volume of traffic through the village.*

a stream of traffic (=a long continuous series of cars, trucks etc) *There was a constant stream of traffic.*

the roar/rumble/hum of traffic *The only noise was the distant rumble of traffic.*

traffic jam *n*

a long line of vehicles on a road that cannot move or can only move very slowly

ADJECTIVES

a huge/massive traffic jam *There was a huge traffic jam on the main road.*

a long traffic jam *Long traffic jams built up.*

a 5-mile/20-mile etc traffic jam *The road was closed, leading to a 25-mile traffic jam.*

VERBS

be/get stuck in a traffic jam *They were stuck in a traffic jam for an hour.*

cause a traffic jam *The accident caused a huge traffic jam.*

sit in a traffic jam *I hate sitting in traffic jams.*

tragedy *n*

a very sad event that involves a lot of suffering

ADJECTIVES/NOUNS + tragedy

a terrible/great tragedy *His death is a terrible tragedy for his family.*

an awful/appalling tragedy (=very unpleasant and shocking) *This is an appalling tragedy which will affect us for the rest of our lives.*

a personal tragedy (=affecting a particular person) *He suffered a great personal tragedy two years ago when his son died suddenly.*

a human/humanitarian tragedy (=affecting large numbers of people) *The UN wants to see an end to the conflict and the human tragedy involved.*

the real tragedy *The real tragedy is that his death could have been avoided.*

a family tragedy *The boy's operation was a success and a family tragedy was avoided.*

tragedy + VERBS

a tragedy happens/occurs/takes place *The tragedy happened shortly before 5 p.m. on Saturday.*

a tragedy unfolds (=the events of the tragedy happen) *People watching the news reports were horrified at the tragedy that was unfolding.*

tragedy befalls sb *formal* (=it happens to them) *There was no indication of the tragedy that was about to befall the family.*

VERBS + tragedy

avert/avoid a tragedy (=prevent it from happening) *The owners could have done something to avert this tragedy.*

suffer a tragedy *People in the earthquake zone have suffered an appalling tragedy.*

be affected/touched by tragedy *The disease is very common in the region and most people's lives have been affected by tragedy as a result.*

be dogged by tragedy (=suffer several tragedies) *His early life was dogged by tragedy.*

cope/deal with tragedy *We are grateful for the support of friends as we try to cope with this tragedy.*

end in tragedy *The fishing trip ended in tragedy for the four men after their boat overturned.*

PREPOSITIONS

a tragedy for sb/sth *It will be a tragedy for the town if the factory closes.*

tragic *adj* THESAURUS ▶ **sad (2)**

train *n*

a set of carriages pulled along a railway line by an engine

ADJECTIVES/NOUNS + train

an express train (=one that does not stop at many places) *There are express trains to the airport every 20 minutes.*

a slow train (*also* **a stopping train** *BrE*) (=one that stops at a lot of places) *We got on the stopping train by mistake and it took hours to get home.*

a direct train (=one that goes somewhere directly, so you do not have to change trains) *There's no direct train to Berlin - you'll have to change at Hamburg.*

an earlier/later train *Can't you get an earlier train?*

the first/last train *They missed the last train home and had to stay in a hotel.*

the 2 o'clock/5.23 etc train *You could get the 3.21 train to Brighton.*

the overnight train (=that travels through the night) *Edward had arrived on the overnight train and was very tired.*

a passenger train (=for transporting people, not goods) *The tunnel is for passenger trains.*

a freight train (*also* **a goods train** *BrE*) (=for transporting goods, not people) *The freight train was carrying hazardous chemicals.*

T

a commuter train (=that people going to work use) *The crash involved two crowded commuter trains.*

a subway train (=one that goes under the ground in a city) *The subway trains run all night.*

a tube/underground train (=one that goes under London) *Tube trains get very hot in the summer.*

a steam train (=powered using steam) *Railway enthusiasts have the opportunity to take a nostalgic trip on a steam train.*

VERBS + train

go by train *The quickest way is to go by train.*

take/get/catch a train *I took the first train home.*

get on a train (*also* **board a train** *formal*): *At the next station, a few more passengers boarded the train.*

get off a train *She got off the train in Paris.*

change trains (=get off one train and onto another) *You'll have to change trains in Paris.*

wait for a train *Sarah spent half an hour waiting for a train.*

miss a train (=be too late to get on it) *I just missed the last train.*

train + VERBS

trains run (=take people from one place to another at fixed times) *Trains run from Victoria station every few minutes.*

a train arrives *The train arrived on time.*

a train leaves (*also* **a train departs** *formal*): *This train will depart in five minutes.*

a train pulls into/out of a station (=arrives at a station or leaves a station) *The train pulled into the station and I got off.*

a train terminates somewhere (=ends its journey there) *All trains will terminate in Oxford.*

a train derails/is derailed (=comes off the rails) *Most of the passengers escaped injury when their train was derailed.*

train + NOUNS

a train journey *BrE*, **a train trip** *AmE*: *They were not looking forward to the long train journey.*

a train ticket/fare *How much is the train fare to Derby?*

a train driver *The train driver apologized for the late departure.*

a train crash (*also* **a train wreck** *AmE*): *Ten people were killed in the train crash.*

a train station *I'll meet you at the train station.*

a train timetable *BrE*, **a train schedule** *AmE*: *According to the train timetable, the next train is due in five minutes.*

a train set (=a toy train with railway tracks) *A little boy was playing with his train set.*

PREPOSITIONS

a train to/for sth *Is this the train for Birmingham?*

a train from sth *Betty arrived on the train from Boston.*

on a train *He called me to say he was on the train.*

by train *We decided to go by train.*

⚠ Don't say 'go by the train' or 'travel by the train'. Say **go by train** or **travel by train**.

PHRASES

a train is due (=it is expected to arrive) *The next train is due in 11 minutes.*

training *n*

the process of teaching or being taught the skills for a particular job or activity

ADJECTIVES/NOUNS + training

special/specialist training *Oil workers receive special training in safety procedures.*

formal training (=you study something at a college, rather than just learning as you do it) *She had no formal training in art.*

basic training *The new police officers have 12 weeks of basic training.*

on-the-job training (=while doing a job rather than in a classroom) *On-the-job training was seen as more important than formal education.*

in-service training (=while working for an employer) *Most employees take advantage of our in-service training programme.*

intensive training (=doing a lot of work in a short time) *You get a week of intensive training before going on your first placement.*

staff training *Not enough priority is given to staff training.*

teacher training *Applications for teacher training have increased by nearly 50%.*

management training *Her company provides management training to some of the UK's top organizations.*

vocational training (=teaching students how to do a job) *The college provides vocational training for nurses and hospital technicians.*

professional training *He doesn't have any professional training.*

VERBS

give sb/provide training *Employees should also be given adequate training in fire safety precautions.*

get/receive/have training *I don't think we get enough training at work.*

undergo training (=be given training) *Hundreds of Nigerian soldiers are undergoing training at the academy.*

do/carry out training (=teach someone how to do something) *Someone from the HR department will be doing the training.*

need/require training *The team will need extra software training.*

lack training *Most of the workers lacked the training to use this equipment.*

training + NOUNS

a training course (*also* **a training programme** *BrE*, **a training program** *AmE*): *Staff will be sent on a training course on using the new system.*

a training scheme *The company has over 50 young people on its training schemes.*

a training session *Make sure you attend the computer training sessions.*

a training manual *She has written a training manual for social workers.*

a training centre *BrE*, **a training center** *AmE*: *She runs a training centre for young people leaving prison.*

PREPOSITIONS

training for sth *She received five years' training for a career as a minister of religion.*

training in sth *He had no formal training in interior design.*

tranquil *adj* THESAURUS ▸ quiet (3)

transcribe *v* THESAURUS ▸ write (1)

transform Ac *v*

to completely change the appearance, form, or character of something

ADVERBS

completely/totally transform sth *The city has been totally transformed and there are a lot of modern office buildings.*

radically/fundamentally transform sth *Our aim is to radically transform the education system.*

rapidly transform sth *Computers are rapidly transforming the world as we know it.*

successfully transform sth *The teachers have successfully transformed this school into a high-achieving institution.*

gradually/slowly transform sth *The old industrial part of town is gradually being transformed into an attractive residential area.*

magically/miraculously transform sth (=in a sudden and impressive way) *Rain magically transforms the desert into a green paradise.*

PREPOSITIONS

transform sth into sth *She has transformed the company into a thriving modern business.*

transform sth from sth to/into sth *He transformed these young people from unknown theatre actors into stars.*

PHRASES

help (to) transform sth *He promised to help transform the company into an internationally famous brand.*

the power/ability to transform sth *A book can have the power to transform someone's life.*

THESAURUS: transform

alter, adapt, adjust, turn sth up/down, reform, revise, restructure, transform, revolutionize, distort, twist, misrepresent → **change[1] (2)**

transformation Ac *n*

a complete change in something

ADJECTIVES

a complete/total transformation *He had plastic surgery and underwent a complete transformation.*

a great/major transformation *We've seen a major transformation in the appearance of the town centre.*

a radical/fundamental/profound transformation *There has been a radical transformation of the country's political system.*

a rapid transformation *He called for a rapid transformation to a market economy.*

a dramatic transformation (=having a very strong effect) *A change of wallpaper can bring about a dramatic transformation in a room.*

a miraculous transformation (=sudden and very impressive) *The billionaire chairman has achieved a miraculous transformation in the club.*

a remarkable transformation (=very great) *There has been a remarkable transformation in him since he started his new job.*

a political/economic etc transformation *He is the leader who brought about the political transformation of the country.*

social/cultural transformation *This period was one of profound social transformation in Europe.*

VERBS

undergo a transformation (*also* **go through a transformation**) *She seems to have undergone a complete transformation since she went to university.*

result in a transformation (*also* **lead to a transformation**) *The award resulted in the transformation of her life.*

bring about a transformation *A small sum of money could bring about a complete transformation of the park.*

achieve a transformation *He has achieved a complete transformation of the business.*

involve/require a transformation *Meeting these targets would involve a transformation of the way the school is run.*

see/witness a transformation *We are currently witnessing a dramatic transformation in the way we communicate.*

a transformation takes place (*also* **a transformation occurs/happens**) *The next time I visited the house, a complete transformation had taken place.*

T

PREPOSITIONS

a transformation from sth into/to sth *We've seen her transformation from shy little girl to confident woman.*

a transformation in sth *What brought about this transformation in his performance?*

THESAURUS: transformation

alteration, reform, shift, swing, fluctuation, transformation, revolution, shake-up, U-turn → **change²**

transient *adj* THESAURUS **temporary**

transition Ac *n*

when something changes from one form or state to another

ADJECTIVES

a gradual transition *These experiences are part of the gradual transition from childhood to adulthood.*

a successful transition *Will the country be able to make a successful transition to democratic government?*

a smooth/orderly transition (=happening without any problems) *The country managed a fairly smooth transition to independence.*

a peaceful transition *We all want to see a peaceful transition to democracy.*

a seamless transition (=done so well that people do not notice the change) *Managers did not expect a completely seamless transition to the new IT system.*

a difficult/painful transition *Her son was making the difficult transition from junior school to senior school.*

VERBS

make a transition *The biggest problem will be making the transition from one system to the other.*

undergo a transition *European society was undergoing a major transition during that period.*

mark a transition (=be a sign that it is happening) *The death of the leader marked the country's transition into a modern nation.*

ensure a transition *We want to ensure a smooth transition to the child's new school.*

manage a transition *She managed the restaurant's transition into a profitable business.*

ease a transition (=make it happen without problems) *Someone leaving hospital after a long stay may need help to ease the transition.*

a transition occurs (*also* **a transition takes place**) *We cannot expect that a rapid transition to democracy will take place.*

transition + NOUNS

a transition period (*also* **a period of transition**) *The major industrial nations are in a transition period.*

a transition process (*also* **a process of transition**) *He will deal with any problems that might arise during the transition process.*

transition arrangements *Following an election, sensible transition arrangements have to be put in place.*

a transition team *AmE* (=a group of politicians who will form a new government) *The president will announce his transition team tomorrow.*

PREPOSITIONS

a transition from sth to sth *That year was the beginning of France's transition from a monarchy to a republic.*

a transition to sth *We want to help her make the transition to independent living.*

a transition into sth *These developments marked Europe's transition into the industrial age.*

a transition between sth and sth *The transition between childhood and adulthood is often a difficult time.*

in transition (=in the process of changing from one form or state to another) *The committee is in transition, with new officials elected but not yet in place.*

translate *v*

to change written or spoken words into another language

PHRASES

be difficult/hard to translate *The German word Gemütlichkeit is difficult to translate into English. It means something like 'a friendly atmosphere'.*

PREPOSITIONS

translate sth into English/Chinese etc *Can you translate this into French?*

translate sth from English/Chinese etc *The book had been translated from Italian.*

translation *n*

the act of translating something, or something that has been translated

ADJECTIVES

an accurate/exact translation *The most accurate translation of the word would be 'master'.*

a rough/free/loose translation (=one that is not very exact) *It's a rough translation, but I think the meaning is clear.*

a literal translation (=one in which each word is translated exactly) *A literal translation of the phrase would be 'What age have you?'*

an English/Japanese etc translation *He wrote the first English translation of this famous Greek text.*

NOUNS + translation

machine translation (=done automatically, using a computer program) *Machine translation is not always very reliable and produces some interesting mistakes.*

VERBS

do/make/produce a translation *Students are asked to do a translation of a poem.*

translation + NOUNS

translation work *He does some translation work in his spare time.*

translation problems *First, we read the text and identify possible translation problems.*

PREPOSITIONS

a translation of sth *She is working on a new translation of the Bible.*

a translation from sth *The phrase is a translation from Arabic.*

a translation into sth *The first paper in the exam is a translation into French.*

PHRASES

be/get lost in translation (=losing its meaning or effect after being translated) *Jokes are often lost in translation.*

read sth in translation (=not in the original language) *I have only read her poems in translation.*

transparent *adj* THESAURUS **clear[1] (4)**

transport Ac *n especially BrE*

a system or method for carrying passengers or goods from one place to another

ADJECTIVES/NOUNS + transport

road transport *Buses are the safest form of road transport in this country.*

rail transport *Freight delivery costs could be reduced by using rail transport.*

air transport *The air transport industry is going through a period of change.*

public transport (=buses, trains etc that are available for everyone to use) *We recommend that you travel by public transport.*

private transport (=a vehicle that you own and drive) *Most people in this country have access to private transport.*

local transport *Local transport is poor here, so you really need a car.*

passenger/freight transport *Aircraft now provide over 90% of international passenger transport.*

motorized transport *For around a decade, horse-drawn carriages existed on our roads alongside motorized transport.*

transport + NOUNS

a transport system *We need a better public transport system.*

transport costs *A business needs to keep transport costs low.*

transport links *The region has good transport links to the capital.*

transport policy *We would like to see a more environmentally responsible transport policy.*

transport infrastructure (=roads, railways etc) *The existing transport infrastructure cannot cope with population growth.*

transport users *Severe weather is causing problems for transport users around the country.*

a transport company/operator/provider *An increase in the number of transport operators has not brought improvements to the service.*

a transport hub (=an airport, railway station etc that connects many transport routes) *We aim to transform the city into a major European transport hub.*

VERBS

arrange/organize transport *Her company organizes transport for major sporting events.*

provide transport *We will provide transport to and from the hotel.*

PREPOSITIONS

transport to a place *Bus transport to the train station is available.*

transport from a place *Will transport be provided from the airport?*

without transport *The car was being repaired, leaving us without transport.*

PHRASES

a means/mode/form of transport *Horses and carts were the only means of transport.*

have your own transport (=have a car or have access to one) *The supermarket offers a bus service for customers who do not have their own transport.*

In American English, the usual word is **transportation**.

transportation *n*

the activity of taking people or things from one place to another, or ways of doing this

transportation + NOUNS

a transportation system/network *The country now has an efficient transportation system.*

transportation links *The city has good transportation links.*

transportation costs *Because of the distances involved, transportation costs are high.*

ADJECTIVES/NOUNS + transportation

public transportation *The number of commuters using public transportation has increased to 29.6 percent.*

air/rail/road transportation *We can make air transportation safer.*

PHRASES

a means/mode/form of transportation *Horses and boats were the main means of transportation.*

Transportation is more common in American English. In British English, people usually say **transport**.

T

trap *n*

1 something that catches or tricks someone unexpectedly

VERBS

set/lay a trap *She set a trap for him and he fell straight into it.*

fall into/walk into a trap *You walked into his trap when you agreed to go.*

lead/lure sb into a trap (=encourage someone to go into a trap) *The rebels had lured the soldiers into a trap.*

catch sb in a trap *They were caught in a trap and it seemed like there was no way out.*

avoid a trap *You can avoid these traps by following our advice.*

escape (from) a trap *They need proper training to help them escape the poverty trap.*

ADJECTIVES

an obvious trap *I didn't answer this question as it was an obvious trap.*

2 a piece of equipment or hole in the ground for catching animals

VERBS

set/lay a trap *My father taught me how to hunt and set traps.*

put traps down *We had a problem with mice so we put traps down.*

be caught in a trap *The fox got caught in a trap, but luckily we managed to save it.*

trash *n AmE* things that you throw away

VERBS

take out the trash (=take it outside the house to be collected) *She asked her son to take out the trash.*

throw/put/dump sth in the trash (=throw it away) *He tore the letter up and threw it in the trash.*

pick up the trash *The playground was dirty because nobody picked up the trash.*

trash + NOUNS

a trash can (=a container for putting trash in) *He carried the bag outside and dumped it in the trash can.*

PREPOSITIONS

in the trash (=in a container for trash) *She claims to have found the money in the trash.*

> **Trash** is used in American English. British speakers say **rubbish**.

travel[1] *v*

to go to a place, especially one that is far away

ADVERBS

often/frequently travel *She frequently travels to Europe on business.*

travel abroad *My dad sometimes has to travel abroad for his job.*

travel everywhere *Ashley travels everywhere by bicycle.*

travel widely/extensively (=to many places) *David had travelled extensively throughout Europe.*

travel light (=not take many things with you) *I usually try to travel light, so that there is less to carry.*

travel alone/on your own/independently *It is not safe for women to travel alone.*

PREPOSITIONS

travel by train/car/air etc *Emily hated travelling by plane.*

travel to somewhere *I've always liked the idea of travelling to exotic places.*

travel across somewhere *We travelled by train across Eastern Europe.*

travel with sb *They are travelling with their two children.*

PHRASES

go travelling *BrE*, **go traveling** *AmE*: *He plans to go travelling for a year before university.*

travel the world (=go to many parts of the world) *They wanted to travel the world together.*

travel the country (=go to many parts of a country) *The band travelled the country singing in festivals and competitions.*

travel far and wide (=to many places, especially in order to find something) *The chef has travelled far and wide to find recipes for his new book.*

travel[2] *n* the activity of travelling

ADJECTIVES/NOUNS + travel

air travel *Air travel has become more popular in the last few years.*

rail travel *The changes were introduced to make rail travel safer.*

bus/coach/car etc travel *The price includes coach travel to and from the airport.*

foreign/international/overseas travel *Her job involves a lot of foreign travel.*

long-distance travel *Long-distance travel is becoming much more common these days.*

business travel *People should share cars more for business travel.*

space travel *He was interested in the history of space travel.*

travel + NOUNS

the travel industry *The storms have affected the country's travel industry badly.*

travel arrangements *I'll make all the travel arrangements.*

travel expenses/costs *The company offered to pay my travel expenses.*

travel restrictions (=rules controlling who is allowed to travel) *The journey would be difficult because of travel restrictions imposed by the government.*

a travel ban *The spread of the disease could lead to a travel ban.*

travel documents (=passport, tickets etc) *Make sure you keep your travel documents in your hand luggage.*

travel insurance *Will the travel insurance pay out if you miss the flight?*

a travel book/guide *Bali looks so lovely in the travel books.*

a travel writer *He's an award-winning travel writer.*

a travel brochure (=giving details of available holidays) *We spent the evening looking through a pile of travel brochures.*

a travel agent (=a shop or company that arranges travel for customers) *We booked the flight through a travel agent.*

travel sickness (=a sick feeling caused by travel) *The tablets can be useful for people who suffer from travel sickness.*

PREPOSITIONS

travel to a place *Do US citizens need a visa for travel to India?*

travel from a place *The tickets are also valid for rail travel from the airport.*

> **Travel, journey, or trip?**
> Don't confuse **travel** and **journey** or **trip**. You use **travel** about the activity of going to different places: *I've always been interested in the idea of space **travel**.* You use **journey** or **trip** about one time when you go from one place to another: *Did you have a **good trip/journey?*** Don't say 'Did you have a good travel?'

PHRASES

a form/mode/method/means of travel *I find the train a more comfortable mode of travel.*

traveller *BrE*, traveler *AmE n*

someone who is on a journey, or someone who travels often

ADJECTIVES/NOUNS + traveller

a business traveller *Business travellers are offered special deals.*

air/rail/coach travellers *Air travellers suffered long delays because of the storms.*

a frequent traveller *She was a frequent traveller to Europe.*

a seasoned/experienced traveller *This is the sort of information that every seasoned traveller knows.*

an independent traveller *They provide maps for independent travellers wishing to explore France by car.*

a keen traveller (*also* **an inveterate traveller** *formal*) (=someone who likes travelling very much) *He is an inveterate traveller who has spent much time in Asia.*

an intrepid traveller (=one who likes risk and adventures) *Intrepid travellers can take a boat down the Mekong River.*

a solo/single traveller (=someone who is travelling alone) *Single travellers often have to pay extra.*

a fellow traveller (=someone who is travelling on the same vehicle or boat) *He got into conversation with a fellow traveller.*

a budget traveller (=someone who wants to travel cheaply) *The book lists cheap simple accommodation which will appeal to budget travellers.*

a foreign traveller *Foreign travelers contributed about $2.3 billion to the US economy.*

a world traveller *He is a writer and a world traveller.*

a weary traveller (=one who is tired) *Weary travellers would be given food, drink, and a bed for the night.*

PREPOSITIONS

a traveller from/to a place *The riches of these Indian rulers were admired by travellers from the West.*

treacherous *adj* THESAURUS ▸ **dangerous**

treasure *n*

valuable things, especially gold, silver, and jewels

ADJECTIVES

buried treasure *They were digging for buried treasure.*

hidden treasure *People were drawn there by stories of hidden treasure.*

sunken treasure (=lost under the sea) *The divers were looking for sunken treasure.*

VERBS

find/discover treasure *You won't find the treasure without the map.*

look for/search for treasure *He returned to search for the treasure.*

treasure + NOUNS

a treasure trove (=a group of valuable or interesting things) *A treasure trove of fossils has been found in China.*

a treasure house (=a place containing lots of valuable things) *The Hall is a treasure house of antiques.*

a treasure chest (=a large box for storing treasure) *They had no idea where the treasure chest was buried.*

a treasure hunter *Coins are often found by treasure hunters with metal detectors.*

treasured *adj* THESAURUS ▸ **valuable (2)**

treat[1] *v*

1 to behave towards someone or something in a particular way

ADVERBS

treat sb well *The majority of workers are well treated.*

treat sb badly *Why did he treat me so badly?*

treat sb fairly/unfairly *I just want to be treated fairly.*

treat sb equally *All people should be treated equally, whatever their age.*

treat sb differently *Should girls be treated differently from boys in school?*

treat sb harshly (=in a severe or unkind way) *The guards treated the prisoners harshly.*

treat sb kindly *The world had not treated him kindly.*

treat sb sympathetically *A victim of crime should be treated sympathetically by the police.*

treat sb accordingly (=in a way that is suitable to them or to their situation) *She is a senior officer and should be treated accordingly.*

treat sb leniently (=less severely than is possible) *We were surprised that the judge treated him so leniently.*

treat sb shabbily (=very unfairly) *He feels that the company has treated him rather shabbily.*

treat sb favourably *BrE*, **treat sb favorably** *AmE* (=treat one person or group better than another one, in a way that seems unfair) *Some children were treated more favourably than others.*

PHRASES

treat sb with respect/contempt/suspicion etc *When you treat the kids with respect, they act responsibly.*

treat sb as a friend/an equal/an adult etc *We have worked together for years and we treat each other as friends.*

treat sb like dirt *informal* (=very badly and with no respect) *He's a horrible man who treats his wife and children like dirt.*

2 to use drugs or medical care in order to deal with a medical problem that someone has

ADVERBS

treat sb/sth effectively/successfully *Experts say the illness can be treated successfully, but has to be spotted in its early stages.*

PREPOSITIONS

treat sb for sth *The doctors are treating him for high blood pressure.*

treat sb/sth with sth *Pneumonia can usually be successfully treated with antibiotics.*

PHRASES

sth is effective in treating sth *The cream is effective in treating a wide range of skin conditions.*

treat[2] *n*

something special that you do or buy for yourself or someone else, that gives pleasure

ADJECTIVES/NOUNS + treat

a special treat *As a special treat he was allowed to stay up late to watch the game on TV.*

a real/great treat *Going to the zoo was a real treat for the children.*

a little treat *You can give your dog a biscuit as a little treat.*

a birthday/Christmas/holiday treat *We took her out to dinner as a birthday treat.*

an occasional treat *I don't usually eat sweet foods, but I sometimes let myself have the occasional treat.*

a rare treat *It was a rare treat to see the band perform in Europe.*

VERBS

give sb/yourself a treat *I wanted to give you a special treat.*

deserve a treat *Everyone deserves a treat from time to time.*

get a treat *Jazz fans will get a treat when they listen to this CD.*

PREPOSITIONS

as a treat *Dad let me borrow his car as a treat.*

for a treat *I bought myself some flowers for a treat.*

PHRASES

be in for a treat (*also* **have a treat in store**) (=will get a treat) *Justin Bieber fans have a treat in store when he appears in a special Christmas show.*

treatment *n*

1 something that is done to cure someone who is injured or ill

ADJECTIVES/NOUNS + treatment

medical treatment *She could not afford to pay for medical treatment.*

hospital treatment *Several people needed hospital treatment for burns.*

emergency/urgent treatment *The driver needed emergency treatment.*

the right treatment *He will get better soon, if he has the right treatment.*

an effective treatment *The most effective treatment is to stay in bed.*

further treatment (=more treatment) *The patient does not require further treatment.*

dental treatment (=for your teeth) *Children get free dental treatment.*

cancer treatment *He returned to France to continue his cancer treatment.*

psychiatric treatment *He underwent psychiatric treatment after a period of severe depression.*

laser treatment (=done with a laser) *Laser treatment can be technically difficult.*

alternative treatments (=treatments that are

not part of normal scientific medicine) *She found out all she could about alternative cancer treatments.*

fertility/infertility treatment (=for helping someone who is unable to have children) *Mrs Smith received fertility treatment using donor eggs.*

VERBS

give sb treatment (*also* **administer treatment** *formal*): *He was given treatment at a local hospital.*

provide treatment *The Health Service provides excellent treatment.*

get/have/receive treatment (*also* **undergo treatment** *formal*): *Two boys received treatment for gunshot wounds.*

need treatment (*also* **require treatment** *formal*): *All three were beaten so badly that they needed hospital treatment.*

respond to treatment (=become better when given treatment) *He got a lung infection which did not respond to treatment.*

refuse treatment (=say you do not want it) *Everyone has the right to refuse medical treatment.*

PREPOSITIONS

the treatment of sth *There have been great advances in the treatment of cancer.*

a treatment for sth *What is the best treatment for a cold?*

PHRASES

a course of treatment (=treatment that lasts for a period of time) *They have started her on a new course of treatment.*

2 a way of behaving towards someone

ADJECTIVES/NOUNS + treatment

special/preferential treatment (=one person is treated better than others) *Although I was the boss's daughter, I didn't get any special treatment.*

equal/the same treatment *Everyone should get equal treatment under the law.*

harsh treatment (=severe, cruel, or unkind) *They do not deserve such harsh treatment.*

VIP treatment (=special treatment, which very important people get) *We were given VIP treatment.*

star treatment (=special treatment, which famous people get) *Winners get star treatment from the media.*

the silent treatment (=refusing to speak to someone because you are angry with them) *He's been giving me the silent treatment ever since our argument.*

VERBS

get/have/receive a treatment *Harper described the treatment he had received in prison.*

suffer a treatment (=receive bad treatment) *I've suffered worse treatment than that in the past.*

put up with a treatment (=accept it, even though it is bad) *Employees often put up with such treatment rather than risk losing their jobs.*

deserve a treatment *Disabled people deserve equal treatment.*

single sb out for a treatment (=give it to them and only them) *He was hoping he wouldn't be singled out for special treatment.*

PREPOSITIONS

the treatment of sb *They are complaining about the harsh treatment of prisoners.*

treaty *n*

a formal written agreement between two or more countries or governments

ADJECTIVES/NOUNS + treaty

an international treaty *The US refused to sign any international treaty on cutting carbon emissions.*

a peace treaty *Jordan signed a peace treaty with Israel.*

an extradition treaty (=one which says that people can be brought back to a country for trial) *The United States has had an extradition treaty with Mexico since 1978.*

a bilateral treaty (=one signed by two countries) *Uzbekistan and Russia signed a bilateral treaty of friendship.*

a draft treaty (=one that has been written but not yet signed) *The committee produced a draft treaty on arms limitation.*

VERBS + treaty

sign a treaty *The treaty was signed by eight European countries.*

negotiate a treaty (=discuss the conditions in order to reach agreement) *They are trying to negotiate a treaty to end the war.*

conclude a treaty *formal* (=successfully agree it) *In 1875 Japan and Russia concluded a treaty.*

enter into a treaty (=agree to it) *We hoped that they would be willing to enter into a treaty with the Palestinian authority.*

draft a treaty (*also* **draw up a treaty**) *The six countries began drafting a treaty.*

ratify a treaty (=make it official by signing it or accepting it) *The government cannot ratify the treaty without Parliament's consent.*

breach/violate a treaty (=break it) *If their troops crossed the border, they would be breaching the treaty.*

amend/renegotiate a treaty (=make changes to it) *All parties have agreed to amend the treaty.*

treaty + VERBS

a treaty bans/prohibits sth *The three countries signed a treaty banning the sale of whale meat.*

a treaty requires sth (=says that someone must do something) *The new treaty requires the national banks to support each other.*

a treaty provides for sth (=says that something can or should happen) *The treaty provided for the destruction of half of these missiles.*

a treaty governing sth (=one that controls or affects something) *They had signed a treaty governing the use of US military bases overseas.*

be bound by a treaty (=have to obey it) *They refused to be bound by any treaty that controlled troop movements.*

a treaty expires/runs out (=it ends) *Once the treaty has expired, flights over the area can resume.*

PREPOSITIONS

the Treaty of Rome/Versailles etc *The Treaty of Amiens in 1802 brought a brief peace.*

a treaty on sth *These nations are drafting a treaty on fishing in their waters.*

a treaty with sb *They could never imagine signing a treaty with their old enemy.*

a treaty between sb and sb *A treaty between the Soviet Union and Finland was concluded.*

under/according to a treaty *The European Investment Bank (EIB) was set up under the Treaty of Rome in 1958.*

PHRASES

the terms/provisions of a treaty *Under the terms of the treaty, the two sides agreed to a ceasefire.*

be in breach of a treaty (=do something that breaks it) *By sending their military forces to sea, they are in breach of the treaty.*

a treaty comes into force (=it starts) *Until the treaty comes into force, foreign troops will remain in the country.*

tree *n*

a very tall plant that has branches and leaves, and lives for many years

ADJECTIVES/NOUNS + tree

a pine/oak/chestnut/palm etc tree *We sat in the shade of a big oak tree.*

a fruit/apple/olive etc tree *He has a large garden with fruit trees.*

a Christmas tree (=a real or artificial tree that people put in their houses and decorate for Christmas) *Many families put presents under the Christmas tree.*

a tall tree *The tallest tree in the world is a Californian redwood.*

a tree is bare (=it does not have any leaves) *In winter the trees are bare.*

a dead tree *There is a dead tree that needs cutting down.*

a fallen tree *A fallen tree lay across the road, blocking their way.*

a hollow tree (=empty inside) *Some birds make their nests inside hollow trees.*

a gnarled tree (=old, rough, and twisted, with lumps on the trunk and branches) *An old gnarled tree stood next to the house.*

an evergreen tree (=that does not lose its leaves in winter) *These small evergreen trees are ideal for gardens.*

a deciduous tree (=that loses its leaves in winter) *The oak tree is deciduous and loses its leaves late in the year.*

VERBS + tree

climb a tree *Children enjoy climbing trees.*

chop down/cut down a tree (*also* **fell a tree** *formal*): *He chopped down the tree because it was blocking the view.*

plant a tree *She planted a plum tree in the backyard.*

grow a tree *You can grow small fruit trees in containers.*

prune a tree (=cut back some of its branches) *I normally prune the apple trees in the winter.*

tree + VERBS

a tree grows *These trees can grow to a height of 15 metres.*

a tree stands *An ancient oak tree stood in front of the cottage.*

a tree produces sth (*also* **a tree bears sth** *formal*): *The tree produced a few small apples.*

trees line sth (=form a line along the edge of a place) *Palm trees line the beach.*

a tree sways (=moves from side to side) *The tree was swaying in the wind.*

a tree falls *A tree fell on a car and injured the driver.*

tree + NOUNS

a tree trunk (=the main central part of a tree, from which the branches grow) *I leaned against a tree trunk.*

a tree stump (=the part remaining in the ground when the rest has been cut down) *She sat on a tree stump to rest.*

a tree house/treehouse (=a house built in a tree, usually for playing) *He built a tree house for the children.*

a tree surgeon (=someone who treats damaged trees, especially by cutting off branches) *The tree was sawn up by a team of tree surgeons.*

Treetops (=the tops of the trees) is usually written as one word.

PHRASES

an avenue of trees (=a road with trees on both sides) *An avenue of trees led up to the house.*

a clump of trees (=a group of trees growing close together) *There was a clump of trees at the far end of the lake.*

a grove of trees (=a small area of land with trees growing on it) *The hill could easily be seen through a grove of trees.*

tremble *v*
to shake slightly in a way that you cannot control, especially because you are upset or frightened

ADVERBS

tremble slightly *He found himself trembling slightly.*
tremble violently *She was trembling violently from head to foot.*
tremble uncontrollably *The disease makes people tremble uncontrollably.*

NOUNS

sb's body trembles *Her whole body was trembling with anger.*
sb's knees/legs tremble *She was terrified and could feel her knees trembling.*
sb's voice trembles *He was nervous and his voice was trembling.*
sb's hand/fingers tremble *Her fingers trembled with excitement as she opened the envelope.*
sb's lip/mouth trembles *His mouth was trembling as he gave us the bad news.*

PREPOSITIONS

tremble at sth *He trembled at the thought of having to tell his dad.*
tremble with anger/rage/fear/excitement *Before walking on stage to receive the prize I was trembling with excitement.*

PHRASES

tremble from head to toe/foot (*also* **tremble all over**) (=your whole body is shaking) *The shock of the accident made her tremble from head to foot.*
tremble like a leaf (=tremble a lot because you are very frightened or worried) *The frightened child was trembling like a leaf.*

T

tremendous *adj* THESAURUS **huge**

trend *n*
a gradual change or development in a situation, or in what many people do

ADJECTIVES/NOUNS + trend

a recent/new trend *The recent trend has been for people to rent rather than buy their own home.*
the current/latest trend *If current trends continue, the amount of carbon dioxide in the atmosphere will double by the year 2030.*
a general trend (=one followed by most people or happening in most places) *There was a general trend towards marriage at an older age.*
a growing/increasing/rising trend *The show is part of a growing trend towards violence on TV.*
an alarming/worrying/disturbing trend *I have noticed a worrying trend in attitudes to older workers.*
the underlying/long-term trend (=the trend over a long period of time) *The underlying trend is for rich economies to get richer.*
a downward/upward trend (=a tendency for something to increase or decrease) *The downward trend in population growth was not seen as a problem.*
economic/market trends *This forecast is based on current economic trends.*
the national trend *Crime rates in the city fell, in contrast to the national trend.*
the international/worldwide/global trend *There is a global trend towards caring more for the environment.*
a trend is evident (=is easy to notice or identify) *A trend towards marrying later in life was becoming evident.*

VERBS

a trend continues *The trend for more twin births is continuing.*
a trend emerges *A new trend towards openness in politics had begun to emerge.*
start a trend *The younger generation started a trend toward living in the downtown area.*
follow a trend *Divorce rates in Scotland are following the general trend.*
reverse a trend (=make something start to change back) *The new manager succeeded in reversing the downward trend in the team's fortunes.*
halt a trend (=make it stop) *We need government policies that will halt this downward economic trend.*
buck the trend (=do something that is not what is generally happening) *Many small companies are struggling in the recession, but we are bucking the trend.*
show/indicate a trend *These reports indicate a new trend in how the public thinks of politicians.*
reflect a trend (=follow what is generally happening) *More people in the city are living alone, reflecting a national trend.*

PREPOSITIONS

a trend towards/toward sth *There has been a trend towards bigger farms.*
a trend away from sth *We are seeing a trend away from relying on government for these services.*
a trend in sth *Challenging the decisions of officials is a disturbing trend in professional sport.*
a trend for sth *This development seems to be following the trend for smaller homes with smaller gardens.*

THESAURUS: trend

vogue, trend, craze/fad, sth is all the rage → **fashion (2)**

trial *n*
1 a legal process in a court of law

ADJECTIVES

a fair trial *Everyone has the right to a fair trial.*

an unfair trial *Human rights groups claim that his trial was unfair.*

a criminal trial (=dealing with a crime) *There are several stages in a criminal trial.*

a civil trial (=dealing with disagreements between people, rather than crimes) *The court mainly deals with civil trials.*

NOUNS + trial

a murder/fraud etc trial *She was a witness in a murder trial.*

VERBS

stand/face trial (=be judged in a court of law) *His doctors said he was unfit to stand trial.*

be awaiting/facing trial (=be going to be judged in a court of law soon) *He spent five months in prison awaiting trial.*

a trial is held *The trial will be held sometime next month.*

a trial opens (=officially begins) *The trial opened five weeks ago.*

a trial is adjourned (=it is officially stopped for several days, weeks, or months) *The trial was adjourned until November.*

a trial collapses (=it ends without a verdict) *The trial collapsed after it emerged that the victim had drunk so much wine she could not remember what happened.*

NOUNS

a trial judge *The trial judge told the jury to ignore this evidence.*

a trial lawyer *He is regarded as one of the finest trial lawyers in the state.*

a trial court *The case will return to the trial court in May.*

a trial date *No trial date has been set.*

a trial verdict (=a decision about whether or not someone is guilty) *His lawyers have said they will appeal the trial verdict.*

PREPOSITIONS

a trial for sth *His trial for murder began yesterday.*

at a trial *She will have to give evidence at the trial.*

during a trial *During the trial, the man claimed he had never met Max.*

without trial *He was imprisoned for two years without trial.*

PHRASES

be on trial (=be being judged in a court of law) *Her son is on trial charged with murder.*

go on trial *Taylor went on trial accused of killing his wife.*

put sb on trial *Eight people were arrested and put on trial.*

bring sb to trial *The people who were responsible for this crime must be brought to trial.*

be sent for trial (*also* **be committed for trial** *BrE*): *Smith's lawyer battled to stop him being sent for trial in Britain.*

a case goes/comes to trial *If the case ever went to trial, he would probably lose.*

2 a process of testing something or someone

ADJECTIVES

clinical trials (=of a new drug or medical device on humans) *Clinical trials of the drug will begin soon.*

extensive trials (=a lot of thorough trials) *Extensive trials have been carried out on the product, to make sure that it is safe.*

initial trials (=the first ones) *Information from these initial trials will be very useful.*

NOUNS + trial

field trials (=of a new product in the conditions in which it will be used) *The company is currently carrying out field trials of new mirrors for heavy vehicles.*

time/speed trials (=in order to see how fast someone or something goes - used in sport) *A series of time trials decides who will take part in the final race.*

VERBS

do/carry out a trial (*also* **conduct/perform a trial** *formal*): *Before a drug company can sell a new drug, it has to carry out trials to see how well it works.*

take part in a trial (*also* **participate in a trial** *formal*): *Eight schools are taking part in the trial.*

undergo trials (=be tested) *A new aircraft is currently undergoing trials for the Royal Air Force.*

trial + NOUNS

a trial period *Any new laws should be given a trial period of a year.*

a trial run *Many couples have a trial run the day before their wedding day.*

PREPOSITIONS

on trial (=in order to test something) *They let me have the computer on trial for a few days.*

a trial for sth *Trials for the Olympics started on July 1st.*

PHRASES

on a trial basis (=in order to see whether something is successful) *Smith was hired on a 12-month trial basis.*

by/through trial and error (=in order to find out which is the best of several possible methods) *I learnt most of what I know about gardening through trial and error.*

tribute *n*

1 something that shows your respect or admiration for someone

ADJECTIVES

a special tribute *He wrote the song as a special tribute to his wife.*

a fitting tribute (=very suitable) *A set of special postage stamps honouring the artist will make a fitting tribute to his work.*

a warm tribute *He paid a warm tribute to Steve, saying that he was one of the kindest people he had ever met.*

a moving tribute *Bob's speech was a moving tribute to his son who had been killed in a road accident.*

a final tribute (=to someone who has died) *A church service was held as a final tribute to the soldiers who died for their country.*

a lasting tribute (=that will last for a long time) *The garden is meant to be a lasting tribute to celebrate the life of John Lennon.*

a silent tribute (=when people show respect silently) *The crowd stood in silent tribute to all those who had lost their lives in the war.*

a floral tribute *formal* (=flowers given as a tribute) *At her funeral the church was decorated with floral tributes.*

VERBS

pay tribute to sb/sth (=praise someone publicly and thank them for what they have done) *In his speech the headmaster paid tribute to Mrs Green.*

offer a tribute *Many actors have offered tributes to the film star who died yesterday.*

write a tribute *She wrote a tribute to him in the local newspaper.*

tribute + NOUNS

a tribute album/concert (=a record or a concert to show respect for someone) *A group of musicians recorded a tribute album to Amy Winehouse.*

PREPOSITIONS

a tribute to sb/sth *The new university building was named 'The Frank Thompson Centre' as a tribute to the professor.*

2 something that shows that someone or something is very good

PHRASES

sth is a tribute to sb/sth *The improvement in results is a tribute to the hard work of students and their teachers.*

trick *n*

1 something you do in order to deceive or surprise someone

ADJECTIVES/NOUNS + trick

a dirty/mean/nasty trick (=a very unkind and unpleasant one) *That was a dirty trick to play on someone!*

a cruel trick *It was a cruel trick to let them think he was dead.*

a con trick (*also* **a confidence trick** *formal*) (=when someone is deceived in order to get their money) *She was the victim of a con trick and lost all her savings.*

VERBS

play a trick (on sb) *The other boys played a nasty trick on him.*

fall for a trick (=be deceived by a trick) *I'm not going to fall for that old trick again.*

trick + NOUNS

a trick question (=one that is hard to answer correctly because it is a trick) *I thought it was a trick question so I refused to answer it.*

PHRASES

use every trick in the book (=do anything, however bad, to try to get something) *She's prepared to use every trick in the book to improve her chances of winning.*

2 something difficult or apparently impossible that you do to entertain people

ADJECTIVES/NOUNS + trick

a magic/conjuring trick (=a clever trick in which you seem to make things appear, disappear, or change by magic) *A magician must never give away the secret of how he did a magic trick.*

a clever trick *He taught the dog to do some clever tricks.*

a card trick (=a trick done with playing cards) *For this card trick you start by asking someone to pick any card from the pack.*

a party trick (=something clever you do to impress or entertain people at parties) *His party trick is guessing strangers' birthdays.*

VERBS

do/perform a trick *The magician performed several tricks to entertain the children.*

learn a trick *I'd like to learn a few card tricks.*

teach sb a trick *She taught me a trick in which you make a coin seem to disappear.*

tricky *adj* THESAURUS ▸ **difficult**

trip *n*

a visit to a place that involves a journey

ADJECTIVES/NOUNS + trip

a business trip *She's away on a business trip.*

a school trip (=when children and teachers from a school go somewhere) *My daughter went on a school trip to Washington.*

a shopping/fishing/skiing etc trip *He was exhausted after an all-day shopping trip.*

a boat/coach/bus trip *They took a boat trip to see the seals.*

a road trip (=a long journey by car or other road vehicle) *The book is about a road trip across the US.*

a day trip (=when you go somewhere for pleasure and come back the same day) *York is close enough to visit as a day trip.*

a round trip (=a journey to a place and back again) *She makes a 150-mile round trip to see her mother every week.*

the return trip (=the journey back to a place) *Two days later she began her return trip to Chicago.*

a wasted trip (=a trip in which you do not achieve what you wanted to) *I had a wasted trip because they didn't have the shoes in my size.*

VERBS

go on a trip *They've gone on a trip to Greece.*
take a trip *We decided to take a trip on the Santa Fe railway.*
make a trip *He had to make the long trip to Minneapolis alone.*
book a trip *She's booked another trip to Florida.*
cancel a trip *He had to cancel the trip because his mother became ill.*
postpone a trip (=decide to make it at a later date) *Bad weather forced us to postpone our trip.*
plan a trip (=intend to make one) *We're planning a trip to see our friends in Germany.*

PREPOSITIONS

a trip to a place *She was planning a trip to Italy later that year.*
a trip by bus/boat/plane etc *He had never taken a trip by boat before.*
on a trip *They were away on a trip, so the house was empty.*

triumph *n*

an important victory or success, especially after a difficult struggle

ADJECTIVES

a great/major triumph *It was a major triumph for us to win the championship.*
a small/minor triumph *The award represents a small triumph for independent film-makers.*
a personal triumph *Coming second in the race was a personal triumph.*
a political/diplomatic triumph *Persuading the two countries to sign a peace agreement was a remarkable diplomatic triumph.*
a final/eventual triumph *The competition ended with the final triumph of the German team.*
the ultimate triumph (=the biggest triumph of all) *The ultimate triumph of his career came at the Olympic Games where Smith won the gold in the 200 metres.*

VERBS

hail sth as a triumph (=consider something to be a triumph) *The film festival was hailed as a triumph.*
celebrate a triumph *The team celebrated their triumph by having a party.*
represent a triumph *The election of President Obama represented a triumph for African Americans.*

PREPOSITIONS

a triumph over sb/sth *He scored two goals in the team's triumph over Chelsea.*
a triumph against sb/sth *Her triumph against her opponent surprised everyone.*
a triumph for sb/sth *The election victory was a triumph for the party.*
a triumph of sth *It is a triumph of modern medicine that few people die of the disease nowadays.*

PHRASES

a sense of triumph *I left the room with a sense of triumph, knowing I had won the argument.*
a moment of triumph *His moment of triumph came at the US Masters Golf Tournament.*
triumph over adversity (=success in a very difficult situation) *The film is about one man's triumph over adversity.*
the triumph of good over evil *In his books, Lewis writes about the triumph of good over evil.*

trivial *adj* THESAURUS ▸ **unimportant**

troops *n*

soldiers in an organized group

> **Grammar**
> Used in the plural, except when used before another noun.

ADJECTIVES/NOUNS + troops

government troops *There are reports of serious clashes between government troops and guerrillas.*
American/French/UN etc troops *This operation was undertaken by British troops.*
enemy troops *His platoon was captured by enemy troops.*
foreign troops *He demanded that all foreign troops be withdrawn from the region.*
armed troops *The city is surrounded by armed troops loyal to the president.*
combat troops *Heavily armed combat troops were deployed on the streets of the capital yesterday.*
ground troops (=who fight on land) *The advancing ground troops were supported by air power.*
regular troops (=those that do not have a special role or skill) *There has been fierce fighting between rebels and regular troops.*
elite/crack troops (=the best soldiers) *The general's headquarters is guarded by crack troops.*
peacekeeping troops *The Secretary General has ruled out sending UN peacekeeping troops into the republic.*
front-line troops (=those in the place where there is fighting) *There was a high casualty rate among front-line troops.*

VERBS + troops

send (in) troops *He hopes to persuade his NATO allies to send more troops to the area. | Johnson wanted to win the war without sending in American ground troops.*
withdraw troops (*also* **pull out troops**) (=make them leave a place) *Both countries have agreed to withdraw their troops.*
deploy troops (=send them to a place to fight

or do something) *UN troops were deployed in order to keep the peace.*

lead/command troops *The troops were led by inexperienced officers.*

mass troops (=bring large numbers of them together) *Both countries have begun massing troops along the border.*

station troops somewhere (=keep them in a particular place for a period of time) *525,000 American troops are still stationed in the south of the country.*

troops + VERBS

troops fight *General Suleiman said his troops would fight to the end.*

troops serve (=do their job) *Thousands of troops who served in the war suffered mental health problems afterwards.*

troops march somewhere *British troops marched north to attack the German forces.*

troops advance (=move forward in order to attack a place) *Government troops advanced on the rebel stronghold.*

troops withdraw (*also* **troops pull out**) (=leave a place) *British troops pulled out of the area last May.*

troops + NOUNS

troop withdrawal (=the act or process of troops leaving a place) *The US plans a troop withdrawal soon.*

troop deployment (=the act or process of putting troops in a place) *The size of the troop deployment in the region has been halved.*

a troop carrier (=a vehicle or ship used to carry troops) *Their troop carrier was hit by a roadside bomb.*

T

trophy *n*

a large object such as a silver cup or plate that someone receives as a prize for winning a competition

ADJECTIVES/NOUNS + trophy

a major trophy *The club has not won a major trophy for several years.*

a prestigious trophy (=one of the best and most important) *The Champions League trophy is one of the most prestigious trophies in soccer.*

a championship trophy *The team was presented with the championship trophy.*

a tennis/football/baseball etc trophy *She is the proud winner of the tennis trophy.*

VERBS

win/take a trophy *He won the school chess trophy.*

award sb a trophy *Uruguay was the first national football team to be awarded the World Cup trophy.*

give sb a trophy (*also* **present sb with a trophy** *formal*): *He presented her with the trophy for winning the race.*

receive a trophy *The winners of the quiz will receive a trophy.*

lift a trophy *The team captain lifted the trophy and the crowd cheered.*

trophy + NOUNS

a trophy winner *His next game is against last year's trophy winner.*

a trophy cabinet (=a cupboard where trophies are kept) *The winner's cup is proudly displayed in the club's trophy cabinet.*

PREPOSITIONS

a trophy for sth *She won the trophy for the best college player.*

tropical *adj*

coming from or existing in the hottest parts of the world

NOUNS

a tropical climate *Queensland has a warm tropical climate.*

a tropical country/area/island etc *The fruit is available throughout the year in tropical countries.*

a tropical beach *I'd like to spend my holiday lying on a tropical beach somewhere.*

a tropical paradise *The island is a tropical paradise.*

a tropical bird/fish *Many tropical fish are brightly coloured.*

a tropical plant/tree/flower *Most tropical plants will die if there is even a small amount of frost.*

tropical fruit *I enjoy eating tropical fruit such as mangoes and pineapples.*

a tropical forest/rainforest/jungle *We must stop the destruction of tropical rainforests.*

a tropical disease (=an illness that occurs in tropical countries) *She had several tests at the Hospital for Tropical Diseases.*

tropical medicine (=the treatment and study of illnesses that occur in tropical countries) *He is a doctor who specializes in tropical medicine.*

a tropical storm *The tropical storm smashed through the Bahamas.*

tropical sun *You should wear a hat to protect yourself from the tropical sun.*

trouble *n* problems or difficulties

ADJECTIVES

great/terrible trouble *I've been having terrible trouble sleeping.*

serious trouble *She was having serious trouble with her teenage son.*

big trouble *When he gets home, he will be in big trouble with his parents.*

real trouble *I had real trouble finding the place.*

endless trouble (=continuing for a very long time) *We had endless trouble selling the house.*

teething troubles *BrE* (=small problems that you have when you first start doing or using something new) *There were a lot of teething troubles with the software at first.*

financial/economic trouble *If the banks get into financial trouble, why should taxpayers bail them out?*

ADJECTIVES/NOUNS + trouble

engine trouble *The plane had to return to Heathrow when it developed engine trouble.*

car trouble *They're very late – perhaps they've had car trouble.*

money trouble *I didn't realise that we had money troubles until it was too late.*

VERBS

have trouble doing sth *He is having trouble getting his message across to the voters.*

cause trouble *I hope the delay hasn't caused you any trouble.*

get into/run into trouble *The company ran into financial trouble and had to close down.*

mean/spell trouble (=be trouble in the future) *He is now fit and well, which can only spell trouble for his rivals.*

avoid trouble *We can avoid trouble by planning carefully.*

be asking for trouble (=be doing something that will result in problems) *You're asking for trouble walking around the yard in bare feet.*

PREPOSITIONS

trouble with sth *We've had lots of trouble with the car this year.*

in trouble *There were rumours that their marriage was in trouble.*

PHRASES

without any/much trouble (=easily) *The work was carried out without any trouble.*

a lot of trouble *We've been having a lot of trouble with the old heating system.*

trouble ahead (=in the future) *These figures point to trouble ahead for the economy.*

in times of trouble *In times of trouble, the family were more united than ever.*

in deep/dire trouble (=having very serious problems) *It seems that the economy is in deep trouble.*

trousers *n especially BrE*

a piece of clothing that covers the lower half of your body, with a separate part fitting over each leg

PHRASES

a pair of trousers *I need to buy a new pair of trousers.*

ADJECTIVES/NOUNS + trousers

short/long trousers *At school we used to have to wear short trousers.*

baggy trousers (=big and not fitting close to your body) *He was dressed in a suit with baggy trousers.*

loose trousers *I need a belt because my trousers are a bit loose.*

tight trousers *He had eaten too much and his trousers felt tight.*

flared trousers (=wide below the knee) *Flared trousers were popular in the 1970s.*

VERBS

wear trousers *He was wearing a pair of black trousers.*

be dressed in trousers *She was dressed in a blue blouse and a pair of white trousers.*

put on your trousers *He put on his trousers and a clean shirt.*

take off your trousers *She took off her trousers and changed into a skirt.*

take down your trousers *The doctor asked him to take down his trousers.*

pull up your trousers *She reached down and pulled up her trousers.*

trousers + NOUNS

a trouser leg *He rolled up his trouser legs and waded into the river.*

a trouser pocket *She took a handkerchief from her trouser pocket.*

a trouser suit *BrE* (=a woman's suit consisting of a jacket and trousers) *She was wearing a smart blue trouser suit.*

a trouser press *BrE* (=a piece of equipment for making trousers flat and smooth) *There was a trouser press in our hotel room.*

> **Trousers** is used especially in British English. American speakers usually say **pants**.

T

truce *n*

an agreement to stop fighting or arguing

VERBS

call a truce (*also* **declare a truce** *formal*): *The two sides agreed to call a truce.*

agree (to) a truce *After long discussions, a truce was eventually agreed.*

negotiate/broker a truce *UN officials are trying to negotiate a truce between the two sides.*

sign a truce *Finally, a truce was signed and the war ended.*

break a truce (*also* **violate a truce** *formal*) (=begin fighting again after a truce has been agreed) *The French accused the English of breaking the truce.*

a truce breaks down *The truce broke down when Tom accused James of lying.*

ADJECTIVES

an uneasy truce (=one in which the situation is not really calm) *There was an uneasy truce between Lily and Stephen at dinner.*

a fragile truce (=one that is likely to fail) *The fragile truce has lasted for only a few weeks.*
a temporary truce *Last month they reached a temporary truce in the dispute.*
a two-day/week-long etc truce *The week-long truce came to an end.*

PREPOSITIONS

a truce between sb and sb *The truce between Britain and France broke down in 1803.*
a truce with sb *The government declared a truce with the rebel army.*

truck *n*

a large road vehicle used to carry goods

ADJECTIVES/NOUNS + truck

a heavy/light truck *Heavy trucks go past the house all day.*
a pickup truck (=a small truck with low sides that is used for carrying goods) *He drives a red pickup truck.*
a delivery truck (=for taking goods from one place to another) *There was a supermarket delivery truck parked in front of the house.*
a flatbed truck (=with a flat open surface for carrying things) *The company uses flatbed trucks to carry heavy equipment.*
a refuse truck *BrE*, **a garbage truck** *AmE* (=for collecting rubbish) *She drives a garbage truck for a living.*
a fire truck *AmE* (=carrying equipment and people that stop fires burning) *Fire trucks rushed to the scene and managed to put out the fire.*

VERBS

drive a truck *He got a job driving a truck.*
load a truck (with sth) *The men loaded the truck and drove off.*
unload a truck *She helped us to unload the truck.*
park a truck *She parked the truck in front of the house.*
rent/hire a truck *When we moved house, we hired a truck to carry the furniture.*
a truck carries sth *The truck was carrying metal pipes.*

truck + NOUNS

a truck driver *He works as a truck driver.*
a truck stop *AmE* (=a cheap place to eat next to a road, used mainly by truck drivers) *We stopped at a truck stop in Toledo.*

PHRASES

a convoy of trucks (=a group of trucks travelling together) *A convoy of 15 trucks brought food and medical supplies to the city.*
a fleet of trucks (=trucks owned by a particular company) *The firm has a fleet of trucks which travel all over the US.*

Truck is more common in American English. British speakers use **truck**, but they also often use the word **lorry**.

true *adj*

1 correct and based on facts

NOUNS

a true story *The film is based on a true story.*
a true picture/reflection *The news reports don't really give you a true picture of what is really happening.*
a statement is true *Students have to decide if the statements are true or false.*
a rumour/accusation/allegation is true *If the rumours are true, then the factory could close.*

VERBS

remain/hold true (=continue to be true) *Many of these general principles still hold true.*
ring true (=seem believable) *There is something about her story that just doesn't ring true.*

ADVERBS

especially/particularly true *It is important to have your heart checked regularly. This is especially true for older people.*
absolutely/completely true *It is absolutely true that the system needs to be modernized.*
quite true *BrE* (=completely true) *What he said was quite true.*
equally true (=true to the same degree or amount) *The same thing is equally true for boys and girls.*
not entirely/exactly/strictly true (=not completely true) *It is often said that young people aren't interested in politics, but that is not entirely true.*
generally/largely true *It is generally true that houses are cheaper in the north.*

PHRASES

sb's dream comes true (=something that you have always wanted really happens) *Then, in 2008, his dream came true and he was hired by CBS News.*
the same is true for sb/sth *People want security for their children, and the same was true for people in the past.*

THESAURUS: true

accurate
information | figures | description | record | account | picture | assessment | measurement
based on facts and not containing any mistakes:
Patients should have accurate information about the risks of their treatment. | He was able to give the police an accurate description of his attacker. | The amazing thing is that Newton's measurements were so accurate.

undeniable/indisputable
fact | truth | evidence | effect | influence
used when something is definitely true, and no one can argue or disagree about it:
*The undeniable fact is that carbon gases are building up in the atmosphere. | Researchers are looking for indisputable evidence of biological activity on Mars. | **It is indisputable that** the situation is getting worse.*

If you want to say firmly and definitely that something is true, you say **It is a fact (that)**: *It is **a fact that** most crime is committed by young men.*
You can also say that a situation **is the case** (=it exists and is true): *It used **to be the case** that there were few women studying science.*
You can also say that what someone says **is the truth** (=they are not lying): *I knew that what she said **was the truth**.*

ANTONYMS **true → untrue**

2 real

Grammar
True is only used before a noun in this meaning.

NOUNS

sb's true feelings/character *Marianne never showed her true feelings.*

sb's true identity *He was worried that someone would discover his true identity.*

the true value/cost of sth *You only understand the true value of freedom when you have it taken away from you.*

the true meaning of sth *The story of 'The Lion and The Mouse' teaches children about the true meaning of friendship.*

sb's/sth's true worth (=how good or valuable they really are) *The players will be keen to show their coach their true worth.*

the true nature/extent of sth *There are different opinions among scientists on the true nature of the problem.*

true love/happiness *I wondered if I would ever find true love, and then I met Jack.*

a true friend *A true friend wouldn't lie to you.*

a true professional (=someone who does their job with a lot of skill) *Her colleagues described her as a true professional who was respected by everyone.*

a true believer *A true believer is prepared to sacrifice everything for the sake of their religion.*

PHRASES

show your true colours *BrE*, **show your true colors** *AmE* (=show your real character) *The regime showed its true colours and arrested the opposition leader.*

THESAURUS: true
genuine, authentic, true, bona fide/bonafide, hard → real (1)

truly *adv*

THESAURUS **very**[1]

trust[1] *v*

to believe that someone or something is good and reliable

ADVERBS

trust sb/sth completely/totally *We need to find someone who we can trust completely.*

not entirely/fully trust sb/sth (=not completely) *We don't entirely trust his reasons for helping.*

trust sb implicitly *formal* (=without any doubts) *I gave him the money because I knew I could trust him implicitly.*

never trust sb/sth *I would never trust him to keep a secret.*

VERBS

be able to trust sb/sth *The friendship will only work if you are able to trust her.*

learn to trust sb *An abused animal must learn to trust people again.*

be afraid to trust sb/sth *After that experience, I was afraid to trust anyone.*

NOUNS

trust your instincts *I thought he looked dishonest – I should have trusted my instincts.*

trust sb's judgment *Don't you trust my judgment?*

PREPOSITIONS

trust in sb/sth *I trusted in his ability to do a good job.*

trust sb with sth (=trust someone to take care of something) *We trusted you with our safety.*

PHRASES

sb/sth is not to be trusted (=you should not trust them) *Be careful – her advice is not to be trusted.*

trust[2] *n*

a firm belief that a person or organisation is honest and good

ADJECTIVES/NOUNS + trust

absolute/complete trust *Children at this age have complete trust in their parents.*

great trust *The others had placed great trust in me and I did not want to let them down.*

mutual trust (=trust that two people have for each other) *In order to reach an agreement, there needs to be an atmosphere of mutual trust.*

blind trust (=trusting someone too much, without asking any questions) *Their blind trust in their president began to fade a little more with every scandal.*

misplaced trust (=wrong because someone

does not deserve it) *His trust in his friend was sadly misplaced.*
public trust *Politicians are beginning to lose public trust.*
consumer/voter trust *The nuclear industry is having problems building consumer trust.*

VERBS

have trust in sb/sth *Patients must have trust in their doctor.*
put (your) trust in sb/sth (*also* **place (your) trust in sb/sth**) *They're putting all their trust in you, so don't disappoint them.*
earn/win/gain sb's trust *An officer has to earn his men's trust.*
abuse/betray sb's trust (=be disloyal to someone who trusts you) *He has completely betrayed the voters' trust.*
lose trust *People have lost trust in the banking system.*
build trust (*also* **build up trust**) *A good teacher builds trust by giving pupils support and encouragement.*
establish trust *formal*: *The company worked to establish trust between workers and managers.*
rebuild/regain/restore trust *formal* (=make someone trust you again) *When a husband or wife has been unfaithful, it can take years to rebuild trust.*
be based on trust *Good business relationships must be based on mutual trust.*
develop trust *It took many years to develop the trust that exists between us.*
inspire trust *She inspired trust in all her supporters.*

PREPOSITIONS

trust in sb/sth *I have enormous trust in his abilities.*
trust between people *Ever since childhood, there has been very little trust between the brothers.*
trust among/amongst people *Our efforts to develop trust among the population are beginning to succeed.*

PHRASES

a breakdown in/of trust (=when you stop trusting someone) *There had been a complete breakdown in trust between the former business partners.*
a breach of trust (=a lack of trust caused by someone's behaviour) *His behaviour was unprofessional and amounts to a serious breach of trust.*
an atmosphere/climate of trust *The talks took place in an atmosphere of trust and cooperation.*

truth *n*

the true facts about something, rather than something untrue, imagined, or guessed

VERBS + truth

tell (sb) the truth *How do we know you're telling us the truth?*

⚠ Don't say 'say the truth'.

speak the truth *literary*: *He always spoke the truth, whether it was popular or not.*
know the truth *At last I knew the truth about my parents.*
find out/discover/uncover the truth *She was determined to find out the truth, whatever it took.*
learn the truth *When she learns the truth, she may decide to help us.*
get at/get to the truth *informal* (=discover the truth) *The police will eventually get to the truth of the matter.*
search for/seek the truth *Claire's father spent years searching for the truth about her death.*
reveal the truth *She'd promised never to reveal the truth to anyone.*
accept/admit the truth *Our pride stopped us from admitting the truth.*
conceal/hide the truth *They tried to conceal the truth from their children.*
bend/distort/stretch the truth (=say or write something that is not completely true) *He has been known to bend the truth when it suits him.*

truth + VERBS

the truth emerges/comes out (=is discovered after being hidden) *When the truth finally emerged, he was forced to resign.*
the truth dawns (on sb) *informal* (=someone realizes the truth) *It was a shock when the truth finally dawned: he was not who he claimed to be.*

ADJECTIVES/NOUNS + truth

the whole/full truth *People only found out the full truth later.*
the simple/plain truth *The simple truth is that there isn't enough money to pay for it.*
the naked/unvarnished truth (=without attempting to hide anything or make something sound better) *The book claims to tell the unvarnished truth about the war.*
the sad/painful truth (=something that is true but that you regret) *The sad truth is that she still misses him.*
the awful/terrible/dreadful truth *She could not bring herself to tell them the awful truth.*
the honest truth (=used to emphasize that you are telling the truth) *We didn't come here to steal anything, and that's the honest truth.*
the gospel truth (=something that is completely true in every way, so that you can depend on it completely) *Don't take everything she says as the gospel truth.*

PHRASES

get the truth out of sb (=make someone tell you the truth) *I'll get the truth out of her, whatever it takes!*

the truth of the matter *The truth of the matter is that we don't know what really happened.*

sth has the ring of truth (about it) (=it seems true) *His account of what happened had the ring of truth about it.*

there is an element of truth in sth (=some of it is true) *There's an element of truth in what you say, but it's a little too simplistic.*

there is a grain/kernel/shred of truth (=a very small amount of it is true) *There isn't a grain of truth in these allegations.*

be/come close to the truth (=tell the truth, especially when someone does not want this) *The company tried to have the book banned because it came a little too close to the truth.*

PREPOSITIONS

the truth about sb/sth *If you don't tell me the truth about what happened, I'm going to tell your father about this.*

the truth behind sth *The truth behind his death may never be known.*

the truth of sth *She kept the truth of her father's disappearance a secret all her life.*

truthful *adj* THESAURUS **honest**

try[1] *v*

1 to use effort so that you can do something, which you may not be able to do

ADVERBS

try hard *She was trying hard not to show her feelings.*

try unsuccessfully/without success *The climbers tried unsuccessfully to reach the top of the mountain last year.*

try in vain/vainly try to do sth (=unsuccessfully) *He tried in vain to quit smoking.*

try desperately/frantically (=extremely hard) *The ambulance crew tried desperately to save his life.*

try your best/hardest (=do as well or as much as you can) *I tried my best to look after her.*

try again/one more time *Let's have a rest and then we'll try again.*

try repeatedly/continually *She repeatedly tried to speak to her manager about the problem.*

VERBS

give up trying *Her novel was rejected by several publishers, but she never gave up trying.*

PHRASES

try as you might (=try as hard as possible to do something, but still not be successful) *Try as he might, he could not get the incident out of his mind.*

it was not for (the) lack of trying (=used to say that someone failed even though they tried very hard) *I didn't persuade her, but it wasn't for the lack of trying.*

Try or attempt?
These words mean the same. **Attempt** is more formal than **try** and is often used about things that are difficult: *They are **attempting** to travel to the South Pole.* **Attempted** is also often used when talking about crimes: *The men were charged with **attempted** murder.*

2 to do something in order to find out if you like it, or if it will work

ADVERBS

have you ever tried sth? *Have you ever tried wind-surfing?*

have never tried sth *I've never tried Vietnamese food before.*

PHRASES

try everything *We tried everything, but we couldn't get the engine to start.*

try[2] *n* an attempt to do something

ADJECTIVES

a good try (=a good or determined attempt) *I don't know if I can win, but I'm going to have a good try.*

a nice try (=a good try that is not successful) *Nice try, Claudia, but not good enough, I'm afraid.*

sb's first/second try *Only half the students passed the test on their first try.*

VERBS

have a try *I decided to have one last try.*

give sth a try *spoken: I knew I didn't have much chance of getting the job, but I thought I'd give it a try.*

be worth a try (=be worth trying because you may succeed) *If you're looking for a room for the night the Swan Hotel is worth a try.*

trying *adj* THESAURUS **annoying**

tuition *n*

teaching, especially in small groups

ADJECTIVES/NOUNS + tuition

college tuition *College tuition is becoming increasingly expensive.*

private tuition *Wealthy parents can afford private tuition for their children.*

extra tuition *He is having extra tuition after school.*

expert tuition (=teaching from someone who knows a lot about a subject) *With hard work and expert tuition, she has made great progress.*

individual/one-to-one tuition (=teaching one person rather than a group) *His father was giving him some one-to-one tuition in how to hold the golf club.*

free tuition *Students from poorer families are able to get free tuition.*

maths/English/chemistry etc tuition *He needs more maths tuition if he is going to pass his exam.*

VERBS

give sb tuition *She was given private tuition in the evenings.*

receive tuition *Over 10,000 young people have been able to receive free tuition in a wide range of sports.*

pay for tuition *His grandparents offered to pay for his tuition.*

offer/provide tuition *The Guitar School's evening classes will offer tuition in a variety of styles.*

tuition + NOUNS

a tuition fee (=money that students pay for teaching) *Students will not have to pay tuition fees if their family's income is below a certain level.*

PREPOSITIONS

tuition in sth *He needs more tuition in maths.*

tumour *BrE*, tumor *AmE n*

a mass of diseased cells in your body that have divided and increased too quickly

NOUNS + tumour

a brain/skin/kidney etc tumour *He died of a brain tumour.*

ADJECTIVES

a cancerous tumour (=caused by cancer) *She had surgery to remove a cancerous tumour.*

a malignant tumour (=dangerous and caused by cancer) *She has a malignant tumour and needs chemotherapy.*

a benign tumour (=not caused by cancer) *To his great relief, the tumour turned out to be benign.*

VERBS

diagnose sb with a tumour (=say as a doctor that someone has tumour) *After he was diagnosed with a tumour, he had to have an operation.*

remove a tumour *A surgeon successfully removed the tumour.*

die of a tumour *She died of a brain tumour.*

a tumour grows *This new drug can prevent a tumour from growing.*

PREPOSITIONS

a tumour in sth *The tumour in his chest has grown.*

a tumour on sth *She has a tumour on her heart.*

PHRASES

the risk of a tumour *There is no proof that mobile phone use increases the risk of tumours.*

the growth/development of a tumour *The drug can slow down the growth of a tumour.*

the removal of a tumour *Complete removal of the tumour is often possible.*

tune *n*

a series of musical notes that form part of a song

ADJECTIVES

a catchy/memorable tune (=one that is easy to remember) *His songs have simple words and catchy tunes.*

a great tune *The Beatles wrote some great tunes.*

NOUNS + tune

a show tune (=a tune from a musical) *The album is a collection of Broadway show tunes.*

the theme tune/signature tune *BrE* (=the tune at the beginning or end of a television programme, film etc) *Do you remember the theme tune from the movie 'Titanic'?*

VERBS

play a tune *He played a tune on the piano.*

sing a tune *What's the name of the tune he's singing?*

hum a tune (=sing it by making a continuous sound with your lips closed) *Alice hummed a little tune to herself.*

whistle a tune (=sing it by blowing air through a small hole made with your lips) *Can you whistle the tune to me?*

write a tune (*also* **compose a tune** *formal*): *They wrote many great tunes together in the 1980s.*

hear a tune *He only has to hear a tune once to be able to play it on his guitar.*

hold/carry a tune (=sing it with the correct musical notes) *I've never been able to carry a tune.*

PREPOSITIONS

to the tune of sth (=using the same tune as another song) *The song was sung to the tune of 'Amazing Grace'.*

tunnel *n*

a passage that has been dug under the ground or through a mountain for cars, trains etc to go through

ADJECTIVES/NOUNS + tunnel

a dark tunnel *He looked into the dark tunnel at the end of the platform.*

a long tunnel *The train entered a long tunnel.*

a narrow tunnel *She ran down the narrow tunnel leading to the exit.*

an underground tunnel *The prisoners escaped through an underground tunnel.*

a rail/railway/railroad tunnel *A bridge and a railway tunnel will soon connect the mainland to the island.*

a road tunnel *They drove through a road tunnel under the river.*

VERBS

dig a tunnel *It took over a year to dig the tunnel.*

build a tunnel *The men will start building the tunnel next month.*

T

blast a tunnel (=create it using explosives) *Railway engineers blasted a tunnel through the mountainside.*

a tunnel leads/runs somewhere *The Greenwich Foot Tunnel leads under the River Thames.*

enter a tunnel (*also* **go into a tunnel**) *The train slowed down as it entered the tunnel.*

emerge from a tunnel (=come out of it) *The train emerged from the tunnel and stopped at the platform.*

tunnel + NOUNS

a tunnel entrance *The tunnel entrance was blocked by fallen trees.*

tunnel walls *At times, the tunnel walls were so tight we had to squeeze through.*

a tunnel system/network *Fortunately, he had a map of the tunnel system.*

PREPOSITIONS

a tunnel through sth *The tunnel through the mountain was completed in the late 1950s.*

a tunnel under/beneath sth *The subway train broke down in a tunnel under the river.*

in a tunnel *Most of the lights in the tunnel were broken.*

PHRASES

the roof of a tunnel *The roof of the tunnel was only inches above his head.*

the entrance to a tunnel *To the right was the entrance to a second tunnel.*

a network/system of tunnels (=a system of connected tunnels) *The network of tunnels beneath the castle dates from the 12th century.*

a maze of tunnels (=a complex and confusing system of tunnels) *He got lost in the maze of tunnels under the prison.*

turn[1] *v*

1 to move around, or make something move around

PHRASES

turn (sth) to the right/left *Put the key in the lock and turn it gently to the right.*

turn sth clockwise/anticlockwise *You have to turn the screw clockwise to tighten it.*

turn + NOUNS

turn a handle/knob *She turned the door handle very quietly.*

turn a key *You turn the key to open the window.*

turn a screw *Which way do you turn the screw to loosen it?*

turn your head/face/body *He turned his head and looked away.*

NOUNS + turn

the wheels turn *The train's wheels began to turn slowly.*

2 to change and become different

THESAURUS: turn

get, grow, turn, go, come → **become**

turn[2] *n*

the time when you may or should do something

PHRASES

it's sb's turn to do sth *Mum says it's your turn to wash the dishes.*

take turns (*also* **take it in turns** *BrE*) (=with each person giving the others a chance to do something) *My mum and dad take it in turns to do the cooking.*

out of turn (=at a time when someone else should do something) *If one player goes out of turn, it just confuses everything.*

VERBS

wait your turn *I'm before you – you'll have to wait your turn.*

miss a turn *If I play this card, the next player has to miss a turn.*

have your turn *Tom hasn't had his turn yet.*

give sb a turn *Don't be selfish – give your sister a turn!*

sb's turn comes *It seemed like hours before my turn came.*

type *n*

one member of a group of people or things that have similar features or qualities

ADJECTIVES/NOUNS + type

this/that type *He is not suited to this type of work.*

different types *I've worked with many different types of people over the years.*

a particular/certain type *Have you driven this particular type of car before?*

a new type *Their engineers designed a new type of engine.*

the same type *I use the same type of software at work.*

various types *We studied how well the plant grows in various types of climate.*

some types *Some types of crime are actually decreasing.*

the main type *There are two main types of gas in the Earth's atmosphere: nitrogen and oxygen.*

blood type (=one of the classes into which human blood can be separated) *Mother and child had the same blood type.*

skin/hair type *The best shampoo for you depends on your hair type.*

personality type (=the particular type of character a person has) *Find out your personality type by answering our simple questionnaire.*

T

PREPOSITIONS

a type of sth *There are various types of rose bush growing in her garden.*

PHRASES

of a/the type *He pulled out a tiny gun of the type you see in cowboy films.*

of this/that/each/every type *I've never seen a car of this type before.*

typhoon *n* THESAURUS wind

typical *adj*

having the usual features or qualities of a particular group or thing

ADVERBS

fairly typical *Her reaction is fairly typical of someone her age.*

absolutely/entirely typical *His own story is absolutely typical.*

sth is by no means typical (=it is not typical at all) *The house is by no means typical of the other houses in the area.*

NOUNS

a typical example/case *This painting is a typical example of the artist's work.*

a typical day/week/month etc *On a typical day, students go to classes from 7.30 a.m. to 1.15 p.m.*

a typical feature *This type of ceiling is a typical feature of Moroccan architecture.*

a typical scenario (=a typical situation that might happen) *I know this doesn't sound like a very typical scenario.*

VERBS

seem typical (of sth) *It seemed typical of the sort of poem we had to read at school.*

PREPOSITIONS

typical of sb/sth *"He was late." "How typical of him."*

tyre *BrE*, tire *AmE n*

a thick rubber ring that fits around the wheel of a car, bicycle etc

ADJECTIVES/NOUNS + tyre

a front tyre *I bought a set of new front tires.*

a rear/back tyre *We had to change one of the back tyres.*

a spare tyre *The spare tyre is in the boot.*

a flat tyre (=one that does not have any air inside it) *I had a flat tyre and had to push my bike all the way home.*

a worn tyre (=one on which the pattern of lines has almost gone) *The car skidded because the tires were badly worn.*

a bald tyre (=one which has worn completely smooth) *Police officers noticed that the car had two bald tyres.*

a punctured tyre (=with a hole in it made by something sharp) *I always carry a bicycle repair kit in case I get a punctured tire.*

a burst tyre *On lap two, Millar had a burst tire and crashed.*

snow tyres (=used when driving on snow or ice) *Most folk switch to snow tires for the winter.*

a car/lorry/bicycle etc tyre *They sell and fit car tyres.*

VERBS

change a tyre *Do you know how to change a tyre?*

check the tyres (=make sure there is enough air in them) *Always check the tires before a long journey.*

puncture a tyre (=make a hole in it - used of something sharp) *I rode over a sharp twig, which punctured the tyre.*

a tyre bursts/blows (=the air suddenly comes out because it gets a hole in it) *I was driving along when suddenly the front tire blew.*

tyre + NOUNS

tyre pressure (=the force of the air in a tyre) *Have you checked the tyre pressure lately?*

tyre marks (*also* **tyre tracks**) (=marks left by tyres) *There were tire marks on the road close to where the crash happened.*

Uu

ubiquitous *adj* THESAURUS **common (1)**

ugly *adj*

1 very unpleasant to look at

NOUNS

an ugly man/woman/girl/person *The general was a big ugly man with a beard.*

an ugly face *This will take the smile off his ugly face!*

an ugly building/town/place *They lived in an ugly industrial town.*

an ugly stain/mark *The wine made an ugly stain on the carpet.*

an ugly colour *BrE*, **an ugly color** *AmE*: *The walls were painted in an ugly brown colour.*

an ugly scar *The knife attack left him with an ugly scar running from his ear to his chin.*

an ugly monster/beast *The story is about an ugly monster who falls in love with a beautiful princess.*

an ugly duckling (=an ugly person or thing – used especially about one that later becomes beautiful) *Felicity revealed she was an ugly duckling and none of the boys at school wanted to kiss her.*

ADVERBS

really/incredibly ugly *I thought I was really ugly when I was a teenager.*

hideously ugly (=extremely ugly) *His face was hideously ugly.*

sth is plain ugly/downright ugly (=very ugly – used when saying strongly that you dislike something) *The yellow plastic chairs were just plain ugly.*

VERBS

look ugly *Do you think the glasses make me look ugly?*

PHRASES

as ugly as sin (=extremely ugly) *These dogs are as ugly as sin but some people find them appealing.*

THESAURUS: ugly

hideous
creature | monster | face | clothes | shirt | jacket | tie | shoes
extremely ugly:
The picture made her look like some kind of hideous monster. | His hideous face twisted into a smile. | Father was wearing a hideous orange tie with white dots.

grotesque
figure | face | mask | creature | character | appearance | image | scene | imitation | parody | caricature
extremely ugly, especially in a strange or unnatural way:
His paintings are full of grotesque figures. | The dancers wore grotesque masks. | She sucked in her cheeks, in a grotesque imitation of a girl in a fashion magazine.

revolting
colour | mess | sight | man | woman
extremely ugly, so that you almost feel sick – used especially when you strongly dislike someone or something:
The door was painted a revolting purple colour. | His neck was covered in blood – it was a revolting sight. | He's a nasty revolting little man.

repulsive
face | man | woman | appearance
extremely ugly – used especially when you feel you cannot look at someone or something:
His repulsive face was hidden under a mass of black hair. | Women ***found*** *him* ***repulsive****. | Snakes were* ***repulsive to*** *her.*

unattractive
man | woman | child | girl | place | location | town | building | colour | person | face | appearance
not pleasant to look at. **Unattractive** sounds more formal and less strong than **ugly**:
In the film she plays an unattractive woman who is trying to find a husband. | They lived in an unattractive modern town. | The water was an unattractive green colour. | She ***found*** *him* ***physically unattractive****.*

unsightly *formal*
building | mark | stain | spot | hair | pile | appearance
unpleasant to look at, and spoiling the appearance of something:
The old city is now full of unsightly office buildings. | The cream is useful for hiding unsightly marks on the skin. | There were unsightly piles of litter in the driveway.

plain
woman | girl | face
a plain woman or girl is not beautiful or attractive:
The photograph was of a plain round-faced woman. | Her rather plain face was white with tension.

homely *AmE*
woman | girl | man | face
a homely person is not beautiful or attractive:
The door was opened by a large homely woman. | He stared at the homely face of his grandmother.

If something looks **ugly** and spoils the view, you can say that it is an **eyesore** or a **blot on the landscape**: *The wind farm is a blot on the landscape.*

ANTONYMS **ugly → beautiful**

2 frightening because people are behaving in a violent way, or are likely to become violent

NOUNS

an ugly situation/incident *It was a very ugly situation and people could have been hurt.*

ugly scenes *There were ugly scenes outside the courtroom.*

an ugly argument/dispute/quarrel *They became involved in an ugly dispute with their neighbours about who owned the land.*

an ugly fight/confrontation *The meeting ended in an ugly confrontation between demonstrators and the police.*

an ugly atmosphere *There was an ugly atmosphere at the game.*

VERBS

become ugly (*also* **get/turn ugly** *more informal*): *We decided to leave before things got ugly.*

ultimatum *n*

a threat to punish someone if they do not do something

VERBS

give sb an ultimatum *My boss gave me an ultimatum: get better results or find another job.*

issue/deliver an ultimatum (=officially give someone an ultimatum) *The authorities issued an ultimatum to the students to end their protest or face arrest.*

present sb with an ultimatum *formal* (=give them one) *The two sides had been presented with an ultimatum to reach an agreement by the weekend.*

receive an ultimatum *They had received an ultimatum to withdraw troops before noon.*

comply with an ultimatum (=do what someone wants) *They complied with an ultimatum to surrender weapons.*

ignore an ultimatum (=not do what someone wants) *He ignored their ultimatum to reveal who had given him the information.*

PREPOSITIONS

an ultimatum from sb *He started to help more around the house, following an ultimatum from his wife.*

PHRASES

the terms of an ultimatum *The terms of the ultimatum required them to leave before Friday.*

umbrella *n*

a thing that you hold up to protect yourself from the rain

VERBS

open/put up your umbrella *It started to rain so I put up my umbrella.*

take down/fold up your umbrella *He took down his umbrella and went into the station.*

take an umbrella (with you) *If you go for a walk, take your umbrella.*

carry an umbrella *A woman carrying an umbrella walked up to the ticket office.*

ADJECTIVES

a rolled umbrella (*also* **a furled umbrella** *formal*) (=an umbrella that is folded because you are not using it) *The woman attacked him with a furled umbrella.*

an open umbrella *There was an open umbrella drying in the hall.*

NOUNS + umbrella

a golf umbrella *They sheltered under his huge golf umbrella.*

umbrella + NOUNS

an umbrella stand *I left my umbrella on the umbrella stand in the hallway.*

PREPOSITIONS

under sb's umbrella *Do you mind if I come under your umbrella?*

THESAURUS: umbrella

parasol
a thing like an umbrella that provides shade from the sun:
She wore a yellow silk dress and carried a parasol.

unable *adj* not able to do something

ADVERBS

completely/totally unable to do sth (*also* **utterly unable to do sth** *formal*): *I was completely unable to work out the answer.*

almost/nearly/virtually unable to do sth *It was so hot I was virtually unable to breathe.*

quite unable to do sth *formal* (=completely unable) *She was quite unable to resist his charm.*

VERBS

feel unable to do sth *After hours of walking, he felt unable to continue.*

leave sb unable to do sth *The accident left him unable to walk.*

find yourself unable to do sth *formal*: *We found ourselves unable to refuse his offer.*

PHRASES

unwilling or unable to do sth *They were unwilling or unable to give us more information.*

unacceptable *adj*

so wrong or bad that it should not be allowed

ADVERBS

completely/totally/wholly unacceptable *We find their attitude completely unacceptable.*

simply unacceptable (=used when you want to emphasize that you strongly disapprove of something) *The child's bad manners were simply unacceptable.*

politically unacceptable *Such a decision was politically unacceptable for the government.*

socially unacceptable *Driving while you're drunk has become socially unacceptable.*

morally unacceptable *It would be morally unacceptable to treat children in that way.*

VERBS

be considered (to be) unacceptable *That sort of behaviour would be considered unacceptable.*

be regarded as unacceptable (=be considered unacceptable) *Taking drugs in sport is generally regarded as unacceptable.*

NOUNS

unacceptable behaviour *BrE*, **unacceptable behavior** *AmE*: *Her unacceptable behaviour caused arguments.*

an unacceptable level/degree *Burning coal produces unacceptable levels of pollution.*

an unacceptable risk *We don't want the company taking unacceptable risks with our money.*

PREPOSITIONS

sth is unacceptable to sb *His views are unacceptable to many people.*

PHRASES

it is unacceptable for sb to do sth *In those days it was unacceptable for women to smoke in public.*

unanimous *adj*

agreed or decided by everyone in a group

ADVERBS

almost/nearly/virtually unanimous *The question produced an almost unanimous response.*

NOUNS

a unanimous decision/choice *The managers made a unanimous decision to spend the money.*

a unanimous vote/verdict *The jury's verdict was unanimous – not guilty.*

unanimous agreement/approval/consent *There has to be unanimous agreement of the members.*

unanimous support/backing *People in the village have given the idea their unanimous support.*

the unanimous view/opinion *This was the unanimous view of club members.*

PREPOSITIONS

unanimous on/about sth *British voters are unanimous on this issue.*

unanimous in doing sth *Parents were unanimous in wanting more information.*

PHRASES

be far from unanimous (=there is a lot of disagreement) *We expected complete agreement but opinion is far from unanimous.*

unattractive *adj* THESAURUS **ugly (1)**

unaware Ac *adj*

not noticing or realizing what is happening

ADVERBS

totally/completely/entirely/wholly unaware *Children were playing next to the railway line, totally unaware of the danger.*

quite unaware *BrE* (=completely unaware) *Kate seemed quite unaware that she had offended me.*

largely unaware *Employers were largely unaware of the changes the government was introducing.*

blissfully unaware (=happy and not realizing something bad) *He laughed, blissfully unaware that he was the target of the joke.*

apparently/seemingly unaware *The man broke into the house, apparently unaware that he was being filmed.*

VERBS

seem/appear unaware *The handsome young man seemed totally unaware of the effect he was having on the girls.*

remain unaware *Most people remained largely unaware of the change to the law.*

PREPOSITIONS

unaware of sth *Tom seemed to go through life totally unaware of the trouble he was causing.*

uncertain *adj*

not sure, clear, definite, or decided

VERBS

remain uncertain *The date of her departure remains uncertain.*

look/seem uncertain *His future career seemed uncertain.*

feel uncertain *Paul felt uncertain about what to do next.*

become uncertain *Many employees have become uncertain about their future.*

ADVERBS

highly/extremely uncertain *The future of the company is highly uncertain.*

NOUNS

an uncertain future/fate *The economy is in trouble and the country faces an uncertain future.*

an uncertain world *We live in an uncertain world.*

uncertain times *In these uncertain times you never know what will happen next.*

PREPOSITIONS

uncertain about sth *He was uncertain about the purpose of the meeting.*

uncertain of sb/sth *Madeleine was very young and uncertain of herself.*

PHRASES

in no uncertain terms (*also* **in no uncertain manner/fashion**) (=in a very clear way that leaves no doubt) *Her father had told her in no uncertain terms that she must not see this man again.*

uncertainty *n*

a feeling of doubt about what will happen

ADJECTIVES

considerable uncertainty/a lot of uncertainty *There is considerable uncertainty about the team's future.*

growing/increasing/increased uncertainty *Party members have expressed growing uncertainty about his leadership.*

continuing uncertainty *There is continuing uncertainty about the best way to tackle the problem.*

economic/financial uncertainty *We are living in a period of financial uncertainty.*

political uncertainty *Political uncertainty often has a negative effect on a country's economy.*

VERBS

cause/create uncertainty *The changes in oil prices have created a lot of uncertainty.*

face uncertainty *Farmers are facing increasing uncertainty about their future.*

feel uncertainty *Ellie felt a strange uncertainty about whether she was doing the right thing.*

uncertainty surrounds sth *Uncertainty surrounds the president's visit.*

PREPOSITIONS

uncertainty about/over sth *There is a lot of uncertainty about the company's future.*

PHRASES

a feeling of uncertainty *The changes resulted in a general feeling of uncertainty.*

a degree/element/note of uncertainty *There is always a degree of uncertainty about the outcome of any military operation.*

an area of uncertainty (=something which people are not certain about) *Many of the issues have been resolved, but there are still some areas of uncertainty.*

a time/period of uncertainty *The country is going through a period of uncertainty.*

a climate of uncertainty *The security scares have created a climate of uncertainty and distrust.*

uncomfortable *adj*

not feeling comfortable or relaxed

ADVERBS

extremely uncomfortable *Her questions made him extremely uncomfortable.*

distinctly uncomfortable (=very clearly uncomfortable) *I began to feel distinctly uncomfortable about the situation.*

slightly uncomfortable *Slater always felt slightly uncomfortable before a performance.*

VERBS

feel uncomfortable *Men often feel uncomfortable when talking about their feelings.*

look/appear/seem uncomfortable *He looked uncomfortable in his formal suit.*

become/grow uncomfortable *She became increasingly uncomfortable in the crowded train carriage.*

make sb uncomfortable *Her praise seemed to make him uncomfortable.*

NOUNS

an uncomfortable feeling *She had the uncomfortable feeling that she had made a mistake.*

an uncomfortable experience *A job interview can be a very uncomfortable experience.*

an uncomfortable atmosphere *The argument had left an uncomfortable atmosphere in the room.*

an uncomfortable silence *There was a long uncomfortable silence.*

an uncomfortable question *The minister had to face some uncomfortable questions from reporters.*

an uncomfortable position/situation *She was put in the uncomfortable position of having to lie to protect her boss.*

an uncomfortable reminder (=something that makes you remember something bad) *The photograph was an uncomfortable reminder of how much weight he had gained.*

an uncomfortable truth/fact *The uncomfortable truth is that not all parents care properly for their children.*

PREPOSITIONS

uncomfortable about sth *She felt uncomfortable about the questions he was asking.*

uncomfortable with sb/sth *He was uncomfortable with the idea of having to borrow money.*

THESAURUS: uncomfortable

awkward, uncomfortable, humiliating → **embarrassing**

uncommon *adj* THESAURUS **rare**

U

unconscious *adj*

1 unable to see, move, feel etc in the normal way because you are not conscious

ADVERBS

completely/totally unconscious *When we found him, he was completely unconscious.*

VERBS

remain unconscious *The patient remained unconscious for several minutes.*

be found unconscious *He was found unconscious lying in a pool of blood.*

be left unconscious *The man had been attacked and left unconscious.*

render sb unconscious *formal* (=make someone unconscious) *The blow rendered him unconscious.*

become unconscious *After the injection, she quickly became unconscious.*

knock/beat sb unconscious *They kicked him and beat him unconscious.*

lie unconscious *The boy lay unconscious on the ground.*

2 not realizing something

ADVERBS

totally/completely/quite unconscious of sth *If I was jealous, I was totally unconscious of it.*

NOUNS

an unconscious desire/wish *She probably did it out of an unconscious desire to shock.*

an unconscious feeling *He may have been suffering from an unconscious feeling of fear.*

the unconscious mind (=things people feel without being aware of it) *Psychologists are interested in how the unconscious mind affects our decisions.*

PHRASES

on an unconscious level *It's possible that on an unconscious level he was trying to get her attention.*

unconventional *adj* THESAURUS ▶ **unusual**

underestimate *v*

to think that something is less big, less important etc than it really is

ADVERBS

seriously underestimate sth *We seriously underestimated how much it would cost.*

massively/grossly/vastly etc underestimate sth *The government massively underestimated the extent of the problem.*

NOUNS

underestimate the size/number/extent etc of sth *They admitted that they underestimated the size of the debt.*

underestimate the importance of sth/sb *It would be hard to underestimate her importance as an American writer.*

underestimate sb's ability *He said he initially underestimated the ability of his opponent.*

ANTONYMS **underestimate → overestimate**

undergo Ac *v*

to experience something, or have something done to you

NOUNS

undergo a change *The country has undergone massive changes in recent years.*

undergo a transformation (=change completely) *After the accident, his personality underwent a complete transformation.*

undergo treatment/surgery/an operation *The cyclist underwent emergency surgery yesterday after a collision with a car.*

undergo tests/trials *He is undergoing tests for pneumonia.*

undergo training *Doctors have to undergo six years of training.*

undergo repairs/restoration *The ship is currently undergoing extensive repairs.*

underlying Ac *adj*

used about causes, reasons, principles etc that are important but are not obvious or not mentioned

NOUNS

the underlying cause/reason *Stress is the underlying cause of many illnesses.*

the underlying motive *She is interested in the underlying motives that guide human actions.*

an underlying assumption (=an idea that is not proved but that someone bases their opinions on) *There is an underlying assumption that new technology is always a good thing.*

the underlying problem *Little is being done to correct the system's underlying problems.*

the underlying theme (=the main subject or idea in a book, speech, film etc) *Death and rebirth are underlying themes in all of his novels.*

the underlying message (=the idea that someone is trying to express) *The underlying message of his speech was that the economic good times are over.*

the underlying meaning *You have to read the poem closely to discover its underlying meaning.*

an underlying principle (=a belief about what is right and wrong) *Their actions go against the underlying principles of the Christian faith.*

the underlying philosophy (=set of ideas that guides behaviour or an activity) *I don't think the company's underlying philosophy has ever changed.*

an underlying idea/aim/intention *The government's underlying aim is to encourage growth in the economy.*

THESAURUS: underlying

fundamental, core, essential, central, underlying → **basic (1)**

understand *v*

to know the meaning of something, or the reasons for something

Grammar

Understand is not used in progressive forms. Don't say 'I am understanding' or 'I was understanding'.

ADVERBS

fully/completely/totally understand sth *Jack was too young to fully understand why his mother had left.*

understand sb/sth perfectly *I understand perfectly what you're saying but I don't agree.*

not really understand *Scientists still don't really understand how the brain processes this information.*

understand sb/sth correctly *If I understand him correctly, Smith is arguing that happiness comes from having a belief in your own ability.*

be little understood/poorly understood (=be something that no one knows much about) *HIV and AIDS were little understood in the mid-1980s.*

be commonly/generally understood (=by most people) *The Bernese Alps is generally understood to refer to the entire mountain range between the Interlaken Valley to the north and the Rhône Valley to the south.*

VERBS

can/can't understand *The woman had a strong accent, and I couldn't understand what she was saying.*

be starting/beginning to understand *Doctors are beginning to understand what causes the disease.*

help sb understand *This chapter will help students understand when to use the present tense.*

PHRASES

be easy/difficult to understand *It is difficult to understand why he refused such a good offer.*

can easily understand *I can easily understand her unwillingness to get involved.*

make yourself understood (=speak in a way that someone else understands) *I'm not very good at German, but I can make myself understood.*

understanding *n*

knowledge about something, based on learning or experience

ADJECTIVES

a good understanding *He seems to have a good understanding of the situation.*

a better/greater/deeper understanding *We now have a better understanding of the causes of the disease.*

a clear understanding *Before you begin, you need a clear understanding of what you want to achieve.*

a complete/thorough/full understanding *The degree gives students a thorough understanding of the subject.*

a deep/profound understanding *As a writer she shows a deep understanding of the human mind.*

a proper/real understanding *They seem to lack any real understanding of the issues involved.*

a basic/fundamental understanding *The aim of the examination is to test basic understanding of the written language.*

sufficient/adequate understanding *Young children do not have sufficient understanding to make a decision like that.*

a limited understanding *We have only a limited understanding of how the brain works.*

a poor understanding *Most people have a poor understanding of the law.*

VERBS

have an understanding *The government doesn't seem to have a clear understanding of the problem.*

gain/develop/acquire an understanding (=get an understanding) *Scientists began to develop a better understanding of our solar system.*

demonstrate/show an understanding *People applying for citizenship will have to demonstrate an understanding of the English language.*

increase/improve sb's understanding (*also* **enhance sb's understanding** *formal*): *The classes really helped to increase our understanding of the subject.*

deepen/broaden sb's understanding *It is hoped that the research will broaden our understanding of the disease.*

need/require an understanding *To do business in a country, you need an understanding of its customs.*

provide an understanding *Cave drawings provide some understanding of how ancient people viewed their world.*

PREPOSITIONS

an understanding of sth *If you lived here, you'd have a better understanding of the problems we face.*

an understanding about sth *My understanding about that period of history was improved by reading the book.*

PHRASES

a lack of understanding *His remarks show an*

incredible lack of understanding about what is actually happening in the region.

a level/degree of understanding (=amount of understanding) *I was impressed by their high level of understanding of the law.*

undertake Ac *v formal*

to start to do something, especially something that needs a lot of time and effort

NOUNS

undertake a task/project *Dr Johnson undertook the task of writing a comprehensive English dictionary.*

undertake work *The work is being undertaken by a team of experts.*

undertake research *Students may undertake full-time research leading to a doctorate.*

undertake a review/analysis *The Court of Appeal decided to undertake a review of the case.*

undertake a journey/voyage *You should not undertake a long journey if you are unwell.*

PHRASES

sth is not to be undertaken lightly (=not to be started without serious thought, for example because it is difficult) *It was not a voyage to be undertaken lightly.*

THESAURUS: undertake

make, give, take, commit, carry out, conduct, perform, undertake, implement → **do**

uneasy *adj*

1 slightly nervous or worried because you think that something bad might happen or might have happened

ADVERBS

a little/slightly/vaguely uneasy *She felt slightly uneasy when she noticed a spot of dried blood on his shoe.*

deeply/extremely/profoundly uneasy (=very uneasy) *The way he looked at me made me deeply uneasy.*

increasingly uneasy *Parents are becoming increasingly uneasy about the influence of the internet.*

VERBS

feel uneasy *Tom began to feel uneasy when she still had not come home the next day.*

make sb uneasy *The behavior of some of the guards towards the prisoners made me uneasy.*

become/get/grow uneasy *She was alone, and as darkness fell, she began to grow a little uneasy.*

NOUNS

an uneasy feeling/sense *I had this uneasy feeling that I was being followed.*

PREPOSITIONS

uneasy about sth *With unemployment rising, people feel uneasy about the future.*

uneasy with sth *Society is understandably uneasy with the idea that doctors should help someone to die.*

2 used to describe a period of time when people have agreed to stop fighting or arguing, but which is not really calm

NOUNS

an uneasy peace *There was an uneasy peace in the region for nearly three years before the conflict started up again.*

an uneasy truce *It was an uneasy truce, and tension was never far from the surface.*

an uneasy calm *Things seemed quiet enough, but it was an uneasy calm.*

an uneasy alliance/relationship *The Christian Democrats formed an uneasy alliance with the Socialists in order to stay in power.*

an uneasy compromise *The result was an uneasy compromise which no-one much liked.*

unemployed *adj* without a job

VERBS

be unemployed *Fifty per cent of the men in this town are unemployed.*

become unemployed *He became unemployed after the factory where he worked closed down.*

NOUNS

unemployed people *Training is an important and effective way of helping unemployed people back to work.*

unemployed workers *There are an estimated 3,000,000 unemployed workers.*

an unemployed man/woman *An unemployed man was jailed for two years yesterday for burglary.*

an unemployed actor/teacher/engineer etc *The firm was started by two unemployed engineers.*

Grammar

Unemployed can also be used as a noun: *The government plans to introduce a new scheme to help* ***the long-term unemployed****.* (=people who have been unemployed for a long time)

THESAURUS: unemployed

out of work
unemployed, especially for a long period of time, when you had a job before:
I've ***been out of work*** *for two years. | Many of the waiters are* ***out-of-work actors****.*

redundant *BrE*
if someone is made redundant, they are told that they no longer have a job:
He was ***made redundant*** *earlier this year. | It can be difficult for* ***redundant workers*** *to find employment.*

U

jobless
total | figures | rate
used especially in news reports, when talking about the number of people who do not have a job:
The jobless total has risen by 6% in the last year. | The latest jobless figures show that the economy is continuing to grow. | The German jobless rate fell below 10 percent.

You can also say that someone is **looking for work**: *How long have you been **looking for work**?* This sounds less direct than saying that someone is **unemployed**.
You say that someone is **on the dole** (BrE) or **on welfare** (AmE) when they are receiving money from the government because they do not have a job: *I didn't want to go back **on the dole**. | Many people **on welfare** don't have anyone to take care of their kids while they train for a job.*

unemployment *n*

a situation in which people cannot get a job

ADJECTIVES/NOUNS + unemployment

high unemployment (=many people do not have a job) *They live in a town where unemployment is high.*
low unemployment (=few people do not have a job) *The area has the lowest unemployment in Europe.*
rising/increasing unemployment *Rising unemployment led to more crime.*
falling unemployment *Politicians want a growing economy with falling unemployment.*
mass/large-scale unemployment (=very large numbers of people are unemployed) *No-one wants a return to the mass unemployment of the 1930s.*
long-term unemployment (=people are unemployed for a long time) *It can be difficult to help people out of long-term unemployment.*
widespread unemployment (=in many places) *The collapse of the currency led to widespread unemployment.*
youth/male/female etc unemployment (=the number of young people/men/women etc unemployed) *Youth unemployment has reached 50%.*

VERBS + unemployment

reduce/cut unemployment *The government's main aim is to reduce unemployment.*
combat/fight unemployment (=reduce or prevent it) *The best way for the unions to combat unemployment was to defend existing jobs.*
face unemployment (=be going to be unemployed) *Hundreds of workers now face unemployment.*
experience unemployment *Anyone who has experienced unemployment knows that it is not pleasant.*

unemployment + VERBS

unemployment goes up/increases/rises *During their term in office unemployment increased by 50%.*
unemployment soars (=increases quickly to a high level) *The economic crisis has seen unemployment soar.*
unemployment goes down/drops/falls *Unemployment continued to fall.*
unemployment stands at sth (=it is at a particular level) *Unemployment stood at over 10%.*
unemployment hits/reaches sth (=it becomes a particular high level) *This year, unemployment hit the one million mark.*

unemployment + NOUNS

the unemployment rate *The unemployment rate was 17%.*
unemployment figures/statistics *They publish monthly unemployment figures for the UK.*
an unemployment blackspot *BrE* (=an area where there is higher unemployment than in other places) *The town became an unemployment blackspot after the factory closed.*

PREPOSITIONS

unemployment among sb *Unemployment among young men is 45% in some areas.*

PHRASES

a rise/increase in unemployment *The crisis meant a sharp rise in unemployment.*
a fall/reduction in unemployment *We are hoping to see a fall in unemployment.*
the level/rate of unemployment *The country is suffering from a high rate of unemployment.*

unfair *adj* not right or fair

ADVERBS

grossly/extremely unfair *The system was grossly unfair.*
most unfair *spoken* (=very unfair) *I think it is most unfair of the court to punish a man for protecting his house from burglars.*
totally unfair *It's totally unfair to blame one player when the team doesn't play well.*
rather unfair *I feel that this criticism is rather unfair.*
a little/slightly unfair (*also* **a bit unfair** *BrE spoken*): *You're being a little unfair on him.*
blatantly/manifestly/patently unfair (=very obviously unfair) *The newspaper called the decision blatantly unfair.*

NOUNS

an unfair advantage *The rich clubs can afford to buy the best players, which gives them an unfair advantage.*
unfair competition/trade (=when not everyone has the same opportunity in

business) *Our industry will suffer from unfair competition if other governments increase their farming subsidy.*

unfair dismissal (=when someone is illegally made to leave their job) *She took the company to a tribunal for unfair dismissal.*

VERBS

think sth is unfair *I think it's unfair that I have to do all the work.*

consider sth unfair/regard sth as unfair (=think that something is unfair - more formal) *She regarded the judgement as unfair and tried to get it overturned.*

PREPOSITIONS

unfair to/towards sb *He shouldn't get special treatment - it would be unfair to the other students.*

unfashionable *adj*

not popular or fashionable at the present time

VERBS

become unfashionable *His work became unfashionable after his death.*

ADVERBS

deeply unfashionable (=very unfashionable) *Marriage was regarded as deeply unfashionable.*

NOUNS

an unfashionable area/part of a place *They lived in an unfashionable part of London.*

an unfashionable view/idea *I know this is an unfashionable view, but I think that children need to have clear rules.*

unfortunate *adj*

used when you think someone or something is unlucky or you wish that something had not happened

ADVERBS

most/highly unfortunate (=very unfortunate) *It was most unfortunate that it rained on the day of the wedding.*

particularly/singularly unfortunate *The timing of the announcement was particularly unfortunate.*

NOUNS

an unfortunate accident/incident/event *There was an unfortunate incident involving a pan of hot oil.*

an unfortunate man/woman *The unfortunate man just happened to be in the wrong place at the wrong time.*

an unfortunate victim *He was the unfortunate victim of a tragic accident.*

an unfortunate consequence/result *What seems like a harmless joke can have unfortunate consequences.*

an unfortunate coincidence *By an unfortunate coincidence, his boss overheard their conversation.*

an unfortunate habit *She had the unfortunate habit of laughing too loud.*

PHRASES

it is unfortunate that *It is unfortunate that so many people were hurt.*

unfriendly *adj*

not kind or friendly - used about people and places

ADVERBS

distinctly unfriendly (=in a way that is very noticeable) *The man's attitude was distinctly unfriendly.*

rather unfriendly *Big cities can be rather unfriendly places.*

extremely unfriendly *The atmosphere was extremely unfriendly.*

NOUNS

an unfriendly voice/tone *"I'm not interested," she said in an unfriendly voice.*

an unfriendly way/manner *Her father often growled at her in an unfriendly way.*

PREPOSITIONS

unfriendly to/towards sb *The local people were rather unfriendly to us at first.*

unhappy *adj* not happy or not satisfied

ADVERBS

deeply/extremely unhappy *Bruno Morenz was a deeply unhappy man.*

desperately/terribly/dreadfully unhappy *It was the first time she had been away from home and she was desperately unhappy.*

clearly/obviously unhappy *The manager was clearly unhappy with the team's performance.*

increasingly unhappy *The poll shows that Americans are becoming increasingly unhappy with the president.*

VERBS

be/feel unhappy *I don't know why I feel so unhappy.*

look unhappy *His parents looked very unhappy when they heard the news.*

make sb unhappy *I knew that leaving would make her unhappy, but I had no choice.*

NOUNS

an unhappy childhood *He moved far away to escape his unhappy childhood.*

an unhappy marriage *Is it better to divorce than to stay in an unhappy marriage?*

unhappy memories *Ruth tried to put these unhappy memories from her mind.*

an unhappy time *He had a fairly unhappy time at boarding school.*

PREPOSITIONS

unhappy about sth *She seemed unhappy about something.*

unhappy with/at sth *Alan was very unhappy with the court's decision. | They are unhappy at the way they have been treated.*

THESAURUS: unhappy

unhappy, homesick, gloomy, glum, dejected/downcast, mournful, wistful, down, miserable, depressed, heartbroken, distressed, devastated
→ **sad (1)**

unhealthy *adj*

1 likely to make you ill

NOUNS

unhealthy food *If you eat unhealthy food you will get fat.*

an unhealthy diet *An unhealthy diet can increase the risk of cancer.*

an unhealthy environment/unhealthy conditions *Working in an unhealthy environment is linked with various diseases.*

an unhealthy lifestyle *She encouraged him to change his unhealthy lifestyle.*

2 not normal or natural and likely to be harmful

NOUNS

an unhealthy fear of sth *He has an unhealthy fear of change.*

an unhealthy interest in sth *Newspapers take an unhealthy interest in the private lives of politicians.*

an unhealthy obsession with sth (=a harmful interest or fear which stops you thinking about anything else) *Does our society have an unhealthy obsession with beauty?*

uniform *n*

a particular type of clothing worn by people who belong to a school or organization

ADJECTIVES/NOUNS + uniform

school uniform *Our school uniform is dark blue and grey.*

army uniform *He wore his army uniform to the wedding.*

police uniform *The two men were in police uniform.*

naval uniform *His naval uniform consisted of white trousers, a blue jacket, and a white cap.*

soldier's/nurse's/police officer's etc uniform *She changed into her nurse's uniform.*

VERBS

wear a uniform *Helen was wearing her new school uniform.*

be dressed in a uniform *In the photograph he was dressed in his army uniform.*

put on/change into a uniform *He feels proud when he puts on his army uniform.*

PREPOSITIONS

in uniform *Two guards in uniform were standing outside the prison gate.*

U

unimportant *adj* not important

VERBS

seem unimportant *His own safety seemed unimportant compared with that of his children.*

see/regard sth as unimportant (*also* **consider sth to be unimportant**) *In those days, women's education was seen as unimportant.*

ADVERBS

relatively unimportant *The differences between the designs are relatively unimportant.*

NOUNS

an unimportant detail *I didn't want to waste time talking about unimportant details.*

PREPOSITIONS

unimportant to sb *Physical beauty was unimportant to her.*

THESAURUS: unimportant

minor
change | problem | injury | accident | damage | offence | difference | detail | role
not important or serious:
She made a few minor changes to her speech. | The driver suffered minor injuries. | The fires caused only minor damage. | He has played only a minor role in decision-making.

small
thing | problem | mistake
not important:
His mind wandered from one small thing to another. | We had a small problem with the car door. | There were a few small mistakes, but the rest of the essay was very good.

trivial
matter | things | incident | detail
very unimportant and not worth worrying about or spending time on:
Boiling a kettle may seem like a trivial matter, but it can cause problems for some people. | She gets annoyed about the most trivial things.

insignificant
amount | number | effect | impact | risk
very small and unimportant, especially when compared to other things:
$2 million is an insignificant amount compared to the total amount that people pay in taxes. | The changes will have an insignificant effect on global warming. | Her own problems ***seemed insignificant****. | The amount of carbon produced is* ***relatively insignificant****.*

negligible
effect | impact | amount | difference | risk | increase
extremely small and not important, and not worth paying attention to:
The wind only had a negligible effect on the runners' times. | The difference in price is negligible.

petty
crime | criminal | argument | dispute | squabble
petty crimes or arguments are not serious:
Teenagers who are involved in petty crime usually get a warning from the police if they are caught. | Petty disputes between neighbours can sometimes turn into something much more serious.

secondary
role | aim | purpose | issue | consideration
not as important as something or someone else:
Grant occupied a secondary role in the leadership. | Helping prisoners find work was a valuable but secondary aim. | They have lots of money, so price is a secondary consideration (=a less important thing to consider). *| The romance is* ***secondary to*** *the main story.*

In more formal English, you can also say that something is **of no importance** or **of little importance**: *The money is* ***of no importance.***
If something is less important than another thing, you can say that it is **of secondary importance**: *The attractiveness of the design is* ***of secondary importance.***

union *n*

1 an organization formed by workers to protect their rights

VERBS

belong to a union *Most teachers belong to a union.*
join a union *Are you planning to join the union?*
form a union *Workers demanded the right to form a union.*

union + NOUNS

a union leader/official *Union leaders criticized the government for failing to tackle the jobs crisis.*
a union member *Union members voted to strike over proposed pay cuts.*
a union representative *Union representatives will meet the industry minister.*
union membership *Union membership rose to 50% by 1948.*

NOUNS + union

a teachers'/miners'/nurses' etc union *The teachers' union has called a series of strikes.*

2 the act of joining two or more things together, or the state of being joined

ADJECTIVES

political/economic union *The two nations have made the first step towards political union.*
full union *Their eventual aim is full political union.*
a close union *The treaty was intended to create a close union between the two states.*

VERBS

form a union *At that time, Russia and Belarus agreed to form a union.*
break up/dissolve a union (=end it) *Some people believed that the best way to settle the dispute was to dissolve the union.*

PREPOSITIONS

a union between sb/sth *He emphasized his support for the continued union between Scotland and the rest of the UK.*
union with sb/sth *They want to be part of a political union with Europe.*

unique *adj*

unlike anyone or anything else. You often use **unique** when saying that someone or something is very unusual or special

NOUNS

a unique opportunity *This is a unique opportunity to stay in a wonderful Austrian castle.*
a unique combination of sth *The rise in temperatures is due to a unique combination of factors.*
a unique way/style *The boss had his own unique way of doing things.*
a unique position *She was in the unique position of being the only daughter among nine sons.*
a unique feature *The building has several unique features, including a medieval clock.*
a unique ability/talent/skill *Lee had a unique ability to bring people together.*

ADVERBS

absolutely/totally/completely unique *Hendrix's style of guitar-playing was absolutely unique.*
hardly/by no means unique (=not unique at all) *Her experience is by no means unique.*

⚠ Don't say 'very unique'. Say **absolutely/totally/completely unique**.

PREPOSITIONS

be unique to sth (=only existing or happening somewhere) *Kangaroos are unique to Australia.*

university *n*

an educational institution at the highest level, where you study for a degree

ADJECTIVES

a top/leading/prestigious university (=one that is important and well respected) *Bregier graduated from one of France's most prestigious universities.*
oldest university *Founded in 1636, Harvard is the country's oldest university and probably its most distinguished.*

U

a private/public university *The average cost of a year at a private university is $24,000 and for a public university $9,200.*

VERBS

go to university *Her daughter was about to go to university.*
be at university BrE: *We were at university together.*
study (sth) at university *She studied law at Edinburgh University.*
apply for university *I applied for university without any real idea of what I wanted to do.*
start university (*also* **enter university** *formal*): *Some people take a year off before they start university.*
leave university *Students often find work soon after leaving university.*
graduate from university (=leave after getting a degree) *She graduated from Liverpool University in 2006.*
drop out of university (=leave before finishing your course) *He dropped out of university in order to join a rock band.*

university + NOUNS

a university course *He studied history at school and was now planning to take a university course.*
a university student *Thirty years ago 33% of university students were female.*
a university graduate (=someone who has completed a university course) *She is a university graduate who speaks three languages.*
a university lecturer/professor *Her father was a university lecturer and her mother a teacher.*
a university degree *He was a qualified engineer with a university degree.*
a university education *I did not have the advantage of a university education.*
a university department *She was working as a research assistant in a university department.*
the university campus (=the area of land containing the main buildings of a university) *There were violent protests on university campuses.*
a university friend (*also* **a friend from university**) *I met an old university friend the other day.*

PHRASES

get/be offered a place at university *She's hoping to get a place at Oxford University to study law.*
admission to university (=the right to go to a university) *A record number of students are seeking admission to the University of California.*
a university entrance exam/examination (=one that you must pass in order to go to university) *Her son is studying for his university entrance exams.*

U

unkind *adj*

treating someone in a way that makes them unhappy or upset

VERBS

seem unkind *It seemed unkind to leave Daisy out, so she was invited too.*
not mean to be unkind (=not intend to be unkind) *I'm sure they did not mean to be unkind.*

NOUNS

unkind words/comments/remarks *She decided to ignore their unkind comments.*
an unkind thing *A lot of unkind things were said.*

PREPOSITIONS

unkind to sb *Lucy was sorry she had been so unkind to him.*
unkind about sb/sth *The newspapers were very unkind about his wife.*

THESAURUS: unkind

mean *especially spoken*
thing | **streak**
unkind:
It was a mean thing to do. | *The boss had a mean streak* (=an unkind part of his or her character). | *Don't be* ***mean to*** *your sister!*

Mean or unkind?
Mean is more informal and is mainly used in spoken English. **Unkind** is more formal and is mainly used in written English.

nasty *especially spoken*
thing | **temper** | **way**
very unkind - used especially when someone is deliberately unkind, and seems to enjoy making people unhappy:
Be careful - she has a nasty temper. | *When they fired her, they did it in a really nasty way.* | *Why are you being so* ***nasty to*** *him?*

hurtful
thing | **comment** | **remark**
hurtful comments and actions make someone upset:
Couples sometimes do hurtful things to each other. | *His comments were* ***deeply hurtful to*** *me and my family.*

spiteful
remark | **attack** | **look** | **glee**
deliberately unkind to someone because you are jealous of them or angry with them:
Other girls, jealous of her looks, made spiteful remarks. | *She watched them fail with spiteful glee* (=spiteful pleasure).

malicious
rumour | **gossip** | **allegation** | **accusation** | **look** | **smile** | **satisfaction** | **act**
done because you want to upset, hurt, or cause trouble for someone:

Someone had been spreading malicious rumours about him on the internet. | *The rules are designed to protect officers from malicious allegations.* | *There was a malicious smile on her face* (=she was smiling because she was enjoying causing trouble).

unsympathetic
not seeming to care about someone's problems, and not trying to help them or make them feel better:
His parents were very unsympathetic, and told him that he deserved to fail his exam. | *Her doctor was* ***unsympathetic to*** *her and told her to pull herself together.*

> **Unsympathetic** is less common before a noun.

hard-hearted
man | woman
not caring at all about other people's feelings – used especially when this is part of someone's character:
Real people are being hurt, and only the most hard-hearted man would find this funny. | *Was he hard-hearted enough to leave his son in jail overnight?*

unintentionally unkind

inconsiderate
not thinking about the effects of your actions on other people, in a way that seems rude:
It was ***inconsiderate of*** *Dan not to say that he would be late.* | *Drivers were criticized for being* ***inconsiderate to*** *other road users.*

insensitive
not seeming to care about other people's feelings, so that you may upset them:
She seems completely ***insensitive to*** *the feelings of others.* | *He later admitted that some of his* ***remarks*** *were* ***insensitive***.

unknown *adj* THESAURUS ▸ famous

unlawful *adj* THESAURUS ▸ illegal

unlikely *adj*

not likely to happen or be true

ADVERBS

highly/extremely unlikely *He is highly unlikely to succeed.*

most unlikely (=very unlikely) *It is most unlikely that the situation will improve.*

rather/pretty/fairly/quite unlikely *It's pretty unlikely that she threw it away by mistake.*

increasingly unlikely *It looks increasingly unlikely that the Bank of England will cut interest rates.*

equally unlikely *He probably won't ask you to go, but he's equally unlikely to ask me.*

VERBS

seem/look/appear unlikely *It seems unlikely that he will change his mind.*

sound unlikely *His story sounds very unlikely to me.*

be thought/considered unlikely *It is thought unlikely that they will find another buyer at this stage.*

find sth unlikely *He claims he found the letter on the floor, but I find that highly unlikely.*

NOUNS

an unlikely possibility/prospect (=something that you do not think could happen) *She was worried about the unlikely possibility that we wouldn't have enough food.*

an unlikely scenario (=a situation that seems unlikely to happen) *The company could be saved by a takeover, but this scenario is increasingly unlikely.*

an unlikely explanation (=one that does not seem believable) *Leaves on the railway line always seems like an unlikely explanation for delays.*

PHRASES

in the unlikely event of sth (=if something which is unlikely happens) *In the unlikely event of an accident, the system will automatically shut down.*

unlock *v* THESAURUS ▸ open² (1)

unlucky *adj*

1 if you are unlucky, something bad happens to you by chance

ADVERBS

desperately unlucky (=extremely unlucky) *He was desperately unlucky not to score when his shot hit the post.*

unlucky enough to do sth *If you are ever unlucky enough to meet a tiger, don't try to run away.*

PREPOSITIONS

unlucky with sth *She is always unlucky with her choice of men.*

> **Unlucky or unfortunate?**
> **Unfortunate** is more formal than **unlucky**.
> **Unlucky** is much less common than **unfortunate** before a noun. You say *an* ***unfortunate*** *accident/incident/coincidence/victim* (not an 'unlucky' one).

2 something that is unlucky is believed to bring bad luck

NOUNS

an unlucky number *Thirteen is an unlucky number.*

PHRASES

it is unlucky to do sth *Some people think it is unlucky to walk under a ladder.*

U

unnecessary *adj*
not needed, or more than is needed

ADVERBS

totally/completely/entirely/wholly unnecessary *His journey had been completely unnecessary.*

quite unnecessary *BrE* (=completely unnecessary) *"I'll give you a lift in my car." "Thank you, but that's quite unnecessary."*

VERBS

seem unnecessary (*also* **appear unnecessary** *formal*): *All this last minute rushing around seems totally unnecessary.*

make sth unnecessary *The condition can now be treated with drugs, making surgery unnecessary.*

be considered unnecessary *He spent his time doing work that many people would consider unnecessary.*

NOUNS

unnecessary suffering/pain *The vet was careful to avoid causing the animal any unnecessary suffering.*

unnecessary worry/anxiety/distress *If you phone his mother now, you'll just cause her unnecessary anxiety.*

an unnecessary risk *There's no point taking unnecessary risks.*

an unnecessary expense/cost *He thinks advertising is an unnecessary expense.*

an unnecessary extravagance (=something that costs more than is necessary or more than you can afford) *The chairman called first-class airline travel an unnecessary extravagance.*

unnecessary work *We need to be more focused and cut down on unnecessary work.*

unpleasant *adj* not pleasant or enjoyable

ADVERBS

extremely/deeply/highly unpleasant *It was an extremely unpleasant experience for us.*

thoroughly unpleasant (=in every way) *He was a thoroughly unpleasant man who nobody liked.*

NOUNS

an unpleasant experience *Being shouted at by my boss was a very unpleasant experience.*

an unpleasant surprise/shock *Tom got a rather unpleasant surprise when he opened the door.*

an unpleasant task *Her husband had the unpleasant task of clearing the blocked drain.*

an unpleasant feeling/sensation *I had the unpleasant feeling that someone was watching me.*

an unpleasant smell/odour/taste *The fish had a rather unpleasant taste.*

an unpleasant situation *Paul found himself in the unpleasant situation of having to admit that he'd spent all the money.*

an unpleasant memory *Seeing that photograph has brought back some unpleasant memories.*

an unpleasant side effect (=an unpleasant effect that a drug has on your body in addition to curing pain or illness) *This drug has a number of unpleasant side effects.*

PREPOSITIONS

unpleasant for sb *This treatment is quite painful and unpleasant for patients.*

unpleasant to sb *He was very unpleasant to his sister, and made her cry.*

PHRASES

make life unpleasant (=cause problems for someone, usually deliberately) *He is a powerful man and can make life very unpleasant for anybody who angers him.*

THESAURUS: unpleasant

poor, disappointing, unpleasant, negative, grim, undesirable, detrimental, unfavourable → **bad (1)**

unpopular *adj* not liked by most people

ADVERBS

extremely/deeply/highly unpopular *His arrogant manner made him deeply unpopular.*

increasingly unpopular *The war was becoming increasingly unpopular.*

widely unpopular (=among many people) *The party promised to abolish this widely unpopular tax.*

politically unpopular (=unpopular with voters) *Cuts in public spending are politically unpopular.*

VERBS

prove unpopular (=be found to be unpopular) *The changes proved unpopular, and the company decided to go back to the old system.*

make sb/yourself unpopular *He made himself unpopular by criticizing his fellow scientists.*

NOUNS

an unpopular president/prime minister/government *The government is extremely unpopular at the moment.*

an unpopular decision *A leader must have the courage to take unpopular decisions.*

an unpopular policy/measure *No minister wanted to be associated with the unpopular policy.*

PREPOSITIONS

unpopular with/among people *The new design for the product was unpopular with customers.*

unreliable *adj* not able to be trusted

ADVERBS

extremely/highly unreliable *The telephone service is extremely unreliable.*

notoriously unreliable (=well known for being

unreliable) *He is notoriously unreliable and often turns up late for work.*

increasingly unreliable *The car became increasingly unreliable as time went by.*

inherently unreliable (=used when saying that this is a basic feature of something and you cannot trust it) *The evidence was regarded as inherently unreliable because it had been obtained under torture.*

VERBS

prove unreliable (=be shown to be unreliable) *These surveys have proved unreliable in the past.*

unrest *n*

a political situation in which people protest or behave violently

ADJECTIVES/NOUNS + unrest

growing/mounting unrest *There was growing unrest in Egypt.*

widespread unrest (=existing in many places or among many people) *As prices soared, there was widespread unrest.*

social unrest *The policy led to rising unemployment and social unrest.*

political unrest *A month of political unrest followed the killing of 12 protesters by the police.*

industrial unrest *The general strike came after weeks of industrial unrest.*

civil/internal/domestic unrest (=between groups of people in a country, or between the people and the government) *Our country is being torn apart by civil unrest.*

racial/ethnic unrest *Ethnic unrest is becoming more frequent and more violent.*

student unrest *Anti-war demonstrations became the focus of student unrest.*

VERBS

cause/provoke/spark unrest *The introduction of new working practices provoked severe industrial unrest.*

lead to unrest *Food shortages led to widespread social unrest.*

PHRASES

an outbreak of unrest *Troops usually respond to outbreaks of unrest with force.*

a period of unrest *The election results were followed by a long period of unrest.*

a wave of unrest (=a sudden increase in unrest) *A wave of unrest had resulted in seven deaths.*

unsafe *adj* THESAURUS **dangerous**

unsuccessful *adj*

not achieving what you wanted to achieve

NOUNS

an unsuccessful attempt/bid/effort *The prisoners made an unsuccessful attempt to escape.*

an unsuccessful application *Unfortunately, on this occasion your application was unsuccessful.*

an unsuccessful candidate/applicant (=for a job or course) *She was an unsuccessful presidential candidate in 2008.*

an unsuccessful campaign *There was an unsuccessful campaign to stop the road from being built.*

ADVERBS

largely unsuccessful (=mostly unsuccessful) *Their efforts to attract support were largely unsuccessful.*

ultimately unsuccessful (=unsuccessful at the end) *His appeal was ultimately unsuccessful.*

singularly unsuccessful *formal* (=very unsuccessful) *The peace talks were singularly unsuccessful and the fighting began again soon afterwards.*

VERBS

prove unsuccessful *formal* (=be shown to be unsuccessful) *The search for life on other planets has so far proved unsuccessful.*

PREPOSITIONS

be unsuccessful in (doing) sth *He was unsuccessful in obtaining a visa.*

THESAURUS: unsuccessful

failed

attempt | marriage | experiment | robbery | uprising | coup | policy | artist | musician

used about things that are unsuccessful, or about people who have been unsuccessful at a type of work. **Failed** sounds stronger and more disapproving than **unsuccessful**:

They were involved in a failed attempt to blow up a plane. | He was almost 50, with two failed marriages behind him. | Her husband was a failed artist.

Failed is always used before a noun.

doomed

attempt | effort | love affair

if something is doomed, you know that it will be unsuccessful and that bad things will happen:

He made a doomed attempt to reach the South Pole. | 'Romeo and Juliet' is the story of a doomed love affair. | Some people say that the government's economic policy ***is doomed to failure*** (=certain to fail).

abortive

attempt | coup

an abortive attempt is unsuccessful and has to be abandoned before it is finished:

Two US marines died in an abortive attempt to rescue the hostages. | He was the leader of an abortive coup against the military government (=an attempt to change the leader or the government by force).

Abortive is always used before a noun.

fruitless
search | attempt | effort | exercise | task
not producing the result you want, especially after you have spent a lot of time and effort:
I spent the next three hours in a fruitless search for my car keys. | The company made a series of fruitless attempts to persuade the banks to lend them money. | The meeting was a fruitless exercise.

Instead of saying that something was **unsuccessful**, you can say that it **was a failure** or it **ended in failure**: *The experiment was* ***unsuccessful****. | The experiment* ***was a failure/ended in failure****.*
You can also say that someone **tried in vain** to do something (=their efforts were unsuccessful): *The firefighters* ***tried in vain*** *to save the house.*

unsuitable *adj*

not having the right qualities for a particular person, purpose, or situation

ADVERBS

totally/completely/quite/wholly unsuitable *The car was totally unsuitable for driving over rough ground.*
highly unsuitable (=very unsuitable) *The climate is highly unsuitable for growing fruit trees.*
clearly/obviously unsuitable *He was clearly unsuitable for this type of work.*

VERBS

be considered unsuitable (*also* **be deemed unsuitable** *formal*): *The job was considered unsuitable for women.*
make sb/sth unsuitable *The pollution makes the water unsuitable for drinking.*

PREPOSITIONS

unsuitable for sb/sth *The film is unsuitable for children.*

THESAURUS: unsuitable

inappropriate
behaviour | conduct | use | clothing | message | language
not suitable for a particular situation or purpose:
Parents should not reward inappropriate behaviour. | This is an inappropriate use of company funds. | Slang is ***inappropriate in*** *an academic essay. | It would be* ***inappropriate for*** *us to comment at this stage.*

the wrong...
way | place | time | person | direction
not the right thing or person for a particular job or purpose:
It seemed to us to be the wrong way to tackle the problem. | This is the wrong place for a private conversation. | Sorry. I think I've called at the wrong time. | She was simply the wrong person for the job.

out of place
not looking or seeming suitable for that place or situation:
The horse-drawn carriage ***looks a little out of place*** *among the busy traffic. | At first I* ***felt a bit out of place****.*

incompatible
two ideas or things that are incompatible cannot exist or be done together. Two people who are incompatible are unlikely to have a successful relationship, because they have very different characters, beliefs etc:
He considered the role of wife and mother to be ***incompatible with*** *a career. | Why do* ***totally incompatible*** *people get married?*

incongruous *formal*
seeming strange and unsuitable, often in a humorous way, because of being unexpected in a particular situation or very different from its surroundings:
It ***seemed incongruous*** *having a dance band at the funeral. | He was dressed in a three-piece suit with an incongruous tie, shaped like a fish.*

inconvenient
time | moment | place
not suitable and causing problems for you:
He always seems to call at inconvenient times. | The new station is inconvenient for pedestrians, because it is a long walk from the centre of town.

unfit
not suitable to be used for something, or not suitable to do something:
The boat is not only unfit to live in but is actually unsafe. | The meat was declared ***unfit for human consumption*** (=not suitable to eat). *| The house was* ***unfit for human habitation*** (=not suitable to live in).

untidy *adj especially BrE* not tidy

VERBS

look untidy *It looks very untidy having cables all over the floor.*

NOUNS

an untidy heap/pile *Her clothes were in an untidy heap on the bed.*

untrue *adj*

not true, because the person does not know the facts, or because they are lying

Grammar
Untrue is much less common before a noun.

ADVERBS

completely/totally/entirely untrue *Mr Carman said the story was completely untrue.*

patently untrue (=obviously untrue) *The allegations are absurd, ridiculous, and patently untrue.*

simply untrue (=used when saying very definitely that something is untrue) *The firm does not use child labour. That is simply untrue.*

THESAURUS: untrue

false
name | address | information | impression | idea
not true and not based on the facts, or not the real one:
He gave a false name and address to the police. | Complaints are frequently based on false information. | The article gives a ***totally false*** *impression of life in China today. | Decide whether these statements are* ***true or false****.*

misleading
impression | picture | statement | information | advertisement
likely to make people believe something that is not true, especially because you do not give all the facts:
The article gives a misleading impression of the situation. | The report contains a number of misleading statements. | The information on the hotel website is ***deliberately misleading****.*

trumped-up
charges | evidence
using information that is not true, in order to make someone seem guilty of doing something wrong:
He was arrested by the secret police on trumped-up charges. | No-one could convict me on such trumped-up evidence.

Trumped-up is always used before a noun.

You can also say that something is **not the case**: *Recent reports suggest that violent crime is increasing, but this* ***is*** *simply* ***not the case****.*

THESAURUS: untrue

incorrect, inaccurate, false, untrue, misleading, misguided, mistaken → **wrong (1)**

unusual *adj*

different from what is usual or normal

ADVERBS

very/most unusual *Gandhi was a most unusual politician.*

extremely/highly unusual *We've not had any snow yet, which is extremely unusual.*

NOUNS

an unusual situation *Nobody was really prepared for such an unusual situation.*

unusual circumstances *Because he died in unusual circumstances, there will be an investigation.*

an unusual event/occurrence *The severe flooding was the result of a series of unusual events.*

an unusual case *The case is unusual because the victim's body has never been found.*

an unusual feature *The most unusual feature of the room is the large round window.*

an unusual name *Rover is an unusual name for a cat.*

PHRASES

something/nothing/anything unusual *Did you notice anything unusual about him?*

take the unusual step of doing sth *The transport ministry took the unusual step of closing the airport.*

THESAURUS: unusual

rare
occasion | opportunity | occurrence | case | instance | event | species | breed | plant | bird
not happening very often, or existing only in small numbers:
He never cried except on rare occasions. | This is a rare opportunity to see examples of life from thousands of years ago. | This is ***one of those rare*** *cases where both sides have won. | In those days, divorce was a* ***relatively rare*** *event. | They found a rare species of butterfly.*

exotic
place | location | destination | setting | lands | plant | flower | animal | bird | wildlife | food | fruit | perfume
something that is exotic seems unusual and interesting because it is in or from a country that is far away:
He enjoys spending his holidays in exotic places. | Tahiti is an exotic setting for a honeymoon. | She dreamt of travelling to exotic lands in the Far East. | The garden is famous for its collection of exotic plants from all over the world. | Nowadays, exotic fruit such as mangoes is available in many European supermarkets.

exceptional
circumstances
very unusual and happening very rarely:
90-day visas can be extended only in exceptional circumstances. | The presence of a jury in a civil trial is now ***quite exceptional****.*

out of the ordinary
unusual and surprising or special:
It was a small village where ***nothing out of the ordinary*** *ever seemed to happen. | Did you* ***notice anything out of the ordinary about*** *his behaviour?*

U

freak
accident | occurrence | storm | wave | wind
extremely unusual and unexpected:
Their car was crushed by a tree in a freak accident. | There is always a risk of a freak occurrence. | A freak wave wrecked most of the seafront.

Freak is always used before a noun in this sense.

unprecedented
number | step
if something is unprecedented, it has never happened before:
An unprecedented number of students have received top grades. | He took the unprecedented step of granting an interview to a Russian journalist (=he did something that had never been done before). *| This kind of deal is* ***completely unprecedented****.*

unheard of
if something is unheard of, it has never happened or been done before - used especially when something seems very surprising to people at that time:
In our small town, this kind of crime was ***almost unheard of****. | Mobile phones were* ***completely unheard of*** *in those days.*

eccentric
behaviour | millionaire | inventor | appearance
behaving in a way that seems rather strange but not frightening:
The students were used to his ***somewhat eccentric*** *behaviour* (=rather eccentric). *| The house was owned by an eccentric millionaire. | He was a small man with white hair and an eccentric appearance.*

unconventional
method | way | approach | idea
very different from the way in which people usually do something, often in a way that seems interesting:
Laing has developed some rather unconventional methods for communicating to his troops. | His approach to business may seem unconventional, but he certainly gets results.

unorthodox
view | opinion | method | way | approach | manner | behaviour | idea
unorthodox ideas or methods are different from the usual ones, and therefore seem surprising to many people:
He is known for his ***highly unorthodox*** *political views. | The school uses some unorthodox teaching methods. | This book takes an unorthodox approach to art criticism.*

U

unwilling *adj*

not wanting to do something and refusing to do it

VERBS

seem unwilling *She seems unwilling to admit that she was wrong.*

prove unwilling *formal* (=show that you are unwilling) *Both sides have proved unwilling to try to reach an agreement.*

ADVERBS

increasingly unwilling *Canadians have become increasingly unwilling to pay for generous social programs.*

PHRASES

unwilling or unable to do sth *He was unwilling or unable to pay the fine.*

THESAURUS: unwilling

reluctant
admiration | smile | agreement | acceptance | decision | hero
unwilling - used especially when someone does not want to do something at first, but is persuaded to do it:
The coach is very strict, but the players have a kind of reluctant admiration for him. | We eventually sold our home, but it was a very reluctant decision. | Hoffman plays the reluctant hero of the film. | He is reluctant to talk about his childhood.

grudging
admiration | respect | approval | support | admission | apology
given unwillingly:
He could not help feeling a kind of grudging admiration for the old lady. | The English fans have a grudging respect for the German team. | The president gave his somewhat grudging approval to the plan. | He persuaded James to give him grudging support. | I received a grudging apology from the company.

Grudging is always used before a noun.

In more formal English you can also say that you are **loath to** do something, when you do not want to have to do it: *He has more staff than he needs, but he is* ***loath to*** *get rid of good people.*

upbringing *n*

the way that your parents care for you and teach you to behave when you are growing up

ADJECTIVES

a strict upbringing *He reacted rebelliously against his strict upbringing.*

a privileged upbringing (=when someone has advantages because their family is wealthy) *Due to his privileged upbringing, he finds it difficult to identify with ordinary people.*

a religious/Muslim/Catholic etc upbringing *Because of her religious upbringing, she would not divorce her husband.*

a sheltered upbringing (=one in which someone is protected from difficult or unpleasant experiences) *Mary had had a very sheltered upbringing and was shocked by some of the things she saw.*

a middle-class/working-class upbringing *She had a comfortable middle-class upbringing.*

a good upbringing *However good their upbringing, young people may still behave badly.*

VERBS

have a ... upbringing *He had a rather unusual upbringing because his father worked in a circus.*

upset[1] *adj*

unhappy and worried because something unpleasant or disappointing has happened

ADVERBS

deeply upset (=very upset) *She's still deeply upset about her uncle's death.*

all upset *spoken* (=very upset) *She got all upset and started crying.*

too upset *Miss Hurley is too upset to speak to anyone at the moment.*

genuinely upset *He sounded genuinely upset on the phone.*

VERBS

get upset (=become upset) *There's no need to get upset - he'll be back very soon.*

seem/sound/look upset *She noticed that her friend looked upset.*

make sb upset *It makes me upset just to think about it.*

PREPOSITIONS

upset about/at/over sth *Her father was upset about losing his licence.*

upset[2] *v*

1 to change something in a way that causes problems

NOUNS

upset the balance *It's important not to upset the balance of nature.*

upset sb's plans *Ken's visit upset her plans for the day.*

PHRASES

upset the apple cart *informal* (=do something which causes problems) *Ministers are anxious not to upset the apple cart by making changes too quickly.*

2 to make someone feel unhappy or worried

NOUNS

upset sb's feelings *I was careful not to upset her feelings.*

urban *adj* relating to towns and cities

NOUNS

an urban area *People often move from the country to urban areas looking for work.*

an urban centre *BrE*, **an urban center** *AmE* (=a city or large town) *There are good railway connections from all urban centres in the UK.*

urban regeneration/renewal (=improving poor areas of towns or cities by making new jobs, homes etc) *The government has spent a lot of money on urban renewal.*

urban growth/development *Rapid urban growth meant a lot of green spaces were lost.*

urban decay (=a situation in which the living conditions in a city become very bad) *The city developed a reputation for crime and urban decay.*

urban deprivation (=the problem of people in cities being very poor) *The government should do more to reduce urban deprivation.*

the urban population *In Venezuela, the urban population has grown at a faster rate than has the total population.*

urban planning/design *Urban planning should not favor car drivers over pedestrians and cyclists.*

urban sprawl (=the spread of city buildings and houses into an area that used to be countryside) *Past efforts to control urban sprawl have been largely ineffective.*

ANTONYMS **urban → rural**

urge *n* a strong wish or need

ADJECTIVES

a strong/powerful/great urge *The urge to have some more ice cream was too strong to resist.*

an irresistible/uncontrollable/overwhelming urge (=very strong) *When I saw him, I had an irresistible urge to laugh.*

a sudden urge *She fought back the sudden urge to beg his forgiveness.*

a terrible urge *He had a terrible urge to run away and hide.*

an instinctive/basic/natural urge (*also* **a primal urge** *formal*) (=a natural urge that all people or animals have) *Every animal has an instinctive urge to survive.*

a human urge *There is a fundamental human urge to try to understand the world.*

VERBS

feel/have/get an urge *I still sometimes feel an urge to have a cigarette.*

be overcome by an urge *I was overcome by an irresistible urge to cry.*

resist/fight/suppress an urge *She had to resist a constant urge to look back over her shoulder.*

satisfy an urge (=do what you feel you want to do) *He satisfied his urge to travel by going to India.*

give in to an urge (=do what you feel you want to do, when this is wrong) *I try not to give in to the urge to gossip.*

urgency *n*
the need to deal with or do something quickly

ADJECTIVES

great urgency *The situation is one of great urgency.*

added/increased urgency *The rapid spread of the disease has given added urgency to a national health education campaign.*

new urgency *Following the recent wave of terrorist attacks, senior politicians are working for peace with a new urgency.*

VERBS

understand/recognize/realize the urgency of sth *The rich countries must recognize the urgency of removing the obstacles to development in the poorer parts of the world.*

stress/emphasize the urgency of sth *She stressed the urgency of economic and political reform.*

lend/add urgency to sth (=make it urgent) *Rising fuel prices have lent urgency to the search for alternative electrical power sources.*

PREPOSITIONS

the urgency of sth *Politicians are finally realizing the urgency of the matter.*

PHRASES

sth is a matter of urgency (=it is very urgent) *Dealing with climate change is a matter of urgency.*

sth is a matter of the utmost urgency (=it is extremely urgent) *The crisis is a matter of the utmost urgency.*

a sense/note of urgency *There was a note of urgency in her voice.*

a lack of urgency *There seemed to be a lack of urgency about the team's performance.*

urgent *adj*
needing to be dealt with or done immediately

ADVERBS

extremely urgent *Can you give him the message? It's extremely urgent.*

most urgent spoken (=very urgent) *I need to talk to the principal – it's most urgent.*

increasingly urgent *The situation is becoming increasingly urgent.*

NOUNS

an urgent problem *It is an urgent problem which must be tackled at once.*

an urgent need *There is an urgent need for stricter regulation.*

urgent action *Urgent action is needed to boost employment.*

urgent attention *She believes the nation's drug problem requires urgent attention.*

an urgent task/job *I've got some urgent tasks to finish before I leave tonight.*

urgent business *She told them that she had urgent business on the other side of town.*

an urgent meeting *Health chiefs have called an urgent meeting to discuss the problem.*

urgent talks *The union is seeking urgent talks with management on this matter.*

an urgent message *I have an urgent message for Sam – where is he?*

use[1] *v*
to do something with or in something

NOUNS

use a computer/phone/machine etc *Doctors are using computers to treat patients.*

use a car/bicycle/bus etc *More and more people are using their cars to travel to work.*

use a room/office/house/building etc *He is welcome to use my office.*

use a system/a program/the internet *You need to have special training before you can use the system.*

use a method/technique/approach *The houses are built using traditional methods.*

use your skill/knowledge *I want a job which allows me to use my language skills.*

use information/data *Some people are worried about how this information will be used.*

use a word/term/name/phrase *Advertisers like to use words like 'new' and 'exciting'.*

use a language *The language he uses sounds rather old-fashioned.*

use a reason/excuse/argument *They use the argument that nuclear energy is good for the environment.*

use the opportunity/chance to do sth *You should use the opportunity to meet new people.*

ADVERBS

use sth carefully *The drug needs to be used very carefully.*

use sth sparingly (=be careful to only use a little of something) *We try to use water sparingly.*

PREPOSITIONS

use sth for sth *I often use the internet for my coursework.*

use sth as sth *The room is being used as a store room.*

PHRASES

be easy/difficult to use *The camera is very easy to use.*

ready to use *The sauce is ready to use from the jar.*

> **Use or take?**
> When talking about ways of travelling, you often say **take** instead of **use**: *It's quicker if we **take** the bus.* | *Why don't we **take** the train instead of driving? It's better for the environment.*

U

THESAURUS: use

utilize *formal*
skills | expertise | knowledge | information | data | technology | method | technique | equipment | system | services
to use something that is available to you, for a practical purpose:
She feels that her skills are not being fully utilized. | Companies can utilize this information when making business decisions. | College equipment must not be utilized for personal use.

employ *formal*
method | approach | strategy | technique | means
to use a particular way of doing something:
A number of approaches can be employed to assist this process. | The surgeons employed a technique which has never been used before. | They ***employed every means at their disposal*** (=every available method).

apply
method | approach | theory | technique | technology | knowledge | rule | principle | standard | criterion
to use something such as a method or a principle, in a particular situation:
They applied modern scientific methods to the study of traditional Chinese medicine. | Students will have the opportunity to apply the knowledge they have learned in practical situations. | People are beginning to apply human standards of medicine to the care of their animals.

draw on sth
experience | knowledge | memories | work
to use something that you or other people have learned in the past, in order to help you do something:
He was able to draw on his own experience as a teacher when he was writing the book. | There is a huge amount of existing knowledge for researchers to draw on. | She drew on her childhood memories of her grandparents. | Jung draws on the work of Gerhard Adler, a fellow German psychologist.

exploit
opportunity | situation | potential | resources | weakness
to use something, especially so that you can get advantages for yourself:
Some companies are failing to exploit opportunities in overseas markets, because they believe exporting is too risky. | The country will remain poor unless it can exploit its huge natural resources. | He was quick to exploit any weakness in his opponent's argument.

resort to sth
violence | force | threats | extreme measures | desperate measures | legal action | strike action
to use violence, force, or other extreme methods as a way of achieving something, especially after all other methods have failed:
The protesters say they are willing to resort to violence if necessary. | Some men resorted to extreme measures, in order to avoid serving in the army (=they used extreme methods). | *No one wants to have to resort to legal action* (=take a case to court).

exercise *formal*
power | control | authority | influence | right | privilege | judgment | caution | restraint | self-discipline | discretion | veto
to use your power, influence, rights, judgment etc:
Congress exercised its power to limit government spending. | Only 40% of the population exercised their right to vote. | Doctors have to exercise their professional judgment in these cases. | The police officer can exercise discretion in minor traffic offences (=choose what to do, based on your own judgment).

exert *formal*
influence | pressure | power | control | authority
to use your influence, power, authority etc:
The church still exerts considerable influence over people's lives. | The US exerted pressure on him to resign. | Big supermarkets can exert enormous power in order to keep food prices low. | The government exerts little control in these areas, which are far from the capital city.

You can also say **make use of** something, when talking about using something that is available to you: *Guests can* ***make use of*** *the hotel facilities, including the gym and the swimming pool.*

use[2] *n*

the way that something is used, or how often something is used

ADJECTIVES

good/better/best use *Universities need to make better use of technology.*

efficient/effective use *More efficient use of energy can reduce our heating bills by as much as 50%.*

greater use (=something is used more) *We want to encourage employees to make greater use of the sports facilities.*

widespread/extensive use (=in many places and by many people) *The widespread use of the internet has given ordinary people access to all kinds of information.*

heavy use (=something is used a lot) *Heavy use of chemicals is having a damaging effect on the environment.*

excessive use (=something is used too much) *There was excessive use of force by the police.*

regular use *These drugs are not recommended for regular use.*

occasional use (=something is only used a few times) *The car has only had occasional use.*
proper/correct/appropriate use *They are trained in the proper use of the equipment.*
clever/skilful use *Clever use of make-up can improve your appearance.*
personal/private use *He keeps the helicopter for his own personal use.*
full/maximum use (=something is used as much as possible) *The book shows you how to make full use of your talents.*
optimum use (=the best possible use of something) *The room is designed to make optimum use of the available space.*

VERBS

make use of sth (=use it) *Do the students make use of the library?*
come into use/be brought into use (=start being used) *Computers first came into use in the early 1950s.*
go out of use (=stop being used) *In Britain thousands of railway stations have gone out of use.*
encourage/promote the use of sth *We do not encourage the regular use of sleeping pills.*
ban/prohibit the use of sth *The treaty bans the use of chemical weapons.*

NOUNS + use

energy use *These cookers are more efficient in their energy use.*
land use *We carried out a survey of land use in national parks.*
car use *We can help to reduce car use by providing good public transport.*
drug/alcohol/tobacco use *Drug use is on the increase.*

PREPOSITIONS

the use of sth *There are strict rules concerning the use of weapons by police officers.*

PHRASES

put sth to (good) use (=use it to achieve something useful) *The money you raised will be put to good use.*
in use (=being used) *The car is 50 years old, but it is still in use.*
in constant use (=used all the time) *The meeting room is in constant use.*

useful *adj*

if something is useful, it is good because it helps you to do what you want

NOUNS

useful information *The book is packed with useful information about Paris.*
useful advice *My father gave me some useful advice.*
a useful tip (=a useful piece of advice about the best way to do something) *The website has some useful tips on selling your home.*
a useful source *The internet is a useful source of information.*
(a) useful experience *I thought that the trip would be a useful experience.*
a useful tool (=a useful method) *Videos can be a useful tool for language teaching.*

VERBS

find sth useful *Did you find the book useful?*
come in useful (=be useful) *The extra money will come in useful.*
prove useful *formal* (=be shown to be useful) *His advice proved very useful.*
make yourself useful *He made himself useful around the house by doing chores.*

PREPOSITIONS

be useful for (doing) sth *The cupboard is useful for storing sheets and towels.*
be useful to sb *The money will be useful to me.*

ADVERBS

extremely/really useful *The drug has proved extremely useful in treating the disease.*
especially/particularly useful *I found the pronunciation information especially useful.*
potentially useful (=may be useful in the future) *The data is potentially useful to scientists.*

PHRASES

it is useful to do sth *It is useful to know what to do in case of an emergency.*
serve no useful purpose (=not be useful) *Sending her to prison will serve no useful purpose.*
a useful way of doing sth *Keeping lists of the words you learn is a useful way of remembering vocabulary.*

THESAURUS: useful

handy
hint | tip | way | book | guide
useful and convenient or easy to use. **Handy** is more informal than **useful**:
He gave me some handy hints about what to buy in the local market. | A handy tip is to put the seeds in some water before you plant them. | The map ***came in handy*** *when we were trying to find our hotel* (=it was useful).

helpful
advice | suggestion | hint | tip | information
if something is helpful, it is useful because it helps you to do something:
The leaflet contains plenty of helpful advice on giving up smoking. | Thank you for all your helpful suggestions. | We hope this information will be ***helpful to*** *you in making your decision. |* ***It can be helpful*** *to discuss your problems with a friend.*

worthwhile
experience | job | career | cause | activity | exercise | investment

U

if something is worthwhile, it is useful because it benefits you or other people:
Working with young children can be a very worthwhile experience. | *We decided to give the money to a worthwhile cause* (=one that helps people). | *I* **found** *the course extremely* **worthwhile** *and I learned a great deal.*

very useful

valuable
information | **source** | **help** | **advice** | **contribution** | **experience** | **resource** | **asset** | **insight** | **guide**
very useful:
This information could be valuable to the police. | *Eggs are a valuable source of protein.* | *He made a valuable contribution to the discussion.* | *The archaeological records give us a valuable insight into the life of a medieval village* (=useful information which helps you understand more about something).

invaluable
information | **source** | **resource** | **experience** | **help** | **contribution** | **asset** | **insight** | **guide**
extremely useful:
The letters are an invaluable source of information for researchers. | *The authors would like to thank Theresa Madden for her invaluable help.* | *The drug could be* **invaluable for** *treating cancer patients.*

indispensable
part | **element** | **tool** | **guide** | **source**
someone or something that is indispensable is so useful and important that you cannot do something without them:
He became an indispensable part of the team. | *Market research is an indispensable tool for business success* (=you cannot succeed without it). | *For walkers, a compass is* **absolutely indispensable**.

You can also say that something is **of use** (=it is useful in some way): *I hope you'll* **find** *the book* **of use**. | *The information* **could be of use** *to an enemy.*

ANTONYMS **useful → useless**

useless *adj*
not useful or effective in any way

ADVERBS

completely/totally/absolutely/utterly useless *The map was old and it was completely useless.*

virtually/almost/practically useless *The spray was virtually useless in keeping away the mosquitoes.*

fairly useless (*also* **pretty useless** *BrE*) (=rather useless) *If the knife isn't sharp, it is pretty useless.*

NOUNS

useless information *His mind is full of useless information about sport.*

VERBS

prove useless *formal* (=something is shown not to be effective when you use it) *Police checkpoints proved useless at stopping the suicide bombers.*

render sth useless *formal* (=make it useless) *She was in a terrible accident which rendered her legs virtually useless.*

PREPOSITIONS

useless for sth *Salt water flooded onto the land, making it useless for farming.*

useless to sb *The information was useless to me.*

PHRASES

it is useless trying to do sth *It's useless trying to argue with him.*

worse than useless *My raincoat is so old, it is worse than useless.*

Grammar
Useless is usually used after the verb **be**, or other verbs. The only noun it is commonly used with is **information**. For other nouns, it is better to use the adjectives in the Thesaurus section.

THESAURUS: useless

pointless
exercise | **question** | **argument**
not likely to have any useful result:
Washing his clothes seemed like a pointless exercise, if he was going to get them dirty again the next day. | ***It is completely pointless*** *arguing with him – he always thinks he is right.*

futile
attempt | **effort** | **exercise** | **gesture** | **search**
actions that are futile are not worth doing because they have no chance of being successful:
She shut the door in a futile attempt to keep out the smoke. | *The talks were a futile exercise, because neither side was interested in peace.* | *Averland sent troops to support them, but he knew it was a futile gesture* (=something that you do, even though you know it cannot possibly be successful).

hopeless
task | **situation** | **attempt** | **struggle** | **case**
if something that you try to do is hopeless, there is no hope of being successful:
Trying to stop the fire from spreading was a hopeless task. | *The situation* **seemed hopeless** *and everyone thought that the factory would close.* | *At first, his doctors thought that he was a hopeless case* (=someone who you cannot do anything to help, or a situation that is impossible to change).

fruitless
search | attempt | effort | talks | negotiations | discussions
if something is fruitless, you do not find or achieve what you want:
Hamilton led investigators on a fruitless search of the desert. | *These discussions* ***proved fruitless****, with each side blaming the other.*

You can also say that something is **a waste of time/money/effort** (=it is not worth the time, money, or effort that you use because you do not achieve anything): *The scheme was a* ***waste of money****.*

ANTONYMS **useless → useful**

user *n*
someone who uses a product, service etc

Grammar
Often plural.

NOUNS + user

a computer user *Computer users are being warned to look out for the virus.*

a road user *Signal to let other road users know you are turning right.*

an internet user *Internet users who illegally download music could face large fines.*

a drug user *To her horror, she found out her son was a drug user.*

a wheelchair user *The paths through the park are suitable for wheelchair users.*

a business user (=businesses who use something) *The hotel offers special midweek rates targeted at business users.*

ADJECTIVES

a regular user *If you are a regular sunbed user, you risk long-term skin damage.*

a heavy user (=someone who uses something a lot) *Electricity companies are warning that heavy users face much higher bills.*

a light user (=someone who uses something only a little) *Light users of the service will receive a reduction in their bill.*

user-friendly *adj* THESAURUS **easy**

usual *adj*
happening, done, or existing most of the time or in most situations

NOUNS

the usual way/manner/method *Make a cheese sauce in the usual way.*

the usual time/place *I'll meet you at the usual time.*

the usual pattern *Our conversation followed the usual pattern.*

usual practice (=what is normally considered the right way to do something) *It is our usual practice to ask for payment in advance.*

the usual routine *Everything felt strange because I was away from home and my usual routine.*

the usual number/amount/quantity *The birds produced only half the usual number of eggs.*

the usual sort of sth *Dad gave me the usual sort of advice about studying hard.*

the usual stuff *informal*: *We had all the usual stuff for breakfast.*

the usual suspects (=the people or things that are usually involved in or responsible for something) *When a window was broken, the head teacher called the usual suspects to his study.*

the usual channels (=the usual system or method) *Any complaints must be dealt with through the usual channels.*

PHRASES

as usual (=used for saying what usually happens) *John was late, as usual.*

longer/quicker/worse etc than usual *It is taking longer than usual for orders to reach our customers.*

as big/much etc as usual *I didn't feel as relaxed as usual.*

not your usual self (=behaving differently from usual, especially by seeming worried or upset) *Clare didn't seem her usual self today.*

it's business as usual (=used for saying that something or someone is still working or operating as normal when people think they might not be) *It's business as usual at the White House despite the dramatic events of yesterday.*

utensil *n* THESAURUS **tool (1)**

utilize (*also* **utilise** *BrE*) *v* THESAURUS **use[1]**

U

Vv

vacancy *n*

a job that is available for someone to start doing

NOUNS + vacancy

a job vacancy *He searched the newspapers regularly for job vacancies.*

a staff vacancy *Many officers are working overtime because of staff vacancies.*

ADJECTIVES

a suitable vacancy *We will keep your letter on file in case other suitable vacancies arise.*

an unfilled vacancy (=a job for which no one has been hired) *The teaching unions estimate there are some 10,000 unfilled vacancies.*

VERBS

have a vacancy *We have no vacancies for cleaners at present.*

advertise a vacancy *Where did you see the vacancy advertised?*

fill a vacancy (=find someone for a job, or be the person who takes the job) *I'm afraid that vacancy has now been filled.*

create/leave a vacancy *The vacancy was created when the previous coach resigned.*

a vacancy comes up (*also* **a vacancy arises/occurs** *formal*) (=it happens) *A vacancy has arisen on the committee.*

PREPOSITIONS

a vacancy for sb *She asked if there were any vacancies for salespeople.*

vacant *adj*

empty, or available for someone to have or use

NOUNS

a vacant seat/chair *I was lucky enough to find a vacant seat on the bus.*

a vacant house/apartment/building *Some of these vacant buildings are in a very bad condition.*

vacant land *Nearly all the vacant land has been bought by property developers.*

a vacant lot *AmE* (=an empty unused area of land in a city) *He had watched the area develop from vacant lots to a busy neighborhood full of new apartment blocks.*

a vacant space/site *People have started using vacant spaces in the city to grow vegetables.*

a vacant position/post (=a job that is available) *The company has several vacant positions that need filling.*

VERBS

leave sth vacant *The position was left vacant by the retirement of Ted Anderson.*

become vacant *The house became vacant when the old lady died.*

a job/post falls vacant *formal* (=it becomes available) *When posts fall vacant they should be publicly advertised.*

THESAURUS: vacant

free, vacant → **available**

bare, blank, hollow, free, vacant, deserted, uninhabited, unoccupied → **empty**

vacation *n AmE*

1 a period of time when you travel to another place for pleasure

ADJECTIVES/NOUNS + vacation

a summer vacation *We went to Europe on our last summer vacation.*

a family vacation *We had to cancel the family vacation.*

a long vacation *She decided to take a long vacation.*

a short vacation *We spent a short vacation at the beach.*

a two-week/three-day etc vacation *He went for a two-week vacation in Palm Springs.*

a skiing/golfing/walking etc vacation *We took a walking vacation in Sicily.*

VERBS

go on vacation *Where are you going on your vacation?*

take/have a vacation *We usually take a vacation once a year.*

need a vacation (*also* **could use a vacation** *informal*): *You're working too hard. You need a vacation.*

spend a vacation *We spent most of our vacation on the beach.*

book a vacation *I booked our vacation on the internet.*

plan a vacation *Whenever we plan a vacation our first thought is "Can we take the dogs?"*

vacation + NOUNS

a vacation spot (=a place for a vacation) *The island is my favorite vacation spot.*

a vacation home/house *They have a vacation home near Carmel.*

vacation plans *Do you have any vacation plans this summer?*

a vacation trip *I'm planning a vacation trip to Costa Rica.*

PREPOSITIONS

on vacation *He's on vacation in Hawaii.*

⚠ Don't say 'have vacation'. Say **be on vacation**.

Vacation is used in American English. British speakers say **holiday**.

2 a time of rest from work or school

ADJECTIVES/NOUNS + vacation

paid vacation (=time spent away from your job when you still get paid) *My job allows me three weeks' paid vacation a year.*

school/college vacation *The school vacation starts next week.*

summer vacation *Denise came home during her summer vacation from college.*

VERBS

take vacation *She has not taken any vacation this year.*

have/get vacation *How much vacation do you get in your new job?*

PREPOSITIONS

on vacation (from sth) *He was at home on vacation from his studies.*

in/during a vacation *I went home to stay with my family during the vacation.*

Vacation is used in American English. British speakers say **holiday**.

vaccine *n*

a substance that protects people from a particular disease

ADJECTIVES

an effective vaccine *The vaccine is 95% effective.*

a safe vaccine *Parents were worried that the vaccine wasn't safe.*

a live vaccine (=containing living organisms) *Live vaccines must be used within a short period of time.*

NOUNS + vaccine

a flu/AIDS/malaria etc vaccine *Doctors need more supplies of the flu vaccine.*

VERBS

a vaccine protects sb against sth *The vaccine is used to protect people against polio.*

give sb a vaccine *The vaccine is usually given to young children.*

have had a vaccine (=have been given it) *Have you had your flu vaccine?*

develop a vaccine *Scientists are currently developing a new vaccine against malaria.*

PREPOSITIONS

a vaccine for/against a disease *There is a vaccine for pneumonia.*

PHRASES

a dose/shot of vaccine *Two doses of vaccine are given at an interval of four weeks.*

vague *adj* not clear or definite

NOUNS

a vague idea/notion/concept *The students only had a vague idea of what they were supposed to do.*

a vague sense/feeling *She had a vague feeling that she had missed something important.*

a vague recollection/memory *I have only a vague recollection of what the house looked like.*

a vague impression *Everything happens so quickly that all you are left with is a vague impression.*

a vague suspicion *A vague suspicion began to form in his mind.*

a vague unease/dread (=a feeling that something bad is going to happen) *As I entered the empty building, I felt a vague unease.*

a vague promise *The politicians made vague promises about reforms.*

a vague description *Witnesses gave only a vague description of the driver.*

a vague hint/reference *He gave only a few vague hints about his personal life.*

a vague gesture *When I asked where Ricky was, she made a vague gesture in the direction of the house.*

a vague shape/outline *It was getting light, and she could just make out the vague shape of a building ahead of her.*

vain *adj*

failing to achieve the result you wanted

Grammar
Only used before a noun in this meaning.

NOUNS

a vain attempt/effort/bid *He waved his arms in a vain attempt to scare the dog away.*

a vain hope *Young men moved south in the vain hope of finding work.*

a vain search *Parents have been to every store in town in a vain search for the toy.*

a vain plea/appeal *He made a vain plea for mercy.*

valiant *adj* THESAURUS brave

valid Ac *adj*

good and based on what is reasonable or sensible

NOUNS

a valid point *I think he is making a valid point.*

a valid reason *I had a perfectly valid reason for being there.*

a valid excuse *You must have a valid excuse for any absence.*

a valid argument *He explains why none of these arguments are valid.*

a valid criticism/complaint *If the complaint is valid, the customer should get his money back.*

a valid conclusion *The researcher could not draw any valid conclusions from this data.*

ADVERBS

equally valid *Each of these ways of looking at things is equally valid.*

perfectly valid *It's a perfectly valid question.*

statistically/scientifically valid (=based on correct numbers or good research) *The drug trials were not scientifically valid.*

valley *n*

an area of lower land between two lines of hills or mountains

ADJECTIVES

a deep/steep valley *The river had carved out a deep valley.*

a green/wooded/lush valley (=one with a lot of plants or trees growing in it) *There were cattle grazing down in the green valley.*

a fertile valley (=where crops grow well) *The farm is situated in a fertile valley.*

a peaceful/quiet valley *They sat together, looking out over the peaceful valley.*

a narrow valley *The valley becomes narrower at this point.*

a wide/broad valley *The castle is on a hill, overlooking the wide valley below.*

NOUNS + valley

a river valley *The route passes through beautiful wooded river valleys.*

a mountain valley *The village is in a remote mountain valley.*

the Thames/San Fernando/Loire etc Valley (=a valley with a particular river running through it) *There are beautiful views across the Forth Valley.*

valley + NOUNS

the valley floor *Most of the town is built on the valley floor.*

PHRASES

the side of a valley *He looked across to the far side of the valley.*

the slopes of a valley *They live on the slopes of a wooded valley.*

the head of a valley (=the higher end of a valley) *There is a waterfall at the head of the valley.*

the bottom of a valley *The stream in the bottom of the valley was spanned by a narrow bridge.*

valuable *adj*

1 worth a lot of money

NOUNS

a valuable painting/ring/antique etc *The museum has some extremely valuable paintings.*

valuable jewellery *BrE*, **valuable jewelry** *AmE*: *Thieves stole valuable jewellery and other items.*

a valuable object/item *The most valuable object was a rare Chinese vase.*

valuable land *The estate includes some valuable agricultural land.*

THESAURUS: valuable

precious
metal | stone
very rare and expensive:
The company hoped to find gold or other precious metals. | The bracelet was decorated with diamonds and other precious stones.

priceless
antique | jewel | collection
so valuable that it is impossible to calculate a price:
The big house is full of priceless antiques. | The exhibition features a priceless collection of some of the best examples of African art. | The statue is priceless.

2 very useful and important

NOUNS

valuable information *He was able to provide the police with some valuable information.*

a valuable source of sth *Nuts are a valuable source of protein.*

valuable help *She thanked them for their valuable help.*

valuable advice *The book is full of valuable advice about growing plants.*

a valuable contribution *She made a valuable contribution to the discussion.*

valuable experience/lesson *Nursing students can gain valuable experience of caring for patients.*

a valuable resource/tool (=a very useful thing you can use to do something) *The internet is a valuable tool for research.*

a valuable insight (=a very useful idea about something) *The films provide a valuable insight into what life was like in the early part of the 20th century.*

a valuable asset (=someone or something that is very useful and helps you be successful) *Lisa is a valuable asset to the team.*

a valuable commodity (=a type of person or thing that is considered to be very important and useful) *Skilled workers are a valuable commodity.*

valuable time *Police officers waste valuable time doing paperwork.*

ADVERBS

extremely/highly valuable *The information is highly valuable for people who are making investment decisions.*

VERBS

prove valuable *formal* (=be valuable to someone when they are trying to do something) *His knowledge of Russian was to prove very valuable for his work.*

PREPOSITIONS

valuable for sb/sth *The book will be valuable for students of all ages.*

valuable to sb *This information could be valuable to the police.*

THESAURUS: valuable

precious
possessions | memory | gift | time | moments
if something is precious, it is very important to you and you care about it a lot:
The house was full of precious memories. | I don't want to waste any more of your precious time. | My freedom is very ***precious to*** *me.*

treasured
possessions | memory | gift
very special and important to someone – used especially about something that you keep for a long time:
She kept her most treasured possessions in a box under her bed. | The holiday was now a treasured memory.

irreplaceable
extremely special and important, especially because it is the only one of its kind:
The manuscripts are said to be irreplaceable.

You use **invaluable** about something that is extremely useful: *The data will be* ***invaluable to*** *scientists researching climate change.*

value *n*

1 the amount of money that something is worth

ADJECTIVES/NOUNS + value

the total value *The total value of his computer equipment is around £5,000.*

the real value *The real value of their salaries has fallen.*

sth is good value (=it is worth the money you paid for it) *At ten euros a pair, these jeans are really good value.*

sth is bad/poor value (=it is not worth the money you paid for it) *Ten dollars for a coffee is really bad value.*

high value (=worth a lot of money) *You should insure any goods of high value.*

low value (=not worth a lot of money) *The low value of the dollar will benefit tourists.*

the market value (=the amount something can be sold for) *The mortgage is more than the house's current market value.*

the monetary/cash value (=the value of something in money) *They made an attempt to assess the cash value of the contract.*

face value (=the value printed on something) *The tickets are selling for far more than their face value.*

street value (=the amount that users will pay for illegal drugs) *Drugs with a street value of £1,600 were found in the car.*

property/land values *Property values have fallen sharply.*

VERBS

have a value of sth *The diamond has a value of over $1 million.*

increase/rise/go up in value *The painting has gone up in value since we bought it.*

double in value *The house doubled in value over two years.*

double the value of sth *We doubled the value of the car by filling it with petrol!*

add value to sth *A brand adds value to a product.*

fall/go down in value *There is a risk that the shares may fall in value.*

reduce the value of sth *A new housing development could reduce the value of your home or spoil your view.*

put a value on sth (=say how much it is worth) *It's hard to put a value on something so unusual.*

the value of sth increases/rises *The value of the land had increased by $2 million.*

the value of sth falls *The value of your investment may fall.*

sth holds its value (=its value does not fall over time) *Good quality furniture should hold its value.*

PREPOSITIONS

the value of sth *The value of your investments can go down as well as up.*

PHRASES

a fall/drop in value *There was a sudden drop in the value of oil.*

a rise/increase in value *We saw a rapid increase in the land's value.*

value for money *BrE* (=good value) *Every customer is looking for value for money.*

2 the importance or usefulness of something

ADJECTIVES

great value *These drugs are of great value in treating cancer.*

little value *The information was of little value.*

real/true value *The documents are too short to be of real value.*

lasting value (=for a long time) *He wanted to achieve something of lasting value.*

practical value (=in real situations) *His research has been of little practical value.*

entertainment value (=because of being enjoyable) *In terms of entertainment value, it's a great film.*

sentimental value (=because of being a gift, reminding you of someone etc) *The ring wasn't expensive but had great sentimental value.*

nutritional value (=the amount of things that a food contains, which are good for your health) *The nutritional value of cereals can vary.*

VERBS

be of value (=be important or useful) *The fans' support was of great value to the team.*

have value *All ideas have value and should be listened to.*

realize/recognize the value of sth (=understand it is important or useful) *He did not recognize the value of careful preparation.*

question the value of sth (=say that it is not important or useful) *More and more people are questioning the value of marriage.*

the value lies in sth *The book's value lies in the questions it raises.*

PREPOSITIONS

the value of sth *They talked to us about the value of a good education.*

PHRASES

place/put a high value on sth (=consider something to be important) *Our society places a high value on education.*

3 your values are your ideas about what is right and wrong, or what is important in life

> **Grammar**
> Always plural in this meaning.

ADJECTIVES/NOUNS + value

traditional values *The president called for a return to traditional values.*

moral values (=about right and wrong) *She had her own set of moral values.*

cultural/social values *The films of the time reflected changing social values.*

human values *Society changes, but human values remain the same.*

family values (=traditional ideas about what a family should be like, in which marriage is very important) *The party places a great emphasis on family values.*

core values (=most basic values) *The party needs to express its core values clearly.*

VERBS

hold/have values *People brought up in different times hold different social values.*

share sb's values *They vote for the candidate who shares their values.*

uphold values (=defend or support them) *The new party was dedicated to upholding traditional values.*

value + NOUNS

a value system (=a set of values) *People with different value systems can cause conflict in the workplace.*

PHRASES

a set of values *Young people have a completely different set of values.*

vandalism *n*

the crime of deliberately damaging things, especially public property

ADJECTIVES

mindless/wanton vandalism (=completely stupid and without any purpose) *The head teacher described the damage to the school buildings as mindless vandalism.*

PHRASES

an act of vandalism *The Richmond police department is investigating an act of vandalism at the Reagan Building.*

vanish *v* to disappear or stop existing

ADVERBS

vanish completely/altogether (=stop existing completely) *The ship seemed to have vanished completely.*

vanish forever *Their traditional way of life may soon vanish forever.*

simply/just vanish *There was no sign of any people - they had all just vanished.*

suddenly/quickly vanish *The man suddenly vanished into the crowd.*

mysteriously vanish (=in a way that cannot be explained) *Amelia Earhart's plane mysteriously vanished somewhere over the South Pacific.*

PREPOSITIONS

vanish from somewhere *These birds have almost vanished from the wild.*

PHRASES

vanish without (a) trace (=disappear completely) *The driver of the car had vanished without a trace.*

vanish from sight/view *She turned a corner and vanished from sight.*

vanish into thin air (=suddenly and completely disappear) *My wallet had vanished into thin air.*

vanish from the face of the earth (=no longer exist anywhere on the earth) *Nobody really knows why the dinosaurs vanished from the face of the earth.*

sth has all but vanished (=almost stopped existing) *The community my grandparents grew up in has all but vanished.*

vanish into the darkness/night/mist/fog *As mysteriously as he had appeared, he vanished into the night.*

> **THESAURUS: vanish**
> vanish, go away, fade (away), melt away, die out → **disappear**

variation Ac *n*

a difference between similar things, or a change from the usual amount or form of something

ADJECTIVES

great/huge/wide variation *There is a wide variation in the colour of the fruit.*

considerable/significant variation *At this age children's language ability shows considerable variation.*

minor/slight/small variation *We noticed some slight variations in the test results, but nothing significant.*

possible variation *There are several possible variations on the basic plan.*

individual variation *Their average intake is 1,500 calories, but there is great individual variation.*

local variation *In the last election local variations in the way people vote could clearly be seen.*

regional/geographical variation *The research shows that regional variations exist as regards what people eat.*

seasonal variation (=variations between different times of the year) *The research studied seasonal variation in the number of people who caught the disease.*

genetic variation (=variation caused by genes) *Biologists are interested in the genetic variation between people.*

VERBS

there is some variation *There is some variation in size.*

variation occurs/exists *formal* (=there is some variation) *Variations in price occur across the country.*

cause variation *Many factors cause variations in the weather.*

show variation *The test results show considerable variation in ability among the students.*

find variation *We found a wide variation in people's opinions.*

study variation *She is studying regional variations in pronunciation of certain words.*

explain variation (*also* **account for variation** *formal*): *How can the variations in behaviour be explained?*

NOUNS + variation

a temperature variation *Astronauts wear special suits to protect themselves from extreme temperature variations.*

a price variation *The report shows gas price variations within the state.*

PREPOSITIONS

a variation in sth *We expect seasonal variations in the number of passengers.*

a variation of sth *He played us a few variations of the song.*

a variation on sth *The chef came up with a new variation on a traditional recipe.*

a variation between sth *There is a lot of variation between individuals when it comes to height.*

a variation among sth *There is some variation among cultures regarding the age at which a child is considered adult.*

varied Ac *adj*

consisting of or including many different kinds of things or people, especially in a way that seems interesting

ADVERBS

widely/highly varied (=very varied) *We offer a widely varied range of activities. | His musical tastes are highly varied.*

richly varied (=varied in many different ways) *England is a richly varied country.*

NOUNS

a varied range/selection *This book offers a varied selection of realistic business English writing tasks.*

a varied diet *Experts agree that a varied diet is the key to good health.*

a varied career *He had a long and varied career.*

varied needs *Teachers have to consider the varied needs of their students.*

a varied group *The exhibition will show a wide range of works by a varied group of artists.*

a varied collection *The zoo has a varied collection of animals.*

varied forms *Discrimination can take many varied forms.*

a varied programme *BrE*, **a varied program** *AmE*: *She entertained the audience with a varied programme of songs.*

PHRASES

rich and varied *She has led a rich and varied life.*

many and varied *His interests are many and varied.*

variety *n*

1 a lot of things of the same type that are different from each other in some way

ADJECTIVES

a wide/great/large variety *Our school has students from a wide variety of backgrounds.*

a huge/enormous variety *Fruit is eaten by a huge variety of animals and birds.*

an infinite/endless variety (=that seems never to end) *There is a seemingly infinite variety of beers to choose from.*

a rich variety (=of many interesting types) *A rich variety of plants grow here.*

a bewildering variety (=so many that you feel confused) *There is a bewildering variety of software available.*

an amazing variety *The market has an amazing variety of fresh fish.*

sheer variety (=used when emphasizing that

V

there are lots of different types) *It is the sheer variety of Italian cuisine that makes it so special.*

VERBS

offer a variety of sth *The college offers a variety of courses.*

contain a variety of sth *There is a library containing a variety of books.*

include a variety of sth *Researchers took care to include a variety of women in their study.*

cover a variety of sth (=deal with a lot of different types of things) *The book covers a variety of topics.*

PREPOSITIONS

a variety of sth *A variety of techniques were used.*

2 if something has variety, it seems interesting because it contains several different things, and is not always the same

VERBS

add/give/bring variety to sth (=make something seem more interesting because it contains different things, not just the same thing) *Add variety to your exercise routine by trying new sports.*

have variety *I wanted a job that had more variety.*

lack variety *His films lack variety – they always seem to have the same plot.*

3 a particular type of thing

ADJECTIVES

a new variety *A new variety of banana has been developed.*

a rare/unusual variety *She is suffering from a very rare variety of the disease.*

a common variety *The most common variety of wild rat is the Norway rat.*

different varieties *They have a huge selection of wines, with over 500 different varieties on offer.*

NOUNS + variety

a grape/crop/apple etc variety *Different grape varieties produce wines of different characters.*

a language variety (=a type of a language spoken in a particular area) *British and American English are different varieties of English.*

PREPOSITIONS

a variety of sth *The lake has more than 20 varieties of fish.*

vary Ac *v*

to be different from each other, or different in different places, situations etc

ADVERBS

vary considerably/greatly/widely *The amount of food available varies considerably from season to season.*

vary enormously *Farm sizes vary enormously within Europe.*

vary significantly *The software is the same, but performance can vary significantly on different machines.*

vary wildly (=a lot) *Prices varied wildly from store to store.*

vary slightly *The cooking time may vary slightly depending on your oven.*

NOUNS

varying degrees *She was involved in a number of car accidents of varying degrees of seriousness.*

varying levels *Children with varying levels of ability can still be taught together.*

varying sizes *Make sure you have pieces of wood of varying sizes to keep your fire going.*

varying amounts *Fruits contain varying amounts of natural sugar.*

PREPOSITIONS

vary in size/shape/quality etc *The hotel's bedrooms vary in size.*

vary between things/people *Guidelines on internet use vary between companies.*

vary with/according to sth *The method of training varies with the type of work involved.*

PHRASES

vary from place to place/person to person/year to year etc *The acidity of soil varies from place to place.*

vary from 10 to 100/25 cm to 60 cm etc *The temperature of the water in the river varies from 65°F to 86°F.*

vary between 10 and 100/25 cm and 60 cm etc *The castle had walls varying between three and four feet in thickness.*

vast *adj* THESAURUS ▶ huge

vegetable *n*

a plant such as a potato or cabbage that is eaten raw or cooked

ADJECTIVES/NOUNS + vegetable

fresh vegetables *Fresh vegetables taste best just after they have been picked.*

raw vegetables *Some vegetables are better eaten raw.*

organic vegetables (=grown without using chemicals) *Most supermarkets sell organic fruit and vegetables.*

green vegetables *Eat plenty of green vegetables.*

leafy vegetables *Leafy vegetables contain iron.*

root vegetables (=vegetables whose roots you eat, such as carrots) *Excellent soups can be made from root vegetables.*

salad vegetables (=that you eat raw in a salad) *You can buy ready-prepared salad vegetables.*

canned vegetables (*also* **tinned vegetables** *BrE*): *Do canned vegetables have as many vitamins as fresh ones?*

frozen vegetables *There are packets of frozen vegetables in the freezer.*

baby vegetables (=vegetables that are eaten before having grown to their full size) *Baby vegetables can be delicious, but it is important not to overcook them.*

VERBS

grow vegetables *If we had a garden, we could grow our own vegetables.*

vegetable + NOUNS

vegetable soup *I think I'll have the vegetable soup.*

vegetable oil *She uses vegetable oil instead of butter.*

a vegetable garden/patch/plot (=where you grow vegetables) *Anna was digging in the vegetable garden.*

PHRASES

fruit and vegetables *They buy fruit and vegetables at the market.*

vegetarian *n, adj*

someone who does not eat meat or fish

NOUNS

a vegetarian restaurant *There are some good vegetarian restaurants in New York.*

a vegetarian dish/meal *They have a small selection of vegetarian dishes on the menu.*

a vegetarian diet *Research shows that a vegetarian diet is good for your health.*

ADJECTIVES

a strict vegetarian *A strict vegetarian wouldn't eat fish.*

VERBS

become (a) vegetarian *More and more people are becoming vegetarian.*

PHRASES

sth is suitable for vegetarians *Is this soup suitable for vegetarians?*

vehicle *n formal*

a car, bus, truck, or similar machine

ADJECTIVES/NOUNS + vehicle

a motor vehicle (=a car, truck etc) *The company is a leading manufacturer of motor vehicles.*

a heavy goods vehicle (=a large truck) *Drivers of heavy goods vehicles need a special licence.*

an off-road vehicle (=designed for driving on rough ground) *Most off-road vehicles are fitted with bigger tyres.*

a commercial vehicle (=used for business) *We sell vans, trucks, and other commercial vehicles.*

a stolen vehicle *Police have found the stolen vehicle.*

an abandoned vehicle *The abandoned vehicle is thought to have been used in the robbery.*

a parked vehicle (*also* **a stationary vehicle** *formal*): *The bomb was hidden in a parked vehicle.*

an oncoming vehicle (=a vehicle moving towards you) *I was dazzled by the lights of an oncoming vehicle.*

a military vehicle *There have been attacks on military vehicles in the area.*

an armoured vehicle *BrE*, **an armored vehicle** *AmE* (=with thick metal to protect it from bullets and bombs) *Their armoured vehicle was hit by a bomb.*

VERBS + vehicle

drive a vehicle *Driving a vehicle while drunk is a serious crime.*

park a vehicle *The driver had parked the vehicle near traffic lights.*

hire/rent a vehicle *Customers may want to hire their own vehicle.*

own a vehicle *Police are asking who owns the vehicle.*

stop a vehicle *The driver stopped the vehicle outside the bank.*

vehicle + VERBS

a vehicle breaks down (=stops working) *Police helped the driver of a vehicle that had broken down on the motorway.*

a vehicle collides with sth (*also* **a vehicle crashes into sth**) (=hits something by accident) *Her vehicle collided with a tree.*

vehicle + NOUNS

vehicle emissions (=gases from vehicles' engines) *The new engines are designed to reduce vehicle emissions.*

vehicle crime *Police are pleased that vehicle crime has come down.*

vengeance *n*

the act of doing something harmful to someone because they harmed you

VERBS

take vengeance on sb (*also* **wreak/exact vengeance on sb** *formal*) (=do something harmful to someone, because they have harmed you) *He decided to take vengeance on his wife's killer.*

swear/vow vengeance on/against sb *formal*: *At that moment she swore vengeance on her enemies.*

seek vengeance on/against sb *formal*: *The main character seeks vengeance against his former business partner.*

ADJECTIVES

a terrible vengeance *He exacts a terrible vengeance on his daughter's murderer.*

PHRASES

an act of vengeance *The man smashed his boss's car in an act of vengeance.*

venomous *adj* THESAURUS **poisonous**

V

venture *n*

a new business activity that involves taking risks

ADJECTIVES

a commercial/business venture *Companies have less money for business ventures than they used to have.*

sb's new/latest venture *Her latest commercial venture is a new Chinese restaurant.*

a joint venture (=by two or more businesses, working together) *The new service is a joint venture between two software companies.*

a successful/profitable venture *Running an internet company can be a highly profitable venture.*

a failed/unsuccessful venture *The organisation couldn't survive another failed venture.*

an ambitious/bold venture *The new magazine is another ambitious venture by the millionaire businessman.*

a private venture (=using money from people and businesses, not the government) *The airport is operated as a private venture.*

a financial/money-making venture *As a successful businessman, he's always looking for other money-making ventures.*

VERBS

set up/start/launch a venture *Banks can give advice on setting up new business ventures.*

undertake/embark on a venture *formal* (=start a new venture) *The company can't undertake another major venture at the moment.*

fund/finance/support a venture (*also* **invest in a venture**) (=provide money for it) *They need other businesses to help fund the venture.*

join in a venture/enter into a venture *We're joining in the venture with several local groups.*

venture + NOUNS

venture capital/funds/funding (=money used for new business ideas) *Banks are making more venture capital available.*

a venture capitalist (=someone who lends money to people who are starting new businesses) *The company is having talks with a venture capitalist.*

venture partners *They can't sign a contract without speaking to their venture partners.*

venue *n*

a place where a concert, party, sports event etc takes place

ADJECTIVES

a popular venue *The hotel is a popular wedding venue.*

a suitable venue *We discussed suitable venues for the meeting.*

an ideal/perfect venue *The hall is an ideal venue for a birthday party.*

a big/large venue *A huge event like a conference requires a large venue.*

a major venue *Stadiums have now become major venues for rock concerts.*

top/premier venue (=most important venue) *The game will be played at the country's premier sports venue.*

a small/intimate venue (=with space for only a small audience) *The band plays jazz clubs and other intimate venues.*

NOUNS + venue

a music/concert venue *The hall makes an excellent music venue.*

a sports/sporting venue *The stadium is the most impressive sporting venue in the country.*

an entertainment venue *A singer of his standard will demand a top-class entertainment venue.*

a conference/exhibition venue *The hotel is also widely used as a conference venue.*

a wedding venue *Church halls can make perfectly good wedding venues.*

VERBS

book/hire/arrange a venue *First set a date for the wedding and then book the venue.*

find/choose a venue *Choosing a venue for such a large party will be difficult.*

change the venue for sth *We had to change the venue for the meeting.*

PREPOSITIONS

a venue for sth *We couldn't find a suitable venue for the meeting.*

at a venue *There were a lot of people at the venue.*

verb *n*

a word that is used to say what someone or something does, for example 'come' or 'see'

ADJECTIVES

a transitive verb (=needing an object) *'Produce' is a transitive verb.*

an intransitive verb (=not needing an object) *'Bleed' is an intransitive verb.*

a regular/irregular verb (=following a regular pattern, or not following one) *I try to learn the forms of all the irregular verbs.*

an active verb (=with the person or thing doing the action as the subject) *Active verbs make your writing lively, personal, and direct.*

a passive verb (=with the person or thing that the action is done to as the subject) *Passive verbs are used a lot in scientific writing.*

a singular/plural verb (=showing whether the subject is one thing or person or more) *In British English, you can use a singular verb or a plural verb after 'team'.*

a main verb *If a sentence does not have a main verb, it is not a full sentence.*

a finite verb (=showing tense) *'Was' is a finite verb.*

an auxiliary verb (=a verb that is used with another verb, for example to form a tense) *In*

English the auxiliary verbs are 'be', 'do', and 'have'.

a linking verb (=a verb that connects the subject of a sentence with a word that describes the subject) *In the sentence 'They look silly', 'look' is a linking verb.*

a modal verb (=a verb such as 'can' or 'may' that is used with other verbs to express possibility, permission, intention etc) *'May' and 'might' are modal verbs.*

a phrasal verb (=a verb with an adverb or preposition after it, for example 'set off' or 'look after') *The phrasal verb 'give up' has several different meanings.*

verb + NOUNS

a verb form *You have to choose the appropriate verb form.*

a verb ending (=the end part of a verb, which changes to show tense or person) *The regular past tense verb ending in English is '-ed'.*

VERBS

a verb agrees with the subject *In Arabic, all verbs agree with their subjects in gender and number.*

a verb inflects (=has different forms, for example to show tense and number) *Greek verbs inflect for tense, person, and number.*

PHRASES

the subject of a verb (=the noun or pronoun that comes before it) *In the sentence 'I like pizza', 'I' is the subject of the verb.*

the object of a verb (=the noun or pronoun that comes after it) *'The ball' is the object of the verb in 'I hit the ball.'*

verbal *adj* THESAURUS ▸ spoken

verdict *n*

1 an official decision made in a court of law about whether or not someone is guilty or about how someone died

ADJECTIVES/NOUNS + verdict

the final verdict *He was not in court to hear the final verdict.*

a unanimous verdict (=the whole jury agrees) *The jury found him guilty by a unanimous verdict.*

a majority verdict *BrE* (=most of the jury agrees) *They were finding it difficult to reach a majority verdict.*

a guilty/not guilty verdict *Everyone was expecting a guilty verdict.*

an open verdict *BrE* (=stating that the facts about someone's death are not known) *As there was no medical evidence on the cause of death, he recorded an open verdict.*

VERBS

arrive at/reach a verdict (=agree on a decision) *It took the jury 16 hours to reach a verdict.*

return/give/announce/deliver a verdict (=officially say what it is) *The jury returned a verdict of unlawful killing.*

record a verdict (=officially say what it is – used especially about the cause of someone's death) *The coroner recorded a verdict of accidental death on all four victims.*

consider your verdict (=think about what it should be) *The jury retired to consider their verdict.*

appeal (against) a verdict (=formally ask for it to be changed) *His lawyers will almost certainly appeal against the verdict.*

overturn a verdict (=officially say that it was wrong) *He was convicted of spying, but the verdict was later overturned.*

uphold a verdict (=officially say that it was right) *This verdict was upheld at the appeal court.*

PREPOSITIONS

a verdict of sth *He recorded a verdict of accidental death.*

a verdict against sb *The appeal court overturned the verdict against him.*

2 someone's opinion about something after they have seen what it is like

ADJECTIVES

sb's final verdict *The audience's final verdict was encouraging.*

a unanimous verdict (=one that everyone agrees about) *The unanimous verdict was that it was an excellent hotel.*

a favourable verdict *BrE*, **a favorable verdict** *AmE* (=people think something is good) *They are hoping for a favourable verdict when their cooking skills are judged next week.*

a damning verdict (=people think something is bad) *Inspectors gave a damning verdict on the school.*

VERBS

give a verdict *Visitors have been giving their verdict on the new parking charges.*

get a verdict *He went to get the players' verdict on the game.*

PREPOSITIONS

sb's verdict on sth *What's your verdict on the movie?*

versatile *adj*

having many different skills or uses

ADVERBS

highly/extremely/incredibly versatile *He is a highly versatile musician and can play a range of instruments.*

NOUNS

a versatile performer/actor/musician/player *She is a versatile actress who has played a wide range of roles.*

a versatile design *The car's versatile design*

means that it can be used for a variety of purposes.

a versatile system *We needed a more versatile software system.*

version Ac *n*

one form of a story, piece of writing, piece of software etc

ADJECTIVES/NOUNS + version

a new version *They are working on a new version of a Greek play.*

the old version *You couldn't do this with the old version of the software.*

the final version *The final version of the report omitted these criticisms.*

a different version *The two groups listened to different versions of the story.*

the original/first version *The original version was in Latin but later editions were in English.*

an earlier/later version *The president vetoed an earlier version of the bill.*

the latest version *The company will soon release the latest version of its network operating system.*

a modern version *He created the modern version of baseball.*

an online/electronic version *They are developing an online version of the magazine.*

the film/television version (=a film or programme based on a book or play) *He appeared in the film version of 'Harry Potter and the Half-Blood Prince'.*

a cover version (=a recording of a song that was originally recorded by someone else) *She has just released a cover version of the Beatles' song 'Help!'*

an improved/better version *The manufacturers come up with new improved versions each year.*

a modified version *The company later produced a modified version of the aircraft.*

a revised version (=a changed version of something written) *In a revised version of the script, this scene was cut.*

an updated version (=changed to include the latest information) *An updated version of the 'Best Restaurant' guide has just been published.*

a simplified version *This simplified version of Shakespeare's play is intended for younger children.*

an abridged version (=a shorter version of a piece of writing) *'Reader's Digest' published abridged versions of many popular novels.*

the full version *You can read the full version of this article online.*

the unabridged version (=not shortened – used when this version is long) *We read the unabridged version of 'Moby Dick'.*

the uncut version (=used about a film that includes parts that were not in the film when it was shown in cinemas) *We watched the uncut version of the film 'Blade Runner'.*

VERBS

produce/make a version *They produced a new version of the software.*

create a version *People can create a version of themselves online.*

develop a version *We are developing an electronic version of the dictionary.*

PREPOSITIONS

a version of sth *This is a version of the card game Trumps.*

very *adv* to a great degree

ADJECTIVES

very good/big/happy/tired etc *I thought it was a very good idea.*

very few/little *In those days, very few people had telephones.*

the very best/worst/poorest/simplest etc *We use the very best materials that are available.*

ADVERBS

very much *I liked the town very much.*

very well/quickly/often etc *The fire spread very quickly.*

very very... especially spoken: *I'm feeling very very tired.*

⚠ Don't use **very** with adjectives that already mean "very". For example, don't say 'It was very huge/terrible/terrifying/fascinating/delicious'. Just say **It was huge/terrible/terrifying/fascinating/delicious** or **It was absolutely huge/terrible/terrifying/fascinating/delicious**.

Using other words apart from very

Students overuse **very**, because it is the safe word to use. It can make your writing sound more authoritative if you can use another adverb such as **highly** or **deeply**, with the right adjective.

THESAURUS: very

highly

successful | popular | profitable | desirable | unlikely | unusual | likely | probable | significant | important | skilled | intelligent | respected | educated | effective | efficient | reliable | complex | sensitive | dangerous | risky | toxic | suspicious | critical

very – used with these adjectives:

Now Williams is a highly successful businessman. | Was he a terrorist? It seemed highly unlikely. | These findings are highly significant. | US scientists have developed highly effective treatments for many diseases. | This waste is highly dangerous and can be damaging to the local environment.

V

deeply
concerned | worried | disturbed | troubled | shocked | saddened | upset | unhappy | ashamed | embarrassed | involved | committed | unpopular | suspicious | grateful | interested | influenced | divided | moving | worrying | disturbing | troubling | shocking | offensive
very – used with these adjectives:
She is deeply concerned about the health of her unborn baby. | He became deeply involved in politics at university. | The war has been deeply unpopular in this country. | I found the film deeply moving.

> **Deeply** or **highly?**
> **Deeply** is often used when your emotions are strongly affected by something. You say that you are ***deeply*** *concerned/saddened/shocked etc*, or that something is ***deeply*** *moving/worrying/offensive etc.*
> **Highly** often has a more positive feeling than **deeply**. For example, you say that something is ***highly*** *successful/important*, or that someone is ***highly*** *intelligent/educated/respected*. On the other hand, **highly** is also used when saying that something is very unusual or dangerous.

absolutely
right | correct | free | essential | vital | crucial | necessary | sure | certain | delicious | brilliant | gorgeous | fantastic | ridiculous | terrible | awful | impossible
used with adjectives that already contain the meaning 'very', for example **delicious** or **awful**, and with other adjectives that cannot be graded, for example **necessary** or **free**:
You are, of course, absolutely right. | It is absolutely essential to wear a helmet. | The cake tastes absolutely delicious. | Heavy snow made travel by road absolutely impossible.

truly
remarkable | amazing | magnificent | spectacular | memorable | astonishing | sorry | happy | grateful | honoured
really – used especially with adjectives that mean very impressive or good, or when saying that you are very sorry or happy:
Winning five gold medals was a truly remarkable achievement. | There is some truly spectacular scenery. | I'm truly grateful to him for what he has done.

greatly
encouraged | distressed | relieved | disappointed | surprised | influenced
a lot – used with adjectives ending in **-ed** and past participles:
They are greatly encouraged by the success of the scheme. | I was greatly relieved when the trip was canceled. | He was greatly influenced by Picasso.

veteran *adj* THESAURUS **experienced**

veto[1] *v*
to officially refuse to allow something that other people have agreed

NOUNS

veto legislation/a bill (=stop something becoming a law) *The president could still veto the bill.*

veto a plan/idea/proposal *It only needs a single member to veto the plan.*

veto a measure (=veto something that has been planned) *Council leaders are intending to veto the measure.*

veto a decision *She can veto any decision the committee takes.*

veto a budget *The leader of the council might veto their budget.*

VERBS

threaten to veto sth *A number of senators have threatened to veto the proposal.*

PHRASES

have the power/right to veto sth *Does the chairman have the right to veto any decision?*

veto[2] *n*
an official refusal to allow something, or the right to do this

VERBS

use your veto (*also* **exercise your veto** *formal*): *Russia used its veto to reject the plan.*

PHRASES

the power/right of veto *The president has the right of veto over any legislation.*

viable *adj*
something that is viable is able to be successful

ADVERBS

economically/commercially/financially viable (=producing enough money, or not costing too much money) *New projects must be economically viable.*

NOUNS

a viable alternative *We want to make public transport a viable alternative to using cars.*

a viable option *Moving the company was not a viable option.*

a viable solution *Perhaps the only viable solution is to merge the hospitals.*

a viable method/means/way of doing sth *In some cities the traffic is so bad that cycling is the only really viable means of transport.*

a viable proposition (=something that may be

or is successful) *Winter tourism is not a viable proposition for us.*

a viable business *He turned the farm into a viable business.*

a viable plan/strategy *They have failed to come up with a viable plan.*

a viable candidate *He remains the only viable candidate the party has.*

vibrant *adj* THESAURUS ▸ **bright (2)**

vicious *adj* THESAURUS ▸ **cruel (1)**

victim *n*

someone who something bad happens to

ADJECTIVES

an innocent victim *Children are the innocent victims of war.*

an unfortunate/hapless victim *He was the unfortunate victim of a computer error.*

a helpless/passive victim *The people are seen as passive victims of their government's decisions.*

an unsuspecting/unwitting victim (=not realizing what is happening) *He crept up behind his unsuspecting victim.*

the intended victim *The police believe that it was his brother who was the intended victim.*

NOUNS + victim

a crime/murder/rape etc victim *The parents of the murder victim said they were glad her killer had been caught.*

an accident/crash victim *The crash victims were rushed to hospital.*

a flood/earthquake/tsunami etc victim *Earthquake victims were living in tents in the city's parks.*

a famine victim (=someone in a place where there is too little food to eat) *Aid is being shipped to famine victims.*

a cancer/AIDS etc victim *He helped raise money for AIDS victims.*

VERBS

fall victim to sb/sth (=be harmed by someone or something) *Thousands of people fall victim to internet criminals every day.*

portray sb as a victim (=show someone as a victim) *She was portrayed as the victim of a loveless marriage.*

blame the victim (=say that someone is responsible for bad things that happen to them) *Asking a woman what she did to provoke an attack is blaming the victim.*

victim + NOUNS

a victim mentality/culture (=when someone always thinks of themselves as a victim) *Many of us fall into a victim mentality, and blame all our troubles on other people.*

PREPOSITIONS

a victim of sth *At least half the students know someone who has been the victim of violence.*

PHRASES

a victim of circumstance (=someone who suffers because of something they cannot control) *She was a victim of circumstance, born at a time when women had no power.*

be/become a victim of your own success (=suffer in some way as a result of being successful) *The festival has become a victim of its own success and it is difficult to find a place that is big enough.*

victorious *adj* THESAURUS ▸ **successful (2)**

victory *n*

a situation in which you win a battle, game, election, or dispute

ADJECTIVES/NOUNS + victory

a great/major victory *The British army won a great victory.*

an easy victory *The team were expecting an easy victory over their opponents.*

a decisive victory (=definite and clear) *The battle was a decisive victory for the US.*

a landslide victory (=won by a very large number of votes in an election) *The Democrats won by a landslide victory.*

a crushing victory (=defeating your opponent by a very large amount) *Australia won a crushing 139-run victory over the West Indies.*

a narrow victory (=won by a small amount) *A general election produced a narrow victory for the People's Progressive Party.*

a surprise victory *He is £1 million richer after his surprise victory in a TV talent show.*

an election/electoral victory *The Democrats were celebrating their election victory.*

a military victory *Napoleon won many military victories.*

a moral victory (=showing that your beliefs are right, even if you lose the argument) *The victims' families claimed the verdict as a moral victory.*

VERBS

win/score a victory *Today we have won an important victory.*

lead sb to victory *She led her team to victory in the finals.*

clinch (a) victory (=finally win) *Adams scored a last-minute goal to clinch victory.*

pull off a victory (=win when it is difficult) *Martin pulled off a surprise victory in the semi-final.*

sweep to victory (=win easily) *Nixon swept to victory by 47 million votes to 29 million.*

scent victory (=know that you could win soon) *Faldo is ruthless when he scents victory.*

taste victory (=know what it is like to win) *He tasted victory on only two occasions as England captain.*

celebrate a victory *They celebrated their victory by drinking all night.*

victory + NOUNS

victory celebrations *The victory celebrations went on all night.*

a victory parade *They intend to hold a victory parade.*

a victory speech *In his victory speech, he thanked his team.*

a victory lap (=when a winning runner or player runs around the playing area) *He then took a victory lap around the arena.*

PREPOSITIONS

a victory over sb *It was Murray's first victory over Federer.*

a victory against sb *He once scored three goals in a 5–2 victory against Ireland.*

a victory for sb *The court's decision represents a victory for all women.*

a victory in sth *Victory in the World Cup is something all football teams dream of.*

PHRASES

a string of victories (=a series of victories) *The team won a string of victories.*

video *n*

moving pictures of someone or something, which are recorded

NOUNS + video

a music/pop video *He has directed several music videos for top British bands.*

a wedding video *Many couples have a wedding video as well as photographs.*

VERBS

record sth on video *She had no idea that the interview was being recorded on video.*

make/shoot a video *They made a video of the performance.*

be captured/caught on video (=recorded on video) *The crime was captured on video.*

watch a video *They were at home that evening, watching a video.*

show/play a video *The students were shown a video of an experiment.*

rewind/fast-forward a video (=so that you can see an earlier or later part) *I rewound the video and watched the beginning of the film again.*

download/upload a video *She filmed her friends singing and then uploaded the video onto the internet.*

stream video (=play it on your computer while you are downloading it) *How fast a connection do you need to stream video?*

video + NOUNS

a video camera/video equipment *The reporters used a secret video camera.*

a video screen/monitor *The game was shown live on a giant video screen.*

a video image *Video images of the volcanic eruption were broadcast.*

a video recording *Can a video recording of a police interview be used in a court as evidence?*

a video clip (=a short video) *You can download video clips from the internet.*

video footage (=a piece of video film) *Police are currently studying video footage to identify the rioters.*

video evidence (=a recording of events, used in a court) *Video evidence of illegal activities can later be used in court.*

a video diary (=a record someone makes of their activities on video) *While on the trip, he kept a video diary.*

a video message *She was unable to attend the awards ceremony, but she had recorded a video message.*

a video game *Many kids sit and play video games all day.*

a video recorder (=for recording television programmes or showing videos) *I set my video recorder so that I could watch my favourite programmes when I got back from holiday.*

PREPOSITIONS

on video *His performance is on video.*

view[1] *n*

1 an opinion

ADJECTIVES

political views *Throughout his long life, his political views have not changed.*

sb's personal view *My own personal view is that the plan will succeed.*

a widely held view (=a view that many people have) *There is a widely held view that young people eat too much junk food.*

the general view (=what most people think) *The general view is that the government could do more to help poor people.*

strongly/deeply held views (=strong views that someone is unwilling to change) *He is known for his strongly held views on modern art.*

conflicting/opposing views (=completely different views) *There are conflicting views about the best way to teach reading.*

extreme/extremist views *She was a politician with extreme views on immigration.*

strong views *Teachers usually have strong views on education.*

traditional/old-fashioned views *They have very traditional views about the role of women.*

different views *Different people have different views about fairness.*

a view is popular/unpopular *The view that girls are cleverer than boys has become increasingly popular.*

right-wing/left-wing views *She belongs to a political group with extreme left-wing views.*

VERBS + view

tell sb your views/let sb have your views *We want customers to tell us their views.*

V

air your views (=tell someone in public about your views, especially when you may want to complain or disagree) *There was a meeting, at which local people were allowed to air their views about the new airport.*

express/give a view (*also* **articulate/present a view** *formal*) (=say what you think) *The politician expressed a view that is held by many people.*

have/hold a view (*also* **subscribe to a view** *formal*): *He has very strange views about people from other cultures.*

take a view (=make a decision based on your opinion) *The government took the view that the law should be changed.*

a view is shared (=people agree with it) *The views of the manager are not shared by most workers.*

reflect/represent the view of sb (=show what someone's view is) *The article reflects the views of many young people.*

challenge/reject/oppose a view (=say that you disagree) *Our organisation challenges the government's view that the problem is not serious.*

welcome/invite/seek views (=ask people to give their views) *We're inviting views from people who regularly use the service.*

affect sb's view (*also* **colour/shape sb's view** *formal*): *His years in prison have clearly shaped his views on the justice system.*

support a view (=agree with it) *It is worrying that many people support his racist views.*

discuss/exchange views *Meetings are a chance for members to exchange views.*

hear a view (*also* **listen to a view**) *The committee will be hearing people's views on a range of subjects.*

view + VERBS

sb's view changes *When did your views on education change?*

sb's view differs from sth *My own view differs from that of the previous speaker.*

PREPOSITIONS

views about/on sth *What are your views on the money paid to footballers?*

according to a view *According to this view, there is no such thing as bad publicity.*

PHRASES

in my view (=used when giving your opinion) *In my view, the system needs to be improved.*

an exchange of views (=when people say what they think, especially when they disagree) *There was a frank exchange of views at the meeting.*

be consistent with a view *formal* (=contain ideas that are similar to a view) *The decision was consistent with the minister's view that the country needs more troops.*

be of the same view *formal* (=agree) *All members of the panel were of the same view.*

2 the things that you can see from a place

ADJECTIVES/NOUNS + view

a good/great/fabulous view *From here we get a good view of the castle.*

a breathtaking/wonderful view *The hotel also offers breathtaking views of the palace.*

a panoramic view (=when you can see in many directions) *There was a spectacular panoramic view from the top of the hill.*

a sea/ocean view (=a view of the sea) *I'd like a room with a sea view.*

a mountain view (=a view of mountains) *We loved the clean air and the mountain views.*

VERBS

enjoy/admire the view (*also* **take in the view**) *They sat enjoying the view down the valley.*

⚠ Don't say 'watch the view'.

spoil the view (=make it look bad) *Some local people think the tower spoils the view.*

have/give a view (*also* **afford/command/boast a view** *formal*): *The dining room had an excellent view of the river.*

PREPOSITIONS

a view across/over sth *The restaurant has fabulous views over the river.*

the view from sth *Everyone admires the view from this window.*

view² *v formal*

to have a particular opinion or attitude

Grammar
Often passive.

ADVERBS

view sth favourably/positively (=think it is good or acceptable) *I think the committee will view her suggestion favourably.*

view sth unfavourably/negatively *formal* (=think it is bad or unacceptable) *Any school would view such violent behaviour very unfavourably.*

view sth objectively (=without personal feelings affecting your opinion) *You should try to view the situation objectively.*

view sth cautiously/suspiciously *The plan was viewed cautiously by the company.*

be generally/widely viewed as sth (=by many people) *He's widely viewed as the best player on the team.*

be traditionally/historically viewed as sth *Britain has been traditionally viewed as a rich country.*

view sth largely/primarily as sth *The event was viewed largely as a success.*

VERBS

tend to view sth *Teenagers tend to view their parents as old-fashioned.*

try to view sth *We should try to view the problem differently.*

PHRASES

view sth with dismay (=think it is sad) *Her recent behaviour was viewed with dismay.*

view sth with concern (=be worried about it) *News of her disappearance is being viewed with concern.*

view sth with alarm/horror (=be shocked or upset by it) *News of the attack was viewed with horror.*

view sth with caution/suspicion (=think it might not be good) *The first results are positive but we should still view them with caution.*

sth depends on how you view sth *The result of the election depends on how people view the present government.*

viewed from sb's perspective *Viewed from a child's perspective, the courtroom is a frightening place.*

viewpoint *n*

a way of thinking about something

ADJECTIVES

a different/alternative viewpoint (*also* **another viewpoint**) *Managers wanted a longer working day but staff had another viewpoint altogether.*

a particular viewpoint *The report doesn't express any particular viewpoint.*

a personal viewpoint *She's adopting a purely personal viewpoint in her article.*

a scientific/political viewpoint *Let's consider the situation from a political viewpoint.*

a critical viewpoint *He looks at the issue from a very critical viewpoint.*

VERBS

have/hold a viewpoint (*also* **take/adopt a viewpoint**) *Other people may hold a different viewpoint from mine.*

express/offer/present a viewpoint *She expressed this viewpoint in a letter to the local newspaper.*

share a viewpoint (=have the same viewpoint as someone else) *I'm afraid I don't share your viewpoint on this issue.*

reflect/represent a viewpoint (=show that you have a viewpoint) *Does the statement represent the viewpoint of all the workers?*

NOUNS + viewpoint

the majority viewpoint (=the viewpoint that most people have) *One member of the team does not share the majority viewpoint.*

PREPOSITIONS

from a viewpoint *Seen from a child's viewpoint, the situation looks very different.*

sb's viewpoint on sth *What is the church's viewpoint on the issue of abortion?*

PHRASES

be written from a particular viewpoint *The story is written from a religious viewpoint.*

tell a story from a particular viewpoint *He tells the story from the viewpoint of a foreign visitor.*

vigorous *adj*

using a lot of energy and strength or determination

NOUNS

vigorous exercise/activity *Try to do 20 minutes of vigorous exercise every day.*

a vigorous campaign *There was a vigorous campaign by local people to stop the new airport.*

vigorous debate *There needs to be open and vigorous debate about the future of our country.*

a vigorous defence/attack *The prime minister offered a vigorous defence of the government's decision.*

vigorous action/efforts *The college is making vigorous efforts to attract the best teachers.*

vigorous opposition *There has been vigorous opposition to the new law.*

vigorous growth *The company has shown vigorous growth in recent years.*

vigorous competition *There is vigorous competition among students for a place on this course.*

vile *adj* THESAURUS > **terrible**

village *n*

a very small town in the countryside

ADJECTIVES/NOUNS + village

a small/little/tiny village *They come from a small village in Laos.*

a pretty/picturesque/charming village *There are many pretty villages to visit in the area.*

a quiet/sleepy village (=one where there is not a lot of activity) *I had grown up in a sleepy little village and wasn't used to city life.*

a remote/isolated village (=one that is far away from larger towns) *We need to get food aid to the more remote villages.*

an old/ancient village *After an hour, we arrived at the lovely old village of Kinver.*

a quaint village (=old and pretty or interesting) *Tourists come and take photographs of the quaint little villages.*

an unspoiled village (=not made more modern and less attractive) *It was a pleasant unspoiled village with pretty stone cottages.*

a fishing/mining village *The tiny fishing village became a major seaside resort.*

a rural village *Young people from rural villages move to the cities.*

a mountain/hilltop village *The paths lead to picturesque mountain villages.*

a coastal/seaside village *Coastal villages have been battered by storms.*

village + NOUNS

the village hall/school/shop/church *A meeting will be held at the village hall on Tuesday.*

the village green (=an area of grass for everyone to use) *They played cricket on the village green.*

village life (=all the activities in a village) *She had always taken an active part in village life.*

vintage *adj* THESAURUS ▸ **old (1)**

violate *v* THESAURUS ▸ **disobey**

violation Ac *n*

an action in which someone breaks a law, agreement, principle etc

ADJECTIVES/NOUNS + violation

a serious violation *The committee said there had been serious violations of Senate rules.*

a gross violation (=a very serious violation) *The minister had been dismissed for gross violation of arms export controls.*

a clear violation *This is a clear violation of their privacy.*

a flagrant/blatant violation (=a very clear violation that shows someone does not care about a law, agreement etc) *Shooting down a civilian aircraft was a flagrant violation of international law.*

a minor violation *Even minor violations of this principle were punished.*

human rights violations *There have been protests about human rights violations at the prison.*

a traffic violation *Speeding is one of the most common traffic violations.*

a ceasefire violation *Each side accused the other of ceasefire violations.*

VERBS

commit a violation *Several soldiers were suspected of committing human rights violations.*

constitute a violation *formal* (=be a violation) *The actions may constitute a violation of the treaty.*

report a violation *It is your duty to report any violation to the Environmental Protection Agency.*

investigate a violation *The organization is investigating possible human rights violations.*

PREPOSITIONS

in violation of sth *They had fired several missiles, in violation of the ceasefire agreement.*

violence *n*

behaviour that is intended to hurt other people physically

ADJECTIVES

physical violence *They were threatened with physical violence.*

domestic violence (=between a couple in their home) *She left her husband because of domestic violence.*

racial violence (=between people of different racial groups) *There were outbreaks of racial violence in some cities.*

ethnic violence (=between people of different ethnic groups) *Thousands of civilians were killed in ethnic violence in the Congo.*

terrorist violence (=bombs, shooting etc to obtain political demands) *The nation has suffered terrorist violence for many years.*

gratuitous violence (=unnecessary violence in films, on television programmes etc) *These films are full of gratuitous violence.*

mindless violence (=stupid and without any purpose) *His son was the victim of mindless violence by a group of youths.*

escalating/growing violence (=becoming worse) *There have been reports of escalating violence in the region.*

VERBS

use violence *He denied using violence.*

resort to violence (=use it, especially when other methods have failed) *They were willing to resort to violence to achieve their ends.*

threaten violence (=say you will use it) *It is a crime to use or threaten violence to get into a place.*

experience/suffer violence *Some women even suffer physical violence.*

witness violence (=see it) *Many people witnessed the violence.*

incite/provoke violence (=do or say something to cause it) *The opposition leader was accused of inciting violence against the president.*

quell the violence (=stop it) *The National Guard was brought in to quell the violence.*

violence breaks out/erupts/flares (=suddenly starts) *Violence erupted during the demonstration.*

violence escalates (=becomes worse) *The violence escalated as youths turned over a bus and began smashing shop windows.*

PREPOSITIONS

violence against sb *He has a history of violence against women.*

violence towards/toward sb *No type of violence toward another person is acceptable to me.*

violence between sb *Violence between Muslims and Hindus claimed 300 lives.*

PHRASES

an act of violence *There have been many acts of violence during this conflict.*

an outbreak of violence *There was a fresh outbreak of violence on March 24th.*

an end to violence *Politicians on both sides are calling for an end to violence.*

the use of violence *The use of violence is never justified.*

the threat of violence *The threat of violence is often enough to make people hand over their money.*

a victim of violence *She lives in a home for victims of domestic violence.*

violent *adj*

involving or showing actions intended to hurt people physically

NOUNS

(a) violent crime *There has been a big increase in violent crime.*

a violent attack *Her son was the victim of a violent attack.*

a violent protest/demonstration *There were violent demonstrations outside the US embassy.*

a violent clash/confrontation (=a violent fight – used especially in news reports) *There were violent clashes between police and protesters.*

a violent death *The king died a violent death.*

a violent struggle *There was a violent struggle and someone was stabbed.*

a violent incident *Violent incidents such as kidnapping dropped sharply last year.*

violent behaviour (*also* **violent conduct** *formal*): *The fans were arrested for violent behaviour outside a soccer game.*

a violent film/movie/TV programme *Do violent films cause violent behaviour?*

VERBS

turn/become violent *The demonstration turned violent when police arrived.*

PREPOSITIONS

be violent towards/toward sb *He had been violent towards his wife on several occasions.*

THESAURUS: violent

vicious
attack | thug | killer
violent and dangerous, and seeming to enjoy hurting people for no reason:
It was a vicious attack on an unarmed man. | We were surrounded by a gang of vicious thugs, armed with knives (=violent people – used when you strongly disapprove of them). | *French police are trying to find the vicious killer of an elderly couple.*

rough
treatment | handling
using force or violence, but not causing serious injury:
There were complaints about rough treatment by the police. | The teenager's rough handling by the guards was shown on videotape. | Some of the boys were being a bit **rough with** *the younger kids.*

brutal
murder | attack | dictator | crackdown
behaving in a way that is very cruel and violent, and showing no pity:
The judge said that it was a particularly brutal murder. | He was lucky to survive such a brutal attack. | Idi Amin was a brutal dictator. | The government launched a brutal crackdown on the opposition (=they used violence to stop anyone from opposing the government).

savage
attack | killer | killing | fighting | violence
attacking people in a particularly cruel way – used about people and fighting, especially in news reports:
He was sentenced to life in prison for a savage attack on a young boy. | There was savage fighting in the capital Mogadishu.

bloody
war | battle | fighting | conflict | violence
a bloody battle or war is very violent and a lot of people are killed or injured:
The country has just had a bloody civil war. | The Russians were engaged in a bloody battle against the German army. | There has already been five months of bloody violence.

ferocious
attack | defence | battle | gunbattle | dog | beast
a ferocious attack or battle is extremely violent. A ferocious animal is likely to attack people in a very violent way:
It was the most ferocious attack I have ever seen. | The two armies fought a ferocious battle for control of the city. | The house was guarded by two ferocious-looking dogs. | I was frightened that I would be attacked by some ferocious beast (=animal).

fierce
dog | battle | fighting
a fierce animal or person looks frightening and likely to attack people. A fierce battle is very violent:
A fierce dog stood growling at the gate. | A fierce battle broke out, lasting into late Sunday morning. | The bodyguards **looked** *very* **fierce**.

bloodthirsty
story | tale | monster
a bloodthirsty story contains a lot of violent scenes. A bloodthirsty person likes violence or likes watching violence:
The film is a bloodthirsty tale of revenge. | The terrorists are shown as bloodthirsty monsters. | The ancient Britons **were a bloodthirsty lot** (=they were very violent people – a rather informal use).

gory
movie | film | photograph | book | scene
showing or describing injuries, blood, death etc clearly and in detail:

V

She likes watching gory horror movies | The book was too gory for many readers. | The report showed the gory scenes after the crash.

virgin *adj* THESAURUS ▸ **natural (1)**

virtual Ac *adj*

1 very nearly a particular thing

NOUNS

a virtual certainty *It is a virtual certainty that he will win.*

a virtual necessity *In rural areas, a car is a virtual necessity.*

a virtual impossibility *Victory was now a virtual impossibility.*

a virtual standstill (=when almost nothing is moving) *Heavy snow brought the city to a virtual standstill.*

a virtual unknown (=someone who is not very famous) *Most of the actors in the film are virtual unknowns.*

a virtual stranger *I didn't want to give my phone number to a virtual stranger.*

a virtual prisoner (in your own home) *Her illness makes her a virtual prisoner in her own home.*

the virtual disappearance of sth *The report mentions the virtual disappearance of fish from the river due to pollution.*

a virtual absence of sth (=when there is almost none of it) *The virtual absence of jobs in inner cities has caused a lot of social problems.*

virtual collapse *The company was in a state of virtual collapse.*

virtual silence (=when people hardly speak at all) *They drove back home in virtual silence.*

2 made, done, seen etc on the internet or on a computer

NOUNS

virtual reality (=an environment produced by a computer that looks and seems real to the person experiencing it) *He likes playing virtual reality games on his computer.*

a virtual community *Virtual communities allow people from all over the world to communicate with each other.*

a virtual world/environment *'Second Life' is a virtual world in which characters are controlled by people over the internet.*

a virtual gallery/office/library *Welcome to our virtual gallery, where you can find examples of our artists' work.*

THESAURUS: virtual

man-made, synthetic, imitation, fake, false, simulated, virtual → **artificial**

virtue *n*

something that is good about something or someone

ADJECTIVES

a great/considerable virtue *One of the great virtues of this software is that it is very easy to use.*

the traditional/old-fashioned/ancient virtues *The traditional virtues of fair play and loyalty are disappearing from professional sport.*

the main/chief/supreme virtue *The chief virtue of the automobile is the personal independence it gives the owner.*

the simple virtues *The story is about the simple virtues of kindness and friendship.*

a rare virtue *Such honesty is a rare virtue these days.*

the added virtue *This delicious recipe has the added virtue of being extremely simple to make.*

a cardinal virtue *formal* (=very important) *Honesty is a cardinal virtue in this job.*

VERBS

have a virtue (*also* **possess a virtue** *formal*): *The instructions have the virtue of being very clearly written.*

preach/extol/expound the virtues of sth *formal* (=praise them) *She likes to extol the virtues of healthy eating.*

embody the virtues of sth (=be a very good example of something good) *He is someone whose life embodies the virtues of kindness and simplicity.*

PREPOSITIONS

the virtue of sth *The virtue of booking flights early is that you can often get them at a reduced price.*

THESAURUS: virtue

benefit, merit, virtue, the good/great/best thing about sth, the beauty of sth is that → **advantage**

virtuoso *adj* THESAURUS ▸ **skilful**

virtuous *adj* THESAURUS ▸ **good (3)**

virus *n*

1 a very small living thing that causes infectious illnesses

ADJECTIVES/NOUNS + virus

a deadly/killer virus (=that kills people) *A killer virus has already been responsible for the deaths of hundreds of people.*

a nasty virus (=that makes people very ill) *This is a particularly nasty virus.*

a virulent virus (=causing many people to become ill) *The AIDS virus is very virulent.*

the AIDS/flu/polio etc virus *They are trying to stop the spread of the flu virus.*

VERBS

have a virus *Mary had a virus and was not at school that day.*

get/catch a virus (*also* **contract a virus** *formal*): *He does not know when he contracted the virus.*

be infected with/carry a virus (=have a virus, which you may then give to other people) *A nurse at the clinic was found to be carrying the virus.*

be exposed to a virus (=meet it and risk catching it) *Some people who are exposed to the virus will never become ill.*

fight a virus (=have it and be trying to recover from it) *Your body is still trying to fight the virus.*

pass on/transmit a virus (=pass it from one person or animal to another) *The rabies virus is transmitted when one animal bites another.*

recover from a virus *She's at home recovering from a virus.*

a virus causes sth *HIV is the virus that causes AIDS.*

a virus attacks sth *This virus attacks different cells in the body.*

a virus kills sb *The flu virus kills many elderly people every year.*

a virus goes round/spreads *The virus spread throughout the population.*

a virus mutates (=changes slightly) *Viruses can mutate to new forms against which existing vaccines are not effective.*

PHRASES

a strain of a virus (=one type of it) *Doctors fear that a new strain of the virus will appear.*

2 something that can destroy information in a computer

NOUNS + virus

a computer virus *A computer virus made me lose all my work.*

an email virus *How can you protect yourself against email viruses?*

VERBS

be infected by/have a virus *I got a message saying my computer was infected by a virus.*

create/write a virus *Why do people create computer viruses?*

contain a virus *The email may contain a virus.*

a virus wipes sth (off) (=deletes or clears data off something) *The new virus could wipe everything off your hard disk.*

Software that stops your computer being infected by viruses is called **anti-virus** software: *Does your computer have* ***anti-virus*** *protection?*

V

visa *n*

an official mark put on your passport that gives you permission to temporarily enter or leave a foreign country

ADJECTIVES/NOUNS + visa

a 14-day/six-month etc visa *They gave me a three-month visa at the airport.*

a British/US etc visa *He was refused a British visa.*

a tourist/travel/visitor's visa *She applied for a tourist visa.*

a work/student visa *They had sent their daughter abroad on a student visa.*

an entry/exit visa (=to enter or leave a country) *All foreigners need an entry visa.*

a transit visa (=that allows you to pass through a particular country) *Transit visas will be issued at the airport.*

a valid visa (=one that is officially acceptable) *His student visa is only valid as long as he is at college.*

VERBS + visa

apply for a visa *I applied for a visa to visit China.*

get a visa (*also* **obtain a visa** *formal*): *He was having difficulties getting a visa.*

give sb a visa (*also* **grant sb a visa** *formal*): *She has been granted a special visa.*

issue a visa *The Consulate has the power to issue work visas.*

need a visa *Canadians don't need a US visa.*

refuse/deny sb a visa *The embassy refused him a visa.*

revoke/cancel a visa (=say that someone no longer has permission to be in a country) *The authorities revoked his visa and sent him back to Australia.*

overstay your visa (=stay longer than you are allowed to) *Some people enter the country legally and then overstay their visas.*

extend/renew sb's visa (=allow a visa to continue for longer) *He hoped that his visa might be extended.*

visa + VERBS

sb's visa expires/runs out (=it ends) *I had 14 days to leave the country because my visa had expired.*

visa + NOUNS

a visa application *US immigration authorities have turned down their visa application.*

visa requirements *Check the visa requirements with your travel agent.*

visible Ac *adj*

something that is visible can be seen

ADVERBS

clearly/plainly/easily visible (=easy to see) *The broken bone was clearly visible on the X-ray.*

highly visible (=very easy to see) *Cyclists should wear highly visible colours.*

barely/hardly visible (=almost impossible to see) *The parked car was barely visible in the darkness.*

just visible (=only just able to be seen) *There was thick fog, and the outline of the road was just visible.*

still visible *The bullet holes are still visible in the walls.*

VERBS

become visible *It will be several weeks until your pregnancy becomes visible.*

stay visible (*also* **remain visible** *formal*): *The marks may remain visible for several months.*

leave/make sth visible *The tide went out, leaving the top of the rocks visible above the water.*

visible + NOUNS

a visible sign *Check the plant for any visible signs of disease.*

a visible improvement *You can expect to see a visible improvement within a few weeks.*

a visible difference *There is no visible difference between the two types of flour.*

visible symptoms *Some diseases have no visible symptoms.*

a visible means of sth (=a way of doing something that is clear to see) *The prison cell had no visible means of escape.*

PREPOSITIONS

visible to sb *The sign was clearly visible to passing motorists.*

visible from sth *The house wasn't visible from the road.*

PHRASES

visible to the naked eye (=able to be seen without using special equipment) *The comet is now visible to the naked eye.*

vision Ac *n*

1 the ability to see

ADJECTIVES/NOUNS + vision

good vision *He is blind in one eye, but has good vision in the other.*

normal vision *Someone with normal vision should be able to see those numbers.*

perfect vision *Babies aren't born with perfect vision.*

20-20 vision (*also* **twenty-twenty vision**) (=perfect vision, with no need for glasses) *A pilot must have 20-20 vision.*

poor vision (*also* **defective/impaired vision** *formal*): *Her vision was quite poor and she always wore glasses.*

blurred vision (=not clear, for example because of illness) *He complained of headaches and blurred vision.*

night vision (=the ability to see when it is dark) *Cats have good night vision but can't see colour very well.*

peripheral vision (=the ability to see things at the edges of what you are looking at) *After her illness she could still read, but her peripheral vision was poor.*

VERBS

blur sb's vision (=make someone not see clearly) *Tears blurred her vision.*

clear your vision *She blinked to clear her vision.*

correct sb's vision *Some people wear contact lenses to correct their vision.*

2 someone's idea about what something is like, or how something should be

ADJECTIVES

a new/different/alternative vision *In his speech he said that he had a new vision for our country.*

a clear vision *The engineers at BMW had a clear vision of what they wanted to achieve.*

ambitious vision *Jeffrey outlined an ambitious vision of the future for the club.*

a radical vision *His plans are based on a radical new vision of space and the future.*

a personal vision *The role of the artist is to present a personal vision of the world.*

a shared vision *The two men had a shared vision of the future of the organization.*

sb's overall vision *What is your overall vision for the company?*

sb's long-term vision *Europe's major leaders need to talk in terms of their long-term vision, not a short-term fix.*

an idealistic vision *Marxists have an idealistic vision of a perfect society.*

a disturbing vision *In his book 'Nineteen Eighty-Four', Orwell offered a disturbing vision of the future.*

VERBS

set out/outline/put forward your vision (=explain it) *The principal set out her vision for the college.*

offer/provide a vision *The party seemed to offer an alternative vision of society.*

create/develop a vision *Winkelmann created a vision of Greece as the birthplace of European civilisation.*

achieve/realize/fulfil your vision *We want to achieve our vision of helping every child to get a world-class education.*

PHRASES

sb's vision for the future *In his speech, the chairman talked about his vision for the future of the company.*

turn sb's vision into (a) reality (=make it really happen) *As an architect, my job is to turn the client's vision into a reality.*

3 the ability to have great ideas about what people can achieve

ADJECTIVES

great vision *He was a politician of great vision, who helped to establish the welfare state.*

little/no vision *The trouble with these people is that they have no vision.*

VERBS

lack vision *This approach lacks vision.*

PHRASES

a man/woman of vision *We need a president who is a man of vision.*

lack of vision *He criticized them for their lack of vision.*

visit *n*

an occasion when someone goes to spend time in a place or goes to see a person

ADJECTIVES

a brief/short visit *Apart from a brief visit to Mexico, she's never been out of the US.*

a flying visit *BrE* (=a very short visit) *I'm only here for the weekend – just a flying visit this time.*

a surprise/unannounced visit (=not expected) *Naomi paid a surprise visit to an old school friend.*

an official/state visit (=that an important person makes as part of their work) *The president made an official visit to France this week.*

a return visit (=to a place you have visited before, or by someone you visited previously) *George was already planning a return visit.*

regular/frequent visits *He became impatient with his wife's frequent visits to his office.*

occasional visits *Except for occasional visits from her daughter, she sees no-one.*

VERBS

pay sb a visit (=visit someone) *I decided to pay him a visit at his office.*

make/pay a visit *The king made an official visit to Poland last year.*

have/receive a visit from sb *I've just had a visit from the police.*

come for a visit *Why don't you come for a visit this summer?*

arrange/organize/plan a visit *We can arrange a visit as soon as you like.*

cancel a visit *She had to cancel her visit because she was ill.*

postpone a visit (=arrange it for a later time) *We may have to postpone our visit.*

cut short a visit (=leave before you planned to) *He had to cut short his visit because his wife was ill.*

PREPOSITIONS

a visit to sth *We enjoyed our visit to the museum.*

a visit to sb (*also* **a visit with sb** *AmE*): *After my visit with John, I went straight home.*

a visit from sb *I'm expecting a visit from my son.*

on a visit *We're just here on a short visit.*

during a visit *What did you do during your visit to Prague?*

PHRASES

be worth a visit *Las Palmas, the lively capital, is well worth a visit.*

visitor *n*

someone who comes to visit a place or a person

ADJECTIVES

a frequent/regular visitor (=who visits somewhere often) *He was a frequent visitor to the art gallery.*

an occasional/rare visitor *My daughter is a rare visitor to our house these days.*

an important visitor *The school is expecting an important visitor today.*

a surprise/unexpected visitor *A surprise visitor is waiting to see you downstairs.*

a foreign/overseas visitor *Many foreign visitors come to the city every year.*

a casual visitor (=someone who does not visit in a regular or planned way) *The museum is of interest both to experts and to casual visitors.*

a first-time visitor *First-time visitors are always impressed by the town's clean quiet streets.*

a welcome visitor (=someone who you are happy to see) *She was always a welcome visitor to the cottage.*

an unwelcome visitor *The house was surrounded by a high fence to keep unwelcome visitors out.*

NOUNS + visitor

a museum/gallery/park etc visitor *The exhibition is very popular with museum visitors.*

a winter visitor (=a bird that comes to a country in the winter) *Some winter visitors stay on until mid-April.*

VERBS + visitor

have/get a visitor *She lives alone, and doesn't get many visitors.*

attract/draw visitors *The Eiffel Tower attracts visitors from all over the world.*

expect a visitor (=a visitor will be arriving soon) *I have to clean the house because we're expecting visitors.*

greet/welcome a visitor *He stood at the front gate and greeted the visitors as they arrived.*

receive a visitor (=meet and greet a visitor) *Visitors are received by a guide who will show them around the castle.*

allow visitors (*also* **admit visitors** *formal*): *The hospital doesn't allow visitors after six o'clock.*

entertain a visitor *How are you going to entertain your visitors?*

visitor + VERBS

visitors come *Twelve million overseas visitors came to the UK last year.*

visitors flock (=come in large numbers) *Visitors flocked to see the exhibition.*

visitor + NOUNS

a visitor attraction *The park is the most popular visitor attraction in the northwest.*

a visitor centre *BrE*, **a visitor center** *AmE* (=a building containing information, toilets etc for visitors) *The Visitor Centre includes a display about the town's history.*

PREPOSITIONS

a visitor from sth *Venice attracts visitors from all over the world.*

a visitor to sth *Visitors to the cathedral numbered more than 2.25 million last year.*

vital *adj*

extremely important and necessary

ADVERBS

absolutely vital *It's absolutely vital that you tell the police everything you know.*

NOUNS

a vital role/part *Richardson played a vital role in the team's success.*

a vital part/element *Learning to play with other children is a vital part of growing up.*

a vital ingredient/component (=a vital part) *One vital ingredient was missing from the team's performance: confidence.*

vital information *The radio was a source of vital information on sea and weather conditions.*

a vital clue (=something that gives you vital information) *The bombers may have left behind vital clues.*

vital evidence *Vital evidence contained in the file had disappeared.*

a vital witness (=someone who has vital information about a crime) *Police are trying to find a vital witness who may have seen what happened.*

a vital source of sth *My mother's job was a vital source of income for the family.*

vital organs (=the parts of your body that are necessary to keep you alive, for example your heart and lungs) *Fortunately, the bullet missed his vital organs.*

PREPOSITIONS

vital to sth *These measures are vital to national security.*

vital for sth *Regular exercise is vital for your health.*

PHRASES

it is vital to do sth *It is vital to be honest with your partner.*

it is vital that... *It is vital that you keep accurate records.*

be of vital importance *Reading is of vital importance in language learning.*

THESAURUS: vital

big, significant, major, notable, key, essential, vital, crucial/critical, paramount, historic, landmark, momentous → **important (1)**

vitamin *n*

a chemical substance in food that is necessary for good health

ADJECTIVES

vitamin A/B/C etc *Oranges contain a lot of vitamin C.*

an essential vitamin (=one that is very important for your body) *These pills have a carefully balanced range of essential vitamins.*

VERBS

take a vitamin (=swallow vitamins in the form of a pill etc) *She takes vitamins every day.*

contain a vitamin *Carrot juice contains many vitamins.*

include a vitamin *The cream includes vitamin E which helps protect the skin.*

vitamin + NOUNS

a vitamin pill/tablet *He was taking large quantities of vitamin pills.*

a vitamin supplement (=extra vitamins that you take in addition to your food) *There is no evidence that vitamin supplements actually improve health.*

vitamin deficiency (=a lack of necessary vitamins) *If you have a balanced diet, you are unlikely to suffer vitamin deficiency.*

PHRASES

a source of vitamins (=something you can get vitamins from) *Fish is a good source of vitamins.*

a lack of vitamins *The illness is caused by a lack of vitamins.*

rich/high in a vitamin *Spinach is rich in vitamins.*

vivid *adj*

vivid memories, dreams, descriptions etc are so clear that they seem real

NOUNS

a vivid memory (*also* **a vivid recollection** *formal*): *I have a very vivid memory of going there as a child.*

a vivid dream *He had a vivid dream about being attacked by a shark.*

a vivid imagination (=a tendency to imagine a lot of things, which may not be accurate) *He has a very vivid imagination – you can't believe everything he says.*

a vivid description/account *She gave us a vivid description of the fight.*

vivid detail *I remember the accident in vivid detail.*

a vivid example of sth (*also* **a vivid illustration of sth** *formal*) (=something that shows very clearly what something is like) *New York City provides a vivid example of the changes taking place in many cities across the US.*

a vivid picture/image *He had a vivid picture of her in his mind.*

a vivid impression/sense of sth *The book gives the reader a vivid impression of life on the island.*

a vivid reminder *The violence is a vivid reminder of how strongly people feel about the issue.*

ADVERBS

particularly vivid *The writer's descriptions of his family are particularly vivid.*

remarkably vivid *She has a remarkably vivid recollection of her early life.*

VERBS

remain vivid *Her memories of living in Vienna remain vivid.*

THESAURUS: vivid

brilliant, vivid, vibrant, dazzling, garish → **bright (2)**

vocabulary *n*

all the words that someone knows or uses

ADJECTIVES

a large/wide/extensive vocabulary *Shakespeare had a very large vocabulary.*

a limited/small vocabulary *He had just started learning English and his vocabulary was fairly limited.*

basic/essential vocabulary *The book teaches you the basic vocabulary that you need to know when you're on holiday.*

technical/specialized vocabulary *The instructions were full of technical vocabulary.*

French/Chinese/Russian etc vocabulary *Some American English vocabulary is different from that of British English.*

an active vocabulary (=the words someone can use) *Children of this age have an active vocabulary of about 1,000 words.*

a passive vocabulary (=the words someone can understand but does not use) *Your passive vocabulary is much larger than your active vocabulary.*

VERBS

have a vocabulary *By 18 months of age, the girl had a vocabulary of around 300 words.*

use a vocabulary *Try to use a wider vocabulary in your writing.*

build/develop a vocabulary *Children need to develop a specialized vocabulary to describe the features they find.*

expand/improve your vocabulary (=learn more words) *Reading helps to expand your vocabulary.*

enrich your vocabulary (=make it better) *Teaching students proverbs and idioms can help enrich their vocabularies.*

learn vocabulary *What's the best way of learning new vocabulary?*

enter the vocabulary (=become part of a language) *New terms began to enter the vocabulary.*

vocabulary + NOUNS

a vocabulary test *The teacher gave us a vocabulary test.*

a vocabulary exercise *There is a vocabulary exercise at the end of each chapter.*

a vocabulary item *formal* (=a word, especially in a coursebook or a language class) *The difficult vocabulary items are explained at the bottom of the page.*

vogue *n* THESAURUS **fashion (2)**

voice *n*

the sounds that you make when you speak, or the ability to make these sounds

ADJECTIVES

a loud voice *Why are you talking in such a loud voice? I'm not deaf.*

a quiet/low/soft voice (=not loud) *When he spoke, his voice was soft and gentle.*

a deep/low voice (=near the bottom of the range of sounds) *She heard the deep voice of her father downstairs.*

a high voice (=near the top of the range of sounds) *They used to repeat her words in silly high voices.*

a clear voice *Natalia's clear voice rang out.*

a small voice (=quiet and not strong or confident) *She answered in a small voice, "I think I was afraid."*

a booming voice (=very loud) *This big booming voice said "Hello, my dear."*

a trembling/shaking voice (=because you are nervous or afraid) *He stood up and began to speak in a trembling voice.*

a silly voice *Stop talking in that silly voice!*

a squeaky voice (=very high and not strong) *The puppet mouse talks in a little squeaky voice.*

a husky voice (=low and slightly rough in an attractive way) *Marilyn Monroe said the words in a husky voice.*

a gravelly voice (=very deep and slightly rough) *He sang to her in his famous gravelly voice.*

a sing-song voice (=going high and low in a pleasant musical way) *She began to recite the poem in a sing-song voice.*

a monotone voice (=boring because the tone does not change) *He just carried on talking in a monotone voice.*

sb's singing/speaking voice *She has a beautiful singing voice.*

VERBS + voice

raise your voice (=speak more loudly) *She did not raise her voice, or express any anger.*

lower your voice (=speak more quietly) *He lowered his voice to a whisper.*

keep your voice down (=not speak loudly) *Keep your voice down, they'll hear you!*

project your voice (=make it be heard far away from you) *Singers have to learn to project their voices.*

lose your voice (=lose the ability to speak loudly or clearly, for example when you have a cold) *I can't give the presentation because I've lost my voice.*

hear sb's voice *I could hear angry voices.*

recognize sb's voice *He recognized her voice instantly.*

put on a voice (=speak in a particular voice) *We would put on silly voices and tell jokes.*

voice + VERBS

sb's voice rises (=becomes louder or higher) *Her voice rose in panic.*

sb's voice drops (=becomes lower) *Len's voice dropped so that it could only just be heard.*

sb's voice breaks/cracks (=becomes higher or unsteady because they are upset) *Her voice broke and she was unable to continue.*

a boy's voice breaks (=becomes deep as he becomes a man) *His voice had only recently broken.*

sb's voice trembles/shakes (=sounds unsteady) *His voice shook with anger.*

sb's voice trails off/away (=becomes quieter until you cannot hear it) *"It's just that...," his voice trailed away uncertainly.*

a voice speaks/calls/answers etc *Then a voice spoke and he realized he was not alone.*

PREPOSITIONS

in a loud/soft/deep etc voice *"Come here," he said in a kind voice.*

PHRASES

have a good/great/fabulous voice (=have a good, great etc singing voice) *To be a star it's not enough to have a great voice.*

sb's tone of voice *His tone of voice was aggressive.*

at the top of your voice (=in a very loud voice) *She shouted "Help!" at the top of her voice.*

volcano *n*

a mountain with a large hole at the top, through which ash or hot liquid rock is sometimes forced out

ADJECTIVES

an active volcano (=it may erupt at any time) *Mount Etna is an active volcano.*

a dormant volcano (=it has not erupted for a long time) *Volcanoes can remain dormant for hundreds of years.*

an extinct volcano (=it does not erupt any more) *The town is near an extinct volcano.*

VERBS

a volcano erupts (=it sends out ash, hot rock etc) *The volcano last erupted 50 years ago.*

volume Ac *n*

1 the amount of sound produced by a television, radio etc

ADJECTIVES

full volume (=as loud as possible) *She turned the TV right up to full volume.*

high volume *The CD player gives excellent sound quality even at high volume.*

low volume *Can we have the volume a little lower please?*

loud volume *The volume of the music was very loud.*

VERBS + volume

turn the volume up (*also* **increase the volume** *formal*): *I turned up the volume on the microphone.*

turn the volume down (*also* **decrease the volume** *formal*): *The neighbours asked her to turn down the volume, because they couldn't sleep.*

PREPOSITIONS

at high/low/full volume *The stereo was playing at low volume.*

2 the total amount of something

ADJECTIVES

high/large volume (*also* **considerable volume**) *formal*: *We are pleased with the high volume of sales.*

huge/enormous/great volume *A huge volume of water poured down the main street.*

low volume *The low volume of production makes the cars very expensive.*

the total volume *The total volume of consumer spending has increased.*

the average volume *What is the average volume of production per month?*

the sheer volume of sth (=used when saying that there is a surprisingly large amount of something) *The sheer volume of information available on the internet is overwhelming.*

VERBS

produce volumes of sth *Factories used to produce huge volumes of smoke.*

increase/decrease the volume of sth *Brazil and Argentina have increased the volume of trade between them.*

PHRASES

the volume of traffic *Local people are worried about the high volume of traffic passing through the village.*

the volume of work *They are unable to cope with the volume of work.*

THESAURUS: volume

quantity, volume, level, proportion, quota, yield → **amount**

3 a book

ADJECTIVES/NOUNS + volume

a small/slim volume *She published a slim volume of poetry.*

the first/second/final volume *This is the final volume of the Harry Potter series.*

a companion volume (=a book that goes together with another one) *'Dogs in the News' is the companion volume to 'Cats in the News'.*

PREPOSITIONS

a volume of essays/poems/stories etc *I'm reading a volume of essays by Montaigne.*

voluntary Ac *adj*

1 if something is voluntary, you do it because you want to do it, not because you have been paid, or because you feel you have to do it

NOUNS

voluntary work *She does voluntary work for a cancer charity.*

a voluntary agreement/arrangement *Voluntary agreements can be more effective than government intervention.*

voluntary worker *Voluntary workers are at the heart of any political campaign.*

voluntary contributions (=money that people give to help an organization do its work) *The animal rescue centre is supported entirely by voluntary contributions.*

voluntary redundancy (=when a worker offers to leave his or her job, in return for money from his or her company) *The company wants to get rid of 800 jobs through voluntary redundancy.*

PHRASES

on a voluntary basis *The charity workers work on a voluntary basis.*

THESAURUS: voluntary

optional
class | course | extra | excursion
if something is optional, you can choose whether to do it or have it:
This class is optional for second year students. | You can choose to do an optional study skills course. | Optional extras include leather seats and a sun roof (=other things you can choose to have when you buy something). | *There is an optional excursion to the Taj Mahal* (=a trip that you can choose to go on).

2 voluntary organizations exist in order to help people. They exist because people give them money, rather than getting it from the government

NOUNS

a voluntary organization/group/body/agency *Meals for homeless people are often provided by voluntary groups.*

the voluntary sector (=voluntary organizations in general in a country, and the work that they do) *The voluntary sector has an important role in sport.*

vote[1] *v*

to show which person or party you want, or whether you support a plan, by marking a piece of paper or raising your hand

PHRASES

vote yes/no *Most people voted yes.*

vote Democrat/Republican/Conservative etc *My father usually votes Republican.*

vote by a large/small majority *The party voted by a large majority to cut taxes.*

be eligible/entitled to vote (=be legally allowed to vote) *All those aged 18 or over are eligible to vote.*

register to vote (=put your name on the list of voters) *We must encourage people to register to vote.*

ADVERBS

vote unanimously (=everyone votes for the same person or thing) *The committee voted unanimously in favour of the proposal.*

vote overwhelmingly (=by a large majority) *Union members voted overwhelmingly to strike.*

vote narrowly (=by a small majority) *The Senate narrowly voted to pass the bill.*

vote tactically *BrE* (=vote for a person or party that you do not usually support, in order to stop another person or party from winning) *Many people decided to vote tactically, to prevent the socialists from getting in again.*

PREPOSITIONS

vote for sth/in favour of sth *A majority of the islanders voted for independence.*

vote for sb *Are you going to vote for Obama?*

vote against sth *His party voted against the reforms.*

vote on sth (=about something) *MPs will vote on the issue tomorrow.*

THESAURUS: vote

cast your vote *formal*
to vote in an election:
People will cast their votes to choose the next leader of the United States. | The first votes have been cast in the country's general election.

go to the polls
if the people in a country go the polls, they vote in an election. **Go to the polls** is used especially in news reports:
*Tomorrow **voters go to the polls** to choose a new government. | The **country** will **go to the polls** on January 21st.*

elect
leader | president | prime minister | governor | government | representative | official | member of parliament | chairman
to choose a leader, representative, or government by voting:
*Obama was elected president of the United States. | He will lead the country's first **democratically elected** government. | The **newly elected** leader will take office today* (=start his or her official job). *| She was the first woman to be **elected to** Congress.*

re-elect
to elect someone again:
He was re-elected president with 49% of the vote.

ballot
members | workers | employees
to ask the members of an organization to vote on something in order to decide what to do:
The union will ballot its members on whether to go ahead with the strike action.

veto
bill | legislation | law | decision | proposal
to vote against something that other people have agreed on, so that it cannot happen:
The governor threatened to veto the bill. | The president has the right to veto any piece of legislation (=any law or part of a law). *| China can veto any decision made by the other members of the Security Council.*

vote² *n*

an occasion when a person or a group of people vote in an election

VERBS

get/receive votes *The party which receives the most votes will be elected to govern the country.*

win/lose the vote *She won the vote and became president.*

have the vote (=have the right to vote in an election) *Women in New Zealand have had the vote since 1893.*

cast a vote (=vote in an election) *After all the votes have been cast, they have to be counted.*

have/take a vote (on sth) (=organize a vote to decide something) *They took a quick vote on what to do next.*

count the votes *The votes were counted and the result of the election was announced.*

sb's vote goes to sb/sth *My vote will go to the party that does the most for the environment.*

ADJECTIVES/NOUNS + vote

a majority vote (=when most people vote for someone or something) *A change in the law would need a two-thirds majority vote.*

a unanimous vote (=when everybody votes the same way) *The vote in favour of the proposal was unanimous.*

an electoral vote (=a vote in an election) *He needed 270 electoral votes to win.*

a decisive vote (=a vote that decides the result of an election) *The Green Party may have the decisive vote in the next election.*

the popular vote (=the votes of the people of the country in an election) *The Conservative Party won 42.9% of the popular vote.*

a parliamentary vote (=a vote in parliament) *He voted against the government in a parliamentary vote.*

a postal vote (=when you send in your vote by post) *She applied for a postal vote because she is too ill to travel to the polling station.*

PREPOSITIONS

a vote for sth/in favour of sth *He said that a vote for his party would be a vote for change.*

a vote for sb *There were only three votes for the other candidate.*

a vote against sth *Thirty votes were cast against the proposal.*

by a vote *The matter was decided by a vote of committee members.*

PHRASES

put sth to the vote (=have a vote in order to decide something) *The issue was put to the vote in the House of Commons.*

sb's share of the vote *The Social Democrats' share of the vote fell by 5%.*

a vote of (no) confidence (=an official vote to show that people support or do not support a government, leader etc) *The government won a vote of confidence by 339 votes to 207.*

voter *n*

someone who has the right to vote in an election, or who votes in a particular election

ADJECTIVES/NOUNS + voter

a Conservative/Labour/Republican etc voter *He has been a Labour voter all his life.*

a first-time/new voter (=someone who has not voted in an election before) *Many students will be first-time voters.*

male/female voters *The party was successful in attracting female voters.*

young voters *College fees are a big issue for young voters.*

an average/ordinary voter *Over the past 50 years, the average voter has become better educated.*

a floating voter (=someone who is not sure who to vote for) *The party was trying to win the support of floating voters.*

registered/eligible voters (=someone on the official list of people who have the right to vote) *The Liberal Democrats had the support of no more than 9% of registered voters.*

VERBS + voter

appeal to/attract voters *A reduction in tax is likely to appeal to many voters.*

convince/persuade voters *The party struggled to convince voters to support them.*

put off voters (*also* **alienate voters** *formal*): *They risk putting off voters because of the extreme views of some of their members.*

voter + VERBS

voters elect/choose sb/sth *More than 60% of the voters chose Nixon.*

voters support/back sb/sth *The majority of women voters support the president.*

voters favour sb/sth *BrE*, **voters favor sb/sth** *AmE*: *Tennessee voters favored Clinton over Bush in 1992.*

voters reject sb/sth *California voters rejected the new law.*

a voter registers (=puts his or her name on the official list of people with the right to vote) *More young voters have registered than ever before.*

voter + NOUNS

voter turnout/participation (=the number of people who vote in an election) *Voter turnout has been dropping in France.*

voter apathy (=a lack of interest in voting) *There were signs of voter apathy at the last election.*

vow *n* a serious promise

ADJECTIVES/NOUNS + vow

a solemn vow (=very serious) *He took a solemn vow to accept whatever duties he was given.*

marriage/wedding vows *She wrote her own marriage vows.*

a holy/sacred vow *When we get married in church we are making sacred vows.*

VERBS

make a vow *I made a vow never to go near the place again.*

take a vow (=make a vow at a formal ceremony) *The monks had taken a vow of silence.*

keep a vow (=do as you promised) *She kept her vow not to tell anyone about their affair.*

break a vow (=not do as you promised) *She accused him of breaking his marriage vows.*

exchange vows (=make promises to each other as part of a wedding ceremony) *They wanted to exchange vows before their family and friends.*

renew your vows (=have a second wedding ceremony to repeat your promises) *They will renew their marriage vows in a private ceremony.*

PHRASES

a vow of silence/poverty/obedience etc *People close to him have finally broken their vow of silence.*

be bound by a vow (=to have promised seriously to do something) *She told him she was bound by a vow not to tell any other person.*

voyage *n*

a long journey in a ship or spacecraft

ADJECTIVES/NOUNS + voyage

a sea/ocean voyage *The book is about a 19th-century sea voyage to Tasmania.*

a ship's maiden voyage (=the first one which a ship makes) *The 'Titanic' was a luxury ship that sank on its maiden voyage.*

a great voyage *The explorer's first great voyage took him to Australia.*

an epic voyage (=a very long one that involves brave or exciting actions) *On August 2nd 1492, Columbus finally set off on his epic voyage to cross the Atlantic Ocean.*

a long voyage *The ship began its long voyage across the Indian Ocean.*

a dangerous voyage *He was sent on a dangerous voyage to West Africa.*

VERBS

go on/make a voyage (*also* **undertake a voyage** *formal*): *The two ships made a 52-day voyage across the Pacific Ocean.*

begin/set out on a voyage (*also* **embark on a voyage** *formal*): *They began the long voyage home.*

PREPOSITIONS

a voyage to/from/across sth *The voyage to Tonga took three weeks.*

on a voyage *He described all the things that happened on the voyage.*

during a voyage *During the voyage several of the sailors became ill.*

PHRASES

a voyage of discovery *Between 1768 and 1779, Captain Cook made various voyages of discovery.*

vulnerable *adj* easy to harm or attack

ADVERBS

highly/extremely vulnerable *The bridge was extremely vulnerable to attack.*

particularly/especially vulnerable *The team looked especially vulnerable towards the end of the game.*

increasingly vulnerable *The government has become increasingly vulnerable to electoral defeat.*

PHRASES

be vulnerable to attack/criticism/damage etc *Many women feel vulnerable to attack if they go out at night.*

be in a vulnerable position/situation *The country is in the vulnerable position of producing barely half its own food.*

wage *n*

money you earn for doing your job

> **Grammar**
> Often plural.

ADJECTIVES

high wages *The workers are demanding higher wages.*

low wages *Farmworkers receive low wages for long hours.*

good wages *In general, IT jobs pay good wages.*

a decent wage (=a fairly good one) *Jobs in the factories used to pay a decent wage, but those jobs are gone now.*

the hourly/daily/monthly etc wage *She earns an hourly wage of $11.*

the minimum wage (=the lowest wage that a company can pay someone according to the law) *Most of the new jobs in the area only pay the minimum wage.*

the basic wage (=before extra amounts are added) *Overtime is one way in which workers can increase their basic wage.*

lost wages (=the amount you lose by not being able to work) *You may be able to claim on your insurance for lost wages.*

VERBS

earn a wage (*also* **be on a wage** *BrE*): *He earns a wage of £300 a week.*

get/receive a wage *The housewife receives no wage for her work.*

pay a wage *Some firms still paid lower wages to female workers.*

supplement your wages (=earn extra money) *He supplements his wages by working in a bar in the evenings.*

dock sb's wages (=give someone less money as a punishment) *You'll get your wages docked if you're late to work again.*

push up/raise wages (=increase them) *A shortage of workers is pushing up wages.*

hold down/keep down wages (=keep them at a low level) *The government wants to hold down wages in the public sector.*

wages increase/rise *Currently, wages are rising by about 3% per year.*

wages fall *Profits increased but wages fell.*

wage + NOUNS

a wage increase/rise *The rail workers demanded a 20% wage increase.*

a wage reduction/cut *Those who kept their jobs had to take large wage cuts.*

a wage freeze (=wages stay the same) *The wage freeze was part of a plan to bring down inflation.*

wage levels/rates *Wage levels remained low during the 1930s.*

the wage bill (=the amount a company has to pay in wages) *The firm says it cannot find the cash to pay its wage bill.*

a wage earner (=someone who earns a wage) *I am the only wage earner in our house.*

PHRASES

a cut/drop in wages (=someone's wages are reduced) *Would you accept a 5% cut in your wages?*

a fall/decline in wages (=wages become lower generally) *Workers experienced a fall in wages.*

an increase/rise in wages *The company had refused to give miners a real increase in wages.*

> **THESAURUS: wage**
> pay, wages, income, earnings, the money → **salary**

waist *n*

the middle part of someone's body, which is usually narrower than their chest or their hips

ADJECTIVES

a slim/narrow waist (*also* **a slender waist** *literary*): *His shoulders were broad and he had a slim waist.*

a small/tiny waist *The dress draws attention to her tiny waist.*

waist + NOUNS

sb's waist size/measurement *Her waist size is 26 inches.*

waist height/level *The grass grew in some places to waist height.*

PREPOSITIONS

around sb's waist *She was wearing a belt around her waist.*

PHRASES

up to sb's waist *Every now and then the explorers would sink up to their waists in snow.*

from the waist down/up *She was paralysed from the waist down.*

stripped to the waist *He was stripped to the waist, wearing only an old pair of jeans.*

waist deep *She was standing waist deep in the ocean.*

wait[1] *v*

to stay somewhere or not do something until something else happens, someone arrives etc

ADVERBS

wait patiently *They waited patiently for the rain to stop.*

wait anxiously/nervously *All his friends were waiting anxiously for their exam results.*

wait expectantly (=because you are hoping that something good or exciting will happen) *He took out his camera and waited expectantly.*

wait forever *informal* (*also* **wait ages** *BrE informal*) (=wait a long time) *I had to wait ages for a bus.*

not wait long (=not wait for a long time) *She did not have to wait long for a train.*

wait around (*also* **wait about** *BrE*) (=stay in the same place and do nothing while you are waiting) *I can't wait around any longer.*

wait up (=wait for someone to return before you go to bed) *Don't wait up for me; I may be late.*

wait + NOUNS

a waiting list (=a list of people who are waiting for something) *If you don't get the class you want, you can put your name on a waiting list.*

a waiting room (=a room at a station, doctor's etc where people wait) *Take a seat in the waiting room until the dentist calls your name.*

PREPOSITIONS

wait for sb *I'll wait for you outside.*

wait for sth *There were a lot of people waiting for the bus.*

wait until/till sth *I waited until the end of his speech before I left the room.*

PHRASES

wait two hours/20 minutes etc *William waited an hour for his sister to arrive.*

keep sb waiting *The doctor kept us waiting for half an hour.*

wait with bated breath (=while feeling very anxious or excited) *She waited with bated breath to see what he would say.*

wait in vain (=wait for something that never happens) *They waited in vain for him to come back.*

wait and see (=used when saying that you will find out about something soon) *I don't know what he's going to say – we'll just have to wait and see.*

wait your turn (=wait until it is your turn to do something) *Patrick joined the back of the queue and patiently waited his turn.*

wait a minute/second/moment (=used for telling someone to not do something immediately) *Wait a second – I'll drive you home.*

Can't wait

If you say that you **can't wait** to do something, you mean that you feel very excited about it: *I* ***can't wait*** *to see my family again.*

W

wait[2] *n*

a period of time in which you wait for something to happen, someone to arrive etc

ADJECTIVES/NOUNS + wait

a long/lengthy wait *He rang her hotel, and after a long wait she came to the phone.*

a short/brief wait *He had a short five-minute wait at the bus stop.*

a one-hour/30-minute etc wait *They was a 20-minute wait for a table at the restaurant.*

an anxious/nervous wait *She now faces an anxious wait to see if she has been picked for the school team.*

the average wait *The average wait for patients at the clinic is about 25 minutes.*

VERBS

have a wait *We had a long wait at the doctor's.*

face a wait *The students face an anxious wait until their exam results are published.*

PREPOSITIONS

a wait for sth *They will now face a six-week wait for the results of the tests.*

PHRASES

be worth the wait *The meal was excellent and worth the wait.*

walk[1] *v*

to move forward by putting one foot in front of the other

ADVERBS

walk away *She turned and walked away.*

walk back *They walked back to the car in silence.*

walk backwards *He was walking backwards down the hill to relieve the strain on his legs.*

walk together *They walked together for a short distance.*

walk quickly/fast *Ella could hear the footsteps of somebody walking quickly.*

walk briskly/swiftly (=quickly – more formal) *Without speaking, he walked briskly into the office.*

walk slowly *She took his hand and they walked slowly along the path.*

walk barefoot (=without shoes or socks) *The boys never walked barefoot for fear of broken glass.*

PREPOSITIONS

walk down/along a street/road etc *She was walking down King's Road.*

walk into/out of a place *If you're famous, everyone turns to look at you when you walk into a restaurant.*

walk up to sb/sth *I walked up to the door and rang the bell.*

PHRASES

walk five miles/300 metres etc *We must have walked ten miles today.*

walk all the way to a place *I walked all the way to the next town, which was over 20 kilometres away.*

within walking distance (=that are near enough to walk to) *There are plenty of bars and restaurants within walking distance of the hotel.*

walk² *n*

a journey that you make by walking

ADJECTIVES/NOUNS + walk

a long walk *We went for a long walk in the woods.*

a short walk *The house is only a short walk from local shops.*

a little walk *I just felt like a little walk.*

a brisk walk (=fast) *A brisk walk will improve your circulation.*

an easy walk *From here it is an easy walk to the top of the hill.*

a strenuous walk (=needing a lot of effort or strength) *It was quite a strenuous walk and the next day my legs were aching.*

a five-mile/ten-kilometre etc walk *He began the five-mile walk back to town.*

a five-minute/two-hour etc walk *There's a good restaurant a five-minute walk away.*

a country/forest/coastal etc walk *There's a pleasant woodland walk nearby.*

a sponsored walk *BrE* (=done by many people in order to get money for charity) *The school organized a sponsored walk and raised £500.*

VERBS

go for a walk *Let's go for a walk on the beach.*

⚠ Don't say 'make a walk'.

take/have a walk *I try and have a little walk every lunchtime.*

take the dog for a walk *Could you take the dog for a walk?*

PHRASES

have a walk around (=walk in a place in order to find out what it is like) *Feel free to have a walk around the school.*

a walk around the block (=a short walk in that part of the city) *I took the dog for a short walk around the block.*

the walk back/home *The walk home took 20 minutes.*

PREPOSITIONS

a walk in the park/country/countryside/forest/mountains etc *We went for a walk in the countryside near Oxford.*

a walk along the river/beach/street etc *How about a walk along the river?*

a walk through the town/forest/fields etc *Take a walk through the town, and you will find a good choice of restaurants.*

a walk around the town/grounds/lake etc *They went for a walk around the castle grounds.*

on a walk (=while you are walking somewhere) *What did you see on your walk?*

wall *n*

an upright flat structure made of stone or brick, that divides one area from another or surrounds an area

ADJECTIVES/NOUNS + wall

a high/low wall *The prison is surrounded by high walls.*

a thick wall *The castle has thick walls.*

a bare wall (=with no decoration or pictures) *There was no furniture – just four bare walls.*

the outer/inner wall *The outer walls of the house looked very solid.*

the external/internal wall *We knocked down one of the internal walls to make the bedroom bigger.*

the kitchen/bathroom etc wall *She wants to paint the kitchen walls yellow.*

the city walls *You can walk along the ancient city walls.*

VERBS

climb/jump over a wall *The thieves must have climbed over the wall.*

PREPOSITIONS

against a wall *He leaned his bike against the wall.*

wallet *n*

a small flat case, carried in a pocket especially by men, for holding paper money, bank cards etc

VERBS

take out/get out your wallet *He took out his wallet to see if he had enough money.*

open your wallet *The man opened his wallet and took out a £5 note.*

steal sb's wallet *Someone has stolen my wallet!*

lose your wallet *I think I've lost my wallet – I must have dropped it somewhere.*

a wallet contains sth *The wallet contained all his credit cards.*

wander *v*

to walk slowly somewhere, usually without a clear direction or purpose

PREPOSITIONS/ADVERBS

wander around (sth) *We wandered around the old town.*

wander through sth *I wandered through the empty rooms.*

wander down/across/over *Helen wandered down to the river.*

wander off (=away from the place where you are now) *Her son had wandered off to the other end of the garden.*

wander aimlessly (=with no idea of where you should be going) *She wandered aimlessly around the house.*

NOUNS

wander the streets *The boy was found wandering the streets of Paris.*

want *v*

to have a desire for something

ADVERBS

very much want sth/want sth very much *She very much wanted to go back to Japan.*

really want sth *I really want to go to college.*

want sth badly (=a lot) *The person who stole the photograph obviously wanted it badly.*

desperately want sth (=a lot, so you will feel very sad if it does not happen) *He desperately wants his mum and dad to get back together.*

particularly want sth *I particularly want to hear about the African part of your trip.*

just want sth (*also* **simply want sth** *formal*): *I just want to be left alone.*

PHRASES

whatever/whenever/wherever sb wants *Now he can do whatever he wants.*

anything/anywhere/anytime sb wants *You can come back anytime you want.*

if you want (to) *You can go if you want.*

get what you want *You've got what you wanted, so you can leave now.*

do what you want *At college, you can do what you want, instead of being told what to do.*

all I want is... *All I want is a normal life.*

it's (just) what I've always wanted *I love my new garden – it's what I've always wanted.*

want sth for your birthday/Christmas etc *What do you want for your birthday?*

war *n*

fighting between countries using soldiers and weapons

ADJECTIVES/NOUNS + war

a world war (=involving many countries) *No-one wants another world war.*

a nuclear war (=involving nuclear weapons) *The possibility of nuclear war is very frightening.*

a civil war (=between opposing groups within a country) *The English Civil War started in 1642.*

the Iraq/Vietnam/Korean etc War *People were protesting against the Vietnam War.*

World War I/World War II *He was a pilot in World War II.*

a bloody war (=in which many people are killed) *Which was the bloodiest war in history?*

a just war (=one that you believe is right) *They believe that they are fighting a just war.*

all-out war (=one in which armies fight each other and thousands of people are killed) *They are worried that the dispute could turn into an all-out war.*

a guerrilla war (=involving a small unofficial military group) *The rebels are fighting a guerrilla war against the government.*

a conventional war (=not nuclear) *In conventional wars, it is mainly soldiers who are killed.*

a religious war *How many people have died in religious wars?*

VERBS

fight a war *King Henry VII was fighting a war in Scotland.*

fight in a war (=take part as a soldier) *Her grandfather fought in the war.*

win/lose a war *Why did Franco win the Civil War?*

declare war (on sb) (=say you are at war with a country) *In 1941, Britain and the US declared war on Japan.*

wage/make war (=start and continue a war) *Their aim was to destroy the country's capacity to wage war.*

go to war (=become involved in a war) *Are we prepared to go to war over this?*

prevent war (*also* **avert war** *formal*): *Their first objective was to prevent war.*

war breaks out (=it starts) *They married just before war broke out.*

a war rages (=continues in a very violent way) *A civil war is still raging there.*

⚠ Don't say 'do the war'. Say **go to war** or **make war**.

PHRASES

devastated/ravaged by war (=very badly damaged by it) *They were born in an area ravaged by war.*

be on the brink of war (=be about to be involved in one) *The country was on the brink of war.*

the outbreak of war (=the time when it starts) *A week after the outbreak of war, he joined the army.*

the horrors of war *They wanted to forget the horrors of war they had witnessed.*

a prisoner of war (=a soldier who is caught by the enemy during a war and kept prisoner) *He ended up in a camp for prisoners of war.*

war + NOUNS

the war years *The couple spent most of the war years apart.*

a war hero *John McCain was a war hero, who flew combat missions in Vietnam.*

a war veteran (=someone who took part in a war) *Many war veterans still suffer from psychological problems.*

a war criminal (=someone who behaves very cruelly in a war, in a way that is against international law) *Many Nazi war criminals were never punished.*

a war correspondent (=a reporter sending reports from a war) *Being a war correspondent is a dangerous job.*

a war zone (=an area where a war is fought) *The country had turned into a war zone.*

a war crime (=a cruel act in a war which is against international law) *General Mladic was charged with war crimes, after his troops killed thousands of Bosnian civilians.*

a war wound *He still suffered pain from an old war wound.*

PREPOSITIONS

in/during a war *Her father served as a pilot during the war.*

at war (with sb) *Russia was at war with Poland.*

a war with/against sb *Many people opposed the war against Iraq.*

a war between sb and sb *War between Venice and Turkey broke out in 1571.*

wardrobe *n* THESAURUS ▸ **clothes**

wares *n* THESAURUS ▸ **product**

warfare *n*

fighting between groups of people, usually in a war

ADJECTIVES/NOUNS + warfare

modern warfare *Computer technology is an important part of modern warfare.*

chemical warfare (=using chemicals as weapons) *The factory produced poison gas used in chemical warfare.*

biological/germ warfare (=using dangerous bacteria or disease as a weapon) *These bacteria might be used in biological warfare.*

nuclear warfare *How can we protect the world from nuclear warfare?*

conventional warfare (=not nuclear) *In conventional warfare, it is soldiers who are usually the target.*

guerrilla warfare (=involving small unofficial military groups) *The organization used guerrilla warfare and started blowing up bridges and roads.*

jungle warfare *The Japanese had been trained in jungle warfare.*

gang warfare (=fighting in groups of young people) *Gang warfare is wrecking the neighborhood.*

> **Open warfare**
> This phrase is often used when saying that people become so angry with each other that they say or do very unpleasant things, without trying to hide their feelings: *The two sisters had a difficult relationship and at times there was* ***open warfare*** *between them.*

VERBS

engage in/wage warfare (=take part in it) *Rebels waged guerrilla warfare against the occupying army.*

PREPOSITIONS

in warfare *How are these weapons used in warfare?*

PHRASES

a method/means/form of warfare *Tanks were first used as a means of warfare in 1917.*

warm *adj*

1 slightly hot in a pleasant way

NOUNS

warm weather/climate *The weather has been nice and warm.*

a warm day/evening/summer etc *We often eat outside on warm evenings.*

warm sun/sunshine *They relaxed in the warm sunshine.*

a warm temperature *Tropical plants grow best in warm temperatures.*

warm water/air *Wash the shirt in warm water.*

a warm place *Cats always find a warm place to sleep.*

a warm bed *He wanted to be at home in his nice warm bed.*

a warm bath *A warm bath helps to relax the muscles.*

warm clothes/clothing (=clothes that keep you warm in cold weather) *You'll need warm clothes on a cold day like this.*

VERBS

stay/keep warm *I kept moving in order to stay warm.*

get warm *We sat by the fire to get warm.*

wrap up warm (=wear clothes that keep you warm in cold weather) *In winter, make sure your children wrap up warm.*

keep sth warm *Keep the vegetables warm while you make the sauce.*

ADVERBS

pleasantly warm *The sun was pleasantly warm on his skin.*

unusually/exceptionally warm (*also* **unseasonably warm** *formal*) (=used for describing weather that is warmer than usual) *The weather has been unusually warm for April.*

PHRASES

nice and warm *It's nice and warm by the fire.*

nice warm *I think I'll have a nice warm bath.*

lovely and warm *The weather's freezing but it's lovely and warm in the house.*

> **THESAURUS: warm**
>
> **lukewarm/tepid**
> only slightly warm:
> *The* ***coffee*** *was only* ***lukewarm*** *when it finally arrived. | Add two cups of* ***lukewarm water*** *to the yeast. | Soak the dried fruit in* ***tepid water*** *for about ten minutes.*

THESAURUS: warm

warm, boiling, scorching, humid, feverish → **hot**

2 friendly

NOUNS

a warm welcome/reception *Visitors can be sure of a warm welcome.*

a warm smile *She always greets us with a warm smile.*

a warm atmosphere *People like the club because there's a very warm atmosphere.*

ADVERBS

genuinely warm *Her smile was genuinely warm.*

THESAURUS: warm

nice, warm, welcoming, hospitable, amiable, genial, cordial, approachable → **friendly**

warn *v*

to tell someone that something bad or dangerous may happen, so that they can avoid it or prevent it

ADVERBS

always/constantly/repeatedly warn sb (=often or many times) *Parents repeatedly warn children about the dangers of crossing roads.*

officially warn sb *He was officially warned that he could lose his driving licence.*

PREPOSITIONS

warn sb about/of sth *Patients were not warned of the health risks of having this treatment.*

warn sb against sth *The government has warned people against travelling to the island because of the fighting.*

warning *n*

something that tells you something bad or dangerous might happen so you can be ready for it

ADJECTIVES

advance/prior warning (=before something happens) *Workers were given no advance warning that the factory was going to close.*

fair warning (=enough to be reasonable) *He was given fair warning that such behaviour would not be tolerated.*

a stern warning (=serious and strict) *I got a stern warning against giving false information to the police.*

a stark warning (=unpleasantly clear) *Cigarette packets carry the stark warning 'Smoking kills'.*

NOUNS + warning

a health warning (=a warning that something is bad for your health) *All tobacco products must carry a health warning.*

a flood/gale/tornado/typhoon etc warning *A flood warning has been issued for those who live near the river.*

VERBS

give a warning *His manager gave him a warning that if he was late again he would lose his job.*

issue a warning (=officially warn people) *Police have issued a warning about the threat of terrorism.*

deliver/sound a warning (=mention something in an official speech or statement, which is intended to warn people about something) *The minister sounded a warning about the country's economic situation.*

listen to a warning (*also* **heed a warning** *formal*) (=take notice of it) *Drivers failed to heed warnings about fog.*

ignore a warning *He had ignored their warning to stay in the car.*

carry a warning (=have a warning printed on it) *By law, cigarette packets carry a warning about the dangers of smoking.*

be a warning (*also* **serve as a warning** *formal*): *The judge said the long sentence should serve as a warning to others.*

a warning comes *The warning came too late.*

warning + NOUNS

a warning sign/signal (=something that shows you that something bad could happen) *Don't ignore the warning signs of stress.*

a warning light *Red warning lights were flashing.*

a warning label *All packs of cigarettes now carry a warning label.*

a warning shot *Troops fired warning shots over the heads of demonstrators.*

a warning look/glance/gesture *My boss gave me a warning look.*

PREPOSITIONS

a warning about/of sth *They chose to ignore warnings about bad weather.*

without (any) warning *The soldiers fired into the crowd without warning.*

PHRASES

a word of warning (=used before telling someone to be careful about something) *A word of warning: don't use too much glue.*

an early warning system (=a system that warns people about something dangerous, a long time before it happens) *An early warning system failed to prevent widespread damage by the tsunami.*

wash¹ *v*

to clean something with water and usually soap

NOUNS

wash the dishes (=wash all the plates, pans, spoons etc, especially after a meal) *It's my turn to wash the dishes.*

wash clothes/socks etc *This shirt needs washing.*

wash your hair/hands/face/feet *I wash my hair every other day.*

wash a car *The car needs washing – it's really dirty.*

wash the floor *I washed the floor and cleaned the windows.*

wash vegetables/a lettuce etc *The salad leaves are washed in spring water.*

PREPOSITIONS/ADVERBS

wash off the dirt/mud/blood etc *She had a shower to wash off the dirt.*

wash away the dirt/mud etc *The rain had washed away all the mud.*

wash out the soap/blood/dirt etc *He washed out the blood from his clothes.*

wash up *BrE* (=wash the plates, cups, spoons etc, especially after a meal) *I'll wash up.*

wash sth thoroughly *Make sure that you wash the vegetables thoroughly.*

PHRASES

wash sth clean *He scraped the mud off his boots and washed them clean under a tap.*

THESAURUS: wash

to wash something

rinse
hair | **hands** | **mouth** | **clothes** | **cloth** | **plate** | **dish** | **glass** | **cup** | **vegetables** | **lettuce**
to wash something quickly by pouring water on it, in order to remove soap, shampoo, dirt etc:
Rinse your hair thoroughly to get rid of the shampoo. | *He quickly rinsed his dirty clothes in the sink.* | *Polly went into her little kitchen and* ***rinsed out*** *two glasses.* | *I* ***rinsed off*** *the soap.*

> You use **rinse out** about using water to clean the inside of a cup, pan etc.

do the dishes (*also* **do the washing-up** *BrE*)
to wash all the plates, pans, spoons etc, especially after a meal:
Sarah was in the kitchen doing the dishes.

do the laundry (*also* **do the washing** *BrE*)
to wash clothes:
We usually do the laundry once week.

to wash yourself

have a bath/shower *BrE*, **take a bath/shower** *AmE*
to wash your body in a bath or shower:
She went home and took a shower.

have a wash *BrE*
to quickly wash yourself, especially your hands or face:
I had a quick wash and changed into some clean clothes.

freshen up
to wash your face and hands so that you feel more comfortable, for example after you have been travelling or working:
She hoped there would be time to freshen up before the interview.

wash² *n*

1 if you give something a wash, you clean it using soap and water

ADJECTIVES

a good wash (=a thorough wash) *His football socks always need a really good wash after a game.*

a quick wash *I'll just give my hair a quick wash before we go.*

VERBS

give sth a wash *The car looks pretty dirty. I'll give it a wash this morning.*

sth needs a wash (*also* **sth could do with a wash** *informal*): *That shirt needs a wash – it's filthy!*

2 if you have a wash, you clean your face or body

ADJECTIVES

a quick wash *Have I got time for a quick wash?*

VERBS

have a wash *BrE*: *Haven't you had a wash this morning?*

get a wash *I like to get a wash before dinner.*

waste¹ *v*

to use more of something than is useful or sensible, or not use something fully

NOUNS

waste time *We wasted a lot of time arguing about who was to blame.*

waste money *They wasted a lot of money on unnecessary things.*

waste energy/electricity/water *Leaving lights switched on at night wastes energy.*

waste resources *We should not waste our country's natural resources.*

waste space *How can I make use of the wasted space under the stairs?*

waste effort/energy *Don't waste your effort trying to make him change his mind.*

waste a chance/opportunity *She wonders why they are wasting their chance to get an education.*

waste your life *He felt that he had wasted his life instead of doing something useful.*

PREPOSITIONS

waste sth on sth/sb *Don't waste your money on those stupid magazines!*

waste² *n*

1 unwanted materials or substances that are left after you have used something

ADJECTIVES

household/domestic waste (=from homes) *Newspapers and magazines make up 10% of household waste.*

industrial waste (=from factories) *A lot of pollution is caused by industrial waste.*

agricultural waste (=from farms) *Scientists are trying to develop fuels from agricultural waste.*

chemical waste *There should be stricter controls over chemical waste.*

hazardous/toxic waste (=dangerous because it is poisonous) *They were fined for illegal dumping of hazardous waste.*

nuclear/radioactive waste *Radioactive waste must be safely transported.*

organic waste (=from plants, fruits, and vegetables) *Organic waste can be used to make compost for your garden.*

human waste (=from people going to the toilet) *The prison was full of the smell of human waste.*

VERBS

recycle waste *How much of our household waste is recycled?*

get rid of waste (*also* **dispose of waste** *formal*): *One way of disposing of waste is to burn it.*

dump waste *They were fined for illegally dumping waste.*

create/produce waste *This process produces a lot of waste.*

reduce/minimize waste *We need to minimize waste and encourage recycling.*

waste + NOUNS

waste disposal (=getting rid of waste) *There are strict rules about hazardous waste disposal.*

a waste product (=an unwanted substance which is produced as part of a process) *Your kidneys separate water and waste products from the blood.*

waste paper (=paper that has been used and thrown away) *We recycle all our waste paper.*

2 a failure to use something in an effective, useful, or sensible way

ADJECTIVES

a complete/total waste *That was a complete waste of effort.*

a terrible waste *It would be a terrible waste if you didn't become a writer.*

a tragic waste (=used especially after someone young has died) *Police described her death as "a tragic waste of a young life".*

an unnecessary/needless waste *The meeting was an unnecessary waste of time.*

VERBS

be a waste *He is so talented it would be a waste if he didn't join a band.*

go to waste (=not used and therefore wasted) *Don't let all this food go to waste.*

PHRASES

a waste of money/time/effort/space etc *She thinks make-up is a waste of money.*

watch¹ *v*

to look at something for a period of time

NOUNS

watch television *We watched television all evening.*

watch a film/a show/the news etc *All the parents came to watch the school concert.*

watch a game/fight/race etc *I'm going to watch the game on TV.*

watch football/tennis/cricket etc *He likes watching baseball.*

ADVERBS

watch carefully *Watch carefully. You might learn something.*

watch closely (=very carefully) *I watched him closely to see what he would do next.*

watch intently/attentively *formal* (=with a lot of attention) *Her father was watching her intently as she worked.*

watch anxiously/nervously *His mother watched anxiously as he was put into the ambulance.*

watch helplessly (=without being able to do anything to stop a bad situation) *He watched helplessly as Paula fell into the icy water.*

watch impassively (=without showing any emotion, especially when this is surprising) *She watched impassively as the prisoner was brought into the courtroom.*

PREPOSITIONS

watch sth on TV/television/the internet *We watched the game on TV.*

watch from sth *Kate was watching from the window.*

watch for sth (=in order to see if something happens) *The judges are always watching for mistakes.*

PHRASES

can't/couldn't bear to watch sth (=you do not want to watch something, because it makes you feel very uncomfortable) *Ruth could not bear to watch her parents arguing.*

sit/stand and watch (=watch and do nothing) *Everyone just sat and watched me struggling.*

watch with interest/amusement/dismay etc *Harriet watched him with interest.*

watch in horror/amazement/disbelief etc *He watched in horror as the house burnt down.*

watch[2] *n*

1 a small clock that you usually wear on your wrist

VERBS + watch

wear a watch *He was wearing a gold watch.*

look at/check your watch (*also* **consult your watch** *formal*): *I looked at my watch. It was 4.30.*

glance at your watch (=look at it quickly) *"I must go," he said, glancing at his watch.*

set your watch (=make it show the correct time) *She set her watch and put it on her wrist.*

put/set your watch forward (=make it show a later time) *The passengers were reminded to put their watches forward three hours.*

put/set your watch back (=make it show an earlier time) *On Saturday night, don't forget to put your watch back an hour.*

watch + VERBS

a watch says... *My watch says twenty past one.*

a watch stops *Her watch had stopped after getting wet in the sea.*

a watch ticks (=makes short regular sounds as the seconds pass) *It was so quiet you could hear her watch ticking.*

ADJECTIVES

a watch is fast (=it shows a later time than the real time) *No, it's only 12.15 - your watch must be fast.*

a watch is slow (=it shows an earlier time than the real time) *My watch is three minutes slow.*

a digital watch (=that gives the time in numbers) *I think digital watches are easier to see.*

> **Wristwatch** and **stopwatch** are written as one word.

2 the act of watching someone or something carefully

ADJECTIVES/NOUNS + watch

a close watch *We are keeping a close watch on the situation.*

a careful watch *It is important to keep a careful watch on students' progress.*

a constant watch (=all the time) *My father kept a constant watch on the road ahead while I was driving.*

a 24-hour/round-the-clock watch (=all day and night) *Police officers are keeping a 24-hour watch on his home.*

neighbourhood watch *BrE*, **neighborhood watch** *AmE* (=a system in which neighbours watch each other's houses to prevent crime) *Since the neighbourhood watch scheme started, there have been fewer burglaries.*

VERBS

keep/maintain a watch on sb/sth *The police kept a careful watch on the soccer fans.*

stand watch (=watch something carefully in order to protect it) *Armed guards stand watch outside his room.*

PREPOSITIONS

watch on sb/sth *Keep a watch on how much your daughter eats.*

watch over sb/sth *They never relaxed their constant watch over the prisoners.*

watch for sb/sth *They kept a careful watch for any signs of the enemy.*

on watch (=watching something carefully because it is your period of time to do it as part of your job) *Who's on watch tonight?*

PHRASES

be on the watch for sth (=be looking and waiting for something, especially to avoid trouble or danger) *Visitors are advised to be on the watch for anything suspicious.*

water *n*

the clear liquid that falls as rain and can be used for drinking, washing etc

ADJECTIVES/NOUNS + water

drinking water (=water that you can drink safely) *There is no source of drinking water on the island.*

tap water (=water that comes out of a tap) *The tap water is not safe to drink.*

running water (=water that comes out of a system of pipes in a building) *Only half the city's houses had running water.*

fresh water (=water in lakes, rivers etc that does not contain salt) *This bird is usually found near fresh water.*

salt water (=sea water, or water to which salt has been added) *The waves splashed his face with salt water.*

deep/shallow water *The plant grows in shallow water in pools and ponds.*

clear water *They walked along the beach and swam in the clear blue water.*

clean water *Millions of people do not have access to clean drinking water.*

dirty water *She poured the dirty water down the drain.*

contaminated/polluted water (=that has harmful substances in it) *They became ill from drinking contaminated water.*

hot/boiling water *The tiny house had no heating or hot water.*

cold/freezing water *He dived into the freezing water to save the child.*

lukewarm/tepid water (=only slightly warm) *Stir the yeast into lukewarm water.*

bottled water (=water to drink that you buy in bottles) *Sales of bottled water go up in the summer.*

mineral/spring water (=water that comes naturally out of the ground, usually sold in bottles) *This mineral water comes from the Scottish mountains.*

sparkling/fizzy water (=bottled water with bubbles in it) *You can mix sparkling water with fruit juice to make a refreshing drink.*

hard/soft water (=containing a lot of calcium, or not much calcium) *Hard water is formed as rainwater passes down through layers of limestone.*

water + NOUNS

the water supply *A dam was built to improve the water supply.*

the water level *People who live near the river are worried that the water level is still rising.*

a water shortage *There is a severe water shortage in many parts of the country.*

VERBS

boil/heat water *He was boiling some water to make tea.*

water flows *We watched the water flow under the bridge.*

water runs *I let the cool water run down my back.*

water drips *Water dripped from his coat onto the floor.*

water leaks *Water had leaked into the cellar.*

water evaporates (=changes into a gas) *Most of the water in the pond had evaporated and there was hardly any left.*

PHRASES

a glass of water *She poured herself a glass of water.*

a drink of water *He asked for a drink of water.*

a drop of water *I drink the last few drops of water from my flask.*

a pool/puddle of water *There were pools of water on the ground.*

a bucket of water *I went to get a bucket of water and a scrubbing brush.*

waterfall *n*

a place where a river falls down over a cliff

ADJECTIVES

a spectacular/magnificent waterfall *Thousands of people visit this spectacular waterfall every year.*

W

VERBS

a waterfall plunges/cascades *formal* (=the water goes very quickly downwards) *A great waterfall plunges down the hillside.*

a waterfall thunders *formal* (=makes a very loud noise) *At this point, the waterfall thunders over huge rocks.*

form/create a waterfall *As the land drops away, the river forms a dramatic waterfall.*

wave[1] *n*

1 a line of raised water that moves across the surface of the sea

ADJECTIVES/NOUNS + wave

a big/great wave *The storm sent great waves crashing into the cliffs.*

a tidal wave (=a very large wave that flows over the land and destroys things) *The winds and a tidal wave killed 45 people.*

a tsunami wave (=a very large wave, usually caused by an earthquake, that causes a lot of damage when it reaches land) *A tsunami wave hit Japan, destroying whole towns.*

VERBS

waves break (=fall onto the land or a boat) *We watched the waves breaking on the shore.*

waves crash (=fall noisily) *Huge waves crashed down on us.*

waves lap (=hit something gently) *He could hear the sound of waves lapping against the boat.*

waves pound (=hit something hard) *The waves pounded the rocks.*

waves roll in (=move continuously towards the shore) *You can sit on the cliffs and watch the waves roll in.*

sink/vanish beneath the waves *The ship sank beneath the waves.*

wave + NOUNS

wave energy/power (=electricity from the movement of waves) *Wave energy can then be converted into electricity.*

PHRASES

the crest of a wave (=the top of the wave where it begins to fall) *He had a photograph of a surfer riding on the crest of a wave.*

on the ocean waves (=on the ocean) *They spent a week on the ocean waves on a cruise ship.*

2 a side-to-side movement of your hand

ADJECTIVES

a quick wave *A quick wave and then she was gone.*

a friendly wave *He ignored her friendly wave and carried on walking.*

VERBS

give (sb) a wave *I looked across and gave them a wave.*

PHRASES

a wave of the hand *He interrupted her with an impatient wave of the hand.*

3 a sudden increase in a particular type of behaviour, activity, or feeling

NOUNS + wave

a crime wave (=a sudden increase in crime) *Police are trying to deal with a crime wave that has swept the city.*

a heat wave (=a period of unusually hot

weather) *California is in the middle of a heat wave.*

ADJECTIVES

a great wave of sth *She felt a great wave of love and affection for him.*

a sudden wave *Peter felt a sudden wave of pain.*

a fresh wave of sth (=another wave) *A fresh wave of fighting erupted in the region yesterday.*

the current/present wave of sth *The current wave of strikes began in November.*

VERBS

a wave hits sb/sth *He was hit by a wave of nausea every time he tried to stand up.*

feel a wave of sth *For a second Maggie felt a wave of fear.*

a wave sweeps sth (=it affects the whole of something) *It is the latest in a wave of job cuts that is sweeping the industry.*

a wave sweeps/washes over sb (=someone suddenly experiences a feeling or emotion) *A sudden wave of joy swept over her.*

PREPOSITIONS

a wave of sth *The incident triggered a wave of violence.*

in waves *The pain came in waves.*

wave² *v*

1 to move your hand from side to side to say hello or make someone notice you

NOUNS

wave your arms/hands *Excited fans were waving their arms in the air.*

ADVERBS

wave frantically/wildly/madly (=with quick movements, especially to get someone's attention) *We waved frantically to get the police officer's attention.*

wave cheerfully/happily *Crowds of people waved happily as the princess drove past.*

wave sb on/through (=move your hand to show them they can continue going somewhere) *A soldier opened the gate and waved us through.*

PREPOSITIONS

wave at/to sb *The singer waved at the crowd.*

PHRASES

wave goodbye to sb *At the station, people were waving goodbye to each other.*

turn to wave (*also* **turn and wave**) *The king turned to wave before climbing onto the plane.*

2 to hold something in your hand and move it from side to side

NOUNS

wave a flag/banner *The president's supporters cheered and waved flags.*

wave a gun *Armed men ran through the streets shouting and waving their guns at terrified people.*

wave a piece of paper *He burst into my office waving a piece of paper excitedly.*

way *n*

1 a method for doing or achieving something

> **Grammar**
> You can say a **way to do something** or a **way of doing something**.

ADJECTIVES

the right/wrong way *He showed me the right way to hold the racket.*

a good way *Running is a good way of keeping fit.*

the best way *What's the best way to learn a language?*

a different way *There are many different ways of borrowing money.*

a new/fresh way *Companies are constantly thinking of new ways to improve their products.*

a quick way *Looking on the internet is usually the quickest way to find information.*

an effective/sure way (=certain to be successful) *Improving your diet is the most effective way to lower your risk of heart disease.*

the only way *The only way is to tell him what he is doing wrong.*

an easy way *I know an easy way to make bread.*

the hard way (=the most difficult way) *I learned the hard way – there are many easier ways of doing it.*

a roundabout way (=not direct, or not simple) *It was a roundabout way of asking us to leave.*

VERBS

have a way *Companies have lots of ways of finding out information about people.*

think of/come up with a way *I've thought of a good way of making money.*

find/discover a way *We must find a better way of dealing with the problem.*

look at/explore ways *The government is looking at new ways of encouraging reading.*

change the way *Recently we have changed the way we organize our accounts.*

improve the way *They want to improve the way in which patients are treated.*

transform/revolutionize the way (=change it completely) *Einstein's discovery transformed the way we think about space and time.*

PREPOSITIONS

a way of doing sth *I wish there was a way of making him stop crying.*

in a way *Animals communicate in various ways.*

a way around sth (=a way of avoiding or dealing with a problem) *Can you think of a way around the problem?*

a way out of sth (=a way of getting out of a bad situation) *There seems to be no way out of the current economic crisis.*

PHRASES

there is a way *Actually, there is a way you can help.*

there is no way (=used when speaking very firmly and definitely) *There's no way of knowing if the treatment will work.*

there are ways and means (=there are different ways of doing something, especially ones that most people do not know about) *There are ways and means of raising the money that we need.*

2 a road, path, direction etc to a place

ADJECTIVES

the quickest way *She told us the quickest way to the hospital.*

the shortest way *The shortest way is to go across the field.*

the right way *Are you sure this is the right way?*

the wrong way *I think we've gone the wrong way.*

the other way (=from the opposite direction) *A big truck was coming the other way.*

this/that way (=used when showing someone the direction to go somewhere) *The conference room is that way.*

both ways (=left and right) *Look both ways before you cross the road.*

VERBS

go this way/that way/the wrong way etc *You go that way and I'll go this way.*

ask sb the way *He asked me the way to the police station.*

tell sb the way *Can you tell me the way to the nearest post office, please?*

show sb the way *If you can show me the way, I'll take you by car.*

know the way *Does anyone know the way from here?*

lose your way (=become lost) *He lost his way in the fog.*

find your way (=discover the right way to get somewhere) *I managed to find my way home.*

go sb's way (=go in the same general direction as them) *If you're going my way, can you give me a lift?*

ADVERBS

the way in *She looked all around the building, but couldn't find the way in.*

the way out *Which is the way out?*

the way back *Can you find your way back to the car park?*

the way home *I'm sure this isn't the way home.*

PREPOSITIONS

the way to sth *Could you tell me the way to the station?*

PHRASES

on my/her etc way (=while you are going somewhere) *I can get some milk on my way home.*

all the way (=all the time while you are going somewhere) *There are speed restrictions all the way to London.*

3 distance

ADJECTIVES

a long way *I was feeling tired because I had walked a long way.*

a short/little way *The house is just a little way up the track.*

PREPOSITIONS

a long/little/short way from sth *I was a long way from home.*

PHRASES

all the way from/to sth (=used when you are talking about a long distance) *Hank has come all the way from the US.*

quite a way (=a fairly long distance) *It's quite a way to the beach – you'll have to get a bus.*

a long way away/off (=far away from somewhere) *Bombs exploded a long way away.*

weak *adj*

1 not physically strong – used especially when someone is unhealthy or cannot lift something

NOUNS

a weak heart/chest/stomach etc *My brother had a weak heart and he died very young.*

weak arms/legs/back etc *Her legs were weak and she could only walk with difficulty.*

a weak voice *"Can I have some water?" he said in a weak voice.*

VERBS

feel weak *He suddenly felt weak and asked if he could sit down.*

PREPOSITIONS

weak from sth *She was weak from lack of sleep.*

weak with hunger/exhaustion *The animal was weak with hunger.*

PHRASES

too weak to do sth *My aunt was too weak to leave her bed.*

THESAURUS: weak

frail
man | woman | lady | body | arms | health
weak and thin, especially because you are old:
She was a small frail old lady in her late seventies. | My grandparents were unable to travel because of their frail health.

shaky
voice | hand
weak and unsteady, especially because you are ill or nervous:

W

"I'm okay," she said in a shaky voice. | He held out a shaky hand. | I still ***feel*** *a little* ***shaky*** *after the operation.*

delicate
child | woman | constitution
weak and becoming ill easily:
Hilary was rather a delicate child, and her parents were always worried that she would catch cold. | She had rather a delicate constitution (=her body was weak and she became ill easily).

feeble
attempt | effort | voice
very weak, especially because you are very tired, ill, old, or young:
She made a feeble effort to move her leg. | "Can someone help me?" said a rather feeble voice behind me. | For a week she was too feeble to get out of bed.

puny *disapproving*
kid | boy | man | arms | appearance
small, thin, and weak-looking. **Puny** sounds rather informal:
He was a puny kid who was often bullied at school.

infirm *formal*
weak or ill for a long time, especially because you are old:
The home is for people who are elderly and infirm.

Infirm is often used as a noun: *Everyone had to join the army, except* ***the old and the infirm***.

ANTONYMS **weak → strong (1)**

2 not having any power or influence, or not successful

NOUNS

a weak leader/ruler/king *His opponents claim that he is a weak leader who cannot make his own decisions.*

a weak government *The government is weak and relies heavily on the US for support.*

weak management *The company's problems are mainly caused by weak management.*

a weak economy *The economy was weak and inflation was too high.*

sb's/sth's weak point (=the thing that is likely to make someone or something likely to fail) *His weak point is lack of experience.*

ADVERBS

financially/economically/politically/militarily weak *The war left Britain economically weak.*

inherently weak (=used when the basic character of something is weak) *The country's political system is inherently weak and unstable.*

PHRASES

be in a weak position *The unions are in a weak negotiating position.*

weak and ineffective/indecisive *Under his leadership, the government looked weak and ineffective.*

ANTONYMS **weak → strong (4)**

3 not strong enough to be effective or believable

NOUNS

a weak argument/excuse *Their arguments seem weak and unconvincing.*

weak evidence *The judge decided the evidence was too weak for a successful prosecution.*

a weak joke *He was always making weak jokes about women drivers.*

a weak plot *The film is let down by a weak plot and some awful acting.*

THESAURUS: weak

feeble
attempt | effort | excuse | justification | argument
very weak:
I ignored his feeble attempts at humour. | The newspaper hid behind the feeble argument that they were only reflecting the views of ordinary people.

lame
excuse
a lame excuse is very weak and not at all believable:
He came up with some lame excuse about missing his train.

pathetic
attempt | excuse
extremely weak – used when you strongly disapprove of what someone says or does and have no respect for them:
This is just a pathetic attempt to twist the facts. | He made some pathetic excuse about forgetting to call her.

4 not strong and likely to break

NOUNS

a weak material *Silicon is normally quite a weak material.*

PHRASES

sth is too weak to support sth *The branch was too weak his weight.*

THESAURUS: weak

delicate, brittle, breakable, flimsy → **fragile**

ANTONYMS **weak → strong (2)**

5 not bright

THESAURUS: weak
faint, weak, pale, poor/bad, soft, low → **dim**

weaken *v*

to make someone or something weaker

Grammar
Often passive.

ADVERBS

seriously/severely weaken *The economy was seriously weakened by the war.*

greatly/considerably/significantly weaken sth *The power of the president was considerably weakened.*

further weaken sth (=even more) *Many industries had been further weakened by the world recession.*

fatally/gravely weaken (=in a way that makes someone or something certain to fail) *The arms scandal had fatally weakened his leadership.*

already weakened *His body was already weakened by his illness.*

NOUNS

weaken sb's position *The stories in the press weakened his position as leader.*

weaken sb's power/authority/influence *The power of the courts has been considerably weakened.*

weaken sb's resolve (=make someone less determined) *Nothing will weaken our resolve to deal with the current economic crisis.*

weakness *n*

a problem or fault that someone or something has

ADJECTIVES

a major/serious/fundamental weakness *There was a major weakness in the design of the plane.*

main/biggest/greatest weakness *The novel's greatest weakness is that it doesn't have a proper ending.*

human weakness *Greed is a common human weakness.*

a glaring weakness (=a very obvious weakness) *There is a glaring weakness in this argument.*

a fatal weakness (=which makes something certain to fail) *There was one fatal weakness in the plan – they did not have enough money.*

a possible/potential weakness *The lack of a strong leader is one potential weakness.*

an inherent weakness *formal* (=one that is part of the way in which something has been designed or organized) *There are some inherent weaknesses in the current system.*

VERBS

have a weakness *If she has one weakness, it is her lack of patience.*

find/discover/identify a weakness *Experts have identified several weaknesses in the structure of the building.*

highlight/expose/reveal a weakness (=show that it exists) *The report highlights a number of weaknesses in the running of the school.*

exploit a weakness (=get an advantage from it) *Don't give your opponent a chance to exploit your weaknesses.*

a weakness lies in sth *Her main weakness lies in her lack of experience.*

PREPOSITIONS

a weakness in sth *There were some obvious weaknesses in the proposal.*

PHRASES

strengths and weaknesses (=good and bad aspects) *A good politician will understand his own strengths and weaknesses.*

a sign of weakness *His political enemies were watching closely for any sign of weakness.*

wealth *n*

a large amount of money or possessions

ADJECTIVES

great/vast/huge/enormous wealth (*also* **untold wealth** *formal*): *The kings used their vast wealth to build enormous palaces.*

personal/private wealth *He is a man of great private wealth.*

national wealth (=owned by a country) *As national wealth increased, people felt more confident about the future.*

material wealth (=money and valuable things that you own) *The people are not rich in material wealth but they are extremely happy.*

natural wealth (=oil, coal, wood, and other things that a country has) *The country's natural wealth includes natural gas and minerals.*

VERBS

acquire wealth (=get wealth) *There is nothing wrong with acquiring wealth – it's what you do with it that matters.*

inherit wealth (=get it from someone who dies) *He inherited all his wealth from his grandfather.*

accumulate/amass wealth (=get a lot of wealth) *A successful businessman, he amassed enormous wealth.*

create/generate/produce wealth (=do or make things that earn money) *Poor countries need governments with policies that generate wealth.*

flaunt your wealth *disapproving* (=show it to other people so that they can see how rich you are) *We dislike rich people who flaunt their wealth.*

wealth + NOUNS

wealth creation (=doing or making things that earn money) *The purpose of the economy is wealth creation.*

PHRASES

the distribution of wealth *Society would be more equal if there was a fairer distribution of wealth.*

wealthy *adj* THESAURUS ▸ rich (1)

weapon *n* a knife, bomb, gun etc

ADJECTIVES/NOUNS + weapon

nuclear/atomic weapons *The country is thought to be developing nuclear weapons.*

conventional weapons (=not nuclear) *The aircraft are designed to carry either nuclear or conventional weapons.*

chemical weapons (=using chemicals such as poisonous gases, or dangerous germs) *Troops may have been exposed to chemical weapons.*

biological weapons (=using dangerous germs) *He believes they were planning a biological weapons attack using anthrax.*

an offensive weapon (=one that can be used to attack someone illegally) *He was charged with carrying an offensive weapon.*

a lethal/deadly weapon (=that can kill) *A knife is a lethal weapon.*

the murder weapon (=the weapon used to kill someone) *Police found a knife at the scene that is believed to be the murder weapon.*

an automatic weapon (=one that can fire a lot of bullets very quickly) *The shots were fired from an automatic weapon.*

VERBS

fire a weapon (=shoot a gun or missile) *Police were told not to fire their weapons.*

be armed with/carry a weapon *The suspect is believed to be carrying a weapon.*

use a weapon *He says he used the weapon in self defence.*

use sth as a weapon (=use it to harm someone or something) *The government was trying to use starvation as a weapon against its own people.*

brandish/wield a weapon *formal* (=wave it around in a threatening way) *The police say the man was brandishing a weapon and that they had no choice but to shoot him.*

PHRASES

weapons of mass destruction (=weapons intended to kill a lot of people and cause a lot of damage) *They wrongly believed Iraq had weapons of mass destruction.*

wear[1] *v*

to have something such as clothes, shoes, or jewellery on your body

NOUNS

wear clothes/jeans/a shirt/a dress etc *What kind of clothes was he wearing?*

wear a tie *I have to wear a tie for work.*

wear a uniform *A man wearing a police uniform approached the car.*

wear glasses/contact lenses *I didn't know you wore glasses.*

wear a watch/a ring/jewellery etc *We're not allowed to wear jewellery at school.*

wear make-up/lipstick/perfume *She always wears a lot of make-up.*

wear black/red/green etc (=black, red etc clothes) *He often wears blue.*

PREPOSITIONS

wear sth for/to sth *What are you wearing for the wedding?*

PHRASES

what to wear *I can't decide what to wear.*

something to wear *She looked in the wardrobe for something to wear.*

have nothing to wear *I've nothing to wear – can I borrow your black dress?*

comfortable/uncomfortable to wear *Make sure you choose shoes that are comfortable to wear.*

wear[2] *n*

1 a particular type of clothes

> **Grammar**
> Don't use **wear** on its own to refer to clothes. **Wear** is always used with a noun or adjective before it.

ADJECTIVES/NOUNS + wear

evening wear (=for formal events in the evening) *The band were dressed in evening wear.*

casual/everyday wear (=not formal) *We sell stylish casual wear for men and women.*

designer wear (=made by well-known and fashionable designers) *I can't afford designer wear.*

maternity wear (=for pregnant women) *The shop sells maternity wear.*

> **Menswear**, **womenswear**, **childrenswear**, **sportswear**, and **leisurewear** are written as one word.

> **THESAURUS: wear**
> clothing, garment, dress, wear, gear, wardrobe → **clothes**

2 damage caused by being used over a period of time

VERBS

show wear *The hotel is beginning to show some wear.*

cause wear *Braking suddenly causes a lot of wear on your tyres.*

reduce wear *The toes of the shoes have metal caps to reduce wear.*

minimize wear *Oil minimizes wear on the machine.*

prevent wear *To prevent wear, cover the sofa with a rug.*

ADJECTIVES

excessive wear *Heavy trucks are causing excessive wear on the road.*

PHRASES

wear on sth *The sweater had some wear on the elbows.*

PHRASES

signs of wear *Replace your running shoes when they start to show signs of wear.*

wear and tear (=damage over a period of time during the normal use of something) *Check the equipment for wear and tear.*

weather *n*

the temperature and other conditions such as sun, rain, and wind

ADJECTIVES/NOUNS + weather

good/nice/lovely weather *We had good weather all week. | Nice weather today, isn't it?*

glorious/beautiful/perfect weather *It was glorious weather, so we decided to go for a picnic.*

bad/poor weather *Several flights were cancelled owing to bad weather.*

awful/dreadful/terrible/atrocious weather *We came home early because of the awful weather.*

hot/cold weather *The weather was cold and grey.*

fine/sunny/fair/dry weather *If the weather is fine, we'll eat outside.*

wet/rainy/damp weather *I'm fed up with all this wet weather.*

mild weather (=not too cold or rainy) *The weather is usually fairly mild in October.*

severe weather (=very bad) *The ship sank in severe weather.*

windy/stormy/snowy/cloudy weather *The windy weather is causing problems for drivers.*

wintry weather (=cold, often with snow) *We stayed indoors because of the wintry weather.*

winter/summer etc weather *People are outside enjoying the beautiful summer weather.*

VERBS + weather

have good/bad etc weather *We had lovely weather all week.*

enjoy the weather *People were out enjoying the sunny weather.*

weather + VERBS

the weather improves/deteriorates (=it gets better or worse) *I hope the weather will improve soon.*

the weather turns colder/warmer/sunny/humid etc (=it becomes colder etc) *The weather usually begins to turn warmer at the beginning of May.*

the weather holds (out) (=good weather continues) *Let's hope the weather holds till the end of the week.*

the weather breaks (=stops being good) *We got almost all the harvest in before the weather broke.*

weather + NOUNS

the weather forecast (=a description of what the weather is expected to be like in the near future) *What's the weather forecast like for the weekend?*

a weather map (=a map showing the current or expected future weather) *The weather map shows a band of rain coming in from the east.*

weather conditions (=whether it is raining or sunny) *The rescue was difficult because of the appalling weather conditions.*

weather patterns (=the usual weather that comes at a particular time each year) *Changes in weather patterns are thought to be caused by global warming.*

PHRASES

weather permitting (=if the weather is good enough) *Breakfast is served on the terrace, weather permitting.*

THESAURUS: weather

climate
the usual weather conditions in a particular country or area:
Queensland has a warm ***tropical climate****. | Britain has a relatively* ***temperate climate*** (=not too severe). *| He is not used to living in a* ***cold climate****. |* ***Climate change*** *will cause sea levels to rise.*

conditions
the weather at a particular time, especially when considering how this will affect a planned event or activity:
It's important to check the ***weather conditions*** *before you go hiking in the mountains. |* ***Conditions*** *are* ***perfect*** *for today's boat race. |* ***Freezing conditions*** *are making the roads extremely hazardous.*

the outlook
what the weather will probably be like for the next few days - used especially on weather forecasts:
The outlook for *the weekend is for continued sunny weather.*

website *n*

a place on the internet where you can find information about something

ADJECTIVES/NOUNS + website

a good/useful website *She showed me a really useful website.*

an official website *I looked at the organization's official website.*

a news/travel/education etc website *I found the hotel on a travel website.*

a company/store website *It says on the company website that they are open till six o'clock.*

a school/college website *Term dates are posted on the school website.*

a personal website (=that someone makes about themselves) *Welcome to my personal website.*

a secure website (=one that is safe to use) *How do you know if a website is secure?*

VERBS

have a website *The school has its own website.*

visit a website *You can visit the university's website to get more information.*

design/create a website *Students learn how to design their own websites.*

put/post sth on a website *She posted the photos on her website.*

launch a website (=make it available for people to use) *The government has launched a website containing information on environmental issues.*

download sth from a website *You can download the software from our website.*

navigate a website (=go from one part to another to find the information you want) *The website is too difficult to navigate.*

update a website (=change it slightly so it contains the latest information) *News websites are updated every few minutes.*

bookmark a website (=mark it so you can get to it easily again) *If you're looking for good local hiking trails, bookmark this website.*

a website contains sth *The website contains a lot of useful information.*

PREPOSITIONS

on a website *There's a photograph of Dan on his website.*

PHRASES

a website gets/receives/has had... hits (=used when saying how many people have visited it) *We have already had 5,000 hits on our website.*

a link to a website *He sent her a link to his website in an email.*

wedding *n*

a ceremony in which two people get married

ADJECTIVES/NOUNS + wedding

a big/huge wedding (=with a lot of guests) *The couple couldn't afford a big wedding.*

a quiet wedding (=with not many guests) *We had a quiet wedding, with just a few close friends and family.*

a white wedding (=a traditional wedding where the bride wears a white dress) *She had always wanted a white wedding.*

a traditional wedding *They had a traditional Indian wedding.*

a church wedding *Her family wants her to have a church wedding.*

a registry office wedding *BrE* (=at a local government office, not in a church) *They decided to have a registry office wedding.*

a civil wedding *AmE* (=a wedding that is not performed by a religious leader) *Civil weddings are becoming more and more popular.*

VERBS

go to a wedding (*also* **attend a wedding** *formal*): *I'm going to a wedding on Saturday.*

come to the wedding *She wrote to say she couldn't come to the wedding.*

conduct a wedding *formal* (=perform the ceremony that marries two people) *Their wedding was conducted by the local priest.*

organize a wedding *My mother helped me organize our wedding.*

invite sb to a wedding *She didn't invite me to her wedding.*

a wedding takes place *The wedding took place in Paris at the weekend.*

wedding + NOUNS

sb's wedding day *She looked beautiful on her wedding day.*

the wedding ceremony *Her uncle, a priest, conducted the wedding ceremony.*

the wedding service (=the ceremony in a church) *It was a beautiful wedding service.*

the wedding reception (=the large formal meal or party after a wedding) *There was lots of dancing at the wedding reception.*

a wedding dress *Who designed the princess's wedding dress?*

a wedding ring *I noticed that the woman wasn't wearing a wedding ring.*

a wedding cake *The bride and groom cut the wedding cake.*

a wedding present/gift *He gave them a painting as a wedding present.*

a wedding guest *All the wedding guests laughed.*

a wedding invitation *They had already sent out all the wedding invitations.*

a wedding photograph/picture *I was looking at our old wedding photographs the other day.*

wedding vows (=the promises made by people who are getting married) *The couple exchanged wedding vows.*

sb's wedding night *We spent our wedding night in a hotel.*

sb's wedding anniversary (=the date on which they got married in a previous year) *They celebrated their tenth wedding anniversary in May.*

PREPOSITIONS

at a wedding *I was a guest at their wedding.*

week *n*

a period of seven days, usually measured in Britain from Monday to Sunday and in the US from Sunday to Saturday

ADJECTIVES/NOUNS + week

this week (=the present one) *I can't see you this week.*

last week (=the one before the present one) *Last week, my washing machine broke down.*

next week (=the one after the present one) *The wedding is next week.*

the previous week (=the week before) *She was thinking about something that had happened the previous week.*

the following week (=the week after) *She booked another appointment for the following week.*

the past week (=the past seven days approximately) *Five soldiers have been killed in the past week.*

the coming weeks (=the next few weeks) *We look forward to working with you in the coming weeks.*

a full/whole week *I can't believe we've been here a whole week already.*

a busy week *I've had a very busy week.*

a quiet week (=not busy or eventful) *This has been a fairly quiet week for the police.*

a good/bad week *Did you have a good week?*

a working week *BrE*, **a workweek** *AmE* (=the amount of time you spend working during a week) *His typical working week is 55 hours.*

VERBS

a week passes (by)/goes by *As the weeks passed, he began to get better.*

spend a week *I spent six weeks in Spain last summer.*

sth takes a week *It will take many weeks to finish this job.*

PREPOSITIONS

for a week *I'm going away for a week.*

in a week *It's too much work to do in one week.*

during the week (=Monday to Friday, but not weekends) *We don't go out much during the week.*

PHRASES

the beginning/end/middle of the week *We get our wages at the end of every week.*

a day of the week *Friday is our busiest day of the week.*

once/twice/three times etc a week *She goes to yoga twice a week.*

week after week (*also* **week in, week out**) (=every week, for a long time) *We keep practising the same dance steps week in, week out.*

for weeks (=for a lot of weeks) *This situation continued for weeks.*

weekend *n*

the period including Saturday and Sunday

ADJECTIVES/NOUNS + weekend

this weekend (=the one closest to now) *What are you doing this weekend?*

next weekend (=the one after this one) *I'm going to Palm Springs next weekend.*

last weekend (=the one before this one) *We were in Glasgow last weekend.*

the previous weekend (=the weekend before) *The talks had been scheduled for the previous weekend.*

the following weekend (=the weekend after) *They had originally planned to meet the following weekend.*

a long weekend (=Saturday, Sunday, and also Friday or Monday or both) *We're going to Paris for a long weekend.*

a holiday weekend (=a weekend that has days before or after it which are public holidays) *The roads are always busy on the holiday weekend.*

a good/pleasant/wonderful weekend *I hope you have a wonderful weekend.*

a busy weekend *We have a busy weekend ahead of us.*

VERBS

have a good/busy etc weekend *I had a lovely weekend with my family.*

spend a weekend... *We spent the weekend working on the garden.*

weekend + NOUNS

a weekend break *BrE* (=a holiday that lasts a weekend) *She was looking forward to her weekend break in Prague.*

PREPOSITIONS

at the weekend *BrE*, **on the weekend** *AmE*: *We're going camping at the weekend.*

at weekends *I only see him at weekends.*

over the weekend (=during the weekend) *I'll think about it over the weekend.*

weep *v*

to cry a lot – used especially in written descriptions

ADVERBS

weep bitterly (=cry a lot, because you are very unhappy) *Helen wept bitterly when she found out that he had gone.*

weep quietly/softly/silently *I heard a woman weeping quietly in another room.*

weep uncontrollably/hysterically *The mother of the dead boy was weeping hysterically.*

weep openly (=without trying to hide your tears) *People in the crowd wept openly when the princess's death was announced.*

PREPOSITIONS

weep for sb/sth *She wept for her children.*

weep at/over sb/sth *He was weeping over the death of his sister.*

PHRASES

weep tears of joy/laughter/frustration etc *His parents wept tears of joy when they heard the news.*

weep with happiness/joy/relief etc *She wept with relief when she heard that he was safe.*

break down and weep (=become very upset and start crying) *When he heard the victims' stories, he broke down and wept.*

weep buckets *informal* (=cry a lot) *I wept buckets, night after night.*

weight *n*

1 how heavy and fat someone is

VERBS

put on weight (*also* **gain weight** *formal*): *He had put on weight since she last saw him.*

lose weight *She lost a lot of weight when she was ill.*

⚠ Don't say 'lose your weight'.

watch your weight (=try not to get fatter, by eating the correct foods) *He has to watch his weight because he has a heart condition.*

get/keep your weight down (=become thinner or stay thin) *I've lost 10 lbs, but how do I keep my weight down?*

get/keep the weight off (=become or stay thinner) *I changed my eating habits so I'd keep the weight off.*

control your weight *It's important for boxers to control their weight.*

maintain your weight (=stay at a weight) *The article gives advice on maintaining a healthy weight.*

sb's weight goes up/increases *My weight seems to go up every time I get weighed.*

sb's weight goes down/falls *People started to notice that his weight had gone down.*

weight + NOUNS

a weight problem (=a tendency to be too fat) *I've always had a weight problem.*

weight gain *The medication can cause rapid weight gain.*

weight loss *After the first month of dieting, weight loss slows down.*

ADJECTIVES

sb's ideal weight (=what someone should weigh, according to their height and body type) *She weighs about 10 lbs more than her ideal weight.*

a healthy weight *It sounds as if you're quite a healthy weight.*

excess weight (=the pounds that make you heavier than you should be) *You'll feel better if you lose the excess weight.*

NOUNS + weight

body weight *The weight of your head is a fraction of your whole body weight.*

birth weight *Babies with a low birth weight may have more medical problems than bigger babies.*

sb's target weight (=the weight someone is trying to be) *I've reached my target weight.*

2 how much something weighs, or something that is heavy

VERBS

carry/support/bear the weight of sth *I didn't know if the roof would support my weight.*

increase/reduce the weight of sth *I don't want to increase the weight of my suitcase. | Engineers have reduced the weight of the plane.*

ADJECTIVES

heavy weight *The crane can lift heavy weights.*

extra weight *The extra weight of the caravan makes driving uphill more difficult.*

weight + NOUNS

a weight limit *The weight limit per bag is 20 kilograms.*

PHRASES

3 tons/75 kg/20 stone etc in weight *Some of these fish are over two kilos in weight.*

sell sth by weight (=sell it according to its weight) *Fruit and vegetables are sold by weight.*

under the weight of sth (*also* **beneath the weight of sth** *formal*) (=because something is heavy) *Karen staggered along under the weight of her heavy backpack.*

welcome *n*

the way in which you greet someone or react to something

ADJECTIVES

a warm/friendly welcome *You always get a warm welcome at Lisa's house.*

a big welcome (=with special things happening) *We're planning a big welcome for the team when they return.*

a great/wonderful/tremendous welcome *Thank you for such a wonderful welcome.*

a rapturous/rousing welcome (=very happy and excited) *He returned to his homeland to a rapturous welcome in 1996.*

a tumultuous welcome (=a very noisy one from a crowd) *The Pope received a tumultuous welcome.*

an official welcome *New students will meet in the hall for an official welcome by the university.*

a cautious/guarded welcome (=used for saying that you are happy about something but also slightly worried about it) *The plan was given a cautious welcome by the Labour Party.*

VERBS

give sb a ... welcome (*also* **extend sb a ... welcome** *formal*): *He was given a great welcome by the crowd.*

get/receive a ... welcome *You are sure to receive a warm welcome.*

outstay/overstay your welcome (=stay longer than someone wants) *We had better go soon – we don't want to outstay our welcome.*

PREPOSITIONS

a welcome to sb *I would like to give a warm welcome to you all.*

in welcome (=in order to welcome someone) *He held out his hand in welcome.*

PHRASES

give sb/get a hero's welcome (=get a big welcome because you have done something very brave or good) *The players will get a hero's welcome when they return.*

a speech of welcome *The Mayor made a brief speech of welcome.*

a smile of welcome *She greets visitors with a warm smile of welcome.*

welcoming *adj* THESAURUS ▶ friendly

well behaved *adj* THESAURUS ▶ good (3)

well-known *adj* THESAURUS ▶ famous

well-off *adj* THESAURUS ▶ rich (1)

west *adj, adv, n*

the direction towards which the sun goes down, or the part of a place that is in this direction

ADJECTIVES

the far west *She travelled to the far west of the country.*

west + NOUNS

the west side/end *The church has a square tower at the west end.*

the west coast *Iona is a tiny island off the west coast of Scotland.*

the west bank *The village is on the west bank of the Hudson River.*

a west wind (=a wind from the west) *A west wind blew the smoke away.*

VERBS

go/travel/head west *He headed west to Nebraska.*

face west *The living room faces west.*

ADVERBS

further west *Prague is further west than Vienna.*

due west (=directly west) *The track led due west.*

PREPOSITIONS

in the west *There is rich farmland in the west.*

to/towards the west *To the west he could see the outline of houses.*

from the west *Cloud will move in from the west overnight.*

the west of a place *He has strong support in the west of the country.*

> When people talk about **the West**, they usually mean western Europe and North America.

wet *adj*

1 covered in or full of water

NOUNS

wet clothes/trousers/socks etc *You need to change out of your wet clothes.*

a wet towel/cloth *Don't leave wet towels on the bed!*

wet hair *She'd been swimming and her hair was still wet.*

wet feet/hands *Make sure you have a good pair of walking boots, because you don't want wet feet.*

wet grass *He slipped on the wet grass and fell.*

a wet patch (=a small wet area) *The car went out of control when she hit a wet patch on the road.*

wet things (=wet clothes) *You'd better take those wet things off.*

ADVERBS

wet through (=with every part very wet) *It never stopped raining and our clothes were wet through.*

soaking/sopping/wringing wet (=very wet) *Her boots leaked and her socks were soaking wet.*

dripping wet (=so wet that water is dripping off) *He ran out of the bathroom, dripping wet.*

slightly wet *My hair was still slightly wet after my shower.*

VERBS

get wet *We got very wet when we tried to give the dog a bath.*

get sth wet *I didn't want to get my feet wet.*

PREPOSITIONS

wet with sth *His cheeks were wet with tears.*

PHRASES

cold and wet *I was too cold and wet to keep going.*

wet and muddy *His boots were wet and muddy.*

> **Wet paint** has not dried yet: *Be careful – the **paint** is still **wet**.*

THESAURUS: wet

soaked

clothes | trousers | shirt

very wet – used about clothes and people: *My clothes were **completely soaked**. | His shirt was **soaked with** blood. | We **got soaked** on the* *way back home.* | *The poor little boy was* ***soaked to the skin*** (=his clothes were completely soaked). | *She was* ***soaked through*** (=her clothes were completely soaked).

Soaked is not used before a noun, except as **rain-soaked/blood-soaked**: *the* ***rain-soaked*** *earth* | *a* ***blood-soaked*** *handkerchief*

drenched
very wet:
Everyone ***got drenched*** *when a huge wave hit the boat.* | *Her clothes were* ***drenched in blood.*** | *She was* ***drenched in sweat.***

Drenched is not used before a noun, except in **rain-drenched/sweat-drenched/blood-drenched**: *the* ***rain-drenched*** *streets* | *his* ***sweat-drenched*** *body*

soggy
ground | **paper** | **handkerchief** | **sandwich** | **bread** | **biscuit** | **vegetables** | **mess**
unpleasantly wet and soft:
It had been raining hard and the ground was soggy underfoot. | *She found a piece of soggy paper in one of her pockets.* | *His aunt pulled out a soggy handkerchief and wiped her eyes.* | *The vegetables will get soggy if you cook them for too long.*

sodden *BrE*
clothes | **ground**
very wet with water:
They just wanted to get out of their sodden clothes. | *The rain had stopped hours ago, but the ground was still sodden.*

boggy
ground | **area**
boggy ground is very wet and muddy:
The soldiers were having difficulty moving across the boggy ground. | *This plant grows in boggy areas.*

saturated
ground | **clothes** | **soil**
extremely wet, and unable to take in any more water or liquid:
Our clothes were saturated. | *His bandage was* ***saturated with*** *blood.*

waterlogged
ground | **field** | **pitch**
if the ground is waterlogged, it has water on its surface because it is so wet that it cannot take in any more:
There could be flooding if it rains, because the ground is waterlogged. | *Last Saturday's game was cancelled because the field was waterlogged.*

ANTONYMS **wet → dry (1)**

2 rainy

NOUNS

a wet day/afternoon/morning etc *One wet weekend, we decided to go for a walk.*

a wet summer/spring/winter etc *It's been a fairly wet summer this year.*

a wet climate *The west of Scotland has a wet climate.*

wet weather *In wet weather, we usually play indoors.*

a wet spell (=a wet period of time) *If there is a wet spell after a dry summer, the plant may flower again.*

the wet season (=the time of the year when it rains a lot) *It's a very dry area and only has rain in the wet season.*

PHRASES

cold and wet *It was cold and wet – not the weather to be sleeping in a tent.*

THESAURUS: wet
wet, damp, showery, drizzly, grey → **rainy**

ANTONYMS **wet → dry (2)**

wheel *n*

1 one of the round things under a car, bus, bicycle etc that turns when it moves

ADJECTIVES

the front wheel *The front wheel went over a big bump.*

the back/rear wheel *The rear wheels of the bus got stuck in the mud.*

VERBS

a wheel turns (*also* **a wheel goes round**) *When you pedal, the wheels turn.*

a wheel spins (=turns around quickly, when the vehicle is not going along) *The rear wheels spun in the sand.*

PHRASES

the spokes of a wheel (=the thin metal bars that connect the outer ring of a wheel to the centre, especially on a bicycle wheel) *Rays of light shine from the centre like the spokes of a wheel.*

2 a steering wheel, which you hold and use for controlling a car or similar vehicle

VERBS

turn the wheel *You need to turn the wheel slowly when the road is icy.*

take the wheel (=start to drive) *Dad pulled over and said it was my turn to take the wheel.*

PREPOSITIONS

behind/at the wheel (=driving a vehicle) *After months without a car, it felt strange to be behind the wheel again.*

wheelchair *n*

a chair with wheels, used by people who cannot walk

wheelchair + NOUNS

wheelchair access *Does the building have wheelchair access?*

a wheelchair user *The hotel is fully accessible to wheelchair users.*

a wheelchair ramp (=a slope for people in wheelchairs) *There is a wheelchair ramp at the entrance.*

VERBS

use a wheelchair *He can't walk very far, and he has to use a wheelchair.*

push a wheelchair *I don't need anyone to push my wheelchair for me.*

ADJECTIVES

an electric wheelchair *When he's outdoors, he uses an electric wheelchair.*

PREPOSITIONS

in a wheelchair *People in wheelchairs should be able to use buses and trains, just like anyone else.*

whiff *n* THESAURUS ▶ smell[1]

whisper[1] *v*

to speak very quietly, using your breath rather than your voice

PREPOSITIONS

whisper (sth) to sb *The man whispered something to a boy standing by the door.*

whisper (sth) about sb/sth *I knew they were whispering about me.*

PHRASES

whisper (sth) in sb's ear *She whispered the answer in my ear.*

whisper[2] *n*

a very quiet voice you make using your breath and very little sound

ADJECTIVES

a low/soft/gentle whisper *When he spoke, it was in a low whisper.*

a hushed whisper (=one in which you are careful not to speak loudly) *They spoke in the hushed whispers of churchgoers.*

a loud whisper *"Where do you think you're going?" I said in a loud whisper.*

a hoarse/husky whisper (=with a voice that sounds a little rough) *Her voice came out as a hoarse whisper.*

a stage whisper (=a loud whisper that you intend everyone to hear) *"What is he talking about?" Rory said, in a stage whisper.*

PREPOSITIONS

in a whisper (=in a very quiet voice) *"Not now!" he said, in a whisper.*

PHRASES

speak/talk in whispers *The two men were speaking in whispers and I wondered what they were saying.*

white *adj, n*

1 the colour of snow

ADVERBS

very white *Agnes noticed that he had very white teeth.*

completely white *Her mother's hair was now completely white.*

pure white *The tree was covered with pure white blossom.*

bright/brilliant white *The gallery has brilliant white walls.*

dazzlingly white (=so bright that something is difficult to look at) *The walls were dazzlingly white in the afternoon sunshine.*

snow white (=very white - often used about hair) *His hair was snow white.*

milky white (=very white - often used about skin or liquid) *She never sunbathed, and was proud of her milky white skin.*

creamy white (=white with a slight yellow colour) *The cheese is a creamy white colour.*

shiny white *The bathroom had shiny white tiles.*

PREPOSITIONS

in white (=in white clothes or white paint) *She wanted to get married in white.*

PHRASES

black and white *A black and white dog was sitting outside the shop.*

⚠ Don't say 'white and black'.

as white as snow (=very white) *Her skin was as white as snow.*

white with frost/snow *In the morning the ground was white with frost.*

2 looking pale, because of illness or strong emotion

VERBS

go/turn white *Anne's face went white. "He can't have gone!" she cried.*

ADVERBS

very white *He looked at her. She was very white.*

PHRASES

as white as a sheet (=very pale) *Do you feel OK? You're as white as a sheet.*

white with shock/anger/fear/pain *My mother's face was white with shock.*

wicked *adj* THESAURUS ▶ bad (4)

W

wide *adj*

1 measuring a long distance from one side to the other

NOUNS

a wide river/lake/valley *We crossed the wide river on a huge suspension bridge.*

a wide road/street/avenue/path *The Champs-Elysées is a magnificent wide road in Paris.*

a wide corridor/staircase *Romanov walked down the wide marble staircase to the great hall.*

a wide field/beach *The hotel is next to a wide sandy beach.*

a wide area *Pieces of metal and wood were scattered over a wide area.*

a wide mouth/face/forehead *He looked handsome, with his wide mouth and perfect teeth.*

a wide grin/smile *"I am glad to hear that!" said Gabriel, with a wide smile.*

wide shoulders/chest/hips *He was of medium height, with wide shoulders and a strong chest.*

wide eyes *She had beautiful wide blue eyes.*

wide feet *I have wide feet and I need to be careful when I'm buying shoes.*

PHRASES

at its/their widest point *The Great Plains are about 600 miles across at their widest point.*

wide open spaces (=a wide area with no mountains, buildings or other features) *The film is set in the wide open spaces of Canada.*

THESAURUS: wide

broad
shoulders | chest | back | grin | smile | leaves | river | street | avenue | path | valley
broad means the same as **wide**:
The man was very tall with broad shoulders. | He came into the room with a broad grin on his face. | This plant has broad leaves up to 25 cms long. | The broad river stretched away beyond them. | The restaurant stood at the corner of a broad street.

Broad or wide?

Broad is much more common than **wide** when talking about someone's **shoulders**, **chest**, or **smile**.

Apart from these cases, **wide** is the usual word to use. **Broad** is used especially in literary descriptions of people and places, often when saying that someone or something looks attractive.

thick
piece | slice | book | volume
if something is thick, there is a large distance between its two opposite surfaces or sides:
I'll need a thick piece of rope. | She cut herself a thick slice of bread. | 'The Letters of Kingsley Amis' is a big thick book of just over 1,200 pages.

ANTONYMS **wide → narrow (1)**

2 including many different kinds of things or people

wide + NOUNS

a wide range/variety *The paint is available in a wide range of colours.*

a wide choice/selection *There is a wide choice of bars, cafés, and restaurants.*

wide knowledge/experience *The staff have a wide knowledge about plants.*

wide powers *The constitution gives the president wide powers.*

a wide audience (=a large number of people) *The book is intended for a wide audience.*

wide agreement/consensus *There is wide agreement that the recent forest damage was caused by pollution.*

PHRASES

have a wide appeal (=be attractive to many different types of people) *Their music continues to have a very wide appeal.*

a wide array of sth *formal* (=a lot of different things) *He answered dozens of questions on a wide array of topics.*

a wide cross-section of sb (=a group that is typical of a much bigger group) *The students come from a wide cross-section of society.*

THESAURUS: wide

broad
range | selection | category | agreement | consensus | audience | alliance | coalition | spectrum | cross-section | generalization
broad means the same as **wide**:
Visitors can choose from a broad range of activities. | The courses offered by the college fall into three broad categories. | There was broad agreement on the need for tougher laws on drugs. | His later work appeals to a much broader audience. | The government was a broad alliance of eight political parties (=a large group of different people, organizations, countries etc). | *Among voters there is a broad spectrum of opinion on this issue* (=a wide range of different opinions - formal use). | *The survey asked a broad cross-section of people about their shopping habits* (=a group that is typical of a much bigger group). | *As a broad generalization, young lawyers have more energy, whereas older lawyers have more experience* (=a general statement that something is true in most cases).

Broad or wide?

With some words, you can only use **broad**. You say a **broad category/alliance/coalition/generalization** (not a 'wide' one).

It is much more common to say a **wide**

variety/choice/selection than a 'broad' one.
Broad is used especially in more formal English.
The abstract meaning of **broad** (=including many different people or things) is much more common than the literal meaning (=measuring a long distance across).

ANTONYMS **wide → narrow (2)**

widespread *adj* THESAURUS **common (1)**

wife *n*
the woman that a man is married to

ADJECTIVES/NOUNS + wife

sb's first/second/third etc wife *His second wife will inherit all of his money.*
sb's former wife/ex-wife *The actor's ex-wife sold her story to the newspapers.*
a devoted/loving wife (=one who loves her husband) *She was a devoted wife and mother.*
a dutiful wife *old-fashioned* (=one who behaves in a loyal and obedient way) *She played the role of the dutiful wife in public, but in private she had a series of affairs.*
a faithful/unfaithful wife *He killed his unfaithful wife and her lover in a fit of passion.*
sb's new wife *He took his new wife to Hawaii for their honeymoon.*
sb's future wife *He met his future wife at university.*
sb's late wife (=someone's wife who is now dead) *His late wife's mother helped to look after the children.*
sb's estranged wife (=someone's wife, who they no longer live with - used especially in newspapers) *His estranged wife, Maggie, refused to say whether she would divorce him.*
sb's common-law wife (=a woman who a man lives with as his wife, without them being officially married) *When he died, the house went to his common-law wife, Pearl.*
a trophy wife *disapproving* (=a beautiful young woman who is married to a rich or successful older man) *He wanted a trophy wife so that he could impress his friends.*

VERBS

have a wife *He has a wife and two children.*
meet your wife *Bruno met his wife when he hired her to work at his theater.*
marry your wife *He married his wife when he was 25.*
find (sb) a wife *His parents wanted to find him a wife.*
leave your wife *Simon left his wife for another woman.*
lose your wife (=your wife dies) *He lost his wife last year.*
be unfaithful to your wife (*also* **cheat on your wife** *informal*) (=have sex with someone who is not your wife) *I would never be unfaithful to my wife - I love her too much.*
divorce your wife *He divorced his wife in order to marry his mistress.*
be separated from your wife *He has been separated from his wife for several years.*

PHRASES

husband and wife *They are no longer living as husband and wife.*

wild *adj*
living in a natural state, not changed or controlled by people

NOUNS

wild flowers/plants/grass *The meadow was full of wild flowers and grasses.*
a wild rose *Wild roses are growing all over the fence.*
a wild animal/creature *There are many wild animals living in the forest, including deer and boar.*
a wild beast (=a large and dangerous wild animal) *The jungle was full of wild beasts.*
a wild bird/horse/dog/cat *This marshland is home to many wild birds.*

THESAURUS: wild
wild, pure, organic, unspoiled, undeveloped, untouched, virgin → **natural (1)**

wildlife *n*
the animals that live in an area

ADJECTIVES

local/native wildlife *The oil is causing problems for local wildlife.*
rare wildlife *The island is home to some rare wildlife.*
endangered wildlife (=very rare types of animal that may soon not exist any longer, because of man's activities) *The animals who live there include some of the world's most endangered wildlife.*

VERBS

protect/conserve wildlife *We need to balance the needs of farmers with protecting local wildlife.*
harm/threaten/endanger wildlife *Pollution in the river is harming wildlife.*
encourage wildlife *What can I do to encourage wildlife in my garden?*

wildlife + NOUNS

wildlife protection/conservation *More money needs to be spent on wildlife conservation.*
a wildlife habitat (=a place where animals can live) *As the population grows, more and more wildlife habitats are being destroyed.*

a wildlife reserve/sanctuary (=an area of land where wild animals are protected) *There are plans to turn the area into a wildlife sanctuary.*

the wildlife population (=the animals that live somewhere) *The wildlife population is constantly under threat from big logging companies.*

will *n*

1 the desire or determination to do something

ADJECTIVES

a strong will *As a small child she had a very strong will.*

an iron will (*also* **a will of iron**) (=an extremely strong will) *Her gentle manner concealed an iron will.*

an indomitable will (=a strong will which means you do not give in) *The most successful athletes have an indomitable will to win.*

a weak will *It's a myth that people are fat because of a weak will.*

political will (=determination on the part of governments and politicians) *There was a lack of political will to do anything about the problem.*

the general/collective will (=what most people want) *It is the role of government to enforce the general will of the nation.*

VERBS

have the will to do sth (=be determined enough to do it) *Do you have the will to win?*

lack the will to do sth *He lacked the will to resist.*

lose the will to do sth *The country's troops had lost the will to fight.*

destroy/break/sap sb's will *These comments were designed to destroy her confidence and sap her will.*

obey sb's will *It was the kind of place where workers were expected to obey the manager's will.*

impose your will on sb (=make someone do what you want) *She was trying to impose her will on the other members of the committee.*

PHRASES

strength of will *She had achieved success by sheer strength of will.*

an effort of will (=a determined effort to do something you do not want to do) *With a great effort of will, she resisted the temptation to look at the letter.*

an act of will (=something that you have to force yourself to do) *For most of us, taking exercise is an act of will.*

a battle/clash/test of wills (=when two determined people oppose each other) *Even the smallest decision could become an exhausting battle of wills.*

Will is also used in many phrases. If you do something **against your will**, you do it even though you do not want to do it: *She was made to sign the letter* ***against*** *her* ***will***. If you do something **of your own free will**, you do it because you want to, without being forced to do it: *He walked into a police station and gave himself up* ***of*** *his* ***own free will***. **Free will** is the idea that we all have the power to make our own decisions: *He believes that God gave us* ***free will*** *to make moral choices.*

2 a legal document stating what happens to your property after you die

VERBS

make a will *My lawyer has advised me to make a will.*

draw up a will (=write one) *We have finally taken the decision to draw up a will.*

leave a will *Who will inherit my property if I don't leave a will?*

leave sb sth in your will *My father left me the house in his will.*

change your will *She changed her will so that he wouldn't get any of her money.*

willing *adj* wanting to do something

ADVERBS

always willing to do sth *Maurice is always willing to give advice.*

perfectly willing/only too willing to do sth (=completely willing) *He told us that he was perfectly willing to help.*

increasingly willing to do sth *People are increasingly willing to spend money on meals in restaurants.*

VERBS

appear/seem willing to do sth *At first the man appeared willing to do what they wanted.*

find sb willing to do sth *We found 20 people willing to take part in the experiment.*

show willing (=show that you feel enthusiastic and want to help) *I was keen to show willing and said that I would be free all day Saturday.*

PHRASES

willing and able to do sth *Managers are willing and able to take a practical approach to problems.*

ready and willing to do sth *The boys were ready and willing to tell us what happened.*

more than willing to do sth (=very willing) *He was more than willing to join the group.*

less than willing/far from willing to do sth (=not willing) *The minister seemed less than willing to answer their questions.*

ANTONYMS **willing → unwilling**

willingness *n*

being prepared to do something or having no reason not to want to do it

ADJECTIVES

great willingness *She demonstrated great willingness to learn new skills.*

little/not much willingness *There was little willingness to talk about the problem.*
a genuine willingness *There is a genuine willingness to find a solution to the problem.*
sb's apparent willingness (=when someone seems to be willing to do something) *He was criticized for his apparent willingness to talk to the terrorists.*

VERBS
show/demonstrate willingness *None of the children showed any willingness to go home.*
express a willingness (=say that you are willing) *The president has expressed a willingness to change the law.*

PHRASES
willingness on sb's part (=willingness by someone to do something) *There was no real evidence of a willingness on their part to end the strike.*

win[1] *v*

1 to be the best or most successful in a game, election, war, argument etc

NOUNS
win a game/match *Our team won the game 2-0.*
win a race *The men's 100 meter race was won by Usain Bolt.*
win a competition *She won the school poetry competition.*
win a championship/tournament/league (=win a competition which consists of many games or stages) *Hamilton is hoping to win the world championship this season.*
win an election *The Democratic Party is expected to win the next election.*
win a battle/war *Who won the battle of Waterloo?*
win a victory *The protesters have won a huge victory against the government.*
win an argument *He won the argument and his suggestion was accepted.*
win a case/appeal *The workers won their case against the company.*
win a title (=be the winner of a sports competition) *India are the favourites to win the title.*

ADVERBS
win easily *He is a much better player - he should win easily.*
win comfortably (=by a large amount, so that you do not have to worry about winning) *The Celtics won comfortably, with a 22-point lead.*
win convincingly (=by a large amount) *United won convincingly by three goals to nil.*
win outright (=clearly and completely) *If one candidate gets more than 50 percent of the vote, he will win the seat outright.*
win narrowly (=by only a small amount) *In 1916 he narrowly won re-election.*

VERBS
be expected to win *The Irish horse is expected to win.*
deserve to win *We played great football and I thought we deserved to win.*

PREPOSITIONS
win by ten points/three metres etc *We won by 23 points.*
win at cards/chess etc *My brother always wins at chess.*
win against sb *We haven't won against them for months.*

PHRASES
a winning streak (=when you win several times one after another) *The defeat ended the team's eight-game winning streak.*
win hands down *informal* (=very easily or by a large amount) *He won hands down, getting 10,000 out of the possible 12,000 votes.*

2 to succeed in getting something as a result of your efforts

NOUNS
win a prize/award/medal *Doris Lessing won the Nobel Prize for Literature in 2007.*
win a contract *The contract to build the power station was won by a French company.*
win the right to do sth *It was a long time before women finally won the right to vote.*
win a reputation for/as sth *Durham won a reputation as a hard worker.*
win a scholarship *She won a scholarship to study ballet in London.*
win a place (on a course) *Louise worked hard to win a place at Leeds University to study German.*
win sb's support/approval *The government needs to win support from voters for its economic reforms.*
win praise *He won praise for helping to end the war.*
win sb's respect/admiration/affection/sympathy *His talent won him respect from the other players.*
win sb's trust/confidence *It takes time to win the trust of the horse.*

THESAURUS: win
receive, obtain, acquire, gain, win, earn, inherit, get hold of sth → **get (1)**

win[2] *n*

a victory, especially in sport

ADJECTIVES/NOUNS + win
a five-point/two-goal etc win *The team had a nine-point win over Arizona.*
an easy win *He had an easy win in the first game.*

W

a comfortable win (*also* **a convincing win** *BrE*) (=by a large amount) *The Manchester side enjoyed a comfortable win against their London rivals.*

a big win (=an important win, or one that you win by a large amount) *This is the biggest win in the young player's career.*

straight/successive/consecutive wins (=one after the other) *This result makes six straight wins for the Canadian.*

VERBS

have/score a win (*also* **notch up a win** *informal*): *We haven't had a win in six games.*

celebrate a win *The American is celebrating her third consecutive win.*

pull off/clinch a win (=win when it is difficult) *The youngster clinched a 9-6 win over the champion late last night.*

cruise to a win (=win easily) *The French side cruised to a win over a poor Spanish team.*

secure/seal a win (=make it certain) *Can they secure the win they need to get into the next round?*

PREPOSITIONS

a win over/against sb *The team ended the season with a win against Manchester United.*

wind *n*

moving air, especially when it moves strongly or quickly in a current

ADJECTIVES

a strong wind *The wind was so strong he could hardly stand up.*

a gentle/light wind (=not strong) *There was a gentle wind blowing through the trees.*

high winds (=very strong winds) *High winds are making driving conditions difficult.*

a cold wind *She wrapped her scarf around her face against the cold wind.*

an icy/biting/bitter wind (=very cold) *She shivered in the icy wind.*

a blustery/gusty wind (=which blows strongly for short periods) *The golfers had to battle against a blustery wind.*

a fresh wind *BrE* (=quite cold and strong) *It will feel colder in places exposed to a fresh northeasterly wind.*

a 20-/40-mile-an-hour wind *The walkers struggled in 35-mile-an-hour winds.*

gale force/hurricane force winds (=very strong) *The island was battered by gale force winds.*

the north/south etc wind (=coming from the north etc) *They sought shelter from the north wind.*

a northerly/southerly etc wind (=coming from the north etc) *A fresh northerly wind was speeding the ship southwards.*

the prevailing wind (=the wind that blows somewhere most of the time) *The prevailing wind comes from the west.*

VERBS

the wind blows *The wind blew from the northeast.*

the wind picks up (*also* **the wind gets up** *BrE*) (=becomes stronger) *The wind started to pick up in the afternoon.*

the wind drops/dies down (=becomes less strong) *The wind had dropped a little.*

the wind howls (=makes a lot of noise) *The wind howled round the house all night.*

the wind moans (=makes a long low sound) *They could hear the wind moaning in the trees.*

the wind changes (=starts blowing from a different direction) *The wind had to change before his fighting ships could sail against the Spanish.*

the wind buffets sth (=the wind hits it with a lot of force) *It was dark and the car was buffeted by the wind.*

wind + NOUNS

wind speed *Wind speeds of up to 80 miles an hour were recorded.*

wind power/energy *The government is looking at alternative sources of energy, such as wind power.*

a wind farm (=a place where wind energy is produced) *Some people think wind farms are just as ugly as power stations.*

a wind turbine (=a modern windmill for producing electrical power) *The electricity is generated by a huge wind turbine.*

wind chimes (=long thin pieces of metal that make musical sounds in the wind) *We hung wind chimes above the door.*

PREPOSITIONS

in the wind *Flags were blowing in the wind.*

against the wind (=in order to protect yourself from the wind) *We huddled together against the wind.*

PHRASES

a gust of wind (=a sudden strong movement of wind) *A gust of wind blew my hat off.*

be blowing/swaying/flapping etc in the wind (=be moving about in the wind) *The trees were all swaying in the wind.*

provide shelter/protection from the wind *The wall provided some shelter from the wind.*

the wind chill factor (=the decrease in temperature caused by the cold wind) *It must have been minus five degrees with the wind chill factor.*

THESAURUS: wind

breeze
a gentle pleasant wind:
The trees were ***moving*** *gently* ***in the breeze.*** *|* ***A gentle breeze*** *was* ***blowing*** *from the sea.*

W

draught *BrE*, **draft** *AmE*
a current of cool air which blows into a room, especially one that makes you feel uncomfortable:
There's a bit of a ***draught*** *in here – can you close the door?*

gale
a very strong wind:
The ship was blown off course in a ***severe gale***. *|* ***Howling gales*** *and torrential rain continued throughout the night.*

hurricane
a storm that has very strong fast winds and that moves over water – used about storms in the North Atlantic Ocean:
The hurricane devastated Florida and killed at least 40 people. | The island was ***hit by a hurricane***.

typhoon
a violent tropical storm – used about storms in the western Pacific Ocean:
A ***typhoon*** *has* ***hit*** *the Philippines, lifting roofs off houses and uprooting trees.*

tornado (*also* **twister** *AmE informal*)
a violent storm with strong winds that spin very quickly in a circle, often forming a cloud that is narrower at the bottom than the top:
The town was ***hit by a tornado*** *that damaged several homes.*

cyclone
a violent tropical storm with strong winds that spin in a circle:
A devastating ***cyclone struck*** *Bangladesh in April that year. | This cyclone was traveling at speeds in excess of 100 miles an hour.*

window *n*

a space or an area of glass in the wall of a building or vehicle that lets in light

ADJECTIVES/NOUNS + window

an open window *She felt a breeze from the open window.*

a window is closed/shut *All the windows were closed.*

a front/back window *I don't want people looking in my front window.*

an upstairs/downstairs window *Someone was waving to me from an upstairs window.*

the rear window (=the back window, especially of a car) *The car's rear window had been smashed.*

a shop/store window *She looked in shop windows.*

sb's bedroom/office window *From his bedroom window he could see two men having an argument.*

the kitchen/car etc window *She had left the kitchen window open.*

a stained glass window (=made of pieces of coloured glass) *The church has fine medieval stained glass windows.*

VERBS

open a window *I opened the window and breathed in the fresh air.*

close/shut a window *It's cold – can we shut the window?*

roll up/down a window (=open or shut the window in a car) *I rolled the window down and waved to him.*

a window overlooks sth (=you can see something from a window) *They gave me a room with a window overlooking the garden.*

window + NOUNS

a window frame *The window frame was rotten.*

a window pane (=the glass part of a window) *There were dirty marks on one of the window panes.*

a window sill (=the bottom edge of the frame of a window) *A bird was sitting on the window sill.*

PREPOSITIONS

through a window *I could see a shadowy figure through the bathroom window.*

out of a window *She lay in bed looking out of the window.*

from a window *From the bedroom window, we could see the hills.*

at/in the window *A woman's face appeared at the window.*

windy *adj*

if it is windy, there is a lot of wind

NOUNS

a windy day/night/morning *It is no fun cycling on a wet and windy day.*

a windy morning/afternoon/evening *It was a cold windy morning in spring.*

windy weather *In windy weather, water from the fountain is blown sideways.*

windy conditions *Golfers are having problems with the windy conditions.*

ADVERBS

really windy *It was really windy, and we could hardly stand upright.*

too windy *It was too windy to take the boat out.*

THESAURUS: windy

breezy
day | **morning** | **afternoon** | **sunshine**
if the weather is breezy, the wind blows fairly strongly:
It was a breezy day, and it was hard to hold the map flat. | They were enjoying the breezy autumn sunshine.

blustery
day | **night** | **morning** | **afternoon** | **evening** | **conditions** | **wind** | **weather**

W

if it is blustery, it is very windy, with sudden strong movements of wind:
It was a cold, blustery day. | Despite the blustery conditions, he finished the race in 10 minutes 29 seconds.

gusty
wind | conditions
gusty wind blows with strong, sudden movements:
The plane was trying to land in a gusty wind. | You need skill to windsurf in gusty conditions.

stormy
weather | night | day | evening | sea | waters
if the weather is stormy, there are strong winds, heavy rain, and dark clouds:
The ship sank in stormy weather 400 years ago. | It was a dark and stormy night. | Rescue helicopters hoisted 11 crew members from the stormy waters.

windswept
island | beach | hill | cliff | plain | plateau | moor
a windswept place is often windy because there are not many trees or buildings to protect it:
Agriculture is difficult on this rocky windswept island. | People were walking their dogs on the windswept beach.

wine *n*

an alcoholic drink made from grapes, or a type of this drink

ADJECTIVES

red/white/rosé wine *The waiter brought some red wine.*

French/Spanish/Italian etc wine *The restaurant has a good selection of French wines.*

dry wine (=not sweet) *I'd like a dry white wine, please.*

sweet wine *A slightly sweet wine goes well with fruit such as pears.*

sparkling wine (=with bubbles of gas in it) *The best-known sparkling wine is champagne.*

strong wine (=containing a lot of alcohol or having a lot of flavour) *This village produces strong wines of good character.*

light wine (=not having a strong taste) *The wine is light and refreshing.*

full-bodied wine (=with a pleasantly strong taste) *This cheese goes well with full-bodied red wines.*

vintage wine (=good quality wine from a particular year) *They keep a collection of vintage wines in the cellar.*

fine wine (=a good and expensive wine) *He was a lover of fine wines and good food.*

cheap wine *I had a big hangover caused by drinking too much cheap wine.*

NOUNS + wine

table wine (=inexpensive wine to drink with a meal) *The vineyard produce table wines for local use.*

the house wine (=the cheapest wine available in a restaurant) *I ordered a glass of the house wine.*

NOUNS + wine

a wine glass/bottle *The wine was served in beautiful wine glasses.*

the wine list (=the list of wines in a restaurant) *I asked to see the wine list.*

a wine buff/connoisseur (=someone who knows a lot about wine) *The website is for wine buffs.*

a wine merchant(s) (=a company or shop that sells wine) *The company was voted Best Organic Wine Merchant.*

VERBS

drink wine *I don't drink a lot of wine – just a couple of glasses a week.*

sip wine (=drink it in small quantities from a glass) *She sipped her wine slowly.*

pour wine *The waiter poured some wine into his glass.*

a wine matures (=its taste improves over time) *The wine is kept in oak barrels to mature.*

a wine breathes (=the air helps to improve the taste after it has been in a bottle) *Some people say you should let the wine breathe for up to half an hour before you drink it.*

the wine is corked (=it tastes bad because the cork has allowed air into the bottle) *This wine has a funny taste – I'm sure it's corked.*

PHRASES

a bottle of wine *Let's open another bottle of wine.*

a glass of wine *I poured myself a glass of wine.*

wing *n*

1 one of the parts of a bird's or insect's body that it uses for flying

VERBS

flap its wings (=move them) *The ducks woke up and flapped their wings.*

beat its wings (=move them in a regular way while flying) *The female beats her wings at up to 500 times a second.*

flutter its wings (=move them quickly) *I heard some birds fluttering their wings outside the window.*

spread/open its wings *The young bird spread its wings and attempted to fly.*

stretch its wings (=open them completely) *The cage was so small the birds could not even stretch their wings.*

fold its wings *The birds fold their wings and dive into the sea in search of fish.*

wings flap *I could hear the swan's huge wings flapping overhead.*
wings beat *Their great wings beat slowly.*

ADJECTIVES

outstretched wings *The eagle descended on outstretched wings.*

2 a group within an organization, especially a political party

ADJECTIVES

the left wing (=that supports socialist policies) *She is known to be on the left wing of British politics.*

the right wing (=that supports companies and business, a strong army etc) *The right wing of the party want to increase military spending.*

the extreme/radical wing (=having opinions that seem unreasonable to many people) *He belonged to the extreme wing of the communist party.*

the political wing (=of a group that also has an unofficial military part) *The government held talks with the political wing of the IRA (Irish Republican Army).*

This meaning of **wing** is often used in the adjectives **left-wing** and **right-wing**: *right-wing politicians | When he was young he was very* ***left-wing****.*

winner *n*

a person or animal that has won something

ADJECTIVES

the clear winner *She was the clear winner, with 150 points more than her nearest rival.*

the overall winner (=after all the parts of the race or competition have finished) *After all the scores are added together, the overall winner will be announced.*

the outright winner (=out of all the people or teams) *She was delighted to be declared the outright winner.*

a convincing winner (=someone who wins easily) *He was a convincing winner, defeating his opponent by 3 sets to 0.*

the lucky winner *The lucky winner of the competition will drive home this car.*

the eventual winner (=at the end of the race or competition) *After an exciting finish, Johnson was the eventual winner.*

joint winners (=two people share the first prize) *The two women were declared joint winners of the competition.*

a worthy/deserving winner *After such a magnificent performance, he was a worthy winner.*

a previous/former winner *She was presented with the trophy by a previous winner of the tournament.*

a likely winner *Chelsea looked likely winners of the match when they scored in the 85th minute.*

VERBS

announce the winner *The winner of the competition will be announced in next month's magazine.*

declare sb/sth the winner *She was declared the winner and given a gold medal.*

choose/pick a winner *Have you ever picked the winner in a horse race?*

emerge as the winner *He emerged as the winner of the country's presidential elections.*

the winner receives sth *The winner will receive a $1,000 prize.*

NOUNS + winner

the competition winner *The competition winners each received a cheque for £5,000.*

an award/prize/medal/cup winner *He was an award winner in this year's photography competition.*

PREPOSITIONS

the winner of sth *She's a former winner of the Young Musician of the Year award.*

winter *n*

the season after autumn and before spring, when the weather is coldest

ADJECTIVES

this/next/last winter *It's not as cold as last winter.*

the previous/following winter *The previous winter he had seen swans flying south.*

early winter *Fresh nuts are at their best in late autumn and early winter.*

late winter *In late winter we sometimes get a lot of snow.*

a cold winter *I hope we don't get another cold winter.*

a severe/hard/harsh winter (=very cold) *In a hard winter, many birds starve.*

a mild winter (=not very cold) *Winters here are generally mild.*

a long winter *The long winter finally came to an end.*

VERBS

winter comes/arrives *He wanted to finish the building work before winter arrived.*

winter + NOUNS

winter coat/winter shoes *It looks cold outside – you'll need your winter coat.*

a winter landscape/scene *The Christmas card had a snowy winter landscape on the front.*

the winter months *During the winter months the town is often cut off.*

the winter term *BrE*, **the winter semester** *AmE* (=the time between October and March at a school, college, or university) *I had just completed the winter semester at university.*

a winter's day/morning/afternoon *One winter's day, we decided to go for a walk in the snow.*

PREPOSITIONS

in (the) winter *It usually snows here in the winter.*

during (the) winter *The caravan was too cold to live in during the winter.*

the winter of 2012/1947 etc *We moved to Montana in the winter of 2011.*

PHRASES

in the depths of winter (=in the middle of the winter) *Even in the depths of winter, the harbour is never completely frozen.*

the onset of winter (=the start of winter) *She dreaded the onset of winter.*

wipe *v* THESAURUS clean[2]

wire *n*

1 thin metal in the form of a thread, or a piece of this

ADJECTIVES/NOUNS + wire

copper/steel wire *The cables that support the bridge are made of steel wire.*

fine/thin wire *Only a piece of fine wire could fit through such a tiny hole.*

thick wire *Curtains hung from a thick wire.*

barbed wire (=wire with a lot of sharp points on it, used for making fences) *The field was surrounded by barbed wire.*

razor wire (=wire with a lot of blade-shaped pieces fitted to it, used for making fences) *The prison wall had razor wire on the top.*

wire + NOUNS

a wire fence *The compound was surrounded by a wire fence.*

wire netting *We put some wire netting around the plants, to protect them from wild animals.*

wire mesh (=a thin wire net) *The fence is made of a thin wire mesh.*

PHRASES

a piece/length/strand of wire *The pieces of wire he'd cut were too short.*

a coil of wire *The coil of barbed wire will be used for a fence.*

2 thin metal thread that carries electricity or electrical signals

ADJECTIVES/NOUNS + wire

electrical wire *He has a roll of electrical wire in the garage.*

telephone wires *A man was up a ladder repairing the telephone wires.*

overhead wires *Don't go fishing anywhere near overhead wires.*

bare/exposed wires *Those exposed wires could give you a serious electric shock.*

VERBS

attach a wire *Attach the red wire to the car battery.*

PHRASES

a tangle of wires (=an untidy mass of wires) *There's an ugly tangle of wires behind the TV.*

wisdom *n*

good sense and judgment, or wise words

ADJECTIVES

great wisdom *She was a woman of great wisdom.*

ancient wisdom *In some cases modern science confirms ancient wisdom.*

political wisdom *As a statesman, he was known for his political wisdom.*

worldly wisdom (=relating to how people behave, usually gained from experience) *I was young and lacking in worldly wisdom.*

accumulated wisdom (=collected over many years from many people) *In these books, there is the accumulated wisdom of mankind.*

VERBS

acquire/gain wisdom *Wisdom is gained through experience.*

impart/dispense wisdom (to sb) *formal* (=give someone good information or advice) *Her followers listened as she imparted wisdom to them.*

share your wisdom (with sb) *often humorous* (=give someone good information or advice) *Would you mind sharing your wisdom with us?*

PHRASES

words of wisdom (=words in which someone says something wise) *He offered his young neighbour a few words of wisdom.*

pearls of wisdom *often humorous* (=very wise and helpful words) *Thank you, Matthew, for those pearls of wisdom.*

a piece of wisdom *When someone asked what to do, he would give them a small piece of wisdom.*

a source of wisdom *To his students, he was a source of wisdom and inspiration.*

give sb the benefit of your wisdom *often humorous* (=give someone some good information or advice) *I was wondering if you could give us the benefit of your wisdom about this.*

wise *adj*

1 sensible and based on good judgment

NOUNS

a wise decision/choice *I told him he had made a wise decision.*

a wise move (=a sensible thing to do) *Getting into an argument with a police officer was not a wise move.*

a wise precaution (=a sensible thing to do in case something else happens) *It is a wise precaution to take a spare set of batteries.*

a wise investment *He had increased his wealth by making wise investments.*

a wise use of sth *We must make wise use of our resources.*

wise advice *My father gave them a lot of wise advice.*

wise words *We should remember the wise words of the philosopher Socrates.*

2 having a lot of knowledge and experience of life

PHRASES

a wise old man/woman *A wise old man once said "Be true to yourself."*

THESAURUS: wise

clever, smart, bright, brilliant, gifted, wise, cunning, brainy → **intelligent**

wish *n*

a desire to do or have something

ADJECTIVES

sb's greatest/deepest wish (*also* **sb's dearest wish** *BrE*) (=what they want most of all) *Her greatest wish was to see her parents again.*

sb's last/final/dying wish (=just before someone dies) *Her last wish was to be buried in her husband's grave.*

a fervent wish *formal* (=a strong wish) *It was always his fervent wish to return to his native land.*

a secret wish *Jane had always had a secret wish to be a dancer.*

VERBS

make a wish (=silently ask for something that you want to happen) *Helen blew out the candles and made a wish.*

get/have your wish (=get what you want) *She wanted him to leave, and she got her wish.*

grant/fulfil sb's wish (=give them what they want) *His parents would now be able to grant his wish.*

express a wish (=say that you want to do something) *He expressed a wish to go to the United States.*

respect sb's wishes (=do what they want) *We have to respect his wishes.*

ignore sb's wishes *It is important not to ignore the wishes of the patient.*

reflect sb's wishes (=show what their wishes are) *The council is the voice of the people so it must reflect their wishes.*

wish + NOUNS

a wish list (=all the things you would like to have) *We all made a wish list of who we would like in the team.*

PREPOSITIONS

a wish for sth *Reporters ignored his wish for privacy.*

PHRASES

sb's wish comes true (=something you want really happens) *One day I hope my wish will come true.*

have no wish to do sth *I have no wish to keep you here for longer than is necessary.*

against sb's wishes (*also* **contrary to sb's wishes** *formal*): *Contrary to her parents' wishes, she decided not to go to university.*

in accordance with sb's wishes *formal* (=following what someone wants) *In accordance with his wishes, the money was used to establish a school.*

wistful *adj* THESAURUS **sad (1)**

wit *n*

1 the ability to say things that are clever and amusing

ADJECTIVES

great wit *Her books describe upper-class life with great wit.*

quick wit *He enjoyed interviews, often displaying his quick wit.*

sharp wit (=able to answer people quickly and amusingly) *You need to have a sharp wit to be a stand-up comedian.*

caustic/acerbic/barbed wit (=unkind but cleverly humorous) *He responded with his usual acerbic wit.*

dry wit (=funny and clever while seeming to be serious) *She is known for her dry wit.*

razor-sharp wit (=very sharp wit) *He made fun of them with his razor-sharp wit.*

2 the ability to think quickly and make the right decisions

Grammar

Usually plural in this meaning.

VERBS

use your wits *Politicians have to use their wits when they're being asked difficult questions.*

gather/collect/recover your wits (=manage to think what to do next after a shock or surprise) *She collected her wits and continued speaking.*

live by your wits (=get money by being clever or dishonest, not by doing an ordinary job) *He didn't want to work, and thought he could live by his wits.*

PHRASES

keep/have your wits about you (=be able to think quickly and do the right thing in a difficult situation) *You have to remain calm and keep your wits about you when you're being interviewed.*

pit your wits against sb (=compete in a test of knowledge or intelligence) *I pitted my wits against him in a game of chess.*

have the wit to do sth (=be clever enough to know what to do) *She had the wit to apologize for her mistake.*

a battle of wits (=a situation in which opposing sides try to win by using their intelligence) *The negotiations had become a battle of wits.*

witness *n*

someone who appears in a court of law to say what they know about a crime

ADJECTIVES/NOUNS + witness

a key witness (=a very important witness) *The defendant's ex-wife will be a key witness at the trial.*

an expert witness (=someone with special knowledge who gives an opinion in court) *An expert witness testified that the injuries were probably caused by a kitchen knife.*

a prosecution witness *During the trial, over 30 prosecution witnesses were called.*

a defence witness *A defence witness said that Carter was not holding a gun when the shot was fired.*

a star witness (=a very important witness who says things that help one side a lot) *It was a major blow to their case when their star witness was arrested.*

the principal witness (=the main witness) *The principal witness was too sick to testify.*

a character witness (=a witness who says that the person being tried is a good person) *He said he would gladly be a character witness for her.*

a reliable/unreliable witness (=whose information can or cannot be trusted) *The woman proved to be an unreliable witness.*

VERBS

call a witness (=require a witness to speak in court) *She was the final witness to be called.*

appear as a witness *He appeared as an expert witness at several government inquiries.*

question a witness *They were not permitted to question government witnesses.*

cross-examine a witness (=ask them questions about what they have said) *His attorney cross-examined the witness.*

a witness testifies (=makes a statement) *Two witnesses testified that they had seen him take the money.*

a witness gives evidence *Child witnesses gave evidence using closed circuit television cameras.*

witness + NOUNS

the witness box/stand (=the place where the witness sits when speaking in court) *He spent three hours in the witness stand.*

a witness statement/account (*also* **witness testimony**) (=what a witness says) *In her witness statement she said that she had left the house around eight.*

PREPOSITIONS

a witness in a case/trial *She was an important witness in a murder trial.*

a witness for sb/sth *The witnesses for the prosecution did not sound convincing.*

PHRASES

a witness takes the stand (=begins to answer questions) *He was the last witness to take the stand.*

witty *adj*

using words in a clever and amusing way

NOUNS

a witty remark/comment *Mike made us all laugh with his witty remarks.*

a witty article/piece/column *She writes witty articles about everyday life for a Sunday newspaper.*

a witty account/tale *The novel is a witty account of his experiences as a journalist in New York.*

witty conversation *The TV presenter was trying to make witty conversation with one of his guests.*

witty repartee/banter (=friendly conversation in which people make a lot of jokes about each other) *I used to love listening to their witty repartee.*

ADVERBS

delightfully/wonderfully witty *John Betjeman wrote some delightfully witty poems about the British way of life.*

THESAURUS: witty

amusing, humorous, light-hearted, witty, comic, comical, hilarious, hysterical → **funny (1)**

woman *n* an adult female person

ADJECTIVES/NOUNS + woman

a beautiful/attractive/pretty woman *Your wife is a very attractive woman.*

a married/single/divorced woman *The king was not allowed to marry a divorced woman.*

a young/middle-aged/old/elderly woman *Who is the young woman in the black dress?*

a strong woman *Some men like strong women.*

a career woman (=who wants to be successful in her job) *I didn't want to be a career woman who only saw her children at weekends.*

woman + NOUNS

a woman president/prime minister *Mrs Thatcher was Britain's first woman prime minister.*

a woman artist *Frida Kahlo is one of my favourite women artists.*

PHRASES

a women's magazine *Women's magazines are full of advice about dieting.*

women's rights *She fought for women's rights.*
the women's movement (=the movement to improve conditions for women in society) *The women's movement started in the early 1960s.*
the women's team *The women's team won a gold medal.*

wonder *n*

1 a feeling of surprise and admiration for something because it seems very impressive

VERBS

fill sb with wonder *The sight of the huge mountains filled her with wonder.*
feel wonder *It's difficult to express the wonder I felt when saw my baby.*

PREPOSITIONS

with wonder *Her eyes opened wide with wonder.*

PHRASES

look/stare/gaze/watch in wonder *They watched in wonder as the magnificent bird flew off into the sky.*
full of wonder *When he first arrived, he was full of wonder about the place.*

> **Wonder** is often used when saying that something surprises you, or does not surprise you: *There are so many children in the class –* ***it's a wonder that*** *she can remember all their names. | It's been raining all day.* **No wonder** *the ground is so wet.*

2 something that impresses you and makes you full of surprise and admiration

> **Grammar**
> Usually plural in this meaning.

PHRASES

the wonders of the world *The Grand Canyon is one of the great wonders of the world.*
the wonders of nature *God gives us intelligence to uncover the wonders of nature.*
the wonders of science/medicine/modern technology *The wonders of modern medical science make it possible for many illnesses to be treated.*
sth is one of the wonders of the age/of its time (=it is one of the most impressive things of its time) *The pyramids were one of the great wonders of the age.*

ADJECTIVES

the great wonders *Science makes us aware of the great wonders that surround us.*
natural wonders *The Great Barrier Reef is one of Australia's great natural wonders.*

PREPOSITIONS

the wonders of sth *People were impressed by the wonders of nuclear energy.*

wonderful *adj* THESAURUS ▸ excellent

wood *n*

1 the material that trees are made of

ADJECTIVES

solid wood *The doors are all made of solid wood.*
bare wood (=not painted or covered) *We decided to paint the bare wood.*
a hard/soft wood *Oak is a hard wood.*

VERBS

be made of wood *The whole house is made of wood.*
chop wood *He was chopping wood for the fire.*
cut/saw wood *A local carpenter cut the wood to the right size.*
carve wood (=used a knife to shape it) *The room was decorated with carved wood.*
paint wood *The wood was all newly painted.*
stain wood (=dye it with a special liquid) *The seats are in a light-coloured stained wood.*
varnish wood (=paint it with a clear substance to make it shiny) *You can varnish the wood or leave it as it is.*
wood splinters (=small sharp pieces break off it) *Soft wood splinters easily.*

wood + NOUNS

wood chips (=small rough pieces) *Cover the soil with wood chips to prevent weeds.*
wood shavings (=thin curly pieces) *He cleared up the wood shavings.*
wood smoke (=smoke from burning wood) *There was a smell of wood smoke.*
a wood carving (=a picture cut from wood) *There are wood carvings all over the church.*

PHRASES

a piece of wood *He made a bench out of pieces of wood.*
a plank of wood (=a long thin flat piece) *The shed was built from some old planks of wood.*
a block of wood *I used a block of wood to knock the pole into the ground.*
the grain of the wood (=the natural lines in it) *The oil enhances the natural grain of the wood.*

2 a small forest

ADJECTIVES

a dense/thick wood (=with a lot of trees growing closely together) *Paul led the way up through the dense woods.*
a dark wood *She found herself lost in a dark wood.*
a pine wood *The pine woods smell lovely as you walk through them.*

PREPOSITIONS

in a wood/in the woods *We went for a walk in the woods.*
through a wood/through the woods *The route then passes through a wood.*

PHRASES

deep in the woods *The noise came from deep in the woods.*

the middle of the woods *They passed a large empty house in the middle of the woods.*

the edge of the woods *We left the car on the edge of the woods and continued on foot.*

a clearing in the woods (=a space where there are no trees) *They decided to camp in a clearing in the woods.*

word *n*

a single group of letters or sounds that have a particular meaning

ADJECTIVES

a new word *Computer technology has brought many new words into our language.*

the right word *He struggled to find the right word.*

a German/Italian/Latin etc word *'Science' comes from a Latin word meaning 'knowledge'.*

a long/short word *Prepositions are usually short words, that show the position or direction of something.*

big words *spoken* (=long and difficult words) *He uses all these big words that I don't understand.*

a five-letter/nine-letter etc word *Can you think of a nine-letter word meaning 'hard'?*

angry/harsh/kind/brave etc words (=something angry etc that is said) *Angry words were spoken, which nearly led to a fight.*

a careless word (=something that is said carelessly) *One careless word could put us all in danger.*

a rude word *Someone had written a rude word on the back of his chair.*

a swear word (=a rude or offensive word, used especially when you are angry) *I've never heard him use a swear word.*

a four-letter word (=a very rude word) *The programme was full of four-letter words.*

VERBS + word

say/speak a word *I have never said the words 'I love you' and not meant it.*

write a word *Edward Thomas wrote these words in 1908.*

use a word *Be very careful how you use the word 'foreign'.*

find words (=succeed in thinking of words to express something) *She couldn't find the words to explain how she felt.*

search for words (=try to think of words to use) *She hesitated, searching for words.*

have a word for sth *The people have more than 40 different words for snow.*

coin a word (=invent it) *Richard Owen was the man who coined the word 'dinosaur'.*

pronounce a word *How do you pronounce this word?*

spell a word *I always find Mississippi a hard word to spell.*

look up a word (=try to find it in a dictionary) *I looked up the word 'lugubrious' in my dictionary.*

word + VERBS

a word means sth *The Spanish word 'matador' means 'killer'.*

a word comes/derives from sth *The word 'plumbing' derives from the Latin word for 'lead'.*

PREPOSITIONS

a word for sth *'Vater' is the German word for 'father'.*

words of encouragement/comfort/wisdom (=encouraging etc things that are said) *He murmured soothing words of comfort.*

PHRASES

the meaning of a word *What is the meaning of the word 'tangible'?*

in the words of sb (*also* **in sb's words**) (=used when repeating someone else's words) *In the words of Rousseau "Man is born free, but everywhere he is in chains."*

in your own words *Describe in your own words what happened.*

in other words (=used when saying the same thing in a different way or explaining it) *He said he couldn't give me answer right now – in other words, he doesn't know.*

have/exchange a few words with sb (=have a short conversation) *He paused to exchange a few words with the guard.*

put your feelings/thoughts into words (=say something that expresses your feelings or thoughts) *The winner said it was hard to put his feelings into words.*

be lost for words (=be so surprised or emotional that you can't think of anything to say) *It was rare for Virginia to be lost for words.*

work[1] *v*

1 to do a job or use effort to do something

ADVERBS

work hard *We have all been working hard to finish the project.*

work part-time/full-time *Some mothers choose to work part-time.*

work late (=carry on working one evening) *He said he had to work late tonight.*

work tirelessly/ceaselessly (=hard, all the time) *They have worked tirelessly to bring about peace in the region.*

work well with sb/together *We work well together and are good friends too.*

work closely with sb/together *I look forward to working closely with you on this task.*

work independently *Students are encouraged to work independently.*

work effectively/efficiently *If we work more efficiently, we can produce more.*

work diligently (=hard and carefully) *He worked diligently in the laboratory.*

PREPOSITIONS

work for sb/a company etc *He works for an insurance company.*

work at/in a factory/office/hospital etc *Dad worked at the local car factory.*

work as a nurse/journalist/teacher etc *She worked as a nurse for six years.*

work in industry/education/publishing etc *He had previously worked in publishing.*

work on sth *The scientists are working on a possible cure for cancer.*

PHRASES

work from home *Technology now allows many people to work from home.*

2 if a machine, medicine, method etc works, it does what it should or produces the result you want

ADVERBS

work well *The system works very well.*

work perfectly *The car was working perfectly when I drove it this morning.*

work properly *The doctors did some tests to find out if her kidneys were working properly.*

work smoothly (=without problems) *The new software seems to be working smoothly.*

work efficiently *If the heart is strong and working efficiently, oxygen will circulate all round the body.*

PREPOSITIONS

sth works on sth (=used when saying that something is effective at dealing with a problem) *The cleaning fluid works on most types of stains.*

sth works for sb (=used when saying that you find that a method is effective) *Have you tried spraying a little oil on the lock? That usually works for me.*

PHRASES

find out if sth works *The drugs are being tested, to find out if they work on a range of different patients.*

work like a dream (=very well) *This strategy worked like a dream, and he started winning games.*

> **THESAURUS: work**
>
> manage, pass, work → **succeed**

W

work² *n*

1 what you do in order to earn money

ADJECTIVES/NOUNS + work

part-time work *He does part-time work at the local library.*

temporary work *Many students look for temporary work during the vacation.*

full-time work *Are you available for full-time work?*

freelance work (=selling your work to different companies rather than being employed by one) *She never took another permanent job, but supported herself with freelance work.*

secretarial/clerical/office work *I have experience in secretarial work.*

manual/physical work (=work done with your hands or body) *It was too hot in the afternoons to do manual work.*

skilled/unskilled work *They could only find low-paid unskilled work.*

paid work *She hasn't done any paid work since she had children.*

voluntary work *BrE*, **volunteer work** *AmE* (=a job you are not paid for) *I do voluntary work in a youth club.*

sb's daily work (=the work someone does every day) *When they finished their daily work they were too tired to do anything.*

dangerous/interesting/rewarding etc work *It's interesting work and I enjoy it.*

VERBS

look for work (*also* **seek work** *formal*): *Young people come to town looking for work.*

find work *It was difficult for them to find work.*

start work *He started work as a trainee accountant.*

return to work/go back to work *His doctor agreed he was fit enough to return to work.*

do ... work *Women should be paid the same as men for doing the same work.*

work + NOUNS

work clothes *He had just got home and was still in his work clothes.*

a work environment *It is important to have a pleasant work environment.*

PREPOSITIONS

out of work (=without a job) *He lost his job and was out of work for six months.*

in work (=with a job) *There has been an increase in the incomes of those still in work.*

off work (=not working temporarily, usually because you are ill) *He had an accident and has been off work for two weeks.*

PHRASES

sb's line of work (=type of work) *I meet lots of interesting people in my line of work.*

sb's place of work *formal*: *They lived very close to their place of work.*

2 activity that involves effort

ADJECTIVES/NOUNS + work

hard work *It's been very hard work, but I've loved every moment of it.*

backbreaking work (=extremely tiring) *Clearing the garden was slow, backbreaking work.*

heavy work (=hard physical work) *The heavy work is done by the gardener.*
arduous work *formal* (=very hard) *In those days coal mining was arduous work.*
light work (=work that is not physically hard) *He had been ill, but she found him some light work to do.*
practical work *Students have to do experiments and other practical work.*
domestic work (=cleaning the house, cooking etc) *Women still do most of the domestic work.*
construction/building work *They appointed a project manager to oversee the building work.*
agricultural/farm work *His sons helped with the farm work.*

VERBS

do work *He was doing some work on his father's car.*
carry out work (=do some work, especially work that has been planned) *The work should be carried out without further delay.*
set to/get to/get down to work (=start work) *They set to work cutting down trees and undergrowth.*
undertake work *Do you have the necessary legal expertise to undertake this work?*
complete work *Once the work is completed, the sports centre will be opened again.*
work starts/begins *Work had already started on the bridge.*
work continues *Work is continuing on three major building projects.*

PREPOSITIONS

work on sth *Work on the project will begin soon.*

PHRASES

a piece of work *This study is a useful piece of work.*
hard at work *The children were hard at work making Christmas decorations.*
Keep up the good work! (=used when telling someone they have done something well) *Well done! Keep up the good work!*

3 something that is produced by a painter, writer, composer etc

ADJECTIVES

a great work *He regarded this book as his greatest work.*
a beautiful/astonishing/exceptional etc work *The trophy is a beautiful work in solid silver.*
sb's early/earlier work *The exhibition includes some of the artist's early work, which was done when he was student.*
sb's late/later work *I prefer her later work.*
a dramatic work (=a play) *'Romeo and Juliet' is one of Shakespeare's best-known dramatic works.*
an orchestral work *He is most famous for his large orchestral works.*

VERBS

produce/create a work *She has also produced works of non-fiction.*
write/compose a work *This piano work was written in memory of a childhood friend.*
perform a work *The work was first performed in Paris.*
commission a work (=ask for it to be produced) *Reed had commissioned works from several leading American painters.*

PREPOSITIONS

a work by sb *He believed the painting was an early work by Picasso.*
the works of sb *Are you familiar with the works of Shakespeare?*

PHRASES

a work of art *She had a collection of paintings and other works of art.*

4 the studies that have been done on a particular subject

THESAURUS: work
work, study, experiment → **research[1]**

worker *n*

1 someone who does a job

ADJECTIVES

a skilled worker *There is a shortage of skilled workers such as electricians and plumbers.*
an unskilled worker *Unskilled workers receive very low wages.*
a full-time worker *The bureau has only two full-time workers.*
a part-time worker *A high percentage of the female staff were part-time workers.*
a temporary worker *Hospitals rely heavily on temporary workers.*
a low-paid worker *Low-paid workers often have to take second jobs.*
a manual/blue-collar worker (=someone who does physical work) *Manual workers often live close to their workplace.*
a white-collar worker (=someone who works in an office, a bank etc) *In the past, white-collar workers worked for one company for a long time.*

NOUNS + worker

a factory/farm/office etc worker *Factory workers threatened to go on strike.*
a rescue worker *Rescue workers searched through the ruins looking for survivors.*
a research worker *Research workers have tried for many years to find a cure for the disease.*
a health worker (=a nurse, doctor etc) *The organization provides training for health workers in Africa.*
a migrant worker (=someone who comes

from another country or region to work) *The strawberries are picked by migrant workers.*

a public sector worker (=someone who works for an organization owned and run by the government) *Nurses and other public sector workers will find out if their pay will be increased.*

a private sector worker (=someone who works for a private company) *Two-thirds of private sector workers do not have a workplace pension.*

VERBS

employ workers *The factory employs 1,000 workers.*

take on/recruit workers (=start employing them) *We are not taking on any more workers.*

lay off workers (*also* **make workers redundant** *BrE*) (=stop employing them) *75 workers have been laid off.*

workers strike/go on strike *Workers may strike for better pay and conditions.*

workers lose their jobs *Many workers are worried about losing their jobs.*

2 someone who works in a particular way

ADJECTIVES

a good/hard worker (=someone who works hard) *She is a hard worker and should do well in her exams.*

a quick/fast worker *If you're a fast worker it will take less time to finish the task.*

a slow worker *She's such a slow worker it takes her forever to get anything done.*

a productive worker (=who does a lot of useful work) *They are keen to get rid of older and less productive workers.*

works *n* THESAURUS > factory

world *n*

1 the planet we live on, and all the people, cities and countries on it

PHRASES

the best/tallest etc in the world *We want to become the best team in the world.*

the world's best/tallest etc *It is the world's largest car manufacturer.*

all over the world (=in every part of the world) *The city attracts visitors from all over the world.*

the world over (=in every part of the world – more formal) *He is known the world over for his poems.*

anywhere in the world *This is the best food you will eat anywhere in the world.*

the rest of the world *How will this affect Britain and the rest of the world?*

part of the world *This part of the world was new to her.*

ADJECTIVES

the whole/entire world *Today the whole world is threatened by pollution.*

VERBS

travel the world *He spent a few years travelling the world.*

see the world (=travel to different parts of the world) *He quit his job to see the world.*

save the world (=help people in the world) *She was a young idealist who wanted to save the world.*

lead the world (=be the most successful in the world) *Britain leads the world in defence electronics.*

rule the world *The Romans wanted to rule the world.*

world + NOUNS

a world war (=involving many countries in all parts of the world) *Humankind would not survive another world war.*

a world record *He holds the world record for the 200 metres sprint.*

a world champion *He returned from the tournament as world champion.*

the world championships *She'll be competing in this year's world championships in Russia.*

the world economy *The price of oil has a huge influence on the world economy.*

world markets (=financial markets) *The prospect of a war in the region has made world markets very nervous.*

a world tour (=visiting or performing in all regions of the world) *The band begins a world tour in April.*

PREPOSITIONS

around/across the world (=in many parts of the world) *We deal with over 100 companies around the world.*

throughout the world (=in all parts of the world) *The company has hotels throughout the world.*

2 society, or life in general

ADJECTIVES/NOUNS + world

the modern world (*also* **today's world**) *Electronic devices are a common feature of the modern world.*

the real world *We want everything to be fair, but the real world is not like that.*

an ideal/perfect world *In a perfect world, there would be no crime.*

the outside world (=society outside a particular place, group etc) *She preferred life in a religious community to life in the outside world.*

a vanishing/disappearing world (=which may soon stop existing) *These proud hard-working farmers belong to a vanishing world.*

W

PREPOSITIONS

in a/the ... world *He is the most respected critic in the art world.*

a world of... *We live in a world of international air travel.*

PHRASES

I don't know/I wonder what the world is coming to *disapproving* (=used in comments about the bad aspects of modern life) *When I see shows like this on TV, I wonder what the world is coming to.*

it's a small world (=used when you unexpectedly meet someone, find out that two people know each other etc) *It turns out my neighbour works with my friend's husband – it's a small world.*

the ways of the world (=the unpleasant realities of life) *She was too experienced in the ways of the world to believe this story.*

3 a particular group of countries

ADJECTIVES/NOUNS + world

the Arab world *The Arab world is in a period of great change.*

the Islamic/Muslim world *These customs are practised throughout the Islamic world.*

the English-speaking/French-speaking etc world *Her books are widely read across the Spanish-speaking world.*

the developing world (=societies that are not modern or industrial) *We must not think of the developing world as constantly needing our help.*

the industrialized/developed world *Most of these problems are caused by the industrialized world.*

the Western world (=areas such as northern Europe and the United States, with modern societies) *People here are suspicious of the Western world.*

The phrase **the Third World** is sometimes used about poor countries, but it is becoming old-fashioned and some people consider it to be offensive. It is better to say **the developing world**.

worried *adj*

unhappy because you keep thinking about a problem, or about something bad that might happen

ADVERBS

very/really worried *She was really worried that she would fail her test.*

seriously/deeply worried *Hazel was now seriously worried. Why hadn't he come back?*

extremely/desperately worried *All this time I was desperately worried about my family.*

increasingly worried (=more and more worried) *The family became increasingly worried about her safety.*

a little/slightly worried (*also* **a bit worried** *BrE*): *I was a little worried at first.*

not unduly worried (=not very worried) *Jerry did not sound unduly worried at the prospect of going to jail.*

VERBS

be/feel worried *I was so worried about you!*

get/become worried *You should have called me. I was getting worried.*

look worried *Her parents looked worried.*

PREPOSITIONS

worried about sb/sth *Many people said they were worried about the economy.*

NOUNS

a worried expression/look/frown *John came in with a worried look on his face.*

PHRASES

worried sick (=extremely worried) *Where have you been? We've been worried sick!*

worry[1] *v*

1 to be so anxious or unhappy about something that you think about it a lot

ADVERBS

really worry *I really worry that I might lose my job.*

worry a lot *They worry a lot about what will happen to their children.*

worry slightly *I do worry slightly about his health.*

worry constantly *We live in a world where people worry constantly about the future.*

worry needlessly/unnecessarily *There is plenty of time left – I think you're worrying needlessly.*

worry unduly (=too much) *Don't worry unduly about the cost.*

PREPOSITIONS

worry about/over sth *Most people worry about money from time to time.*

PHRASES

Don't worry! (*also* **not to worry!**) *spoken*: *"I forgot my umbrella!" "Don't worry, we can use mine."*

sth is nothing to worry about (=you should not worry about it) *The doctor told him the marks on his skin are nothing to worry about.*

have enough to worry about (=used to say that someone does not want to hear about or do something) *I've got enough to worry about without you telling me all your problems.*

worry yourself sick (*also* **worry yourself to death**) *informal* (=worry about something very much) *Why didn't you phone us? We've been worrying ourselves sick!*

2 to make someone so anxious or unhappy about something that they think about it a lot

ADVERBS

really worry sb *What really worries me is the cost of going to university.*

worry sb a lot *The poor state of her health worries me a lot.*

worry sb slightly *The rising cost of the project does worry me slightly.*

PREPOSITIONS

worry yourself about sth *Don't worry yourself about me – I can look after myself.*

worry sb with sth *She didn't want to worry her husband with these problems.*

PHRASES

I don't want to worry you, but... *spoken* (=used for introducing news that might be bad) *I don't want to worry, you but there's black smoke coming from the back of your car.*

not let sth worry you *You're probably older than the other candidates, but I wouldn't let that worry you.*

worry² *n*

a problem that you are anxious about or are not sure how to deal with

ADJECTIVES

sb's main/biggest worry *My biggest worry is that I might forget my speech.*

a major/big/great/considerable worry *Traffic congestion is a major worry in the area.*

a real worry *It's a real worry that my children are so far away.*

sb's only worry *My only worry is that I might not have enough money to finish the course.*

a constant worry *For parents of teenagers, drugs are a constant worry.*

a nagging worry (=one that you keep worrying about) *She had a little nagging worry that she was doing the wrong thing.*

an immediate worry *The immediate worry is that there may be another explosion.*

a particular worry *Safety is a particular worry when you are dealing with children.*

a worry is unfounded (=there is no reason to worry) *Tests proved that worries about chemicals in the water supply were unfounded.*

financial/money worries *The company has considerable financial worries.*

VERBS

have worries *We have some worries about the cost of the building work.*

express/voice worries (=say that you are worried) *Some politicians have expressed worries about sending more troops to the region.*

ease/alleviate worries *formal* (=make someone less worried) *The report has helped to alleviate residents' worries about air pollution.*

dismiss sb's worries (=say that there are no problems and someone should not be worried) *Local people are concerned about increased traffic but the council has dismissed their worries.*

forget your worries *People regard their summer holiday as a chance to forget their worries.*

PREPOSITIONS

worries about/over sth *We still have some major worries about cost.*

a worry to sb *Her children have never been a worry to her in any way.*

amid worries (=used for saying that something happens at a time when people are worried) *The factory was closed amid worries about safety.*

PHRASES

a source/cause of worry *Her children were a constant source of worry.*

be sick/frantic with worry *The girl's mother was sick with worry over her missing daughter.*

no worries *spoken especially BrE* (=used like 'okay' for agreeing or accepting something) *"Can you help me with this table?" "Yeah, no worries."*

worrying *adj* making you feel worried

ADVERBS

very/deeply/extremely worrying *The news was deeply worrying.*

particularly/especially worrying *The situation in rural areas is particularly worrying.*

NOUNS

a worrying situation *The company's financial situation was very worrying.*

a worrying incident *This sounds like a very worrying incident and we will be looking into it.*

a worrying development (=a new event that is worrying) *The police say these attacks are a worrying development.*

a worrying trend *The figures from the survey show an extremely worrying trend.*

a worrying sign *The people who examined the bridge found worrying signs of structural damage.*

worrying news *She had some worrying news about her mother's health.*

the most worrying thing/aspect *The most worrying thing is that she won't eat.*

a worrying time *When the baby was ill, it was a worrying time for the whole family.*

worse *adj*

the comparative form of 'bad' or 'badly'

ADVERBS

much worse/far worse/a lot worse *Conditions were much worse in rural areas.*

considerably/substantially worse *formal: The situation became considerably worse when he lost his job.*

infinitely worse (=very much worse) *My exam results could have been infinitely worse.*

progressively/steadily worse *The violence grew progressively worse.*

even worse *My cooking's even worse than yours.*

no worse (*also* **not any worse**) *Doctors have said that she's no worse this morning.*

slightly worse (*also* **a little worse**) *She's feeling slightly worse today.*

worse off (=in a worse situation as a result of something) *When taxes go up, most people are worse off.*

VERBS

get/become worse (*also* **grow worse** *formal*): *The economic situation was getting worse.*

make sth worse *Getting angry will just make the situation worse.*

PHRASES

worse and worse *The bullying got worse and worse.*

there's nothing worse than... (=used for saying that you dislike something very much) *There's nothing worse than lending something and not getting it back.*

there are worse things (=used for saying that you have accepted a bad situation) *Well, there are worse things than working in the evenings.*

be none the worse for sth (=to not have suffered much as a result of something) *The dog spent the night outside but seemed none the worse for the experience.*

sth could be worse *Cheer up – things could be worse.*

better or worse *I wasn't sure whether his behaviour was getting better or worse.*

make matters/things worse *Then, to make matters worse, I couldn't find the car keys.*

worse luck *spoken* (=used for saying that you are rather annoyed or disappointed) *I'll have to work this Sunday, worse luck.*

ANTONYMS **worse → better**

worship *n*

the activity of praying or singing in a religious building in order to show respect and love for God

ADJECTIVES/NOUNS + worship

religious worship *Do you regularly attend a mosque, synagogue, or other place of religious worship?*

public worship *Music plays an important part in public worship.*

Sunday/Friday worship *About 30 people attended Sunday worship.*

PHRASES

a place of worship *The temple is an ancient place of worship.*

an act of worship *He knelt in an act of worship.*

freedom of worship (=the right to worship in your chosen religion) *The law gave freedom of worship to people of all religions.*

worst *adj, n*

the person, thing, or situation that is worse than all others

Grammar

As a noun, **worst** is always used in the phrase **the worst**.

PHRASES

by far the worst/easily the worst/the absolute worst (=much worse than the others) *He has made several films, but this one is by far the worst.*

the worst in the world/country *The area has some of the worst unemployment in the country.*

the very worst (=the worst – used for emphasis) *He always took the dog for a walk, except in the very worst weather.*

the worst (part) is over *The worst is over, and the journey should be easier from now on.*

the worst (thing) that can happen *I'll give it a try – what's the worst that can happen?*

at its worst (=when it is as bad as it can be) *At its worst, family life can feel like being in a prison.*

VERBS

assume/expect/fear the worst (=be worried something terrible has happened) *When she didn't come home that night, we feared the worst.*

prepare for the worst *We prepared for the worst by drawing up emergency plans.*

avoid/escape the worst of sth *I was fortunate to escape the worst of the rain.*

think/believe the worst of sb (=think someone is bad or does things for bad reasons) *He's very cynical, and always thinks the worst of everyone.*

bring out the worst in sb (=make someone behave very badly) *Power brings out the worst in some people.*

ANTONYMS **worst → best[1]**

worthless *adj*

not worth any money, or not useful at all

ADVERBS

completely/absolutely/utterly worthless *The coins are completely worthless.*

almost/virtually/practically worthless *The shares have become virtually worthless.*

PREPOSITIONS

worthless without sth *Knowledge from books is worthless without practical experience.*

ANTONYMS **worthless → valuable**

worthwhile *adj*

if something is worthwhile, it is important or useful, so that you get something good from it

ADVERBS

sth is well worthwhile (=it is very worthwhile) *It's well worthwhile looking at their website.*

extremely worthwhile *He found living abroad to be an extremely worthwhile experience.*

NOUNS

a worthwhile job *Teaching is a very worthwhile job.*

a worthwhile experience *The project was a worthwhile experience for everybody who took part in it.*

a worthwhile exercise (=something that is useful and worth doing) *I'm not sure if the training course was a worthwhile exercise.*

a worthwhile contribution *Extra lighting would make a worthwhile contribution to road safety.*

a worthwhile cause *She wants to raise money for a worthwhile cause such as a cancer charity.*

a worthwhile investment *The company has proved to be a worthwhile investment for its shareholders.*

VERBS

find sth worthwhile *I found the course very worthwhile, and definitely learnt a lot.*

THESAURUS: worthwhile

handy, helpful, worthwhile, valuable, invaluable, indispensable → **useful**

wound[1] *n*

an injury to your body, especially one that is made by a weapon such as a knife, bullet, or bomb

ADJECTIVES

a serious/severe/bad wound *He was taken to hospital with serious head wounds.*

a deep wound *Surgeons had to put three stitches in a deep wound in his shoulder.*

a minor/superficial wound (=not serious) *His wounds, luckily, were minor.*

a fatal/mortal wound (=causing death) *The second man's knife inflicted the fatal wound.*

multiple wounds (=several different wounds) *The man had multiple wounds to his head and body.*

an open wound (=one which exposes flesh under the skin) *A player should not continue to play with an open wound.*

a gaping wound (=one that is wide and open) *Blood spurted from his gaping wounds.*

NOUNS + wound

a head/leg etc wound *The victim died of chest wounds.*

a stab/knife wound *He was taken to hospital and treated for stab wounds.*

a gunshot/bullet wound *Deaths from gunshot wounds have risen sharply in the city.*

a war wound *He walked with a limp, the result of an old war wound.*

a flesh wound (=one that does not injure bones or parts inside the body) *It's only a flesh wound and will heal in ten days or so.*

VERBS

suffer/receive a wound *The victim had suffered multiple wounds to his back and stomach.*

inflict a wound *These fish can inflict serious wounds.*

dress/bandage a wound (=cover it with cloth) *The nurse dressed my wounds.*

clean/bathe a wound *He finished cleaning the wound and began bandaging the arm.*

a wound heals *The wound is healing nicely.*

PREPOSITIONS

a wound in sth *There's a deep wound in his leg.*

wounds to sth *She has stab wounds to the arms and chest.*

PHRASES

treat sb for wounds *Several people were treated for gunshot wounds.*

wound[2] *v*

to injure someone with a knife, gun, bomb etc

Grammar
Usually passive.

ADVERBS

be badly/seriously/severely wounded (*also* **be gravely wounded** *formal*): *Her husband was seriously wounded in the attack.*

be critically wounded (=be so badly wounded that you might die) *Some of the victims are critically wounded.*

be fatally/mortally wounded (=so badly that you die) *The president was fatally wounded by a gunman in the crowd.*

be slightly/lightly wounded *Two people were shot and slightly wounded.*

You can also say that someone's **pride** is **wounded**, when they feel upset, especially because they are unsuccessful: *His* ***pride*** *was* ***wounded*** *when he was turned him down for the job.*

wrap *v*

to put paper or cloth around something

ADVERBS

wrap sth tightly/loosely *Wrap the sandwiches tightly in plastic film.*

wrap sth loosely *The scarf was loosely wrapped around her neck.*

be beautifully wrapped *He gave her a scarf, beautifully wrapped in pink tissue paper.*

be warmly wrapped *He was warmly wrapped in a blanket.*

NOUNS

wrap a present/gift *She had already bought and wrapped all her Christmas presents.*

PREPOSITIONS

wrap sth in sth *Wrap each banana in aluminium foil and bake in the oven.*

wrap sth round/around sth *She wrapped a towel around her dripping hair.*

wreck *n* THESAURUS ▸ accident

write *v*

1 to put words on paper or on a computer screen

NOUNS

write a letter/email/message/note *Laura wrote a long letter to Ross, saying how much she loved him.*

write a word/phrase/sentence *There have been thousands of words written on this subject.*

write your name/address/phone number *Please write your full name and address.*

write a book/novel/story *She is planning to write a book about her experiences in Washington.*

write a play/poem *Shakespeare wrote more than 30 plays.*

write a report/article/paper/essay *I was interested in history, and enjoyed writing essays.*

write a list *Write a list of the questions you want to ask.*

write a cheque *BrE*, **write a check** *AmE*: *She wrote a cheque for £20 and handed it to him.*

ADVERBS

well/beautifully written *The book is beautifully written and there are some memorable descriptions.*

badly/poorly/terribly written *The menu was badly written, and full of obvious mistakes.*

carefully written *The document was carefully written to avoid admitting any responsibility.*

write sth clearly/neatly *He wrote his name clearly in big letters so that everyone could read it.*

PREPOSITIONS/ADVERBS

write to sb *You should write to the company and complain.*

write about sth *She writes about the lives of ordinary people.*

write of sth *formal* (=mention that something exists) *The ancient historians wrote of a lost continent called 'Atlantis'.*

write of sb/sth (=describe them in a particular way) *His commanding officer wrote of him: '"He was one of the finest characters I have ever met."*

write sth in a book/letter etc *"I have nothing but good wishes for your country," Gandhi wrote in a letter to President Roosevelt.*

write sth in English/German etc *The book was written in French and translated into English.*

write sth on sth *She wrote her name on the form.*

write for a newspaper/magazine *He writes for the Sunday Times.*

write sth down (=write it on paper so that you can remember it) *The police officer wrote down my address in his notebook.*

write sth out *She wrote out the names of all the wedding guests.*

write back *I'm still waiting for them to write back.*

Grammar

You can **write someone a letter**, or **write (a letter) to someone**. In American English, you can also say **write someone**: *He wrote me the following day.*

THESAURUS: write

put

to write something in a particular place, or using particular words:

I'll put the date of the next meeting in my diary. | *She wanted to tell him that she was sorry, but she* ***wasn't sure what to put.*** | *After you have agreed a price, you should ask the company to* ***put it in writing*** (=write what has been agreed, so that there is an official record).

enter

to write something on a computer:

The first thing you need to do is enter your password. | *Some of the information was* ***incorrectly entered*** *into the database.*

type in/key in

to write something on a computer:

After you have typed in a document, it is important to make sure that you have saved it. | *The results of the research are keyed in, so that the data can be analysed.*

Type in, key in, or enter?

These words basically mean the same. **Enter** is often used about **passwords** and instructions to the computer. **Type in/key in** can be used about names and numbers, or about longer pieces of text. **Type in/key in** has the feeling of using your fingers on a keyboard, whereas with **enter** the emphasis is on the computer receiving the information or instructions you have given it.

take

notes | minutes

to write notes while someone is speaking or while something is happening, so that you can use them later:

His lawyer was taking notes during the interview. | *The secretary took the minutes of the meeting* (=write down an official record of what is said).

Instead of saying **take notes**, you can say **make notes**.

sign
name | letter | card | form | agreement | contract | document | cheque
to write your name at the end of something, especially to show that you wrote it or agree with it:
Don't forget to sign your name on the card. | The journal published a letter signed by 18 of the world's top scientists. | The two leaders will meet to sign a peace agreement.

fill out/in
form | application | questionnaire
to write information on a form or other official document:
You have to fill out a form to join the club. | I filled out an application for the job.

transcribe *formal*
words | conversation | interview | notes | evidence
to write something exactly as it was said or written:
She was not absolutely sure that she had transcribed his words with total accuracy. | The interviews will be recorded so that they can be later transcribed. | He was busy transcribing his notes from the lecture.

to write something quickly or untidily

jot down
ideas | thoughts | details | notes | list | figures | name
to write something quickly, especially so that you can remember it and use it later:
I've already jotted down a few ideas for my speech. | She jotted down a list of things she wanted to buy.

scribble
note | name | number | address | word
to write something quickly and in an untidy way:
His lawyer sat behind him scribbling notes. | Mary hastily scribbled her telephone number on the back of an envelope. | She found a notepad and scribbled a few words in it.

scrawl
name | signature | word | note | graffiti
to write something in a careless untidy way, which is often difficult to read:
Caroline scrawled her signature on the form. | Someone had scrawled graffiti all over the walls.

dash off
letter | note | book | story
to write something quickly, especially a letter or note to someone:
He dashed off a quick letter saying that he would be pleased to accept the job.

2 to create a song or a piece of music

NOUNS

write a song *The song was written by Bob Dylan.*

write the music *Paul McCartney wrote the music.*

write the words/lyrics (=the words of a song) *Tim Rice wrote the lyrics for the musical 'Evita'.*

write the score/soundtrack (=the music for a film, musical, or show) *Williams wrote the score for the film 'Star Wars'.*

Write or compose?
You **write** the words of a song, or you **write** a piece of music: *The song was **written** by John Lennon. | He was asked to **write** some music for the film.*
You **compose** a piece of music, especially classical music: *The symphony was **composed** by Beethoven. | Mozart **composed** his first opera at the age of 12.*

writer *n*

someone who writes books, stories, articles etc

ADJECTIVES

a good/great/fine writer *I think Margaret Atwood is a very good writer.*

a modern/contemporary writer *He was one of Japan's most original modern writers.*

a prolific writer (=someone who writes a lot of books, stories etc) *P.G. Wodehouse was a prolific writer who wrote hundreds of books and short stories.*

a freelance writer (=who is paid to write articles etc for various employers) *She now works as a freelance writer.*

NOUNS + writer

a fiction/science-fiction/mystery etc writer *The movie is based on a story by the science-fiction writer Philip K. Dick.*

a travel/history/sports etc writer (=someone who writes articles and books about a subject) *I like to read books by travel writers when I'm on holiday.*

PREPOSITIONS

a writer on sth *He was one of the finest writers on art of the 20th century.*

a writer of sth *She is best known as a writer of short stories.*

writing *n*

1 books, poems, articles etc, especially those by a particular writer or about a particular subject

ADJECTIVES/NOUNS + writing

academic/scholarly writing *In academic writing, you should avoid contractions such as 'don't' or 'aren't'.*

creative writing (=writing stories about imaginary people and events) *He is currently*

W

teaching creative writing at the University of Michigan.

descriptive writing (=in which you describe things or people) *Students are asked to discuss a passage of descriptive writing.*

travel writing *We publish the best travel writing from around the world.*

historical/sociological/scientific etc writing *Historical writing today examines the lives of ordinary people, as well as the rich and powerful.*

writing + NOUNS

writing skills *An English teacher tries to develop children's writing skills.*

writing style *Different newspapers tend to use different writing styles.*

a writing workshop *She attended a writing workshop for aspiring poets.*

a writing career *Her writing career spanned four decades.*

writing ability *Unlike many sportsmen who produce an autobiography, he does have genuine writing ability.*

PREPOSITIONS

writing on/about sth *The latest medical writing on the subject dismisses the use of drugs.*

PHRASES

a piece of writing *It's a brilliant piece of writing.*

2 the style of the letters that someone writes with a pen or pencil

ADJECTIVES

neat writing *Unlike most children her age, she has very neat writing.*

untidy/messy writing *He had written a quick note in his usual messy writing.*

joined-up writing *BrE*, **cursive writing** *AmE* (=in which the letters are joined to each other) *The children were practising joined-up writing.*

VERBS

read sb's writing *It is sometimes difficult to read her writing.*

recognize the writing *I didn't recognize the writing on the envelope.*

written *adj*

written language is put on paper, computer screens etc, rather than being spoken

NOUNS

written language *The written language is difficult for foreigners to learn.*

written English/Arabic/Japanese etc *The spelling of 'its' is one of the most common problems in written English for native speakers.*

a written report/statement *At the end of term, each student receives a written report about their work.*

written consent (=saying that you agree to allow something to happen) *The doctor must obtain written consent from the patient.*

the written word (=things that people write in books, newspapers etc, rather than things people say) *He understood the power of the written word to change society.*

ANTONYMS **written → spoken**

wrong *adj*

1 not correct, true, or acceptable

ADVERBS

completely/totally/quite wrong *I may be completely wrong but I think she's lying.*

hopelessly wrong (=completely wrong in a very surprising way) *In most cases judges are right, but in a few they are hopelessly wrong.*

clearly/obviously/plainly wrong (*also* **demonstrably wrong** *formal*): *The information they gave us was clearly wrong.*

morally wrong *Is it morally wrong for a professor to date a student?*

factually wrong *Some of the information in the book is factually wrong.*

fundamentally wrong *The government's approach to the problem is fundamentally wrong.*

intrinsically/inherently wrong (=wrong in its basic nature) *There's something intrinsically wrong with a world where children die of hunger.*

VERBS

get sth wrong *The person who wrote the article got their facts wrong.*

prove sb wrong *People do not like to be proved wrong.*

look/seem/sound wrong *Don't hang the picture there – it looks wrong.*

PREPOSITIONS

wrong about sth/sb *I was wrong about his name – it's John, not Jim.*

wrong for sb *A job that involves dealing with people would be completely wrong for her.*

PHRASES

it is/would be wrong to... *Do you think it would be wrong to offer him money?*

there is something/nothing wrong with... *There's nothing wrong with asking her to dance if you like her.*

what's wrong with... *I don't understand what's wrong with playing football in the garden.*

be on the wrong track (=have the wrong approach, so that you cannot achieve what you want) *The detectives thought they had found the killer, but unfortunately they were on the wrong track.*

THESAURUS: wrong

incorrect

information | advice | diagnosis | name | spelling

something that is incorrect is wrong because

someone has made a mistake. **Incorrect** is more formal than **wrong**:
I'm afraid that the information they gave you was incorrect. | *He admitted that his staff had made mistakes and given incorrect advice.* | *I checked the document for any incorrect spellings.*

inaccurate
information | **figures** | **data** | **measurement** | **map** | **report** | **picture** | **claim**
something that is inaccurate is not exactly right and contains mistakes. **Inaccurate** is more formal than **wrong**:
The report was based upon inaccurate information. | *The official figures may well be inaccurate.* | *The old maps were often inaccurate.* | *The authorities made inaccurate claims about the shooting.*

false
information | **statement** | **claim** | **accusation** | **allegation** | **impression** | **picture** | **idea** | **assumption** | **premise**
not based on true facts:
He was charged with giving false information to the police. | *Many of the claims made in the book are* ***completely false****.* | *This accusation is* ***totally false****, Your Honour.* | *I hope I haven't given you a false impression of what the job is like.* | *Are the following statements* ***true or false****?*

untrue
not based on true facts, especially because someone is lying or guessing. **Untrue** is much less common before a noun:
I can't believe he said that about me. It's ***completely untrue****!* | *Many of their allegations are untrue.*

misleading
impression | **picture** | **information** | **statistics** | **statement** | **claim** | **advertisement** | **article** | **term**
making people believe something that is wrong, especially because someone or something does not give all the facts:
Statistics can sometimes give you a misleading impression about a situation. | *Companies can be punished if they give misleading information about their products.* | *The advertisement is misleading because it makes it look like the service is completely free.*

misguided
attempt | **belief** | **notion** | **decision** | **policy** | **strategy**
wrong because of being based on bad judgment or a lack of understanding of a situation:
Hundreds of people were put in jail in a misguided attempt to combat terrorism. | *The professor has the misguided belief that science can solve all our problems.* | *Looking back, we can see that this was a misguided decision.* | *The government's policy on drugs seems* ***totally misguided****.*

mistaken
belief | **impression** | **view** | **identity**
wrong – used about ideas and beliefs. Also used about a person being wrong:
People are going out in the sun using creams, in the mistaken belief they are protected against strong sunlight. | *We don't know why he was shot – it may have been a case of mistaken identity* (=people thought that someone was another person). | *She's* ***completely mistaken*** *if she thinks that I don't care about her.*

You're mistaken sounds more polite and less direct than saying **you're wrong**.

ANTONYMS **wrong → right[1] (1)**

2 not suitable for doing something

Grammar
In this meaning, you usually say ***the wrong*** *time/place etc.*

NOUNS

the wrong time/moment *Have I called at the wrong moment?*

the wrong place *Parking in the wrong place gets you a $120 fine.*

the wrong kind/sort of sth *She is eating the wrong kind of food if she wants to lose weight.*

the wrong way/direction *We wanted to go back into the town, but we set off in the wrong direction.*

ANTONYMS **wrong → right[1] (2)**

3 used to describe a situation where there are problems

ADVERBS

very wrong *When she smelled the gas in the house she knew something was very wrong.*

terribly/dreadfully/horribly wrong *Harry felt sure that something was terribly wrong.*

seriously wrong *Doctors didn't think there was anything seriously wrong with him.*

drastically wrong (=involving a very serious problem) *They knew something was drastically wrong in their marriage.*

dangerously wrong *We identified something dangerously wrong with the design.*

VERBS

go wrong *From that moment on, everything went horribly wrong for the team.*

PREPOSITIONS

wrong with sb/sth *I don't know what's wrong with the car.*

PHRASES

there is something/nothing wrong *There's something wrong with this yogurt – it smells funny.*

W

something/nothing/anything (is) wrong *It was several days before they even noticed anything was wrong.*

find something/nothing/anything wrong *She always finds something wrong with my suggestions.*

what's wrong? *You look upset – what's wrong?*

You can also say that **there is something the matter (with sb/sth)**, especially when you do not know what is wrong: *He looks worried – I think **there is something the matter**.* You can also say **what's the matter**: *I don't know **what's the matter** with this machine. It won't print my documents. | You seem very unhappy – **what's the matter**?*

X-ray *n*

a beam of radiation that can go through solid objects and is used for photographing the inside of the body

VERBS

have an X-ray (*also* **go for an X-ray**) *When I injured my hand, I had to have an X-ray.*

send sb for an X-ray *The doctor sent him for an X-ray to see if his thumb was broken.*

take an X-ray (*also* **do an X-ray** *BrE*): *They took an X-ray of his chest.*

an X-ray shows sth *The X-ray showed that she had broken a bone in her leg.*

NOUNS + X-ray

a chest/leg/foot etc X-ray *He went to the hospital for a chest X-ray.*

X-ray + NOUNS

X-ray machine/X-ray equipment *At the airport they put your bags through an X-ray machine.*

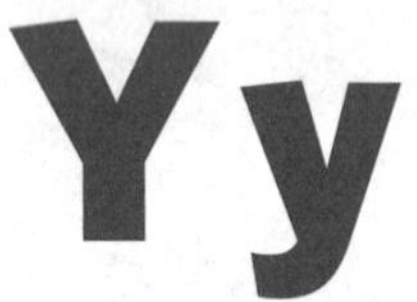

yard *n*

1 *AmE* the area around a house, usually covered with grass

ADJECTIVES

a back yard/backyard *He's watering the plants in the back yard.*

a front yard *She went into the front yard to cut the grass.*

PREPOSITIONS

in the yard *The children are playing in the yard.*

yard + NOUNS

a yard sale (=a sale of used clothes and things from someone's house which takes place in their yard) *You could have a yard sale to raise some money.*

> In British English, people say **garden**: *The kids are out in the* ***garden****.*

2 an enclosed area next to a building or group of buildings, used for a special purpose, activity, or business

NOUNS + yard

a school yard/schoolyard *The children are playing games in the school yard.*

a prison yard *They are allowed out into the prison yard for an hour a day.*

a timber yard (=where wood for building or making things is stored or sold) *He's gone to the timber yard to get some wood for a bookshelf.*

a builder's yard (=where materials for building are stored or sold) *You can get the bricks from your local builder's yard.*

a goods/freight yard (=where goods can be loaded onto or unloaded from trains) *We watched the trains entering and leaving the goods yard.*

yawn *n* an act of yawning

ADJECTIVES

a big/huge yawn *With a huge yawn, she slowly got out of her chair.*

a noisy/loud yawn *A loud yawn was heard from the back of the room.*

VERBS

give a yawn *She gave a yawn and said: "It's time for bed."*

stifle a yawn (=stop yourself from yawning) *He stifled a yawn and looked at his watch.*

hide a yawn *Sue put her hand over her mouth to try to hide a yawn.*

year *n*

1 a period of 365 or 366 days divided into 12 months, beginning on January 1st and ending on December 31st

ADJECTIVES

this/next/last year *She will be eight this year.*

every year *We go to France every year.*

the current year *The budget for the current year is 3 million euros.*

the coming year (=the year that is about to start) *Here are some events to look out for in the coming year.*

the past year *Over the past year everyone has worked extremely hard.*

the previous year *They had married the previous year.*

the following year *The following year he was made captain of the team.*

the new year (=used to talk about the beginning of the next year) *The report is due at the beginning of the new year.*

the school/academic year (=the period of the year during which there are school or university classes) *In British schools, the academic year starts in September.*

the financial/fiscal year (=the 12-month

period over which a company's accounts are calculated) *We submit our accounts at the end of the financial year.*

a leap year (=a year that has 366 days, which happens every four years) *2020 is a leap year.*

VERBS

a year passes (by)/goes by *A year had passed since he first suggested the idea.*

spend a year *I spent two years working in Iran.*

sth takes a year *It took several years before the feeling in his hand returned.*

last a year *The course lasts for three years.*

PREPOSITIONS

in/during/over the year *In the past year, 16 people have been killed.*

in the year 1846/1900 etc *Joe was born in the year 2000.*

for a year/three years etc *I went to live in France for a year.*

PHRASES

the beginning/start of the year *They moved here at the beginning of last year.*

the end of the year *Work should finish around the end of the year.*

all year round (=at all times during the year) *The campsite is open all year round.*

(at) this time of year (=used especially when talking about the season) *There are a lot of bees around at this time of year.*

2 a particular period of time in someone's life or in history

Grammar
Always plural in this meaning.

ADJECTIVES

early years *David remembers the early years of television.*

later/latter years *In his later years, Einstein became involved in politics.*

the last/final/closing years of sth *She was very ill during the last years of her life.*

the intervening years (=between two periods or events) *Little seems to have changed in the intervening years.*

sb's teenage years *Her teenage years were very unhappy.*

sb's formative years (=when someone's character develops) *The writer spent his formative years in Ireland.*

NOUNS + year

sb's childhood years *This is the home in which she spent her childhood years.*

the war years *Orwell worked for the BBC during the war years.*

the boom years (=when an economy or industry is very successful) *In the boom years, thousands of new homes were built.*

sb's retirement years *He enjoyed his retirement years in Wales.*

the Bush/Blair etc years (=when Bush, Blair etc was leader) *Britain changed a lot during the Thatcher years.*

PHRASES

in recent years *The number of cases has risen dramatically in recent years.*

in later years *In later years he regretted their argument.*

in years gone by (=in the past) *The old fort defended the island in years gone by.*

⚠ Don't say 'in ancient years'. Say **in ancient times** or **long ago**.

PREPOSITIONS

the years of sth *He lived in Hungary during the years of Communism.*

sb's years in sth *He has written a book about his years in prison.*

sb's years as sth *In all her years as a doctor, she had never seen anything like this.*

during the years *I first met Max during the early years of the war.*

yellow *adj, n*

the colour of butter or the middle of an egg

TYPES OF YELLOW

pale/light/soft yellow *She wore a pale yellow dress.*

dark/deep yellow *This plant has deep yellow flowers.*

bright/brilliant yellow *He wanted to paint his bedroom bright yellow.*

golden yellow *The wine is a golden yellow color.*

lemon yellow (=light yellow) *A school of lemon yellow fish swam past.*

PREPOSITIONS

in yellow (=in yellow clothes) *I just don't look good in yellow.*

PHRASES

a shade of yellow *I like that shade of yellow.*

yellow with age (=used to describe paper or old white paint) *The map was yellow with age.*

yield *n* THESAURUS amount

young *adj*

a young person or animal has not lived for very long

NOUNS

young people *Some young people leave school without any qualifications.*

a young child/girl/boy *The programme is not suitable for young children.*

a young man/woman/lady *She was a young woman of about 25 years old.*

a young adult *The disease is common in children and young adults.*

a young daughter/son *Tom is married, and has a young daughter.*

a young couple *Outside the church was a young couple who had just got married.*

a young family (=parents with young children) *A lot of young families live in this street.*

a young wife/mother *Mike has a beautiful young wife.*

the younger generation (=young people in general) *It is natural for the younger generation to want to do things differently.*

a young offender (=young person who has committed a crime) *This part of the prison is for young offenders.*

a young player/artist/writer etc *He is a very talented young player.*

VERBS

look young *Bill's wife looked younger than he did.*

feel young *I'm 50 but I feel a lot younger.*

die young *He died young in a road accident.*

marry young *Edith married young, and had two children before she was 20.*

stay young (=feel or look younger than you are) *Looking after her grandchildren helps her stay young.*

ADVERBS

too young *You're too young to get married.*

relatively young *He is only 47, which is a relatively young age for a president.*

PHRASES

the young (=young people as a group) *Unemployment is one of several problems facing the young.*

in sb's younger days (=when someone was younger) *John was a great footballer in his younger days.*

young at heart (=old but thinking and behaving as if you are young – used to show you approve) *For anyone who is young or young at heart, the nightlife in the town is great.*

young for your age (=looking younger than you really are) *He has always looked young for his age.*

THESAURUS: young

small/little
child | boy | girl | kid
used about very young children:
They have two small children. | Two small boys were running up the road. | The little girl asked me a question. | We used to go camping a lot when the kids were little.

> **Small or little?**
> **Small** sounds more neutral. You often use **little** when expressing your feelings about the child: *He's a sweet* ***little*** *boy. | You're a naughty* ***little*** *girl!*

teenage
boy | girl | child | daughter | son | mother | pregnancy | years
between the ages of 13 and 19:
The magazine is intended for teenage girls. | 60,000 babies were born to teenage mothers in England and Wales that year. | He spent his teenage years in Australia.

> **Teenage** is only used before a noun.

adolescent *especially written*
girl | boy | child | male | female | son | daughter | years
at the age when you change from being a child into an adult – used especially when talking about the problems that young people have at this age:
Sudden mood changes are common in adolescent girls. | I spent another day arguing with my adolescent son. | During the adolescent years, many changes happen to your body.

juvenile *formal*
crime | delinquent | delinquency | violence | offender | court
relating to young people who commit crime:
There has been an increase in juvenile crime. | People disagree on how to punish juvenile delinquents (=young people who commit crimes). *| In the 1950s, comic books were blamed for juvenile delinquency* (=criminal behaviour by young people).

> **Juvenile** is only used before a noun in this meaning.

youthful *especially written*
face | appearance | looks | enthusiasm | optimism | energy | exuberance
seeming young, or typical of someone who is young – often used when talking about someone who is no longer young:
Despite his youthful appearance, the actor is actually in his late 40s. | He wanted to keep his youthful looks. | When he started his job, he was filled with youthful enthusiasm.

junior
champion | championship | league
connected with sports played by young people rather than adults:
He was the British junior tennis champion. | The team plays in the junior league.

> **Junior** is only used before a noun.

ANTONYMS **young → old (1)**

youth *n*

the time when someone is young, especially when he or she is a teenager

Y

VERBS

spend your youth *The singer spent his youth in India.*

relive/recapture your youth (=do things you did when young, in order to try to experience youth again) *The band's fans are clearly trying to relive their youth.*

waste your youth *I wasted my youth studying for exams.*

PHRASES

in sb's youth (=when someone was young) *She had been a great beauty in her youth.*

a misspent youth *often humorous* (=spent doing things that were bad or not useful) *He is trying to make up for his misspent youth.*

your lost youth (=the time long ago when you were young) *He wept for his lost youth.*

the days/dreams/friends etc of sb's youth *She has never forgotten the dreams of her youth.*

youthful *adj* THESAURUS ➤ **young**

Zz

zeal *n*

great eagerness to do something

ADJECTIVES

great zeal *She performed her duties with great zeal.*

excessive zeal (=too much) *The police were accused of controlling the protesters with excessive zeal.*

missionary/religious zeal (=great eagerness because you strongly believe that something is right) *He tried with missionary zeal to convince her to become a vegetarian.*

revolutionary/reforming zeal (=eagerness to make big changes) *She was known for her revolutionary zeal in wanting to improve the lives of the poor.*

PREPOSITIONS

with zeal *He approached the task with zeal.*

a zeal for sth *She has shown considerable zeal for getting things done efficiently.*

PHRASES

in sb's zeal to do sth *In his zeal to get the job finished quickly, he can be a bit careless.*

zealous *adj* THESAURUS ➤ **enthusiastic**

zone *n*

a large area that is different from other areas around it in some way

ADJECTIVES/NOUNS + zone

a war zone *Hundreds more troops have arrived in the war zone.*

a danger zone *Civilians were told to leave the danger zone.*

an earthquake zone (=where earthquakes are likely to happen) *It's not advisable to build nuclear reactors in an earthquake zone.*

a disaster zone *The flooding was so bad that the city was declared a disaster zone.*

an economic zone (=an area with special trade or tax conditions) *The area has been made a special economic zone.*

a time zone (=which has a different time from the rest of the world) *Los Angeles is in a different time zone from New York.*

a 20 miles/80 kilometres etc per hour zone (=where vehicles' speed is limited) *He was doing 42 miles per hour in a 30 miles per hour zone.*

a no-parking zone *You can't leave your car here – it's a no-parking zone.*

a pedestrian zone (=only for people walking, not cars) *The main part of the city centre is a pedestrian zone.*

a smoke-free/nuclear-free etc zone (=where smoking, nuclear weapons etc are not allowed) *The office is a smoke-free zone.*

a demilitarized zone (=where soldiers and military activities are not allowed) *The demilitarized zone between North and South Korea was created after the Korean War.*

the euro zone (=the countries where the euro is used as the official money) *The country wanted to leave the euro zone.*

VERBS

enter a zone *Only a few journalists have been able to enter the disaster zone.*

leave a zone *Staff were advised to leave the danger zone.*

set up/establish/create a zone *The government intends to set up an enterprise zone in the region.*

declare/designate sth a zone (=officially make it a zone) *The college was declared a no-smoking zone.*

divide sth into zones *The vast exhibition is divided into zones.*

PREPOSITIONS

in a zone *It was like being in a war zone.*

THESAURUS: zone

region, zone, district, neighbourhood, suburb, quarter, slum, ghetto → **area (1)**

Academic Collocations List

What is the Academic Collocations List?

The Academic Collocations List (ACL) is a list of the most frequent collocations that are found in academic texts. The list of just over 2,400 collocations was created as part of a research project involving Longman Dictionaries, Pearson Language Testing and a team of corpus linguists led by Professor Douglas Biber from Northern Arizona University.

The ACL was compiled using the written section of the Pearson International Corpus of Academic English (PICAE) containing over 25 million words from textbooks and journals. The materials themselves were selected from a range of academic subjects, covering humanities, social sciences, natural and formal sciences, professions and applied sciences.

In order to identify frequent collocations, computer programs were developed to analyse the data automatically and systematically. In order to focus on academic collocation, the following were excluded from the search:

- Proper names (such as *New York, Dow Jones Index*)
- Personal names (such as *Robert, Dr Green*)
- Grammatical function words (such as *of, in, the*)
- Words that appear on the General Service List (GSL) – the 2,000 most frequent words in English as identified by Michael West (1953). GSL words were allowed as collocations of academic words (e.g. **make an observation**) – but not as the main element of the collocation.

This initial list (over 16,000 collocations) was further reduced by identifying part-of-speech combinations that would identify useful chunks of language for learners of English: adjective + noun, adverb + adjective; adverb + verb; verb + noun; noun + noun. Other combinations, such as determiner + noun (e.g. some historians) were considered to be pedagogically less useful. The list was then reviewed by a panel of linguists and reduced further to 2,469.

Why is the ACL important?

In order to answer this question, we first need to ask why collocation itself is important. For many years, teachers and students have acknowledged the benefits of learning language in 'chunks' rather than as individual words. By having access to ready-made chunks of language, learners are able to retrieve language more quickly and accurately and this in turn improves fluency. At the same time, collocations are often difficult to guess in a foreign language. They might be easy to understand, but trying to produce accurate collocations based on translation from your own language is often not successful. Collocations need to be learnt as a single unit of information to ensure that they are always produced accurately. Many learners know this to be true for phrasal verbs (such as **get up**); the same is true for a collocation such as **significant contribution**.

As more and more students continue into further education, and increasing numbers decide to continue their studies in English, so the need to broaden the knowledge of vocabulary to academic registers also increases. A major step forward was made in 2000 when research into academic vocabulary resulted in the creation of the Academic Word List (Averil Coxhead). The ACL builds on this early research to include the most frequent collocations found across a range of academic disciplines – offering learners further support in their academic studies of English.

How is the ACL organized?

The 2,469 collocations that make up the ACL can be presented in a number of different ways – and by going to the online version of the *Longman Dictionary of Collocations and Thesaurus*, you can decide how best to search the list for your own use.

In the following pages, we have followed the organising principles that have been used in the rest of this dictionary: collocations are presented at the entry that the user is most likely to look up, so:

- Adjectives are shown at the **noun** entry (e.g. *brief* ***overview***)
- Verbs are shown at the **noun** entry (e.g. *raise* ***awareness***)
- Adverbs are shown at the **verb** or **adjective** entry (e.g. ***rely*** *heavily (on), relatively* ***few***)

For further information on the Academic Collocations List, go to:
http://www.pearsonpte.com/research/Pages/home.aspx

The creation of the Academic Collocations List was a joint venture between Pearson Language Testing and Longman Dictionaries. Both teams would like to thank Professor Douglas Biber and Bethany Gray for their computational analysis of the source corpus; Andrew Roberts for tagging the initial list and conducting the validation study; and the panel of experts who reviewed and commented on the list during its development: Professor the Lord Quirk, Professor Geoff Leech, Professor David Crystal, Della Summers and Diane Schmitt.

ability (*n*) **adjectives:** cognitive

abuse (*n*) **adjectives:** sexual

accept (*v*) **adverbs:** (be) commonly/generally/universally/widely accepted

acceptable (*adj*) **adverbs:** socially

acceptance (*n*) **adjectives:** widespread

access (*n*) **adjectives:** direct, easy, electronic, equal, free, limited, online, open, public, ready, unlimited| **verbs:** allow/deny/gain/give/have/provide access (to)

accessible (*adj*) **adverbs:** easily, readily

account (*n*) **adjectives:** brief, comprehensive, historical

accuracy (*n*) **adjectives:** great

achievement (*n*) **adjectives:** academic

acquire (*v*) **adverbs:** newly acquired

act (*n*) **adjectives:** sexual

action (*n*) **adjectives:** appropriate, collective, legal, military, positive

activism (*n*) **adjectives:** political

activity (*n*) **adjectives:** commercial, cultural, economic, human, learning, physical, political, professional, related, social| **verbs:** engage in (an), undertake

acute (*adj*) **adverbs:** particularly

adjustment (*n*) **adjectives:** structural| **verbs:** make adjustments

administration (*n*) **adjectives:** public

adopt (*v*) **adverbs:** (be) widely adopted

advances (*n pl*) **adjectives:** technological

advantage (*n*) **adjectives:** major

affairs (*n pl*) **adjectives:** economic, financial, internal

affect (*v*) **adverbs:** adversely, directly, severely, significantly

agency (*n*) **adjectives:** federal, regulatory

agenda (*n*) **adjectives:** political| **verbs:** set

agree (*v*) **adverbs:** generally, strongly

agreement (*n*) **adjectives:** broad, general, international| **verbs:** reach

aim (*n*) **adjectives:** overall, primary

ally (*v*) **adverbs:** (be) closely allied (to, with)

alternative (*n*) **verbs:** provide

amount (*n*) **adjectives:** (a) considerable/huge/significant/substantial/vast amount (of); (an) enormous amount (of)

analysis (*n*) **adjectives:** careful, comparative, critical, detailed, economic, final, full, further, historical, qualitative, quantitative, statistical, subsequent, systematic, textual, thematic, theoretical| **verbs:** conduct, use

ancestor (*n*) **adjectives:** common

answer (*n*) **adjectives:** final

apparent (*adj*) **adverbs:** immediately, particularly| **verbs:** become

appearance (*n*) **adjectives:** physical

apply (*v*) **adverbs:** equally

approach (*n*) **adjectives:** alternative, analytical, common, comprehensive, critical, flexible, general, holistic, integrated, logical, methodological, qualitative, quantitative, similar, standard, systematic, theoretical, traditional| **verbs:** adopt, develop, take, use

appropriate (*adj*) **adverbs:** particularly| **verbs:** consider, deem, seem

area (*n*) **adjectives:** complex, core, geographic(al), key, local, main, major, metropolitan, particular, related, rural, specific, subject, urban, vast, whole, wide| **verbs:** cover, identify

arena (*n*) **adjectives:** political

argument (*n*) **adjectives:** compelling, counter, general, logical, main, similar, valid| **verbs:** develop, make, present, support

arrangement (*n*) **adjectives:** institutional| **verbs:** make arrangements

array (*n*) **adjectives:** (a) vast/wide array (of)

article (*n*) **verbs:** publish

aspect (*n*) **adjectives:** certain, cultural, fundamental, general, key, negative, particular, positive, related, social, specific, technical| (*n pl*) various aspects| **verbs:** consider, focus on (an)

assessment (*n*) **adjectives:** accurate| **nouns:** process| **verbs:** make

assign (*v*) **adverbs:** (be) randomly assigned (to)

assistance (*n*) **adjectives:** financial, medical, technical| **verbs:** provide

associate (*v*) **adverbs:** (be) closely/commonly/positively/strongly associated (with)

assume (*v*) **adverbs:** (be) generally assumed

assumption (*n*) **adjectives:** basic, common, fundamental, underlying | (*n pl*) certain assumptions | **verbs:** make

attempt (*n*) **adjectives:** deliberate

attention (*n*) **adjectives:** careful, considerable, critical | **verbs:** draw attention (to); focus attention (on)

attitude (*n*) **adjectives:** negative, positive | (*n pl*) changing, cultural, public, social attitudes | **verbs:** change

audience (*n*) **adjectives:** wider

author (*n*) **adjectives:** first, original

authority (*n*) **adjectives:** central, local, political, public | **verbs:** exercise

autonomy (*n*) **adjectives:** greater, relative

available (*adj*) **adverbs:** currently, freely, publicly, readily, widely | **verbs:** become, make

average (*n*) **adjectives:** national

aware (*adj*) **adverbs:** acutely, fully, increasingly, keenly, well | **verbs:** become, make

awareness (*n*) **adjectives:** greater, growing, increased, increasing, public | **verbs:** increase, raise

background (*n*) **adjectives:** cultural, diverse, historical, social | **nouns:** knowledge

base (*v*) **adverbs:** (be) largely based (on)

basis (*n*) **adjectives:** legal, theoretical

behave (*v*) **adverbs:** differently

behaviour (*n*) **adjectives:** acceptable, appropriate, human, individual, sexual, social

belief (*n*) **adjectives:** religious, widespread

believe (*v*) **adverbs:** (be) widely believed

benefit (*n*) **adjectives:** (*n pl*) economic, potential benefits | **verbs:** provide

blurred (*adj*) **verbs:** become

body (*n*) **adjectives:** international, professional

bond (*n*) **adjectives:** strong

boundary (*n*) **adjectives:** clear, cultural, national

business (*n*) **nouns:** sector, transaction

call (*v*) **adverbs:** (be) commonly called

capacity (*n*) **adjectives:** limited

capitalism (*n*) **adjectives:** global, industrial

care (*n*) **adjectives:** primary | **verbs:** provide

career (*n*) **adjectives:** academic | **nouns:** development, opportunity

case (*n*) **adjectives:** civil, exceptional, individual, specific

category (*n*) **adjectives:** broad, general, main | **verbs:** fall into (the) category (of)

cause (*n*) **adjectives:** major, underlying

centre (*n*) **adjectives:** urban

challenge (*n*) **adjectives:** major, serious | **verbs:** face, pose, present

change (*n*) **adjectives:** cultural, demographic, dramatic, economic, fundamental, historical, major, minor, radical, significant, structural, technological | (*n pl*) environmental changes

change (*v*) **adverbs:** constantly, dramatically, rapidly

changing (*adj*) **adverbs:** ever, rapidly

chapter (*n*) **adjectives:** final, following, introductory, opening, preceding, previous, subsequent

characteristic (*n*) **adjectives:** common, defining, key, salient, specific | (*n pl*) certain, demographic, individual, main, physical, similar characteristics

charge (*v*) **adverbs:** (be) highly charged

choice (*n*) **adjectives:** individual, personal

chosen (*v*) **adverbs:** (be) randomly chosen

circle (*n*) **adjectives:** (in) academic circles

circumstances (*n pl*) **adjectives:** certain, changing, exceptional, historical, local, personal, political, social, special

cite (*v*) **adverbs:** (be) frequently cited

class (*n*) **adjectives:** lower, ruling | **nouns:** consciousness

clear (*adj*) **adverbs:** entirely, fairly

climate (*n*) **adjectives:** current, political | **nouns:** change

clue (*n*) **verbs:** provide

colleague (*n*) **adjectives:** professional

comment (*n*) **adjectives:** written | **verbs:** make

common (*adj*) **adverbs:** fairly, increasingly, relatively

communicate (*v*) **adverbs:** effectively

communication (*n*) **adjectives:** direct, effective, electronic, personal, verbal, written

community (*n*) **adjectives:** academic, ethnic, international, local, rural, scientific, virtual, wider

competence (*n*) **verbs:** demonstrate

competition (*n*) **adjectives:** increased

competitive (*adj*) **adverbs:** highly

complex (*adj*) **adverbs:** extremely, highly, increasingly

complexity (*n*) **adjectives:** increasing

component (*n*) **adjectives:** basic, essential, fundamental, individual, key, main, major

concentration (*n*) **adjectives:** high

concept (*n*) **adjectives:** abstract, basic, central, defining, key, theoretical | **verbs:** use

concern (*n*) **adjectives:** central, environmental, major, primary

concern (*v*) **adverbs:** (be) mainly/particularly/primarily concerned (with)

conclusion (*n*) **adjectives:** general, logical | **verbs:** draw, lead to (the)

condition (*n*) **adjectives:** (a) sufficient | (*n pl*) appropriate, climatic, economic, experimental, living, natural, normal conditions | **verbs:** create conditions

conference (*n*) **adjectives:** annual, international, national | **verbs:** attend, hold

confine (*v*) **adverbs:** (be) largely confined (to)

conflict (*n*) **adjectives:** armed, internal, political, potential, social | **nouns:** resolution | **verbs:** come into conflict (with), resolve

connect (*v*) **adverbs:** (be) closely/directly/intimately connected (to, with)

connotation (*n*) **adjectives:** negative, positive

consciousness (*n*) **adjectives:** political

consensus (*n*) **adjectives:** general, political | **verbs:** reach

consent (*n*) **adjectives:** informed | **verbs:** give

consequences (*n pl*) **adjectives:** direct, economic, environmental, negative, political, possible, serious, social, unintended | **verbs:** cause, have

consider (*v*) **adverbs:** (be) generally considered

consideration (*n*) **adjectives:** careful, ethical, further, political, practical | **verbs:** give, require, take into

constant (*adj*) **adverbs:** relatively | **verbs:** remain

constraints (*n pl*) **verbs:** impose

construct (*n*) **adjectives:** social

construct (*v*) **adverbs:** (be) socially constructed

contact (*n*) **adjectives:** close, direct, first, personal, physical, sexual, social | **verbs:** come into contact (with), maintain, make

context (*n*) **adjectives:** broader, cultural, economic, global, historical, institutional, international, original, political, present, social, specific, wider | **verbs:** provide

contrast (*n*) **adjectives:** marked, sharp, stark, striking

contribute (*v*) **adverbs:** significantly

contribution (*n*) **adjectives:** major, significant | **verbs:** make

control (*n*) **adjectives:** central, internal, personal

control (*v*) **adverbs:** (be) carefully/tightly controlled

controversial (*adj*) **adverbs:** highly

core (*n*) **adjectives:** central

correct (*adj*) **adverbs:** politically

correlate (*v*) **adverbs:** (be) highly/negatively/positively/significantly/strongly correlated (with)

correlation (*n*) **adjectives:** high, negative, positive, significant, strong

cost (*n*) **adjectives:** additional, rising

country (*n*) **adjectives:** capitalist, industrial, industrialized

coverage (*n*) **verbs:** provide

create (*v*) **adverbs:** newly created

crime (*n*) **verbs:** commit

crisis (*n*) **adjectives:** economic

criteria (*n pl*) **adjectives:** objective | **verbs:** meet, use

critical (*adj*) **adverbs:** highly

critique (*n*) **adjectives:** radical

culture (*n*) **adjectives:** common, dominant, global, local, modern, national, political, popular, traditional

currency (*n*) **adjectives:** foreign, single

customer (*n*) **adjectives:** potential

damage (*n*) **adjectives:** environmental

dangerous (*adj*) **adverbs:** potentially

data (*n pl*) **adjectives:** appropriate, available, empirical, existing, experimental, historical, missing, numerical, original, preliminary, primary, qualitative, quantitative, raw, relevant, reliable, secondary, statistical | **nouns:** gathering, set | **verbs:** collect, extract, gather, interpret, obtain, present, process, provide, record, report, store, transmit, use

database (*n*) **adjectives:** online

death (*n*) **adjectives:** premature

debate (*n*) **adjectives:** academic, considerable, contemporary, heated, ongoing, political, public, theoretical

decade (*n*) **adjectives:** next, previous | (*n pl*) early, recent decades

decision (*n*) **adjectives:** final, major, strategic

define (*v*) **adverbs:** (be) broadly/clearly defined

definition (*n*) **adjectives:** broad, general, narrow, precise | **verbs:** use

degradation (*n*) **adjectives:** environmental

degree (*n*) **adjectives:** varying, (a) considerable/higher/significant degree (of)

demand (*n*) **adjectives:** increased, increasing

democracy (*n*) **adjectives:** liberal, social, western

demonstrate (*v*) **adverbs:** (be) clearly demonstrated

dependent (*adj*) **adverbs:** highly

describe (*v*) **adverbs:** briefly, previously described; (be) best described (as, in terms of)

description (*n*) **adjectives:** accurate, brief

design (*n*) **adjectives:** experimental, urban

design (*v*) **adverbs:** well designed; (be) specifically designed (to, for)

desirable (*adj*) **adverbs:** highly, socially

detail (*n*) **adjectives:** sufficient, technical, (in) considerable detail

determine (*v*) **adverbs:** (be) largely determined (by)

develop (*v*) **adverbs:** (be) fully/highly/ originally developed

development (*n*) **adjectives:** cognitive, further, future, historical, industrial, normal, physical, professional, regional, significant, subsequent, technological, urban | **verbs:** affect/contribute to/encourage/facilitate/ promote the development (of)

differ (*v*) **adverbs:** considerably, significantly, widely

difference (*n*) **adjectives:** crucial, fundamental, major, obvious, radical, sexual, significant | (*n pl*) cultural, ethnic, individual, racial, regional, substantial differences

different (*adj*) **adverbs:** entirely, fundamentally, markedly, qualitatively, radically, slightly, substantially, totally, widely

difficult (*adj*) **adverbs:** increasingly

difficulty (*n*) **adjectives:** (*n pl*) practical difficulties | **verbs:** encounter, experience, face, present difficulties

dilemma (*n*) **adjectives:** ethical, moral | **verbs:** face

dimension (*n*) **adjectives:** cultural, political, social

disagree (*v*) **adverbs:** strongly

disaster (*n*) **adjectives:** natural

discipline (*n*) **adjectives:** academic

discourse (*n*) **adjectives:** academic, dominant, public, scientific

discover (*v*) **adverbs:** newly discovered

discrimination (*n*) **adjectives:** positive, racial | **verbs:** face

discuss (*v*) **adverbs:** briefly, previously discussed; (be) widely discussed

discussion (*n*) **adjectives:** brief, earlier, fuller, preceding, previous

disperse (*v*) **adverbs:** (be) widely dispersed

display (*n*) **adjectives:** public

dispute (*n*) **verbs:** resolve

distinction (*n*) **adjectives:** clear, sharp | **verbs:** draw, make

distribute (*v*) **adverbs:** (be) widely distributed

distribution (*n*) **adjectives:** geographic(al), normal

diversity (*n*) **adjectives:** cultural, ethnic, great

divide (*v*) **adverbs:** (be) further divided (into)

document (*v*) **adverbs:** (be) well documented

domain (*n*) **adjectives:** public
dominance (*n*) **adjectives:** male
doubt (*n*) **verbs:** cast doubt (on)
draft (*n*) **adjectives:** first
duration (*n*) **adjectives:** long, maximum, short
economy (*n*) **adjectives:** advanced, capitalist, global, local, national, political, rural
edition (*n*) **adjectives:** revised
educate (*v*) **adverbs:** well/highly educated
education (*n*) **adjectives:** higher, primary, secondary
effect (*n*) **adjectives:** adverse, beneficial, combined, dramatic, negative, overall, positive, profound, significant, similar
effective (*adj*) **adverbs:** highly, particularly
effects (*n*) **adjectives:** environmental
efficient (*adj*) **adverbs:** highly
effort (*n*) **adjectives:** concerted, considerable
election (*n*) **adjectives:** presidential
element (*n*) **adjectives:** basic, core, essential, individual, key, main, single, structural | (*n pl*) constituent elements | **verbs:** contain
embed (*v*) **adverbs:** (be) deeply embedded
emerging (*adj*) **adverbs:** newly
emissions (*n pl*) **verbs:** reduce
emphasis (*n*) **adjectives:** greater, increasing, particular, special, strong | **verbs:** give, place, shift
employment (*n*) **adjectives:** full, paid | **nouns:** opportunities
encounter (*n*) **adjectives:** first
encounter (*v*) **adverbs:** (be) commonly encountered
energy (*n*) **adjectives:** atomic, nuclear, renewable, solar
enhance (*v*) **adverbs:** greatly
entity (*n*) **adjectives:** separate, single
environment (*n*) **adjectives:** external, immediate, natural, physical, political, social, urban | **verbs:** create
equal (*adj*) **adverbs:** roughly
equality (*n*) **adjectives:** greater, racial, social | **verbs:** promote
equilibrium (*n*) **adjectives:** dynamic
equivalent (*n*) **adjectives:** roughly
error (*n*) **adjectives:** common, random, standard | **verbs:** correct
essay (*n*) **adjectives:** critical
establish (*v*) **adverbs:** once established; (be) clearly/firmly/well established
established (*adj*) **adverbs:** long, newly | **verbs:** become
evaluate (*v*) **adverbs:** critically
evaluation (*n*) **adjectives:** critical
event (*n*) **adjectives:** historical
evidence (*n*) **adjectives:** ample, anecdotal, available, clear, compelling, considerable, convincing, direct, documentary, empirical, experimental, further, historical, little, recent, scientific, strong, substantial, sufficient, supporting | **verbs:** find, give, present, provide, show
evident (*adj*) **adverbs:** clearly, particularly | **verbs:** become
evolution (*n*) **adjectives:** biological
examination (*n*) **adjectives:** critical, detailed, (upon, on) closer examination
example (*n*) **adjectives:** classic, obvious, prime, specific, striking, typical | **verbs:** provide
exception (*n*) **adjectives:** notable
exclusion (*n*) **adjectives:** social
exclusive (*adj*) **adverbs:** mutually
existence (*n*) **adjectives:** continued
expand (*v*) **adverbs:** rapidly
expansion (*n*) **adjectives:** rapid
expectations (*n pl*) **adjectives:** high, social | **verbs:** meet
expenditure (*n*) **adjectives:** public
experience (*n*) **adjectives:** individual, personal, previous, prior, professional, shared
expert (*n*) **nouns:** opinion
expertise (*n*) **adjectives:** technical
explanation (*n*) **adjectives:** alternative, further, plausible, possible | **verbs:** give, provide
explicit (*adj*) **verbs:** make
exploitation (*n*) **adjectives:** economic, sexual
explore (*v*) **adverbs:** further
expression (*n*) **adjectives:** facial

extent (*n*) **adjectives:** (to a) considerable extent

factor (*n*) **adjectives:** critical, crucial, demographic, key, main, major, related, significant, specific | (*n pl*) associated, contextual, cultural, economic, environmental, external, historical, political, relevant, social factors | **verbs:** identify factors

faith (*n*) **adjectives:** religious

family (*n*) **adjectives:** nuclear

feature (*n*) **adjectives:** central, characteristic, common, defining, distinctive, distinguishing, essential, general, key, main, major, particular, positive, prominent, salient, significant, specific, striking, structural | (*n pl*) physical features | **verbs:** identify features

feedback (*n*) **adjectives:** negative, positive | **verbs:** give, provide, receive

few (*adj*) **adverbs:** relatively

field (*n*) **nouns:** research

figures (*n pl*) **adjectives:** significant

find (*v*) **adverbs:** (be) commonly found (in); (be) frequently/generally found

finding (*n*) **adjectives:** key, main, preliminary findings | **verbs:** report findings

flexibility (*n*) **adjectives:** greater

focus (*n*) **adjectives:** central, clear, main, major, particular, primary, specific | **verbs:** become (the) focus (of), provide

following (*adj*) **adverbs:** immediately

force (*n*) **adjectives:** driving, military, powerful | (*n pl*) economic, external forces

form (*n*) **adjectives:** alternative, appropriate, dominant, modified, specific, traditional

form (*v*) **adverbs:** newly formed

format (*n*) **adjectives:** standard | **verbs:** follow, use

formula (*n*) **adjectives:** general

foundation (*n*) **verbs:** provide (a) foundation (for)

fraction (*n*) **adjectives:** small

framework (*n*) **adjectives:** conceptual, institutional, legal, regulatory, theoretical

freedom (*n*) **adjectives:** religious

frequency (*n*) **adjectives:** high(er), low(er)

function (*n*) **adjectives:** basic, essential, main, primary, social, specific | **verbs:** perform, serve

funds (*n pl*) **adjectives:** public

gender (*n*) **nouns:** equality, stereotype

generation (*n*) **adjectives:** first, next, previous, younger

goal (*n*) **adjectives:** common, economic, ultimate | **verbs:** achieve, set

goods (*n pl*) **adjectives:** imported

government (*n*) **adjectives:** central, federal, local, municipal, national, representative | **nouns:** control, department, expenditure, intervention, policy

group (*n*) **adjectives:** distinct, diverse, dominant, ethnic, homogeneous, powerful, racial, religious, vulnerable

grow (*v*) **adverbs:** rapidly

growing (*adj*) **adverbs:** rapidly

growth (*n*) **adjectives:** continued, economic, significant

guidance (*n*) **verbs:** give, provide

harm (*n*) **adjectives:** potential

health (*n*) **adjectives:** mental, physical

help (*n*) **verbs:** seek

heritage (*n*) **adjectives:** cultural

high (*adj*) **adverbs:** relatively

higher (*adj*) **adverbs:** significantly, slightly

history (*n*) **adjectives:** brief, cultural, natural, oral

identical (*adj*) **adverbs:** almost

identify (*v*) **adverbs:** (be) clearly/easily identified

identity (*n*) **adjectives:** collective, cultural, ethnic, national, political, religious, sexual, social | (*n pl*) multiple identities

ideology (*n*) **adjectives:** dominant, political

ignore (*v*) **adverbs:** (be) largely ignored

illness (*n*) **adjectives:** mental

illustration (*n*) **verbs:** provide

image (*n*) **adjectives:** positive, public, visual

impact (*n*) **adjectives:** direct, emotional, enormous, environmental, great, likely, little, major, negative, positive, potential, profound, significant | **verbs:** assess (the)/consider (the) impact (of), make

implementation (*n*) **adjectives:** effective, successful

implications (*n pl*) **adjectives:** major, political, social, wider| **verbs:** consider (the) implications (of)

importance (*n*) **adjectives:** central, critical, crucial, fundamental, increased, increasing, perceived, strategic, (be of) considerable/paramount/vital importance

important (*adj*) **adverbs:** clearly, equally, increasingly

impossible (*adj*) **adverbs:** virtually

impression (*n*) **adjectives:** first| **verbs:** create, give (sb an), make

improvement (*n*) **adjectives:** significant

incidence (*n*) **adjectives:** high

income (*n*) **adjectives:** disposable, low, middle, national, total

increase (*n*) **adjectives:** dramatic, significant

increase (*v*) **adverbs:** dramatically, greatly, significantly

increasing (*adj*) **adverbs:** ever

independent (*adj*) **verbs:** become

indication (*n*) **adjectives:** clear| **verbs:** give/provide (an) indication (of)

individual (*n*) **adjectives:** particular, private, single, unique

inequality (*n*) **adjectives:** economic, social

influence (*n*) **adjectives:** considerable, cultural, major, positive, powerful, significant| (*n pl*) external influences

influence (*v*) **adverbs:** (be) greatly/heavily/strongly influenced (by)

influential (*adj*) **adverbs:** highly, particularly

inform (*v*) **adverbs:** (be) fully informed

information (*n*) **adjectives:** accurate, additional, available, basic, detailed, digital, essential, factual, full, further, given, limited, little, necessary, personal, related, relevant, reliable, specific, statistical, sufficient, useful, valuable| **nouns:** flow, gathering, processing, retrieval, sharing| **verbs:** add, carry, collect, contain, convey, disclose, extract, find, gain, gather, give, obtain, process, provide, receive, seek, share, store, transmit

initiative (*n*) **adjectives:** new| **verbs:** take

innovation (*n*) **adjectives:** technological

inquiry (*n*) **adjectives:** critical

insight (*n*) **adjectives:** new| **verbs:** gain/give/offer/provide insight (into)

inspection (*n*) **adjectives:** (on/upon) closer inspection

instability (*n*) **adjectives:** political

institution (*n*) **adjectives:** academic, cultural, democratic, educational, financial, national, political, public, social

instructions (*n pl*) **verbs:** follow

integrate (*v*) **adverbs:** (be) fully integrated

integration (*n*) **adjectives:** economic, social

intelligence (*n*) **adjectives:** artificial, emotional

intend (*v*) **adverbs:** (be) originally intended

intensity (*n*) **adjectives:** high, low

intent (*n*) **adjectives:** original

interaction (*n*) **adjectives:** complex, human, significant, social

intercourse (*n*) **adjectives:** sexual

interest (*n*) **adjectives:** considerable, increased, increasing, national, personal, renewed, vested| (*n pl*) conflicting, economic, individual interests

internet (*n*) **nouns:** access

interpretation (*n*) **adjectives:** alternative, correct, historical, literal

intervention (*n*) **adjectives:** effective

interview (*n*) **verbs:** conduct

introduction (*n*) **adjectives:** brief, critical

investigation (*n*) **adjectives:** empirical, further, scientific

investment (*n*) **adjectives:** foreign, private

investor (*n*) **adjectives:** foreign

involve (*v*) **adverbs:** (be) actively involved; (be) directly involved (in)

involved (*adj*) **verbs:** become/get involved (with/in)

involvement (*n*) **adjectives:** active, direct

isolation (*n*) **adjectives:** social

issue (*n*) **adjectives:** central, complex, contemporary, controversial, core, critical, cultural, current, ethical, global, key, legal, main, major, methodological, practical, real, related, relevant, similar, single, special, specific, technical, theoretical, wider | (*n pl*) environmental issues | **verbs:** address, consider, deal with (an), discuss, explore, identify, raise

item (*n*) **adjectives:** individual

journal (*n*) **adjectives:** academic, international, online, scholarly | **verbs:** publish

judgment (*n*) **verbs:** make

know (*v*) **adverbs:** previously known; (be) commonly known (as); (be) generally known (as, by); (be) widely known

knowledge (*n*) **adjectives:** historical, personal, previous, prior, professional, specific, tacit, technical | **verbs:** acquire, require

language (*n*) **adjectives:** appropriate, national, natural, verbal

law (*n*) **adjectives:** natural

leader (*n*) **adjectives:** political

learning (*n*) **adjectives:** collaborative, experiential, lifelong | **nouns:** difficulties, environment, objective, outcome, process, resources, strategy | **verbs:** enhance

legislation (*n*) **adjectives:** national, proposed | **verbs:** introduce

level (*n*) **adjectives:** appropriate, high, increased, low, minimum, overall, (at/on a) deeper level

life (*n*) **adjectives:** academic, contemporary, cultural

likelihood (*n*) **adjectives:** greater | **verbs:** increase, reduce

likely (*adj*) **adverbs:** equally, highly

limitations (*n pl*) **verbs:** have, impose

line (*n*) **adjectives:** dividing | **verbs:** draw

link (*n*) **adjectives:** causal, direct, strong

link (*v*) **adverbs:** (be) closely linked (to, with); (be) directly linked (to); (be) directly/inextricably linked (to, with); (be) strongly linked

literature (*n*) **adjectives:** published, relevant, scholarly

little (*adj*) **adverbs:** relatively

living (*n*) **adjectives:** daily | **verbs:** make (a)

location (*n*) **adjectives:** geographic(al)

look (*n*) **adjectives:** closer

low (*adj*) **adverbs:** relatively

majority (*n*) **adjectives:** great, large, overwhelming, simple, vast

management (*n*) **adjectives:** effective, financial, middle, senior, strategic, top

market (*n*) **adjectives:** competitive, domestic, financial, global, internal, national

marketplace (*n*) **adjectives:** global

material (*n*) **adjectives:** published, relevant, useful | **verbs:** provide

meaning (*n*) **adjectives:** literal, original, particular, shared, specific | **verbs:** convey

means (*n*) **adjectives:** alternative, useful

measurement (*n*) **adjectives:** accurate

measures (*n pl*) **adjectives:** legislative

media (*n*) **adjectives:** digital, electronic, global, national, popular, visual | **nouns:** coverage

meeting (*n*) **adjectives:** annual

member (*n*) **adjectives:** prominent

memory (*n*) **adjectives:** collective

mention (*v*) **adverbs:** previously mentioned

merits (*n pl*) **adjectives:** relative

message (*n*) **verbs:** convey

method (*n*) **adjectives:** alternative, common, effective, experimental, modern, qualitative, quantitative, scientific, standard, statistical, traditional | **verbs:** apply, describe, develop, employ, use

methodology (*n*) **verbs:** use

minor (*adj*) **adverbs:** relatively

minority (*n*) **adjectives:** ethnic, small | **nouns:** group

mobility (*n*) **adjectives:** social

mobilization (*n*) **adjectives:** political

model (*n*) **adjectives:** alternative, original, theoretical

motivate (*v*) **adverbs:** (be) politically motivated

movement (*n*) **adjectives:** feminist, free, national, political, religious, social

nation (*n*) **adjectives:** industrialized

nature (*n*) **adjectives:** changing, dynamic, precise

necessary (*adj*) **verbs:** deem

need (*n*) **adjectives:** perceived | (*n pl*) changing, individual, physical, specific needs

network (*n*) **adjectives:** global
new (*adj*) **adverbs:** entirely
norm (*n*) **adjectives:** cultural, social
number (*n*) **adjectives:** finite, increased, infinite, significant, substantial, vast
objective (*n*) **adjectives:** key, primary, strategic | **verbs:** achieve, meet, set
objectivity (*n*) **adjectives:** scientific
obligation (*n*) **adjectives:** legal | **verbs:** fulfil, have
observation (*n*) **adjectives:** direct | **verbs:** make
obvious (*adj*) **adverbs:** fairly, immediately | **verbs:** become, seem
occur (*v*) **adverbs:** frequently, naturally
occurring (*adj*) **adverbs:** naturally
offence (*n*) **adjectives:** criminal, serious | **verbs:** commit
opinion (*n*) **nouns:** leader
opportunity (*n*) **adjectives:** educational, equal, limited, unique | **verbs:** create, offer, provide
oppose (*v*) **adverbs:** (be) strongly opposed
opposition (*n*) **adjectives:** binary
order (*n*) **adjectives:** established, high, natural
organ (*n*) **adjectives:** internal
organism (*n*) **adjectives:** living
organization (*n*) **adjectives:** international, political, social
orientation (*n*) **adjectives:** sexual
origin (*n*) **adjectives:** ethnic
outcome (*n*) **adjectives:** desired, final, likely, negative, positive, possible | **verbs:** achieve, affect
overview (*n*) **adjectives:** brief, comprehensive, general | **verbs:** give/provide (an) overview (of)
panel (*n*) **adjectives:** solar
paradigm (*n*) **adjectives:** dominant
paragraph (*n*) **adjectives:** previous
parameters (*n pl*) **verbs:** set
part (*n*) **adjectives:** central, crucial, integral, major, previous, significant, substantial, vital | (*n pl*) constituent parts
participant (*n*) **adjectives:** active
participation (*n*) **adjectives:** active, effective, full, political
party (*n*) **adjectives:** interested, political, ruling, third | **nouns:** leader
pattern (*n*) **adjectives:** changing, complex, consistent, similar
peace (*n*) **nouns:** treaty
peak (*n*) **verbs:** reach
people (*n*) **adjectives:** indigenous
percentage (*n*) **adjectives:** high, large, low, small
perception (*n*) **adjectives:** public, visual
performance (*n*) **adjectives:** academic, improved, overall, superior | **verbs:** enhance
period (*n*) **adjectives:** brief, earlier, entire, extended, given, historical, initial, short, whole
perspective (*n*) **adjectives:** critical, cultural, global, historical, new, theoretical
phase (*n*) **adjectives:** final, first, initial, next
phenomenon (*n*) **adjectives:** cultural, social
philosophy (*n*) **adjectives:** moral, natural, political
picture (*n*) **adjectives:** accurate, overall
pilot (*n*) **nouns:** study
planning (*n*) **adjectives:** strategic | **nouns:** stage
plausible (*adj*) **verbs:** seem
player (*n*) **adjectives:** key
point (*n*) **adjectives:** appropriate, central, critical, crucial, final, focal, obvious
policy (*n*) **adjectives:** current, economic, educational, effective, environmental, foreign, key, national, public, social | **verbs:** make
pollution (*n*) **adjectives:** environmental
popular (*adj*) **adverbs:** increasingly
populate (*v*) **adverbs:** (be) densely/sparsely populated
population (*n*) **adjectives:** indigenous, rural
portion (*n*) **adjectives:** large, significant, small
position (*n*) **adjectives:** central, dominant, final, initial, legal, original, privileged, unique
possibility (*n*) **verbs:** consider
potential (*n*) **adjectives:** full, great | **verbs:** have

power (*n*) **adjectives:** economic, explanatory, legislative, military, nuclear, predictive, purchasing, solar, unequal

powerful (*adj*) **adverbs:** extremely

practice (*n*) **adjectives:** cultural, established, normal, professional, reflective, religious, traditional | (*n pl*) administrative practices

precedence (*n*) **verbs:** take precedence (over)

preceding (*adj*) **adverbs:** immediately

prediction (*n*) **verbs:** make

premise (*n*) **adjectives:** basic

presence (*n*) **adjectives:** physical

presentation (*n*) **adjectives:** oral | **verbs:** give

press (*n*) **adjectives:** national

pressure (*n*) **adjectives:** competitive, increased, increasing

principle (*n*) **adjectives:** basic, established, ethical, fundamental, general, guiding, key, main, moral, organizing, underlying

priority (*n*) **adjectives:** first, high, low | **verbs:** give priority (to)

probability (*n*) **adjectives:** conditional, high, low

problem (*n*) **adjectives:** additional, central, complex, ethical, financial, fundamental, major, methodological, potential, related, specific, technical | **nouns:** area | **verbs:** create, encounter, experience, face, identify, pose

problematic (*adj*) **adverbs:** highly

procedure (*n*) **verbs:** adopt, describe, follow, use

proceedings (*n pl*) **adjectives:** legal

process (*n*) **adjectives:** complex, continuous, creative, democratic, developmental, due, dynamic, evolutionary, natural, ongoing, slow, underlying | **verbs:** begin, describe, start

product (*n*) **adjectives:** the final product | (*n pl*) imported products

production (*n*) **adjectives:** increased, industrial

productivity (*n*) **adjectives:** increased

profile (*n*) **adjectives:** high, low

programme (*n*) **adjectives:** educational

progress (*n*) **adjectives:** technological

property (*n*) **adjectives:** intellectual | (*n pl*) physical, similar, structural properties

proportion (*n*) **adjectives:** (a) great/high/increasing/large/significant/small proportion (of)

proportional (*adj*) **adverbs:** (be) directly proportional (to)

prospects (*n pl*) **adjectives:** future

prosperity (*n*) **adjectives:** economic

protection (*n*) **adjectives:** environmental, legal

provision (*n*) **adjectives:** educational | **verbs:** make

proximity (*n*) **adjectives:** close, physical

public (*n*) **adjectives:** wider

purpose (*n*) **adjectives:** primary, specific

qualification (*n*) **adjectives:** educational, professional

quality (*n*) **adjectives:** high, low, personal

quantities (*n pl*) **adjectives:** large, small, vast

question (*n*) **adjectives:** central, complex, crucial, ethical, fundamental, reflective, related, specific | **verbs:** pose, raise

range (*n*) **adjectives:** (a) broad/diverse/great/large/limited/narrow/vast/whole/wide range (of); (the) entire range (of); (a, the) full range (of) | **verbs:** cover (a) range (of)

rare (*adj*) **adverbs:** relatively

rate (*n*) **adjectives:** annual, constant, high, overall

reaction (*n*) **adjectives:** adverse, chemical, emotional, strong

read (*v*) **adverbs:** widely

reality (*n*) **adjectives:** historical, objective, political

realize (*v*) **adverbs:** (be) fully realized

reason (*n*) **adjectives:** compelling, major, obvious, primary, underlying

receive (*v*) **adverbs:** well received

recent (*adj*) **adverbs:** relatively

recognition (*n*) **adjectives:** mutual

recognize (*v*) **adverbs:** (be) widely recognized

recommendation (*n*) **verbs:** make

record (*n*) **adjectives:** accurate, historical

reduce (*v*) **adverbs:** (be) greatly/significantly reduced

reduction (*n*) **adjectives:** significant

refer (*v*) **adverbs:** (be) commonly referred (to) (as); (be) frequently referred (to)

reference (*n*) **adjectives:** specific

reflection (*n*) **adjectives:** critical

reform (*n*) **adjectives:** economic, political, social

regard (*v*) **adverbs:** (be) widely regarded (as)

relate (*v*) **adverbs:** (be) clearly/closely/directly/strongly related (to)

relation (*n*) **adjectives:** causal| (*n pl*) economic relations

relationship (*n*) **adjectives:** causal, clear, close, complex, direct, intimate, linear, personal, positive, reciprocal, significant, social, special, strong, symbiotic| (*n pl*) economic, interpersonal relationships| **verbs:** establish

relevant (*adj*) **adverbs:** highly, particularly| **verbs:** consider

rely (*v*) **adverbs:** rely heavily (on)

remarks (*n pl*) **adjectives:** concluding

remove (*v*) **adverbs:** (be) far removed (from)

report (*n*) **adjectives:** annual| **verbs:** publish

representation (*n*) **adjectives:** graphical, political, schematic, visual

requirement (*n*) **adjectives:** functional, legal, minimum| **verbs:** meet

research (*n*) **adjectives:** academic, basic, comparative, considerable, current, earlier, educational, empirical, existing, experimental, extensive, further, future, initial, little, original, past, previous, primary, published, qualitative, quantitative, recent, scholarly, scientific, traditional| **nouns:** effort, evidence, findings, methodology, topic, (for) research purposes| **verbs:** carry out, conduct, publish, undertake

resemblance (*n*) **verbs:** bear resemblance (to)

resemble (*v*) **adverbs:** closely

resources (*n pl*) **adjectives:** additional, available, economic, electronic, financial, limited, natural, scarce, sufficient, valuable| **verbs:** allocate, provide, require, use

respond (*v*) **adverbs:** appropriately

response (*n*) **adjectives:** appropriate, emotional, individual

responsibility (*n*) **adjectives:** individual, personal, primary, social| **verbs:** accept, assume, take

responsible (*adj*) **adverbs:** socially, (be) directly/largely/partly/primarily responsible (for)

restrictions (*n pl*) **verbs:** impose

result (*n*) **adjectives:** final, positive, preliminary, quantitative, similar| (*n pl*) consistent, experimental results| **verbs:** obtain

review (*n*) **adjectives:** annual, brief, comprehensive, critical

right (*n*) **adjectives:** legal, natural| (*n pl*) individual rights

risk (*n*) **adjectives:** increased, potential| **nouns:** assessment

role (*n*) **adjectives:** active, central, critical, crucial, direct, dominant, essential, key, leading, major, minor, pivotal, prominent, significant, vital| **verbs:** assume/consider/examine/take on/take up (the) role (of); play/take (a) role (in)

root (*v*) **adverbs:** (be) deeply rooted

roots (*n pl*) **adjectives:** historical

rule (*n*) **adjectives:** legal

safety (*n*) **adjectives:** personal

sample (*n*) **adjectives:** random

science (*n*) **adjectives:** biological, natural, physical

score (*n*) **adjectives:** average, high, mean

scrutiny (*n*) **adjectives:** close, critical

section (*n*) **adjectives:** concluding, final, introductory, opening, preceding, previous

sector (*n*) **adjectives:** economic, manufacturing, private, public

security (*n*) **adjectives:** national| **nouns:** policy

select (*v*) **adverbs:** (be) carefully/randomly selected

selective (*adj*) **adverbs:** highly

sense (*n*) **adjectives:** specific, (in a) literal sense

sensitive (*adj*) **adverbs:** extremely, highly, particularly

service (*n*) **adjectives:** military| **nouns:** sector| **verbs:** provide

set (*n*) **adjectives:** complex

setting (*n*) **adjectives:** educational, social

sex (*n*) **adjectives:** biological, safe

share (*v*) **adverbs:** widely shared

shift (*n*) **adjectives:** global, major, significant

side (*n*) **adjectives:** negative

significance (*n*) **adjectives:** cultural, great, little, political, practical, social, statistical

significant (*adj*) **adverbs:** highly, particularly, statistically

similar (*adj*) **adverbs:** broadly, remarkably

simple (*adj*) **adverbs:** relatively

situation (*n*) **adjectives:** complex, similar

skill (*n*) **adjectives:** technical, transferable | (*n pl*) academic, appropriate, cognitive, core, interpersonal skills

skilled (*adj*) **adverbs:** highly

society (*n*) **adjectives:** capitalist, civil, contemporary, democratic, human, industrial, modern, rural, traditional, western, wider

solution (*n*) **adjectives:** alternative, optimal

sophisticated (*adj*) **adverbs:** highly, increasingly

source (*n*) **adjectives:** alternative, common, external, key, main, major, original, possible, potential, primary, principal, rich, secondary, single, useful | (*n pl*) multiple sources | **nouns:** material | **verbs:** become (a) source (of), provide, use

space (*n*) **adjectives:** personal, physical

speaker (*n*) **adjectives:** native

species (*n*) **adjectives:** human

specific (*adj*) **adverbs:** culturally, historically

spectrum (*n*) **adjectives:** broad, political

sphere (*n*) **adjectives:** domestic, private, public

stability (*n*) **adjectives:** economic, political

stable (*adj*) **adverbs:** relatively | **verbs:** remain

staff (*n*) **adjectives:** professional

stage (*n*) **adjectives:** developmental, earlier, final, initial

standard (*n*) **adjectives:** high, living, minimum, professional

state (*n*) **adjectives:** democratic, federal, independent, mental, sovereign | **nouns:** sector

state (*v*) **adverbs:** explicitly

statement (*n*) **adjectives:** clear, general, written | **verbs:** make

statistics (*n pl*) **adjectives:** descriptive, official | **verbs:** use

status (*n*) **adjectives:** current, economic, equal, high, legal, low, political, professional, relative, social, socioeconomic, special

step (*n*) **adjectives:** final

stereotype (*n*) **adjectives:** negative, racial

straightforward (*adj*) **adverbs:** fairly, relatively

strategy (*n*) **adjectives:** alternative, coping | **verbs:** develop, have, use

stress (*n*) **nouns:** level | **verbs:** cause, reduce

striking (*adj*) **adverbs:** particularly

structure (*n*) **adjectives:** basic, clear, complex, economic, existing, formal, global, hierarchical, institutional, internal, organizational, overall, political, social, underlying

structure (*v*) **adverbs:** (be) highly structured

study (*n*) **adjectives:** academic, classic, comparative, detailed, earlier, early, empirical, experimental, further, future, historical, intensive, longitudinal, previous, qualitative, quantitative, recent, seminal, subsequent, systematic, theoretical | (*n pl*) numerous studies | **verbs:** conduct, perform, review

success (*n*) **adjectives:** academic, economic

successful (*adj*) **adverbs:** highly, particularly | **verbs:** prove

suggest (*v*) **adverbs:** strongly

suit (*v*) **adverbs:** (be) ideally suited; (be) particularly suited (to)

summary (*n*) **adjectives:** brief, useful | **verbs:** present, provide

support (*n*) **adjectives:** additional, considerable, emotional, empirical, financial, institutional, mutual, professional, technical, widespread | **verbs:** provide

surprising (*adj*) **adverbs:** hardly

survey (*n*) **adjectives:** national, recent | **nouns:** data | **verbs:** conduct

symptom (*n*) **adjectives:** physical

system (*n*) **adjectives:** binary, capitalist, complex, comprehensive, dynamic, economic, educational, integrated, legal, solar

target (*n*) **nouns:** audience| **verbs:** meet, set

task (*n*) **adjectives:** main, primary| **verbs:** carry out (the), complete, perform

teaching (*n*) **nouns:** strategy

technique (*n*) **adjectives:** basic, statistical| **verbs:** develop, employ, use

technology (*n*) **adjectives:** advanced, current, digital, modern

tendency (*n*) **adjectives:** general, increasing, natural, strong| **verbs:** have/show (a) tendency (to)

tenet (*n*) **adjectives:** central

term (*n*) **adjectives:** technical

test (*n*) **adjectives:** diagnostic, statistical| **nouns:** score

text (*n*) **adjectives:** classic, introductory, key, literary, original

theme (*n*) **adjectives:** central, common, key, main, major, recurrent

theory (*n*) **adjectives:** classical, critical, cultural, economic, evolutionary, general, scientific, social| **verbs:** apply, develop, test, use

think (*v*) **adverbs:** differently, previously thought

thinking (*n*) **adjectives:** creative, critical| **nouns:** process

thought (*n*) **adjectives:** careful| **nouns:** process

threat (*n*) **adjectives:** external, perceived| **verbs:** pose (a) threat (to)

tie (*v*) **adverbs:** (be) closely tied

time (*n*) **adjectives:** brief, prime| (*n pl*) earlier times

tool (*n*) **adjectives:** analytical, powerful, useful

topic (*n*) **adjectives:** key, related| **verbs:** cover, discuss

trade (*n*) **adjectives:** global

tradition (*n*) **adjectives:** cultural, literary, western

training (*n*) **adjectives:** professional

transaction (*n*) **adjectives:** commercial

transformation (*n*) **adjectives:** radical, social| **verbs:** undergo

transition (*n*) **verbs:** make

transport (*n*) **adjectives:** public| **nouns:** system

treat (*v*) **adverbs:** differently, equally

treatment (*n*) **adjectives:** appropriate, effective, equal, fair, medical, preferential, unfair| **verbs:** give (sb), receive

treaty (*n*) **adjectives:** international| **verbs:** sign

trend (*n*) **adjectives:** current, general, growing, increasing, social| **verbs:** show

true (*adj*) **adverbs:** equally

trust (*n*) **adjectives:** mutual

turnover (*n*) **adjectives:** high, low

type (*n*) **adjectives:** distinct, specific

unchanged (*adj*) **verbs:** remain

unclear (*adj*) **verbs:** remain

understand (*v*) **adverbs:** clearly, fully

understanding (*n*) **adjectives:** mutual, theoretical, (a) deep understanding (of)

understood (*v*) **adverbs:** (be) easily/poorly/properly/readily understood

unemployment (*n*) **adjectives:** high, low

unlikely (*adj*) **adverbs:** highly| **verbs:** seem

usage (*n*) **adjectives:** common

use (*n*) **adjectives:** continued, widespread

use (*v*) **adverbs:** effectively, sparingly, (be) commonly/extensively/frequently/widely used

useful (*adj*) **adverbs:** extremely, particularly| **verbs:** prove

valid (*adj*) **adverbs:** equally

valuable (*adj*) **adverbs:** extremely, particularly

value (*n*) **adjectives:** core, economic, high, intrinsic, minimum, negative, numerical, positive, potential, traditional| (*n pl*) cultural, shared values

value (*v*) **adverbs:** (be) highly valued

variable (*adj*) **adverbs:** highly

variable (*n*) **adjectives:** dependent, independent, individual, random, single